Pope Clement V, from a fifteenth-century edition of the Clementinae.
(© Archivo Iconografico, S.A./CORBIS)

NEW
CATHOLIC
ENCYCLOPEDIA

NEW CATHOLIC ENCYCLOPEDIA

SECOND EDITION

3

Can–Col

GALE®

Detroit • New York • San Diego • San Francisco • Cleveland • New Haven, Conn. • Waterville, Maine • London • Munich

in association with
THE CATHOLIC UNIVERSITY OF AMERICA • WASHINGTON, D.C.

THOMSON

GALE

The New Catholic Encyclopedia, Second Edition

Project Editors
Thomas Carson, Joann Cerrito

Editorial
Erin Bealmear, Jim Craddock, Stephen Cusack, Miranda Ferrara, Kristin Hart, Melissa Hill, Margaret Mazurkiewicz, Carol Schwartz, Christine Tomassini, Michael J. Tyrkus

Permissions
Edna Hedblad, Shalice Shah-Caldwell

Imaging and Multimedia
Randy Bassett, Dean Dauphinais, Robert Duncan, Leitha Etheridge-Sims, Mary K. Grimes, Lezlie Light, Dan Newell, David G. Oblender, Christine O'Bryan, Luke Rademacher, Pamela Reed

Product Design
Michelle DiMercurio

Data Capture
Civie Green

Manufacturing
Rhonda Williams

Indexing
Victoria Agee, Victoria Baker, Lynne Maday, Do Mi Stauber, Amy Suchowski

While every effort has been made to ensure the reliability of the information presented in this publication, The Gale Group, Inc. does not guarantee the accuracy of the data contained herein. The Gale Group, Inc. accepts no payment for listing; and inclusion in the publication of any organization, agency, institution, publication, service, or individual does not imply endorsement of the editors or publisher. Errors brought to the attention of the publisher and verified to the satisfaction of the publisher will be corrected in future editions.

LIBRARY OF CONGRESS CATALOGING-IN-PUBLICATION DATA

New Catholic encyclopedia.—2nd ed.
    p. cm.
        Includes bibliographical references and indexes.
        ISBN 0-7876-4004-2
        1. Catholic Church—Encyclopedias. I. Catholic University of America.
    BX841 .N44 2002
    282′ .03—dc21
    2002000924

ISBN: 0-7876-4004-2 (set)
0-7876-4005-0 (v. 1)
0-7876-4006-9 (v. 2)
0-7876-4007-7 (v. 3)
0-7876-4008-5 (v. 4)

0-7876-4009-3 (v. 5)
0-7876-4010-7 (v. 6)
0-7876-4011-5 (v. 7)
0-7876-4012-3 (v. 8)
0-7876-4013-1 (v. 9)

0-7876-4014-x (v. 10)
0-7876-4015-8 (v. 11)
0-7876-4016-6 (v. 12)
0-7876-4017-4 (v. 13)
0-7876-4018-2 (v. 14)
0-7876-4019-0 (v. 15)

Printed in the United States of America
10 9 8 7 6 5 4 3 2 1

Foreword

This revised edition of the *New Catholic Encyclopedia* represents a third generation in the evolution of the text that traces its lineage back to the *Catholic Encyclopedia* published from 1907 to 1912. In 1967, sixty years after the first volume of the original set appeared, The Catholic University of America and the McGraw-Hill Book Company joined together in organizing a small army of editors and scholars to produce the *New Catholic Encyclopedia*. Although planning for the *NCE* had begun before the Second Vatican Council and most of the 17,000 entries were written before Council ended, Vatican II enhanced the encyclopedia's value and importance. The research and the scholarship that went into the articles witnessed to the continuity and richness of the Catholic Tradition given fresh expression by Council. In order to keep the *NCE* current, supplementary volumes were published in 1972, 1978, 1988, and 1995. Now, at the beginning of the third millennium, The Catholic University of America is proud to join with The Gale Group in presenting a new edition of the *New Catholic Encyclopedia*. It updates and incorporates the many articles from the 1967 edition and its supplements that have stood the test of time and adds hundreds of new entries.

As the president of The Catholic University of America, I cannot but be pleased at the reception the *NCE* has received. It has come to be recognized as an authoritative reference work in the field of religious studies and is praised for its comprehensive coverage of the Church's history and institutions. Although Canon Law no longer requires encyclopedias and reference works of this kind to receive an *imprimatur* before publication, I am confident that this new edition, like the original, reports accurate information about Catholic beliefs and practices. The editorial staff and their consultants were careful to present official Church teachings in a straightforward manner, and in areas where there are legitimate disputes over fact and differences in interpretation of events, they made every effort to insure a fair and balanced presentation of the issues.

The way for this revised edition was prepared by the publication, in 2000, of a Jubilee volume of the *NCE,* heralding the beginning of the new millennium. In my foreword to that volume I quoted Pope John Paul II's encyclical on Faith and Human Reason in which he wrote that history is "the arena where we see what God does for humanity." The *New Catholic Encyclopedia* describes that arena. It reports events, people, and ideas—"the things we know best and can verify most easily, the things of our everyday life, apart from which we cannot understand ourselves" (*Fides et ratio,* 12).

Finally, I want to express appreciation on my own behalf and on the behalf of the readers of these volumes to everyone who helped make this revision a reality. We are all indebted to The Gale Group and the staff of The Catholic University of America Press for their dedication and the alacrity with which they produced it.

Very Reverend David M. O'Connell, C.M., J.C.D.
President
The Catholic University of America

Preface to the Revised Edition

When first published in 1967 the *New Catholic Encyclopedia* was greeted with enthusiasm by librarians, researchers, and general readers interested in Catholicism. In the United States the *NCE* has been recognized as the standard reference work on matters of special interest to Catholics. In an effort to keep the encyclopedia current, supplementary volumes were published in 1972, 1978, 1988, and 1995. However, it became increasingly apparent that further supplements would not be adequate to this task. The publishers subsequently decided to undertake a thorough revision of the *NCE,* beginning with the publication of a Jubilee volume at the start of the new millennium.

Like the biblical scribe who brings from his storeroom of knowledge both the new and the old, this revised edition of the *New Catholic Encyclopedia* incorporates material from the 15-volume original edition and the supplement volumes. Entries that have withstood the test of time have been edited, and some have been amended to include the latest information and research. Hundreds of new entries have been added. For all practical purposes, it is an entirely new edition intended to serve as a comprehensive and authoritative work of reference reporting on the movements and interests that have shaped Christianity in general and Catholicism in particular over two millennia.

SCOPE

The title reflects its outlook and breadth. It is the *New Catholic Encyclopedia,* not merely a new encyclopedia of Catholicism. In addition to providing information on the doctrine, organization, and history of Christianity over the centuries, it includes information about persons, institutions, cultural phenomena, religions, philosophies, and social movements that have affected the Catholic Church from within and without. Accordingly, the *NCE* attends to the history and particular traditions of the Eastern Churches and the Churches of the Protestant Reformation, and other ecclesial communities. Christianity cannot be understood without exploring its roots in ancient Israel and Judaism, nor can the history of the medieval and modern Church be understood apart from its relationship with Islam. Interfaith dialogue requires an appreciation of Buddhism and other world religions, as well as some knowledge of the history of religion in general.

On the assumption that most readers and researchers who use the *NCE* are individuals interested in Catholicism in general and the Church in North America in particular, its editorial content gives priority to the Western Church, while not neglecting the churches in the East; to Roman Catholicism, acknowledging much common history with Protestantism; and to Catholicism in the United States, recognizing that it represents only a small part of the universal Church.

Scripture, Theology, Patrology, Liturgy. The many and varied articles dealing with Sacred Scripture and specific books of the Bible reflect contemporary biblical scholarship and its concerns. The *NCE* highlights official church teachings as expressed by the Church's magisterium. It reports developments in theology, explains issues and introduces ecclesiastical writers from the early Church Fathers to present-day theologians whose works exercise major influence on the development of Christian thought. The *NCE* traces the evolution of the Church's worship with special emphasis on rites and rituals consequent to the liturgical reforms and renewal initiated by the Second Vatican Council.

Church History. From its inception Christianity has been shaped by historical circumstances and itself has become a historical force. The *NCE* presents the Church's history from a number of points of view against the background of general political and cultural history. The revised edition reports in some detail the Church's missionary activity as it grew from a small community in Jerusalem to the worldwide phenomenon it is today. Some entries, such as those dealing with the Middle Ages, the Reformation, and the Enlightenment, focus on major time-periods and movements that cut across geographical boundaries. Other articles describe the history and structure of the Church in specific areas, countries, and regions. There are separate entries for many dioceses and monasteries which by reason of antiquity, size, or influence are of special importance in ecclesiastical history, as there are for religious orders and congregations. The *NCE* rounds out its comprehensive history of the Church with articles on religious movements and biographies of individuals.

Canon and Civil Law. The Church inherited and has safeguarded the precious legacy of ancient Rome, described by Virgil, "to rule people under law, [and] to establish the way of peace." The *NCE* deals with issues of ecclesiastical jurisprudence and outlines the development of legislation governing communal practices and individual obligations, taking care to incorporate and reference the 1983 *Code of Canon Law* throughout and, where appropriate, the *Code of Canons for the Eastern Churches*. It deals with issues of Church-State relations and with civil law as it impacts on the Church and Church's teaching regarding human rights and freedoms.

Philosophy. The Catholic tradition from its earliest years has investigated the relationship between faith and reason. The *NCE* considers at some length the many and varied schools of ancient, medieval, and modern philosophy with emphasis, when appropriate, on their relationship to theological positions. It pays particular attention to the scholastic tradition, particularly Thomism, which is prominent in Catholic intellectual history. Articles on many major and lesser philosophers contribute to a comprehensive survey of philosophy from pre-Christian times to the present.

Biography and Hagiography. The *NCE*, making an exception for the reigning pope, leaves to other reference works biographical information about living persons. This revised edition presents biographical sketches of hundreds of men and women, Christian and non-Christian, saints and sinners, because of their significance for the Church. They include: Old and New Testament figures; the Fathers of the Church and ecclesiastical writers; pagan and Christian emperors; medieval and modern kings; heads of state and other political figures; heretics and champions of orthodoxy; major and minor figures in the Reformation and Counter Reformation; popes, bishops, and priests; founders and members of religious orders and congregations; lay men and lay women; scholars, authors, composers, and artists. The *NCE* includes biographies of most saints whose feasts were once celebrated or are currently celebrated by the universal church. The revised edition relies on Butler's *Lives of the Saints* and similar reference works to give accounts of many saints, but the *NCE* also

provides biographical information about recently canonized and beatified individuals who are, for one reason or another, of special interest to the English-speaking world.

Social Sciences. Social sciences came into their own in the twentieth century. Many articles in the *NCE* rely on data drawn from anthropology, economics, psychology and sociology for a better understanding of religious structures and behaviors. Papal encyclicals and pastoral letters of episcopal conferences are the source of principles and norms for Christian attitudes and practice in the field of social action and legislation. The *NCE* draws attention to the Church's organized activities in pursuit of peace and justice, social welfare and human rights. The growth of the role of the laity in the work of the Church also receives thorough coverage.

ARRANGEMENT OF ENTRIES

The articles in the *NCE* are arranged alphabetically by the first substantive word using the word-by-word method of alphabetization; thus "New Zealand" precedes "Newman, John Henry," and "Old Testament Literature" precedes "Oldcastle, Sir John." Monarchs, patriarchs, popes, and others who share a Christian name and are differentiated by a title and numerical designation are alphabetized by their title and then arranged numerically. Thus, entries for Byzantine emperors Leo I through IV precede those for popes of the same name, while "Henry VIII, King of England" precedes "Henry IV, King of France."

Maps, Charts, and Illustrations. The *New Catholic Encyclopedia* contains nearly 3,000 illustrations, including photographs, maps, and tables. Entries focusing on the Church in specific countries contain a map of the country as well as easy-to-read tables giving statistical data and, where helpful, lists of archdioceses and dioceses. Entries on the Church in U.S. states also contain tables listing archdioceses and dioceses where appropriate. The numerous photographs appearing in the *New Catholic Encyclopedia* help to illustrate the history of the Church, its role in modern societies, and the many magnificent works of art it has inspired.

SPECIAL FEATURES

Subject Overview Articles. For the convenience and guidance of the reader, the *New Catholic Encyclopedia* contains several brief articles outlining the scope of major fields: "Theology, Articles on," "Liturgy, Articles on," "Jesus Christ, Articles on," etc.

Cross-References. The cross-reference system in the *NCE* serves to direct the reader to related material in other articles. The appearance of a name or term in small capital letters in text indicates that there is an article of that title elsewhere in the encyclopedia. In some cases, the name of the related article has been inserted at the appropriate point as a *see* reference: (*see* THOMAS AQUINAS, ST.). When a further aspect of the subject is treated under another title, a *see also* reference is placed at the end of the article. In addition to this extensive cross-reference system, the comprehensive index in volume 15 will greatly increase the reader's ability to access the wealth of information contained in the encyclopedia.

Abbreviations List. Following common practice, books and versions of the Bible as well as other standard works by selected authors have been abbreviated throughout the text. A guide to these abbreviations follows this preface.

The Editors

Abbreviations

The system of abbreviations used for the works of Plato, Aristotle, St. Augustine, and St. Thomas Aquinas is as follows: Plato is cited by book and Stephanus number only, e.g., Phaedo 79B; Rep. 480A. Aristotle is cited by book and Bekker number only, e.g., Anal. post. 72b 8–12; Anim. 430a 18. St. Augustine is cited as in the Thesaurus Linguae Latinae, e.g., C. acad. 3.20.45; Conf. 13.38.53, with capitalization of the first word of the title. St. Thomas is cited as in scholarly journals, but using Arabic numerals. In addition, the following abbreviations have been used throughout the encyclopedia for biblical books and versions of the Bible.

Books

Acts	Acts of the Apostles
Am	Amos
Bar	Baruch
1–2 Chr	1 and 2 Chronicles (1 and 2 Paralipomenon in Septuagint and Vulgate)
Col	Colossians
1–2 Cor	1 and 2 Corinthians
Dn	Daniel
Dt	Deuteronomy
Eccl	Ecclesiastes
Eph	Ephesians
Est	Esther
Ex	Exodus
Ez	Ezekiel
Ezr	Ezra (Esdras B in Septuagint; 1 Esdras in Vulgate)
Gal	Galatians
Gn	Genesis
Hb	Habakkuk
Heb	Hebrews
Hg	Haggai
Hos	Hosea
Is	Isaiah
Jas	James
Jb	Job
Jdt	Judith
Jer	Jeremiah
Jgs	Judges
Jl	Joel
Jn	John
1–3 Jn	1, 2, and 3 John
Jon	Jonah
Jos	Joshua
Jude	Jude
1–2 Kgs	1 and 2 Kings (3 and 4 Kings in Septuagint and Vulgate)
Lam	Lamentations
Lk	Luke
Lv	Leviticus
Mal	Malachi (Malachias in Vulgate)
1–2 Mc	1 and 2 Maccabees
Mi	Micah
Mk	Mark
Mt	Matthew
Na	Nahum
Neh	Nehemiah (2 Esdras in Septuagint and Vulgate)
Nm	Numbers
Ob	Obadiah
Phil	Philippians
Phlm	Philemon
Prv	Proverbs
Ps	Psalms
1–2 Pt	1 and 2 Peter
Rom	Romans
Ru	Ruth
Rv	Revelation (Apocalypse in Vulgate)
Sg	Song of Songs
Sir	Sirach (Wisdom of Ben Sira; Ecclesiasticus in Septuagint and Vulgate)
1–2 Sm	1 and 2 Samuel (1 and 2 Kings in Septuagint and Vulgate)
Tb	Tobit
1–2 Thes	1 and 2 Thessalonians
Ti	Titus
1–2 Tm	1 and 2 Timothy
Wis	Wisdom
Zec	Zechariah
Zep	Zephaniah

Versions

Apoc	Apocrypha
ARV	American Standard Revised Version
ARVm	American Standard Revised Version, margin
AT	American Translation
AV	Authorized Version (King James)
CCD	Confraternity of Christian Doctrine
DV	Douay-Challoner Version

ERV	English Revised Version	NJB	New Jerusalem Bible
ERVm	English Revised Version, margin	NRSV	New Revised Standard Version
EV	English Version(s) of the Bible	NT	New Testament
JB	Jerusalem Bible	OT	Old Testament
LXX	Septuagint	RSV	Revised Standard Version
MT	Masoretic Text	RV	Revised Version
NAB	New American Bible	RVm	Revised Version, margin
NEB	New English Bible	Syr	Syriac
NIV	New International Version	Vulg	Vulgate

C

CANA OF GALILEE

Cana of Galilee is the home town of Nathaniel (Jn 21.2), where Jesus changed water into wine at a wedding feast (Jn 2.1–11), and where later a Jewish royal official came to Jesus and asked Him to cure his son at Capharnaum (Jn 4.46). This town is certainly distinct from the Cana (modern Qanah) in the tribe of Aser (Jos 19.28), near Sidon. Tradition since 1600 locates it at modern Kefr Kenna on the road from Nazareth to Tiberias. Older tradition locates it, with greater probability, at modern Khirbet Qanah, ten miles north of Nazareth.

Bibliography: F. M. ABEL, *Géographie de la Palestine,* 2 v. (Paris 1933–38) 2:412–413. C. KOPP, *The Holy Places of the Gospels* (New York 1963) 143–154. R. SCHNACKENBURG, *Das erste Wunder Jesu* (Freiburg 1951).

[J. E. WRIGLEY]

CANAAN AND CANAANITES

The term "Canaanite" is historically, geographically and culturally synonymous with "Phoenician." For convenience, Canaanite is used to designate the Northwest Semitic people and culture of Palestine and Western Syria before 1200 B.C., while Phoenician refers to the same people and culture after that date.

The origin of the term Canaanite, which first appears in 15th- and 14th-century texts from Egypt, Alalakh, Nuzi and Ugarit, is not certain. Derivation from a lost Semitic word *kn',* "murex," with later meanings of merchant or purple merchant is possible. The etymology of Phoenician is uncertain also, but since the murex shellfish, which yielded purple dye, was abundant along the Syrian coast, so that Phoenicia became the center of the manufacture of purple dye, the Greek name "Phoenicia" probably refers to this industry (φοῖνιξ, purple or crimson).

Canaanite territory included most of Palestine west of the Jordan and the Lebanon-Syrian coast as far north as Ugarit near modern Latakia. Just how far inland this latter region extended cannot be determined with precision.

History. The Canaanites may have settled in these areas as early as the fourth millennium. This inference is based on the Canaanite names of towns founded before 3000 B.C., such as Jericho, Beth Yerakh and Megiddo. The coastal cities such as Acco (Acre), Tyre, Sidon, and UGARIT have names that are Semitic and in some instances specifically Canaanite. Since there is no clear evidence to show that these names supplanted earlier non-Semitic names, it becomes difficult to accept the theory of S. Moscati [*I Predecessori d'Israele* (Rome 1956) 40–41] that the Canaanites migrated into these parts around 2000 B.C.

Early Period. In the third millennium Canaan was in close commercial and political contact with Egypt. In fact, Egypt claimed political suzerainty over Canaan and *c.* 2600–2200 B.C. BYBLOS was virtually an Egyptian colony. After two centuries of decline and anarchy in Egypt, matched by similar developments in Canaan, there arose the powerful Twelfth Dynasty in Egypt (1991–1786 B.C.), which once again brought Canaan into the Egyptian orbit. The Egyptian execration texts from 1950–1850 B.C. reveal that a new wave of Semitic nomads had moved into Palestine bearing Amorrite names. Though Egypt claimed political control over Palestine, revolts were not infrequent. The second half of the 18th century saw the rise of the Hyksos who ruled Canaan and the Delta of Egypt *c.* 1710–1580 B.C. Further study in the history of the HYKSOS shows that most of the known Hyksos names are certainly or probably Canaanite or Amorrite, not Hurrian nor Hittite, as formerly believed. Concurrent with the Hyksos movement was a great migration of Hurrian and Indo-Iranian tribes from the northeast into Syria and Palestine, so that by the 15th century many cities in Palestine, such as Megiddo, Ascalon and Jerusalem, were ruled by princes with non-Semitic names. It follows that the Canaanites of the Late Bronze Age (*c.* 1550–1230 B.C.) were a much more mixed people than their ancestors

Capture and Punishment of Adoni-Bezek. (©Historical Picture Archive/CORBIS)

of the Middle Bronze Age. The Late Bronze Age is characterized as a period of vigorous commercial activity and trade with the Aegean regions, interior Syria and Egypt. As a result of wealth gathered by trade, Canaanite prosperity—that of Ugarit is a good example—reached an unprecedented level.

Late Period. In the course of the 13th century the Canaanites lost most of their territory to the Israelites who conquered the hill country of Palestine, and to the PHILISTINES who, driven away from the Delta by Ramses III, settled along the coast from Gaza to south of Jaffa (Joppe). Several decades later, Aramaean tribesmen from the Syrian desert occupied the hinterland of Phoenicia from Hauran to the Eleutherus Valley. Phoenicia was thus reduced to the coast and the immediate hinterland from the Ladder of Tyre to just north of Arvad, a distance of about 120 miles. The Phoenicians, however, were later able to extend their southern border as far as Jaffa. Their cities included Tyre, Sidon, Sarepta, Byblos, Arvad and

Amrit. In the early Iron Age, the most important were Byblos and Sidon, but later Tyre assumed the ascendancy (Ez 27). In the Bible (Dt 3.9; Is 23.2) and in Homer's Odyssey the Phoenicians are called Sidonians.

Phoenicia's commercial expansion began in the 11–10th century, when her traders penetrated to all parts of the Mediterranean coast, setting up colonies by 900 B.C. in Cyprus, Sicily, Sardinia, Africa and Spain. In the late eighth and early seventh century Assyrian expansion put an end to the independence of Sidon, while at the same time the rise of Greek colonization weakened Phoenician commerce in the Mediterranean. In 572 B.C., after a siege of 13 years, the Chaldeans destroyed Tyre and with it all serious Phoenician maritime activity. The Greeks and the Punic colonies would fill the void created by the passing of the mainland powers (*see* CARTHAGE).

Culture. Phoenician art was essentially synthetic; it borrowed and combined motifs from Egypt and Mesopotamia, as is evident in the groups of Phoenician ivories found at MEGIDDO, Enkomi in Cyprus, Nimrud, Samaria and Arslan Tash, as well as from the silver bowls discovered in Greece and Cyprus. The chief cultural contribution of the Phoenicians was the invention, sometime before 1500 B.C., of the linear alphabet from which are derived Hebrew, Syriac, Arabic, Amharic and numerous other Oriental scripts. Though there is still some dispute, 800 B.C. is the probable date when the Greeks borrowed the Phoenician alphabet and thus began its spread throughout the West.

Before the hundreds of inscribed clay tablets dating to the 15th and 14th century B.C. were discovered at Ugarit beginning in A.D. 1929, the principal sources of knowledge of the Canaanite language were the Hebrew Bible, since Biblical Hebrew is a Canaanite dialect, and the scores of Phoenician inscriptions, which, though generally brief and formulaic, sufficed to give a substantial idea of the nature of the language. The Azitawwadu Inscription from Karatepe in southern Turkey, discovered in 1946 and dating to the late eighth century B.C., contains 63 lines and is thus the longest and linguistically perhaps the most informative Phoenician inscription yet found.

See Also: AMORRITES.

Bibliography: E. A. SPEISER, "The Name *Phoinikes*," *Language,* 12 (1936) 121–126. B. MAISLER, "Canaan and the Canaanites," *The Bulletin of the American Schools of Oriental Research,* 102 (1946) 7–12. J. GRAY, *The Legacy of Canaan: The Ras Shamra Texts and Their Relevance to the Old Testament* (*Vetus Testamentum,* Suppl 5; 2d ed. 1964). W. F. ALBRIGHT, "The Role of the Canaanites in the History of Civilization," *The Bible and the Ancient Near East,* ed. G. E. WRIGHT (New York 1961) 328–362. J. C. L. GIBSON, "Observations on Some Important Ethnic Terms in the Pentateuch," *Journal of Near Eastern Studies,* 20 (1961) 217–238.

[M. J. DAHOOD]

CANADA, THE CATHOLIC CHURCH IN

The second largest country in the world after Russia, Canada is comprised of the northern half of the North American Continent and adjacent islands, except Alaska. It is bordered on the north by the Canadian Arctic Islands, on the east by the Atlantic Ocean, on the south by the United States and on the west by the Pacific Ocean. Mountainous in its western regions with plains falling to the lowlands in the south, Canada has a climate that varies from temperate in the south, to arctic in the far north. The wealth of natural resources found in the region includes iron ore, nickel, copper, zinc, gold, lead, silver, coal, natural gas and petroleum, while agricultural products grown in its vast plains consist of wheat, barley, tobacco, fruits and vegetables. Dairy farms and a strong fishing industry also contribute to Canada's economy.

Capital: Ottawa.
Size: 3,851,800 sq. miles.
Population: 31,281,100 in 2000.
Languages: English, French.
Religions: 14,076,500 Catholics (45%), 281,530 Muslims (.9%), 11,574,000 Protestants (37%), 375,375 Jews (1.2%), 1,063,555 other, 3,910,140 without religious affiliation.

Self-governing since 1867, Canada retains ties to Great Britain as a Commonwealth nation, despite the fact that the French-speaking province of Québec maintains a civil law based on the French system. Canada is divided into ten provinces, the Yukon Territory and the Northwest Territories. Ontario is the largest and most populous of the principally English provinces, while the Province of Québec is second in both population and industrial production. Canadian provinces are completely autonomous in such things as education, civil law, property rights, exploitation of natural resources and other matters of local interest. The federal government has jurisdiction in matters of national concern, e.g., postal service, customs, shipping, navigable rivers, criminal law and military service. The boundary between the United States and Canada is the longest unfortified border in the world. While friction between Québec and the rest of Canada has traditionally threatened the federation, the flow of professionals to more lucrative employment in the United States also stalled the region's otherwise thriving economy.

Discovery and Colonization. Norsemen from Greenland under Leif Ericson explored North American shores, probably those of present-day Canada, around the 11th century. In 1497 John Cabot sailed from Bristol, England, to either Cape Breton Island or Newfoundland. Thereafter European fishermen flocked to the banks of Newfoundland and to the mainland coasts. In 1534 Jacques Cartier of Saint-Malo, France, reached the Gaspé Peninsula and planted a cross on July 24, taking possession of Canada in the name of King Francis I. The following year he explored the interior, visiting both Stadaconé (Québec) and Hochelaga (Montréal), and preached to the native tribes with the help of interpreters. He planned a settlement with François Roberval, but war interfered with those plans. For the next 60 years colonization ceased, although the fisheries and fur trade continued.

French Rule. In 1603 Samuel de Champlain visited Canada briefly. Upon his return in 1604 the first settlement was established on Sainte-Croix Island, but half of the expedition died of scurvy during the winter. In June of 1605 the colony, with help from France, moved to Port Royal, Acadia (Annapolis, Nova Scotia), where Father Nicolas Aubry began evangelization among the native

Archdioceses	Suffragans
Edmonton	Calgary, St. Paul in Alberta
Gatineau-Hull	Amos, Mont-Laurier, Rouyn-Noranda
Grouard-McLennan	Mackenzie-Fort Smith, Whitehorse
Halifax	Antigonish, Charlottetown, Yarmouth
Keewatin-Le Pas	Churchill-Hudson Bay, Labrador City-Schefferville, Moosonee
Kingston	Alexandria-Cornwall, Peterborough, Sault St. Marie
Moncton	Bathurst, Edmundston, St. John (New Brunswick)
Montréal	Joliette, St. Jean-Longueuil, St. Jerome, Valleyfield
Ottawa	Hearst, Pembroke, Timmins
Québec	Chicoutimi, St. Anne-de-la-Pocatière, Trois-Rivières
Regina	Prince Albert, Saskatoon
Rimouski	Baie-Comeau, Gaspé
St. Boniface	no suffragans
St. John's (Newfoundland)	Grand Falls, St. George's
Sherbrooke	Nicolet, St. Hyacinthe
Toronto	Hamilton, London, St. Catharines, Thunder Bay
Vancouver	Kamloops, Nelson, Prince George, Victoria

Directly subject to the Holy See are the archdiocese of Winnipeg; the Greek Melkite eparchy at St. Sauveur de Montréal; the Maronite eparchy at St. Maron, Montréal; and the Slovak Byzantine eparchy of Sts. Cyril and Methodius in Toronto. The Ukranian Byzantine Church has a metropolitan in Winnipeg, with suffragans Edmonton, New Westminster, Saskatoon, and Toronto. A military ordinariate is also located in Canada.

tribes. Aubry was replaced in 1610 by Jesse Fléché, who died in 1611. Jesuits Pierre Biard and Ennemond Massé continued the missionary work, particularly among the Micmacs. However, in 1613 the British attacked Port Royal, destroying the Jesuit colony at Mount Desert Is-land and causing the Jesuits to abandon the Acadian mission and return to France.

Meanwhile, in 1608 Champlain founded Québec, bringing Franciscan friars Denys Jamet, Joseph Le Caron, Jean Dolbeau and Brother Pacifique Duplessis to work among the native people of Lower Canada. Accompanying Champlain during his exploration of the Great Lakes, they brought the Gospel to the Hurons. In need of assistance, the friars issued a call to the Jesuits and in 1625 Fathers Charles Lallemant, Jean de Brébeuf and Ennemond Massé arrived in Québec. Brébeuf immediately proceeded to Huron country where he was supported by the Company of One Hundred Associates (Company of New France) in settling the area. Meanwhile Québec prospered; it had about 100 inhabitants when it was captured by Scottish-English forces in July of 1629. The 1632 Treaty of Saint-Germain-en-Laye restored France's possessions in America, whereupon the French resettled Acadia and resumed the colonization of Québec. Capuchins sent to that region by Cardinal RICHELIEU worked zealously until 1755, when they were dispersed by the British. Almost 3,000 avoided exile by taking refuge in Canada, Newfoundland and the United States, and when London authorized the return of former inhabitants to Acadia in 1764, many returned. From 1632 to 1659 Québec, Trois-Rivières and Montréal formed the three important centers of the French colony.

In 1632 Jesuit Fathers Paul Lejeune, Anne de Noüe, Antoine Daniel, Ambroise Davost and Brother Gilbert Burel arrived in Québec and reopened the missions within a year. In August of 1634 the missionaries moved to Trois-Rivières, and established a college at Québec the following year, the first north of Spanish America. The Jesuits's success among the Huron angered the Iroquois, resulting in the deaths of the eight NORTH AMERICAN MARTYRS, canonized by Pius XI on June 29, 1930.

The Duchess of Aiguillon founded the Hotel Dieu at Québec, under the direction of the Augustinians from Dieppe, and the Ursulines established a convent directed by MARIE OF THE INCARNATION. Montréal was settled under the aegis of the Paris-based Society of Our Lady of Montréal, and was celebrated with a Mass led by Barthélemy Vimont, SJ, in 1642. The Hotel Dieu at Montréal was founded by Jeanne Mance. In 1657 the Society of Ville-Marie sent the first four Sulpicians to Montréal, and in 1658 Marguerite Bourgeois founded the Sisters of the Congregation of Our Lady for the education of girls. About this time the Church of New France received Bishop François de Montmorency Laval, who reached Québec in June of 1659. He established a seminary of foreign missions in 1663 and a secondary school at Québec in 1668. By 1665 the settlement included 18 secular priests,

31 Jesuits, ten Ursulines, 23 hospitallers and four Sisters of the Congregation. In 1674 Québec was established as a diocese responsible directly to the Holy See.

The colonies had a threefold struggle against the native tribes, the English coastal colonies and the commercial interests of the companies controlling the settlements under a royal grant. In 1663 the king of France appointed an administrator and set up an independent council. The Sulpicians ministered to a new colony established at Kingston in 1673 and constructed a church and a seminary at Montréal. The Franciscans returned to Canada in 1670 and began work in Québec, Montréal, Detroit, the Gaspé, Cape Breton and Newfoundland. The Iroquois agreed to receive Jesuit missionaries, through whom Kateri TEKAKWITHA was converted to Christianity. Claude ALLOUEZ, SJ, the first missionary to the Ottawas, founded the Mission of the Holy Ghost, at the extreme western end of Lake Superior, from which Father Jacques

MARQUETTE and Louis Joliet left for their exploration of the Mississippi in 1673.

Laval resigned his see in 1674. His successor, Jean Baptiste de la Croix Chevrières de Saint-Vallier, was consecrated in Paris on Jan. 25, 1688, and arrived in Québec on August 15. His administration was a controversial one, disrupted by the civil authorities, the clergy and the religious orders. In 1700 he was captured and imprisoned by the British while on his way to France and did not return to Canada until 1713. Before his death in 1727, he founded the general hospital at Québec and convoked the first diocesan synods in 1690. Henri Marie Dubreuil de Pontbriand (d. 1760), who arrived in Québec in 1741, restored and enlarged the cathedral, reorganized the clergy retreats, twice traveled throughout his immense diocese and wrote a considerable number of circulars and pastoral letters. He took a personal interest in the missions of the Louisiana Territory and Detroit. In 1755 he sanctioned

The igloo-shaped Our Lady of Victory Catholic church in Inuvik, Canada. (©Paul Almasy/CORBIS)

the Institute of Mme. d' Youville, the Sisters of Charity of the General Hospital of Montréal (GREY NUNS). The cathedral was destroyed during the Seven Years' War (1756–63).

French Losses of Territory. The Treaty of Utrecht (1713) ceded to England all of Hudson's Bay, Newfoundland and Acadia. France now attempted to extend Canadian boundaries westward, and Pierre Gaultier de La Vérendrye reached Lake Winnipeg in 1733. However, English colonists took advantage of the Seven Years' War to gain control of Québec in 1759 and Montréal in 1760. By the Treaty of Paris (1763), England acquired Canada, Acadia and the eastern part of Louisiana, leaving France only the islands of Saint-Pierre and Miquelon.

By this time the Catholic population—all of French descent—had increased to 65,000 and were distributed throughout Québec, Trois-Rivières, Montréal and the parishes along the banks of the Saint Lawrence. Each city

had its own institutions of charity and elementary schools conducted by nuns, while the rural schools were entrusted to the Sisters of the Congregation of Our Lady, or to lay teachers under the direction of the clergy. In addition, the Jesuits had their college at Québec and the Sulpicians their apostolic works at Montréal. The missionaries pursued their ministry among the indigenous tribes of the eastern and central portions of Canada and the Louisiana Territory. Coming under British control, the Church lacked a bishop; its 196 priests, 88 parishes and six communities of women passed to the control of a country whose laws were openly hostile to Catholics.

English Rule. As a British colony, Canadians enjoyed only those religious freedoms permitted under English law. Control from Rome was illegal and correspondence with the pope forbidden. A shortage of priests resulted when many chose to return to France. After the death of Pontbriand in 1760, the chapter reaffirmed the authority of the vicars-general and a third bish-

QUEBEC, *The Capital of* NEW-FRANCE, *a Bishoprick, and Seat of the Soverain* COURT.

1. *The Citadel.* 2. *the Castle.*
3. *Magazine.* 4. *y͏̎ Recolets.*
5. *Ursulines.* 6. *Jesuits.* 7.

7. *Cathedral of Our Lady.*
8. *The Palace* 9.*y͏̎ Seminary.*
10. *The Hôtel Dieu.*

11. *S͏̎ Charles River.*
12. *The Common Hospital.*
13. *The Hermitage of the Recolets.*

14. *The Bishop's House.* 15. *The Parish Church of the Lower Town.*
16. *The Upper Town* 17. *y͏̎ Lower Town.*
18. *The Platform & Battery of Cannon.*
19. *The Isle of Orleans.* 20. *Point Lievi.*

Quebec in the 18th century, engraving by Thomas Johnston.

op was appointed for the Trois-Rivières area. In 1765 Joseph Olivier Briand, vicar-general and administrator of Québec succeeded in getting a promise that the English government would not actively oppose his consecration. Later Briand obtained permission from London for a co-adjutor with the right of succession, and in 1772 he consecrated Louis Philippe Mariaucheau d' ESGLIS, the first Canadian to become a bishop. Although at first the bishop and his coadjutor were regarded simply as "overseers of the Roman Church," the British eventually gave in and in 1811 the crown lawyers submitted that it would be difficult to deny the bishop the use of his title. The bishops of Québec were accorded the honorary title of archbishop until, in 1844, Archbishop Joseph Signay became the first to bear the title of metropolitan.

The Québec Act. In 1774 England passed the Québec Act, which returned to Canadians their civil and religious liberties. A civil government replaced the military and an oath of loyalty replaced the old oath of renunciation of the Catholic faith. Thus Catholics became eligible for public office and freedom of religion was assured, the single restrictive clause "obedient to the authority of the King" being added to calm fanatics and to reserve the right to install a Protestant bishop at Québec. However, most Canadians were not satisfied with the act, principally because of the unpopularity of the legislative council. In 1791, therefore, two new constitutional governments were created: one for Lower Canada and one for Upper Canada, each with its own governor aided by a legislative council and an executive council chosen by the governor, and by a legislative assembly elected by the people. These changes proved beneficial to the Church, as did the French Revolution, for between 1791 and 1802 about 45 French priests, in exile in England, were permitted to immigrate to Canada.

In 1818 Bishop Joseph Octave PLESSIS regrouped Canada's 500,000 Catholics into four units: the vicariate apostolic of Halifax (1817), Montréal, Upper Canada and the Red River area. When Plessis set out for Rome in 1819 to obtain approval for his plan, he did not know that Québec had been designated an archdiocese (Jan. 12, 1819), and that Rome had established a vicariate apostolic for Upper Canada and New Brunswick, whose titulary was the vicar-general of Québec. Opposition from Lord Bathurst, the Colonial Secretary, led Plessis to renounce his plan for several dioceses and to agree not to assume the title of archbishop, which would have made him senior to the Protestant bishop. He did, however, obtain the government's permission for two regional bishops: Jean Jacques Lartigue for Montréal and Joseph Norbert PROVENCHER for the Red River. But in point of fact, four bishops had been named in 1819 and this state of affairs was eventually sanctioned. After that the Church grew rapidly, due in no small part to the efforts of Bishop Ignace BOURGET of Montréal who enlisted the help of several religious communities in France, established them locally, worked for the education of his people and took an active part in the missionary movement both in Canada and among the Canadians who had immigrated to the United States.

Alexander MacDonell became bishop of Kingston in 1826 and Angus MacEachern bishop of Charlottetown in 1829. There followed the dioceses of Toronto (1841) and Bytown (modern Ottawa; 1847), after which sees multiplied rapidly in Upper Canada, due to the influx of Scottish Catholics and other non-English immigrants. The Church also expanded into the western part of the country. In 1845 the Oblates of Mary Immaculate went to the Red River country and under the leadership of Bishop Alexandre TACHÉ (later archbishop of St. Boniface), the Church made rapid progress among the native tribes even in the northernmost regions.

Confederation. By the early 19th century a movement for the union of all the provinces was slowly gaining favor. In 1864 London approved the plan by the British North America Act, and on July 1, 1867 the Dominion of Canada came into being, comprised of the Provinces of Ontario, Québec, New Brunswick and Nova Scotia, with Ottawa as the capital city. Other provinces were later added: Manitoba in 1870, British Columbia in 1871, Prince Edward Island in 1873, Alberta and Saskatchewan in 1905, the Yukon and Northwest Territories in 1912, and Newfoundland, including Labrador, in 1949. By the Statutes of Westminster (1931) Canada received full and complete independence, with no tie to Britain other than her voluntary allegiance to the Crown.

Bibliography: *Canada and Its Provinces,* eds., A. SHORTT and A. G. DOUGHTY, 23 v. (Toronto 1914–17). J. BRUCHÉSI, *Histoire du Canada pour tous,* 2 v. (Montréal, v.1, 5th ed.; v.2, 4th ed., 1946). W. P. BULL, *From Macdonnell to McGuigan: The History of the Growth of the Roman Catholic Church in Upper Canada* (Toronto 1939). P. F. X. DE CHARLEVOIX, *History and General Description of New France,* tr. J. G. SHEA, 6 v. (New York 1866–72). DOMINIQUE DE SAINT-DENIS, *L'Église catholique au Canada* (6th ed. Montréal 1956), Fr. and Eng. É. M. FAILLON, *Histoire de la colonie française en Canada,* 3 v. (Montréal 1865–66). A. H. GOSSELIN, *L'Église du Canada après la conquête,* 2 v. (Québec 1916–17). L. M. LEJEUNE, *Dictionnaire général . . . du Canada,* 2 v. (Ottawa 1931). A. G. MORICE, *History of the Catholic Church in Western Canada: From Lake Superior to the Pacific, 1659–1895,* 2 v. (Toronto 1910). *Documents relating to Northwest Missions 1815–1827,* ed. and tr. G. L. NUTE, (St. Paul 1942). G. SAGARD-THÉODAT, *Histoire du Canada et voyages que les Frères mineurs recollects y ont faicts pour la conversion des infidèles depuis l'an 1615,* 4 v. (Paris 1866). A. TESSIER, *Histoire du Canada,* 2 v. (3d ed. Québec 1959); *Neuve France, 1524–1763,* v.1. *Mandemants, lettres pastorales et circulaires des èvêques de Québec,* eds., H. TÊTU and C. O. GAGNON, 2 v. (NS, Québec 1889–90).

[G. CARRIÉRE]

The Modern Era. By the first half of the 20th century, Canada had attained full industrial and national maturity. In 1959 Georges Vanier became governor-general, the second Canadian and the first Catholic to hold this office. The period after 1900 was also one in which the Canadian Church came of age. In 1908 it was removed from the jurisdiction of the Congregation for the Propagation of the Faith, signifying that it was no longer regarded by the Holy See as a missionary territory. This recognition of the adulthood of the Canadian Church had been foreshadowed in 1899 by the establishment of an apostolic delegation and the naming of Canada's first cardinal in the person of Archbishop Elzéar TASCHEREAU of Québec. Under the confederation, there was no State religion in Canada; all beliefs enjoyed complete freedom. Relations between the civil authority and the Catholic Church remained both proper and cordial, and in several matters the State collaborated closely with the Church.

The Church's growing vitality was reflected in its numerous clergy, its prosperous religious communities, its agencies for religious and social work, and its colleges and universities. Canadian missionaries worked in all areas of missionary endeavor and initiated a significant effort for the aid of the countries of Latin America. While at the time of the Confederation (1867) Protestants outnumbered Catholics, by the 1970s Catholics had become the predominant religious group.

The Influence of Vatican II. In 1943, two decades before the Second Vatican Council encouraged the establishment of national episcopal conferences, the Canadian bishops had created the Conférence des évêques du Canada/Canadian Conference of Catholic Bishops (CCCB). The presidency alternates between the two linguistic sectors of the Conference, so that when the president is an Anglophone the vice president is a Francophone and vice versa. The CCCB's staff is likewise balanced, and includes offices of Social Affairs, Missions, Liturgy, Religious Education and the Canadian Appeal Tribunal. In addition to the national CCCB, there are four regional episcopal assemblies: the Atlantic Episcopal Assembly, the Assemblée des évêques du Québec, the Ontario Conference of Catholic Bishops and the Western Catholic Conference.

Canadian bishops attending Vatican II included Paul-Émile Léger (b. 1904) of Montréal; Maurice Roy (1905–85), archbishop of Québec City; George Bernard

Flahiff (b. 1905), archbishop of Winnipeg; and Bishop Gerald Emmett Carter (b. 1912). The progressive positions taken by the Canadian bishops at the Council continued to be articulated at the General Assembly of the Synod of Bishops dating from 1967. The Canadian delegation called for service, not power; for communion, not regimentation; for an authentic application of the "principle of subsidiarity" in the Church itself; for the priest's role in the world to extend to a legitimate pursuit of temporal objectives; for the preaching of social and not merely private justice.

After Vatican II, the CCCB provided leadership in many areas of Catholic concern, most notably through the National Episcopal Commission for Social Affairs. Initially, there were both Anglophone and Francophone social affairs commissions, but they were successfully merged in 1973. Social justice issues were also the motivation behind the Church's cooperation with various non-Catholic bodies, both Christian and non-Christian. Although there were ecumenical discussions prior to Vatican II, following the Council the ecumenical climate in Canada warmed considerably. Common projects such as the Toronto School of Theology, the Atlantic School of Theology and the faculty of religious studies at McGill University, Montréal provided a solid ecumenical environment. Similarly, the Ecumenical Forum (Toronto), the Canadian Center for Ecumenism (Montréal) and the Shalom Institute (Vancouver) created a dialogue across the faiths. The premier ecumenical body in the country is the Canadian Council of Churches (CCC), in which the Roman Catholic Church has associate status. The CCC is designed to give expression to the fundamental unity of Christian communions and provide a forum for dialogue and shared action. It works in concert with the World Council of Churches. In addition, Canada is the only country that has a permanent national level committee bringing together representatives of the Canadian Jewish Congress, the Canadian Council of Churches and the Canadian Conference of Catholic Bishops.

Atlantic Canada. During the 1970s many of Canada's Atlantic dioceses experienced serious losses in clerical and religious personnel, resulting in difficulties for the congregations that maintain hospitals and schools in the area. However, the role of the laity was vigorously fostered in much of the area. The contemplative life fostered by Cistercians and Sisters Adorers of the Precious Blood, underwent a modern revival in the Nova Nada (Spiritual Life Institute of America) community in the Diocese of Yarmouth, Nova Scotia. As a sign of both the maturing ecumenical climate following the Council and of the pragmatic leadership of the local Ordinary, when the regional Holy Heart seminary was closed in 1970, the archdiocese of Halifax cooperated with the Anglican and

United Church authorities to establish the Atlantic School of Theology. By the late 1990s the province' nondenominational education system, which had been run by church boards since 1949, was under fire, and in 1998, following a referendum a provincial school system was set in place that would include religious education and observances within its regimen.

Another sign of the times following Vatican II and concurrent with the revival of Québec nationalism was the emergence of Acadian consciousness—religious, political and cultural. The Acadians, French-speaking Roman Catholics, traced their roots back to the pre-Conquest period in Atlantic Canada, and their infamous deportation in the 18th century became the stuff of legend. Religious communities helped preserve Acadian identity. The Holy Cross Fathers established St. Joseph's College (1864), which eventually became the Université de Moncton, and the Eudist Fathers founded the Collège Ste. Anne (1890), Church Point, N.S, which became inter-denominational in 1971. In the post-conciliar period, with the emphasis on the value of indigenous culture and the necessity for liturgical adaptation, the Church's commitment to the Acadian revival was secured.

Catholicism in the Maritime "provinces" remained strongly Celtic as well as French; moreover, the native Micmac and Malecite tribes, were almost all Catholic. In Nova Scotia, the Church helped foster Celtic culture, both at the parish level on Cape Breton Island, and at the academic level at St. Francis Xavier University in Antigonish. Even through the 20th century, the European immigrants who altered the face of Catholicism in Upper Canada had little impact on the ethnic and linguistic mix of the Atlantic provinces. By the year 2000 the Atlantic provinces had 747 parishes tended by 616 diocesan and 117 religious priests. Other religious included approximately 52 brothers and 2,100 sisters.

Québec. The Church in New France was a vigorous and powerful one. Educators, social reformers, mystics and administrators of distinction molded the shape of the new world, among them MARIE DE L'INCARNATION, founder of the Ursuline order in Canada; François de LAVAL de Montmorency, the first bishop of New France; and Marie-Marguerite D' YOUVILLE, founder of the Sisters of Charity of the Hôspital Général de Montréal. Jesuits, Sulpicians, Recollets and Hospitallers served the numerous pastoral needs of the ever-expanding Church.

After France relinquished her holdings to Britain in the Treaty of Paris (1763), the Gallic influence of the Québec Church was weakened, and the Church now looked to Rome as the intellectual and administrative center for French Canadian Catholics. During the French Revolution significant numbers of that country's religious sought refuge in French Canada, and Catholicism became a major factor in preserving the French culture and language from assimilation by the British. While Québec's reliance on Rome helped protect French Catholic integrity, it also inculcated a profound clerical and theological conservatism which served the interests of the state, particularly the early nationalists, and resulted in a unified Catholic voice, a spiritual homogeneity.

The Quiet Revolution. The Quiet Revolution—la révolution tranquille—is generally considered to have commenced with Premier Joseph-Mignault-Paul Sauvé's "désormais" (henceforth), uttered in the provincial legislature in the fall of 1959. Sauvé was responding to a question from the opposition that argued a particular point on the ground that that was the way it was always done in the past. Sauvé's "désormais" was a public declaration of departure from the past of a social and feudal Québec. The Quiet Revolution meant fundamental modifications in the educational and social service institutions of the province; increased participation of French Canadians in the federal civil service and in federal public life; and a stronger involvement of French Canadians in the business community and in the general economic life of the province and the nation. These changes profoundly affected the Church, the principal and most powerful institution in Québec.

Concurrent with the political and social upheaval in the province were the changes created by Vatican II. Rather than concentrate on power and privilege, under the leadership of Léger of Montréal and Roy of Québec City and amid some controversy, the Church gradually divested itself of exclusive ownership and responsibility for hospitals, trade unions, orphanages and cooperatives. Georges-Henri Lévesque, a Dominican friar and founder of the faculty of social science at Laval University; Alexandre Vachon, the first dean of the faculty of science at Laval, and subsequently archbishop of Ottawa; Adrian Puliat, reputedly the founder of engineering education in Québec; renowned educator Alphose-Marie Parent, chairman of the Parent Commission that reorganized Québec's secondary school system and abolished Church-controlled classical colleges; atomic physics professor Larkin Kerwin, first lay president of Laval and president of the National Research Council—these figures and others assisted in the work of the Quiet Revolution, convinced that the diminishment of Church power and the increasing secularization of the province did not herald the end of Christianity in the province. Nonetheless, the insularity, the triumphalism, the enormous energy and large personnel, the privileges and prerogatives of an established and respected institution—all these things passed.

Despite the changes following the Quiet Revolution and Vatican II, and despite a loss of clergy, the Church in Québec remained a stronghold of the faith in Canada. Although the Church relinquished many of its schools, hospitals, orphanages, etc. to the state, Québec's religious and church leaders continued to exercise considerable, though far more modest, influence on their society. Repeatedly, Québec's bishops took a leading role in attending to social and political issues: the problems of inflation and unemployment; the role of trade unions; the dignity of work and the workplace; the role of women in the family, society, and Church; the principle of self-determination as it relates to all people; and the ravages of sexism both in society and in the Church. In the area of women and ministry, the Québec church cooperated closely with such women's groups as L'autre Parole, Femmes en Eglise, Femmes en Ministerem, and Femmes de l'église Populaire. By 2000 the Québec Church had 1,883 parishes tended by 3,010 diocesan and 1,952 religious priests. Other religious included approximately 2,000 brothers and 16,300 sisters.

Ontario. While Ontario traditionally harbored deep reservations concerning the Roman Catholic faith, by the late 1900s its Catholic population was 35 percent and growing. With immigration mostly from historically Catholic countries like Italy, Poland and Portugal following World War II, the Ontario Church moved from being a largely Irish, French and German church to a multiethnic community. To meet the pastoral needs of the new immigrants, the Ontario bishops, and particularly the Archbishop of Toronto, drew upon many ethnic priests and sisters.

Of special concern to Ontario Catholics was their school system. From the Confederation until 1915 primary Catholic schools received public funding, and from 1915 to 1985 they received additional funding for grades nine and ten. Full funding to all Catholic schools in Ontario was granted in 1987, creating one of the wealthiest and most sophisticated Catholic school systems on the continent. However, during the 1990s the system came under fire from minority faiths and was forced to justify the existence of such public funding. In a lawsuit brought by Jewish and Protestant parents who claimed that public funding violated their constitutional right to equality of religion, the court ruled that such constitutional rights to the public funding of religious education were limited to those established at the time of Confederation. The system again came under attack in late 1999 when the United Nations human rights committee ruled that Ontario's funding of Catholic schools was a violation of an international agreement. Although the UN ruling was not binding, it gave the Ottawa government cause for concern and the matter continued to be reviewed into 2000. In addition to its primary and secondary schools, the Church, through various religious congregations, administered several Catholic colleges federated with the provincial universities.

In addition to education, other areas of concern to the Ontario Church included immigration, unemployment, housing, farm subsidies and spiritual alienation in the urban centers. While the Church continued to grow, like other Churches in Canada, it suffered from a decline of clerical personnel that threatened the continued health of the institution. By 2000 the Church in Ontario had 1,273 parishes tended by 1,584 diocesan and 988 religious priests. Other religious included approximately 190 brothers and 3,600 sisters. Of those total parishes and missions, eight were of the Slovakian Church and 75 were of the Ukranian Church.

The West. The Church in Western Canada included the territories—Yukon and the Northwest Territories—the three prairie provinces—Manitoba, Saskatchewan and Alberta—and the Pacific province of British Columbia. The relative youth of the western Church could be seen in the fact that most of the ecclesiastical jurisdictions were accorded the status of dioceses only in the 20th century: Regina, 1910; Edmonton, 1912; Winnipeg, 1915, for instance.

The West was unique in that it had a sizable Ukrainian population with its own ecclesiastical province and metropolitan see. It also had a large Catholic population of native people, who by the 1980s were at the center of various national and provincial social justice initiatives. The political and cultural aspirations of Canada's native peoples were endorsed by many Catholics eager to redress the inequities of the past and resolved to support an indigenous movement toward legitimate self-government, land claim rights and the recovery of authentic native values. Kisemanito (Great Spirit) Center in Grouard, Alberta, founded in 1980, worked to educate a native clergy, while dioceses sought new ways to incorporate native customs and concepts into the public worship of the Church. In 1975 the Church, together with other Christian churches, established "Project North," to mobilize public opinion in favor of the native peoples. The Nishga in British Columbia and the Dene in the Northwest Territories benefited especially from the churches' vigorous defense of aboriginal land claims.

Western Canadian bishops remained vigilant in defending the rights of native people, acutely conscious of its responsibilities but also acutely conscious of its limited clerical resources. Many of the western dioceses relied on lay leadership exclusively, and the few vocations to the religious and priestly life that were fostered were incapable of meeting the mounting needs. In the past, many of the major western dioceses relied on clergy from Atlantic Canada to supply their pastoral needs, but this ceased to be the case by the 1970s. To help meet the needs of a maturing laity, western bishops looked to such bodies as the Newman Theological College, Edmonton; the Catholic Bible College, Canmore; and the Catholic liberal arts colleges: St. Thomas More (Basilian), Saskatoon; Regina (Jesuit), Campion; St. Pauls' (Jesuit/lay), Winnipeg; St. Joseph's (Basilian), Edmonton; St. Mark's (Basilian), Vancouver. British Columbia's Trinity Western University, which trained Catholic teachers for primary and secondary schools, fought to maintain the traditions of the Church in 1999 by successfully overturning an attempt by the British Columbia College of Teachers to remove its requirement that students not engage in homosexual activity during their tenure at the college. Despite a statement from two Supreme Court Justices to the effect that Christianity was discriminatory and intolerant of differences, the university won its case. Although the western Church remained both a minority church within a predominately Protestant society and an evangelizing church, it continued to be concretely involved in social causes, particularly as they pertained to indigenous peoples and to the defense of Catholic values. By 2000 the Western provinces contained 1,691 parishes and missions, tended by 789 diocesan and 574 religious priests. Other religious included approximately 120 brothers and 2,240 sisters. Of these totals, the Ukranian Church had 440 parishes and missions in the region.

Into the 21st Century. By the year 2000 the Church in Canada was seeking to address issues from its past as well as from its future. Beginning in 1997 the bishops attempted to address certain "errors" once committed by Canadian missionaries working in Latin America and promoted the possibility of inter-American episcopal conferences as a way of meeting the needs of an increasing Spanish-speaking population in North America. Similar efforts were made to address the wrongs done to native tribes by early Christian missionaries, one in September of 2000 organized as part of an ecumenical effort in Newfoundland. The government's liberal stance on many social issues continued to concern, and sometimes divide the clergy. Canadian courts and the legislature were proactive in legalizing abortion in 1988, legalizing the abortifacient RU-86 in 1996 and ending the distinction between homosexual and heterosexual couples in 1999. In May of 1999, during the Canadian bishops's ad limina visit, Pope John Paul II encouraged the creation of urban lay ministries to combat the "culture of discrimination and of indifference" taking root in modern cities. He also warned against secularization as a force undermining Catholic identity.

Despite the effects of an increasingly liberal culture and the variety of the land and its people, the Canadian church continued to exercise international leadership in the theology of ministry, co-responsibility, subsidiarity and collegiality; it remained a church that strongly defended the political and cultural rights of its native peoples, and that continued to celebrate the value of religious freedom, the priority of conscience, the principle of "unity in diversity," and loyalty to the Roman and Apostolic See.

Bibliography: G. BAUM, *Catholic and Canadian Socialism* (Toronto 1980). *Gentlemen-Bishops and Faction Fighters: The Letters of Bishops O Donel, Lambert, Scallan and Other Irish Missionaries,* ed. C. J. BYRNE, (St. John's 1984). M. CZERNY and J. SWIFT, *Getting Started on Social Analysis in Canada* (Toronto 1984). D. DONOVAN, *A Lasting Impact: John Paul II in Canada* (Ottawa 1985). J. W. GRANT, *Moon of Wintertime: Missionaries and the Indians of Canada in Encounter since 1534* (Toronto 1984). J. HAMELIN, *Le XX siéle: Tome 2, De 1940 à nos jours. Histoire du catholicisme québècois,* ed. N. VOISINE, (Montrél 1984). J. B. HANNINGTON, *Every Popish Person: The Story of Roman Catholicism in Nova Scotia and the Church of Halifax* (Toronto 1984). M. W. HIGGINS and D. R. LETSON, *Portraits of Canadian Catholicism* (Toronto 1986). *The Man from Margaree: Writings and Speeches of M. M. Coady,* ed. A. LAIDLAW, (Toronto 1971). D. C. MASTERS, *The Coming of Age, CBC International Service History of Canada,* v. 4 (Toronto 1967). H. MOL, *Faith and Fragility: Religion and Identity in Canada* (Burlington 1985). P. O'NEILL, *Upon This Rock: The Story of the Roman Catholic Church in Newfoundland and Labrador* (St. John's 1984). E. F. SHERIDAN, *Do Justice: The Social Teaching of the Canadian Catholic Bishops (1945–1986)* (Sherbrooke 1987). L. K. SHOOK, *Catholic Post-Secondary Education in English-speaking Canada: A History* (Toronto 1971). N. VOISINE and R. CHOQUETTE, "Catholicism," *Canadian Encyclopedia* (Edmonton 1985). J. R. WILLIAMS, *Canadian Churches and Social Justice* (Toronto 1984).

[M. W. HIGGINS/EDS.]

CANADELL QUINTANA, ENRIQUE, BL.

Martyr, religious of the Order of Poor Clerics Regular of the Mother of God of the Pious Schools (Piarists); b. June 29, 1890, Olat, Gerona, Spain; d. in the night Aug. 17–18, 1936. Enrique was a Piarist from the community of Our Lady of Barcelona, who was especially devoted to the Real Presence in the Eucharist. At the start of the Revolution, he fled to his sister's house in Olat. There he spent his days reading and praying. On the night of Aug. 17 some soldiers arrived, arrested him, and took him away in a car. During the journey, the soldiers cruelly beat him with their rifle butts. About ten kilometers down the road, they stopped the car, ordered him out, and shot him near Castelfullit. He was beatified on Oct. 1, 1995 by Pope John Paul II together with 12 other Piarists (*see* PAMPLONA, DIONISIO AND COMPANIONS, BB.).

Feast: Sept. 22.

Bibliography: "Decreto Super Martyrio," *Acta Apostolicae Sedis* (1995): 651–656. *La Documentation Catholique* 2125 (Nov. 5, 1995): 924.

[L. GENDERNALIK/EDS.]

CANAL, JOSÉ DE LA

Historian and apologist; b. Uciedo, Spain, Jan. 11, 1768; d. Madrid, April 17, 1845. He became an Augustinian in 1785 and a priest in 1792. He taught philosophy at Burgos, Salamanca, Toledo, and Madrid. When religious houses in Spain were dissolved in 1809 under the French, he translated several French works in defense of the Church. He was attacked for some of them, replied in 1814, and was confined in a monastery at Ávila for a year. He was released by Ferdinand VII and appointed, with Antolin Merino, to continue the *España Sagrada*, v. 43–44 (*see* FLÓREZ, ENRIQUE). In volumes 45 to 47 Canal treated the dioceses of Gerona and Lérida. He wrote a number of religious works and was director of the Real Academia de la Historia until his death.

Bibliography: G. DE SANTIAGO VELA, *Ensayo de una bibliotecaibero-americana de la Orden de San Agustín,* 7 v. in 8 (Madrid 1913–31) 1:570–595. A. C. VEGA *La España sagrada y los Agustinos en la Real Academia de la historia* (El Escorial 1950). A. ORTIZ, *Dictionnaire d'histoire et de géographie ecclésiastiques* 11:698–700. R. BÄUMER, *Lexikon für Theologie und Kirche* (Freiburg 1957–65) 2:913.

[F. ROTH]

CAÑAS Y CALVO, BLAS

Chilean founder of homes for children; b. Santiago, Feb. 3, 1827; d. there, March 23, 1886. He was the son of José Antonio Cañas and Mercedes Calvo and came from a family that had many priests, among them the first Chilean archbishop, Manuel Vicuña, who baptized him. In 1836 he entered the seminary in Santiago, where he was a brilliant and pious student. He was ordained Sept. 22, 1849. Subsequently, he was professor at the seminary, joining the faculty of theology in 1859. He preached in the capital in a powerful but simple style, dogmatic yet evangelical. He served as a chaplain for nuns and held several other minor ecclesiastical positions. He acquired a reputation for sanctity and was known for his great love for the poor. On Aug. 15, 1856, he founded La Casa de María, a place of asylum and education for girls of poor families, and established a congregation of nuns to run it. A pontifical congregation since 1941, this group had 50 nuns in 1964 and conducted similar houses in Santiago, Valparaíso, and Mendoza (Argentina). In 1872 he founded a similar institution for boys, Patrocinio de San

José, which is now under the care of the Salesians. Cañas y Calvo was expert in obtaining alms for his houses; his humility elicited them even from non-Christians. He shunned honors, and against his will the government presented his name to Rome for the bishopric of Concepciín. However, he died before any appointment was made.

Bibliography: C. FERNÁNDEZ FREITE, *Don Blas Cañas el Vicente de Paul chileno* (Santiago 1936). M. A. ROMÁN, *Vida del señor D. Blas Cañas* (Santiago 1887).

[F. ARANEDA BRAVO]

CANDIDO, VINCENZO

Moral theologian; b. Syracuse, Sicily, 1572 or 1573; d. Rome, Nov. 7, 1654. He became a Dominican at Rome in 1593. Owing to his piety and prudence, he was elected provincial of the Sicilian Province in 1609 and of the Roman Province in 1633. Three times he was prior of the Minerva; twice (1642, 1649), vicar-general of the Order; and intermittently from 1617 to 1642, penitentiary at St. Mary Major. In 1645 Innocent X appointed him Master of the Sacred Palace. His theological opinions expressed about Jansenism and those in his *Illustriorum disquisitionum moralium* (1637–43) have often been classed as laxist (*see* LAXISM).

Bibliography: I. TAURISANO, *Hierarchia Ordinis Praedicatorum* (Rome 1916) 57–58. P. MANDONNET, *Dictionnaire de théologie catholique* (Paris 1903–50) 2.2:1506.

[J. A. FARREN]

CANDIDUS OF FULDA (BRUUN)

Hagiographer, theologian; d. Fulda 845. He entered Fulda under its second abbot, Baugulf (779–802), and was sent by Abbot Ratgar (802–817) for literary and artistic study under EINHARD. He was ordained after his return, but seems to have played no part in the canonical deposition of Ratgar. He enjoyed the confidence of Abbot Eigil (818–822) who assigned him to paint the apse of the new basilica, where the remains of St. Boniface were placed. Bruun was a teacher, but it is not certain that he became head of the monastery school after RABANUS MAURUS was elected abbot (822–842). His chief literary work was a *Life of St. Eigil* in two books, one in prose (*Monumenta Germaniae Historica: Scriptores* 15:221–33) and one in verse (*Monumenta Germaniae Historica: Poetae* 2:96–117). The work, written *c.* 840 with the encouragement of Rabanus, is valuable for the internal history of Fulda. A life of Baugulf, suggested by Eigil, if actually written, remains unknown.

It is another "Candidus," Wizo, the Anglo-Saxon disciple and confidant of ALCUIN who is almost certainly the author of the first section, *De imagine Dei,* of the *Dicta Candidi (Monumenta Germaniae Historica: Epistolae* 5:615), long attributed to Bruun. This section, on man's soul as bearing the image of the Trinity, was taken in part from the *Libellus de dignitate conditionis humanae,* Ch. 2. The rest of the passage is that which is known also as the *Dicta* of Alcuin. Unfortunately, the origin of the *Libellus de dignitate* itself is obscure; but since it was already quoted as a supposed work of St. Ambrose *c.* 790, it is strongly suggested that both parts of Wizo's passage, *De imagine Dei,* are excerpts from this earlier *Libellus.* When B. Hauréau published the *Dicta Candidi* [*Histoire de la philosophie scolastique* (Paris 1872) 1:134–137], he included 11 other items along with the above section, treating all 12 entries as a single treatise; hence, the rise of the misnomer *XII Dicta Candidi.* Special interest has centered on No. XII as an early example of rational argument for the existence of God. However, the actual provenance of these 11 items must still be explored before their place in the history of early medieval speculation and scholastic method can properly be assessed. Like the first *Dicta* of Wizo, with which they appear as anonymous items in the earliest MS tradition, these last 11 dicta undoubtedly belong to a period before 800 A.D.

There is an *Opusculum de passione Domini* (*Patrologia Latina* 106:57–104), a series of Holy Week homilies for a monastic community, and a letter entitled "Whether Christ Could See God with His Bodily Eyes" (*Monumenta Germaniae Historica: Epistolae* 4:557–561) that are both by the same author; but critical opinion is divided as to which "Candidus" it is.

Bibliography: M. MANITIUS, *Geschichte der lateinischen Literatur des Mittelalters* (Munich 1911–31) 1:660–663. F. ZIMMERMANN, "Candidus . . . Geschichte der Frühscholastik," *Divus Thomas* (Fribourg 1914–54) 7 (1929) 30–60. H. LÖWE, "Zur Geschichte Wizos," *Deutsches Archiv für Erforschung des Mittelalters* 6 (1943) 363–373. P. SCHMITZ, *Histoire de l'ordre de saint Benoît* (Maredsous 1942) 2:109–110. W. WATTENBACH, *Deutschlands Geschichtsquellen im Mittelalter* (Weiman 1952–63) 233. S. HILPISCH, *Lexikon für Theologie und Kirche* (Freiburg 1957–65) 2:736.

[J. J. RYAN]

CANDLEMAS

Medieval English word formerly used to designate the Feast of the Presentation of the Lord, on which day candles are blessed. The name itself captured the lighting of candles during Mass to mark the light of Christ coming to the world. Marked for most of Christian history on

Woman praying during a Candlemas service at Westminster Cathedral. (©Hulton-Deutsch Collection/CORBIS)

February 2, the narrative of the presentation of the Lord (Lk 2:22–38) was earlier proclaimed on February 14. Before Rome's nativity date, December 25, was widely received, the celebration of the birth was observed in Eastern churches as one of a few manifestations on the feast of Epiphany, then January 6. The two dates for Candlemas, earlier February 14 and later February 2, were derived from the 40-day span between the nativity of Jesus and the feast of his parents' presentation of him in the Temple. (February 14 marked the forty days between Epiphany and the presentation feast; February 2 marks the same span between Christmas and the presentation.)

The 40-day span between the two is itself based on a wedding of an Old Testament law and a New Testament narrative. The Book of Leviticus (12:2–8) prescribes that "a woman who gives birth to a male child is unclean for seven days and is to remain in the blood of her purification for 33 days." The total, 40 days, is the chronology that is applied to the Lukan narrative of Mary presenting the child Jesus in the Temple. In the Gospel of Luke the themes of purification of Mary and presentation of Christ are presented along with Simeon's "meeting" Christ and his oracle foreseeing suffering in Christ's life (Lk 2:22–40).

Origins. The earliest evidence comes from the late fourth-century travel-diary of the pilgrim Egeria, who testified from Jerusalem:

Note that the fortieth day after Epiphany is observed here with special magnificence. On that day they assemble at the place of the resurrection (the "Anastasis"). Everyone gathers, and things are done with the same solemnity as at the feast of Easter. All the presbyters preach first, then the bishop, and they interpret the passage from the Gospel about Joseph and Mary taking the Lord to the Temple, and about Simeon and the prophetess Anna, daughter of Phanuel, seeing the Lord, and about the sacrifice offered by his parents. When all the rest is done in the proper way, they celebrate the sacrament and have their dismissal (chapter 26).

The original Eastern provenance is further supported by the reception of the Greek name for the feast, *hypapante kuriou*, meaning "meeting of the Lord," in the earliest Latin sources. Later this was rendered into Latin words as *occursus domini*, referring to the meeting of the infant Lord with Simeon and Anna. It took centuries before the feast was received throughout the Western churches.

Customs. In the West, the feast and its procession spread gradually, acquiring candle-blessing prayers in the ninth century, and blessing and distribution of candles with the procession in the tenth. The liturgical sources indicate there was great variety in the way the feast was celebrated. In general, there is a shift in emphasis of the feast, from the presentation of the Lord to the purification of Mary. As the purification theme came to dominate, it acquired a more penitential emphasis in many places.

The reform of the calendar after Vatican II returned to the Christological emphasis of the feast, namely the Presentation of the Lord. It simplified the blessing and procession with candles, added a reading from the Letter to the Hebrews to the lectionary, and restored the full account of Lk 2:22–40, now including Anna.

Bibliography: K. STEVENSON, "Origins and Developments of Candlemas: A Struggle for Identity and Coherence?" *Time and Community,* ed. J. N. ALEXANDER (Washington, D.C. 1990) 43–76. G. MEALO, "Presentación del Señor," *Nuovo dizionario di mariologia* (Turin 1985) 1654–62. H. URS VON BALTHASAR, *The Threefold Garland: The World's Salvation in Mary's Prayer* (San Francisco 1982) 51–57.

[M. F. CONNELL]

CANDLES

Candles were used by the Romans—not only for necessary lighting but also for veneration of the gods, of the dead, and of the emperor. From the earliest Christian times candles were used for the *Lucernarium* (the 2d-century ceremonial light for evening prayer, the ancestor of the paschal candle); borne in funeral processions; burned at the tombs of the dead, especially of the martyrs (from the 3d century); and lighted before relics of the saints and sacred images (4th–5th centuries). From the same period candles in great numbers were used to give splendor in churches and particularly around the high altar.

From the 7th century there is evidence of the use of candles at Mass. They were borne in procession to the altar, carried for the chanting of the Gospel, and placed around the altar. Only in the 11th century did they make their appearance *on* the altar table. From the early 17th century came legislation making obligatory the use of candles at Mass and determining their number. Under the 1917 *Code of Canon Law*, candles had to be of pure beeswax *saltem ex maxima parte* (reckoned as at least 65 percent) for the paschal candle and for Mass, and beeswax in "notable quantity" (reckoned as at least 25 percent) for all other candles burned *on* the altar. Because of local shortages a decree of the Congregation of Rites, given in December 1957, permitted the episcopal conference of any country to determine what was "a becoming part" of beeswax for altar candles if it was difficult to obtain. The previous legislation also prescribed that two candles were to be burned at low mass, six at solemn high mass, and seven for a festal pontifical mass. At solemn Mass two candles were borne in procession and for the chanting of the Gospel, and two or more were carried as torches for the Consecration. Two candles were also lighted on the altar whenever the Blessed Sacrament is taken from the tabernacle; if it was solemnly exposed 20, or at least 12, were used. These provisions are no longer mandated under the present 1983 *Code of Canon Law*.

A blessing has been in use for candles since the 15th century. There is no obligation to bless candles for liturgical use except the paschal candle and the candles used for the liturgy of CANDLEMAS (Feast of the Presentation of the Lord; February 2).

Bibliography: J. B. O'CONNELL, *Church Building and Furnishing* (Notre Dame, Ind. 1955) 208–210. J. P. BEAL, et al., eds., *New Commentary on the Code of Canon Law* (New York 2000).

[J. B. O'CONNELL/EDS.]

CANISIUS, PETER, ST.

Jesuit theologian, writer, apostle, and Doctor of the Church (in the vernacular more properly Kanijs, not de Hondt); b. Nijmegen, Netherlands, May 8, 1521; d. Fribourg, Switzerland, December 21, 1597.

Canisius was born of an aristocratic family of Nijmegen, which belonged to the duchy of Gelderland and was thus at the time still subject to the constitution of the German Empire. His father, a graduate of the University of Paris, became the instructor of the princes in the court of the Duke of Lorraine and was nine times appointed mayor of his native town. Against the will of his father, Canisius chose to take up the study of theology. In Cologne (1536–46, except for the years 1539–40, which he spent in Louvain) he became closely acquainted with a circle of learned and devout priests who labored to effect

Lit candles flickering inside the Cathedral of the Immaculate Conception, Castries, St. Lucia, Windward Islands, West Indies. (©Tony Arruza/CORBIS)

a reform within the Church and who were influenced by the spirit of German mysticism and of the DEVOTIO MODERNA, especially of Nikolaus van Esche, and Gerard Kalckbrenner and Johannes Justus LANSPERGIUS, prior and subprior respectively of the Carthusians of St. Barbara. Canisius' career as a writer, which won him the honor of being one of the creators of a Catholic press and the first of the literary Jesuits, began early. The Cologne 1543 edition of Tauler, edited by ''Petrus Noviomagnus,'' was attributed to Canisius by Braunsberger and Tesser, but this is open to doubt (according to Streicher and Brodrick). However, Canisius is certainly the author of the two-volume edition of the ''Fathers of the Church,'' (Cologne 1546), which contains texts from Cyril of Alexandria and Leo I. This first work of Canisius is at the same time the first book ever published by a Jesuit.

In the meantime, after attending a retreat that (Bl.) Peter FABER, one of the first six companions of IGNATIUS LOYOLA, gave in Mainz in April and May 1543, Canisius joined the Society of Jesus, which had been confirmed by PAUL III in 1540. While in Cologne Canisius became the center of the first Jesuit foundation on German soil. In their controversy with the elector and archbishop, Hermann von Wied, who was inclined to Protestantism, Canisius was chosen to be spokesman for the Catholic clergy and the citizens; and, in 1545, he was called upon three times to represent the rights of the city of Cologne before Emperor Charles V. On one of these occasions Canisius attracted the attention of Cardinal Otto Truchsess of Waldburg, Bishop of Augsburg, and was called by him to the Council of TRENT as his theological consultant. When the council moved to Bologna, Canisius went with it. In September 1547, Ignatius Loyola summoned him to Rome. Canisius was sent to Messina where he taught in the first Jesuit School from spring 1548 to July 1549. Recalled to Rome, he made his solemn profession on September 4, 1549, thus becoming the eighth Jesuit to be professed.

Canisius was called the "Second Apostle of Germany after Boniface" by Leo XIII. It was during the three decades following his return to Germany after his profession that he labored for the reestablishment of the Catholic Church in Germany, which had been greatly shaken by the Reformation. He sought to restore and renew the Catholic faith by teaching and preaching, especially in Ingolstadt, Vienna, Augsburg, Innsbruck, and Munich. He exercised great influence upon the whole ecclesiastical situation in Germany, which grew continuously more favorable owing to his activity.

In June 1556 Canisius was appointed by Ignatius Loyola to be the first superior of the German Province of the Society; in 1562, the Austrian section was separated to form the Austrian Province, but Canisius continued as provincial in South Germany (except for two short interruptions) until 1569. The development of the three already existing colleges of Ingolstadt, Vienna, and Prague was due largely to him, as was also the establishment of new ones in Munich, Innsbruck, Dillingen, Tyrnau, Hall (Tyrol). He also took a leading part in the founding of several Jesuit colleges in the North German Province.

In spite of difficulties and misunderstandings Canisius remained faithful to the society during his life. The contrary opinion of Protestant biographers lacks historical justification and is in contradiction to the evidence.

His personal reputation contributed much to attract new vocations from the native population to religious life in the society. By developing the organization of the Jesuits, Canisius created the necessary basis for a permanent and regular apostolate through which the Society of Jesus in Germany became an important and leading force in the Counter Reformation.

Canisius' influence on the hierarchy and on the general situation of the Church became more and more important. He was in contact with almost all the Catholic leaders of his time and aided in the awakening of a new self-assurance among the German Catholics. Evidence of this is clear in the letters of the saint, of which about 1,400 are known, 1,310 of which have been published. Only a small number are private letters; most of them deal with reforms within the Church, with questions concerning Church government and religious life. He was the adviser of Emperor Ferdinand I (at whose personal wish Canisius was made administrator of the Diocese of Vienna, 1554–55), and of PIUS IV, PIUS V, and GREGORY XIII. He participated in the discussion between Catholic and Protestant divines at Worms (1557), aided in the solution of the crisis in the council (1562–63), and was consulted

PETRVS CANISIVS NEOMAGVS SOC.IESV THEOLÓGVS.

St. Peter Canisius, 17th-century engraving.

in the Reichstag Sessions (1566, 1576). Moreover, Canisius was the adviser of the nunciatures and the papal legates assigned to Germany. Several times the popes conferred special missions upon him. He came forth with numerous admonitions concerning Church reforms and severely criticized the attitude of a large part of the clergy in Germany, including the bishops. For the clergy he demanded better selection and education, and he advocated closer ties between Rome and the Church in Germany. The importance of his recommendations appeared in decisions later taken in Rome under Gregory XIII. The number of nunciatures was increased, papal seminaries were founded in Germany, and the Collegium Germanicum in Rome was enlarged and consolidated. Canisius' suggestion for the abolition of the privileges of the aristocracy with regard to elections to canonries and episcopates failed, however, due to the circumstances of the time.

Writings. Canisius exerted his widest and most permanent influence through his writings. Of primary importance are his catechisms, which appeared in three different forms. The *Summa Doctrinae Christianae,* first published anonymously in Vienna in 1555, contained 213 questions and answers, a number that increased to 223 in the post-Tridentine edition of 1566. It was intended to be a compendium for universities and graduating classes of

Jesuit schools. On the request of Canisius a collection of sources and texts to support the catechism was published in four volumes by Petrus BUSAEUS (de Buys), SJ, *Authoritatum sacrae Scripturae et Sanctorum Patrum, quae in Summa Doctrinae Christianae Doctoris Petri Canisii theologi S. I. citantur . . .* , pars 1, etc. (Cologne 1569–70). In 1556 at Ingolstadt, Canisius' short catechism was printed as a supplement of a Latin grammar, with the title *Summa doctrinae christianae per questiones tradita et ad captum rudiorum accomodata.* It asks 59 questions and gives short answers, thus representing a short summary of the Catholic doctrine intended for the use of the first religious instruction to children. The third edition, with the title *Catechismus Minor seu parvus Catechismus Catholicorum,* first printed in Vienna in 1558 or 1559, appeared in later editions also under the title *Catechismus Catholicus* or *Institutiones christianae pietatis.* It contains, besides a detailed calendar with feasts and saints, 124 questions and short answers, and was introduced into secondary schools as a textbook for religious instruction. All these editions have a certain common format in that they contain concise questions and answers. This method was not invented by Canisius but it was one to which he adhered strictly. Very often illustrations were added to the editions of the catechisms. The "Illustrated Catechism" (published by Christoph Plantin, Antwerp 1589) deserves special attention because of its excellent format.

Though Canisius made no claim to the originality of his ideas and was without literary ambition, his catechisms are his most ingenious achievement. In use throughout Europe and in mission countries, they went through 200 editions even during his lifetime, and were translated into many languages. Hundreds of editions were published from the 17th to the 19th centuries. The fact that until the 19th century the name "Canisius" in German was synonymous with "catechism" is proof of the popularity and importance of his catechetical work.

Moreover, there were exegetical, apologetic, ascetical, and hagiographical works, in which Canisius, obviously not gifted in speculative thought, nevertheless showed learning in the field of Holy Scripture and the writings of the Fathers of the Church.

Last Years. Misunderstandings arose between him and his successor, Paul Hoffaeus. According to reports of Canisius' stepbrother Theodore and others, Canisius' insistence upon extreme accuracy, his tendency to perfectionism, and his careful attention to completeness of documentation seemed to Hoffaeus to lay too heavy a burden upon the province. Hoffaeus therefore reported the case to Rome, hoping to have Canisius relieved of the responsibility of continuing his writing against the CENTURIA-

TORS OF MAGDEBURG, with which he had been charged by Pius V. This was done in 1578. Further misunderstandings arose about lending money at interest, which was a very controversial issue at that time: Hoffaeus favored the licitness of taking interest under the so-called *contractus germanicus.* Canisius did not, and his opposition led to his transfer to Fribourg, Switzerland, where the task of the development of the newly erected college was assigned to him. He gathered the funds, selected the site, and superintended the erection of a college. His main work in Fribourg was preaching, though he continued writing until his death.

The "Spiritual Testament" written during the last years of his life at the end of his "Spiritual Diary," although surviving only in fragments, shows features characteristic of Canisius.

He was indefatigable, strong in faith and in his attitude toward the pope and the Church. Nevertheless he was fully aware of the shortcomings in the lives of ecclesiastics of his time, and he criticized them with a severity and a frankness nearly unprecedented. In his writings one finds such characteristic statements as "Peter sleeps, but Judas is awake." The worship of relics, the doctrine of indulgences, pilgrimages, and the cult of the saints were subject to distortion and abuse, and the awareness of this spurred Canisius continually to do what he could to correct it. Canisius never showed signs of despair or even of discouragement. On the contrary, he encouraged the timid. The secret of his confidence in God was his imperturbable faith of which the following passage of a letter (written in March or April 1561) may be quoted as an example: "The fear of many people is greater than necessary, because they look for human and not for divine help; they act in despair instead of praying with holy confidence for the oppressed Church." Judging from the fragments of his diary, he lived in constant union with God, and this influenced and connected his multiple activities. His religious life was according to the pattern of Christian humanism as this was practiced in his native country. The influence of the Devotio Moderna is discernible to him. His knowledge of Holy Scripture and of the Fathers of the Church was profound. He enjoyed certain privileges of a mystical kind. Although he was often maliciously defamed and vituperated by his adversaries, his language, severe though it appears to us, was remarkably mild when compared to the asperity common in controversy of his time, and he tried also to have his friends use moderation. He clarified the distinction between culpable apostasy and a mere matter-of-fact separation from the Church that did not, in his opinion, necessarily imply fault. When in Rome, Canisius emphasized his conviction that there was no question of formal apostasy in the case of many Protestants. He refused to accept the new

scientific principles of humanism. As is apparent from his hagiographic and historical writings, he lacked the competence of a critical observer of history. This uncritical attitude, furthermore, is to be seen very often in his manner of dealing with cases of personal revelation, obsession, and sorcery. He was intransigent in his views regarding the lawfulness of taking interest for loans; he did not take the changing circumstances of the times sufficiently into account. Nevertheless, these shortcomings do not diminish the importance of his versatile genius for the Church in Germany. His historical greatness lies in the fact that he was entirely aware of the tasks of his time, and with indefatigable zeal he sought to cope with them, devoting his entire life to the work without thought of personal advantage or self-interest.

Soon after his death the veneration of the first German Jesuit began within the German Jesuit provinces, in Switzerland, in the Tyrol, and in South Germany, and it was principally through his catechisms that he remained in the memory of the people. In 1614 the first biography was published by Matthaeus Rader, followed in 1616 by F. Sacchini's, which was appreciated even by L. Ranke. The process of beatification started soon after the publication of these biographies but was interrupted by the suppression of the Jesuit Order. Canisius was beatified in 1864 and canonized by Pius XI in 1925, when he was also declared a Doctor of the Church, an honor that emphasized the importance of his catechisms. He is buried in St. Michael's Church in Fribourg.

Feast: April 27.

Bibliography: *B. Petri Canisii epistulae et acta,* ed. O. BRAUNSBERGER, 8 v. (Freiburg 1896–1923); *S. Petri Canisii catechismi latini et germanici,* ed. F. STREICHER, 2 v. (Rome 1933–36). *Petrus Canisius: Reformer der Kirche,* ed. J. OSWALD and P. RUMMEL (Augsburg 1996). *Petrus Canisius, SJ: Humanist und Europäer,* ed. R. BERNDT (Berlin 2000). C. SOMMERVOGEL et al., *Bibliothèque de la Compagnie de Jésus,* 11 v. (Brussels–Paris 1890–1932; v. 12, suppl. 1960) 2:617–688; 8:1974–83; 12:988. J. BRODRICK, *St. Peter Canisius: 1521–97* (Baltimore 1950; Chicago 1998). K. DIEZ, *Christus und seine Kirche* (Paderborn 1987). J. H. M. TESSER, *Petrus Canisius als humanistisch geleerde* (Amsterdam 1932). F. STREICHER, ''De spirituali quodam libro diurno S. Petri Canisii,'' *Archivum historicum Societatis Jesu* 2 (1933) 56–63. B. SCHNEIDER, ''Petrus Canisius und Paulus Hoffaeus,'' *Zeitschrift fü katholische Theologie* 79 (1957) 304–330. A. DE PELSEMACHER, ''St. Pierre Canisius: La Spiritualité d'un apôtre,'' *Revue d'ascétique et de mystique* 35 (1959) 167–193. J. LECLER, ''Die Kirchenfrömmigkeit des hl. Petrus Canisius,'' *Sentire Ecclesiam,* ed. J. DANIÉLOU and H. VORGRIMLER (Freiburg 1961) 304–314.

[B. SCHNEIDER]

CANO, MELCHIOR

Spanish Dominican and theologian; b. Tarancón (Cuenca), Jan. 6, 1509; d. Toledo, Sept. 30, 1560. His *De*

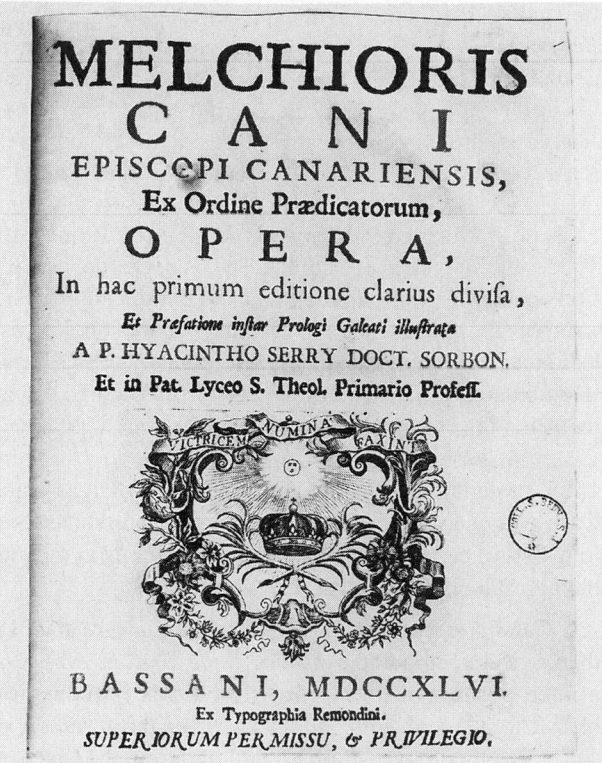

Title page from Collected Works, 1746, by Melchior Cano.

locis theologicis entitles him to be regarded as the founder of modern FUNDAMENTAL THEOLOGY. After entering the DOMINICANS in 1523, he studied from 1527 to 1531 under Francisco de VITORIA at SALAMANCA. Cano always remained grateful to his old master, who inspired him to attempt a new, methodical treatment of theology based on the sources and expressed in literary language.

In 1533 his brilliant but stormy career began with his appointment as a lecturer in philosophy at the Dominican College of St. Gregory in Valladolid. There too he obtained the second chair in theology in 1536, having for his senior colleague Bartolomé de CARRANZA. From this period dates the rivalry between these two utterly incompatible characters, which ended only with Cano's death. His outstanding ability won for him the principal professorship of theology at the University of ALCALÁ in 1542 and the succession to De Vitoria at Salamanca in 1546. Two of his courses from this period (1546–52), the *Relectio de sacramentis in genere* and the *Relectio de paenitentia,* were printed in 1550. His reputation as a theologian was enhanced during his attendance (1551–52) at the Council of TRENT as theologian of the Emperor CHARLES V. He was rewarded with the bishopric of the Canary Islands, but he did not take up residence and resigned the see in 1554. He then became involved in the religious politics of the Spanish court, and his impetuous disposi-

tion gained him many enemies. As the theological adviser of PHILIP II in his dispute with Pope PAUL IV, he fell into deep disfavor at Rome. Further causes of contention were his implacable hostility to the newly founded Society of Jesus and his campaign against the immunities and privileges of powerful cathedral chapters. Although twice (1557, 1559) elected provincial of the Castile Dominicans, he was denied confirmation in office by Rome until 1560, after the death of Paul IV. The leader of the opposition against him among the Spanish Dominicans was his old rival Carranza, since 1557 archbishop of Toledo. Less brilliant as a theologian and more tolerant of new currents in spirituality, Carranza differed also from Cano in his esteem for the JESUITS and papal theologians. Carranza's *Commentarios sobre el Catecismo Cristiano* (Antwerp 1588) brought him into conflict with the INQUISITION, and Cano was charged to examine the book. He produced two long lists of censured propositions. His attitude in this unhappy affair is still a matter of controversy.

Cano's epoch-making and influential treatise on theological method, the *De locis theologicis,* was first printed posthumously in 1563. Book 1 is introductory; bks. 2 to 11 deal with the authority of the ten *loci,* or sources of theology: Scripture, oral tradition, the Catholic Church, the councils, the Roman Church, Fathers, theologians, natural reason, philosophers, and human history. Book 12 treats of the use of the *loci* in scholastic disputation; bks. 13 and 14 were planned to discuss their use in the exposition of Scripture and in controversy with adversaries of the Catholic faith; these, however, were never written. The work is a skillful application to theology of the methodological principles expounded by Rodolphus Agricola in his *De inventione dialectica* (Cologne 1548).

Bibliography: The *De locis theologicis* has had about 30 editions, most recently in J. P. MIGNE, *Theologiae cursus completus,* 28 v. (Paris 1837–66) 1:58–716; since the Cologne edition of 1605 the two *Relectiones* have been included. F. A. CABALLERO, *Melchior Cano,* v.2. of his *Conquenses ilustres,* 4 v. (Madrid 1868–75). J. QUÉTIF and J. ÉCHARD, *Scriptores Ordinis Praedicatorum* (Paris 1719–23) 2.1:176–178. P. MANDONNET, *Dictionnaire de théologie catholique* 2.2:1537–1540. *Dictionnaire de théologie catholique,* Tables générales 513–514. A. LANG, *Die Loci Theologici des Melchior Cano und die Methode des dogmatischen Beweises* (Munich 1925); *Lexicon für Theologie und Kirche,* new eds. J. HOFER and K. RAHNER (Freiburg 1957–65) 2:918. E. MARCOTTE, *La Nature de la théologie d'après M. Cano* (Ottawa 1949). A. DUVAL, *Catholicisme* 2:465–467.

[F. COURTNEY]

CANON, BIBLICAL

1. Introduction

Understanding of the canon of Sacred Scripture in general requires clarification of the terminology used in this matter, the relationship between inspiration and canonicity, the criterion of the canon for the Catholic Church, and the criteria used in other Christian Churches.

Terminology. The Greek word κανών, from which the English word canon is a direct borrowing, signifies (1) a cane, a straight rod; (2) a measuring rod; and (3) a norm, a law. In the last sense the term is used for a law, or canon, of CANON LAW. In regard to the Bible the term was first used to designate the idea of the Sacred Scripture as the norm of true religion, but it was soon employed also in the sense of norm or list defining what books constitute the Sacred Scriptures. It is in the last sense that the term is used throughout this article. The Catholic canon of the Bible is the list of books that the Catholic Church officially declares to be inspired by God and presents as such to the faithful.

Disagreement on which books are inspired already existed among the early Jews; the Palestinian Jews accepted a shorter list than did the Alexandrian Jews. In the first Christian centuries those books that were recognized by all were called ὁμολογούμενοι, the books "agreed upon"; those not accepted by all were called ἀντιλεγόμενοι, "contradicted" or ἀμφιβαλλόμενοι, "doubtful." Since the 16th century the terms introduced by SIXTUS OF SIENA have superseded the old terms, so that the ὁμολογόνμενοι are now called protocanonical, and the ἀντιλεγόμενοι are called deuterocanonical. Catholics today accept both protocanonical and deuterocanonical books as inspired and part of the canon. Protestants generally reject the deuterocanonical books and call them apocryphal. Catholics reserve the term apocryphal for books other than the deuterocanonical books, e.g., the Gospel of James. This latter category of books, which Catholics call apocryphal, are called pseudepigraphical ("falsely titled") by Protestants.

Inspiration and Canonicity. All the books in the canon are inspired, but it is debated whether or not there is or could be any inspired book that, because of its loss, is not in the canon. The Church has not settled the question. The more general opinion is that some inspired books probably have been lost. In 1 Cor 5.9, St. Paul refers to a previous letter of his, and in 2 Cor 2.3–9; 7.8–12 he refers to an earlier letter different from 1 Corinthians. However, not all agree on these conclusions. In Col 4.16 Paul speaks of a letter that he wrote to the Laodiceans, which as such is not extant, although it may possibly be our Ephesians. The OT, too, mentions lost books, which may have been inspired (1 Chr 29.29; 2 Chr 9.29; 12.15).

Catholic Criterion of Canonicity. The problem of the criterion of the canon remains only partially solved. Catholics hold that the proximate and ultimate criterion is the infallible decision of the Church in listing its sacred

and canonical books. St. Augustine says (*C. epist. fund.* 5.5; *Corpus scriptorum ecclesiasticorum latinorum* 25:197): "I would not believe the Gospel, if the authority of the Catholic Church did not move me."

But the question remains: By what means did the Church determine the matter? The testimony of Christ and the Apostles, who cite the OT as a sacred work, is indicative of the inspiration of the books they cite. Their testimony may suffice for the entire OT, inasmuch as they often quote from the Septuagint (LXX), which contained both protocanonical and deuterocanonical books. Once the inspiration of 2 Peter is established, the fact that 2 Pt 3.16 refers to certain Pauline Epistles in conjunction with other Scriptures (i.e., the OT) suffices to show the inspiration of genuinely Pauline writings. Some hold that the Church in determining the canon preserves a revelation left by the Apostles on this matter. It is difficult to suppose, however, that the Apostles left behind an explicit tradition about the canon. The history of the canon shows too many doubts and fluctuations for this theory to be plausible.

M. J. Lagrange and S. Zarb hold that apostolic authorship suffices to establish inspiration for the NT, and prophetic authorship for the OT. In this case, although Mark and Luke were not Apostles, they wrote down the gospel as preached respectively by Peter and Paul, who thus became the ultimate authors of the second and third Gospels. Christ gave the Apostles a special understanding of the kingdom (Mk 4.11) and promised special guidance (Jn 14.16; 16.13) so that their word was received as the word of God (Lk 10.16; 1 Thes 2.13). Thus, although apostolicity and inspiration are not the same, yet, when the Apostles wrote, they were inspired. Tradition supports this theory. The MURATORIAN CANON excludes the Shepherd of HERMAS as not apostolic. St. Justin (*Apol.* 1.67; *Patrologia Graeca* 6.429) says the Gospels are "memoirs" of the Apostles. Origen (*Peri archon* 1.4; *Patrologia Graeca* 11:118) says: "It is manifestly preached in the churches . . . that that Spirit inspired each of the holy prophets and Apostles." St. Irenaeus (*Adv. haer.* 3.1.1; *Patrologia Graeca* 7:844) says of the Apostles: "They then preached it, but afterwards, by the will of God, handed it down to us in the Scriptures." Tertullian (*Adv. Marc.* 4.2.1; *Corpus Christianorum. Series latina* 1:547) says: "The evangelical instrument has the Apostles as authors, on whom this duty of promulgating the gospel was imposed by God Himself." St. Augustine (*C. adv. leg.* 1.20.39; *Patrologia Latina* 42:626) says that if the apocrypha attributed to Andrew and John "were really theirs, they would have been accepted by the Church."

Opponents of this view note that not all books of the OT are by prophets and say the patristic texts merely

Page from 12th-century Gelati Gospel, Museum of Fine Arts, Georgia. (©Dean Conger/CORBIS)

show that these books were traditionally accepted, but they do not make apostolicity a criterion. K. Rahner suggests that the NT is willed by God as a constituent element of the Church and is inspired in that sense and that the Church is able to recognize its own constituent elements. Although Y. M. J. Congar accepts this view in general, he objects that it minimizes the role of Apostles and prophets. He admits that inspiration was a grace of the primitive Church, but he holds that it was primarily a personal grace of the Apostles.

Protestant Criteria of Canonicity. Early Protestant attempts to solve the problem made the criteria subjective: Luther made the criterion consist in the intensity with which Christ is preached according to the principle of justification by faith alone, and therefore he excluded James from the canon. Others, especially Calvin, appealed to the interior testimony of God given to each reader, or to the edifying nature of the matter, or to its sublimity and simplicity.

More recent Protestant attempts have sought a more objective criterion. T. Zahn tried to explain the origin of the canon by saying that the early Christians used the present canonical books in public worship and eventually came to revere them as sacred. The liturgical reading of the words and acts of Jesus strengthened the religious life

Folio from a fragment of an Arabic Bible, 8th or 9th century (Cod. Vat. Arabic 13, fol. 73 v).

of the Assembly. To this one may object: why was canonical acceptance not given to works like the Shepherd of Hermas, or to the first Epistle of Clement (which also was read at public worship)? A. von Harnack suggested that all the men of the first generation had charisms, and so all that they wrote was considered inspired. The Roman Church, to defend itself against Montanists and other dissidents, in A.D. 180 drew up a closed list of inspired works. Against von Harnack's view is the objection that the Church never put charismatic utterances on the same plane as apostolic teaching. R. H. Grützmacher tries to find a middle way between the historical and authoritative approach. According to him, historical criticism chooses a number of books, as early as possible in origin, from which each Christian by an inner light chooses those on which to found his faith. The Church aids this choice, having worked on the canon for centuries and having settled on those books that experience shows useful for salvation. Another Protestant, G. B. Smith, concludes that only when one admits a divine authority in the Church

can there be an infallible canon. Liberal Protestants, because of a loose concept of inspiration, show little concern with the problem of the criterion of the canon.

Bibliography: H. OPPEL, KANΩN: *Zur Bedeutungsgeschichte des Wortes und seiner lateinischen Entsprechungen (regulanorma)* (Leipzig 1937). L. WENGER, ''Canon in den römischen Rechtsquellen und in den Papyri: Eine Wortstudie,'' *Sitzungsberichte der Akademie der Wissenschaften in Wien* 220.2 (1942). H. HÖPFL, *Dictionnaire de la Bible,* suppl. ed. L. PIROT, (Paris) 1:1022–45. S. ZARB, *De historia canonis utriusque testamenti* (2nd ed. Rome 1934). K. RAHNER, *Inspiration in the Bible,* tr. C. H. HENKEY (New York 1961). Y. M. J. CONGAR, ''Inspiration des écritures canoniques et apostolicité de l'Eglise,'' *Revue des sciences philosophiques et théologiques* 45 (1961) 32–42. G. B. SMITH, ''Can the Distinction between Canonical and Non-canonical Writings be Maintained?'' *Biblical World,* NS 37 (1911) 19–29. J. VAN DODEWAARD, *Encyclopedic Dictionary of the Bible,*tr. and adap. by L. HARTMAN (New York 1963) 308–314. T. VON ZAHN, *Geschichte des neutestamentlichen Kanons,* 2 v. (Erlangen 1888–92) 1:83; *Einige Bemerkungen zu A. Harnacks Prüfung der Geschichte des neutestamentlichen Kanons* (Leipzig 1889). A. VON HARNACK, *Die Entstehung des Neuen Testaments und die wichtigsten Folgen der neuen Schöpfung* (Beiträge zur Einleitung in das N.T. 6; Leipzig 1914). R. H. GRÜTZMACHER, *Die Haltbarkeit des Kanonbegriffes: Theologische Studien Th. Zahn dargebracht* (Leipzig 1900).

[W. G. MOST]

2. History of Old Testament Canon

The broad phases of this topic can best be treated by a consideration of the history of the development of the OT canon among the Jews and then treating of the history of this canon in the Christian Church. The particular treatment of each of these is noted below.

CANON OF THE OLD TESTAMENT AMONG THE JEWS

In the development of the OT canon among the Jews, note should be taken of the early stages in the formation of the three parts of the Hebrew canon, of the motives for the canonization of the sacred books, of the formal closing of the canon, and of the collections of the sacred books among the Jews of the Diaspora and among the Jewish sectaries at Qumran.

Early Formation. The formation of the OT books themselves is a matter distinct from the formation of the OT canon. The former was the material growth of the OT, book by book; the latter was the origin and development of the special attitudes toward these books that saw in them works inspired by God. These two aspects of the story of the OT are so closely akin that they tend to fuse with one another in any discussion of the development of the OT. There is, nevertheless, a true distinction between them, and it is useful to take note of it at the very outset.

The first clear harbinger of Jewish convictions toward the canon of Scripture is met with in Josephus (*Con-*

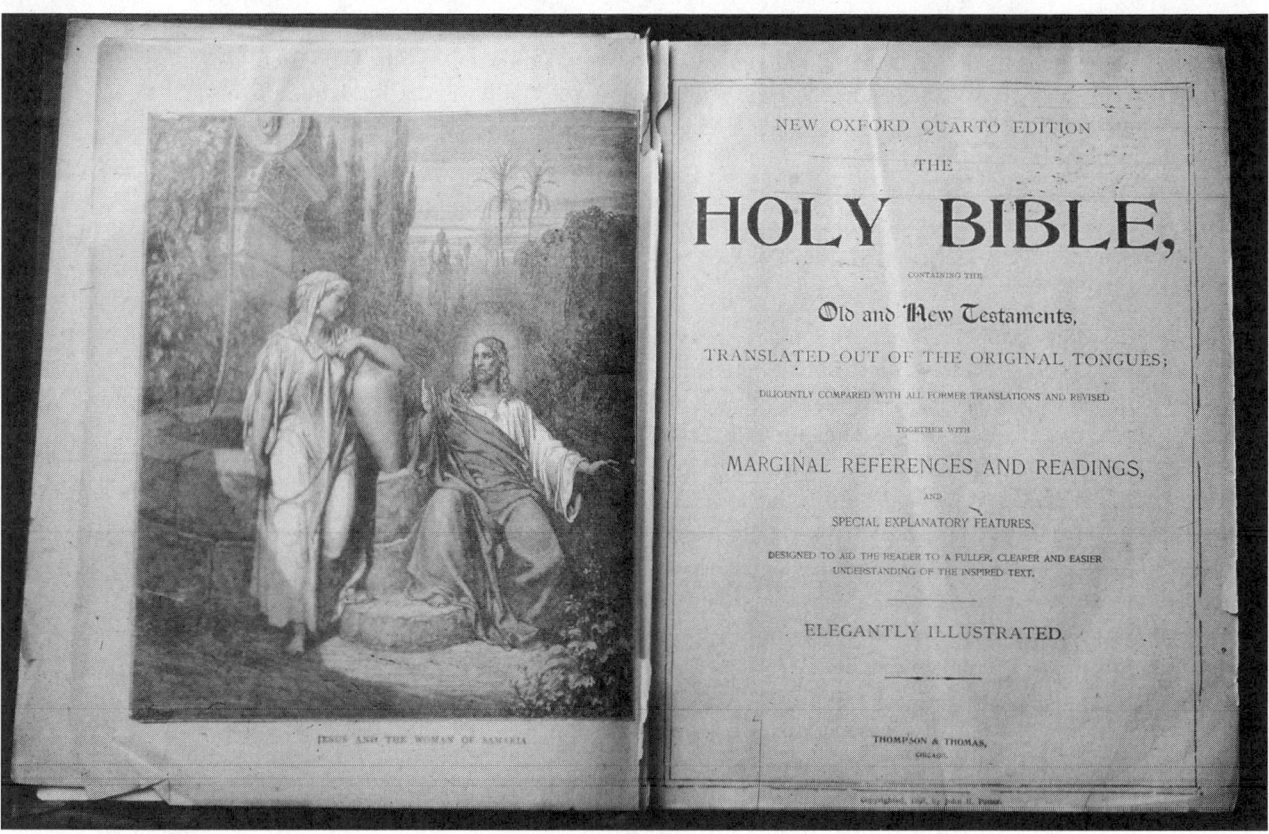

Bible, open to an illustration of "Jesus and the Woman of Samaria."

tra Apion 1.38–42). He held the hallmarks of the canonical books to be: that their number is fixed, that they are sacred and as such are to be distinguished from all other books, that they are of divine origin and therefore enjoy supreme authority, and that they were written in the span of time between Moses and Artaxerxes I. On this last point Josephus was obviously mistaken, because several of the OT books were demonstrably written after the time of Artaxerxes I (d. 423 B.C.).

The Hebrew collection of sacred books evolved over several centuries. Of this historical process there is not very much definite information at hand. Some have supposed that the threefold division of the Hebrew canon into the Law, the Prophets, and the Writings really marks three stages in the development of the collection. According to this view, the first canon was the Law, the second the Prophets, and the third the Writings. There is another point of view favored by Hölscher that sees the Law, the Prophets, and the Writings growing more or less concurrently, with no fixation of the three sections being effected separately at different times. The determination would have been made for the tripartite whole at one time.

The Law. In 2 Kgs 22.8 it is reported that the high priest Helcia (*c.* 621 B.C.) discovered the book of the Law

in the Temple. This was probably the nucleus of Deuteronomy as it is now known (Dt ch. 12–26). It was recognized as divinely authoritative, for it was taken as the foundation of a fresh dedication of the people to God (2 Kgs 23.1–14). The growth of the Torah entered upon a new stage with the arrival of Ezra in Jerusalem *c.* 397 B.C. He promulgated a book of law that is identified by some with the Priestly Code. It agrees with the latter in requiring that the Feast of Booths (Tabernacles) be celebrated for eight days, rather than seven as prescribed by Deuteronomy (Dt 16.13).

Frequently the Samaritan schism is introduced as a help in fixing the dates of the Pentateuch. The argument runs thus: The SAMARITANS have a Pentateuch that agrees in substance with that of the Hebrews. The Pentateuch must have achieved its final form and have been acknowledged as inspired at some time before the Samaritan break with the Jews, since it is unlikely that the Samaritans would have taken anything from the Jewish community after they separated from it. The difficulty comes, however, in ascertaining the dates of the Samaritan breach from the available data. The probable conclusion is that the Pentateuch was a complete collection received as inspired at least by the middle of the 4th century B.C., when it is estimated the Samaritan schism took place.

The Prophets. Around the Law as center there soon began to cluster other books that were held in veneration by the people. The Former Prophets, as the Hebrews referred to the books of Joshua, Judges, Samuel, and Kings, are known to have been grouped together with the five books of the Law from as early as the mid-4th century B.C. The fact that they were associated in this fashion with the Torah seems to indicate that in the minds of the people these books too were sacred.

As to the Latter Prophets, Isaiah, Jeremiah, Ezekiel, and the Twelve (Minor Prophets), these books were being produced since the 8th century B.C. Eventually they were brought together in a collection. A letter reproduced in 2 Mc 1.10–2.18 speaks of the formation of a library containing, among others, prophetical books (2 Mc 2.13). Nehemiah (*c.* 425 B.C.; Neh 13.6–7) is credited with founding this library. Some understand its establishment as marking an early stage in the collection of prophetical books that were accepted as inspired. Even if all credit is denied to this letter, it is justifiable to conclude that, at the time when 2 Maccabees was written, the Prophets were known as a collection of sacred books. In Sirach (Ecclesiasticus) Ben Sirach (*c.* 180 B.C.) alludes to the books of the Twelve Prophets besides the three great Prophets (Sir 48.22; 49.7–10). He appears to know the Prophets as a collection. Daniel (167–164 B.C.) makes mention of "the books" and then cites from Jeremiah (Dn 9.2). This can be taken as an oblique testimony to the author's acceptance of Jeremiah's work as inspired. It seems, therefore, safe to conclude that, at least by the beginning of the 2nd century B.C., the Prophets were received as an inspired collection.

The Writings. In the preface, which is usually not considered canonical, to the Greek translation of Sirach there are allusions that imply the existence of the Writings as a collection. These references date from the time when Sirach was translated into Greek (*c.* 132 B.C.). The translator speaks of "the Law and the Prophets and the later authors," and of "the Law itself, the Prophets and the rest of the books." It appears from this that the third division of the canon was only falling into place at the time, since it had not yet been named. From these words in the preface to Sirach it is obviously not possible to establish the precise number of books or which ones were contained in the collection.

By the beginning of the Christian Era the third group was definitely recognized as inspired, since certain passages in the NT presuppose the Writings as part of the OT by that time. In Lk 24.44, for example, Christ speaks of what is written in "the Law of Moses, the Prophets and the Psalms" as having to come true. The sacred character of these books is obviously assumed. Though some are

dubious about understanding the term in this way, it is very probable that the whole collection of the Writings is referred to under the name of the first book in it, the Psalms.

Josephus, writing at the end of the 1st Christian century, alludes to an OT canon that included the Writings (*Contra Apion* 1.38–42). Philo too is familiar with the tripartite division of Scripture (*De Vita Contempl.* 25). There is an explicit reference to the Writings in the Talmud (*Baba Bathra* 14b–15a). Though this would have been written down only after A.D. 200, it probably stems from an earlier tradition.

The Writings do not seem to have been accepted as readily as the Law or the Prophets. Perhaps this is to be explained in terms of the liturgical usage noted below. Though gradually both the Prophets and the Writings found a place in the Hebrew canon, neither of these two was considered to enjoy the same importance as the Law.

Motive for Canonization. The formation of the OT as sketched above marks the stages along the way to final canonization. Canonization in the strict sense came later and involved not only the acceptance of some books but also the exclusion of others. There is no general agreement among scholars about the motives that impelled the Jewish community to accept the OT books as canonical. Some have supposed that certain books were received as canonical because of their legal character; they contain "the canons," the Law. Others maintain that it is an inspired quality of this literature that led to its canonization. These books were regarded as sacred because they contained the Word of God. Östborn's theory proposes that a book was held to be canonical if it had a specific motif, i.e., if in some way it celebrated or at least reported Yahweh's activity. This underlying idea endowed the book with a cultic value, so that it could be employed in the Jewish liturgy of the synagogue. A book in which Yahweh's activity was memorialized was held to be canonical, i.e., religiously right and suitable for worship. Östborn's hypothesis has not convinced many, because his endeavor to discover a fundamental theme throughout the whole OT is forced and open to question at several points.

Closing of Old Testament Canon. From the earliest times the people of Israel held certain writings in the highest regard as having originated from God. In Dt 31.26, for example, the Levites are enjoined to reserve the book of the Law beside the ark of the covenant. Although there are frequent references to the early collecting of books [Dt 31.9–13, 24–26; Jos 24.26; 1 Sm 10.25; 2 Chr 29.30; Ps 71(72).20; Prv 25.1], there is no explicit evidence of an official closing of the OT canon in pre-Christian times. The absence of such information has encouraged speculation. It was believed for a time that the collection of OT books was fixed conclusively by Ezra. The proponents of this theory relied largely on the apocryphal 4 Ezra 14.19–48, written *c.* A.D. 90, about 500 years after Ezra lived. But when carefully examined this passage does little more than ascribe to Ezra some role in the preservation of the OT texts. It does not unequivocally affirm that he was the final arbiter of the OT canon.

At another time it was believed that the OT canon was determined by Ezra together with his associates, "the men of the Great Synagogue." Elias Levita first suggested this in *Massoreth ha-Massoreth* (1538). The view was approved by Johannes Buxtorf the Elder in *Tiberias sive Commentarius Masorethicus* (Basel 1620). Buxtorf's endorsement helped the theory gain wide acceptance for a time. Brian Walton also wrote concerning the men of the Great Synagogue: "Their work of establishing the Canon possessed truly divine authority . . ." (*Polyglott. Proleg.* 4.2, London 1657).

The very existence of the Great Synagogue, to say nothing of its alleged canonizing function, is open to question. One grave objection to its existence is the complete silence about it in the OT itself, as well as in Josephus, Philo, and the Apocrypha. The earliest reference to such a group is in the Mishnaic treatise, *Pirke Avoth* (c.1), which dates only from the 2nd or 3rd Christian century.

The canon of the OT was not formally and authoritatively defined during the pre-Christian era. It was the threat of the Christian "heresy" with its wide diffusion of Christian writings that led Judaism to make certain decisions about its sacred canon. The books of the Law and the Prophets were exactly known, having been established as sacred by fairly long liturgical use. At least by the beginning of the Christian Era, lessons from the Law and the Prophets were read in the synagogue (Lk 4.16–19; Acts 13.15, 27). The Writings were credited also with a sacred quality. They were not, however, in general use in the synagogue, except for the Psalms. Thus the people could not have accepted from liturgical practice the books that were in the third part of the canon.

Other factors in the final settlement of the Jewish canon may have been the developing rivalry between Greek and Jewish culture and the rise and spread of apocalyptic literature. The influence both of Greek philosophy and of the proliferating Jewish apocalypses was viewed with alarm by Jewish religious leaders. They moved to neutralize this threat to the faith by establishing a collection of books that Jews could accept as authoritative. The decision taken at Jamnia (Jabneel) *c.* A.D. 100 by a Jewish synod was the issue of a longstanding discussion about which books, particularly among the Writings, belonged to the canon. Though the action of the synod was given as final and decisive, the canonicity of Esther, the Song of Songs, and Ecclesiastes continued to be doubted after Jamnia.

Alexandrian Canon. It is problematical whether one may speak of a LXX canon in the sense of a formally authorized list of books. There appears to be little warrant, direct or implied, for concluding that in the Jewish DIASPORA any authorized group ever independently took a stand on the canon. All too commonly it is assumed that great differences of opinion divided Palestinian Jews from those of the Dispersion and that the differences sprang from divergent theories of inspiration prevalent in Alexandria and Jerusalem. This is a purely gratuitous inference [see Peter Katz, *Zeitschrift für die neutestamentliche Wissenschaft und die Kunde der äteren Kirche* 47 (1956) 209]. The Hellenistic Jews before the fall of the theocracy in Palestine looked reverently toward Jerusalem and favored religious currents coming from it. Doubts were referred there for solution (Josephus, *Contra Apion* 1.30–36). They turned to Jerusalem for their Scriptures (2 Mc 2.13–15) and for its translation [Est 11.1 (Vulg); 10.31 (LXX)]. If they used the deuterocanonical books in the Diaspora, it was because they had received them from Palestine. Moreover, it is not patent that these books gained anything in transit, as though they came to enjoy a canonical status in Alexandria that they had never possessed in Palestine. Canonicity could not have been a problem at that time, for a rigid concept of it had not yet emerged. Palestine, then, was the source of the esteem for the deuterocanonical works. The OT, as it is found in the LXX, reflects, therefore, a tradition older than the present Hebrew Bible in regard to its list of sacred books.

Canon of the Qumran Community. The bearing of the writings of the QUMRAN COMMUNITY upon the question of the OT canon remains a matter for discussion. Although fragments of some of the deuterocanonical books (Tobit and Sirach) have been found among the DEAD SEA SCROLLS, not everyone thinks that this is sufficient evidence to establish their acceptance as canonical by the Qumran community. The Qumran scribes apparently adhered to a particular script and format in copying unquestioned canonical works; the deuterocanonical books did not receive this special treatment. This treatment of Biblical texts, however, was not invariable; and therefore hard and fast conclusions cannot be drawn from it.

One must keep in mind that the notion of a strict canon was not fully developed at this time. That the deuterocanonical books were copied at all at Qumran would indicate that the sectarians saw them as works of some special religious value. That they were not copied in the precise way as were the Law and the Prophets may merely point to the lesser degree of veneration in which they were held. The Qumran collection, then, was similar to the Greek collection. Neither was absolutely fixed, and both displayed considerable variation regarding their number and arrangement. Both reflected a tradition antedating the Masoretic canon and one less restrictive in recognizing books as sacred.

CANON OF THE OLD TESTAMENT AMONG CHRISTIANS

In the history of the OT canon among Christians, note should be taken of the use of the OT in the NT, of the attitude of the Fathers and writers in the Western Church until the Council of Trent, of the OT canon in the Eastern Churches, and of the divergences between the Catholic and the Protestant canons of the OT.

In the New Testament. An examination of the NT use of the OT shows that the NT writers had the same broad view of the sacred books as the Hellenist and Qumran Jews had of them. The NT writers knew and used a fuller collection that included the so-called deuterocanonical books. The OT of the early Church was not the Masoretic Text (MT), but the Septuagint (LXX), which contained the deuterocanonical as well as the protocanonical books. In the LXX the former were not, as in some later versions, relegated to a limbo of doubt by being grouped together in a place apart. Rather, they were interspersed throughout the whole OT and assigned to places where they seemed best to fit. For example, historical books such as 1 Esdras, Tobit, and Judith found their place following Chronicles and Nehemiah. Books of a poetical character such as Wisdom and Sirach followed Job, Canticles, Ecclesiastes, and Proverbs. This led to the acceptance of these books as an integral part of the OT used by the early Church in the West.

Canon of the Western Church. The consensus of the Church through the 2nd and 3rd centuries was favorable to the full OT catalogue. It is supported by Pope St. CLEMENT I, St. POLYCARP, the Shepherd of HERMAS, St. IRENAEUS, and TERTULLIAN, all of whom employ the deuterocanonical writings as Scripture.

Doubts began to develop in the East in the 4th century. These doubts seem to have emerged as an aftermath of the Christian polemic with the Jews. Since the Jews from the time of the Synod of Jamnia no longer recognized the deuterocanonical literature, it would have been futile for Christian apologists to make use of them. JUSTIN MARTYR says this expressly (*Dial. Tryphon*). These hesitations gradually evolved into misgivings about the canonicity itself of the books. Attitudes toward the canon through the next several centuries were marked by a curious discrepancy between statement and practice. Several writers express themselves in favor of the restricted He-

brew canon; yet, in practice, they freely employ the deuterocanonical books as Scripture. The people who lapsed into this ambiguity, again, did not have a clearly thought out concept of canonicity and consequently did not express themselves with precision. Though they seem to imply that the deuterocanonical works were of lesser authority than the protocanonical books, they nonetheless admit that they were received by the Church, and thus they implicitly attest to their authoritative status.

St. JEROME (A.D. 340–420) distinguished between ''canonical books'' and ''ecclesiastical books.'' The latter, he judged, were circulated by the Church as good ''spiritual reading,'' but were not recognized as authoritative Scripture. St. AUGUSTINE, however, did not recognize this distinction. He accepted all the books in the LXX as of equal value, noting that those designated as apocryphal by Jerome were of either unknown or obscure origin. Augustine's point of view prevailed and the deuterocanonical books remained in the Vulgate, the Latin version that received official standing at the Council of Trent.

The situation remained unclear in the ensuing centuries, although the tendency to accept the disputed books was becoming all the time more general. In spite of this trend some, e.g., John Damascene, Gregory the Great, Walafrid, Nicholas of Lyra and Tostado, continued to doubt the canonicity of the deuterocanonical books. St. THOMAS AQUINAS has for a long time been listed as a dissenter because of his supposed doubts about Wisdom and Sirach, but P. Synave has argued convincingly to clear him of this imputation [*Revue biblique* 21 (1924) 522–533]. The Council of Trent definitively settled the matter of the OT Canon. That this had not been done previously is apparent from the uncertainty that persisted up to the time of Trent.

Canon of the Oriental Church. The Syrian Church employed only the Hebrew canon in the Peshitta translation. Subsequently, under the influence of the LXX, it used a canon substantially the same as the LXX. The Nestorians, however, refrained from this adjustment.

M. Jugie has shown conclusively that from the earliest times through the Middle Ages there was general agreement in the Byzantine Church that the disputed books were canonical. The disputations between Latins and Greeks in the years following the breach show no disagreement centering on the OT canon. In presenting to the Greeks theological arguments that they should find relevant and decisive, the Council of Florence did not hesitate to make free use of texts from the deuterocanonical books to bolster the doctrines on purgatory and the FILIOQUE.

Only in the 17th century, because of Protestant influence, was the canonicity of the deuterocanonical books first seriously questioned in the Oriental Churches. Zachary Gerganos (1627), a Greek who had studied at Wittenberg, was the first to dissent from the traditional Byzantine teaching. Such views, aired by others in the East, drew the fire of significant persons both in the Slavic and Greek churches. In Russia, throughout the 18th century, opinion was fluid regarding the deuterocanonical works. Finally, in the 19th century Russian Orthodox theologians universally excluded them from the canon.

The misgivings about the traditional Greek canon in Russian Orthodoxy gradually filtered into the Greek Church, and traditional canonicity became an open question.

Divergences between Catholic and Protestant Canon. Differences between Catholic and Protestant views on the OT canon are the result of differing attitudes toward the deuterocanonical books. The Wyclif Bible (1382), under Jerome's influence, reproduced only the books found in the Hebrew canon. The Coverdale Bible (1535) included the deuterocanonical works. Luther's translation (1534) grouped them together at the end of the OT under the caption: "Apocrypha: these are books which are not held equal to the sacred Scriptures and yet are useful and good for reading." The Thirty-Nine Articles of Religion (1563) of the Church of England asserted that they were to be read "for example of life and instruction of manners," though they ought not to be employed "to establish any doctrine." The King James Bible of 1611 printed the books between the OT and the NT. John Lightfoot (1643) spoke out against this arrangement because he feared that "the wretched Apocrypha," so placed between the OT and NT, might give the mistaken impression that they form a link between the two Testaments. The Westminster Confession (1647) decreed that the books, "not being of divine inspiration, are no part of the canon of Scripture, and therefore are of no authority in the Church of God; nor to be in any otherwise approved, or made use of than other human writings." The British and Foreign Bible Society decided (1827) to omit the controverted books in future publications, except for some pulpit Bibles, with this statement: "The Principles of the Society exclude the circulation of those Books or parts of Books which are usually termed Apocryphal." On the Continent the Protestant position does not seem to have changed essentially from what it was shortly after the Reformation.

Edmond Jacob expressed a current of thought in modern Protestantism when he describes the Apocrypha as a "bridge" between the OT and NT and a "link" in the chain of the unity of revelation. He adds that, though

their witness is secondary, they should be inserted at the end of the OT as was done at the time of the Reformation [E. Jacob, "Considerations sur l'Autorité canonique de l'Ancien Testament," *Le Problème Biblique dans le Protestantisme,* ed. J. Boisset (Paris 1955) 81–82].

Bibliography: *Encyclopedic Dictionary of the Bible,* tr. and adap. by L. HARTMAN (New York 1963) 308–313. E. MANGENOT, *Dictionnaire de théologie catholique,* ed. A. VACANT et al. (Paris 1903–50) 2.2:1569–82. H. HÖPFL, *Dictionnaire de la Bible,* suppl ed. L. PIROT et al. (Paris) 1:1022–45. J. HASTINGS and J. A. SELBIA, eds., *Dictionary of the Bible,* rev. in 1 v., ed. F. C. GRANT and H. H. ROWLEY (New York 1963) 121–123. W. R. SMITH, *The Old Testament in the Jewish Church* (London 1902). M. JUGIE, *Histoire du canon de l'Ancien Testament dans l'église grecque et l'église russe* (Paris 1909). M. L. MARGOLIS, *The Hebrew Scriptures in the Making* (Philadelphia 1922). S. ZEITLIN, *An Historical Study of the Canonization of the Hebrew Scriptures* (Philadelphia 1933). G. ÖSTBORN, *Cult and Canon: A Study of the Canonization of the OT* (Uppsala 1950). H. H. ROWLEY, *The Growth of the Old Testament* (New York 1950). F. V. FILSON, *Which Books Belong in the Bible? A Study of the Canon* (Philadelphia 1957). W. BARCLAY, *The Making of the Bible* (New York 1961). B. J. ROBERTS, "The Dead Sea Scrolls and the Old Testament Scriptures," *The Bulletin of the John Rylands Library* 36 (1953) 75–96. A. C. SUNDBERG, "The Old Testament of the Early Church," *Harvard Theological Review* 51 (1958) 205–226. P. KATZ, "The Old Testament Canon in Palestine and Alexandria," *Zeitschrift für die neutestamentliche Wissenschaft und die Kunde der äteren Kirche* 47 (1956) 191–217.

[J. C. TURRO]

3. History of New Testament Canon

The complete list of NT books was recognized as sacred and canonical only after a protracted history. The nature of this history and its theological implications will be discussed first. Then consideration will be given to the actual formation of the collection of NT books, the final fixation of the canon, and the criteria of NT canonicity.

PROBLEM OF THE NEW TESTAMENT CANON

The development of the NT canon is an example of the development of dogma. Its history was locally vague and varied and not definitively completed until the Council of Trent.

Historical Summary. Before the middle of the 2nd century the question had never been raised as to what books were sacred or how many sacred books there were. The canon, already implicitly present in the apostolic age, gradually became explicit through a concatenation of providential factors forming and fixing it. God works slowly through men's minds and historical events to produce His ultimate purpose.

The Church in the early postapostolic age was aware of but three authorities: the OT, the spoken word of Christ, and the oral testimony of the Apostles. Only gradually and obscurely did the words of Christ as recorded by His disciples assume the authority of Scripture. Then, as people's memory of the Apostles dimmed, their writings along with the letters of St. Paul, came into prominence as sacred.

To give a summary glance, the 27 NT books may be divided into two categories. (1) The protocanonical books, or books of the "first list": the four Gospels, the 13 Pauline Epistles (excluding Hebrews), 1 John, and 1 Peter. These books were universally accepted from the middle of the 2nd century with practically no doubts or hesitations. (2) The deuterocanonical books, or books of the "second list": Hebrews, Revelation, 2 Peter, 2 John, 3 John, James, and Jude. These suffered awkward moments, both locally and universally. The last five had an obscure and fluctuating history of acceptance, especially among the Latins and the Syrians. The Latins doubted the Pauline authorship of Hebrews and therefore also its canonicity. The Greeks and the Syrians, after the 2nd century, doubted the Johannine authorship of Revelation and thus also its canonicity. Besides the protocanonical and deuterocanonical books, there were many rival books for which canonicity was claimed, particularly among the Greeks.

In the East the canon was fluid and extended to many books not now recognized as canonical. Justin's εὐαγγέλιον, for instance, was any proclaiming of the good news, and many writings could have fulfilled this definition. In the West the canon was more juridical and normative, tending to exclude rather than include sacred books. Only in the 5th century did the Church come to a universal stabilization of the canon, and not until the Council of Trent did the canon receive its dogmatic definition.

Church's Relationship to Canon and Inspiration. Before the history of the canon is traced from its apostolic formation to its fixation among the Latins, Greeks, and Syrians, it must be placed into proper relationship to both inspiration and the Church [see INSPIRATION, BIBLICAL]. The history of the canon was a dramatic recognition by the Church that the living Word of God (God's activity as a revealer of divine truth) is intrinsically joined to the inspired written word of God. NT Scripture is the original self-representation in written concretization of what the early Church lived and believed. Sacred writings developed and formed as its very life processes, the distilled essence of itself. Whether Gospel, letter, or sermon, these writings were the intrinsic expression of its life—in a unique way.

God definitively and eschatologically formed the Church in a historical process, "the Christ Event." The mysteries of Christ, His life, death and Resurrection (with His Ascension and gift of the Spirit) were God's revelation of Himself to man, His Word in the Christ Event.

These mysteries have been continued in the MYSTICAL BODY OF CHRIST, the Church. Scripture was thus a constitutive element of the early Church, and through it the living Word of God became objectivized in the written word of God wherein His saving activity is contained and expressed. Scripture, therefore, came into existence, not only on the occasion of the founding of the early Church, but also as an inner moment of its formation under God's direction. In the process of the canonization of the NT canon the Church, the prolongation of the Christ Event, rediscovered itself in the written concretization of its very essence.

Yet, it seems, the fact of the inspiration of Scripture could have become known only by a revelation given by God in the apostolic age. Otherwise it would be impossible to ensure the historical plausibility of this revelation in view of the uncertainties and doubts involved in the proclamation of the canon.

Two things must be considered: first, the original revelation contained in the inspired writings, which was initially and essentially the self-knowledge of the Church; second, the reflex knowledge and expression of this revelation wherein the Church claimed and proclaimed what had always belonged to it. The first revelation, the inspired content of the NT Scriptures, was complete with the death of the last Apostle. The reflex knowledge, however, involved a subsequent, divinely guided historical process.

FORMATION OF THE COLLECTION OF NEW TESTAMENT BOOKS

Through the ages the Church connaturally recognized within its sacred writings something consonant with its nature. It recognized itself. The historical process of this recognition began with the Church of the first postapostolic age, which held three authoritative sources of revelation; the OT, Christ, and the Apostles.

Authoritative Sources in the Early Church. From its very beginning and as a part of its essence the Church possessed a canon of inspired writings: the OT. Humanly and psychologically speaking, Jesus "discovered" Himself in the OT by uniting in Himself all the OT paradoxical themes of SALVATION HISTORY. He found His coming, His work, and His death foretold there (see Lk 4.16–22; 24.24–27, 44–46; Jn 5.39). Further, He used the OT as the incontestably authoritative word of God to prove, for instance, the indissolubility of marriage (Gn 1.27; 2.24; see Mk 10.6–9), the resurrection of the dead (Ex 3.6; see Mk 12.26–27), the superiority of the Messiah over David [Ps 109(110). 1; see Mk 12.35–37]. As eschatological fulfillment, He transformed what was temporary and changeable into the eternal and unchangeable. This is exemplified by His position on divorce (Mk 10.2–12) and by the so-called antitheses of the Sermon on the Mount: "You have heard that it was said to the ancients. . . . But I say to you . . ." (Mt 5.21–46). He had not come to destroy, but to complete the Law and the Prophets (Mt 5.17).

The apostolic Church, following its Master, held the OT as absolute authority in demonstrating the Christ Event. This conviction stemmed fundamentally from the fact that the OT was revered as the inspired word of God (2 Pt 1.19–21; 2 Tm 3.14–17). NT writings are full of "proof texts" from the OT; especially Romans, Galatians, Hebrews, and the Petrine sermons in Acts.

The Fathers of the postapostolic age likewise considered the OT as authoritative, but with notable variations. The letters of IGNATIUS OF ANTIOCH, for instance, contain only two explicit OT quotations, both from Proverbs (*Ad Ephes.* 5.2; *Ad Magn.* 12). The Gospels, which he significantly calls "the flesh of Christ," dominate his letters. The Prophets are important because "they foretold the gospel of Christ, hoped in Him, and awaited His coming" (*Ad Philad.* 5.2). The Shepherd of HERMAS, on the other hand, indicates no acquaintance at all with the OT. Yet 1 Clement, composed about 40 years earlier in Rome, gives more than 100 citations from the OT and only two from the Gospels. For Clement, God speaks to Christians through the OT. This Father continuously reinforces his teaching by citations from the OT, but with an unquestionably Christian interpretation. According to the Epistle of BARNABAS the Christians were the first to understand the OT correctly.

The very fact that a Christian interpretation was given to the OT accredits supreme authority not primarily to the OT Scriptures but to Christ whose person, in word and work, was glimpsed shining through these Scriptures. The Apostles preached not so much the OT as Christ and His work of redemption. The Gospels give witness to Him in whom alone are hidden all the treasures of wisdom and knowledge. St. Paul considers Christ's word the supreme norm that decides matters without further discussion (1 Cor 7.10; 9.41; Acts 20.35).

Authorized by Jesus and endowed with the power of the Holy Spirit to preach the gospel and establish the Christian community, the Apostles were regarded, not only as "the eyewitnesses and ministers of the word" (Lk 1.2), but also as the final authority on the traditions in which the authentic words of Christ and their interpretation were found. To resist false teachers was the duty of the Apostles (Jude 17–19; 2 Pt 3.1–2).

In the early postapostolic age the authority of the Apostles was further enhanced. Ignatius exhorts the Mag-

nesians to hold fast to the teachings of the Lord and His Apostles (13.1), and Polycarp sets before the Philippians the example of "Paul . . . and the other Apostles" (9.1; 3.2; 11.2–4). The letter known as 2 Clement put "the Apostles" (i.e., the writings of the Apostles) on the same level as "the sacred books" of the Prophets (14.2). However, the authority of the Apostles was not equated with that of Christ, and they were quoted much less often. Yet, as early as 200, Serapion of Antioch said, "We accept Peter and the other Apostles as we accept Christ" (Eusebius, *Hist. Eccl.* 6.12.3).

A canon of Christian-inspired writings was inevitable. At first the remembered words of the Lord were preached. But very early they began to be committed to writing. As missionary territory expanded, the Apostles sent letters to individual churches as a substitute for preaching. These were regarded not merely as private letters but as official communications. Yet a considerable time had to elapse before these were gathered together and acknowledged as a second canon of incontestable authority along with the OT.

Development of a Canon of Christian Writings. There was a substantial continuity and development of the Christian Church from its birth until the time when its emergence into full relief in the latter part of the 2nd century was witnessed to by profane history. Although from a historical viewpoint the early moments of the Church and its inspired books are shrouded in obscurity, Luke (1.1–2) nevertheless indicates that there was much careful investigation and that many undertook to write of Christ. These endeavors, which produced the collection of the four Gospels and the collection of the 13 Epistles of St. Paul, formed the basis for the eventual full canon of 27 NT books.

The Gospels. Probably each of the four canonical Gospels was primarily composed for liturgical reading. From the part of the world where each of these was originally written in the second half of the 1st century, copies were soon circulated to other parts of the Christian world, and to some extent the earlier writings seem to have affected the later ones (*see* SYNOPTIC GOSPELS). The four Gospels, however, did not have the canonical authority of the OT before the middle of the 2nd century. In the writings of the APOSTOLIC FATHERS there are only three places where the words of Christ as found in the Gospels are introduced by the phrase that is used for the introduction of quotations from the OT, "it is written": Barnabas 4.14 (quoting Mt 22.14), 2 Clement 2.4 (quoting Mt 9.13) and 14.1 (quoting Mk 11.17). Generally, the words of Christ, though known from the canonical Gospels, are introduced by the phrase, "the Lord says" or "the Lord has said." Therefore, they are cited, not so much under the authority of Scripture as under that of Our Lord. Further, in the DIDACHE 8.3 and 2 Clement 8.5 we find the expression, "the Lord directed in His gospel," where the last word refers to the "good news" as preached by Christ rather than to a written Gospel. This can be seen in the fact that the quotations are often not in the precise form as they occur in the canonical Gospels (see, e.g., 1 Clement 13.1–2; 46.7; Polycarp 2.3). Moreover, the Apostolic Fathers cite a few sayings of Christ that are not contained in the canonical Gospels but stem apparently from oral tradition or from apocryphal books (see, e.g., Ignatius, *Ad Smyrn.* 3.2; 2 Clement 4.5; 5.2–4; 8.5; 12.2). These citations, however, are not numerous, and although Justin Martyr uses traditions about Christ that are not in the canonical Gospels, he never introduces them with the formula, "Scripture says." Probably he had a noncanonical Gospel, possibly the so-called Gospel of the Hebrews, from which he quotes the words of Christ (see 5. Apocrypha of the NT). He also mentions the custom of reading "the Memoirs of the Apostles" or "the Prophets" in the liturgy (*1 Apol.* 67.3–5).

Although the Apostolic Fathers speak of the Gospel in the singular only, Justin almost always speaks of the Gospels in the plural, the only exception being in *Dial.* 100.1. This indicates that in his time written accounts of the Gospel were assuming importance. However, he still uses the formula, "the Lord says," which shows that the written Gospels were not yet given an authority in their own right as the word of God.

TATIAN, a disciple of Justin, composed *c.* 170 his DIATESSARON, or "harmony" of the four Gospels (see Eusebius, *Ecclesiastical History* 4.29.6). Although he incorporated some apocryphal material, his work is based substantially on the four canonical Gospels and is thus a witness to the special authority that these had now acquired.

Pauline Epistles. Collections of the writings of St. Paul, at first of varying size, were made at a very early period, long before the four Gospels were gathered together. Probably by the end of the 1st or the beginning of the 2nd century, the full corpus of the 13 Pauline Epistles (not including Hebrews) was known in most of the Christian communities. In 2 Pt 3.15–16, reference is made to the "epistles" of Paul as already well-known to the faithful to whom 2 Peter is sent, but there is no way of knowing which of Paul's Epistles were included in this collection. Ignatius of Antioch (*c.* 110) used 1 Corinthians, Romans, Ephesians, and Galatians, and probably also Colossians, 1 Timothy, and 1 Thessalonians.

The letter of POLYCARP to the Christians of Philippi is important in determining the time in which the Epistles of St. Paul were known and recognized as having special authority. This letter, which is usually dated between 107 and 117, although ch. 1 through 12 have been recently dated as late as the 4th or 5th century, makes use of almost all the 13 Pauline Epistles, the only ones (perhaps accidentally) not referred to being 1 Thessalonians, Titus, and Philemon. Polycarp often introduces the words of Paul with the phrase, "You already know," thus indicating the acknowledged authority of Paul's letters. Justin uses Romans, 1 and 2 Corinthians, Galatians, Ephesians, Philippians, Colossians, 2 Thessalonians, 1 Timothy, and also Hebrews, although he does not name Paul as the author of these writings.

Full NT Canon. MELITO OF SARDES (*c.* 170–180) speaks of the "books of the OT," thereby implying that there were also "books of the NT" that were recognized as inspired Scripture. Justin introduces his numerous quotations from the Gospels with the technical formula for introducing Sacred Scripture, "It is written," as also does Tatian in citing Jn 1.5. When MARCION broke with the orthodox Church in 140, he drew up his own list of sacred books, in which he rejected the whole OT and accepted only a mutilated version of Luke and ten of the Pauline Epistles (excluding the three Pastoral Epistles). According to D. de Bruyne and A. von Harnack, it was in reaction to Marcion that the Church established and fixed its NT canon between 160 and 180. (For the NT canon of the Roman church at this time *see* MURATORIAN CANON.) In 180 the Christian martyrs at Scillium in Numidia, when asked what they had in their satchel, replied: *"Libri et epistolae Pauli,"* the *libri* no doubt including the Gospels, if they also had the Pauline Epistles. During this period also Revelation, 1 John, and 1 Peter reached full canonical stature.

FIXATION OF NEW TESTAMENT CANON

At the beginning of the 3rd century the NT canon had passed the first major step toward fixation. Further doubts would center on other than the Gospels and the main Pauline corpus. Since the history of the NT canon at this time differed somewhat from place to place, the process of final fixation will be treated here as this took place separately among the Greeks, the Latins, and the Syrians.

Among the Greeks. The two main centers of the Greek Church at this time were at Alexandria in Egypt and at Caesarea in Palestine. Disputes about the doubtfully authoritative books took different forms at these two places.

In Egypt. Before CLEMENT OF ALEXANDRIA (d. after 217) the history of the NT canon in Egypt is obscure. Clement apparently knew all the 27 books of the later-defined NT canon, with the possible exception of James, 2 Peter, and 3 John. But he also attributed a high degree of authority to several other books. Some of these he considered even divinely inspired, such as the Didache, Shepherd of Hermas, Kerygma of Peter, and probably 1 Clement.

ORIGEN (185–255) largely reflects the view of the Egyptian Church as given by Clement, but he is also aware of controversies regarding the canonical status of 2 Peter, James, Hebrews, 2 and 3 John. He likewise speaks of Jude with reservations.

The Egyptian Codex D contains a canon, known as the *Canon Claramontanus,* probably drawn up in the 3rd century, that lists OT and NT books. It has the complete NT canon, including all seven of the CATHOLIC EPISTLES as well as the Epistle of Barnabas, Shepherd of Hermas, Acts of Paul, and Apocalypse of Peter. However, the last four (noncanonical) books are marked with a horizontal stroke indicating that they were not accepted as Scripture either by the copyist of the manuscript or in the practice of his community. On the other hand, the Egyptian collection of the Chester Beatty Papyri, dating from the 3rd century, does not have the seven Catholic Epistles included in its otherwise correct canon.

ATHANASIUS lists, in his well-known *Paschal Epistle* of 367, the present complete NT canon of 27 books, concerning which he says: "These are the sources of salvation, for the thirsty may drink deeply of the words to be found here. In these alone is the doctrine of piety recorded. Let no one add to them or take anything away from them." Egypt was thus the first province of the Church to have a fixed and definite canon of 27 NT books.

In Palestine. EUSEBIUS OF CAESAREA (d. 340), who is important as a witness to the Palestinian canon, but even more so for his abundant information on the state of the canon in various other Christian communities, gives the following classifications. (1) *Homologoumena,* "agreed on," i.e., books accepted everywhere. These are the four Gospels, Acts, the 14 Pauline Epistles, 1 John, 1 Peter, and, "if it seems right," Revelation (*Ecclesiastical History* 3.25). In regard to the Pauline Epistles he says: "Definitely and certainly the 14 Epistles are by Paul, but it must be noted that some have opposed the Epistle to the Hebrews, appealing to the Roman Church, which does not acknowledge it as Pauline" (3.3, 5). (2) *Antilegomena,* "disputed," i.e., books whose canonicity is challenged. Some of these are books that are revered by a majority, but rejected by a minority: "the so-called Epistle of James, the Epistle of Jude, the Second Epistle of Peter, and the so-called Second and Third Epistles of John that were written either by the Evangelist or by another John." Therefore, Eusebius puts in this group five of the seven so-called Catholic Epistles. Of the Epistles

of James and Jude he says that, even though they are not well-attested in antiquity, "they have been publicly read in most churches" (2.23, 24–26). In connection with the *antilegomena* Eusebius lists the *notha,* "spurious" works: Acts of Paul, Shepherd of Hermas, Revelation of Peter, Epistle of Barnabas, Didache, and "if it seems right," the Revelation of John. Because of the influence of St. DIONYSIUS OF ALEXANDRIA, who judged the Revelation of John as unauthentic on literary grounds, Eusebius is personally inclined to include it with the *notha.* He also mentions that "the Gospel of the Hebrews" could be listed with the *notha* because it is held by some as sacred. (3) Heretical writings, mostly apocryphal gospels, to be completely rejected; no ecclesiastical writer of recognized authority deemed these writings worthy of the slightest notice (3.25).

Among the Latins. Consideration of the canon among the Latins can be well divided into two periods, because there is a distinct change of attitude after the middle of the 4th century.

Before the Middle of the 4th Century. In Gaul St. IRENAEUS (d. 202), who was familiar with the traditions of the churches not only in Gaul but also in Italy and Asia Minor and was closely connected through his teachers with the apostolic age, explicitly names and accepts at least 21 NT books as canonical. He uses the four canonical Gospels in about 625 quotations, and he rejects the apocryphal gospels; he quotes the Acts (54 times), 12 of the Pauline Epistles (280 times), accepts Revelation as Johannine (quoted 29 times) and quotes the Catholic Epistles of 1 Peter and 1 and 2 John (15 times); but he never quotes James. References are uncertain about the others. He does not refer to Philemon and, though he knows Hebrews, he does not admit its Pauline origin. He introduces the Shepherd of Hermas with the formula "Scripture says." He does not use the name New Testament for the Christian canonical writings but describes them as the "evangelical and apostolic writings."

In Italy the canon of the Muratorian Fragment, probably composed *c.* 180 to 190 (possibly by Hippolytus), is our earliest ecclesiastical list of the NT canon (if we except the anti-Marcionite prologues to the Gospels). It lists 22 (or 23) NT books; for details *see* MURATORIAN CANON.

St. HIPPOLYTUS OF ROME (d. 235), a disciple of Irenaeus, calls the Scriptures of the two Testaments "the two breasts of Christ," indicating the intimacy of nourishment in the inspired word. His NT includes at least 21 books. Hebrews he regards as not Pauline, and therefore, to him uncanonical. He does not use Philemon, 2 or 3 John, James, or Jude.

The Edict of Diocletian (303) that the Sacred Books should be sought out and burned must have led the various churches to determine more sharply which books constituted Sacred Scripture.

In Africa, Tertullian used all of the NT books except 2 Peter and 2 and 3 John. He ascribes Hebrews to Barnabas and excludes it from Scripture, although he admits it is widely used by the various churches. Difficulties persisted with Hebrews and the Catholic Epistles. Even St. CYPRIAN of Carthage (d. 253) never used Hebrews; of the Catholic Epistles, he quoted only from 1 Peter and 1 John. In the North-African Monsen Canon, written around 360, Hebrews, James, and Jude were still missing.

After the Middle of the 4th Century. The middle of the 4th century is a turning point in the history of the canon for the Latin Church. Intensive exchange of ideas and closer contact with the East, caused principally by the Arian struggle, had a far-reaching effect in bringing the Western canon up to the level of the Eastern. Then, too, translating the Greek Fathers into Latin and Jerome's Vulgate (containing all 27 NT books) helped to unify and stabilize a universal canon. The so-called Decree of Gelasius, reputedly written in 382, contains a list of all 27 NT books. Its authenticity, however, is disputed. Under Augustine's influence three African synods, one at Hippo (393) and two at Carthage (397 and 419), accepted all 27 books as canonical. In the first two synods, Hebrews is not listed as Pauline, even though it is regarded as canonical, but the last of the three councils considers it to be Paul's. The letter of Pope St. INNOCENT I to Exuperius in 405 officially lists all 27 NT books.

Among the Syrians and in Asia Minor. In the Greek-speaking part of Syria St. LUCIAN OF ANTIOCH (d. 312), founder of the Antiochian School [*see* EXEGESIS, BIBLICAL, 4] rejected Revelation, 2 Peter, 2 and 3 John, and Jude. With minor variations, this represents the attitude of the Syrian Church from THEOPHILUS OF ANTIOCH (d. 186), who, however, accepted Revelation, to the time of St. JOHN CHRYSOSTOM (d. 407). During the 5th century all 27 books except Revelation were accepted, but the Catholic Epistles were considered second-rank authorities. In the Syriac-speaking parts, prior to the publication of the PESHITTA, all the Catholic Epistles and the Apocalypse are missing from the canon, but a third (apocryphal) Epistle of Paul to the Corinthians is accepted, St. EPHREM even censuring those who question its canonicity. [This apocryphal Epistle is not listed in the Syrian Catalogue (*c.* 400) discovered by A. S. Lewis in St. Catherine's Monastery, Mt. Sinai.] With the publication of the Peshitta, James, 1 Peter, and 1 John were accepted. The Syrian Jacobite canon is practically limited to the 22 books of the Peshitta; Revelation, 2 Peter, 2 and 3 John, and Jude

are omitted. In the 2nd half of the 4th century, the Council of Laodicea in Asia Minor and St. GREGORY OF NAZIANZUS list the full canon except Revelation, although this is included in the canon of St. BASIL, St. GREGORY OF NYSSA, and Epiphanius of Constantia.

Final Stabilization. Since the 5th century, the NT canon of 27 books has been universally accepted by the Greek and the Latin Church alike. Yet during the Middle Ages, Hebrews, Revelation, and the Catholic Epistles except 1 Peter and 1 John were still the subject of some controversy. The Shepherd of Hermas and the third Epistle to the Corinthians are also found in some medieval MSS. CAJETAN (TOMMASO DE VIO) (d. 1534) doubted the authenticity of Hebrews, James, Jude and 2 and 3 John, and considered them less authoritative. Luther was bolder. His interpretation of Paul was the criterion for all the NT books. On this basis he formed three groups: Romans, Galatians, and John; the other NT books, including the Synoptics, he relegated to second place; he severely censured Hebrews, Jude, 2 Peter, and Revelation, while he called James "a straw epistle." Despite this, all Protestants have the same NT canon as Catholics.

In the 16th century both literary and dogmatic criticism of the traditional canon became so intense that the Council of Trent dogmatically defined the canon on April 8, 1564. This dogmatic decree, *De Canonicis Scripturis,* lists by name the sacred and canonical books of both Testaments: 45 for the OT, 27 for the NT. According to the minutes of the Council, it was merely repeating, after a month of heated debate, the list given at the Council of Florence (1442) in the decree for the Jacobites. The decree of Trent, repeated by Vatican I on April 24, 1870, is the infallible decision of the magisterium. In the decree, certain doubtfully authentic deuterocanonical sections are also included with the books (*cum omnibus suis partibus*): Mk 16.9–20; Lk 22.19b–20, 43–44; and Jn 7.53–8.11.

CRITERIA OF CANONICITY

Distinction must be made between the internal criterion and external criteria.

Internal Criterion. The internal criterion lies in the mysterious nature of the Church, which recognizes in Scripture something intrinsic to its nature and canonizes it as a normative constitutive element of its existence. Inspiration, which links the personal Word of God to His written word, is a supernatural charism. It thus lies beyond human deduction. The Church, as supernatural, simply recognizes itself in Scripture. Time and history become dramatic elements in this sublime perception.

External Criteria. These helped articulate its act of recognition, especially apostolicity and liturgy. Every book of the NT was either written or guaranteed by an Apostle. This, then, was the reason why each was accepted as sacred and normative, for doctrinal apostolic authority is the foundation of the Church: "You are built upon the foundation of the apostles and prophets" (Eph 2.20; see Mt 28.18–20). In practice the Church also showed its reverence for the NT as holy and canonical by sanctioning its use in public worship. The liturgy made the community participate in the Mystery of Christ, proclaiming it through the word. Thus, in various regions the apostolic Church guided the faithful to acceptance of the apostolic, inspired word. In this process other nonapostolic traditions were added, which accounted for the doubts and disputes of the early years. But the Church needed only to apply the principle of apostolic approbation to solve the doubts. When called upon to do so at Trent, through its infallible, apostolic magisterium, it decisively recognized what God had given it through the Apostles—the 27 NT books, the written embodiment of its existence.

Bibliography: H. HÖPFL *Dictionnaire de la Bible*, suppl. ed. L. PIROT et al. (Paris) 1:1022–45. *Encyclopedic Dictionary of the Bible,* tr. and adap. by L. HARTMAN (New York 1963) 312–313. E. MANGENOT, *Dictionnaire de théologie catholique*, (Paris 1903–50) 2:1550–69, 1582–1605. J. MICHL and K. RAHNER, *Lexicon für Theologie und Kirche,* (Freiburg, 1957–66) 5:1280–84. E. JACQUIER, *Le Nouveau Testament dans l'église chrétienne* (Paris 1911) v.1. M. J. LAGRANGE, *Histoire ancienne du canon du Nouveau Testament,* v.1 of *Introduction à l'étude du N.T.* (Paris 1933). G. M. PERRELLA, *Introducción general a la Sagrada Escritura* (Turin 1954). A. WIKENHAUSER, *New Testament Introduction* (New York 1958). A. ROBERT and A. TRICOT, *Guide to the Bible,* tr. E. P. ARBEZ and M. P. MCGUIRE (Tournai–New York 1951–55) 1:87–103. C. F. D. MOULE, *Birth of the New Testament* (New York 1962). H. RIESENFELD, *The Gospel Tradition and Its Beginning* (London 1957).

[F. SCHROEDER]

4. Canon Criticism

Traditionally, the term "canon" has designated the list of books that belong to the Bible, both OT and NT. In recent times the canon has entered into Biblical theology as a vital factor, and not merely as an official list. Two directions can be distinguished: canon as process, and canon as the (canonical) shape given to the books of the Bible.

Canon as Process. James A. Sanders has described his views explicitly as "canonical criticism." By this he means that the canon must be viewed as a process, an examination of the way in which the canon came to be formed. The formation of the Torah (Law, or the Pentateuch) within the Hebrew Scriptures provides an illustration. This Bible is called the *Tanakh,* after its threefold division: Torah (T, Genesis to Deuteronomy); Prophets (N, for *Nĕbí'îm,* which includes earlier [Joshua to Kings]

and later [Amos to Ezekiel] prophets; finally, the Writings (K, for *Kĕtûbîm,* which includes the rest of the books, Psalms to Chronicles). These three parts of the Hebrew Bible were formed over a long period of time, and all received their present form after the exile (begun in 587 B.C. when Jerusalem fell to Nebuchadnezzar).

The Torah provides the clearest example of canonical criticism. The question is: Why and how do these five books form a distinct unity? Logically and historically the storyline of the people of God extends from Abraham (Gn 12) through Deuteronomy to the book of Joshua. The promise to Abraham is fulfilled in the takeover of Palestine by Joshua. But the Torah ends with Deuteronomy, which describes the three discourses of Moses to the Israelites in the plains of Moab before entering the Promised Land. The story line has been broken by the insertion of Deuteronomy at this point. Why? Because the Jewish community that formed the canon recognized the necessity (and the pre-eminence) of Moses and the Law for their own self-understanding and preservation in the postexilic era. That was the reason they placed Deuteronomy ("the book of the law" found in the Temple under Josiah, 2 Kgs 22) in its present position, sealing off the Torah, as it were. It is canon as process and helps to explain why the Bible took the shape it did.

Many aspects of this approach remain to be worked out, especially the formation of the rest of the Bible, and what does the process have to say to the present communities of faith which are nourished by the Bible? Sanders' interpretation of the canonical process is an exciting glimpse into the way in which certain Biblical books may have functioned within the believing community as the canon was in process of formation. Two observations should be kept in mind. First, the construal remains a hypothetical inference, since there are no hard historical facts about the process. Second, the bearing of the process upon the ongoing use and interpretation of the canonical books remains secondary, in that it sets down no obligatory use or meaning for the modern community of faith. Nonetheless, it is useful in pointing up various levels of meaning that have emerged from the Biblical text.

Canonical Shape. Brevard S. Childs avoids the phrase "canonical criticism" and the "process" that this involves. Instead, he speaks of "canonical shape," emphasizing the final form of the Biblical books as they have been edited and promulgated in the Jewish tradition at the beginning of the Christian era (*c.* 100). While he is aware of the larger canon that prevailed in the early Church and in Roman Catholicism (Council of Trent), he limits himself to the Hebrew (and also Protestant) Bible for ecumenical purposes.

Childs begins with the results of historical critical methodology as applied to the Bible (both OT and NT, as will be seen). These results have been hypothetical and uncertain in that little unanimity has been achieved, and the concentration has been on the prehistory of the Biblical text (e.g., what was the "original" reading and meaning of Is 6:1–13, or 7:1–25 before these chapters assumed their present form?). Childs insists that the meaning of the Hebrew Bible is to be found in its present final form, as this was established by the Jewish community and inherited from them by the early Church.

Thus, for example, one is not to be preoccupied with the various traditions (JEPD) that combined to form the Pentateuch. These never existed as canonical Bible; they are the (hypothetical) sources that eventually formed the Pentateuch, but it is the "five books" in their final canonical shape that constitute the Biblical word. The same approach is applied to the rest of the OT. Childs eschews all hypothetical reconstruction in favor of the final form. By no means does he deny that the Biblical text was edited and increased by later additions. Instead, he insists on the supreme validity of the interpretation of the final shape (e.g., he grants that chapters 40–66 were added to Is 1–39, in the post-exilic period, but he insists that it is precisely chapters 1–66 that must be interpreted as a whole in order to arrive at the Biblical meaning).

With remarkable expertise Childs extends his explorations to the NT canon as well. Here again he seeks the holistic meaning as opposed to the fragmented and hypothetical reconstruction of NT sources (e.g., the "original" sayings of Jesus, or the Q source of the SYNOPTIC GOSPELS). He readily grants that Luke–Acts was written and conceived as one work. But in the canon these works are separated, and thus a particular canonical shape and function is given to each. The purpose of the Gospel of Luke is to enlarge its original witness to Christ (for Theophilus, Lk 1:3) by making it part of the fourfold Gospel witness. Similarly, Acts now functions as an interpretive guide for the understanding of the letters of Paul.

The views of Childs have met with a warm reception, both pro and con. One basic difficulty is the establishment of a fixed point for the canonical, and hence binding "shape." Indeed, for the Christian, the OT has itself received a new canonical shape by being joined to the NT. Moreover, one cannot simply pass over the fact that an enlarged canon, which includes the so-called apocrypha that are absent from the Hebrew/Protestant Bible, is accepted in Latin and Greek Christian tradition. Finally, the canonical interpretation should not be allowed to override other levels of meaning that appear within the text. Thus one must also read and understand Isaiah 40–66 against its unmistakable background of the exilic and postexilic era. Similarly, one must evaluate carefully the Infancy Narratives in the Gospels of Matthew and Luke on their own level, and not only as part of a Gospel. In other words, there are various levels of meaning in the text that need not be sacrificed for the sake of the final, canonical meaning.

The emphasis of Childs and Sanders upon canonicity and a holistic approach to the Biblical text is welcome. They have called attention to a neglected area of Biblical interpretation; the Bible is a product of tradition, editing and revision on the part of the community.

Bibliography: Canonical Criticism. J. A. SANDERS, *Torah and Canon* (Philadelphia 1972); *Canon and Community* (Philadelphia 1984); *From Sacred Story to Sacred Text* (Philadelphia 1987). Canonical Shape. B. S. CHILDS, *Introduction to the Old Testament as Scripture* (Philadelphia 1979); *The New Testament as Canon* (Philadelphia 1984); *Old Testament Theology in a Canonical Context* (Philadelphia 1985). Reactions to Canon Criticism. *Journal for the Study of the Old Testament* 16 (1980) 1–76. J. BARR, *Holy Scripture: Canon, Authority, Criticism* (Philadelphia 1983). H. VON CAMPENHAUSEN, *The Formation of the Christian Bible* (London 1972). J. BLENKINSOPP, *Prophecy and Canon* (Notre Dame 1977).

[R. E. MURPHY]

CANON LAW, 1983 CODE

The *Code of Canon Law for the Latin Church*, incorporating many of the reforms of Vatican II, was promulgated on January 25, 1983, by Pope JOHN PAUL II. The apostolic constitution *Sacrae disciplinae leges* described the procedures and guiding principles of the revision. A parallel text was also proposed for the oriental Catholic Churches.

Preparation. Announced on January 25, 1959, by Pope JOHN XXIII, and undertaken in earnest in 1966 after the conclusion of Vatican II, the task of revision spanned almost a quarter century. In 1971, the commission began distributing draft texts for comments and observations. The draft of the *Lex ecclesiae fundamentalis* (LEF), or Fundamental Law of the Church, was the first sent out for study; it was followed by a text on administrative procedure. Later, *schemata* on crimes and penalties, sacramental law, and procedures for the protection of rights were distributed at regular intervals. In 1978, the remaining parts of the proposed code were printed and distributed. After all the comments had been reviewed, a consolidated version of the law was prepared (1980) for the members of the commission. Their observations were then incorporated into a *relatio* (report), distributed in 1981, which became the basis for work during the final plenary session of the commission held in October of 1981. At this meeting, a number of major issues upon which general unanimity was lacking were selected for discussion. These included norms on marriage tribunals, the sharing of jurisdiction by laypersons, and membership in Masonic societies. The commission was also called upon to address some 30 additional issues proposed by the members.

A final version of the text was presented in 1982 to Pope John Paul II. With the assistance of a select committee, he examined the draft, invited further suggestions from Episcopal Conferences, and eventually introduced a number of additional changes in the light of suggestions received. The final text was then duly promulgated. Contrary to the norms in effect under the 1917 code, translations of the new code were permitted, and according to special norms issued by the Secretariat of State, on Jan. 28, 1983, such texts are to be approved by Episcopal Conferences, not by the HOLY SEE. Only the promulgated version in Latin, however, is regarded as authentic. Translations have been published in various languages, including two different English translations; one approved by the Episcopal Conference in the United Kingdom and the other by the National Conference of Catholic Bishops in the United States.

On Jan.2, 1984, Pope John Paul II, by the *motu proprio* entitled *Recognito iuris canonici codice,* established the pontifical commission for the authentic interpretation of the Code of Canon Law, under the presidency of then Archbishop (later Cardinal) Rosalio Castillo Lara, SDB. The commission handed down its first authentic interpretation on June 26, 1984. When the Pontifical Commission for revision of the Code had completed its work and was dissolved, the Commission for Interpretation of the Code assumed responsibility for the publication of *Communicationes.*

Plan. Instead of following the plan of the 1917 code that modeled itself closely on that of the Roman Civil Law (General Norms, Persons, Things, Trials, Crimes and Penalties), the 1983 code follows a model based on the threefold mission of the Church: to teach, sanctify, and serve. The code is now divided into seven books: I. General Norms; II. The People of God; III. The Function of Teaching; IV. The Function of Sanctifying; V. Temporal Goods; VI. Delicts and Penalties; VII. Procedures. While Books III and IV treat of the prophetic (Word) and priestly (Sacrament) missions of the Church, no one specific book treats of the royal mission, that of governing; rather, these norms are found in the remaining parts of the code.

Throughout the revision process, there was question of another book, the Fundamental Law of the Church, applying equally to Latin and Oriental rite Catholics. Opposition to such a document was strong, however, because of the risk of expressing doctrine in legislative form; it was therefore decided not to proceed at this time with the promulgation of the LEF. Because of this, a number of general norms had to be incorporated into the Code of Canon Law itself; among such were those on the rights and obligations of the faithful and many of those treating the papacy, ecumenical councils, and other issues.

Two particular problems regarding the plan concerned the place of personal prelatures and of institutes of consecrated life. While the drafts had placed personal prelatures within the canons on the particular Church, strong objections were raised against this on theological grounds, and prelatures were eventually moved to the first part (The Christian Faithful) of Book II, under a distinct heading. Similarly, at one point in the process it was proposed to place the canons on institutes of consecrated life alongside those treating of associations in the Church. Again, for theological reasons, Book II was divided into three parts: the Christian faithful; the hierarchical dimension of the Church; and institutes of consecrated life and societies of apostolic life, thus highlighting the charismatic dimension of consecrated life alongside the hierarchical dimension of Church structures. This new division was well received in general.

The Vision of the Church. Book II, c. 204, begins with the recognition that the Church is the people of God, comprising all the baptized. Baptism makes a person a member of the Church and the subject of rights and obligations. But the Church is not only a people; it is also a hierarchically organized community. Thus, the unifying factor is ecclesial communion with the successor of Peter and the bishops in communion with him. The code recognizes various degrees of communion (cc. 205; 844, etc.). Other Christians, who are not in full communion with the Catholic Church, may nevertheless share in some of the Sacraments and sacramentals of the Church in virtue of their Baptism. The theme of "communion" is one that ties together many parts of the legislation; those who place themselves outside of ecclesial communion are known as the "ex-communicated" (c. 1331). The ecumenical dimension of the law is evident, particularly in c. 11, which no longer extends merely ecclesiastical laws to all the baptized, but limits their scope to those who have been baptized in the Catholic Church or received into it. Many other canons speak of the importance of fostering true ecumenism (cc. 383; 755, etc). The code also recognizes that persons might leave the Church by a formal act, with certain consequences in law.

On a third level, communion leads to mission, since the Church by its nature is missionary (c. 781). This mission is threefold: to teach, sanctify, and serve. The laity, in virtue of their Baptism, are called upon to share in all these functions (c. 204). The code focuses on the Sacrament of Baptism as the unifying factor, rather than primarily on the Sacrament of Orders. These three missions are carried out through the apostolate. Canon 298 spells out seven possibilities of apostolic endeavors: promoting the perfection of Christian life, divine worship, teaching the faith, evangelization, works of piety, works of charity, and animating the world with a Christian spirit. These possibilities have been the object of further reflection in the meetings of the Synod of Bishops. For an apostolic endeavor to be truly such, however, it must be carried out in communion with the diocesan bishop (cf. c. 675).

On a fifth level, we could note that the apostolate presupposes an apostle. In various ways, the code invites those called to the apostolate to make a whole-hearted effort to lead a holy life (c. 210), to serve the Lord with an undivided heart (cc. 277; 599), to be models of holiness (c. 387), and so forth. In other words, there is no minimum; rather, there is an ideal toward which all apostles are to strive.

This vision of the Church is complemented by the recognition of the role of the Holy Spirit as soul of the Church. In seven well-chosen canons (cc. 206–879; 369–375; 573–605; 747), the action of the Holy Spirit is emphasized: the awakening of individual faith and the response, the establishment and guiding of the hierarchy, the charismatic dimension of Church life, and the unity of teaching and doctrine.

Major Features. Many factors distinguish the 1983 code from its 1917 counterpart. In the introduction to the legislation, Pope John Paul II outlines one specific feature of the code: not surprisingly it is "the Church's fundamental legislative document," based on the "juridical and legislative heritage of revelation and tradition." The code, then, flows from the doctrine of the Church as a whole. Indeed, it has more doctrinal norms than did the previous law. As was the case with the LEF, however, there is a risk in applying civil law interpretative standards to the 1983 canons. The canons themselves, because they are more pastoral in outlook, are necessarily written in a particular style; expressions such as, "showing an apostolic spirit," "being a witness to all," "acting with humanity and charity" (c. 383), "showing special concern," (c. 384), being "an example of holiness," "knowing and living the paschal mystery" (c. 385), and so forth, cannot be applied literally in all instances. Rather, the code promotes a renewed attitude of heart and mind, one that Pope Paul VI called for when he spoke of a *novus habitus mentis,* a new mentality [cf. *Acta Apostolicae Sedis* 57 (1965): 988]. Otherwise, to use his words again, the code risks becoming simply "a rigid order of injunctions" [*Origins* 3 (1973–74): 272]. The code necessarily has a juridical characteristic, but one that is tempered by the very nature of the Church itself. Indeed, the last words of the code to the effect that the ultimate norm

is the salvation of souls—*salus animarum, suprema lex* (c. 1752), based on Cicero's *De lege* (III 3.8)—express clearly the difference between this law and other codes that might at first sight be similar.

A second characteristic flows from this. Since the new code has as one of its basic purposes to translate the teachings of Vatican II into terms of daily life for Catholics, it is not surprising to find that many of the conciliar prescriptions are repeated textually in the law. The various decrees are thus a major source of material. Since the code implements the council, and not the converse, it is of primary importance to return to the conciliar context as a whole for the interpretation of the law. Otherwise, there would be the danger of reducing Vatican II to those prescriptions retained for incorporation into the code.

A third major feature of the legislation is its reliance on complementary norms. A number of the canons refer explicitly to particular norms to be elaborated by the Holy See (cf. cc. 335, 349, 569, 997, 1402, 1403, etc.), norms that would be too detailed or changing to be placed in a code. Many other canons refer to the decrees of Episcopal Conferences (about 100 in all), to decisions of diocesan bishops (about 300), or finally, to the proper law of institutes of consecrated life (approximately 100 canons). This means, in practice, that almost one-third of the canons allow for adaptation of some sort at the local level. A number of Episcopal Conferences have begun the task of preparing this complementary legislation (cf. c. 455). At the diocesan level, the process will usually take place within a diocesan synod; for this reason, many dioceses are presently organizing synods to prepare for the appropriate local legislation. In religious and secular institutes, although the task of revising constitutions is almost completed, many institutes are now turning their attention to complementary "codes" or specialized directories (c. 587 n.4) to apply the general legislation in more detail.

Some other features of the revised legislation are inclusion of a fundamental charter of rights and obligations, the recognized importance of the particular church, the implementation of consultation on various levels, flexibility to promote the Church's mission, an increased role recognized for lay members of the Church, and accountability in regard to financial matters.

There are, however, a few weaknesses in the code (in particular, certain norms on procedures, perhaps too great an insistence on hierarchical dimensions of Church life, and an overly cautious vision of the laity), but these are far outweighed by the advantages of the new legislation, particularly its fidelity to Vatican II and its reliance on local legislation. The code, as a universal document, often leaves the door open for future developments (cc. 129; 1055, etc.). Through this code and the *Code of Can-*

ons for the Eastern Churches, the Church has completed the major task of translating Vatican II's insights into norms of practical conduct, providing a basis for healthy and orderly Church development in the years ahead.

Bibliography: *Codex Iuris Canonici auctoritate Joannis Pauli PP. II promulgatus,* in *Acta Apostolicae Sedis* 75 (1983): II, xxx–324. J. A. ALESANDRO, "Law and Renewal: A Canon Lawyer's Analysis of the Revised Code," *Canon Law Society of America Proceedings* 44 (1982): 1–40. L. CASTILLO, "La communion ecclésiale dans le nouveau Code de droit canonique," *Studia Canonica* 17 (1983): 331–355. J. A. CORIDEN, et al., *The Code of Canon Law. A Text and Commentary* (New York 1985) xxvi–1152. T. J. GREEN, "Persons and Structure in the Church: Reflections on Selected Issues in Book II," *Jurist* 45 (1985): 24–94. F. G. MORRISEY, "The New Code of Canon Law: The Importance of Particular Law," *Origins* 11 (1981–82): 421–430; "Decisions of Episcopal Conferences in Implementing the New Law," *Studia Canonica* 20 (1986): 105–121.

[F. G. MORRISEY]

CANON LAW, HISTORY OF

The nature of the Church as a visible society existing in the world demands that there be a formal legal structure guiding and coordinating the faithful to the attainment of a common goal. The body of these ecclesiastical laws is called CANON LAW. Since there is continual change in society, there is constant change in Canon Law. The history of Canon Law is, in fact, the history of continual borrowing from and adaptation to the milieu in which the Church found herself. The discussion in this article is treated under the following main headings: (1) Early Church, (2) Carolingian Era, (3) False Decretals to Gratian, (4) Classical Period, (5) The Corpus Iuris Canonici to the Council of Trent, (6) The Council of Trent to the Code of Canon Law, and (7) The Code of Canon Law to the Present.

1. Early Church

From the beginning of the 3d century at least, the local Christian community—wherever it was established—possessed adequate and necessary machinery for its government. It had certain stable and universal characteristics: oneness of faith, of ethics, and of cult (especially Baptism and the Eucharist), a monarchial and indivisible episcopacy, the notion of apostolic succession, the distinction between clergy and laity, and finally an awareness of the principle of a *ius ecclesiasticum* (ecclesiastical law). There were as well factors that assured coordination among Christian communities and promoted supralocal unity: the consecration of the bishop by several neighboring bishops; episcopal assemblies; the drawing up of the constitutions of the Church; ex-

change of episcopal letters; collections of conciliar canons; and, after the advent of the Roman Emperor CONSTANTINE I (313), the support of imperial power. Although it cannot be said that a juridical society in the strict sense existed as yet (for in fact the code of laws was concerned mainly with matters of worship), the bases of the organization of a community were ready at hand in New Testament writings (cf. Mt 16.18–19; 18.18; 28.18; Jn 10.21; 21.15–17), where the beginnings of a regulatory system can be seen; the Apostolic Council of Antioch of 51 (Acts 15.23–29), matrimonial legislation, excommunication, justice within a community (Mt 18.15–18; 1 Cor 5–7).

The internal organization of Christian communities before the end of the 3d century must be reconstructed from sources not specifically juridical: the New Testament, apocryphal and antiheretical literature of the 2d century, and the writings of the apostolic Fathers and apologists. The most important of these are the letter of the Roman community to the community of Corinth, known as the *Prima Clementis* (Rome, *c.* 96), the Epistle of BARNABAS (Alexandria, 96 to 130), the apocryphal apocalypse known as the *Shepherd of HERMAS* (Rome, *c.* 96 to 140), the letters of IGNATIUS OF ANTIOCH (d. *c.* 110), and the letter of POLYCARP of Smyrna (d. 167?) to the community of Philippi.

With the 3d century, the Africans Tertullian and Cyprian molded the framework and the vocabulary of Western Law (*institutio, disciplina, regula, successio, sacramentum, ordo, plebs, ius, primatus, cathedra,* etc.). Besides, there were the pseudo-Apostolic Constitutions of the Church, juridico-didactic or juridico-liturgical documents. Written primarily in Greek, these constitutions were soon translated into Arabic, Syriac, Ethiopian, Coptic, and Latin, and constantly corrected and reedited. They were widely diffused and became the foundation of the discipline of the communities. They included the *Doctrina XII Apostolorum* or the DIDACHE (*c.* 100), which originated in Syria or Palestine; the *Traditio Apostolica* of HIPPOLYTUS OF ROME (*c.* 218), which is fundamental for the cult and discipline of the Church of Rome (again written in Greek) and which is the basis for subsequent constitutions; the *DIDASCALIA APOSTOLORUM* (*c.* 250 or 300, Syria or Palestine), the first attempt at a canonical corpus; the *Constitutiones Apostolorum* in eight books (*c.* 400, Syria or Palestine), whose influence was widespread despite subsequent reprobation of QUINISEXT, the Council in Trullo (691); the 30 *Canones ecclesiastici Apostolorum* (*c.* 300, Syria or Egypt); the 85 *Canones Apostolorum* (which are books of *Constitutiones Apostolorum*), the first 50 of which are known in the West (notwithstanding their rejection by the *Decretum Gelasianum*); the 38 *Canones Hippolyti,* which were an

The "Novella," of Joannes Andreae (d. 1348), book 2, in a Bolognese manuscript (MS Vat. lat. 1456, fol. 179r, detail). The miniature is signed by the artist Nicholas of Bologna and is dated 3 June 1353.

enlargement of the *Traditio Apostolica* of Hippolytus; the nine *Canones pseudo-synodi Antiochenae apostolorum* (*c.* 350 to 400, Palestine? Antioch?); the *Constitutiones per Hippolytum* or *Epitome* (post-5th-century); the *Testamentum Domini* (400 to 500, Syria); the 18 and the 25 *Canones paenitentiales apostolorum* (4th century); the *Octateuchus Clementis* (512 or 518? 8th-century Syriac version).

Development of Canon Law in the East to the 7th Century. The first Greek canonical collection preserved in the original text was the *Synagoge Canonum* in 50 titles by John the Scholastic III (*c.* 570). The Oriental collections before this date are accessible only in reconstructions from Latin or Syriac versions. These are conciliar texts that became sources of law by reason of the authority attributed to them by the Churches. Including translations, the Oriental collection prior to the 6th century consists of the following documents: (1) The first deposit embraces the decrees of the Councils of ANCYRA (314), NEOCAESAREA (314 to 25), GANGRA (341 to 42), Antioch (*c.* 341), and Laodicea (343 to 380), compiled under Bishop Meletios of Antioch (*c.* 342 to 381), and known as the *Corpus canonum* of Antioch. To this were subsequently added (2) the canons of the Councils of NI-CAEA I (325) and CONSTANTINOPLE I (381); this is the collection to which the Fathers of CHALCEDON (451) referred. (3) Finally, after 451, the canons of CHALCEDON were added to the above mentioned documents. The whole collection (1, 2, 3) is known as the *SYNTAGMA CANONUM ANTIOCHENUM,* or the primitive foundation upon which all the ancient collections rested. In about 500 the *Syntagma* was translated into Syriac at Mabbug. During the 6th century (soon after 519), the canons of the Councils of Ephesus (431), Africa (419), and SARDICA (343) and the 85 *Canones Apostolorum* were added. The Council in Trullo, or the Quinisext Council (691), limited the sources of law to the general and local councils, the

Patristic canons, and the Canon of Cyprian (c.2). It is, indeed, this list in the *Collectio Trullana* that constitutes the common foundation of Oriental law.

After the era of Constantine, the emperors often legislated on ecclesiastical matters, as protectors of the Church (e.g., in the *Codex Theodosianus* of 438, books 3, 9, and 16). But it was Justinian who exercised a capital, formal, and decisive influence on the development of Canon Law by his religious legislation in the *Corpus Iuris Civilis,* from which excerpts or summaries were soon drawn for the special use of the Church. The imperial laws were added as appendixes to the systematic canonical collections, such as the *Collectio LX titulorum* (*c.* 535) and the *Collectio L titulorum* of John the Scholastic (*c.* 570), to make up mixed collections that prepared the way for a new type of collection, the NOMOCANON. These latter were collections *utriusque iuris,* combining civil laws and conciliar canons on the same subject.

Pre-Carolingian Law in the West. In the West the history of the most ancient canonical collections is mixed up with the history of the versions. Very early (probably under Julius I, 337 to 352? and Innocent I, 401 to 417?), the canons of Nicaea (325) and of Sardica were translated and gathered in the collection *Vetus Romana,* which certainly was in use at the beginning of the 5th century. The so-called *Isidoriana,* or *Hispana Collectio-Versio,* known in three recensions, was probably prepared in Rome between *c.* 419 and 451. The so-called *Prisca,* or *Itala Collectio-Versio,* differs from the *Isidoriana* with respect to the ordering of the canons.

Under the pontificates of Gelasius I (492 to 496) and his successors until Hormisdas (514 to 523), there was a fruitful and original juridical activity, born of the Gelasian renaissance. The work no longer consisted merely of translations, but was an ordering of the councils and decretals into a single corpus, with the purpose of unifying and coordinating legislation under the authority of the Roman pontiff and of making it universally obligatory. The most famous work is the *collectio-versio* of DIONYSIUS EXIGUUS, the so-called *Dionysiana,* known in at least three editions: the *Prima* (*c.* 497 to 500), the *Secunda* (beginning of 6th century), and the *Tertia* (before 523). The same Dionysius completed his *collectio-versio* with a Collectio decretalium (*c.* 498 to 514), consisting of decretals from Siricius (384 to 399) to Anastasius II (496 to 498), taken either from the archives of the Lateran or from earlier collections. The two Dionysian works, known also as *Liber canonum* and *Liber decretorum (Zacharias* to Pepin in 747) are now called the DIONYSIANA COLLECTIO. Together with the *Dionysiana,* in the same period are (*c.* 495 to 500) the QUESNELLIANA COLLECTIO, known especially in France, the Freising Collection (after

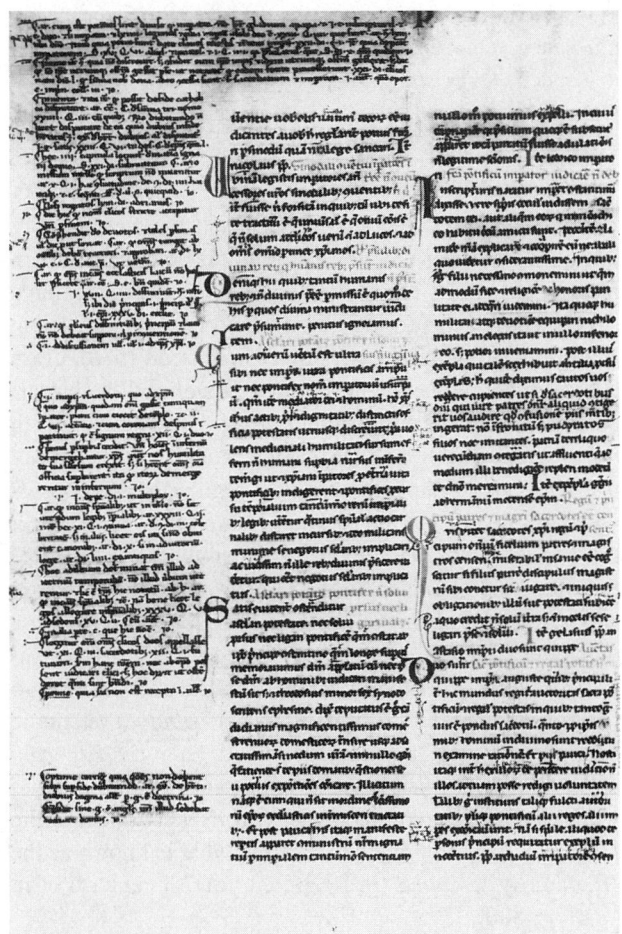

"Glossa ordinaria" of Joannes Teutonicus on Decretum 96, in a 13th-century MS (MS Pal. lat. 624, fol. 69v).

495), the *Vaticana* (under Hormisdas), the *Sanblasiana,* and the Teatina or *Collectio Ingilrami* (soon after 523), all of which pursue the same goal as the *Dionysiana* with varying degrees of success, i.e., the collecting of ancient law and the unifying of it.

The researches of W. H. Peitz call into question the history of the earlier collections up to the 6th century. According to Peitz (1) all the ancient versions, with the exception of the *Vetus Romana,* were prepared by Dionysius Exiguus. The *Prisca* and the *Isidoriana* were thus successive corrections of the same work by the same author. (2) Before Dionysius, there was no collection at all, in either Greek or Latin. Even the *Syntagma canonum antiochenum* is a work of Dionysius circulating in the East. The same applies to the *Corpus canonum* of the African Church. (3) Collections such as the *Frisingensis* or the *Quesnelliana* derive from the *Dionysiana* in varying degrees. If these conclusions are accepted, they will necessitate the rewriting of the history of the sources anterior to the 6th century.

The Italian collections subsequent to the Gelasian renaissance (*Dionysiana*) and prior to the Carolingian renaissance (*Dionysio-Hadriana*) are of minor importance, except for the following collections of decretals: the *Thessalonicensis* (*c.* 531), the AVELLANA (*c.* 555) and the *Mutinensis* (*c.* 601).

Canon Law in the Spanish Church. Juridical activity in Spain was characterized from its origins by a concern for unification. Few documents (versions, decretals) have survived from the period before the Visigothic invasion. Beginning with the conversion of Recaredo (586), close ties were forged between the civil power and the hierarchy, favoring the establishment of solid institutions. With the Council of TOLEDO (589) there began a conciliar activity unique in the Church for its regularity and conservatism. It resulted in the *Collectio Hispana chronologica*, the so-called *Isidoriana* (falsely attributed to Isidore of Seville, d. 636). Based on the *Dionysiana*, this collection was drawn up at the Council of Toledo (633); between then and the 17th Council of Toledo (694) it was increased by 104 decretals (from Damasus, 366 to 384, to Gregory I, 604). To facilitate its use, a *Tabula* (systematic summary) was composed, followed later by *Excerpta* along the same lines. When the extracts in the *Excerpta* were replaced by complete texts from the Collectio, the *Hispana chronologica* then became what is known as the *Hispana systematica* (in Spain, end of 7th century; or in Gaul, *c.* 800).

Systematic Collections of the African Church. The African Church, particularly in the persons of Tertullian and Cyprian, molded the vocabulary of law. Versions were always held in honor there, such as the *Caeciliani Versio* (beginning of 5th century) and the two versions established at the time of the Apiarian controversy: the *Attici Versio* and the *Cyrilli Versio*. The *Corpus canonum orientale* was translated for the first time in Africa (*Corpus canonum Africanum*). Among the canonical collections there may be noted the *Breviarium* of Hippo (393) and the *Collectio concilii Cartaginensis* 17 (419), known also as the *Codex canonum Ecclesiae Africanae*. Both the West and the East owed their acquaintance with African canons to the text of this collection. The Vandal invasion and persecution (after 429) put an end to the vitality of the African Church; even after the restoration of the hierarchy under Justinian (534), conciliar activity did not revive. Production was confined to systematic compilations: the *Breviatio canonum* of Fulgentius Ferrandus in 232 chapters (*c.* 546), and the *Concordia canonum* attributed to a bishop, Cresconius, but actually compiled in the 6th or 7th century. The latter is a systematic classification of the chronological collections of Dionysius Exiguus (according to Peitz, this would in fact be

one of Dionysius' works). The Arabian invasion permanently destroyed the African Church.

Gallic Collections. In Gaul, as in the Spanish Church but with less continuity and centralism, the conciliar activity was active until the end of the 7th century (Council of Saint-Jean-de-Losne, 673 to 675). During the troubled years of the accession to power of the mayors of the Palace of Austrasia (the future Carolingians) toward 740, the Frankish Church went through a period of profound decadence. The Gallic collections up to the Carolingian renaissance are as follows: the *STATUTA ECCLESIAE ANTIQUA* (*c.* 476 to 485), the *Collectio Arelatensis* or the (pseudo) Council of Arles II (442 to 506), the *Andegavensis I* (after 450), and perhaps the *Quesnelliana*. In the 6th century there was the *Liber auctoritatum,* or *Liber canonum,* of the Church of Arles (*c.* 560 to 595), as well as various collections: the *Corbeiensis,* the *Coloniensis,* the *Albigensis,* the *Lugdunensis,* the *Remensis I,* the *Lauresheimensis* (Lorsch), the *Pithouensis,* the *Bigotiana,* the *Collectio S. Mauri,* and the Collection of Saint-Amand. To the period immediately preceding the Carolingian period belong the Andegavensis II, which is relatively well ordered, and the *Herovalliana* (*c.* 740), which is badly ordered and corrupt. Neither collection was of a quality to arrest in any way the deterioration that law was undergoing.

Decline and Decentralization of Discipline. In fact, from the end of the paleo-Christian era (late 6th century) until the Carolingian renaissance (from the 2d half of the 8th century), a period of anarchy and decadence reigned in the Church, as a result of the breaking up of the *Imperium* after the invasions, and of the progressive and turbulent rise of the national kingdoms. The sources of law reflect this situation: there are local peculiarities and a confusion in discipline and in worship.

From the time of the invasions the new law of the conquerors had been juxtaposed to Roman law. However, because of the personal character of the Roman laws, the *Lex romana* continued to be applied to the persons and things of the Church, which were considered as "Roman." Hence special collections were compiled for the use of persons subject to Roman law: the *Lex romana Visigothorum* or the *Breviarium* of Alaric (*c.* 506), the *Edictum Theodorici* (beginning of the 6th century), the *Lex romana Burgundionum* (beginning of 6th century), and the *Lex romana Curiensis* or *Raetica* (8th century). *See* LEGES ROMANAE BARBARORUM.

From the 6th to the 12th centuries Germanic law contributed increasingly to the formation of Canon Law, because of the ascendancy of the Franks and later of the Empire in the life of the Church. The collections of Germanic law, which were all composed after the conversion of the peoples to Christianity, already reflected the influence of the Church: the *Lex Salica* (*c.* 500, and versions until *c.* 750), the *Lex Ripuaria* (6th–8th centuries), the *Lex Francorum Chamavorum* (c. 802 or 803), the *Lex barbara Burgundionum* or *Lex Gundobaldi* (end of 5th century), the *Lex Alamannorum* (beginning of 7th century), the *Lex Baïwarorum* (*c.* 750), the *Lex Frisonum* (8th or 9th century), the *Lex Saxorum* (beginning 9th century), the *Lex Thuringorum* or *Lex Anglorum* (beginning 9th century), the *Lex barbara Visigothroum* (466 or 485 to 649 or 672), the *Leges Langobardorum* (whose first collation of 643 is known as the *Edictum Rothari*).

To these documents should be added the acts emanating from the royal power, such as the CAPITULARIES and the *Diplomata*. A very concrete source of law is provided by the formularies, collections of formulas used for the authentic production of civil or ecclesiastical acts. Such for example were the 400 *Formulae* of the Ostrogothic Kingdom collected by Cassiodorus *c.* 537 under the name of *Variae,* and the *Formulae* of Marculf (*c.* 660). All the other collections of Formulae, including the famous LIBER DIURNUS ROMANORUM PONTIFICUM (from 590 to 795) are not from this period.

Penitentials. From the Insular Churches (i.e., those of the British Isles: England, Wales, Scotland, Ireland), where there prevailed juridical peculiarities in organization and discipline, a penitential system based on a scale of penances, and differing from the ancient *Paenitentia* of the Church, spread to the Continent through missionary monks and the numerous *libri paenitentiales* that appeared from the 6th century onward. These PENITENTIALS contain catalogues of sins and the corresponding scales of penances and were of great importance both for penitential discipline and for the history of morals and customs. The penitentials were also an effective instrument of civilization through their regulations on hygiene and food.

Bibliography: F. MAASSEN, *Geschichte der Quellen und der Literatur des canonischen Rechts im Abendlande bis dem Ausgang des Mittelalterrs* (Graz 1870; repr. Graz 1956). P. FOURNIER and G. LEBRAS, *Histoire des collections canoniques en occident depuis les fausses décrétales jusqu'au Décret de Gratien,* 2 v. (Paris 1931–32). S. KUTTNER, *Repertorium der Kanonistik* (Rome 1937); *Studi e Testi,* 71. I. A. ZEIGER, *Historia iuris canonici,* 2 v. (Rome 1940–47). B. KURTSCHEID and F. A. WILCHES, *Historia iuris canonici,* 2 v. (Rome 1941–43). A. VAN HOVE, *Commentarium Lovaniense in Codicem iuris canonici 1,* v.1–5 (Mechline 1928–). A. M. STICKLER, *Historia iuris canonici latini:* v.1, *Historia fontium* (Turin 1950). W. M. PLÖCHL, *Geschichte des Kirchenrechts,* 3 v. (Vienna 1953–59). H. E. FEINE, *Kirchliche Rechtsgeschichte,* v.1, *Die Katholische* Kirche (3d ed. Weimar 1955). J. GAUDEMET, *L'Église dans l'Empire romain* (Paris 1958). J. J. RYAN, "Observations on the Pre-Gratian Canonical Collections," *Actes du Congràs de Droit Canonique médiéval* (Louvain 1958). W. M. PEITZ, *Dionysius Exiguus-Studien,* ed. H. FOERSTER (Berlin 1960). A. COUSSA, *Epitome praelectionum de iure ecclesiastico orientali,* 3 v. (Grottaferrata-Rome 1948–50; supplement 1958). G. LE BRAS et al., eds., *Histoire du droit et des institutions de l'Église en Occident* (Paris 1955–) v.1, *Prolégomenès.* E. SCHWARTZ, *Zeitschrift der Savigny-Stiftung für Rechtsgeschichte, Kanonistische Abteilung* 25, 56 (1936) 1–114.

[C. VOGEL]

2. Carolingian Era

In about the middle of the 8th century, the Franks began to take over the protection of the Latin Church. Spain was Arab, England isolated, and the Eastern Roman Empire, alienated from the Western Church after the Trullan Council (692) and weakened by the iconoclast controversy, had quarreled with the papacy, which in turn sought support among the Franks against the Lombards. The consolidation of the Frankish Church had been intimately connected with the development of the Austrasian Carolingians. Imbued as he was with Germanic notions of a private church, the major-domo Charles Martel (d. 741) had parceled out Church lands and offices to laymen; he did indeed support missionary activity (of Willibrord, Pirmin, Boniface), but he did not trouble himself with Canon Law or constitutions. The last known conference of bishops had been in about 680, and there was no longer any metropolitan organization.

When he took over the duties of a king, Martel's son Pepin (742 to 768), together with his brother Carloman until 747, and in accord with the ideas of the Pope, set about strengthening ecclesiastical organization. Though Pepin may have disappointed the pope after his acquisition of the royal title in 751, a title and legitimation for which he had the Pope to thank, he did lay the groundwork of a Rome-oriented Canon Law, and this was of importance for the future.

Canon Law of the Merovingian Period. Under the Merovingians, the independence of the national churches had come strongly to the fore, both in the field of liturgy and in the field of Canon Law; the universal collections (e.g., DIONYSIANA, later HISPANA) had been supplemented since as early as the 6th century (perhaps stemming from Arles) by works of a more local coloring. There had indeed been attempts to combine the two principles, the universal and the local [cf. the *Collectio Andegavensis,* probably initiated by Leodegar of Autun (d. 679 or 680) and the *Herovalliana* from the first half of the 8th century]. But hope of success was assured only when the Monarch began to interest himself in a unification of Canon Law. Pepin himself requested from Pope Zacharias a rescript on Canon Law in 747.

The insular PENITENTIALS, brought by the Irish-Scottish and Anglo-Saxon missionaries, exercised an influence on the Frankish Church, independently of the general collections. With their highly developed casuistry and their tendency to replace protracted mild penances by short strict ones (redemption principle), these insular penitentials became widely disseminated and began to supplant the comparatively meager penitential instructions of the ancient Church.

Carolingian Ecclesiastical Reform. The aim of the Carolingian ecclesiastical reform initiated by Pepin was to reduce the divergent institutions and tendencies of Canon Law into a unity dictated by the Carolingian monarchy and supported by the clergy and imperial nobility. Anyone who, like U. Stutz or H. E. Feine, speaks of an ''irruption of Germanism into canon law'' and a period of ''Germanically cast canon law'' extending down to Gratian (1140), simply because the lower echelons of the Church were being reorganized according to the idea of the private church is looking at a broad reform in a way that narrows it to a mere portion of itself and then regards it from a merely modern legal-dogmatic point of view. For the ecclesiastical organization as a whole was restored; every diocese was given a bishop to whom monasteries and foundations were subordinated; the metropolitan constitution was renewed—so that Charlemagne (768 to 814) could already list 21 metropolitans in the Empire as a whole in his testament of 811.

Implementation. The monarchs used reform councils and legislation to raise the level of ecclesiastical life; the bishops used diocesan synods and *capitula episcoporum.* The series of reform councils began in Austrasia with the *Concilium Germanicum* (probably 743), continued in Neustria (Soissons) in 744 and by 745 to 747 embraced the entire Empire. The important reform councils were: imperial Councils of Heristal (779) and Frankfurt (794), where Charlemagne tackled questions of dogmatic theology and recognized the institution of the private church; the Council of Aachen (816 to 817), which newly defined the status of canons; the Council of Paris (829).

On many occasions, ecclesiastical CAPITULARIES were promulgated in connection with the conciliar decisions. The *Admonitio generalis* of 798 was of fundamental importance for the discipline of the Church; and the *Capitulare* of 802, for the program of the new Emperor. There appears to have been no official collection of the numerous capitularies. From 829 it was customary to refer in the capitularies to the private collection of Abbot St. ANSEGIS of Fontenelle (d. 833), which had come into existence shortly before but which included barely 30 percent of the capitularies from the preceding 50 years; the Pseudo-Isidorean collection of capitularies of BENEDICT THE LEVITE claimed to be a continuation of this Ansegis collection. Of importance for the life and practice

of the Church were the *capitula episcoporum,* episcopal instructions to the diocesan clergy that often exerted an influence far beyond the time and diocese of the promulgator (THEODULF OF ORLÉANS, Chaerbald of Lüttich, Hincmar of Reims).

Collections of Canon Law. When ecclesiastical regulations had been unified, the general collections regained prestige. This no doubt was due to their practicability and suitability, as well as to a newly awakened esteem for ecclesiastical authority, particularly that of the ancient plenary councils and papal decretals. Capitularies and councils made extensive reference to the general collections, and Pope Adrian I delivered to Charlemagne in 774 a model code that contained the councils and the collection of Decretals of DIONYSIUS EXIGUUS (i.e., *Dionysio-Hadriana*). The QUESNELLIANA can be traced in Carolingian capitularies in 755 (*Monumenta Germaniae Historica: Capitularia* 14); from 789 (*Monumenta Germaniae Historica: Capitularia* 22), and perhaps even from 779, until about 830 the *Dionysio-Hadriana* or the *Dionysiana* was the almost exclusive source; in West Frankish capitularies, the *Hispana* appeared before the middle of the 9th century. Similarly in the councils after 800, the *Dionysio-Hadriana* was evidently the standard collection (Aachen 836, perhaps also the DACHERIANA); but it is doubtful whether the HADRIANA was granted official recognition at the Council of Aachen of 802. Pope Nicholas I (858 to 867) certainly spoke of the *Hadriana* as the *Codex Canonum* (P. Jaffé, *Regesta pontificum romanorum ab condita ecclesia ad annum post Christum natum 590–882,* ed. P. Ewald, 2785). *Dacheriana* was compiled about the year 800(?) from the *Hadriana* and the *Hispana,* and is considered to be the real achievement of the Frankish reform, whose efforts slackened about 830. Among the reform collections must finally be listed the FALSE DECRETALS (PSEUDO-ISIDOREAN FORGERIES), which, however, together with the Roman law brought to light in the 9th century, had but little influence on Carolingian Canon Law.

With the return to the ancient Canon Law, there was a corresponding revision of the penitential regulations. The provincial synods of Reims, Arles, Châlon-sur-Saône, and Tours were held at the command of Charlemagne in 813 and their decisions were officially compiled (this being the only known instance of a systematic collection of decisions of Carolingian reform synods). They were attempting to counteract the confusion created by the various contradictory penitentials, and to direct attention back to the general collections. In 829 a direct order was given to do away with the penitentials, and attempts were made to replace them with new ones. Witness to this reform effort is the penitential of Bishop Haltigar of Cambrai (817 to 831), compiled probably about 829. RABANUS MAURUS (d. 856), whose special concern was the canonical instruction of the clergy, compiled two penitentials of a similar character (841 to 847; 853), based mainly on the *Hadriana* and the *Hispana*. But the influence of the old penitentials could not be eradicated, and the attempt as well to reinstate the *poenitentia publica* that had been supplanted by private confessional practice had only a short-lived success.

Carolingian Theory of Canon Law. There was no ecclesiastical jurisprudence as such in Carolingian days. A start was made on a theory of the sources of law, but there was a lack of theoretical and systematic investigation and of scholarly institutions. Writings on Canon Law were occasioned usually by ecclesiastical and political controversies; and it is significant that it was precisely men involved in politics and in theological controversy who occupied themselves with Canon Law.

The older generation (centering around Charlemagne), under the stimulus of newly flourishing theology, began to devote attention to the role of authority (*auctoritas*) and reason (*ratio*), and was chiefly interested in reform, thereby collaborating with the monarch. The Spanish-born Bishop THEODULF OF ORLÉANS (d. 821), a man well informed in legal process, produced influential capitularies; Bishop Remedius of Chur (d. *c.* 806) attempted in his *Capitula* to effect a synthesis of Roman, Germanic, and Frankish penal law; Bishop Ghaerbald of Lüttich (d. 809), put the instructions of Charlemagne into practice.

The faltering regime of Louis the Pious and numerous lay encroachments divided the empire into factions. Some men, e.g., the theologically trained Bishop Jonas of Orléans (d. 843), felt themselves protectors and guides of the King; Jonas remained loyal to Emperor Louis when the Emperor's elder sons rose against him. On the opposing side stood Archbishop Agobard of Lyons (d. 840), a representative of "Carolingian rationalism." He called upon Emperor Louis to extend the law of the Franks to the entire Empire in order to eliminate the multiplicity of indigenous tribal laws (principle of personal law). For him, to act against the canons meant to act against God, and he earnestly called for the restitution of all ecclesiastical property held by laymen. Agobard supported Louis's sons and lost his archdiocese, in which, however, his faithful assistant, Deacon Florus (d. *c.* 860), a man thoroughly familiar with Canon Law and Roman law, continued to be active. He was certainly echoing his master when he demanded the *privilegium fori* for clerics and episcopal jurisdiction. The most prolific scholar in questions of Canon Law seem indeed to have been Archbishop HINCMAR OF REIMS (d. 882). Despite the considerable number of his writings on the subject of Canon Law, he

does not present an accurate picture of the Canon Law of that time. His chief concern was to strengthen the power of metropolitans and synods, and it was only reluctantly that he allowed Pope Nicholas I the last word in their controversy. The achievement of the Carolingian canonists was that they again enhanced the prestige of the canonical traditions of the ancient Church. They did indeed mold tradition according to their ideas, but without them the Latin Church might have dissolved into individual churches; at least the ties of unity would have been dangerously loosened.

Bibliography: General. Maassen. É. LESNE, *La Hiérarchie épiscopale 742–882* (Lille 1905); *Histoire de la propriété ecclésiastique en France,* 6 v. in 8 (Lille 1910–43), v.2. A. WERMINGHOFF, *Verfassungsgeschichte der deutschen Kirche im Mittelalter* (2d ed. Leipzig 1913). H. VON SCHUBERT, *Geschichte der christlichen Kirche im Frühmittelalter* (Tübingen 1921). R. SOHM, *Das altkatholische Kirchenrecht und das Dekret Gratians,* ed. E. JACOBI and O. MAYER (Munich 1918). P. FOURNIER and G. LEBRAS, *Histoire des collections canoniques en occident depuis les fausses déscrétales jusqu'au Décret de Gratien,* 2 v. (Paris 1931–32). E. RÖSSER, *Göttliches und menschliches, unveränderliches und veränderliches Kirchenrecht bis zur Mitte des 9. Jahrhunderts* (Paderborn 1934). A. VAN HOVE, *Commentarium Lovaniense in Codicem iuris canonici 1,* v. 1 (Mechlin 1928–). A. M. STICKLER, *Historia iuris canonici latini:* v.1, *Historia fontium* (Turin 1950). W. WATTENBACH, *Deutschlands Geschichtsquellen im Mittelalter. Vorzeit und Karolinger,* Hefte 1–4, ed. W. LEVISON and H. LÖWE (Weimar 1952–63) supplement. *Die Rechtsquellen,* ed. R. BUCHNER (1953). G. LE BRAS et al., eds., *Histoire du droit et des institutions de l'Église en Occident* (Paris 1955–) v.1 *Prolégomènes.* G. LE BRAS, *Institutions ecclésiastiques de la chrétienté médiévale (Histoire de l'église depuis les origines jusqu'à nos jours* 12; 1959). W. M. PLÖCHL, *Geschichte des Kirchenrechts,* v.1 (2d ed. Vienna 1960). H. E. A. FEINE, *Kirchliche Rechtsgeschichte* (4th ed. Cologne 1964–) v.1. J. J. RYAN, "Observations on the Pre-Gratian Canonical Collections: Some Recent Work and Present Problems," *Congrès de Droit Canonique Médiéval Louvain et Bruxelles, 22–26 Juillet* (Louvain 1959) 88–103. **8th Century.** E. LOENING, *Geschichte des deutschen Kirchenrechts,* 2 v. (Strasbourg 1878) v.2. F. ZEHETBAUER, *Das Kirchenrecht bei Bonifatius* (Vienna 1910). H. NOTTARP, "Sachkomplex und Geist des kirchlichen Rechtsdenkens bei Bonifatius" in *Sankt Bonifatius: Gedenkgabe zum zwölfhundertsten Todestag* (Fulda 1954). T. SCHIEFFER, *Winifried-Bonifatius und Die christliche Grundlegung Europas* (Freiburg 1954). G. LE BRAS, "Pénitentiels," *Dictionnaire de théologie catholique,* ed. A. VACANT et al., 15 v. (Paris 1903–50) 12.1:1160–79. J. T. MCNEILL and H. M. GAMER, trs., *Medieval Handbooks of Penance* (New York 1938). L. BIELER, ed., *The Irish Penitentials,* app., D. A. BINCHY (Scriptores Latini Hiberniae 5; Dublin 1963). **Reform.** U. STUTZ, "Das Karolingische Zehntgebot," *Zeitschrift der Savigny-Stiftung für Rechtsgeschichte, Germanistische Abteilung* 29 (1908) 180–224. H. FICHTENAU, *Das karolingische Imperium* (Zurich 1949). É. DELARUELLE, "Charlemagne et l'Église," *Revue d'histoire de l'Église de France* 39 (1953) 165–99. H. BARION, *Das fränkisch-deutsche Synodalrecht des Frühmittelalters* (Bonn 1931). C. DE CLERCQ, *La Législation religieuse franque . . . ,* 2 v. (Paris-Antwerp 1936–58). J. SEMMLER, "Reichsidee und kirchliche Gesetzgebung," *Zeitschrift für Kirchengeschicte* 71 (1960) 37–65. F. L. GANSHOF, *Was waren die Kapitularien?* (Weimar 1961). H. HÜRTEN, "Alkuin und der Episkopat im Reiche Karls des Grossen," *Historisches Jahrbuch der Görres-Gesellschaft* 82 (1963) 22–49. W. A. ECKHARDT, *Die Kapitularien-*

sammlung Bischof Ghaerbalds Von Lüttich (Göttingen 1955). J. RAMBAUD-BUHOT, "Une Collection canonique de la réforme carolingienne," *Revue historique de droit français et éranger* 33 (1956) 50–73. **Theory.** For individual authors, see W. WATTENBACH, *Deutschlands Geschichtsquellen im Mittelalter. Vorzeit und Karolinger*, Hefte 1–4, ed W. LEVISON and H. LÖWE (Weimar 1952–63), with extensive bibliography. J. FLECKENSTEIN, *Die Bildungsreform Karls des Grossen* (Freiburg 1953). L. WALLACH, *Alcuin and Charlemagne* (Ithaca, New York 1959), reviewed by H. LÖWE in *Göttingische gelehrte Anzeigen* 214 (1962) 144–53. H. DÖRRIES, "Die geistigen Voraussetzungen und Folgen der Karolingischen Reichsteilung 843" in *Der Vertrag von Verdun 843*, ed. T. MAYER (Leipzig 1943). J. DEVISSE, *Hincmar et la loi* (Dakar 1962). H. BACHT, "Hinkmar von Reims" in *Unio Christianorum: Festschrift für Erzbischof Dr. Lorenz Jaeger* (Paderborn 1962).

[H. FUHRMANN]

3. False Decretals To Gratian

The Carolingian reform had striven to unify and restore Canon Law: composite collections had been for the most part eliminated; and the return to the ancient texts of the universal law, approved by the Church of Rome (Dionysio-Hadriana) had restored to their place of honor the traditional rules respecting the ecclesiastical hierarchy, penitential discipline, the institution of marriage, and judicial order. However, the Church was still undergoing many trials: seizure of ecclesiastical property by secular rulers, abuses of the privilege of the forum, and all sorts of obstacles to the exercise of episcopal power.

It was in this context that the Isidorian forgeries (FALSE DECRETALS) were put into circulation (847 to 857) alleging incontestable authorities for texts decreeing much needed reforms. Generally faithful to traditional law, the False Decretals innovated on certain points and exercised a considerable influence on canonical literature. They reinforced the episcopal power, generalized the principle of appeal to Rome in important cases, broadened the privilege of the forum, regularized judicial procedure (*Spoliatus ante omnia est restituendus*), and reemphasized the sacred character of ecclesiastical property.

From the 10th to the middle of the 11th century, Canon Law underwent a period of decline; it suffered, in effect, from the weakening of the authority of the Holy See, which resulted from the interference of the Roman aristocracy and the Germanic emperors. It was characterized by an extreme fragmentation, as was the political power of the day, which was bound up with the parceling out of feudal lands, the contemporary culture, which was then sheltered in monasteries, and the economy itself, which was essentially tied to the land and was domestic and stagnant. The Church and its law were narrowly dependent on these concrete conditions; it underwent a partial laicization through the system of private churches (*Eigenkirchen*) and had to depend on the local authorities to carry out its moral mission, slowly and with difficulty. This latter function had to be accomplished in the most diverse areas: in struggles against superstition, immorality and violence; in the defense of the lower classes; etc. Progress was neither uniform nor constant, often being compromised by upheavals, wars, primitive customs, and such calamities as famines and epidemics.

In the absence of an active and respected central power, the most noteworthy canonical works of this era were the local collections, of limited scope, composed by private authors. These generally manifest no critical sense in the choice of texts, which they treat with extreme liberty (by interpolations, false attributions, composition of apocrypha) with a view to adapting them to local needs or their own reforming intentions. In the midst of an abundant but uneven output, several works merit particular mention: in Italy, the collection called *ANSELMO DEDICATA, COLLECTIO*, dedicated to Archbishop Anselm of Milan (882 to 896) and the *Collectio libri quinque* (1015 to 1020); in Germany, the *Libri duo de synodalibus causis et disciplinis ecclesiasticis*, dedicated by Regino of Prüm (d. 915) to Archbishop Atto of Mainz; in France, the Collection of ABBO OF FLEURY (988 to 996), addressed to King Hugh and King Robert. But the most celebrated work of this period is the *Decretum* of BURCHARD, bishop of Worms (1000 to 1025), which sets forth the principles that should govern imperial reform. A protegé of Emperor Henry II, Burchard relied on the support of the secular powers for reorganizing the Church and maintaining the discipline of the clergy and of the Christian people.

The Gregorian Reform. The optimism of Burchard nonetheless lacked foresight, for a true reform of Christian society could not be effectively brought about unless it was begun from the very center, free from self-interested interventions of secular powers, and carried out in line with the spiritual mission of the Church.

Such would be the principles animating the GREGORIAN REFORM: the primacy of the Holy See, the independence of the Church, and fidelity to tradition. The decree of Nicholas I (1059) confining papal elections to the cardinals constituted a decisive step in the emancipation of pontifical power. Now that the Church was free at the summit and the supreme authority of the sovereign pontiff was restored, indispensable reforms could be progressively extended to all Christendom.

Gregorian teaching made the sovereign pontiff the primary source of ecclesiastical law (*Dictatus Papae* 17). He exercises authority through councils, over which he presides and whose decisions he approves, and through written responses (decretals), which he gives whenever he is consulted on a disputed point. The pope also guarantees the authority of the texts expressing the common law of the Church. In order to restore to honor the authentic sources of a canonical tradition that they claimed was continuous, the Gregorians carried out research in libraries and archives in Rome and throughout Italy. They unearthed a great number of new fragments, favorable to the rights of the Roman Church (*LIBER DIURNUS*, *Ordines Romani*, and, above all, decretals, collected in the *Britannica*) or capable of providing support for reforming measures [ancient councils, patristic texts, Roman law (the *Authentica* and *Pandecta*)]. These texts supplemented the Gregorian collections, the best known of which are the *DICTATUS PAPAE*, attributed to Gregory VII; the *Breviarium* of ATTO OF VERCELLI; the *Collectio Libri Duo;* the *Collection of SEVENTY-FOUR TITLES*; and the collections of ANSELM II OF LUCCA and of Cardinal Deusdedit (DEUSDEDIT COLLECTION).

The controversies over the burning issues of the day (the power of the papacy, the validity of Sacraments conferred by simoniacal clergy, law investiture, oaths, reordination, etc.) provoked an abundant polemical literature. Many theological questions are treated in these writings, and the argumentation is rarely objective and dispassionate, but the discussions favored the progress of canonical science. Authorities are discussed, compared, interpreted; their particular force is evaluated and related to the jurisdictional primacy of Rome.

Urban II to Gratian. After the reign of Gregory VII (1073 to 1085), precisely because the principle of the primacy had triumphed to such an extent that it had obscured the original doctrinal aspects of the reform, it became possible to moderate the overly rigorous measures of the Gregorian reform by the frequent use of dispensations and the reconciliation of guilty clerics, particularly in the pontificates of Urban II (1088 to 1099) and Paschal II (1099 to 1118). But the initial indulgence of Urban II was not approved by some, such as BONIZO OF SUTRI, who in his *Liber de vita christiana* (1089 to 1095) showed himself a partisan of the rigorist Gregorian position, or by the anonymous author of the *Britannica* (c. 1090).

On the other hand, the *POLYCARPUS* of Cardinal Gregory (1104 to 1013), while Gregorian in tendency, reflects the more conciliatory influence of IVO, bishop of Chartres (1091 to 1116), the classic representative of the French canonical tradition. Favorable to reform, respectful of the papal primacy, Ivo was no less careful to maintain peaceful relations between Church and State, with prudence, moderation, and realism. He accepted lay investiture on condition that it be limited to temporalities and conferred only after legitimate election and consecra-

tion; he suggested thereby the solution that had been adopted in England (1102) and in France (1107), and which at Worms (1122) would reestablish peace between the papacy and the Empire. An enlightened pacifist, Ivo wanted to limit recourse to war and to extend the machinery of peace (PEACE OF GOD), while admitting the right of recourse to arms to defend rights unjustly violated. The divorce of King Philip I (1092) and other cases that were submitted to him gave him an opportunity to develop more precisely the doctrine of marriage (*Decretum,* VIII–IX; *Panormia* VI–VII). With regard to ecclesiastical law, Ivo counseled tempering strict justice with mercy, for the supreme law of ecclesiastical government is of the pastoral order: the salvation of souls and the building up of the kingdom of God in charity, which is the fulfillment of the law (*Prologue, Patrologia Latina*, ed. J. P. Migne, 161:47C, 58D). The *Liber de misericordia et de justitia* of ALGER OF LIÈGE (c. 1105) expressed the same ideal.

A conservative and moderate spirit, Ivo did not reject indiscriminately the traditional texts of the methodical collections (the *Decretum* of BURCHARD and the PENITENTIALS) condemned by the Gregorians, but strove to bring them into harmony with the new trends and authorities, drawing inspiration from and adapting rules laid down by BERNOLD OF CONSTANCE (1054 to 1100). The latter had set forth excellent principles on the sources of Canon Law and the rules of interpretation and concordance of texts. He urged canonists to reject apocrypha, analyze each fragment according to circumstances of time, place, and persons that occasioned its composition; then to determine the nature of the rule laid down, its permanent or temporary character. To these rules, as adopted and developed by the prologue of Ivo (*Patrologia Latina* 161:47–60), the preface to Abelard's *Sic et Non* (*Patrologia Latina* 178:1339–49), c. 111 to 1117, added remarks of a semantic and dialectic order that were to profit canonists and theologians alike. In this manner, canonical science was gradually organized, arming itself with a method suitable for resolving the conflicts of authorities. The choice of texts and arguments became rigorous, and juridical rules were formulated with more precision. Besides, the renaissance of Roman law at Bologna at the end of the 11th century exerted a happy influence on canonists.

Byzantine Law to 1054. From the 7th century until the break of July 16, 1054, the history of the Canon Law of the Byzantine Church was dominated by three factors: the fixing of legislation, the composition of systematic collections, and the growth of canonical science.

In 691 to 692 the QUINISEXT SYNOD (in Trullo) met at Constantinople to revise and complete the legislation of the fifth and sixth ecumenical councils (Constantinople, 553, 680 to 681). The 102 canons then promulgated were for the most part a repetition of previous legislation, but canon two was of decisive importance for the Canon Law of the Oriental Churches; it enumerated the sources of this law to the exclusion of all other documents, so much so that the collections produced according to its specifications constitute the common *fontes* of Oriental Canon Law. After the councils of Nicaea (787) and Constantinople (869) the Orient had no general councils; ecclesiastical questions were henceforth decided by the patriarch of Constantinople (with his synod of bishops located in, or visiting, the capital), or by the secular authorities (legislation of the basilicas).

The composition of systematic collections, begun *c.* 535 with the *Collection in 60 Titles* and the various *Nomocanones,* was continued in new collections. The most important of these collections is the *Nomocanon in 14 Titles,* composed *c.* 630 by the jurisconsult Enantiophanes. As its name indicates, the work resembles both the civil laws (third part) and ecclesiastical documents (second part); the first part gives the titles that divide the canonical material. A second edition of this work dates from 883; it is generally attributed to the patriarch PHOTIUS (857 to 886) and was recognized in 920 as the official collection of the Church of Constantinople. It was brought up to date by Theodore Bestès in 1080. (*See* NOMOCANON.)

The canonical science of the Oriental Church is noteworthy for the composition of systematic commentaries, expounding the ensemble of legislation then in force, both canonical and imperial. The first commentator seems to have been Theodore Prodramus (8th century); the most famous are John Zonaras, Alexis Aristenes (beginning of the 12th century), and Theodore BALSAMON. The method followed by these authors was inspired by the rules of jurisprudence of Justinian. After the paraphrase, giving the general sense of the text, come the *scholia:* explanations of difficult terms, and circumstances of composition. Then the author compares, if need be, decisions relative to the same topic and points out their application. He proposes questions and cases and gives their solutions, illustrated by patriarchal decrees and imperial constitutions. It is incontestable that the canonical science manifested by the great Oriental commentators surpasses that of contemporary Western canonists, who were still seeking a properly scientific method.

Bibliography: P. FOURNIER and G. LEBRAS, *Histoire des collections canoniques en occident depuis les fausses décrétales jusqu'au Décret de Gratien,* 2 v. (Paris 1931–32) 1:127–456; 2:1–352. A. VAN HOVE, *Commentarium Lovaniense in Codicem iuris canonici 1,* v.1–5 (Mechlin 1928–) 1:157–64, 216–33, 293–342. A. M. STICKLER, *Historia iuris canonici latini:,* v.1, *Historia fontium* (Turin 1950) 67–72, 117–95, 407–10. S. KUTTNER, "Liber Canonicus: A Note on Dictatus Papae c. 17," *Studi gregoriani,* ed. G. B. BORINO 2 (1947) 387–401. *Monumenta Germaniae Historica: Libelli de lite* (Berlin 1826–). Sacred Congregation for the Eastern Church, *Codificazione canonica orientale: Fonti* (Vatican City 1930–), ser.1, fasc. 8. *Studi storici sulle fonti del diritto canonico orientale.* C. DE CLERCQ. *Dictionnaire de droit canonique,* ed. R. NAZ, 7 v. (Paris 1935–65) 2:1170–84. A. WUYTS, *Catholicisme* 3:1109–16. *Traditio,* an annual with summary of recent bibliography.

[C. MUNIER]

4. Classical Period

The time from the *Decretum* of GRATIAN (*c.* 1140) to the death of the canonist JOANNES ANDREAE (1348) was the classical period in the history of Western Canon Law; for the scientific study of the canons of the Church was begun by Gratian and reached its climax in the works of Joannes Andreae. During this period the Church, for the first time, promulgated official collections of universally binding laws: the *Decretals of GREGORY IX* in 1234; the *LIBER SEXTUS* in 1298; and the *CLEMENTINAE* in 1317. These remained the only authenticated collections of decretal legislation and became the center of the CORPUS IURIS CANONICI that governed the Western Church from 1582 until the CODE OF CANON LAW of 1917.

Before the *Concordia discordantium canonum* or *Decretum* of Gratian there was available the confusing wealth of written traditions described in the preceding sections of this article. Time and again efforts had been made to reform and unify this tradition (*see* CANONICAL COLLECTIONS BEFORE GRATIAN), most strikingly in the *Decretum* of BURCHARD OF WORMS (*c.* 1023), but none of these was regarded as adequate by the reforming party that came to the fore in the Church of the 11th century. Coherence and universality were lacking, and the reformers turned to more ancient sources (*see* GREGORIAN REFORM). However, the preoccupations of these reformers led them to suppress as contradictory of papal authority a great portion of the Franco-Germanic tradition. This led to greater confusion. Most of the *Decretum* of Burchard reappeared in the influential *Decretum* (*c.* 1096) of IVO OF CHARTRES; the situation was complicated by competition between varying types of collections and by numerous contradictions between texts appealed to by champions of reform and those advanced by their opponents. At the turn of the 11th century, as the fires of the investiture controversy died away and the reformers began to understand that the enforcement of full reform would be impossible in practice, there was a search for a workable system of interpretation of texts that would at once make for unity within the Church and allow a reconciliation between the Roman and the suspect Franco-

Germanic traditions. The chief figures in this movement were BERNOLD OF CONSTANCE (*De excommunicatis vitandis, c.* 1091), Ivo of Chartres (prologue "De consonantia canonum" to his *Panormia, c.* 1096), and ALGER OF LIÈGE (*Liber de misericordia, c.* 1105). Adapting certain principles of Biblical and rhetorical hermeneutics to the study of the canons, they separated precept from counsel and principles of eternal validity from those affected by conditions of time, place, or person.

This quest of a sure way through the thickets of canonical tradition was paralleled by efforts of theologians with respect to their sources; as had been made clear by LANFRANC in his criticism of the Eucharistic theology of BERENGARIUS OF TOURS, the problem of the authenticity, reconciliation, and interpretation of sources was crucial also to theology. It was, in fact, a theologian who gave the final sheen to the rules of interpretation and principles of textual criticism adumbrated by Bernold and Ivo and practiced to some extent by Alger. About 1115 to 1117 Peter ABELARD developed these principles in a theological setting in the preface of his *Sic et Non* (*Patrologia Latina* 178:1344–49), a treatise in which patristic texts are played off dialectically against one another in order to arrive at a balanced, coherent tradition. A method of scientific theology was now set, and it was claimed at once for the canonical field. Whether or not Gratian decided in or about 1120, independently of Abelard, to compile a rigorous *summa* of canonical tradition along the lines suggested by his predecessors, he undoubtedly received a stimulus at some point from Abelard's incisive rendering of their principles, and in particular from Abelard's insistence, apparently original, on working out from context, phraseology, etc., the precise meaning of a term or an idea in a given text. Applying Abelard's dialectical method to the mass of texts provided by existing collections, Gratian proposed texts for and against chosen propositions and sought to penetrate textual divergences by defining terms and applying relentlessly the rules of interpretation. The result (*c.* 1140) was his *Concordia discordantium canonum,* the foundation of the classic law of the Church. To arrive at this first scientific formulation of the teaching of the canons, Gratian doubtlessly was spurred on by the presence in Bologna of a vigorous school of civil law, which, under IRNERIUS, had since 1100 contributed to the revival of the study of classical Roman law. Gratian then demonstrated in the *Decretum* that it was possible to mold a seemingly amorphous mass of canons into a system of jurisprudence that could compare with the enviable order of the civilian corpus.

Stages of the Classical Period. As a synthesis of the patristic, conciliar, and papal teaching on the organization of the Church (the hierarchy, clerical discipline, excommunication), on the social structure of Christianity (matrimony, usury, relations of spiritual and secular authorities), and on the Sacraments, worship, and liturgy, the *Decretum* provided canonists with a mine of solid information and provided the Church with sure bases on which to build an ordered array of institutions. By 1150 it was in use in schools and synods; although never "received" by the Church as an authentic collection, from the time of Alexander III (1159 to 1181) onward it was the manual of the Roman Curia. The first impact of the *Decretum* was on the scholastic centers. Commentaries and glosses on and summaries of the *Decretum* began to appear, first at Bologna, then in France and England (*see* DECRETISTS), notably, to mention only a few, from PAUCAPALEA, Gratian's own disciple; Roland Bandinelli (ALEXANDER III); Stephen of Tournai; RUFINUS; SICARDUS OF CREMONA; also many anonymous authors (e.g., the *Summa Parisiensis, Summa Monacensis*); and HUGUCCIO (HUGH OF PISA). If the *Decretum* set in motion a wave of canonistic writing, it no less occasioned a flood of questions. On many points the solutions Gratian offered were fragmentary or hesitant and called for development; in some areas of Europe confusion was caused by a lack of harmony between local custom and the tradition of the Church as represented in the *Decretum*. The papacy, as a result of the Gregorian Reform and of the tradition mirrored in the *Decretum* itself, had emerged as the undisputed guardian and master of Church law, and was now called upon to offer solutions to these problems. From the mid-12th century onward thousands of replies to cases appeared from the papal chancery, particularly between 1159 and 1216 (from Alexander III through Innocent III); in the meantime the masters in the schools posed new questions, suggested solutions other than those advanced by Gratian, and provided the papacy with arguments upon which to draw.

This papal and canonistic activity introduced the second phase of the classical period. In order to implement the *Decretum* and to continue its *concordia,* canonists began about 1160 to make collections of papal, conciliar, and patristic material overlooked by or unknown to Gratian and, in particular, of the new papal replies or DECRETALS. These collections of *Decretales extravagantes* (i.e., circulating distinct from the *Decretum*) were put together in most parts of Europe, the best known coming from Spain, Portugal, France, Italy, and England (*see* DECRETALS, COLLECTIONS OF). Many were of a private nature and loosely ordered; the first semisystematic collection was that of Bernard of Pavia between 1177 and 1179 (*Collectio Parisiensis II*), covering decretals from Honorius II (1127 to 1130) to Alexander III. After the Third Lateran Council more systematic collections made their appearance, notably, in England (*Appendix Concilii Lateranensis III*), France (*Bambergensis*), and Italy (*Lipsien-*

CANON LAW, HISTORY OF

sis). The high point was reached (1191 to 1192) when Bernard of Pavia published his *Breviarium extravagantium,* an arrangement in five books of about 900 decretals issued between 1140 and 1191; the headings given the books, *iudex, iudicium, clerus, connubia, crimen,* originally were a mnemonic aid for memorizing the main subject of the books. This was soon accepted by the schools as a definitive collection and became the *Compilatio Prima* of the QUINQUE COMPILATIONES ANTIQUAE.

The third phase of classic canonistics began with canonists who, in preference or in addition to making glosses on the *Decretum,* composed commentaries on the ''new'' decretals of the *Compilatio Prima* and kindred compilations. Peter of Spain wrote an apparatus on Bernard of Pavia's collection as early as 1193, the Englishman RICHARD DE MORES four or five years afterward, and Bernard himself in 1198. Apparatuses followed from ALANUS ANGLICUS, LAWRENCE and VINCENT OF SPAIN, Tancred JOHN OF WALES, etc., and were joined by writings on the later compilations. Although there was a lull in decretist activity as such after 1191 to 1192, studies on Gratian's *Decretum* resumed with a new vigor when it was perceived that a harmony had to be established between the *Decretum* and the new compilations, glosses, and apparatuses. The period from 1210 to 1220 was in fact one of intense decretist as well as decretalist production at Bologna, many of the decretalists mentioned above being the authors also of decretalist writings, e.g., Alanus Anglicus, Lawrenc of Spain, and John of Wales. It proved to be the final, brilliant moment of the decretist epoch. In 1216 JOANNES TEUTONICUS, the author also of an apparatus on the *Compilatio tertia antiqua* and one on *Compilatio quarta antiqua,* published the gloss on the *Decretum* that became the *ordinaria.* Summing up more than a half-century of decretist learning, this gloss announced in effect the end of the period of canonistic research. The range of the decretal legislation of Innocent III (1198 to 1216) and of the constitutions of the Fourth Lateran Council (1215) had shown once and for all that there was now a living law of the Church and that this called for the same canonistic attention that hitherto had been given to the traditions enshrined in the work of Gratian.

It was also becoming clear that the time had come for a new *concordia*—not, as in Gratian's day, of *discordantium canonum,* but of *collectionum discordantium.* By 1230 there was such a profusion of decretals and variety of collections that Gregory IX commissioned and then authenticated (1234) a definitive collection of decretals not included in or coming after Gratian's *Decretum* (*see* GREGORY IX, DECRETALS OF). Gratian's *Decretum,* however, retained its place, and BARTHOLOMEW OF BRESCIA brought the *glossa ordinaria* of Joannes Teutonicus into line with the ''new'' universal law from about 1240

to 1245. The spread of a uniform law of the Church was now possible and henceforth juridical activity concentrated on the consolidation of a strongly hierarchical, centralized, closely regulated society. There was a great flowering in the next half-century of glosses, commentaries, *summae, lecturae,* and *reportoria* on the decretals, chiefly from Sinibaldus Fieschi (INNOCENT IV), Godfrey of Trani, BERNARD OF PARMA (*glossa ordinaria,* before 1241), BERNARD OF MONTMIRAT (*Abbas antiquus*), HOSTIENSIS, and William DURANTI THE ELDER (*see* DECRETALISTS).

Of course decretal legislation was continued after 1234: Gregory IX himself published decretal letters, as did most of the succeeding popes. Besides, the two Councils of Lyons (1245, 1274) published constitutions. From time to time collections of this new material were made (e.g., three collections of his own decretals by Innocent IV), and special glosses were composed (e.g., by BERNARD OF COMPOSTELLA the Younger on the *Novellae* of Innocent IV; by Duranti the Elder on the *Novellae* of Gregory X); but until the *Liber Sextus* (also called the ''Sext'') of Boniface VIII cleared the air in 1298, there was an ever-increasing problem of the relationship of these new decretals to the universal legislation established by Gregory IX. A great part of the Sext was legislation especially composed to meet new needs or in mitigation of decretal and conciliar legislation since 1234. Canonical science, which had tended to rest on its laurels after the masterly *Summa* (1253) and the exhaustive *Lectura* (*c.* 1270) of Hostiensis and *Speculum iudiciale* of Duranti the Elder (1272; 1287), now stirred itself once more. With the Sext, in fact, the classical period of Canon Law entered its final phase. Although the *CLEMENTINAE,* promulgated some 19 years later by John XXII, also occasioned much canonical activity, the Sext was in effect the last great collection of the classical age, and it led to a flow of brilliant glosses, apparatuses, etc., from such canonists as GUIDO DE BAYSIO, JOHN LE MOINE, William of Mont Lauzun, Zenzelinus de Cassanis, Petrus Bertrandus, and ALBERIC OF ROSATE.

With Joannes Andreae the golden age of canonistic scholarship came to an end. The great Bolognese lay canonist produced, among other works, two *glossa ordinaria* (one on the Sext, *c.* 1301, and on the *Clementinae,* 1322). Moreover, in his *Novella Commentaria* on the *Decretals* of Gregory IX, completed in 1338, Joannes Andreae surveyed the whole of decretalist literature from the *Quinque Compilationes Antiquae* onward and arranged a century of glosses on the decretals into a coherent, enduring apparatus. The classical period was at an end, and in Joannes it had its last representative and its first literary historian. The black death, which claimed Joannes Andreae in 1348, thinned the ranks of canonists and of scholarship in general; and the Great Schism soon disrupted that unity of Christendom that the classic age had labored to build. Canonical science never quite recovered afterward.

Aspects of the Classical Period. The ideal of a *concordia discordantium canonum* so succesfully pursued by Gratian at Bologna soon attracted a following all over Europe. By the end of the 12th century there were flourishing schools of Canon Law in France (especially at Paris) and in England (chiefly at Oxford, where John of Tynemouth, Simon of Southwell, and Master Honorius were the leaders, but also to some extent at Northampton and in the cathedral schools of Exeter and Lincoln). From the early 13th century on a faculty of Canon Law was a normal part of the *studia generalia* then coming to life in France (Orleans, Angers, Montpellier, Toulouse), and Spain (Palencia, Salamanca, Valladolid), and Italy (Padua, Vercelli, Siena, and Piacenza). Bologna, the nursery of canonists, never yielded her position, although powerful centers (e.g., Padua in the 14th century) were to constitute a challenge. Bologna's fertility is best seen, perhaps, around 1200, when a host of decretists and decretalists—Italians, Germans, Spaniards, Anglo-Normans, Welsh—worked side by side to produce numerous collections and apparatuses.

For most of the 13th century the *Decretum* was the basic or ordinary text in these schools, and lectures on it took place in the morning period. When the *Decretals of Gregory IX* appeared, they were read *extraordinarie* in the afternoon sessions and generally did not achieve the "ordinary" status of the *Decretum* until the Sext (1298) and *Clementinae* (1317) were introduced as "extraordinary" books. In some studia, however, e.g., Oxford, there was a changeover from the *Decretum* to decretals before 1300, the *Decretum* being relegated to the former "extraordinary" place of the decretals. Lectures on the ordinary text were given by professors and regent doctors; but when regent doctors were scarce, exceptional bachelors might be enlisted to conduct "quasi-ordinary" lectures; as a rule, the extraordinary texts were entrusted to the bachelors. In some universities there were endowed chairs, or at least a fixed stipend, for the ordinary teachers, but in others each professor had to negotiate a contract with his students as a body; bachelors, however, were not entitled at any point to a fee. The course for the license to lecture *extraordinarie* or *cursorie* (baccalaureate) generally comprised three years of civil law, two years on the *Decretum,* and a complete study of the decretals; for the doctorate a further three or four years were required, during which the bachelor *extraordinarie,* engaged in public disputations, and stood in as *ordinarius* at least once for each regent doctor. After the final doctorate examination there was a compulsory period, normally two years in duration, of ordinary teaching as a regent doctor.

The statutes of Canon Law faculties generally echo those of the faculties of the older (though to canonists, inferior) science of civil law. Canon Law, indeed, owed an immense debt to Roman law; civilians, on the other hand, armed with a code of laws stabilized in the 6th century, depended little on canonists, although they did not ignore the principles underlying Canon Law and ecclesiastical institutions. Classic Roman law had enjoyed the favor of the Roman Curia from the earliest days, and in time many popes came to look on it as part of their heritage. However, the use to which it was put by imperial jurists, such as Peter Crassus during the investiture contest, occasioned a certain ecclesiastical reserve, which is to some extent reflected in Gratian's *Decretum.* But as glosses and commentaries multiplied on the *Decretum,* canonists often found it to their advantage to adopt techniques from the civilian glossators; and as questions increased and situations grew more complex, it became widely recognized that the classic Roman law could be profitably exploited in the interests of the public law of the Church for its theory of laws, its approach to justice, its teaching on contracts and pacts, its sense of the privileges of priesthood and of sacred places, its maxims and reflex principles. By 1220 canonists were studying Roman law as a matter of course; by mid-century the complete canonist was a *doctor utriusque iuris;* by 1300 a civil law degree was desirable before proceeding to Canon Law studies. With the development of ecclesiastical courts a knowledge of civil law procedures became imperative (*see* ORDINES JUDICIARII), and from 1170 onward various summaries and expositions of procedure were written for canonists, the most influential being those of Tancredus (1214 to 1216; later adapted by Bartholomew of Brescia about 1236), WILLIAM OF DROGHEDA (Oxford 1239), and William Duranti the Elder (*Speculum iudiciale,* 1272, 1287; later reworked by Joannes Andreae, Baldus, and others). The spread of the universal law, the growth of papal provisions, the development of episcopal curias, etc., naturally created a demand for canonists well versed in both laws. To counter career-seeking, Honorius III prohibited in 1219 the study of civil law to monks, priests, and beneficed clerks, but papal dispensations were not too difficult to obtain afterward. The ordinary canonist who attended Roman law schools probably would not be more than a simple clerk at the time, and would not come under the ban.

Relations between Canon Law and theology were on another footing. At the beginning of the 12th century the canons were regarded as a part of theology, and Gratian himself taught them at Bologna as "external theology."

But in establishing Canon Law as a science, Gratian, for all the theological source material in his *Decretum,* opened the way not only to a distinction of the science of Canon Law from that of theology, but also to a separation. There were, of course, decretists in the early period who were both canonists and theologians: Roland Bandinelli (Alexander III), Gandulpus, LABORANS, Huguccio (the latter a prime source for the theological learning of his day). Toward the end of the 12th century, however, canonists and theologians alike contributed to a widening gap between the two fields. If Sicardus of Cremona abandoned a discussion of the Eucharist "to the theologians," there were theologians who omitted to speak of Matrimony (on which there had been a cascade of decretals from Alexander III) and of Orders. From 1200 onward canonistic science concentrated more and more on institutional aspects of the Church, deriving little from the vigorous theological speculation that began to sweep Europe. The theologians, for their part, seemed content to allow that Canon Law govern worship, the administration of the Sacraments, the functioning of the ecclesial body. Richard Fishacre, who wrote the first commentary on Peter Lombard's *Liber Sententiarum* at Oxford (*c.* 1240 to 1243), borrowed freely from Raymond of Peñafort; St. Albert and St. Thomas were indebted to the *Decretum* and decretals.

One genre of canonical literature to which the classic age gave rise was to play a large part in the emergence of later moral theology. Through *summae* of penitential practice (later called *Summae confessorum*), the decrees of popes and councils and the doctrines developed by canonists on all aspects of domestic, social, and economic life were made available to priests often far removed from scholastic circles. The movement began about 1210 with ROBERT OF FLAMBOROUGH, an English penitentiary at St. Victor in Paris, and grew in strength after the pastoral reforms of the Fourth Lateran Council (1215). Its greatest exponents were the Dominicans RAYMOND OF PEÑAFORT (*Summa de casibus, c.* 1225; revised *c.* 1234) and JOHN OF FREIBURG (*Summa confessorum,* 1298). These *Summae* in turn inspired a host of manuals of the general pastoral care and of sacramental practice, such as the *Oculus sacerdotis* of WILLIAM OF PAGULA (*c.* 1320), the *Manipulus curatorum* of Guido de Monte Richerii (1333), and the *Summa praedicantium* of John of BROMYARD (1348). All these contributed in no small way to the spread of a knowledge of the universal law of the Church and to its universal observance.

Bibliography: G. LEBRAS, "Canon Law," in *The Legacy of the Middle Ages,* ed. C. G. CRUMP and E. F. JACOB (Oxford 1926) 321–61; *Institutions ecclésiastiques de la Chrétienté médiévale* (A. FLICHE and V. MARTIN, eds., *Histoire de l'église depuis les origines jusqu'à nos jours* (Paris 1935–) 12; 1959) 21–119. P. FOURNIER and G. LEBRAS, *Histoire des collections canoniques en occident depuis les fausses décrétales jusqu'au Décret de Gratien,* 2 v. (Paris 1931–32) 2:334–52. A. VAN HOVE, *Commentarium Lovaniense in Codicem iuris canonici 1,* v.1–5 (Mechlin 1928–); v.1, Prolegomena (2d ed. 1945) 1:343–77, 412–65. A. M. STICKLER, *Historia iuris canonici latini:,* v.1, *Historia fontium* (Turin 1950) 1:188–268. C. MUNIER, *Les Sources patristiques de droit de l'Église du VIIIe au XIIIe siècle* (Strasbourg 1957). S. KUTTNER, *Repertorium der Kanonistik* (Rome 1937); *Studi e Testi,* 71. S. KUTTNER, *Harmony from Dissonance: An Interpretation of Medieval Canon Law* (Latrobe, Pennsylvania 1960); "Papst Honorius III. und das Studium des Zivilrechts," *Festschrift für Martin Wolff,* ed. E. VON CAEMMERER (Tübingen 1952); "Bernardus Compostellanus Antiquus," *Traditio* 1 (1943) 277–340; "Notes on a Projected Corpus of Twelfth-Century Decretal Letters," *ibid.* 6 (1948) 345–51. S. KUTTNER and E. RATHBONE, "Anglo-Norman Canonists of the Twelfth Century," *ibid.* 7 (1949–51) 279–358. C. DUGGAN, *Twelfth-Century Decretal Collections and Their Importance in English History* (London 1963). S. KUTTNER'S introduction to reprinted edition of JOANNES ANDREAE, *In quinque decretalium libros novella commentaria,* 5 v. in 4 (Venice 1581; repr. Turin 1963). B. KURTSCHEID, "De utriusque iuris studio saeculo XIII," in *Acta Congressus iuridici internationalis Romae, 1934,* v.2 (Rome 1935) 315–24. H. RASHDALL, *The Universities of Europe in the Middle Ages,* ed. F. M. POWICKE and A. B. EMDEN, 3 v. (new ed. Oxford 1936) 1:87–175, 585–89. E. FOURNIER, "L'Enseignement des décrétales à la Faculté de Paris au moyen âge," appendix to *L'Origine du vicaire-général et des autres membres de la curie diocésaine* (Paris 1940) 367–75. J. DE GHELLINCK, *Le Mouvement théologique du XIIe siècle* (2d ed. Bruges 1948) 416–510. A. M. LANDGRAF, "Diritto canonico e teologia nel secolo XII," *Studia Gratiana* 1 (1953) 373–413. S. STELLING-MICHAUD, *L'Université de Bologne et la pénétration des droits romain et canonique en Suisse aux XIIIe et XIVe siècles* (Geneva 1955). C. G. MOR, "Il 'miracolo' bolognese: La diffusione del metodo scientifico della scuola di Bologna nel secolo XII," *Studi e memorie per la storia dell'Università di Bologna,* new series 1 (1956) 161–71. P. MICHAUD-QUANTIN, *Sommes des casuistique et manuels de confession au Moyen Âge (XII–XIV siècle)* (Louvain 1962). L. E. BOYLE, "The Curriculum of the Faculty of Canon Law at Oxford in the First Half of the 14th Century," in *Oxford Studies Presented to Daniel Callus* (Oxford 1964) 135–62. P. LEGENDRE, *La Pénétration du droit romain dans le droit classique de Gratien à Innocent IV* (Paris 1964). Valuable bibliographies and notes in the *Bulletin of the Institute of Research and Study in Medieval Canon Law* in *Traditio* 11– (1955–). G. LE BRAS et al., *L'Age classique, 1140–1378. Sources et théorie du droit* (Histoire du droit et des institutions de L'Église en Occident 7; Paris 1965).

[L. E. BOYLE]

5. The *Corpus Iuris Canonici* to the Council of Trent

The publication of the CLEMENTINAE and *Extravagantes Ioannis XXII* during John XXII's lifetime and of the *Extravagantes Communes* at the end of the 15th century opened up a new field of study to canonists, who had already written several works on the other collections of CORPUS IURIS CANONICI. Many of these new publications stem from the study of law pursued in the great university centers of Europe as well as at the University of the Pontifical Curia. Thus originated the *commentaria, summae, quaestiones, repetitiones, consilia* or *responsa,* etc. The didactic and practical nature of the works contributed to the lack of originality of the majority of canonists of this period.

Besides the usual commentaries or works of a practical nature, the literary output is marked by the publication of works that reflect the problems of the time. Treatises on schism appeared in order to prove the legitimacy of a specific pope or the supremacy of the sovereign pontiff or of the general councils, during the crucial phase of CONCILIARISM. The reports of civil and ecclesiastical authorities on the modality of the origin of the power of the emperor or of kings in relation to the pope were notable; so were those that dealt with the independence of kings from the emperor, with corollaries on the so-called ecclesiastical liberties. In addition to the treatises there appeared several works that were concerned with international law. They were occasioned by the wars of conquest against the Saracens in Africa and against the Turks, and the discovery of new, distant lands, such as India and America.

Councils of Constance and Pisa. Many canonists wrote on schism, taking a stand either for or against the pope. Besides his commentaries on the *Decretales* of Gregory IX and the *Clementinae, Repetitiones,* and *Consilia,* Cardinal Francis ZABARELLA, legate to the Council of Constance, wrote *De schismate,* which was published in several editions and later forbidden by the Council of Trent. Petrus de Ancherano, legate to the same Council and author of commentaries on the *Decretales* of Gregory IX, *Liber Sextus,* and *Consilia,* had participated in the Council of Pisa, where he wrote the *Repetitio* on the war on the infidels against HOSTIENSIS and composed the *Allegationes iuris pro Concilio Pisano.* Antonius de Butrio, author of commentaries on the *Decretales of Gregory IX* and *Liber Sextus,* and of *Consilia, Repertoria iuris, De iure patronatus, De symonia,* and *De acquisitionibus,* besides being engaged by pontifical commission in negotiations for the extirpation of schism, wrote a treatise on the subject in 1408.

Among the writers participating in the Council of Constance who wrote on schism and the general councils was Master André Dias with treatises on: *De schismatibus, Gubernaculum conciliorum,* and *De civitate ecclesiastica,* and the canonical-pastoral works *Confessio generalis maior, Confessio generalis minor* or *Modus confitendi, De decimis,* and *Lumen confessorum.* Jean Gerson and Pierre d'Ailly wrote theologico-juridical works and treatises on the supremacy of a council over the pope. Paulus Vladimirus, Rector of the University of Cracow, presented to the Council his *Demonstratio Cruciferis de Prussia seu Ordini Teutonico opposita Infideles armis et bello non esse ad Christianam fidem converten-*

dos. He also wrote *Tractatus de potestate papae et imperatoris respectu infidelium.* Defending the opposite side was the treatise *De bello* by the contemporary Iacobus episcopus Laudensis.

An important treatise on the schism is that of Ioannes de Lignano, commentator on the *Decretum, Decretales* of Gregory IX, and *Clementinae,* and author of *De bello, De pace, Repetitiones, Concordantia decreti et decretalium,* etc. Like Baldus de Ubaldi he wrote twice in defense of Urban VI. Against J. Lignano's treatise *De fletu Ecclesiae,* St. Vincent Ferrer wrote *De moderno Ecclesiae schismate,* in which he defended the antipope Clement VII. Baldus, having lectured on the three first books of the *Decretales* of Gregory IX, after his first *Allegationes* in favor of Urban VI, published under the title *Quaestio Baldi de schismate,* wrote *Allegationes secundae pro Urbano VI.* Ioannes de Imola, lawyer, canonist and author of commentaries on the *Decretales* of Gregory IX, *Liber Sextus,* and *Clementinae, Consilia* and *Repetitiones,* produced also a *Tractatus super schismate.* Bartholomew de Saliceto, civil lawyer, left a *Consilium pro Urbano VI;* and Nicholas de Fakenham, the *Determinatio pro Urbano VI.* Concerning Clement VII and Benedict XIII, Jean Le Fèvre wrote *Tractatus de schismate,* or *De planctu bonorum;* the works of Cardinal Petrus Flandrin and Peter Barriere were directed against Ioannes de Lignano; and Boniface Ferrer issued his *Tractatus pro defensione Benedicti XIII.* Cardinal Petrus Amelii wrote a treatise against the calling of a council to dissolve the schism; and Laurentius Ridolfi, a Florentine canonist, wrote a *Consilium* and *Allegationes* to justify the Council of Pisa. Robertus de Fronzola and Iacobus de Camplo, compiler of *Decisiones novae* of the Sacred Rota, also wrote the treatises *De schismate* concerning the Council of Pisa. Besides the tract on the legitimacy of his election, Benedict XIII wrote a reply to William d'Ortolan's treatise written to refute the first mentioned.

Council of Basel-Ferrara-Florence. Various canonists who took part in the Council of Basel-Ferrara-Florence produced works on Canon Law. John de Torquemada, commentator on the *Decretum,* was the first to appear in defense of the pope against the Council in his *Summa de Ecclesia, Tractatus in favorem Eugenii IV contra decreta Concilii Constantiensis et contra gesta in Concilio Basiliensi,* and *Tractatus de potestate papae et Concilii generalis auctoritate.* Nicholas de Tudeschis, the King of Aragon's ambassador at the Council of Basel, has a place among the best canonists of his time for his commentaries on the *Decretum, Decretales* of Gregory IX, *Liber Sextus, Clementinae,* and *Flores utriusque iuris.* Rodrigo Sanchez de Arevolo wrote *Defensorium Ecclesiae et status ecclesiastici, De libera et irrefragabili auctoritate Romani Pontificis, De conciliis generalibus,*

De origine ac differentia principatus imperialis et regalis, De pace et bello, etc. Of no small importance was St. John Capistran's *Tractatus de papae et concilii sive Ecclesiae auctoritate,* as well as his commentaries on the *Decretales* of Gregory IX and *Extravagantes* and his work of a pastoral nature, *Speculum conscientiae.* Petrus de Monte, defender of the pope against the Council of Basel, wrote *De potestate papae et concilii.* Joannes de Podio, author of *Lectura super decretales,* also wrote *De potestate Summi Pontificis et concilii;* and Marcus Mantuanus, *Dialogus de concilio.*

Church and State. Besides the common commentaries and works already mentioned, which refer to war, the spread of the gospel, and the power of the pope in relation to civil authority, one should remember the *Consilia* on the legitimacy of the Portuguese war against the Saracens, by Antonio de Pratovecchio and Antonio Rosellis. Rosellis, author of commentaries on the *Decretales* of Gregory IX, *Repetitiones,* and *Tractatus legitimationum,* issued also the *Monarchia seu Tractatus de potestate Imperatoris et Papae.* The same subjects are treated by Petrus Quesvel in *Directorium iuris;* Joannes Quaglia, in *De Civitate Christi:* Master Adam, in *Defensorium Ecclesiae;* Alvarus Pelagii, in *Speculum Regum* and *De planctu Ecclesiae;* Ludovicus de Cividale, in *Dialogus de papali potestate;* Aeneas Silvii Piccolomini, in *Tractatus de ortu et auctoritate Imperii Romani;* Franciscus Zoanettus, in *De Romano Imperio ac eius iurisdictione;* Guillelmus de Monserrat, in *Tractatus de successione regum;* Restaurus Cataldus Perusinus, in *De imperatore;* Michael Ulcurrunus, in *Opus imperiale;* and Alphonsus Alvares Guerreiro, in *Thesaurus Christianae Religionis et Speculum Sacrorum Summorum Pontificum, Imperatoris ac regum.* Antonius Corsetus Siculus was the author of *Repetitiones* and *De potestate et excellentia regia.* Aegidius Bellamera commented on the *Decretum, Decretales* of Gregory IX, and *Clementinae* and authored *Consilia,* which copies the statements made by Oldrado de Ponte on the total independence of kings from the emperor. These arguments are treated, though not always *ex professo,* by Petrinus Belli Albensis in *De re militari;* by Joannes Lupi Segobiensis, in *De bello;* by Paris a Puteo, in *De re militari;* or by Martinus Laudensis, in *De bello.*

General Commentaries. Other commentators on one collection or other of the *Corpus Iuris Canonici* not yet mentioned were Guido de Baysio, Henricus Bohic, Dominicus de Sancto Geminiano, Joannes Fantuzzi, Marianus Socinus, Benedictus Capra de Benedictis, Bonifatius de Vitalinis, Paulus de Aretio, Guilelmus Bonte, Philipus Franchus de Franchis, Ioannes de Prato, Alexander de Nevo, Angelus de Castro, Franciscus de Accoltis, Ioannes Antonius de Sancto Georgio, Laurentius de Pinu, Ioannes Franciscus de Pavinis, Stephanus

Costa, Felinus Sandeus, Augustinus Beroius, Prosdocimus de Comitibus, Andreas Alciati, Iacobus de Zocchis de Ferraria, Andreas de Barbatia, Ioannes de Anaia, Laurentius Pulbericus, Andreas Tartagnus, Decius, Iacobus Ioannes de Canis, Ioannes de Vico Mercato, Ioannes de Palaciis Rubeis, Iacobus Radwicz, Guido Papa, Ludovicus Gomesius, and Ioannes Koelnet de Vanckel. Several authors developed both Canon and civil law, and some indicated their points of contact and their differences; e.g., Bartolo di Sassoferrato, in his *Tractatus inter ius canonicum et civile;* Ioannes Baptista de S. Blasio, in his *Contradictiones iuris civilis cum canonico;* Galvanus de Bettino de Bononia, in *Contrarietates et diversitates seu differentiae inter ius canonicum et romanum;* Ioannes Milis, in *Repertorium utriusque iuris:* Ioannes Berberius, in *Viatorium utriusque iuris;* Felinus Sandeus; Franciscus de Accoltis; Antonius Corsetus; Iacobus Fontanus; and Petrus Maurocenus, author of *Concordantiae iuris civilis et canonici.*

The pastoral aspect of canonist publications is represented in *Summae confessorum,* or cases of conscience, such as *Summa Astesana* by Astesano, OFM, brought up to date in regard to sources of law by Gomes de Lisboa; the *Summa Pisana,* by Bartolomew a Sancto Concordio, OP, and added to by Nicolaus ab Auximo, OFM; the *Summa,* by Saint Antonine of Florence, OP; the *Summa iuris,* by Antonio de Bitonto; the *Summa Angelica,* by Angelus de Clavasio, OFM; the *Summa Rosella,* by Ioannes Baptista Trovamala, OFM; the *Summa Tabiena,* by Ioannes Cagnazzo de Tabia; the *Summa Sylvestrina,* by Sylvester Prierias, OP; and the *Summa Armilia,* by Bartholomeus a Fumo, OP. Finally, worth recalling in the beginning of the 16th century are the merit and influence of Ioannes de Chapuis and Vitalis de Thebis on future editions of the *Corpus Iuris Canonici.*

Bibliography: A. VAN HOVE, *Commentarium Lovaniense in Codicem iuris canonici 1,* v.1–5 (Mechlin 1928–); v.1, Prolegomena (2d ed. 1945) 1:466–81. R. H. TRAME, *Rodrigo Sánchez de Arévalo, 1404–1470* (Washington 1958). A. D. DE SOUSA COSTA, *Canonistarum doctrina de Judaeis et Saracenis tempore Concilii Constantiensis* (Rome 1965). N. DEL RE, ''Il 'Consilium pro Urbano VI' di Bartolomeo da Saliceto,'' *Studi e Testi* 219 (1962) 213–63.

[A. D. DE SOUSA COSTA]

6. The Council Of Trent To The Code Of Canon Law

The decrees of the Council of Trent had the controlling influence on the Canon Law of the Church until the promulgation of the Code of CANON LAW in 1917. New canonical institutes that developed in the period had their foundation in the reform in the Church that the Council inspired.

Council of Trent. The Council of Trent (19th ecumenical, 1545 to 1563) laid the dogmatic and canonical bases for the internal reform of the Church, anchoring the Church still more in the papacy. It gave the Church a new direction in its development, toward being no longer the Western Church but rather the Catholic Church. Tridentine Canon Law did not abolish the older Canon Law but rather restored, supplemented, and renewed it, and thereby created the basis for the modern development. Dogma and discipline were discussed together. The reform decrees were primarily canonical in content, dealing with the position and duties of clerics, regulations on ordinations, benefices and patronages, religious orders, criminal proceedings and penitential discipline, synods, and, in a particularly detailed fashion, marriage.

These regulations concentrated ecclesiastical faculties in the hands of the pope and in the hands of the bishop with regard to the diocesan clergy. But the implementation of the reform decrees encountered opposition in individual states, which led to legal confusion and legal disparities, especially for Catholics in Protestant territories where the council decrees were not recognized at all. Since many points of the agenda had not been completed at the Council, certain important matters were left to the personal regulation of the pope: Creed, Index, catechism, Missal, editions of the Bible, Breviary.

Since the interpretation, implementation, and dispensation of the council decrees had been entrusted to the pope, the Congregatio Cardinalium Concilii Tridentini Interpretum (now Congregation of the Council) was established in 1564.

In order to cope with all the assignments, the Roman CURIA was expanded and thoroughly reformed. The College of Cardinals (which since 1586 to 1587 included 70 members, of whom six were cardinal bishops, 50 were cardinal priests, and 14 were cardinal deacons) began the reform. Congregations of cardinals (initially 15 in number) were established to supplement the old curial offices, and each of these new congregations had its own area of competency; this entailed a fundamental and systematic reorganization of the curial administration. Thus there came into existence the Congregation of the Index (1571), the Congregation of the Inquisition (1542, 1564; later Holy Office), the Congregation of the Consistory (1587), the Congregation of Bishops and Regulars (1601), Propaganda (1622), etc. The work of codifying Canon Law was begun under Gregory XIII (1572–85). The text of the *Corpus Iuris Canonici* was reviewed by a commission of cardinals and *periti* (*Correctores Romani*), and an official Roman edition was published (1580–1582). Clement VIII (1592–1605) had all the scattered decretals of the remaining common Canon Law collected into a Liber Septimus of the *Corpus;* but this book was not approved, because some states did not recognize all the regulations of Canon Law. Only the most important canonist among the popes, Benedict XIV (1740–1758), had his decrees collected and published (1746, 1751) as authentic sources of Canon Law.

Missions. The discovery of new continents with heathen inhabitants and the defection of entire peoples of the Old World from the Catholic Church made necessary an organizational separation of the areas that had remained Catholic from the countries that were only gradually to be encompassed by the missions to the heathens and Protestants (*terrae missionis*). Of radical importance for the organization of the missions was the institution of the Congregation for the Propagation of the Faith (1622) as a central Roman office. The area of the missions (organizational forms were mission stations, mission parishes, apostolic prefectures, apostolic vicariates, missionary dioceses) was placed under the Congregation, whose prefect (the "red pope") acquired extensive plenary powers.

Diocesan Constitution. Trent strengthened the position of bishops by giving them papal plenary powers as ordinary jurisdictional powers in their capacity as *delegati sedis apostolicae*. The *Pontificale Romanum* prescribed for bishops an oath of obedience to the pope. The jurisdictional power of the ordinary over cathedral and collegiate chapters and monasteries was restored. The orderly episcopal constitution that had been breached before the Council by exemptions was again implemented.

The Council deprived the office of archdeacon of all ordinary jurisdiction; all disputes were to be referred to the episcopal court. The archdeacon was replaced in judicial matters by the OFFICIALIS and in matters of administration rights were strengthened. The auxiliary bishop came to the fore as the assistant to the bishop, especially when the bishop was encumbered with political duties.

The Council of Trent ordered that provincial synods be held every three years and diocesan synods annually, but the command was never implemented. The parish clergy was bound to the bishop because the *approbatio pro cura* was granted for only a limited time. The ordinary was given supervision of the clergy and their theological training to ensure that ecclesiastical offices were filled worthily. There was an intensification of the parochial pastorate, a strict enforcement of celibacy and residence requirement, a limitation of plurality of benefices (only one benefice could be awarded to each cleric), and a reorganization of the law on patronage and incorporation.

Religious Institutes. Religious life acquired new importance because of the new orders and congregations that were founded. These were the Theatines (1524), the Capuchins (1528), and the Jesuits (1534) with their monarchically centralist constitution and sterner obligation to obedience. There was a general reform of the old orders and the foundation of numerous congregations, adapted by specialized assignments to the individualism of the modern age. They constituted a mobile element in ecclesiastical assignments in virtue of the disappearance of the cloister, the concept of stability, and the profession of solemn vows. The papal rights of supervision over exempt monasteries were delegated by Trent to the bishops.

Marriage Law. The Council of Trent's decree TAMETSI established exact norms for the form of marriage, namely, the solemnization of the marriage before the pastor and two witnesses. It corrected the abuses that had arisen through clandestine marriages and prescribed the entry of the marriage in ecclesiastical marriage registries. These regulations were not uniformly implemented; they came into force only in the parishes in which they were officially proclaimed, and they were not proclaimed uniformly everywhere.

The papal decree NE TEMERE (1907–1908) declared that the decree *Tametsi* was universally binding and made the participation of the pastor active rather than passive; i.e., he was to obtain the consent of the bridal couple. A new impediment to marriage, that of MIXED MARRIAGES, arose as a result of the Protestant Reformation.

Procedure and Penal Law. In procedural Canon Law, the *iudices in partibus* appeared as the court of third appellate instance, instead of a papal court; and the competency of circuit courts was renewed. The old procedure for accusations gradually gave way to the inquisitorial procedure. In official procedure there developed the office of the public prosecutor (*promotor fiscalis*), modeled on French trial law (*procureur du roi*).

In penal law the *Cenacle* bull collated the censures reserved to the pope, and these were raised in 1568 to the status of penal law with legal force in perpetuity. The Protestants were still considered members of the Catholic Church, but they were held to be heretical and therefore excommunicate. The necessity of daily coexistence led to the ban from all communication with only those excommunicated by name (*excommunicati vitandi*).

Currents dangerous to the papal system arose within the Church in the 17th century in France in GALLICANISM and JANSENISM. Gallicanism was a form of national State-Church sovereignty supporting CONCILIARISM, and had a basis in the canonicodogmatic and religiotheological area. A general assembly of Catholic clergy (1682) set the four slogans of Gallicanism: (1) princes are unlimited in matters of secular government; (2) the pope is limited in matters of spiritual government by the general council (in accord with decrees of the Council of Constance); (3) the pope is specially limited by the Gallican privileges; (4) in matters of faith, the pope is limited by the episcopate as a whole. These articles were condemned by Pope Alexander VIII in 1690, but it had descendants in the FEBRONIANISM founded by Nicholas of Hontheim in 1763 and JOSEPHINISM in Austria and Belgium. These theories formed, together with the theory of natural law of the Enlightenment, the bases for the system of State-Church sovereignty. According to this system, the State claims the right to make the Church subject to the power of the State (*iura circa sacra*): *ius advocatiae, ius inspectionis, ius cavendi, ius placeti, ius exclusivae, ius appellationis ab abusu, ius dominii supremi, ius reformandi*. The radical tendencie of the Enlightenment led during the French Revolution to the legal abolition of Christianity.

Neither the French Revolution nor the Napoleonic era led to the collapse of the Church; rather they contributed to its spiritual renewal. The papacy centralized in itself, in ever-increasing measure, all ecclesiastical power. The episcopalistic currents of the *ancien régime* receded in favor of the common law. With many European states concordats were concluded that mitigated State-Church sovereignty. Conferences were held by the bishops in individual states to discuss improvement of the state of the Church and the means to a universal implementation of the Canon Law. The Church's desire to strengthen its rights so as to attain independence for the fulfillment of its divine commission led to the convocation of Vatican I (20th ecumenical council, 1869 to 1870). The definition of the universal papal primacy and papal infallibility in matters of faith anchored the Canon Law on the infallible supreme episcopacy of the pope; political conditions prevented the Council from concluding its deliberations on the place of the bishop in the Church. Thus the question of the reform of Canon Law remained unresolved.

It was not until the reign of Pius X (1903–1914) that this thought was revived. In 1904 a commission of cardinals was established to elaborate a draft of a code of Canon Law. Meanwhile, difficult and urgent areas had been regulated experimentally: rights of religious orders and pastors, appointment of bishops, solemnization of marriages, penal and procedural law, election of the pope, and reorganization of the Roman Curia.

Bibliography: R. NAZ, *Dictionnaire de droit canonique*, ed. R. NAZ, 7 v. (Paris 1935–65) 4:1446–1520. A. M. STICKLER, *Lexikon für Theologie und Kirche*, ed. J. HOFER and K. RAHNER, 10 v. (2d, new ed. Freiburg 1957–65) 5:1296–1300. H. E. FEINE, *Kirchliche Rechtsgeschichte*, v.1 *Die katholische Kirche* (4th ed. Cologne 1964). A. M. KOENIGER, *Grundriss einer Geschichte des Katholischen Kirchenrechts* (Cologne 1919). W. PLÖCHL, *Geschichte des Kir-*

chenrechts, 3 v. (Vienna 1953–59; 2d ed. 1960–) v.3. P. HINSCHIUS, *Das Kirchenrecht der Katholiken und Protestanten in Deutschland,* 6 v. (Berlin 1869–97; repr. Graz 1959). R. VON SCHERER, *Handbuch des Kirchenrechts,* 2 v. (Graz 1886–98). U. STUTZ, "Kirchenrecht" in *Encyklopädie der Rechtswissenschaften,* ed. F. VON HOLTZEN-DORFF and J. KOHLER, 5 v. (2d ed. Berlin 1913–15) 5:279–390. J. F. VON SCHULTE, *Die Geschichte der Quellen und der Literatur des kanonischen Rechts,* 3 v. in 4 pts. (Stuttgart 1875–80; repr. Graz 1956), v.3. A. M. STICKLER, *Historia iuris canonici latini:* v.1, *Historia fontium* (Turin 1950). A. VAN HOVE, *Commentarium Lovaniense in Codicem iuris canonici 1,* v.1–5 (Mechlin 1928–); v.1, *Prolegomena* (2d. ed. 1945).

[P. LEISCHING]

7. The 1917 Code Of Canon Law

On March 19, 1904, Pope Pius X in the *motu proprio Arduum sane munus* [*Acta Apostolicae Sedis* 36 (1904), 549] announced his determination to refine the laws of the Church into a single volume. At that time ecclesiastical law had to be ferreted out of a bewildering number of sources. In addition to the Corpus iuris canonici and the decrees of Trent were the constitutions of later Roman pontiffs (collected in the Bullaria) as well as the instructions, decrees, and decisions of the Roman congregations. In those sources the material was arranged chronologically rather than systematically. The texts were verbose including, as they did, narration and exposition. Later provisions had superseded numerous rulings. The commission of cardinals established by the pope to carry out this project, under the direction of Cardinal Gasparri, used as a model the 19th-century civil codes of Europe. There the law was stated in abstract formulations totally cut off from the particular cases and concrete situations in which the principles had been worked out.

Beginning in March 1912, when a draft of the Code had been completed, there began a consultation with the bishops of the Latin Church and superiors of religious orders. Their suggested modifications were studied and the text amended. Meanwhile, World War I erupted and Pius X died (1914), to be succeeded by Benedict XV. Finally, on May 27, 1917, Pentecost Sunday, the pope promulgated the *Codex Iuris Canonici Pii X Pontificiis Maximi iussu digestus Benedicti Papae XV auctoritate promulgatus* (Vatican City 1917). The Code, he noted, had been requested by many bishops at the First Vatican Council and was 12 years in the making. It was to take effect the following Pentecost (May 19, 1918).

The 2,414 canons of the 1917 Pio-Benedictine Code are arranged in five books subdivided into parts, titles and chapters. Book I (cc. 1–86) establishes general norms. Book II "On Persons" (cc. 87–725) treats clerics, religious, and lay persons. Book III "On Things" deals with Sacraments (cc. 731–1153); sacred times and places (cc. 1154–1254); divine worship (cc. 1255–1321); the ecclesiastical magisterium (cc. 1322–1408); benefices (cc. 1409–1494); and ecclesiastical goods (1495–1551). Book IV "On Processes" concerns the judicial system (cc. 1552–1998) and the beatification and canonization of saints (cc. 1999–2141). Book V "On Crimes and Penalties" (cc. 2195–2414) lays down the penal law of the Church. The footnotes, organized by Cardinal Gasparri to indicate the sources from which the canons were drawn, do not have the same authority as the canons themselves. Cardinals Gasparri and Seredi (1923 to 1939) reproduced all the documents referred to in the notes (except the *Corpus iuris canonici,* the Council of Trent, and liturgical books) in nine volumes of fontes.

Post-Code Developments. Just as there was provision for an authorized interpretation of the decrees of the Council of Trent, so on Sept. 15, 1917 the Holy Father, implementing canon 17 of the Code, instituted the Commission for the Authentic Interpretation of the Code of Canon Law. The decisions of this commission, as indeed all laws promulgated by the Holy See, were to be published in the official journal, the *Acta Apostolicae Sedis* (canon 9). The commission in 1935 and 1950 made available collections of its responsa.

In the course of the next 40 years, the code itself was modified slightly in only four or five instances by dropping a phrase or substituting a term, but legislative activity by no means came to a halt. The 20th-century popes accommodated discipline to the needs of the time. The Canon Law Digest was founded to provide English translations of various documents affecting the code such as: "replies of the Code Commission; declarations of the Supreme Pontiffs in Encyclicals, Letters, or Apostolic Constitutions; Replies, Decrees, and Instructions of the Sacred Constitutions; and even decisions of the Sacred Tribunals in particular cases." Five volumes of approximately 600 pages each were required for the years 1917 to 1962. The canon law was modified in such areas as papal elections, marriage, confirmation, religious life (secular institutes), military chaplaincies, procedures, and the Communion fast.

Bibliography: Codex iuris canonici Pii X Pont. Max. iussu digestus Benedicti Papae XV auctoritate promulgatus, praefatione, fontium annotatione et indice analytico-alphabetico ab Emo. Petro Card. Gasparri auctus (Vatican City 1917). T. BOUSCAREN, J. O'CONNOR, and E. PFNAUSCH, eds. *Canon Law Digest,* 11 v. (Milwaukee, Mundelein, Illinois, Washington 1934–1991). M. CONTE A CORONATO, *Institutiones iuris canonici,* 5 v. (Turin 1950–61). E. EICHMANN, *Lehrbuch des Kirchenrechts,* ed. K. MÖRSDORF, 3 v (9th ed. Paderborn 1959–60). J. ABBO and J. HANNAN, *The Sacred Canons: A Concise Presentation of the Current Disciplinary Norms of the Church,* 2 v. (St. Louis 1952). T. BOUSCAREN and A. ELLIS, *Canon Law: A Text and Commentary,* 4th rev. ed. (Milwaukee

1963). S. KUTTNER, "The Code of Canon Law in Historical Perspective," *The Jurist* 28 (1968) 129–48.

[J. E. LYNCH]

8. The 1983 Code of Canon Law to the Present

The Second Vatican Council. On Jan. 25, 1959, a few months after his election, Pope John XXIII surprised the Catholic world by announcing his intention to convoke an ecumenical council, which would lead "to the desired and long awaited modernization (aggiornamento) of the Code of Canon law." [*Acta Apostolicae Sedis* 51 (1959) 68]. The pope waited until the completion of the first session of the council before appointing on March 28, 1963, the members of the Pontifical Commission for the Revision of the Code of Canon Law. Since the commission decided to postpone any activity until the council adjourned, it did not formally undertake its task until Nov. 20, 1965. At that session the then reigning pope, Paul VI, insisted that canon law must be reformed in accord with a "new way of thinking proper to the Second Ecumenical Council of the Vatican." The commission identified ten discrete areas of the law and established study groups of experts or consultors to assist in the actual formulation of the new code. Conferences of bishops throughout the world were invited to nominate additional consultors, as well as to make proposals for the renewal of the law.

Paul VI, however, did not delay the implementation of conciliar resolutions. Even while the council was still in session, he decreed a number of changes in the law. His first notable enactment, *Pastorale munus* of Nov. 30, 1963, for example, granted to bishops extensive faculties which had hitherto been reserved to the Holy See. From the close of the council to the end of his pontificate (1966 to 1978) Pope Paul VI promulgated at least 219 documents which effected change in the Church He revised extensively its liturgical and sacramental life and established many structures called for by the council, such as the synod of bishops and episcopal conferences. He sought to infuse the law with the new spirit of collegiality. When the new code finally did appear, therefore, its canons did not seem all that new to most Catholics because they embodied and systematized the reforms Pope Paul VI had already introduced.

Revision Process of the 1983 Code. In April 1967 Cardinal Pericle Felici, the president of the Commission for the Revision of the Code, assembled a central committee of consultors to elaborate principles to guide in the work. Among the ten principles drawn up and later approved by the First Synod of Bishops in the fall of 1967, the most notable were that the code should be animated by a spirit of pastoral care, that ecclesiastical penalties be kept to a minimum, that the office of bishop be enhanced, and that SUBSIDIARITY at all levels be respected.

From 1972 to 1977 as the ten study groups gradually completed their first drafts or schemata of the proposed new law, they sent them for evaluation to the conferences of bishops throughout the world, to the unions of superiors general of religious and secular institutes, to the various departments of the Roman Curia, and to pontifical universities and faculties. By the end of 1978 these bodies had returned their written comments to the commission. In light of the observations received, a second draft with the canons arranged sequentially in a single volume was prepared and presented to the cardinals of the commission on June 29, 1980. The pope increased the number of cardinal members and asked that each submit a written report in preparation for a plenary session of the commission. Then, in response to a request for a second worldwide consultation, the pope added 15 representatives of episcopal conferences bringing the commission membership to 74. Its staff in a document entitled the *Relatio* dated July 16, 1981, summarized the written observations of the expanded commission. The plenary session, based on the 1980 draft of the code and the proposals in the *Relatio*, was held in Rome Oct. 20 to 28, 1981. At the conclusion of the session the commission voted unanimously to submit the amended canons to the pope for promulgation. For a year the pope with a small group of canonists reviewed the commission's final draft and made a number of changes of his own.

Promulgation of the 1983 Code. On Jan. 25, 1983, exactly 24 years after Pope John XXIII had called for an aggiornamento, Pope John Paul II promulgated the new *Code of Canon Law for the Latin Church* to take effect Nov. 27, 1983, the First Sunday of Advent: *Codex iuris canonici auctoritate Ioannis Pauli PP.II promulgatus* [*Acta Apostolicae Sedis* 75.2 1983] xxx + 317. Although only the Latin text is official, translations into the vernacular languages, are permitted, unlike with the 1917 Code, provided they are approved by the episcopal conferences. *The Code of Canon Law in English Translation* prepared by The Canon Law Society of Great Britain and Ireland in association with The Canon Law Society of Australia and New Zealand and The Canadian Canon Law Society was published in 1983. The Canon Law Society of the United States also prepared a translation, which was approved by the National Council of Catholic Bishops. It appeared in 1983 with facing pages of Latin and English texts. A new translation was published by the Canon Law Society of America in 1999 to take account of corrections made in the Latin text as well as to present a more accurate English version. All of the above publications have translations of the pope's Apostolic Constitution *Disci-*

plinae Leges promulgating the text and the American version also includes the Preface in both Latin and English.

Comparison of the Two Codes. The 1983 Code is about three-quarters the size of the 1917 Code, 1,752 canons to 2,414. The reduction was accomplished mainly by eliminating certain sections and by combining several canons into one canon with several paragraphs. The section on the beatification and canonization of saints, about 150 canons, was completely omitted and the treatment of the Roman curia was reduced from 24 canons to two. (New sets of norms pertaining to the canonization process and to the curia, promulgated respectively in 1983 and 1988, are now published as appendices to the 1983 Code). The 85 canons dealing with benefices have been eliminated. Other sections have been considerably reduced: ecclesiastical crimes and punishments, from 220 canons to 88; sacramental law, from 425 to 325, sacred times and places, from 100 to 48, and judicial processes from, 450 to 320.

Far more significant than the relative size of the two codes are the different ecclesiologies undergirding them. The 1917 Code reflected a Church viewed in political categories, that is, as a perfect society, which was monarchical in structure. The Second VATICAN COUNCIL envisioned the Church as a theological mystery existing in hierarchical communion. Pope John Paul II in *Sacrae disciplinae leges*, the decree of promulgation, observed, "in a certain sense this new Code could be understood as a great effort to translate this same conciliar doctrine and ecclesiology [of Vatican II] into canonical language."

Even the ordering of the 1983 Code resonates to the new spirit. Whereas the books of the earlier code were organized according to the civil law of the Emperor Justinian (persons, things, and actions), the outline of the new code is based on the mission of the Church, with its threefold munera or offices of teaching, sanctifying, and pastoring. In the 1917 Code, furthermore, all authority above the level of the diocese was labeled delegated papal power, while in the new Code all jurisdiction is episcopal the purpose of papal jurisdiction being the inner unity of the college of bishops.

Significant Innovations. Among the notable features of the new code is the attention given to the laity. Canon 208 insists on the equality of all those who belong to the Church. For the first time in church law "the obligations and rights of all the Christian faithful" are spelled out (cc. 208–223). All have the right, for example, to free association for charitable or pious purposes or to further the Christian calling in the world (c. 215) and to vindicate their rights before an ecclesiastical court (c. 221). The lay faithful have the right and obligation, among others, to participate in the apostolate (c. 225), to assume ecclesiastical offices for which they are qualified (c. 228), and the right to a decent remuneration for their services (c. 231). More specifically, they can be in charge of parishes (c. 517.2), preach in churches (c. 766), assist at marriages if no priests or deacons are available (c. 11112.1), and serve on the diocesan finance council or even as finance officer of the diocese.

Another new feature of the code, recognition of the principle of subsidiarity, is the delegation of legislative authority to provide for local circumstances. In the 1983 Code 84 canons require or permit episcopal conferences to legislate. The conference in each region, for instance, is to set the amounts at which special permission is needed to alienate church property (c. 1292), to determine more precisely the observance of fast and abstinence (c. 1253), and to enact norms for the catechumenate (c. 788.3). Besides episcopal conferences, the Code in a number of places also leaves it to the judgment of the local diocesan bishop to issue norms, such as for parish finance boards (c. 537), for preaching in the diocese (c.772.1), for catechetics in the diocese (c. 775.1) and for sacramental sharing (i.e., allowing non-Catholics to receive certain sacraments, c. 844.5).

Canon law, to be sure, is much more extensive than the legislation contained in the 1983 Code. Liturgical law and concordat legislation ("agreements entered into by the Apostolic See with nations or other political societies"), though not part of the code, have legal force (cc. 2 and 3).There is, furthermore, the CODE OF CANONS OF THE EASTERN CHURCHES promulgated by Pope John Paul II Oct. 18, 1990. Additional papal legislation, to be treated below, has also appeared since the 1983 Code. As was just noted, episcopal conferences may implement or give specificity to provisions of the 1983 Code as well as enact norms of their own. Each diocese or religious institute may have particular law for its subjects.

Interpretation of Canon Law. As with the 1917 Code, provision was made for the authentic interpretation of the new law. On Jan. 2, 1984, Pope John Paul II established the Pontifical Commission for the Authentic Interpretation of the Code of Canon Law with competence over all the universal laws of the Latin Church. With the new law on the Roman curia, *Pastor bonus* of June 25, 1988, its name was changed to the Pontifical Council for the Interpretation of Legislative Texts. The council is now charged to interpret all laws of the Church, both Eastern and Latin. The general decrees of the conferences of bishops are to be submitted to the council and examined from a juridical perspective. At the request of those concerned, the council determines whether particular laws and general decrees of legislators (below the pope) are in conformity or not with universal church law. In the 1995 issue of its journal, *Communicationes* (27:195–209), the council (or commission) listed the 26 authentic interpretations it had issued to date. Such interpretations have since become rather infrequent, only one in 1998 and another in 1999.

Post-Code Developments. Besides the apostolic constitutions *Divinus perfectionis magister* on the causes of saints (1983) and *Pastor bonus* on the reorganization of the Roman curia (1988), now printed as appendices to the code, other significant documents have affected canon law. The apostolic constitution EX CORDE ECCLESIAE on Catholic universities and other postsecondary institutions of Aug. 15, 1990, complemented canons 807–814 of the Code. The apostolic constitution *Universi dominici gregis* of Feb. 22, 1996, established new norms for the election of a pope. The Pontifical Council for Promoting Christian Unity issued a Directory for the Application of Principles and Norms on Ecumenism on March 25, 1993, which was promulgated by authority of the pope. On Aug. 15, 1997, six congregations and two pontifical councils issued an "Instruction on Certain Questions Regarding the Collaboration of the Non-Ordained Faithful in the Sacred Ministry of Priests," approved by the pope *in forma specifica*. Pope John Paul II in an apostolic letter AD TUENDAM FIDEM issued *motu proprio* May 18, 1998, modified the code by adding a second paragraph to canon 750. Accordingly, Catholics are obliged to assent to "each and every thing which is proposed definitively by the magisterium of the Church concerning the doctrine of faith and morals." Canon 1371, which lists those who are to be "punished with a just penalty," is also adjusted to include one who" pertinaciously" rejects the doctrine mentioned in the expanded canon 750. On May 21, 1998, Pope John Paul II issued an apostolic letter *motu proprio Apostolos suos* entitled "The Theological and Juridical Nature of Episcopal Conferences." At the end of the document were four complementary norms, more restrictive than the codal text on the legislative competence of these bodies.

Bibliography: Codex iuris canonici auctoritate Ioannis Pauli PP. II promulgatus, fontium annotatione et indice analytico-alphabetico auctus (Vatican City 1989). X. OCHOA, *Index verborum ac locutionum Codicis iuris canonici,* 2nd ed. (Vatican City 1984). J. BEAL, J. CORIDEN, and T. GREEN, *New Commentary on the Code of Canon Law* (New York 2000). A. MARZOA et al., eds., *Comentario exégetico al Código de derecho canónico,* 6 v. (Pamplona 1996). J. FOX, "A General Synthesis of the Work of the Pontifical Commission for the Revision of the Code of Canon Law," *The Jurist* 48 (1988) 800–40. For annual review, *Ephemerides theologicae Lovanienses* (Bruges 1924–).

[J. E. LYNCH]

CANON LAW SOCIETY OF AMERICA

The Canon Law Society of America (CLSA) is a professional association, dedicated to the promotion of both the study and the application of CANON LAW in the Catholic Church. It was incorporated as a non-profit corporation in the District of Columbia on Feb. 13, 1981. It actively promotes canonical and pastoral approaches to significant issues within the Catholic Church, both the Latin or Roman Catholic Church and the Eastern Catholic Churches. After Vatican Council II, the society offered its services to dioceses in the United States for the revitalization and proper application of church law.

HISTORY AND STRUCTURE

History. A group of canonists in the United States established the CLSA on Nov. 12, 1939 at The Catholic University of America in Washington, DC during the early days of World War II. The Reverend William Doheny was elected the first president and the Reverend Clement Bastnagel became the first general secretary. Other notable presidents include John Cardinal Krol (1948); John Cardinal Carrberry (1955); Archbishop John Quinn (1957); and Adam Cardinal Maida (1968). Sister Lucy Vazquez became the society's first female president in 1990. The archives of the CLSA are available for research at the University of Notre Dame Archives, South Bend, Indiana.

Structure. The CLSA organizes its activities through an annual general meeting of the society, at which time it elects officers and determines resolutions for future study and activity by the society. A Board of Governors that oversees the operations of the CLSA is composed of elected officers: president, vice-president who is president-elect, a secretary, a treasurer, and seven consultors, one of whom is *ex officio* the immediate past president.

The society organizes its study and activities around three types of committees. There are constitutional committees created by the CLSA Constitution. Ongoing committees are a second type whose members carry out tasks deemed essential to the ongoing life of the society. A third type is the project committee created for a specific task.

An executive coordinator, appointed from the active membership of the society by the Board of Governors for a three-year term of service, serves the membership and the Board of Governors under the direction of the president and the Board of Governors. Created in 1965, the Office of Executive Coordinator assists the operations of the society on a daily basis. The executive's task is the general implementation of the board's policies and decisions, as well as the fulfillment of specific duties as mentioned in the bylaws of the society. A listing of executives includes Paul Boyle, CP (1965–1967); Thoms J. Lynch (1968–1972); Donald E. Heinschel (1973–1979); James H. Provost (1980–1985); Edward G. Pfnausch (1986–1990); James M. Carr (1991); Patrick Cogan, SA (1992–1998); and Arthur J. Espelage, OFM (1999–).

Membership. The CLSA's membership includes men and women in 43 countries. Membership in the Canon Law Society of America is open to interested persons who wish to collaborate in the promotion of the pastoral ministry of the Church within the context of its legal/canonical structures. Membership of non-Catholic persons is also welcomed.

ACTIVITIES

Annual general meeting. In an effort to promote a better understanding of church law and its pastoral application, the society convenes an annual convention and other symposia. Collaboration with other professional church organizations and learned societies is yet another area of the society's involvements. The minutes of the annual meetings were recorded in *The Jurist* until 1968. Beginning with the 31st annual convention in 1969, the society has published the complete proceedings in a separate series, *CLSA Proceedings.*

Role of Law award. Each year since 1973, the Board of Governors chooses a recipient for the CLSA Role of Law Award. The recipient is a member of the society whose life and ministry represent service to the Church through the ministry of law. The criteria used in the nomination and selection process look for embodiment of a pastoral attitude; commitment to research and study; participation in the revision of law; facilitation of dialog and interchange of ideas within the society and with other groups. The first recipient was the Rev. Frederick McManus. Dr. Stephan G. Kuttner, who taught the history of canon law for decades, was the first layperson to receive the Role of Law award in 1978. Other notable recipients include the Reverends Lawrence G. Wrenn (1976); Donald E. Heintschel (1982); Francis G. Morrisey, OMI (1990); Victor Pospishil (1994); Sister Sharon L. Holland, IHM (1999) and the Most Reverend Raymond L. Burke (2000).

Publication services. The society developed CLSA Publications as a means to promote greater understanding and application of canon law. The society sponsored and published with permission English translations of the *Code of Canon Law* (1983) and the *Code of Canons of the Eastern Churches* (1990), as well as the *New Commentary on the Code of Canon Law.* Several series of canonical resources appear: *Canon Law Digest, CLSA*

Proceedings, Roman Replies, CLSA Advisory Opinions and the *CLSA Newsletter,* as well as specialized studies on marriage and tribunal ministry.

Bibliography: R. G. CUNNINGHAM, ed., *Reflections on the Occasion of the 50th Anniversary* (Washington, DC 1988).

[A. ESPELAGE]

CANONICAL COLLECTION BEFORE GRATIAN

Three main periods are distinguished in the history of the sources of Canon Law prior to the Code of CANON LAW: (1) the collections prior to the *CORPUS IURIS CANONICI,* (2) the formation of the *Corpus Iuris Canonici,* and (3) the collections between the *Corpus Iuris Canonici* and the Code of Canon Law. The first period extends from the beginnings of the Church to the *Decretum of GRATIAN* (about 1140) and contains a great number of collections of the most varied sort and structure: those of universal and regional law; collections whose norms owe their origin and authority to councils, popes, secular legislators; those containing genuine and spurious statutes ascribed to their real or alleged authors; collections that arrange the material chronologically or systematically. All these are to be considered as private collections in the technical sense of the word.

Pseudoapostolic Collections. The exigencies of the first years of the Church's history gave rise to the pseudoapostolic collections that contain, together with other material, disciplinary decrees that in one way or another go back to the apostolic tradition or appeal to it. The content is to a large extent genuine, but the ascription to the apostles is spurious. Of particular significance among such collections are the DIDACHE, the *DIDASCALIA APOSTOLORUM,* the *Constitutiones* and the 85 *Canones Apostolorum,* and also the *Tradito Apostolica* of HIPPOLYTUS, all of which have been subjected to more or less numerous reworkings and imitations.

Regional Collections. A further group of collections came into existence from the fourth to sixth centuries in various regions: in the Orient, the *SYNTAGMA CANONUM ANTIOCHENUM,* or *Corpus Canonum Orientale,* containing the norms of the general and local Oriental councils; in Africa, the *Codex Canonum Ecclesiae Africanae* (419); in Gaul, the *STATUTA ECCLESIAE ANTIQUA* (in the last quarter of the fifth century, probably by Gennadius of Marseilles) and various translations of the canons of the Greek councils and collections of papal decretals (*Arelatensis, QUESNELLIANA COLLECTIO*); in Italy, the various editions of the famous *DIONYSIANA COLLECTIO,* containing canons and papal decretals, of the end of the fifth and early sixth centuries, as well as far less important ones such as the *Coll. Frisingensis* (after 495), *Vaticana,* etc. In Spain, there was a merging of the collections of Italy, Africa and Gaul. In all these collections, despite their regional variety, is expressed the uniform Catholic legal code.

Regional-National Collections. In the mid-sixth century, a political fragmentation and particularization began, bringing with it a variety of national and regional disciplines and a plethora of collections expressing regional particularism. This situation lasted until the end of the seventh century. In the East the individual churches developed their own codes which were used in conjunction with the latest edition of the *Syntagma.* Among these there were notable systematic collections, in particular the *Collectio L titulorum* (550–570) of John Scholasticus and the NOMOCANON (amalgamation of civil and ecclesiastical laws). In Africa there was the *Breviatio Canonum Fulgentii Ferrandi* (mid-sixth century) and the *Concordia Canonum Cresconii* (sixth–seventh century). The only Italian collection of substantial importance is the *Avellana* (*c.* 555), containing papal decrees. In the most widely scattered dioceses and provinces of Gaul, a plethora of *libri canonum* appeared. The PENITENTIALS (above all the *Columbani, Cumeani, Theodori Cantauriensis*) gave expression to the discipline prevailing in the insular churches (Ireland and England); from these churches at this period came only a few collections in the wider sense, for example, the HIBERNENSIS COLLECTIO (*c.* 700). But the Church of Spain continued the ancient tradition of universal disciplinary norms especially in the continually supplemented *Hispana* (*chronologica* and later also *systematica*), containing conciliar canons and papal decretals.

Collections of the Frankish Reform. Efforts at reform in the territory of the politically unified Frankish kingdom and its sphere of influence led to a compilation drive that initially effected the acceptance of the large ancient collections of universal and papal norms: the *Dionysio-Hadriana* (transmitted in 774 by Pope Adrian I to Charlemagne as an expression of the Roman discipline) and the HISPANA COLLECTIO, as well as the combination of the two, the DACHERIANA COLLECTIO (*c.* 800). There were also new penitentials of this sort and the episcopal capitularies. This authentic reform movement was partially successful. It was followed by the efforts of a group of reformers in France to use collections in order to assure the victory of a rather genuine ecclesiastical discipline. At this time there appeared the so-called FALSE DECRETALS (PSEUDO-ISIDOREAN FORGERIES) of mid-ninth century: the *Hispana* of Autun, the *Capitula Angilramni,* the *Capitularia Benedicti Levitae,* the *Decretales Pseudo-Isidorianae* (*see* BENEDICT THE LEVITE).

Collections from the Frankish to the Gregorian Reform. In the transitional period of the late ninth century and the tenth century there were, aside from the smaller collections, in Germany the *Libri duo de synodalibus causis* of REGINO OF PRÜM (*c.* 906), in France the *Collectio* of ABBO OF FLEURY (988–996), in Italy the *Collectio Anselmo dedicata* (*c.* 882). In the wake of the reform of the first half of the 11th century, supported by bishops and princes, new collections were made; they included two of special importance: in Italy, the *Collectio V Librorum* (between 1015 and 1020); in Germany, the *Decretum of BURCHARD* in 20 books (1020–25).

Gregorian Reform Collections. The Gregorian Reform based itself deliberately, as a disciplinary reform, on new collections that stressed the appropriate norms of the past and the prerequisite of a central ecclesiastical authority, the Roman primacy. The most important of these numerous collections were: in Italy, the *Collection of SEVENTY-FOUR TITLES* (*c.* 1175), the *Collectio canonum* of Anselm of Lucca (*c.* 1082), the collection of DEUSDEDIT in four books (between 1083 and 1086), the *Liber de vita christiana* of Bonizo of Sutri (*c.* 1090), the *Coll. Britannica* (*c.* 1090), the POLYCARPUS of Cardinal Gregory (*c.* 1104–06); in France, the *Liber Tarraconensis* (between 1085 and 1090), and above all, continuing the reform in a manner aimed at compromise, the important *Collection of IVO OF CHARTRES*: *Tripartita, Decretum, Panormia;* in Spain was compiled the *Collectio Caesaraugustana* (between 1110 and 1120). This same period produced numerous compilations of lesser importance.

Collections Immediately before Gratian. The great number of the above-mentioned collections and especially the variety of the norms they contained occasioned canonical uncertainty that had inconvenient consequences. Efforts to harmonize the norms therefore became more and more pronounced. They expressed themselves not only in the elaboration of rules of interpretation and concordance, such as the *Prologus* of Ivo of Chartres and the *Sic et Non* of Abelard, but also in concordance treatises and collections such as that of BERNOLD OF CONSTANCE (end of the 11th century), the *Liber de misericordia et iustitia* (*c.* 1105) of Alger of Liège and the *Sententiae Sidonenses* (between 1130 and 1135). All these prepared the way for Gratian's work, which not only brought together the past norms in one collection, but also harmonized them one with another and so became the *terminus ad quem* of the preceding and the *terminus a quo* of the subsequent canonical collections.

Bibliography: LIJDSMAN, *Introductio in ius canonicum,* 2 v. (Hilversum 1924–29). B. KURTSCHEID and F. A. WILCHES, *Historia iuris canonici,* 2 v. (Rome 1941–43). A. VAN HOVE, *Commentarium Lovaniense in Codicem iuris canonici 1,* v.1, Prolegomena (2d ed. 1945). A. M. STICKLER, *Historia iuris canonici latini:* v.1, *Historia* *fontium* (Turin 1950). F. MAASSEN, *Geschichte der Quellen und der Literatur des canonischen Rechts im Abendlande bis dem Ausgang des Mittelalters* (Graz 1870; repr. Graz 1956). P. FOURNIER and G. LEBRAS, *Histoire des collections canoniques en occident depuis les fausses décrétales jusqu'au Décret de Gratien,* 2 v. (Paris 1931–32). *Histoire du droit et des institutions de l'Église en Occident,* ed. G. LEBRAS et al. (Paris 1955–) v.1. W. WATTENBACH, *Deutschlands Geschichtsquellen im Mittelalter. Vorzeit und Karolinger,* Hefte 1–4, ed. W. LEVISON and H. LÖWE (Weimar 1952–63), Suppl: *Die Rechtsquellen.* A. M. STICKLER, *Lexikon für Theologie und Kirche,* eds., J. HOFER and K. RAHNER, 10 v. (2d, new ed. Freiburg 1957–65) 6:253–256. J. J. RYAN, "Observations on the Pre-Gratian Canonical Collections," in *Actes du Congrès de Droit canonique mediéval, 1958* (Louvain 1959) 88–103. *Bulletin of the Institute of Research and Study in Traditio,* 12 (1956) 616–620; 13 (1957) 510–513; 14 (1958) 510–511; 15 (1959) 500–504; 16 (1960) 564–571; 17 (1961) 545–552; 18 (1962) 482–490; 19 (1963) 538–553; 20 (1964) 513–524.

[A. M. STICKLER]

CANONIZATION OF SAINTS (HISTORY AND PROCEDURE)

Canonization is a solemn declaration by the pope in which a deceased member of the faithful is proposed as a model and intercessor to the Christian faithful and venerated as a saint on the basis of having lived a life of heroic virtue or having remained faithful to God through martyrdom [W. J. Levada, "Glossary," *Catechism of the Catholic Church,* 2d ed. (Washington 2000)].

History. The faithful of the primitive Church believed that martyrs were perfect Christians and saints since in imitation of Christ they had shown the supreme proof of charity by giving their lives for the sake of the Gospel and the good of the Church; by their sufferings they had attained eternal life and were perfectly conformed to Christ, the Head of the Mystical Body. The faithful invoked their intercession before God to obtain on earth the grace to imitate the martyrs in their unquestioning and complete profession of faith.

From its very beginning, the remembrance of the martyrs had the characteristics typical of a true veneration. It was distinguished clearly from the memory of other deceased persons in that the date and place of martyrdom or of the martyr's burial were held sacred not only by relatives but by the whole Christian community and the anniversary of their martyrdom was added to the public calendar of the Church. Furthermore, whereas the usual commemoration of the dead was marked by a sense of mourning and intercession for eternal rest of the deceased, the remembrance of the martyrs evidenced a feeling of joy and the conviction that being united to Christ they were now intercessors on behalf of the living.

Toward the end of the great Roman persecutions, this phenomenon of veneration, formerly reserved to

Father Ronald Pytel announcing a miracle attributed to Blessed Sister Faustina Kowalska, who was canonized the following April. (AP/Wide World Photos)

martyrs, was extended to those confessors who, without dying for the faith, had nonetheless defended it and suffered for it (*confessores fidei*). Within a short time, this same veneration was extended to those who had been outstanding for their exemplary Christian life especially in austerity and penance (ascetics), as well as those who had excelled in Catholic doctrine (doctors) or in apostolic zeal (bishops and missionaries).

Episcopal Canonization. Between the sixth and tenth centuries, the number of deceased who were included in the cult of the saints notably increased. The faithful were often satisfied with the reputation of a holy life or with an extraordinary spirit of charity, and, most of all, the fame of miracles. New names were added to liturgical calendars and martyrologies; the number of feasts rapidly increased; often lives, legendary in character, were written. As a consequence, abuses arose that required correction. The urgent need of regulating this matter, so important in the life of the Church, called for a certain uniformity of practice.

In the first centuries the popular fame or the *vox populi*, sometimes called canonization by acclamation, represented the only criterion by which a person's holiness was ascertained. A new element was gradually intro-

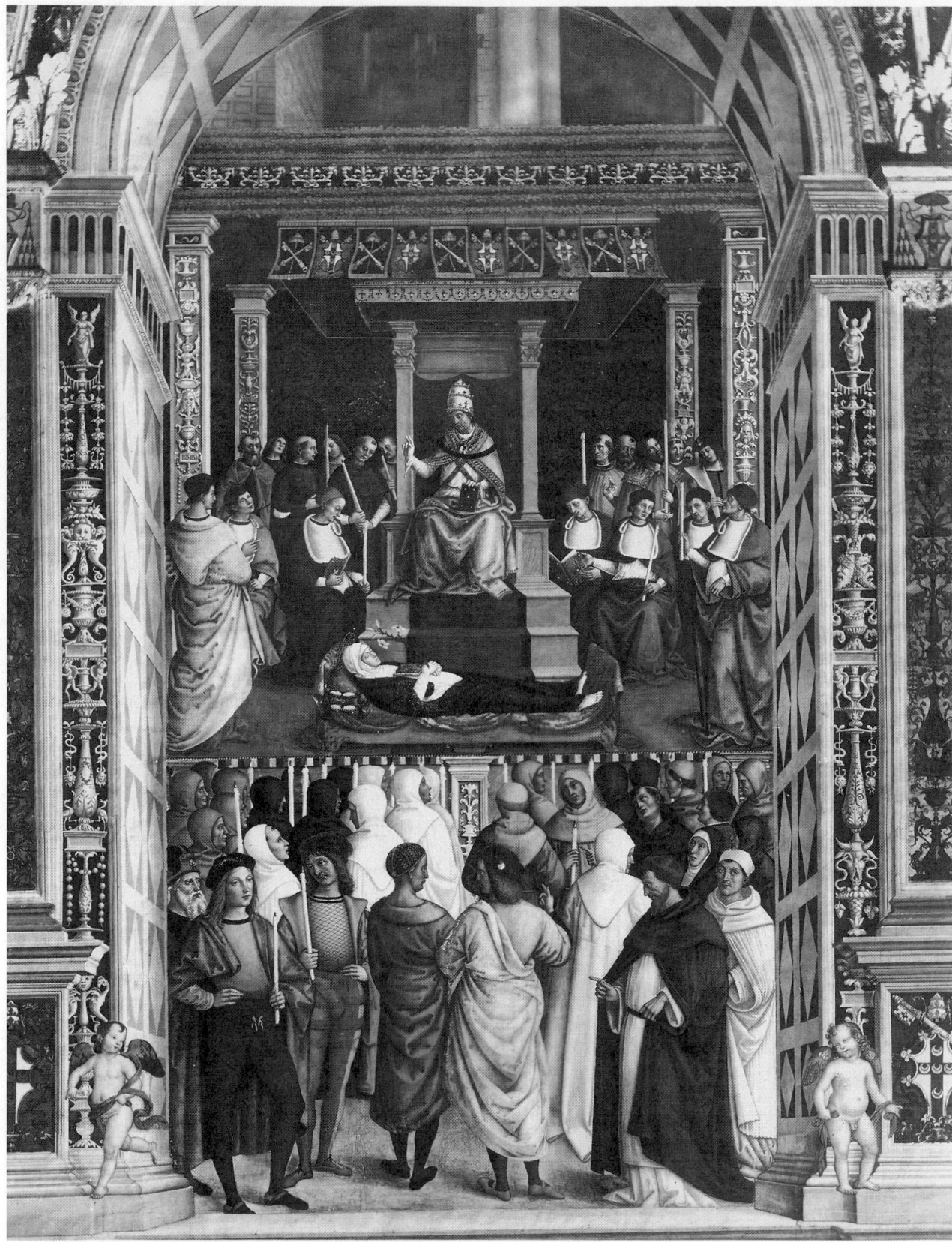

Pope Pius II canonizes St. Catherine of Siena, fresco by Pinturicchio (1454–1513), the Piccolomini Library, Siena, Italy.

duced, namely, the intervention of ecclesiastical authority, i.e., of the competent bishop. However, the fame of sanctity, as a result of which the faithful piously visited the person's tomb, invoked his intercession and proclaimed the healing effects of it, remained the starting point of those enquiries that culminated with a definite pronouncements on the part of the bishop. A biography of the deceased person and a history of his alleged miracles were presented to the bishop. Following a judgment of approval, the body was exhumed and transferred to an altar. Finally, a day was assigned for the celebration of the liturgical feast within the diocese or province.

Through a gradual multiplication of interventions by the Roman pontiffs, papal canonization developed a more definite structure and juridical value. Procedural norms were formulated and such canonical processes became the main avenue of investigation into the saint's life and miracles. Under Gregory IX this practice became the only legitimate form of inquiry (1234). From this time on, papal canonization acquired an exclusive and more distinguished value. Further developments of this doctrinal and historical process were contained in the provisions of the constitution *Immensae aeternae Dei*, promulgated by Sixtus V in 1588. This document provided the guidelines for a new organization of the work of the Roman Curia. The task of preparing papal canonizations was entrusted to the Congregation of Rites. During the period of transition, from 1588 to 1642, the Congregation developed its own method of action and uniform practice. In 1642, Urban VIII ordered a single volume to be issued that would contain all the decrees and subsequent interpretations on the canonization of saints promulgated during his pontificate. The work appeared under the title *Urbani VIII Pont. O. M. Decreta servanda in canonizatione et beatificatione sanctorum*.

In the following century, when Benedict XIV wrote his masterly treatise *De Servorum Dei beatificatione et Beatorum canonizatione*, he relied heavily on the experience of the Congregation of Rites. He illustrated, in a clear and definitive manner, all the elements that had been used in these processes and clarified the fundamental concept of the heroic degree of virtue.

Procedure. The reform of the formal process for beatification and canonization was begun when in 1913 St. Pius X divided the Congregation of Rites into two departments: one to deal with matters liturgical and the other devoted to the canonization of saints. While not completely taken up into the 1917 Code of Canon Law, this division of labor was affirmed by Pius XI in the 1930 creation of a historical section to the Congregation of Rites (*Gia da qualche tempo*, Feb. 6, 1930) and definitely established by the motu proprio *Sanctitatis clarior* (Mar. 19

1969) of Paul VI which created two new dicasteries in place of the one Sacred Congregation of Rites, namely, the Sacred Congregation of Rites and the Sacred Congregation for the Causes of Saints. A complete revision of the norms for canonization, set in motion by Paul VI, was completed during the pontificate of John Paul II and promulgated by the apostolic letter *Divinus perfectionis magister* (Jan. 25, 1983) which provides directives for the organization and working of the Congregation and norms for carrying our the process for canonization. The norms published by the Congregation for the Causes of Saints in that same year (*Normae servandae in Inquisitionibus ab Episcopis faciendis in Causis Sanctorum*, Feb. 7, 1983) and the new *Code of Canon Law* complete the modern legislation governing causes for sainthood.

Structure of the Process. The 1983 norms were formulated in the light of modern notions of history, contemporary methods of research and newly available means of communication. The process for canonization is conducted in two distinct phases, namely, the diocesan and the Roman or apostolic. Following the death of a person who has lived an exemplary Christian life and enjoys a reputation for holiness (*fama sanctitatis*) or for martyrdom (*fama martyrii*) any Catholic, even the bishop himself, can initiate a formal process for canonization. The diocesan phase is guided by the "Norms to be Observed in Inquiries Made by Bishops in the Causes of Saints" (*Normae*, Feb. 7, 1983). These norms, read in the context of the procedural law of the 1983 *Code of Canon Law*, provide a clear outline for the diocesan investigation. It is the diocesan bishop who formally opens the cause and conducts the "instruction" (*instructio*), as it is called, of a canonization process within his own diocese, ordinarily the place where the candidate for sainthood died.

A cause is considered "recent" if the virtues or martyrdom of the candidate for sainthood can be proved through the deposition of eye-witnesses. Such a cause can only begin five years after the death of the servant of God. An "ancient" cause, sometimes referred to as "historical," is one wherein the proofs for martyrdom or virtues can be brought to light only from written sources. There is no time limit for ancient causes.

Central to the entire process of canonization is the person of the postulator. While requiring the approval of the bishop, the postulator is formally appointed by the "actor," that is, the person or group that presents the cause to the local bishop and that agrees to bear the moral and financial responsibility for the cause. The primary task of the postulator is to oversee the investigations into the life, work and holiness of the servant of God, and to provide evidence to the bishop of the authenticity of the cause and its importance for the Church. Once the diocesan phase is completed the postulator continues in his role during the apostolic process and must take up residence in Rome where he collaborates with the Congregation for the Causes of Saints in the creation of the *Positio*, a printed volume that contains a lengthy exposition of the life and virtue of the servant of God, that, in effect, becomes the formal argument for canonization.

Diocesan phase. The purpose of the diocesan process is to gather information and documentation regarding the life, work and holiness of the candidate sufficient to prove the validity of the petition for canonization and to uncover both the positive and negative aspects of the life and virtue of the servant of God, a title permitted once the formal process has begun. For the cause to advance, all the candidate's published writings must be submitted to the judgment of two theological censors, appointed by the bishop, regarding matters of doctrine and moral teaching. The other writings by or about the servant of God are gathered and reviewed by a historical commission, also established by the bishop and their judgment, particularly in ancient causes, is an important element in bringing the diocesan process to a successful conclusion. The focus of this investigation is the quality of the life and virtue of the man or woman under consideration. Did the person persevere in the Christian faith until death? Did the candidate live a life of heroic virtue? Clear evidence must be available that the individual exhibited a life of faith, hope and charity beyond that expected of the ordinary Christian.

The deposition of witnesses must be carried out carefully under the watchful eye of the promoter for justice, another appointment by the local bishop, who supervises the entire diocesan process for canonical accuracy and faithful adherence to the norms. The bishop, or his delegate, must personally ensure that the diocesan process is properly carried out because "a positive outcome of a cause depends to a great extent on his good instruction." (*Norms*, no. 27).

It falls to the bishop as well to investigate the possible existence of any public cult of devotion to the candidate that may be contrary to the norms of the Church. For this reason, prior to closing the diocesan process, the tomb of the servant of God, the room in which the servant of God lived or died and any other place where there might be a display of public cult must be visited and examined.

The results of this complex process must be gathered together to form the "acts" of the diocesan cause of canonization. The original copy of the acts is kept sealed in the archives of the diocese. Two authenticated copies of the acts, together with copies of the published works of the servant of God, are forwarded to Rome, one to be kept in the archives of the Congregation for the Causes of Saints and the other to serve as the "public copy" available to those responsible for composing the *Positio*.

This focus on the diocesan process under the leadership and supervision of the bishop is the most significant change from earlier legislation regarding causes for canonization. The second phase is completely under the direction of the Congregation for the Causes of Saints in Rome.

Roman or apostolic phase. When the acts of the diocesan process have been delivered to the Congregation for the Causes of Saints they are carefully examined for their fidelity to the norms of law. Once declared "valid," a "relator" is named for the cause. The relator, an official of the Congregation, studies a particular cause in detail and collaborates with an assistant from outside the Congregation, often the postulator, in creating the *Positio* according to the accepted norms for Christian HAGIOGRAPHY.

The *Positio* includes the *Informatio* and the *Summarium*. The *Informatio* is the clear and systematic exposition of the life and virtue of the servant of God. The theological and moral virtues form a structure or outline for presenting the evidence for heroic virtue or for martyrdom. The *Summarium* is a summary of the depositions of witnesses questioned on specific points during the diocesan investigation. This structure is aimed at demonstrating that the life of the servant of God, particularly the non-martyr, was so governed by the demands of Christian charity towards God and neighbor that in daily life the theological and moral virtues were practiced in an exemplary and heroic manner. If the subject of the cause is a martyr, the report is intended to prove that the servant of God was killed because of his or her Christian faith, *in odium fidei* and that the servant of God intended to offer his life for Christ and for his Church.

The "promoter for the faith," another official of the Congregation, serves as an overseer in the examination of the cause by the historical and theological consultants to whom the *Positio* may be submitted for evaluation and judgment. In ancient causes, the judgment of historical consultants precedes that of the theological experts. At this point in the process any controversial theological questions must be examined thoroughly.

The opinions of the experts, together with the written report of the promoter for the faith, are submitted to cardinals and bishops who make up the formal membership of the Congregation for the Causes of Saints. Their judgment is then forwarded to the pope for his judgment. Ordinarily, a "decree of heroic virtue" is the first formal step towards beatification. In this declaration the Church recognizes the extraordinary virtue of the servant of God and the title "venerable servant of God" is used when speaking of the candidate. The pope alone makes the decision regarding beatification and canonization.

Miracles Required for Canonization. As the Church discerns the holiness of life of a servant of God through the process of research, historical study and theological reflection, the decision to beatify or canonize a non-martyr requires a confirmation on the part of God, a miracle. One MIRACLE is required to proceed to beatification and another to proceed from beatification to canonization. Divine intervention in a miracle, the "finger of God" (*digitus Dei*) points out, as it were, the authenticity of the holiness of the servant of God and the correct judgment of the Church. When miracles occur in connection with the intercession of the particular candidate whom some of the faithful have invoked in prayer, the Church sets about an investigation similar in structure to the process for the life and virtue of the servant of God already described, to discover whether God has indeed performed this extraordinary act and whether it can by truly ascribed to the intercession of this candidate for sainthood.

In the case of martyrs no miracle is required for beatification or canonization. This is because the very act of sacrificing one's life is seen as proof of heroic virtue, the perfection of charity. "Greater love than this no one has, than to lay down one's life for one's friend." From the earliest days of the Church the MARTYR has been considered as one who is given immediate entry into heaven.

The "instruction" of a reported miracle, while following the same structure as the earlier diocesan process concerning the life of virtue, must be carried out separately. In the late 20th and early 21st century, the majority of reported miracles are healings. All of the medical evidence, the eye-witness reports and the documentation, often voluminous given modern medical procedures and technology, must be gathered and carefully reviewed by a medical expert who is part of the diocesan process. The Church does not ask of such experts a theological judgment (that is, whether or not this is a miracle) but a scientific judgment. Is there any medical or scientific explanation for this cure or this change in a person's physical condition? It is the theologians who make the theological judgment.

If the conclusion of the diocesan process is positive, the acts are forwarded to the Congregation for the Causes of Saints just as in the case of the investigation into the life and virtue of the servant of God. The examination of the diocesan acts of a reported miracle undergoes a rigorous scrutiny within the Roman Congregation. In addition to the theological consideration, a college of medical experts is employed to carefully review the account of the reported miracle and the documentation provided. Again a medical/scientific opinion is rendered and presented in a General Congregation, that is, a meeting of all the bishop and cardinal members of the Congregation for the Causes of Saints. A positive judgment suggests that "it is possible to safely proceed to the beatification of the servant of God."

Beatification. Although it is not mentioned in the current norms for canonization or in the *Code of Canon Law*, BEATIFICATION is, in fact, required before the non-martyr can be declared a saint by canonization. When the pope declares someone "blessed," conferring that title on a venerable servant of God, he declares that for the pastoral good of the Church this person is worthy of emulation and can enjoy a public cult of praise within the confines of a particular diocese, region or religious family.

Once the decision for beatification is announced, the postulator of the cause must supervise the opening of the tomb of the venerable servant and take a portion of the remains to be presented to the Holy Father during the ceremony of beatification as a "relic" of the newly beatified. Thus begins the public cult of authentic relics for this candidate for canonization. In addition, the Holy See authorizes a proper prayer to be used in celebrations of the Eucharist or the Liturgy of the Hours on the feast of the new *beatus*.

The beatification is normally celebrated in Rome at St. Peter's basilica within a Pontifical Mass. After the penitential rite and before the Gloria, the bishop who instructed the cause, together with the postulator, makes a formal request for the beatification of the venerable servant of God. After a brief biography of the candidate is read, the pope makes the solemn pronouncement enrolling the venerable servant among the blessed and assigns a date for the annual feast day within the proper region, diocese or religious community. The congregation responds "Amen." The relics of the newly named blessed are then brought forward, the bishop makes a formal statement of thanks to the pope and the sign of peace is exchanged between the pontiff, the bishop and the postulator. The Mass continues with the Gloria in usual manner.

Canonization. The progression from beatification to canonization requires a second miracle that must be "instructed" in the same manner as the first miracle. Once a reported miracle has been successfully instructed, the Congregation for the Causes of Saints informs the pope of their positive *votum* with regard to the canonization of a particular blessed. The pope is not bound to move forward to canonization, but would ordinarily do so. Canonization is the goal of all causes and represents the definitive declaration on the part of the Church that the one to be canonized is before the throne of God in heaven and the public cult of the new saint is formally extended to the universal Church. The bull of canonization infallibly declares the exemplariness of the saint's life and recognizes his or her role as a heavenly intercessor.

As with the beatification, the ceremonies of canonization normally take place in Rome at St. Peter's basilica within a Pontifical Mass. Inserted between the penitential rite and the Gloria, this simple ceremony is marked by great solemnity. The prefect of the Congregation for the Causes of Saints, together with the postulator, makes the formal request for canonization. Once the short biography of the blessed servant of God is read, the litany of the saints is sung. This is followed by the solemn pronouncement of sainthood by the pope and the congregation responds "Amen." The prefect makes a formal act of thanks to the pontiff and the sign of peace is exchanged with the bishop and the postulator.

See Also: SAINTS AND BEATI.

Bibliography: L. HERTLING, *Dictionnaire de spiritualité ascétique et mystique. Doctrine et histoire,* ed. M. VILLER et al. (Paris 1932–) 2:77–85. H. DELEHAYE, *Les Origines du culte des martyrs* (2d ed. Brussels 1933); *Sanctus: Essai sur le culte des saints dans l'antiquite* (Brussels 1927). F. GAGNA, *De processu canonizationis a primis ecclesiae saeculis usque ad Codicem juris canonici* (Rome 1940). G. GIAQUINTA, *Ricerche sull'istituto giuridico della canonizzatione dale origini alle decretali di Gregorio IX* (Rome 1947). A. VAUCHEZ, *Sainthood in the Later Middle Ages* (Cambridge 1997). F. ANTONELLI, *De inquisitione medico-legali super miraculis in causes beatificationis at canonizationis* (Rome 1962). K. WOODWARD, *Making Saints* (New York 1996). F. VERAJA, *Le Cause di Canonizatione dei Santi: Commento alla Legislatione e Guida Pratica* (Rome 1992). R. RODRIGO, *Manuale per Istruire I Processi di Canonizatione* (2d ed. Rome 1998).

[P. MOLINARI/G. B. O'DONNELL]

CANONS, CHAPTER OF

The chapter is a college of priests, called canons, whose primary function is to give God solemn worship in a cathedral or collegiate church (*Codex Iuris Canonicis* c. 503). This purpose is common to all chapters of canons, but a cathedral chapter has additional duties.

History. The word "chapter" is found for the first time in pontifical documents of the 12th century, although it was already used in the correspondence of the popes and in private documents. The word indicates the function of serving as the bishop's counselor. In the primitive Church, the bishop, priests, and deacons took part in the government of the cathedral church, which was the only church in the diocese. Later, with the increase in the number of priests and churches, it became necessary for the priests of the episcopal city, and in particular for those of the cathedral church, to participate more closely in the government of the church together with the bishop. They were readily available on occasions of solemn liturgical ceremonies performed at the cathedral.

It was the cathedral clergy who assumed the government of the diocese during vacancy of the see and elected the new bishop. Until the 12th century the laity participated with the clergy in the election, but the Church soon reserved the election exclusively to the clergy of the cathedral. The chapter came to claim wider powers: to impose excommunications and interdicts; to confer benefices; to require the bishop to consult it; and to participate in provincial councils. This prompted the councils, and in particular the Council of Trent, to intervene in order to correct abuses and exaggerations. The primary sources of historical information concerning chapters are therefore the decrees of the councils and in particular the decretals.

Canonical legislation. According to the *Codex Iuris Canonicis* (c. 504), the erection, alteration, or suppression of a cathedral chapter is reserved to the Apostolic See. Certain members within a chapter have titles that involve both rights and duties. One of the canons must preside over the chapter, but the code does not specify how this person is to be designated. This matter is left to the chapter's statutes, as is the possibility that other offices may be established. Every cathedral chapter must have a canon penitentiary, who has ordinary jurisdiction to remit in the sacramental forum certain *latae sententiae* censures not reserved to the Apostolic See (*Codex Iuris Canonicis* c. 508).

In an ordinary assembly convoked by its president, the chapter must, at the very beginning, vote on a number of statutes for itself. These statutes are approved by the diocesan bishop (*Codex Iuris Canonicis* c. 505), and they establish rules of procedure for deliberations and other norms concerning liturgical and administrative functions (*Codex Iuris Canonicis* c. 506).

Diocesan College of Consultors. In the United States there exists no cathedral chapter. At the end of the 19th century, the American bishops did not deem it opportune to petition for the establishment of such chapters, but at the Second and Third Councils of Baltimore they decreed the institution of diocesan consultors. The Consistorial Congregation later recognized this institution and the 1917 *Code of Canon Law* included it in the universal legislation (1917 *Codex Iuris Canonicis* cc. 423, 428). The 1983 code has transferred many of the functions formerly assigned to the cathedral chapter to the college of consultors. Other functions formerly belonging to the cathedral chapter are now given to the diocesan presbyteral council.

Bibliography: J. P. BEAL et al., *New Commentary on the Code of Canon Law* (New York 2000). H. A. AYRINHAC, *Constitution of the Church in the New Code of Canon Law* (New York 1925). D. BOUIX, *Tractatus de capitulis* (3d ed. Paris 1882). É. FOURNIER, *Nouvelles recherches sur les curies, chapitres et universités de l'ancienne Église de France* (Paris 1942). G. H. COOK, *English Collegiate Churches of the Middle Ages* (New York 1960). F. LOT and R. FAWTIER, eds., *Histoire des institutions françaises au moyen âge*, 3 v. (Paris 1957–62). P. TORQUEBIAU, *Dictionnaire de droit canonique*, ed. R. NAZ (Paris 1935–65) 3:530–595, contains a complete bibliog. For information specific to cathedral chapters, see: H. NOTTARP, "Ehrenkanoniker und Honorarkapitel," *Zeitschrift der Savigny-Stiftung für Rechtsgeschichte, Kanonistiche Abteilung* 45 (1925) 174–335. P. HOFMEISTER, *Bischof und Domkapitel nach altem und nach neuem Recht* (Württemberg 1931). G. BARRACLOUGH, "The Making of a Bishop in the Middle Ages," *American Catholic Historical Revue* 19 (1933–34) 275–319. C. R. CHENEY, *English Bishops' Chanceries, 1100–1250* (Manchester, Eng. 1950). K. EDWARDS, *The English Secular Cathedrals in the Middle Ages* (Manchester, Eng. 1949). S. L. GREENSLADE, "Sede vacante Procedure in the Early Church," *Journal of Theological Studies* 12 (1961) 210–226. R. I. BURNS, "The Organization of a Mediaeval Cathedral Community: The Chapter of Valencia (1238–1280)," *Church History* 31 (1962) 14–23. M. BIERBAUM, *Lexikon für Theologie und Kirche*, ed. J. HOFER and K. RAHNER (Freiburg 1957–65) 3:496–500.

[R. LATRÉMOUILLE, J. GILCHRIST]

CANONS REGULAR OF ST. AUGUSTINE

One of the largest monastic families of the medieval Church; called also Austin Canons.

Origin. Unlike that of so many other religious orders, the origin of the Austin canons was not closely tied to the work of a single saint or the work of a single house, but was the result of a complex process. After his conversion St. AUGUSTINE displayed an immense attachment to the full common life, and when bishop of Hippo he insisted that the clergy living at his cathedral should live under a common rule and hold no private property. The disordered condition of the times prevented his example having considerable immediate effect, but records of his deep interest in the religious life were preserved for posterity in his writings and in his biography written by POSSIDIUS.

The continuous existence of the regular canons as an organized body is now known to date from the middle decades of the 11th century and to have begun with the adoption of what was in effect a monastic regime by certain communities, largely communities of clergy, in Italy and southern France. To the often neglected obligation of CELIBACY, and the equally neglected life with a common dormitory and refectory, both of which ancient canons had demanded of clergy living in collegiate or cathedral churches, there was now added acceptance of an obliga-

tion to hold no private possessions, i.e., to follow apostolic precedent and "be of one heart and mind and have all things in common." Inevitably this radical form of life struck some clerics as both novel and questionable, and its legitimacy was hotly challenged. The matter was brought up at the Lateran Synod of 1059 by no less a person than Hildebrand, the future Pope GREGORY VII, who, like so many leaders of the GREGORIAN REFORM, saw the value of the movement in an age of considerable ecclesiastical corruption. The synod gave this form of clerical life full approval, though it was not made in any way compulsory; this decision was confirmed in almost identical wording at the Lateran Synod of 1063. Surviving evidence does not give a complete and precise list of the houses that first followed the form of life thus approved, but it is certain that it was early adopted at Rome and in Tuscany, where Lucca seems to have soon become a major center of the new way of life. Other houses were to be found in certain parts of northern Italy and southern France, the former owing something to the influence of the CAMALDOLESE and VALLOMBROSANS. Especially important in these early stages were the houses of San Frediano at Lucca, San Lorenzo of Ulcio near Turin, and Saint-Ruf near Avignon. PETER DAMIAN gave the order vigorous and valuable support at this time.

Early Expansion. In the last decades of the 11th century and in the early 12th century, the new order made very considerable progress in western Europe, the chief areas of expansion being Lombardy, Tuscany, Burgundy, Aquitaine, and northeastern France, where the Province of Reims was a major center. Important foundations of this period included Santa Croce, Mortara; Santa Maria in Porto (Ravenna); GREAT SAINT BERNARD; Rottenbuch, REICHERSBERG; Toulouse Cathedral; SAINT-QUENTIN in Beauvais; and Mont-Saint-Elois. ALTMANN, Bishop of Passau (1091), had been an early pioneer and a keen reformer in southern Germany and Austria, but major progress came only in the early 12th century, notably with the support of Abp. Conrad of Salsburg (d. 1147). The effective spread of the order in England began under King Henry I (1100–35) and proceeded rapidly, as it did also in Ireland but on a smaller scale somewhat later. In Scotland little progress was made for local reasons; expansion in the Spanish peninsula and Scandinavia was also limited. But by the mid-13th century the total number of houses of regular canons in Europe was certainly very considerable. It cannot be precisely estimated, and in any case houses of the order varied so greatly in size that any such figure by itself would be misleading. But in England alone about 206 houses had been founded by the late 13th century.

The Adoption of the Rule of St. Augustine. In the early years of the regular canons it was not regarded as necessary for any monastic order to adopt a specific rule, but experience quickly showed the value of this practice. At first regular canons appealed to the "apostolic life," but for legal and other reasons and by an obscure and piecemeal evolution they fairly quickly came to adopt the so-called Rule of St. AUGUSTINE. The first major signs of this adoption are to be found mostly in France, about the time of Pope URBAN II (1088–99); by the second quarter of the 12th century the rule seems to have been almost universally adopted by the order. The Rule of St. Augustine itself has a very complex history, which has not yet been fully revealed despite much modern research. Most of the document is a masculine version of a number of precepts given by St. Augustine *c.* 423 to a community of nuns of which his sister was superior, but to these precepts was prefixed a short list of injunctions of a very practical nature generally known as the *Ordo monasterii.* The date and authorship of the latter and that of the adaptation of Augustine's *Letter 211* are in dispute, but not a few authorities regard both as having been drawn up by a follower of Augustine shortly after, or possibly just before, the saint's death (430). The early regular canons found much of the *Ordo monasterii* archaic, and it is clear that from the early 12th century they abbreviated the text of the Rule in the interests of practicality.

The Observances of the Order. The early regular canons found no ready-made corpus of observances completely suitable for their purpose but gradually built up their own from a variety of sources. The Rule of St. Augustine was very brief and largely concerned with spiritual precepts. It was to some extent augmented by the *Institutio canonicorum* drawn up in 816–817 for houses of canons throughout the Carolingian Empire, though these latter were seculars not regulars and so their rules were not completely suitable. The customs of the BENEDICTINES, built up over the centuries, proved a valuable quarry for the new order; a section of the order drew also on the observances of the new contemporary orders, notably the CISTERCIANS. For a long time there was no very close uniformity of observance within the order, individual houses picking and choosing fairly freely, subject only to the approval of the local ordinary. But the leading houses of the order soon compiled observances that were widely adopted, the more influential customs being those of Saint-Quentin at Beauvais, Saint-Ruf, SAINT-VICTOR of Paris, and MARBACH. As time went on, attempts were made to secure a greater uniformity of detail. Thus, in the late 13th century the General Chapters of the English Austin Canons, after much effort, produced a uniform code of observances for their members, the Statutes of Healaugh Park (*Statuta de Parco*), though their adoption was slow and partial. Furthermore, at an early date individual congregations of canons had developed their own

particular customs, which in certain cases were much more severe than those followed by the rest of the order, principally owing to the influence of the Cistercians. Then in 1339 Pope BENEDICT XII promulgated a code of observances for the order in the bull *Ad decorem.*

Basically, however, most of the regular canons had adopted from early times observances whose temper, they claimed, was a *via media* between that of the clergy and the monks. In effect they did not differ greatly from many Benedictine observances, though they were somewhat less exacting over silence, fasting, and the length of Matins.

Organization. The regular canons were clerical in origin and always generally retained this quality of personnel, lay brethren forming only a minor element in the order. Their houses were normally subject to visitation by the ordinary, only a small minority aquiring the privilege of EXEMPTION from episcopal inspection. On the Continent a fair sprinkling of houses ranked as abbeys, but in England almost all were PRIORIES. The Cistercians having early demonstrated the utility of general chapters, these were instituted for all orders not already possessing them by LATERAN COUNCIL IV (1215). Those of the regular canons were subsequently organized on a regional basis normally meeting every three years.

An important if not large minority of medieval regular canons early belonged to independent congregations that had their own customs and an independent machinery of government. One of the first of these, the Order of the Holy Sepulcher of Jerusalem, begun by 1114, gave extensive powers to the motherhouse, in imitation of the venerable Order of CLUNY, but later congregations usually adopted a system of general chapters of their own on Cistercian lines. Most of these formal orders of regular canons were small, with some widely scattered houses that tended to drift away as time went on. The various independent orders were mostly in their heyday in the 12th century. The Order of Arrouaise, originating *c.* 1090, followed a severe, contemplative regime; that of Saint-Victor of Paris, whose motherhouse was founded in 1108 by Abelard's teacher WILLIAM OF CHAMPEAUX, was closely connected with the rise of the University of PARIS and produced an important group of writers that included HUGH OF SAINT-VICTOR and RICHARD OF SAINT-VICTOR. The PREMONSTRATENSIANS, whose motherhouse of PRÉMONTRÉ near Laon was founded in 1120 by NORBERT OF XANTEN, showed great vitality from the first; some of its houses were contemplative, others were early involved in missionary work, notably in eastern Germany. The Order of the Holy Sepulcher of Jerusalem, which owed its existence to the crusading movement, declined when this collapsed. In the Spanish peninsula the Order of SANTA CRUZ

(COIMBRA), begun in 1132, was of some importance and owed much in its origin to the Order of Saint-Ruf near Avignon, whose own reputation was considerable. The Order of Sempringham (the GILBERTINES), the only medieval order of English origin, was not of more than local importance, and had double MONASTERIES. Its motherhouse was founded in 1131, but the Augustinian Rule was not followed for some years.

Houses of Austin Canons in the Middle Ages and long after varied greatly in size. Few of them rivaled the largest Benedictine houses, but many were of moderate size. For largely unavoidable reasons, the order was early saddled with a sizable minority of very small houses, whose lack of resources and personnel rendered their life liable to considerable strains and were a cause of anxiety to those in authority. As time went on a number of these were either suppressed or made cells of larger houses. A number of houses, especially in early times, were founded in parochial or collegiate churches, but later it was often found preferable to establish them either just outside residential areas or more rarely in "places remote from human habitation," like Cistercian houses. A notable feature of the order was its connection with HOSPITALS, including those of the Great Saint Bernard, and of St. Bartholomew's and St. Thomas' in London.

Recent research strongly suggests that the earliest regular canons seldom tried to carry out pastoral work in the modern sense: such activity would have interfered greatly with the complex liturgical regime they early adopted. Occasionally one of the brethren might serve a parish in, or near, the conventual church, and a house was usually authorized to put a canon in charge of souls at any of its churches provided he were living in community with other brethren. But generally speaking, regular canons in charge of souls in the Middle Ages were not numerous, though their number seems to have increased somewhat after the plague epidemics of 1347–50. Like the Benedictines, the medieval regular canons gradually established some contacts with medieval universities, but these were not, on the whole, very vigorously exploited.

Recent History. By the end of the Middle Ages the regular canons were reduced in number and influence, though signs of continued vitality were not lacking, notably the foundation of the Congregation of WINDESHEIM in Holland, whose motherhouse was founded in 1386 under the influence of the mystic Gerard GROOTE and which flourished in Germanic lands. Its most famous member was THOMAS À KEMPIS, the probable author of the *IMITATION OF CHRIST*. Rather later came the Congregation of the Lateran, begun at Fregionaia, near Lucca, under BARTHOLOMEW OF ROME. Confirmed by the pope in 1421, its brethren were given charge of the Lateran Basilica by Pope EUGENE IV but were replaced there by seculars in 1471.

The religious changes of the 16th century led to considerable numbers of houses of the order being suppressed, and the secularizations of the 18th and 19th centuries caused much further damage. As time went on old machinery was modified; e.g., the French houses of the order were regrouped to form a French congregation. Austria and Switzerland were the only major areas where the order's life went on without interruption: in 1907 the surviving houses in Austria were formed into the Austrian Congregation of Canons Regular; in Switzerland the venerable house of SS. Nicholas and Bernard, the Great Saint Bernard Hospice, despite much adversity, continues as the head of a congregation, as does the other leading Swiss house of the order, SAINT-MAURICE. Also maintaining continuity with the medieval world are the Canons Regular of the Holy Cross, originally founded in Belgium *c.* 1210, and the Military Order of the Red Star Crucifers, which long worked extensively in eastern Europe (*see* BRETHREN OF THE CROSS). The largest of the medieval orders today, however, is that of the Premonstratensians. The Canons Regular of the Immaculate Conception, founded by Dom Adrien Gréa in 1871, now have their chief house in Rome. The modern regular canons are engaged in a very wide range of pastoral, educational, and social activities. Recently the smaller congregations have been considering coordinating their common activities.

Bibliography: E. AMORT, *Vetus disciplina canonicorum regularium et saecularium,* 2 v. (Venice 1747), old but valuable. J. C. DICKINSON, *The Origins of the Austin Canons and Their Introduction into England* (London 1950). P. FRANK, *Canonicorum regularium sodalitates* (Vorau, Austria 1954). C. DEREINE, *Dictionnaire d'histoire et de géographie ecclésiastiques,* ed. A. BAUDRILLAT et al. (Paris 1912–) 12:353–405; "Coutumiers et ordinaires de chanoines réguliers," *Scriptorium* 5 (1951) 107–113; 13 (1960) 244–246. *La vita commune del clero nei secoli XI e XII,* 2 v. (Milan 1962).

[J. C. DICKINSON/EDS.]

CANORI-MORA, ELISABETTA, BL.

Patroness of abused spouses, mystic and Trinitarian Tertiary; b. Rome, Italy, Nov. 21, 1774; d. Rome, Feb. 5, 1825. Elisabetta was the daughter of a wealthy, Christian family headed by Tommaso Canori and Teresa Primoli. Under the tutelage of the Augustinian Nuns of Cascia (1785–88), she grew spiritually. In 1796, she wedded Cristoforo Mora (d. 1845), a lawyer who abused her and eventually abandoned her and their two children (Marianna and Luciana; two others had died in infancy), reducing the family to poverty. Elisabetta provided for her children and paid her husband's debts by working as a maid, laundress, and seamstress. While earning a living and raising her family, Elisabetta ministered generously to the poor and sick. Following a grave illness in 1801, she was favored with many spiritual gifts, and she became a member of the secular third order of the Most Holy Trinity in 1807. Her home was always open to those in need of spiritual or material comfort. She offered the sufferings of her life for the conversion of her husband, who, after her death, became a Trinitarian tertiary and Conventual Franciscan priest. Her body rests in the Trinitarian San Carlino alle Quattro Fontane Church in Rome. A miracle attributed to Elisabetta's intercession was approved, July 6, 1993, which led to her beatification by John Paul II, April 24, 1994.

Feast: Feb. 4.

Bibliography: *La mia vita nel cuore della Trinità. Diario della Beata Elisabetta Canori Mora, sposa e madre* (Vatican City 1996). P. GIOVETTI, *Madri e mistiche: Anna Maria Taigi ed Elisabetta Canori Mora* (Milan 1991); *Elisabetta Canori Mora: Sposa, madre e mistica romana* (Milan 2000). P. REDI, *Elisabetta Canori Mora: un amore fedele tra le mura di casa* (Rome 1994). *Acta Apostolicae Sedis* (1994): 501–503.

[K. I. RABENSTEIN]

CANOSSA, MADDALENA GABRIELLA, ST.

Foundress of the Daughters of Charity of Canossa; b. Verona, Italy, March 2, 1774; d. Verona, Italy, April 10, 1835. After the death (1779) of her wealthy father, Marquis Ottavio of Canossa, Maddalena's mother, Marchesa Teresa Szluha, remarried in 1781. Maddalena was then raised by an uncle and given a private education. In 1799 she dedicated herself to caring for poor girls, and in 1800 she began to house some of them. In 1803 she opened a charity school, but when she attempted to dwell there herself (1805), she was constrained to return to her family. In 1808 she founded her religious congregation, dedicated to educational and hospital work. By the time of her death the Canossian Sisters had five houses. Maddalena, whose remains are housed in a marble sarcophagus in Verona, was beatified by PIUS XII on Dec. 7, 1941. During her canonization on Oct. 2, 1988, Pope JOHN PAUL II related that when she saw the material and moral misery around her "she saw that she could not love her neighbor 'as a lady,' that is, by continuing to enjoy the privileges of her social class, and merely sharing her possessions without giving herself."

Feast: May 8 (formerly May 14).

Bibliography: D. BARSOTTI, *Dio solo e Gesù crocifisso: teologia di un carisma* (Milan 1985). M. FARINA and F. RISPOLI, *Maddalena di Canossa* (Turin 1995). I. GIORDANI, *Maddalena di Canossa*, 4th ed. (Brescia 1957). L. LIBERA, *Lettere di direzione spirituale alla marchesina Maddalena Gabriella di Canossa*, supplement to A. CATTARI, *Maddalena Gabriella di Canossa, gli anni decisivi di un itinerario spirituale* (Milan 1982). A. BUTLER, *The Lives of the Saints*, rev. ed. (New York 1956), 2:309–311. T. PICCARI, *Sola con Dio* (Milan 1965).

[A. MENATO]

CANTERBURY, ANCIENT SEE OF

Principal metropolitan see of England, founded *c.* 600 by AUGUSTINE OF CANTERBURY. Pope St. GREGORY THE GREAT had envisaged LONDON as the ecclesiastical metropolis of southern England, but instead Augustine chose the capital of Kent, the most powerful and civilized Anglo-Saxon kingdom of the time, whose King ETHELBERT had become a Christian. Canterbury itself was a Roman city, a small replica of Rome in ecclesiastical organization, architecture and church-dedications (for example, *see* SAINT AUGUSTINE, ABBEY OF). The See of Canterbury has always been small in extent: eastern Kent with several "peculiars" elsewhere; but the Province of Canterbury came to include the whole of England south of the Humber, along with Wales. Before his death (*c.* 604), Augustine had founded the suffragan Sees of ROCHESTER and London.

History. Until 653 Canterbury was ruled by Augustine and his Italian companions: LAWRENCE, MELLITUS, JUSTUS and HONORIUS. The first Anglo-Saxon archbishop was Frithonas (Deusdedit of Canterbury, 655–664). A new impulse was given to the Church in England by Archbishop Theodore (668–690), who held councils; appointed bishops to new sees, even in the north; and placed Irish missionary centers under episcopal control. With the African monk HADRIAN, he refounded the Canterbury school, which trained scholars and future bishops and outshone the Irish schools of the time.

In 753 YORK, in accordance with Gregory the Great's plan, became a metropolitan see. About 40 years later King Offa of Mercia tried to make Lichfield a Midland metropolitan see, but in 802–803, the supremacy of Canterbury was confirmed by both the Pope and a provincial council. After the disasters of the ninth-century Danish invasions the see recovered under Odo of Canterbury and DUNSTAN, who worked in close association with the Kings of the time. In the later Danish invasions, Canterbury gained its first martyr, St. ALPHEGE, archbishop from 1005 to 1012.

After the Conquest, LANFRANC, who replaced the simoniacal Stigand, worked very closely with King WILLIAM I at the reform of the English church. SIMONY, and

"The Miracle Window," stained glass window depicting St. Thomas Becket saving Adam the Forester, who has been shot by an arrow, Canterbury Cathedral, Canterbury, England, 12th century. (© Angelo Hornak/CORBIS)

eventually marriage for the higher clergy (*see* CELIBACY, HISTORY OF) were abolished, the monasteries were reformed by the introduction of Norman abbots and a more vigorous intellectual and spiritual life, and monks sometimes replaced canons as chapters of cathedrals. This latter practice, almost unique in Christendom, had already started under Dunstan. Soon after his death the cathedral CHAPTER of Christ Church, Canterbury, had become monastic, and under Lanfranc, its observances (codified in his *Monastic Constitutions*) and its literary and artistic activities strongly influenced other monasteries. Lanfranc also regained lost Canterbury estates from Odo of Bayeux and established a temporary ascendancy over the northern province of York. However, in spite of EADMER's claims and the Canterbury forgeries, Lanfranc's position was reversed by a papal decision in 1121 and York regained permanent independence.

The disputes over INVESTITURE between Archbishop ANSELM OF CANTERBURY and King WILLIAM II and King HENRY I brought importance to Canterbury and exile to the most original theological thinker ever to occupy Augustine's chair. The dispute over the Constitutions of CLARENDON, including the treatment of criminous clerks and the right of appeal to Rome, between Thomas BECKET and HENRY II culminated in the former's martyrdom. This shocked all Europe and a cult of the archbishop rapidly sprang up over most of Europe, while in England the pilgrimage to Becket's tomb retained its immense popularity throughout the Middle Ages.

The later 12th century was marred by disputes between archbishops, who wanted to establish a collegiate church at Hackington whence archbishops might draw trained curialists for administering the diocese, and monastic chapters whose monks regarded this projected church as their rival. The monks were successful in the prolonged litigation that followed, though at a high cost, financially and in diminution of religious spirit.

Archbishops from 1200 to the Reformation. The disputed election of 1205 to 1207, which ended in the nomination of STEPHEN LANGTON by Pope Innocent III, was the most famous in English ecclesiastical history. After the end of the interdict that followed King JOHN's rejection of Langton, Canterbury enjoyed a series of remarkably able and intellectual bishops for most of the 13th century. These included St. EDMUND OF ABINGDON, BONIFACE OF SAVOY, ROBERT KILWARDBY, JOHN PECKHAM and ROBERT OF WINCHELSEA who put into effect the decrees of the reforming Councils of the LATERAN and of LYONS. They visited the province as well as the diocese systematically and efficiently, and promulgated a code of laws about clerical discipline, administration of the Sacraments and preaching.

The 14th- and 15th-century archbishops were generally civil servants or canon lawyers rather than scholars; often their promotion reflected the growing control of the Church by the crown. SIMON OF SUDBURY (1375–81), for example, was killed by the mob in the Peasants' Revolt as the King's principal reactionary adviser. These archbishops, often of aristocratic families, took a prominent part in politics and sometimes were translated by the Pope at the King's request to remote and unimportant sees in punishment for their political activities.

Through most of the Middle Ages England was remarkably free from heresy, but when the LOLLARDS arose Archbishops William COURTENAY, Thomas ARUNDEL and Henry CHICHELE were zealous in suppressing them with the help of the secular arm. However, they excluded the INQUISITION.

From the 12th century, archbishops of Canterbury were so frequently papal LEGATES that they enjoyed the name of *legatus natus*. A few were promoted to be cardinals in Rome, but John KEMP, BOURGCHIER and MORTON (1452–1500) were all cardinals while remaining archbishops of Canterbury. William WARHAM (1503–32) was a friend of COLET and ERASMUS, and toward the end of his reign began the crisis that was to lead to the Reformation in England. Thomas CRANMER (1533–56), tool of HENRY VIII, pronounced the king's marriage with CATHERINE OF ARAGON null after its validity had been upheld by the Pope, and rejected papal supremacy, substituting for it the doctrine that the king was supreme head of the Church in England. Under Cranmer, all the monasteries and chantries and several hospitals were suppressed, four of the diocesan manors were ceded to the King, the relics of Thomas Becket were destroyed and his name, together with that of the Pope, was removed from all the service books.

The accession of MARY TUDOR brought reconciliation with Rome and the appointment of Cardinal Reginald POLE as archbishop and legate (1556–58). But the deaths of Mary and of Pole on the same day ended all hope of a permanent Catholic restoration. Under ELIZABETH I the Acts of Supremacy and UNIFORMITY were renewed, England became Protestant and Canterbury was made the headquarters of the Anglican Church (*see* ANGLICANISM).

Cathedral. The first cathedral of Canterbury, begun by Augustine and completed by his successors, had been burned in 1067. Eadmer describes it as a miniature of Old St. Peter's, Rome. It was rebuilt by Lanfranc on a much bigger scale with a nave of nine bays, but a choir of only two. From 1100 to 1130, under Anselm and priors Ernulf and Conrad, the eastern limb was rebuilt and enlarged for processions and the display of exceptionally numerous relics of Canterbury saints. This part was badly burned in 1174, and the choir was rebuilt by two architects named William, one French and the other English (1174–84). The relics of Thomas Becket were translated to the chapel of the Holy Trinity, to the east of this choir. The nave was rebuilt from 1379 onward in perpendicular style under the architect Henry Yevele and the fine tower ("Bell Harry") under John Wastell, c. 1500. Architecturally, it is one of the finest cathedrals in England, and it is enriched by stained glass dating from 1180 to 1280, especially the theological windows of Old and New Testament types and antitypes and the martyrdom of St. Thomas. There are also many tombs of saints and archbishops. A Norman crypt and part of the monastic buildings still survive.

Bibliography: BEDE, *Ecclesiastical History* ed. H. SPELMAN, i, 25–33; ii, 5–8; iv, 1–2. *Councils and Ecclesiastical Documents Relating to Great Britain and Ireland,* ed. A. W. HADDAN and W. STUBBS, 3 v. (Oxford 1869–78) v.3. *Registers of archbishops of Canterbury* pub. by Canterbury and York Society. I. J. CHURCHILL, *Canterbury Administration,* 2 v. (New York 1933). R. WILLIS, *The Architectural History of Canterbury Cathedral* (London 1845). H. LOXTON, *Pilgrimage to Canterbury* (Newton Abbot, England 1978). P. COLLINSON, et al., *A History of Canterbury Cathedral* (Oxford/New York 1995). P. BRETT and J. DOYLE, *Canturbury* (Norwich, England 1997).

[H. FARMER/EDS.]

CANTICLES, BIBLICAL

Biblical canticles are liturgical hymns taken from the books of the Bible other than the Book of Psalms and resembling the Psalms in form and content. The use of the Biblical canticles in the Christian liturgy began in the East, where it may have been borrowed from a Jewish custom; but it was known in the West as early as the 4th century. In some Biblical manuscripts (e.g., the Codex Alexandrinus) the canticles are inserted immediately after the Book of Psalms. According to the Roman rite, three New Testament canticles are used each day in the Divine Office: the BENEDICTUS or Canticle of Zechariah (Lk 1.68–79) at Lauds; the MAGNIFICAT or Canticle of the Blessed Virgin Mary (Lk 1.46–55) at Vespers; and the NUNC DIMITTIS or Canticle of Simeon (Lk 2.29–32) at Compline. The pre-1970 Roman Breviary used several Old Testament canticles as the fourth "psalm" at Lauds, two different ones for each day of the week, one for "first" Lauds (on most days) and another for "second" Lauds (on penitential days). These were (in the order of the Bible): the first Canticle of Moses, also known as the Canticle of Miriam (Miriam; Ex 15.1–18), second Lauds of Thursday; the second Canticle of Moses (Dt 32.1–43), second Lauds of Saturday (but since 1960 only Dt 32.1–18); the Canticle of Anna (1 Sm 2.1–10), second

Lauds of Wednesday; the Canticle of David (1 Chr 29.10–13), first Lauds of Monday; the Canticle of Tobit (Tobias; Tb 13.1–8), first Lauds of Tuesday; the Canticle of JUDITH (Jdt 16.13–17), first Lauds of Wednesday; the Canticle of Sirach (Sir 1.1–13), first Lauds of Saturday; the first Canticle of Isaiah (Is 20.1–6), second Lauds of Monday; the second Canticle of Isaiah (Is 45.15–25), first Lauds of Friday; the Canticle of Ezekiel (Is 38.10–20), second Lauds of Tuesday; the Canticle of Jeremiah (Jer 31.10–14), first Lauds of Thursday; the Benedicite Dominum or the Canticle of the Three Youths in the Fiery Furnace (Dn 3.52–88), divided into two hymns— Dn 3.52–57, second Lauds of Sunday, and Dn 3.57–88, first Lauds of Sunday; and the Canticle of Habakkuk (Hab 3.2–19), second Lauds of Friday. Many of these canticles have been retained in the 1970 Liturgy of the Hours.

Bibliography: H. SCHNEIDER, *Die altlateinischen biblischen Cantica* (Beuron 1938); "Die biblischen Oden im christlichen Altertum," *Biblica* 30 (1949) 28–65, 239–272, 432–452, 479–500.

[L. F. HARTMAN/EDS.]

CANTOR IN CHRISTIAN LITURGY

With its roots in Hebrew liturgical worship (*see* CANTOR IN JEWISH LITURGY), the role of the cantor, or leading singer of prayer, in the liturgy of the Christian church, grew from a volunteer activity to a complex ritual involvement in only a few hundred years. Later historical movements within the church saw a decline of the cantor until the time of the Second Vatican Council, which brought about its renaissance.

Early Christian Tradition. Early Christian ritual assumes an ambiguity in the development of music as an independent element, as "Hebrew and Greek have no separate word for music. The frontier between singing and speaking was far less precise" (J. Gelineau). Ritual utterances, a form of cantillation, were closer to speech and thus less technically demanding. This practice allowed a volunteer prayer leader to fill the role. Volunteer leadership in worship was also encouraged by a basic theological belief, coming from the prophets, that God dealt directly with Israel, and that every person had an equal right to approach God directly (A. Z. Idelsohn). Historical evidence suggests that readers and singers did much the same work at liturgy, sharing the different types of scripture so the action of reading or chanting was foremost. No specific rank or title of cantor emerged until the end of the third and beginning of the fourth century.

Fourth Century and After. The cantor, as a title, appears in canon 15 of the Council of Laodicea (*c.*

Illumination, letter D, at beginning of canticle, "Book of Habacue," Chapter 3, from "Saint Alban Psalter," 12th century.

344–360) that states, "No other shall sing in the assembly except the cantor who has been canonically chosen to ascend the ambo and chant from the parchment." Further, canon 23 addresses singers in the generic: "The readers and singers have no right to wear the orarium or to read or sing thus vested." Canon 24 continues: "No one of the clergy, from presbyters to deacons, and so on in ecclesiastical rank from subdeacons, readers, singers, exorcists, doorkeepers, or any of the order of ascetics, ought to enter a tavern" (J. D. Mansi, *Sacrorum Conciliorum nova et amplissima collectio* [Florence-Venice 1757–98] 2:567). St. John Chrysostom (347–407) observes that in church the lector speaks alone and even the seated bishop listens in silence; in the same way the cantor chants alone, and when all reply, they sound as a single voice (Hom. In 1 Cor 36.6).

This development reflected the spread of Christianity. As E. Foley explains, "As this was a time of ecclesiastical expansion, so was it one of ritual complexification. The eucharistic perspective of *Apostolic Tradition* (chapter 4), with its servant Christology and pneumatic ecclesiology in which the community was identified with the servant-son, gave way to a developing Roman prayer which emphasized the presence of Christ as priest and victim, downplayed the role of the community, and presented an almost monophysitic Christology in court rhetoric. This change in liturgical perspective and evolution in liturgical language in the west is mirrored by euchological language in the east which increasingly emphasizes fear and awe."

The arrival of the office of cantor brought an expansion of musical artistry and craft. Soloists, alternating with one another or with the choir, offered new opportunities for sophistication in technique and performance. This opened the door to the growth of the SCHOLA CANTORUM. By this time, more musicians were needed to provide music for the daily schedule of services in Rome. The music of this group of cantors altered the style of the previous chant to reflect the increasing splendor of papal celebrations and gave birth to the Gregorian chant repertoire (L. Johnson).

Separation of Title and Function. The leader of the schola, called the precentor, was a minor cleric who supervised the details of the readings and chants for the Mass, helped the pope vest, and gave the intonations for the chants. It was one of the precentor's assistants, the archcantor, who was music teacher and director of formation for the *schola cantorum*. He was also a traveling teacher who spread the Roman method of the chant. Bede, in the early part of the eighth century, related that John, the Archcantor, was brought to England in 678 specifically to teach Roman chant. (L. Johnson)

As part-singing became more prominent in the liturgy, the role of the cantor as a solo singer diminished in importance, and over time the cantor was replaced by the schola cantorum. What had been the music book of the cantor, the cantatorium, was eventually subsumed into the antiphonary of the schola. Within the course of historical events, the use of polyphonic music, with its intricacies and dramatic effects, eclipsed the less compelling sound of the single voice. As a part of this evolution, the office of cantor or precentor became an honorary position with duties limited to supervisory or nominal functions.

The Reformation Period. Following the Reformation, the title of cantor was given to the director of music in the Lutheran Church, who was also a leader of sung prayer. For example, J. S. BACH was cantor to St. Thomas Church and to Leipzig. In this capacity, Bach was responsible for all the music of church and town: for weddings and funerals, feasts and festivals, and each week, the four hour Sunday service. He composed, performed, taught, stage-managed, and directed the Kantorei, always around the centrifugal force of the people's song. In the Roman Catholic Church, the role of the cantor continued its descent into disuse. Charged with merely intoning psalms, responsories, and antiphons, and with singing litanies, they were further reduced to lighting the lamps in choir, distributing music, sweeping, and cleaning up after others (Decrees of Pius VI, 1781 and 1783, see R. F. Hayburn).

Twentieth Century Revival. Vatican II's Constitution on the Sacred Liturgy, *Sacrosanctum Concilium* (Dec. 4, 1963) asserted, among other things, music's integral ministerial function in worship and issued fundamental principles for the revision and renewal of the Church's liturgy. The 1967 Instruction on Music in the Liturgy, *Musicam Sacram* (March 5, 1967, n.33) underlined the importance of the RESPONSORIAL PSALM and initiated a revival of the role of cantor. As early as March 1968, a plenary session of the National Catholic Music Educators Association, meeting in Houston, Texas, celebrated Mass with a cantor.

The promulgation of the *General Instruction of the Roman Missal* (1969) initiated a flurry of documents which, in turn, contributed to the revival of the cantor as a leader of sung prayer in the Mass. These writings included the U.S. Appendix to the General Instruction, the documents *Music in Catholic Worship* (1972), and *Liturgical Music Today* (1982). The 2000 revision of the *General Instruction of the Roman Missal* continues to support the leadership role of the cantor in sung prayer.

Bibliography: S. CORBIN, *L'Eglise a la conquete de sa musique* (Paris 1960). L. DEISS, *Spirit and Song in the New Liturgy, Revised* (Cincinnati, OH 1976). E. FOLEY, *Ritual Music: Studies in Liturgical Musicology* (Portland, OR 1995). *Foundations of Chris-*

A boy in a bar mitzvah at Adath Jeshuran, attended by Rabbi Morris Garden and Cantor Morris Amsel. (©Minnesota Historical Society/CORBIS)

tian Music: The Music of Pre-Constantinian Christianity *tian Music: The Music of Pre-Constantinian Christianity* (Collegeville, MN 1996). ''The Cantor in Historical Perspective,'' *Worship* 56 (1982) 194–213. J. GELINEAU, ''The Animator'' *Pastoral Music* 4 no. 1 (October–November 1979) 19–22. *Learning To Celebrate: The Mass and Its Music* (Washington, DC 1985). J. HANSEN, *Cantor Basics* (Washington, DC 1991). R. F. HAYBURN, *Papal Legislation on Sacred Music* (Collegeville, MN 1979). L. J. JOHNSON, *The Mystery of Faith: The Ministers of Music* (Washington, DC 1983). D. KODNER, *Handbook for Cantors, Revised Edition* (Chicago 1997). J. QUASTEN, *Music and Worship in Pagan & Christian Antiquity* (Washington, DC 1983).

[J. HANSEN]

CANTOR IN JEWISH LITURGY

The role of the cantor, called *hazzān* in Hebrew, as the leader of sung congregational prayer in Jewish liturgical services came into prominence with the destruction of the Second Temple in Jerusalem in A.D. 70, resulting in local synagogue liturgies replacing Temple liturgies of animal sacrifice, public prayer, and choral psalm-singing. Originally the term *hazzān* meant supervisor, and it was applied both to a person having charge for a building and attending to its ritual readiness, as well as to a bailiff of the court who executed punishments, especially flogging.

According to the Talmud his function was to take out from the holy ark the Torah (Pentateuch) scroll, open it at the appointed reading for the week, call the weekly portion, and return it to the ark after the service was completed. The oldest mention of the *hazzān,* though not by this name, is in Lk 4.20, where he is called a ὑπηρέτης (attendant).

The post–Second Temple period witnessed the emergence of the synagogue liturgy with its ever-growing repertoire of liturgical poetry that went beyond the capabilities of the average Jew, thus necessitating the musical leadership of a professional cantor. In the gaonic period after the 5th century, the reading from the Torah and the recitation of the prayers were as a rule duties of the cantor, who in this function was called the *sheliah tzibbur* (agent of the congregation). The position of cantor became more important as the art of composing liturgical poetry, *piyyutim* evolved. A skilled cantor could create both the piyut itself and its melody.

In the course of time, the musical performance became so demanding that the *hazzān* had to be assisted by other singers called *tomechim* (supporters), especially on festival days. This applied to richer communities. Poorer ones, unable to afford two officials, gave preference to a *hazzān* rather than to a rabbi, according to the directive given by Asher ben Yehiel (*c.* 1250–1327), one of the leading rabbinical authorities of his time. Nevertheless, both in late medieval and in early modern times, in the measure that the authority of the rabbi was in ascendancy in the synagogue as against the former lay leadership, there was a tendency to relegate the *hazzān* to a position completely under the rabbi's control. The rabbis demanded that all candidates be examined for piety as well as for voice and insisted that piety and learning count above musical distinction, in reaction to charismatic cantors who held sway over the congregation, and cantors whose vanity exceeded their piety. Nonetheless as long as the Jews have revered their sacred texts, they have required the offices of skilled precentors. This remains the case today as ordained cantors are in much demand throughout the Jewish world.

Bibliography: A. Z. IDELSOHN, *Jewish Music in Its Historic Development* (New York 1929; repr. 1946). A. M. ROTHMÜLER, *The Music of the Jews* (London 1953; repr. Gloucester, Mass. 1962).

[M. J. STIASSNY/B. OSTFELD]

CANTWELL, JOHN JOSEPH

First archbishop of Los Angeles, Calif.; b. Limerick, Ireland, Dec. 1, 1874; d. Los Angeles, Oct. 30, 1947. He was the son of Ellen (O'Connell) and Patrick Cantwell.

After attending Sacred Heart College, Crescent, Limerick, and St. Patrick's College, Thurles, he was ordained on June 19, 1899. He then went to the United States, where he was stationed at Berkeley, California, from 1899 to 1904. While assistant at St. Joseph's Church there, he founded the Newman Club at the University of California. From 1905 to 1914 he was secretary to Abp. Patrick Riordan of San Francisco, and in 1914 was made vicar-general. Having been appointed bishop of Monterey-Los Angeles on Sept. 21, 1917, he was consecrated and installed that December. With the separation of Monterey-Fresno on June 1, 1922, Cantwell's see became Los Angeles-San Diego. He was made metropolitan of the new Province of Los Angeles on July 11, 1936.

Cantwell's 30-year episcopate in Los Angeles coincided with a phenomenal growth in the area. In 1917 the population of Los Angeles was less than 500,000; at his death it exceeded 2,000,000. The number of Catholics in 1917 was estimated at 178,233; in 1947, even after two dioceses had been detached, the Los Angeles see had 600,000 Catholics. They were served by two auxiliary bishops and 688 priests, of whom 362 were diocesan; there were 217 parishes with resident pastors, two diocesan seminaries, three seminaries for religious, four colleges, 35 high schools, and 115 parochial schools with 42,877 pupils. The Confraternity of Christian Doctrine was organized in 1922, and from 1943 on it utilized released time authorized by the state at the archbishop's request. At the archbishop's invitation, 14 communities of priests, six of lay brothers, and 36 of nuns established themselves in his see. Despite the 1929 Depression and the 1933 earthquake, progress continued as Catholic hospitals and charitable institutions were founded or enlarged.

Under Cantwell, synods were held in 1927 and 1942. In 1931 he received the Golden Rose of Tepeyac in gratitude for hospitality to exiled Mexican bishops and their flock during persecution. His solicitude for aliens led to the foundation of Mexican, Italian, Portuguese, Chinese, Russian, and Maronite chapels. Cantwell also inspired the organization of a Catholic Actors' Guild, the Thomas More Club for lawyers, and the Bellarmine group for industry and labor. The Legion of Decency (1934) grew out of Cantwell's appeal for a curb on abuses in the movie industry.

Bibliography: Archives, Los Angeles Chancery. J. B. CODE, *Dictionary of American Hierarchy* (New York 1940). M. P. O'DONNELL, *Effect of John J. Cantwell's Episcopate on Catholic Education in California* (Washington 1952).

[N. C. EBERHARDT]

CANUTE, KING OF ENGLAND AND DENMARK

Reigned: 1017–1035. Canute came to the throne amidst great turmoil in the aftermath of AETHELRED II's long reign (978–1013 and 1014–1016), which had been marred by a protracted struggle against Canute's father Swegn Forkbeard of Denmark and his Viking host. Swegn forced Aethelred to flee to the Norman court of his brother-in-law in December 1013, but Swegn's death in February 1014, prevented the consolidation of his power and the undisputed succession of his son Canute. Confusion resulted when some magnates chose Canute as lord, but others invited Aethelred to return and resume the crown.

Canute temporarily left England to seek help from his brother, who had become king of Denmark upon Swegn's death. When Canute returned in September 1014, he faced not only the aging Aethelred, but the formidable and indefatigable son of Aethelred, Edmund "Ironside." Aethelred died on April 23, 1016, and Canute and Edmund negotiated an end to their fighting later that year following the Battle of Ashingdon. They agreed to a north-south division of the kingdom that followed a traditional pattern. Edmund took the south portion that included Wessex, and Canute took Mercia and presumably Northumbria. When Edmund died the same year on November 30, Canute succeeded to the whole realm. Cunning and ruthless, Canute forestalled possible counter claims of other heirs of the House of Wessex by banishing Edmund's brother Eadwig, later killed, and by sending Edmund's infant sons to the court of Sweden. Then in the summer of 1017 Canute married Aethelred's widow Emma to prevent her brother, the duke of Normandy, from pursuing any military action on behalf of her sons, half-brothers to Edmund and Eadwig.

Canute's marriage to Emma was clearly driven by political exigency, for earlier Canute had entered into *marriage danicum* with Aelfgifu of Northampton, daughter of a prominent northern magnate. The House of Wessex had used marriage to establish alliances between southern kings and their northern subjects, and Canute, a foreigner, also used the relationship with Aelfgifu and her family to attract northerners to his cause. Although the north seemed solidly behind him by 1017, Canute did not repudiate the Danish marriage when he made Emma his Christian wife. He acknowledged and provided for Aelfgifu of Northampton's sons, but he made an agreement that any of his sons by Emma would have the superior claim on the succession

Canute's reign had begun violently and had proceeded well into 1017 with the murderous purging of any magnates Canute suspected of deceit or treachery. Yet Canute proved himself an able ruler capable of delegating power and of attracting men he could trust. Canute's most notable recruit was Godwin, whose power increased until he was second only to Canute in the kingdom.

A baptized Christian when he became king, Canute was at pains to win the Church's approval, but he obviously ignored its teachings when they inconvenienced him. Church leaders must have found his maintenance of two marriages repugnant, but they were tactfully silent concerning the matter. Their endorsement of him through the coronation ceremony brought with it an implied sanction from God and gave him a legitimacy that conquest did not. He strove to enhance that legitimacy, and to lessen any hostility still residual among churchmen who might have suffered directly from the struggle to establish Danish rule. He gave lavishly to monasteries and to the poor on a journey to Rome in 1027. He visited the pilgrimage sites and negotiated for his English archbishops to receive their palliums from the pope at a reduced cost. His piety and humility grew over the years, but they did not inhibit his political astuteness.

Having taken advantage of English war weariness, he brought the realm its first political stability in decades, although he often acted as a tyrant. Following his brother's death, Canute was able to expand his rule to Denmark in 1019 and to create a regency in Norway under Aelfgifu of Northampton for their son Swein in 1030. The size and strength of his empire placed him among the most powerful rulers in Christendom, but in 1035 he died without clearly designating an heir. His empire disintegrated in a power struggle between half-brothers, Aelfgifu's second son, Harold Harefoot and Emma's son, Harthacnut.

Bibliography: G. N. GARMONSWAY, *The Anglo-Saxon Chronicle* (Rutland, Vermont 1992) 144–158. R. R. DARLINGTON and P. MCGURK, *The Chronicle of John of Worcester* (Clarendon, Oxford 1995) 473–521. A. CAMPBELL, *Encomium Emmae Reginae* (Camden, 1949). M. K. LAWSON *Cnut: The Danes in England in the Early Eleventh Century* (London 1993) 117–222.

[P. TORPIS]

CANUTE IV, KING OF DENMARK, ST.

Reigned 1080 to July 10, 1086; b. *c.* 1043; d. Odense, Denmark. He was the son of King Sweyn Estrithson and the grandnephew of King Canute the Great of England and Denmark. Before succeeding his brother Harold Hen to the throne, Canute had spent his youth in Viking expeditions to England and the Baltic countries.

He proved to be an energetic, reforming king, seeking to extend the royal tax laws at home and to challenge William the Conqueror's hold on England. After his marriage to a Flemish princess, Adele, he attempted to organize the Danish Church on a Continental pattern. His donation to the cathedral of Lund is the first recorded act of a Danish king. He established an abbey of English Benedictines at Odense. The rural aristocracy resented his fiscal policy, and in 1085 a revolt broke out as he was about to sail for England. He was captured and killed in the church he had founded in Odense (today, Sankt-Knud). Miracles at the tomb of this "martyr" led King Erik Evergood to request his canonization, and this was granted in 1099 by Pope Paschal II. The monks at Odense fostered his veneration and wrote his life. Traditionally the patron of Denmark, he was also popularly regarded as the patron of numerous guilds until eclipsed by Canute Lavard. His relics are still at Odense in a 12th century wooden reliquary. Canute was the father of Bl. Charles the Good, Count of Flanders.

Feast: Jan. 19; July 10.

Bibliography: *Knuds-bogen 1986: studier over Knud den Hellige*, ed. T. NYBERG, H. BEKKER-NIELSEN, and N. OXENVAD (Odense 1986). M. C. GERTZ, *Vitae sanctorum danorum* (new ed. Copenhagen 1908–12) 27–168, 531–558; *Knud den Helliges Martyrhistorie* (Copenhagen 1907). B. SCHMEIDLER, "Eine neue Passio S. Kanuti regis et martyris," *Gesellschaft für altere deutsche Geschichtskunde/Neues Archiv* 37 (1911–12) 67–97. P. D. STEIDL, *Knud den Hellige* (Copenhagen 1918). A. BUTLER, *The Lives of the Saints*, ed. H. THURSTON and D. ATTWATER (New York 1956) 1:121. T. GAD, *Kulturhistorisk Leksikon for nordisk Middelalder*, ed. J. DANSTRUP (Copenhagen 1956–) 8:596–600.

[L. MUSSET]

CANUTE LAVARD, ST.

Danish noble; b. Roskilde, *c.* 1096; d. Haraldsted, Jan. 7, 1131. Son of the Danish King Erik Evergood, he was baptized Gregory. The surname "Lavard" is equivalent to the English "Lord." As a youth he was at the court of Saxony with the future Emperor Lothair III. His uncle, King Niels (Nicholas), named him duke of Schleswig *c.* 1115. Through the protection of Lothair, whom he tried to evangelize, he became, *c.* 1129, prince (Knés) of the Wends in eastern Holstein. Put forward as eventual successor to King Niels, he constituted a rival to the latter's son, Magnus, whose entourage assassinated Canute at Haraldsted, near Ringsted, Denmark. This crime brought on a civil war that lasted until the accession of Canute's son, Waldemar I the Great. Reports of miracles at Canute's tomb at Ringsted led to the building of a chapel on the site of the murder. Pope Alexander III canonized Canute in 1169; the solemn translation of his remains took place on June 25, 1170. Canute became the patron saint of the Danish guilds, and his cult spread throughout Denmark and Schleswig. His present tomb at Sankt-Bendt church, Ringsted, dates only from the 17th century.

Feast: Jan. 7; June 25.

Bibliography: *Vitae sanctorum danorum,* ed. M. C. GERTZ (new ed. Copenhagen 1908–12) 169–247. L. WEIBULL, *Nordisk historia* 2 (1948) 415–432. A. BUTLER, *The Lives of the Saints*, ed. H. THURSTON and D. ATTWATER (New York 1956) 1:49. T. GAD, *Kulturhistorisk leksikon for nordisk middelalder,* ed. J. DANSTRUP (Copenhagen 1956—) 8:600–603, with bibliog.

[L. MUSSET]

CAO DAI

Literally, "high tower" or "high altar," a Daoist expression for the Supreme One. Cao Dai is a syncretic and esoteric Vietnamese new religious movement that combines aspects of DAOISM, BUDDHISM, CONFUCIANISM and Roman Catholicism. It was founded by Ngo Van Chieu (1878–1926), a minor official in the French colonial civil service in Vietnam in 1919. In a traditional Daoist table-moving spirit séance, he claimed to have received the "Third Revelation" that would unite and complete the earlier two revelations that had produced Buddhism, Daoism, Confucianism, and Roman Catholicism. The founders and deities of these four religions (e.g., Sakyamuni Buddha, Laozi, Confucius, Moses, Jesus Christ) are clustered in the "upper" Cao Dai pantheon of deities that its adherents worship daily. Adherents also venerate an open-ended "lower" pantheon of "patron saints" that includes Pericles, Julius Caesar, St. Joan of Arc, Voltaire, Victor Hugo, J. Jaurès, Winston Churchill, Sun Yat-sen, Li Thai Po and Tranh Thinh.

From its Daoist roots, Cao Dai inherits the spirit séances and divination ceremonies. Its ethical vision, precepts of daily living and ancestor veneration ceremonies are taken from Confucianism. For its teachings on karma and reincarnation, it draws upon Buddhism. Its hierarchical leadership structure (i.e., the ordering of the movement as a "Holy See" with a "pope" as supreme leader, a college of "cardinals" as his advisers and "archbishops" as local leaders), its ideal of universal love and its colorful rituals are adapted from Roman Catholicism. The representation of the Supreme One as an eye in a triangle that appears in all its religious art and architecture is influenced by early 20th-century French theosophical esotericism.

The movement experienced much growth under the charismatic leadership of Le Van Trung, a former gov-

Caodaists attending Mass. (©Françoise de Mulder/CORBIS)

ernment functionary who reorganized the movement along the hierarchical leadership structure of the Roman Catholic Church. Van Trung created a "Holy See" in Tay Ninh, a southern provincial city by the banks of Vam Co Tay River, some 65 miles (105 km) northwest of Ho Chi Minh City (formerly Saigon). He was also responsible for building the landmark Cao Dai "cathedral" in Tay Ninh, a highly eclectic edifice patterned after St. Peter's Basilica in Rome, and fusing Buddhist, Daoist, Confucian and Roman Catholic architectural elements. The formal reorganization was completed in 1926, and Van Trung became the movement's first "pope."

Originally an urban movement of nationalist intellectuals in Saigon, it soon captured the imagination of Vietnamese peasants in the rural districts of the south and southwest. At its peak, Cao Dai counted some two million members, and had a strong political and military presence in the south. It espoused a militant and nationalist ideology in its anti-colonial insurrection against French rule. The sect operated a parallel government and had its own militia until the mid-1950s, when Ngo Dinh Diem disbanded its militia and forced its "pope," Pham Cong Tac, into exile. After the 1975 communist victory, Cao Dai's influence was curtailed, and attempts were made to integrate them within a reconstructed communist society. Although the communist authorities have al-

---

Capital: Praia, São Tiago.
Size: 1,557 sq. miles.
Population: 401,310 in 2000.
Languages: Portuguese, Crioulo (a mix of Portuguese and West African).
Religions: 385,290 Catholics (96%), 8,820 Protestants (2%), 7,200 other.
Diocese: Santiago de Cabo Verde, immediately subject to the Holy See.

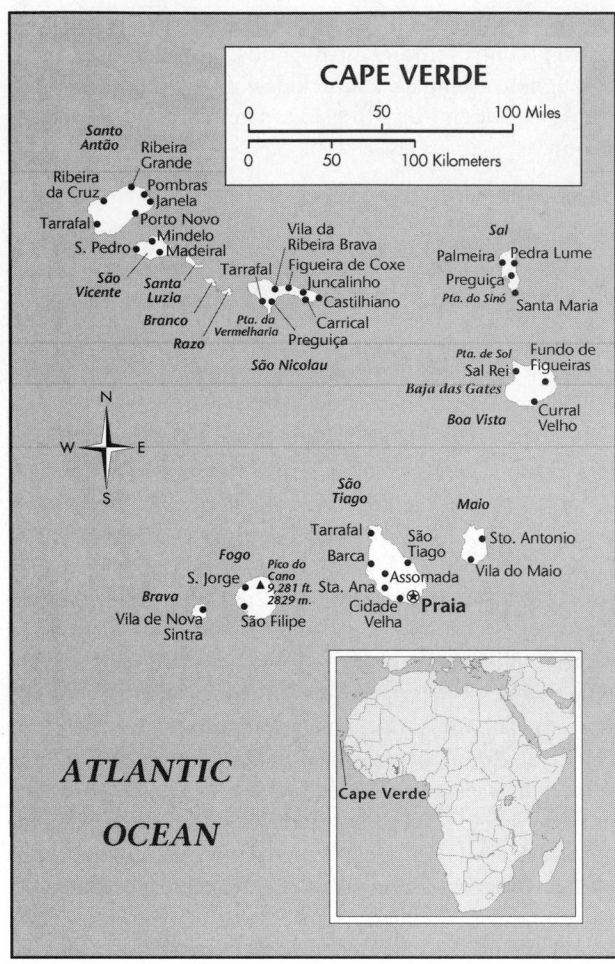

lowed the "Holy See" in Tay Ninh to operate, there are reports of sporadic harassment of the sect's adherents. Many adherents have fled abroad, establishing large overseas Cao Dai communities in Australia, France and the United States.

Bibliography: *The Religious Constitution of Caodaism: Religious Constitutional Laws*, explained and annotated by His Holiness Pope Hô-Pháp, L. DAVEY, tr. (Wiley Park, New South Wales, Australia 1992). E. H. BÙI, *Caodaism: A Novel Religion* (San Jose, Calif. 1992). K. E. FIELDS, "Culture and Politics in Vietnamese Caodàism," in S. A. ARJOMAND, ed., *The Political Dimensions of Religion* (Albany, New York 1993) 205–18. G. GOBRON, *History and Philosophy of Caodaism; Reformed Buddhism, Vietnamese Spiritism, New Religion in Eurasia*, PHAM-XUÂN-THÁI, tr. (Saigon 1950). K. PHAN, *Caodaism* (London 2000). V. L. OLIVER, *Caodai Spiritism: A Study of Religion in Vietnamese Society* (Leiden 1976). J. S. WERNER, *Peasant Politics and Religious Sectarianism: Peasant and Priest in the Cao Dai* (New Haven, Conn. 1981).

[V.T. PHAM]

CAPE VERDE, THE CHURCH IN

The Republic of Cape Verde is comprised of a chain of ten volcanic islands and five islets in the North Atlantic Ocean off the coast of Africa, 300 miles west of Senegal. The Cape Verde islands are characterized by volcanic activity, steep, rocky terrain, violent winds, and prolonged droughts; desertification and deforestation have become major threats to the little land suitable for agriculture. Uninhabited until their discovery by the Portuguese in the 15th century, the islands are now home to an ethnic Creole majority as well as Europeans and Africans. The islands, which include Săp Tiago, Santo Antão, São Vicente, São Nicolau, Sal Rei, Boa Vista, Fogo, Maio, Brava, and Santa Luzia, contain few natural resources; fishing is a substantial industry.

Discovered in 1456 by Venetian navigator Ca Da Mosto and colonized by the Portuguese as a trading center for African slaves, the islands became important to Portugal's trade with Africa, Asia, and South America. The islands remained a colony of Portugal until 1951, when they became an overseas territory. Fighting along-side nationalists in Portuguese Guinea (now Guinea-Bissau), Cape Verde obtained its political independence on July 5, 1975.

Franciscans were the first to minister on the islands, brought by Portuguese traders. In 1532 the Diocese of Santiago de Cabo Verde was created, its jurisdiction at first extending to the African coast from the Gambia River to Cape Palmas (in modern Liberia). Such large geographical demands seriously hindered the Church's development, and between the 17th and 19th centuries the mission languished. Twice for long periods (1646–72, 1826–45) there was no resident bishop. A minor seminary was established in 1866, but Portugal's anticlerical government closed it in 1910.

In 1941 the islands saw a resurgence in missionary activity, with the arrival of Holy Ghost Fathers who reinvigorated the diocese. Capuchins came in 1946, followed by Salesians, to work among a population described as dechristianized. By 2000 Cape Verde contained 31 active parishes administered to by 15 secular and 32 religious priests, six brothers, and 104 sisters.

The ruins of a Portuguese fortress on Sao Vicente, Cape Verde. (©Dave G. Houser/CORBIS)

While the Church's evangelization efforts in Cape Verde continued to be successful, the population as a whole became increasingly threatened by the encroachment of the Sahara desert, and younger citizens were emigrating to escape drought and poverty by 2000. Beginning in February 1984 Pope John Paul II, through his personal charity Cor Unum, established "John Paul II for the Sahel," to combat poverty, hunger, and health risks as well as develop alternate agricultural methods in Cape Verde and the eight other nations in the Sahel region threatened by the encroachment of the Sahara's sands. In 1999 $5.5 million was donated to this cause, followed in 2000 by $1.6 million. A representative from the Holy See also participated in an international conference in Bonn, Germany in December 2000 to address the loss of arable land in the Sahel.

Bibliography: "A religião em Cabo Verde," in *Portugal em Africa* 13 (1956). J. PEREIRA DE OLIVEIRA, "Actividades dos padres do Espirito Santo em Cabo Verde," *ibid.* 14 (1957) 303–. "A acção dos padres do Espirito Santo em Cabo Verde," *Boletim Geral do Ultramar* 392 (Lisbon 1958) 111–115. R. PATTEE, *Portugal na Africa contemporânea* (Coimbra 1959) with full bibliography. *Bilan du Monde* 2:205–206. A. MENDES PEDRO, *Anuário Católico do Ultramar Portugues* (1960): *Annuaire Catholique de l'Outre-Mer. Portugais* (Estudos de ciéncias políticas e sociais 57; 1962), Fr. and Port. on opposite pages. Centro de Estudos Políticos e Sociais, Lisbon. Missão para o Estudo da Missionologia Africana, *Atlas missionário português* (Lisbon 1962).

[R. PATTEE/EDS.]

CAPECELATRO, ALFONSO

Cardinal, author; b. Marseilles, Feb. 5, 1824; d. Capua, Italy, Nov. 14, 1912. He was born in France, whence his father Francesco, Duke of Castelpagano, had gone into exile to escape the tyranny of Ferdinand I, King of the Two Sicilies. In 1830, the family returned to Italy, residing at S. Paolo Belsito, Province of Nola. In 1840 Alfonso entered the ORATORIANS in Naples. Shortly after ordination (1847), he was chosen pastor of St. Philip Neri parish in Naples, devoting himself to studies and religious duties. He was of great service to the Oratorians when he succeeded in having the church of the Girolomini, with its cloisters and rich library, declared a national monument with all the privileges and guarantees appertaining thereto. Leo XIII appointed him assistant librarian of the Vatican Library (1879). He became archbishop of Capua (1880), cardinal (1885), and prefect of the Vatican Library (1899). His close relations with the royal court, and his support of TOSTI may account for his

Bernard Capelle.

not receiving the See of Naples in 1898. Capecelatro's vast literary production includes several biographies distinguished for their historical and scholarly qualities, wealth of information, and classical style. These qualities are especially evident in his *Storia di S. Caterina da Siena* (1856). He also published *Newman e la religione cattolica in Inghilterra* (1859); several well-known prayer books; a life of Christ; biographies of SS. Peter Damian, Alphonsus Liguori, and Philip Neri. The last work has appeared in English. Capecelatro also published his autobiography *I miei venticinque anni di episcopato* (1905). His *Carteggio* contains the correspondence he exchanged with outstanding men of the period.

[H. R. MARRARO]

CAPELLE, BERNARD

Liturgist; b. Namur, Belgium, Feb. 8, 1884; d. Louvain, Oct. 12, 1961. Born to a family of magistrates and baptized Paul, he followed the course of studies at the Collège Notre Dame de la Paix at Namur. In 1906 he was ordained for the Diocese of Namur and for six years served as assistant pastor at Gembloux. He then went to Rome, where he earned doctorates in philosophy and theology at the Gregorian University, and in 1912 he re-

ceived the first doctorate bestowed by the Biblical Institute. His dissertation concerned the text of the Latin psalter in Africa. On Oct. 14, 1918, he entered the Abbey of Maredsous and made his profession on Oct. 15, 1919. He was immediately given the direction of the library and charged with editing the *Revue Bénédictine*. In 1922 he was assigned by his Abbot, Dom Columba Marmion, to teach dogmatic theology at the Abbey of Mont-César in Louvain. So great was the enthusiasm with which the monks there received the new professor that they chose him on Jan. 23, 1923, as coadjutor abbot to Abbot Robert de Kerchove (1846–1942).

Mont-César had retained since 1909 the leadership of the liturgical movement in Belgium. Capelle strengthened this leadership by his energetic collaboration on the abbey's review, *Questions liturgiques et paroissiales*, and through the influence he exercised over many liturgical study weeks and circles. From 1936 to 1956 he occupied the chair of liturgy at the University of Louvain and later taught for the Institut Supérieur de Liturgie at Paris. He was consultor for the Congregation of Rites, a member of the Henry Bradshaw Society and the preparatory liturgical commission of Vatican Council II.

An erudite historian of ancient Christian liturgies, he was also a popular writer and preacher. Most of his writings have been gathered into three volumes of *Travaux liturgiques de doctrine et d'histoire* (Louvain 1955).

Bibliography: F. VANDENBROUCKE, *Revue d'histoire ecclésiastique* 56 (1961) 1024–25; "Dom Bernard Capelle," *Ephemerides liturgicae* 76 (1962) 43–49. A. G. MARTIMORT, *Maison-Dieu* 68 (1961) 203–207. *Revue Bénédictine* 71 (1961) 231–232.

[N. N. HUYGHEBAERT]

CAPÉRAN, LOUIS

Theologian; b. Saint-Gaudens, France, April 15, 1884; d. Toulouse, Jan. 9, 1962. He was named canon at the Cathedral of Toulouse. At first, he wrote works that pertained to contemporary thought such as: *Foi laïque et foi chrétienne: La Question du surnaturel* (Paris 1938); *L'Anticléricalisme et l'affaire Dreyfus (1897–1899)* (Paris 1948); *Histoire contemporaine de la laïcité française* (La Roche-sur-Yon 1957); *France nouvelle et Action Catholique* (Toulouse 1942). Then, his books concerning practical evangelization were published: *La Méthode du prêtre: Leçons et lectures sur les preuves de la religion* (Toulouse no date); *Manuel à l'usage des écoles, des catéchismes et des mouvements de jeunesse* (Paris no date). He also made translations of the Gospel for the use of the faithful: *Évangile de Saint Jean: La Lumière et la vie* (Paris 1950); *Évangile de Saint Luc: Le*

Sauveur des hommes (Paris 1951); *Évangile de Saint Marc: Le Fils de Dieu* (Paris 1951); *Évangile de Saint Matthieu: Le Roi Messie* (Paris 1951).

[G. MOLLAT]

CAPERNAUM

A town in Galilee, at the site of modern Tell Hûm, on the north-northwest shore of the Sea of Galilee. The transliteration Capharnaum, rather than Capernaum, appears in the Douai-Rheims translation of the Bible and became the traditional Catholic spelling. Capernaum, the standard English transliteration of the name, was adopted by the New American Bible (1970), following the Revised Standard Version (RSV) and the King James Version (KJV). The name comes from the Aramaic or late Hebrew *kᵉpar-nāḥûm,* "village of Nahum." Capernaum was "by the sea, in the territory of Zabulon and Nephthalim" (Mt 4.13), about three miles southwest of the Jordan's entrance into the Sea of Galilee. Although unmentioned in the Old Testament, it is referred to 16 times in the Gospels. Using it as the center for much of His ministry, Jesus worked many miracles there. It was there, too, that St. Matthew, the publican, was called to follow Jesus. Because of its unbelief (Mt 11.23; Lk 10.15), Jesus threatened severe judgment on Capernaum. It is mentioned also by Flavius Josephus, who was brought there when he was wounded in a battle near the Jordan.

Excavating the Ancient City. Nineteen seasons of archaeological excavations, in Capernaum, were conducted by the Franciscans between 1968 and 1986. Capernaum is one of a number of biblical sites that fell within the Franciscan Holy Land Custody. Chief among the finds is a limestone synagogue, dating somewhere between the 2nd and the 5th centuries A.D. Beneath this synagogue are the ruins of an older structure, the remains, perhaps, of the synagogue where Jesus taught (Mk 1:21–28; Jn 6:71).

These excavations continued an earlier archaeological expedition undertaken in 1921 by Gaudenzio Orfali. In addition to unearthing the synagogue, Orfali found the remains of an octagonal church, which had been built probably on the traditional site of the house of St. Peter. There is evidence that in very early times the Judeo-Christians converted the house of Peter into a place of worship. Later excavations appear to have identified the remains of Simon Peter's house (Mk 1:29–34).

Bibliography: G. ORFALI, *Capharnaüm et ses ruines d'après les fouilles accomplies à Tell–Houm par la Custodie franciscaine de Terre Sainte (1905–1921)* (Paris 1922). *Biblical Archaeologist,* 46 (1983) 198–204. *Biblical Archaeology Review,* 8 (6, 1982) 26–37; 9 (4, 1983) 50–53.

[S. MUSHOLT/EDS.]

CAPGRAVE, JOHN

Historian, theologian; b. Lynn, Norfolk, England, April 21, 1393; d. Lynn, August 12, 1464. Probably the most important of the English AUGUSTINIANS, Capgrave became a doctor of theology at Cambridge *c.* 1430 and served as Augustinian provincial of England from 1453 to 1457. His *Chronicle of England* to 1417 (ed. F. C. Hingeston, *Rerum Brittanicarum medii aevi scriptores*), dedicated to King Edward IV, was the first history of England not written in Latin. In his same Norfolk dialect he also wrote *Ye solace of pilgrimes* (ed. C. A. Mills, London 1911), an excellent description of classical and Christian Rome done in 1450; the *Lives of St. Augustine, St. GILBERT OF SEMPRINGHAM* and a *Sermo* (*Early English Text Society* 1910); and the metrical lives of *St. Catherine of Alexandria* (*Early English Text Society* 1893) and *St. NORBERT* (not yet edited). In Latin he wrote commentaries on almost all the books of the Bible, of which only those on Genesis, Exodus, and Acts of the Apostles are extant in manuscript; the *De fidei symbolis;* and the *Liber de illustribus Henricis* (ed. F. C. Hingeston, *Rerum Brittanicarum medii aevi scriptores*), dedicated to King Henry VI; as well as other works now lost, such as a life of Humphrey of Gloucester, his chief patron. The *Nova legenda Anglie* (London 1901), Capgrave's most famous work, is actually only a rearrangement of the *Sanctilogium* of John of Tynemouth, OSB.

Bibliography: E. M. THOMPSON, *The Dictionary of National Biography from the Earliest Times to 1900,* 63 v. (London 1885–1900; repr. with corrections, 21 v., 1908–09, 1921–22, 1938; suppl. 1901–) 3:929–931. W. DIBELIUS, "John Capgrave und die englische Schriftsprache," *Anglia* 23 (1901) 153–194, 323–375, 427–472; 24 (1901) 211–263, 269–308. A. DE MEIJER in *Augustiniana* 5 (1955) 400–440; 7 (1957) 118–148, 531–575, bibliog.

[A. DE MEIJER]

CAPILLAS, FRANCIS DE, BL.

Dominican protomartyr of China; b. Bacquerin de Campos, Spain, Aug. 18, 1607; d. Fujian (Fukien), China, Jan. 15, 1648. From Spain he went to Manila (1631), where he was ordained and was active from 1633 to 1641 in Cagayan and Babuyanes. In 1642 he was sent to China via Formosa, joining Francisco Diaz, OP, a missionary returning to his former work in Fujian. They arrived just at the time that the Manchu Tartars were overthrowing the Ming dynasty. During the Tartar invasions, heavy demands were made on the Dominicans, and it was difficult to maintain the peace. Christianity was outlawed on Aug. 9, 1647. Francis, apprehended by mistake on the following day in Fujian, was beaten, and his ankles were stretched on the rack. He was suspected of sorcery because of his patience in suffering. Later he was beheaded as "the leader of the traitorous Christians." His body was eventually taken away by his followers; his head is still venerated at the Dominican house in Valladolid. The process for beatification was begun immediately; resumed in 1901, it was completed Sept. 2, 1909.

Feast: Jan. 15.

Bibliography: J. RECORDER DE DORDA, *Vida del protomartir de China, beato Francisco de Capillas* (Avila 1909). J. M. GONZÁLEZ, *Historia de las misiones dominicanas de China*, v.1 (Madrid 1964). A. BUTLER, *The Lives of the Saints* (New York 1956) 1:98–99. B. M. BIERMANN, *Die Anfänge der neueren Dominikanermission in China* (Münster 1927).

[B. M. BIERMANN]

CAPITAL PUNISHMENT

The execution of a criminal under death sentence imposed by competent public authority. Unlike the act of a private person exacting revenge for a wrong done to himself or to his family, this penalty manifests the community's will to vindicate its laws and system of justice, to atone for wrongful conduct, and to deter criminal acts by others in the future. Among some primitive peoples, a popular assembly might order death not only to retaliate for murder or treason, but also to appease spirits offended by sorcery, incest, or sacrilege.

Ancient Practices. Capital punishment existed in the legal codes of the ancient Middle Eastern kingdoms. These codes commonly prescribed death for homicide and for some religious or sexual offenses. Thus, for Israel, it was declared that "whoever sheds the blood of man, by man shall his blood be shed" (Gn 9.6) and further that "you shall not let the sorceress live. Anyone who lies with an animal shall be put to death. Whoever sacrifices to any god, except to the Lord alone, shall be doomed" (Ex 22.17–19). The law of the Israelites at one time or another listed as capital crimes homicide, bearing false witness in a capital charge, kidnapping, insult or injury to a parent, sexual immorality, witchcraft or magic, idolatry, blasphemy, and sacrilege. Hebrew law clearly distinguished between voluntary and involuntary manslaughter: "When a man kills another after maliciously scheming to do so, you must take him even from my altar and put him to death" (Ex 21.14). It likewise embraced the *lex talionis:* "If injury ensues, you shall give life for life, eye for eye, tooth for tooth, hand for hand" (Ex 21.23–24). It is generally understood that this principle of retribution was enunciated not only to sanction stern penalties, but also to protect offenders from excessive punishments. When death was prescribed, the sentence was more often carried out by stoning, although

hanging, beheading, strangulation, and burning were also used. Among the Babylonians, the Code of HAMMURABI distinguished between manslaughter and willful homicide and also proclaimed the *lex talionis.* Death and mutilation were frequent penalties. The Assyrian Code likewise mentioned death and mutilation, but it remains questionable how often such penalties were inflicted. In the Hittite kingdom, death was reserved mainly for crimes committed by slaves or for special crimes against the king.

The term capital punishment derives from *caput,* a word used by the Romans variously to mean the head, the life, or the civil rights of an individual. Roman law also knew the death penalty as the *summum supplicium.* In addition to death, Roman law looked on perpetual hard labor and banishment (*interdictio aquae et ignis et tecti*—denial of fire, water, and shelter) as lesser capital punishments. Banishment meant in effect a grave loss of one's civil rights or status (*deminutio capitis*). During the Republic, death was imposed mainly for crimes among the military. Under the emperors, it became increasingly common as the penalty for a much wider range of offenses. Rome early embraced the *lex talionis* in its Law of the Twelve Tables (450 B.C.). Ancient Greece and Rome generally looked on homicide, treason, and sacrilege as capital offenses. Later Roman law put other crimes, such as arson and false coining, in the same category. The Greeks imposed death in several ways, e.g., sometimes a free man would be permitted to take poison, and a slave would be beaten to death. Roman usages included strangulation, exposure to wild beasts, crucifixion, and the *culeus* (drowning a condemned man tied up in a sack with a cock, a viper, and a dog).

Christian Attitudes Towards Capital Punishment. Ancient Israel had prescribed capital punishment for some crimes, but the Old Testament spoke also of divine mercy: "As I live, says the Lord God, I swear I take no pleasure in the death of the wicked man, but rather in the wicked man's conversion, that he may live" (Ez 33.11). Few took these words, however, as a restriction on the community's power to execute a justly condemned criminal. The same proved true of Christ's new teaching on the *lex talionis:* "You have heard that it was said, 'An eye for an eye,' and, 'A tooth for a tooth.' But I say to you not to resist the evil-doer; on the contrary, if someone strike thee on the right cheek, turn to him the other also" (Mt 5.38–39). Christians tended to hear in these words an exhortation to be quick to waive lawful rights out of love even for an erring neighbor. Along with it, however, they have recalled St. Paul's defense of civil authority: "For it is God's minister to thee for good. But if thou dost what is evil, fear, for not without reason does it carry the

Sister Helen Prejean and a fellow death penalty opponent address members of the media; photograph by Kuni. (AP/Wide World Photos)

sword. For it is God's minister, an avenger to execute wrath'' (Rom 13.4).

Over time the essence of this traditional concept of the state as the upholder of justice and of its competence to punish with measures it deems necessary and reasonable has been accepted by the Church. At the same time, the reasons for and outlook upon capital punishment have differed over the centuries. For ease of presentation this article focuses on five more or less distinct periods.

From the Time of Jesus to the 4th Century. The earliest Christian experience at the height of the Roman Empire was chiefly that of victim. Every execution recorded in the New Testament is seen as an unjust abuse of power — the beheading of John the Baptist, the crucifixion of Jesus, the stoning of Stephen, the death of Antipas of Pergamum; not to mention the martyrdom traditions of Peter and Paul and so many others under Roman emperors from Nero to Diocletian. Capital punishment was an un-

savory institution used as a blunt instrument of power-politics. Its most memorable function was providing the early Christian community with a crowd of witnesses ('martyres') who were revered for their faith and courage in shedding their blood at the hands of unjust imperial agents.

The relatively few Christian records that survive from this first period reflect the utter distaste with which the practice was generally viewed. Athenagoras of Athens declared executions to be intolerable even if in accordance with the code of justice, and Tertullian held there could be no exception to God's law against taking human life. The *Apostolic Tradition,* usually dated in the third century, forbade any Christian in authority from imposing a death penalty. Canon 56 of the Council of Elvira (A.D. 306) prohibited Christian magistrates from attending church services during their term of office because of the danger of their having been involved in legal bloodshed. Lactantius (*c.* 240–320), though ultimately inconsistent, at least in his early work insisted that no Christian could kill either in war or by being involved in capital trials, both of which were unacceptable actions for any follower of Christ, even though he generally acknowledged the right of the state to use the sword.

The Emperor Constantine to the 10th Century. With the conversion of Constantine in the fourth century leading to the adoption of Christianity as the state religion of the Roman Empire, Christians found themselves cast—willy-nilly—in the role of potential executioners. The problems this created were monumental and the stances adopted were diverse. A classical event for the study of this transitional era is the execution of Priscillian, heretical Bishop of Avila, by Emperor Maximus in Trier in 385. It is the first documented instance of Christians killing fellow Christians for heresy. Carried out with the collusion of Bishop Ithacius, it provoked outrage. Bishops Martin of Tours, Ambrose of Milan, and Sergius of Rome severed communion with Ithacius and the other bishops involved. Their protest may have had more to do with the fact that a church leader was executed by the civil authority for a religious offence than with the execution as such. In any event, the ominous event was to cast a long shadow for centuries to come.

Ecclesiastics like Ambrose and Augustine and John Chrysostom never lost sight of the fact that ''the Church abhors bloodshed.'' In reply to a Christian governor who asked for his advice, Ambrose made it clear that, in his opinion, a Christian magistrate should avoid killing, noting that ''even pagan governors commonly boast of never having executed a man'' (Dudden, 1:121, n.2). This ideal was even more pronounced in AUGUSTINE, although later misinterpretations long obscured this fact. Commenting on Rom 13.4, he defended severity for the sake of social order, but praised the Christian instinct to moderate juridical sternness. His advice to Christian magistrates judging heinous murder cases was to ''let your indignation be tempered by considerations of humanity.'' As long as ''the violent excess of savage men be restrained, why do you not commute your sentence to a more prudent and more lenient one?'' (Ep. 133 and 134).

Despite the chaos and violence that followed the collapse of the Roman Empire and the centuries of migrations of peoples all over Europe and beyond, the ideal, though often obscured, was never obliterated. The penitential books of the 8th and 9th centuries, in dealing with capital crimes, considered them as sins to be expiated according to their seriousness, but never to be avenged by use of the death penalty. In mid-ninth century Pope Nicholas I, in a letter to the recently-converted Bulgars, actually recommended abolition as the Christian ideal: ''You

should save from death not only the innocent but also criminals, because Christ has saved you from the death of the soul'' (quoted by Compagnoni, p. 47).

Vestiges of the earlier attitude of aversion to the use of capital punishment, even when it was theoretically justifiable, survived in church canons declaring unfit for sacramental ordination anyone who had ever imposed, carried out, or otherwise assisted in carrying out an execution.

The Hildebrandine Reform through the Middle Ages. In the 11th century the Hildebrandine (GREGORY VII) Reform brought with it certain readiness to incorporate the use of force into the service of the church. The Augustinian conditions and restraints on using violence and waging justified war were offset by church indulgences guaranteeing that this newly authorized kind of killing, done in the interests of the church, was not only ethically unobjectionable but was in fact the special work of God—*Deus vult* (''God wills it'').

The two centuries from 1050 to 1250 saw significant change in church acceptance and endorsement of violence. GRATIAN recognized and grappled with the problem in his *Decretum* (*c.* 1140). In his famous Causa 23, he tried to reconcile the earlier ideal and the current developing practice. He cited the advice of Jesus to ''turn the other cheek'' no less than six times in this single Causa, and went back to ponder the commandment, ''Thou shalt not kill,'' three different times. In the end, Gratian adopted the Augustinian suggestion that these precepts of Christ were to be observed ''in the preparation of the heart, not the conduct of the body.'' He concluded that executions could be lawfully carried out by Christians in certain circumstances. By the 13th century canonist generally agreed that the ''hard sayings'' of Jesus about loving one's enemies, doing good to those who hate you, endlessly forgiving sinners, and never taking revenge were best presented as spiritual advice to private individuals. In the legal forum, a more useful principle was to be found in Roman law — ''vim vi repelleret.'' It affirmed the legality of using proportionate violence to counter unjust aggression — tit for tat, an eye for an eye, a life for a life.

On the theological side Peter the Chanter (d. 1197) was a lonely voice objecting to the trend toward justifying the killing of all manner of offenders.

This change of church policy can also be traced gradually in the formal documents of the period. In 1184 Pope Lucius III issued the decretal *Ad abolendam*, sometimes called the ''founding charter of the Inquisition,'' that opened the way for the use of capital punishment as the standard remedy for dealing with recalcitrant heretics, while identifying at the same time a long list of diverse groups designated as heretics including, for the first time, the Waldenses.

It was in this same period that a group of Waldenses in 1210 seeking to be reconciled with the Church were required to affirm that: "the secular power can, without mortal sin, exercise judgment of blood, provided that it punishes with justice, not out of hatred, with prudence, not precipitation" (Denzinger, 257).

The fact that the canonists had found a way to obviate earlier ambivalence helped clear the way for Canon 3 of the Fourth LATERAN COUNCIL in 1215, endorsing as official policy henceforth that heretics were to be handed over to the secular power for punishment after the bishops had applied all the sanctions of canon law (which itself prohibited bloodshed). Sixteen years later, Pope Gregory IX in his constitution, *Excommunicamus* (1231) incorporated into canon law the 1224 imperial constitution of Frederick II, acknowledging burning at the stake by the secular arm as the appropriate punishment for a recalcitrant heretic.

On the theoretical plane, in medieval times, St. THOMAS AQUINAS made his classic defense of the death penalty on the ground that "if a man be dangerous and infectious to the community, on account of some sin, it is praiseworthy and advantageous that he be killed in order to safeguard the common good" (*Summa Theologiae* 2a2ae, 64.2). Citing Aristotle, he argued that "by sinning man departs from the order of reason and . . . falls into the slavish state of the beasts" (*ST* 2a2ae, 64.2 ad 3). Aquinas, however, also proposed as a working jurisprudential norm that "in this life penalties should rather be remedial than retributive" (*ST* 2a2ae, 66.6). Thus, while upholding capital punishment in principle on grounds of retribution, social defense, and deterrence, he sounded an interestingly modern note by the priority he gave to rehabilitation as a penal aim.

The Rise of the National State to Modern Times. With the rise of the national state, the practice of capital punishment continued unabated and unscrutinized. The countries of Europe invoked the death penalty when heresies and non-conformity appeared to threaten national unity and used it to punish more offenses.

Martin LUTHER harked back to the Augustinian position that execution of heretics was wrong, but otherwise he actually reinforced its broad use by the state for all other offenses with his doctrine of the two kingdoms. The sacralization of the executioner as God's avenger in the secular order was more indispensable than ever. Five years after Luther's death, John CALVIN executed Michael Servetus in Geneva for heresy (1553). When he

wrote to explain himself to the leading Lutheran theologian, Philip Melanchthon, to the surprise of many, Melanchthon completely approved of Calvin's action, saying that since Servetus denied the Trinity, he was not so much a heretic as a blasphemer, and blasphemy was a capital crime according to Roman Law. Except for a few relatively small pacifist groups like the Quakers, Protestants like Catholics questioned neither the theory or the practice.

The so-called "Roman Catechism" drafted and published by order of the Council of TRENT (1566) summarized the official Catholic position. Its treatment of the Commandment "Thou shalt not kill" is, for the most part, an eloquent affirmation of the gift of life, filled with the spirit of Jesus and the Gospel. But in explaining the Commandment the Catechism acknowledges some exceptions, among them killing in self-defense, in a just war, and capital punishment. With regard to the last, it says:

> Even among human beings there are some limitations to the extent of this prohibition of killing. The power of life and death is permitted to certain civil magistrates because theirs is the responsibility under law to punish the guilty and protect the innocent. Far from being guilty of breaking this commandment, such an execution of justice is precisely an act of obedience to it. For the purpose of the law is to protect and foster human life. This purpose is fulfilled when the legitimate authority of the state is exercised by taking the guilty life of those who have taken innocent life . . . . [Part III, c. 5]

The practical consequences of this acceptance and approval of capital punishment can be seen in an extreme example at the end of the 16th century. In a concerted effort to stamp out brigandage in the Papal States, Sixtus V (1585–1590) in his first five months as pope, had over 7,000 Roman bandits beheaded and had the heads of many posted on the Ponte Sant'Angelo. He celebrated his 'success' by having a medal struck bearing his image and the inscription 'Securitas Perfecta.' Meanwhile England was witnessing executions that were even more bloody if fewer in number carried out in the name of religion. In Paris the "grand gibbet" of Montfaucon that could hang up to 60 people simultaneously, rivaled Notre Dame Cathedral as an architectural marvel.

Few at the time seriously contested the state's right to execute criminals or the essential reasonableness of capital punishment. It was a young Italian, Cesare Beccaria, who opened the modern debate on the institution itself with his essay *Dei delitti e delle pene* (1764). On the basis of his own theory of society, he rejected the state's right to take a citizen's life. Far more influential, however, was his critique of the death penalty as cruel, unreasonable, and ineffective. Within two years his essay had appeared in French translation and had become known all over Europe. Beccaria spoke of Montesquieu's influence on his thought, but he himself merits the title of father of modern penal reform.

Many trace the abolition of capital punishment in Tuscany (1786) and Austria (1787) to Beccaria's challenge to "enlightened" rulers. His essay also stimulated Samuel Romilly and other leaders of the crusade to reform England's penal code, a movement that reduced British capital offenses to four crimes by 1861. In the U.S. at the end of the 18th century, Dr. Benjamin Rush and others led a campaign for the abolition of capital punishment in Pennsylvania and elsewhere. By the dawn of the 20th century, philosophers and theologians were beginning to join social reformers in their critique of capital punishment.

The Twentieth Century. The symbolic dawn of a new age opened with the formation of the United Nations. The words of the UN's Universal Declaration of Human Rights (1948) echo in Pope John XXIII's *Pacem in Terris* (1963), where he stated,

> Any human society . . . must lay down as a foundation this principle: every human being is a person . . . By virtue of this he has rights and duties of his own . . . which are universal, inviolable, and inalienable. If we look upon the dignity of the human person in the light of divinely revealed truth, we cannot help but esteem it far more highly. (nn. 9–10).

In 1972 the U.S. Supreme Court ruled against the death penalty because of inequities in imposing sentences (*Furman v. Georgia*). A number of states and the federal government set about passing laws to get around the accusation of a capricious selection process and thus get around the Eighth Amendment's ban on cruel and unusual punishment. In November 1974, the National Conference of Catholic Bishops, in a decision that was far from unanimous, made a simple declaration in opposition to the death penalty. Two years later, their position was far more clear and effective. They took as guidelines: 1) the sovereignty of God over life; 2) the duty to aid the criminal and not merely punish; 3) the awareness of human fallibility; 4) the need of reconciliation; and 5) the growing awareness of the complexity of criminal actions and motivations. Their pastoral conclusion was that the death penalty should be abolished, a position articulated in terms resonant with the Church's opposition to abortion and euthanasia, and the bishops urged Catholics to range themselves at the side of the Quakers, who had a long tradition of struggle in behalf of life.

About the same time (March 1976), the Canadian bishops, for pastoral reasons, passed a resolution favoring the abolition of the death penalty and calling for prison reform and the reform of the entire justice system. Its action was taken in respect for life, while it termed the death penalty a violent measure which begets violence. Writing in the *Osservatore Romano* (Feb. 20, 1977), G. Concetti stated forthrightly that the right to life is "primordial and inviolable" and that the state lacks the right to take it away. In the modern understanding the state is viewed not as having absolute rights, like the divine right of kings, but more accurately as a limited mechanism with rights and powers limited even as are the rights of the citizens it represents.

In 1978 French theologian Jean-Marie Aubert, a pioneer in moving the spotlight away from the theoretical issue of the state's right to kill and to focus it rather on the sordid practice itself, affirmed that "at the level of historical analysis, we can only conclude that capital punishment is . . . an evil, barbaric institution, unworthy of any and every society today" (*Chrétiens et Peine de Mort*, p. 90). Aubert's book appeared the same year in which Pope JOHN PAUL II was elected and launched his continuing campaign to change minds, hearts and policies so as to end the practice of deliberately killing human beings, no matter how heinous their crimes.

John Paul addressed "the problem of the death penalty" in his encyclical *Evangelium vitae* (March 25, 1995). He noted that "there is a growing tendency, both in the Church and in civil society, to demand that it be applied in a very limited way or even that it be abolished completely." John Paul acknowledged that public authority must "redress the violation of personal and social rights by imposing on the offender an adequate punishment for the crime . . . while at the same time offering the offender an incentive and help to change his or her behavior and be rehabilitated." And he adds,

> for these purposes to be achieved, the nature and extent of the punishment must be carefully evaluated and decided upon, and ought not go to the extreme of executing the offender except in cases of absolute necessity: in other words, when it would not be possible otherwise to defend society. Today however, as a result of steady improvements in the organization of the penal system, such cases are very rare, if not practically non-existent (n. 56).

The *Catechism of the Catholic Church* quotes *Evangelium vitae* verbatim, but it prefaces the section on capital punishment saying, "the traditional teaching of the Church does not exclude recourse to the death penalty, if this is the only possible way of effectively defending human lives against the unjust aggressor" (n. 2267). Taking their cue from the Pope John Paul, the U.S. Catholic

Bishops in November 2000 included in a statement on crime and criminal justice an appeal for all Americans to "join us in rethinking the difficult issue (of capital punishment) and committing ourselves to pursuing justice without vengeance. With our Holy Father we seek to build a society so committed to human life that it will not sanction the killing of any human person."

Bibliography: NCCB Statement on Capital Punishment, *Origins* 6 (1976) 389–395. *Responsibility & Restoration: A Catholic Perspective on Crime and Criminal Justice,* A STATEMENT OF THE CATHOLIC BISHOPS OF THE UNITED STATES. (Washington, DC, 2000). J. MEGIVERN, *The Death Penalty. An Historical and Theological Survey* (New York, 1997). J-M. AUBERT, *Chrétiens et Peine de Mort* (Paris, 1978). G. H. STASSEN, ed., *Capital Punishment: A Reader* (Cleveland, 1998). F. COMPAGNONI, "Capital Punishment and Torture in the Tradition of the Roman Catholic Church," *Concilium* 120 (10/1978). N. BLAZQUEZ, *Pena de Muerte,* #3 in Series Teologia Siglo XXI (Madrid, 1994).

[D. R. CAMPION/E. J. DILLON/J. MEGIVERN]

CAPITANIO, BARTOLOMEA, ST.

Cofoundress of the SISTERS OF CHARITY of Lovere; b. Lovere, Lombardy, Italy, Jan. 13, 1807; d. Lovere, July 26, 1833. At the age of 11 she entered the convent of the Poor Clares in Lovere, but she returned to her family in 1824, and in her home opened a school for youth. She received spiritual and practical guidance from Don Angelo Bosio. Her inclination led her to forgo entering the Poor Clares. At Lovere in 1826 she started a hospital, where she was prodigiously active as directress and in other positions, even tending the sick in their own homes. By her letters, about 300 of which are extant, she continued to counsel the youth of Lovere and neighboring towns. Local pastors esteemed this correspondence very highly. Her writings include also many devotional pieces; programs for pious associations; prayers for various feasts; and norms for life, even for priests. In the spiritual combat she fought especially against pride. Bartolomea conceived a religious institution dedicated to all types of charitable work. After she and Vincenza GEROSA had dedicated themselves completely to God (Nov. 21, 1832), they founded the first house of the new congregation. The youngest among religious foundresses, she died the following year. She was beatified on May 30, 1926; and canonized, together with Vincenza Gerosa, on May 22, 1950.

Feast: July 26.

Bibliography: S. C. LORIT, *Bartolomea Capitanio* (Rome 1982). L. MAZZA, *Della vita e dell'Istituto della venerabile Bartolomea Capitanio,* 5 v. (Modena 1905). A. STOCCHETTI, *Le Sante Bartolomea Capitanio e Vincenza Gerosa* (Vicenza 1950).

[M. C. BIANCHI]

CAPITO, WOLFGANG

Swiss reformer; b. Hagenau in Alsace, 1478; d. Strassburg, Nov. 4, 1541. Capito (Köpfel) was educated at Ingolstadt, Freiburg, and Basel, where he was professor of theology and cathedral preacher (1515–20). He held degrees in law, theology, and medicine and was in addition a distinguished Hebraist. From 1520 to 1523 he was chaplain and chancellor to the archbishop of Mainz. After his arrival in Strassburg in May 1523 he worked tirelessly for the propagation of the Reformation in the city. Some of the ideas and emphases in his early theology approximate to a striking degree those of the ANABAPTISTS, with a few of whom he was on friendly terms, but this unusually sympathetic position altered after 1532, and in a vernacular pamphlet of 1534 he repudiated the Anabaptists decisively.

Bibliography: J. W. BAUM, *Capito und Butzer* (*Leben und ausgewählte Schriften der Väter und Begründer der Reformirten Kirche,* ed. K. R. HAGENBACH, v.3, Elberfeld 1860). O. E. STRASSER, *La Pensée théologique de Wolfgang Capiton dans les dernières années de sa vie* (Neuchâtel 1938). *The Mennonite Encyclopedia,* 4 v. (Scottdale, Pa. 1955–60) 1:512–516. R. STUPPERICH, *Die Religion in Geschichte und Gegenwart* (Tübingen 1957–65) 1:1613.

[C. GARSIDE, JR.]

CAPITULARIES, IMPERIAL AND ECCLESIASTICAL

Imperial and ecclesiastical capitularies is the name given to the body of legislation, in the form of short articles (*capitula*), issued by the Carolingian kings and emperors during the second half of the 8th and 9th centuries. The term *capitulare* for such a royal or imperial ordinance occurs in contemporary sources.

Capitularies were sometimes concerned with one particular matter, e.g., church organization or defense, but more often they dealt with a variety of topics; some articles were in the nature of true legislation, others were of a more administrative and executive kind. The capitularies are the hallmark of the Carolingian attempt at ordered government.

Area and Period. Most capitularies were issued for people of all of the lands under Frankish rule; some, for the Franks or the Lombards only ("Frankish" and groups only, such as the Salic Franks or the Bavarians. Their validity was on a personal basis and its duration is hard to generalize. They sometimes contained specific references to duration, e.g., the capitulary of Quierzy (A.D. 877), which was to be in force only during the Italian expedition of Charles the Bald. But usually there was no explicit indication; duration depended on the nature of the capitulary and the circumstances of its promulgation. Capitularies of a real legislative character had permanent validity unless expressly changed or abolished; those inspired by temporary situations naturally had only a temporary validity. There are some extant capitularies from the time of Carloman and Pippin III, but the main body comes from the period of Charlemagne and Louis the Pious. After the division of 843 there were no more capitularies in the East Frankish kingdom, or in the realm of Lothair I, except for Italy where they continued until the late 9th century (A.D. 898). In the West Frankish kingdom capitularies continued to be issued to a considerable extent until the death of Charles the Bald (877); they stopped altogether after A.D. 884.

Promulgation and Conservation of the Text. Although sometimes sent out in the form of official circular letters, capitularies were not usually drafted in official full texts by the royal chancery, but were notes or title lists set down to recall the contents of royal commandments made orally; hence, the allusive and elliptical character of most of them. The form was often that of orders and prohibitions. Since there was no one authoritative text, manuscript tradition shows an exceptional number of variant readings.

The royal *bannum,* i.e., the ruler's right to command, was the basis of the authority of the capitulary. The spoken word of the prince was the ultimate legal basis for his contemporaries. Consultation with and consent given by lay and ecclesiastical magnates was a feature of annual meetings though the impact of this advice and consent differed from time to time. The real meaning of the consent has been much discussed. It may be assumed that until the reign of Louis the Pious the term meant little more than a formal recognition of the validity of the royal edicts, and a promise to stand by them and see to their execution. This is clear in texts where people are to be ordered to ''consent'' to certain capitularies. Certainly there is no textual evidence to warrant a theory of the necessity of popular consent for the validity of royal legislation, let alone a theory of popular sovereignty. During the latter part of Louis the Pious's reign and after it, the aristocracy gained power from the weakening of royal authority and turned their ''consent'' into something that could be withheld and could, therefore, be a factor of real importance in the promulgation of the capitulary.

When the prince issued a new set of capitularies they were distributed throughout the realm either by royal envoys (*missi dominici*) or by the counts in their respective domains (*pagi*). Copies were made and preserved not only in the royal archives but throughout the realm. From the beginning individuals made collections of capitularies for practical purposes, often combining them with other legal material in a single manuscript. Most copies of capitularies that have come down to us (from the 9th, 10th, and 11th centuries) are of that nature; no original text has been preserved. One of the most influential collections was made under Louis the Pious by Abbot Ansegisus of Saint-Wandrille. It follows a systematic order, and was frequently in official use. The so-called Benedict the Levite, well-known through the False Decretals, made a collection of capitularies as a continuation of those gathered by Ansegisus, probably in 847–852. Benedict's collection contains many spurious elements.

Contents and Types. Capitularies dealt with diverse matters: legal, ecclesiastical, military, fiscal, administrative, and commercial. Even though matters in several of these categories were often treated in the same set of capitularies, it is nevertheless possible to distinguish certain types on the basis of their form or contents. The distinction between *ecclesiastica* and *mundana* is made in the texts; the former deal with church matters, the latter with a variety of legal, military, and administrative topics. *Capitula mundana* are further divided into: (1) *capitula legibus addenda,* or capitularies adding some legislation to various existing national bodies of law, such as the *Lex Salica;* (2) *capitula per se scribenda,* or autonomous royal edicts; and (3) *capitula missorum,* or instructions given to royal envoys on their departure from the royal palace. This threefold division goes back to Carolingian times.

Capitularies dealt with monastic and canonical organization and discipline: such liturgical topics as stipulations concerning church chant and computation of the date of feast days; access to Holy Orders; and the veneration of (new) saints and image worship. They were valid in areas where Church and civil law might both claim some jurisdiction such as: restoration of church buildings and the benefices of their incumbents; church tithes; wandering monks and pilgrims; competence of courts, procedure, and punishment of criminous clerks; crimes committed by laymen for which church courts were competent; protection of churches and churchmen. They also treated of the role of the *advocatus,* i.e., the layman responsible for various temporal functions of ecclesiastical institutions; the special attention to be given in the law courts to actions brought by churches; the belief in ordeals; and numerous other religious and ecclesiastical matters.

All preserved capitularies are in Latin, although very imperfect Latin, and it is improbable that any were written in other languages. The Latin is interspersed with Germanic or Romance words and is sometimes very difficult to understand precisely. The capitularies were conceived in one of the Germanic or Romance dialects of the time and then literally translated into Latin. They present the phenomenon of vernacular thought and speech patterns using Latin words. The situation improved under Louis the Pious as a consequence of the so-called Carolingian Renaissance, and the Italian capitularies were always better written than the Frankish ones. The absence of a precise technical language was particularly felt in legal matters where there was little or no influence of Roman law.

Bibliography: F. L. GANSHOF, *Was waren die Kapitularien?* (Weimar 1961). G. SEELIGER, *Die Kapitularien der Karolinger* (Munich 1893). C. DE CLERCQ, *La Législation religieuse Franque . . . ,* 2 v. (Paris-Antwerp 1936–58). R. BUCHNER, "Die Rechtsquellen," Wattenbach-Levison (1953) Beiheft, a recent survey of editions and literature.

[R. C. VAN CAENEGEM]

CAPITULATIONS

Capitulations are agreements by electors limiting in advance the powers of a prelate to be chosen from among themselves. Such capitulations were frequently entered into by episcopal electors in the Middle Ages, although Pope NICHOLAS III in 1280 declared invalid any oath by which a future prelate bound himself to fulfill conditions that were "illicit or impossible or contrary to the liberty of the church" (*Corpus iuris canonici* VI° 2.11.1). The most important capitulations were those by which the cardinals sought, from the 14th century onward, to limit the powers of future popes. The right of the cardinals to be sole electors of the pope was established by a canon of 1179. Subsequently their role in the general work of ecclesiastical government became increasingly important and, in the 13th century, it was commonly maintained that the sacred college was a divinely established element in the government of the Church. The election capitulations of the 14th and 15th centuries brought this development to a climax, for they were essentially attempts to establish an oligarchic headship for the Church in place of a papal monarchy. In laying down conditions to be observed by future popes, the cardinals were especially concerned with enhancing their own status. The first recorded capitulations (1352) stated that the number of cardinals was to be limited to 20 and that no new ones were to be created until the number had fallen to 16. No cardinal was to be deposed or excommunicated without the unanimous consent of the others, and none appointed without the consent of two-thirds of them. Similarly, consent of two-thirds of the cardinals was required for any alienation of church property by the pope, and, finally, half the revenues of the papacy were to be assigned to the sacred college. INNOCENT VI, who was elected in this conclave of 1352, subsequently denounced the pact as contrary to the provisions of the canon *Ubi periculum,* which had regulated the conduct of the election of POPES (1274), and as an illicit infringement of the pope's plenitude of power. During the WESTERN SCHISM cardinals of both obediences swore that, if elected, they would seek to end the schism, by resigning if necessary. Subsequently, detailed capitulations were drawn up at the conclaves of 1431, 1458, and 1464. During the 1460s the theologian Teodoro de'Lelli and the canonist Andreas de BARBATIA denounced the recent capitulations as contrary to the divinely willed PRIMACY of Peter's successor. Nevertheless the practice continued into the 15th and 16th centuries. All pacts and promises among the cardinals during election CONCLAVES were forbidden by Pius IV in the bull *In eligendis* (1562) and again by Gregory XV in the bull *AETERNI PATRIS* (1621).

Bibliography: J. LULVÈS, "Die Machtbestrebungen des Kardinalkollegiums gegenüber dem Papsttum," *Mitteilungen des Instituts für österreichische Geschichtsforschung* [(Innsbruck) Graz–Cologne 1880–] 35 (1914) 455–483. W. ULLMANN, "The Legal Validity of the Papal Electoral Pacts," *Ephemerides iuris canonici* (Rome 1945–) 12 (1956) 246–278. H. JEDIN, *History of the Council of Trent,* tr. E. GRAF, v. 1–2 (St. Louis 1957–60); *Geschichte des Konzils von Trient,* 2 v. (Freiburg 1949–57; v. 1, 2d ed. 1951) 1:76–100.

[B. TIERNEY]

CAPRANICA, DOMENICO AND ANGELO

Brothers, notable in the ecclesiastical life of the 15th century.

Domenico, humanist and cardinal; b. Capranica (near Palestrina), Italy, May 31, 1400; d. Rome, Aug. 14, 1458. After being educated at Padua and Bologna, he entered papal service, where he won the admiration of POGGIO and other humanists. MARTIN V created him bishop of Fermo (1425) and cardinal (1426; published November 1430). He failed to receive his hat before Martin's death. Excluded from the conclave, he was driven from Rome to plead his cause before the Council of BASEL. EUGENE IV recognized him as cardinal (1434). His intelligence, integrity, and wholehearted service made him the confidant of NICHOLAS V, who appointed him grand penitentiary; he was also a stern critic of the NEPOTISM of CALLISTUS III. His zeal and generosity found expression in the foundation (1458) of the Collegio Capranicense for poor scholars in theology and Canon Law.

Angelo, bishop and cardinal; b. Capranica, c. 1400; d. Rome, July 3, 1478. Educated in philosophy and law, he was appointed archbishop of Siponto-Manfredonia (1438) and bishop of Ascoli (1447). He played a significant role in the canonization of JOHN CAPISTRAN. He was appointed bishop of Rieti in 1450. PIUS II made him governor at Bologna (1458), where he displayed both personal integrity and ability as an administrator and diplomat. Created cardinal (1460), he labored unceasingly for the revival of the religious life and the improvement of clerical education.

Bibliography: J. TOUSSAINT, *Dictionnaire d'histoire et de géographie ecclésiastiques* 11:932–941. R. MOLS, *ibid.*, 11:928–932. J. WODKA, *Lexikon für Theologie und Kirche* (Freiburg 1957–65) 2:930, recent literature.

[J. G. ROWE]

CAPRARA, GIOVANNI BATTISTA

Cardinal, papal diplomat; b. Bologna, May 29, 1733; d. Paris, June 21, 1810. He owed his rapid rise to noble birth and competence in Canon Law. After serving as vice-legate to Bologna (1758–66), he went as titular archbishop of Iconium and nuncio to Germany (1767–75), where he had to contend with the FEBRONIANISM of HONTHEIM; combat the prince-bishops of Cologne and Mainz, who were hostile to the nuncio's religious action and to the interventions of Rome; and face resistance to the application of Clement XIV's brief, *Dominus ac Redemptor* (1773), suppressing the Jesuits. His period as nuncio to Lucerne (1775–85) was happier. He was then (1785–93) promoted to the nunciature of Vienna at the request of Catholic Austria. Careful to avoid a rupture between Austria, with its JOSEPHINISM, and the Holy See, Caprara was patient to the point of weakness. This accounted for his passivity when the Congress of EMS (1786) voted the famous Punctation challenging papal authority, and when the Diet of Frankfort (1791) imposed on the new Emperor Leopold II a capitulation contrary to the rights of the sovereign pontiff. He waited eight days after the close of the Diet to raise an ineffectual protest. Created cardinal (1792), he returned to Rome (1793) in disgrace with Pius VI because of his failure at Vienna and the Jacobin tendencies that were attributed to him as a result of his admonitions concerning the policy to be adopted toward the French Revolution.

NAPOLEON I, aware of this, demanded Caprara as papal legate *a latere* to regulate the application of the CONCORDAT OF 1801. The cardinal arrived in Paris (Oct. 4, 1801), although the Concordat was not promulgated until April 18, 1802. The legate anticipated the use of his powers to obtain the resignation of bishops and to establish a new division of dioceses. In this delicate, complex situation he had to resolve with the French minister Portalis the many problems connected with the reorganization of the Church in France. Counseled by BERNIER, who acted as his adviser and duped him in the process, he wanted to be above all else a peacemaker. Rome reproached him for giving way and permitting constitutional bishops to be named to the new sees set up by the Concordat; for the retractions by bishops and priests who had supported the CIVIL CONSTITUTION; for not preventing the organic articles; and for having taken an oath to the First Consul, although the version attributed to him differed from the one he actually made.

Caprara participated in the negotiations for the Italian Concordat and Bonaparte's coronation in Paris. He received the See of Josi in 1800 and that of Milan in 1802. As archbishop of Milan he crowned Napoleon King of Italy. His policy of conciliation placed him more and more in the bad graces of Pius VII, who resolved in 1806 to resist caesaropapism. Caprara was excluded from the negotiations undertaken in 1807 and confided to Cardinal de Bayanne. Despite the papal order (December 1807) that he ask for his passport, Caprara remained in Paris. In 1809 he made one last effort to obtain concessions from the Pope, who was imprisoned at Savona. Ill, deaf, and almost blind, he died at Paris. Napoleon had him buried in the Pantheon.

Bibliography: R. MOLS, *Dictionnaire d'histoire et de géographie ecclésiastiques* (Paris 1912–) 11:944–957.

[J. A. M. LEFLON]

CAPREOLUS, JOHN

Scholastic theologian; b. Rodez, France, *c.* 1380; d. Rodez, April 6, 1444. Little is known of this most celebrated Thomist of the Middle Ages. He entered the Dominican Order at Rodez for the province of Toulouse, and in 1407 was assigned by the Dominican general chapter at Poitiers to lecture on the *Sentences* of Peter Lombard at the University of Paris. In 1408 and 1409 he composed the first part of his *Libri defensionum theologiae divi Thomae de Aquino,* familiarly called the *Defensiones.* He took his degree at the University of Paris (1411 and 1415) in theology. He was made regent of studies at Toulouse, but by 1426 was back at Rodez, where he spent the rest of his life.

Capreolus completed parts two, three, and four of the *Defensiones,* his only known work, in 1426, 1428, and 1433, respectively. Although it is cast in the form of a commentary on the *Sentences,* the content is a penetrating exposition and defense of Thomistic teaching. Isidore de Isolanis (d. 1528), who summarized the work, honored Capreolus no less than Aquinas, and he was then and later known as "the soul of St. Thomas" and the "prince of Thomists." With clarity and erudition he systematically defended the Thomistic doctrine against DUNS SCOTUS, HENRY OF GHENT, JOHN OF RIPA, Ockham (*see* OCKHAMISM), and lesser theologians.

After his death his work was published at Venice in four folio volumes (1483, 1514, 1519, 1589); the first volume was edited by Thomas de St. Germain, a colleague of Capreolus. Isidore de Isolanis, Paul Soncinas (d. 1494), and Sylvester Prierias (d. 1523) published abridgments, and a modern edition in seven quarto volumes was published in Tours (1900–07), edited by Ceslaus Paban and Thomas Pègues.

Bibliography: J. QUÉTIF and J. ÉCHARD, *Scriptores Ordinis Praedicatorum* (Paris 1719–23) 1:795–796. F. C. COPLESTON, *History of Philosophy* (Westminster, Md. 1946–1963) v.3. T. M. PÈGUES, ''Capréolus 'Thomistarum Princeps' à propos de la nouvelle édition de ses oeuvres,'' *Revue thomiste* 7 (1899) 63–81; ''La Biographie de Jean Capréolus,'' *ibid.* 317–334; ''Pouvons nous sur cette terre arriver à connaître Dieu,'' *ibid.* 8 (1900) 50–76; ''Théologie Thomiste d'après Capréolus: De la voie rationelle que nous conduit à Dieu,'' *ibid.* 288–309; ''L'idée de Dieu en nous,'' *ibid.* 505–530. M. GRABMANN, ''Johannes Capreolus O. P. der 'Princeps Thomistarum' († 1444), und seine Stellung in der Geschichte der Thomistenschule,'' *Mittelalterliches Geistesleben,* v.3 (Munich 1956) 370–410. G. BEDOUELLE, R. CESSARIO, and K. WHITE, eds. *Jean Capreolus et son temps* (Paris 1997). J. CAPREOLUS, *On the Virtues,* tr. and ed. R. CESSARIO and K. WHITE (Washington, D.C. 2001).

[J. A. WEISHEIPL]

CAPTIVITY EPISTLES

The term ''captivity epistles'' has been applied to four letters traditionally attributed to Paul: Philippians, Philemon, Ephesians, and Colossians. Though each of these letters is claimed to be by Paul, and each makes reference to his imprisonment, in fact it seems the designation ''captivity epistles'' was always a ''leftover'' category, the other groups consisting of the great epistles (Rom, Gal 1 and 2 Cor), the pastorals, and the Thessalonian correspondence. In fact, 2 Timothy has several references to Paul's imprisonment (2 Tm 1:16–17, 2:9, 4:16–17), and yet its themes and vocabulary have placed it in the category of the pastorals.

On the basis of themes and vocabulary, Philippians and Philemon fit well together, as do Ephesians and Colossians, but the four taken together are not so homogeneous. For Philippians and Philemon, the place of imprisonment is not certain. Four possibilities have been suggested for Philippians: Corinth, Rome, Caesarea, and Ephesus, with the latter three also possibilities for Philemon.

Most contemporary scholars do not accept Paul as the author of Ephesians and Colossians, although in his recent commentary J. D. G. Dunn takes the position that Colossians most likely comes from a hand other than Paul's, but that it was written around the same time as Philemon, possibly with Paul's knowledge and approval. In his monograph on the disputed Paulines, Raymond F. Collins points out that a number of scholars find indications that Colossians was used as a source for Ephesians.

Bibliography: M. BOCKMUEHL, *The Epistle to the Philippians* (Black's New Testament Commentary 11; London 1998). R. F. COLLINS, *Letters That Paul Did Not Write* (Good News Studies 28; Wilmington 1988). J. D. G. DUNN, *The Epistles to the Colossians and to Philemon* (Grand Rapids, Mich. 1996). M. Y. MACDONALD, *Colossians and Ephesians* (Sacra Pagina 17; Collegeville, Minn. 2000).

[V. KOPERSKI]

CAPUTIATI

Members of a religious confraternity of laymen organized *c.* 1182 in the neighborhood of Le Puy, France, to restore peace by combating roving bands of mercenaries who were ravaging the countryside. Their name derived from the white hood (*caputium*) worn by the members, to which was attached a picture or medal of the Virgin and Child, bearing the inscription *Agnus Dei qui tollis peccata mundi dona nobis pacem.* The founder of the movement, Durand Chaduiz, was a woodcutter or carpenter who claimed to have received his mission from the Blessed Virgin in a vision. The brethren bound themselves to refrain from cursing and swearing, gaming, drunkenness, and ostentation in dress. They undertook to live in harmony and to proceed against disturbers of the peace. The movement spread rapidly through Auvergne and the neighboring provinces and received support from the clergy. It succeeded in pacifying Auvergne and in reducing the exactions of feudal lords from their subjects. In 1183, with the assistance of the army of King Philip II, the Caputiati massacred a great number of mercenaries. They are said to have subsequently developed revolutionary and heretical ideas, demanding absolute liberty and equality for all. Whatever the truth of these charges, within a year or two they were ruthlessly suppressed by the feudal nobility assisted by the hated mercenaries.

Bibliography: E. SEMICHON, *La Paix et la trève de Dieu,* 2 v. (2d ed. Paris 1869). A. MENS, *Dictionnaire d'histoire et de géographie ecclésiastiques,* ed. A. BAUDRILLART et al. (Paris 1912–) 11:970–973. G. MARSOT, *Catholicisme. Hier, aujourd'hui et demain,* ed. G. JACQUEMET (Paris 1947–), 2:520. A. BORST, *Lexikon für Theologie und Kirche,* ed. J. HOFER and K. RAHNER, 10 v. (2d, new ed. Freiburg 1957–65) 2:932.

[F. COURTNEY]

CARABANTES, JOSÉ DE

Spanish Capuchin missionary; b. June 27, 1628; d. April 11, 1694. He entered the order on Oct. 11, 1645, and was ordained on Sept. 21, 1652. In 1657 he went to the missions in Venezuela, and in 1660 he went into the interior to catechise the Native Americans there. After nine years of intense and effective work, he returned to Spain to report to the Council of the Indies about the mission and the Native Americans. A year later he personally presented to the Pope the submission of five caciques, written in the Chaima language. Unable to return to his favorite field of missions among the pagans, he dedicated the rest of his days to preaching the gospel in Spain, working great wonders and accomplishing many spiritual rejuvenations, which gained him the title of Apostle of Galicia. He was also a successful writer, publishing books for spiritual reading and many volumes of sermons, homilies, and instructions. Of particular importance is *Práctica de las misiones* (2 v. León-Madrid 1674–78), from which modern missiologists have taken methods for the conversion of the native peoples. Also attributed to him is *Arte y vocabulario de la lengua de los caribes de Nueva Andalucía*. In 1666 in Seville he published an account of his missionary work in Venezuela. He died with a reputation of sanctity, and a movement for his beatification began in 1729. The cause was introduced in 1910, and in 1920 the apostolic processes began.

Bibliography: A. DE VALENCINA, *Vida del V. P. José de Carbantes* (Seville 1908). P. M. DE MONDREGANES, *Problemas misionales* (Madrid 1960). B. DE CARROCERA, *Los primeros historiadores de las misiones capuchinas en Venezuela* (Caracas 1964).

[I. DE VILLAPADIERNA]

CARACCIOLO

Perhaps the oldest of the Neapolitan noble families. Its history in Naples dates back to the 8th or 9th century. For the most part its members are noteworthy for their loyalty to the rulers of Naples and to the Church. Outstanding figures include *Sergianni,* or Giovanni (d. Naples, 1431), who fought under King Ladislaus of Naples in 1411 and became the seneschal of his successor, Joanna II. Out of favor and then returned to power, he oppressed the nobles and acted arrogantly toward the queen. He was murdered, probably at her orders. *Giovanni* (b. 1487; d. Susa, 1550) was a general in Florence in 1529, then marshal of Kings Francis I and Henry II of France. *Galeazzo* (b. Naples, 1517; d. Geneva, 1586), a nephew of Pope PAUL IV, was influenced by the new religious teachings and in 1551 became a follower of Calvin in Geneva, where he remained. *Domenico* (b. in Spain, 1715; d. Naples, 1789) was educated at the Caracciolo College

in Naples. After brief diplomatic experiences in Florence and Paris, he represented Naples at Turin (1754–64). Advanced to the major courts of London (1764–71) and Paris (1771–81), he was well liked and praised by the French. In 1781 he was appointed viceroy of Sicily, where his reforms were the finest work of his career, according to Croce. In 1786 he was recalled to be the chief minister in Naples, an office he held until his death. *Francesco* (b. Naples, 1752; d. Naples, 1799) obtained naval experience by serving on a British ship, fighting the pirates of North Africa, participating in the Battle of Toulon, and commanding a Neapolitan ship that supported the English blockade of the French coast (1795). When Ferdinand IV and Maria Carolina fled from Naples to Sicily at the approach of the French army, December 1798, Francesco commanded one of the ships, Nelson the other. In January, Francesco obtained permission to return to Naples, where he joined the Republicans. During Cardinal Fabrizio RUFFO's siege of Naples in June, Francesco escaped from the city but was captured and turned over to Nelson by the cardinal. He was tried and hanged on board ship, and his body was thrown into the sea, June 29, 1799.

The cardinals in the family (the first date given being that of their cardinalate) included *Bernardo* (1244; d. 1255) and the Dominican theologian *Nicolò* (1378; d. 1389). *Marino* (1535; d. 1538) represented the Duke of Milan at Lateran Council V (1515) and later Pope LEO X, first at Augsburg (1518), then at Worms (1521). During Pope CLEMENT VII's pontificate he favored a league with Emperor CHARLES V against King Francis I of France. Charles V appointed him governor of Milan in 1536. *Innico* (1667; d. 1685) was an energetic archbishop of Naples. His nephew *Innico* (1715; d. 1730) spent 33 years as bishop of Aversa. *Nicolò* (1715; d. 1728) was nuncio to Florence and vicegerent of Rome. *Giovanni Costanzo* (1759; d. 1780) was a member of several congregations in Rome. *Diego Innico* (1800; d. 1820) accompanied Pope PIUS VI into exile and remained with him until he died. He negotiated a concordat with Naples in 1818.

Landolf (d. 1351) was a distinguished Franciscan theologian. The Augustinian *Giacomo* (d. 1357) was a philosopher, theologian, and preacher. *Roberto* (d. 1495), a Franciscan Conventual, was perhaps the greatest preacher of the school of BERNARDINE OF SIENA. St. *Francis Caracciolo* (d. 1608) founded the Congregation of Clerks Minor Regular (Caracciolini) in 1588.

Bibliography: F. DE'PIETRI, *Cronologia della famiglia Caracciolo* (Naples 1605). G. MORONI, *Dizionario de erudizione storico-ecclesiastica,* 103 v. in 53 (Venice 1840–61) 9:231–235. P. LITTA, *Famiglie celebri italiane,* 11 v. (Milan 1819–99); 2d ser., 78 fasc. (Turin 1902–23), fasc. 6. M. SAGLIOCCO, *Compendio delle virtù del cardinale I. Caracciolo già vescovo d'Aversa* (Rome 1738). B.

CROCE, *Uomini e cose della vecchia Italia,* 2 ser. (Bari 1927), ser. 1, 143–182; ser. 2, 83–112. M. SCHIPA, *Nel regno di Ferdinando IV Borbone* (Florence 1938) 77–323. H. M. ACTON, *The Bourbons of Naples, 1734–1825* (New York 1958) 92–94, 198–206, 364–366, 398–401. G. FUSSENEGGER et al., *Lexikon für Theologie und Kirche,* ed. J. HOFER and K. RAHNER, 10 v. (2d, new ed. Freiburg 1957–65) 2:933–934.

[M. L. SHAY]

CARACCIOLO, FRANCIS, ST.

Cofounder of the Congregation of Clerks Regular Minor; b. Villa Santa Maria, Abruzzi, Italy, Oct. 13, 1563; d. Agnone, Italy, June 4, 1608. The early life of Francis (baptized Ascanio) Caracciolo del Leone o Pisquizi was exemplary, and after being miraculously cured of a kind of elephantiasis, then called leprosy, the 22-year-old youth vowed himself to an ecclesiastical life. He quietly slipped off to Naples and in 1587 was ordained there. He joined the Confraternity of the White Robes of Justice, organized to give spiritual assistance to condemned criminals. In 1588 he mistakenly received a letter addressed to an uncle also named Ascanio Caracciolo. Father John Augustine Adorno, former Genoese ambassador to Spain, and Father Fabricius Caracciolo Marsicovetere of the Church of St. Mary Major in Naples were begging Ascanio's participation in the founding of a new religious institute. Young Ascanio accepted the invitation as providentially meant for himself and helped to formulate the rules of the Clerks Regular Minor approved by Sixtus V (July 1, 1588) and confirmed by Gregory XIV (February 18, 1591) and Clement VIII (June 1, 1592). The members of the congregation took a fourth vow not to aspire to ecclesiastical dignities. Their ministry comprised numerous works of charity, and one of their distinctive characteristics was their practice of perpetual adoration of the Blessed Sacrament. The original intention was to honor the Mother of God with the title of Clerks Regular Marian, but Sixtus V, a Friar Minor, preferred Clerks Regular Minor, and so the name remained.

At his profession Ascanio took the name of Francis. Adorno had been superior of the new community, but upon his death in 1591, the office devolved on Francis. He remained rector general until 1598. During his administration, the Clerks Regular Minor became established in Rome and in Spain. He personally founded the house and Church of St. Joseph in Madrid and of the Annunciation in Valladolid, as well as a house of studies near the University of Alcalá. As rector general, then as novice master, local superior, and vicar-general in Italy, Francis was distinguished for humility, mortification, unflagging toil, purity, and devotion to the Eucharist and the Blessed Virgin. In 1607 Francis was finally relieved of administrative offices. He begged for an obscure room under a staircase, and there he devoted himself anew to contemplation and redoubtable penances. He interrupted his retirement to negotiate with the Oratorians for the transfer of one of their houses in Agnone to the Clerks Regular Minor. He went to Agnone by way of Loretto, where he spent an entire night in prayer, seemingly with a premonition of his end. After a brief illness he died at Agnone. His body had to be transferred secretly to Naples because the popular cult of Francis Caracciolo had already begun.

Caracciolo's extant writings include some letters and a work of devotion, *Le sette stazioni sopra la Passione di N.S. Gesu Christo* (Rome 1710). He was beatified by Clement XIV in 1769 and canonized by Pius VII on May 24, 1807. In 1838 St. Francis Caracciolo was chosen patron of the city of Naples; and in 1925 patron of Eucharistic Congresses held in Abruzzi. The Pia Unione Famiglia Caracciolo was organized in 1925. Comprising representatives of all the branches of the ancient noble Caraccioli, the union serves as a lay auxiliary organization of the Clerks Regular Minor; propagates devotion to the Holy Eucharist and to St. Francis Caracciolo; and sponsors the review 'S. Francesco Caracciolo,' which appears several times during the year.

Feast: June 4.

Bibliography: A. B. FRASSONI, *La gente e la famiglia di S. Francesco Caracciolo* (Rome 1943). G. ROSSI, *Il precursore dell'adorazione perpetua* (4th ed. Rome 1951). I. FELICI, *Il principe mendicante* (Rome 1959). A. BUTLER, *The Lives of the Saints,* ed. H. THURSTON and D. ATTWATER (New York 1956) 2:470–472.

[M. P. TRAUTH]

CARACCIOLO, LANDOLF

Franciscan theologian, *Doctor collectivus;* b. Naples, *c.* 1287; d. Amalfi, 1351. He studied arts, probably at the University of Naples, *c.* 1305 to 1310, and theology at the University of Paris, *c.* 1315, where he commented on the *Sentences, c.* 1322, and later became master. He returned to Naples, where he became minister provincial, 1324–25. In 1326 he was sent to Bologna as the legate of Robert of Naples. On Aug. 21, 1327, he was consecrated bishop of Castellammare, but was transferred on Sept. 20, 1331, to the See of Amalfi. From 1343 onward he was frequently entrusted with diplomatic missions by Queen Johanna I of Anjou (d. 1382), for which he was honored with the titles of *Logotheta* and *Protonotarius* of the Kingdom of Naples.

At least 35 MSS of his *Commentary on the Sentences* are known to be extant [*Repertorium commentariorum in*

Sententias Petri Lombardi 1:n.514; V. Doucet, "Supplement," *Archivum Franciscanum historicum* 47 (1954) 58]. He also wrote *Commentaria moralia in quatuor Evangelia* (ed. Naples 1637), *Postilla super Evangelia dominicalia* (Florence MS Laurenziana, Plut. 8 dext. 12, fol. 5–98v), *Sermones, Tractatus de arte sermocinandi* (Cracow, Univ. Library MS 1295, fol. 294–808), and lost commentaries on Zacharias and on Hebrews (*Repertorium biblicum medii aevi* 3:nn. 5365–67). The *Tractatus de Conceptione B. M. V.* attributed to him is unauthentic, and the *Extracta ex Landulphi de Immaculata Conceptione B. M. V.* is a posthumous version of his doctrine (*In 3 sent.* 3).

PETER OF CANDIA, later Alexander V, enumerated him with Francis of Meyronnes and Francis of Marchia as the most notable followers of DUNS SCOTUS in the first half of the 14th century. Caracciolo himself declares that he follows the Subtle Doctor in many points: "Doctorem Subtilem ut plurimum sequimur" (Naples, Bibl. Naz. MS VII. C. 49). Nevertheless, in the same MS there are several marginal notations indicating that the doctrine proposed is contrary to that of Scotus: "Loquitur contra Scotum." Similarly an Assisi MS (Bibl. Munic. 199) of Peter of Candia's lectures contains a marginal note expressing amazement that Caracciolo should thus deviate from the Subtle Doctor, whom he always follows (fol. 13r).

In *In 3 sent.* 3 Caracciolo defends the IMMACULATE CONCEPTION in a way that suggests the doctrinal development between 1320 and 1325. Although he adopted many of the ideas and arguments in favor of the privilege from Scotus and WILLIAM OF WARE and opposed the Dominican view proposed by JOHN OF NAPLES, he is often too oratorical and lacking in critical judgment. More notable in his teaching are the "quinque regulae" for disputing with an opponent both from authority and from reason; in this he seems to have been influenced by the treatise *Nondum erant abyssi* of PETER AUREOLI (ed. Quaracchi 1904, 78–94).

Caracciolo's writings notably influenced later theologians, such as Peter of Aquila, Alphonsus of Toledo (fl. 1344), WILLIAM OF VAUROUILLON, St. BERNARDINE OF SIENA, John Vitalis (fl. 1390), Juan de TORQUEMADA, Ludovicus a Turre (fl. 1486), and Bernardine of Busti (fl. 1490).

Bibliography: A. EMMEN, "Testimony of Landulf Caracciolo on Scotus' dispute in favour of the Immaculate Conception," *Doctor Subtilis* ('s Hertogenbosch, Netherlands 1946) 92–129. J. H. SBARALEA, *Supplementum et castigatio ad scriptores trium ordinum S. Francisci a Waddingo* (Rome 1906–36) 3: 163–165. *Hierarchia Catholica medii* 1:84, 462. D. SCARAMUZZI, *Il pensiero di Giovanni Duns Scoto nel Mezzogiorno d'Italia* (Rome 1927) 67–75; "L'Immacolato Concepimento di Maria," *Studi Francescani* 28 (1931) 33–69. H. MAISONNEUVE, *Dictionnaire d'histoire et de géographie ecclésiastiques* 11:980.

[A. EMMEN]

CARAFA (CARAFFA)

A noble Neapolitan family that first came into notice during the 14th century, and in its several branches has had a remarkable history in the annals of the Church. Almost exclusively during the 16th and 17th centuries it provided prelates for Naples and Aversa, exerting great influence there and throughout Europe. The apex of its fame was the elevation of Gian Pietro Carafa to the papacy as Paul IV (1555–59), followed soon after in the reign of Pius IV by the lowest ebb of its fortunes, the trial and execution of Paul IV's nephews Cardinal Carlo and Giovanni, Duke of Paliano, for treason and other crimes.

Oliviero. Diplomat; b. Naples, 1430; d. Rome, Jan. 20, 1511. He descended from the counts of Maddaloni (Caserta), became a jurist, was consecrated archbishop of Naples on Dec. 29, 1458, and created a cardinal on Nov. 18, 1467, at the insistence of King Ferdinand of Naples, whom he had served faithfully as president of his council of state and as special envoy. He helped end the war between Ferdinand and Sixtus IV and was sent to draw up the peace treaty. He founded the magnificent crypt chapel in the cathedral of Naples and had the body of St. Januarius (San Gennaro) brought there from Montevergine. Oliviero became cardinal bishop of Ostia, Nov. 29, 1503, and dean of the Sacred College. A generous and pious patron of literature and the arts, he erected for his family the chapel of St. Thomas Aquinas in the church of Santa Maria sopra Minerva at Rome and commissioned Filippino Lippi to decorate it with frescoes, one of which depicts the saint presenting the cardinal to the Virgin. Another monument is the cloister of Santa Maria della Pace, built by Donato Bramante in 1504. Oliviero's palace at Rome, alongside of which stood the statue of Pasquino, was a circumspect retreat for artists and writers. In its cultured atmosphere Oliviero's nephew, Gian Pietro, the future Paul IV, received his education.

Carlo. Adventurer; b. Naples, 1517; d. Rome, March 4, 1561. He was the youngest son of Gian Alfonso, Count of Montorio, and nephew of Paul IV, and he was made a cardinal, June 7, 1555. A debauched and scheming military adventurer without even the requisite education for a simple clerk, he rapidly acquired influence over his uncle and was the guiding spirit of the anti-Spanish policy, which ended in an unsuccessful war against Philip II. While the Pope was pursuing with fierce energy the work of Church reform, unknown to him his nephew was leading a dissipated life in the pontifical court. Only toward the end of his reign did Paul IV learn of his immorality, crimes, and double-dealing with the foreign powers. Indignant, he banned the cardinal and his brothers with their families from Rome on Jan. 27, 1559. This ban undermined the prestige of the Carafa and led to their downfall in the next pontificate. At the death of Paul IV Carlo believed that he could regain his position in the Curia by working for the election of Cardinal de' Medici. Once elected, however, Pius IV arrested the nephews of his predecessor (June 7, 1560), probably yielding to pressure from certain cardinals and Philip II. Following the murder of the Duchess of Paliano, Carlo's sister-in-law, by members of the Paliano family who suspected her of infidelity, an inquest was held in which Carlo's devious political career was investigated. He and his brother Giovanni, Duke of Paliano, and others were condemned to death for high treason. The cardinal was executed by strangulation in the Castel Sant' Angelo. His reputation was at least formally rehabilitated in a consistory held Dec. 26, 1567, by Pius V, early intent on restoring the prestige of his revered predecessor's family. It is to be noted that only the charges of *laesa maiestas* and *fellonia* were examined and revised, not that of murder.

Antonio. Scholar; b. Naples, March 25, 1538; d. Rome, Jan. 13, 1591. He was the cousin of Carlo and a learned Greek scholar who had as his teacher Cardinal Guglielmo SIRLETO. He received a canonry at St. Peter's from his uncle, Paul IV, but was deprived of his benefice when other members of his family were exiled. He was eventually recalled to Rome by Pius V, restored to his canonry, and created a cardinal in 1568. Prefect of the Congregation of the Council, he was also a member of the congregations charged with the correction of the Missal, the Breviary, and the Vulgate. Gregory XIII appointed him *bibliothecarius* (librarian) of the Vatican Library. He prepared an edition of the Septuagint published at Rome in 1586. He left some manuscript notes of an apologetic nature on the life of Paul IV, later used by Antonio Caracciolo in his *Collectarna historica de vita Pauli IV.*

Alfonso. Librarian; b. Naples, 1540; d. there, Aug. 26, 1565. As the favorite nephew of Paul IV, he was made a cardinal when 17 years old (March 15, 1557) and named *bibliothecarius* of the Vatican Library. Alfonso was the only member of the family whom Pius IV allowed near him after the expulsion of the Carafas from Rome. His promising career was ended by an early death. He is the subject of an important recent study by De Maio, who complains that Alfonso has been altogether neglected by biographers or confused with his cousin Antonio, a later *bibliothecarius.*

Carlo II, Ven. Social apostle; b. Mariglianella (Naples), 1561; d. Naples, Sept. 8, 1633. After a short stay

Oliviero Carafa, 17th-century engraving.

with the Jesuits he entered the Spanish military service. Although a brilliant officer, his earlier interest, the religious life, again took hold of him. From the time of his ordination in Naples, Jan. 1, 1599, he dedicated himself to an apostolate among the masses. After giving his possessions to the poor, he and eight companions organized missions for the people (1601) and in 1606 opened a house at Naples for his *Pii Operarii* (Pious Workers), the origin of the congregation surviving to the present. After his death several miracles were attributed to him. His cause was reintroduced at Rome in 1894 to 1895.

Vincenzo. Jesuit general; b. Andria, May 9, 1585; d. Rome, June 8, 1649. The third son of the Duke of Andria, he entered the Jesuit novitiate on Oct. 4, 1604. After his ordination he taught philosophy and engaged in social works. Under his direction the congregation of the nobles at Naples became a center of social action for the diffusion of charity. He was provincial of Naples when elected to succeed Mutius Vitelleschi on Jan. 7, 1646, as seventh general of the society. His firmness in governing was tempered by his charity for the sick and poor, suggesting the ways of St. Ignatius. During the famine and plague that ravaged Rome (1648–49) he personally saw to the feeding of thousands for two months. The plagues provided him the opportunity of fulfilling a vow made in 1624, to dedicate himself to the care of the plague-ridden.

In their service he contracted the disease from which he died. Under the pseudonym of Luigi Sidereo he left a series of ascetic writings: *Fascetto di Mirra* (Rome 1635) and *Camino del cielo* (1641). He instituted in all the churches of his order the con-fraternity of *Bona Mors* (A Good Death), at once approved and favored by the popes and still in existence today.

Pierluigi. Papal nuncio; b. Naples, July 31, 1581; d. Rome, July 15, 1655. After studies in Venice, Rome, and a doctorate in law from the University of Naples, he became vice legate to Ferrara, governor of Fermo, and bishop of Tricarico (Potenza) on March 29, 1624. As nuncio to Cologne he effected reforms, founded colleges throughout lower Germany and a university at Münster, and introduced the Capuchins and Jesuits into the Palatinate and the Dioceses of Trier, Fulda, and Constance. He returned to his diocese and rebuilt the cathedral. When he received the cardinalate in 1645 he resigned his see to become legate to Bologna and prefect of the Congregation of the Council. He died during the conclave that elected Alexander VII.

Carlo III. Papal nuncio; b. place and date uncertain; d. April 1644. He became bishop of Aversa (Naples) on July 19, 1616, and then nuncio to the imperial court (1621), where he became well acquainted with the religious problems in Germany and Bohemia. He aided Emperor Ferdinand II in selecting candidates for sees, reforming colleges, and arranging for the restitution of churches and abbeys taken by the Protestants. He published the *Commentaria de Germania sacra restaurata* in 1641.

Carlo IV. Papal nuncio; b. Naples, 1611; d. Rome, Oct. 19, 1680. He was the nephew of Carlo III and succeeded to the See of Aversa, then was made nuncio to Switzerland (1653), Venice (1654), and the court of Emperor Leopold (1658–64). When he was created cardinal (1664), he renounced his see to his brother, Paolo, a Theatine.

Rosa di Traetto, Ven. Franciscan tertiary; b. Naples, April 6, 1832; d. there, May 2, 1890. She was a descendant of the dukes of Traetto, a branch of the Carafas, and joined the Order of the Servants of the Sacred Heart (Franciscan Tertiaries), founded by Caterina Volpicelli. Her life was marked by continual, painful illness and extraordinary gifts of prayer. She won many vocations to her order by her example and direction. The cause of her beatification was introduced on Aug. 28, 1907.

For Gian Pietro Carafa, *see* PAUL IV, POPE.

Bibliography: L. JADIN, *Dictionnaire d'histoire et de géographie ecclésiastiques,* ed. A. BAUDRILLART et al. (Paris 1912–) 11:986–95, bibliog. E. MANGENOT and A. PALMIERI, *Dictionnaire de théologie catholique,* ed. A. VACANT et al., 15 v. (Paris 1903–50) 2.2:1709. P. AUVRAY et al., *Catholicisme. Hier, aujourd'hui et demain,* ed. G. JACQUEMET (Paris 1947–) 2:524–27. F. SCANDONE, "I Carafa di Napoli," *Famiglie celebri italiane* of P. LITTA et al, 2d ser., 2 v. (Naples 1902–23). For Carlo I, see L. PASTOR, *The History of the Popes From the Close of the Middle Ages,* 40 v. (London-St. Louis 1938–61): v.13–40, from 1st German ed. *Geschichte der Päpste seit dem Ausgang des Mittelalters,* 16 v. in 21. (Freiburg 1885–1933; repr. 1955–) v.14 *passim*; 15:131–78, 415–29. For Alfonso and contemporaries R. DE MAIO, *Alfonso Carafa, Cardinale di Napoli 1540–1565* (*Studi e Testi* 210; Vatican City 1961), bibliog. and documentation.

[H. H. DAVIS]

CARAMUEL, JUAN LOBKOWITZ

Cistercian bishop, moral theologian, and mathematician; b. Madrid, Spain, May 23, 1606; d. Vigevano, Italy, Sept. 8, 1682. He studied philosophy at Alcalá, entered the Cistercians at Palencia in 1623, continued his sacred studies at Salamanca, and taught for three years in monasteries of his order. He was missioned to the monastery of Dunes, Spanish Flanders, and in 1638 he received his doctorate in theology from the University of Louvain.

He then became titular abbot of Melrose, Scotland, and vicar for the Cistercian abbeys of Ireland, England, and Scotland. Later named abbot of Dissembourg in the Diocese of Mayence, he drew much attention by his preaching and became suffragan to the bishop of Mayence. The King of Spain then sent him to the court of the Emperor, Ferdinand III, who gave him the Benedictine Abbeys of Montserrat and Vienna. At the same time he became vicar general to the archbishop of Prague. During a siege he organized the ecclesiastics and was praised for helping to defend the city.

In 1655 he was cited to Rome to answer for some of his writings but is said to have satisfied and amazed Pope Alexander VII with his learning. He became bishop of Compagna-Satriano in the Kingdom of Naples in 1657. This see he resigned in 1673; he was then named bishop of Vigevano (Pavia) in central Italy.

Caramuel was a man of extraordinarily broad learning. He spoke 24 languages and wrote more than 250 works in grammar, poetry, mathematics, astronomy, physics, politics, Canon Law, logic, metaphysics, theology, and asceticism. However, he had a penchant for the singular and even the bizarre. In dogma he engaged in speculation that was regarded as temerarious, and a number of his works were put on the Index. In moral theology he tried to reduce everything to mathematical formulas, and he maintained that even the most difficult problems relating to grace could be resolved with ruler and compass. He appeared to use probabilism as a means of attenuating the obligation of law and was dubbed by St. Alphonsus Liguori with the unenviable title, "Prince of Laxists." The restless energy of his mind and laxity of his moral thought are illustrated in the following passage from his *Theologia fundamentalis:*

> I am a man of sharp and fervid intelligence. One moment I am in the heavens, the next in the depths. A fly cannot move in chapel without distracting me. . . . I do not avoid distractions; they come by the thousands and sometimes they are voluntary. Yet I suffer no scruple on that account, for I reasonably suppose that I am obliged to no internal activity [in prayer]. . .To have it is good, yet to lack it involves not even a slight fault. [n.442; cited by D. Prummer, *Manuale Theologiae Moralis* (Freiburg im Br. 1928) 2.302.

Bibliography: V. OBLET, *Dictionnaire de théologie catholique* 2.2:1709–12. R. BROUILLARD, *Catholicisme* 2:527–528. L. F. O'NEIL, *The Catholic Encyclopedia* 3:329–330. *Nomenclatur literarius theologiae catholicae* 4:604–610.

[P. F. MULHERN]

CARAVARIO, CALLISTO (KALIKST), ST.

Missionary priest, Salesian martyr; b. Cuorgne near Turin, Piedmont, Italy, June 8, 1903; d. Lin-Chow Tsieu, southern China, Feb. 25, 1930. Callisto was educated by the SALESIANS, including Vicenzo Cimatti (1879–1965), who inspired Callisto's missionary spirit. Callisto entered the order in 1918, was professed in 1919, and fulfilled his dream of evangelizing foreign lands when he was sent to the mission in Macau (1924), then to Shanghai (China), and Timor (Indonesia), where he labored for two years. He returned to Shiu Chow, China, in March of 1929 and was ordained two months later in Shanghai by Luigi Versiglia (1873–1930). Thereafter he was assigned to the growing mission at Lin Chow.

Six months later he returned to Shiu Chow to report his progress to Bishop Louis VERSIGLIA, who decided to visit the mission. The party, including the Salesians and several young Chinese, was ambushed en route. One of the female catechists earlier had rebuffed an attacker's marriage proposal. When he showed his determination to take the aspiring nun by force, the priests intervened, were beaten, and shot. The bodies of the martyrs were recovered and buried at the door of the church of Saint Joseph in Lin Kong How. Pope John Paul II beatified Caravario on May 15, 1983 and canonized him on Oct. 1, 2000 as one of the 120 martyrs of China (*see* CHINA, MARTYRS OF, SS.).

Feast: Nov. 13 (Salesians).

Bibliography: G. BOSIO, *Monsignor Versiglia e Don Caravario* (Turin 1935). T. LEWICKI, *"Ten kielich mam wypełnić krwią": opowieść o pierwszych męczennikach salezjańskich* (Warsaw 1985). *Acta Apostolicae Sedis* 78 (1986): 140–42. *L'Osservatore Romano*, English edition, no. 21 (1983): 11.

[K. I. RABENSTEIN]

CARAYON, AUGUSTE

Jesuit bibliographer; b. Saumur (Maine-et-Loire), France, March 31, 1813; d. Poitiers (Vienne), France, May 15, 1874. After ordination, he joined the Jesuits (1841) and spent his life as a procurator and librarian. Despite weak eyesight, he loved books and manuscripts. In addition to reediting some books on asceticism and ecclesiastical history, he edited a list of 4,370 works on the Society of Jesus in *Bibliographie historique de la Compagnie de Jésus* (1864) and a collection of *Documents inédits concernant la Compagnie de Jésus* (23 v. 1863–70, 1874–86).

Bibliography: C. SOMMERVOGEL et al., *Bibliothèque de la Compagnie de Jé* 11 v. (Brussels-Paris 1890–1932) 2:714–718. L. KOCH, *Jesuiten-Lexikon: Die Gesselschaft Jesu einst und jetzt* (Paderborn 1934) 299.

[M. DIERICKX]

CARBONARI

One of the most influential of the numerous secret societies in 19th-century Italy aiming at political and social betterment.

Origin, Organization, Membership. Many obscurities remain concerning the Carbonari (literally charcoal burners). Legends have connected them with Philip of Macedonia (383–336 B.C.), with St. Theobald, an 11th-century monk who was proclaimed patron of the Carbonari, with a medieval benevolent group of German charcoal workers, and with the Good Cousins, a late medieval association in France. It is doubtful, however, that the Carbonari anteceded the late 18th century, and it is possible that the society was introduced to Naples early in the 19th century by returning exiles or by French troops. In rites and organization the Carbonari resembled the *charbonnerie* of Franche Comté. Native Italian secret societies of the 18th century or the Illuminati in Germany are also possible forerunners. Freemasonry influenced the Carbonari, perhaps in its origin; but significant differences existed between the two in their type of members, program, and religious outlook. Most Carbonari were middle class, military, petty bureaucrats, or peasants. Their aim was to win national independence, institute

Early meeting of Carbonari. (Bettmann/CORBIS)

constitutional and democratic reforms, and broaden the franchise. Professedly they were Christians, although anticlerical, and they utilized Christian symbolism.

The Carbonari were organized into numerous local cells, each one being bound in obedience to a central hierarchy. Individual members referred to one another as *buoni cugini* (good cousins) and to their opponents as *pagani* (heathens). Meetings were held in a *baracca* (hut), whose interior was referred to as the *vendita* (shop), whereas the surroundings were designated as the *foresta* (forest). The hierarchy consisted of a regent, two assistants, an orator or preacher, a secretary, a treasurer, and an archivist. Periodic general or partial assemblies met to implement policy and to preserve discipline. Carbonari were joined regionally in a *vendita madre* and an *alta vendita*. Organization, rites, and aims differed widely according to place and time. Originally there were, it seems, only two grades, apprentices and masters. No limits appear to have been placed on the number of apprentices who could be admitted. In their initiation ceremony, some pious generalities were uttered and an oath of secrecy was imposed. The role of apprentices was that of disciplined, obedient fieldmen. The initiation rites of a master involved a pseudoreligious ceremony, during which Jesus Christ was revealed as the first victim of tyranny and as the ''great carbonaro.'' The candidate for master,

in imitation of Christ, had to submit to a mock trial that ended with Pilate's washing of his hands. New Testament expressions were used frequently during these proceedings. Little information is available concerning the higher ranks of the Carbonari. There is some indication that the ceremony for a grand master, or cavalier of Thebes, included a mock crucifixion. Perfect masters were obligated to destroy Caesar, Herod, and Judas, the murderers of Christ, who may have been taken as figures for lay tyrants, autocratic ecclesiastics, and malefactors of wealth, the political and religious enemies of the Carbonari. As many as seven or nine grades may have existed, but even their names are a source of some confusion. Detailed knowledge of conspiratorial aims seems to have been reserved for the higher echelons.

History. By 1802 mention was made of Carbonari. Joachim Murat wrote to Napoleon I in 1809 that they existed in the chief Italian cities. They were especially strong in Abruzzi and Calabria and sought first to end the French dominance there (1808–14). After the restoration of the Bourbon monarchy in the Kingdom of Naples, they pressed for constitutional reforms, but Ferdinand I issued instead a stringent edict (April 14, 1814) against them and backed up the measure with arrests, imprisonments, and even executions. When Carbonari forged a papal document approving them, Pius VII put an end to rumors by issuing an edict condemning them. Some members then fled throughout the Mediterranean area, especially to France, Spain, or Portugal, taking the society's aims with them. Other splinter groups emerged, such as the *Confederazione Latina,* the *Adelfia,* and the *Guelfia.* Meanwhile Carbonari had infiltrated the Neapolitan army and took part in minor uprisings in 1816 and 1817. When mutiny erupted at Monteforte (July 1, 1820), the Neapolitan Carbonari encouraged rebellion for ''God, King, Constitution.'' At that time Carbonari membership in the Kingdom of Naples alone was reputed to be 100,000; and for all Italy, perhaps 300,000 or even 640,000.

In northern Italy the organization's headquarters were in Genoa. The rise of Austria to dominance in the Italian peninsula after 1815 roused the resentment of many nationalists in the STATES OF THE CHURCH and in Lombardy. Most prominent leaders of the RISORGIMENTO were Carbonari at one time or another. Thus the Carbonari were implicated in an uprising in Piedmont (March 1821) that Austrian troops had to suppress. The Holy See continued its opposition in more stringent terms. In the constitution *Ecclesiam* (Sept. 13, 1821) Pius VII condemned the society specifically and applied to its members the penalty of excommunication and the other censures contained in earlier disapprovals of Freemasonry. In reply to inquiries by some Neapolitan bishops, the Sacred Penitentiary stated that the teachings and proceedings of the Carbonari were prohibited and that the condemnation was to be rigorously enforced (Nov. 8, 1821). These strictures were confirmed by Leo XII in the constitution *Quo graviora* (March 13, 1825). To counteract the Carbonari within the States of the Church, the SANFEDISTS were employed.

Despite this, the Carbonari remained strong. Around 1830 they were directed from Paris by a veteran revolutionary and Freemason, Filippo Buonarroti (1761–1837), who had founded the Perfect Sublime Masters to coordinate the revolutionary activities of all secret societies throughout Italy and Europe. Rebellions fomented by Carbonari in the States of the Church (in Romagna and the Marches) and in the Duchies of Parma and Moderna (1831) were again repressed by Austrian arms. This led to the society's rapid decline. Giuseppe Mazzini, a carbonaro since 1827, questioned the Carbonari aims and methods and organized a rival secret society, Young Italy. The two movements occasionally concerted their action, especially during uprisings in the Romagna (1843) and at Rimini (1845). Pius IX, however, condemned both societies in the encyclical *Qui pluribus* (Nov. 9, 1846). Carbonari groups probably participated in the revolutionary movements of 1848, 1860, and 1870. Leo XIII renewed all previous condemnations in the encyclical *Humanum genus* (April 20, 1884).

Outside of Italy the Carbonari proved something of a threat in France until 1830. A revival of the society in Portugal (1907) was partially responsible for the establishment there of a republic. On the whole the Carbonari never posed the threat to public order that Metternich claimed. For the most part they did not go beyond seeking national independence and moderate constitutional reforms. Only in the Papal States and in Lombardy, where ANTICLERICALISM was strong, is there evidence that the society might have sought the destruction of religion and civil authority.

Bibliography: A. LUZIO, *Giuseppe Mazzini Carbonaro* (Turin 1920). E. MORELLI, *Giuseppe Massini: Saggi e Ricerche* (Rome 1950), esp. 5–25, "Mazzini nella recente storiografia: Note ed appunti." E. L. EISENSTEIN, *The First Professional Revolutionist: Filippo Michele Bounaroti, 1761–1837* (Cambridge, Mass. 1959). R. J. RATH, "The Carbonari: Their Origins, Initiation Rites and Aims," *American Historical Review* 69 (1964) 353–370. F. S. MARANCA, *Enciclopedia Italiana di scienzi, littere ed arti*, 36 v. (Rome 1929–39; suppl. 1938–) 8:962–963.

[M. P. TRAUTH]

CARCELLER GALINDO, FRANCISCO, BL.

Martyr, religious of the Order of Poor Clerics Regular of the Mother of God of the Pious Schools (Piarists);

b. Oct. 2, 1901 in Forcall, Castile, Spain; d. Oct. 2, 1936. Carceller was a priest assigned to the Collegium of Our Lady of Barcelona. In addition to his regular classes, he devoted himself to the religious formation of the older students who both loved and admired him. He fled to his parent's home on July 17, 1936 for protection. On July 29 he was arrested and imprisoned at Castellon. In the middle of the night on Oct. 2, the soldiers removed from the prison thirty-five priests, among whom was Carceller. They were lined up and executed by machine gun. Carceller was beatified on Oct. 1, 1995 by Pope John Paul II together with 12 other Piarists (*see* PAMPLONA, DIONISIO AND COMPANIONS, BB.).

Feast: Sept. 22.

Bibliography: "Decreto Super Martyrio," *Acta Apostolicae Sedis* (1995): 651–656. *La Documentation Catholique* 2125 (Nov. 5, 1995): 924.

[L. GENDERNALIK/EDS.]

CÁRDENAS, BERNARDINO DE

Bolivian Franciscan missionary, writer, and bishop of Paraguay; b. La Paz, 1579; d. near Santa Cruz de la Sierra, Bolivia, Oct. 20, 1668. In 1594 he entered the Jesuit Colegio de San Martín in Lima and later entered the Franciscan Order in that city. Cárdenas grew up speaking Spanish and two native languages, Quechua and Aymará. This advantage, combined with his zeal, helped him become a noted missionary. In 1621 he almost lost his life working among the tribes to the east of La Paz. From 1624 to 1625, he was able to quell a dangerous rebellion of the native peoples who were threatening La Paz itself. In 1629 the bishops of the province of Bolivia in provincial council named Cárdenas official delegate and visitor to all the native peoples of their jurisdictions, a task that he completed with great zeal and to almost universal approval. One result of this experience was his noteworthy *Memorial y relación verdadera . . . de cosas del Reyno del Perú* (Madrid 1634). His success moved Pedro Villagómez, then Bishop of Arequipa, to name him visitor to the important mining center of Cailloma. There, as in Bolivia, Cárdenas's condemnation of the sale of coca and alcoholic beverages to the native peoples brought the censure of some and the approval of many. By Feb. 27, 1638, the king had presented Cárdenas for the bishopric of Paraguay; the Holy See approved on Aug. 13, 1640. Impatient to get to work, Cárdenas did not await the arrival of his bulls and was consecrated in Tucumán on Oct. 14, 1641, an act that the Holy See later judged valid, even though illicit. His enemies had declared that he was not a bishop. The Jesuit REDUCTIONS OF PARAGUAY were the most important institutions in the bishopric. In the beginning, relations between Cárdenas and the Jesuit superiors were cordial, but by the end of 1644 a scandalous disagreement broke out that resulted in violence on both sides and lasted until Cárdenas was finally driven from his see in 1651. After long litigation the Council of the Indies disapproved of the actions against him and in 1660 ordered that he be escorted to his see. However, he was too old to return, and in 1662 he was transferred to the See of Santa Cruz de la Sierra, where he died in the sanctuary of Araní, the common opinion being that he was a saint.

The figure of Cárdenas has become a symbol of controversy similar to that of Bishop PALAFOX Y MENDOZA of Mexico, of whom he was a contemporary. At the time of the expulsion of the Jesuits, their enemies at court published three volumes of the memorials and countermemorials of the case. In the 19th century, the Peruvian priest VIGIL resurrected Cárdenas's reputation as a bishop, and in the 20th century Augusto Guzmán wrote a novelized version of his life. The Jesuits still continue their defense of their actions. Cárdenas's life has not yet received objective treatment. Yet his pectoral cross, smashed by a bullet fired while he was besieged in his cathedral by the native peoples of the Reductions and still carefully preserved with due authentication, is mute testimony that the bishop had many opponents.

Bibliography: A. GUZMÁN, *El kolla mitrado: Biografía de un obispo colonial, fray Bernardino de Cárdenas* (2d ed. La Paz 1954). A. YBOT LÉON, *La iglesia y los eclesiásticos españoles en la empresa de Indias,* 2 v. (Barcelona 1954–63). P. PASTELLS, ed., *Historia de la Compañía de Jesús en la provincia del Paraguay,* 8 v. in 9 (Madrid 1912–49).

[L. G. CANEDO]

CÁRDENAS, JUAN DE

Jesuit moral theologian; b. Seville, 1613; d. there, June 6, 1684. He entered the Society of Jesus at the age of 14, and for many years he held various administrative offices, including those of novice master, rector, and provincial. He wrote many short ascetical treatises, but his fame comes chiefly from his work in moral theology. His *Crisis theologica bipartita* (Lyons 1670) examined many of the moral opinions prevalent at his time, especially those involving laxism and rigorism. This work was strongly attacked by the French Dominican James of St. Dominic, and in the 1680 edition Cárdenas reasserted his position in a supplement that defended moderate probabilism. Although he presented a clear and strong line of argumentation, and although his opinions were moderate and sound, the work was weakened by constant digressions referring to his rigorist adversaries, who included

Vincent BARON and Jean Baptiste GONET. The Venetian editions of 1694, 1700, and 1710 also contained an explanation of the 65 propositions condemned by Pope Innocent XI in 1679. This part was also published as a separate volume entitled *Crisis theologica in qua plures selectae difficultates ex morali theologia ad lydium veritatis lapidem revocantur ex regula morum posita a SS. D.N. Innocentis XI P.M. . . .* (Seville 1687). Cárdenas holds an important place in the history of casuistry and of probabilism.

Bibliography: P. BERNARD, *Dictionnaire de théologie catholique* (Paris 1903–50) 2.2:1713–14. *Nomenclatur literarius theologiae catholicae* 2.1:231. C. SOMMERVOGEL et. al, *Bibliotèque de la Compagnie de Jésus* (Brussels-Paris 1890–1932) 2:734–737.

[F. C. LEHNER]

CARDIEL, JOSÉ

Missionary and geographer of Paraguay; b. La Guardia, Spain, March 18, 1704; d. Faenza, Italy, Dec. 6, 1781. He entered the Jesuit Society on April 8, 1720, and was already a priest when he arrived in Buenos Aires in 1729. Two years later he was sent to the Guaraní Reductions (*see* REDUCTIONS OF PARAGUAY.) He took part in various attempts to establish new missions among the Mocoví, Abipón, Charrua, Pampa, and Serrano tribes, and also explored the Patagonian Coast. In 1768 he was deported to Italy, where he lived until his death, preparing studies and maps for the history and geography of Paraguay. His cartographic work has been almost completely reproduced and analyzed by G. Furlong (*Cartografía jesuítica del Río de la Plata,* 2 v. Buenos Aires 1936). Cardiel's most important writings are *Carta-relación* (1747), *Declaración de la verdad* (1758), and *Breve relación* (1771).

Bibliography: G. FURLONG, *José Cardiel, S.J., y su Carta-relación (1747)* (Buenos Aires 1953).

[H. STORNI]

CARDIJN, JOSEPH

Cardinal, champion of the working class; b. Schaerbeek, a suburb of Brussels, Nov. 13, 1882, of working-class Flemish parents; d. Louvain, July 24, 1967. His father opened a small coal business in Hal, Belgium, depending on Joseph for manual assistance. In 1897 he entered the minor seminary at Malines and became aware of the gulf which separated him from his boyhood friends who had entered factories. At his father's deathbed in 1903, the young seminarian vowed to consecrate his priesthood "to end the scandal which brings death to millions of young workers, separating them from Christ and the Church.'' He was ordained by Cardinal Mercier in 1906. During one year of study at Louvain and five years of college teaching, he spent his vacations examining working-class conditions in Belgium, Germany, France, and England.

His opportunity to apply his social principles came in 1912, when he became assistant in the parish of Laeken, a Brussels suburb. He spent his time making the acquaintance of young workers, interesting himself in their material conditions. He gathered a band of young men and women to engage in the social apostolate, and developed his technique of allowing the workers to analyze their environment and discover their own mission. His principle was that religion must not be separated from life and that every Christian is called to be an apostle of Christ to his fellows.

During World War I his nascent organizations were disrupted and Cardijn was imprisoned by the German occupiers. In 1919 he reassembled his followers and the work began to spread. Cardinal Mercier was uncertain about the autonomy of working-class associations, but in a visit to Rome during the Holy Year of 1925 Cardijn managed to intrude into the study of Pius XI and completely won his approval. His movement, now called ''Jeunesse ouvrière chretiénne'' (Young Christian Workers, in English-speaking countries) spread rapidly; and in 1935 at a joint rally of the Belgian and French sections in a Parisian stadium, 80,000 enthusiastic working youth celebrated the liturgy with materials entirely fabricated by themselves. World War II again interrupted a work that had spread to most European countries, and Cardijn was imprisoned by the German Gestapo, managing to escape only in the confusion of liberation. After the war Cardijn undertook 24 intercontinental trips to developing countries to spread his belief in a humanity united in justice and peace. He played a prominent role in the Second Vatican Council, where his volume *Laïcs en premières lignes* (1963) helped to shape the decisions on the role of the laity. He was elevated to the episcopate and cardinalate in 1965.

Cardijn united a burning faith in the Church and in the ordinary worker with a dynamic personality. A seeker and a visionary until the end, he could say after 61 years of intense priestly activity: ''An old man is always tired; but a good priest is never old.''

Bibliography: A. ARBUTHNOTT, *Joseph Cardijn* (London 1966). M. DE LA BEDOYERE, *The Cardijn Story* (Milwaukee, 1958). J. CARDIJN, *Laymen into Action,* tr. of *Laïcs en premières lignes* (London 1964). M. FIEVEZ, J. MEERT, and R. AUBERT, *Cardijn* (Brussels 1969). M. WALCKIERS, *Sources Inédites relatives aux débuts de la Joc* (Louvain-Paris 1969).

[J. N. MOODY]

CARDINAL

Cardinals are prelates of the Roman Catholic Church, second in hierarchy only to the pope, who constitute a special college and who have the exclusive right to elect the Roman pontiff, to advise him either as a group or individually and to represent him on solemn occasions as legates or special representatives.

The term ''cardinal'' or *cardinalis* was initially an adjective used to referred to every priest permanently attached to a church or every clergyman who belonged to a titular church (*intitulatus* or *incardinatus*). It also became the common designation of every priest who belonged to a central or episcopal church, an ecclesiastical *cardo* (hinge). It was synonymous of principal, excellent, superior. The term *cardinalis* means, according to a usage in existence since Pope St. Gregory the Great (590–604), a cleric who had been assigned to serve in a church other than the one he was ordained for. These clerics were referred to as ''priest cardinals.'' By the 11th century, the adjective ''cardinal'' had become a noun and they were referred to as cardinal priests.

DEVELOPMENT OF THE OFFICE

Cardinal Priests. The historical origin of the office of cardinal goes back to the presbyterate of the bishop of Rome. As early as the 1st century, the *Liber Pontificalis* says that Pope St. Cletus or Anacletus (76–88), following St. Peter's instructions ordained 25 presbyters for the City of Rome. Pope St. Evaristus (97–105), the fifth successor to St. Peter, divided the Roman churches (titles) among the priests. In the 3d century, Pope St. Dionysius (260–268), was faced with the disarray of the Roman Church caused by Valerian's persecution, and then by the problems created by Emperor Gallienus's (260–268) reversal of his father's policies and restoration of the church's confiscated property and cemeteries. Dionysius carried out a thorough reorganization of the church, as may be seen in the report of the *Liber Pontificalis,* allocating the parishes and cemeteries to the several priests, and delimiting new episcopal units in his metropolitan area.

In the 4th century, Pope Marcellus, (308–309), ordained 25 priests for the City of Rome and authorized the administration of baptisms, penance, and funerals in the titles. A century and a half later, Pope St. Simplicius (468–483) arranged for priests from some of the Roman titular churches to assist with the services at the major basilicas of St. Peter, St. Paul, and St. Lawrence. Thus was initiated the praxis of incardination.

Following a very old custom of the Eucharistic celebration by the bishop together with his presbyterate, the heads of the Roman titular churches celebrated the main

Angelo Cardinal Sodano (center), the Vatican's Secretary of State, during the ceremony of sanctification of a newly renovated Roman Catholic church, Moscow, 1999. (AP/Wide World Photos)

liturgies in the patriarchal basilicas of the city in weekly turns, *hebdomadaries.* The most ancient document in existence containing the names of the Roman titles is the constitution *Ut si quis papa superstite,* issued by Pope St. Symmachus (498–514) during the Roman synod of March 1, 499. At the end of the document appear the names of the 72 bishops who participated as well as those of the titular priests of Rome with the names of their titles. The titles (of property) were those of early Christian families who had given their homes to the Church for worshiping and instruction. A century later, in the Roman synod of 595, convoked by Pope St. Gregory I, 24 titular priests signed the documents issued. This list is the second catalog of the titular churches of Rome, all of them appearing by then under the denomination of a saint.

The number of titles rose from 18 in pre-Constantinian times to 25 in the 6th century and then to 28 in the mid-9th century. Until the 8th century there were most probably five titular churches assigned in each area to each one of the patriarchal basilicas. They were rearranged in the 8th century and the seven heads of the neighboring titular churches were called to the liturgy in the Lateran basilica, the cathedral of the pope as bishop of Rome, and the heads of the titular churches celebrated the liturgy in the four other patriarchal basilicas: St. Peter, St. Paul, St. Lawrence, and St. Mary the Major (or Liberian).

The first time that the term ''cardinal'' appears in the *Liber Pontificalis* is in the biography of Pope Stephen III (IV) when in the Roman Synod of 769, it was decided that the Roman pontiff should be elected from among the deacons and cardinal priests and later, during the same pontificate, the weekly liturgical celebrations in the major basilica Saint John Lateran of Rome were assigned to the cardinal bishops. With the passing of time and their involvement in ecclesiastical affairs of the Universal

Church because of their proximity to the Bishop of Rome, the main functions of the cardinals evolved from purely liturgical and pastoral to more administrative and judicial.

Cardinal Bishops. Since the early centuries there were several dioceses in the vicinity of Rome known as "suburbicarian" sees. The role of these bishops originated from the need for assistance that the popes had. As the amount of ecclesiastical and temporal matters that the popes had to attend to increased, they called on the bishops of the dioceses that had existed in the vicinity of Rome since the early centuries of the Church to represent them at liturgical functions in the Lateran basilica and to assist them with their counsel. These suburbicarian bishops eventually became the cardinal bishops. The *Liber Pontificalis,* in the pontificate of Pope Stephen III (768–772), calls them "episcopis cardinalibus" and says that they, according to an ancient custom, celebrated solemn mass every Sunday at St. Peter's altar at the Lateran basilica. Their number was always seven although their sees varied through the centuries. One of them, the bishop of Ostia, has been the consecrator of the new bishop of Rome, if necessary, since the pontificate of Pope St. Mark (336). In 1150, Pope Bl. Eugenius III granted the deanship of the College of Cardinals to the bishop of Ostia, a decision that is still in effect.

Cardinal Deacons. There were two kinds of deacons: Palatine and regional. The former are the seven original deacons of the City of Rome (established in the 3d century by Pope St. Fabian [236–250], who divided Rome into seven regions and provided for each a deacon and a subdeacon), and who took part in the liturgy of the Basilica of St. John Lateran. The latter were the 12 regional deacons who took part in the liturgy of the other basilicas. By the 12th century, the distinctions between these two classes of deacons had disappeared. The first time that a deaconal monastery is mentioned in the *Liber Pontificalis,* is in the biography of Pope Benedict II (684–685). From the times of Pope Hadrian I (772–795) there had been 18 deaconries or agencies charged with the material assistance to the needy of Rome and that had a church as the center point of its activities. Since the 12th century, a cardinal was in charge of each of the deaconries.

FROM 1059 TO 1946

In 1059, Pope Nicholas II, continuing the effort of the Church to free the election of its head from all secular influence, published the decree *In Nomine Domine* in which he gave the cardinal bishops the right to be the sole electors of the Roman pontiff. The other cardinals and the Roman clergy were to assent to the election. The emperor was to be informed as a courtesy.

The College of Cardinals was organized in its present form and categories of membership in 1150 when Pope Bl. Eugene III (1145–53) appointed a dean (the bishop of Ostia) and a camerlengo or administrator of the college's wealth. Traditionally, the clerics created cardinals were required to reside in Rome. This custom was changed in 1163 when Pope Alexander III (1159–81) allowed the archbishop of Mainz, Conrad of Wittelsbach, to return to his see after having being created a cardinal. In order to make him a member of the Roman clergy, Alexander named him to a church in the city, making him a titular pastor. In 1179 Alexander reserved the election of the pope exclusively to the cardinals of the three ranks by the decree *Licet de vitanda.* The decree required two-thirds of the votes for a valid election.

Since the 12th century, the cardinals have had precedence over archbishops and bishops, and since the 15th century, even over patriarchs (bull *Non Mediocri* of Pope Eugene IV, 1431–47). They could vote in ecumenical councils even if they were only deacons. Their number, which usually did not exceed 30 from the 13th to the 15th centuries (the Councils of Constance and Basle decreed that the cardinals must be 24), was fixed by Pope Sixtus V with the constitution *Postquam verus* Dec. 3, 1586) at 70 on the model of the 70 elders of Israel: six cardinal bishops, 50 cardinal priests, and 14 cardinal deacons. The Council of Trent urged the internationalization of the college, but the cardinals from the Italian peninsula constituted the absolute majority of the membership for centuries.

Pope Innocent IV (1243–54) granted the use of the red hat to the cardinals during the Council of Lyon in 1245 and the red cassock was granted to the cardinals in 1294 by Pope Boniface VIII (1294–1303). In 1965 Pope Paul VI abolished the red hat. The red biretta, red skullcap (calotte or zucchetto), red cloak or mantle, were bestowed upon the cardinals in 1464 by Pope Paul II (1464–71). Pope Urban VIII (1623–44) granted the title of eminence to the cardinals in a secret consistory celebrated on June 10, 1630.

During the pontificate of Pope Clement V (1305–14), the creation of the favorites of secular princes as cardinals increased. From the 15th century on, the emperor and the kings of France, Spain, and Portugal abrogated themselves the "right" to name crown cardinals. Oftentimes, these became the diplomatic representatives of their princes before the papal court and were also known as cardinals protector. Since the 16th century, those secular princes also started practicing the "right of exclusion," by which through the crown cardinals, they could veto the election of any pope. The right, exercised in several conclaves, was abolished by Pope St. Pius X in 1904. Cardinal protectors of religious orders had been in existence since the pontificate of Honorius III (1216–27) when one was appointed as protector of the Franciscans. The system of cardinal protectors for orders and congregations was abolished in 1964.

DEVELOPMENTS IN THE 20TH CENTURY

The second half of the 20th century saw substantial changes take place in the office of the cardinalate. A marked trend toward the internationalization of the College of Cardinals was initiated in 1946 by Pope Pius XII. Not only did he appointed the first cardinals of several nations such as Chile, China, Colombia, Cuba, Ecuador, Mozambique, and Peru, but also for the first time in centuries the Italian cardinals did not constitute the absolute majority of the college. This trend continued in successive pontificates until, following the consistory of 2001, there were 185 cardinals from 69 different countries.

The maximum number of members of the College of Cardinals remained at 70 from 1586 until John XXIII set aside this rule and raised the membership to 75 in 1958 (even more in subsequent consistories). The number continued to grow during the pontificates of Paul VI and John Paul II. In his consistorial allocution of March 5, 1973, Pope Paul VI announced that the number of cardinals entitled to participate in papal elections was limited to 120. The total number of cardinals (electors and nonelectors) has never been fixed since 1958. The highest has been 185, after the consistory of 2001 celebrated by Pope John Paul II.

For centuries, the cardinals have exercised power of governance, administration, and discipline over the suburbicarian dioceses, titles, and deaconries that they headed. These powers were abolished by John XXIII and Paul VI by their *motu proprios Suburbicariis sedibus* (April 11, 1962) and *Ad hoc usque tempus* (April 15, 1969). Now the cardinal is only to further the good of the diocese or church by counsel and patronage.

Another innovation introduced by Pope John XXIII in his *motu proprio Cum gravissima* of April 15, 1962, was that those cardinals who are not already bishops must receive episcopal consecration. Until then they were required to have been ordained priests.

Pope Paul VI effected essential changes in the office of cardinals. By his *motu proprio Ad purpuratorum patrum,* issued on Feb. 11, 1965, he decided that Eastern patriarchs named to the College of Cardinals would keep their patriarchal see as a title. Accordingly, there will be members of the college who are not even symbolically incardinated to a church in Rome. Moreover, on Nov. 21, 1970, Paul VI decreed (*motu proprio Ingravescentem aetatem*) that the cardinals lose the right to participate in papal elections upon reaching 80 years of age. Also, that cardinals heading organs in the Roman Curia were asked to submit their resignation to the pope upon reaching 75 years of age and ceased as members of the same at 80. For the first time since they became the exclusive electors of the pope, cardinals in good standing were deprived from exercising their electoral function because of age. The document that Paul VI issued on Oct. 1, 1975, regulating the papal election, *Romano Pontifice eligendo,* kept the language of the constitution *Ne Romani electione,* issued by Clement V in 1311. The Pauline document stated that no cardinal elector could be "excluded from active and passive participation in the election of the Supreme Pontiff because of, or on pretext of, any excommunication, suspension, interdict or other ecclesiastical impediment. Any such censures are to be regarded as suspended as far as the effect of the election is concerned"(n. 35).

The new Code of Canon Law (1983) addresses the topic of the cardinals in Chapter III: "The Cardinals of the Holy Roman Church" (canons 349–359). Its main innovations are the definition of the College of Cardinals as a special college, no longer referring to it as the "Senate of the Roman Pontiff," as in the 1917 code, whose prerogative it is to elect the Roman pontiff in accordance with the norms of a special law. This law is the apostolic constitution *Universi dominici gregis,* promulgated by Pope John Paul II on Feb. 22, 1996.

Besides codifying the changes decreed since 1917, the new code, (1) established the naming of special papal envoys (while keeping the practice of "Legatus a latere") entrusted with a particular pastoral task. In 1998 Pope John Paul II started the practice of naming as special envoy prelates who are not cardinals; (2) eliminated the list of 24 cardinalitial privileges; and (3) established the celebration of ordinary and extraordinary consistories, replacing the praxis of secret, semipublic, and public consistories. Both kinds of consistory are secret except when an ordinary consistory deals with certain solemn acts such as canonizations or creation of new cardinals.

Consistories. The cardinals assist the pope in collegial fashion in meetings called consistories. They are gathered by order of the pope and under his presidency and address important ecclesiastical matters. The consistory was instituted by Pope Leo IV (847–855) with a decree issued in the Roman synod of Dec. 8, 853. It mandated the cardinals to meet weekly in the pontifical palace to deliberate with the pope. As the Roman synod dwindled in importance, the consistory became the most important collegial organ of the pope, with an advisory function. With the establishment of the Roman Congregations by Pope Sixtus V in 1588, by which the activities of the commissions of cardinals were institutionalized, the consistory became less important and those cardinals who headed these new organs of the Roman Curia became very influential figures in the government of the universal Church. Pope John Paul II called five extraordinary consistories between 1979 and 2001. All cardinals, electors, and nonelectors were invited to participate in these gatherings.

Orders. The College of Cardinals is still divided into three orders: the episcopal order, to which belong those cardinals to whom the Roman pontiff assigns the title of a suburbicarian Church, and the Eastern-rite Patriarchs who are made members of the College of Cardinals; the presbyteral order; and the diaconal order. The suburbicarian churches are Ostia (reserved for the dean of the college who unites it to his own suburbicarian see), Albano, Frascati, Palestrina, Porto-Santa Rufina, Sabina-Poggio Mirteto, and Velletri-Segni. In 1965, Pope Paul VI, by his motu proprio *Sacro Cardinalium Consilio,* established that the dean and sub-dean of the Sacred College of Cardinals should be elected to their posts by and from among the cardinal bishops instead of succeeding by order of seniority as had been the practice for centuries and as was legally stipulated by the 1917 Code of Canon Law (c. 237, §1). This election by the cardinal bishops requires papal confirmation to be valid. At the beginning of 2001, there were 136 titular churches and 57 deaconries. Cardinals also have the right of "option" to another title or deaconry. The practice as started by the antipope Alexander V (1409–10). Until then, the cardinals kept until death the sees, titles, or deaconries that they had originally received. Pope Eugenius IV (1431–47) authorized the practice and Sixtus V (1585–90) codified it with precise regulations in his constitution *Religiosa sanctorum.* The cardinal deacons may opt to the rank of priests after 10 years of their elevation to the college. The senior cardinal deacon, or protodeacon, announces the name of the newly elected pontiff to the people and imposes the pallium on him on the day of the inauguration of the new pontificate. Acting in place of the pope, he also confers the pallium on metropolitan bishops or gives the pallium to their proxies, usually the day of the Feast of SS. Peter and Paul.

Requirements for the Cardinalate. Those to be promoted to the cardinalate are men freely selected by the pope, who have at least received the priestly ordination (until the 1917 code, the cardinals needed only to be deacons; the last one was Cardinal Teodulfo Mertel who died in 1899) and are outstanding in doctrine, virtue, piety, and prudence in practical matters; those who are not already bishops must receive episcopal consecration. From the moment of publication, they are bound by the obligations and they enjoy the rights defined in the law. In the 14th and 15th centuries some canonists and theologians

unsuccessfully advanced the idea of the divine institution of the cardinalate. Instead, the nomination of cardinals is referred to as "creation," signifying that the office of cardinal is of ecclesiastical institution and could be abolished by the pope.

Cardinals "in pectore." A person promoted to the dignity of cardinal, whose creation the pope announces, but whose name he reserves *in pectore* (in his bosom), is not at that time bound by the obligations nor does he enjoy the rights of a cardinal. When the Roman pontiff publishes his name, however, he is bound by these obligations and enjoys these rights, but his right of precedence dates from the day of the reservation *in pectore.* This practice of reserving the name of a cardinal was started during the pontificate of Martin V (1417–31). Pope John XXIII created three cardinals *in pectore* in 1960 and died without ever publishing their names. John Paul II reserved the names of one cardinal in the consistory of 1979 and two in the consistory of 1998. All three were published at later consistories.

Vacancy of the Apostolic See. When the Apostolic See is vacant because of the death or resignation of the pope, the College of Cardinals exercises the limited powers granted to it in the special legislation that provides for the election of the successor. In 1996 Pope John Paul II issued the apostolic constitution *Universi dominici gregis* to regulate the vacancy and the election.

Bibliography: M. ANDRIEU, "L'origine du titre de cardinal," *Miscellanea Giovanni Mercati.* 6 v. (Vatican City 1946) 5:113–144. *The Book of Pontiffs (Liber Pontificalis): The Ancient Biographies of the First 90 Roman Bishops to A.D. 715,* tr. R. DAVIS (Translated Texts for Historians, Latin Series V; Liverpool 1989). J. F. BRODERICK, "The Sacred College of Cardinals: Size and Geographical Composition (1099–1986)," *Archivum Historiae Pontificiae* (1986) 7–71. F. CLAEYS BOUUAERT, "Dioceses Suburbicaires," *Dictionnaire de droit canonique,* 4:1267–71. A. DE LA HERA, "La reforma del colegio cardenalicio bajo el pontificado de Juan XXIII," *Ius canonicum,* 2 (1962) 677–716. J. FORGET, "Cardinaux," *Dictionnaire de Théologie Catholique contenant l'exposé des doctrines de la théologie catholique, leurs prevues et leur histoire.* ed. A. VACANT et al., 15 v. (Paris 1903–50), continué sous celle de E. AMANN et al. (Paris 1903–50 [i.e., 1899–1950]) 2, pt. 2, cols. 1717–24. H. G. HYNES, *The Privileges of Cardinals. Commentary with Historical Notes* (Catholic University of America Canon Law Studies, no. 217; Washington 1945). S. KUTTNER, "Cardinalis. The History of a Canonical Concept," *Traditio,* 3 (1945) 129–214. C. LEFEBVRE, "Les origines et le rôle du cardinalat au moyen age," *Apollinaris,* 41 (1968) 59–70. *The Lives of the Ninth-Century Popes (Liber Pontificalis). The Ancient Biographies of Ten Popes from A.D. 817–891,* tr. R. DAVIS (Translated Texts for Historians, 20; Liverpool 1995). C. MESINI, "Origine della prelatura cardenalizia," *Apollinaris,* 45 (1972) 339–351. J. P. BEAL, J. A. CORIDEN, and T. J. GREEN, eds., *New Commentary on the Code of Canon Law* (Commissioned by the Canon Law Society of America; New York 2000). T. J. REESE, "The College of Cardinals," *Inside the Vatican: the Politics and Organization of the Catholic Church*

(Cambridge, Mass. 1996). J. B. SÄGMÜLLER, "Cardinal," *The Catholic Encyclopedia* (New York 1913) 3:333–341.

[S. MIRANDA]

CARDONA MESEGUER, MATIAS, BL.

Martyr, priest of the Order of Poor Clerics Regular of the Mother of God of the Pious Schools (Piarists); b. Dec. 23, 1902, in Vallibona, Castile, Spain; d. Aug. 20, 1936. Matias had just been ordained on Apr. 11, 1936. A member of the San Anton community in Barcelona, he went to his home town of Vallibona at the beginning of the religious persecution. On Aug. 17, he left his sister's house where he was staying to seek asylum at his uncle's farm in the mountains. He was arrested shortly thereafter by soldiers sent by the Revolution Committee. He turned himself in, and they imprisoned him. In the early morning of Aug. 20, soldiers took him from the prison in a truck along with a diocesan priest; the two were shot along the side of the road near his hometown. He was beatified on Oct. 1, 1995 by Pope John Paul II together with 12 other Piarists (*see* PAMPLONA, DIONISIO AND COMPANIONS, BB.).

Feast: Sept. 22.

Bibliography: "Decreto Super Martyrio," *Acta Apostolicae Sedis* (1995): 651–656. *La Documentation Catholique* 2125 (Nov. 5, 1995): 924.

[L. GENDERNALIK/EDS.]

CAREY, WILLIAM

Baptist missionary pioneer; b. Paulers Pury, Northamptonshire, England, Aug. 17, 1761; d. Serampore, India, June 9, 1834. Born in humble circumstances and baptized an Anglican, he was apprenticed to a shoemaker (1779) and during this period became a Baptist. He was ordained and supplemented a meager income as a pastor by making shoes and teaching school. Impressed with the importance of giving the gospel to the non-Christian world, he stimulated the organization of the Baptist Missionary Society (1792). Under its appointment he went to India (1793), where he became eminent as a missioner, linguist, translator, educator, and scientist. To make a living and to avoid deportation by the East India Company, then opposed to missions, he was for a time manager of an indigo plantation. Gaining a foothold in Serampore, at that time a Danish possession, he and two colleagues translated the Bible in whole or in part into 44 Indian languages and dialects. By means of a press, which they established at Serampore, copies were manufactured and distributed. Carey also translated some of the Sanskrit classics into English. He and his colleagues established schools and capped them with a degree-granting college. As recreation he developed a botanical garden and won fame in India and Europe as a naturalist.

Bibliography: E. CAREY, *Memoir of William Carey, D.D.* (2d ed. London, 1837). M. DREWERY, *William Carey: Shoemaker and Missionary* (London, 1978). G. SMITH, *The Life of William Carey—Shoemaker and Missionary* (London, 1885). F. D. WALKER, *William Carey* (London 1926).

[K. S. LATOURETTE]

CARIBBEAN, CATHOLIC CHURCH IN THE

This essay presents a discussion of the development of the Catholic Church in the Caribbean islands in general and in specific areas not covered elsewhere in the encyclopedia. For further discussion of the Church in CUBA, HAITI, and the DOMINICAN REPUBLIC, see those individual entries.

The Spanish Period. Of the four Greater Antilles only Jamaica and the western part of Hispaniola were lost to the Spanish Empire. By contrast, of the Lesser Antilles, only Trinidad remained in Spanish hands until 1797, while the Venezuelan islands of Cubagua and Margarita remain Spanish speaking until today. Even before the Spanish discovery of the Lesser Antilles on the second voyage of Columbus (1493) this chain of volcanic and limestone islands, that circles the Caribbean Sea on the East, was already diverging both in culture and inhabitants from the bigger Antilles. The Carib people that migrated from the South American mainland had exterminated the Arawak-speaking less bellicose Taino inhabitants from all the inhabitable islands except Trinidad. The Caribs were in the process of invading eastern Puerto Rico when the Spanish conquest interrupted the process.

Since the first encounter when the little Spanish fleet anchored off Guadalupe and Marie Galante (named after Columbus' flagship) in October of 1493, the Spaniards encountered fierce resistance from the indigenous peoples. Claiming the islands for Spain was easy; settling them effectively was altogether different. Most of the islands were named after saints or titles of the Virgin Mary to which Columbus had devotion: Our Lady of Guadalupe in Extremadura, Our Lady of Nieves (of the Snows) now deformed to be Nevis, Our Lady of la Antigua, Our Lady of Monserrat in Catalonia, St. Martin of Tours (now the island of St. Marteen), St. Ursula and her 11,000 Virgins and Martyrs (thus the Virgin Islands), the Holy Cross (St. Croix), the Most Holy Trinity (Trinidad) etc. The first evidence of Catholicism is to be found in the

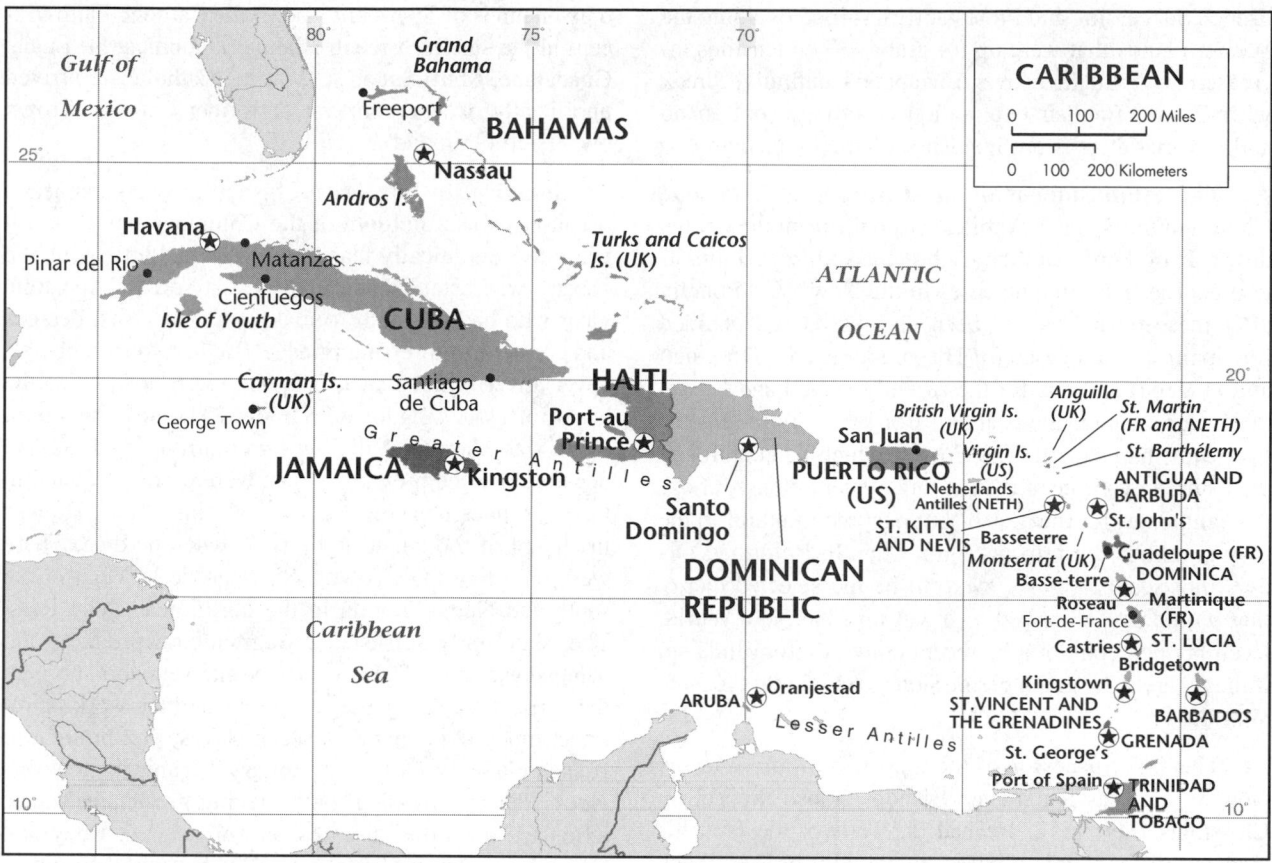

pious names that the islands were given even if their first effective European settlers were rapacious, not very religious and largely Protestant (first the Dutch, then the French and English, and finally the Danes).

The Spaniards did not settle any of these islands, except Cubagua, which was rich in pearls, and neighboring Margarita which supplied the former. Various reasons explained this abandonment by the earliest Europeans who came to visit. First, the process of conquering and settling was very difficult and was delayed in Hispaniola until 1508. Secondly, most of the Europeans who came died from hunger and the West Indian disasters; hurricanes and droughts specially took their toll on the foreigners who had little capacity to adapt to the new and little food that the natives could offer them. Most of the smaller islands did not have water and had a very limited capacity to sustain more than a band of dwellers. This would continue to be true up to the middle of the 17th century for the new English and French settlers on the Eastern North American seaboard as well. Some of the islands are very dry and desert like (especially the Dutch islands off South America, the Bahamas and Barbados). Thirdly, on the islands where the Caribs lived, there was great resistance to the interlopers. Fourthly, they did not have any significant natural wealth or deposits. Lastly,

these islands were always on the frontier: a sort of no-man's land raided first by the Caribs, then by the pirates of various nationalities, personalities and intentions that roamed these seas after 1525. European conflicts always echoed in the Antilles, wrecking security. Many islands changed hands more than once. To summarize: climate, lack of food, natural disasters (hurricanes, volcanoes, sea and earthquakes), later the diseases brought by African slaves, dangers of attacks and lack of natural resources made the white Europeans liable to infirmity, death or insecurity. European settlements in these Lesser Antilles were always precarious and transient. Few descendants of the white Europeans remain in these islands even today.

The 16th century was characterized by raids and punishing expeditions on the part of the Spaniards. Some Caribs were enslaved and taken off to work in Puerto Rico by the settlers, who faced a labor shortage after disease and epidemics killed off the bulk of the Taino population in the Greater Antilles. The Bahamas were also raided to take the more peaceful Lucayos into forced service in Hispaniola and Puerto Rico. The French in turn were venturing into the unknown waters of the Caribbean vying for the wealth they had heard about. The Wars between Spain and France over Italy and then over the

French Succession and Protestantism spilled over into the Western lands that were up for grabs. When tensions increased with England over Elizabeth's definitive break with Rome, English explorations, raiding, contraband and terrorist attacks on Spanish settlements increased.

The establishment of the Church. The Catholic Church in the Spanish Antilles was built from the Crown down. King Ferdinand the Catholic asked Pope Julius II to erect the first three dioceses in the New World barely after these territories had been discovered and claimed for Spain: two dioceses for Hispaniola (Santo Domingo and la Vega) and one for the recently settled and "pacified" San Juan (as the island of Boriken or future Puerto Rico was then called). The Crown, which had control of the Church by virtue of the Patronato, meticulously chose the candidates for the new bishoprics: men faithful to the Crown and to the reform of the Church. Reformed Orders, not secular priests, were to be the selected clergy that would be authorized to travel into the New World. Even laymen could not be recent converts from Judaism if they were to be given permission to travel into the New World.

The first Successor of the Apostles to arrive in the New World was San Juan's Bishop Alonso Manso, on Christmas Day, 1512. He had barely two priests at his disposal in the whole diocese. Eventually he went back to Spain and made ecclesiastical rearrangements to make his diocese viable. The Diocese of San Juan's territory was augmented with the Lesser Antilles and eastern Venezuela and the Guyanas. The bishop of Puerto Rico was thus in charge of these fierce islands inhabited by Caribs. But not much was done to further the Evangelization of the difficult places. The friars that would spearhead the spreading of the Gospel in heathen lands more or less avoided these islands and went on to the Cumaná coast of Venezuela and also to the Guyanas where some of them were martyred.

The establishment of the Catholic Church in the Lesser Antilles and Jamaica, the Bahamas and the Dutch islands off Venezuela (Curacao, Aruba and Bonaire) would be entirely different from their Spanish sister Churches. In these islands, the Church was built not from the Crown down but from trickles of indentured servants who were Catholics in the English islands and from adventuresome planters in the case of the French islands, and only the slaves themselves (as was the case in Curacao). The late dates for the establishment of bishoprics in these islands contrasts dramatically with the first bishoprics in the Americas. The Spanish Crown's argument that the Holy See could not erect new bishoprics in territories claimed (even though not effectively occupied) by her was partly to blame. Most of the interlopers were not only enemies of Spain but also of the Catholic Faith. Except in the smaller French islands (Dominica, St. Lucia, Guadalupe, Martinique, St. Martin) Catholicism arrived unofficially or as a remnant of former Catholic Crown ownership (Trinidad).

Jamaica. In Jamaica no bishopric was established because it was a fiefdom of the Columbus family and it was not economically feasible since it had little gold. An abbacy was established. This was a sort of Apostolic vicar who had the right to make pastoral visits, decrees and corrections of erring priests. The first four "abbots" never arrived in Jamaica, only the fourth made it to the island of Don Amador de Samono. The next important abbot was Marqués Villalobos who arrived in 1582 and declared that the previous vicars were more interested in their revenues than in their clerical obligations. He was in charge of the island until 1606 when he died. There were only two main towns: Santiago de la Vega in the south and Nueva Sevilla in the north, near Ocho Ríos. The island only subsisted on agricultural products and some sugar cane. There were few natives who survived the germs brought by the Europeans and the working regime imposed by them, so black slaves, first brought to Hispaniola in the early 16th century, became the real survivors. Their "blessing" was having greater resistance to malaria and other diseases, as well as greater physical strength to work in the tropics. This became their curse. Jamaica supplied ships going on expeditions to the mainland with water, hides and other meat products. Pigs, goats and cattle were released in the countryside to reproduce for themselves and so as to guarantee the locals easy food resources.

In 1608 a very well known and scholarly cleric, a Baroque poet, don Bernardo de Balbuena was named Apostolic vicar of Jamaica. In 1610 his confirmation arrived from Rome (where the Crown presented its candidates for ecclesiastical offices). The Crown paid his traveling expenses. He finally embarked for Jamaica with his voluminous library, one priest, four servants and four black slaves. The war of Dutch independence started up again and crossing the seas was most dangerous, given the formidable presence of many Dutch vessels in open waters. The English were aiding the Dutch against the Spanish (who had also acceded to the Portuguese Crown) who had virtual European and American hegemony. Not many ships plied the route, especially to forlorn Jamaica, but he arrived safely. His parishioners were few and far between. He despaired at the difficult lives led by the Jamaicans. In 1620 he was promoted to a bishopric, that of San Juan de Puerto Rico. He now had greater hopes for a dignified life, but the Dutch got to him there. Fired by their successful excursions in northern Brazil and the East Indies, taking away some Portuguese trading posts, the

Dutch arrived in San Juan in 1625 and burned the city and Balbuena's library as well. The poet who was a bishop died in 1627.

It was now the English's turn to attack Spanish dominions. They had already attacked Santo Domingo, Puerto Rico and Portobello in Panama in the late 16th century and had gone from transient stopovers for refreshments to their first permanent settlements (in uninhabited Barbados in 1625 and in Antigua in 1635). The Spaniards did not extricate them from these islands that were of no use to them. The Puritans now in power in London were very much eager to settle their own colonists in the New World. They had already tried New England, and after a near disaster, had managed to economically salvage the situation for the Pure Christian Commonwealth they hoped to establish in order to secure true religion against the unreformed Anglican Church, which they were fleeing. A post closer to Spanish quarters, on Providence island off Nicaragua, proved to be a disaster: the Spaniards did not tolerate this close intrusion into Cuban waters and they massacred the colonists who had dared to settle Spanish lands.

As a vengeance Cromwell decided to take over Santo Domingo. In 1654 a fleet sailed from Plymouth and after picking up recruits of ambitious arrivals in Barbados and St. Kitts, sailed for Hispaniola. In the failed attack more than a thousand died. As an afterthought and so as not to return empty handed they decided to attack Jamaica (1655). The frail governor surrendered to the scared Englishmen. All priests and the friars of the Dominican convent in Santiago la Vega, as well as lay Catholics were deported and could not carry their goods or belongings with them. But some of the lay settlers did not go along with the surrender and they freed their slaves and made them their guerrilla companions in the mountains of the interior. Thus began the long Jamaican experience of runaway slaves living on the mountain, a group that became known as the Maroons (from the Spanish word for runaway slaves). The guerilla war lasted for three years after which the Spaniards were finally vanquished. Their freed slaves did not lay down their arms. The treaty of Madrid on July 8, 1670, officially ceded Jamaica to England. Although it was not the first island to be occupied by European interlopers on the Spanish Main it was the first of the Greater Antilles lost by Spain.

After the restoration of the monarchy in England a Spanish settler in Kingston a certain Mr. Castillo, a slave merchant for South American customers, seems to have succeeded in getting permission from the pro Catholic King James II to have his private chapel. Father Thomas Churchill was allowed into Jamaica in early 1688 and not only officiated at Mr. Castillo's chapel, but seems to have gathered four parishes, including one in the former Dominican convent in Spanish Town. With the overthrow of James II, Catholicism was once again prohibited.

Port Royal, the new capital, became the center of Caribbean piracy, once Santiago la Vega (now Spanish town) was moved closer to the seaport. Henry Morgan made it his base of operations to raid Spanish shipping. It was very hard to properly survey the vast empire and keep it together. In 1671 Panama City was captured and so utterly destroyed by pirate Henry Morgan (d. 1688) that it had to be reestablished elsewhere. But Port Royal's reputation as an island Babylon came to an end with a seaquake that sunk it in 1692.

Jamaica was developed in the latter 17th and early 18th centuries as a great sugar cane plantation. It was also an entrepot for slave reshipments to the Spanish mainland. After the English learned the techniques of sugar cultivation from the Dutch, who themselves had learned them from the Portuguese in Brazil, they started to exploit its relatively fertile soil with great economic success. Barbados, which was a completely Protestant island, was the first to implement this changeover from the early tobacco experiments as a viable consumer cash crop. The changeover also meant abandoning the practice of indentured servants, poor white folks from Ireland, Scotland and England, who came for three or six years of labor intensive service and then would be freed to pursue their own livelihood. Massive slave labor was imported in order to feed the sugar cane plantation. Not until the middle of the 18th century were the nonconformist clergymen allowed with great hesitation to preach Christianity to the slaves. There was fear that conferring Christian Baptism and teachings to the slaves might empower them to fight for their dignity.

Some Catholics seemed to have lived in Jamaica at least covertly during the next century and a half. The only official priest on the island was the chaplain of the captured French soldiers defeated off St. Lucia. The penal laws were finally abolished in England in 1791, and for the first time the Catholics were allowed to have their rites and Mass celebrated legally. The State authorities had to approve a Catholic priest who would still have to be supervised very carefully. The Catholic bishop of London was given the charge of finding priests for Catholics resident in Kingston. Most of these were Spanish slave merchants. Franciscan Fr. Anthony Quigly was sent in 1792 to care for the souls of Catholics in Jamaica. By 1797 there were some more Catholics on the island.

Neighboring Haiti's massive slave revolt caused panic and obliged many slave owners to flee to Jamaica. Father Le Cun, apostolic vicar for Haiti arrived in Jamaica in 1799 in this manner. Father Quilgy had just died.

These French Catholics played a significant part in the history of the Catholic Church on the island. Some regiments of North American blacks that had been given their freedom by the British, when they fought against the 13 colonies, were brought to Jamaica as free blacks. They organized the first Baptist churches in Jamaica.

In 1811 a Spanish merchant in Kingston built a Church at his own expense for Catholics, and also brought Joao Rodríguez, a Portuguese Augustinian priest from Veracruz, Mexico to tend the flock, which consisted of French refugees from Haiti, Spanish émigrés from Cuba and a few Irish and Dutch Catholics. In 1821 there were only two priests in Jamaica. One of them, Father Blake, complained to the new apostolic vicariate of the English West Indies, Bishop Buckley, that the other did not share the emoluments with him. But the bishop confirmed Father Rodríguez and gave him ample faculties to name worthy priests in case he had to leave the island.

In 1838, when slavery was abolished in Jamaica very few slaves had owners who were Catholic and thus very few were Catholic. Most were non-conformist Moravian, Baptists and Methodists, as well as Anglicans. Catholics, though, had been a significant minority in Jamaica. When Spanish born Franciscan Father Benito Fernández fled the war of Independence in New Granada (future Colombia) he came to Kingston and helped Father Juan Araujo take care of his flock. After Father Araujo returned to Portugal in 1824 Father Fernández had lots of problems with itinerant diocesan priests and he asked the Holy See to send religious priests to help him. He was also named apostolic vicar (1837) for Jamaica and two other British territories: Bahamas and British Honduras (future Belize).

These are other very pervasive realities in all the Antilles throughout much of its last three hundred years: foreign-born religious clergy have been the predominant Evangelizers, not the diocesan clergy. Also the Holy See has tried to follow Church connections through the dominant colonial master. In Cuba and Puerto Rico, for example, it was through the Spanish government and Church that the Holy See worked. Rome tried to tie both islands ecclesiastically (since Puerto Rico was dependent on Santiago de Cuba until 1901), following the political bonds between them. Catholics in English islands were entrusted to London, and Dutch religious orders worked in Dutch islands. In extreme cases language connections were followed, with the young Baltimore Diocese taking charge of some of the English islands during turbulent times.

With the arrival of the Jesuits in Kingston, sent by the Holy See in December of 1837, the pastoral situation changed dramatically and for the better: Catholicism could be cultivated in the countryside, outside of the pressing needs of urban Kingston. In 1850 other Colombian Jesuits came to help and founded St. George's College in Kingston, a well known educational institution in Jamaican life which was to be the school of many important leaders of the future nation. After the death of Father Fernández in 1855 all apostolic vicars were to be Jesuits. Indeed the first bishop of Jamaica (consecrated on August 15, 1889) was a Scottish-born Jesuit, Bishop Charles Gordon. He brought sisters from Great Britain to take charge of an orphanage. When he died, Father John J. Collins, SJ, was made bishop in 1907. By then the American Jesuit province of Maryland-New York was in charge of Jamaica. Kingston was to have a succession of Jesuit bishops until Archbishop Samuel Carter, a Jamaican Jesuit of black and East Indian extraction, in 1970.

After the refusal of many freed slaves to continue to work as sugar cane laborers, and their preference to live as subsistence farmers in the countryside, the British decided to go back to their first solution: indentured servants. But Europeans were not willing to do this anymore. In order to stave the economic downturn of ever rebellious Jamaica, the colonial authorities decided to import workers from two other parts of their far flung empire: Hindu and Muslim East Indians and Chinese. This new policy of labor exploitation was to especially transform the island of Trinidad and the South American enclave of British Guyana. Blanche Aquee, the first Chinese convert girl in Jamaica (1904) was the instrument for the conversion of two thirds of the Chinese to Catholicism. As in Trinidad, fewer East Indians converted to Catholicism. The East Indians kept their traditions and their religious practices. This has meant that the English Caribbean has a very complex ethnic, religious and cultural diversity. In 1929 Bishop Dinand started the first native congregation for women. Others have since sprouted, aside from foreign congregations that are also helping on the island.

Efforts to increase native presence in the clergy also bore fruit with the foundation of St. Michael's Seminary in 1952, especially with the degree granting faculties given to it by the University of the West Indies. Many earlier priests had been trained by religious orders or in diocesan seminaries in Great Britain or the United States. Jamaican native priests were to become bishops all throughout the English islands. Social work with lepers has also been a particular feature of Jamaican Church life.

After the Second Vatican Council permanent deacons have become a feature of Jamaican Church life, as have special lay ministries. There is a very serious and well-planned effort to reach out and convert unchurched Christians. Certain features of Evangelical enthusiastic charismatic life have been blended in Jamaican Catholicism, where some features of Latin American Catholicism (e.g., Marian devotions) are not salient. In this and other English islands where Catholics are a minority excellent relations with other Christian denominations prevail. Indeed in some of the British Virgin Islands Catholic parishioners aren't sufficient in number and wealth to have their own Church buildings, so they celebrate Mass at different hours than the local Anglican congregations in the Anglican Church. As in all other islands, big or small, among the varied pastoral problems some are in the forefront: family life tends to depend on mothers, since fathers tend to abscond or leave the household. Also there is a resurgence of traditional African religious and syncretic sentiments and practices (such as the Rastafarian movement which began in Jamaica in the 1930s, which have also found followers in other English-speaking islands like Grenada, Trinidad and Guyana or the Kumina cult or the Jordanite Movement) and a Pentecostal attack on Catholic parishioners.

The high hopes and expectations for a better life that independence brought in 1962 have largely disenchanted most of the population and many thousands of Jamaicans and other West Indians have migrated first to Great Britain (until the gates were practically closed in the early seventies) and especially to the United States. Endemic poverty has bred violence (especially in crime ridden Kingston, some sections of which are dominated by gangs) and drug trafficking. In Jamaica the recent killing of some foreign-born Catholic priests involved in social work has been very disturbing. Most of the economies of the Lesser Antilles depend on tourism, which can be a source of income but also a ghetto experience for the locals, ''distanced'' as they are from these very wealthy places where the idyllic Caribbean is evoked in immediate proximity with abject poverty. Tourism has also brought with it prostitution and lifestyles which bring radically different values to the countryside people. In these islands there is a very definite search for a peculiar identity. They have deep African roots but nonetheless they are very different from the Africa that their forefathers let behind many years before. This is evident when they encounter African priests who occasionally help out in the West Indies: they are very different from the West Indians just as the Creoles are from their European forbearers.

The Diocese of Montego Bay was created in 1967 and had Bishop Clarke, a St. Michael's Seminary alumnus, as bishop. He was later promoted to the Kingston Archdiocese and Bishop Charles Dufour, also Jamaican and former rector of St. Michael's was made bishop of Montego Bay. The Apostolic vicariate of Mandeville was created in 1997 and has Monsignor Michael Boyle, an American Passionist, as bishop. Vocations remain critically low in order to meet the demands of parish life in the country. Seminary formation has recently been moved to the St. John Vianney and Martyrs of Uganda Seminary in Tuna Puna, Trinidad, combining the ecclesiastical resources of all the English-speaking islands. But localism prevails in the Catholic populations of the islands. The French islands, for example, have always been rather aloof from the rest of their neighbors, be they Spanish, English or Dutch.

Trinidad. Columbus discovered Trinidad on July 31, 1498 on his third voyage. Like contemporaneous Puerto Rico, it was a battleground between Carib and Arawak. The Spaniards raided it to get slaves for the neighboring island of Cubagua's pearl business. In response to both of these attacks the Arawaks moved their settlements inland. Attempts to settle the island were made in 1532-34 and again in 1569 from Puerto Rico but these failed. Only in 1592 was the first settlement of a permanent nature founded: the present day Saint Joseph (San José). Antonio de Berrio, its founder, was not authorized by the Crown to settle so he was ordered to leave, which he refused. The Crown authorities in the Audiencia or Royal courts in Santo Domingo, which had civil jurisdiction over the island, were impotent to do anything. For 20 years no Spanish ships arrived on the island.

Not having any particular interest for the Spanish, who themselves were overstretched over the two continents and the Philippines as well, the island lead, like other Greater and Lesser Antilles a rather sad subsistence. Isolation was the best way to describe the situation in Trinidad throughout the 17th and 18th century. Contraband sales of tobacco were the only ways its dwellers could survive. The bishop of Puerto Rico, which had ecclesiastical jurisdiction over the island, argued that the natural right of people to survive overrode human laws making a trade, which brought food and clothing illegal. He himself was also involved with the trade. Starvation or serious poverty was the other option. Spanish shipping had a monopoly of commodities but the system did not work: it could not supply the Antillean domains. However, this illegal tobacco trade with the Dutch, French and English could not compete with the Virginia and Barbados tobacco production.

The native villages produced tobacco for themselves and for the vecinos (householders). The Dutch took neighboring Tobago in 1632. From 1613 onwards a Spanish ship was supposed to visit Trinidad every year. In 1687 Capuchin missionaries from Catalonia, who had been working in neighboring mainland Cumaná came to Trinidad and gathered ten native villages or self-contained reducciones (segregated entities) also called misiones de viva conversión. In these towns the friars had absolute authority over the converts. The locals, however, wanted native labor for their cocoa plantations. This contradiction surfaced again and again: could there be authentic evangelization with forced labor? As had happened in virtually all situations where friars evangelized the natives apart from the Europeans or Creole (be it California or Paraguay) the civilian authorities got the Crown to eventually expel the priests and incorporate the natives into the colonial administration so that they could be subject to the exploiters more directly. In 1708 the missions were transformed into misiones de doctrina and thus the secular clergy was in charge of the affairs of the former misiones de viva conversión. The Capuchins argued the natives were not ready for the change, but their appeal was lost. The friars left. After their departure only four of the missions survived. The secular clergymen did not know the native language and they were not trained to supervise the daily lives of so many new parishioners.

Starting in 1727 the cocoa trees, from which chocolate was extracted, started to fail in their production. The locals migrated and only 250 free men remained on the island. The Franciscan convent in Port of Spain withered and the last Franciscan died in 1790. The convent was then turned into a hospital.

It was only after the reformist King Charles III came to the throne in Spain that the economic development of these dormant islands took place. The Empire was reorganized in 1776 and Trinidad was put under the jurisdiction of the newly created Viceroyalty of New Granada, whose capital was Bogotá, and under the immediate tutelage of the intendencia or administration of Venezuela. In 1765 there were 2,503 inhabitants in Trinidad: half were natives and the others free whites. In 1783 a Royal decree (cédula) was issued encouraging efforts to populate Trinidad with French settlers that had been displaced from their islands now handed over to the British. A year later they and their slaves accounted for more than twice the number of original settlers. British subjects of Irish extraction (supposedly Catholics) followed the French. From 1785–1787 the population grew rapidly, half of it being the black slave population brought by the wealthier planters who moved in (especially from 1777–1783) or bought from the British islands and even from Africa itself. In the new capital, Port of Spain, French was the more commonly used language. Trinidad cotton was being exported via Grenada to England. Even older Spanish planters relied on English credit not only to provide machinery and equipment for the sugar cane plantations but also to supply their basic needs. Militias were finally organized.

Slave mortality was impressive: in 1788 alone some 893 slaves died. British traders controlled Trinidad henceforth. In 1782 the British tried to negotiate with Spain proposing an exchange of Western Florida for Trinidad but Spain refused. The British had their covetous eyes on Trinidad, especially after acquiring the neighboring former French islands of St. Lucia, and in particular because of its proximity to British Guiana. In order to defend itself the Spanish government relied on the British traders to loan money and buy rations and military equipment. In 1794 this frontier island had close to 16,000 people, with the great majority of inhabitants being non-Spanish foreigners and their slaves.

In 1790 Pope Pius VI created the new Diocese of Guyana, a suffragan see to Santo Domingo, removing Trinidad and eastern Venezuela from the Diocese of Puerto Rico. A Venezuelan was named bishop, but there was no effective supervision of Trinidad.

British Trinidad. In 1796, under pressure from France, Spain declared War on Britain. Trinidad and Puerto Rico were immediately put on the lists of priority for a British attack. On Feb. 16, 1797 a British naval expedition landed more men than there were inhabitants on the island. British desires were fulfilled when they captured the unprepared island of Trinidad in military action, followed by a quick surrender by the Spanish governor. Puerto Rico repulsed the same invaders later in the year. In the peace negotiations that took place in March of 1802 Trinidad was ceded to Britain. Many French and Spanish settlers left for the mainland, but most stayed on.

The British governor of Trinidad, Picton, wanted English priests to be sent to Trinidad. He made this known to the Roman Catholic vicar apostolic of London. But the Congregation of the Propaganda Fide in Rome wanted to make sure the island was to be severed from Spain and thus from the Guyana Diocese: ''the Church is not accustomed to change easily the limits of dioceses with changes made by the civil authorities'' wrote Cardinal Gerdil to Bishop Douglass in London on May 8, 1802. The governor was very displeased with the Spanish priests ministering to Catholics in Trinidad and he dismissed from his duties the vicar forane (or principal priest on the island). It was a strange situation with a Protestant governor acting as Royal vice-patron of the Catholic Church while mingling in the affairs of the local Catholic Church. The next governor, Woodford, also acting as vice-patron, would also suspend priests and even issue approvals of marriage cases for Catholics.

Finally the British governor contacted the bishop of Guyana and the bishop ordered the reinstating of the vicar forane in Port of Spain. In the meantime the governor was encouraging Venezuelans to revolt against Spain. No episcopal visits were ever made to Trinidad during this time that it officially belonged to the Guyana Diocese.

The upcoming wars of independence of Venezuela and the disruptions of ecclesiastical life that followed would leave the Guyana Diocese vacant until 1841.

During the Revolution many French priests were either expelled or fled the country, some came to North America, but they did not come in significant numbers to the Antilles. Their presence was also discouraged by the British even if they were to minister to the French-speaking planters because the British feared that they would be tainted with republican ideas. In 1802 there were eight priests in all of Trinidad; they were all Spanish. Baptisms and weddings usually took place in private homes. By 1817 there were no more native churches.

The declaration of the war of independence in 1810 by Simon Bolivar in Venezuela caused serious problems of an upsurge of royalists and insurgent refugees in Trinidad. Almost 6,000 refugees came to Trinidad from 1814 to 1819. About 12 priests came over as well, but since their political ideals (in favor of insurgence) were not always in conformity with those of the bishop of Guyana, they were not granted faculties to serve as priests and thus worked as unpaid assistants. The problem with these priests was that they could not hear confessions in French, and many parishioners spoke only French. Some were mere adventurers. Most of the lay people were not very instructed in the Faith. No Spanish ecclesiastical monument in Trinidad has survived into our times, a small sign of the precarious nature of the Faith on the island.

In the meantime Protestant settlers and Anglican minister were encouraged to move in, but they never became a significant force in the land. In 1809 Methodist and Presbyterian ministers came to Trinidad, but they complained that the government did not give them full freedom to evangelize. Not until 1835 did these denominations come to stay with a more permanent presence. In 1815 a disbanded regiment of North American black slaves who had been given their freedom by the British for having fought against their revolutionary masters was brought to Trinidad; most of these were Protestants. In 1822 another group of disbanded former slaves were given lands in Trinidad and settled there.

British rule would totally and substantially transform Trinidad, though the basic formative years of Spanish domination would keep it from becoming another Antigua or Jamaica: slave islands dominated by absentee Europeans and a few local merchants and supervisors. Trinidad was so late in the English fold that it could not be transformed, as had happened with their other possessions, into massive sugar cane producing islands. The slave trade would be abolished in 1810 and thus the traditional labor force needed to clear the relatively untouched lands of this largest of the Lesser Antilles was closed off. Two thirds of the free population was composed of native peoples. Some English settlers wanted immediate transfer of the legal system to a British system, but the free natives were in such a majority that representative government would fall in their hands, thus the Spanish law was upheld. By 1807, however, the colony was bankrupt. And to complicate matters further, a fire in 1808 destroyed most of Port of Spain.

After the Napoleonic upheavals of the Roman Curia subsided and before the Propaganda Fide began its work, the situation of Catholics in the former islands that belonged to Spain or France and were now British was difficult. London had no diplomatic linkage with the Holy See and Catholics in Britain itself were only tolerated. Finally in 1818 Pope Pius VII appointed Father Thomas Gillows as vicar apostolic for the English and Danish Antilles. Due to his health problems he could not assume his office and Father James Buckley replaced him. In June of 1819 he was ordained the first Catholic bishop for the English West Indies. He wisely chose to reside on the island with the highest Catholic population of the English Antilles: Trinidad.

Aside from being tolerated by the British government and its representatives (who mostly suspected Catholics of being covert enemies of the Crown and subjects of a foreign potentate called the pope), Bishop Buckley's major problem was to find priests to staff his parishes. He first tried to find priests from neighboring islands who could speak French and English but this did not produce the desired results. In 1823 there were two priests in St. Thomas, Virgin Islands, one each in Monserrat, Grenada and St. Vincent, two in Jamaica and three each in Dominica and St. Lucia. He had nine priests in Trinidad. He appointed Abbé Le Goff, a French expatriate who had spent time in England and Martinique, as vicar general in Trinidad. He then went on to visit his islands (1822) and found that Spanish-speaking priests who had fled the mainland manned most of them. They usually did not have any assigned salary but some were rather well off given the fact that most of the islanders (be they free, manual laborers or slaves) were Catholics, while the merchants and government employees were Protestants. The only priest in some of the islands made his living off the stole fees that are received on the occasion of the celebrations of Sacraments. The situation was particularly difficult in Monserrat, visited in 1822, where the Catholics (mostly descendants from Irish indentured servants) had retained their faith in spite of the fact that had heard no Mass and had not seen a Catholic priest for 26 years. Some of the upper class girls had been sent to study in English convent schools and knew their doctrine quite well. In order to solve this problem the bishop left Trinidad in 1825 for London and Rome. One of the issues that took him there was recruiting priests, especially from Ireland. He managed to get a Spanish priest and an English priest to come. But the British authorities saw Irish priests, like French priests before them, as untrustworthy and dangerous. They were deemed unfit and potentially rebellious, coming, as they did from the lower classes. Only two priests were allowed to come from Ireland: one to Grenada and later to Montserrat, and a Dominican, Father Hynes, to Guiana, where he was later to become bishop.

The second problem he faced was the issue of mixed marriages. Since Trent Catholic law required an oath on the part of the non-Catholic party to raise all the children as Catholics. The bishop urged that only a promise be required. A very high pastoral risk was to be taken if the oath would be demanded of Protestant partners. The good relations with the government officials and the government paying salaries of some priests, as well as Catholics abandoning their faith in order to marry Protestants unwilling to make the oath would be some of the sad consequences of such a strict requirement. Finally Rome consented and relaxed the oath from Protestants, making it a promise. A third problem Bishop Buckley encountered was the construction of decent parish churches. There was also the issue of the cost of religious instruction, which he tried to convince the Colonial Office to subsidize. As was the case in Jamaica, the Catholic Church would have a significant impact in the education of 19th and 20th century Trinidadians.

The British government's solution for the faltering economies of the other islands that depended on sugar cane cultivation was to bring indentured servants from Africa and the Indian subcontinent. The two British possessions that received a larger proportional share of East Indians were Trinidad and Guiana. From 1838 to 1914 Trinidad received almost 144,000 East Indian laborers who would come over on a five-year contract. After ten years of residence they would receive a subsidized return ticket to India. Many of the owners did not provide much of housing or medical care and not all paid their workers the same wages given the Creole workers. Certainly, the white-black-Arawak mixture was complicated with Chinese and East Indian indentured servants. Most of them retained their traditional religions: Hindu sects and Islam, but some were converted to the Catholic faith and others came into it by mixed marriages.

Religious orders, especially from Great Britain and Ireland, would eventually bring the pastoral solution for the scarcity of priests in the Lesser Antilles. The Dominicans and Benedictines from England and Holland would establish themselves in Trinidad, Jamaica, Curacao and St. Marteen. The American Jesuits and Passionists would also come to Jamaica. Other religious orders would take over in the smaller islands, like the Redemptorists in the Danish Virgin Islands. Not only did they start recruiting native West Indians as novices and eventually as religious priests, but they would also sponsor the St. John Vianney and Ugandan Martyrs Seminary in Tuna Puna, Trinidad, an institution first associated with a Benedictine Abbey, as a formation place for native diocesan priests. Female religious orders also increasingly became staffed and lead by native West Indian sisters.

Anthony Pantin was made Archbishop of Port of Spain in 1967. In 1976 Trinidad and Tobago got their independence from Britain.

Curacao and the Dutch Islands. The Dutch Islands were colonized under the auspices of the West India Company, which ruled these places until 1791, when the Crown took over the direct rule of the islands from the Company. According to the Spaniards Curacao, Bonaire and Aruba were useless islands. In the 1630s, however, salt ponds attracted the Dutch. Smuggling goods and slaves into Spanish America (Puerto Rico, Cuba, Venezuela and Colombia) was to become their big business. Only they had the fleet to accomplish this, and they had also developed the African contacts to provide them with their human cargo. Jews had a very significant part in this trade as well. No cash crops could really grow well in these dry islands: they became the slave entrepot of the New World.

The reformed Church officially banned Catholics from living on the islands, but just as the Dutch merchants in the Indies specialized in smuggling, they also learned to tolerate Catholics as part of sound business. The Coro Diocese in neighboring Venezuela (founded in 1531) claimed jurisdiction over these islands that lay so very close. When the Diocese of Caracas succeeded the Coro Diocese as the north Venezuelan See, it also claimed the islands. The Bishop of Caracas gave faculties to resident priests in Curacao to be vicar generals there. Priests from Venezuela came over to care for the flock. Occasionally religious priests would work in Curacao, such as Jesuit Father M. Schabel from 1704–1713. The Propaganda Fide in Rome made an apostolic prefecture of the islands in 1767. From 1776 to 1820 Dutch Franciscans occupied this prefecture. In 1842 it was elevated to the status of apostolic vicariate. Father Mathinus Niweindt, a Dutch secular priest was the vicar until 1860, although he had begun his service as prefect in 1824. In 1843 he became the first bishop of Curacao. The anomalous and unique situation with the slaves in Curacao was that the Calvinist and Jewish businessmen did not allow blacks to become their coreligionists. Even the Jewish merchants, breaking their long-standing Sephardic traditions did not circumcise their slaves, rather allowing them to become Catholics. Catholicism was a sign of being black and a slave.

One of the conflicts that arose was the issue of slave marriages, which were supposed to take place before civil magistrates before going to the religious ceremony. The slave masters and merchants did not want to allow the slaves to be married because this impeded their sale or transfer to other estates. Many slaves fled to Venezuela to earn their freedom and practice their faith more freely. Around the city of Coro many former Curacao slaves who earned their freedom by fleeing ended up forming whole barrios of freemen. In 1785 the Dutch authorities prohibited the apostolic prefect from performing marriages of slaves. In the 1795 slave rebellion Franciscan Father Schinck, acted as a mediator between the civil authorities and the slaves. The slaves convincingly argued that they should be recognized as human beings, and not be treated worse than animals. In 1817 Franciscan Father J. Stöppel argued before the Dutch king that slaves ought to be allowed to marry in the Catholic faith with civil recognition and to baptize and raise their children in the Catholic Faith. This, however, was deemed dangerous by the authorities.

But the Catholic Church, in a curious turn of history, had little to do with the abolition of slavery in the Dutch Antilles, an abolition that benefited only the Catholics on the island. Bishop Niewindt himself, it was noted by Father J. Putman, was a slave owner. This priest who criticized the bishop was asked to resign his post and he returned to Holland in 1853. The bishop was in favor of a gradual abolition of slavery; Father Putman was in favor of an immediate abolition. As Cuba and Puerto Rico, latecomers to the sugar cane trade, prospered in the 19th century, the Lesser Antilles deprived of their forced labor (slaves), withered. After 1815, the islands were bankrupt. Trade with Venezuela, exchanging Venezuelan products for European manufactured goods, was henceforth the only significant economic activity carried on in these islands up the arrival of the Shell Oil refinery in 1915. There was no more slave trade after the British started enforcing the trade ban in 1814. Many Dutch colonists moved to the new Republics in North and South America. Slavery was abolished in Curacao at a rather late date (1863). The slaves at St. Marteen mutinied after the French side of the island (St. Martin) abolished slavery in 1848. There the slaves forced the authorities to grant them legal freedom on their own initiative. Not so in Curacao.

Catholics in the Netherlands were an oppressed significant minority. When in 1870 the Dutch Dominicans arrived in Curacao they brought with them the concern that the Irish had had with the English: complete equality as opposed to second-rate citizenship. In Curacao this demand for equality before the law was compounded by the fact that Catholics were mostly blacks. The Dominicans worked very hard at organizing the Catholic workers into cooperatives and following the Dutch model, a workers union was formed in 1919. The Shell refinery had established itself in Curacao in 1915. Catholic schools, newspapers and even a Catholic party were founded. In 1922, under Catholic inspiration, workers on the island held a first general strike. In 1948, though, the Catholic party was defeated.

By 1958 Curacao was made a bishopric but it still mostly depended on foreign and religious clergy. The first native-born priest to be elevated to the Curacao bishopric was consecrated in 1973. Catholic schools comprised 75 percent of all primary and secondary schools on the island.

The British plundered St. Eustatius in 1781 because it was a smuggling colony within sight of British St. Kitts, which supplied North American colonists in their rebellion against the British. After this most merchants from St. Eustatius moved into neutral Danish St. Thomas. St. Marteen lived off cattle raising and salt ponds. After the slaves got their emancipation in 1848 the local economy collapsed on this island. Subsistence farming and more recently, tourism have been the mainstay of the economy of these Leeward Dutch islands.

The French Islands: Martinique, Guadalupe, Dominica and St. Lucia. Columbus discovered Guadalupe on his second voyage in 1493. Abandoned like all the Lesser Antilles by the claimant, it was raided by the Spaniards so as to chastise Carib Indians. It was not until 1635 that the French occupied it. Some of the planters that came from St. Kitts took the initiative. In 1627 the French Company, the Compagnie des Indes, which was in charge of making a profit, sold Grenada and St. Lucia to Sieur du Parquet and more French planters arrived there as well. The pioneers in Guadalupe and Martinique were Normans, Bretons and Gascons, later joined by Irishmen who were fleeing British terror in their native land and had gone to France seeking refuge. At first they turned it into a tobacco plantation island. But then the shift to the more profitable and more labor consuming sugar cane plantations took place.

The French experiment with island colonies was similar to the British and Dutch experiences: commercial companies. These private entrepreneurs, like their English and Dutch counterparts, had little desire to establish bishoprics (and indirectly royal control) in the West Indies. This not only meant that the local civil authorities would have more power over priests but also that the local planters tended to diminish the influences of priests over their slaves. Profit, not evangelization, was the main concern of the early settlers that came to these difficult forsaken places. Religious life was not a paramount concern for them.

When the first French priests arrived they were quite concerned with the evangelization of the fierce Caribs in Martinique, Guadalupe and Dominica. During the early period the natives helped supply the European settlers. But some of the black slaves brought to the young plantations ran away and joined the Caribs. In 1632 Father Raymond Breton wrote a Carib dictionary and catechism. In 1666 Father du Tertre, a Dominican friar, began his ministry in St. Lucia as Abbé Jean Baptiste Labat, another Dominican, would do at the end of the 17th century. They learned the Carib language in order to preach the Gospel to them in their own tongue. Up to 1685 the missionaries tried to teach the Caribs but there was very little success in converting many to the Catholic faith.

As the Caribs were driven away from Martinique and Guadalupe and took refuge in Dominica, a peace treaty was signed with them (1660), but planters still needed laborers, who were recruited in Paris, Brittany and Normandy. These ''engagés'' or indentured servants usually had three years of obligatory labor for those who brought them over. But as tobacco planting was substituted by the more difficult sugar cane planting, black slavery substituted indentured French servants. Already by the second half of the 17th century the black slaves were more than half the population of the island of Guadalupe, even while 3,083 whites still remained as settlers. In 1664 Governor De Tracy ordered the evangelization of the black slaves under penalty of a fine. By 1685 King Louis XIV had issued the Code Noir in order to further direct the incorporation of African slaves into West Indian society as Catholic subjects. Blacks seem to have been eager participants in catholic ceremonies: Sunday was the only day they could rest and get together. Priests insisted on black slaves' right to marry, even if this made their master's ability to exchange or sell them more difficult. During the first decade of their adaptation to their new home their death rate was very high.

Religious orders, like the Capuchins, and later the Jesuits, Dominicans and Carmelites were active on the islands. They were very subservient to the Crown that paid their passage and their salaries once in the West Indies. The Jesuits were especially active among the slaves, having learned their language: a blend of Spanish, French, Dutch and English. In contrast with the Spanish islands, in the English and Dutch islands the European languages were transformed into patois or altogether different languages, as was the case with Creole in Haiti.

Some Huguenots and Jews also came over to these islands. The economic connections of both these groups were necessary if the colony was to survive. Benjamin de Costa, a Sephardic Jew, was one of those who introduced sugar cane cultivation to Martinique in 1654. Also the few Europeans had to stand united against the Carib threat. French Protestants controlled the financing and the main sugar cane mills. At one point Protestants owned two-thirds of the Company fleet ships. There was a certain rivalry between these religious groups in the French Indies. This was a constant feature of the religious diversity that all the Lesser Antilles experienced to a lesser or greater extent; an extreme contrast to the purely European Catholic Quebec and Puritan New England.

During the Seven Years War, from 1759 to 1762, Britain occupied all the French islands in the Lesser Antilles. French planters insisted on maintaining their laws even under British domination. When this war was over, France had to choose between the racially homogenous model colony of Quebec or the economically more prosperous islands of Martinique and Guadalupe. Such was the importance of these little islands to the Mother Country that France chose to abandon Quebec with a serious British insistence. The expectations to take over all of Saint Domingue (Haiti and the Spanish Santo Domingo) would soon prove the fatal mistake French politicians had made. It was a great stroke of British diplomacy and war. After the French Revolution, Saint Domingue rebelled and the French were never able to recover this, the most prosperous of the slave colonies.

Some of the priests who were fleeing revolutionary France came to Martinique and Guadalupe. Abbé Le Goff was one who came to Martinique after spending some time in England, and also helped the newly elected bishop of Trinidad, Bishop Buckley.

Between 1852 and 1887 Guadalupe planters received 45,000 East Indian and 5,800 African laborers, while Martinique received 29,400 East Indians and 10,500 Africans. Most of the East Africans stayed. After 1870 the islands were integrated into France, and the people given privileges to study in France like other French citizens and also to elect their own home rule. These islands were treated as a special departments of France itself.

St. Lucia, discovered in 1506, along with Dominica was Carib territory. The French tried variously to dominate it. It became the focal point of the French Caribbean navy. It was lost to the French after a naval battle in 1797 and passed on to the hands of the British who officially controlled it from 1803 to 1979 when it became independent. Tobago, Granada, Dominica and St. Vincent also passed permanently into British hands. In 1850 Roseau,

Dominica, was made a diocese, which included the Leeward and Virgin Islands. Presently it has an American Redemptorist as bishop. It is a suffragan see of Castries, St. Lucia.

The Virgin Islands. Discovered by Columbus on his second trip in 1493, St. Croix harbored fierce Caribs that assailed Columbus. Their warriors raided various villages in eastern Puerto Rico and eventually attacked San Juan itself in 1530. Spanish expeditions launched from Puerto Rico depopulated their inhabitants. As with most other Lesser Antilles they could not sustain nor attract the Spanish claimants, so both the French and the English tried to occupy them during the late 17th century. They were too close to Puerto Rico for the Spaniards to lay still. Only upon sale of the islands to the Danes, a minor European power, were the Spaniards at ease. After 1754 these islands came under the direct rule of the Danish Crown and St. Thomas was declared a free port. But even so, after the 1830s foreign trade declined, as did sugar cane plantations. Slaves were resold in Fajardo and Puerto Rico, and St. Thomas supplied the latest European goods to Puerto Rico's young consumer market in an official trade. English was adopted as the local language of schools after 1850. Occasionally slaves would run away to Puerto Rico to gain their freedom. The roots of Catholicism in the Danish Virgin Islands date to Spanish merchants as well as French planters and entrepreneurs living there.

In March of 1804 Bishop Carroll of Baltimore was instructed by the Propaganda Fide to minister to the needs of Catholics in the Danish Islands. He did indeed send some priests to help. In 1818 Rome put these islands under the jurisdiction of the newly created apostolic vicar for the English speaking islands.

In 1848 as they were expecting emancipation a slave rebellion broke out in St. Croix. With the help of Spanish troops from Puerto Rico, it was quelled. Freedom was promised, but like in contemporary Puerto Rico, compulsory work was required of the technically free blacks. Even though liberty was given to 17,000 slaves in St. Croix on July 3, 1848, full legal freedom came only in 1878. Many decided to leave for the neighboring islands, both Spanish and British. From 1835 to 1911 the Danish Virgin Islands' population declined almost by half in St. Croix, by two thirds in St. John and by a third in St. Thomas.

In 1850 the Danish Virgin Islands and the Leeward Islands were separated from the Trinidad Diocese and belonged to the new Diocese of Roseau in Dominica. In December of 1855 the papal legate who was visiting Charlotte Amelia, Monsignor George Talbot, encountered a schism among the parishioners of Saints Peter and Paul Church in St. Thomas, the only Catholic Church on the island. The bishop at Roseau was not able to solve the dispute. The Propaganda Fide was asked by the legate on behalf of Pope Pius IX to entrust this mission to the Redemptorists, who were versed in English, Spanish and French, which were the languages used on the Danish Virgin Islands. It was the first foreign mission outside of Europe and continental United States given to the Redemptorist Fathers. One of the founders of the Redemptorist Province of North America, Father Joseph Prost, was in charge of the two brothers and the other priest who were to take charge of the St. Thomas Parish. He presented his credentials to the bishop in Dominica in 1858. The bishop reassigned the Redemptorists to the Holy Cross Parish in Christiansted, St. Croix. The three other Redemptorists arrived a little later (on April 24, 1858) from New York, but one brother died of smallpox before disembarking and they were quarantined.

On June 1, 1858 Father Louis Dold, a member of the American province was named pastor of Saints Peter and Paul in St. Thomas. The lack of personnel was a serious problem for the small band of Redemptorists, even after the arrival of two new members from the American province and one from England. Eventually Rome decided they should have just one parish, the one in St. Thomas, and after other deaths due to typhoid the first superior, Father Prost returned to Austria. The new superior in St. Thomas, a Belgian Redemptorist by the name of Father Louis De Buggenoms, would eventually be entrusted the Dominican Republic as vicar apostolic in 1866. The Redemptorists established schools for the poor so as to educate them first of all in the Faith. In 1874 De Buggenoms established an academy of higher studies called St. Thomas College.

Some vocations started to come from St. Thomas for the Redemptorist Congregation. Charles Warren Currier was the first native of St. Thomas to be ordained a priest in Amsterdam on Nov. 24, 1880. The St. Thomas Redemptorists preached missions in the neighboring islands of Tortola (British Virgin Islands), Montserrat, Antigua, St. Kitts, Dominica and Saba. In 1873 the bishop named the local Redemptorist superior as vicar general of the diocese. In 1880 the secular priest, pastor of St. Patrick's in Fredericksted in St. Croix was consecrated as bishop for the Diocese of Roseau. His former parish was given over to the Redemptorists from Canada who arrived in 1891. Belgian, American, English, Austrian, Canadians and Dutch Redemptorists worked in the Virgin Islands those last years of the 19th century, but another native priest, Father William Cletus Stafford, also served and died there.

Being economic liabilities for the Danish government, it approved the sale of the islands to the United

States as early as 1867. This did not become a reality until 1917, during World War I. When the Diocese of Ponce was created in 1924, the Danish and British Virgin Islands were separated from the Roseau Diocese and placed under the jurisdiction of the American bishops in San Juan, Puerto Rico. The Virgin Islands became a prelature on April 30, 1960 and became a part of the suffragan see of San Juan when that archdiocese was created in April of 1960. Its first bishop was understandably a Redemptorist, Father Edward Harper. He founded a Catholic High School in St. Croix and founded new parishes in both St. Croix and St. Thomas (outside the capital of Charlotte Amelia). After April of 1977, when Charlotte Amelia became a diocese it was attached to the Archdiocese of Washington, D.C. as a suffragan see. Bishop Harper was its first resident bishop, who retired in 1985 and was succeeded by Capuchin Bishop O'Malley. This diocese has mostly depended on transient priests and religious orders and has had no native born bishops. It now has a diocesan bishop. In 1989 the Redemptorists left their important St. Thomas Parish, but to this day, they still have Christiansted under their care.

The Redemptorists took care of Tortola Catholics from their St. Thomas base. In 1957 the first Catholic Church was constructed on the island. The British Virgin Islands are now part of the Diocese of Antigua. In Virgin Gorda Catholics have used the Anglican church for their own Masses until recently, for they still have no Church of their own.

Other islands. Barbados, the oldest English Caribbean colony was occupied in 1623. St. Kitts followed shortly thereafter. By 1645 there were 11 Protestant parishes on the island. Most of the migrants there were indentured servants. Tobacco was the cash crop that made the island prosper. Nevis and Barbuda were occupied in 1628, Antigua and Monserrat in 1632.

French and English colonists, jointly occupied St. Kitts in 1626. They feared both Carib and Spanish attacks. By 1671 firmly in British hands, Protestant parishes were established in St. Kitts as they were established in Nevis and Montserrat. But there always remained a group of French Catholic planters that demanded their own Catholic pastors. A similar situation reigned in Monserrat, where many of the original planters had come from Ireland. The most serious problem of these small islands with mixed religion and national origins was the absence of Catholic clergy and the ignorance of their Catholic faith.

At first there was a policy of toleration of Catholics in the face of a superior Spanish fear. But with increasing Puritan intolerance Catholics were not to be tolerated. Quakers and other Protestant dissidents were to migrate elsewhere. There was also a problem of staffing these islands with Protestant clergy. These island churches were technically controlled by the very distant London bishop. The Spanish solution of central organization for early control did not exist in these islands. The local planters tended to control the pastors and their preaching and influence over the slaves. The pastors had little spiritual and moral influence over the pretentious colonists. Only in 1824 was an Anglican bishop, William Coleridge, named for these islands, and he was to be stationed in Barbados. Pastors were really subjects of the local officials of the Company or the Crown. Slaves were not to be evangelized. Barbados finally got a Catholic bishop in the person of Anthony Dickson, bishop of Bridgetown in 1971.

The Antigua Diocese that includes Montserrat, Nevis, St. Kitts, Barbuda, Anguilla and British Virgin Islands was created even later on, when Jamaican Donald Reece, former rector of St. Michael's Seminary, was made Antigua's bishop in 1981.

Granada is 65 percent Catholic, has its own Antillean bishop, Sydney Charles, since 1975. St. Vincent and the Grenadines form another diocese, with Trinidadian Robert Rivas, O.P., as bishop.

St. Lucia was mostly Catholic, since it had been developed by the French, but it lacked priests. Eventually, though, the importance of this Catholic population was recognized when it was made a diocese in 1956 and an archdiocese (Castries) in 1974, and was given in the person of Bishop Kelvin Felix a native Dominica-born archbishop. The island population at present is 86.7 percent Catholic.

The Bahamas are not on the Caribbean, but on the Atlantic seaboard. This long chain of rather dry islands was the first place to be visited by Columbus on his discovery of America on Oct. 12, 1492. The Spanish depopulated them by waving slave raids of the native Arawaks called the Lucayos. The islands were spurned because they lacked mineral resources, foodstuffs and even fresh water. The process of incorporation of these difficult islands into the British colonial system in the New World followed this route: first came the Company of Adventurers, then the Proprietors from the Carolinas and finally the Crown took full control of the colony (1718–1787).

Dissenters from Bermuda were the first to settle the islands with permanence, in particular the island of Eleuthera. Bermudans dumped their social undesirables in the Bahamas. These dwellers were rather poor and depended more on the sea than on the land resources. A salt industry was developed in the Turks and Caicos part of the Bahamian chain. In the early 18th century the Crown governors themselves were traders in slaves, although the majority of Bahamians were still white. Since the Bahamian whites were quite remiss about their own practice of the Christian faith, they were even less eager to share it with their new slaves. In 1776 they were briefly taken over by the rebellious North American colonists. In 1781 the Spanish briefly captured them. Many North American loyalists settled in the Bahamas. In 1810 there were 4,232 Whites and 11,477 slaves. Thanks to the poor fertility of the soils Bahamian slaves were not as concentrated as others in English islands. They were employed in all sorts of occupations, since the islands were not primarily for agricultural exploitation. In 1834 slavery was abolished there.

But the Catholic Church was conspicuously absent up to these times in Bahamian history. The Apostolic Prelature of the Bahamas was created at a rather late date, in 1929. It was elevated to an apostolic vicariate in 1941. The Nassau bishopric was established in 1960 and it was a suffragan see to the Kingston Archdiocese until it was made a metropolitan Archdiocesan See in June of 1999. Its present bishop is a Jamaican-born Jesuit.

The Turks and Caicos Islands are still part of Britain's dominion in the West Indies. The Hamilton Diocese in Bermuda was first an apostolic prefecture (1953) and an apostolic vicariate in 1956. On June 12, 1967 it became a diocese and has an American-born religious bishop. It is a suffragan see of Nassau.

The Antillean Episcopal Conference. In the 1960s many islands started to gain their independence. The Holy See has provided for the dismemberment of the larger inter island dioceses into local "national" dioceses. There was a notable increase in the number of native-born originally diocesan priests as West Indian bishops. This had also happened in the Greater Antilles as well. Only the smaller islands, which usually had smaller Catholic populations anyways, have been grouped in with larger island dioceses (e.g., Antigua has the British Virgin Islands, Saba, St. Kitts, Montserrat). The older dioceses have been made archdioceses. The archdiocese of Port of Spain (Trinidad) has as suffragan sees the Dioceses of Paramaribo, Georgetown in Guyana and Willemstad in Curacao; the Archdiocese of Castries (in St. Lucia), has Kingstown in St. Vincent and St. Georges in Grenada as suffragan sees; the Archdioceses of Roseau (in Dominica), Nassau (Bahamas) and Kingston (Jamaica), has Belize in Central America as a suffragan see; finally there is the Archdiocese of St. Pierre-Fort de France (Martinique), which has Basse-Terre in Guadalupe and Cayenne in South America as suffragan sees.

The Antillean Bishop's Conference gathers all the non-Spanish West Indies except Haiti and also mainland countries like British Guyana, Dutch Guyana (Suriname) and French Guyana (Cayenne) as well as Belize and English-speaking islands in the North Atlantic region (Bahamas, Bermuda).

Some of the islands, however, remain attached to their former colonial masters: Turks and Caicos, Cayman Islands, British Virgin Islands, St. Marteen. Efforts on the part of CELAM (Latin American Episcopal Council) to include the various language groups in the fragmented Caribbean have lead to an insistence on the peculiarity of the Caribbean region within CELAM. More meetings are being held in the non-Spanish islands and some efforts at the level of seminary formation have succeeded in strengthening the feeble ties between the Caribbean islands which after such an important part of their history have been separated not by spatial distances but by national colonial interests.

Conclusions. If we are to synthesize we should say that the non-Hispanic West Indies had a very different ecclesiastical history from their Spanish neighbors. The Catholic Church, except in the French islands, existed as a minority within a plurality of religious denominations. It was not Episcopal from its inception, but took a long time to have its local bishops. The first efforts to colonize began in the 17th century. Scarcity of priests with diverse national origins and a mere transitory service would be common even unto the 19th century. Religious orders were the ones involved in the evangelization of the native remnant populations: some, like the Spanish Capuchins in Trinidad, were more successful than others (e.g., the French in Dominica, Martinique, Guadalupe, St. Lucia). Diocesan priests usually did not fare as well as Religious priests in the pastoral work on the islands. The parishioners tended to be of different linguistic groups. Religious ignorance was rampant. Many islands changed colonial masters and this created a peculiar situation: British or Dutch official intolerance combined with actual accommodation.

These islands had a very unsettled population as well as European high mortality rates and absentee ownerships of huge estates. A very frequent feature in Caribbean Catholic history is that lay and priest refugees from neighboring countries in turmoil tend to take over "permanent residence" and work in their tentative home. Intra island migration is also a consistent feature of pastoral reality on these islands: even slaves were resold in neighboring islands when sugar plantations were no longer viable in the older, soil depleted islands. Freed blacks sometimes preferred to leave the island where they had been slaves and get other employment in other islands. Such was the case in the Danish Virgin Islands after the abolition of slavery in 1848. Spanish laws in the late 18th century allowed for runaway slaves from English, Dutch and French islands to get their freedom once they professed the Catholic Faith on Spanish territory. This was a significant problem in Curacao, where many slaves fled to Venezuela to gain their freedom. Refugees from the wars of Venezuelan independence also came to Trinidad. Jamaicans looking for work went to Cuba in the 19th and 20th century to work in sugar plantations there. Jamaicans also worked in the construction of the Panama Canal. Many also went to the Caribbean coasts of Costa Rica, Guatemala, Honduras and Nicaragua, where they keep their eminently Protestant and English distinctiveness in a Hispanic context of young countries that are still trying to integrate these differing Caribbean coastal areas to their national identity and to their political and social integrity. Even today Colombians fleeing violence in their native country have sought employment in the smaller islands: in the Cayman Islands, for example, the Bishop of Montego Bay has to find Spanish speaking priests for them. Priests and other religious fleeing religious persecution in recently established Communist rule in Cuba and the later years of the Dictatorship of Trujillo in the Dominican Republic went to Puerto Rico, as had previously been the case with some loyalist clerics (including one of its 19th century bishops) fleeing the revolt against Spain in Venezuela and Peru.

After the natives were excluded, exterminated or absorbed the two great problems were the uneducated whites, not much inclined to religion, exposed to heterodox neighbors and the issue of slavery. When the semi private commercial Agencies that took over the islands could not depend on indentured servants as a labor force that was increasingly employed in sugar cane cultivation they resorted to massive importation of African slaves. The Spanish and French Crowns had a serious interest in christianizing the African slaves, not so the British (especially the established Church of England). The Dutch slave merchants had no interest at all. But Baptism was more an instrument of domination and pacification than of liberation. The Catholic Church as an institution was not very prominent in the fight for the abolition of the slave trade and slavery as such. The Church grew and prospered in the 19th century, especially with the arrival of new religious orders that belonged to the different colonial masters. The Holy See was active in the organization of the local churches only after the second quarter of the 19th century and it tended to follow the colonial structures, trying to get English priests for English islands and also for the formerly French and Spanish islands than had come under British domination. But it was hampered by its lack of influence in British colonial policies.

No significant ecclesiastical monuments remain from before the 19th century. But Catholicism made a significant contribution to the education of many Catholics and non-Catholics alike in the islands. Especially after 1960, it has become a more diocesan-run institution, with an increasing number of native diocesan West Indian bishops. Many pastoral situations continue to be a challenge, especially the disintegration of the family and the education of the faithful in their own Faith in order to withstand the Pentecostal and neo-African syncretic religious movements. Poverty continues to be a serious problem in the islands among many segments of the population. Migration to the larger islands and to the United States is an escape valve, but evidences the graveness of the problem. Independence has not brought the significant improvement that it promised and the economies continue to be frail and ever dependent on outside factors. Communion has much room to grow among these islands.

Bibliography: J. A. NOEL, *Trinidad, Provincia de Venezuela* (Caracas 1972). V. LEAHY, O.P., *Catholic Church in Trinidad, 1797–1820* (Port of Spain 1980); *Bishop James Buckley, 1820–1828* (Port of Spain 1980). F. OSBORNE, "La Iglesia Católica en el Caribe de habla inglesa,"; A. LAMPE, "La Iglesia Católica y la esclavitud en Curacao"; L. HURBON, "La Iglesia Católica y la esclavitud en las Antillas francesas durante el siglo XVII"; K. HUNTE, "Las iglesias protestantes y la esclavitud en el Caribe inglés"; all in *Historia General de la Iglesia en America Latina IV, Caribe* (Universidad de Quintana Roo, 1995). J. ROGOZINSKI, *A Brief History of the Caribbean* (New York 1999). C. V. BLACK, *History of Jamaica* (Kingston 1983). D. BISNAUTH, *A History of Religions in the Caribbean* (Kingston 1993). M. CRATON and G. SAUNDERS, *Islanders in the Stream, a History of the Bahamian People,* v. 1 (Athens, Ga. 1999). J. GAUCI, CSSR, *Redemptorist Apostolates in the Caribbean of the Nineteenth Century* (Santo Domingo, 1989).

[F. B. FELICES]

CARILEFFUS, ST.

Hermit; b. Aquitaine; d. *c.* 540. According to the two 9th-century lives, the only written evidence, Carileffus (Calais) was a monk at the Abbey of Ménat or at the Abbey of Micy. He set out with a companion, AVITUS, and he was ordained by Maximin of Micy (d. 520), bishop of Orléans. Leaving Avitus, he adopted a solitary life in the Diocese of Le Mans on the river Anille. The Abbey of Anille, later Saint-Calais, from evidence in royal charters of the eighth century, seems to have been built in his honor. It took his name perhaps in the ninth century when his cult is well attested. A diploma of 760 suggests that his body was buried at Saint-Calais, where, after its translation to Blois during the course of the Norman invasions, it was again returned in 1663.

Feast: July 1.

Bibliography: *Monumenta Germaniae Historica: Scriptores rerum Merovingicarum* 3:386–394, earliest life, fragments only. J.

MABILLON, *Acta sanctorum ordinis S. Benedicti* (Venice 1733–40) 1:621–633. A. M. ZIMMERMANN, *Lexikon für Theologie und Kirche,* ed. J. HOFER and K. RAHNER (Freiburg 1957–65) 2:941. *Bibliotheca hagiograpica latina antiquae et mediae aetatis* (Brussels 1898–1901) 1:1568–72. A. M. ZIMMERMANN, *Kalendarium Benedictinum,* (Metten 1933–38) 2:389. R. AIGRAIN, *Catholicisme* 2:369–370. J. HAVET, *Questions mérovingiennes,* 6 pts. in 1 v. (Paris 1885–90) pt. 4 *Les Chartes de Saint-Calais,* 5–58, 209–247.

[V. I. J. FLINT]

CARISSIMI, GIACOMO

Italian composer; b. Marino, April 18, 1605; d. Rome, Jan. 12, 1674. Nothing definite is known about his early training. After having served as a singer and organist at the cathedral in Tivoli and as *maestro di cappella* at the cathedral in Assisi, he became *maestro di cappella* on Dec. 15, 1629, at the church of San Apollinare (attached to the German College) in Rome, where he remained until his death. He was also active at the Oratory of San Marcello and, in July 1656, was named *maestro di cappella del concerto di camera* at the Roman court of Christina of Sweden. Such eminent musicians as M. A. CHARPENTIER, Bernhard, Kerll, and G. P. Colonna were his students, and the wide dissemination of his music, especially in Germany and France, won him an international reputation. Attempts were made to persuade him to work in Venice and in the Low Countries, but Carissimi refused to leave Rome. He was influential in introducing into sacred music techniques of the *stile moderno* employed in secular music, thus hastening the demise of the *stile antico.* Very little of his liturgical music (Masses, motets, psalms, *sacrae contiones*) is available in modern editions, but the use of *concertato* devices and monody is seen in the few examples that are at hand. His contribution to the nonliturgical Latin oratorio was of fundamental importance for that form, which he was the first to make artistically significant. (In fact HANDEL borrowed whole scenes from his work.) His 16 oratorios are not only important historically, they are also excellent music.

Bibliography: F. GHISI, *Die Musik in Geschichte und Gegenwart,* ed. F. BLUME (Kassel-Basel 1949–) 2:842–845. R. EITNER, *Quellen-Lexikon der Musiker und Musikgelehrten,* 10 v. (Leipzig 1900–04; New York n.d. [1947]) 2:332–335. J. LOSCHELDER, "Neue Beiträge zu einer Biographie Giacomo Carissimis," *Archiv für Musikforschung,* 5 (1940) 220–229. M. F. BUKOFZER, *Music in the Baroque Era* (New York 1947) 123–126. P. H. LÁNG, *Music in Western Civilization* (New York 1941). A. C. LEWIS, *Grove's Dictionary of Music and Musicians,* ed. E. BLOM, 9 v. (5th ed. London 1954) 2:70–73. P. M. YOUNG, *The Choral Tradition* (New York 1962). T. CULLEY, *A Documentary History of the Liturgical Music at the German College in Rome, 1573–1674* (Ph.D. diss. Harvard University 1965). R. W. ARDREY, *The Influence of the Extended Latin Sacred Works of Giacomo Carissimi on the Biblical Oratorios of George Frederic Handel* (Ph.D. diss. Catholic University of America 1964). F. CRUCIANI, "Il motetto *O Stupor et Gaudium* attribuito a Giacomo Carissimi," *Esercizi: Musica e Spettacolo* 16–17 (1997–98) 77–86. G. DIXON, *Carissimi* (Oxford 1986). G. MASSENKEIL, "Giacomo Carissimi," in *The New Grove Dictionary of Music and Musicians,* ed. S. SADIE, v. 3 (New York 1980) 785–794. D. M. RANDEL, ed., *The Harvard Biographical Dictionary of Music* (Cambridge, Mass. 1996) 135–136. N. SLONIMSKY, ed., *Baker's Biographical Dictionary of Musicians* (8th ed. New York 1992) 293. B. A. STEIN, *Between Key and Mode: Tonal Practice in the Music of Giacomo Carissimi* (Ph.D. diss. Brandeis University 1994).

[T. CULLEY]

Sheet music manuscript "Cantabo Domino," solo cantata by Giacomo Carissimi.

CARLISLE, ANCIENT SEE OF

The Ancient See of Carlisle was an English bishopric established by Henry I in 1133 with its seat at Carlisle, county Cumberland (Latin, *Carleolensis*). Originally the area was part of the kingdom of Strathclyde, having been Christianized by St. NINIAN and other Celtic missionaries from Glasgow. Later it was placed under the jurisdiction of the bishops of LINDISFARNE. Considerably impoverished during the Scandinavian invasions, it was then captured by King WILLIAM II (RUFUS) in 1092 and placed under the archbishopric of YORK. This aroused opposition from the bishops of both Glasgow and DURHAM, which may have prompted Henry I to establish Carlisle as a separate diocese. Henry's visit to Carlisle in 1122 was followed by a series of royal endowments for the priory of CANONS REGULAR, which he had founded there in 1102; in 1133 the PRIORY was raised to CATHEDRAL status, the king's confessor, Aethelwulf, being consecrated as its first bishop.

As a frontier see between England and Scotland Carlisle had a later history that was frequently turbulent, its bishops often being called upon to settle border disputes. Nevertheless, much construction work was carried on under great bishops such as John de Halton (1292–1324) and Thomas Appleby (1363–95), as their diocesan constitutions show. Among the religious orders introduced into the diocese were the Benedictines at Wetheral (1106–12) and St. Bees (1120), the Cistercians at Calder (1134) and Holmcultram (1150), another house for the canons regular of St. Augustine at Lanercost (1169), and the Premonstratensians at Preston, Kendal, c. 1180. As for the Mendicants, both the Franciscans and Dominicans arrived in Carlisle in 1233; the Carmelites, in Appleby in 1281; and the Augustinian friars, in Penrith by 1300. There were also six hospitals and two colleges in the diocese.

The Wars of the Roses, and later the Anglo-Scottish wars, contributed considerably to the spiritual decline of the diocese. The dissolution of its monasteries was completed with some difficulty between 1536 and 1540, but in general neither the religious nor the secular clergy offered much resistance to the ecclesiastical reforms of HENRY VIII, who refounded the see in 1541. Its present cathedral is one of the smallest in England.

Bibliography: *The Victoria History of the County of Cumberland,* ed. J. WILSON (London 1901–) v.2, basic. J. C. DICKINSON, *The Origins of the Austin Canons and Their Introduction into England* (London 1950) 245–251. D. KNOWLES and R. N. HADCOCK, *Medieval Religious Houses: England and Wales* (New York 1953) 132. F. POWICKE and E. B. FRYDE, *Handbook of British Chronology* (2d ed. London 1961) 212–214. A. PENN and E. MALLETT, *Carlisle Cathedral: The Stained Glass and the Carved Capitals* (Much Wenlock, England 1996).

[L. MACFARLANE]

CARLOMAN

Frankish mayor of the palace; b. before 714; d. Vienne, France, Aug. 17, 754. The assembly of nobles accepted CHARLES MARTEL's division of the Frankish kingdom between his eldest son Carloman, who received Austrasia, Alamannia, and Thuringia, and his younger son PEPIN III, who ruled in Neustria, Burgundy, and Provence, and the two brothers soon united to dispossess Grifo (d. 753), an illegitimate son of their father, of his rather meager inheritance. They then reduced revolts in Aquitaine and Bavaria and collaborated against rebellions of Aquitanians, Alans, Bavarians, and Saxons. They crowned the last Merovingian, the so-called son of Theuderich IV (d. 737), who became Childeric III. Carloman took the initiative in supporting the reform of the Church in Gaul, which was carried out by St. BONIFACE, and he established bishoprics in Würzburg, Erfurt, and Eichstätt. He arranged for reforming councils in 742 and 743 and secured metropolitan dignity for Boniface. The opposition of the nobles and the perils of war made it impossible for him to restore the church property confiscated by his father, but he gave new lands to the Church and endowed the Abbey of FULDA for Boniface. In 747 Carloman entrusted his lands and his children to his brother Pepin and went to Rome to become a monk. He built the monastery of St. Sylvester on Mt. Soracte, but later retired to MONTE CASSINO to escape the attentions of affectionate Frankish pilgrims. Later when Aistulf, King of the LOMBARDS, menaced the safety of Rome, Pope STEPHEN II, having asked in vain for aid from the eastern Roman Emperor CONSTANTINE V, turned to Pepin, who had with papal support declared himself king of the Franks. To counteract this appeal, Aistulf sent Carloman (whether willing or not is unknown) to intervene on his behalf or to rouse his former subjects in opposition to Pepin's policy of papal alliance. As Monte Cassino lay in the territory of the Duke of Benevento, a vassal of the Lombard king, it is probable that Carloman was under pressure to perform this difficult mission. He was entirely unsuccessful, however, as Pepin forced him into a monastery at Vienne, where he died the next year. His sons were deprived of their inheritance and were also confined to a monastery. Carloman was buried at Monte Cassino, and he was considered a saint during the centuries immediately following his death. He is still remembered in the BENEDICTINE calendar on August 17.

Bibliography: *Monumenta Germaniae Historica: Scriptores* 1:292, 329; 7:581. *Liber pontificalis,* ed. L. DUCHESNE (Paris 186–1958) 1:448. *Patrologia Latina,* ed. J. P. MIGNE (Paris 1878–90) 173:498. G. DRIOUX, *Dictionnaire d'histoire et de géographie ecclésiastiques,* ed. A. BAUDRILLART et al. (Paris 1912) 11:1058–60, with extensive bibliog. B. GEBHARDT, *Handbuch der deutschen Geschichte,* ed. H. GRUNDMANN (Stuttgart 1954–60) 1:125–27. T. SCHIEFFER, *Lexicon für Theologie und Kirche,* ed. J. HOFER and K. RAHNER (Freiburg 1957–65) 5: 1362–63; *Winfrid-Bonifatius und die christliche Grundlegung Europas* (Freiburg 1954); ''Angelsachsen u. Franken,'' *Abhandlungen der Akademie der Wissenschaften und der Literatur Mainz* 20 (1950) 1431–1529.

A. M. ZIMMERMANN, *Kalendarium Benedictinum: Die Heiligen und Seligen des Benediktinerorderns und seiner Zweige* (Metten 1933–38) 2:584–586. R. MACAIGNE, *L'Église mérovingienne et l'état pontifical* (Paris 1929) 287–292. J. MABILLON, *Acta sanctorum ordinis S. Benedicti* (Venice 1733–40) 4:112–118. J. DUBOIS, *Catholicisme* 2:561–562.

[C. M. AHERNE]

CARMEL, MOUNT

Mountain range stretching from Haifa, Israel, southeastward for about 15 miles and reaching a height of 1,800 feet above sea level. It separates the Plain of Saron (Sharon) on the south from the Plain of Aser on the north. The lofty headland of Carmel, with its church and Carmelite monastery, juts into the Mediterranean and can be seen for miles from a ship approaching the port of Haifa. Its Hebrew name *karmel* ordinarily means orchard, but here connotes a pleasant woodland. The range, which is still heavily wooded, but now mostly with scrub growth, was noted in antiquity for its magnificent forest (Am 1.2; Is 33.9; 35.2), symbolic of a land blessed by God (Jer 50.19).

Since antiquity Carmel has been regarded as a holy mountain. In the middle of the 2d millennium B.C. the geographical lists at Karnak called Carmel "the sacred cape"; Iamblichus (*De vita Pythagorica* 3.15) wrote that it was "the most holy of all mountains and forbidden of access to many," and Tacitus (*Hist.* 2.78) related that Vespasian, after offering sacrifice at Carmel's open–air altar, received the favorable oracle that hinted he would become emperor (see also Suetonius, *Lives of the Caesars* 8.5). This sacred mountain was chosen by Elijah as the site for the altar in the contest between him and the prophets of BAAL (1 Kgs 18.17–46). Tradition locates the place of Elijah's sacrifice on the rocky plateau of el–Muḥraqa on the southeast flank of the range. Carmel is now known in Arabic as Jebel Mâr Elyâs (Mountain of Lord Elijah).

Bibliography: *Encyclopedic Dictionary of the Bible* 324–325. F. M. ABEL, *Géographie de la Palestine* 1:350–353. D. BALY, *The Geography of the Bible* (New York 1957) 136–137. M. DU BUIT, *Géographie de la Terre Sainte* (Paris 1958) 65–66, 107. M. AVI-YONAH, "Mount Carmel and the God of Baalbek," *Israel Exploration Journal* 2 (1952) 118–124.

[C. MCGOUGH]

CARMELITE RITE

Until the liturgical reforms of Vatican II, CARMELITES had their own rite in the sense that they celebrate the liturgy according to liturgical books that were edited on their own authority, with approval granted by the Holy See.

The Franco-Roman liturgy, brought to Jerusalem by the Crusaders (1099) and adapted to the particular needs of the Holy City, was probably imposed on the Carmelites by Albert, Patriarch of Jerusalem, when he wrote their rule (*c.* 1207). However, when the Carmelites moved to Europe and their order changed from an eremitical to a mendicant one, the new situation brought a need for uniform liturgical celebration. The Jerusalem rite was too local in character; it could hardly be followed outside the Holy City itself. In the beginning there was disagreement as to what adaptation should be made. The solution imposed by authority in 1281 and 1294 prescribed the rite of Jerusalem according to the old Ordinal, with exceptions only for whatever was universal practice. It seems that these exceptions were indicated by special rules for simplification. Very likely, the old Ordinal, together with these rules, was at the basis of the new Ordinal, which was composed by Sibertus de Beka in 1312 and was the official code for the Carmelite liturgy until 1580. A more radical solution, however, was proposed in another Ordinal, made probably in England. This Ordinal greatly reduced the local elements of the Jerusalem rite and presented a structure of the Divine Office that was both strictly canonical and clearer. Though not accepted by the order at first, except perhaps in England, this Ordinal was adopted in 1584 and has remained the basic form of the Carmelite liturgy ever since.

Sibert's Ordinal followed the Jerusalem rite rather closely but eliminated some of its characteristic elements, such as processions. While the Ordinary of the Mass was similar to that of the Dominicans, the Proper reproduced the Jerusalem rite. However, there was an important difference: from being a memorial to the Holy Land, the rite became an expression of Carmelite spirituality, especially its devotion to the Mother of God. Uniformity was difficult to maintain because of varying devotions and the influence of local customs. After several attempts to reintroduce uniformity, Carmelite service books after 1544 tended to follow the Roman rite more closely.

The General Chapter of 1580 finally decreed a radical reform, which Petrus ab Apostolis implemented by adopting the Ordinal elaborated in England in the 13th century. Historians have claimed that this Ordinal was taken over from the Dominicans. Although the Carmelite and Dominican rites are similar, there are too many differences to allow such a simple solution. Some saints proper to the Jerusalem rite, its commemoration of the Resurrection, and many of its liturgical texts have been retained in the Carmelite rite. The structure of the 1580 rite was completely different from that in Sibert's Ordinal. The 1580 reform resulted in a new and more logical Office: superfluous texts were eliminated, commemorations of the Resurrection were reduced, and a better correspondence between liturgical texts was worked out. Few changes were made in the Missal: The Italian text (unfortunately, not the best tradition) was adopted, the order of the Gospels after Trinity Sunday was changed, and the rubrics were further adapted to the Roman rite. But despite the alterations introduced, one can still speak of continuity with earlier Carmelite tradition. There was a constant endeavor on the part of the order's authorities to adopt the Roman rite as the Discalced Carmelites did, but the Congregation of Rites was opposed. Yet in 1648 the Order was obliged to observe all feasts introduced into the Roman Missal.

From the beginning of the 20th century the authority of the prior general over the liturgy of the order was recognized. Roman feasts were no longer automatically introduced. New service books were printed, one of which, the Ceremonial of 1906, eliminated all the changes made since 1580. The reform of Pius X gave the order the opportunity to return to its calendar of 1580 with but a few exceptions. After Vatican II a decision was made to adopt the Roman Rite in place of the Carmelite Rite.

Bibliography: A. A. KING, *Liturgies of the Religious Orders* (Milwaukee 1955) 235–324. J. BOYCE, *Praising God in Carmel: Studies in Carmelite Liturgy* (Washington, D.C. 1999). P. KALLENBERG, *Fontes Liturgiae Carmelitanae* (Rome 1962).

[H. SPIKKER/J. SULLIVAN]

CARMELITE SISTERS

From the 13th century onward there are instances of women taking the habit and making vows according to the Carmelite Rule (*see* CARMELITES). The institution of Carmelite nuns, however, may be said to date from the bull *Cum nulla,* granted by Nicholas V on Oct. 7, 1452, to (Bl.) John SORETH. This bull, which gives permission to receive into order devout women of celibate life, was obtained in connection with the founding of the monastery of Our Lady of the Angels in Florence, Italy, later rendered illustrious by St. Mary Magdalene de' PAZZI. Carmelite nuns, who lead a strictly contemplative life, are found in 13 countries. Besides the cloistered nuns, 15 active sisterhoods are affiliated with the order and are represented in 29 countries.

[J. SMET]

Carmelite Nuns, Calced (OCarm). Official Catholic Directory #0300. Examples of the affiliation of professed women with the Carmelite Order already occured in Italy in the 13th and 14th centuries. *Conversae,* or oblates, made vows and were subject to the prior of the local friary, though they continued to live at home. Instances occur in Messina, 1283 (Bonaventura di Misano); Bolo-

gna, 1304 (Benvenuta Venturoli); Florence, 1309 (Diana Buzzadelli); Florence, 1374 (Santa Saluccio); Pisa, 1390 (Bonuccia Sardi). Eventually, in Florence, two communities of *conversae* were formed: the Nunziatina (1453) and St. Mary of the Angels (1454), rendered famous by its most illustrious member, St. Mary Magdalen de' Pazzi. Only in the following century did these monasteries receive the cloister.

On Oct. 7, 1452, the prior general, Bl. John Soreth, obtained from Pope Nicholas V the bull *Cum nulla* authorizing him to enroll women in the order. The institution of cloistered Carmelite nuns was thus canonically established.

Under Soreth's initial patronization, cloistered monasteries flourished in the Netherlands: Guelders (1453), Nieukerk (1455), Liège (1457), Dinant (1459), Huy (1466), Namur (1468), Vilvorde (1469, still extant). Outside Wallonia, other monasteries were founded in Flanders, but this early development was arrested by the Wars of Religion.

With the assistance of Bl. Frances d'Amboise, duchess of Brittany (1427–1485), who later entered the order, Soreth introduced Carmelite nuns into France: Bondon (1463), Les Couëts (1476). In France, too, growth was impeded by the religious wars.

In Italy, early growth was promoted by the reformed Congregation of Mantua: Parma (1465), Reggio Emilia (1485), Brescia (1486), Ferrara (1489), Mantua (1492), Trino (1493), Florence (1508). Illustrious members of this group of monasteries were Bl. Archangela Girlani (d. 1495) and Bl. Joan Scopelli (1428–1481). With Spain, Italy was to prove the most fertile soil for the development of Carmelite cloistered life.

The Spanish monasteries did not accept cloister until it was imposed by the Council of TRENT. An exception is the Incarnation of Valencia, which was enclosed from its foundation (1502). From the life of St. Teresa it is abundantly clear that the Incarnation of Avila, founded in 1479, was not obliged to the cloister. In Teresa's time, the order counted seven communities of nuns in Andalusia, one in Aragon, and three in Castile. Catalonia acquired Carmelite monasteries only in the 17th century.

The supressions of monasteries by Catholic monarchs who did not believe in the contemplative life, by Napoleon, and by the 19th-century liberal governments wreaked havoc among the Carmelite nuns. In the Spanish civil war, 1936–1939, three Carmelite nuns lost their lives: Mary of the Patronage of St. Joseph Badía Flaquer (1903–1936), Trinity Martínez Gil (1893–1936), and Josepha Ricard Casabant (1889–1936).

At present there are monasteries located in Italy, Spain, Portugal, Germany, the Netherlands, Brazil, Vene-

"Pope Honorius III Approves the Carmelite Order," painting by Pietro Lorenzetti, 14th century. (©Archivo Iconografico, S.A./ CORBIS)

zuela, the Dominican Republic, Puerto Rico, the Philippine Islands, Indonesia, and the United States.

From the monastery of Santa Croce, in Naples, the Carmelite nuns came to the United States in 1930. In that year, two nuns arrived in New York and founded their first monastery in Allentown, Pennsylvania. Three other foundations followed in subsequent years: Wahpeton, North Dakota, in 1954; Hudson, Wisconsin, in 1963; and Christoval, Texas (2000, moved from San Angelo, Texas).

Bibliography: C. CATENA, *Le Carmelitane: Storia e spiritualità* (Rome 1969). J. SMET, *Cloistered Carmel: A Brief History of the Carmelite Nuns* (Rome 1986). A. M. MARTINO, "Monasteri femminili del Carmelo attraverso i secoli," *Carmelus* 10 (1963) 263–312. See also the special number of the review *Carmelus* 10 (1963) 1–312.

[P. H. OTTERSON]

Carmelite Nuns, Discalced (O.C.D., Official Catholic Directory #0420); founded in Spain in the 16th century by St. TERESA OF AVILA, the Discalced Carmelite nuns are probably the best known of all cloistered orders of women. From the original foundation at Avila, this branch of the Carmelite reform movement spread throughout the world, and has numbered in its ranks many illustrious members.

Teresa of Avila entered the Carmelite convent of the Incarnation at Avila in 1533, but 20 years passed before she embarked on a completely generous program of spiritual living. As part of her own plan for a more dedicated life, she petitioned her superiors for permission to establish a single convent where a few nuns could follow the primitive Carmelite Rule and eliminate some of the abuses then existing at the Incarnation convent. There was much resistance and reluctance on the part of her own Carmelite superiors, the local ecclesiastical authorities, and the townspeople who feared that another convent would prove a financial burden to the area. But finally, on Aug. 24, 1562, Teresa and three other nuns occupied a small stucco building in Avila, which became known as the convent of St. Joseph. During her difficulties before and following the foundation at Avila, she was greatly aided by the Franciscan PETER OF ALCANTARA and the Dominican Pedro Ibáñez (d. 1565). Teresa originally intended to found only one convent, but her private revelations and the requests of bishops in Spain encouraged her to establish additional convents for cloistered Carmelite nuns. She spent the remainder of her life traveling through Spain organizing these convents, 15 of which she had founded by the time of her death in 1582. In 1600 there were 47 convents of Discalced Carmelite nuns.

ANNE OF JESUS was the dominant personality among the nuns after Teresa's death, and it was she who established the first foundation in the Low Countries at Brussels. Bl. ANNE OF ST. BARTHOLOMEW is credited with having saved the city of Antwerp by her prayers during the siege of 1622. Barbe Acarie (1566–1618), a noblewoman and mother of six children, introduced the nuns into France in 1604. She herself entered one of the convents in 1614, after her husband's death. Adopting the name of Mary of the Incarnation, she died after only four years in the convent of Pontoise, and was beatified in 1791.

In the 18th century, the order was distinguished by Bl. Mary of the Angels, daughter of a noted Italian family, who died at the Carmel of Turin in 1717; St. TERESA MARGARET, who died at the age of 22 at the Carmel of Florence; and the 16 nuns from the Carmel of Compiègne who were guillotined during the French Revolution in 1794, and beatified by Pius X in 1906. The 19th-century Carmelite from the French province of Normandy, St. THÉRÈSE DE LISIEUX, added new luster to her order. Her memoirs, published after her death, became a bestseller in spiritual literature, and Pius XI called her the greatest saint of modern times. A contemporary of Thérèse, a young French nun from the Carmel of Dijon, Sister ELIZABETH OF THE TRINITY, has also attracted considerable attention by her writings.

The first Discalced Carmelite convent in the United States was founded at Port Tobacco, Maryland, in 1790 by a group of nuns from the Carmel of Antwerp. This was also the first foundation of female religious in the original 13 colonies. In 1830 the Port Tobacco community moved to permanent quarters in Baltimore. At the beginning of the 21st century, there were 64 convents in the United States.

The life and work of the Carmelite nun is exclusively one of prayer and penance. There is no active apostolate, since the nuns dedicate themselves to praying for the work of the Church and for the sanctification of priests. Perpetual abstinence is observed, as well as a yearly fast from September 14 until Easter. The Divine Office is recited in choir each day, and two hours are devoted daily to formal meditation. The nuns are cloistered; they speak to visitors only through a grillwork in the convent parlor. A nun remains all her life in the convent she first enters, except when she is sent to join a newly established convent.

Bibliography: W. NEVIN, *Heirs of St. Teresa of Avila* (Milwaukee 1959). ANDRÉ DE STE. MARIE, *The Order of Our Lady of Mt. Carmel* (Bruges 1913).

[P. T. ROHRBACH/EDS.]

Carmelite Sisters for the Aged and Infirm. (Ocarm, Official Catholic Directory #0330); a congregation founded in 1929 by Mother M. Angeline Teresa to meet the need for modern methods of caring for the aged. The congregation, distinctively American in spirit, strives to preserve the dignity and independence of the individuals whom it serves. Mother Angeline Teresa, together with six companions who had gained experience in working with the indigent aged as Little Sisters of the Poor, began the community with the approval of Cardinal Patrick Hayes of New York. From 1929 to 1931 the sisters lived in the old rectory of St. Elizabeth's Church in New York City, where they prepared themselves spiritually and planned their new type of work. Toward the end of that period they accepted seven elderly guests and looked for larger quarters. The Catholic Charities of the Archdiocese of New York presented the religious with the downpayment for the property located at 66 Van Cortlandt Park South in the Bronx. Here the sisters maintained the mother-house and novitiate until 1947 when they transferred the headquarters of the community to Avila-on-the-Hudson in Germantown, New York.

The first home, named St. Patrick's, became the prototype of the homes the sisters founded in subsequent years. The sisters plan each new home with a view to providing the best geriatric care for persons 65 years of age and over, without distinction as to race, color, or creed. Affiliated with the Carmelite Order, the sisters live a community life according to the Rule of St. Albert and their own constitutions, which received the initial approval at Rome, July 16, 1957.

Bibliography: B. DE LOURDES, *Where Somebody Cares* (New York 1959); "Allies of the Aging," *Catholic Nurse* 5 (1956) 28–32. *Dizionario degli Istituti di Perfezione* (Rome 1974–) 2:402–403. J. MEAD, *The Servant of God, Mother M. Angeline Teresa, O.Carm (1893–1984)* (Petersham, Mass. 1990).

[M. P. LAPORTE]

Carmelite Sisters of Charity. (C.a.Ch., Official Catholic Directory #0340); a religious congregation with papal approval (1870, 1880), founded at Vich (Barcelona), Spain, in 1826 by St. Joaquina de VEDRUNA, assisted by Esteban de Olot (1774–1854), a Capuchin priest. The scope of the institute, whose members assume simple perpetual vows, is education and the care of the sick. Governing the congregation is a superior general, who is elected by a general chapter and who resides in Rome, together with her council. Provincial and local superiors are appointed for three-year terms by the superior general and council. By the 20th century, the congregation had spread from Spain to Italy, England, India, Argentina, Brazil, Chile, Peru, Venezuela, Cuba, Dominican Republic, Puerto Rico, and the United States. (1955).

In the United States, the sisters engage in the ministry of healthcare, nursing, academic education, parish ministry and pastoral work among Hispanics, immigrants and the homeless. The U.S. provincialate is in Silver Spring, Maryland.

[D. MCELRATH/EDS.]

Carmelite Sisters of Corpus Christi. (OCarm, Official Catholic Directory #0350); a congregation begun in 1908 when five English converts opened a school at the request of the Bishop of Leicester, England. The foundress was Clare Ellerker, later Mother Mary of the Blessed Sacrament. She remained the head and moving spirit of the community until her death in 1949.

In the beginning, Vincent MCNABB, who took an interest in their work, had formed them into Dominican Tertiaries. When the group grew to 50, they were invited to work in the British West Indies and in Duluth, Minnesota (1920). They then petitioned the Holy See to become a religious congregation, but Rome refused because they were too few in number. Invited a few years later to become Carmelites, they accepted and became an active community in that order, to be known as Corpus Christi Carmelites. In 1958 the community received its final approval from Rome. They have 19 houses in North America, England, and the West Indies. In the United States their headquarters are at Middletown, New York. The motherhouse and novitiate of the congregation is in Tunapuna, Trinidad. The sisters engage in varied work—homes for the aged and for children, Cana retreats, high schools and elementary schools, kindergartens, work with retarded children, and catechetical work.

Bibliography: K. BURTON, *With God and Two Ducats* (Chicago 1958). A. MULLINS, *The Corpus Christi Carmelites* (Dublin 1963). *A Great Adventure: The Story of Corpus Christi Carmel, by Some Corpus Christi Carmelites* (Trinidad, 1944; repr. Tunapuna, 1976). *Dizionario degli Istituti di Perfezione* (Rome 1974–), 2:406–407.

[K. BURTON]

Carmelite Sisters of St. Thérèse of the Infant Jesus. (C.S.T.; Official Catholic Directory #0380); an American diocesan congregation begun in Bentley, Oklahoma, in 1917. The founder, Agnes Cavanaugh, was born and educated in Schuylerville, New York. In its early years, the community worked in great poverty and hardship among the Choctaw tribe. Gradually, teaching became its most important work, and the congregation now staffs schools in Oklahoma and California. The sisters primarily engage in academic education, catechetics and parish ministry. The motherhouse is in Oklahoma City.

[C. T. CARTER/EDS.]

Carmelite Sisters of the Divine Heart of Jesus. (Carmel D.C.J., Official Catholic Directory #0360); a pontifical congregation affiliated with the Order of Discalced Carmelites, founded in Berlin, Germany, in 1891 for the rescue of orphaned and abandoned children. The foundress, Mother Mary Teresa of St. Joseph (Anna Maria Tauscher van den Bosch), a convert from Lutheranism, extended the work to Czechoslovakia, Hungary, Austria, Italy, Switzerland, and Holland. During her eight years in the United States and Canada (1912–20), she established 18 St. Joseph Homes for the children of the poor and for the aged of the middle class.

In 1930 the foundress obtained final approbation from the Holy See for constitutions that correspond with the original Rule of Carmel and prescribe a life of contemplation and active reparative charity. Besides homes for children and the aged, the sisters conduct nurseries, kindergarten and day centers. They also offer facilities for weekend retreats and days of recollection, and do house visiting.

The congregation has established houses in Europe, the United States, Canada, and Central America; the general motherhouse is in Sittard, Holland. In the United States, the congregation has three provinces: Northern (headquartered in Milwaukee), Central (headquartered in St. Louis) and Southwestern (headquartered in La Mesa, California).

Bibliography: *The Servant of God, Mother Mary Teresa of St. Joseph,* tr. B. BITTLE (Pewaukee, Wis. 1953).

[M. A. ENCK/EDS.]

Congregation Of Our Lady Of Mt. Carmel. (OCarm; Official Catholic Directory #0400) A religious community of women devoted to teaching, nursing, and social service work, founded in 1825 in Tours, France, by Charles Boutelou and Mother St. Paul Bazire. Within a decade, because of persecution, the sisters were forced to disband in France. Mother Teresa Chevrel and Mother Augustine Clero, having volunteered for a foreign mission, had come to the United States in 1833. In 1839 Bp. Anthony BLANC of New Orleans invited them to teach in that city. Gradually other schools were established. By 1961 the sisters conducted nine schools and administered one hospital in the Archdiocese of New Orleans and five schools in the Diocese of Lafayette, Louisiana. At the New Orleans motherhouse they also conduct Mt. Carmel Junior College for the education of their young religious. The congregation was aggregated to the Carmelite Order in 1930. In 1951 the sisters changed from the Rule of St. Augustine to that of St. Albert. They take simple perpetual vows. In 1957 the congregation became a pontifical institute, and in the following year its constitutions were revised accordingly. After 1960 applicants from the Philippine Islands were accepted. and in 1962 the first band of missionaries was assigned to the Philippines. In 1999, the congregation counted 21 foundations with 105 professed sisters.

Bibliography: C. NOLAN, *Bayou Carmel: The Sisters of Our Lady of Mount Carmel of Louisiana (1833–1903)* (Kenner, La. 1977). N. J. PERCHÉ, *Détails sur le mort et les obsè de M. l'abbé É Rousselon* (Lyon 1867).

[M. E. ROMAGOSA]

Congregation of the Mother of Carmel (Syro-Malabar). The first religious community for women in the SYRO-MALABAR CHURCH, founded in 1866 by Bl. Cyriac Elias Chavara at Koonammavu, Kerala. Rev. Fr. Leopold OCD, an Italian missionary and the delegate of the DISCALCED CARMELITES collaborated in the foundation. After the death of Bl. Chavara in 1871, Fr. Leopold directed the community until his transfer from India. In the beginning, the institute admitted members belonging to both Syro-Malabar and Latin Churches. The community was divided into Oriental and Latin groups, following the ritual separation in 1887 of the Catholics under the Archdiocese of Varapuzha. The Oriental group had to face a number of difficulties during the following years until Aloysius Pazheparambil became director of the convents and, in 1896, vicar apostolic of Ernakulam. He strengthened the organization, provided it with a written constitution, and helped in the establishment of many convents. The Congregation continued as independent diocesan communities in various Syro-Malabar dioceses until 1963, when all were united into one Papal Congregation with one superior general residing at the Mt. Carmel Generalate in Aluva.

At that time, the original rules, modeled on those of the Italian Carmelite Sisters of the Third Order Regular, were radically revised and the name of the community changed from the Third Order of Carmelites. The rules underwent further revision in the light of Vatican II and the 1990 CODE OF CANONS OF THE EASTERN CHURCHES.

Members of the Congregation take simple perpetual vows and wear a brown or white habit, scapular and veil.

In addition to their principal ministries of education and Christian formation, especially of women and children, the sisters also care for the sick and destitute, engage in social and family welfare, and other similar activities. Their charism is defined as "to remain united to God in contemplátion and consecrated to him in action."

From a small community within Kerala, the territorial boundaries of the Syro-Malabar Church, the Congregation has grown and expanded in Asia, Africa, Europe and the United States. By the end of 2000, there were about 6,000 members distributed in 19 provinces (12 in Kerala, 7 in other states of India) and 3 regions (all in India outside Kerala). The Generalate is at Aluva, India.

Bibliography: *C. M.C. Constitution* (Aluva 1998). *C.M.C. Directory* (Aluva 1996). JOSSY, C.M.C., *In the Shadow of the Most High* (Aluva 1997). *Indian Christian Directory* (Kottayam 2000) 1218.

[A. M. MUNDADAN]

CARMELITE SPIRITUALITY

Carmelite spirituality is rooted in the Vita Apostolica movement of the 12th and 13th centuries and flowers with a particular brilliance in the 16th-century Spanish Reformation, 17th-century France and again in the late nineteenth and twentieth centuries. Traditionally Carmelite spirituality has focused very narrowly, interpreting its experience through the writings of the two great mystical Carmelite Doctors of the Church, saints Teresa of Jesus (TERESA OF AVILA) and JOHN OF THE CROSS. Scholarship has extended the field in two directions. There has been a serious study of the medieval tradition preceding the two Spanish mystics, a study which has not only shown the Carmelite roots of the two great Doctors but which can stand on its own as a valued mystical tradition. There has also been a serious theological reevaluation of the works of Thérèse of Lisieux, a 19th-century French Carmelite named Doctor of the Church in 1997, a reevaluation that has moved her teaching from popular piety to serious mystical theology. Other contemporary Carmelite writers, most notably St. Edith (Teresa Benedicta of the Cross) Stein, Blessed Elizabeth of the Trinity, and Blessed Titus Brandsma, have added to the substance of this rich tradition.

Origins: The Primitive Carmelite Spirit. The Carmelites must be located in the context of the lay hermit movements that arose in Europe during the late 12th and early 13th centuries. These movements, typified by the disciples of Francis of Assisi and by the various hermit groups of central Italy that were united in 1256 to form the Augustinian Hermits, were a product of the great

12th-century renewal of the Church called the *Vita Apostolica* movement in which devout men and women strove to live in imitation of Christ and his twelve apostles. Central to this scheme was a radical poverty in which the hermit imitated the apostles sent out to preach with no bag, no spare tunic, no walking stick (Mt 10:10). Although the lay hermits were essentially contemplative, their identity cannot be separated from a mission of witnessing to the Gospel by both deeds and words. The medieval imagination did not dichotomize the apostolic and contemplative lives; the overflow of prayer was seen to be apostolic preaching. The hermits' zeal to imitate the poverty of Christ led them to a profoundly incarnational spirituality by which they approached the Divine Mystery through the humanity of Christ, a feature that has always remained central in the Carmelite tradition.

The phenomenon of lay hermits was by no means limited to Italy; the Latin Crusader kingdom was a particularly fertile ground for those who wished to live like the desert fathers. Sometime after 1193 with the peace that concluded the Third Crusade, hermits began to gather in the wadi 'ain es-Siah on the south-western slopes of Mount Carmel within sight of the Mediterranean. The names and origins of these hermits have not survived. Some were pilgrims to the Holy Land who decided to stay in the land of Christ as an expression of their religious conversion. Some had probably been hermits before Saladin's victory at Hattin (1187) forced the Latin population to evacuate the majority of the kingdom they had held since the First Crusade. Some perhaps were adventurers who had come to the Holy Land and there experienced a conversion. There is no evidence that the hermits living on Mt. Carmel had any sort of organization prior to the time that they chose a leader and approached the Latin patriarch, Albert of Vercelli (also known as Albert of Avogardo d. 1214), and asked him for a Way of Life (*formula vitae*) sometime between 1206 and 1214.

It is arguable whether Albert gave them their *formula vitae* or whether he ratified a proposal they presented to him. The document shows some evidence of two hands, and perhaps the *formula vitae* was actually a composite of precepts that expressed the simple form of life which they proposed to lead and Albert's spiritual exhortation to them about living a life of discipleship to Jesus Christ (*in obsequio Ihesu Christi*).

The Way of Life which Albert gave to the hermits is extremely simple with only a minimum of prescriptions. There is no mention of a habit. Albert mandated perpetual abstinence and a great fast from the Feast of the Holy Cross until Easter. The hermits were to hear mass daily, but pray the psalms alone in their cells. As was characteristic of hermits in the *vita apostolica* tradition,

Carmelite friar carving a crucifix. (©Philip Gould/CORBIS)

they were to have no private possessions. They were to submit themselves in obedience to their prior whom— Albert reminded them—Christ had placed over them. The prior, on his part, was to remember the scriptural injunction about the one who would be greatest serving the needs of the others. Unless they were legitimately occupied elsewhere, they were to remain in their cells meditating day and night on the Law of the Lord. This last injunction has been seen by many as being at the heart of Carmelite spirituality, but scholarship suggests that perhaps this is too narrow an interpretation. What is certainly central in the spirituality outlined in the Carmelite's Way of Life is attentiveness to the Word of God. Albert exhorted them: "Let the Sword of the Spirit, that is the Word of God, dwell in your hearts and on your lips, that all that you do you may do with the Word of the Lord for accompaniment." Carmelite spirituality is a spirituality of the Word of God. It was this immersion in the Word of God that generated the dynamism of their spirituality.

The rhythm of Carmelite life, established by these first hermits, is marked by collective and individual solitude, which creates an atmosphere in which union with God is achieved through continuous prayer. Specific religious discipline mandates silence, fasting, perpetual abstinence, manual work, vocal recitation of the psalms, the chapter of faults, and hearing mass. They were exhorted, in Albert's paraphrase of Eph 6:11–17, to don the spiritual armor of the moral virtues.

Jacques de Vitry, bishop of Acre from 1216 to 1228, testifies to this primitive vision writing: "(The hermits)

. . . after the example of the holy prophet, Elijah live on Mount Carmel—on that part of the mountain that is near Haifa, by the fountain of Elijah, close to (the Abbey of) St. Margaret of Carmel. They live as hermits. And there like bees they store their honey, offering the Lord the sweetness of their spirit in their little cells'' (Jacques De Vitry, *La Traduction de l'Historia Orientalis de Jacques De Vitry*, ed. Claude Buridant [Paris 1986], p. 96.)

Adaptation of the Ideal to the Mendicant Life. Life for the first generations of Carmelites was not static. In 1226 they sought the blessings of the Apostolic See on their project and Honorius III acknowledged that they lived a quasi-religious life as penitents. Many lay hermits were penitents, that is men and women dedicated to living what would be called a countercultural life in witness against the empty values of the secular society around them. In 1229 Gregory IX imposed a strict communal poverty on the hermits of Carmel so that they would be more free of worldly concerns and able to give themselves to contemplation. Various other papal bulls made modifications in their life until Innocent IV in 1247 named two Dominicans, Cardinal Hugh of St. Cher and Bishop William of Tortosa, to rework Albert's *formula vitae* into a proper religious rule. Innocent issued this rule by the Papal Bull *Quae honorem Conditoris* on Oct. 1, 1247, making the lay hermits canonical religious. The modifications of Albert's text introduced the common office, common refectory, and other details of conventual life, as well as the canonical requirements of the three vows of religion. At the same time, and with some bending of the text, the Carmelites were able to settle in cities and towns, undertake the ministry of mendicants, especially preaching and the hearing of confessions. The order quickly clericalized for these ministries, but was slower to move into academics. It became clear to all, however, that if the Carmelites were to preach and undertake the cura animarum, they would have to pursue proper theological education. By the end of the 13th century, they were at the universities along with the other mendicant orders.

These changes—ministry, clericalization, and education—affected the development of the spirituality of the order, not always for the better. Nicholas Gallicus, prior general of the order in the 1260s wrote a circular letter to the order, the *Ignea Sagitta*, lamenting the spiritual losses which the order suffered as a result of abandoning the life of rural hermits for urban mendicants. Nicholas's letter is a powerful description of the ideals of Carmelite spirituality that he was anxious to preserve for future generations and ranks only after the rule as the second foundational text for Carmelite spirituality. The letter extols the silence and solitude of the hermitage and while it speaks of the desert, it is not a dry and arid place,

but a lush refuge where nature turns the heart and the mind towards God. The *Ignea Sagitta*, known in English as the *Fiery Arrow*, contains the theme of bridal mysticism, in which the soul finds union with its Divine Spouse. This theme, which the Carmelite tradition takes from older sources, flowers richly in the *Spiritual Canticle* of Saint John of the Cross. Bede Edwards says that the *Ignea Sagitta* contains almost all the sanjuanist themes. He mentions the absolute transcendence of God, the theological virtues by which the soul comes into union with God, purity of conscience, attention to God alone, prayer, and mortification of the senses and the tongue. To Edward's list should be added the themes of the nuptial spirituality between God and the soul and the importance of self-knowledge in the spiritual life, and the blessedness of solitude. Nicholas also articulates the theme that Christ himself is the Mountain of our ascent to God, a theme which John of the Cross will develop fully in the *Ascent*.

Noteworthy also in the *Ignea Sagitta* is the allegorical and mystical use of scripture interpreted to critique the concrete issues which Nicholas believed his listeners needed to examine. It gives us a valuable insight on how rooted in the Word of God the actual spiritual experience of this outstanding Carmelite was.

Nicholas's eloquent testimony to the primitive Carmelite ideal ironically is a masterpiece of academic argument. Strewn with patristic and literary sources, artfully constructed, and elegantly argued, Nicholas clearly demonstrates the potential for spirituality to be articulated from head and heart together.

Nicholas was not unique in his call to return to the primitive vision of the founder. Contemporaneous with the *Ignea Sagitta*, the Franciscan Order was experiencing the tension between the Spirituals, a reformist faction who wished to preserve the radical vision of St. Francis, and the Conventuals, who were anxious to update that vision to contemporary circumstances that would enable them to better serve the Church ministerially. Among the Carmelites, however, there was to be no established movement to conserve the primitive charism. While some hermit communities continued to exist, Nicholas seems to have found no organized response to his call for the order itself to return to its eremetical character. Although Nicholas lamented Carmel's undertaking the urban mendicant life, it is doubtful that the Carmelites would have survived suppression at the Second Council of Lyon in 1274 had the order not shown some potential for pastoral usefulness. An interesting compromise is seen in that although Carmel embarked full sail on the sea of apostolic ministry, its spirituality retained the language of the desert.

The Elian Character. Their connection with Carmel, the mountain famous from antiquity for its connection with the proto-prophet, Elijah, made it only natural that the Carmelites would turn to him for inspiration. The testimony of Jacques de Vitry informs us that there was, from the earliest period of development, a clear identification of the hermits on Mount Carmel with the great prophet of that mountain. Sometime prior to the 1281 Constitutions of the Chapter of London, the Carmelites had developed an understanding of themselves as having descended from the "Schools of the Prophets" established by the Prophet Elijah on Mount Carmel. They chronicled this descent in the *Rubrica Prima* traditionally affixed to the Constitutions of the Order. This legend did not sound as outrageous to medieval ears as it does to moderns as a tradition going back to Cassian and other early monastic sources called Elijah the *Pater Monachorum* and attributed the development of the monastic life to the Old Testament prophet. The Carmelites, since they came from the mountain on which the prophet lived, simply asserted that they were the channel by which the monastic charism had passed down from the Hebrew prophet to the Christian desert-dwellers.

The Marian Character. There also has traditionally been a strong Marian theme to Carmelite Spirituality. Although Mary is mentioned neither in the rule nor the Fiery Arrow, Carmelites were devoted to her from the beginning. The original oratory on Mount Carmel was dedicated to her and the hermits themselves known as the Brothers of Saint Mary from Mount Carmel. A very old icon, perhaps dating from the end of the thirteenth century, is preserved in Cyprus and shows the brothers gathered under Mary's mantle for protection. The Carmelites espoused devotion to the Immaculate Conception, weighing in to the great theological debates of the Middle Ages on the Franciscan side in favor of the doctrine. By the early fifteenth century the Carmelites had invented a number of legends associating Mary's protection with the scapular of their habit. From the fifteenth century onward they spread devotion to the Blessed Virgin Mary by encouraging the laity to wear a miniscule version of their scapular.

The English Carmelite JOHN BACONTHORPE (d. 1348) who had studied at Paris and wrote extensively on a wide variety of medieval theological subjects, is the first of the order's great Marian authors. He is the first to explain the origins of the order's name being connected to the chapel on Mount Carmel and goes so far as to say that the order was founded for the purpose of venerating Mary. (Smet, *The Carmelites* I, p. 55). His commentary on the Carmelite rule seeks to demonstrate that the rule reflects the life and virtues of the Virgin. The title of the order, The Brothers of the Blessed Virgin Mary from

Mount Carmel, creates a curious devotion within the order to Mary as Sister alongside her more traditional title of Mother. In 1479 the Flemish Carmelite Arnold Bostius (1445–1499) wrote his work, the *De Patronatu et patrocinio BVM in dicatum sibi Carmeli ordinem*, which synthesizes Marian devotion (Smet, *The Carmelites*, I, p. 117).

Carmelite mystical writers of the period include Henry of Hane (1299) whose work showed the influence of Ekhardt, The Provençal Guido Terreni (d. 1342), the Bolognese Michael Aiguani (d. 1400) and the German Sibert de Beka (d. 1332).

Crystallization of the Spirituality: The Decem Libri. Carmel received a third foundational document in the *De Institutione primorum monachorum* which first appeared in the *Decem Libri* of Philip Ribot *c.* 1380. This book alleged itself to be the work of a fourth-century bishop of Jerusalem, John XLIV, chronicling the evolution of the order from the time of Elijah until the conversion of the proto-Carmelites at the preaching of the apostles on Pentecost. The work, while it draws on a variety of older sources, is a fourteenth-century work, presumably compiled by Ribot (d. 1391) himself. Its value, while not historical, is its rich exposition of the Carmelite spiritual tradition, outlining the traditional characteristics of Carmelite Spirituality. It develops a four-step process of growing into union with God based on a mystical interpretation of God's command to Elijah in 1 Kgs 17:3–4:

1. Turning away from the world and towards God
2. Mastering one's passions
3. Immersing oneself in charity, which is understood here to be primarily love of God, secondarily love of neighbor
4. And, strengthened by charity, vanquishing sin and being restored to original innocence. Once we have been so purified, we are ready to enjoy the Presence of God in contemplation.

The numerous printings, editions, and translations of Ribot's work (English by Thomas Bradley; French by Thomas de Lemborch; Spanish, anonymous in the Codex of Avila), in the century after its publication testify to its quick spread and its influence. The stories of Elijah's journey from the solitude of Carith to fulfilling the mission given him by God and of the evangelical role attributed to the mythical Carmelites who heard the preaching of the apostles, also brilliantly reconcile the apostolic life with the contemplative vocation of Carmel.

Efforts at Reform. The Institute of the First Monks can be seen not only as a creative mythology of its past, but as an inspiration for reform and renewal. While most of the other orders were already experiencing the rise of observant movements to counteract the laxity of the 14th century, the Carmelites were slow to reform. Their life had been somewhat relaxed with the mitigation of the rule by Eugene IV in 1432. Ironically, that was the very time that reform began to blossom, originating in the Tuscan convent of Le Selve near Florence and spreading to Mantua, which became the center of the first great Reform of the Carmelite Order. Le Selve was the convent of Nicholas Calciuri (d. 1466) who wrote the *Vita de santi e romiti del Monte Carmelo and the Vita fratrum del Sancto Monte Carmelo* to inspire members and affiliates of the order to recapture the spiritual vision of the founders (Smet, *The Carmelites* I. 74, 116). The Mantuan Reform produced several notables, most especially the great Italian humanist Blessed Baptist of Mantua (1447–1516). In addition to his elegant Latin poetry, he wrote a number of spiritual texts including *De vita beata* and *De patientia*. Contemplation is not achieved by legislation; nevertheless, the Mantuan Reform was effective in refocusing its adherents on the contemplative nature of the Carmelite tradition.

The fifteenth century saw several other reforms of the order in addition to Mantua. In 1456 the General Bl. John Soreth (1395–1471) promulgated a set of reform constitutions that eliminated private property, revoked all privileges exempting religious from the common life, restricting access and egress from the house, and imposing minimum ages for the novitiate and for ordination. Houses that chose the reform were given certain rights and privileges to protect the reform from those who did not want to accept its strictures. For those who did not accept the reform, known as the Conventuals, Soreth promulgated a new set of constitutions in 1462. This legislation eliminated the grosser violations of private property and imposed some measure of the common life on all, including academics and officials who had become used to a great measure of independence. While hardly observant, these constitutions set at least a minimal standard to reinforce against the breakdown of the common life. Soreth instituted a program of regular visitations to make sure that the constitutions were followed.

More serious attempts for reform were made in the sixteenth century. The eremetical life according to the unmitigated rule was introduced at Monte Oliveto near Genoa in 1516. This was followed by reform legislation proposed by Prior General Nicholas Audet in the *Isagogicon* of 1523 and incorporated into the *Caput Unicum* of the General Chapter of 1524.

The reforms of the fifteenth and sixteenth centuries were all concerned with the establishment of an evangelical life, a return to the purity of the ideals of the *Vita Apostolica* movement in which the order had been conceived. They were anxious to correct the many abuses regarding poverty that had crept into religious life. They were also, for the most part, concerned with establishing appropriate boundaries between the religious and the laity, especially regarding the monastic enclosure. Overall, reform focused on the structures of religious life; it was more an attempt to create the situations conducive to the spiritual life rather than to teach the spiritual life. Reform writing more often concentrates on concrete legislation rather than spiritual doctrine.

One of the tensions that appeared in the Reform movements was the dichotomy between the contemplative and the apostolic life. This tension grew much stronger after the Council of Trent when religious orders were increasingly forced to make a choice that would have been foreign to medieval religious and declare themselves either apostolic or contemplative, the later requiring the monastic enclosure. As long as this dichotomy was maintained—and that would be into the modern era—Carmel had a difficult time of keeping the balance that marked its original vision.

The *Devotio Moderna* and Carmel. A marked development of this period is the introduction of specified periods of mental prayer into the daily routine. For the first centuries of Carmel, mental prayer was the reflecting on the Word of God as it came to the Carmelite in the choir, in the refectory, in the chapter-room, and throughout his day. The friar ruminated on this word as he went about the tasks of the day. By in the fifteenth century various provinces, beginning with Portugal, introduced the custom of one or more daily periods reserved for mental prayer. This was at the same time that the practice of discursive meditation, made popular in the *devotio moderna*, was becoming popular. Meditation was seen to be a good preparation for the grace of contemplative prayer.

The mediation methods of the *Devotio Moderna* of the 14th and 15th centuries made popular once again the emphasis on the humanity of Christ, especially as it manifested itself in Christ's passion and death. While Carmelites were not prominent in this movement, this renewed emphasis had an impact on the whole Church and the work of many of the great Rhineland mystics was to pass down through the Franciscan spiritual writer Hendrik Herp (d. 1477) to the Spanish mystics, particularly to St. John of the Cross.

The Introduction of Nuns. It was in the mid-fifteenth century that Carmel finally received its first nuns. In May of 1452 Prior General John Soreth received into the order the beguines of Ten Elsen in the Netherlands. Later that same year the prior of Florence received the bull *Cum Nulla* from Nicholas V, permitting the prior general or provincials to receive women as Carmelite nuns. It was Soreth's hope that the nuns would be a tremendous boost in encouraging both reform and contemplation among the friars. It was a hope that only realized its potential a century later when a Spanish nun captured the imagination of the order in a way that no male reformer had been able.

St. Teresa. The reform of Saint Teresa of Avila can only be understood in the context of the Spanish Reformation instituted by the Catholic Monarchs Ferdinand and Isabella at the end of the *reconquista*. The Spanish Church anticipated many of the reforms of Council of Trent, and most of the religious orders generated observant branches as their members sought to embrace what they understood to be the primitive vision of their founders. The observants put a particular stress on poverty, penitential practices, and the contemplative life. Many of these movements, such as the discalced Franciscans of Peter of Alcántara, went barefoot as a sign of their commitment to return to unmitigated religious rules.

Teresa de Cepeda y Ahumada was born in 1515, the daughter of Alonso de Cepeda, son of a Jewish merchant of Toledo who had been forced to convert to Christianity, and Alonso's second wife, Beatriz de Ahumada. In 1535 she entered the Carmelite monastery of the Encarnación in Avila. Teresa learned about mental prayer early in her Carmelite life and she was profoundly influenced by Francisco de Osuna's *Third Spiritual Alphabet*. Although drawn to contemplative prayer, she lacked the discipline to persevere in it through periods of aridity. In 1554 she was profoundly moved by an encounter with a statute of Christ being scourged, and this experience proved to be the beginning of her mystical life (*The Book of Her Life* 9.1.9). From this mystical life came her great spiritual energy that directed the reform of Carmel and the great renewal of Carmelite spirituality.

When she initiated the reform of Carmel (Aug. 24, 1562) Teresa put before her eyes the model of the holy hermits from whom Carmel took its origin (cf. *Way of Perfection* 11.4), even though the structure she adopted for her nuns was cenobitic in form in conformity with the requirements of the Council of Trent (Efrén de la Madre de Dios, "El ideal de S. Teresa en la fundación de San Jose," *Carmelus* 10 [1963] 206–230). Looking back to the early hermits for inspiration, Teresa's contemplative ideal came forth from the atmosphere of solitude, silence, and prayer as demanded by the Carmelite Rule. In her first book written for the instruction of her discalced nuns, she centered the whole observance around mental prayer (cf. *Way of Perfection* 4.2,3). By mental prayer Teresa means an intimate sharing between friends—the soul and God (*The Book of Her Life* 8.5). The mystical life described in her autobiography is based on personal experiences that occurred only when she committed herself totally to God. The discalced Franciscan, Saint Peter of Alcántara, had a particularly strong effect on shaping her vision of observant life, even as her Jesuit spiritual directors facilitated her interior development. Through the years, Teresa received advice from many confessors and learned men of the secular clergy and of different religious orders. They did not change her Carmelite spirit but rather helped her shape it into a vital part of the renaissance of spirituality that was energizing the whole Church during the Catholic Reformation.

From its beginning, Teresa's reform of Carmel was scheduled by long periods of mental prayer each day. The constitutions of the discalced friars, written in 1567, prescribed three hours of solitary prayer. At least one of them was to be spent reading aloud the point to be meditated on during the mental prayer that followed (*Bibliotheca Mist. Carm.* 6 [Burgos 1919] 400). The interest in the contemplative life was not limited to the discalced reform and spiritual literature; even among the friars following the unmitigated observance, it showed signs of renewal. Miguel de Carranza wrote *Camino del cielo en siete jornadas para los siete diacute;as de la semana* (Valencia 1601). And Juan Sanz excelled as a master of contemplation (J. Pinto de Vitoria, *Vida del V. M. Fr. Juan Sanz* [Valencia 1612]).

St. John of the Cross. When the confessors and learned men were Teresa's own friars, their voice had the sound of her own traditions and of the doctrines and teachings of the *Institutio*. They approached and explained the reformed life and Carmelite spirituality in theological, scientific, and historical categories, bringing Carmel from isolation into dialogue with both the Church and the academy. Among them St. John of the Cross displayed a particular genius. According to his first biographer, José de Jesús Maria (Quiroga, 1562–1629) he had studied the spiritual heritage of Carmel in the light of patrology, history, and Bible in order to articulate the substance of contemplation, (*Historia . . . del V. P. Fr. Juan de la Cruz* [Brussels 1628] 1.4.37–38).

John of the Cross was not the inventor of a new doctrine but a wise man who framed his doctrine in principles so diaphonous that their ultimate consequences are seen at a glance to follow from them. For St. John the supernatural life pivots on two hinges: the soul and God. God is like a seed infused in the depths of the soul, where God dwells and whence God governs the soul and with it the whole body, so that God and the soul constitute in a sense one thing, thus making it possible to say with St. Paul "It is no longer I that live, but Christ lives in me" (Gal 2.20). The will is in charge of this supernatural metabolism. This transforming union takes place when the will submits itself completely to God's will. And it is achieved by an absolute turning away from everything that does not come from God. Although this is spoken of as negation, it is positive in its significance, for it is made up of acts of the love of God. The Triune God is not an abstract concept but a spiritual reality implanted in the apex of the human spirit, which, in its turn, is surrounded by many corporal crusts, like a dwarf fan-palm, to use the metaphor of St. Teresa (*Interior Castle* I.2.8).

John of the Cross begins his elaboration of the doctrine of perfect union of the soul with God by analyzing the characteristics of the body and of the spirit or soul, whether intellectual or sensitive. Like many others in the sixteenth century, John drew his underlying philosophical concepts from the lineage of Neoplatonic thought that came down from antiquity through—among others—Clement of Alexandria, Augustine, the Victorines, and Bonaventure, to give modes of expression to Christian thought. The abstract concepts of Aristotelian thought, theologically represented by Thomism, could not adequately convey the clear exposition of the spiritual realities of which John wrote and which he intended to be not so much subjects of theological reflection as guides for the spiritual life. The first fruit of the doctrinal influence of St. John of the Cross appears in the *Interior Castle* of St. Teresa. She tells of the opportune intervention of a "learned man," who was, in fact, John (*Interior Castle* IV, 1.8). Teresa's detailed analysis of the soul, pointing out potencies, passions, imaginations, thoughts, soul and spirit, is a superb treatise that shows the influence of John of the Cross (cf. Efrén de la Madre de Dios, *San Juan de la Cruz y el misterio de la Santísima Trinidad en la vida espiritual* [Saragossa 1947]).

Influence of St. John of the Cross in the 17th Century. The first disciples of St. John of the Cross, unaffected by the scholasticism which was to prevail afterward, follow his Trinitarian schema: José de Jesús Maria (Quiroga) wrote *Subida del alma a Dios* (Madrid 1656–59) and Inocencio de San Andrés (d. 1620) wrote *Teologiá mística y espejo de la vida eterna*. Cecilia del Nacimiento (1570–1646) wrote *De la transformación del alma en Dios*.

Others who did not depend as closely on John of the Cross were nevertheless outstanding and influential in their own right. Among them were Juan de Jesús Maria (Aravalles d. 1609) who redacted the *Instrucción de Novicios* for the discalced Carmelites. The great mystic Juan de Jesús Maria (Sampedro 1564–1615) played an important role in the spiritual formation in the Italian discalced congregation. His three volume *Opera omnia*, was edited by Ildefonso de S. Luis (Florence 1771–74). More eclectic and somewhat influenced by St. John of the Cross was Tómas de Jesús (Díaz Sánchez de Avila

1564–1627), author of numerous and profound mystical treatises, such as *De contemplatione divina libri sex*. (Jerónimo) Gracián de la Madre de Dios (d. 1614), although without scientific pretensions, was a most effective interpreter of Carmelite spirituality. He was devoted to the eremitical origins of Carmel and fond of the "cave" of Pastrana. To his contemplative fervor he added an indefatigable zeal in preaching and writing (*Obras del p. Jerónimo Gracián de la Madre de Dios*, 3 v., Burgos 1932–33). Driven from the Discalced, he spent his final years in the Ancient Observance where, at the request of the Prior General, Enrique Silvio, he wrote *Della disciplina regolare . . . dell perfettione e spirito con che si ha de osservare la regola . . . particolarmente quella sotto la quale vive l'Ordine della gloriosa Vergine del Carmine* (Venice 1600). This work had a wide diffusion among the Italian Carmelites, partly because of the interest Silvio took in it. For many years it was standard reading in the refectory.

St. John of the Cross also had eminent followers in the Ancient Observance, most notably Miguel de la Fuente (1574–1626), who borrowed his psychological structure in *Las tres vidas del hombre: corporal, racional y espiritual* (Toledo 1623). Another Carmelite of the Ancient Observance who showed himself a follower of St. John of the Cross was Pablo Ezquerra (1626–96), author of *Escuela de perfección, formada de espiritual doctrina de filosofía sagrada y mística theología* (Saragossa 1675; new edition, Barcelona 1965).

The French School and the Touraine Reform. Cardinal de Bérulle and the *parti devôt* that gathered in the salon of Mdme. Acarie were responsible for the revival of French spirituality at the close of the sixteenth century. While this revival extended far beyond Carmel, the cardinal's introduction to France of the Discalced Reform with Anne of St. Bartholomew and Anne of Jesus created a fortuitous blend of Carmel with French spirituality. Of particular note are the nuns Marie de l'Incarnation (Barbe Acarie d. 1618) and Madeleine de Saint Joseph (d. 1637). Avoiding the heresies of Jansenism and Quietism, prevalent at the time, the French tradition put a strong emphasis on the humanity of Christ, consistent with the teachings of Teresa and John.

An important figure in the French Carmel of the period is Brother Lawrence of the Resurrection (Nicolas Herman 1614–1691). Lawrence's work, consisting of various letters, maxims, and memories of conversations with him, was edited and published after his death by a French secular priest, Joseph de Beaufort. The doctrine is best summarized by the short treatise *Practice of the Presence of God*, which Beaufort drew from Lawrence's letters and conversations. Because Archbishop Fénelon recommended Lawrence to his Quietist followers, many orthodox Catholics overlooked him. Lawrence, however, enjoyed a wide popularity among Protestants. The Protestant pastor Pierre Poiret (1646–1719) published Lawrence's works in a French edition and a German edition, popular among the Pietists. Various English translation were well known in 18th-century Anglican circles, and no one did more to popularize Lawrence than John Wesley, the founder of Methodism.

Due in no small part to the example of the discalced, reform and renewal was to develop in the ancient branch of Carmel in France, producing a rich harvest of mystical writings. At Rennes, Philip Thibault (1572–1638) led a new and powerful revival of interest in stricter observance. Thibault avoided using the word "reform" to prevent a schism, such as had occurred in Spain. The best exponent of the mysticism that accompanied this revival of Carmelite ideals in France was the lay-brother John of Saint-Samson (1571–1636). His principal works are: *Les Contemplations sur les mysterieux effets de l'amour divin; De l'effusion de l'homme hors de Dieu, et de sa refusion en Dieu par voye mystique; La Vraye espirit du Carmel; Le Miroir et les flammes de l'amour divin; De la souverain consommation de l'âme en Dieu par amour (Les Oeuvres spirituelles et mystiques du divin contemplatif fr. Jean de St. Samson,* Rennes 1658). He treated the classic themes of the presence of the Trinity in the soul and the human form of God in Jesus Christ. Union with God is achieved through introversion, beginning by mastering the senses, until one gets to the spiritual potencies, whose vertex is God's dwelling place. Tourraine provided other important writers. Dominque de Saint-Albert (1596–1634) wrote *Théologie mystique, Traicté de l'oraison mentale,* and *Formulaire de l'oraison unitive.* León de Saint-Jean (1600–71) wrote a work called *Théologie mystique* (Paris 1654) as well as *L'ouverture des trois cieux de S. Paul* (Paris 1633). Pierre de la Résurrection, master of novices, authored *Le manuel des religieux profez pour servir à la conduite des seminaires et études des religieux de la province de Tourraine* (4 v. Nantes 1666), *De l'amour et de la connaissance de Jésus et de Marie* (2 v. Rennes 1664), and *Le gouvernement des passions* (Nantes 1662). Maur de l'Enfant Jésus (1618–90) wrote *L'Entré à la divine sagesse* (Bordeaux 1652), *Théologie chrétienne et mystique* (Bordeaux 1651); and *Le Royaume intérieur de Jésus-Christ dans les âmes* (Paris 1668). Daniel de la Vierge-Marie (1615–1678) while primarily remembered for his historical writings, made notable contributions to the spiritual literature of the order; his *Art of Arts* (Antwerp 1646) is a treatise on prayer according to Saint Teresa. But the most outstanding of all, with the exception of John of Saint-Samson, is the Venerable Michael of St. Augustine

(1621–84) for his *Institutionum mysticarum libri quatuor,* (ed. Antwerp 1671) containing his *Mary-form and the Marian Life in Mary* which anticipates the Marian spirituality of St. Louis Grignon de Montfort. Michael's emphasis on a spirituality that very much has Mary as its center and organizing principle marks a strong departure from the classically Christocentric Carmelite mystical doctrine.

Influence of Scholasticism. Meanwhile, in the discalced Carmel there emerged a powerful school of Carmelite mysticism reshaped by scholastic influences. Defending St. John of the Cross and crediting him with the doctrine of St. Thomas, who after the Council of Trent was the oracle of Catholic doctrine, the Discalced Carmelites built up their master's mystical doctrine with the stones of Thomism. At the same time, they formed the three great *cursus*: the *Complutensis* (University of Alcalá de Henares) in philosophy and the *Salmanticenses* (University of Salamanca) in dogmatic and moral theology. Diego de Jesús (Salablanca, 1570–1621) edited the works of St. John of the Cross with luminous *Apuntamientos* (explanatory notes) justifying his doctrine. Nicolás de Jesús María (Centurión d. 1655) defended it also in 1631 with his *Elucidatio theologica circa aliquas phrases et propositiones theologiae mysticae, in particulari V. P. N. Joannis a Cruce.* In a more positive form the Portuguese José del Espíritu Santo (Baroso 1609–74) wrote *Cadena mística: Enucleatio mysticae theologiae S. Dionysii, Primera parte del camino espiritual de oración y contemplación.* Antonio del Espíritu Santo, also a Portuguese, wrote *Directorium mysticum,* published in 1677, three years after its author's death. Antonio de la Anunciación (d. 1713) wrote *Manual de padres espirituales para almas que tratan de oración* (Alcalá 1679); *Disceptatio mystica de oratione et contemplatione* (1683); and *Quodlibeta mystica* (1712). In France Philippe de la Trinité published his *Summa theologiae mysticae* (1656), and Cyprien de La Nativité de la Vierge (1605–80), his *Traité de l'oraison mentale* (1650). Honorée de Sainte-Marie (1651–1729), a learned and polemic writer, defended his mystical school with *Tradition des pères et des auteurs ecclesiastiques sur la contemplation.* In Italy Baldassaro di S. Catarina di Siena (d. 1673) wrote an excellent commentary on the *Interior Castle,* illuminated with the doctrine of St. Thomas: *Splendori riflessi di sapienza celeste vibrati dá gloriosi gerarchi Tommaso d'Aquino e Teresa di Gesù* (Bologna 1671). In Spain Francisco de San Tómas (1707) made a summary of Carmelite mysticism in his *Médula mística, sacada de las divinas letras, de los santos padres y de los más clásicos doctores míticos y scolásticos* (1691). But the summit of this scientific ascent was achieved by the eminent Andalucian José del Espíritu Santo (d. 1736) with his *Cursus* *theologiae mystico-scholasticae*, which remained incomplete because of its author's death. This work put an end to the scholastic cycle of Carmelite mysticism. At this point, mystical writing had arrived at so insipid a conceptualistic analysis that it was necessary to abandon it and look for new horizons of greater relevance.

Postscholastic Development. Once the scholastic influence had run its course, Carmelites were left with two possibilities: either to defend the past, selecting texts and writing new commentaries, or to reopen the psychological route, which had been abandoned when the second generation of discalced mystics turned from the methodology of St. John of the Cross toward Thomistic scholasticism. Confronted with this dilemma, Carmelite spirituality both in the Ancient Observance and the Discalced Reform suffered a crisis of indecision, almost of sterility. (*El estado actual de los estudios sobre espiritualidad entre los carmelitas*, Trabajos del I Congreso de espiritualidad [Salamanca 1954; Barcelona 1957]). Fortunately, the modern era has seen the Carmelite heritage break free of the strictures of scholasticism and recover the vitality of its 16th- and 17th-century pinnacle.

St. Thérèse of the Child Jesus (Thérèse of Lisieux). Thérèse Martin, known as Thérèse of the Child Jesus or THÉRÈSE OF LISIEUX (1873–1897), marks a revitalization of the Carmelite tradition and its advancement into the modern era, recognized when John Paul II declared her Doctor of the Church, referring to her as the "Doctor of the Science of Love." Born in Normandy, the youngest child of a large family in which several siblings had died in infancy, Thérèse was surrounded with an extraordinary familial love from her birth. She was deeply affected by the death of her mother when she was four years old and it seems to have opened a wound in her psyche that only God could salve. That hurt provided the path of entry for an extraordinary grace that would transform Thérèse and through her touch countless people in the century after her death. She had a profound awareness of the tender mercy of God, a tenderness and forgiveness that seems to be related to her memories of her mother. A precocious child, she received permission to enter Carmel at the extraordinarily youthful age of 15.

Two of her sisters had preceded her into the monastery, and a third followed after the death of her father. By all outward signs, there was nothing that should have marked her for the extraordinary impact she made in her brief life. Her spirituality, deeply rooted in expressing Love of God through concrete acts of love towards neighbor, led her to a Christocentricity in which she lived out the death and resurrection of Christ in the midst of life's everyday occurrences. She recognized that true asceticism is not a matter of ferocious penance, but the far more difficult surrender of self-will. She instinctively practiced the prayer of the Presence of God, declaring that not three minutes could go by without her thinking of her beloved. Diagnosed with tuberculosis at the age of 23, she entered into a period of great spiritual darkness for the last seventeen months of her life. This was a great trial of faith in which she confessed she was in such spiritual darkness that she well understood the unbelief of the atheist. Despite the inner turmoil, her exterior manner was so cheerful and loving that not even her closest intimates knew the purgation through which she was going.

Thérèse would most likely have been forgotten to history except that her sisters had asked her to write down her memories of their childhood. Far from producing a collection of anecdotes, Thérèse related her memories as a narrative of the extraordinary grace that God had worked throughout her life. The journal, originally written in three different sections, was published the year after her death as *Histoire d'une âme* (*The Story of a Soul*) and became an outstanding spiritual classic of the twentieth century. Theologians began to look anew at Thérèse's writings and interpret them as serious writings in mystical theology. Modern editions of her autobiography, as well as her letters, poetry, and several short plays were edited and published, along with the records of her conversations in the final months of her life.

Blessed Elizabeth of the Trinity. Elizabeth of the Trinity (Catez) (1880–1906) was born in the district of Farges-en-Septaine, France. After the death of her father in 1887, Elizabeth, her mother, and her sister lived in modestly genteel circumstances in Dijon. Elizabeth was an accomplished pianist but chose to enter the Carmel of Dijon rather than pursue a career in music. Her choice of vocation did not delight her mother, who would have preferred to arrange a prestigious marriage. In accordance with her mother's wishes, she delayed entering until she was 21. In Carmel she took the title "of the Trinity" as the indwelling of the Trinity in the Soul was a very important theme for her, a spiritual gift that she was already experiencing. As she would later write, "our soul is indeed heaven where God dwells, where we must seek him and where we must remain." Her time in Carmel was brief; she developed Addison's Disease and died in 1906. In the months before she died she wrote several small treatises: *Heaven in Faith, Last Retreat, The Greatness of Our Vocation,* and *Let Yourself Be Loved* (all 1906). Although written as private reflections—one for her sister, one for a friend, and two for her superior in Carmel—they provide a spirituality as uniquely profound as it is compact. Her letters, her diary, and her poetry have also been edited and published.

Elizabeth had read Thérèse of Lisieux's *Story of a Soul* even before entering Carmel, and while she approaches many of the same topics, she does so from a distinct perspective and with a different style. Her work is marked by strong Pauline themes, at times having an almost evangelical flavor. Elizabeth understood the need for conformity to Christ in his suffering and death—a particularly poignant theme in a young woman terminally ill. In its silent surrender the soul is subject to the touch of the Holy Spirit so that consecrated to God's love it may become a "Praise of Glory (Eph 1:12)."

Saint Edith (Teresa Benedicta of the Cross) Stein. Edith STEIN (1891–1942) was born the youngest child in a large, prosperous, and orthodox Jewish family in Breslau Germany (now Wroclaw, Poland). Her father died when she was a toddler. An unusually gifted child, she briefly dropped out of school, but returned not only to finish basic studies but to go on into academic levels that had previously been restricted to men. She began her studies in psychology, but switched to philosophy under the influence of Edmund Husserl, the father of phenomenology, whose leading student and academic assistant she became. In 1916 she submitted her doctoral thesis, *Zum Problem der Einfühlung* (*On the Problem of Empathy*). While still an adolescent, Edith had ceased believing in the faith of her family, but a series of experiences caused the young phenomenologist to move beyond agnosticism and reexamine religious ideas with her keen philosophical insight. She converted to Catholicism after reading the *Vida* of Saint Teresa of Avila. She desired to enter Carmel, but under the influence of her spiritual directors she instead took an active role as a Catholic intellectual and feminist in between-the-wars Germany. Her research explored the possibilities of a dialogue between phenomenology and Thomism. While she taught at a teacher-training college run by Dominican nuns in Speyer, she traveled extensively, lecturing on Catholicism and modern philosophy as well as on the role of Christian women in the world. When the racial laws of the Third Reich made it impossible for her to teach or lecture, she finally received permission to enter Carmel. She entered the Cologne monastery in 1933. By her own admission, not being much good for housework, she was encouraged to continue her research and writing, which she now applied to Carmelite themes, particularly undertaking a contemporary analysis of John of the Cross.

In 1938 Edith and her sister Rosa, a convert to Catholicism, fled to the Carmelite convent in Echt, Holland. This escape from danger proved only temporary, and in August of 1942 they were arrested along with monks, nuns, and other religious of Jewish blood and deported. Edith lived out her science of the Cross during her brief imprisonment, transport, and death in Auschwitz. Calm and recollected to the end, she spent her energy comforting the women and children targeted for extinction because they, like her, belonged to the race of the Messiah.

Although Edith had lectured for years before entering Carmel and had done considerable research and writing after entering, very little of her work was published before her death. In addition to her dissertation, the most import of her works are *Endliches und Ewiges Sein* (*Finite and Eternal Being*) and *Kreuzeswissenschaft* (*The Science of the Cross*), both published in 1950. Editions of her collected works have been produced in most modern languages in the final decades of the twentieth century.

Blessed Titus Brandsma. Titus Brandsma (1881–1942) has been less studied than Edith Stein and Elizabeth of the Trinity because much of his writing has yet to be translated from the Dutch. Brandsma, a Carmelite friar of the Ancient Observance, mixed careers in academics and journalism. It was in the later role that he took the stance against Nazism that led to his arrest and eventual death at Dachau in 1942. However, it was in his distinctive academic career—he was on the founding faculty of the Catholic University of the Netherlands at Nijmegen in 1923 and later served as its *rector magnificus*—that he wrote and lectured extensively in mysticism, specializing both in the Lowlands and the Carmelite traditions. Although he wrote extensively for both popular and academic audiences, he produced no comprehensive synthesis of his spiritual doctrine. Touring the United States in 1935, he gave a series of lectures that, while intended to be more popular than scholarly, was the first attempt to present a historical synthesis of Carmelite Spirituality. It was published the following year as *Carmelite Mysticism: Historical Sketches*.

Other Twentieth Century Carmelite Figures. The rich spiritual treasures represented by Thérèse, Elizabeth, Edith, and Titus mark a definite advance of the tradition beyond its 16th- and 17th-century heritage. Their writings are only now being synthesized into a new school of Carmelite Spirituality. Among other authors who should not be overlooked in that process is the American poet Jessica Powers (Miriam of the Holy Spirit, 1905–1988).

There were many other Carmelites of the modern era whose lives testify to the depth of their spirituality as they served God by serving their neighbor in the midst of daily, but often extraordinary, lives. Most did not leave much in the way of written sources, but their biographies will be rich examples of the applied spiritual theologies—Père Jacques Bunel, the Admiral Georges (Louis de la Trinité) Thierry d'Argenlieu, Bl. Raphael Kalinkowski, Bl. Hilary Januszewski, Bl. Teresa of the Andes, the Carmelites of the Mexican Revolution, the Carmelites of the Spanish Civil War, Bishop Donal Lamont and the Carmelites of Rhodesia/Zimbabwe. These are only the most famous. The modern era will provide as rich sources for Carmelite Spirituality as any era in the order's past.

Bibliography: *Acta capitulorum generalium Ordinis fratrum B. V. de Monte Carmelo,* ed. G. WESSELS, 2 v. (Rome 1914–34). *Albert's Way: The First North American Congress on the Carmelite Rule,* ed. M. MULHALL. T. BRANDSMA, *Carmelite Mysticism, Historical Sketches,* (Chicago 1936). *Bullarium carmelitanum,* 4 v. (Rome 1715–68). E. CARROLL, ''The Marian Theology of Arnold Bostius, *Carmelus* (1962) 197–326. J.-B. CATHANEIS, *Speculum Ordinis fratrum Carmelitarum* (Venice 1507). C. CICCONETTI, *La Regola del Carmelo: origine, natura, significato* (Rome 1973). C. DE JESÚS SACRAMENTO, *La escuela carmelitana* (Avila 1923). D. A VIRGINE MARIA, *Speculum carmelitanum* (Antwerp 1680). B. EDWARDS, H. CLARK, *The Rule of St. Albert* (Aylesford, Kent) 1973. *Ephemerides carmeliticae* (Florence 1947). *Carmelus: Commentarii ab Instituto Carmelitano editi* (Rome 1954). *L'Eremitismo in Occidente nei secoli XI e XII; Atti dei seconda settimana internazionale di studio, Mendola 30 Augusto–6 Settembre 1962* (Milan 1965). E. FRIEDMAN, *The Latin Hermits of Mt. Carmel; A Study in Carmelite Origins* (Rome 1979). K. HEALY, *Methods of Prayer in the Directory of the Carmelite Reform of Touraine* (Rome 1956). V. HOPPENBROUWERS, *Devotio mariana in Ordine fratrum B. V. M. de Monte Carmelo a medio saeculi XVI usque ad finem saeculi XIX.* C. JANSSEN, *Les Origines de la réforme des Carmes en France au XVIIᵐᵉ siècle* (La Haye 1963). P. KALLENBERG, *Fontes liturgiae carmelitanae* (Rome 1962) W. MCGREAL, *At the Fountain of Elijah: The Carmelite Tradition* (1999). NICHOLAS OF FRANCE, *Ignea Sagitta,* ed. STARING, (*Carmelus* 9 1962) 3–52. P. RIBOT, ''De institutione et peculiaribus gestis Carmelitarum,'' *Speculum.* L. SAGGI, *La congregazione mantovana dei Carmelitani sino alla morte del B. Battista Spagnoli,* (Rome 1954). SILVERIO DE SANTA TERESA, *Historia del Carmen Descalzo,* 15 v. (Burgos 1935–52). J. SMET, *The Carmelites: A History of the Brothers of Our Lady of Mt. Carmel,* 4. v. (Darien IL, 1975). J. SMET, *Cloistered Carmel.* A. E. STEINMANN, *Carmel vivant* (Paris 1963). O. STEGGINK, *La reforma del Carmelo espanol, le vísita canónica del general Rubeo y su encunetro con santa Teresa (1566–67)* (Rome 1965). A. STARING, *Medieval Carmelite Heritage: Early Reflections on the Nature of the Order* (Rome 1989). C. DE VILLIERS, *Bibliotheca carmelitana* (Orleans 1752; Rome 1927). K. WAIJMAN, *The Mystical Space of Carmel* (1999). J.WELCH, *The Carmelite Way: An Ancient Path for Today's Pilgrim,* (New York 1996). B. ZIMMERMAN, *Monumenta historica carmelitana,* v. 1 (Lérins 1907).

[P. T. MCMAHON]

CARMELITES

(O.Carm, Official Catholic Directory #0270); the Fathers and Brothers of the Blessed Virgin Mary of Mount Carmel (OCarm), one of the MENDICANT ORDERS, originated on Mount CARMEL in Palestine.

Origin and Development. The conquest of the Holy Land by the crusaders (1099) brought to the Kingdom of Jerusalem, besides Latin religious orders, numbers of hermits who flourished in the West. During the 12th century, these settled especially in the sites traditionally associated with the life of the Savior: the Jordan Valley, Mount Quarantena, the flatlands in Galilee near the mount of the multiplication of loaves and fishes, the valley of Kedron beside Jerusalem, and even the walls of the city itself. The disastrous Battle of Hattin (1187) destroyed the military forces of the Latins, who were driven back to a strip of coastland, eventually extending from Tyre to Jaffa. Latin clergy and religious took refuge in Acre, which the Third Crusade restored to Latin hands (1191). The only site suitable for the eremitical life left in the Holy Land was Mount Carmel, and in the 13th century pilgrim accounts and chronicles begin to mention Latin hermits at the fountain of Elijah in the wadi 'ain essiah, a narrow valley opening into the sea on the western flank of Mount Carmel at the Bay of Haifa. These hermits were no doubt, partially at least, refugees from the other eremitical sites in Palestine. They received a rule, or *formula vitae,* from Albert, patriarch of Jerusalem, during the years he lived in the Holy Land, 1206–14. The date of origin of the order, long the subject of acrimonious debate, can thus be determined with relative accuracy as occurring 1192–1214.

The rule of St. Albert, a medieval rule that has been little noticed by historians, shows the Carmelites leading an eremitical life and practicing perpetual abstinence, fasts, and silence. In the midst of the cells stood an oratory where the religious assisted at daily Mass ''when this can conveniently be done.'' Those who could read recited the psalms that ''the institutions of the holy fathers and the approved custom of the Church assigned to each hour.''

The hermits dwelling on Mount Carmel had a particularly keen sense of the continuity of monasticism with the way of life of Elijah and of others of the Old Testament. The statement prefixed to the constitutions of 1281 may be taken to reflect the viewpoint of the primitive Carmelites: ''From the time when the prophets Elias and Eliseus dwelt devoutly on Mount Carmel, holy fathers both of the old and new testament . . . lived praiseworthy lives in holy penitence by the fountain of Elias in a holy succession uninterruptedly maintained'' (*AnalOCarm* XV, 208).

Mount Carmel, however, did not prove as safe a haven as expected, and the hermits began drifting back to the West in search of asylum. In 1238 some migrated to Frontaine (site unknown) on Cyprus, Messina, Marseilles, and Aylesford and Hulne in England. In Palestine they established sites in the suburb of Acre and ultimately in Tyre.

The Carmelites brought with them from the Holy Land their own liturgical rite, a form of the rite of the Holy Sepulchre in Jerusalem. It received definitive form in the *Ordinal* of Sibert de Beka (*c.* 1312). The Carmelite rite was abandoned and the Roman rite adopted in 1972.

Many of the new foundations were no longer located in remote places, the proper habitat of hermits, and the Carmelites felt obliged to request the Holy See to be allowed also to settle in populated areas. Permission to this effect was granted by Pope Innocent IV by his letter, *Quae honorem,* Oct. 1, 1247. By this document, also, the *formula vitae* of St. Albert became a canonical rule.

The Carmelites gradually moved into the cities and began to engage in the apostolate after the manner of the mendicant orders. They managed to survive the Second Council of Lyons (1274), which abolished all mendicant orders, except the Franciscans and Dominicans, but granted provisional approval to the Carmelites and Augustinians. Later (1298), Boniface VIII extended unconditional approval to the latter two. In 1326 John XXII extended the *Super cathedram* of Boniface VIII to the Carmelites, thereby making them partakers of all the privileges and exemptions of the Franciscans and Dominicans. This act completed the gradual process by which the Carmelites became mendicants. Their original striped mantle was replaced by a white one in 1287.

Carmelite life in Palestine was totally extinguished with the fall of Acre and the other Latin strongholds in 1291, but the province of the Holy Land, reduced to the houses on Cyprus, continued to exist until 1570, when the Turks took the island. The Discalced Carmelites returned to Mount Carmel in the 17th century and are there today. Excavations begun in 1958 uncovered the foundations of the monastery and chapel near the fountain of Elijah.

By the end of the 13th century the order numbered over 150 houses, divided into 12 provinces scattered through Cyprus, Sicily, England, Scotland, Ireland, France, Italy, Germany, and Spain. During the 14th century the number of houses doubled, and the provinces reached a total of 21. In the 15th century the order underwent a final phase of expansion in Scandinavia, Eastern Europe, and Portugal.

Medieval Growth and Decline. The entry of the Carmelites into the ranks of the mendicants brought with it the need for learning. The constitutions of 1281 established a *studium generale* at Paris, but only in 1309 did the Carmelites move from a site on the way to Charenton (outside Paris) to the left bank of the Seine to a house provided by PHILIP (IV) the Fair in the Place Maubert. By 1294 houses for philosophy were established in Toulouse, Montpellier, London, and Cologne. By 1324 the *studia generalia* included also Bologna, Florence, and Avignon. Oxford and Cambridge, though never officially designated *studia generalia,* were highly regarded, and

Aerial view of Aylesford Monastery, Kent, England.

drew students from overseas. The Carmelites arrived too late in the scholastic period to establish a distinct school. Noteworthy Carmelite scholastics were: Gerard of Bologna (d. 1317); Guy Terrena of Perpignan (d. 1342); JOHN BACONTHORP; Michele AIGUANI; and Thomas NETTER of Walden, author of the *Doctrinale antiquitatum fidei Catholicae* against the Lollards.

The original oratory on Mount Carmel had been dedicated to the Blessed Virgin, and the Carmelites made their vows to God and Our Lady. In Europe, Carmelite devotion to Mary underwent rapid development and became characteristic of the order. Everywhere the Carmelites dedicated their new churches to the Blessed Virgin and established Marian confraternities. The Marian title of the order was often defended in the early writings of the Carmelites; the constitutions of 1294 declared that the order was to be identified by the name of the Blessed Virgin. In the course of time, Marian devotion was especially promoted through the brown scapular of Our Lady of Mount Carmel.

During the Western Schism (1378–1417) the Carmelites, like other religious orders, followed pope and antipope according to regional loyalty. The general of the time, Bernard Oller, a native of Minorca and residing with his curia in Avignon, followed Clement VII. The Ur-

Eremitical convent at Wölfnitz, Austria.

banist portion of the order elected Michele Aiguani of Bologna in 1381. Both groups abided by the Council of Pisa (1409) and adhered to Alexander V and John XXII. In 1411 the order was unified under one general, John Grossi.

In 1432 the rule underwent a second mitigation that authorized the use of meat three days a week and walking in the cloisters at suitable times. The regulations for fast and abstinence were later modified still further. Today the prior general has full powers in this matter.

By the 15th century religious observance had considerably declined. Reaction to abuses produced movements of reform, Observantine groups, typical of the times. Some time before 1413 the reform of Mantua arose in northern Italy. In the Rhineland and in the Low Countries reforms originated in the convents of Mörs (1441) and Enghien (*c.* 1447). These movements achieved official status with the election of Bl. John SORETH, who issued new constitutions in 1462, eliminating the more serious abuses. In addition, his reform prescribed the renunciation of temporal goods and privileges, observance of the common life, curtailment of outside activity, and exclusion of seculars from the monastery. The reform of Soreth was effective especially in Germany, the Low Countries, and northern France.

Another pre-Tridentine reform was inaugurated in Albi by the reforming Bishop Louis d'Amboise in 1499. Under the leadership of Louis de Lire (d. *c.* 1522) it spread to the convents of Rouen and Melun and to the *studia generalia* of Paris and Toulouse. In Italy the re-

formed convent of Monte Oliveto, founded at Multedo (Pegli) near Genoa in 1514, followed the rule of 1247.

During the Renaissance the order produced a number of noteworthy humanists, including the Florentine painter Fra Filippo Lippi; John Crastone (fl. 1475), author of an early Greek lexicon and psalter; and Bl. BAPTIST OF MANTUA, whose many poems appeared in more than 500 editions.

The Protestant Reformation wiped out the provinces of Saxony, Denmark, England, Scotland, and Ireland. The remaining provinces of Germany, the Low Countries, and France suffered much from the wars of religion. Outstanding in the defense of the Catholic faith were Povl HELGESEN, in Denmark; Eberhard BILLICK, in the Archdiocese of Cologne; and Andreas Stoss (d. 1540), son of Veit Stoss, the sculptor, in the Diocese of Bamberg (Germany). At the head of the order in those parlous times was Nicholas Audet, prior general from 1524 to 1562. Besides his labors in doctrine and discipline at the Council of Trent, Audet carried on the reform of the order, neglected since the death of Soreth. In 1524 he published newly revised constitutions.

The Reforms of the Counter Reformation. Giovanni Battista Rossi (1507–88), better known by the Spanish form of his name, Rubeo, carried on the reform of the order in the spirit of Trent. In the quickened atmosphere of the Counter Reformation, with its strongly mystical bent, the order hearkened back to its eremitical origins. St. Teresa of Ávila, during her lifetime, founded convents where the cloistered contemplative life was led, and with the help of St. John of the Cross, inaugurated a reform among the friars. The reform group became involved in a conflict with the order over jurisdictional rights, and was censured by the general chapter of 1575. Eventually peace was restored, and in 1593 the discalced friars became a separate order (*see* CARMELITES, DISCALCED).

In France, during the 17th-century spiritual revival, a movement emphasizing the contemplative ideal began in the convent of Rennes in the province of Touraine. Under the leadership of Philippe Thibault (1572–1638) it spread throughout the province and all of France, the Low Countries, and Germany. In Italy several independent movements arose: in northern Italy, the reform of Piedmont; in Naples, the reform of Santa Maria della Vita; in Sicily, the reforms of Santa Maria della Scala del Paradiso and of Monte Santo, trends that spread also to the Papal States. Reformed convents and provinces sprang up in Poland, Brazil, Portugal, and Spain. The general chapter of 1645 amalgamated all these convents under one discipline, called the Stricter Observance, to be ruled by uniform constitutions. These constitutions (1650), basically those of Touraine, emphasized the contemplative character of Carmelite life.

The renewed religious fervor gave the order new vitality. Old convents were repopulated and restored, and many new foundations were made, among them a number of hermitages. A flourishing spiritual literature was developed by such writers as JOHN OF SAINT-SAMSON, Michael of St. Augustine, MARK OF THE NATIVITY, Maur of the Child Jesus, and Michael de la FUENTE. In the other theological sciences a number of *summae* and compendia were produced. An attempt to make John Baconthorp's doctrine the official teaching of the order met with little success.

Interest in the origins of the Carmelites produced an abundant historical literature, not always of a critical nature. Juan Bautista de LEZANA wrote the official history of the order, *Annales* (4 v. Rome 1645–56). Daniel of the Virgin Mary edited early texts in his *Speculum Carmelitanum* (4 v. Antwerp 1680). The appearance of the *Acta Sanctorum*, which called into question the Carmelite claim that the prophet Elijah had founded the order, was the signal for a violent debate with the BOLLANDISTS. In 1698 Innocent XII imposed silence on both parties.

Carmelite devotion to Mary found expression in numerous works by authors, such as Lezana, Matthias of St. John, Daniel of the Virgin Mary, and Andrea Mastelloni. It was principally through popular devotional works and sermons that the order spread devotion to the Blessed Virgin. The brown scapular of Our Lady of Mount Carmel became one of the most widespread Marian devotions in the Church. In Michael of St. Augustine and the Carmelite tertiary Mary of St. Theresa Petijt, Marian devotion achieved mystical proportions.

In the period after Trent the missionary activity of the order took definite form. Although individual Carmelites labored in Spanish America (for example, Antonio VÁZQUEZ DE ESPINOSA), the organizing of work there was rendered impossible by the restrictions of Philip II and his successors. The province of Portugal founded a mission in Brazil (1580) from which the provinces of Bahia, Pernambuco, Rio de Janeiro, and Maranhão-Para developed. The province of Touraine founded a mission in the West Indies in 1646 that lasted until the French Revolution.

Destruction and Renewal. As in the case of other orders, the century between 1770 and 1870 was disastrous for the Carmelites. During the earlier part of this period absolutist governments suppressed convents and interfered in the internal government of the order. In 1766 the provinces of France were organized into a national order; in 1804 a similar arrangement was decreed in Spain. The French Revolution swept away the provinces in France and Belgium, while the Napoleonic hegemony led to suppression in Germany, Italy, and Spain. After 1815 absolutist and liberal governments alike continued the war on religious orders. The general chapter of the Carmelite order in 1788, on the eve of the French Revolution, was the last to be held for half a century. During the 19th century only four general chapters were convened, whereas these are normally held every six years.

With the relaxation of oppressive laws, the revival of the order became possible. In 1889 the province of Spain was erected. In Italy by 1909 the remnants of the order had been gathered into the provinces of Tuscany, Rome, Naples, and the commissariate of Sicily. In 1879 Straubing (Bavaria) was added to Boxmeer and Zenderen in Holland to make the province of Germany and the Netherlands. From Straubing in 1864, the American province of the Most Pure Heart of Mary was founded. The province of Ireland had been reestablished as early as 1738 and in 1840 numbered seven houses. Ireland originated provinces in Australia (1881) and New York (St. Elias, 1889). Spanish and Dutch friars helped revive the Brazilian provinces of Rio de Janeiro and Pernambuco early in this century. In 1900 the International College of St. Albert was opened in Rome. In 1904 the prior General, Pius Mayer, issued new uniform constitutions, uniting the whole order under one observance. He also ordered the publication of a ritual (1903) and ceremonial (1906) of the Carmelite rite. In 1909 he inaugurated the journal for scientific studies, *Analecta Ordinis Carmelitarum*. His successor, Elias Magennis, published constitutions in 1930, which governed the order until the Second Vatican Council. The most recent constitutions are those of 1995.

Present Status. The order consists of 19 provinces, two commissariats general, and three delegations, situated in Italy, Malta, Spain, Portugal, France, Germany, Austria, Poland, the Czech Republic, the Netherlands, the United Kingdom, Ireland, Brazil, Peru, Venezuela, Colombia, Bolivia, Zimbabwe, Australia, Indonesia, the Philippines, Puerto Rico, Mexico, and the United States. The order numbers 2,019 members (1999).

The order is governed by a prior general and his council, consisting of a procurator general and four assistants general. The general chapter, held every six years and attended by the priors provincial and commissaries general and their *socii,* elect the general and his council and enact general laws. Between general chapters, Councils of Provinces and General Congregations are held. Within each nation the order is divided into provinces, each governed by a prior provincial and four definitors. Commissariats general are jurisdictions preliminary to becoming provinces. Individual houses or convents are governed by a local prior and his council. Priors and provincials are elected every three years at the provincial chapter for a maximum of two terms. The prior general and his council reside in Rome, via Sforza Pallavicini, 10, 00193, Rome.

The *studium generale* of the order, the International Center of St. Albert in Rome, houses graduate students from all the provinces for the priesthood. The Institute for Carmelite Studies, founded in 1951, publishes the review, *Carmelus,* as well as monographs on Carmelite spirituality, Mariology, and history.

The Carmelite order proposes to its members a life of contemplation, community, and apostolate. The habit consists of a brown woolen tunic with leather belt, scapular, and hood. On certain occasions a white mantle is worn.

Lay Carmelites (Third Order Secular). The female branches of the Carmelite second and third orders are treated elsewhere (*see* CARMELITE SISTERS). In addition, men and women living in the world have adopted the Carmelite spiritual ideal by following the rule in accordance with their state in life. For the benefit of such persons the Carmelite Third Order was created by the bull *Dum attenta* of Sixtus IV (1476). The taking of vows by Carmelite tertiaries is optional. There is also a Carmelite SECULAR INSTITUTE, the Leaven, which has its headquarters at Chislehurst, Kent, in England.

Bibliography: J. SMET, *The Carmelites,* 4 v. in 5 (Darien, Ill. 1976–88). A. STARING, *Medieval Carmelite Heritage* (Rome 1989). C. CICCONETTI, *La regola del Carmelo* (Rome 1976). V. MOSCA, *Alberto, patriarcha di Gerusalemme* (Rome 1996). B. M. XIBERTA Y ROQUETA, *De scriptoribus scholasticis saeculi XIV ex ordine Carmelitarum* (Louvain 1931). T. BRANDSMA, *Carmelite Mysticism: Historical Sketches* (Englewood Cliffs, N.J. 1936). K. HEALY, *Methods of Prayer in the Directory of the Carmelite Reform of Touraine* (Rome 1956). V. HOPPENBROUWERS, *Devotio mariana in Ordine Fratrum B.M.V. de Monte Carmelo, saec. XVI–XIX* (Rome 1960). E. M. ESTEVE, *De valore spirituali devotionis s. scapularis* (Rome 1953). *Ordinaire de l'Ordre de Notre Dame du Mont-Carmel par Sibert de Beka (vers 1312),* ed. B. ZIMMERMAN (Paris 1910). P. KALLENBERG, *Fontes liturgicae Carmelitanae* (Rome 1962). A. M. FORCADELL, ''Ritus Carmelitarum Antiquae Observantiae,'' *Ephemerides liturgicae,* 64 (1950) 5–52. T. M. NAVARRO, *Tertii carmelitici saecularis Ordinis historico-iuridica evolutio* (Rome 1960). *Bullarium carmelitanum,* ed. E. MONSIGNANO and J. A. XIMENEZ, 4 v. (Rome 1715–68). J. BATTISTA LEZANA, *Annales sacri, prophetici, et Eliani Ordinis Beatissimae Virginis Mariae de Monte Carmelo,* 4 v. (Rome 1645–56). DANIEL A VIRGINE MARIA, *Specilum carmelitanum,* 4 pts. in 2 v. (Antwerp 1680). C. DE VILLIERS, *Bibliotheca carmelitana,* ed. G. WESSELS, 2 v. in 1 (Rome 1927). *Analecta Ordinis Carmelitarum Calceatorum* (Rome 1901-). *Analecta Ordinis Carmelitarum Discalceatorum* (Rome 1926-). *Carmelus: Commentarii ab Instituto Carmelitano editi.*

[J. SMET]

CARMELITES, DISCALCED

The Order of Discalced Friars of the Blessed Virgin Mary of Mount Carmel sprang from the 16th-century reform inaugurated by St. Teresa of Avila and St. John of the Cross. The Discalced Carmelites, whose mode of life was a return to the observance of the primitive Carmelite rule, had their origin in Spain, but soon spread to Italy, the rest of Europe, and across the world.

Reform Movement. Five years after Teresa of Avila had successfully launched the reform of the Carmelite nuns, she obtained permission, in 1567, from the prior general of the Carmelite friars, Giovanni Battista Rossi (1507–88), for the foundation of two monasteries of men who would follow the primitive rule. She acquired a small piece of property at Duruelo, a place equidistant between the Spanish towns of Salamanca and Avila, and there on Nov. 28, 1568, the first monastery was officially started. The original community comprised only three members: Joseph of Christ, a deacon; Anthony of Jesus, who had resigned as prior of the Carmelite monastery at Medina del Campo to become the new prior at Duruelo; and John of the Cross, then a young priest ordained only a year previously. Soon new members joined the reform in great numbers; some came from the Carmelite Order itself, while others were new recruits. Under the sponsorship of PHILIP II, king of Spain, the Discalced Carmelites enjoyed an instant popularity and new monasteries were rapidly founded. By the time of Teresa's death (1582), there were 15 monasteries.

Teresa of Avila's purpose in sponsoring the reform of the Carmelite friars was to reestablish Carmelite objectives and disciplines that had become weakened over the two preceding centuries. The official mitigations in the rule allowed by Eugene IV in 1432, as well as the other unofficial mitigations of the pre-Tridentine era, were eliminated. Perpetual abstinence from meat and the yearly fast from September 14 to Easter were reinstated, and more time was given to the exercises of the spiritual life, particularly mental prayer. Members of the reform were originally called Contemplative Carmelites, but soon became known as Discalced Carmelites, because of their custom of wearing sandals. The older group hence came to be known, by way of contrast, as the Calced Carmelites.

Despite its rapid development, the reform movement was involved in severe difficulties at the outset. The initial permission for the reformed monasteries was granted by the prior general on the condition that the new monasteries be founded only in the province of Castile in Spain and that the whole reform movement remain within the original Carmelite Order. The discalced, however, began to found monasteries outside Castile, and there developed a desire to separate themselves from the original order. The difficulty between the calced and the discalced was based on the dual ecclesiastical jurisdiction that regulated the activities of the reform. Philip II, intensely interested in the regulation of the religious orders of Spain, had obtained from the Holy See apostolic visitators for the various orders. The visitators appointed for the Carmelites, Pedro Fernández de Recalde (d. 1580) and Francisco Vargas, both Dominicans, possessed more authority over the order than the general himself. The difficulty was compounded in 1573 when Vargas delegated his faculties to a young Discalced Carmelite priest, Jerome GRATIAN. In 1574 Gratian received even wider faculties from the apostolic nuncio, Niccolò Ormaneto (d. 1577). In this peculiar jurisdictional arrangement, the discalced made new foundations with permission granted by Gratian. Primitive systems of communication and the uncertainty of both parties regarding the exact nature of Gratian's faculties produced a tense struggle.

At the general chapter conducted at Piacenza, Italy, in 1575, stern measures were adopted to curtail the activities of the discalced and limit them to a few monasteries in Castile. It was during the execution of these decrees that John of the Cross was apprehended by the calced friars in 1577 and imprisoned by them for eight months in the monastery at Toledo. Ultimately, through the mediation of Philip II and the apostolic nuncio, the difficulties were settled, and the discalced were established as a separate province within the order in 1581. Finally, on Dec. 20, 1593, Clement VIII established the Discalced Carmelites as an independent religious order with their own superior general and administration.

Expansion and Subsequent History. In 1582 the discalced friars sent their first missionaries to the Congo, but the entire expedition was lost at sea. A second group suffered the same tragic consequences, but finally a third group reached the Congo successfully. The Spanish discalced, however, were not enthusiastic about the spread of the order beyond the confines of Spain. The worldwide expansion of the order thus fell to the Italian branch. Monasteries of the reform had already been founded in Genoa, Venice, and Rome, when Clement VIII in 1600 separated the three monasteries and their 30 priests from the Spanish Carmelites, thus creating two separate congregations within the reform, Spanish and Italian, a division that lasted until 1875. From the Italian group the reform spread throughout Europe in the early 17th century—to Belgium, France, Germany, Poland, Lithuania, and even to missions in England.

THOMAS OF JESUS (Díaz Sánchez de Avila), whose work influenced the establishment of the Congregation for the PROPAGATION OF THE FAITH, promoted missionary activity among the discalced. One of their more important mission endeavors was in Persia. In Sumatra two Discalced Carmelites, Bl. DIONYSIUS OF THE NATIVITY and Bl. Redemptus of the Cross, suffered martyrdom (1638). Prosper of the Holy Spirit led a small group to Palestine (1634) and reoccupied Mt. CARMEL, the ancient seat of the order, which had not been inhabited by Carmelites since their expulsion by the Saracens in 1291. The monastery newly reconstructed there was twice destroyed by the Turks in 1720 and 1821. The present monastery on Mt. Carmel, completed in 1853, houses the international school of philosophy for the order. The superior general who resides at Rome, is, according to the legislation of the order, the prior of the monastery on Mt. Carmel.

The European provinces of the order were largely destroyed during the revolutions and suppressions of the 18th and 19th centuries. The restoration of the provinces took place after the middle of the 19th century, and in 1875 Leo XIII united the Spanish and Italian congregations. A new missionary movement ultimately brought Discalced Carmelites to Asia, South America, and the United States. In 1907 there was founded in Rome the College of St. Teresa and St. John of the Cross, an international house of theology for members of the order; in 1957 the Institute of Spiritual Theology was established there.

The first permanent foundation in the U.S. was made at Holy Hill, Wis., in 1906 by friars from the Bavarian province. In 1916 friars from the province of Catalonia founded a monastery in Washington, D.C. These two groups were united in 1940, and in 1947 the monasteries of this union were established canonically as the Province of the Immaculate Heart of Mary. In 1915 Spanish friars exiled from Mexico established themselves in Oklahoma, and ultimately made additional foundations in Texas and Arkansas. These monasteries of the southwestern section of the U.S. were constituted as the Province of St. Therese (1935). Since 1925 friars from the Irish province have staffed monasteries in California. In 1983, the monasteries in the Western states were constituted as the California-Arizona Province.

Carmelite Way of Life. The daily life of the Discalced Carmelite combines prayer and apostolic activity. The Divine Office is recited in common, and two hours are devoted to meditation each day, one in the morning and the other in the afternoon. Silence is maintained in the cloisters throughout the day, except for an hour of recreation in the afternoon and an extra hour in the evening during the summer. Perpetual abstinence is maintained, as well as the yearly six-month fast. The friar lives in a cell, a small room containing only a simple desk and bed made of planks. Apostolic activities, such as preaching, administration of the Sacraments, and spiritual direction, are undertaken insofar as they are considered comformable to the contemplative ideal of the order. Discalced Carmelites teach their own friars who are studying for the priesthood but do not conduct schools for lay people. The order has always considered itself the custodian of the writings and doctrine of St. John of the Cross and St. Teresa of Avila, and the four centuries of its existence have witnessed a large production of books and periodicals concerning spiritual theology.

One of the early institutions of the reform was the ''desert,'' a monastery of complete eremitical life where the friars could retire for a year at a time to engage in a life of solitude and silence. The first desert was founded by Thomas of Jesus at Bolarque in Spain (1592). The deserts were destroyed during the revolutions, but a number have since been rebuilt. Friars of any province may, with permission of the superior general, spend a year in one of these deserts.

Bibliography: O.C.D., Official Catholic Directory #0260. BRUNO DE JÉSUS-MARIE, *St. John of the Cross*, ed. B. ZIMMERMAN (New York 1957). E. A. PEERS, *Handbook to the Life and Times of St. Teresa and St. John of the Cross* (Westminster, Md. 1954). SILVERIO DE SANTA TERESA, *Historia del Carmen Descalzo en España, Portugal y América*, 14 v. (Burgos 1935–49). JOACHIM DE L'IMMACULÉE CONCEPTION, *L'Ordre des Carmes* (Paris 1910). H. PELTIER, *Histoire du Carmel* (Paris 1958). *Analecta Ordinis Carmelitarum Discalceatorum* (Rome 1926–). *Ephemerides Carmeliticae* (Rome 1947–).

[P. T. ROHRBACH/EDS.]

CARMELITES OF MARY IMMACULATE

The Carmelites of Mary Immaculate (CMI; Official Catholic Directory #0275) is a religious congregation of priests and brothers of the Syro-Malabar Church, founded at Mannanam, Kerala (India), in 1831 by Thomas Palackal, Thomas Porukara, and Blessed Kuriakose Elias CHAVARA, three native diocesan priests. Palackal and Porukara soon died, and Chavara had to carry on the work alone. It was the first religious institute among the Malabar Catholics. Members, who are mostly clerics, take simple perpetual vows. Blessed Kuriakose, who took his religious vows with ten other priests when the institute was canonically erected in 1855, was superior until his death in 1871. During his lifetime seven monasteries were established. The following eight decades saw the Carmelites spread throughout Kerala.

In the beginning their rule/constitution was a modified version of that of the Discalced Carmelites. Through various revisions radical changes were introduced so much so that the original rule finds only a very distant echo in the present constitution. The Holy See approved the first constitution in 1885 and 1906, and a revision of them in 1958. A more radical revision started after Vatican II and the new constitution was approved by Rome in 1983. Slight modifications were made in 1996 and 1997. Governing the congregation is a prior general, assisted by four councillors and an auditor general, all of whom are elected every six years. Each provincial superior and his four councilors and provincial auditor are chosen for three-year terms. The Generalate is located in Ernakulam, Kerala (India).

From its inception, the congregation has always labored to serve the church in Kerala, focusing on preaching retreats, training clergy and lay ministers; educating the youth and disseminating Christian literature; laboring for the conversion of non-Christians and for the reunion of all Christians; undertaking works of mercy and operating charitable institutions. As the congregation grew, it was divided into three provinces in 1953. The number of provinces increased during the last fifty years and at present there are 13 provinces (six in Kerala, seven in other states of South India and North India, and one mission region in West India). In 1962 the congregation was entrusted with a mission territory in the Archdiocese of Nagpur in central India. After that four more mission dioceses were entrusted: Sagar (MP), Rajkot (Gujarat), Jagadalpur (MP), Bijnor (UP/Uttaranchal).

Since the 1950s, the CMI has experienced tremendous growth. By the end of the 20th century, membership was over 2,300 with 224 houses and 130 mission stations.

Outside of India, the congregation has an active presence in Africa (Ghana, Kenya, Madagascar, Namibia, South Africa, Tanzania), Australia, Canada, Papua Guinea, Europe, South America and the USA. The North American headquarters is located in Brooklyn, NY.

Bibliography: K. C. CHACKO, *Father Kuriakose Elias Chavara: Servant of God* (Mannanam, India: 1959). *The Carmelite Congregation of Malabar* (Trichinopoly 1931). *The Syrian Carmelite Congregation of Malabar* (Kottayam 1955). *(CMI) Constitutions and Directory* (Kochi 1997). *Carmelites of Mary Immaculate (CMI) Directory* (Kochi 1997). "Carmelites of Mary Immaculate (CMI)," in *Indian Christian Directory* (Kottayam 2000, 1249–1250).

[A. M. MUNDADAN]

CARNAP, RUDOLF

Philosopher; b. Ronsdorf, Germany, 1891; d. Los Angeles, Calif., Sept. 14, 1970. Carnap was the most prominent representative of logical empiricism (also called logical positivism and neopositivism). He was *privat-dozent* at Vienna from 1926 to 1931, professor at Prague from 1931 to 1936, at Chicago from 1936 to 1952, and at Los Angeles from 1954 to 1961. His principal contributions were in the areas of meaning, logic, philosophy of science, and philosophy of probability.

In the theory of meaning, his work centered on the verification theory of meaning, the view that the meaning of sentences consists in the conditions of their verification. Carnap's initial formulation identified verifiability with translatability into phenomenalist language (not, however, using visually oriented "sense-data" as primitive) and the task of philosophy with the "logical construction" of all human knowledge. As a by-product of this analysis, he deduced the meaninglessness of metaphysics as a result of its untranslatability.

Convinced in the early 1930s by his research and by discussions with his colleagues of the Vienna Circle (of which he was a leading member) of the untenability of his original position, Carnap rejected phenomenalism for physicalism, reinterpreting the empirical basis of protocol statements concerning physical observations and measurements and rejoining translatability—being able to eliminate theoretical terms—in favor of testability—being able to test derived observations—as the criterion of meaning. This he liberalized further in the 1950s, finally arriving at the requirement that a sentence is meaningful if it really adds to the observation statements derivable from a theory. Carnap nevertheless felt that the more liberal criterion ruled out metaphysics while retaining established science.

In logic, Carnap developed logical syntax, which he hoped could be used to establish his philosophical view

but whose influence has proved greater in pure logical theory. He also contributed substantially to formal semantic theory. More important yet was his work on modal logic, which introduced the semantic treatment later developed by Kripke.

Much of the work of his last decades was devoted to establishing the possibility of constructing the logical concept of probability by semantic concepts. This work, successful technically, failed to have the philosophical impact he anticipated because of his inability to establish convincingly a unique probability concept.

Carnap's intellectual honesty and his demonstration of the power of modern logic has had an overwhelming influence on a whole generation of philosophers.

Bibliography: Carnap's most influential studies: *Die logische Syntax der Sprache* (Vienna 1934), tr. *The Logical Syntax of Language* (London 1937). "Testability and Meaning," *Philosophy of Science* 3 (1936) 419–471, 4 (1937) 1–40. *Meaning and Necessity* (Chicago 1947). *Logical Foundations of Probability* (Chicago 1950). "The Methodological Character of Theoretical Concepts," in FEIGL et al., *Minnesota Studies in the Philosophy of Science* 1 (Minneapolis 1956) 38–76. *Philosophical Foundations of Physics* (New York 1966). Other important works: *Der Raum, Logical Construction of the World, Pseudo-Problems in Philosophy, Philosophy and Logical Syntax, Introduction to Semantics and Introduction to Symbolic Logic.* Significant books on Carnap: KRAUTH, *Die Philosophie Carnaps* (Vienna 1970). P. A. SCHILPP, ed., *The Philosophy of Rudolf Carnap* (La Salle, Ill. 1963). BARONE, *Filosofia* 4.353–392. CAPONIGRI, *Les grandes courants de la pensée mondiale contemporaine,* ser. 3, 1.267–295.

[N. M. MARTIN]

CARNESECCHI, PIETRO

B. Florence, Dec. 24, 1508; beheaded and burned as a heretic, Rome, Oct. 1, 1567. He was the son of a Florentine merchant and was well versed in the classics. He became the secretary of Clement VII, Cardinal Giulio de Medici. Between 1536 and 1540 he made the acquaintance of Juan de Valdés, Bernardino Ochino, and Peter Martyr Vermigli; in 1541 he was in the circle of Reginald Pole in Viterbo. The apostasy of Ochino and Vermigli in 1542 brought Carnesecchi under suspicion, but in 1546 he was acquitted of heresy for lack of evidence. He then was the guest of Catherine de Médici in France. In 1552 he was in Venice, where with D. Grimani he favored the Lutheran attitude toward the Reformation. He rejected Paul IV's demand that he appear in Rome and was condemned for contumacy in 1558; but on the death of Paul IV, he secured an annulment of the condemnation. He remained under suspicion, however, and Pius V reopened the case. After a trial lasting a year he was condemned and executed.

Bibliography: G. K. BROWN, *Italy and the Reformation to 1550* (Oxford 1933). *Dizionario ecclesiastico* 1:524. J. LENZENWEGER,

Lexikon für Theologie und Kirche (Freiburg 1957–65) 2:953. O. OR-TOLANI, *Pietro Carnesecchi* (Florence 1963).

[E. A. CARRILLO]

CARO, JOSEPH BEN EPHRAIM

Talmudic authority and codifier of Jewish law; b. Spain, 1488; d. Safed, Palestine, 1575. His family, after being exiled from Spain by the 1492 expulsion of the Jews, migrated to Turkey, where, for a time, Caro headed the Rabbinical Academy in Nicopolis. He finally settled in Safed in 1536. Even before his arrival at this center of Cabalistic activity (*see* CABALA), he was already strongly influenced by Jewish mystical speculation. His tendencies to martyrdom and asceticism, and his dreams in which his Maggid (the spiritual mentor believed by him to be the Mishnah personified) appeared and instructed him, were major obsessions of his life. Although he was a strong supporter of the efforts of Jacob Berab (*c.* 1475–1546) to reinstitute the Semikhah (traditional ordination) and was among the first to enjoy its revival, he himself succumbed to the opposition created by this attempt to centralize Rabbinical authority after he conferred the honor on one disciple.

Caro's best-known work is his code of Jewish law, the *Shulhan 'Arukh* (Prepared Table), published from 1564 to 1565, an abridgment of an earlier massive undertaking, the *Beth Yoseph* (1550–59). While the former presents the simple statement of the law without exposition, the latter is a thorough analysis and critique of the Talmudic and post-Talmudic sources that serve to provide an authoritative basis for his conclusions. Intended to establish standards of legal interpretation and procedure in order to obviate the chaotic multi-authority method then prevalent, the *Beth Yoseph* was originally conceived as a commentary to the *Arba'ah Turim* of Jacob ben Asher (*c.* 1270–*c.* 1343), retaining its outline but surpassing the model in comprehensiveness and decisiveness. Although he often tended to impose his own opinion in areas of dispute, he relied mainly on Alfasi (1013–1103), Maimonides, and Asher ben Yehiel (*c.* 1250–1327) as his standards, deciding the law in accordance with any two of the three in agreement. While these three were representative of the Ashkenazic (Franco-German-Polish) and Sephardic (Spanish-Near Eastern) currents in Jewish religious practice, the frequent agreement of Alfasi and Maimonides tended to favor the Sephardim. Much Ashkenazic opposition to Caro's code centered in the concern of the Askenazim for the priority of local custom, a matter ignored by him. But, unlike their rejection of Maimonides's *Mishneh Torah* for its failure to cite the sources of its decisions, his achieve-ment gradually gained acceptance for its success in this regard. However, approval was assured only after the rules of the *Shulhan 'Arukh* were interpolated with the comments of Rabbi Moses Isserles (*c.* 1525–72) of Poland, who vigorously upheld the authority of Ashkenazic practice.

Among Caro's other works are *Maggid Mesharim* (uncertainly ascribed to him), an account of his discussions with the personified Mishnah; *Keseph Mishnah,* a commentary on Maimonides's code defending the author's compilation; *Bedek ha-Bayit,* a supplement to the *Beth Yoseph* and a rejoinder to its critics; and *Kelale ha-Talmud,* a methodology of the TALMUD.

Bibliography: *The Jewish Encyclopedia* 3:583–588. S. GANZ-FRIED, *Code of Jewish Law (Kitzur Schulchan Aruch): A Compilation of Jewish Laws and Customs,* tr. H. E. GOLDIN (New York 1928), tr. of an abridgment of the *Shulhan 'Arukh.* H. L. GORDON, *The Maggid of Caro* (New York 1949). R. WERBLOWSKY, *Joseph Karo: Lawyer and Mystic* (New York 1962).

[R. KRINSKY]

CARO RODRÍGUEZ, JOSÉ MARÍA

Cardinal, archbishop of Santiago de Chile, supporter of social reform and social action; b. San Antonio de Petrel, Province of Colchagua, 1866; d. Santiago, 1958. Born of poor but cultured parents, Caro Rodríguez was educated at home and in public school. At 15 he entered the seminary of Santiago in the St. Peter Damian section for poor students. He was sent to Rome to study theology, and he received the doctorate and was ordained in 1890. There he contracted tuberculosis, from which he suffered throughout his life. From 1891 to 1911 he was professor of grammar, Greek, Hebrew, philosophy, and dogmatic theology at the seminary of Santiago. He was appointed apostolic vicar of Tarapacá in 1911 and titular bishop of Milas the next year.

Iquique, the city where the bishop resided, had an antireligious atmosphere, and he was attacked in the press and from the lecture platform. To teach and defend the faith, he published a weekly news sheet, *La Luz,* which was distributed free of charge. To counteract the general atmosphere, he sponsored a series of public ceremonies: a celebration in honor of Constantine's Edict of Toleration, a Palm Sunday procession (during the course of which 300 men attacked the faithful, who defended themselves with blessed palms), and a Corpus Christi procession (for which he placed on trucks the altars he was not permitted to erect in the streets). His energetic spirit reassured the Catholics, and their numbers increased. On his pastoral visits he toured small towns in the high plateaus and deserts of the interior, traveling by truck, horse, or mule. In each town he walked about among the faithful and taught catechism to the children. He was welcomed here more cordially. He and his clergy were as poor as the people, and he defended the position of the workers in the disputes at the saltpeter works.

In 1925 he was transferred to La Serena. He continued his work as religious propagandist, catechist, and missionary. Again he was in an area indifferent to religion, and the Freemasons attacked him harshly; he replied with his polemical book, *Misterio*. The poverty of the prelate and the clergy was aggravated by a fire at the episcopal residence in which everything, including his library, was lost. One Catholic school had to close because of lack of funds. Caro Rodríguez continued his visitations of the interior and fostered piety by holding Eucharistic congresses. On his visitations his first stops were the hospitals and the jails; throughout his life he visited patients in the hospitals daily. In 1939 the Diocese of La Serena was elevated to an archbishopric, but that year he was transferred to Santiago as archbishop.

In Santiago he was faced with new problems in the needs of a growing urban population. He established 67 parishes, most of them within the city. To solve the problem of vocations, he fostered the recruitment of clerical students; built a new seminary in Apoquindo; sought the collaboration of male religious orders, who worked in the schools and parishes; and increased by 25 the number of religious congregations for women dedicated to teaching and charitable works. He continued the work of the Sacred Heart, Marian, and Eucharistic congresses, opened the votive shrine of Maipú (dedicated to the Virgin del Carmen), and presided at the first Chilean Provincial Council. His deep concern with social problems led him to originate or support Christian Social Aid, the Institute of Rural Education, the ASICH (an association of Catholic labor unions), Young Catholic Workers, and the USEC (Union of Catholic Employers). He was very interested in modern methods of communication applied to the apostleship and founded Radio Chilena and the newspaper *Luz y Amor*. He was made a cardinal in 1945.

Caro Rodríguez, a holy, humble, and simple man, was very popular, especially among the poor. He devoted his strong will and active intelligence to searching for, and carrying out personally, new methods for the apostleship. A prolific writer, he published 33 books and pamphlets of Catholic propaganda, instruction, and apologetics written for the general reader. He produced a great deal for the newspaper and sent out a number of pastoral letters. His works were published in inexpensive editions so they could be given out generously. At his death about 400,000 copies of his works were in circulation.

Bibliography: J. VANHERK MORIS, *Monseñor José María Caro: Apóstol de Tarapacá* (Santiago de Chile 1963).

[W. HANISCH]

CAROCCI, HORACIO

Jesuit missionary and linguist; b. Florence, Italy, 1579; d. Tepotzotlán, Mexico, July 14, 1662. Having entered the Society of Jesus on Oct. 23, 1601, he was sent to Mexico in 1605. He was ordained in 1608 and after tertianship was sent to Tepotzotlán, where the society maintained a school for the natives who spoke only Mazahua (Mazagua), Nahuatl, or Otomí. Carocci became a specialist in Otomí. In 1625 a report sent by Diego de Torres to Jerónimo Díez, the provincial procurator appointed to Rome and Madrid, noted that the priests sent to Tepotzotlán to study Otomí learned only to hear confessions, poorly at that, for they did not wish to become proficient in the language for fear of being stationed permanently among the natives; only Carocci knew Otomí well. Torres requested that Carocci be allowed 100 pesos annually to pay the native peoples who helped with the linguistic labors of preparing a grammar and vocabulary of Otomí. Carocci prepared also a grammar and vocabulary of Nahuatl, published in 1645, and he was familiar with Mazahua. He was rector of the major seminary from 1649 to 1653 and then rector of the school and novitiate in Tepotzotlán until his death. The Jesuit historian Francisco Javier ALEGRE felt that Carocci's brilliant qualities, enhanced by humility and a zeal for souls, were stifled in the loneliness of an inhospitable village and sacrificed to his relations with the ungrateful Otomí.

Bibliography: F. J. ALEGRE, *Historia de la provincia de la Compañía de Jesús de Nueva España*, ed. E. J. BURRUS and F. ZUBILLAGA, 4 v. (new ed. Rome 1956–60). A. M. GARIBAY KINTANA, *Historia de la literatura náhuatl*, 2 v. (Mexico City 1953–54).

[F. ZUBILLAGA]

CAROL

There are almost as many definitions of the word as there are collections of carols or books about them: "a carol is a song of joy accompanying a dance" (Julian's *Dictionary*); "a hymn of praise, especially such as is sung at Christmas" (*Encyclopedia Britannica*); "songs with a religious impulse that are simple, hilarious, popular, and modern" (*Oxford Book of Carols*). It is a relief to find that from *c.* 1300 until the Reformation, at least, the word carol bore a definite and accepted meaning: in his now standard work, *The Early English Carols* (Oxford 1935), R. L. Greene defined it as a poem "intended,

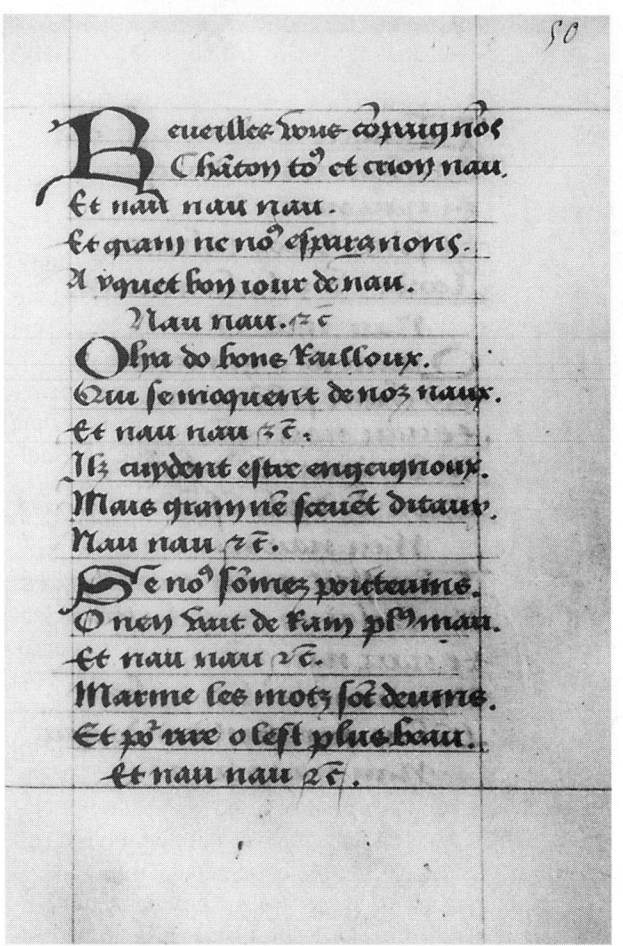

A portion of one of the oldest known French carols, c. 1483 (Bibl. de l'Arsenal MS 3653).

or at least suitable for singing, made up of uniform stanzas, and provided with a burden [that is, an external refrain], which begins the piece and is to be repeated after each stanza."

Essentially English Character. The carol, although associated with the medieval French *carole,* is essentially English, the English representative of a family of European poetic and musical *formes fixes,* such as the *rondeau, ballade,* and *virelai.* The closest analogy to the carol on the Continent is the 13th-century *lauda spirituale* of Italy (*see* JACOPONE DA TODI). Both carol and *lauda* manifest the homely didacticism and devotional fervor of vernacular religion, such as the Franciscans propagated; both are by origin popular songs for alternating chorus and solo singer, but they later undergo sophisticated musical treatment; both are probably to be associated with popular litanies and processions and give special honor to the Blessed Virgin, the Holy Family, and the saints of Christmas week. Whether the development of the carol owes most to this association (Sahlin derives "carol" ultimate-

ly from "kyrie eleison") or to the "godlification" of courtly or pagan round dances (Greene) is still a matter for scholarly dispute. About 500 English medieval carol texts survive, some of them in several versions; more than 100 of these have musical settings, ranging from simple melodies to elaborate polyphonic settings in the late 15th and early 16th centuries.

There is little connection between the medieval carol and the folk ballad (the Corpus Christi carol is an exception), though a background of folk custom can often be sensed (the traditional strife between the Holly and the Ivy, for example). Nor, musically speaking, do medieval carol settings derive from folk song; their idiom is related to that of the *conductus,* one of the simpler styles of medieval art music. The carol tradition, in words and music, is a *written* one. Finally, despite the frequent occurrence of the word "nowell" as an exclamation of joy in the carol, the English medieval carol has no traceable links with the French *noël.* Although the *noël* is, like the carol, essentially a popular religious song drawing imaginative strength from the same world—apocryphal legend, the lives of the saints, the best-loved Latin hymns, the miracle and mystery plays—its vogue begins later, at the end of the 15th century, and continues for a long time after the Reformation. Most importantly, the *noël* was never a *forme fixe* as the English medieval carol was.

Disfavor during the Reformation. At the time of the Reformation the carol fell into disfavor, chiefly because it was associated with the "papist" and "superstitious" practices of "unreformed Catholicism." If the latest medieval carols were often processional songs sung in honor of the saints of Christmas, then the decline in the popularity of the carol is not surprising. Nor is it surprising to find that the nearest literary equivalents to the medieval carol survive in collections of Recusant poetry, where the spirit of the old faith is dominant (*see* RECUSANT LITERATURE). The carol lost much of its vitality with the gradual changes in religious temper and outlook. Nevertheless it continued to develop. Related to the elaborate polyphonic carols of the early Tudor period are William BYRD's two consort songs in carol form, "Lullaby, my sweet little baby" and "An earthly tree." As a popular religious song the carol was replaced to some extent by the metrical psalm, especially in the version of Thomas Sternhold (d. 1549) and John Hopkins (d. 1570). But some Christmas themes found their way into the broadside ballads, cheaply printed and hawked about the streets to be sung to popular tunes of the day. The purely jovial and festive side, often present in the medieval carol (The Boar's Head carols; "Goday my lord, Sir Christemasse"; etc.), is now usually predominant ("drawe hogsheads drye / Let flagons flye / Make fires nose high"). But printed collections of the 17th century also contain crude, maudlin, and verbose carols of the saints (e.g., "A Carrol for St. Stephen's Day," to the tune of "Where is my true love"). These carols are in the familiar, jog-trot meters of the broadside ballad; the traditional form of burden and verse is seldom or never found.

During the 18th century the carol eked out a precarious existence as a broadside, possibly becoming more and more provincial and unfashionable, even as a type of popular song. As an art song it continued the lines established earlier by such songs as Henry Lawes's "'Tis Christmas now, 'tis Christmas now / When Cato's self would laugh" (in a tuneful contemporary style) and his pastoral verse anthem, "Hark, shepherd swains." Characteristic Augustan collections contain triumphal Christmas anthems (e.g., *A Collection of Psalms and Hymns for the Use of Bedford Chapel,* 1791) and elegant solo arias (e.g., J. F. Lampe's *Hymns on the Great Festivals,* 1746). Both these collections contain settings of Christmas hymns by the brothers Wesley (*see* WESLEY, CHARLES; WESLEY, JOHN). This was appropriate and right, but it does not make these fine hymns into carols in the true sense of the word.

Revival in the 19th Century. The 19th century rediscovered the carol and its meaning. The modern habit of forming collections of carols seems to date from Davies Gilbert's *Some Antient Christmas Carols, with the Tunes to which They Were Formerly Sung in the West of England* (1822). He looked upon carol singing as a thing of the past and attempted, as a good antiquarian, to rescue the traditional songs from oblivion. Among his carols were "Whilst Shepherds Watched" (originally published in a supplement to Tate and Brady's psalms) and "The Lord at first did Adam make." Gilbert's work was supplemented by W. Sandys' *Christmas Carols, Ancient and Modern,* (1833): "Hark, the herald angels," "God rest you merry," "The first Nowell," etc. Not all early editors were in love with the traditional broadside carol. The editor of *Christmas Carols or Sacred Songs* (1833) intended his carols, "breathing proper sentiments of piety," to "supersede the rude strains which are current throughout the country"; in fact they breathed Gothic poeticisms and superseded nothing.

It was in stark reaction to this "sentimental" and pietistic view of the carol that Edmund Sedding published his *Collection of Antient Christmas Carols* (1860). For him carols were part of Catholic truth and Catholic worship, and in him we see the connection between the carol revival and the OXFORD MOVEMENT. One of his translators was J. M. Neale (1818–66), a great hymn-writer, translator, and a leading figure in the liturgical revival that followed the Oxford Movement. With a friend he had already produced two now famous carol collections: *Car-*

Title page of Richard Kele's "Christmas Carolles Newly Imprinted," a collection published in London (1550).

ols for Christmas-Tide, Set to Ancient Melodies by the Revd. T. Helmore. . .; the Words, Principally in Imitation of the Original, by the Revd. J. M. Neale (1853) and a similar *Carols for Easter-Tide.* In these books are summed up two great characteristics of the revival—the debt to the past and the rich Swedish collection of the late 16th century, *Piae Cantiones* (1582). It was to a Latin springtime carol from this book, "Tempus adest floridum," that Neale wrote the words of "Good King Wenceslas."

Folk songs and broadside balladry, Protestant piety, Gothic taste, doctrinal hymns and foreign carols, ancient Latin song, antiquarian scholarship, and the revival of Catholic worship have all found a place in the revival of the carol that began about mid-19th century and is still vigorous. The paradox of it all is that the music of the English carol in its golden age, the 15th century, has remained almost completely unknown. Medieval carol poems, on the other hand, have been the favorite stand-by for 20th-century composers. Peter Warlock and Benjamin Britten are among those who have found inspiration in this rich field.

Bibliography: R. L. GREENE, ed., *The Early English Carols* (Oxford 1935); *A Selection of English Carols* (Oxford 1962), an indispensable suppl. to the earlier book. J. STEVENS, ed., *Medieval Carols* (Musica Britannica, 4; 1952), a "musical companion" to Greene's literary collections. M. R. SAHLIN, *Étude sur la carole médiévale* (Uppsala 1940). P. DEARMER et al., eds., *The Oxford Book of Carols* (New York 1928), the most comprehensive modern collection, but not scholarly.

[J. E. STEVENS]

CAROLINE DIVINES

A term applied to a succession of theological writers, mostly of the 17th century, many of them under Charles I; they maintained that Catholicity, Biblical but non-Roman, rather than Puritan Protestantism, was the chief feature of the Reformed Church of England in its organization and government (episcopal and not presbyterian) and in its ritual and theology, particularly on the Eucharist.

Such ideas as these emerged during the reign of James I and became prominent under Charles I. The pioneers were Richard HOOKER (1553–1600); Thomas Bilson (1547–1616), Bishop of Winchester, who declared that the Anglican disagreement with Rome on Holy Communion was not concerning the fact, but only the manner of Christ's Presence; Lancelot ANDREWES (1555–1626); and John Overall (1560–1619), Bishop of Norwich, who pointed out that his church no longer spoke of the bread and wine as "creatures" after the consecration.

Principal Early Divines. Their terminology recalled the old traditional Catholic theology rather than the new Protestant theology. Chief among them were the following:

Christopher Sutton (1565–1629) of Westminster, author of the devotional works, *Dise Vivere* and *Godly Meditations upon the Most Holy Sacrament.*

William LAUD (1573–1645), Archbishop of Canterbury, most prominent of the divines.

Richard Montague (1577–1641), Bishop of Chichester, historian of Christian origins from which he tried to show that the Anglican position derived. He said his aim was "to stand in the gapp against puritanism and popery." He wrote on the Eucharistic Sacrifice.

Gregorio PANZANI, papal agent at the court of Charles I, reported to Rome that Montague admitted the authority of the pope, and accepted the body of Catholic dogmas except transubstantiation. He suggested a conference in France to bring about reunion, which he thought would be easy.

Thomas Jackson (1579–1640), president of Corpus Christi College, Oxford, and Dean of Peterborough, moved from a Puritan to a Catholic position through his studies, which produced 12 books of *Commentaries on the Apostles' Creed.*

William Forbes (1585–1634), Bishop of Edinburgh, whose writings on purgatory and the Eucharist were published posthumously in 1658 as *Considerationes Modestae et Pacificae.*

George Herbert (1593–1640), a typical country parson, was the poet of the Carolines who taught sacramental doctrine in verse *(The Temple: Sacred Poems)* and in prose *(The Priest to the Temple).*

Nicholas Ferrar (1592–1637), a deacon who founded, at the manor house of Little Gidding, Huntingdon, a family religious house where the piety of Caroline theology was put into practice with genuine fervor.

John Bramhall (1594–1663), Archbishop of Armagh, who upheld the Anglican doctrine of the real presence, repudiated the charge that the Church of England was in schism, and, in reply to the Catholic Bishop Richard Smith, published his *Replication* (1656), a prayer that he might live to see the reunion of Christendom.

John Cosin (1594–1672), Bishop of Durham who, at both Cambridge and Durham, introduced ornate altars with crucifix, candles, and vestments. He also put together a *Collection of Private Devotions,* in effect, the Catholic Breviary. For all of these he was charged by the Puritans with popery, but in fact he was anti-Roman and repudiated the doctrine of transubstantiation.

Herbert Thorndike (1598–1672), Canon of Lincoln and later of Westminster, wrote, among other similar works, the *Epilogue to the Tragedy of the Church of England,* a plea for return to the primitive Church, and the *Reformation of the Church of England better than that of the Council of Trent.* He stated that separation from Rome made a church schismatic before God (cf. Albion, 172.3).

Henry Hammond (1605–60), Archdeacon of Chichester, public orator at Oxford, Biblical critic and voluminous writer, tolerant rather than polemical, whose best-known work is the *Practical Catechism.*

Jeremy TAYLOR (1613–67), Bishop of Down and Connor, perhaps the greatest Catholicizing influence among the Carolines because of the quality of writing in his *Worthy Communicant, Holy Living,* and *Holy Dying.* Yet he defended the penal laws against papists and wrote a *Dissuasive from Popery.*

Later Divines. Among the later Caroline divines, so called because of the same school of thought, were the following:

Dr. Richard Sherlock (1612–89), "accounted by precise persons popishly affected," who wrote the *Principles of the Holy Catholick Religion,* as well as a work entitled *The Practical Christian.*

Thomas Wilson (1663–1755), nephew of Sherlock and trained by him for the ministry. As Bishop of Sodor and Man, which was exempt from English law, he introduced "the ancient discipline of the Church." His *Instruction for the Lord's Supper* and *Sacra Privata* have remained popular devotional works.

Anthony Sparrow (1612–55), Bishop of Norwich, whose *Rationale* of the Book of Common Prayer, illustrated from Catholic sources, was reprinted by John Henry NEWMAN in 1837.

Thomas Ken (1657–1711), Bishop of Bath and Wells, best known for his morning and evening hymns.

John Johnson (1662–1725), Vicar of Cranbrook, Kent, author of *The Propitiatory Oblation in the Holy Eucharist* and *The Unbloody Sacrifice,* aroused considerable opposition.

The aim of all these writers was to show the Church of England as reformed yet still Catholic, steering a middle course between Romanism and Presbyterianism and so providing support for the *via media* argument of the TRACTARIANISM and the OXFORD MOVEMENT of the 19th century. All are pertinent to the ecumenical dialogue between Anglicans and Catholics in England following Vatican Council II. (*See* ANGLICANISM.)

Bibliography: *The Library of Anglo-Catholic Theology,* 83 v. (Oxford 1841–63) republished the works of the divines mentioned. *The Dictionary of National Biography from the Earliest Times to 1900* (London 1885–1900) lists their works in articles under their names. G. ALBION, *Charles I and the Court of Rome* (London 1935). D. CARTER, *Die Religion in Geschichte und Gegenwart* (Tübingen 1957–65) 1:1620–21.

[G. ALBION]

CAROLINGIAN ART

The art of the Carolingian period (later 8th and early 9th centuries) has a particular importance in that it reflects, for the first time, the Germanic North's critical interest in Latin culture and emotional concern over the interpretation of Scripture. The achievement of this era is known mostly through the illuminated book and the crafts of ivory carving and metal work. Much building, however, was done—especially of monasteries—under royal patronage. Carolingian art was an aristocratic expression, but it laid the foundation for the great popular expression of the later Middle Ages.

The impetus of the whole movement was CHARLEMAGNE, who was impressed by the sumptuousness of By-

"The Lothair Crystal," crystal pendant engraved with scenes from the story of "Susanna and the Elders," matching chain, 9th century, Carolingian, in the collection of the British Museum.

zantium and even had diplomatic relations with the Muslims. He allied himself, however, to the papal throne at the accession of Adrian I in 772. As a result of the iconoclastic struggle in the East (*see* ICONOCLASM), Charlemagne became concerned for the use of images in religious art and wrote to Adrian recommending pictures for their commemorative and decorative value. Aware of the mistakes that were being made in copying Scripture, he admonished the clergy to establish schools.

He himself founded the palace school at Aachen, with ALCUIN of York as its head. To this beginning must be attributed the later development of such scholars as RABANUS MAURUS, abbot of Fulda; Hincmar, archbishop of Reims; and JOHN SCOTUS ERIGENA of Saint-Denis. Thus the influence of the schools was widely scattered, and distinctive styles developed in different localities.

Sculpture. The revival of the antique style is attested to by the casting of the great bronze doors at Aachen. Also of great interest is the bronze equestrian statuette, formerly in the Musée Carnavalet in Paris but now in the Louvre. While this object has no documentation prior to the 16th century, it is known that Charlemagne caused a mounted statue of Theodoric to be removed from Ravenna and set up in front of his palace at Aachen. The style of this small statue is certainly in keeping with work that Einhard, the director of the imperial workshops, might have accomplished.

Louis I, Holy Roman Emperor.

Manuscript Illumination. The first book known to have been executed at the palace in Aachen is the Gospels of Godescalc (781–783). It is on purple vellum, and though somewhat crude, it originated an aristocratic style that was later developed under the Abbess Ada at Trèves and of which the Gospels of Saint-Médard-de-Soissons is the finest example. Both books are now in the Bibliothèque Nationale, Paris. Several works of this general type reveal a strong Syrian influence, whether in the Hellenistic treatment of landscape, the theatrical backgrounds, or the portrait effigies recalling the consular diptychs.

The school of Tours is best exemplified by the Vivian Bible, or the First Bible of Charles the Bald (Bibliothèque Nationale). This is an extraordinary work of the middle of the 9th century; like other books from Tours, it uses subjects from the Old Testament that were popular in early Christian art. The dedication page is highly original, as is a page showing the dance of David, a Biblical figure to whom Charlemagne was likened. But the MSS done at Tours, where Alcuin had worked on the Vulgate, are most distinctive for their narrative scenes and the beauty of their script. It was this clear, minuscule lettering that inspired the Roman type of the 15th century.

Perhaps the most creative manuscript of the 9th century is the Utrecht psalter, which was written at Hautvil-lers, near Reims (*c.* 832). The text is in rustic capitals that derive from Western books of *c.* A.D. 400. The lively pen drawings were much admired; their influence can be detected not only in manuscript illumination, but in ivory book covers and silver work—done probably at Saint-Denis—and in the exquisite narrative scenes on the crystal of Lothair, which is now preserved in the British Museum.

Another work of great originality is the Sacramentary, now in Paris, executed before 855 for DROGO, bishop of Metz. In it, scenes taken mostly from the life of Christ are combined with richly foliated initial letters. In this work the beauty of the silhouette was fully achieved while maintaining a certain subservience to the classical tradition. Its ivory covers are in the same spirit and serve as important documents in the development of the liturgy. The taste for the silhouette, combined with the flowing line, undoubtedly derives from the linear animal style of the period of the racial migrations. Several examples exist that show creative adaptations of this style to the art of the Latinized West. Especially fine are the Gospels of Francis II and the Second Bible of Charles the Bald, both in the Bibliothèque Nationale. They come probably from the monastery of SAINT-VAAST at Arras.

Much uncertainty exists as to work that may have been executed either at CORBIE near Amiens or at Saint-Denis. The fact that Charles the Bald assumed the abbacy of Saint-Denis in 867 is not without significance, and much work is attributed to the monk Liuthard on stylistic grounds. At that time scenes of the Crucifixion appeared, probably as a result of the poem by Rabanus Maurus, *De laudibus Sanctae Crucis.* (*See* CRUCIFIXION [IN ART].) The Codex Aureus from St. Emmeram of Regensburg, now at Munich, is dated 870 and belongs to this northern school. Less original than some, it sums up the Carolingian tradition in magnificent fashion.

There can be no doubt but that France in the 9th century became the radiating center for the arts. Whether the golden altar of S. Ambrogio in Milan, which must date before 835, was executed in France or in Italy is uncertain, but in any case it reflects the spirit of Carolingian art, as does the Bible of St. Paul-outside-the-Walls, Rome, which was executed in 880 for Charles III, the Frankish king and German emperor, and the latter may be said to mark the termination of the tradition.

Architecture. In Carolingian architecture there are echoes of the two traditional styles, Roman and Byzantine, but fused as conditions dictated to form the basis of the great medieval development.

The Palatine chapel at Aachen was begun in 792 and dedicated in 805. The plan is that of S. Vitale at Ravenna, from which monument Charlemagne plundered columns, but the construction was heavy Roman vaulting. (*See* RAVENNA.*)

The church of Germigny des Prés near Saint-Benoîtsur-Loire was consecrated in 816 by Theodulf, a Goth from Spain. The quatrefoil plan with a center tower has many prototypes in the East, but the direct influences must have come from the Visigothic tradition. The apsidal mosaic is crude but reveals a desire to emulate the Byzantine style.

Of the Abbeys of S. Riquier near Abbeville and SANKT GALLEN in Switzerland there are no remains. The former, dedicated in 799, was basilican in plan with two great round towers reaching a height of almost 180 feet, one over the crossing, the other above an imposing façade. Other towers were composed with these, establishing a relationship that became traditional. The upper sections and spires were of wood. The entire length of the church (with atrium) measured some 340 feet. Something is known of Sankt Gallen from the famous plan of *c.* 820, preserved in the monastic library. Its most distinctive characteristic was an apse at either end, a feature that was used in an early Christian church in North Africa and was greatly developed in later German churches. Sankt Gallen, which had been founded in the 7th century by Irish monks, later came under Benedictine rule. There the stimulus from the great Western monastic centers of Carolingian culture had a final flowering.

See Also: CHURCH ARCHITECTURE; MANUSCRIPT ILLUMINATION.

Bibliography: General. C. R. MOREY, *Medieval Art* (New York 1942). R. P. HINKS, *Carolingian Art* (London 1935; repr. pa. Ann Arbor 1962). M. L. W. LAISTNER, *Thought and Letters in Western Europe, A.D. 500 to 900* (2nd ed. New York 1957). P. LEPRIEUR et al., "L'Art de l'époque mérovingienne et carolingienne en occident," in A. MICHEL, *Histoire de l'art*, 8 v. in 17 (Paris 1905–29) 1.1:303–427. E. KITZINGER, *Early Medieval Art in the British Museum* (2nd ed. London 1955). A. M. FRIEND, "Carolingian Art in the Abbey of Saint Denis," *Art Studies,* 8 v. in 9 (Princeton 1923–31) 1:67–75. J. M. K. CLARK, *The Abbey of Saint Gall as a Centre of Literature and Art* (Cambridge, Eng. 1926). M. BUCHNER, *Einhard als Künstler* (Strasbourg 1919). J. VON SCHLOSSER, *Schriftquellen zur Geschichte der Karolingischen Kunst* (Vienna 1896). Architecture. A. K. PORTER, *Medieval Architecture: Its Origins and Development*, 2 v. (New York 1909) v. 1. K. J. CONANT, *Carolingian and Romanesque Architecture, 800 to 1200* (Pelican History of Art, ed. N. PEVSNER [Baltimore 1953–] Z13; 1959). Decorative Arts. A. MASKELL, *Ivories* (London 1905). A. GOLDSCHMIDT, *Die Elfenbeinskulpturen*, 4 v. (Berlin 1914–26) v. 1. G. H. LEHNERT et al., *Illustrierte Geschichte des Kunstgewerbes*, 2 v. (Berlin 1907–09) v. 1. É. MOLINIER, "L'Évolution des arts mineurs du VIIIᵉ au XIIᵉ siècle," in A. MICHEL, *op. cit.* 1.2:815–881. O. K. WERCKMEISTER, *Der Deckel des Codex Aureus von St. Emmeram* (Strasbourg 1963). Manuscripts. J. A. HERBERT, *Illuminated Manuscripts* (London 1911). A. C. L. BOINET, *La Miniature carolingienne* (Paris 1913). Plates only. A. GOLDSCHMIDT, *The Carolingian Period,* v. 1 of his *German Illumination* (New York 1928). W. R. W. KÖHLER, *Die Karolingischen Miniaturen,* 3 v. in 4 (Berlin 1930–60). E. K. RAND, *A Survey of the Manuscripts of Tours,* 2 v. (Cambridge, Mass. 1929). F. F. LEITSCHUH, *Geschichte der Karolingischen Malerei* (Berlin 1894). J. EBERSOLT, *La Miniature byzantine* (Paris 1926); *Orient et occident,* 2 v. (2nd ed. Paris 1954). E. T. DEWALD, *The Illustrations of the Utrecht Psalter* (Princeton 1932). E. H. ZIMMERMANN, *Die Fuldaer Buchmalerei in Karolingischer und Ottonischer Zeit* (Halle 1910). J. O. WESTWOOD, *The Bible of the Monastery of St. Paul near Rome* (Oxford, Eng. 1876). K. MENZEL et al., *Die Trierer Ada-Handschrift* (Leipzig 1889).

[W. R. HOVEY]

CAROLINGIAN REFORM

An effort made during the period extending from about 740 to 900 by the Carolingian rulers and their supporters to strengthen ecclesiastical structures and to revitalize spiritual life in the Frankish kingdom. In its early stages the reform movement was spearheaded by the Carolingian rulers, who recruited important elements of the episcopacy and the monastic world to support reform. With the passing of time royal leadership of the reforming effort became less prominent, especially when royal power began to decline after the death of Louis the Pious in 840 and the agreement reached by his successors in the Treaty of Verdun of 843 to divide the Frankish empire into three separate entities. Thereafter the reforming effort was led by bishops whose concerns tended to be local. The reform movement began as an effort to correct conditions afflicting the Frankish church during the later Merovingian period, including corruption, ignorance, and immorality within the clergy, the widespread survival of pagan practices, diversity in liturgical practice, and the massive seizure of church property. Under the influence of more sophisticated concepts of the nature of society and its governance and of expanding intellectual horizons generated by the CAROLINGIAN RENAISSANCE, the movement took on new dimensions that moved it from an emphasis on what contemporaries called *correctio* (correction) to a concern for *renovatio* (renewal).

The original model for the correction of the Frankish church was drawn from the missionary effort that unfolded on the eastern frontier of the Frankish kingdom in the late 7th and early 8th centuries under the leadership of Anglo-Saxon monks. The most influential figure in that missionary field was BONIFACE, who between 718 and 741 succeeded in winning numerous converts in Hesse, Thuringia, and Bavaria. Boniface established a solid ecclesiastical organization built around a series of newly established bishoprics, including Salzburg, Passau, Freising, Würzburg, and Erfurt. Supporting this diocesan structure were several newly founded monasteries (the chief of which was Fulda), which served as educational centers training a disciplined, literate clergy to continue missionary work, to occupy the key positions in the emerging church organization, and to take up the pastoral work required to sustain effective Christian life. Always mindful of the way in which Christianity had come to England in the time of Pope GREGORY I (THE GREAT), Boniface constantly turned to Rome for authorization to act and for guidance in the substantive aspects of his work; clearly he sought to create a religious establishment that would be subordinate to Rome.

Carloman and Pepin III. During the period of their joint rule as mayors of the palace, CARLOMAN and PEPIN III launched a reforming movement intended to embrace the entire Frankish kingdom. Due primarily to the initiative of Carloman, whose portion of the Frankish kingdom faced the missionary frontier, the Frankish rulers turned to Boniface, who in his capacity as papal legate was given a key role in directing the assault on corruption in the Frankish church. The program was spelled out in a series of synods held in the 740s whose enactments were given the force of law by the rulers. Drawing on experiences in the missionary field that program emphasized bringing order to the ecclesiastical hierarchy, improving the education and the conduct of the clergy, suppressing paganism, and safeguarding ecclesiastical resources. In its initial stages it contained elements which envisaged a goal dear to Boniface: the creation of a Frankish church subordinate to Rome. But that dream met considerable resistance in Francia. With the abdication of Carloman in 747, Boniface lost his prime supporter, and his influence on the Frankish reforming activity gradually eroded until finally in 753 he returned to missionary work in Frisia, where he met a martyr's death in 754. Leadership of the reform movement devolved on Pepin III, king of the Franks after 751, and his Frankish advisers, the chief of whom was CHRODEGANG, bishop of Metz. During the remainder of his reign, Pepin III was a strong promoter of reform down lines defined in the acts of the early synods, but he proceeded in a way that left no doubt that reform was a royal undertaking intended to achieve ends that would strengthen royal authority.

Charlemagne's Reform Efforts. As was the case in most aspects of Carolingian society, CHARLEMAGNE gave new energy to the reform movement and expanded its scope in significant ways. The quickening and broadening of reforming activity were in part consequences of his conviction that he as ruler was personally responsible for shaping the spiritual life of his subjects in a way that would assure their salvation, a responsibility that greatly increased matters about which the king must be concerned. No less important was a firmer grasp of Christian traditions that resulted from the cultural renewal patronized by Charlemagne. That backward look led to an expansion of the norms used to guide the correction of the religious establishment and the addition of new elements to the reforming agenda. As a result, from its early stages the Carolingian reform movement was marked by a spirit of restoration in religious matters rather than by a spirit of innovation.

The particulars of Charlemagne's reforming program were set forth in a barrage of ecclesiastical legislation which was circulated in conciliar enactments and in capitularies carrying the force of law. Exemplary of the first were the *acta* of the Council of Frankfurt in 794 and of the latter were the *Admonitio generalis* of 789 and the *Capitularia missorum generalis* of 802. Much of this legislation emerged from royal assemblies and synods in which lay and ecclesiastical potentates were called upon to weigh and find solutions to the problems facing the Church; their expanded participation in deliberations on religious matters meant that reform became a central matter on the political agenda of the kingdom. The reforming legislation focused on a variety of topics: the reestablishment of the metropolitan structure; the definition of episcopal power and responsibility; the extension of the parish structure; the improvement of the intellectual and moral life of the clergy; the protection and enlargement of ecclesiastical resources, including the imposition of the tithe; the standardization of liturgical practices; more effective pastoral activity aimed at deepening knowledge of the faith and raising the moral standards of the laity; the destruction of pagan remnants; and the improvement of the physical facilities related to religious life. As Charlemagne's reform program unfolded it began to reach out in new directions. The duties of royal subjects were increasingly given a positive turn that equated acceptable civic behavior with the practice of Christian virtues conducive to peace and concord as well as simply refraining from sin. Safeguarding doctrinal orthodoxy became a matter of royal concern, as witnessed by the effort reflected in a statement entitled the *Libri Carolini*, prepared by THEODULF OF ORLÉANS on orders from Charlemagne to define the orthodox position on ICONOCLASM, even to the point of correcting the papacy, and in writings by ALCUIN commissioned by the king aimed at exterminating the heresy of ADOPTIONISM not only in Francia but also in Spain. Establishing the norms which defined morality and doctrinal orthodoxy increasingly drew the intellectual establishment into the reform movement.

Charlemagne took significant measures to make his program effective. Enforcement of reforming legislation was made the responsibility of all public officials, but the chief burden fell to the bishops of the realm. The *missi dominici* were charged with seeing to it that all responsible parties knew about the reforming legislation and that each did his part in enacting the program. But Charlemagne was not content merely to command reform by fiat. He sought to provide the tools that would supply the substantive components required to deepen spiritual life. Reforming clerics, such as Alcuin and Theodulf, were given crucial positions at the royal court from which to give visibility to the religious component to royal policy. Reform concerns became a criterion in determining fitness for appointment to the office of bishop or abbot and for monitoring their behavior. The ruler took the lead in increasing the number of schools dedicated to elevating the educational level of the clergy to the point where bishops and priests could adequately discharge their pastoral functions. The royal court concerned itself with providing books crucial to spiritual formation, including a correct version of the Bible, standardized guides to the performance of the liturgy, penitentials, homilaries geared to instruction of the laity, and collections of canon law. Frequently, the papacy was asked for guidance in these matters and often responded with copies of key liturgical works and canon law collections; notable examples of such works were *Sacramentarium Gregorianum (Hadrianum)* and the *Dionysio-Hadriana* provided by Pope Adrian I. As a consequence, the Carolingian reform movement took on a strong Roman complexion, without however extending to the pope a directive role in shaping it. As the Carolingian Renaissance took shape, reforming leaders came into possession of a wide range of scriptural commentaries, theological texts, church histories, canon law collection, and hagiographical texts that provided an enriched understanding of what Christianity was and how to live the Christian life. That heightened awareness was reflected in reforming legislation, in textbooks compiled by masters in episcopal and monastic schools to educate the clergy for pastoral duties, in homilaries to aid priests in improving their sermons, and in compendia (*florilegia*) compiled to provide *exampla* useful in guiding Christians in understanding how they should behave and what they should believe. In brief, during Charlemagne's reign an infrastructure began to be shaped to turn reforming commands into effective actions aimed at redirecting the lives of all Christians.

Louis the Pious and the Height of Reform. The Carolingian reform movement reached is greatest intensity during the first fifteen years of the reign of Louis the Pious (814–840). Louis himself had a strong commitment to improving the ecclesiastical establishment and deepening spiritual life. He surrounded himself with clerical advisers deeply committed to reform; the most dedicated of these advisers was a monk, BENEDICT OF ANIANE, who until his death in 821 played a decisive role in shaping Louis' religious program. In general terms, Louis' reforming effort followed the basic lines set down by his father. Under the influence of BENEDICT special attention was given to monastic reform. Important legislation enacted in 816 and 817 sought to require the adoption by all monasteries of the BENEDICTINE RULE, slightly modified to fit a new age. An effort was also made to impose on all canons who served in cathedral chapters a form of common life outlined earlier by Bishop Chrodegang of Metz. However, in important ways reform under Louis the Pious went beyond that promoted by Charlemagne. Advocates of reform increasingly insisted that affairs in a true Christian society must be conducted in a way that not only recognized that spiritual matters constituted an autonomous realm in human existence but also that spiritual affairs must take priority over secular concerns. In the minds of the most dedicated reformers guiding Louis' reform, it followed from these premises that spiritual leaders must guide the Christian community and that secular leaders must defer to their opinion in shaping policy and must accept clerical judgment of their suitability to rule. Within this ideological framework religious reform took on a particular political coloration; reform became a means through which actions must be taken to maintain the unity of the Christian empire that Charlemagne had founded. The reforming party became a unity party. The implications of reform oriented in this direction were so threatening to many interests in Louis' realm that a reaction set in which had major implications not only for the reform movement but also for the political regime that the Carolingians had fashioned.

After the Treaty of Verdun. The Carolingian reform movement took on new complexities after the death of Louis the Pious in 840 and the signing of the Treaty of Verdun of 843 which divided the Carolingian empire into three independent kingdoms. The reforming effort lost its chief animating force: a single king mandating the improvement of religious life. The sons of Louis the Pious, especially Charles II the Bald, continued to support reform as defined by their predecessors, but their conflicting political concerns and their declining power and resources limited their effectiveness. The burden of reform increasingly fell on a shrinking number of archbishops and bishops who out of memory of the past and of personal conviction felt a compulsion to use their offices as a means of improving Christian life. Their reforming actions, often summarized in episcopal legislation and capitularies, echoed the goals of Pepin III, Charlemagne, and Louis the Pious: strengthening ecclesiastical organization; improving the quality of the clergy; organizing more effective pastoral activity; protecting church property; standardizing the liturgy; and improving lay morality. Concerns about protecting the Christian community from heterodox views remained a matter engaging reformers, as evidenced by the major theological disputes over the nature of the Eucharist and predestination involving such luminaries as PASCHASIUS RADBERTUS, HRABANUS MAURUS, GOTTSCHALK, HINCMAR OF REIMS, and JOHN SCOTUS ERIGENA. The reforming bishops of the later Carolingian era continued their search for instruments and techniques that would serve to deepen understanding of the faith and of the moral obligations attached to being a Christian. They often called on theologians, scriptural exegetes, moralists, hagiographers, and historians produced by the Carolingian Renaissance, especially in monasteries, to provide the guidance in gaining a better understanding of Christianity.

But it was a losing cause for these reformers. Their ability to act collectively was limited by lack of institutional structures embracing the entire Christian community in the West and by the increasing political fragmentation of the late Carolingian world. Some hoped perhaps that the bishop of Rome, widely accepted as the titular head of the Church, could provide unified leadership in inspiring and guiding religious reform. Pope NICHOLAS I (858–867) certainly acted on occasion as if he were ready to play that role. But in examining his career in detail it seems clear that he was more concerned with defining ecclesiastical jurisdictions than with deepening spiritual life. In fact, some evidence suggests that by the last half of the 9th century the Carolingian reform effort had become a movement centered on establishing the legal bases that defined jurisdictions within the ecclesiastical structure. Nicholas I's letters to various ecclesiastical and lay leaders reflected this preoccupation. So did the actions and the writings of one of the most ardent reformers of the 9th century, Hincmar, archbishop of Reims, who seldom missed an opportunity to remind those whose lives he touched, including the kings, bishops, priests, and assorted members of the laity, of his legal right to judge their behavior and of their obligation to accept his authority. The collections of canon law of the era, including especially the famous FALSE DECRETALS OF PSEUDO-ISIDORE, gave major attention to jurisdictional relationships within the ecclesiastical establishment and between the clergy and lay leaders. Reform had become a matter of defining the proper structure of the Christian community rather than of seeking ways to enhance spiritual life.

The End of the Carolingian Reform. So by the end of the 9th century the Carolingian reform had run its course. Developments were afoot pushing the Christian establishment toward a condition not unlike that existing at the time the reform began. There existed no single figure who could spur all western Christendom to seek renewal along common lines; the last Carolingian emperors were shadowy figures, and the papacy was increasingly victimized by local Roman potentates. Bishops became progressively intertwined in feudal arrangements which demanded their concentration on secular affairs. Private churches controlled by powerful landowners produced a new crop of uneducated priests who were ill equipped to provide effective pastoral care. Church property increasingly fell under the control of laymen or secularized clergymen who exploited it for private gain. Viking and Magyar raids took a heavy toll on the monasteries, which had long generated materials invaluable in defining Christianity and deepening its spiritual components. The Frankish church drifted toward the chaos of the feudal age to await a new monasticism heralded by the founding of CLUNY in 910 and a revitalized papacy which together would generate from within the Church itself the GREGORIAN REFORM of the 11th century,

Despite is ultimate end, the Carolingian reform was of great historical significance. It did much to define the norms upon which later reforms would be built. In large part those norms resulted from a recovery of the heritage of the early Church and its redefinition to fit the needs of a society influenced strongly by Germanic institutions and customs. To the degree that it encouraged the reestablishment of contact with a more intellectually sophisticated past and the appropriation of the intellectual and artistic treasures of that past, the Carolingian effort to correct and renew Christian life played a prime role in establishing the foundations for the future cultural life of western Europe. It also made considerable progress in establishing a uniform pattern of worship across much of western Europe. That common ritual in turn produced ways of marking the fundamental events in human life reaching from birth to death, thereby creating powerful social bonds extending across the entire Christian community; and it generated modes of expression in architecture, art, and music that became powerful forces undergirding a common Christian culture. Furthermore, the reform effort played a major role in giving permanent form to an organizational structure based on a system of dioceses and parishes that allowed the Church to play a significant role in shaping ordinary life in the West and in creating a consciousness of the Church as a self-defining corporate entity capable of determining its own destiny. The Carolingian reformers promoted missionary activity that greatly reduced the remnants of paganism existing in the world the Carolingians inherited, substantially expanding the boundaries of western Christendom and marking the initial stage in the transition from a western European world under siege to one of growing influence. Although the Carolingian reform has sometimes been criticized for its failure to deepen the piety and the knowledge of Christian teaching and morality among the mass of common people, there is some evidence suggesting that ritual life was changed, that the basic tenets of the faith were better understood, that the sacramental system was more widely observed, and that Christian regulations pertaining to such matters as marriage, burial, oath-taking, and criminal behavior were observed more carefully. While the task of fully Christianizing western European society lay in the future, the Carolingian reform marked a significant preliminary step toward that end.

Bibliography: *Capitularia regum Francorum*, 2 v., ed. A. BORETIUS and V. KRAUSE, *Monumenta Germaniae Historica, Leges, Sectio II* (Hannover 1893–97; repr.1980–84). *Capitula Episcoporum*, v. 1–3, ed. P. BROMMER, R. POKORNY, and M. STRATMANN, *Monumenta Germaniae Historica* (Hannover 1984–1995). *Concilia aevi karolini*, 2 v., ed. A. WERMINGHOFF, *Monumenta Germaniae Historica, Leges, Sectio III: Concilia 2*, 1/2 (Hannover 1906–08; repr. 1997–99). *Die Konzilien des karolingischen Teilreiche 853–859 (Concilia aevi Karolini DCCCXLIII–DCCCLIX)*, ed. W. HARTMANN, *Monumenta Germaniae Historica, Concilia 3* (Hannover 1984). *Die Konzilien des karolingischen Teilreiche 869–874 (Concilia aevi Karolini DCCCLX–DCCCLXXIV)*, ed. W. HARTMANN, *Monumenta Germaniae Historica, Concilia 4* (Hannover 1998). *Die Briefe des heiligen Bonifatii*, ed. and tr. M. TANGL, *Monumenta Germanicae Historica, Epistolae Selectae 1* (Berlin 1916; reprinted 1978), English translation as *The Letters of St. Boniface*, tr. E. EMERTON, intro. T. F. X. NOBLE, (New York 2000). *Vita sancti Bonifatii archiepiscopi Moguntini*, ed. W. LEVISON, *Monumenta Germaniae Historica, Sriptorum rerum Germanicarum in usum scholarum 57* (Hannover and Leipzig 1905; repr. 1999), English translation as "Willibald, The Life of Saint Boniface," tr. C. H. TALBOT in *Soldiers of Christ. Saints and Saints' Lives from Antiquity and the Early Middle Ages*, ed. T. F. X. NOBLE and T. HEAD (University Park, Penn. 1985) 107–40. *Vita Benedicti Abbatis Anianensis et Indensis auctore Ardone*, ed. G. WAITZ, *Monumenta Germaniae Historica, Scriptores 15/1* (Hannover 1887; reprinted, 1963), 189–220, English translation as "Life of Saint Benedict, Abbot of Aniane and of Inde," tr. A. CABANISS in *Soldiers of Christ. Saints and Saints' Lives from Antiquity and the Early Middle Ages*, ed. T. F. X. NOBLE and T. HEAD (University Park, Penn. 1985) 213–54. *Les idées politico-religieuses d'évêque du IXe siècle: Jonas d'Orléans et son "De institutione regia," étude et texte*, ed. J. REVIRON (Paris 1930).

[R. E. SULLIVAN]

CAROLINGIAN RENAISSANCE

A revival of interest in classical learning in the Carolingian Empire (France, Germany, and Italy). Beginning under the patronage of CHARLEMAGNE (768–814), it continued to the end of the 9th century. In its involvement with classical and patristic literature, the movement was similar to the Isidorian renaissance in 7th-century Spain, the OTTONIAN RENAISSANCE of the 10th century, and the 12th-century renaissance in France and England. It differed from the Italian RENAISSANCE of the 14th and 15th century in its emphasis on clerical reform as originally inspired by St. BONIFACE with the encouragement of PEPIN III (741–768) and as incorporated by Charlemagne into civil law (e.g., *Monumenta Germaniae Capitularia* 1:22). The revived interest in learning is exemplified by Charle-

magne's important "mandate" (not a capitulary; cf. L. Wallach), the *Epistola de litteris colendis* (tr. M. L. W. Laistner, *Thought and Letters in Western Europe, A.D. 500 to 900* 152–153) written to Baugulf, Abbot of Fulda between 794 and 796, urging him to promote education in the area around his abbey. The primary interest of the Carolingian revival, however, was not in the classics as such, but rather in their use as a means of studying the Latin language and culture—an attitude the Carolingian scholars inherited from the patristic period; it was the Fathers of the Church who were read for content. Yet a love of learning for its own sake was bred in such men as the Spanish-born THEODULF OF ORLÉANS, who as a political prisoner wrote to his former colleague, Bp. Modoin of Autun, "Death is better than life without study, teaching, or worship." Carolingian poetry (*Monumenta Germaniae Poetae* v. 1–4), more than other literary forms, demonstrates the influence of the Latin classics on the Carolingians; the prose compositions of the period, however, reflect the classical mood only incidentally (*see* MEDIEVAL LATIN LITERATURE).

Charlemagne and the Court Circle. Charles, King of the Franks (768–814), emperor of the Romans from 800, was head and patron of the movement for education and reform that was the heart of the renaissance (*see* CAROLINGIAN REFORM).

Alcuin. Charlemagne found in ALCUIN of York (*c.* 735–804) the man to organize and systematize his educational program, and it was as an administrator (781–796) that Alcuin made his mark, though he wrote a number of poems in classical meters, some of considerable lyric power. He composed and edited texts for the education of clerics and authored textbooks on Latin grammar, rhetoric, dialectic, and orthography. He knew at first hand Vergil, Ovid, and Lucan. Alcuin, or "Horace," his nickname within the court circle, seems to have known Horace through quotations. Charlemagne initiated the PALACE SCHOOL—which lasted till the death of his grandson, Charles the Bald—when he attracted a galaxy of scholars to assist Alcuin: Paul the Deacon (in 782), Dungal (in 787), and Theodulf, the future bishop of Orléans (sometime after 787). PAUL THE DEACON (730?–799?) came to Charles' attention when he wrote a plea in fine elegiac verses for the release of his brother, imprisoned for a political offense. He also wrote a poem in praise of Lake Como in epanaleptic verses and an abridgment of Festus' *De verborum significatione*, which was important for archaic Latin.

The Irishmen. DUNGAL (d. after 827) was one of many wandering Irishmen who contributed greatly to the revival of learning on the Continent; Dungal knew the Fathers and was expert in astronomy (*Monumenta Ger-*

maniae Epistolae 4:570). CLEMENT OF IRELAND (d. after 828) succeeded Alcuin as master of the palace school (796), but was probably there earlier. He wrote an *Ars grammatica,* which he dedicated to Emperor LOTHAIR I (840–855). Another Irishman who contributed to the first generation of Carolingian scholarship is Colman (fl. early 9th century), who wrote a poem in fine Latin to a fellow countryman returning to Ireland. SMARAGDUS OF SAINT-MIHIEL was probably Irish; he wrote poetry (*Monumenta Germaniae Poetae* 1:602–619; 2:918–924) and taught Latin grammar, composing a commentary on DONATUS.

Theodulf of Orléans. The greatest scholar and author of the court circle was undoubtedly a Visigoth in the Isidorian tradition, Theodulf of Orléans (*c.* 770–821), whose writings (e.g., *Ad Carolum regem, Contra judices, GLORIA, LAUS ET HONOR*) show his classical training. His deep political insight reflects the Hispano-Roman sophistication that had been developed through the Councils of TOLEDO. He tried in vain to persuade Charles not to divide his empire according to the Frankish principle of equal inheritance (*Monumenta Germaniae Poetae* 1:526). Emperor Louis the Pious' attempt to maintain the primacy of his firstborn, Lothair I, over the two younger sons may have been an effect of Theodulf's hitherto unheeded advice. The results were disastrous in the 9th century, but ultimately (987) primogeniture became the rule in France. PAULINUS OF AQUILEIA was another poet-member of the court circle (*Monumenta Germaniae Poetae* 1:123–128), while PETER OF PISA, a grammarian, instructed Charles himself and illustrated his teaching—as was customary—with examples from ancient pagan and Christian authors. The only Frank to belong to the circle was ANGILBERT, a disciple of Alcuin, who wrote *Ecloga ad Karolum regem.* Through an affair with Bertha, one of Charlemagne's daughters, he had two sons; one was the lay historian Nithard. Angilbert later (between 796 and 802) became a monk and abbot of SAINT-RIQUIER, where he introduced the *laus perennis.*

The Second Generation. EINHARD (*c.* 770–*c.* 840) bridges two generations of the palace school. He was educated at Fulda and later at Aachen under Alcuin. His *Life of Charlemagne* is the best biography of the Middle Ages, and its strong classical orientation is evident in his use of SUETONIUS as a model. Nithard continued the biographical tradition in his history of the sons of Louis the Pious (*Historiarum libri 4*). Some time earlier LEIDRADUS OF LYONS (d. 814) had established an episcopal school in accord with Charlemagne's prescription, and there FLORUS OF LYONS (d. 860), who was possibly Spanish, continued to be the leading figure of the school.

Rabanus Maurus and His Circle. The royal monastery of Fulda was an important educational and cultural center of the Carolingian renaissance, especially under its great abbot, RABANUS MAURUS (776–856). Sent to Tours in 802 to study under Alcuin, he returned to Fulda the following year to direct the monastic school. He was abbot from 822 until 842, when he became archbishop of Mainz. His *De arte grammatica* and *De rerum naturis* do not show great originality, but he unquestionably deserves his title of preceptor of Germany. His student WALAFRID STRABO (809–849), later abbot of REICHENAU, was the tutor of Emperor Charles the Bald (840–877). Although Strabo was acquainted with most of the Latin meters, he preferred the hexameter (*Monumenta Germaniae Poetae* 2:259–472). Another of Rabanus's students, LUPUS (*c.* 805–*c.* 862), later abbot of Ferrières, was sent to study at Fulda *c.* 828. His letters (*Monumenta Germaniae Scriptores* 6:1–26) and MS collection reveal his interests in the classics, for of the 20 MSS that are certainly from his scriptorium at Ferrières, perhaps ten are Lupus's own transcriptions. Another student, GOTTS-CHALK OF ORBAIS (*c.* 805–869), was dedicated as a child to the monastic life at Fulda by his parents but later wished to withdraw. His request was denied; he was transferred to Orbais, and finally, because of his views on predestination, he was imprisoned for the rest of his life in Hautvillers. He wrote a poetical *conflictus,* or debate, between the Old Testament as represented by Alethea, a shepherdess, and the New, represented by Pseustis. Further works included 17 original and very human poems and several excellent hymns. His rebellion against dedication as a child to monastic life was an important—though personally disastrous—step in the Church's insistence on absolute freedom in choosing the religious life. Wandelbert of Prüm, a member of the same circle of writers, wrote hymns in Sapphic meters.

Hincmar of Reims. In the zeal and uprightness that characterized his episcopate, HINCMAR OF REIMS (d. 882) might be considered the fruition of Charlemagne's reforming efforts. His verses and letters mark him as a product of the Carolingian renaissance. His political theory is expressed in his *De ordine palatii* and *De institutione regis;* his course of action regarding the divorce of LOTHAIR II confirms his position that the emperor was subject to the Church *ratione peccati* (*Patrologia Latina,* 125: 623–772).

Two Irishmen also grace the second generation of the Carolingian renaissance: Sedulius Scotus (fl. 848–858) and JOHN SCOTUS ERIGENA (*c.* 810–*c.* 877). The former was the leading figure among his compatriots at LIÈGE; the latter, at the court of Charles the Bald. Sedulius was an accomplished poet, a master of all types of classical verse, who was reluctant to depart from classical precedents in any of his 83 poems; he was also a grammarian who wrote commentaries on Eutyches and

Priscian. He knew Cicero, Vegetius, Frontinus, Valerius Maximus, Macrobius, and Seneca.

The Court and Charles the Bald. Charles II the Bald is often condemned—probably quite unjustly—for buying off the piratical NORMANS. However, he appears in a much better light when one examines the patronage of learning at his court. The leading scholar in Charles' entourage was John Scotus Erigena, who wrote Greek verses and Latin poetry filled with Greek words and taught grammar and dialectic—rejecting absolute predestination on the basis of logic alone (*De predestinatione*). He was a commentator on Scripture and proved himself the first original philosopher of the Middle Ages (Gilson) in his *De divisione naturae,* which was based on the Greek and Latin sources of Platonism (*see* NEOPLATONISM). Milo of Saint-Amand, who also belonged to the same court circle, used patristic writers (e.g., Prudentius), as well as Macrobius. RADBOD OF UTRECHT (d. 917) was educated in Cologne and at Charles' court. As bishop of Utrecht he was forced to flee from the Northmen to Deventer, where he established an intellectual center. Radbod was the author of poems (*Monumenta Germaniae Poetae* 4:160–173), homilies, and historical works. HUCBALD OF SAINT-AMAND (840–930), another member of Charles' circle (*Ecloga de calvis*), was a humanist who listed the books in his library (many of which are still preserved at Valenciennes). He wrote a work on chant, *De institutione harmonica,* in which he tried to bring Greek and Boethian musical theory to bear upon chant and to establish definite pitch. Micon of Saint-Riquier (d. 865) compiled one of the better medieval FLORILEGIA in which he arranged authors alphabetically. HAGIOGRAPHY flourished in the time of Charles the Bald under Florus of Lyons, USUARD, ADO OF VIENNE, and others.

Medieval libraries were small but were probably used exhaustively, given the monastic stipulation of meditative reading. At the beginning of the Carolingian period only a few places (Rome, Bobbio, York) had libraries, but in its course libraries were developed at CORBIE, LUXEUIL, LORSCH, Fulda, FONTENELLE (SAINT-WANDRILLE), SAINT-AMAND-LES-EAUX, and SAINT-RIQUIER. The Carolingian SCRIPTORIUM saw the full development of a distinctive half-uncial script now named Carolingian minuscule, the basis of the modern book and cursive hands (*see* PALEOGRAPHY, LATIN). As a result of Carolingian stimulation, cathedral schools flourished in Utrecht, Würzburg, Magdeburg, Laon, REIMS, Blois, Orléans, CHARTRES, Bourges, and Lyons.

The classical character of Carolingian art is evident in the revival of bronze-casting and the use of Roman and Byzantine elements in the small, octagonal royal chapel at AACHEN, based on San Vitale in RAVENNA from which its columns were taken. The church built by Theodulf at Germigny des Prés (near Orléans) has a quatrefoil plan; mosaics in the Byzantine tradition adorn the interior.

See Also: CAROLINGIANS; CAROLINGIAN ART; LIBRI CAROLINI.

Bibliography: *Monumenta Germaniae Poetae aevi Carolini,* 4 v. (1884–1923). M. MANITIUS, *Geschichte der lateinischen Literatur des Mittelalters,* 3 v. (Munich 1911–31) v. 1, 3. C. H. BEESON, *Lupus of Ferrières as Scribe and Text Critic: A Study of His Autograph Copy of Cicero's De oratore* (Cambridge, Mass. 1930). P. LEHMANN, "Die handschriftliche Überlieferung der römischen Literatur," *Philobiblion* 7 (1934) 209–238. J. DE GHELLINCK, *Littérature latine au moyen-âge,* 2 v. (Paris 1939): v. 1, *Depuis les origines jusqu'à la fin de la renaissance carolingienne à saint Anselme; Bibliothèque catholique des sciences religieuses* 85–86. F. L. GANSHOF, "Charlemagne," *Speculum* 24 (1949) 520–528. M. HÉLIN, *A History of Medieval Literature,* tr. J. C. SNOW (rev. ed. New York 1949) 27–49. L. WALLACH, "Charlemagne's *De litteris colendis* and Alcuin," *Speculum* 26 (1951) 288–305. M. L. W. LAISTNER, *Thought and Letters in Western Europe, A.D. 500 to 900* (2d ed. New York 1957). H. LIEBESCHÜTZ, "Theodulf of Orleáns and the Problem of the Carolingian Renaissance," *Fritz Saxl Memorial Essays* (London 1957) 77–92. F. L. GANSHOF, *Lexikon für Theologie und Kirche,* ed. J. HOFER and K. RAHNER, 10 v. (2d, new ed. Freiburg 1957–65) 5:1377–79. E. S. DUCKETT, *Carolingian Portraits* (Ann Arbor 1962). *Corbie, abbaye royale* (Lille 1963). R. P. HINKS, *Carolingian Art* (London 1935; repr. pa. Ann Arbor 1962). J. SZÖVÉRFFY, *Die Annalen der lateinischen Hymnendichtung. Ein Handbuch,* 2 v. (Berlin 1964–65) 1:167–312. D. T. RICE, ed., *The Dawn of European Civilization* (New York 1965) 197–218, 269–326.

[C. M. AHERNE]

CAROLINGIANS

A Frankish family from which emerged a succession of rulers of the kingdom of the FRANKS who played a decisive role in shaping the course of western European history during the period from *c.* A.D.700 to *c.* A.D.1000.

Origin and Rise to Power

The rather elusive evidence on the dynasty's origin, most of it slanted to throw favorable light on the family, establishes that it stemmed from the union of two Frankish families, which during the sixth century amassed huge land holdings and extended followings in Austrasia, one of the kingdoms that emerged from the partition of the original kingdom of the Franks created by CLOVIS I (481–511) and his successors. The leaders of these two families, Arnulf and Pepin I the Elder of Landen, came into prominence in the first decade of the seventh century as influential figures serving the MEROVINGIAN king of Austrasia. Eventually, in 613 they led a revolt which overthrew Brunhilde, the dowager queen who had aroused aristocratic ire by her attempt to increase the

Golden Book of Prüm, engraved cover showing Christ with the kings of the Carolingian dynasty, first half of the 12th century.

power of the monarchy and her ruthless actions to safe-guard the interests of the offspring of her marriage to King Sigibert I (561–575) of Austrasia. As a reward for their role in ridding him of his Austrasian rival, King Chlothar II of Neustria, now sole king of the entire Frankish realm, appointed Arnulf as bishop of Metz and Pepin I as mayor of the palace in Austrasia. These offices provided their holders with opportunities to add to their wealth, their following, and their prestige during the reigns of Chlothar II (584–629) and his son and successor, Dagobert I (623–639). Although the evidence is not totally convincing, the sources propagating the official Carolingian version of family history claimed that with the marriage of Arnulf's son to Pepin's daughter the two families were joined to establish a single dynasty whose history began with the offspring of the marriage, PEPIN II of Herstal. Thus the family is often referred to as the Arnulfians or the Pippinids. Eventually, however, it came to be known as the Carolingians in honor of its most illustrious member, Carolus Magnus (CHARLEMAGNE).

Pepin II. Following the death of Pepin I in 639 or 640, the family suffered a temporary setback resulting from an aborted attempt in 656 of Grimoald, Pepin's son and successor as mayor of the palace, to arrange the election of his son as king in place of a member of the Merovingian dynasty. For his challenge to the right of the Merovingian family to hold the royal office, Grimoald was executed by Neustrian aristocrats eager to check the Pippinids. In the tumultuous two decades that followed, marked chiefly by the efforts of the mayor of the palace in Neustria, Ebroin, to establish his control over the entire Frankish kingdom, Pepin II quietly guarded his family's holdings and following, both substantially increased by his marriage in 670 to Plectrude, a member of another powerful Austrasian family. His opportunity to repair his family's fortunes came when the Neustrian aristocracy sought his aid in ridding themselves of the tyrannical rule of Ebroin and his successors as mayors of the palace. Pepin II and his Austrasian following won a victory over the Neustrian followers of Ebroin in the Battle of Tertry in 687. That victory put Pepin II in a position to dominate the entire Frankish kingdom by controlling the office of the mayor of the palace serving the Merovingian kings of both Neustria-Burgundy and Austrasia. Skillfully playing aristocratic factions against each other, Pepin was able not only to strengthen his position in Austrasia but also to build a following and expand the family land holdings in Neustria-Burgundy. He attained his goal in part by using the authority of his titular masters, the Merovingian kings, to appoint counts, bishops, and abbots loyal to the Pippinids and to reward them with lands pertaining to the royal domain. As a result of internal problems afflicting the Merovingian kingdoms in the late 7th

century, leaders of aristocratic families in Aquitaine, Thuringia, and Bavaria, territories previously conquered by Clovis I and his sons, sought to establish themselves as rivals of the Pippinids by leading movements to throw off Frankish rule. Pepin employed force and diplomacy to maintain Frankish dominance in those regions. He also successfully defended the Frankish kingdom against attacks by Gascons, Frisians, and Saxons, external foes always eager to raid Frankish territory.

Consolidation of Power

During the first half of the eighth century the Carolingian family built on the successes of Pepin II to soldify its position in the Frankish kingdom to the point tha allowed it to assume the Frankish crown. That success was due chiefly to the effective leadership of CHARLES MARTEL and PEPIN III the Short.

Charles Martel. The death of Pepin II in 714 led to a struggle to find a successor. Eventually, Pepin's illegitimate son, Charles, emerged victorious by overcoming the opposition of his stepmother, Plectrude, and of an anti-Pippinid coalition made up of Neustrian-Burgundian aristocratic families and pagan Frisians. From then until his death in 741 Charles took actions that greatly expanded his family's dominance over the Frankish kingdom. Although he held no office except that of mayor of the palace serving the Merovingian royal dynasty, so successful was he in exercising real power that he felt no need to replace a "do-nothing" Merovingian king who died in 737. His success was due in part to his continuation of his father's policy of filling key offices in the royal administration and the ecclesiastical establishment with loyal followers. To increase the number of followers Charles expanded the use of vassalage and benefice. Vassalage involved an act of commendation whereby a freeman voluntarily accepted a position of dependence with respect to another freeman who became his lord; implicit in the act was the obligation of the vassal to serve his lord. In return the vassal received the protection of his lord and was granted a benefice which consisted of something of material value, such as an office or land. It has long been alleged that Charles engaged in a systematic confiscation of church property to reward his vassals, especially in return for military service. There is scant evidence to support that charge; perhaps he did grant to his followers some church property that he had confiscated from worldly bishops and abbots who themselves were using the wealth and power gained from church property to further their own political ends. In his own day Charles won ecclesiastical favor by lending his support to Christian missionaries, including WILLIBRORD, BONIFACE, and PIRMIN, who were seeking to win converts and establish organized Christian life along the eastern frontier of the

Frankish kingdom in Frisia, Thuringia, Hesse, Alemannia, and Bavaria.

Charles also enhanced the reputation of his family by his military feats, successes that owed much to his ability to expand his military resources by rewarding vassals with grants of land which permitted them to provide military service at their own expense. While he was able to repel raids by pagan Frisians and Saxons on his northern and eastern frontiers, his main success came in southern Gaul, where a crisis emerged in the form of Muslim raids from Spain, recently taken from the VISIGOTHS by Muslim forces which had been advancing across the Mediterranean world since the death of MUḤAMMAD in 632. Although Duke Eudo of Aquitaine valiantly resisted the Muslim raiders, he was finally forced to call on the Franks for aid. Charles responded with a force that inflicted a major defeat on the Muslims at a battle fought near Poitiers in 732, a triumph which earned Charles the epithet *Martellus* (the Hammer). Although this triumph by no means ended Muslim raids in southern Gaul, it prompted contemporaries to credit Charles Martel with saving Christendom by stopping what seemed to be the irresistible advance of Islam. No less significantly, his intervention in southern Gaul provided the opportunity to strengthen Frankish control over Aquitaine, Provence, and Burgundy, where the Franks had long claimed overlordship. A measure of Charles' expanding reputation came in 739, when Pope GREGORY III sought his assistance in defending the papacy from the LOMBARDS. Charles declined that plea, but it would not be long before the papacy received a different response from the new power emerging north of the Alps, the Pippinid dynasty.

Pepin III. Before his death in 741 Charles Martel divided the realm between his two sons, CARLOMAN and Pepin III the Short. During the years of their joint reign the brothers cooperated in quelling rebellions in Bavaria, Aquitaine, and Alemannia, where there continued to be an unwillingness among local aristocratic leaders to accept a position inferior to the Pippinid family. In 743 Carloman and Pepin III sought to quiet that opposition by filling the vacant throne of the Frankish kingdom with a member of the Merovingian dynasty, a clear demonstration that despite its weakness that ancient family still commanded respect among the Franks. While protecting the integrity of the kingdom of the Franks and defending its borders, Carloman and Pepin III won favor by lending their support to a reform movement led by Boniface and approved by the papacy. The reform program, aimed at correcting a wide range of abuses that beset the religious establishment under the late Merovingians, was spelled out in a series of church councils held in the 740s whose enactments were given the force of law to be enforced by the mayors of the palace.

In 747 Carloman abdicated his office as mayor of the palace to become a monk. Pepin moved immediately to assume control of the entire Frankish realm, but some were not ready for that eventuality, including those loyal to Carloman's heirs and Pepin's half-brother, Grifo, who sought to foment rebellion in Bavaria and Aquitaine as a means of making good his claim to his share of the inheritance of his father, Charles Martel. Even before these threats were completely resolved, Pepin took a step that was decisive in the history of his dynasty: He decided to assume the title of king of the Franks. Perhaps that decision was prompted by his need to find a way of enhancing his status in the face of opposition within his own family and from other rival families. In order to justify replacing the Merovingian dynasty, which had held the kingship of the Franks for more than 250 years, in large part because their subjects believed that their blood carried with it a divine entitlement to the royal office, Pepin took a momentous step. In 750 he sent an embassy to Rome to inquire whether it was good or bad that the kings in Francia were powerless. Pope ZACHARIAS responded that it was better to call king one who held power than one who lacked power and commanded that Pepin be made king. Taking this response as a mandate to assume the royal office, Pepin turned to the notables of the kingdom who in 751 elected him king of the Franks. That action was followed by an innovation in Frankish history: The new king was anointed by the bishops; perhaps Boniface was among them. So fortified, Pepin III, "king by the grace of God," relegated the last Merovingian king to a monastery.

The position of the new king, viewed as a usurper by some, soon received additional sanction from the papacy. In the face of a mounting threat from the Lombards to Rome and to papal authority over the city and its surrounding territory and no longer able to count on aid from the emperor in Constantinople, the traditional protector of the papacy, Pope STEPHEN II (III) journeyed to Francia in 754 to meet with Pepin. The result was a series of negotiations which led to a pact of friendship between the king and the pope entailing mutual responsibilities deeply rooted in religious convictions. Pepin promised to serve as protector of the pope and the people of St. Peter and to restore to papal control specific territories which the papacy claimed. That claim was likely based on a document recently forged at the papal court, the famous DONATION OF CONSTANTINE, which stated that the first Christian emperor granted Pope SYLVESTER I possession of the western part of the Roman Empire. In return for Pepin's promise Stephen II anointed the king, his queen, and his sons, Carloman and Charles. He also bestowed on the father and the sons the title of *patricius Romanorum*, which implied some kind of authority in Rome, and proclaimed that none but members of Pepin's family should ever wear the Frankish crown.

Pepin upheld his part of the agreement by conducting military campaigns into Italy in 755 and 756, which ended in victories over the Lombard king and the granting to the papacy of considerable territories in central Italy, most of which previously had been claimed by the emperor in Constantinople. This so-called DONATION OF PEPIN constituted a landmark event in papal history by establishing the Papal States (*see* STATES OF THE CHURCH) as an independent entity, a state whose security was now linked with the destiny of God's special people, the Franks, and the dynasty that led them.

In the years between 756 and his death in 768 Pepin spent much of his energies on a series of campaigns that resulted in the incorporation of Aquitaine into the Frankish realm. He also actively promoted religious reform. In his reign the leadership of the reform movement slowly shifted from Rome, where Boniface had originally sought to place it, to the north, where the new king became the key figure in shaping the religious life of his subjects. That role was still another factor enhancing the power and the prestige of the Carolingian dynasty.

Charlemagne

As had been the custom with his Merovingian predecessors, the first Carolingian king divided his kingdom between his sons, Charles and Carloman. Their co-rulership was marked by mounting rivalry which threatened the internal unity that Pepin had established and the agreement he had made to protect the papacy and the Papal States, especially after Charlemagne sought advantage over Carloman by accepting a Lombard bride in return for an alliance with Desiderius, the Lombard king. Then in 771 Carloman died. Charlemagne immediately seized his brother's inheritance, assumed sole control over the entire kingdom, and repudiated his Lombard alliance and his recent bride. Thus began a remarkable reign that brought the Carolingian dynasty to the apogee of its power and influence and led contemporaries to call the king Charles the Great, Charlemagne.

Conqueror, Diplomat, Governor. Charlemagne was first of all a successful war leader, a key factor in holding the allegiance of his followers. During the first 30 years of his reign very few seasons passed without a campaign somewhere. Although Frankish armies sometimes suffered defeat, usually they were victorious, in part because of Charlemagne's skill in recruiting, supplying, and maneuvering his troops. One result of his campaigns was the solidification of Frankish control over territories that the Franks had long claimed, especially Aquitaine and Bavaria. Other triumphs resulted in the submission of extensive new areas to Frankish rule, including Frisia, Saxony, Lombard Italy, the Avar empire, and a portion of Muslim Spain lying between the Pyrenees and the Ebro river. An administrative structure manned by trusted Frankish aristocrats was imposed on these conquered territories as a means of assuring their assimilation into the Frankish realm. And those same triumphs produced booty and tribute which allowed Charlemagne to strengthen his claim on the allegiance of his followers, both lay and ecclesiastical, by bestowing rich rewards on them. The victories over the pagan Saxons and Avars was accompanied by their conversion to Christianity, often achieved by the use of force, especially in Saxony. Christianization proved to be an effective tool in incorporating conquered peoples into the Frankish realm.

As the frontiers of his kingdom were extended, Charlemagne sought to assure their defense by establishing heavily militarized territories, called marches, at strategic points around the periphery of his realm. He also mounted a successful effort combining military action and diplomacy aimed at winning allies and neutralizing potential threats to his kingdom posed by such neighbors as the Danes, various Slavic tribes, the Byzantine emperors, the Lombard dukes of Benevento in southern Italy, the Papal States, the Muslim caliphs ruling in Baghdad and Cordoba, the Christian rulers of the kingdom of the Asturias in northwestern Spain, the Gascons and Bretons in Gaul, and the Anglo-Saxon kings of Mercia and Northumbria. By the end of his reign his military and diplomatic successes won the Frankish kingdom recognition as a major world power.

In the midst of his military and diplomatic activities Charlemagne found time to concern himself with the governance of his expanding realm. In general, he was not a political innovator; rather, he ruled within the institutional framework inherited from the Merovingians. His chief concern was with utilizing traditional political institutions and techniques more effectively to establish order and maintain concord among his subjects. The king's authority continued to be represented at the local level by counts and bishops, charged with acting in the name of the king to administer justice, collect taxes, raise armed forces, and keep the peace in each of the more than 400 counties and 200 dioceses into which the kingdom was divided. As had long been the case, the central government was made up of the king and his personal entourage, called the *palatium* (palace). In addition to the royal family, the palace was composed of trusted lay and ecclesiastical companions of the king who discharged a variety of functions, including managing the royal resources, leading armies, conducting diplomatic missions, producing written documents related to royal administration, counseling the king on policy issues, directing religious life, and taking part in activities that entertained the king and his family. Charlemagne's powerful personality was a prime factor in making this rather primitive administrative structure effective. Equally important was his success in filling offices at all levels with competent individuals drawn from a limited number of powerful aristocratic families, especially from Austrasia, eager to serve the king in return for the prestige, the power, and the material rewards derived from holding office.

Charlemagne was most innovative as a political leader in strengthening linkages between his person and his *palatium* and the local centers of power spread across his huge realm. He utilized several means to achieve this end: asserting influence through a network of office holders drawn from a limited number of families with shared interests; summoning power wielders of the kingdom to annual assemblies for consultation and approval of royal policies; regularizing and extending the use of *missi dominici*, royal agents sent out in pairs to tour specifically defined territorial entities to announce and enact the royal will locally; improving communication between the central government and local organs of government by expanding the use of written documents, especially CAPITULARIES, royal orders dispatched across the kingdom to inform all concerned what the king willed and how his commands were to be achieved; expanding the use of vassalage to create personal bonds linking important subjects to him and of benefices to provide material benefits on a basis that encouraged the vassal to remain loyal to his royal lord; and requiring all free men in his realm to swear an oath obliging them to be faithful in obeying and serving the ruler.

Charlemagne's efforts to make more effective traditional political institutions were accompanied by a subtle change in the concepts defining the purpose of government and the role of the king. To the traditional view of king as warlord there was added a religious dimension defined by ideas drawn from Old Testament models of kingship and from the vision of the city of God articulated by St. AUGUSTINE. The evolving concept of governance imposed on the king who ruled ''by the grace of God'' an obligation to shape the spiritual and material lives of his subjects according to the commands of God. Kingship took on a ministerial dimension which mandated that a ruler be both priest and king, thereby blurring the distinction between the sacred and the secular, between the Church and the state, and greatly expanding the responsibilities and the political priorities of the ruler not only in religious matters but also in a wide range of social affairs related to eradicating sin, keeping order, protecting the weak, and providing justice for all.

Religious Reformer and Cultural Patron. Changing concepts of the function of kingship and the ends of governance gave impetus to two interrelated developments associated with the Carolingian dynasty: a religious reformation and a cultural renewal. The effort to reform religious life, already begun under Pepin III and Carloman, was expanded and given fresh impetus by Charlemagne, whose efforts were prompted at least in part by his personal belief that he as ruler had a responsibility for the spiritual well being of his subjects. His reforming program was complex, worked out by the king and his close advisers, enacted in a succession of church councils, publicized through capitularies which carried the force of law, and enforced by royal agents, especially bishops, who supported the correction of religious life. Reform focused on certain key problems: imposing a hierarchical structure on the ecclesiastical system, especially by strengthening episcopal authority; extending that organization into the rural areas of the kingdom in the form of a parish structure; mandating better training for the clergy as a means of improving the intellectual and moral capabilities required to discharge their offices; improving pastoral care so as to deepen understanding of the true faith and its behavioral norms; protecting and expanding the material resources of the Church, including the imposition of tithes; regularizing and standardizing liturgical practices; rooting out all traces of paganism; and suppressing deviations from the orthodox faith. The quest for norms that defined the right way to be Christian led to a vigorous exploration of Christian tradition defining canon law, theology, cult practices, and morality. The reformers were quick to turn to the papacy for guidance, especially in the realms of liturgy and canon law. Consequently, Charlemagne's religious *reformatio* took on a strong Roman complexion and marked an important step in establishing Roman Catholicism as a unifying force in western Europe. As Charlemagne's reform unfolded, it thrust the king into an ever more powerful role in controlling religious life, especially in terms of filling key ecclesiastical offices, managing church resources, and deciding what constituted the proper way to be Christian and to run the Christian community.

Charlemagne's efforts to improve the royal government and the religious establishment created a need for better educated individuals to serve the monarchy and the Church. The response to that need produced a cultural renewal, known as the Carolingian Renaissance, that reached its full force after Charlemagne's reign but which in its beginning owed much to his initiative and which constituted one of the most enduring contributions of the Carolingians dynasty. Charlemagne's cultural revival was given its original impetus and shape by a circle of scholars he gathered at his court from Italy, Spain, Ireland, and England; the most important of these foreigners was ALCUIN of York. Their intellectual interactions at the royal court in which the king was personally involved eventually led to measures taken with royal support to achieve the basic objectives of the king's cultural program: the establishment of an educational system equipped to improve Latin literacy as a means of enhancing the performance of those charged with imposing order on the Frankish society and with guiding the souls of the faithful to salvation.

Like his religious reform, Charlemagne's cultural program was essentially corrective, designed to renew cultural norms that had fallen into neglect in the Frankish kingdom. Court scholars soon began to produce textbooks to serve as tools in teaching Latin and to search out texts required to assure competency in interpreting Scripture, explaining doctrinal fundamentals, applying canon law, performing the liturgy, and teaching Christian morality. Attention was given to increasing book production and collection so as to make copies of those texts widely available. The answer was the establishment at the royal court of a copy center, called a *scriptorium*, and a library. Emphasis on book production prompted the adoption of a system of handwriting known as Carolingian Minuscule that was easier to write and to read and the search for techniques and motifs useful in decorating books.

Prompted by royal command and guided by literary and artistic activity at court, cultural life quickened across Charlemagne's realm. Existing cathedral and monastic schools, scriptoria (*see* SCRIPTORIUM), and libraries were reenergized and new ones came into existence. In some of these schools skilled masters expanded the curriculum to the point where a full-scale education in the liberal arts comparable to that of the late classical world became available. Library collections began to include not only writings of church fathers but also the works of classical Latin authors; many classical texts have survived only in manuscripts produced in Carolingian scriptoria. The impact of cultural revival became evident in many areas: the increasing number of schools, scriptoria, and libraries; the increased honor paid to masters in these schools; the increased number and improved quality of written documents pertaining to civil and ecclesiastical administration; the increasing sophistication of writings devoted to explaining scripture and resolving complex theological issues; innovations in art and architecture spurred by the effort to improve religious facilities and deepen piety; stylistic creativity manifested in letter writing, history, hagiography, and poetry; the articulation of fresh ideas about the nature of society and its governance, the structure and practice of Christian life, and the responsibilities of those who wielded power.

Emperor. This impressive list of achievements during the first 30 years of Charlemagne's reign provided the background for the culminating event of his career, his elevation to the office of emperor on Christmas Day, 800. A decisive factor leading up to this event was a growing consciousness among Charlemagne's advisers, and perhaps in the king's own mind, that a new community was evolving under the aegis of the Carolingian dynasty. Increasingly referred to as the *imperium christianum*, that community was envisioned to consist of all who professed the orthodox faith proclaimed by the Roman church and its Carolingian protectors. Its formation and its welfare owed much to Charlemagne, whose traditional titles seemed to many to convey inadequately the true role of the ''new David,'' and the ''new Constantine'' as leader of the society of true believers. And it was increasingly perceived that the future of the Christian community depended on leadership by one who could be trusted to give priority to the guardianship of orthodox Christendom. The concern for the welfare of the *imperium christianum* was acerbated in the eyes of many by the demonstrated unfitness of the heretical emperors in Constantinople to lead the Christian community; that unfitness was made especially manifest to many when a woman, IRENE, became emperor in 797.

The concern about the direction of the Christian community reached crisis proportions when papal leadership of the *imperium christianum* came under assault. In 799 a faction of Roman aristocrats rebelled against Pope LEO III, seeking to depose him on the grounds of tyranny and personal misconduct. Leo III escaped with his life by fleeing to Charlemagne's court. Long accustomed to protecting the papacy and the Papal States from external foes, Charlemagne was now called upon to deal with internal foes of the papacy in a situation where the king's rights to take action in judging the successor of St. Peter were far from clear. Creative action was in order. Acting through delegates Charlemagne restored Leo III to office in late 799 and then made an extended tour of his realm to consult with various advisers, finally ending in Rome in late 800 to settle matters. After carrying out extensive discussions during December of 800, arrangements were made that avoided judging Pope Leo III by allowing him to clear himself before an assembly of dignitaries by swearing under oath that he was innocent of the accusations against him. Two days later, on Christmas Day, as Charlemagne prepared to celebrate Mass in the basilica of St. Peter, Pope Leo III placed a crown on his head while the assembled crowd acclaimed him emperor. Then the pope performed the ritual act of obeisance due an emperor.

Although the evidence surrounding the coronation is confusing, there can be little doubt that Charlemagne and Leo III collaborated in reaching the momentous decision to revive the Roman Empire in the West. Some evidence suggests that plans for the event began to take shape as early as the meeting of Charlemagne and Leo immediately after the attack on the pope, with the king taking the leading role. Each stood to gain from the restoration of the empire. Aside of ridding himself of his enemies, Leo III put himself in Charlemagne's debt by lending authenticity to a still another new title that further exalted the Carolingians but was not enthusiastically accepted by all the new emperor's subjects. Papal participation in the imperial coronation marked another step in establishing papal involvement as a constitutive factor in authenticating the election of secular rulers. Charlemagne's status was elevated among his subjects by a title that took into account the diverse peoples he had conquered, his efforts to establish peace and concord, and his services on behalf of Christianity. And he could now claim equality with the emperors in Constantinople. His position as emperor gave greater clarity to his legal status in Rome and the Papal States, especially in terms of taking legal actions against those who had conspired to depose Leo III.

Less clear is what the new title meant to Charlemagne in governing his own realm during the last years of his reign. Some evidence suggests that being emperor had little or no impact on his political program. For example, he kept his old titles as king of the Franks and of the Lombards to which were added an enigmatic phrase to the effect that he was "emperor governing the Roman Empire," and in 806 he made provisions for his own succession that divided his kingdom into three portions without any reference to his imperial title or the idea of political unity implicit in that title. Other testimony indicates that the imperial title added new dimensions to his concept of his role as leader of the *imperium christianum*. For example, he intensified his efforts to reform the Church in terms that emphasized unity, peace, and concord, took steps to bring greater uniformity into a legal system marked by excessive diversity, engaged in a successful military and diplomatic campaign to gain acceptance of his imperial title from the emperor in Constantinople, and in 813 bestowed with his own hands the imperial crown on his only surviving son, Louis I the Pious. Perhaps it would not be amiss to suggest that Charlemagne was not quite sure what his new office meant. In the final analysis, he seems to have viewed the imperial office as an honor extended to him in recognition of his personal accomplishments, an award to be used as he pleased but not to be set aside lightly in view of its potential for enhancing his authority as a Christian ruler and his status among other rulers in his world. In any case, what happened on Christmas Day of 800 bestowed on the Carolingian dynasty the honor of renewing the Roman Empire in the West, thereby creating an institution that would play an important part in western European history for centuries to come.

Louis I

When Charlemagne died in 814, the destiny of the Carolingian dynasty whose cause he had served so well fell to his son, Louis I the Pious. Although Louis I has often been dismissed as a political weakling whose policies set the Carolingian family on the course of ruin, recent scholarship has provided a more positive evaluation of his reign and demonstrated that his apparent failures were a consequence of problems inherent in the system he inherited rather than of his faulty leadership. Well educated, deeply religious, and politically experienced as a result of serving as subking of Aquitaine since 781, Louis came to the throne with definite ideas about the nature of Christian society and the responsibilities of its leadership. One of his first acts was to adopt the title of "Emperor and Augustus", dropping all reference to his kingship of Franks and Lombards, an act that heralded his dedication to establishing and maintaining the unity of the realm he had inherited. He gave notice that it was his aim to raise the moral tone of his regime by launching an attack on corruption and immorality which led to the purging the royal court of many of his relatives as well as several of his father's chief advisers. In their place he installed advisers committed to his program of unity, including especially the monk BENEDICT OF ANIANE.

Collectively, these new advisers were products of the religious reform and the cultural renaissance that had taken shape during Charlemagne's reign; their education instilled in them a conviction that the imperial office and the emperor must serve as instruments for shaping the earthly city of God in which all stood united under a Christian emperor who directed them in a common effort to conduct themselves according to the norms defined by the Christian religion. That conviction, to which Louis enthusiastically subscribed during the early years of his reign, spawned a vigorous effort to intensify the reform movement begun by his predecessors. In the legislation that emerged from that effort emphasis was on establishing uniform rules governing clerical life, imposing on the monastic establishment a uniform regime defined by the Rule of St. Benedict (*see* BENEDICTINE RULE), and bringing all the faithful together in observing common moral standards and liturgical practices. As Louis' reform progressed, its clerical leaders increasingly pressed upon the emperor his accountability before God for giving priority to spiritual issues in his actions and his obligation to accept the guidance of spiritual leaders.

Louis did not neglect his worldly duties entirely. For example, he defended the imperial frontiers vigorously, continued his father's diplomatic efforts, promoted missionary activity in Scandinavia, and patronized cultural activities. But even in these matters he acted in ways that reflected his determination to serve the political, social, and cultural ends implicit in the concepts undergirding the Christian empire. He took steps to make governmental institutions more effective in identifying and correcting injustice and corruption and in formulating laws that would unify God's people.

Louis sought to unite his regime more closely with the papacy by welcoming Pope STEPHEN IV to Francia in 817, receiving from the pope an imperial crown and a papal anointment that his father had denied him when he with his own hands bestowed the imperial office on his son in 813. Louis worked out with Stephen IV and his successor, Pope PASCAL I, the *Pactum Ludovicianum,* which reaffirmed the friendship pact between the pope and the Frankish ruler first established in 754 by Pope Stephen II and Pepin III and confirmed the role of the emperor as guarantor of territorial integrity of the Papal States. In 824 Louis' government reached an agreement with Pope EUGENIUS II called the *Constitutio Romana* which sought to integrate the Papal States more closely into the structure of the empire by defining more precisely the relationship between the emperor and the pope in terms that allowed the emperor greater authority over what happened in Rome. The ultimate statement of Louis' effort to ensure unity came in the *Ordinatio imperii,* issued in 817 to define succession to Louis. Contrary to Frankish custom, it designated his oldest son, Lothair, as co-emperor with the right to succession to the imperial office. Louis' other sons, Pepin and Louis, were assigned subkingdoms but were subordinated to Lothair, who would have ultimate authority over the entire empire.

Despite the concerted efforts of Louis and his advisers to create and perpetuate a unified Christian empire, their program encountered growing difficulties. The ehtnic, linguistic, and legal diversity existing within the Empire constituted a formidable obstacle to effective unity. Louis' effort to set aside the tradition of partition of the realm among all the royal heirs aroused opposition, as evidenced by the revolt of the grandson of Charlemagne, Bernard, king of Italy, whose rights to succession were totally bypassed in the *Ordinatio imperii.* Although Louis succeeded in ending this rebellion in a way that led to Bernard's death, he was by no means able to win support for his idea of succession from many of his subjects whose material welfare was associated with one or another possible heirs to the throne.

In his effort to celebrate unity and concord Louis took a step that discredited him in the eyes of many. In 822 he summoned the lay and ecclesiastical magnates of his realm to join him in reconciling their differences by admitting their sins and joining in an act of public penitence. The emperor himself confessed and did penance for a series of acts carried out in the performance of his office, including his part in exiling key advisers who had served his father and in bringing about the death of King Bernard of Italy. This bizarre episode, highly charged with religious overtones reflecting the ideals of imperial unity, convinced many powerful aristocrats that Louis not only had belittled his imperial office but also had fallen completely under the influence of his clerical advisers. Many aristocrats were concerned about Louis' regime for other reasons. Although he acted decisively to defend his empire, he undertook no wars of conquest, thus ending the flow of booty with which Charlemagne had rewarded his powerful supporters. The prospect of a central government dominated by clerics determined to hold those in positions of authority to moral standards defined by the Christian religion posed a threat to the power that many self-serving noble families had long been accustomed to wielding at the local and regional level, including the license to reduce powerless subjects to a position of dependence.

The resistance to the creation and perpetuation of a unified imperial regime eventually found a focus around a particular event: the birth in 823 of a son, Charles, to Louis by his second wife, Judith. This well-educated and gifted queen immediately set about assuring an inheritance for her son, a cause that she sought to aid by advancing the role of her family at court. Before long Louis I began to accede to her wishes, taking actions that raised questions about his commitment to the imperial ideal and the *Ordinatio imperii* of 817 and that threatened to diminish the territories assigned to Louis' older sons in that ordinance. The redirection of royal policy led the champions of imperial unity to shift their allegiance to Lothair, whose own ambitions added a disturbing element to the gathering storm. The ensuing jockeying for position ended in revolts in 830 and 833 in which Louis' three older sons joined hands against their father and his wife, each seeking to better his own position while preventing an inheritance for their half-brother, Charles. As a result of the second revolt, Louis was forced to surrender his office on the grounds that faults he had committed as ruler, including his failure to uphold the *Ordinatio imperii* of 817, proved his unfitness to rule as a Christian emperor. Although that harsh measure, shaped primarily by a group of church leaders committed to the cause of imperial unity and the interests of Lothair, was overturned in 834 and Louis was restored to power, the circumstances that brought about the emperor's deposition placed important constraints on the concept of authority which had prevailed under earlier Frankish rulers. The last years of Louis' reign witnessed continued maneuvering, chiefly at the instigation of Queen Judith, to provide a substantial inheritance for Charles, an end that was achieved just before Louis died. In the process much of the passion for imperial unity was dissipated; of greater interest among conflicting factions were concerns with what form the ultimate division of Louis' empire would take and who would benefit most.

The Dissolution of the Empire and the End of the Carolingian Dynasty

Upon Louis' death in 840 LOTHAIR I moved immediately to assert his authority as emperor over the entire realm of his father. His brothers, Louis the German and Charles the Bald, joined forces in opposition and inflicted a major setback on his ambitions at the Battle of Fontenoy in 841. In the extended negotiations that ensued the three brothers agreed on the Treaty of Verdun in 843. It provided for a division of the empire into three autonomous political entities. To Louis went everything east of the Rhine and north of the Alps to create an entity henceforth called the kingdom of the East Franks. Charles was assigned everything west of a line following the Scheldt, Meuse, Saône, and Rhône rivers, a territory soon known as the kingdom of the West Franks. Lothair I received the territory between the other two kingdoms, stretching from the North Sea south into Italy. While retaining the imperial title, Lothair I gave up all claim to effective authority over his brothers.

After the Treaty of Verdun went into effect the three Carolingian rulers sought to sustain some semblance of unity by periodic efforts at brotherly cooperation in resolving common problems. Due in part to their efforts, some aspects of the Carolingian program continued to evolve, including religious reform and cultural renewal. But gradually the idea of political unity eroded, leaving it to the Church to nurture the concept of unity based on membership in a single ecclesiastical structure, adherence to a common faith, and observance of a common cult practices. Universalist concepts within the Church were represented with particular vigor by popes NICHOLAS I (858–867) and JOHN VIII (872–882).

Each of the independent kingdoms created by the Treaty of Verdun went its own way, but each proceeded toward the same end insofar as the Carolingian dynasty was concerned: the weakening of royal authority and the eventual replacement of Carolingian rulers with new ruling families. Along the path toward the extinction of the family, the last Carolingians had to cope with the same fundamental challenge that had faced their Merovingian predecessors: the claim of powerful aristocrats to political autonomy in their local setting. Their response to that challenge led to the emergence of a new monarchical system based on the lord-vassal relationship that defined governance in terms of personal political services promised by vassal to the lord-king in return for benefices (fiefs) in the form of offices or grants of land which provided the resources used by royal vassals to establish dominance over their own vassals and dependent serfs. The collapse of effective monarchy was hastened by the damage heaped upon the Carolingian world by outside invaders, including Vikings, Muslims, and Magyars, against whom the Carolingian kings were incapable of organizing effective defense.

The Middle Kingdom. The most vulnerable of the kingdoms created by the Treaty of Verdun was the Middle Kingdom of Emperor Lothair I, who continued with little success his claim to superior authority over his brothers. Upon his death in 855 his realm was divided into three separate kingdoms. Lothair II inherited the northernmost part, Lotharingia or Lorraine, where he ruled until his death in 869. Thereupon his kingdom came to an end, replaced by a vaguely defined principality which for many generations remained a bone of contention between the rulers of the West and the East Frankish kingdoms, then of France and Germany. Another of Lothair's sons, Charles, received Burgundy and Provence as a kingdom; eventually two separate kingdoms, Burgundy and Provence, were carved out of this territory, each ruled over by kings with remote or no ties with the Carolingian family. Lothair I's oldest son, Louis II, crowned king of Italy in 844 and emperor in 850 by his father, proved to be an effective ruler, but only in Italy. He was especially noted for his efforts to defend Italy against Muslim attacks and for continuing the Carolingian policy of protecting the papacy, albeit in a fashion that put severe limits on papal autonomy. But after his death without an heir in 875, Italy slipped toward political chaos. The papal search for a successor to Louis II as emperor resulted in the coronation of successive Carolingians, first Charles the Bald (875) and then Charles III the Fat (881), neither of whom was effective in ruling Italy. Thereafter, a series of petty princes, some distantly related to the Carolingians and others non-Carolingians, competed for the kingship of Italy and the imperial title. As their rivalry proceeded, the imperial title grew increasingly meaningless and the kingdom of Italy fragmented into local lordships whose impotence set the stage for a long succession of intruders into Italy. By 900 any effective Carolingian presence in Italy had ended. A major victim of that development was the papacy which increasingly fell under the dominance of local aristocratic families interested in ensconcing family members on the papal throne as a means of pillaging the wealth of the Roman Church and the Papal States.

The Kingdom of the East Franks. In the kingdom of the East Franks Louis the German ruled until 876. His realm was composed of several semi-autonomous duchies that had been shaped by leaders of the powerful Frankish families whom Charlemagne had entrusted with establishing Frankish rule over fractious ethnic groups that had long resisted Frankish overlordship. As the ninth century proceeded the leaders of these families played on ehtnic memories and their ability to exploit royal resources and functions to carve out virtually independent principalities. Included among those duchies were Bavaria, Saxony, Thuringia, Franconia, and Alemannia; added later to that list was Lotharingia and Swabia. Despite troubles within his own family and raids on his kingdom by Slavs and Vikings, Louis the German ruled with some effectiveness. His authority was based primarily on his success in arranging marriage alliances that strengthened his position in several of the duchies and his success in gaining the support of key ecclesiastsical figures. Prior to his death he divided his kingdom among his three sons, the most notable of whom was Charles III the Fat, who through the efforts of Pope John VIII was crowned emperor in 881, became the sole ruler of the kingdom of the East Franks in 882 after the untimely deaths of his brothers, and then was elected king of the West Frankish kingdom in 884. However, Charles the Fat was not successful in any of these roles; under pressure from all sides, he finally abdicated in 887, the last Carolingian to rule over the entire realm created by Charlemagne. The magnates of the East Frankish kingdom then elected as king Arnulf, an illegitimate son of a brother of Charles III. Arnulf (887–899) proved to be a modestly effective ruler, winning some support from the powerful ducal families and defending the realm against Slavic, Viking, and Magyar raiders. In 898 Pope FORMOSUS persuaded him to accept the imperial office and the kingship of Italy, but he was able to achieve little in terms of controlling Italy. On his death in 899 he was succeeded as king of the East Franks by his son, Louis IV the Child, who ruled until 911. Thereupon the lay and ecclesiastical magnates of the East Frankish kingdom chose as king a non-Carolingian, Duke Conrad of Franconia. His election signaled that a new, non-Carolingian political entity, Germany, was coming into existence.

The Kingdom of the West Franks. The reign of Charles the Bald (843–877) in the kingdom of the West Franks was marked by major challenges and mixed results. A fundamental problem facing the new king involved safeguarding of royal authority against the ambitions of powerful aristocratic families who were successfully exploiting their land holdings, military followings, and fortified castles to establish local enclaves of dominance. In dealing with this challenge Charles sought to establish with these local potentates a lord-vassal relationship in which each vassal pledged to respect his lord's

royal prerogatives in return for concessions in the form of offices, lands, and immunities from royal authority, concessions increasingly viewed as permanent possessions of their recipients, to be handed down to their descendants. This policy provided the means for dukes and counts to hasten the creation of principalities in which they assumed an ever larger share of public authority and built followings of subordinates who became their vassals. In dealing with aristocratic claims Charles had some success in playing one faction against another, a tactic that allowed him to gain the support of various noble families interested in limiting the success of other families. Charles was also successful in enlisting the support of the ecclesiastical establishment, especially that of Archbishop HINCMAR OF REIMS, in defending royal authority. His ecclesiastical policy entailed generous grants to bishops and abbots of land and immunity from royal authority, efforts to protect the Church's resources from greedy laymen, support of religious reform, and patronage of cultural activity associated with enriching religious life. For all his skill in rallying support for the royal cause, royal rights and royal resources diminished, basically as a consequence of the royal decision to concede both in return for support and of the growing perception that royal authority rested on a contract defined by what lay and ecclesiastical potentates promised to do in exchange for concessions made by the king. Charles' efforts to prevent the erosion of royal authority were complicated by his inability to muster an effective defense against the ever more destructive Viking incursions into his kingdom, a challenge that local potentates, utilizing their private armies and their fortified castles, met more successfully than did the king.

Amidst his trials in defense of his kingdom and his royal authority, Charles still found time and energy to play a role in the larger world which earned him recognition as the most efffective of the late Carolingians. He was able to fend off an invasion of his kingdom by his brother, Louis the German, to play a role in thwarting the efforts of his nephew, King Lothair II of Lotharingia, to gain a divorce that would have provided Lothair with a legitimate heir to his kingdom, and to claim a share of Lotharingia after Lothair II's died without an heir. As a consequence of his patronage his court became the cultural center of western Europe, producing literary and artistic works that represented the most mature products of the Carolingian Renaissance. The culminating event of Charles' career came in 875, when through the efforts of Pope John VIII he was elected emperor, an honor that brought him little political gain anywhere in the Carolingian world, least of all in his own kingdom.

Charles was succeeded by his son, Louis II the Stammerer (877–879), and his grandsons, Louis III (879–882) and Carloman (879–884), under whose rule royal power continued to erode. The magnates of the West Frankish kingdom then selected Charles the Fat as king. Already king of the East Frankish kingdom and emperor, Charles was an inept ruler who was forced to abdicate in 887. Thereupon, a non-Carolingian, Odo, count of Paris and a member of one of the most powerful West Frankish families, the Robertines, was elected king, in part on the basis of his role in defending Paris against Viking attacks. Despite his efforts, Odo enjoyed little success against a variety of powerful figures whose loyalty, real or pretended, to the Carolingian dynasty provided an excuse for resisting him. To offset their opposition Odo finally agreed to the restoration of the Carolingian line in the person of Charles III the Simple, grandson of Charles the Bald.

During his reign Charles III (898–923) struggled valiantly to defend and even expand royal authority in the face of pressure exerted by the nobility to limit the king's authority. In this struggle he continued to rely on and receive the support of the Church. Charles III took a major step toward ending the long-standing Viking menace by reaching an agreement with the Viking leader Rollo in 911 in which Charles III granted to Rollo and his Norman followers a territory in the lower Seine valley, eventually known as the duchy of Normandy, to serve as their permanent home. In return Rollo became the vassal of Charles III and agreed to become a Christian, actions which marked important steps in integrating the Vikings into the mainstream of western Christendom. Charles III also conducted a skillful diplomatic campaign that led to the restoration of Lotharingia to the West Frankish kingdom.

Despite these successes, Charles was unable to retain the loyalty of key power wielders in his West Frankish realm. Their rebellion led to Charles' imprisonment and his replacement by a new king, Robert I (922–923), who after a brief reign was succeeded by Ralph (Raoul), duke of Upper Burgundy (923–936), both non-Carolingians connected with the Robertine dynasty that earlier had produced King Odo. Ralph continued the traditional Carolingian effort to defend royal authority against ambitious dukes and counts. Most of them eventually accepted him as their lord but who as vassals conducted affairs in their domains in a fashion that allowed little room for royal authority. Ralph suffered a setback as king when he was forced to surrender control over Lotharingia to Henry I, king of the East Franks. When Ralph died without heirs in 936, the leader of the Robertine family arranged for the election of a Carolingian, Louis IV, the son of Charles III the Simple, who had been living in exile in England since the overthrow of his father in 923.

With the reigns of Louis IV d'Outremer (from overseas) (936–954), his son, Lothair IV (954–986), and his grandson, Louis V (986–987), the Carolingian dynasty approached its end. Their reigns unfolded in a setting where the leaders of the various principalities that had been taking shape in the kingdom of the West Franks at least since the Treaty of Verdun had gained ascendancy in political life. These princes recognized the kings as their overlords and accepted their place as vassals, a position that gave the kings a theoretical right to command their allegiance and to claim certain services from them. These powerful royal vassals in turn surrounded themselves with their own vassals who owed their prime allegiance and services to their local lords rather than to the king; an extensive network of intermediaries had been created between the king and his subjects, limiting his ability to assert power over them directly. This feudal order had evolved because it proved effective in establishing local order in an era of political instability and persistent outside invasions. Because of the willingness of their predecessors to buy support by granting their powerful vassals lands, offices, and the rights to exercise public functions, the last Carolingians were left with dwindling resources with which to support their political actions. They had become little more than first among equals, still guarding what little remained of the prestige that their Carolingian predecessors had gained for the royal title, but limited in their ability to direct affairs within their realm.

On Feb. 2, 962 an event unfolded that signaled that during the course of the 10th century the role long played by Carolingians had passed into other hands. The non-Carolingian king of the East Franks and of Italy, OTTO I the Great, received from Pope JOHN XII the imperial crown bestowed earlier on Charlemagne by Pope Leo III and held by several of his descendants but vacant since 924. Like Charlemagne, Otto I earned that honor through his deeds in defending Christendom, supporting the Church, and rescuing the papacy from its oppressors. Perhaps the sequence of events that led to Otto I's election as emperor made it easier for the magnates of the West Frankish kingdom to reach their decision when in 987 King Louis V was killed in an accident; they elected as his successor a member of the Robertine family, Hugh Capet, whose elevation marked the beginning of a new dynasty, the Capetians, to lead a political entity that would soon be called France. For the first time since Pepin II's victory at Tertry three centuries earlier in 687 no member of the Carolingian dynasty was in a position of power.

Afterword

The fact that the last Carolingians suffered a fate much like that of their Merovingian predecessors at the hands of powerful aristocrats bent on establishing local centers of power might tempt one to conclude that the history of the Carolingian dynasty represented little more than an inconsequential interlude in western European history. That similarity should not veil the large mark the family made on western European society. Perhaps that mark was best described by a contemporary of Charlemagne who hailed his hero as *Europae pater* ("father of Europe"). In a real sense the dynasty of Charlemagne had generated a widely shared consciousness of membership in a new entity called Europe. That entity embraced a distinctive territory and a unique human community with its own political, religious, economic, social, and cultural features that set it aside from other contemporary communities. The Carolingian dynasty could rightfully lay claim to an important role in establishing the foundations for that community. Although there were limitations on the achievements of the Carolingians as political leaders, religious reformers, and cultural patrons, their programs in these realms were crucial in defining ideological parameters and institutional structures which succeeding generations employed to bring to maturity western European civilization as a potent force in world history.

See Also: CAROLINGIAN REFORM; CAROLINGIAN RENAISSANCE; LIBERAL ARTS; MONASTIC SCHOOLS.

Bibliography: Sources. The reconstruction of the history of the Carolingian dynasty depends on a wide range of literary sources, including chronicles and annals, biographies, letters, capitularies, charters, Germanic law codes, acts of church councils, canon law collections, theological and philosophical tracts, poetry, saints' lives, scriptural commentaries, moral admonitions, educational manuals, and even forged texts. Recent scholarship has demonstrated clearly that there is also much to be learned about the Carolingian world from its archaeological and artistic record. The Latin versions of most of the literary texts have been published in such great collections as the *Monumenta Germanicae Historia*; J. P. MIGNE, ed., *Patrologia Cursus Completus, Series Latina*: and the *Corpus Christianorum, Series Latina* and *Corpus Christianorum, Continuatio Medievalis*. A full list of Carolingian literary sources with citations to published editions can be found in *The New Cambridge Medieval History*, Volume 2: *c. 700–c. 900*, ed. R. MCKITTERICK (Cambridge, New York, and Melbourne, 1995) 867–885. A useful brief description of the main sources for Carolingian history is provided by R. COLLINS, *Charlemagne* (Toronto and Buffalo, 1998) 1–15. For fuller treatment, see W. WATTENBACH, W. LEVISON, and H. LÖWE, *Deutschlands Geschichtsquellen im Mittelalter: Frühzeit und Karolinger*, Parts 1–6 and Beiheft: *Die Rechtsquellen*, by R. BUCHNER (Weimar, 1952–1973); a revised version of this work, somewhat simplified in organization, has been edited by F. HUF and published in 2 vols. under the same title in 1991. Helpful introductions to the Carolingian artistic record are J. HUBERT, J. PORCHER, and W. VOLBACH, *Carolingian Art*, trans. J. EMMONS, S. GILBERT, and R. ALLEN, *The Art of Mankind* (London 1970); F. MÜTHERICH and J. E. GAEHDE, *Carolingian Painting* (New York 1976); and C. HEITZ, *Le France pré-romaine: Archéolgie et architecture religieuse du haut Moyen Âge du IVe siècle à l'an mil* (Paris 1987). Some sense of the material world in which Carolingian life unfolded is provided by the illustrations in D. BULLOUGH, *The Age of*

Charlemagne (London and Toronto, 1963), and H. ROTH, *Kunst und Handwerk im frühen Mittelalter: archäologische Zeugnisse von Childerich I. bis zu Karl dem Grossen* (Stuttgart 1986). **Literature.** J. F. BÖHMER and E. MÜHLBACHER, *Regesta Imperii*: v. 1: *Die Regesten des Kaiserreichs unter den Karolingern*, (2d ed. Innsbruck 1908; reprinted, Hildesheim 1966). H. PIRENNE, *Mahomet et Charlemagne* (Paris 1937); Eng. tr. *Mohammed and Charlemagne* by B. MIALL (New York 1939). E. AMANN, *Histoire de l'Église depuis les origines jusqu'à nos jours* 6, ed. A. FLICHE and V. MARTIN (Paris 1947). L. HALPHEN, *Charlemagne et l'Empire carolingien* (Paris 1947); Eng. tr. as *Charlemagne and the Carolingian Empire*, by G. DE NIE (New York 1977). E. PATZELT, *Die karolingische Renaissance* (Graz 1965). R. DOEHAERD, *Les haut moyen âge occidental: Écomies et sociétés* (2d ed. Paris 1971); Eng. tr. as *The Early Middle Ages in the West: Economy and Society* by W. G. DEAKIN (Amsterdam 1978). P. RICHÉ, *La vie quotidienne dans l'Empire carolingien* (Paris 1973); Eng. tr. as *Daily Life in the World of Charlemagne)* by J. MCNAMARA (Philadelphia 1983). S. FONAY WEMPLE, *Women in Frankish Society. Marriage and the Cloister, 500 to 900* (Philadelphia 1981). R. MCKITTERICK, *The Frankish Kingdoms under the Carolingians, 751–987* (London 1983). P. RICHÉ, *Les Carolingiens: une famille qui fit l'Europe* (Paris 1983); Eng. tr. as *The Carolingians: A Family who Forged Europe* by M. I. ALLEN (Philadelphia 1993). W. HARTMANN, *Die Synoden der Karolingerzeit im Frankenreich und in Italien* (Paderborn 1989). A. ANGENENDT, *Das Frühmittelalter. Die abenddländische Christenheit von 400 bis 900* (Stuttgart 1990) 233–460. R. SCHIEFFER, *Die Karolinger* (2d ed. Stuttgart 1997). R. HODGES, *Towns and Trade in the Age of Charlemagne* (London 2000).

[R. E. SULLIVAN]

CARON, REDMOND

Irish Franciscan theologian, the first to publish a systematic course on missiology; b. near Athlone, Westmeath, Ireland, *c.* 1605; d. Dublin, May 1666. He studied for the priesthood in Drogheda, Salzburg, and Louvain and then taught philosophy and theology in St. Anthony's College, Louvain. His mission (1649) as canonical visitor of the Irish Franciscan province was disastrous and his acts were annulled. Subsequently, he served in Ghent and Antwerp (1651–52), in Paris (1652), in Flanders as chaplain to Spanish troops (1653–54), again in Paris (1655–61), in Britain (1661–65), and, finally, in Dublin. Meanwhile, he cared for refugee Irish Poor Clares (1655). He supported the Remonstrance (1661), a formal statement of grievances and allegiance to King Charles II written by Anglo-Irish laymen and championed by Peter WALSH, and in its defense wrote his *Loyalty Asserted* and *Remonstrantia Hibernorum contra Lovanienses*. In 1653 he published a manual of apologetics and another of missiology for regular clergy and, in 1659, a general work on missiology.

Bibliography: T. F. HENDERSON, *The Dictionary of National Biography from the Earliest Times to 1900* (London 1885–1900) 3:1062. F. Ó BRIAIN, *Dictionnaire d'histoire et de géographie ecclésiastiques* (Paris 1912–) 11:1140–41. E. D'ALENCON, *Dictionnaire* *de théologie catholique* (Paris 1903–50) 2.2:1799. B. MILLETT, *The Irish Franciscans 1651–1665* (Rome 1964), *passim.* M. O. N. WALSH, "Irish Books Printed Abroad 1475–1700," *The Irish Book* 2 (1963) 9. *Archivium Hibernicum* 24 (1961), *passim;* 25 (1962), *passim;* 26 (1963), *passim.*

[B. MILLETT]

CARPANI, MELCHIORRE

Barnabite missionary to Burma; b. Lodi, Italy, 1726; d. there, July 8, 1797. At the age of 18, he entered the BARNABITES, and in 1764 he departed for the missions of Ava and Pegù in Burma. There he was the first to study the characters of the Burmese alphabet, which he attempted to set in type for a printing press. In 1774, after an attempt upon his life, he was recalled to Rome. During his term as superior of the College of San Giovanni at Lodi (1775–85) he published the *Alphabetum Burmanum* (1776) and the *Memorie sopra la vita di Hyder Ali Kan* (1782). The latter biography of an Indian general is an important source for the modern history of India.

Bibliography: L. GALLO, *Storia del cristianesimo nell'Impero birmano,* 2 v. (Milan 1862), *passim.* G. BOFFITO, *Scrittori Barnabiti,* 4 v. (Florence 1933–37) 1:424–426.

[U. M. FASOLA]

CARPOCRATES

Early second century Gnostic teacher in Alexandria. Clement of Alexandria (*Strom.* 3.5–9) states that Carpocrates's son Epiphanes founded the sect of Carpocratians, wrote a work *On Justice,* and died at the age of 17, highly revered by his followers. Other sources mention only the name of Carpocrates (Irenaeus, *Adv. haer.* 1.25, and Hippolytus, *Philos.* 7.32). Origen (*C. Cels.* 5.62) speaks of a sect of Harpocratians, and many modern authorities deny the existence of a heresiarch Carpocrates and assume that the name originated in the adoption by the sect of the Egyptian god Horus-Harpocrates [see H. Kraft, "Gab es einen Gnostiker Karpokrates?" *Theologische Zeitschrift* 8 (1952) 434–443]. A disciple, Marcellina, brought the sect to Rome in the reign of Anicetus. The Carpocratians taught the creation of the world by lower angels and successive reincarnations until the soul ascends to God. Strongly influenced by Hellenistic philosophy, the sect was noted for its magical practices and its antinomianism.

See Also: GNOSTICISM.

Bibliography: Texts. W. VÖLKER, ed., *Quellen zur Geschichte der christlichen Gnosis* (Tübingen 1932) 33–38. **Studies.** H. LIBORON, *Die karpokratianische Gnosis* (Leipzig 1938). G. BAREIL-

LE, *Dictionnaire de théologie catholique,* ed. A. VACANT et al., 15 v. (Paris 1903–50; Tables générales 1951) 2.2:1800–03. G. SALMON, *A Dictionary of Christian Biography,* ed. W. SMITH and H. WACE, 4 v. (London 1877–87) 1:407–409.

[G. W. MACRAE]

CARPZOV

An eminent Saxon family of orthodox Lutheran theologians and jurists of the 17th and 18th centuries.

Benedikt, b. Wittenberg, May 27, 1595; d. Leipzig, Aug. 30, 1666. He was a man of deep religious convictions. From 1620 on he was a member of the bench at Leipzig, serving as professor of law (1645), privy councilor at Dresden (1653), and again judge at Leipzig (1661). A judge for more than 40 years, he became the father of German penal law, and in *Jurisprudentia ecclesiastica* (1649) he systematized Lutheran episcopal polity and church law.

Johann Benedikt (I), brother of Benedikt; b. Rochlitz, June 22, 1607; d. Leipzig, Oct. 22, 1657. He was a pastor and professor of theology at Leipzig (1645), the author of *Isagoge in libros ecclesiarum luth. symbolicos* (1665), and a forerunner of the specialized study of symbolics. In the Syncretistic controversy he was a mediating influence, strictly Lutheran in principle, though respectful of the opinions of Georg CALIXTUS.

Johann Benedikt (II), son of Johann Benedikt; b. Leipzig, April 24, 1639; d. Leipzig, March 23, 1699. He was a professor of ethics (1665) and of theology (1684), and a pastor of St. Thomas church (1679). He was a violent opponent of PIETISM; and against Philipp Jakob SPENER, August Hermann FRANCKE, and Christian Thomasius he wrote *De jure decidendi controversias theologicas* (Leipzig 1696).

Samuel Benedikt, son of Johann Benedikt (I); b. Leipzig, Jan. 17, 1647; d. Dresden, Aug. 31, 1707. As a student at Wittenberg (1668), he became a friend of Abraham CALOV. He was court preacher at Dresden (1674), superintendent (1680), and successor of Philipp Spener as senior court preacher (1693). He wavered in his public attitude toward Pietism.

Johann Gottlob, son of Samuel Benedikt; b. Dresden, Sept. 26, 1679; d. Lübeck, April 7, 1767. He was the most learned of the family, an orthodox Lutheran OT scholar and an opponent of Pietists and Moravians (*see* PIETISM; MORAVIAN CHURCH). He served as professor of Hebrew at Leipzig (1713) and as superintendent at Lübeck (1730). His *Introductio ad libros canonicos bibliorum VT* (1714–21) vigorously defended the orthodox Lutheran view of verbal inspiration against the rising progressive Biblical criticism.

Johann Bendikt (III), grandson of Johann Benedikt (II); b. Leipzig, May 20, 1720; d. Königslutter, April 28, 1803. He was one of the last representatives of old Lutheran orthodoxy, an authority on the NT and patristics as well as on theology. Professor of philosophy at Leipzig (1747) and of Greek at Helmstedt (1748), he wrote *Liber doctrinalis theologiae purioris* (1767) to combat the rationalistic theology of W. A. Teller.

Bibliography: E. BEYREUTHER, *Die Religion in Geschichte und Gegenwart,* 7 v. (3d ed. Tübingen 1957–65) 1:1623–24. F. SCHÜHLEIN et al., *Lexikon für Theologie und Kirche,* ed. J. HOFER and K. RAHNER, 10 v. (2d, new ed. Freiburg 1957–65) 2:955–956. H. LEUBE, *Die Reformideen in der deutschen lutherischen Kirche zur Zeit der Orthodoxie* (Leipzig 1924).

[R. H. FISCHER]

CARR, HENRY

Educator, superior general of the Basilian Fathers (1930–42), and founder of the Pontifical Institute of Mediaeval Studies, Toronto, Canada; b. Oshawa, Canada, Jan. 8, 1880; d. Vancouver, Nov. 28, 1963. Carr graduated from the University of Toronto in honor classics in 1903, after interrupting his studies to enter the Basilian novitiate at Toronto in 1900. From the first year of his priesthood, 1905, Carr planned to make St. Michael's the Catholic college in the University of Toronto, and he fashioned a working partnership between a Catholic college and a state university that has since been widely copied in English-speaking Canada. From 1915 to 1925 he was superior of St. Michael's College. In 1929 Carr founded the Institute of Mediaeval Studies and served as its president until 1936. He later established St. Thomas More College at the University of Saskatchewan, Saskatoon, where he was principal from 1942 to 1948. At the age of 71 he organized St. Mark's College at the University of British Columbia, Vancouver; he remained as its head until his retirement in 1961. During these and other activities, his qualities of heart made him the center of an immense circle of friends. Carr held honorary degrees from every institution at which he had taught: the University of Toronto, 1912; the University of Saskatchewan, 1952; Assumption University of Windsor, 1955; and the University of British Columbia, 1956.

Bibliography: "Father Henry Carr: A Symposium," *Basilian Teacher* 8 (1963–64) 287–334. *Basilian Annals* 3 (Nov. 1964) 295–297.

[R. J. SCOLLARD]

CARR, THOMAS MATTHEW

Founder of the Augustinian Order in the U.S.; b. Dublin, Ireland, 1755; d. Philadelphia, Pa., Sept. 29, 1820. As the son of Michael and Mary (McDaniel) Carr, he was baptized Matthew. He was professed in the Augustinian Order in Dublin, Nov. 6, 1772, taking the name Thomas. He attended the order's house of studies in Toulouse, France, and was ordained there on June 13, 1778. After holding several offices in Dublin, including that of prior (1795), he answered Abp. John Carroll's plea for priests in America. He arrived in Philadelphia early in 1796, and spent the rest of his life in two main endeavors: mission work in the Philadelphia area and founding an American province of the Augustinians.

Upon his arrival Carr set about establishing the parish of St. Augustine. A tract of land was bought and construction began in September 1776. Despite financial help obtained from a state-approved lottery and from such prominent Philadelphia residents as George Washington, various difficulties delayed the dedication of St. Augustine until June 1801. In the meantime Abp. Carroll made Carr vicar-general for all of Pennsylvania east of the Susquehanna River (1799). In this capacity he healed the trustee schism at Holy Trinity Church in Philadelphia. On Aug. 27, 1796, his superior general in Rome appointed him prior of the Philadelphia community and superior of the American Augustinian missions, with the title of vicar-general. He was empowered to found new houses and to establish a novitiate. Legal recognition was obtained in 1804 when Gov. Thomas McKean of Pennsylvania signed the act of incorporation of the Brothers of the Order of Hermits of St. Augustine. Carr then spent some time in retirement at Conewago, Pa., and St. Mary's Seminary, Baltimore, Md., but he returned to St. Augustine and, in 1811, opened St. Augustine Academy, a secondary school of classical and religious studies. In 1812 he published a devotional book, *The Spiritual Mirror.* Before his death Carr willed all properties held in his name to the Order of St. Augustine, thus guaranteeing the order's permanency in the U.S.

[A. J. ENNIS]

CARRANZA, BARTOLOMÉ

Theologian; b. Miranda de Arga (Navarra), Spain, about 1503; d. Rome, May 2, 1576. Because of his place of birth, Carranza was called Fray Bartolomé de Miranda. He studied at Alcalá (1515–20) and entered the Dominican Order. He continued his studies at Valladolid, taught the liberal arts and theology in the same city (1530), and was promoted to master of theology at Rome (1539). He was present at the Council of Trent as the imperial theologian (1545–47; 1551–52) and served as a consultant during the Inquisition. He was named prior of Palencia (1549) and provincial of Castile (1550). He worked actively for the Catholic restoration in England (1554–57) and in Flanders. Offered the bishoprics of Cusco, Peru (1542) and the Canary Islands (1549), he refused them both, but Philip II constrained him to accept the archbishropic of Toledo (1557). In his life and works he showed himself a zealous reformer; he put his reforms into practice in his archdiocese until August of 1559 when his apostolic activities were interrupted by his imprisonment by the Inquisition.

From prison he exercised great influence against a strong anti-Protestant reaction in Spain, the hatred and scheming of the Grand Inquisitor, Don Fernando de Valdes, and the theological formalism and passion of Melchior Cano. His trial began with the approval of Philip II and under the authority of Paul IV; it continued during the reign of Pius IV, who succeeded in naming special legates. His refusal to accept the presence of the Grand Inquisitor was honored (1560), and he was defended by Martin de Azpilicueta, an eminent jurist. He was accused of teaching Lutheran doctrine in his books and sermons, and hundreds of propositions, allegedly heretical, were extracted from his works. Pius V ordered the prisoner to be brought to Rome (1566), but died as he was about to pronounce an acquittal (1572) after which Philip II and the Inquisition worked harder to obtain his condemnation. Gregory XIII made him retract 16 theological propositions as "vehemently suspicious of heresy" in April 1576. On his tomb in Santa Maria sopra Minerva, Gregory XIII ordered a laudatory inscription: "Viro genere, vita, doctrina, contione atque elemosinis claro."

Carranza's published works are: *De necessaria residentia episcoporum* (Venice 1547), *Summa Conciliorum . . . Quatuor Controversiae* (Venice 1546), and *Commentarios sobre el Catechismo Christiano* (Antwerp 1558; critical edition by José I. Tellechea Idígoras [Madrid 1972]).

Bibliography: J. I. TELLECHEA IDÍGORAS, *Lexikon für Theologie und Kirche*, ed. J. HOFER and K. RAHNER (Freiberg 1957–65) 2:957; *Fray Bartolomé Carranza: Documentos Históricos*, 2 v. (Archivo Documental Español 18.19; Madrid 1962–63); *Bartolomé Carranza, Arzobispo . . . de Toledo* (San Sebastián 1958); "Los prolegómenos jurídicos del proceso de Carranza," *Anthologica Annua* 7 (Rome 1959) 215–336; "Censura de Fray J. de la Peña sobre proposiciones de C.," *ibid.* 10 (1962) 399–449; "Melchor Cano y Bartolomé Carranza," *Hispania Sacra* 15 (1962) 5–93.

[J. I. TELLECHEA IDÍGORAS]

CARRIÈRE, JOSEPH

Sulpician moral theologian; b. Panouze-de-Cernon, near Rodez, France, Feb. 19, 1795; d. Lyons, April 23, 1864. He attended the Sulpician seminary at Issy, where he taught theology even before ordination. Immediately after ordination in 1817 he was assigned to teach the postgraduate course in moral theology at the seminary in Paris. Here he composed a remarkable course, *Praelectiones theologicae majores in seminario Sancti Sulpitii habitae* (1837–47), of which he published three sections: *De matrimonio* (2 v. Paris 1837); *De justitia et jure* (3 v. Paris 1839); and *De contractibus* (3. v. Paris 1844–47). These treatises went through several editions and won him great acclaim. He was the first writer of note to treat of theology in its relations to the Napoleonic Code, and his expositions of French law were accepted as authoritative by the jurists of his time, who admired him greatly for his knowledge, clarity, fairness, and decisiveness of judgment and his simplicity and modesty of character. Extant correspondence with bishops, priests, and laymen show how highly his advice was esteemed. As official visitator of the Sulpician houses in the U.S. in 1829 he attended the First Council of Baltimore. In 1850 he became the 13th superior general of the Society of Saint Sulpice.

Bibliography: E. LEVESQUE, *Dictionnaire d'histoire et de géographie ecclésiastiques*, ed. A. BAUDRILLART et al. (Paris 1912), 11:1131–32. *Dictionnaire de théologie catholique*, ed. A. VACANT et al., 15 v. (Paris 1903–50; Tables générales 1951), 2.2:1804–05. L. BERTRAND, *Bibliothèque sulpicienne*, 3 v. (Paris 1900), 2:272–281. P. H. LAMAZOU, *M. Carrière, supérieur de Saint Sulpice* (Paris 1864). H. HURTER, *Nomenclator literarius theologiae catholicae*, 5 v. in 6 (3d ed. Innsbruck 1903–13) 5.1:1389.

[M. J. BARRY]

CARROLL, CHARLES

Statesman, signer of the Declaration of Independence; b. Annapolis, Md., Sept. 19, 1737; d. Baltimore, Md., Nov. 14, 1832. The only son of Charles and Elizabeth (Brooke) Carroll, he used "of Carrollton," the name of one of his estates, to distinguish himself from his father, "of Annapolis," and his grandfather, "the Attorney General." The first Charles Carroll had immigrated to Lord Baltimore's tolerant palatinate because of English religious discriminations; these extended to Maryland after 1688 and he lost his attorney general's commission. Disbarred from political life, he so concentrated on amassing wealth that his grandson, Charles Carroll of Carrollton, was born to the greatest fortune in the American colonies.

Early Life. Bohemia Manor Academy, secretly conducted by the Society of Jesus in defiance of Maryland law, prepared Carroll and his cousin John, afterward Archbishop CARROLL, for the English Jesuit college of St. Omer, in French Flanders. Following his studies there, Carroll attended the Collège Louis-le-Grand in Paris. Although religious disability would prevent his practicing in Maryland, he studied law in Bourges, Paris, and London. After 16 years of European education, he returned to Annapolis on June 5, 1768, and married Mary Darnall. All but three of their seven children died young.

The Stamp Act had had violent repercussions in Maryland, and Carroll's father was one of those who, on the passage of the Townshend Acts, set up manufactories. However, a provincial matter was responsible for Carroll's entry into public life. Under Governor Robert Eden, the assembly and council of 1770 were bitterly opposed on the question of regulating officers' fees and stipends of the clergy of the Established Church. On Jan. 7, 1773, a dialogue in the *Maryland Gazette*, unsigned but generally believed to be the work of Secretary Daniel Dulany, received wide attention. It presented a "First Citizen" whose arguments against the official position were demolished by a "Second Citizen's" replies, at least for the time being.

"Second Citizen," however, did not have the last word. In the *Gazette* of Feb. 4, 1773, "First Citizen" was the victor in another dialogue, written obviously by another author. Dulany, replying, signed "Antilon"; Carroll, replying in turn, signed "First Citizen"; and so the exchange continued until midsummer. Resorting finally to sneers at Carroll as a disfranchised Catholic, Dulany's weapon boomeranged as feeling in favor of the discriminated-against "First Citizen" mounted. The controversy established Carroll's preeminence in Maryland, where citizens publicly thanked him for defending their liberties. [*See* CHURCH AND STATE IN THE U.S. (LEGAL HISTORY), 1].

Public Career. Carroll became a member of the Committee of Correspondence for Annapolis in 1774 and was active in the Peggy Stewart affair. Suspecting that anti-Catholic sentiment engendered by the recent Quebec Act would mar his usefulness, he declined as delegate to the first Continental Congress but accompanied the Maryland delegation as unofficial consultant. Although his religion was unpopular, his Catholicism was the chief reason for his appointment to the first American diplomatic mission to try to ingratiate the French Canadians. His fellow members were Benjamin Franklin and Samuel Chase, and his cousin John Carroll, SJ, was asked to accompany them. The mission was sent too late to be successful, but it established Carroll as a national figure. On July 4, 1776, he was elected to Congress from Maryland. He took his seat on July 18, and on August 2 signed his customary "Charles Carroll of Carrollton" to the Declaration of Independence, which his efforts had influenced Maryland to support.

Carroll was placed on the Board of War, which during the Conway Cabal "investigated" George Washing-

ton at Valley Forge. He resigned from Congress in 1778, after the consummation of the French alliance; he also refused to accept reelection later in the year, and he did not return to national politics until 1789, when he became a U.S. senator under the new constitution. He had refused, moreover, during a Maryland political emergency, to go as a delegate to the Constitutional Convention in Philadelphia, but he worked for ratification, becoming strongly and permanently identified with the new Federalist party. His senate service ended in 1792 when Congress passed a law forbidding state legislators from serving in Congress. Carroll's service in the Maryland body continued until 1800, the year of the Federalist overthrow. He viewed with alarm the election of Thomas Jefferson and opposed most Republican measures. He later reprobated the War of 1812.

Carroll spent his old age in studious pursuits, one of his extensive projects being a comparative study of religions. He also interested himself in charitable and educational movements and served as president of the American Colonization Society, which founded Liberia. He was identified with companies promoting westward expansion and, as a director, laid the cornerstone of the Baltimore and Ohio's new railroad on July 4, 1828. This was his last appearance in public. He lived four years longer. At the time of his death at the age of 95, he was the last surviving signer of the Declaration of Independence.

Bibliography: E. H. SMITH, *Charles Carroll of Carrollton* (Cambridge, Mass. 1942).

[E. H. SMITH]

CARROLL, DANIEL, II

American patriot, delegate to the Continental Congress and Constitutional Convention, signer of the U.S. Constitution; b. Upper Marlborough, Md., July 22, 1730; d. Rock Creek, Md., May 7, 1796. He was the son of Daniel and Eleanor (Darnall) Carroll and brother of John, the future archbishop of Baltimore. The family was related to the Darnalls, Digges, Lees, and Horseys of Maryland, and to the Carters and Brents of Virginia. Daniel Carroll II, who also married an Eleanor Darnall, daughter of Ann Rozier Darnall of England, was a first cousin by marriage to Charles Carroll of Carrollton. With his successful ventures into the business of merchant, plantation owner, and tobacco farmer, and with the large inheritances from both his father and wife, Daniel Carroll II early became a prosperous aristocrat of great wealth.

He entered political life in 1777, at a time when Maryland, of all the colonies, was most opposed to independence. Despite the stern opposition of the proprietary government, Carroll realized the need for more democratic legislation if unity was to be assured in the colony. For 18 years, in both state and national affairs, he fought the prevailing conservative, political, and religious views of his day: in the Maryland Senate and Council (1777–80); in the Continental Congress (1780–84); in the Constitutional Convention (1787–88); as member of the U.S. House of Representatives (1780–91); and as a commissioner for planning the capital in Washington (1791–95).

Carroll believed that a strong, centralized federal government was necessary for the preservation of the nation. He favored federal control of western lands and believed that the growing radicalism in state governments should be checked and religious toleration practiced in all states. In his view, reserved powers should be given to the people if not delegated to the central government. Despite divided opinion on the issue in his own state, he strongly urged Maryland's ratification of the Constitution, of which he was one of the two Catholic signers.

Though frequently overshadowed by his more famous cousin, Charles Carroll of Carrollton, eclipsed by his brother John, first archbishop of Baltimore, and confused with his distant relative, Daniel Carroll of Duddington, Daniel Carroll II of Upper Marlborough made a lasting contribution in his emphasis on the value of strong, centralized government and the recognition of the dignity of man and his need for religious liberty.

Bibliography: M. V. GEIGER, *Daniel Carroll* (Washington 1943); "Daniel Carroll," *Catholic World* 163 (May 1946) 163–166.

[M. V. GEIGER]

CARROLL, HOWARD JOSEPH

Bishop, administrator; b. Pittsburgh, Pa., Aug. 5, 1902; d. Washington, D.C., March 21, 1960. He was educated at Duquesne University, Pittsburgh; St. Vincent's College, Latrobe, Pa.; and the University of Fribourg, Switzerland, from which he earned a doctorate in sacred theology. Carroll, ordained on April 2, 1927, was a curate at Sacred Heart Church, Pittsburgh, from 1928 to 1938, and also taught philosophy at Mt. Mercy College, Pittsburgh, during that period. During World War II he held high offices in the National Catholic Community Service, and he was an original member of the board of directors of the United Service Organizations (USO). He also served as Chairman of the Overseas Committee of the USO. From 1944 to 1957 he was the general secretary of the National Catholic Welfare Conference (NCWC). In this office he assisted in the organization of the NCWC

Catholic Relief Services, Departments of Youth and Immigration, Office for United Nations Affairs, Catholic Resettlement Committee, Foreign Visitors Office, Bureau of Health and Hospitals, National Council of Catholic Nurses, and Bureau of Information. He also helped establish *Noticias Catolicas,* the Spanish and Portuguese translations of the National Catholic News Service. In 1955 he became the U.S. representative of the Supreme Council for Emigration of the Consistorial Congregation, and two years later he was consecrated as the first bishop of Altoona-Johnstown, Pa. As bishop he undertook an ambitious building program that included a new cathedral in Altoona.

[P. F. TANNER]

CARROLL, JOHN

First Catholic bishop of the U.S., Archbishop of Baltimore; b. Upper Marlborough, Md., Jan. 8, 1735; d. Baltimore, Dec. 3, 1815. The third of seven children of Daniel and Eleanor (Darnall) Carroll was born of a distinguished family. Through his father he descended from Keane Carroll of Ireland, the elder brother of Charles Carroll who migrated to Maryland and served there as attorney general. Through his mother he was related to the Darnalls, whose American branch was founded by Col. Henry Darnall, brother-in-law of Lord Baltimore.

Early Years. Carroll's education began at home with his mother, who had been educated in France; later he attended Bohemia Manor, a short-lived Jesuit school in northern Maryland. In 1748, with his cousin Charles, a signer of the Declaration of Independence, he went to St. Omer, conducted by English Jesuits in French Flanders. He entered the Jesuit novitiate at Watten in 1753 under Father Henry Corbie and in 1755 became a Jesuit scholastic. Completing the scholasticate at Liège, he taught philosophy there, made his profession in 1771, and then taught at the Jesuit college in Bruges. The exact dates of his ordination and renouncing of his father's legacy cannot be documented, but the former probably took place in 1769 and the latter between 1764 and 1771.

After teaching a few months at Bruges, with his superior's consent he toured the Continent as tutor to Charles Philippe, son of the English Lord Stourton. His journal of the tour (1771–73) offers interesting comment on the central and southern Europe of that time. In the summer of 1773, he became prefect of the sodality at Bruges, where he received news of the dissolution of the Society of Jesus by papal action on July 21, 1773. In October, Austrian officials invaded the college and he was arrested. On the intervention of the English Lord Arundell of Wardour Castle, he was released and went to Wardour as family chaplain until the spring of 1774.

Return to America. Carroll returned in 1774 to live with his mother at Rock Creek, Md. In 1776, the Continental Congress persuaded him to accompany Charles Carroll, Samuel Chase, and Benjamin Franklin to Canada in an effort to win the province to the side of the Colonies in their revolt against England. Arriving in Montreal in April, he was shown no courtesies on the order of Bp. Joseph Briand and had to offer Mass privately in the house of Father Pierre Floquet, a former Jesuit. After the commission's failure, he went to Philadelphia with the ailing Franklin, earning his gratitude for his "friendly assistance and tender care."

After his return to Rock Creek, his zealous ministry soon necessitated the building of St. John's Chapel at Forest Glen on the property of his brother Daniel, one of the framers of the Constitution; he also had to travel 60-mile journeys to reach a Virginia congregation.

Desiring to protect former Jesuit properties in the new nation and to organize the clergy for a more effective ministry, in 1782 he devised a plan that was in substance adopted in 1784, creating a "Form of Government, Rules for the Select Body of Clergy, and Regulations for the Management of Plantations." The American clergy petitioned Rome to name Father John Lewis their superior; but when a vicar-general was appointed, Carroll, on Franklin's recommendation, was made "head of the missions in the provinces . . . of the United States" on June 9, 1784. During the next six years he visited his territory, reported to Rome on conditions (March 1, 1785), and publicly defended the beliefs and rights of Catholics in the new Republic.

In 1784, he published the *Address to the Roman Catholics of the United States of America,* defending the Faith against the attacks of the apostate Jesuit Charles Wharton, whose *Letter to the Roman Catholics of Worcester* had appeared in Philadelphia earlier that year. In the Philadelphia *Columbian* of December 1787, he answered attacks on religious liberty made in its pages, saying: "Freedom and independence acquired by the united efforts, and cemented with the mingled blood of Protestants and Catholic fellow-citizens, should be equally enjoyed by all." In the *United States Gazette,* June 10, 1789, under the name "Pacificus," he reiterated the principle that the Republic had been created by the "generous exertion of all her citizens to redress their wrongs, to assert their rights, and to lay its foundations on the soundest principles of justice and equal liberty." In December 1789, he composed an "Address of the Roman Catholics" to President Washington, congratulating him on his office and reasserting that Catholics had a well-founded title to justice and equal rights in return for their exertions in the nation's defense.

Archbishop John Carroll.

First U.S. Bishop. In 1788 Rome had decided to create the first diocese in the U.S., and on Sept. 17, 1789, Pius VI ordered the bull prepared naming Carroll bishop of Baltimore, thereby confirming the choice of the American clergy. (*See* BALTIMORE, ARCHDIOCESE OF.) His consecration took place Aug. 15, 1790, in Lulworth Chapel on the estate of Thomas Weld in Dorset, England, with Bp. Charles Walmesley presiding and Father Charles Plowden preaching the sermon.

As first Catholic bishop, Carroll set a precedent for cordial relations between the government and the hierarchy. In 1791 at his first synod, he initiated the custom of public prayers for the president and the government. He influenced Washington to ask Congress for an appropriation to support the work of two priests among the native people of the Northwest Territory. Carroll also visited Washington in retirement at Mount Vernon and preached the first president's eulogy at St. Peter's Church in Baltimore on Feb. 22, 1800.

His relations with Jefferson were equally cordial, and when the Louisiana Territory was purchased in 1803, he secured Jefferson's protection for the Ursuline nuns and their properties. In return, he appointed to Louisiana priests devoted to American principles, eliciting Jefferson's comment that he had perfect confidence in Carroll's "patriotism and purity of views." Although opposed to the War of 1812, he defended Madison for his religious principles and his endeavors to preserve peace. In tribute to his patriotism, Carroll was invited to speak at the laying of the cornerstone of the Washington Monument in Baltimore but had to decline because of illness.

Interest in Education. Carroll was also a promoter of culture. From its founding until his death, he was president of the Baltimore Library Company and instituted its printed catalog. Under his auspices Catholic colleges for men were founded in Maryland at Georgetown (1788), Baltimore (St. Mary's, 1799), and at Emmitsburg (Mt. St. Mary's, 1808). Academies for girls were begun at Georgetown (Visitation, 1799), Emmitsburg (St. Joseph's, 1809), and Bardstown, Ky. (Nazareth, 1814).

Although primarily concerned with religious education, he had so deep a conviction that education must flourish in the Republic that he became famous in Maryland as a patron of secular schools as well. In 1784 he became a member of the board of directors of the newly chartered St. John's College at Annapolis and was elected president of the board four years later. In 1785 at the second annual commencement of Washington College, Chestertown, Md., honorary degrees were conferred on both George Washington and Carroll. The next year he presided at the public meeting held to initiate a boys' academy for Baltimore. In 1801 he began serving as director on the board of the nonsectarian Female Humane Association Charity School. Two years later he was elected president of the board of trustees for the newly founded Baltimore College open to all denominations. When the University of Maryland was rechartered in 1812 he was elected provost, but had to decline because of ecclesiastical burdens. A monument to Carroll's cultural influence is the old Cathedral of the Assumption in Baltimore, whose cornerstone he laid on July 7, 1806, and whose design he influenced by collaborating with the architect, Benjamin Latrobe.

Ecclesiastaical Administration. Carroll possessed a genius for organization. To him are due the formulation of the principles and the foundations that made possible the later expansion and status of the Church in the U.S. As first bishop, and later first archbishop of Baltimore, he deserves full credit for the vitality of the faith in the early years of the Republic.

After his consecration, faced with the task of coordinating the work of his clergy he called the first national synod in 1791. Under his guidance, rules were drawn up governing the administration of the Sacraments of Baptism, Holy Eucharist, Penance, and Matrimony for a country where the Catholic minority were scattered, often far from priests, and frequently parties to mixed marriages. The problem of his successor was also discussed and the synod recommended to Rome that the diocese be divided, with a second bishop at Philadelphia, or that a coadjutor with the right of succession be appointed. When Rome adopted the second alternative, he was given a coadjutor in 1794, but it was not until December 1800 that the first coadjutor bishop, Leonard NEALE, was consecrated.

In 1802 Carroll again suggested a division of his diocese and received Rome's permission to recommend boundaries, episcopal cities, and candidates for the new dioceses. He then recommended four sees: Boston, comprising the five New England states of that time; New York, with jurisdiction over that state and eastern New Jersey; Philadelphia, controlling the rest of New Jersey, Pennsylvania, and Delaware; and Bardstown, Ky., embracing Kentucky and Tennessee. For bishop of Boston, he recommended Jean CHEVERUS; for Philadelphia, Michael EGAN; for Bardstown, Benedict FLAGET; for New York, however, he made no recommendation, believing that no worthy candidate could be found in that city. When, on April 8, 1808, Pius VII created the sees, Carroll's candidates were appointed and Richard Concanen was named bishop of New York. Carroll continued his jurisdiction over Maryland and the South; and because Concanen, who was in Italy when he was consecrated, could not find transportation to New York, Carroll made Anthony Kohlmann vicar-general until the bishop should arrive. He consecrated the other new bishops in Baltimore in 1810. The hierarchy then drew up an agreement for the uniformity of Catholic discipline throughout the country. Together with the regulation of the Synod of 1791, this agreement constitutes the earliest codification of Canon Law for the church in the U.S. Carroll and his suffragans also drafted, on Nov. 15, 1810, a solemn protest against Napoleon's captivity of Pius VII and sent it with their first joint encyclical to the hierarchy of Ireland.

Carroll received the PALLIUM brought by the British minister, Augustus Foster, on Aug. 18, 1811. By this time he believed that Louisiana and Florida warranted another diocese and recommended the president of St. Mary's College in Baltimore, Louis Dubourg, who went to New Orleans in 1812 as apostolic administrator of the diocese and was consecrated bishop in 1815.

Religious Foundations. Deeply concerned for the spiritual and educational needs of the laity, he encouraged foundations of religious orders for women: the Carmelites, who settled at Port Tobacco, Md., in 1790; the Poor Clares, who first settled at Frederick, Md.; the Sisters of Loretto at the Foot of the Cross, founded in 1812 at Hardin's Creek, Ky.; and the Sisters of Charity of Nazareth, also founded in Kentucky in 1812.

The foundation of the first distinctly American community of religious women, the Sisters of Charity of St. Joseph, was due to his encouragement of their founder, Bl. Elizabeth SETON. He had first heard of Mrs. Seton through the Filicchi brothers of Leghorn, Italy; the younger, Antonio, interested him in her conversion in 1804. Carroll confirmed her in New York on May 25, 1806. Two years later he encouraged her to start a school for Catholic girls in Baltimore. In March 1809, he permitted her to take vows, insisting, however, that she accept a dispensation from complete poverty so that she might provide for her five children. During her first difficult years as superior of the small community in Emmitsburg, Carroll was her support and mentor. When on Jan. 17, 1812, he confirmed the rules for her community, although they were substantially those of the French Daughters of St. Vincent de Paul, he saw to it that modifications allowed for conditions in the United States and for Mother Seton's peculiar situation as religious superior and mother of five children.

Carroll encouraged religious orders of men as well. An Augustinian monastery was established in Philadelphia in 1796 under Thomas Matthew CARR, with George Washington among the contributors to the building fund for St. Augustine's Church. The Dominicans, arriving in 1804, hoped to start a monastery under Edward FENWICK in Maryland, but were persuaded to go to Kentucky where Carroll saw greater need for them. By 1807 they had opened St. Thomas School for boys there.

Having been himself a Jesuit, Carroll hoped to see the Society restored in the U.S. Moreover, rather than see the Jesuits divested of any part of their original strength, he opposed in 1800 the affiliation of the former Jesuits of the U.S. with a pseudo-Jesuit society calling themselves the PACCANARISTS. On March 7, 1801, when a pontifical brief granted canonical existence to the Society in Russia, he sought means of aggregating the American group to the Russian; and on June 21, 1805, he named Robert MOLYNEUX to head the qualified restoration. On Dec. 7, 1814, he had the pleasure of receiving a copy of the bull that restored the Society throughout the world. He was too old to rejoin, but cherished "the greatest sensation of joy and thanksgiving" that the Society of Jesus would flourish in the U.S.

To foster the increase of a secular clergy, he supported the establishment of St. Mary's Seminary. While still in England for his consecration in 1790, he had begun negotiations with the French Society of Saint Sulpice to found a seminary in Baltimore, which opened the following year; and in 1802 he vigorously opposed the recall of the Sulpicians to France.

Dissension and Controversy. Thirty priests were trained at St. Mary's between May 25, 1793, when Carroll ordained Stephen BADIN, the first graduate, and Carroll's own death in 1815. The growth of a native clergy was slow, however, and he had to rely increasingly upon priests from Ireland, France, and Germany—clergy whose temperaments and nationalistic leanings created problems. Germans in Philadelphia and Westmoreland County, Pa., disputed his jurisdiction in 1798; in the former case causing his arrest, and in the latter taking him to court, where Judge Alexander Addison vindicated him, declaring him "the sole episcopal authority . . . of the United States." The next year in Baltimore, a German priest and congregation at St. John's Church began open opposition that resulted in four years of controversy and another court action in which he was again vindicated.

In Norfolk, Va., Charlestown, S.C., and Augusta, Ga., Irish priests allied themselves with trustees to resist his authority. Although the majority of the French clergy proved invaluable, three of their number becoming his suffragan bishops, a few caused scandal and a few returned to France when the position of the Church there improved after 1802. And while Carroll appreciated the ideals and labors of the priests in religious orders, he nevertheless suffered opposition from some of their superiors, among them Charles Neale and John Grassi of the Jesuits.

Significance. Carroll's leadership and administration of the Church in the U.S. fixed traditions that later enhanced its prestige. His devotion to religious freedom and his delineation of the relations of the Church with Rome in spiritual matters defined and gave proof of the compatibility of Catholicism and democracy. His charity was endless. In these difficult years he measured each crisis by the ultimate and common good not only of the Church but also of the nation. He lived to see independence declared, won, and again preserved in the War of 1812; the Catholic population quadrupled and the clergy doubled. As Cardinal Gibbons expressed it: "His aim was that the clergy and people should be . . . identified with the land. . . . From this mutual accord of Church and State there could but follow beneficent effects for both." Enfeebled by age and illness, Carroll received the last Sacraments on Nov. 23 and died on Dec. 3, 1815. He was buried in the chapel of St. Mary's Seminary, but in 1824 his body was removed to the Cathedral (later Basilica) of the Assumption.

Bibliography: D. BRENT, *Biographical Sketch of the Most Rev. John Carroll,* ed. J. C. Brent (Baltimore 1843). P. GUILDAY, *The Life and Times of John Carroll, Archbishop of Baltimore, 1735–1815* (Westminster, Md. 1954). J. D. SHEA, *Life and Times of the Most Rev. John Carroll, Bishop and First Archbishop of Baltimore* (New York 1888). A. M. MELVILLE, *John Carroll of Baltimore* (New York 1955).

[A. M. MELVILLE]

John Patrick Carroll.

CARROLL, JOHN PATRICK

Bishop; b. Dubuque, Iowa, Feb. 22, 1864; d. Fribourg, Switzerland, Nov. 4, 1925. He was the son of Martin and Catherine (O'Farrell) Carroll. After completing his primary education at St. Raphael's School, Dubuque, he entered the secondary department of St. Joseph's College (later Loras) in the same city. He attended the Grand Seminary, Montreal, Canada, for philosophical and theological studies and was ordained in 1889. He served as professor of philosophy at St. Joseph's until 1894, when he was appointed president of the college. In 1904, Carroll succeeded John B. Brondel, first bishop of Helena, Mont. His first concerns as bishop were the erection of a larger cathedral and the establishment of a diocesan college. He laid the cornerstone of the new cathedral in 1908, formally dedicated it in 1914, and arranged its formal consecration in 1924. Construction of Mount St. Charles College in Helena (later named Carroll College in his honor) was begun in 1909.

In 1908, Carroll was proposed as successor of Bp. Denis J. O'Connell as rector of The Catholic University of America, Washington, D.C., but the Holy See did not make the appointment. Carroll served in 1910 and 1912 as national chaplain of the Ancient Order of Hibernians. He was nationally known as an orator, and he delivered the principal address at the Washington Celebration in Portland, Ore.; preached at the dedication of the cathedrals in Cheyenne, Wyo., and Seattle, Wash.; delivered the oration of the Catholic Day at the Alaska-Yukon Pacific Exposition; and addressed the national convention of the American Federation of Labor at Seattle in 1913. In 1925, during the crisis aroused by the Oregon School Case, he opposed an Oregon statute, which was ultimately declared unconstitutional, requiring public school attendance of all children between eight and 16. Carroll died while en route to Rome for his ad limina visit.

[T. A. CLINCH]

CARROLL, WALTER SHARP

Papal diplomat; b. Pittsburgh, Pa., June 18, 1908; d. Washington, D.C., Feb. 24, 1950. He received his B.A. (1930) from Duquesne University, Pittsburgh, and his Ph.D. (1933) from the University of Fribourg, Switzerland, before being ordained on Dec. 8, 1935. He subsequently attended the Universities of Tours, France, and of Florence, Italy, and obtained his S.T.L. (1936) from the Gregorian University and his J.C.D. (1939) from the Pontifical University of the Lateran in Rome. Following a brief assignment as curate at St. Basil's Church, Pittsburgh, in 1940, he served from 1944 to 1950 as attaché in the Vatican Secretariate of State and as U.S. military vicar delegate. In 1943–44 he was sent to North Africa to facilitate its communications with the Holy See and to assist war prisoners. He performed a similar mission in Austria and Germany during 1944–45. When Rome was captured by the Allies in June 1944, he improvised a Vatican press office and instituted press conferences to inform the world of Vatican events. He was also instrumental in arranging audiences with Pius XII for Americans in military service. After the war, he represented the Holy See at the 1947 meeting of the International Refugee Organization in Geneva, Switzerland. His wartime efforts were honored by his appointment as papal chamberlain (1943) and domestic prelate (1944).

[P. F. TANNER]

CARTER, WILLIAM, BL.

English printer and martyr; b. place and date unknown; d. Tyburn, Jan. 11, 1584. In 1563 he was apprenticed to John Cawood, Queen's printer, and later he became amanuensis to Nicholas Harpsfield in Fleet prison. He married and had children. Carter was imprisoned "divers times" for printing "lewd [i.e., anti-Protestant] pamphlets," and was put on surety for good behavior. He was finally detained in the Tower (July 1582), tortured, and brought to trial for printing Gregory Martin's *Treatise of Schisme* (issued 1578 with a false imprint), an action that he had earlier confessed. The prosecution alleged that the book contained a passage concerning Judith and Holofernes that urged the killing of Queen Elizabeth. He was condemned at the Old Bailey on Jan. 10, 1584, and executed the next day. He was beatified on Nov. 22, 1987, as one of the martyrs of ENGLAND, SCOTLAND AND WALES.

Feast: May 4.

Bibliography: E. H. BURTON and J. H. POLLEN, eds., *Lives of the English Martyrs,* ser. 2, v.1 (London 1914), no further v. pub. A. F. ALLISON and D. M. ROGERS, *A Catalogue of Catholic Books in English . . . 1558–1640*, 2 v. (London 1956).

[D. M. ROGERS]

CARTESIANISM

A philosophical doctrine initiated by René DESCARTES and subsequently developed by a number of his disciples and later philosophers. Although the term is used in a general way to designate the fundamental tenets of RATIONALISM, it is more properly applied to the movement that was closely associated with Descartes and consciously sought to propagate his thought. In this article, such terminological usage is first explained and then a survey given of the development of the movement, in its stricter sense, as this took place in Holland, France, and England.

Terminological usage. The specialists who were collaborators on the classic *Vocabulaire technique et critique de la philosophie* (ed. A. Lalande, Paris 1st ed. 1926, 8th ed. 1960) refused to authorize an article setting out the theses of Cartesianism because, in their view, the editorial committee could not agree on the thinkers, or the characteristics of the doctrine, that could be properly called Cartesian. This incident illustrates the change of climate in the historical exegesis of authors since the time when E. Caird (1835–1908) wrote the article "Cartesianism" for the eleventh edition of the *Encyclopaedia Britannica* (1910–11) and gave simply a masterly exposition of Descartes, N. MALEBRANCHE, G. W. LEIBNIZ and B. SPINOZA.

If by the term "Cartesian" is meant a thinker who accepts the fundamental theses of Descartes himself, then it must be objected that the extent to which Leibniz and Spinoza withdrew from the principles radically weakens their affiliations with him. Despite the important formative influence Descartes exercised upon their thought, it is only by a traditional "historical" usage that they can

René Descartes.

be called Cartesians, a usage that presents many opportunities for misunderstanding. It is true that Leibniz insisted that Spinoza's philosophy was an exaggerated Cartesianism, but he equally denied that he himself was a Cartesian. In some ways, the fourth book of Locke's *Essay* has more claim to be called Cartesian than any work of Leibniz or Spinoza. Malebranche alone, of the important thinkers, both in his expressed intentions and in much of his doctrine, would perhaps qualify as a disciple.

Possibly owing to the influence of G. W. F. HEGEL, in his *Lectures on the History of Philosophy,* it has become customary to divide the seventeenth century into two schools—the rationalist, of which Descartes was the founder, and the empiricist, with John LOCKE as its progenitor. Moreover, it has been widely accepted that the French *philosophes* of the eighteenth century (Voltaire, Diderot, etc.) based their theories on the empiricist doctrines of Locke and Newton and brought about the downfall of the rationalist doctrines of Cartesianism. As has been suggested, rationalism is as an essential element of Locke's theories, as it is of Descartes's theories. The conventional linkage between Newtonianism and French materialism, accepted by F. Bouillier (1813–99) in his *Histoire de la philosophie cartésienne* (Paris 1854), can no longer be regarded as acceptable in view of recent scholarship. It is therefore more accurate to restrict the term "Cartesian" to those thinkers, mostly minor figures, who claimed the title for themselves and attempted to be, in varying degrees, disciples of Descartes.

Holland. It is natural that the first Cartesians were to be found in Holland, where Descartes was living and where most of his works were first published. Their activities were centered at the Universities of Utrecht and Leyden.

Utrecht. At the University of Utrecht, Henri Reneri (1593–1638), professor of philosophy, was one of the first to defend publicly the new doctrine, as did his successor, Regius (Henri de Roy, 1598–1679), who was in frequent communication with Descartes and read through the manuscript of the *Meditations.* Voëtius (Gijsbert Voët, 1589–1676), professor of theology at the same university, was a bitter opponent of the new theories, which were forbidden by a university decree. Descartes himself feared that Regius might become "the first martyr of his philosophy." When Regius published his own *Fundamenta Physices* in 1646, there was a break in the close friendship. The fundamental criticism that Descartes made of Regius's views was that he reversed the order of his philosophy, putting his metaphysics after, and not before, his physics. The *Notae in programma quoddam,* published by Descartes in 1647, are a refutation of certain theses elaborated by Regius as an attack on the nature of soul as this is expounded in the *Meditations.*

Leyden. At the University of Leyden, as early as 1647 there were bitter attacks on the doctrine of Descartes, mainly on the use of methodological doubt and the guarantee of human veracity based on the proof of the existence of God. The chief exponents of these attacks were Revius (Jacques de Rèves, d. 1658), who was the regent of the theological faculty and a pastor, and Triglandius (Jacobus Trigland, d. 1654), professor of theology. The first publicly accused Descartes of Pelagianism; the second damned him as an atheist. There were a number who replied on behalf of Descartes. Among them was J. Clauberg (1622–65), who was professor in several German universities and wrote *Defensio Cartesiana adversus Jacobum Revium* (1652), as well as several commentaries on the major works of Descartes. In his latter works, he gave his attention especially to the problem of the relations of body and soul and denied that there could be any real interaction between the two: the interaction he described as "procatarctic," after a theory akin to occasionalism. Other defenders were Andriaan Heereboord (1614–61); C. Wittich (1625–87), who later attacked Spinoza in terms of orthodox Cartesian doctrine; and Heldanus (A. van der Heiden, 1597–1678), who protested so strongly that he lost his professorial chair.

Arnold GEULINCX was professor at the University of Louvain, but he went to Leyden in 1658 and there became a Protestant. His most important work is his *Ethica,* which was not published in complete form until after his death. Starting from the dualistic division of matter and mind, he argued that a material thing cannot be a true cause, since it cannot know that it acts. It follows then that the soul does not really produce the effects on bodies that it thinks it does. Descartes, it may be noted, had denied action in the sense of causing the existence of a change or movement, but he admitted that action could determine the character a change could assume or the direction of a motion. Regius and Clauberg follow their master in allowing the second sense of action: Geulincx, and later Malebranche, deny action in both senses. The denial of interaction, even in the second sense, leads Geulincx to the theory of OCCASIONALISM. When one perceives a certain change occurring in his body and wills a certain action designed, for instance, to ensure its alteration, and then performs the action willed, the occurrence of the perception and the occurrence of the bodily behavior are both effects of divine intervention. A person's act of will is due wholly to himself; the perception is caused by God. The self-caused volition is the occasion on which God caused the bodily behavior (Malebranche differs here in attributing both volitional and bodily states to God). The volitional act itself is accordingly an occasional cause. The analogy of the two clocks, synchronized by God to keep perfect time, is found to be the most apt illustration. For Geulincx, then, only two substances manifest their essential nature in real causal activity, that is, finite selves and God.

France. The reaction to Descartes's philosophy in France, if not so openly violent, was equally mixed. A typical composite of opinions is to be found in the *Objections* published as an appendix to the *Meditations,* the manuscript having been circulated to various individuals and groups by Father Marin Mersenne, of the Order of Minims, who was aptly called "the great businessman of letters" of the seventeenth century. Descartes published a series of replies to each set of objections.

The third set of objections is by Thomas HOBBES, but they merely serve to show that the English philosopher, rather characteristically, was rooted in his own radical EMPIRICISM and understood little of the text he was criticizing.

The fourth set are due to Antoine ARNAULD, who was to prove himself one of the most ardent defenders of the Cartesian doctrine, and one of the authors, together with Pierre NICOLE, of the textbook known as the *Logic of Port Royal,* an attempt to formulate a logic according to Descartes's principles (*see* LOGIC, HISTORY OF). Even when official opposition to the new doctrine was widespread, especially after Descartes's works had been placed on the Index *donec corrigantur* in 1663, he continued his polemic in their favor and was forced to flee to Holland later before the threat of civil intervention. Despite his general acceptance of the main doctrine, Arnauld was the only critic to call attention to the confusion caused by Descartes's theory of representative ideas and to note the essential difference between his view and the scholastic doctrine of SPECIES.

Pierre GASSENDI, the author of the fifth set of objections, was a canon of Dijon and later professor of mathematics in Paris. Although he was himself opposed to Aristotelian scholasticism, he nevertheless was a bitter opponent of Descartes. His own doctrine was a revival of ATOMISM, akin to that of Epicurus, but essentially empirical in outlook. He rejected entirely the dualistic distinction of body and soul. Locke was very sympathetic to his views.

Jesuit Reaction. The seventh set of objections, published only in the second edition of the *Meditations,* were made by a Jesuit professor, Pierre Bourdin (1595–1653). The objections in themselves were not notably pertinent, but they illustrate the effort Descartes made to stay on good terms with his previous teachers at La Flèche. Father Jacques Dinet (1580–1653), who had taught Descartes, was instrumental in keeping good relations with the philosopher. At the college of La Flèche, where Descartes had been a pupil, he found two fervent advocates in Fathers Antoine Vatier (1591–1659) and Pierre Mesland (1596–1639); but this was exceptional and, on the whole, the Society of Jesus showed reserve, if not open hostility, to him. A general congregation of 1682 forbade the teaching of any Cartesian doctrines. Other religious orders had adepts of the Cartesian philosophy in their midst, notably, of course, the Oratorians with Malebranche. In the famous Benedictine monastery of St. Maur was the erudite Jean MABILLON, who recommended the study of Descartes in his treatise on monastic studies.

Other Views. At the University of Paris were other exponents of Cartesian doctrine. Jacques Rohault (1620–75), a professor of physics, was one of the most successful. His weekly lectures were attended by all the leading personalities of the time, and his *Traité de Physique* (Paris 1671) became the textbook of most European universities. He also published *Entretiens de philosophie* (Paris 1671), a philosophical work of almost literal Cartesian orthodoxy. His pupil, Pierre Sylvain RÉGIS, first taught in Montpellier and Toulouse but came to Paris in 1680, where he continued to expound his views, published in his *Système de Philosophie* (Paris 1690). He differed from Descartes in maintaining that the existence of bodies is as evident as the existence of selves, and that ideas arise from the union of body and soul and are not

innate. Mention should also be made of Claude Clerselier (1614–84), who edited the letters of Descartes, as well as the posthumous works of Rohault, a pious Catholic whose main concern was to defend the doctrines of Descartes against accusations of atheism and libertinism.

In the 1660s, two works appeared that had a short-lived but widespread influence in France. The first was the *Traité de l'esprit de l'homme* (Paris 1661) by Louis de la Forge; the second, by Géraud de Cordemoy (1620–84), was *Le discernement du corps et de l'âme* (Paris 1666). Cordemoy, a lawyer by profession, had been chosen by J. BOSSUET as tutor to the elder son of Louis XIV. He was thoroughly convinced of the dualistic distinction between soul and body, although he introduced atomic divisions into the definition of matter; in attempting to solve the problems thereby raised, he arrived at a theory of interaction that presupposes the instrumentality of God as its efficient cause, a form of occasionalism akin to that developed later by Malebranche. For De la Forge, a doctor who had edited Descartes's posthumous *Traité de l'homme,* Cartesian dualism was a vital innovation and most important discovery, although he insisted that it was in principle identical to the doctrine of St. AUGUSTINE. He also defended the doctrine of representative ideas and placed the cause of the substantial union of body and soul in the will of God, arriving then at a theory of psychophysical parallelism. According to De la Forge, the difference between the philosophy of Descartes and that of his spiritual forebears was that Descartes alone had given an adequate definition of matter. (*See* SOUL-BODY RELATIONSHIP.)

England. The works of Descartes were translated rapidly into English. Cambridge was slightly sympathetic toward the new doctrine. Henry More, a fellow of Christ's College and a correspondent of Descartes, professed himself an ardent disciple but later publicly renounced his adhesion. Ralph Cudworth, professor of Hebrew and master of Christ's College, while making a distinction between the conscious object and unconscious tendency of Descartes's doctrine, denounced it as a mechanistic atheism. Although these and other CAMBRIDGE PLATONISTS read Descartes's works, it cannot be asserted that their views are colored, except negatively, by his philosophical principles.

At Oxford, Anthony Legrand (d. 1699) published *Institutio Philosophiae* (London 1672), but he was violently opposed by Samuel Parker (1640–88), bishop of Oxford, who confounded Descartes and Hobbes in the same imprecation. Despite this condemnation, the works of Descartes were widely read at the university, and Locke began to study them immediately after his graduation; the extent of his debt can be measured by the great number of references in his notebooks and journals.

Growth and decline. The doctrine of Descartes spread among the society of Paris, as well as among the Cartesians of Port Royal, in the midst of whom Blaise PASCAL was an outstanding exception. De la Forge noted the names of four Cartesian "salons," later to be satirized by Molière in *Les Femmes Savantes*. Descartes's funeral in 1667, at the church of Saint-Étienne-du-Mont, became a kind of manifestation on behalf of the new doctrine. But official opposition grew, especially after the publication of the decree of 1663 which placed his works on the Index; in 1669, candidates for doctorates were obliged to defend anti-Cartesian theses at the Sorbonne; in 1671, the archbishop of Paris forbade the teaching of Descartes's opinions, and a further decree of the Parlement of Paris was stopped only by a clever satire of N. Boileau-Despréaux. Pierre Daniel HUET, bishop of Avranches, who had himself professed Cartesian views, made an elaborate attack in his famous *Censura* (Paris 1689), and Father Gabriel Daniel, in his *Voyage du monde de Descartes* (Paris 1690), presented a semiserious novel deriding the philosophy and science of Descartes.

The heyday of the new doctrine can be placed between 1660 and 1690. Afterward there was a steady decline of Descartes's influence, which became almost—at least directly and openly—a dead letter in the eighteenth century. It is noteworthy that no work of Descartes was printed in France between 1724 and 1824, when Victor COUSIN once more drew attention to the greatest of French philosophers.

See Also: PHILOSOPHY, HISTORY OF; DESCARTES, RENÉ; DUALISM; INNATISM; SUBJECTIVISM.

Bibliography: C. L. THIJSSEN-SCHOUTE, *Nederlands Cartesianisme* (Amsterdam 1954). A. G. A. BALZ, *Cartesian Studies* (New York 1951). E. J. DIJKSTERHUIS et al., *Descartes et le cartésianisme Hollandais* (Paris 1950). G. COHEN, *Écrivains français en Hollande* (Paris 1920). W. H. BARBER, *Leibniz in France* (Oxford 1955). R. PINTARD, *Le Libertinage érudit*, 2 v. in 1 (Paris 1943). G. SORTAIS, *La Philosophie moderne*, 2 v. (Paris 1920–22). J. B. BORDAS-DEMOULIN, *Le Cartésianisme*, 2 v. (Paris 1843). R. LENOBLE, *Mersenne* (Paris 1943). M. MERSENNE, *Correspondence,* ed. C. DE WAARD, 4 v. (Paris 1945–55).

[L. J. BECK]

CARTHAGE

Carthage is a town on the Gulf of Tunis, 12 miles northeast of Tunis, capital of TUNISIA. Carthage, founded by Tyre *c.* 841 B.C., long dominated the western Mediterranean, which it contested with Rome. Destroyed (146 B.C.) and rebuilt (29 B.C.) by Rome, it came under the VANDALS (439), Byzantium (533), and the Arabs (698);

it was held by Spain (1535–74) but yielded to the Ottoman Turks and then became part of the French protectorate (1881), which gained its independence (1956).

Christianity was introduced into Carthage by A.D. 150, from both Rome and the East, and flourished quickly (more than 20 known basilicas); but it suffered repeatedly from persecution and heresy. The acts of the 12 Scillitan martyrs (d. July 17, 180) is the oldest document of Christian North Africa. Christian Latin letters in the area were distinguished by TERTULLIAN (who was inclined to MONTANISM), MINUCIUS FELIX, ARNOBIUS THE ELDER, LACTANTIUS, the poet Commodian (probably 3rd century), MARIUS VICTORINUS, Dracontius, FULGENTIUS OF RUSPE, FERRANDUS, and, above all, AUGUSTINE. Carthage's first known bishop, Agrippinus, presided over 70 bishops in a council (*c.* 220) that declared baptisms administered by heretics invalid. Carthage's greatest bishop, the martyr St. CYPRIAN, from whose episcopacy (248–258) dates Carthage's ecclesiastical primacy in Africa, condemned NOVATIAN but disputed with Rome about rebaptism; a council of 87 bishops under him defended the traditional African practice of rebaptism (256), which was not abandoned until the Council of Arles (314). Donatists, with their bishops, afflicted Carthage from 311 until after the time of St. Augustine, who studied in Carthage and became there an advocate of MANICHAEISM. DONATISM was occasioned by the DISSIMULATION of Bp Mensurius of Carthage in the persecution of Diocletian (303), by the unorthodox reconciliation of LAPSI, and by the ever available dispute over rebaptism.

Pelagianism (*see* PELAGIUS AND PELAGIANISM) appeared in Carthage in 411, the year a council of 286 Catholic and 275 Donatist bishops broke the strength of Donatism. Pelagianism was condemned in a council of more than 200 bishops held in 418 under Bishop Aurelius (391–429), who had a codex of canons of the African Church compiled; the council's canons on original sin, grace, and the necessity of prayer show the influence of Augustine, Aurelius's close friend and collaborator. After the death of Aurelius, heterodox elements rose and sided with the Arian Vandals, who took Carthage (439), sacked Rome (455), and all but ended Carthage's ecclesiastical primacy in a persecution that had but few respites. VICTOR of Vita describes the Vandal persecution. From 439 to 454 the see was vacant, Genseric installing an Arian bishop who was patriarch of the Vandal Church; as in other barbarian Arian Churches, neither the bishop nor his clergy had any influence in affairs of state. The Vandals used their vernacular in their liturgy, as opposed to the orthodox liturgy of Carthage, which was almost identical with that of Rome. Bishop Deogratias (454–457), known for his charity to captives from the sack of Rome, was succeeded after 24 years by Eugene,

Remains of Circular Punic Gate, ca. 1985–1998, Carthage, Tunisia. (Sandro Vannini/CORBIS)

a saintly bishop also known for charity. Eugene was condemned to hard labor by the Vandals (484–487) and then exiled to ALBI in France (496), where he died (505). There was no successor until 523.

Although Justinian rebuilt churches and protected orthodoxy, and although Carthage became a Byzantine exarchate along with RAVENNA, the city declined under Byzantine rule. Bishop Reparatus, because of his defense of the THREE CHAPTERS, was exiled to Asia Minor and died there (563). After Justinian's death (565) weak bishops could not prevent abuses by imperial officials and Catholics turned to Rome, which intervened even in administrative affairs. Christian refugees from the Arab conquest of Syria and Egypt brought MONOPHYSITISM and MONOTHELITISM to Carthage *c.* 640. A council of 646 condemning Monothelitism is the last known event of the Church in Carthage before the Arab conquest (698). *See* NORTH AFRICA, EARLY CHURCH IN.

The Church survived after 698, though its status was inferior. A monk from the monastery of St. Sabas in Jerusalem found the Church of "Africa" suffering from the attacks of "tyrants" *c.* 850, and he continued to Spain in search of stipends for his monastery. In 990 Carthage sent its elected bishop to Rome for consecration, and popes wrote to bishops and the Church of Carthage (1053, 1073, and 1076), as well as to local rulers of North Africa concerning Christians there. CONSTANTINE THE AFRICAN was born in Carthage (1010–20). After the Norman conquest of Sicily (1061–91) and the Almohad conquest of North Africa (1160), Christianity almost disappeared in Carthage. From the 13th century, Europe sought to regain Christian North Africa. St. LOUIS IX of France died besieging Tunis (1270), which had replaced Carthage in importance. Christian merchants and mercenary troops in the region required chaplains. Trinitarians and Mercedarians ransomed Christian slaves. Franciscans and Dominicans carried on missionary work. Raymond LULL'S school for Arabic studies was in Tunis.

The Congregation for the PROPAGATION OF THE FAITH sent Capuchins (1624) and Vincentians (1645) to Carthaginian Africa. The Vincentians, chaplains of French consuls, were regarded as vicars by the Holy See, as if the See of Carthage still existed. Jean LE VACHER, vicar apostolic (1650–66), was succeeded by Italian Capuchins (who cared for French, Italians, and Maltese) as provicars under the Vincentian Vicariate of ALGERIA and TUNISIA (in Algiers). In 1741 Carthage was made a vicariate apostolic. A chapel of St. Louis in Carthage (1839), French sisters (1840) who expanded beyond Carthage, and Brothers of the Christian Schools (1855) were followed by White Fathers (1875), who carried the apostolate to the Muslims. Under the French protectorate, Carthage was restored as a metropolitanate without suffragans (1884) and primate of Africa (1893) under Cardinal Charles M. A. LAVIGERIE. The Church was governed by a concordat between France and the Holy See (1894–1964) until the See was suppressed, made titular, and replaced by a prelacy *nullius* of Tunis comprising the same jurisdiction (Tunisia).

Bibliography: P. MONCEAUX, *Histoire littéraire de l'Afrique chrétienne,* 7 v. (repr. Brussels 1963). H. LECLERCQ, *L'Afrique chrétienne* (2d ed. Paris 1904); *Dictionnaire d'archéologie chrétienne et de liturgie,* ed. F. CABROL, H. LECLERCQ, and H. I. MARROU, 15 v. (Paris 1907–53) 2.2: 2190–2330. G. LAPEYRE, *L'Ancienne église de Carthage,* 2 v. (Paris 1933). C. COURTOIS, "Histoire de l'Afrique du Nord des origines à la fin du Moyen–Âge," *Revue historique* 198 (1947) 228–249; *Les Vandales et l'Afrique* (Paris 1955). G. LAPEYRE and A. PELLEGRIN, *Carthage latine et chrétienne* (Paris 1950). P. HUBAC, *Carthage* (Paris 1952). J. FERRON and G. LAPEYRE, *Dictionnaire d'histoire et de géographie ecclésiastiques,* ed. A. BAUDRILLART et al. (Paris 1912–) 11: 1149–1233. P. KAWERAU, *Die Religion in Geschichte und Gegenwart,*³ 7 v. (3d ed. Tübingen 1957–65) 3:1160–61. A. STUIBER et al., *Lexicon für Theologie und Kirche,*² ed. J. HOFER and K. RAHNER, 10 v. (2d, new ed. Freiburg 1957–65); suppl., *Das Zweite Vatikanische Konzil: Dokumente und Kommentare,* ed. H. S. BRECHTER et al., pt. 1 (1966) 6:1–4. G. BARDY and E. JARRY, *Catholicisme,* 2:602–607. *Paulys Realenzyklopädie der klassischen Altertumswissenschaft,* ed. G. WISSOWA et al. (Stuttgart 1893–), suppl. 10:957–992.

[E. P. COLBERT]

CARTHAGE, COUNCILS OF

Many councils were held in CARTHAGE (3d to 6th centuries). Under Agrippinus 70 bishops in 225 considered the validity of Baptism by heretics. Donatus called a council in 235. Of many councils called by CYPRIAN, Bishop of Carthage (*c.* 249–258), those of 251, 252, 253, 255, and 256 dealt with the LAPSI, Christians defecting in the fearful Decian persecution. Unwilling to absolve them through the Sacrament of Penance, the Church granted forgiveness if a confessor awaiting martyrdom interceded for them with the bishop. Cyprian decided to permit the *lapsi* sacramental absolution, a practice ultimately universal. In 252, 253, and 256 the councils also reexamined the validity of Baptism by heretics. Under Gratus (349) and Genethlius (390), disciplinary measures were enacted for clergy and bishops. A canon of Scripture (397) included a prohibition against all other reading in the churches (*Enchiridion symbolorum,* 186). Aurelius, Bishop of Carthage (391–429), held councils frequently and dealt with problems of Donatism and Pelagianism (*see* PELAGIUS AND PELAGIANISM). In 411 a confrontation of Donatist and Catholic bishops (June 1, 3, 8) resulted in complete defeat for the Donatists—imperial legislation strengthening the orthodox position.

The most important councils in Carthage dealt with Pelagius, a Celtic monk denying the necessity of grace, whose tergiversations successfully deceived the Council of Diospolis (Palestine), where he was exonerated after his African condemnation. A meeting of 67 bishops in Carthage and 18 at Milevis in Numidia (416) sent letters (Augustine, *Epist.* 175; *Patrologia Latina* 33:758–762) to Innocent I begging him to secure a disavowal from Pelagius himself. Innocent I wrote in reply (Augustine, *Epist.* 181–183; *Patrologia Latina* 33:779–788), insisting on man's daily need of grace, but willing—even eager—to pardon a repentant Pelagius (Jan. 27,417). He wrote again to Carthage, where another council sat (417), emphasizing his own primacy (*Corpus scriptorum ecclesiasticorum latinorum* 44:715–723; *Regestapontificum romanorum ab condita ecclesia ad annum post Christum natum 1198* 321). Zosimus, his successor (417–418), wrote a similar letter (*Regesta pontificum romanorum ab condita ecclesia ad annum post Christum natum 1198* 342) the following year (*Corpus scriptorum ecclesiasticorum latinorum* 35:115–117). Meantime Pelagius and his disciple Celestius convinced the pope of their innocence, the former being reinstated and Celestius tentatively approved. Zosimus ordered Carthage to reexamine its position. Put on the defensive, Augustine spent the most painful year of his episcopate. Celestius, however, behaving disgracefully, came under the censure of Emperor Honorius and fled. Nine articles (*Enchiridion symbolorum,* 222–230) on grace and original sin were formulated by 214 African bishops in council (May 1, 418). [Canon 3, condemning unbaptized infants to hell on the principle "Whoever is not on the right hand is doubtless on the left," does not appear in Mansi (4:326–334) or in Roman collections.] Zosimus finally condemned Celestius and excommunicated Pelagius. From May 25 to 30, 419, 217 bishops met; canons of previous councils were read before papal representatives; thus they received a quasi-ecumenical validity.

The Arian VANDALS invaded North Africa (429), persecuting the Church and setting up rival bishops. Thus 466 bishops met in Carthage (Feb. 1, 484) before Huneric, the Vandal king. The Catholic bishops were exiled. Justinian's African conquest (534) made possible a Carthaginian council in that year, dealing with policies regarding converted Arians, cleric and lay.

See Also: GRACE, CONTROVERSIES ON; SALUTARY ACTS; GRACE, ARTICLES ON.

Bibliography: CYPRIAN, *Epistolae* 44, 45, 48, 57, 59, 61, 64, 70, 71, 72. J. D. MANSI, *Sacrorum Conciliorum nova et amplissima collectio,* 31 v. (Florence-Venice 1757-98) 1:840–851, 863–866, 868–872, 881–882, 897–900, 900–902, 923–926, 951–992; 3:143–158, 671–678: 7:1056–59, 1171–74. A. STUIBER, *Lexikon für Theologie und Kirche,* ed. J. HOFER and K. RAHNER, 10 v. (2d new ed. Freiburg 1957–65) 6:1–2. P. FRANSEN, *ibid.* 3–4. A. AUDOLLENT, *Dictionnaire d'histoire et de géographie ecclésiastiques,* ed. A. BAUDRILLART et al. (Paris 1912–) 1:747–750, 811–822, lists all councils of Carthage. G. BARDY, *Catholicisme* 2:606–607. C. J. VON HEFELE, *Histoire des conciles d'après les documents originaux,* tr. and continued by H. LECLERCQ, 10 v. in 19 (Paris 1907–38) 1.1:165–176; 1.2:837–841, 1101, 1105–06, 1107–18; 2.1:76–78; 2.2:1136–39. L. DUCHESNE, *The Early History of the Christian Church,* 3 v. (New York 1909–24) 1:282–313. H. LECLERCQ, *L'Afrique chrétienne,* 2 v. (2d ed. Paris 1904).

[C. M. AHERNE]

CARTHUSIAN RITE

This entry traces the origins and history of the Carthusian Rite and its unique characteristics in Mass and Office. It seems certain that the predominant and exclusive influence in the formation of the Carthusian liturgy was the rite of the primatial See of Lyons, of which Grenoble was a suffragan. This is true of the Mass and very largely of the Office, though for the latter the order of psalmody (which governs the form of the Hours) laid down by the Rule of St. Benedict was adopted; for the other variable parts of the Office, the Antiphonary of Lyons was drawn upon.

There is considerable evidence for these assertions. One of the earliest Carthusian liturgical manuscripts (MS 33 at St. Hugh's Charterhouse, Parkminster, England) shows that the octave day of Pentecost was celebrated with the Mass of the feast, so that the series of Masses for the Sundays after Pentecost are one behind the corresponding series in the Roman rite; the last of the series is *Si iniquitates* instead of *Dicit Dominus.* This, the versicle *Pone, Domine, custodiam ori meo,* said before the Confiteor at Mass, and the prayer at the mixing of the wine and water (*De latere,* etc.) are all features common to the early Carthusian liturgy and to that of Lyons. Similar influences may be seen in the Antiphonary. Guigo I,

the fifth prior of Chartreuse, who compiled both books, followed the principle advocated by Agobard, archbishop of Lyons (d. 840), that only Scripture and sermons from the Fathers could be used at the Office or Mass. As a consequence "ecclesiastical compositions" were excluded from the rite: Mass for the dead had as Introit *Respice* instead of *Requiem,* and many well-known pieces found no place. Although at a later date some nonscriptural matter found its way into the Missal and Office, the Carthusians were conservative in this matter; there were no "historical" second nocturn lessons in the Carthusian Office. Hymns were allowed in the Office, though at Lyons there were none until a late date. Guigo's work is to be found in the *Consuetudines Cartusiae;* his successors coordinated successive enactments of general chapters in a collection known as *Statuta Antiqua* (c. 1222), which remained in force until 1582, when a reform of the rite produced the *Ordinarium.* However, little real change was effected in the rite. From the Council of Trent to Vatican II the Carthusian Rite was largely as it was codified by Guigo.

Mass. The celebrant of a high Mass was attended by a deacon (there is no subdeacon). Mass began below the step at the Gospel side, where the celebrant sang the versicle *Pone, Domine,* etc., to which the choir responded, and the Confiteor follows (a short form). Introit, Kyrie, and Gloria were recited by the celebrant while they are sung by the choir; after the Collect he went to his seat at the Epistle side and listened to the Epistle sung by a monk from the choir; meanwhile the deacon prepared the offerings. Immediately after the Gospel (or Credo), the celebrant washed his hands and received the paten and chalice from the deacon. As the drop of water is poured into the chalice, the celebrant said *De latere Domini nostri Jesu Christi exivit sanguis et aqua, in nomine Patris,* etc. Paten and chalice were offered simultaneously with the prayer *In spiritu humilitatis.* The priest then washed his hands again. Meanwhile the deacon incensed the altar, walking around it, swinging the thurible at the full length of its chains. During the Canon the celebrant held out his arms in the form of a cross, unless some manual act was necessary. The kiss of peace was given with an instrument. The deacon communicated with the priest on Sundays and certain feasts. Having drunk the ablutions, the celebrant left the chalice for the deacon to purify and went to the Epistle corner to sing the *Complendae* (Postcommunions). There was no blessing or *Placeat.* The blessing of candles, ashes, and palms takes place after the preparatory prayers at the foot of the altar, but the Carthusians had no liturgical processions.

Office. The Carthusian Office followed the general pattern of the monastic Breviary, but the lessons at Matins were very long compared to those of other monastic

Exterior of portico underside in Cloister of Carthusians, Rome, Italy. (©Michael Maslan Historic Photographs/CORBIS)

orders (e.g., two or three chapters of a book of Scripture comprised the three lessons of a ferial night). All the day Hours concluded with long ferial preces before the Collect. The Carthusian Breviary, used only by those unable to go to choir, contained short lessons on the pattern of the modern Roman Breviary. Simplicity and sobriety are the chief characteristics of the historical Carthusian liturgy.

Bibliography: A. A. KING, *Liturgies of the Religious Orders* (Milwaukee, Wisc. 1955). L. C. SHEPPARD, *The Mass in the West* (New York 1962); "How the Carthusians Pray," *Thought* 4 (1929) 294–311. J.-B. MARTIN, *Bibliographie liturgique de l'ordre des Chartreux* (Ligugé, Austria 1913). J. HOGG, *Mittelalterliche Caerimonialia der Kartäuser* (Berlin 1971). H. BECKER, *Die Kartause: liturgisches Erbe und konziliare Reform: Untersuchungen und Dokumente* (Salzburg 1990). E. CLUZET, *Particularités du missel cartusien: contribution à l'étude des origines du missel cartusien* (Salzburg 1994). A. DEVAUX, *Les origines du missel des chartreux* (Salzburg 1995). E. CLUZET, *Sources et genèse du missel cartusien* (Salzburg 1996).

[L. C. SHEPPARD/EDS.]

CARTHUSIAN SPIRITUALITY

That no specific school of Carthusian spirituality comparable to Ignatian or the French School (Pierre de Bérulle) exists has frequently been asserted. The first Carthusians sought simply to live apart solely for God. WILLIAM OF SAINT THIERRY's encomium to the early Carthusian hermits, the *Golden Epistle* to the Carthusians of Mont-Dieu, testifies to the degree to which they patterned themselves on the desert fathers, whose spirituality they knew through JOHN CASSIAN and JEROME and the Latin translations of JOHN CLIMACUS, the Rule of ST. BASIL, and the lives and sayings of the desert fathers. At its most basic level Carthusian spirituality consists of the Greek and Latin patristic spiritual theology focused on the reformation of the image of God in man deformed by sin (see Ladner) and the reintegration of the passions disintegrated by sin, with *discretio*—as it was for John Cassian and the early tradition—the governor of all the other spiritual virtues. Carthusian spirituality differed little in general

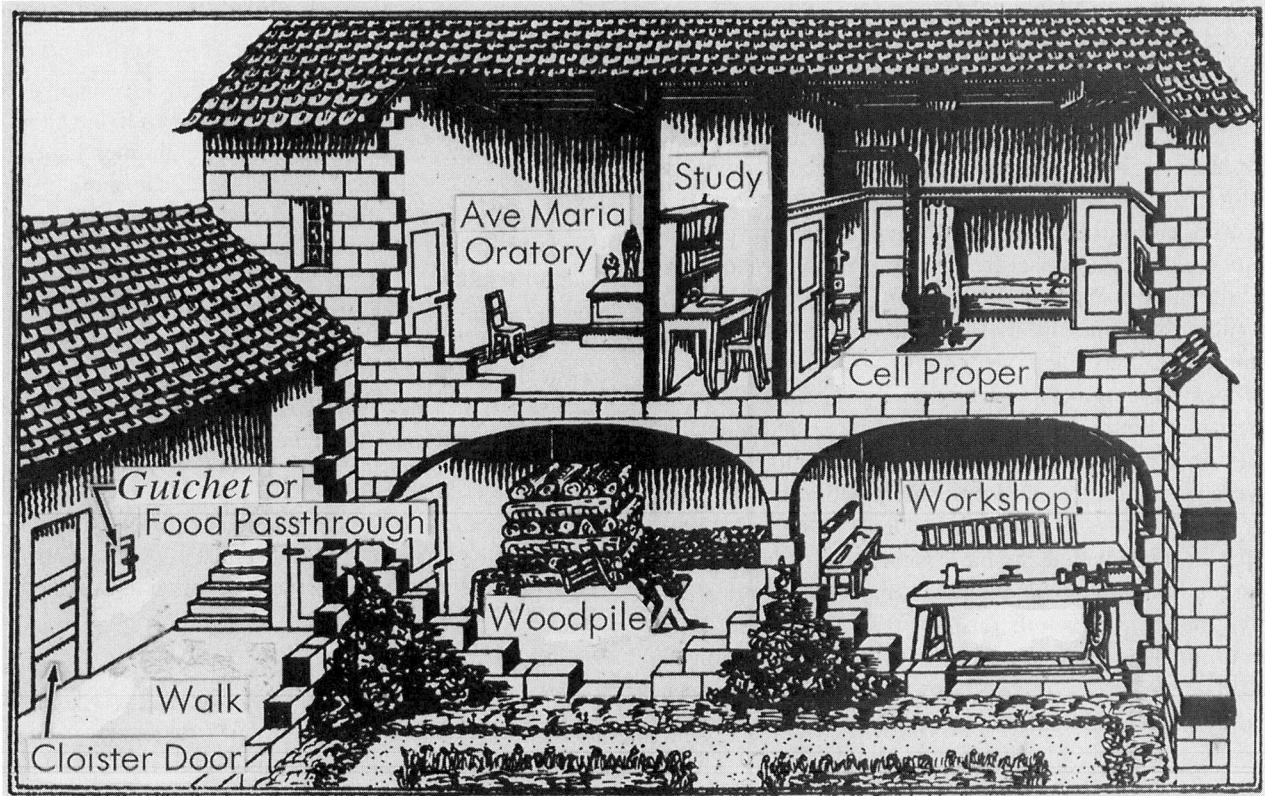

The Interior of a Carthusian cell.

content from that of other monastic renewal movements of the eleventh and early twelfth century, including the CAMALDOLESE, CISTERCIANS, and GRANDMONTINES.

However, from the beginning the Carthusians set out to pursue this spirituality by making themselves utterly free for God (*vacare Deo*) in solitude. Only after more than 50 years were they transformed into a religious order of eremitic-coenobitic monasteries. In the process they developed unique customs and structures to preserve their original purpose. Their liturgy was drawn pragmatically from the cathedral practices of five dioceses in the Dauphiné, especially Grenoble and Vienne, and from the liturgical practices of the canons regular of St. Ruf (see Devaux). The Carthusians sought liturgical simplicity in many ways, for instance, in the first centuries choosing readings only from three or four of the greatest of the Latin church fathers and, even in the late 20th century, limiting their music exclusively to unaccompanied Gregorian chant.

The Carthusians may be said to have developed a distinctive spirituality in the sense that their legislation aimed not so much at prescribing the content of spiritual theology as establishing the conditions under which a monk could singlemindedly free himself for God alone by sitting sedulously in his cell (a small cottage). They left the world in order to know it more truly by gaining distance from it and by reordering both knowledge and love of God and neighbor in a way someone distracted by mundane responsibilities and attractions could not. This in turn required them to establish a way of life that dealt pragmatically and realistically with the temptations to leave the cell and the obstacles to living joyously in it. As more communal functions were added to Carthusian practice (e.g., daily conventual Mass) over subsequent centuries, their aim was precisely that served by the limited communal elements at the founding: to make it possible to live as healthily in solitude as possible, to maintain the Carthusian purpose (*propositum*). Manual labor (largely copying books during the medieval period) was not an end in itself but a crucial supporting structure for the sole purpose of the Carthusian life: to give oneself to God in prayer and contemplation and thereby to know and love the world better. The outline for the famous manual for contemplation of Guigo II (d. 1178), widely known for its four steps of *lectio, meditatio, oratio*, and *contemplatio*, came to him while engaged in manual labor.

Carthusians were prohibited from leaving the monastery to preach or do pastoral work, although from ST.

BRUNO onward, individual Carthusians such as St. Anthelm of Belley and ST. HUGH OF LINCOLN were reluctantly convinced by ecclesiastical leaders to leave contemplative solitude and became exemplary bishops. From the first Carthusians did permit themselves to "preach with their hands" by writing and copying, as GUIGO I's *Consuetudines* explain (ch. 28). From the first two centuries of Carthusian life have survived several letters of spiritual counsel from the pen of St. Bruno (most of the other works attributed to him appear to have been written by non-Carthusians), the remarkable *Meditationes* of Guigo I, and the *Scala Claustralium (Ladder of Monks)* of Guigo II as referred to above. All of these reflect the simple cell-sitting life of prayer and reflection described above. Only with the later thirteenth century do we find specific manuals on contemplation and mystical union by HUGH OF BALMA and GUIGO DU PONT (d. 1297). Hugh's fundamental emphasis is on short aspirative "upsurges" into unknowing union, a major step in the affective Western assimilation of the Pseudo-Dionysian tradition. Hugh's work may have had some impact on the 14th-century *CLOUD OF UNKNOWING* in England and certainly influenced Spanish spirituality in the early modern era. The Carthusians also served as important transmitters of the mystical spirituality of JAN RUYSBROEC both locally and internationally.

From the late 13th century onward a broadening stream of categories of spiritual writings may be found emanating from the charterhouses of France, Germany, the Low Countries, England, Spain, Italy, Slovenia, Moravia, Bohemia, and Poland. They include the visions of Marguerite d'Oingt (d. 1310) and Beatrice d'Ornacieux (d. 1303/1309), Carthusian nuns in Provence; a very popular 14th-century life of Mary (and Jesus) written in German verse by Philip of Seitz (d. 1345–46), transmitted in the houses of the Teutonic Knights and taken up into world history chronicles by the 15th century; the "bestselling" compendium of patristic and medieval spiritual commentary on the life of Christ by LUDOLF OF SAXONY; some of the best Latin hymns and poetry of the later Middle Ages, written by Conrad Haimburg of Gaming (d. 1366) celebrating the lives of the saints and the Virgin Mary arranged according to the liturgical cycle; biblical commentaries, including a cycle of commentaries on Old Testament women by Johannes Brewer of Hagen (d. 1475) at Erfurt; manuals for biblical exegesis; treatises on monastic life, monastic formation, and monastic leadership, above all *discretio* (e.g., in the writings of Heinrich Egher van Kalkar [d. 1308], Nikolaus Kempf of Gaming [d. 1497], Jakob Kunike of Paradies [d. 1465]); works on monastic and general church reform; the spiritual journals of DOMINIC OF PRUSSIA; and writings in many other areas. Juan de Padilla (d. 1520) wrote devo-

tional poetry in early modern Spanish (Castilian) about the life of Christ.

Two authors in particular wrote encyclopedically on all these topics and more, including how to live a Christian life as, e.g., a city clerk, lawyer, grain merchant, or farmer: Denys of Ryckel (Denis the Carthusian) in the Netherlands and the aforementioned Johannes Brewer of Hagen at Erfurt. Stephen Maconi (d. 1424) and Bartolomeo [Serafini] de Ravenna (d. 1413) championed the canonization of CATHERINE OF SIENA; Cardinal Nicholas Albergati (d. 1443) combined Renaissance philology and classical literature with the Carthusian eremitical tradition. At Paris in the 16th century, Godfrey Tillmann (d. 1561) published important editions of the Church fathers.

Two Carthusians of Trier, Dominic of Prussia and Adolf of Essen (d. 1439) developed the meditative Rosary devotion (popularized by Dominicans). Other Carthusians contributed to the emerging devotion to the Sacred Heart.

During the era of the Protestant Reformation, Carthusians at Cologne and Paris wrote spiritual and dogmatic works intended to counter Protestantism. Peter Blomevenna (d. 1536), Dietrich Loher (d. 1554), Laurentius Surius, Johann Justus LANSPERGIUS, Gerard Kalckbrenner (d. 1566), Nicholas van Essche (d. 1578), Richard Beaucousin (d. 1610) and others influenced (by their writings and by offering spiritual direction) and were in some instances influenced by the spirituality of e.g., PETER CANISIUS, Ignatius of Loyola, Benedict Canfield, and Pierre de Bérulle, and the Rhineland Beguine mystic Maria van Hout of Oisterwijk (d. 1547). The great 17th-century prior general of the order, Innocent Le Masson issued a post-Tridentine manual for the formation of Carthusians, the *Disciplina Ordinis Cartusiensis*. His *Avis spirituels et meditations* were republished by the Carthusians at Tournai in 1911.

Recovering from the external pressures of the late 18th- and early 19th-century turmoil in France, Spain, and Italy, in the 20th century some Carthusian spiritual writers became known outside the houses of the order, where the centuries-old patterns of novice formation and a life of steady cell-sitting continued. In the middle of the 20th century writings on spirituality by Augustin Guillerand, François de Sales Pollien, Jean-Baptiste Porion, Benoît Lambres (Benoît de Moustier), and Thomas Verner Moore appeared in French, English, and other languages. More recently a variety of writings by Cyril Pierce, André Poisson and others have appeared, usually anonymously, in French, Spanish, Italian, and German. Maurice LaPorte's research into the spirituality of the initial Carthusian movement circulated in six volumes within the order, with portions published in three volumes in the

Sources Chrétiennes series. Basic descriptions of the life and spirituality of the Chartreuse by anonymous Carthusians (as well as one by the Cistercian Thomas MERTON) have been staples in French, English, and other European languages throughout the last two centuries.

Bibliography: G. VAN DIJCK et al., *Nouvelle Bibliographie Cartusienne* (2002), v. 1, sect. 12: "Spiritualité," bibliography. Un Chartreux [M. LAPORTE], ed., *Lettres des premiers chartreux*, v. 1: *S. Bruno, Guiges, S. Anthelme* (*Sources Chrétiennes* 88; Paris 1962); v. 2: *Les moines de Portes* (*Sources Chrétiennes* 274; Paris 1980, reprinted 1999); *Coutumes de Chartreuse*, (*Sources Chrétiennes* 313; Paris 1984), contains a thorough discussion of the original spirituality of the Carthusians in its introduction. H. DE BALMA, *Théologie mystique*, ed. F. RUELLO and J. BARBET (*Sources Chrétiennes* 408–409; Paris 1995–96). G. DU PONT, *Traité sur la Contemplation*, 2 v., ed. P. DUPONT (*Analecta Cartusiana* 72; Salzburg 1985). *Carthusian Spirituality: The Writings of Hugh of Balma and Guigo de Ponte*, trans. and ed. D. D. MARTIN, Classics of Western Spirituality (New York 1997). M. D'OIGNT, *Oeuvres*, ed. by A. DURAFOUR, P. GARDETTE, and P. DARDILLY (Paris 1965). N. KEMPF, *Tractatus de Mystica Theologia*, 2 v., ed. K. JELLOUSCHEK, J. BARBET, and F. RUELLO (*Analecta Cartusiana* 9; Salzburg 1973). G. KALCKBRENNER, *Mélanges de Spiritualité*, ed. A. DEVAUX (*Analecta Cartusiana* 158; Salzburg 1999). **Studies.** A. DEVAUX, *Les origines du missel des Chartreux* (*Analecta Cartusiana* 99.32; Salzburg 1995). B. RIEDER, *Deus locum dabit: Studien zur Theologie des Kartäuserpriors Guigo I. (1083–1136)* (Paderborn 1997). G. MURSELL, *The Theology of the Carthusian Life in the Writings of St. Bruno and Guigo I* (*Analecta Cartusiana* 127; Salzburg 1988). *The Mystical Tradition and the Carthusians*, v. 4 (*Analecta Cartusiana* 130.4; Salzburg, 1995), 5–157, 16–25. D. D. MARTIN, *Fifteenth-Century Carthusian Reform: The World of Nicholas Kempf* (*Studies in the History of Christian Thought* 49; Leiden 1992). C.- M. BOUTRAIS, *Ancient Devotions to the Sacred Heart of Jesus by Carthusian Monks of the XIV–XVII Centuries* (4th ed.; London 1953).

[D. D. MARTIN]

CARTHUSIANS

The Carthusian Order is a purely contemplative monastic order that was founded in 1084 by St. Bruno (*see* BRUNO THE CARTHUSIAN, ST.). The name Carthusian is derived from *cartusia*, the Latin word for the French *chartreuse*. The English word "charterhouse" is a corruption of this French term.

Origin. In 1084 Bruno and six companions, under the guidance of St. HUGH OF GRENOBLE, arrived in the Chartreuse mountains, a section of the French Alps about 30 miles from Grenoble. The solitary and austere site, together with the severe climate, profoundly influenced the life and growth of the young community. When Urban II (1088–99) called Bruno to Rome in 1090, the new order passed through a severe crisis and the Carthusian foundation was temporarily abandoned. After a short time, the community reformed under Landuin the new

Carthusian nun, 18th-century France, Bibliothèque des Arts Decoratifs, Paris, France. (©Gianni Dagli Orti/CORBIS)

prior (d. 1100) and resumed its solitary life. At the papal court Bruno still longed for the solitary life, and after some months the pope permitted him to withdraw to Calabria in southern Italy, where he founded a second Carthusian monastery similar to the one in France. While returning from a visit to Bruno in Calabria, Landuin fell into the hands of the forces of the antipope Clement III (1084–1100) and perished in prison because of his allegiance to the true pope; he was thus the first of many Carthusian martyrs.

Rule. Since Bruno did not intend to found a new monastic order, he wrote no rule. The example of his life entirely "hidden in the Face of God" served, however, as the source of inspiration for all the succeeding generations of Carthusians. As the community of La Grande Chartreuse flourished and its reputation for austerity and sanctity became known, other groups of hermits desired to adopt the Carthusian way of life. It was for these new communities that Guigo, the fifth prior, at the request of Hugh of Grenoble, compiled in 1127 the *Consuetudines* (customs) according to which the Carthusians lived. This primitive legislation was supplemented by ordinances of the general chapters. On several occasions the ordinances were gathered together in a single edition, such as that of 1581, when the *Nova Collectio* was published. The latest revision (1924) brought the statutes into conformity with the *Code of Canon Law* and was approved *in forma specifica* by Pius XI in the apostolic constitution *Umbratilem* (July 8, 1924). In the wake of Vatican II, the statutes were revised as the *Statuta Renovata* (1971, 1973), and again, very slightly, to conform to the 1983 *Code of Canon Law,* approved by the General Chapter of 1987 as the *Statuta ordinis Cartusiensis.*

The supreme authority of the order is vested in the general chapter, which meets every two years at the Grande Chartreuse and is composed of the priors of all the monasteries and the professed members of the community of the Grande Chartreuse. The business of the chapter, however, is transacted by a definitory elected for each session. The prior of the Grande Chartreuse is elected by the community, but then has to be approved by the other priors and prioresses of the order. He is the minister general of the order. His authority is supreme between the sessions of the general chapter. Although each monastery is *sui juris* and its prior a major superior according to Canon Law, the government of the order is nonetheless highly centralized.

History. Under Guigo, the fifth prior (1109–36), seven more charterhouses were founded. In the following years still other groups of hermits requested copies of the *Consuetudines* in order to become affiliated to the sons of St. Bruno. In all, 38 charterhouses, including two for nuns, were opened during the 12th century and extended as far as Denmark. In 1178 the first charterhouse in England was opened at Witham in Somerset. As the result of a vow made after the murder of Thomas Becket, King Henry II invited the Carthusians to establish a foundation and promised them large grants of land in Selwood Forest. Henry, however, failed to provide for the people who were already living off the donated land, and the foundation almost ended in tragedy. The ability of Hugh, the prior of Witham, in dealing with Henry saved the foundation and the Carthusians became firmly established in England. Hugh later became the celebrated bishop of Lincoln and because of his firmness in defending the rights of the Church became known as ''The Hammer of Kings'' (*see* HUGH OF LINCOLN, ST.).

In the beginning the new foundations remained under the jurisdiction of the local bishop; but as the order expanded, the need of a central governing body became evident and a general chapter of all the priors was held in 1140 at the Grande Chartreuse under the leadership of St. ANTHELM OF CHIGNIN. The priors, released from the authority of their bishops, promised obedience to the general chapter. The exemption from episcopal jurisdiction was approved by Rome. The expansion of the order continued throughout the 13th century, when 34 monasteries were founded, including a brief experiment in Ireland between 1280 and 1321. The Carthusian foundation in Ireland has never been renewed.

Growth and Vicissitudes. The 14th century marked an extensive development of the order with 107 new foundations. Charterhouses were opened for the first time in Germany and Prussia. In the same century, however, the order also suffered severe reverses. In 1349, during the ravages of the Black Death, more than 400 Carthusians perished. In one house, Montrieux, all but the prior were victims of the plague. After the plague the order regained its vigor; in 1371 there were 150 monasteries spread throughout Europe. It is interesting that during these first four centuries of the order's history there were no less than 26 pontifical bulls exempting the Carthusians from the payment of all tithes because of their poverty. Toward the end of the century the WESTERN SCHISM divided the order in two; the houses of Italy and Germany adhered to the pope of Rome, Urban VI, while the monasteries of Spain and France gave their allegiance to Clement VII at Avignon. The division gave rise to the election of two generals, both claiming the rights of the prior of the Grande Chartreuse. Although many attempts were made at unification during the schism, it was only after the election of Alexander V (1409) that a reunion was effected through the resignation of the two contending priors general. Despite the difficulties experienced throughout the Church in the 15th and early 16th centuries, the Carthusian Order continued to grow; 43 foundations were made in the 15th century, and an additional 13 in the 16th. By 1521 the order numbered 195 houses; never before or since have the Carthusians been so flourishing.

A serious decline set in during the Reformation, when 39 houses were suppressed and more than 50 Carthusians gave their lives for the faith. Notable among these martyrs were the 18 English monks who were tortured and killed in the period from 1535 to 1540 (*see* ENGLAND, SCOTLAND, WALES, MARTYRS OF). Carthusian blood flowed also in Yugoslavia and Austria at the hands of the heretics and of the Turks; in Holland and France the Reformers destroyed charterhouses and massacred the monks. In 1562 the Grande Chartreuse itself was completely destroyed by the Huguenots. In spite of wars and persecutions, however, the Carthusians continued to attract numerous vocations; during one period of 13 years in the 16th century the book of profession at the Grande Chartreuse registered the vows of 115 novices. In the first half of the following century, 21 foundations were made, and these were the last new charterhouses to be founded before the French Revolution. Carthusians were once more put to death by the Huguenots in France and by the Turks in Yugoslavia.

17th and 18th Centuries. In 1676 the order numbered 173 charterhouses with 2,300 choir monks, 1,500 lay brothers, and 170 nuns. In that same year the Grande Chartreuse, destroyed by fire for the eighth time, was completely reconstructed by Innocent LE MASSON, one of the most outstanding generals of the order (d. 1703). In addition to the traditional eremitical and conventual buildings, spacious pavilions were provided to receive the priors coming to the general chapter. The proponents of JANSENISM, prevalent during this period, tried to infiltrate into the order under the appearances of a higher spirituality. Because of the traditional simplicity of solitaries, the Jansenists expected no obstacle in spreading their doctrines. The vigorous action of Le Masson in banning Jansenist books from all charterhouses and in writing a dogmatic treatise on the questions under dispute did much to save the Carthusians from the contamination of this heresy. In 1710 the general chapter required all the monks to sign the formulary of Alexander VII (1656) and decreed that no one would be admitted to profession who had not done so. In only one of the seven Carthusian provinces of France was the submission incomplete. After a prolonged and patient procedure, 31 monks were excommunicated and separated from the order. They took refuge in Holland, where, with the exception of a few who repented and returned to the order, they remained until their deaths in the most miserable circumstances, both spiritual and material. These religious represented less than one percent of the entire order, which maintained a remarkable fidelity to orthodoxy.

The 18th century was characterized by a nationalist spirit according to which many of the Catholic rulers desired to exercise complete control over the Church within their realms. Upon the insistence of the royal power, the two Carthusian provinces of Spain were erected as an autonomous congregation by Pius VI in 1784. Shortly afterward the court of Naples published a decree uniting all the Neapolitan houses as a separate body. The Republic of Venice and Emperor Joseph II of Austria suppressed all the charterhouses in their states under the pretext of need of monastic property for public education. In Tuscany the grand duke closed the two houses in his territory. At the beginning of the French Revolution the general chapter had authority over only 126 houses, 75 of which were in France. The decrees of the revolutionary government confiscated all the French houses, and these were subsequently thoroughly pillaged by the army. During the bloody days of the revolution many Carthusians were imprisoned; some died in prison, and others were put to death or exiled. During the Napoleonic era all but five of the houses of the order were suppressed.

Recent History. The restoration of the former monarchies favored the religious orders. Without returning their property, King Louis XVIII of France permitted the monks to live at the Grande Chartreuse (1816). The order immediately attracted large numbers of postulants, who after their formation were sent to other charterhouses that were repurchased as the number of subjects increased. Gradually, monasteries were also reacquired in Italy and Savoy. While the Carthusians were experiencing a rebirth in France and in Italy, the revolution of 1834 in Portugal suppressed all the charterhouses in that kingdom. The following year the Spanish government dispersed the Carthusian congregation and seized its property. The houses of the order in Switzerland were likewise suppressed. In the last quarter of the 19th century, as the antireligious spirit subsided, the Grande Chartreuse repurchased monasteries in Germany, Italy, Switzerland, Spain, and England, as well as in France. Several of these houses were for Carthusian nuns. At the end of the century the order, divided into three provinces, numbered about 700 monks and brothers, and 100 nuns.

Because of the anticlerical laws of the early 20th century, the Carthusians once more were exiled from France and ten charterhouses were confiscated. The community of the Grande Chartreuse, together with the prior general, was established at Farneta in Italy. The monks remained in exile until 1929, when the first French house, Montrieux, was reopened. It was only in 1940, during the confusion of the war, that they were able to reoccupy the Grande Chartreuse.

Carthusian Life. The Carthusian family is comprised of two types of monks—the fathers and the brothers—to which is added the female branch of the order, which is comprised of the nuns.

Monks. The choir monks, all of whom must become priests, are bound to the sung, canonical Office in choir. In addition, each monk says the Office of Our Lady in his cell. With the prior's permission, however, this Office can be replaced with another form of Marian devotion. The monk lives in a hermitage consisting of a covered walkway, private garden, and workshop on the ground floor; above is the *cubiculum,* or living room, where he prays, studies, eats, and sleeps. Here he passes the greater part of his life. The cells, entirely separated from one another, open on the main cloister, which connects with the church and other conventual buildings. Toward midnight, the monk rises to go to the church to sing Matins and Lauds, after which he returns to his cell for a second period of sleep of about three hours. In early morning he leaves his cell for conventual Mass and then says his solitary Mass (which can be celebrated later in the day with the agreement of the prior); he leaves once again in the late afternoon for Vespers. The remainder of the day, spent in solitude, is given to the recitation of the Office, contemplative prayer, spiritual reading, study, and manual labor. In winter one meal is taken at noon, and a collation of bread and beverage is taken in the evening; in summer there are two meals. There is no breakfast, and meat is never allowed, even in cases of sickness. A fast on bread and water is kept once a week (normally on Friday). Within the monastery silence is strictly observed. Once a week the monks take a hike of three or four hours in the surrounding countryside, during which they converse freely in a spirit of fraternal charity. Besides the walk, a recreation permitting monks to speak casually with each other takes place each Sunday, and, for those who so desire, also at each liturgical feast of the rank of Solemnity.

Lay Brothers. Brothers were among St. Bruno's first companions and have always formed an integral part of the Carthusian family. They are religious contemplatives like the choir monks but are called to a solitude less exacting, and enjoy a well-balanced life in which prayer and spiritual reading alternate with periods of work. They attend the night office of the fathers and can participate in the chant of the Psalms and the reading of the lessons. Otherwise they have the option of reciting their own office made up of "Our Fathers" and "Hail Marys" or of simply praying in silence. They can also serve at conventual Mass as either lector or acolyte. Their day begins with a time of prayer or spiritual reading, which is then followed by the Mass. Each brother has his own simple cell where he says his Office, reads, sleeps, and takes his meals, except on Sundays and certain feasts when meals are taken in the refectory. Devoted to the service of the fathers, who by their rule may not leave their cells to work, the brothers care for the material needs of the monastery. When possible they work alone; when obliged to work with others, they observe silence so far as practicable. Thus, whether in their cells or at work, they live as solitary contemplatives. They benefit, moreover, from the atmosphere of peace and tranquility created by the more secluded life of the choir monks.

Nuns. Female religious have been affiliated to the order since the 12th century. They follow a rule similar to the fathers, but their life was traditionally less solitary. In the post-Vatican II era, the life of Carthusian nuns more closely resembles that of the monks. After profession of solemn vows they receive the consecration of virgins and possess the unique privilege of the ancient blessing of DEACONESSES. Lay sisters lead a life of humble service similar to the brothers and like them aspire to a life of contemplative union with God. In the wake of Vatican II, the nuns received for the first time a set of statutes distinct from those of the monks (1973, 1991). Since 1973 the prioresses have assembled in a general chapter, meeting in conjunction with the general chapter of the

order. In recent years a greater degree of solitude has been permitted the nuns.

Current Status. Vocations to Carthusian solitude are relatively rare. In 2001 the order had five houses in Spain, four in France, two in Italy, and one each in Slovenia, Germany, Switzerland, England, the United States, and Brazil. A new foundation has been emerging in Argentina since 1997. There were five houses of nuns (two in France, two in Italy, and one in Spain). The Carthusian emblem is a globe surmounted by a cross and seven stars with the motto "While the world changes, the cross stands firm."

Bibliography: A three-volume general history of the order is being compiled by an international team of scholars led by J. HOGG, D. LE BLÉVEC and others, to be published by Éditions Honoré Champion (2002ff). G. VAN DIJK et al., *Nouvelle Bibliographie Cartusienne* (forthcoming 2002). *The Evolution of the Carthusian Statutes from the Consuetudines Guigonis to the Tertia Compilatio, Documents* (Analecta Cartusiana 99.1–20; Salzburg 1989–1993). B. TROMBY, *Storia critico-cronologica diplomatica del patriarca S. Brunone e del suo ordine cartusiano,* 10 v. (Naples 1773–79). C. LE COUTEULX, *Annales ordinis cartusiensis* (1084–1429), 8 v. (Montreuil 1887–91). J. L. HOGG and P. DINZELBACHER, ed., *Kulturgeschichte der christlichen Orden* (Stuttgart 1997), 274–296. A. P. F. LEFEBVRE, *St. Bruno et l'ordre des Chartreux,* 2 v. (Paris 1883). C. M. BOUTRAIS, *La Grande Chartreuse* (Grenoble 1881; rev. 1964), Eng., *The History of the Great Chartreuse,* tr. E. HASSID (London 1934). T. MERTON, *The Silent Life* (New York 1957). E. M. THOMPSON, *The Carthusian Order in England* (New York 1930). ADAM, CHAPLAIN OF ST. HUGH, *Magna vita Sancti Hugonis: The Life of St. Hugh of Lincoln,* ed. D. L. DOUIE and H. FARMER, 2 v. (London 1961–62), Latin and Eng. Un Chartreux [M. Laporte of the Grande Chartreuse], *Coutumes de Chartreuse* (*Sources Chretiennes* 313; Paris 1984). *The Chartae of the Carthusian General Chapter* (Analecta Cartusiana 100; Salzburg 1982–). M. ZADNIKAR and A. WIENAND, *Die Kartäuser: Orden der Schweigenden Mönche* (Cologne 1983). B. BLIGNY and G. CHAIX, eds., "La Naissance des chartreuses," *Actes du VIe Colloque Internaitonal d'Histoire et de Spiritualité Cartusiennes, Grenoble, 12–15 Septembre 1984* (Grenoble 1986). A. GIRARD and D. LE BLÉVEC, eds., "Les Chartreux et l'art: XIVe–XVIIIe siècles," *Actes du Xe Colloque International d'Histoire et de Spiritualité Cartusiennes* (Villeneuve-lès-Avignon, 15–18 Septembre 1988; Paris 1989). J. HOGG, "Everyday Life in the Charterhouse in the Fourteenth and Fifteenth Centuries," in *Klösterliche Sachkultur des Spätmittelalters,* Internationaler Kongress Krems an der Donau 18. bis 21. September 1978, in the series *Veröffentlichungen des Instituts für Mittelalterliche Realienkunde Österreichs* 3 (Vienna 1980), 113–46. H. RÜTHING, "'Die Wächter Israels'—ein Beitrag zur Geschichte der Visitationen im Kartäuserorden," in *Die Kartäuser: Der Orden der schweigenden Mönche,* ed. M. ZADNIKAR with A. WIENAND (Cologne 1983), 169–83; *Der Kartäuser Heinrich Egher van Kalkar, 1328–1408* (*Veröffentlichungen des Max-Planck-Instituts für Geschichte 18/Studien zur Germania Sacra* 8; Göttingen 1967). G. CHAIX, *Réforme et Contre-Reform Catholique: Recherches sur la Chartreuse de Cologne au XVIe siècle,* 3 v., (Analecta Cartusiana, 80; Salzburg 1981). D. MERTENS, *Iacobus Carthusiensis: Untersuchungen zur Rezeption der Werke des Kartäusers Jakob von Paradies* (*Veröffentlichungen des Max-Planck-Instituts für Geschichte 50/Studien zur Germania Sacra* 13; Göttingen 1976). D. D. MARTIN, *Fifteenth-Century Car-*

thusian Reform: The World of Nicholas Kempf (Studies in the History of Christian Thought 49; Leiden 1992).

[A MONK OF THE GRANDE CHARTREUSE/G. VAN DIJCK]

CARTWRIGHT, THOMAS

PURITAN Controversialist; b. Herts, 1535; d. Warwick, Dec. 27, 1603. Thomas, son of a yeoman, studied at Clare and St. John's Colleges, Cambridge (1547–53), where he absorbed Reformation ideas. At Mary's accession he left the university to read law. Between 1558 and 1570, except for two years in Ireland, he held fellowships at St. John's and Trinity Colleges, becoming Lady Margaret Professor in 1569. He used this chair primarily to promote the Puritan cause, to which he had committed himself in the Vestiarian Controversy of 1566. He became identified more closely with nonconformity by actively preaching reform of the constitution and ecclesiastical polity of the Established Church along Presbyterian lines, proposing that the bishops and the crown governing the church be replaced by ministers and elders. Although these views deprived him of his professorship and enforced, over the next 15 years, periodic exile in Geneva, Antwerp, and Middelburg, he remained the most articulate spokesman for the Puritans in the Admonition Controversy against Abp. J. WHITGIFT. Cartwright urged, especially in his three *Replies* to Whitgift's *Answere and Defense of the Aunswere* [sic], the restoration of the Established Church to the simplicity of doctrine and practice of Apostolic Christian times; he advocated sweeping Calvinist reforms of religious ceremonies extending to many ceremonies prescribed in the BOOK OF COMMON PRAYER. Contemporaries regarded him as the leading 16th-century Puritan. He authored the Millenary Petition (1603) but died before the Hampton Court Conference.

Bibliography: A. F. S. PEARSON, *Thomas Cartwright and Elizabethan Puritanism, 1535–1603* (Cambridge, Eng. 1925). D. J. MC-GINN, *The Admonition Controversy* (New Brunswick, N.J. 1949). C. H. and T. COOPER, comps., *Athenae canta-brigienses*, 3 v. (Cambridge, Eng. 1858–1913) 2: 360–366. J. B. MULLINGER, *The Dictionary of National Biography from the Earliest Times to 1900*, 63 v. (London 1885–1900) 3:1135–39.

[M. J. HAVRAN]

CARVAJAL

Uncle and nephew, both cardinals. Juan de Carvajal, cardinal bishop and papal legate; b. Trujillo, Estremadura, Spain, *c.* 1400; d. Rome, Dec. 6, 1469. An auditor of the Rota and governor of Rome in 1440, he was sent to persuade Emperor Frederick III and the German princes to abandon the neutrality they had assumed in the struggle between Eugene IV and the Council of Basel, and he appeared before the Diet of Mainz in 1441 and the Diet of Frankfort in 1442. In the later Diet of Frankfort in 1446 he was associated with Tommaso Parentucelli (later Pope Nicholas V); their work culminated when the emperor and the princes went into opposition to the Council of Basel. Later in 1446 Carvajal and Parentucelli were both made cardinals. In the same year Carvajal was named bishop of Plasencia in Spain. In 1448 he negotiated the Concordat of Vienna regulating German relations with the papacy. He served also as legate to Bohemia, where the Hussite problem continued, and on missions to Hungary (1455–61) and Venice (1466–67) he sought to stiffen resistance against the Turks. In Hungary he was accompanied by JOHN CAPISTRAN, and while he was there, John Hunyadi defeated the Turks at Belgrade. Carvajal became bishop of Porto in 1461 and chamberlain of the College of Cardinals in 1469.

Bernardino Lopez de Carvajal, cardinal bishop, member of the uncanonical council of Pisa-Milan, nephew of Juan; b. Plasencia, Estremadura, 1456; d. Rome, Dec. 16, 1523. He became bishop of Astorga in 1488, of Badajoz in 1489, of Cartagena in 1493, and of Sigüenza from 1495 to 1519. He was made a cardinal in 1493 and sent as legate to Germany in 1496. As one of the Spanish cardinals favored by Alexander VI, he did not get on well with Julius II. In 1504 he was entrusted with the custody of Cesare Borgia, whom he allowed to escape. Following the negotiation of peace between Venice and the papacy, the withdrawal of the pope from the League of Cambrai, and the dispatch of a papal army against Ferrara (whose duke was supported by the French), Carvajal and other dissident cardinals assembled at Pisa and proclaimed a council, summoning Julius II to appear. They were excommunicated, and Julius convoked the Fifth Lateran Council. When Leo X became pope, Carvajal recognized the Fifth Lateran Council and, having pledged obedience, was absolved and restored to his honors. In 1521 he became bishop of Ostia.

Bibliography: T. MINGUELLA Y ARNEDO, *Historia de la diócesis de Sigüenza y de sus obispos*, 3 v. (Madrid 1910–13). P. PASCHINI, *Roma nel Rinascimento* (Bologna 1940). L. GÓMEZ CANEDO, *Un español al servicio de la S. Sede: don J. da C.* (Madrid 1947). P. ALONSO and M. ALAMO, *Dictionnaire d'histoire et de géographie ecclésiastiques*, ed. A. BAUDRILLART et al. (Paris 1912) 11:1239–42. J. WODKA, *Lexikon für Theologie und Kirche*, ed. J. HOFER and K. RAHNER (Freiburg 1957–65) 2:959–960.

[D. R. CAMPBELL]

CARVAJAL, GASPAR DE

Dominican explorer and missionary; b. Trujillo, Estremadura, Spain, *c.* 1504; d. Lima, Peru, 1584. According to his own testimony, he came from Spain with Bp. Vicente VALVERDE to establish the Order of St. Dominic in Peru. He arrived there in 1538 and in November of that year, while established in a convent in Lima, he had to defend the rights of his community. In 1539 he was in Cuzco, where he became the legal guardian of two of the sons of Atahualpa, Francisco Ninancuro and Diego de Ilaquita. Early in 1541, as vicar-general appointed by Bishop Valverde, he went to Quito where, as a chaplain, he joined the expedition organized by Gonzálo Pizarro to explore the province of Canela. Once in the eastern forests, he joined Francisco Orellana in the discovery and the navigation of the Amazon River. He was the chronicler of that expedition, on which he lost an eye. When he arrived in Cubagua and heard of the deaths of Valverde and Francisco Pizarro, he returned to Lima at once. His personal prestige enabled him to mediate first in the dispute between the *oidores* and Viceroy Núñez Vela, then in the actions of La Gasca in Cuzco, and finally in the disagreements between Viceroy Andrés Hurtado de Mendoza and Bravo de Saravia. He was prior of Lima and of Cuzco, and in 1557 was elected provincial of the Dominicans in Peru. His jurisdiction then included Quito, Lima, Cuzco, Guamanga, and Chile. In his late years he wrote his eyewitness account of the discovery of the Amazon River to correct some of the reports of that discovery that had already appeared.

Bibliography: G. DE CARVAJAL, *Descubrimiento del río de las Amazonas,* ed. J. T. MEDINA (Seville 1894; reprint Cáceres 1953).

[J. M. VARGAS]

CARVAJAL, LUISA DE

Spanish ascetic who ministered to persecuted English Catholics; b. Jaraicejo (Cáceres), Spain, Jan. 2, 1568; d. London, Jan. 2, 1614. Luisa, of noble birth, was orphaned at the age of 6, and raised by her aunt and uncle at Pampeluna (Pamplona), where she showed early evidence of sanctity. She refused either to marry or to become a nun; instead, after the death of her aunt and uncle, she vowed herself to poverty and prayer with a group of women from her uncle's household. After 12 years she was permitted by her Jesuit confessor to fulfill a long-cherished desire to minister personally to persecuted English Catholics. Upon reaching London (1606) she gathered helpers, who lived in poverty and visited sufferers in their homes and in prison. She feasted the prisoners John ROBERTS and Thomas Somers the night before their martyrdom (1610). The government, complaining that she did more to convert Protestants than 20 priests, twice imprisoned her. She was released only at the request of

the Spanish ambassador, who probably could not have prevented her eventual deportation, had she not died in his residence on her 46th birthday. Her body was taken back to Spain. Among her numerous charities were funds to found the English Jesuit novitiate in Flanders.

Bibliography: G. FULLERTON, *Life of Louisa de Carvajal* (London 1873), based on a full-length contemporary biog. by L. MUÑOZ (Madrid 1632).

[D. M. ROGERS]

CASA, GIOVANNI DELLA

Italian priest and poet; b. Mugello (Florence), June 28, 1503; d. Montepulciano, Nov. 14, 1556. Della Casa had a good classical education at Florence and Bologna. After taking minor orders—he delayed final ordination for some years—he entered the clerical bureaucracy at Rome, meanwhile leading the rather dissipated life reflected in the verses he wrote at that time. In 1544 he was named archbishop of Benevento, but he never resided in that see. Instead Paul III appointed him apostolic nuncio to Venice, the chief duties imposed on him being to ward off the influence of Charles V over that city and to repress any nascent Protestantism. He prosecuted both tasks with skill and resolution. His indictment of Vergerio, Bishop of Capodistria, for heresy caused the bishop to flee from Italy. Vergerio composed a scathing denunciation, on moral grounds, of Della Casa, a document that may have helped to impede the archbishop's ecclesiastical advancement. His nunciature ceasing upon the death of Paul III (1549), Della Casa retired to the country and to his books. In 1555 Paul IV recalled him to Rome and made him secretary of state, but not, to Della Casa's disappointment, a cardinal. Yet it was the failure of his worldly ambitions that in fact brought out his best capacities as a poet. The whole theme of his last and finest sonnets—poems that place him high among the Italian masters of this form—is bitter reflection on the vanity of human wishes and the need for humble conversion to God.

Galateo (1551–54), his elegant treatise on good manners, was a compliment to Galeazzo Florimonte, Bishop of Sessa, who had suggested its composition. While stressing external civilities, the work also insinuates the claims of conscience; and it is perhaps this discreet edge of moral teaching, along with the polished style, that has kept the work alive. But it is on his small output of Italian poems, mostly sonnets, that Della Casa's reputation ultimately rests. He is a minor poet, but a very remarkable one, and this for reasons both of content and of style. Della Casa's chief theme was the old Augustinian and Petrarchan one: the desperate need of the soul for the peace to be found in God alone. The poet treated his material with a certain adult gravity; his stress on the insufficiency of the ''world'' rather than the ''flesh'' struck a distinctly new note in 16th-century Italian poetry. To this relative novelty of theme Della Casa brought a distinctive style, at once weighty and musical, involved and delicate. His last poems mark a saturation point; here the Italian sonnet has received all it can from classical influences without losing its native grace.

Bibliography: Works. *Opere,* ed. G. PREZZOLINI (Milan 1937). *Lirici del Cinquecento,* ed. L. BALDACCI (Florence 1957). Studies. B. CROCE, *Poesia popolare e poesia d'arte* (Bari 1933) 375–384. L. BALDACCI, *Il petrarchismo italiano nel Cinquecento* (Milan 1957) 181–268.

[K. FOSTER]

CASANATE, GIROLAMO

Cardinal, founder of Casanatense Library; b. Naples, Feb. 13, 1620; d. Rome, March 3, 1700. After law studies at the University of Naples, he began, under Innocent X, a long career in various ecclesiastical offices. From 1648 to 1658, he governed Sabina, Fabriano, Ancona, and Camerino; then he was inquisitor at Malta and after 1666 a consultor to several of the Congregations, including the Propagation of the Faith. He was assigned to the Supreme Tribunal of the Apostolic Signature and later was assessor of the Holy Office as well as secretary to the Congregation of Bishops and Religious, as it was then known.

In 1673 Casanate received the title of cardinal deacon and after his ordination in 1686, cardinal priest. Innocent XII bestowed on him the title Librarian of the Holy Church in 1693. Casanate is an example of the profound learning of his century. In dealing through his official capacities with the controversial issues of his day (including quietism, Gallican liberties, and foreign missions), he displayed remarkable knowledge. His library was renowned. By augmenting the private library inherited from his father with purchases, in some cases whole library collections from major European countries, and with his own scholarly papers, he left at his death a collection estimated at more than 25,000 volumes. The library was endowed and placed under the direction of the Dominicans at Santa Maria sopra Minerva. At that time it ranked second to the Vatican Library in size and value of manuscripts and volumes. It was one of the first libraries opened for general public use (1701). Its collection contained examples of both contemporary scholarship and early Latin and Greek works on the Church. A special papal dispensation allowed heretical works to be kept there for consultation by a theological faculty of six Dominicans chosen from England, France, Germany, Italy, Poland, and Spain, who were commissioned by the Casanate endowment to teach and to defend the faith with the writings of Thomas Aquinas. The library holdings were increased and catalogued in the 18th century. In the 19th century it was taken over by the state and today remains as state property.

Bibliography: M. D'ANGELO, *Il Cardinale Girolamo Casante, 1620–1700* (Rome 1923).

[P. D. SMITH]

CASANI, PIETRO (PETER), BL.

Priest, assistant to founder of Pious Schools, educator, and preacher; b. Lucca, Italy, Sept. 8, 1570; d. Rome, Italy, Oct. 17, 1647. Of noble birth, Pietro was 20 years old when he decided to dedicate himself completely to the service of God and entered the Congregation of the Mother of God in Lucca, founded by St. John LEONARDI, for whom Casani served as secretary. After Casani was ordained a priest (1600), he centered his services especially on hearing the confessions of and doing pastoral work with youth. In Lucca, he established a congregation of Our Lady of the Snows. His way of life was marked by his enthusiasm for priestly and religious vocations, which he fostered by word and example.

In the union of the Luccan Congregation with the Pious Schools founded by St. Joseph Calasanctius in 1614, Casani served as secretary general and rector of St. Pantaleon in Rome. When the union was dissolved in 1617, Casani remained a Piarist and dedicated himself to the Christian education of poor children and the life of poverty. Casani worked closely with JOSEPH CALASANCTIUS, who appointed him the first rector of the motherhouse of St. Pantaleon in Rome, first assistant general, first novice master, and first provincial of Genoa and Naples and commissioner general for the foundations in Central Europe. Casani traveled throughout Tuscany, Lombardy, Liguria, Germany, and Poland where he founded schools and novitiates. A theologian, he wrote fluently in both Latin and Italian, and he left manuscripts that credit him as a writer and mathematician. His last few years were spent in Rome at the side of Calasanctius, bearing with him the suffering and troubles of the order.

He died at the motherhouse, where his body was interred in the church. His cause was opened shortly after his death by Calasanctius, but Calasanctius's death and loss of significant documents delayed the process until it was introduced in 1922. Pope John Paul II beatified him on Oct. 1, 1995.

Bibliography: *Epistolario di Calsanzio,* ed. L. PICANYOL, 9 v. (Rome 1950–1956). G. SÁTHA, *San José de Calasanz, su obra . . . ,* tr. C. AGUILERA and J. CENTELLES (Madrid 1956). *Memorie* *storiche . . . P. Casani* by an anon. Piarist (Rome 1904); *Acta Apostolicae Sedis* (1995): 721–22.

[L. MESKO/R. P. MATEO]

CASANOVAS PERRAMÓN, IGNACIO, BL.

Martyr, priest of the Order of Poor Clerics Regular of the Mother of God of the Pious Schools (Piarists); b. June 15, 1893, Igualada (near Barcelona), Spain; d. Sept. 16, 1936. Ignacio taught at the Collegium of Our Lady of Barcelona from 1921 until his death. A good priest, he was also skilled in various kinds of woodworking. Following the outbreak of civil unrest, he went to his family home in July 1936 in Can Brunet where he stayed with his widowed mother. Soldiers arrested him on Sept. 16. They marched him out of town, ordered him to stop, and shot him while he prayed. He was beatified on Oct. 1, 1995 by Pope John Paul II together with 12 other Piarists (*see* PAMPLONA, DIONISIO AND COMPANIONS, BB.).

Feast: Sept. 22.

Bibliography: "Decreto Super Martyrio," *Acta Apostolicae Sedis* (1995): 651–656. *La Documentation Catholique* 2125 (Nov. 5, 1995): 924.

[L. GENDERNALIK/EDS.]

CASAROLI, AGOSTINO

Cardinal; Vatican Secretary of State; b. Nov. 24, 1914, Castel San Giovanni, in the province of Piacenza (Italy); d. June 9, 1998, Rome.

Agostino Casaroli was born into a pious, middle-class family and attended the minor seminary of Bedonia. He studied theology in the exclusive Alberoni College of Piacenza and canon law in Rome at the Lateran University (1936–40). Ordained a priest in 1937, he began his life-long career in the Vatican diplomatic service as an archivist in the Secretariat of State.

In February of 1961 Pope John XXIII appointed Casaroli under-secretary at the Vatican Foreign Office and the Department for Extraordinary Church Affairs. Casaroli initiated a new style in dealing with the Communist bloc that came to be known as the Vatican *Ostpolitik*. The new approach situated Vatican diplomacy in the context of a policy of active neutrality between existing international blocs of nations. Although *Ostpolitik* was roundly criticized in some circles, it was manifestly in line with the approach of Pope John XXIII toward world problems. With patience and ingenuity he worked to insure the con-tinued existence of the Church in hostile Communist-run countries. By accepting compromises on nonessentials, Casaroli secured conditions of passably normal life for Catholic communities, even though it was largely limited to worship and the administration of sacraments.

Casaroli's first inroads behind the Iron Curtain came about in 1963. By order of Pope John XXIII, he went to Czechoslovakia and Hungary, where the Cold War had created very complex situations for the Catholic Church. Vienna's Cardinal Franz König had done much to pre-pare the ground. In 1964 Casaroli signed a "secret" agreement with Hungary. In 1965 in Prague, he con-vinced the government to allow Joseph Beran, just named a cardinal by Paul VI, to go to Rome to receive the red biretta. For the archbishop it meant going into exile, but it also allowed the appointment of a worthy successor, a confessor of the faith and later cardinal, Frantisek To-masek, who lived to see the end of Communism in Czechoslovakia. More dramatic was Casaroli's part in gaining the release of Hungarian Cardinal Josef Minds-zenty in 1971, who fifteen years before had taken refuge in the American Embassy in Budapest. Mindszenty's de-liverance ended in exile in Vienna.

In Belgrade in June of 1966, Casaroli signed the first of a series of agreements that gave some degree of legali-ty to the Catholic Church in several countries in Central and Eastern Europe. The following year he was able to visit all Catholic dioceses in Poland for an onsite analysis of the situation. In 1970 he went back in Belgrade to sign the establishment of normal diplomatic relations with a Communist country where the Catholics were a minority. By then he had been made an archbishop with the titular church of Carthage and appointed to head the Vatican Congregation for Extraordinary Church Affairs. About that time he addressed his activity toward Moscow, the center of world Communism. He went there for a week at the end of February of 1971 to express the adhesion of the Holy See to the pact of non-proliferation of nuclear arms. Casaroli was given a chance to meet, for the first time in half a century, officials responsible for religious affairs in the Soviet Union. Two years later he was for the second time able to visit Czechoslovakia, where he was also allowed to ordain new Catholic bishops. The following year (March to April of 1974), Casaroli was in Cuba, meeting most of the bishops and some clergy, as well as President Fidel Castro.

By 1975 Casaroli's contacts with Eastern European leaders had become routine. On June 5 he was in East Germany, and on June 26 the Bulgarian leader Todor Zhivkov was received in the Vatican, while from July 30 to August 1 Casaroli met most of them in Helsinki on the occasion of signing the final document on security and cooperation in Europe, when he also presided over the first and final sessions of the conference. It was an event seen by observers, including Casaroli himself, as the beginning of political and military detente in Europe, leading finally to the collapse of the Iron Curtain and of Communism fifteen years later. By 1978 Cardinal Casaroli was acknowledged as a world leader in political affairs. In June he addressed the Assembly General of the United Nations in New York, reading a message from Paul VI to the world organization.

Casaroli served as Secretary of State during the short reign of John Paul I. In April of 1979 Pope John Paul II confirmed him in the position, named him a cardinal on June 30 of that year, and assigned him the duties of prefect for the Council for Public (i.e., foreign) Affairs of the Church, and president of the Pontifical Commission for the Vatican City State. He continued to travel widely: to Lebanon and Hungary (1980); to Poland, just afer the attempted assassination of John Paul II (1981); and to Washington for meetings with President Ronald Reagan and other high administration officials (December of 1981). On the Italian scene, he negotiated important changes and additions to the Lateran Pact, the concordat between the Holy See and Italy (February of 1984), and the following year he assisted at the signing of a treaty of peace and friendship between Argentina and Chile after a year-long territorial conflict. He saw the fruits of his *Ostpolitik* when Mikhail Gorbachev initiated a policy of *glasnost* and *perestroika* in the Soviet Union (1985). In 1988 Casaroli took part in the celebrations for the Millennium of the conversion of the ancient Kievian Rus to Christianity (988–1988) and was received at the Kremlin. The following year the Secretary General of the Soviet Communist party, Mikhail Gorbachev, was in the Vatican for the "audience of the century" (Dec. 1, 1989).

Casaroli asked to be freed from his official responsibilities when he turned seventy-five, the age limit for service in the Roman Curia; in due course his request was accepted (Dec. 1, 1990). Retirement allowed him more time for his cherished projects in the field of pastoral and humanitarian work, particularly among the youth in the Casal del Marmo (formerly Porta Portese), a school-prison for teenage detainees. He had been engaged there all his priestly life, preaching to them, hearing their confessions, preparing them for the sacraments, and following some even after they had left prison. At one point he also agreed to act as editor-in-chief of their magazine *La Tradotta*. At Casal del Marmo he was known simply as "Don Agostino." In retirement he wrote an autobiography published posthumously under the title, *Il martirio della pazienza* (*Martyrdom of Patience*). In it the cardinal evaluated with objectivity his own role in the important events in which he played a part.

Agostino Cardinal Casaroli. (Catholic News Service)

At the time of his death John Paul II issued a statement praising Cardinal Casaroli for "courageous steps to improve the situation of the Church in Eastern Europe." Cararoli was buried in the Basilica of the Twelve Apostles in the center of Rome.

Bibliography: A. CASAROLI, *Il martirio della pazienza* (Torino 2000); *Nella Chiesa per il mondo. Discorsi* (Rusconi 1988); "La Santa Sede e l'Europa," *La Civiltà Cattolica* (Feb. 19, 1971); "Il discorso pronunciato nell'Università di Parma," in *L'Ossservatore Romano* (March 18, 1990); "La Santa Sede si è sempre impegnata per un obiettivo: affermare in concreto i diritti di Dio ed i diritti degli uomini," in *L'Osservatore Romano* (June 4–5, 1990); "Paolo VI e il dialogo," *Il Regno* 19 (1984); *Nella Chiesa per il mondo. Omelie e discorsi* (preface by J. GUITTON) (Milano 1987); *Der Heilige Stuhl und die Völkergemeinschaft. Reden und Aufsätze* (Berlin 1981); *Glaube und Verantwortung. Ansprachen und Predigten* (Berlin 1989); *Wegbereiter zur Zeitenwende. Letzte Beitrage* (Berlin 1999). A. SANTINI, *Agostino Casaroli, hombre de dialogo* (Madrid 1993); L. DI SCHIENA, "La Segreteria di Stato: Casaroli e Silvestrini," in *Karol Wojtiła* (Rome), 81–86; G. WEIGEL, "After the Empire of Lies," chapt. in *Witness to Hope* (New York 1999), 582–627; G. ALBERIGO, "Verso la Ostpolitik," in *Papa Giovanni (1881–1963)* (Bologna 2000) 151–57; C. KRAMER VON REISSWITZ, "Rome's Kissinger," *Inside the Vatican* 7 (1998): 48–49; V. FAGIOLO, "Reciproca collaborazione. L'evoluzione dei rapporti tra Chiesa e Stato italiano dopo la revisione del Concordato firmata da Bettino Craxi e Agostino Casaroli nel 1984," *30 Giorni* 1 (2000): 40–47; "La morte del Cardinale Agostino Casaroli," in

L'Osservatore Romano (June 10, 1998) (Editorial commemoration).

[G. ELDAROV]

CASAS MARTÍNEZ, FELIPE DE JESÚS, ST.

Mexican protomartyr of Japan; b. Mexico City, May 1, 1572; d. Nagasaki, Japan, Feb. 5, 1597. His Spanish parents, Alonso de las Casas, a rich merchant, and Antonia Martínez, went to Mexico in 1571. Felipe entered the Franciscans in Puebla in 1589, but he did not persevere. He decided instead to become a merchant and went to the Philippines. In Manila he took the habit once more in May of 1593 and made his profession the next year. He embarked for Mexico on July 12, 1596. A storm damaged the ship and took it to the shores of Japan on Oct. 18, 1596. Felipe received lodgings at the Franciscan convent of Miyako, Kyoto. On Dec. 11, 1596, the order to imprison and crucify the Christian missionaries of the district of Miyako was given. Felipe was not included on the list, but by his vehement desire for martyrdom he managed to become one of the group. The 26 missionaries were taken from Miyako to Nagasaki, where they were martyred. Each cross had five iron rings for the neck, hands, and feet, and a pedestal. Raised on the cross, Felipe could not rest his feet because the pedestal was low; the neck ring choked him. He cried out three times, "Jesus." His body was pierced by three lances, and in this manner he who was the last to arrive was the first to die. He was beatified on Sept. 14, 1627, and declared patron of Mexico on Feb. 5, 1629, in ceremonies that his mother witnessed. Felipe was canonized on June 8, 1862.

Feast: Feb. 5.

Bibliography: M. CORTINA PORTILLA, *Una biografía en grabados* (Mexico City 1994). X. ESCALADA, *Felipe de Jesús: México bravío y artista* (Mexico City 1991). H. MAGARET, *Felipe, Being the Little-known History of the Only Canonized Saint Born in North America* (Milwaukee 1962). J. A. PICHARDO, *Vida y martirio del protomártir Mexicano san Felipe de Jesús las Casas* (Guadalajara, Mex. 1934). E. E. RIOS, *Felipe de Jesús: El santo criollo* (Mexico City 1954).

[E. GÓMEZ TAGLE]

CASEL, ODO

Liturgy scholar; b. Koblenz-Lützel, Sept. 27, 1886; d. Herstelle-Weser, March 28, 1948. Casel became a Benedictine monk in 1905; studied at Maria Laach, Rome, and Bonn; and earned doctoral degrees in both theology and philology. He was spiritual director for the Benedictine sisters at Herstelle from 1922 until his death during the Easter Vigil, 1948.

Casel attained prominence as a liturgical scholar through his editorship of the *Jahrbuch für Liturgiewissenschaft*. His special achievement, however, was to bring out the meaning of liturgy as a celebration of the mysteries of Christ and His Church: the ritual and sacramental deed of the Church makes present Christ's act of salvation.

Casel obtained his first insights from the liturgy and the Fathers of the Church, whose traditional teachings he wished merely to hand on faithfully; but he took formal elements also from the history of religions, which, especially the Hellenistic mystery cults, were a sort of preparation for Christ. Although he in no way intended to dispute the uniqueness of Christian cult he encountered opposition. In the course of the ensuing controversy Casel perfected his conception of the liturgy, especially through the inclusion of scriptural teaching and a more positive evaluation of Old Testament worship. After Casel's death, his rich insights were further developed. Thus his doctrine, with light nuances and corrections, became one of the most valuable elements of contemporary theology on the liturgy, the Sacraments, and the Church. (*See* MYSTERY THEOLOGY.)

His principal works are: *Das Gedächtnis des Herrn in der altchristlichen Liturgie* (Freiburg 1918), *Die Liturgie als Mysterienfeier* (Freiburg 1922), *The Mystery of Christian Worship* (Westminster, Md. 1962), *Faitesceci en mémoire de moi* (Paris 1962), *La Fête de Pâques dans l'Eglise des Pères* (Paris 1963), *Das Mysterium des Kommenden* (Paderborn 1952), *Das Mysterium des Kreuzes* (Paderborn 1954), and *Mysterium der Ekklesia* (Mainz 1961). He also published numerous original contributions in the *Jahrbuch für Liturgiewissenschaft* (Münster 1921–41).

Bibliography: T. FILTHAUT, *Die Kontroverse über die Mysterienlehre* (Warendorf 1947). *Maison-Dieu* 14 (1948) 1–106. *Das Paschamysterium. P. Odo Casel zum Gedächtnis,* Liturgie und Mönchtum 3 (1949). A. MAYER et al., eds., *Vom christlichen Mysterium* (Düsseldorf 1951), containing a complete bibliography. T. KAMPMANN, *Gelebter Glaube* (Warendorf 1957) 105–115. A. SCHILSON, *Theologie als Sakramententheologie: Die Mysterientheologie Odo Casels,* 2nd ed. (Mainz 1987). A. SCHILSON, "Die Gegenwart des Ursprungs: Überlegungen zur bleibenden Aktualität der Mysterientheologie Odo Casels," *Liturgisches Jahrbuch* 43 (1993) 6–29. M.-J. KRAHE, *"Der Herr ist der Geist": Studien zur Theologie Odo Casels,* 2 vols. (St. Ottilien 1986). A. A. HÄUSSLING, "Odo Casel – noch von Aktualität? Eine Rückschau in eigener Sache aus Anlaß des hundertsten Geburtstages des ersten Herausgebers," *Archiv für Liturgiewissenschaft* 28 (1986) 357–387. A. GROZIER, *Odo Casel – Künder des Christusmysteriums,* ed. Abt-Herwegen-Institut der Abtei Maria Laach (Regensburg 1986).

[B. NEUNHEUSER]

CASEY, SOLANUS

Capuchin priest, b. Nov. 25, 1870, Oak Grove, Wisconsin; d. July 31, 1957, Detroit, Michigan. His parents, Bernard James Casey and Ellen Elizabeth Murphy, both immigrated from Ireland in the 1850s. They were married in Salem, Mass., in 1863. In 1865 they moved to an 80-acre farm near Prescott, Wisconsin. Bernard Francis was the sixth child in a family of ten boys and six girls. When he turned 17, he moved to Stillwater, Minnesota, and worked in a lumber mill, as a part-time prison guard, and as one of Stillwater's first streetcar operators. In 1891 Bernard entered Saint Francis de Sales Seminary in Milwaukee, where he began his secondary education. As a young seminarian, he visited the Capuchins. In 1897 he was invested as a novice at St. Bonaventure Monastery in Detroit, receiving the religious name Francis Solanus. Solanus pronounced his simple vows on July 21, 1898 and returned to Milwaukee where at St. Francis Seminary he began his studies for the priesthood. Studies were extremely difficult for the young friar and questions arose among his professors and superiors as to his qualifications for ordination. His religious example eventually persuaded his superiors to permit his ordination and Solanus was ordained on July 24, 1904. However the young priest was not given faculties to preach or to administer the sacrament of penance.

Over the next twenty years Casey served at several parishes in New York—in Yonkers, the lower east side of Manhattan, and Harlem. In each of these parishes, Solanus served in unassuming ministries as sacristan and porter, and offered Mass each day without being able to preach. In Harlem, however, the provincial minister, Benno Aichinger, directed him to begin keeping records of "favors" he was influential in obtaining through enrollments in the Capuchin Seraphic Mass Association. His advice to those who came to him for help was simple. After encouraging them to make a sacrifice for the foreign missions, that is, be enrolled in the Seraphic Mass Association, he would tell them to thank God ahead of time for granting the favor they requested.

Casey returned to Saint Bonaventure's in Detroit in 1924, and ministered there until 1945. He became known for his charity to the poor; the image of him in the soup kitchen offering food, clothing, or simple advice to the poor was quite well known. During the war years the number of his "favors" steadily grew as people flocked to have a moment of his time or to receive his blessing. Because his health was failing, he was sent in 1945 to Saint Michael's Friary in Brooklyn, NY, and later to the Capuchin novitiate in Huntington, Indiana, where he remained until his return to Detroit in 1956. Suffering from skin cancer and a chronic skin disease, he spent much of

Odo Casel.

the following year, until his death, in Detroit's St. John Hospital.

Shortly after Casey's death, the process of gathering information about his life, work, and the favors granted through his intercession was begun. On July 11, 1995 he was declared a "servant of God." The decree states: "While [Casey's] example is relevant for all priests and religious, it would seem to be such in a particular manner for all Americans. They will be able to derive from his life an inspiration entirely based on faith and charity and, at the same time, deeply human: sociable, optimistic and cheerful, compassionate and active in trying to alleviate the spiritual and material suffering of others."

Bibliography: J. P. DERUM, *The Porter of Saint Bonaventure* (Detroit 1968). M. H. CROSBY, *Thank God Ahead of Time* (Chicago 1985). C. ODELL, *Father Solanus: The Story of Fr. Solanus Casey, O.F.M. Cap.* (Huntington 1988).

[R. J. ARMSTRONG]

CASIMIR, ST.

Patron saint of Poland and Lithuania; b. Cracow, Poland, Oct. 5, 1458; d. Grodno, Belorussia, March 4, 1484. He was the third son of King Casimir IV of Poland and Elizabeth, an Austrian princess. For his teacher he had the learned historian Jan DŁUGOSZ. At the age of 13, Casimir was asked to accept the throne of Hungary from a faction opposed to King Matthias Corvinus, but the plan never materialized. After his brother Władysław became ruler of Bohemia, Casimir became heir apparent to the Polish crown. While his father was in Lithuania on affairs of state from 1481 to 1483, Prince Casimir governed Poland in his stead with conspicuous prudence and justice. Not wishing to renounce his celibacy, he rejected his father's plans for him to wed the daughter of Emperor Frederick III of Germany. He died while on a trip in Lithuania, of which he was also Grand Duke, and was buried in the cathedral at Vilna. Casimir was noted for his deep piety, chastity, and a spirit of prayer with special devotion to the Blessed Virgin. The number of attributed miracles caused him to be venerated as a saint, and he was canonized in 1521. Pope PAUL V extended his feast to the entire Church.

Feast: March 4.

Bibliography: *Acta Santorum* March 1:334–355. F. JAROSZEWICZ, *Matka Świetych Polska* (Cracow 1767; repr. in 4 pts. Poznań 1893) 1:209–216. F. PAPÉE, *Święty Kazimierz królewicz polski* (Lemberg 1902); *Studya i szkice z czasów Kazimierza Jagielloń-czyka* (Warsaw 1907). J. DUBOIS, *Catholicisme* 2:614. B. STASIEWSKI, *Lexikon für Theologie und Kirche,* ed. J. HOFER and K. RAHNER, 10 v. (2d, new ed. Freiburg 1957–65) 6:12.

[L. SIEKANIEC]

CASONI, FILIPPO

Cardinal, papal secretary of state; b. Sarzana (La Spezia), Italy, March 6, 1733; d. Rome, Oct. 9, 1811. After completing his studies in Rome at the *Sapienza,* where he became *doctor utriusque juris* (1767), he was governor of Narni and Loreto, in the States of the Church, and the papal vice-legate to AVIGNON. In this city and in the county of Venaissin, Casoni at first appeased (March 1789), by free distribution of grain, the popular movements provoked by the food shortage after the poor harvest of 1788. In vain, however, he did attempt to calm those who were enthused by the FRENCH REVOLUTION and the propaganda of local patriots and wanted to attach Avignon and Venaissin to France. He instituted a national guard and established new municipalities that greatly reduced the authority of the pope and the vice-legate; but Pius VI disavowed these concessions, and the local revolutionaries remained dissatisfied. Far from remedying the situation, which the pope ascribed to Casoni's weakness, the dispatching of an apostolic commissioner charged with restoring the former state of affairs and reestablishing order met with failure. So agitated did matters become that Casoni had to leave Avignon (June 1790), and

he retired first to Carpentras and then to Chambéry. After being vice-legate to Nice he became titular archbishop of Perge and went as nuncio to Madrid (1794–1800), where he clashed with the regalism of the Spanish government. Conflict became acute when Urquijo, the prime minister, profited from Pius VI's death by publishing a decree that attributed to bishops the plenitude of faculties, and reserved to the crown whatever concerned episcopal consecration and to the Spanish Rota what pertained to the Roman tribunals. With the support of Manuel Godoy, who aspired to power, Casoni obtained from King Charles IV the recall of the decree, the publication of the apostolic constitution *AUCTOREM FIDEI,* and on Dec. 13, 1800, the dismissal of Urquijo. Casoni was created cardinal (Feb. 23, 1801) and succeeded CONSALVI as secretary of state (June 1806–February 1808). Charles Alquier, the French ambassador to Rome, appreciated his moderation, but Casoni played an unobtrusive role, since PIUS VII assumed responsibility for papal policy concerning NAPOLEON I. Old and ill, he retired in 1808 and died three years later.

Bibliography: J. BECKER, *Relaciones diplomáticas entre España y la Santa Sede durante el Siglo XIX* (Madrid 1909). A. MATHIEZ, *Rome et le clergé français sous la Constituante* (Paris 1911). L. SIERRA, "La Caída del Primo Ministro Urquijo en 1800," *Hispania* 23 (1963) 556–580; "La Reacción del Episcopado español ante los decretos de matrimonio del ministro Urquijo de 1799–1813," *Estudios de Deusto* 11 (1963); 12 (1964).

[J. LEFLON]

CASSANDER, GEORGE

Humanist and liturgist; b. Pittem, Belgium, Aug. 15, 1513; d. Cologne, Feb. 3, 1566. His family name was Casant. At the Collège du Château in Louvain, he earned a master of arts in 1533. At Ghent and Bruges he taught literature. In 1544, after a tour of Italy, he enrolled in the theological faculty of Cologne and in 1549 undertook both the teaching of theology and the direction of the newly founded Academy of Duisberg. He bent his efforts to bring the Anabaptists back to the Catholic faith, and between 1561 and 1566 joined forces with the programs launched by the Emperors Ferdinand I and Maximilian II to reestablish unity in the Church. In his principal work, *De Officio Pii ac Publicae Tranquillitatis vere Amantis Viri in hoc Religionis Dissidio* (1561), he showed that abuses in the Church though real were insufficient grounds for leaving it. Later his *Consultatio de Articulis Religionis inter Catholicos et Protestantes Controversis* (posthumously published in 1577) tried to put a Catholic interpretation on Protestant tenets. These works met with strong opposition from both sides; he was accused of excessive tolerance, of being too ready for compromise. The fact is he realized that there were mistakes on the part of all concerned and refused to believe that the rupture within Christianity was definitive. While he defended the Church's stand regarding the rites of the Mass and the practice of infant Baptism [*De Baptismo Infantium* (1563)], he showed that the contemporary movement for return of the chalice to the laity also had a genuine tradition behind it [*De Sacra Communione Christiani Populi in utraque Panis et Vini Specie* (1564)]. His life and works (placed on the Index in 1617) have been a sign of contradiction for many. The strength of his convictions has often been called into question, without reason, however, for he died confessing to Novimula, the rector of Cologne, his truly Catholic sentiments.

Bibliography: J. BAUDOT, *Dictionnaire d'archéologie chrétienne et de liturgie*, ed. F. CABROL, H. LECLERCQ, and H.I. MARROU, 15 v. (Paris 1907–53), 2.2:2333–40. R. KOPER, *Lexikon für Theologie und Kirche*, ed. J. HOFER, and K. RAHNER, 10 v. (2d, new ed. Freiburg 1957–65) 2:968–969. R. STUPPERICH, *Die Religion in Geschichte und Gegenwart*, 7 v. (3d. ed. Tübingen 1957–65), 1:1625–26. R. HAASS, *Neue deutsche Biographie* (Berlin 1953) 3:166. H. DE VOCHT, *History of the Foundation and the Rise of the Collegium Trilingue Lovaniense, 1517–1550*, 3 v. (Louvain 1951–54) v.3 *The Full Growth* (University of Louvain, Recueil de travaux d'histoire et de philologie 4.5), 296–303. J. LECLER, *Toleration and the Reformation*, tr. T. L. WESTOW, 2 v. (New York 1960), 1:270–296.

[N. N. HUYGHEBAERT]

CASSANT, MARIE JOSEPH

Trappist Cistercian; b. Casseneuil-sur-Lot, France, March 6, 1879; d. Abbey of Notre Dame du Désert, June 17, 1903. Joseph desired intensely to become a priest, but was handicapped by an almost total lack of the necessary intellectual endowments. At the age of 15 he entered the Trappist Cistercian Abbey of Notre Dame du Désert (Dec. 5, 1894), where he received the habit of a choir religious, made his simple profession in 1897, and was solemnly professed on May 24, 1900. Weak in body, prone to discouragement, and unresponsive by nature to many aspects of monastic culture, this seemingly ungifted monk lived in a constant and vivid awareness of the essential Christian and monastic realities. Less articulate than Thérèse of Lisieux or Charles de Foucauld, Joseph nevertheless had the same thirst for the absolute, the same poverty of spirit, and the same intense charity. With the help of his spiritual father, André Malet (later abbot of the monastery), Joseph had the joy of being ordained on Oct. 12, 1902, and of living the last eight months of his life as a priest. His cause for beatification was introduced at Rome, Feb. 19. 1956.

Bibliography: M. E. CHENEVIÈRE, *L'Âme cistercienne du Père Marie-Joseph Cassant d'après ses notes inédites* (Abbey of Sainte-Marie-du-Désert 1938); *L'Attente dans le silence: Le Père Marie-Joseph Cassant* (Bruges 1961), definitive biog.

[C. WADDELL]

CASSIAN, JOHN (JOHANNES CASSIANUS)

Monk and ascetical writer; b. Scythia Minor (modern Rumania), probably 360; d. Marseilles, between 432 and 435. While still a youth, John was initiated into asceticism at a monastery in Bethlehem. Toward 386 with his friend Germanus he undertook a trip to Egypt, where they made contact with Egyptian monasticism; at the end of a seven-year period they returned to Palestine. A short while later they again went to the Nile regions and visited various monastic communities, perhaps going as far as the THEBAID. It is difficult to determine the duration of this second sojourn, but certainly toward 399 or 400 the two friends were in Constantinople in contact with St. JOHN CHRYSOSTOM, by whom Cassian was ordained a deacon.

In 404 Germanus, then a priest, and Cassian arrived at Rome with a letter from the Constantinopolitan clergy in favor of their exiled bishop, John Chrysostom. In 414 or 415 on the occasion of the Schism of Antioch, a priest by the name of Cassian was invited to Rome from Alexandria; it is not certain that this was really John Cassian. In any case he was certainly a priest when, about this time, he went to Marseilles. There he founded two monasteries, one for men under the title of SS. Peter and Victor, and the other for women under the title of St. Savior. Nothing is known of the organization of these monasteries, but the type of ascetical life led there can be easily deduced from the works of their founder. After his death the cult of a saint was attributed to him in that region.

Works. All three of Cassian's works have been preserved. The *De Institutis coenobiorum et de octo principalium vitiorum remediis libri XII* was written in 417–418 at the solicitation of Bishop Castor. It is an integrated work divided in two parts as is indicated by the title. The first part (bks. 1–4) treats of the external institution of the monastery: the clothing of the monk (1), the nocturnal, canonical prayer (2), the daily monastic prayer (3), and the organization of the common life (4). The second part constitutes a description of the actual life, the spiritual doctrine of the battle to obtain *puritas cordis* (purity of heart) and the perfection of the cenobitic life. This is contained in the struggle against the principal vices (bks. 5–12): gluttony (5), luxury (6), avarice (7), wrath (8), sloth (9), *acedia* (discouragement) (10), vainglory (11), and pride (12).

Manuscript folio from "Collatio IV," 8th century, by John Cassian (Cod. Vat. Lat, 5766, fol. 4r.)

Collationes XXIV was written in three parts at the suggestion of Honoratus of Lérins, later bishop of Arles. The first part was published in 419–420; it is an organic treatise and contains a general idea of the problem of the spiritual life (nos. 1–10): the notion of Christian perfec-tion (1); the fundamental disposition, discretion (2); vocation (3); obstacles, particularly concupiscence (4); vices (5); sin (6); the elimination of the obstacles—the spiritual battle (7); angels and demons (8); prayer and its forms (9–10). The second part (nos. 11–17), written before 426, treats of diverse arguments of spiritual theology distributed without apparent logical connection: charity (11); *apatheia* (12); the relation between grace and liberty, Cassian's SEMI-PELAGIANISM being most manifest there (13); spiritual science (14); charisms and miracles (15); friendship among the perfect (16); the essential and the accidental in the spiritual life (17). The third part was published between 426 and 429 and continues the method of the second by making a collection of ascetical problems: three kinds of monks (18); the cenobitic life and the anchoritic life (19); the purgative way (20); the liberty that comes from evangelical perfection (21); temptations against the flesh and their proper remedies (22); impeccability as not possible on this earth (23); and the advantages and demands of anchoritism (24).

De Incarnatione Domini contra Nestorium, libri VII, written perhaps originally in Greek at the request of a Roman archdeacon, later Pope LEO I, is the least interesting of Cassian's works. It treats the problem of Nestorianism, affirming that this doctrine is derived from PELAGIANISM. It defends the legitimacy of the title THEOTOKOS attributed to the Virgin Mary and concludes with expressions of recognition and veneration toward John Chrysostom. The documentation for this tract was sent to Cassian by Leo from Rome and included the letters of accusation against Nestorius from CYRIL OF ALEXANDRIA.

Doctrine. On the theological plane the name of Cassian is connected with the doctrine of Semi-Pelagianism, which he explicitly defended and explained in various parts of his spiritual writings, though most clearly in the *Collatio XIII.* Semi-Pelagianism teaches that original sin is more a punishment than a true sin in the descendants of Adam and that man with original sin still has a capability of achieving his own justification, particularly at the beginning, and can desire it as a sick man can desire his own health. The grace of God is necessary for salvation but is rendered efficacious by concourse with the human will, so that in a certain sense grace is a recompense for the use of one's own will, which thus concludes by meriting salvation. There is thus no such thing as a predestination to glory (*ante praevisa merita*). This doctrinal notion was condemned at the Council of Orange (529), although the name of Cassian was not mentioned; however, in the Middle Ages the doctrine of Semi-Pelagianism was known under his name.

To understand how Cassian arrived at these conclusions in the theological field, although St. AUGUSTINE attacked Pelagius and JULIAN OF ECLANUM for their theories on grace, it is necessary to be aware that Augustine's term *gratia victrix* was considered by Cassian as perilous for ascetical practice. He was concerned above all to safeguard the rights of liberty and of human responsibility even in the field of justification.

The spiritual works of Cassian have a double merit. From the point of historical interest, they constitute the most interesting documents for monasticism in the 5th century; from a doctrinal point of view they form the first *summa* of spiritual theology in the West; and what is even more remarkable, the statements of the problems of spiritual life as they are exposed by Cassian in his *Institutiones* and in his *Collationes* remained, with few variations, identical along the course of the history of Christian spirituality down to contemporary times.

The keystone of this structure of the spiritual life is exposed by Cassian in his *Collatio I*: the final end of monastic life consists in the acquisition of the reign of God; the immediate end is an entrance into the reign of God and a spiritual struggle that conducts to purity of heart.

Kingdom of God and Contemplation. By the kingdom of God Cassian understood, without doubt, heavenly recompense, that is, eternal life that is expected after death. But it is not necessary to await the end of earthly life to be incorporated into the kingdom of God. In some manner the achievement of the kingdom of God is possible even during earthly life if the monk orders his life in such fashion as to tend as far as possible toward unity with God. This union can be realized by contemplation. Man is placed between God's simplicity and the multiplicity of material things. With his knowledge he can penetrate the essence of known objects and can lose himself in the multiplicity of material; but he can also elevate himself to perfect simplicity by contemplating God alone. This attention directed to God progressively transforms man in God, until it reestablishes the image of God in the human spirit. The acquisition of the kingdom of God is thus attained by means of meditation. According to Cassian, this is perfectly realized in the life of the hermit.

Spiritual Combat and Purity of Heart. The state described as contemplation is the final plane to which Christian asceticism aspires. To arrive there, it is necessary to have a positive approach to life (*vita actualis*), which consists in the reordering of one's actions and the achievement of the perfect life. But this cannot be realized without combat, a battle against vices, sin, and the demons. This spiritual combat brings to the soul the virtues necessary for the perfect cenobitic life; and the result of a well-conducted campaign is purity of heart "which casts fear out" (*Coll. XI*). Whoever reaches the state of loving purity is on the borders of contemplation.

Among the explicit sources cited by Cassian, other than the Scriptures, which he quotes at least 1,800 times, are SS. Basil, Jerome, John Chrysostom, Athanasius, Palladius, Rufinus of Aquileia, and Evagrius Ponticus. Of the later writers who used or reflected Cassian's thought, SS. Benedict, Isidore of Seville, and Fructuosus of Braga indicate the wide diffusion of his writings in the 5th and 6th centuries; Alcuin, Rhabanus Maurus, Peter Damian, and St. Thomas Aquinas testify to his great influence on the Middle Ages; and the authors of the Devotio Moderna, as well as Ignatius of Loyola, Scupoli, Rodriguez, and Bernardino Rossignoli, assured his survival in modern times.

Bibliography: S. MARSILI, *Giovanni Cassiano e Evagrio Pontico* (*Studia anselmiana* 5; 1936). L. CRISTIANI, *Jean Cassien*, 2 v. (Paris 1946). O. CHADWICK, *John Cassian: A Study in Primitive Monasticism* (Cambridge, Eng. 1950). M. OLPHE-GALLIARD, *Dictionnaire de spiritualité ascétique et mystique Doctorine et histoire*, ed. M. VILLER et al. (Paris 132–) 2:214–276. P. T. CAMELOT, J. HÖFER and K. RAHNER *Lexicon für Theologie und Kirche.* (Freiburg 1957–65) 5:1016–17. P. GODET, A. VACANT et al, ed. *Dictionnaire de théologie catholique* (Paris 1903–50) 2.2:1823–29. B. ALTANER, *Patrology*, tr. H. GRAEF (New York 1960) 537–540. C. STEWART, *Cassian the Monk* (New York 1998). B. RAMSEY, tr., *John Cassian: The Conferences* (New York 1997); *John Cassian: The Institutes* (New York 2000).

[F. CHIOVARO]

CASSIAN OF NANTES, BL.

Capuchin missionary and martyr; b. Nantes, France, Jan. 15, 1607; d. Condar, Ethiopia, Aug. 7, 1638. He was born of a Portuguese merchant family. His early acquaintance with the Capuchins led him to enter their novitiate in 1623. In 1633 he was sent to the Cairo mission, where he joined his Capuchin confrere, Father Agathangelus. When their efforts to convert the dissidents were thwarted by the scandalous lives of Catholics living there, they left for Ethiopia (1637). To make entrance easier, they donned the habit of the dissident Coptic monks, but were discovered, taken prisoner, and hauled to Condar for trial. After a three-day public ordeal, they were given the choice of accepting dissident doctrines or death by hanging. They chose the latter. Their untiring zeal for the reunion of the dissident Coptic Church with Rome led to their deaths. On Oct. 23, 1904, Pius X beatified them.

Feast: Oct. 7.

Bibliography: *Lexicon Capuccinum* (Rome 1951) 361. C. MALONEY, "Missionaries and Martyrs, Bl. Agathangelus and Cassian," *Round Table* 21 (1956) 136–145.

[J. SCHARDT]

CASSIANO DA MACERATA

Capuchin priest, missionary, and scholar; b. Macerata, Italy, 1708; d. there, Feb. 4, 1791. Little is known about his early life. He received the religious habit in 1728. In 1738 he was sent to the Tibetan missions and on Jan. 6, 1741, arrived at Lassa, Tibet. Approximately two years later Cassiano left Tibet and entered Nepal in northern India. His missionary activities were beset with typical mission problems, i.e., the bad example of local Christians, misunderstandings, and persecution. The Holy See recalled him in 1756. He remained at Rome, where he devoted himself to writing accounts of his missionary activities. His work is used as a source by other authors, some drawing heavily from his unpublished works. Cassiano also spent time working on a Tibetan grammar, which was printed by the Holy See in 1773.

Bibliography: *Lexicon Capuccinum* (Rome 1951) 361. CLEMENTE DA TERZORIO, *Le Missioni dei Minori Cappuccini,* 10 v. (Rome 1913–38) 8:418; 9:600. *Analecta Ordinis Fratrum Minorum Cappucinorum* (Rome 188) 50 (1934) 47–49.

[M. CRAIG]

CASSIODORUS SENATOR, FLAVIUS MAGNUS AURELIUS

Sixth-century statesman, author, and scholar; b. Scyllacium, Calabria, *c.* 485; d. Vivarium, *c.* 580. Of a Calabrian family in the Ostrogothic civil service, Cassiodorus received an excellent classical education, entered the employment of the Ostrogothic kings, and became quaestor and secretary (507) to THEODORIC THE GREAT (474–526), consul (514), and a little later master of offices, the equivalent of prime minister. In this position he worked for a reconciliation between the conquered Romans and the barbarians. In 533 he was made a praetorian prefect by Athalaric and under Vitiges received the title of patrician.

After the Byzantine invasions of northern Italy, the Ostrogothic kingdom crumbled and Cassiodorus attempted to found a school for theology in Rome under Pope Agapetus (535–536); failing, he retired to his villa at Vivarium in Calabria. There he founded a monastery whose monks devoted themselves to studying and copying books of both sacred and profane learning. Though not a monk himself, he followed the religious services as patron.

Writings. The writings of Cassiodorus reflect his interests as statesman and educator. His *De origine actibusque Getarum* is a history of the Gothic peoples compiled for Theodoric but completed under Athalaric.

The text is lost, but the work is cited frequently by Jordanis. Since the Goths were nomads without a written tradition, Cassiodorus collected the tribal legends and arbitrarily identified material found in the classic authors, which referred to the Scythians and Getes, with the Goths in order to compose 12 books in classic style.

His panegyric for Theodoric and other discourses are preserved only in fragments, but the *Chronicle* that he composed at the request of Eutharic (519) is a world history concentrating in later sections on the achievements of the Goths. Its purpose is apologetic.

About 537 Cassiodorus published his *Variae,* a collection in 12 books of official letters written while he was in service to the Ostrogothic kings. Composed as models of correspondence rather than as source material for historians, they frequently omit dates and personal names. Books one to five are from the reign of Theodoric; six to eight contain chancellery formulas; eight to ten give the edicts published under Athalaric, Theodahat, and Vitiges; 11 and 12 contain letters Cassiodorus wrote as praetorian prefect and display his love of erudition, human interests, and observations on nature.

Of *Ordo generis Cassiodororum,* a family genealogy, only fragments remain. Finally, his *De anima* was written at the end of his public service and represents his leave-taking of the world. Influenced by Augustine and CLAUDIANUS MAMERTUS, he discusses in it the problems connected with a knowledge of the soul from its origin to its immortal destiny.

Monastic Instructions. For the monks, Cassiodorus composed a series of instructions. His *Commentary on the Psalms* is a useful, mainly allegorical, explanation based on St. AUGUSTINE but exhibiting personal opinions also. His *Expositio epistolae ad Romanos* is a corrected version of the originally heretical work composed by PELAGIUS, in which Cassiodorus established the characteristic readings of the Vulgate text, apparently extending his revision to the whole Bible as is witnessed in the *Codex Amiatinus,* copied directly from a Cassiodoran manuscript. His *Complexiones in epistolis apostolorum* is a brief commentary on selected passages from the Gospels and Acts.

The *Institutiones divinarum et humanarum lectionum* is his most influential work. After deploring the lack of theological schools in the West (preface), the first book gives the monks an account of the theological treatises monks should have read in order to understand Scripture and appreciate the Church's teachings. It enumerates the older commentaries and the works of historians, and remarks that even monks who are educated enough to read or copy manuscripts should be made aware of the Christian heritage. The second book enumerates the secular (liberal) arts necessary for a comprehension of the Scriptures: grammar, rhetoric, dialectic, arithmetic, music, geometry, and astronomy. It lists also the authors dealing with these subjects. The *Institutes* is thus a catalogue of the books contained in the library at Vivarium.

Cassiodorus is responsible also for the compendium of the ecclesiastical histories written by Theodoret of Cyr, Socrates, and Sozomen, as translated and condensed by the monk Epiphanius and called the *Historia ecclesiastica tripartita*. Finally, in his 92d year he wrote a *De orthographia* at the request of monks seeking rules for copying manuscripts.

Intent on preserving the Church's culture, Cassiodorus performed an invaluable service in supervising translations from the Greek and in recopying all the books he had gathered in his long career. Unlike the monks of St. BENEDICT at MONTE CASSINO, who combined physical labor with spiritual contemplation, he insisted on preserving the materials for the intellectual life of the Church. Thus he had an incalculable effect on the Middle Ages even though after his death the library at Vivarium was destroyed, most of its manuscripts finding their way to the papal library in the Lateran. He was not the author of the *REGULA MAGISTRI*, and the Benedictine rule was not observed at Vivarium. Only later did the Benedictines take over the intellectual interests cultivated by Cassiodorus.

Bibliography: *Opera Omnia,* 2 v. *Patrologica Latina,* ed. J. P. MIGNE (Paris 1878–90) 69–70; *Chronica,* ed. T. MOMMSEN (*Monumenta Germaniae Historica: Auctores antiquissimi,* 11; 1894) 109–161; *Variae,* ed. T. MOMMSEN and L. TRAUBE (*ibid.* 12; 1894); *Institutiones,* ed. R. A. B. MYNORS (Oxford 1937). E. K. RAND, "The New Cassiodorus," *Speculum* 13 (1938) 433–447. W. A. BAEHRENS, *Texte und Untersuchungen zur Geschichte der altchristlichen Literatur* (Berlin 1882), 42:186–199, Vivarium and its MSS. W. WEINBERGER, "Handschriften von Vivarium," *Miscellanea Francesco Ehrle,* 5 v. (*Studi e Testi,* 37–41; 1924) 4:75–88. P. COURCELLE, "Le Site du monastère de Cassiodore," *Mélanges d'archéologie et d'histoire* 55 (1938) 258–307; *Les Lettres grecques en Occident: De Macrobe á Cassiodore* (rev. ed. Paris 1948) 313–388. G. BARDY, *Catholicisme* 2:618–621. D. M. CAPPUYNS, *Dictionnaire d'histoire et de géographie ecclésiastiques,* ed. A. BAUDRILLART et al. (Paris 1912), 11:1350–1408. R. HELM, *Reallexikon für Antike und Christentum,* 3:915–926. F. BLATT, "Remarques sur l'histoire des traductions latines," *Classica et Mediaevalia* 1 (1938) 217–242. L. SZYMANSKI, *The Translation Procedure of Epiphanius-Cassiodorus* (Catholic University of America, *Studies in Medieval and Renaissance Latin, Language and Literature* 24; 1963), with bibliog.

[F. X. MURPHY]

Ernst Cassirer.

CASSIRER, ERNST

Neo-Kantian philosopher; b. Breslau, Poland, July 28, 1874; d. New York, April 13, 1945. At the age of 18 Cassirer entered the University of Berlin and in 1894 began studying I. KANT under Georg Simmel (1858–1918). In 1896, now at the University of Marburg, he worked directly with Hermann Cohen (1842–1918), the guiding force of the neo-Kantian movement. Cassirer married in 1901 and established himself in Munich; later he moved to Berlin, where he became a *Privatdocent*. He accepted a full professorship in 1917 at the newly founded University of Hamburg, where he later became rector. By this time he had broken from Cohen's interpretation of Kant and had received the inspiration for his master work on symbolic forms. In 1933 he lectured at Oxford, and in 1935 he removed his family to Göteborg, Sweden. Cassirer went to Yale University as a visiting professor in 1941. In 1944 he left New Haven for Columbia University.

The philosophy of Ernst Cassirer has been characterized as idealistic naturalism, a characterization that perhaps accents best the line of advance Cassirer made beyond neo-Kantianism. His major work, *The Philosophy of Symbolic Forms* (tr. R. Manheim, 3 v., New Haven 1953–57), attempts to locate the exact place of mind in the framework of nature. Here he uses culture as the locus of mind in nature. The symbolic function is given as the ground of the possibility of a world. The sign relation in its office of organ of reality brings about, rather than indicates, the object. In this Cassirer's true debt to Kant can be seen. Somewhat in the manner that Kant assumed synthetic a priori judgments, Cassirer assumes the function of the symbolic relation, and proceeds to concern himself with the possibility of this alone. Cassirer felt that Kant's transcendental critique had not gone far enough. Its limitations could be found in the consideration of the theoretical sciences alone: the objectivity of Euclidian geometry and Newtonian physics had been reached, but not objectivity as such. For this a broader interpretation of knowledge was needed to include the intuition and expression of language, myth, religion, and art. From Kant's critique of reason the transition had to be made to a critique of culture.

Cassirer distinguishes three modal forms of the symbol function: the expressional, the intuitional, and the conceptual. The expressional function stems from emotive or affective experience and is found in such expressions of culture as art and myth. In this perspective there is a certain mingling of the sign and the signified. The intuitional function is on the level of volitional and teleological concerns. On this level there is a greater systemization of the sensuous, even though the data may be expressed in commonsense language. The final form is the conceptual function. Here theoretical interests have full play and the expression is that of science, the highest development of relational thinking. It may be questioned whether the formulation of the three modalities of symbolic representation is completely exhaustive of the varieties of experience. Cassirer offers no justification of these, merely presenting them as the actual situation of knowledge forms. Nor does he argue for the symbolic form concept; he cites empirical data from the evidence of the *Kulturwissenschaften* alone. The question of what reality is apart from the symbolic forms is considered irrelevant by Cassirer—there is no encountering of a world except in the mythical, artistic, perceptual, or scientific forms. These are the contexts of the object that is experienced and known. Space, time, cause, number, etc., constitute the objectivity of these symbol relations.

Among Cassirer's major works is his history of epistemology, *Das Erkenntnisproblem in der Philosophie und Wissenschaft der neueren Zeit,* 3 v. (Berlin 1906, 1907, 1920; Eng. *The Problem of Knowledge,* tr. W. H. Woglom and C. W. Hendel, New Haven 1950). Cassirer presented the directing lines of his philosophy of science in his early work (1910), *Substance and Function* (tr. W. C. Swabey and M. C. Swabey, Chicago 1923). Later works include *The Platonic Renaissance* in England (tr.

J. P. Pettegrove, Austin, Texas 1953); *The Philosophy of the Enlightenment* (tr. J. P. Pettegrove and F. C. A. Koelln, Princeton 1951); an analysis of the most complicated problems of quantum theory in physics and knowledge, *Determinism and Indeterminism in Modern Physics* (tr. O. T. Benfey, New Haven 1956); and *Essay on Man* (New Haven 1944) and *Myth of the State* (New Haven 1946).

See Also: NEO-KANTIANISM.

Bibliography: P. A. SCHILPP, ed., *The Philosophy of Ernst Cassirer* (Evanston, Ill. 1949). C. H. HAMBURG, *Symbol and Reality* (The Hague 1956). R. ALLERS, ''The Philosophy of Ernst Cassirer,'' *The New Scholasticism* 25 (1951) 184–192. J. M. KROIS, *Cassirer, Symbolic Forms, and History* (New Haven 1987). S. G. LOFTS, *Ernst Cassirer: A 'Repetition' of Modernity* (Albany 2000).

[M. J. M. REGAN]

CASSOCK

A close-fitting robe with long sleeves worn by clergy in ordinary life and by clergy and laymen as well when taking part in religious functions. This name was originally given to the dress of soldiers and horsemen but survives today in ecclesiastical use only.

The ordinary cassock varies in color and trim, as a signification of different degrees of ecclesiastical dignity: that of the pope is entirely white without trimmings of any color; that of cardinals is black trimmed with scarlet; that of archbishops and bishops is black trimmed with amaranth red, and that of pastors and curates is black without any trim.

The cassock reserved for choir and public ceremonies of the Church is more colorful but without contrasting trim. The pope wears white silk. Scarlet is worn by cardinals at ordinary times, and purple in penitential season. Bishops wear purple, and pastors retain black. Laymen wear black when they are permitted to take the place of those in the minor orders of the clergy. The use of red for the cassock of laymen dates from the 19th century and should not be tolerated.

[M. MCCANCE]

CASTAÑEDA, FRANCISCO DE PAULA

Franciscan journalist and defender of the Church in Argentina; b. Buenos Aires, 1776; d. Paraná, May 12, 1832. He was ordained in 1800 and, after teaching at the University of Córdoba, returned to Buenos Aires. In May 1815, when no one dared to speak patriotically because the revolution was thought to have failed, he did so and fought the disillusionment that was beginning to disturb the people. Chiefly during the government of Martín Rodríguez, when RIVADAVIA initiated a religious persecution with the so-called reform of the clergy, Castañeda published simultaneously as many as six newspapers. Unfortunately, he found that he was forced to employ the same vulgar and even scurrilous language used by his enemies, who were also those of the Church. As a result of his publications, he was exiled six times. No one defended the religious orders as he did when Rivadavia took over the convents and the other possessions of the orders. Castañeda was vitally concerned with ending illiteracy and founded schools wherever he could, not only in Buenos Aires but also in Santa Fe and Entre Ríos. He established art classes everywhere, believing that there was nothing like drawing to refine a spirit and set it on the path of knowledge and virtue. The fact that Rivadavia did not commit greater excesses against the Church was due above all to Castañeda. His death was from natural causes, not, as his enemies wrote, from the bite of a rabid dog. The Italian Josí Ingenieros wrote shockingly false pages about Castañeda, but another liberal writer, Arturo Capdevila, has written an enthusiastic and well-documented volume on his life and virtues.

Bibliography: A. CAPDEVILA, *La santa furia del padre Castañeda* (Madrid 1933). A. SALDÍAS, *Vida y escritos del P. Castañeda* (Buenos Aires 1907).

[G. FURLONG]

CASTE SYSTEM, INDIAN

In ancient India society was divided into four classes (*varna,* meaning literally "color"): Brahmins (priests), Kshatriyas (warriors), Vaiśyas (merchants and peasants), and Śūdras (servants). The caste system does not seem to have been derived from these classes, but rather to have been grafted upon them. It arose among the non-Aryan peoples of India and was the means by which different racial, religious, and social groups were assimilated within Hinduism. In the course of time the number of castes and subcastes has grown to over 2,000. The basic principle of caste is that no one may marry or entertain in his or her home a person of another caste. Thus, all the different castes are kept permanently separate, even though they may live together in the same village. Further, certain trades and habits of life were considered unclean, so that those who practiced them could not come within a certain distance of a member of another caste or drink from the same well. This prohibition is based on ritual purity and shows the fundamentally religious basis of caste. In modern times the extremes of "untouchability" have been legally abolished and many caste distinctions

Pope John Paul II wearing white papal cassock with capelet. (AP/Wide World Photos)

are breaking down, especially in the towns. But in the villages they remain in force, and it is still very rare for anyone to marry outside his or her caste.

See Also: HINDUISM.

Bibliography: J. H. HUTTON, *Caste in India: Its Nature, Function and Origins* (Cambridge, Eng. 1952). B. RYAN, *Caste in Modern Ceylon* (New Brunswick, N.J. 1953).

[B. GRIFFITHS/EDS.]

CASTEL GANDOLFO

Town with population of 3,000 18 miles southeast of Rome on the west shore of Lake Albano; it is known for the villa used as an occasional papal residence since the 17th century. A large necropolis nearby indicates a population in prehistoric times. The ruins of a villa of the Emperor DOMITIAN can be seen in the garden of the present papal villa. A castle or villa *Gandulfi,* mentioned in 816, came into the possession of the Savelli family (1285), who, after losing it several times, ceded it to the Holy See for financial considerations (1596). The present villa, begun in 1629 by Urban VIII, who commissioned the work to Carlo Maderno, served many popes as a late spring or fall residence and as a place for the reception

Lower-caste Hindus line a road in the eastern Indian state of Bihar to protest their inability to take part in Indian general elections, September 18, 1999; photograph by Vikram Kuman. (AP/Wide World Photos)

of distinguished guests. Giovanni Lorenzo BERNINI built the cupola Church of St. Thomas of Villanova in a Greek cross (1661).

Although the Law of GUARANTEES (1871) granted the popes use of the villa, they did not visit it again until 1934. Under Pius IX two communities of nuns, deprived of their convents, were lodged at the villa. Giovanni Battista de ROSSI died and Cardinal Rafael MERRY DEL VAL recuperated there. The LATERAN PACTS of 1929 accorded the Holy See extraterritorial rights over Castel Gandolfo and the nearby villas of Bernini and Cybò, all three of which are part of Italy; the villas cover about 100 acres. During World War II, Castel Gandolfo sheltered 12,000 refugees, most of them from the fighting at Anzio. Pius XII died in Castel Gandolfo (1958).

Bibliography: R. MOLS, *Dictionnaire d'histoire et de géographie ecclésiastiques*, ed. A. BAUDRILLART, et al. (Paris 1912–) 11:1417–18.

[A. RANDALL]

CASTEL SANT' ANGELO

Roman citadel, famed in the history of the city and the papacy. Its construction was begun in 130 by Emperor Hadrian (117–138) as a mausoleum for himself and family (*moles Hadriani*) and was completed by Antoninus Pius (138–161) in 139. Situated at the Tiber in the gardens of Domitian (81–96), it was composed of a square substructure (275 ft. wide and 164 ft. high) that supported a cylindrical tower (210 ft. in diameter) faced with marble. The tower was surmounted by a tumulus of earth, planted with cypresses surrounding a square altar and probably a bronze quadriga, guided by the sun-god, symbolic of the extent of imperial power. In the chambers of this tomb were sarcophagi that contained the ashes of Hadrian, his wife Sabina, and his sons, as well as other emperors to Septimus Severus (193–211). Aurelian (270–275) transformed it into a bastion at the head of a fortified bridge, and by the 5th century it had become important in the defense of Rome. Its side facing the river was fortified with a wall, six towers, windows for archers, and battlements to mount catapults. It was used as a prison for the first time by Theodoric the Great (489–526).

Castel Sant' Angelo and bridge, Rome, Italy. (©John Heseltine/CORBIS)

According to legend Pope Gregory I, while crossing the Aelian bridge during the plague of 590 in a penitential procession, saw an angel on the summit of the citadel sheathing his sword as a sign that the plague was ended. From that time it was known by its present name. In the 10th century during the ascendancy of the House of Theophylact, Alberic and MAROZIA made it their stronghold. Pope JOHN X (928) was imprisoned there and smothered by order of Marozia, who assumed the title, *Donna Senatrix;* BENEDICT VI (974) was strangled in its dungeons by the faction of Crescentius and the deacon Boniface Franco (antipope Boniface VII); John XIV (984) after four months' imprisonment died either from starvation or poison administered by his successor, BONIFACE VII. In 1277 a passageway (*passetto Vaticano*) was built by Nicholas III to connect the fortress with the papal palace. After the fateful election of Urban VI in 1378, it fell under the control of the French pope, Clement VII (*see* WESTERN SCHISM). The Romans stormed the castle, cut off the hands of the defenders, and stripped the marble from the walls. Restoration was begun by Boniface IX (1389–1404) and continued by Nicholas V (1447–55) according to plans drawn by the Florentine Bernardo Rosselino (1409–64). Alexander VI (1492–1503) entrusted the further work to the architect and military engineer,

Antonio da Sangallo (1463–1534), who designed the octagonal dungeons at the corners. Julius II (1503–13) added a frontal loggia, and Leo X (1513–21) erected a chapel and extensive apartments for feasts and plays. When mutinous imperial troops sacked Rome (1527), CLEMENT VII (1523–34) sought its safety and remained there a virtual prisoner for seven months. From the time of Urban VIII (1623–44) it was used primarily as a foundry and barracks, though its dungeons were still used. In the 18th century, the adventurer Alessandro Cagliostro (1743–95) was condemned by the Inquisition to life imprisonment within its walls. Here too Lorenzo RICCI, general of the Society of Jesus at the time of its suppression, was confined during the two years before his death (Nov. 24, 1775). In 1752 the marble angel on the castle's summit, carved by Giacomo della Porta (1541–1604), was replaced by the bronze statue of St. Michael by the Flemish sculptor Pierre Verschaffelt (Pietro Fiammingo, 1710–93), which is there today. In 1886 excavations and restorations were performed under the direction of Mariano Borgatti. The Castel Sant' Angelo is now a national monument and military museum.

Bibliography: S. B. PLATNER, *A Topographical Dictionary of Ancient Rome,* cont. and rev. T. ASHBY (Oxford 1929). R. A. LANCIANI, *The Ruins and Excavations of Ancient Rome* (Boston 1897).

P. PAGLIUCCHI, *I castellani del Castel S. Angelo di Roma* (Rome 1906–). M. BORGATTI, *Castel Sant' Angelo in Roma* (Rome 1931). G. LUGLI, *Roma antica, il centro monumentale* (Rome 1946).

[E. D. MCSHANE]

CASTELLINO DA CASTELLI

Italian priest-apostle of religious instruction; b. Menaggio (Diocese of Como), *c.* 1476; d. Milan, Sept. 21, 1566. In 1536 he founded the first school in Milan for instructing children in Christian doctrine. Its name, *Compagnia della reformatione in carità*, aroused suspicion and was changed in 1546 to *Compagnia dei servi de' puttini in carità*. In the same year the Council of Trent approved the *Compagnia* and enriched its work with an indulgence of seven years. At first Castellino had difficulty gaining the support of diocesan authority, but when Niccolò Ormaneto, vicar-general appointed by St. Charles BORROMEO (the temporarily absent archbishop of Milan), arrived in 1564, he found 15 such schools; within two years their number doubled, and soon they were diffused throughout northern Italy. When Borromeo returned to Milan in 1566, he established in his diocese the Confraternity of Christian Doctrine in order that children might be carefully and systematically instructed. His fame has eclipsed that of Castellino, who was his precursor in this work and therefore an important though little-known figure in the Counter Reformation.

Bibliography: A. TAMBORINI, *La Compagnia e le scuole della dottrina cristiana* (Milan 1939).

[M. S. CONLAN]

CASTELLIO, SEBASTIAN (CHÂTEILLON)

Protestant humanist and Biblical scholar; b. St.-Martin-du-Fresne (Department of Ain), Burgundy, France, 1515; d. Basel, Switzerland, Dec. 29, 1563. After his student days in Lyons, he became a Protestant and left for Strasbourg, where he made the acquaintance of John CALVIN (1540). The following year he was called by Calvin to Geneva, where he was made rector of the college. When he was denied ordination to the ministry because of his liberal exegesis, he moved to Basel (1545). Here, after several years of poverty, he was appointed professor of Greek at the university (1553). At Basel he had more controversies with Calvin and Theodore BEZA over exegetical matters and such theological questions as the Trinity and predestination. His opposition to the Calvinist execution of Michael SERVETUS (1553) inspired his book *De haereticis, an sint persequendi?* (Basel 1554) and marked him as one of the few men of his age in favor of religious liberty.

Castellio, however, is best known as a Bible translator. A master of Latin, Greek, and Hebrew, he translated the whole Bible from the original languages into both Latin and French. Although his Latin version (Basel 1551) was done in elegant Ciceronian language, his French version, one of the most original of the 16th century, was written in the popular vernacular of his time and place.

Bibliography: J. HOMEYER, *Lexikon für Theologie und Kirche,* ed. J. HOFER, and K. RAHNER, 10 v. (2d, new ed. Freiburg 1957–65) 2:973. H. LIEBING, *Die Religion in Geschichte und Gegenwart,* 7 v. (3d. ed. Tübingen 1957–65) 1:1627. F. BUISSON, *Sébastien Castellion,* 2 v. (Paris 1892). S. L. GREENSLADE, ed., *The Cambridge History of the Bible* (Cambridge, Eng. 1963), 8–9, 71–72, 116.

[A. M. MALO]

CASTI CONNUBII

In the encyclical *Casti Connubii*, issued on Dec. 31, 1930, Pope PIUS XI sought to reaffirm the sanctity and dignity of Christian marriage, uphold the integrity of the family and warn against various errors against conjugal union. According to Pius XI, while one may freely choose to marry or not, because marriage is a divine instituted sacrament, the nuptial union is subject to the laws laid down for it by its Divine Author. The right to beget children imposes a corresponding duty to educate them for life here and hereafter, and thus clearly restricts the exercise of this right to the married state, wherein alone this duty can be adequately fulfilled. It is moreover a way of life in which husband and wife sanctify each other through that conjugal fidelity which deserved to be compared to the union between Christ and His Church which He loves ''not for the sake of His own advantage, but seeking only the good of His spouse.''

Pope Pius XI also warned that the nuptial bond must never be subject to the whims of man or woman to allow them the unbridled liberty of those purely human unions, variously described as ''temporary,'' ''experimental,'' or ''companionate.'' Nor may the obligations arising from the use of the marital right be avoided by the sins of contraception, direct sterilization, and abortion. Without prejudice to the dignity of woman but in support of it, Pius XI condemned the errors of those who profess to free her from what they regard as the burdens of conjugal fidelity, obedience, and love.

Bibliography: PIUS XI, ''Casti connubii'' (encyclical, Dec. 31, 1930) *Acta Apostolicae Sedis* 22 (1930) 539–592, Eng. *Catholic Mind* 29 (Jan 1931) 21–64. J. L. THOMAS, *The Catholic Viewpoint on Marriage and the Family* (Garden City, N.Y. 1958). E. W. O'ROURKE, *Marriage and Family Life* (Champaign, Ill. 1956). J. E. KERNS, *The Theology of Marriage* (New York 1964).

[S. KARDOS/EDS.]

CASTIGLIONE, BALDASSARE

Italian writer; b. Casatico, Mantua, December 6, 1478; d. Toledo, Spain, February 2, 1529. He was trained from early childhood in the amenities of courtly life, and studied Greek and Latin in Milan under George Merula and Demetrius Calcondila. In 1499 he entered the service of his lord and relative Francis Gonzaga, under whose leadership he fought against the Spaniards. In 1503 he moved to Urbino where he spent 11 important years enjoying the full confidence first of Duke Guidobaldo da Montefeltre and then of his successor, Francis della Rovere. During this period he carried out many important diplomatic missions for his patrons.

Diplomat and Nuncio. His activity spans the height of the Italian Renaissance during the papal reigns of Julius II, Leo X, and Clement VII. He was sent as ambassador from Urbino to Julius II and fought under this fiery pontiff at the siege of Mirandola in 1511. With both Julius II and Leo X he shared a passionate love for the fine arts, and he cultivated the friendship of artists, especially Raphael. Castiglione had an active interest in archeology. He was fond also of pageants and public spectacles. He was ambassador from Mantua to Leo X and to Clement VII, who, in 1524, made him prothonotary and sent him to Spain as his nuncio. As a convinced sympathizer of Charles V, Castiglione tried in vain to have the wavering Pope support the Emperor's cause in his struggle with Francis I. Since communications with the Curia had become strained and difficult, he could do nothing to prevent the sack of Rome (May 6, 1527), a failure for which Pope Clement sharply reproached him. Castiglione died without having witnessed the much-desired reconciliation between the Pope and Charles V. The Emperor, who esteemed Castiglione greatly, had obtained for him the bishopric of Avila.

Castiglione's letters, written during the difficult mission to Spain, express a keen discernment of events and people, a dignified defense of his actions, and a serene confidence of having accomplished his duty. His habitual poise gives way to indignation only once: when he condemns the *Dialogue on the Sack of Rome* —itself a sharp attack on the corruption of the clergy, the veneration of false relics, and other abuses—a work written by the young secretary of Charles V, Alphonse of Valdes. The violence of the nuncio's reaction marks the last phase in the spiritual development of one of the foremost representatives of the Renaissance on the eve of the Counter Reformation.

Literary Activity. During most of his life Castiglione had devoted himself to secular and literary pursuits. He wrote Latin and Italian verses and, in honor of the Duchess and the court of Urbino, composed *Tirsi,* an ec-

Baldassare Castiglione.

logue in octaves, which was recited during the carnival of 1506. His long and intimate familiarity with the classics, his experience at several courts, especially the enlightened and orderly court of Urbino, his courage in battle and in loyalty to his lords, his respect for women, and his friendship with the most outstanding personalities of his time were among the influences that gave shape to his most famous work, *Il Libro del Cortegiano*. This book, considered by some of his contemporaries to be his autobiography, was conceived after the death of Duke Guidobaldo in 1508; the author intended it as a memorial to a great ruler and friend. It was written for the most part between 1513 and 1518, and published in Venice (1528) when Castiglione, then in Spain, decided to thwart its clandestine publication by others. The work was placed on the Index in 1590.

His Masterwork. In spite of the lack of a final revision and the many linguistic problems involved in publishing a modern critical edition, *Il Libro del Cortegiano* (*Book of the Courtier*) is a stylistic masterpiece. Castiglione's severest critics, who charge him with spiritual shallowness and insincerity, cannot deny the formal perfection of his work, in which the harmony of Ciceronian prose shines through the vernacular, the learned subject matter is fused with personal reminiscence, and a great variety of material is subtly blended into a graceful whole.

Taking the medieval knight as paradigm, Castiglione creates the 16th-century gentleman, in much the same manner as the architect Laurana transformed the medieval castle of Urbino into a Renaissance palace. Written with a characteristic *sprezzatura,* the *Book of the Courtier* is modeled on Cicero's *De oratore.* It takes the form of a conversation among real characters who contribute in turn their opinion on the main subject, the formation of a perfect courtier, a man of noble lineage, skilled in the use of weapons and in the laws of chivalry, carefully trained in letters and fine arts, graceful and polished in demeanor, accomplished and poised in conversation. Among the long digressions there is one on wit, which is based on the *De oratore* and illustrated with a collection of jokes, and another, by the lady of the court, on love. A fourth section, subsequently added to the original scheme, deals with the duties of the courtier as a mentor of princes, and with the rules of good government. The book closes with a Neoplatonic exaltation of spiritual over sensual love.

Castiglione's work had extraordinary influence, especially at the beginning of the Renaissance in England and Spain. In 1534, it was translated and published by Juan Boscan. Twelve more editions appeared in Spanish before the end of the 16th century. Its wide acceptance in Catholic Spain during this period shows that value was attributed to Castiglione's work in spite of his almost total lack of explicit reference to Christian teaching.

Bibliography: *Opere,* ed. C. CORDIÉ (Milan 1960); *Il cortegiano, con una scelta delle opere minori,* ed. B. MAIER (Turin 1955); *Il libro del cortegiano,* ed. V. CIAN (Florence 1894; 4th ed. 1947); *Lettere,* ed. P. SERASSI, 2 v. (Padua 1769–71); *Poesie volgari, e latine,* ed. P. SERASSI (Rome 1760); *The Book of the Courtier,* tr. T. HOBY (London 1928; ed. W. H. D. ROUSE, New York 1956). G. C. FERRERO, "Studi sul Castiglione," *Rivista di sintesi letteraria* 2 (1935) 473–480. V. CIAN, *Un illustre nunzio pontificio del Rinascimento: Baldassar Castiglione* (Studi e Testi 156; 1951); "Un episodio della storia della censura in Italia nel secolo XVI: La censura ecclesiastica del Cortegiano," *Archivio storico lombardo,* ser. 2, 14 (1887) 661–727. E. LOOS, *Baldassare Castigliones Libro del cortegiano: Studien zur Tugendauffassung des Cinquecento* (Frankfurt a. M. 1955). W. SCHRINNER, *Castiglione und die englische Renaissance* (Berlin 1939). M. MORREALE DE CASTRO, *Castiglione y Boscán: El ideal cortesano en el renacimiento español,* 2 v. (Madrid 1959). P. BURKE *The Fortunes of the Courtier* (University Park PA 1996). R. W. HANNING and D. ROSAND, (eds.) *Castiglione* (New Haven 1983). R. W. HANNING and D. ROSAND, (eds.) *La corte el Cortegiano* (Rome 1980).

[M. MORREALE]

CASTIGLIONE, GIUSEPPE

Jesuit missionary in China, where he painted for the emperors at Beijing and became a principal member of the Imperial Painting Bureau; b. Milan, July 19, 1688; d. Beijing, China, July 16, 1766. After initial schooling in art, Castiglione was attracted to religious life and entered the Jesuit novitiate in Genoa (1707). He executed a number of paintings in Genoa and completed his novitiate in Portugal before he was finally sent by the superior general, M. TAMBURINI, to Beijing. He arrived in Beijing on Dec. 22, 1715; there he became known as Lang Shihning and a favorite artist and architect in the imperial court. He was active under three emperors: the grand Kang Xi (d. 1722); his son Yong Zheng (d. 1735); and the nephew of Kang Xi, Qian Long (d. 1795). Qian Long was an atrocious persecutor of Christians, but his high esteem for Castiglione afforded opportunity to the painter to intercede for his fellow Christians.

Castiglione is of little importance in the history of Chinese painting but emerges as a symbol of Western influence in 18th century China; apparently Chinese sophistication of the 18th century had an admiration for European-like painting somewhat similar to Europe's interest at that time in Chinoiserie. Castiglione brought with him a competence in European painting ability and was able to please his imperial patrons with "realistic" portraits, narrative accounts of imperial conquests, and studies of nature (flowers, animals). He produced few paintings in a thoroughly Chinese style. His fusion of Western and Chinese elements may be seen in a wide handscroll, about 30 feet long, representing 100 horses (National Palace Museum, Taiwan). In this work the mixture of light and shade with Chinese convention in composition and the more delicate Chinese brushwork produces a strong, almost surrealistic effect that is neither Chinese nor European in style.

Another scroll, "The Feast of Victory at the Purple Light Hall" (collection S. Kriger, Washington, D.C.), was painted to represent a victory feast (April 18, 1760) in celebration of the subjugation of the Eleuths. The painting, about 25 feet long, displays easy facility of delineation with a Western touch particularly marked in the rendering of the Emperor, which may very well be a true portrait likeness of Qian Long.

Castiglione served also as architect (in collaboration with the Jesuit M. Benoist) for the Emperor's Old Summer Palace (Yüan Ming Yüan), a European styled structure that gave the Emperor (Qian Long) his wish to have a Chinese equivalent of Versailles.

Castiglione is the only European painter recorded in the Chinese work *History of Painting,* composed in 72 chapters by Peng Songjian in about 1800. Other missionaries who were active artists in China during this period were Ignatius Sichelbarth (1708–80) and Denis Attiret (1708–68).

Emperor Qian Long, scroll painting detail, 1760, by Giuseppe Castiglione.

Bibliography: L. PFISTER, *Notices biographiques et bibliographiques sur les Jésuites de l'ancienne mission de Chine 1552–1773,* 2 v. (Shanghai 1932–34), 2:635–639. G. R. LOEHR, *Giuseppe Castiglione* (Rome 1940), with bibliog. and catalogue of paintings.

[R. J. VEROSTKO]

CASTILLO Y GUEVARA, FRANCISCA JOSEFA DEL

Nun and author; b. Tunja, Colombia, 1671; d. there, 1742. She came from a distinguished Christian family and entered the convent of the Poor Clares of Tunja at 18. She held several positions as sexton, doorkeeper, and mistress of novices and was abbess in three different periods. Very spiritual, she was favored with visions and ecstasies, was able to foresee future events, and endured many mortifications. At the order of her confessors, she wrote several books: *Autobiografía* (Philadelphia 1817); *Sentimientos espirituales* (v.1, Bogotá 1843; v.2, Bogotá 1942). In her writings one can perceive the influence of her reading of the works of St. Teresa of Jesus. Her own work shows soundness of doctrine, a knowledge of the Bible, and an ardent love of God. She has been considered one of the best writers of the 18th century in Colombia. Even centuries later her exemplary life and her writings remain a source of pride, since they depict an exceptionally high moral level in a period of the history of New Granada.

Bibliography: J. M. VERGARA Y VERGARA, *Historia de la literatura en Nueva Granada,* ed. A. GÓMEZ RESTREPO and G. OTERO MUÑOZ, 3 v. (Bogotá 1958). R. M. CARRASQUILLA, "Francisca Josefa del Castillo," *Obras completas,* ed. J. E. RICAURTE, 5 v. in 6 (Bogotá 1956–61) 2:257–277.

[J. RESTREPO POSADA]

CASTNER, GASPAR

Missionary to China; b. Munich, Oct. 7, 1665; d. Beijing (Peking), Nov. 9, 1709. He entered the Society of Jesus on Sept. 17, 1681, and, after distinguishing himself in his theological studies at Ingolstadt, he was named professor of philosophy at Regensburg in 1695. The following year he set out for China from Lisbon, arriving in Macau in 1697. For five years he preached in the neighborhood of Guangzhou (Canton). He also directed the construction of a memorial church on the island of Shangchuan (Sancian), where St. Francis Xavier had died in 1552. He was sent to Rome with Father Francis Noël in 1702 to represent the bishops of Nanjing (Nanking) and Macau concerning the CHINESE RITES. Together with Noël he composed a memorial on the suitability of the Chinese words Tian (T'ien) and Shangdi (Shang-ti) as the equivalent for God. Before returning to China in 1707 he convinced the Portuguese that ships sailing for China should strike out from the Cape of Good Hope directly for Timor, without passing through the Straits of Malacca, thereby cutting the journey to Macau to less than a year. After his return to China, Castner was ordered to Beijing, where word of his skill in mathematics had already been received. The Emperor Kangxi (K'ang Hsi) named him president of the bureau of mathematics and tutor to the imperial prince. He was also a noted cartographer and did excellent work mapping the Chinese empire.

Bibliography: L. PFISTER, *Notices biographiques et bibliographiques sur les Jésuites de l'ancienne mission de Chine 1552–1773,* 2 v. (Shanghai 1932–34), 1:486–489. L. KOCH, *Jesuiten-Lexikon: Die Gesellchaft Jesu einst und jetzt* (Paderborn 1934); photoduplicated with rev. and suppl., 2 v. (Louvain-Heverlee 1962), 1:959–960. C. SOMMERVOGEL et al., *Bibliothèque de la Compagnie de Jésus,* 11 v. (Brussels-Paris 1890–32; v.12, suppl. 1960), 2:853–854.

[J. H. CAMPANA]

CASTORENA Y URSÚA, JUAN IGNACIO DE

First Mexican journalist and bishop of Yucatán; b. Zacatecas, July 31, 1668; d. Mérida, Yucatán, July 13, 1733. He was a member of a noble, wealthy family, the son of Capt. Juan de Castorena Ursúa y Goyeneche and Teresa de Villarreal. He studied in Mexico City under the Jesuits and received a doctorate in law from the university and a doctorate in theology from the University of Ávila, Spain. For some time he lived in Madrid, where he was attached to the nunciature as a theologian. He was also an honorary chaplain and preacher at the court of Charles II. When he returned to Mexico, he received a royal appointment as canon of the cathedral of Mexico City. He served as censor of the Inquisition and as rector of the University of Mexico. In 1721 he founded a school for girls in Zacatecas, the Colegio de los Mil Angeles. He became bishop of Yucatán in 1729. Castorena y Ursúa is best known as the founder of *Gaceta de México.* Although news sheets had been published sporadically in Mexico since 1541 and gazettes since 1666, this was the first news periodical. It began on Jan. 1, 1720, and came out once a month. It contained religious, commercial, maritime, and social news and book reviews. On the occasion of the National Journalism Exposition in 1944, the Mexican government published a series of postage stamps honoring Castorena y Ursúa and a bio-bibliography on him.

Bibliography: M. OCHOA CAMPOS, *Juan Ignacio María deCastorena Ursúa y Goyeneche: Primer periodista mexicano* (Mexico City 1944). A. AGÜEROS DE LA PORTILLA, *El periodismo en México durante la dominación española* (Mexico City 1910). X. TAVERA ALFARO, ed., *El nacionalismo en la prensa mexicana del siglo XVIII* (Mexico City 1963).

[E. GÓMEZ TAGLE]

CASTRO, AGUSTÍN PABLO

Mexican Jesuit, scientist, and humanist; b. Córdoba, Mexico, Jan. 24, 1728; d. Bologna, Nov. 23, 1790. A brilliant student, he had such easy success in his studies in Puebla that he became somewhat conceited, so that he was criticized for indolence during his philosophy studies. His zeal did not wane again. He was ordained in Mexico City in October 1752 and from then on devoted himself to teaching and the ministry, finding time also to write humanistic studies and poetry. He served in Puebla, Veracruz, and Mexico City, always available to help in the confessional, to preach, and to assist the dying. From 1756 to 1763 he taught philosophy in Querétaro, was vice rector of San Ildefonso in Mexico City, worked in Guadalajara and Valladolid, and finally, taken ill, went to Tepotzotlán. During that period, somewhat influenced by the philosophical ideas of the Enlightenment, he devoted himself to philosophy and wrote his three-volume *Cursus philosophicus.* In May 1763 he went to Veracruz, where, as a result of coming in contact with business and commerce, he wrote some works in the field of economics. The next year he was assigned to the University of Mérida, Yuán, where he taught moral theology, Canon Law, jurisprudence, and law, contributing effectively to the growth of the university. At the end of 1766 he went to Córdoba and then to Mexico City where he was stationed when the expulsion of the Jesuits was decreed on June 25, 1767. He and his companions went to Bologna. He resumed his literary activities, was named superior, went to Ferrara in 1773, and later returned to Bologna, again as superior. A great literary and scientific figure of his age, he was drawn into diverse fields by his intellectual curiosity. His writings show influence of the superficiality of the times.

Bibliography: M. VALLE PIMENTEL, *Agustín Pablo de Castro, 1728–1790* (Mexico City 1962). J. L. MANEIRO and M. FABRI, *Vidas de mexicanos ilustres del siglo XVIII,* ed. and tr. B. NAVARRO (Mexico City 1956).

[F. ZUBILLAGA]

CASTRO, MATEO DE

First Brahman bishop of the Latin rite; b. Divar, near Goa, India, c. 1594; d. Rome, 1668 or 1669. Castro, converted by the Theatines, studied under the Franciscans in Goa. Then, convinced that his aspirations for the priesthood could not be realized under the Portuguese *padroado* (royal control of ecclesiastical appointments), he went to Rome, where he completed his theological studies under the Propaganda of the Faith. After ordination he was named missionary apostolic and entrusted with the evangelization of the Brahmans of India. He was already known as a critic of the Portuguese and of the Jesuits and other orders working in the *padroado,* and what was to be a long and bitter conflict between the *padroado* and the Propaganda began. Following a prolonged dispute with the bishop of Goa over the exercise of his faculties, Castro returned to Rome to present his case. In order to promote the more effective evangelization of peoples outside the patronage jurisdictions of Spain and Portugal, the Holy See was formulating its plan for erecting vicariates apostolic, and Castro was the first vicar apostolic so appointed. As titular bishop of Chrysopolis *in partibus infidelium* he was sent to Bidjapur in the native state of Idalkan, bordering directly on Portuguese Goa. There he established a seminary and consecrated a native Brahman clergy affiliated with the Oratory of St. Philip Neri. Although in accordance with the instructions of Propaganda, this move intensified the struggle between himself and the Portuguese, who resisted any encroachment upon their *padroado* rights. Charges of personal irregularities were levied against him in order to undermine his work. These difficulties led to Castro's making subsequent trips to Rome. Although aware that his conduct was at times intemperate and imprudent, Propaganda maintained its confidence in him. As a result of these storms, Castro spent his last years in Rome at the College of the Propaganda. His turbulent career highlights one of the tragic chapters in the history of the Church's missions. His zeal and sincerity are unimpugned, and the charges that he was plotting against the Portuguese political power have not been substantiated. Unfortunately, under the impact of opposition, he resorted to diatribe and imprudent conduct. His failure, and that of his two cousins, Custodio de Pinho and Thomas de Castro, who also became vicars apostolic, served to postpone efforts of the Holy See to foster a native episcopacy in mission lands until the policy was once more vigorously renewed by Pius XI, Pope of the Missions.

Bibliography: S. DELACROIX, ed., *Histoire universelle des missions catholiques,* 4 v. (Paris 1956–59), 2:138, 194–197. T. GHESQUIÈRE, *Mathieu de Castro, Premier vicaire apostolique aux Indes* (Louvain 1937). A. HUONDER, *Der einheimische Klerus in den Heidenländern* (Freiburg 1909). A. JANN, *Die katholischen Missionen in Indien, China und Japan: Ihre Organisation und das portugiesische Patronat vom 15. bis 18. Jahrhundert* (Paderborn 1915). E. D. MACLAGAN, *The Jesuits and the Great Mogul* (London 1932). B. DE VAULX, *History of the Missions,* tr. R. F. TREVETT (New York 1961).

[A. M. CHRISTENSEN]

CASUISTRY

The term casuistry comes from the Latin *casus,* case. In general, casuistry denotes the method that applies the principles of a science to particular facts. Thus, there are casuistries proper to civil and canonical law (jurisprudence), to psychology (casework), to commerce (case system). In theology, casuistry signifies that part of moral theology, or that method, that treats of the application of moral principles to singular cases. In the past, some Protestant theologians incorrectly called the whole of Catholic moral theology by the name casuistry. In any event, since the issuance in 1993 of the encyclical letter *VERITATIS SPLENDOR,* the casuistry of the Schools, developed after the Council of Trent, no longer enjoyed standing in Catholic moral theology.

Basic Approach. The approach of Post-Tridentine casuistry is basically one which conceives the unity of the singular reality through a multiplicity of general and abstract ideas. While the moral laws are known with sufficient certitude in their abstract formulation, the concrete act, unique and singular, to which one would apply them, remains difficult to analyze because of its complexity. Casuistry allowed one to bridge the gap between the concrete action and the abstract norms. Thanks to it, conscience, which must base its judgments on an objective morality, had access to principles already particularized and more easily applicable to the singular. Nevertheless, despite their high degree of particularization, the enunciations of casuistry remained general, in the sense that they were of value, not just for a particular individual, but for every person placed in the same circumstances. They did not take into consideration, therefore, strictly personal factors that may be apposite in a case of conscience.

Necessity. Casuistry, essentially a science of application, was judged to be needed because of the imperfection itself of our knowledge. While casuistry exhibited limitations and dangers, it was thought to assist our human condition subject to sin and error. Even Aquinas, whose own moral theology centers on teleology and virtues not cases and consciences, was cited to support the need of casuistry. "Anyone who perfectly knew the principles according to all their virtualities," says St. Thomas, "would not need any conclusions proposed to him separately. But, because those who know principles do not know them so as to consider everything that is found virtually contained in them, it is necessary for them that, in the sciences, the conclusions be deduced from principles'' (*Summa Theologiae* 2a2ae, 44.2).

Function. Casuistry served a double function: to illustrate principles (case casuistry found in the manuals of cases of conscience) and to study moral problems of concrete life (practical casuistry found in the various treatises on special moral theology).

Case Casuistry. Through means of typical examples, real or fictitious, future confessors and counselors were taught the correct way to handle moral principles. They were initiated into the prudent and judicious solution of cases of conscience. This scholastic exercise was deemed necessary for the formation of future priests.

Practical Casuistry. By the very logic of its development, moral theology should be perfected by some casuistic rules that bring it closer to the singular reality. Since it is a normative science, it demands not only a clarification of Christian principles, but also their application to contemporary life. It ought to "make real" the Christian ideal in the various spheres of individual, family, social, and professional life. Since it is the purpose and end of moral investigation, practical casuistry performs a "realizing" function in moral theology. It, therefore, presupposes in the moralist perspicacity, a decisive mind, and sure judgment. Even after *Veritatis splendor*, moral theologians are obliged to engage in some forms of practical casuistry.

Limitations. Casuistry was not intended to replace either conscience or prudence. It was not meant to free conscience from its responsibilities by giving it ready-made answers that could be applied without personal reflection. Its role was to clarify conscience by showing why a particular solution is obligatory or better. It aided conscience to decide for itself. It was not able to foresee all possible cases. The better practitioners of moral theology understood that prudence must complete the work of casuistry. Especially when absolutely obligatory norms were not involved, prudence aided in weighing with care all the circumstances of the case.

Casuistry and the Moral Minimum. It was customary to distinguish between the casuistry as applied to an action already done and as applied to an action not yet performed. The first, known as the merciful casuistry of the confessional, was adapted to the judgment of a past action. It easily contented itself, as a result, with the formulation of a moral minimum. Taking its inspiration from the words of Jesus to the adulterous woman, "Neither will I condemn thee" (Jn 8.11), it was designed especially for the confessor who must make an objective yet merciful judgment of his penitent, and even hold him innocent, if possible, in doubtful cases. Casuistry even in its application to the future, in order to avoid rigorism, had also to indicate the lower limits of the love of God set forth in the commandments, i.e., the precise point where sin begins. By doing this, it inculcated respect and fidelity toward the law. Once the minimum was indicated, it should also have considered the opportunity, the utility, and even the comparative perfection of particular acts. If it sought to help the person resolve his cases of conscience in a Christian way, something of counsel and a certain evangelical plenitude was expected to have found a place in it.

History. Beginning with the Gospel, the morality of the New Testament focused on concrete life. It therefore may be considered as the beginning of Christian casuistry (Lk 20.20–26; 6.7; Mk 2.23–28). Applying the Christian ideal to a pagan surrounding quickly posed cases of conscience that had to be resolved. St. Paul solved several of them (eating sacrificial food, work, virginity).

Patristic Age. Casuistic elements are also found in the Fathers, particularly in Origen, Clement of Alexandria, and St. Augustine. These concerned, for example, military service, persecutions, lying, the Sabbath, and dress. It is therefore inaccurate to claim that casuistry invaded Christianity through the influence of Stoicism or the Jewish law. At the end of the patristic age, from the 6th to the 11th century, a casuistry of sin was formed, which was connected with the development of auricular confession. It is contained in the PENITENTIALS.

The Middle Ages (13th–16th Century). The Fourth Lateran Council (1215) made annual confession and Communion obligatory. This accentuated the practical character of clerical studies and gave a new importance to casuistry. Clerics were initiated into cases of conscience by the *Summae confessorum,* which replaced the Penitentials. These works contained a résumé of morality from the practical and limited point of view of the confessor. They coexisted with the great commentaries on the *Liber Sententiarum* of P. Lombard.

16th–17th Century. The significant contribution of this period was the *Institutiones Theologiae Moralis.* In the 16th century, a particular circumstance, the creation of a course in cases of conscience, gave a new spirit to casuistry and made it more scientific. Tridentine legislation insisted on the pastoral formation of clerics and on the obligation of the penitent to accuse himself of sins according to number and species. As a result there was instituted, along with the course in scholastic theology (destined for those who wished to obtain the title of doctor), a course in cases of conscience (destined first for those who took only two years of theology, then made obligatory for all clerics). As a manual for this course, the *Institutiones Theologiae Moralis* (Azor, Laymann) were created, as a sort of a compromise between the *Summae Confessorum,* which were henceforth considered to be insufficient, and the great commentaries (*Summae*), which omitted the practical and pastoral aspect. These works, oriented especially toward practical morality, besides assuring all clerics a better pastoral preparation, enriched moral theology by giving it clarity, precision, and a high degree of accuracy in analysis.

This was the golden age of casuistry. Progress was interrupted in the middle of the 17th century by the quarrels concerning Jansenism and probabilism. Absorbed by these polemics, moralists neglected the deepening of principles so much that moral theology was reduced practically to the knowledge required of a confessor and was oriented toward a minimalist casuistry. It was forgotten that casuistry could not be perfectly autonomous and that it must rest on a solid moral system. It was sometimes cultivated for itself, like a mental puzzle, on the level of pure dialectic without any relation to concrete life. The most improbable hypotheses were imagined and discussed. By splitting hairs about how far one could go and where one must stop, certain authors fell into laxism. Casuistry, as a result, had to submit to the attacks of Pascal. Henceforth it had a bad name, which it never completely lost.

18th–19th Century. If one excepts the beginning of reform at Tübingen, Germany, about the middle of the 18th century, one may say that at the beginning of the 18th century moral theology was contained almost exclusively in predominantly casuistic manuals. The *Medulla* of Busenbaum (d. 1668), commented upon by Lacroix (d. 1714) and St. Alphonsus (d. 1787), left a profound mark upon moral theology and, through St. Alphonsus and J. P. Gury (d. 1866), exercised its influence up to the beginning of the 20th century.

20th Century. In the first half of the twentieth century, the adversaries of casuistry no longer, as they did in Pascal's day, accused it of laxism but reproached it rather for turning toward rigorism. Thus, certain partisans of situational morality sought to free moral theology from the subtleties and sophisms of the casuistic method. According to them the proper field of casuistry is law. When it is brought into morality, they contended, it brings with it an atmosphere that is too juridical. In short, the very legitimacy of this method for morality was called into question by these authors. The renewal that moral theology experienced after World War II brought casuistry back into fashion by emphasizing its value and utility, and by indicating its dangers and its limitations. But immediately following the Second Vatican Council, the sort of ca-

suistry that had been practiced since the sixteenth century rapidly lost currency among Catholics.

Conclusion. According to a most favorable view, casuistry, when it is well used, remains indispensable; it is an art that demands flexibility and awareness of the concrete. But, while keeping to its method and its proper purposes, it must remain connected to the more elevated parts of moral theology. Conscious of its own limitations, it must allow itself to be complemented by prudence, not forgetting the other aids at the disposal of a Christian for finding the correct solution of his doubts of conscience, prayer, and docility to the inspirations of the Holy Spirit. In the late 1960s, Servais Pinckaers began a strong critique of casuistry and its late-medieval antecedents. His subsequent work influenced the moral teaching of *Veritatis splendor* and the *Catechism of the Catholic Church.*

Bibliography: E. HAMEL, "Valeur et limites de la casuistique," *Sciences ecclésiastiques* 11 (1959) 147–173. M. PRIBILLA, "Klugheit und Kasuistik," *Stimmen der Zeit* 133 (1938) 205–216. J. VIALATOUX, "Réflexions sur les idées de casuistique et de loi morale," *Mémorial J. Chaine,* ed. Faculté Catholique de Théologie (Lyon 1950). R. EGENTER, "Kasuistik als christliche Situationsethik," *Münchener theologische Zeitschrift* 1 (1950) 54–65. M. REDING, "Situationsethik, Kasuistik und Ethos der Nachfolge," *Gloria Dei* (1951) 290–292. Y. CONGAR, "Die Kasuistik des heiligen Paulus," *Verkündigung und Glaube: Festgabe für Franz X. Arnold,* ed. T. FILTHAUT and J. A. JUNGMANN (Freiburg 1958). R. M. WENLEY, *Encyclopedia of Religion and Ethics,* ed. J. HASTINGS, 3:239–247. K. GOLDAMMER et al., *Die Religion in Geschichte und Gegenwart.* (3d ed. Tübingen 1957–63) 3:1166–71. R. BROUILLARD, *Catholicisme* 2:630–637. S. PINCKAERS, *The Sources of Christian Ethics* (Washington 1995). R. CESSARIO, *Introduction to Moral Theology* (Washington 2001).

[E. HAMEL/R. CESSARIO]

CATACOMBS

Ancient Christian subterranean cemeteries found in Naples, Syracuse, Malta, Tunisia, and various parts of the Roman Empire, but particularly in the environs of Rome. The name comes from the accidental location of the cemetery of Callistus on the Via Appia near the circus of Maximus and the basilica of St. Sebastian in a depression (κατὰ κήμβας, near the low place) between two hills. The term was used to locate the cemetery of Callistus in the 3d century. As this was the only underground cemetery known during the Middle Ages, upon the rediscovery of the early Christian cemeteries in the 16th century the word catacomb was applied generally to all such subterranean burial places.

Christian Cemeteries. The primitive Christians interred their dead in the pagan burial places. Gradually, however, they obtained control of sections of these burial sites that they called cemeteries (κοιμητήρια, place of

Entrances to two tombs in the "ad catacumbas" under the basilica of St. Sebastian. (Alinari-Art Reference/Art Resource, NY)

rest) as an indication of their belief in a final resurrection. Roman law forbade burial within populated areas; hence cemeteries were located outside the city walls, particularly alongside the main or consular roads. Roman families constructed mausoleums and funeral monuments in rows on the large thoroughfares, where they could be seen by passersby and could be used for memorial services and banquets. The ashes of infants, slaves, freedmen, clients, and relatives of a family were buried in these usually commodious structures; the poorer classes, particularly when inhumation became more general (during the 1st century A.D.), used obscure parts of the terrain for simple graves in the cemetery areas, and there were also various types of funeral monuments placed at ground level.

Christian Burial. Since the Christians were opposed to cremation, under the influence of Jewish practice and in imitation of the burial of Christ, they apparently used the simplest types of ground burial at first. Information revealed by the excavations of the tomb of St. Peter in the Vatican and details regarding the care for the remains of the martyr POLYCARP OF SMYRNA (d. *c.* 156) indicate that during the 2d and early 3d centuries special attention was paid to preserving the identity of Christian martyr graves, and memorial ceremonies were held on occasion

in the cemeteries in keeping with the customs of Roman society. During this period likewise, Christians were buried in the large vaults of the nobler families to which they were attached by relationship or service.

The earliest catacombs as such date from the 3d century; they appear to be extensions of the family-type mausoleum that could no longer accommodate new burials, although they were continually in process of reuse from generation to generation. Despite the fact that the Christian religion was not officially tolerated in the Roman Empire, the family ownership of burial sites was not generally challenged, and cemeteries were protected by law as *loca religiosa,* or religious places. Evidently a number of Christian family-owned sites were joined together, and as space on the ground level became inadequate, caves were dug out beneath the soil after the fashion of the Etruscan burial sites. These were linked together eventually by networks of passages, a yard or so wide, and about six feet in height; and graves (called *loculi*) were dug in the tufa walls, between one-and-a-half and two feet high and four to five feet in length, one on top of the other. Some were wide enough to hold two or three bodies (*locus bisomus, trisomus*). These individual graves were closed with rectangular slabs of slate, marble, chalk, or earthenware. The name of the defunct person was chiseled or scratched on this cover, frequently with the age, date of death, and a symbol or blessing formula. Sometimes a representation of the deceased in a gold, glass, coin, ivory, or metal figure was affixed. Often small vessels with perfume or oil lamps were found in or near these graves, but the majority lack identification and appear to be the burial places of the unknown or of abandoned children.

The nature of the soil in the Roman countryside made this type of cemetery possible, since the low hills are composed of tufa, a soft clay that on drying becomes hard as stone. The digging was done by *fossores,* a corporation of grave diggers who apparently plotted the direction of their excavations and dug two, three, or four levels, going further into the earth for expansion, but respected the property rights of surrounding owners and understood basic geological principles for safety. In the 3d century Christian places of burial came under the ownership of the local community. The cemetery of Callistus on the Via Appia had been confided to the charge of the Deacon Callistus (later pope) by Pope ZEPHYRINUS (199–217); and under Pope FABIAN (236–250) the seven (regionary) deacons had control of the cemeteries attached to the churches of their regions. In the 4th century, they came under the charge of the priests attached to the title churches, each of which had its own cemetery along the nearest consular road outside the city.

Loculi walls of the catacombs of St. Sebastian, Rome. (Alinari-Art Reference/Art Resource, NY)

There is no evidence for the construction or use of the catacombs as refuges during the periods of persecution. It was only in the 4th century, when the cult of martyrs became general, that they were used for memorial services. Within the complex of the net of corridors constituting the catacombs, rectangular or round rooms were also constructed and used for burial; bodies were buried in the walls, or in sarcophagi, sometimes placed in a recess or niche with an arched top called an *arcosolium.* The walls of these rooms, called *triclia,* as in the cemetery beneath the basilica of St. SEBASTIAN, were decorated at first with figured motifs similar to pagan ornamentation, then gradually with specifically Christian symbols. Only toward the middle of the 3d century is there evidence of the introduction of definitely Christian scenes. The figures used are borrowed from contemporary art.

In the 4th century both on the walls of the catacombs and on the sides of the sarcophagi, representations of the Good Shepherd, the Orans, the Zodiac, Daniel, Noah, Jonah, catechetical and baptismal scenes appear. Scenes from the Old and New Testaments, particularly the Eucharistic banquet, become somewhat common; and after the 4th century and the construction of the basilicas, Christ is depicted among the Apostles and the Christian faithful.

In estimating the place and extent of use of the catacombs by the early Christians, it must be remembered that, as they disappeared from sight from the 9th to the 16th century, and despite the removal of many of the remains authorized by the 9th-century popes, they were preserved almost intact, while the ground and open air level cemeteries were destroyed by the ravages of time. It would seem that before the Constantinian Peace of the Church (313) the catacombs were considered an integral part of the Christian cemetery. They were confiscated during the Valerian (258) and Diocletian (303) persecu-

An engraving on the wall of catacombs in Rome. (©Charles & Josette Lenars/CORBIS)

tions, but they were later restored to Christian control (specifically, in 260 and 311, respectively).

Rediscovery. The catacombs were rediscovered in the 16th century by Renaissance humanists whose primary aim was a search for ancient inscriptions and artifacts. Antonio Bosio described his findings in his *Roma sotterranea.* His immediate successors pillaged the catacombs for works of art and the relics of the martyrs, frequently using false criteria in their attempts to utilize their discoveries for apologetic purposes.

In the 19th century the Jesuit G. Marchi (1795–1860) and G. B. de ROSSI (1822–94) undertook a scientific study of the Roman catacombs, using for guidance evidence furnished by the calendars, martyrologies, legends, liturgical texts, and patristic writings, as well as the itineraries of pilgrims from the Byzantine and Carolingian ages and sylloges or collections of inscriptions. Thus they were able to identify and give chronological and cultic placement to the main factors of early Christian life to which the catacombs witness. This work of discovery and identification is still being pursued.

The Principal Roman Catacombs. The excavations beneath St. Peter's Basilica in the Vatican revealed a number of burial sites, mainly rows of mausoleums

along the roads that bifurcated the original bill. These had been originally pagan monuments that were gradually utilized by the Christians; and from the 3d century, Christian symbols and decorations appear in some of the tombs. Peter had apparently been buried in a simple grave in a clear space that had other, mainly primitive-type, graves; and in the late 2d century a small monument was erected in a wall that passed over the Petrine grave. The 2d- and early 3d-century popes seem to have been buried in the vicinity of Peter's grave. There is no indication of catacomb construction in this area; but the information supplied by these discoveries proved most useful in interpreting findings in other Christian cemeteries and catacombs.

On the Via Appia there were three cemeteries, each with its catacombs: Callistus, with its crypt of 3d-century popes and St. Cecilia; Praetextatus, near the Roman Jewish catacombs and the syncretist hypogeums; and the *Ad Catacumbas* under the basilica of St. Sebastian. On the Via Ostiensis were the tombs of St. Paul and St. Timothy; and the cemeteries of Commodilla and of St. Thecla. The cemetery *Ad Duas Lauras* on the Via Labicana has preserved some of the better 3d- and 4th-century Christian art, including agape banquet scenes and depictions of New Testament incidents from the Constantinian age.

On the Via Tiburtina were the cemetery of Cyriacus, where St. LAWRENCE had been buried; the cemetery of HIPPOLYTUS; and an anonymous cemetery, discovered in 1927 almost intact, with the tomb of the martyr Novatian. The Via Nomentana had the cemetery of SS. Alexander, Eventius, and Theodulus at the 10th milestone. It contained a *memoria* over which was built a basilica honoring these martyrs. It was the site likewise of the cemetery and basilica of St. AGNES, of the cemetery of St. Nicomedes, of the *Coemeterium maius* with the picture of four saints, and an *arcosolium* in which a cathedra and benches had been carved out of tufa.

On the Via Salaria were the catacombs of Priscilla and of the Giordani; of Maximus and Felicitas; and of Traso or St. Saturninus. The Via Aurelia contained the cemeteries of St. Pancratius, SS. Processus and Martinian, and Calepodius, where St. Callistus was buried. The last was discovered in 1960 and contains paintings that represent the martyrdom of the saint. A similar new discovery was made at the conjunction of the Via Salaria with the modern Via Dino Compagni. Its contents were explored by A. Ferrua.

The cemetery of Pamphilus was discovered on the Via Salaria Vetus in 1920. One of the oldest catacombs is that of Domitilla on the Via Ardeatina, with its reminiscences of the ancient Roman family of the Flavii. The names given these catacombs reflect the earliest owners

Crypt of the Popes in the catacomb of St. Callistus. The memorial inscription dates from the 4th century, Rome. (Pontifica Commissione di Archeologia Sacra)

of the property, the title churches or locations in which they were found, or the names of martyrs actually or allegedly buried in them.

Bibliography: P. TESTINI, *Archeologia cristiana* (Rome 1958). A. BOSIO, *Roma sotterranea,* ed. G. SEVERANO (Rome 1632). G. MARCHI, *Monumenti delle arti cristiane primitive . . . ,* v.1 *Architettura cimiteriale* (Rome 1844–47). P. STYGER, *Die römischen Katakomben* (Berlin 1933). L. HERTLING and E. KIRSCHBAUM, *The Roman Catacombs and Their Martyrs,* tr. M. J. COSTELLOE (2d ed. London 1960). A. FERRUA, *Le pitture della nuova catacomba di Via Latina* (Rome 1960). M. J. JOHNSON, ''Pagan-Christian Burial Practices of the Fourth Century : Shared Tombs?'' *Journal of Early Christian Studies* 5 (Spr 1997) 37–59. J. B. BARCLAY, ''The depiction of figures from the Hebrew Scriptures in the art of the Roman catacombs,'' in *Prayer and Spirituality in the Early Church,* ed. P. ALLEN (Everton Park, Queensland, Australia 1998) 97–110.

[F. X. MURPHY/EDS.]

CATAFALQUE

From the Italian *catafalco,* derivation of which is uncertain, a catafalque is a wooden or steel structure that was historically used particularly for the absolution after REQUIEM MASSES. It designated (1) a framework support-ing the coffin at funerals when the corpse is physically present; or (2) more commonly the structure used to simulate the presence of a corpse, a practice of questionable meaningfulness. Originally the catafalque was nothing but the bier or support for the corpse. The use of a catafalque to represent an absent body seems to have originated later with the introduction of absolutions for the dead. Gradually the structure was increased in size, and frequently it was covered with a baldachin so that it came to assume monumental proportions when used for persons of high rank. In some countries the size of the catafalque was commensurate with the deceased's rank and wealth. The place for the catafalque was before the altar outside the sanctuary. It was covered with a black cloth or pall (except for little children for whom white is used), and surrounded by candles.

The liturgical reforms of Vatican II rendered the catafalque obsolete in many places. While it was never expressly forbidden, the desire for authenticity in liturgical celebration and the authoritative suggestion that absolution be given only in the actual presence of the corpse in the reformed funeral rites brought about its demise.

Bibliography: *Notitiae* 7–8 (1965). P. BAYANT, ''Le Mobilier d'Église,'' *Liturgia,* ed. R. AIGRAIN (Paris 1930) 256–257. J. B.

Arcosolium tomb in the catacomb of the Giordani, with paintings of the ''Raising of Lazarus'' and the ''Good Shepherd,'' Rome. (Pontifica Commissione di Archeologia Sacra)

O'CONNELL, *Church Building and Furnishing* (South Bend, Ind. 1955) 239–242. G. MALHERBE, ''Le Castrum Doloris ou catafalque des services funèbres'' *Paroisse et Liturgie* 33 (1951) 116–121. J. B. O'CONNELL, *The Celebration of Mass* (new ed. Milwaukee 1956) 634–636.

[A. CORNIDES/EDS.]

CATALDINO, JOSÉ

Jesuit missionary; b. Fabriano, Italy, April 1571; d. Reduction of San Ignacio Miní, Paraguay, June 10, 1653. He was already a priest when he entered the Society of Jesus on March 1, 1602. On April 30, 1604, he left Spain for Peru in the expedition of Father Diego de Torres; they arrived in Lima on Nov. 22, 1604. Cataldino was immediately appointed to the mission of Tucumán and Paraguay, arriving in Asunción for the first time on Dec. 13, 1605. In 1609, he and Father Mascetta, also an Italian, began their evangelical work in the large area of Guairá. Cataldino's years among these tribes were long and painful. After he founded the Reductions of San Ignacio Miní and Loreto, Cataldino was named superior of all the Paraguayan missions. This appointment induced him to work harder, and he created the new Reductions of San Pablo, San José, and Encarnación. After 11 years in this position, he was in charge of the Indians at Villarica, and subsequently worked for the conversion of the natives of Uruguay (*See* REDUCTIONS OF PARAGUAY).

Bibliography: F. XARQUE, *Vida apostólica del ven. p. Josef Cataldino* (Zaragoza 1664). P. PASTELLS, ed., *Historia de la Compañia de Jesús en la provincia del Paraguay* (Madrid 1912–15).

[H. STORNI]

CATALDO, JOSEPH MARY

Jesuit missionary; b. Terracina, Italy, March 17, 1837; d. Pendleton, Ore., April 9, 1928. He was the son of Antonio and Sebastiana (Borusso) Cataldo. He became a Jesuit novice on Dec. 23, 1852, and was ordained on Sept. 8, 1862, in Liège, Belgium. Two days later he departed for the U.S., where he studied and taught at Santa Clara College, Calif., until 1865. From 1865 to 1877 he worked among the Nez Percé, Coeur d'Alène, and Spokane native peoples, whose languages he mastered. Before his death he had learned eight native tongues and two Alaskan languages in addition to French and English.

Appointed superior of the Jesuit Rocky Mountain Mission in 1877, Cataldo sent missionaries to the Gros Ventres, Crow, Blackfoot, Assiniboine, and Arapaho tribes in Montana; to the Cheyenne in Wyoming; the Okanogan in Washington; the Umatilla in Oregon; and the Alaskan Eskimos. He founded Gonzaga College, Spokane, Wash. (1883), and approved the establishment of Immaculate Conception College, Seattle, Wash. (1892). After he was replaced as superior in 1893, he worked with the native people of Montana, Idaho, Oregon, and Alaska and with the settlers in the Pacific Northwest. His greatest attachment was to the Nez Percé at St. Joseph's Mission, Culdesac, Idaho, for whom he wrote a prayerbook and a life of Christ in the Nez Percé language.

Bibliography: W. N. BISCHOFF, *The Jesuits in Old Oregon* (Caldwell, Idaho 1945). R. C. CARRIKER, ''Joseph M Cataldo, SJ: Courier of Catholicism to the Nez Percés,'' in *Churchmen and the Western Indians*, ed. C. A. MILNER, II and F. A O'NEIL (Norman, Okla. 1985) 109–139.

[W. N. BISCHOFF]

CATALDUS OF RACHAU, ST.

Bishop and patron of Taranto; b. Ireland, early seventh century; d. Taranto, Italy, *c.* 671. Everything known concerning him is based on legends dating from the 12th century. He was born close to the monastery of Lismore, became a monk there, and then later became bishop of Rachau. On the return from a pilgrimage to the Holy Land, he was shipwrecked off the Gulf of Taranto. Supposedly he then became bishop of Taranto, where he was considered a great reformer and builder of churches. He is venerated as a miracle worker in Italy, especially at his see city, where his body was buried in the cathedral, and also at Sens and Auxerre in France.

Feast: May 10.

Bibliography: *Acta Sanctorum* May 2 (1863) 568–577. F. UG-HELLI, *Italia sacra,* ed. N. COLETI, 10 V. in 9 (2d ed. Venice 1717–22) 9:121. B. MORONE, *Vita e miracoli di S. Cataldo . . . ,* 2 pts. (Naples 1779). C. STORNAJOLO, ''Crocetta aurea opistografa della cattedrale di Taranto,'' *Nuovo bollettino di archeologia cristiana* 21 (1915) 83–93. G. BLANDAMURA, *Un cimelio del s. VII esistente nel duomo di Taranto* (Lecce 1917). J. F. KENNEY, *The Sources for the Early History of Ireland,* v. 1, *Ecclesiastical* (New York 1929) 185. F. LANZONI, *Le diocesi d'Italia dalle origini al principio de sec. VII (an. 604),* 2 v. (Faenza 1927) 1:79. A. M. TOMMASINI, *Irish Saints in Italy,* tr. J. F. SCANLAN (London 1937) 401–432. J. L. BAUDOT and L. CHAUSSIN, *Vies des saints et des bienhereux selon l'ordre du calendrier avec l'historique des fêtes* (Paris 1935–56) 5:196. *Martyrologium Romanum,* ed. H. DELEHAYE (Brussels 1940) 183.

[R. E. GEIGER]

CATANOSO, GAETANO (CAJETAN), BL.

Priest of Reggio Calabria, founder of the Congregation of the Sisters of St. Veronica of the Holy Face (*Congregazione delle Suore Veroniche del Volto Santo*); b. Chorio di San Lorenzo, Reggio Calabria, Italy, Feb. 14, 1879; d. Reggio Calabria April 4, 1963. Gaetano's parents were landowners who encouraged his faith and vocation. Ordained in 1902, he gained a reputation for holiness while serving as a parish priest. In 1920, he founded a parish confraternity and newsletter devoted to the Holy Father. He also used the bulletin to promote the Poor Clerics Association and to encourage vocations. Catanoso was appointed pastor of Santa Maria della Candelora, Reggio Calabria (1921), where he founded the Missionaries of the Holy Face and built a shrine in honor of the Holy Face. The first members of the congregation—dedicated to charity, prayer for reparation, and catechesis—were clothed in 1935 and their constitutions were approved by the diocese in 1958. To renew spirituality among his flock, Catanoso promoted eucharistic and Marian devotions, catechesis, and parish missions. He organized teams of priests to conduct these missions in the region. In addition to his parish work (1921–50), Catanoso served as chaplain to religious institutes, a prison, a hospital, and the archdiocesan seminary. He was immedi-

Vestments hanging in the backroom of the Cataldo Mission, built by Jesuit missionaries, Coeur D'Alene, Idaho, 1995. (© Kevin R. Morris/CORBIS)

ately venerated after his death. An inexplicable healing at his intercession, approved as a miracle June 25, 1996, led to his beatification by John Paul II on May 4, 1997.

Feast: April 4.

Bibliography: A. SORRENTINO, *Il Tuo Volto, Signore, io cerco* (Reggio Calabria 1996). *Acta Apostolicae Sedis,* 12 (1997): 599.

[K. I. RABENSTEIN]

CATECHESIS, I (EARLY CHRISTIAN)

In the New Testament the word catechesis (κατη-χεῖν) is used to signify teaching or instruction in the law of God (Acts 18.25; Rom 2.18; Gal 6.6). It differs from the KERYGMA, or announcement of the kingdom of God, and from the *didascalia,* or doctrinal teaching of the homily for the baptized. The practice of catechesis is referred to by the author of the Epistle to the Hebrews (5.12–14; cf. 1 Cor 3.1–3) as feeding children with milk rather than the solid food of justice.

The primitive catechesis as revealed in the Epistles of Paul, Peter, and James in particular seems to have developed in two forms. The first, addressed to converts from Judaism, was based on the Holiness Code of Leviticus (17–19) and followed the lines of the Jerusalem apostolic decree that had prescribed Baptism and abstention from uncleanliness and idolatry (Acts 15.19–21) as essential for entrance into the Church of Christ. This early catechesis emphasized adherence to the Word of God as truth in contrast with idolatry and stressed the requirements of fraternal charity. It contained an instruction on worship and was completed with an exhortation that, as children of light (Lk 16.8), Christians should excel in virtue. There are numerous indications in the NT of the use of catechetical formulas based on Christ's Sermon on the Mount and of lists of vices and virtues (Mt 5.3–11; Lk 6.20–23) that seem to have been formed into groups of texts for teaching.

With the expansion of the Church to Syria, Asia Minor, and Greece, a different emphasis appeared, directed toward the Hellenistic proselytes and converts from paganism. Although the title of the early 2nd century work DIDACHE suggests it is a summary of the evangelical preaching of the Apostles, it is in fact a compendium of moral precepts, directives for the organization of Christian communities, and instructions regarding Baptism and Eucharist. The moral instruction, based on Jewish teaching in the Psalms and Proverbs, introduced along with it catalogues of virtues that were common to both the Hellenistic (Aristotle, *Eth. Nic.* 2.7) and Jewish ethical codes (Deuteronomy ch. 30). Both the Didache and the Letter of BARNABAS supply examples of the primitive catechesis in the guise of the two ways, of life and of death (Did.), or of light and darkness (Bar.), and were based on Jewish synagogue practice. The Didache proclaimed the law of the love of God and of neighbor taken by Christ from the Old Testament (Dt 6.5; Lv 19.18) and the golden rule (Did. 1.2). It described the virtues (1.3–4.14) and vices (5–6.3) that characterize respectively life and death by way of preparation for Baptism (7), and described participation in the Eucharist (9.1–5).

The Letter of Barnabas inculcated the virtues of wisdom, prudence, understanding, and knowledge (2.1–5), and described the two ways (18–20) on an eschatalogical background (4.1–14), insisting on the imitation of Christ in His Passion (5, 6). It explained the significance of Baptism in connection with the cross (9.1–11), and exhorted to familial and social virtue (19.4–12), encouraging its hearers by a reminder of the Resurrection and final retribution (21.1).

Catechesis along the line of the Didache became standard in the 2nd century in the preparation for Baptism and was accompanied by exorcisms and the scrutiny of sponsors as well as fasting. On POLYCARP's letter to the Philippians, IRENAEUS remarked (*Adv. haer.* 3.3, 4) that

"those seeking salvation can apprehend the nature of the faith and the teaching of the truth." On a background of hope in the Resurrection and of Our Lord's commands (2.1–3), Polycarp stressed the imitation of Christ in His patience (8.2, 9.1) and inculcated the virtues that lead to holiness (9.1–12). Christians must flee avarice (2.1, 11.2–3); husbands, wives (2.2), widows (2.3), deacons (5.2), young men, virgins (5.3), and priests (6.1–3) are to practice kindness, forgiveness of injuries, and moderation toward the culpable (6.2), praying for all, particularly civil rulers (12.3).

The APOLOGISTS of the 2d century combined the kerygma and the catechesis in the enunciation of the CHRISTIAN WAY OF LIFE (JUSTIN, ATHENAGORAS, THEOPHILUS OF ANTIOCH). With the rise of the catechetical schools toward the end of the century, the bishops prepared the candidates for Baptism (*catechumenoi*) by a series of moral instructions accompanied by exorcisms and fasting. This took place in the house churches and followed a pattern leading to the handing over of the CREED (*traditio*). With the emancipation of the Church (313), these instructions assumed a more formal character as is exemplified in the *Catechetical Lectures* of CYRIL OF JERUSALEM, AMBROSE's *De Sacramentis* and *De Mysteriis,* and the *Cateches* of THEODORE OF MOPSUESTIA. AUGUSTINE discussed the method in his *De catechizandis rudibus,* linking it with salvation history, which leads the catechumen from faith to hope and from hope to charity. With the spread of infant Baptism, the formal structure of the early catechumenate gave way to more informal catechesis by way of liturgical homilies in church and instruction in the home.

Bibliography: P. CARRINGTON, *The Primitive Christian Catechism* (Cambridge, Eng. 1940). G. SLOYAN, ed., *Shaping the Christian Message* (New York 1958) 3–37. F. X. MURPHY, *Studia moralia,* v.1 (Rome 1963) 54–72. L. BOPP, *Lexikon für Theologie und Kirche,* ed. J. HOFER and K. RAHNER (Freiburg 1957–65) 6:27–29. C. H. DODD, *The Apostolic Preaching and Its Developments* (London 1936; repr. 1963); *Gospel and Law* (New York 1951). J. DANIÉLOU, *La Catéchese aux premiers siècles.* (Paris 1968). J. I. H. MCDONALD, *Kerygma and Didache: The Articulation and Structure of the Earliest Christian Message.* (Cambridge/New York 1980). O. C. EDWARDS and J. H. WESTERHOFF, eds., *A Faithful Church: Issues in the History of Catechetics.* (Wilton, CN 1981).

[F. X. MURPHY/EDS.]

CATECHESIS, II (MEDIEVAL)

This essay surveys catechetical practice during the period—about 1000 years—between the decline of the catechumenate in the 5th century to the eve of the REFORMATION in the 15th. In the first five centuries of the Church's history, catechesis focused primarily on the instructions given to adults as they prepared for baptism. By the 6th century, the organized catechumenate had all but disappeared. In places where Christianity had taken root the baptism of infants was common practice, and baptism of adults became the exception rather than the rule. With the mass conversions of the FRANKS and Germanic peoples, individuals were baptized after a preparation of only a few weeks, or with little or no instruction. From this time the Church in Europe faced the challenge of educating in the faith large groups of rude, unlettered people and their children. A new concept and style of catechesis emerged as entire tribes were brought en masse into the Church.

To gain an idea of the content and flavor of the oral catechesis in the period from the 5th to the 11th centuries, study of the pastoral treatises, liturgical texts, hagiography, and directives of local councils is necessary. The pastoral treatises written by bishops and missionary monks reflect the characteristics of an oral method and aim at practical education in Christianity, not as speculation but as a way of life. The history of liturgy, the development of religious art, and records of local councils also reveal something of catechetical practice. Medieval penitentials are another written source shedding light on methods of teaching Christian morality to peoples of tribal culture.

Gregory the Great. Pope GREGORY I (590–604) stands out as the most important single influence on pastoral catechesis in the early Middle Ages. He recognized the inner relationship between missiology, liturgy, and catechesis and proposed a form of catechesis wonderfully adapted to his times. His *Liber regulae pastoralis*, a pastoral manual for bishops, was widely distributed even during Gregory's lifetime. The work firmly established in Europe the ideal of the bishop as teacher and father of his flock. If the *Liber regulae pastoralis* is not important for catechetical content, it is nonetheless most significant for its concept of the bishop's teaching office. Gregory's *Homilies* give a picture of his own idea of the essence of the Christian message. A major theme is the Person of Christ, Mediator between God and men, who in His holy Church pours out on the world the gift of the Holy Spirit.

In a letter to a monk who was going to join St. Augustine of Canterbury, Gregory outlined important principles of missionary catechesis. He wrote that the temples of the idols should be converted to places of Christian worship, ''that the nation, seeing their temples are not destroyed, may remove error from their hearts, and knowing and adoring the true God, may the more familiarly resort to the places to which they have been accustomed'' (St. Bede, *Hist. Eccl.* 1.30). Gregory followed the same principle with regard to pagan festivals, directing that

Christian feasts be gradually substituted for the pagan celebrations.

In much the same vein, one of Gregory's early successors, Pope BONIFACE V (619–625), in a letter to King Edwin of Northumbria dated A.D. 624 outlined a program of fundamental catechesis. The pagans were to be taught the emptiness of idols, and the importance of belief in a Creator God, who sent His Son to redeem the human race. As a consequence, they were called to embrace the Gospel and to be reborn as children of God by Baptism (*Patrologia Latina* 80:438). Throughout this period of evangelization among the barbarians, Christ was seen especially as an opponent of their heathen gods. He was the true God to whom they had vowed their loyalty, and it was their duty to live out that loyalty according to the pattern set down for them by the ministers of His Church.

Another work attributed to Gregory the Great, *The Books of Dialogues on the Life and Miracles of the Italian Fathers (Libri dialogorum)*, illustrates another means common in medieval times for handing on the faith. The author's intention was to show that holiness was not a thing of past, but that God continues to raise up saints in the present. In describing the activities of these saintly figures, he provided much information about religious attitudes and practice of the time. Similarly, the works of St. GREGORY OF TOURS, especially his *Historia Francorum*, are an invaluable source of information about the history and evangelization of 6th century Gaul. He reports the lives and miracles of St. Martin, who had preceded him by almost two centuries as bishop of Tours, as well as scores of other Gallic saints. These collections of tales of the marvelous and miraculous became a major source of the Christian cult of the saints. For centuries it was to their local saints that Europeans looked for a vivid illustration of the Christian life and for a bond with the next world.

Missionary Catechesis. A discourse linked to St. GALL (d. 627), the Irish monk who had emigrated to Switzerland, contained a catechesis faithful to the tradition established by St. AUGUSTINE OF HIPPO in his *De catechizandis rudibus*. Gall's discourse gave a resume of the religious history of the world from the Fall to the Redemption and treated the mission of the Apostles, the vocation of the gentiles, and the divine constitution of the Church (PL 87:13–26).

St. BONIFACE (d. 754), the apostle of Germany, who had joined the BENEDICTINES in England, provided a link between the Romano-Anglo-Saxon religious tradition and the religious culture that flowered in the next century under the early CAROLINGIANS. Boniface's missionary efforts in Frisia were characterized by fidelity to Rome, a spirit of adaptation to local customs where this could be harmonized with the Christian life, and an understanding of the need to establish permanent monastic centers for the preservation and diffusion of Christianity. The correspondence of St. Boniface shows that he always looked to Holy Scripture for the substance of his teaching.

A letter from Gregory II in 719 approved his method. "You are to teach [the pagans] the service of the kingdom of God by persuading them to accept the truth in the name of Christ, the Lord our God. You will instill into their minds the teaching of the Old and New Testaments, doing this in a spirit of love and moderation, and with arguments suited to their understanding. Finally, we command you that in admitting within the Church those who have some kind of belief in God you will insist upon using the sacramental discipline prescribed in the official ritual formulary of the Holy Apostolic See" [C. H. Talbot, tr. and ed., *The Anglo-Saxon Missionaries in Germany* (New York 1954) 68]. In 735 St. Boniface wrote to the Abbess Eadburga in England, "I beg you to continue the good work you have begun by copying out for me in letters of gold the epistles of my lord, St. Peter, that a reverence and love of the Holy Scriptures may be impressed on the minds of the heathens to whom I preach, and that I may ever have before my gaze the words of him who guided me along this path" (*ibid.* 91).

Fifteen sermons traditionally once attributed to St. Boniface are important as indicating a medieval catechesis that is faithful to the Christocentric synthesis handed down from the age of the Fathers. The moral teaching of these sermons is noteworthy for its consistent development of the law of charity (PL 89:843–872).

Indicative of the prevailing pattern in Germany is the work of one of Alcuin's disciples, RABANUS MAURUS (d. 856). His treatise *De disciplina ecclesiastica* (PL 112:1193–1262) aimed to show a method of instructing pagans who asked for Baptism. The work is divided into three short books, of which the third is an amplification of the teaching of the two ways of the *Didache*.

Parental Responsibility. Usages of the ancient catechumenate were incorporated in the rite of Baptism, regularly administered to infants. There is no trace of a formal, ecclesiastical postbaptismal catechesis for children. It was assumed that the task of their education in the faith was the responsibility of their parents. A work attributed to St. ELIGIUS (d. c. 658), bishop of Noyon, shows him insisting on parental responsibility in handing on the truths of faith. "Know by memory the Symbol and the Lord's Prayer, and teach them to your children. Instruct and admonish the children, whom you have received as newborn from the baptismal fount, to live ever in the fear of God. Know that you have taken an oath on their behalf before God" (PL 87, 527).

By the 8th century, synods were decreeing that parents and godparents were obliged to know by heart the Our Father and the Creed, and to teach these to their children. These two formulas, essential elements in the ancient catechumenate, were considered the basic statements of Christian doctrine.

De institutione laicali by Bishop JONAS OF ORLEANS, a contemporary of Alcuin, emphasizes the responsibility of parents and godparents in the training of their children (PL 106:121–278). From the same period is a fragment attributed to a Christian woman, Dodena, entitled *Liber manualis.* The treatise illustrates the way a home catechesis might have been carried on at its best (PL 106:109–118).

Other Works. A 9th-century work, *Disputatio puerorum per interrogationes et responsiones,* illustrates a more formal, systematic catechesis in a somewhat stilted, dialogue form. The work shows clearly an analytical approach to the teaching of Christian doctrine that was later to become a dominant method for many centuries. In its 9th-century context, however, it can hardly be taken as typical of popular catechesis, which was not yet generally directed to children or centered in schools (PL 101:1097–1144).

Legislation. Ecclesiastical legislation of this early period makes it clear that the minimum aimed for, sometimes evidently in circumstances of great difficulty, was the universal memorization of the Creed and the Our Father, together with a basic understanding of Christian morality. It was consistently held that around these two formulas could be developed a fuller understanding of the Christian life. The Council of Clovesho in 747 instructed bishops to visit the outlying districts of their dioceses annually, to teach the people who rarely heard the word of God to avoid pagan practices. Boys were to be chosen for the study of Holy Scripture. Above all it was necessary to teach the essentials of the Faith—the doctrine of the Trinity and the Creed—and to see that godparents knew these truths (J. D. Mansi, *Sacrorum Conciliorum nova et amplissima collectio* 12:396–398). The Council of Frankfort (794) decreed that all Christians should be taught the Creed and the Our Father (Mansi 13:908). The Council of Arles (813) insisted on the duty of parents to instruct their children (Mansi 14:62).

A letter from St. BEDE (*c.* 672–735) to Egbert, Archbishop of York, recommended that those, priests included, who understood only their native tongue, be taught the Creed and the Our Father in the language they understood, though Bede also insisted that Latin was to be preferred for those who could manage it (PL 94:659). A similar policy was advocated by King Alfred the Great in the 9th century. (The single instance during this period of a policy of adopting the vernacular for liturgical use was the effort of SS. CYRIL AND METHODIUS among the Slavs.)

Defects. A number of abuses resulted when certain elements of medieval cultural catechesis were carried to a logical extreme. Memorization and analysis of the Creed and the Our Father was sometimes overemphasized to the exclusion or neglect of the biblical narrative method, which had been so favored by the Fathers. The medieval fascination for numbers, coupled with a recognition of the need for memory aids, fostered another abuse in the ordering of the truths of the Faith according to artificial and arbitrary classifications. Thus, the number seven was used as a teaching aid: seven Sacraments, seven works of mercy, seven petitions of the Lord's Prayer, seven capital sins. Such a methodology easily distorted the inner logic, coherence, and symmetry of the Christian mystery.

Liturgical Practice. Liturgical texts indicate that despite wide variances and notable changes, catechesis continued to be linked to sacramental practice. Two documents of the Carolingian era, the one known the GELASIAN SACRAMENTARY, dating from the 8th century and the other as *Ordo Romanus XI* dating from the 9th century, show that the Roman rite of initiation had been adapted in northern Europe and adjusted to the fact that infant baptism was the general rule. There are some vestiges of the ancient scrutinies and exorcisms in the Gelasian Sacramentary during lent in preparation for baptism that would take place at Easter, but the emphasis seems to have been on the latter as a means of purifying those who were not old enough to be examined as to their knowledge and behavior.

A development not anticipated by these early sacramentaries was the fracturing of the unity of the sacraments of initiation. It was to have a lasting impact on catechesis. First, the fear that a child might die without baptism made parents and pastors alike reluctant to wait for Easter or Pentecost when the rite was normally celebrated. Then the inaccessibility of bishops, especially away from Rome, led to a lengthening of the period between baptism and confirmation. Finally, concern for the health of the infant during long ceremonies in dank and cold churches one the one hand and reverence for the sacrament led to postponing the reception of the Eucharist. Thus the Paschal significance of the sacraments of initiation and catechesis lost its focal point. In 1215 the Fourth Lateran Council in the canon *Utriusque sexus* sought a partial remedy by insisting that everyone, upon reaching the age of discernment (*ad annos discretionis*), receive the Eucharist at least at Easter.

The same canon also prescribed that all the faithful should "confess all their sins . . . to their own priest at least once a year." The annual confession, usually during lent, became, as witnessed by the *The Lay Folks Catechism* (1357), the occasion for parish priests to examine penitents on their knowledge of the faith. Should a penitent be unable to recite the six basic tenets found in the catechism (the 14 points of the Creed; the Ten Commandments; the seven sacraments; the seven works of mercy; the seven virtues; and the seven deadly sins), the confessor was to impose an additional penance. On the other hand, the Archbishop of York offered an indulgence of 40 days to every who could recite "the six things."

Some of the manuals used by confessors, the *Libri penitentiales,* directed that penitents be examined on their knowledge of the creed and be asked to recite the LORD'S PRAYER from memory. As auricular confession became the common practice, the sacrament of penance became an occasion for more catechesis. Penitents were instructed regarding virtues to be cultivated and vices to be avoided as well as their Christian responsibilities.

The fact that certain didactic elements of the liturgy developed into miracle, mystery, and morality plays is an indication of the strength of social and cultural elements in handing on the Christian tradition. Throughout the medieval period, innumerable religious customs and works of religious art created an atmosphere that supported a vital Christian society.

12th to 15th Centuries. From about the mid-11th century, the revival of commerce, with its accompanying growth of town life and urban institutions, affected the religious orientation of European civilization and the traditional modes of catechesis. The function of community custom in religious education was recognized as inadequate. Local councils in the 13th century imposed on parish priests the obligation of explaining to the people on Sundays the articles of faith in simple and clear fashion. The Council of Lambeth (1281) provided a brief summary of the instructions priests were to give their people (Mansi 24:410–413).

In the rise of the new orders, especially the DOMINICANS and FRANCISCANS, can be seen a remarkable effort to adapt catechetical methods to the needs of urban society. The mendicants brought about a revival of popular preaching, but they were not exempt from the intellectual influences that had affected the traditional structure of the Christian message. The history of catechesis here followed closely the development of philosophy and theology. The recovery of the Aristotelian corpus and the development of systematic theology in the high Middle Ages had a profound influence on catechetical methodology, though this influence was not fully realized until the discovery of printing made it widespread. A key difference between the catechesis of the early Middle Ages, as exemplified by St. Gregory in the late 6th century, or Rabanus Maurus in the 9th, and that of the period marked by the rise of the universities was in the change from a historico-narrative to a logical organization of the content of the catechesis. Popular catechesis still emanated chiefly from the pulpit, but as the analytic method of the universities tended to carry over into the methods of the preacher, the purposes of theology and catechesis were not always clearly distinguished. That there was a significant difference between the two was clear to St. THOMAS AQUINAS (d. 1274), as a study of his catechetical sermons reveals [see St. Thomas Aquinas, *The Catechetical Instructions,* tr. J. B. Collins (New York 1939)]. Even in these sermons, however, St. Thomas reveals how controlling were the intellectual and social influences of his age. The traditional framework of SALVATION HISTORY had all but disappeared in the writings of the 13th century.

Among writers who have exercised the greatest influence on the development of catechesis must be numbered be the sometime chancellor of the University of Paris (1409–12), Jean GERSON (1363–1429). Trained as a theologians and often invited to preach at court, even while he was university chancellor, he taught catechism to children. The five volumes of Gerson's written works, a goodly number in French, give evidence of his interest in reform, including the reform of theological studies, and include many treatises on the care of souls. Early in the 15th century he compiled *ABC des Simples Gens*, an outline of the basic teachings of the Christian faith that "simple folk" should commit to memory. Another work of the same period, is *Tractatus de parvulis trahendis ad Christum,* in which Gerson emphasized the need of teaching in terms a child could understand. He tried to persuade university theologians to produce simple treatises of the essentials of religion for common folk, and proposed that the treatises be made in the form of posters to be displayed in public places where people could gather to read and ponder them. Another of his works was *De confessione mollicei,* a manual for confessors describing children's sexual habits. The catechetical work that was to have the most lasting and widespread influence was Gerson's *Opusculum tripertitum* (c. 1395). One of the first works printed in the New World (Mexico 1544), it provides pastoral explanations of the Decalogue, Confession, and preparation for death. Gerson is a significant transition figure to the next period of catechesis which, with the invention of printing, came to be dominated by catechetical manuals and the printed word.

Bibliography: P. GÖBL, *Geschichte de Katechese im Abendlande vom Verfalle des Katechumenates bis zum Ende des Mittelalters* (Kempten 1880). C. HEZARD, *Histoire du catéchisme depuis la naissance de l'église jusqu'à nos jours* (Paris 1900). G. S. SLOYAN, ed.. *Shaping the Christian Message* (New York 1958). A. E. CRUZ, *Historia de la Catequesis* (Santiago de Chile 1962). J. H. WESTERHOFF and O. C. EDWARDS, eds. *A Faithful Church: Issues in the History of Catechesis* (Wilton, CT 1981). J. D. C. FISHER,*Christian Initiation: Baptism in the Medieval West* (London 1965). M. M. GATCH, *Preaching and Theology in Anglo-Saxon England: Aefric and Wulfstan* (Toronto 1971). J. A. WEISHEIPL,*Friar Thomas d'Aquino: His Life, Thought and Work* (Garden City, NY 1974).D. DOUIE,*Archbishop Pecham* (Oxford 1952). D. C. BROWN,*Pastor and Laity in the Theology of Jean Gerson* (Cambridge 1987).

[M. E. JEGEN/EDS.]

CATECHESIS, III (REFORMATION)

The classical Renaissance stirred new interest in educational methods and gave rise to schools for the upper classes. Among the prominent educators at the end of the 15th and beginning of the 16th centuries, men like John Colet in England, Erasmus and Juan Luis Vives on the continent, were mindful of the place of religious formation in the humanistic education they proposed.

On the popular level, the 15th and 16th centuries saw a proliferation of devotional works, many containing a kind of catechesis. A 16th-century Austrian work, *Road to Heaven,* exhorted the head of the family to attend the sermon and recall it after dinner with his family. He was also supposed to question them on the Ten Commandments, the seven deadly sins, the Our Father, and the Creed. Finally, he should have a little drink brought in for the group and lead them in singing a hymn referring to God, Our Lady, or the Saints [P. Janelle, *The Catholic Reformation* (Milwaukee 1949) 23].

A decree of the Fifth Lateran Council (1514) recognized a general need for better religious instruction. Schoolmasters were to teach religious truths: the divine precepts, the articles of faith, sacred hymns and psalms, and the lives of the saints (J. D. Mansi, *Sacrorum Conciliorum nova et amplissima collectio* 32:881).

Luther's Catechism. Preaching and formal catechesis were not enough to stem the abuses that prepared the way for the Lutheran movement. Martin LUTHER's teachings captured the popular mind in large areas of Germany through the medium of a highly effective catechesis. Luther's catechism first appeared in 1528 in the old medieval form of *tabulae,* or wall charts. This was followed within a year by a printed version. The arrangement of Luther's 1529 catechism—commandments first, then the Creed, followed by prayer and the Sacraments—threw the doctrine of grace out of context, thereby destroying the vital synthesis of the divine message of salvation. The organization of the work revealed Luther's own religious and spiritual problems, and marked the beginning of a long history of catechisms that used the threefold division of creed, code, and cult, with a major emphasis on code. This arrangement was logical in the light of Lutheran theology, but it ill suited a Catholic catechesis.

It was only with Luther that the term catechism came to refer to a book, both to the manual used by the catechist and to the simpler text placed in the hands of a child. Until this time, the term catechism referred only to the content of the catechesis. The period of the REFORMATION coincided, therefore, with the significant transition to that period in which the catechism manual began to play a dominant part in forming both the theory and practice of catechesis. Luther left detailed directions for the use of his catechisms, insisting on rote memorization of the exact text as a means of preserving his teaching intact. Memorization was to precede an analysis of the material.

Catholic Reaction. Of necessity, in the face of heresy, Catholic catechesis reacted to PROTESTANTISM by becoming greatly concerned with theological accuracy, as this was necessary to keep clear the essential differences in doctrine that separated the Church from the new sects. The Catholics in their reaction to the propagation of LUTHERANISM did not immediately recognize the implications and consequences of Luther's innovations in catechesis. Catholic catechisms countered by an imitation of Luther's short question and answer method, satisfied for the most part that so long as orthodoxy was guaranteed a satisfactory solution to the problem posed by Luther's catechism had been found.

The first Catholic catechism written as a reaction to Luther's was published in Augsburg in 1530, and was followed by a series in German and Latin. The first efforts were not very successful because they lacked clarity and conciseness. Many were too long and learned for popular use. They differed in wording of essential matters, a decided weakness in the face of the lucid and uniform presentation provided by Luther's rapidly spreading catechism.

St. Peter Canisius. St. Peter CANISIUS (1521–97) produced three catechisms that remedied many of the weaknesses of the earlier Catholic efforts. In 1555 his large catechism, *Summa doctrinae christianae* appeared. He had been asked to gloss it with references to Holy Scripture, the Fathers and Doctors, and Canon Law, as an aid to preachers and school masters. Realizing the impossibility of satisfying the needs of theologians, parish priests, and youthful students with a single work, Canisius published the *Catechismus minimus* (1556), which first appeared as the appendix to a Latin grammar. This small work contains only 59 questions divided into six short chapters, treating in order: (1) faith and the Creed, (2) hope and the Lord's Prayer, (3) charity and the decalogue, (4) the Sacraments, (5) the avoidance of sin, (6)

good works. A few months later a German version of the little catechism appeared. Canisius added to this book a series of prayers for all occasions: morning and evening, before and after meals, and a daily prayer for all the needs of Christendom. Almost 40 years later he prepared an edition of the *Catechismus minimus* with the words divided into syllables to make mastery of the text easier for small children.

The third catechism of Canisius, the *Parvus catechismus catholicorum* (1558), was intended for youths of about 14 years. This book set the tone of catechesis in Germany for the next 200 years. By 1597, 134 editions of the work had been published. It underwent many revisions and additions at the hands of the author himself, who enriched it with prayers and meditations on the life of Christ. Some of the editions were richly illustrated.

The catechisms of Canisius were written to defend the faith against heresy, and therefore they necessarily had a strong intellectual quality. They were admirably devoid of polemics, however, and although they are written in question and answer form, they retained much of the spirit and even the language of Scripture and the Fathers.

Other Efforts. In France, Edmund AUGER, SJ, produced catechisms in 1563 and 1568, similar in approach to the works of Canisius. During the same period, Gaspar Astete and Juan Martínez de RIPALDA, Jesuits, wrote catechisms which were still in use in the 20th century in Spain. In England, Dr. Laurence Vaux's *A Catechisme of Christian Doctrine necessarie for children and ignorante people* (1562) also showed the influence of Canisius.

The Roman Catechism. During the Council of TRENT there was an effort to provide for the drafting of two catechisms: one in Latin for the learned, and one to be translated into vernaculars for the unlettered and children. Only the first was attempted and completed by a postconciliar commission in 1566. Using the catechetical works of Canisius as a model, the *Catechismus ex decretis Concilii Tridentini ad Parochos,* or *Catechismus Romanus,* was intended as a reference book for pastors and a norm on which subsequent texts were to be based.

The preface of the work notes that catechesis is not the same as theology, but treats only those things "that belong peculiarly to the pastoral office and are accommodated to the capacity of the faithful." The pastor is urged to keep before his mind the general plan of the catechesis that is summed up in three points: (1) all Christian knowledge and eternal life is to know Jesus Christ; (2) but to know Christ is to keep His Commandments; (3) and charity is the end of the Commandments and the fulfillment of the law. The pastor is also reminded of the importance of the manner of imparting the truths of faith. He should adapt his instruction to the age, capacity, and condition of those being instructed. Further, since all the doctrines of Christianity are derived from the word of God, the pastor should devote himself to the study of the font of catechesis. Pastors are expected to correlate their instructions with the homily on the Sunday Gospel, and for this purpose the catechism provides a supplement giving references to the sections in the catechism which could be related to the Gospel for each Sunday of the liturgical year.

The *Roman Catechism* was approved by Pius V in 1566, and by Gregory XIII in 1583. It has since enjoyed continual recommendation. Leo XIII, Pius X, and Pius XI recommended its use by the clergy in more recent times.

The *Catechismus Romanus* was translated immediately into Italian by order of Pius V, and within the next three years into German, French, and Polish. A Spanish translation was resisted by some influential Spaniards who were opposed to the publication of religious books in the vernacular, and also because some theologians objected to the catechism's interpretation of a passage in St. Matthew regarding Baptism (Mt 28.18–19).

The Council of Trent also promoted the progress of catechesis by decreeing that the people, and especially the children, be carefully instructed. ''The bishops shall also see to it that at least on Sundays and other festival days, the children in every parish be carefully taught the rudiments of the faith and obedience toward God and their parents by those whose duty it is, and who shall be compelled thereto, if need be, even by ecclesiastical censures'' [H. J. Schroeder, *Canons and Decrees of the Council of Trent* (St. Louis 1941) 196].

Local Legislation. Diocesan statutes further specified the Tridentine decrees. The Synod of Besançon (1571) directed that the prayers that every Christian should know were to be recited at the Sunday sermon. In rural areas the pastors were obliged to gather the children one day a week in order to have them recite their prayers in Latin and in French (*Dictionnaire de théologie catholique,* 2:2.1919).

This same period saw a council in Lima, Peru, approve a catechism authorized by Philip II of Spain. This catechism was translated into the Quechua and Aymara languages. The Council of Mexico in 1585 called for a short and simple catechism containing the LORD'S PRAYER, the HAIL MARY, APOSTLES' CREED, SALVE REGINA, 12 articles of the faith, the Ten Commandments of God and five precepts of the Church, the seven Sacraments, and the seven capital sins. A translation was to be made for the native peoples of each diocese, and the text was to be explained on the Sundays of Advent and during Lent. Before receiving Baptism, adults were to know the Our Father, the Creed, and the Ten Commandments in their language.

The CONFRATERNITY OF CHRISTIAN DOCTRINE, approved by Pius V in 1571, was a significant agency of catechesis. A cooperative work of clergy and laity from the beginning, the confraternity, founded in Milan and fostered by St. Charles BORROMEO, was especially widespread in Italy and spread to France and Germany. Members of the confraternity undertook the responsibility of furthering the work of religious instruction among the members of their own families.

Bellarmine's Catechisms. St. Robert BELLARMINE's catechisms, written at the order of Clement VIII for use in the PAPAL STATES, were the most influential of the catechisms written shortly after the Council of Trent. The *Dottrina cristiana breve* is a short summary of Christian doctrine for pupils (1597). The following year Bellarmine produced a teacher's manual in catechetics, *Dichiarazione piu copiosa della dottrina cristiana* (1598). These books do not present so synthesized a catechesis as do those of Peter Canisius, but they are of great doctrinal clarity and rich in psychological insights. In the short catechism the questions avoid abstractions and are placed in a context a child can understand. In the larger catechism the usual question and answer pattern is reversed and the questions are put in the mouth of the pupil, while it is the teacher who answers. Here, Bellarmine had in view a method of helping the inexperienced catechist anticipate his pupil's questions, and a guide for clear, complete, and adequate explanations. The catechesis was to be built around the theological virtues: faith centered in the Creed, hope expressed in the Our Father, and charity in the Commandments of God and of the Church. The Sacraments are treated as sources and means of the Christian life.

In a brief of 1598 Clement VIII exhorted bishops throughout the world to ''use their utmost endeavors to have this catechism, written at Our command, adopted and followed in their respective churches, dioceses, and parishes'' [J. Brodrick, *The Life and Work of Blessed Robert Bellarmine* (New York 1928) 395]. The catechism was translated eventually into more than 60 different tongues and dialects, including editions in Arabic, Hindustani, Chinese, Congolese, Ethiopian, Hebrew, and Peruvian. It was the only catechism St. Francis de Sales allowed in his diocese. Urban VIII in 1633 recommended its use in the missions; a century later Benedict XIV, in a special constitution to all the bishops of the Church, advised its adoption as the official manual of every diocese. When at Vatican Council I a uniform and universal catechism was proposed, it was Bellarmine's catechism that was recommended as a model.

The catechisms engendered as part of the Catholic reformation provided excellent summaries of doctrine in relatively simple language. Thus, they satisfied a critical need, and were a major factor in checking the spread of heresy and preserving the purity of doctrine. Today, writers active in the catechetical renewal hold that these catechisms also had the less desirable effect of fostering a catechesis that ran counter to the inherent dynamism of the Biblical narrative approach in teaching Christian doctrine. According to these writers, in the post-Reformation catechisms the relation between the parts of Christian doctrine was not established, and thus the message was not presented as an integrated whole, the good news of salvation centered in Christ (see Hofinger, Jungmann, Sloyan).

Important advances were made in school catechesis, though this remained subordinate to the teaching of religion in the Church and in the home. Charles Borromeo's work in fostering schools was imitated by other dioceses throughout Italy. Besides the Jesuits, other religious congregations that made notable contributions to the theory and practice of school catechesis were the Ursulines, Somaschi, Barnabites, and the Clerks Regular of the Christian Schools.

17th-Century Efforts. Diocesan catechisms, special children's catechisms, and treatises on catechetics multiplied during the 17th century. FRANCIS DE SALES personally instructed children of his diocese. In 1602 in Toulouse, a 14th-century work of Jean GERSON was reprinted as part of a teacher's manual. Adrien Bourdoise opened a school in Paris in 1622 especially for the purpose of bringing religious influence into families through teaching young children. He also produced an original book on catechetical pedagogy, *Les rudiments de la foi en faveur des simples fidèles.* Among the contributions of Bourdoise was the division of the pupils into age groups, with particular adaptations for each group. This practice became customary in the large cities of Europe, where lay catechists sometimes assisted as instructors. It was widely taken for granted that catechesis meant an explanation of the text of a catechism followed by recitation of questions and answers.

St. VINCENT DE PAUL (1581–1660) incorporated a catechesis as an integral part of the missions preached by his priests in rural areas. During their missions his priests were to teach catechism twice a day. In the afternoon they were to catechize the children for an hour in a simple manner. In the evening the same material was to be taught to adults. The catechesis was never to be replaced by a sermon. Guided by Vincent de Paul, St. Louise de Marillac provided a special manual for teaching catechism to the poor in their homes.

The Sulpician Method. In the Sulpician method, inaugurated by Jean Jacques OLIER (1608–57), seminarians were the principal catechists. Distinctive features included the care to adjust the catechesis to the age level of the child, and a concern for helping children live in accord with the doctrine taught. In promulgating the method, great emphasis was given to the qualifications of teachers, who were supposed to reflect a strong love of God and of children. Sulpician techniques did not shun an appeal to a spirit of competition. Teachers made use of a point system for correct answers, gave places of honor in class, and awarded prizes for outstanding recitations. Hymn singing in the course of a catechism lesson was intended to keep a happy atmosphere. There was a conscious effort to supplement the analytical approach, though there was still much stress on memorization. Children were to memorize the Sunday Gospel as preparation for the catechism lesson. The class, regularly held on Sunday afternoon, included a homily on the Gospel by the catechist and an attempt to make an application of the day's lesson to the everyday life of the child. Much of the catechetical practice since the 17th century bears the mark of the influence of the Sulpician method.

St. John Baptist de la Salle. The method of St. John BAPTIST DE LA SALLE (1651–1719) brought a renewed appreciation of the use of narrative in catechesis, although one of his chief catechetical works, *Duties of a Christian,* makes little or no advance over the customary arrangement of the text, which proceeded from Creed to Commandments, Sacraments, and prayer. De la Salle's method was unusual at his time in holding that memorization should follow the explanation of the text, not precede it. Formulas were to be memorized as summaries only after a careful development of the lesson. Though a biblical-liturgical approach was lacking, the method did emphasize the value of teaching the life of Christ and the lives of the saints. Passages from Scripture were used, but chiefly as illustrations of a point of dogma.

Other Influences. Among the other figures who contributed significantly to the theory and practice of catechesis in the 17th century were St. John EUDES, BOSSUET, Charles Thuet, and Claude FLEURY. Thuet produced a manual showing three distinct methods for effectively using the *Roman Catechism:* in sermons, dialogues, and meditations. Claude Fleury published a catechism containing an abridgement of sacred history, one of a growing number of catechisms seeking to make a closer correlation between Holy Scripture and the question and answer treatment of dogma by this time considered standard.

All the methodological weaknesses of the 16th and 17th centuries were countered by the fact that catechesis was still given in a Christian environment. Formal catechesis was enforced and supported by the religious orientation of family and society well into the 18th century. It was only then that secular values began to set the tone of European culture.

Bibliography: C. HEZARD, *Histoire du catéchisme depuis la naissance de l'église jusqu'à nos jours* (Paris 1900). G. S. SLOYAN, ed.. *Shaping the Christian Message* (New York 1958). A. E. CRUZ, *Historia de la Catequesis* (Santiago de Chile 1962). J. H. WESTERHOFF and O. C. EDWARDS, ed.. *A Faithful Church. Issues in the History of Catechesis* (Wilton, CT 1981). J. BRODRICK,*Saint Peter Canisius* (Baltimore 1950). *The Life and Work of Blessed Robert Bellarmine* (London 1928) J-C. DHOTEL,*Les Origines du Catechisme Moderne* (Paris1966). B.L. MARTHALER,*The Catechism Yesterday and Today* (Collegeville, MN 1995).

[M. E. JEGEN]

CATECHETICAL DIRECTORIES, NATIONAL

Catechetical directories are a new genre of writings in Roman Catholic religious education that furnish guidelines delineating pastoral principles, set goals, and suggest means for religious education. The directories were mandated by Vatican II in *Christus Dominus.* They are pastoral in purpose and "deal with the fundamental principles of such [catechetical] instruction, its arrangement, and the composition of books on the subject" (art. 44). There are two kinds: a general directory for the universal Church and particular directories which address special needs of the faithful required by "the different circumstances of particular nations or regions" (for a discussion of the former, see *GENERAL DIRECTORY FOR CATECHESIS*).

The French hierarchy promulgated a directory for use in the dioceses of France in 1964. The Argentine bishops published a similar one in 1967, and in 1971 the Mexican bishops issued a directory *ad experimentum.* The Italian hierarchy commissioned a foundational document, *Il rinnovamento della catechesi* (1970), which in effect is a catechetical directory, thought its guidelines are implicit rather than explicit. In April 1972 the National Conference of Catholic Bishops initiated a process to produce a catechetical directory for use in the United States. Working under the direction of the Bishops' Committee of Policy and Review was a directory committee composed of 12 persons: four bishops, two laywomen, one layman, two women religious, one brother, one religious priest, and one diocesan priest. The result of their work, *Sharing the Light of Faith: National Catechetical Directory for Catholics of the United States,* was approved by the NCCB in 1977 and by the Congregation for the Clergy in Rome in October 1978; its authority comes from this approval.

Sharing the Light of Faith is a handbook containing directives (norms, standards) and guidelines (recommendations, suggestions) for the catechesis of Catholics of all ages (cradle to grave) and in all circumstances of life. It is designed to serve as a foundation or base for the development of catechetical materials appropriate for every time and circumstance of life in contemporary U.S. society.

Not all parts of the document are of equal weight. Only those parts that deal with the teaching of the Church in regard to revelation (chap. III) and the Christian message (parts of chaps. V and VI), and the norms and criteria for teaching these (art. 47) are normative and are thus to be observed by all. The other portions of the directory are also important, but the treatment of such matters as stages of human development, methodology, catechetical roles and training, organization and structures, and resources is subject to change in light of new knowledge or different circumstances.

Bibliography: B. L. MARTHALER, *Catechetics in Context: Notes and Commentary on the General Catechetical Directory* (Huntington, Ind. 1973); *The Living Light* 9 (1972) 7–20; *Religious Education* 66 (1971) 357–363.

[B. L. MARTHALER/W. H. PARADIS]

CATECHISM, IMPERIAL

Name given to the *Catéchisme à l'usage de toutes les Églises de l'Empire français*, published by order of Emperor NAPOLEON I (May 1, 1806). When the CONCORDAT OF 1801 was promulgated, the French government promised in the organic articles (art. 39) attached to it a single liturgy and a single catechism for all dioceses in the country. Unification had previously been urged in the *cahiers* of the clergy in 1789, and its need became more evident with the Concordat's new division of dioceses. Pre-Revolutionary sees were accustomed to their own catechisms. New dioceses often comprised portions of three or four former ones, with the result that there were instances of several different catechisms in use within a single diocese. The task of composing a uniform catechism was confided to the Director of Cults Portalis, and to the worthy Abbés d'Astros and Jauffret, who drew inspiration from the catechism composed for the Diocese of Meaux by Bossuet.

Between the completion of the draft copy (1803) and the published version (1806), Napoleon proclaimed the French Empire. To gain a populace submissive to such innovations as military conscription and the novel taxes suggested by his ambitious policies, and to heighten his authority, he sought more and more to utilize the Church.

At his insistence the chapter in the new catechism on the Fourth Commandment contained audacious statements concerning the respect and affection due to authority, and specifically to Napoleon's person and dynasty. When Pius VII refused to grant needed ecclesiastical approval, Napoleon turned to the compliant CAPRARA, papal legate to Paris, and pretended that his approbation was that of the Holy See.

This catechism's deviation from traditional Catholic teachings on submission to authority, and its endeavor to remove from bishops liberty to establish the text of the catechism caused lively emotion among French Catholics, and in Rome. Despite the Emperor's injunctions, episcopal submission was merely nominal. On one pretext or another bishops avoided use of the catechism. In Belgium, opposition was open; in France, it kept increasing with Napoleon's persecution of Pius VII. In 1814, with Napoleon in defeat, King Louis XVIII hastened to suppress the Imperial Catechism, and to restore to each bishop the power to provide a catechism for his own diocese.

Bibliography: A. LATREILLE, *Le Catéchisme impérial de 1806* (Paris 1935).

[A. LATREILLE]

CATECHISM OF THE CATHOLIC CHURCH

The *Catechism of the Catholic Church,* promulgated by Pope John Paul II on December 8, 1992, is a compendium of Catholic doctrine that serves as a reference text for teaching and particularly for preparing local catechisms. Modelled on the so-called "Roman Catechism," promulgated in 1566 by the Council of Trent, the *Catechism of the Catholic Church* is divided into four parts of unequal length: the profession of faith, the celebration of the Christian mystery, life in Christ, and Christian prayer. Part one introduces the reader to God's revelation and is organized around the tenets of the Creed. Part two explains how God's plan for salvation is made present in the sacred actions of the Church's liturgy, especially in the sacraments. Part three presents Catholic tradition on law and grace and the principles of Christian morality found in the Commandments. Part four outlines the meaning and importance of prayer in Christian life and explains the petitions of the Lord's Prayer.

The Catechism of the Catholic Church consists of 2,865 numbered paragraphs, with extensive cross-references in the margins and an analytical index. The text itself is distinguished by the use of large and small print. The body of the text, in large print, presents the

teaching of the Church; passages in small print offer supplementary explanations, generally historical or apologetic, and quotations from patristic, liturgical, magisterial, and hagiographic sources. Further, at the end of each thematic unit, there is a series of condensed formulas that summarize the main points of the foregoing section. The original French edition ran 676 pages; the English edition published in the United States, 803 pages.

History. The development of the *Catechism of the Catholic Church* began with a recommendation by Bernard Cardinal Law, archbishop of Boston. In the course of the proceedings of the Extraordinary Assembly of the Synod of Bishops in 1985 to celebrate the twentieth anniversary of the Second Vatican Council, Law proposed "a Commission of Cardinals to prepare a draft of a Conciliar Catechism to be promulgated by the Holy Father after consulting the bishops of the world." The proposal was endorsed by the Synod and accepted by Pope John Paul II, who, in 1986, appointed a commission of twelve cardinals to oversee the work. It was chaired by the prefect of the Congregation for the Doctrine of the Faith, Joseph Ratzinger, and included American cardinals Bernard Law and William Baum. The actual drafting of the Catechism was delegated to a committee of seven residential bishops, assisted by Christoph Schönborn, O.P., of the University of Fribourg, Switzerland, and later cardinal archbishop of Vienna.

In the initial drafts, prepared through 1987–88, the *Catechism* had three parts and an epilogue. The drafting of part one, the explanation of the Creed, was entrusted to Bishops José Estepa (Spain) and Alessandro Maggiolini (Italy); part two on the sacraments to Bishops Jorge Medina (Chile) and Estanislao Esteban Karlic (Argentina); part three, the section on morals to Jean Honoré (France) and David Konstant (England). Once it was decided to make the section on prayer an integral part of the Catechism, the task of drafting part four was given to an Eastern theologian, Father Jean Corbon of Beirut, a member of the International Theological Commission. The seventh member of the committee, Archbishop William Levada, then of Portland, Oregon, and later of San Francisco, was charged with producing a glossary. In November 1989 the Commission sent the draft text to all the bishops of the world for their consultation. While the text received a generally positive evaluation, the Commission did examine and evaluate over 24,000 amendments suggested by the world's bishops. On June 25, 1992, John Paul II officially approved the definitive text. The formal promulgation of the Catechism came on December 8, 1992, with the publication of the apostolic constitution *Fidei depositum.*

The Interdicasterial Commission that supervised translations into other modern languages approved the

Sister Concepcion teaches a catechism class at the Immaculate Conception Church, Havana, Cuba, 1998. (AP/Wide World Photos)

English language text in February 1994. By 1998 the English edition published under the auspices of the National Conference of Catholic Bishops had sold two and a half million copies.

With the apostolic letter *Laetamur magnopere,* dated August 15, 1997, Pope John Paul II introduced the *editio typica,* the official version in Latin. The new edition incorporated a number of modifications in the text approved by the Pope, which bishops' conferences throughout the world were asked to include in future editions of the *Catechism.* The most notable change to the text was the section on capital punishment, which was changed to reflect Pope John Paul's arguments against the death penalty in his 1995 encyclical *Evangelium vitae.*

In March 2000, the United States bishops' conference published a second edition of the *Catechism* for the United States. This second edition incorporates the modi-

fications promulgated in *Laetamur magnopere,* and includes an English translation of the more extensive analytical index that appeared in the Latin edition and a glossary developed by Archbishop Levada.

Nature and Purpose. The Catechism does not include pedagogical or methodological considerations. The Prologue states:

> By design, this Catechism does not set out to provide the adaptation of doctrinal presentations and catechetical methods required by the differences of culture, age, spiritual maturity, and social and ecclesial conditions among those to whom it is addressed. Such indispensable adaptations are the responsibility of particular catechisms and, even more, of those who instruct the faithful (n. 23).

The Catechism seeks to respond to an authentic need expressed by many for a clear, intelligent, and coherent presentation of the Catholic faith for the present age. According to the prologue of the Catechism:

The Catechism of the Catholic Church is intended primarily for bishops. As teachers of the faith and pastors of the Church, they have the first responsibility in catechesis. Through the bishops, it is addressed to redactors of catechisms, priests, and catechists. It will also be useful reading for all other Christian faithful (n. 12).

Bibliography: Editorial Commission of the *Catechism of the Catholic Church, Informative Dossier* (Vatican City 1992). M. SIMON, *Un Catéchisme universel pour l'église catholique du Concile de Trente à nos jours* (Louvain 1992). J. RATZINGER, "The Catechism of the Catholic Church and the Optimism of the Redeemed," *Communio* 20 (Fall 1993): 469–84. B. L. MARTHALER, *The Catechism Yesterday & Today: The Evolution of a Genre* (Collegeville, Minn. 1995).

[J. POLLARD/D. KUTYS]

CATECHISM OF THE COUNCIL OF TRENT

Also called the Roman Catechism, projected as early in the council as 1546, was completed only after the council, in 1564, and published in Latin in 1566. As its full title indicates—*Catechism of the Council of Trent for Parish Priests Issued by Order of Pope Pius V*—it is not a manual for the faithful but for priests, "a book issued by the authority of the Holy Synod from which pastors and others who hold the office of teaching could seek sure doctrine and then set it forth for the building up of the faithful" (preface). Its authoritative character, comprehensive scope, and irenic tone set it apart from most other catechisms of the time that were the compositions of individuals and often in question-answer form.

The catechism's division into four parts concerned with the Creed, the Sacraments, the Commandments, and the Lord's Prayer, continues the tradition of the medieval catechesis. Its Scripture-steeped structure and content, a distinguishing feature of the Roman Catechism, is reinforced by its constant recourse to the Church Fathers (especially St. Augustine). The catechism's use of the Scholastics, though evident in its definitional and analytical methodology, is relatively minor. The influence of St. THOMAS AQUINAS is obvious, but only as the "Common Doctor" of the tradition. Because it was mandated by the Council of TRENT and issued by order of Pope Pius V, the Tridentine Catechism served as a norm of orthodoxy. Although it was quickly translated into most of the principal European languages, the first English translation, by J. Donovan, was published at Maynooth College in 1929.

Bibliography: P. RODRIGUES et al., eds., *Catechismus Romanus seu Catechismus ex decreto Concilii Tridentini ad parochos Pii V Pont. jussu editus [Editio critica]*(Vatican City 1989). R. BRADLEY and E. KEVANE, eds., *The Roman Catechism: Translated and Annotated in accord with Vatican II and Post-Conciliar Documents and the New Code of Canon Law* (Boston 1985). P. RODRIGUEZ and R. LANZETTI, *El Catecismo Romano: fuentes e historia del texto y de la redaccion* (Pamplona 1982). G. BELLINGER, *Der Catechismus Romanus und die Reformation: die katechetische Antwort des Trienter Konzils auf die Haupt-Katechismen der Reformation* (Paderborn 1970). R. BRADLEY, *The Roman Catechism in the Catechetical Tradition of the Church: The Structure of the Roman Catechism as Illustrative of the "Classical Catechesis"*(Lanham, MD, 1990). B. L. MARTHALER, *The Catechism Yesterday & Today* (Collegeville, MN 1995). HOFINGER, *Lexikon für Theologie und Kirche*, ed. J. HOFER and K. RAHNER (Freiburg 1957–65) 2:977–978.

[P. DE LETTER/R. I. BRADLEY]

CATECHISMS

From the Greek κατηχεῖν (to speak so as to be heard, hence to instruct orally; cf. Lk 1.4; Act 18.25; Rom 2.18; Gal 6.6). A catechism according to an English-speaking and German usage is a manual of Christian doctrine, often in question and answer form (German, *Katechismus*). In Romance languages, the term also signifies the act of catechizing, the work of presenting Christian doctrine or an individual lesson, especially to the young (French, *catéchisme;* Italian, *catechismo*).

Patristic and Early Medieval Periods. Catechisms (*catecheses*) in the patristic era were traditionally prebaptismal and adult in orientation (e.g., Cyril of Jerusalem, Κατηχήσεις John Chrysostom, Ὁμιλίαι κατηχητικαί; Augustine, at the end of *Catech. Rud., Sermones* 212–215; Rufinus of Aquileia, *Commentarius in symbolum apostolorum*). At times these lectures and homilies dealt with the immediately postbaptismal doctrinal needs of new Christians, in which case they were called "mystagogic" or simply "paschal" (e.g., Cyril of Jerusalem, Κατηχήσεις μυσταγωγικαί; Augustine, *Selected Easter Sermons,* ed. P. Weller, St. Louis 1959). Throughout the CAROLINGIAN and early and high medieval periods, numerous handbooks were produced that had the Christian formation of clergy and laity as their aim. Among these might be named the *Disputatio puerorum per interrogationes et responsiones* attributed doubtfully to Alcuin (d. 804; *Patrologia Latina* [PL] 101:1097–1144), the 9th-century *Catechesis Weissenburgensis* by a monk of that monastery (ed. G. Eckhard, Hanover 1713), the 12th-century *Elucidarium* attributed to Honorius of Autun (PL 172:1109–76; cf. Y. Lefèvre, *L'Elucidarium et les lucidaires,* Paris 1954), and the ingenious compendium of Hugh of Saint-Victor in that same century, *De quinque septenis seu septenariis* (PL 175:406–414). These treatises might be called the second layer of adult catechetical formation, suitable for those who could read Latin.

More basic were the catechisms proposed by bishops, emperors, and Church synods to be spoken orally to the unlettered faithful by those who had the *cura animarum*. Among these, which invariably assumed phrase-by-phrase expositions by the clergy of the two baptismal prayers, Apostles' Creed and Our Father, and a list of vices to be avoided, might be mentioned the *Capitularia* of Charlemagne (A.D. 802; PL 97:247) and his letter (15) to Garibaldus (PL 98:917–918); the synods of Leipzig (A.D. 743; PL 89:822, c.25), Clovesho (A.D. 747; J. D. Mansi, *Sacrorum Conciliorum nova et amplissima collectio* 12:398, c.10), Frankfurt (A.D. 794; Mansi 13:908, c.33), Aachen (A.D. 802; PL 97:247, c.14), Arles (A.D. 813; Mansi 14:62, c.19), Mainz (A.D. 813; Mansi 14:74, c.45, 47), and Trier (A.D. 1227; Mansi 23:31, c.8). The synod of Albi (A.D. 1254; Mansi 23:836, c.17, 18) required pastors to explain the articles of the creed simply each Sunday, and children to be brought to Mass from the age of seven onward, and at the same time to have the *Pater, Ave,* and *Credo* explained to them. The Council of Lambeth demanded that this instruction be given by pastors four times a year on feast days, "without any fantastic weaving of subtle adornment," and that it include "the fourteen articles of faith [i.e., the Creed], the Ten Commandments of the Decalogue, the precepts of the gospel, namely the two concerned with charity, the seven works of mercy, the seven capital sins and their progeny, the seven principal virtues, and the seven Sacraments of grace" (A.D. 1281; Mansi 24:410). In 1357 the Convocation of York approved a series of ordinances very similar to the canons of the Council of Lambeth published in 1281 that outlined the contents and frequency of catechetical instruction. They were expanded and translated into English verse for the benefit of the clergy who could not understand Latin. Despite the fact that the work became known as *The Lay Folks' Catechism*, it was written primarily to help parish priests instruct the faithful who in turn were to teach their children. About the same time a council in Lavaur, France issued a similar catechism (A.D. 1368; Mansi 26:486). In the Lavaur catechism a summary of the necessity of faith comes first; next, a severe charge to the clergy on its obligations to catechize; third, the 14 articles and seven Sacraments, "on which the whole Christian religion is based." Seven virtues and their opposing vices come after these "truths to be believed." These, together with the seven gifts of the Spirit and the beatitudes that correspond to them, are the "things that are to be loved," and the seven petitions of the Our Father describe the "things to be hoped for." In the 14 articles of the Creed, seven are said to pertain to the Deity proper, seven others to the humanity of Christ.

Influence of St. Augustine. The scheme of multiples of seven seems to have originated with Augustine's treatise on the Sermon on the Mount (PL 34:1229–1308), in which he reduces the beatitudes to seven by identifying the last one in Matthew's Gospel with the first, then compares them with the seven gifts of the Spirit from the Vulgate version of Is 11 in reverse order that in turn correspond to the seven petitions in the Lord's Prayer. This mnemonic device emerged as supreme in medieval practice via popularizers such as Isidore of Seville, Rabanus Maurus, and especially Hugh of St. Victor's *De quinque septenis seu septenariis*. Hugh's "five sevens" are the seven deadly sins, seven petitions of the Lord's Prayer, seven gifts of the Holy Spirit, seven virtues, and the seven Beatitudes.

A second insight of Augustine was his threefold division of all doctrine in his *Faith, Hope, and Charity* (c. A.D. 422; known as the *Enchiridion;*). In it the "confession of faith is briefly summed up in the Creed. . . . But of all those matters which are to be believed in the true spirit of faith, only those pertain to hope which are contained in the Lord's Prayer" (114), while "all the divine commandments hark back to charity . . . . Of course the charity meant here is the love of our neighbor" (121). Augustine's extended treatment of the creedal articles (9–113) is in the speculative vein. The petitions of the Lord's Prayer (114–116) are seven in number, "three of which request eternal goods, the remaining four, temporal goods necessary for the attainment of the eternal." The Holy Spirit, it is pointed out, "diffuses charity in our hearts" (121).

Although Augustine entirely subordinates the Decalogue to the twofold commandment of love of God and love of neighbor in the *Enchiridion* (117–122), he is often said to have pioneered in presenting the Ten Commandments as a framework for Christian morality (*Catech. Rud.* 35.41). The convenient ten headings prevailed, and indeed in a Mosaic spirit of observance, while Augustine's stress on the Holy Spirit as the finger of God who wrote on the stone tablets and again at Pentecost was largely forgotten (cf. P. Rentschka, *Die Dekalogkatechese des hl. Augustinus, Kempten* 1905).

Paradoxically, Augustine's best insight survived least well, namely, the *narratio* of the story of salvation in six epochs (*aetates*), of which the seventh was eternity, the Day of the Lord. This idea is developed in two sample introductory catecheses at the end of *De catechizandis rudibus*. The landmark figures of the six ages are Adam, Noah, Abraham, David, the Babylonian captivity, and Christ, "from [whose] coming the sixth age is dated" (39). Augustine was still in a millenarian phase at this writing (*c.* 405), but the important matter was his presentation of the Church's faith in a historical framework. He was the first to deal with the life of the Church (the sixth *aetas*) as sacred history in the same sense as the events described in Scripture.

Augustine's greatness as a catechist resided in his musings on the relation between symbol and reality, word and truth, speech and thought. The psychological optimum for the reception of an idea figured largely in his catechetical theory. Lesser teachers, unable to handle his poetic diction or his psychology, gravitated to his reasoned reflections on the mysteries. The result was a rationalized Christianity cut off from its Biblical sources despite the massive use of the Bible made by Augustine (42,816 citations from both Testaments according to P. de Lagarde). The catechisms derived from his writings set the tone of Christianity in the West for 1,000 years. In departing from his Biblical and liturgical concerns and concentrating on his rationale of the mysteries, they created a vacuum of evangelical preaching and catechizing that the Reformers filled.

Middle Ages. Treatises on Christian life, such as Alcuin's *De virtutibus et vitiis* on perfection for the soldier (PL 101:613–638), continued into the Middle Ages as a genre on the art of living and dying. Among these were *L'Art de mourir* attributed to Matthew of Cracow, Bishop of Worms (1478), *Tafel der kerstlygken Levens* (1475), and various shepherd's almanacs filled with secular and sacred information, such as the *Compost ou Kalendrier des bergiers* (Paris 1492). From the invention of printing onward, and even before, woodcut illustrations were used both in books and as wall charts (*tabulae*).

St. Thomas Aquinas. St. THOMAS AQUINAS in his various adult catechetical treatises had not been guilty of an imbalanced concern with Christian behavior. These works were chiefly his *Compendium theologiae,* done on Augustine's pattern of faith, hope, and charity (1272–73, broken off when he was only ten chapters into hope and the petition "thy kingdom come") and the *reportatum* in Latin of 57 of his Italian sermons delivered at Naples during Lent 1273 on the Creed (15), the Lord's Prayer (10), and the law, i.e., charity and the Decalogue (32), to which should be added his earlier conferences on the Hail Mary and a treatise on the Church's Sacraments done for the archbishop of Palermo in 1261. In these lectures, fully scholastic in tone though they were, there was at least a healthy concern for the revealed mysteries.

Jean Gerson. The next major figure in the history of medieval catechesis is Jean GERSON (1363–1429). Forcibly retired as chancellor of Paris in his last years (1409–12), Gerson taught catechism in Lyons and continued to write. He is best known for *L'ABC des simples gens,* for a personal apologia for his engagement in the work of catechizing entitled *Tractatus de parvulis trahendis ad Christum* [*Opera Omnia* (Antwerp 1706) 3.278–291], and an *Opus tripertitum* (*ibid.* 1.426–450) on the Commandments, confession, and dying well. In the last- work the attention given to moral precepts is so considerable that the writer's initial concern with the mysteries of faith has shrunk to a kind of prologue.

Pre-Reformation. The lectures survived in medieval pulpit preaching until Trent, but the strain represented by Gerson's writing continued much stronger. Thus, Dietrich Kolde's influential *Christenspiegel* of 1480 (ed. C. Drees, Werl 1954) was extremely moralistic, as was Johannes Herolt's *Liber discipuli de eruditione Christi fidelium* (Strasbourg 1490). The latter devotes six pages to the Creed, three to the Our Father, and 101 to morality under the headings Commandments, deadly sins, and various moral precepts [cf. P. Bahlmann, *Deutschlands katholische Katechismen bis zum Ende des 16 Jahrhunderts* (Münster 1894) 12; also P. Göbl, *Geschichte der Katechese im Abendland vom Verfall des Katechumenates bis zum Ende des Mittelalters* (Kempten 1880)].

From the close of the patristic period (i.e., from the 9th or 10th century) through the whole Tridentine era, little was done to relate beatitudes, works of mercy, evangelical counsels, fruits of the Holy Spirit, prayer, and almsgiving to the story of salvation as it culminated in the redemptive deed of Christ. They are lumped together with *effectus divinitatis or bona redemptionis,* i.e., related in a most general way to the works of the Spirit that conclude the Apostles' Creed. Although Jungmann's studies (*Pastoral Liturgy,* New York 1962) show the conservative force of medieval culture on folk piety, Rudolf Padberg (*Erasmus als Katechet,* Freiburg 1956) is quite right in describing the entire medieval period as a catechetical vacuum.

Humanism. Late in the fifteenth century a number of humanists, including Erasmus, tried another tack. Among their attempts were the brief *Cathecyzon* (*c.* 1510) by John Colet, Dean of St. Paul's and founder of its school, and Erasmus' adult catechism of 1533 [*Dilucida et pia explanatio symboli . . . decalogi praeceptorum, et dominicae praecationis; Opera Omnia* (Leyden 1706) 5.1133–96]. By the onset of the REFORMATION the Catholic catechisms in commonest use included books of piety such as the *Liber Jesu Christi pro simplicibus* (1505) and the catechisms of J. Dietenberger (Cologne 1530) and G. Witzel or Vicelius (Leipzig 1535).

Luther. The catechism genre took definitive form in the 16th century and became a powerful instrument in the cause of reform. In 1529 Martin Luther published two catechisms, the *Der kleine Katechismus,* his Small Catechism, and his *Deutsch Katechismus* that came to be known as *Der grosser Katechismus,* his Large Catechism. Luther's preface to the Small Catechism clearly stated that it was intended to be in the hands of the lower clergy an instrument to instruct the uneducated laity. It was in the tradition of medieval catechesis, but Luther introduced three notable innovations: First he reordered the sequence, treating the Ten Commandments before explaining the Creed. Second, instead of dividing the Creed into 12 or 14 articles, he focused on three, the salvific work of the Father, Son, and Holy Spirit. And third, influenced by the Bohemian Brethren, he introduced the question-answer method that was to become in a staple in Protestant and Catholic catechisms alike. Luther's Large Catechism is distinguished chiefly by its insight into the daily life of the peasant, its concern with the "existential" character of the gospel, and its reliance on God's action rather than man's as ultimately effective in the work of salvation.

St. Peter Canisius. Canisius, the apostle of Catholic Germany in the Reformation period, produced three handbooks of Catholic faith: a *maior catechismus* (Vienna 1555), a *minimus* bound in with a Latin grammar, as Colet's had been (Ingolstadt 1556), and a *parvus* or *minor* (Cologne 1558). All three were done in Latin first, then in German (*S. Petri Canisii Cat. Lat. et Germ.,* ed. F. Streicher, Munich 1933–36). The intermediate one, entitled *Capita doctrinae christianae compendio tradita . . .*, became normative in many countries. It was composed of 124 questions and two appendices, one of Scripture texts against heretics and the other a quotation from Augustine on steadfastness in faith. There were five parts, three on the theological virtues and the matching prayers (or law), a fourth on the Sacraments, and a fifth on "duties of Christian holiness" (the smallest catechism had featured sins and the opposing goods in this fifth place). The first four doctrinal sections taught *sapientia;* the last, *justitia.* Canisius claimed authorship of the books only in 1566, although publishers had attributed it to him as early as 1559. In 1569 a fellow Hollander named P. de Buys (*see* BUSAEUS) produced with Canisius' help a work that supplied more than 4,000 references to Scripture and the Fathers for the *Catechismus maior* (4 v. Cologne 1569–70); this work is generally known as *Opus catechisticum,* a title given it in its revision by J. Hase (Cologne 1577).

St. Robert Bellarmine. Bellarmine produced his *Dottrina cristiana breve* in 1597 [*Opera omnia* (Paris 1874) 12:261–282], a brief handbook deriving from his instruction of Jesuit brother cooperators at Rome. It began with the sign of the cross, then went on to Creed, Our Father, Hail Mary, Ten Commandments, precepts of the Church, counsels, Sacraments, virtues, gifts, works of mercy, gifts of the Spirit, four last things, and mysteries of the rosary.

A year later (1598), motivated by the demands of office in his brief archbishopric of Capua, Bellarmine produced what might be called a teacher's manual of doctrine, *Dichiarazione più copiosa della d.c. (ibid.,* 283–332). The student is the questioner here, and the teacher, the respondent at length. Bellarmine follows Augustine's three virtues as the way to know what things are *credenda, speranda,* and *amanda.* The Sacraments that follow the threefold listings of obligations (cf. above) are those means "by which the grace of God is acquired." All the matters that come after "the four principal parts of doctrine," i.e., from the theological and moral virtues onward, "help greatly in living in conformity with the will of God."

Other Efforts. The Jesuits Edmond AUGER writing in France (1530–1591) and Jerónimo Martinez de RIPALDA, in Spain (1536–1618) produced handbooks similar to the above two.

The Tridentine Catechism. The Council of TRENT adjourned in 1563, and the catechism its Fathers asked for was ready in Latin (having been composed in Italian) by 1566. A trio of Dominicans led by a certain Foreiro wrote it; a secular priest humanist named Poggianus was the polisher of its phrasing. The CATECHISM OF THE COUNCIL OF TRENT, a manual for parish priests, running to more than 400 pages, is popularly known as *Catechismus Romanus,* though the full title in its first edition (Rome 1566) was *Catechismus ex Decreto Concilii Tridentini ad parochos Pii V Pontificis Maximi iussu editus.* Its fourfold division is: (1) faith and the Creed, (2) the Sacraments, (3) the Decalogue and the laws of God, (4) prayer and its necessity, chiefly the Lord's Prayer. The restoration of the Sacraments to an integral place in the plan of Redemption rather than as aids to observing the precepts is important; so is the book's heavy reliance on Scripture and the Fathers in place of the metaphysically tinged vocabulary of the scholastics. The general tenor of doctrinal exposition is Augustinian.

Attempts such as that of Trent in a humanist vein had been made by Cardinal Stanislaus HOSIUS, *Confessio catholicae fidei christianae vel potius explicatio quaedam confessionis* (Vienna 1561), and by Bp. Friedrich NAUSEA, *In catholicum catechismum libri sex* (Cologne 1543); but all three were fated to lose out in popular exposition to the medieval lists or "truths." Canisius genuinely admired Trent's catechism but his neater summaries and classifications prevailed. Bellarmine said it was his model, but it is doubtful that he understood the attempt it represented. In fact, the little use (more accurately, the highly selective use) made of it by catechism authors since 1566 is perhaps the most notable feature about it. There is reason to think this handbook was quite influential in the pulpit over the years, but again, in proportion to the capacities of the priests who used it. It is quite unmarked by a polemical tone once it has mentioned "pernicious errors" in the introduction. The same introduction gives high promise of a throughgoing evangelical or kerygmatic theology that is never realized. The times were simply incapable of it, the more especially as a genuine evangelical release was overtaking the Church in tandem with unmistakably heretical positions.

After Trent. Post-Tridentine catechisms were in the mold of those by Bellarmine, Canisius, Auger, and Ripalda in the four chief language groups or in translations from one of the first two.

English and American. Laurence Vaux translated and adapted Canisius in 1567 as *A Catechisme of Christian doctrine necessarie for Children and ignorante people* (Louvain 1567; repr. Manchester 1885), deriving additional help from Pedro de SOTO's *Methodus confessionis. . . seu epitome* (Dillingen 1567). What came to be known as the Doway Catechism was produced by Henry Turberville, a professor at the English College there, sometime before 1649, the date of a third edition (*An Abridgment of the Christian Doctrine: with Proofs of Scripture on Points Controverted*). The order is Bellarmine's, but the treatment is Turberville's own. Its tenor is Bible-quoting, polemical, allegorical, adult. Two other British efforts were those of Richard CHALLONER of London (*The Catholic Christian Instructed,* 1737) and George Hay of Edinburgh (*The Sincere Christian,* 1781; *The Devout Christian,* 1783). John LINGARD wrote *Catechistical Instruction on the Doctrines and Worship of the Catholic Church* in 1836 (London 1840). All the above-mentioned were being published in the United States until well into the 19th century. Abp. John CARROLL abridged Hay's larger works (1772) in a form that contributed verbally to the Baltimore catechism. Meanwhile, in Ireland Abp. James Butler of Cashel produced a catechism (1775) that was revised by order of a Synod of Maynooth (1875) and in that form (1882) recommended itself to substantial borrowings in the United States. Archbishop John McHale oversaw a bilingual *Christian Doctrine* (1865) for his Irish-speaking Diocese of Tuam. Among those in the United States who produced catechisms in the 19th century, all of them European-derived, were J. H. MCCAFFREY (Baltimore before 1865) and J. P. A. VEROT (Augusta 1864). The English-language efforts described above were all lineal descendants in the tradition of the "four principal parts of doctrine." When they halted to make a brief explanation, it was generally in the spirit of a work such as Rufinus of Aquileia's *Commentarius in symbolum* or a similar Augustine-derived source.

French. Attempts were made in France in the Enlightenment period to follow through on Augustine's two

Biblical catecheses in *De catechizandis rudibus*. They included Claude FLEURY's *Catéchisme historique* (Paris 1683), which is prefaced by a claim of the superiority of the Bible's method of storytelling and a fairly mild disquisition against the usefulness of theology's method in catechetics. Methodologically Fleury presented material in expository lesson form with prayers from the liturgy interspersed and questions at the end.

François POUGET, an Oratorian, produced a similar Bible-oriented catechism, *Instructions générales en forme de catéchisme où l'on explique en abrégé, par ecriture sainte et par la tradition, l'histoire et les dogmes . . . la morales . . . les sacraments, les prières . . .* (Paris 1702). Fleury subsequently went on the Index as a Gallican; Pouget, too, because his patron Bp. Colbert of Montpellier was a Jansenist. Both catechisms were unexceptional.

Jacques Benigne Bossuet, bishop of Meaux, produced the Biblical *Le second catéchisme* before his formal doctrinal one [*Oeuvres complètes* (Bar-le-Duc 1687) 10].

Italian. Italy broke away from the Bellarmine mold somewhat with the *Compendio della dottrina cristiana* by Bp. Casati of Mondovì (1765). It was in the spirit of the catechisms of Montpellier and Meaux and was probably the work of Canon G. M. Giaccone.

German. Similar forerunners of modern Biblical catechisms appeared in Germany in the 19th century, beginning with the *Biblische Geschichte des Alten und Neuen Testaments* by Bernard von OVERBERG (Münster 1804). J. I. von FELBIGER (1785), C. von SCHMID (1801), I. Schuster (1845), G. MEY (1871), and F. J. Knecht (1880) all produced "Bible histories" in which virtuous conduct was excerpted from the Scriptures to illustrate and augment the catechism lesson. Overberg had the larger vision, seeing the Bible as the "history of God's gratuitous concern for man's salvation." The same idea was found in the *Biblische Geschichte der Welterlöserung durch Jesum der Sohn Gottes* (Augsburg 1806) by B. Galura, Bishop of Brixen. Overberg was the reformer of the schools of Westphalia and a friend of Goethe; he rightly deserves to be named with educators such as Pestalozzi and Herbart. Galura studied at the University of Vienna for a year before his ordination—uncommon enough—and tried to come to terms with the spirit of the *Aufklärung* in his *Grundsätze der sokratischer Katechisiermethode* (1793). In a six-volume reform of the plan of theology, *Neueste Theologie de Christentums* (Augsburg 1800–04), he identified as the *Grundidee* of the Bible the kingdom of God or the kingdom of heaven. Other important figures were Augustin Gruber, Archbishop Of Salzburg (1823–35), who gave lectures to his priests on the

Augustinian technique of the sacred *narratio* and the necessity of inductive explanation before any memory is required (*Katechetische Vorlesungen,* 1830–34); Johann Baptist HIRSCHER, who tried to bridge the gap between sacred history and doctrinal formation in his theoretical essay *Katechetik* (Tübingen 1831) and his larger and smaller Catholic catechisms (Freiburg 1842, 1845); and another professor of the new discipline pastoral theology, J. M. SAILER, whose lectures on that subject (Munich 1788) demanded instruction based on the Bible for pedagogic reasons of concreteness and immediacy, so as to "form man in the divine life rather than instruct him intellectually." It is evident that in German-speaking lands the demands of child nature were being heard for perhaps the first time. France had known something similar through the efforts of the clergy at the parish of Saint-Sulpice, Paris, and of Bp. Dupanloup of Orléans (cf. J. Colomb, "The Catechetical Method of St. Sulpice" in *Shaping the Christian Message,* ed. G. Sloyan, New York 1958); but the pedagogic efforts of the Germans, Austrians, and Swiss were much more realistic in their developmentalist theories on the nature of the child.

A number of 19th-century catechisms tried to depart from subject matter orientation and to center on the individual's natural concern for himself with questions like "Why did God make you?" The only clear result was an anthropocentricism in a pejorative sense. Very shortly the authors were back at the business of a summary of doctrine in theological form with a largely apologetic concern. The great figure in Germany who updated Canisius, but without his Biblical or patristic unction, was Josef DEHARBE, SJ, whose catechism, or *Lehrbegriff* (1847), based on the theological manual of G. Perrone, had a vigorous history (in German-speaking America, among other places). His work was subsequently revised by Josef Linden, SJ (1900), and T. Mönnichs, SJ (1925), the latter the so-called German *Einheitscatechismus.*

Towards a Universal Catechism. With every passing year the number of catechisms grew so that already in 1742 Pope Benedict XIV recommended that Bellarmine's catechism become standard throughout the Catholic world. In 1761 Pope Clement XIII protested against the rationalism of the ENGLIGHTENMENT. He urged a uniform catechetical method that would employ the same words and expressions. In the 1770s Empress Maria Teresa directed Johann Ignaz von Felbiger to edit a series of catechisms for use in the schools throughout Austria and Bohemia. Emperor Napoleon I commissioned and ordered an *imperial CATECHISM,* to be used "in all the churches of the French empire." There was much support for a uniform catechism at the First Vatican Council. After much debate (and some compromise) the Council Fathers approved the *Schema constitutionis de parvo cat-*

echismo(1870). It directed that a short catechism be drawn up, "modelled after the Small Catechism of the Ven. Cardinal Bellarmine." The stated intention was to "facilitate the disappearance in the future of the confusing variety of other short catechisms."

Because of the hasty adjournment of the council, the decree was not promulgated and the project was never heard of again.

There were brief, abortive efforts in the same direction by Pope Pius X in favor of his own *Compendio della dottrina cristiana* (1905) and likewise by Cardinal Gasparri with his three-level *Catechismus catholicus,* which Pope Pius XI praised faintly.

National Catechisms. In the United States the bishops made repeated attempts to reach agreement on a uniform catechism for the whole country. In the wake of Vatican I, they achieved their goal. The *Catechism of the Third Plenary Council of Baltimore* (1885), was the fruit of the labors of J. de Concilio, priest of Newark, and J. L. SPALDING, Bishop of Peoria, Ill. It had 421 questions in 37 chapters and more than 72 pages. There are no "parts"; the order is Creed, Sacraments (gifts, fruits, and beatitudes after Confirmation), prayer, Commandments, and last things. A revision of 1941 by the bishops' committee of the Confraternity of Christian Doctrine, with which the name of F. J. Connell, CSSR, is most closely associated, returned to the order Creed, Commandments, Sacraments, prayer. Both are theological summaries (the latter testifying to little of the theological progress of the intervening 55 years). Neither professes any pedagogical concern.

In a similar vein, France produced a national catechism in 1938 that was much criticized for its length and technical vocabulary. A national commission for its revision was set up in 1941, and in 1947 under the authorship of Canons Camille Quinet and André Boyer a much-improved catechism in the form of a pupil text was produced. It is composed of lessons and has a general Biblical-liturgical orientation, though "doctrines of faith" provide the *Leitmotiv.* Belgium received a revised national catechism unmarked by distinctive features in 1947. The German national *Katholischer Katechismus* appeared in 1955 (Freiburg) after having been begun in 1938 and interrupted by World War II. It is intended for children of the upper elementary years and is in four parts, following the schema of the Creed in 12 articles. Almost half the lessons fall under the heading "The Forgiveness of Sins," including temptation, sin, the Sacraments, and grace. A multivolume teacher's manual, at present incomplete, accompanies it. The initial claims in its favor that it fulfilled all the hopes of the kerygmatic renewal have been tempered somewhat by closer examination, but it is unquestionably a modern watershed. It was translated into 22 languages within five years of its appearance. Although the catechism is anonymous, the men most closely connected with its production included G. Fischer, H. Fischer, F. Schreibmayr, and K. Tilmann. Austria produced a national catechism conceived along similar lines in 1960, guided by Vienna's director of religious education, L. Lentner. England's bishops have one in preparation.

In 1963 and 1964 the Australian bishops published a *Catholic Catechism* for the upper four elementary grades in two volumes with matching teacher's manuals (Sydney). J. Kelly of the Archdiocese of Melbourne was its chief architect. The trend begun in the German catechism is brought to a relative perfection in the two pupil's books of the Australian product. So much is this so that national hierarchies now have to face the question of the merit of expressing the Church's faith in a single, fixed form for school children in these sensitive years. Modern universal literacy is a major consideration. The "official" catechism took its rise in a period of near illiteracy, and its commitment to memory was largely predicated on that fact. Ecclesiologically, the position that saw in the fixed formularies of the catechism a faithful reflection of the *fontes revelationis,* to be coupled, after the Scriptures, with liturgies, creeds, and councils, prevailed for 15 centuries.

In Holland plans for a new catechism were being laid in the 1950s, but under the influence of the Second Vatican Council, the focus changed. *De nieuwe Katechismus,* published by the Dutch hierarchy late in 1966, was designed for adults. A maelstrom of controversy swirled about the "Dutch Catechism" because its critics, friendly and unfriendly, saw it as reshaping the catechism genre and redefining the task of catechesis. Aimed at adults, it sought to bring the Christian message into dialogue with issues of the contemporary world. When a second edition was published (1968), it had a supplement that addressed the points that Church authorities found ambiguous in the original edition.

Despite the controversy that surrounded it, the Dutch Catechism became a model for other national catechisms in that it was directed toward at adults. In 1985 the German Episcopal Conference published a *Katholischer Erwachsenen-Katechismus* (English translation, *The Church's Confession of Faith: A Catholic Catechism for Adults,* San Francisco, 1987). In 1986 the bishops of Spain published *Esta es nuestra fe. Esta es la fe de la iglesia*, a work intended for both young people and adults, especially people responsible for catechesis. The following year the Belgian hierarchy issued *Livre de la foi* (English translation, *Belief and Belonging,* Col-

legeville, 1991), a catechism for adults that the bishops intended as an instrument to aid in the re-evangelization of the country. In 1991 the bishops of France published *Catéchisme pour adultes,* five years in the making. The Catholic Bishops Conference of the Philippines approved a *Catechism for Filipino Catholics* that is described as an "adult catechism" in so far as "it provides *a sourcebook* for those who address the typical Sunday Mass congregation of an ordinary Filipino parish" (par. 16).

In the years following the Second Vatican Council many Church leaders, citing the precedent of the Roman Catechism published after the Council of Trent, called for a new "conciliar catechism." In response to a formal proposal made at the Extraordinary Synod of Bishops assembled to commemorate the 20th anniversary of Vatican II, Pope JOHN PAUL II appointed a commission of 12 cardinals to oversee the compilation of a new catechism. When John Paul introduced the new *Catechism of the Catholic Church* with the apostolic constitution *Fidei depositum* in 1992, he acknowledged that the arrangement of the Four Pillars (Creed, Sacred Liturgy, Christian Way of Life, and Prayer) followed the traditional order found in the Tridentine Catechism. The purpose of the new Catechism is manifold: John Paul wrote that it is "to serve as a sure norm for teaching the faith." It is to provide "the Church's Pastors and the Christian faithful" with "a sure and authentic reference text for teaching Catholic doctrine and particularly for preparing local catechisms." It is a means whereby the faithful can deepen their knowledge of "the unfathomable riches of salvation," an instrument "to support ecumenical efforts" by presenting "the content and wondrous harmony of the Catholic faith," and finally, a reference work for everyone "who wants to know what the Catholic church believes."

The publication of the *Catechism of the Catholic Church* shifts emphasis from uniformity to unity. It signals the abandonment of the quest for a single catechetical text that would be standard throughout the Catholic world. Towards the conclusion of the apostolic constitution *Fidei depositum*, Pope John Paul reiterates the point that the Catechism "is meant to encourage and assist in the writing of new local catechisms, which take into account various situations and cultures, while carefully preserving the unity of faith and fidelity to Catholic doctrine." Thus, as the number of Catechisms continues to grow, they are marked by variety in style and presentation while at the same time witnessing to the unity of faith transmitted by the Scriptures and proclaimed in the Church's liturgy.

Bibliography: E. MANGENOT, *Dictionnaire de théologie catholique,* ed. A. VACANT et al. (Paris 1903–50) 2.2:1895–1968. J. A. JUNGMANN, *Lexikon für Theologie und Kirche,* ed. J. HOFER and K. RAHNER (Freiburg 1957–65) 6:27–54. L. CSONKA, "Storia della catechesi,'' *Educare III* (3d ed. Zurich 1964) 61–190. J. HOFINGER, ''The Right Ordering of Catechetical Material,'' *Lumen Vitae* 2 (1947) 718–746; J. A. JUNGMANN, *Die Frohbotschaft und unsere Glaubensverkündigung* (Regensburg 1936); *Glaubensverkündigung im Lichte der Frohbotschaft* (Innsbruck 1962). R. PADBERG, *Erasmus als Katechet* (Freiburg 1956). G. S. SLOYAN, ed., *Shaping the Christian Message* (New York 1958). P. BRAIDO, *Lineamenti di storia della catechesi e dei catechismi* (Rome 1989). R.BRODEUR, ed., *Les Catéchismes au Québec 1702–1963* (Sainte-Foy/Paris 1990). B. L. MARTHALER, *The Catechism Yesterday and Today* (Collegeville, MN 1995). J.-C. DHOTEL, *Les origines du catéchisme moderne* (Paris 1967).

[G. S. SLOYAN/EDS.]

CATECHISMS IN COLONIAL SPANISH AMERICA

The essence of a Spanish American catechism during the colonial period was the *doctrina cristiana,* and hence the small treatises designed to teach the basics of Christianity were generally known by this title (*see* ENCOMIENDA-DOCTRINA SYSTEM).

Primitive Catechisms. The need for a catechism was felt from the very beginning in the evangelization of the natives of the New World. Father Ramón Pane, the first missionary to Española (*c.* 1495), described the failure of his efforts. He had not used any form of catechism, but apparently relied only on teaching the natives the Our Father and other customary prayers. There is no mention of systematic instruction. With the conquest of Mexico, the first formal catechisms appeared. The earliest known catechisms were written in the picture language of the Aztecs. A fragment of one of them was probably among the Mexican manuscripts collected by Lorenzo BOTURINI BENADUCI. Rediscovered in Mexico (1806) by Alexander von Humboldt and presented to the Royal Library at Berlin, it has since been lost. Another example is the complete catechism of Pedro de GANTE, still preserved in the Biblioteca National of Madrid. Other early catechisms date from the decade after the conquest of Peru. These are generally written in Spanish. One feature of these primitive catechisms is their diversity. The first archbishop of Lima, Jerónimo de LOAYSA, declared that almost every missionary in the diocese had written his own catechism, a situation to which the archbishop objected highly. These catechisms did not merely confine themselves to eternal truths, but also touched on many aspects of earthly existence. They included advice on the need and methods of personal cleanliness for the natives, especially if they were going to confession or Communion; instructions on how to bring in running water and how to take care of bridges; discussions on the obligation of the native peoples to keep roads in repair; and so on.

As the conquest of the Americas was consolidated, pressure mounted for the complete destruction of the old catechisms. There was too much diversity in their doctrinal teaching, and as order was established, counsels governing the personal and civic life of the natives were gradually taken care of by the civil government. As a result, few of the primitive catechisms are extant. The work of their radical revision was facilitated by the Council of TRENT, which issued the Roman catechism. This was used by the Council of Lima (1583), the Council of Mexico (1585), and by Luis ZAPATA DE CÁRDENAS, Archbishop of Bogotá, as the basis for new catechisms for Spanish America.

Printing. Because of the need for dictionaries of the native languages and for catechisms, the Church was responsible for the introduction of the printing press in the New World. Of the 223 titles of works printed in 16th-century Mexico, more than 85 percent were connected with the Church's proselytizing work. In 1544 the *Doctrina breve* was published. Written in Spanish, it contained the elements common to all catechisms of the era: the Ten Commandments, the Creed, the Sacraments, the laws of the Church, the capital sins, works of mercy, and prayers. The first catechism in a native language was that of Alonso de Molina, printed in 1546. Both he and the chronicler-explorer Bernardino de SAHAGÚN wrote in Nahuatl; other works were printed in the Tarasco, Otomi, Pirinda, Mixteco, and Zapoteca dialects. In Peru the *Doctrina christiana y catecismo para instrucción de los indios,* written in Spanish, Quechua, and Aymara, was printed in 1584 by Antonio Ricardo on the first type brought to Mexico. That same type was later passed on to the Jesuits, who took it to the Paraguayan Reductions and were using it there in the 18th century.

Attitudes Shown in Catechisms. In presenting dogmas, such as the Trinity and Incarnation, in the native languages, there was the danger that using native-language terms would cause the pagan meaning to linger. Therefore, if paraphrasing of the concept was impossible, some European words were introduced. The Dominican Martín de León used a combination of native language and Spanish to signify God, saying ''Teotl Dios.'' Others retained the entire Spanish word, such as ''Dios'' or ''Cristo.'' Bishop Zumárraga urged that the Scriptures be translated into the native languages, disagreeing with those who feared putting the Sacred Books in the hands of the newly converted. The catechisms reveal that the Spaniards regarded the native peoples as having the mentality of children. Zumárraga continually advised his priests to use simple language and concepts. The Peruvian catechism of sermons of 1585 warned the missionaries not to preach as if they were in a court or a university, for to do so would overwhelm and confuse their audience. Priests

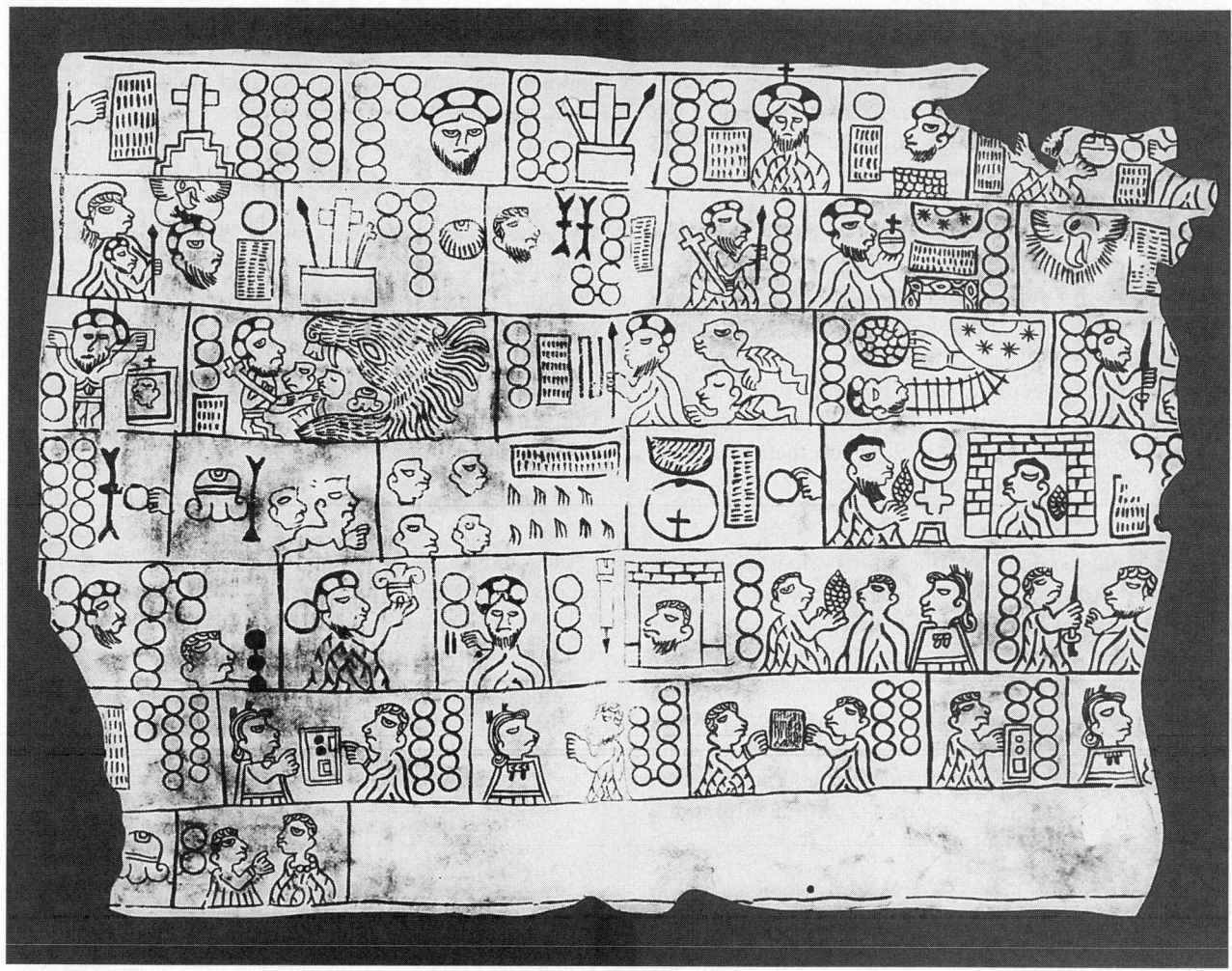

Fragment of a catechism in Mexican picture writing, black ink drawings on agave paper, probably dating from the first half of the 16th century. The pictures read alternately from left to right and right to left. The first picture in the top row is the beginning of an exposition of the Fourteen Articles of Faith; the last picture in row four is the beginning of an explanation of the Ten Commandments.

adapted some native customs to the Christian faith. Pedro de Gante, upon seeing how the natives sang in praise of their pagan gods, composed songs about God, Christ, and the Virgin Mary. Father Lucerno placed great drawings of the Last Judgment in public places to arouse the curiosity of the people and cause them to seek explanations.

The Church was conscious of the danger that mass conversions could result in a superficial knowledge of the Catholic faith. Zumárraga warned in the *Doctrina christiana* of 1546 that some natives were Christians in name and appearance only, but were not well versed enough in their religion to explain it when questioned by nonbelievers. He often stressed the need of real understanding, rather than ceremony and memorization.

Methods and Problems of Teaching. The catechisms were not in a question-and-answer form, but arranged according to themes that were then explained.

Applications were made to daily situations. The Seventh Commandment was explained as prohibiting the use of false weights, mixing bad products with good in order to deceive the buyer, and wrapping tamales in many leaves so as to make them appear larger. Zumárraga presented as violators of the Fourth Commandment those parents who neglected their children, kings who passed unjust laws, and Church officials who cared more for the temporal than the spiritual. Masters who treated their servants badly or who did not pay them fairly were breaking the Seventh Commandment. The Dominican catechism of 1548 explained that because woman was made from man, she should not be regarded as a slave, but rather loved and respected. The concept of the Trinity was explained in native terms with the comparison being made to the rugs they made. The rug could be folded three, four, five times; it was still the same rug. So it was with the Trinity.

Idolatry. The two main obstacles in the initial conversion of the native peoples were idolatry and polygamy. To combat idolatry, the friars utilized reason, fear, and love. Sahagún offered the natives the argument that the pagan gods were unable to free them from the Spaniards because the conquerors were servants of the true, all-powerful God who had helped them. Legendary heroes, such as Quetzalcóatl, were false deities, now dead and burning in hell. The God of the Christians was one of kindness who did not want human sacrifices, wishing instead the reverence and love of the people. The Peruvian catechism demonstrated that upon rejecting their false gods, the natives could love, rather than fear, the grandeur of nature. They should not worship the sun because, as human beings with souls, each one of them was better than the sun, who could not speak, sense, or know about God.

To avoid the danger of the return of paganism, each catechism stressed the difference between honoring Christian images and adoring pagan idols. The natives were warned that drink endangered their souls because it occasioned memories of idolatry. Pedro de Gante separated the upper-class children from their parents, believing that by living in the boarding school they would forget their pagan ways. The educated youths were then sent out to preach Sunday sermons in the surrounding towns.

Polygamy. In the Aztec culture women, besides being wives, were also servants. Consequently, the limitation to one partner in the Christian religion was an economic hardship. This was an impediment in the conversion of the upper class. The promiscuous example of the Spaniards also gave the natives the opportunity to counter the missionaries' reprimand with the observation that many conquerors did not obey the Christian precept.

When a native convert did renounce polygamy and prepared to receive the Sacrament of Matrimony, the problem arose concerning which woman should be his wife: the present partner, his first mate, or his favorite woman. In 1537 it was decided that the legal wife would be the first partner or the woman at the time of conversion. As time progressed and the natives were educated in the faith from early childhood, the difficulties in connection with idolatry and polygamy decreased.

Confession. The catechisms dealt extensively with confession. In the pagan religion there had been a form of confession which dealt with corporal transgressions and carried a judicial pardon. The act of telling sins to the Catholic priest, therefore, was not too different, but the concept of its supernatural character was new. In addition to corporal sins, the friars had to emphasize in their catechisms the sins of thought. Sins committed while intoxicated could no longer be blamed on the liquor rather than on the responsibility of the individual. Most of the books had a formal series of questions that the priest asked the penitent so as to make confession easier and more orderly. Some native penitents experienced difficulty concerning the number of their sins. They did not intend to lie, but because of confusion or fear were not accurate. Martín de León advised confessors to be very patient and not pressure them for exact numbers. Motolinía, one of the original Franciscan priests in Mexico, read a list of sins, and the penitent would signify the number by putting aside a seed or pebble for each transgression. God's mercy and His desire that the sinner change his life were stressed. Generally confession was received once a year in Lent, and Communion, once during the Easter season.

The early catechisms presented the Church in the image of the fatherhood of God. This gave equality to all people in the eyes of God, no matter what their condition on earth. Those who were patient in their sufferings, no matter how conquered or humiliated, would be rewarded with the eternal joys of heaven.

Bibliography: J. G. DURAN, *Monumenta Catechetica Hispano-American* (Buenos Aires 1984). L.RESINES, *Catecismos Americanos del siglo XVI.* (Madrid 1992). E. GARCIA AHUMADA, *Comienzos de la catequesis en America y particularmente en Chile* (Santiago 1991).

[D. E. TANCK]

CATECHIST

From its earliest days the Church recognized that the entire Christian community has the responsibility for catechesis. Modern Church documents, notably the *General Directory for Catechesis* (1997), have assigned this responsibility to individuals according to their position in the Church and their state of life. The bishop has the primary responsibility for catechesis in the local church and presbyters, parents and educators have specific duties and ministries in accord with pastoral needs.

The laity who are called and given this mission from the Church assume different levels of dedication and commitment. Full-time catechists devote their lives to this ministry and are publicly recognized as such. Part time catechists, often volunteers, offer a more limited but very important contribution to parish life.

Formation of Catechists. The General Directory insists that "diocesan pastoral programs must give absolute priority to the formation of lay catechists" (234). Bishops are to be scrupulously attentive to the catechetical formation of priests both in seminary training as well as ongoing clergy formation. Catechetical centers and institutes in many parts of the world, some under the aegis of Catholic universities, some organized by dioceses, have provided opportunities for ongoing catechist formation in the form of courses in scripture, theology or liturgy, retreats and days of prayer, and workshops or seminars on special topics.

The vocation of the catechist is both communal and individual. The Church fosters and discerns this ecclesiastical vocation and confers on the individual the mission to catechize, that is, to foster and strengthen the faith of Christian believers by means of the experience of Christian life as well as by doctrinal formation. The GDC lists three dimensions of the formation of catechists: being, knowing, and 'savoir-faire." These three aspects must be seen as integral aspects of formation and developed in a holistic way.

Being. The formation of catechists begins with the personal formation of the catechists themselves (GDC, 239). They must attend to their maturity as persons, believers, and evangelizers.

Knowing. To be successful the catechist needs to have sufficient knowledge of the message that they seek to communicate, and as well as some knowledge of the background of those to whom they communicate. With regard to the first, formation includes both a biblical-theological foundation and a study of the human sciences such as psychology, sociology and pedagogy (GDC, 243). The doctrinal material is presented within an organic vision that respects the "hierarchy of truths"(241). The program should enable the catechists to articulate their own faith and should enable them to interpret their life experience in light of the gospel message. With regard to the second, it is necessary for catechists to be informed about the social contexts in which they work. Catechesis is effective only when it takes into consideration the actual people to whom it is addressed. Catechists must appreciate and respect their language, customs, symbols, and questions.

Savoir-faire. Knowledge in itself is not enough. In addition, the General Directory stresses the importance of *savoir-faire*, of "knowing how" to hand on the message in a manner adapted to the capacity of those being catechized. It is based on sound educational theory, the ability to organize learning activities and lead effective discussions. The catechists'*savoir-faire* is strengthened by the opportunity to observe the sessions of those more experienced, to plan with and be mentored by other catechists.

Commissioning Catechists. The vocation of the catechist is supported by the witness of the whole Christian community because "catechesis is a work for which the whole church must feel responsible and must wish to be responsible" (CT, 16; GDC, 220). Although faith is a personal act—the free response of the human person to the initiative and self-revelation of God—it is not an isolated act. One can not give oneself faith, nor can one believe without being carried by the faith of others (CCC, 166).

Catechesis is effective to the extent that the Christian community becomes a "point of concrete reference for the faith journey of individuals" (GDC, 158). Since 1935, by the Decree of the Sacred Congregation of the Council (now the Congregation for the Clergy), "On the Better Care and Promotion of Catechetical Education," it has been the practice in many places to observe "Catechetical Sunday" as a way of focusing on the importance of catechesis and to recognize the role of the catechist in the community. It is an occasion to commission catechists within the context of the Eucharist in order to sanction and confirm their call to service in the faith community.

Bibliography: CONGREGATION FOR THE CLERGY, *General Directory for Catechesis* (Washington, DC: United States Catholic Conference, 1997). INTERNATIONAL COUNCIL FOR CATECHESIS, *Adult Catechesis in the Christian Community: Some Principles and Guidelines.* (Washington, DC 1992). CONGREGATION FOR THE EVANGELIZATION OF PEOPLES, *Guide for Catechists* (Washington, DC 1993). C. BONIVENTO, ed., *"Going, Teach . . ."* Commentary on the Apostolic Exhortation Catechesi Tradendae of John Paul II* (Boston 1980). T. H. GROOME and M. J. CORSO, eds., *Empowering Catechetical Leaders* (Washington, DC: National Catholic Educational Association, 1999).

[C. DOOLEY]

CATECHUMENATE

A process by which catechumens, whether adults or children of catechetical age, are prepared for Baptism according to an organized method, which includes liturgical rites as well as instruction; also the state or Order of catechumens, carrying canonically defined privileges.

Beginnings. The origins of the catechumenate can perhaps be found in Judaism, for instruction was required before an adult gentile was admitted to circumcision and proselyte baptism, and similarly before the initiatory washing practiced by the Qumram community. Mention of the catechumen (*katēchoumenos*) and the catechist (*katēchōn*) occurs already in Paul (Gal 6.6). In the Christian Church, Acts contains several examples of instruction given immediately before baptism (e.g. Acts 8.35). The moral teaching of the *Didache* (probably first century) on the 'Two Ways' (1–6) was apparently intended for pre-baptismal recitation (7.1: "having first recited all these things, baptize . . ."). However, there is no evidence for a catechumenate spread over a period of time before the second half of the second century, when its existence is implied by Justin's link of fasting and prayer with instruction (1 *Apology* 61.2). Subsequently a considerable amount can be discovered about the catechetical practices of the early Church, though one must beware of assuming a uniform pattern. Tertullian (d. *c.* 220), writing in Latin, adopted the Greek term *catechumeni* when he reproached heretics for not making a clear distinction between the faithful (i.e. the baptized) and the catechumens (*De praescr. adv. haer.* 41); he recommended the postponement of baptism until the candidate was old enough to receive instruction (*De bapt.* 18). Although the catechetical school in Alexandria was perhaps more of a Christian university than an organization for providing preparation for baptism, both Clement (*Stromata* 2.95–96; *Die griechischen christlichen Schriftsteller der ersten drei Jahrhunderte* pp. 164–5) and Origen (*In Jo.* 6.144–5; *Sources Chrétiennes* 157.240) attest a three-year catechumenate in that city. P. Bradshaw has established that there was diversity in the Alexandrian practice, with evidence of a 40-day catechumenate. The so-called APOSTOLIC TRADITION (17 [ed. B. Botte, *Sources Chrétiennes* 11*bis*]) appears to offer similar evidence for Rome, though allowing the time to be shortened in exceptional cases. *Apostolic Tradition* sets out detailed provisions: members of the community had to vouch for the candidate's way of life (there was a list of prohibited professions) and motives (especially necessary when Christianity was a forbidden religion); we have here the first signs of sponsors and godparents (15–16). The *Ap. Trad.* (18–19) also gives rules for the conduct of catechetical classes, concluding with prayer and the laying on of the hand by the catechist (*doctor*). At the end of the catechumenate the candidates underwent a second investigation as to their observance of Christian morals, again with the support of the testimony of the persons who introduced them; if they passed this test, they were allowed to "hear the gospel" (a phrase which perhaps means receiving systematic instruction on the mysteries of the faith), and after a more intensive final preparation, consisting of a two-day fast, hand-layings, and exorcisms, including a final exorcism performed by the bishop "to ascertain whether (s)he is pure" (the first sign of the Scrutinies: see below), they were allowed to proceed to baptism (*Ap. Trad.* 20). Thus two distinct stages must be differentiated: the actual catechumenate and the final preparation for baptism. In the East those in the latter stage were subsequently called those "given light" (*phōtizomenoi*), since baptism is an enlightenment (Heb 6.4; 10.32; Justin 1 *Apol.* 61.12); in the West "seekers" (*competentes*) or "chosen" (*electi*).

Though Catechumens were not admitted to the Mass of the Faithful or Eucharist proper, they listened to the readings and sermons at the Mass of the Catechumens or Service of the Word. In addition to this instruction, the catechist took the catechumens through the Bible, especially the books that presented the principles of the Christian life and were within the capacity of a beginner. Origen referred to Esther, Judith, Tobias and the Sapiential books (*in Num. hom.* 27.1; *Patrologia Graeca* 12:780–1); in the fourth century Athanasius set out a similar list with the addition of the *Didache* and the *Shepherd of Hermas* (*Ep. fest.* 39; *Patrologia Graeca* 26:1177).

4th and 5th Centuries. At the beginning of this period the Council of Elvira (A.D. 305) provides evidence for the existence of a two-year catechumenate in Spain (can. 42; Hefele-Leclercq 1.245). However, once the conversion of CONSTANTINE brought the period of persecution to an end, there came a new phase in the history of the catechumenate. With the increasing number of conversions it proved impractical to retain the old system. Moreover, partly because of the severity of the penitential discipline for those who relapsed into serious sin after baptism, partly because the obligations of baptism were taken very seriously, it became common in these centuries to postpone the baptism even of the children of Christian parents; Augustine quotes the saying "Let him do what he wants: he is not baptized yet (*sine illum, faciat; nondum enim baptizatus est*)" (*Conf.* 1.11.18). To fill the gap created by the postponement of baptism a child could be admitted into the catechumenate early in life and remain indefinitely in this state, which involved a degree of attachment to the Church and entitlement to the name "Christian" (Augustine, *in Jo.* 44.2; *Patrologia Latina* 35:1714), but not yet the name "faithful," which was reserved to the baptized. Each year as Easter approached there were frequent exhortations for candidates to give in their names (*nomen dare*) for baptism.

Adult pagans who wished to become Christians first received an introductory catechesis, which would be adapted to the candidate's personal needs. Examples can be found in Augustine's *De catechizandis rudibus* (*Patrologia Latina* 40:309–348), which develops the principles for this kind of catechesis and presents two model instructions, a longer and a shorter. If the catechist, a deacon or a priest, was satisfied with the candidate's motives, he was to lead the candidate to faith, from faith to hope, and from hope to love; his instruction was to be characterized by cheerfulness (*hiliaritas*), and would present the divine plan for redemption by telling the story of salvation from the creation of the world and the Fall to the work of Christ and the Last Judgment. The example that Gregory of Nyssa provides in the East in his *Oratio catechetica* (*Patrologia Graeca* 45:9–105) takes a more systematic form. After this preliminary instruction the applicant was admitted into the catechumenate by a rite, which might include the tracing of the sign of the cross on the candidate's forehead, exorcism, the imposition of hands, and (in the West) the administration of salt; Augustine alludes to some of these details in his own reception (*Conf.* 1.11.17). It appears that catechumens could be given salt repeatedly, perhaps as a substitute for the Eucharist (Third Council of Carthage, canon 5: CCSL 149.330; Augustine, *De pecc. merit. et remiss.* 2.26.42; *Patrologia Latina* 44:176). These rites were later combined in the West to form the *Ordo ad catechumenum faciendum.*

In addition to the postponement of baptism discussed above, the freedom from persecution in the fourth century brought about other changes in the catechumenate. Candidates might offer themselves for baptism with inadequate motivation (Cyril of Jerusalem, *Procat.* 3–7). Systematic formation, instead of being spread over two or three years, was now crammed into the few intense weeks between enrollment and baptism (cf. M. Dujarier, pp. 94–7). However, due weight should be given to the instruction the catechumens acquired from their many years listening to homilies, especially at the Sunday Eucharist (cf. W. Harmless, pp. 56–7, 156–7).

Several examples of baptismal catechesis survive from the fourth and fifth centuries. Notable among these are the three sets of sermons delivered by Cyril, bishop of Jerusalem from about 350 to 387: the *Procatechesis,* given at the beginning of Lent to the candidates who had just given in their names for baptism; eighteen Lenten *Catecheses,* most of which are devoted to the exposition of the Creed, which provided a convenient summary of Scripture (*Cat.* 5.12); and five *Mystagogic Catecheses,* given during Easter week, interpreting the meaning of baptism, chrismation, and first communion after they had been received at the Easter Vigil without being explained in advance. Other examples of baptismal catechesis are St. Ambrose's sermons *De Elia et Ieiunio* (*Patrologia Latina* 14:697ff) and *De Abraham* (*Patrologia Latina* 14:419ff) and his instructions *De Sacramentis* and *De Mysteriis* (*Sources Chrétiennes* 25*bis*), St. Augustine's Sermons 56–9 and 212–6 (*Patrologia Latina* 38:377ff and 1058ff), John Chrysostom's *Baptismal Instructions* (*Ancient Christian Writers* 31; *Sources Chrétiennes* 50 and 366), Theodore of Mopsuestia's *Catechetical Homilies* (*Studi e Testi* 145); and at Rome the frequent instructions (*frequentibus praedicationibus*) to which Leo the Great refers (*Epist.* 16.6; *Patrologia Latina* 54:702).

The cultivation of secrecy, called by later historians the *Disciplina arcani* (*see* SECRET, DISCIPLINE OF THE), required knowledge of certain central doctrines, prayers and rites to be withheld until candidates had given in their names for baptism, or even until after baptism. The secre-cy contributed to an aura of sacred dread, which was systematically fostered in the "awe-inspiring mysteries"—a term perhaps borrowed from the pagan mystery-religions on the initiative of Constantine. As an inducement to seek baptism, preachers dangled before the eyes of the catechumens hints of secrets to be revealed only to the initiated: "Those who are initiated understand what I mean" (Chrysostom, *In Gen.* 27.8; *Patrologia Graeca* 53:251). The pilgrim Egeria (*Peregrinatio* 47.2) describes the excitement which Cyril (or possibly his successor John) generated among his hearers by his catechetical preaching. Similar practices are evident elsewhere. At Milan Ambrose explained the meaning of the rites in six instructions entitled *De sacramentis* delivered in the week after baptism. In the region of Antioch, however, John Chrysostom and Theodore of Mopsuestia thought it better to prepare the candidates by explaining the baptismal rites shortly before they were received, though even they deferred the explanation of the Eucharist until after first Communion.

A common feature of the Lenten catechumenate was the Handing Over or Presentation of the Creed (*traditio symboli*), at which the candidate for the first time heard from the bishop the words of the Creed, for they were generally not revealed until a person had been accepted for baptism; sermons preached during this rite by Cyril of Jerusalem, Ambrose and Augustine have come down to us. After learning the words with the help of the godparents (for it was forbidden to write them down), the candidates on a later occasion had to repeat them to the bishop at a ceremony called the Recital or Giving Back of the Creed (*redditio symboli*). In some Churches, e.g. St. Augustine's Hippo, there were similar rites of Presentation and Recital of the Lord's Prayer (cf. Harmless pp. 274–93).

Another rite celebrated in the West from the time of the *Apostolic Tradition,* though not apparently in the East, was the Scrutinies, which seem originally to have been solemn exorcisms overseen by the bishop to ascertain whether the candidates would show by their humble acquiescence that they had been truly delivered from the devil's power, or by signs of resistance that the demonic influence still continued ("we have determined that you are free [from the evil powers]": Augustine *Serm.* 216.11; *Patrologia Latina* 38:1082. Cf. A. Dondeyne, "La discipline des scrutins"). Some texts describe the candidate standing on goat skin during this rite. Both the ritual and the interpretation of the Scrutinies gradually evolved: in Rome at the beginning of the sixth century, according to John the Deacon, three times "we scrutinize their hearts through faith, to ascertain whether since the renunciation of the devil the sacred words have fastened themselves on his mind" (*ad Senarium* 4: *Studi e Testi*

59 [1933] 171, 173). In the same century the Gelasian Sacramentary gives rites for scrutinies on the third, fourth, and fifth Sundays of Lent (*Liber Sacramentorum* [Mohlberg] nn.193–257). Before the end of the sixth century the number of scrutinies has increased to seven (*Ordo Romanus XI*, Andrieu pp. 417–47), by which time they seem to have become little more than solemn exorcisms. This shift, which came about as an elaborate rite for adults, was now used for infants and children. The whole process that was meant to nurture conversion was now transformed into exorcism, an indication that perhaps parents might have benefited from it.

Subsequently, as adult baptism became a rarity except in missionary situations, the adult catechumenate was progressively reduced and ultimately fell into disuse. There is, however, evidence that the parents had to undergo instruction before the baptism of their child (Caesarius of Arles, Serm. 84.6: *Corpus Christianorum* 103.348). Although Gregory the Great still demanded a preparation of 40 days before the baptism of adults, the Apostle of the Suevians, Martin, bishop of Braga in Portugal, recorded a canon that set the requirement at only three weeks (*Capitula* c.49; Mansi 9:855), and even this was not always followed in the case of mass Baptism. In the first printed edition of the *Rituale Romanum* (1487) and in the Sarum Ritual all the preliminaries were compressed into one complicated but inconsistent rite, eventually celebrated at the church door immediately before baptism (Henry Bradshaw Society 99.25ff; Fisher 158–179).

Modern Times. The impetus towards the restoration of a prebaptismal catechumenate came originally from the missionary field. Provincial councils of Mexico and Peru demanded a 40-day period of instruction before baptism; in other places, e.g. the East Indies, a minimum of 20 days was the rule. The directives of the Congregation for the Propagation of the Faith were not consistent, although they did attempt to exercise greater strictness along the lines of the ancient catechumenate. Towards the end of the of nineteenth century some features of the early Christian catechumenate were reintroduced in Africa by Cardinal LAVIGERIE, founder of the Society of Missionaries of Africa ("White Fathers"), who established a four-year preparation for Baptism divided into stages of *postulantes*, *catechumeni* and *electi*; in other parts of Africa a catechumenate of two years was thought sufficient. In addition, the catechetical movement made religious educators conscious of the excessive intellectual emphasis in catechisms, while liturgical studies recalled that the early Church had placed catechesis in a liturgical context.

Consequently, in April of 1962, on the eve of the Second Vatican Council, the Sacred Congregation took a first step towards the revitalization of the baptismal liturgy by publishing a new "Order of Baptism divided into various steps" (*Acta Apostolicae Sedis* 54 [1962] 310–338), which allowed the existing prebaptismal rites to be spread over a more prolonged process of catechetical preparation. The first step linked fundamental catechesis with rites signifying a turning away from error: a renunciation and adhesion, an exorcism by means of the sign of the cross, and the giving of a new name; in the second, salt was administered; in the third, fourth, and fifth steps solemn exorcisms were performed, making the process one not just of instruction but of total conversion; the sixth step comprised the rites which prepared immediately for Baptism, namely the recital of the Creed, a last exorcism, the "opening" of the candidate's ears (cf. Mk 7.34), another renunciation, and anointing with the oil of catechumens; the seventh and final step consisted of Baptism itself followed by chrismation of the candidate's head. Neither confirmation nor first Communion formed part of the process.

There had scarcely been time to implement this reform when the Second Vatican Council resolved to carry it further. The Constitution on the Sacred Liturgy *Sacrosanctum Concilium* (1963) laid down the general directives:

> 64. The catechumenate for adults is to be restored (*instauretur*) and broken up into several steps (*gradibus*), and put into practice at the discretion of the local ordinary. In this way the time of the catechumenate, which is intended for appropriate formation, can be sanctified through liturgical rites to be celebrated successively at different times.

> 65. In mission territories, in addition to what is available in the Christian tradition, it should also be permitted to incorporate ceremonies (*elementa*) of initiation which are found to be customary in each society, provided they can be adapted to the Christian rite . . . .

In 1965 the Council set out more detailed pastoral guidelines in the Decree on Missionary Liturgy (*Ad gentes*). It is stated clearly that the catechumenate is a period not only of instruction but also of gradual spiritual development and introduction to the life of the local community. The catechumen embarks on a "spiritual journey" involving deepening conversion and a "progressive change of sensibility and morals (*sensus et morum*)" which carries "social implications" (n.13). The catechumenate is not

> a mere exposition of dogmas and precepts, but a training in the Christian life as a whole and a probation (*tirocinium*), to be prolonged as need be, by means of which disciples become united with

Christ, their Master. Catechumens, therefore, should be initiated in a suitable way into the mystery of salvation and the practice of the moral teaching of the gospels, and introduced into the life of faith, liturgy, and charity of the people of God through sacred rites to be celebrated successively at different times (n.14).

This process calls for the cooperation not only of clergy and catechists, but of godparents (*patrini*) and the whole community. Subsequently, the U.S. National Statutes for the Catechumenate required the process to be extended for at least a year (n.6).

These directives were put into effect when *Christian Initiation, General Introduction* was published in 1969, followed by the *Rite of Christian Initiation of Adults* (RCIA) in 1972. Baptism, Confirmation, and Eucharist form a unified process as the "sacraments of Christian initiation." The rite is divided into four "periods (*tempora*) for making inquiry and maturing" and three "steps (*gradus*) marking the catechumens' progress as they pass, so to speak, through another doorway or ascend to the next level." The programme is devised as follows (RCIA 6–7):

First period: Evangelization and Precatechumenate. A period of inquiry.

First step: Acceptance into the Order of Catechumens. Conferred when the candidate has reached "initial conversion" and the desire to become a Christian.

Second Period: Catechumenate. The candidate's faith and conversion develop by a process which is not merely intellectual but "directs the heart towards God, fosters participation in the liturgy, inspires apostolic activity, and nurtures a life completely in accord with the spirit of Christ" (U.S. edition 78 [Latin edition 99]). Blessings, exorcisms and other rites are celebrated not merely to mark and encourage progress but also as instruments of formation. Catechumens are already connected to the Church though not yet incorporated into it; they are admitted to the blessings of the faithful and granted a Christian burial (*Codex iuris canonici* 206.1; 1183.1). They are, however, normally dismissed from the eucharistic assembly after they have been prayed for in the Intercessions.

Second step: Election or Enrollment, which ideally takes place at the beginning of Lent. On the basis of the recommendation of the godparents and catechists the local community vouches for the candidate's readiness for baptism (RCIA 119 [22, 133]), and their names are recorded in a book.

Third period: Purification and Enlightenment. This is intended not for instruction but to "purify the minds and hearts of the elect" (RCIA 139 [22,153]). A key element is the Scrutinies, celebrated on the third, fourth, and fifth Sundays of Lent. Instead of being an opportunity for the bishop to judge the effectiveness of the exorcisms, as in the early Church, they have become "rites for self-searching and repentance," designed to "complete the conversion of the elect" (RCIA 141 [25, 154]). Later in this period the "Presentations" of the Creed and the Lord's Prayer are celebrated; on Holy Saturday the candidates recite the Creed they have learned; the public recitation of the Lord's Prayer takes place at the baptismal Eucharist.

Third step: the three sacraments of Baptism, Confirmation, and first Communion, ideally celebrated during the Easter Vigil.

Fourth period: Mystagogy. This is "a time for the community and the neophytes together to grow in deepening their grasp of the paschal mystery and in making it part of their lives through meditation on the Gospel, sharing in the Eucharist, and doing works of charity" (RCIA 244 [37]).

Particular Circumstances. The Ordo provides for adaptation for children who were not baptized as infants and have attained catechetical age. They are enrolled as catechumens, and after a formation of several years if needed (USA RCIA no. 253) they are fully initiated through the sacraments of Baptism, Confirmation, and Eucharist as are adults.

The revised OICA has also influenced the formation of adult Catholics who were baptized as infants but not catechized, and the reception of candidates into the full communion of the Catholic Church, namely those who were initiated in other Christian churches but now seek to join the Roman Catholic Church. Because they have already been baptized, their status differs significantly from the catechumens, who have not been baptized. The rite insists that "no greater burden than necessary is required" (U.S. 473, R 1) for their formation. It insists that "anything that would equate candidates for reception with those who are catechumens is to be absolutely avoided" (US 477, R 5). The U.S.A. provides liturgical rites to mark the candidate's formation, but these are distinct from the rite for catechumens. The high point of reception is eucharistic communion. This is preceded by the profession of faith and an act of reception, followed by confirmation if required.

Thus much of the ritual and the terminology of the early Church has been reintroduced, though sometimes, as with "Scrutinies" and "Mystagogy," not only the rites but also the meaning of the terms has undergone change.

Bibliography: *Rite of Christian Initiation of Adults* (Study Edition, Chicago 1988). H. LECLERCQ and P. DE PUNIET, *Dictionnaire d'archéologie chrétienne et de liturgie* 2.2: 2530–2621. A. DONDEYNE, "La Discipline des scrutins dans l'église latine avant Charlemagne," *Revue d'histoire ecclésiastique* 28 (1932) 5–33, 751–787. T. MAERTENS, *Histoire et pastorale du rituel du catéchuménat et du baptême* (Bruges 1962). J. D. C. FISHER, *Christian Initiation: Baptism in the Medieval West* (London 1965). *Concilium* (UK) 54 (1967) 72–88, "Evangelization and Catechumenate in the Church around the World." M. DUJARIER, *A History of the Catechumenate: The First Six Centuries* (New York etc. 1979). A. BUGNINI, *The Reform of the Liturgy 1948–1975* (Collegeville 1990). E. J. YARNOLD, *The Awe-Inspiring Rites of Initiation* (2nd ed. Edinburgh and Collegeville 1994). W. HARMLESS, *Augustine and the Catechumenate* (Collegeville 1995). M. E. JOHNSON, *The Rites of Christian Initiation: Their Evolution and Interpretation* (Collegeville 1999).

[E. YARNOLD]

CATEGORICAL IMPERATIVE

The Kantian categorical imperative follows from a conception of rational morality that is valid and binding for all rational minds. Just as KANT, in his *Critique of Pure Reason*, considered rational science as knowledge valid and binding for all rational minds, so in his *Critique of Practical Reason*, he considered morality as comparable to science in the sense of being true necessarily and universally without qualification. The categorical imperative is categorical not because of a divine command, nor because of a conformity with nature, nor because of any consensus, however large; rather it has the category of an a priori. Once rational knowledge and rational morality are agreed to, according to Kant's reasoning, their universality and validity give evidence of their a priori character.

Explanation. The principle of Kantian rational morality is that an act is moral if and only if the principle in the act is capable of universalization without an internal contradiction. Even more fundamental for Kant, however, is the deontological primary principle that "there is nothing in the world or even out of it that can be called good without qualification except a good will." The principle on which the good will wills its acts must not contain any implication of circumstances or pragmatic consequences, because these would introduce contingencies that Kant wished to avoid. The right act is determined, for him, by a principle that is the same for every individual regardless of circumstances. To admit contingent circumstances would destroy the purely rational and categorical nature of the imperative.

First Formulation. Such reasoning led Kant to the first formulation of his categorical imperative: "Act only on that maxim which you can at the same time will to become a universal law." This categorical imperative is present in every moral act that is obligatory in itself without reference to any other end. In this way the categorical imperative is distinguished from the hypothetical, which represents the practical necessity of a possible act as a means to something else that is willed or might be willed. An act that is good only as a means to something else is commanded by a hypothetical "ought" or imperative, but an act that is conceived to be good in itself without any ordination to a further end is commanded by a categorical "ought" or imperative. The hypothetical imperative asserts only that an act is good for some purpose, actual or possible. The categorical imperative declares an act to be binding and exacting in itself, without reference to any purpose or end beyond itself.

If nothing can be called good without qualification except a good will, the good will is good in itself and not because of what it accomplishes or the uses to which it is put. Even if a good will achieves nothing, for Kant it is comparable to a jewel that would shine by its own light as something with intrinsic value. This good will operates solely from the motive of duty, not because God commands the act, but because it is good in itself. This deontological strain in Kant leads him to consider the good will as the will to do what ought to be done on the presupposition that man is free. Freedom and duty are reciprocal terms for Kant, although he admits that morality requires man only to be able to think freedom without self-contradiction, not to understand it. Freedom is postulated by the moral law, but human intelligence will never fully uncover how freedom is possible.

Other Formulations. Kant stated the categorical imperative in two other forms in addition to the one enunciated above. The second form was "Treat every rational being including yourself always as an end, and never as a mere means." The third form asserted that "a principle of moral conduct is morally binding on me if and only if I can regard it as a law which I impose on myself." The latter form stresses the autonomous morality of Kant, which denies that the moral law is something imposed upon man *ab extra*.

Critique. All three formulations of the Kantian categorical imperative have been criticized on the grounds of their ETHICAL FORMALISM, which would in application lead to conclusions opposed to established moral judgments. Refusing to repay borrowed money, for example, does not seem to involve a contradiction that is purely logical or formal, but it is dependent upon social and economic conditions in which people would not lend money if there were no assurance of repayment. A good will seems to require definition in terms of content as well as form. Again, a formal principle or categorical imperative to obey laws that are universal and necessary leaves out of the moral sphere the performance of unique acts in particular existential circumstances. It implies a consistency and uniformity in good acts that is not borne out in practice, where moral life is rich in diversity.

Kantian formulations of the categorical imperative are to be criticized as much on grounds that they cannot be validly applied as on grounds of their formalism. In addition there is a rigidity, an inflexibility, and a harshness in the application of these principles. They restrict morally good acts to those done out of respect for the moral law; and yet it is good to help others from motives of compassion and love when duty and obligation are not clearly present. These motives have independent moral value according to most moralists, but Kant seems to consider all inclinations other than that to duty as morally irrelevant. He also confuses the goodness of an act with the merit one receives in performing it.

For the philosopher with theistic presuppositions there is a further criticism of the autonomous, rather than the heteronomous, nature of Kantian morality. The human reason does not create morality; it merely articulates morality in practical prudential judgments of conscience, which may be termed the ''prismatic analysis'' through which the law of God is transmitted. Obligation is not self-imposed; it is heteronomously imposed through the mediation of law in the individual conscience of man. Circumstances and motives are required for the existential consideration of the moral act, and the moral act is good if motivated by charity as well as by duty.

Kant's dissatisfaction with a theistic ethics arose both from his own moral philosophy and his epistemology. For him a theistic ethics would imply a theological voluntarism, because the divine perfection in such an ethics would be God's will considered as independent of His goodness and wisdom. However one may criticize theological voluntarism, even Kant would not conclude that in such an ethic *every* moral law would depend exclusively on God's will alone. Kant's fundamental objection to a theistic ethics arose from his epistemological position that God is accessible neither to intuition nor to demonstrative knowledge. Thus any critique of the Kantian categorical imperative is reductively a critique of Kant's philosophical position on the possibility of man's speculative knowledge of God and of the nature of the moral ''ought.''

See Also: DEONTOLOGISM; ETHICS, HISTORY OF.

Bibliography: I. KANT, *The Moral Law; or, Kant's Groundwork of the Metaphysic of Morals,* tr. and ed. H. J. PATON (New York 1948). W. T. JONES, *Morality and Freedom in the Philosophy of Immanuel Kant* (London 1940). J. D. COLLINS, *A History of Modern European Philosophy* (Milwaukee 1954).

[T. A. WASSMER]

CATEGORIES OF BEING

The categories of being are defined variously as the most general predicates expressive of real BEING or as pure conceptions of the understanding. The most important and influential doctrines on the categories are those of ARISTOTLE and KANT. Since Aristotle's elaboration of a doctrine of categories is prior to Kant's and may well have been the first (*see* Plato, *Soph.* 254B, for a possible adumbration), it is granted priority of exposition here.

The Greek term κατηγορίαι, meaning predicates, links the doctrine of categories with the PROPOSITION. This simple fact has been the cause of a number of different views on the origin and nature of the doctrine of categories in Aristotle. Some have maintained that the doctrine arose from a consideration of grammar; others that it is a logical doctrine that came to have ontological import; others that, originally an ontological doctrine, it came to be expressed in logical terminology. Since there was no developed grammar in the relevant sense for Aristotle to rely on and since the doctrine of categories makes distinctions where grammar would not and does not honor possible grammatical distinctions, the first view is implausible. The other views involve a problem that, as applied to Aristotle, is often anachronistic. For when it is asked whether the doctrine of categories is logical or metaphysical, it is not always clear whether the question turns on the meaning these adjectives might have had for Aristotle or on the meaning they have today. Yet, even when restricted to the Aristotelian perspective, one cannot always grasp the precise import of a given statement about the categories. If the categories are predicates and genera, it is not the case that every predicate falls within a category. Indeed, Aristotle broaches the problems of metaphysics by way of the categories, thereby indicating that the categories are not a list of just any uses of being, but are rather the highest genera predicable of real being as opposed to accidental being. Therefore, if the categories, since they are genera, are logical, they are logical relations that attach to real being. In short, they are not classifications derived from language simply, but classifications found in language expressive of real being.

Aristotle's treatise on categories. Although its authenticity has been questioned, most scholars now accept the *Categories* as the work of Aristotle. This treatise prefaces the actual listing of the supreme genera with a number of distinctions that indicate what the author intends to do. First it notes that some verbal expressions are complex while others are incomplex. A complex verbal expression is one that admits of truth or falsity; for example, ''The man runs.'' Incomplex expressions are neither true nor false and can be components of complex expressions. Examples of incomplex expressions are ''man'' and "runs." The categories themselves are incomplex expressions.

Aristotle then distinguishes being predicable of a subject and being present in a subject. To be present in a subject means to pertain to the subject accidentally and not essentially; thus what is present in a subject in this sense is not part of the subject's QUIDDITY. The author adds that what is present in a subject is incapable of existence apart from a subject. What is predicable of a subject, on the other hand, means whatever can be said of a subject whether essentially or accidentally. Predicability involves universality and on this assumption, Aristotle divides things themselves as follows: (1) Some things are predicable of a subject but are never present in a subject; the author has in mind universal expressions of what a thing is, such as "man". (2) Some things are present in a subject but are never predicable of a subject; such are singular accidents, for example, a particular whiteness. (3) Some things are both predicable of a subject and present in a subject; these are accidents considered universally, for example, whiteness. (4) Finally, some things are neither present in a subject nor predicable of a subject; for example, the individual man or the individual horse.

Substances are precisely things of this fourth kind. Aristotle calls such singular entities first substances; second substances are all predicates that can be affirmed essentially of first substances, that is, things falling in the first class. Examples of second substance, accordingly, are: man, horse, animal, living organism and finally, substance itself.

If man can be predicated of Socrates and animal can be predicated of man, then animal can be predicated of Socrates. This observation indicates that a hierarchy of predicates can be found that will end ultimately with such terms as substance.

Aristotle then lists his categories: "Incomplex expressions signify either substance, quantity, quality, relation, place, time, situation, condition, action or passion" (*Cat.* 1b, 25–27). Aristotle offers the following examples of things of which these are predicated as supreme genera: of substance, man or horse; of quantity, two inches long; of quality, white and grammatical; of relation, double, half and greater; of place, in the market, in school; of time, last year and yesterday; of situation, lying and sitting; of condition, shod and armed; of action, to lance, to cauterize; of passion, to be lanced, to be cauterized. Such expressions are neither true nor false, although true or false expressions are composed from them.

Categories and real being. Aristotle's intention in enumerating these ten highest predicates or supreme genera is not made explicit in the *Categories,* as it is else-

where. That he was not merely classifying all possible predicates is evident enough from the *Metaphysics* (1017a, 7–1017b, 9). Acutely aware of the variety of uses and meanings of "is" and "being," Aristotle emphasizes that not every use of these terms is relevant to the science of being as being. Some uses do not purport to assert that what is said "to be" exists independently of human knowledge. Yet even when interest is confined to real being, "being" and "is" do not have a unique sense. "On the other hand, the varieties of essential being are indicated by the categories; for in as many ways as there are categories, may things be said to be. Since predication asserts sometimes what a thing is, sometimes of what sort, sometimes how much, sometimes in what relation, sometimes in what process of doing or undergoing, sometimes where, sometimes when, it follows that these are all the ways of being" (1017a, 22–27; tr. Hope).

In an effort to understand the things that are, man arrives at knowledge that expresses itself in such propositions as "Socrates is man," "Socrates is seated," "Socrates is five feet tall." Predicates attributed to such entities as Socrates are not all of a piece, however, though some (for example, "man," "animal" and "living thing") are related as more and less general. To say of Socrates that he is seated is not an expression of what Socrates is essentially, but of something "present in him." Since for a thing to be is for it to be something or other and what it is said to be relates to it, either essentially or accidentally, the categories are the logical arrangement of predicates expressive of modes of real being.

Logic vs. ontology. Is Aristotle's teaching on the categories a logical or metaphysical doctrine? To be a SUBSTANCE or an ACCIDENT is a mode of real being; the names of the supreme genera, like the names of subordinate genera and of the ultimate species, are not logical terms. Moreover, Aristotle speaks of the categories of *being.* On the other hand, to be a predicate is no more an ontological characteristic than to be a GENUS, SPECIES or difference and yet these terms figure prominently in the elaboration of the doctrine (*see* PREDICABLES).

Such considerations have led a significant number of scholars to say of the doctrine of categories that it lies in the shadowy region between logic and ontology. Perhaps it is more accurate to say that what is categorized is real being, but that to be categorized, to be a genus or species, is to take on a logical relation. If it is generally true that logical relations attach to real things because of our way of knowing them, the apparently anomalous character of the categories also furnishes a general view of the nature of the logical. There is nothing merely logical about being a substance, but to say of substance that it is a supreme genus is to relate the content of one concept to the meanings of a number of predicates subordinate to it, and like it, expressive of the natures of things like Socrates and Alcibiades. To say of substance that it is a category, then, is like saying of horse that it is a species; in both cases one is asserting of something real a kind of predicability that is consequent upon man's abstractive manner of knowing real things (*see* ABSTRACTION).

The reluctance to call the doctrine of categories logical is based on the recognition that substance, quantity, quality, etc., signify modes of real being; the reluctance to call the doctrine ontological is based on the recognition that the ascending series of predicates, man-animal-living substance, does not answer to any real division in the thing of which all these terms are predicated. Moreover, it would be fallacious to argue as follows: Substance is a supreme genus; man is a substance; therefore, man is a supreme genus. For real being to fall into the schema of the categories, it must be universal, but universality and predicability are not ontological characteristics. Therefore the correct conclusion is this: only real being falls under the categories; but, in order to be in a category, real being must be considered as the subject of such logical relations as predicability, genus and so forth.

Kantian categories. Kant arrives at his categories, which are principles of pure or a priori synthesis on the part of the understanding, by a consideration of classes of judgment (*Kritik der reinen Vernunft*). These classes are more reminiscent of Aristotle's *On Interpretation* than of his *Categories,* for they involve the comparison of propositions with respect to their quantity, quality and modality, together with the notion of simple and complex propositions. Kant suggests that, if one abstracts from the content of judgments and concentrates on their form alone, he finds that the function of thought in a judgment can be brought under four headings: quantity, quality, relation and modality. Each heading comprises three "moments." With respect to quantity, judgments are universal, particular or singular; with respect to quality, they are affirmative, negative or infinite; with respect to relation, they are categorical, hypothetical or disjunctive; with respect to modality, they are problematical, assertorical or apodictical. Kant gives at this point a hint as to why he has called these trichotomies moments. Speaking of modalities of judgment, Kant says that problematical judgments are those in which an affirmation is accepted as merely possible; in assertorical judgments the affirmation is regarded as true; in the apodictical it is regarded as necessary. In a note he suggests that it is as if thought were in the first instance a function of UNDERSTANDING, in the second of JUDGMENT and in the third of REASONING.

Kant connects what he chooses to call categories with these divisions of the form of judgments: by a category he means a pure conception of the understanding applicable a priori to objects of INTUITION. Since the table of judgments exhausts the function of the understanding, one should be able to arrive at an exhaustive enumeration of categories. The categories of quantity are unity, plurality, totality; those of quality are reality, negation and limitation; the categories of relation are substance and accident, cause and effect and reciprocity between agent and patient; those of modality the pairs: possibility-impossibility, existence-nonexistence, necessity-contingency. The function of the categories is to render the manifold of sensuous intuition conceivable; they are, so to speak, the a priori patterns of understanding that constitute the OBJECTIVITY of objects. Kant compares his own results with Aristotle's and observes that the Greek philosopher, not having a guiding principle, hit upon his categories in a haphazard and adventitious manner.

Criticism of the categories. Kant's doctrine of categories is neither the same sort as Aristotle's, as he misleadingly suggests, nor a relevant criticism of the earlier doctrine. The term category functions so differently in these authors that no direct comparison of the two lists of categories is illuminating. One must rather go to the most general presuppositions of Aristotelian and Kantian philosophy. Depending on which basic option one prefers, one of these doctrines will be regarded as hopelessly wrongheaded; in more sanguine moments, one will doubtless find some remote glimmer of plausibility in the other view, though not think of it as a doctrine of categories.

Difficulties of much the same kind arise when one turns to contemporary discussions of categories that are influenced by the theory of types (*see* ANTINOMY). Such discussions often suggest that Aristotle intended to formulate a general theory of types of predicate, and find, of course, that the Aristotelian categories are woefully inadequate. Here, too, the initial impression that wholly opposed views are being juxtaposed soon gives way to the thought that the views may after all be complementary. Such an irenic moment is achieved, however, at the expense of any genuinely common meaning of the term category, since agreements are not reached under the aegis of what either side would be willing to call categories.

The main complaint of J. S. MILL against the Aristotelian categories was that they left out of account such realities as man's feelings. One is tempted to see as akin to Mill's more recent suggestions that, since the categories are classifications of things and man is not a THING, "existentials," or categories of human being, must be devised.

The fate of the Aristotelian doctrine of categories depends on one's ability to resist the anachronistic impulse to see what adumbrations of familiar procedures can be discovered in Aristotle and to regain the more basic kind of thinking underlying science and logic that permeates Aristotelian philosophy. From a variety of quarters, notably from PHENOMENOLOGY, philosophers are being urged to recognize the continuing and fundamental validity of a knowledge that requires taking the knower into account. Perhaps it is only by heeding these suggestions that one can grasp the nature of the Aristotelian categories.

See Also: SUBSTANCE; ACCIDENT; QUANTITY; QUALITY; RELATION; PLACE; SITUATION (SITUS); ACTION AND PASSION; TIME.

Bibliography: L. M. DE RIJK, *The Place of Categories of Being in Aristotle's Philosophy* (Assen, Netherlands 1952). M. SCHEU, *The Categories of Being in Aristotle and St. Thomas* (Catholic University of America, Philos. Stud. 88; Washington 1944). R. J. BLACKWELL, "The Methodological Function of Categories in Aristotle," *The New Scholasticism,* 31 (1957) 526–537. J. A. OESTERLE, *Logic, the Art of Defining and Reasoning* (2d ed., Englewood Cliffs, N.J. 1963). L. DE RAEYMAEKER, *The Philosophy of Being,* tr., E. H. ZIEGELMEYER (St. Louis 1954). R. E. MCCALL, *The Reality of Substance* (Catholic University of America, Philos. Stud. 168; Washington 1956). G. RYLE, "Categories," *Logic and Language,* ed., A. G. N. FLEW (2d series; New York 1953) 65–81. E. FREEMAN, *The Categories of Charles Peirce* (Chicago 1934).

[R. M. MCINERNY]

CATENAE, BIBLICAL

Biblical catenae (from *catena,* chain; fuller name, *catenae patrum*) are commentaries made up of short excerpts from the Fathers or other ancient writers, strung together like the links of a chain to form a continuous exposition of a passage of Scripture. The first use of the name *catena* in this sense appears to be in the *editio princeps* of the *Catena Aurea* (1484) of St. THOMAS AQUINAS, although he himself had described this work as an *expositio continua* of the four Gospels. Among earlier names were exegetical eclogues, collected explanations and simply interpretations. Some catenae are drawn from one Father exclusively; others from two or three, with an evident attempt to give equal place to the Antiochene and Alexandrian schools of exegesis; still others are based on as many as 80 or more sources. In the better catenae each excerpt is introduced by the name of the commentator or by an identifying abbreviation. Where this is not the case, some excerpts can only be tentatively ascribed to a given Father or be left as of unknown authorship. As this suggests, much research remains to be done in this field. In typical appearance the manuscript has either only relatively few words of text in large letters in the center of the page surrounded by abundant commentary, or the text is immediately followed by the commentary written in parallel columns. There are Greek, Latin and Eastern (mostly Syriac) catenae.

Greek Catenae. These are valuable to both the exegete and the textual critic. For the former, they possess a unique importance in that they offer him a vast storehouse of otherwise unknown patristic exegesis. It is estimated that over half of the commentaries of the Fathers have been preserved through catenae, including passages from heretical writers otherwise doomed to possible oblivion. To the textual critic, as so far studied, catenae reveal many variant readings of the HEXAPLA text. In both these respects Latin catenae are far less important than Greek ones, since they present the Biblical text and much of the commentary only in translation.

Greek catenae first appeared as the golden age of patristic exegesis came to a close at the end of the fifth century. Original, creative commentators gave way to compilers of exposition culled from their predecessors. At the same time the very mass of accumulated commentary created the need for some sort of analysis and methodical classification, if it was to be made generally available. The earliest known Greek to compile extensive catenae is PROCOPIUS OF GAZA (d. 538), who edited a commentary on the Octateuch (the Pentateuch plus Joshua, Judges and Ruth) drawn from the writings of CYRIL OF ALEXANDRIA, BASIL THE GREAT and GREGORY OF NYSSA. He compiled catenae also on 1 and 2 Samuel, 1 and 2 Kings, 1 and 2 Chronicles, Isaiah and Song of Songs. Among other Greek catenists are Olympiodorus of Alexandria (6th century), John Drungarios (7th century), Andreas the Presbyter (7th century) and Nicetas of Heraclea (11th century).

Latin Catenae. With roots going back to BEDE's commentaries, Latin catenae came to flower during the 11th century as part of the CAROLINGIAN RENAISSANCE. This medieval revival of learning gave a place of preeminence to the Bible and its patristic exegesis. The compilation of catenae was encouraged, and by the end of the ninth century virtually every book of the Bible had its commentary pieced together from the Fathers. Outstanding among early catenists were ALCUIN (d. 805), CLAUDIUS OF TURIN (d. 827), RABANUS MAURUS (d. 865) and WALAFRID STRABO (d. 849). For two centuries following their first appearance, Latin catenae went through a period of deterioration. Compilers were unlearned, their work careless and uncritical, and their exegesis often inconsistent if not in contradiction with itself. Spurred on perhaps by the reform in theological FLORILEGIA (for example, Peter ABELARD's *Sic et non*), scripturists undertook to remedy this confused state of affairs. Thus, by degrees, out of the chaos of the 11th century just described and as a by-product of scholasticism, came improvement culminating in the *expositio continua* of St. Thomas on the four Gospels, later known as the *Catena Aurea,* a model for all future labors. Its excerpts, drawn from over 80 sources, are gracefully interlocked to produce pleasant as well as instructive reading (repr. Turin 1938; Eng. tr. 4 v., Oxford 1841–45).

Among modern works akin to the medieval catenae are: J. M. Péronne, *La Chaine d'or sur les psaumes,* 3 v. (Paris 1879); J. M. Neale and R. F. Littledale, *Commentary on the Psalms from Primitive and Medieval Writers . . . ,* 4 v. (London 1860–74); and G. Bellino, *Gesù Cristo nelle S. Scritture e nei SS. Padri e Dottori,* 9 v. (Turin 1911–15).

Syriac Catenae. Of Eastern catenae, the following Syriac ones may be mentioned: (1) an anonymous compiler known as *Garden of Delights* (7th century), (2) Severus, an Antiochene monk (9th century), (3) Bishop Dionysius bar Ṣalībī (12th century) and (4) BAR-HEBRAEUS, a commentary on both the Old Testament and the New Testament titled *Storehouse of Mysteries.*

For the publication of the various catenae, see bibliography below.

See Also: EXEGESIS, BIBLICAL.

Bibliography: R. DEVREESSE, *Dictionnaire de la Bible,* suppl. ed., L. PIROT, et al. (Paris 1928–) 1:1084–1233. K. STAAB, *Lexikon für Theologie und Kirche,* eds., J. HOFER and K. RAHNER, 10 v. (2d, new ed. Freiburg 1957–65) 6:56–57. W. ELTESTER, *Die Religion in Geschichte und Gegenwart,* 7 v. (3d ed. Tübingen 1957–65) 1:1627–28. G. BARDY, *Catholicisme* 2:860–862.

[C. O'C. SLOANE]

CATHARI

Members of a medieval sect adhering to a dualistic heresy of Oriental origin that became widespread in Western Christendom after 1150 (*see* HERESY, HISTORY OF, 2). The present study covers its origins, history, organizations and disappearance.

Origins. Beginning with the 11th century, religious life in western Europe had difficulty maintaining its equilibrium, despite the GREGORIAN REFORM movement and the new monastic trends (for example, *see* CLUNIAC REFORM; CISTERCIANS). Some sought to satisfy their aspirations by a return to evangelical poverty (*see* POVERTY MOVEMENT) and simplicity, from which it was easy to fall into heresy. This was the origin of many sporadic movements superficially labeled Manichaean by contemporaries, but of which little is actually known (*see* PETER OF BRUYS; HENRY OF LUSANNE; ARNOLD OF BRESCIA). It was Bogomilism that provided these indistinct currents with the doctrinal framework they lacked. Bogomilism itself traced its origin to those Paulician colonies settled in Thrace by the Emperor Nicephorus I (802–811), through

which a dualistic and iconoclastic heresy, originally of Armenia, took root in the Balkans. It penetrated into Bulgaria and during the reign of Czar Peter (927–969) inspired the preaching of the priest Bogomil, who taught contempt for the official Church, held the Sacraments to be useless, rejected the Old Testament and retained but one prayer, the Our Father. The world, which was the creation and domain of the devil, was evil. But the dualism of the BOGOMILS was not radical, inasmuch as the devil was a rebellious and fallen angel inferior to the principal of Good. This heresy is known principally through the *Treatise* of Cosmas the Priest, written in 972. In the early 11th century, the Bogomils in Constantinople developed a more radical doctrine that admitted complete equality between the principal of Good, that is, the creator of the invisible world, and the principal of Evil, the creator of the material world. This doctrine was characteristic of the Church of Dragovitsa.

History in Europe. This Eastern heresy was not found in the West until the middle of the 12th century when its adherents are called Cathari from καθαροί, a traditional name for Manichaeans. Transferred from the Balkan Peninsula principally by knights returning from the second CRUSADE, the heresy spread rapidly in northern France, through the Rhine countries where Cathari were mentioned in 1163, to southern France (the *Boni homines* of Lombers in 1165). They also spread into Italy *c.* 1176, especially Milan where many heretics resided. However, there could not have been a Catharist bishop in Italy before 1170.

At first all Cathari in Italy were subject to Bishop Mark, who professed the moderate dualism of the Catharist church of Bulgaria. The arrival of Nicetas, Catharist bishop of Constantinople and an absolute dualist, in Italy soon after 1174, led Mark to transfer to the order of Dragovitsa, which Nicetas represented. Under Mark's successor, John the Jew, the Cathari divided into separate groups. The first was composed of the partisans of absolute dualism, called Albanenses, organizing themselves in the church of Desenzano, south of Lake Garda. They were particularly numerous in Verona. Those who remained faithful to the moderate Bulgarian dualism, the Garatenses, constituted the church of Concorezzo, near Milan. Moderate dualists also came together around the church of Bagnolo, near Mantua, adhering to the order of Esclavonia. Like these, the Catharist churches of Vicenza, Florence and Spoleto rejected absolute dualism.

In northern France, Catharism was practically limited to CHARITÉ-SUR-LOIRE, but heresy made extraordinary strides in the south. Through contact with the Albanenses absolute dualism was quickly accepted. Soon all heretics in the Midi, both Cathari and WALDENSES, came to be known as ALBIGENSES. By the end of the 12th century there were four Albigensian bishops, with sees at Carcassonne, Toulouse, ALBI and Agen. Around 1225, a church of Razès in the Limoux region was added. The capture of Montségur (1244) precipitated the rapid decline of Catharism within France.

Organization. There was no real unity of doctrine among the Cathari, excepting their agreement on the principle that the visible world was evil. They rejected the Sacraments of the Church, particularly the Baptism of water and Matrimony. Although absolute dualists recognized a portion of the Old Testament, the great majority of Cathari accepted only the New Testament, which they read in its Catholic version.

Absolute dualists held that Good and Evil constituted two distinct spheres; one the kingdom of the good god who was spiritual and suprasensible; and the other, the kingdom of the evil god, creator of the material world. For the moderate dualists, or monarchists, the supreme god had created the invisible heaven, the heavenly spirits who inhabited it and the four elements, whereas the devil was merely the organizer of the sensible world. The Cathari explained the creation of man by myths: the evil god, or Satan, had imprisoned spirits in material bodies. The only salutary way to escape this evil world, was by the reception of the *consolamentum,* the Cathari's unique sacrament administered by the imposition of hands. Christ had come to reveal to men the means of salvation. His earthly life had been simply an appearance.

The Catharistic church considered as its members only the Perfect, who had received the *consolamentum.* They were subject to strict poverty and a rigorous asceticism, their diet being completely vegetarian except for fish. They observed three Lents each year. The Perfect, who for the most part were poor peasants or artisans, were accorded great veneration. In the hierarchy of the Perfect, deacons were above the ordinary Perfect, and at the head was the bishop who was assisted by a "major son" and a "minor son." The major son succeeded the bishop.

The ordinary Cathari, the Believers, lived according to their beliefs, without fixed rules of morality. It was sufficient for them to believe that the *consolamentum* assured their salvation. During the ceremony of the *melioramentum* the Believers "worshipped" the Perfect and listened to their preaching; their chief concern was the reception of the *consolamentum* when in danger of death. Catharism was well received by the lesser nobility, who were poor and turbulent, by peasants and artisans and above all by the burghers of the cities who profited from USURY that the Cathari had legalized.

Catharism has long been known only by the refutations found in the works of Catholic authors, for example, ALAN OF LILLE's *Summa,* prior to 1200, the compilations attributed to Bonacursus and Prepositinus of Cremona and the *Summa* of Rainier of Sacconi, 1250. The *Liber de duobus principiis,* written by an Italian dualist *c.* 1230 [ed. A. Dondaine, *Un Traité néomanichéen . . .* (Rome 1939)], is now available as well as the anonymous Catharist treatise ed. by C. Thousellier, *Un Traité cathère inédit. . .* (Louvain 1961).

Disappearance of the Cathari. Long before 1250, the church of the Cathari in France was fragmented and before 1260 the Catharistic bishops of Toulouse sought refuge in Italy. There, the entire hierarchy disappeared before the end of the 13th century. In the Midi, the last strongholds of the heresy, which were in the upper valley of Ariège and in the Carcassonne region, disappeared before 1330; in Italy Catharism died out quietly toward the end of the 14th century. In addition to the inherent weakness of the Catharist principle of passivity the most vital factor in its disappearance was the example of the MENDICANT orders. The DOMINICANS and FRANCISCANS had presented an effective alternative to Catharism, and this rather than the INQUISITION was probably most responsible for its disappearance.

Bibliography: C. G. A. SCHMIDT, *Histoire et doctrine de la secte des Cathares ou Albigeois,* 2 v. (Paris 1849). A. BORST, *Die Katharer* (Stuttgart 1953). J. GUIRAUD, *Histoire de l'Inquisition au moyen âge,* 2 v. (Paris 1935–38) v.1. E. G. A. HOLMES, *The Albigensian or Catharist Heresy* (London 1925). S. RUNCIMAN, *The Medieval Manichee* (Cambridge, Eng. 1947; repr. 1955). COSMAS LE PRÈTRE, *Le Traité contre les Bogomiles,* ed. and tr., H. C. PUECH and A. VAILLANT (Paris 1945). D. OBOLENSKY, *The Bogomils: A Study in Balkan Neo-Manichaeism* (Cambridge, Eng. 1948). A. DONDAINE, "La Hiérarchie cathare en Italie," *Archivum Fratrum Praedicatorum,* 19 (1949) 280–312; 20 (1950) 234–324. T. KAEPPELI, "Une Somme contre les hérétiques de S. Pierre Martyr (?)," ibid. 17 (1947) 295–335. *The Summa contra haereticos: Ascribed to Praepositinus of Cremona,* ed. J. N. GARVIN and J. A. CORBETT (Notre Dame, Ind. 1958). ILARINO DA MILANO, "Il *Liber supra stella* del piacentino Salvo Burci contro i Catari e altre correnti ereticali," *Aevum,* 16 (1942) 272–319; 17 (1943) 90–146; 19 (1945) 281–341.

[Y. DOSSAT]

CATHEDRAL

The principal church of a diocese in which the bishop has his *cathedra* or seat and where he preaches, teaches, and conducts religious services. The term is derived from the Greek καθέδρα, which passed into Latin as *cathedra.* In the early Christian era the *cathedra* was a symbol of authority (*see* CHAIR OF PETER), and the expression *ex cathedra* signifies the solemn teaching authority of the pope as the successor of St. Peter (*see* H. Denziger, *Enchiridion symbolorum* 3074). Although the bishop may set up a temporary *cathedra* in any church within his diocese, one particular edifice, usually in the city in which he resides, is designated for the establishment of a permanent *cathedra* and is called the diocesan cathedral. Only a diocesan bishop may establish a cathedral; titular bishops are not authorized one.

The cathedral is not necessarily the largest or most splendid religious edifice in the diocese, for at Rome St. John LATERAN is the cathedral proper of the pope as bishop of Rome, rather than the more magnificent ST. PETER'S BASILICA. Many of the cathedrals throughout the world, however, represent the very best architectural developments of the periods in which they were constructed (*see* CHURCH ARCHITECTURE). The highly developed iconographical cycles in many of the medieval cathedrals served both a didactic and a decorative purpose, and they have been justly termed ''the Bibles of the illiterate.'' Often the BAPTISTERY was a separate building, and there was also a bishop's palace, bell tower, and accommodations for monks, or for the canons serving in the chapter. The cathedral complex found at Pisa is representative of this development.

The juridical character of a cathedral does not depend on its form, dimensions, or decoration. Without undergoing any physical change beyond the erection of a *cathedra*, a parish or mission church may become a cathedral, as is often the case when a new diocese is formed. What properly constitutes a cathedral is its assignment by proper authority—the Holy See in most cases—as the residence of a bishop in his hierarchical capacity. Such official designation is known as canonical erection and is usually included in the Apostolic Letters by which a diocese is formed, although the Third Council of BALTIMORE authorized bishops in the U.S. to select the location themselves.

The cathedral may be transferred from one location to another within a city or from one city to another within a diocese, but there is usually only one cathedral, just as there is only one diocesan bishop. In exceptional circumstances, when two dioceses are united, such as in the ancient See of BATH AND WELLS, each will retain its right to maintain a permanent *cathedra* for the bishop in separate cathedrals, known as co-cathedrals. By special indult of the Holy See, when a new cathedral was built in the Archdiocese of BALTIMORE, the old cathedral and the new cathedral were given the status of co-cathedrals. A pro-cathedral is one temporarily used by a bishop until a more suitable structure can be built. No differentiation is made between the cathedrals of patriarchal, primatial, metropolitan, and other episcopal sees. Cathedrals rank

The nave of Saint-Pierre-et-Saint-Paul Cathedral, Troyes, France, built between 1208 and 1429. (©Vanni Archive/ CORBIS)

immediately after the four major Roman BASILICAS (St. John Lateran, St. Peter's, St. Paul-Outside-the-Walls, and St. Mary Major).

The codes of canon law declare that cathedral churches should be dedicated by a solemn consecration (*Codex iuris canonici* c. 1217 §2; *Codex Canonum Ecclesiarum Orientalium* [CCEO] c. 871 §1). The feasts of the dedication and of the titular patron are celebrated in all churches of the diocese. The Latin code requires that the cathedral be the usual location for ordinations (c.1011 §1). This code strongly encourages a new diocesan bishop to take canonical possession of his diocese within the context of a liturgical act in the cathedral, with the diocesan clergy and other members of the faithful gathered (c. 382 §4). A bishop may also be buried in his cathedral church.

Bibliography: M. A. FRANCES DE URRUTIGOYTI, *Tractatus de ecclesiis cathedralibus earumque privilegiis et praerogativis* (Venice 1698). A. D. SERTILLANGES, *La Cathédrale: Sa Mission spiritu-*

Interior of a Roman Catholic cathedral, Alba Lulia, Romania, 18th Century. (©Sandro Vannini/CORBIS)

elle, son esthétique, son décor, sa vie* (Paris 1922). C. A. BACHOFEN (C. Augustine), *Rights and Duties of Ordinaries according to the Code and Apostolic Faculties* (St. Louis 1924). L. SYLVESTRE, *Le Cathédratique* (Quebec 1946). P. AHEARNE and M. LANE, *Pontifical Ceremonies* (London 1947). N. DIDIER, *Les Églises de Sisteron et de Forcalquier du XIᵉ siècle à la Révolution: Le Problème de la "concathédralité"* (Paris 1954). R. NAZ, *Dictionnaire de droit canonique,* ed. R. NAZ (Paris 1935–65) 5:228–233. F. L. CROSS, *The Oxford Dictionary of the Christian Church* (London 1957) 248–249.

[B. J. COMASKEY]

CATHEDRAL AND EPISCOPAL SCHOOLS

Medieval institutions usually connected with the cathedral church. The cathedral school arose from the bishop's desire to prepare men for the priesthood, and it admitted both laymen and clerics; the episcopal school, which was chiefly for clerics, was generally conducted by the bishop himself.

Origin of the School. In the first three centuries the Church prescribed no training for men who desired to be clerics. Christians received their elementary and literary education in pagan schools. A youth wishing to become a cleric was usually apprenticed to a bishop who taught by action the functions of a church's minister, imparted a minimum of sacred doctrine and guided the youth's moral formation. After the Christians gained legal rights in 313 (Edict of MILAN), the Church experienced a wave of conversions that created the need for more clerics. EUSEBIUS OF VERCELLI in 354 and AUGUSTINE OF HIPPO in 394 introduced formal courses in Scripture and theology into the training of clerical candidates. Until the suppression of the pagan schools under Justinian I in 529, however, no change occurred in the elementary or literary education of clerical aspirants.

With the suppression of the pagan schools and the general political and social turmoil of the sixth century, bishops could no longer presume that candidates had received preliminary elementary and literary training. Thus, from the sixth century the cathedral schools assumed the role of teaching grammar and literature. The school thereafter offered all levels of instruction from reading and writing to formal theology and courses in Sacred Scripture.

Curriculum of the School. Before 313 there was very little formal schooling. The young men received an apprenticeship training in performing the sacred functions and in governing the Church; the bishop gave some informal instruction in reading, understanding and explaining the Scriptures. After 313, however, more formal education, especially in Scripture and theology, was possible.

When the cathedral schools assumed the task of elementary education, they accepted the regular courses offered in the schools of the late Roman Empire, a combination of the trivium and quadrivium, or liberal arts (*see* LIBERAL ARTS). From the trivium came grammar, how to read and write Latin correctly and some reading in pagan and Christian classics; and rhetoric, some principles of correct speaking and preaching. From the quadrivium came arithmetic, how to count and compute dates, especially that of Easter; and music, how to sing the Psalms and the liturgy. The cathedral schools, however, also offered higher education, a training in Sacred Scripture, apologetics and some dogmatic theology.

Teachers in the School. Until 313 usually the only teacher in the cathedral school was the bishop, who shared his knowledge and experience with the young candidates. With the new freedom after 313, however, the bishop could travel more extensively in his diocese and to compensate for his absence, generally appointed a cler-

Salisbury Cathedral and School, 1220–1250, Salisbury, Wiltshire, England. (©Michael Nicholson/CORBIS)

ic called *scholasticus* to preside over the six or seven men apprenticed to the Church.

In time, others came forward to aid and, later, to supplant the bishop's direct work in the school. CHRODEGANG, bishop of Metz from 742 to 746, wrought the most radical change throughout Europe by introducing canonical life into episcopal sees. Henceforth, a group of priests dedicated to performing the liturgy at the cathedral lived with the bishop. Since they followed a community life based on a rule or canon, they were called "canons." In addition to performing the liturgy, the canons were also responsible for educating the young men living with the bishop. The priest governing the canons was called the dean or archdeacon; the canon in charge of the grammar school was the *scholasticus* or headmaster; and the music school was ruled by the *precentor*. Most European dioceses adopted this mode of cathedral life. It was generally from these cathedral schools and from the ruling canons

that the universities and their officials developed in the 12th century.

Famous Cathedral Schools. In Rome in 190, Pope Eleutherius appointed Victor, the archdeacon, to conduct a school; by 220 the school had grown into a formal organization. After 313 the school moved into the Lateran palace where it established a famous library. In 394, Augustine, bishop of Hippo, organized a formal school with a schedule similar to that of the monasteries of the East. This organization of the cathedral and its school served as Chrodegang's model in 742.

In 598 Augustine, the apostle of England, founded King's School as an integral part of Christ Church Cathedral at Canterbury. The school, which had a section for grammar and another for song or chant, served as a model for England. The school at York educated ALCUIN, and in 767 named him chancellor or *scholasticus*. Alcuin followed the organization of York's school in his educational reform of Charlemagne's kingdom in 781 (*see* PALACE SCHOOLS).

Lubin, consecrated bishop of Chartres in 544, first taught in his own school but later appointed Caletric to conduct it. This school gained its title to fame under a series of gifted scholars and teachers, such as, John of Salisbury and Bernard of Chartres, who led a classical renaissance in the early 12th century. The cathedral school of Norte Dame in Paris, which dates from the 11th century, was the nucleus of the University of PARIS.

Bibliography: M. L. W. LAISTNER, *Thought and Letters in Western Europe, A.D. 500 to 900* (2d ed. New York 1957). E. S. DUCKETT, *Carolingian Portraits: A Study in the Ninth Century* (Ann Arbor 1962). H. I. MARROU, *A History of Education in Antiquity,* tr. G. LAMB (New York 1956). H. RASHDALL, *The Universities of Europe in the Middle Ages,* ed. F. POWICKE and A. B. EMDEN, 3 v. (new ed. Oxford 1936) v. 1. P. RICHÉ, *Education et culture dans l'Occident barbare, VIe–VIIIe siècles* (Paris 1962).

[E. G. RYAN]

CATHERICK, EDMUND, BL.

Priest and martyr, *alias* Huddleston; b. Carlton, near Richmond, North Riding, Yorkshire, England, *c.* 1605; d. hanged, drawn, and quartered at York, April 13, 1642. Edmund was born into a recusant Catholic family, educated at the English College of Douai, and ordained abroad. Thereafter he ministered for seven years in Yorkshire until he was arrested near Watlas. He was examined by Justice Dodsworth, a close relative, to whom he made admission of his priesthood under the guise of kinship. Catherick was convicted, arraigned at York, and condemned to death together with Bl. John LOCKWOOD. His mortal remains were buried at Toft Green, but later translated to St. Gregory's Monastery, Downside. The skull, which had been displayed on Micklegate Bar to discourage other Catholic sympathizers, is now at Hazlewood Castle. He was beatified by Pius XI on December 15, 1929.

Feast of the English Martyrs: May 4 (England).

See Also: ENGLAND, SCOTLAND AND WALES, MARTYRS OF.

Bibliography: R. CHALLONER, *Memoirs of Missionary Priests,* ed. J. H. POLLEN (rev. ed. London 1924; repr. Farnborough 1969). J. H. POLLEN, *Acts of English Martyrs* (London 1891).

[K. I. RABENSTEIN]

CATHERINE II (THE GREAT), EMPRESS OF RUSSIA

Reign 1762 to Nov. 17, 1796; b. Stettin, Prussia, May 2, 1729; d. 1796, St. Petersburg. Sophia Augusta Frederica was the daughter of Christian Augustus, Prince of Anhalt-Zerbst, and his wife, Johanna Elizabeth of Holstein-Gottorp. When selected by the Empress Elizabeth Petrovna to be the bride of the future Peter III, Princess Sophia abandoned Lutheranism to embrace the Orthodox religion and took the name Catherine Alexeyevna. Her marriage to Grand Duke Peter on Sept. 1, 1745, was unsuccessful from the start; his talents and interests were childish and contrasted with Catherine's ambitions, self-will, and intelligence. During her 17 years as grand duchess, she was estranged from her husband and took several lovers, although a son, the future Czar Paul I (reign 1796–1801) was born on Oct. 2, 1754. At the death of Empress Elizabeth on Jan. 5, 1762, the grand duke ascended the throne as Peter III, but because of his imprudent pro-Prussian policies and his threat to divorce Catherine, he aroused opposition. Gregory Orlov and his three brothers swore allegiance to Catherine on July 9, 1762, and with the help of the regiments of the guard, seized Peter, obtained his abdication, and imprisoned him in the Castle of Ropsha, where he and Ivan VI, son of Anna Petrovna, died violently shortly after.

Uprisings and National Reforms. Catherine corresponded with DIDEROT, VOLTAIRE, and the ENCYCLOPEDISTS, and in the beginning of her reign she inclined to their "enlightened absolutism." In 1767 she published her famous *Nakaz* (instruction) for law reform in which she urged the equality of all before the law and the freedom of all under the law, whose function is to protect, not oppress. Her demand that punishment should never be torture and that death sentences should be rare was acclaimed throughout Europe. However, the deputies assembled to codify the laws were inept. In fact even Catherine's equality before the law did not apply to serfs and peasants, who were openly bought, sold, and exploited as sheep and cattle. In the 1760s, at least 40 uprisings occurred; they culminated in the Ural Cossack Uprising or Peasant Rebellion (1773–75), led by Yemilyan Pugachev, who pretended to be Peter III. Pugachev was executed, but this uprising, added to the French and American Revolutions, blunted the desire for enlightened reform. Catherine's *Nakaz* became a dead letter. She now turned to a stricter control of her domestic administration. She created 80 provinces (*guberniya*) in which she allowed a limited measure of democracy and permitted the local gentry to elect the councilors of the district (*uyezd*) director. But as Catherine enlarged and ensured the privileges of the gentry, she paved the way for a more permanent and oppressive serfdom. To her, a privileged gentry meant a closer supervision of the popular mood and a tighter control over incipient unrest. Little came of her attempts to democratize the cities, since the poor quality of urban education did not prepare the people for civic responsibility.

Foreign Policy. Catherine's activity in foreign affairs led to the successful pursuit of the war against the Turks to secure better trade routes on the Black Sea. She also strengthened Russia's strategic position in the West. The Lithuanian-Polish state, she felt, must be either brought under the influence of, or conquered by Russia. Through manipulation of the "liberum veto," Poland became so weak that Russia, Austria, and Prussia were able to partition this state in 1772, 1792, and 1795. Catherine thus extended the Russian border further west. She also encouraged the colonization of Alaska. The two Turkish wars (1764–74, 1781–91) ensured safe trade routes and fertile farm lands and secured the southern borders against the Turks and Crimean Tatars. These wars called attention to the genius of her generals, P. A. Rumyantsev, A. V. Surorov, A. Galitsin, P. Panin, and G. A. Potyomkin, whose military ability was mediocre but whose talent for organization and colonization of these areas was more noteworthy.

Catherine's personal life was lonely. She did not marry a second time, and her son Paul lived apart from the court. History seems to have forgotten the daughter born to her in 1758. While she cultivated leaders of European thought, she assiduously made favoritism a quasi-official institution. During her reign of 34 years she had more than 10 favorites, who were handsomely rewarded, and some (G. Orlov, G. A. Potyomkin, P. L. Zubov, and S. Poniatowski) were of importance to Russian and Polish history.

Catherine and the Jesuits. As Emperor Peter I before her, Catherine saw the need for education in Russia. She founded the Academy of Fine Arts, the Academy of Sciences, the Moscow and Smolny Institutes for Young Ladies, and facilities for the study of medicine. This interest also ensured the continuity of the Society of Jesus in the Catholic Church. At the first partition of Poland (1772), four Jesuit colleges and two residences—201 Jesuits—passed under Russian rule. Because she was pleased with the Jesuit methods of teaching youth, she refused to allow Pope CLEMENT XIV's Brief of Suppression of the Society of Jesus (July 21, 1773) to be promulgated in Russia. Pius VI granted permission to the Jesuits in White Russia to receive into the society former confreres living in other countries. At Catherine's urging, the Latin bishop of White Russia ordained 20 Jesuit scholastics in 1777, and two years later he authorized a novitiate in Polotsk. When Gabriel Gruber, later general of the Jesuits, came to St. Petersburg in 1785, he found 10,000 Catholics in the capital. It was at the request of Paul I that Pope Pius VII restored the Society of Jesus on March 7, 1801.

Although the Jesuits found protection with Catherine, the Eastern Rite Catholics were persecuted. After the

Catherine II, Empress of Russia.

first partition of Poland, she sent missionaries, accompanied by soldiers, to restore the "renegades" to Orthodoxy. She did agree to the nomination of a new bishop for the Eastern Rite diocese at Polotsk, but later, after the second partition of Poland and despite her promise to protect Catholics of both rites, Catherine suppressed all other Eastern Rite dioceses, forcibly united over 1.5 million Eastern Rite Catholics to Orthodoxy, and dispersed the Order of Basilians.

Her Importance. Catherine left a Russia whose boundaries were the Neman River, the Dniester River and the Black Sea. She is significant in the history of the Catholic Church for her protection of the Society of Jesus. Intellectual circles and the courts of Europe admired her brilliance and grandiose political projects. She wrote much: memoirs, comedies, comic operas, and fairy tales for her grandchildren. Catherine was the real successor to Peter the Great. Yet by her stratification of classes in Russia, she perhaps did more to prepare the coming of the 1917 revolution than any other single Russian monarch.

Bibliography: CATHERINE II, *Memoirs of Catherine the Great,* tr. K. ANTHONY (New York 1927). G. S. THOMSON, *Catherine the Great and the Expansion of Russia* (London 1947). F. D. DAVID and M. L. KENT, *Rome and Russia: A Tragedy of Errors* (Westminster, Md. 1954). B. VON BILBASSOFF, *Katharina II, Kaiserin von*

Russland im Urteile der Weltliteratur (Berlin 1897). G. P. GOOCH, *Catherine the Great and Other Studies* (New York 1954). M. E. VON ALMEDINGEN, *Catherine, Empress of Russia* (New York 1961). O. HÖTZSCH, ''Catherine II,'' *Cambridge Modern History,* (London–New York 1902–12) 6:657–701.

[W. C. JASKIEVICZ]

CATHERINE DE MÉDICIS

Queen of France, wife of Henry II (1547–59), daughter of Lorenzo de' Medici, Duke of Urbino, and of Madeleine de la Tour d'Auvergne, Countess of Boulogne; b. Florence, April 13, 1519; d. Blois, Jan. 5, 1589. In 1533 Catherine married Henry (then Duke of Orléans), second son of Francis I of France; she later became Queen of France on her husband's accession to the throne in 1547. Three of her four sons became kings of France. She was kept out of politics during the reigns of Henry II and Francis II (her eldest son), but after being declared regent during the minority of Charles IX, her second son, she remained in virtual control to the end of his reign (1574).

Political Policy. Her chief traits were her ''possessive maternalism'' and her devotion to politics. Her outlook was essentially political: even in promoting the careers of her children she found an outlet for political machinations. An admirer of Machiavelli, she worked toward the goal of national unity. Deeply involved as she was in the problems of the Huguenots, the warring religious factions, and the ambitions of the nobility, she showed ability in retaining power and defending the crown. The only principle to which she adhered in her religious policy was GALLICANISM: she considered matters of faith to be under royal prerogative. She was not a fanatic, but was notoriously unscrupulous in her actions—her weapons included intrigue, duplicity, violence, and perjury. Antidoctrinaire, she pursued a piecemeal, pragmatic policy in the form of a series of expedient moves, and she thought in terms of ''a temporary policy leading to a permanent solution'' (J. E. Neale), an expedient with disastrous consequences. Her vision as a ruler was limited; she was often erratic and inconsistent, and consequently she never rose to the stature of a statesman.

Religious Controversy. Catherine began with designs for partial toleration toward the Huguenots and advocated coexistence of the two religions. Indifferent to dogmas, she professed a liberty of doctrine that was unacceptable to contemporary theologians, and she was inclined to regard religious rifts mainly as court intrigues amenable to personal conciliation. In July 1561, together with Louis I de GUISE, Cardinal de Lorraine, she launched the Colloquy of Poissy, which she hoped to turn into a National Council of the Gallican Church to foster reconciliation between the HUGUENOTS and Catholics. Her inability to grasp the importance of doctrinal matters caused the failure of this meeting. She found an abyss separated Cardinal de Lorraine and Theodore de Bèze (or BEZA), the Huguenot theologian, and the debate at Poissy aroused religious feelings and widened the gap between the two groups, thus preparing a way for armed conflict. Tension was further increased when the Edict of January 1562, designed to grant the Huguenots civic status and abolish the death penalty for heresy, came up for registration before the Paris high court of justice (*parlement*). Finally, the Massacre of Vassy (March 1, 1562) began the religious wars. Catherine's policy of expediency proved ineffective. Trying to keep in check the Catholic Triumvirate (Duke Francis de Guise, Constable Anne de Montmorency, and Marshal de Saint-André) and forestall its armed uprising, she encouraged the strengthening of the Huguenot party and completion of the Huguenot military organization. Catherine, captured with the king by the Triumvirs on March 27, entered the war on their side. She curtailed the liberties of the Huguenots and, while negotiating with their chiefs, sought external allies—the pope, Spain, and Savoy. The Huguenots were aided by ELIZABETH OF ENGLAND, to whom Louis I Condé ceded Le Havre. Catherine besieged Rouen (September). The war freed her from the Triumvirs' control: Guise was assassinated at Orléans and Saint-André at Dreux; and Montmorency was captured. Catherine had Condé and Montmorency (each a prisoner of the other side) conduct negotiations leading to the Pacification of Amboise (March 19, 1563). Liberty of conscience was achieved, but serious restrictions were imposed on freedom of worship. Catherine recaptured Le Havre from the English (July 28) and on signing the Treaty of Troyes (April 12, 1564) regained Calais, lost by the Treaty of Cateau-Cambrésis (March 1559).

She then undertook a long tour of France lasting until May 1566. At Bayonne she met her daughter Elizabeth (married to Philip II) and some members of the Spanish court, including the Duke of Alva, to discuss a possible league between France, Spain, and the Emperor. The suspicions of the Huguenots were soon aroused by Alva's rule of terror in the Netherlands; they feared concerted action, led by Catherine, against the Protestants. New hostilities broke out in September 1567 with an abortive attempt by the Huguenots to seize the king. The second religious war ended officially with the Treaty of Longjumeau (March 23, 1568), but sporadic hostilities and atrocities continued. Catherine's policy toward the Huguenots became aggressive: already in 1567 she had dismissed Chancellor Michel de l'Hôpital (who had previously guided her policy of moderation) and then planned to seize the Huguenot leaders Louis I Condé and

Gaspard de Coligny. Coligny rose in defense in August 1568, and the third religious war began. Catherine took offensive action against the Huguenots grouped in Poitou. Her army, commanded by Tavannes, defeated Coligny at Jarnac (May 13, 1569), where Condé was killed, and at Moncontour (October 3). She outlawed Coligny in September 1569, and on Aug. 8, 1570, she signed a peace treaty at Saint-Germain. Influenced by the moderately inclined *politiques,* she tried to establish a balance between the parties. She decided to marry her daughter Margaret to Henry de Navarre, the titular head of the Huguenot party, and made unsuccessful plans for the marriage of her son, Henry, the Duke of Anjou, to Elizabeth I of England. At court, the Huguenots replaced the Guises as the influential party. A project was born for a united Huguenot-Catholic force to challenge Spain in the Netherlands; Coligny was to cooperate with William of Orange, the leader of the Dutch uprising. Dreading the might of Spain and resentful of Coligny's unprecedented influence over Charles IX in the planning of the campaign, Catherine stopped the expedition. When Coligny's attitude became threatening, she ordered Maurevel to assassinate him. Coligny was wounded in Paris on Aug. 22, 1572. Fearing revenge, Catherine obtained from the king permission to massacre the Huguenots who were assembled in Paris for the wedding of Henry de Navarre.

Her subsequent moves were ineffectual. For the Massacre of ST. BARTHOLOMEW'S DAY she never found a plausible excuse. She resorted to a short-lived expedient of legal toleration, which involved bribing Huguenot nobles with titles and sinecures. But her grip over national affairs was lost: she was never able to impress Henry III with her counsels.

Appreciation. Catherine was a woman of superior intelligence and prodigious energy and was well read and eloquent; she had a fine taste for the arts and constructed, among others, the palace of Tuilleries and the castles of Monceaux and Chenonceaux. Despite the shortsightedness of her political plans, as Neale put it, "she was a woman of great qualities, if not a great woman."

Bibliography: J. HÉRITIER, *Catherine de Médicis* (Paris 1959), Eng., tr. C. HALDANE (New York 1963). J. E. NEALE, *The Age of Catherine de Medici* (London 1943; new ed. London 1957). P. VAN DYKE, *Catherine de Médicis,* 2 v. (New York 1923). L. ROMIER, *Le Royaume de Catherine de Médicis,* 2 v. (Paris 1922). J. H. MARIÉJOL, *Catherine de Médicis* (Paris 1920). R. ROEDER, *Catherine de Medici and the Lost Revolution* (New York 1937).

[W. J. STANKIEWICZ]

CATHERINE DE' RICCI, ST.

Dominican contemplative of the Counter Reformation; b. Florence, Italy, April 23, 1522; d. Prato, Feb. 2, 1590. She was a child of patrician lineage and spiritually formed by her aunt, a Benedictine abbess, but she entered the Dominican convent of San Vincenzio, Prato, founded 1503 in the spirit of SAVONAROLA's reform. At age 14 she was professed, taking her deceased mother's name. From the first she endured physical afflictions and spiritual raptures that her sisters doubted until they were won over by her humility and holiness. During Holy Week of 1542 her ecstasies began; thereafter for 12 years from Thursday noon to Friday at 4 P.M. she relived Christ's Passion. Among her other supernatural gifts were mystical visits with St. Philip Neri and St. Mary Magdalen de' Pazzi, neither of whom she had met. She led an uncommonly effective life, advising bishops, cardinals, generals of orders, and three future popes; directing disciples in person and in letters of great charm; looking after the poor and distressed; and, as prioress (1560–90), administering the convent with wisdom and energy. Her spirituality was that of Savonarola, softened by her optimism and compassion; she promoted frequent Confession and Communion, and a spirit of joy, peace, and energetic action (*gagliardo combattimento*). She composed a *lauda* in honor of Savonarola and a Bible-based canticle of the Passion, *Amici mei,* used in the Dominican Liturgy of Good Friday. The *promotor fidei* in the process of her beatification was Cardinal Prospero Lambertini (later Benedict XIV), who afterward made frequent reference to her in his classic *De servorum Dei beatificatione.* Her iconography includes a death mask made by her brother, a portrait probably by Naldini (*c.* 1570), and an unfinished sketch of her miraculous crucifix by H. Besson, OP.

Feast: Feb. 13.

Bibliography: *Le lettere di S. Caterina de' Ricci,* ed. A. GHERARDI (Florence 1890). *Lettere inedite di S. Caterina de' Ricci,* ed. S. PARDI (Florence 1912). *Compendio della vita della beata Caterina de' Ricci: Estratto da' processi fatti per la sua beatificazione* (Florence 1733). S. RAZZI, *La vita della reverenda serva di Dio, la Madre Suor Caterina de' Ricci* (Lucca 1594). F. M. CAPES, *St. Catherine de' Ricci* (London 1905). A. BUTLER, *The Lives of the Saints,* ed. H. THURSTON and D. ATTWATER (New York 1956) 1:328–331. G. DI AGRESTI, *S. Caterina de' Ricci: Fonti* (Florence 1963).

[M. E. EVANS]

CATHERINE OF ALEXANDRIA, ST.

Martyr. Data of her life derive from two works without historical value. A *Conversio* recounts her royal birth and her mystical espousal with Christ in a vision just after her baptism. A *Passio* reports her discourses at Alexandria before the Emperor with pagan philosophers whom she converted. When she persuaded the Empress to become a Christian, Catherine was tortured on the wheel

"Saint Catherine of Alexandria," panel painting by Fernando Yanez de la Almedina, 16th century, Museo del Prado, Madrid, Spain. (© Archivo Iconografico, S.A./CORBIS)

and decapitated (Nov. 24 or 25, 305). The *Passio* ends with angels translating her relics to Mt. Sinai, where, however, nothing seems to have been known of her *c.* 820. The earliest evidence of her cult, apparently introduced by Eastern monks who had fled from ICONOCLASM, appears in a painting of the early 8th century in Rome. After the 10th century her cult became very popular, especially in Italy. She is one of the FOURTEEN HOLY HELPERS; is the patroness of some 30 groups, including philosophers and maidens; and is portrayed with a book (knowledge), a crown (royal birth), and a wheel.

Feast: Nov. 25.

Bibliography: *Lexikon für Theologie und Kirche*, ed. J. HÖFER and K. RAHNER (Freiburg 1957–65) 6: 60–61. D. BALBONI, *Bibliotheca sanctorum* (Rome 1961–) 3:954–965. K. LEWIS, "Pilgrimage and the Cult of Katherine of Alexandria in Late Medieval England," in *Pilgrimage Explored* (Woodbridge, England 1999), 145–160. S. NEVANLINNA and I. TAAVITSAINEN, *Katherine of Alexandria: The Late Middle English Prose Legend in Southwell Minster Ms 7* (Woodbridge, England 1993). S. JEFFERIS, "The 'Saint Catherine Legend' of the Legenda Aurea Traced through its German Translations and Other German Versions in Prose, Verse, and as a Play," in *Legenda Aurea* (Montreal 1986), 253–265.

[M. J. COSTELLOE]

CATHERINE OF ARAGON

Queen of England, daughter of Ferdinand of Aragon and Isabella of Castile; b. Alcalá, Spain, December 1485; d. Kimbolton, England, Jan. 7, 1536. In October 1501, she arrived in England for her marriage to Arthur, Prince of Wales, the eldest son of Henry VII. The marriage took place in November 1501, at St. Paul's Cathedral, London. Unfortunately, Arthur died in April 1502, but in 1503 Catherine was betrothed to Prince Henry, Henry's sole surviving son. Because of consanguinity, a papal dispensation was obtained for the proposed union. Catherine was for years a mere pawn in a shabby diplomatic game played between her own father and Henry VII, and she suffered accordingly; but soon after HENRY VIII's accession in 1509, he married Catherine, and her life was for some time a comparatively happy one. The king was a devoted husband and Catherine bore him four children; the court was brilliant.

Catherine was an able regent while Henry was at war in France in 1513, and she took every possible means of maintaining the Anglo-Spanish alliance. But the capture of the French king, Francis I, by CHARLES V (1525) upset the balance of power in Europe, and early in 1527 England offered her support to France against Spain.

Meanwhile, probably in the latter part of 1526 or the beginning of 1527, Henry began to feel an attraction for Anne Boleyn, one of Catherine's ladies-in-waiting, and in the spring, 1527, he professed doubts about the validity of his marriage. He commenced to think of its dissolution by the pope. In May, Cardinal WOLSEY and William Warham, Archbishop of Canterbury, arranged a collusive suit, and Henry was cited to answer a charge of having lived for 18 years in incestuous relationship with his brother Arthur's widow.

The international situation complicated English affairs. The armies of Charles V sacked Rome in May 1527, and made Pope CLEMENT VII their prisoner. Eventually a commission was issued to the papal legates, Wolsey and Cardinal CAMPEGGIO, to hear the divorce suit in open court in England and to pronounce a decision, if necessary. This legatine court first met in May 1529. Catherine appeared before it in June, refused to recognize its jurisdiction, and appealed to the pope. On July 23, 1529, Campeggio adjourned the court until October. It never met again. In 1530, Thomas CRANMER appealed to the European universities about the validity of the marriage. The pope, in November 1532, warned Henry not to divorce Catherine or to remarry. But in January 1533, he married Anne Boleyn secretly, and in May, Cranmer, as the new Archbishop of Canterbury, pronounced sentence of divorce. At length (in March 1534) the pope declared Catherine's marriage to Henry to be valid. Catherine, after her final separation from the king in July 1531, was subjected to increasingly harsh treatment, until she died at Kimbolton, having previously been imprisoned at a number of other places. *See* REFORMATION, PROTESTANT (IN THE BRITISH ISLES).

Bibliography: G. CAVENDISH, *The Life and Death of Cardinal Wolsey,* ed. R. S. SYLVESTER (1st ed. pub. 1641; Early English Text Society 243; London 1959). G. MATTINGLY, *Catherine of Aragon* (Boston 1941). P. HUGHES, *The Reformation in England,* 3 v. in 1 (5th, rev. ed. New York 2963), [5]. J. E. PAUL, *Catherine of Aragon and Her Friends* (London 1965).

[J. E. PAUL]

CATHERINE OF BOLOGNA, ST.

Poor Clare, mystic, writer, and artist; b. Bologna, Italy, Sept. 8, 1413; d. there, March 9, 1463. She was the daughter of John de Vigri and Benvenuta Mammolini. As companion to Margaret d'Este she was educated at the ducal court until Margaret's marriage. Catherine, then 14, joined a group of Franciscan tertiaries in Ferrara who later adopted the Rule of St. Clare. She served first as convent baker and portress, then as mistress of novices. During this time she wrote an important treatise on what she called the seven spiritual weapons; the treatise reflects the mystical quality of her interior life. It was also during this period, according to her own statement, that she was visited one Christmas Eve by Our Lady, who placed the newborn Christ in her arms. In 1456 Catherine was made abbess of a new convent of Clares in Bologna, and she remained in that office almost without interruption until her death. Clement XI canonized her May 22, 1712. Her body, seated and richly garbed, is incorrupt but blackened by age and dampness. Usually represented as a Poor Clare holding the Infant, she is also honored as patron of artists. Paintings and miniatures of hers, notably her illuminated Breviary, are extant. Writings include *Le sette arme necessarie alla battaglia spirituale,* in many editions and translations, from 1475 (Bologna) to 1922 (Florence); *Sermones ad sacras virgines* (Bologna 1522, 1635); *Rosarium metricum de mysteriis Passionis Christi Domini et de Vita BVM;* and minor works in verse and prose.

Feast: March 9.

Bibliography: *The Seven Spiritual Weapons,* trans. H. FEISS and D. RE (Ontario 1998). J. WOOD, *Women, Art and Spirituality:*

Catherine of Aragon, Queen of England. (Archive Photos)

The Poor Clares of Early Modern Italy (Cambridge 1996). *Le sette armi spirituali,* C. FOLETTI, ed. (Padua 1985). S.-S. MARTINELLI, "La Canonizzazione de Caterina Vigri: un problema cittadino nella Bologna del Seicento," in *Culto dei santi, istituzioni e classi sociali in eta preindustriale* (Rome 1984), 719–33. J. R. BERRIGAN, "Saint Catherine of Bologna: Franciscan Mystic," in *Women Writers of the Renaissance and Reformation,* K. M. WILSON, ed., (Athens, Ga. 1987), 81–95.

[F. LAUGHLIN]

CATHERINE OF GENOA, ST.

Widow, mystic, heroic servant of the poor and sick in her native city, hospital administrator; b. Genoa, toward the close of 1447; d. probably Sept. 15, 1510; canonized May 18, 1737.

Life. Catherine was the youngest of five children in the Fieschi family, then the most powerful of the Guelph families of Genoa. She was a descendant of Robert, brother of Innocent IV. Her father was Viceroy of Naples; her mother, Francesca di Negro, belonged to an ancient, noble family of Genoa. They had three sons, then two daughters: Limbania, who became a nun, and Caterinetta. Reliable details of Catherine's early years are scarce. At age 13 (1460) she attempted unsuccessfully to enter religious life. Late in 1461 her father died, and in

St. Catherine of Genoa.

the ensuing political realignments Catherine became an unhappy family pawn in the union of the Guelph Fieschi with the Ghibelline Adorni. On Jan. 13, 1463, at only 16, she was married to Giuliano Adorno, a wayward, self-indulgent man. Neglected by her husband, the lively, sensitive Catherine spent ten dreary years, the first five in utter loneliness and the rest in futile, if innocent, worldly gaieties, while her inner depression deepened to desperation. On March 20, 1473, while attempting to make her confession to a priest, she felt herself suddenly overwhelmed by the immense love of God, lifted above her miseries, enlightened by grace, and radically changed. The experience lasted for some time and was followed at home shortly after by a first (and last) vision of the Crucified. She made a general confession on March 24 and entered a new life. Almost simultaneously Giuliano's affairs had moved toward bankruptcy. This misfortune, together with Catherine's prayers, brought about his conversion. He agreed to a life of perpetual continence and became a Franciscan tertiary, although Catherine, in spite of her devotion to the Franciscan mystic Jacopone da Todi, did not. Giuliano disposed of valuable properties and together with Catherine lived in a small house near the hospital of the Pammatone to serve the sick and help the poor of the district. In this humble work they persevered until Giuliano's death on Jan. 10, 1497.

From 1479 on, they occupied two small rooms within the hospital, serving without pay and at their own expense. From 1479 to 1490 Catherine worked as an ordinary nurse. From 1490 to 1496 she was administrative head (*rettora*) of the hospital. During the epidemic of deadly fever of 1493, which is said to have carried off as much as 80 per cent of the population, her heroism and efficiency intensified. Her remarkable friendship with Ettore Vernazza, a young Genoese lawyer, began that same year. Much of the authentic information known about Catherine is due to this intimate friend and associate.

For almost 25 years up to 1479 Catherine's life, so interiorly rich, so externally fruitful in charitable works, developed solely under the impulse of grace without human help. It was marked by frequent ecstatic absorptions and by long, mysterious fasts, during which she was unable to take food—apparently an operation of God in which (as she said) her will had no part and to which she attached no great significance. With the death of Giuliano, this middle period came to a close and with it her fasts and spiritual isolation. Shortly after, she came under the spiritual direction of a priest, Cattaneo Marabotto, to whose firsthand knowledge of her spirit, doctrine, and interior life, history is much indebted. Catherine appreciated Marabotto's presence and help, his capacity to understand and not interfere with the work of God's grace in her soul. She continued her hospital work, managed the detailed finances of Giuliano's estate, and extended her influence in conversations with disciples. Becoming more expansive and communicative, she opened up to share with them her intense love and mystical insight. From 1506 until her death in 1510, gathering infirmities took their toll, and she was incapacitated for increasing periods of time, but she continued at her work almost to the end.

Cult and Relics. A popular cult began 18 months after her death when her body was exhumed to be placed in a marble sepulcher and was found almost perfectly preserved. In response to popular demand, her remains were exposed for eight days. Cures attributed to her intercession began to occur, and popular veneration continued. Official efforts to have her canonized began in 1630, but her canonization did not take place until May 18, 1737, when she received that honor together with Vincent de Paul, Francis Regis, and Giuliana Falconieri. Her portrait without nimbus found in the sacristy of the hospital church may be the picture mentioned in the hospital accounts less than two years after her death and approved by Marabotto.

Writings. The works commonly attributed to Catherine present a problem. There is no solid evidence that Catherine ever wrote down her thoughts and sayings. All extant biographies, editions, and translations of her works go back to the *Vita e Dottrina,* published in Genoa by Jacobo Genuti in 1551. It is the joint production of Catherine's confessor, Marabotto, and her spiritual son Ettore Vernazza, both of whom faithfully recorded her sayings, but with interspersed interpretations of their own. Thus the luminous, fascinating, spontaneous utterances of Catherine, obviously born of intense experience and insight, rest in a matrix of dull comment.

The *Treatise on Purgatory* ascribed to her is a collection of her sayings first written down (as part of the *Vita*) by Vernazza, but later enlarged by theological additions that convey little of Catherine's fresh and lively spirit. The *Spiritual Dialogues* depend on the *Vita* but chiefly convey Battista Vernazza's version of Catherine's spirit, learned at second hand. They make a solid, intelligent, and well-organized treatise, but one that contains little of Catherine's rich spontaneity. Nevertheless, the words of Catherine scattered through these works constitute a precious record of her spiritual doctrine and mystical insight.

Doctrine. Although Catherine's authentic teaching drew its nourishment from the pre-Reformation Church, it has nevertheless a remarkably contemporary, or perhaps timeless, ring and resonance. In spirit it is open, positive, joyous, trustful of the all-embracing goodness of God. It shows the unstudied spontaneity of a saintly soul's personal experience; there is a soaring and yet sober quality in it, a refinement at once of holy liberty and of docility to the Holy Spirit. It is a rich mystical realization of the immense, tireless love of God, always expressed in new turns, applications, and rediscoveries. Lift sin, she said, from a man's shoulders, then allow the good God to act. God seems to have nothing else to do but to unite Himself to men. Everything she said is a variation on this theme.

Theologians and spiritual writers have singled out her thoughts on purgatory for special notice, but these with other eschatological texts are part of the larger intuition of God's loving way with souls. The historical emphasis on her *Treatise on Purgatory* (originally but a chapter in the *Vita*) derived in part from the Lutheran controversy shortly after her death. There are indications that early editors conventionalized some of her phrases. But the central thought comes through: purgatory is the projection beyond of that mystical purgation which also takes place in this world in souls open to God's action. Frederick William Faber approved her concept of purgatory; Cardinal H. E. Manning wrote a preface to an English translation; Cardinal J. H. Newman enshrined it in his *Dream of Gerontius;* Aubrey de Vere wrote a poetic paraphrase of it.

According to Catherine, the imperfect soul at death plunges willingly into its purgation with joy and pain.

The same law of purification is at work Here-and-Now and Beyond—there is essential continuity of the interior life; the difference is rather in extent and intensity. The fundamental and universal experiences of the soul Here also have their place There. Hence her eschatology focuses on those features that she can forecast on the basis of her experience. She speaks of the holy soul, still in the flesh, placed in the purgatory of God's burning love so that it might, at the time of death, go straight to God. In this way one is to understand how it is with the souls in purgatory, abiding content in the fire of divine love.

Initial experience and act. In passing out of this life the soul to be purged perceives its sinful self as cause of its purgatory just once, never to dwell on the fact again, since it would be a self-centered thought. Then, wholly centered on God, it plunges eagerly into the ocean of purifying fire. The motive force is impetuosity of the "love which exists between God and the soul and tends to conform the soul to God." The soul seems to find God's great compassion in being allowed to remove the impediment within.

Subsequent process. This involves the dispositions, joys, and sufferings of the soul during its purgation, and finally comes the conclusion of the process. It is the story of Catherine's own mystical experience of purgation and her interpretation of that experience. The souls in purgatory simply accept the consequence of their epoch-making choice to deliver themselves to purgation. They do not dwell on their past sins; they do not compare themselves with others. They see themselves in God only; otherwise they would be letting self come in. Though the pain of purgatory is "horrible as hell," yet these souls are content, cannot find the pain to be pain. There is no joy comparable to that of a soul in purgatory, except the joy of the blessed in paradise. Because the soul has an instinct for God and its own perfection, an extreme fire springs up within it. As it approaches its original purity and innocence, that instinct of God releases increasing happiness, "for every little glimpse that can be gained of God exceeds every pain and every joy that man can conceive without it." The joy of the soul in purgatory continually increases because of the inflowing of God into it as the impediments diminish. The soul becomes progressively impassible. The fire burning within it without opposition is like the fire of life eternal. The soul purified remains in the fire, and the fire remains what it was, God. Thus, the pain of purgatory arises from the discord of spirit with Spirit and ends when they are in complete concord.

Feast: Sept. 15.

Bibliography: P. U. B. DA GENOVA, *S. Catherine Fieschi Adorno,* 2 v. (1960–62). *Catherine of Genoa: Purgation and Purgato-

ry, the Spiritual Dialogue, ed. S. HUGHES (New York 1979). D. C. NUGENT, ''Saint Catherine of Genoa: Mystic of Pure Love,'' in *Women Writers of the Renaissance and Reformation,* ed. K. M. WILSON, (Athens, Georgia 1987) 67–80. K. JORGENSEN, '''Love Conquers All': The Conversion, Asceticism, and Altruism of St. Caterina of Genoa,'' in *Renaissance Society and Culture,* eds. J. MONFASANI and R. MUSTO (New York 1991) 87–106. C. BALDUZZI, *Il Soprannaturale in Santa Caterina da Genova: patrona degli ospendali* (Udine 1992). F. DE MARTINOIR, *Catherine de Genes, La joie du Purgatoire: Caterina Fieschi Adorno, 1447–1510* (Paris 1995).

[P. L. HUG]

CATHERINE OF RACCONIGI, BL.

Mystic; b. Racconigi, province of Cuneo, Piedmont, Italy, June 24?, 1486; d. Caramagna, Piedmont, Sept. 4, 1547. Catherine was the youngest of seven children of a blacksmith. She worked as a weaver and distributed her wages to the poor. She loved solitude and contemplation and was vowed to virginity; she is known to have been favored with many mystical graces and prophecies as well as being privileged with the stigmata. From her Dominican confessor she received the habit of a tertiary on Dec. 22, 1513. Although she was esteemed and consulted by illustrious personages, she was also persecuted by the envious. When forced to take refuge in Caramagna, Catherine offered herself as a victim for sinners and for the maintenance of peace. Pius VII authorized her Mass and Office on April 9, 1808. She is commemorated in the Order of Preachers and in the dioceses of Turin and Mondovì, and is particularly venerated in Racconigi, where her house was made into an oratory and chapel in the Dominican church, in Caramagna, and in Garessio (Cuneo), where there is a chapel in her honor.

Feast: Sept. 4.

Bibliography: G. F. PICO DELLA MIRANDOLA and P. M. MORELLI, *Compendio delle cose mirabili della beata Caterina da Racconigi* (Chieri-Turin 1858). G. BONETTI, Vita. . . . (Turin 1876). A. FERRARIS, *Beata Caterina Mattei da Racconigi* (Alba 1947). A. GUARIENTI, *La Beata Caterina da Racconigi* (Alba 1964).

[I. VENCHI]

CATHERINE OF SIENA, ST.

Dominican tertiary and mystic, doctor of the church; b. Siena, probably in 1347; d. Rome, April 29, 1380.

Life. Catherine was the 23rd child (a twin) of Jacopo Benincasa, a dyer, and his wife, Lapa Piagenti. Jacopo was a good Christian and was to prove a true father to Catherine in her struggle for freedom to follow her unusual vocation. Lapa was an average Italian housewife;

she was hardworking, maternally affectionate, but spiritually rather obtuse. Catherine grew up intelligent, cheerful, and intensely religious. It is reported that at the age of 7, following a vision of Christ in glory, she vowed her virginity to him. Later on, her mother repeatedly urged her to care more for her appearance with a view to marriage. Catherine at first yielded a little but then proved intractable, and to show her resolution she cut off her hair. This led to persecution from her family, which was ended when Jacopo ordered that Catherine be left in peace and allowed her a room of her own for prayer and meditation. Catherine was already being guided in her spiritual life by the Dominicans, and she greatly desired to become a tertiary of the order. This was accomplished, after some difficulty, in 1364 or 1365. The next three years she spent in seclusion from the world, devoting herself to prayer and the practice of severe austerities. It proved to be a preparation for the active apostolate that was to follow, and it ended, probably in the spring of 1368, with a vision that convinced Catherine that Christ had accepted her as his ''bride.'' She received his command to carry her love for him out into the world and so give full scope to the charity within her.

Catherine's life from that time until her death fell into three somewhat clearly marked periods: from 1368 to the summer of 1374; from this date to November 1378; and then the year and a half until her death in 1380. The first period was spent entirely in Siena and is marked by four important developments. First, there gathered around her the nucleus of the group of friends and disciples with which her name is associated: men and women; priests both secular and religious, among whom Dominicans naturally predominated; and the laity; most of them her seniors, but all in some measure her spiritual pupils, and all accustomed to calling her ''mother.'' The formation of this ''family'' led in turn to the beginning, not later than 1370, of the great series of Catherine's letters. Probably she could already read, and later would learn to write, but she dictated nearly all her letters to secretaries chosen from her ''family.'' At first simply vehicles for spiritual instruction and encouragement, the letters soon began to touch on public affairs. The first public issue to receive her attention was a projected Crusade against the Turks. Meanwhile, in the little world of Siena, it was inevitable that her personality and influence should arouse some opposition and even slander. She was a saint who mixed fearlessly in the world and spoke with the candor and authority of one completely committed to Christ. At the same time she was a woman, young and with no social position. She was accused of hypocrisy and presumption. At this critical point it was her Dominican affiliation that saved her. Summoned to Florence to give an account of herself to the general chapter of the order held there in May and June of 1374, she satisfied the rigorous judges, and her work was given official Dominican protection. The chapter appointed Bl. RAYMOND OF CAPUA (1330–99) as director of Catherine and her followers; from then on he was very closely associated with her activities.

The next four years saw Catherine's influence on public affairs at its greatest. Two issues in particular led her into church politics: the Crusade already mentioned and the war between Florence and her Italian allies against the papacy (1376–78). Catherine's political achievements should not, however, be overestimated. She had no interest in secular politics as such and often showed herself naïve and ingenuous when involved in them. Such influence as she had was due to her manifest holiness, to her Dominican connection, and to the impression she made on Gregory XI and, to a lesser degree, on his successor, Urban VI. She first saw Gregory at Avignon in June 1376. She had gone there at the request of the Florentines, hoping to make peace between them and the pope. This effort was in vain, but she did have much to do with Gregory's decision to bring the Curia back to Rome in that same year. She had persisted also in her efforts for the Crusade, the project that so often recurs in her letters and that had brought her to Pisa in 1375. This visit is worth recording because it was during an ecstasy in a church in that city that Catherine received the stigmata, though the wounds were visible only to herself. By January 1377 Catherine was back in Siena. During the next two years she continued her tireless apostolate in that city and in the Tuscan countryside and, with less success, her efforts for peace in Florence. Gregory had died in March of 1378, and his successor was the well-meaning but often harsh and tactless Urban VI. In the autumn the Great Schism began.

This disaster overshadowed and saddened the last phase of Catherine's life. From November 1378 until her death she was in Rome, occupied chiefly with her prayers and pleading on behalf of Urban VI and the unity of the Church, and with the composition of her book, the *Dialogue,* written in four treatises, which she intended as her spiritual testament to the world. Early in 1380 her agony over the state of the Church, for which she had offered herself as a victim to God, brought on a seizure, the prelude to her death. She died, surrounded by her "children," and was buried in the church of the Minerva at Rome. Her head is at S. Domenico in Siena.

Spirituality. Spiritually, Catherine ranks high among Catholic mystics and spiritual writers. Her spirituality is markedly Christocentric: gifted by nature with a fine intelligence and intense vitality, she surrendered herself to the Incarnate Word. The basic theme of her teach-

Jesus Christ presenting St. Catherine of Siena with crown, painting by Pier Francesco Bissolo. (©Hulton Getty/Liaison Agency)

ing is God's creative and recreative (redemptive) love, expressed and symbolized in the Precious Blood. Her stress on the importance in Christian living of clear, exact knowledge shows her Dominican training, but her teaching derives at least as much from SS. Augustine and Bernard as (indirectly in any case) from St. Thomas. Venerated in her lifetime as a saint, she was canonized by Pius II in 1461. In 1939 Pius XII declared her and St. Francis of Assisi the chief patron saints of Italy, and, on Oct. 1, 1999, she was declared patron of Europe by John Paul II. In 1970, she was declared Doctor of the Church.

Feast: April 29 (formerly April 30).

Bibliography: Works. The standard complete edition of Catharine's letters is *Le lettere di s. Caterina da Siena,* ed. N. TOMMASÈO, 4 v. (Florence 1860), rev. ed. P. MISCIATTELLI, 6 v. (Siena 1913–21; repr. Florence 1939–40). E. DUPRÉ-THESEIDER, *Epistolario da Santa Caterina da Siena* (Rome 1940). *Saint Catherine of Siena as Seen in Her Letters,* tr. V. D. SCUDDER (New York 1905), a selection. *Dialogue or Libro della divina dottrina,* ed. M. FIORILLI (2d ed. Bari 1912), rev. S. CARAMELLA (1928), Eng. tr. A. L.

THOROLD (London 1896). *I, Catherine: Selected Writings*, ed. and tr. K. FOSTER and M. J. RONAYNE (London 1980). *The Letters of Catherine of Siena*, tr. S. NOFFKE (2d ed. Tempe, Ariz. 1999). Literature. *Fontes vitae s. Catharinae Senensis historici*, ed. M. H. LAURENT et al. (Siena 1936–). The most authoritative early life is RAYMUND OF CAPUA'S *Leggenda Major*, Eng. tr. G. LAMB, *The Life of St. Catherine of Siena* (New York 1960). A. LEVASTI, *My Servant Catherine*, tr. D. M. WHITE (Westminster, Md. 1954). A. GRION, *Santa Caterina da Siena: Dottrina e fonti* (Brescia 1953). G. CAVALLINI, *Catherine of Siena* (London 1998); *Things Visible and Invisible: Images in the Spirituality of St. Catherine of Siena*, tr. JEREMIAH (New York 1996), SR. M. *The Secret of the Heart: A Theological Study of Catherine of Siena's Teaching on the Heart of Jesus* (Front Royal, Va. 1995). A. CURTAYNE, *Saint Catherine of Siena* (New York 1935). S. UNDSET, *Catherine of Siena*, tr. K. AUSTIN-LUND (New York 1954). S. NOFFKE, *Catherine of Siena: Vision Through a Distant Eye* (Collegeville, Minn. 1996). R. FAWTIER, *Sainte Catherine de Sienne et la critique des sources*, 2 v. (Paris 1921–30), v. 1 *Sources hagiographiques*, v. 2 *Les Oeuvres de s. C. de S.* R. FAWTIER and L. CANET, *La Double expérience de Catherine Benincasa* (Paris 1948). Fawtier's radical criticism of the sources was examined by E. JORDAN in *Analecta Bollandiana* 40 (1922) 365–411. E. DUPRÉ-THESEIDER, ''La Duplice esperienza di S. C. da S.,'' in *Rivista storica italiana* 62 (1950) 533–574.

[K. FOSTER]

CATHERINE OF SWEDEN, ST.

Bridgettine; b. 1331 or 1332; d. Vadstena, March 24, 1381. She was the daughter of St. BRIDGET OF SWEDEN. In early youth she married the nobleman Eggard von Kürnen, with whom she lived in continency. In 1350 she joined her mother in Rome, sharing as daughter and companion Bridget's life of prayer, pilgrimage, and charitable works. After her husband's death (1351), Catherine refused many offers of marriage. Having accompanied her mother's remains to Sweden (1375), she devoted herself to the interests of the community founded by Bridget at Vadstena, becoming its first superior. From 1375 to 1380 she was in Rome to further her mother's canonization and the approbation of the Bridgettine rule. At this time she became the friend of CATHERINE OF SIENA. Though not formally canonized, she is listed in the Roman martyrology. A chapel in the Piazza Farnese is dedicated to her. Her devotional writings, including The *Consolation of the Soul,* have not survived.

See Also: BRIGITTINE SISTERS.

Feast: March 24.

Bibliography: A. BUTLER, *The Lives of the Saints*, ed. H. THURSTON and D. ATTWATER (New York 1956) 1: 669–671. A. L. SIBILIA, *Bibliotheca Sanctorum* 3:994–996.

[M. J. FINNEGAN]

CATHERINE THOMAS, ST.

Canoness Regular of Saint Augustine; b. Valdemuzza, Majorca, Spain, 1533; d. Palma, Majorca, 1574. Catherine, orphaned at the age of seven, already showed signs of great piety and gifts of prayer. She went to work as shepherdess for an uncle, who beat and starved her. In spite of this treatment she made great strides in the spiritual life. At the age of 16 she was accepted at the convent of St. Mary Magdalen in Palma, at her confessor's insistence, for she had no dowry. Here she tried to hide her spiritual gifts under a cloak of stupidity. Strange phenomena soon made her the center of controversy. She apparently had the gift of prophecy and also conversed with angels. She was said to have been attacked by devils who filled the cloisters with fearful shrieks and who once tossed her into a cistern full of muddy water. Distinguished visitors came continually to see her. She foretold the day of her own death at the age of 41. She was beatified in 1792 and canonized in 1930.

Feast: April 1.

Bibliography: A. BUTLER, *The Lives of the Saints*, ed. H. THURSTON and D. ATTWATER (New York 1956) 2:6–7. J. L. BAUDOT and L. CHAUSSIN, *Vies des saints et des bienhereux selon l'ordre du calendrier avec l'historique des fêtes* (Paris 1935–56) 4:135–136.

[M. J. DORCY]

CATHOLIC

The word catholic means general or universal (from the Greek καθολικός). Originally applied to the universal care and providence of God (by Tertullian), to the general resurrection (by Theophilus of Antioch), it is still used of those Epistles addressed to the Church at large and not to particular communities.

But today the term is more often applied to the Church founded by Christ, which is of its nature intended for all races and all times. The Prophets of the Old Law announced the universal reign of the Messiah, and this was established by Christ, who spoke of the kingdom as being destined for all men and who sent out His disciples to teach all nations. The reception of Cornelius marked an important step in the realization of this ideal; St. Paul in his day could already speak of the faith as being known throughout the whole world (Rom 1.8). Early Church documents (Didache, St. Polycarp) speak of universality as one of the characteristics of Christianity, and St. Ignatius of Antioch (*Smyrn.* 8.2) was the first to use the expression the Catholic Church. The growth of the Church in the first two centuries is often taken as a sign of its divine origin, since up to the time of Constantine there were very few material advantages to be obtained by a profession of Christianity; yet persecution increased rather than diminished the spread of the Church [*see* MIRACLE, MORAL (THE CHURCH)]. The struggle with the Donatists helped to clarify catholicity as a mark of the Church. The claim of the Donatists to be the one true church of Christ was seen to be inadmissible, since they were but a sect in a small corner of the globe. Optatus of Mileve and St. Augustine particularly insisted on this aspect of the Church of Christ spread throughout the world. Throughout history, as new lands and peoples have been discovered, the one and same Church has been extended to all parts of the world.

The word Catholic is also applied to the teaching and the faith of the Church of Christ, and in this sense it means what is believed by the whole Church. Thus Catholic teaching becomes a test of orthodoxy. It is sound doctrine as opposed to heresy, or, as Vincent of Lérins said, "that which has been believed everywhere, always, and by all. This is what is truly and properly Catholic" (*Common.* 1.2; *Enchiridion patristicum,* ed. M. J. Rouët de Journel [21st ed. Freiburg im Breisgau 1960] 2168). What is believed by the universal Church must be true, otherwise there would be a total defection from the teaching of Christ.

Finally the word Catholic is used of individual Christians insofar as they belong to the Catholic Church and are orthodox in their belief.

See Also: CATHOLICITY; ROMAN CATHOLIC; CHURCH, ARTICLES ON.

Bibliography: K. RAHNER and F. MUSSNER, *Lexikon für Theologie und Kirche,* ed. J. HOFER and K. RAHNER, 10 v. (2d, new ed. Freiburg 1957–65) 6:88–90. G. W. H. LAMPE, ed., *A Patristic Greek Lexicon* (Oxford 1961–). "Catholicus" in *Thesaurus linguae Latinae* (Leipzig 1900–) 3:614.53–618.35. Y. M. J. CONGAR, *Divided Christendom,* tr. M. A. BOUSFIELD (London 1939) 93–144. H. DE LUBAC, *Catholicism,* tr. L. C. SHEPPARD (New York 1958); *The Splendour of the Church,* tr. M. MASON (New York 1956). G. THILS, *Les Notes de l'église dans l'apologétique catholique depuis la réforme* (Gembloux 1937) 214–254. A. DULLES, *The Catholicity of the Church* (Oxford 1985). GARCIA Y GARCIA, H. LEGRAND, and J. MANZANARES, "The Local Church and Catholicity," *The Jurist* 52 (1992) 1:1–582.

[M. E. WILLIAMS]

CATHOLIC ACTION

A term used to designate both a concept and an organization of laity, and having a variety of meanings depending upon the decade and the region to which reference is made. This article treats (1) the definition of the term, (2) its origins and development, (3) organizational forms of Catholic Action, and (4) its theological significance.

Definition. At one extreme Catholic Action was used to refer to any external action of a Catholic layman

"The Children's Crusade," by Gustave Doré. (©Bettmann/ CORBIS)

inspired by his faith. This is Catholic Action only in a loose or accommodated sense. At the other extreme, Catholic Action referred only to such actions of lay groups as were so defined, and mandated by the local ordinary. In this sense, the term denotes a tightly structured organization that served as an arm of the hierarchy in lay life. The mandate is essential. Between these extremes were the multiple types of organization which may or may not have been classified as Catholic Action depending upon the concept prevailing in a particular country at a particular time.

This ambiguity of concept became apparent during the pontificate of Pius XII. As late as 1957 he acknowledged "a regrettable and rather widespread uneasiness which arises from the use of the term 'Catholic Action.'" The pope proposed "to restore to the term 'Catholic Action' its generic sense and to apply it simply to all organized movements of the lay apostolate recognized as such, nationally or internationally, either by the bishops on a national level or by the Holy See for movements desiring an international status. It would then be sufficient for each movement to be designated by its name and characterized by its specific form, and not by a common term." Further, he suggested an organizational reform: "All groups would belong to Catholic Action and would

Pope Pius XII is carried to the site from which he will address the 1947 Convention of Catholic Action groups, Rome, Italy. (©Bettmann/CORBIS)

preserve their own autonomy, but together they would form, as Catholic Action, a federated unit. Every bishop would remain free to accept or reject a movement, to entrust it or not entrust it with a mandate, but he could not refuse it recognition on the ground that it does not belong to Catholic Action by its nature" [*Six ans se sont, Acta Apostolicae Sedis* 49 (1957) 929–30].

This juridic and hierarchical concept of Catholic Action underwent further refinement after the death of Pius XII. However, John XXIII showed little concern for the tight legal categories of his predecessors. Meanwhile, during the 1950s, the term LAY APOSTOLATE received wide usage. It offered a practical way of avoiding the problem of definition. It was generic. It could be used to refer to all Catholic lay activity, whether organized or unorganized, episcopally mandated or simply of Christian inspiration, without danger of quibbles over terms or ecclesiastical jurisdiction.

Origins and Development. The term "Catholic Action" is a literal translation from the Italian, "Azione Cattolica," a specific national organization or movement. Saint Pius X seems to have been the first pope to use the term, stressing its importance in several encyclicals. Pius XI, however, gave to it its classical definition as "the participation of the laity in the apostolate of the Church's hierarchy." The concept was implicit in the encyclical *Ubi Arcano Dei* [*Acta Apostolicae Sedis* 14 (1922) 695] and later the pope remarked that the definition was "delivered after due thought, deliberately, indeed, and one may say not without divine inspiration" (Discourse to Italian Catholic Young Women, *L'Osservatore Romano*, March 21 to 22, 1927). Through his voluminous writings and addresses, Pius XI gave Catholic Action a charter, a spirit, and an apocalyptic urgency. While he did not deny that the term could be used in a broader sense, he tended throughout his pontificate to restrict it to (1) action or work of the laity, which was (2) organized, (3) apostolic, and (4) done under a special mandate of the bishop. A spate of manuals developed each of these points. Theorists tended to be juridical and pedantic in their discussions, while the priests and laity engaged in the work of Catholic Action developed their organized activities with less rigidity as a consequence of their encounter with the needs of the world. The most outstanding practitioner was Canon Joseph CARDIJN of Belgium, whose work Pius XI regarded as a model of Catholic Action and whom Paul VI elevated to the College of Cardinals in 1965.

Cardinal Saliège, archbishop of Toulouse, less concerned with theory than with contemporary conditions of life that many found unworthy of human beings, viewed Catholic Action in terms of institutional change, having for its task "to modify social pressure, to direct it, to make it favorable to the spread of the Christian life, to let the Christian life create a climate, an atmosphere in which men can develop their human qualities, can lead a really human life, an atmosphere in which the Christian can breathe easily and stay a Christian." It would, he said, "lift up the mass, not a couple of individuals; the mass, prompted and set in motion by a natural leader chosen from the mass and remaining part of the mass" [*Documentation catholique* 42 (1945) 266].

Organization. Each country gave to Catholic Action specific and varied forms. Italian Catholic Action and Belgian JOCISM are probably the polar types. The former, which had its origins in movements beginning as early as 1863, was intended to overcome open hostility to the Church. Six divisions were organized, for men, women, young men, young women, male students at universities, and female students. It was viewed at times by the Italian government as a political threat and was defended by Pius XI in a concordat and an encyclical, *Non abbiamo bisogno* (1931). Its main concerns were to establish better relations between the Church and the government and to revive Catholic practice among the negligent. Jocism, on the other hand, was concerned with changing or Christianizing economic and social institutions through a technique expressed in the formula, "see, judge, act," applied in small groups in a specialized or like-to-like apostolate.

Between the extremes of the monolithic Italian structure and the specialized forms there developed many movements directed to specific tasks such as the teaching of religion or the amelioration of conditions in a single area, e.g., motion pictures, literature, or the labor movement. In the United States there are, on the one hand, the highly centralized National Councils of Catholic Men and Women and the Confraternity of Christian Doctrine that are professedly the arm of the bishop in each diocese. On the other are activities of such diverse groups as the Christian Family Movement, the Sodality, Serra International, Labor Guilds, Catholic Interfacial Councils, and study clubs that, while usually not mandated by the local bishop, nevertheless exist with his approval. This variety of organizations, methods, and objectives compounded the confusion of those struggling with the concept of Catholic Action.

Theological Significance. Pius XI claimed that Catholic Action had its origins in the New Testament. Saint Paul, for example, referred to his lay helpers who "have toiled with me in the gospel" (Phil 4.3). Although social conditions in an industrial society call for different approaches to the world and new forms of collaboration between clergy and laity, Pius XI saw the layman essentially as an extension of the priest. He wrote that, "especially in our times, when the integrity of the faith and of morals is daily approaching a more dangerous crisis, and when we lament such a scarcity of priests that they seem to have proven unequal to caring for the necessities of souls, more reliance must be placed on Catholic Action" [*Quae Nobis, Acta Apostolicae Sedis* 20 (1928) 384–85]. It was his genius to see that the layman's life in the world must be related in a dynamic way to the mission of the Church. Catholic Action, he insisted, "is also social action, because it promotes the supreme good of society, the Kingdom of Jesus Christ. It is not unmindful of the great problems which vex society and which are reflected in the religious and moral order, but under the guidance of the hierarchy, it studies them and proposes to solve them according to the principles of justice and Christian charity" [*Con singular complacencia, Acta Apostolicae Sedis* 34 (1942) 256]. The "Pope of Catholic Action" also developed the theology of the priesthood through his many references to the priest as "the soul of Catholic Action."

The concept that a hierarchical mandate was necessary for Catholic Action was questioned anew by the developing theology of the laity. In the militant language of Catholic Action, in the sense of Pius XI, the layman may have been said to receive his commission from his bishop. If his role was to act as a soldier whose chief virtue was obedience rather than initiative, there was no difficulty. If, on the contrary, the mark of the authentic layman was a spirit of discovery and autonomy in lay life, issuing from competence based upon the development of his natural talents, it is difficult to see how his ministry could have been conceived as an extension of the clerical or hierarchical Church.

Catholic Action as a movement or a theological concept was laid to rest by Vatican II. The Catholic Action movements were a successful accommodation or bridge between an ecclesiology that rooted all ministry of the Church in the hierarchy and a growing awareness of the gifts of each person to the world as a witness to the gospel. The major VATICAN II documents, on the Church, *Lumen gentium*, and on the Church in the modern world, *Gaudium et spes*, witness the shift by omitting even any reference to Catholic Action. The shift can be found especially in chapter 4 of *Lumen gentium*.

Bibliography: J. NEWMAN, *What Is Catholic Action?* (Dublin 1958). L. MATHIAS, *Catholic Action, Theory and Practice* (Madras 1952). J. FITZSIMONS and P. MCGUIRE, eds., *Restoring All Things: A Guide to Catholic Action* (New York 1938). W. FERREE, *Introduction to Catholic Action* (Washington 1942). T. M. HESBURGH, *The Theology of Catholic Action* (Notre Dame, Ind. 1946).

[D. J. GEANEY]

CATHOLIC ALMANAC

Designed as a ready-to-hand reference work, the *Catholic Almanac* is a documentary, factual, and current annual publication covering a wide range of information about the Church, its members, and organizations. The almanac, carefully researched and indexed, is compiled from authoritative sources (all cited) and original surveys. Coverage of timely topics includes complete or excerpted texts of encyclicals and significant Church documents, features on subjects of topical interest, and a month-by-month review of news of the year with coverage of the activities of the pope, other Vatican actions, and national and international news of Catholic interest. Factual material includes statistics in many categories concerning the Church in the United States, Canada, and all other countries; and biographical sketches of the pope, cardinals, bishops of the United States from 1789 to the present, and bishops of Canada. Standard information on the Church covers doctrine, the Bible, liturgy and Sacraments, the Church calendar and saints' days, Marian doctrine, Eastern Catholic Churches, up-to-date information on the ecumenical movement and Catholic-Jewish relations.

Church history in general is presented in a century-by-century review of significant events from the first Pentecost to the present; the history of the Church in the United States is given in summary form and in a listing of background dates of each state. Information on the Church in the United States includes religious orders and congregations, secular institutes, home and foreign missions, social services, retreat houses, organizations, societies and movements, Catholic newspapers and periodicals, and awards. The almanac also contains an extensive glossary of terms.

The *Catholic Almanac* originated remotely from *St. Anthony's Almanac,* a 64-page annual with calendar, feature, and devotional contents, published by the Fran-

ciscans of Holy Name Province from 1904 to 1929. Completely revised and enlarged, the publication was issued under the title *The Franciscan Almanac,* by the *Franciscan Magazine* from 1921 to 1933, and by St. Anthony's Guild from 1936 to 1971. From 1940 to 1969, its title was *The National Catholic Almanac.* The present title was adopted in 1969. Felician A. Foy, OFM, has been editor since 1952. The 1959 to 1971 editions were produced jointly by St. Anthony's Guild and Doubleday & Co., Inc. The *Catholic Almanac* was acquired in 1971 by Our Sunday Visitor, Inc., Huntington, Ind.

[R. M. AVATO]

CATHOLIC APOSTOLIC CHURCH

Originated when a group of Christians in England in the early 19th century concluded that the Second Coming of Jesus Christ (*see* PAROUSIA) would be preceded by a restoration of the original college of 12 Apostles. They belonged to a prayer circle that, beginning in 1826, met once a year at the country estate of Henry Drummond, a devout and wealthy London banker. The rationalism of the age and the spiritual lethargy of the established church led them to pray for a revival of the gifts of the apostolic church. These Christians came under the influence of Edward IRVING (1792–1834), pastor of a Presbyterian church in London, who had joined the Drummond group. Because of Irving's leading role in the movement, the members of the Catholic Apostolic Church were often called "Irvingites." Irving became convinced that Christ would return in 1864, in preparation for which there should be a revival of the offices of the early Church— apostles, prophets, evangelists, pastors, and teachers, to which angels (bishops) and deacons were added later. He himself was removed from his pastorate by the Church of Scotland in 1832 because he encouraged speaking in tongues in his congregation. The first apostle of the Catholic Apostolic Church was appointed in 1832 and the second in 1833. Before his early death, Irving was made an angel, or bishop, but not an apostle. The organization of the new church was completed in 1835, when the other apostles were selected and held their first council in London. These 12 men spent a year in prayer and then left England for their missionary assignments around the world. In general their evangelistic labors were fruitless, but they did win some followers in Germany; a Catholic Apostolic Church was opened in Berlin in 1848. A schism in North Germany in 1863 led to the formation of the NEW APOSTOLIC CHURCH.

As a revival movement with a strong millennialist focus, it had much success in the late 19th century. But when the last of the apostles died in 1903, and the Second

NEW CATHOLIC ENCYCLOPEDIA

Coming was not imminent, the movement underwent a gradual decline. Over time, the movement shed its millennialism, and drew closer to Roman Catholic and Orthodox doctrinal and liturgical practices. Its liturgy developed along Catholic lines and emphasized the sacrificial character of the Eucharist. Its priests wore vestments, and soon veneration of the Mother of God, anointing of the sick, and the use of a tabernacle, sanctuary lamp, and holy water were introduced. Its doctrine was based on the NICENE, Apostles, and ATHANASIAN CREEDS (*see* CREED).

With the loss of their distinctive brand of millennialism, the raison d'être for the movement's existence was called into question. Many of their members joined the Church of England and the Roman Catholic Church, while those who remained splintered into competing sects.

Bibliography: P. E. SHAW, *The Catholic Apostolic Church* (New York 1946). K. W. STEVENSON, "The Catholic Apostolic Church: Its History and Its Eucharist," *Studia Liturgica* 13 (1979) 21–45. S. GILLEY, "Edward Irving: Prophet of the Millennium," in *Revival and Religion Since 1700* (London 1993) 95–110.

[W. J. WHALEN/EDS.]

CATHOLIC CHARITIES USA

Catholic Charities USA is a national association of local and diocesan Catholic agencies founded by 17 laymen and nine clerics at the Catholic University of America in 1910. Its former name was the National Conference of Catholic Charities (NCCC), which it kept until 1986. In 2001, it was the largest private network of social service organizations in the United States. It works to support families, reduce poverty, and build communities through a threefold mission: to provide service for people in need; to advocate for justice in social structures; and to call the entire Church and other people of good will to do the same.

Establishment and Early Years. In 1900, there were more than 800 Catholic institutions providing care to needy people, dependent children, prisoners, elders, sick people, and people with disabilities. Gradually, these individual institutions perceived a need to organize. Lead agents in establishing the old NCCC were the lay leadership of the St. Vincent de Paul Society. All the 17 laymen in the founding group were members of the Society. The principal framers included Thomas M. Mulry, President of the Superior Council of New York City in 1910, and Edmond J. Butler, a member of the same Council. Clerical founders included Msgr. William J. Kerby of The Catholic University of America; Rev. Francis Foy of Nutley, N.J.; Msgr. D. J. McMahon of New York City; Rev. M. J. O'Connor of Boston, Mass.; and Msgr. William J. White of Brooklyn, N.Y. The initiative, however, for establishing the Conference came from Brother Barnabas of The Brothers of the Christian Schools in New York. Long active in the service of youth, he had become convinced that the work of Catholic charitable organizations was impaired by a lack of regular communication among themselves and of opportunity for the interchange of ideas. Associated for years with Mulry, he had repeatedly discussed with him the desirability of an annual meeting of Catholic charity workers from all over the U.S. When the Society of St. Vincent de Paul at its meeting in Richmond in 1908 warmly endorsed such a conference, Brother Barnabas wrote to Bishop Thomas J. Shahan, Rector of the Catholic University of America, urging him to sponsor it. Shahan agreed and an organizational meeting was held on Feb. 19, 1910.

This organizing group agreed to found a national conference, and its first general meeting, attended by about 400 delegates, was held at the Catholic University of America, Sept. 25 to 28, 1910. Bishop Shahan was elected president and held that office until 1929. Monsignor Kerby served as secretary until 1920, when he was succeeded by Monsignor John O'Grady.

Catholics involved in charitable and social work at the time viewed their activities as calling for immediate relief for the needy, as well as concerted efforts at removing conditions that caused poverty and destitution. This view marked a transformation of social work, both in methods and ends. Caring was not enough. Social science was used to influence policies that affected the most vulnerable populations. Training for this apostolate became more rigorous and systematic. The NCCC aimed to improve standards for those engaged in Catholic social work. To promote its goals, the Conference sponsored local, regional, and national conferences of Catholic agencies; encouraged establishment of Catholic schools of social work, established the *Catholic Charities Review* (1916); and carried on a program of information service, research projects, and occasional publication dealing with specific problems.

The Conference met biennially at Catholic University until 1920. Thereafter it met annually in various cities across the U.S. Establishment in 1916 of a committee of diocesan directors of charity as one of the permanent national committees of the Conference was the beginning of the close relationship between diocesan directors and the Conference and gave a marked impetus to integration of Catholic charitable activities at the local and diocesan levels.

An obvious obstacle to the success of the Conference during its early years was the inadequate representation at the biennial meetings of the Catholic sisterhoods who at the time provided about 75 percent of the Catholic charitable activities in the U.S. Monsignor O'Grady arranged for a meeting of representative religious communities to coincide with the Conference meeting of 1920. From this meeting developed the National Conference of Religious.

1930 to 2000. The federal social legislation enacted to counter the devastating effects of the Great Depression of the 1930s was almost universally endorsed by the NCCC. The Conference, however, opposed the means test (that is, making aid depend upon proof of need), and in its support of benefits for elderly citizens argued for a program that would distribute these benefits as a matter of right, rather than on proof of need. Moreover, in its support of legislation, the Conference constantly took the position that government, in all its welfare programs, should foster and develop private agencies, rather than supplant them. The NCCC returned to this stance consistently throughout the 1940s and 1950s. Within the NCCC itself during that decade, Mr. Robert Biggs, of the St. Vincent de Paul Society in Baltimore, and Dr. Charles P. Neill, of Catholic University, were foremost in stressing the need of training not only for relief of distress but for elimination of its causes. This decade also saw deliberations at the annual meeting reflecting the concern that professionalization of social work may have been accompanied by a loss of its "spiritual component," and leaders of the Conference emphasized the importance of Christian charity as the guiding beacon and standard in Catholic social work. These concerns were also developing at the local and regional level, whose meetings began to inform the national assembly.

The original mission was reaffirmed in the 1972 report known as the *Cadre Study* and continues today, although local charitable agencies began to diversify the types of services they offered as times changed. Where housing, soup kitchens, adoption, and prison ministries would be examples of outreach in the 1960s, or job training, counseling, and elderly services the focus in the 1970s, more wide-ranging and creative services arose in the 1980s and 1990s. These included services for pregnant women, refugee and immigration assistance, services to persons with HIV/AIDS, drug treatment, and emergency disaster relief. For the last several years prior to the turn of the millennium, more than 9.5 million people were helped each year by Catholic Charities USA. In 1999 it accounted for every dollar spent, nearly 2.3 billion dollars. The national office is an advocate for social policies that aim to reduce poverty, improve the lives of children and families, and strengthen communities. Its Disaster Response Office organizes the Catholic community's response to disasters in the United States.

Publications. From the outset the Conference had hoped to foster a strong program of research. The publication of a *Directory of Catholic Charities* (Washington 1922) was the result of a long and continuing effort to get a factual picture of Catholic charities in the United States. Kerby's *The Social Mission of Charity* (New York 1921), O'Grady's *Catholic Charities in the United States* (Washington 1931), and Msgr. John M. Cooper's *Children's Institutions* (Philadelphia 1931) began to meet the need for a literature on Catholic social work. The Conference's committee on Standards of Family Case Work in Diocesan Agencies in 1926 published a useful report entitled "A Program for Family Service in Diocesan Agencies." In 1934 the Conference began publication of an information bulletin that would keep diocesan directors aware of the rapidly developing social legislation and its provisions, and circulated a series of informational bulletins among Catholic child-care institutions. After World War II it began circulation of a new information bulletin dealing with such topics as child-welfare legislation, socialized medicine, international relief, housing, and juvenile delinquency. Since 1950 the Conference has sponsored a series of studies on particular aspects of social work.

Bibliography: NATIONAL CONFERENCE OF CATHOLIC CHARITIES, *Proceedings* (Washington 1911–1972). J. O'GRADY, *Catholic Charities in the United States: History and Problems* (Washington 1931). M. T. BOYLAN, *Social Welfare in the Catholic Church* (New York 1941). D. T. MCCOLGAN, *A Century of Charity,* 2 v. (Milwaukee 1951). D. P. GAVIN, *National Conference of Catholic Charities, 1910–1960* (Milwaukee 1962). V. P. MAINELLI, ed., *Call to Action: A Casebook on Convening for Awareness and Action* (Washington, D.C. 1975). NCCC, *250 years of Service: A Chronicle of the Catholic Charities Movement* (Washington, D.C. 1979). Journals: *Catholic Charities Review* (a Vincentian journal published from 1895–1916 and then undertaken by NCCC, 1917–1974). *Social Thought* (Washington 1975-). Archives for the National Conference of Catholic Charities/Catholic Charities USA for the years 1920–1992 are located at the Catholic University of America.

[D. P. GAVIN/P. J. HAYES]

CATHOLIC COMMISSION ON INTELLECTUAL AND CULTURAL AFFAIRS

A collaborative organization founded in 1946 with ecclesiastical approval to encourage Catholic intellectual life and activities both in the United States and abroad. In the words of one of its founders, Jesuit Father John Courtney MURRAY, the Catholic Commission on Intellectual and Cultural Affairs (CCICA) seeks to provide "a ministry of clarification" on urgent matters of the day. In 1994 the membership stood at about 400. The organization is unique insofar as it is not defined by any one specialty. Membership is open to those outside the academy, though it is comprised primarily of full-time scholars.

The CCICA is governed by an executive board and its operations are overseen by an executive director. The longest serving executive director was Father William Rooney, a professor of English at the Catholic University of America. He served the CCICA from 1954 to 1982, after replacing Augustinian Father Edward Stanford (1946–54), the former president of Villanova University. It was under Rooney's tenure that thousands of dossiers on Catholic intellectuals were collected for use by the CCICA's membership committee, a project that proved to be unwieldy. All of these records were destroyed. The CCICA continues to publish an annual of its proceedings that is circulated privately among the members. Subject matter for these have included such topics as "Unity and Diversity in the Church" (1992), "The Young Catholics" (1993), and "The Future of Catholic Intellectual Life in the United States" (1999). In 2001 the CCICA's archive was located at the College of the Holy Cross in Worcester, Massachusetts.

[P. J. HAYES]

CATHOLIC DAUGHTERS OF THE AMERICAS

The Catholic Daughters of the Americas (CDA) is a charitable organization of Catholic lay and religious women who "strive to embrace the principle of faith working through love in the promotion of justice, equality, and the advancement of human rights and human dignity for all." Incorporated in Utica, NY, June 18, 1903, as a parallel organization to the Knights of Columbus, the organization assumed the name "Catholic Daughters of America" in 1921 to distinguish it from another offshoot of the Knights of Columbus called the "Daughters of Isabella." Recognizing its members in Mexico and the Caribbean, the 1978 CDA convention delegates changed the name from "America" to "Americas."

From the outset members organized into groups at the local level called "courts." Their early goals included "the propagation and preservation of the Faith, the intensification of patriotism, the spiritual and intellectual development of Catholic womanhood and the promotion of Catholic charitable projects." The CDA grew quickly in membership, developing a nationwide structure. According to its constitution and bylaws, the local and state courts, and the national court meet periodically under the leadership of a regent. Members elect delegates to a national biennial convention. National officers and directors assist the national regent (formerly called supreme regent) in the spiritual, philanthropic, legislative, patriotic, and social activities of the CDA. Under the jurisdiction of the state courts, girls ages six to eighteen comprise the Junior Catholic Daughters of the Americas (JCDA). A national youth chairman works with state and local courts to support their meetings and activities.

From the beginning the CDA had a publication to inform the membership about issues of interest and significance to women. The national publication has held various titles: the *Herald* (1904), *Woman's Voice* (1930), *News and Views* (1952), and *Share* (1970).

Initially, the Knights of Columbus guided the women, helping them draft their original bylaws and their ceremonial and initiation rites. For a few years Knights occupied several leadership positions at the national level and assisted at CDA initiation rituals and the establishment of new courts. Members used secret passwords for several decades to verify their eligibility to attend meetings as members in good standing.

The years of greatest growth and change were during the long-time regency of Mary C. Duffy (1923–1950) when she led the CDA to national, and eventually to international, recognition. She moved CDA headquarters from Utica to New York City and increased dues to establish a national fund for philanthropic action. Duffy organized the activities of the CDA into departments led by national directors and loosened the ties with the Knights of Columbus, giving the CDA greater autonomy. She was the first regent to choose a national chaplain from the American hierarchy. In the 1920s and 1930s the CDA promoted catechetical work and other pastoral ministries. During the World War II years, under Duffy's leadership, the CDA participated in war-relief efforts, and after the war vigorously supported post-war charitable and rehabilitative projects.

Working closely with American bishops in the decades after World War II, the CDA partnered projects with the National Catholic Relief Services, Catholic Charities USA, and the National Catholic Education Association. Courts at all levels supported the construction of chapels, and the educational work of the Catholic University of LOUVAIN (Leuven) in Belgium, The CATHOLIC UNIVERSITY OF AMERICA in Washington, D.C., and the NORTH AMERICAN COLLEGE in Rome.

In its first hundred years the Catholic Daughters developed a close relationship with Catholic bishops and church leaders in the Americas and abroad. The national regent became an *ex officio* observer at the fall meeting of the United States Conference of Catholic Bishops. Her membership on the board of Morality in Media indicates the CDA's long-time concern about the impact of the entertainment medium in American culture.

CDA membership rose from 60 in 1903 to 214,092 in 1962. It totaled 107,600 by the year 2001, with courts throughout the United States, the Dominican Republic, Guam, Puerto Rico, Saipan, and the Virgin Islands. At one time courts also met in Canada, Cuba, and Panama.

Bibliography: The papers and publications of the CDA are in the archives of The Catholic University of America, Washington, D.C. Of particular note are the issues of *Share* commemorating the fiftieth, sixtieth, seventieth, and seventy-fifth anniversaries of the CDA. Other important sources of information about the CDA include: M. DVORACEK, "Glorious History: Joy in the Beginning," *Share* (summer 1993) 32–35; R. MCLAUGHLIN, "Down Memory Lane in CDA History," *Share* (fall 1999) 11–13; S. RYTLEWSKI, "JCDA/Youth: Reviewing the Past, Looking to the Future," *Share* (fall 1999) 16–17; G. J. HEBERT and H. JOYCE, *The Catholic Daughters of the Americas: 1903–1986*, revised and updated by Edna Jane Nolte and Thomas Finney (1986).

[C. D. CLEMENT]

CATHOLIC DIRECTORY, OFFICIAL

Published annually by P. J. Kennedy & Sons, New York, the Official Catholic Directory provides up-to-date information about the Roman Catholic Church in the United States, organized diocese by diocese in alphabetical order, including the dioceses of the various Eastern Catholic Churches. The listings give the names, addresses, and telephone numbers of the ordinary, past and present, and auxiliary bishops; the clergy, parishes, diocesan offices and commissions, educational institutions within the diocese, religious orders and congregations represented, medical facilities; in short, all Catholic organizations that have diocesan recognition. The information is derived from reports submitted to the publishers by the ecclesiastical authorities of each diocese.

Preceding the main body of the directory are sections devoted to the organization of the papacy and the Roman Curia, the College of Cardinals, the Apostolic Nunciature, the National Conference of Catholic Bishops, and the United States Catholic Conference. In the back of the book, following the listing of the dioceses, is a brief summary of the organization of the Catholic Church in Canada and Mexico. There is a detailed directory of all the American foreign missions. A page is devoted to the United States Conference of Secular Institutes. There is also a directory with the address and phone numbers of the headquarters of the male and female religious orders in the United States. There are listings of mission churches in the U.S.; the cardinals, archbishops, and bishops in the U.S.; an alphabetical index of all the secular and regular clergy; and a necrology for the previous year. An appendix provides information on places of pilgrimage in the U.S.

Although the word "official" in the title dates only from 1905, this directory began in 1886. Until 1899 it was called *Hoffmann's Catholic Directory, Almanac and Clergy List*. However, this directory had three predecessors and is considered to be their direct successor. In 1817, the *Catholic Laity's Directory to the Church Service* was published. This was followed in 1822 by *The Laity's Directory to the Church Service*. Both these items served as directories for the Church in the U.S. From 1833 until 1896 this purpose was served by *Sadlier's Catholic Directory, Almanac and Ordo*.

[R. B. MILLER]

CATHOLIC EDUCATIONAL REVIEW

The *Review* was a journal of import and interest to Catholic education published ten times a year between January 1911 and November 1969. In 1907 Thomas E. Shields of The Catholic University of America had started the "Catholic Educational News Service," in which, until 1910, he had published a series of articles on teaching religion. Response led to him establishing the Catholic Education Press to publish Catholic elementary school textbooks. He saw no successful Catholic periodical to meet the challenge of nonreligious theories in the field of education. (In the 1890s the *Review of Catholic Pedagogy* had lasted one year; *Mooker's Magazine*, about two years; and *Catholic School Work*, seven months in 1909.) On June 15, 1910, he and Edward A. Pace petitioned Thomas J. Shahan, Rector of the University, to have the Catholic Education Press publish such a journal under Catholic University's Department of Education. The three agreed to pick up the deficit themselves for five years if there was one, then either to cease publication or ask for outside help.

Shields and Pace wrote a prospectus indicating as the journal's purpose attention to the needs of Catholic teachers; it would bring to their attention the connection between principles and practice, improvements in method, and standards of criticism of current theories. The initial intent was to have each issue contain a survey of the field: one article each on the history of education from the Catholic standpoint, methods, management or policy, a practical phase, the philosophy or psychology of education, the international struggle between materialism and religion in education, the contributions of teaching communities, and practical schoolroom difficulties, as well as worthwhile news and book reviews. The first article, by Pace, was on "The Papacy and Education." Many of the early articles were contributed anonymously by nuns. In the first 40 years there were 413 articles on curriculum (especially the role of religion; curriculum reconstruction; such phases as social studies, Latin, and vocational education; but content was deficient in the physical sciences, mathematics, and modern languages); 354 on methodology (mostly in religion, but also in English, social studies, Latin, and arithmetic); 271 on history (especially Catholic); 207 on administration (especially supervision and affiliation); 178 on philosophy; 163 on psychology; 119 on teacher training; 109 on Federal relations; 88 on guidance; 22 on library matters; and 201 on miscellaneous literary, political, scientific, sociological, and other noneducational subjects. At first the emphasis was on elementary schools, but in the 1920s it included more of secondary interests, and later increasingly more of college and university interests. Dissertation abstracts brought research to the reader's attention. There were few editorials.

Shields served as editor until his death in 1921. Some other prominent editors and associate editors were Bp. Patrick J. McCormick; George Johnson; Felix M. Kirsch, OFMCap; Michael J. McKeough, OPrem; James E. Cummings; Francis P. Cassidy; Frank J. Drobka; Urban J. Fleege; and Sister Mary Vernice, SND. Joseph A. Gorham was editor from 1949 until his death on July 7, 1966; under him the *Review* was honored by the Catholic Press Association with gold medals for excellence in 1953 and 1955. In Sept. 1966 an editorial board was appointed from Catholic University's School of Education faculty; and in 1968 a new editorial board was appointed from a University-wide basis.

By April 1911 there were 3,670 subscriptions to Canada, Panama, Europe, and Australia, as well as the United States. By 1921 there were about 4,000 subscriptions, which decreased in the Depression to 1,870, about where they remained until after World War II. Campaigns during the 1950s brought them up to 4,675 in 1960, about where they leveled off. At Shields's death, all but 20 shares of the *Review's* stock were given to Catholic Sisters College. In Dec. 1947 Vincent Shields, nephew of the founder, was succeeded as managing editor by James A. Magner of Catholic University, and in 1948 the general administration of the *Review* was transferred to the University. The issue of Nov. 1969 was the last, because of a feeling in some quarters that the impact of the journal had recently not been sufficiently significant and because of a lack of financial resources to meet spiraling costs.

Bibliography: J. A. GORHAM, "Looking Back Fifty Years," *Catholic Educational Review* 59 (1961) 145–154. J. J. CUDDY, "A Critical Analysis of the Contents of the First Forty Years of the Catholic Educational Review," unpublished M.A. dissertation, The Catholic University of America (Washington, D.C. 1953).

[H. A. BUETOW]

CATHOLIC EPISTLES

Seven short epistles in the NT (James; Jude; 1 and 2 Peter; 1, 2 and 3 John) have traditionally been grouped under the heading "Catholic Epistles." In this context, "catholic" seems to have been used to reflect their supposed general or universal audience, and to distinguish them from the letters attributed to St. Paul which were addressed to individual churches or persons. But there is nothing about Jude and 2 Peter that precludes them from having been addressed to specific communities. Further, E. Kasemann had the notion that, when compared to Paul, they reflect traits of "early catholicism," that is to say, they manifest a heightened concern for Church order, domesticated ethics, and diminished eschatological expectation. The texts of these letters, taken in themselves, do not sustain Kasemann's position. Moreover, it is possible that not all seven letters are later than the Pauline epistles.

The grouping is still used as a matter of convenience and they continue to be studied together as, for example, in the edition of the papyrus texts of the NT (Grunewald) and the Syriac manuscripts (Aland and Juckel). Although they share some similarity because of common parenetic traditions, there is no demonstrable literary dependence among them with the exception of 2 Peter and Jude (Brox). In short, each deserves treatment on its own terms. In this volume, 1, 2 and 3 John are considered in connection with the JOHANNINE WRITINGS. The others are described in detail in earlier volumes; this article is a report on current thought regarding the authors, structures and some themes in James, 1 Peter, Jude and 2 Peter (in probable chronological sequence).

Bibliography: R. A. MARTIN and J. H. ELLIOTT, *James, I - II Peter, Jude* (Minneapolis 1982). R. J. BAUCKHAM, *Jude, 2 Peter* (Waco, Tex. 1983). F. W. DANKER, *Invitation to the New Testament Epistles,* v. 4 *A Commentary on Hebrews, James, 1 and 2 Peter, 1, 2 and 3 John and Jude With Complete Text from the Jerusalem Bible* (Garden City, N.Y. 1980). R. KUGELMAN, *James and Jude* (Wilmington, Del. 1980). D. SENIOR, *1 and 2 Peter* (Wilmington, Del. 1980). J. NEYREY, *First Timothy, Second Timothy, Titus, James, First Peter, Second Peter, Jude* (Collegeville 1983). W. G. HUPPER, "Additions to a 2 Peter Bibliography" *Journal of the Evangelical Theological Society* 23 (1980) 65–66. J. SNYDER, "A 2 Peter Bibliography," *ibid.* 22 (1979) 265–267. G. WAGNER, ed., *Bibliographical Aids: Exegetical Bibliographies of the Writings of the New Testament,* First Series Nos. 10–14: Gal., Phil., Eph., Col., Phlm., Thes., Pastorals, Catholic Epistles, Heb., Rev. (1977–79). D. SYLVA, "A 1 Peter Bibliography," *Journal of the Evangelical Theological Society* 25 (1982) 75–89. R. J. BAUCKHAM, "2 Peter: A Supplementary Bibliography," *ibid.* 25 (1982) 91–93. W. GRUNEWALD with K. JUNACK ed., *Das Neue Testament auf Papyrus,* v.

1 *Die katholischen Briefe* (Berlin 1986). B. ALAND with A. JUCKEL, ed., *Das Neue Testament in syrischer Überlieferung,* v. 1 *Die grossen katholischen Briefe* (Berlin 1986).

[M. KILEY]

CATHOLIC HEALTH ASSOCIATION

An organization founded in Milwaukee, Wis., in 1915 as the Catholic Hospital Association, "for the promotion and realization of progressively higher ideals in the religious, moral, medical, nursing, educational, social, and all other phases of hospital and nursing endeavor and other consistent purposes especially relating to the Catholic hospitals and schools of nursing in the United States and Canada." Because the national health system of Canada differs from that of the United States, Canadian Catholic hospitals in 1945 formed their own hospital council that, in 1954, became the Catholic Hospital Association of Canada.

By 1914, the American College of Surgeons was establishing minimum standards for the practice of surgery in hospitals and the American Medical Association was beginning to insist that only hospitals with adequate facilities should be entrusted with internships and residencies. Aware of these developments, Charles B. Moulinier, SJ, regent of the Marquette University Medical School (Wis.), took the occasion of a retreat that he had given to the Sisters of St. Joseph of Carondelet in St. Paul, Minn., to discuss with the hospital sisters of that order how Catholic hospitals should best meet these new standards. They agreed that an effective means would be the formation of an association of Catholic hospitals.

With the encouragement of Sebastian G. Messmer, archbishop of Milwaukee, Moulinier took the initiative for forming such an association and prepared a constitution for it. The association's first convention, held in Milwaukee in 1915, adopted the constitution and elected Moulinier president, a position he held until 1928. Moulinier worked assiduously at the CHA's immediate objective—preparing Catholic hospitals for standardization. The existence of the CHA and its cooperation with the American College of Surgeons contributed significantly to the success of his efforts.

The association became the Catholic Health Association in 1979 and today represents the combined strength of its members, more than 2,000 Catholic health care sponsors, systems, facilities, and related organizations. CHA unites members to advance selected strategic issues that are best addressed together rather than as individual organizations. It strengthens the Church's healing ministry in the United States by advocating for a just health care system, convening leaders to share ideas and foster collaboration, and uniting the ministry voice on critical issues. In 2001, the association issued a "Shared Statement of Identity for the Catholic Health Ministry."

In 2001, Catholic health care in the United States included 61 health care systems, 637 hospitals, 518 long-term care nursing facilities, 122 home health agencies plus hospital based home care, 36 hospice organizations, and 694 other services along the care continuum (e.g., adult day care, assisted living, and senior housing).

The association is governed by 25 elected members of its Board of Trustees. Its national office has been in St. Louis, MO, since 1929. It also has an office in Washington, DC, which is dedicated in part to advocacy, public policy, and governmental relations.

[R. T. SHANAHAN/R. STEPHENS]

CATHOLIC LIBRARY ASSOCIATION

The Catholic Library Association (CLA) was founded in 1921. Since then it has actively pursued its originally stated purpose: to coordinate the exchange of ideas among librarians; to provide a source of inspirational support and guidance in ethical issues related to librarianship; and to foster fellowship for those who seek, serve, preserve, and share the word in all its forms. The association carries out its mission by encouraging the establishment of religion-oriented libraries; promoting accepted standards of library service; serving as an educational resource for professional librarianship, and fostering research and development in the field. Membership is open to individuals who share the values of the association regardless of the types of libraries in which they serve. Organizational membership is open to institutions and libraries that support the mission and goals of the association.

The association supports and provides for the creation, compilation, publication, and use of religious reference tools and develops cooperative relationships with associations having mutual interests. Its official publication is the *Catholic Library World.* Published quarterly, the journal includes topics of interest to children's, high school, and academic libraries as well as parish and community libraries, archives, and library education. The journal reviews books of interest to professional librarians as well as library users. The CLA also publishes the *Catholic Periodical and Literature Index,* a quarterly index of Catholic periodicals, national Catholic newspapers, essays, book reviews, and monographs. Coverage began in 1930 and since 1981 the reference resource has been available in both print and electronic formats.

The association established the Regina Medal in 1959 to honor an individual's continued distinguished contribution to children's literature. Other awards made annually include: the Aggiornamento Award (established 1980), presented by the Parish and Community Libraries Section to recognize contributions made by an individual or an organization for the renewal of parish and community life in the spirit of Pope John XXIII; an annual Certificate of Merit (established 1966) is presented by the High School Libraries Section in recognition of an outstanding contribution to the growth of high school librarianship; the Jerome Award (established 1992) is given by the Academic Libraries Section in recognition of outstanding contributions and commitment to excellence in scholarship that embody the ideals of the association. The John Brubaker Memorial Award recognizes an outstanding work of literary and professional merit published in *Catholic Library World.* Two scholarship awards are made each year: the Reverend Andrew L. Bouwhuis Memorial Scholarship for graduate study toward a master's degree in library science and the World Book Award for scholarships for continuing education in school or children's librarianship.

The CLA holds its annual conference in conjunction with the National Catholic Educational Association, underscoring the strong and consistent commitment of the organization to religious education. Headquarters of the CLA are located in Pittsfield, Massachusetts.

Bibliography: CATHOLIC LIBRARY ASSOCIATION, *Handbook and Membership Directory, 1999–2001* (Pittsfield, Mass. 1999).

[A. R. CHWALEK]

CATHOLIC MEDICAL ASSOCIATION

The Catholic Medical Association (CMA), formerly the National Federation of Catholic Physicians' Guilds, traces its genesis to a meeting of Catholic doctors in 1932 in New York City. The CMA, which underwent the name change in 1997, continues to be a national organization of Catholic physicians dedicated to upholding the principles of the Catholic faith and morality as related to the science and practice of medicine. It is also a member of the International Federation of Catholic Medical Associations (FIAMC). The CMA works closely with the Catholic Health Association, the Catholic Press Association, the National Council of Catholic Laity, and all National Right-to-Life groups. It supports all worthwhile medical mission programs, and is particularly supportive of the Mission Doctors Association, headquartered in Los Angeles, California. It frequently serves as a consultant for the USCCB Health Affairs Committee, as well as for local ordinaries.

The purposes of the Catholic Medical Association are (1) to uphold the principles of Catholic faith and morality as related to the science and practice of medicine; (2) to cooperate in leading the Christian community, especially with the particular medical expertise and experience of the Catholic physician, to understand, develop, and apply Christ's principles of faith and morality to modern medical science and practice; (3) to lead the Christian community in the work of communicating Catholic medica ethics to the medical profession and the community-at-large; (4) to uphold Catholic hospitals in the application of Catholic moral principles in medical practice; and (5) to enable Catholic physicians to know one another better and to work together with deeper mutual support and understanding.

Local chapters or guilds are urged to participate widely in parish and diocesan activities—sex education or awareness, natural family planning and pre-Cana programs, Birthright, pro-life activities, defense of the family and of marriage, and of chastity itself. The CMA collaborates with the National Catholic Bioethics Center in Boston, Massachusetts, which lends its doctrinal expertise on health-care issues and disseminates that information throughout the country in a monthly newsletter, *Ethics and Medics,* and a journal *The National Catholic Bioethics Quarterly.*

Although CMA is not a policy-making body, it lends its name and professional standing to those issues that lie at the intersection of medicine and morals. It has adopted resolutions advocating universal HIV-testing for pregnant women (1996), non-cooperation in the production of vaccines derived from cells harvested from aborted fetuses (1996), condemnation of so-called ''morning-after pills'' (1998), encouragement of ethical medical school curricula related to terminal illness (1998), and a moratorium on any attempt to achieve human cloning in the laboratory (1998). Through all these resolutions is a tacit adherence to biblical and natural-law principles.

The CMA publishes the *Linacre Quarterly,* named for Thomas Linacre, a distinguished physician of the 16th century. A journal of the ethics and philosophy of medical practice in support of the magisterium, it serves the needs of the increasing number of physicians who have had minimal exposure to Catholic teaching and assists all readers through its medico-moral discussions.

Each local guild is autonomous. Efforts have been made to form independent guilds in each major hospital in some of the larger cities. Activities include retreats or a Mass, usually in connection with the feast of St. Luke, the CMA patron, on October 18, health care of religious, fostering Catholic medical student groups, and cooperating with local charity organizations in the care of the sick and the poor.

[W. A. LYNCH/P. J. HAYES]

CATHOLIC NEAR EAST WELFARE ASSOCIATION

Commonly known by its acronym, CNEWA, an agency of the Holy See established to support the pastoral mission and institutions of the Catholic Churches of the East and to provide humanitarian assistance to the needy and afflicted without regard to nationality or religion. The Holy Father also has entrusted it with responsibility for promoting the union of the Catholic and Orthodox churches.

CNEWA works on behalf of the Christian East—that is, those lands in which, from ancient times, the majority of Christians are members of the various Eastern churches. Its mandate extends to the churches and peoples of the Middle East, Northeast Africa, India and Eastern Europe and to Eastern Catholics everywhere. It raises and distributes funds to help meet the material and spiritual needs of the people it serves.

Establishment and early history. During the years following World War I, Popes Benedict XV and Pius XI sought to bring material and spiritual aid to the countries and peoples afflicted by the war. They were supported generously by the faithful of the whole world and in particular by the Catholics of United States. Various American associations were organized to assist the needy in Russia and the Near East.

On March 11, 1926, Pius XI merged these American Catholic associations into one—*The Catholic Near East Welfare Association*, a pontifical organization incorporated in Pennsylvania on Sept. 30, 1924 to support the pastoral, relief and ecumenical activities of the Greek Catholic Exarchate in Constantinople. The fledging association was placed under the immediate direction of the Archbishop of New York, who was charged to form a governing body for it selected from the U.S. hierarchy. On Sept. 15, 1926, at their eighth annual meeting, the Catholic bishops of the United States expressed ''their full approval and adoption'' of the pope's plan and declared that the new Catholic Near East Welfare Association ''shall be the sole instrumentality authorized to solicit funds for Catholic interests in those regions and shall be so recommended to the entire Catholic population of the United States.''

On June 28, 1930, the pope established regulations to clarify the objectives of CNEWA and to strengthen its

bonds with the Holy See, emphasizing that CNEWA was to conduct its activities under the immediate and personal direction of the Archbishop of New York, who would function as president and treasurer. The archbishop was to select a secular priest and entrust him with the day-to-day administration of the organization with the title of secretary. CNEWA continued to operate under its Pennsylvania civil charter until Dec. 14, 1942 when it was reincorporated under the Religious Corporations Law of the State of New York.

Later developments. On June 18, 1949, the Holy See's humanitarian and charitable assistance to Palestinian refugees and displaced persons was consolidated and formalized with the establishment of the PONTIFICAL MISSION FOR PALESTINE. Pope Pius XII entrusted its direction to the Secretary of CNEWA with the mandate of coordinating aid from the entire Catholic world for the suffering people of the Holy Land. Offices were established first in Beirut, Lebanon, and later in Jerusalem and Rome; after the 1967 Arab-Israeli war, another office was opened in Amman, Jordan.

CNEWA support of India's Eastern Catholic churches—the Syro-Malabar and the Syro-Malankara Churches—increased after Indian independence in 1947. The establishment in the 1960s of CNEWA's sponsorship programs for the support of needy children, seminarians, and religious sisters strengthened its presence in India as well as in Northeast Africa, particularly Egypt, Eritrea, and Ethiopia. An Addis Ababa office was established in 1993, and an Asmara office, in 1999.

CNEWA informs people about the peoples and faiths of the East, especially through its bimonthly magazine, *CNEWA World*. The governing body of CNEWA is a board of nine trustees, chaired by the Archbishop of New York. CNEWA's principal office is located in New York City. The following have served as secretary (general): Father Edmund A. Walsh, S.J., (1926–31); Msgr. James B. O'Reilly (1931–41); Msgr. Bryan J. McEntegart (1941–43); Msgr. Thomas J. McMahon (1943–55); Msgr. Peter P. Tuohy (1955–60); Msgr. Joseph T. Ryan (1960–66); Msgr. John G. Nolan (1966–87); and Msgr. Robert L. Stern (1987–).

[M. J. L. LA CIVITA]

CATHOLIC STUDENTS MISSION CRUSADE

The Catholic Students Mission Crusade (CSMC), a mission education organization, sprang from a vision of two Society of Divine Word seminarians, Clifford J. King and Robert B. Clark, who wanted to establish an organization similar to the highly successful Protestant Student Volunteer Movement for Foreign Missions that John Mott had founded. The first meeting took place in 1918 at Techny, outside Chicago, Illinois, with over 100 clergy, seminarians, laity and a few bishops attending. The organization grew quickly under the leadership of Frank A. Thill, its national director who later became Bishop of Salinas, Kansas in 1938. Thill edited the organization's national magazine, *The Shield*, and traveled the country challenging students to imitate the zeal and dedication of the medieval Crusaders for their faith.

Two parallel themes permeated the organization: imagery surrounding the medieval crusaders and the promotion of missions at home and abroad. By the 1930s, the CSMC had enrolled a half-million members. In the next decade, it began compiling U.S. Catholic missionary statistics and in the 1950s it drew on the experience and knowledge of member mission societies to produce *Fundamentals of Missiology* and *Perspectives in Religion and Culture*. Other books in the 1960s drew attention of U.S. Catholics to the church and cultures in Africa and Asia.

At biennial national conventions, except during World War II, several thousand youth and adult leaders rallied for a summer conference, where they listened to talks by missionaries, walked through large-as-life mission displays, and took part in liturgical services aimed at inspiring young people to read, support missionaries in prayer and to consider a mission vocation themselves. Locally the CSMC was conducted in school units on the junior and senior high school level, as well as in colleges and seminaries. The units used the many audio-visual resources produced by the national office in Cincinnati, Ohio, and attempted to infuse a mission spirit throughout the schools. "Round Table" discussions, talks by returned missionaries, prayer, song and mission kits provided information and formation about missions at home and abroad. For half a century, the Catholic Student Mission Crusade became one of the most effective and pervasive mission education and promotion programs.

Almost as quickly as the organization had begun, the CSMC closed its national doors in 1972. New understandings of mission which surfaced at the Second Vatican Council, the demise of crusade themes and medieval imagery, and a plethora of liturgical and catechetical developments following the Council, and social and political issues of the 1970s directed the attention of U.S. Catholic youth elsewhere.

Bibliography: A. DRIES, "Whatever Happened to the Catholic Students Mission Crusade," *The Living Light* 34.3 (Spring 1998) 61–64. A DRIES, *The Missionary Movement in American Catholic History* (Maryknoll, N.Y. 1998).

[A. DRIES]

CATHOLIC THEOLOGICAL SOCIETY OF AMERICA (CTSA)

Founded, 1946, as a professional and learned society, and legally incorporated as a nonprofit corporation in the State of New York. Its first president was Francis J. Connell, C.Ss.R.

According to the society's constitution, its purpose, "within the context of the Roman Catholic tradition, shall be to promote studies and research in theology, to relate theological science to current problems, and to foster a more effective theological education, by providing a forum for an exchange of views among theologians and with scholars in other disciplines." Since its founding, the CTSA has sought to assist those entrusted with a teaching ministry in the Church, to develop in the Christian people a more mature understanding of their faith, and to further the cause of unity among all people through a better appreciation of the role of religious faith in the life of human beings and society. It seeks to achieve its purpose chiefly through its annual convention in early June, through the publication of the convention *Proceedings*, through a program of scholarly publication, and a variety of ad hoc committees for research and inquiry into specific questions.

The CTSA also publishes, either in the *Proceedings* or separately, various reports of special study groups or research teams which it sponsors. Examples of such publications include *The Renewal of the Sacrament of Penance* (1975), *Human Sexuality* (1977), *Woman in Church and Society* (1978), *Catholic Perspectives on Baptism, Eucharist, and Ministry* (1986), and *Report of the CTSA Committee on the Profession of Faith and Oath of Fidelity* (1990).

Each year the CTSA presents an award to a member for outstanding achievement in theology. Originally called the Cardinal Spellman Award, it is now known as the John Courtney Murray Award.

In keeping with the change and renewal occurring in the Church as a result of Vatican Council II, CTSA has also experienced change and renewal in its own activity and in its ministry to the church. In the early 1970s the CTSA revised its Constitution. The requirements for membership were raised so that ordinarily the doctorate in theology is required for active membership and the completion of doctoral course work is required for associate membership. At the same time during the years since Vatican II, CTSA membership has increased and broadened to include a number of non-Catholic theologians, a growing number of women and lay persons, and a greater number of graduates from European and non-Catholic universities. Women religious and lay members have served on the board of directors and the presidency. From the early 1980s onward, membership became more culturally and ethnically diverse, with an increasing number of African-American, Hispanic/Latino(a) and Asian theologians joining as members. This was a far cry from its early days as a bastion of theologians who were white, male and clerical.

The CTSA came of age in 2001, when a Vietnamese-American theologian, Peter C. Phan, the Warren-Blanding Professor of Religion and Culture at The Catholic University of America, assumed the office of CTSA president, becoming the first Asian-American, indeed, the first non-Caucasian to assume this position. Picking up on this momentum for change and diversity, the members of the Society elected M. Shawn Copeland, an African-American woman theologian, as vice-president at the 2001 annual convention. She assumes the presidency of CTSA in 2003, the first African-American theologian to do so.

[C. L. SALM/E. H. KONERMAN/J. Y. TAN]

CATHOLIC THEOLOGICAL UNION AT CHICAGO

The Catholic Theological Union at Chicago was founded in 1967. In response to the renewal of the Second Vatican Council, three religious orders—the Franciscans of Sacred Heart Province, the Servites of the Eastern U.S.A. Province and the Passionists of Holy Cross Province—chose to unite their seminaries in order to more creatively educate for the religious priesthood. It was also their decision to locate the school near other graduate schools of theology and the University of Chicago in order that students and faculty may benefit from and contribute to theological scholarship and ministerial formation in an urban, ecumenical and university setting. Classes began in the fall quarter of 1968, with a faculty of 24 and an enrollment of 108.

After its founding, other religious communities designated Catholic Theological Union as their official theologate: the Augustinians (1968), the Norbertines (1968), the Cincinnati Province and Kansas City Province of the Society of the Precious Blood (1968), the Missionaries of the Sacred Heart (1969), the Society of the Divine Word (1970), the Eastern Province of the Congregation of the Holy Ghost (1971), the Claretians (1972), the Viatorians (1972), the Xaverian Missionaries (1973), the Crosiers (1974), the Comboni Missionaries of the Heart of Jesus (1976), the Pontifical Institute for Foreign Missions (1976), the St. Nicholas Diocese in Chicago for Ukrainian Catholics (1978), the Priests of the Sacred

Heart (1979), the Assumption Province of the Franciscans (1980), the Congregation of the Blessed Sacrament (1980), the St. Paul of the Cross Province of the Passionists (1981), the Capuchins (1982), the Society of St. Columban (1984), the Redemptorist Fathers and Brothers (1984), the Central United States Province of the Missionary Oblates of Mary Immaculate (1985), the Western Province of the Congregation of the Holy Ghost (1985), the Oratorians (1987), the Maryknoll Missioners (1988), the St. John the Baptist Province of the Missionary Oblates of Mary Immaculate (1988), the St. Bonaventure Province of the Franciscan Conventuals (1988) and the Missionaries of St. Charles-Scalabrinians (1992).

The Catholic Theological Union is not a coalition of independent schools. Rather, the participating orders closed their individual theologates and merged their resources into one school, with one administration and faculty. Control is vested in the Board of Trustees. The primary mission of the Catholic Theological Union is the academic and pastoral formation of students preparing for priesthood and for a variety of other ministries in the United States and around the world. The school also provides continuing theological education for clergy, religious and lay persons. The Catholic Theological Union is committed to theological education and scholarship within a community of faith in interaction with a living Catholic tradition and ecumenical, interfaith and cross-cultural perspectives and resources. Through its degree programs and other educational and formational opportunities the Catholic Theological Union strives to educate effective leaders for the church whose mission is to witness Christ's good news of justice, love and peace to people of all nations. Reflecting the diverse cultures, nationalities and races of the women and men who make up the Catholic Theological Union community, the school sees the pursuit of justice, inclusivity and collaboration as integral to its ethos.

See Also: WASHINGTON THEOLOGICAL UNION.

[K. HUGHES]

CATHOLIC TRADITIONALISM

Catholic traditionalism is defined as an international movement to preserve religious, ideological, organizational, and cultic patterns of pre-Vatican II Catholic identity. Catholic traditionalism emerged in a diffuse and segmented manner. The movement was initially part of the conservative Catholic discontent with the reform initiatives of the Second VATICAN COUNCIL. With the spread of conflict and polarization in the wake of the Council, and following the prohibition of the Tridentine Liturgy after November 1971, Catholic traditionalism became a more organizationally and ideologically distinct movement.

Distinguishing ideological characteristics of Catholic traditionalism include tendencies toward a literalistic and ahistorical reading of pre-Vatican II Church documents and decrees (especially those associated with the Council of TRENT, Vatican I, and papal anti-modernist encyclicals and pronouncements) and a strong conspiracy orientation embued with apocalyptic imagery. The most extreme element in the movement (*sede-vacantists*) asserts that Vatican II was a "false council," that recent popes are deposed and excommunicated, and that the *Novus Ordo* Mass is an intrinsically invalid rite. More moderate elements accept the authority of the Magisterium, but assert that the pope and bishops have erred in judgment. These traditionalists have also focused attention on alleged "contradictions" between the pre- and post-Vatican II Church doctrine and discipline. As a sectarian-like movement, traditionalists have openly defied Church hierarchy by establishing illicit chapels and Mass centers in a campaign to "save" the Latin TRIDENTINE form of the Mass—the culture symbol of the traditionalist discontent with *aggiornamento*.

The first traditionalist organization, the Catholic Traditionalist Movement, Inc., was publicly launched in the United States in March of 1965, when the Reverend Gommar De Pauw, a professor of theology and canon law at Mount St. Mary's Seminary in Emmitsburg, Maryland, issued a "Catholic Traditionalist Manifesto" warning against the Vatican II "Protestantizing" of the Roman Catholic faith. By the early 1970s, other traditionalist organizations had formed under various names in the United States. The best known are the Orthodox Roman Catholic Movement, Traditional Catholics of America, Roman Catholics of America, and St. Pius V Association; and in Europe the Society of St. Pius X, Catholic Counter Reformation, and Association of St. Pius V. These groups, along with the support of unaffiliated traditionalist priests, established a world-wide network of traditionalist publications, schools, chapels, and Mass centers promoting pre-Vatican II theology and liturgical and sacramental practice.

The most visible figure in the traditionalist movement is the Archbishop Marcel Lefebvre. After the Second Vatican Council, the former Archbishop of Dakar (Senegal) and of Tulle (France) allied himself with those forces resisting *aggiornamento*. In 1968, he resigned as head of the Holy Ghost Fathers in a dispute over reform of the order in keeping with Vatican II directives. Lefebvre moved to Rome to retire but, by his own account, was sought out by young men desiring direction in priestly formation. In October 1970, Lefebvre opened a seminary in Econe, Switzerland. The next month, the Bishop of Fribourg canonically established Lefebvre's *Fraternité Sacerdotale de Saint Pie X* (Society of St. Pius X).

Following a canonical investigation of his seminary in 1974, the French archbishop issued an acerbic "Declaration" (November 21) repudiating the "neo-modernist" and "neo-Protestant" tendencies manifest in the documents of Vatican II. For the next several months, a series of meetings, negotiations, and an exchange of letters took place between Lefebvre and the Vatican. In June of 1975, Pope Paul VI removed the canonical approval of the Society of St. Pius X and all its establishments, including the seminary at Econe. In July of 1976, following public defiance of an explicit Vatican directive prohibiting new ordinations, Lefebvre was deprived of the canonical authority to exercise his priestly powers.

Subsequent negotiations failed to resolve the conflict between the French archbishop and Rome and the status of the traditionalist movement in general. Lefebvre's priestly fraternity currently operates an international network of seminaries, chapels, schools and religious foundations and remains the flagship organization in the traditionalist cause.

The number of seminarians grew from a handful in 1970 to over 350 ordained priests by the mid-1990s. In 1987, at age 82, Archbishop Lefebvre made known his intention to perpetuate the movement by consecrating episcopal successors. In order to forestall the threat of schism, the Vatican made several attempts at rapprochement, but all fell through. Finally, on June 30, 1988, Archbishop Lefebvre ordained four bishops, all members of the Society of St. Pius X, including Richard Williamson, rector of the Society's seminary in Ridgefield, Connecticut. Because he proceeded in defiance of papal directives, Archbishop Lefebvre and the four bishops he consecrated automatically incurred excommunication.

See Also: LEFEBVRE, MARCEL.

Bibliography: Y. CONGAR, *Challenges to the Church: The Case of Archbishop Lefebvre* (Huntington, Ind. 1976). M. W. CUNEO, *The Smoke of Satan: Conservative and Traditionalist Dissent in Contemporary Catholicism* (New York 1997). M. DAVIES, *Apologia Pro Marcel Lefebvre*, v. I & II (1980, 1983). W. D. DINGES, "Roman Catholic Traditionalism," in *Fundamentalisms Observed*, ed. M. E. MARTY and R. S. APPLEBY (Chicago 1991). J. HANU, *Vatican Encounter: Conversations with Archbishop Marcel Lefebvre*, tr. E. SHOSBERGER (Kansas City 1978). M. J. WEAVER and R. S. APPLEBY, eds., "We Are What You Were: Roman Catholic Traditionalism in America," in *Being Right; Conservative Catholics in America* (Bloomington 1995).

[W. D. DINGES]

The Catholic University of America in 1923. (©CORBIS)

CATHOLIC UNIVERSITY OF AMERICA, THE

Incorporated in 1887 under the laws of the District of Columbia and canonically erected with pontifical status by Leo XIII in 1889, The Catholic University of America, Washington, D.C., was the first Catholic institution of its kind to be established in the U.S.

Pontifical Status Action for the establishment of a national Catholic university was successfully initiated in 1884 at the Third Plenary Council of Baltimore by the efforts of Bp. John L. SPALDING of Peoria. His proposal gained force when the council learned that Mary Gwendolyn CALDWELL had offered $300,000 as a founding endowment.

The need for a university had been mentioned as early as 1819 by an Irish-born Augustinian missionary to the U.S., Robert Browne. In succeeding years the idea had interested such men as Abp. Martin J. SPALDING of Baltimore, Bp. Thomas A. BECKER of Wilmington, and Isaac T. HECKER. There was persistent opposition to the plan from some of the hierarchy, including Bp. Bernard J. MCQUAID of Rochester and Abp. Michael A. CORRIGAN of New York, as well as from certain representatives of

the German Catholics, some members of the Society of Jesus, and a segment of the Catholic press.

Despite these opposing forces, the bishops meeting during the Third Plenary Council of Baltimore in 1884 authorized their Apostolic Delegate, Abp. James GIBBONS, to appoint a committee to initiate the project. During the next few years plans were formulated at committee meetings. The Catholic University of America was decided upon as the name and Washington, D.C. selected as the site. At the meeting of October 1886, Bp. John J. KEANE of Richmond was chosen as the first rector after Bishop Spalding of Peoria had declined the post.

In 1885 Pope LEO XIII had sent his private approval of the project and in 1887 gave his endorsement in a letter to Gibbons and his fellow bishops. On April 19, 1887, the university was incorporated by Congress under the laws of the District of Columbia. On March 7, 1889, in the apostolic letter *Magni Nobis Gaudii* the pope formally approved the statutes and accorded the institution pontifical status. The university was formally opened on Nov. 13, 1889, with Pres. Benjamin Harrison among the many guests who attended the ceremony, which was the final event in the centennial celebration of the U.S. hierarchy.

Besides Keane as rector and Philip J. Garrigan as vice rector, the faculty numbered ten. Of these, two were Sulpicians, John B. Hogan, the librarian, and Alexis Orban, the spiritual director. Two were Paulists, Augustine F. HEWIT, lecturer in church history, and George M. SEARLE, lecturer in science. The only layman, Charles W. Stoddard, was lecturer in English. Five of the faculty were European-born: Henri HYVERNAT, professor of Scripture; Joseph POHLE, philosophy; Joseph SCHROEDER, dogmatic theology; Thomas J. BOUQUILLON, moral theology; and Joseph Graf, music. The 46 students who enrolled initially were drawn from 21 dioceses, one was a Sulpician, and nine were from the Paulist house of studies.

Early in 1889 Cardinal Gibbons had been asked by Hewit, Superior General of the Paulists, if his community might establish a house of studies near the university. Gibbons replied on February 19 that the trustees would permit and would also invite other communities to establish such houses. The Paulists were thus the first of many orders to found houses of study in the neighborhood.

Although the university had opened as a graduate school of theology for the clergy only, it was not long before the need was felt for additional academic disciplines as well as for the increased revenue that would accrue from an enlarged student body. In October 1895 the school of philosophy and the school of social sciences were opened to all qualified male applicants.

The new students included three African Americans, of whom Bishop Keane said, "They stand on exactly the same footing as other students of equal calibre and acquirements." When the newspapers reported, however, that women would also be enrolled and some began to apply, the university announced that it regarded the matter as too important for hasty decision and therefore "it has not yet been considered by the Board of Directors, and nothing will be done except as they decide." Although later years saw a certain variation in policy regarding the admission of both groups, properly qualified women have been admitted since 1928 and black students since 1937.

Finances and Growth. In its early years the university depended entirely on student fees, gifts, and a meager investment income. The total was too small to permit the university to fulfill its purpose as an institution of graduate instruction. Finances proved still to be the chief problem facing the third rector, Denis J. O'CONNELL, who assumed office in March 1903. At O'Connell's suggestion, strongly supported by Cardinal Gibbons as chancellor, Pius X in September of that year gave public authorization for an annual collection to be taken up throughout the dioceses of the U.S.

Another change hastened by the financial crisis was the introduction of undergraduate lay students in the fall of 1905. The step was taken both to increase income and to bring the university's facilities to more students. The first 15 years had proved there were too few students either prepared for or interested in graduate studies to warrant continuing on that level alone. Nonetheless, as new programs and departments were added and a few suppressed, the university continued to emphasize in its mission statement and stated priorities its predominantly graduate character.

Bishop Spalding's proposal for an advanced teachers college, similar to that at Columbia University in New York City, began to take shape in 1911 with the founding of Catholic Sisters College. Established as a separate corporation (1914), it was located apart from the main campus, but its degrees were conferred by the rector of the university. Parallel courses and instruction were given in Brady Hall, erected for that purpose, because the policy of the university did not allow the sisters to attend classes and lectures on the main campus nor to mingle with the male student body there. Beginning with graduate students, the students enrolled in Sisters College were gradually integrated with the general student body of the university. By 1964 it had been incorporated into the university administratively, and in 1968 the trustees voted it out of existence.

Change and Reorganization. World War II had a major impact on the university with regard to both the size and the character of the student body. The outbreak of hostilities in Europe in 1939 meant that many priests and seminarians who would have previously pursued graduate studies in Europe, a majority in Rome, came to Washington. The large proportion of clerics and religious—exempted from the draft—among the student body somewhat attenuated the drop in enrollment that affected most colleges and universities in the country. In the years immediately following the war lay students taking advantage of the GI Bill swelled the enrollment, while the number of religious students began to decline. Unlike in the early decades when enrollment was often far below the number that could be accommodated, after the war the university was at times strained to provide for the number of applicants. This was particularly true during the time of Bishop William J. McDonald when total enrollment grew from 3,858 in his first year as rector (1957–58) to 6,779 in his last (1967–68).

In 1964 the Catholic University joined with four other universities in the District of Columbia (American, George Washington, Georgetown, and Howard) to form the D. C. Consortium of Universities. This arrangement enabled the participating institutions to coordinate their respective graduate programs and permitted graduate students, with certain restrictions, to enroll in courses at the other universities. The university's Mullen Library is a member of the Washington Research Library Consortium that enables seven universities in the Washington, D.C. metropolitan area to cross-list their holdings and share resources through a digital library system.

Bishop McDonald's rectorship was a watershed in the history of the university. Preoccupied with building, the production of *The New Catholic Encyclopedia*, and a desire to appease a number of constituencies with conflicting expectations, he did not cope well with the momentous cultural and religious changes signaled by the Second Vatican Council taking place at the time. He secretly expunged sections of the report that the Canon Law faculty had prepared for the council's Ante-Preparatory Commission and tightly controlled who could speak on campus, banning a number of respected Catholic theologians. Internal tensions, caused in part by the rector's disregard for established academic procedures, came to a head in the spring of 1967 when the board of trustees, ignoring the recommendations of the faculty, voted to terminate the services of the Reverend Charles E. Curran, an assistant professor in the school of theology. Faculty and students, in public protest, absented themselves from the classroom and took the issue to the media. The unwanted publicity caused Cardinal O'BOYLE, the chancellor of the university, to intervene. Father Curran was reinstated, but the incident was to have lasting consequences for the protagonists as well as the institution. Bishop McDonald resigned shortly afterwards, Father Curran emerged as a major voice in the U.S. church, and new instruments for the governance of the university were adopted.

In the wake of Bishop McDonald's departure, the board of trustees hired outside consultants and set up a series of committees that led to a thorough rewriting of the university bylaws and the formulation of new statutes for the ecclesiastical schools (theology, philosophy, Canon Law). The new documents reaffirmed the university's ties to the Catholic Church, made provision for an elected board of trustees that would be made up of an equal number of clerical and non-clerical members, and adopted titles for the administrative officers more in accordance with American usage. The rector was replaced by a president who did not need to be a priest, and in fact, the first two presidents appointed under the new bylaws were laymen, Clarence Walton (1970–78) and Edmund D. Pellegrino (1978–82). Pellegrino was succeeded by William J. Byron, S.J., the first member of a religious order to head the university.

The new statutes enacted for the ecclesiastical faculties in 1968 followed the general norms of the apostolic constitution *Deus Scientiarum Dominus* of 1931, and they have been interpreted to comply with subsequent directives of the Holy See (*Normae quaedam* (1968), *Sapientia Christiana* (1979), and *Ex corde ecclesiae* (1990). The norms in these and related documents provided the context for the protracted litigation, canonical and civil, that ended in the withdrawal of Father Charles Curran's *missio canonica* and his departure from the university. The issues, many and complex, divided the campus and brought much unwanted notoriety to the university. The Congregation for the Doctrine of the Faith examined Curran's writings and questioned his theological method as well as the position he took on certain issues, chiefly in the area of sexual ethics. While defending his orthodoxy Curran maintained that the overarching issue was academic freedom. For the board of trustees and the university administration the overarching issue was their right to credential teachers of Catholic theology according to Church norms and procedures. The civil courts decided in favor of the university under principles of contract law in March 1989.

Throughout its history the university has sought to bring the Catholic intellectual tradition into conversation with the pursuits and priorities of the American academe. The mission is not unique to The Catholic University of America, but its pontifical status and singular relationship to the Church presents an ongoing challenge to the institution to find ways and create structures that safeguard its Catholic character and insure academic freedom in the tradition of American universities.

Bibliography: P. H. AHERN, *The Catholic University of America, 1887–1896: The Rectorship of John J. Keane* (Washington 1949). C. J. BARRY, *The Catholic University of America, 1903–1909: The Rectorship of Denis J. O'Connell* (Washington 1949). R. J. DEFERRARI, *Memoirs of the Catholic University of America, 1918–1960* (Boston 1962). J. T. ELLIS, *The Formative Years of the Catholic University of America* (Washington 1946).P. E. HOGAN, *The Catholic University of America, 1896–1903: The Rectorship of Thomas J. Conaty* (Washington 1949). C. J. NUESSE,*The Catholic University of America: A Centennial History* (Washington, DC 1990).

[J. T. ELLIS/EDS.]

CATHOLICITY

Alhough the idea of universality was highly developed in the Bible, catholic (καθολικός) is not a scriptural word. The term appears for the first time in Saint Ignatius of Antioch (*Smyrn.* 8.2).

History. In the first two centuries, two ideas of catholicity were predominant: first, geographical universality (with all its consequences, including universality of people, of conditions of life, etc.); then, in a subsidiary way, universality of truth and orthodoxy. See A. Göpfert, *Die Katholizität der Kirche* (Würzburg 1876) and R. Söder, *Der Begriff der Katholizität der Kirche und des Glaubens nach seiner geschichtlichen Entwicklung* (Würzburg 1881). Saint Augustine, particularly, in opposing the Donatist schism, developed the notion of geographical catholicity. See P. Batiffol, *Le Catholicisme de saint Augustin* (5th ed. Paris 1929). In Saint Augustine also—and sometimes in Saint Optatus of Milevis—one finds the word *catholica* as a noun; it denotes the Church, the *magna catholica*, and not the *fides* or the *religio*. See O. Rottmanner, "Catholica," *Revue Bénédictine* 17 (1900) 1–9. However, the Fathers gladly explain catholicity by all the aspects of the Church capable of being universal: it is spread over all the earth; it brings the true religion to all men; it speaks to people of all conditions; it heals all kinds of sin; it offers men the most varied spiritual gifts. Thus, for example, Saint Cyril of Jerusalem (*Catech.* 18.23; *Patrologia Graeca*, ed. J. P. Migne, 33:1044) explains it.

The Middle Ages were to gather and synthesize all that the Fathers had written; hence the long lists of aspects of catholicity that one finds especially in the commentaries on the ninth article of the Creed, *et unam, sanctam, catholicam et apostolicam ecclesiam.* See, for example, James of Viterbo, *De regimine christiano* (1301–02), in *Le Plus ancien traité de l'église*, ed. H. Arquillière (Paris 1926), or Juan de Torquemada (d. 1468), *Summa de ecclesia* (Venice 1561). An unpublished text characteristic of the abundance of the aspects of the idea of catholicity is one by John of Ragusa, *Tractatus de ecclesia* (Basel, University Library, MS A I 29, folio 302v–431r). The Church is catholic, he says; it extends to all places, over all times, from Abel to the end of the world; it has spread among all peoples (Rv 7.9); it propounds all the universal precepts, and not the particularist obligations of Judaism; it possesses every sacramental remedy, for every ill and every fault; it teaches a complete doctrine, which gives to all men all that is necessary for salvation; it is the means of universal salvation, for outside the Church there is no salvation; it is catholic in virtue of its worship, which is set forth in every way and at all times; finally, it embraces all men, the good and the wicked (*Tractatus de ecclesia* 2.11–12).

In modern times, the development of controversial theology gave some vitality to the question of the notes of the Church, but they were understood in a very apologetic sense. The Church is catholic, it was said, because it extends over all the earth; this diffusion, without being absolute, is greater than that of the other Christian communions and progressively tends toward absolute universality. The catholicity of time—uninterrupted continuance since antiquity—is of secondary importance. Fi-

nally, a universality of doctrine appeared, particularly in Suárez in his controversy with James I. For three centuries quantitative catholicity was emphasized for an apologetic purpose; see G. Thils, "La Notion de catholicité de l'église à l'époque moderne," *Ephemerides theologicae Lovanienses* 13 (1936) 5–73.

At the end of the 19th century, attention was given to a notion of qualitative catholicity. In the beginning there was reference to the transcendence of the Church in comparison with all the particularisms of nation, language, race, etc.; see A. de Poulpiquet, "La Notion de catholicité," *Revue des sciences philosophiques et théologiques* 3 (1909) 17–36. Later was stressed the fundamental capacity of the Church to touch and to transfigure all things in restoring them to unity in Christ; see Y. M. J. Congar, *Christianity Divided*, tr. M. Bousfield (Philadelphia 1939) 93–114. At present, there is insistence on diversity in unity, catholicity being the opposite of uniformity; see G. Thils, *Histoire doctrinale du mouvement oecuménique* (2d ed. Louvain 1963) 262–75. Since Vatican II the idea of the Church as *communio* has come into prominence, basing ecclesiology on the ontology of communion revealed in the Trinity and the Incarnation.

Theology. A historical survey shows sufficiently how complex is the catholicity of the Church. By catholicity one understands the Church itself insofar as it is constituted in the plenitude of Christ and is capable of expanding totally and universally in all its elements and according to all its dimensions.

One may distinguish, first of all, catholicity as note, as a distinctive sign permitting the discernment of the true Church—the universal extension of the Church, its transcendence in comparison with all that is particularized, and its multiform incarnation in all reality. There is also catholicity as property, which is an essential constitutive element of the Church.

Catholicity, like the Church itself, involves an interior and divine aspect, and an exterior, visible and social aspect. As for the invisible aspect, God the Father has made His Son the Christ, the one in who dwells and is incorporated all the plenitude of the divinity (cf. Col 2.9). And Christ has sent the Spirit, who pours into men's hearts a varied abundance of gifts. Thus engendered by the Holy Trinity, the Church is "the Body of Christ, the fullness of Him who fulfills Himself in and by all things" (Eph 1.22); it ought to attain the whole new universe, recreated in embryo in the Resurrection of the Lord. But there is also a visible and social aspect. The extension of the Church, the active presence of the Lord to all the world, the universal epiphany of the gifts of the Spirit are sensible and visible both in the Church—the institution of salvation—and in men and the effects achieved by its spiritual work.

Catholicity may also be considered as a gift and as a mission: *Gabe und Aufgabe*. A gift, since it is one of the constitutive dimensions of the Church itself, which is a gift of God, instituted by Christ, engendered by the power of the Spirit. But also a mission. The grace of the Lord ought to be applied to all men of all times "in order that they may enter into all the plenitude of God" (Eph 3.19). Thus is achieved the fullness of the total Christ, the Church, which visibly manifests this spiritual plenitude in a world itself in a state of perpetual becoming. The mission is the very expression of this catholicity.

The Church is thus a mystery of unity and of diversity. As for diversity, it should realize concretely in its structure and in its daily life all legitimate diversity and variety out of regard for the Holy Spirit and the multitude of His gifts: diversity in spirituality and in rites; in languages and institutions; in doctrinal categories and philosophical systems. But this marvelous diversity would be only chaos without the cement of the essential unity of the Spirit, of dogma, and of structure.

See Also: MYSTICAL BODY OF CHRIST; RESURRECTION OF CHRIST; CHURCH, ARTICLES ON; CATHOLIC.

Bibliography: Y. M. J. CONGAR, *Catholicisme. Hier, aujourd'hui et demain,* ed. G. JACQUEMET (Paris 1947–) 2:722–25. J. L. WITTE, "Die Katholizität der Kirche," *Gregorianum* 42 (1961) 193–241. W. STÄHLIN, *Allein. Recht und Gefahr einer polemischen Formel* (Stuttgart 1950). Y. CONGAR, *After Nine Hundred Years* (New York 1959); *Dialogue Between Christians* (London 1966); *Vraie et fausse réforme dans l'Église* (2d ed., Paris 1969). H. VOLK, *Gott Alles in Allen* (Mainz 1961). H. ASMUSSEN et al., *The Unfinished Reformation* (Notre Dame 1961). P. ALTHAUS, "Sola Fide Numquam Sola," *Una Sancta* (1961) 227–35. J. MEYENDORFF, *Orthodoxy and Catholicity* (New York 1966). J. PELIKAN, *The Emergence of the Catholic Tradition* (Chicago 1971). R. EVANS, *One and Holy* (London 1972). H. URS VON BALTHASAR, *Katholisch* (Einsiedeln 1975). K. RAHNER, *Grundkurs des Glaubens* (Freiburg 1976).

[G. THILS/R. KRESS/EDS.]

CATHOLICOS

The title of the heads of the Armenian Apostolic Church, Orthodox Church of Georgia, and the Assyrian Church of the East. Catholicos in its first usage signified the head of a church who was dependent on a patriarch but also acted as his vicar. Later, the titles of patriarch and catholicos had the same denotation. The leader of the Armenian Church at Etshmiadzin bears the title Supreme Patriarch and Catholicos of All Armenians. The Church of Georgia, formerly under the Armenian catholicos, separated in 609 and later became autocephalous. Its primate also is called Catholicos—Patriarch of All Georgie.

The title of catholicos was given the leader of the bishops of Seleucia during the fourth century. When a distinct church, the Assyrian Church of the East emerged, the Catholicos received the additional title of Patriarch.

Bibliography: D. ATTWATER, *The Christian Churches of the East,* 2 v. (rev. ed. Milwaukee 1961–62). R. ROBERSON, *The Eastern Catholic Churches: A Brief Survey,* 6th ed. (Rome 1999).

[S. J. BEGGIANI]

CATHREIN, VIKTOR

Jesuit moral philosopher and spiritual writer; b. Brig, Switzerland, May 8, 1845; d. Aachen, Germany, Sept. 10, 1931. He entered the Jesuits in 1863 and became a professor in the scholasticate of the German province. Cathrein was a leading neo-Thomist and was distinguished for his vigorous attack upon positivism in ethics and jurisprudence and for his opposition to the idea that morality can be separated from religion. His criticism of socialism was influential in shaping Catholic thought upon the subject. His *Der Sozialismus* (Freiburg 1890) went through 23 editions up to 1923 and was translated into the principal modern languages. Among his other philosophical works were: *Moralphilosophie* (2 v. Freiburg 1890–91; 20th ed. 1955); Grundbegriffe des Strafrechts (Freiburg 1905); *Die Einheit des sittlichen Bewusstseins* (3 v. Freiburg 1914); *Die Grundlage des Völkerrechts* (Freiburg 1918). Cathrein also took an interest in spirituality, and some of his last writings are in this field: *Die Verheissungen des göttlichen Herzens Jesu* (Freiburg 1919); *Die Christliche Demut* (Freiburg 1919); *Eucharistische Konvertitenbilder* (Leipzig 1923); *Die lässliche Sünde* (Freiburg 1926); *Lust und Freude, ihr Wesen, ihr sittlicher Charakter* (Innsbruck 1931).

Bibliography: L. KOCH, *Jesuiten-Lexikon: Die Gesellschaft Jesu einst und jetzt* (Paderborn 1934); photoduplicated with rev. and suppl., 2 v. (Louvain-Heverlee 1962), 307. W. SCHÖLLGEN, *Lexikon für Theologie und Kirche,* ed. J. HOFER, and K. RAHNER, 10 v. (2d, new ed. Freiburg 1957–65); suppl., *Das Zweite Vatikanische Konzil: Dokumente und Kommentare,* ed. H.S. BRECHTER et al., pt. 1 (1966) 2 2:980. E. RAITZ VON FRENTZ, *Dictionnaire de spiritualité ascétique et mystique. Doctrine et histoire,* M. VILLER et al. (Paris 1932–) 2:352.

[L. B. O'NEIL]

CATRIK, JOHN

Bishop, royal envoy; b. Catterick, Yorkshire; d. Florence, Dec. 28, 1419. He graduated bachelor of Canon and Civil Law and licentiate of Canon Law at Oxford by 1406. After having held many benefices, mostly in the Diocese of Lincoln, he was papally provided to the bishopric of SAINT DAVID's, April 27,1414. He was translated to COVENTRY AND LICHFIELD by papal bull on Feb. 1, 1415, and then to EXETER, Nov. 20, 1419. He was chancellor to Cardinal Henry BEAUFORT, and later served Kings Henry IV and Henry V as a diplomat in France and Burgundy from 1405 to 1411 and in 1416. On May 22, 1414, he was appointed the king's proctor at Rome. In October 1414 he was an envoy to the Council of CONSTANCE, and headed the English delegation there from April to May 1415, and again from Sept. 24, 1416, to the end of the Council. He left Constance with MARTIN V and remained at the Curia until his death.

Bibliography: C. L. KINGSFORD, *The Dictionary of National Biography from the Earliest Times to 1900,* 63 v. (London 1885–1900) 11:78–79. A.B. EMDEN, *A Biographical Register of the University of Oxford to A.D. 1500,* 3 v. (Oxford 1957–59) 1: 371–372.

[G. WILLIAMS]

CATROU, FRANÇOIS

Jesuit historian, littérateur, and preacher; b. Paris, Dec. 28, 1659; d. there, Oct. 18, 1737. He was admitted to the Jesuit novitiate, Oct. 28, 1678, and during his studies he showed a marked ability for eloquence and literary expression. He preached with success at Rouen, Bourges, Tours, Orléans, Paris, and elsewhere for seven years. In 1701 he gave up this career to become the first editor of the *Mémoires de Trévoux pour servir à l'histoire des sciences et des beaux-artes* (often shortened to *Journal de Trévoux*); he remained in this office for 12 years. The *Mémoires* continued in the hands of the Jesuits until their suppression in France (1762), by which time 265 volumes had been published. Articles by Joseph René Tournemine (1661–1739), Pierre François de Charlevoix (1682–1731), Guillaume François BERTHIER, Charles Merlin (1678–1747), Étienne Souciet (1671–1744), Jean HARDOUIN, Édouard Vitry (1666–1730), and others made it a powerful voice against Jansenists, Protestants, and the ENCYCLOPEDISTS. In 1768 it was continued as the *Journal des beaux-arts et des sciences,* ed. Abbé Aubert (32 v. 1768–75) and brothers Castilhon (18 v. 1776–78), and as the *Journal de littérature, sciences et arts,* ed. J. B. Grosier (6 v. 1779–82).

During these years Catrou began the research that prepared him for his three major historical works: *Histoire général de l'Empire du Mogul depuis sa fondation* (2 v. Paris 1705; Eng. tr. 1826); *Histoire du fanatisme dans la religion protestante* (2 v. Paris 1733), a study of several Anabaptist sects (parts published separately as *Histoire des anabaptistes,* Paris 1705) and Quakers; and *Histoire romaine* (21 v. Paris 1725–37). This last work,

Viktor Cathrein.

though criticized often as more pompous than precise, had much influence. It was reedited by Pierre Rouillé, SJ (1737), with extensive notes and translated into English by R. Bundy (6 v. London 1728–37). It also became the basis for Nathaniel Hooke's (d. 1764) *The Roman History from the Building of Rome to the Ruin of the Empire* (4 v. London 1757–71). Catrou's translation of Vergil, *Les oeuvres de Vergile, traduction nouvelle . . .* (Paris 1716), in spite of inaccuracies, was in wide use.

Bibliography: C. SOMMERVOGEL et al., *Bibliothèque de la Compagnie de Jésus,* 11 v. (Brussels-Paris 1890–1932) 2:882–889; 8:227–229; 9:11–12. H. CHÉROT, *Dictionnaire de théologie catholique,* ed. A. VACANT et al., 15 v. (Paris 1903–50; Tables générales 1951), 2.2:2012–13. M. PREVOST, *Dictionnaire de biographie française* (Paris 1929), 7:1428. For the *Mémoires de Trévoux,* see G. DUMAS, *Histoire du Journal de Trévoux depuis 1701 jusquén 1762* (Paris 1936). P. C. SOMMERVOGEL, *Table méthodique des Mémoires de Trévoux 1701–1775,* 3 v. (Paris 1864–65). J. P. GRAUSEM, *Dictionnaire de théologie catholique,* ed. A. VACANT et al., 15 v. (Paris 1903–50; Tables générales 1951), 15.1: 1510–16.

[E. D. MCSHANE]

CATTANEO, LAZZARO

Jesuit missionary to China; b. Sarzana, near Genoa, 1560; d. China, Jan. 19, 1640. He entered the Society of

Jesus at Rome in 1581. After being ordained he sailed from Lisbon in 1588 for Goa. The next year he was made superior of the mission for the Malabar coast. In 1593 he went to Macau, and from there into China. He studied Chinese at Chaoking with Matteo RICCI, and in 1598 he joined Ricci in a journey to Beijing (Peking). After labors in Nanjing (Nanking) and Macau, he became the first missionary to Shanghai, arriving there in 1608 at the invitation of a famous and influential Chinese convert, Hsü Kuang-chi. Cattaneo's work took him also to Hangzhou (Hangchow) in 1611, and later to Loshan (Jiangsu province), where he founded a new mission. In 1622 he retired to Hangzhou and spent his remaining years writing spiritual treatises in Chinese and working in linguistics.

Bibliography: L. PFISTER, *Notices biographiques et bibliographiques sur les Jésuites de l'ancienne mission de Chine 1552–1773,* 2 v. (Shanghai 1932–34), 1:51–56. P. M. D'ELIA, ''Arrivo del Cattaneo,'' in *Fonti Ricciane,* ed. M. RICCI, 3 v. (Rome 1942–49), 1:331–334.

[J. C. WILLKE]

CAULET, FRANÇOIS ÉTIENNE

Bishop of Pamiers, staunch opponent to the *régale* of Louis XIV; b. Toulouse, May 19, 1610; d. Pamiers, Aug. 7, 1680. He was the Jesuit-educated son of a well-to-do parliamentary family. Caulet first came into prominence as director of the seminary of Saint-Sulpice in Paris in 1642. Having been appointed bishop of the small and heavily Protestant Diocese of Pamiers in 1644, he attracted wide attention by his sweeping program of reform and the austerity of his life. In 1655 he was one of five French bishops who refused to sign the formulary condemning Jansenism, but this was probably as much a matter of principle as it was a sign of adherence to Jansenist doctrines. A decade later, he became the central figure in the opposition to the king's efforts to extend the *régale* into hitherto exempt dioceses. His appeal to Innocent XI for assistance was answered with alacrity, but for three years the diocese was in a state of siege, with Caulet, deprived of his temporalities, holding out the best he could against the combined forces of king, parliament, intendant, and even his own metropolitan. He maintained this stubborn resistance until his death at the age of 70.

Bibliography: L. BASSETTE, *Jean de Caulet* (Grenoble 1946). M. DUBRUEL, *Innocent XI et l'extension de la Régale* (Paris 1907). J. CARREYRE, *Dictionnaire d'histoire et de géographie ecclésiastiques,* ed. A. BAUDRILLART et al. (Paris 1912), 12:7–10.

[L. L. BERNARD]

CAULITES

Extinct French monastic order, named after the motherhouse, Val-des-Choux (Vallis Caulium), founded in 1193 in a remote wilderness by Ven. Viard (Guy), a Carthusian lay brother of Lugny. Land for the foundation was granted by the Duke of Burgundy. The order's life and discipline were based on the Rule of St. Benedict as interpreted by Cîteaux, but the monks wore the habit of the Carthusians. They lived a rigid community life, and observed strict silence and perpetual abstinence. Their source of livelihood was agricultural labor, but the Caulites never accepted or cultivated land beyond the immediate neighborhood of the monastery. The prosperous organization spread quickly and incorporated about 30 houses in France, Scotland, Spain, and Portugal during the 13th century. The head of the order was the grand prior of Val-des-Choux; priors governed the subordinate houses and convened each year for a general chapter. The first constitution was approved by Innocent III in 1205, but it was moderated in 1226 by order of Honorius III. In the 16th century wars and the commendatory system weakened the order to such an extent that by the 18th century only a few depopulated houses remained. After vain efforts at reform, the Grand Prior, Chevenet, with the approval of Dorothée Jalloutz, the abbot of SEPT-FONS, merged with the flourishing community of reformed Cistercians of that monastery. In 1761 the union was sanctioned by Clement XIII. The Cistercians rebuilt and repopulated Val-des-Choux, renamed it Val-Saint-Lieux, but in 1791 it was suppressed, as were all monastic establishments, by the Revolution. During the 19th century the monastic buildings housed various industrial projects while the church was left in ruins.

Bibliography: BEAUNIER, *Abbayes et prieurés de l'ancienne France,* ed. J. M. L. BESSE, 12 v. (Paris 1905–41). P. VERMEER, ''Cîteaux: Val-des-Choux,'' *Collectanea Ordinis Cisterciensium Reformatorum* 15 (1954) 35–44. H. WOLTER, *Lexikon für Theologie und Kirche* 2 6:95.

[L. J. LEKAI]

CAUNTON, RICHARD

Papal chaplain, English royal servant; b. Pembrokeshire, Wales; d. June or July, 1465. He became principal of Haberdash Hall, Oxford, in 1428, and by 1450 was a doctor of canon and civil law. He held a number of livings, mostly in southwest Wales, and was archdeacon of Salisbury from 1446 to 1465, and of Saint David's from 1459 to 1465. Richard was king's clerk under Henry VI in 1437 and was probably appointed king's proctor at Rome in 1441, a position he held for many years. He was also employed on a number of royal embassies to France

(1439), to Denmark (1449), and to Poland, Denmark, Prussia, and the Hanse towns in 1464. He became a clerk of the Apostolic CAMERA in 1443 and was a papal chaplain by 1453. Between 1442 and 1446 he was proctor at Rome for a number of English bishops, and in December 1445 acted as the envoy of EUGENE IV to King Henry.

Bibliography: A.B. EMDEN, *A Biographical Register of the University of Oxford to A.D. 1500*, 3 v. (Oxford 1957–59), 1:373–374. C. L. SCOFIELD, *The Life and Reign of Edward the Fourth*, 2 v. (New York 1923) v.1. E. YARDLEY, *Menevia Sacra*, ed. F. GREEN (London 1927).

[G. WILLIAMS]

CAUSALITY

In a general sense causality designates anything that has the character of a cause; more specifically it describes the relationship between cause and effect. Sometimes it is distinguished from causation, which is taken to mean any type of causative action (*see* ACTION AND PASSION). Cause (Gr. αἰτια, αἴτιον; Lat. *causa*) is itself defined by scholastics as, that from which something else proceeds with a dependence in being. It is related to PRINCIPLE, which is that from which something proceeds in any way whatsoever; to CONDITION, which is a prerequisite factor needed to make causal action effective; and to OCCASION, which is an opportunity that may induce a free agent to act.

This article first exposes Greek and scholastic teaching on causality, furnishing a brief historical survey of its development to medieval times, together with an analysis of the nature of causality and the corollaries it entails. It then recounts and criticizes views on causality held by some of the principal philosophers of the modern and contemporary periods.

Greek and Scholastic Teaching

The origins of causality in Greek thought are summarized in various works of ARISTOTLE (esp. *Meta.* 983a 25–984b 20). Aristotle notes that while none of the previous philosophers had furnished a systematic exposition of causality, their separate and sometimes confused treatments give evidence of four different types of causes.

CLASSIFICATION AND HISTORY

The four causes enumerated by Aristotle are "the matter, the form, the mover, and 'that for the sake of which'" (*Phys.* 198a 20–25). These have became known as the material, formal, efficient and final causes.

Basic definitions. By MATTER or material cause Aristotle means "that out of which a thing comes to be and

which persists." Examples would be the cloth out of which a suit is made and the tobacco of a cigar. By FORM or formal cause he refers to "the form or archetype, that is, the statement of the essence." In art, the shape of a bowl would constitute its formal cause; in nature, the soul of a living thing would be its formal cause. By mover, AGENT, or efficient cause Aristotle understands the "primary source of the change or coming to rest" (*see* EFFICIENT CAUSALITY). Thus a carpenter is the efficient cause of a house's being built, or wind is the cause of the motion of waves on water. By final cause, he means that "in the sense of end or that for the sake of which a thing is done" (*see* FINAL CAUSALITY). For example, one studies in order to become learned, or the natural camouflage of animals is for the sake of protecting them from their enemies. Final cause may also refer to the object of desire or the desire of the object. (Confer, *Phys.* 194b 20–35.)

Pre-Socratics. The earliest of the causes, sought by the pre-Socratics although not formally recognized as such, was the material cause. All the Ionians searched for one or more types of matter composing the cosmos, some opting for water (Thales), others for air (Anaximenes) or an indeterminate *apeiron* (Anaximander). Later philosophers enquired into the material and the efficient causes of things. EMPEDOCLES, for example, posited friendship and strife as the forces uniting or dissolving the combination of the elements, thus accounting for order and chaos respectively. Such forces can be interpreted along the lines of efficient causality. ANAXAGORAS also apparently hinted at efficient causality in his doctrine of Nous, although, as Aristotle observed, this offered more promise that it gave (*see* GREEK PHILOSOPHY).

Socrates and Plato. SOCRATES may be said to have searched for the final causes of human conduct in his quest for the virtuous life. The Pythagoreans and especially PLATO, made further advance into the quest for causes by investigating formal causality. For Plato, these forms or archetypes in the world of ideas are the patterns participated and imitated by sensible reality. Analogously, as a shadow has its meager reality from the tree that casts it and the sun that makes this possible, so the sensory world has its reality by virtue of the ideas (forms) it imitates and the One above the ideas. This theme of PARTICIPATION runs throughout many of Plato's middle and later works. Plato also makes use of efficient causality when he speaks of the demiurge (confer, *Timaeus*) as forming the world below.

Aristotelian and other usage. Aristotle not only presented a thorough enumeration and description of the various causes, but went on to employ them extensively in his works. He viewed all SCIENCE (*SCIENTIA*) as a search for causes, for only causal knowledge is scientific knowledge. His theory of proof or DEMONSTRATION (confer, *Posterior Analytics*) is rooted in this doctrine of causes. The connecting link between a subject (*S*-term) and its attribute (*P*-term) is a cause (*M*-term). Thus the cause (*M*-term) always tells why *P* belongs to *S* or how one knows that *P* belongs to *S*. Hence, all science is "a search for the middle term." Both in the *Physics* and in the *Metaphysics*, Aristotle comes to the conclusion of the existence of an Unmoved Mover or an Uncaused Cause. The Uncaused Cause is commonly viewed as an object of desire and thus as a final cause, while the Unmoved Mover is often interpreted as an efficient cause. To sum up the importance of Aristotle's contribution on the subject of causality, this lay in his showing to others what to look for when seeking scientific knowledge and how to proceed in such investigation. His systematic treatment and delineation of the causes changed the search for truth from a random groping to a systematic enquiry.

Later Greek thought. After Aristotle, there was comparatively little stress on formal recognition and use of causes. Skeptics rejected them and the Stoics were primarily interested in the ethical life of virtue amidst a pantheistic setting. The latter did, however, stress the immanent causality of the *logos* in the world and of "seeds" in things as active forms from which reality emerges. The Epicureans accepted ATOMISM with its consequent denial of teleology or final causality. Neoplatonists were principally noted for their attempt to merge Aristotelian and Platonic teachings on causality. They gave further impetus to recognition of a fifth cause, the exemplary cause (*see* EXEMPLARY CAUSALITY).

Scholastic development. Although Aristotle laid the essential groundwork for the doctrine of causality, it was mainly the scholastics who further clarified, refined and applied his doctrine. Nearly all employed the Aristotelian terms, but many offered various interpretations and applications of the doctrine.

Since the most notable Aristotelian in the medieval Latin West was St. THOMAS AQUINAS, his views will be summarized here. St. Thomas defines cause in a number of ways, but two of his definitions contain the essential elements. A cause is "that upon which something else follows of necessity" (*In 5 meta.* 1.749). Again, a cause is that which "brings some influence on the being of the thing caused" (*ibid.* 751). The key to understanding causality, for Aquinas, is to see that it always involves a positive principle exerting some influence on a perfection or thing that is coming to be, that is, an influx into being. His definitions are necessarily obscure, for the notion of causality is fundamentally analogical and no analogical term admits of a strict DEFINITION (*see* ANALOGY). One error of present-day thinkers in appraising causality is to ignore this analogical character of the causes and attempt to reduce all causality to some type of efficient cause. This preoccupation leads automatically to MECHANISM.

JUSTIFICATION OF CAUSALITY

Virtually no philosopher has denied the practical utility and necessity of the concept of causality, although frequent efforts have been directed toward showing that, in the real order, this concept is speculatively unverifiable. Yet man can and does regularly verify the extramental existence of causal influences. His starting point, most evident in experience, is the fact of CHANGE. He observes change in nature and experiences himself as capable of producing it. Explanation of the obvious fact of change and MOTION thus leads to explicit knowledge of the doctrine of causes.

In the most commonplace examples of change, for example, the sculpting of a statue, an agent (efficient cause) does something to a marble subject (material cause). As a result of the agent's activity, the marble comes to possess actually a new shape or determination (formal cause). What prompted this action on the part of the agent was the fact that he sought to produce something: he had some goal at which he aimed (final cause). Briefly, then, in changes produced by ART, one observes that there must be a substratum (material cause), a determination (formal cause) that comes to be actually present in the substratum through the activity of an agent (efficient cause), for some purpose (final cause).

Making an analogous transition from art to the order of NATURE, one sees that the material cause accounts for the continuity that is evident in all changes in the universe; the formal cause is the principle of novelty, without which no change would be manifest; the efficient cause initiates and makes this novelty to come about actually; and the final cause accounts for the action's tending to a determinate effect. The principles involved in this explanation apply then, not merely to art, but to nature and to physical change as such. Consequently and in analogous fashion, one can understand that such causes are also required for any change in the physical world, whether these be substantial or accidental.

St. Thomas summarizes this line of reasoning as follows:

> There must of necessity be four causes: because when a cause exists, upon which the being of another thing follows, the being of that which has the cause may be considered in two ways. First, absolutely; and in this way the cause of being is a form by which something is a being-in-act . . . . It follows of necessity that there are two other causes, namely the matter and the agent that reduces the matter from potency to act. But the action of an

agent tends to something determinate, just as it proceeds from some determinate principle, for every agent does what is in conformity with its nature. That to which the action of the agent tends is called the final cause. Thus, there are necessarily four causes. [*In 2 phys.* 10.15.]

Since change is an objective occurrence in the real order, the principles without which it would be unintelligible are clearly objective as well; hence the foregoing explanation is not to be construed as psychological, but as ontological in character. It requires, moreover, an intellectual insight into the nature of real beings and their operations. Hence, nominalists and empiricists, denying the intellect's ability to grasp natures, also reject this explanation. The exposition above is predicated on the indemonstrable first principle that being is intelligible and accordingly, that man can know (in the sense of understand) reality itself (*see* FIRST PRINCIPLES).

ANALYSIS OF CAUSALITY

Because the rejection of scholastic views on causality by modern philosophers is based largely on a misunderstanding of what is meant by causality and how it occurs, some refinements of the explanation already given are now attempted.

One or more effects. In a certain sense, the effect of the various causes is but one effect of all four—each contributing to this effect in its own special manner. Yet the following distinctions obtain. Material and formal causes may be regarded as intrinsic, for they enter into the composition of the thing. Efficient and final causes are said to be extrinsic. The material cause influences the being of the effect through its role as subject, recipient and passive principle, thereby limiting the act that it receives. The formal cause has for its effect the determination or specification of the being of the effect, thereby making it to be this kind of thing rather than that. The efficient cause has for its effect the coming-to-be of the new determination (form) in the subject. Lastly, the final cause has for its effect the perfection itself that has come to be, formally considered as a term of the intention of the agent. It should be noted that this intention need not be conscious or cognitive in the agent; it can be simply a tendency of the agent.

Reciprocity of causes. Reciprocity is often evident between causes. The final cause explains why the agent causes, while the agent makes the final cause or end come to be. When the final cause is considered in the order of intention, it is what moves the agent to act. When it is considered in the order of execution, it is what the agent has produced. Thus, as Aristotle observes, health is the final cause of walking, but walking in turn produces or contributes to health. Hence, the final cause may be

termed first in the order of intention and last in the order of execution. It is also termed the highest of the causes for without it none of the other causes could actually cause.

Nature of causal action. No agent loses anything in causing. To cause is itself a perfection; for an agent to necessarily lose in causing would be for it to become increasingly less perfect and this implies a contradiction. It must be noted, therefore, that there is no transfer in causing as such—a position St. Thomas calls *ridiculum* (*C. gent.* 3.69)—as though the agent causes by "giving up" its own form or perfection, thereby entailing its loss. Leibniz apparently misunderstood the scholastic doctrine in this manner.

Instead, causing by finite beings involves an eduction of the form from the potency of the matter (*see* MATTER AND FORM). Strictly, the form does not come from the agent. Rather, by means of the action of the agent, the form that was already potentially in the matter comes to be present there actually. Thus water in becoming warm does not literally receive heat from the fire. It is because the flame is actually hot that water, which is potentially hot, comes to be actually so.

It is nonetheless true to say that finite causes lose in causing, although this is not because they are causing as such. Their loss is due to the presence of other causes acting reciprocally upon them. Since in the physical order every action involves a reaction, it is impossible to separate physically the activity of an agent from its being acted upon by a reciprocal agent. A physical agent, when acting, is always a patient with respect to something else. What is required to understand causality, therefore, is an intellectual abstraction whereby one considers separately two distinct but inseparable elements as these occur in the physical order.

Priority of nature. The priority of the cause to the effect, considering both in the order of act, is not a priority of time but one of nature. The effect flows from the cause and not conversely. Although parents, as human beings, exist temporally before their offspring, they do not do so strictly qua parents. They become parents only at the moment of conception. In the order of act, therefore, a cause and its proper effect are simultaneous. For this reason the effect continues to be only so long as its cause(s) continue to act. It is important to distinguish, therefore, the proper effect of a cause from its general effect. One can say that a tailor is the cause of the suit, as his general effect, but not that the suit is the proper effect of the tailor, for obviously the suit can continue to be when the tailor has died. Rather the proper effect of the tailor is the suit in its coming-to-be. Thus, the suit begins to become, continues becoming and ceases to become only so long as the tailor begins, continues and stops working on it. The suit continues to be, therefore, not because of the tailor—who no longer exerts causal influence with respect to it—but because its material and formal causes effect this conjointly.

Action and passion. With respect to efficient causality, there is only one motion or action, but this gives rise to two CATEGORIES OF BEING: passion, from the viewpoint of the patient; and action, from the viewpoint of the agent. There is then but one actuation and the change as such is in the patient, not in the agent. This can be more easily stated by saying that the effect is a prolongation of the act of the agent in the patient. There are not two separate acts that somehow must be connected by a third, essentially the mistaken view of Hume; there is but a single act.

Causes of being and becoming. The distinction between a cause in the order of becoming (*in fieri*) and a cause in the order of being (*in esse*) must also be noted. A creature's causality is limited to the order of becoming, while only God can cause in the order of being. The limitation of a creature's causality is shown by the fact that EXISTENCE (*esse*) proceeds from the form and no creature is a total cause of any form. Rather, creatures are causes of a form's eduction from the potentiality of matter. If creatures do not cause the form as such, much less are they causes of the *esse* resulting from the form. God's unique causality in the order of being is also clear from the fact that only what is *esse* can cause it. Since creatures merely have *esse*, they cannot cause it in the strict sense.

From these notions a number of corollaries follow. One is that nothing can escape the universal causality of God. Since becoming proceeds from being as its principle and tends toward being as its term, becoming always presupposes causality in the order of being. Another corollary is that the causality of any creature presupposes the concurrent causality of God (*see* CONCURRENCE, DIVINE). This should not be viewed as prohibiting genuine secondary causality by creatures, as proposed by occasionalism. Rather it is the very thing that makes creatures capable of exercising their own causality (*See* CAUSALITY, DIVINE).

Subdivisions of causes. Among the many distinctions that can be employed to render causality intelligible are those that subdivide the various causes. Thus, material cause may refer to primary matter or secondary matter in physical things, depending on whether one is concerned with substantial or accidental change. Formal cause may be subdivided into substantial formal cause, that is, the soul of an animate being, or accidental formal cause, that is, quantity or various qualities. Efficient cause may be divided in many ways. The most important

of these would be the divisions into primary and secondary; principal and instrumental; necessary and free; ultimate, intermediate and proximate; and total and partial. The final cause may be viewed as either the object of desire or the desire of the object, the end of generation or the end of the generated thing, etc. A fifth cause, of which Aquinas makes fruitful use, is the exemplary formal cause. Briefly, it is "a form, in imitation of which something comes into being from the intention of an agent that determines its end for itself" (*De ver.* 3.1). This is like a blueprint in the mind of an artificer, according to which some artifact is fashioned.

Causality in Modern Thought

Entering the era of modern philosophy, one experiences a consensus that is definitely antithetic to the traditional doctrine of causality. In what follows, the principal teachings of philosophers who have been most influential in this area, namely, empiricists, rationalists, and positivists, will be sketched.

BACON AND DESCARTES

Francis BACON is representative of this movement in its early stages. He appears to be interested primarily in formal causes, although these for him often serve as nothing more than laws of nature. However, at times his formal causes bear a resemblance to efficient causes. He removes final causality from the realm of natural philosophy and bequeathes it to metaphysics. For all practical purposes, he seems to have regarded final causes as an anthropomorphism that had best be purged from the field of science.

René DESCARTES added further impetus to this general opposition to traditional causes. In making matter inert and in reducing all motion to local motion, he prepared the way for mechanism. The Cartesian view does not admit that things have intelligibility or necessity in their own right, because, as J. Maritain has rightly observed, Descartes made things depend for their intelligibility upon a divine will and not upon divine ideas. Hence, for him, final causes lead to a fruitless search and can be dismissed from human enquiry.

LOCKE AND HUME

John LOCKE and David HUME were both empiricists and nominalists, Hume being the more consistent of the two. Their rejection of causality could easily have been anticipated. However, in Locke's case, rather than reject causality outright, he preferred to relegate it, as he did substance, to the realm of the unknowable. For both Locke and Hume, all that man can know are successive phenomena.

It is primarily by Hume that the major attack is launched upon efficient causality. According to Hume, man knows only his ideas and images directly and not the world of reality. Mind is, for him, simply a state of successive phenomenal impressions and judgment is replaced by association. In asking whether causality can be justified, Hume requests that one show how its most important characteristic, necessary nexus, is grounded in experience. Not finding it rooted there, he concludes that the necessary connection between cause and effect is psychological, having its ground in custom and the association of ideas. Cause thereupon becomes a relationship among ideas and no longer an influence of one thing upon the other in the real world. However, Hume never berated the practical utility of the notion of cause; he simply maintained its speculative unverifiability. Again, for Hume, instinct is more to be trusted than reason.

The principal shortcoming of Hume's view stems from his EMPIRICISM and NOMINALISM. He attempted to have the senses detect, in a formal way, causality and necessity per se—something that those powers are incapable of doing. Aquinas had himself observed that not even substance is sensible per se, but only *per accidens*. Since he did not admit abstraction of an intellectual nature, Hume was consistent within his own system in rejecting causality and substance. And, unable to justify causality ontologically, he did the next best thing in justifying it psychologically. Yet Thomas REID, of the ''Common Sense'' school of philosophy, disagreed violently with Hume's conclusions and reacted by making causality a first principle of knowledge.

KANT'S CRITIQUE

Immanuel Kant, awakened by Hume from the ''dogmatic slumber'' of Wolffian rationalism, saw Hume's problem but was not content to accept his solution. For Kant, Hume's was no solution and so he himself faced the thorny problem of justifying causality. Kant's faith in Newtonian physics and mathematics required him to find an answer that would preserve the status of those disciplines. He felt no such concern for metaphysics, however.

Briefly, Kant's position is this. Man knows but the order of appearance or PHENOMENA, not the order of things-in-themselves or NOUMENA. Now, to know means to change the datum by locating it within a spatio-temporal relationship, whose structure is supplied by the knower through the a priori forms of sensibility. Next man must impose upon this spatio-temporal datum certain other categories that are also rooted in the knower a priori. These are the categories of the understanding (*Verstand*): Quantity, Quality, Relation and Modality. Causality is contained as a subdivision of Relation. Together with the forms of space and time, these categories are constitutive of experience, as opposed to the ideas of reason (*Vernunft*), which can only be regulative of experi-

ence. Previous philosophy erred in confusing the regulative function of ideas with the constitutive functions of the categories. The categories (including causality) are valid when applied to the phenomenal order, but not valid when applied beyond this to the noumenal order. To attempt the latter is to court transcendental illusion (or metaphysics, as Kant understood it). Nevertheless, such a tendency is natural to man and he must always be wary lest he give in to it.

Since Kant allowed a valid but restricted use of causality and other categories within the phenomenal order, he felt that he had preserved the legitimate character of the positive sciences. But maintaining the inapplicability of such categories to the noumenal order led Kant to conclude that metaphysics was impossible as a science. For Kant, then, man does not discover causality in the order of things; rather, he prescribes it and imposes it upon the phenomena in order to render them intelligible (*Prolegomena to Any Future Metaphysics,* a. 36). Interestingly enough, Kant himself refers causality to the noumenal order, an error he specifically warns against (confer, *Prolegomena,* a. 13, Remark 2, and *Critique of Pure Reason,* Introduction, 1). While Kant's general position is understandable in the light of his conceptualism, it is not amenable to a philosophy of moderate realism.

Hegel renders Kantian thought more idealistic, accounting for causality by an unfolding of Absolute Mind, although the process is somewhat obscure. To a considerable extent, the Cartesian demand for clear and distinct ideas and for certitude is at the root of the denial or misunderstanding of causality in modern philosophy. It is true that causality is fundamentally a mystery and therefore lacks the clarity one might desire as an optimum. But opaque though it may be, its certitude is guaranteed by man's direct insight into the real. That this insight is limited can readily be granted.

POSITIVISM AND MODERN SCIENCE

In the main, contemporary philosophy follows the pattern set by its predecessors. POSITIVISM accepts causality only as invariable sequence, and this is really to deny its acceptance. PRAGMATISM, while granting the usefulness of the concept of cause, remains close to positivism. Current scientific empiricism generally regards causality as a convention. Representative of both positivism and scientific empiricism, Moritz Schlick of the Vienna Circle says, ''The sentence: 'A follows necessarily from B,' so far as content is concerned, is completely identical with the sentence: '*In every case* where the state A occurs, the state B follows,' and says nothing more whatsoever'' (*Philosophy of Nature,* tr. A. Van Zeppelin, New York 1949, 89). Charles Sanders PEIRCE reduced efficient cause to its effect and its effect to an irreducible

NEW CATHOLIC ENCYCLOPEDIA

301

fact. Thus, for him, there are only facts. ''The existence of a fact is equivalent to the existence of its consequence. Thus if the consequences of a supposed fact exist, then, so does the supposed fact for the pragmatist'' (*Values in a Universe of Chance,* ed. P. Wiener, Garden City, N.Y. 1958, 129). Rudolf Carnap and Phillip Frank look upon cause as a convention; A. S. Eddington, L. Boltzmann, and E. Mach see nature as acausal.

With the increasing mathematization of the sciences, causality is rapidly losing all dynamical significance and becoming more statistical. Contributing to this view is the current tendency among modern scientists to investigate logical constructs, instead of the world of reality itself. Yet there are indications of a resurgence of interest in causality among philosophers of science such as Mario Bunge and perhaps the future will see a reinstatement of traditional notions.

CONCLUSION

The principle of causality must be seen and grasped in the sensory order, but by an intellectual rather than by a sensory act (*see* CAUSALITY, PRINCIPLE OF). Consequently, nominalism and empiricism, in denying such an ability to man, are logically forced to deny causality as having no more than psychological value. Conceptualism is itself little more than a refined ASSOCIATIONISM, a position whose depths were adequately plumbed by Hume. Hence, unless one grants the epistemological position of moderate REALISM, they will be led to reject causality as metaphysically and scientifically unverifiable. Yet the doctrine of causes is of greatest importance, not only for philosophy and theology, but for the sciences as well. Causality is precisely what enables these disciplines to discern connections and acquire CERTITUDE, instead of merely accumulating facts. The manipulation of nature does not require such a doctrine, but an understanding of nature does. For without causality, man necessarily becomes limited to the order of OPINION and thereby hopelessly frustrated in his quest for knowledge.

See Also: METAPHYSICS; METAPHYSICS, VALIDITY OF; INSTRUMENTAL CAUSALITY

Bibliography: G. B. KLUBERTANZ and M. R. HOLLOWAY, *Being and God* (New York 1963). J. F. ANDERSON, *The Cause of Being* (St. Louis 1952). F. X. MEEHAN, *Efficient Causality in Aristotle and St. Thomas* (Washington 1940). M. A. BUNGE, *Causality* (Cambridge, Mass. 1959). V. F. LENZEN, *Causality in Natural Science* (Springfield, Ill. 1954). E. NAGEL, *The Structure of Science* (New York 1961). A. GUZZO and F. BARONE, *Enciclopedia filosofica,* 4 v. (Venice-Rome 1957) 1:957–975. A. E. MICHOTTE, *La Perception de la causalité* (2d. ed. Louvain 1954).

[G. F KREYCHE]

CAUSALITY, DIVINE

God, however conceived by those who speak of Him, is generally thought of as in some way the cause of the world. His CAUSALITY has in fact been expressed in terms of all four causes, pantheists seeing God as immanent and identical with the world, others seeing Him as an extrinsic source affecting the universe through EFFICIENT CAUSALITY and FINAL CAUSALITY. This article restricts itself to God's influence as the AGENT, or efficient cause, of the existence and activity of His creation and the relationship of secondary causes to His primary causality.

Antiquity. Historically it is quite evident that until God was known through Christian revelation as the Creator, the divine causality was only partially and hesitatingly grasped. Early Greek philosophers simply assumed the existence of the world and attempted to explain it through material principles. Only with ANAXAGORAS was a type of divine causality introduced to explain the universe. This philosopher's concept of the Nous, the intelligent source of the ORDER in things, was a giant step beyond the theories of his materialist predecessors. While recognizing in such an Intelligence the source and continuator of order, however, Anaxagoras still thought in terms of a causal contact that was somehow physical and local; his Nous was a kind of WORLD SOUL, a demiurge. The concept of the demiurge is to be found too in SOCRATES, for whom God is the organizer of the cosmos and the provident cause of ordered finality.

The concept of God advanced by PLATO has been variously evaluated by historians. The demiurge seems to perdure in his explanation of the actual causality of the sensible world. This is the supreme efficient cause of the world of appearances, but it is subordinated to its exemplar in the world of Ideas and to the Idea of the Good as to a final cause. The kind of efficient causality conceived is imperfect; it seems to include a localized contact with effects, making God again a world soul and dependent on higher causes. In his perception of the exemplarity of Ideas, however, and in the notion of efficient causality producing participations in the world of Ideas, Plato provided themes that were later to be fruitfully developed.

ARISTOTLE had an exalted concept of God, but one conditioned by (and perhaps derived from) his conception of the eternity of the heavenly bodies. Because such bodies are perfect and eternal, they require a First Mover who is the source of such perfection and thus is PURE ACT. The life of this First Mover is described as the activity of subsistent intelligence contemplating itself (*Meta.* 1074b 15–1075a 11). But the relations of such an intelligence to the material world are very remote. His causality is primarily final, since all tendency in nature is toward

God as end. Simply because of the divine perfection, providence is so impersonal as to be nonexistent; there is no contact with the world, and the finalism averred is fatalistic. God is efficient cause of the movement of the first heaven; from its movement the rest of the universe revolves, obeying in its processes the rigid laws of finality. Both Plato and Aristotle were seen by St. Thomas Aquinas, however, as having conceived the problem of the universe in terms of the causality of its very existence (*Summa Theologiae* la, 44.1–2).

The Stoics assumed much of the terminology of their predecessors but used it in a basically materialist sense (*see* STOICISM). Their God was a Logos whose fundamental attribute is providence; but they described Him literally as the soul of the corporeal world, entering into composition with its effects. Providence is the inexorable and immutable unfolding of the necessary laws of being of the Logos. Opposed to their view was the teaching of EPICURUS, who posited the clinamen, or principle of deviation within the atomic realm. For him, motion in the cosmos is an effect of pure chance, stable enough for practical living, but prevented by the clinamen from being a rigid destiny oppressing men.

These influences were synthesized and refined by the Romans, who were largely eclectic in their philosophizing but who favored Stoic doctrines, particularly in the fatalistic aspects of their philosophies (*see* FATE AND FATALISM).

The final significant phase of ancient thought on God's causality was NEOPLATONISM. The presuppositions of this movement were avowedly theological, since it considered the visible world only in its relationship to God. Neoplatonist thinkers regarded God as utterly transcendent, and thus it became necessary for them to posit intermediaries to allow for some type of contact with the cosmos. PHILO JUDAEUS was a precursor, naming the angels of the Old Testament as such intermediaries. With PLOTINUS, however, the doctrine of EMANATIONISM characteristic of Neoplatonism came to be fully articulated. God is the One, from which Intelligence emanates as a kind of necessary creation; then Soul proceeds in its turn, and finally matter. It is from Intelligence that the world emanates, corresponding to Intelligence's contemplation of the Platonic Ideas. The entire explanation, being based on a necessary emanation from the perfection of the One, leaves the system open to the charge of PANTHEISM. Nor does Plontius explain the kind of causality exercised on the world, except as an inevitable consequence of the perfection of the One and as an influence of Intelligence, its immediate cause.

Thus the Greco-Roman world, in various ways, recognized a causal relationship between God and the uni-verse. The primary emphasis was not so much on the concept of source or origin as it was on providence. Nor was the causality explained in very precise terms, and this for want of knowledge of the manner of origin of things from God the Creator.

Patristic Era. In the Christian Era the creative causality of God was explained by St. JUSTIN MARTYR, among others; he used but corrected Platonic concepts. He maintained the idea of CREATION *ex nihilo* and avoided so exaggerating the divine TRANSCENDENCE as to cut God off from His creatures. Like Justin, St. IRENAEUS opposed GNOSTICISM, with its Neoplatonic emanationism and its hierarchy of eternal intermediaries or aeons that went to form the pleroma. By the doctrine of creation Irenaeus excluded both pantheism and the conception of God as cause of the continued existence of creation. CLEMENT OF ALEXANDRIA, while employing Platonic elements in his writings, defended the doctrine of creation. ORIGEN rejected the eternity of matter, but his maintaining the eternal creation of spirits gave occasion for error. TERTULLIAN, also denying the eternity of matter, was a strong defender of the creation of the world in time.

In St. AUGUSTINE is to be found the fullest explanation of the divine causality by any Father of the Church. Augustine saw all being, unity, truth, goodness, and beauty as participations of the Subsistent Word. These participations are not Neoplatonic, necessary emanations, but a true creation as taught by Scripture, *ex nihilo* and beginning at a definite point in time. Time itself is a part, a mode, of this creation. No change in God is implied, for God is above time and is its cause, planning through all eternity for creation to take place and for time to begin. Augustine saw divine CONSERVATION as the continuation of creation, with all things continuing in existence as dependent reflections of Uncreated Truth. Typical of Augustine is the EXEMPLARISM he taught as part of the divine causality. The Ideas of Subsistent Truth are the exemplars of all beings in the universe. They are not the separated Ideas of Plato, consulted by the demiurge; they are the content of the divine mind itself. They are at once exemplary and efficient, since God puts them into existence in His creatures. Augustine also defended divine providence as the conscious source of the order and goodness of all things; God wills their perfection and His will is effective. Vexed by the problem of EVIL, he formulated his basic principle for addressing the problem: "The cause of evil is not efficient but deficient, for evil is a defect, not an effect" (*Civ.* 12.7). (*See* PATRISTIC PHILOSOPHY.)

Early Scholasticism. In the centuries before the zenith of SCHOLASTICISM, there were reflections both of Neoplatonism and of Aristotle. JOHN SCOTUS ERIGENA represents the Neoplatonic line. Creation is the evolving of the being of God (*natura increata creans*), first in Intelligence (*natura creata creans*), then in the visible world (*natura creata non creans*). God, as it were, creates Himself in the world by these necessary emanations, and the world, in its turn, returns inevitably to Him (*natura nec creata nec creans*). The Arab philosophers were important for their interpretation of Aristotle. In AVICENNA there was a reassertion of the Neoplatonic hierarchy, but now expressed in terms of the Aristotelian heavenly spheres. The Avicennian concept of providence is fatalistic. AVERROËS reaffirmed the necessary eternity of the universe, holding that the heavenly spheres and matter are coeternal with God, who is the cause of their movement as final cause exclusively. God has no knowledge of anything outside Himself, and the laws of the universe are expressions of a deterministic finality. (*See* ARABIAN PHILOSOPHY.)

Among the scholastics, it was primarily Augustinian teaching that served to express the theology of God's causality. St. ANSELM OF CANTERBURY restated the doctrine of creation and conservation as found in Augustine. St. BONAVENTURE significantly developed Augustine's concept of exemplarity. But it was in the grand synthesis of St. THOMAS AQUINAS that the fullest and most satisfying analysis of divine causality was finally achieved.

Thomistic Analysis. God's causality as efficient, or productive, is required by Aquinas on three counts: the initial production of the universe, the conservation of all things in their existence, and the actual exercise of causality by all agent causes.

Production and Conservation. As to the initial production, St. Thomas deals first with the procession of all beings from God (*Summa Theologiae* 1a, 44) and then with creation itself (1a, 45). God is the efficient cause of all, including matter; He is the exemplar above whom there is no further model; and He is the final cause of all. There is here an obvious echo of positions adopted throughout history, an echo that is particularly pronounced in the treatment of efficient causality. The argument Aquinas uses, found in various forms in Plato, Aristotle, and Augustine, is briefly, this. All being apart from God must come from Him, for God is Subsistent *Esse; esse* is uniquely an effect of God, and therefore all other beings must participate in *esse* from Him. While invoking both Plato and Aristotle in support of this argument, Aquinas is more profound—if only because of his knowledge of the revealed truth of creation. From this truth comes his insight into the meaning of God as Subsistent *Esse* and the implications of this concept for an understanding of divine causality.

Creation is the production of the total being of the universe from nothingness, that is, from no subject that exists anteriorly. This total production is not a necessary emanation; rather it is a free act accomplished by the divine fiat. It is not eternal but takes place in time. The implications of this for clarifying what is meant by God's own perfection and causality are clear. The very being of things is conferred on them from God as from a primal source; whereas there formerly was God and nothing else, other beings suddenly began to exist. God as the source is the fullness of being—His own an unreceived, limitless being; the being of all else an effect that He produces. Thus what the divine causality explains is the very fact of EXISTENCE. This means that God alone is the first and proper cause of *esse*. It means that the divine causality does not work physically on a preexistent matter, that God's causality does not require His physical contact or His IMMANENCE in creation. Rather this causality is a pure communication; the First CAUSE is perfective of its effects without being itself perfected or changed in any way. On the other hand, the creature is totally dependent on such divine causality; this dependence makes all the difference between its existing and its not existing.

Through his concept of creation, Aquinas was able to clarify the nature of creatural dependence on God. The pagan philosophers, it is true, were able to discern the relationship between limited being and a primary unlimited source, but they did not appreciate its significance or the precise dependence it implied. Once the revealed fact of the absolute emergence of all existents from God was understood, on the other hand, the concept of God as Subsistent *Esse,* with all its implications, became clear. God alone is His being; He created other existents from nothingness. This revealed truth thus guided the Christian interpretation of the meaning of God's subsistence. If any other being exists apart from God, it can only be a participated being and must receive its *esse* from the One who is being without limitation. When God causes, His initial causality must be a bestowal of existence as such. There is no other source, nor can anything be presupposed to the divine causality.

The knowledge of creation thus led to a formulation that applies to the whole range of divine causality, viz, "*esse* is the proper effect of God." That God did produce the universe from nothingness makes clear the basis of the statement that God is His own *esse,* that "to be" is, as it were, the very nature of God. Therefore *esse,* wherever it is found outside of God, is an effect—an effect that God alone can produce. Every existent, as a consequence, actually and continually depends on God. Thus could Aquinas adopt and explain in his own way Augustine's teaching that conservation is the continuation of creation. Any effect that is dependent on its cause not only for its coming-to-be but also for its actual being is continually dependent on such a cause. All creatures, because they exist and for as long as they exist, actually and continually receive their existence from God (*Summa Theologiae* la, 104.1).

Exercise of Causality. The teaching that *esse* is the proper effect of God need not entail a rejection of creatural causality. St. Thomas was at pains to preserve the reality of both divine and created causality, rejecting an error of his own times that would eliminate either type and even refuting a position later to be adopted by DURANDUS OF SAINT-POURÇAIN (*De pot.* 3.7; *Summa Theologiae* 1a, 105.5). The production of creatures, for Aquinas, means the communication of being in various and limited ways. Since God willed to create, His creatures must be limited and cannot themselves be Subsistent Being. Their limitation is in their essence, which is made to be actualized by *esse;* in this way God is the cause of the entire being of His creatures. But the perfection of the divine causality precisely as communicative embraces the production of certain creatures that are more perfect than others in that the former can contribute actively to the development of creatures, whereas the latter cannot. Stated somewhat differently, God makes at least some things to be efficient causes (*Summa Theologiae* 1a, 103.6).

Aquinas explains, moreover, how God's causality does not eliminate the causality of secondary causes but rather causes them to be themselves causes actually causing. Efficient causality is always the active communication of existence to an effect. Because *esse* is the proper effect of God, every other agent in causing must participate in the influence of divine causality. Not only does it do this in view of its essence and its power to operate, received initially from God, but also in actual subordination to God's influx in the very exercise of its causality. The power actually to share in God's proper causality is communicated as a passing force, one that can be received only transiently and subordinately to God. But it is this power that is the ultimate completion of every created cause and renders it capable of actually causing. Only through this power can it impress its proper likeness on its effect, thus functioning on its own level of causality. The completion of its power to cause enables it to make its effect exist, since it communicates *esse,* the ultimate actuality of all perfections. The particular kind of existence is made actual by *esse,* and the power received from God to enter into this communication makes the secondary cause actually the cause of its own effect. Because this ultimate power derives from its subordination to God, both God and the secondary cause are total causes of the entire reality of the effect—God as primary, the created agent as secondary, cause.

Aquinas explains the subordination of secondary causes to God by teaching also that God "applies" the power of the secondary cause to its exercise. This point became the occasion for acrid controversy between Thomists and Molinists in the 16th and 17th centuries (*see* CONGREGATIO DE AUXILIIS; BÁÑEZ AND BAÑEZIANISM; MOLINISM; PREMOTION, PHYSICAL; CONCURRENCE, DIVINE). St. Thomas maintains simply that God applies all causes to their actual operation because they are moved movers and He is the First Mover. Yet even this is but another facet of the dependence of the creature, as composed of essence and existence, on the unique Subsistent *Esse.* It is because, in their ontological structure as substances, created causes are so composed that they cannot be identical with their own operation (*Summa Theologiae* la, 54.1–2). Their exercise of operation is the acquisition of a new accidental *esse* to which, as created, they are merely in potency. This potentiality cannot be actualized unless through the intervention of God, who is First Mover and Pure Act precisely because He is Subsistent *Esse.* The communication of MOTION by God is not the bestowal of a reality distinct from the transient power by which the created agent participates in the production of *esse.* It is simply another facet of the dependence of creatural causality on God's causality.

The causality of God, particularly with regard to conservation and concurrence with secondary agents, is considered by Aquinas an effect of God's government (*Summa Theologiae* la, 103). This, in turn, is simply the execution of divine providence (*ibid.* la, 22). God acts intelligently, and His causality follows a plan. In defending the rightness and goodness of this causality as it extends to every single entity and to every mode of being, Aquinas treats also the problem of evil. He does so by invoking and elaborating upon the teaching of Augustine noted above (*ibid.* la, 49; 1a2ae, 79). Arguing that the whole of creation and the causality of God is an act of His intelligence and free will, he further rejects all types of fatalism and DETERMINISM from God's causal influence on creatures.

Later Scholasticism. Apart from those who continued and explored the insights of Aquinas (*see* THOMISM), several notable figures in the era before the age of modern philosophy contributed to thought on the divine causality. In his critical assaults on Thomistic teaching, Duns Scotus maintained that St. Thomas's insight to the effect that God is the sole proper cause of *esse* is indefensible; he likewise rejected the notions of the ubiquity of the divine causality and the action of God on all created causes. He did not, however, offer any positive rational substitute for the Thomistic positions on these subjects (*see* SCOTISM). WILLIAM OF OCKHAM also introduced a skeptical theme concerning reason's power to know God and His action on His creation (*see* OCKHAMISM). F. SUÁREZ, while professing to comment on Aquinas, actually sought a middle way between Thomism and Scotism; in his eclecticism, however, he rejected the key notion, the real distinction between essence and existence. His theories of divine causality are built rather on what may be called the factual or contingent aspect of the creature and on the grandeur of the universe, leading him to accent the notion of divine providence (*see* SUAREZIANISM).

Modern Thought. Two features regulate the conceptions of the divine causality in modern philosophy. One is that the object of thought is the IDEA; the other, that the content of knowledge matches only sensible PHENOMENA, which are usually explained mechanistically. These assumptions, in various combinations and applications, run throughout modern philosophical systems and so qualify them that in fact they are not concerned with problems of the real but with problems of thought. This general concern conditions and often characterizes what is said about divine causality.

Rationalism, Empiricism, and Idealism. The God of R. DESCARTES is one of his clear and distinct ideas, postulated a priori by the very existence of the thinking self. God is involved in the creation of movement—the local movement typical of Descartes's concept of the corporeal universe. This movement is initiated when created by God in a constant and determined degree; through it the corporeal world develops according to mechanical laws, which guarantee the conservation of this constant energy.

In the spirit of Descartes, N. MALEBRANCHE developed his OCCASIONALISM, according to which God alone is a true cause. This basic concept follows from the clear idea of God as infinite, since in Malebranche's view the finite is utterly dependent on the infinite. Further, for him all corporeal creation is contained in the idea of EXTENSION, which is pure passivity. God acts where His creatures are present; they do not truly act, and thus they are not causes.

For B. SPINOZA, God is the sole substance. Spinoza explains the world as a series of emanations from the divine attributes, which proceed from God by natural necessity and are coeternal with Him. There is no efficient causality; creatures are formal effects of a fatalistic evolution. G. W. LEIBNIZ, on the other hand, stays within the world of ideas. His MONAD is the primordial substance of all being. From the order of possibles in the divine mind, God chooses the best possible world; this is the only sufficient reason for His action (*see* SUFFICIENT REASON, PRINCIPLE OF).

The phenomenalistic strain is particularly stressed by T. HOBBES, who is agnostic with regard to God and thus puts any knowledge of Him beyond the reach of mind. Hobbes is content simply to call God the omnipotent source of all the mechanistic movement by which the world of impressions is explained. Caught up also in an examination and classification of ideas, J. LOCKE presents an argument for God's creative power, but the very notion of causality is so invalidated by his system that the argument reduces to mere assertion. I. KANT has in fact nothing positive to say about the divine causality; rather his critique renders any such affirmation impossible (*see* AGNOSTICISM).

For G. W. F. HEGEL, the extreme idealist, everything real is rational. The world is but the evolution—through a dialectic of thesis, antithesis, and synthesis—of the Infinite Idea. The world is distinguished from this Idea only as a step in its evolution. Since the evolution is conceived as rigidly deductive through the process of dialectic, Hegel's system is one of determinism. God is in truth measured by the necessity of the laws of Hegelian logic.

Positivism, Evolutionism, and Subjectivism. On the positivist level, the influence of F. BACON is important because of the mentality his scientific method engendered. The sound procedures of experiment, hypothesis, and verification he proposed, when extended to the investigation of metaphysical problems by later thinkers, led to agnosticism. So too did the success of I. NEWTON in applying the laws of mathematics to nature; from this arose the conviction that scientific knowledge is alone valid knowledge. These positivist beginnings matured into the materialism and naturalism of the Deists, both French and English, of the 17th and 18th centuries (*see* DEISM). God was acknowledged only as a blind impersonal force behind a purely mechanistic universe. POSITIVISM itself has its foremost spokesman in Auguste COMTE, whose system, if not atheistic, is at best a materialistic pantheism—although later positivists preferred to classify themselves as agnostic.

With C. R. DARWIN and his theory, EVOLUTIONISM came into ascendancy as a monistic explanation of the universe through the development of matter. Herbert SPENCER, its outstanding spokesman, explained everything by the law of evolution; for him an Absolute exists and is the object of religion, but it is for the human mind completely unknowable. Another evolutionary thinker whose view of divine causality is noteworthy is the French Jesuit Pierre TEILHARD DE CHARDIN. Although professing orthodoxy in matters of faith, Teilhard seems to limit God's causality to that of the "Omega Point"—a type of final cause that terminates the evolutionary process [*The Phenomenon of Man,* tr. B. Wall (New York 1959) 271]. He speaks of the universe as "a mysterious product of completion and fulfillment for the Absolute Being Himself" [see C. Tresmontant, *Pierre Teilhard de Chardin—His Thought* (Baltimore 1959) 93]. Again, his attitude toward evil is somewhat unorthodox, for he sees this as physically inevitable in the world, arising through a type of statistical necessity (*ibid.* 94).

An attempt to escape the positivist and the materialist spirit of modern science characterized the Modernist movement of the 19th century. MODERNISM avers an absolute agnosticism with respect to intellectual efforts to reach God but asserts an immediate experience of divinity immanent within the soul. Such experience is regarded as the source of all philosophy and theology. Affirmations about God have no absolute value; their value is their meaningfulness to the person. Another philosophical system that relies heavily on subjective elements is that of H. BERGSON. For Bergson, the real is pure becoming; in such becoming, INTUITION discovers the explanation of all things. God is the Creator by a loving energy that must express itself and must produce creatures, especially men, who are able to love. Like the thought of Teilhard de Chardin, which it undoubtedly inspired, that of Bergson seems to favor a form of pantheistic evolution.

Conclusion. From the foregoing survey of the concept of divine causality, it becomes clear that the full grasp of the concept depends on two factors. First, only with the revelation of the fact of creation can the tentative insights, even the most profound metaphysical discoveries, of philosophers receive their full understanding and application. It was the concept of creation that enabled Aquinas to see the full import of God's being the unique Subsistent *Esse,* and thus to appreciate the subordination of all creation to Him in being and action. Second, modern philosophers cut themselves off from the real problem and from a genuine metaphysical insight simply by so distorting the power of intelligence as to turn it away from being and concentrate it on itself. Certainly, to evaluate the dependence of the world on God pertains to the highest reaches of human wisdom; it needs not only the assistance of God's revelation but also every resource to be found in the soundness of human reason.

See Also: GOD IN PHILOSOPHY; CREATION; PROVIDENCE OF GOD (THEOLOGY OF).

Bibliography: R. GARRIGOU-LAGRANGE, *God: His Existence and His Nature,* tr. B. ROSE, 2 v. (St. Louis 1934–36); *The Trinity and God the Creator,* tr. F. C. ECKHOFF (St. Louis 1952). J. D. COLLINS, *God in Modern Philosophy* (Chicago, Ill. 1959). J. F. ANDERSON, *The Cause of Being: The Philosophy of Creation in St. Thomas* (St. Louis 1952). L. R. WARD, *God and World Order* (St. Louis 1961). N. DEL PRA DO, *De veritate fundamentali philosophia christianae* (Fribourg 1911).

[T. C. O'BRIEN]

CAUSALITY, PRINCIPLE OF

The principle of CAUSALITY has been variously stated in the history of philosophy. Among such formulations are the following: Every effect has a cause. Every contingent being has a cause. Whatever is reduced from potency to act is reduced by something already in act. Whatever comes to be has a cause. What is, has sufficient reason for its existing (*see* SUFFICIENT REASON, PRINCIPLE OF).

Different Evaluations. With the exception of empiricists, nominalists, and skeptics, the vast majority of philosophers have all agreed on the validity of the principle of causality. However, dispute has taken place with respect to the limits of its valid use. For example, I. KANT accepted the proposition as synthetic a priori, hence as capable of extending man's knowledge, as well as being universal and necessary. Nonetheless, he restricted its employment to the order of PHENOMENA, refusing to permit it a legitimate role in the interpretation of NOUMENA. Others have argued as to whether the law of causality is a self-evident principle, or a demonstrable conclusion. Still others have viewed the proposition as analytic or synthetic or both.

All agree that the casual proposition is not established by the presentation of evidence that this effect was produced by that cause—an individual fact easily verified empirically. Rather, the proposition is one that asserts necessity and claims universality. Usually, however, it is not viewed as applicable to being as such, but only to created or finite being.

Many positivist philosophers, as well as a number of linguistic analysts, admit the universality of the causal proposition, but only because they view it as a tautology. From the viewpoint of the formulation, ''Every effect demands a cause,'' if effect and cause be taken as correlatives, the proposition does seem to differ in no way from the statement, *''A is A''*. Such thinkers claim the proposition is certain only because of the syntax of language. Accordingly, for them, its certainty can be guaranteed only at the expense of sacrificing content.

Initially, perhaps the most basic question that can be asked about the causal proposition is this: Is it necessary that when something comes to be, it does so under the influence of another? This question should be understood as applying to the coming to be of any ACT, substantial or accidental; to any CHANGE; and even to CREATION. Those maintaining the validity of the causal proposition answer this question in the affirmative. Immediately, the subsequent problems arise. Why is such a necessity demanded, and how does one know this? The necessity cannot be simply a psychological necessity, i.e., one on the part of the knower, as propose by David HUME; rather, it must be an ontological necessity.

Some seek this necessity through an analysis of the concept of cause, as though a conceptual analysis of contingent being could reveal its relation to a cause. Yet neither the concept of being nor its contraction to that of finite being implies dependence upon a cause. The reason is quite clear. As St. THOMAS AQUINAS puts it, "Relation to its cause if not part of the definition of a thing caused" (*Summa Theologiae* 1a, 44.1 ad 1). Causality is thoroughly existential, and since existence is not contained in the concept—which pertains to the essential order—no amount of conceptual analysis can reveal the exercise of causality. Hume's rejection of causality as real may well be explained by his having searched for it where it could not be found, i.e., in the order of conceptual analysis.

Justification of the Principle. To justify the causal proposition, then, one must show that he being of a finite thing is from another and that this is necessarily so. This truth is comprehended in the real order through judgment and reasoning, not through mere logical analysis. Thus St. Thomas continues: "Still it [the relation to the cause] follows as a result of what belongs to its nature. For from the fact that a thing is a being by participation, it follows that it is caused. Hence, such a being cannot be without being caused, just as a man cannot be without having the faculty of laughing" (*ibid*). But how does one know that a creature is a "being by participation"? This follows from the fact that its essence and existence are really distinct principles. In short, whatever a finite being possesses, it has from its essence or what results from its essence (as a property), or from something nonessential and extrinsic to it. Since creatures are many, since there is in each a composition of potency and act, and since no creature has its existential necessity from itself, its existence must be from another. Its being therefore is *ab alio* (*see* ESSENCE AND EXISTENCE; PARTICIPATION).

When it has been established that the being of a creature comes necessarily from without, the causal proposition is itself established. "Whatever participates in something, receives what it participates from that from which it participates; and to this extent that from which it participates is its cause" (*De subs. sep.* 3; *C. gent.* 2.15). Because only God has existence in virtue of His essence, whatever else has existence has it through the action of another, i.e. God. This consequent then is the causal proposition states on the highest metaphysical plane. To put it differently, the moment one sees that the essence of creatures manifests an indifference to existence, at that moment he can grasp that any creatural act demands influx from another. This again is to state the causal principle, not merely as applying in a particular

case, but as having universal validity for the realm of finite being.

Although the validity of the causal proposition is seen in concrete experience, INDUCTION and ABSTRACTION are required to render its formulation universal. Summing up the views of J. Owens (see bibliography), one can state that the causal proposition is not analytic with respect to a consideration of the ere concept of contingent being; however, it is analytic with respect to a judgment wherein one comes to grips with the existential order. Thus, the nominalist, in refusing to accept an intellectual insight into the real, is consistent in denying real meaning to the universal validity of the causal proposition. For the causal principle is no more sensible per se than is SUBSTANCE.

In light of the causal proposition one sees that all things, either ultimately or proximately, bear some relationship to each other; that there is an existential bond in the order of BEING; and that the sciences, and especially metaphysic, possess validity.

See Also: METAPHYSICS, VALIDITY OF; FIRST PRINCIPLES.

Bibliography: M. J. ADLER, ed., *The Great Ideas: A Syntopicon of Great Books of the Western World*, 2 v. (Chicago 1952) 1:155–178. L. DE RAEYMAEKER, *The Philosophy of Being*, tr. E. H. ZIEGELMEYER (St. Louis 1954). B. GERRITY, *Nature, Knowledge and God* (Milwaukee 1947). J. OWENS, "The Causal Proposition—Principle or Conclusion?" *The Modern Schoolman* 32 (1954–55) 159–171, 257–270, 323–339.

[G. F. KREYCHE]

CAUSE, FIRST

The concept of first cause, by which, in the absolute sense, God is understood, is derived from the metaphysical demonstration of the necessity of an ultimate efficient per se (direct) cause of the existence of multiple and diverse finite realities (St. Thomas, *Summa theologiae,* 1a, 2.3). The first cause is the ultimate uncaused cause, the one cause of all other reality. In the relative sense, the first cause may be the cause that is first in any order of created causes.

Finite reality, in which essence and existence are distinct, requires an efficient proper cause of its being, for its nature is not sufficient reason for its finite existence. A proper effect demands the actual operation of the cause of which it is the effect and ceases with the cessation of that cause (St. Thomas, *Summa theologiae* 1a, 104.1). Whatever demands a cause of its becoming (*in fieri*), demands also a cause of its existence (*in esse*), since the first of all effects is being, which is presupposed to all other effects, and does not presuppose any other effect (St. Thomas, *Summa contra gentiles,* 2.21). Continued existence, therefore, is a present effect that must be due to the operation of the present cause of that existence.

The argument proceeds from the premise, an obvious fact of sensory and intellectual experience, that realities, both substance and accidents, come into existence through the action of a series of essentially subordinated efficient causes. But it is a contradiction in terms that such a series should proceed to infinity. The existence of a first cause, itself uncaused and self-subsistent, must be admitted necessarily.

The same conclusion follows an argument proceeding from the consideration of contingent realities (that may either exist or not exist). It is evident that such realities are not the reason for their own existence, otherwise they would be self-existent. Their existence, therefore, must be the effect of the proper efficient first cause of existence. The existence of all being, therefore, is the direct proper effect of the per se causality of the first uncaused cause.

All causes, other than the first cause, whether they be properly principal or instrumental, are secondary causes whose very existence as causes, as well as whose operations as causes, is an effect of their proper direct cause, God Himself.

The concept of first cause, therefore, signifies not only the primary causality of all causal activity in the created universe, but the primary causality of the very being of all causes. Moreover, the conservation of all created reality in existence is the proper effect of the first cause, whether the reality be of the material or spiritual order, or the composite of the two. Whatever is, or can be, is an effect of the first, efficient, causality of the first cause.

See Also: EXEMPLARISM; EXEMPLARITY OF GOD; GOD IN PHILOSOPHY; GOD, PROOFS FOR THE EXISTENCE OF; GOOD, THE SUPREME.

Bibliography: *Dictionnaire de théologie catholique,* ed. A. VACANT et al., 15 v. (Paris 1903–50; Tables générales 1951–), Tables générales 1:557–560. J. DE VRIES et al., *Lexikon für Theologie und Kirche,* ed. J. HOFER and K. RAHNER, 10 v. (2d, new ed. Freiburg 1957–65) 6:96–100. I. M. DALMAU, *Sacrae theologiae summa,* ed. Fathers of the Society of Jesus, Professors of the Theological Faculties in Spain, 4 v. (Madrid), v. 1 (5th ed. 1962), v. 2 (3d ed. 1958), v. 3 (4th ed. 1961), v. 4 (4th ed. 1962); *Biblioteca de autores cristianos* (Madrid 1945–) 61, 90, 62, 73, 2.1:1–36.

[M. R. E. MASTERMAN]

CAUSSADE, JEAN PIERRE DE

Jesuit spiritual writer; b. Cahors, capital of Quercy, March 7, 1675; d. Toulouse, Dec. 8, 1751. He studied at the Jesuit university in Cahors, where Fénelon had also been a student. On April 16, 1693, he entered the novitiate of the Society of Jesus at Toulouse. For more than 20 years he taught the classics, philosophy, and the sciences in the various colleges in his province. He was ordained in 1704 and added to his responsibilities as a teacher those of confessor and preacher, besides acting as spiritual director for his confreres. He gave up teaching in 1724 to become a member of a team of preachers working in "urban missions." In 1729 or 1730 he was sent to Lorraine and became acquainted with the Visitation nuns at Nancy. He was publicly denounced, probably by a Jansenistic pastor, for imprudence of language in one of his sermons, and was sent back to his province where he spent two years in semidisgrace in the seminary at Albi. His spiritual correspondence with the Visitation nuns at Nancy, which extended over a period of about ten years, is the major evidence of his spiritual guidance. From Albi, Caussade was recalled to Nancy, where he divided his time between retreats given at the house of St. Ignatius and the spiritual direction of sisters, especially those of the Visitation and the Good Shepherd. Already deeply influenced by Fénelon's spirituality, Caussade then became familiar with the writings of Bossuet and studied especially the *Instruction sur les états d'oraison.* He wrote a work in the form of dialogues in which he treated the teaching of the two prelates whose controversy had divided the Church in France at the end of the 17th century. This book was published in 1741 at Perpignan when Caussade was rector of the college in that city. He had left Nancy in 1739 and later was rector of the College at Albi. In 1746 he returned to Toulouse.

The work printed at Perpignan in 1741 was titled: *Instructions Spirituelles en forme de Dialogues sur les divers états d'oraison, suivant la doctrine de M. Bossuet, évêque de Meaux* (Spiritual Instructions in the Form of Dialogues on the Various States of Prayer according to the Doctrine of Bishop Bossuet of Meaux). Since the author was not named, the work was attributed to Paul Gabriel ANTOINE, a theologian of repute, whose name appeared in connection with the imprimatur. It would seem that the work caused no stir when it appeared. The *Journal de Trévoux,* edited by Jesuits, referred to it in moderate terms in 1745. In 1752, a short time after his death, Caussade was attacked by the *Nouvelles Ecclésiastiques,* a Jansenistic publication.

Caussade is known especially for a work called *Abandon à la Providence divine,* for which he was not directly responsible. Henri Ramière, SJ, who published it in 1861, tells how the Visitation nuns had kept the letters received from their spiritual director. One of them, Mother Sophie de Rottembourg, had made a kind of treatise of them by grouping into 11 chapters certain passages from his correspondence and from notes taken at his conferences. Ramière learned of this manuscript from the Religious of Nazareth, who had a copy of it. He reworked the text and arranged it according to what seemed to him the dominant theme. He divided it into two parts, the first dealing with the virtue and the second with the state of abandonment. It was printed in Le Puy and enjoyed a considerable success. The treatise was completed in later editions, by the addition of a series of letters gathered from collections preserved at the Visitation convent of Nancy.

Caussade's doctrine is dominated by the idea of peace. A disciple of St. Francis de Sales and of Fénelon, he remained faithful to Ignatian spirituality as interpreted by Louis LALLEMANT. He relates all spirituality to interior peace, obtained by fidelity to the order of God, by faith in the universal and ever actual working of the Creator, by accepting one's cross, and by a confidence in God's fatherly goodness. This is the Salesian ideal of evangelical simplicity and of absolute docility to the will and pleasure of God.

Bibliography: H. BREMOND, *Apologie pour Fénelon* (Paris 1910). M. OLPHE-GALLIARD, *Dictionnaire de spiritualité ascétique et mystique. Doctrine et histoire,* ed. M. VILLER et al. (Paris 1932), 2.1:354–370. "Le Père de Caussade, directeur d'âmes," *Revue d'ascétique et de mystique* 19 (1938) 394–417; 20 (1939), 50–82. "L'Abandon à la Providence divine et la tradition salésienne," ibid. 38 (1962), 324–353.

[M. OLPHE-GALLIARD]

CAVALCANTI, GUIDO

Italian poet; b. Florence, *c.* 1259; d. there, August 1300. He was prominent in the political conflicts between factions of the GUELFS and died of a fever contracted in political exile. Dante called him "the first of my friends" and dedicated the *Vita Nuova* to him. Guido's name appears several times in the *Divina Commedia* as the poet who had stolen the glory of G. Guinizelli's style, and Guido's poems are praised in Dante's *De vulgari eloquentia* as "most subtle and smooth." These references led to the conclusion that Cavalcanti's poetry sprang from the same conceptual and poetic sources, the same atmosphere, from which the *Vita Nuova* arose, and that he manifests the qualities generally judged characteristic of the *dolce stil nuovo*—mainly the idea that poetry is inspired by love and that the mystic conception of beauty is the source of nobility and perfection and a ladder to God. There is indeed considerable insistence in Cavalcanti's poetry on the destructive force of love and on the fear and torment caused by the approach of the beloved; these aspects were considered personal quirks of his pessimistic and melancholy mind.

It is clear now, however, that these views have to be abandoned. There can be no doubt that when Dante speaks of himself and of the *dolce stil nuovo* in the famous lines "I mi son un che quando Amore spira noto. . . ," he does not speak of love that inspires, but of the spirits, the movements of love that he and his friends are able to detect and describe. In fact, the most important of Guinizelli's and Cavalcanti's poems are a kind of scientific analysis of love, with no reference to personal sentiment. Considered without reference to background, these poems seem inspired by Christian MYSTICISM, but Guinizelli's key thought clearly derives from Avicenna's pagan conception of beauty as an emanation from a higher Intelligence and as a ladder to perfection. Cavalcanti speaks of love in conformity with Averroes' thought; he explains it as a passion of the sensitive appetite and holds that "from its power death often originates," because it prevents rational activity, the true life of man. Cavalcanti's conception of love as something that alienates the soul from the "supreme good" and brings death to man is to be found in the Averroist treatise *De summa felicitate* by G. da Pistoia, which is significantly dedicated "to Guido, most beloved friend." Cavalcanti's *canzone* "Donna mi prega" clearly expresses the repudiation of love by a philosopher who praises contemplation of the truth above all and rejects the fears and mutability of lovers.

It must be added that Cavalcanti is not simply a rigorous Averroistic philosopher. He is a poet first of all; he strove to create pure intellectual poetry, excluding every hint of sentiment or personal experience. His is a stern, sententious language, obscure, aphoristic, making no concession to common speech. It was a necessary cloak to hide his atheism, but it sprang primarily from the disdain of the philosopher (clearly expressed in a polemic against Guido Orlandi) for all ordinary people unable to understand his "scientific demonstration." Further, Cavalcanti conceived of poetry as something difficult and subtle. He was a versatile poet, however, and wrote in the *dolce stil nuovo* some pieces not inferior to Dante for grace and limpidity, and also some delicate, fresh pastorals. His *ballata* "Perch'io non spero," written during his exile from Florence in 1300, expresses with deep sincerity and moving tenderness his sorrow and nostalgia.

If at times Cavalcanti reverts to the themes and modes of Guinizelli, it is clear that he is not speaking of a real woman whom he adores, but of philosophy, his true lady. It is of her that he spoke in a sonnet to Guido Orlandi, opposing her to the Blessed Virgin and praising her for her power to heal and other miracles. Dante implies that Cavalcanti was excluded from the way to God because he had been a follower of Aristotelian naturalism and had disdained the help of Vergil, the poet of the divine mission of Rome. Cavalcanti mirrors the last years of the secularism of the 13th century. With him the religious superficiality of the troubadours turns into a pronounced repudiation of religion. He was dedicated to poetry, philosophical rigor, and a treatment of love on a purely psychological level, to the complete exclusion of moral and religious values.

Bibliography: G. CAVALCANTI, *Le rime,* ed. G. FAVATI (Milan 1957). M. CASELLA, ''La Canzone d'amore di Guido Cavalcanti,'' *Studi di filologia italiana* 7 (1944) 95–160. O. BIRD, ed., ''The Canzone d'amore of Cavalcanti according to the Commentary of Dino del Garbo,'' *Mediaeval Studies* 2 (1940) 150–203; 3 (1941) 117–160. B. NARDI, ''L'averroismio del primo amico di Dante,'' *Studi danteschi* 25 (1940) 43–79; ''Noterella polemica sull'averroismio di G. Cavalcanti,'' *Rassegna di filosofia* 3 (1954) 47–71. J. E. SHAW, *Guido Cavalcanti's Theory of Love* (Toronto 1949). G. FAVATI, ''La Canzone d'amore del Cavalcanti,'' *Letteratura moderne* 3 (1952) 422–453. P. O. KRISTELLER, ''A Philosophical Treatise from Bologna Dedicated to G. Cavalcanti and His Questio de Felicitate,'' in *Medioevo e Rinascimento: Studi in onore di Bruno Nardi,* 2 v. (Florence 1955) 1:425–463. R. MONTANO, *Storia della poesia di Dante,* v.1 (Naples 1962).

[R. MONTANO]

CAVALLI, FRANCESCO

Baroque opera and church composer (original name, Pier Francesco Caletto-Bruno); b. Crema (Lombardy), Italy, Feb. 14, 1602; d. Venice, Jan. 17, 1676. He received musical training under his father, G. B. Caletto, an organist, and in March 1616 undertook studies with MONTEVERDI in Venice, adopting the surname of Federigo Cavalli, the patrician who made his education possible. He spent his life in Venice, serving at San Marco as singer, organist, or *maestro di cappella.* While he was the leading exponent of early Venetian opera, he composed also a number of Masses and motets in various forms, from solo monodies to two-choir works, all in the *stile moderno.* These works, though dramatic, are not operatic, and it is clear that Cavalli distinguished between church and stage music. In the smaller ones there are devices common to less pretentious *concertato* music, and in the polychoral works there is the fullness of sound characteristic of Venetian religious music of that time. Like almost all his sacred music, his unpublished Requiem, reputedly a work of great solemnity, is still unavailable in a modern edition.

Bibliography: A. A. ABERT, *Die Musik in Geschichte und Gegenwart,* ed. F. BLUME 10 v. (Kassel-Basel 1949–) 2:926–932. E. J. WELLESZ, *Grove's Dictionary of Music and Musicians,* ed. E. BLOM 9 v. (London 1954) 2:128–132. W. S. NEWMAN, *The Sonata in the Baroque Era* (Chapel Hill, N.C. 1959). P. H. LÁNG, *Music in Western Civilization* (New York 1941). M. F. BUKOFZER, *Music in the Baroque Era* (New York 1947). D. J. GROUT, *A Short History of Opera* 2 v. (New York 1965). M. N. CLINKSCALE, ''Pier Francesco

Manuscript folio from book of poems, 14th century, by Guido Cavalcanti (Cod. Chigiano 1, VIII. 305, fol. 56r).

Cavalli's *Xerse*'' (Ph.D. diss. University of Minnesota, 1970); ''Francesco (born Pietro Francesco Caletti) Cavalli'' in *International Dictionary of Opera* 2 v. ed. C. S. LARUE (Detroit 1993) 229–232. J. GLOVER, *Cavalli* (London 1978). P. G. JEFFREY, ''The Autograph Manuscripts of Francesco Cavalli'' (Ph.D. diss. Princeton University, 1980). D. M. RANDEL, ed., *The Harvard Biographical Dictionary of Music* (Cambridge, Massachusetts 1996) 146–147. N. SLONIMSKY, ed. *Baker's Biographical Dictionary of Musicians, Eighth Edition* (New York 1992) 309. T. WALKER, ''Francesco Cavalli'' in *The New Grove Dictionary of Music and Musicians, vol. 4,* ed. S. SADIE (New York 1980) 24–34.

[T. CULLEY]

CAVANAUGH, JOHN JOSEPH

President of the University of Notre Dame, Ind.; b. Owosso, Mich., Jan. 23, 1899; d. Notre Dame, Ind., Dec. 28, 1979. In 1925, Cavanaugh left a very promising business career to enter the Congregation of the Holy Cross. Ordained a priest in 1931, he received the S.T.L. degree from the Gregorian University in Rome in 1933. He returned to Notre Dame where he succeeded John F. O'Hara as Prefect of Religion. In 1938, Cavanaugh became assistant provincial of the Congregation's U.S. Province and in 1940 was appointed vice-president of the University of Notre Dame. He succeeded J. Hugh O'Donnell as president in 1946.

Cavanaugh presided over the transition of Notre Dame from an enclosed compound with most students living on campus to an institution serious about integration into the mainstream of the American academic community. Cavanaugh structured the university, encouraged new programs in teaching and research, and laid the foundation for the fund raising machinery which would build an endowment and make expansion possible.

When canonical requirements forced him to step down as president in 1952, Cavanaugh became director of the Notre Dame Foundation, the university's development program. Ill health caused his retirement in 1960, but he held a number of public service posts, participated in the 1965 Civil Rights March in Selma, Ala., and from 1968 to 1973 worked as chaplain at Saint Mary's College, Notre Dame, Ind.

A 1958 speech on the failure of American Catholics to exercise intellectual leadership brought Cavanaugh much criticism at the time. A longtime friend of the Kennedy family, he offered Mass in the White House the morning after the president's assassination in 1963, and at the family's home in Hyannis Port, Mass., in 1969, when Joseph P. Kennedy, the president's father, died.

See Also: NOTRE DAME DU LAC, UNIVERSITY OF.

Bibliography: University of Notre Dame Archives, biographical file, "J. J. Cavanaugh." T. STRITCH, "A Hero of Transition," *Notre Dame Magazine* 9 (Feb. 1980) 3–5.

[J. T. CONNELLY]

CAVAZZONI, GIROLAMO

Renaissance organist and polyphonist; b. Urbino, Italy, *c.* 1520; d. Venice, 1560. He was a son of Marco Antonio Cavazzoni, godson of Cardinal Bembo, and pupil of Willaert. His fame rests today on his extensive volume of keyboard music, *Intavolatura cioè Ricercari, Canzoni, Hinni, Magnificati* (Venice 1542), comprising four *ricercari*, two *canzone*, twelve hymns, and settings of the odd-numbered verses of the Magnificat in tones I, IV, VI, and VIII. This was followed in 1543 by a similar work containing three organ Masses: *Missa Apostolorum, Missa Dominicalis,* and *Missa de Beata Virgine.* His collections contain many marks of originality. The *ricercari* received the first polyphonic treatment of this form, and his two *canzoni* initiated a new distinct *canzona* literature for keyboard. In the *Gloria* and *Credo* settings of his Masses, the alternation plan is clearly regular; e.g., "Gloria" (celebrant), "Et in terra" (organ), "Laudamus Te" (choir), "Benedicimus Te" (organ), "Adoramus Te" (choir).

See Also: LITURGICAL MUSIC, HISTORY OF.

Bibliography: Modern eds. of selections from the *Intavolatura* in L. TORCHI, ed., *L'arte musicale in Italia,* 7 v. (Milan 1897–1908) v.2–3. G. BENVENUTI, ed., *I classici della musica Italiana,* v.6 (Milan 1919). G. TAGLIAPIETRA, ed., *Antologia di musica antica e moderna per pianoforte,* 14 v. (Milan 1931–32) v.1. I. FUSER, ed., *Classici italiana dell'organo* (Padua 1955). A. SCHERING, ed., *Geschichte der Musik in Beispielen* (Leipzig 1931) 103. A. T. DAVIDSON and W. APEL, *Historical Anthology of Music,* rev. ed. 2 v., (Cambridge, Mass. 1975) 1:121–127, general. H. KLOTZ, *Die Musik in Geschichte und Gegenwart,* ed. F. BLUME 10 v. (Kassel-Basel, 1949–) 2:934–937. J. A. FULLER-MAITLAND, *Grove's Dictionary of Music and Musicians,* ed. E. BLOM 9 v. (London 1954) 2:132. D. M. RANDEL, ed., *The Harvard Biographical Dictionary of Music* (Cambridge, Mass. 1996) 147. C. H. SLIM, "Girolamo Cavazzoni" in *The New Grove Dictionary of Music and Musicians, vol. 4,* ed. S. SADIE (New York 1980) 35–36. N. SLONIMSKY, ed. *Baker's Biographical Dictionary of Musicians, Eighth Edition* (New York 1992) 310.

[M. T. HYTREK]

CAVE, WILLIAM

Anglican scholar, b. Pickwell, Leicestershire, England, Dec. 30, 1637; d. Windsor, England, Aug. 4, 1713. Educated at Cambridge (1653–60), where he received his master's degree, he was vicar at Islington (1662–79), All Hallows the Great (1679–89), and Isleworth (1690–1713). In 1674 he published *Tabulae ecclesiasticae,* a catalogue of Church authors in the tradition of Jerome's *De viris illustribus* and Bellarmine's *De scriptoribus ecclesiasticis.* Expanded into an ecclesiastical archive in 1685, Cave's *Tabulae* served as a basis for his monumental *Scriptorum ecclesiasticorum historia literaria* (1688–99), which dealt by epochs with the whole of Church literature to Luther. Cave also published a series of historical monographs: *Primitive Christianity* (1672); the *Apostolici* (1677), covering the chief figures of the first three centuries; and the *Ecclesiastici* (1683), on the Fathers of the fourth century. In 1685 he published a tract on Church government in which he attacked the Roman primacy. Although logical and erudite, he lacked a critical sense and was censured by continental Protestants as well as by Catholics for his attempt to identify the Anglican Church with the primitive Christian Church. All of Cave's works were placed on the Index of Forbidden Books in 1693.

Bibliography: J. OVERTON, *The Dictionary of National Biography from the Earliest Times to 1900,* 63 v. (London 1885–1900; repr. with corrections, 21 v., 1908–09, 1921–22, 1938; suppl. 1901), 3:1250–52. C. CONSTANTIN, *Dictionnaire de théologie catholique,* ed. A. VACANT et al., 15 v. (Paris 1903–50; Tables générales 1951–), 2.2:2044–45.

[F. X. MURPHY]

CAVO, ANDRÉS

Mexican historian; b. Guadalajara, Jan. 21, 1739; d. Rome sometime after 1794, although some biographers give 1800. He entered the Society of Jesus at the age of 20 and a few years later was sent to the missions in the northwest, where he performed excellent service as a catechist until the expulsion of the Jesuits (1767) compelled him to leave Mexico. Cavo went to Veracruz to take passage, and there he formed a close friendship with Father José Julián Parreño, a distinguished citizen of Havana, former rector of the College of San Ildefonso in Mexico City, and one of the highest authorities in the Province of Mexico. Both established their residence in Rome. Since expatriation became unbearable to both Cavo and Parreño, they decided to be secularized; therefore, their names do not appear in the catalogues made up at that time of the Mexican Jesuits resident in Italy. Cavo wrote *De vita Josephi Juliani Parreni, Havanensis* (Rome 1792), a tract written in good Latin that contains some details of the calamities suffered by the expelled Jesuits on their voyage to Rome, and *Historia civil y política de Méjico,* left in manuscript form and dedicated to the municipal government of Mexico City. The only evidence of the existence of the latter work was the brief mention of it by Beristaín in his *Biblioteca,* until Carlos María Bustamante found a copy in the library of the bishop of Tenagra and published it in Mexico in 1836, under the title *Los tres siglos de Méjico durante el gobierno español.* It covers the period from the conquest of Mexico by Cortés in 1521 to the end of the Vice-royalty of the Marquis of Cruillas, who preceded Croix, in 1766. It is written in an easy simple style, without pretension or presumption. Cavo appears to have been a person of a gentle and peaceful nature, sincerely pious, studious, modest, faithful, and constant in his friendships.

[M. DELA PAZ PANI CARRAL]

CAVOUR, CAMILLO BENSO DI

Italian statesman, leader in the *RISORGIMENTO*; b. Turin, Aug. 10, 1810; d. there, June 6, 1861. Camillo, Count of Cavour, was the son of Michele, a marquis and Turin's police chief, and of Adele (de Sellon) Cavour, a devout convert from Calvinism. During his youth Cavour developed a rationalistic attitude toward religion, influenced by visits to his mother's family and perhaps by his travels in England and France. Cavour was educated for a military career but resigned his commission in 1831 and then occupied himself for several years in the successful management of his family's properties. The July Revolution of 1830 in France greatly influenced Cavour's political outlook and led him to hope that a constitutional

Camillo Benso Di Cavour. (Archive Photos)

monarchy could be established also in Piedmont. In 1847 he founded in Turin the newspaper *Il Risorgimento* to represent the moderate liberal party and wrote for it chiefly on economic and financial questions. He was elected to the legislature in 1848. In the cabinet of Massimo d'Azeglio he served as minister of agriculture, industry, and commerce, and later as minister of finance. He broke with d'Azeglio in 1852 and traveled in France and England for several months. As premier of Piedmont (1852–59, 1860–61) Cavour distinguished himself for his financial and economic reforms and diplomatic maneuvers against Austria to promote the power of Piedmont and then to unite Italy politically.

Ecclesiastical Policies in Piedmont. Cavour was secular in mentality and believed that in Church-State conflicts the interests of the latter must prevail. In 1850 he joined the radical deputies in support of the Siccardi laws, which were contrary to the concordat of 1841 between the Holy See and Piedmont, and sought to abolish clerical immunities in civil courts, to suppress certain feast days of obligation (which were also civil holidays), to restrict the property rights of religious congregations, and to introduce civil marriage. As premier he defended the Rattazzi bill of 1855 to suppress all religious communities except those dedicated to preaching, teaching, or care of the sick. The bill proposed also to utilize the revenue derived from the sale of confiscated religious properties to increase the stipend for the lower clergy. Cavour claimed that religious orders might have been useful during the Middle Ages but had no utility in his day. As proof he contrasted the progress of England, France, and Prussia with the stagnation of Naples and Spain where religious were numerous. To defeat the Rattazzi bill, the bishops offered to contribute money to increase the stipend of the lower clergy. Cavour resigned as premier because of his cabinet's hesitancy, but he soon returned to office, and the Rattazzi bill was enacted. Cavour was excommunicated for his promotion of the legislation.

Italian Unification. As Cavour's ambitions widened, he sought to unify all Italy under VICTOR EMMANUEL II. To gain help against Austria he allied Piedmont with France. At Plombières, France, NAPOLEON III and Cavour agreed to wage a joint military campaign in Lombardy against Austria. Cavour resigned as premier in 1859 when France withdrew from the war, but he continued, through the Italian National Society, to encourage the revolutionaries in the central duchies and the Romagna district of the STATES OF THE CHURCH to seek annexation to Piedmont. When Cavour returned to the premiership in 1860, he annexed Romagna and the duchies after plebiscites. The action against Romagna caused Cavour to be excommunicated anew. To prevent an advance on Rome by GARIBALDI, Cavour dispatched Piedmontese troops into the Marches and Umbria. After the papal forces were defeated at Castelfidardo, these papal lands were also annexed.

In 1861 the new Kingdom of ITALY was officially proclaimed, with Victor Emmanuel II as king, Cavour as premier, and Rome as capital. PIUS IX, however, still retained the government of Rome and the surrounding territories under the protection of a French garrison. Cavour sought to win this prize through diplomatic negotiation. His representatives, Diomede Pantaleoni and Carlo Passaglia, offered the pope complete freedom of spiritual jurisdiction, the right to maintain diplomatic relations, possession of the Roman basilicas, an annual income, and protection. Pius IX refused to abdicate his temporal power, and Cavour's previous attitudes toward the Church and his extension of the Rattazzi laws to all the Italian states created suspicion concerning his future actions. Negotiations abruptly broke off. In June Cavour died, and the ROMAN QUESTION remained a major problem until 1929.

Mystery continues to surround Cavour's deathbed religious sentiments. It was stated officially that he received the last rites of the Church. Father Giacomo da Poirino was summoned from the local parish church shortly before Cavour's death. Later Pius IX questioned the priest, but the latter did not explain the details of his ministrations, nor did he reveal whether Cavour was conscious and went to confession, or merely received conditional absolution while unconscious.

Cavour never shared the extreme anticlericalism of the leftists and seemed often to be motivated by political expediency in his ecclesiastical policies. He was fond of justifying his actions by quoting the phrase, ''a free Church in a free State,'' but he interpreted this motto to justify unilateral despoliations of Church rights guaranteed by concordats. Cavour was the outstanding figure in the *Risorgimento.*

Bibliography: A. C. JEMOLO, *Church and State in Italy, 1850–1950,* tr. D. MOORE (Philadelphia 1960). D. MACK SMITH, *Cavour and Garibaldi, 1860: A Study in Political Conflict* (Cambridge, Eng. 1954); *Italy: A Modern History* (Ann Arbor 1959). E. PASSERIN D'ENTRÈVES, *L'ultima battaglia politica di Cavour: I problemi dell'unificazione italiana* (Turin 1956). R. AUBERT, *Le Pontificat de Pie IX* (Fliche-Martin 21; 2d ed. 1964). R. GREW, *A Sterner Plan for Italian Unity: The Italian National Society in the Risorgimento* (Princeton 1963). M. MAZZIOTTI, *Il conte di Cavour e il suo confessore* (Bologna 1915).

[M. L. SHAY]

CAYET, PIERRE VICTOR

Theologian; b. Montrichard, France, 1525; d. Paris, either March 10 or July 22, 1610. He studied arts and law at Paris under P. Ramus and followed him into Calvinism. He left Paris for Geneva and devoted himself to the study of theology. After a tour of German universities, he was named pastor of the Calvinist church at Montreuil-Bonnin near Poitiers. Having been created an official of the court of Henry of Navarre, Cayet followed that king to Paris, where he came into contact with Cardinal Du Perron. Accusations of practicing sorcery and magic caused him to lose favor with the Calvinists. On Nov. 9, 1595, he abjured Protestantism, returned to the religion of his birth, and, in a letter, told of the reasons for his return. This document was violently attacked by the Calvinists, and their provocations occasioned Cayet's vigorous defense of Catholicism in a fusillade of works published between 1596 and 1599. In 1598 he was named rector of the University of Paris, a post he never accepted, since he was not a doctor of theology. After his ordination in 1600, he continued to publish works of an apologetic nature. His *Chronologie septennaire* (Paris 1605) was placed on the Index for its denial of the authority of the pope over bishops. He defended this work, and, at his death, his religious loyalties were suspect.

Bibliography: E. MANGENOT, *Dictionnaire de théologie catholique,* ed. A. VACANT et al., 15 v. (Paris 1903–50; Tables générales 1951–), 2.2:2046–48. H. HURTER, *Nomenclator literarius* theologiae catholicae, 5 v. in 6 (3d. ed. Innsbruck 1903–13) 3:412–414.

[C. R. MEYER]

CECILIA, ST.

Virgin and martyr. Though she is one of the most celebrated Roman martyrs, there is no trace of a cult of Cecilia in early times. She is not mentioned by the CHRONOGRAPHER OF 354 or by Ambrose, Damasus, Jerome, or Prudentius; nor is she represented in any of the early Christian decorated ''gold glasses''. A fragmentary inscription dated by G. B. de ROSSI between 379 and 464 refers to a church (*titulus*) named after her. On Nov. 22, 545, her feast was celebrated in the basilica of St. Cecilia in Trastevere. According to a legend of the fifth or sixth century, Cecilia was a young Christian of high rank betrothed to the noble Valerian, whom she converted to Christianity, and who was executed, together with his brother Tiburtius, by the Roman prefect, Turcius Almachius.

Cecilia, though ordered to be suffocated in a hot bath, escaped unharmed. After being struck three times on the neck with a sword, she lived for three days and asked Pope Urban to convert her house into a church. These events are connected with a persecution under either Marcus Aurelius or Diocletian. Cecilia was buried in a crypt next to that of the popes in the Catacomb of Calixtus. It is possible that a pious Christian woman of the old Caecilian family, but not a martyr, obtained this site for Cecilia's burial. In April 821 her body was removed from the crypt by Pope Paschal I and placed under the altar of the basilica of St. Cecilia, though the Liber pontificalis states that the body was found in the Catacomb of Praetextatus. In 1599 this tomb was reopened, and Maderna carved the statue of the saint that is now seen beneath the altar. From the time of the Renaissance, St. Cecilia is usually portrayed with a small organ or viola. She is the patron of musicians.

Feast: Nov. 22.

Bibliography: T. CONNOLLY, *Mourning into Joy: Music, Raphael, and Saint Cecilia* (New Haven 1994). V. L. KENNEDY, *The Saints of the Canon of the Mass* (Rome 1938). N. PIRROTTA, *Ceciliana*, ed. M. A. BALSANO and G. COLLISANI (Palermo 1994). R. PUSCHMANN, *Heinrich von Kleists Cäcilien-Erzählung: Kunst- und literarhistorische Recherchen* (Bielefeld 1988). E. JOSI, *Bibliotheca sanctorum* 3:1226–29.

[M. J. COSTELLOE]

CECILIA ROMANA, BL.

DOMINICAN nun; b. Rome, *c.* 1200; d. Bologna, Italy, 1290. Cecilia Cesarini began her religious life in the

St. Cecilia. (Archive Photos)

monastery of S. Maria in Tempulo, Rome. In 1221 she moved with her community to S. Sisto, a reformed monastery founded in that year by St. DOMINIC, from whom the group received the Dominican habit and in whose hands they renewed their vows. In 1225 Cecilia and three other S. Sisto nuns were sent to Bologna to the monastery of S. Agnese, newly founded by (Bl.) JORDAN OF SAXONY and (Bl.) Diana d'Andalo, in order to establish the Dominican life there. Cecilia was prioress of S. Agnese in 1237. Her reminiscences of Dominic, embodying much information about the foundation of S. Sisto, and including the only eyewitness description of Dominic's features, were preserved in writing by another nun *c.* 1280. Her cultus was confirmed in 1891.

Feast: June 9.

Bibliography: A. M. WALZ, ed., ''Die *Miracula Beati Dominici* der Schwester Cäcilia,'' in *Miscellanea Pio Paschini, Studi di storia ecclesiastica*, 2 v. (Rome 1948–49) 1:293–326. H. M. CORMIER, *La Bienheureuse Diane d'Andalò et les bienheureuses Cécile et Aimée* (Rome 1892). H. WILMS, *Geschichte der deutschen Dominikanerinnen* (Dülmen 1920) 25–28.

[J. A. DOSHNER]

CEDD (CEDDA), ST.

Northumbrian monk, missionary bishop; d. Oct. 26, 664. He was the brother of St. CHAD and a disciple of AIDAN OF LINDISFARNE. He was sent from Northumbria to assist King Peada of Mercia in the evangelization of his kingdom (653). He was then sent to help the recently converted King Sigebert of Essex to Christianize his people and was consecrated bishop of the East Saxons (654) by FINAN OF LINDISFARNE. He founded two monasteries among the East Saxons, one at Bradwell-on-Sea, where a contemporary church still survives, and the other at Tilbury. He also founded a monastery at Lastingham, Yorkshire (658). BEDE describes the elaborate ritual, the fasting and prayers that Cedd and Chad used in consecrating this site. In 664 Cedd attended the Council of Whitby to act as interpreter for the Irish party, though he accepted the council's "Roman" decision. Shortly afterward he died of plague and was buried in the churchyard at Lastingham; his remains were later translated to the stone church there. Bede is the main authority for his life.

Feasts: Oct. 26, March 2 (English Benedictines), Jan. 7 (translation).

Bibliography: BEDE, *Ecclesiastical History* 3.21–26; 4.3.

[B. COLGRAVE]

CEILLIER, REMI

Patristic scholar, b. Bar-le-Duc, France, May 14, 1688; d. Flavigny, France, May 26, 1761. He entered the Benedictine monastery of Moyen-Moutier in the Vosges in 1704, where he was ordained in 1710 and taught theology until 1716. In 1718 he became prior of St. Jacques de Neufchâteau and in 1733 of Flavigny-sur-Moselle, where he is buried. His first work was the *Apologie de la morale des Pères* (1718), a defense of the moral doctrine of the Fathers from Athenagoras to Augustine against the strictures of Jean Barbeyrac of Lausanne. The *Nouvelle bibliothèque des auteurs ecclésiastiques,* published by Louis Dupin in 1686, inspired Ceillier to begin a collection of sacred writers. In 1729 the first volume of his annotated *Histoire générale des auteurs sacrés et ecclésiastiques* appeared. Aided by his confreres he completed 23 volumes in the next 34 years. The series begins with the Old Testament and extends to the middle of the 13th century. Supplied with a two volume index in 1782, the work was re-edited by Armand Caillau, and republished in 17 volumes by L. M. Bauzon (1858–69). Although suspected of Jansenistic tendencies, even in passages quoting or explaining the Fathers on grace and free will, Ceillier was highly regarded by Benedict XIV.

Bibliography: A. BEUGNET, *Étude biographique et critique sur Dom Remi Ceillier* (Mémoires de la Société des Lettres, Sci-

ences et Arts de Bar-le-Duc 2.10; Bar-le-Duc 1891). *Dictionnaire de théologie catholique,* ed. A. VACANT et al., 15 v. (Paris 1903–50; Tables générales 1951–), 2.2:2049–51.

[F. X. MURPHY]

CELEBRET

The popular name for the document called a "commendatory letter," obtaining for a priest admission to the celebration of the eucharist in a church other than the one to which he is attached. By means of these letters the competent superior bears witness to the bearer's legitimate ordination to the priesthood, his good moral standing in his own diocese or religious group, his freedom from any ecclesiastical penalty that excludes the celebration of the eucharist, his freedom from any irregularity, and his consequent commendable status in general. Since the beginning of the Church, clerics traveling for one purpose or another were furnished with such introductory letters. These ensured their hospitable reception in other places and enabled them to exercise their respective orders. Various names have been used for these documents: "letters," "canonical letters," and "testimonial letters"; but the most commonly used term was "commendatory letters." The term celebret, a Latin word meaning "let him celebrate," has been commonly used since the latter part of the 19th century. The exact origin of this term is not determinable. It may have been taken from the primary purpose of commendatory letters, namely, the admission of the bearer to the celebration of Mass. The earliest legislation concerning commendatory letters appeared in the 4th century, implying that they were used to some extent before that time. The present Church law concerning the celebret is found in canon 903 of the 1983 Code of Canon Law.

[G. F. SCHORR/EDS.]

CELESTINE I, POPE, ST.

Pontificate: Sept. 10, 422 to July 27, 432. The *Liber Pontificalis* says that he was by birth a Campanian, son of Priscus; he was probably born between 375 and 380. He apparently migrated to Rome and became a member of the city clergy, serving as deacon under Innocent I (401–417). In his Ep. 192, which was written in 418, Augustine mentions a letter Celestine wrote to him. Significantly, the letter was written during the pontificate of Zosimus (417–418), when Roman-African relations had descended to a new low. The deacon Celestine was clearly a man of some influence. He remained loyal to Boniface I (418–422) in his struggle with Eulalius and succeeded him in 422.

Celestine took a very hard line against heresy. He used the civil authority to help him confiscate the churches of the Novatianists, and he supported the imperial policy of expelling the Pelagians. He opposed Nestorius, patriarch of Constantinopole (428–431) when he gave sanctuary to the Pelagian leaders, Caelestius and Julian Eclanum. This struggle against Pelagianism would have far-reaching consequences later in his pontificate.

Celestine had an elevated view of Roman primacy. This view was gaining ground in the West, but the Africans rejected the validity of any external authority. A deposed African bishop named Antoninus had appealed to Boniface I, who had died before the matter could be settled, and Celestine inherited the problem. Augustine (Ep. 209) made a strong case against Antoninus to his old acquaintance, and Celestine apparently let the matter drop. However, when a second African, the rogue priest Apiarius, appealed to Rome, Celestine heard the appeal and ordered the Africans to reinstate him, sending a legation headed by the overbearing bishop Faustinus to see that this was done. Later at an African council in 426 Apiarius confessed his misdeeds. The triumphant African bishops wrote to the pope to remind him of their right to handle their own affairs and told him never again to send Faustinus to Africa.

Celestine had more success in Gaul, where he weakened the metropolitan status of the bishops of Arles and countered the monks of Lérins who proposed a modified Pelagianism (Semi-Pelagianism) to ward off Augustinian predestinationism. The pope also got the bishops of Illyricum (in the Balkan Peninsula) to accept the authority of his vicar, thus checking the influence of Constantinople in that area.

The central event of his pontificate was the Nestorian controversy. The patriarch of Constantinople had denied that Mary, the mother of Jesus, could be called *Theotokos* ("God-bearer"), on the logical grounds that no human could be the parent of the deity. However, the title had been in use for centuries among the Eastern Christians, and Cyril, patriarch of Alexandria (412–444) and a great theologian, argued that the human and divine were so united in the person of Christ that Mary could indeed be called the Mother of God. Unfortunately for Nestorius and Celestine, Cyril was also a consummate and brutal ecclesiastical politician who saw a chance to depose a hated rival, just as his uncle Theophilus of Alexandria had deposed another Constantinopolitan patriarch, John Chrysostom, in 403. Cyril moved quickly to revive the Rome-Alexandria alliance, so prominent in the fourth century.

Nestorius proved an easy target. His sanctuary for the Pelagians had infuriated the pope, who also resented Constantinople's primatial claims. Nestorius wrote to Celestine in Greek, which he could not read, while Cyril sedulously wrote in Latin, listing Nestorius's many errors, a view supported by the papal representatives in the Eastern capital. In 430 a Roman synod condemned Nestorius, and Celestine entrusted the execution of the synod's decision to Cyril, who was delighted to have papal support.

However, Nestorius was the emperor's appointee, and the eastern bishops knew Cyril's concerns were not just theological. The Emperor Theodosius II (408–450) thought it best to call an ecumenical council to meet in Ephesus in 431. Celestine found himself in a bind. In his view the Roman condemnation had settled the matter, but Roman primacy carried little weight with the Eastern bishops and none with the emperor. Celestine had to send legates, but he instructed them to work with Cyril, to watch for any threat to papal primacy, and to reject the council's decisions if they differed from Rome's.

Cyril soon showed what he really thought of Roman primacy. Tired of waiting for the legates, he opened the council on June 22, and engineered Nestorius's condemnation for heresy and deposition from office. The Syrian bishops, opponents of Cyril, arrived soon after and held their own council, which rehabilitated Nestorius. When the papal legates finally arrived, they learned that two councils had been held without them. Cyril diplomatically held a third session, which repeated the results of the session on June 22, and with which the legates agreed. Since the Council of Ephesus agreed with the Roman synod, Celestine tactfully ignored Cyril's machinations.

Celestine's concern for heresy had great importance for the British Isles. Pelagius was a Briton, and Rome feared that his teachings had spread to his home church and that the British bishops could not stop it. In 429 a deacon named Palladius urged the pope to send Bishop Germanus of Auxerre to Britain to combat Pelagianism. He enjoyed marginal success because he had to return in 447 during the pontificate of Leo I (440–461). In 431, Celestine sent a bishop named Palladius to be the first bishop of the few Irish faithful. Scholars conjecture that he was the deacon who had urged the sending of Germanus to Britain, reasoning that Rome was concerned that Pelagianism could spread from Britain to the incipient church in Ireland and that this deacon was already experienced in dealing with the heresy. Palladius thus anticipated the famous Bishop Patricius (Saint Patrick) by a few years, but nothing is known of his work in Ireland.

Celestine saw to the rebuilding of the basilica of Santa Maria in Trastevere, damaged in the Gothic pillage of 410, and he urged the building of Santa Sabina on the Aventine Hill, probably the finest example of classical architecture in the Late Roman period. He also introduced psalmody into the Roman liturgy, according to the *Liber Pontificalis.*

Feast: April 6.

Bibliography: *Patrologia Latina*, ed. J. P. MIGNE (Paris 1878–90) 50:417–553; *Patrologia Latina*, Suppl. 3:18–21, editions. *Clavis Patrum latinorum*, ed. E. DEKKERS (Streenbrugge 1961) 1650–54. *Liber pontificalis*, ed. L. DUCHESNE (Paris 1958) 1:230–231; 3:84–85. E. CASPAR, *Geschichte de Papsttums von den Anfängen biz zur Höhe der Weltherrschaft* (Tübingen 1930–33) 1:381–416, 609. G. BARDY, *Histoire de l'élise depuis les origines jusqu'à nos jours*, ed. A. FLICHE and V. MARTIN (Paris 1935—) 4:256–258; *Dictionnaire d'histoire et de géographie ecclésiastiques*, ed. A. BAUDRILLART et al. (Paris 1912—) 12:56–58. H. LECLERCQ, *Dictionnaire d'archéologie chrétienne et de liturgie* (Paris 1907-53) 13.1:1203–04. R. U. MONTINI, *Le tombe dei Papi* (Rome 1957) 99–100. R. VIELLIARD, *Recherches sur les origines de la Rome chrétienne* (Rome 1959) 87–88. T. G. JALLAND, *The Church and the Papacy* (Society for Promoting Christian Knowledge; 1944) 295–300. E. FERGUSON, ed., *Encyclopedia of Early Christianity* (New York 1997) 1:228. H. JEDIN, *History of the Church* (New York 1980) 2:100–107, 262–263. J. N. D. KELLY, *Oxford Dictionary of Popes* (New York 1986) 41–42. A. DIBERARDINO, *Patrology* (Westminster, MD 1986) 4:587–589. C. PIETRI, *Roma Christiana* (Rome 1976) 2:955–966, 1026–1043, 1130–1139. H. VOGT, "Papst Cölestin und Nestorius," in *Konzil und Papst* (Munich 1975) 85–101. L. DAVIS, *First Seven Ecumenical Councils* (Wilmington 1983) 134–169.

[J. F. KELLY]

CELESTINE II, POPE

Pontificate: Sept. 26, 1143 to Mar. 8, 1144; b. Guido de Castellis, presumably at Macerata in the March of Ancona. An admirer and former student of ABELARD and a learned scholar himself, he was also a friend of PETER THE VENERABLE of Cluny. Under CALLISTUS II, he was brought to Rome, and he was named cardinal deacon in 1127 and cardinal priest in 1134. As legate and vigorous supporter of INNOCENT II during the schism with Anacletus (*see* PIERLEONI), he was present with BERNARD OF CLAIRVAUX in his championship of the pope's claims before ROGER OF SICILY. His election without controversy two days after the death of Innocent II was widely acclaimed. Celestine, already an old man, was destined to govern the Church only six months. As cardinal he had opposed Innocent's concessions to Roger of Sicily made in the Treaty of Mignano (1139), but was apparently seeking new negotiations at the time of his death. Following LOUIS VII's abandonment of opposition to the incumbency of Pierre de la Châtre in the See of Bourges, he removed the interdict placed by his predecessor on certain French lands because of Louis VII's attempt to depose the archbishop of Bourges.

Bibliography: *Patrologia latina* 179:761–820. *Pontificum romanorum . . . vitae*, ed. J. M. WATTERICH, 2 v. (Leipzig 1862)

2:276–278. *Liber pontificalis*, ed. L. DUCHESNE (Paris 1886–1958) 2:385, 449. P. JADFFÉ, *Regesta pontificum romanorum ab condita ecclesia ad annum post Christum natum 1198* (Graz 1956) 2:1–7. H. K. MANN, *The Lives of the Popes in the Early Middle Ages from 590 to 1304* (London 1902–32) 9:102–112. P. BREZZI, *Roma e l'Impero medioevale 774–1252* (Bologna 1947). F. X. SEPPELT, *Geschichte der Päpste von den Anfängen bis zur Mitte des 20. Jh.* (Munich 1954–59) 3. W. KURZE, "Minute nel fondo del monastero di S. Salvatore al Monte Amiata. Annotazioni critiche sulla tradizione del privilegio di Celestino II del 23 febbraio 1144 (CDA 344)," *Rivista di Storia della Chiesa in Italia* (1997) 451–62. W. PETKE, *Lexikon für Theologie und Kirche*, 3d. ed. (1995). J. N. D. KELLY, *Oxford Dictionary of Popes* (New York 1986) 167.

[M. W. BALDWIN]

CELESTINE II, ANTIPOPE

Pontificate: Dec. 15/16, 1124. He died in 1125 or 1126. Born into a Roman family, Teobaldo Boccapecci (or Boccapecorini) was made cardinal deacon of St. Maria Nuova by Paschal II (1099–1118) *c.* 1100. Callistus II (1119–24) promoted him to cardinal priest of St. Anastasia in 1122. After Callistus' death there was a chaotic election in the church of St. Pancratius. First a Cardinal Saxo was put forward by the majority of cardinals, only to be dropped for Teobaldo, who was subsequently elected as Celestine II. Both candidates had been supported by the Pierleoni family. While Teobaldo-Celestine was being invested and after he had received the pallium, troops under the leadership of Robert Frangipani broke into the church and proclaimed Cardinal Lambert of Ostia as pope. Fighting broke out in which Celestine received serious wounds. He resigned as pope and Lambert became Honorius II (1124–30). Celestine is considered an antipope because his consecration was not completed and he was never formally enthroned. Nonetheless, he was canonically elected, even if he resigned immediately and under some duress. Nothing substantive is known of his last days; he was probably at least in his late fifties when he received his wounds and it is assumed that he died of them no later than 1126.

Bibliography: J. P. MARCH, ed. *Liber Pontificalis completus ex codice Dertusensi* (Barcelona 1925) 204–11. I. M. WATTERICH, *Pontificum Romanorum* (Leipzig 1862) 2.157–59. PETER THE DEACON, *Chronica monasterii Cassinensis* 4.83; 4.108–09 in *Monumenta Germaniae historica, Scriptores* 34.546, 572–74 (also in older MGH SS edition, 7.804, 821–22). R. MOLS, *Dictionnaire d'histoire et de géographie ecclésiastiques* (Paris 1953) 12.58–59. J. N. D. KELLY, *The Oxford Dictionary of Popes* (Oxford 1986) 167.

[P. M. SAVAGE]

CELESTINE III, POPE

Pontificate: March 21?, 1191, (ordained priest March 30, consecrated April 14, 1191) to Jan. 8, 1198; born Giacinto (Hyacinthus) of the Boboni-Orsini family, in the Arcula district of Rome, *c.* 1105–06; died Rome; buried in St. John Lateran *iuxta S. Mariam de Reposo*; subdeacon of the Lateran Basilica (1126); ABELARD'S fellow student at Paris *c.* 1138, and his staunch defender against St. Bernard at the Council of SENS (1140); promoted cardinal deacon of Santa Maria in Cosmedin (Feb. 13, 1144) by Celestine II or (Dec. 22, 1144) by Lucius II, a position he held for 47 years.

His outstanding diplomatic skills were utilized in numerous legations and missions and his intellectual qualities brought him into a close relationship with eminent contemporaries such as Gerhoh of Reichersberg and Thomas BECKET. He acted on behalf of Eugenius III (1149) to facilitate Louis VII's return to France after the Second Crusade and preached the crusade for Anastasius IV in Iberia (1154–56). Following the Diet of Besançon (1157), Adrian IV appointed him (1158) as one of two mediators deputed to negotiate with Frederick Barbarossa. A supporter of Alexander III, his intelligence and integrity proved invaluable to the exiled pope (1162–65), on whose behalf he wrote no fewer than 14 letters to the French king; he also won over to the papacy the allegiance of Genoa. A second legation (1172–74), involving crusade preaching, collection of *census* and affairs in Leon, confirmed his exceptional curial expertise in Iberian affairs. As a respected negotiator, he contributed to the Treaty of Venice (1177) that ended the papal schism of 1159–77. Subsequently he participated in various commissions concerning territorial questions between pope and emperor and undertook an important legation to North Italy (May-June 1181).

The octogenarian pope, 85 years old at his election, is frequently represented as the compromise candidate of the College of Cardinals. However, his elevation is far more likely to have marked a renewed determination for thorough reform, demonstrated by his promotion (1193) of six cardinals of the highest moral integrity to fight against corruption. He sought to impose celibacy on all subdeacons whilst attempting unsuccessfully to reconcile the marital problems of the kings of France and Leon. He performed four canonizations; the bishops Ubaldus of Gubbio (1191) and Bernward of Hildesheim (1192); the abbots, John Gualbert of Vallombrosa (1193) and Gerald of Sauvemajeur (1197). In particular, Cencius, whom he created papal *camerarius*, was instrumental in systematizing the finances of the Church through the *Liber Censuum* and in the determined struggle against forgeries.

Tense relations ensued with Henry VI over his desire to unify Sicily and the Empire. Clement III had promised him an imperial coronation in 1189 but constantly procrastinated; the new pope crowned the emperor on Easter Sunday, April 15, 1191, on the day following his own consecration. Celestine, however, supported the claim of Tancred of Lecce to the *Regno*, creating him papal vassal by the Concordat of Gravina, but on Tancred's death in 1194, the union became a reality. Relations with Henry further deteriorated over the assassination of Albert, bishop of Liège, and the captivity and ransom of Richard I of England. However, the German crusade of 1195–96, Henry's proposal of Dec. 18, 1196 that one prebend in every cathedral of the Empire should be put at the pope's disposal and the emperor's death on Sept. 27, 1197, combined to prevent immediate conflict.

In Celestine's relations with Rome, he achieved a brief respite following an agreement with a Senate of 56 and the concession of Tusculum but Benedict Carushomo, the single senator, soon began to restrict his influence, not only within the city but also throughout Sabina and Marittima. By June 1197, John, cardinal priest of Santa Prisca, was reported as acting in the place of the now seriously ill pope, undertaking every one of his duties save that of consecrating bishops. Celestine may even have expressed his willingness to abdicate, but the cardinals resisted this unprecedented diminution of their rights and he died in office.

Bibliography: *Patrologia Latina* 206:863–1280; *Regesta Pontificium Romanorum*, ed. P. JAFFÉ and G. WATTENBACH et al., 2 (Leipzig 1888) 577–644, 771–72. *Codex constitutionum quas summi pontificium ediderunt in solemne canonizatione sanctorum a Johanne XV ad Benedictum XIII*, ed. G. FONTANINI (Rome 1729) 27–34. J. M. BRIXIUS, *Die Mitglieder des Kardinalskollegiums 1130–1181* (Berlin 1912) 52, 104. B. ZENKER, *Die Mitglieder des Kardinalskollegiums 1130–1159* (Würzburg 1964) 161–67. R. MOLS, "Celestin III," *Dictionnaire d'histoire et de géographie ecclésiastiques*, ed. A. BAUDRILLART et al. (Paris 1912—) 12:62–77. R. AUBERT, "Hyacinthe, *Iacinthus Bobonis*," *ibid.* 25:504. C.-E. PERRIN, "Les negotiations de 1196 entre l'empereur Henri VI et le pape Célestin III," *Mélanges d'histoire du Moyen Age dédiés à la mémoire de Louis Halphen* (Paris 1951) 565–72. W. HOLTZMANN, "La *Collectio Seguntina* et les Décretales de Clément III et de Celestin III," *Revue d'Histoire Ecclésiastique* 50 (1955) 400–53. W. MALECZEK, *Papst und Kardinalskolleg von 1191 bis 1216. Die Kardinäle unter Coelestin III und Innocenz III.* (Vienna 1984). K. BAAKEN, "Zu Wahl, Weihe und Krönung Papst Cölestins III," *Deutsches Archiv* 41 (1985) 203–211. V. PFAFF, "Die Kardinäle unter Papst Coelestin III.," *Zeitschrift der Savigny-Stiftung für Rechtsgeschichte*, Kanonistische Abteilung 41 (1955) 58–94; "Analekten zur Geschichte Papst Coelestins III.," *Historisches Jahrbuch* 109 (1989) 191–205; "Die Kardinale unter Papst Coelestin III. (1191–1198). Dritter Teil, Nachtrage, Berichtigungen und Register," *Zeitschrift der Savigny-Stiftung für Rechtsgeschichte*, Kanonistische Abteilung 106 (1989) 401–407; "Celestino III," *Enciclopedia dei Papi* (Rome 2000) 2: 320–26. *Lexikon für Theologie und Kirche* (Freiburg 1994), col. 1247.

[B. M. BOLTON]

CELESTINE IV, POPE

Pontificate: Oct. 25, 1241 to Nov. 10, 1241; b. Goffredo Castiglioni. A Milanese, he was the nephew of URBAN III. For a time archpriest and chancellor of Milan, he entered the CISTERCIANS of HAUTECOMBE in 1187. In 1227 he became cardinal priest of S. Marco; in 1239, cardinal bishop of Sabina. When GREGORY IX died (August 1241), the Roman Senator Matteo Rosso ORSINI, in order to forestall FREDERICK II's influence and secure a quick papal election, at once enclosed in the Septizonium, a run-down palace, the ten cardinals then in Rome, including, however, John COLONNA, Frederick's ally. On Oct. 25, 1241, this divided "first CONCLAVE" finally elected Colonna's candidate, the aged, infirm Goffredo, as Celestine IV. He died within the month, possibly before he was crowned.

Bibliography: A. POTTHAST, *Regesta pontificum romanorum inde ab a. 1198 ad a. 1304* (Graz 1957) 1:940–941. H. K. MANN, *The Lives of the Popes in the Early Middle Ages from 590 to 1304* (London 1902–32) 13:440–450. K. WENCK, "Das erste Konklave der Papstgeschichte, Rom, August bis Oktober 1241," *Quellen und Forschungen aus italienischen Archiven und Bibliotheken* 18 (1926) 101–170. E. KANTOROWICZ, *Frederick the Second, 1194–1250,* tr. E. O. LORIMER (New York 1957). R. MOLS, *Dictionnaire d'histoire et de géographie ecclésiastiques,* ed. A. BAUDRILLART et al. (Paris 1912) 12:77–79. F. X. SEPPELT, *Geschichte der Päpste von den Anfängen bis zur Mitte des 20. Jh.* (Munich 1954–59) 3:449–451, 616, G. SCHWAIGER, *Lexicon für Theologie und Kirche,* ed. J. HOFER and K. RAHNER (Freiburg 1957–65):1255. M. CLELIA FERRARI, "1243: L'operato di Gregorio da Montelongo a Vercelli," *Studi di storia medioevale e di diplomatica* 17 (1998) 109–118. J. N. D. KELLY, *The Oxford Dictionary of Popes* (New York 1986) 191–192.

[W. H. PRINCIPE]

CELESTINE V, POPE

Pontificate: July 5 to Dec. 13, 1294. Peter of Morrone, Born 1209/10 most probably in the village of S. Angelo Limosano (county of Molise, Kingdom of Naples-Sicily) to a family of peasants. He became a Benedictine monk in the nearby monastery of S. Maria di Faifula before 1230, then a hermit in the Morrone mountains near Sulmona (about 1235–40) where he founded his principle abbey of S. Spirito del Morrone living in his cell of S. Onofrio in the mountains above. About 1240 he moved eastward to found another abbey, S. Spirito a Maiella. There he organized a community of hermits that Pope GREGORY X recognized as a congregation within the Order of St. Benedict. He structured his Celestinians according to the CISTERCIANS and, although without theological education, he proved to be an efficient head of his monks. He encouraged donors so that his community soon spread from the Abruzzi to Rome and Apulia at-

tracting the attention of the Papal Curia and the kings Charles I and Charles II of Anjou, rulers of the Kingdom of Naples-Sicily. He was said to heal the sick and work miracles. After the death of Pope NICHOLAS IV (1291), due to divisions within the college of cardinals who were unable to elect a new pope, the Holy See remained vacant for almost three years. King Charles II when visiting Perugia where the cardinals then were in residence mentioned Peter of Morrone's name as a candidate which led to his election by inspiration (i.e. without a formal scrutiny) on July 5, 1294. He was annointed and crowned at L'Aquila August 29, choosing the name of Celestine ('the heavenly one'). King Charles II prevented him from moving to Rome and organized his transfer to Naples to keep him under his control. Apparently inspired by the eschatological speculations of Joachim of Fiore about the forthcoming Age of the Holy Spirit which was to be the Age of the Monks, on September 18 he created twelve new cardinals, the number of the apostles, among them five monks.

In October, accompanied by the king, he traveled to Naples where he requested a small wooden cell to be built for him in the residence of Catelnuovo. By then it was evident that he was incapable of governing the Church. Some cardinals and others abused his ignorance for their own profit, and soon there was widespread corruption at the Curia. All this clearly disturbed Celestine, who began seriously to consider abdicating. Cardinal Benedict Caetani and canonists of his entourage such as Guido of Baisio and Johannes Monachus correctly informed him that canon law permitted a pope to renounce his office even without the participation of the college of cardinals who, however, were afraid that such an act without precedence might endanger the Church, and King Charles would also have regretted such a step that would have deprived him of his influence. After Cardinal Matteo Rosso Orsini had drafted a pertinent constitution, Celestine abdicated in a consistory on Dec. 13, 1294, in a touching ceremony taking off his papal garments and putting on the rough and simple gray habit of his monks. The cardinals swiftly elected his successor, Benedict Caetani (BONIFACE VIII), on December 24.

On his way back to Rome, the former pope, now again Peter of Morrone, fled to his hermitage at S. Onofrio and from there, pursued by papal envoys, to Apulia. There he unsuccessfully tried to escape to Greece following the example of some Franciscan Spirituals whom he had protected from the persecutions by the majority of their order permitting them to live in a community bearing his name. When his boat stranded at Vieste near the Gargano mountains he was arrested by the Anjou authorities in May 1295 and brought back to Anagni where Boniface was then in residence and who held him in light custody in the nearby castle of Fumone. There Peter-Celestine died of natural causes on May 19, 1296 (ever since his feast), aged about 86. He found his final rest in the Celestinian church of S. Maria di Collemaggio at L'Aquila. Soon his personality was instrumentalized in the struggle between Boniface VIII and King Phillip the Fair of France, and through the efforts of his brethren, some Spirituals and the French enemies of Boniface VIII who was accused of having forced the hermit-pope to resign, he was canonized on May 5, 1313, by Pope Clement V at Avignon. (In 1969 his name was canceled from the official calendar of saints since he had been venerated only locally in his Abruzzi-Molise homelands). Peter-Celestine, who had occasionally shown some harsh traits of character, e.g. by banishing monks of Montecassino who had been unwilling to become members of his congregation, soon became the object of eschatological speculations as the "angelic pope" figuring in prophecies as late as Pseudo-Malachias. In reality, he had been unable to reform and even adequately to govern the Church, and his resignation, an act of responsibility, had prevented the papacy from being afflicted by further harm.

Bibliography: H. K. MANN, *The Lives of the Popes in the Middle Ages* (London 1931). *Dizionario biografico delgi Italiani* (Rome 1979) 27: 402–415. *Dictionnaire historique de la papauté* (Paris 1994) 319–323. *Enciclopeida dei papi* (Rome 2000) 2:460–472. P. HERDE, *Cöestin V. 1294. Peter vom Morrone. Der Engelpapst* (Stuttgart 1981); *Storia della Chiesa*, ed. D. QUAGLIONI (Milan 1994) 11:93–127.

[P. HERDE]

Manuscript illustration depicting Pope Celestine V dedicating his life to Cardinal Stefaneschi, 14th century.

CELESTINES

A branch of the BENEDICTINES, called also Hermits of St. Damian or Hermits of Morrone. They were founded by the hermit Peter of Morrone, later Pope Celestine V. Peter became a Benedictine monk at Faifoli (Benevento diocese) in 1235 and spent the next years in seclusion on Monte Morrone. His asceticism attracted several companions; and though originally the group followed no set religious practice after their approval by Urban IV in 1264, they adopted the BENEDICTINE RULE. The Hermits, who were noted for the severity of their way of life (e.g., perpetual abstinence), were approved again by Gregory X in 1274 and by Peter, once he became pope. From 1240 to 1243 Peter and his companions were temporarily at Monte Maiella, but after a short period they returned to their original site. All Celestine priories were subject to visitation by the abbot of the monastery of the Holy Ghost on Monte Morrone at Sulmona, Italy. The abbot general was elected for a three-year term by the annual general chapter. As pope, Peter ordered that lay brothers be admitted into the congregation. The Celestines, who

numbered 150 monasteries on the Continent at their height in the early 15th century, weathered the Reformation and the Wars of Religion, but became extinct in the late 18th century because of a decline in membership and a general hostility on the part of society toward monasticism. The choir dress was black, and the working habit was a white tunic with black scapular and hood. The lay brothers wore a brown habit. The symbol of the order was a cross entwined with the letter "S" sewn on the scapular.

The name Celestines was given also to some of the radical Franciscan SPIRITUALS. This group derived their name from the fact that Celestine V placed them under his special protection, but they were distinct from the Benedictine Celestines. In 1294 Pietro da Macerata and several companions approached the pope and asked permission to live as monks under the rule of St. Francis, but directly under papal authority rather than under the superior of the Franciscans. This new group was called the Poor Hermits of the Lord Celestine and, after papal jurisdiction, were subject to their leader, Macerata, who changed his name to Liberato. Their official protector was Cardinal Nicholas Orsini, and their houses were obtained from the Benedictine Celestines. When Celestine resigned in 1294, his successor, Boniface VIII, revoked the privileges of these Franciscan Celestines. His action caused several of them to move to the island of Trixoma in the Gulf of Corinth and later to Thessaly. In 1303 they returned to Rome in an unsuccessful attempt to have their rights restored. The remaining members gathered at Narbonne (the Franciscans of Narbonne) in 1308 to live a strict, cloistered life.

See Also: CELESTINE V.

Bibliography: A. FRUGONI, *Celestiniana* (Rome 1991). D. DOUIE, *The Nature and the Effect of the Heresy of the Fraticelli* (New York 1978).

[C. L. HOHL, JR.]

CELIBACY, CLERICAL, HISTORY OF

The practice of celibacy in the Church, or the renunciation of marriage undertaken implicitly or explicitly for the purpose of practicing perfect chastity, is an almost uniquely Christian institution whose history reflects the idealism and, at times, the contradictions of Christian asceticism.

Antiquity and the Old Testament. Among ancient peoples celibacy, especially female celibacy or VIRGINITY, was given a sacral value but was not considered to be a way of life. Temporary continence was often imposed as a form of corporal purification (*lustratio*), but only in relation to worship. Virgins, moreover, were consecrated to a female deity—the six Roman Vestals for 30 years—but perpetual celibacy was ordinarily not practiced. In Sparta, the unmarried lost civic rights (ἀτιμία) and were given menial tasks. After the time of Camillus (402 B.C.), Roman bachelors had to pay special taxes (*aes uxorium*); during the imperial period, they were deprived of parental inheritance (*caducariae leges*).

In the Old Testament, sexual acts, even when not sinful, were considered defiling (Lv 15). Virginity in the bride was the object of high praise (Dt 22. 14–29), and, in practice, a girl who had been violated was unable to find a husband (2 Sm 13.20). But the state of virginity was not to be permanent; to be unmarried and childless was to be the object of shame (Gn 30.23; Is 4.1; 54.4; Jg 11.37–40). Marriage was considered honorable and compulsory for all, and to have many children was viewed a sign of divine favor (Gn 22.17). Thus, in Old Testament times, virginity as a state of life consecrated to God was unknown, except in the period of the ESSENES.

The New Testament. In the New Dispensation, on the contrary, especially in discussion of the higher aspects of morality, the New Testament emphasizes the value of virginity as a means of worshiping God. This is apparent in the example of Christ, Mary, John the Baptist, as well as in the teaching of the Lord. Virginity is presented as a state of eschatological beatitude. In heaven men will not marry because they will not die; in this respect they will be like the angels (Lk 20.36; also Mt 22.30 and Mk 12.25, texts that are still more significant for the traditional comparison of angelic life with that of the unmarried). Prior to beatitude, however, celibacy is the way of consecrating oneself to God, if it is accepted freely for the sake of the kingdom of heaven (Matthew 19.12, 19). Nevertheless, it is a special grace and vocation; "not all can accept this teaching" (Matthew 19.11–12).

Paul did not underestimate marriage, nor, with the Gnostics, did he consider it useless in view of the world's imminent destruction. He was generous in his advice to married Christians, helping them in their special vocation (Col 3.18; 4.1; Eph 5.22; 6.9; 1 Tm 4.3; 5.14). In any event, he stated that "it is better to marry than to burn" (1 Cor 7.2–6, 9, 27–28, 36); but for him, marriage, like all created things, is secondary if compared to the life in Christ (1 Cor 7.29–31). With this in mind, Paul praised celibacy and virginity as a more perfect state, since it is the condition for a more fervent consecration to God, avoids earthly concerns, and prepares for the possession of eschatological goods (1 Cor 7.26–35). The unmarried are able to concentrate only on God, while married persons must think on each other. Paul's teaching, however, is not a universal law. He presented it as a counsel, as a grace or as an individual charism, as a special vocation (1 Cor 7.6–7, 25). This charism, however, does not seem to have been granted to all the leaders of the Pauline churches. Besides, it is difficult to find a peremptory argument in favor of a universal law in view of 1 Corinthians 9.5 and of the matrimonial status of Peter, of the other Apostles, and of the brethren of Christ there cited. The question is controversial, but the pastoral Epistles give clear evidence that the Pauline churches were ruled by married *episcopoi, presbyteroi,* and *diakonoi.* Ministers of the New Testament were not obliged to celibacy, but only to what would traditionally be called *boni mores.* Duties in this regard were presented in stereotype form (1 Tm 3.2–13; Ti 1.6–9), with emphasis on three points: the bishop should be married but once; he should rule well his own household, keeping his children under control and perfectly respectful; for, as Paul asked, if a man cannot rule his own household, how is he to take care of the Church of God?

The Patristic Age. During the first three or four centuries, no law was promulgated prohibiting clerical marriage. Celibacy was thus a matter of choice for bishops, priests, and deacons. Under certain conditions, as shall be evident below, they were permitted to contract marriage and live as married men.

Clerical Marriage Permitted. CLEMENT OF ALEXANDRIA (*c.* 150–*c.* 215), commenting on the Pauline texts, stated that marriage, if used properly, is a way of salvation for all: priests, deacons, and laymen (*Stromata* 1.3.12; *Patrologia Graeca*, ed. J. P. Migne, 8:1189). The Synod of Gangra (*c.* 345) condemned manifestations of false asceticism, among others the refusal to attend divine worship celebrated by married priests (c.4; J. D. Mansi, *Sacrorum Conciliorum nova et amplissima collectio* 2:1101). The APOSTOLIC CONSTITUTIONS (*c.* 400) excommunicated a priest or bishop who left his wife "under pretence of piety" (*Sacrorum Conciliorum nova et amplissima collectio* 1:51). Socrates (*Ecclesiastical History* 1.1.11; *Patrologia Graeca* 67:101), Sozomen (*Ecclesiastical History* 1.1.23; *Patrologia Graeca* 67:925), and Gelasius of Cyzicus (*Hist. concilii Nicaeni* 1.2.32; *Sacrorum Conciliorum nova et amplissima collectio* 2:906) stated that new tendencies at the beginning of the 4th century had tried to prohibit clerical marriage, but until that time individual choice had been the rule. They reveal that when Bishop Hosius (Ossius) of Córdoba sought to have the First Council of NICAEA (325) pass a decree requiring celibacy, the Egyptian Bishop PAPHNUTIUS, himself unmarried, protested that such a rule would be difficult and imprudent. He further emphasized that celibacy should be a matter of vocation and personal choice. The Council accepted this point of view and took measures to prohibit clandestine marriages with consecrated virgins (*agapete;* see John Chrysostom, *Fem. reg., Patrologia Graeca* 47:513–32; *Subintr., Patrologia Graeca* 47:495–514). Gregory the Elder of Nazianzus (*c.* 274–374) was bishop of that city when his son and successor, GREGORY OF NAZIANZUS the Younger, was born (*c.* 330). GREGORY OF NYSSA lived with his wife after his consecration (372), and the succession of GREGORY THE ILLUMINATOR (*c.* 240–332), the first Catholicos of Armenia, remained in his family for four generations, passing from father to son.

However, there is evidence to show that a great number of clerics in the early Church were unmarried or else left the married state after ordination. The testimony of TERTULLIAN (*De exhortatione castitatis* ch. 13; *Patrologia Latina* 2:390) and ORIGEN (*In Levit. hom.* 6.6; *Patrologia Graeca* 12:474) may be suspect in that both authors were sympathetic to the sect of the Encratites (it may be noted that Origen castrated himself); but many other authors, cited by Eusebius (*Demonstratio evangelica* 1.9; *Patrologia Graeca* 22:81) and Jerome (*Adversus Vigilantium* ch. 2; *Patrologia Latina* 23:341), testify to clerical renunciation of marriage. During the 4th century most of the bishops in Thessaly, Greece, Macedonia, Egypt, Italy, and western Europe were unmarried or left their wives after consecration. But for priests and deacons

clerical marriage continued to be in vogue. A famous letter of SYNESIUS OF CYRENE (d. *c.* 414) is evidence both for the respecting of personal decision in the matter and for contemporary appreciation of celibacy. Elected bishop of Ptolemais, he noted that many Egyptian bishops were unmarried. For himself, Synesius declared that he would refuse consecration if it meant abandoning his wife and the prospect of rearing many children. He was permitted to retain his status (*Epist.* 105; *Patrologia Graeca* 66:1485).

Conditions of Clerical Marriage. Legislation concerning the marriage of bishops, priests, and deacons is a valuable source of information for these practices in the early Church. First, it was declared that marriage could precede but not follow ordination. This general rule was applied according to circumstances of age and person. If a married candidate for major orders had been baptized as an adult (as was the case with many bishops of the period), he might keep his wife; unmarried candidates were free to marry before consecration or to remain unmarried. Other candidates, however, were baptized as children. Ordinarily, they became clerics while yet quite young, and upon ordination as lector or cantor they were permitted to choose between marriage and continence. Thus, the Council of Hippo in 393 (*Sacrorum Conciliorum nova et amplissima collectio* 3:922) declared that lectors might function until the age of puberty; "thereafter, however, unless they had married while enjoying a good reputation, or unless they vowed continence, they are not permitted to read." The condition of "good reputation" (*custodita pudicitia*) was understood to mean chaste; if the young man committed a sin against chastity, he could not be accepted into the clerical state without renouncing his right to marry; for, according to INNOCENT I (*Patrologia Latina* 20:477), "any baptized, but defiled [*corruptus*] person wishing to become a cleric, must promise that he will never marry." The canonical reason for this decision was that the marriage of a *corruptus* would not have been officially blessed by the Church and would therefore become the object of popular derision. Monks, however, if they became clerics, were not permitted to marry even if they were *incorrupti* (Siricius, *Epist.* 1; *Patrologia Latina* 13:1137). Accordingly, the practice may be summed up as follows: generally speaking, marriage was permitted before the diaconate. One exception, however, must be mentioned. In 314 the Council of ANCYRA (c.10; *Sacrorum Conciliorum nova et amplissima collectio* 2:517) permitted deacons to marry after ordination if they had previously declared their intention to marry.

Secondly, the marriage must be monogamic, in accord with the words of Saint Paul, that a bishop be *unius uxoris vir.* Even though variously interpreted, these words were given at least one universal application: if a married cleric should lose his wife, he was not permitted to marry again. The *Apostolic Constitutions* (*Sacrorum Conciliorum nova et amplissima collectio* 1:462), for example, declared that after ordination bishops, priests, and deacons were not permitted to contract marriage if they had no wife, nor to cohabit with another if they had one; they were to be satisfied with the wife they had had at ordination. The attitude of the early Church, which looked with disfavor upon second marriages, was a sufficient reason for this law. If second marriages were considered inexcusable even for allaying the passions of youth, for a cleric they would have been scandalous. More lenient interpretations of this Pauline text, e.g., that of THEODORET OF CYR (*Patrologia Graeca* 82:805), stated that since Saint Paul was aware of the polygamy practiced by both Jews and Gentiles, he was merely reminding clerics of the general law of monogamous Christian marriage. Consequently he forbade only simultaneous polygamy. Ordinarily, however, this interpretation was not accepted and monogamy was understood to exclude successive polygamy as well. Second marriages were considered contemptible and without blessing, and a man who had twice been married could not be accepted into the clergy. Later casuistry led many authors to distinguish between marriages contracted before and after baptism. Thus JEROME (*Epist. 69, ad Oceanum; Patrologia Latina* 22:654) stated that several bishops and priests had been ordained after a second marriage, if the first had been performed before baptism. This distinction was no longer admitted after INNOCENT I and LEO I, when any man twice married was refused ordination. By extension, the same popes refused ordination to a man who had been married but once, whose wife, however, had lived with another man either legitimately or illegitimately.

The Eastern Church. During the 4th century, as a result of the diversity of practice, the Church felt the need for legislation in this field of clerical activity. The growth of monastic influence, moreover, promoted the cause of virginity and celibacy, as is evident in the letters and sermons of AMBROSE and Jerome. When the opposition of Jovinian and Vigilantius brought on a reaction to the monastic spirit, the Church was forced to take cognizance and to act decisively. Neoplatonic ideas also were at work. Laws passed in the East and in the West generally followed regional custom. Eastern practice and law were usually more liberal than those of Rome, Gaul, or Africa, and were codified by THEODOSIUS II and JUSTINIAN I, both Christian Emperors enjoying great authority in the Church. Urging national custom, both codes forbade bishops to marry; the Justinian code even denied episcopal consecration to the father of a family; if the married man were without children, he might be consecrated pro-

vided he separated from his wife. In all cases, unmarried men were preferred for episcopal consecration (*Corpus iuris civilis, Codex Iustinianus,* ed. P. Krueger 1.3.47; *ibid.* Nov 6.1; 123.1).

Priests, deacons, and other clerics, however, were permitted to live in marriage contracted before ordination but were forbidden to take another wife if the first should die. If they did so, they were to be degraded; the second marriage was judged invalid, and the children were considered illegitimate and even incestuous (*Corpus iuris civilis, Codex Iustinianus* 1.3.44). The Trullan Synod in 692 (*see* QUINISEXT SYNOD) passed similar laws. Bishops were to observe absolute continence; if the bishop-elect was married, his wife had to live in a remote monastery (at her husband's expense). She was permitted to become a deaconess.

For all other clerics, however, the Synod permitted marriage before ordination and the use of marriage rights afterward; it further condemned all forms of bigamy. The Synod, by indirection, criticized Latin marriage legislation: if anyone should attempt to deprive a married priest, deacon, or subdeacon of his marriage rights, or if one of the aforesaid should renounce his wife ''on the pretense of piety,'' he was to be condemned and deposed. Several concessions, however, were made to Latin usage: sexual relations were prohibited prior to the celebration of the liturgies (in practice, on Saturday); a Greek priest was not to have relations with his wife while traveling in barbarian (Latin) countries (cc.3, 13). No further legislation on celibacy and clerical marriage was issued by the EASTERN CHURCH throughout its history.

From these laws varying usages grew, both before and after the EASTERN SCHISM, as well as after partial reunions with Rome. In the Byzantine and Russian Church, bishops had usually been monks; if an unmarried priest was elected bishop, he ordinarily took vows similar to those of the monk, before consecration. Many priests, moreover, who were immediate assistants of the bishop, were unmarried. On the other hand, a priest attached to a country parish was required to marry. If his wife died, he was compelled to renounce his office and retire to a monastery. The Coptic Church followed canon ten of the Council of Ancyra, allowing all deacons to marry except those who explicitly promised to live as celibates. Among the Ethiopians and Chaldeans, priests were permitted to marry after ordination.

The Eastern Catholic churches, in theory, follow the legislation of 692, which has been approved by several popes (Clement III, Innocent III, and Benedict XIV); in practice, however, Latin influence has altered the situation. Priests and deacons of the SYRO-MALABAR CHURCH must remain unmarried; the same is true for the ETHIOPI-

AN (GE'EZ) CATHOLIC CHURCH, except that the bishop might dispense in the matter. The Syrians (1888) and the Copts (1899) demand celibacy, except for a convert from Orthodoxy. Melkite, Maronite, and Armenian priests and deacons, however, may be married before ordination. Many priests stationed in towns remain unmarried after seminary training. Lacking priests for rural parishes, bishops have often ordained pious married laymen without benefit of full clerical studies. Among the Ruthenians and the Romanians priests are generally married, even in city parishes.

Legislation and Practice in the West. Celibacy became a canonical obligation for the clergy in the West through the combined efforts of popes and regional councils. It is the earliest example of general legislation based on the papal authority of decretals and the collaboration between Rome and the bishops acting collectively. About 300, a Spanish council at ELVIRA (near Granada) required absolute continence for all its clergy under pain of deposition (c.33): "We decree that all bishops, priests, deacons, and all clerics engaged in the ministry are forbidden entirely to live with their wives and to beget children: whoever shall do so will be deposed from the clerical dignity" (*Sacrorum Conciliorum nova et amplissima collectio* 2:11). One of the Spanish bishops, Hosius of Córdoba, who had been present at Elvira, tried in vain for the same decision at the First Council of Nicaea. This legislation, however, did not enter the Western Church until the second half of the 4th century and was effected through the decretals of various popes: DAMASUS I (*Ad Gallos episcopos,* 366–84); SIRICIUS (*Ad Himerium Tarraconensem,* 385; *Ad episcopos Africae,* 386); Innocent I (*Ad Vitricium Rothomagensem,* 404; *Ad Exuperium Tolosanum,* 405; *Ad Maximum et Severum,* 401–417); Leo I (*Ad Anastasium Thessalonicum,* 446?; *Ad Rusticum Narbonensem,* 458). Councils issued the same decrees for Africa (Carthage, 390, 401–19; cf. cc.3–4 of 419), France (Orange, 441; Tours, 461), and Italy (Turin, 398). No longer could priests, deacons, and (after Leo I) subdeacons be married.

The first letter of Damasus I (wrongly ascribed to Siricius in *Patrologia Latina* 13:1181–96; cf. *Clavis patrum* Number 1632) gave the classic arguments of the period urging celibacy. How can a cleric advise perfect continence to widows and virgins if he does not observe celibacy? Ministers of Christ must obey the Scriptures, which authoritatively require them to live in celibacy (cf. Rom 8.9; 1 Cor 7.29; Rom 13.14; 1 Cor 7.7). Marital acts were repugnant to the sacred ministry; pagan and Jewish priests were aware of the necessity of refraining from sexual relations. Saint Paul counseled abstinence even for laymen, whose duty it was to bear children (1 Cor 7.5). The statement of Damasus, "that since intercourse is a defilement, surely the priest must undertake his duties

with heavenly aid," may appear to favor Encratism; but it seems that the pope, in alluding to Saint Paul and to the Old Testament, understood defilement (*pollutio*) to mean a legal impurity and not a sin.

In practice, before ordination the candidate was required to take a vow of chastity (*professio conversionis*). This *conversio* legally placed him in the state of public penitents who were forbidden the use of marriage. Thus, married candidates were required to promise continence in the legislation of the Councils of Orange (441, c.22), Arles (*c.* 450, c.2; 524, c.2), and Orléans (537, c.6). GREGORY I (*Patrologia Latina* 77:506) made this profession the general rule for the subdiaconate, and the Fourth Council of Toledo (663), presided over by ISIDORE OF SEVILLE, decreed this profession for priests and deacons assigned to parishes. Before the subdiaconate, moreover, the candidate had to declare under oath that he had not committed the four major sins of sodomy, bestiality, adultery, or the violation of consecrated virgins (*Ordo Romanus* 34; M. Andrieu, *Les 'Ordines Romani' du haut moyen-âge,* 3:549, 607).

Custom and legislation provided for the status of clerical wives. On the day of the husband's ordination, the wife received a special blessing. Such wives, known as *presbyterissae (presbyterae)* and *diaconissae (diaconae),* wore a distinctive garb and were not permitted to remarry, even after the death of their husbands (Orléans, *c.* 573, c.22; *Les 'Ordines Romani' du haut moyen-âge* 4:140–41). At the time of Leo I, clerics were not obliged to dismiss their wives, but could live with them in celibacy. Writing to Bishop Rusticus of Narbonne, Leo stated that married clerics should not give up their wives but should live together in wedded love, without the acts of love, so that a spiritual marriage might replace a carnal one (*Patrologia Latina* 54:1204). Later, however, such cohabitation appeared to be overly difficult and suspicious, and canonical legislation proceeded more cautiously. A bishop was required to provide another household for his wife. Each day she might come to the bishop's house and carefully look after its needs; but she was not to bring her servants, and, as a safeguard, the bishop was always to be attended by clerics. A priest, on the other hand, was permitted to keep his wife in his home (probably for reasons of economy), but they were not to share a common room (Orléans, 541, c.17). The archpriest was always to be attended, especially at night, by his clerics (*canonici clerici*), and one of them, or if necessary a layman, was to sleep in his room. Other priests and deacons slept alone, but were expected to provide a female servant who should sleep in the wife's room to warrant her virtue. Married clerics who disregarded these precautions were branded with the heresy of Nicolaitism (Tours 557, c.20). Priests were forbidden to have other women in their household, and VIRGINES SUBINTRODUCTAE were especially suspect (Bordeaux, 663, c.3). In the cities, common sleeping quarters were to be provided for priests and for lesser clerics (Tours, 567, c.15).

The Gregorian Reform. The period following the decline of the Carolingian Empire was a time of crisis for clerical celibacy. The disorganization of society and the concomitant destruction of churches and monasteries by the Northmen and other invaders of the Empire, and the progressive secularization of Church lands led to the demoralization of the clergy. Councils in the 10th and 11th centuries regularly protested against the two chief vices of the clergy; simony and clerical marriage (Nicolaitism) [see H. Maisonneuve, *La morale chrétienne d'après les conciles des Xᵉ et XIᵉ siècles* (Namur 1950–)]. Thus, e.g., the Council of Trosly (Soissons, 909) stated that in the monasteries enclosure had been abandoned and many priests were married. The Synod of Augsburg (952) and the Councils of Anse (994) and Poitiers (1000) all decreed the law of celibacy. BURCHARD OF WORMS in his *Decretum* (*c.* 1110) recalled the ancient law prohibiting the marriage of priests (*Patrologia Latina* 140:645–646). About 1018 BENEDICT VIII protested against the current subversion of celibacy and strengthened the legislation of the Church, especially by imposing penalties for offenders. Priests, deacons, and subdeacons were forbidden to marry or to cohabit with a woman. Their children were declared to be forever serfs of the Church and could not be freed or granted rights of property and inheritance. The purpose of these canons (similar to that, perhaps, of the Justinian *Corpus*) was to prevent the secularization of ecclesiastical property by the families of priests.

Disorder existed not only in the practice of the period but even in the field of doctrine. Arguments circulated against celibacy were answered by PETER DAMIAN in his *Liber Gomorrhianus* and in *De coelibatu sacerdotum ad Nicolaum II* (*Patrologia Latina* 145:159–90, 379–88). He in turn was answered by Ulric, Bishop of Imola (*c.* 1060), in his *Rescriptum seu epistola de continentia clericorum* (*Monumenta Germaniae Historica: Libelli de lite* 1), a pamphlet once attributed to Saint ULRIC OF AUGSBURG and condemned by GREGORY VII (1079). Ulric appealed to the texts of Saint Paul and to the freer practices of the first several centuries, forgetting the power of the Church to initiate new laws. These errors were renewed in the *Tractatus pro clericorum connubio*, the enlarged Norman edition of Ulric's work, and by the *An liceat sacerdotibus inire matrimonium* (*Monumenta Germaniae Historica: Libelli de lite* 3). These writings claimed that celibacy was a personal vocation, not a canonical state, and that marriage in itself was not evil. In the next century the Goliards appealed to the natural law as an argument for greater freedom.

Against these conditions, many popes in the 11th century proceeded with vigor. LEO IX (1049) assigned the wives and concubines of priests to servitude as *ancillae* to the Lateran palace. NICHOLAS II (1059) deprived married priests, even in the external forum, of the right to perform liturgical acts of worship, and they were forbidden to live in the *presbyterium* of the churches. They were also denied all further rights to ecclesiastical prebends. To further his effort, the pope tried to enlist the support of the laity by prohibiting them to attend Mass offered by a married priest or by one who lived in concubinage. Many laymen, indeed, were gravely scandalized by clerical immorality and supported the program of papal reform. Some of these, however, belonging to the sect of the PATARINES, fell under the influence of MANICHAEISM and became CATHARI.

GREGORY VII issued no new decretals on the subject, but energetically applied existing law through the action of his legates and by extensive correspondence with bishops. Writing to Otto of Constance, the pope summarized his actions and intentions: "Those who are guilty of the crime of fornication are forbidden to celebrate Mass or to serve the altar if they are in minor orders. We prescribe, moreover, that if they persist in despising our laws, which are, in fact, the laws of the Holy Fathers, the people shall no longer be served by them. For if they will not correct their lives out of love for God and the dignity of their office, they must be brought to their senses by the world's contempt and the reproach of their people" (*Patrologia Latina* 148:646; *Regesta pontificum romanorum ab condita ecclesia ad anum post Christum natum*, ed. S. Löwenfeld, 4932). By his courage and zeal, Gregory must be credited with being the true restorer of sacerdotal celibacy in those disturbed times.

The last stage in the struggle against clerical marriage, until that time considered only illicit in the Western Church, was to declare such marriages invalid. This action was taken at the First and Second LATERAN COUNCILS of 1123 and 1139. In the latter (cc.6–7; *Conciliorum oecumenicorum decreta* 174), the impediment of orders was definitively declared to be a diriment impediment. In explaining this decision, canonists commonly state that the candidate for ordination to the subdiaconate tacitly takes the vow of celibacy; thus BONIFACE VIII (*Corpus iuris canonici*, ed. E. Friedberg, VI° 3.15). This theory recalls similar vows taken in the Merovingian period and in the Russian Church. Other explanations are based on the power of the Church to annul marriages contracted contrary to her laws, or on arguments that clerical marriage is contrary to the divine law (e.g., Sanchez, *De sancto matrimonii sacramento* 7.27). This latter explanation came up for further discussion at the Council of TRENT.

The Age of the Reformation. By the end of the Middle Ages the Church again experienced a period of decline in clerical morality, occasioned by the BLACK DEATH, the Hundred Years' War, the WESTERN SCHISM, and the pagan spirit of the RENAISSANCE. Most historians of this period point to clerical marriage as a common practice and to the sons of priests who were legitimated, and, as in the case of ERASMUS, even ordained to the priesthood with a dispensation from the Roman Curia (at the cost of 12 gros tournois). In his *Commentary on the Galatians* (4.30; 1535), LUTHER stated that his movement would have made little headway against the papacy if clerical celibacy had then been observed as it was in the time of Jerome, Ambrose, and Augustine; that "celibacy was something remarkable in the eyes of the world, a thing that makes a man angelic."

At the time of his break with the Church (1517), Luther did not promote sacerdotal marriage, and, in a letter of Jan. 17, 1522, refused to encourage it. But by the end of that year he condemned celibacy in his *De votis monasticis,* and in April 1523 he officiated and preached at the wedding of Wenzeslaus Link, the late vicar general of the AUGUSTINIANS. Finally, Luther himself was married on the evening of June 13, 1525, to the scandal of many of his friends and the applause of many married priests of his day. Luther then attempted a doctrinal justification based on the authority of the Pauline texts, denial of the Church's authority to issue new laws (he burned the books of Canon Law in 1530 as the work of the devil), denial of the Sacrament of Holy Orders, the futility of good works, and the necessity of marriage for fallen nature (cf. Luther, *Werke* 6:442, 550; 8:654; 10.2:276). CALVIN was perhaps less radical than Luther; for, while requiring marriage as the general rule, he admitted (commenting on Mt 19.12 and 1 Cor ch. 7) that celibacy may be an acceptable means of serving God. But Calvin claimed that celibacy as a personal vocation cannot be judged of greater value than the common way of life. The Geneva reformer protested against the despising of marriage, found in the writing of Saint Jerome and, in his opinion, in the average treatise on theology (cf. Calvin, *Commentaires sur le Nouveau Testament* 1561; Mt ch. 19 and 1 Tm 4.3).

The Council of Trent. Opposition to the Protestant position, by popes, bishops, priests, and kings, failed to agree on the methods to be used or on the nature of true reformation within the Church. Several of the princes, e.g., Emperor Ferdinand I, thought it opportune to grant Germany a married priesthood as well as Communion under both species. Duke Albert V of Bavaria suggested that only married men be ordained and that the Church be indulgent to priests who sinned. According to L. von Pastor, PIUS IV did not altogether refuse to examine the matter, but distinguished the possibility of practical and individual grants of dispensation (such as were given later in the case of the UTRAQUISTS) from the general problem, which was submitted to the Council of Trent.

In its 24th session, the Council studied these questions together with others related to marriage. On Feb. 2, 1563, the cardinal of Mantua presented the theologians with a list of Protestant theses for their examination. Here were found (C. J. von Hefele, *Histoire des conciles d'après les documents originaux,* translated and continued by H. Leclercq, 10:507; *Concilium Tridentinum. Diariorum, actorum, epistularum, tractatuum nova collectio,* ed. Görres-Gesellschaft, 9:376) the statements equating virginity and marriage (No. 5), and the legitimacy of marriage for priests in the Latin Church and for everyone who has not received the grace of perfect chastity; otherwise marriage would be degraded (No. 6). Discussion of No. 5 was neither difficult nor protracted. Theologians brought arguments to bear from Matthew chapter 19 and 1 Corinthians ch. 7, from the Fathers and the example of the Blessed Virgin, leading to the definition of the superiority—objectively speaking—of virginity dedicated to God (sess. 24; c.10; *Conciliorum oecumeniorum decreta* 731). From the psychological point of view, however, for those who are not called to celibacy, a vow is neither proposed nor advised as something better. Many opponents of the Council's definition, both then and now, forget this distinction. To understand Tridentine thinking, reference must be made to 1 Corinthians ch. 7: the Council did not go beyond the words of Saint Paul.

Discussions on sacerdotal celibacy, however, were longer and of greater moment. In general, theologians and canonists expressed opinions that were more severe than canon 9, which was finally voted by the Fathers of the Council. Concerning the suitability of celibacy to the sacerdotal vocation, the Council cited texts from Scripture (1 Cor 7.5, 33), the Fathers (e.g., Jerome), and various papal decretals. In the first place, it was argued, celibacy is the condition of God's service in the apostolate. A married minister of religion is too preoccupied with his wife and family to give such service. Secondly, the priesthood, even in the Old Testament, requires a form of sanctity that implies the curbing of carnal desires. In the Old Testament, priests were obliged only to a limited time of worship; but now they were totally consecrated to God. These arguments were presented by Jean Peletier, Jean de Lobera, Claude de Sainctes, and Miguel de Medina. Regarding the nature of the obligation and the possibility of general or individual dispensation, two opposing views were introduced. The more rigid view, expressed by De Sainctes and De Lobera, claimed that marriage and the priesthood were incompatible. While good in itself, marriage nevertheless rendered one unfit for the ministry. Consequently, celibacy for the priest was a duty based on divine law. Since Holy Orders obliged the candidate to celibacy as Baptism did to the Christian life, a vow was unnecessary.

Such views were difficult to reconcile with historical evidence, and De Sainctes was content to gloss over such evidence. For him, the early Church had always required celibacy—only the Trullan Synod had permitted marriage for incontinent Greek priests, and Rome had tolerated its decision to avoid greater evil. But this was not a true dispensation, for none could be given by the pope.

Fortunately, other theologians were historically better informed and proposed more realistic views. The majority claimed that clerical celibacy was required by ecclesiastical law (Jean Peletier, Antonius Solisius, Richard du Pre, Lazaruss Broychot, Francisco Foriero Ferdinand Tritius, John de Ludegna, and Sanctes Cinthius). In their opinion, a priest was unable to contract marriage either by the will of the Church or by reason of an implicit vow involved in ordination to the subdiaconate. Despite the suitability of celibacy to the sacerdotal state, the pope might fundamentally dispense from the law, or, as some thought, at least dispense from the vow. At length, the debate was resolved into the question of whether it was opportune to dispense priests at that time. The Portuguese Dominican, Francisco Foriero, argued in the affirmative, stating that the Church might allow clerical marriage for such grave reasons as combating schism or heresy in a particular country. Three other Dominicans, John Valdina, Cinthius, and De Ludegna, and the Franciscan Lucius Angusiola, agreed with this opinion. Others, however, such as Broychot and Tritius, denied the utility and prudence of such a dispensation.

In voting to accept canon 9 (H. Denzinger, *Enchiridion symbolorum*, ed. A Schönmetzer, 1809), the Council rejected the opinion that celibacy was of divine law. It taught, first, that the Church had the right to prohibit and invalidate sacerdotal marriage by reason of ecclesiastical law or of vow. If the Church should change its legislation or not require the vow, priests would not be obliged to celibacy. Thus, the canon did not distinguish between the Eastern and the Western Church; for both, the fundamental law was the same. Secondly, the Church taught that in holding sacerdotal celibacy in such high regard, it wished in no wise to minimize its regard for marriage. Both vocations were distinct and each had its distinctive obligations. Thirdly, the Council rejected the claim of those priests who held that celibacy was impossible. Since priests had accepted celibacy by vow, they should implore the grace of God, which would be sufficient to reinforce them in their resolve. Implicitly, therefore, the Church refused to grant a dispensation for the clergy of Germany.

Current Position. The common opinion today may be summed up as follows: clerical celibacy is considered most proper to the sacerdotal ministry; it is in no sense a depreciation of marriage, but is the condition for greater freedom in the service of God. The law of celibacy is of ecclesiastical origin and may therefore be abrogated by the Church. In the early Church and in the East the marriage of bishops, priests, and deacons was permitted for good reason. Recent popes have found similarly good reason to dispense from celibacy in the case of married Protestant pastors who converted and desired ordination. VATICAN COUNCIL II, at the request of the bishops from many countries, permitted a married diaconate, admitting married men of mature years.

Bibliography: E. VACANDARD, *Dictionnaire de théologie catholique*, ed. A. VACANT et al., 15 v. (Paris 1903–50) 2.2:2068–88; ''Les Origines du célibat ecclésiastique,'' in *Études de critique et d'histoire religieuse*, 4 v. (Paris 1909–23) v.1. H. C. LEA, *History of Sacerdotal Celibacy in the Christian Church*, 2 v. (3d ed. London 1907), uncritical in details. H. LECLERCQ, *Dictionnaire d'archéologie chrétienne et de liturgie*, ed. F. CABROL, H. LE-CLERCQ, and H. I. MARROU 2.2:2802–32. G. LE BRAS, *Dictionnaire de théologie catholique* 9.2:2123–2317. A. FLICHE, *La Réforme grégorienne,* 3 v. (Louvain 1924–37). E. JOMBART and É. HERMAN, *Dictionnaire de droit canonique*, ed. R. NAZ, 7 v. (Paris 1935–65) 3:132–56. C. SPICQ, *Les Épîtres pastorales de Saint Paul* (Paris 1947). P. RENARD, *Dictionnaire de la Bible* ed. F. VIGOUROUX, 5 v. (Paris 1895–1912) 2.1:394–96. P. DELHAYE, ''Le Dossier anti-matrimonial de l'*Adversus Jovinianum* et son influence sur quelques écrits latins du XIIᵉ siècle,'' *Mediaeval Studies* 13 (1951) 65–86. F. SPADAFORA, *Temi di esegesi (1 Cor 7.32–38) e el celibato ecclesiastico* (Rovigo 1953). P. VAN IMSCHOOT, *Théologie de l'Ancien Testament,* 2 v. (Tournai 1954–56). J. CHRYSOSTOM, *Les Cohabitations suspectes,* ed. and tr. J. DUMORTIER (Paris 1955). A. BIELER, *L'Homme et la femme dans la morale calviniste* (Geneva 1963), often erroneous. *Encyclopedic Dictionary of the Bible*, tr. and adap. by L. HARTMAN (New York 1963) from A. VAN DEN BORN, *Bijbels Woordenboek* 2548–49. P. H. LAFONTAINE, *Les Conditions positives de l'accession aux ordres dans la première législation ecclésiastique, 300–492* (Ottawa 1963).

[P. DELHAYE]

CELLES-SUR-BELLE, MONASTERY OF

Former Augustinian foundation near the village of Melle, France, Diocese of Poitiers. It was founded early in the 11th century, on property originally given to the BENEDICTINES of SAINT-MAIXENT by William of Aquitaine, as a priory of CANONS REGULAR OF ST. AUGUSTINE dependent on the Abbey of Saint-Pierre de Lesterp. It was created an abbey by Bp. William II Adelelme of Poitiers in 1140 with Jean de Uzon as the first abbot, and had its independence from Lesterp ratified under Bp. GILBERT DE LA PORRÉE in 1148 through a bull of EUGENE III. The abbey was dedicated to Our Lady, and the fame of the miracles attributed to her intercession at Celles made it a pilgrimage center from *c.* 1095, although the great annual pilgrimage, the *Septembresch,* or the Feast of the Nativity of the Virgin Mary, is first mentioned only in 1395. The pilgrimage flourished into the 15th century, reaching its apogee in the reign of Louis XI, who visited the abbey about ten times, left lavish gifts, and had the 12th-century monastery church reconstructed during the years 1470 to 1477. The pilgrimage was restored in 1899, and Bishop Durfort of Poitiers solemnly crowned the venerated statue of Notre-Dame de Celles on Sept. 26, 1926. The practice of COMMENDATION was introduced in 1515 with the nomination of Geoffroy d'Estissac, later abbot-bishop of Maillezais. The monastery was pillaged by the HUGUENOTS and abandoned by the monks in 1568. It was besieged again in 1569 by Admiral Coligny, but defended by the Barbeziére family, on whom King Charles IX of France (d. 1574) subsequently bestowed its income. Following attempts by Cardinal F. de La Rochefoucauld and Henri-Louis II de La Rochefoucauld to wrest the control from the Barbezières, the abbey was finally united to the Congregation of France in 1651. The church was rebuilt in 1669, and new cloisters were constructed in 1682. Its income in 1787 was estimated at 14,000 livres, and it had several priories, 12 parishes, and some chapels dependent on it. The last titular abbot was C. TALLEYRAND-PÉRIGORD. The monks were expelled in 1791, and the property served as a prison for the Vendée rebels. Today the church serves parish needs and is administered by the MONTFORT FATHERS, who in 1921 established a novitiate in the former cloisters of the abbey.

Bibliography: L. H. COTTINEAU, *Répertoire topobibliographique des abbayes et prieurés,* 2 v. (Mâon 1935–39) 1:649. P. CALENDINI, *Dictionnaire d'histoire et de géographie ecclésiastiques,* ed. A. BAUDRILLART et al. (Paris 1912–) 12:116–118. R. GAZEAU, *Catholicisme. Hier, aujourd'hui et demain,* ed. G. JACQUEMET (Paris 1947–) 2:773. A. LARGEAULT, *Notre-Dame de Celles, son abbaye, son pèlerinage* (Parthenay 1900).

[G. E. GINGRAS]

CELSUS

Greek philosopher, author of the *True Discourse* (Ἀληθὴς Λόγος), the most important pagan intellectual opponent of Christianity before Porphyry; fl. second half of the second century A.D. No details on his life and place

Celsus. (Bettmann/CORBIS)

of his activities are extant. The original text of the *True Discourse* (*c.* A.D. 178) is lost, but about nine-tenths of the treatise can be reconstructed with practical certainty from the extracts and arguments found in ORIGEN's elaborate refutation, *Against Celsus* (Κατὰ Κέλσου) in eight books, composed nearly 70 years later (A.D. 246). Celsus was an adherent of Middle Platonism, but was, above all, a champion of Hellenic culture in all its aspects. In his polemic he showed a marked familiarity with the Old and the New Testaments and Christian teachings in general. However, he was not always aware of the precise differences between Judaism and Christianity, nor of those between Christian orthodoxy, heresy, and Gnosticism. While showing some appreciation for the Christian concept of the Logos and for Christian ethics, he rejected the Christian concept of God as the absolute Creator, and branded the teachings on the Incarnation and Crucifixion as absurd. He ridiculed likewise many of the Biblical narratives and miracles. On the political side, he accused the Christians of being unpatriotic because of their attitude toward the religious policy of the state. Celsus was not so much a philosopher as an ardent champion of Hellenism as expressed in a long and venerable tradition. On the twin pillars of *logos* and *nomos,* to which antiquity had given authority, he erected a philosophy of history. Christianity was rejected as being new and outside the

Muirdach's Cross from 10th century, detail showing two sections telling stories from the Bible, Monasterboice, County Louth, Republic of Ireland. (©Michael St. Maur Sheil/CORBIS)

Hellenic tradition, indeed even a repudiation of it. This argument against Christianity was resumed by Porphyry and the Emperor Julian.

Bibliography: F. L. CROSS, *The Oxford Dictionary of the Christian Church* (London 1957) 256. H. HUHN, *Lexikon für Theologie und Kirche,* ed. J. HOFER, and K. RAHNER, 10 v. (2d, new ed. Freiburg 1957–65) 6:108–109. C. ANDRESEN, *Die Religion in Geschichte und Gegenwart,* 7 v. (3d. ed. Tübingen 1957–65) 1:1630–31. *Logos und Nomos: Die Polemik des Celsus wider das Christentum* (Berlin 1955). J. QUASTEN, *Patrology,* 3 v. (Westminster, Md. 1950), 2:52–57, with good bibliography. P. C. DE LA-BRIOLLE, *La Réaction païenne* (6th ed., Paris 1942) 109–169.

[M. R. P. MCGUIRE]

CELTIC RELIGION

The ancient Celtic-speaking peoples were distributed over a wide area from Ireland to Asia Minor, and their religious ideas and practices reflect in part borrowings from other early or contemporary cultures. Greek and Roman writers supply valuable information on Celtic religion from the 3d century B.C., but they tend to be superficial and to be satisfied with rough identifications of Celtic divinities with their own gods and goddesses. Much information is furnished also by a critical sifting of the pagan traditions preserved in medieval Latin, Irish, and Welsh sources. A fairly rich mythology can be reconstructed especially out of the Irish literature in Latin and in Old and Middle Irish.

The gods in the historical period were largely anthropomorphic, and several of them corresponded to Mars, Mercury, and Apollo. However, many of the gods were local or tribal or, at least, given different names in different areas. Celtic personal and place names frequently reflect divine associations. Thus, Lugdunum (modern Lyons) was "the town of Lug," a divinity found on the Continent and in Ireland. Mother goddesses, the *Matronae* or *Matres,* were worshiped, especially in the region of the Rhine, by both Celts and Germans, and the cult of a horse goddess Epona was widespread and popular. Sacred plants (especially the mistletoe), trees, hills, mountains, rivers, springs, and remote open places, played a special role in Celtic religion. Major or minor divinities were associated with such sacred objects or places. In Ireland the belief in the *Sid*-folk or fairies, originally divine beings affecting various aspects of human life, is very old. They were thought to dwell chiefly under hills. Animals also were assigned divine attributes, especially bulls, horses, boars, and bears. Magic, magical formulae, spells, and curses are frequently mentioned and their effects described. Old Irish literary remains, with their emphasis on *geis* (taboo), reflect the important place of taboos in pagan Celtic religious and social life. The pagan Celts are thought to have had a vivid belief in a life beyond the grave and even a belief in transmigration of souls, but on this point there are no certain details.

On the Continent, in Britain, and in Ireland, the priestly class, the druids, played a major part in religion, law, education, and the determination of public policy. They were of royal blood and had to undergo a long period of training. There seem to have been divisions or grades among the druids, but the evidence is in part vague and conflicting. They were specialists in divination and were regarded as having prophetic powers. They performed certain religious rites and presided at sacrifices. In the historical period at least, there were sacrifices of animals and offerings of various kinds. Although there are references to human sacrifice in Gaul and Britain, it must have been rare. At any event, there is no evidence that this practice was approved or conducted by the druids.

Like the Roman *pontifices,* the druids had charge of the calendar, which, as all early calendars, was religious in character and indicated the days on which ordinary business could be carried out and those on which all or some actions were forbidden. As champions of Celtic traditions in all phases of life, the druids were deprived of their authority in Gaul by the Romans from the time of Claudius. However, they continued to flourish in Ireland until the triumph of Christianity. In Irish tradition much stress is placed on their wondrous powers as diviners and magicians. The brehons and bards of Christian Ireland became the heirs of the druids and, like them, were the tenacious preservers and champions of national cultural traditions.

Bibliography: F. N. ROBINSON, *The Oxford Classical Dictionary,* ed. M. CARY et al. (Oxford 1949) 758–759. J. A. MACCULLOCH, J. HASTINGS ed., *Encyclopedia of Religion and Ethics,* 13 v. (Edinburgh 1908–27) 3:277–304. J. RYAN, F. KÖNIG, ed. *Christus und die Religionen der Erde: Handbuch der Religionsgeschichte,* 3 v. (2d ed. Vienna 1961) 2:245–265. R. HERTZ, *Die Religion in Geschichte und Gegenwart,* 7 v. (3d ed. Tübingen 1957–65) 3:1238–41. T. G. E. POWELL, *The Celts* (New York 1958). J. ZWICKER, *Fontes historiae religionis Celticae (Fontes historiae religionum,* ed. C. CLEMEN, 5.1–3; Bonn 1934–36). R. LANTIER, ''Keltische Mythologie,'' *Wörterbuch der Mythologie,* ed. H. W. HAUSSIG (Stuttgart 1961–) Abt. 1.2.1, fasc. 5, 100–162. J. VENDRYÈS et al., *Les Religions des Celtes, des Germains, et des anciens Slaves* (''Mana'' ser. 2.3; Paris 1948) 235–320. J. DE VRIES, *Keltische Religion* (Die Religionen der Menschheit 18; Stuttgart 1961).

[M. R. P. MC GUIRE]

CELTIC RITE

Lack of evidence about liturgical practice in the localities in which the Celtic rite is said to have existed precludes arriving at a clear picture. There has never been a distinct Celtic rite in the strict sense of the term ''rite'' as we apply it to the MOZARABIC or AMBROSIAN rites.

Origins. The Celtic monks, tireless missionaries who traveled widely, did not intend to draw up a new liturgy. They seem to have chosen elements from different rites and combined them. The Celtic rites, therefore, were an eclectic composition of foreign customs, Roman and Gallican. We know indeed that in Scotland, Ireland, Wales, Cornwall, and Brittany—the regions to which the Saxon invasion had confined the remains of Celtic culture and Christianity—there were certain disciplinary differences from Roman customs and those introduced by St. AUGUSTINE of Canterbury, who landed in Kent in the summer of 597. These differences applied principally to the form of the TONSURE, the date of Easter, and the general form of ecclesiastical organization, heavily influenced by the monastic element. After the abortive synod to which the Celtic Christians were summoned by St. Au-

Celtic Cross. ((c) Paul Almasy/CORBIS)

gustine in 603, the Synod of Whitby (664) witnessed their complete submission. Yet traces of an independent liturgy lingered on for about 500 years in parts of Ireland and Scotland until the Synod of Cashel (1172) when the Anglo-Roman liturgy was introduced into Ireland. Brittany probably lost its distinctive rites at the time of Louis I, the Pious (817), and Scotland lost its rites in the 11th century through the efforts of Queen Margaret (d. 1093, canonized 1250).

Sources. The principal sources are to be found in three liturgical books—the Bangor Antiphonary, the Bobbio Missal, and the Stowe Missal, all of monastic origin. As its name implies, the Bangor Antiphonary is a collection of antiphons, versicles, hymns, canticles, etc., and was compiled probably for the use of the abbot of the famous monastery of Bangor in Ireland. The book dates from the end of the 7th century (between 680 and 690); it is now in the Ambrosian Library at Milan. The Bobbio Missal, a 7th-century manuscript discovered by J. Mabillon at Bobbio, Italy, is one of the earliest witnesses for the history of the Roman Canon; it represents a local liturgy influenced by Rome and includes certain borrowings from Rome, despite a different Mass order. Lastly, the Stowe Missal, a manuscript of the late 8th or 9th century, was composed probably for the abbey of Tallaght near Dublin. It contains, in addition to part of the Gospel of St. John (with which it is bound), the Ordinary of the Mass, three Mass Propers, and the rites of Baptism, Anointing, and Communion of the Sick. In addition there are various liturgical fragments to be found in several manuscripts of Irish origin. From the slender evidence at our disposal, the most that can be asserted is that the Gallican rite was the principal formative factor of the Celtic liturgy, which in course of time became increasingly Romanized.

Characteristics. The preparation of the oblations took place before the celebrant's entrance, as in the GALLICAN RITES. The introductory prayers include a confession of sins and examples of lengthy apologies, as well as a litany of Irish saints. The first part of the Mass, in its later form in the Stowe Missal, follows the Roman form: Gloria, one or more Collects, Epistle, Gradual, and Alleluia. At this point was said a litany, borrowed from the East, the *Deprecatio Sancti Martini* (which occurs also in the Ambrosian rite). After two prayers and the partial unveiling of the offerings with a threefold invocation over them, the Gospel was sung, followed by the Credo (including the FILIOQUE). At the Offertory, after the complete unveiling of the offerings, the chalice, and sometimes the paten, were elevated. There followed a commemoration of the dead and reading of the DIPTYCHS. The Preface with the usual preliminary dialogue and followed by the Sanctus came next with, usually, a post-Sanctus. Though the Canon in the Stowe Missal is headed *Canon dominicus papae Gilasii*, it is in fact the Gregorian Canon with several Irish saints named in it. It is evidence of the use of the Roman Canon in the Celtic Church at the beginning of the 9th century. After the Memento of the living occurs a list of more than 100 holy people (Old Testament and Irish saints among them). Various chants were designated for Communion, including (in the Bangor Antiphonary) the beautiful hymn *Sancti venite.*

Great latitude appears to have been allowed to individual monasteries in the arrangement of the Divine Office, and details of it are to be found in the various monastic rules. The Celtic monks exerted their greatest influence in the evolution of the Sacrament of Penance, for it was largely through them that the practice of private (as opposed to public) satisfaction for sin became popular.

Bibliography: L. GOUGAUD, *Dictionnaire d'archéologie chrétienne et de liturgie*, ed. F. CABROL, H. LECLERCQ, and H. I. MARROU, 15 v. (Paris 1907–53) 2.2:2969–3032 treats the subject exhaustively with full bibliographical references. A. A. KING, *Liturgies of the Past* (Milwaukee 1959) 186–275 has full bibliography and list of sources, including those of liturgical fragments in various MSS. *Bobbio Missal*, ed. A. WILMART, et al. (Henry Bradshaw Society 61; London 1924). *Antiphonary of Bangor*, ed. F. E. WARREN (Henry Bradshaw Society 4, Pt. 1, 1893; 10, Pt. 2, 1895). *Stowe Missal*, ed. G. F. WARNER, (Henry Bradshaw Society 32; 1915). F. E. WARREN, *Liturgy and Ritual of the Celtic Church* (Oxford 1881).

[L. C. SHEPPARD]

CEMETERIES, CANON LAW OF

From the beginning the Church has followed the practice of burying its dead. Where it is possible, the Church is to have its own cemeteries [*Codex Iuris Canonicis (CIC)*, c. 1240 §1; *Codex Canonum Ecclesiarium Orientalium (CCEO)*, c. 874 §2]. It allows that each parish have its own cemetery (*CIC*, c. 1241 §1; *CCEO*, c. 874 §4). Religious institutes of men and women, other juridic persons, and even private families, may have their own cemeteries (*CIC*, c. 1241 §2; *CCEO*, c. 874 §4).

Blessings of Cemeteries. The Church prescribes that the cemeteries it owns should be blessed. The blessing of a cemetery is conducted according to the appropriate rite. By such a blessing, the cemetery is designated a sacred place, and becomes subject to the canons regarding sacred places in general.

In cases where the Church *cannot* (e.g., because all cemeteries are government owned) or *does not* (e.g., because of religious prejudice, bigotry, the poverty of the people) own its cemeteries, the law makes provision. Consistent with the Church's desire that every Catholic be buried in blessed ground, the law provides: (1) where Catholics are permitted to have use of a separate section of the community or municipal cemetery, this special Catholic section is to be blessed; (2) when Catholics cannot have their own section in a community cemetery, each individual grave is to be blessed before the body of the deceased is lowered into it (*CIC*, c. 1240 §2; *CCEO*, c. 874 §2).

Bibliography: H. LECLERCQ, *Dictionnaire d'archéologie chrétienne et de liturgie*, (Paris 1907–53) 3:1626–65. J. GULEZYNSKI, *Catholic University of America Canon Law Studies 159: The Desecration and Violation of Churches* (Washington 1942). S. MANY, *Praelectiones de locis sacris* (Paris 1904). F. J. MOULART, *De sepultura et coemeteriis* (Louvain 1862). C. M. POWER, *Catholic University of America Canon Law Studies 185: The Blessing of Cemetaries* (Washington 1943). A. C. RUSH, Catholic University of America, *Studies in Christian Antiquity 1: Death and Burial in Christian Antiquity* (Washington 1941).

[C. M. POWER]

CENACLE

Traditional site of the room in which Jesus had His Last Supper with His Apostles. The term comes from the

Latin *coenaculum* (dining room), which is used in the Vulgate as the translation of two different Greek words. The first of these, ἀνάγαιον (upper room), used in Mk 14.15 and Lk 22.12, refers to the large furnished upper room chosen by our Lord for the celebration of His Last Supper and the institution of the Holy Eucharist. The average ancient-Palestinian home was one storied and flat roofed. The homes of the wealthy, however, often included a guest room, penthouse-fashion, on the second or upper floor, often having an outer staircase leading up to it. The other word, ὑπερῷον, also meaning upper room, was applied by St. Luke in Acts 1.13 to the place where Mary and the Apostles stayed in prayer after the Ascension of Jesus into heaven, presumably until Pentecost day. Since both Greek words are practically synonymous, as shown by the single term *coenaculum* of the Latin Vulgate for both and by their use in the Septuagint, where the two words are employed interchangeably, it seems probable that Luke wished to identify the "upper room" of the first Christian Pentecost with that of the Last Supper.

Today, southwest of the present walls of the Old City of Jerusalem, in Israel, the memory of the Cenacle is attached to a large (45 by 29½ feet) Gothic room of the 14th century on the second floor of an ancient building. This is a reconstruction of an older chapel that had been left in a dilapidated condition at the departure of the Crusaders (A.D. 1187). A cenotaph of David is venerated on the ground floor and has become, since 1948, a favorite pilgrimage spot.

The history of this site, according to St. Epiphanius (d. 403), goes back to the first century of the Christian era. According to him, a small church that had been built here in apostolic times survived the destructions inflicted by Titus and Hadrian. About A.D. 350 this old church was given needed restoration, and in 390 a great basilica, known as Holy Zion, was erected near it. The basilica is clearly represented on the famous sixth-century mosaic map of Medaba and was lovingly referred to by the Byzantines as "The Mother of All Churches." As early as the fourth century, and more generally in the sixth, this church was clearly identified as the site of the Last Supper. The Crusaders, when they captured Jerusalem in 1099, found both churches in ruins. They restored the basilica in Romanesque style, but of this construction nothing was left after the destruction ordered by the Sultan of Damascus in 1219.

The title of Holy Zion contributed to an erroneous identification of the hill of the Cenacle with the Davidical Zion, which actually was on the opposite hill to the east, Mt. Ophel, beyond the Tyropeon Valley. A tomb of David, therefore, made its appearance here in the 12th

Catholic priest at funeral, Northern Ireland. (©David & Peter Turnley/CORBIS)

century and prompted the Muslims' desire to possess the site. In 1342 the Franciscans received from Pope Clement VI the care of the Cenacle in perpetuity. It was then that they built the small Gothic chapel described above. In 1523 the Muslims transformed the chapel into a mosque and finally, in 1551, expelled the Franciscans from the site.

Today's Cenacle building cannot evidently be anything but a commemoration and an approximate localization, yet it clearly deserves reverence and respect. The Franciscans were able to return to a new monastery *ad coenaculum* (near the cenacle) on March 26, 1936, but were obliged to evacuate during the troubles in 1948. In 1960 they were allowed to reoccupy their monastery and chapel, which had been badly damaged by mortar fire.

Bibliography: C. KOPP, *The Holy Places of Gospels,* tr. R. WALLS (New York 1963) 321–334; L. H. VINCENT and F. M. ABEL, *Jérusalem Nouvelle,* 2 v. (Paris 1922) 1:421–481. E. POWER, *Dictionnaire de la Bible,* suppl. ed. L. PIROT, et al. (Paris 1928–) 1:1064–84. D. BALDI, *Enchiridion locorum sanctorum* (2d ed. Jerusalem 1955) 597–675. F. H. DALMAIS, "La Sainte Sion, mère de toutes les églises," *Bible et Terre Sainte* 11 (May 1958) 3–5.

[E. LUSSIER]

CENACLE, RELIGIOUS OF THE

Religious of the Cenacle, officially known as the Congregation of Our Lady of the Retreat in the Cenacle (RC), a congregation of women religious with papal approbation, founded in 1826 at Lalouvesc, France, by Saint Thérèse COUDERC. The constitutions of the community are based on the Rule of St. Ignatius of Loyola, whose *Spiritual Exercises,* together with the spiritual heritage of the founder, constitute the bases for the formation and training of the religious.

The Cenacle sisters engage in both contemplative and active ministries, employing spiritual retreats and instructions in Christian doctrine as means of educating people in the interior life. The word Cenacle comes from the Latin *coenaculum* (supper room) and designates the place of retreat, the upper room, in Jerusalem, where Our Lady, the Apostles, and the followers of Our Lord met in prayer in the days preceding the first Pentecost. Modeling their life and work on that first spiritual retreat of early Christian times, the Religious of the Cenacle find in it the inspiration for the interior life and spirit of their congregation and their ministries.

At the end of 2000, the congregation was found in Europe (Belgium, Croatia, England, France, Ireland, Italy, The Netherlands, and Switzerland), North America (Canada and the United States), South America (Brazil), Africa (Madgascar and Togo), Asia (The Philippines and Singapore) and Oceania (Australia and New Zealand). The congregation established their first house in the U.S. in 1892. The Generalate is in Rome.

Bibliography: H. M. LYNCH, *In the Shadow of Our Lady of the Cenacle* (New York 1941).

[T. HALL]

CENOBITES

Cenobites are religious who, by contrast with hermits or anchorites, live their life in common. In precise usage, however, "cenobite" (Gr. κοινός, common, and βίος, life) is limited to members of monastic communities whose lives are spent primarily in the monastic *cenobium* and not in apostolic work of a kind that leads the religious outside. Thus among contemporary religious, the Benedictines, Cistercians, and Oriental monks are properly termed cenobites; and religious of orders such as the Carthusian, Camaldolese, and Valambrosians, may be called cenobites because their life consists of a blend of the eremitic and cenobitic lives. Though the early hermits of the East occasionally convened for common worship, the religious life in common actually had its origin at the beginning of the 4th century with the monasteries of St. Pachomius, where the essential features of cenobitism were established: life together according to a rule under the supervision of a recognized religious superior. In the East, the Pachomian type of monasticism gave way in the course of the 5th century to that of St. Basil, who replaced the militarism of Pachomius with a more domestic spirit and corrected the overemphasis on manual labor by carefully subordinating work to prayer. In the West, after a century and a half of experiment (400–550) based on various Eastern precedents, the Rule of St. Benedict appeared and, in the course of the next two centuries, replaced virtually every vestige of earlier forms of monasticism. Whereas the cenobitic rules of the period of experiment had often emulated the most striking and excessive elements of Eastern asceticism, the cenobitism of St. Benedict developed the discretionary spirit of St. Basil, strengthening it with a wisdom derived from Roman governmental experience. St. Benedict contributed to the cenobitic institution especially by his emphasis on stability, the vow and virtue that binds the monk to one particular community, and in his development of St. Basil's ideal of the monastery as a family under the abbot as a father and representative of Christ. The Rule of St. Benedict outlines a form of cenobitism that has proved remarkably durable. Among the monks of the West, it has never been replaced, while all the newer institutions, which for the most part have been directed to some kind of specific apostolic work, have not strayed far from the spirit of St. Benedict in those aspects of their lives that have remained cenobitic.

Bibliography: H. LECLERCQ, *Dictionnaire d'archéologie chrétienne et de liturgie,* ed. F. CABROL, H. LECLERCQ, and H. I. MARROU 15 v. (Paris 1907–53) 2.2:3047–3248. J. OLPHE–GALLIARD, *Dictionnaire de spiritualité ascétique et mystique. Doctrine et histoire,* ed. M. VILLER et al. (Paris 1932–) 2:404–416.

[A. DONAHUE]

CENOBITISM

An early form of monastic organization. Although the monastic ideal began primarily as a flight from the world in search of inwardness, recollection, and a life hidden in God, the dangers of solitude and its temptations quickly became apparent. The gathering of hermits into loosely knit groups with a free and personal relationship to a spiritual father, the abbot, did not eliminate these dangers. Gradually a tendency toward communal institutions became manifest since these provided a material and spiritual support for the interior life.

St. Pachomius. The earliest communal monastic foundation was located in the Thebaid (northern Egypt), where St. PACHOMIUS organized large communities with heads and deputy heads. They were federated into a congregation whose superior had authority over all the houses and whose members met in two annual chapters. Well-organized and financially remunerative work was combined with silence to frame and support prayer; and this was regulated partly as a common exercise and partly house by house; spiritual instructions followed a similar plan. The asceticism was reasonable; and though the discipline of the individual will was its essential goal, nevertheless the system left scope for personal initiative. The charismatic gifts of the founder were not stabilized in juridical structure, and after his death tendencies to disintegration manifested themselves; some of his imitators, such as Shenoute, had to resort to outright violence to maintain order. But the first rules created remarkably balanced formula that exercised a profound influence, especially in the West. In the East, BASILIAN monasticism is an independent initiative; in it the common life is based on sociological and ecclesiastical considerations.

Lower Egypt. The ideal of solitude indulged by hermits in lower Egypt was tempered by the proximity of other cells, the meeting every Sunday for the Office, and the moral authority of the elders. It is here that the term *coenobium* and the classification of the monks into different kinds are encountered. These distinctions must not be absolutized or made into antithetical categories. They existed side by side, and the same monk passed from one category into another.

In 5th-century Palestine the laura was a synthesis; it had an organized center where the young monks were trained and isolated cells for the full-fledged monks who maintained regular relations with the community. These institutions did not prevent the monks, among whom there were saints, from passing from one community to another with a freedom that may surprise the legal-minded men in the West.

A return to the strict Basilian conception, actualized on the scale of large communities, can be seen in the Studite reform of the late 8th century. But this was never an absolute ideal in the East, where order did not eliminate CHARISM. Colonies of hermits and lauras (not to be identified with the Palestinian lauras) remained licit. The price of this liberty was *idiorythmia,* or a type of monastic independence that tolerated the retention of some private property and called only for limited obedience; it became an abuse in the 14th century, beginning at Mt. ATHOS. It gradually spread and was finally legitimized.

In the West, the strict cenobitic rule instituted by St. BENEDICT became the norm, and the reformers always saw in it the touchstone of observance. There is nothing contradictory in recognizing that this has been combined through the centuries with an aspiration to solitude, for inwardness and sociability complement each other. In modern religious congregations, cenobitism has been assimilated into centralized juridical structures that render pointless the notion of stability, understood as a bond to a certain definite house.

See Also: CENOBITES; HERMITS.

Bibliography: H. LECLERCQ, *Dictionnaire d'archéologie chrétienne et de liturgie*, ed. F. CABROL, H. LECLERCQ, and H. I. MARROU, 15 v. (Paris 1907–53) 2.2:3047–3248. J. OLPHE-GALLIARD, *Dictionnaire de spiritualité ascétique et mystique. Doctrine et histoire*, ed. M. VILLER et al. (Paris 1932–) 2:404–416. C. LIALINE and P. DOYÈRE, *ibid.* 4:936–982, s.v. érémitisme. A. PLÉ, ed., *Communal Life* (The Religious Life 8; Westminster, Md. 1957).

[J. GRIBOMONT]

CENSER

A vessel for holding glowing coals on which IN-CENSE is strewn for the sake of producing a fragrant smoke. It is known also as a thurible, from the Latin word for censer, *thuribulum.*

When incense was introduced into the Christian liturgy in the 4th century, the censer was of the same form as that commonly used in pagan worship, i.e., a small metal pot hanging from three relatively short chains, which were joined at the top in a metal ring. This type of censer without a cover is represented in several mosaics and paintings from the 5th and later centuries. In the early Middle Ages, however, a perforated metal cover was often placed over the pot to prevent the coals from falling out when the censer was swung. A fourth chain was then added to facilitate the raising of the cover when incense was put on the coals. All the chains could then be made longer. This soon became the prevalent form throughout Christendom.

Both the pot and its cover were often plated with gold or silver and adorned with symbolic figures or with elaborate architectural designs representing small castles, churches, arcades, etc.

The auxiliary cup (with a flat base or a foot) for holding the incense to be used in the censer was originally of hemispherical form and called in Latin by such words as *pyxis, busta, capsella,* and *acerra.* From the 12th century on this was often made in an oblong or boatlike shape and therefore is known in Latin as *navis* or *navicula;* hence the English word "boat" for the incense holder.

Bibliography: A. WECKWERTH, *Lexikon für Theologie und Kirche,* ed. J. HOFER and K. RAHNER, 10 v. (2d, new ed. Freiburg 1957–65) 8:1012–13. H. LECLERCQ, *Dictionnaire d'archéologie* *chrétienne et de liturgie*, ed. F. CABROL, H. LECLERCQ, and H. I. MARROU, 15 v. (Paris 1907–53) 5.1:21–33. R. LESAGE, *Catholicisme. Hier, aujourd'hui et demain*, ed. G. JACQUEMET (Paris 1947–) 4:109. P. MORRISROE, *The Catholic Encyclopedia*, ed. C. G. HERBERMANN et al., 16 v. (New York 1907–14; suppl. 1922) 3:519.

[J. J. MCGARRAGHY/EDS.]

CENSORSHIP OF BOOKS (CANON LAW)

The censorship of books is the control of literature that is exercised by the Church for the salvation of souls. It is a judgment made by ecclesiastical authority whether a book adheres to Catholic teaching on faith and morals. This control is deemed censorship in its strict sense when it is exercised prior to the publication of a literary work.

History. Ecclesiastical censorship began with St. Paul at Ephesus and the burning of pagan books (Acts 19.19). The early Church acknowledged as morally and doctrinally sound some works contained in the Muratorian Fragment (2d century), the *Constitutiones Apostolorum* (4th or 5th century), the *Decretum Gelasianum* (5th century), and the writings of St. Jerome (d. 420). There also existed antecedent disapproval of anonymous and/or apocryphal works.

Some of the early Fathers voluntarily practiced individual censorship. St. Ambrose (d. 397) and St. Augustine (d. 430) are two who submitted their works to others for prior censorship. Baronius (1538–1607) held that censorship was customary as early as the 5th century. Two later instances of censorship, the letter of Pope Nicholas I (867) and the citation of Abelard (1079–1142) before the Council of Soissons (1121), indicate that censorship had become obligatory through custom.

The Franciscan Order first legislated concerning censorship under the influence of St. Bonaventure (d. 1274) in the *Constitutiones Narbonnenses* (1260). The medieval universities enacted similar laws in the same century, and by the 15th century diocesan synods had passed laws of censorship also.

The invention of the printing press in 1453 hastened the need of legislation for the entire Church; such legislation first appeared in the 1487 bull *Inter multiplices* of Pope Innocent VIII (1482–92). This bull was re-issued in 1501 by Pope Alexander VI (1492–1503) and was included in the Fifth Lateran Council (1512–17). The Council of Trent (1543–63) dealt with the censorship of books, and Pope Pius IV (1559–65) published the constitution *Dominici gregis* in 1564, reaffirming the need of censorship. Although many popes had issued subsequent legislation concerning the censorship of books, it was not until the reign of Pope Leo XIII (1878–1903) that this entire field of law was reorganized in the constitution *Officiorum ac munerum* (Jan. 25, 1897). Many of the provisions of this constitution appeared in the Code of 1918. Pope Pius X (1903–14) strengthened the regulations of censorship in the encyclical *Pascendi dominici gregis* (Dec. 8, 1907). He did this in order to halt the spread of Modernism.

Current Law. The Church's discipline on the censorship of books changed dramatically after the Second Vatican Council with the publication of the decree of the Congregation for the Doctrine of the Faith on March 19, 1975, "On the Vigilance of the Church's Pastors Regarding Books" [*Acta Apostolicae Sedis* 67 (Rome 1975) 281–228; *Canon Law Digest* 8, 991–999], which reflected a new awareness of the Church's dialogic relationship with the modern world. These norms were included in the revised *Code of Canon Law*, promulgated by Pope John Paul II in 1983 (c. 823–832).

The most significant change is the much narrower scope of publications which are subject to mandatory censorship. The 1917 Code required that all writings concerned with religion or morals be submitted for prior censorship. The newer norms affect only a few categories of more or less "official" Church publications, namely, the Sacred Scriptures, liturgical books and prayer books, catechisms, textbooks of theology and related subjects for use in schools, and religious publications which are distributed in churches.

Another notable change is the description of the doctrinal criteria which are to guide the censor in making a judgment that nothing stands in the way of publishing the writing *nihil obstat*. The earlier norm (actually from the decree of Benedict XV in 1753) was stated in terms of "the dogmas of the Church and the common teaching of Catholics" and included the "common positions of learned persons" (c. 1393 of the 1917 Code). The revised legislation says that the censor "is to consider only the teaching of the Church about faith and morals as it is proposed by the ecclesiastical magisterium" (c. 831). It seems to be a more confining and rigorous standard. However, in practice it should not be. The censor is not to demand that all writings be in complete and exact conformity with magisterial teachings, but only to consider those teachings in making an evaluative judgment about the writings.

The local ordinary whose permission to publish (*imprimatur*) is required may be either that of the author or of the publisher. In some instances the approval may be given after the publication of the book rather than before (c. 827). Censors are no longer required to be clerics; they are simply persons whom the local ordinary approves.

The censorship of books is a function of the Church's teaching office. Its pastoral purpose is the preservation of the integrity of faith and morals as well as the prevention of harm to the Christian faithful (c. 823). The process in not intended to stifle creativity or to hinder legitimate freedom of theological inquiry and expression (c. 218). It is to assure the accuracy and reliability of a relatively narrow range of official Church publications.

Bibliography: D. H. WIESK, *The Precensorship of Books* (*Catholic University of America Canon Law Studies 329*; Washington, 1954). H. C. GARDINER, *Catholic Viewpoint on Censorship* (New York 1958; rev. ed. 1961). J. A. GOODWINE, "Problems Respecting the Censorship of Books," *Jurist* 10 (1950) 152–183. E. BARAGLI, "Una constante preoccupazione pastorale della Chiesa," *La Civilta Cattolica* 2 (1975) 436–449. L. ECHEVARRIA, "La vigilancia episcopal sobre la publicacion de libros," *Revista española de Derecho canonico* (1975) 341–372. F. J. URRUTIA, "De limitibus libertatis scribendi fidelium iuxta legem canonicam," *Periodica* 65 (1976) 529–583. J. CORIDEN, "The End of the *Imprimatur*," *Jurist* 44 (1984) 339–356.

[J. C. CALHOUN/J. A. CORIDEN]

CENSURE, THEOLOGICAL

A pejorative judgment that indicates that a proposition is in some way opposed or harmful to faith or morals. Theological censures were already used in the Middle Ages by John XXII against the errors of the FRATICELLI, and by the Council of Constance against the errors of Wycliff and Hus. One of the most extensive lists of such censures was put forth by Clement XI in his condemnation of many propositions of François Quesnel (H. Denzinger, *Enchiridion symbolorum,* ed. A. Schönmetzer [32d ed. Freiburg 1963] 2502). All these censures seem reducible to three general categories: heretical, erroneous, and rash. A proposition is censured as heretical if it contradicts a truth of divine and Catholic faith; as erroneous in Catholic doctrine or in theology if it contradicts a truth that is Catholic doctrine or theologically certain; as rash if it contradicts a proposition that is not a strict theological conclusion but is well grounded and commonly held by theologians.

See Also: NOTES, THEOLOGICAL.

Bibliography: *Sacrae theologiae summa,* ed. Fathers of the Society of Jesus, Professors of the Theological Faculties in Spain, 4 v. (Madrid), v. 1 (5th ed. 1962) 1.3:884–913.

[E. J. FORTMAN]

CENSUS (IN THE BIBLE)

In the Old Testament the practice of taking a census, though in opposition to the older Israelite amphictyonic traditions, arose with the monarchy in connection with the centralization of military organization; in postexilic times the priestly editors incorporated the census lists into their writings according to certain then-prevalent notions and thus, at times, outside the original historical context of the particular census; in the New Testament Saint Luke mentions two distinct Roman censuses, the first in dating the birth of Christ, the other in alluding to a temporary rebellion led by Judas, the Galilean.

Censuses in the Old Testament. The census lists of the Old Testament represent genuine sources, though colored and interpreted by later redactors according to the latter's understanding and aims. In its historical origin the census served the purpose of ascertaining the military strength of the tribes. When the monarchy began its program of centralizing the nation's military organization by a census, there was religious and political opposition, since the census was understood to be an impingement upon Yahweh's kingship, as well as upon the autonomous liberty of the tribe. The documents, uncovered at Mari, attest the widespread Semitic antipathy to the census (see E. A. Speiser, 24–25). The power of the people was in the hands of its god; hence, taking a census implied lack of confidence in the nation's god and incurred guilt. In the light of census-incurred guilt, the law of Exodus 30.11–16 is to be understood: each person registered in the census had to pay a half shekel to be used for cultic atonement made to Yahweh. The law shows postexilic redaction in that the sanctuary shekel referred to (Ex 30.13) is of postexilic terminology; also, this law, claiming Mosaic institution, gave additional authority to the Temple tax that was necessary in postexilic times to support the Temple (Mt 17.24). Besides its military motive, the Old Testament census served also as a basis for taxation and the state-imposed corvée (2 Sm 20.24; 1 Kgs 5.13; 9.15; 2 Chr 8.8; 10.18).

Censuses in the Book of Numbers. The Pentateuchal PRIESTLY WRITERS used two census lists in the Book of Numbers (Nm 1.1–46; 26.1–51) to underline the sacerdotal functions of the tribe of Levi (1.47–54) and to preface the allotment of the Promised Land to the individual tribes; "Among these groups the land shall be divided as their heritage in keeping with the number of individuals in each group" (Nm 26.52). The lists follow the tribes (Nm ch. 1) and clans (ch. 26) of Genesis ch. 46 with some slight discrepancies, e.g., Becher, son of Benjamin (Gn 46.21) is said to be the son of Ephraim (Nm 26.35). The only ones alive for both censuses, the one at Sinai and the one on the Plains of Moab 40 years later, are said to be Moses, Joshua, and Caleb (Nm 26.63–65). In both censuses the number for half the tribes is more than 50,000. The changes in the numbers of each tribe between the two censuses probably indicates their changing relative importance. The main problem raised by both these censuses is the sum total of more than 600,000 fighting men in each census, which implies a total population well over two million. When one considers that the Israelites subsisted for 40 years in a barren desert, marched as a group (with 25 abreast and a yard apart, as stated, the column would be 44 miles long), could all be summoned by the sound of two trumpets, and could gather at one Tent of Meeting (Numbers 10.2), it is evident that the figure is grossly exaggerated. According to G. E. Mendenhall, the census lists of Numbers are anachronistic in their present context; historically they represent traditions from the time of the amphictyony that record the military. Units (*'ălāpîm*) of each tribe ready for war in case the common welfare of the tribes is threatened. The original, premonarchical *'elep* was the technical term of a subsection of a tribe that the later priestly editor, in his redaction of preexisting sources, interpreted in the light of the later military *'elep* of the monarchy that comprised about 1,000 men. Thus the extravagant census figures of Numbers would lie in a postexilic misunderstanding of earlier terminology. W. F. Albright suggests that figures in Numbers may be based on actual figures found in the Davidic census that the priestly writers adapted for their purpose; if the 603,550 of Numbers 1.46 and the 601,730 of Numbers 26.50 represent the total population and not just the warriors, these figures would not be incredible for the time of David. A possible, but unlikely, solution, suggested by A. Bentzen, is that the figures are arrived at by gematria, giving a numerical equivalent to the Hebrew letters for "Sons of Israel."

Census in the Book of Samuel. The figure of 1,300,000 warriors given for the census of David in 2 Samuel 24.9 is also incredibly high, while the figure of the Chronicler for the same census, reckoned over less territory, is even higher (1 Chr 21.5). These figures can only be due to the exaggeration or misunderstanding of a later age; it would give the semibarren land of Israel a population density twice that of any modern European country. The horror engendered by David's census and the punishment that follows seem to indicate not only the usual Semitic antipathy to a census but also an antipathy for the centralizing policies that came with the monarchy. Previously, Yahweh was king (1 Sm 8.7); great numbers did not matter, since He had led the people in the holy war (Jg ch. 7); but now, under the monarchy, what had been cultic and religious was being arrogated by the civil and military authority. By putting trust in numbers as other kings did (Prv 14.28), David showed a lack of faith in Yahweh. Moreover, the census, administered by a central authority, violated the tribal freedom formerly enjoyed under the amphictyony (see G. E. Mendenhall, 56). The people were reluctant to surrender tribal freedom that

David was encroaching upon little by little. A census would also lead to more taxes (1 Sm 8.10–18) and forced labor, of which an official was already in charge (2 Sm 20.24). The Chronicler, in his account of the census (1 Chr ch. 21), is interested primarily in glorifying the piety of the king and emphasizing the high price paid for the Temple site. A later theology is reflected in that it is Satan and no longer Yahweh who incites David to take the census (2 Sm 24.1; 1 Chr 21.1).

Postexilic Census Lists. The census lists found in Ezra 2.1–67 and Nehemiah 7.6–69 are almost identical. The one in Nehemia, used for underscoring the importance of having pure Jewish ancestry, seems to be original and apparently shows the actual population at the time of NEHEMIA (2d half of the 5th century B.C.). As reused in Ezra, it has for its purpose to make it appear that vast numbers returned immediately after the edict of Cyrus. Neither here nor in the apocryphal 3 Esdras do the figures add up to the given total of 42,360 (Neh 7.66; Ezr 2.64). The list contains, not only personal names, but also names of clans and cities, and in some cases it is difficult to say which is which.

Censuses in the New Testament. Saint Luke mentions two Roman censuses: the first in connection with the birth of Christ, which took place when Cyrinius (Quirinius) was governor of Syria (Lk 2.2), the other as occasioning the short-lived rebellion led by Judas the Galilean (Acts 5.37). Josephus (*Bell. Jud.* 2.8.1; 7.8.1) makes explicit mention of Judas's rebellion against Rome, when the Romans, upon reducing Judea to the status of a province in A.D. 6, took a census. Also, according to the chronological date of Josephus (*Ant.* 18.1.1, 2.1; 17.13.2), Cyrinius was governor of Syria in A.D. 6, and seemingly for the first time.

The difficulty caused by the reference to the census of Cyrinius in Luke's Gospel lies in the fact that in profane sources there is no explicit record corroborating his statement that Cyrinius was legate in Syria when a census was taken in Judea before the death of Herod the Great (4 B.C.). According to Josephus, Cyrinius held power as a legate, with authority over Judea, *c.* A.D. 6 to 7. Yet, the nativity narratives place Christ's birth in the reign of Herod the Great. A possible solution may lie in the fact that Cyrinius was in Syria with special powers waging the Homonadensian War also between 12 B.C. and 9 to 8 B.C. at the time when Saturninus was the legate there (see Tacitus 3.48; Strabo 12.6.5). Tertullian (*Adv. Marc.* 4.19) dates the birth of Christ by a census that he says took place under Saturninus (see W. Ramsay, *The Bearing of Recent Discovery. . . ,* 243–45). Thus, Cyrinius, in Syria with Saturninus at this time, could very well be credited with carrying out or at least initiating a census at the earlier date (perhaps completed only in A.D. 6 when he became legate). This would be compatible with the thought of most scholars that Christ was born *c.* 8–7 B.C. A frequent objection that Rome would not take a census in Herod's territory is not compelling when it is remembered that Herod, though a *rex socius,* held his authority and its exercise at the discretion of the emperor. Although no extra-Biblical record mentions this census (if it is completely distinct from that of A.D. 6), there is evidence of periodic Roman census-taking in Egypt and Gaul during the 1st Christian century (see W. Ramsay, *Was Christ Born at Bethlehem?,* 131–48). The "census of the whole world" does not mean that it was accomplished in all parts of the empire simultaneously. Although a return to the place of family origin is unknown in other Roman censuses, it is a fact that the Romans respected the customs of subjugated peoples, and to the Jews, one's tribe and place of origin had great importance. Despite these concurrences, Luke's citation still raises questions. He calls it the first under Cyrinius and feels that it is so well known, that he can date the birth of Christ by it. Yet, there is no notice of it in Josephus, who is rather detailed for the reign of Herod. Josephus calls the census of A.D. 6 "the first." The attempt to solve the discrepancy by giving the adjective πρώτη a comparative force and translating: "This census took place earlier than that which occurred when Cyrinius was governor of Syria" is not supported by any similar use of πρώτη in Luke (see A. N. Sherwin-White, 171). Other possible solutions are that Josephus had gotten his facts wrong, or that Luke, knowing the early Christian tradition that the Davidic origin of Christ had been established by an official census, took it for granted that the census was at the time of his birth, when actually it was the same census of A.D. 6, which he already shows himself familiar with in Acts.

Bibliography: G. A. BUTTRICK, ed., *The Interpreters' Dictionary of the Bible,* 4 v. (Nashville 1962) 1:547. *Encyclopedic Dictionary of the Bible,* tr. and adap. by L. HARTMAN (New York 1963), from A. VAN DEN BORN, *Bijbels Woordenboek* 335–38. R. DE VAUX, *Ancient Israel, Its Life and Institutions,* tr. J. MCHUGH (New York 1961) 65–67. E. A. SPEISER, "Census and Ritual Expiation in Mari and Israel," *The Bulletin of the American Schools of Oriental Research* 149 (1958) 17–25. G. E. MENDENHALL, "The Census Lists of Numbers 1 and 26," *Journal of Biblical Literature* 77 (1958) 52–66. W. F. ALBRIGHT, "The Administrative Divisions of Israel and Judah," *The Journal of the Palestine Oriental Society* 5 (1925) 20–25. A. BENTZEN, *Introduction to the Old Testament,* 2 v. (2d ed. Copenhagen 1952) 2:34. W. M. RAMSAY, *Was Christ Born at Bethlehem?* (3d ed. London 1905); *The Bearing of Recent Discovery on the Trustworthiness of the New Testament* (4th ed. London 1920). M. J. LAGRANGE, "Où en est la question du recensement de Quirinius?," *Revue biblique* 18 (1911) 60–84. A. DEISSMANN, *Light from the Ancient East,* tr. L. R. M. STRACHAN (rev. ed. New York 1927) 270–71. T. CORBISHLEY, "Quirinius and the Census," *Klio* 29 (1936) 81–95; "The Date of Our Lord's Birth," *Scripture* 1 (1946) 77–80. A. N. SHERWIN-WHITE, *Roman Society and Roman Law in the New Testament* (Oxford 1963) 162–71. H. U. INSTINSKY, *Das Jahr der Geburt Christi* (Munich 1957).

[S. C. DOYLE]

Peter Kloeckner, prominent citizen and member of the Center Party, photographed while on his way to a public luncheon tendered by Chancellor Wirth, 1922. (©Bettmann/CORBIS)

CENTER PARTY

The Center was one of the leading parties in the Reichstag in Germany between 1871 and 1933. Its achievements in uniting Catholics of widely different social backgrounds, defending Catholic interests, and promoting social reform had a marked influence on Catholic parties elsewhere in Europe.

Definition. The Centrist leaders always insisted that it was a nonconfessional party open to non-Catholics; its founders made serious efforts to attract Protestant members in the early 1870s. But the substantial failure of the initial attempt, the ability of the party to play an important political role on a Catholic basis, and extensive Catholic opposition to the Center's conversion into a real interconfessional party made the leadership cool to anything but a formal definition of nonconfessionalism in its later history. The party name described its favorite position in the Reichstag—between the conservative parties (chiefly Prussian and representative of authoritarian monarchical traditions, Prussian hegemony, and state control over the churches) and the democratic parties (desirous of a secular and centralized democratic state). The pre-1918 Center regarded constitutional monarchy and a federal-state system as necessary safeguards against a possible democratic majority that would separate Church and State, secularize education, and tend toward socialism. The party placed itself on a factual basis after the overthrow of monarchical institutions in November 1918 and collaborated with the liberal and democratic parties in trying to create a viable republic. Its leaders justified their change of course on the grounds that the Weimar Republic liberated the Church, provided support for the clergy and ecclesiastical institutions, and ensured Catholics of complete civic equality. In the later 1920s and early 1930s the party's basic concern with Catholic cultural objectives and its social structure drove it toward the right and to a consideration of the advisability of supporting constitutional changes along semiauthoritarian lines.

Origins and Early History. Neither the party name nor its basic position from 1871 to 1918 were new, since three of its first leaders, Peter Reichensperger, his brother August, and Hermann von Mallinckrodt, had helped to found in 1852 the Catholic fraction in Prussia, later renamed the Center fraction, after the Protestant monarchy withdrew some of the Church's constitutional liberties. The party, however, foundered in 1862–63 when many Catholic voters, especially in the liberal Rhineland, chose to back the liberal parties in their conflict with the Bismarck ministry over expansion of the Prussian army rather than the Center, which sought to preserve the constitutional status quo in the contest. A more basic cause of its failure was the absence of any deep Catholic concern about the Church in a state in which it still enjoyed considerable freedom and in which the monarchy and liberal majority seemed to be hopelessly at odds with each other.

The action by representative personalities throughout Catholic Germany to create new Center parties in the Reichstag and Prussian Landtag sprang essentially from their fear of an anti-Catholic alliance between the hegemonic Prussian government and the liberal parties after the unification of Germany (1870–71). Catholics in Prussia and southern Germany alike had not concealed their dismay over Prussia's replacement of Catholic Austria as the leading state in Germany; their acceptance of the defi-

nition of papal infallibility by VATICAN COUNCIL I led secular and nationalistic liberals to believe that Catholics could not be loyal Germans while under papal authority. The appearance of 57 Catholic Centrists in the first Reichstag session indicates that many Catholics shared the fears of the party's founders regarding the freedom and rights of the Church. The prime factor, however, in the party's growth from a respectable 57 members in 1871 to 100 in 1881 was Bismarck's major error in associating his person and the Prussian state with the liberal parties in a massive legislative and administrative assault on the Catholic Church, which he believed to be the source of the Center's strength and a part of a general Catholic alliance trying to weaken the Protestant empire.

The Center met its severest test not in the KULTUR-KAMPF but in the 1880s when Bismarck became fully conscious of its legislative power following the disintegration of the National Liberal party. By negotiating a settlement with the Vatican and appealing to the monarchical sentiments of the Center's aristocratic conservative wing, the chancellor hoped to split the party in two. WINDTHORST, the Center's leader since 1874, was deeply discouraged by his exclusion from the negotiations between Bismarck and the Vatican that ended the Kulturkampf, but he was able to preserve his party's unity. His colleagues and followers substantially backed him when he twice refused papal requests that the Center support the chancellor in his military legislation (1887). After the 1890 elections, even Bismarck recognized that the government would have to work with the Center Party unless it was willing to abolish universal and equal suffrage.

The Center from 1890 to 1918. After Bismarck's forced retirement (1890), the Centrist leadership envisioned considerable domestic influence. Bismarck's successors rejected all suggestions of a *coup d'état* against the constitution and sought a working relationship with the Center. But Windthorst's sudden death (March 1891) deprived the Center of the one personality able to draw the Catholic electorate into the new course without serious difficulty. The task was all the greater because the government sought the Center's support for heavy military expenditures and for legislation favorable to labor, industry, and commerce in a time of deep agricultural depression. Ernst Lieber, Windthorst's successor, was too uncertain about his own position and too worried about party unity in the face of serious agrarian disaffection to support wholeheartedly the government's policies before the later 1890s. Deep concern lest reactionary advisers convince Emperor William II that the monarchy could not govern with a Reichstag under Centrist leadership led Lieber to move his party steadily in the government's direction after 1895. Before his premature death (1902), Lieber received credit for the passage of the new national civic code, two major naval bills, and legislation supporting Germany's colonial program.

Insurgency by younger Centrists who opposed the colonial administration's treatment of natives and of Catholic missions disrupted the party's relationship with the government (1906). It was restored in 1909 because the Conservative Party found it more comfortable to collaborate with the Center than with democratic liberals who wanted political reforms in Prussia, the Conservative stronghold.

Before 1918. The gradual improvement of the position of German Catholics after 1895 justified the Center's course. All religious orders, except the Jesuits, regained corporative rights. The Church regained some supervisory influence over Prussian confessional schools. Some concessions were made toward parity for Catholics in the Prussian and imperial civil service. But Catholic support of the party declined from 85 percent during the Kulturkampf to 55 percent in the 1912 elections. Much of the defection occurred in the working classes. The Center had not been late in its awareness of the humane and political necessity of social action. It had supported Bismarck's insurance legislation for the aged, injured, and ill in the 1880s and assisted in the introduction of the six-day workweek, labor courts, better working conditions, and pensions for widows and orphans. It had cooperated in the formation of Catholic unions and, later, of interconfessional ones. The Center had also helped to establish and to direct the People's League for Catholic Germany, which promoted Christian social reform among middle-class German Catholics and educated Catholic labor leaders. These efforts did much to keep large numbers of Catholic workers loyal to the party and to the Church. But the predominant influence of urban and rural propertied elements in the Center, its conservative policy on taxation and tariffs, its silent opposition to democratic suffrage in Prussia, and its initial inability to win general ecclesiastical approval for interconfessional unions alienated all but devoutly Catholic workers.

World War I. During this war of total mobilization, the question of workers' rights in Prussia and of Catholic labor's place in the Center assumed new significance. Throughout most of the war, the Centrist leadership, concerned about the future of Church-State relations and confessional education in Prussia, and under heavy pressure from Catholic business and agrarian groups, refused to sponsor Prussian electoral reform. Catholic labor leaders, in heavy competition with the Social Democratic unions for the allegiance of Catholic workers, insisted on labor suffrage in Prussia. Even the major representatives of Catholic labor followed Matthias Erzberger without enthusiasm when he argued convincingly in 1917 that the

war was at best a stalemate and that the Center should join with the democratic parties in an effort to secure a compromise peace. Early in 1918, when Germany's war prospects had brightened, the old leaders isolated Erzberger by pledging support of electoral reform in Prussia. But they had to follow Erzberger's lead when Ludendorff informed the government (September 1918) that the war was lost and that the emperor should appoint a democratic cabinet to negotiate peace with the U.S. and its allies. All the Centrist leaders were taken unawares by the November revolution that they considered unnecessary in view of recent constitutional changes. Nevertheless, they accepted the revolution and aided the early convocation of a democratically elected constitutional assembly that would restore parliamentary government and the rule of law.

The Center in the Weimar Republic (1919–33). In postwar Germany the Center party achieved influence and assumed responsibilities beyond anything it had known in its earlier history. Despite heavy criticism from Catholic rightists and conservatives, it collaborated with the Social Democrats and Democrats in providing Germany with a moderate constitution and a responsible government in this critical period. Under Erzberger's direction the party insisted that Germany must accept the Versailles Treaty. Later it supported Stresemann's policy of reconciliation with the other Western powers, though concern for its conservative supporters made the party do so cautiously. But the Center's responsible conduct and the frequency with which prominent Centrists held the chancellor's office did not satisfy the party's Bavarian wing, which had broken away in 1920, and other Catholic critics of the Center's course prior to the later 1920s. Internally, the party was increasingly wracked by disagreements among agrarians, laborites, and civil servants over economic policy. The German bishops were disturbed over the Center's inability to win the support of its democratic allies for a national confessional school law, placing confessional schools on the same legal plane as the interconfessional schools of the Weimar constitution. The election of a priest, Ludwig KAAS, as party chairman (1928) reflected the belief of many members that only a clergyman could restore party unity. The concern with unity, the desire for a school law, and the essential weakness of the party's democratic elements were important factors in the Center's steady movement toward political alliance with the non-Nazi right. Kaas's efforts in this direction were thwarted by the intransigence of the conservative Nationalist leader, Alfred Hugenberg, and by President Hindenburg's replacement of Chancellor Heinrich Brüning, a moderate conservative Centrist, by the Catholic reactionary Franz von Papen (June 1932).

Dissolution of the Center. Both anger against von Papen and fear of his intentions led the Center's leaders to seek a coalition with national socialism, which they underestimated as a threat to parliamentary government. They were bitterly disappointed when Hitler was appointed chancellor by Hindenburg in January 1933 after the failure of von Papen's successor, General von Schleicher, and did not invite the Center to join his coalition cabinet. Two months later the party voted for the Enabling Act, which gave legal sanction to Hitler's dictatorship. The party leadership had decided that it was hopeless to resist Hitler and hoped that their action would cause him to preserve the Reichstag, respect the rights of the Church, and permit Catholic civil servants to continue in office. Most scholars believe there was a connection between the Center's approval of the Enabling Act and Kaas's interest in a German concordat with Rome. It is also the preponderant opinion that the sudden dissolution of the party in early July 1933 stood in direct relationship to the concordat negotiations then reaching their high point in Rome. But Hitler's possession of total power and the flight of members from the party between March and July would in any case have made it virtually impossible to avoid dissolution. The Nazi dictator was wise enough to focus his attack on the party and not on the Church as Bismarck had done.

See Also: PIUS XII.

Bibliography: C. BACHEM, *Vorgeschichte, Geschichte, und Politik der deutschen Zentrumspartei,* 9 v. (Cologne 1927–32). K. EPSTEIN, *Matthias Erzberger and the Dilemma of German Democracy* (Princeton 1959). R. MORSEY, *Staatslexikon,* ed. Görres-Gesellschaft, 8 v. (6th, new and enl. ed. Freiburg 1957–63) 8:966–970. J. ROVAN, *Le Catholicisme politique en Allemagne* (Histoire de la démocratie chrétienne 2; Paris 1956). E. ALEXANDER, "Church and Society in Germany," *Church and Society,* ed. J. N. MOODY (New York 1953).

[J. K. ZEENDER]

CENTESIMUS ANNUS

Pope John Paul II's ninth encyclical, issued on May 1, 1991, commemorating the hundredth anniversary of Pope LEO XIII's encyclical *RERUM NOVARUM.* John Paul's major social encyclical is divided into six sections. Chapter one, "Characteristics of *Rerum Novarum,*" pays tribute to Leo, who faced the social problems generated by a new form of property (capital) and a new form of labor (simply for wages). Work is part of the human vocation, but when labor becomes a commodity to sell, new injustices can and did arise. In *Rerum Novarum,* Pope Leo defended the essential dignity and rights of workers, together with the principle of solidarity (under its classical name "friendship"). Criticizing both socialism and liberalism, he stated that "the defenseless and the poor have a claim to special consideration."

In chapter two, "Toward the New Things of Today," John Paul sketches the history of the last 100 years, including two world wars, the consolidation of Communist dictatorship, the arms race and the Cold War. These movements were complicated outside Europe by decolonization. He also refers to three types of response to the Communist threat: (1) the European social market economies tried to end the situations of injustice that fueled revolutionary movements by building a "democratic society inspired by social justice"; (2) others set up repressive systems of national security, which risked destroying the very freedoms they were intended to protect; and (3) affluent Western societies tried (successfully) to compete with Marxism at its own level, by demonstrating a superior ability to meet human material needs.

With this the pope comes to "The Year 1989" (chapter three), and his analysis of the fall of Communism, which he traces to the recovery and application of the principles of Catholic social teaching by Polish workers in the name of solidarity, faced with the inefficiency of the economic system and the spiritual and cultural void brought about by Communism. The consequences of 1989 apply to the Third World, in that they enable the Church to affirm "an authentic theology of integral human liberation" (no. 26), and to Europe, where a great effort is now needed "to rebuild morally and economically the countries which have abandoned Communism." Disarmament should make possible a greater "mobilization of resources" for "economic growth and common development," both in Europe and in the Third World. But development is threatened by resurgent totalitarianism, materialism, and religious fundamentalism.

The fourth chapter, "Private Property and the Universal Destination [i.e., purpose] of Material Goods," is the heart of the encyclical. An individual right to property exists but is limited by nature: it is created by human work, and since the earth as a whole was given to man in common, all possession should be subordinated to the common good. These days, the possession of "know-how, technology and skill" are just as important as material resources in the creation of wealth. This leads to new types of exclusion and poverty, especially in the Third World. To an unjust economic system where fundamental human needs remain unsatisfied and development impossible, one must oppose not socialism but a "society of free work, of enterprise and of participation," in which "the market is appropriately controlled by the forces of society and by the State." In such a system, profit is not the only regulator of the life of business, monopolies are broken down, unpayable debts are deferred or canceled, and every effort is made to create conditions under which the poorer nations may share in development (no. 35).

In advanced economies, the need for basic goods is replaced by the "demand for quality," leading to the danger of consumerism: lifestyles directed not towards "truth, beauty, goodness and communion with others for the sake of common growth" but towards acquisition for the sake of "enjoyment as an end in itself," where the definition of human needs has been distorted by a false anthropology. Consumerism alienates man from his true self, which can only be attained by self-transcendence and self-gift. It leads to the disordered consumption of natural resources and irresponsible destruction of the environment and the creation of "structures of sin" that impede human development (to which the pope opposes the structures of "human ecology," starting with the family as sanctuary of life).

Despite its advantages, the market has limits. There are "collective and qualitative needs which cannot be satisfied by market mechanisms" and human goods which must not be bought and sold, but need to be defended by the State and society (no. 40). Marxism has failed, but marginalization, exploitation, and alienation persist. The Church endorses the "free economy," but only if economic freedom is "circumscribed within a strong juridical framework which places it at the service of human freedom in its totality," which is ethical and religious at its core (no. 42). She offers her social teaching, however, not as a model but as an "indispensable and ideal orientation" towards the common good.

In chapter five, "State and Culture," the pope warns that human freedom depends on the recognition of an ultimate truth, without which "the force of power takes over," and democracy slides into totalitarianism (44–45). Human rights, starting with the right to life and culminating in religious freedom, must be protected, and the security of stable currency and efficient public services assured by the State. Families and other intermediate communities and "networks of solidarity" on which the culture of a nation depends should be supported. The principle of subsidiarity, however, militates against excessive State interference and control, as occurs in the "Social Assistance State."

The Church contributes to "a true culture of peace" by promoting the truth about human destiny, creation and Redemption, and about our shared responsibility for avoiding war. Peace is promoted by development, which in turn depends on "adequate interventions on the international level" and "important changes in established life-styles," especially in the more developed economies (51–52, 58). Chapter six, "Man Is the Way of the Church," emphasizes that the Church's social doctrine is inspired by her care for each human being, and forms a part of her evangelizing and salvific mission, revealing man to himself in the light of Christ. Though primarily theological, it is interdisciplinary, and rather than being merely a theory is a basis for action. With the help of grace, "Love for others, and in the first place love for the poor, in whom the Church sees Christ himself, is made concrete in the promotion of justice" (58).

Bibliography: For the text of *Centesimus annus,* see: *Acta Apostolicae Sedis* 83 (1991): 793–867 (Latin); *Origins* 21, no. 1 (May 16, 1991): 1–23 (English); *The Pope Speaks* 36 (1991): 273–310 (English). For commentaries and summaries of *Centesimus annus,* see: R. CHARLES, *Christian Social Witness and Teaching,* vol. 2, *The Modern Social Teaching: Contexts: Summaries: Analysis* (Leominster, 1998). S. GREGG, *Challenging the Modern World: Karol Wojtyła/John Paul II and the Development of Catholic Social Teaching* (Lanham, 1999). D. L. SCHINDLER, *Heart of the World, Center of the Church: Communio Ecclesiology, Liberalism and Liberation* (Grand Rapids, 1996). G. WEIGEL, ed., *A New Worldly Order: John Paul II and Human Freedom-A "Centesimus Annus" Reader* (Washington, D.C., 1992). J. P. DOUGHERTY, "The Ecology of the Human Spirit," *L'Osservatore Romano,* English edition (October 16, 1996).

[S. CALDECOTT]

CENTRAL AFRICAN REPUBLIC, THE CATHOLIC CHURCH IN

The Central African Republic is a landlocked country positioned almost precisely at the center of the African continent. Located on a plateau about 2,500 feet in elevation, it is bordered on the north by Chad, on the east by Sudan, on the south by Congo and the Democratic Republic of Congo (formerly Zaire), and on the west by Cameroon. The dense forests covering the country's southern region thin out to a savanna in the north that is frequently buffeted by hot, dry harmattan winds. Considered one of the last refuges for Africa's wildlife, the Central African Republic is threatened by encroaching desert conditions, deforestation in the south, and chronic water shortages. While natural resources include diamonds, uranium, gold, and oil reserves, the country has suffered through government mismanagement and social and economic adversity. More than two-thirds of Central Africans—predominately members of the Banda, Baya, and Mandjia tribes—live in outlying areas and engage in subsistence agriculture; the average life expectancy of an adult male was 42 years in 2000.

The Central African Republic was politically tied with Chad to form the colony of Ubangi Shari, and was once part of French Equatorial Africa. After gaining independence from France on Aug. 13, 1960, the Central African Republic suffered under a series of military governments before a civilian government rose to power in 1993.

Capital: Bangui.
Size: 240,376 sq. miles.
Population: 3,512,750 in 2000.
Languages: French (official); Sangho, Arabic, Hunsa, and Swahili are also spoken.
Religions: 878,190 Catholics (25%), 526,910 Muslims (15%), 874,900 Protestants (25%), 846,350 indigenous beliefs (24%), 386,400 other (11%).
Archdiocese: Bangui, with suffragans Bambari, Bangassou (1964), Berbérati (1955), Bossangoa (1964), Bouar, Kaga–Bandoro, and Mbaiki.

While archaeologists determined the region to have been inhabited by man since the paleolithic period, little is know of these early peoples. Part of the African Gaoga empire during the 16th century and likely the home of pygmy tribes as late as the 18th century, the Central African Republic was used by African slave traders as a convenient place to relocate conquered tribes from neighboring Chad and the Congo, as well as from nearby Somalia and the lakes region. French explorers appeared in the1880s, establishing the city of Bangui in 1889 and uniting the Central African Republic with Chad to form the colony of Ubangi Shari. The region's first mission, founded with great difficulty by Prosper Augouard at Saint-Paul-des-Rapids near Bangui in 1894, was a precarious one standing alone amid a hostile population given to cannibalism.

Reflecting the area's political ties to Chad, the Vicariate of the French Upper Congo and Ubangi (now Brazzaville) was created from the Vicarate of the French Congo in 1894. The region's first three missions were created the Prefecture of Ubangi Shari in 1909, and would become the Vicarate of Bangui in 1940. The nearby Prefecture of Berbérati would be made a vicariate in 1952. Meanwhile, the French government's institution of forced labor to expand its rubber enterprise causing an exodus of natives from the Ubangi Shari, which was incorporated into French Equatorial Africa in 1910. Although a lack of missionaries hurt the Church's evangelical efforts during World War I, an influx of personnel after the war allowed missions to expand beyond the borderland rivers into the region's interior. In 1938 the first African priest was ordained.

French Capuchins driven from Ethiopia began to labor in Berbérati in 1938, and after World War II they were joined by Italian Capuchins, also driven from Ethiopia. Dutch Holy Ghost Fathers received Bangassou in 1954, and the following year the region's Church hierarchy was formally established. Protestant missions, mainly from the United States, began working in the area in 1920 and gained most converts in Bangassou and Bossangoa.

The country's minor seminaries, located in Sibut and Berbérati, had 114 seminarians in 2000. The region contained 115 parishes and numerous primary and secondary schools. The Church had 138 secular and 145 religious priests, as well as 59 brothers and 370 sisters, to administer to the faithful of the Central African Republic in 2000. Continued political unrest and threats to the republic's democratic government by members of the military were the concern of many in the Church, prompting Bangui's Archbishop Joachim Ndayen to host peace talks beginning in 1996. In 1999 Pope John Paul II spoke to Central African Republic bishops about their "difficult and complex situation," but commended evangelization efforts that had resulted in the creation of two new diocese and the promotion of the Christian family in the region.

[J. LE GALL/EDS.]

CENTRAL SENSE

In scholastic psychology, the central sense (*sensus communis*) is an internal organic power for acquiring sense knowledge, distinct from the external and other internal SENSES. Its function is to grasp all the stimuli known through the external senses, to compare them, unifying or distinguishing among them, and to know the very activity of the external senses, that is, to be conscious of sensation. Its organ is to be found in the sensory and psychosensory zones of the cerebral cortex, in the associative cortical zones, and in the long and short associative fibers that link these zones.

Necessity. At the close of his study on the external senses, Aristotle concluded that there was need for a superior function of sense knowledge to explain certain activities closely associated with external sensation, but not themselves reducible to the operations of the external senses. These activities are (1) consciousness of the operation of the external senses and (2) knowledge of the similarities and differences between the objects of the various external senses. Each sense knows only the SENSIBLES that are proper to it. Sight is aware of color but not of sound, just as hearing is aware of sound but not of color. Again, sight is not audible and therefore is unknowable through hearing. Hearing is not colored and cannot be grasped by sight. No direct exchange is then possible between the external senses, either at the level of their proper object or of their specific activity. Moreover, no external sense can know its own sensation. In fact, not being colored, sight is not visible. The same is true of the other senses. For to know its own sensation, the sense would have to double itself in such a way that the sensory organ would become detached from itself as knowing subject to consider itself as object of its knowl-

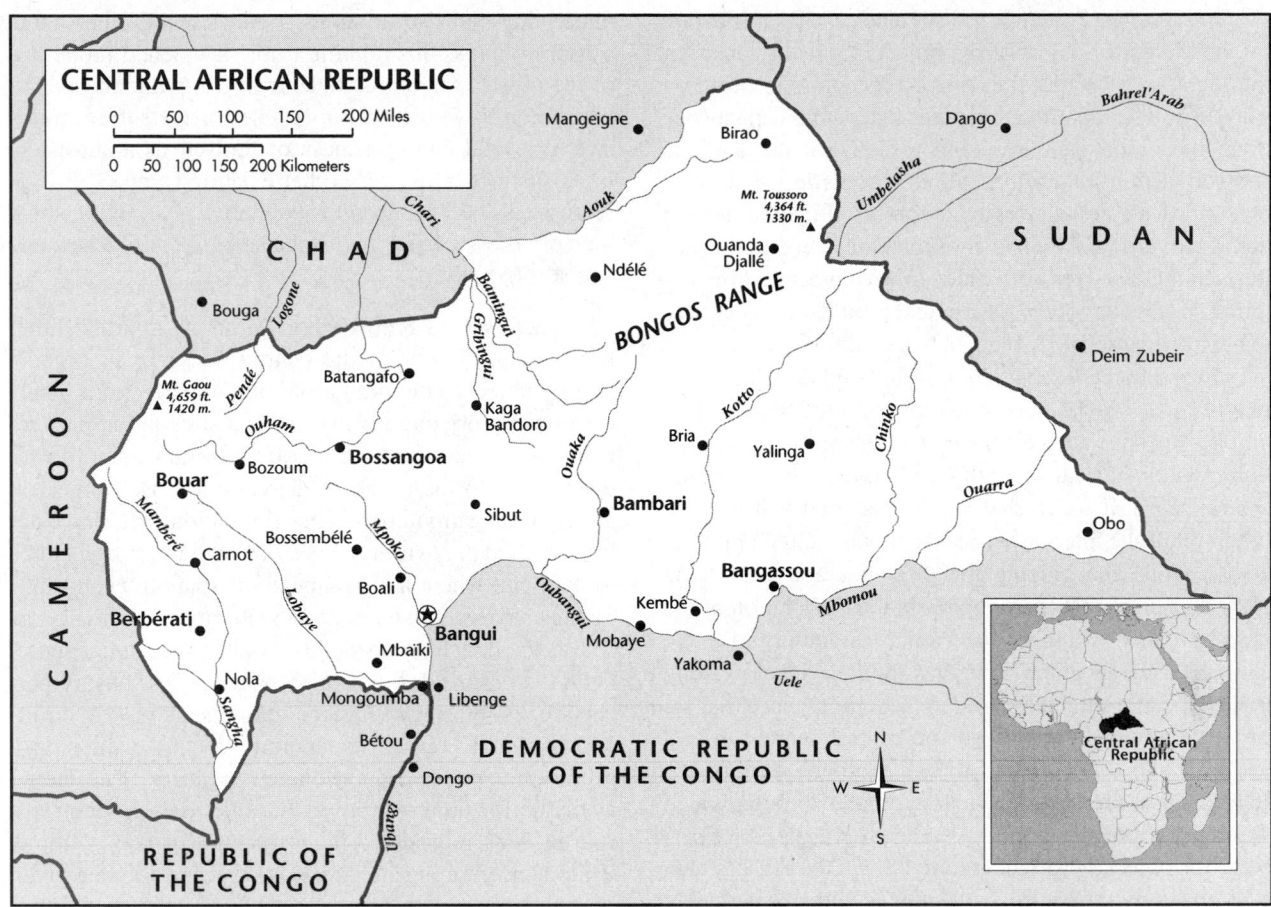

CENTRAL AFRICAN REPUBLIC

edge—an impossible dissociation at the level of organic operative powers. Therefore these two kinds of operations—discerning among the sensible objects of the various senses and being conscious of sensation—require an organic cognitive power superior to the external senses, common to all, and central as regards their specific operation. This is the central sense.

Operation and Functions. The roles of the central sense in elaborating sense knowledge can best be discussed in terms of its various functions in sensation, in perception, and in consciousness.

Sensation. SENSATION here is understood as knowledge of the action exerted upon sensory receptors by a specific stimulus, whatever be the nature of the object causing the stimulation. According to St. THOMAS AQUINAS (*In lib. de sensu* 19.282–296) the central sense, as a superior power, uses the external senses as instruments to know sensible things. For it is from the central sense, as from a common source, that the power to sense (*vis sentiendi*) diffuses itself into the external senses. This explains why the stimulations of all the senses converge and terminate at the central sense (*In 3 de anim.* 3.599–613). Therefore no expressed species is needed in the *sensus*

communis (*see* SPECIES, INTENTIONAL). The central sense collects the data of the various external senses in a global way. From this comes its aptitude for comparing the stimulations of the various senses, for grouping and synthesizing these, as well as for distinguishing and dissociating them.

To explain how the central sense operates in the distinction and synthesis of sensation, St. Thomas takes a rather obscure Aristotelian comparison and likens the central sense to a point toward which various lines converge (*In 3 de anim.* 3.599–613, 12.773). Just as the point can be considered indivisible in itself, or as multiple as the terminus of various lines, so it is with the central sense. To the extent that it integrates explicitly and actually the activity of each of the external senses, giving it special attention, the central sense can discern the likenesses and differences among sensations and among objects of the various external senses. To the extent that it operates at its own level, which surpasses that of the external senses (*De ver.* 15.1 ad 3; *Summa Theologiae* 1a, 57.2), it can synthesize the objects of the various senses and reconstitute the unity of the stimuli affecting the knowing subject.

Perception. Perception designates the identification by the knowing subject of the object that is the source of the stimulus affecting the sensory receptors to bring on sensation. The identification takes place with dependence upon the global cognitive and affective context of the subject, within which it acquires a specific meaning. It presupposes a holistic organization of all qualitative and quantitative data supplied by sensation. Perception thus implies the discovery of values in the object that the external senses cannot recognize, and permits the establishing of a functional contact between the object and the knowing subject. Given this unifying and discriminating function, the central sense plays an important role in elaborating the knowledge that makes perception possible. Some scholastics attribute this elaboration entirely to the central sense. It seems that St. Thomas makes it the task rather of all the internal senses (without excluding INTEL-LECT), while recognizing the preponderant role of the COGITATIVE POWER (particularly in the elaboration of the *experimentum,* with the concurrence of memory). For the cogitative power alone perceives the individual existing in its ineffable singularity and detects in it values that escape the external senses and the central sense (*In 2 de anim.* 13.396–398). Thanks to its organizing activity, the central sense prepares the sensory matter through which the superior powers (cogitative, then intellect) better perceive the object's profound reality. Since the sensory data centralized by the *sensus communis* in some way already reveal, as impressions produced by the accidents of the object, the nature of that object, there can be no doubt of the importance of this first organization of knowledge effected by the central sense.

Consciousness. The central sense initiates the conscious awareness of the whole object and begins perceiving the distinction existing between subject and object. This awareness, however, remains as frail and as limited as the sensation upon which it is based. In fact, the central sense grasps in sensible objects only the forms of energy (qualities affected with a certain quantity) that stimulate the sensory receptors, without perceiving the singular existent being as such, for this is the proper object of the cogitative power. It follows that the distinction recognized by the central sense between sensations and their specific content is again found at the accidental level, qualitatively and quantitatively, without reaching the level of the concrete substance, which is perceived only by the cogitative power. This occurs whether the substantial reality of the object or that of the subject, the ego, is concerned. The contribution of the central sense to the total consciousness of the subject is thus constituted by the perception of the distinction between, on the one hand, the continuing flux of sensations (as activities following each other, without implying the grasping of an underlying, subsisting subject) and, on the other hand, sensory impressions relating to the accidental properties of the objects affecting the senses. But without this first distinction, it would be impossible for the subject to arrive at a total consciousness of himself as a subsistent being distinct from every other existing being. This consciousness is deepened at the cogitative level (with which memory is associated) and at the level of intelligence. (*See* CONSCIOUSNESS.)

Unconscious Knowledge. Although a partial function of consciousness, the central sense is an organic power subject to the limitations and imperfections inherent in every organic faculty. Thus a stimulation may remain below the threshold required to transmit sufficient disturbance to the organ of the central sense to make it aware of the stimulation. The stimulation will, however, have excited the external sense in which it leaves its trace to the point where a subsequent stimulation, even subliminal, may reactivate it, and, by summation, finally arrive at the threshold needed to awaken the central sense. On the other hand, the energy available for sensory perception, as for every vital operation, is necessarily limited; thus an increased expenditure of this energy on a given perception proportionately reduces the energy available for other purposes that play only a secondary role in consciousness (cf. *De ver.* 13.3). For example, while concentrating its attention on the work of a given sensation, the central sense is not able to give equal attention to another sensation. The latter escapes its vigilance, even though it is perceived confusedly. It may, in its turn, emerge at the level of consciousness if it becomes the object of special attention. Consequently, even though in principle the central sense can perceive all sensations, the beam of its clear and distinct attention cannot be simultaneously applied with equal effectiveness to all sensations. A goodly number thus remain at the edge of conscious perception. Further research on the organic structure of the central sense is needed before the phenomenon of unconscious sensations can be more fully explained.

Role in Sleep. To the degree that it implies a loss of consciousness, sleep requires a corresponding inhibition of the central sense and of all the senses whose thresholds increase as a result. If a sensory stimulation is strong enough, it can go beyond the threshold of sensation without reaching consciousness as a sensation, because the central sense is bound in sleep and does not perform its proper functions. Such a stimulation is eventually integrated in disguised fashion within some oneiric content of the imagination. Reducing the inhibition of sensitiveness can bring a corresponding freedom to the central sense. This allows the subject a certain discrimination between dream images and sensations brought on by stimuli coming from extrasubjective reality. However, as long as some inhibition persists, perception from the central sense remains proportionately handicapped. The subject still confuses dreams and reality, not clearly distinguishing between reality and its representation in the IMAGINATION (*Summa Theologiae* 1a, 84.8 ad 2).

See Also: SENSE KNOWLEDGE; KNOWLEDGE, PROCESS OF.

Bibliography: M. STOCK, "Sense Consciousness according to St. Thomas," *Thomist* 21 (1958) 415–486. B. J. MULLER-THYM, "Common Sense, Perfection of the Order of Pure Sensibility," *Thomist* 2 (1940) 315–343. E. J. RYAN, *The Role of the "Sensus Communis" in the Psychology of St. Thomas* (Carthagena, Ohio 1951). M. DE CORTE, "Notes exégétiques sur la théorie aristotélicienne du 'Sensus communis'," *New Scholasticism* 6 (1932) 187–214. E. BARBADO, "La conciencia sensitiva según S. Tomàs," *Ciencia tomista* 30 (1924) 169–203.

[A. M. PERREAULT]

CENTURIATORS OF MAGDEBURG

The *Centuries,* 16th-century Lutheran account of Church history, were conceived by Matthias FLACIUS ILLYRICUS, a devout and strict follower of Martin Luther. The work was begun in 1559 and completed in 1574. It was originally published under the title *Ecclesiastica historia . . . ,* but the third edition printed at Nürnberg in 1757 entitled the work *Centuriae Magdeburgenses,* and it has been known by that title ever since. Flacius was aided by a number of prominent Protestants, among whom were Aleman, Wigand, Judex, and Copus. This group conceived their project to be a treatment of Church history that would prove the veracity of the Lutheran Church and disprove the theological claims of Rome. As a result the *Centuries* are passionate Lutheran polemics. The work consists of 13 volumes, each representing a century of ecclesiastical history. Flacius rejected the humanistic view of history as an all encompassing study of the phenomena of man and concentrated upon Church affairs. In the Augustinian manner, the *Centuries* view history as the eternal struggle between the forces of good and evil, of God and the devil. History is consequently the story of God's will.

A central theme runs throughout the work: the pure, pristine doctrines of Apostolic Christianity have been perverted by the Romanists, while the Lutherans have rediscovered the true doctrines of God. Many critical and uncomplimentary anecdotes are used to undermine Catholic doctrine and worship. As an example, the legend of Pope Joan is accepted as historically accurate. The papacy consistently appears as the anti-Christ, which has diverted God's teachings.

The role of the *Centuries* in historiography in general, and in Reformation historiography in particular, is

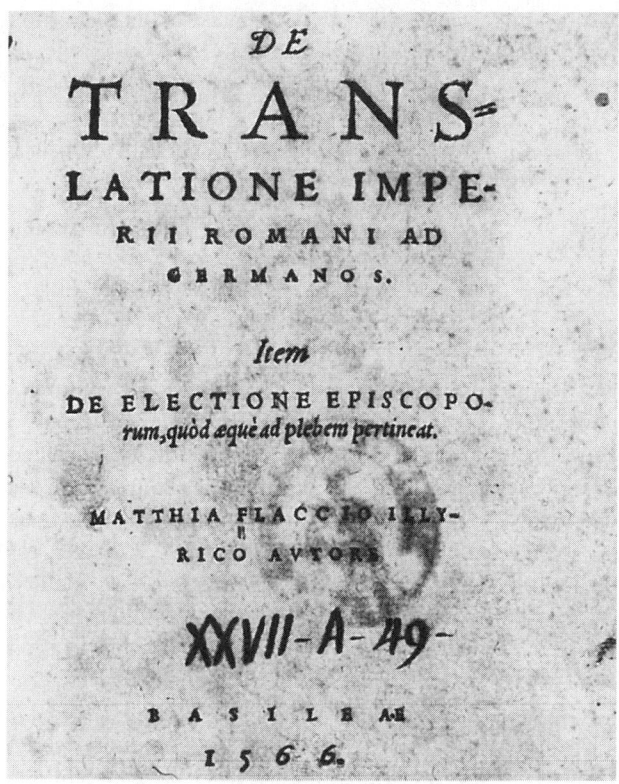

Frontpiece page from Ecclesiastica historia, Vol. 9, 1566, printed in Basel, written by Matthias Flacius Illyricus.

most important. The *Centuries,* with their obvious Lutheran tone, passed into the stream of ecclesiastical literature many legends that persist to the present day. The uncritical use of spurious sources beclouded the true sources of Church history. Many miracles, at least those that proved Flacius's thesis, were presented as historically verified. Historical writing became a tool that could be utilized for partisan causes and for a prolonged mechanical and chronological study of facts. However, the very purpose of the work was indirectly to aid the cause of sound ecclesiastical scholarship. Flacius's attack upon the sources and documents of the Catholic Church forced her to return to the very same sources and documents to verify her position. The Catholic historians were required to use profane history in their own defense. Thus ecclesiastical history became historically minded. Research, always the most valuable method in any intellectual confrontation, assumed new proportions and importance.

Each century was assigned a volume divided into 16 basic titles and subjects under such headings as rites, Church doctrine, schisms, heresies, and political changes—all of which had taken place within that century. Thirteen volumes were printed by 1574; the three remaining volumes appeared in MS but were never published. The most effective Catholic response to the

Centuriators was written by Cardinal Caesar BARONIUS in his famous *Annales Ecclesiastici* (1588–1607).

Bibliography: W. PREGER, *Matthias Flacius Illyricus und seine Zeit,* 2 v. (Erlangen 1859–61). R. BÄUMER, *Lexikon für Theologie und Kirche,* ed. J. HOFER and K. RAHNER, 10 v. (2d, new ed. Freiburg 1957–65) 6:1274.

[C. L. HOHL, JR.]

CENTURION

Roman military officer in command of a "century," nominally 100 foot soldiers; ten centuries constituted a cohort; and 60, a legion. The centurion's duties consisted in training, inspecting, and disciplining the troops in his charge (cf. Mt 8.9) and leading them in battle. At times he was the highest-ranking official in a particular area, especially in the provinces. The NT mentions five centurions. Three remain unnamed: one at Capharnaum (Mt 8.5–1.3; Lk 7.2–10), one in charge of Jesus' execution (Mt 27.54; Mk 15.39, 45; Lk 23.47), and another in Jerusalem at the time of Paul's arrest (Acts 22.25–26; 23.17, 23). The names of the other two are Cornelius, whom Peter received into the Church (Acts 10.1), and Julius, who brought Paul safely to Rome (Acts 27.1, 11, 43).

Bibliography: *Encyclopedic Dictionary of the Bible,* tr. and adap. by L. HARTMAN (New York 1963), from A. VAN DEN BORN, *Bijbels Woordenboek,* 338–339. F. D. GEALY, G. A. BUTTRICK, ed., *The Interpreters' Dictionary of the Bible,* 4 v. (Nashville 1962) 1:547–548. J. HASTINGS and J. A. SELBIA, eds., *Dictionary of the Bible,* 5 v. (Edinburgh 1942–50) 1:366–367.

[R. MERCURIO]

CENTURIONE BRACELLI, VIRGINIA, BL.

Foundress of the Brignoline Sisters; b. Genoa, Italy, April 2, 1587; d. Genoa, Dec. 15, 1651. At age 15, Virginia complied with the wish of her father, the doge of Genoa, and married Gasparo Grimaldi Bracelli. She was left a widow with two daughters when she was 20 years old. During a famine she opened her palace, which she called *Santa Maria del Refugio dei Tribolati,* to abandoned children and those in distress. In 1619, the women who worked with her in the apostolate bound themselves by a solemn promise of perseverance to a common life under the Franciscan Rule. The Daughters of Our Lady of Mount Calvary, known as the Brignoline Sisters, opened their second house (1641) through the munificence of the Marquess Emmanuele Brignole and soon spread throughout northern Italy. The sisters were invited to Rome in 1815 and moved the motherhouse to the Es-

quiline Hill near St. Norbert's Church in 1833. In addition to founding the Brignolines, Mother Virginia organized a group to maintain Genoa's *Madonnette,* about 900 sacred images of the Virgin Mary recessed into the outer walls of guild halls and houses throughout the city. She was beatified at Genoa by John Paul II, Sept. 22, 1985.

Feast: Dec. 15.

Bibliography: R. MAGAGLIO, *Una patrizia genovese antesignana della moderna assistenza sociale: cenni biografici sulla serva di Dio Virginia Centurione Bracelli (1587–1651) nel centenario della sua traslazione dal Convento di Brignole alla Chiesa del conservatorio di Marassi (1872–1972)* (Genoa 1972). *Acta Apostolicae Sedis* (1986): 968–971. *L'Osservatore Romano,* Eng. ed. 40 (1985): 5,8.

[K. I. RABENSTEIN]

CEOLFRID OF WEARMOUTH, ST.

Benedictine abbot; b. *c.* 642; d. Langres, France, Sept. 25, 716. Born of a noble family, he entered the monastery of Gilling at the age of 18 but in 664 moved to Ripon, where the BENEDICTINE RULE had been introduced under WILFRID OF YORK. Benedict Biscop brought him to Wearmouth as prior in 674, and together they traveled to Rome (678–680) to obtain books, pictures, architects, stonemasons, and glassmakers for England. They also brought John, archchanter of St. Peter's, from Rome to teach and write music at Wearmouth. When Benedict founded the abbey at Jarrow in 681, Ceolfrid, together with Easterwine (d. 686), was made deputy abbot under the founder. The dedication stone from this monastery, dating from 685, is the oldest written record in Northumbria. The twin foundation of Wearmouth-Jarrow was very rich and had one of the best schools and libraries in England. The *Codex Amiatinus,* the oldest and best Vulgate Bible extant, may have been made at Wearmouth-Jarrow *c.* 700, and Ceolfrid, taking it to Rome as a gift, died on his journey through France. His relics were translated to Wearmouth-Jarrow and later to Glastonbury. Ceolfrid's influence was especially important in the Romanization of the Celtic Church and in the cultural renaissance of Europe in the eighth century. The two chief vitae of the saint are an anonymous *Vita abbatum* (tr. Douglas S. Boutflower, Sunderland 1912) and the *Vita beatorum abbatum* of BEDE.

Feast: Sept. 25.

Bibliography: *Acta Sanctorum* Sept. 7:113–126. BEDE, *Historia Ecclesiastica* 2:79–103, 325–361, 375–389. P. H. BLAIR, *An Introduction to Anglo-Saxon England* (Cambridge, Eng. 1959). *Bibliotheca sanctorum* 3:1126–27. I. N. WOOD, *The Most Holy Abbot Ceolfrid* (Jarrow, Durham 1995). A. BUTLER, *The Lives of the*

Saints, ed. H. THURSTON and D. ATTWATER (New York 1956) 3:635–637.

[H. E. AIKINS]

CEPEDA, FRANCISCO

Dominican missionary and grammarian; b. Spain, 1532; d. Guatemala, 1602. He entered the Dominicans in the Convent of Santo Domingo de Murcia of the province of Andalucía. He went to America and to Chiapas, Guatemala, before 1560 and worked as a missionary. He became prior of the Zacapula convent and was a definitor at the provincial chapters of 1580, 1587, 1591, and 1602. He also served as commissary of the Holy Office. On May 16, 1593, he was elected provincial. He is best known as a grammarian. From the writings of his Dominican comissionaries he composed a uniform simplified grammar of various native languages in the area, *Artes de las lenguas de Chiapa, Zoques, Cendales (Celdales), y Cinacantecas.*

Bibliography: A. DE REMESAL, *Historia general de las Indias occidentales y particular de la gobernación de Chiapa y Guatemala*, 2 v. (2d ed. Guatemala City 1932). F. XIMÉNEZ, *Historia de la provincia de San Vicente de Chiapa y Guatemala de la Orden de predicadores*, 3 v. (Guatemala City 1929–31).

[A. B. NIESER]

CERBONIUS, ST.

Bishop of Populonia (Piombino, Tuscany, Italy); d. island of Elba, late sixth century. When in the sixth century the Vandals drove the bishops out of Africa, Cerbonius went with St. Regulus (d. 542) to Tuscany and was made bishop of Populonia, where he lived a communal life with his clergy. Totila (d. 552), king of the Ostrogoths, ordered Cerbonius exposed to a bear in punishment for sheltering Roman soldiers, but when the bear did not attack, the bishop was freed. Because of this legend he is often pictured in art with a bear. The Lombards exiled him on Elba, where he died 30 years later. His body was buried at Populonia. He is the patron of Massa Marittima, the diocese into which his see was later incorporated. A later and even more legendary life asserts that he was denounced and summoned by Pope VIGILIUS for celebrating Mass too early on Sunday, but the marvels attending his trip to Rome moved the pope to meet him on the road and send him back to Populonia with honor.

Feast: Oct. 10.

Bibliography: *Acta Sanctorum* Oct. 5:87–102. A. BUTLER, *The Lives of the Saints*, ed. H. THURSTON and D. ATTWATER (New York 1956) 4:80. GREGORY I (the Great), *Dialogus* 3.11.

[B. CAVANAUGH]

CEREMONIAL OF BISHOPS

The Ceremonial of Bishops, or *Caeremoniale Episcoporum* was a logical outcome of the ordinal–pontifical evolution as a ceremonial for bishops. The first edition, promulgated by Clement VIII, July 14, 1600, was not an innovation. Such a ceremonial guide found its immediate sources in the compilations of the masters of ceremonies of the papal household. Several of their works have been edited, notably ordinal 14 of Mabillon, compiled by Cardinal Stefaneschi. Such papal custom books eventually end in the *Caeremoniale Romanum* prepared by Patrizzi in 1488, edited in 1516 by Marcellus, and reedited with a famous commentary by Catalani in 1750. Paris de Grassi, master of ceremonies in Bologna and Rome, edited a book in 1564 intended for bishops in their own sees, but only after vehemently opposing others who earlier had made papal ceremonies available to bishops. A revised edition of the Ceremonial of Bishops was promulgated in 1984 (U.S. edition, 1989) and supersedes all previous editions.

Bibliography: J. NABUCO, "La Liturgie papale et les origines du Cérémoniel des évêques," *Miscellanea Liturgica in Honorem L. Cuniberti Mohlberg* (Rome 1948) 1:283–300; *Ius pontificalium: Introductio in caeremoniale episcoporum* (Tournai 1956). A. TEGELS, "Caeremoniale episcoporum," *Worship* 59 (1985) 528–532.

[R. T. CALLAHAN/EDS.]

CEREMONIES, CONGREGATION OF

Known since 1967 as the Prefecture of the Papal Household, the Congregation of Ceremonies was traditionally responsible for the direction of the liturgical and diplomatic ceremonial of the papal court.

The existence of this congregation dates back at least to the early years of the 17th century. Concerning its history prior to that time, there is some disagreement. Most authors hold that the congregation had its origin in the Sacred Congregation of Rites and Ceremonies founded by Sixtus V in his constitution *Immensa dei* of 1588. Subsequently, either by another decree of Sixtus V or through a gradual evolution, the Congregation of Ceremonies broke off from the parent congregation and assumed a separate existence. Another theory places the beginnings of the congregation in a cardinalatial commission formed by Gregory XIII in 1572 to reform the ceremonies of the papal chapel. This commission was absorbed by the new Congregation of Rites and Ceremonies established by Sixtus V, and then later once again resumed its independent status.

Historically, the congregation was responsible for the regulation of the protocol, formalities and ceremonies that were observed in the papal chapel and court. It regulated the dress and insignia of cardinals, bishops, prelates, and members of the papal court and household. It also organized public and private papal audiences, and handled questions of diplomatic etiquette and protocol. Chief among its diplomatic duties was the organization and direction of the solemn reception by the pope of heads of state, prime ministers, and ambassadors.

By decree dated Aug. 15, 1967, Pope Paul VI reorganized the congregation and gave it a new name: the Prefecture of the Papal Household. Following a subsequent restructuring of March 28, 1968, the Prefecture is now responsible for managing the papal chapel, organizing private and public papal audiences, overseeing and preparing non-liturgical elements of papal ceremonies, coordinating itineraries and other arrangements for papal visits and trips throughout the world, and determining protocol regarding papal audiences, state visits and presentation of diplomatic credentials.

Bibliography: M. LALMANT, *Dictionnaire de droit canonique*, ed. R. NAZ, 7 v. (Paris 1935–65) 3:258–60. N. DEL RE, *La Curia Romana* (2d ed. Rome 1952). P. C. VAN LIERDE, *The Holy See at Work*, tr. J. TUCEK (New York 1962). J. ABBO and J. HANNAN, *The Sacred Canons*, 2 v. (2d ed. St. Louis 1960) 1:254.

[R. J. BANKS/EDS.]

CERFAUX, LUCIEN

New Testament scholar; b. Presles, Belgium, June 14, 1883; d. Lourdes, France, Aug. 11, 1968. Before matriculating at the Belgian College in Rome, Cerfaux studied at the minor seminary of Good Hope in the diocese of Tournai. He received a Ph.D. and an S.T.D. from the Gregorian University (1903–10) and studied for one year in the Pontifical Biblical Institute (1910–11). He served as professor of Sacred Scripture in the seminary of Tournai for the next 20 years (1911–30), a period enriched by his friendship with the Dominican Antoine Lemonnyer and with Léonce de Grandmaison, S.J. He was named a part-time instructor at the Catholic University of Louvain in 1928 and was appointed to the chair of New Testament studies at the university in 1930. Among his disciples were Joseph Thomas, Jacques Dupont, Archbishop Maxime Hermaniuk, and Bishop Albert Descamps, the secretary of the Pontifical Biblical Commission. Cerfaux was named to the Biblical Commission in 1941 and served as a *peritus* for the Second Vatican Council. He founded *Studia Hellenistica* and served on the editorial board of several other journals, including the *Ephemerides theologicae Lovanienses,* of which he was coeditor until his death. He cofounded (1949) the Colloquium Biblicum Lovaniense and served as its first president.

Cerfaux's scholarly activity falls into two periods. In his first period, Cerfaux was principally interested in the New Testament environment. He devoted his time and writing to Gnosticism, the mystery religions, Alexandrine Judaism, and the Apostolic Fathers. After 1936, his main interest was New Testament exegesis. This period is marked by the appearance of his Pauline trilogy: *The Church in the Theology of St. Paul* (1942), *Christ in the Theology of St. Paul* (1951), and *The Christian in the Theology of St. Paul* (1962). Cerfaux's interest in the Synoptics resulted in several books and many articles, as well as in the posthumous publication of *Jésus aux origines de la tradition.*

Bibliography: J. DUCULOT, ed., *Recueil Lucien Cerfaux,* 3 v. (Gembloux 1954–62). F. NEIRYNCK, ed., "Bibliographie Lucien Cerfaux," *L'Évangile de Luc: Biblioteca Ephemeridum Theologicarum Lovaniensium* 32, ed. J. DUCULOT (Gembloux 1973) 71–90. A. DESCAMPS, "La carrière scientifique de Monseigneur Cerfaux," *Ephemerides theoligicae Lovanienses* 30 (1954) 683–696; "Monseigneur Lucien Cerfaux: Ébauche d'un portrait," *L'évangile de Luc* 9–21. J. COPPENS, "La carrière et l'oeuvre scientifique de Mgr. Cerfaux," *L'évangile de Luc* 23–59.

[R. F. COLLINS]

CERIOLI, COSTANZA, BL.

Religious foundress; b. Soncino (Cremona), Italy, Jan. 28, 1816; d. Comonte di Seriate (Bergamo), Dec. 24, 1865. She was the daughter of the wealthy Count Francesco Cerioli. After attending the school run by the Visitandines in Bergamo (1826–32), she married the sexagenarian Gaetano Buzzechi Tassis, a noble and wealthy widower (1835). The disparity in age and spiritual outlook between wife and husband, the latter's ill health, and the premature deaths of their three children, only one of whom reached adolescence, were trials that Costanza bore patiently. After Gaetano's death (1854), his widow dedicated her wealth and energies to works of charity. She began caring for rural orphan girls in her home and kept increasing the number of persons who supervised their formation as the number of children grew. In 1857 she founded the Sisters of the Holy Family of Bergamo to carry on this work and took Paola Elisabetta as her name in religion. To care for orphaned boys she founded, with the help of Giovanni Capponi, the Brothers of the Holy Family. Costanza wrote the rules for both congregations, which were approved by the Holy See. She was beatified March 19, 1950.

Feast: Dec. 24.

Bibliography: E. FEDERICI, *Suor Paola Elisabetta Cerioli, Vedova Buzecchi-Tassis* (Comonte di Seriate 1948). A. BUTLER, *The Lives of the Saints,* ed. H. THURSTON and D. ATTWATER (New York 1956) 4:606–607.

[V. A. LAPOMARDA]

CERQUEIRA, LUÍS DE

Bishop of Japan; b. Vila de Alvito, Portugal, 1551 or 1552; d. Nagasaki, Feb. 16, 1614. On July 14, 1566, he entered the Jesuit novitiate in Evora, where he studied philosophy and theology. About the end of 1575 he was attached to the secretariate of the Jesuit general curia in Rome. There he worked until early 1577. From 1585 to 1586 he was professor of theology in Coimbra; from 1586 to 1589, socius of the Portuguese provincial; and thereafter, again professor of theology. While teaching theology in Evora, he learned, in January of 1592, of his appointment as coadjutor to the bishop of Japan. The papal bulls did not arrive until early 1594, and in the meantime he took his doctorate in theology at Evora (November 1593). Finally, on March 30, 1594, he set out for Asia. On Sept. 22, 1594, he arrived in Goa, whence he proceeded on April 21, 1595, to Macau, arriving Aug. 7. He became bishop of Japan in February of 1598 upon the death of Bishop Pedro Martins just before the latter reached Malacca on a journey from Macau to India. Despite the threatening situation in Japan, Cerqueira risked sailing for Japan on July 16, 1598, in company with the visitator Alessandro VALIGNANO; they landed on Aug. 5, 1598. On that same day Toyotomi Hideyoshi, the military dictator of Japan who issued an edict against Jesuits, was stricken with a fatal illness and died in September. Cerqueira remained in Japan, mainly in Nagasaki, until his death.

Cerqueira was a gentle and zealous pastor whose practical capacities had been sharpened by his work in the Jesuit general curia and as socius of the provincial. He was prudent and energetic and managed to maintain a dignified independence even vis-à-vis such a commanding personality as his fellow worker and visitator Valignano. Cerqueira's impressive conscientiousness made him insist energetically on the observance of the directives in papal communications, even in cases in which the effort was made (for example, by the Franciscans from the Philippines) to present him with a *fait accompli.* He also gave proof of remarkable diplomatic talent in his dealings with the Japanese princes. A deeply religious man, he sought zealously to intensify religious life in Japan.

At the very beginning of his reign, he created, at a meeting in October of 1598, the legislative basis for his activity. He opened the first seminary for Japanese candidates for the secular priesthood and installed the first Japanese pastors in Nagasaki. Cerqueira undertook a series of apostolic journeys; in 1606 he paid an unofficial visit to the former Shōgun, Tokugawa Iyeyasu, in Fushimi (near Kyōto); at this time he became personally acquainted with the Christian communities in central Japan. Cerqueira's term coincides with the flowering of the early Japanese Church; there were many conversions, including those of influential feudal lords. There were also local persecutions (Ōmura, 1606; Arima, 1612). In 1612 there began the great persecution that was to lead to the decline and fall of the Japanese Church. Cerqueira was dead before the definitive expulsion of the missionaries (November 1614).

Cerqueira as professor wrote various treatises (*De legibus, De gratia,* preserved in manuscript), and as bishop he wrote extensive reports on the state of the Japanese Church, memoranda and apologia for Pope and King, a report on the martyrs of Higo (1603). In 1605 there appeared in Nagasaki his work *Manuale ad Sacramenta Ecclesiae ministranda,* with a Japanese appendix.

Bibliography: H. CIESLIK, "Zur Geschichte der kirchlichen Hierarchie in der alten Japanmission," *Neue Zeitschrift für Missionswissenschaft,* 18 (1962) 42–58, 81–107, 177–195. J. F. SCHÜTTE, "A história inédita dos 'Bispos da Igreja do Japão' do Pe. João Rodriguez Tçuzu, S.J.," *Congresso Internacional de História dos Descobrimentos, Actas,* 5.1 (Lisbon 1961) 297–327. C. SOMMERVOGEL et al., *Bibliothèque de la Compagnie de Jésus,* 11 v. (Brussels–Paris 1890–1932) 2:1000–02; 9:23. A. FRANCO, *Imagem da virtude (Noviciado de Evora)* (Lisbon 1714) 461–477.

[J. F. SCHÜTTE]

CERTITUDE

The term certitude derives from the Latin, *cernere* (Gr. κρίανειν), which means to resolve, decide after seeing the evidence. St. Thomas Aquinas defines certitude as "the firmness of the adherence of a knowing power to the thing known" (*In 3 sent.* 26.2.4). Primarily a quality of the JUDGMENT, certitude can be considered positively to indicate the firmness of the mind in its assent and negatively, the exclusion of all prudent fear of ERROR. It is distinguished from other states of mind such as DOUBT, which is an inability either to affirm or deny; and OPINION, which is the acceptance of a judgment as probable. Since the INTELLECT is made for knowing TRUTH, and its perfect actuation is had only when the truth is known with evidence, formal certitude is had when what is known presents itself as objectively evident.

Historical Development

Among the early Greek philosophers the question of certitude was not formally considered, although the reasonings of the early cosmologists implied the view that ordinary certitudes were not reliable. With the rise of the SOPHISTS there developed an explicit questioning of the ability of the human mind to arrive at true and certain knowledge. For some, such as HERACLITUS, Protagoras and Gorgias, reality was in such flux that it could never be known as it is.

CLASSICAL GREEKS AND MEDIEVALS

Against these, SOCRATES and PLATO contended the possibility of the human mind's arriving at true certitudes. While Plato fostered a skepticism relative to sense perception, he claimed certitude to be attainable in the intelligible sphere, where knowledge is had of Ideas or Ideal Forms. These are the ultimate realities and the only objects of knowledge in the strict sense. For ARISTOTLE first principles are self-evidently certain and hence indemonstrable. He held that sensible beings can be known by virtue of the FORM (the inner principle of determination) and that all the materials of intellectual knowledge are somehow derived from and through the senses.

After Aristotle, speculative philosophy made little progress. For the Epicureans the one thing necessary was pleasure, in the sense of a lack of perturbation ('αταραξία); and truth, virtue and all else are of value only insofar as they promote this. The Stoics implied that (subjective) certitude is attainable, especially in the knowledge of what constitutes an ethically good and wise life. Against the alleged certitude of this position the Skeptics reacted and for about five hundred years (c. 300 B.C.–A.D. 200) SKEPTICISM exercised great influence in Greek and Roman thought.

St. Augustine's *Contra academicos* is a refutation of the skeptical positions of the New Academy; and in general the Church Fathers and the scholastics through the Middle Ages discouraged skepticism and affirmed the ability of the mind to know with certitude. They distinguished between what the mind knows by the natural light of reason and what it accepts on testimony and between intrinsic and extrinsic evidence; the latter being important for Divine Revelation (confer St. Augustine, *C. acad.* 2.7; St. Thomas, *In 3 sent.* 26.2.4; ST 2a2ae, 2.1.) In the NOMINALISM of WILLIAM OF OCKHAM, however, skepticism did find some expression.

MODERN PHILOSOPHERS

From its beginning, modern philosophy was characterized by the firm conviction that if the true object of the mind is philosophically determined, or if its proper limits are faithfully respected, man is capable of certitude. One may be asked to admit that the object of reliable knowledge is the unique divine substance (SPINOZA), or the Absolute Spirit in itself and in its self-manifestations (HEGEL); true knowledge may be limited to ideas and their interrelation (British EMPIRICISM), or to sense presentations as informed by the categories of the understanding (KANT); but with these qualifications settled, the outstanding thinkers are convinced that truth and certitude are attainable.

Thus, DESCARTES, facing the anti-intellectualism of the Renaissance and the atheism and skepticism of his day, sought to find a new and firm foundation for certitude in metaphysics. Beginning with the self and using the technique of doubt, he was convinced that his reflections finally overcame doubt, gave him true knowledge of his own existence, of God and of the external world. RATIONALISM glorified the power of the mind to know and to build systems, but it has been accused of vastly exaggerating man's capacity for certain knowledge. While the empiricists limited the immediate objects of human knowledge to ideas or impressions, they (apart from David HUME) were convinced that in this narrow area certitude was to be had. Kant, impressed by the success of the physical sciences, decided that only scientific truth and certitude were reliable; hence metaphysics, which deals with "questions such as cannot be answered by any empirical employment of reason, or by principles thence derived," is not available with the certitude of evidence (*Critique of Pure Reason,* Introd. A3; B6). So questions on the nature of the soul, of the world and of God lead only to illusion.

SCHOLASTIC AND CONTEMPORARY THOUGHT

As a result of the works of modern philosophies, scholastic philosophers have devoted much time to questions of truth and certitude. In the 19th century many of them, influenced by the thought of J. BALMES, held that man naturally possesses some absolutely certain truths that need no justification whatsoever. Later, Cardinal Désiré MERCIER and others taught that man's many spontaneous certitudes need further philosophical reflection in order to establish the human capacity for truth and to arrive at reflex certitudes. Others admit some naturally known certitudes, and since these are known implicitly in each judgment, one needs merely to become explicitly aware of them.

Leaving SCHOLASTICISM aside, one can say that the contemporary philosophical scene is very complex, but that one of its outstanding features is an antimetaphysical attitude that becomes an outright skepticism for many. This is due in no small measure to the skepticism of Hume, who paved the way for most of contemporary empirical philosophy and for the antimetaphysical views of POSITIVISM, PHENOMENALISM and pragmatism. Developments in scientific method and studies in the nature of language and logic have contributed much to the skeptical mood of LOGICAL positivism and LINGUISTIC analysis. When there is admission of truth, it is often with a relativistic twist, in terms of scientific VERIFICATION, utility (personal or public) or adaptation to an evolving environment.

Kinds Of Certitude

That there may be intellectual convictions or firm assents of the mind of various kinds, can be seen by brief reflection. One may be certain that Julius Caesar was stabbed to death; that the human soul is immortal; that another person loves him; that God exists; and that he himself exists. In all these areas certitude may be claimed and yet it is obvious how different are the assents, for example, to one's own existence and to Caesar's murder. Moreover, whether because of prejudice or training, men do at times assent to a false doctrine or position with a dedication worthy only of the truth. Hence it has become usual and necessary to distinguish various kinds of certitude.

SUBJECTIVE VS. OBJECTIVE

Since certitude is primarily a characteristic of human assent, it can be said that all certitude is subjective. However, it is called purely subjective when evidence is lacking, or is not known to be present, for the firm assent then given is in reality only an affective disposition of the subject, who believes without doubt and without proper motivation that he possesses the truth. Objective certitude means a firm assent of the mind to a known truth, an assent motivated by the evidence, and wherein the known motive for assent excludes all prudent fear of error.

ABSOLUTE VS. CONDITIONAL

This division, common in scholastic manuals, is made in view of the foundation on which the certitude rests. The former is said to rest on the natures or essences of things; the latter on the connection between finite natures and their operations. Absolute (or metaphysical) certitude is had in the knowledge of self-evident truths, such as the proposition that a thing cannot simultaneously be and not be; of demonstrated conclusions, such as the spirituality of the soul; or even of the contingent fact of one's own existence. When any given truth is known with metaphysical certitude, this means that the denial of that truth would be a denial of the very nature of what is known; hence its opposite is excluded as utterly impossible. However, in the operations of finite beings, it is possible that the nature, while remaining essentially unchanged, may be impeded in the production of its natural operation or effect, and thereby a note of the conditional or hypothetical enters in. Since finite agents are divided into the two classes of (1) free—man in his deliberate acts—and (2) determined—all other material beings and even man in his nonfree operations such as growth—conditional certitude is of two kinds, physical and moral.

PHYSICAL CERTITUDE

This certitude characterizes assent to concrete applications of PHYSICAL LAWS. Such laws come to be known through INDUCTION and they tell how nonfree natures operate. Presupposing the accuracy of observation and the correct use of induction, such laws are themselves meta-

physically certain, since they reveal the natures of things. In simple examples, it is of the nature of fire to burn, of unsupported heavy bodies to fall, of hydrogen and oxygen to unite to form water. However, when it comes to the operation of these laws in concrete instances, some defect of matter or agent may impede such operation from taking place. The law is still certain conditionally, however, on condition that such defects do not occur.

Scholastic manuals usually insist here that divine cooperation is also necessary and that God can (for some special reason) suspend a physical effect without at all changing the nature of the agent (see MIRACLES). Hence, although absolute certitude is not to be had, one can and does give a firm assent without prudent fear of error in given instances. One can be certain that food will nourish him and that fire will burn a dry log. This assent is motivated by the knowledge of how the given nature operates and granting no indication of divine intervention, it provides a certitude that is called physical.

MORAL CERTITUDE

This is said to be had in some concrete applications of moral laws. The laws are arrived at by induction and they enunciate truths about how human beings freely operate. Traditional examples have to do with maternal love, the natural veracity of men and the reliability of historical testimony. Since exceptions to such "laws" can be had by the abuse of free will, it is clear that the necessity found in this area is far less rigorous than in the working of the laws of nature; so certitude here is not easily had and when had, is of a very different kind. However, presupposing knowledge of the apposite law of human conduct and knowing from the circumstances that there need be no fear of an exception, one can have moral certitude about his friend's loyalty, his wife's fidelity or a particular person's veracity.

Some philosophers have been willing to call only metaphysical certitude true certitude; and they speak of physical and especially of moral certitude as only very high probabilities. However, for others this places too stringent limitations on the nature of certitude and fails to recognize that scientific progress presupposes physical certitude and that human life and communication presuppose the reliability of moral certitude.

SPECULATIVE VS. PRACTICAL

Certitude is divided also into speculative and practical. The former is taken to refer either to what is theoretically valid or to the sphere of being in general. The latter means either a high degree of probability that is sufficient for the ordinary activity of daily living, or refers to particular judgments applying law to a specific case, to what actually ought to be done (see PRUDENCE).

NECESSARY VS. FREE

Considering the role of the will in assents, one can speak of necessary and free certitude. The former is had in response to truths so immediately evident that the intellect, having once adverted to them, cannot refuse its assent. Here the will merely directs attention to the proper consideration. Examples are: one's own existence, one's immediate experience, the principle of contradiction. However, most truths are not so immediately evident and the will usually has a more important role in the exercise of judgments. Truths such as the existence of God, of the spirituality of the soul and those deriving from human testimony may indeed be assented to firmly and securely; but they can be, and have been, doubted, and they do not force the mind's assent. These are free certitudes.

NATURAL, REFLEX AND SUPERNATURAL

Natural certitude is sometimes taken to mean the spontaneous, pre- reflective convictions of men relative to such truths as one's own existence, the existence of other beings or the need of living a morally good life; in this sense it is distinguished from reflex certitude, which is known to be based on objective evidence and which presupposes awareness of the powers and limits of the human mind. However, from the point of view of the means whereby truth is acquired, natural certitude refers to truths that are legitimately acquired by the natural powers of the human mind in the light of objective evidence; and is thus distinguished from supernatural certitude, which is had in truths that are accepted on the authority of God's revealing.

Objective Natural Certitude

Of special importance for philosophy are firm assents that are acquired by the natural operations of the human mind (hence not in virtue of revelation) and are based on the self-manifestation of what is known. Whenever this sort of certitude is had, no matter what the process through which the being that is known manifests itself in one or other intelligible aspect, it is always characterized by the note of NECESSITY. In this sense what is assented to with this sort of certitude must present itself as infallibly and necessarily true. Only in this way can the intellect be perfectly actuated in its natural drive for truth and find that satisfaction and joy that results only from the secure possession of its proper good, which is the truth.

FIRST PRINCIPLES

This sort of certitude can be had by the intellect in either its immediate or mediate assents. In the knowledge of FIRST PRINCIPLES one is dealing with truths that can be recognized and affirmed by a sort of natural instinct or INTUITION, once the meaning of the subject and predicate has been grasped. Thus, if a person knows the meaning of "whole" and of "part," he can immediately affirm the relation between them. As St. Thomas says, first principles "are not acquired by reasoning, but from the sole fact that their terms are known" (*In 4 meta.* 6.599). This holds for such truths as the principles of CONTRADICTION, of IDENTITY, of FINALITY, etc. In these cases there is a recognition of truths that are infallibly, necessarily and evidently true; whose evidence, in fact, is self-manifesting; and whose truth is so totally and so evidently present that there can be no room for doubt, hesitation or any sort of incertitude.

While these principles are grasped with supreme evidence and certitude, it must be admitted that they are vague in content and come far from satisfying man's desire for truth. St. Thomas looks on them as a sort of seed-bed (*De ver.* 18.4.) wherein truths are contained in an imperfect manner and must be brought to flower in the actual and certain knowledge of what is virtually contained in the principles. By this is meant the vast area of mediately known truths that are acquired by DEMONSTRATION.

CERTITUDE OF DEMONSTRATION

Demonstrated truths are all conclusions of science and philosophy derived from premises that are certain and evident, so that the new truths themselves are, by the process of demonstration and through the mediating function of some middle term between subject and predicate, rendered evident and certain. Unlike the evidence and certitude of first principles, the evidence and certitude of conclusions are themselves mediate and derived. Yet, even in these truths, it is the object known, that thus mediately manifests itself to the mind and specifies the intellectual act. It does reveal itself as necessarily and infallibly true and it can be justified in the light of first principles; hence this sort of scientific certitude also results in the perfect satisfaction of the mind in its quest for truth.

As St. Thomas points out, the certainty of the conclusions rests ultimately on the evidence and certitude of first principles; hence the function of demonstration is to render the evidence of the conclusion present to the intellect by showing its connection with first principles. "The whole certainty of scientific knowledge arises from the certainty of principles. For conclusions are known with certainty when they are reduced to principles. Therefore, that something is known with certainty is due to the light of reason divinely implanted within us . . ." (*De ver.* 11.1 ad 13).

Church Teaching On Certitude

In this matter the Catholic Church has consistently and officially taken a clear stand. Its expressed views are: (1) The human mind is capable of arriving at truth. (2) Of itself it is incapable of arriving at knowledge of supernatural truths concerning God and man. (3) Even with regard to some truths about God that can be naturally known, it is not easy for man to arrive at them and so it is fitting that God should come to man's aid by revealing them to him.

HUMAN CERTITUDE

While these themes can be illustrated from the whole history of Church teachings, a few brief references to the documents will suffice. On the ability of the human mind to know truth and to know it with certitude: "The reasoning process can prove with certitude the existence of God, the spirituality of the soul and the freedom of man" [H. Denzinger, *Enchiridion symbolorum*, ed. A. Schönmetzer (32d ed. Freiburg 1963) 2812; confer, 3004, 3026]. Pope Pius XII presents the abiding views of the Church in this matter when he says: "It is well known how highly the Church esteems human reason for its function to demonstrate with certainty the existence of God, personal and one; to prove beyond doubt from divine signs the foundations of the Christian faith itself; to express properly the law which the Creator has imprinted in the hearts of men; and finally to attain to some understanding, indeed a very fruitful one, of mysteries" (*Enchiridion symbolorum*, 3892). Speaking of SCHOLASTIC PHILOSOPHY he continues: "This philosophy, acknowledged and accepted by the Church, safeguards the genuine validity of human knowledge, the unshaken metaphysical principles of sufficient reason, causality and finality; in a word, the possibility of attaining certain and unchangeable truth" (*ibid.*).

SUPERNATURAL TRUTHS

However, the Church has been fully aware also of the fact that what man can learn by his own natural powers is quite limited. These limitations are found in two areas, the natural and the supernatural. With an eye to constant Church teaching, Vatican Council I clearly points out that there is an order of knowledge entirely beyond the natural powers of man, a supernatural order, wherein revelation is required if man is to learn anything at all about it: The Church has always held and holds "that there are two orders of knowledge, distinct not only in origin but also in object. They are distinct in origin, because in one we know by means of natural reason; in the other, by means of divine faith. And they are distinct in object, because in addition to what natural reason can attain, we have proposed to us as objects of belief mysteries that are hidden in God and which, unless divinely re-

vealed, can never be known" (*Enchiridion symbolorum*, 3015). This position is reinforced by a corresponding canon (*Enchiridion symbolorum*, 3041).

DIVINE REVELATION

Even in those matters pertaining to God that the human mind can learn by the natural light of reason, the same Council explicitly states that such truths have also been revealed by God so that they may "easily be known by all men with solid certitude and with no trace of error" (*Enchiridion symbolorum*, 3005).

Relative to the acceptance of the fact of revelation, the Council teaches that God provides all the means necessary for (moral) certitude in this matter. To ensure the reasonableness of our assent, "God has willed that external proofs of His revelation, namely divine acts and especially miracles and prophecies, should be added to the internal aids given by the Holy Spirit" (*Enchiridion symbolorum*, 3009). This position is reaffirmed in the corresponding canons and the possibility of knowing miracles with certitude is restated in the words: "If anyone says . . . that miracles can never be recognized with certainty . . . let him be anathema" (*Enchiridion symbolorum*, 3034).

While the certitude respecting the fact of revelation is normally moral, the certitude had in the supernatural act of faith itself, made by divine GRACE and having the authority of God Himself as its motive, is of a higher quality than any natural certitude.

Certitude And Faith

Supernatural certitude, having as its motive not the evidence of what is assented to, but the authority of God revealing and being informed by grace, has special pertinence in the matter of the virtues of faith and hope. Revelation, by providing the believer with the opportunity for a secure assent to new truths, is a source of new certitudes and of renewed security in assents to some naturally knowable truths about God's existence and nature.

In the process of passing from unbelief to belief, we can distinguish various steps and indicate briefly the role of certitude in each. The initial steps, which help to turn the person towards the acceptance of faith, concern things that are naturally known and for which natural certitude can be had. As initial steps towards faith, these natural acts are motivated by divine grace. In the process one must come to know and admit the credibility of God as witness to truth; and as this rests on the demonstrated existence and veracity of God, it is known in an evident and certain judgment. There must then follow the knowledge that God has actually revealed some particular truth; and the acceptance of this, in order to be reasonable, must rest on such proofs as will render it evident and certain to the human mind. Finally, in making the act of faith itself, one assents firmly and with certainty, to what God has revealed, motivated only by the knowledge that He has so revealed. In this assent the mind does not see or understand what it believes—the object of faith, for example, the Holy Trinity—but it recognizes with certitude that it should assent for motives that are now evident. In making the full act of assent, the will has an important role to play, since the object is not evident and therefore cannot determine the intellect.

Certitude And Hope

The supernatural virtue of HOPE is a habit whereby man confidently expects eternal happiness as well as the means necessary to arrive at it. Thus the acts of this virtue have as their object the possession and enjoyment of God by vision and love, as well as the supernatural help to attain this end; they have as their motive God's fidelity, power and mercy. In addition to this divine side, there is the human side, man's cooperation with grace and his fidelity to the will of God. Insofar as hope rests on the firm foundation of God's fidelity to His promises, it is characterized by complete certitude, since God will most certainly fulfill His promises. However, insofar as hope includes the human element of man's cooperation with, and fidelity to, grace and his final perseverance—and of these one cannot be so sure—it is always colored by some uncertainty. As St. Paul says, "work out your salvation with fear and trembling" (*Phil* 2.12) and this must be because we may fail and not because God can fail us. St. Thomas points out that "filial fear is not opposed to the virtue of hope, for thereby we do not fear that what we hope to obtain through God's help will fail us, but rather we fear that we may withdraw ourselves from that help" (ST 2a2ae, 19.9 ad 1). So hope, as an act of the will elicited under divine grace, does not have the same sort of certitude as an act of faith.

Rejection Of Certitude

Only a radical skepticism positively rejects all certitude and gives up in despair when faced with the problems of human knowledge. Still, very many schools of philosophy do, at least implicitly, reject the possibility of certitude in one area or another. Such schools have flourished not only in the ancient, but also in the modern world and are treated in detail elsewhere in the *Encyclopedia* (*see* SKEPTICISM; KNOWLEDGE, THEORIES OF).

Summarily it can be said that in many contemporary philosophies there is either a skepticism about SENSE knowledge and a consequent rejection of the noetic role of SENSATION, or a skepticism about intellectual KNOWL-EDGE and a consequent limitation of valid knowledge to the empirically verifiable. Concretely what is needed is an analysis of both knowledge and certitude that recognizes the complexity of the knowledge process. In the attainment of knowledge one finds aspects of singularity and universality, of necessity and contingency, of materiality and spirituality and of identity and diversity between knower and known. These elements are not easily harmonized in any theoretical exposition of the nature of knowledge. However, an adequate explanation must preserve all the experienced elements, even those difficult to reconcile. Because knowledge is of the universal and necessary, one cannot reject the singular and the contingent. Knowledge means an identity between knower and known; still, the diversity between them cannot be denied.

Since man is a composite unity of body and soul, of mind and matter, his cognitional situation reflects this; he is limited neither to pure sense perception nor to a purely intellectual vision entirely divorced from the senses. The human contact with experienced being occurs at various levels. One has sense knowledge of sensible beings; one also has intellectual knowledge of these same beings according to one or another aspect of their intelligible structure. With these as a foundation, one can go on to a deeper intellectual knowledge of material things and their operations, of one's own mental and volitional activities as spiritual and finally of God.

The problem of human certitude is identical with the general problem of human knowledge, with the study of its proper object and of its nature. The doubt that characterizes skepticism is self-defeating, whether as a general theory or as limited to some area of inquiry and results in despair and the abandonment of inquiry rather than a fruitful investigation and evaluation of the facts.

See Also: EPISTEMOLOGY; KNOWLEDGE; TRUTH.

Bibliography: THOMAS AQUINAS, *Truth,* tr. R. W. MULLIGAN et al., 3 v. (Chicago 1952–54). R. F. O'NEILL, *Theories of Knowledge* (Englewood Cliffs, N.J. 1960). L. M. RÉGIS, *Epistemology,* tr. I. C. BYRNE (New York 1959). I. TRETHOWAN, *Certainty, Philosophical and Theological* (Westminster, Md. 1948). W. A. WALLACE, *The Role of Demonstration in Moral Theology* (Washington 1962). *Philosophy of Knowledge,* eds. R. HOUDE and J. MULLALY (Philadelphia 1960). J. OWENS, *An Elementary Christian Metaphysics* (Milwaukee 1963). F. A. CUNNINGHAM, "*Certitudo* in St. Thomas Aquinas," *The Modern Schoolman,* 30 (1952–53) 297–324. S. HARENT, *Dictionnaire de théologie catholique,* ed. A. VACANT et al., 15 v. (Paris 1903–50) 6.1:201–215. H. DENZINGER, *Enchiridion symbolorum,* ed. A. SCHÖNMETZER (32d ed. Freiburg 1963).

[R. F. O'NEILL]

CERTITUDE OF FAITH

Unlike the motives for CERTITUDE that characterize the natural and philosophical sciences, the certitude of faith is based on the fact that a truth is revealed by God, who can neither be deceived nor deceive. Such certitude is not based on evidence that is internal to the truth in question but rather on the omniscience and veracity of God, who has revealed. It is of the nature of moral-historical certitude in that it depends upon testimony, but is elevated above this type of certitude since the Person testifying is God. The certitude of faith does not depend upon the certitude surrounding the preambles of faith. Regardless of the rigor of the reasoning employed in arriving at the judgment of credibility or even of credendity regarding the DEPOSIT OF FAITH, the act of faith itself transcends such reasoning and remains entirely free, since an act of supernatural faith cannot be made on the basis of natural reason alone. Faith is a mutual and free gift that is exchanged between God and the believer. The act of faith is congenial to the truths of natural reason that are used in explanation or amplification of it but does in no way depend upon them.

Apart from scattered remarks in several of the Fathers, dealing with God's fidelity, the question of the certitude of faith did not receive serious theological consideration until the early Middle Ages. With the scholastics, and especially the commentators on St. Thomas Aquinas, the doctrine of the formal object of faith began to develop until it achieved final form in the definition of Vatican Council I. According to Vatican I, the certitude of faith depends upon two facts: that God has revealed and that He can neither deceive nor be deceived. Once the fact of revelation is recognized (H. Denzinger, *Enchiridion symbolorum* ed. A. Schönmetzer (32d ed. Freiburg 1963) 428, 3004, 3420–26), and the fact that God cannot be deceived nor deceive (ibid., 3008), there results in the believer a freedom from the fear of error that forms the basis for a loving COMMITMENT to the content of revelation. The fact that this commitment is free, however, means that it is not compelling in the way that conclusion compels assent once the premises are known. A number of intellectual, nonintellectual, or even unconscious influences may interfere with man on his way to the certitude of faith (ibid., 3876) or in his possession of it. Faith depends on the action of grace both for its inception and for the certitude that follows from it (ibid., 3004, 3015).

See Also: FAITH; FAITH, BEGINNING OF.

Bibliography: A. CHOLLET, *Dictionnaire de théologie catholique,* ed. A. VACANT et al., 15 v. (Paris 1903–50; Tables générales 1951–) 2.2:2155–68. M. C. D'ARCY, *The Nature of Belief* (New York 1931; new ed. 1958). R. AUBERT, *Le Problème de l'acte de foi* (3d ed. Louvain 1958). A. GARDEIL, *La Crédibilité et l'apologetique* (Paris 1908). J. PIEPER, *Belief and Faith,* tr. R. and C. WINSTON (New York 1963).

[J. P. WHALEN]

CESARINI

Impoverished noble family of Rome that achieved importance and wealth after 1400. When the family became extinct in 1686, four members had been cardinals and for nearly 200 years it had had hereditary right to the office of gonfalonier, flagbearer of the people. *Giuliano*, cardinal 1426 (d. Nov. 10, 1444), taught at the University of Padua (where he knew NICHOLAS OF CUSA and Domenico CAPRANICA) and was nuncio in France and England before being created cardinal. Legate to the Council of BASEL, he served as its president until the extremists became radically antipapal (1437). At the Council of FLORENCE his work and exemplary character impressed his contemporaries. His successful mission in Hungary (1442), activated Pope EUGENE IV's crusade against the Turks. King Ladislaus III of Poland and John Hunyadi defeated the Turks in 1443 but were then overwhelmed by them at Varna (1444), where Ladislaus and Cardinal Cesarini were killed. For years historians believed the cardinal guilty of making Ladislaus break his oath to the Turks by renewing the war, but recent research has disproved this charge. *Giuliano*, cardinal 1493 (d. 1510), set an example by opening his collection of antiquities to the public. *Alessandro*, cardinal 1517 (d. Feb. 13, 1542), served under Pope PAUL III as legate to Emperor CHARLES V, as legate to France, and as member of the commission preparing for the Council of TRENT.

Bibliography: V. DA BISTICCI, *Vite di uomini illustri del secolo XV*, ed. P. D'ANCONA and E. AESCHLIMANN (Milan 1951). P. LITTA et al., *Famiglie celebri italiane*, 14 v. (Milan 1819–1923) v.5. L. PASTOR, *The History of the Popes from the Close of the Middle Ages*, 40 v. (London-St. Louis 1938–61): v.1 6th ed.; v.3-6, 5th ed., 1:282–328; 4; 5. R. A. LANCIANI, *The Golden Days of the Renaissance in Rome* (Boston 1906). O. HALECKI, *The Crusade of Varna* (New York 1943). T. V. TULEJA, ''Eugenius IV and the Crusade of Varna,'' *American Catholic Historical Review* 35 (1949–50) 257–275. F. L. CROSS, *The Oxford Dictionary of the Christian Church* (London 1957) 258. R. MOLS, *Dictionnaire d'histoire et de géographie ecclésiastiques*, ed. A. BAUDRILLART et al. (Paris 1912–) 12:216–250.

[M. L. SHAY]

CESLAUS OF SILESIA, BL.

Dominican missionary priest; b. Kamien, Poland, *c.* 1184; d. Wrocław, Poland, July 15, 1242. He was probably of the noble Polish family of Odrowaź, a relative of St. HYACINTH and the famous Bishop Iwo Odrowaź of

Cracow. Hyacinth and Ceslaus, both canons of the cathedral of Cracow, joined the DOMINICANS in Rome *c.* 1218. Ceslaus established the first house of his order in Prague, Bohemia, and preached throughout the neighboring countries. The center of his activity was in Poland, where about 1224 he founded the Dominican priory at Wrocław and became its prior. He also served as spiritual director of St. HEDWIG. Through his prayers, Ceslaus is credited with saving Wrocław from the siege of the Tartars (*c.* 1240–41). His long-standing cult was confirmed by Pope CLEMENT XI in 1713.

Feast: July 17, July 20 (Wrocław).

Bibliography: *Acta Sanctorum* July 4:182–199. B. ALTANER, *Die Dominikanermissionen des 13. Jhs.* (Habelschwerdt 1924) 212–218. A. ZAHORSKA, *Illustrowane Żywoty Świętych Polskich* (Potulice, Pol. 1937) 143–151. M. NIWIŃSKI, in *Polski Słownik biograficzny* (Cracow 1938) 4.4:357. P. DAVID, *Dictionnaire d'histoire et de géographie ecclésiastiques,* ed. A. BAUDRILLART (Paris 1912–) 12:252–253. J. KLOCZOWSKI, *Dominikanie polscy na Śląsku w XIII–XIV wieku* (Lublin 1956) 147.

[L. SIEKANIEC]

CEVOLI, FLORIDA, BL.

Baptized Lucrezia Elena, Poor Clare mystic; b. Pisa, Italy, Nov. 11, 1685; d. Città di Castello (Perugia), Umbria, Italy, June 12, 1767. As the daughter of Curzio Cevoli and his wife, Countess Laura della Seta, Lucrezia was born into a life of privilege. During her schooling under the Poor Clares of San Martin Convent, Pisa (1780–85), she discerned a call to religious life and contemplation. On June 7, 1703, despite opposition from her family, Lucrezia became Florida upon entering the Poor Clares at Città di Castello, where Saint Veronica GIULIANI was her novice mistress. Following her profession (June 10, 1704), Sister Florida held various offices, including cook, novice mistress, pharmacist, and vicaress. She succeeded Veronica as abbess in 1727 and was re-elected to that office for the next thirty years, with some breaks. Mother Florida was distinguished by her spirit of prayer and fidelity to the Rule. As abbess she is remembered for reforming the community and encouraging her sisters to receive the Eucharist weekly. At her beatification on May 16, 1993, Pope John Paul II noted that her sharing in the problems of contemporary society while cloistered is attested "by the correspondence she maintained with some influential individuals of her time and her authoritative mediation for peace."

Feast: June 12.

Bibliography: L. DE ASPURZ IRIARTE, *Beata Florida Cevoli, discepola di santa Veronica Giuliani* (Siena 1993).

[K. I. RABENSTEIN]

CHABHAM, THOMAS

English canonist; educated about 1190 at Paris, where he studied under Peter the Chanter. He spent a period in the service of the bishop of London before becoming, on Oct. 15, 1206, perpetual vicar of Sturminster Marshal, Dorset, in the diocese of Salisbury. Shortly afterward he became subdean of Salisbury, an office he filled until at least 1239. He is the author of a *Summa de arte predicandi* and of many sermons, still unpublished, but is chiefly known for a *Summa* for confessors that was written about 1222, possibly as a pendant to the synodal statutes of his diocesan, Richard Poore. This *Summa* is extant in some 85 manuscripts, and has been printed twice, at Cologne and Louvain in 1485. It was so celebrated that it was often ascribed to writers such as Rabanus Maurus, John of Salisbury, Innocent IV, or Thomas Aquinas. Chabham, breaking away in the *Summa* from the cut–and–dried schemata of the traditional penitential literature and from a too juridical approach to the confessional, gives valuable advice to priests on their lives as pastors, telling them what they should know and do, and what virtues they should inculcate in their penitents. Hence, while professing to be nothing more than a *Summa de poenitentia,* Chabham's *Summa* is in effect a manual of the pastoral care in general, the first of a new style of pastoral manual.

Bibliography: H. F. RUBEL, "Chabham's Penitential and Its Influence in the 13th Century," *Publications of the Modern Language Association,* 40 (1925) 225–239. J. C. RUSSELL, *Dictionary of Writers of Thirteenth Century England* (New York 1936) 159. C. R. CHENEY, *English Synodalia of the 13th Century* (Oxford 1941) 49, 54. T. KAEPPELI, "Un Recueil de sermons prêchés à Paris et en Angleterre," *Archivum Fratrum Praedicatorum,* 26 (1956) 161–191. P. MICHAUD–QUANTIN, *Sommes des casuistique et manuels de confession au Moyen Age* (Louvain 1962).

[L. E. BOYLE]

CHABOT, JEAN BAPTISTE

Orientalist; b. Vouvray, France, Feb. 16, 1860; d. Paris, Jan. 7, 1948. He was ordained on May 30, 1885, and studied at the École des Hautes Études and at Louvain, where he obtained his doctorate of theology in 1892 with a brilliant thesis on the seventh century ascetic Isaac of Ninive. He continued Syriac studies at the Collège de France under R. Duval, whom he succeeded. In 1903 he founded the *Corpus scriptorum christianorum orientalium,* with H. HYVERNAT and J. Forget, a collection of texts and Latin translations of the works of Syriac, Coptic, Arab, and Armenian Fathers. He was the sole director of this enterprise for ten years and continued until shortly before his death as chief editor and general manager after the Catholic universities of Louvain and Washington assumed financial and administrative responsibility of the *Corpus.* In and apart from the *Corpus* he published many texts, translations, and studies of early Syrian theology and history: Denis Tell-Mahre, Elias of Nisibis, Michael the Syrian, the *Synodicum orientale,* THEODORE OF MOPSUESTIA, CYRIL OF ALEXANDRIA, James of Edessa, the Hexaemeron, etc. He became a member of the Académie des Inscriptions et Belles Lettres in 1917 and edited Phoenician and Aramaean inscriptions for the Institute's *Corpus inscriptionum Semiticarum.* He published works of a more popular nature on inscriptions of Palmyra (1922) and the history of Syriac literature (1934). His valuable library and personal papers were left to the University of Louvain.

Bibliography: G. RYCKMANS, "Jean–Baptiste Chabot," *Muséon,* 61 (1948) 141–152. G. BARDY, *Catholicisme,* 2:855.

[T. PETERSEN]

CHAD (CEADDA), ST.

Northumbrian monk, bishop of Lichfield; d. 672. Chad was a disciple of St. AIDAN and one of four brothers who were priests. Although a native of Northumbria, he later studied in Ireland. When his brother CEDD died in 664, he succeeded him as abbot of Lastingham, Yorkshire. While Bp. WILFRID OF YORK was in Gaul, King Oswiu of Northumbria had Chad uncanonically consecrated bishop and placed him over all or part of Wilfrid's Diocese of York. When Abp. THEODORE OF CANTERBURY made his first visitation in 669, he reconsecrated Chad and restored Wilfrid to York. Chad was soon made bishop of Mercia with his see at Lichfield, but he died three years afterward of the plague. Bede, the main authority for his life, vividly describes his last days. Many miracles reportedly took place at his tomb. His relics are said to be in St. Chad Cathedral, Birmingham.

Feast: March 2.

Bibliography: BEDE, *Ecclesiastica historica* 3.23, 28; 4.3.

[B. COLGRAVE]

CHAD, THE CATHOLIC CHURCH IN

Also known as Tchad, the Republic of Chad is located in north central Africa, and borders Libya on the north, Sudan on the east, the Central African Republic on the south and southeast, and Cameroon, Nigeria and Niger on the west. The landlocked region has a landscape that forms a shallow basin within its borders. Its northern deserts evolve into forested lowlands in the southern region, where most of the population resides, while the Tibesti

Capital: N'Djamena.
Size: 495,752 sq. miles.
Population: 8,424,504 in 2000.
Languages: French, Arabic; Sara, Sango, and numerous tribal languages are spoken in various regions.
Religions: 1,433,106 Catholics (17%), 4,043,792 Muslims (48%), 1,009,940 Protestants (12%), 1,937,666 practice indigenous faiths (23%). Three religious traditions exist equally within Chad: indigenous African religions and Christianity predominate among the tribal farmers to the south, while the northern section of the country is Islamic.
Archdiocese: N'Djamena, with suffragans Doba, Moundou, Pala, Sarh, Goré, and Lai.

Mountains extend along Chad's eastern boundary. Cotton, peanuts, salt, millet and fish are among Chad's major agricultural products; natural resources include yet-untapped petroleum reserves, uranium, natron and fish from Lake Chad, the largest body of water in the Sahel region. Dry harmattan winds visit the north, sometimes causing droughts, and locust plagues are also not uncommon. The southern climate is tropical. Three fourths of Chadians rely on subsistence agriculture or herding livestock, and monies loaned by the World Bank and other international sources have been invested in improving the country's agricultural technology.

A former territory of French Equatorial Africa, Chad gained its independence in 1960 while remaining a member state of the French Community. Decades of war, as well as invasions from Libya followed, with a final peace achieved only in 1990. Unfortunately, that peace did not hold and by 2000 Chad was once more wracked by rebel violence. In addition to warfare, Chad is also threatened by the encroachment of the Sahara, a situation that has resulted in famine throughout much of the Sahel region. Through Pope John Paul II's private charity, Cor Unum, the pontiff established a program to address the problems caused by the encroachment of the desert in this part of Africa in 1996.

History. First explored by the French in 1892, Chad was made a part of French Equatorial Africa in 1910. Almost a decade after it became a French colony, Catholic evangelization began in the region with the arrival of the Holy Ghost Fathers in the south in 1929. In 1938 two Capuchins, expelled from Ethiopia, took charge of the mission. Not until Chad's reclassification as a French overseas territory in 1946 did Jesuits and Oblates of Mary Immaculate begin organized mission activity. The Prefecture Apostolic of Fort-Lamy, embracing all but the southernmost part of the country, was created in 1947 and was confided to the Jesuits. Oblates were entrusted with the section in the southwest that became the Prefecture Apostolic of Pala in 1956. French Capuchins worked to

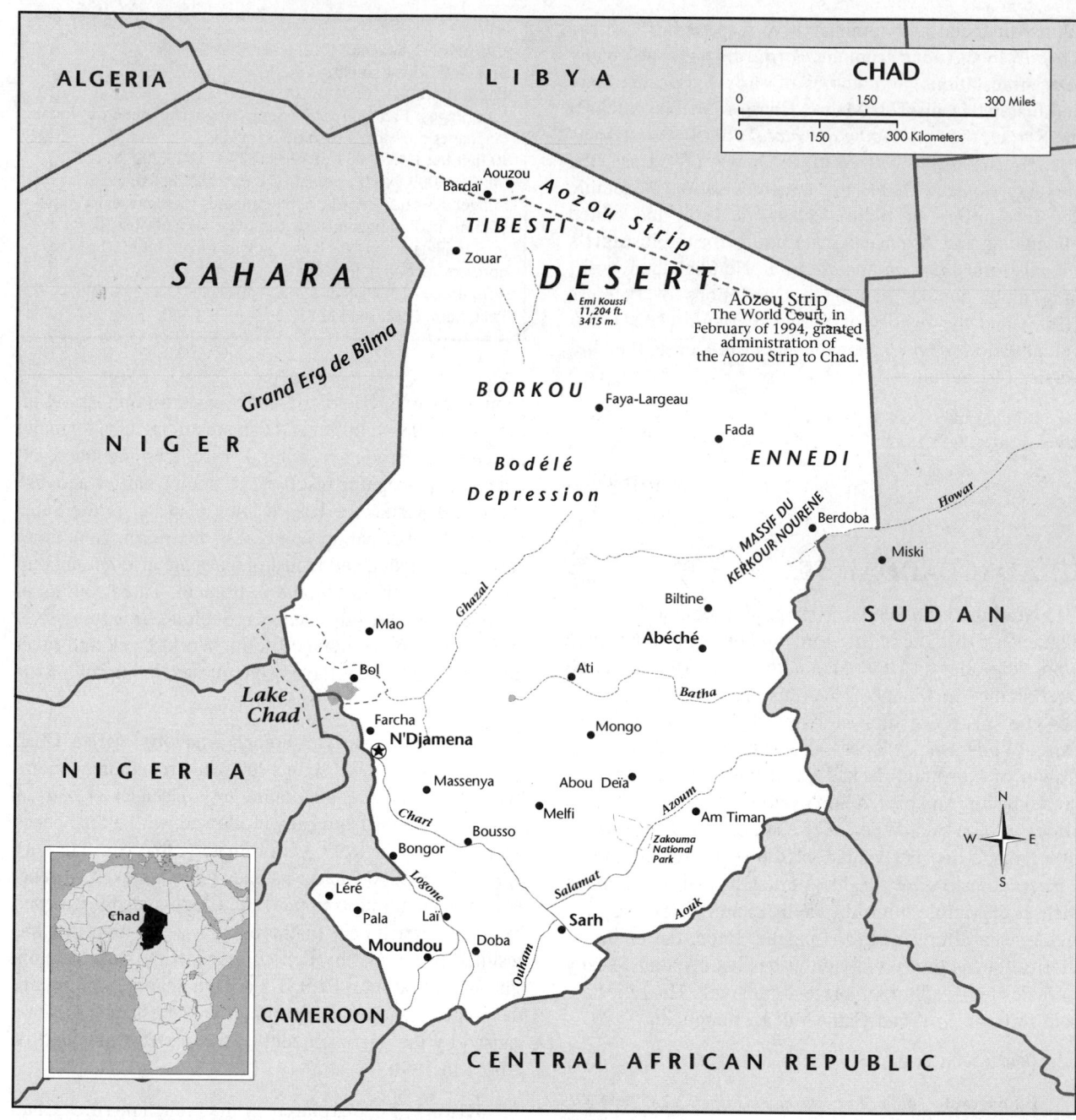

CHAD

0   150   300 Miles

0   150   300 Kilometers

ALGERIA

LIBYA

Aouzou
Bardaï

Aozou Strip

TIBESTI

Zouar

DESERT

SAHARA

▲ Emi Koussi
11,204 ft.
3415 m.

Aozou Strip
The World Court, in
February of 1994, granted
administration of
the Aozou Strip to Chad.

Grand Erg de Bilma

NIGER

BORKOU   Faya-Largeau

Fada

ENNEDI

Bodélé
Depression

Howar

MASSIF DU
KERKOUR NOURENE   Berdoba

Miski

SUDAN

Biltine

Ghazal

Mao

Abéché

Bol

Ati

Batha

Lake
Chad

Farcha   Mongo
N'Djamena

NIGERIA

Massenya   Abou Deïa

Azoum   Am Timan

Melfi

Chari   Bousso   Zakouma
National
Park

Bongor   Salamat

Logone   Aouk

Léré

Lai

Sarh

Pala   Doba

Moundou   Ouham

CAMEROON

CENTRAL AFRICAN REPUBLIC

Chad

N
W   E
S

the east of Pala in the area that became the Prefecture Apostolic in 1951 and the Diocese of Moundou in 1959. Fort-Lamy became a diocese in 1955 and an archdiocese in 1961, when Fort-Archambault was created as a diocese from its southernmost territory and confided to the Jesuits. By the end of the 20th century three-fourths of the country's Catholics resided in the Moundou diocese.

Chad became a republic in the French Community in 1958, and was granted full independence two years later, on Aug. 11, 1960. Its constitution was drafted in 1962. Ethnic and political tensions continued to build

over the next two decades, and in 1982 civil war erupted in Chad. One of the targets was the Church, and many Catholics who were actively involved in ending the fighting became political targets and were killed. By 1987 the government stabilized, and by 1990 peace had been achieved. In an effort to preserve such stability the Vatican established diplomatic relations with the new Chadian government in 1988. Unfortunately, under transitional president Lieutenant General Idriss Deby, the secular government began to curtail certain freedoms in early 1990, prompting Church leaders once again to take an active and vocal role in bridging the religious, political and ethnic differences that continued to simmer. Despite resolving a border dispute with Libya and implementing a new democratic constitution in March of 1995, the government remained in disarray, and by 1998 violence had once again broken out in the northern region.

Into the 21st Century. By 2000 Chad had 99 parishes tended by 109 diocesan and 130 religious priests. The 38 brothers and 285 sisters focused on the administration of the nation's 54 primary and seven secondary schools, as well as operating hospitals, shelters and other agencies providing social services to the nation's people. Although amicable relations existed between the country's many faiths, tensions between Protestants and Muslims had increased due to active evangelical efforts by several churches. During a meeting with a delegation of Chadian bishops led by Archbishop Charles Vandame, Pope John Paul II encouraged efforts at fostering "better mutual understanding," adding his hope that "all believers will put aside their antagonisms, and unite their efforts to fight against everything that stands in the way of peace and reconciliation." In 1999 representatives of the Church participated in a government-sponsored team to develop a Family Code designed to resolve family law disputes by taking into account the customs and religious doctrines surrounding such things as marriage and divorce and inheritance. Church members also remained actively involved in human rights issues stemming from the continuing war, prompting the government to intermittently ban assemblies addressing such concerns.

Bibliography: *Bilan du Monde,* 2:833–836. *Annuario Pontificio* has data on all diocese. For additional bibliography, *see* AFRICA.

[J. BOUCHAUD/EDS.]

CHAIN OF CAUSATION

Sanskrit, *Pratītyāsamutpāda,* or the doctrine of Dependent Origin, a basic tenet of Early and all Hīnayāna Buddhism. It is contained essentially in the Buddha's Second and Third Noble Truths, which explain the cause of suffering and point the way to the cessation of suffering, respectively. There are 12 links in the Chain of Causation, or 12 spokes in the Wheel of Dependent Origin, representing three consecutive existences. The first two, ignorance of the way to salvation (*avidyā*) and the karma-forming forces that determine the form of the next existence (*saṃskāra*), refer to the former life. Three to ten, namely, the initial consciousness of the embryo (*vijñāna*), the psychophysical organization comprised in the five elements of existence (*nāma-rūpa*), the six senses including the mind (*saḍāyatana*), the contact of the

senses with the world, beginning at birth (*sparśa*), sense experience (*vedanā*), thirst for things of the world (*tṛṣṇā*), clinging to the world of sense (*upādāna*), and becoming or the will to be born (*bhava*)—refer to the present life. Eleven and twelve, new birth (*jāti*), and old age and death (*jarāmarana*), refer to future life. The Chain of Causation can be destroyed only when ignorance, its initial and fundamental cause, is destroyed, and this can be accomplished only through the knowledge that gives liberation. The cause of suffering is ignorance, and the cessation of suffering is found by entering into *nirvāna.*

See Also: BUDDHISM; ELEMENTS OF EXISTENCE; NIRVĀNA.

Bibliography: C. SHARMA, *Indian Philosophy: A Critical Survey* (New York 1962) 60–63. H. L. FRIES, *Non–Christian Religions* (New York 1963) 34–38. C. REGAMEY, F. KÖNIG, ed. *Christus und die Religionen der Erde* (Vienna 1961) 3:229–303, esp. 271–274.

[M. R. P. MCGUIRE]

CHAIR OF PETER

As a theological expression, signifies the authority, especially the teaching authority, of the pope. The chair in which a bishop presides over his people was from early times regarded with respect as symbolizing his authority, since it was from his official chair (in which he sat, facing his people) that he gave the homilies by which he instructed his flock in the word of God. Hence the Feast of St. Peter's Chair, whether at Antioch or Rome, commemorated his authority there. Since the teaching power of the pope is not merely that of a bishop but that of the successor of St. Peter, the chair of Peter indicates the authoritative doctrinal power of the pope as the successor of St. Peter. This is the origin of the expression *ex cathedra* definition; such a papal pronouncement (very rarely made) is one in which the pope infallibly defines a doctrine that is irrevocably binding on all the faithful.

The Feast of the Chair of Peter is an ancient liturgical feast that is celebrated on February 22 in the Church's liturgical year.

[B. FORSHAW/EDS.]

CHAISE-DIEU, ABBEY OF

Former BENEDICTINE abbey, Haute-Loire department, France, in the Diocese of Le Puy, but formerly in the Diocese of Clermont. Founded in 1046 by Robert of Chaise-Dieu, the abbey was endowed by Popes GREGORY VII, PASCHAL II, and EUGENE III. After a first "century of saints," it reached the height of its influence during the

Abbey bell tower at La Chaise-Dieu, France. (©Marc Garanger/ CORBIS)

second half of the 13th century, when it was second in power and prestige only to CLUNY as the head of a highly centralized congregation of more than 300 abbeys and priories in France, Spain, and Italy. The congregation began to decline in the 14th century, but this was a period of seigneurial expansion and of reconstruction for the abbey. A new church was built there by Pope CLEMENT VI, a former monk of Chaise-Dieu. The GOTHIC structure with three naves of equal height was completed in 1352 and still survives as a parish church. In 1640 Chaise-Dieu was affiliated with the MAURISTS through the influence of RICHELIEU, who held the abbey in COMMENDATION. Plundered during the WARS OF RELIGION, it was suppressed during the FRENCH REVOLUTION. The church still contains magnificent sculptured choir stalls, a 15th-century *danse macabre*, and a collection of early 16th-century tapestries. A notable part of the archives is preserved at Le Puy.

Bibliography: L. H. COTTINEAU, *Répertoire topo-bibliographique des abbayes et prieurés* (Mâcon 1935–39)

1:667–669. R. VAN DOREN, *Dictionnaire d'histoire et de géographie ecclésiastiques*, ed. A. BAUDRILLART et al. (Paris 1912–) 12:264–266. P. DESCHAMPS and J. LECLERCQ, *La Chaise-Dieu* (Paris 1946). U. ROUCHON et al., *La Chaise-Dieu, commemoration du IXᵉ centenaire* (Le Puy 1952). H. GLASER, *Lexikon für Theologie und Kirche* [2] ed. J. HOFER and K. RAHNER (Freiburg 1957–65) 2:1001. P. R. GAUSSIN, *L'Abbaye de la Chaise-Dieu 1043–1518* (Paris 1962).

[A. H. TEGELS]

CHALCEDON

Modern-day Kadiköy in Turkey, founded in *c*. 678 B.C. by the city of Megara in Bithynia across the Bosporus from Byzantium on the site of a former Phoenician trading post. It shared the fate of Byzantium, passing under the domination of Athenians, Persians, and Romans. It seems to have had a Christian bishop at the end of the 2d century, and Constantine considered establishing his capital there. The scene of the Fourth Ecumenical Council, it was made a metropolitan see without suffragans by Marcian and Pulcheria in 451. After being destroyed by the Persians in A.D. 616, it fell in 1350 to the Turks, who changed its name to Kadiköy.

Its most famous church was the basilica of St. EUPHEMIA, where the Council of CHALCEDON was held, and the city proper boasted of its St. George and Holy Redeemer churches as well as of six monasteries. Along the coast toward the east in Hiereia (modern Phanaraki) were the church of the Virgin, the chapel of St. Elias, and the Eutropius monastery; still farther out were the settlement of the Oak (Drys, modern Djadi-Bostan), famous for the church of the Apostles SS. Peter and Paul, where St. JOHN CHRYSOSTOM was condemned in 403, and three monasteries, including that of St. Satyrus. During the Middle Ages the nearby hills were settled by monks dependent on the monastery of St. Auxentius, which is surrounded by the ruins of Christian monasteries.

Chalcedon is the seat of a Greek Orthodox Metropolitan and a Latin titular archbishopric.

Bibliography: *Paulys Realenzyklopädie der klassischen Altertumswissenschaft,* ed. G. WISSOWA et al. (Stuttgart 1893–) 10.2:1552–59. H. LECLERCQ, *Dictionnaire d'archéologie chrétienne et de liturgie,* ed. F. CABROL, H. LECLERCQ, and H. I. MARROU, 15 v. (Paris 1907–53) 3.1:90–130. R. JANIN, *Dictionnaire d'histoire et de géographie ecclésiastiques,* ed. A. BAUDRILLART et al. (Paris 1912–) 12:270–277; *Lexikon für Theologie und Kirche,* ed. J. HOFER and K. RAHNER, 10 v. (2d, new ed. Freiburg 1957–65) suppl., *Das Zweite Vatikanische Konzil: Dokumente und Kommentare,* ed. H. S. BRECHTER et al., pt. 1 (1966) 2:1005–06. A. M. SCHNEIDER, A. GRILLMEIER, and H. BACHT, *Das Konzil von Chalkedon: Geschichte und Gegenwart,* 3 v. (Würzburg 1951–54) 1:291–302.

[P. T. CAMELOT/EDS.]

CHALCEDON, COUNCIL OF

The Fourth Ecumenical Council, held at Chalcedon Oct. 8 to 31, 451. Considered here are its historical antecedents, history, dogmatic decisions and canons, historical and doctrinal significance.

Historical Antecedents. The Council of Chalcedon marks a final episode in the quarrels over doctrine and policy that followed the Council of EPHESUS (431) and the *Latrocinium,* or Robber Council of EPHESUS (449). The Robber Synod resulted in the triumph of DIOSCORUS OF ALEXANDRIA and EUTYCHES and the defeat of those who (e.g. FLAVIAN OF CONSTANTINOPLE and THEODORET OF CYR) were labeled Nestorians because they acknowledged two natures in Christ.

Leo I was informed of the errors of Eutyches by letters from Flavian, Eusebius of Doryleum, and Theodoret of Cyr and through communication with his deacon Hilary. Leo protested strongly to Emperor THEODOSIUS II and his sister PULCHERIA, requesting (Oct. 13, 449) the convocation of a general council in Italy. No reply was made to his letters or to those Leo wrote on December 24. The intervention of the Western emperor VALENTINIAN III (February 450) likewise had no effect. Theodosius abided by the decisions taken at the Robber Synod and brushed aside any intervention by the Roman pontiff in Eastern affairs. Later (July 16, 450) in writing to the emperor concerning the election of ANATOLIUS to the See of Constantinople, Leo maintained his position as arbiter of the faith: Anatolius should make a profession of the Catholic faith as it had been set forth in Leo's *Tome* to Flavian.

The sudden death of Theodosius (July 28, 450) brought about a reversal of the situation. Pulcheria came to power and immediately married the senator Marcian, who thereupon became emperor (Aug. 24, 450). The all-powerful eunuch Chrysaphius, the god-child of Eutyches, was put to death, and Eutyches was exiled and interned. Writing to the pope to announce his accession to the throne, Marcian suggested calling a council, which a short while later (September 22) he decided should be held in the East. But Leo temporized in his reply of April 451, and in another letter (June 9) he asserted that the peril of invasion by the Huns appeared to make a convention of the bishops inopportune. Leo preferred a council in Italy rather than in the East, where there would be political intrigues and influences. But on May 23 Marcian convoked a council to meet on Sept. 1, 451, at Nicaea in Bithynia.

On the conciliar agenda was an important doctrinal problem. It now seemed necessary to complete the work of the Council of Ephesus by settling the question as to the one or two natures in Christ; only thus could an end

be made to the error of Eutyches and of those who restricted and deformed the thought of St. CYRIL OF ALEXANDRIA. Leo believed that his *Tome* should suffice without a council, which would risk a renewal of the disorders caused by the Robber Synod. Marcian, on the other hand, though adhering firmly to the orthodox position, desired a council in the East, where the imperial authority could adjudge the doctrinal question. Beyond the theological problem, there was a problem of a possible quarrel between the pope and the emperor.

History. On receiving the news of the convocation, Leo replied that he would not oppose the decision of the emperor and would send legates to preside in his place. It was necessary, however, to maintain the faith as defined at Ephesus and as set forth in his *Tome* to Flavian. The bishops summoned to the council first met at Nicaea, but were soon transferred to Chalcedon so that Marcian could more easily supervise the debates. They actually numbered 350 or 360, although later tradition mentions 600 or 630. These bishops were almost all from the East. The West was represented by three Roman legates and two African bishops.

The council commenced on Oct. 8, 451, in the basilica of St. EUPHEMIA in the presence of 19 imperial commissioners under the effective presidency of the Roman legates (Bps. Paschasinus of Lilybeum and Lucentius of Ascoli, and Boniface the priest). The first four sessions (October 8–17) constituted a trial of the instigators of the Robber Synod of Ephesus, and from the outset Paschasinus demanded the condemnation of Dioscorus, who in fact was deposed at the third session (October 13). The two synodical letters of St. Cyril were solemnly approved but no mention was made of the 12 anathemas. Likewise, Leo's *Tome* was accepted with the cry, "Peter has spoken through Leo."

Although the bishops were reluctant to add anything to what had been set forth at the Councils of Nicaea I and Ephesus, Marcian wanted a doctrinal definition that would abolish the controversy, the more so when he discovered that there were some who hesitated to speak of two natures in Christ in the same manner as Leo.

At the fifth session (October 22) a text was presented to the bishops; it had been edited by a commission under the chairmanship of Bp. Anatolius of Constantinople and has been preserved in the conciliar acts. It was approved by the bishops but opposed by Paschasinus, who did not think it did justice to the doctrine of Leo. Since this matter dealt with two natures in Christ and touched immediately on the authority of the Apostolic See, Paschasinus threatened to leave if Leo's thought was not given proper consideration. To avoid an impasse the imperial commissioners proposed that a new commission of six bishops

Illumination from "Collectio canonum," depicting events at Council of Chalcedon, 11th century (Cod, Vat. Lat. 1339, fol. 9r).

produce a new version and gave the bishops a choice of siding with either Leo or Dioscorus. The commission developed a new formula of faith, which conformed to Leo's thought by explicitly defining the two natures in Christ. This statement was accepted by the bishops and was solemnly approved on October 25 in the presence of Marcian and Pulcheria. The emperor confirmed all that had been done by the council.

In the ten (or 11) remaining sessions (October 26–31) the cases of Theodoret of Cyr, Ibas of Edessa, and DOMNUS OF ANTIOCH were considered, and a number of disciplinary canons were promulgated. After dispatching a long letter to the pope explaining their actions and asking his confirmation of the council's decrees, the bishops departed.

Dogma and Canons. The formula of faith is based expressly on Scripture, the definitions of Nicaea and Constantinople I, and on the teachings of the Holy Fathers, and takes particular note of the synodical letters of St. Cyril and the *Tome* of Leo. It is opposed to those who would destroy the mystery of the Incarnation by partitioning Christ and refusing to call Mary THEOTOKOS (the Nestorians), to those who claim that divine nature is capable of suffering, and to those who confuse or amalgamate the two natures and speak of only one nature after the union (Eutyches). The council defined one Christ, perfect God and man, consubstantial with the Father and consubstantial with man, one sole being in two natures, without division or separation and without confusion or change. The union does not suppress the difference in natures; their properties, however, remain untouched, and they are joined together in one Person, or *hypostasis.*

This definition was elaborated from formulas of Cyril, Leo I, John of Antioch, Flavian of Constantinople, and Theodoret of Cyr in remarkable balance, and it put an end to the Christological uncertainties of the 4th and 5th centuries. It excluded the "one nature of the Incarnate Word," which was an Apollinarian formula that St. Cyril had employed in a sense that could be accepted, but to which Eutyches had given a clearly heterodox meaning. It distinguished between nature and person. It stated that in Christ there were two distinct natures whose individual properties had not been destroyed in the union. They subsisted in the unity of one Person, or *hypostasis.* This precision of vocabulary gave the word *prosopon* (person) a much stronger significance than it had in the thought of Theodore of Mopsuestia or Nestorius. It completed the theology of Cyril with that of Leo and definitively proclaimed the unique Person of Christ, son of God, and son of Mary, true God and true man.

On October 25 the council, in response to the invitation of Marcian, promulgated 27 canons devoted to ecclesiastical discipline and to the direction and moral conduct of the clergy and monks. It defined the individual rights of bishops and metropolitans: priests were to be under the authority of the bishop; monks were to reside in their monasteries and were to be under the jurisdiction of the bishop; they were both to observe celibacy under pain of excommunication. All these regulations were justified by events preceding the council.

On October 29, however, another canon gave to the See of Constantinople privileges equal to those of ancient Rome and granted its bishop jurisdiction over the Metropolitans of Pontus, Asia, and Thrace. This primacy in the Orient was based on the political position of the "new Rome," in which the emperor and senate now resided. The following day the Roman delegates protested vigorously in the name of the pope and called attention to the canons of Nicaea that had determined the hierarchical order of the patriarchal sees.

Leo put off his reply to the letter of the council that requested him to confirm its decrees. Letters from Marcian and Anatolius also went unanswered. Then on May 22, 452, the pope annulled everything that had been done in disregard of the canons of Nicaea. It was not until March 21, 453, that Leo confirmed the decrees of the council, and then only regarding matters of faith. This incident was a significant episode in the opposition that was to increase between Rome and Constantinople in the following centuries.

Significance. The Council of Chalcedon represented a culmination in the history of the dogma of the Incarnation. Beyond dealing with the diverse theological tendencies that confronted each other, it stated the Catholic doctrine that preserved indissolubly the two facets of the mystery: the unity of person in the Incarnate Word and the perfect integrity of His two natures. The theology of St. Cyril and that of Leo, as inheritor of St. Augustine and Tertullian, are merged in these formulas; and they do justice also to what was of value in the Antiochene theology. Nevertheless the Cyrillan partisans remained absolutely opposed to two natures, in which they were determined to see a form of Nestorianism. MONOPHYSITISM, even though frequently only verbal, was about to be born and to provoke many quarrels and schisms, which still remain unresolved.

From another point of view, the Council of Chalcedon marked an important step in the development of the Roman primacy. The authority of Celestine had been affirmed at Ephesus; that of Leo was imposed with still greater vigor at Chalcedon. The doctrine of the primacy of the Apostolic See, as opposed to a "Church of the Empire" held by the emperors of Constantinople, was affirmed. Even though this primacy was unanimously recognized at Chalcedon, it still ran the risk of being questioned, and the unity of the Church was compromised by the dangerous political principle that was invoked to justify the primacy of Constantinople in the East. On this problem further disputes and schisms were in the offing; all was not settled in 451.

The acts of Chalcedon are preserved in several ancient collections. In Greek there are three compilations of letters and a record of the minutes in which the order of the second and third sessions is reversed. In Latin, documents are contained in the *Collectio Novariensis de re Eutychis* (before 458) and *Coll. Vaticana* (*c.* 520). There are three recensions of translations of the acts from Greek (6th century) and several collections of the letters of Leo. All these documents are published (*Sacrorum Conciliorum nova et amplissima collectio*, 6). There is a more recent edition by E. Schwartz (*Acta conciliorum oecumenicorum* 2.2–5).

Bibliography: B. ALTANER, *Patrology*, tr. H. GRAEF from 5th German ed. (New York 1960) 291–293. *Gesta de nomine Acaci*, ed. O. GUENTHER (*Corpus scriptorum ecclesiasticorum latinorum* 35.1; Vienna 1895) 440–453. EVAGRIUS, *History ecclesiastical*, *Patrologia Graeca*, ed. J. P. MIGNE, 161 v. (Paris 1857–66) 86.2:2415–2886. LIBERATUS OF CARTHAGE, *Breviarium causae Nestorianorum et Eutychianorum* (*Acta conciliorum oecumenicorum* [Berlin 1914–] 2.5; Berlin 1936) 98–141. A. GRILLMEIER and H. BACHT, *Das Konzil von Chalkedon: Geschichte und Gegenwart*, 3 v. (Würzburg 1951–54) v. 1–3. PIUS XII, "Sempiternus Rex" (Encyclical, Sept. 8, 1951) *Acta Apostolicae Sedis* 43 (1951) 625–644. R. V. SELLERS, *The Council of Chalcedon* (London 1953). F. X. MURPHY, *Peter Speaks through Leo* (Washington 1952). H. M. DIEPEN, *Douze dialogues de christologie ancienne* (Rome 1960); *Les Trois chapitres au Concile de Chalcédoine* (Oosterhout, Neth. 1953). A. GRILLMEIER, *Lexikon für Theologie und Kirche*, ed. J. HOFER and K. RAHNER, 10 v. (2d, new ed. Freiburg 1957–65) suppl., *Das Zweite Vatikanische Konzil: Dokumente und Kommentare*, ed. H. S. BRECHTER et al., pt. 1 (1966) 2:1006–09; *Christ in Christian Tradition*, tr. J. S. BOWDEN (New York 1965) 480–495. P. T. CAMELOT, *Éphèse et Chalcédoine*, v. 2 of *Histoire des Conciles Oecuméniques* (Paris 1962). P. T. R. GRAY, *The Defense of Chalcedon in the East* (Leiden 1979) 451–553. A. BAXTER, "Chalcedon, and the Subject of Christ," *Downside Review* 107 (1989) 1–21. J. S. ROMANIDES, "St. Cyril's 'One Physis or Hypostasis of God the Logos Incarnate' and Chalcedon," in *Christ in East and West*, ed. P. FRIES and T. NERSOYAN (Macon, Ga. 1987) 15–34.

[P. T. CAMELOT]

CHALDEAN CATHOLIC CHURCH (EASTERN CATHOLIC)

The contacts that the Holy See made with the Assyrian Church of the East from the time of the Latin Crusades resulted in the gradual emergence of a fledging Chaldean Catholic community. The first Patriarch of the Church of the East known to have made contact with Rome was Sabrishō'ibn-al-Masīḥī (1226–57). Latin missionaries commended him to Innocent IV, and the pope in turn addressed a letter of good wishes and encouragement to the patriarch. In 1247 Rabban Ara, the Patriarchal Vicar, acknowledged receipt of the pope's letter and thanked him in terms indicative of respect for the papal authority. Rabban Ara's letter was accompanied by two others, one brought from China by Rabban Ara himself, and the other containing the profession of faith of Ishō'yab bar Maldon, Metropolitan of Nisibis, two other metropolitans, and three bishops. It seems that a collective union was being sought. The letter that Ya-balāhā III (1281–1317) addressed to Pope Benedict XI on May 18, 1304, indicated his desire to enter into communion with the See of Rome.

Circumstances of time, place, and persons played a controlling part in the instability of the union. In Cyprus, dispositions made by the Holy See impelled the faithful of the Church of the East to resist union for 120 years and to oppose and repudiate members of their clergy who favored it. For example the bull of Honorius III of Feb. 12, 1222, had commanded the Latin patriarch of Jerusalem, the Latin archbishop of Caesarea, and the bishop of Bethlehem to bring the Christians to obedience to the Latin archbishop of Nicosia; and the bull of John XXII of Oct. 1, 1326, had ordered the patriarch of Jerusalem to extirpate heresies by whatever means he chose. A brief union was effected in 1340 by Elias, Bishop of Cyprus. Several of those converted during the union achieved in 1445 by Timothy, Bishop of Cyprus, abjured five years later. A rigid policy of Latinization was applied by the Doge of Venice, who succeeded the Lusignans as ruler of the island in 1489.

Communion with Rome. The definitive union that brought forth the Chaldean Catholic Church took place in the 16th century. Simon III Basidi (1480–93) and his successors introduced a hereditary succession to the patriarchate, from uncle to nephew or cousin. Since the Assyrian Church of the East reserved to metropolitans the right to consecrate the patriarch, the Basidis, known as the "Abuna" (patriarchal family, sought to create metropolitans only from among their own number, as a precaution. This reduced the number of metropolitans until under Simeon V bar Māmā there was only one, his eight-year-old nephew. The practice brought ignorant and unworthy minors to patriarchal rank, for which they were unprepared, and imposed celibacy on them. The conscience of the hierarchy was aroused; they sought a radical remedy in communion with Rome.

The movement was led by the three bishops of Irbīl, Salamas, and Azerbaijan. They met at Mosul with the clergy, the monks, and three or four lay delegates from each of ten regions to elect a patriarch. Their choice was Sulāqā, a religious priest since 1540 and superior of the Convent of Rabban-Hormizd, near Alkosh, approximately 25 miles from Mosul. He refused, even after a second ballot. After a third ballot, in which he still led, the assembly decreed that force be used, if necessary, to oblige the candidate to present himself. Sulāqā was hailed before the assembly, and his election was proclaimed amid cries of joy and applause. The bishops among the electors seem to have excluded themselves to avoid any suspicion of self-interest.

Armed with the proper documents and accompanied by three notables, Adam, Thomas, and Khalaph, Sulāqā left Mosul for Rome, with an escort of 70 as far as Jerusalem. On Nov. 15, 1552, he arrived in Rome, accompanied only by Khalaph. One companion had died on the way, and another had been detained by illness. On the basis of a report by Cardinal Maffei, Pope Julius III promulgated his bull of Feb. 20, 1553, proclaiming Sulāqā Patriarch of Mosul. This was the official establishment of the Chaldean Catholic Church.

Sulāqā was consecrated a bishop on April 9, 1553, by Pope Julius III in the Basilica of Saint Peter and received the pallium from the hands of the pope at a secret consistory held at the Vatican on April 28. At Sulāqā's request for help in his ministry, the pope appointed the Dominican Ambrose Buttigeg as representative of the Holy See to the fledging Chaldean Catholic Church. In July Sulāqā left Rome, accompanied by A. Buttigeg; Antoninus Zahara, a Dominican from Malta; and a certain Matthew; as well as by his first companion Khalaph. He arrived in Diarbekir, his patriarchal residence, on Nov. 12, 1553, where he was received triumphally by clergy and people, as evidenced by his letter to Julius III (one of two letters remaining of his correspondence). On November 19, seven days after his return, he consecrated Bishop Ḥabīb Elias Asmar. In December he obtained in Aleppo from the Sultan documents that acknowledged him head of the Chaldean nation, "after the example of all the Patriarchs." In 1554 he consecrated Metropolitan 'Abdīshī' of Jezireh. Elias Asmar later identified five bishops and metropolitans consecrated by Sulāqā.

With the help of a hierarchy of eight bishops, assisted by Ambrose and Antoninus, and armed with documents from the Sultan, Sulāqā initiated the expected reform. As was quite natural, opposition to his efforts soon made itself felt. In fact, the Assyrian Patriarch Simeon Denḥā, now Sulāqā's rival and bitter enemy, prevailed upon the Pasha of Amadya to invite Sulāqā there under the pretext that his presence in that region could contribute to the union of the Assyrians and Chaldean Catholics. Once in Amadya, Sulāqā was imprisoned and subjected to every sort of torture for four months. Finally, by order of the Pasha, he was put into a sack and thrown into a lake to drown, about Jan. 12, 1555.

Three Centuries of Conflict. Mar 'Abdīshô of Jezireh succeeded Sulāqā. He was not able to leave for Rome until 1561; he was confirmed there on April 17, 1562, and received the pallium on May 4. In haste to return to his threatened flock, he did not attend the Council of Trent. In 1578 'Abdishô died in the Convent of Saint James the Recluse, where he had established his residence. The electoral synod was prevented by great difficulties from meeting until 1579, when it elected as patriarch the aged Mar Yabalāhā IV, Bishop of Jezireh and administrator of the vacant patriarchate. The new patriarch died in 1580, before confirmation of his appointment could be sent to Rome.

His successor was Simeon IX, Bishop of Gelu, Seert, and Salamas. He and all his flock had recently been converted through the zeal of Elias Asmar, Metropolitan of Diarbekir. The electoral synod commanded Elias Asmar to go to Rome to seek confirmation and the pallium. Simeon IX made the mistake of residing in the Convent of Saint John, near Salamas, where he was the butt of vigorous attacks by the Assyrians. The mountainous terrain and the conflict between Turks and Persians made communication difficult, thereby inhibiting contacts between this patriarch and Rome. Leonard Abel, Archbishop of Sidon and envoy of Pope Gregory XIII since January 1584, unable to reach the patriarch at his residence, sent him the profession of faith, which he signed once again in 1585. Simon IX died in 1600.

As a result of the continuing difficulties, the electoral synod was unable to meet, and the election of Simeon X took place in accordance with hereditary law. The profession of faith that the new patriarch sent to Rome by Thomas, Metropolitan of Diarbekir, was not deemed satisfactory. The Franciscan Thomas Obicini brought the patriarch another formula to sign. He received a most cordial welcome, and the formula was signed on July 28, 1619.

Professions of faith were sent to Rome by Simeon XI in 1653, Simeon XII in 1658, and Simeon XIII in 1670. The last-named besought Pope Clement X to leave the ancient liturgical rites and ecclesial customs intact. The pressure of serious local difficulties made frequent contacts with Rome impossible. Simeon XIII finally felt obliged to return to Assyrian Church. He established himself at Kotchannes, where, ensconced among impenetrable mountains, he became the first of a new series of Assyrian patriarchs.

The Chaldean Catholic Church of Diarbekir was thus left without a shepherd; and an Assyrian bishop, dependent on Rabban-Hormizd, resided in Diarbekir. Yet the Chaldean Catholic community remained favorable to union, as it had been since 1552. It was supported in its loyalty by the work of the Capuchin John Baptist of Saint Aignan. Conversions continued, the most famous being that of Joseph, the Assyrian Bishop of Diarbekir. Opposed, cruelly persecuted, and several times imprisoned at the instigation of the Assyrian Patriarch Elias X, Bishop Joseph received a brief of felicitations from Pope Clement X, dated Jan. 25, 1677. Soon afterward the Sultan acknowledged his right to the title of patriarch of Diarbekir, Mardin, and other places. Joseph besought Rome for confirmation of this title and also for the pallium. At first Rome hesitated, but it granted them to him on Jan. 8, 1681, under the title *Patriarchatus nationis chaldaeorum patriarchae regiminis destitutus.* Rome did not grant him the title of Patriarch of the Assyrian Church of the East, reserved out of diplomacy for the Assyrian patriarchs, successors of Sulāqā, who resided at Kotchannes, or the title of patriarch of Babylon, reserved for the Assyrian Patriarchs of the Abūna-Basidi family, who resided at Rabban-Hormizd.

The Chaldeans thus had their own patriarch in the person of Joseph I, the first of the *ad interim* series of patriarchs of Diarbekir. In 1691 Joseph I, having grown old and wanting to assure the patriarchal succession and thus avoid all possible intrigue after his death, dared to consecrate his coadjutor, Joseph Şlībā, as patriarch, even before he himself resigned. Because of this irregular procedure, the Holy See did not recognize Joseph II Şlībā until June 18, 1696. Discouraged by persecutions and difficulties of all sorts, Joseph II asked to retire to Rome. However, stricken with the plague, he died in 1713 before he could leave for Rome.

Timothy Mār Eugene, Bishop of Mardīn since 1691, succeeded him under the name of Joseph III. His patriarchate was marked by great progress. On the occasion of his official visit to Mosul, 3,000 Assyrian Christians were converted, and 3,000 others followed later. The fury of the Assyrian Church knew no bounds, and they had the patriarch imprisoned several times. To make things worse, a decree by the Sultan had just granted Mosul and Aleppo to the Assyrians, giving the Catholics Diarbekir and Mardīn. This made the situation of the Chaldean Catholics in Mosul and Aleppo very critical.

When Joseph III arrived in Rome on Jan. 1, 1732, he offered his resignation, but it was not accepted. The war between the Turks and the Persians obliged him to remain in Rome until the end of 1741, when he returned to his anxious flock. He died on Jan. 23, 1757.

His successor was Lazarus Hindi, Joseph IV. Rome first recognized him by the title of archbishop of Amīd,

then as patriarch of the united Chaldeans on March 24, 1759. His resignation, presented on Aug. 21, 1780, was not accepted until Dec. 7, 1781. But not finding anyone to take his place, Rome turned again to Joseph IV and named him patriarchal administrator *ad interim.* On March 21, 1791, Joseph was called to Rome, and John Hormizd, the neoconvert bishop of Mosul, of the Abūna family, was designated apostolic administrator. Joseph and the clergy of Diarbekir forsaw serious danger for Catholicism in the naming of this neoconvert. In 1792 Joseph went to Rome, and on Feb. 3, 1793, he succeeded in annulling the nomination of John Hormizd and reestablishing himself as Patriarchal administrator of Aīd, with Joseph Attar as his vicar-general. Joseph IV died in 1796.

The 19th and 20th Centuries. In 1802 the priest Augustine Hindi was named administrator of the Patriarchate of Diarbekir. On Sept. 8, 1804, he was consecrated bishop at Mardīn. Following the suspension of John Hormizd (1812), Augustine Hindi was named apostolic delegate for the Chaldeans, a post he held for 15 years. Rome did not want to name him patriarch, for there was hope of one day winning over one of the two Assyrian patriarchs of Kotchannes or Rabban-Hormizd, who had been in correspondence with Rome since 1770 to 1771. The aim was to unite the Chaldeans under a single patriarchate. Meanwhile, Rome rewarded Hindi by granting him the pallium, which it sent to him on Nov. 2, 1818. Seeing in this act his recognition as patriarch, Augustine declared himself Patriarch Joseph V. Rome corrected his error by pointing out to him that the pallium signified nothing more than the rank of archbishop. Augustine died in Diarbekir on April 3, 1827, putting an end to the series of patriarchs of Diarbekir, begun 147 years earlier.

Immediately after Hindi's death, Rome was ready to grant the pallium and patriarchal authority to John Hormizd, the 74-year-old metropolitan of Mosul. The party opposed to John, then represented in Rome by Gabriel Dambo, founder of the Catholic Chaldean Monastic Institute of Rabban-Hormizd, was able to delay the execution of this plan until July 5, 1830. From that date on, John Hormizd, the last of the Abūna family, was the sole representative of the Chaldean Catholic Church, under the name of John IX Hormizd, Chaldean Patriarch of Babylon. He continued the succession that had originated with Addai and Mari in subapostolic times and from which Sulāqā had separated in 1553 to form a union with Rome. To the Assyrians there remained only the Patriarchate of Kotchannes, which continued the succession of Sulāqā that had reverted to the Assyrian Church.

John died on Aug. 16, 1838, after a long and checkered life. His successor was Nicholas Zaya, formerly bishop of Salamas, and coadjutor of John Hormizd, with the right of succession. Nicholas was confirmed on April 27, 1840. The Chaldean bishops were displeased with this choice, which deprived them of their right to a free election. Zaya resigned in 1847 and retired to his former diocese, where he died in 1855.

Joseph Audo, administrator of the patriarchate, was elected patriarch in 1847 and confirmed on Sept. 11, 1848. His long pontificate was marked by many conversions and also by great dissension with Rome, which began in 1860, on questions of jurisdiction, especially over the status of the SYRO-MALABAR CHURCH. The national synod that he held June 7 to 21, 1858, at the Convent of Rabban-Hormizd, was never approved by Rome. Joseph Audo died on March 14, 1878. Speaking of him at the consistory of Feb. 28, 1879, Leo XIII said, ". . . Quem eximius pietatis et religionis sensus ornabat."

His successor, Elias Peter Abūlyonan, Bishop of Jezireh, was confirmed on Feb. 28, 1879, and died of typhoid fever on June 27, 1894. Elias Peter was succeeded by Abdisho V Khayyāth, who was elected on Oct. 28, 1894, and confirmed on March 28, 1895, and who died in Baghdad on Nov. 6, 1899. Joseph Emmanuel II Thomas, who was unanimously elected on July 9, 1900, and confirmed on Dec. 17, 1900(?), died on July 21, 1947, at age 97; in a decree of July 3, 1902, the Holy See named him apostolic delegate for the Assyrians. He was a member of the Iraqi Senate for 25 years, and his long pontificate was tumultuous, with the massacres of 1918 (World War I), when four bishops, many priests, and 70,000 Chaldean Catholics died.

The spiritual leader of all the Chaldeans in the world is the Chaldean Patriarch of Babylon, who is assisted: (1) by the Chaldean hierarchy, in the administration of the eparchies, (2) by the patriarchal synods of the entire hierarchy, and, (3) by the permanent synod, which is part of the patriarchal curia. The patriarch is elected by the Chaldean hierarchy and enthroned even before he submits his request to enter into communion with Rome. Canonical election confers on the patriarch the right to the patriarchal office. The patriarch resides in Baghdad, Iraq.

Bibliography: S. GIAMIL, *Genuinae relationes inter Sedem Apostolicam et Assyrorum Orientalium seu Chaldaeorum Ecclesiam* (Rome 1902). J. M. VOSTÉ, "Mar Iohannan Soulaqa: Premier Patriarche des Chaldéens," *Angelicum* 8 (1931) 187–234. G. BELTRAMI, *La chiesa caldea nel secolo dell'unione* (Orientalia Christiana 83; 1933). R. RABBAN, *Shahīd al-Ittihad* (Martyr of Union; Mosul 1955), a biography of Sham'un Yohannan Sulāā. ABDOULAHAD, ARCHBISHOP OF AMID, "Vie de Mar Youssef Ier: Patriarche des Chaldéens," ed. and tr. J. B. CHABOT, *Revue de l'Orient Chrétien* 1.2 (1896) 66–90. S. BELLO, *La Congrégation de S. Hormisdas et l'Église chaldéene dans la première moitié siècle* (Orientalis Christiana Analecta 122; Rome 1939). D. ATTWATER, *The Christian Churches of the East*, 2 v. (rev. ed. Milwaukee 1961–62).

V.1. R. ROBERSON, *The Eastern Christian Churches: A Brief Survey* (6th ed. Rome 1999).

[R. RABBAN/EDS.]

CHALDEANS

Chaldeans are an Aramaic-speaking people called in Akkadian *kaldu* (the Babylonian form of a presumed original *kašdu*), in Hebrew *kaśdîm,* in Aramaic *kaśdāi,* and in Greek χαλδῖιοι. The Chaldeans made their first appearance in history around the end of the 2nd and the beginning of the 1st millennium B.C. as raiders (cf. Jb 1.17) and later settlers in the semi-swampy regions at the head of the Persian Gulf. Apparently they had come from the western coast of the Persian Gulf, where they seem to have been in contact with people using a form of South Arabic script [see W. F. Albright, *The Bulletin of the American Schools of Oriental Research* 128 (1952) 39–45]. In periods when Assyrian control of southern Mesopotamia was weak, the Chaldeans were able to establish small independent kingdoms, of which the most important was Beth-Yakin. In the 8th century B.C. even the city of Babylon was held for short periods by Chaldean princes, e.g., by Mukîn-Zêri (731–728) and Merodach-Baladan (722–710, 703) of Beth-Yakin, who, around the time of his revolt against Sennacherib of Assyria in 703, sent an embassy to King Hezekiah of Juda (2 Kgs 20.12–19; Is 39.1–8; 2 Chr 32.31). The speedy decline of Assyria after the reign of Assurbanipal (668–627) allowed the Chaldean Nabopolassar to make himself independent king of Babylon (626–604). In 612 the allied forces of the Medes and the Chaldeans captured Ninive and destroyed the Assyrian Empire. Nabopolassor's son NEBUCHADNEZZAR (604–561) continued the work of his father in conquering all of northern Mesopotamia and then proceeded to incorporate into the Chaldean Neo-Babylonian Empire all of Syria and Palestine. However, with the capture of Babylon by the Persian King Cyrus the Great (539) from Nabu-na'id (Nabonidus) the Chaldean Empire came to an end. (On the history of Babylonia during this period, *see* MESOPOTAMIA, ANCIENT.)

In the Bible the terms Chaldeans and the land of the Chaldeans (Chaldea) become synonymous with Babylonians and Babylonia from the 7th century B.C. on (2 Kgs 25.4, 25.13, 25.24–26; Is 13.19, 23.13, 43.14; Jer 21.4, 22.25, 24.5, 25.12; Ez 1.1–3, 11.24, 16.29; Hab 1.6). According to Gn 11.28, 11.31, and 15.7 (See also Neh 9.7; Jdt 5.6; and Acts 7.4), ABRAHAM came originally from "Ur of the Chaldeans"; since the Chaldeans could hardly have been in the ancient Sumerian city of UR as early as the time of Abraham, the phrase "of the Chaldeans" must apparently be taken as an anachronism.

The name Chaldean was commonly employed by Greek and Roman writers, following the death of Alexander, to signify astrologers or diviners. It is used in this sense in the pseudohistorical stories of the Book of DANIEL (2.5, 2.10, 4.4, 5.7, and 11). The astrology of Babylonia spread to Egypt and throughout the cities of the Greek and Roman world. Its practitioners ranged from learned men, well versed in mathematics—hence the name ''Mathematicians'' (Greek, μαθηματικοί; Latin *mathematici*) for astrologers—to mere charlatans. Under the Roman Empire, many of the leading writers and thinkers in East and West were profoundly influenced by the Chaldean astrology and were convinced that it could ascertain the will of the gods and man's destiny. The Chaldeans were repeatedly attacked and refuted in the writings of the Church Fathers.

Bibliography: *Paulys Realenzyklopädie der klassischen Altertumswissenschaft,* ed. G. WISSOWA et al. (Stuttgart 1893–) 3:2045–62. A. DUPONT-SOMMER, *Les Araméens* (Paris 1949). K. F. KRÄMER, *Lexikon für Theologie und Kirche*[2], ed. J. HOFER and K. RAHNER, 10 v. (2d, new ed. Freiburg 1957–65) 2:1002–04. *Encyclopedic Dictionary of the Bible,* tr. and adap. by L. HARTMAN (New York 1963), from A. VAN DEN BORN, *Bijbels Woordenboek* 341–342.

[J. B. WHEATON/T. A. BRADY]

CHALICE, PATEN, AND VEIL

The chalice and paten are vessels used in the Eucharistic liturgy; the veil, a covering for them. This article treats of their development and use.

The most essential of all the liturgical vessels is the chalice in which the wine at Mass is consecrated. It is the only vessel mentioned in all four scriptural accounts of the institution of the Eucharist. Early chalices were akin to the drinking vessels normally in use and were distinguished from these only by ornamentation. They were made from any metal, and chalices of glass, wood, or horn were not unknown; since the 9th century, however, only precious metals have been used. Besides the chalice there have existed at various times in history the *calix ministerialis,* a cup without a base and with two handles, used for giving communion to the faithful; and also the *calix offertorialis,* which was a larger form of the same shape, into which the faithful poured their contributions of wine at the Offertory procession. By the 9th century these chalices for the faithful had fallen into disuse; there remained only the priest's chalice, to which a base was added. The bowl became hemispherical; next a stem was introduced between bowl and base; then a node (knob) was made in the middle of the stem. During the Middle Ages the base became large, the bowl smaller, eggshaped, and (later) conical. Under baroque influence the base was made larger still, the node pear-shaped, the cup shaped like a lily. Decorations of engraved patterns on early chalices gradually became more complicated by the 8th century and sometimes included texts on the base or around the bowl. Later decorations became even more lavish, often incorporating inlaid precious stones, pearls, and enameled medallions. The modern chalice, under the influence of functional design, concentrates on gracefulness of line, balance of proportion, and excellence of material rather than applied ornament, and its shape is inspired chiefly by forms in vogue during the 1st millennium. It is prescribed that the cup be of gold, of silver, or even of tin, but goldplated within; its neck should be designed in a way that does not impede handling by the priest, and its base, wide enough to ensure relative stability.

Until the Middle Ages it was customary for each church to have but one chalice; since Masses have become more numerous, most churches have several chalices, and a great many priests possess their own.

The paten is a shallow plate on which the large host rests at times both before and after consecration. It may be of gold or silver, gilt on the concave surface. Originally, a paten was a very large dish, sometimes of metal but often of wood, from which the Eucharist was distributed to the faithful in the days when unleavened bread was in use. By the 9th century, when Communion of the faithful had become infrequent, the paten was reduced in size and in time assumed its present form.

The veil covering the chalice and paten as they are carried to the altar is, at least in the Latin rite, of comparatively recent origin. Not until 1570 was it prescribed for the Roman Rite. Since the reforms of Vatican II, its use is now optional.

Bibliography: J. BRAUN, *Das christliche Altargerät in seinergeschichtlichen. Entwicklung* (Munich 1932). H. LECLERCQ, *Dictionnaire d'archéologie chrétienne et de liturgie,* ed. F. CABROL, H. LECLERCQ, and H. I. MARROU, 15 v. (Paris 1907–53) 2.2:1595–1645. J. BAUDOT, *ibid.* 1646–51. V. H. ELBERN, *Der eucharistiche Kelch im frühen Mittelalter* (Düsseldorf 1961). M. RIGHETTI, *Manuale di storia liturgica,* 4 v. (Milan): v.1 (2d ed. 1950) 1:461–71.

[C. W. HOWELL/EDS.]

CHALLONER, RICHARD

Bishop, vicar apostolic of the London district, author; b. Lewes, Sussex, Sept. 29, 1691; d. London, Jan. 12, 1781. Challoner, the resolute leader of English Catholics during the 18th century, combined a firm administration with spiritual prudence necessitated by the times. His pastoral leadership, devotional writings, and exemplary life of prayer and mortification have made him one of the most venerated vicars apostolic of England. Challoner was converted from Presbyterianism to Catholicism in his youth while living at Lady Anastasia Holman's Warkworth Manor, where his widowed mother was housekeeper. He was tutored by the Holman's chaplain, John Gother, apologist and missionary, who arranged for Challoner's admittance to the English College at Douai (1705). He spent 25 years at Douai as student, teacher, and administrator, completing the 12 year course in eight years. After entering the seminary, he taught poetry, rhetoric, and philosophy. He was ordained (1716) and received his bachelor of divinity degree (1719), whereupon college officials appointed him vice president, professor of theology, and prefect of studies. He later earned a doctorate in divinity (1727).

Receiving a long-awaited missionary assignment, Challoner returned to England (1730). Although the penal laws were not as rigorously enforced as in former times, he was nevertheless compelled to live under layman's disguise, celebrate Mass secretly, and conduct religious meetings in obscure inns. Success as a missionary priest and ''controversial writer'' led to his appointment as vicar-general. Controversy over a pamphlet by Challoner, in part refuting an attack on Catholicism by Dr. Conyers Middleton, a prominent Anglican divine, forced him to return to Douai (1738). Anticipated papal appointment of Challoner to the Douai College presidency prompted vigorous intervention by Bp. Benjamin Petre, vicar apostolic of the London district, who pleaded to Rome that Challoner be made his coadjutor bishop. After difficulties and delay, Challoner returned to England and was consecrated titular bishop of Debra and nominated coadjutor with right of succession to Petre (1741). He assumed much of the work of the aging Petre and succeeded him in 1758. For the next 23 years he successfully administered the London district, which included ten counties, the Channel islands, and British North America.

Challoner's pastoral achievements are especially noteworthy when it is recalled that, due to existing laws, he spent his life in clandestine service. A zealous preacher particularly devoted to the poorer classes, he made numerous conversions in the London slums. He founded the ''Benevolent Society for the Relief of the Aged and Infirmed Poor'' and established three schools. Although Jacobite in sympathy, Challoner eventually recognized George III as *de jure* sovereign. He unsuccessfully sought practical solutions for Catholics forced by law to marry under Anglican rite. He defended episcopal authority over regular clergy and instituted conferences that increased clerical unity during a period of threatened imprisonment for ''exercising the functions of a popish priest.'' In general, Challoner's episcopacy was marked

Page from the the 13th-century ''Missal of St. Corneille de Compiègne,'' shows the celebration of a Mass with the chalice partially covered by a folded veil; in the Bibliothèque Nationale, Paris (MS Latin 17318, folio 173r).

by efforts to infuse into the ancient faith a spirit of resistance to the anti-Catholic forces prevalent in the 18th century. He labored to save Catholicism in England from extinction; his writings and preachings served to strengthen the faith of the Catholic minority and to condition them to the possibility of a permanently hostile society. Challoner lived to see official signs of Catholic toleration, however, in the Catholic Relief Act (1778). During the Gordon Riots he fled London temporarily. He died several months later.

Challoner wrote numerous books and pamphlets. His major literary efforts were *Think Well On't* (1728), a book of meditations; *The Garden of the Soul* (1740), the most popular of his devotional writings, although subsequent editors radically altered the original; *Memoirs of the Missionary Priest* (2 v. 1741–42); *Britannia Sancta* (1745), a treatise depicting lives of English, Scottish, and Irish saints; *Meditations for Every Day in the Year* (1753); and *British Martyrology* (1761). Moreover, he revised the English Catechism, made several translations, e.g., *The Imitation of Christ* and St. Augustine's *Confessions,* and provided English Catholics with a more readable Bible by revising the Douay-Rheims. Although unsuccessful in making English Catholics steady readers of Scripture, Challoner's Bible (1749–52) was the standard Catholic version until recent times.

Bibliography: E. H. BURTON, *The Life and Times of Bishop Challoner, 1691–1781,* 2 v. (London 1909). M. TRAPPES-LOMAX,

Richard Challoner.

Bishop Challoner (New York 1936). T. COOPER, *The Dictionary of National Biography from the Earliest Times to 1900,* 63 v. (London 1885–1900; repr. with corrections, 21 v., 1908–09, 1921–22, 1938; suppl. 1901–), 3:1349–52. D. MATTHEW, *Catholicism in England* (2d ed. New York 1950). E. I. WATKIN, *Roman Catholicism in England* (New York 1957). J. CARTMELL, ''Richard Challoner,'' Clergy Review 44 (1959), 577–587. E. DUFFY, ed., *Challoner and His Church: A Catholic Bishop in Georgian England* (London 1981).

[J. T. COVERT]

CHALMERS, THOMAS

Scottish Presbyterian theologian; b. Anstruther, Fifeshire, Scotland, March 17, 1780; d. Edinburgh, May 30, 1847. After studying at the University of St. Andrews, he taught mathematics and was ordained a minister. In 1810 he experienced a conversion and adhered to the evangelical party of the Church of SCOTLAND. His preaching was highly praised by William Wilberforce and others of the Clapham Sect. His *Astronomical Discourses* (1817), a series of lectures on the relations between astronomy and Christian revelation, gained wide popularity. Chalmers also won a respected reputation as a political economist and philosopher. In 1815 he was appointed to the Tron Church, one of the leading churches in Glasgow, but he transferred to the largest and poorest parish in the city, St. John's Church, where his success was remarkable. He became professor of moral philosophy at St. Andrews (1823) and professor of theology at Edinburgh (1828). After his election to the General Assembly of the Church of Scotland (1832), he supported the ''veto act'' of 1833, restricting the rights of laymen to nominate candidates for ecclesiastical positions. Together with the evangelical party, Chalmers advocated that ministers be selected by the congregations. The civil courts declared this procedure illegal (1838–39). When Parliament did not take action on the matter, Chalmers led nearly a third of the clergy and laity of the Church of Scotland into a schism known as ''the Disruption'' (May 1843), which lasted until 1929. Chalmers was chosen first moderator of the Free Protesting Church of Scotland (later the Free Church of Scotland) and was responsible for establishing it on a solid financial basis. He acted also as professor of divinity in the Free Church's New College at Edinburgh. Chalmers also published numerous works, which have been collected in 34 volumes.

Bibliography: W. HANNA, *The Life and Writings of Thomas Chalmers,* 4. v. (Edinburgh 1849–52). H. WATT, *Thomas Chalmers and the Disruption* (Edinburgh 1943). W. G. BLAIKIE, *The Dictionary of National Biography from the Earliest Times to 1900,* 63 v. (London 1885–1900) 3:1358–63.

[T. P. JOYCE]

CHALMERS, WILLIAM (CAMERARIUS)

Theologian; b. Aberdeen, Scotland, date unknown; d. Paris in 1678. After training for the priesthood at the Scots' College in Rome, he became a Jesuit. In 1625, following a brief sojourn in England, he left the Jesuits and became an Oratorian. He published his *Selectae disputationes philosophicae* in Paris in 1630. He edited several opuscula of Augustine, Anselm and Fulgentius in 1634. A work on moral theology, *Disputationes theologicae de discrimine peccati venialis et mortalis* (Fastemburg), appeared in 1639. He published a short ecclesiastical history of Scotland, *Scotianae ecclesiae infantia, virilis aetas, senectus* (Paris 1643). He is, however, known mostly for his spirited rejection of MOLINISM and vigorous defense of physical premotion in his *Antiquitatis de novitate victoria* (Fastemburg 1634) and his *Dissertatio theologica de electione angelorum et hominum ad gloriam* (Rennes 1641).

Bibliography: A. INGOLD, *Dictionnaire de théologie catholique,* ed. A. VACANT et al., 15 v. (Paris 1903–50) 2.2:2211.

[C. R. MEYER]

CHALON-SUR-SAÔNE, COUNCILS OF

Various national (Merovingian), provincial, and diocesan councils held at the former diocesan seat of Chalon-sur-Saône (Latin, *Cabillonum*) in the Province of Lyons. In 579 Guntram, King of Orléans, convoked there a national council that deposed the bishops of Embrun and Gap for armed violence. In 603 another national council, held at the instigation of Queen Brunhilde of Austrasia and Abp. Aridius of Lyons, deposed Bp. DESIDERIUS OF VIENNE. Another national council, held sometime between 643 and 652, promulgated 20 disciplinary canons, prescribing fidelity to the Nicene Creed and the ancient canons and making provision for the election and authority of bishops, the administration of Church property, the government of monasteries, and Christian morals. It prohibited abbots and monks from going to the king without episcopal permission; it forbade simony, selling slaves outside the realm, and farm labor on Sunday; and it recommended private sacramental confession with imposed penances. In 813 CHARLEMAGNE ordered reform councils to be held throughout his empire, at Mainz, Reims, Tours, Arles, and Chalon-sur-Saône. The 66 bishops and abbots of the Lyonnais who met at Chalon urged CATHEDRAL schools for future clerics; forbade simony; recommended the BENEDICTINE RULE for monasteries, the restoration of public penance, private confession to God and a priest and the imposition of canonical penance; forbade masters to dissolve slaves' marriages; required Communion by all on Holy Thursday; and prescribed for monasteries of women. The canons appeared in the second capitulary of the Diet of Aachen (813); Gratian's *Decretum* also contains some of them. Other provincial councils were held at Chalon in 873, 894, and 1056. In 1064 a provincial council under PETER DAMIAN who had been sent by Pope Alexander II at the request of HUGH OF CLUNY, ended the claims of the Bp. Drogo of Mâcon by confirming Cluny's exemption from diocesan authority. In 1072 Alexander II's legate held a council there to oppose simony, with prelates from the Provinces of Vienne and Besançon in attendance.

Bibliography: C. PERRY, *Histoire civile et ecclésiastique . . . de Chalon-sur-Saône* (Chalon-sur-Saône 1659). C. J. VON HEFELE, *Histoire des conciles d'après les documents originaux*, tr. and continued by H. LECLERCQ, 10 v. in 19 (Paris 1907–38) 3:201, 246–247, 282, 1143; 4:104, 636, 687, 697, 733, 1122, 1231, 1283. P. GRAS, *Dictionnaire d'histoire et de Géographie ecclésiastiques*, ed. A. BAUDRILLART et al. (Paris 1912–) 12:294. *Dictionnaire de théologie catholique*, Tables générales, ed. A. VACANT et al., 15 v. (Paris 1951–) 704.

[A. CONDIT]

Thomas Chalmers.

CHAMINADE, GUILLAUME JOSEPH, BL.

Founder of the Marianists and the Marianist Sisters; b. April 8, 1761, Périgueux (Dordogne), France; d. Jan. 22, 1850, Bordeaux. Chaminade was the youngest of the 15 children of a textile merchant. After ecclesiastical studies in Périgueux, Bordeaux, and Paris, he was ordained (1784) and earned a doctorate in theology (1785). He then joined his two brothers as a teacher in the seminary of Mussidan. During the French Revolution he refused to take the oath in support of the Civil Constitution of the Clergy. As a nonjuring priest he exercised his ministry in disguise at Bordeaux until forced into exile in Spain (1797–1800). At the shrine of Our Lady of the Pillar in Saragossa he was inspired to found sodalities and religious societies. Upon his return to France he centered his activities in Bordeaux for the remainder of his life. He acted as administrator of the Diocese of Bazas (1800–1802) before his appointment as canon of the Bordeaux cathedral (1803). Chaminade was responsible for the return of many of the constitutional clergy and for the reestablishment of various religious societies. In 1816 he founded the Marianist Sisters; and in 1817, the Marianists. The origins of almost all pious works and benevolent institutions in Bordeaux during the first half of the 19th century have been traced to Chaminade's efforts. The *Manuel du Serviteur de Marie* (Bordeaux 1801) was Chaminade's sole published work, but his numerous writings are extant in MS form, and together with the notes taken by those attending his conferences, they supply a complete picture of his spirituality. A monument, topped by a statue of Mary Immaculate, marks his grave in Bordeaux. His cause was opened in 1909 and he was beatified by Pope JOHN PAUL II, Sept. 3, 2000, following the instantaneous, miraculous cure of an Argentinian woman's tumor.

Feast: Jan. 22.

Bibliography: H. ROUSSEAU, *William Joseph Chaminade* (Dayton 1914). G. ANGELI, *Dottrina mariana del p. Chaminade* (Subiaco 1976). K. BURTON, *Chaminade, Apostle of Mary* (Milwaukee 1949). M. CHAMINADE, *Our Lady's Tinker* (St. Meinrad, Ind. 1950). M. DARBON, *Guillaume-Joseph Chaminade* (Paris 1946). G. DOIG KLINGE, *Dos maestros espirituales: Guillermo José Chaminade y Fray Luis de Granada*, 2d. ed. (Lima 1990). G. GOYAU, *Chaminade, fondateur des Marianistes, son action religieuse et scolaire* (Paris 1914). H. LEBON, *Dictionnaire de Spiritualité Ascétique et Mystique*, 2:454–459. A. L. SEEBOLD, *Social-Moral Reconstruction according to the Writings and Works of William Joseph Chaminade* (Washington 1948). A. M. WINDISCH, *The Marianist Social System according to the Writings of William Joseph Chaminade* (Fribourg, Switz. 1964).

[G. J. RUPPEL]

CHAMPAGNAT, MARCELLIN JOSEPH BENOÎT, ST.

Baptized Joseph Benoît Champagnat, priest and founder of the MARIST BROTHERS (Little Brothers of Mary); b. the hamlet of Rosey, Marlhes (south of Lyon) in the Loire Valley, France, May 20, 1789; d. Notre Dame de l'Hermitage, Loire, France, June 6, 1840. Champagnat was the ninth of ten children born to Jean-Baptiste, a farmer who also ran a wheat mill, and Marie-Thérèse. His mother and an older sister, Louise, a nun who returned home when her convent was destroyed during the French Revolution, shared with him their devout faith.

Champagnat had no formal education until he was fifteen when he was tutored by his brother-in-law, Benedict Arnaud, so that he could enter the junior seminary of Verrieres. At the major seminary in Lyons his fellow seminarians included St. Jean Baptiste VIANNEY (the Cure of Ars), St. Peter CHANEL, and Ven. Jean Claude COLIN. Champagnat was one of the original group of seminarians at Lyons who discussed with Colin the foundation of the Marist Fathers. They planned the Society of Mary to encompass both teaching brothers, organized by Champagnat, and priests.

After ordination (1816) Champagnat was assigned as a curate in LaValla (Loire). An encounter there with a dying boy who was totally ignorant of Catholic teachings convinced him of the need for teachers who could provide excellent education in rural areas. This incident expedited the foundation of the Marist Brothers (Jan. 2, 1817) with Jean Marie Granjon and Jean-Baptiste Audras as its first members. They opened their first school in Marlhes (1818). The archbishop of Lyons blessed their work and gave it financial support. In 1824, Champagnat was relieved of parish duties to devote himself to organizing and directing his institute.

Meanwhile, he continued to collaborate with Colin in establishing the Marist Fathers. He pronounced his vows as a member in 1836 when Rome approved the congregation. Champagnat was inclined to have the brothers subject to the superior of the Marist Fathers, but Colin, superior of the society, overruled him, making him the superior of the brothers. Champagnat published his pedagogical ideas in *Guide des Écoles* (1853), a work that has been reprinted many times and that serves as a norm for the Marist Brothers. In addition to instilling in students a sense of the transcendent, the need for social values, and commitment to fraternal and divine service, his principles stressed new methods of teaching literacy. Many of his letters to his brothers also survive. He died after dictating his "spiritual testament," and was buried in the cemetery at Notre Dame de l'Hermitage.

At the time of his death, 180 Marists taught 7,000 students in 43 schools in France. In 1852 they opened a school in Britain, the first outside France, and by 1860 there were 379 schools with a total of 50,000 pupils. Today about 5,000 Marists operate schools in 72 countries.

Champagnat was declared venerable by BENEDICT XV in 1920 and beatified by Pope PIUS XII, May 29, 1955. During the canonization ceremony in St. Peter's Square on April 18, 1999, Pope John Paul II praised Champagnat's sensitivity to the spiritual and educational needs of his time and his efforts to overcome the prevailing religious ignorance and the abandonment that youth were experiencing. A statue of Champagnat holding a child on his shoulders can be found in the transept of St. Peter's Basilica, Rome.

Feast: June 6.

Bibliography: *Acta Apostolicae Sedis,* 10 (1999): 459–461. *L'Osservatore Romano,* English edition, no. 16 (1999). *Vatican Information Service* (19 April 1999). BR. JEAN BAPTISTE, *Life and Spirit of J. B. M. Champagnat* (Paris 1947). G. CHASTEL, *Marcellin Champagnat* (Paris 1939). J. COSTE and G. LESSARD, eds., *Origines maristes*, 4 v. (Rome 1960–66). M. A. DORADO SOTO, *El pensamiento educativo de la Institución Marista* (Valencia 1984). J. ÉMILE,

Dictionnaire de spiritualité ascétique et mystique, 2:459–461. BR. IGNACE, *Le Bx. Marcellin Champagnat* (Paris 1955). BR. LEÓ, *Valor actual de la pedagogía del beato Marcelino Champagnat* (Bogota 1956). S. D. SAMMON, *A Heart that Knew No Bounds: The Life and Mission of Saint Marcellin Champagnat* (New York 2000). J. VIGON, *Le Père Champagnat* (Paris 1952).

[L. A. VOEGTLE/EDS.]

CHANCE

The term chance (Lat. *casus*) is used in a variety of ways. In some contexts it is considered as that which is entirely without cause; this was the view of DEMOCRITUS and LUCRETIUS. Other writers count chance as a cause, but differ as to the kind of causality it exercises. Thus some modern scientists, such as Max Born, maintain that chance is the cause of all things; A. EINSTEIN, on the other hand, protested against this thesis by saying that God does not play dice. Others call chance a cause, but insist that it is indeterminate, either because it is the result of a basic indeterminism in nature or because the human intellect cannot encompass the various lines of causality that exist. What these various notions have in common can be clarified by a proper definition of chance, and this is the burden of the present article.

Aristotle's Analysis. ARISTOTLE attempted such a clarification in bk. 2 of the *Physics* (195b 30–198a 13), where he made use of several distinctions in his search for a definition of chance. Of things that come to be, some come to be always in the same way, whereas others do not. Of the latter, some come to be often, whereas others come to be seldom. Chance is found among those things that happen seldom; however, since not everything that happens seldom is by chance, other divisions are necessary to manifest the definition. A further division considers events that happen for a purpose and those that do not. Of the former, some are the result of an intention—whether this be the intention of an intelligent agent or simply what is intended by nature—whereas others are not.

Apart from these distinctions, Aristotle also proposes a division based on causes, since most thinkers agree that chance is in some way a cause. Thus he holds that just as beings are either *per se* or *per accidens,* so also are causes. For example, assuming that a white, musical builder constructs a house, the builder is the *per se* cause of the house, whereas white and musical are its *per accidens* causes. Among *per accidens* causes, some are such by reason of something accidentally associated with the cause, as in the example mentioned, and others are such by reason of something accidentally associated with the effect—for example, an argument that might arise over the house already built. The difference is shown in the accompanying diagram. Chance itself is a kind of *per accidens* cause that results from something accidentally associated with an effect, as the builder just chances to be the cause of the argument over the house. (Notice that in this case one *per se* cause is also a *per accidens* cause; in the case of a *per accidens* cause that is such by reason of something accidentally associated with a per se cause, the latter cause is itself composite, namely, the white builder.)

Utilizing these divisions, Aristotle defines chance as a *per accidens* cause in things that are for an end and that happen seldom. As something happening seldom, the effect in chance is something neither intended nor expected by the agent. Aristotle's example is a man who collects money by going to market for some purpose other than collecting money. If such a man always or usually collected money by going to market, this event would not be by chance.

A further clarification of the notion of chance is achieved by Aristotle's contrasting the chance with the vain. An action is vain when that which was intended does not happen. Aristotle shows that actions can be (1) vain and chance, (2) vain and not chance, (3) chance and not vain, and (4) neither vain nor chance. Suppose that Socrates goes to market to buy cabbage. It might happen that the store is out of cabbage but that Socrates does meet his friend who owed him a debt: vain and chance. Again, he might neither get the cabbage nor meet his friend: vain and not chance. Yet again, he might get the cabbage and meet his friend: chance and not vain. Finally, he might get the cabbage and not meet his friend: neither vain nor chance.

The failure to distinguish between the chance and the vain has led some to hold that chance happens only when the intended end is not achieved. However, as has been seen, there can be chance whether the intended end is achieved or not. What is necessary is that some end be intended. If an agent who acts by intelligence and will attains the unintended end, this is usually called FORTUNE. Among Aristotelians, the term chance is reserved for agents who act by nature.

Causal Intersections. From this definition of chance, it is possible to explain the various positions held concerning it. In the first place, philosophers who hold that all things happen of necessity deny that chance exists. Even among philosophers who admit the existence of chance, there are those who hold that chance causes nothing since it is a *per accidens* cause. It is certainly true that there is an accidental unity in whatever results from chance. It is also true that two or more *per se* causes will be found to have been acting in the production of such an event. St. THOMAS AQUINAS thus says that "a cause which hinders the action of a cause so ordered to its effect as to produce it in the majority of cases, clashes sometimes with this cause by accident: and the clashing of these two causes, inasmuch as it is accidental, has no cause. Consequently what results from this clashing of causes is not to be reduced to a further pre-existing cause, from which it follows of necessity" (*Summa theologiae* 1a, 115.6). The last statement, that the *per accidens* intersection of two lines of causality is not to be reduced to a further preexisting cause, must be understood of a cause preexisting in nature. Aquinas notes in another place: "Let us suppose that a man is prompted to dig a grave by the influence of a celestial body, working through his emotions, as was said. Now the grave and the location of the treasure are united only accidentally, for they have no intrinsic relation to each other. Thus, the power of the celestial body cannot directly give an inclination to this entire result, namely, that this man should dig this grave and that it should be done at the place where the treasure is. But an agent working by intellect can be the cause of an inclination to this entire result, for it is proper for an intelligent being to order many things toward one" (*C. gent.* 3.92). Aquinas further observes that man's intellect can cause an event that in nature would be by chance. He continues, "Fortuitous events of this kind, when referred to their divine cause, lose their fortuitous aspect; but when referred to a celestial cause, they do not" (*ibid.*). Thus chance remains even when the combined effect might be caused by the ordering of a higher cause. The reason is that nature, in this case the celestial body as a natural cause, produces effects that are *per se* one. It cannot have, as a proper effect, something that is only accidentally one. Of such it can be only the *per accidens* cause. This also shows that chance is more than mere ignorance of the concatenation of causes and that chance results from the inability of the lower cause to control causal intersections.

Accidental Causality. The notion that chance is the cause of all things results from a different kind of confusion over the *per accidens*. In the *Metaphysics* (1013b 34–1014a 20) Aristotle again discusses the causes and their division into *per se* and *per accidens*. St. Thomas's commentary on this point is illuminating (*In 5 meta.* 3.789). He states that the *per se* cause can become a *per accidens* cause by reason of something happening to the effect in one of three ways. (1) It may come about in such a way that what is added to the *per se* effect has a necessary order to it, as happens when the primary effect removes an obstacle to the secondary effect. This may happen when a contrary is removed, as when food is spoiled by removing it from a refrigerator, not because heat itself spoils the food, but because the refrigerator's

cold opposed the growth of bacteria that is a cause of the food's spoiling. There can also be a necessary connection of effects when there is no contrariety, as when an arch falls because a pillar is removed. When the secondary effect follows the primary in this way, the *per accidens* cause is not called chance, since such added effects follow always or often. (2) Again, the secondary effect can follow the primary effect, not as something necessary or often, but as happening seldom, as the argument over the house or the finding of a treasure by one digging a grave. The *per accidens* cause of such a secondary effect is called chance or fortune. (3) Finally, the connection between two events may be only in the mind, as one might imagine that his opening a door was the cause of an earthquake, because a tremor occurred just as he was opening the door.

Chance and Luck. Thus not every intersection of lines of causality is to be attributed to chance. If a person decides to cross a muddy street, he should not attribute the soiling of his shoes to chance merely because he did not intend this effect. Such would be chance only if it happened seldom to one who crossed a muddy street. In spite of this, many use the term chance in such indiscriminate fashion. They speak of taking a chance on the horses or of luck in a dice game. Chance in a strict sense is not found in such actions. Suppose, for example, a person bets on a horse and loses. This is not chance but vain. Similarly, if he bets on a horse and wins, to call this chance is to overlook the fact that the winning was what was intended, whereas chance is something that is not intended but is accidentally associated with a primary effect. There is justification for the use of the term chance in such instances, however, because the mind, seeing the general rule, counts what departs from this only slightly as something that has already happened. For example, a person calls the lost wager bad luck because he has carefully considered the factors and come to the firm belief that the possibility of this horse's losing the race is so small that it can be ignored. In other words, he considers the connection of primary and secondary effects to be that of (1) above. The winning is attributed to chance in a similar way. The person bets on the horse, keenly aware that he seldom wins; considering this, he in effect forgets or ignores the fact that he actually intends to win. When he does win, it is something that happens seldom and is, in a way, unintended.

Randomness and Probability. Chance is used improperly in another way when applied to RANDOMNESS or probability. For example, it might be said that an even distribution of sand and cement comes about by chance since it is the result of a random mixing. Again, the killing of a bird by one or two of the many shot pellets fired is said to be accounted for by the laws of chance. This overlooks the fact that the end was intended and, more important in this example, is something probable, whereas chance is what happens seldom. Yet nature is also said to use chance in this way to accomplish her ends. In her production of great numbers of seeds and of many individuals of each species, she intends the preservation of such species. In the circumstances, this seems to be the most economical means of achieving her ends.

That such a use of the term chance is that of Democritus, of Lucretius, and of many modern scientists seems further evidenced by the latters' reference to the laws of chance as laws of probability. Even the term law, when used here, indicates a regularity that is foreign to the proper definition of chance. On the other hand, Einstein's maintaining that God does not play dice is well founded. If God is throwing dice to achieve His effects, He does not do so as a casual player awaiting a fortunate turn of a seven or eleven. Rather, He is more like the scientist investigating probabilities, who throws the dice countless times with the firm assurance that these numbers will occur with a definite frequency.

This last consideration seems to be the basis of the denial of chance by such thinkers as B. SPINOZA, and G. W. LEIBNIZ. They hold that chance results only from the fact that man's intellect cannot encompass the causes at work in any event. Thus, for a greater intellect, chance would not exist. However, although it is true that for a greater intellect there are fewer effects owed to chance and that for the divine intellect nothing is by chance, chance is nonetheless a reality. In effect, these last thinkers are denying indeterminism in nature. Such a solution ignores the fact that something ordained with certainty by a higher cause can still be contingent when considered in its relation to lower causes.

See Also: FATE AND FATALISM; CONTINGENCY; NECESSITY.

Bibliography: H. J. FREEMAN, *The Problem of Chance* (Doctoral diss. unpub. River Forest, Ill. 1963). M. BORN, *Natural Philosophy of Cause and Chance* (Oxford 1949). C. DE KONINCK, "Abstraction from Matter, III," *Laval Théologique et Philosophique* 16 (1960) 169–188. A. ALIOTTA, *Enciclopedia filosofica* (Venice-Rome 1957) 1:921–927. R. EISLER, *Wörterbuch der philosophischen Begriffe* (Berlin 1027–30) 3:667–670. M. J. ADLER, ed., *The Great Ideas: A Syntopicon of Great Books of the Western World* (Chicago 1952) 1:179–192.

[R. A. KOCOUREK]

CHANCELLOR, DIOCESAN (EPARCHIAL)

The chancellor of a diocese is a person whose principal work is to care for the archives of the diocese. The word "chancellor" comes from the Latin *cancellarius.* In ancient Rome the *cancellarius* was the doorkeeper who stood at the latticework or chancel, which separated the magistrate in the law courts from the people, and admitted petitioners. He gradually assumed the work of a kind of secretary or notary with judicial powers. The term chancellor was later given to the civil notaries whom the bishops were empowered to appoint by the legislation of Charlemagne.

As the curias of the bishops began to develop, the need grew for repeated use of authentic documents and written testimony drawn up by a public person of ecclesiastical authority. The Fourth Council of the Lateran (1215) ordered bishops to have a public person or two other competent men for the work of drawing up both judicial and extrajudicial acts [*Corpus iuris canonici,* ed. E. Friedberg (Leipzig 1879–81; repr. Graz 1955) X 2.19.11; cf. J. D. Mansi, *Sacrorum Concilorum nova et amplissima collectio,* 31 v. (Florence–Venice 1757–98); repr. and cont. by L. Petit and J. B. Martin 53 v. in 60 (Paris 1889–1927; repr. Graz 1960–), 23.154]. These officials came to be termed variously: chancellors, notaries, actuaries, and *tabelliones.*

The Third Provincial Council of Milan (1573), besides designating the chancellor as notary, also made him custodian of the archives. One of its decrees ordered the curial documents to be preserved in the episcopal archives under the care of the chancellor, who was to keep the key to them. This and other local legislation and custom gradually produced the general law setting up the office of chancellor with his double function of public notary in the curia and custodian of the diocesan archives.

Under present law [*Codex iuris canonici* (Rome 1918; rep. Graz 1955) c. 482 §1; *Codex Canonum Ecclesiarium Orientalium, c.* 252 §1], the chancellor is the authorized official whose chief functions are to preserve in the archives the acts of the curia, to arrange them in order, and to compile an index of them. By reason of office the chancellor is also a notary (*Codex iuris canonici c.* 482 §3; *Codex Canonum Ecclesiarium Orientalium, c.* 252 §3).

As to qualifications, the chancellor must be of good reputation and above all suspicion. In the Eastern Churches, the chancellor must be a deacon or a priest (see *Codex Canonum Ecclesiarium Orientalium, c.* 252 1); this is not the case in the Latin Church.

The diocesan bishop can freely remove the chancellor from office. A diocesan administrator may not remove a diocesan chancellor without the consent of the college of consultors (*Codex iuris canoninci c.* 485; CCEO *c.* 255). If necessary, the chancellor may be given an assistant with the name of vice-chancellor (*Codex iuris canonici c.* 482; §2; CCEO *c.* 252 §2). The chancellor's duties are performed in subordination to the bishop and the vicar-general.

In many dioceses, particularly in the U.S., the chancellor has additional functions. These are not given, however, by the general law, which defines his duties merely as those of archivist-notary. In such instances the chancellor receives delegated jurisdiction, in whole or in part, from the bishop, and not by virtue of office (*Codex iuris canonici c.* 981 §1).

Bibliography: L. MATHIAS, *The Diocesan Curia* (Madras 1947) 35–39. J. E. PRINCE, *The Diocesan Chancellor* (Catholic University of America, *Studies in Medieval and Renaissance Latin, Language and Literature* 167; Washington 1942). F. X. WERMZ and P. VIDAL, *Ius canonicum,* 7 v. in 8 (Rome), v. 1 (2d ed. 1952), v. 2 (3d ed. 1943), v. 3 (1933), v. 4.1 (1934), v. 4.2 (2d ed. 1936), v. 5 3d ed. 1946), v. 6 (2d ed. 1949), v. 7 (2d ed. 1951) 2:644–645.

[E. A. FORBES/EDS.]

CHANDLER, JOSEPH RIPLEY

Member of U.S. Congress, journalist; b. Kingston, Mass., Aug. 25, 1792; d. Philadelphia, Pa., July 10, 1880. He was the son of Joseph and Saba (Ripley) Chandler. Although largely self-educated, he conducted a girls' seminary in Philadelphia from 1818 until 1826, when, with a small group of associates, he purchased the newspaper *Gazette of the United States.* He eventually became sole proprietor and made the *Gazette* one of the most influential Whig journals until 1847, when he sold it to the *North American.* In 1848 he became an editor of *Graham's American Monthly Magazine of Literature.*

Chandler was a member of Philadelphia's common council (1832–48) and a delegate to the state constitutional convention of 1837; he was also president of the first board of trustees of Girard College, Philadelphia, and grand master of the Pennsylvania Freemasons. He had married a Catholic in 1833 and in 1849 was received into the Church. Elected to Congress in 1848 as a Clay Whig, he was twice reelected. His speech "The Temporal Power of the Pope," delivered in the House in 1855, answered Rep. Nathaniel Banks's charge that Catholicism was incompatible with political liberty. In 1858 Chandler was appointed U.S. minister to the Kingdom of the Two Sicilies, where he served until 1861. Returning to Philadelphia, he renewed an earlier interest in penology. A member of the board of inspectors of the county prison (1861–80), he represented the Philadelphia Society for Alleviating the Miseries of Public Prisons at an international congress in London in 1872.

Several of Chandler's orations were published in pamphlet form, but the elegant and highly moral fugitive

St. Peter Louis Marie Chanel.

pieces upon which his literary reputation rested have never been collected. His other works include *A Grammar of the English Language* (1821, rev. ed., 1848), a text widely used in public schools, and *The Beverly Family or the Home Influence of Religion* (1875), a didactic novel preaching religious tolerance.

Bibliography: M. SHAVER, *Dictionary of American Biography,* ed. A. JOHNSON and D. MALONE, 20 v. (New York 1928–36; index 1937; 1st suppl. 1944; 2d suppl. 1958), 3:614–615.

[F. GERRITY]

CHANEL, PETER LOUIS MARIE, ST.

Missionary; b. Cuet (Ain), France, July 12, 1803; d. Futuna Island, Oceania, April 28, 1841. After ordination he joined the recently founded MARIST FATHERS (1831) and sailed (1836) with Bishop Pompallier as provicar and superior of the seven Marists to whom was entrusted the vicariate of Western Oceania, established that year. When still 1,500 miles from his eventual headquarters in New Zealand, the bishop left Pierre BATAILLON and one brother on Wallis Island, and Chanel and Brother Nizier on neighboring Futuna (1837). Pompallier proposed to return in six months, but circumstances delayed him for five years. In his isolation Chanel struggled with an unknown language and was wholly dependent on inconstant chiefs for material needs, but he made the difficult adjustment to a world of whalers, traders, and warring tribes of savages. His serene, gentle character endured with profound faith, patience, and fortitude the frustrations of apparent failure, severe privations, and finally, active persecution by the principal chief. A few had been baptized, a few more were being instructed, when Chanel was surrounded in his hut and clubbed to death, becoming thereby Oceania's first martyr. In 1843 the whole island became Catholic and has remained so. Chanel was beatified November 17, 1889, and canonized June 12, 1954.

Feast: April 28.

Bibliography: L. LAURAND, *La Croix au bout du monde* (Brussels 1968). J.-C. MARQUIS, *St. Pierre Chanel: de l'Ain au Pacifique* (Bourg-en- Bresse 1991). C. ROZIER, *Écrits du Père Pierre Chanel* (Paris 1960), with full bibliog. W. SYMES, *Life of St. Peter Chanel* (Bolton, Eng. 1963).

[J. E. BELL]

CHANNING, WILLIAM ELLERY

Unitarian clergyman and author; b. Newport, Rhode Island, April 7, 1780; d. Bennington, Vermont, Oct. 2, 1842. He belonged to a prominent New England family. Five years after his graduation (1798) from Harvard, he was ordained a minister in the Congregational Church. Shortly afterward he became pastor of Federal Street Church in Boston, Massachusetts, where he remained until his death. In 1814 he married his cousin Ruth Gibbs. Channing's sermon at Jared Spark's ordination (1819) in Baltimore, Maryland, earned him the title "apostle of Unitarianism." He soon became involved in the controversy that divided the Congregationalists of New England into the so-called orthodox Calvinists and the opposition group, or Unitarians. In 1820 he organized a conference of liberal Congregational ministers, and five years later he formed the American Unitarian Association (*see* UNITARIAN UNIVERSALIST ASSOCIATION). Channing's form of religious liberalism emphasized humanitarianism and toleration rather than doctrinal novelties. His sermons and writings exercised considerable influence over American authors such as R. W. Emerson, W. C. Bryant, H. W. Longfellow, J. R. Lowell, and O. W. Holmes. For Channing, all questions were moral questions. He was ahead of his time in his views on temperance, labor problems and public and adult education. He considered slavery an evil to be wiped out at the earliest possible opportunity. A pacifist, Channing organized the Massachusetts Peace Society to destroy the romantic glamour of war.

William Ellery Channing.

Bibliography: D. P. EDGELL, *William Ellery Channing: An Intellectual Portrait* (Boston 1955).

[J. Q. FELLER]

CHANT BOOKS, PRINTED EDITIONS OF

The first Catholic liturgical book was the Bible, from which the Lessons were read and the Psalms chanted, until at least the fourth century when the codifying of Catholic ritual and ritual music began. This article covers only printed collections of Gregorian chant used in the Latin Mass and Divine Office.

Medicean Edition. The first important printed edition of Gregorian chant, the Medicean, published by the Medici press at Rome in 1614–15, has been incorrectly associated with PALESTRINA. In 1577 he and Zoilo had been commissioned by Gregory XIII to systematize the chants contained in the Missals and Breviaries newly revised in conformity to the decrees of the Council of Trent. Zoilo had corrected the sanctoral cycle of Masses, and Palestrina, the Sunday Masses, but both of their MSS were lost after the death of Palestrina in 1594 and were never published. The Roman printer, Giovanni Battista Raimondi, had contracted with Palestrina to complete the

Opening page of "Liber Gradualis," chant book published in 1883, Solesmes, France.

work, but after Palestrina's death and the deceitful intrigues of his son Iginio, nothing was done until 1608. On May 31 of that year, Paul V gave Raimondi permission to undertake the printing of new chant books. Six editors were appointed to prepare the MSS: G. B. Nanino, C. Mancini, F. Soriano, R. Giovanelli, P. Felini, and F. Anerio; and the resulting Medicean edition appeared only in 1614–15, after the death of Raimondi. This edition contains a mutilated and truncated melody. The editors considered it barbaric to allow many notes on syllables not containing the tonic accent of the Latin word, nor would they allow long notes over the grammatically short syllables, or vice versa. Moreover, they eliminated many of the melismatic passages in the Graduals and Alleluias.

Ratisbon Edition. The most important editions printed in the 19th century were those of Ratisbon and Solesmes. The Ratisbon work was edited by Msgr. F. X. Haberl and published in 1869 by F. PUSTET of Ratisbon (Regensburg), Germany. Haberl had found a copy of the Medicean edition in the seminary library at Freising and

was convinced that it was based on the MS that Palestrina had prepared for Gregory XIII. Subsequent researches of R. Molitor, C. Respighi, and R. C. Casimiri proved that Haberl's claim was unfounded. In 1868 Pustet received permission for the exclusive printing of chant books for 30 years. This was followed by a long series of decrees and approbations by Pius IX and Leo XIII that in effectively gave an "official" character to this edition. Thus Haberl's work prolonged the errors of the Medicean edition.

Vatican Edition. The Vatican edition was based on paleographic researches by the monks of Saint-Pierre de SOLESMES, Solesmes-sur-Sarthe, France. It was initiated under Abbot GUÉRANGER and carried out by Dom Pothier, and Dom MOCQUEREAU; the Liber Gradualis of 1883 and 1895 was the work of Pothier, and the Liber Usualis of 1903 that of Mocquereau. In 1904 Pope St. Pius X appointed a commission under the presidency of Pothier to prepare an official edition of the chant books. Since the commission decided to base the new edition on the Pothier works of 1883 and 1895, and not that of 1903 by Mocquereau, the Solesmes monks withdrew from the work. The books of the Vatican edition appeared as follows: Kyriale, Aug. 14, 1905; Cantus Missae, June 8, 1907; Graduale Vaticanum, Aug. 7, 1907; Officiorum Defunctorum, May 12, 1909; Cantorinus, April 3, 1911; and Antiphonale Diurnum Romanum, Dec. 8, 1912. Even though the Solesmes monks did not officially participate in this edition, Pothier incorporated more than 2,000 improvements in the 1907 Graduale Vaticanum that he had taken from the Liber Usualis prepared by Solesmes in 1903. Since 1913 all Propers for new feasts and new saints have been entrusted to the monks of Solesmes.

The Vatican edition was available with or without the Solesmes rhythmical signs that represent devices and letters found in some tenth-century MSS (they appear in the Desclée editions of Tournai Belgium). At first the Solesmes monks attached them to the notes and even altered the shape of certain notes in order to reproduce them. Many musicians did not accept the Solesmes interpretation, and a decree of the Congregation of Sacred Rites, dated Feb. 14, 1906, directed that all reproductions of the Vatican edition must reproduce the notes exactly; if any rhythmical signs are added they must be separate from the neums and not alter their shape in any manner. The *Instruction on Sacred Music and Sacred Liturgy* (Sept. 3, 1958) stated that rhythmical signs may be admitted, provided that the nature and arrangement of the notes as given in the Vatican editions of chant be preserved intact.

Bibliography: A. GASTOUÉ, *Musique et liturgie: Le Gradual et l' Antiphonaire romains: Histoire et description* (Lyon 1913). F. X. HABERL, *Giovanni Pierluigi da Palestrina und das Graduale Ro-*

manum Officiale der Editio Medicaea von 1614 (New York 1894). A. MARCHESAN, "L'Opera di Pio X nella restauratione della musica sacra," *Bollettino Ceciliano* 5 (1910) 209–224. R. MOLITOR, *Die Nach-Tridentinische Choral-Reform zu Rom,* 2 v. (Leipzig 1901–02). A. PONS, *Droit ecclésiastique et Musique sacrée,* 4 v. (St. Maurice 1958–61). C. RESPIGHI, *Giovanni Pier Luigi da Palestrina e l'Emdazione del Graduale Romano* (Rome 1899). F. ROMITA, *Jus musicae liturgicae* (Turin 1936); *La preformazione del Motu Proprio di S. Pio X sulla musica sacra* (Rome 1961). A. FORTESCUE, *The Catholic Encyclopedia,* ed. C. G. HERBERMANN et al. (New York 1907–14) 9.1:296–304. R. HAYBURN, *St. Pius X and the Vatican Edition of the Chant Books* (Los Angeles 1964).

[R. F. HAYBURN/EDS.]

CHANTAL, JANE FRANCES DE, ST.

Foundress of the Order of the Visitation of Holy Mary; b. Dijon, France, Jan. 23, 1572; d. Moulins, Dec. 13, 1641.

When Jane was 18 months old, her mother, Marguerite de Berbisey, died. Her father, Bénigne Frémyot, councilor and afterward president of the parliament at Dijon, became the main influence in her formation. She was educated at home by visiting tutors in reading, writing, dancing, and playing musical instruments—the usual subjects for girls of her station. She developed into a woman of beauty and quality, with good judgment and a lively, gay temperament.

At the age of 21 she married Baron Christophe de Rabutin-Chantal. At their residence, the castle of Bourbilly, near Semur-en-Auxois, she reestablished the custom of daily Mass, introduced other communal practices of piety, and engaged in works of charity. Of the couple's six children, two died at an early age; a boy and three girls survived. After seven years of marriage her husband was killed in a hunting accident. She returned to her father's home, where, desiring to make progress in the spiritual life, she sought priestly guidance. Her director encouraged her in a piety that was already excessive and austere.

Under threat of disinheriting her children, her father-in-law required her to return in autumn 1602 to live with him at Monthelon. There she spent seven-and-one-half years exercising the virtues of patience and humility, and working on the education of her children.

In 1604 on a visit to her father she met Francis de Sales and wished to place herself under his direction. After some hesitation he consented and began her spiritual formation according to his principles. She made a double vow—to remain unmarried and to obey him. The fulfillment of her wish to enter the religious life was deferred and she was counseled to have patience. In 1607

St. Jane Frances de Chantal.

he disclosed to her his plan for founding a group of women who would especially imitate the virtues exemplified in Mary's visit to Elizabeth and secondarily engage in works of mercy toward the poor and sick. On June 6, 1610, she and two companions assisted at Mass, which he celebrated in his chapel, received their rule from him, and afterward retired to their convent, known as the Gallery House. First vows were pronounced a year later.

Both the name and the constitutions of the institute underwent various changes. The official title became the Visitation of Holy Mary. A second revision of the rule in 1613 established its general plan, which was further modified when the external works of charity were eliminated and the cloister adopted under the influence of the bishop of Lyons, Denis Simon de Marquemont. On 23 April 1618, Paul V elevated the institute to the dignity of a religious order.

After the foundation of the Visitation, Jane de Chantal was concerned both with perfecting herself and her followers in its spirit and with establishing new monasteries. By the time of her death there were 80 houses. Benedict XIV beatified her on August 21, 1751; canonization took place under Clement XIII on July 16, 1767.

Feast: December 12.

Bibliography: *Sa Vie et Ses Oeuvres,* 7 v. (Paris 1874–79). *Jeanne de Chantal: Zeugnisse ihrer Zeitgenossen,* ed. L. MARIL (Einsiedeln 1967). FRANCIS DE SALES, *Jane de Chantal: Letters of Spiritual Direction,* tr. P. M. THIBERT, ed. W. M. WRIGHT and J. F. POWER (New York 1988). É. BOUGAUD, *St. Chantal and the Foundation of the Visitation,* tr. A. Visitandine, 2 v. (New York 1895–1902). G. PAPÀSOGLI, *Come piace a Dio* (Rome 1981). A. RAVIER, *Jeanne-Françoise Frémyot, baronne de Chantal* (Paris 1983) and Eng. tr. M. E. HAMILTON *Saint Jeanne de Chantal: Noble Lady, Holy Woman* (San Francisco 1989); *Petite vie de Jeanne de Chantal* (Paris 1992). E. K. SANDERS, *Saint Chantal* (New York 1928). E. STOPP, *Madame de Chantal* (Westminster, MD 1963), with bibliography; *Hidden in God: Essays and Talks on St. Jane Frances de Chantal,* ed. T. O'REILLY (Philadelphia 1999). W. M. WRIGHT, *Bond of Perfection: Jeanne de Chantal and François de Sales* (New York 1985); *A Retreat with Francis de Sales, Jane de Chantal, and Aelred of Rievaulx: Befriending Each Other in God* (Cincinnati, Ohio 1996).

[E. J. CARNEY]

CHAPEL

A miniature church, established originally as a place of prayer or *oratorium,* in royal or episcopal residences. With the extension of Christianity to the rural areas, the establishment of an oratory as a place of worship for a local population gave the chapel a public function. In some sections the *martyrium* or *memoria,* a shrine erected to house the relics of a saint or to honor the place of his martyrdom, became a center for religious services. In the 5th century the councils gave these private centers of worship an official character by bringing them under the jurisdiction of the local bishop. The chapel remained, however, the possession of the founder and his heirs. Clerics attached to a private church often became subject to the will of the owner rather than to the jurisdiction of the bishop, and the clergy of the king's chapel played a major role in the management of the realm.

The etymology of the word ''chapel'' is based upon the *capella* of St. MARTIN OF TOURS, which the Merovingian kings kept in the oratory of their palace. This precious relic was the legendary cape Martin divided with a beggar and later beheld in a vision as worn by Christ Himself. The *capella* was carried into battle as a pledge of victory and used as a surety for the verification of oaths. Confusion between the *oratorium,* where the oath was administered, and the *capella,* upon which it was sworn, caused the oratory of the palace to become known as the *Capella s. Martini,* the chapel of St. Martin. The priest in charge of the royal oratory came to be called the chaplain from his office as *capellanus,* guardian of the cape. Under CHARLEMAGNE this office gained important status and was sometimes exercised by a bishop.

At the same time the famous church of AACHEN was built as the royal chapel, setting the model for a type of ecclesiastical institution whose office and influence far exceeded the meaning of its name. The great architectural developments of the medieval centuries found original and characteristic expression in chapels independently constructed or integrally attached to a cathedral or monastic church. Notable examples may be found in the abbey church of SAINT-DENIS and the Sainte-Chapelle of LOUIS IX. In modern times the word is applied to a variety of ecclesiastical buildings, smaller than churches and attached to universities, colleges, and hospitals. The papal chapel (*capella pontificia*), originally the site of liturgical service within the LATERAN or the Vatican (*see* SISTINE CHAPEL), is today the assembly of the sacred college of cardinals and of other dignitaries, both clerical and lay, meeting with the pope in solemn liturgical ceremonies.

Bibliography: Sources. *Monumenta Germaniae Historica: Capitularia* (Berlin 1826–) v.2. HINCMAR, *De ordine palatii,* ch. 15 in *Monumenta Germaniae Historica: Capitularia* (Berlin 1826–) 2.3:523. EINHARD, *The Life of Charlemagne,* tr. S. E. TURNER (Ann Arbor 1960). *Vita Betharii, Monumenta Germaniae Historica: Scriptores rerum Merovingicarum* (Berlin 1826–) 3:615. SUGER, *Abbott Suger on the Abbey Church of St. Denis and Its Art Treasures,* ed. and tr. E. PANOFSKY (Princeton 1946). Literature. H. LECLERCQ, *Dictionnaire d'archéologie chrétienne et de liturgie,* ed. F. CABROL, H. LECLERCQ, and H. I. MARROU, 15 v. (Paris 1907–53) 3.1:406–428; 10.2:2512–23. A. VILLIEN and H. LECLERCQ, *ibid.* 3.1:390–399. W. HENRY, *ibid.* 1.1:1039–42. G. JACQUEMET et al., *Catholicisme. Hier, aujourd'hui et demain,* ed. G. JACQUEMET (Paris 1947–) 2:933–939. E. H. SWIFT, *Roman Sources of Christian Art* (New York 1951). H. SAALMAN, *Medieval Architecture* (New York 1962). O. VON SIMSON, *The Gothic Cathedral* (2d ed. New York 1962). F. L. CROSS, *The Oxford Dictionary of the Christian Church* (London 1957) 263.

[P. J. MULLINS]

CHAPELLE, PLACIDE LOUIS

Diplomat, archbishop;. b. Runes, France, Aug. 28, 1842; d. New Orleans, Louisiana, Aug. 9, 1905. He was educated at Mende, department of Lozère, and at Enghien, Belgium. At age 17 he immigrated to the United States and entered St. Mary's Seminary, Baltimore, Maryland. Before his ordination in June of 1865, he taught at St. Charles College, Catonsville, Maryland. His first years as a priest were spent as assistant at St. John's Church, then pastor of St. Joseph's, both in Baltimore; in 1882, he became pastor of St. Matthew's, Washington, D.C. In November of 1891, he was consecrated titular bishop of Arabissus and coadjutor with right of succession to Archbishop J. B. Salpointe of SANTA FE, New Mexico. When Salpointe resigned, Chapelle became archbishop in 1894 and ruled Santa Fe until 1897.

On Dec. 1, 1897, shortly before the outbreak of the Spanish–American War, Chapelle was transferred to the

Interior of the Palatine Chapel. (©Archivo Iconographico S.A./CORBIS)

Archdiocese of NEW ORLEANS as its sixth archbishop. In 1898 he was appointed apostolic delegate to Puerto Rico and Cuba and chargé d'affaires of the Philippine Islands. Early in 1899, he visited the Caribbean area, returning to his see in April to receive the pallium from Bishop Edward Fitzgerald of Little Rock, Arkansas. Later that year, he went to the Philippines and while in Manila secured the release of priests and religious taken prisoner by Aguinaldo. He later helped in solving the many problems pertaining to Church properties and parochial rights of the Spanish clergy in the islands. Leo XIII, in a pontifical brief, praised the archbishop's work; he was named an assistant to the pontifical throne and count of the Roman Court. Although Chapelle asked to be relieved of diplomatic duties in order to devote his energies to New Orleans, he continued temporarily as apostolic delegate to Cuba and Puerto Rico, directing the redistribution of dioceses and parishes there.

Despite frequent and lengthy absences from New Orleans, Chapelle founded 12 parishes and missions, brought the Dominican fathers to the archdiocese, and opened the St. Louis theological seminary in Faubourg Bouligny. One of his main concerns throughout his tenure in New Orleans was the reduction of the diocesan debt that had burdened three of his predecessors. He succeeded in liquidating the debt but not without alienating some of his priests, who claimed that the tax imposed by the archbishop, in addition to the normal assessments, was excessive. Another cause of complaint was the number and length of his absences from the archdiocese on diplomatic missions. As if to answer his critics, the archbishop scheduled a series of parish visitations in 1905, reaching the farthermost parish, Lake Charles, in July. There he learned that an epidemic of yellow fever had broken out in New Orleans. He hastened back to the city, but a few days later he died, a victim of the disease.

Bibliography: F. J. TSCHAN, *Dictionary of American Biography,* ed. A. JOHNSON and D. MALONE, 20 v. (New York 1928–36) 4:11–12.

[H. C. BEZOU]

CHAPMAN, JOHN

Benedictine historian and exegete; b. Ashfield, England, April 25, 1865; d. Downside, Nov. 7, 1933. He was educated at Christ Church, Oxford, and took Anglican orders in 1889 but joined the Catholic Church in 1890. In 1892 he became a Benedictine at MAREDSOUS, and was ordained in 1895. He was master of novices and prior at ERDINGTON (1895–1912), superior at CALDEY (1913–14), and a chaplain in England, France, and Switzerland during World War I. After the war he worked on the commission for the Vulgate in Rome (1919–22), and became prior (1922) and then abbot (1929 to his death) of DOWNSIDE, to which he had transferred his residence in 1919. He contributed numerous articles on patrology and Church history for the *Revue Bénédictine,* the *Dublin Review,* the *Catholic Encyclopedia,* and the *Encyclopedia of Religion and Ethics.* The most important of his early works are *Notes on the Early History of the Vulgate Gospels* (Oxford 1908) and *John the Presbyter and the Fourth Gospel* (Oxford 1911). He wrote several treatises on problems of the spiritual life and on mysticism. After his death his *Spiritual Letters* (London 1935) and *Matthew, Mark and Luke* (London 1937) were published; the latter argues that the Greek text of Matthew is earlier than that of Mark.

Bibliography: F. L. CROSS, *The Oxford Dictionary of the Christian Church* (London 1957) 264. G. R. HUDLESTON, *Dictionnaire de spiritualité ascétique et mystique. Doctrine et histoire,* ed. M. VILLER et al. (Paris 1932—) 2:488–492. R. GAZEAU, *Catholicisme* 2:946–947.

[F. X. MURPHY]

CHAPPOTIN DE NEUVILLE, HELÉNÈ DE

Founder of the Franciscan Missionaries of Mary; b. Nantes, France, May 21, 1839; d. San Remo, Italy, Nov. 15, 1904. Helénè, the daughter of Sophie Caroline (du Fort) and Paul Charles Chappotin, displayed interest in the missions early on. She entered the Society of MARY REPARATRIX in 1864 and took the name Mother Mary of the Passion. From 1865 to 1876 she labored in the Madura missions of India, and was appointed provincial superior there at the age of 29. In 1877 Pope Pius IX authorized her to found the Institute of Missionaries of Mary. The founder had been interested in the Franciscan mode of life since her brief association with the POOR CLARES in 1860. She was received into the third order of Franciscans in 1882, when her own institute became permanently affiliated with the FRANCISCANS and took the name Franciscan Missionaries of Mary. Mother Mary of the Passion received final approbation of her constitutions from the Holy See (May 11, 1896). Her *Meditations liturgiques et franciscaines* (5 v. Paris 1896–98) constitutes a legacy of spiritual writings for her missionary sisters. Her cause for beatification was introduced in 1923.

Bibliography: T. F. CULLEN, *Mother Mary of the Passion* (abr.ed. North Providence, Rhode Island 1942). G. GOYAU, *Valiant Women: Mother Mary of the Passion* . . . , tr. from French by G. TELFORD (London 1936).

[M. F. CONDON]

CHAPPUIS, MARIA SALESIA, VEN.

Visitation nun; b. Soyhières, France (now Switzerland), June 16,1793; d. Troyes (Aube), France, Oct. 7, 1875. Maria was the sixth of ten children of Catherine (Fleury) and Pierre Chappuis, a judge. After attending a school (1805–08) run by the VISITATION NUNS at Fribourg, Switzerland, Marie entered this order in 1811 but soon left. She returned in 1814 and pronounced her first vows in 1816. Soon after this she was assigned to Metz to start a new Visitation convent, but ill health compelled her return to Fribourg. At Troyes she was chosen superior in 1826 and held this office for 11 terms. From 1838 to 1844 she was superior in Paris. In both Troyes and Paris she served also as mistress of novices. At Troyes she was associated with Louis BRISSON and collaborated with him in the foundation of the OBLATE SISTERS OF ST. FRANCIS DE SALES (1866) and the OBLATES OF ST. FRANCIS DE SALES (c. 1871). Her cause for beatification was introduced in 1897. Questions have since been raised concerning her spiritual doctrines, which did not, however, profess to inaugurate a new school.

Bibliography: L. BRISSON, *Vie de la vénérée Mère de Sales Chappuis* (Paris 1891). P. DUFOUR, *Dictionnaire de spiritualité ascétique et mystique. Doctrine et histoire,* ed., M. VILLER et al. (Paris 1932) 2:496–498. H. WAACH, *Marie de Sales* (Kriens 1969).

[E. J. CARNEY]

CHAPT DE RASTIGNAC, ARMAND, BL.

Theologian; b. the Périgord, France, Oct. 2, 1729; d. Paris Sept. 3–15, 1792. He received his doctorate at the Sorbonne, was appointed pastor at Saint-Mesmin d'Orléans, and eventually took the post of vicar-general of the Diocese of Arles. He was a deputy at the assembly of the French clergy in 1755 and 1760. He participated in the meetings of the Estates General in 1789 and tried to forestall action against ecclesiastical property. Because of the weakness of his voice, he wrote out and published two of his most important statements: *Question sur la propriété des biens ecclésiastiques* (Paris 1789) and *Accord de la révélation contre le divorce* (Paris 1791). In addition he translated and published with notes the famous synodal letter of Patriarch Nicholas III (d. 1111) of Constantinople to the Emperor Alexius I Comnenus (d. 1118) regarding the authority of emperors with relation to the erection of ecclesiastical sees, *Lettre synodale de Nicolas* (Paris 1790). He signed protests against the arbitrary anticlerical laws of the Constituent Assembly. He fell sick and was bedridden for many months; when finally arrested for his views, he could scarcely walk. After a short imprisonment, he was killed in the September massacres. His beatification took place on Oct. 17, 1926.

Helénè De Chappotin De Neuville.

Feast: Sept. 2.

Bibliography: C. TOUSSAINT, *Dictionnaire de théologie catholique,* ed. A. VACANT, 15 v. (Paris 1903–50; Tables générales 1951–) 2.2:2215–16. G.JACQUEMET, *Catholicisme* 2:949. H. HURTER, *Nomenclator literarius theologiae catholicae,* 5 v. in 6 (3d ed. Innsbruck 1903–1913); v.1 (4th ed. 1926)[3] 5:306.

[C. MEYER]

CHAPTER OF FAULTS

Chapter of faults is a meeting of the members of a religious community, held at an appointed time and place (usually the chapter house or room), at which those members guilty of some transgression of the rule publicly confess their faults. The custom serves, on the one hand, to guard the religious discipline of the house, and on the other hand, to exercise the members in humility and mutual understanding. From its beginnings in the 3rd century, monasticism has included in its daily or weekly schedule some kind of public confession. Precepts in St. Basil's *Rules,* observed by contemporary Eastern monks, provide for a confession comparable to the modern Western form of the chapter; and from the 4th to the 9th century, both in the East and the West, customs similar to the modern chapter were practiced wherever monasticism was found. But the *Rule of St. Benedict,* though it provided for public acknowledgment of faults, did not specifically provide for a chapter. The chapter in its contemporary form did not appear until the time of the customaries of the 8th and 9th centuries. In customaries, such as those of Cluny and Hirschau, the modern chapter is prescribed in detail; even the verbal formulas are still in use: the monks were to confess their faults in turn before the community and receive their penances from the abbot. The *clamatio* or *proclamatio,* the accusation of one monk by another in chapter, was generally included as an essential part of the chapter. This custom was more or less uniform and universal throughout the later Middle Ages. The monastic reforms and new institutions of each generation incorporated it into their constitutions. Notable among them in the 12th century were the Cistercians and the new orders of friars—the Dominicans, Carmelites, and Franciscans. It was preserved also by the new institutions of the Counter Reformation, with the exception of the Society of Jesus, which substituted other forms of discipline. The influence of Jansenism in ascetical theology helped to ensure the preservation of this custom into the 20th century; but with the widespread modern reaction against Jansenist tendencies, the chapter of faults (along with other ascetical practices misunderstood by the Jansenists) has tended to play a less serious role in monasticism than that envisioned by the early medieval constitutions. In most—though by no means in all—religious congregations the *proclamatio* has fallen into disuse.

Bibliography: P. SCHMITZ, *Dictionnaire de spiritualité ascétique et mystique. Doctrine et histoire,* ed. M. VILLER et al. (Paris 1932–) 2:483–488.

[A. DONAHUE]

CHAPTERS, RELIGIOUS

The *chapter* is an organ of governance within a religious institute constituted in accord with the proper law of the institute with the authority to make decisions and set direction. In religious institutes belonging to the Eastern Churches the comparable organ of governance is called a *synaxis* (*Codex Canonum Ecclesiarum Orientalium,* 441, 511, and 512). The primary work of a chapter is to preserve the spiritual patrimony or heritage of the institute; it carries out this general mandate by promoting suitable renewal, electing superiors and councils as determined by its proper law, treating matters of major importance to the institute, and issuing norms which bind members. Chapters may be *general,* representing the entire institute; *provincial,* representing a province of the institute; or *local,* representing an individual religious house. A *chapter of elections* deals exclusively with elections while a *chapter of affairs* deals with other matters. A chapter is *ordinary* when it occurs at the regular intervals established in the institute's proper law; chapters convoked at other times are *extraordinary.*

The proper law of each religious institute specifies the frequency with which the chapter meets, how its members (*capitulars*) are selected and the manner of conducting business. The chapter body usually includes both *ex officio* members, i.e., participants by reason of office held, and elected members. Constitutions of some institutes also give the highest superior or the chapter itself the faculty, for serious reasons, to appoint additional members with full capitular rights. Chapters of monastic institutes, of very small institutes, and of local houses are usually coextensive with their membership. Each chapter, however, regardless of size, authority or composition, should be representative of the whole institute or of that part of the institute for which it acts.

The formal divisions of a chapter are convocation, celebration, and confirmation, each governed by the proper law of the institute. Convocation is the authoritative announcement to all who have the right to participate of the assembling at a definite place at a definite time. The person competent according to proper law convokes a chapter; ordinarily this is the superior who acts after obtaining either the advice or consent of the council as indicated by proper law. Many institutes require convocation of general chapters 6 to 12 months prior to the actual convening.

A chapter convenes at the time it is formally opened by the person competent according to the institute's proper law, and it is celebrated in accord with the provisions of proper law. Celebration encompasses that series of actions, including prayer, discussion, and voting, by which the chapter conducts its affairs. Absent applicable norms in the proper law of the institute, universal law governs (*Codex Iuris Canonicis* 631–632 on chapters, 119 and 164–179 on elections, and 124–126 on juridic acts; *Codex Canonum Ecclesiarium Orientalium,* 511–512 on synaxes, 947–956 on elections, and 931–933 on juridic acts). By its nature the chapter functions collegially, i.e., although presided over by designated authority, each member including the presiding officer votes on an equal basis with every other member. In addition, all individual members of the institute, provinces, and houses are free to send suggestions to the general chapter, in accord with the norms of proper law.

Confirmation is the action by which the competent superior approves the acts of the chapter and by this approval renders them binding. Because religious institutes, provinces and formally erected houses enjoy public juridic personality by law, actions taken by such chapters ordinarily are complete and effective in themselves. Confirmation is required for the acts of a chapter only when either universal or proper law expressly requires it or the nature of the matter warrants it.

The term *chapter* derives from early monastic usage. Monks gathered daily as a community to listen to a reading (*caput*) from the rule. Gradually this gathering included discussion and decisions concerning the application of the rule; the room came to be known as the chapter house and the assembly itself as the chapter. By the thirteenth century general chapters were required for all religious institutes. Other forms of life closely allied to religious institutes, such as societies of apostolic life, existing since the seventeenth century, and secular institutes, recognized in law in 1947, may, but are not required to, incorporate this organ of governance into their proper law.

The institute's proper law determines the competence of a chapter. While in session chapters hold extraordinary legislative authority, but the ordinary executive authority of the superior vis-à-vis members perdures while the chapter is in session. Chapters are commonly understood to participate in the exercise of jurisdiction when they take definitive action on such matters as the administration or alienation of church property, election of superiors, and enacting of certain policies affecting members of the institute or its apostolate.

[R. SMITH]

CHARACTER

A term derived from the Greek χαρακτήρ, meaning engraving. Since the engraving on an object originally showed the worth of the thing, moralists use the term character to designate the moral worth or value of a human PERSON. In a wider sense, character has come to mean any distinctive sign; psychologists use the term in this sense to designate particular dispositions of an individual or of a group that account for their distinctive modes of behavior.

In a broad sense, character signifies a strong adherence to principles that can be morally good or bad. Taken in this meaning, a strong character enables a person to do what he wants and to dominate over his environment and other individuals; in this understanding, a person with a strong character can be morally objectionable. More properly, however, character signifies the good moral values manifested in a person's deliberate actions. An individual has a strong character if his responsible actions are in accord with objectively good moral principles. A man of character consistently lives up to moral norms as

he knows them. His subjective knowledge of what is morally acceptable concurs with objective norms given by nature and God's revelation. The remainder of this discussion is concerned with character in this more proper meaning.

Role of Will. In character, the WILL plays a leading role. Although the will is a spiritual faculty of the soul, it is nevertheless indirectly influenced by an individual's physical DISPOSITION and TEMPERAMENT. Native physical endowments of temperament affect the acquisition of a good character. Moreover, the environment of family and other social relationships, by affording favorable opportunities, provides wholesome influences in the formation of character. Although heredity and environment can give a suitable background, the formation of a good character develops from personal efforts required in doing what is known to be right. Undoubtedly an individual can surmount the unfavorable moral circumstances of family and environment and acquire a strong moral character.

The will is the faculty of CHOICE. In its act of choosing, the will prefers one course of action from the several motives proposed by the INTELLECT (*see* MOTIVE). When the choice of the will is expressed externally, the character of the person is manifested. If the choices are consistently bad morally, the character is noted as bad; if the choices are good, the character is likewise good. If a choice is a departure from the usual pattern of morality, it can be said that the act is not characteristic of the individual.

Frequently the will is presented with several possible courses of action of which some may be morally bad. It is the will that must choose either to follow an easier but morally wrong course or to adhere to principles that assure good moral conduct. This dilemma of the will takes place under TEMPTATION when there are alternatives either of pursuing the advantage of the moment when to do so is not morally good or of choosing what CONSCIENCE dictates as morally right. Although actual grace from God gives supernatural assistance in such a choice, the inherent strength of will provides the natural dispositions for God's grace. The choice that the will makes remains the responsibility of the individual. A strong moral character enables the person to cooperate more easily with the helping grace of God.

Character Formation. Because the will is the most important factor in the formation of a good moral character, the will must be made strong. Strength of will is acquired through the practice of virtues, while natural virtues result from repeated and consistently good actions. It is the purpose of a VIRTUE to give an added power and inclination to a faculty. The will is given this power when it has become qualified by the four cardinal virtues of prudence, justice, fortitude, and temperance. Growth in these virtues is essential for building a strong and good character. Catholic theology rightly asserts that the cardinal virtues are infused and remain with sanctifying grace; however, promptness and facility in the use of these virtues comes only from putting them into practice.

PRUDENCE is a virtue of the practical intellect that inclines one to choose the most suitable means to effect a good result. However, prudence also has a definite effect on the choices of the will. It trains one to think before making decisions, and it inclines him to be firm in carrying out what has been sufficiently deliberated. Prudence is the director for the other cardinal virtues. This direction makes a person's choices reasonable so that they escape the pitfalls of both foolish excess and regrettable deficiency. A good moral character must have the balance afforded by prudence.

JUSTICE plays an important part in character, for it directly inclines the will to respect the rights of other persons. The man of character is truthful and honest because others have the right to be dealt with truthfully and honestly. He is habituated to act justly: this course of action is his mark or characteristic. Temperance brings to the will an added impetus to control the concupiscible emotions that pull toward isolated sense pleasures that sometimes are contrary to the total moral good of the person (*see* TEMPERANCE, VIRTUE OF). Although the desires and aversions of the senses tend to what is good, their goals are limited goods that must be reconciled with the entire pattern of life. A man of character is strong enough to resist the advantage of the moment. Fortitude, or COURAGE, when it has been acquired through practice, enables the will to use the strong irascible emotions rather than take the line of least resistance (*see* FORTITUDE, VIRTUE OF). This virtue urges a person to pursue a good course of action despite the difficulties encountered.

See Also: HABIT.

Bibliography: THOMAS AQUINAS, *Summa Theologiae* 1a2ae, 49–89. R. ALLERS, *Psychology of Character,* tr. E. B. STRAUSS (New York 1939). G. W. ALLPORT, *Pattern and Growth in Personality* (New York 1961). E. B. BARRETT, *Strength of Will* (New York 1915).

[J. A. BURROUGHS]

CHARBONNEAU, JOSEPH

Archbishop; b. Lefaivre, Ontario, Canada, July 31, 1892; d. Victoria, British Columbia, Canada, Nov. 19, 1959. He studied at the Sulpician College and at the Grand Seminary, Montreal, where he was ordained June 24, 1916. He continued his studies at The Catholic University of America, Washington, D.C., and later at the Canadian College, Rome, receiving the degrees of D.D.C., Th.D., and Ph.D. He was appointed superior of the major seminary at Ottawa, Ontario, and served as vicar-general of the Ottawa diocese. He was consecrated first bishop of Hearst, Ontario (Aug. 15, 1939), and named titular archbishop of Amorio and coadjutor with the right of succession to Abp. Georges Gauthier of Montreal (May 18, 1940); he succeeded to the see (Aug. 31, 1940). As archbishop of Montreal he was renowned for his work in welfare, education, and immigration. He came into conflict with the provincial government, the Union Nationale, headed by Premier Maurice DUPLESSIS, especially in 1949 when the archbishop opposed the labor legislation on the grounds that it was deficient in social justice. In the same year he threw his support to the laboring class in the famous strike at Asbestos. On Feb. 9, 1950, he resigned his see "for reasons of health," was appointed titular archbishop of Bosphorus by Pius XII, and retired to the convent of the Sisters of St. Anne, Victoria, British Columbia, where he died.

[J. T. FLYNN]

CHARBONNEL, ARMAND FRANÇOIS MARIE DE

Missionary, educator; b. Monistrol-sur-Loire, France, Dec. 1, 1802; d. Crest, Drome, France, March 29, 1891. Educated at the Basilian College, Annonay, he joined the Society of the Priests of Saint Sulpice in Paris and was ordained in 1825. He volunteered for missionary work and was sent to Montreal, Canada, where he served from 1840 to 1847. After refusing several bishoprics in France, Canada, and the United States, he was consecrated bishop of Toronto on May 26, 1850. There he founded St. Michael's College (1852) and led a successful struggle for Tax–supported Catholic schools. In 1856 he brought about the division of his jurisdiction by the erection of dioceses at Hamilton and London. He resigned from his see on April 29, 1860, and entered the Capuchin Order at Rieti, Italy. He was named titular bishop of Sozopolis in 1869, and made titular archbishop in 1881. The last years of his life were spent in France preaching on behalf of the Society for the Propagation of the Faith.

Bibliography: C. CAUSSE, *Vie de Monseigneur de Charbonnel: Évêque de Torento* (Paris 1931).

[R. J. SCOLLARD]

CHARDON, LOUIS

Dominican mystical theologian and spiritual director; b. Clermont (Oise), March 12, 1595; d. Paris, Aug.

17, 1651. As a member of a well-to-do family, he pursued his higher studies at Paris, where, attracted by the order's intellectual apostolate, he became a Dominican in the Annunciation Priory, taking the habit and the name Louis in May 1618. In 1632 he went to Toulouse as "ordinary preacher," but in 1645 returned to Paris where he devoted his remaining years to writing and spiritual direction. All his works were written during the last four years of his life. His French translations of the *Dialogue of St. Catherine of Siena* (1648) and the *Institutiones divinae* of John Tauler (1650) were followed by his most popular work, *Meditations on the Passion of Our Lord Jesus Christ;* another treatise on the art of meditation is extant. His principal work, *The Cross of Jesus* (1647), is a precise theology of Christian suffering, especially of fervent souls; its main theme is the spiritual progress of the Christian through the cross. It is both a speculative and practical work, a perfect blend of the theologian's knowledge and the mystic's experience. Though some consider his spirituality Carmelite, owing to his emphasis on the way of negation, his doctrine is in complete harmony with the teachings of Dominican spiritual theology (unity of the spiritual life, the mystical state as a development of the life of grace and virtue) especially of the German Dominican school with its doctrine of purification, all of which Chardon explains by means of the Thomistic doctrine concerning the nature and function of sanctifying grace.

Bibliography: H. BRÉMOND, *Histoire littéraire du sentiment religieux en France,* 11 v. (Paris 1916–33) v.8. L. CHARDON, *The Cross of Jesus,* tr. R. T. MURPHY and J. THORNTON, 2 v. (St. Louis 1957–59). F. FLORAND, *Dictionnaire de spiritualité ascétique et mystique. Doctrine et histoire,* ed. M. VILLER et al. (Paris 1932) 2.1:498–503.

[C. HAHN]

CHARDON, MATHIAS CHARLES

Theologian; b. Yvois-Carignan (Ardennes), Sept. 22, 1695; d. Abbey of St. Arnoul, Metz, Oct. 20, 1771. He was a Benedictine of the Abbey of St. Vannes, Verdun, where he served as novice master and later taught philosophy and theology until he was deposed by the general chapter of the Congregation of St. Vannes in 1730 for refusing to submit to the constitution *Unigenitus.* His great work, which still has value, is a history of the celebration and administration of the Sacraments from apostolic times to his own day, *Histoire des sacrements* (6 v. Paris 1745). It is to be found in Migne's Cursus *Theologiae completus* (v.30).

Bibliography: B. HEURTEBIZE, *Dictionnaire de théologie catholique,* ed. A. VACANT et al., 15 v. (Paris 1903–50) 2.2:2216.

[A. ROCK]

CHARISM

The word charism or charisma (from Gr. χάρισμα) denotes a gift freely and graciously given, a favor bestowed, a grace. Charism as understood in the Bible is first treated, then its relation to the individual possessing it, and finally its meaning for the corporate Church.

In The Bible

Except for two variants in the Greek Version of Sirach (Sir 7.33; 38.30) and Theodotion's translation of Psalms 30(31).22, the use of the word charism in the Bible is confined to the New Testament, in which it occurs 17 times, principally in Romans and 1 Corinthians. The usage, however, is not uniform, varying between a general meaning equivalent to grace (χάρις) and the technical meaning, which is treated here.

Technical Usage. In its technical meaning, a charism is a spiritual gift or talent granted by God to the recipient not primarily for his own sake but for the benefit of others "in order to perfect the saints for a work of ministry, for building up the body of Christ," i.e., the Church (Eph 4.12; see also 1 Cor 14.26). Saint Paul gives it a quasi definition in 1 Cororinthian, 12.7 as a "manifestation of the Spirit for profit," i.e., for the profit of others.

Some eight lists of charisms occur more or less clearly in the New Testament: (1) Rom 12.6–8; (2) 1 Cor 12.4–10; (3) 1 Cor 12.28–31; (4) 1 Pt 4.10, and, without mention of the term, (5) 1 Cor 14.6, 13; (6) 1 Cor 14.26 and (7) Eph 4.11 as well as (8) Mk 16.17–18. Although these lists are neither uniform nor complete, it is possible to group the charisms contained in them according to similarity of function and to arrive at their probable meaning, as follows.

Various Kinds of Charisms. Teaching charisms comprise those of APOSTLES ('απόστολοι) or itinerant missionaries (Didache 11.3–6), evangelists (εὐαγγελίσται; *see* EVANGELIST) or preachers of the gospel, prophets (προφῆται) who spoke in God's name under the inspiration of the Holy Spirit, and teachers (διδάσκαλοι) who instructed the Christians and catechumens. To the teaching charisms one may also conjoin those of exhorting (παρακαλεῖν), speaking (λαλεῖν), and hymnody (ψάλλειν), as well as the more important, yet more indefinable, utterances of knowledge and wisdom (λόγος γνώσεως and λόγος σοφίας), i.e., of different grades of supernatural understanding.

Service charisms include gifts for governing and guiding as well as serving, since administration is interchangeable with ministration among Christ's followers, e.g., presiding (προστασία), governing (κυβέρνη σις), ministering (διακονία), giving (μετάδοσις), mercy (ἔλεος), and services of help (ἀντιλήμψεις). The exercise of Holy Orders might possibly be included here as well.

Extraordinary or miraculous charisms embrace the gifts of healing (ἴαμα), miracles (δυνάμεις), faith (πίστις), such as would "move mountains," exorcism ('εξόρκωσις), and immunity from harm arising from deadly things such as serpents or poison. Among miraculous charisms of the intellectual order would be included PROPHECY (προφητεία), in as far as it involved revelation ('ατόκάλυψις), reading of hearts, or prediction of future events, and the gift called Discernment of Spirits (διάκρισιτ πνευμάτων), i.e., the supernatural ability to distinguish between true and false spiritual phenomena (see DISCERNMENT, SPIRITUAL). Finally, the popular Gift of Tongues or glossolalia (γένη γλωσσῶν), and the related interpretation, or possibly translation, of tongues ('ερμηνεία γλωσσῶν) complete the lists.

Value. Although the phenomenon, if not the name, of charismatic gifts was evident in the Old Testament (e.g., in Moses, the Prophets), the full outpouring of the Spirit was reserved for messianic times [Ps 67(68).19; Eph 4.7–13]. This was particularly true of the Church's early years, when it needed special helps for its consolidation, survival, and expansion. Human pride, however, tended to overemphasize the spectacular gifts such as tongues, and it became necessary for the Church's leaders, e.g., in 1 Corinthians ch. 12–14, to remind Christians of (1) the common source of all gifts, the Holy Spirit; (2) the comparative value of the charisms, e.g., prophecy far surpassing tongues; (3) the superiority of love ('αγάτη) over all charisms; and (4) what should be the orderly interaction of hierarchical and charismatic functions in the Church.

Bibliography: *Encyclopedic Dictionary of the Bible*, tr. and adap. by L. HARTMAN (New York 1963), from A. VAN DEN BORN, *Bijbels Woordenboek*, 350–51. A. LEMONNYER, *Dictionnaire de la Bible*, suppl. ed. L. PIROT, et al. (Paris 1928–) 1:1233–44. É. OSTY, *Les Épîtres de St. Paul aux Corinthiens* [*Bible de Jérusalem*, 43 v., each with intro. by the tr. (Paris 1948–54) 37; 1949] 52–60. G. RICCIOTTI, *Paul the Apostle*, tr. A. ZIZZAMIA (Milwaukee 1953) 171–79. J. BONSIRVEN, *Theology of the New Testament*, tr. S. F. L. TYE (Westminster, Md. 1963) 324–31. F. PRAT, *The Theology of Saint Paul*, tr. J. STODDARD, 2 v. (London 1926) 1:127–33, 423–28.

[W. F. DICHARRY]

In the Church

In accordance with the technical meaning of the word charism as found in the New Testament and particularly in Saint Paul, theology defines charism as a gratuitous gift from God, SUPERNATURAL, transitory, given to the individual for the good of others, for the benefit of the CHURCH. This section discusses: (1) the nature of this gift, namely, what it consists of and what it implies in the individual receiving it; and (2) the different types of charisms as theology views them.

Nature. The early Fathers and ecclesiastical writers used the word loosely in the sense of GRACE or gift. Saint Thomas Aquinas stated that it is a grace given by God not for the personal justification or sanctification of the individual, but for the spiritual welfare of others. It differs essentially from the type of grace that renders the individual pleasing to God or holy in His sight (*gratia gratum faciens*). All grace, as the very name implies, is gratuitously given (*gratis data*) by God; yet, since charism lacks the added perfection of rendering the individual holy, it retains for its name the merely generic term of gratuitously given grace (*gratia gratis data; see Summa theologiae* 1a2ae, 111.1 ad 3). In this sense charisms differ from sanctifying or actual grace, from VIRTUES, gifts of the Holy Spirit (*see* HOLY SPIRIT, GIFT OF), and from graces of state of life. All these graces are entitative or operative HABITS or dispositions that inhere in the subject and have as their primary purpose the subject's perfection.

Charisms on the other hand may be given to the individual in a purely instrumental manner to accomplish some salutary effect in others. Thus a charismatic person might not necessarily be a holy person, although ordinarily God will use as His instrument one who is close to Him. As a matter of fact at times there might exist a correlation between certain gifts of the Holy Spirit and certain charisms, for instance, between the gifts of wisdom and counsel on the one hand, and the charisms of supernatural understanding and discernment of spirits on the other. In these cases the individual is instrumentally empowered with extraordinary ability to communicate to others that which he had received permanently through a gift.

The superiority and permanency of those graces that render the individual holy do not detract from the ontological and supernatural perfection of charisms. Charisms are the product of special intervention of God in man's faculties and operation. Metaphysically speaking, they may be reduced to the category of accidents, of transitory qualities or instrumental operative powers by which man's faculties are elevated to behavior beyond their natural capacity. They consist in different types of intellectual illuminations, in facility of communication with others, in ability to perform miraculous deeds, etc.

In the strictest sense charisms stand only for extraordinary gifts such as prophecy, glossolalia, etc. Yet, gifts such as ecclesiastical jurisdiction, exercise of Sacred Orders, and infallibility also fulfill the definition, for all these are supernatural, freely given gifts ordained for the benefit of the Church. These latter gifts, however, are more permanent in nature.

Types. Arrangements or classifications made by theologians are somewhat arbitrary. Saint Thomas, visualizing the role of these gifts in the Church precisely in a doctrinal and apologetic function, states that "they are ordained for the manifestation of faith and spiritual doctrine" (*Summa theologiae* 3a, 7.7). With this criterion in mind he divides charisms into three categories (*Summa theologiae* 1a2ae, 111.4). First, there are those charisms that empower the apostle with extraordinary knowledge of divine things. This is done by special faith, by word of wisdom (cognition of divine things, λόγος σοφίας), and word of knowledge (cognition of human affairs, λόγς γνώσεως). Second, he numbers those charisms by which one may efficaciously confirm in the eyes of his audience the divine origin of his teachings. Through these he instrumentally performs deeds that are proper to God—prophesies, discerns spirits, heals, and works miracles. Finally he considers those charisms concerned with the actual deliverance of the gospel, by which the minister of it is enabled to present efficiently the divine doctrine to his audience. To this realm of charisms belong glossolalia and the related interpretation.

See Also: PROPHECY (THEOLOGY OF).

Bibliography: *Dictionnaire de théologie catholique: Tables générales*, ed. A. VACANT et al., 15 v. (Paris 1903–50) 1:582–83. J. GEWIESS and K. RAHNER, *Lexikon für Theologie und Kirche*, ed. J. HOFER and K. RAHNER, 10 v. (2d, new ed. Freiburg 1957–65) 2:1025–30. H. LECLERCQ, *Dictionnaire d'archéologie chrétienne et de liturgie*, ed. F. CABROL, H. LECLERCQ, and H. I. MARROU, 15 v. (Paris 1907–53) 3:579–98. X. DUCROS, *Dictionnaire de spiritualité ascétique et mystique. Doctrine et histoire*, ed. M. VILLER et al. (Paris 1932–) 2.1:503–07. C. PESCH, *De gratia*, v.5 of *Praelectiones dogmaticae*, 9 v. (Freiburg 1910–22), app., "De gratiis gratis datis."

[R. J. TAPIA]

CHARISMATIC PRAYER

A style of Christian prayer now widespread in the Catholic Church in the wake of the charismatic movement. Related to an initial experience of the Holy Spirit, it is rooted in the conviction that prayer is a gift of God (Gr. χάρισμα; 3:460) and not the product of human striving. In the NT, the Holy Spirit, the Gift of God (Acts 2.38; Rom 5.5; Jn 4.10; 7.37–39) gives inspired utterance, whether this be such basic acclamations as "Jesus is Lord!" (1 Cor 12.3), "Come, Lord Jesus!" (Rv 22.20) and "Abba, Father!" (Gal 4.6), or inspired intercession (Rom 8.26–27), or prayer in tongues (1 Cor 14; Acts 2.1–11).

Glossolalia, or tongue-speaking, is the most celebrated aspect of charismatic prayer. As practiced among charismatics, it is used both in personal prayer and in public prayer meetings, where most often it is a spontaneous choral singing without intelligible words. Less frequently it is used in a proclamatory way by an individual, followed by an "interpretation" by someone else or sometimes by the speaker himself. As a prayer-gift, speaking in tongues is generally explained by theologians and biblical scholars who have experienced or studied the movement as a form of preconceptual prayer, that is, vocalization of a prayer of the heart (or of the spirit, as distinct from the mind, 1 Cor 14.15–16) prior to conceptualization and shaping into understandable language—a phenomenon not without parallels in other traditional forms of prayer. That it is not, except in very rare instances, the speaking of a real human language is supported by cross-cultural linguistic studies of tongue-speaking and by Paul's teaching that the "interpretation" is equally inspired and not simply the work of a translator (1 Cor 14.13). The tongue-speaking by the Apostles on Pentecost may be understood as their actually speaking the various languages of their hearers. However, one should not overlook the emphasis in the text of Acts upon the miraculous hearing. Three times the text says *each one* (singular) heard *them* (plural) speaking *his own* (singular) language (Acts 2.6, 8, 11). This, coupled with the accusation of drunkenness to which Peter addresses his response (rather than to an unusual brilliance in languages) suggests to some scholars that Luke used the early Pauline tradition of a preconceptual prayer language and, combining it with current Jewish Pentecost traditions about the gift of the Law amid wind and fire, saw the first Christian Pentecost as the new covenant of the Spirit destined for "every nation under heaven." In any case, charismatics view the experience as one in which they yield to the Spirit praying within them. This prayer, which is essentially praise and thanksgiving (1 Cor 14.16), also disposes to a hearing of a "word of the Lord," whether this be in a scriptural reading, an interpretation, or a prophecy (usually uttered in an oracular "I" form). All of these have Pauline antecedents. Prediction is not the primary function of prophecy. Its primary function as inspired speech is the community's "upbuilding, encouragement and consolation" (1 Cor 14.3).

A further aspect of charismatic prayer is prayer for healing, whether physical or emotional, and occasional prayer for "deliverance," though in the latter case there is considerable divergence of both theory and practice within the movement (see HEALING, CHRISTIAN).

Elements of biblical and early Christian spirituality that the charismatic approach to prayer has pointed up are thus: (1) prayer as a gift of the Holy Spirit; (2) the primacy of praise; (3) the importance of expecting to hear God speaking in prayer; (4) the healing ministry of the Church and the role of prayer in the healing process.

Bibliography: E. ENSLEY, *Sounds of Wonder; Speaking in Tongues in Catholic Tradition* (New York 1977). F. S. MACNUTT, *Healing* (Notre Dame, Ind. 1974); *The Power to Heal* (Notre Dame, Ind, 1977). D. GELPI, *Pentecostal Piety* (New York 1972). G. T. MONTAGUE, *The Holy Spirit: Growth of a Biblical Tradition* (New York 1976); *The Spirit and His Gifts* (New York 1974). W. J. SAMARIN, *Tongues of Men and of Angels* (New York 1972).

[G. T. MONTAGUE]

CHARISMATIC RENEWAL, CATHOLIC

The movement for Catholic charismatic renewal, though international in scope, is not a single, unified effort but rather a highly diverse collection of individuals, groups, and activities, in quite different stages of development, sometimes with diverse emphases. It fosters a continual personal and social conversion to Jesus Christ and openness to the power and charisms of the Spirit. The source of its life is the baptism in the Holy Spirit, understood as the full appropriation of the graces of Christian initiation.

The growth of the charismatic renewal coincided with enthusiasm stirred by the Second Vatican Council. In the early years it reinforced the judgments of Pope Paul VI that it is "a chance for the church," and of Yves Congar that it constitutes "a grace for the church." In the United States, the place of its origin, its early growth has not been sustained, but it is still a growing movement in places such as Brazil, Colombia, France, Lithuania, Italy, and India. Eastern Europe has shown itself especially receptive.

Covenant Communities. The movement is populist in character, largely, though not exclusively, lay. It still has a considerable number of prayer groups internationally, though the leadership has been largely exercised by covenant communities and by international fellowships of covenant communities, which are now officially recognized by the Holy See. Two such fellowships had their origin in France and Australia. Though the Bishops' Committee on Charismatic Renewal in the United States had warned of the danger of over-control in 1984, some covenant communities suffered negative publicity for authoritarian postures. Covenant communities continue to be a significant part of the international movement, but they are absent in some countries, such as Poland. Internationally, prayer groups continue to be the mainstay of the renewal, though, where informed leadership is lacking, many do not survive.

The internationalization of French communities, such as the Community of the Beatitude and the Emmanuel Community, and of the American Mother of God Community (Gaithersburg, MD) has provided anchors for the movement. The covenant communities, especially in France, have been a source of vocations to the priesthood. In recent years priests have taken over the ideals of the Oratorians and have formed communities engaged in the pastoral ministry while living a measure of community life. Such communities of priests exist in places like St. Paul, MN, Detroit, MI, and Ottawa, Canada.

As a movement the Catholic charismatic renewal has projected a theologically conservative image, which is verified in fact partly because of its populist character. This conservatism is often less ideological and more the attempt of persons reawakened spiritually to recover the sources of Catholic spirituality: the Scriptures, daily Mass, confession, spiritual direction, retreats, eucharistic adoration, Marian piety, and retreats. The movement has retained a contemplative quality noted from its earliest days. While it still has pietist expressions, its social engagement is slightly greater than that of the general Catholic population. Some covenant communities have made outstanding contributions to social transformation. El Minuto di Dios, centered in Bogota, Columbia, is involved in a major housing project for the poor, education, radio evangelization, and ministry among prostitutes and has erected an art museum. ECCLA, the Latin American umbrella organization for the renewal, begun in 1973, has had its 14th conference, with delegates from 20 countries, discussing such themes as New Evangelization, human development, and the formation of a Christian culture. The Hispanic renewal is marked by a determination to unite the power of conversion with the power to change social structures, demonstrating that personal conversion is also social conversion. French Cardinal Lustiger confided a center for AIDS patients in Paris to the Emmanuel Community.

In September 1993 the International Catholic Charismatic Renewal Services, the Roman office, was granted ecclesiastical status with a juridical personality, which gave the Catholic renewal recognition of a more official and structural kind. This development was announced in a retreat held in Assisi, Italy, in September 1993 with 1,000 delegates from 90 countries present, including ecumenical representatives from various Protestant, Anglican, and Orthodox churches. The conference reinforced the biblical and contemplative character of the renewal, with a series of conferences on the Epistle to the Romans by the patristic scholar Raniero Cantalamessa.

Ecumenical Ties. The ecumenical dimensions of the renewal, which were present from its inception, continue to be an important part of its on-going life. The dialogue between the Pontifical Council for Promoting Christian Unity and some Pentecostal churches has been an instrument of bringing Catholics and Pentecostals into a new appreciation of the other's spiritual heritage. An expression of this new relationship is the formation of a charismatic consultation in Italy, made up of Pentecostals, Waldensians, Baptists, and Roman Catholics, a development unthinkable a few years ago. Meetings of the renewal at Rimini, which twice have numbered 65,000, have representatives of the Pentecostal churches present.

Baptism in the Spirit. New life has been infused into the renewal internationally by the publication in 1991 of the scholarly Christian Initiation and Baptism in the Holy Spirit: Evidence from the First Eight Centuries by Kilian McDonnell and George Montague, now in five languages. The research shows that what is called baptism in the Holy Spirit, the principle cause of the growth both of classical Pentecostalism and the Catholic charismatic renewal, was, in the early centuries of the Church, an integral part of the sacraments of initiation (baptism, confirmation, Eucharist). Among other sources the evidence comes from five Doctors of the Church, persons especially reliable in identifying the faith and practice of the church (Cyril of Jerusalem, Hilary of Poitiers, John Chrysostom, Basil of Caesarea, and Gregory Nazianzus). Therefore, baptism in the Holy Spirit does not belong to private piety, but to the public, official liturgy of the church, and it is normative for all. Baptism in the Holy Spirit does not belong to any one movement. The baptism in the Spirit is not tied in any necessary way to an enthusiastic style of communal prayer. Finally, one can choose the baptism in the Holy Spirit and not choose the charismatic renewal. They are separable.

This book was the basis of a theological consultation in May 1990, consisting of 10 theologians and three pastors, which issued "Fanning the Flame," a popular document that contains the core of the biblical and patristic research and applies it pastorally. This document has wide distribution and is in 18 languages. The two publications, the scholarly book and the popular document, have been the basis of theological discussions in universities in Amsterdam and Paris. International Charismatic Renewal Services in Rome under the direction of British Charles Whitehead and the American Ken Metz, has a mandate to promote the baptism in the Holy Spirit internationally and has used the two publications as the focus of its efforts.

After 25 years of existence the renewal is assessing both its identity and its relation to the mainstream of Catholic life. While reaffirming the central theological reality of the renewal, the baptism in the Spirit as an integral part of Christian initiation, it wants both to maintain its special charism and to answer the question, "What is the normal Christian life of grace?" Most leaders are well aware of the danger of becoming isolated from the sources of Catholic life. Such isolation would make it difficult for the renewal to live at the heart of the Church, which it understands is its truest vocation.

Bibliography: K. MCDONNELL and G. MONTAGUE, eds., *Fanning the Flame: What Does Baptism in the Holy Spirit Have to Do with Christian Initiation* (Collegeville MN 1991); *Christian Initiation and Baptism in the Holy Spirit: Evidence from the First Eight Centuries* (Collegeville MN 1991); *Toward a New Pentecost, For a New Evangelization* (Collegeville MN 1993). H.I. LEDERLE, *Treasures Old and New: Interpretations of the Baptism in the Holy Spirit* (Peabody MA 1988). F.A. SULLIVAN, "Catholic Charismatic Renewal," in S. M. BURGESS and G. G. MCGEE, *Dictionary of Pentecostal and Charismatic Movements* (Grand Rapids MI 1987) 110-126.

[K. MCDONNELL]

CHARISMS IN RELIGIOUS LIFE

High interest in the concept of charism (3:460) as a focal element in the renewal of religious life followed closely on the promulgation of the documents of Vatican Council II. A simple reference in *Lumen gentium* (42) to the evangelical counsels as constituting a gift of God to the Church was elaborated in *Perfectae caritatis* (1) and developed still further by Paul VI's 1971 apostolic exhortation on religious life (Paul VI *Evangelica Testificatio* 7–29). References in these documents to the "proper character of each institute," "the charisms of the founders," and "the dynamism proper to each religious family" prompted religious congregations to develop a new sense of their origins. The deepening understanding of the spirit of the founder, a renewed study of Scripture, and a keener sensitivity to the signs of the times, have become the triadic impetus for revitalizing the religious institute.

Religious Life as Gift within the Church. Vatican Council II's Dogmatic Constitution on the Church first situates religious life ecclesially (*Lumen gentium* 43–47), then a separate decree turns to the specific renewal of religious institutes (*Perfectae caritatis*). The study of the charism that religious life is, or, of the charisms of particular founders is, accordingly, best done in the context of the general theology of charism within the life of the Church. Seen thus organically related to the life of the Church, the renewal proper to religious life avoids either narrow concern for superficial differences or a diminished appreciation of the place of religious life among the rich variety of gifts given for the building up of the Body of Christ.

From the theology of charism, some principles are of particular value in reflecting on the charism of religious life. These are: (1) that charisms are universally present in the Church; (2) that charisms are frequently of quite an ordinary character; (3) that charisms are apostolic: related, that is, to the building up of the Kingdom of God and given for the benefit, not only of the recipient, but also for others; and (4) that charisms appear in constantly new forms. These principles provide a sound basis on which a religious institute might ground the work of research and reflection on its proper charism.

Prior to the awakened awareness of religious life as a charism, it was common to speak of the call to religious life. Sometimes the connotation was that this call to religious life carried strong meanings of duty or obligation or even of unwelcome intrusion into ordinary life. Viewed as a charism, however, religious life is seen as both a gift and a call. That it is a gift implies that there is a grace given as a power to fulfill joyful religious commitment for the sake of the Kingdom. The screening of candidates for religious life should include discernment of gifts that will enable the candidate to respond. That response is not merely a matter of a good and disciplined will determined to live up to an intellectualized Meal, but rather a response made with a certain ease and freedom of spirit.

Discernment of Charisms. Several ideas are used interchangeably in discussing the charism of religious life. These are "the spirit of the founder," "the spirit of the institute," "the charism of the founder," and the "founding charism." It is more useful, however, to broaden the appreciation of the various dimensions of a community's self-image by distinguishing among the aspects just named, and even to add others, rather than to make them terms interchangeable with charism. In other words, the gift that a particular institute is to the Church is a composite of interrelated qualities. The charism of the founder is the gift and call given enabling the founder to institute a particular religious family. The events of a historical period, the particular geographic location, the cultural milieu, the ecclesial setting, the other persons who joined at the founding of the community—all of these contribute toward the characteristic spirit of the institute. The dynamism of the charism throughout the history of the institute can be explored through the lived experience of the members, the decisions made, the roads taken and not taken. Understanding its charism requires, therefore, that an institute explore it as a continuing operation within a corporate entity in history and not as a static quality inhering in the founder alone. The charism of the present institute, the ensemble of its gifts, are organically related to the founding persons, but it may and probably should exhibit some differences.

The sources for understanding and explicating the charism of religious life or of a particular institute are Scripture, theology of charism, foundational texts, histories, and other archival materials. To these sources must be added an examination of the contemporary needs of the People of God and a realistic assessment of the present members' capacities to respond to these needs. A search process that is reflective, discerning, and dialogic will illumine the meaning of the charism of the institute so that it might be anointed and freed for the service of God and his people.

Bibliography: L. CADA and R. FITZ, "The Recovery of Religious Life," *Review for Religious* 34 (1975) 690–718. J. C. FUTRELL, "Discovering the Founder's Charism," *The Way Supplement* 14 (Autumn 1970) 62–70. P. KAUFMAN, "The One and the Many: Corporate Personality," *Worship* 42 (1968) 546–556. W. KOUPAL, "Charism: A Relational Concept," *Worship* 42 (1968) 539–545. PAUL VI, *Evangelica testificatio,* tr. *On the Renewal of Religious Life* (USCC Publ. Office, Washington, D.C. 1971). K. RAHNER, "Observations on the Factor of the Charismatic in the Church," *Theological Investigatons* 12, tr. D. BOURKE (New York 1974) 89–97.

[G. FOLEY]

CHARITÉ-SUR-LOIRE, ABBEY OF

The former Benedictine priory of *B. Maria de Caritate ad Ligerim,* near Nevers, France, Diocese of Nevers. The basilican monastery founded in 706 was devastated in 771. At the request of Bp. Geoffrey of Auxerre and Count William of Nevers, it was restored (1056) by the monks of CLUNY under the direction of St. HUGH OF CLUNY. As one of the five "daughter" monasteries immediately dependent on Cluny, it in turn governed 52 monasteries. Pope PASCHAL II consecrated the church in 1107. By 1343 it numbered 80 monks, but this number had dropped to 18 in 1436. Jean de Bourbon, abbot of Cluny (1456–85), tried to reform the monastery but he could not stem the monastic and economic decline. Having been progressively ruined by the rule of commendatory abbots imposed in 1538, it was united to the Cluniac Congregation of Strict Observance March 13, 1634. It was suppressed in 1790. Most of the buildings of the cloister are still standing. The church, despite later changes, remains a model of Roman Burgundian architecture.

Bibliography: L. H. COTTINEAU, *Répertoire topobibliographique des abbayes et prieurés,* 2 v. (Mâcon 1935–39) 1:705–706. R. VAN DOREN, *Dictionnaire d'histoire et de géographie ecclésiastiques,* ed. A. BAUDRILLART et al. (Paris 1912–) 12:419–421. H. H. HILBERRY, "La Charité-sur-Loire Priory Church," *Speculum. A Journal of Mediaeval Studies* 30 (1955) 1–14.

[R. GRÉGOIRE]

CHARITY

Charity (from Old French *charité,* Latin *caritas*) stands in general for the state of being in and responding to God's love and favor, more specifically for our whole-hearted love of God, who reveals Himself in the Scriptures, and for the love of our neighbor as ourselves there inculcated, and most specifically for the third and greatest of the theological virtues. These senses are kept in the vocabulary of English-speaking Catholicism, although there, and even more elsewhere, the word has gone down in the world and is applied to an active benevolence toward those in need and sometimes to a dutiful or even a patronizing regard for those one finds socially and psychologically taxing. This decayed usage, however, will be neglected in this article, which summarizes the teaching of (1) the Scriptures; (2) the Fathers; and (3) St. Thomas Aquinas, whose theological formulation is at once more systematic than that of his predecessors and less confined by the concept of obligation than that of most of his successors. There is need to avoid the two extremes: making charity an ineffable impulse, defying description, and isolating it as a technical way of loving God or of treating one's neighbor with supernatural kindliness.

Sacred Scripture. Words from the Hebrew root verb *'āhēb* are rendered to mean, first, God's love for men; second, men's love for God; and third, the love between men in this religious setting. Such love involving a special choice, as in the Latin *dilectio,* is called ἀγάπη, a word adopted by the NT and later Church writers to signify the love of God for Christ (Jn 17.36) and for men (Rom 5.8), of Christ for men (Rom 8.35), of men for God (Jn 2.5) and for one another (Jn 12.35); there is no clear instance of its employment in a non-Christian context. Ἔρως, a sexual love, is not referred to in the NT, which speaks of ἐπιθυμία i.e., *concupiscentia;* there also φιλία means ordinary friendship or natural affection.

Agape was translated by the Vulgate Bible as *caritas,* possibly because *amor* had impure associations and *dilectio* and *amicitia* were too secular. Charity is the word consistently used by the Reims and Douay versions, and often by the Authorized and Confraternity Versions; and it never occurs in Revised Version, though the Revised Standard Version adopts it for Acts 9.36; it seems less ambiguous than "love" and will not go flat while kept close to the etymology *carus,* French *cher,* and to the idea of holding dear and cherishing.

The dominant theme is that God first loves us (1 Jn 4.9) and commends His charity toward us in the death of His Son (Rom 5.8–10). Our love in return springs from the new man who is now dead to sin and born afresh to life in Christ (Jn 3.3; Rom 6.6; 2 Cor 5.17; Col 3.10; 1

Pt 1.23). We are now members of God's family, like little children (Mt 8.2), receiving the spirit of adoption whereby we cry "Abba! Father!" (Rom 8.15; Gal 4.6). The Trinity dwells in us (Jn 14.23); we are members of the same body of Christ (1 Cor 12.27), branches of the same vine (Jn 15.4); and Christ lives in us (Gal 2.20). We form one body and one spirit in the hope of our calling (Eph 4.4), to become partakers of the divine nature (2 Pt 1.4).

To live in this way goes with loving God with our whole heart and soul and mind and loving our neighbor as ourselves; such is the fulfillment of the law, the summing up of all the Commandments and prophecies (Mt 22.36–40; Rom 13.9–10). This is charity, that we walk according to God's Commandments (2 Jn ch. 6); and the thought was related by St. John to the key ideas of God as light (Jn 1.4; 8.12; 1 Jn 1.5; 2.8), and life (Jn 1.4; 5.26; 14.19), and Father (Jn 4.14; 14.21–23; 15.10; 2 Jn 4), and to the revelation of God as charity itself (1 Jn 4.16). To St. Paul it was the bond of union (Rom 12.10; Eph 4.15; Col 1.4; 3.14) and the most excellent and lasting activity of immortal life (1 Cor 13.1–13). St. Peter preached the same message of charity born from incorruptible life and receiving salvation in the final issue (1 Pt 1.8–9; 22.23; 3.8; 4.8).

The Fathers. The early writers of the Church devoted no set treatise to the virtue of charity. For them, it was the way of Christian life; and their teaching, which appeared in their comments and homilies on the Scriptures, was directed to maintaining the unity of the faithful, realized in the Eucharistic communion, and to fostering their practical love for one another. Thus SS. Ignatius of Antioch, Clement of Alexandria, and Polycarp. Clement of Alexandria was more speculative; charity is bound up with the gnosis, or knowledge of God freeing us from the material world. SS. Basil, Gregory of Nazianzus, and John Chrysostom brought out what it means to love one's neighbor as oneself. It was not until St. Augustine, named the *Doctor Caritatis,* that one sees the first sketches, somewhat darkly edged by the contrasts between the laws of nature and grace, of a systematic treatment. Charity is the perfect justice that obeys the sovereign law of love; the essence of sin is to go against it. The *De diligendo Deo,* though wrongly attributed to him, represents his doctrine; the classical synopsis of it is St. Thomas's three questions on the gospel law (*Summa Theologiae* 1a2ae, 106–108). Gregory the Great wrote as a pastoral theologian; and the topic of charity, although elaborated in terms of literature and spiritual direction by the great monastic writers, notably St. Bernard, and interpreted according to the Platonist mystical tradition, notably by the Victorines, received no strictly theological development until the 13th century, when the great scholastics, having girded up the loins of their understanding (1 Pt 1.13), set about analyzing the concepts in the Christian mind.

St. Thomas. Here St. Thomas offers the best theological centerpiece, for apart from the fact that he has been declared an authentic exponent of what the Church thinks, his treatment, which is profoundly scriptural, draws together the strands of many different traditions—Platonist, Aristotelean, Stoic, patristic, and even romantic—into the best pattern of reference for later discussions and disagreements. The *ex professo* treatise of the *Summa Theologiae* on charity (2a2ae, 23–46), which is followed here, should be complemented (1) by the questions on the nature of love (1a2ae, 26–28), on the gospel law already referred to, which introduced the treatise on grace, on the life of perfection (2a2ae, 184); and (2) by the debates *De caritate*.

Friendship. Charity itself (2a2ae, 23) is introduced as the kind of love called friendship (23.1), in agreement with Our Lord's words, ''No longer do I call you servants, but friends'' (Jn 15.15). It goes beyond the love of what is good for us, as in the theological virtue of hope, and the disinterested love for another (*benevolentia*) and the doing of good to another, to a condition of mutual loving between persons who are sharers. This sharing (*communicatio, participatio*) is God's granting to us His own happiness, *beatitudo*. The teaching of *Nicomachean Ethics* book 8 on the association implied in all friendship is equably assumed into the apostolic preaching; our citizenship is in heaven in fellowship with God's Son (1 Cor 1.9; Phil 3.20) and is invested with the NT κοινωνία. This is the basis that makes charity different from other forms of friendship and the friendliness that is part of social justice (2a2ae, 114); indeed all friendship that has this glow from within imparted by God's own joy is charity, and any religious account that excludes it may be talking about some sort of love of God, but not about charity (*see* FRIENDSHIP).

This relationship between persons means that the charity of God poured forth in our hearts by the Holy Spirit, who has been given to us (Rom 5.5), is still our own act of loving (23.2). We are not, as it were, swamped, for the first cause maintains secondary causes as principals (cf. 1a, 105.5); and were we to be merely God's instruments, then our active friendship with God would lack the spontaneity, ease, and delight to be expected of godlike operations. The argument against the singular opinion of Peter Lombard that charity is the Holy Spirit in us was confirmed at Trent (H. Denzinger, *Enchiridion symbolorum* [Freiburg 1963] 1529). It is wholly the effect of God's power, giving us a power, or *virtus,* of activity by which we pass from what we were to what we want to be. It is not one of the moral virtues enabling

us to live according to right reason, but a theological virtue, conjoining us, as St. Augustine says, to God Himself (22.3). His goodness lies beyond the immediate objectives of all the other virtues; and consequently charity, through which we reach it, is a special virtue, although not in the limited sense that other virtues are, since its objective, which is not one among many particular kinds of good, embraces them all while holding them distinct and subordinate (23.4). Moreover, charity is a single virtue, for despite its manifold activities, its end and basis remain always the same, namely, God's sharing His goodness in everlasting happiness (23.5). It rests on God for Himself, not for what He gives to us, and therefore it is the greatest of all the virtues (23.6; cf. 1 Cor 12.8, 13).

St. Augustine spoke of virtue as the ordering of love; and although we may be well ordered with respect to particular and limited ends, we are not fully virtuous unless our charity bears us to the ultimate end of the whole of life (23.7); ''if I distribute all my goods to feed the poor, and if I deliver my body to be burned, yet do not have charity, it profits me nothing'' (1 Cor 13.3). From this principle is developed the theology of charity as the ''form'' of all the virtues (23.8). The term is used teleologically rather than typologically, for it is not that charity gives to each virtue its own specific interest, which is largely abstract, but that in the concrete it makes each virtue serve the final blessedness of being in love with God and His friends—hence St. Paul's injunction, ''Let all that you do be done in charity'' (1 Cor 16.14). Here again, it is not that behavior has to become stilted or interrupted by an extrinsic ordination, as seems suggested by spiritual writers who have not grasped the theology of God's universal causality, but that it should well up unaffectedly from our friendship with God. ''For his workmanship we are, created in Christ Jesus in good works'' (Eph 2.10). There is a distinction between intention and attention; God can be actually, though implicitly, loved without being thought of, and He is virtually loved in all the activities, except sin, of those who continue to set their heart on Him. ''For the rest, brethren, whatever things are true, whatever honorable, whatever just, whatever holy, whatever lovable, whatever of good repute, if there be any virtue, if anything worthy of praise, think upon these things'' (Phil 4.8).

Charity in Relation to Us. Charity is an immortal love (2a2ae, 24), and therefore its seat is the will (*appetitus intellectivus*), not the emotional powers (*appetitus sensitivus*). It ranges beyond our present environment and breaks through the obscurities of faith to reach the mystery of God; ''so that, being rooted and grounded in love, you may be able to comprehend with all the saints what is the breadth and length and height and depth, and to know Christ's love which surpasses knowledge in order that you may be filled unto all the fullness of God'' (Eph 3.18–19). This Pauline concept of being filled runs throughout this part of the theological study. For as charity is not limited by the knowledge furnished by the mind, so it lies more deeply in the will than at the level of its choices (24.1) and comes to us not through our own efforts but by God's gift, or ''infusion'' (24.2). And like his other supernatural gifts, ''these are the work of one and the same Spirit, who allots to everyone according as he will'' (1 Cor 12.11). And charity is not measured by natural capacity (24.3), nor is it because of temperament or force of circumstances that some become better lovers of God than others, but ''according to the measure of Christ's bestowal'' (Eph 4.7).

That charity can grow was declared at Trent (sess. 6, ch. 10), and theology draws analogies between bodily and spiritual increase through nourishment and exercise. The preoccupation of later scholastic writers with the amount (*quantitas*) of charity and the effects on it of acts that are below strength (*actus remissi*) may appear quaint to the modern reader, but the theory that it grows, not by addition, but by intensification, a deepening participation or possession (*per majorem radicationem in subjecto*), accords with the psychology of disposition or ''habits'' (1a2ae, 52–53) and the thought of St. Paul (Eph 3.17). To this growth no term can be fixed in this present life, because the love it shares, namely, the Holy Spirit, is infinite and so is the power of God who causes it; and man's questing heart can always love more than it does (24.4–7). On the other hand, venial sin does not reach deep enough directly to effect or cause a weakening of charity, although it may dispose to its being lost (24.10) through grave sin, for according to the teaching of the Church, charity in fact does not make a man impeccable (24.11–12).

Charity, then, is an analogical idea in that a single meaning may exist at different strengths, and charity allows for a difference of degrees (*secundum magis et minus*). This raises the question in spiritual theology whether and when charity in this life can be called perfect (24.8); and the discussion, which may be regarded as an extension of St. Thomas's fourth proof for the existence of God, proceeds according to the traditional Platonist terms of participation and of drawing closer to God. If love matches the beloved, then God alone can love Himself as much as He can be loved, and no creature can ever hope to attain such perfection. If love is in proportion to the lover, then different degrees are possible. God may be wholeheartedly and actually loved always, but this is the condition of charity as it is in heaven (*caritas patriae*); until we see Him in vision and so long as we hold Him by faith, He does not always engage our attention and expressed affection. As for our love in the pres-

ent life (*caritas viae*), it is possible for us to set aside all other things, except insofar as the necessities of life require them, and devote ourselves to divine things. Yet such perfection is rare; what is common to all who are in God's friendship is that their whole heart is steadily (*habitualiter*) given to God in such sort that they neither harbor nor will anything contrary to His love. This is sane and generous doctrine, and it avoids the division, of which the classical theologians of the Church have always been suspicious, between a mystical elite and plain Christians who are well content if they can keep the Commandments. The precepts of charity are first and foremost, not of the Decalogue (cf. 1a2ae, 100, 107; 2a2ae, 44); and it should be remembered that the ''state'' of perfection constituted by vows and the episcopal order is directly a category of canon law, not of spiritual theology (cf. 2a2ae, 184).

The progress possible in this life is stated according to three stages—beginners (*incipientes*), those who are advancing (*proficientes*), and those who are well advanced (*perfecti*)—which may be taken as corresponding approximately to the purgative, illuminative, and unitive ways (24.9). The distinction should be made to represent not three different compartments, but rather three emphases in principal occupations. At first we strive to keep alive our friendship with God, afterward seek to deepen it, and finally may come so to cling as to ''desire to depart and to be with Christ'' (Phil 1.23). The process is continuous; the end is in the beginning, the first grace of Baptism is the seed of glory, and holiness in this life is never so secure as not to be fearful of a fall; ''work out your salvation with fear and trembling'' (Phil 2.13).

The Objects of Charity. An esoteric treatment of such a high virtue is forestalled by the scriptural and patristic insistence on its social force: ''If anyone says that he loves God, and hates his brother, he is a liar. For how can he who does not love his brother, whom he sees, love God, whom he does not see? And this commandment we have from Him, that he who loves God should love his brother also'' (1 Jn 4.20–21).

God is loved, first of all, not merely as integrating our human experience, but as revealing Himself and pledging the communication of His joy. That He is loved for His own sake was taken quite simply, until with the refinement of abstractions in theology and their isolation as representing concrete situations, coupled with a spiritual theory of abnegation and practice of introspection to bring about the purification of motives, men began to ask themselves whether the pure and disinterested love of God was compatible with thoughts of self or indeed with images of His Incarnation and Sacraments. The question, which came to a head in the troubles between Fénelon and Bossuet, is summed up by R. A. Knox [*Enthusiasm* (Oxford 1957) 249]: "When I meditate about God I seldom lose sight of what *he is for me,* whereas when I use the prayer of contemplation my mind is more easily directed to the thought of what God is *in himself.* The contrast should not be overstressed; if it had not been, Quietism would probably have ended with Molinos, and the Church in France would have been spared a long and painful controversy." Knox also draws attention to a certain Platonism separating pure forms from the rich complex of God's loving action in us. Moreover the theological sense of symbolism seems to have been lost (cf. 3a, 8.3 ad 3; 23.3) in an attempt to strip love down to one element. Certainly there was a movement against the pregnant words of Scripture: "If thou didst know the gift of God, and who it is who says to thee, Give me to drink, thou, perhaps, wouldst have asked of him, and he would have given thee living water" (Jn 4.10). God gives Christ to us, and has given us to Christ (Jn 17.6). "How can he fail to grant us also all things with him?" (Rom 8.32). The ordinary teaching authority of the Church was quick to keep charity related to the ordinary works of virtue and quite properly expecting its reward not, as it were, by a quasi-juridical grant of a prize, but by the demand of love that it should find what it seeks (cf. 1a2ae, 114.4); "If anyone love me he will keep my word, and my Father will love him, and we will come to him and make our abode with him" (Jn 14.23).

The same movement of God goes to God and to all who are or can be His friends; it is not, as sometimes suggested, that we love God and because of this by a further and imperated act love our neighbor, as if one were our end and the other our means. Our love is elicited from charity (25.1), other persons being taken in God and as companions in His happiness; underlying this is the theology that creatures are true principal agents, though secondary, and true ends, though nonultimate. Notice also that we are bidden to do to our neighbor as we do to ourselves, and how unforced, and in a sense "undutiful," that is. It is to love our neighbor as a sharer in happiness, and this charity itself, not to make too fine a point, is itself lovable; for like happiness itself, it is not so much a virtue itself as a total condition (25.2).

And who is my neighbor? As in the story of the good Samaritan, charity is not restricted to a circle formed by one's customs, tastes, prejudices, or religious or cultural training; but as an impulse, it knows no limits: All creatures of mind and heart who can share in the fellowship of eternal life are the proper objects of its love, and other things too can be cherished as existing for divine honor and human benefit; so by charity does God love them (25.3). Strictly speaking we cannot be friends with ourselves. Yet as belonging to God, who is our friend, we should love ourselves, and also our bodies; an unearthly love that disdains the material world as evil is rejected (25.4–5). It will be noticed how sound Catholic tradition has excluded from this love in Christ neither the self nor the whole of creation that will be restored in Christ, "the firstborn of every creature, things visible and things invisible, and in him all things hold together, and through him he should reconcile all things, whether on earth or in the heavens" (Col 1.15–20), "who will refashion the body of our lowliness, conforming it to the body of his glory, by the power by which he is able to subject all things to himself" (Phil 3.21).

"I say to you, love your enemies" (Mt 5.44). It would be perverse to force oneself to cherish an enemy as such. One may hate the sin, but not the sinner (25.7). As contained potentially at least in the divine goodness that charity loves, an enemy must be regarded with fundamental good will by a Christian and may not be denied a place among those whom one wishes well. Moreover, one must be prepared to love his neighbor effectively should the occasion arise and to do him the good of which he is in need. "If your enemy be hungry, give him food to eat, if he be thirsty, give him to drink" (Prv 25.21). The more we love God, however, the less we shall wait for this need or be blocked by any enmity (25.8–9); "If you salute your brethren only, what are you doing more than others? You therefore are to be perfect, even as your heavenly Father is perfect" (Mt 5.47, 48).

Priorities in Charity. Charity is not an attitude of generalized affection but has its predilections and special occasions (2a2ae, 26), according to two principles: (1) what is better (*melior*), and therefore more like to God, and (2) what is nearer to us (*conjunctior*); for as we have seen, such polarization is essential to charity as it is to friendship. God's love comes above all, for even in natural love the part loves the whole even more than itself; much more in charity, then, is He loved as the fount of all that shares His happiness (26.1–3). The only break with this rule comes from that kind of self-love called sin. For the rest, after God we should first love ourselves, not in any self-regarding sense, but with a sober recognition that unless we are friends with God we cannot be in charity with others, even though we set their eternal welfare above our temporal good (26.4–5).

Charity also responds to the varieties in companionship (*consociatio*). It would be unreasonable to expect us to bear an equal affection for all; some do not enter into our life, and of those who do, some are better and therefore more lovable in themselves. Yet charity goes past esteem, and to others we warm because we are closer, and therefore love them with more intensity (26.6–12); there is no reason to suppose that any good reason for loving will be taken away in heaven (26.13).

Main Act of Charity. This is called *dilectio* (2a2ae, 27). "Dilection" is now a pallid translation, and there is no single equivalent term in English for this committed love that picks out its beloved. It seeks rather to love than to be loved; yet when it is mutual, all is well (27.1). It is not simple benevolence, although this is comprehended; but according to the dialectic of the deepest loving, often referred to in the *Summa,* this love, unlike knowing, transforms itself into the condition of its object—the beloved is treated as the self, and the practical axiom of morality, that we should do to others as we would be done by, takes on a new dimension in the friendship of charity (27.2).

The loving is on account of (*propter*) God, and nothing else. If one takes "on account of" in terms of final, formal, and efficient causality, then He is the ultimately, wholly, and underivatively lovable good; if it is taken in terms of material or dispositive causality, then rightly He is loved on account of other things, the blessings that draw us to Him gratefully, and even the penalties that make us fearful of losing Him (27.3). Moreover this love takes over where our knowledge leaves off, for faith is only a mediate and partial possession; whereas charity cleaves immediately "to God Himself and to other things only as being in Him," there is nothing in God that cannot be loved and nothing we can love that cannot be for Him (27.4–5). Finally, there is no limit to be set to this loving, and no excess is possible as there is in the moral virtues (27.6).

It may be observed parenthetically that although the terms of causality have been applied to charity and, by implication, to grace, both are constituted by the special presence of God as an object of knowledge and love, not by the general presence of His power (cf. 1a, 8.3). If we have to use the Aristotelean categories, it is to *relation* that we should look, and treat the life of divine grace and friendship within us as the coming forth into us of the life of the Blessed Trinity (cf. 1a, 43.3).

Corollaries. There is an abandon about charity—more congenially in the sense of being unconstrained than surrendered to outside control—and its interior effects are joy, peace, and mercy (2a2ae, 28–30). "These things I have spoken to you that my joy may be in you, and that your joy may be made full" (Jn 15.11); and again, "Peace I leave with you, my peace I give to you" (Jn 14.27). Both are the consequences of virtue, rather than virtues in themselves, and are considered among the beatitudes and the fruits of the Spirit (cf. 1a2ae, 69.70). "Rejoice with those who rejoice, weep with those who weep" (Rom 12.15); *misericordia* seems to be a special virtue, although it is wider in meaning than the English "mercy," but includes all gracious, familiar, compassionate loving-kindness [cf. E. Hill, *Blackfriars,* 46 (1965), 411–417].

External Acts. External acts of charity are benefaction, almsgiving (*see* ALMS AND ALMSGIVING), and fraternal correction (2a2ae, 31–35). "Therefore while we have time let us do good to all men" (Gal 6.10), beginning with those who are nearest to us. "He who has the goods of this world and sees his brother in need and closes his heart to him, how does the love of God abide in him?" (1 Jn 3.17); the giving we are charged with is conveniently summarized under the headings of the corporal and spiritual works of mercy. "Do not regard him as an enemy, but admonish him as a brother" (2 Thes 3.15); such a benefaction of charity is perhaps the most difficult to perform.

Sins against Charity. The sin against the principal act of charity is hate (2a2ae, 34). The sins against joy are ACEDIA and ENVY (2a2ae, 35, 36). The first, well diagnosed by Cassian, is commonly translated as sloth, but it means rather a boredom with divine things, no more to be confused with the spiritual dryness described by the spiritual writers than the steady choice of charity is to be confused with sensible devotion (*see* ARIDITY, SPIRITUAL). Envy, too, is not desire, but sadness about another's good. The sins against peace are discord in the heart, contentiousness in speech, and schism, strife, and rebellion in deed (2a2ae, 37–42). Most of the sins against the external acts of charity are forms of injustice, but SCANDAL in a special manner is a sin against the loving-kindness we should show to one another (2a2ae, 43); it does not mean shocking another, but providing the occasion for his spiritual ruin.

Precepts. There are two great commandments of charity, that we should love God with our whole heart and our neighbor as ourself (2a2ae, 44). All other precepts are subordinate to these; Christian perfection consists mainly in their observance and not in the counsels (2a2ae, 184.3). Such is the law of love, but it is not an ordinance in the juridical sense, for it is not directed to the well-being of a group, but only to the happy intercommunication of persons in friendship [cf. T. Gilby, *Between Community and Society* (London and New York 1953) 194–202].

Gifts. The classical theological teaching culminates in the consideration of the gift of the Holy Spirit called WISDOM (2a2ae, 45). There the great mystical writers see how our knowledge shaped by love can rise to an experience of God that has gone beyond all concepts: "We speak a wisdom of God, mysterious, hidden which God foreordained before the world to our glory . . . to us God has revealed them through his Spirit. For the Spirit searches all things, even the deep things of God. . . .

The spiritual man judges all things, and he himself is judged by no man. For who has known the mind of the Lord that he might instruct him? But we have the mind of Christ'' (1 Cor 2.7–16). It is noteworthy that St. Thomas, revising a previous judgment that made of this gift a sort of gnosis, took it also into the practical business of intelligent living (45.3) and related it especially to the seventh beatitude (45.6), ''Blessed are the peacemakers, for they shall be called the children of God'' (Mt 5.9).

Bibliography: F. PRAT et al., *Dictionnaire de spiritualité ascétique et mystique. Doctrine et histoire,* ed. M. VILLER et al. (Paris 1932—) 2:507–691. C. SPICQ, *Agape in the New Testament,* tr. M. A. MCNAMARA and M. H. RICHTER (St. Louis 1963). J. E. VAN ROEY, *De virtute caritatis quaestiones selectae* (Mechlin 1929). G. GILLEMAN, *The Primacy of Charity in Moral Theology,* tr. W. F. RYAN and A. VACHON (Westminster, Md. 1959). B. HÄRING, *The Law of Christ,* tr. E. G. KAISER (Westminster, Md. 1961—).

[T. GILBY]

CHARITY, BROTHERS OF

Official Catholic Directory #0290; a religious congregation of brothers (*Fratres a Caritate,* FC) with papal approval (1888, 1899), founded at Ghent, Belgium, in 1807 by Canon Peter Joseph TRIEST. After Triest assigned the first members to a hostel for elderly men, his congregation received local episcopal approval in 1809 ''for works of charity, service of the poor and destitute.'' The institute spread to Canada (1865), the U.S. (1874), England (1881), Ireland (1883), and the Netherlands (1894). Missions were established in the Congo (1911), Transvaal (1928), Rwanda and Indonesia (1929), India (1936), Cuba (1950), and Peru (1962). The apostolate encompasses the care of aged men and of the mentally ill; the education of retarded, deaf, mute, blind, and disabled children; and teaching in primary, secondary, and technical schools. The generalate is located in Rome.

Bibliography: C. REICHGELT, *Les Frères de la Charité,* v.1 (Ghent 1957), covers 1807–76.

[L. C. DE BEUCKELAER/EDS.]

CHARITY, WORKS OF

The word ''charity'' derives from the Latin *caritas,* which meant family affection, friendship, patriotism. It was used by Cicero to express love for humankind, an important tenet of Stoic doctrine (*see* STOICISM). But the Christians used *caritas* to translate the Greek AGAPE—impregnating the Latin word with all the meaning of the Greek term in Holy Scripture and in particular in the teaching of Jesus—love of God and love of men with all

the duties that this rich concept implies [see H. Petré, *Caritas. Étude sur le vocabulaire latin de la Charité chrétienne* (Louvain 1948) 96–]. Works of charity are the practical embodiment of those duties of love for one's neighbor. They will be considered historically in this survey as they existed in Christian antiquity and in the Middle Ages, and as they continue in modern times.

In Christian Antiquity

The dynamic concept of charity that was to flower in works of charity was implanted in His Church by Jesus Christ.

The teaching of Jesus. In the mind of our Lord, the precept of loving God is inseparable from that of loving our neighbor: they are two aspects of the same virtue. Christ places these two precepts of love at the center of His teaching. Loving God means striving to become like Him—reproducing His universal goodness to men who, as a consequence, have a right to our love and, if necessary, to our pardon (Mt 5:43–48). Christ calls his teaching on charity a ''new commandment'' (Jn 13:34). Under the Mosaic Law one's neighbor was a Hebrew and the love of others was primarily negative; it consisted in seeking to avoid all that could provoke reprisals according to the terms of the laws of retaliation. Even when the law of love was translated into positive acts, the precept always remained self-interested, inspired by self-love. Even the most humane of the Hebrew moralists, Hillel, understood this when he said: ''Do not to your neighbor what you do not want done to you.''

Christ denounced this narrow interpretation of the Scribes (Mt 5:43), thereby defining the law of charity as a law of social relations. It is not enough to love one's friends; one must do good to one's enemies (Mt 5:46–48; Lk 10:25–37). The new commandment obliges one, as well, to love the neighbor as Christ has loved him—to the point of giving one's life for him (1 Jn 3:16). Love of neighbor in Christ's teaching (Jn 15:17) is not something optional, but a categorical imperative that all disciples must obey in order to belong to the Master. Jesus calls it ''my commandment''; it is not just one of the precepts of His code but His favorite one—the mark of those who believe in Him (Jn 13:35). The command (at the same time a privilege) will make charity in the sight of heaven the touchstone for discerning Christ's own (Mt 25:34–45). Protestations of love for God will not be acceptable to God if they are not translated into acts beneficial to the neighbor in the form of assistance, material aid, etc. The two precepts are in fact one. Jesus is not content with declaring the second similar to the first. He wished to bestow on it a high dignity and stress its serious importance. He even gives it precedence over public worship:

"Charity (Aiding Mother and Children)," 1857, *engraving.* (©Bettmann/CORBIS)

"To love one's neighbor as oneself is more precious than all holocausts and sacrifices" (Mk 12:33).

The transition from the love for man to love for God, besides revealing the originality of Christ's teaching, is the secret of all Christian works of charity and makes them transcend even the most impressive secular humanitarian achievements. The message of Christ, rooted in the universal fatherhood of God, has swept away national and religious differences, attacked racial and caste discrimination (Gal 3.:8), and inspired heroic dedication.

The apostolic tradition. Christ's message of brotherly love constantly leavened the preaching and teaching of the Apostles and the first believers. St. John, the apostle of charity, never tired of recommending it and delighted in insisting (1 Jn 4:20–21) on the fusion of the two precepts into one. St. Paul synthesizes the essence of Christianity into charity (Gal 5:14; 6:2; Rom 13:8); reiterates the equality of the master and slave (Phil ch. 16)

and the obligation of the rich to supply the wants of the poor (2 Cor 8:12); and points out the free character of charity in the example of Christ (2 Cor ch. 7–8). St. James proclaims: "Religion pure and undefiled before God the Father is this: to give aid to orphans and widows in their tribulation, and to keep oneself unspotted from this world" (Jas 1:27).

This teaching was immediately translated into action. The author of the Acts thus pictures the first Church of Jerusalem:

> Now the multitude of the believers were of one heart and one soul, and not one of them said that anything he possessed was his own, but they had all things in common. And with great power the apostles gave testimony to the resurrection of Jesus Christ our Lord; and great grace was in them all. Nor was there anyone among them in want. For those who owned lands or houses would sell them and bring the price of what they sold and lay

it at the feet of the apostles, and distribution was made to each, according as any one had need. [Acts 4:32–34; also 2:44]

A concrete example of this practice is seen in the Cypriote Barnabas (Acts 4:35). It is true that community ownership of goods was unique to the Church in Jerusalem, and even there it tended to disappear as circumstances were modified.

This thirst for an enthusiastic sharing was not strange in the state of endemic misery that the Mother Church was enduring, tried by hunger, persecution, and political agitation. Moreover, it was necessary to beg constantly in Antioch (Acts 11:29), in Galatia (1 Cor 16:1), and in Macedonia (2 Cor 8:1–15; Rom 15:26), for the faithful in Jerusalem.

As the Christian community grew the first difficulties arose. The author of the Acts tells of the discontent among the Greek-speaking Jews because they felt that the widows of their group were being neglected in the daily ministrations (Acts 6:1–6). The problem sprang from a lack of personnel; the Apostles accordingly ordered the election of seven men to whom they confided the work of helping the poor. Until that time it had been done by the Apostles themselves. The very fact of the election of these deacons (as they were later called by St. Irenaeus) shows the supreme importance the Apostles attached to charitable works.

The special task of the deacons was to assist at the common meal or agape, originally connected with the Eucharistic celebration. According to the tradition, which persisted even later on, the poor had to receive food and drink since a common table, to which all contributed according to their means, united rich and poor alike. However, even here difficulties arose and were denounced by St. Paul (1 Cor 11:18–22). The agape very soon lost its importance.

To aid the poor was not simply a public duty assigned to deacons. They were assisted by widows possessing special qualities precisely outlined by St. Paul: "Let a widow who is selected be not less than 60 years old, having been married but once, with a reputation for good works in bringing up children, in practicing hospitality, in washing the saints' feet, in helping those in trouble, in carefully pursuing every good work" (1 Tm 5:9–10). Private charity thus stood side by side with public charity and Paul frequently emphasized the obligation of each Christian to practice it (Gal 6:10). He held out the example of Tabitha (Dorcas) at Joppa (modern Jaffa) who had "devoted herself to good works and acts of charity" (Acts 9:36). When she died the Christians sent for Peter, who was in nearby Lydda, and on his arrival, "all the widows stood about him weeping and showing

him the tunics and cloaks which Dorcas used to make for them" (*ibid.*).

Charity in the persecuted Church. Thus the gospel was transformed into a social message that stimulated it and gave it a special character harmonizing with the growth of the new faith in time and space.

There are reliable proofs from both Christian and pagan sources, of the increasing charity of the generations of Christians that followed the Apostolic age. Lucian writes: "Their law-giver has taught them that they are all brothers; as soon as something happens which touches their common interests nothing is too difficult for them and they are capable of incredible activity" (*Peregr.* 10). Tertullian says: "Our care for the derelict and our active love have become our distinctive sign before the enemy. . . . See, they say, how they love one another and how ready they are to die for each other" (*Apol.* 39). Justin in his *Apologia* to the emperor affirms: "We, who loved above all else the ways of acquiring riches and possessions, now hand over to a community fund what we possess and share it with every needy person; we, who hated and killed one another, now, after the coming of Christ, live in community, and pray for our enemies" (*Apol.* 1.14). Already in the year 96, Pope Clement, sketching the ideal picture of a Christian community, as Corinth was before it was torn by internal strife, stressed the spirit of charity: "Who, living among you, has not heralded abroad your reputation for unbounded hospitality? You were all happier to give than to receive . . . , day and night you kept up your efforts on behalf of the whole brotherhood" (1 Clem 1:2). Christian practice was seen against a transcendent background as in the following passage from the *Letter to Diognetus* (ch. 10): "Any man can be an imitator of God, if he takes on his own shoulders the burden of his neighbors, if he chooses to use his advantage to help another who is underprivileged, if he takes what he has received from God and gives to those who are in need—for such a man becomes God to those who are helped. Then, even though you are on earth, you will see that God rules in heaven."

Prescriptions for the Practice of Charity. Almsgiving, in particular, was considered spiritual ransom, as Clement stated in his second letter to the Corinthians: "Almsgiving is good as a penance for sin; fasting is better than prayer, but almsgiving is better than both, and charity covers a multitude of sins" (2 Clem 16). For this reason the exercise of charity was intimately connected with worship; every Sunday in fact (2 Cor 16:2), or every month, or whenever they wished (Tertullian, *Apol.* 39), the believers brought their gifts (in money or kind) during the celebration of the Mass and presented them to the bishop (Justin, *Apol.* 1:67) who placed them on the altar table, as offerings to the Lord. Thus the needy received them from the hand of the Lord. "The grace and kindness of the Lord supported all the poor," writes Pope Cornelius (Eusebius, *Ecclesiastical History* 6:43). The task of distributing the offerings belonged to the deacons who at the end of the divine service divided them among those present. A part of the offerings was reserved for the needy who were not at the service and later was brought to their homes; the remainder was used for the agape feast. The deaconesses (*Const. Apost.* 2:17) continued helping them. However, the entire work of assistance was directed by the bishops (*Const. Apost.* 1:1; 2:25, 26, 27) who "have made their ministry a perpetual refuge for the needy and widows" (*Shepherd of Hermas*); in the Didache they were considered as fathers of the poor (ch. 1, 3, 4) and by St. Ignatius of Antioch as "guardians of widows" (*Ad Polycarp* 4).

The *Apostolic Constitutions* are filled with detailed prescriptions for the practice of charity in the first centuries—prescriptions for the ministers and the beneficiaries, and details about the means, the abuses, and the value of sacrifice (see ch. 1, 2, 4, 8). Origen has handed down valuable principles to guide the Church in aiding the poor (*Comm. Ser. 16 in Mt.*).

> Let us be prudent, so that we may come to the aid of everyman according to his dignity, recalling the words: "Blessed is he who is wise in dealing with the needy and the poor." We must not give away too easily the goods of the Church, caring only not to destroy or steal them. Rather we must make distinctions regarding the causes of poverty, the dignity of each indigent person, his education and the degree of his need. . . . Therefore, we must not treat equally one, who from his infancy, has led a hard and straitened life and one, who accustomed to ease and wealth, has fallen into poverty. Nor must we give the same things to men and women, to the aged and the young, to the sick who can provide nothing for themselves and those who can help themselves in some small way. It is important also to inquire about the needs of large families, especially those who are industrious but still cannot make ends meet. In short, he who wishes to use the goods of the Church well must be very wise.

The same writer, in accord with St. Paul (1 Cor 9:14), vindicating the right of the clergy to live on the revenues of the Church, states: "Our food must be simple and our clothing plain so that we do not keep for ourselves more than we give the naked and thirsty or those who suffer a lack of material things."

It was this prudent spirit of wise administration and a fear of abuses that led the deacons to keep lists and records of the names and conditions of those they assisted.

Accordingly, it is known that in the year 250 the Roman Christian community had about 100 ecclesiastics and 1,500 poor; the result was a heavy demand on the common treasury. The funds kept in this treasury were not only the regular offerings of the faithful made during the sacred liturgy, but also periodic contributions, gifts of money or valuables given on special occasions such as Baptism or death, tithes (*Const. Apost.* 5:20), alms collected in time of emergencies (Cyprian, *Epist.* 60; *Patrologia Latina* 4:359), and almsgiving united to fasting to make this good work valuable for salvation (*Shepherd of Hermas* 5:3; Origen, *Hom 10 in Lev;* Chrysostom, *Sermo de ieunio;* Augustine, *Sermo 208 in quadrag.,* etc.).

Widows and Orphans. These "deposits of piety" as Tertullian (*Apol.* 39) called them, were distributed according to a scale—the first places being reserved, as we see from ancient church sources, for widows and orphans. The reason for this was the real poverty of these two groups in ancient times, as well as the esteem widows enjoyed in the primitive community (1 Tm 5:16). St. Polycarp called them "altars of God" (*Ad Philipp.* 4). They formed a category apart, performed special tasks, and were enrolled in a separate register [see J. Danielou, "Le Ministère des femmes dans l'Église ancienne," *Maison Dieu* 61 (1960) 70–96].

Prisoners and Captives. In a period when Christians paid for their faith in Christ by prison and forced labor, the Church could not be indifferent to the lot of her children. Prisoners were the special objects of both public and private charity (Tertullian, *Ad Mart.* 1). It was a duty to visit and care for a prisoner and to work for his liberation—this duty was repeatedly inculcated by the *Apostolic Constitutions* (7:1, 3) and by St. Cyprian (*Epist.* 37; *Patrologia Latina* 4:326). St. Ignatius wrote to those in Smyrna: "When the Christians become aware that one of their number is a prisoner or suffering for the name of Christ, they take upon themselves all his needs and, if possible, they free him" (*Ad Smyr.* 6). It is said of Origen that "he was with the holy martyrs not only while they were in prison, and not only while they were being examined up to the last sentence, but also after this when they were led away to death, displaying great boldness and coming into close contact with danger" (Eusebius, *Ecclesiastical History* 6.3–4).

Although it was one of the duties assigned to the deacons, the visiting of prisoners was done also by private individuals as a duty of charity, and no one hesitated to bribe the jailor to that end (Lucian, *Peregr.* 12; Eusebius, *Ecclesiastical History* 6.61). The example of the deacons Tertius and Pomponius in Africa, and the charity shown to the martyrs Perpetua and Felicity is well known [see

O. Gebhardt, *Acta martyrum selecta* (Berlin 1902) 66]. The writings of early Christians are filled with histories of this kind and they indicate the double aim of the visits—to console and to sustain the prisoners and to be consoled by their blessing.

Christian charity also reached the brethren condemned to forced labor in the mines. The Christian community tried to keep in touch with them and obtain their liberty. Examples of this type of charity are recorded about the Roman community at the time of Pope Soter (Eusebius, *Ecclesiastical History* 6:23; Hippolytus, *Philos.* 9:12) and the Egyptian community during the persecution of Diocletian (Eusebius *De mart. palest.* 10:1; 11:5).

Besides alleviating the sufferings of prisoners, the Christians sought to ransom them. Episodes of this kind were probably not rare, even though today it is difficult for the historian to say in individual cases whether it was a question of freeing prisoners or ransoming slaves. It would seem, though, that the initiative fell to some courageous individuals rather than to the community. There were numerous occasions of real heroism. "We know that many among ourselves have given themselves up to chains in order to redeem others; many have surrendered themselves to slavery and provided food for others with the price they received for themselves," notes St. Clement of Rome (*Ad Cor.* 1:2). When, in 253, Numidian brigands seized a number of Christians, the community of Carthage quickly collected 100,000 sesterces for ransom, declaring that they were ready to raise more if necessary. In 255 the Christians of Rome contributed money when the Goths captured some members of the Christian community in Cappadocia (Basil, *Epist. 70 Ad Damasum, Patrologia Graeca* 32:435–436). Such liberation of prisoners by ransom is often mentioned in 4th- and 5th-century Gallic epitaphs.

Slaves. Particular care was taken of slaves, and Christianity had a decided influence in ameliorating their condition. Converted slaves were accepted as brothers and in the face of this reality their social condition took second place (*Iren.* 4:21:3; Tertullian, *De Corona* 13). "Nor is there any other reason," wrote Lactantius, "why we take for ourselves the name of brothers one to another, unless it is that we believe that we are equal; for since we measure all human things, not by the body, but by the spirit, and although the condition of the bodies may be diversified, there are not slaves among us, but we regard them and speak of them as brothers in spirit and as fellow slaves in religion." Slaves participated fully as members of the community and could become clerics and even bishops. As persons, in the moral sense, they enjoyed the same esteem as free men. The honesty and chastity of slaves could not be violated. Since they were expected to practice the same virtues as free men, their virtues were likewise recognized and extolled. The *Acts of the Martyrs* offers its ample proof of this in frequent praise of the heroism of Christian slaves.

Such presuppositions underlie the recommendations to masters to treat their slaves kindly and not to forget that they are brothers. On their part slaves—conforming to the Pauline teaching prevalent in the ancient Church—were to endure their slavery for the glory of God and obtain true liberty, which is that of the spirit (1 Cor 7:21–24). This did not prevent Christian masters from freeing their slaves, and in some instances community funds were used to purchase their freedom, but those so released were not to regard their liberty as a right (Ignatius, *Ad Polyc.* 4:3). The Synod of Elvira in 300 denounced ill treatment of slaves (c:5:41; also Origen, *Comm. in Rom.* 3:4).

The Sick and the Dead. The community assisted the sick, especially the incurable, with the consolation of their prayers, their visits, and material help (Tertullian, *Ad Uxor* 2:4). But Christian charity was not limited to the living; according to Emperor Julian one of the factors that favored the growth of Christianity was the great care the faithful took to bury the dead (Sozomen, *Ecclesiastical History* 5:15). This pious task was performed willingly even by individuals (Aristides, *Apol.* 15); but usually the Church as a community took charge and entrusted the work to the deacons (*Const. Apost.* 3:7) and expenses for the burial of the poor were paid by the community (Tertullian, *Apol.* 39). The Christians did not limit their burial duties to members of their own faith; Lactantius writes: "We will not therefore allow the image and workmanship of God to lie as prey for beasts and birds, but we shall return it to the earth, whence it sprang; although we will fulfill this duty of kinsmen on an unknown man, humaneness will take over and fill the place of kinsmen who are lacking" (*Instit.* 6.12). Their concern for the dead led the Christians to pray and make offerings for the repose of their souls. This ancient custom had important repercussions on the living, bringing them comfort and strengthening the cause of Christianity.

These pious duties became very impressive in the event of public disasters. During the plague that devastated Alexandria in 259 Bishop Dionysius bore witness to the conduct of the faithful:

> Most of our brethren, in their surpassing charity and brotherly love did not spare themselves and clinging to one another fearlessly visited the sick and ministered to them. Many, after having nursed and consoled the sick, contracted their illness and cheerfully departed this life. The best of our

brethren died in this way, some priests and deacons, and some of the laity. The conduct of the pagans was just the opposite; they would drive away those beginning to fall sick and people fled from their dear ones; they threw the dying into the street and bodies were left unburied. [Eusebius, *Ecclesiastical History* 7:22:9–10:1]

St. Cyprian recorded much the same regarding the plague in Carthage in 252 (*De Mortalitate* 14; *Patrologia Latina* 4: 591–593); while others fled, he gathered his own congregation and reminded them of their duty, setting them the example (*Vita Cypriani, Patrologia Latina* 3:1489). During the plague that raged in the reign of Maximinus "all the pagans were aware of the zeal and piety of the Christians. They alone, in such evil surroundings, showed their compassion and love for all men by actual deeds. Some dedicated themselves to caring for the sick and burying the dead. Others gathered together crowds of hungry people and fed them. These glorified the God of the Christians and confessed that only the Christians were pious and religious" (Eusebius, *Ecclesiastical History* 9:8:14–15).

Travelers. Outside their own community the Christians sought to provide for strangers, especially for their brothers in the faith. This assistance was not left to the good will of individuals; although hospitality was widely practiced by Christians as a duty (Rom 12:13; 1 Pt 4:9; Didache 12; *Hermas* 8:10; Tertullian, *Ad Uxor* 2:4; Cyprian, *Epist.* 7, etc.), it also had a community character. In his first letter to the Corinthians, Clement stresses, among the other virtues that had signalized the Church, the splendid and noble custom of hospitality (1 Cor 1:2). The example of the Roman community is particularly worthy of note. In a letter written during the time of Marcus Aurelius, Dionysius, Bishop of Corinth, mentions the ancient custom of receiving any of the brothers who passed through Rome: "You keep up the ancestral custom of the Romans, a custom which your blessed bishop Soter has not only maintained but even increased, providing abundant help to the saints and, with blessed words, encouraging the brethren who come to Rome as a loving father his own children" (Eusebius, *Ecclesiastical History* 4:23:10). The great regard in which the Roman community was held did not depend so much on its being the center of apostolic activity in the West, as on its charity. In a period when Christianity existed in scattered communities, the infrequent trips of some of the brethren were the only contact between them. For this reason hospitality was of vast importance and was the subject of a treatise (now lost)—*Peri filoxenias*—by an oriental writer, Melito, bishop of Sardis (Eusebius, *Ecclesiastical History* 4:26). Clement never tired of extolling hospitality (1 Cor 10:7; 11:1; 12:1).

This spirit of welcome occasioned some abuses: heretics, tricksters, and vagabonds could infiltrate and jeopardize the community. However, measures were taken to forestall this: the new arrival had to prove that he was a Christian; if he possessed the gift of prophecy his works had to correspond to his words. Hospitality was limited to two or three days, after which the guest had either to leave or earn his own living (Didache 11, 12). Later, a traveling Christian had to present a kind of passport issued by the community he was leaving (Council of Elvira, c. 25).

Beginning of Union among Scattered Church Communities. The care lavished on a wayfaring brother in the faith formed a bridge, as has been stated, between the scattered communities. What the guest had to tell of the sufferings or the good fortune of his own church was of common interest. The ancient churches felt a strong bond between them and reacted according to the Pauline rule: "If one member suffers anything, all the members suffer with it, or if one member glories, all the members rejoice with it. Now you are the body of Christ, member for member" (1 Cor 12:26–27). Such a spirit made brotherly love dynamic and the most distant people neighbors. "They know each other and love each other by invisible signs even before they meet," exclaims the pagan Cecilius (Minutius Felix, *Octav.* 9:3).

The knowledge of belonging to a holy society very early took deep roots in the minds of individuals and it was linked with a sense of responsibility toward the whole company, even toward all mankind. "Pray for all the saints," Polycarp counseled, following St. Paul (1 Cor 59:2), "pray for the emperors, and authorities and rulers, for those who persecute and hate you, and for the enemies of the cross" (*Ad Phillip.* 12:3). The bishops worked to put this concept of charity into action, intervening in particular circumstances to eliminate the motives for dispute and to create a climate of common understanding. But charity shone with a special light in extraordinary cases when one community would make its own the suffering of another community.

St. Paul had worked from the beginning of his missionary life among the pagans to foster these bonds of charity, promoting the idea of helping the Church in Jerusalem. A generation later, the persecutions began, and those who lived in relative tranquility worried about those who were threatened or stricken. Dionysius, Bishop of Corinth, affirmed this, writing to the Romans about the year 170: "It has been your custom from the beginning to do good in various ways to all the brethren, sending help to the Christians in the mines" (Eusebius, *Ecclesiastical History* 4:23:10). A hundred years later, another Dionysius, Bishop of Alexandria, in a letter to Pope Stephen mentioned, almost in passing, the assistance given by the pope to the Churches in Syria and Arabia (*ibid.* 7:5:2). Basil of Caesarea narrated that at the time of Pope Dionysius (259–269) the Church of Rome sent money to Cappadocia to liberate the Christians who had fallen into the hands of the barbarians. This fact was remembered with gratitude in that country as late as the 4th century (*Epist.* 70 *Ad Damasum Patrologia Graeca* 32:435–436). Eusebius recalled also that the Roman Church kept alive the custom of helping suffering communities even during the last persecution of Diocletian (Eusebius, *op. cit.*, 4:22:9).

From the satire on Peregrinus (*Peregr.* 13) by Lucian, we learn how lively and active the interest and preoccupation of all the communities were for their distant sister-communities during the persecution under Marcus Aurelius. The letters of Ignatius to the various churches are also an eloquent commentary. From this source we learn of the sincere interest of the communities of Asia Minor and Rome in the fate of a bishop they had never seen and the care they took of his church at Antioch, left without a shepherd. Monetary aid took second place to the personal interest that led whole communities, bishops and faithful alike, to console and encourage one another and bear each other's sufferings.

From the edict of Constantine to Gregory the Great. The conversion of some of Roman society to Christianity was not immediately followed by a flowering of evangelical ideals. However, from the 4th century Christianity introduced new notions even into secular civilization; one of these is the concept of charity in the social sense of the word, of the fellowship and responsibility of man toward his brothers, the disinherited, the poor, the homeless, the vagabonds, the sick, and the mentally ill. There is no text of Roman law that is inspired by *caritas*. This concept remained foreign to the juridical order of the classical Roman age. But once *caritas* became a fundamental Christian virtue, it inspired juridical texts of the postclassical age and texts inserted by the Justinians [E. Albertario, "'Caritas' nei testi giuridici romani" in the *Rendiconti dell'Istituto Lombardo di scienze e lettere* 64 (1931) 375–392]. Respect for the human person, founded on the religious conviction that he is an object of the merciful love of God, was unknown to the pagan world. The liberality of the master toward his slaves was a very different thing, as were the benefits—bread and circuses—which the people received from the government: dividends of the spoils of conquests.

Liberty of worship, the juridical right to own property, and the restoration of the wealth confiscated by Diocletian (Lactantius, *De morte persecutorum* 48) allowed the Church a more liberal and substantial organization of charity. And it was a providential coincidence that as the end of persecution brought an influx of conversions to the Church so it also brought an increased number of needy converts who had to be assisted. The Church was able to raise money from the large fortunes of converts from aristocratic families. In 367 the consul Lampadius, on taking office, made large donations for the needy (Ammianus Marcellinus 27:3:5) and the prefect Nebridius, at Constantinople, did the same from his annual income (Jerome, *Epist.* 85). Placilla, the wife of Theodosius (Theodoret, *Ecclesiastical History* 5:18), engaged in works of charity and many noble Roman women followed her example, e.g., Pauline, daughter of Paula; Fabiola; and Melania. St. Jerome bore witness to this in his writings (*Epist.* 77, 108; *Patrologia Latina* 22:690, 878), as did St. Paulinus of Nola (*Epist. 29 ad Severum; Patrologia Latina* 61:315). At the death of his wife Paulina in 396, the senator Pammachius gave a banquet in the Vatican basilica for all the poor of Rome. St. Jerome noted: "The precious stones which once adorned her neck now serve to feed the poor" (*Epist.* 66; *Patrologia Latina* 22:641). The name of Pammachius was connected with a hospice he founded at the port of Rome, near Ostia; and the name of Fabiola was linked to a hospital in the city where she gave personal service as well as financial aid to the poor. Paulinus of Nola, who knew all these instances well, summed up the complete change in social values when he called the beggars "patrons of our souls" (*Epist. 13 ad Severum; Patrologia Latina* 61:313). It was now the rich who appeared in the place of servants.

But the principal source of charitable endeavors was the possessions of the Church, which had come to her through imperial favor and which, besides covering the expenses of the clergy, were used to carry on charitable works. "The possessions of the Church are the patrimony of the poor," said St. Ambrose (*Epist.* 18:16; *Patrologia Latina* 16:1018). The bishops, as usual, assumed the leadership. From the time of Constantine the emperors gave them authority to administer the provision of food for orphans and widows, and later for prisoners (Theodoret, *Ecclesiastical History* 1:10). The councils reminded them of their obligation to care for the needy. From their ranks came some of the most representative apostles of charity both in the East and the West.

The Rise of Church-sponsored Charitable Institutions. In Caesarea of Cappadocia, St. Basil, not content with having provided food for an entire year (368) to a region devastated by famine, began to construct (372) on the edge of the city a group of buildings (church, monastery, school of arts and trades, hospices, and hospital) destined to receive wayfarers, sick persons, and especially lepers, and staffed them with qualified personnel (Sozomen, *Ecclesiastical History* 6:34; Allard, *St. Basil* 109–111). Such "homes for the poor" (*ptochotrophia*) were not isolated phenomena. During the same period many others could be found, for example, at Amasya in Pontus and elsewhere. The Church of Alexandria had a group of nurses (*parabolani*) under the protection of the bishop; their number in the period from 416 to 418 exceeded 500. Another organizer of charitable works in Constantinople was St. John Chrysostom, who was aided by some generous souls of the aristocracy [C. Baur, *Johannes Chrisostomus und seine Zeit,* 1 (Munich 1929) 130, 303; 2 (Munich 1930) 55, 73]. Such was his ardor in condemning the avarice of the wealthy that in many texts he seemed to doubt the right of individuals to own private property. He did not, however, sanction the right of the poor to revolt against the rich. Rather he intended to incite the rich to the practice of charity.

In the West it is sufficient to name such bishops as Ambrose of Milan, Epiphanius of Pavia, Maximus of Turin, Paulinus of Nola, Martin of Tours, Nicetius of Lyons, and Sidonius Apollinarius. Ambrose was interested in everyone without distinction of rank; anyone could approach him, wrote St. Augustine (*Conf.* 6:3), unless the crowds of needy formed an impenetrable barrier around him. As soon as he was consecrated bishop, he gave all the gold and silver he possessed to the Church and to the poor; later on he bequeathed all he owned to the church in Milan (*Vita Ambr.* 38; *Patrologia Latina* 14:42). In the second book of his *De Officiis,* he insisted on the duties of charity, good works, and hospitality, and when in 378, after the defeat of Adrianople, many Christian soldiers fell into the hands of the Goths, Ambrose ordered all the vessels that had not yet been used for the sacred rites to be melted down and used as ransom. To justify his action he said: "It is better to conserve the living chalices of souls than those of metal! How beautiful is the sight of a procession of prisoners of whom it can be said: Christ has ransomed them. Here is useful gold, the gold of Christ that frees from death, the gold that ransoms modesty and saves chastity" (*De Off.* 2:28:136–143; *Patrologia Latina* 16:148).

It can be affirmed without a doubt that many of the bishops were very much aware of the urgent need for charity in all areas: from providing food and clothing to protecting the poor against the avidity of tax collectors and defending debtors from the mercilessness of usurers; from combating the rigors of the law to the guardianship of the rights of the poor of whom the bishops were, by their office, the defenders. In tragic times, such as those of the 5th century, when, according to St. Jerome, on account of the incessant wars "satis dives est, qui pane non indiget, nimium potens, qui servire non cogitur" (he is rich enough who does not lack bread; he is strong enough

who is not compelled to be a slave; *Epist. 120 ad Rusticum*; *Patrologia Latina* 22:1085), the preoccupations of a bishop could not differ from those of Peter Chrysologus: "Where are the barns . . . kept for the hunger of the poor?" (*Sermo* 122; *Patrologia Latina* 52). By this time the organized charity of the bishops had passed beyond the simple stage of a private duty and assumed a public character. The continual increase of the needy and the growing lack of those who could care for them conferred on the bishops a kind of investiture, which the events of the time made quite natural.

Development of Charitable Institutions under Church Administration. The bishops' work assumed a particular importance in regard to hospitality; the numerous hospices and hospitals erected during this period, although administered autonomously, were the property of the Church and as such headed by the bishops. The laws of the later empire recognized their position and entrusted the control to them, leaving to the heirs of the benefactors and their executors the tasks of administration. In the time of Justinian the juridical picture of hospital administration under the vigilance of the bishop was traced in its essential lines. These, it may be noted, were institutions that are today in the hands of the laity and have become an essential characteristic of every civilized state. But the historian of civilization must stress the fact that they are derived from a Christian inspiration and developed for many years under the protection of the Church. Herein lies the value and importance of the first two centuries of the free Church. Instead of being amazed at the length of time it took for the Christian ideal to penetrate human society, the historian must recognize the Christianization of social institutions that later expanded into the medieval city. In fact, Emperor Julian the Apostate testified to the influence of Christian charity on society when he wrote in 362 to the priest Arsacius: "Why do we not turn our eyes towards those institutions to which the impious religion of the Christians owes its growth, towards the help it gives to aliens? Build many xenodochia in every city. It is a shame for us that the inhuman Galileans sustain not only their poor but ours as well" (Sozomen, *Ecclesiastical History* 5:16).

Active assistance was already considered a fundamental element of monastic life as early as the 4th century, the heroic era of the Fathers of the desert. There is, in the technical language of the Egyptian monks, evidence that the strong disciplinary organization of the cenobite community tended to centralize the gathering and distribution of alms to the needy in a specialized service that was called diaconia. Cassian was the first to explain the meaning of this word, which was the name given to the almshouse of the Egyptian monastery of Diolco, supplied by the faithful and headed by a monk with the title of *diaconetès* [H. I. Marrou, "L'origine orientale des diaconies romaines," *Mélanges d'Archéologie et d'histoire* 57 (1940) 95–142]. Cassian's text brings us back to the middle of the 4th century. Little by little as they developed, the monastic diaconias tended toward autonomy. Almsgiving was made possible more by the contributions of the faithful than by the work of the monks. When larger offerings, such as lands, possessions, etc., were added to the fruits of the earth brought by the peasants, the diaconia became a proprietor, and had to receive juridical recognition. This autonomy was the first step toward independence, which probably was realized at Aphroditus from 573 to 574. Favored by the imperial government, the diaconias soon spread widely in Egypt, in Palestine (Marrou, *op. cit.* 9), in the Greek East (*ibid.* 10–11), and after the Justinian reconquest, in the Italian peninsula and even in Rome (*ibid.* 11–14).

Papal Patronage. At Rome, for that matter, thanks to the solicitous vigilance of the popes, the practice of charity always held first place. Reference has already been made to Pope Cornelius's interest in the poor. The pope as "Father of the Poor" meets us in the persons of Leo the Great and Gelasius. Symmachus founded three homes for the poor. Pelagius I was anxious that the patrimony of the Church should always be sufficient to care for the needy (*Lib. pont.* 1:263). But the service of the poor reached its peak under Gregory the Great.

Gregory had scarcely ascended the pontifical throne when he made his first concern the assuring of provisions for the city. He therefore warmly recommended to Peter, administrator of the patrimony of Sicily, that he not permit the consignments of grain to decrease. In the absence of civil authority and even contrary to it, Gregory felt it his imperative duty to protect the interests of the needy. "We have no wealth of our own, but the care and administration of the goods of the poor have been confided to us" (*Registrum Epistolarum* 13:23). This was his aim in the wise administration of the wealth of the Church and he stressed it to his administrators: "Have the Judge before your eyes for He will come; and remember you gather the best treasure for me, not when you acquire new riches but when you bring me the blessings of Heaven through your service to the poor" (*ibid.* 13:37).

The term "goods of the poor" is often used to indicate the patrimony of the Church, which by that time had developed to a notable degree. Gregory took charge of this patrimony energetically and made it a masterpiece of administration as well as an important organ of ecclesiastical government. The saint did not distribute alms at random; a special register listed the names of the persons aided and the date and amount of the alms donated (Giovanni Diacona, *Vita Gregorii* 2:30), but when there was

a famine he opened the granaries of the Church to the poor. His charity was clothed with delicacy and is sometimes quite touching. Wracked with pain on his deathbed, he remembered a bishop who suffered from the cold and sent him a cloak, insisting that the messenger go at once because of the rigor of the season (*Epist. Reg.* 14:15). According to the well-known saying of John the Deacon, Gregory was "the father of the family of Christ" [H. Grisar, *San Gregorio Magno* 65 (Rome 1928) 324].

The Middle Ages

By the Middle Ages the Church had spread throughout the Western world and its charitable works and institutions flourished under the influence of Rome.

Charity in the Western Church. Many churches in the West were inspired by the Roman example that "charity resides in the bishop." This was especially true of the Frankish Church, which for all of the 5th and part of the 6th centuries was one of the most glorious of the ecclesiastical provinces, known both for its men of virtue and its fervor in good works. The bishops led exemplary lives and were distinguished for their doctrine and piety. Many of the bishops carried out the ideal of charity, first realized by Martin of Tours, the great anticipator, whose glory increased as his example encouraged. The Church, in fact, continued that tradition and felt honored to dedicate her strength to all kinds of poverty and need. Lists of the needy were kept and the *matricularii* formed a kind of association of the poor of Christ who had the privilege of begging from door to door, of receiving regular subsidies and of living in "a house of the poor." The bishop was the official protector of both the poor and the oppressed, and defended them in the courts.

An analogous situation existed in the British Isles at the time of Gregory the Great, but we do not know how far the results fulfilled the wishes of the Pontiff (*Epist.* 12:21). It would seem that the ancient rivalry between Britons and Anglo-Saxons injured discipline as well as charitable efforts. It was only later, at the time of Pope Vitalian, that the monk Theodore of Tarsus skillfully succeeded in bringing about peace. A new spirit then appeared in the field of charity. Bishops and abbots took great interest in the lower classes whom they protected against the power of the wealthy. Sometimes they acted as a curb, sometimes as a spur through penitential discipline, encouraging good works and pious foundations, liberating slaves, improving roads, aiding the peasants who were reduced to hunger by wars, and reconstructing destroyed dwellings.

In the Iberian Peninsula charity suffered as a result of the political and religious activities of the Arian government, which harassed the Church and confiscated its possessions. Only after the conversion of the Visigoths did Spain slowly accept the discipline and institutions already in use in other Western churches. St. Leander of Seville made his influence felt in the reorganization of charity under the protection of the bishops. According to the prescriptions given by the Council of Chalcedon, the bishops were obliged to appoint an *econome* to administer the goods of the Church [*Conc. Hisp.* (*c.* 590) c. 6]. From the end of the 6th century, through the urging of wise and saintly men such as the above-mentioned St. Leander, and Isidore of Seville, Masona of Emerita, John of Gerona, and Fulgentius of Astigi, the bishops were established as fathers of the poor and defenders of the goods of the Church, which were considered as the patrimony of the poor [*Conc. Tolet.* (*c.* 589) c. 3, 5, 6; (*c.* 638) c.15].

The influence of the councils. The most prominent bishops of the time did not limit their work to their own dioceses. By encouraging regional councils they gave greater influence to the tenets of the Church and established uniformity in practice throughout an entire kingdom. This was true in Merovingian France, where from 511 to 614 more than 30 national synods were held. During these synods the issue of church discipline was discussed and questions regarding the practice of charity periodically recurred.

The documents of the time recall the dignity of the poor to whom a quarter of the tithes belonged, according to the Roman custom mentioned by Gregory the Great (*Epist.* 11:64). The synods recommended assistance for those unable to work and the infirm [*Conc. Aurel.* (*c.* 511) c. 16]; for wayfarers and pilgrims; for abandoned children and lepers. This latter category of unfortunates attracted the particular attention of all the saints of the period, e.g., Romain of Luxeuil (d. 653), Aregus, Bishop of Gap (d. 604), Radegunde, Odile, etc. The West did not possess, as did the East, different types of institutions to aid various classes of needy. In the East, from the 4th century, rich and populous cities could boast of hospitals and other institutions adapted to the types of unfortunates who needed help. In the 9th century the *xenodochium* or hospice, principally for pilgrims and the poor, appeared, and sometimes, like the one in Lyons founded by King Childebert and mentioned in the Council of Orléans [(*c.* 549) c. 15], accepted also the aged and infirm.

The Status of Slaves. The synods definitely brought about the penetration of Christian ideals into legislation and morals. The problem of slaves is an example. Among the pagans during the early Middle Ages, the condition of slaves was no better than it had been in ancient times. The Church did not remain insensible to their fate and acted in various ways to alleviate it, for example, by en-

couraging emancipation, as happened in England through the work of those monasteries that received slaves in order to free them. This practice influenced the conduct of private citizens. Adopting a solution offered by German law, which recognized servitude as an intermediate condition between liberty and slavery, the Church transferred a number of slaves into this category, prescribing at the same time that the "servants of the family of God, through motives of justice and mercy, should be obliged to work less than the servants of private individuals" [*Conc. of Eauze* (*c.* 551) c. 6; *ibid.* 114]. The synod of Agde (*c.* 506) obliged the bishops to give these servants wages, in money or in kind. Many laws of the councils took pains to make the condition of servants as humane as possible, forbidding labor on feast days, upholding the right of slaves to indissoluble matrimony and—in some cases—even recognizing their right to receive Holy Orders. Finally, codifying a Roman law on the right of asylum, the Council of Orléans (*c.* 511) offered slaves recourse to a privilege that saved them from torture and unjust condemnation to death (cc. 1–3; *ibid.* 2).

The Status of Women and Children. Another important step in the progress of charity was the slow transformation of the position of women. The Council of Mâcon (585) assured to widows and orphans the assistance of the bishop in judgment (*Monumenta Germaniae Historica,* c. 12, *Concilia aevi merovingici,* 169). Particular protection was given to those widows who intended to live in a state of religious consecration [*Conc. Paris.* (*c.* 556–573) c. 6; *ibid.* 144]. The Church also ruled against the German custom of repudiating a wife, and the synod of Orléans (533) forbade the breaking of the marriage contract for reasons of illness (c. 11; *ibid.* 63). The actions of queens, such as St. Radegunde and St. Bathilde, contributed to mitigating the violence of the period, and the example of consecrated virgins, such as St. Genevieve and St. Odile, who delighted in serving the poor and infirm, "precious members of the Lord," was of great influence.

Greater protection was assured also to abandoned children. Roman legislation, amended in the 5th century under Honorius and Theodosius II, had given ample powers to the Church in this matter. This law protected the Church in her actions even after the new peoples in France, England, and Spain had come under its influence [*Monumenta Germaniae historica Leges Visigothorum,* ed. Zeumer, 193; *Formulae merovingici et Karolini aevi,* ed. Zeumer, n. 49, 21; n. 11, 241].

The Status of Prisoners. Another Roman law inspired prescriptions in favor of prisoners. The Council of Orléans (*c.* 549) decreed that the archdeacons should pay a weekly visit to prisoners to provide for their needs and console them (*Conc. aevi merovingici,* c. 20, 107). The Church frequently paid the prisoners' expenses, and bishops ransomed prisoners of war. The public was particularly influenced by these works of mercy.

Decentralization. After Gregory the Great the religious and political scene of the Christian world changed rapidly. Byzantium lost its hold on the West; Africa and Spain became Muslim camps, and Christianity turned to the Germanic peoples. The affairs of the Church were more and more discussed in national diets and councils, where the decisive word was often left to the secular power.

The very organization of charity among the new peoples mirrored social and economic conditions very different from those of the preceding epoch. In the ancient Church, most of the poor were urban and all charitable works stemmed from the bishop; but the Germanic people were rural. To adapt to this situation, a process of administrative decentralization slowly developed through the erection of rural churches (parishes) served by resident clergy to whom were confided those charitable works that had been the concern of the bishops [see G. Forchielli, *La pieve Rurale* (Bologna 1938)].

The evolution is especially clear in Merovingian France of the 6th century. With the increase of conversions in the country and the expansion of dioceses, the relations between the rural community and the bishop became more and more difficult. A need for churches that would be religiously and economically independent, though still under the authority of the bishop, consequently arose. A step toward decentralization of administration was occasioned by the prohibition to transfer ecclesiastical possessions [*Conc. Epaon.* (*c.* 517) c. 12 in *Conc. aevi merovingici* 22]. The rapid growth of the bishops' patrimonies made efficient administration impossible, and distribution of assistance to the poor declined. A solution was found in the free transfer or rent of small properties to poor laymen (the *precaris*) or ecclesiastics. When the Council of Orléans (*c.* 538) forbade the bishops to take back the grants already made to ecclesiastics (c. 20; *ibid.* 79) the foundations of the regime of BENEFICES was laid. The Council of Carpentras (*c.* 527) went further and authorized rural churches to accept legacies (*ibid.* 41). As a consequence canonical legislation regarding the role of bishops in patrimonial matters was extended to the parish priests. The decentralization of the administration of Church funds was accompanied by the decentralization of charitable work as well. This took place toward the middle of the 6th century and was sanctioned by the synod of Tours in 567, which imposed on each ecclesiastical community or parish the obligation of taking care of its own poor: "Each city shall nourish its poor and needy with suitable food—according to its means" (c. 5 *ibid.* 123). This new approach to charity was authorized in all the states of the Carolingian Empire and even beyond: in Spain, England, and even in Rome during the time of Adrian I (772–795).

Before Charlemagne, the practice of charity involved the Church in great difficulties under the last of the Merovingian kings. Clovis claimed and obtained the right to name the higher clergy (*Conc. Aurel.* c. 4 in *Conc. aevi merovingici,* 4). As a result, the dioceses were soon occupied by men from the court who used the goods of the poor for their personal needs. The golden age of charity was only a memory.

Decadence reached its peak under Charles Martel, who handed over Church property to his own vassals. Their misuse of it brought on the impoverishment and demoralization of the clergy. The strenuous efforts of St. BONIFACE, the apostle of Germany, succeeded in obtaining the recognition of Church property and the promised payment of an annual rent by the new beneficaries [Synod of Lestinnes (*c.* 743) *Monumenta Germaniae historica, Conc. Aevi Karolini,* 1.7, iii]; but with Pepin the Short secularization of Church revenues returned.

The work of Charlemagne and feudal decadence. A renewal took place under Charlemagne, who, although holding firmly to the idea that the sovereign had a right to dispose of Church property, was faithful to his program of becoming the refuge of the needy [*Monum. Germ. Hist. Capitulare Missorum* (*c.* 802) in *Capitularia Regum Francorum* 1:93]. He sought to stop abuses and both supported and encouraged ecclesiastical benefices; decisions in this matter can be found in the *capitularia* of Charlemagne. They contain norms for providing shelters [*Cap. Franc.* (*c.* 783)], assistance to widows and orphans [*Cap. Saxon.* (*c.* 797)], and hospitality to strangers [*Cap. Missorum* (*c.* 802)]. At the Chapter of Nimwegen (806), which regulated the practice of begging and the repression of vagabondage, the duties of the nobles toward the poor of their domains was also fixed as well as the obligation of running the *xenodochia* according to the intentions of the founders. The *missi dominici,* charged with controlling the administration of the nobles, had to watch over and respect the rights of the poor and the correct use of revenues and resources destined for them.

Under Louis the Pious another strong impulse toward charitable action on the part of the clergy was attempted in the synod of Aachen (*Aquisgranum, c.* 817). In the spirit of the canonical reform introduced by Chrodegang of Metz, some decisions of the synod referred to the organization of charity: each bishop was obliged to maintain a hospice for the needy, and the clergy was obliged to contribute to its support by paying a tax on their income. The direction of the hospice was to be in the hands of a canon. Monks were obliged to erect a hospital outside the cloister, but within the monastery, and were required to shelter widows and destitute women in a suitable house.

The influence of the Carolingian legislation was felt in England where, as in the imperial dominions, the economic basis for charity was the payment of tithes [*Canones Aelfrici* (*c.* 960) in D. Wilkins, *Concilia Magnae Britanniae et Hiberniae* (London 1737) 1:253] imposed on the nobles of the kingdom as well as on the clergy [*Constit. Regis Aethelstani* (*c.* 928); *Canones sub Edgaro Rege,* (*c.* 960); Wilkins, 1:205, 238]. Even after the decadence caused by the Lombards in Italy, the Carolingian influence was felt. Old hospices were restored to their original use after the secularization of Charles Martel [*C. Mantuanum* (*c.* 782) c. 12; *Pippini capitulare italicum* (*c.* 801–810) in *Capitularia Regum Francorum* 1:195:3; 210:9]. Others arose in the course of the next century. The foundation by the archpriest Datheus in Milan of a hospice for abandoned children was characteristic (Muratori, *Antiquitates Italicae* 3:587). In Rome the charitable activity of the popes was noteworthy: Paul I, a worthy emulator of Gregory the Great (*Lib. pont.* 1.463); Adrian I, (772–795); Leo III (795–816); and Pascal I (817–824). The *Liber pontificalis* stressed the interest and charity of Pascal I toward distant communities like those in Spain, to which he sent help for the ransom of prisoners (*Lib. pont.* 2:60).

The principal means the popes employed in Rome to administer "alms to our brethren in Christ—the poor" (*Liber diurnus,* form. 95) were the diaconias, which from the end of the 7th century to the 9th kept their specific character of public institutions for charitable aid. Popes, clergy, and laity contributed to their upkeep [G. Ferrari, OSB, *Early Roman Monasteries* (Rome 1957) 355–361].

Decline of Charitable Institutions. After Charlemagne, notwithstanding the precautions sanctioned by Louis the Pious, charitable organizations underwent another decline. In fact, the general historical situation did not leave much room for charity. Europe was again in conflict and countries were devastated; on the north by the Normans and Danes; on the east by the Magyars; on the southwest by the Saracens. The struggle between the successors of Charles increased the feudal anarchy, and the insecurity of the country and the difficulties of transport greatly reduced agriculture and trade.

The Church in councils frequently raised its voice on behalf of the oppressed: first through the "PEACE OF GOD," which obliged belligerents to respect the rights of the innocent; then through the "Truce of God," which attempted to limit wars by making the belligerents respect Sunday as a holy day; later, the truce extended from Wednesday to the following Monday.

Effect of Feudalism on Charity. The exercise of charity was impeded also by the complex structure of feudal society. In principle, the Church maintained the supervision of public assistance but the spiritual power was limited by a network of privileges annexed to the land of a parish or a diocese; the clergy themselves were divided by diverse obediences. Besides, the feudal lord was obliged to assist the poor who lived on his lands and depended on him. In addition, trade associations, confraternities, and similar groups carried on works of charity. Hence, the exercise of charity was no longer the exclusive task of the Church. A common characteristic, however, signalized the most diverse initiatives, namely, the religious inspiration that was faithful to the teaching of the Church and a lively faith that put its resources at the service of the poor and suffering.

The breakdown of the practice of charity continued during the feudal period. In fact, except for England, the care of the poor by the Church does not reappear even in the 11th century, when a new spirit of religious reform began that was to establish itself strongly in the following century. The absence of the Church's voice from the *Decretals* of Gratian is symptomatic. The task of caring for the poor was left to individual institutions—the monasteries, hospital orders, and secular associations.

The monasteries. The charitable preoccupation of Eastern monasticism permeates the rule of St. Benedict and the customs of the great medieval abbeys. Almsgiving was traditionally one of the fruits of monastic labor. St. Basil, Cassian, the *Regula Magistri*—principal sources of St. Benedict's rule—taught that the monk should not only support himself but also give the fruit of his labor to the poor. St. Benedict lists comforting the poor (*pauperes recreare*) as an example of good works, and he confides this task to the particular attention of the *cellerarius,* stating that "in them we minister to Christ." Following his example the medieval abbeys practiced great charity toward the poor, often devoting a large part of the monastery's income to that purpose. In one year, for example, the monastery of Cluny provided for 17,000 needy persons, and that of Saint-Riquier daily supplied the needs of 300 destitute persons, 150 widows, and 60 members of the clergy.

The reception of guests in the Middle Ages was an indirect form of giving alms to anyone who had need of a bed or a meal or was infirm or unable to work. St. Benedict dedicated a chapter of his rule to hospitality (*Regula* ch. 53). The guest house (*hospitale hospitum*), designed to receive travelers, pilgrims, clerics, monks, and nobles both secular and ecclesiastic, was separated from the hospice for the poor (*xenodochium*), which received beggars, invalids, the aged, and the infirm. After the reform of Charlemagne, CLUNY encouraged hospitality in all its forms and exemplified it throughout Europe. The Council of Mainz (1261) explicitly mentions that such hospices are usually annexed to every monastery [P. Schmitz, OSB, *Histoire de l'Ordre de Saint Benoit* 2 (Maredsous 1942) 34–50].

In the 12th century the Cistercians, wishing to live the Benedictine Rule in its original purity, gave a new impulse to charity. Outstanding among the members of this order was St. BERNARD OF CLAIRVAUX whose abbey practiced almsgiving in all its forms. During a famine in Burgundy (1125) 2,000 poor were cared for by the saint. Every Cistercian abbey had a guest house where pilgrims, travelers, and the infirm received lodging and care. The abbot himself waited on them after having welcomed them by prostrating himself at their feet [E. Vacandard, *Vie de Saint Bernard* v. 1 (Paris 1910) 454)]. The monastery of HEISTERBACH in 1197 distributed food daily to 1,500 poor people.

Canons regular and secular associations. If the exercise of charity and, in particular, of hospitality was considered in the Benedictine monasteries as a function subordinated to the contemplative ideal, the inherent value of this service was stressed by the CANONS REGULAR who, in the renewed religious climate of the 12th and 13th centuries, were responsible for the renewal of *hospitalitas* in its widest social implication, viz, assistance to pilgrims and travelers, permanent and occasional care of the sick, the poor, expectant mothers, the aged, and abandoned children. Bound to cathedral chapters during the time of the Gregorian reform, they were genuine religious orders. The laity cooperated in providing hospices. The geographical location of these foundations—at a river crossing, in the heart of a forest, or an alpine pass—symbolized this intention to aid travelers and pilgrims. Together with the monks of Cluny, the Canons Regular played an important part in the organization of pilgrimages to the shrine of St. James in Compostella. The vogue of the legend of St. Julian the Hospitaler illustrates this movement in which the laity played an important part (C. Dereine in *Dictionnaire d'histoire et geographie eccl.* 12:385–386).

Augustinian hospital work flourished from the beginning of the 12th century, when many communities, all living under the rule of St. Augustine, devoted themselves to the care of the sick. Among the first were the Hospitalers of St. John of Jerusalem whose motto was: "Defense of the Faith and Service to the Poor." In the rule, written by Raymund of Puis, the sick man is defined as "quasi dominus" of the house [L. Le Grand, "Les maisons-Dieu," *Revue des questions historiques* 16 (1896) 134)].

The TEUTONIC KNIGHTS added the obligation of serving the sick and pilgrims to military service. The Antonines directed the hospital of Mota (Vienne) and became the largest order of hospitalers in Europe. The order of the Holy Spirit was founded between 1170 and 1180 at Montpellier; to its founder, Innocent III confided the direction of the Roman hospital of S. Spirito in Sassia built in 1204.

The possession of hospitals by secular associations began in the 12th century when the Canons ceased to live a common life. Hospitals belonging to them were little by little taken over by groups other than religious orders. Thus, the Hôtel Dieu of Paris, which had been the hospital of the Chapter of Notre Dame, was confided (1217) to a corporation of four priests, 30 lay brothers, and 25 lay sisters. Although not bound by religious vows, this and similar autonomous communities of hospitalers lived a common life under the direction of a prior or prioress, and obeyed a rule of life based on that of a religious order, usually the rule of St. AUGUSTINE. The latter was adapted to the particular circumstances and was completed by special statutes. Associations of this kind prospered everywhere: the Brothers of Penance in Brussels, the Beghards, the Alexians, the Hospitalers of Aubrac, Rodez, etc. Some joined an already existing order of hospitalers: for example, the Brothers of the Holy Spirit became associated with the order of the same name [M. Heimbucher, *Die Orden und Kongregationen der Katholischen Kirche* (3d ed. Paderborn 1933–34) 1:611–620].

Under the impulse of both the hospital orders and the autonomous associations, the network of new foundations spread rapidly in the 13th and 14th centuries. At first, these, too, were under the direction of the bishops, but the movement for emancipation of the cities, which tended to centralize public works in the hands of the city government, brought about the exclusion of the bishops from charitable institutions. The intervention of city magistrates did not limit itself to controlling the financial direction of the institutions but extended even to the choice of hospital personnel. Charity became the business of the state. The aim of this intrusion was not to remove pious works from religious influence but to avoid the guardianship of the bishops. This movement was felt particularly in Italy where bishops and abbots found themselves involved as temporal princes in a bloody rivalry between citizens and feudal authority. Nothing damaged charity so much as the quest for wealth and power. Because the Church was so intimately bound to the structure of medieval society it did not escape this pitfall, especially when peace brought wealth and well-being to the West. The luxury and worldly spirit displayed by many bishops and prelates provoked protests, one of the strongest being that of St. Bernard, who contrasted the hunger and nakedness of the poor with the pomp of bishops (*De moribus et officio episcoporum* 2 in *Patrologia Latina* 182:810) and even with the luxury displayed by monks in their churches: "The Church shines with walls, but is lacking in care for the poor" [*Apologia* 12:28 in *S. Bernardi Opera III* (Rome 1963) 105].

The influence of the mendicants. It is not surprising that when heretical movements arose in revolt against this neglect of the poor (WALDENSES, BROTHERS AND SISTERS OF THE FREE SPIRIT, ALBIGENSES) St. FRANCIS OF ASSISI's call to poverty and penance served as an exorcism (1182–1226). He does not belong to the heroes of charity for any external acts: he was not an innovator in works of charity; he did not found any charitable institutions. But the influence of the Poverello was extraordinary; his mysticism of poverty gave a new character to the exercise of charity. Medieval mysticism saw Christ in the poor; Franciscan spirituality gave this mysticism an intimate, fraternal spirit.

St. Francis has been perpetuated not only in the order he founded but also in the Third Orders and the Confraternities that incorporate his spirit. The same may be said of St. DOMINIC. The Third Orders Regular for women prepared the way for the modern congregations of charity. They still exist in great numbers under Franciscan and Dominican titles. The Beguines also participated in this religious renewal and led many women to the practice of charity. (*See* BEGUINES AND BEGHARDS.) Living a religious life in small communities, although not bound by vows, these women dedicated themselves to pious works and the care of the sick both in hospitals and in their own homes. The movement had notable success in the Rhine Valley and the Low Countries. (*See* SPIRITUALITY, RHENISH; SPIRITUALITY OF THE LOW COUNTRIES.)

The increasing numbers of lay people of both sexes serving in health and welfare institutions can be explained by the growth of cities in which poor hygienic conditions contributed to illness, and inadequate sources of food supply created hunger. Preachers did not fail to encourage the alleviation of these conditions. Best known was the Franciscan Berthold von Reichensberg (d. 1272) who in his missions throughout Europe constantly extolled works of mercy as a true service of God. The response of the people is evident in the number of legacies to pious works and charitable foundations. In 1244 Pier Luca Borsi, head porter of a wool guild in Florence, founded the Company of Mercy with money he collected by taxing his colleagues for swearing. The Company of

Bigallo (1256) in the same city developed into a powerful charitable institution. Symbols of the age's pious emulation are the hospitals in Chartres, Florence, Cologne, Lübeck, Milan, and Rome. But their grandiose exteriors were more impressive than their interior development and the services offered. In this respect the West had nothing to compare with contemporary Byzantine hospitals. The monastery of Pantocrator of Constantinople, which made such an impression on Anselm of Havelberg (1134–36), had annexed to it a series of charitable-social institutions. Beside the hospital itself, there was a home for the aged, a section for special diseases (the mentally ill and epileptics), a pharmacy run by laymen, and a school of medicine that carried on the tradition of AESCULAPIUS. A century later James of Vitry called attention to the hospitals of St. Anthony and St. Sanson, worthy to be numbered among the principal hospitals of Christianity [G. Schreiber, *Gemeinschaften des Mittelalters* (Regensberg, Münster 1948) 3–80].

Special charitable activities. In the West, although hospitals admitted those suffering from almost every kind of sickness, for sanitary reasons they did not accept those with diseases considered contagious, such as leprosy. Hospitals for lepers (*leprosaria*) were organized outside the cities and were financed by legacies and donations. They were staffed by communities of lay brothers and sisters, such as the Franciscans and the Knights of St. Lazarus. The latter group founded a large number of *leprosaria*, possibly 3,000, throughout Europe.

From the time of St. Louis IX hospitals for the blind had been established in Paris (L'Hôpital des Quinze-Vingts), Hanover (1256), Tournai (1351), and Padua (14th century). Toward the end of the Middle Ages conditions for the care of the mentally ill, who until then had been treated as prisoners or worse, were greatly improved and hospitals were erected in Hamburg (1375) and Mirandola (1400). Special hospices for orphans and foundlings increased in number, especially in Italy as early as the 15th century. One of the most famous was the Hospital of the Innocents founded in Florence in the 15th century.

Special concern was shown for prostitutes. Their number had multiplied after the Crusades through the dissoluteness of the soldiers and the development of the towns. Innocent III in 1198 called attention to this social calamity. A house of refuge, the first nucleus of a religious congregation, was founded in Paris in 1204 by Folcus of Neuilly. His example soon found imitators in Marseilles, Bologna, Rome, and Messina. In Germany the Congregation of the Penitents of St. Mary Magdalen was founded. Its inspiration grew out of the Council of Mainz (1225) and the congregation was constituted an order for penitents by Gregory IX as a result of their favorable influence in various cities. In the 13th century there were 50 houses of the order.

Special hospices for the assistance of travelers greatly increased. From the 11th century hospices were established near mountains, forests, and rivers—special hazards for the traveler. Hence arose the mountain refuges (Roncesvalles, Grand-Saint-Bernard, Aubrac, Vallombrose, etc.); the work of the "Fratres Pontifices" (Bridge Builders) in Provence and Spain, who constructed bridges and roads, and the Congregation of Altopascio, in Italy, whose members transported travelers across the marshes of Lucca; and the forest refuges in the North (Flône, Affligem, Vicogne, etc). Associations for the maintenance of roads and bridges were protected by kings and lords and favored with indulgences by the bishops.

Another work prompted by charity was the ransoming of prisoners captured in the long struggle against the Moors in Spain. The first to dedicate himself to this work was St. JOHN OF MATHA. The TRINITARIANS, founded by St. John and approved (1198) by Innocent III, ransomed prisoners and labored to alleviate the condition of those who remained in slavery. The Order of Mercy, founded by St. PETER NOLASCO, was also dedicated to this work. It began as a military order but soon became a mendicant order.

Toward the end of the Middle Ages the shortcomings of the charitable institutions became many and evident. The cause of the poor suffered from the consequences of the Great Western Schism, the worldly spirit of many spiritual leaders, and the piling up of benefices and the system of giving *in commendam* that converted so many charitable institutions into sources of easy gain for those who held them. Added to this was the misery of the age: destitution caused by wars and the endless calamities that accompanied them. Charity, it is true, still had at its disposal resources and an organization: confraternities increased in number; the instinct for charitable giving, as is shown by the number of legacies and bequests, remained alive in individuals. But charity lost its luster because it was no longer in intimate touch with the misery of the poor; it took on bourgeois attitudes and its very instruments became fossilized. In the 16th century the revival of the Church in its better representatives moved toward a revival of charity. Meanwhile, the Church had to meet the new era under unfavorable conditions, giving ground in some regions to the attacks of the Protestant REFORMATION and surrendering a large part of its position to the civil power.

Modern Times

The secularization of charity, which began during the period of the communes, spread considerably at the beginning of the 16th century and achieved a complete separation from the Church because of the Reformation. The process was closely related to contemporary socioeconomic developments and to the new spiritual movements inherent in humanism. The object of charitable assistance was no longer the poor man as a brother in Christ but the citizen as such. Charity was divested of its transcendent quality. Currents of the new orientation were strong in the Flemish cities, in the Rhineland, in other sectors of the Empire, and in Italy.

It was not that the Church relegated, even temporarily, her charitable action to convents and religious sodalities. The intervention of the Church continued to leave its mark on social institutions; e.g., the measures it took against the abuses of usurers, and in particular the erection of public pawnbroker establishments, MONTES PIETATIS, protected by the Franciscans. These developed especially in Italy in the 15th century through the initiative of Barnabas of Terni, St. James of the Marches, Louis of Verona, St. John Capistran and, above all, by Bl. Bernadine of Feltre [M. Weber, *Les Origines des Monts-de-Piété* (Rixheim 1920)]. In countries not yet touched by heresy there was beneficial collaboration between civil and religious authorities. Thus in Italy, Pius II in 1458 issued a bull recognizing the statutes of hospitals founded by the state in Milanese territory. In Portugal the popes were always disposed to collaborate with secular authority for the expansion of charitable institutions: e.g., Alexander VI, who (1499) authorized King Don Manuel to incorporate small hospitals in Coimbra, Evora, and Santarem into the larger hospitals of the same locality, and finally extended the permission to other places; Leo X, who at the request of the king (1516) provided benefices for All Saints' Hospital in Lisbon. Since most charitable institutions were of ecclesiastical origin, jurisdiction over many of them was given to the clergy. [F. de Almeida, *Historia da Igreja em Portugal*, v. 1 (Coimbra 1915) 2:467–470].

Where the secular power violently attacked the rights and works of the Church, as in Protestant countries, there were grave results. "Under the Popes," LUTHER admitted, "there was a strong drive to give alms to the poor, but now everyone has become cold and insensible" [H. Grisar, *Martin Luthers Leben und sein Werk* (Freiburg 1926) 497]. It was really Luther himself who contributed to this situation by his doctrine on the inefficacy of good works for salvation, at a time when there was a fresh outbreak of poverty largely as a result of the confiscation by secular authority of monasteries and other sources of Catholic charity.

The work of the Council of Trent. The Council of TRENT contributed greatly to improving the spirit of charity. The earnest entreaties of that synod had antecedents that cannot be ignored. Such, for example, was the initiative of the bishop of Verona Gian Matteo Giberti (1495–1543). Assisted by Louis di Canossa, bishop of Bayeux, Giberti founded (1528) a large Xenodochium Misericordiae for orphans and the infirm; the following year he founded a society of charity; he reopened many *Montes Pietatis* and provided for the rehabilitation of prostitutes; he named visitors for each parish to make a census of the poor in order to assist them with public funds. At his death he left 6,000 gold florins for charitable works. Many of his recommendations to the clergy were included in the canons of the Council of Trent.

At the same time, numerous charitable associations were carrying on important works: the Company of St. Jerome and the Company of Divine Love, founded respectively at the end of the 15th century and the beginning of the 16th, did much to revivify charitable endeavors. From the Company of Divine Love sprang a new institution to assist those afflicted with syphilis, for which there was then no cure. Syphilitics were always refused by hospitals for fear of contagion. Thanks to the generosity of Ettore Vernazza, the first hospital for such incurables was erected in Genoa (1499); Rome, Naples, and other cities followed suit [P. Cassiano da Langasco, *Gli ospedali degli incurabli* (Genoa 1938)].

New Charitable Orders. Charity was revived with the rise of new religious orders that either made charity a primary end or gave it an important place. Among the first group were the Congregation of Clerks Regular of Somascha founded about 1530 by St. Jerome EMILIANI for the care of orphans; the Brothers of St. John of God, and the Ministers of the Sick of St. Camillus for the care of the sick and for hospital service. The second group included the Barnabites, Capuchins, Jesuits, Clerks Regular of the Religious Schools, and the Theatines.

Through the Council of Trent the Church not only reaffirmed the validity and the indispensability of good works for salvation but even promulgated a juridical order for the development of this position, proclaiming indirectly, by numerous works of mercy, the primacy of charity.

The Influence of the Bishops. Both the means approved by the council for the administration of pious works and the powers of control confided to the bishops influenced more or less extensively the bishops' actions. There was almost no activity in the countries won over to Protestantism; episcopal action was fettered in France, where civil authority was dominant, but functioned freely in Spain and Italy, where the authority of the bishops was

recognized. A noble example was St. Charles BORROMEO in Milan who devoted himself to putting the spirit of Trent into practice. He lived so much like the poor that in his funeral oration it was said: "Charles had of his wealth what the dog had of the wealth of his master; a little water and a little straw." The 11 diocesan synods and the six provincial synods over which he presided regulated the care of the needy with a real sense of pastoral responsibility. He approved the new society of Ursulines in Brescia, founded to educate the children of the poor, and he aided in every possible way the development of numerous houses already existing in Milan for the rehabilitation of wayward girls. To the Oblates of St. Ambrose, which he founded in 1578, he assigned the care of souls in charitable institutions. During a plague in 1576, he replaced the governor who had fled and went about among the stricken, consoling and assisting them. He exhorted his clergy to aid the victims of the plague even to the point of sacrificing their lives [*Delle cure della peste. Istruttione di s. Carlo card. di Santa Praesede ed arciv. di Milano* (Venice 1630)].

Charity in mission lands. The missionary work of religious orders opened new fields for Christian charity and enlarged others already initiated by the hierarchy. After the conquest of New Spain, institutions for the relief of the natives had been established under the direction and with the cooperation of the Church. Vasco de QUIROGA, Bishop of Michoacán (1537–65), was one of the pioneers of charity. While still a layman and a member of the second tribunal of Mexico he learned of the extreme misery of the native peoples and with his own money built a hospital, Santa Fé, which he later completed by adding a home for abandoned children. In 1533 he was sent on a mission to the Province of Michoacán and built another Santa Fé on the banks of Lake Pátzcuaro near Vayámeo. When he returned to Michoacán in 1538 as bishop, he began, with the favor of the crown, the organization of work in common, the equal division of the fruits of labor, civil and religious education, and the eradication of begging and vagabondage. Before Quiroga, others had begun similar institutions such as the hospital of Jesus Nazareno, founded (*c.* 1521) by Fernando Cortés. Later, in 1534, Bishop ZUMÁRRAGA founded an institution of charity in Mexico, called Amor de Dios, which grew through revenues from Charles V. Toward the middle of the 16th century, the hospital of St. Joseph was founded for the natives. In 1564 Dr. Pedro Ortiz founded the hospital of St. Lazarus for lepers. This was followed by another, Nuestra Señora de Los Desamparados, for blacks, mulattoes, and poor children. The FRANCISCANS and AUGUSTINIANS were energetic hospital builders in New Spain, especially in Michoacán, where charitable institutions developed rapidly. This work was especially necessary because of the severe epidemics. In 1555 the provincial synod of Messino decreed that there should be a hospital next to the church in every village. This decree bore fruit in the following decade.

Charitable works had other promoters as well—among them viceroys, governors, confraternities, and private citizens. They met the most diverse needs and populated the southern provinces with hospitals, hospices for the poor and penitents, maternity homes, and homes for abandoned children. *Montes Pietatis* were established at Darien and Bogota in Colombia (1555); Lima (1538), Cuczo (1538), Huamanga (1555), and Juli (1570) in Peru; Santa Cruz de la Sierra (1612) and La Paz (1617) in Bolivia; Quito (1565) in Eucador; Santiago (1540) and La Imperial (1570) in Chile. The work developed from Mexico to Argentina and from the Antilles to the Philippines.

In the Portuguese colonies overseas, the practice of charity flowed naturally from the tradition of the mother country. In addition to the usual relief given to beggars by the secular and religious clergy particular help was given during epidemics or other public calamities. Such, for instance, were the famine (1564–76) in Braga; the plague (1569, 1579, 1598) in Lisbon, in Braga (1569) in Evora (1580), and at other times in Algarve, Santarem, and Coimbra. In these crises the generosity and heroism of priests and religious and particularly of Bps. Bartolomeo dos Mártyres and Theotonio de Braganza were exemplary. Among works begun by the clergy were the hospital of St. Mark in Braga, the orphanages of Our Lady of Grace and Our Lady of Hope in Oporto, the Pietà hospital and orphanage in Evora, the retreats of St. Mary Magdalen in Castillo Branco and Coimbra, the orphanage of Jesus and the retreats of Our Lady of the Incarnation and Our Lady of the Angels in Lisbon [F. De Almeida *Historia de Igreja en Portugal*, v. 3 (Coimbra 1915) 2:467–488].

During the Middle Ages many religious associations of the laity in Portugal were dedicated to charitable practices, e.g., Espíritu Santo, Nossa Senhora de Rocamador, Nossa Senhora de Piedade, Penitêncîa, and Santissima Trinidade. Queen ISABELLA greatly influenced these organizations and in her will she mentioned "Santa Misericordia de Rocamador." The name "Misericordia" is especially connected with two persons: Queen Eleanor, wife of John II, and Fra Miguel Contreras, a Spanish Trinitarian. On the advice of the latter, the Queen founded (1498) the Confraternity of Misericordia in Lisbon, which spread rapidly throughout Portugal and across the ocean. The statutes (*compromisso*) of this pious association (issued 1516) bound the 100 members, half of whom belonged to the nobility and half to the working class, to the practice of the 14 works of mercy. Members

went in pairs to visit the sick, prisoners, and poor people in their homes to discover their needs and supply them with food, money, dwellings, beds, etc. The many privileges that King Manuel granted to the association occasioned its rapid spread. At the death of Queen Eleanor (1525), 61 branches of the Misericordia had taken solid root in metropolitan territory [see V. Ribeiro, *A santa casa da Misericordia de Lisboa* (Lisbon 1902)].

From the 17th to the 19th centuries the Misericordia spread to Portuguese dominions overseas. In Asia there were more than 25, some of which still exist (Goa, Ormuz, Diu, Damâo, Chaul Cannanore, Cochin, Quilon, Nagatapam, Colombo, Mannar). The Misericordia at Goa, the first (1519) and most important branch, added to the general charitable program outlined by the *compromisso* of Lisbon the establishment of the Hospital del Rei (1542) and the Hospital dos pobres (1568) for Christian natives and the care of needy young girls, especially orphans. Another social and religious problem arose—that of the prostitutes whom the confraternity sought to help by founding homes for penitents, such as Nossa Senhora da Serra (1605) and Santa Maria Magdalena (1609). Furthermore, in the East the Misericordia took on the functions of a bank and became the guardian of legacies and inheritances which, after the death of the owners, were transferred to their heirs in the mother country.

Pietro della Valle summed up the work of the Misericordia in Goa: ". . . almost all the works of mercy which elsewhere are performed by diverse institutions and societies are carried on here by the Misericordia, which keeps deposits, handles letters of credit, helps the poor, the sick, hospitals and prisoners, protects children, arranges marriages, looks after converted prostitutes, redeems slaves; in short, does all the works of mercy of which a city or country has need. Surely it is a holy thing and of infinite service to the public . . ." [J. Wicki, SJ, "Die Bruderschaft der 'Misericordia' in Portugiesisch-Indien," *Das Laienapostolat in den Missionem* (Beckenried 1961) 79–97].

In the 16th century offsprings of the Portuguese Misericordia were found even in Japan (Nagasaki, Sakai). But the activity of the famous institution did not cover all charitable work in the Far East when missionaries entered the scene. The Jesuits in Japan began a hospital at Oita (Kyushu) with the help of a Portuguese doctor, Luis d'Almeida (*c.* 1555); foundations of the same kind for men, women, and lepers multiplied in the following decade at Nagasaki, Sakai, and Urakmi. Through the work of the Franciscans, who had erected St. Anne's Hospital in Manila (1580–81), two others were built (1594–97) at Miyako [D. Schilling, OFM, *Hospitäler der Franziskaner in Miyako* (Beckenried 1950)]. The Jesuits also founded hospitals in India for the natives at Margão (Salsete) and especially in the Pescadores and Mannar, where there were seven by 1571 (*Mon. Hist. S.J., Documenta Indica* 8:32–33).

In Brazil, the Misericordia worked in Baía, Maranhão, Santos, and Rio de Janeiro, and missionaries ran hospitals in all the great centers. The Jesuits were especially active [S. Leite, *Historia da Companhia de Jesus no Brazil* (Lisbon 1938) 2:570]. The college at Rio had a hospital annexed to it and provided two large rooms where slaves and their families were cared for. The colleges in general were centers of charitable work. In every college there was a priest who was "procurator of the poor." The work of assistance included another beneficial social function: the workmen were the first to benefit from the harvest on the estates connected with the missions.

Mention must be made of those who tried to limit the effects of the commercial organization of slavery after the conquest of South America. If, notwithstanding the abominable crimes of which they were victims, the slaves embraced the religion of their oppressors, it was because of the charity of its missionaries. Peter CLAVER (1580–1654), "the slave of the Negro slaves," is a symbol; for 40 years he was the incarnation of heroic charity. Other protectors of the natives and slaves were Bartolomé de LAS CASAS (1474–1566) and Antonio Vieira (1608–97), who dared to condemn the iniquity of government officials and slave traders.

The problem of begging and St. Vincent de Paul. Economic and political factors at the beginning of modern times brought about an almost permanent state of pauperism for large segments of the population and led to the consequent problem of begging. The Spanish humanist Juan Luis Vives had studied the problem in *De subventione pauperum, sive de humanis necessitatibus* (Bruges 1526). The Benedictine Juan MEDINA published *De la orden que en algunos pueblos de España se ha puesto en la limosína para remedio de los verdaderos pobres* (Salamanca 1545). Both books advocated the suppression of begging and the gathering of the genuinely poor into public institutions. Practical application of these principles was attempted in Flanders and the Spanish countries, but protests arose, e.g., D. de Soto's authoritative *Deliberacion en la causa de los pobres* (Salamanca 1545). [On this question see A. Muller, *La querelle des fondations charitables en Belgique* (Brussels 1909).] The secular power intervened to repress begging, first by general prohibitions and then by threats of corporal punishment, including death (as in England, the Low Countries, and Flanders).

The prohibitions were useless; the necessity of offering asylum to the homeless, the sick, and the unemployed remained. Attempts to solve the problem were made by housing beggars in buildings destined for this purpose and providing work for them. Hospices of this kind appeared everywhere. Sixtus V founded one in Rome; it soon closed for lack of funds, but was reopened by Innocent XII and Clement XI. In Spain shelters (*albergues*), extolled by Christoval Perez de Herrera in *Discursos del amparo de los legitimos pobres y reducción de los fingidos . . .* (Madrid 1598), multiplied but without significant results. In England workhouses developed around the end of the 17th century. Fruitless attempts to cope with the problem were made in France, where in Paris alone there were about 40,000 beggars.

St. VINCENT DE PAUL came on the scene at this juncture. He is considered the most characteristic representative of Catholic charity in modern times, justly called "Le ministre de la charité nationale, le grand aumônier de la France." The confraternity of charity that he organized (1617) among his parishioners of Chatillon-les-Dombes to visit the sick poor in their homes was the seed from which a remarkable number of charitable institutions grew. He brought women into charitable works more completely and more independently than ever before. For members of the nobility he founded the Ladies of Charity, who soon spread to all the provinces of France. Since they were unable to cope with all the needs of the poor, the saint, with the aid of St. LOUISE DE MARILLAC, founded (1633) the Daughters of charity, a religious congregation devoted entirely to the service of the poor. Similar institutions were founded under the influence of the Daughters of Charity: the Daughters of St. Géneviève, founded by Françoise de Blosset; the Daughters of the Holy Family, by Maria Miramion; the Daughters of Providence, etc. Pauperism was reduced in France by the untiring work of these institutions. In 1653 the hospital of the Holy Name of Jesus was founded in Paris (the modern Hospital of the Incurables) to take care of the aged. In 1656 the General Hospital was founded to care for and give work to beggars. Louis XIV donated a number of buildings for this purpose, thus enabling the hospital to receive as many as 10,000 needy persons and foundlings. With the help of the clergy, especially the Jesuits, other general hospitals were founded in the provinces. Père Chaurand alone founded about 123 and Père Guevarre, who succeeded him after his death, continued the work in various parts of France and in Piedmont [C. Joret, *Le P. Guevarre et la fondation des bureaux de charité du XVII siècle* (Toulouse 1899)].

Specialized assistance. Failing in their aim to eliminate begging, the general hospitals took up their original role of helping the really poor, the infirm, orphans, and destitute women. In France the Hôtels-Dieu, open to all types of unfortunates, spread throughout the country, though often the help they gave was more generous than wise. Every year 25,000 persons passed through the HÔTEL-DIEU in Paris. The same was true of Rome's hospital of St. James in Augusta. But certain categories of needy were taken care of in specialized houses. Hospitals for strangers in Rome have been mentioned: there were 22 of these, seven of which were founded after the 15th century [Piazza, *Opere pie di Roma* (Rome 1697)]. Through the initiative of St. Philip NERI, the hospital of the Trinity for pilgrims was founded in Rome; another of the same type was started in Naples. Orphans found asylum with the SOMASCAN FATHERS (an order founded by St. Jerome Emiliani *c.* 1528 for the care of orphans), while other institutions provided for the moral preservation of young girls; 17 in Rome, 22 in Naples, etc. Refuges for the rehabilitation of prostitutes were numerous in Palermo, Naples, Florence, etc.

The Mentally Ill. Vives in his *De subventione pauperum* had given wise counsel for the treatment of these unfortunates, but his contemporaries continued to consider the mentally ill as possessed or sorcerers. They were interned in common prisons, not with a view to cure but to assure public safety. They were treated like animals until the end of the 18th century, and very few asylums were provided for them in any country before the 19th century. In Spain there were asylums at Valencia, the Association of the Innocents (1409) founded by a member of the Order of Mercy; at Saragossa, the hospital of Our Lady of Grace (1425) founded by Alfonso of Aragon; and other institutions at Seville (1436), Valladolid (1489), and Toledo (1483). In Italy the care of the insane was confided to the Roman confraternity of S. Maria della Pietà, which rose under Pius IV (1561) and which in the 18th century came under the direction of the Hospital of the Holy Spirit. In England, an ancient priory in London (Bedlam) was transformed into a mental hospital at the time of Henry VIII. In the 18th century, similar asylums rose in York, Nottingham, Manchester, Norwich, and Liverpool. At the same period, there were houses for the insane in Frankfurt, Amsterdam, and Ghent. Coercive methods used with the violent were often nothing less than torture; and patients were chained, not only during their violent seizures, but permanently. It was only at the end of the 17th century that courageous doctors in France began using the straight jacket.

Deaf Mutes. As early as the 16th century serious efforts had been made to rehabilitate deaf mutes. This problem greatly interested the former Jesuit L. Hervás y Panduro toward the end of the 18th century [see his *Escuela española de sordomudos,* 2 v. (Madrid 1795) 1:8]. Spain was the first country to provide educators for these unfortunates: the Benedictine Pedro Ponce de León (d. 1584) taught speaking, writing, arithmetic, and religion

to deaf mutes (Hervás y Panduro, *op. cit.,* 1:297–305). His example bore fruit and in 1620 Juan Pablo Bonet of Aragon suggested in *Reducción de las letras y arte para enseñar a hablar los mudos* grammatical instruction according to the inductive method. Attempts of this kind multiplied everywhere: in England, by an Oxford professor, John Wallis (1660–61); in Holland, at Amsterdam, by a Swiss doctor Johan Konrad Amman (*Surdus et mutus loquens,* 1692); in Italy, by Fabrizio d'Acquapendente at Padua and by the Jesuit F. Lana-Terzi at Brescia; in France, by the Spanish Jew Jacob Rodriguez Pereira. But it was Abbé Charles-Michel de l'Épée (*c.* 1712–89) who opened institutions for these unfortunates, teaching them by a method of imitation. Abbé Tommaso Silvestri, who opened a similar school in Rome in 1784; Abbé Stork, who perfected the one already existing in Vienna; and Henri Daniel Guyot, who in 1790 started a like institution in Groningen, Holland, all studied and used the method of Charles-Michel. Religious and priests were pioneers in this difficult field of education.

Prisoners and Captives. Christian charity placed special emphasis on aid to the incarcerated. Prison conditions were atrocious and cruelty was commonplace. But protesting voices offered concrete suggestions: in Spain, Cristóforo Pérez de Herrera (1598) called for prison inspection to correct negligence and limit the absolute power of those in authority; in Italy, G. Battista Scanaroli of Modena (1655) published a work rich in interesting proposals, and in France D. Mabillon (1695), referring to the imprisonment of religious, proposed an excellent program that seemed to be a forerunner of the penal reform of the 19th century [Thuiller, *Ouvrages posthumes de D. Mabillon* (Paris 1724) 2:321–335]. But public attention was especially awakened in the 18th century when an Englishman, John Howard, revealed the condition of European prisons after firsthand inquiry in different countries.

In the meantime the Church supplied these deficiencies as best she could. Hundreds of confraternities with this specific aim developed. A few examples will suffice: in Rome, the Archconfraternity of Charity founded in 1519 by Cardinal Giulio de Medici (later Pope Clement VII); in Milan (where work for the imprisoned was quite ancient and greatly influenced by Charles Borromeo), the confraternities of Pietà and Our Lady of Loreto, which constituted, according to the judgment of G. Toniolo "a reform school for penal law and prisons much older and more efficacious than the writings of Beccaria" [*L'Histoire de la Charité en Italie* in *Congrès scientif. des Catholiques* (Brussels 1895)]. There were numerous confraternities of this kind in France: at Aix, the White Penitents (1517) and the Sisters of the Dominican Third Order, who took care of female prisoners; at Marseilles, the Work of Prisons (1674); at Lyons the Confraternity of Mercy (1636). In France the intervention of St. Vincent de Paul on behalf of those condemned to the galleys was particularly effective.

This latter group of unfortunates calls to mind another great social problem. After the defeat of the Moors in Spain, piracy became organized. Pirate ships from the Mediterranean ports of North Africa sacked the coasts of Spain, France, and Italy, and carried men, women, and children into slavery. Their sufferings awakened heroic dedication all over the West. Trinitarians and MERCEDARIANS continued their mission, although the difficulties of the time obliged them to modify their primitive rule. The Trinitarians organized confraternities to gather funds for the ransom of captive Christians. Other societies performed the same tasks, e.g., the Roman confraternity of the Gonfalone. The Lazarists in Tunis and Algiers sacrificed themselves for the material and spiritual comfort of Christian slaves. Lack of documentation makes it difficult to determine the number of persons ransomed. In the 18th century the Trinitarians and Mercedarians united their efforts and special missions went abroad every three or four years. In 1720 about 1,000 prisoners were liberated.

Charity after the French Revolution. Works of charity in the second half of the 18th century dried up at the source in many European countries after the suppression of MORTMAIN and the secularization of public help. States confiscated the property of pious foundations and used it for other purposes. In France this confiscation was carried out on a large scale during the Revolution of 1789; the goods of the clergy were seized (Nov. 2, 1790) and religious congregations suppressed (Aug. 18, 1792). Hospital funds were declared national property (1794) and all assistance centralized in the state. The repercussions in the field of charity were disastrous. On the eve of the Revolution the poor and sick found help from 35,000 religious, in 2,000 hospitals, capable of receiving 100,000 unfortunates and spending annually 30 million lire (R. Herrman, *La Charité de l'Église,* 149). When private charity was abolished by the Revolution as being humiliating, the poor fell into the most complete destitution.

Resurgence of Religious Institutions. But the state had to retreat. By 1796 it became necessary for the French government to give back to charitable institutions all property that had not been sold or given away; an effort was made in the towns to organize offices of assistance and committees for the poor; nursing sisters had to be called upon to staff hospitals while awaiting Napoleon's decree of 1804, which reestablished religious teaching congregations. Charitable congregations of women were then aided by the state.

In the 19th century the resurgence of charity was so great that it is impossible to measure its achievements. The growth of charitable institutions already in existence was significant (the Daughters of Charity in less than 50 years increased from 1,500 members to 8,000). A great number of new institutions, especially those for women, made the service of the poor the principal aim of their vocation. They spread rapidly in countries like Germany, where after the secularization of relief and the near disappearance of local hospitals, a rebirth of religious congregations was evident. The Daughters of Charity, the Franciscan Sisters of the Poor, and the Sisters of St. Charles may be instanced. Even important personages in the political and cultural fields wrote their names in the annals of charity: Antonio ROSMINI-SERBATI (1797–1855), for example, was the founder of the Institute of Charity (1828) and the Sisters of Providence (1833).

Needs of the Period Met by New Foundations. Works of charity proliferated to such an extent as to pose a problem of wise administration. In Turin, for example, the Little House of Divine Providence, founded by St. Giuseppe COTTOLENGO (1786–1842), formed a city within a city with its 8,000 unfortunates of all classes (aged, sick, insane, retarded) who were cared for by hundreds of nuns and priests [P. Gastaldi, *I prodigi della carità cristiana* (Turin 1910)]. St. John BOSCO (1815–88) assured the continuity of his institutions for needy youth by founding the Salesian Fathers (1859) and the Daughters of Mary Help of Christians (Salesian Sisters, 1874).

There was no type of misery that did not find a vocation to succor it: in France a young servant girl, Jeanne Jugan, founded the Little Sisters of the Poor and Aged (1840) to provide homes for the aged; Anna M. Jahouvey founded the Sisters of St. Joseph of Cluny in 1807 (*see* ST. JOSEPH, SISTERS OF) to care for infants; Father Ludovico da Casoria in Naples founded the Grey Brothers and the Sisters of St. Elizabeth for the care of the blind and deaf mutes; St. M. Euphrasia PELLETIER founded the Sisters of the GOOD SHEPHERD (1835) to aid women with criminal records or who had fallen into vice; and the Marchesa Giulia Falletti Barolo founded the Daughters of Anne of Providence. Don L. ORIONE (1872–1940), who with Don Bosco and Cottolengo, forms the Italian triumvirate of great apostles of charity, founded the Daughters of Divine Providence and the Little Missionary Sisters of Charity. "Convinced that the world would be conquered by love," he created in Italy and beyond an immense network of foundations.

The introduction of the Catholic laity. In the first half of the 19th century a new phenomenon arose in the history of charity—the organized participation of Catholic laymen. In 1801 in Paris, under the direction of the former Jesuit Delpuits and through the initiative of some medical and law students, the Congregation of Maria Auxilium Christianorum was founded; it is recognized as the source of modern French charity [G. de Grandmaison *La Congregation* (Paris 1902)]. It was destroyed by the revolution of 1830, but three years later it was replaced by another group of lay apostles, the nucleus of the Conference of Charity, called, after 1836, the Conference of St. Vincent de Paul. This group was composed of six university students in Paris led by A. Frédéric OZANAM (1813–53) who, envisioning a vast association of charity for the relief of the lower classes in every country, saw his work spread rapidly through the whole Christian world. In the mid-1960s the membership numbered more than 210,000, divided into more than 15,000 working groups in 80 nations aiding all types of unfortunates with no distinction of religion and employing no humiliating investigations [Ozanam, *Le Livre du Centenaire* (Paris 1913)]. The work has female branches, such as the Society of St. Elizabeth in Germany and the Female Society of St. Vincent de Paul founded in 1856 by Celestine Scarabelli in Italy.

The plan of Ozanam was to put a group of selected Catholics at the service of the poor and thus establish bonds of brotherhood among those separated by rank and fortune. Using different means, others aimed at the same end: In Italy there were those who listened to the voices of Bruno Lanteri and Rosmini; in England a great number were mobilized by H. E. MANNING, the cardinal of the poor, in his war against misery. The very birth of Catholic socialism is associated with this movement of charity. In Germany, A. KOLPING and W. von KETTELER, before being social reformers, were men of charity for the essence of charity is the desire to raise one's neighbor from his misery. One of the admirable features of the St. Vincent de Paul Society is that it avoids bureaucracy by direct and personal contact with the needy.

With the industrial revolution and the consequent accumulation of wealth by the few and the misery of the many, it became evident that the old idea of pure charity could not offer an adequate solution unless it were associated with the goals of "social justice." A few isolated attempts were made to infuse charity with the concepts of social justice. Such were, for example, Ozanam's advocacy (1840) of a "natural wage" that would assure the workingman and his family enough money to live and be educated; the beginnings of Christian socialism promoted by Père J. B. LACORDAIRE, Abbé H. L. C. MARET, and Ozanam in 1848; the "Union of Fribourg" (1886), which gathered a nucleus of interested Catholics from various countries in order to find a just solution for social problems. Some prelates, such as Ketteler, the bishop of

Mainz in Germany, and Cardinal Manning in England, addressed themselves to the problem. But it was Pope Leo XIII, who wrote the Magna Carta of Christian social activity in the encyclical *RERUM NOVARUM* (1891). Pius XI's encyclical *QUADRAGESIMO ANNO* (1931) reaffirmed and updated Leo's teaching.

One essential point emerges from these solemn pontifical documents: the coexistence of two leading principles, social justice and social charity. Social justice must erect "a juridical and social order which can penetrate all economic life"; social charity "must be the soul of this order and public authority must work to protect it" (*Quadragesimo anno*).

When social questions are discussed, temporal society and its common well-being are directly concerned. In this field the charity of the Church cannot indefinitely operate alone. Its role is sometimes temporary, until public authority takes necessary measures; at other times the Church assumes a complementary role, helping those who, for one reason or another, are not protected by laws that must be generalized and are sometimes too slow to meet cases of immediate need.

See Also: CATHOLIC NEAR EAST WELFARE ASSOCIATION; HOSPITALS, HISTORY OF; MERCY, WORKS OF; CATHOLIC CHARITIES USA; PONTIFICAL MISSION FOR PALESTINE .

Bibliography: E. T. DEVINE, *Practice of Charity* (New York 1901). G. NEYRON, *Histoire de la charité* (Paris 1927). Union des oeuvres catholiques de France, 65th, 1950, *L'Église, éducatrice de la charité* (Paris 1951). F. ZOEPFL, *Mittelalter Caritas im Spiegel der Legende* (Frieburg 1929). A. BAUDRILLART, *La Charité aux premiers siècles du christianisme* (Paris 1903). G. SUHR, *Volksnot und Kirche* (Gütersloh 1948). M. W. JERNEGAH, *Laboring and Dependent Classes in Colonial America, 1607–1783* (Chicago 1931). C. R. HENDERSON, *Modern Methods of Charity* (New York 1904). F. D. WATSON, *The Charity Organization Movement in the U.S.: A Study in American Philanthropy* (New York 1922). R. GUARDINI, *Der Dienst am Nächsten in Gefahr* (Würzburg 1956). International Labor Office, *Approaches to Social Security* (Montreal 1942). F. R. SALTER, ed., *Some Early Tracts on Poor Relief* (London 1926). G. UHLHORN, *Christian Charity in the Ancient Church* (New York 1883). K. WOODROOFE, *From Charity to Social Work in England and the United States* (Toronto 1962). W. J. MARX, *Development of Charity in Medieval Louvain* (New York 1936). H. F. WESTLAKE, *Parish Gilds of Medieval England* (New York 1919). H. BRANDENBURG, *Caritas und Wohlfahrtspflege* (Freiburg 1959). H. WOLFRAM, *Vom Armenwesen zum heutigen Fürsorgewesen* (Greifswald 1930). K. DE SCHWEINITZ, *England's Road to Social Security* (New York 1961). F. M. EDEN, *The State of the Poor* (London 1928). W. K. JORDAN, *Philanthropy in England, 1480–1660* (New York 1959). H. BOLKESTEIN, *Wohltätigkeit und Armenpflege im vorchristlichen Altertum* (Utrecht 1939). E. L. CHASTEL, *Charity of the Primitive Churches* (Philadelphia 1857). L. LALLEMAND, *Histoire de la charité*, 4 v. in 5 (Paris 1902–12). W. LIESE, *Geschichte der Caritas,* 2 v. (Freiburg 1922). A. C. MARTS, *Man's Concern for His Fellow Man* (Geneva, N.Y. 1961). E. ABBOTT, ed., *Some American Pioneers in Social Welfare* (Chicago 1937). V. D. BORNET, *Welfare in*

America (Norman, Okla. 1960). N. E. COHEN, *Social Work in the American Tradition* (New York 1958). A. DE GRAZIA, *American Welfare* (New York 1961). W. A. FRIEDLANDER, *Introduction to Social Welfare* (New York 1955). F. E. LANE, *American Charities and the Child of the Immigrant* (Washington 1941).

[M. SCADUTO]

CHARLEMAGNE

Charlemagne (or Charles the Great) was king of the FRANKS from 768 to 814, king of the LOMBARDS from 774 to 814, and emperor from 800 to 814. The son of King PEPIN III and Bertrada, he was born in 747 or 748 and died on Jan. 2, 814. Little is known about Charlemagne's youth. He received religious training from his mother and from Abbot Fulrad of St. Denis, a confidant of his father. He learned to read Latin but never to write. While he was still a child, his father was elected king by the Frankish nobles, a momentous step taken with papal approval that led to the deposition of the last Merovingian king. Charlemagne first appeared in the historical record in late 753 and early 754, when he played a role in the ceremonies organized to welcome pope STEPHEN II on the occasion of the pope's visit to Francia. That visit resulted in an alliance between the papacy and the Franks that would play an important role in Charlemagne's future career. During the course of his stay in Francia in 754 Stephen II anointed King Pepin III, Queen Bertrada, Charlemagne, and his younger brother, CARLOMAN, thereby providing further legitimacy for the newly founded royal dynasty. Along with his father and brother Charlemagne also received from the pope the title *patricius Romanorum*, which implied an imprecise obligation to serve as protector of Rome and the Romans. Infrequent bits of information in the sources suggest that while growing up Charlemagne and his brother were involved in their father's military campaigns and court life, learning from those experiences what was needed to prepare them for their future role as kings.

In accord with Frankish custom the kingdom of the Franks was divided between Charlemagne and Carloman when Pepin III died in 768. A period of rivalry between the brothers ensued which threatened to undo Pepin III's work in unifying the Frankish kingdom. One consequence of this fraternal rivalry was the marriage of Charlemagne to the daughter of DESIDERIUS, king of the Lombards, a union negotiated by Bertrada that some viewed as a move to isolate Carloman and as a threat to the papacy and the Papal States whose chief enemy was the Lombard king and whose well-being Pepin III and his sons had pledged to defend. But the potential crisis stemming from fraternal rivalry ended with the death of Carloman in 771. Charlemagne moved decisively to set aside

Charlemagne.

the claims of Carloman's heirs and to assume sole kingship over the entire Frankish kingdom.

Charlemagne's Military Accomplishments. As sole ruler Charlemagne launched an extraordinarily active career which involved him in a wide range of activities. Central to his 45-year reign were his military activities, continuing a tradition in Frankish history that reached back to CLOVIS (ruled 481–511). Some of his wars ended with the submission to Frankish rule of peoples over whom the Franks had long claimed lordship but who constantly sought autonomy, such as the Aquitainians and the Bavarians. Others were aimed at subduing external peoples perceived to threaten the Frankish kingdom. Most notable among those were the Saxons, whose repeated raids had long menaced the eastern frontier of the kingdom. Beginning in 772 Charlemagne set out to end that threat by subjugating the Saxons and incorporating them into the Frankish kingdom. That end, not achieved until 804, required repeated campaigns, many prompted by Saxon repudiation of peace treaties. Some of the Frankish expeditions ended in defeat, and others witnessed mass killings and forced deportation of rebellious Saxons. Saxon resistance was stiffened by the Frankish insistence that the Saxons accept Christianity, a demand that was accompanied by forced conversions and by draconian laws punishing those who refused to convert or who after conversion resisted such Christian practices as tithing. In the course of the long Saxon wars the neighboring Frisians became involved and were conquered.

At intervals during the Saxons wars Charlemagne conducted other military operations. One of them drew him into Italy. Shortly after he became sole king of the Franks, he repudiated his Lombard wife, thereby breaking his alliance with the Lombard king, Desiderius. In response to appeals from Pope Adrian I beseeching him to live up to the promise made by his father to protect the Papal States, Charlemagne invaded Italy in 773–774, forced Desiderius to surrender, and assumed the title of king of the Lombards. That victory gave him possession of most of Italy, but required subsequent campaigns to retain control. In 778 he led an expedition into Spain in an attempt to take advantage of internal dissension among the ruling Muslims by establishing a Frankish presence south of the Pyrenees that would hinder Muslim incursions into Frankish territories in southern Gaul. That venture ended in a disastrous Frankish defeat at the hands of Gascon (Basque) forces at Roncevalles, an episode immortalized in *The Song of Roland*, an epic poem composed later. But Charlemagne persisted and eventually succeeded in conquering an Frankish enclave, called the Spanish March, between the Pyrenees Mountains and the Ebro River. The final submission of the Bavarians in 788 brought the Franks into contact with the Avars to whom the Bavarians allegedly had turned for assistance against the Franks. The Avar Empire had originally been shaped north of the Danube in the sixth century by Asiatic nomads who established dominance over the indigenous Slavic population and who often proved to be a formidable challenge to the eastern Roman Empire during the seventh century. By the eighth century the Avar power was in decline, providing an inviting target for the Franks. A succession of brilliantly conducted campaigns in 791, 795, and 796 destroyed the Avar state, allowed the victors to seize vast booty, and opened the way for the annexation of a large bloc of territory in the Middle Danube Valley. Military victory was accompanied by the effective extension of a missionary effort, already begun by the Bavarian clergy, aimed at converting the inhabitants of the Avar Empire.

Charlemagne's military victories greatly extended the frontiers to be defended and raised concerns among peoples faced with the arrival on their borders of an aggressive major power. In protecting Frankish frontiers and in dealing with apprehensive neighbors Charlemagne combined military means with effective diplomacy. The conquest of Saxony brought the Franks into contact with several Slavic tribes living east of Elbe and with the Danish kingdom. Against any Slavic tribe which showed hostility toward the Frankish state Charlemagne directed punitive raids which usually ended up with the exaction of tribute; those who preferred peace were permitted to become vassals of the king with some assurance of Frankish protection. During the first stages of the Saxon wars the Danes often lent aid to the Saxons; Charlemagne responded by strengthening the fortifications in the frontier area facing Denmark. Before his death internal problems in the Danish kingdom lessened the Danish threat and provided opportunity for diplomatic exchanges that led to peaceful relations and the promise of increasing Frankish influence in Denmark. The most ominous development on the northern frontier was the beginning of raids on Frankish territory along the North Sea coast by seagoing Danes, a threat Charlemagne sought to counter by creating a Frankish fleet. To protect the new frontier mapped out by the victories over the Avars Charlemagne created militarized marches under the command of trusted officials based in Bavaria and northern Italy. The interactions between the Franks and the Slavic peoples along a frontier extending from the Baltic Sea to the Balkan peninsula set in motion a chain of events that would soon transform the Slavic world. The creation of marcher zones was also adopted against the Muslims facing the Frankish enclave in Spain and the hostile Bretons and Gascons in Gaul. Charlemagne's annexation of the Lombard kingdom did not assure complete control of Italy. In the southern part of the peninsula independent Lombard princes, especially the dukes of Benevento, continued to threaten peace in the Frankish kingdom of Italy and had to be restrained with military campaigns. The Papal States, whose boundaries remained problematic and whose political status with respect to Charlemagne' kingdom of Italy was not clearly defined, complicated the Italian scene. The Frankish position in Italy also led to confrontations with the Byzantine Empire. A complex series of diplomatic negotiations, sometimes punctuated by military encounters in Italy and along the Dalmatian coast, ensued. In general, Charlemagne's diplomatic encounters with the emperors in the East allowed him to strengthen his position vis-à-vis the Byzantine Empire. Charlemagne established diplomatic ties with the Abbasid caliph in Baghdad, Harun-al-Rashid, a relationship nurtured by the fact that these two rulers shared common enemies, the Byzantine emperors and the Umayyad caliphs in Spain. Charlemagne enjoyed a vague role as protector of the Christian establishment in Jerusalem. And his presence was felt in the affairs of Anglo-Saxon kings of Mercia and Northumbria in England. Through successful warfare and effective diplomacy Charlemagne had become a world figure.

Government Structure. Military and diplomatic concerns did not distract Charlemagne from concerns about the governance of his realm. In general, he was not a political innovator, being content to retain the political institutions and techniques inherited from his MEROVINGIAN predecessors. His aim was to improve these institutions and to adapt them to serve a more sophisticated concept of the nature and purposes of government than had guided his predecessors. The royal government continued to be served at the local level by counts, each charged with acting in the name of the king in a specific territory to administer justice, raise troops, collect revenues due the king, and keep the peace. Steps were taken to improve the administration of justice at the local level by attaching individuals learned in the law, called *scabini*, to each court under the jurisdiction of the count to assure judgments in accord with law. Counts were rewarded for their services by income from lands attached to their offices, charges made for public services performed, fines, and royal gifts. Bishops continued to be entrusted with important political functions, particularly in administering justice, caring for the poor, and restraining law breakers. The central government consisted of the king's personal entourage, called the *palatium* (palace), made up of trusted lay and ecclesiastical companions of the king who discharged a variety of functions associated with managing the royal resources, mustering and leading armies, conducting diplomatic missions, producing written documents required for carrying on administrative activities, rendering justice in major cases, and counseling the king in shaping policy. At both the local and central levels of government careful attention was given to assuring a regular royal income, derived primarily from the produce of royal estates, war booty, tolls on commercial activity, and obligatory gifts imposed on rich subjects, and only secondarily from direct taxation. Income from war booty was especially valuable in allowing Charlemagne to attract as officials at all levels individuals drawn from a limited number of aristocratic families interlocked by kinship ties who were eager to serve the king in return for the prestige, the power, and the material rewards derived from holding office and enjoying royal favor.

Charlemagne was most innovative as a ruler in extending and strengthening the linkages between his person and his court and the local centers of power. He exploited the shared interests and the kinship ties of powerful aristocratic families, chiefly from Austrasia where the Carolingian dynasty had its roots, from which most office holders were drawn as a means of establishing consensus within the ruling elite whose reach extended across the entire realm. He continued the traditional annual assemblies which brought together in the presence of the king himself most of the counts, bishops, abbots, and powerful aristocrats of the realm in a setting where complaints could be aired, advice sought, new policies announced, and personal ties cemented. He regularized and extended the use of *missi dominici*, royal agents sent out in pairs to make regular circuits around specifically defined territorial entities embracing several counties for the purpose of making the king's will known, ascertaining how well local officials were discharging their duties, correcting abuses by those officials where necessary, trying particularly difficult judicial cases, and meting out punishment to lawbreakers. To improve communications between his court and local units of government Charlemagne sought to expand the use of written documents in dealing with administrative matters. Especially important were his CAPITULARIES, written documents dispatched across the kingdom to inform interested parties of the king's will and to direct how his programs were to be carried out. He greatly expanded the use of vassalage and benefices as a means of establishing personal bonds between the king and powerful subjects. Those willing to accept vassalage swore under oath to accept the king as their overlord and to be loyal to him; in return they were rewarded with benefices in the form of offices or grants of land to be exploited for their personal benefit as long as they remained loyal and served their lord. Charlemagne even required all free men in his realm to swear an oath obligating them to be faithful in obeying and serving the ruler.

Managing Subjugated Lands. Although conquest was not new in Frankish history, Charlemagne's success as a conqueror gave some urgency to the governance of conquered peoples. He was certainly aware that diversity was a reality in his vast realm, precluding the possibility of a unitary system of governance, with one notable exception: his conquered subjects must accept Christianity, which meant that the ruler must do whatever was needed to mount a missionary effort, to put in place an ecclesiastical organization, to recruit and train clergy to meet the spiritual needs of the new converts, and to provide the physical and monetary resources required to sustain Christian worship. Charlemagne's acceptance of diversity was evidenced by the fact that everywhere in his realm he allowed his subjects to be judged by the law under which they were born. In 781 he created the subkingdoms of Italy and Aquitaine, each ruled by one of his sons, a step that clearly recognized the unique traditions prevailing in those areas. With the passing of time he sought to efface that uniqueness by filling secular and ecclesiastical offices with Frankish aristocrats and by making inhabitants of Italy and Aquitaine subject to royal legislation. In Saxony Charlemagne sought to put in place political and religious structures that duplicated those prevailing in Francia, a policy that led to the rapid assimilation of the Saxons into the Frankish world. In the somewhat ill-defined border regions facing the Bretons, the Muslims, the Slavs in the Danube Valley, and the Danes, Charlemagne established marches directed by dukes who were entrusted with considerable political autonomy, especially in military affairs; the powerful officials were drawn from the king's most trusted followers. Taken together, these measures allowed a considerable number of people to be incorporated into the Frankish realm without serious threat to the internal order. But the system also created a situation where local potentates entrenched in various regions for the purpose of ruling them in the name of the Frankish king could develop a power base that eventually enabled them to resist the royal government.

Charlemagne Redefines Kingship. Charlemagne's efforts to improve traditional techniques of government were accompanied by a subtle change in the concepts defining the purpose of government and the role of the king. Charlemagne inherited from his Merovingian predecessors a concept of kingship based on the king as a warlord who had the power to command his subjects to do what he willed as long as he retained the power to enforce his commands. He did not abandon that model of rulership, especially insofar as his power to command was concerned. But as his reign progressed, the scope of that power was extended. His own legislation and the pronouncements of his chief counselors on the art of ruling began to add a religious dimension to what it meant to rule and to be a subject. Increasingly prominent was the idea that in a Christian society he who ruled ''by the grace of God'' had an obligation to rule according to the commands of God, and his subjects had a duty to respect the law of God in their conduct. By that definition the ruler must become an agent serving to realize the will of God, a duty that required that he direct his efforts toward assuring the salvation of his subjects. Kingship began to take on a ministerial dimension which mandated that a ruler be both priest and king, dedicated to assuring both the spiritual and material well-being of his subjects. This concept of kingship, which drew its substance chiefly from the Old Testament model of kingship and from St. Augustine's ideas on the nature of the city of God, began to blur the distinction between the sacred and the secular, between the Church and the state, and to bestow on the secular leader the authority to direct both spheres.

Despite the boldness of Charlemagne's political program, there were signs by the end of his reign that it was overly ambitious. Those signs suggested that during his reign the scope of government greatly expanded due to his conquests and to the new range of responsibilities emerging from a redefinition of the function of government and its leader, but that the means of coping with that expansion did not materialize. The human resources needed to enact his political program were lacking, being limited to a narrow range of families that had long enjoyed a central place in the Carolingian world. The material resources to support royal enactments were insufficient, especially after the cessation of military conquests during the last part of Charlemagne's reign and the consequent shrinking of booty available for distribution to loyal followers. The infrastructure undergirding the central administration was too primitive to reach out across a vast and diverse realm to explain and enforce measures aimed at creating order and providing justice. As a consequence of these limitations, political power began to escape royal control into private hands, as it had done earlier during the Merovingian chapter in the history of the Frankish kingdom. Without dubbing him a political failure, it can perhaps be said that in the context of his age Charlemagne simply tried to do too much by way of establishing effective government on a permanent basis.

Charlemagne's Religious Reform Efforts. Despite the magnitude of the problems facing him in the political realm and of the effort made to solve those challenges, Charlemagne found the time and energy to leave his mark on other facets of his world. He won widespread praise in his age as a religious reformer. His efforts in this realm represented a continuation of the reforming effort begun in the 740s by his father, Pepin III, and his uncle, Carloman. Charlemagne expanded and intensified their reforming program and placed the full power of the state behind its realization. His concern for religious reform was motivated in part by his personal piety. But he was keenly aware of the importance of the ecclesiastical establishment to his political program. And he became increasingly convinced that he as ruler had a duty imposed by God to see to it that his subjects gained eternal salvation. The result was a series of councils that enacted reforming measures given the force of public law in royal capitularies, the most important of which were the *Capitulare generalis* of 789 and the *Capitulare missorum speciale* of 802. Responsibility for enforcing this legislation was given to all public officials, but bishops were the chief agents in realizing meaningful reform. But in the final analysis it was the ruler's responsibility to purify the religious life of his subjects. Consequently, Charlemagne's reform effort served to place the direction of the Christian community into the hands of the secular ruler.

The reforming legislation promulgated by Charlemagne was traditional in its spirit and its content. It was inspired by an awareness of defects in contemporary religious life that needed correction in accordance with norms laid down by earlier church councils and encoded in collections of canon law. A few major concerns dominated Charlemagne's reform program: instituting a hierarchal church organization involving metropolitan archbishoprics, bishoprics, and parishes; defining the authority and responsibilities of the archbishops, bishops, and priests serving this hierarchy, especially bishops; improving the moral and intellectual quality of the clergy; protecting church property and income; regularizing and standardizing liturgical practices; providing physical facilities required for the proper conduct of religious life; intensifying pastoral care in order to deepen understanding of the faith and to root out all traces of paganism; improving moral behavior among all Christians in a variety of areas, such as criminal activity, marriage practices, treatment of the powerless, and property transactions. As the reform movement gained momentum, its scope began to broaden. Charlemagne and his chief religious advisers began to assume responsibility for defining and guaranteeing orthodox doctrine. That dimension of reform was evident in the famous *LIBRI CAROLINI*, compiled by THEODULF at Charlemagne's command to correct the decisions on icons enacted by the Council of NICAEA in 787, and in the pronouncements of the Council of Frankfurt in 794 and the subsequent writings of ALCUIN condemning ADOPTIONISM. These facets of Charlemagne's religious policy suggest that the Frankish king was charting a course that would give the West its own version of CAESAROPAPISM, not unlike that exemplified by Roman emperors from CONSTANTINE THE GREAT to emperors ruling in Constantinople in Charlemagne's own day.

Charlemagne's aggressive domination of religious life in his realm proceeded without alienating the Frankish episcopacy which generally gave its full support to the ruler's program. Perhaps that support owed much to the fact that Charlemagne controlled episcopal appointments and had the resources to extend valuable favors to supportive clerics. However, the record seems to indicate clearly that the king filled episcopal offices with men who took their religious responsibilities seriously, who believed in the royal reform program, and who possessed the skills to give substance to that program. Neither did two popes who held office during his reign, ADRIAN I (773–795) and LEO III (795–816), resist the caesaropapist course followed by Charlemagne. Although by the end of the 8th century the papacy was extended recognition as the titular head of Christendom, both Adrian I and Leo III were fully aware of the extent to which the survival of the Papal States and of the pope's authority over those who inhabited the Papal States depended on the protection of the Frankish ruler; thus, neither was inclined to challenge his religious policy. In fact, Adrian I repeatedly proclaimed his approval of Charlemagne's efforts to purify religious life and to lead in the spread of Christendom among the pagans. The king in turn was moved by the deepest respect for the spiritual head of Christendom. He

was especially bound to Adrian I by personal ties, and, as we shall see, took major steps to rescue Leo III from his enemies. On numerous occasions he sought papal advice and sanction for his religious program. On two different occasions he reaffirmed the friendship pact that Pepin III had established with Pope Stephen II. And he extended the territorial boundaries of the Papal States by restoring to the pope lands that were part of his kingdom of Italy.

The Carolingian Renaissance. Charlemagne's efforts to improve the royal government and the religious establishment posed the need for better-educated secular and religious officials. The response to that need was a cultural renewal, known as the "CAROLINGIAN RENAISSANCE," which in its beginning owed much to Charlemagne's initiative and which constituted one of his most enduring achievements. Charlemagne's renaissance was given its original impetus by a circle of educated men from outside Francia whom Charlemagne gathered at his court in the 780s and 790s. Included were the Italians PAUL THE DEACON, PAULINUS OF AQUILEIA, and PETER OF PISA, the Visigoth Theodulf, the Irishman DUNGAL, and above all the Anglo-Saxon Alcuin of York, all products of an intellectual revival that had occurred in their lands during the 7th and 8th centuries. It was not long after they joined the royal court that their ranks began to be complemented by natives of Francia who were the disciples of these outsiders. The interactions of the members of the court circle with each other and with the king eventually found expression in royal commands, which together spelled out the fundamental features of the Carolingian cultural renewal; especially exemplary were a capitulary entitled *Admonitio generalis* of 789 and a royal letter entitled *Epistola de letteris colendis* ("Letter Concerning the Cultivation of Letters") circulated sometime during the 790s. These texts provided for the establishment of schools equipped to improve Latin literacy; the production of accurate copies of books basic to understanding Christian teachings; the assemblage of libraries that would allow studies beyond the elementary level; measures to assure the proper performance of the liturgy; and steps aimed at deepening among all Christians a knowledge of the basic tenets of the faith. Members of the court circle began to produce textbooks required to improve literacy, to convey the basic tenets of the faith, and to perform the liturgy properly. They collected copies of books that would make possible the deeper exploration of the Christian religion, including the writings of the Latin church fathers and selected classical authors. As a consequence an important royal library was created. A royal copy center, called a *scriptorium*, developed where books were copied and sometimes decorated with painted miniatures which set their creators in search of models for the art of book decorating. The royal *scriptorium* played an important role in propagating a new style of writing, the Carolingian minuscule, which made copying and reading much easier. The combination of royal commands on educational matters and the example set by the court scholars soon began to have an influence across the entire kingdom. Existing episcopal and monastic schools were revived and new ones founded; some of these schools produced masters who were able to expand the curriculum to the point where they could provide a broad education based on the traditional liberal arts. The number of *Scriptoria* and libraries increased, especially in monastic centers, where some libraries featured a wide range of books, including many classical writings, the only surviving copies of which came from these libraries. The fruit of Charlemagne's effort to renew culture was soon evidenced in the increased use of writing in the conduct of royal government and ecclesiastical administration, the improved competence in Latin, an enriched level of discourse reflected in the literary production of the era, especially in poetry, history writing, biblical commentaries, and letter writing, and in church building and decoration. Perhaps there was some truth to a boast that a ''new Athens'' was in the making, especially at Aachen after it became the favorite royal residence and the center of a building program that embodied many of the major features of the Carolingian revival in architecture and art. In fact, the full fruits of the Carolingian cultural renewal did not emerge until after Charlemagne's reign, but his patronage had given cultural renewal a form and a purpose that would leave a long-lasting mark on the cultural face of western Europe.

Charlemagne Is Crowned Emperor. The impressive list of accomplishments associated with the first 30 years of Charlemagne's reign provided the background for the culminating event of his regime: his coronation as emperor. As his reign progressed there were increasing signs that in the minds of many, perhaps including Charlemagne himself, his feats as warrior, governor, religious reformer, and cultural patron elevated him to a status inadequately conveyed by his traditional titles, king of the Franks and the Lombards and *patricius Romanorum*. He was a universal leader, uniquely endowed to safeguard the spiritual and material well-being of the community of true believers, a community increasingly conceived as an *imperium Christianorum* whose members included those who adhered to the true faith of Rome and whose leader needed a title befitting his role in creating, directing, and sustaining such an entity. The increasing knowledge of classical history in the court circle emerging from the Carolingian Renaissance suggested comparisons with great Roman emperors. The situation in Constantinople, where a succession of emperors had fostered the heresy

of ICONOCLASM and where after 797 a women, IRENE, held the imperial office, pointed up the unfitness of the Greek emperors to lead the *imperium Christianorum*.

A development in Rome provided the occasion for giving substance to this line of thinking, which at its essence had to do with locating responsibility for the direction of orthodox Christian society. In 799 a crisis developed in Rome that raised serious doubts about the ability of the pope to guide the *imperiium christianorum* and posed a major challenge for Charlemagne. A faction of Roman aristocrats rebelled against Leo III (795–816) and sought by force to render him unfit for office by blinding him; the rebels charged Leo III with tyranny and with serious personal misconduct. Leo III escaped with his life by fleeing to Charlemagne's court, placing Charlemagne in a position of deciding how he would proceed in a situation that involved judging the vicar of St. Peter and restoring order within the Papal States where the pope was ruler. The Frankish ruler acted decisively. He took steps to restore the pope to his office and then, after wide consultation, made a journey to Rome in late 800 to settle matters. After extensive discussions during December of 800, Charlemagne arranged an assembly of dignitaries on December 23 at which Leo III was allowed to clear himself of the charges brought against him by swearing under oath that he was innocent. Two days later on Christmas day as Charlemagne prepared to celebrate Mass in the basilica of St. Peter, Pope Leo III placed a crown on his head while the assembled crowd acclaimed him emperor and then the pope performed the ritual act of obeisance due an emperor.

Charlemagne's coronation as emperor posed two problems, the answers to which eluded not only his contemporaries but also many later historians. The first involved assigning responsibility for this momentous step. Although EINHARD, the biographer of Charlemagne, wrote later that the king would never have gone near St. Peter's on that fateful day had he known what was going to happen, the evidence makes it more likely that the coronation was jointly planned by Leo III and Charlemagne as a means of serving ends useful to each party; given the pope's tenuous position at the moment, one suspects that Charlemagne played the leading role in charting the course of events in December of 800. In his moment of need Leo III was undoubtedly pleased to play a role in proceedings that would strengthen his ties to his protector by allowing him to sanction an important new title for the Carolingians just as his predecessors had done a half-century earlier in approving the assumption of the Frankish kingship by Pepin III. The pope's role in the bestowing the imperial crown on Charlemagne implied that papal participation was in some way a requisite to authentic election to the imperial office. Given the long connection of the papacy with the protocol of the imperial court in Constantinople, it is likely that Leo III played the decisive role in arranging the ritual proceedings that occurred on Christmas Day, 800. Charlemagne very likely welcomed a clarification of his legal position in passing judgment on those who had attacked the pope, a power he soon used to condemn the conspirators. He could as emperor claim equality with his counterpart in Constantinople. Above all else, he was granted recognition for his accomplishments in carrying out God's will more successfully than anyone else. Such recognition pleased his advisers and gave them fresh ammunition with which to flesh out their concept of ministerial kingship.

The Final Years of Charlemagne's Reign. A second, more intractable problem centered around what the imperial title meant to Charlemagne and what effect it had on his actions as ruler. The answer to that question must be sought in his actions during the last years of his reign. Some evidence suggests that the imperial title meant little to him. He continued to call himself "king of the Franks and the Lombards," to which was joined the enigmatic designation "emperor governing the Roman empire." In 806 he provided for the future division of his realm among his three sons without any consideration of the unity implicit in the idea of empire or any mention of the imperial title. In his lifestyle he continued to dress, eat, and play in the fashion of a typical Frankish noble with little concern for modes of conduct or protocols associated with the imperial dignity. Some evidence suggests that in the last years of his life he increasingly turned away from the clerical advisers who played a role in securing his imperial coronation in order to give a larger share in wielding power to the powerful noble families that had played a part in establishing the royal power of the Carolingian dynasty and who had little interest in promoting the imperial ideal. But other pieces of evidence suggest that Charlemagne took the imperial title seriously. He undertook a long military and diplomatic effort aimed at winning recognition of his title from the emperor in Constantinople, an end he finally realized in 812. He sought to reenergize his reform program in the years after 800 in a context that suggested he felt that his new title mandated renewed concern for the spiritual welfare of his subjects. The terminology used to convey imperial orders, the protocol adopted for the conduct of court life, the symbols used on royal coinage, and the motifs employed in creating and decorating the main structures of his new residence in Aachen all suggest that a "new Rome" was being built and reflected an awareness that the imperial office was a source of ideological elements which strengthened Charlemagne's authority. In 813 Charlemagne with his own hands bestowed the imperial crown on his only surviving son, Louis the Pious.

That act suggested that he believed that the imperial title had some value to a successor faced with holding together the vast empire that he and his Carolingian predecessors had put together. And it also indicated that he wished to exclude the papacy from any role in providing legitimacy for the imperial title. Taken together, this evidence points to the conclusion that Charlemagne saw the imperial crown as a unique award extended to him in recognition of his personal accomplishments, an award to be used as he pleased but not to be set aside lightly lest its potential for enhancing his authority as a ruler and his and his family's status among other rulers in his world be wasted.

When Charlemagne died in 814, one author wrote that "Rivers of tears now flow unceasing, / for the world bewails the death of Charlemagne," while another writing somewhat later remembered with longing that when his life ended he "left all Europe filled with every goodness." However much deserved on the basis of his many accomplishments, these sentiments do not speak to his personal qualities which must not be overlooked in assessing his career. His powerful personality was a vital force in a setting in which institutional structures were fragile and personal relationships played a fundamental role in maintaining order. Although he gained the admiration of an elite circle of nobles and clergymen for his interest in learning, his new political concepts, and his progressive religious ideas, to most of his subjects Charlemagne was preeminently an ideal warrior chief, companion, and family man. He was a giant man blessed with extraordinary energy and vitality. He loved the active life—military campaigning, hunting, and swimming. He was no less at home at the banquet table, where quantities of food and drink, storytelling, and spirited verbal thrusts created an atmosphere of joviality among his numerous companions. He was naturally gregarious, loquacious, and intellectually inquisitive, allowing him to be the dominant person in his court circle. But he could be brutal on occasion; for instance, after a disastrous defeat at the hands of the Saxons in 782, he ordered the slaughter of 4,500 Saxon prisoners of war in an effort to terrorize that truculent people into submission. Never far from his mind were the interests of his large family. In the course of his reign he was married five times; after his last wife died in 800, he remained unmarried but shared his life with several concubines. These liaisons produced at least eighteen children. The royal sons counted as legitimate began early to learn the arts of being king, Pepin as king of Italy, Louis as king of Aquitaine, and Charles at his father's court. Charlemagne refused to allow his daughters to marry, keeping them with him to adorn his court and perhaps to dote on their loving father. Two of them bore illegitimate children fathered by court officials. One of the tragic episodes in Charlemagne's life was marked by the death of four of his children in a two-year span from 810 to 812, including Pepin and Charles, both destined to succeed their father. Despite behavior that those living by different moral standards might hold in disdain, Charlemagne was a model of piety in the eyes of his subjects. He attended Mass daily, prayed frequently, gave generously to the support of the Church, and acted frequently in the interests of the poor and oppressed. These qualities and traits made him a figure capable of commanding the respect, loyalty, and affection of his subjects; on these feelings rested much of his authority.

Charlemagne's reign represented an important chapter in western European history. His empire did not long survive him, but the ideal of a politically unified Europe inspired some western Europeans until the present, sometimes with unhappy consequences. Charlemagne served as the model prince during most of the Middle Ages. The goals he pursued—orderly government, religious reform, cultural renewal, Christian expansion—influenced the programs of many later medieval kings. What he actually achieved during his reign laid a firm basis upon which an orderly, civilized society was later built in western Europe. For these accomplishments, he justly deserved to be called "the Great" and *Europae pater*.

See Also: 'ABBĀSIDS; BYZANTINE EMPIRE; CAROLINGIAN REFORM; STATES OF THE CHURCH; UMAYYADS.

Bibliography: *Einhardi vita Karoli Magni,* ed. O. HOLDER-EGGER, (*Monumenta Germaniae Historica, Scriptores rerum Germanicarum in usum scholarum* 24 Hannover 1911; reprinted, 1965). *Notker der Stammler, Taten Kaiser Karls des Grossen (Notkeri Balbuli Gesta Karoli Magni imperatoris),* ed. H. F. HAEFELE, (*Monumenta Germaniae Historica, Scriptores rerum Germanicarum in usum scholarum* 12 Munich 1959; reprinted, 1980), English translation of both biographies as *Two Lives of Charlemagne,* trans. L. THORPE, (London and New York 1969). *Annales regni Francorum, a. 768–814,* ed. F. KURZE, (*Monumenta Germaniae Historica, Scriptores rerum Germanicarum in usum scholarum* 6 Hannover 1895; reprinted, 1950) 26–141, English translation in *Carolingian Chronicles. Royal Frankish Annals and Nithard's Histories,* trans. B. W. SCHOLZ (Ann Arbor, MI 1970) 46–97. *Capitularia regum Francorum,* ed. A. BORETIUS and V. KRAUSE, 2 v., (*Monumenta Germaniae Historica, Leges, Sectio II* Hannover 1893–1897; reprinted, 1980–1984), 1:44–259. *Concilia aevi karolini,* ed. A. WERMINGHOFF, 2 v., (*Monumenta Germaniae Historica, Leges, Sectio III: Concilia* 2, 1/2 Hannover 1906–1908; reprinted, 1997–1999), 2/1:74–306. *Epistolae karolini aevi,* v. 2–3, ed. E. DÜMMLER, et al (*Monumenta Germaniae Historica, Epistolae* 4–5 Berlin 1892–1935, reprinted 1985–1995), 3:494–567; 4:1–34. *Codex Carolinus,* Epp. 49–97, ed. W. GUNDLACH. (*Monumenta Germaniae Historica, Epistolae,* v. 3: *Epistolae Merowingici et Karolini,* v. 1 Berlin 1892) 567–648, 654–655. *Alcvini sive Albini Epistolae,* ed. E. DÜMMLER, (*Monumenta Germaniae Historica, Epistolae,* v. 4: *Epistolae Karolini Aevi,* v. 2 Berlin 1899) 1–493. *Die Urkunden Pippins, Karlmanns und Karl des Grossen (Pippini, Carlomanni, Caroli Magni Diplomata),* ed. E. MÜHLBACHER (*Monumenta Germaniae Historica, Diplomata Karolini* 1 Hannover 1906; reprinted, 1991) 77–478. *Poetae latini aevi carolini,* ed. E. DÜMMLER (*Monumenta Germaniae Historica, Poetae* 1 Berlin 1881; reprinted, 1997). *Karolus Magnus et Leo Papa. Ein Paderborner Epos von Jahre 799,* ed. J. BROCKMANN, with studies by H. BEUMANN, F. BRÜNHÖLZL, and W. WINKELMANN, (*Studien und Quellen zur westfälischen Geschichte* 5 Paderborn 1966). *Opus Caroli regis contra synodum (Libri Carolini),* ed. A. FREEMAN with P. MAYVAERT (*Monumenta Germaniae Historica, Legis, Sectio II: Concilia, Supplement* 1 Hannover 1998).

[R. E. SULLIVAN]

CHARLES, PIERRE

Jesuit priest, missiologist and theologian, b. Brussels, Belgium, July 3, 1883; ordained as a Priest Aug. 24, 1910; d. Louvain, Feb. 11, 1954. Throughout his teaching career (1914–1954) he was professor of dogmatic theology at the College theologique S.J de Louvain. During these same years he was frequently a lecturer or visiting professor at other institutions: the University of Louvain, the Gregorian University in Rome, Fordham University in New York, the University of Rio de Janeiro and others. He also visited many sites where missionaries were working.

Charles is best known for his missiology, the field that inspired his principal writings after 1923. From that year he became a frequent contributor to the "Missiology Weeks" (annual except during World War II) which he directed at Louvain until 1950. In 1926 he began publishing his *Dossiers de l'Action Missionnnaire,* which eventually became a textbook correlating missionary history and theological reflection. His central position was that "the formal purpose of missions is not first of all to save souls but to establish, to constitute, the visible Church in those countries where this is lacking." He emphasized that it should be the responsibility of the local church, once established or planted, rather than the foreign missioners, to continue and complete the work of conversion. In accord with this principle he strongly supported the positions of Popes Benedict XV and Pius XI "that the first task of missioners is the creation of an indigenous clergy." He was an early proponent of the need for inculturation of the Church among its new peoples. His conception of the Church deepened through the years: "It is not only with souls that the church is concerned; it is the equilibrium of the world as a whole and its eternal value that [the Church] conserves and consecrates." (*Etudes missiologiques, p. 37*). It was a tribute to his vision that in 1948, when Pope Pius XII was considering convoking an ecumenical council, he named Pierre Charles general secretary for the preparations. In 1951, however, Pius decided not to continue the project. In his writings, Pierre

Charles anticipated many missionary aspects of Vatican Council II. Some of his more important writings include: *Dossiers de l'action missionnaire,* 2nd edition (Louvain 1939); *Missiologie (Louvain 1939); Etudes missiologiques* (Bruges 1955); *The Prayer for all Times (Westminster, Md. 1949);* and *The Prayer for all Things* (New York 1964).

Bibliography: J. LEVIE, "In Memoriam: Le Pere Pierre Charles, S.J. (1883–1954)," *Nouvelle Revue Theologique* 76 (March 1954) 254–273. J. MASSON, "Pierre Charles, S.J. 1883–1954 : Advocate of Acculturation," in *Mission Legacies,* ed. G.H. ANDERSON et al. (Maryknoll, N.Y. 1994), 410–415.

[W.D. MCCARTHY]

CHARLES V, HOLY ROMAN EMPEROR

Reigned 1519 to 1558; b. Ghent, Flanders, Feb. 24, 1500; d. San Jerónimo de Yuste, Province of Estremadura, Spain, Sept. 21, 1558. As the son of Philip the Handsome, Duke of Burgundy, and Joanna, third child of Ferdinand of Aragon and Isabella of Castile, he was heir presumptive to an empire vaster than Charlemagne's, and over which the "sun never set." It included the Netherlands and claims to the Burgundian circle, which came to him at the death of his father (Sept. 25, 1506); it included Castile, Aragon, the conquered kingdoms of Navarre and Granada, Naples, Sicily, Sardinia, the conquests of the New World, and possessions in North Africa, all of which after the death of Ferdinand (Jan. 23, 1516) he ruled jointly with his mad mother; and it included the Hapsburg duchies of Austria with rights over Hungary and Bohemia, inherited from his paternal grandfather, Emperor Maximilian I (Jan. 12, 1519).

Education in Flanders. Charles, 6 years old at the death of his father, was placed in the guardianship of his aunt, Archduchess Margaret of Austria, who, as regent of the Netherlands, proved a shrewd ruler and a firm but devoted foster-mother to Charles and his sisters, Eleanor, Isabella, and Mary. His brother Ferdinand and his sister Catherine were reared in Spain. Among his tutors at Mechlin (Malines) were Robert of Ghent, Adrian Wiele, Juan de Anchiata, and Charles de Poupet, but it was Adrian of Utrecht (Pope ADRIAN VI, 1522 to 1523) who taught him piety and also won his lifelong affection. The ways of the court he learned from the experienced politician Guillaume de Croy, Lord of Chièvres, appointed his governor by Maximilian in 1509. Mercurino Arborio di GATTINARA, Margaret's jurisconsult and an admirer of Dante's ideals of universal monarchy, instructed him to transcend dynastic nationalism for the universalism connected with the imperial office to which he was destined.

Charles V, Holy Roman Emperor.

On Jan. 5, 1515, Charles was declared of age by the Estates at Brussels. The next year he succeeded Ferdinand, and as Charles I of Castile and Aragon he traveled to Spain to accept this new power from the 80-year-old viceroy, Cardinal XIMÉNEZ DE CISNEROS, who died of fever at Roa on his way to meet the king. At Tordesillas, Charles visited his insane mother, whom he had never known, and met his brother Ferdinand (age 15), whom he had never seen. In the first months of his reign, Charles, through his ministers, arbitrated the grievances of the grandees and the demands of the *Cortes* and appointed Gattinara his grand chancellor to succeed the unpopular Jean de Sauvage, who died June 7, 1518. These first steps in government were accelerated by the news of the death of Maximilian; Charles was now Archduke of Austria and a candidate for the vacant imperial throne.

Imperial Election. Though his choice was opposed by Pope Leo X, who feared the union of the imperial and Neopolitan crowns on the head of the same sovereign, and by Francis I, Henry VIII, and Frederick the Wise of Saxony, his rivals for the title, Charles won the votes of the seven electors, partly through intrigue and liberal bribery (it cost the Hapsburgs 850,000 gulden, borrowed from the banking house of the Fuggers). Scarcely 20 years old, Charles swore to the exacting terms of the coronation oath before the electoral college, and on Jan. 23,

1520, he was crowned in Charlemagne's cathedral at Aachen. The empire that came to Charles was held together by a net of dynastic marriages; hence the dictum,

Bella gerant alii, tu felix Austria nube, Namque Mars aliis, dat tibi regna Venus.

Let others make wars, you happy Austria make marriages; While Mars gives kingdoms to others, Venus gives them to you.

The first objective of his reign was not new conquest but the protection and consolidation of his inheritance. To this end he arranged strategic matrimonial alliances: Isabella was married to Christian II of Denmark (1514); Ferdinand to Anne, daughter of Ladislaus of Hungary and Bohemia (1521); Mary to Louis II of Hungary (1522); Catherine to John III of Portugal (1524); Eleanor, widow of Emmanuel of Portugal, was betrothed to Francis I, king of France (1530); Charles himself, after numerous engagements, married Isabella of Portugal (1526). His aunt, CATHERINE OF ARAGON, was already the wife of HENRY VIII OF ENGLAND, and his son Philip was later joined in a hapless marriage to MARY TUDOR (1554). His niece Christina of Denmark was wed to Duke Francesco Sforza II of Milan; his sister-in-law Beatrice of Portugal, to the Duke of Savoy; other relatives were married into the families of the Medici, Farnese, and Gonzaga.

Opposition and War. The maintenance of his wide power brought him into conflict from the inception of his reign.

Spain. Charles, with his French speech, Flemish background, and Burgundian councilors, was looked upon as a foreigner in Spain, and he had to face attempts to seize or limit his royal right. These he thwarted by defeating the *comuneros* in the Battle of Villalar (April 23, 1521) and executing their leader, Juan de Padilla; the next year he captured Vicente Pirez, captain general of the *Germanía;* in 1525 he put down the Valencian *Moriscos.*

France. Charles's relations with the king of France narrowed into a contest for the control of the Italian peninsula and the hegemony of Burgundy. He challenged Francis I rights to Milan, which had been reconquered by the French king at the Battle of Marignano (1515), as well as his dynastic claims to Naples. Four wars followed, interrupted by inconclusive and violated truces. On Feb. 24, 1525, the imperial army, commanded by the *condottiere,* Fernando Pescara, captured Francis at Pavia. By the terms of the Treaty of Madrid (Jan. 14, 1526), Francis relinquished his titles to Italy and his suzerainty over Artois and Flanders, ceded Burgundy, and surrendered his two sons to Charles as hostages. The French king, upon liberation, repudiated the treaty and entered the Holy League of Cognac (May 22, 1526) with CLEMENT

VII, Venice, Florence, and the deposed Duke of Milan, Francesco Sforza II; he was also allied with Henry VIII of England. The next year imperial troops under the command of Constable Charles de Bourbon sacked Rome (May 7, 1527) and besieged Clement VII in the CASTEL SANT' ANGELO. Charles made peace with the pope (Treaty of Barcelona, June 29, 1529) and with Francis (Peace of Cambrai, Aug. 2, 1529), winning favorable terms and a ransom of two million gold crowns for Francis' sons. At Bologna, on Feb. 23, 1530, Charles was crowned King of Lombardy and Holy Roman Emperor by Clement VII. He was the last Holy Roman Emperor to be crowned by a pope. When Sforza, who had been reinstated as Duke of Milan, died childless in 1535, the contest was reopened. Francis invaded Savoy and Piedmont in his third attempt to capture Milan, but his early successes were checked by Charles' invasion of Provence (1536). This war terminated with the Treaty of Nice (June 18, 1538), which reaffirmed the conditions of the Treaty of Cambrai, but left Francis in occupation of two-thirds of Piedmont. In 1542 Francis tried again, this time with the aid of Süleyman I, Ottoman emperor. His victory at Ceresole (1544) was again nullified when Charles invaded the valley of the Marne and marched on Paris. By the Treaty of Crépy (Sept. 18, 1544), Francis abandoned claims on Italy, Flanders, and Artois, and Charles renounced Burgundy. In secret clauses of the treaty Francis promised to help the Emperor fight Protestantism, regain Calvinist Geneva for the Duke of Savoy, and further the Council of TRENT.

German Estates. The element of universalism in Charles' political conception met its strongest test from the German Estates. When he outlawed Martin LUTHER at the Diet of Worms (1521), he believed he was removing not only an innovator in doctrine, but an opponent to authority, his own and LEO X's. In effect he established the reformer as a mustering-point for anti-Romanists and for German princes who sought territorial independence and chafed under the annoyance of heavy imperial taxation. While Charles proceeded to the French Wars, his brother Ferdinand, whom he appointed president of the *Reichsregiment* (council of regency), faced the problems of religious and political unrest. The Knights' Revolt (1522 to 1523), in which Franz von Sickingen and Ulrich von HUTTEN led troops against the ecclesiastical princes, was followed by the PEASANTS' WAR (1524 to 1525). In 1526 princes sympathetic to the reformers formed the League of Torgau and at the second Diet of Speyer (1529) they protested against its strict reaffirmation of the terms of the Diet of Worms. Thus, when Charles returned to Germany after his coronation to preside in splendor at the Diet of Augsburg (1530), he confronted an assembly factionally divided. Conciliatory religious formulas failed (*see* INTERIMS), and on Feb. 27, 1531, the Protestant princes and representatives of the free cities met in the town hall of Schmalkalden to form the league that provoked the Schmalkaldic Wars (1546 to 1547). The emperor's victory at Mühlberg (April 24, 1547) and the capture of John Frederick of Saxony and Philip of Hesse were high points of power, but they later faded in the French capture of Metz, Toul, and Verdun, and in the great triumph of territorialism, effected by the Peace of AUGSBURG (Sept. 25, 1555), which gave recognition to Lutherans (but not Calvinists) within the Empire, provided they followed the religion of their prince (*cujus regio, ejus religio*).

Ottoman Empire. From his Spanish and Austrian forebears Charles inherited a traditional hostility toward Islam. The reconquest of lands taken by the Turks in Hungary and along the Mediterranean became a chivalric ideal. Under Süleyman I, Belgrade (1521) and Rhodes (1522) fell, and King Louis of Hungary was defeated in the Battle of Mohács (1526), which led to a disputed dynastic succession and the siege of Vienna (1529) by a Turkish army. In 1532 Charles was able to organize resistance, and although the small fortress of Güns in western Hungary withstood assault (Aug. 7 to 28), and German troops overcame the Turkish rear guard in Styria, little was achieved beyond moving the locale of the war to the Mediterranean. In North Africa, Khair ed-Din (Barbarossa), corsair and since 1533 admiral of the Ottoman fleet, had seized the Peñon (1516) and Algiers (1518), making the Barbary States a strong garrison for Mediterranean piracy. When diplomacy failed to win Khair ed-Din away from allegiance to the Sultan, Charles risked a maritime expedition. Commanded by the Genoese admiral, Andrea Doria, it drove the Turks from La Goletta (1535) in an engagement that cost Khair ed-Din 75 sail. Tunis was taken on July 31, and 20,000 Christian slaves were liberated. In 1538 Charles entered a Holy League with PAUL III and Venice, but it was ineffective; the Venetian fleet was defeated at Prevesa, and Ferdinand was forced to a truce with Süleyman, after the latter's successes in Hungary in 1547.

Abdication. By 1555 Charles saw how far his policies had fallen from their mark. His vision of a united Germany was permanently blurred by the terms of the Peace of Augsburg; his proposal of the succession of his son Philip to the imperial title was rejected at the Diet of Augsburg (1550 to 1551); Henry II of France continued to harass Italy (the ten-year conflict between Spain and France was not settled until the Treaty of Cateau-Cambrésis in 1559); Gian Pietro Carafa, strong opponent to Spanish interests, was elected PAUL IV (1555–59); Turkish power was undiminished; and the imperial treasury was drained through continuous warfare. Fatigue,

frustration, and long suffering from gout led Charles to surrender the weight of office. On Oct. 25, 1555, in the great Hall of the Golden Fleece at Brussels, he gave the government of the Netherlands to Philip; the next year Spain and Sicily. To Ferdinand he relinquished the Hapsburg Empire (1556), but not the title of Emperor, which he retained until 1558. In September 1557, old beyond his years, he retired to a house that edged the Hieronymite monastery of San Yuste, where he lived until his death, not as a recluse, but quietly giving advice, receiving dispatches, and performing pious acts.

Sobriety, reserve, humorlessness, and self-conscious plainness placed him in contrast to contemporary Renaissance monarchs. Charles, well named the "last of the medieval emperors" (P. Rassow), was loyal to the interests of the Church, but he was also convinced that Rome had scant comprehension of his problems in ruling an Empire that contained a body of subjects stubbornly adhering to popular heresy. Thus, he was initially cool to the idea of a general council at Trent, since he feared that it would end his attempts at conciliation with organized Lutheran churches, sheltered by princes whose support he needed for his warfare. This explains his disregard for Rome in his promulgation of the Augsburg Interim, when he presented the document to the papal legate, Francesco Sfondrati, to be sent to the pope not for opinion or approval, but as a simple announcement of its contents. When criticized, he replied that he was not acting beyond his competence as a Catholic prince. Charles was faithful to his wife during her lifetime. His natural daughter, Margaret of Austria, was born of a liaison with Johanna van der Gheynst five years before his marriage; his natural son, Don Juan, who led the Christian fleet to victory at LEPANTO (Oct. 7, 1571), was born to him and Barbara Blomberg in 1545, six years after his wife's death.

While Charles's regime in Europe was reduced to a policy of uneasy containment, he was the true parent of a new empire in America. He encouraged Spain's *conquista,* thereby securing the economic and fiscal advantages of exploration: Ferdinand Magellan, the Portuguese navigator, was commissioned to chart a western route to the Spice Islands (1519); Hernando Cortés entered Mexico City (1519); Juan Ponce de León made his second expedition to Florida (1521); Pedro de Alvarado conquered Guatemala and Salvador (1523); Sebastian Cabot, the Emperor's pilot, explored the Rio de la Plata (1526–30), on whose estuary Santa María de Buenos Aires was founded by Pedro de Mendoza (1536); Francisco Pizarro founded Lima, the capital of Peru (1535), after seizing large quantities of gold at Cuzco; Hernando de Soto crossed the Mississippi River (1539); and Francisco Vásquez de Coronado explored the California coast (1540). During his reign, two viceroyalties, 29 governorships, four archbishoprics, and 24 bishoprics were formed; universities were founded at Santo Domingo (1536), Mexico (1551), and Peru (1551); and at Seville the *Casa de contratación* (bureau of trade) and the *Consejo de Indias* (council of the Indies) were set up for the central administration of the growing colonies. Merchant cargoes and—most important for the subsidy of Charles's wars—silver bullion from the mines of Zacatecas (Mexico) and Cerro Rico de Potosí (Bolivia) reached the ports of Spain. The wealth of the New World and the complication of its colonial government became the heritage of PHILIP II (*see* PATRONATO REAL).

Bibliography: W. BRADFORD, ed., *Correspondence of the Emperor Charles V . . .* (London 1850), also contains his itinerary from 1519 to 1551. K. LANZ, ed., *Correspondenz des Kaisers Karl V*, 3 v. (Leipzig 1844–46); *Staatspapiere zur Geschichte des Kaisers Karls V* (Stuttgart 1845). L. GROSS, ed., *Die Reichsregisterbücher Kaiser Karls V* (Vienna–Leipzig 1930). A. DE SANTA CRUZ, *Crónica del Emperador Carlos V*, 5 v. (Madrid 1920–25). P. MEXÍA, *Historia del Emperador Carlos V*, ed. J. DE MATA CARRIAZO (Madrid 1945). G. DE LEVA, *Storia documentata di Carlo V in correlazione all'Italia*, 5 v. (Venice 1863–94). H. BAUMGARTEN, *Geschichte Karls V*, 3 v. (Stuttgart 1885–92); *Karl V und die deutsche Reformation* (Halle 1889). W. ROBERTSON, *The History of the Reign of the Emperor Charles V*, 3 v. (Philadelphia 1902), with his life after abdication by W. H. PRESCOTT. P. RASSOW, *Die Kaiser-Idee Karls V* (Berlin 1932); *Die politische Welt Karls V* (Munich 1942); *Karl V, der letzte Kaiser des Mittelalters* (Göttingen 1957). A. HENNE, *Histoire du règne de Charles-Quint en Belgique*, 10 v. (Brussels 1858–60). F. CHABOD, *Lo stato di Milano nell'impero di Carlo V* (Rome 1934); *Per la storia religiosa dello stato di Milano durante il dominio di Carlo V* (Bologna 1938), heavily documented study of Counter Reformation in Milan. G. CONIGLIO, *Il regno di Napoli al tempo di Carlo V: Amministratione e vita economico-sociale* (Naples 1951). C. HARE, *A Great Emperor, Charles V, 1519–58* (New York 1917). H. JEDIN, *History of the Council of Trent*, tr. E. GRAF, 2 v. 1–2 (St. Louis 1957–60); *Geschichte des Konzils von Trient*, 2 v. (Freiburg 1949–57; v.1, 2d ed. 1951), 1 and 2. R. B. MERRIMAN, *The Rise of the Spanish Empire in the Old World and the New*, 4 v. (New York 1918–34) v. 3. M. SALOMIES, *Die Pläne Kaiser Karls V für eine Reichsreform mit Hilfe eines allgemeinen Bundes* (Helsinki 1953). H. HOLBORN, *A History of Modern Germany: The Reformation* (New York 1959). W. FRIEDENSBURG, *Kaiser Karl V und Papst Paul III* (Leipzig 1932). R. TYLER, *The Emperor Charles V* (Fair Lawn, N.J. 1956). P. RASSOW and F. SCHALK, eds., *Karl V: Der Kaiser und seine Zeit* (Cologne 1960), essays for the quadricentennial of his death. K. BRANDI, *The Emperor Charles V: The Growth and Destiny of a Man and a World-Empire*, tr. C. V. WEDGEWOOD (New York 1939).

[E. D. MCSHANE]

CHARLES I, KING OF ENGLAND

Second Stuart king of England; reigned 1625 to 1649; second son of James VI of Scotland (became James I of England, 1603) and Anne of Denmark; b. 1600, in Dunfermline, Scotland; executed, Jan. 30, 1649, in Whitehall, London, England. Charles was the younger of James's two sons, and became heir apparent to the thrones of Scotland and England when his older brother Henry died of typhus in November 1612. He was acclaimed Prince of Wales in 1616 and succeeded to the throne upon his father's death in March 1625.

Charles I was the inheritor of James I's confused religious and political policies. In 1623, James's desire for an alliance with Catholic Spain led him to dispatch Charles, and James's favorite, Buckingham, on a covert mission to the Spanish court to seek the hand of a Spanish princess. English support, however, for the Protestant side in the Thirty Years' War, plus the princess's decisive rejection of Charles's suit—she retired to a nunnery rather than meet the prince—ended the proposed alliance. Instead, shortly after his father's death, Charles married Henrietta Maria, daughter of the king of France. As part of the marriage pact, he secretly agreed to allow English Catholics to worship at the queen's private chapel and to raise his children as Catholics until they were at least 13. In doing so, however, he alienated Parliament, which passed anti-Catholic legislation in response. Charles also alienated the Catholic faction by dismissing Henrietta Maria's Catholic entourage and sending them back to France. By 1627 the religious conflict had led England into war with both France and Spain.

Charles favored the Anglican High Church and promoted many High churchmen to prominent offices in ecclesiastical and secular government. His most prominent appointee was William Laud, made archbishop of Canterbury in 1633, who was passionately opposed to the radical Protestant Puritans and used his position as privy counselor and judge of the Court of High Commission to suppress all Protestant forms of worship other than Anglicanism. Charles's support of his archbishop and administrator alienated both radical and moderate Protestants, who saw High Church love of ritual and display as a first step toward reconciliation with the Catholic church. Laud's policies, especially his enforcement of a Book of Common Prayer, led directly to the "Bishops' War" in Scotland and to the eventual Royalist defeat in the English Civil War.

Bibliography: M. HAVRAN, "The Character and Principles of an English King: The Case of Charles I," *Catholic Historical Review*, LXIX (April 1983) 169–208. L. J. REEVE, *Charles I and the Road to Personal Rule* (Cambridge, Eng. 1989). P. DONALD, *An Uncounselled King: Charles I and the Scottish Troubles, 1637–1641* (Cambridge, Eng. 1990). C. RUSSELL, *The Fall of the British Monarchies, 1637–1642* (Oxford 1991). J. DAVIES, *The Caroline Captivity of the Church: Charles I and the Remoulding of Anglicanism, 1625–1641* (Oxford 1992). K. M. SHARPE, *The Personal Rule of Charles I* (New Haven, Conn. 1992). C. CARLTON, *Charles I, the Personal Monarch* (2d ed. New York 1995). M. B. YOUNG, *Archives Photographiques* (New York 1997).

[K. R. SHEPHERD]

CHARLES II, KING OF ENGLAND

Reigned 1660 to 1685, second son of Charles I, of the royal house of Stuart, and Henrietta Maria; b. London, May 29, 1630; d. London, Feb. 6, 1685. The education of the young prince was cut short by the outbreak of the English Civil War in 1642. Young Charles took an active role in the struggle and witnessed a number of battles during the war. When his father's cause collapsed he fled the country and found a refuge on the Continent.

Following the execution of his father, Charles was proclaimed king in Scotland in February 1649. After extensive negotiations Charles accepted the condition of the Scots that he become a Presbyterian, and landed in that country in June 1650; he was finally crowned king at Scone on Jan. 1, 1651. The defeat of the Presbyterian forces by Oliver CROMWELL allowed Charles to assume command of the army, and he invaded England. Defeated at Worcester in September 1651 by Cromwell, Charles was forced to flee for his life. After some 40 days of wandering, he arrived safely in France. Often destitute, the king spent the next few years moving about the Continent seeking support. The death of Cromwell paved the way for his restoration. Charles landed at Dover in May 1660 to resume his throne. In May of the following year Charles married Catherine of Braganza, the daughter of the king of Portugal. They had no children; and although Charles showed the queen respect, he became notorious for the large number of mistresses he maintained.

It is doubtful whether Charles was ever deeply touched by any belief, but he was virtually a Catholic by the time he returned to England. In order to grant relief to the Catholics in England and to win the support of the Dissenters, Charles issued two Declarations of Indulgence in 1662 and 1672. Both of these met intense opposition in Parliament and resulted in the passage in 1673 of the Test Act, which was intended to bar Catholics from all governmental offices. The Popish Plot, a supposed conspiracy of Catholics to kill the king and other officials, was set off in 1678 by Titus Oates and other informers (*see* OATES PLOT). The news that the king's brother and heir-apparent, the Duke of York, later JAMES II, had become a Catholic led to an attempt in Parliament to exclude him from the throne. The exclusion failed, but the Whig and Tory political parties were born out of the struggle.

Charles triumphed over his opponents when public opinion switched to support the king and his brother with the discovery of the Rye House Plot, a Whig effort to assassinate the royal pair. John HUDDLESTON, OSB, Queen Catherine's chaplain, received Charles into the Roman Catholic Church on his deathbed.

Bibliography: J. A. WILLIAMS, "English Catholics under Charles II: The Legal Position," *Recusant History,* 7 (1963–64) 123–143. J. MILLER, *Popery and Politics in England, 1660–1688* (Cambridge Eng. 1973). A. FRASER, *Royal Charles: Charles II and the Restoration* (New York 1979). K. H. D. HALEY, *Politics in the Reign of Charles II* (New York 1985). J. R. JONES, *Charles II: Royal Politician* (London 1987). P. SEAWARD, *The Cavalier Parliament and the Reconstruction of the Old Regime* (Cambridge Eng. 1988). R. HUTTON, *Charles the Second: King of England, Scotland and Ireland* (Oxford 1989).

[A. M. SCHLEICH]

CHARLES MARTEL

A ruthless and successful warlord who played a pivotal role, as mayor of the palace (714–741), in the rise to royal and imperial rank of the CAROLINGIAN dynasty which carried his name (lat. *Carolus*); b. *c.* 688; d. Quierzy, Oct. 22, 741.

Charles Martel was the son of Pepin II by Alpaida, his concubine, or possible wife. Nothing is known of the first 26 years of Charles's life. In the turmoil following Pepin II's death, Charles was seen as a threat within the family by Plectrude, Pepin's widow, who had him imprisoned. He escaped from captivity and embarked on a career that the sources reveal in outline, but do not give enough detail to explain fully his remarkable success. We know that between 715 and 717 he consolidated his power in Austrasia, and that he did the same in Neustria between 718 and 719. During the years 720–741 he was able to assert his power in the outer regions of the Frankish kingdom and its neighbours.

Under a new MEROVINGIAN king, Chilperic II (715/6–721), Ragamfred, the Naustrian mayor of the palace, attacked Austrasia in association with his Friesian allies. Charles led the resistance to Radbod, but suffered his only recorded defeat. The Neustrian invaders reached Cologne and only withdrew after being given a large amount of treasure by Plectrude. On their return, they were ambushed successfully by Charles at Ambleve, near Malmedy, in the heart of Pepinid territory. Early in the following year, Charles took the war to Ragamfred, defeating the Neustrians at Vinchy, near Cambrai (April 717). He secured control of his father's treasure from Plectrude and raised up Chlothar IV, a Merovingian of questionable ancestry, as the first Austrasian king in four decades. Charles was now the undisputed leader of Austrasia and the Pepinids.

Over the next two years, Charles extended his control over Neustria. On the convenient, if suspicious, death of the Austrasian king Chlothar IV in 718, Charles acted as mayor of the palace to a single Merovingian ruler,

Chilperic II, claiming hegemony over the whole Frankish kingdom. Charles was helped in strengthening the central authority by three factors: the residual strength of the idea that the kingdom was a single political community, fears among the regional nobility at a breakdown of social order, and the threat of Muslim attack. Nevertheless, the sheer size of the territory he aspired to control meant that Charles was committed to constant and repetitive campaigning on the periphery of the Frankish kingdom.

Charles and his successors earned much prestige by their campaigns against non-Christian groups (Muslims, Frisians, and Saxons) that combined military success with religious zeal. Traditionally, the greatest of Charles's military achievements was held to be his defeat of a Muslim army at Poitiers in October 732. For Edward Gibbon, it was one of the world's decisive victories for having saved Western Christendom from a seemingly relentless Muslim advance from recently-conquered Visigothic Spain. Recent research has questioned the location, date, and significance of the battle. Raids into Frankish territory continued for some years until they were effectively stopped during the 740s by civil war in Spain while Septimania, the region between the Rhone delta and the Pyrenees that had been part of the Visigothic kingdom, remained under Muslim control until 759, in the reign of Charles's son, PEPIN III. The immediate consequence of Charles's victory was that it asserted his power in Aquitaine. This advance was not entirely welcome to some local Christian rulers, such as Maurontus of Marseilles, who were prepared to cooperate with Muslim allies in resistance. Nevertheless, in the nineth century, Charles's military success earned him the title 'the Hammer' (lat. *Martellus*).

In 739 Charles's reputation as an outstanding warrior prompted Pope Gregory III (715–731) to send him embassies, bearing such valuable relics as the keys to Saint Peter's tomb and links from his chains, in order to solicit aid against the encroaching Lombard king, Liutprand. Nothing seems to have come of this. Charles may well have preferred to retain the Lombards as allies in view of the help they had recently given him during his campaign against the Muslims in Provence. The close alliance between the papacy and the Franks, with its momentous consequences for western Christianity, was not to be forged until the time of Pepin III (751–768).

Like his father, Charles Martel offered support to missionaries, especially those from England. There were two Anglo-Saxon groups, one led by WILLIBRORD, active in Frisia from 690 to 739, and the other by BONIFACE, active in Friesia, Hesse, and Thuringia from 716 to 753. Their missionary work produced social and religious changes that smoothed the integration of peripheral areas into the Frankish world. Perhaps their greatest achievements lay in reorganizing the Church in nominally Christian areas. From the 660's the papacy had been more active in its relations with Europe beyond the Alps, but it now came into closer contact with Charles Martel, his sons, and the whole Frankish kingdom through these missionaries. From Boniface, too, there is a sharply critical picture of a lax Frankish church, which is not entirely justified.

From the time that he achieved supreme power in the Frankish kingdom, Charles was identified by various titles such as 'duke' (lat. *dux*) or 'prince' (lat. *princeps*), but never as king (lat. *rex*). He took great care to legitimize his position by acting under the nominal authority of a Merovingian ruler: Chlothar IV (717–718), Chilperic II (716–721), and Theuderic IV (721–737). From 737 until his death in 741, Charles operated without a Merovingian on the throne.

Any assessment of the career and significance of Charles Martel is complicated by the nature of the sources, which are overwhelmingly written with a bias that justifies the end of the Merovingian dynasty and glorifies the rise of the Carolingians. Charles is celebrated, paradoxically, as a champion of Christianity against nonbelievers, but also as a great despoiler of Church property. As a way of reconciling these opposing views, the German historian Heinrich Brunner argued, in 1887, that Charles had taken land from the Church in order to lease it to his followers, giving them the resources to create a more costly cavalry army that was superior to its opponents. A more modern twist has been to take the introduction of stirrups as a technological stimulus to this change. The social and economic consequences were profound, giving birth to a society based on the holding of land in return for military service.

Recent work has shown, however, that there is no evidence to support these views. Charles's reputation as a despoiler of Church lands was developed in the mid-ninth century by Archbishop Hincmar of Rheims (845–882), who used earlier sources to castigate the Carolingian rulers of his own time for their abuses. The rise of Charles Martel can be explained through his success on the battlefield, his ruthless political skill and the consequent accumulation of resources, especially through the reunification of Austrasia and Neustria, which attracted supporters in increasing numbers. While Charles was prepared to punish opponents and reward allies with Church land, there is no evidence that he systematically followed such a policy, nor that he was the first to do so. Charles consolidated his power by alliances with key bishops, abbots and magnates. If the age of Charles Martel ushered in change, there were, nevertheless, fundamental continuities between the Merovingian and Carolingian worlds. Charles was buried at the royal monastery of St. Denis among the Merovingian kings.

Bibliography: P. FOURACRE, *The Age of Charles Martel* (London and New York 2000). R. A. GEBERDING, *The Rise of the Carolingians and the Liber Historiae Francorum* (Oxford 1987). R. MCKITTERICK, *The Frankish Kingdom under the Carolingians* (London and New York 1983). I. N. WOOD, *The Merovingian Kingdoms 450–751* (London and New York 1994).

[J. WREGLESWORTH]

CHARLES OF BLOIS, BL.

Claimant of the Duchy of Brittany, Franciscan tertiary; b. *c.* 1319; d. Auray, Sept. 29, 1364. He was the son of Guy of Châtillon, Count of Blois, and Margaret of Valois, Philip VI's sister. Charles married Joan of Penthièvre (Brittany), and they had five children. Supported by France, he was engaged from 1341 in constant war for his wife's and his own succession to Brittany against the de Montforts aided by Edward III of England. From 1347 to 1356 he was an English captive; when he was killed in 1364, his wife surrendered her claim to John IV de Montfort in 1365. Charles supported vigorously the cause of St. IVO of Brittany, canonized 1347. His contemporaries respected him as a saint and wonder-worker. After his death an extraordinary cult developed, propagated by the Franciscan Order; but in 1368, at Duke John de Montfort's urging, it was condemned by URBAN V as premature and uncanonical. Investigations of his cause were interrupted by the Great Schism; the cult was authorized only in 1904. Charles is buried at Graces near Guicamp.

Feast: Sept. 29; June 20 (Blois); Oct. 14 (Vannes).

Bibliography: J.-C. CASSARD, *Charles de Blois* (Brest 1994). L. MAÎTRE, ''Répertorium analytique des actes du règne de Charles de Blois'' in *Bulletin de la Société archéologique de Nantes* (1904). F. PLAINE, ed., *Monuments du procès de canonisation du bienheureux Charles de Blois* (Saint-Brieuc 1921). B. A. POCQUET DU HAUT-JUSSÉ, ''La *Sainteté* de Charles de Blois,'' *Revue des questions historiques* 105 (1926) 108–114. E. DÉPREZ, *La ''Querelle de Bretagne'' de la captivité de Charles de Blois à la majorité de Jean IV de Montfort, 1347–1362* (Rennes 1926). F. BAIX, *Dictionnaire d'histoire et de géographie ecclésiastiques,* ed. A. BAUDRILLART (Paris 1912–) 9:223–228.

[V. I. J. FLINT]

CHARLES OF SEZZE, ST.

Franciscan lay brother and ascetical writer; b. Sezze, Italy, Oct. 19, 1613; d. Rome, Italy, Jan. 6, 1670. Raised by devout parents, Gian Carlo Marchionne had only a few years' schooling, followed by farmwork, before joining the Reformed Franciscan province in Rome in 1635. In ten years of extreme asceticism and intense interior life at small friaries in Latium, he advanced through acquired and infused contemplation into the prayer of ecstatic union. During a Mass in 1648 he received the mystical grace of the Wound of Love: a dart of light from the consecrated Host pierced his heart. From 1646 until his death, he resided at San Francesco a Ripa or San Pietro in Montorio, Rome. Under obedience he wrote five long treatises on the spiritual life in a relatively simple and clear style. His major published works were *Trattato delle tre vie della meditazione* (Rome 1654, 1664, 1742); *Camino interno dell'anima* (Rome 1664); and *Settenari sacri* (Rome 1666). From 1661 to 1665, when his soul had attained the transforming union, he wrote an autobiography, *Le grandezze delle misericordie di Dio,* which has been compared favorably with that of St. Teresa of Avila for its masterful analyses of the successive phases of mystical union. His eminently Franciscan ascetical and mystical theology have been judged sound, substantial, and practical. Innocent X, Alexander VII, and Clement IX valued his company and counsel. A hard nail-shaped growth of flesh was observed under his left breast after his death and was eventually accepted as one of the two miracles required for his beatification (1882). He was canonized by John XXIII on April 12, 1959.

Feast: Jan. 19.

Bibliography: *Opere complete,* ed. R. SBARDELLA, v. 1–2 *Le grandezze delle misericordie di Dio* (Rome 1963–65), with important introd., biog., and extensive bibliog; *Autobiography* (abr.), tr. L. PEROTTI (Chicago 1963). V. VENDITTI, *S. Carlo da Sezze* (Turin 1959). R. BROWN, *The Wounded Heart: St. Charles of Sezze* (Chicago 1960).

[R. BROWN]

CHARLES OF THE ASSUMPTION (CHARLES DE BRYAS)

Theologian; b. Saint-Ghislain, Belgium, 1625; d. Douai, France, Feb. 23, 1686. He entered upon a military career, was captured in a battle against the French near Lens, France, and was taken as a prisoner to Paris. After his release he was inspired, perhaps by the death of his uncle, to join the Discalced Carmelites at Douai (1653). After his ordination in 1659, he requested permission to become a missionary in Persia, but he was assigned to teach theology at Douai instead. He became prior of this community and served two terms as provincial superior of the Carmelites in Belgium and France. His first works, published under the pseudonym Germanus Philalethes Eupistinus, placed him in the middle of the fray over predestination and grace. His first book, *Auctoritas contra praedeterminationem physicam pro scientia media* (Douai 1669), defended the *scientia media*, that is, the doctrine that teaches that God sees not merely all possible and actual situations in the universe He created, but also what a person would do if placed in various circumstances with different graces; He then predestines by merely actualizing one of these orders. Charles's second work, *Scientia media ad examen revocata* (Douai 1670), manifests some of his doubts about the *scientia media*. Charles, attacked by the Dominican Jerome Henneguier for his defense of MOLINISM, reversed his position in his third book, *Thomistarum Triumphus* (2 v. Douai 1670–73), and defended the idea of the *praedeterminatio physica*, that is, God predestines not by means of the *scientia media* but through a modality of grace that infallibly brings the subject to whom it is given to cooperate freely with it. Having been confronted with an attack by the Jesuit Fourmestraux, he published two new works, *Thomistarum Triumphus in perpetuum firmatus* (Douai 1674) and *Funiculus triplex* (Cambrai 1675), indicating his firm adhesion to the Bañezian doctrine of *praedeterminatio physica* (*see* BÁÑEZ AND BAÑEZIANISM). In 1678, as provincial, he published, without the permission of higher superiors, his famous *Pentalogus diaphoricus* in which he declared that a penitent who confesses the same mortal sins week after week ought to be absolved without any hesitation by the confessor. This book was publicly burned by the superior general of the Carmelites, Emmanuel of Jesus, and in 1684 it was placed on the Index until it should be corrected. The reason for the condemnation was brought out by the theologians who attacked it. Among these was the Bishop of Tournai, Gilbert de CHOISEUL DU PLESSIS PRASLIN. He stated that sufficient emphasis was not placed on the idea that a penitent must sincerely intend to avoid sin and take what measures he can to carry out this purpose of amendment. In an exchange of publications with Gilbert, Charles, with permission of the general, published a further explanation of his doctrine, *Éclaircissement* (Lille 1682). This attracted the attention of the famous Jansenist Anthony ARNAULD and elicited from him a sharp response. In his final works, seeking approval for his doctrine, Charles made appeals to the bishop of Arras and the king of France.

Bibliography: E. MANGENOT, *Dictionnaire de théologie catholique* 2.2:2272–74. H. HURTER, *Nomenclator literarius theologiae catholicae* 4:325–327.

[C. MEYER]

CHARLES OF VILLERS, BL.

Abbot; b. Cologne, Germany; d. Hocht near Maastricht, Netherlands, *c.* 1215. He entered the CISTERCIAN Abbey of HIMMEROD *c.* 1184–85 and visited the monastery of Stromberg in 1188, and in 1191 he was at the Abbey of HEISTERBACH, where he served as prior. The Abbey of VILLERS enjoyed its golden age from 1197 to 1209 under Charles, although he is not responsible for the construction of the great abbey church there. He resigned his office as abbot in 1209 and returned to Himmerod, but he was soon summoned from retirement to make the foundation at Hocht, where he is buried.

Feast: Jan. 29.

Bibliography: *Monumenta Germaniae Historica: Scriptores* 25:220–226. É. DE MOREAU, *L'Abbaye de Villers-en-Brabant* (Brussels 1909) 40–50. A. ZIMMERMANN, *Kalendarium Benedictinum: Die Heiligen und Seligen des Benediktinerordens und seiner Zweige* 1:141–143. K. SPAHR, *Lexikon für Theologie und Kirche*[2] 5:1362.

[B. D. HILL]

CHARLEVOIX, PIERRE FRANÇOIS XAVIER DE

Jesuit educator and historian; b. Saint-Quentin, France, Oct. 24, 1682; d. La Flèche, France, Feb. 1, 1761. The son of François de Charlevoix, deputy attorney general, and Antoinette (Forestier) de Charlevoix, he entered the Society of Jesus in Paris in 1698. He was sent to Canada, where he taught in the Jesuit college at Quebec from 1705 to 1709. After returning to France in 1709, he was assigned to the College of Louis-le-Grand, Paris. In 1720 he was commissioned by the French government to return to New France to seek a new route to the Western sea. In the pursuit of this goal, he journeyed through the Great Lakes and down the Mississippi River, reaching New Orleans early in 1722. He returned to France the following year to report his lack of success, but expressed his readiness to continue the mission, an offer that was not accepted. He resumed his teaching career for a time and then served as editor (1733–55) of Mémoires de Trévoux, a monthly journal published by the Jesuits from 1701 to 1762.

Charlevoix's published works include *Histoire de l'éstablissement, des progrès et de la décadence du christianisme dans l'empire du Japon* (Paris 1715), revised as *Histoire et description générale du Japon* (Paris 1736); *La vie de la Mère Marie de l'Incarnation* (Paris 1724); *Histoire de l'Isle Espagnole ou de Saint Domingue* (Paris 1730); *Histoire et description générale de la Nouvelle France* (Paris 1744); and *Histoire du Paraguay* (Paris 1756). *His Histoire de la Nouvelle France,* the first general history of Canada to be published, was translated into English by J. G. Shea (6 v. New York 1866–72; new ed.

New York 1900). The appendix of the original contained the journal of his American voyage in the form of a series of letters to the Duchess de Lesdiguières, compiled to describe the country through which he journeyed as well as the lives and customs of the inhabitants, both native and European-born. It had a separate title, *Journal historique* (1744); it was first translated into English and published in London (1761), and later edited by Louise P. Kellogg (Chicago 1923).

Bibliography: J. E. ROY, "Essai sur Charlevoix," *Transactions of the Royal Society of Canada,* ser. 3, v.1 (1907). C. SOMMER-VOGEL et al., *Bibliothèque de la Compagnie de Jésus,* 11 v. (Brussels-Paris 1890–1932) 2:1075–80.

[R. N. HAMILTON]

CHARLOTTE, DIOCESE OF

The Diocese of Charlotte (*Dioecesis Charlottensis*), encompassing the forty-six counties of western North Carolina, was canonically erected on Nov. 12, 1971 as a suffragan see of the Archdiocese of Atlanta, Georgia. The territory of the new diocese was taken from that of the Diocese of Raleigh, and its first bishop, Michael J. Begley, a priest of the new diocese, was consecrated on Jan. 12, 1972. At the time of its foundation, the diocese included only 35,585 Catholics in a total population of 2,727,500, served by 45 diocesan and 27 religious priests. By the beginning of the new millennium more than 129,000 Catholics were registered in the parishes and missions of the diocese (in a general population of nearly four million persons), and there were 57 diocesan, 11 extern, and 64 religious priests constituting the local presbyterate. In addition, 66 permanent deacons were serving within the diocese. Some of the increase in the number of religious priests is explained by the fact that prior to Begley's retirement in 1984, the *abbatia nullius* status of Belmont Abbey (Benedictine) had been suppressed (1977).

John F. Donoghue, former vicar general of Washington, D.C., was consecrated the second bishop of Charlotte in December of 1984. During his administration, the diocese established its own newspaper, the *Catholic News and Herald*, thus ending its joint venture with the Diocese of Raleigh's *North Carolina Catholic*, in 1991. When Donoghue was named the archbishop of Atlanta in 1993, he was succeeded in February 1994 by William J. Curlin, an auxiliary bishop of the Archdiocese of Washington, D.C., who thus became the third bishop of Charlotte.

The most significant growth in population within the diocese has been focused in the Charlotte metropolitan area, the area of the "Triad" (i.e., the region formed by Greensboro, High Point, and Winston-Salem), and the mountainous region of Asheville and its surrounding communities. Hispanic migrant workers and immigrants, responding to the labor opportunities caused by economic and population expansion, entered the diocese in large numbers, especially during the last twenty years of the century. The diocese has responded with a variety of initiatives in Hispanic ministry. There are also apostolates organized for Korean and Vietnamese Catholics. In 2000 there were 67 parishes and 24 missions, one college (Belmont Abbey), two high schools, and 15 elementary schools.

In marked contrast to the numeric and institutional growth is the decline in the number of women religious in the diocese. In 1971, there were 249 Sisters, while in 2000 there were only 123 women religious in the diocese, 37 of who were in residence at the motherhouse of the Sisters of Mercy of the Americas, Regional Community of North Carolina. One of the only two new foundations of women religious in recent years was established by Mother M. Teresa, M. C., and Bishop Curlin in 1996, when four Missionary of Charity Sisters arrived to serve the needs of the poor in the city of Charlotte. In 1999 the Sisters of St. Vincent, another religious community of women with its roots in India, was founded at Christ the King Parish in High Point, N.C.

[J. F. GARNEAU]

CHARNEL HOUSE

In the Middle Ages, a structure (called *carnarium, oss[u]arium*) attached to a church, to the churchyard wall, or free standing, used for depositing bones, especially painted or inscribed skulls, that might be thrown up when new graves were being opened. The use of charnel houses was obligatory in certain parts of Germany (synods of Münster, 1279 and Cologne, 1280), and customary throughout Christian Europe. Very early, chantry chapels were attached to the charnel houses, sometimes as an upper story, where Masses for the dead were read and a sanctuary light was kept burning. The walls were usually painted with scenes representing purgatory, the Last Judgment, and similar subjects. The chapels were usually tended by members of pious societies or brotherhoods. There were several architectural forms for charnel houses: chapels, niches, and crypts. Many of them were destroyed during the Reformation, and then rebuilt in the 17th and 18th centuries, but during the Enlightenment they fell into desuetude. In popular belief, charnel houses were the meeting place of the poor souls who were supposedly freed from purgatory from Saturday night until Monday morning and during Embertide.

See Also: CEMETERIES, CANON LAW OF.

Bone–covered floor of the charnel house of Monastery of Saint Catherine, Sinai, Egypt. (©Jeffrey L. Rofman/CORBIS)

Bibliography: H. BÄCHTOLD-STÄUBLI, ed., *Handwörterbuch des deutschen Aberglaubens,* 10 v. (Leipzig 1927–42) 5:1427. *Reallexikon zur deutschen Kunstgeschichte,* ed. O. SCHMITT (Stuttgart 1937–) v. 2. W. PESSLER, *Handbuch der deutschen Volkskunde,* 3 v. (Potsdam 1938). A. L. VEIT and L. LENHART, *Kirche und Volksfrömmigkeit im Zeitalter des Barock* (Freiburg 1956) 138. H. SCHAUERTE, *Lexikon für Theologie und Kirche,* ed. J. HOFER and K. RAHNER, 10 v. (2d, new ed. Freiburg 1957–65) 2:133–134.

[M. F. LAUGHLIN]

CHARPENTIER, MARC ANTOINE

Baroque composer noted for his oratorios; b. Paris, *c.* 1634; d. Paris, Feb. 24, 1704. He was a versatile and artistic man who had intended to become a painter, but he studied music in Italy with CARISSIMI and became the leader of the Italian camp in the war between French and Italian tastes. His career included posts with the Princesse de Guise and the Duc d'Orléans (later regent), then at the Jesuit College, and finally, in 1698, at Sainte-Chapelle.

A fecund composer, Charpentier produced both sacred and secular forms, including Masses, motets, *Leçons de ténèbres,* a Magnificat, a *Te Deum,* cantatas, many theater works (an opera, *Medée,* was produced in Paris in 1693), songs, and occasional pieces, in addition to the two dozen oratorios (*Histoires sacrées*), of which *La Reniement de St. Pierre* (The Denial of St. Peter) is best known. Although the grand motet was to become the great form of the "spiritual concerts" of the next century, the motets of M. R. de Lalande, J. J. de Mondonville, and others owe much to Charpentier's oratorios, works of rare delineation and power.

Bibliography: P. PINEAU, ed., *Musique d'Église des XVIIᵉ et XVIIIᵉ siècles,* ser. A. of *Repertoire de musique religieuse et spirituelle,* ed. H. EXPERT (Paris 1913). C. CRUSSARD, *Un Musicien français oublié, Marc-Antoine Charpentier* (Paris 1945). R. W. LOWE, *L'Oeuvre dramatique de Marc-Antoine Charpentier* (Paris 1964). H. W. HITCHCOCK, *The Latin Oratorios of Marc Antoine Charpentier* (Doctoral diss. microfilm; University of Michigan 1954); "The Latin Oratorios," *Musical Quarterly* 41 (1955) 41–65. *Histoire de* *la musique*, ed. ROLAND-MANUEL, 2 v. (Paris 1960–63) v. 1; v. 9, 16 of *Encyclopédie de la Pléiade*. C. STAINER et al., *Grove's Dictionary of Music and Musicians*, ed. E. BLOM, 9 v. (5th ed. London 1954) 2:187–189. J. DURON, "Marc-Antoine Charpentier: *Mors Saülis et Jonathae-David et Jonathas*, de l'histoire sacrée à l'opéra biblique," *Revue de Musicologie*, 77 (1991) 221–268. W. H. HITCHCOCK, "Marc-Antoine Charpentier: Mémoire and Index," *Recherches sur la Musique française classique*, 23 (1985) 5–44; *Marc-Antoine Charpentier* (Oxford 1990). D. OGLESBY, "Marc-Antoine Charpentier," in *International Dictionary of Opera*, ed. C. S. LARUE 2 v. (Detroit 1993) 241–243. J. S. POWELL, "La *Sérénade* pour *Le Sicilien* de M. A. Charpentier et le crépuscule de la comédie-ballet," *Revue de Musicologie*, 77 (1991) 88–96. G. SADLER and S. THOMPSON, "Marc-Antoine Charpentier and the Basse Continue," *Basler Jahrbuch für Historische Musikpraxis*, 18 (1994) 31–45.

[E. BORROFF]

CHARRON, PIERRE

Philosopher and theologian, whose writings are important in the development of modern philosophical skepticism; b. Paris, 1541; d. Paris, Nov. 16, 1603. He was one of 25 children. He studied at Paris, Orléans, Bourges, and Montpellier, receiving a law degree in 1571. Earlier he had become a priest; he was renowned as a preacher and theologian, serving Queen Marguerite of Navarre as preacher-in-ordinary, as theological adviser in several dioceses, and as canon in Bordeaux. In 1589 he tried to retire to a monastic life, but was refused because of his age. He met M. E. de MONTAIGNE in the 1580s, and became his close friend and disciple.

Charron's major writings are *Les trois vérités* (1593), *Discours Chrétiens* (1600), and *De la Sagesse* (1601). The first is primarily an attack on Calvinism, arguing against atheists, non-Christians, and non-Catholics. Charron contended that man cannot have rational knowledge of God because of man's limitations and God's immensity. Hence, he asserted, He can be known only by faith. Atheists, non-Christians and non-Catholics all presume, he claimed, to possess actually unattainable rational knowledge. The *Discours Chrétiens* consists of pious discussions of theological and religious questions. *De la Sagesse*, his most famous work, presents Montaigne's skepticism about knowledge in didactic form. Wisdom, Charron argued, leads to complete doubt, and prepares man to receive revelation by freeing him from all prejudices and wrong opinions. The highest wisdom, prior to receiving revelation, is doubting all rational claims, and living according to nature, like the "noble savage." *De la Sagesse* was extremely popular in the 17th century, and greatly influenced modern philosophical thought by its critique of knowledge, its "method of doubt," and its presentation of a natural morality.

See Also: SKEPTICISM

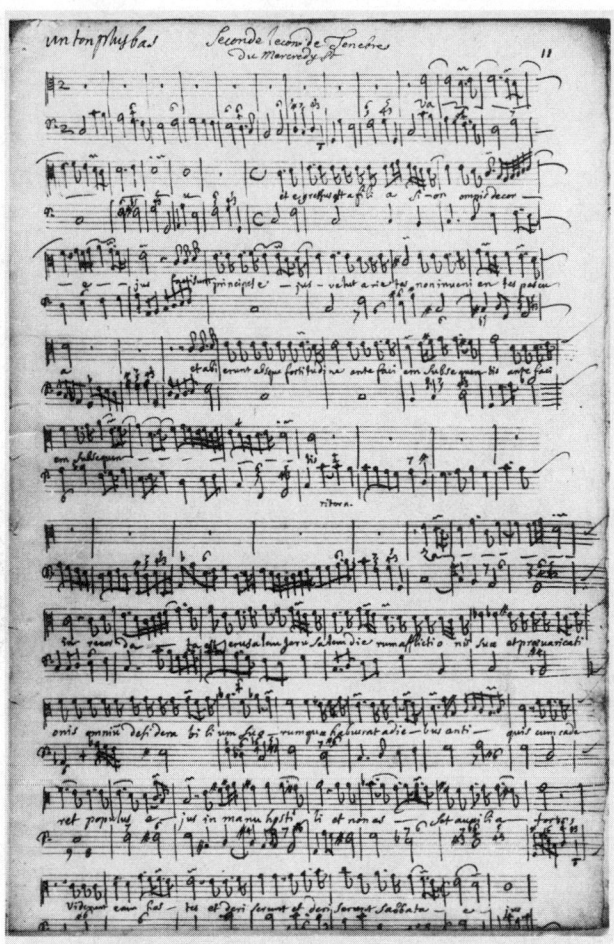

Manuscript page of sheet music from "Second Lesson of Tenerae for Holy Wednesday," holograph, by Marc Antoine Charpentier.

Bibliography: *Oeuvres* (Paris 1635). R. H. POPKIN, *History of Scepticism from Erasmus to Descartes* (Assen 1960). J. B. SABRIÉ, *De l'humanisme au rationalisme: Pierre Charron* (Paris 1913).

[R. H. POPKIN]

CHARTRES [CATHEDRAL]

Nôtre-Dame de Chartres, one of the supreme monuments of Gothic architecture, embodies in its different sections a history of this style from the 12th through the 16th century, with outstanding examples of architecture, sculpture, and stained glass, for the most part well preserved.

Erected above a grotto associated with the legend of the Druidic shrine of a *Virgo paritura*, the cathedral is the successor of several early Christian structures. It occupies the highest elevation in the town and dominates the countryside of Beauce; the contrasting 12th- and 16th-

Scene from the "Life of Saint Eustace," lancet window, Chartres Cathedral, Chartres, France, 13th century. (© Dean Conger/ CORBIS)

century towers of its west façade are visible for miles around the town.

Although the main body of the structure, including nave, transept, and chevet, dates from the 13th century, the west façade remains from a 12th-century church destroyed by fire in 1194. It retains the extraordinary sculptural ensemble of the Royal Portal, dominated by solemn, elongated figures representing Old Testament figures of Kings and Queens of Juda, royal ancestors of Christ. Above the three doorways of the portal are three stained glass windows (*c.* 1150), whose subject matter echoes the main themes of the sculpture, the royal genealogy and life of Christ and the Virgin Mary. These windows, depicting the Tree of Jesse, the Life of Our Lord, and the Passion, constitute, with the rose window above (*c.* 1200), the finest group of early Gothic windows in existence.

The interior, 428 feet by 105 feet (150 feet at the transepts), and 120 feet high, creates an overwhelming impression. No other cathedral possesses a comparable ensemble of 12th- and 13th-century stained glass. The subdued light, rich with the reds and blues of the windows, creates a mystical atmosphere consonant with the faith and its liturgical forms. Notable among the 176 windows are the rose of France of the north transept, donated by Blanche of Castille, and the rose of the south transept (the Triumph of Christ), a gift of the Count of Dreux, both dating from the early 13th century. The "Nôtre-Dame de la Belle Verrière," a window saved from the 12th-century church, is now in the south ambulatory.

The sculpture of the portals of the north and south transepts, with figures drawn from the Old and New Testaments and from the *Golden Legend* (1300–35), marks a tendency in Gothic art toward greater naturalism in proportion and bodily movement, without forsaking strong idealism. Completing the encyclopedic range of sculpture in the cathedral are numerous scenes from the life of

Christ and the Virgin on the choir screen between the sanctuary and the ambulatory, examples of the *détente* style which was popular in the early 16th century.

North of the chevet is the old episcopal palace (17th century), now a museum of art and history. The nearby church of St. Pierre (12th–13th centuries) contains good examples of 14th-century stained glass (*see* STAINED GLASS).

Bibliography: H. ADAMS, *Mont Saint Michel and Chartres* (Washington 1904). Y. DELAPORTE and E. HOUVET, *Les Vitraux de la cathédrale de Chartres*, 4 v. (Chartres 1926). L. GRODECKI, *Chartres*, tr. K. DELAVENAY (New York 1963). A. E. KATZENELLEN-BOGEN, *The Sculptural Program of Chartres Cathedral* (Baltimore 1959).

[J. R. JOHNSON]

CHARTRES [HISTORY]

Town on the Eure River, 48 miles southwest of Paris; capital of Eure-et-Loire Department, which comprises the Diocese of Chartres (*Carnutensis*). The state of the Carnutes, which included Orléans (*Genabum*) and Chartres (*Autricum*), was reorganized before 400 to form the *civitas Aurelianorum,* while Chartres came under SENS, to which the see was suffragan until 1622; thereafter it was suffragan to Paris.

Chartres was sacked by Burgundy (600), by Aquitaine (743), by Normans (858) and after sustaining a Norman attack in 911, by the Duke of Normandy in 963. Its counts, in the tenth century, ruled Blois and Champagne. As an intellectual center in the 11th and 12th centuries, Chartres was united to the crown of France (1286) and given a town charter. The English held Chartres from 1417 to 1432. It was made a duchy in 1528, survived a Huguenot siege in 1568 and then lost its particular history with the accession of the Bourbons; Henry IV was consecrated king in Chartres (1594). Although the French Revolution was not violent in Chartres, documents were systematically destroyed; the library was destroyed in World War II.

The Church was organized in Chartres probably with the peace of Constantine (311–313), but paganism was still a problem at the time of the first known bishop, Valentinus (*c.* 400). St. Solemnis has been associated with the conversion of CLOVIS; St. LEOBIN (*c.* 550) was the first to fix the borders of the diocese, and Pappolus thwarted an attempt to detach Chateaudun as a separate see (573). The Merovingians founded a number of monasteries in the diocese, which by 1272 had 921 parish churches. Blois was detached as a see in 1697. In the Diocese of Chartres, 810 parishes had been formed by 1789.

It was a rich town in Carolingian days and counts of Chartres shared lordship of the town with its famous bish-ops and the powerful cathedral chapter. The chapter, which benefited from pilgrimages and fairs, contested authority with the bishops (1300–1700). The number of religious houses increased through the Middle Ages and religious practice in Chartres seems to have been active at the time of the Reformation. Protestantism, which appeared in 1523, was strong enough to warrant a church in Chartres (1559). Reorganization of Huguenots after the Edict of NANTES (1598) was countered by the establishment of more religious houses and a seminary (1659). By 1789 materialism and the lack of pastoral care had weakened religious life; 82 percent of the clergy accepted the CIVIL CONSTITUTION OF THE CLERGY. The Concordat of 1801 assigned Chartres to Versailles, but the see was restored in 1821.

The schools of Chartres may have been well known at the time of St. Betharius (*c.* 600), whose ninth-century vita lacks credibility. An episcopal school dating from the tenth century became famous under Bishops FULBERT (d. 1028) and IVO (d. 1116). For its chancellors it had BERNARD, GILBERT DE LA PORRÉE and THIERRY; and educated students such as BERENGARIUS, WILLIAM OF CONCHES, BERNARD SILVESTRIS and CLARENBAUD OF ARRAS. By the late 12th century Chartres was in the shadow of the University of PARIS but through its *magistri* retained its importance; JOHN OF SALISBURY and PETER OF CELLE were bishops of Chartres. Humanism based on the study of classical authors and the philosophy of PLATO, BOETHIUS and MACROBIUS characterized Chartres, which inclined to REALISM in the UNIVERSALS controversy; ARISTOTLE's logic was also studied. With translations by CONSTANTINE the African, and Herman of Dalmatia available, medicine and natural science, too, were studied. Secular studies in general were pursued to confirm the harmony between faith and reason, between Biblical revelation and Platonic cosmology. Holy Scripture and the Fathers were also read.

According to a legend based on a chronicle of 1389 and works of 1609 and 1664, Druids in Chartres had a statue on an altar in a grotto dedicated to a *Virgo paritura c.* 100 B.C. They were evangelized by martyrs *c.* A.D. 44, and sent an embassy to the Blessed Virgin, who, in a letter written in Hebrew, was said to have accepted coronation as their queen. A 1389 statue of her, burned in 1793, was replaced in 1855. Chartres also has possessed a "tunic" of the Blessed Virgin, which, according to 12th-century tradition, was given to the cathedral by Charles the Bald in 876 and enclosed in a casket in the 11th century. The relic was cut up and dispersed in 1793, but part of it has been recovered. Pilgrimages, at a peak in the 12th and 13th centuries, came to an end with the Revolution. The crypt was restored in 1860, and the pilgrimages, especially among students, have revived. A miraculous well in Chartres, reputedly the resting place of martyrs in the 1st century and victims of the Normans in 858, had a hospital associated with it from the 11th century, where sisters cared for pilgrims and the sick until the Revolution.

Bibliography: U. TURCK and L. OTT, *Lexikon für Theologie und Kirche*, eds., J. HOFER and K. RAHNER, 10 v. (2d, new ed. Freiburg 1957–65) 2:1034–35. T. DELAPORTE, *Dictionnaire d'histoire et de géographie ecclésiastiques*, ed. A. BAUDRILLART et al., (Paris 1912–) 12:544–574. A. CLERVAL, *Les Écoles de Chartres au moyen-âge* (Chartres 1895). M. MANITIUS, *Geschichte der lateinischen Literatur des Mittelalters,* 3 v. (Munich 1911–31) 3:196–220. E. JARRY et al., *Catholicisme,* 2:999–1006.

[E. P. COLBERT]

CHARTULARY

A medieval manuscript register or volume containing the muniments of the owner, i.e., copies of original title deeds and other documents relating to the foundation, property, privileges, and legal rights of ecclesiastical establishments, municipal and other corporations, colleges, universities, or private parties (also cartulary, Lat. *cartularium, pancarta, codex diplomaticus*). The great majority of such documents are in the diplomatic form of the charter (*carta*), hence the name chartulary for such a collection. The typical chartulary is a businesslike manuscript, written in an ordinary charter hand similar to that of the original documents and containing few or no illustrations, rubrications, or decorated initial letters. However, some chartularies (often later ones that are copies of earlier chartularies rather than immediate copies of original documents) are written in fine book hands and provided with elegant illuminated decorations and illustrations.

There are several types of chartularies. General chartularies were intended to contain all of the archives of the owner, often arranged chronologically but sometimes according to the places to which documents refer, or else according to subject matter or to the grantors of the charters. Most frequently some combination of these factors governs the internal arrangement. Because general chartularies, especially those of ecclesiastical houses, tended to be unmanageably large—extending to several volumes or being contained in a single volume of enormous dimensions—they were often replaced or supplemented by special chartularies. These contain documents of one particular nature, sometimes corresponding with a specific chest or receptacle employed for storage of the originals. Thus a special chartulary might be reserved for all papal, episcopal, royal, or other privileges, or for all documents relating to a single place or endowment. Other special chartularies contain records (plus memoranda) pertaining

to recurring administrative problems or legal disputes. Their contents vary according to the nature of their purpose: privileges, title deeds, compositions, ordinations, material relating to tithes, pensions, rents, surveys and extents, extracts from plea rolls, other records of legal proceedings, etc. Another type is the combination chronicle-chartulary, in which the documents serve to illustrate a running account of the foundation and subsequent growth of the house. In some sections (usually the earlier parts) the narrative will be little more than some brief notes between the charters, in others the narrative almost supersedes the records.

Some form of chartulary may have existed as early as the 6th century (GREGORY OF TOURS refers to *chartarum tomi*), but the oldest surviving chartularies date from the 11th or, in a very few cases, from the 9th and 10th centuries. The great majority of extant manuscripts are of the 13th century and later.

Chartularies by their very nature are extremely rich historical sources; nevertheless, they must be used with caution. Forgeries, which often sought to bolster immemorial rights, were frequent. As copies of original documents, chartularies were subject to error through carelessness, or through the well-intentioned efforts of copyists to correct MSS that they did not understand.

Bibliography: H. BRESSLAU, *Handbuch der Urkundenlehre für Deutschland und Italien,* 2 v. (2d ed. Leipzig 1912–31). A. GIRY, *Manuel de diplomatique* (new ed. Paris 1925) v.1. G. R. C. DAVIS, *Medieval Cartularies of Great Britain* (New York 1958) xi–xvi. F. ZOEPFL, *Lexikon für Theologie und Kirche*, ed. M. BUCHBERGER, 10 v. (Freiburg 1930–38) 10:444–447.

[R. S. HOYT]

CHASTITY

Translating the Latin *castitas,* chastity is the moral virtue that moderates and regulates the sexual appetite in man.

The Natural Virtue of Chastity. Man is by nature a sexual being, endowed with specifically sexual desires or drives. Some regulation of his sexual appetite is required by the nature of human life, both personal and social. When self-moderation and self-regulation in sexual life are apprehended and practiced by man as inherently right or good they assume a moral character and become the natural virtue of chastity. The forms of sexual self-moderation that are concretely apprehended as good or morally necessary have varied greatly in history and still vary among men. They are to a large extent determined by sociological patterns. The principle of sexual self-moderation is, however, an absolute of human morality.

"The Triumph of Love" (detail showing Cupid) from a cassone painted by Francesco Pesellino, c. 1450. Cupid and the steeds of lust pass unnoticed by chaste lovers. (©Burstein Collection/CORBIS)

It is the foundation of natural law and natural virtue in the sexual sphere. Ideally, a rational analysis of human sexuality in terms of this basic principle should lead to the apprehension of the truth of all that Christian ethics places under the heading of natural chastity. In practice this conclusion is rarely reached on rational grounds alone. Christian ethics tacitly benefits by the higher light of revelation in positing the natural conjugal act as the only good fulfillment, in the moral sense, of the genital impulse in man.

Anatomically, physiologically, and emotionally sexuality is profoundly rooted in human nature and in the human person. This is a fact of general human experience that has been scientifically pursued and analyzed in modern sexological studies. The moderating virtue of chastity thus involves a rectification and harmonization of the whole man at the different levels of sexual experience, physical, emotional, and mental. Mere conscious rejec-

tion or unconscious repression of sexuality is not chastity, for neither constitutes a moral moderation of sexuality but only warps and frustrates it.

The modern psychological distinction between sexual fulfillment in a broad, or generic, sense and genital (or, in scholastic terminology, venereal) fulfillment in the strict organic sense clarifies the moral issue at this point. The conjugal act is the moral act of genital fulfillment, but sexuality in the general sense can be and is fulfilled in a well-ordered personal and social life. This is verified in conjugal life, where general sexual fulfillment in everyday relationships is at least as important for husband and wife as genital fulfillment. A satisfactory single life fulfills sexuality in another way. Basic personal energies, including basic sexual energy (i.e., the basic masculine energy of a man, the basic feminine energy of a woman), are channeled into the pursuit of life-enhancing goals. The urge toward genital fulfillment is transcended in the self-realization achieved through general personal and social fulfillment. Chastity, whether practiced in forms appropriate to conjugal life or in those required by single life, always maintains its character as virtue. It is the positive moral moderation and regulation of sexuality.

Chastity in Scripture and the Fathers. The Yahwistic creation narrative sets sexuality within the divine design of creation; sacred and purposeful, the sexual differentiation of mankind leads to monogamous sexual union (Gn 2.18–24). This highly religious and moral vision of sexuality underlies the Judeo-Christian theology of chastity, though in practice it was greatly blurred in the OT by the tolerance of polygamy and divorce (Mt 19.8). Moral chastity in married life is praised in the later wisdom literature (Sir 26.14–18; Wis 3.13; 4.1–2), and there are outstanding individual examples of chastity—Joseph (Gn 39.9), Susanna (Dn 13.22–23), and Sarah and Tobias (Tb 3.14–18; 8.4–9).

In the NT the full sacredness and the full moral ideal of chastity are repeatedly stressed. Chastity (ἐγκράτεια in the sexual sphere) and purity (ἁγνεία) denote the general integration of sexuality with the life of the spirit. Chastity resides above all in the heart and spirit (Mk 7.14–23; Mt 15.10–20) but embraces also the sphere of conduct (Phil 4.8: "whatever is pure," ἁγνά). It is a God-given adornment of man, a fruit of the presence and action of the Spirit (Gal 5.23; 1 Thes 4.3–8).

Patristic teaching on chastity—except when given an antisexual slant by Neoplatonic and Stoic ideas—develops the Biblical theology of chastity as the sanctification of sexuality. The Eastern Fathers emphasize its mystical and transcendent character; the Western, its practical aspects. Chastity is a radiance of the divine beauty (Gregory of Nyssa), makes men akin to God (John Climacus), is divinely fertile (Origen). It belongs to the order of love (Augustine, *Civ.* 15.22) and requires purification from all sensuality (Cassian, *Collationes* 12.7). With Ambrose the three forms of chastity—conjugal, widowed, and virginal—become an established schema in Western theology.

St. Thomas's Theology of Chastity. St. Thomas Aquinas, accepting sexuality as a normal constituent of human nature, makes its moderating virtue, chastity, a subjective part of the cardinal virtue of temperance (*Summa theologiae* 2a2ae, 141.4). Its subject is the sense appetite and involves both body and soul, or in other words the whole man. Thus chastity involves more than the strengthening of the spirit against the assaults of passion: this is the imperfect virtue of continence (*ibid.* 155.1). Chastity moderates and tranquilizes the genital impulse itself. Its highest form is VIRGINITY, which demands complete immunity from coital pleasure (*ibid.* 152.3 ad 5).

There is also a spiritual or metaphorical chastity that consists in the due regulation of experiences of pleasure in the mind (*mens*) of man. To delight in God is an act of chastity in this spiritual sense (*ibid* 151.2).

St. Thomas did not distinguish a form of chastity that is not metaphorical but truly sexual and is yet not genital. Modern psychological findings require a supplementation of his theology of chastity on this point. There is a chastity of the emotions that regulates and sanctifies sexuality in the general sense even where the exercise of genital, or venereal, chastity is not called for. Feminine possessiveness, for instance, can enter deeply into mother-love, especially toward a son. Genital chastity is not in question here; but there is a definite want of sexual moderation and therefore of chastity at the emotional level. St. Thomas is not concerned with emotional chastity. Following St. Augustine, he relates sexuality to the genital act (*commixtio venerea*) in firmly biological terms. Sex belongs to man's animal life, whereas his life in society belongs to the rational and strictly human aspect of being (ST 1a2ae, 94.2). But chastity in moderating genital sexuality moderates and sanctifies the human person, and in marriage the human couple.

The Asceticism of Chastity. Chastity is both a gift of the Holy Spirit and a task of self-discipline. The asceticism of chastity forms an important theme of Christian spirituality in all ages (see LUST). In practice the subject has often been befogged by the predominance of fear of sexuality in the manner of treating it (*see* MODESTY). In modern times the training of youth in chastity has become more positive and realistic.

Chastity in Modern Catholic Theology. The trend of modern Catholic theology has been toward a closer integration of sexuality with the distinctively personal life of man. Sexuality in the general sense is a form, sign, and expression of the human personality itself. Man is man and woman is woman at every level of personal life from the humblest to the most exalted. In this sense—and it is a very far-reaching one—sexuality affects the entire individual, social, and religious life of mankind. It derives its morality (chastity in the generic sense) from the positive and constructive function it should exercise in personal and social life as a whole, in accordance with each one's calling in life. Genital sexuality on the other hand—the specific sexuality proper to married life—is the specific form, sign, and expression of conjugal love. It derives its morality and chastity from its authentic love function in married life, to which it belongs exclusively. The procreative function of genital sexuality is in no way overlooked in this synthesis but assigned its rightful and necessary place within it. At the supernatural level sexuality is integrated with charity. Conjugal genital union stands as specific form, sign, and expression of conjugal charity, which is also procreative charity.

Bibliography: L. M. WEBER, *Lexikon für Theologie und Kirche,* ed. J. HOFER and K. RAHNER (Freiburg 1957–65); suppl., *Das Zweite Vatikanishe Konsil: Dokumente und Kommentare,* ed. H. S. BRECHTER et al. (1966) 6:133–136. W. E.MÜHLMANN and F. BLOEMHOF, *Die Religion in Geschichte und Gegenwart,* 7 v. (3d ed. Tübingen 1957–65) 3:1257–61. A. WILLWOLL, *Dictionaire de spiritualité ascétique et mystique. Doctrine et histoire,* ed. M. VILLER et al (Paris 1932–) 2:787–809. A. AUER, H. FRIES, ed. *Handbuch theologischer Grundbegriffe,* 2 v. (Munich 1962–63) 1: 498–506. J. FUCHS, *De castitate et ordine sexuali* (Rome 1959), standard modern textbook with good bibliog.; *Die Sexualethik des heiligen Thomas von Aquin* (Cologne 1949), analyzes St. Thomas's concept of sexual order. P. LAFÉTEUR, "Temperance," *The Virtues and States of Life,* ed. A. M. HENRY, tr. R. J. OLSEN and G. T. LENNON (*Theology Library* 4; Chicago 1957) 533–613, on St. Thomas's theology of chastity. Modern expositions of personalized chastity. É. MERSCH, *Love, Marriage and Chastity,* tr. from Fr. (New York 1939). D. VON HILDEBRAND, *In Defense of Purity* (New York 1931; repr. Baltimore 1962). H. DOMS, *Der Einbau der Sexualität in die menschliche Persönlichkeit* (Cologne 1959). P. RICOEUR et al., *Esprit* 28 (1960) 1665–1964, on different aspects of sexuality. J. CAZENEUVE, *Les Rites et la condition humaine d' après des documents ethnographiques* (Paris 1958), on sexual ethnology. On the psychology of chastity. L. C. SHEPPARD, tr., *Chastity* (Westminster, Md. 1955). VIIᵉ Congrès international de psychologie religieuse, *Mystique et continence* (Bruges 1952). A. PLÉ, *Vie affective et chasteté* (Paris 1964). A. AUER, "Eheliche Hingabe und Zeugung," *Theologische-praktishe Quatalschrift* 112 (Linz 1964) 121–132, on current theories on the subordination of *opus naturae to opus personae* in conjugal chastity.

[S. O'RIORDAN]

St. Boniface wearing chasuble.

CHASUBLE

The outermost vestment normally worn over the alb by the priest celebrant of Mass. The original chasuble, a genuine everyday garment of Greek-Roman times, was conical in shape, reaching close to the feet on all sides. Its use was not at first restricted to priests or to the celebration of Mass. The restriction came about with the gradual introduction of an investiture ceremony as part of the rite for ordination. The first clear evidence of the chasuble's presentation to the newly ordained priest appeared in the 9th-century Roman Ordinal 35 (27.31; M. Andrieu, *Les 'Ordines Romani' du haut moyen-âge* 4:38–39).

Reverence for the garment explains the existence of ornate chasubles from early times. This very ornamentation was responsible for the first alteration of the original vestment's appearance. The orphreys on the chasuble were at first bands of material used to hide and strengthen the seams. Often a vertical orphrey was applied to the front and back. In the medieval period oblique side bands were joined to the central vertical orphrey to form a Y.

Orphreys became more elaborate with the use of embroidered figures of the Lord and the saints. Since medieval Christians placed greater emphasis on the sacrificial rather than on the meal aspect of the Mass, it is not surprising that the customary image was that of the crucified Lord, causing the Y to be squared off to form a Latin cross.

The second alteration in the form of the chasuble came about as a result of the use of brocades. Medieval and Renaissance love of color prompted vestment makers to employ what were considered at the time the very best weaves. Unfortunately many of the great brocades were heavy and unwieldy. This led to a reduction of the material falling over the arms. Eventually only the front and back panels remained, the back one being decorated with a large cross. By the end of the 18th century particular models of the abbreviated vestments were favored in different countries and were known as the French, Italian, and Spanish chasubles. The last, which broadened toward the bottom, was the most imperfect of all.

The 19th-century renewal of interest in the Middle Ages led to an attempt to restore a more ample style vesture to liturgical functions. Unfortunately, the Gothic revivalists did not offer a restoration of the original chasuble at all, but a garment quite different and imperfect in form, which they called "Gothic." Its use gradually spread despite the opposition of the Congregation of Rites (1863, 1925).

In the wake of Vatican II, the skimpy design and heavy ornamentation has given way to a more ample and noble vestment that is more faithful to the dignity of the original Greco-Roman vestment. In addition to a revival of the Greco-Roman style, the Vatican II liturgical reforms also introduced the chasuble-alb (*casula sine alba*), a long and ample vestment developed for the presider in accordance with the norms of the General Instruction of the Roman Missal. The use of the chasuble-alb removes any need for an alb. With this new vestment the stole is worn outside; it thus makes more evident the sign that the presiding minister acts *in persona Christi*. Only the stole need be of the color required for the day or season.

Bibliography: E. J. SUTFIN, "The Chasuble in the Roman Rite," *Liturgical Arts* 24 (1956) 76–104; "How to Make a Chasuble," *ibid.* 25 (1957) 66–86.

[M. MCCANCE/A. D. FITZGERALD]

CHATARD, FRANCIS SILAS

Fifth bishop of Vincennes (now INDIANAPOLIS), Ind.; b. Baltimore, Md., Dec. 13, 1834; d. Indianapolis, Sept. 7, 1918. Both his father, Ferdinand, and his paternal grandfather, Pierre, an emigrant from Santo Domingo, West Indies, were physicians in Baltimore; his mother was Eliza Anne Marean of Massachusetts. Chatard attended St. Francis Xavier Institute, Baltimore, and Mt. St. Mary's College, Emmitsburg, Maryland, from which he graduated in 1853. He received his degree in medicine from the University of Maryland, College Park, in 1856, and served for a year as resident physician in the Baltimore Alms House, which later became the City Hospital.

Chatard abandoned medicine to enter the Urban College of Propaganda Fide, Rome, Nov. 5, 1857, as a student of the Archdiocese of Baltimore. He was ordained in Rome by Cardinal Constantine Patrizi June 14, 1862; he received his doctorate in theology in 1863 and was appointed vice rector of the North American College, Rome, assisting William McCloskey. In 1868 Chatard became prorector of the college and in 1871 was officially named rector. Pius IX appointed him papal chamberlain in 1875. Although Chatard was a capable college administrator, he encountered financial difficulties under the new Italian regime, and made a visit to the United States in 1877 to appeal for support. The following year Leo XIII named him to the diocese of Vincennes, and he was consecrated in the North American College chapel on May 12, 1878. Extensive reorganization marked his episcopal administration. He summoned synods in 1878, 1880, 1886, and 1891; raised the status of the clergy; improved the schools; encouraged the founding of hospitals and religious institutions; and established 47 new parishes and missions. After the title of his see had been changed to Indianapolis (1898), he built SS. Peter and Paul Cathedral, in the crypt of which he is buried.

In the ecclesiastical controversies of the day, among which the question of secret societies was of particular concern to him, Chatard was classed among the conservatives. He represented the Province of Cincinnati in the Roman meetings preliminary to the Third Plenary, Council of Baltimore, and also wrote numerous articles for American magazines, chiefly the Paulist periodical *Catholic World*. Some of his formal lectures were published as *Occasional Essays* (1881) and *Christian Truths* (1881), and he translated Abbé G. Chardon's *Memoirs of a Seraph* (2 v. 1888).

Bibliography: H. J. ALERDING, *A History of the Catholic Church in the Diocese of Vincennes* (Indianapolis 1883). C. BLANCHARD, ed., *History of the Catholic Church in Indiana*, 2 v. (Logansport, Ind. 1898). R. F. MCNAMARA, *The American College in Rome: 1855–1955* (Rochester 1956).

[R. GORMAN]

CHATEAUBRIAND, FRANÇOIS RENÉ DE

French writer and politician; b. Saint-Malo, Sept. 4, 1768; d. Paris, July 4, 1848. His isolated tomb is on a tiny island off Saint-Malo, le Grand Bé. He was the last of an old Breton family—his eldest brother, who inherited the title of count of Chateaubriand, having died on the scaffold during the Revolution. One of his sisters, Lucile, a woman of fine but morbid sensitivity, wielded a strong influence on his poetic imagination. He grew up first at Saint-Malo, then at his father's château of Combourg, then in various Breton schools (Dol, 1778–80; Rennes, 1781–82; and Dinan, 1784–86). Destined first to a career as a seaman, for which he studied briefly and unsuccessfully at Brest (1783), he received in 1786 a lieutenancy in the regiments of Navarre and spent several years in garrisons (Cambrai, Dieppe). He passed his vacations with his sisters at Fougères, and led a dissipated existence in Paris among men of letters and philosophers such as Évariste Désiré de Parny, Ponce Écouchard Lebrun, Sébastien de Chamfort, and Pierre Ginguené. After watching the first bloody days of the Revolution he left for the U.S. on April 8, 1791.

His account of this journey, published in 1827 as *Voyage en Amérique,* has aroused well-founded doubts (especially concerning his intention of discovering a Polar Sea, his unlikely itinerary, and the account of a visit to George Washington) and critics have looked into accounts of various missionaries, naturalists, and historians for its sources. Whatever the case, after arriving in Baltimore on July 10, 1791, he left suddenly on December 10 and arrived at Le Havre on Jan. 2, 1792. He married Celeste Buisson de Lavigne at Saint-Malo on March 19, 1792, then, after a stay with old friends, men of letters at Paris, he joined a company of émigrés and finally went to England (May 17, 1793). He knew the miseries of emigration, in spite of meager resources augmented by his compatriot J. Peltier and by the French lessons he gave during 1795. He did not give up his literary ambitions, however, but worked on *Les Natchez,* translated English poetry (Milton's and Gray's), and published the *Essai sur les Revolutions,* his first book (1797).

Genesis of Génie du Christianisme. This essay on revolutions, edited by Deboffe at London, proposes an ingenious parallel between the revolutions of antiquity and the French Revolution. It reveals a troubled 30-year-old Chateaubriand torn between the irreligious skepticism of the 18th century and the need for faith. In confidential notes, scribbled a little later in the margins of this work, the author stresses more boldly his doubts and denials. In a new edition (1826), he inserted severe notations on his unbelieving youth, while emphasizing the religious torment that had then begun.

He soon recovered his faith, however, moved particularly by the death of his mother and of one of his sisters, Mme. de Farcy. Under the urging of his friend Louis de Fontanes, he began the preparation of an apology of Christianity. Whatever doubts have been raised about the account he gave of the genesis of this work, and of the circumstances of his conversion, he appeared, on his return to France (May 1800), as the most brilliant member of the group of social and religious reformers whose organ was the *Mercure de France.* His reputation grew further by his refutation of Mme. de Staël's *De la Littérature,* and by the publication (1801) of *Atala,* an episode of his *Génie du Christianisme. Atala* is an "American" nouvelle in the genre of the exotic tales so popular in the 18th century; its defense of the "noble savage," echoing the thought of ROUSSEAU, ends with an idyllic sketch of the primitive world. Christianity and its benefits, however, are represented in it by an old missionary, Father Aubry. A year later (April 1802), *Atala* appeared in its proper place in *Génie du Christianisme.*

This work is divided into four sections, *Dogmes et Doctrines, Poétique du Christianisme, Beaux Arts et Lit-*

François René de Chateaubriand.

térature, and *Culte.* The first part examines the mysteries and the Sacraments, the virtues and the moral law founded on the Decalogue; it affirms the superiority of the Mosaic tradition over all the other cosmogonies; finally, following many apologists of the 18th century, it searches among the wonders of nature for proofs of the existence of God. The second and third parts are given over to the poetry of Christianity and to the philosophical theories it evoked; the epics, the dramatic characters, the portrayal of the passions (and here one chapter is devoted to the "evil of the century" under the title *Vague des passions*), the Christian feeling for nature ("The mythology of the Ancients," says Chateaubriand, "depreciates nature"), the music, especially of Gregorian chant, the architecture, particularly of the Gothic churches—all are called forth as witnesses. In addition, the thinking of Pascal, the eloquence of Bossuet, the "harmonies" of art and nature, which Chateaubriand understood as Bernardin de Saint-Pierre had understood them, all are pressed into service. The last part recalls the beauty of the liturgy, the song of the bells, the solemnities of the Church, Christian festivals; the spectacle of the tomb, sad but at the same time comforting; the role of the clergy and the work of the missions; the humanitarian generosities that manifest themselves in hospitals, schools, legislation, and civilization.

Two novels of love and sin, *Atala* and *René*, appear in this religious apologetic, to show the harmonies a religious soul may establish between the beauties of nature and the human heart, and the remedy Christianity proposes to the *vague des passions*. *René* is autobiographical in large part and concludes with a thought put into the mouth of a missionary priest (but surely Chateaubriand's own): "Solitude is bad for him who does not live with God."

Political Embroilments. The *Génie du Christianisme* corresponded with Bonaparte's views in that year of the Concordat (1802), and Chateaubriand was sent to Rome as secretary to the French ambassador. His discovery of Italy and the Roman countryside is recounted in *Voyage en Italie* (1826). On his return to Paris in 1804, he was preparing himself for a new diplomatic post as minister of France in the Valais, when he learned of the execution of the Duke of Enghien; he then resigned. Two years later he went to Greece, the Orient, Africa, and Spain. This trip provided him with the elements for a novel begun in 1802 or 1804, *Les Martyrs de Dioclétien,* which became the prose poem *Les Martyrs* (March 1809). In its picture of Roman decadence, *Les Martyrs* is partly Chateaubriand's own confession and partly an attack on Napoleon. But its general design, the clash between dying paganism and nascent Christianity, is an illustration of the thesis of the *Génie du Christianisme.*

Napoleon recognized the polemic intent that had been directed against him. To be sure, Chateaubriand admired the great man; but even though he admitted this, it pleased him to be defiant, to "feel his claws." He had served the political aims of the First Consul in his work toward social restoration; but the aristocratic connections of the author of the *Martyrs* turned him against the Emperor who had attacked the very life of the old France in the person of a prince of the blood, the Duke of Enghien, that is, the last of the line of Condé. And Napoleon, who had cherished the idea of turning to his own ends the genius of Chateaubriand, sensed in him the daily growth of a rebellious and rival force. Chateaubriand had clearly aimed at Napoleon, under the names of Neron and Sylla in an article in the *Mercure* (July 1807). Nevertheless the Emperor nominated him to the French Academy (1811), but the rebellious genius wanted to make his reception speech a new weapon against the Emperor, and therefore the talk was never given.

In 1811 the *Itinéraire de Paris à Jérusalem* recounted Chateaubriand's pilgrimage from April 23, 1806, to March 19, 1807, during which he became a knight of the Holy Sepulchre. Only 3 days out of 332 had been spent in Jerusalem, and such haste, the borrowings from numerous books, and the contradictions between the *Itin-*

éraire and the journal edited by Chateaubriand's servant, Julien, published in 1904, have cast doubt on the authenticity of Chateaubriand's work. But a *Journal de Jérusalem* by Chateaubriand, found and published in 1950, but probably contemporaneous with the journey, restores confidence in the account.

When the Empire fell, Chateaubriand zealously championed the restoration of the Bourbons with *De Buonaparte et des Bourbons* (1814) and *Reflexions politiques* (1814). With the return of Napoleon during the Hundred Days, he followed Louis XVIII to Ghent and acted as minister of state for political affairs. But when the King again ascended the throne, Chateaubriand judged himself to have been poorly rewarded for his services in spite of his elevation to the title of peer of France (Aug. 17, 1815). He fought against the ministry in *De la Monarchie selon la Charte* (1816), was active in the campaign of the ultraroyalists in *Le Conservateur* (1818–20), and shared their triumph following the assassination of the Duke of Berry (Feb. 13, 1820). He was in turn minister to Berlin (January–July 1821) and ambassador to London (January–September 1822), and he was sent to Congress of Verona and entered the ministry with a portfolio of foreign affairs (Dec. 28, 1822–June 6, 1824). He pushed for French intervention in Spain (1823) and had a part in its success. But the animosity of the head of the ministry, Joseph de Villèle, and of Louis XVIII, threw him into opposition. His implacable war against the government was sustained in the *Journal des Débats*. After the fall of Villèle (1827) he became ambassador of France to Rome (June 2, 1828) and tried to play a role in the conclave that elected Pope Pius VIII (1829). During the same period, he undertook the edition of his *Oeuvres complètes* (28 v., 1826–31), in which appeared a few new works: *Les Aventures du dernier Abencérage* (1826), a Spanish novella on the 16th century; *Les Natchez* (1826), both an exotic novel and a prose epic; and the *Voyage en Amérique* (1827).

The politics of Charles X and the formation of the Polignac ministry caused Chateaubriand to resign his ambassadorship (Aug. 30, 1829). He reaffirmed, however, his loyalty to the King, who had fled from France in the revolution of July 1830, and his opposition to the new regime of Louis Philippe, against whom he entered the service of the monarchy exiled in Prague, and the Duchess of Berry, daughter-in-law of Charles X. Chateaubriand was on trial twice in 1832; the first time charges were dismissed and the second time he was acquitted.

His last works are *Études historiques* (1831), a large, though incomplete and uneven fresco, in which he describes the advent of the modern world and in which his philosophy of history, always faithful to a Christian perspective, and aware of the action of Providence, shows his faith in human progress; the *Essai sur la littérature anglaise* (1836), in which he sums up his opinion of a literature that profoundly influenced him; *Le Congrès de Vérone* (1838), an apology of his political activity from 1822 to 1823; and the *Vie de Rancé* (1844), a biography of the great Trappist reformer Armand RANCÉ.

Mémoires d'Outre-tombe. Above all he devoted the rest of his life to altering a great work, the *Mémoires d'Outre-tombe* (begun 1803, published posthumously). These *Mémoires* passed through various stages in the course of 45 years. From 1833 an initiated public heard it read in Mme. Récamier's salon at the Abbaye-auxbois. Chateaubriand wanted it to be the poem of his life and his time; he made it above all the poem of his friendships, of his loves (Mme. de Beaumont, Mme. de Custine, Mme. de Noailles, Hortense Allart, and especially Mme. Récamier), and of his hates (Fouché, Talleyrand, Decazes, Thiers, and others). Published in series form in *La Presse* (Oct. 21, 1848–July 5, 1850), and collected in 12 volumes from January 1849 to October 1850, these *Mémoires* are his most lively work, the one that contributed most powerfully to perpetuate his influence on French poetic expression, imagination, and sensitivity from Flaubert and Renan to Maurice Barrès and Marcel Proust. This influence survived French Romanticism, of which, more than any other work, it had revived themes and style, enriched horizons, and shaped thought in several general areas—religious, poetic, and aesthetic.

Bibliography: *Oeuvres complètes,* 14 v. (Paris 1864–73); *Les Martyrs de Dioclétien,* ed. B. D'ANDLAU (Paris 1951); *Itinéraire de Paris à Jérusalem,* ed. E. MALAKIS, 2 v. (Baltimore 1946); *Journal de Jérusalem,* ed. G. MOULINIER and A. OUTREY (Paris 1950); *Les Aventures du dernier Abencérage,* ed. P. HAZARD and M. J. DURRY (Paris 1926); *Les Natchez,* ed. G. CHINARD (Baltimore 1932); *Mémoires d'outre-tombe,* ed. M. LEVAILLANT, 4 v. (Paris 1948). Various editions of correspondence, notably the *Lettres de Chateaubriand à Madame Récamier,* ed. E. BEAU DE LOMÉNIE (Paris 1929). C. A. SAINTE-BEUVE, *Chateaubriand et son groupe littéraire sous l'Empire,* 2 v. (Paris 1861). A. CASSAGNE, *La Vie politique de François de Chateaubriand* (Paris 1911). G. CHINARD, *L'Exotisme américain dans l'oeuvre de Chateaubriand* (Paris 1918). V. GIRAUD, *Le Christianisme de Chateaubriand,* 2 v. (Paris 1928). M. J. DURRY, *La Vieillesse de Chateaubriand,* 1830–1848, 2 v. (Paris 1933). P. MOREAU, *La Conversion de Chateaubriand* (Paris 1933); *Chateaubriand: L'Homme et l'oeuvre* (Paris 1956). M. LEVAILLANT, *Chateaubriand: Prince des songes* (Paris 1960). P. CHRISTOPHOROV, *Sur les Pas de Chateaubriand en exil* (Paris 1961).

[P. MOREAU]

CHATEL, FERDINAND TOUSSAINT

French priest, founder of the Église catholique française; b. Gannat (Allier), Jan. 9, 1795; d. Paris, Feb. 13, 1857. Chatel, who came from a poor family, was ordained (1818) after seminary training under the Sulpicians. He served three years in parish work and then acted as a military chaplain until 1830. In that year he was reprimanded by the archbishop of Paris for unorthodox opinions expressed in periodical articles. In 1831 in Paris Chatel started his own sect, l'Église catholique française (French Catholic Church), which gained a limited following for a few years. It was redolent of DEISM and RATIONALISM and abolished auricular confession, fasting, and clerical celibacy and substituted the vernacular for Latin in the liturgy. Chatel assumed the title "primate of the Gauls" after going through a ceremony of episcopal consecration performed by Bernard Fabré-Palaprat, who falsely claimed to be a bishop. Before long Abbé Auzou, one of the members, parted company with Chatel and took most of the members of the cult with him. Later differences led to further splinterings. The group's political radicalism caused the police to close the temple in Paris (1842). Chatel was imprisoned for a time and then fled to Belgium, but by 1843 he was back in Paris, where he agitated for the emancipation of women, divorce, and socialism. By the time of his death, unreconciled with the Church, Chatel was impoverished and almost alone.

Bibliography: E. MANGENOT, *Dictionnaire de théologie catholique,* ed., A. VACANT et al. (Paris 1903–50) 2.2:2339–50. R. LIMOUZIN-LAMOTHE, *Dictionnaire de biographie française* (Paris 1929–) 8:784–785.

[L. P. MAHONEY]

CHAUCER, GEOFFREY

Greatest English poet of the Middle Ages; b. London, *c.* 1340–45; d. there, Oct. 25, 1400. From surviving official records, Chaucer would appear to have been a moderately successful public servant. He was bourgeois by birth, the descendant of a prosperous family long associated with London and the wine trade. The first records (1357) place him as a member of the household of Elizabeth, Countess of Ulster and wife of Lionel, third son of the reigning king, Edward III. Chaucer's father, John Chaucer, had already made a beginning in service to the crown, and the presence in a noble household of the son of a well–to–do bourgeois was not unusual during that period.

Life. The exact nature of Chaucer's early schooling is uncertain, but another form of his education is not. He accompanied the expedition to France in 1359, probably as a member of the company of Lionel, and was captured and ransomed. He probably rejoined the army and was present at the Peace of Brétigny (1360). The timing of Chaucer's military service is important, because the cam-

Geoffrey Chaucer.

paign of 1359 marked the turning point in English arms for his century. After the stunning defeats of Crécy (1346) and Poitiers (1356), French military policy consisted almost solely in refusal to give battle. The result was a devastated French countryside and a devastated English army. Little in what Chaucer had seen of war inclined him toward the profession of arms.

From 1360, when Chaucer is recorded as still in the service of Ulster, to 1366, when he received a safe–conduct for travel in Navarre—a document difficult to dissociate from the Black Prince's campaign of the following year—Chaucer's life is a blank. With the *Book of the Duchess,* however, Chaucer emerges as an accomplished and confident poet, well read in the polite French literature of the day. Since the most persuasive evidence one has from this period is precisely this poetic ability, the rather slightly founded theory that Chaucer was a favorite of Alice Perrers is not without some probability. Patronesses were not sparing in their demands for poetic tribute, and the court of Edward would have afforded the kind of reading with which Chaucer shows himself familiar. The composition of the numerous amatory lays he dimly remembers in the *Retraction* could most easily be assigned to this period. In addition there is the important evidence of the annuity of 20 marks granted Chaucer in 1367, by Edward III. Since the annuity specifically connects him with the household of Edward, rather than with that of Lionel, the theory of pragmatic poetical devotion to the highly pragmatic Alice seems not impossible.

Marriage. An advantageous marriage seems to have been one of the perquisites of an esquire attached to the court, and Chaucer's career in this respect parallels that of other esquires of the court. In 1366 or before, Chaucer married Philippa Roet, daughter of Sir Payne Roet, who had come to England with her younger sister Katherine in the entourage of Philippa of Hainault at the time of the latter's marriage to Edward III. If Chaucer's marriage is to be regarded as one of love, it conformed to the adage: it was not smooth. Chaucer's bride Philippa retained her position of attendant (*domicella*) upon Queen Philippa, just as her sister Katherine, who had from a very early age been attached to Blanche of Lancaster, retained her position in the Lancastrian household after her marriage to the short–lived Sir Hugh Swynford. In 1372, some three years after the death of the Queen (1369), Philippa joined her sister Katherine in the Lancastrian household, where Katherine's position was undoubtedly strengthened by the death, in the same year, of the Duchess Blanche, wife of John of Gaunt. It is certain that after the death of Blanche, Katherine Swynford was the acknowledged mistress of John of Gaunt, but at what point she became his mistress is uncertain. In any case, Philippa's attachment was to the Lancastrian household and Chaucer's to the king's. Because of this mutual and conflicting complex of loyalties and duties, it is likely that it was not until 1374, with Chaucer's appointment as Comptroller of Customs that Philippa and Geoffrey were able to set up something approaching a normal household. Even so connubial life must have been difficult, for Philippa did not abandon her connections with Lancaster, and-Chaucer's diplomatic services were becoming increasingly in demand. Hence, perhaps, a certain absence of domesticity in Chaucer's self–portraits.

Italy and Humanism. The date of outstanding importance in Chaucer's intellectual life is 1372. Although it is possible that Chaucer could have gotten to Italy as early as 1368 or 1370, it is unquestionable that in 1372 he was appointed to a commission to treat with the Genoese regarding the establishment of a commercial center in an English port. Chaucer not only reached Genoa, but spent some time in Florence, almost certainly as negotiator for a much–needed loan to England. The mission is important in showing the trust that Chaucer enjoyed, but its real significance lies in the fact that from this journey dates Chaucer's knowledge of DANTE, BOCCACCIO, and PETRARCH, and of Italian humanism in general. A second mission in 1378 must have deepened their impression on him.

The Public Servant. With rare exceptions, the remaining records reveal the vicissitudes of a public servant who wished to be a poet. In 1372 Philippa received a life pension of £10 from John of Gaunt, and in 1374 Chaucer received a like pension, but in terms indicating that it was Philippa's services, rather than his own, for which he was being rewarded. Chaucer's financial situation further improved in 1374, when he obtained the positions of Comptroller of Customs on wool and of the Petty Customs on wine, and on other merchandise in the Port of London. The difficulty was, however, that the duties of the Comptroller involved an independent audit of the Collectors' accounts, and therefore had to be kept in Chaucer's own hand. The position was lucrative, but hardly a sinecure. In addition, Chaucer was engaged in two diplomatic missions in 1377 and 1378: the first probably concerning a projected French marriage for Richard II; the second, in regard to an attempt to gain military aid in Italy. However beneficial these activities may have been to Chaucer the man of affairs, they left little time for Chaucer the poet. In 1385 he successfully petitioned for leave to exercise his office through a permanent deputy. To what extent political factors affected his decision is uncertain. Henceforth, he resided in Kent.

One would wish that this well–timed withdrawal had led to a prolonged period of literary productivity, but absolute detachment from the world of affairs did not come easily to Chaucer. From 1385 to 1389 he was a Justice of the Peace in Kent, and in 1386, Member of Parliament for Kent. In 1387, Philippa died, with the consequent loss to Chaucer of her royal and Lancastrian annuities. The extent to which Chaucer's finances were actually affected by this event is problematical, but it is clear that during this period he was involved in numerous law suits, mostly for debt, and that in 1388 he assigned both his exchequer annuities, probably for a cash sum. Public office seems again to have become a necessity. In 1389, he was appointed Clerk of the Works, a position he held until 1391. Possibly he resigned this demanding and hazardous task in favor of a less demanding one as subforester of the King's Park in North Petherton, Somersetshire, but the date of this latter appointment is highly uncertain. Further favors were forthcoming from Richard, but the poet seems nevertheless to have remained in difficult financial circumstances. The deposition of Richard II in 1399 could have been disastrous, entailing as it would the loss of these favors, but Richard's successor was Henry IV, son of John of Gaunt, who had both family and personal reasons for assisting Chaucer. Henry's actions were generous, and in 1399 Chaucer was able to take a lease on a house in the garden of St. Mary's Chapel, Westminster Abbey. The action seems singularly appropriate: Chaucer's withdrawal from the world shows an awareness of

Page from an illuminated manuscript of Chaucer's "Troilus and Criseyde," written in the first decade of the 15th century (Morgan MS 817, fol. 1).

mortality characteristically medieval, while the length of the lease (53 years) suggests a characteristically Chaucerian optimism. Whatever kind of work he intended to write in his last years, the uninterrupted time to create, which throughout his life he had so earnestly sought, had finally come. Some 10 months later, he died.

Works. At the center of any consideration of Chaucer's works is the date 1372. Previous to his first Italian journey, Chaucer's sources had been French. After his return, it is obvious that he became an avid reader of Italian literature, especially of Boccaccio. Hence, he has in the past been said to have had a French, an Italian, and curiously enough, from the point of view of sources, an English (*Canterbury Tales*) period. More recently, influences have remained the basis for establishing Chaucer's periods of composition, but judgments as to maturity or lack of maturity of a poem have been allowed a greater scope. However, it is questionable whether the term "influence" is with Chaucer not more confusing

Page from the first illustrated edition of Chaucer's "Canterbury Tales," published by William Caxton, Westminster, 1484.

than useful. For example, Chaucer may be said to have devoured Boccaccio's romances and meditated upon the philosophy of Boethius. In the *Knight's Tale,* the latter is imposed upon the former. Both are influences, but hardly of the same sort. Thus it has seemed preferable to abandon the conception of "influence" as an organizing principle and to consider the various periods of Chaucer's works in terms of those activities or attitudes that were sufficiently dominant during the various periods of his life to make division meaningful.

Court Poems (1361?–80). As noted above, Chaucer's earliest works were probably court poems of a rather simple variety. Although the invariable principles of court poetry were well established, what is interesting about Chaucer is a certain artistic waywardness. It was acceptable, if not obligatory, to translate the conventionalized process of enamorment in the first part of the *Roman de la Rose,* but the sexual naturalism of the second part, no matter how Christian and philosophic, was not acceptable to the court for which Chaucer wrote. It

is known from the "Prologue" to the *Legend of Good Women* that Chaucer translated the objectionable second part, but of the acceptable first part no mention is here made. So well known were the allegorical personages of the Garden of Love in the *Roman de la Rose* that Chaucer could not have avoided making their acquaintance; yet he could, and did, avoid taking them seriously. The most one can say is that a part of a Middle English translation may be attributed to him (cf. *Roman de la Rose* with Chaucer's "Romaunt of the Rose" in *Works*).

When the Black Death of 1369 took from England one of its most beloved women, the Duchess Blanche of Lancaster, Chaucer seems to have been urged or commissioned to write an elegy, presumably as a consolation directed to her husband, John of Gaunt. This elegy, *The Book of the Duchess,* is a literary masterpiece, the finest of all his early poems. Blanche stands out as if alive in all her native beauty, goodness, and intelligence. Yet the poem bestowed upon its creator no immediate rewards—probably because its success depended upon the highly daring and unconventional device of introducing humor into an elegy. It is Chaucer's first–known use of the "persona," or mask, and in the *Book of the Duchess* its function is central; for it is the bemused stupidity of the persona–Chaucer that evokes from the Black Knight the lyrical praise of his departed lady, Blanche. But the stupidity of the oaf is humorous, and unconventional in an elegy. Almost as unconventional is the failure to present a vision of the subject of the elegy among the joys of heaven. In a complex way, which accepted the convention of the mistress as well as that of the wife, John of Gaunt was highly conventional, and Chaucer must have known it. Yet he refused to sacrifice his own personal vision of the earthly Blanche to a conventionally pious one.

The same is true of the incomplete *House of Fame.* It seems inescapable that the court poet was expected to prepare a romantic poem culminating in the announcement of a forthcoming wedding of no small consequence. But the poem prepared is pure parody—parody of Dante; parody of a second persona–Chaucer, the overfed and underrewarded servant of Venus; parody even of the set beginning of the metrical romance. Yet in the wildness and unevenness of the parody, as in the portrait of Geoffrey seeking to overcome the fatigue of the day in order to read yet another book, one senses not so much comedy, as a strongly implied appeal for relief from his customs duties, and for the opportunity to acquire the learning he considers necessary to the kind of poetry he wishes to write.

Philosophic Period (1380–85). Throughout his life Chaucer was never without an interest in ideas. In this brief period, however, one would judge that much of the reading he had been seeking to do had in fact been accomplished. The *Parlement of Foules* is an occasional poem (perhaps for St. Valentine's Day), cast in the familiar form of the love–debate. However, its questioning of the function of love in the universe, and its debating of the values of the various forms of love by a wide range of social classes, seem to indicate a philosophical interest both in an abstract concept and in its operation throughout society. Chaucer's most explicit philosophical venture, however, is his Herculean struggle to translate Boethius's *De consolatione philosophiae*. It must be kept in mind that the nonexistence of a philosophical vocabulary in English inevitably forced Chaucer into a heavily circumlocutional style, but, with the aid of a massive use of explanatory phrases, Chaucer, who left so much unfinished, indomitably struggled through. One may presume that the labor could not have been as painful as it would appear, for it is the Boethian view of the world that dominates *Troilus and Criseyde,* the most ambitious poem Chaucer ever completed. This story of a noble Trojan prince who finds his goddess in the beautiful and gentle Criseyde, who loves her with a love in which sheer adoration exceeds passion, yet is betrayed by her and gives his life for the loss of his love, has a magnitude and artistic perfection Chaucer never attained before or after. Yet it has a fault. It has to be read by human beings. The human being likes to believe in love, himself falls in love with the exquisite Criseyde, forgets the opening statement that flatly states Criseyde's ultimate falseness, and himself experiences the anguish of Troilus over an event he, as reader, has foreknown since the poem began. Nor can he, like Matthew Arnold in "Dover Beach," take refuge from the treacherous world in human love. It is precisely because Criseyde's love is human that it fails. Only God's love will betray no one.

At the end of the poem, Chaucer calls *Troilus and Criseyde* his "tragedye" (ed. Robinson, V, 1786). It is a ruthlessly logical working–out of the Boethian–Christian view of the nature of the world, and of the nature of the human soul. Chaucer has expressed the view with a completeness that leaves very little further to be said: its precision is almost too absolute. When Chaucer begs of God strength to create an undefined "comedye" (V, 1788), there is more than a suggestion that a kindlier, more complex, more expansive treatment of the phenomenon of human nature is forthcoming.

Canterbury Tales. "Chaucer," says Dryden, "must have been a man of a most wonderful comprehensive nature, because, as it has been truly observed of him, he has taken in the compass of his *Canterbury Tales . . .* the whole English nation, in his age. Not a single character has escaped him. All his pilgrims are severally distinguished from each other" (Spurgeon, 1.278). Dryden's

statement is important not only because it emphasizes the comprehensiveness of Chaucer's art, but because, by the phrase "severally distinguished," he points to Chaucer's method of imparting particularity to generality, a literary method perhaps drawn from the SUBSTANCE and ACCIDENT of medieval philosophy. Thus the Miller and Reeve share the common acquisitive instincts of their class, but their physical and temperamental attributes are exact opposites. The comprehensiveness of class coverage was not an idea entirely new with Chaucer, but the matching of tale to teller, apparent as early as the first two tales of the Pilgrimage, was new, and remains sufficiently new to cause difficulties even for present–day readers.

The question inevitably arises: Why should a respected author like Chaucer include such "low" tales as those of the Reeve and the Miller? The answer would appear to be relatively simple. If Chaucer was to achieve the comprehensiveness for which he has been consistently praised, he had to include uncultured as well as cultured classes, and with them, the tales they might naturally be expected to tell. The Miller, drunk before the pilgrimage even begins, is not a likely narrator for a saint's legend. Furthermore, it cannot be overemphasized that in including such tales, Chaucer, dependent upon court favor, is activated by no profit motive. On the contrary, he knows the risk he is running, as is apparent from his remarks preceding these tales [I(A) 725; 3170]. For the court poet, profit lay in the forms of literature known to be in favor at court—romances, chronicles, moralities—certainly not the "vileinie" of the classes living close to the land. Characteristically, Chaucer took the chance of court disapproval, and in the high comedy of his so–called "low" tales, he demonstrates an artistic skill and, more important, an artistic conscience unequalled in his time.

Artistic Devices. Numerous devices are used in the *Canterbury Tales.* Two have already been mentioned— the breadth of class and attitude included, and the imposing of individual characteristics and attitudes upon those of the class. The latter technique at its best creates the illusion of immediate experience; the former—together with Chaucer's almost complete suppression of references to the events of his age—tends to remove the pilgrims from time and to make of them universal figures. A further device, related to both of the above, is that of the "persona" or mask. Behind his chosen mask—in the *Canterbury Tales* that of the ingenuous bourgeois— Chaucer withdraws from the stage and leaves it open for the dramatic interplay of the pilgrims. It is one of the major contributions of modern criticism to have made a sharp distinction between this Pilgrim Chaucer, as much an artistic creation as any of his characters, and Chaucer, man and poet. The most extensive opportunity for failure to observe this distinction is offered by the *Prioress's Tale.* Even so reputable a historian as Cecil Roth believes that anti–Semitism had penetrated the soul of "gentle Geoffrey Chaucer," apparently because the *Prioress's Tale,* which he considers simply an imitation of the Hugh of Lincoln legend, is included in the *Canterbury Tales* [*History of the Jews in England* (3d ed. Oxford 1964) 57, 89].

However, it is not Chaucer, nor even the fictive Pilgrim Chaucer, who tells the tale. It is the Prioress. Like Browning's monk in the *Soliloquy in a Spanish Cloister*—with whose attitudes Browning himself seems customarily not to have been identified—the Prioress is an artistic creation, and it is her own attitudes and her own personality she is exposing. It is essential to observe that the Prioress's personality is plastic; she conveys no sense of the energy and vocation of the otherwise colorless Second Nun. It may be presumed that the Prioress was the younger daughter of a well–to–do bourgeois family, where one imitated both the manners and the customs of the nobility. One of the latter was to attempt the provision of adequate land and dower for elder children, and positions of distinction in the Church for younger. The Prioress has dutifully imitated polite manners, and this imitation she has brought with her into the cloister; but once inside the cloister, she has adopted the ideal of the cloister—the ideal of virginity, and its conception of virginity as involving participation in the Incarnation. Thus, she thinks of Christ as the infant Christ, and of Mary as mother [VII(B²) 467]. In her tale, the principal figure is a "litel clergeon" who goes to a "litel scole" where he reads a "litel boke" (453, 495, 516). Furthermore, the "cursednesse" of the Jews when finally defined is that of Herod—the attempted murderer of Christ, and the actual murderer of the Holy Innocents, with which latter the "litel clergeon" is, in the Prioress's mind, associated (574, 566). It is important to realize that the Prioress has never seen a Jew—they were expelled from England in 1290—and that the death of "yonge" Hugh of Lincoln, mentioned as a recent outrage (686), happened about a century and a half earlier.

Nevertheless, the Prioress is persuaded that the Jews are bad people and should therefore be executed like other bad people. Her description of the execution of the Jews, horrible though it is, actually contains only the rudest elemental basics—which anyone could have heard or read—of the fine and much appreciated art of execution. It is just as unlikely that the Prioress ever saw an actual execution as that she ever saw a Jew. One has no real basis for assuming that she would have felt less pain over the tearing apart of a human being than over the sufferings of a mouse. She simply loves what, in her position, it is conventional to love, and hates what it is convention-

al to hate—without any knowledge of either. What is really important is that her hate as well as her love are deferentially accepted by the Pilgrims. The *Prioress's Tale* is prophetic, in that it deals with an aspect of the problem of evil that mankind has met again and again, and is still far from solving. Chaucer, who broke his self–imposed silence on contemporary happenings to permit the Nun's Priest's satirical allusion to the mass murder of the Flemings [VII(B²) 3397], is not a likely supporter of genocide, no matter how conventional.

Philosophy of the Tales. The preceding section has dealt with some of Chaucer's literary techniques and some of the misunderstandings to which they have given rise. At least one major question concerning the *Canterbury Tales* remains: Did Chaucer in his "comedye" have in mind any philosophical conception such as that which informed his "tragedye," *Troilus and Criseyde?* Or was he content simply to present a great panorama of human personalities and attitudes? The answer to this question is made difficult by the simple fact that Chaucer, at the time of his death, left the *Canterbury Tales* in a very incomplete state, so incomplete that even the order of the tales has furnished material for extensive controversy. Thus it has become customary, as in the present article, to cite the order of the generally authoritative Ellesmere Manuscript as I, II, III, etc; to include parenthetically (A, B¹, B², etc.) the order long ago created by the Chaucer Society to render consistent the geographical references in the *Tales;* and to return to the Ellesmere MS for line references. However neither order is devoid of objections, and much recent work has been devoted to establishing a definitive order (see Manly, Dempster, Pratt).

The *General Prologue,* however, is highly finished and might be expected to give some indication of the presence or absence of some unifying conception. At first glance, the pilgrims of the Prologue appear to be a highly world–oriented group—prosperous, concerned with the pleasures and profits of life. Furthermore, the company is dominated by the Host of the Tabard, Harry Bailly, whose plan, accepted by the pilgrims, would place the emphasis of the pilgrimage on the pleasure of exchanging stories and would make the climactic event not the arrival at Canterbury, but the return to London and the festive dinner at the Tabard. Yet among the worldly pilgrims there is a distinctly different group: the Knight, the Plowman, and the Parson. Rather interestingly, they represent the old feudal economy—the Knight, who protects Church and people; the Plowman, who provides material food; the Parson, who provides spiritual food. These three are old also in a deeper sense. None of them is materially motivated; each performs his feudal duty as a duty owed in a universe of which God is the author. It is evident that Chaucer intends to give this group positions of the highest dignity in the order of Tales. Although the *Plowman's Tale* is never told, the first of the tales is the Knight's, and the last, which is explicitly stated as knitting up the whole matter of the pilgrimage, is the Parson's.

Paradoxically, it is equally evident that the old are presented as pale and shadowy, while the new are burgeoning with color and energy. It is here that the extraordinary aptness of the pilgrimage fiction becomes evident. In its origin, the pilgrimage had been an act of piety carried out under great hardship and danger; by Chaucer's day, it had become generally, though not necessarily, more pleasurable than devotional. These two attitudes toward the pilgrimage correspond very closely with the attitudes of the worldly and unworldly pilgrims toward life. The central problem posed by Chaucer in the *Canterbury Tales* may possibly be stated thus: Is life in fact the traditional Christian pilgrimage through trial and temptation toward a future eternal city (Heb 11.13; 13.14); or is it a forward movement toward a new and better earthly city, a simple historical change in which an old set of values inevitably yields to a new? Or finally—an idea dear to the 14th–century humanist—are the temporal and eternal worlds not really antithetical, but in fact complementary, the logical movement from a lesser good to a greater good?

The "Marriage Group." If this problem is ever argued out, it is in the so–called "Marriage Group," comprising fragments III(D), IV(E), and V(F). The device of argumentation used in the Group is, of course, not new. It is a dramatic device used constantly; but only in the Marriage Group is the argument so carefully structured and the subject so consistently adhered to. The first speaker is Alice of Bath, Chaucer's greatest, because most lovingly wrought, personality. As she reveals herself, the Alice of the *General Prologue,* with her well–rewarded profession of wool weaving in a prosperous wool country, disappears: Alice is first and foremost a professional wife, the respectability of whose profession has been called into question. Alice's career has embraced five husbands, and she is seeking to continue that career with a sixth. However, someone has recently intimated to her that, according to authoritative scriptural (Jn 2.1) interpretation, her profession of multiple wifehood could be construed as a considerably less respectable one—and a sixth husband (Jn 4.18) as particularly compromising (*Sources and Analogues* 209).

Alice's counterarguments are revealing. To "auctorite," or "gloss," as she prefers to call it [III(D) 26, 119], Alice opposes the "express word" of Scripture (27, 61). Alice finds the gentle text "increase and multiply" (Gn 1.28) literally comprehensible, and she intimates that a

careful literal reading of Christ's remarks about the Samaritan woman's five husbands would remove any opprobrium from her own career (19–20). Alice thus purports to discard the ancient allegorical in favor of the modern literal. However, she is more than slightly self–contradictory. She not only comically misreads on the literal level—as, for instance, that St. Paul (1 Cor 7.4) explicitly confers upon her the power to govern her husbands—but her completely perverted interpretation of 1 Cor 7.7 indicates that she not only does not reject the old allegorical and authoritarian, but seeks to place it on her own side in a fashion so ruthless as again to be comic. In accord with her position as practicing wife of Bath, her Prologue is a tale of the practical values of dominating husbands; but the tale itself is not one of experience. It is Arthurian, drawn, one is led to suppose, from the Arthurian lore surrounding Bath, where Arthur won perhaps his most famous victory.

The tale Alice tells is strikingly different from the *Prologue* in several respects. For one, although the tale accords superficially with Alice's customary theme of practicality and female dominance, there is none of the preoccupation with sex made so explicit in the *Prologue,* and the Hag, whose transformation into youth and beauty is the central event of Alice's story, lives happily ever after with a single husband. Finally, the Hag's discourse shows an awareness of the conflict of grace and sin (1173–76) that is quite surprising—until one recalls that, in her Prologue, Alice's lyrical praise of past sexual delight is accompanied by her outcry: "Alas! Alas! that evere love was sinne!" (614). Alice, like Bath, is an uneasy compound of new and old, and perhaps this is why Chaucer becomes progressively more deeply interested in her.

Though Alice has, almost unconsciously, revealed a sort of indefeasible Christian heritage, every pronouncement she has made concerning the inevitability of female dominance is heresy. The reader expects these pronouncements to be answered, but instead is carried away by two masterpieces of invective, the tales of the Friar and Summoner, in which each reveals the corrupt practices of the other. By the time the Clerk of Oxford has been called upon, the reader has rather forgotten Alice, but it is clear that the Clerk of Oxford has not. What the story of the Clerk does is to set up against the husband–crushing Alice the portrait of the humble, patient, loving Griselda, the medieval ideal of womanhood, whose perfection is reflected in her horror at remaining anything but a "widwe clene" (836). Before Alice can retort, the tale of the Merchant and the incomplete tale of the Squire intervene, widening the subject of the debate from marriage to love—the first questioning whether love is not in fact simply lust, and the second questioning (though fragmentarily presented) whether the ideal relationship is not COURTLY LOVE. The *Franklin's Tale,* which concludes the Group, seems at first glance a model of balance among the positions presented. It is old in that it insists on the basic rightness of the marriage relationship. It is new in that love, which marital constraint can never drive from Griselda, the Clerk's medieval ideal, is presented as something that vanishes at constraint—a "thing as any spirit free." Love within marriage is indeed dependent upon the virtue of patience, as the Clerk has maintained, but it is neither the patience demanded by Alice of her husbands, nor that demanded by the Clerk of the ideal wife—it is a mutual patience demanded as much of the husband as of the wife. The husband is to retain his realm of sovereignty in the world of affairs, but to the woman is accorded sovereignty in the realm of love.

Old and new seem neatly balanced in the *Prologue,* but what upsets the balance is the view of the nature of man expressed in the *Tale.* Medieval theology regarded human nature as corrupted by the Fall, and the manifestation of its flawed state as a certain likeness to him whose lies caused the Fall (Jn 7.44). Truth is an attribute of God; lying, a characteristic of man (Rom 3.4). In grace lay the only means to truth. Yet in the *Franklin's Tale* every man keeps to truth, and woman also—though the scene is pagan Brittany to which grace has yet to come. As in traditional Christian symbolism, woman (Emotion) needs the control of man (Reason), but in the *Tale* both man and woman are essentially good. If mankind is essentially good, then the ideal of the Knight and the raw energy of Alice of Bath have something in common. They are not really antithetical, but complementary. As humanity and its ideals progress, a progressively better world becomes possible. This is the highest point of Chaucer's humanism.

Religious Contrition (1399–1400). Chaucer's last works, the *Parson's Prologue and Tale* and the *Retraction,* are probably best understood in terms of the medieval attitude toward the activities proper to the ages of men. Traditionally, as the early years of one's life were devoted to action, the later and final were devoted to meditation and prayer. This was not only a theory but a practice. For those whose life had been letters itself, declining years posed a particular problem. Why had they not applied their talent to glorifying God, rather than to attracting the praises of men? Both Boccaccio and Petrarch had religious experiences that profoundly affected the nature of their last works. In England, the strictures of St. Paul on any form of writing not conducive to moral instruction had great currency, especially as stated in the opening of Rom 15.4: "All that is written is written for our instruction." One may find this passage cited in any

number of explicitly devotional works, or even attached to works of doubtful moral content, such as Caxton's pious prologue to the *Morte Darthur.* The prevalence of Rom 15.4 is apparent also in the *Canterbury Tales.* When the Nun's Priest suddenly senses that pure comedy does not befit his calling and urges his listeners to seize the miniscule morality of his great satire, it is this same admonition of St. Paul that he quotes [VII(B^2) 3441].

Chaucer too knew the passage and its meaning. In his *Retraction,* he states that his intention is in accord with St. Paul: "Al that is writen is writen for our doctrine" [X(I) 1083]. The grand comedy of his life is past, and he is eager to have his readers note his moral works but is unable to enumerate as many as he would wish. He therefore strives to add to the list of devotional works he has already composed or translated a relatively new type of religious work that was becoming very popular at the end of the 14th century. This was a kind of handbook containing an exposition at greater or lesser length of various matters of doctrine. Originally, these manuscripts had been written in Latin and were designed for use by the parish priest. Later they began to be written in English or translated into English, in part to aid the parish priest's Latin, but principally to meet the demand for works of piety and meditation that was rising within a society that was becoming increasingly literate.

Although Chaucer's *Parson's Tale* was almost certainly translated from Latin tractates designed for use within the Church, there can be little doubt that Chaucer intended it for the same audience as that of the rest of the *Tales.* He earnestly wished it to circulate with the other *Canterbury Tales* and to offset the effects he feared of some tales, as Boccaccio feared the effects of the *Decameron.* The *Parson's Tale* itself represents an apparently hasty and awkward attempt to incorporate an extensive treatise on the Seven Deadly Sins into a rather small one on penitence. However artistically inept it may be, the *Parson's Tale* does communicate, and what it communicates is Chaucer's uncompromising acceptance of medieval Christian doctrine. Heaven is worth striving for, as Chaucer is striving to complete the number of works he believes his calling as poet demands of him. Human nature is worth very little striving for. It is "roten and corrupt" (461). Salvation is not to be found in faith in humanity, any more than in poetic excellence. Art in and for itself has no standing. It is a talent in the scriptural sense (Mt 25.14), and Chaucer at the end of his life is much concerned with the use he has made of it.

Character and Accomplishment. Chaucer has traversed the whole span of human experience, and he ends as human as he began. One meets him first in the *Book of the Duchess* as a rebel against conventional religiosity;

next as the philosopher–artist, inquiring in the *Parlement,* positive in *Troilus,* tentative again in the great debate of the *Canterbury Tales,* but strongly inclined toward a humanistic view of man and his relation to eternity; finally, like Petrarch and Boccaccio, ending his life very unsure of man and the world he inhabits, and very sure of the traditional religious beliefs of his age and the ages before him. Chaucer's powers of observation have never failed to be observed, nor the artistic mastery that transformed observation into character, and character into drama. However, it is perhaps not simply the great art he strove for and attained, but the passion for ideas—the ceaseless striving for a comprehension of the relationship of man to man and man to God—that enabled him to endow his characters and particularly the Canterbury pilgrims with so great a range of attitude that they seem humanity itself. It is true that humanity never changes, but neither does the search for ideas. Perhaps it is in this sense that one may understand Blake's marvelously simple statement: ''Every age is a Canterbury Pilgrimage.''

Bibliography: Editions. *Complete Works,* ed. W. W. SKEAT, 6 v. and suppl. (Oxford 1894–1900); ed. F. N. ROBINSON (2d ed. Boston 1957); *Poetry,* ed. E. T. DONALDSON (New York 1957); *Major Poetry,* ed. A. C. BAUGH (New York 1963); *Text of the Canterbury Tales,* ed. J. M. MANLY and E. RICKERT, 8 v. (Chicago 1940); *Canterbury Tales,* ed. R. D. FRENCH (New York 1948); *Book of Troilus and Criseyde,* ed. R. K. ROOT (Princeton 1926). Criticism. G. L. KITTREDGE, *Chaucer and His Poetry* (Cambridge, Mass. 1915). N. COGHILL, *The Poet Chaucer* (New York 1949). J. S. TATLOCK, *Mind and Art of Chaucer* (Syracuse 1950). D. BETHURUM, ed., *Critical Approaches to Medieval Literature* (New York 1960). R. SCHOECK and J. TAYLOR, eds., *Chaucer Criticism,* 2 v. (Notre Dame 1960–61). W. W. LAWRENCE, *Chaucer and the Canterbury Tales* (New York 1950). E. T. DONALDSON, essays in D. BETHURUM and R. SCHOECK, *op. cit.* W. F. BRYAN and G. DEMPSTER, eds., *Sources and Analogues of Chaucer's Canterbury Tales* (Chicago 1941). G. DEMPSTER, ''Manly's Conception of the Early History of the Canterbury Tales,'' *Publications of the Modern Language Association* 61 (Baltimore 1946) 379–415. R. A. PRATT, ''Order of the Canterbury Tales,'' *Publications of the Modern Language Association* 66 (Baltimore 1951) 1147–67. R. K. GORDON, *Story of Troilus* (London 1934). A. DENOMY, ''Two Moralities of Chaucer's *Troilus and Criseyde,*'' *Transactions of the Royal Society of Canada,* ser. 3, v.44.2 (1950) 35–46. R. A. PRATT, ''Note on Chaucer's Lollius,'' *Modern Language Notes* 65 (1950) 183–187. Literary and other relationships. C. S. LEWIS, *The Allegory of Love: A Study in Medieval Tradition* (Oxford 1936). W. A. PANTIN, *The English Church in the Fourteenth Century* (Cambridge, Eng. 1955). W. FARNHAM, *Medieval Heritage of Elizabethan Tragedy* (Berkeley 1936; repr. Oxford 1956). C. F. SPURGEON, *Five Hundred Years of Criticism and Allusion,* 3 v. (Cambridge, Eng. 1925). C. MUSCATINE, *Chaucer and the French Tradition* (Berkeley 1957). R. D. FRENCH, *Chaucer Handbook* (2d ed. New York 1947). R. S. LOOMIS, *A Mirror of Chaucer's World* (Princeton 1965). M. M. CROW and C. C. OLSON, *Chaucer: Life–Records* (Oxford 1966).

[A. L. KELLOGG]

CHAUMONT, HENRI

Ascetical theologian and spiritual director; b. Paris, Dec. 11, 1838; d. Paris, May 15, 1896. While attending the seminary of Saint-Sulpice in Paris, Chaumont constantly studied the works of St. FRANCIS DE SALES and after his ordination in 1864 made the teaching and spirit of the bishop of Geneva the basis of his preaching and direction. His major work, *Directions spirituelles de Saint François de Sales,* (Paris 1870–79), a series of small treatises, proved tremendously successful, and Chaumont was soon in constant demand as a preacher and spiritual director. He founded three societies dedicated to St. Francis de Sales, which had as their chief objective the sanctification of their members within the framework of their particular ways of life. The women's organization, founded in 1872 with the co-operation of Mme. Carré de Malberg, grew rapidly and soon included many of the highest social class. The society of priests, begun in 1876, to which that of the laymen was soon amalgamated, spread more slowly; but it proved very effective in instilling in the diocesan clergy the spirit of Francis de Sales, and within a few years it numbered in its ranks the elite of the French clergy. For all three groups, Chaumont provided spiritual direction by a priest of the society; a carefully worked-out method of probation during which a regular plan of meditations, readings, and religious exercises was followed; and spiritual reading lists, monthly meetings, and the study of the works of Francis de Sales, which helped to maintain a high level of spirituality. The diocesan groups were autonomous, but a director general and a general council elected by the total membership preserved unity within the organization.

Bibliography: H. DEBOUT, *Dictionnaire de spiritualité ascétique et mystique. Doctrine et histoire,* ed. M. VILLER et al. (Paris 1932–) 2:813–818; *Le Chanoine Henri Chaumont et la sanctification du prêtre* (Paris 1930). A. LAVEILLE, *L'Abbé Henri Chaumont, fondateur des trois sociétés salésiennes* (Tours 1919). S. HECQUET, *Catholicisme. Hier, aujourd'hui et demain,* ed. G. JACQUEMET (Paris 1947–) 2:1029–30.

[M. J. BARRY]

CHAUTARD, JEAN BAPTISTE

Reformed Cistercian abbot, ascetical theologian, and writer; b. Briançon, March 12, 1858; d. Sept-Fons, near Moulins, Sept. 29, 1935. Chautard entered the Trappist monastery at Aiguebelle, near Valence, at the age of 19. In 1897 he was elected abbot of Chambarand, near Grenoble, and two years later abbot of Sept-Fons, a position that he held until his death. In addition to the heavy spiritual and temporal responsibilities of his own monastery,

Chautard had the direction and control of several other monasteries of the order. In 1903 he pleaded so well before the senate and G. Clemenceau the cause of the Trappist communities threatened with dissolution that the government reversed its decision and the order was allowed to continue in France. A man of action with little time for writing, Chautard exercised his great influence within the monastery by his daily conferences to his monks and outside by his tremendous correspondence. Among his various writings he is noted particularly for *L'Âme de tout apostolat* (1910, English translation "The Soul of the Apostolate"). This book, written without regard for style, but filled with the fire of Chautard's spirit, became immensely popular at once. Its great success in spite of its austere tone proved the value of Chautard's central theme that to be fruitful in the ministry of souls one must lead a truly interior life and keep close contact with God. Chautard based his teaching on the Rule of St. Benedict and the writings of St. Bernard. The means that he recommended for a fruitful apostolate are those of these two great masters of the spiritual life: personal prayer, full liturgical life, and self-renunciation.

Bibliography: Abbaye de Sept-Fons, *Dom-Jean-Baptiste Chautard, Abbé de Sept-Fons* (Paris 1937). E. MAIRE, *Images de dom Chautard, abbé de Sept-Fons* (Paris 1938).

[M. J. BARRY]

CHAUTAUQUA MOVEMENT

The first Chautauqua Sunday School Assembly opened in August 1874 at Fair Point on Chautauqua Lake, New York. Lewis Miller, an Akron inventor and farm equipment manufacturer, and John Heyl Vincent, a Methodist Episcopal minister (later bishop), initially intended that the assembly provide summer training for Sunday school teachers. The assembly rapidly broadened to include academic subjects, music, art, and physical education. By 1880 the Chautauqua platform had achieved prominence as a national forum on public issues, international relations, literature, and science. Nine U.S. presidents have visited or spoken at Chautauqua, including Franklin Delano Roosevelt, who gave his "I Hate War" speech in 1936. Between 1985 and 1989 the institution initiated a series of exchanges with the Soviet Union during the time of *perestroika*. Today some 150,000 attend its scheduled summer programs in the arts, education, religion, and recreation.

The founders' purpose was to make education "once the privilege of the few the valued possession of the many." In 1878 Vincent and his associates established the Chautauqua Literary and Scientific Circle (CLSC), the oldest continuing book club in North America. The CLSC was a pioneer in adult education, summer schools, and correspondence courses. It gave hundreds of thousands of readers, particularly women, who had been deprived of a formal education, the opportunity to experience something like a college career. Over 8,400 were enrolled in the first year; 1,718 received diplomas four years later. In 1883 the various educational departments of the institution were reorganized into a university, later designated the College of Liberal Arts. William Rainey Harper, who was principal of the college, became president of the University of Chicago in 1892. Melvil Dewey started a library school in 1901. In 1902, a new charter changed the name of the assembly to the Chautauqua Institution. Chautauqua is a National Historic District; in 1989, it was designated a National Historic Landmark.

From early in the twentieth century, music became increasingly important at Chautauqua. The School of Music was organized in 1889. The New York Symphony Orchestra began a residency in 1920. In 1929 the Chautauqua Symphony Orchestra, under Albert Stoessel, began the summer series that continues to the present. George Gershwin composed his *Concerto in F* in a practice shack on the grounds. Also in 1929, Stoessel created a professional opera company.

The influence of the original assembly gave rise to many independent or permanent Chautauquas—more than 150 by 1904—set up in natural surroundings similar to Chautauqua Lake and organized to advance education among the masses. A separate development from 1903 to the 1920s—the circuit or tent Chautauquas—brought programs of inspiration, culture, entertainment, and lectures to communities throughout the country. By one estimate in 1919, one out of 11 people in the country were attending a Chautauqua every year. *The New Republic* reported in 1924 that more than 10 million people bought 35 million tickets in one year to various Chautauqua performances. Whatever the accuracy of the estimates, Chautauqua and the movement it inspired has had a profound impact on the social and cultural life of the nation.

Bibliography: J. H. VINCENT, *The Chautauqua Movement* (Boston 1886). R. RICHMOND, *Chautauqua: An American Place* (New York 1943). V. and R. O. CASE, *We Called It Culture* (New York 1948). L. J. WELLS, *A History of the Music Festival at Chautauqua Institution from 1874 to 1957* (Washington 1958). J. E. GOULD, *The Chautauqua Movement* (New York 1961). T. MORRISON, *Chautauqua: A Center for Education, Religion, and the Arts in America* (Chicago 1974). M. F. BESTOR CRAM, *Chautauqua Salute: The Bestor Years* (Chautauqua 1990). J. SIMPSON, *Chautauqua: An American Utopia* (New York 1999).

[R. MACKENZIE]

CHAVARA, KURIAKOSE (CYRIAC) ELIAS, BL.

Priest, cofounder of the Syro-Malabar CARMELITES OF MARY IMMACULATE and the Congregation of the Mother of Carmel (*see* CARMELITE SISTERS CONGREGATION OF THE MOTHER OF CARMEL), and a pioneer figure in the Catholic Press in India; b. Kainakary, Kerala (Malabar), India, Feb. 10, 1805; d. Changanacherry, Koonammavu, Kerala, India, Jan. 3, 1871. Ordained in 1829, Chavara founded an institute that was canonically erected as a Carmelite congregation in 1855, when he was confirmed as its superior. He was appointed vicar-general of the Vicariate Apostolic of Verapoly in 1861. Two printing presses, set up by early Portuguese missionaries to Kerala in South India, had disappeared, and in 1844 Chavara was determined to reactivate this apostolate. He designed his own press and used type made by a local blacksmith, and a few years later he was able to send to the Congregation of the PROPAGATION OF THE FAITH in Rome copies of ten devotional and catechetical books that he had published. He also edited the liturgical books of the Syro-Malabar Church. In 1887, his press first issued *Deepika*, now the oldest daily paper in Malayalam, and in 1902, the *Flower of Carmel*, the most widely circulated Catholic magazine in Kerala. In 1963, the Syro-Malabar Church in Kerala maintained approximately 20 publishing establishments, issuing four Catholic dailies, 12 weeklies or monthlies, and a large volume of other Catholic literature.

Chavara died after a long illness. In 1889, his body was transferred to Mannanam. The diocesan process for Chavara's beatification was inaugurated by the archbishop of Changanacherry on Jan. 3, 1958, and he was beatified by John Paul II Feb. 8, 1986, in Kerala together with Blessed Alphonsa MUTTATHUPANDATU.

Feast: Jan. 3 (Carmelites).

Bibliography: *Chavara carama'sathabdi*, ed. H. PERUMALIL (Alleppey 1971). *Acta Apostolicae Sedis* 78 (1986): 1076–1078. *L'Osservatore Romano*, English edition, no. 7 (1986): 6–7. W. HERBSTRITH, *Begegnung mit Indien und einem seiner grossen christlichen Pioniere Kuriackos Elias Chavara* (Trier 1969). J. KANJIRAMATTATHIL, *The Pastoral Vision of Kuriakos Elias Chavara* (Bangalore, India 1986). K. MATHOTHU, *Blessed Father Kuriakose Elias Chavara* (Palai, India 1988).

[F. MAURILIUS/K. I. RABENSTEIN]

CHAVES DE LA ROSA, PEDRO JOSÉ

Spanish bishop and reformer; b. Cádiz, Spain, June 27, 1740; d. there, Oct. 26, 1821. He went to Peru as bishop-elect of Arequipa and was consecrated in Lima on Jan.

John Heyl Vincent. (Archive Photos)

23, 1788. When he took over the diocese, it was in a state of neglect and decadence, but he was prompt in launching a major reform which, although it caused him serious difficulty, was one of the most successful in the history of Peru. He had the special virtue of carrying out his duties with a clear vision of the future at a crucial moment for Latin America. The buildings, discipline, and curriculum of his seminary he restored in accordance with the latest standards of the time; there he prepared a generation of men whom he infused with the desire for reform. These men played an outstanding role in politics, education, and religion during the first years of the republic. Chaves de la Rosa's progressive and firm determination was not well understood by those who should have been his closest collaborators. Vexed at encountering opposition from his own chapter, the clergy, and some religious orders, he sent his resignation to the pope, who accepted it on Aug. 9, 1805. Upon his return to Spain in 1809, he participated in some sessions of the cortes of Cádiz, which honored him with various titles. In 1813 he was appointed Patriarch of the Indies, but two years later he also resigned this honor. Just before he died, he donated his library to the seminary of Arequipa and the rest of his possessions to the orphan asylum he founded in his episcopal city, which still exists as the Instituto Chaves de la Rosa.

César Chávez.

Bibliography: M. DE MENDIBURU, *Diccionario históricobiográfico del Perú* (2d ed. Lima, 1931–34) 4:344–346. R. VARGAS UGARTE, *Historia de la Iglesia en el Perú* (Lima 1953–62).

[E. T. BARTRA]

CHÁVEZ, CÉSAR ESTRADA

Champion of migrant workers, labor organizer; b. southwestern Arizona, March 31, 1927; d. San Luis, Arizona, April 23, 1993. Chávez never distanced himself from the land he and his ancestors so assiduously worked for a livelihood. In 1939, the Chávez family lost their farm and were forced to become migrant farm workers in California.

From an early age, Chávez manifested a burning interest in issues of discrimination and social justice. At school, in cinemas and theaters, and in the U.S. Navy, he experienced anti-Mexican prejudice. In the late 1940s, while living in the Sal Si Puedes area of San José, he met a group of priests on the Spanish Mission Band of the Archdiocese of San Francisco: Donald McDonnell, Thomas McCullough, and Ralph Duggan. McDonnell introduced Chávez to Catholic social teaching on the rights and dignity of workers. McDonnell introduced Chávez to the lives and thought of St. Francis of Assisi, Mahatma Gandhi, and Emiliano Zapata.

Direction of Chávez's Work. Perhaps the most decisive event in Chávez's life was his encounter in 1952 with Fred Ross, a community organizer employed by the Community Services Organization and trained in the Saul Alinsky School of Organizing. He joined Ross as an employee of the CSO and became a professional community organizer. For the next ten years, Chávez gained much experience and rose to become national director of the CSO.

In 1962, Chávez resigned his position with the CSO and formed his own farmworkers' union. The United Farmworkers' (UFW) negotiations, strikes, boycotts, and fasts became the normal tactics they used in their efforts to organize and secure contracts for workers. An intense period of organizing eventually resulted in the passage of a comprehensive law on the rights of farmworkers.

A whole generation of Chicano and Anglo social justice leaders were nourished on the vision and organizational effectiveness of César Chávez's *La Causa.* Several important American politicians, such as Robert and Edward Kennedy and California Governor Jerry Brown, closely followed and supported the struggle.

The most characteristic note of César Chávez was his complete dedication to the cause of migrant farmworkers. He had powerful enemies, among them many with agricultural interests in California, who fought him in every conceivable way—in the courts, on the fields, and even with threats to his physical safety. Chávez was imprisoned more than once. He fasted, marched, picketed, and traveled tirelessly to every part of the nation to promote the cause.

Remaining faithful to his Catholic heritage, Chávez was exemplary in the practice of Catholic faith. He resisted the temptation to criticize publicly what some perceived to be the Church's institutional apathy in the face of injustice. He frequently referred to Our Lady of Guadalupe as patroness of *La Causa.* He linked the best elements of Mexican popular Catholicism with politics and the struggle for socioeconomic justice. César Chávez was arguably the single most significant United States Latino leader of his time.

Bibliography: C. CHÁVEZ, ''The Mexican American and the Church,'' in *Prophets Denied Honor,* ed. A. M. STEVENS-ARROYO (Maryknoll NY 1980). D. GOODWIN, *César Chávez: Hope for the People* (New York 1991). J. LEVY, *César Chávez: Autobiography* of *La Causa* (New York 1975). F. ROSS, *Conquering Goliath: César Chávez at the Beginning* (Keene CA 1989).

[A. F. DECK]

CHÁVEZ OROZCO, MARÍA VICENTA OF SANTA DOROTEA, BL.

Baptized Dorotea (Dorothy), also known as Mother Vicentita, foundress of the Servants of the Poor (now called the Servants of the Holy Trinity and the Poor); b. Cotija, Michoacán, Mexico, Feb. 6, 1867; d. Santísima Trinidad Hospital, at Guadalajara, Jalisco, Mexico, July 30, 1949. The fourth and youngest child of a family that lived amid poverty, Dorotea was drawn to caring for the sick through the work of her parish priest, Fr. Agustín Beas, who established a six-bed infirmary in the rectory tended by members of the St. Vincent de Paul Society. She became his patient when she fell ill with pleurisy in 1892. At that time she discerned her vocation for ministering to the sick and poor, and began her service in the infirmary immediately upon her recovery later that year. She took private vows with Catalina Velasco and Juana Martin del Campo (1895). When her nursing companions abandoned her and their patients in 1898, she conceived the idea of a congregation. It was realized May 12, 1905 with the first sisters professing canonical vows in 1911. Beginning in 1913, she wisely guided her spiritual daughters for thirty years as superior general, refusing to discontinue her work in spite of dangers and calamities. Mother Vicentitia was threatened by revolutionaries (1910–20), and harassment by anti-clerical soldiers in 1926 forced the closure of the motherhouse chapel. In addition, a major earthquake rocked San Vicente Hospital (Zapotlán). She is lauded not only for her charity, but also for her heroic obedience, a virtue that she considered the highest form of sacrifice. Prior to the heart attack that caused her death, Mother Vicentita saw her congregation grow into an important charitable institution that supported eighteen hospitals, clinics, and nurseries.

At her beatification (Nov. 9, 1997) John Paul II proclaimed that she "built her work on the foundation of the suffering Christ, caring with the balm of charity and the medicine of comfort for the wounded bodies and afflicted souls of Christ's favorite ones: the destitute, the poor, and the needy."

Feast: July 30.

Bibliography: *Acta Apostolicae Sedis* 21 (1997): 1049. *L'Osservatore Romano,* English edition, no. 46 (1997): 1–3.

[K. I. RABENSTEIN]

CHEATING

Here understood to mean the use of fraud or deceit, or the violation of the rules of honesty, as, for example, in competitive games and examinations.

In amateur sports of a competitive type there is a tacit agreement on the part of the competitors to observe the rules of the game. Otherwise the whole purpose of the game is defeated, except in that kind of play in which the attempt to circumvent the rules is considered a part of the fun. Normally, therefore, cheating involves what fault there is in the violation of an agreement of this kind. The agreement would rarely be considered to involve a serious commitment on the part of the competitors, and consequently its violation would not be gravely sinful. This is not to say, however, that it is a matter of little consequence, for attitudes and tendencies can be developed by resort to petty dishonesty that can lead to graver offenses.

In professional sports there are frequently explicit standards of behavior required of the competitors. Because of the advantages to be gained by success, there is also an unexpressed agreement to follow the rules. It would be dishonest to break the rules, to resort to unfair practices, or to make an unjust attempt to control the score, especially when money is wagered on the outcome. A violation of rules if aimed at or seen as resulting in monetary loss to another would seem to be an offense against commutative justice.

The acceptance of admission to an educational institution includes a tacit promise to abide by the rules of the school. One can assume that there is a rule against cheating in examinations and in performing assignments, even if it is not explicitly mentioned. Cheating not only interferes with the proper operation of the grading system, which is considered essential to the educational process, but also with competition, which is a normal motivational device used by educators. Cheating also puts the honest student at an unfair disadvantage.

In some types of examination there is also a specific monetary advantage involved for those who succeed with special distinction, e.g., a civil service examination, examinations for scholarships, etc. In such situations an element of commutative justice is involved, and one who succeeds by unfair means deprives another of a valuable consideration. Cheating in these circumstances is not only a grave sin but could also involve an obligation to make restitution to the party or parties injured by the dishonesty.

Some educational institutions dispense with procedures of policing examinations and put the students on their honor not to cheat. The honor system as such does not add to the moral obligation of following the rules of

José Ignacio Checa Y Barba.

the school, unless the students in accepting the system are understood to bind themselves by a special, though implicit, promise to abstain from cheating.

[J. D. FEARON]

CHECA Y BARBA, JOSÉ IGNACIO

Archbishop of Quito; b. Quito, Aug. 4, 1829; d. there, March 30, 1877. The son of Col. Feliciano Checa, one of the founders of Ecuadorean independence, he studied in Quito and in Rome. He was ordained in 1855, and he was named auxiliary bishop of Cuenca in 1861, bishop of Ibarra in 1866, and archbishop of Quito in 1868. Of a quiet and studious nature, Checa y Barba labored throughout his life to raise the spiritual and intellectual level of his clergy. He convoked the second and third councils of Quito, as well as two diocesan synods. His pastorals were noted for their calm charitable tone. He brought the Daughters of Charity and the Vincentians to Ecuador. On March 25, 1874, he led the official consecration of Ecuador to the Sacred Heart, even though his relations with Pres. García Moreno were not particularly warm.

The manner of his death has made Checa y Barba memorable. García Moreno had been assassinated on Aug. 6, 1875. His immediate successor was Borrero, a Catholic liberal. He in turn was overthrown on Sept. 8, 1876, by Gen. Ignacio Veintemilla, a liberal who got firm support from *El Comercio,* a Guayaguil newspaper. In February 1877 the bishop of Riobamba, José Ignacio Ordoñez, censured this paper for its heretical attacks on the Church. Checa y Barba stood with his suffragan when the government objected. On March 1, 1877, Father Gago, a Franciscan, preached to a large gathering in the church of San Francisco on the Syllabus of Errors of Pius IX and on Liberalism. Spies carried the news to Veintemilla, who inspired the police to try to arrest the friar. When Gago protested against the attempt, stating that he was just practicing some of the freedom of thought so highly praised by the Liberals, the bungling, puzzled police captain withdrew to consult his superiors. By the time they arrived, the rumor that the friars were to be expelled had brought about 6,000 people to the church, so that soldiers were called to save the police. The Liberals cried that the clergy had stirred up the people and took occasion from the police stupidity to subject all sermons to complete censorship. On March 7, Checa y Barba, who in the past had tended to remain aloof from all quarrels with the government, protested against this measure as unjust and uncalled for. The protest was rejected. On March 10, the archbishop issued a pastoral warning the faithful against heretical publications. This time the government protested (March 12). Checa y Barba answered in a note of March 17, in which he refused to give to Caesar what did not belong to Caesar. A visit from Veintemilla on March 24 failed to change the archbishop's mind. On Good Friday (March 30) after consuming the Host during the Mass of the Presanctified, the archbishop took some wine to purify the chalice. At the time he remarked to the deacon on the bitter taste. He completed the services but died amid horrible convulsions a short while after. The autopsy revealed that he had been poisoned by strychnine. No one was ever punished for the crime.

Bibliography: J. TOBAR DONOSO, *El Ilmo. Sr. Dr. José Ignacio Checa* (Quito 1937).

[W. LOOR]

CHEFFONTAINES, CHRISTOPHE DE

Theologian; b. near Saint-Pol-de-Léon, Brittany, 1512; d. Rome, May 26, 1595. He was born to the noble Breton family Penfentenyou, joined the Franciscan Observants in 1532 at Cuburien, near Morlaix, and studied in Paris. In both preaching and writing he quickly became a powerful adversary of the Huguenots. After having been guardian at Cuburien and provincial of Brittany in 1565, he was elected minister general of his order

(1571–79). This was a critical period in the history of the Franciscan Observants, for the triumph of Protestantism in northern Europe had inspired a move toward independence among religious of weakened fervor. In accordance with Pius V's (d. 1572) program of reform, Cheffontaines dedicated his eight years as general to visiting the houses of his order with the hope of leading his confreres back to a better observance of the religious spirit. Upon the expiration of his term of office as minister general in 1579, he was named auxiliary bishop of Sens. His theological activity was considerable. So vigorous was his opposition to the errors of the day, that he fell into error himself or at least came close to it. The novelty of some of his opinions caused him to be denounced at Rome. Three of his works were put on the Index, while the rest were prohibited until corrected. His principal work, *Deffence de la foi de nos ancêtres* (Paris 1570), concerned the Eucharistic Presence.

Bibliography: E. D'ALENÇON, *Dictionnaire de théologie catholique*, ed. A. VACANT et al. (Paris 1905–50) 2.2:2352–53. É. LONGPRÉ, *Catholicisme. Hier, aujourd'hui et demain*, ed. G. JACQUEMET (Paris 1947–) 2:1032–33.

[J. CAMBELL]

CHELIDONIA, ST.

Virgin and recluse; b. Abruzzi, Italy; d. Subiaco, Oct. 13, 1152. All information on Chelidonia (the forms of the name as Cledonia or Cledona are incorrect) is based on the vita composed by Guglielmo Capisacchi, a monk of SUBIACO who was professed in 1525 and who completed the chronicle of Subiaco to the year 1573. He claims that he used an early anonymous vita, but he is the sole authority for its existence. According to his vita, Chelidonia was a virgin and anchoress. She received the veil in the Church of St. Scholastica and became an abbess in a convent near Subiaco. She returned, however, to her life as a recluse. She was distinguished for her virtues, prophecies, and miracles. In 1578 her remains were deposited in a shrine under the altar of the Blessed Virgin in the abbey church of Subiaco. She is one of the patrons of Subiaco.

Feast: Oct. 13.

Bibliography: *Acta Sanctorum* Oct. 6:362–377. A. M. ZIMMERMANN, *Kalendarium Benedictinum*, (Metten 1933–38) 3:177.

[M. R. P. MCGUIRE]

CHELLES, CONVENT OF

Former royal Benedictine abbey, in the canton of Lagny, arrondissement of Meaux (Seine-et-Marne),

France; in the old Diocese of Paris, modern Meaux (Latin, *Calae*). It was founded in 656 by Queen BATHILDIS; its first abbess was BERTILLA, who came with nuns from JOUARRE-EN-BRIE (658–659), a foundation following the rule of St. COLUMBAN. Chelles was a double MONASTERY and represented a step in the progress of Columbian monasticism into Burgundy. The abbey early attracted many young women from England; its scriptorium was notable. Having become Benedictine, it was often ruled by Carolingian princesses; after being plundered by the NORMANS, it was restored. St. Elizabeth Rose (d. 1130) was professed a religious there. Reforms in the 12th and 14th centuries culminated in the reform of FONTEVRAULT (1498–1500), which Chelles, with its 90 nuns, had in large part propagated. In 1543, however, its abbesses began once again to be appointed for life. Chelles was suppressed in 1792; only vestiges of the cloister, some tombstones, and several buildings bought by private individuals remain.

Bibliography: L. H. COTTINEAU, *Répertoire topobibliographique des abbayes et prieurés*, 2 v. (Mâcon 1935–39) 1:753–755. R. VAN DOREN, *Dictionnaire d'histoire et de géographie ecclésiastiques*, ed. A. BAUDRILLART et al. (Paris 1912–) 12:604–605. R. GAZEAU, *Catholicisme. Hier, aujourd'hui et demain*, ed. G. JACQUEMET (Paris 1947–) 2:1033–35. E. A. LOWE, *Codices latini antiquiores. A Palaeographical Guide to Latin Manuscripts prior to the Ninth Century* (Oxford 1934–) 6:xxi–xxii. B. BISCHOFF, "Die Kölner Nonnenhandschriften und . . . Chelles," *Karolingische und Ottonische Kunst*, v. 3 of *Forschungen zur Kunstgeschichte und christlichen Archäologie* (Baden-Baden 1952–) 395–411.

[H. TARDIF]

CHEMNITZ, MARTIN

Lutheran theologian; b. Treuenbreitzen, Nov. 9, 1522; d. Braunschweig, April 8, 1586. Educated despite his lack of financial resources, at Magdeburg (1539–42), Frankfurt (1543), Wittenberg (1545), and Königsberg (M.A. 1547), Chemnitz was librarian to Albert of Prussia, Königsberg (1550). Returning to Wittenberg (April 1553), he entered the ministry in December 1553 as pastor of St. Aegidi and assistant to Superintendent Mörlin in Braunschweig. Chemnitz, a fellow student of MELANCHTHON, replied to the attack on LUTHERANISM by young JESUITS of Cologne in his *Theologiae Jesuitarum praecipua capita* (1562). In answer to attacks by the Portuguese Jesuit Andradius, Chemnitz worked eight years on his *Examen concilii Tridentini* (1565–73). His four-volume scholarly analysis of Trent's decisions, based on Scripture, the Fathers, and the history of Catholic dogma, enhanced his reputation far beyond Germany and elicited Jesuit respect for a formidable opponent and scholar. Chemnitz was then in demand as a consultant in doctrinal disputes.

In 1567, upon the request of Duke Albert, Chemnitz accompanied Superintendent Mörlin to Prussia to reorganize the church after the Osiander confusion. Chemnitz's role in drafting the *Corpus doctrinae Prutenicum* (1567) and a similar church ordinance for Braunschweig-Wolfenbüttel, the *Corpus doctrinae Julium* (1569), secured his reputation as a church organizer. Although defending Melanchthon against FLACIUS in earlier vain attempts to straighten out the *Adiaphora Streit,* Chemnitz maintained his more conservative orthodox Lutheran position. He contributed significantly to the final draft (1580) and later defense of the *Konkordienformel,* and was particularly effective in clarifying the doctrines on the Person of Christ and His place in the Lord's Supper. Chemnitz's *De duabus naturis in Christo, de hypostatica earum unione, de communicatione idiomatum,* etc. (1570) laid the foundation for article eight in the Formula of Concord (1580). His "Postilla" likewise exemplified clear and excellent Biblical exposition. Chemnitz was by nature a reflective if eclectic theologian, a profound scholar, and an accomplished linguist, but withal a practical churchman. His goal was to set forth in simple, concise form what the Word of God taught. Doubtless, Chemnitz's inclination toward the reduction of his beliefs to a *corpus doctrinae* tended to crystallize and formalize the *Grundsätze* of the Reformers. Also his insistence in creating a definite church polity with the accompanying purist forms, such as black attire without ornamentation for women at communion, tended to standardize church customs.

Bibliography: T. PRESSEL, *Martin Chemnitz* (*Leben und ausgewählte Schriften der Väter und Begründer der Lutherischen Kirche,* ed. J. HARTMANN, v.8; Elberfeld 1862). P. J. RECHTMEYER, *Der berühmten Stadt Braunschweig Kirchenhistorie,* v.3 (Braunschweig 1710) 273–536, best source of his life. E. W. ZEEDEN, *Lexikon für Theologie und Kirche,* ed. J. HOFER and K. RAHNER (2d, new ed. Freiburg 1957–65) 2:1043–44. F. LAU, *Die Religion in Geschichte und Gegenwart* (3d ed. Tübingen 1957–65) 1:1647–48. G. NOTH, *Grundlinien der Theologie des M. Chemnitz* (n.p. 1930). E. WOLF, *Neue deutsche Biographie* (Berlin 1953–) 3:201–202.

[E. G. SCHWIEBERT]

CH'EN, ROSE AND TERESA, SS.

Lay martyrs, b. Feng, Qi County, Hebei (Hopeh) Province, China; d. near there, July 5, 1900. Serious Teresa Ch'en Jinjie (also called Ch'en Chin-chieh, Chen Qingjieh, Kinn-Tsie, b. 1875) and her vivacious younger sister Rose Ch'en Anjie (also called Ch'en Ai-chieh, Chen Aijeih, Tch'Enn-Kai-Tsie, b. 1878) were among the ten Christians captured by the Boxers as they sought refuge from persecution by fleeing to a neighboring village. The cart driver, who begged for the women and

children to be spared, was beheaded immediately, as were two of the Ch'ens' cousins (ages 12 and 17). Three of the group escaped and the two mothers were seriously injured. Although their captors contemplated taking the two sisters with them, Rose and Teresa refused to move. Instead they dropped to their knees in prayer. Teresa was stabbed to death in a struggle. Rose, already weakening, was offered her life in exchange for denying the faith. Reinvigorated by repeating, "Jesus, have mercy on me!," she remained resolute. After being mortally stabbed, she said her Rosary as she slowly died. Rose and Teresa were among the 2,072 killed between June and August of 1900 whose causes were submitted to the Vatican, of which 56 were beatified by Pope Pius XII (April 17, 1955) and canonized (Oct. 1, 2000) by Pope John Paul II with Augustine Zhao Rong and companions.

Feast: July 20.

Bibliography: L. MINER, *China's Book of Martyrs: A Record of Heroic Martyrdoms and Marvelous Deliverances of Chinese Christians during the Summer of 1900* (Ann Arbor 1994). J. SIMON, *Sous le sabre des Boxers* (Lille 1955). C. TESTORE, *Sangue e palme sul fiume giallo. I beati martiri cinesi nella persecuzione della Boxe Celi Sud-Est, 1900* (Rome 1955). *L'Osservatore Romano,* English Edition 40 (2000): 1–2, 10.

[K. I. RABENSTEIN]

CHEN XIMAN, SIMON, ST.

Lay Franciscan martyr, servant; also known as Simon (Ximan) Tseng or Tceng; b. 1854, Anyang, Lucheng Xian, Shanxi Province, China; d. July 9, 1900, Taiyüan, Shanxi Province, China. Simon was the middle child of the three sons of Joseph Chen and Anotonia Li, who themselves had been born into Catholic families and had worked for the Church. Although illness prevented Simon from completing his seminary studies in Taiyüan, it did not hinder his commitment to celibacy and service to God as a catechist. During his decades as footman to Bishop Fu (Francesco Fogolla), he organized the bishop's trip to the 1897 International Exhibition in Turin, Italy, and traveled with him. During the Boxer Uprising, he was trapped with several dozen Christians in the Taiyüan cathedral. They were arrested and imprisoned prior to execution. His relics were collected by Fr. Fang Ho and taken to the shrine in Peng Chiao, Taipei, Taiwan, in the mid-twentieth century. Simon was beatified by Pope Pius XII (Nov. 24, 1946) and canonized (Oct. 1, 2000) by Pope John Paul II with Augustine Zhao Rong and companions.

Feast: July 4.

Bibliography: L. M. BALCONI, *Le Martiri di Taiyuen* (Milan 1945). *Acta Apostolicae Sedis* 47 (1955) 381–388; *Vita del b. A.*

Crescitelli (Milan 1950). M. T. DE BLARER, *Les Bse Marie Hermine de Jésus et ses compagnes, franciscaines missionnaires de Marie, massacrées le 9 juillet 1900 à Tai-Yuan-Fou, Chine* (Paris 1947). *Les Vingt-neuf martyrs de Chine, massacrés en 1900, béatifiés par Sa Sainteté Pie XII, le 24 novembre, 1946* (Rome 1946). L. MINER, *China's Book of Martyrs: A Record of Heroic Martyrdoms and Marvelous Deliverances of Chinese Christians During the Summer of 1900* (Ann Arbor, MI 1994). J. SIMON, *Sous le sabre des Boxers* (Lille 1955). C. TESTORE, *Sangue e palme sul fiume giallo. I beati martiri cinesi nella persecuzione della Boxe Celi Sud-Est, 1900* (Rome 1955). *L'Osservatore Romano*, Eng. Ed. 40 (2000): 1–2, 10.

[K. I. RABENSTEIN]

CHENOBOSKION, GNOSTIC TEXTS OF

The circumstances surrounding the discovery of the Coptic Gnostic library from the region of Nag Hammadi, Egypt, are set forth in detail by J. M. Robinson in the introduction to *The Facsimile Edition of the Nag Hammadi Codices* (Leiden 1972). Recent study of the codices at the Coptic Museum in Old Cairo shows that the library should be described as consisting of 12 codices and one unbound tractate, "The Discourse on the Three Appearances," formerly Codex XIII, which in antiquity had been placed inside the front cover of Codex VI. Of Codex XII only 9 folios and some loose fragments survive. The covers of Codices I-XI are extant, though many of the papyrus leaves are fragmentary. At least parts of 1,139 inscribed pages have been identified. The tendency of scholars to date the codices in the 4th century receives support from a preliminary study of documentary fragments in the *cartonnage* of the cover of Codex VII: the papyrologist J. W. B. Barns has assigned the dates A.D. 339 and 342 to two such documents. Under the auspices of the Department of Antiquities of the Arab Republic of Egypt and in conjunction with UNESCO, volumes of a photographic facsimile edition of the papyri are now appearing at regular intervals. Editions of a number of tractates have appeared in various languages, and a complete English-language edition is being published in the series "Nag Hammadi Studies" (Leiden).

The contents of the library, numbering 53 tractates, have been considerably clarified by editing and analysis, calling attention to a wide diversity of writings, some of them not Gnostic at all. For example, tractate 5 of Codex VI, untitled but provisionally called "The Discourse on Injustice," was identified by H. M. Schenke as a passage from the *Republic* of Plato poorly translated into Coptic; also, F. Wisse identified the first tractate of Codex XII, despite its fragmentary nature, as a Coptic version of the *Sentences of Sextus*. There are other works of doubtfully Gnostic character that were previously unknown, e.g.,

"The Teachings of Silvanus" (VII.4), a Christian wisdom document, and "The Exegesis on the Soul" (II.6), a myth of the imprisoned soul, supported by biblical and Homeric quotations. Of the literature of Christian or Christianized Gnosticism a variety of literary genres are represented: gospels "of Truth" (I.2 and XII.2), "of Thomas" (II.2), "of Philip" (II.3), "of the Egyptians" (III.2 and IV.2); secret books "of James" (I.1) and "of John" (II.1, III.1, and IV.1); acts "of Peter and the Twelve Apostles" (VI.1) and "The Letter of Peter to Philip" (VIII.3), despite its title; apocalypses "of Paul" (V.2), "of James" (V.3 and 4), "of Peter" (VII.3). There are several apparently non-Christian Gnostic works of great importance for the problem of Gnostic origins, including treatises such as "The Allogenes" (XI.3), apocalypses such as "The Paraphrase of Shem" (VII.1) or "The Apocalypse of Adam" (V.5), prayers such as "The Three Steles of Seth" (VII.5), and revelation discourses such as "The Thunder: Perfect Mind" (VI.2). In one case there is strong evidence for the Christianizing of a Gnostic treatise, "Eugnostos, the Blessed" (III.3 and V.1), by transformation into a revelation of the risen Jesus to his disciples, "The Sophia of Jesus Christ" (III.4 and Berlin Codex 8502). A large number of tractates retell, with variations, the familiar Gnostic myth of the origin of the world and of man; "The Nature of the Archons" (II.4) is a good example. The tendency to classify the bulk of the collection as "Sethian" is being called into question. Some works are recognizably Valentinian (e.g., several in Codex I, also V.3 and XI.1 and 2) and others Hermetic (VI.6, 7, 8), but it s difficult to classify the remainder in terms of a known Gnostic sect.

Research on the documents thus far has tended to stress the importance of the Jewish material in them and the view that Gnosticism in its origins was independent of Christianity.

Bibliography: D. M. SCHOLER, *Nag Hammadi Bibliography 1948–1969* (Nag Hammadi Studies 1; Leiden 1971), with annual bibliographic supplements in *Novum Testamentum. The Facsimile Edition of the Nag Hammadi Codices* (Leiden 1972–). **Texts and translations.** M. MALININE et al., *Epistula Iacobi Apocrypha* (Zurich 1968).R. KASSER et al., *Tractatus Tripartitus* (Bern 1973–).J. E. MÉNARD, *L'Évangile selon Philippe* (Paris 1967). R. A. BULLARD, *The Hypostasis of the Archons* (Patristische Texte und Studien 10; Berlin 1970).M. KRAUSE and P. LABIB, *Gnostische und hermetische Schriften aus Codex II und Codex VI* (Glückstadt 1971). A. BÖHLIG and F. WISSE, *The Gospel of the Egyptians* (Nag Hammadi Studies 4; Leiden 1973).W. FOERSTER, ed., *Die Gnosis 2* (Zurich 1971). **Studies.** A. BÖHLIG, *Mysterion und Wahrheit* (Arbeiten zur Geschichte des späteren Judentums und des Urchristentums 6; Leiden 1968). M. KRAUSE, ed., *Essays on the Nag Hammadi Text's in Honour of Alexander Böhlig* (Nag Hammadi Studies 3; Leiden 1972). G. MACRAE et al., *Essays on the Coptic Gnostic Library* (Leiden 1970). H. C. PUECH, "Gnostic Gospels and Related Documents," in E. HENNECKE and W. SCHNEEMELCHER, eds., *New Testament Apoc-*

rypha v.1, tr. R. M. WILSON (Philadelphia 1963) 231–362. R. M. WILSON, *Gnosis and the New Testament* (Philadelphia 1968).

[G.W. MACRAE]

CHENU, MARIE-DOMINIQUE

Dominican theologian and medievalist; b. Soisy-sur-Seine, France, Jan. 7, 1895; d. 1990. After entering the Dominican Order (1913) at Le Saulchoir, then in Belgium, he was forced by the outbreak of war to study in Rome (1914–20) at what is now called the Pontifical University of St. Thomas Aquinas. Assigned to teach theology at Le Saulchoir (1920), he at once set himself the task of replacing what he took to be the non-historical exposition of the Thomist system (*see* THOMISM) by his teacher in Rome, R. GARRIGOU-LAGRANGE with a reading of Thomas Aquinas in his historical context. His first essay in historical reconstruction of an Aquinas text (1923) was followed by many others, eventually collected in *La Parole de Dieu I—La foi dans l'intelligence* (Paris 1964). His notes toward a medieval philosophical lexicography (never completed), as well as his research on minor figures such as Robert Kilwardby, soon established him as a respected medievalist.

Having become regent of studies at Le Saulchoir, he published (privately) *Une école de théologie: Le Saulchoir* (1937), little more than a pamphlet, justifying the historical emphasis in theological studies and including some caustic asides about "Baroque Scholasticism." Immediately delated to the Dominican authorities in Rome for "Modernism," it was finally placed on the Index in 1942. Chenu continued to teach and to publish the results of his research, the bulk of which appeared in his three magisterial books, *Introduction à l'étude de saint Thomas d'Aquin* (Montreal and Paris 1950), *La théologie comme science au XIIIe siècle* (Paris 1957) and *La théologie au XIIe siècle* (Paris 1957). During the occupation he became increasingly involved in projects to rejuvenate urban Catholicism. He was in effect chief theological adviser to the nascent priest-worker movement in France. Papal anxieties about this movement emerged in the apostolic exhortation *Menti nostrae* (1950), while the encyclical *Humani generis* (1950) reaffirmed official disapproval of theologians who were dismissive of Scholasticism. By 1953 Chenu found himself relieved of all teaching duties and even exiled to Rouen for a time.

He continued to write, publishing *Saint Thomas d'Aquin et la théologie* (Paris 1959), but from this point onward his energies went increasingly into preaching. He was theological adviser to French-speaking African bishops at Vatican II, when, not surprised at the general abandonment of Thomism, he worked behind the scenes to have his ideas about Thomas Aquinas' "evangelical humanism" incorporated into such conciliar texts as *Gaudium et spes*. His later years, back in Paris, were devoted to communicating, in lectures and sermons, his optimistic interpretation of the significance of Vatican II. He had the satisfaction of seeing *Une école de théologie* republished (Paris 1985), but he would have been the first to concede that younger theologians had almost as little interest in his work on Thomas Aquinas as in that of Garrigou-Lagrange. His unfailing optimism, as well as his historian's perspective, assured him that Aquinas would eventually return to the center of Catholic theology. While not an original thinker, and the author in his middle years of much perishable journalism, Chenu remains, with his friend Étienne GILSON, a major figure in the history of the study of Thomas Aquinas.

Bibliography: A. DUVAL, "Bibliographie du P. Marie-Dominique Chenu (1921–1965)," *Mélanges offerts à M.-D. Chenu* (Paris 1967). O. DE LA BROSSE, *Le père Chenu: La liberté dans la foi* (Paris 1969).

[F. KERR]

CHERUBIM

An order of angelic spirits usually ranked after the SERAPHIM. Although the Hebrew word k^e *rûbîm* (plural of k^e *rûb*) may be connected with the Akkadian verb *karābu*, "to bless, to praise," there is no evidence that the Israelites ever considered cherubim as intercessors or praisers of Yahweh. Nor were cherubim thought to be angels, i.e., God's messengers. Cherubim were closely linked with God's glory. As representations in gilded wood and in relief carvings (1 Kgs 6.23–29; 2 Chr 3.7, 10–13), in gold and woven into cloth trappings of the TENT OF MEETING and the veil of the Holy of Holies (Ex 25.18–20; 26.1, 31; 2 Chr 3.14), they were prominent figures where God's glory was believed to dwell [*see* GLORY (IN THE BIBLE)]. They were humanlike in aspect but double-winged and were apparently reminders and guardians of Yahweh's glory.

Yahweh enthroned upon cherubim became a common concept in Israelite cultic lore [1 Sm 4.4; 2 Sm 6.2; 2 Kgs 19.15; 1 Chr 13.6; Is 37.16; Ps 79(80.2); 98(99.1)]. Once they were assigned "to guard the way to the tree of life" in God's garden (Gn 3.24). Perhaps a guarding function was normal for them, but there is no other explicit evidence. In 2 Sm 22.11 and [Ps 17(18.11)] a cherub was Yahweh's flying steed that He mounted to come swiftly to the psalmist's rescue and may have been symbolical of God's ubiquity and agility.

Ezekiel described God's chariot as supported and moved by "figures resembling four living creatures" (Ez

Stone carvings detailing cherub faces, Convent of Santo Domingo. (©Jeremy Horner/CORBIS)

1.4–28) and in 10.20 recognized them as cherubim. He saw them as human in form but four-winged and four-faced. Their wings were outstretched and supported the firmament above which God was enthroned in splendor. When they moved, their wings clapped like thunder, and they sounded like an army shouting a battle cry. They symbolized, then, God's power and mobility.

The part human and part animal mythical creatures of the ancient Middle East may have been the source of the much-modified Israelite conception of cherubim. In Phoenician culture a *krb* had the function of ushering worshipers to the deity and representations of *krb* guarding an enthroned king have been found. In the more ancient Akkadian culture a *kāribu* was an adviser to the gods and an advocate for devotees. In Israelite religion they had no direct role concerning the faithful, nor were they God's advisers. Their attendance on God's glory, their terrifying superhuman mobility, and in general the development of ANGELOLOGY in the postexilic period led to their identification with God's heavenly courtiers.

In the New Testament they are alluded to as celestial attendants in chapters four to six of the Revelation, where the author used imagery derived from Ezekiel. Catholic tradition describes them as angels who have an intimate knowledge of God and continually praise Him. This seems to be a theological development stemming from the four living beings of the Book of REVELATION.

Bibliography: M. HARAN, "The Ark and the Cherubim: Their Symbolic Significance in Biblical Ritual," *Israel Exploration Journal* 9:1 (1959) 30–38; 9:2 (1959) 89–98. W. B. BARRICK, "The Straight-legged Cherubim of Ezekiel's Inaugural Vision (Ezekiel 1:7a)," *Catholic Biblical Quarterly* 44 (1982) 543–550. R. GILBOA, "Cherubim: An Inquiry Into An Enigma," *Biblische Notizen* 82 (1996) 59–75. F. STRICKERT, "Philo on the cherubim," *The Studia Philonica Annual* (Atlanta 1996) 40–57. S. L. COOK, "Creation Archetypes and Mythogems in Ezekiel: Significance and Theological Ramifications," *Society of Biblical Literature Seminar Papers* v. 38 (Atlanta 1999) 123–146.

[T. L. FALLON/EDS.]

CHERUBIN OF AVIGLIANA, BL.

Augustinian friar; b. Avigliana (in Piedmont), 1451; d. Avigliana, Sept. 17, 1479. Of the noble Testa family, Cherubin entered the Augustinian monastery at Avigliana in his youth and from the beginning gave evidence of great holiness. He had ardent piety (which expressed itself particularly in devotion to the crucified Savior), a deep spirit of obedience, and a purity that impressed itself

Luigi Cherubini.

sensibly on those with whom he dealt. The usual *mirabilia,* reported in medieval hagiography, contributed to the development of his cult: at the time of his death, it is said, the church bells rang unaided by human hands; his body continued to give off a sweet odor long after he died. Perini identifies a sermon printed *c.* 1477 as probably his. He was beatified in 1865.

Feast: Dec. 17.

Bibliography: J. LANTERI, *Postrema saecula sex religionis Augustinianae,* 3 v. (Tolentino-Rome 1858–60) 2:58–59. G. B. IMPEROR, *Cuor-Giglio ossia il beato Cherubino da Avigliana* (Turin 1880). D. A. PERINI, *Bibliographia Augustiniana,* 4 v. (Florence 1929–38) 1:71.

[J. E. BRESNAHAN]

CHERUBINI, LUIGI

Composer of classical church music and opera; b. Florence, Italy, Sept. 14, 1760 (baptized Maria Luigi Carlo Zenobio Salvatore); d. Paris, March 15, 1842. Cherubini's catalogue is headed by a Mass in F which he composed at 13, after study from the age of six with his father and later with B. Felici and his son. In 1778, through the Grand Duke of Tuscany (later Emperor Leopold III), he began studies under Giuseppe Sarti at Milan

and then Bologna, which resulted in 20 Palestrina-styled motets. From 1780 to 1806 he concentrated on opera, and in his eight serious Paris operas (he had settled there in 1788) extended the reforms initiated by GLUCK. In 1795 he was appointed professor of counterpoint at the newly founded Paris Conservatory, and became director in 1822. Meanwhile, since Napoleon disliked his music, he moved in 1805 to Vienna, where he met BEETHOVEN (who regarded him as preeminent among living composers) and F. J. HAYDN, and was warmly received by the public; but he returned to Paris after the outbreak of war between Austria and France. Ill and depressed, he ceased composing altogether, until, while he was recuperating at the chateau of the Prince of Chimay, the local music society pleaded with him to compose a Mass for their church; thus began the great series of church music he produced between 1808 and 1836. Outstanding are the two orchestral Requiems, in C-minor and in D-minor (composed for his own funeral). In a memorable phrase about the C-minor's *Agnus Dei,* Cardinal J. H. Newman spoke of "the lovely note C, which keeps recurring as the *Requiem* approaches eternity." In both operatic and sacred forms he combined classic severity of style (tempered by modern harmonic resources and colorful orchestration), great contrapuntal skill, and dramatic power.

See Also: LITURGICAL MUSIC, HISTORY OF

Bibliography: E. BELLASIS, *Cherubini* (enl. ed. Birmingham, Eng. 1912). E. BLOM, "Cherubini in Church," *Stepchildren of Music* (London 1925). G. CONFALONIERI, *Prigiona di un artista: Il romanzo di Luigi Cherubini,* 2 v. (Milan 1948). M. QUATRELLES L'EPINE, *Cherubini, 1760–1842: Notes et documents inédits* (Lille 1913). A. LOEWENBERG, *Grove's Dictionary of Music and Musicians,* ed. E. BLOM, 9 v. (5th ed. London 1954) 2:198–201. N. SLONIMSKY, ed., *Baker's Biographical Dictionary of Musicians* (5th ed. New York 1958) 282–283. R. CARNESECCHI, "Cherubini, chantre de la Révolution," *Rassegna Veneta di Studi Musicali,* 4 (1998) 177–200. B. DEAN, "Luigi Cherubini," in *The New Grove Dictionary of Music and Musicians,* ed. S. SADIE, v. 4 (New York 1980) 203–213. P. GRIFFITHS, *The String Quartet: A History* (New York 1983) 116–118. M. HOHENEGGER, "Themenstrukturen in Orchesterwerken von Luigi Cherubini," *Studien zur Musikwissenschaft,* 43 (1994) 159–189; "Formstrukturen in den Ouverturen von Cherubinis frühen Opern," *Studien zur Musikwissenschaft,* 46 (1998) 95–142. A. JACOBSHAGEN, "*Koukourgi (1792–1793):* à propos d'un opéra-comique inconnu de Luigi Cherubini," *Revue de Musicologie,* 78 (1992) 257–287. S. C. WILLIS, "(Maria-) Luigi (-Carlo-Zenobio-Salvatore) Cherubini," in *International Dictionary of Opera,* ed. C. S. LARUE, 2 v. (Detroit 1993) 246–250; "*Médée (Medea),*" in *International Dictionary of Opera* ed. C. S. LARUE, 2 v. (Detroit 1993) 840–842.

[A. ROBERTSON]

CHESTER, ANCIENT SEE OF

The city of Chester in Cheshire, northwest England, south of Liverpool, may have been, at times, the seat of those bishops of the Anglo-Saxon kingdom of Mercia who are usually associated with Lichfield (*see* COVENTRY AND LICHFIELD, ANCIENT SEE OF). Medieval Chester became important when it was fortified in 907 by Queen Ethelfleda, becoming the site of a royal palace and the scene (973) of the submission of the kings of Britain to King EDGAR THE PEACEFUL. There were two collegiate churches at Chester by the 10th century: St. Werburgh, which was first attested in a document of King Edgar dated 958, and St. John the Baptist. These collegiate churches were restored by Leofric of Mercia *c.* 1057, and are both mentioned as having considerable endowments in the DOMESDAY survey. This same survey indicates that the bishops of Lichfield had retained a strong position in Chester until the time of the Conquest. Then in 1075 the Council of London, under the primacy of Abp. LANFRANC OF CANTERBURY, decreed the removal of the See of Lichfield to Chester. Bishop Peter of Lichfield moved there accordingly, and the collegiate church of St. John the Baptist became the cathedral. In 1102, however, the second bishop of Chester, Roger de Limesey (1086–1117), transferred his see to St. Mary's, Coventry, perhaps because of the hostility of the Welsh. The Abbey of St. Werburgh, refounded with Benedictine monks from BEC by Earl Hugh of Chester (1092), remained important, and it seems that Chester still gave the bishop his title, although no bishop seems to have lived there until the founding of the new see under HENRY VIII in 1541. At that date the abbey church of St. Werburgh became the cathedral.

Bibliography: C. HIATT, *The Cathedral Church of Chester* (London 1897). J. TAIT, ed., *The Domesday Survey of Cheshire* (Edinburgh 1916). D. JONES, *The Church in Chester, 1300–1540* (Manchester 1957) 4–5. R. V. H. BURNE, *Chester Cathedral, from its Founding by Henry VIII to the Accession of Queen Victoria* (London 1958). A. BRUCE, *The Cathedral 'Open and Free': Dean Bennett of Chester* (Liverpool 2000). A. THACKER, *Medieval Archaeology Art and Architecture at Chester* (Leeds 2000).

[V. I. J. FLINT/EDS.]

CHESTERTON, GILBERT KEITH

Writer, journalist, apologist, and illustrator; b. London, May 29, 1874; d. Beaconsfield, June 14, 1936. The Chestertons were of the middle class, "liberal" in politics and religion, and reasonably well to do. From their father, Edward, who "knew all his English literature backwards" and who "never made a vulgar success of all the thousand things he did so successfully," Gilbert and his brother Cecil (1879–1918) learned a love of literature. The Chestertons, in the noblest and most literal sense, were amateurs. From St. Paul's School, where he had been chairman of the junior debating club, and edited its journal (called, significantly, the *Debater*), Chesterton

Gilbert Keith Chesterton, February 1930. (Archive Photos, Inc.)

went (1891) to the London Slade School of Art, and, somewhat later, to lectures in English literature at University College, London.

First Three Periods. Chesterton's career falls into four periods. Before 1900 his work was sporadic, intuitive, and romantic. Swayed by idealism, he rebelled against decadent *fin de siècle* pessimism by adopting a Whitmanian optimism. He had not yet learned to distinguish rationalism (which he continued to abhor) from reason (which he came to rely upon in all judgments less than *de fide*); he had not become, as he labeled himself in his *St. Thomas,* a "moderate realist." Realizing that his work of these years was often unbalanced and antirational, Chesterton destroyed many early MSS and left "an absolute command" that his solipsistic juvenilia never be published.

In 1900 Chesterton emerged from obscurity. His periodical essays, collections of verse, and fantasies transformed him from publisher's reader to a Fleet Street legend. He had published his first poem in 1891, but it was not until 1901, the year of his marriage to Frances Blogg, that he settled in "the Street" for good and began his 12–year long weekly column in the *Daily News*. The first of his approximately 1,500 essays in the *Illustrated London News* appeared in 1905. The Chesterton of these years—a huge man, equipped with a sombrero, a sword-stick, a cape, and attended by an ever-waiting hansom cab—remained the public's image of "G. K. C. "

The forerunner of Chesterton's third period (1908–21) was *Heretics* (1905). A critic's challenge led to Chesterton's rebuttal, and his career as a Christian, but not yet Catholic, apologist opened in 1908 with *Orthodoxy*. These were the years when the two Chestertons, Hilaire BELLOC, H. G. Wells, and G. B. Shaw were influencing each other and England. The debate leading up to and following World War I hit Chesterton hard: the Marconi scandal of 1912–13, a nearly fatal physical and emotional breakdown in 1914, and the death of his brother Cecil in 1918 were the crises he faced.

The Final Period. Chesterton entered his final period by being received into the Catholic Church in 1922. His conversion, at 48, had been gradual, carefully reasoned, and deeply felt. His work in these last years was less gay and more polemic, perhaps less imaginative, but more serious and lasting than much of his earlier writing. Although his illustrations and prefaces became less numerous in the 1920s and 1930s, his contributions to journals were virtually innumerable. As one of the most prolific writers in modern times (especially in this last period), he wrote more than 3,000 prose and verse pieces for *G. K.'s Weekly* alone—sometimes as many as 10,000 words a week. His social, economic, and political propaganda became more searching, and in order to find an even wider audience for "orthodoxy," he turned to weekly broadcasts over the BBC. It was partly his lifelong success in finding new audiences that led Pius XI to bestow upon him (1936) the title of Defender of the Catholic Faith.

His Unique Achievement. Chesterton was neither conventional nor reactionary. He was, to put it bluntly, a rebel. His very reliance upon tradition was original and creative. Almost alone in the midst of the pessimists, agnostics, materialists, and aesthetes of the earliest years of the 20th century, Chesterton "came home." He rediscovered England, Rome—and the Occident. The Thomism latent in his early writings became manifest. (*See* THOMISM.) He taught the primacy of idea and a teleology of limits, and his religious teaching attacked doubt with commitment. He sought to undermine secularism with an apologia that took religion as the guide and goal of all thought and action. The core of Chesterton's moral thought was the vow; of his social thought, the family.

The enemies were eleutheromania and slavery. He fought capitalism and socialism with distributed ownership (*see* DISTRIBUTISM); industrialism and the "servile state" (the phrase is Belloc's) with the concept of the craftsman; imperialism and cosmopolitanism with nationalism; the expert and the misanthrope with the Common Man. He found sanity and creativity in a God-centered, not man-centered, universe; in an informed heart, not in rationalism or irrationalism.

Chesterton's aesthetics stressed art as a rational craft, as meaning. His literary theory was intellectual and antiromantic: literature is secondary—and never "autotelic." Chesterton might be called a metaphysical-moral critic: art is inseparable from creation and from morality. His styles followed his dogmas as conclusions follow premises.

In later life Chesterton's judgments became firmer. He attacked unreason and irrationalism with a style of topsy-turvy that was wholly conscious and wholly controlled. His was not an intuitive, but an individuating-synthesizing mind. The essence of Chesterton and his thought is balance, a balance seen in his dynamic syntheses of reason and faith, the real and the ideal, optimism and pessimism, the urgent and the absurd, the prose and the poetry of life. Because he related the ephemeral to the eternal, issue to principle, few of his writings will date. Not a few thinkers, among them C. S. LEWIS and Ronald KNOX, have acknowledged their intellectual and spiritual debt to this man, whom Étienne Gilson has called "one of the deepest thinkers who ever existed."

A selection of Chesterton's most significant works includes: poetry—*The Wild Knight* (1900), *The Ballad of the White Horse* (1911), *The Queen of the Seven Swords* (1926), *Collected Poems* (1927); novels and fantasies—*The Napoleon of Notting Hill* (1904), *The Man Who Was Thursday* (1908), *Manalive* (1912), *The Flying Inn* (1912); essays—*The Defendant* (1901), *Twelve Types* (1902), *Heretics* (1905), *Tremendous Trifles* (1909), *What's Wrong with the World* (1910), *Fancies versus Fads* (1923), *The Thing* (1929), *The Well and the Shallows* (1935); criticism and biography—*Robert Browning* (1903), *Charles Dickens* (1906), *George Bernard Shaw* (1909), *William Blake* (1910), *The Victorian Age in Literature* (1913), *William Cobbett* (1925), *Robert Louis Stevenson* (1927), *Chaucer* (1932); Christian apologetics and religious biography—*Orthodoxy* (1908), *St. Francis of Assisi* (1923), *The Everlasting Man* (1925), *The Catholic Church and Conversion* (1926), *St. Thomas Aquinas* (1933); plays—*Magic* (1913), *The Judgement of Dr. Johnson* (1927), *The Surprise* (1952); shorter fiction—*The Father Brown Stories* (omnibus ed. 1929), *The Poet and the Lunatics* (1929); travel, memoirs—*The New Je-*

rusalem (1921), *What I Saw in America* (1922), *The Resurrection of Rome* (1930), *Autobiography* (1936).

Bibliography: J. SULLIVAN, *G. K. Chesterton: A Bibliography* (London 1958). M. WARD, *Gilbert Keith Chesterton* (London 1944). C. E. CHESTERTON, *G. K. Chesterton: A Criticism* (London 1908). R. AROCENA, *El sembrado de Chesterton* (Montevideo 1934). E. CAMMAERTS, *The Laughing Prophet: The Seven Virtues and G. K. Chesterton* (London 1937). H. BELLOC, *On the Place of Gilbert Chesterton in English Letters* (New York 1940). R. A. KNOX, *Captive Flames* (New York 1941). V. J. MCNABB, *The Father McNabb Reader* (New York 1954) 82–93. G. WILLS, *Chesterton: Man and Mask* (New York 1961). *G. K. Chesterton: The Man Who Was Orthodox,* ed. A. L. MAYCOCK (London 1963). J. SULLIVAN, ed., *G. K. Chesterton: A Centenary Appraisal* (London 1974). M. COREN, *Gilbert: The Man Who Was Chesterton* (London 1989). J. PEARCE, *Wisdom and Innocence: A Life of G. K. Chesterton* (San Francisco 1996).

[A. HERBOLD]

CHEVALIER, JULES

Religious founder; b. Richelieu (Indre-et-Loire), France, March 15, 1824; d. Issoudun (Indre), Oct. 21, 1907. Because of his family's poverty he was apprenticed early to a shoemaker, but in 1841 he entered the preparatory seminary at Saint-Gauthier. After studies in the major seminary in Bourges he was ordained (1851) and spent the remainder of his life working in that archdiocese. He served in several parishes until in 1854 he became a curate in Issoudun. From 1872 until his death he was pastor and archpriest in Issoudun. With the encouragement of Father Maugenest, who had been a fellow seminarian, he founded the SACRED HEART MISSIONARIES (1854) and acted as their superior general until 1901. In 1882 he collaborated with Marie Hartzer to found the Daughters of OUR LADY OF THE SACRED HEART. Devotion to the SACRED HEART, around which his spirituality centered, formed the subject of all his writings. His two principal works, reprinted several times, are: *Notre-Dame du Sacré-Coeur de Jésus* (1895) and *Le Sacré-Coeur de Jésus* (1900). Chevalier was one of the leading promoters of devotion to the Sacred Heart in the 19th century.

Bibliography: C. PIPERON, *Le Très Révérend Père Jules Chevalier* (Lille 1924). K. SCHNEIDER, *Wege Gottes R. P. J. Chevalier* (Schwann 1928). H. VERMIN, *Le Père Jules Chevalier* (Rome 1957). R. LIMOUZIN-LAMOTHE, *Dictionnaire de biographie française* (Paris 1929–) 8:1064–65. A. BONDERVOET, *Dictionnaire d'histoire et de géographie ecclésiastiques,* ed. A. BAUDRILLART et al. (Paris 1912–) 12:647–648. L. DESPRESSE, *Dictionnaire de spiritualité ascétique et mystique. Doctrine et histoire,* ed. M. VILLER et al. (Paris 1932–) 2:829–831.

[L. F. PETIT]

CHEVALIER, ULYSSE

French bibliographer and historian; b. Cyr Ulysse Joseph Chevalier, at Rambouillet, Seine-et-Oise, France, Feb. 24, 1841; d. Romans, Drôme, France, Oct. 27, 1923. Chevalier was ordained in 1867, and was later named professor of archaeology at the major seminary at Romans (1881) and then of Church history at the Institut catholique of Lyons (1887). He was the recipient of academic honors and a member of many learned societies, including the Académie des inscriptions et belles-lettres. Guided by the great Léopold Delisle, Chevalier followed a life of scholarship, and by 1912 his publications totaled 512. Among the most important are: *Répertoire des sources historiques du moyen âge:* part one *Bio-bibliographie* (2d ed. 1905–07) and part two *Topo-bibliographie* (1894–1903; repr. New York 1962); *Gallia christiana novissima* in seven volumes (begun by J. H. Albanès but published with additions by Chevalier, 1899–1920); and *Repertorium hymnologicum* in six volumes, a catalogue of more than 30,000 hymns and chants used in the Roman rite (1892–1921). He wrote also numerous works on the history of Dauphiné. His name is associated with famous controversies over the authenticity (which he denied) of the Holy SHROUD of Turin (1900) and the Holy House of Loreto (1907). Chevalier's works are somewhat uneven in performance and some of them have become outdated. However, they have rendered appreciable service in the past and remain useful today, especially for the medievalist.

Bibliography: *M. le Chanoine Ulysse Chevalier, correspondant de l'Institut: Son oeuvre scientifique, sa bio-bibliographie* (new ed. Valence 1912). H. LECLERCQ, *Dictionnaire d'archéologie chrétienne et de liturgie,* ed. F. CABROL, H. LECLERCQ, and H. I. MARROU, 15 v. (Paris 1907–53) 9:1743–44. P. THOMÉ DE MAISONNEUFVE, *L'oeuvre scientifique du chanoine U. Chevalier* (Grenoble 1933). G. BARDY, *Catholicisme. Hier, aujourd'hui et demain,* ed. G. JACQUEMET (Paris 1947–) 10:1048–49. R. LIMOUZIN-LAMOTHE, *Dictionnaire de biographie française* (Paris 1929–) 8:1071–72.

[M. I. J. ROUSSEAU]

CHEVERUS, JEAN LOUIS LEFEBVRE DE

First bishop of BOSTON, Mass., bishop of Montauban, France, and cardinal archbishop of Bordeaux; b. Mayenne, France, Jan. 28, 1768; d. Bordeaux, July 19, 1836. He was the eldest of six children of Jean Vincent and Anne Charlotte (Lemarchand) Lefebvre de Cheverus. Educated first at the local *collège* of Mayenne, he was awarded a scholarship in 1781 for Louis-le-Grand in Paris. He subsequently entered Saint-Magloire Seminary and was ordained in Paris on Dec. 18, 1790, just as the

FRENCH REVOLUTION was gathering momentum. Returning to Mayenne he became (1791) an assistant to his uncle Louis René de Cheverus, pastor of Notre Dame de Mayenne. He refused to take the oath required by the CIVIL CONSTITUTION OF THE CLERGY and fled to England in 1792. He first taught French and mathematics in a Protestant school in Wallingford and offered Mass at Overy until he learned enough English to serve a congregation. In 1794 he founded Tottenham Chapel, one of three *émigré* foundations in the London suburbs that endured.

In 1796 he went to Boston at the invitation of Francis A. Matignon, pastor of Holy Cross Church. Submitting to the authority of Bp. John Carroll, he was first destined for the Detroit mission, but Matignon's protests retained him for the Boston area. In Maine he did yeoman service among the scattered white Catholics and the Passamaquoddy and Penobscot tribes, receiving for his missionary efforts among the Native Americans an annual stipend from the state of Massachusetts. Owing to the prejudice against Catholic clergy in New England, he was brought to court in 1800 to 1801 in both civil and criminal actions for having officiated at the marriage of a Maine couple, but was exonerated in both suits. His labors in Boston won the affection of Protestants and Catholics alike, particularly after his fearless and charitable efforts during the yellow fever epidemic of 1798. He was instrumental in the conversion of Elizabeth Bayley Seton, of New York; Dr. Stephen C. Blyth, of Salem; Thomas Walley, of Boston; Calvin White, of Connecticut; and Daniel Barber, of Vermont. His defense of the Church against an attack by John Lowell in the *Monthly Anthology and Boston Review* in 1807 earned him the respect and lifelong friendship of Anthology Club members Harrison Gray Otis, Josiah Quincy, John Kirkland, and Theodore Lyman. To the club's Athenaeum Library, he left his personal library on leaving Boston.

When Boston was created a diocese in 1808 he was named first bishop and was consecrated in Baltimore on Nov. 1, 1810. During his American episcopate (1810–23) he traveled ceaselessly, "more priest than bishop," in the pastoral care of a diocese that included all of New England. A fine preacher, he graced the pulpits of New York, Philadelphia, and Baltimore on his wider travels. In 1815 he dedicated old St. Patrick's Cathedral in New York. In Boston he founded an Ursuline convent (1817) and a second Catholic church, St. Augustine's (1819). His greatest contribution was fostering genuinely friendly relations between the Catholic minority and the non-Catholic majority. Protestant ministers, notably William Ellery CHANNING, Edward Everett, and Thaddeus M. Harris, remained his warm friends for life. When in 1823 Louis XVIII summoned Cheverus back to France, 226 Protestants framed a petition to the king pleading that Cheverus be left in Boston, saying, "We hold him to be a blessing and a treasure in our social community which we cannot part with." Among the signers were Elbridge Gerry, Daniel Webster, Josiah Quincy, and John Lowell.

Returning to France he became bishop of Montauban, a strong Protestant city, rebuilding from 1824 to 1826 a diocese that had suffered the ravages of the Revolution and the Napoleonic era. In 1826 he was made archbishop of Bordeaux and peer of France, serving in the upper chamber of the French legislature from 1827 to 1830. In 1828 Charles X made him councilor of state and in 1830 conferred the office of Commander of the Order of the Holy Spirit. In 1829 Cheverus instituted the first retirement plan for the clergy in the diocese of Bordeaux. Although devoted to the Bourbon monarchy, he nevertheless became a supporter of the Orleanist regime after the July Revolution of 1830. On the recommendation of Louis Philippe he was named cardinal in the consistory of Feb. 1, 1836, with the king himself conferring the red hat in the Tuileries Chapel on March 9, 1836. One of his last pastoral acts was the creation of an association for the care of 167 children left fatherless by a fishing disaster at the Teste in April 1836.

Bibliography: A. J. HAMON, *Life of the Cardinal Cheverus, Archbishop of Bordeaux,* tr. R. M. WALSH (Philadelphia 1839). A. M. MELVILLE, *Jean Lefebvre de Cheverus, 1768–1836* (Milwaukee 1958). W. M. WHITEHILL, *A Memorial to Bishop Cheverus* (Boston 1951).

[A. M. MELVILLE]

CHEVETOGNE, MONASTERY OF

Benedictine foundation outside Rochefort, Diocese of Namur, southeast Belgium; dedicated to the exaltation of the Holy Cross. Founded in 1925 at Amay-sur-Meuse (Diocese of Liège) by Lambert BEAUDUIN in response to Pius XI's *Equidem verba* (1924) inviting Benedictines to work for Christian unity, it became a priory (1928) and moved to Chevetogne (1939). It seeks to establish a *rapprochement* between Rome and other Eastern Christian churches, especially Russian and other Orthodox churches, working for corporate reconciliation rather than for individual conversions. The community celebrates divine services in the Latin and Byzantine (Greek and Slavonic) liturgical rites and pursues studies in the history, theology, and spirituality of non-Catholic groups. The "irenic" method has been presented in the review *Irénikon* since 1926. Works on history, ecclesiology, the liturgy, and comparative theology and spirituality appear in *Editions de Chevetogne.* Byzantine and Russian religious art are reproduced. Annual conferences have been held since 1942. The monastery, which has directed the Pontifical

Greek College in Rome since 1956, depends on the Congregation for the EASTERN CHURCHES. The monastery church (1957) is in Byzantine style. A center for ecumenical training was established in 1964.

Bibliography: *Le Monastère de Chevetogne: Notice historique* (Chevetogne 1962). L. BOUYER, *Dom Lambert Beauduin, un homme d'Église* (Paris 1964). G. CURTIS, *Paul Couturier and Unity in Christ* (Westminster, Md. 1964). R. GAZEAU, *Catholicisme. Hier, aujourd'hui et demain,* ed. G. JACQUEMET (Paris 1947–) 1:406–407. N. EGENDER, *Lexikon für Theologie und Kirche,* ed. J. HOFER and K. RAHNER, 10 v. (2d, new ed. Freiburg 1957–65) 1:421. O. L. KAPSNER, *A Benedictine Bibliography: An Author-Subject Union List,* 2 v. (2d ed. Collegeville, Minn. 1962): v. 1, author part; v. 2, subject part, 2:196–197.

[N. EGENDER]

CHEVRIER, ANTOINE MARIE, BL.

Priest, Franciscan tertiary, and founder of the priests and sisters of the Institute of the Prado; b. Lyons, France, April 16, 1825; d. Lyons, Oct. 2, 1879. The son of silk industry workers in Lyons, Chevrier was ordained in 1850 and immediately began serving the poor in Saint-André parish in the Guillotière, a working class suburb of Lyons. His ministry was transformed in 1856 when he discerned a call to help victims of the Rhône flood and share in their disinheritance. In 1857, he consulted with John VIANNEY who encouraged him to become chaplain of the "Ville de Jesus Infant," a massive charitable organization founded by Camille Rambaud. In 1860, Chevrier acquired the infamous dance hall called "The Prado" and converted it into "the Providence of the Prado," which included lodgings and classrooms for poor children and adolescents, as well as a clinic for the sick. While continuing to live at the Prado, Chevrier was assigned to the parish of Moulin-à-Vent nearby (1867), but was relieved of this duty in 1871 in order to devote himself full time to establishing a congregation to continue the Prado.

He wrote thousands of pages of commentary, including treatises and a training manual, to assist those who followed him. The Society of the Priests of the Prado came to fruition in 1877, when the first four men had completed their studies in Rome and received ordination. The Institute consists of priests, religious, and lay collaborators. Chevrier died at age fifty-four and was buried in the chapel of the Prado. He was beatified by John Paul II (Oct. 4, 1986, in Lyons) who called Chevrier "the apostle of the poorest working class neighbors outside Lyons at the moment in which great industry was born" (beatification homily).

Feast: Oct. 2.

Bibliography: M. ALLIOD, *Un fondateur d'action sociale, Antoine Chevrier* (Paris 1992). A. ANCEL, *Le Prado: la spiritualité apostolique du Père Chevrier* (Paris 1982). A. C. B. ARTS, *De eerbeid waardige Père Antoine Chevrier* (Bussum 1946). P. BERTHELON, *Le message du père Chevrier* (Le Puy 1960); *A. Chevrier, un carisma per evangelitzar els pobres* (Montserrat 1986); *Antoine Chevrier: prêtre selon l'Evangile* (Paris 1986). A. LESTRA, *Le maréchal Pétain chez le père Chevrier.* . . . (Lyon 1941); *Le père Chevrier, avec lettres de Son éminence le cardinal Pacelli et de Son éminence le cardinal Maurin* (Paris 1944). *L'Osservatore Romano,* English edition, no. 42 (1986): 2–4. J. F. SIX, *Vie du père Chevrier, prêtre selon l'Evangile* (Paris 1986). H. WALTZ, *Un pauvre parmi nous, le Père Chevrier* (Lyon 1941). *Acta Apostolicae Sedis* 79 (1987): 301–10.

[K. I. RABENSTEIN]

CHEZAL-BENOÎT, ABBEY OF

Saint-Pierre de Chezal-Benoît (known also as Chazeau-Benoist; Latin, *Casale Malanum, Casale Benedictum*), a Benedictine abbey, located in the Diocese of Bourges, parish and township of Chezal-Benoît, department of Cher, France. The abbey was founded in 1093 by Andrew of Vallombrosa (d. 1112) in a deserted spot. Nothing certain is known of the abbey's history before 1479, when Peter of Mas, the prior of Castres in the Diocese of Albi, became abbot and introduced the reform of the Congregation of St. Justina (Padua) (*see* BENEDICTINES). He abolished the long offices, fasts, and severe punishments, and established a three-year term for the abbots who were elected by a general chapter. The reform, ratified by the Holy See in 1491, was adopted by the following abbeys: Saint-Sulpice of Bourges in 1499, Saint-Allyre of Clermont in 1500, and Saint-Vincent of Mans in 1502. The religious of Chezal-Benoît were formed into a congregation in 1505. There was a continuous line of abbots regularly elected from 1515 to 1763. The following abbeys were attached to Chezal-Benoît: Saint-Martin of Sées in 1511, SAINT-GERMAIN-DES-PRÉS in 1514, Brantôme in 1541, Sainte-Colombe of Sens in 1580, and JUMIÈGES in 1515 and 1580. Several monks were outstanding for their virtue or for their contributions as historians or men of letters: Charles Fernand, Guido Jouvenaux, Jehmann Bondonnet, and Jacques du Breul, who contributed to the MAURIST tradition of learning and industry. When the congregation fell into decline, it was absorbed by Saint-Maur (May 2, 1636). The name of Chezal-Benoît was given to the Maurist houses (numbering about 25) in the region between the Loire and the Dordogne. The abbey was abolished in February 1790, but the abbey church remains.

Bibliography: Sources. Archives Nationales, Paris, LL. 1328–32. Bibliothèque Nationale, Paris, MS Lat. 12787. Bibl. Bourges MSS 184, 187, 191. *Gallia Christiana* 2:162–168. L. V. DELISLE, ed., *Rouleaux des morts du IX ͤ au XV ͤ siècle* (Paris 1866) 168–171. U. BERLIÈRE, "La Congrégation de Chezal-Benoît," *Mélanges d'histoire bénédictine,* 4 v. (Maredsous 1897–1902)

3:97–198. F. DESHOULIÈRES, "L'Église abbatiale de Chezal-Benoît," *Bulletin monumental* 71 (1907) 287–306; "L'Abbaye de Chezal-Benoît," *Mém. soc. antiq. centre* 32 (1909) 149–229. J. LAPORTE, "Aperçu des déclarations de la congrégation de Chezal-Benoît sur la Règle," *Revue Mabillon* 29 (1939) 143–157. L. H. COTTINEAU, *Répertoire topo-bibliographique des abbayes et prieurés* 1:766–767.

[J. LAPORTE]

CHÉZARD DE MATEL, JEANNE MARIE

Foundress of Sisters of the Incarnate Word and the Blessed Sacrament; b. Matel, France, November 1596; d. Paris, 1670. She was a mystic and writer, known for her elevated states of prayer and her infused knowledge of Latin. Although she was an almost illiterate person, she wrote letters and a spiritual journal that have caused her to be compared with Saint Gertrude the Great. Because her devotional writings were framed in technical theological terms, doubts of her authorship were aroused in the mind of Cardinal Alphonse Richelieu. He removed all of her references and then commanded her to write her autobiography and spiritual history. She produced a work of lofty style, replete to an astonishing degree with mystical speculations and liturgical texts. Her institute was authorized in 1633 but not formally begun until 1639 at Matel; it was finally approved in 1644. Her second monastery was erected at Grenoble, and the third, at Paris. Here, on her deathbed, she received the habit of the institute she had founded and made her profession of vows. American branches of her foundation spring from an original foundation in Brownsville, Tex.

Bibliography: L. CRISTIANI, *Dictionnaire de spiritualité Ascétique et mystique. Doctrine et histoire,* ed. M. VILLER (Paris 1932–) 2:837–840. H. WAACH, *Lexikon für Theologie und Kirche,* ed. J. HOFER and K. RAHNER (Freiburg 1957–65) 2:1049. M. HEIMBUCHER, *Die Oerden und Kongregationen der katholischen Kirche,* 2 v. (3d ed. Paderborn 1932–34) 2:427–428. ST. PIERRE OF JESUS, *Life of the Reverend Mother Jeanne Chézard de Matel,* tr. H. C. SEMPLE (5th ed. San Antonio 1922).

[M. J. DORCY]

CHI-RHO

The Chi-Rho is a symbol for the Greek ΙΗΣΟΥΣ ΧΡΙΣΤΟΣ (Jesus Christ) constituted by the abbreviation of the first letters of the two words, I and XP (X or chi, and P or rho) respectively. The first dated use is 269. In the pre-Constantinian use, the chi and iota were combined, almost always as part of an inscription with ἐν (in Christ) or with δοῦλος (servant of Christ). The Chi-Rho form stood for I and XP (Jesus and Christ), but the symbol had been in use among the pagans as an abbreviation for many words beginning with XP, such as χρόνος (time) and χρυσός (gold). However, the vision of CONSTANTINE I in 312, as reported by LACTANTIUS (*De morte* 44) and EUSEBIUS OF CAESAREA in the *Vita Constantini,* led to the use of the symbol of the name or cross of Christ on the soldiers' shields, on the LABARUM, and on coins, apparently in the Chi-Rho form, as well as in the so-called Egyptian *tau* form; alternate forms with the vertical axis placed at an angle and the loop of the rho reversed became common also.

The earliest Christian employment of the Chi-Rho monogram dates from the reign of Constantine. During the 4th and 5th centuries its use on coins, on the exterior and interior of churches and basilicas, as well as on sarcophagi and funeral monuments in the catacombs and cemeteries, became widespread. It was used also as a decorative emblem on glasses and cups, on the exterior of homes, particularly in Syria, and on medals, rings, furniture, and utensils. St. JOHN CHRYSOSTOM mentions its use in epistles [*Patrologica Graeca*, ed. J. P. Migne, (Paris 1857–66) 62:364]. During this period it was likewise used in combination with other symbols. It is found flanked with the alpha and omega (A and Ω) standing for Christ in the midst of the divine eternity, or with the A and Ω pendant from the cross-bar. In Gallic inscriptions and decorations the Chi-Rho is almost always surrounded by a wreath or palm or other leaves, symbolizing the Lord's victory; and occasionally the Chi-Rho is found in the midst of an N, meaning Christ conquers. During the Middle Ages it appeared at the beginning of charters; Merovingian scribes distorted it with flourishes. The imperial chancery used it until *c.* 1200. It appeared in papal documents frequently until the pontificate of LEO IX (d. 1054); after the time of GREGORY VII (d. 1085) the chrismon was used only in private charters. In the late Middle Ages the Chi-Rho symbol was gradually replaced by the combination IHS, derived from the first three Greek letters of the name Jesus. By popular etymology the IHS was interpreted as *In hoc signo* (In this sign, namely, the sign of the cross of Christ), or as *Jesus hominum Salvator.* The Chi-Rho was used, particularly in the East, as an amulet to ward off sickness or danger from evil spirits.

Bibliography: I. SAUER, *Lexikon für Theologie und Kirche* 2:1177, with bibl. F. CABROL, *Dictionnaire d'archéologie chrétienne et de liturgie,* ed. F. CABROL, H. LECLERCQ, and H. I. MARROU, 15 v. (Paris 1907–53) 1.1:1–25. H. LECLERCQ, *ibid.* 3.1:1481–1534. L. TRAUBE, *Nomina sacra* (Munich 1907). V. GARDTHAUSEN, *Das alte Monogramm* (Leipzig 1924). A. WREDE, in *Handwörterbuch des deutschen Aberglaubens,* ed. H. BÄCHTOLD–STÄUBLI, 10 v. (Berlin 1927–42) 2:76–82.

[D. KELLEHER/C. M. AHERNE]

CHIBCHA RELIGION

The Chibcha, a group of South American natives, occupied the high valleys surrounding the modern cities of Bogotá and Tunja in Colombia before the Spanish conquest. The Chibcha religion was of both state and individual concern. Each political division had its own set of priests. Apparently some kind of hierarchy was recognized and the priests were a professional hereditary class. Priests, who were clearly distinguished from shamans, had as their functions the intercession at public ceremonies for the public good, the dispensing of oracles, and consultation with private individuals. Shamans served the individual more than the state and cured illnesses, interpreted dreams, and foretold the future. The Chibchas had an elaborate pantheon of gods headed by Chiminigagua, the supreme god and creator. In addition to the state temples and idols, many natural habitats were considered to be holy places. Ceremonial practices included offerings, public rites, pilgrimages, and human sacrifice. Human sacrifice was said to be fairly common and was made primarily to the sun.

Bibliography: A. L. KROEBER, "The Chibcha," *Handbook of South American Indians*, ed. J. H. STEWARD, 2 v. (Bureau of American Ethnology, Bulletin 143; Washington 1946) 2:905–909. J. PÉREZ DE BARRADAS, *Los Muiscas antes de la conquista*, 2 v. (Madrid 1950–51) 2:435–511.

[J. RUBIN]

CHICAGO, ARCHDIOCESE OF

A metropolitan see (*Chicagiensis*) comprising Cook and Lake counties, IL, an area of 1,411 sq. miles, with a population (1999) of 5,682,000, of whom 2,358,000 (41%) were Catholics; the diocese was erected Nov. 28, 1843; the archdiocese, Sept. 10, 1880. The suffragan dioceses of Belleville, Joliet, Peoria, Rockford, and Springfield constituted, with Chicago, the territory of the original see.

Since 1673, when Jacques Marquette, S.J., and Louis Jolliet (Joliet) passed through what is now Chicago on their return after exploring the Mississippi River, the area has had Catholic associations. A year later, fulfilling a promise he had made to the Kaskaskia natives, Marquette left Green Bay, WI, with two French *voyageurs* and reached the south branch of the Chicago River, where severe weather and serious illness forced him to remain several months. During their stay he offered Mass daily. Subsequently the area was visited by other missionaries and *voyageurs* including, in 1696, François Pinet, S.J., first resident priest and founder of the Mission of the Guardian Angel, which for unknown reasons closed in

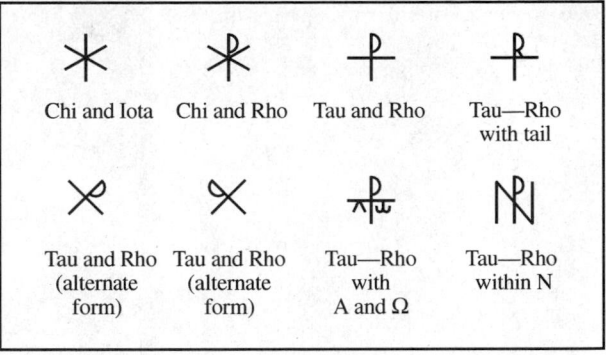

Chi and Iota	Chi and Rho	Tau and Rho	Tau—Rho with tail
Tau and Rho (alternate form)	Tau and Rho (alternate form)	Tau—Rho with A and Ω	Tau—Rho within N

1700. Originally part of the Quebec diocese, Chicago was transferred in 1784 to the prefecture apostolic of the U.S., which became the Baltimore diocese in 1789; in 1808 it passed under the jurisdiction of the new Diocese of Bardstown, KY. Thereafter Chicago was visited by Gabriel Richard, S.S., who arrived from Detroit in September 1821 to offer Mass and preach to the garrison at Ft. Dearborn, and Stephen Badin, the first priest ordained within the U.S., who came in October 1830 from his Potawatomi mission near Niles, MI. In 1834, when the Diocese of Vincennes was erected, eastern Illinois was included in its territory. When Chicago was incorporated as a town in 1833, its 130 Catholic inhabitants, under the impression that they belonged to the St. Louis diocese, petitioned Bp. Joseph Rosati for a resident pastor. To the distant mission was sent the newly ordained John Mary Irenaeus St. Cyr, who built the first Catholic Church, St. Mary's, on the southwest corner of Lake and State Streets. (It was later moved to Madison Street and Wabash Avenue).

Diocese

At the request of the Fifth Provincial Council of Baltimore (1843), Gregory XVI on Nov. 28, 1843, created the new Diocese of Chicago, embracing the entire state of Illinois.

Quarter. The first bishop of Chicago was William QUARTER, pastor of St. Mary's Church, New York City, who was consecrated by Bp. John Hughes in New York on March 10, 1844. The new bishop, with his brother, Father Walter Quarter, arrived in Chicago on May 5 where he soon learned that all but eight of the 24 priests who had been serving throughout the state had been recalled to their respective dioceses by the bishops of St. Louis and Vincennes. Undaunted by the shortage of clergy and the poverty of the settlers, Quarter first opened the College of St. Mary's as a boys' school and seminary and then petitioned the Illinois legislature, which passed an act on Dec. 19, 1844, incorporating the University of St. Mary of the Lake. In New York the following April, he

"Religious Service in Holy Family Parish Church in Chicago" by Franklin McMahon. (©Franklin McMahon/CORBIS)

begged funds to provide this first institution of higher learning in Chicago with a suitable university building; this was dedicated July 4, 1846. At his invitation, the Sisters of Mercy established St. Xavier's Academy for girls in September 1846.

St. Mary's was Chicago's only church when Quarter arrived. In 1846 St. Patrick's was built for the West-side Irish; St. Peter's, for the South-side Germans; and St. Joseph's, for the North-side Germans; while English-speaking Catholics on the North side used Holy Name, the university chapel. By the end of his four-year episcopate he had built 30 churches; ordained 29 priests; traveled extensively throughout the diocese preaching and administering the Sacraments; convened the first diocesan synod in April 1847, preceding it by a three-day retreat for all priests; successfully petitioned the state legislature to enact a law (1845) constituting the Catholic bishop of Chicago and his successors a corporation sole to hold property in trust for religious purposes; and ar-

ranged what was reputed to be the first theological conference held in the U.S., which assembled Nov. 12, 1847 in the university chapel. On Passion Sunday, April 9, 1848, the bishop preached with his usual vigor at the cathedral, but died the following morning. All his property was willed to St. Mary of the Lake University.

Van de Velde. To succeed Quarter, Pius IX appointed the Belgian, James Oliver van de Velde, who had entered the Society of Jesus when he immigrated to the U.S. in 1817 at the age of 22. After completing his studies he had served at St. Louis University, where he was in turn professor, vice president, and president. Despite his efforts to decline the episcopal honor, he was released from his vows and persuaded by Abp. Peter Kenrick of St. Louis and a board of three theologians to receive consecration on Feb. 11, 1849, in St. Louis. On his way to Chicago for installation on Palm Sunday, April 1, 1849, the new bishop visited many parishes of his diocese. Upon learning that his predecessor's will left property, including the episcopal residence, to the University of St. Mary of the Lake, Van de Velde ordered that it be completely restored to him. A serious disagreement resulted when the university faculty failed to accede to all his demands, insisting that the property had been purchased with the personal funds of the two Quarter brothers. This disagreement plus his desire to become a Jesuit again, the rigors of the northern Illinois climate, and his declining health led Van de Velde in 1852 to tender his resignation as bishop. A year later he was restored to the Society of Jesus, and Pius IX transferred him to the see at Natchez, MS, at the same time dividing Chicago by creating Quincy, a diocese for the southern half of Illinois. At his departure, Nov. 4, 1853, there were 119 churches in the state, 70 of them having been commenced by him. Of these, 53 were in places where no church had previously existed. The first Catholic hospital, the first orphanage, and ten new parochial schools, likewise, owe their origin to this prelate.

O'Regan. The third bishop, Anthony O'Regan, of County Mayo, Ireland, had been educated at St. Patrick's College, Maynooth, Kildare, Ireland, and then made professor and later president of St. Jarlath College, Tuam, Galway, Ireland. At the invitation of Kenrick of St. Louis, O'Regan became first president of the new theological seminary at Carondelet, MO, from which post he was called to head the Chicago diocese. Consecrated in St. Louis on July 25, 1854, he was installed in his see city the following September. Within five months, misunderstandings concerning finances led him to dismiss the four diocesan priests who constituted the faculty of St. Mary of the Lake. The four priests, whose withdrawal was lamented by the students, subsequently rendered distinguished service in the dioceses of Trenton and New York. After O'Regan's unsuccessful efforts to induce the Jesuits to assume direction of the university, the building was rented to Father Edward Sorin, founder of Notre Dame University, IN, for a high school.

The success of a series of parochial missions conducted by the Jesuit, Arnold Damen, in 1856 in Chicago led to the establishment of Holy Family Church, which later developed into a large parish with St. Ignatius College and High School on its property. To provide for the French-speaking people of Illinois, Van de Velde had admitted into the diocese Charles CHINIQUY, a Canadian priest in trouble with his bishop. In 1856 O'Regan was forced to suspend and excommunicate the priest for his unorthodox sermons and strange conduct. The prelate's difficulties with the university faculty and with Chiniquy prompted him to resign. In 1858 he went to Rome, was appointed titular bishop of Dora, and retired to Brompton, London, England, where he died Nov. 13, 1866. Meanwhile in 1857 the Alton diocese (later Springfield)

was erected, and Quincy, established in 1853 but never occupied, was joined to it, thus separating central and southern Illinois from Chicago's jurisdiction.

Duggan. Chicago's fourth bishop was well-acquainted with the diocese. Born in Maynooth, County Kildare, James Duggan had left Ireland at 17 to study philosophy and theology at St. Vincent's, Cape Girardeau, MO; was ordained by special dispensation at 22; and six years later was made administrator of Chicago following Van de Velde's departure in 1853. Only ten years after he was ordained, he was consecrated bishop of Antigone and coadjutor to Kenrick of St. Louis. Upon O'Regan's resignation he again became administrator of Chicago, succeeding to the see on Jan. 21, 1859.

Chicago's growth was temporarily interrupted during the first two years of the Civil War, but thereafter parishes began to multiply; 16 were founded during Duggan's tenure. His negotiations with Sorin for the return of the university property culminated in July 1861 when the Holy Cross Fathers left Chicago, and the institution reopened under Father John McMullen. Two years later the seminary department was established under Rector James McGovern. The university, affiliated in 1863 with Rush Medical College and the City Law School, flourished until January 1866, when it was closed abruptly and turned into an orphanage. Duggan, whose inconstancy of purpose and action began to indicate incipient insanity, closed the seminary in August 1868 and ordered the faculty to leave the diocese. By spring 1869 his mental collapse was complete and he was confined to an asylum conducted by the Sisters of Charity near St. Louis, where he lived until 1899 without showing any improvement.

Foley. For the difficult position of administrator, Rome chose Thomas Foley, long-term rector of Baltimore's (old) Cathedral of the Assumption and, at different times, chancellor, vicar general, and administrator of the Baltimore archdiocese. Appointed titular bishop of Pergamus and coadjutor bishop and administrator of Chicago with right of succession, he was consecrated Feb. 27, 1870, in Baltimore and installed in Holy Name procathedral the following month. During his first year 15 new parishes, a hospital, and several new schools were founded. When Chicago's great fire of Oct. 9, 1871, gutted the whole center of the city, seven churches and adjoining rectories and schools were destroyed at a loss of $1 million. In the work of restoration, more substantial and modern structures were built; the cathedral was moved to Holy Name parish, where the new structure was dedicated on Nov. 21, 1875. To help care for the immigrants streaming into Chicago during these years, Foley welcomed many religious orders, including the Franciscans, Lazarists, Servites, Viatorians, and Resurrectionists. At his suggestions, the Peoria diocese was established in 1877.

Archdiocese

When Foley died on Feb. 19, 1879, it was evident that the ailing Duggan would not recover, so Rome rectified the situation by creating Chicago an archdiocese, with Bp. Patrick A. FEEHAN of Nashville, TN, as first archbishop.

Feehan. After being educated at St. Patrick's College, Maynooth, Ireland, and the seminary at Carondolet, MO, Feehan was ordained in 1852. Being a man of unusual administrative ability for which he was subsequently noted, he was an obvious choice for Chicago. He was named on Sept. 10, 1880, and installed in Holy Name Cathedral on November 28. During the next 20 years he worked to provide clergy, churches, and schools for the waves of Catholic immigrants descending upon Chicago. Under him Chicago's churches increased to 298; the number of priests to 538; grammar schools to 166, with 62,723 pupils; and the Catholic population to 800,000.

The first archdiocesan synod was held on Dec. 13, 1887, when the decrees of the Third Council of Baltimore were promulgated and the first diocesan consultors and permanent rectors appointed. When Feehan's advanced age and increasing burdens made an assistant necessary, Alexander J. McGavick, pastor of St. John's church, was appointed titular bishop of Narcopolis and auxiliary bishop of Chicago. Soon after his consecration on May 1, 1899, he became incapacitated and was replaced by Peter J. Muldoon, pastor of St. Charles Borromeo, who was appointed titular bishop of Tamassus and consecrated by the apostolic delegate, Cardinal Sebastian Martinelli, on July 25, 1901. Some Irish-born Chicago clergy resented the choice of Muldoon, a native-born American who had been Feehan's chancellor for many years. One of the malcontents, Jeremiah J. Crowley, pastor of St. Mary's Church, Oregon, IL, was excommunicated for his stubborn opposition, and this situation clouded the last year of Feehan's life. He died suddenly on July 12, 1902, from an apoplectic stroke.

Quigley. On Jan. 8, 1903, Pope Leo XIII transferred James Edward Quigley, bishop of Buffalo, to Chicago where he was installed on March 10. Born in Canada, he had moved as a youth to Buffalo; and had studied at the seminary in Niagara, NY, at Innsbruck, Austria, and at the Propaganda College in Rome, where he was ordained April 12, 1879, and received a doctorate in theology. Upon his return to the U.S. he was pastor of St. Vincent's, Attica, NY, for five years, rector of the cathedral for 12 years, and pastor of St. Bridget's for a few months. On Feb. 24, 1897, he was consecrated bishop of Buffalo, where he won recognition for his administrative ability and for his part in settling the Buffalo dock strike of 1899.

Soon after his installation as Chicago's second archbishop on March 10, 1903, Quigley realized the need for increased facilities for training the clergy and, in October 1905, he opened Cathedral College of the Sacred Heart as a preparatory seminary. During his episcopate the second archdiocesan synod was held on Dec. 14, 1905; a missionary congress met in Chicago Nov. 16–18, 1908; Paul P. Rhode, the first priest of Polish lineage to be elevated to the U.S. hierarchy, was consecrated on July 29, 1908, as one of Quigley's auxiliary bishops; and Rockford was established as a diocese on Sept. 23, 1908, with Bishop Muldoon as first ordinary. With the assistance of the archbishop, the Catholic Church Extension Society for home missions was founded in 1905 in Chicago by Francis C. KELLEY, pastor of Immaculate Conception Church, at Lapeer, MI. When he died on July 10, 1915, Quigley's administration had restored peace to the archdiocese where, in 12 years, parish churches had increased to 326 and clergy to 790, despite the loss of 55 parishes and 74 priests to the new Rockford diocese in 1908.

Mundelein. Rome again looked to New York in selecting George William MUNDELEIN, auxiliary bishop of Brooklyn, to be Chicago's third archbishop. He was installed Feb. 9, 1916, by the apostolic delegate, Abp. (Cardinal) John Bonzano. Finding the facilities of Cathedral College inadequate, the archbishop initiated Quigley Preparatory Seminary in May 1916, and made plans for the erection of a theological seminary on the shores of Lake Eara in Lake County near Area, IL. Under the charter for the University of St. Mary of the Lake, which had been closed since 1866, Mundelein had 14 separate buildings of uniform Georgian style erected there from 1920 to 1934 to constitute St. Mary of the Lake Seminary. After Mundelein was made a cardinal by Pius XI on March 24, 1924, the town of Area changed its name to Mundelein and, with Chicago, was host to the 28th International Eucharistic Congress (June 20–24, 1926).

Catholic Charities was founded in January 1918 to organize the welfare work of the archdiocese. From World War I to the Depression of the 1930s, churches, schools, convents, rectories, and hospitals multiplied rapidly. In 1930 Mundelein directed his auxiliary, Bp. Bernard J. Sheil, to establish the Catholic Youth Organization for the spiritual, mental, and physical development of Catholic youth. Despite the Depression, the finances of the archdiocese were so carefully managed that Bishop of Chicago bonds remained at par during these years. Under Mundelein's vigorous administration, Chicago also attained international recognition. In 1929 the archdiocese contributed $1.5 million toward the new Propaganda College in Rome; and in 1934 for his silver episcopal jubilee, the cardinal acquired the Collegio S. Maria del Lago, a residence for postgraduate students in Rome. When Mundelein died suddenly on Oct. 2, 1939, 82 new parishes had been established and the clergy in the archdiocese had increased to 1,779.

Stritch. On Dec. 27, 1939, Rome announced the transfer of Samuel Alphonsus STRITCH, archbishop of Milwaukee, to Chicago where he was installed on March 7, 1940, by the apostolic delegate, Abp. (Cardinal) Amleto Cicognani. A firm believer in the Catholic press, Stritch promoted the diocesan paper, the *New World*, which increased its circulation from 10,000 in 1940 to 210,000 in 1958. In 1941 he established the Confraternity of Christian Doctrine for teaching released-time programs, parish high schools of religion, lay teacher training courses, parish information classes, and home study courses. He reorganized the Archdiocesan Council of Catholic Women in 1942 and affiliated it with the National Council of Catholic Women; added to Catholic Charities specialized services for the deaf and blind, a guidance center for children, and a house for alcoholics; opened the Catholic Action Federations Office to coordinate the Young Christian Students (YCS), the Young Christian Workers (YCW), and the Christian Family Movement (CFM); set up the Catholic Council on Working Life in 1943; formally recognized the Cana movement, begun in Chicago in 1944, by the appointment of a full-time chaplain in 1946; opened Cardinal Stritch Retreat House for diocesan priests on St. Mary of the Lake Seminary grounds in 1951; appointed an archdiocesan commission on sacred music in 1953; and four years later set up an archdiocesan office for radio and television.

The post-World War II years witnessed the phenomenal growth of the African-American population in Chicago and the movement to the suburbs. Stritch founded a Catholic Interracial Council in 1945; he insisted upon racial integration and kept all parishes functioning in African-American neighborhoods. A group of parish priests formed the Cardinal's Conservation Council to meet the problem of changing neighborhoods. To keep pace with the population explosion on the city's periphery and in the suburbs, 77 new parishes were founded and the Diocese of Joliet was established on Dec. 11, 1948, leaving Chicago with only two counties, Cook and Lake.

Elevated to the College of Cardinals by Pius XII on Feb. 18, 1946, Stritch was appointed pro-prefect of the Congregation for the Propagation of the Faith in 1958. Shortly after his arrival in Rome, he suffered a stroke and died there on May 27, 1958. He was buried on June 3 in Mt. Carmel Cemetery, Hillside, IL.

Meyer. Chicago's fifth archbishop, Albert Gregory MEYER, was born in Milwaukee, WI, March 9, 1903; he attended St. Mary's Parochial School, Marquette High School, and St. Francis Preparatory Seminary in Milwaukee, and the North American College in Rome, where he was ordained by Cardinal Basilio Pompilj on July 11, 1926. After receiving the licentiate in Sacred Scripture from the Roman Pontifical Biblical Institute, he returned to the U.S. where he was curate for a year, then professor, and later rector of St. Francis Seminary until he was named bishop of Superior, WI, on Feb. 18, 1946. He was consecrated in Milwaukee by Abp. Moses E. Kiley on April 11, 1946, and enthroned in Superior the following month. Seven years later he was summoned back to be archbishop of Milwaukee and installed on Sept. 24, 1953. His transfer to Chicago came on Sept. 19, 1958, and he was enthroned there by the apostolic delegate Cicognani, on November 16. John XXIII created him cardinal in the consistory of Dec. 14, 1959.

Shortly after Meyer's arrival in Chicago, a fire in Our Lady of the Angels School on Dec. 1, 1958, resulted in the deaths of 92 children and three Sisters of the Blessed Virgin Mary. He immediately initiated a campaign for greater school safety that involved the expenditure of millions of dollars for fire-protection devices. His high school expansion plan provided for a continuous building program over a ten-year period. The inadequacies of Quigley Preparatory Seminary led to the opening in September 1961 of Quigley South at 79th Street and Western Avenue for a four-year preparatory course, and of St. Mary of the Lake Seminary, Junior College Division, in the completely remodeled St. Hedwig's Orphanage in Niles.

To keep the church abreast of urban renewal, he appointed a full-time priest director to the Archdiocesan Conservation Council, established under Stritch. At a clergy conference on Sept. 20, 1960, Meyer exhorted all of his priests to assume leadership roles in integrating African Americans into Chicago's parishes, schools, hospitals, and other institutions. He endeavored to care for the expanding suburbs by founding 14 new parishes. Its school system then included six Catholic higher institutions: De Paul and Loyola universities and Barat, Mundelein, Rosary, and St. Xavier colleges.

Cardinal Meyer was one of the 12 presidents of Vatican Council II; by the end of the third session he had addressed the Council more often than any other American bishop and had become the intellectual leader of the U.S. hierarchy. His untimely death on April 9, 1965, following brain surgery, was a misfortune for the Universal Church, as well as for the archdiocese. On June 16, 1965, Abp. John P. Cody of New Orleans, LA, was transferred to Chicago as its sixth archbishop.

Cody. John Patrick Cody was born in St. Louis, MO, on Dec. 24, 1907. He was ordained a priest Dec. 8, 1931. From 1933 to 1938 he served on the staff of the Secretariat of State under Giovanni Battista Montini (later Paul VI), and later served as bishop of St. Joseph, MO (1954–56) and Kansas City-St. Joseph (1956–61), before being appointed coadjutor (1961) and then archbishop (1964) of New Orleans.

Cody reorganized the archdiocese of Chicago, first into seven vicariates under vicars selected by him, and later into 12 vicariates under vicars nominated by the clergy. He raised money for the modernization of parishes and schools and undertook much-needed renovations of the Cathedral of the Holy Name.

In the late 1960s and early 1970s he found himself the target of increasing criticism from associations of clergy, first the independent Association of Chicago Priests, then the archdiocesan presbyteral senate. His decision to close four inner-city schools in the summer of 1975 was protested, both to the local press and to the apostolic delegate and the pope. Allegations—denounced by Cody as slanders—of improprieties in the use of church funds culminated in a grand-jury investigation in 1981. Cody died April 25, 1982, and was succeeded by Archbishop Joseph Bernardin of Cincinnati.

Bernardin. Joseph Louis Bernardin was born April 2, 1928, in Columbia, SC. Ordained to the priesthood on April 26, 1952, he was consecrated auxiliary bishop of Atlanta in 1966 before being appointed archbishop of Cincinnati on Dec. 19, 1972. Installed as archbishop of Chicago on Aug. 25, 1982, he was created cardinal the next year, the first American cardinal created by Pope John Paul II.

Bernardin became known as a conciliator and mediator. His work on peace and life issues established the terms in which these issues were discussed nationally. He chaired the NCCB ad hoc committee that produced the pastoral letter, *The Challenge of Peace* (1983). Speaking on this letter at Fordham University later that year, he emphasized the need for a ''consistent ethic of life.'' The following year he coined the term ''seamless garment'' to refer to the Catholic teaching on such issues as abortion, capital punishment, nuclear war, and poverty.

Bernardin gained the stature of the leading spokesman for the Church in the U.S. His reflections on the last years of his life, *The Gift of Peace* (published posthumously), became a bestseller, and he was extolled by Catholics and non-Catholics alike for his courage and grace in dealing forthrightly with terminal (pancreatic) cancer. He died on Nov. 14, 1996, and was succeeded by Archbishop Francis George of Portland, OR.

George. The first native son of Chicago to be named its archbishop, Francis George was born in Chicago on Jan. 16, 1937. He entered the Missionary Oblates of Mary Immaculate (OMI) on Aug. 14, 1957, and was ordained a priest on Dec. 21, 1963. In 1970 he received a Ph.D. in philosophy from Tulane University. From 1973 to 1974 he was provincial superior of the Midwestern province, headquartered in St Paul, MN, and from 1974 to 1986 he served in Rome as vicar general of the Oblates of Mary Immaculate. Pope John Paul II named George, bishop of Yakima, WA, in 1990, and in 1996 made him archbishop of Portland, OR, before transferring him to Chicago on April 8, 1997. He became known as a prolific writer, publishing several books and many articles on religious life, inculturation, and pastoral issues.

Catholic Institutions of Higher Learning. Chicago is home to DePaul University, the largest Catholic university in the U.S. Established in 1898 by the Vincentians, DePaul has an enrollment of more than 20,000 students in eight campuses (Barat, Lake Forest (Conway Park), Lincoln Park, Loop, Naperville, Oak Forest, O'Hare, and Rolling Meadows). Established in 1870 by the Jesuits, St. Ignatius College was renamed Loyola University of Chicago in 1909, when it received the authority to grant professional and graduate degrees. Other universities and colleges within the archdiocesan boundaries are Saint Xavier University in Chicago and Dominican University in River Forest. St. Xavier's College for women was established in 1846 by Mother Francis Xavier Warde, a Sister of Mercy, the first Catholic women's college in Chicago. In 1969, the college went coeducational, and in 1992, the name was changed to Saint Xavier University. Dominican University was founded originally as St. Clara's College, a women's college, by the Dominican Sisters in Sinsinawa, WI in 1901. In 1922, the college was moved to River Forest, IL, and the name was changed to Rosary College. In 1970, Rosary College went coeducational, and in 1997, the name was officially changed to Dominican University. Established in 1968 and sponsored by 25 religious congregations, the Catholic Theological Union at Chicago is the largest Roman Catholic school of theology and ministry in the U.S.

Bibliography: C. J. KIRKFLEET, *The Life of Patrick Augustine Feehan* (Chicago 1922). B. L. PIERCE, *A History of Chicago* (New York, v.1–3, 1937–57; v.4 in progress). J. E. MCGIRR, *The Life of the Rt. Rev. Wm. Quarter*, D.D. (Des Plaines, IL 1920). M. M. QUAIFE, *Checagou: From Indian Wigwam to Modern City, 1673–1835* (Chicago 1933). G. J. GARRAGHAN, *The Catholic Church in Chicago, 1673–1871* (Chicago 1921). J. T. ELLIS, *The Life of James Cardinal Gibbons*, 2 v. (Milwaukee 1952). J. J. THOMPSON, *The Archdiocese of Chicago: Antecedents and Development* (Des Plaines, IL 1920). C. W. DAHM, *Power and Authority in the Catholic Church: Cardinal Cody in Chicago* (Notre Dame, IN 1981). H. C. KOENIG, ed., *Caritas Christi Urget Nos. A History* of the Offices. Agencies, and Institutions of the Archdiocese of Chicago, 2 v. (Chicago 1981).

[H. C. KOENIG/R. TRISCO/EDS.]

CHICHELE, HENRY

Archbishop of Canterbury; b. Higham Ferrers, Northhamptonshire, England *c.* 1361; d. Canterbury, April 12, 1443. Educated at Oxford, he became doctor of laws, 1396. At this time he was ordained and had already held a number of minor ecclesiastical benefices. In 1404 he became chancellor of the diocese of Salisbury. Henry IV employed him on several diplomatic missions. It was while Chichele was at the Curia of GREGORY XII, that he was appointed bishop of St. David's (Wales). The pope consecrated him June 17, 1408, though he was not enthroned until May 11, 1411. In the meantime he was a member of the English embassy (together with Bp. Robert HALLUM) to the Council of PISA. When Abp. Thomas ARUNDEL died, Henry V proposed Chichele for the archbishopric of Canterbury, where he was duly elected March 4, 1414. He governed the province for nearly 40 years. The edited archiepiscopal registers prove Chichele a first-class administrator, lawyer and lawgiver. In his judicial functions he was greatly assisted by the canonist, William LYNDWOOD, whom he appointed his vicar-general. Chichele was anxious to raise the standard of both the clergy and the laity. He took effective steps to prevent the spread of the LOLLARDS.

Chichele was permanently estranged from the papacy when MARTIN V made the bishop of Winchester, Henry BEAUFORT, a cardinal in 1426. Domestically, Chichele sided with Beaufort's opponents, notably Duke Henry of Gloucester, who was instrumental in bringing a charge of PRAEMUNIRE against Beaufort. When Abp. John KEMP (KEMPE) of York was appointed a cardinal in 1439 and by reason of this appointment claimed public precedence over the archbishop of Canterbury, Chichele took the matter before EUGENE IV, who upheld Kempe. Chichele's career is not considered outstanding. His generosity to Oxford, especially All Souls College, is noteworthy.

Bibliography: A. DUCK, *The Life of H. Chichele, Archbishop of Canterbury* (London 1699). W. F. HOOK, *Lives of the Archbishops of Canterbury* (London 1860–84) v.5. E. F. JACOB, "Two Lives of Archbishop Chichele," *Bulletin of the John Rylands Library* 16 (1932) 428–481. F. L. CROSS, *The Oxford Dictionary of the Christian Church* (London 1957) 271. A. B. EMDEN, *A Biographical Register of the University of Oxford to A.D. 1500*, 3 v. (Oxford 1957–59) 1:410–412. *The Register of Henry Chichele: Archbishop of Canterbury, 1414–1443*, ed. E. F. JACOB and H. C. JOHNSON (Oxford 1937–47). W. ULLMANN, "Eugenius IV, Cardinal Kemp, and Archbishop Chichele" *Medieval Studies Presented to Aubrey Gwynn, S.J.* (Dublin 1961) 359–383.

[W. ULLMANN]

CHICHESTER, ANCIENT SEE OF

Medieval diocese of England, coterminous with the County of Sussex, suffragan of CANTERBURY. Neither ETHELBERT of Canterbury's missionary success in Kent nor BIRINUS's in Wessex had any effect on the neighboring South Saxons, and their conversion to Christianity came much later, under WILFRID OF YORK, who successfully preached the gospel to them while exiled from YORK (*c.* 681–686). He founded the first diocese there, with its see at Selsey. However, when he returned to York, Cadwalla, King of Wessex, who had conquered the South Saxons in 685, attached Selsey to his See of WINCHESTER, and Selsey regained its autonomy only in 709. In accord with the decrees of the Council of London (1075) that all sees must be in towns, not villages, the bishop's seat was transferred from Selsey to Chichester in 1082 with no changes in the diocesan boundaries. There the energetic Norman Bishop Ralph de Luffa (1091–1123) reorganized the diocese and began the Norman cathedral, while Bishop Seffrid II (1180–1204) introduced Early English elements into the structure. Chichester's best known medieval bishop was RICHARD OF CHICHESTER (1245–54), friend and chancellor of St. EDMUND OF ABINGDON and BONIFACE OF SAVOY, both archbishops of Canterbury. In the 14th and 15th centuries the bishops of Chichester were often men of substance but were primarily involved with nondiocesan projects; for example, John Langton (1305–37) and ROBERT OF STRATFORD (1337–62) were both chancellors of England. However, the scholar-bishop WILLIAM REDE (1369–85), who collected the early records of the see, helped revive the diocese, which had been hard hit by the BLACK DEATH. The Dominican Bishop Robert Rede (1397–1415) compiled the earliest extant Episcopal register, and the controversial Reginald PECOCK, bishop from 1450 to 1456, was succeeded by John ARUNDEL (1459–78). Bishop Edward Storey (1478–1503) spiritually revitalized the diocese. Robert Sherborn (1508–36) protested against King HENRY VIII, but in the end he resigned his see to the king's man, Richard Sampson (1536–43), under whom the diocese became Anglican. George Day (1543–47) was instituted by Henry VIII, but he was subsequently imprisoned on account of his resistance to the king. He regained his see under Queen MARY. John Christopherson (1557–59) was the last Roman Catholic bishop. Under Elizabeth I, Chichester became a see of the Church of England. BATTLE ABBEY and LEWES PRIORY were the chief monasteries in the diocese.

Bibliography: F. G. BENNETT et al., *Statutes and Constitutions of the Cathedral Church of Chichester* (Chichester 1904). L. F. SALZMANN; v.3, W. H. GODFREY, J. W. BLOC and H. C. CORLETTE, *Catholic Church of Chichester* (London 1911). A. S. DUNCAN-JONES, *Story of Chichester Cathedral* (London 1933). *Chartulary of the High Church of Chichester*, ed. W. D. PECKHAM (Sussex Record Society 46; 1946). K. EDWARDS, *The English Secular Cathedrals in the Middle Ages* (Manchester, Eng. 1949). W. K. L. CLARKE, *Chichester Cathedral: Its History and Art* (London 1962). CHICHESTER DIOCESAN RECORD OFFICE, *Ancient Charters of the Dean and Chapter of Chichester, 689–1674*, 2nd. ed. (Chichester 1976). A. MCCANN, *A Short History of the City of Chichester and its Cathedral* (Chichester 1985). M. HOBBS, *Chichester Cathedral: An Historical Survey* (Chichester 1994).

[M. J. HAMILTON/EDS.]

CHIDWICK, JOHN PATRICK

Chaplain, educator; b. New York City, Oct. 23, 1862; d. New York City, Jan. 13, 1935. He was ordained at Troy, N.Y., Dec. 17, 1887. Chidwick gained fame as chaplain of the U.S. battleship *Maine* when it was blown up in Havana harbor, Cuba, in 1898. His heroism on that occasion was praised in a dispatch from Captain Charles Sigsbee, the *Maine*'s commander, to John Long, Secretary of the Navy. Chidwick was interested in young people, and his youth organizations were most successful. He filled also various offices in the archdiocese of New York, serving as police chaplain, pastor, founder of a high school, and president of the College of New Rochelle in Westchester County, N.Y. From 1909 to 1922, he was rector of St. Joseph's Seminary, Dunwoodie, Yonkers, N.Y., where he exercised a lasting influence on the students confided to his care. He was appointed a papal chamberlain and served as pastor of St. Agnes parish, New York City, until his death.

[J. P. MONAGHAN]

CHIEF PRIESTS

The chief priests are a specific group of temple priests, administrators of the temple's liturgy, buildings, and finances. The Greek plural ἀρχιερεῖς (chief priests), occurring 62 times in the New Testament books and often in Josephus, refers to this important priestly group; whereas the singular ἀρχιερεύς (high priest, chief priest), appearing 38 times in the Gospels and Acts, refers to the HIGH PRIEST, president of the Sanhedrin.

The chief priests are sometimes mentioned alone as acting for the whole Sanhedrin (Mt 26.14; Mk 15.3; Lk 23.4; Jn 18.35; Acts 9.14—the Sanhedrin) or with "the whole Sanhedrin" (Mt 26.59), the SCRIBES (Mt 2.4; Lk 20.19), the ELDERS (Mt 21.23; Acts 4.23), the scribes and

elders (Mt 16.21; 28.41; Mt 15.1; Lk 22.66), the captains or overseers (Lk 22.4), the rulers (Lk 23.13), or the PHARISEES (Mt 27.62; Jn 7.45, 11.47, 18.3). From these passages it is clear that the chief priests were prominent and influential members of the Sanhedrin. According to some scholars (E. Schürer, 2.1:204–206) the chief priests comprised the ruling high priest, former acting but deposed high priests, and leading members of the families from which the high priests were selected. But according to others (J. Jeremias, 38; G. Schrenk, 271) it appears more probable that this group was composed of administrators of the Temple, its buildings, and its treasures, e.g., in descending rank, the Temple governor or captain (στρατηγὸς τοῦ ἱεροῦ), who was next in dignity after the high priest (Acts 4.1, 5.24, 36; Schrenk, 271); the heads of the 24 priestly classes conducting the weekly services (cf. Lk 1.9); the leaders of those conducting the daily services; the overseers (Heb. ʼămarkᵉlîn; Gr. στρατηγοί Lk 22.4, 52), the treasurers (Heb. *qizbārîm*).

Bibliography: G. SCHRENK, in G. KITTEL, *Theologisches Wörterbuch zum Neuen Testament* (Stuttgart 1935–) 3:270–272. E. SCHÜRER, *A History of the Jewish People in the Time of Christ*, division 2, v.1, tr. S. TAYLOR and P. CHRISTIE (Edinburgh 1898) 203–206. J. JEREMIAS, *Jerusalem zur Zeit Jesu* (Göttingen 1958).

[J. E. STEINMUELLER]

CHIEREGATI, FRANCESCO

Papal nuncio and bishop of Teramo; b. Vicenza, 1478: d. Bologna, Dec. 6, 1539. Chieregati (Chieregato) studied law at Padua, Bologna, and Siena, where he received the degree of *doctor utriusque juris*. During his early career he held various positions dealing with the secretarial and diplomatic work of the Church. In 1516 he was sent as papal nuncio to England to notify HENRY VIII that the Concordat of Bologna between the papacy and Francis I of France had been concluded. Subsequently, he represented the papacy at the courts of Spain and Portugal. While in Spain, he became acquainted with Cardinal Adrian Florensz, Bishop of Tortosa, later Pope ADRIAN VI, the Dutch teacher of CHARLES V. Adrian VI created Chieregati bishop of Teramo in the kingdom of Naples. As an indication of the pope's esteem for his virtue, learning, and diplomatic skill, Chieregati was sent as papal nuncio to represent the pope at the Diet of Nuremberg in the fall of 1522. He was entrusted with the task of obtaining obedience to and enforcement of the bull *Exsurge* and the Edict of Worms against LUTHER, as well as of persuading the German princes to take a stronger stand against the Turks in Hungary. The reaction of the Diet was not favorable. After three unsuccessful exhortations, Chieregati, on Jan. 3, 1523, took the step of reading publicly a papal brief issued on Nov. 25, 1522, to the members of the Diet. At the same time, he read instructions prepared for him at least in substance by the pope himself and bearing the same date as the brief. The brief was an appeal to the Diet to suppress religious sedition and to force Luther and his followers to stop their disruptive activities. In essence, Chieregati's instructions constituted a public confession by the pope that the shortcomings of the Curia and the clergy were in a large part responsible for the religious problems of the day. The document also set forth the pope's determination to effect reforms. This public confession was without precedent and both a German and a Latin version were printed for further dissemination in 1523, but did not provoke a sympathetic response. Individual reaction at the Diet was skeptical about the pope's ability to implement his promises, and on February 5 the Diet demanded that the pope, with the approval of the emperor, call a council to meet in a German border city, a council that would operate independently of the pope. It also prepared a list of financial grievances for submission to the pope. Chieregati failed to soften the Diet's position and left Nuremberg in February 1523. With the death of Adrian VI, he lost his diplomatic standing and he spent the rest of his life in relative obscurity.

Bibliography: H. JEDIN, *History of the Council of Trent*, tr. E. GRAF, v.1–2 (St. Louis 1957–); *Geschitchte des Konzils von Trient* (Freiburg 1949–57; v.1, 2d ed. 1951) 1:210–213. L. PASTOR, *The History of the Popes from the Close of the Middle Ages* (London-St. Louis 1938–61): v.9–10, 4th ed.; 9:127–141. B. MORSOLIN, *Francesco Chieregati* (Vicenza 1873). *Deutsche Reichstagsakten unter Kaiser Karl V* (Gotha 1893–1935) v.3. L. VAN MEERBEECK, *Dictionnaire d'histoire et de géographie ecclésiastiques*, ed. A. BAUDRILLART et al. (Paris 1912–) 12:676–678.

[V. H. PONKO, JR.]

CHIGI

An important family of Siena, Italy, mentioned in sources since the 13th century; ennobled in 1377. About that time it was distinguished by two and perhaps three members who were beatified in the era of *Fabio* Chigi, who became Pope ALEXANDER VII.

Bl. Giovanni da Lecceto, b. Maciareto, near Siena, 1300. He entered the order of the AUGUSTINIANS of Lecceto as a lay brother and lived an exemplary life, first in Vallaspra, then in Siena, and Pavia, and again in Siena, where he died Oct. 28, 1363.

Bl. Angela, niece of Giovanni da Lecceto, also belonged to a congregation of hermits of St. Augustine. She lived in Siena where she died a holy death in 1400. She was never officially beatified. (See the *Vitae synopsis,* supplements to the Roman editions of Hoyerus, cited below.)

Monument of Sigismondo Chigi, executed after a design by Raphael, in the church of Santa Maria del Popolo, Rome. (Alinari-Art Reference/Art Resource, NY)

Bl. Giuliana was recently affiliated (rightly or wrongly) with the Chigi family. After being widowed four times, she spent her remaining years as a tertiary of St. Augustine, and died in Siena in 1400 (A. Mercati and A. Pelzer, *Dizionario ecclesiastico* 1:609).

The head of the family is said to have been *Agostino,* known as the Elder, from whom the various branches of the family descended: the Chigi-Albani; the Chigi Camollia, later the Chigi-Saracini; the Chiga *di citta,* or of Siena, extinct in 1758: the Chigi of Rome, extinct in 1573; the Chigi of Viterbo, later the Chigi-Montoro and the Montoro-Patrizi; and the Chigi Zondadari. *Mariano* (1439–1504) was the most prominent of Agostino's sons. He was a prosperous banker in Siena, the founder of a banking house, and on occasion an ambassador of Siena to the court of Pope ALEXANDER VI and to the Republic of VENICE. He became a humanist and patron of the arts.

Agostino the Magnificent (1464–1520) was the most outstanding among Mariano's sons. As the representative of his father's banking house, he established himself in Rome and embarked on a successful career. Having won the confidence of three successive popes (Alexander VI; JULIUS II, who adopted him into his family; and LEO X, who honored him with his visits), he obtained several monoplies (on grain, salt, alum, and right of entry), and carried on an international trade, using the Porto d'Ercole, obtained from the Republic of SIENA. As a patron of the arts, he showed favor to men of letters, such as P. Bembo, Giovio, and P. Aretino; and to architects, especially Baltasar Peruzzi who built his superb palace, the Farnesina; as well as to the painters RAPHAEL SANZIO, Perino del Vaga, Julius Romano, and J. A. Bazzi, who decorated the Farnesina and the chapel of the Chigi in Santa Maria del Popolo. Agostino founded a printing establishment and a library. At his death in 1520, his enterprises were liquidated; his lineage became extinct in 1575.

The Chigi of Siena returned to Rome through the descendants of *Sigismondo* (1479–1525), second son of Mariano, prosperous banker. His great grandson, *Fabio,* a young ecclesiastic, came to Rome, where he made his career. When he became Pope Alexander VII (1655), he practiced nepotism, giving his family every sort of advantage. His nephew *Agostino,* the founder of the Chigi-Albani family, obtained for himself and his family the title of marshal of the Church and guardian of the Conclave. His niece *Agnes* married Ansano Zondadari, and founded the Chigi-Zondadari family. Beginning with the pontificate of Alexander VII, the Chigi were cardinals. First, there were his three nephews: *Flavio* (1631–93), legate, librarian; *Sigismondo* (1649–78) of the Order of Malta, legate; and *Antonio* Bichi (1614–90), son of one of the Pope's half-sisters, internuncio at Brussels, and Bishop of Osimo. Later there were also the following cardinals: *Flavio the Younger* (1711–71), prefect of the Congregation of Rites; *Flavio* Chigi-Albani (1801–73), nuncio in Bavaria and France; and two members of the Chigi-Zondadari family, *Antonio Felice the Elder* (1665–1737), nuncio in Spain, and *Antonio Felice the Younger* (1740–1823), internuncio at Brussels and Archbishop of Siena.

The Chigi Library was one of the glories of the Chigi family. Fabio Chigi began the collection in his palace in Rome and took advantage of his pontificate to enlarge it. The Chigi cardinals, especially *Flavio the Elder,* continued its growth. It now contains about 3,000 MSS (86 with miniatures, 56 Greek, 190 Latin, and many volumes of archival materials). Purchased by the Italian Government in 1918 and ceded to the Vatican in 1923, it has been integrated into the VATICAN LIBRARY. Besides the Greek MSS, described by Pio Franchi de Cavalieri (Rome 1927), the other MSS also have been well catalogued.

Bibliography: M. HOYERUS, *Vita b. Joannis Chisii* (Antwerp 1641; Rome 1655–75). *Acta Sanctorum* Oct. 12:724–735. A. MASSERON, *Les "Exemples" d'un ermite siennois* (Paris 1924). G. CUGNONI, "Agostino Chigi il magnifico," *Archivio della società romana di storia patria,* 2–4 (1879–81), 6 (1883). U. FRITTELLI, *Albero genealogico della nobile famiglia Chigi* (Siena 1922). P. PASCHINI, *I Chigi* (Le grandi famiglie romane 3; Rome 1946). M. H. LAURENT, *Dictionnaire d'histoire et de géographie ecclésiastiques,* ed. A. BAUDRILLART et al. (Paris 1912–) 12:684–685.

[L. CEYSSENS]

CHILE, THE CATHOLIC CHURCH IN

The Republic of Chile occupies the southwestern part of the continent of South America. It is bound on the east by Argentina and on the west by the South Pacific Ocean. The Atacama Desert, extremely hot and barren and a source of copper and nitrates, occupies the northern portion, while to the south a temperate, fertile valley occupies the center of the country, with low mountains running along the coast. The southern region is heavily forested, and in the Tierra del Fuego, cold, wet conditions make the region less conducive to agriculture. Chile is separated from Argentina by the more rugged Andes mountain range. Natural resources include copper, iron ore, molybdenum and some precious metals. Agricultural products consist of wheat, corn, grapes, beans, sugar beets, potatoes and fruits. Timber is another important resource, with the manufacture of wood products being one of Chile's chief industries. While Chile claimed the Antarctic Peninsula in 1940, that claim was not recognized internationally; Argentina laid claim to the same region two years later.

Formerly a Spanish viceroyalty of Peru, Chile declared its independence from Spain in 1810 and achieved it after the Battle of Maipo in 1818. During the 17th and 18th centuries the basic wealth was in agriculture; later, mining predominated, especially that of saltpeter (19th century) and of copper (20th century). Chile extended its territory northward during wars with Peru and Bolivia between 1879 and 1883 that resulted in its present boundaries. Increasing economic problems following World War II resulted in the historic 1970 election of Salvador Allende as the first popularly elected Marxist president in the world. A military coup three years later resulted in the brutal regime of Augusto Pinochet, during which 15,000 Chileans lost their lives and one tenth of the population fled the country. By the 1980s Chile had the largest per-capita debt in the world, and Pinochet, unable to turn the economy around, resigned in 1989. Civilian government returned with the election of Patricio Aylwin and continued through 2000. Over 90 percent of Chileans are mestizo, while surviving Araucanians account for less than seven percent of the population.

Early History. Part of the Incan empire, the region was home to the Araucanian people, a group whose fierce independence caused problems for Spanish explorers when they arrived in 1536. Among those Catholics who arrived with the conquistadores was Rodrigo González de Marmolejo, who founded the first parish in 1547. Overshadowed by Peru to the north, Chile became a viceroyalty to that region. The native population was forced south, and colonization limited itself to the central region, where Santiago was founded in 1541, La Serena in 1544 and Concepción in 1550. Priests soon entered the region: the Mercedarians in 1550, the Franciscans in 1553, the Dominicans in 1557, the Jesuits in 1593, the Augustinians in 1595 and the Hospitallers of St. John of God in 1617. Similarly, convents of nuns were established, such as Limpia Concepción in Santiago (1574), as well as the lay order of Isabelas de Osorno. The hospital of St. John of God was founded in Santiago in 1541. The bishopric of Santiago was created in 1561, and González became its governor.

Although a shortage of priests and the remoteness of the region continued to hamper the missions, the situation was somewhat remedied by the arrival of Bishop Diego de Medellín and Bishop Antonio de San Miguel in 1569 and 1576 respectively, who organized the Church. It was decided at that time that the *doctrina* would be supported by the native people themselves; that one *doctrinero* would serve several towns at the same time; and, finally, that a Spaniard or mestizo would take charge of simple missionary duties during the absence of the *doctrinero* (*see* ENCOMIENDA DOCTRINA SYSTEM IN SPANISH AMERICA). These authorities became the ''sayapayos,''—later called ''fiscales,''—who achieved a certain amount of importance in Santiago and great influence in Chiloé. Bishops San Miguel of Santiago and Medellín, of the Diocese of La Imperial (created in 1563) attended the Third Council in Lima in 1581, and collaborated so that the decrees of the council on Sacraments, doctrine, catechism for natives and reform and discipline of the clergy would have rapid application in Chile. Following the loss of the southern cities between 1599 and 1602, the bishop of La Imperial moved his see to Concepción.

In the diocese of Santiago and to the north, evangelization efforts met with success. Between 1579 and 1621, the number of baptized Christians rose from 36 to over 90 percent. By 1650 almost all non-aggressive tribes in this region had been baptized, resulting in the replacement of the doctrinas by a parish system that lasted until 1810. In the diocese of Concepción, on the other hand, there were more serious problems; except for Chiloé, the region between the Maule and Bío Bío Rivers and some regions near the forts, the Araucanian rejected Christianity, in part because of the war that was being waged against them. The Jesuit Luis de VALDIVIA maintained that to convert them it would be necessary that the war against the Araucanian initiated in 1553 be suspended

Capital: Santiago.
Size: 286,397 sq. miles.
Population: 15,153,790 in 2000.
Languages: Spanish.
Religions: 11,818,980 Catholics (78%), 2,753,300 Evangelical Protestant (18%), 30,800 Jews (.2%), 452,460 follow indigenous faiths (3%), 98,250 without religious affiliation.

and the entrance of missionaries without military aid should be permitted. Although his ideas were accepted only for a brief period (1610–15), the Jesuits and the Franciscans continued to dedicate themselves to establishing missions among the native tribes through the 19th century.

In spite of clashes with civil powers and conflicts between religious orders in the 17th century, the prelates were able to give a solid base to the clergy and to construct churches, cathedrals and seminaries. The Jesuits founded the Colegio de Castro in Chiloé and developed a system of circulating missions in both bishoprics in order to reach isolated places. In 1700 they created the Colegio de Naturales de Chillán. Still, the Araucanian rebellion waged in the south, continuing on through the 19th century, and Church buildings were frequently destroyed by earthquakes and by invasions of native rebels.

The synods, especially those of Bishop Carracso in 1688, Bishop Alday in 1763 (both in Santiago) and Bishop Azúa in Concepión in 1744, dealt with such problems as the conduct of priests, parochial schools, observance of holidays, catechisms and teaching of the lower classes. After the expulsion of the Jesuits throughout South America in 1767, the Franciscans shouldered all mission activity, as well as the operation of Jesuit colleges. They centralized their activities in the Colegio Misiones in Chillán (1756), from there establishing 16 doctrinas from Chillán to Chiloé. Baptism and other Sacraments were administered, teaching was carried out and native languages were learned to better spread the word of God to native tribes.

An Independent Chile. In the pattern of much of South America, Chile declared itself independent of Spain on Sept. 18, 1810, although its autonomous status would not be recognized for seven more years. In 1817, José de San Martin, the liberator of South America, led 3,200 troops across the Andes and defeated the Spanish at the Battle of Chacabuco and Maipo, forcing the colonial government from the region in 1818. During the struggle for emancipation (1810–18), the Church suffered a grave recession. Bishop Rodríguez of Santiago was exiled because of his royalist sympathies, and the mission college in Chillán was disbanded for similar rea-

Archdioceses	Suffragans
Antofagasta	Arica, Iquique
Concepción	Chillán, Los Angeles, Temuco, Valdivia
La Serena	Copiapó
Puerto Montt	Osorno, Punta Arenas, San Carlos de Ancud
Santiago de Chile	Linares, Melipilla, Rancagua, San Bernardo, San Felipe, Talca, Valparaíso.

There are two prelatures, two apostolic vicariates, and a military ordinariate in the country.

sons. As the new government grappled with Chile's future as a free nation, the division of the clergy increased, reaching a high point between 1824 and 1830. Vicar MUZI was sent by the pope to settle ecclesiastical matters, but was unsuccessful and returned to Rome. Despite the fact that Catholicism was the state religion under the 1810 constitution, the government decreed the sequestration of the property of the regular clergy in 1824. Religious services decreased and numerous parishes had no one to serve them; the orders were disorganized and many priests were secularized during the stay of Vicar Muzi.

In 1830, following the stabilization of the Chilean economy due to the discovery of mineral wealth in the Atacama Desert, order was restored and Church institutions were reestablished. The sequestered properties were returned and normal relations were resumed between the government and Rome. Santiago was made an archdiocese, its first archbishop Manuel VICUÑA LARRAÍN. The Dioceses of La Serena and Ancud were created in 1840. Five years later the archdiocese of Santiago was occupied by Rafael Valentín VALDIVIESO ZAÑARTU, and in 1854, that of Concepción by José Hipólito Salas Toro, who, both, like their forerunners of the 16th century, carried out far-reaching reforms. The work of Valdivieso in matters relative to offices of the Curia, religious orders, restoration of the seminary, parish schools, etc., gave the Church in Chile a very solid base for the modern period. At the end of the century, with the effective occupation of Antofagasta and Tarapacá, corresponding apostolic vicariates were created.

During the colonial period ethnicity had limited vocations in Chile. While 17 percent of the region's priests were mestizos in 1565, an order from Philip II prohibited the ordination of non-Europeans thereafter. During the colonial period, due to the shortage of priests, men with one-quarter or less Amerindian blood could be ordained, but the general order prevailed until independence; an exception was made when four natives were ordained in 1794 in the Colegio de Naturales de Chillán. After 1810 the new spirit and the greater racial homogeneity caused the prohibition against such ordinations to disappear. Education, which had been exclusively in the hands of the Church throughout the colonial period, was revived after independence, especially with the arrival of new religious orders, and it began to compete with the state in the field of education. In 1888 the Catholic University of Chile was created, approved by Pope Leo XIII on July 28, 1889, and erected canonically by Pius XI, Feb. 11, 1930.

Throughout the 1800s Chile continued to extend its territory, expanding south to Magallanes (1843), Llanquihue (1848) and Araucania (1884), while in the north adding the provinces of Tarapacá and Antofagasta after the War of the Pacific (1879–84) against Peru and Bolivia. The propagation of the faith to the south of Chile was also advanced through the work of Salesians and Capuchins. The six missions of the Colegio de Jesús, in the heart of the Araucanian territory, where no missionary work had been done since the 16th century, had a Christian population of 29 percent in 1892. The Salesians founded missions in the Autral region, aided in their efforts by the Daughters of Mary who had centers in Punta Arenas, Dawson Island and Tierra del Fuego. The Apostolic Prefecture of Araucania, created in 1848, became an apostolic vicariate in 1928.

Non-Catholic Christians appeared in Chile following independence. The first proponents of Protestantism, such as James Thompson in 1821, were agents of the British and Foreign Bible Society and carried out their mission by traveling through the country on foot. The first Anglican church was built in Valparaiso and was inaugurated in 1858. In the south of the country, among German immigrants, there was already a Lutheran group. However, these churches made no great progress because of the limited number of Germans or Englishmen living in Chile. The Methodist Church had greater importance; it grew in Chile from the preaching of the Spaniard Juan Bautista Canut de Bon at the end of the 19th century, for which reason they were called "canutos."

The Modern Church. Prior to 1810 the Church was organized under the *patronato*, a system of royal patronage exercised by the Spanish sovereigns who took for themselves the right to present prelates, the right to make rules in religious matters, power before tribunals, the *placet* or permission to receive bulls and pontifical documents, etc. Following independence, the Chilean government also made use of these same prerogatives, without the acceptance of the Holy See. This situation created a crisis after 1850, which lasted until a 1925 agreement was reached through the efforts of President Arturo Alessandri and Archbishop Crescente ERRÁZURIZ of Santiago. The constitution was reformed, establishing a division between Church and State, and, in consequence, the definitive disappearance of patronage. In addition Alessandri and the Holy See reconfirmed the future ability of the Church to govern itself, and endowed it with *derecho publico* status whereby its independent status could not be challenged by a court of law.

Through the first decades of the 20th century, Chile underwent an economic turnaround when its saltpeter reserves were no longer needed due to advances in modern technology. Now dependent upon the export of copper, its economy declined, resulting in unemployment and social unrest. The Church remained stable during this period due to its ability to now govern itself outside of government influence. The Catholic University of Valparaiso was established in 1928 and the Catholic University of the North, in Antofagasta, was recognized by the state in 1963.

After the constitutional reform of 1925, the Protestants, particularly the Methodists, Pentecostals and Baptists, increased noticeably, their growth attributable to the evangelical character of such churches and the ignorance of Catholic doctrine and the desire for spiritual guidance. In part because of Protestant—particularly Pentacostal—inroads, a serious falling away from the Church became apparent; it would be especially visible in urban centers during the second half of the 20th century. Another major problem faced by the Church was the shortage of priests in the country.

In 1970 Chileans elected Marxist leader Salvador Allende as president, and a coalition government of communists and socialists made increasing efforts to reduce the power of the Church in Chile. Allende's efforts to nationalize industry and reform land ownership won him opposition not only from conservative Chileans but from the United States as well, as the nation's economy faltered. In September of 1973 Allende was deposed by the military regime of Augusto Pinochet; Allende was killed, along with thousands of others, while many of his supporters fled the country. During the Pinochet regime human rights abuses escalated due to the continued repressions of organized labor and other opposition by the government. Chilean bishops were outspoken in their opposition to Pinochet, and formed the Vicarate of Solidarity to deal with the thousands of imprisoned, tortured or disappeared. When a still-failing economy destabilized Pinochet and a plebecite was scheduled, Church leaders

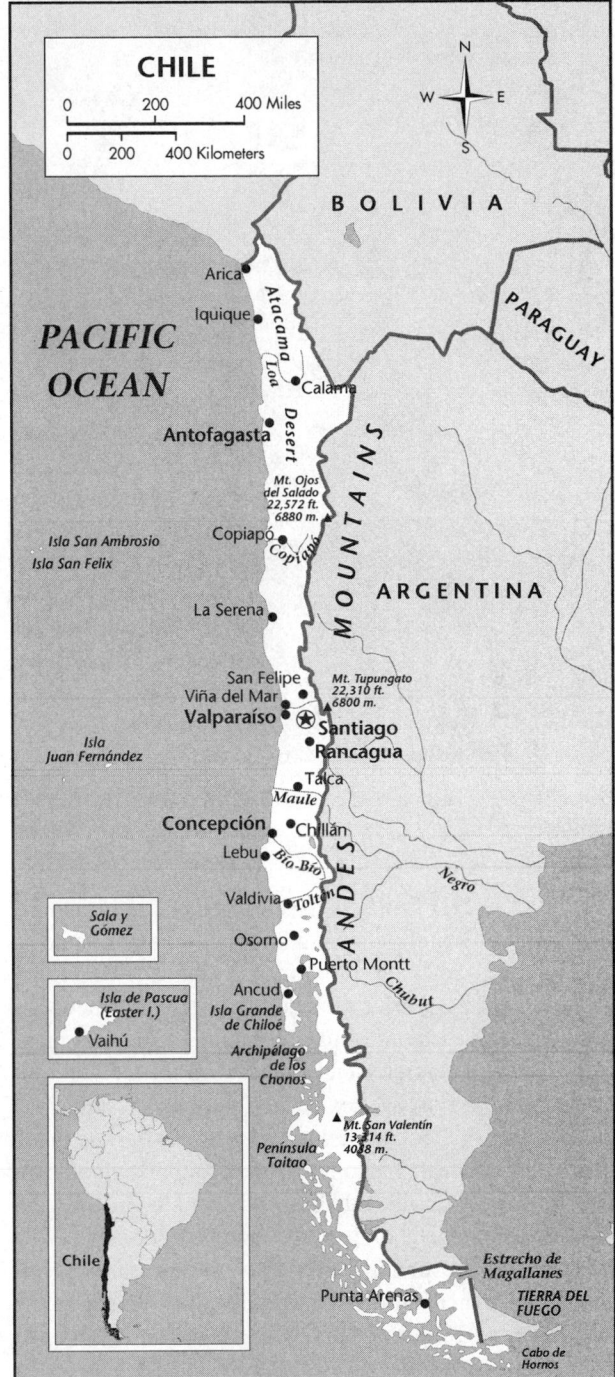

actively educated the public and encouraged voting through registration drives and arrangement for transportation to and from the polls. Pinochet was rejected during the 1988 referendum, and two years later, in 1990, a freely elected government returned to Chile. Grave sites of ''disappeared'' missing since the Pinochet era continued to be discovered.

Easter Week procession, LaSarena, Chile. (©Richard T. Nowitz/ CORBIS)

Into the 21st Century. As the nation approached the millennium, Church leaders addressed several concerns. In 1997 a law legalizing divorce was passed, prompting Chilean Cardinal Carlos Oviedo to state that the new law would "make all families unstable since it creates a mentality of indifferent conscience" toward the Catholic institution of marriage. A sex education program started by the Ministry of Education was withdrawn after the intercession of Chilean bishops. More positively, President Ricardo Lagos abolished the death penalty in Chile in May of 2001, balancing that Church-supported action with stiffer punishments to counter the increase in violent, drug-related crimes. In addition, the Vatican's efforts to mediate long-running land disputes between Bolivia and Chile were supported by the Church when they were proposed in 1996.

By 2000 Chile had 926 parishes tended by 1,060 diocesan and 1,200 religious priests. Other religious included approximately 500 brothers and 5,600 sisters, many of whom attended to the education of more than one third of the country's young people, who are enrolled in the over 1,000 primary and secondary Catholic schools in Chile. Many hospitals, orphanages and other social service agencies were also under the administration of the Church. The Catholic population in Chile continued to come from the more affluent sectors of society and many government leaders and members of the military were of the Church.

Bibliography: R. POBLETE, *La Iglesia en Chile* (Madrid 1961); "La situación religiosa en Chile," *Teología y vida* 3 (1962) 229–235. I. VERGARA, *El protestantismo en Chile* (2d ed. Santiago de Chile 1962). L. GALDAMES, *A History of Chile,* ed. and tr., I. J. COX (New York 1964).

[J. A. DE RAMÓN/EDS.]

CHILIASM

From Greek χιλιάς (1,000) or MILLENARIANISM, from Latin *mille* (1,000) teaches the visible personal rule of Christ on Earth for a millennium before the END OF THE WORLD. Its most ancient form, based on a literal interpretation of Revelation 20, speaks of the resurrection of the just and that of the damned. The first will be followed immediately by the millennium; the second will precede the last judgment. The Holy Office censured a recent revival of the idea: "A system of mitigated millenarianism cannot safely be taught" (H. Denzinger, *Enchiridion symbolorum,* ed. A. Schönmetzer [32d ed. Freiburg 1963] 3839).

Bibliography: J. MICHL and G. ENGLHARDT, *Lexikon für Theologie und Kirche,* ed. J. HOFER and K. RAHNER, 10 v. (2d, new ed. Freiburg 1957–65) 2:1058–62. G. GILLEMAN, "Condamnation du millénarisme mitigé," *Nouvelle revue théologique* 67 (1945) 239–241.

[G. J. DYER]

CHILLENDEN, THOMAS

Prior of Christ Church, Canterbury; d. Aug. 15, 1411. He was professed a Benedictine at Christ Church in 1365 and was a scholar at Canterbury College, the cathedral priory's college in Oxford, becoming bachelor of Canon Law by 1378 and doctor by 1383. He also studied Canon Law at the Roman Curia in 1378 to 1379. He wrote a number of canonical studies, one of which, the *Sexti libri decretalium reportorium,* presumably had some reputation, since five copies still exist. Chillenden was an outstanding administrator. He became treasurer of Christ Church in 1377 and retained the office after his election as prior in 1391. He abandoned the policy of direct exploitation of the conventual estates and leased them all, a program being forced on every great landowner as a result of the decline in population following the BLACK DEATH. He secured good terms for these leases and thereby greatly increased the revenues of the house. In consequence he was able to undertake an extensive rebuilding program for Canterbury; he employed the great mason Henry Yevele to rebuild the cathedral nave, which, together with the choir screen and chapter house, justifies Leland's tribute of Chillenden as "the greatest Builder of a Prior that ever was in Christes Chirche." Other building projects were carried out on conventual properties and at Canterbury College. Chillenden declined his election to the see of Rochester in 1400. In 1409 he attended the Council of PISA as a delegate of the province of Canterbury.

Bibliography: D. KNOWLES, *The Religious Orders in England* (Cambridge, Eng. 1948–60) 2:189–190. A. B. EMDEN, *A Biographical Register of the University of Oxford to A.D. 1500* (Oxford 1957–59) 1:415–416.

[R. L. STOREY]

CHIMAYÓ, SANTUÁRIO DE

A chapel dedicated to Our Lord of *Esquipulas* (Chorti Indian, "springs of water"), Chimayo, N. Mex., built between 1813 and 1816. The devotion originated from Esquipulas, Guatemala, where a famed statue of the Crucifixion has attracted pilgrims from all of Central America since 1595. Pilgrims took home from the shrine cakes of earth, which were believed to have healing powers. The cult reached New Mexico c. 1805, when a small oratory was built near Chimayo on the site of ancient volcanic hot springs, visited by prehistoric peoples for therapeutic purposes. The oratory was then incorporated into the present Santuario, a splendid example of southwestern Spanish colonial architecture built of sun-dried brick and hand-carved timbers. Willa Cather's *Death Comes for the Archbishop* features this chapel and its *santos* (religious images), among which are the Holy Child of Atocha, patron of prisoners, and Santiago de Chimayó.

New Mexico's 200th Coast Artillery, captured by the Japanese on Bataan in 1942, made pilgrimage vows to the Holy Child of Atocha should they survive. On April 28, 1946, 500 persons accompanied the Bataan survivors, walking 30 miles across country to attend a Thanksgiving Mass at the Santuário. The Santuário attracts visitors from many states and countries. Its annual feast is celebrated on the last Sunday in July.

See Also: SANTO.

Bibliography: S. F. DE BORHEGYI, *The Miraculous Shrines of Our Lord of Esquipulas in Guatemala and Chimayo, New Mexico* (Santa Fe, N. Mex. 1956). O. LA FARGE, *Santa Fé: The Autobiography of a Southwestern Town* (Norman, Okla. 1959).

[E. BOYD]

Capital: Beijing

Size: About 3,700,000 square miles (including Tibet).

Population: 1,261,832,482 in 2000. Ethnic (Han) Chinese comprise about 90% of the total population. Minority communities in China include (in the order of size from the largest to smallest): Zhuang (Chuang), Manchu, Hui (Chinese Muslims), Miao (Hmong), Uygur (Uighur), Yi, Tuchia, Mongolian, Tibetan, Buyi (Puyi, a.k.a. Chuang-Chia), Tung, Yao, Korean, Pai, Hani, Kazak, Tai and Li.

Languages: Standard Chinese or Mandarin (Putonghua, based on the Beijing dialect), Yue (Cantonese), Wu (Shanghaiese), Minbei (Fuzhou), Minnan (Hokkien-Taiwanese), Xiang, Gan, Hakka dialects, minority languages.

Religions: Although China is officially an atheist country, a significant proportion of the Chinese population practice a mixture of Taoism, Buddhism and Confucianism. An increasing number of Chinese are joining new religious movements, the best known of which is the Falun Gong movement. The Muslim population comprises about 4-5% of the total population and is mainly concentrated in the interior, especially in the Xinjiang (Sinkiang) region which is overwhelmingly Muslim. Chinese Catholics are estimated to number about 1% of the total Chinese population, with slightly more than half claiming allegiance to the Underground Catholic Church.

CHINA, CHRISTIANITY IN

Since 1949, the communist government of the People's Republic of China has controlled mainland China from its capital in Beijing (Peking). The non-communist Republic of China with its capital in Taipei has governed Taiwan and other offshore islands. On June 30, 1997, and December 20, 1999, respectively, Hong Kong and Macau were returned to mainland Chinese control. This entry covers the history and present status of Christianity in mainland China. For discussion of the Church in Hong Kong, Macau, and Taiwan, see those separate entries.

The Christian presence in China has a long but broken history, shrouded by the mystery of time. Legend has it that St. Thomas traveled to China from India, converted some Chinese, and then returned to Meliapur on the southeast coast of India, where he died. But no evidence has been found to substantiate this claim.

The "Luminous Religion." The arrival of an Assyrian (Nestorian) monk Alopen (Aluoben) in the Chinese capital of Chang'an (modern Xi'an) in 635, during the Tang dynasty, is the first known Christian presence in China. This event is recorded on the so-called Assyrian (Nestorian) Christian monument of Xi'anfu, discovered in 1625. The marble stele, 9 feet high by 3 feet 4 inches wide, was erected in 781 to celebrate "the propagation of the Luminous Religion in the Middle Kingdom." Under this acculturated name the monument in fact retraces the development of the ASSYRIAN CHURCH OF THE

Metropolitan Sees*	Suffragans
Anqing (Anking)	Bengbu (Pengpu), Wuhu (Wuhu)
Beijing (Peking)	Anguo (Ankwo), Zhaoxian (Chaohsien), Zhengding (Chengting), Qingxian (Kinghsien), Baoding (Paoting), Xingtai (Shunteh), Xianxian (Sienhsien), Xuanhua (Suanhwa), Daming (Taming), Tianjin (Tientsin), Weixian (Yungnien), Lulong (Yungping)
Changsha (Changsha)	Changde (Changteh), Hengyang (Hengchow), Yuanling (Yuanling)
Chongqing (Chungking)	Chengdu (Chengtu), Kangding (Kangting), Leshan (Kiating), Xichang (Ningyuan), Nanchong (Shunking), Yibin (Suifu), Wanxian (Wanhsien)
Fuzhou (Foochow)	Xiapu (Funing), Xiamen (Hsiamen-Amoy), Changting (Tingchow)
Guangzhou (Canton)	Meixian (Kaiying), Jiangmen (Kongmoon), Beihai (Pakhoi), Shaoguan (Shiuchow), Shantou (Swatow), Xianggang (Hong Kong)
Guiyang (Kweyang)	Anlong (Lanlung)
Hangzhou (Hangchow)	Lishui (Lishui), Ningbo (Ningpo), Linhai (Taichow), Yongjia (Yungkia)
Hankou (Hankow)	Hanyang (Hanyang), Yichang (Ichang), Qichun (Kichow), Laohekou (Laohokow), Puqi (Puchi), Enshi (Shihnan), Xiangyang (Siangyang), Wuchang (Wuchang)
Hohot (Suiyuan)	Yinchuan (Ningsia), Chongli-Xiwanzi (Siwantze), Jining (Tsining)
Jinan (Tsinan)	Zhoucun (Chowtsun), Linyi (Ichow), Heze (Tsaochow), Qingdao (Tsingtao), Yanggu (Yangku), Yenchow (Yanzhou), Yantai (Yentai)
Kaifeng (Kaifeng)	Zhengzhou (Chengchow), Zhumadian (Chumatien), Shangqiu (Kweiteh), Luoyang (Loyang), Nanyang (Nanyang), Xinyang (Sinyang), Jixian (Weihwei)
Kunming (Kunming-Yunnan)	Dali (Tali)
Lanzhou (Lanchow)	Pingliang (Pingliang), Tianshui (Tsinchow)
Nanchang (Nanchang)	Ganzhou (Kanchow), Ji'an (Kian), Nancheng (Nancheng), Yijiang (Yukiang)
Nanjing (Nanking)	Haimen (Haimen), Shanghai (Shanghai), Suzhou (Soochow), Xuzhou (Suchow)
Nanning (Nanning)	Wuzhou (Wuchow)
Shenyang (Mukden-Fengtien)	Chifeng (Chihfeng), Fushun (Fushun), Jinzhou (Jehol), Jilin (Kirin), Siping (Szepingkai), Yanji (Yenki), Yingkou (Yingkow)
Taiyuan (Taiyuan)	Fenyang (Fenyang), Hongdong (Hungtung), Changzhi (Luan), Shuoxian (Shohchow), Datong (Tatung), Yuci (Yutze)
Xi'an (Sian)	Zhouzhi (Chowchich), Fengxiang (Fengsiang), Hanzhong (Hanchung), Sanyuan (Sanyuan), Yan'an (Yenan)
Apostolic Prefectures:	Ankang (Hinganfu), Baojing (Paoking), Guilin (Kweilin), Hainan (Hainan), Haizhou (Haichow), Jiamusi (Kiamusze), Jian'ou (Kienow), Lingling (Yungchow), Linqing (Lintsing), Lintong (Lintung), Lixian (Lichow), Qiqihar (Tsitsihar), Shashi (Shasi), Shaowu (Shaowu), Shiqian (Shihtsien), Suixian (Suihsien), Tongzhou (Tungchow), Tunxi (Tunki), Weihai (Weihaiwei), Xiangtan (Siangtan), Xining (Sining), Xinjiang (Kiangchow), Xinjiang-Urumqi (Sinkiang), Xinxiang (Sinsiang), Yangzhou (Yangchow), Yiduxian (Iduhsien), Yixian (Yishien), Yueyang (Yochow), Zhaotong (Chaotong); Haerbin (Harbin) is a Russian Byzantine Catholic Exarchate Apostolic directly under the jurisdiction of the Holy See

* The names are given in modernized pinyin form, their historical (pre-communist) equivalents in parentheses

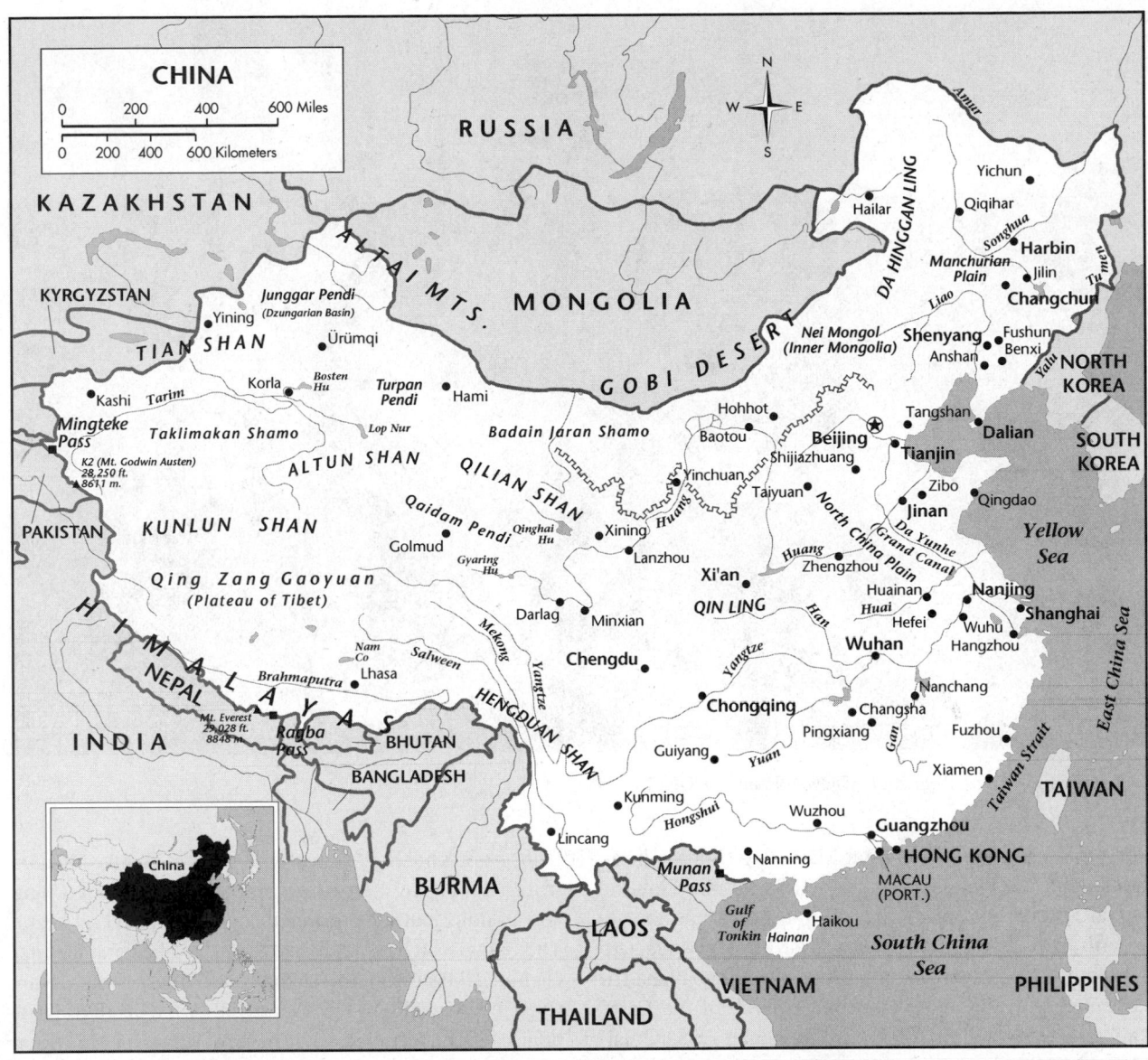

CHINA

0 200 400 600 Miles
0 200 400 600 Kilometers

RUSSIA

KAZAKHSTAN

KYRGYZSTAN

Junggar Pendi
(Dzungarian Basin)

Yining

TIAN SHAN

Ürümqi

Kashi   Tarim   Korla   Bosten Hu   Turpan Pendi   Hami

Mingteke Pass

K2 (Mt. Godwin Austen)
28,250 ft.
8611 m.

Taklimakan Shamo   Lop Nur

ALTUN SHAN

PAKISTAN

KUNLUN SHAN

Qaidam Pendi   Qinghai Hu

Golmud

Gyaring Hu

Qing Zang Gaoyuan
(Plateau of Tibet)

Darlag   Minxian

Nam Co   Salween

NEPAL   Brahmaputra   Lhasa

Mt. Everest
29,028 ft.
8848 m.   Ragba Pass

INDIA

BHUTAN

BANGLADESH

China

BURMA

MONGOLIA

ALTAI MTS.

GOBI DESERT

Badain Jaran Shamo

QILIAN SHAN

Xining   Huang   Lanzhou

Xi'an

QIN LING

Chengdu

HENGDUAN SHAN   Yangtze   Chongqing

Mekong   Guiyang   Yuan

Kunming   Hongshui

Lincang

Munan Pass

Gulf of Tonkin   Hainan   Haikou

THAILAND   VIETNAM

DA HINGGAN LING   Amur

Yichun   Qiqihar   Songhua   Hailar

Harbin   Manchurian Plain   Jilin   Tumen

Changchun

Nei Mongol
(Inner Mongolia)   Shenyang   Fushun   Benxi   Anshan

Hohhot   Baotou   Tangshan   NORTH KOREA

Beijing   Dalian   Liao   Yalu

Shijiazhuang   Tianjin   SOUTH KOREA

Yinchuan   Taiyuan   Zibo   Qingdao

North China Plain   Jinan

Da Yunhe   Grand Canal

Huang   Zhengzhou   Nanjing

Huai   Huainan   Shanghai

Han   Hefei   Wuhu   Hangzhou

Wuhan

Nanchang

Changsha   Fuzhou

Pingxiang   Gan

Wuzhou   Xiamen   TAIWAN

Nanning   Guangzhou   HONG KONG   Taiwan Strait

MACAU (PORT.)   East China Sea

Yellow Sea

South China Sea

PHILIPPINES

LAOS

EAST in China. It also presents the principal points of a unique blend of Christian doctrines with Confucian and Buddhist precepts, and records the names and titles of 70 saints and monks of the Assyrian Church in China.

Generally enjoying the favor of the Tang emperors, the "Luminous Religion" prospered. Soon churches and monasteries existed in all the provinces. Records or architectural remains of at least 15 of these monasteries survive. Modern researchers have ascertained the past existence of Assyrian Christian communities in at least 22 cities and have unearthed medals and crosses as well as sarcophagi and tombs with Christian inscriptions in Syriac. Most intriguing of all is the "Da Qin," an ancient pagoda dedicated to the "Luminous Religion" in Lou Guan Tai (dated 638), with the oldest depiction of the Na-

tivity scene in China. By the turn of the ninth century, China had its own metropolitan and a number of bishops. The xenophobic imperial decree of 845, which ordered the destruction of all "foreign" religions, dealt a grievous blow to both Buddhism and the "Luminous Religion" alike.

Assyrian Christianity also prospered in Central Asia among the Uighurs, the Naimans and the Onguts, and gradually spread among the Keraits and the Mongols. In 1271, the advent of the Mongol Yuan dynasty in China marked the beginning of a strong comeback for the "Luminous Religion." The Italian traveler Marco Polo found adherents in northern, central, and southern China. The most compelling sign of the vitality of the Assyrian Church in China during the Mongol period is perhaps the

Easter Mass at Beijing Cathedral. (©Owen Franken/CORBIS)

story of Rabban Sauma and Mar Mark, two Chinese-born monks of Turkish descent, who in 1278 left the Chinese capital Khanbaliq (present-day Beijing) on a pilgrimage to Jerusalem. During the journey, Mar Mark was elected Patriarch of Baghdad. He took the name of Yaballaha III and ruled over the entire Assyrian Church of the East. Rabban Sauma was, in 1287, sent on behalf of Khubilai Khan and Ilkhan Arghun on a diplomatic mission to Rome and the major capitals of Europe. Yet, as under the Tang dynasty, Assyrian Christianity in thirteenth-century China lacked a strong Han Chinese base and was most active among foreigners and minority residents. It is not surprising therefore that with the demise of the Yuan dynasty in 1368, Assyrian Christianity lost the imperial protection and patronage it had enjoyed for some one hundred years, and again disappeared from the Chinese public scene.

Franciscan Mission. Between 1245 and 1254 Pope Innocent IV dispatched several missions that had meager results to the court of the Great Khan in Karakorum. The Franciscans Giovanni dal Piano del Carpini and Willem van Rubroek and the Dominican André de Longjumeau led the major missions. Despite the return of the Italian travelers Maffeo and Nicolò Polo from the East with a

letter from Khubilai asking for 100 Catholic missionaries in 1269, a papal interregnum and the difficulty of a long and arduous journey prevented contacts for several years. The Franciscan JOHN OF MONTECORVINO became the first Catholic missionary to set foot on Chinese soil. He arrived in Khanbaliq in 1294 shortly after the death of Khubilai but was befriended by the new Khan, Timur. Soon after his arrival he built in the capital the first Catholic Church in China. As papal envoy to the Great Khan, friar Giovanni hoped primarily to convert the emperor and the cosmopolitan non-Chinese court. He was successful in converting Prince George of the Onguts, son-in-law of the emperor, and several Alan chiefs from Nestorianism to Catholicism. Emulating their leaders, many Ongut and Alan tribesmen followed suit. By 1305, friar Giovanni had administered some 6,000 baptisms, erected three churches, and trained a group of boys in the Latin chant and liturgy. He learned the Mongolian language and translated the New Testament, the liturgy of the Mass and the Psalter into that language.

In 1307, upon learning of Giovanni da Montecorvino's achievement, Pope Clement V appointed him archbishop of Kanbaliq and dispatched six Franciscan bishops to help him. Only three arrived at their final destination. The leader of the group was Andrea da Perugia whom Giovanni appointed bishop of Zaitun (modern Quanzhou), a busy city on the coast of southern China. Over the years, the friars benefitted from the protection of the rulers and the largesse of rich foreign benefactors. They built churches in several localities including the prosperous cities of Hangzhou and Yangzhou. Chinese converts were few compared to those belonging to the affluent foreign community.

Heavy casualties caused by the perils and privations of the voyage from Europe to the Far East kept Franciscan reinforcement to a trickle. In 1328, three years after his arrival in Khanbaliq, ODORIC da Pordenone made the long trip back to recruit missionaries for China. He provided a detailed account of the life of Giovanni da Montecorvino and his companions in the capital and other cities of China. The archbishop died around 1328 and no successor reached China to replace him. The papal envoy, Giovanni de Marignolli, entered the Chinese capital in 1342 with handsome gifts and a retinue of 32 people but stayed only three years. On his return, he urged Pope Innocent VI to send more Franciscans to China. However, due to the plagues that had begun to decimate the European population, missionaries were not available.

Meanwhile hostility toward the foreign Mongol Yuan dynasty and those associated with it rose and turned to violence. When the Franciscan bishop of Zaitun was slain in 1362, he was one of the last Catholic missionaries on Chinese soil. At the time of the establishment of the Chinese Ming Dynasty in 1368, Catholics in China may have numbered as many as 30,000, although the majority were probably not Han Chinese. The Franciscan Catholic mission, like its Assyrian (Nestorian) counterpart, was for the most part a religion of foreigners. Both lacked the native leadership and the Chinese following necessary for their survival in this new environment and disappeared almost without a trace. Some Chinese Catholics, however, persevered and handed down their faith in an unbroken tradition until missionaries discovered them at the turn of the twentieth century.

Although the Holy See continued for some time to name titulars to the See of Khanbaliq, it lost all contacts with its Chinese mission. No missionary expeditions seem to have reached China again until the 16th century when Pope Gregory XIII, in 1576, raised the Portuguese concession-port of Macau into a diocese with jurisdiction over the whole of China and Japan.

Jesuit Mission. In the early 16th century, Portuguese navigators reopened the sea route to China. St. Francis XAVIER, one of the members of the newly founded Society of Jesus, soon became interested in the Far East. During his stay in Japan (1549–51), he discov-

Thomas Tien Ken-Hsin (Tian Gengxin), first Chinese cardinal.

ered the importance of China, and he decided to enter the empire. His plan of accompanying a Portuguese embassy to Beijing failed. He died on Dec. 3, 1552, on the island of Shangchuan (Sancian), just a few miles from the coast of Guangdong (Kwangtung) province. His death, however, brought the importance of China to the attention of the West. During the 30 years that followed, Jesuits, Franciscans, Augustinians, and Dominicans tried in vain to gain a foothold in China. The empire's doors were closed to foreigners and traders could stay only at the port of Guangzhou (Canton) for short periods and under strict supervision.

Francis Xavier had come to understand the need to reach native people on their own terms. This meant becoming an integral part of the culture, although without compromise to Christian belief. Alessandro VALIGNANO, the Jesuit Visitor to the East, turned the vision into an effective method of penetrating China. He advocated a thorough preparation that included learning the language and adapting to the culture and customs of the Chinese. He summoned two Italian Jesuits from India, Michele Ruggieri, and Matteo RICCI to Macau. In September 1583, they succeeded in taking up residence at Zhaozhou (Shiuhing). Dressing first as Buddhist monks and later as Confucian scholars when they discovered that the most respected class in China was the Confucian literati, the

Plaster figurines made by the Luoyang Crafts Institute, including Shou-xing, a Chinese god of longevity, and a distinctly Chinese Jesus on a cross. (©Lowell Georgia/CORBIS)

two Jesuits displayed scientific instruments from the West, engaged in discussion with the literati and gained their respect. To strengthen their foothold, they sought to establish themselves in the capital of the empire, Beijing.

While Ruggieri returned to Europe in an unsuccessful effort to solicit an embassy from the pope, Ricci moved north and finally settled in Beijing in 1601, 18 years after entering China. With indefatigable zeal, he exercised a fruitful apostolate, both by the spoken word and by numerous writings. His method quickly won friends and admirers among prominent officials and scholars. He was influential in the conversion of Li Zhizao (Li Chih-tsao), a director in the Board of the Public Works and Xu Guangqi (Hsü Kuang-ch'i, 1562-1633), a member of the Hanlin Academy who later rose to be a grand secretary. Together with Yang Tingyun (Yang T'ing-yün), another learned convert from Hangzhou, they later became known as the "Three Pillars of Christianity in China."

Two years before his death in 1610, Ricci wrote that Beijing counted 2,000 Christians, among whom many were literati.

In 1612 a Belgian Jesuit, Nicolas TRIGAULT, was sent to Europe on a multiple mission. Besides recruiting missionaries and obtaining financial support and books, he obtained approval from Pope Paul V for priests to pray the Divine Office and celebrate the Mass in Chinese. The Jesuits hoped that the substitution of Chinese for Latin as the liturgical language would help the recruitment of vocations, especially among the mature and respected literati who were not able to learn enough Latin to be ordained. Unfortunately the privilege was never used, first because no Chinese translation of these texts existed and then because the Congregation for the Propagation of the Faith withdrew the permission.

One achievement responsible for the success of the Jesuit mission was the reform of the imperial calendar,

Head Bishop Liu Yuanren of the Official Chinese Bishops College, second from right facing camera, presiding over a bishop ordination ceremony at Beijing's Nantang (Southern) Cathedral. (AP/Wide World Photos)

which had accumulated many serious errors that Chinese astronomers had not been able to rectify. In reply to Ricci's request for trained astronomers, the Italian Giacomo Rho, the Swiss Johann Schreck (Terrentius), and the German Johann Adam Schall von Bell sailed to China. In 1629, after proving their competence by accurate predictions of eclipses, they were officially entrusted with the reform of the calendar. Due to the premature death of Schreck, Rho and Schall did the work with the help of the Christian scholar Xu Guangqi (Hsü Kuang-ch'i). When the new calendar was presented to the emperor in 1634, it greatly increased the prestige of the missionaries throughout the empire.

Arrival of Other Missionary Groups. In response to a request by the Portuguese king and to ensure a uniform missionary method in the early stage of evangelization, Pope Gregory XIII, in 1585, had granted the Society of Jesus the exclusive right to preach in Japan and China.

Moreover all missionaries had to embark at Lisbon. Subsequent popes gradually lifted the restriction. In 1635, to the dismay of the Jesuits, the Franciscan Antonio Cabarello de Santa Maria and the Dominican Angelo Cocchi da Fiesole and Juan Bautista de Morales arrived from the Philippines. They settled in the province of Fujian where they were soon joined by more confreres. The first Augustinians arrived in 1680, and the first members of the newly founded PARIS FOREIGN MISSION SOCIETY(MEP), in 1684. The Dominicans retained Fujian as their main area of activity; the Franciscans, Jiangxi, Shandong, and Shanxi and Shaanxi; the Augustinians, the southern provinces; and the MEP, Sichuan and other southern and southwestern territories.

Change of Dynasty. Toward the end of the Ming dynasty, the gospel was being preached in almost all the provinces of the empire. By 1636, the Christian influence of the Jesuits in Beijing was also showing results with

Worship service in the Muen Christian Church, Shanghai, Peoples Republic of China. (©AFP/CORBIS)

140 Catholics among the princes and 70 to 80 among the ladies in attendance at the court. But the last few Ming emperors were weak and powerless to control rebellion and increasing Manchu incursions. The vigorous Manchus, attacking from the north, easily took Beijing in 1644 and established a new dynasty. Gradually, they took control of the whole empire by chasing Ming loyalists southward.

The disorder caused by the change of dynasty temporarily halted the progress of Christianity. Several missionaries lost their lives and the flourishing mission of Fujian was devastated. The Dominican (later St.) Francis de CAPILLAS was decapitated in 1648. Some Jesuits kept their allegiance to the Ming court and accompanied it in its retreat to the south. In 1648, the wife of Prince of Yongming, the last pretender to the throne, along with his son, his mother, and the empress dowager, were baptized by the Jesuit Andreas Xavier Koffler. Ultimately, the last

remnants of the Mings were captured and executed by Manchurian forces.

Under the Manchu Dynasty. Schall, who first helped the unfortunate Chong Zhen (Ch'ung-chen) emperor (1627-1644) to resist the Manchus to the extent of casting cannons for him, remained in Beijing after the takeover and soon found favor with the new rulers. The first Manchu emperor was still a boy, and the regent, respecting the scientific abilities of Schall, reinstated him in his former position as imperial astronomer. The Jesuit exercised great influence over the young Shunzhi (Shun-chih) emperor (1644-61) who called him ''grandpa'' and often summoned him for conferences on religion and politics, and even allowed him to build a church in Beijing.

After the untimely death of Shunzhi in 1661 at the age of 23, an antiforeign reaction led by astronomer Yang Guangxian set in. He accused Schall of treason and of teaching false astronomy. In late 1664 Schall was condemned to death and replaced by Yang as president of the Imperial Board of Astronomy. The death sentence was not carried out but the Jesuit, old and sick, died shortly after his release from prison. After Yang's own downfall in 1669, the Belgian Jesuit Ferdinand Verbiest became the court astronomer and obtained from the Kangxi (K'ang-hsi) emperor (1661-1722), a new investigation that led to Schall's full rehabilitation.

The Kangxi emperor, the second emperor of the Qing (Ching) Dynasty, proved to be a great protector of Christianity. Fond of Western thought and science, the emperor welcomed Jesuits to his court as astronomers, linguists, and artists. Two of them, the Portuguese Tomé Pereira and the French Jean-François Gerbillon played important roles in the conclusion of the Treaty of Nerchinsk (1689), which determined the border between China and Russia. In 1692, in gratitude for all the services rendered by the missionaries, the Kangxi emperor issued an edict of religious freedom permitting the Christian religion to be preached freely in Beijing and in the provinces. Bolstered by the prestige acquired by the Jesuits at the court, the Church, by 1700, counted about 200,000 Chinese Catholics.

Jurisdictional Problems. Since the creation of the diocese of Macau in 1576, China had been under its jurisdiction, and the right of royal patronage, i.e. the Portuguese Padroado, regulated all missionary activities. Portuguese control of missionary activities was slowly eroded when the Congregation for the PROPAGATION OF THE FAITH (Propaganda Fide) began to intervene directly in China from the 17th century onward. In 1660, Propaganda Fide sent three vicars apostolic, all cofounders of the MEP, to the Far East: François PALLU, Pierre LAMBERT DE LA MOTTE and Ignace Cotolendi. In 1674, the Chinese Dominican Luo Wenzao, also known in Western sources as Gregorio López, was appointed vicar apostolic of Nanjing (Nanking) in replacement of Cotolendi who died on his way to China. Consecrated in 1685, Luo became the first local Chinese bishop, but unfortunately China would not see another Chinese bishop for 241 years.

Propaganda Fide's creation of vicariates apostolic in China provoked a violent reaction from Portugal. Missionaries sent by Rome without the consent of Lisbon were often harassed or imprisoned if caught by Portuguese authorities. In 1690 the Holy See and Portugal reached a compromise with the creation of the two bishoprics of Beijing and Nanjing as suffragans of the Portuguese Metropolitan See of GOA, as was the case with Macau. Pope Alexander VIII conceded to the Portuguese crown the right of patronage over the three Chinese dioceses and even permitted Portugal to determine their boundaries. This settlement left little room for the cre-

Beitang (Northern) Cathedral, the largest church in China. (©Marc Garanger/CORBIS)

ation of vicariates apostolic. As a result of complaints from Propaganda Fide, in 1696 the Pope limited the jurisdiction of the three dioceses to one or two provinces while the rest of China was divided into vicariates apostolic.

Chinese Rites Controversy. The Chinese names for God as well as the rituals used to honor ancestors and Confucius were at the core of the bitter 17th- and 18th-century debate known as the CHINESE RITES CONTROVERSY. On one side stood mostly accommodative Jesuits. On the other was a large array of Franciscan, Dominican, Augustinian and MEP clergy who argued against the Jesuits that the native Chinese terminology for God and the Chinese rites to ancestors and CONFUCIUS violated Christian teachings. The controversy took a turn for the worse for the Jesuits when in 1704 Bishop Charles Maigrot, who had already prohibited the Chinese Rites in his vicariate apostolic of Fujian, convinced the Holy Office of the Inquisition to issue a universal condemnation. The ruling was promulgated in Nanjing in 1707 by the papal legate

Charles Maillard de TOURNON. Later it also served as the basis for papal decrees *Ex illa die* of 1715 and *Ex quo singulari* of 1742 that banned the Chinese Rites and prohibited further debate on the controversy. This decision has often been considered as one of the main causes of the lack of development of Christianity in China at that time. It was not until 1939 that the condemnation was annulled in the decree *Plane compertum est*.

Persecutions. In 1692, the Kangxi emperor had issued the Edict of Toleration protecting existing Christian church buildings throughout the provinces and allowing freedom of worship, but he became angered by Rome's condemnation of the Chinese Rites. In 1706 and again in 1720 he prohibited the preaching of Christianity and ordered the deportation of missionaries who did not conform to Ricci's views on the Chinese Rites. These decrees were not fully carried out, but under his successors persecutions periodically flared up and sometimes engulfed the whole of China. At the start of his reign, the Yongzheng (Yung-cheng) emperor (1722-35) ordered the closure of all churches and that Christians renounce their faith. While Jesuits in Beijing, such as Giuseppe Castiglione, remained in the service of the court, most other missionaries in the provinces were deported to Guangzhou and Macau. The Qianlong (Ch'ien-lung) emperor (1735-96) began his reign with a decree proclaiming the death penalty for preaching and embracing Christianity. Numerous lay Christians were killed in the persecution of 1748-1785. In 1748, two Jesuits (António-José Henriques and Tristano d'Attimis) were martyred in Jiangsu and five Dominicans—Pedro Sanz Jorda, Francisco Serrano Frias, Joaquín Perez, Juan Alcober Figuera and Francisco Díaz del Rincon——were put to death in Fujian.

The missions suffered further losses with the imprisonment and deportation of missionaries from Macau in 1762 and with the suppression of the Society of Jesus in 1773. The Lazarists (also known Vincentians) took over the Jesuits' cultural work in Beijing and Propaganda Fide tried to fill the gap in the provinces with missionaries who entered China in secret. But the French Revolution and the Napoleonic War diverted European interest from the missions. Only a dwindling number of European missionaries and Chinese priests continued to minister in China, led by a handful of bishops such as Eugenio Piloti in Shanxi-Shaanxi, Gottfried von Laimbeckhoven in Nanjing and François Pottier in Sichuan.

Early 19th-Century Developments. The dawn of the 19th century found the missions in a deplorable situation. European missionaries numbered no more than 25 and Chinese priests stood at around 50. The Catholic population had fallen to about 135,000 in a total Chinese population of 150 to 200 million. The Church in Sichuan and Guizhou in particular was the target of frequent persecutions. Among the 120 Martyrs of China canonized on October 1, 2000, nine were martyred in these two provinces between 1815 and 1839, including one bishop, Jean Gabriel Dufresse, four Chinese priests and four catechists.

The French Protectorate of Missions. A change occurred in 1842 when, by the Treaty of Nanjing marking the end of the Opium War, England acquired Hong Kong and forced China to open five ports to foreign trade. In 1844 the United States and France followed suit and obtained the same commercial privileges in the open ports as well as the rights to preach and maintain churches and hospitals. At the insistence of the French plenipotentiary Théodore de Lagrené, the Daoguang (Tao-kuang) emperor (1820-1850) in 1846 issued a decree permitting the Chinese to profess the Catholic faith. It also ordered the restitution of previously confiscated church properties and the punishment of local officials who persecuted Catholics. But the decree was never published and thus remained largely ineffective. In the 1858 Treaty of Tianjin (Tientsin), religious liberty for all Christians was reaffirmed and extended to the interior of China. Protection was also guaranteed to missionaries traveling to the interior, provided they carried valid passports. All anti-Christian legislation was revoked. While these measures were directed at the Chinese Catholic community they also greatly benefited Protestants. Meanwhile, as the sole Catholic power among the signatories, France assumed the protection of all Catholic missionaries of whatever nationality. The Beijing Convention of 1860 gave missionaries the right to buy property for religious purposes. The Berthémy Convention of 1865 further regulated this matter. With the tacit consent of the Holy See, France effectively exercised between 1860 and 1880 an exclusive protection over all Catholic missionaries, Chinese Christians and church properties in China. In 1882 Germany claimed the right to protect German missionaries and in 1888 Italy did the same for its own nationals.

Catholic Mission Activities in the 19th Century. Decrees and treaties guaranteeing religious freedom did not put an end to anti-Christian sentiment. When missionaries became involved in legal cases on behalf of Christians, it further irked the non-Christian population. Occasionally violence erupted as in the killing of Fr. Auguste Chapdelaine in 1856; the massacre at Tianjin (Tientsin) of the French consul, two priests, 10 Sisters of Charity, and eight lay persons; and the slaying of two German missionaries in Shandong (Shantung) in 1897. Most serious of all was the Boxer Uprising of 1900. Several of these incidents were utilized by Western powers to justify launching military actions against China, forcing it to make further concessions and fueling Chinese resentment against Christianity.

After 1842 the number of Catholic missionaries increased rapidly with the return of the Franciscans, the Dominicans, the Lazarists, the MEP and the Jesuits whose order had been restored 1814. New groups also joined in. The first members of the Foreign Mission Institute of Milan (PIME) arrived in 1858 and those of the Congregation of the Immaculate Heart of Mary (CICM or Scheut Fathers) in 1865. A Trappist monastery was founded at Yangjiaping, Hebei, in 1883. The opening of hospitals, orphanages, and, above all, schools created great opportunities for an apostolate by women religious. The first to arrive in 1847 were the Daughters of Charity of St. Vincent de Paul followed by the Sisters of St. Paul of Chartres in 1848, the Daughters of Charity of Canossa in 1860, the Helpers of the Holy Souls in 1867, the Franciscan Missionaries of Mary and the Dominican Sisters in 1886. Many other congregations of women followed.

In 1856 the Holy See began to reorganize ecclesiastical divisions. It suppressed the two bishoprics of Beijing and Nanjing still nominally under the Portuguese Padroado and divided their territory into vicariates apostolic. The 22 vicariates apostolic in 1865 increased to 44 by 1900. By early 1900, the condition of the Catholic Church in China seemed rather healthy. With a total membership of about 700,000, it had grown almost sevenfold in the course of the 19th century. At the service of that community were of 900 male missionaries, 59 foreign sisters, and 400 Chinese priests.

Protestant Mission Activities in the 19th Century. In 1807, Robert Morrison of the London Missionary Society became the first Protestant missionary to set foot in Guangzhou. In 1813 William Milne joined him. Faced with the task of preaching the Gospel in a vast and unknown country, they concentrated on the translation of hymns and prayer and in 1819 published the entire Bible in Chinese. They also began the publication of tracts, one of the most characteristic Protestant methods of evangelization in China. The first baptism of a Chinese in the Protestant Church occurred in 1814. In 1816 Liang Fa was received in the Church and a few years later became the first ordained Chinese evangelist. His pamphlet ''Good Words to Admonish the Age'' deeply influenced Hong Xiuquan (Hung Hsiu-ch'üan, 1814-64), the future leader of the Taiping Rebellion.

Education was to be one of the great contributions of the Protestants to the development of modern China. In 1818 Morrison and his colleague founded the Anglo-Chinese College which remained in Malacca until its move to Hong Kong in 1842. Medical work was also to become another major means of contact with the Chinese.

Dr. Peter Parker, in 1835, opened a hospital in Guangzhou and three years later helped found the Medical Missionary Society.

As an interpreter and a medical practitioner, Karl Friedrich Gützlaff made three voyages along the China coast between 1831 and 1833. Finally he succeeded in entering the mainland where he remained as a freelance missionary. Through the publication of his activities in almost every Protestant missionary magazine in America and in Europe, he inspired missionaries and home supporters with a vision of the conversion of China's millions. One of them was James Hudson Taylor, the founder of the China Inland Mission. David Abeel and Elijah Bridgeman sent by the American Board of Commissioners of Foreign Missions were the first American missionaries to arrive in Guangzhou in 1830. Samuel Wells Williams came in 1833 and collaborated with Bridgeman in the production of the Chinese Repository, designed to acquaint outsiders with all facets of Chinese life. Yet for the next twenty years, Chinese Protestants remained a small urban community of less than 300 believers.

Protestant missionary activity did not began in earnest until about 1860 when, in major cities, Anglican, Presbyterian and Methodist denominations began to establish mission stations composed of a chapel, a school and a dispensary or even a small hospital. A major exception was the China Inland Mission (CIM) founded in 1865. CIM concerned itself more with penetrating the remotest parts of China than with establishing permanent mission stations. By 1900, Protestant Christians numbered 100,000 with almost two-thirds of them living in the coastal provinces of Zhejiang, Fujian and Guangdong.

In 1877 the first all-China General Missionary Conference of the Protestant Church stressed the need to bring up a generation of educated Christians of spiritual and moral maturity. In 1879, St. John's College opened in Shanghai followed by Nanjing and Beijing Universities in 1888. Other schools offering a similar Western-style of education were to follow led by prominent missionaries such as the American Presbyterian W. A. P. Martin. By 1890, the total enrollment had reached almost 17,000. The high standard of these schools contrasted sharply with the more than two thousand primary schools for boys and girls established by the Catholic Church all over China with an enrollment of 50,000 students.

Catholic and Protestant missionaries alike considered medical work an important tool of evangelization, but they made use of it differently. While the Catholic Church continued to emphasize the need of small dispensaries and clinics in mission stations, the Protestant

Church quickly focussed on strategically placed hospitals and on the training of Chinese doctors.

Rebellion and Chaos. The 20th century opened with a test of faith for Chinese Christians. The antiforeign Boxer uprising led, in the late spring and early summer of 1900, to the slaughter of many thousands of Catholic, Protestant and Orthodox Christians as well as several missionaries in northern China and Inner Mongolia. Attacks culminated in June 1900 with the Boxers rampaging through Beijing, burning churches and foreign homes, and killing Christians. In the Catholic Church alone, some 30,000 people lost their lives; 86 were later canonized.

The first half of the 20th century brought tremendous changes to China as traditional institutions disappeared. In 1911 the Qing (Ching) dynasty collapsed and a republic was proclaimed. Lacking a strong central unifying authority, the country soon fell prey to factions and warlords. When unity was finally restored, the Sino-Japanese War of 1937-45 and the Civil War that followed threw the nation back into turmoil. But in spite of all these disturbances, the Catholic and Protestant churches both registered a tremendous growth during the period.

The Catholic Church, 1900-1949. Since 1881, because of increasing unfavorable political repercussions emanating from the French Protectorate, the Holy See had wanted to put more distance between missionary interests and France. Its attempts at establishing direct diplomatic relations with the Chinese government were repeatedly thwarted by France until 1922 when Bishop Celso Costantini became the first apostolic delegate to China. Although not officially a member of the diplomatic corps, Costantini became the de facto religious representative of the pope to supervise the entire Catholic Church in China. This, for all practical purposes, brought to an end the French protectorate over Catholic missions in China. Finally, in 1943, the Chinese government dispatched an ambassador to the Vatican and three years later Rome sent an internuncio to China.

At this time, a group of missionaries led by Father Vincent LEBBE and Bishop Jean-Baptiste Budes de Guébriant had called not only for the Catholic Church to relinquish the protection of foreign powers but also to have its own indigenous leadership. Impetus for indigenous leadership came from Pope Benedict XV's apostolic letter *Maximum illud* (1919), and Costantini's own campaign for the establishment of a local Chinese hierarchy. The First Plenary Council of China held in Shanghai in 1924 saw the participation of the first two Chinese prefects apostolic and established fourteen major seminaries to provide a high standard formation for the Chinese clergy. In 1926, Costantini accompanied to Rome the first six

Chinese bishops to be ordained since the days of Bishop Luo in the 17th century. Twenty years later, Pope Pius XII appointed the first-ever Chinese cardinal, Thomas Tian Gengxin of the Society of the Divine Word. The same year, the pope replaced vicariates apostolic in China with 20 archdioceses and 79 dioceses while maintaining 38 prefectures apostolic.

Another important decision of the Holy See that greatly facilitated mission work was the 1939 decree *Plane compertum est of Propaganda Fide* declaring the veneration of Confucius, ceremonies in honor of deceased ancestors, and other national customs to be purely civil in character and therefore permissible to Chinese Catholics.

In the 20th century, three Catholic institutions of higher education were established in China. Renowned Catholic scholar Ma Xiangbo and French Jesuits opened Aurora University (Zhendan University) in 1903. In 1922, the Jesuits also began an Industrial and Commercial College in Tianjin that later became Jingu (Tsinku) University. In 1925, American Benedictine monks established the Catholic University of Beijing (Fujen University); they handed it over to the Society of the Divine Word (SVD) in 1933. After 1936, the number of Catholic secondary schools for male and female students began to grow, reaching a total of 190 by 1949. But the major educational emphasis still remained primary education in rural areas with an enrollment of over 400,000 students.

By 1938, when the Sino-Japanese War began to seriously hamper the development of most Christian churches, membership in the Catholic Church had more than quadrupled to a total of about 3,000,000. Growth resumed in 1946 and by 1949 China had 3,300,000 Catholics. Among the 5,700 priests, almost half were Chinese. Meanwhile 60 percent of the 978 brothers and 70 percent of the 6,927 sisters were also Chinese. Yet the sinization of the hierarchy was still lagging behind. In 1950, the main episcopal seats of Beijing, Nanjing, Shanghai, Shenyang and Guangzhou were headed by Chinese bishops, but out of a total of 146 ecclesiastical divisions, 111 were still in the hands of foreigners.

The Protestant Church, 1900 to 1949. The Protestant Church continued its rapid expansion through the mid-1920s. It passed the half million mark in 1914 and by 1920 totaled over 800,000, divided mostly among Presbyterians, Methodists, Baptists, Lutherans, Congregationalists, Anglicans and CIM. The publication in 1922 of the book *The Christian Occupation of China* marked the peak of missionary self-confidence.

The Student Volunteer Movement founded in 1888 recruited thousands of young Europeans and Americans under the slogan "The Evangelization of the World in This Generation." By 1919, over 2,500 volunteers had sailed to China. This led to the founding of the Chinese Young Men's Christian Association (YMCA) in 1889 and of the Young Women's Christian Association (YWCA) in 1899. Concentrated in the city ports, these institutions catered mainly to Chinese students. In 1922, the announcement in the YMCA magazine of the forthcoming conference in Beijing of the World Student Christian Federation led nationalistic-minded Chinese intellectuals to attack Christianity as a tool of the West for the colonization China.

In response to these charges, a Chinese Christian movement for a Chinese Christianity free from the taint of imperialism began to emerge. This led to the formation of the National Christian Council in 1922 and the Church of Christ in China in 1927. These organizations were attempts to overcome denominational divisions and among the first efforts to establish a self-supporting, self-governing and self-propagating church.

Besides the traditional Christian denominations, independent churches led by charismatic indigenous pastors had already come into being by the 1920s. The Chinese Independent Church began in 1906, the True Jesus Church in 1917, the Jesus Family in 1921, and the Little Flock in 1922. These groups maintained strict standards of social control guided by theologies that were as idiosyncratic as they were fundamentalist. In terms of both numbers and influence, the indigenous churches were a force to be reckoned with. In 1949, these four groups alone drew a membership of over 230,000 out of nearly one million Chinese Protestants.

Despite disruption during the war years, Protestant work in medicine and education remained considerable. By 1949, there were a total of 13 Protestant-run universities and 240 secondary schools. Protestant hospitals numbered 322 while Catholics ran 216.

The Russian Orthodox Church in the Early 20th Century. The Russian Orthodox mission in China had begun in 1727. However, active proselytizing was not its style, and the Church consisted mainly of small Russian enclaves within areas where the Russians settled. As a result of the influx of White Russians who fled the 1917 Russian Revolution, the Church grew to more than 200,000 members in the early 20th century. By 1939, the Russian Orthodox Church had established five bishoprics and a university in Haerbin (Harbin) in northeast China. Many departed China in 1949, leaving only scattered small communities. The East Asian Exarchate of the Moscow Patriarchate of Moscow existed until 1956, when Moscow granted it autocephalous status. The ordinary of the autochepalous Orthodox Church of China resides in Haerbin (Harbin), where a thriving Russian Orthodox community continues to exist.

Early Communist Rule, 1949-1966. The civil war in China between the Nationalist forces of Jiang Jie-shī (Chiang Kai-shek) and the Communists led by Mao Zedong (Mao Tse-tung) resulted in victory for Mao and the founding of the People's Republic of China in October 1949. Initially, the populist tenets of the Communists appealed to some Chinese Protestants actively involved in preaching the social gospel. They believed that the Christian gospel could be combined with the gospel of Chinese communism, especially the teaching on serving the poor. Several Church leaders headed by Wu Yaozong (Y. T. Wu) began to meet with Premier Zhou Enlai to discuss the role of churches in the new China. In July 1950, a Christian Manifesto was issued. Even though the manifesto was at first slow in gaining momentum, eventually over 400,000 signatures were gathered. It urged the Protestant Church to cut off ties with the imperialist powers, to support national reconstruction, and to build a Chinese Church managed by Chinese. This called for a church that was self-governing, self-propagating, and self-supporting—a "Three-Self" church. Organized into committees at the national, provincial, and municipal levels, the Three-Self Movement was the liaison between the Churches and the government organ of the Religious Affairs Bureau and ensured the Church's participation in common national goals as determined by the United Front of the Chinese Communist Party. Citing the need for the Protestant Church to consolidate resources, personnel, finances, and church facilities in order to survive, the Three-Self Movement organizational machinery gradually replaced denominational structures and even the National Christian Council.

In reaction to the Communist victory, the Catholic Church organized for survival. A primary instrument in this task was the Legion of Mary established in 1948. Despite persecutions in some places during 1950, the Catholic Church as a whole remained strongly anti-Communist and continued to flourish. The first sign of a movement similar to the Protestant Three-Self was a manifesto published in November 1950 under the leadership of the Chinese priest Wang Liangzuo. The document contained the three autonomous principles and called for the severance of all ties with the forces of imperialism. Yet with regard to self-governance, it spoke of political independence from the Vatican while maintaining a "religious connection" with the pope. The bishops responded by insisting that no alliance existed between the Church and imperialism and by strongly condemning the formation of a national or independent Catholic Church.

Meanwhile the Oppose America-Aid Korea Movement intensified the campaign against the churches. Denunciations of missionaries and Chinese Christians led to punishment, imprisonment, and expulsions. Because of the definite stand of the Catholic Church against communism, the Communists persecuted and detained a larger number of Catholics than Protestants. The majority of Protestant missionaries had left by the end of 1951 and Catholic missionaries by the end of 1955. Their institutions and properties, such as universities, hospitals, orphanages, were taken over and nationalized or confiscated by the government. After the Papal Nuncio Antonio Riberi was forced to leave in September 1951, relations between the Chinese government and the Vatican were severed. In 1952 Pope Pius XII published his Apostolic Letter *Cupimus imprimis* to strengthen the faith of Chinese Catholics, and in 1954 another Apostolic Letter entitled *Ad Sinarum gentem* discouraged the Chinese Church from proclaiming autonomy and independence from the Holy See. The Chinese government, offended by the critical tone of the letters, confronted the Church even more boldly with more arrests of church leaders opposed to the independent Church movement. At this juncture, Catholic bishops decided to send most of their seminarians abroad to continue their studies.

In 1954 a change in emphasis, characterized by the adoption of the term ''patriotic,'' began to take place in the native movement for the reform of both the Protestant and Catholic Churches. Instead of speaking of the ''independent Church'' or ''reforming the Church,'' which could be interpreted as aiming to change the structure or the nature of the Church, the emphasis was placed on patriotism, which no Chinese Christian could reject. Protestants changed the name of their organization to Three-Self Patriotic Movement (TSPM) while ''progressive'' Catholics established ''patriotic associations'' that resulted, in 1957, in the founding of the national Chinese Catholic Patriotic Association (CCPA). The Catholic Association in its first meeting declared it would thenceforth take charge of its own affairs without any outside interference and maintain a purely religious relationship with the Vatican.

By 1955 the Catholic resistance movement, crushed by mass arrests and condemnations to forced labor, went underground. The witness of Bishop Gong Pinmei (Ignatius Kung) of Shanghai and many others who chose jail, labor camps, and even death for the sake of their faith and their loyalty to the pope would sustain the faith in the years ahead. Meanwhile several Protestant groups, mostly Evangelical Christians, also refused to submit to Communist pressure and continued to carry out their activities in their own ways in spite of the imprisonment of their pastors and leaders. This progressively led to the development of the Protestant and Catholic underground churches. At the same time, more and more Protestants and Catholics began to rally to the cause of the patriotic movements.

The general picture after 1957 is that of a steady decline in church activity as a result of government constraint and lack of church personnel and resources. On the Protestant side the situation hastened the change towards unification of the various denominations, although there is little doubt that the process was not truly voluntary. The Catholic Church felt the urgency of filling up some one hundred episcopal vacancies because Chinese priests who were appointed administrators prior to the departure of the foreign bishops remained for the most part in prison. In 1958, the Holy See, which had only appointed 18 Chinese bishops since 1949, refused to endorse names proposed by bishops who had joined the CCPA. Considering the times to be extraordinary, these bishops went ahead and began to perform ordinations of bishops without papal approval. Saddened by the news, Pope Pius XII in his encyclical *Ad apostolorum principis* expressed his disapproval of the CCPA and stated that the authority for making episcopal appointments was his alone. Not unexpectedly, the government reacted by forbidding Catholic authorities to have further recourse to the Holy See. Thus began the ordinations of ''patriotic'' bishops chosen by the CCPA and ordained without the approval of Rome. By 1962, their number had reached 42 while those formerly appointed by Rome had fallen to about 20. Bishops who supported independent episcopal ordinations had to declare that they had broken off all relations with Rome; those who refused were imprisoned. The Catholic underground church was born of this confrontation.

The Cultural Revolution, 1966–1976. The Red Guard assault on religion that began in August 1966 was, in one sense, merely the culmination of the process that had begun in 1957. Ten years of Cultural Revolution plunged all Christians into a de facto clandestinity and resulted in the closure of churches, the destruction of religious artifacts and the burning of Bibles and Christian books. The few Protestant seminaries that had managed to remain open were also shut down. Both the TSPM and the CCPA stopped functioning. Clergy, nuns and numerous Christian workers were publicly humiliated, tortured, and then sent to prisons and labor camps to join their colleagues who had previously refused to join the Christian patriotic associations. No public church activities were tolerated until 1971 when two churches reopened in Beijing for the benefit of foreign Protestant and Catholic students and diplomats.

Post Revolution and Revival. In 1976, the 10-year nightmare of the Cultural Revolution came to an end. Religious leaders were set free and resumed their ministry while the ban on religious belief and practice was relaxed. A further sign of a more benevolent attitude toward religion came in 1978 with the reappearance of representatives from the five officially recognized religions—Taoism, Buddhism, Catholicism, Protestantism, and Islam—at the meeting of the Chinese People's Political Consultative Conference. This consultative body has no political power but serves as a bridge between the constituencies of the delegates, the Communist party, and the government. The TSPM and the CCPA resurfaced and became instrumental in the return of church properties to their former religious purposes. In 1982, China's new constitution dropped the ultra-leftist content of the preceding ones and recognized the freedom of religious belief for all Chinese people. The right to engage in "normal" religious activities was also affirmed but has remained strictly controlled by the Religious Affairs Bureau since only what the government permits is considered normal and what it does not permit is not only considered not normal but can even be construed as illegal. This submission of the churches to government control is therefore not done without danger of putting the integrity of the faith at some risk and, as a consequence, of jeopardizing authentic Christian living.

"Cultural" Christians. The 1980s also brought the rise of the "Cultural" Christians phenomenon. These Chinese academics and intellectuals read the Bible, studied Christian philosophy and theology, and wrote extensively on religious topics, but for the most part they did not seek baptism or join a church. Thanks to their translation efforts, important patristic and theological works soon became available in Chinese.

Meanwhile the government, wary of the popular interest in Christianity and the substantial increase in church attendance, spoke of "Christian fever." It was also worried by the resilience of the Catholic and Protestant underground churches which steadfastly refused to submit to the control of the TSPM or the CCPA. This led the government in 1989 to introduce a number of administrative measures to enact a stricter control over the membership and leadership of religious activities, including the registration of places of worship. The ban against the Falun Gong spiritual movement in July 1999 further intensified the nationwide crackdown on all unauthorized religious activities. Arrests of Protestants and Catholics who gathered without official permission increased. Even harsher was the treatment of Protestant Evangelicals whose illegal gatherings the police construed as prohibited cults rather than services belonging to one of the five recognized religions. As of 2001, the Communist regime still pursued a policy of allowing registered Christian communities to develop while eradicating all the others. That year, there were over 22,000 registered Protestant and Catholic churches, but this number fell short of meet-

ing the needs of the widely spread and growing Christian communities.

Even with the reopening of China to the West, religious activities of foreigners within China remained strictly controlled. The issuance in September 2000 of a new set of government regulations added fresh measures to restrictions already spelled out in 1994 and 1995. Except for the attendance at religious services at lawfully registered monasteries, temples, mosques and churches, foreigners were prohibited from engaging in religious activities or friendly cultural and academic exchanges with Chinese religious circles without the prior approval of Chinese religious bodies. For Protestants and Catholics this meant the permission of the TSPM or the CCPA at the county or even the provincial level. The 12 articles made it difficult for foreigners to contact underground communities and further curtailed their influence in government-approved religious bodies.

The Protestant Church after 1980. In the Protestant Church, a meeting held in October 1980 resulted in the creation of a new structure called the China Christian Council parallel to the TSPM. The TSPM heeds to the United Front policy of the government by ensuring the Church active participation in the socialist modernization of the country. The China Christian Council helps the Church to further its religious and pastoral duties. The two organizations have interlocking committees, with many of the people holding dual offices in the two organizations. It can be inferred from the dual arrangement that, while the Church is prepared to fulfill its pastoral calling, it is also obliged to reckon with the policy of the Communist party. The Bureau of Religious Affairs is the government agency that executes the religious policy of the state and is the body that the Church must deal with in matters of church-state relations.

The Chinese Protestant Church is nondenominational in character and the China Christian Council is the umbrella organization under which all the congregations are subsumed. A common catechism has been adopted. Although formal denominations no longer exist, traces of different customs and beliefs survive in everyday Church life. The National Union Theological Seminary in Nanjing was the first seminary to reopen in 1981. Since then more than a dozen seminaries and theological schools with male and female students have been established in major Chinese cities.

In addition to the more than 12,000 officially registered churches, countless groups that identify themselves as Protestant Christians meet in homes or other places. The name "house churches" is sometimes used in the West to designate those groups that meet for prayer in defiance of the China Christian Council. However it is an oversimplification to say that there are two large segments diametrically opposed to each other. Extra-church gatherings are part of the Protestant Church life, while many communities still without churches have no other place to meet but in individual homes. Many of the tens of thousands of these "meeting points" are registered and recognized by the China Christian Council. Nonetheless there are as many groups that still convene in defiance of government regulations and refuse all forms of collaboration with the TSPM and the China Christian Council. These Christians, many belonging to fundamentalist indigenous churches, live under the constant threat of being fined and arrested for illegal gathering and of having their unregistered meeting places torn down. Since the beginning of the campaign against the Falun Gong in 1999, such instances of prosecution have increased.

Many in the main Protestant body consider that self-imposed isolation among indigenous groups of recent origin has resulted in serious doctrinal deviations. This has led to a debate as to whether the followers of some of these Christian-inspired movements should still be regarded as Christians. Estimates of the total number of Protestant Christians therefore vary widely. Most reliable sources inside and outside China put the figure at about fifteen million adherents in the registered Church and at least as many in the underground. They are ministered by more than 1,400 pastors and several thousands of evangelists and lay church workers.

The Amity Foundation is remarkable evidence of Chinese Protestant spirit of service to the society. Established in 1985 on the initiative of the Anglican Bishop K. H. Ting and other concerned Christians, Amity Foundation represents a new and successful form of Christian involvement in Chinese society. The foundation concentrates its energy on areas of special needs in education, health and welfare, carrying out projects in impoverished western China and assisting the growing number of elderly people and unemployed workers. Since its inception, Amity has also invited friendly church agencies overseas to participate in its projects through grants, supply of equipment, and recruitment of experts and foreign language teachers. The other major activity of the Amity Foundation is its printing press. Prior to its establishment, Protestant publications had to rely entirely on government-owned presses. Since July 1995, it has published over ten million Bibles in Chinese. Besides the production of Bibles and Christian pamphlets and journals, it also prints materials of other major religious faiths and of general service to society. *Tian Feng (Heavenly Wind)* is the official publication the TSPM and the China Christian Council. Religious literature produced by the Protestant Church or by any religious group for that matter,

remains strictly controlled and cannot be made available in commercial bookstores. With the authorization of the government, it can however be distributed on church premises and through subscription or mail order.

A Divided Catholic Church. At the beginning of the 21st century, the situation of the Catholic Church in China remains very complex and still evolving, but contrary to some reports there has never been a schism within that Church. There is rather one Church that exists in two forms. One is approved by the government and linked to the CCPA. It is often referred to as the Open Church because it functions openly in churches registered with the government. The other group, often referred to as the Underground Church, refuses any control from the Communist regime and therefore operates in private homes or public buildings without seeking government approval.

The Open Catholic Church. Although its roots can be traced back to the emergence of the CCPA in 1957, the division itself became really apparent only after the clergy returned to their dioceses in 1978 and 1979. Since the new policy of the government allowed them to function in public, rather than in hiding, many did so. With less than 30 bishops still alive, some who had been imprisoned for their unswerving loyalty to the pope and had refused any relationship with the CCPA were now more willing to cooperate with the association for the future of the Catholic Church in China. After 1981, the requirement that both consecrators and consecrated ones should swear their independence from Rome was dropped and resulted in more priests willing to accept the episcopal ordination. Several of these bishops secretly obtained legitimization of their status from the pope. Some even actively sought higher positions within the CCPA in order to influence its decision and curb its tendency toward unilateral control.

In late May 1980 more than two hundred delegates representing the government-registered Catholic Church gathered in Beijing to attend the Third National Convention of the CCPA and the National Catholic Representatives Assembly. These two meetings held back-to-back resulted in a major reorganization of structures within the Church with the creation of two additional national organizations: the Chinese Catholic Church Administrative Commission and the Chinese Catholic Bishops Conference. From this point forward, the CCPA relinquished its role as overseer of all Church concerns, relegating itself to look after external affairs and church-state relations. Responsibility for doctrinal and pastoral affairs was given over to the clergy and church leaders. In 1992, further reorganization placed the Bishops Conference on an equal footing with the CCPA while reducing the Church Administrative Commission to a committee responsible for pastoral affairs under the control of the Bishops Conference. Five additional committees were also set up to oversee Seminary Education, Liturgy, Theological Study, Finance Development, and International Relationships. Initiatives in the areas of pastoral work, training of clergy and in the social apostolate of the Church indicate that the new structures are effectively implemented. Since the 1990s, selected seminarians and clergy from the Open Church have been allowed to leave China for further theological training in Catholic seminaries and universities in the United States. As a result, a potential channel has been opened for future reconciliation between the Holy See and the Open Church.

With many ups and downs, the Open Church's attitude toward papal primacy has gradually improved. The prayer for the pope that had been removed from the book of *Collection of Important Prayers* was reintroduced in 1982. In February 1989, the government issued a document, known as *Document 3,* allowing spiritual affiliation with the Holy See and at its meeting, in April of the same year, the Bishops Conference promptly acknowledged the pope as the spiritual leader of the Chinese Church. By the end of the decade, most congregations had also restored the prayer for the pope in the Eucharistic Prayers of the Mass.

The Underground Catholic Church. Many clergy released at the end of the Cultural Revolution were still unwilling to join any Catholic organization registered with the government. They refused to live at a church with other priests who had married, had betrayed others, or had publicly denied the primacy of the pope. Therefore they carried out religious activities in private, and gradually attracted a great number of Catholics to join with them. Bishop Fan Xueyan of Baoding diocese in Hebei province was released in 1979 and acted as the leader of the Underground Church. Recognizing the urgent need for bishops in several dioceses, he ordained in 1981 three bishops without recourse to government or Open Church approval. When Pope John Paul II learned of the circumstances that prompted such a procedure, he legitimized the new bishops and granted them and Bishop Fan special faculties to ordain successors a well as bishops for vacant seats of neighboring dioceses. By 1989 the Underground Church had more than 50 bishops who set up their own episcopal conference. Rome also gave underground bishops the authority to ordain priests without the required lengthy seminary training. This has accounted for the overall poor doctrinal instruction of many priests in the Underground. Moreover, signs of excess and lack of coordination have appeared with some dioceses having as many as three bishops claiming to be the legitimate ordinary.

Since 1989, the Underground Church has been the target of mounting pressure from the government. The same government document of February 1989 that recognized the spiritual leadership of the pope also delineated the steps to be taken in dealing with the members of the Underground Church. Communist cadres were asked to differentiate between underground forces that clung to their hostility and stirred up believers and those who did not join the Open Church because of their faith in the pope. The former category, said the document, must be dealt with severely while patience should be used with the latter. Accordingly the government regarded the setting up of an episcopal conference by the clandestine bishops in November 1989 as a provocation. It resulted in the arrest of several leaders including Bishop Fan. At the local level the implementation of that policy has remained vague and vacillating, resulting in sporadic destruction of unregistered religious buildings, temporary detention and the levy of heavy fines. However, since the ban of the Falun Gong in July 1999, repressive measures against unregistered Catholic communities have also greatly increased.

Toward Reconciliation. This situation has pitted those who chose to worship under the supervision of the government and those who refused to do so. Since 1980 the two sides have gradually moved away from mistrust and bitter accusations to an attitude of understanding respect and to concrete acts of cooperation and genuine efforts at reconciliation. The dividing lines between the two are becoming increasingly blurred. Fidelity to the Holy See has become less an issue since Pope John Paul II has legitimized most of the bishops in the Open Church and most of the new ones are being ordained with his tacit approval. For an ever-growing number of clergy, sisters and ordinary Christians, the division does not make much sense. Many in a courageous and prophetic manner act as bridges between both sides of the Church.

Sino-Vatican Relations. Pope John Paul II has made repeated pleas to the Catholics of China to display toward one another ''a love which consists of understanding, respect, forbearance, forgiveness and reconciliation.'' A complete normalization of diplomatic relations between China and the Vatican cannot happen unless reconciliation first occurs within the Chinese Catholic Church. Informal talks between the Vatican and the Chinese Government have taken place intermittently since the late 1980s. Beijing realizes that it has much to gain from restoring such ties but insists that Rome should first sever its relations with Taiwan. The Vatican sees in the diplomatic normalization a greater freedom and potential for further growth of the Chinese Catholic Church. While progress has been made in finding common ground between them, two events in 2000—the Open Church's ordinations of bishops without papal mandate on January 6 and 25, and Rome's canonization of 120 Martyrs of China on October 1—seriously undermined the negotiations. These misunderstandings highlighted the gulf that continues to separate the Holy See and the Chinese government.

The Catholic Church at the Beginning of the 21st Century. By 1980, it was estimated that less than 1,300 Chinese priests were actively engaged in ministry, and many of those were elderly. The fate of Chinese sisters had not been less terrible than that of priests and seminarians and by 1980, just over one thousand remained. The training of new church leaders and the reopening of seminaries and novitiates was a most urgent priority. Sheshan Regional Seminary near Shanghai was the first Catholic house of formation to reopen in 1982. By 2000, 24 seminaries had been allowed to operate with government permission and another 10 existed in the Underground Church. Formation programs for women religious were carried out in 40 novitiates in the Open Church and 20 in the Underground Church.

In a country where Church educational activities have been drastically curtailed, the Catholic presses of Beijing, Shanghai, and Shijiazhuang in Hebei province are, together with the Protestant Amity Press, important means for reaching out to Christian and non-Christian Chinese. They publish Bibles, Christian literature and journals. They have also reprinted in simplified characters many Chinese translations coming from Taiwan and Hong Kong such as the documents of Vatican II, the liturgy of the Mass, the new code of Canon Law and the new Universal Catechism. The official journal of the CCPA is *Zhongguo Tianzhujiao (The Catholic Church in China).* The Hebei Catholic press also publishes *Xinde (Faith),* a biweekly newspaper with a distribution of 45,000 copies. Distributed in most of the provinces of China it has a readership of over half a million people in the Underground and Open Churches as well as among non-Christians. Besides relaying news of the Church within and outside China, the newspaper also encourages readers to send funds for various charitable causes. Responses have been so enthusiastic that it has led to the establishment of a Catholic social service center called Jinde (Progress) to handle donations for Catholic charity work.

Bibliography: Extensive bibliography in R. STREIT, ed. *Bibliotheca Missionum* vol. IV (Aachen 1928; repr. Rome, 1964); vol. V (Aaachen 1929, repr. 1964); vol. VII (Aachen 1931; repr. Rome 1965). R. STREIT, J. DINDINGER, J. ROMMERSKIRCHEN and N. KOWALSKY, eds. *Bibliotheca Missionum* vols. XII-XIV (Rome 1958–). For a comprehensive study of Christianity in China until 1800, see N. STANDAERT, ed. *Handbook of Christianity in China, 635–1800* (Leiden 2001). Other important references include G. H. ANDERSON, ed., *Biographical Dictionary of Christian Missions* (New York 1998). *Annuaire de l'Église catholique en Chine 1948–1949* (Shanghai 1949). *Annuaire des missions catholiques de Chine* (Shanghai 1924–1940). M. APREM, *Nestorian Missions* (Maryknoll, NY 1980). A. ATIYA, *A History of Eastern Christianity* (London 1968). S. W. BARNETT and J. K. FAIRBANK, eds., *Christianity in China: Early Protestant Writings* (Cambridge 1985). D. H. BAYS, ed. *Christianity in China: From the Eighteenth Century to the Present* (Stanford 1996). T. A. BRESLIN, *China, American Catholicism, and the Missionary* (University Park, PA 1980). G. T. BROWN, *Christianity in the People's Republic of China* (Atlanta 1986). A. CAMPS and P. MCCLOSKEY, *The Friars Minor in China, 1294–1955* (Rome 1995). C. CARY-ELWES, *China and the Cross: A Survey of Missionary History* (New York 1957). T. C. CARINO, ed., *Christianity in China: Three Lectures by Zhao Fusan* (Manila 1986). K. K. CHAN, *Towards a Contextual Ecclesiology: The Catholic Church in the People's Republic of China, 1979–1983* (Hong Kong 1987). J. CHARBONNIER, *Guide to the Catholic Church in China* (Singapore 2000); *Histoire des chrétiens de Chine* (Tournai 1992); *Les 120 martyrs de Chine canonisés le 1er octobre 2000* (Paris 2000). *China Christian Yearbook, 1938–1939,* n.p., n.d. J. CHING, *Confucianism and Christianity: A Comparative Study* (Tokyo 1977). M. CHU, *The New China: A Catholic Response* (New York 1977). P. A. COHEN, *The Missionary Movement and the Growth of Chinese Antiforeignism, 1860–1870* (Cambridge 1963); "Christian Missions and Their Impact until 1900," in *The Cambridge History of China, X: Late Ching, 1800–1911, part 1* (Cambridge 1978). R. R. COVELL, *Confucius, the Buddha and Christ: A History of the Gospel in Chinese* (Maryknoll, NY 1986). A. R. CROUCH et al., eds. *Christianity in China: A Scholar's Guide to Resources in Libraries and Archives of the United States* (Armonk, NY 1989). J. S. CUMMINS, *A Question of Rites: Friar Domingo Navarete and the Jesuits in China* (Manila 1993). C. DAWSON *The Mongol Mission* (New York 1955). J. DE LA SERVIÉRE *Les anciennes missions de la Compagnie de Jésus en Chine, 1552–1814* (Shanghai 1924). I. DE RACHEWILTZ, *Papal Envoys to the Great Khans* (London 1971). P. M. D'ELIA, *Catholic Native Episcopacy in China: Being an Outline of the Formation and Growth of the Chinese Catholic Clergy* (Shanghai 1927). *Documents of the Three-Self Movement* (New York 1963). G. H. DUNNE, *Generations of Giants* (Notre Dame 1962). J. K. FAIRBANK, *The Missionary Enterprise in China and America* (Cambridge 1974). FANG HAO, *Zhongguo Tianzhujiaoshi renwuzhuan (Biographies of the Chinese Catholic Church),* 3 vols. (Taichung 1967, 1970, 1973). R. C. FOLTZ, *Religions of the Silk Road* (New York 1999). R. FUNG, *Households of God on China's Soil* (Maryknoll, NY 1982). J. M. GONZALES, *Historia de la Misiones Dominicanas de China,* 2 vols. (Madrid 1962 and 1964). J. GERNET, *China and the Christian Impact* (Cambridge 1985). GU WEIMIN, *Jidujiao yu jindai Zhongguo shehui (Christianity and Modern Chinese Society)* (Shanghai 1996). E. J. HANSON, *Catholic Policy in China and Korea* (Maryknoll, NY 1980). J. HEYNDRICKX, ed., *Historiography of the Chinese Catholic Church, Nineteenth and Twentieth Centuries* (Leuven 1994). D. HICKLEY, *The First Christians of China* (London 1980). S. HONG, *The Dragon and the Net: How God Has Used Communism to Prepare China for the Gospel* (Old Tappan, N J 1976). A. HUNTER and KIM-KWONG CHAN, *Protestantism in Contemporary China* (Cambridge 1993). H. KÜNG and J. CHING, *Christianity and Chinese Religions* (New York 1989). A. LAM, S. K. *The Catholic Church in Present-Day China through Darkness and Light* (Hong Kong 1997). J. LANGLAIS, *Les Jésuites du Québec en Chine, 1918–1955* (Laval 1979). K. S. LATOURETTE, *A History of Christian Missions in China* (New York 1929; repr. Taipei 1966). A. LAUNAY, *Histoire des Missions de Chine,* 3 vols. (Vannes and Paris 1907–20). A. S. LAZZAROTTO, *The Catholic Church in Post-Mao China* (Hong Kong 1982). B. LEUNG, *Sino-*

Vatican Relations: Problems of Conflicting Authority, 1976–1986 (Cambridge 1992). J. LEUNG, *Wenhua Jidutu: Xianxiang yu lunzheng (Cultural Christian: Phenomenon and Argument)* (Hong Kong 1997). K. C. LIU, ed. *American Missionaries in China: Papers from Harvard Seminars* (Cambridge 1966). Lutheran World Federation/Pro Mundi Vita. *Christianity and the New China* (South Pasadena 1976). L. T. LYALL, *New Spring in China?* (London 1979). J. G. LUTZ, ed. *Christian Missions in China: Evangelist of What?* (Boston 1965). D. E. MACINNIS, *Religion in China Today: Policy and Practice* (Maryknoll, NY 1989). D. MACINNIS and X. A. ZHENG, *Religion under Socialism in China* (Armonk, NY 1991). R. MADSEN, *China Catholics: Tragedy and Hope in an Emerging Civil Society* (Berkeley 1998). R. MALEK and M. PLATE *Chinas Katholiken suchen neue* (Freiburg 1987). *Missiones Catholicae cura S. Congregationis de Propaganda Fide descriptae statistica* (Rome 1901, 1907, 1922, 1927). J. METZLER, ed. *Sacrae Congregationis de Propaganda Fide Memoria Rerum, 1622–1972* (Rome 1976). *Nanjing 86, Ecumenical Sharing: A New Agenda* (New York 1986). J. M. PLANCHET, *Les Missions de Chine et du Japon* (Beijing, 1916-1933). REN JIYU, *Zhongjiao cidian (Dictionary on Religion)* (Shanghai 1981). A. C. ROSS, *A Vision Betrayed: The Jesuits in Japan and China, 1542-1742* (Maryknoll, NY 1992). Y. SAEKI, *The Nestorian Documents and Relics in China* (Tokyo 1951). S. SHAPIRO, *Jews in Old China* (New York 1984). *Shijie Zhongjiao Yanjiu (Studies on World Religion)* (Beijing 1979–). *Shijie Zhongjiao Ziliao (Materials on World Religion)* (Beijing 1979–). C. SOETENS, *L'Église catholique en Chine au XXe siècle* (Paris 1997). J. D. SPENCE, *The Memory Palace of Matteo Ricci* (New York 1984). *The Chinese Recorder* (Shanghai 1935-1941). A. THOMAS (= J. M. PLANCHET) *Histoire de la Mission de Pékin* 2 vols. (Paris, 1923, 1925). B. TOWERY, *The Churches of China: Taking Root Downward, Bearing Fruit Upward* (Hong Kong 1987). E. TANG and J. P. WIEST, eds. *The Catholic Church in Modern China: Perspectives* (Maryknoll, NY 1993). P. A. VARG, *Missionaries, Chinese and Diplomats: The American Protestant Missionary Movement in China, 1890-1952* (Princeton 1958). L. T. S. WEI, *La politique missionnaire de la France en Chine, 1842-1856* (Paris 1957); *Le Saint-Siège et la Chine de Pie XI à nos jours* (Paris 1968). B. WHYTE, *Unfinished Encounter: China and Christianity* (London 1988). P. WICKERI, *Seeking the Common Ground: Protestant Christianity, The Three-Self Movement, and China's United Front* (Maryknoll, NY 1988). J. P. WIEST, *Maryknoll in China* (Armonk, NY 1988). E. WURTH, ed. *Papal Documents Related to the New China* (Maryknoll, NY 1985).

[J.-P. WIEST/EDS.]

CHINESE PHILOSOPHY

Chinese literary sources trace the foundations of China's long, rich and complex philosophical tradition to the mythical Yellow Emperor (Huangdi) who lived earlier than 2,500 B.C. and who laid the framework for Chinese civilization. After him came the reign of the legendary sage-kings, three of whom—Yao, Shun and Yu were idealized in Chinese philosophical writings as model rulers with integrity and upright conduct. As civilization advanced, the obscure Xia (Hsia) dynasty emerged. Not much is known about the Xia dynasty beyond extant literary writings. Some archaeologists would identify the Xia dynasty with the early bronze age civilization excavated at the Erlitou site.

EARLY HISTORY

Shang Dynasty (c.1600–c.1045 B.C.). Chinese philosophical thought took definite shape during the reign of the Shang dynasty in Bronze Age China. During this period, the primeval forms of ancestor veneration in Neolithic Chinese cultures had evolved to relatively sophisticated rituals that the Shang ruling house offered to their ancestors and to *Shangdi*, the supreme deity who was a deified ancestor and progenitor of the Shang ruling family. A class of shamans emerged, tasked with divination and astrology using oracle bones for the benefit of the ruling class. Archaeological excavations have uncovered elaborate bronze sacrificial vessels and other paraphernalia for ancestor veneration rites, which were carried out in temples. The primordial forms of filiality evolved during this period together with the ancestor veneration ceremonies.

Zhou (Chou) Dynasty (c. 1045–221 B.C.). Historically, the Zhou was a semi-nomadic group who conquered their more refined overlords and opted to assimilate themselves into Shang culture and way of life, including ancestor veneration sacrificial ceremonies and their foundations in the concept of filiality. The Zhou ruling house came into power when King Wu, the first Zhou king overthrew Wicked King Jie, the last Shang ruler who would become the paradigmatic figure in Chinese philosophical thought for a tyrannical and incompetent ruler. To justify the overthrow of the last Shang king and to legitimize their rule, the Zhou kings developed the notion of the Mandate of Heaven (*Tianming*) as the basis for the moral-ethical right to rule.

Mandate of Heaven (*Tianming*). The Mandate of Heaven (*Tianming*) is a moral-ethical imperative that states that the legitimacy of a ruler to govern vests in *Tian* (Heaven), which expresses its views in signs, portents and rebellions. A ruling house retains the Mandate of Heaven insofar as it constantly acted morally and for the good of the people. If it strayed from the path of virtue and benevolence, it would lose the right to rule. Wicked King Jie, the last Shang ruler had lost the Mandate of Heaven to the Zhou King Wu because of his evil ways. The successful rebellion that swept the Zhou to power was interpreted as the ultimate portent from *Tian* of a change in mandate. All Chinese emperors, from the first Zhou king onwards became known as *Tianzi* (T'ien-tzu, "Son of Heaven"), the earthly representatives of *Tian* vested with *Tianming* (Mandate of Heaven) to look after the well-being of their subjects. As a political philosophy, the *Mandate of Heaven* is a two-edged sword. While it legitimized a dynasty's right to govern, it also imposed a burden on the ruling house to justify the continuance of this right. Dissatisfied rivals would seize power on grounds that an existing ruling house had lost the Mandate of Heaven by the bad treatment of its subjects.

Itinerant Scholars (*ru*). The Mandate of Heaven would also have another impact on Chinese philosophy—to ensure that they remain in power, rulers began to employ scholars (*ru*) to advise them on good government. Itinerant scholars presented themselves at the court, offering their services. Two of China's most well-known scholars are CONFUCIUS (KONGFUZI) and MENCIUS (MENGZI), who would later become the two pillars of the *Rujiao* ("Traditions of the *Literati*," known in the West as CONFUCIANISM. It was from these wandering scholars that the Hundred Schools (*Bai jia*) of Chinese philosophy would later emerge during the period of the Warring States (*Zhanguo*).

Emergence of classical texts. King Wu was succeeded as regent by his brother, the Duke of Zhou (Zhou Gong), a man of great intelligence, energy, and character whose reign was regarded as the golden age of Zhou rule by Confucius (Kongfuzi) and his followers. The classical texts and historical records that gradually emerged during the Zhou dynasty would later become important sources of precedents for the emergence of classical Chinese philosophical thought. Early forms of the classic texts of the Book of Poetry (*Shijing*), the Book of History (*Shujing*) and the Book of Changes (*Yijing*) first emerged during this period. The Spring and Autumn Annals (*Chunqiu*), a historical chronicle of the State of Lu from 722 to 481 B.C. is an important witness to the twilight years of Zhou rule and the emergence of the Hundred Schools (*Bai jia*), a diverse plurality of Chinese philosophical schools competing for socio-political influence.

***Yin-yang* Philosophical worldview.** The Book of Changes (*Yijing*) is significant as evidence for the systematization of an earlier, ancient Chinese philosophical world view of life within a cyclical and complementary framework. As Chinese cosmology developed, this cyclical framework became known as the *yin-yang*—two opposite but complementary energies that manifest and differentiate the myriad things that come into existence from undifferentiated primordiality or *Dao* (*Tao*). Chinese cosmology maps all phenoma in the universe in pairs of bipolar complementary opposites according to the *yin-yang* matrix, e.g., production-destruction, hot-cool, sun-moon, bright-dark, active-passive, odd-even, male-female, etc. The dynamic interaction of *yin* and *yang* gives rise to the production and destruction of diverse forms of things in the cosmos. Proper and harmonious living would be understood as a balance of *yin-yang*, an imbalance of which leads to disorder, disunity, disharmony, chaos and wars. Later philosophers would combine the yin-yang cosmology with the Five Elements (*Wu*

xing)—the Chinese metaphysical conceptualization of all things (*wan wu*) in terms of the five "phases" (*xing*) of earth, wood, metal, fire, and water.

Decline of the Zhou Dynasty. To control the hostile subjects within their empire, and in the face of difficulties in communication, the Zhou rulers parceled out lands to friends and former foes, thus setting up a feudal system in which the political allies became feudal lords and the commoners were serfs. In theory, all land belonged to the king, who bestowed it on his vassals; they in turn parceled it out to those below them. Arable land was divided into nine well-field units (*tian*), and one out of nine plots was cultivated by the tenants for the feudal lord. Feudal lords were responsible for keeping the peace within their territory, supplying conscripts to the Zhou imperial army and paying an annual tribute to the Zhou king. As the feudal vassals became powerful rulers in their own right, the fiefdoms became *de facto* independent states and the feudal lords gradually arrogated titles and honors that formerly belonged to the Zhou monarch alone.

PERIOD OF THE HUNDRED SCHOOLS (*BAI JIA*)

Major developments took place during the tumultuous period of the Hundred Schools (*Bai jia*), straddling the latter part of the Spring and Autumn Period (722–481 B.C.), the twilight years of the Zhou dynasty, and the Warring States period (481–221 B.C.), when Zhou rule collapsed and feudal states vied for power. This was a period of terrible suffering for the ordinary folk caught in the crossfire of marauding armies. The old cultural-religious order had collapsed and created a spiritual vacuum. Philosophers and scholars from rival schools offered competing solutions to the existential questions on human suffering and social disorder. The diversity and vitality of these schools that emerged resulted in this period being known as the period in Chinese history of the Hundred Schools. Promoters of the two emerging traditions of Confucianism and Daoism battled one another and with other rivals such as the Legalists, Moists and Egoists.

Confucius (Kongfuzi). Confucius (551–479 B.C.) lived during the Spring and Autumn period, the twilight years of the Zhou dynasty. A firm believer in education as the *sine qua non* for one's self-cultivation, he achieved fame by establishing China's first school of learning more than a century before Plato had established his academy in Athens. Confucius firmly believed that everyone could benefit from self-cultivation and insisted that everyone could aspire to be leaders by proper training and education. For him education was more than mere acquisition of knowledge or a means of acquiring power. Rather, education is primarily about character building and self-cultivation, and only secondarily about acquiring skills for career advancement. His twofold legacy of proper education as a cornerstone of socio-political transformation, and teaching as the highest and most noble calling continues to animate the East Asian societies that venerate him as teacher and philosopher *par excellence*. The core of Confucius' teachings centers on the self-cultivation of *li, xiao (hsiao), yi (i)* and *ren (jen)*, commonly translated as propriety, filiality, appropriateness and humanness. The objective of such self-cultivation is to become a *junzi (chün-tzu)* or "superior person." While he claimed to be a transmitter rather than an innovator (see Analects 7:1), the originality and vitality of his overarching vision of life, characterized by a threefold principle—the love of tradition, the love of learning, and the love of self-cultivation was to transform China and the other East Asian societies of Korea, Japan and Vietnam indelibly. Although he personally did not found any mass movement, his teachings were disseminated by his admirers among the *ru (literati)* and co-opted by them, gradually evolving to become the foundational tenets of the *rujiao* ("Teachings of the *Literati*," commonly but inaccurately translated as Confucianism). Confucius himself did not appear to have written anything that can be clearly attributed to him. The only extant collection of his sayings is the *Lun Yu* (Analects), a later compilation by his disciples of sayings attributed to him.

Mencius. The most important contribution that Mencius (372–289 B.C.) made to Chinese philosophy is his assertion on the goodness of the *benxing* ("original human nature"). This assertion would not only undergird his entire philosophy and vision of life, but would eventually become the classical Confucian formulation on human nature (*renxing*). For Mencius, strictly speaking, a human is not a static sort of being, but a dynamic *becoming* striving toward sagehood. In his understanding, an infant is not born as an "individual," but rather, born into a framework of familial and socio-cultural relations that would shape and nurture that infant's *benxing* (original human nature). At birth, the *benxing* comprises the four virtuous tendencies of commiseration, shame, deference and preference that are incipient, underdeveloped and fragile. With proper education and self-cultivation, these tendencies could mature into the four cardinal virtues of "humanness" (*ren*), appropriateness (*yi*), propriety (*li*) and wisdom (*zhi*) in a fully developed human nature (*renxing*) (see Mencius 2A:6). What is meant here is a relational, rather than an essential understanding of personhood that understands the progressive maturing of human nature within an interlocking matrix of *reciprocal relations* that, over a lifetime, defines one's character.

Moism (*Mojia*). Mozi (Mo-tzu), a.k.a. Mo Di (circa 479–381 B.C.) had advocated impartial and universal love of all *without* any distinction, and condemned all expres-sions of human emotions. Mozi was also an austere and disciplined utilitarian, who condemned all forms of extravagance, especially lavish funerals and elaborate musical performances. Mencius' opposition to Mozi was centered on his accusations that Mo-tzu's universal love is too cold, too logical, devoid of human emotion and goes against instinctive human love for one's parents and other members of the family. He argued that it went against the natural order of things to love everyone alike, because it would deny the claim of one's parents to the greatest degree of love through the obligation of filiality. Instead, love for people outside of one's family ought to be an extension of the love for members of one family, and is differentiated according to the type of relationship and the degree of reciprocity (*shu*) within that relationship. Consequently, for Mencius, love and the obligation to love was to be differentiated according to the proximity and distance of such relationship, as stipulated by the principles of propriety (*li*).

Egoism (*wei wo*) of Yang Zhu. Yang Zhu (Yang Chu, circa 440–360 B.C.), an advocate of egoism (*wei wo*) had argued that since everyone, good and bad alike, faces the same death, one might as well live for oneself and enjoy the moment in whatever good that comes one's way. Not surprisingly, his teachings were condemned by Mencius and other scholars as hedonistic, selfish and anti-social. The Mencian critique of Yang Zhu became the classical summary of the School of Egoists: "The principle of philosopher Yang was 'each for himself' [*wei wo*]. Though he might have benefitted the whole country by plucking out a single hair, he would not have done it." (Mencius 7:1). No written works of Yang Zhu are extant, although many scholars think that chapter 7 of the *Liezi (Lieh-tzu)* probably contains some of his ideas.

Legalism (*Fajia*). Legalism (*Fajia*) was an important and very attractive political philosophy that arose in the Hundred Schools (*Bai jia*) period, and was adopted as state ideology by the First Emperor *Qin Shi Huangdi (Shih Huang-ti*, 259–210 B.C.) of the *Qin (Chin)* dynasty. Legalists argued that everyone is inclined to do evil because human nature is basically evil. Therefore, it was necessary for the ruler to rule with an iron fist, promulgating strict laws, and adopting a "carrot-and-stick" approach of harsh punishments to enforce the strict laws and attractive inducements that took advantage of the selfishness of human nature to goad people into proper behavior. The ultimate goal of Legalism was the autocratic ruler's ability to sit back, "do nothing" (*wuwei*) and enjoy the security and prosperity of a society where the fear of the Law coerced everyone into acquiescence. The two most prominent Legalists of the Hundred Schools period were *Han Feizi* (*Han Fei-tzu*, circa 280–233 B.C.) and *Li Si* (*Li Ssu*, circa 280–208 B.C.)

Philosophical Daoism (*Daojia*). Philosophical Daoism (*Daojia*) emerged during the Hundred Schools (*Bai jia*) period as an advocate of a naturalistic philosophy that emphasized the artificiality of human institutions, and promoted the abandonment of worldly pursuits in favor of an accommodation with the natural flow of things in the world. Although its principal goal is the attainment of *wuwei* ("non-action"), which it shared in common with Legalism, Daoist philosophers interpreted *wuwei* as the mode of being and action that seeks to flow with the grain of the *Dao* (*Tao*, "Way") in bringing manifest forms into actuality from primordial flux. *Wuwei* ought to be understood not as the total lack of activity, but rather *active inactivity* that would allow the *Dao* (*Tao*) to run its course and unveil all potentialities to their fullest without any human interference. Thus, *wuwei* is the opposite of "calculated or intentional action" that limits the fullest range of potentialities. While it is true that some Daoists were attracted to the eremitical lifestyle of permanent contemplation of nature of the type that the Daoist philosopher Zhuangzi (Chuang-tzu) had advocated, many Chinese intellectuals found in philosophical Daoism (*Daojia*) a source of spiritual comfort and renewal in the stressful pressures of Confucian officialdom, especially in the midst of socio-political upheavals.

Revival of Confucianism in the Han Dynasty. After the Qin dynasty's disastrous flirtation with Legalism (*Fajia*), which gave rise to the infamous burning of books, the suppression of rival philosophical schools and the execution of rival scholars, the founding of the Han dynasty by Liu Bang in 206 B.C. heralded the beginning of a new imperial era that would last for two millennia until 1911. The Han dynasty became the yardstick by which subsequent Chinese dynasties, intellectual achievements, socio-cultural and philosophical developments, and political institutions would invariably be judged by. At the Imperial Academy (*Taixue*) established in Chang'an in 124 B.C., scholars engaged in a study of both Confucian and Daiost texts as they trained for the Chinese civil service. Under the reign of Emperor Wudi, Confucianism was adopted as the national ideology in 141 B.C. A rudimentary form of the later civil service examination system based on the Five Classics (*Wu jing*, comprising: *Shijing*, the Book of Poetry; *Shujing*, the Book of History; *Liji*, the Book of Rites; *Yijing*, the Book of Changes and the *Chunqiu*, the Spring and Autumn Annals) was instituted to select the best scholars for service as governors and imperial functionaries.

[J. Y. TAN]

BUDDHIST PHILOSOPHY

Early History. Buddhism first entered China sometime during the first century A.D., probably with foreign traders who came into China via the Silk Road or from the maritime route along the southeastern seaboard. For the first two centuries or so, it existed primarily among immigrant settlements. With the fall of the Han dynasty in the early third century, interest in Buddhism among the Chinese increased as the unstable political situation inspired people to seek for new answers. The Central Asian monk Kumārajīva arrived in 402 A.D. and opened his translation bureau in the north, producing some of the finest translations from Sanskrit, many of which are still considered the standard. His rendering of Indian Mādhyamika texts led to the foundation of the Sanlun (or "Three Treatise") school that specialized in Mādhyamika philosophy. Also, the dissemination of Buddhist texts and teachings among the educated elite led to a prolonged exchange of ideas between Buddhism and Taoism, and Buddhism absorbed and modified many Taoist ideas.

Golden Age of Buddhism. Buddhism flourished during the Tang dynasty, although it also suffered severe setbacks. Increased affluence and patronage enabled many original thinkers and practitioners to establish schools of Buddhism more in keeping with Chinese cultural and intellectual patterns and less dependent upon pre-existing Indian schools of thought. Examples include Zhiyi (538–597), who founded the Tiantai school; Fazang (643–712), who consolidated the Huayan school; and the various meditation masters who established Chan as a separate school that transmitted the Buddha-mind directly from master to disciple "outside of words and scriptures." Daochuo (562–645), Shandao (613–681), and others continued building up the Pure Land movement, extending Tanluan's teaching further. During this time Xuanzang (ca. 596–664) traveled in India for sixteen years and brought back many texts which he translated into Chinese. After Kumārajīva, he is considered the second of the greatest translators in Chinese Buddhist history. He concentrated on Indian Yogacāra thought, and, building on the foundation laid by Paramārtha, founded the Faxiang school.

Rivalry and Conflicts with Confucians and Daoists. Success brought its own difficulties. Ever since Buddhism's inception in China some traditional Confucian scholars had decried it as a foreign religion that violated basic Chinese values, especially the loyalty that all citizens owed to the state and the filial piety that sons and daughters owed their parents. In addition, Daoists sometimes saw in Buddhism an antagonist and competitor rather than a colleague. In the past, the government instituted ordination examinations and state-issued certificates to control the size of the *sangha*, and twice during the Northern and Southern Kingdoms period the state had suppressed Buddhism (in 446 and 574). In the year 845, the Tang court was incited to suppress Buddhism once again, and for three years it pursued this policy of razing monasteries and temples, forcing clergy back into lay life or even killing them, and burning books, images, and properties. Unlike the previous two persecutions, this suppression happened in a unified China and affected all areas. Scholars are in agreement that this event marked the end of Buddhism's intellectual and cultural dominance, as the *sangha* never recovered its former glory. The Tiantai and Huayan schools experienced some revivals thereafter, but lost most of their vigor. The Pure Land and Chan schools, being much less dependent upon patronage and scholarship, fared better and became the two dominant schools of Buddhism in China thereafter. After the persecution, Chan communities experimented with new teaching methods that circumvented conventional teaching and inculcated a dramatic, instantaneous experience of enlightenment. The leading figures in this movement were Mazu Daoyi (709–788), Baizhang Huaihai (749–814), Huangbo (d. 850), Linji Yixuan (founder of the Linji school, d. 866), Dongshan Liangjie (807–869), and Caoshan Benji (840–901), the two founders of the Caodong school.

Competition. After the Tang, the intellectual vigor of Buddhism was eclipsed by the rise of Neo-Confucianism in the Song dynasty. Nevertheless, there were significant figures and movements during this time. Many figures worked to reconcile the very different outlooks and methods of the Chan and Pure Land schools, notably Yongming Yanshou (904–975) and Yunqi Zhuhong (1532–1612). The latter was also part of a revival of Chan in the latter half of the Ming dynasty that also included Cipo Zhenke (1543–1603), Hanshan Deqing (1546–1623), and Ouyi Zhixu (1599–1655). All agreed that Pure Land and Chan, though differing in method, strove toward the same goal, though Hanshan and Cipo still tended to define this goal in Chan terms. Zhixu, however, emphasized Pure Land teaching almost exclusively and came to be regarded as one of the patriarchs (*zu*) of this school.

[C. B. JONES]

NEO-CONFUCIANISM

The term "Neo-Confucianism" is often used to refer to the developments in Confucian philosophical thought from the Song dynasty to the collapse of the Qing dynasty (1644–1911). It has been similarly criticized for its misleading portrayal of a unified and normative movement, overgeneralizing the reality of a diverse plurality of vi-

brant, competing schools of thought in China during the period that included *Daoxue* (School of the Way), *Lixue* (School of Principle), and *Xinxue* (School of the Mind), to name a few. These schools regarded Confucius as their inspiration and his teachings as a common cultural-philosophical heritage, but developed his ideas in innovative ways that he would never have recognized. The problem is compounded by the fact that the Chinese themselves never saw fit to coin a single term to describe the diversity of competing schools.

Emergence of Neo-Confucian Schools. After centuries of competing intellectually and spiritually with Daoism (Taoism) and Buddhism, Confucian scholars in the Song Dynasty initiated a process of reinterpreting traditional Confucian classical texts to formulate new answers that responded to the challenges brought by Daoism and Buddhism. This process gave rise to new innovative schools of thought. This revival and revitalization of Confucianism started with the writings of the Northern Song scholars Zhou Dunyi (Chou Tun-i, 1017–1073), Shao Yong (Shao Yung, 1011–1077), Zhang Zai (Chang Tsai, 1020–1077), and the brothers Cheng Hao (Ch'eng Hao, 1032–1085) and Cheng Yi (Ch'eng I, 1033–1077).

Early Neo-Confucian Developments. While overtly condemning Buddhism and Daoism, these scholars were busy combining metaphysical elements borrowed from those two religions with traditional themes from Confucian classics such as the Analects (*Lunyu*), the Mencius (*Mengzi*), the Book of Changes (*Yijing*), and the Book of Rituals (*Liji*). What emerged from the ruminations of these scholars was a novel and innovative metaphysical framework for Confucianism that was designed to counter the attractiveness of rival Daoist (Taoist) and Buddhist metaphysical systems. Zhou Dunyi (Chou Tun-i) and Shao Yong (Shao Yung) had reinterpreted Daoist (Taoist) metaphysical diagrams to offer a nascent metaphysical cosmology for Confucianism. Zhang Zai (Chang Tsai) proposed a materialist understanding of *qi* (*chi*, "energy") as the building block of everything (i.e., spirit, matter and energy) in the universe. The two brothers Cheng Hao and Cheng Yi formulated the theory of "principle" (*li*) as the universal and primordial potentiality from which all living things are ordered.

Zhu Xi and the School of Principle (*Lixue*). It was the great Neo-Confucian scholar Zhu Xi (Chu-Hsi, 1130–1200) who synthesized the efforts of these five Neo-Confucian scholars into a coherent metaphysical framework that later became the foundational tenets of his rationalist School of Principle (*Lixue*). The starting point for Zhu Xi is "principle" (*li*) as predictable and observable patterns of potentialities in the world upon which *qi* (energy) crystallizes and forms all living things. There was one universal and primordial *li* (principle) that is *objectively descriptive* (i.e., it describes *why* things are) and *morally prescriptive* (it prescribes *what* can be done to these things). Adapting the Mencian assertion that "original human nature" (*benxing*) is wholly good, Zhu Xi claimed that *li* (principle) is wholly good, and evil arises not from *li* (principle) but turgid *qi* (bad energy), which can be clarified through disciplined self-cultivation. The purpose of education is to acquire knowledge of the descriptive and prescriptive aspects of *li* (principle) through the "investigation of all things" (*ge wu*).

Wang Yangming and the School of the Mind (*Xinxue*). Wang Yangming (1472–1529), the idealist Neo-Confucian scholar of the Ming dynasty who synthesized the principal teachings of the School of the Mind (*Xinxue*), rejected the rationalist approach of Zhu Xi. He propounded a doctrine of the "unity of knowledge and action" (*zhi xing he yi*) based on the notion that principle (*li*) is found wholly within the mind (*xin*), because the mind is the repository of the innate knowledge of all goodness (*liangzhi*). To investigate these moral principles is to "rectify the mind" (*chengyi*). Thus, for Wang Yangming, the "investigation of things for attaining knowledge" (*ge wu zhi zhi*) is unnecessary, all that is needed is a contemplative and introspective "rectification of the mind" (*chengyi*).

See Also: BUDDHISM-CHINA; CHINESE RELIGIONS; CHINESE RITES CONTROVERSY; CONFUCIANISM AND NEO-CONFUCIANISM; CONFUCIUS (KONG FUZI); DAOISM (TAOISM); LAOZI (LAO-TZU); MENCIUS (MENGZI); MOZI (MO-TZU); ZHUANGZI (CHUANG-TZU).

[J. Y. TAN]

Bibliography: D. BODDE, *Chinese Thought, Society, and Science* (Honolulu 1991) W. T. CHAN, *A Sourcebook in Chinese Philosophy* (Princeton 1963) K. CH'EN, *Buddhism in China: a Historical Survey* (Princeton 1964) W. T. DE BARY, et al., eds. *Sources of Chinese Tradition* (New York 1960) W. T. DE BARY, et al, *The Unfolding of Neo-Confucianism* (New York 1975) W. T. DE BARY, *The Trouble with Confucianism* (Cambridge, MA 1991) A. C. GRAHAM, *Later Mohist Logic, Ethics and Science* (Hong Kong 1978) A. C. GRAHAM, *Disputers of the Tao: Philosophical Argument in Ancient China* (La Salle, IL 1989). A. C. GRAHAM, *Studies in Chinese Philosophy and Philosophical Nature* (Albany, NY 1990) D. L. HALL and R. T. AMES, *Thinking Through Confucius* (Albany, NY 1987) D. L. HALL and R. T. AMES, *Anticipating China: Thinking Through the Narratives of Chinese and Western Culture* (Albany, NY 1995) D. L. HALL and R. T. AMES, *Thinking from the Han: Self, Truth and Transcendence in Chinese and Western Culture* (Albany, NY 1997) J. B. HENDERSON, *The Development and Decline of Chinese Cosmology* (New York 1984) L. M. JENSEN, *Manufacturing Confucianism: Chinese traditions & universal civilization* (Durham 1997) B. I. SCHWARTZ, *The World of Thought in Ancient China* (Cambridge, MA 1985).

CHINESE RELIGIONS

A generic term often used to indicate the various religious traditions that emerged in China over its long history. There are four basic categories of Chinese religions: (1) CONFUCIANISM, (2) DAOISM, (3) BUDDHISM and (4) Chinese folk religions. Throughout China's history, these religious traditions have interacted with, shaped and transformed each other. The boundaries of these religious traditions have remained fluid, with a significant amount of mutual interaction and sharing of common elements. In their later developed form, Neo-Confucianism and Neo-Daoism resembled each other to the extent that it was difficult to tell where one ended and the other began. The traditional Chinese term *sanjiao* ("Three Ways") best exemplifies this complex interaction. *Sanjiao* refers to the three Chinese great religious traditions of Confucianism, Daoism and Buddhism. A person can practice any one or more, or even all three religious traditions simultaneously, according to the specific needs in the course of one's life. One could be a Confucian in public life, a Daoist adept searching for immortality, and offering sacrifices to local deities for good fortune.

Neolithic Origins. The earliest Chinese settlements emerged during the Neolithic period (circa 5,000 B.C.) and the Bronze Age (circa 3,000 B.C.). No unified Chinese civilization existed during these two periods, merely pockets of Chinese settlements known as Yangshao Culture, Dawenko Culture, Liangche Culture, Hungshan Culture, Longshan Culture and Erligang Culture, named after their archaeological sites. Archaeological excavations have uncovered burial sites with graves arranged hierarchically. Remains of graveside ritual offerings of food and drink and pig skulls were unearthed at some sites, while primitive amulets and statues were found at others. These discoveries point to rudimentary forms of ancestor veneration in ancient Chinese religious practice.

Shang Dynasty (circa 1751–1045 B.C.). The period of the Shang dynasty witnessed the emergence of a distinct class of shamans tasked with oracle bone divination (*jiagu*). These shamans inscribed questions to the spirits on pieces of tortoise or oxen bones using the earliest extant form of the Chinese script. These questions were phrased in a way that could be answered by a "yes" (i.e., auspicious) or "no" (i.e., inauspicious). The two possible answers were also inscribed, and the bones heated to induce splitting. The split-line nearest the word "auspicious" or "inauspicious" was taken as the answer. Although some of the questions were addressed to either the supreme deity *Shangdi* (the Most High Lord) or other lesser deities of the wind and grain, celestial bodies, mountains and rivers, the majority of the questions were directed at the ancestors of the Shang ruling family. Other evidence indicates that the Shang ruling house also offered sacrifices to their ancestors and to *Shangdi*. Taken together, the oracle bones and ancestral sacrifices indicate the emergence of a state-sanctioned religious framework that was built upon ancestral veneration. Scholars think that the concept of *Shangdi* originated as a deified primeval ancestor spirit or spirits.

Zhou Dynasty (1045–249 B.C.). The Zhou dynasty introduced the cult of sacrifices to *Tian* ("Heaven"). Researchers remain uncertain whether *Tian* was an anthropomorphic or impersonal entity. Scholars who argue for the anthropomorphic origin of *Tian* have pointed to the fact that etymologically, the ideography for *Tian* is a person with outstretched arms and wearing a hat, perhaps evocative of a deified primordial ancestral guardian protecting the ruling house. During this period, large scale ancestral veneration rituals evolved and took root.

The "Three Ways" (*Sanjiao*). Major developments took place during the tumultuous period of the Hundred Schools (*Bai jia*), straddling the latter part of the Spring and Autumn Period (722–481 B.C.), the twilight years of the Zhou dynasty, and the Warring States period (481–221 B.C.), when Zhou rule collapsed and feudal states vied for power. This was a period of terrible suffering for the ordinary folk caught in the crossfire of marauding armies. The old cultural-religious order had collapsed and created a spiritual vacuum. Philosophers and scholars from rival schools offered competing solutions to the existential questions on human suffering and social disorder. Promoters of the two emerging traditions of Confucianism and Daoism battled one another and with other rivals such as the Legalists, Mohists, and the Naturalists. During this chaotic period, the Daoist classic *Daodejing (Tao Te Ching)* was written. The two eventual victors, Daoism and Confucianism would face a third religious force, BUDDHISM that arrived on Chinese soil in the 2nd century A.D.

Chinese Folk Religions. The popular level witnessed the gradual evolution of vibrant Chinese folk religious traditions that combine elements from the three great religious traditions. A defining characteristic of all Chinese folk religious traditions is its large pantheon of provincial, city and clannic deities, ancestral spirits and ghosts, presided over by the Jade Emperor (*Yuhuang*). Some of the more popular folk religious traditions include the cult of the Kitchen God (who makes an annual report to the Jade Emperor on the behavior and conduct of the family), the ubiquitous cult of the Earth God (*Tudigong*) who protects households from wandering malevolent ghosts, and the cult of the City God (*Chenghuang*) who guards the city and escorts departed souls to the subterranean netherworld realm of the Yellow Springs. Deities are sometimes adopted from the great religions, e.g., the bodhisattva Avalokitesvara becoming the "goddess of mercy" *Guanyin* in Chinese folk religious tradition. Devotees offer prayers, incense, sacrifices and other rituals, in return for favors, good fortune, divination, as well as protection from malevolent or hungry ghosts.

Central to the Chinese folk religious traditions is the annual cycle of religious feasts that combines elements from popular customs, Daoism, Confucianism and Buddhism. Highlights of this cyclical calendar include the Spring Festival or Lunar New Year (first day of the first moon), the Feast of the Earth God (second day of the second moon), the birth of the goddess of mercy, *Guanyin* (19th day of the second moon), the day of "sweeping the ancestral graves," *Qingming* (105 days after winter solstice), the birth of Sakyamuni Buddha or *Vesak* day (eighth day of the fourth moon), the Festival of the Dragon Boats and Dumplings (fifth day of the fifth moon), the hungry ghosts' month (seventh moon), the Festival of the Two Lovers – the Cowherd and Weaving Maid (seventh day of the seventh moon), the Mid-autumn Festival or the Festival of the Moon (15th day of the eighth moon), the Winter Solstice, and the Feast of the Ascension of the Kitchen God to Heaven (a week before the Spring Festival).

See Also: LAOZI (LAO-TZU).

Bibliography: A.P. WOLF, ed., *Religion and Ritual in Chinese Society* (Stanford, Calif. 1974). J. BERLING, *Pilgrimage to Lion's Head Mountain: The Many Levels and Layers of Chinese Religious Life* (Macomb, IL 1993). J. CHING, *Chinese Religions* (Maryknoll, NY: 1993). D. SOMMER, *Chinese Religion: An Anthology of Sources* (New York 1995). D. S. LOPEZ, *Religions of China in Practice* (Princeton 1996). M. SHAHAR and R.P. WELLER, *Unruly Gods: Divinity and Society in China* (Honolulu 1996). M.-C. POO, *In Search of Personal Welfare: A View of Ancient Chinese Religion* (Albany, NY 1998) K. M. SCHIPPER and J. DE MEYER, eds. *Linked Faiths: Essays on Chinese Religions and Traditional Culture in Honor of Kristofer Schipper* (Leiden 2000). S. FEUCHTWANG, *Popular Religion in China: The Imperial Metaphor* (Richmond 2001).

[J. Y. TAN]

CHINESE RITES CONTROVERSY

Spanning three centuries from the 1630s to 1939, the Chinese Rites Controversy arose from a disagreement between the Jesuits on the one hand, and the Dominicans, Franciscans and the Paris Foreign Missionaries, on the other, on the various rituals that were used in the cult of Confucius and the veneration of ancestors (the so-called "Chinese rites"). The dispute centered on whether these rites were purely civil in nature, or religious and therefore amounted to superstition.

The Rites. The ancestral veneration rituals are commonly associated with the cult of Confucius and his teachings, even though they predate Confucius. They consist of prayers, solemn prostrations (*kowtow*), and offerings of incense, food and drinks to one's ancestors that were performed at ancestral shrines, tombs, and ancestral tablets. At the core of these rituals is filial piety (*hsiao*), a virtue that children cultivate toward their parents while they are alive and continue to do so after their death.

The cult of Confucius is a specific form of ancestor veneration, viz., the veneration of Confucius as ancestor *par excellence* by magistrates and scholars. This takes one of two ritual forms. The simple rite was performed on the first and fifteenth of each month. The solemn rite, which included the ritual slaughter of animals and offerings of food and drinks, was performed on the birthday of Confucius and auspicious days in spring and autumn.

Matteo RICCI and his confreres held that the ancestor veneration rituals and the cult of Confucius were civic rituals that enabled the Chinese to show respect and gratitude to their ancestors and *chih sheng hsien shih K'ung Tzu* (Master K'ung the most holy teacher of antiquity). At the same time, they were cautious of some elements in the rites which appeared to be superstitious. They organized conferences in 1603 and 1605 and issued a set of guidelines governing the permissible and prohibited aspects of the rites. In the veneration of ancestors, they forbade the Chinese Christians to pray to the dead ancestors, to burn paper money for the dead, and to believe that the dead would eat the food offerings. They permitted the usage of ancestral tablets inscribed with names and titles of the dead, and of candles, flowers and incense. In the cult of Confucius, the Jesuits allowed Christian scholars to participate in the simple rite, but refused to allow them to take part in the solemn rite on the basis that certain elements, e.g., the ritual slaughter of animals, were superstitious.

Development of the Controversy and Church Decrees. The Chinese Rites Controversy began with the arrival of the Dominican, Juan Bautista MORALES in China in 1633. He was highly critical of the Jesuits, attacking them for allowing the Chinese Christians to continue the practice the cult of Confucius, ancestor veneration rituals and other traditional Chinese customs and practices, which he regarded as erroneous and mere superstitions. Upon his expulsion from China during the persecution of 1637, Morales first reported the issue to the Archbishop of Manila and then to Rome in February 1643. His formal complaint to the Congregation for the Propagation of the Faith (*Propaganda Fide*) was structured as 17 questions on: (1) fast, yearly confession, communion and observance of feast days; (2) use of sacramentals in administering baptism and extreme unction; (3) interest of 30 percent on loans; (4) and (5) usury and usurers; (6) contri-

butions to pagan sacrifices and festivals; (7) Cult of the "guardian deity of the city" (8) Cult of Confucius; (9) ancestor veneration; (10) serving and feeding the dead as though they were living; (11) use of ancestral tablets; (12) funerals; (13) instruction of catechumens on the illicit nature of such rites; (14) the use of the adjective *sheng* (holy); (15) veneration and obeisance (*kowtow*) before the tablet set in honor of the emperor; (16) licitness of prayers and sacrifices for non-Christian relatives; and (17) preaching Christ crucified. In his complaint, words such as "altar," "temple," "sacrifice," "priest," and "genuflection" were used, creating an impression that the Chinese rites were religious and superstitious.

On Sept. 12, 1645 Pope Innocent X approved the resolutions and the decree of the *Propaganda Fide* which responded to Morales' 17 questions by prohibiting the cult of Confucius, ancestor veneration, and ancestral tablets, "until His Holiness or the Holy See will provide otherwise." This decree did not reach China until 1649. The Jesuits were not satisfied with the decree and accordingly in 1651 sent a delegation led by Martin Martini to Rome to present their case. In Rome, Martini presented to the Holy Office of Inquisition, instead of *Propaganda Fide*, four propositions which corresponded to four questions (1st, 2nd, 8th and 9th) in Morales' complaint. Among other things, Martini said that priests did not preside at the cult of Confucius, the cult was celebrated in a hall (*aula*) and not in a temple, the prostrations at the funeral were made in front of a table (*tabula*) and not before an altar. He concluded that Chinese rites were not religious but merely civil and political.

On March 23, 1656, the Holy Office issued a decree with the approval of Pope Alexander VII in favor of the petitioner because the rites appeared to be "merely civil and political." This decree allowed the Chinese Christians to practice their rites provided that superstitious elements were eliminated. Juan de Polanco, O.P., asked whether the 1656 decree abolished that of 1645. On Nov. 20, 1669 the Holy Office answered him in a decree approved by Pope Clement XI that the recent decree did not abolish that of 1645, but that both decrees were in force and that they had to be observed "according to the questions, the circumstances and all that is contained in the proposed doubts."

On March 26, 1693, Charles Maigrot, Vicar Apostolic of Fujian, issued a mandate with seven articles against the Chinese rites that missionaries operating in his vicariate had to comply with. The first and second articles banned the use of *T'ien-chu* (Lord of Heaven) and *Shang-ti* (Lord on High) as names for God; the third article prohibited missionaries from making use of the 1656 decree on the ground that Martini had obtained that decree fraudulently; the fourth article forbade Chinese Christians from taking part in the solemn rite of the cult of Confucius, although it permitted the simple rite; the fifth article banned the use of ancestral tablets; and the sixth and seventh articles dealt with the religious and moral ideas of the Chinese. This mandate caused much indignation among the Jesuits, many Augustinians and Franciscans, and a few Dominicans. The ensuing uproar resulted in Maigrot's mandate being sent to Rome for examination. As a result, in 1697 a particular congregation was established to reopen the case of the Chinese rites. After seven years of studying the case, Pope Clement XI issued a decree dated Nov. 20, 1704 that not only upheld the seven articles in Maigrot's mandate, but went further in banning even the simple rite which Maigrot had tolerated.

In an attempt to resolve the controversy, Pope Clement XI sent his legate, Carlo Tommaso Maillard de TOURNON, who arrived in Beijing in December 1705. Negotiations between Tournon and the Kangxi (K'ang-hsi) emperor (1661–1722) broke down after three meetings, and he was ordered to leave Beijing. Tournon made his way to Nanjing, where he heard that the Kangxi emperor had issued an edict dated Dec. 17, 1706, that expelled all missionaries who were against the Chinese rites and required all missionaries to obtain the imperial permit (*piao*) to remain and work in China. In retaliation, Tournon issued a mandate on his own authority forbidding the cult of Confucius and ancestor veneration and threatening excommunication for those who dared to disobey his mandate. In doing so, he based his mandate on the 1704 decree which, at that time, had not yet reached China. On June 30, 1707, Tournon was escorted by two imperial officials to Macau where he was confined until his death on June 8, 1710.

The missionaries faced a crisis of conscience in choosing between the imperial *piao* or Tournon's mandate. A number of missionaries preferred the *piao* to the mandate, not wishing to jeopardize their existing missionary endeavors. Hearing this, Pope Clement XI issued a decree dated Sept. 25, 1710 which reiterated both the 1704 decree and Tournon's mandate. This decree forbade all kinds of publications regarding the Chinese rites, unless there was the permission of the pope. In addition, the decree included the sentence of excommunication for those who violated this prohibition.

On March 19, 1715 Pope Clement XI published the bull *Ex illa die* with the intention of bringing the controversy to an end. In this bull, the pope reiterated that all missionaries in China were bound to observe the 1704 and 1710 decrees, as well as the mandate of Maillard de Tournon. He allowed the use of the word *T'ien Chu* to designate God, but not *Shang Ti, Tien* (Heaven), and *King Tien* (adore Heaven). The bull imposed the sentence of excommunication for those who disobeyed it. In addition, it included an obligatory oath of observance for all missionaries. The bull became the cause for the persecution of Christians.

In 1719, Pope Clement XI sent Carlo Ambrogio MEZZABARBA to the Chinese court as his legate to defuse the tension and uproar that ensued the implementation of *Ex illa die* in China. The mission was not successful. On the way back to Rome, Mezzabarba stopped for six months at Macau, where on Nov. 4, 1721, he wrote a pastoral letter to all missionaries, reaffirming that the bull *Ex illa die* was still in force. In an effort to defuse the tensions, he granted eight permissions regarding the Chinese rites. This pastoral letter engendered much confusion among missionary personnel in China. A small minority clung onto the bull *Ex illa die*, while the majority made full use of the permissions that Mezzabarba had granted in his pastoral letter.

In 1733, Bishop of Beijing, François de la Purification, wrote two pastoral letters ordering that the bull *Ex illa die* be observed in accordance with Mezzabarba's permissions. The new pope, Clement XII, annulled the two pastoral letters of Bishop of Beijing on Sept. 25, 1735, ordering that the bull *Ex illa die* be observed without any exceptions.

On July 5, 1742, Pope Benedict XIV issued the bull *Ex quo singulari* with the intention of settling the question of the status of the Chinese rites by confirming the authority of Rome on the issue, reinforcing the efficacy of the 1704, 1710, and 1715 decrees and the mandate of Maillard de Tournon, and nullifying the eight permissions of Mezzabarba and the two pastoral letters of the Bishop of Beijing. In addition to removing all exceptions which had been tolerated or permitted in previous periods, the pope prohibited any further discussion of the rites. With this bull, Pope Benedict XIV brought the one-century-and-a-half controversy to an end but the issue unresolved.

20th Century Resolution of the Controversy. Two incidents took place outside China which led to the resolution of the Chinese rites controversy. In the first incident on May 5, 1932, some 60 Catholic students at the Jesuit Sophia University in Japan refused to salute the war dead at the Yasukuni Shrines. To defuse a potentially devastating situation, Bishop Johannes Ross, interpreting c. 1258 of the 1917 Code of Canon Law, allowed Japanese Catholics to visit the Shinto Shrines to pay their respects to the war dead. Later, Bishop Ross presented this case to the archbishop of Tokyo, Jean Alexis Chambon, who verbally permitted the Catholic students to participate in visiting the shrines that honored the war dead. On

Sept. 22, 1932, Archbishop Chambon wrote a letter to the Japanese government, inquiring whether participation in the shrine ceremonies were religious or not. On September 30, he received the answer that the participation was only an act of "manifesting the sentiments of patriotism and loyalty." In January 1933, Bishop Edward Mooney, the Apostolic Delegate to Japan, issued the statement allowing Japanese Catholics to participate in *Jinja Sanpai* (veneration at the shrine) with "a grave reason approved by the judgment of the ordinary."

The second incident occurred in Manchukuo (Manchuria), a new state established by the Japanese Kwantung army on Feb. 25, 1932. The new government implemented the policy of *Wangtao* (the Way of the King). This policy mandated that Manchurian Catholics were required to bow to the picture or statue of Confucius in the Confucian shrine. Augustin Ernest Pierre Gaspais, Bishop of Kirin, officially inquired the Ministry of Foreign Affairs on Feb. 27, 1935, of the meaning of the honor given to Confucius. On March 5, 1935, the Ministry of Education gave the answer that the honor did not have "any religious character" rather than to show the "spirit of loyal patriotism."

On March 12, 1935, Bishop Gaspais called for a conference of the Ordinaries of Manchukuo at the new capital, Ksinking, to re-evaluate the Chinese rites on the participation of Catholics in the non-Catholic ceremonies in the light of the 1917 Codex Iuris Canonicis c. 1258 §2. The results of the conference were personally submitted to *Propaganda Fide* by Bishop Gaspais himself. While in Rome, Bishop Gaspais met with Pope Pius XI on May 16.

On May 28, 1935, Cardinal Fumasoni-Biondi, the Prefect of *Propaganda Fide*, with the approval of the pope, responded to Bishop Gaspais that the Ordinaries of Manchukuo had to make known to the faithful that the ceremonies in honor of Confucius "have absolutely no religious character" and that priests, while awaiting for instructions of the Ordinaries, had to avoid all questionings and controversies of the Chinese rites. This document from the *Propaganda Fide* showed a shift in the Church's viewpoint on the Chinese rites since the bull *Ex quo singulari* of 1742, leading to a reconsideration of the Shinto rites controversy in Japan. On May 26, 1936, *Propaganda Fide* issued the instruction *Pluries instanterque* to Paul Marella, the Apostolic Delegate to Japan, allowing Japanese Catholics to fulfill their duties toward the country and to participate in marriages, funerals and other aspects of the Confucian rites as part of the Japanese socio-cultural fabric.

The instructions of 1935 for Manchukuo and of 1936 for Japan became the basic principle for the instruction *Plane compertum est* of Dec. 8, 1939, approved by Pope Pius XII, for China regarding the Chinese rites. Its preamble clearly stated that, due to changes in customs and ideas in the course of time, the rites now had no more than mere civil or social significance. The instruction allowed Catholics: (1) to participate in honoring Confucius; (2) to set up an image or a tablet of Confucius and to bow to it; (3) to passively participate in public ceremonies which appeared to be superstitious in accordance with the norms of the 1917 CIC c. 1258, and (4) to bow to the deceased, the picture or even the tablet of a deceased person. The instruction also abolished the obligatory oath against the Chinese rites. This was a new element in the instruction in comparison with the two previous instructions. However, the instruction still prohibited discussions of the controversy. The term "questions" was not mentioned in this instruction. This instruction officially ended the Chinese rites controversy.

On Feb. 28, 1941, *Propaganda Fide* issued a despatch entitled *Mens* to the apostolic delegate to China, Archbishop Mario Zanin, on the implementation of *Plane compertum est*. This *Mens* required that no composition of a list of permitted or forbidden ceremonies be made, that the ordinaries give rules and general norms of behavior, not details, in the time of transition, and that individual Catholics were to follow their own conscience in particular cases.

It took almost three centuries, beginning with the first decree of Sept. 12, 1645 and ending with the dispatch of Feb. 28, 1941, to resolve the Chinese rites controversy. This controversy arose as a result of misunderstanding of customs and cultures, methods of evangelization, and politics. It was a clash between two cultures of the European West and of China. Within the Chinese sociocultural milieu, filial piety is the *grundnorm* of ethics in China. As a public ritual manifestation of filial piety, ancestor veneration was the *sine qua non* of Chinese socioethical fabric, the violation of which was considered the most heinous crime. Ironically, the explanation of the Kangxi Emperor on Nov. 30, 1700, that the rite of ancestor veneration was not a superstition but a ceremony honoring one's ancestors in a spirit of filial piety became the basis for *Propaganda Fide*'s 1939 instruction that paved the way for Catholics to take part in ancestor veneration rites. Indeed, the instruction *Plane compertum est* justified the permission that was granted on the basis that these rites were not superstitious or religious, but merely forms of filial piety and respect for one's elders.

Bibliography: *Acta Apostolicae Sedis; commentarium officiale* v.28 (1936); v.31 (1939); v.32 (1940). BENEDICT XIV, *Bullarium* (In quo continentur constitutiones, epistolae, aliaque edita ab initio pontificatus usque ad annum MDCCXLVI), v.1. (Venice 1768). *Collectanea Commissionis Synodalis* (Peiping: Commissio

Synodalis in Siniis) v.9 (1936); v.13 (1940); v.14 (1941). *Magnum Bullarium Romanum* v.16 (complectens constitutiones Benedicti XIV, ab initio Pontificatus usque ad annum 1746) (Luxembourg 1752). J. S. CUMMINS, *Jesuits and Friar in the Spanish Expansion to the East* (London 1986). *A Question of Rites: Friar Domingo Navarrete and the Jesuits in China* (Hants, England 1993). G. H. DUNNE, *Generation of Giants: The Story of the Jesuits in China in the Last Decades of the Ming Dynasty* (Notre Dame, Ind 1962). L. J. GALLAGHER, *China in the Sixteenth Century: The Journal of Matthew Ricci (1583–1610)* (New York 1942). K. S. LATOURETTE, *A History of Christian Missions in China* (London 1929). G. MINAMIKI, *The Chinese Rites Controversy from Its Beginning to Modern Times* (Chicago 1985). D. E. MUNGELLO, *The Chinese Rites Controversy: Its History and Meaning* (Nettetal 1994). R. R. NOLL, ed., *100 Roman Documents Concerning the Chinese Rites Controversy (1645–1941)* (San Francisco 1992). A. S. ROSSO, *Apostolic Legations to China of Eighteenth Century* (South Pasadena 1948).

[P. D. T. VO]

CHINIQUY, CHARLES PASCAL

Author, anti-Catholic polemicist; b. Kamouraska, Quebec, Canada, July 30, 1809; d. Montreal, Canada, Jan. 16, 1899. He was the son of Charles, a sailor, and Marie (Reine) Chiniquy and was orphaned in 1821. After study at the seminary of Nicolet, Quebec, he was ordained Sept. 21, 1833, and then served as curate at Saint-Charles de Bellechasse (1833), officiating minister at Charlesbourg (1834), curate at Saint-Roch of Quebec (1834–38), and chaplain of the naval hospital. He offered his services to Bp. Norbert Provencher for the Northwest missions and was refused. In 1838 he became pastor of the important parish of Beauport. Two years later he began preaching on temperance, founding a temperance society (1840) and becoming known as "Father Mathew of Lower Canada" (*see* MATHEW, THEOBALD). He was transferred to the parish at Kamouraska (1842), where he scandalized the population by his conduct and was obliged to leave the Diocese of Quebec (1846). He joined the Oblates of Mary Immaculate but was dismissed and took up temperance preaching in the Diocese of Montreal. Bishop Ignace Bourget of Montreal revoked Chiniquy's powers (1851), giving him his exeat to the Diocese of Chicago, Ill. As a schismatic after 1852, he attracted a number of French-speaking faithful and even attempted to attract a group of initiates from Canada to Illinois. Denounced by Bps. J. O. Vandervelde, A. O'Regan, and J. Duggan of Chicago, he was placed under interdict in August 1856 and excommunicated in September of the same year. He then founded the Christian Catholic Church and joined the Presbyterian Church in Chicago, from which he was later expelled. Accepted by the Presbyterian synod of Canada, he became an official preacher in Canada and moved to Montreal with his family in 1875.

Caroline Chisholm. (The Catholic University of America)

Chiniquy made many trips abroad. He published several anti-Catholic works that enjoyed great success and were translated into many languages. Among these were his autobiography *Cinquante ans dans l'Eglise de Rome* (1885) and *Quarante ans dans l'Eglise du Christ,* for the period from 1859 to 1899, which was published posthumously; and *La Femme, le prêtre, et le Confessional* (1878). *Mes Combats, Autobiographie de Charles Chiniquy, Apôtre de la Tempérance* was published in Montreal (1946). In 1844, while still a Catholic, Chiniquy published a short work, *Manuel ou Règlement de la Société de Tempérance.* Six days before his death he published in the Montreal *Gazette* his religious testament, replete with blasphemy against the Catholic Church.

[G. CARRIÈRE]

CHISHOLM, CAROLINE (JONES)

Philanthropist, social worker, assisted migration to and settlement in eastern Australia; b. at or near Northampton, England, 1808; d. Fulham, England, March 25, 1877. She was the daughter of William Jones, a yeoman farmer, and she grew up with a strong evangelical sense of duty in social service. In 1830 she married Capt. Archibald Chisholm of the East India Company and became a Catholic. Catholic fervor thereafter reinforced her humanitarian zeal. The couple spent some years in India before settling in Sydney (1838). At that time arrangements for the reception and dispersal of free immigrants in eastern Australia were unsatisfactory. Mrs. Chisholm became concerned for the moral welfare of young unmarried women in a population composed partly of convicts and former convicts, and in 1841 she established a hostel where they could stay until they found employment. From this beginning grew her later social work. She recognized that New South Wales was deficient in "God's police"—women and children. She therefore strove, in several trips through the country in the 1840s, through the Family Colonization Loan Society, which she established in London (1849), and through her pamphlets on colonization, to facilitate the immigration of the better sort of working-class people, especially single women, family groups, and the wives and children of emancipists. Approximately 5,000 people seem to have settled in Australia as a result of her efforts. Her headstone at Northampton is fittingly inscribed "The Emigrant's Friend."

Bibliography: M. KIDDLE, *Caroline Chisholm* (Melbourne 1950).

[L. GARDINER]

CHIVALRY

Term that "denotes the ideals and practices considered suitable for a noble." Deriving its origins from the long military tradition of the Germanic peoples, chivalry reached fruition during the 12th century. The typical noble of that epoch was a knight or mounted warrior, usually bound by feudal ties to his lord and vassals. As knights became increasingly self-conscious, they thought of themselves as forming a clearly defined class, the order of chivalry, with its distinctive ceremony of admission, known as dubbing, and with its appropriate rules of conduct. The true knight was expected to be courageous in battle, loyal to his lord, honest and generous toward his fellow knights and subordinates. Such ideals found their characteristic expression in the *chansons de geste*, but they were ideals that were not always attained in contemporary society.

Christian Influence. Although Christian influence on the origins of chivalry was slight, the Church always sought to inculcate right standards of morality among the nobility and to ameliorate the worst aspects of feudal behavior. For this reason churchmen emphasized the solemn and sacred character of the contract between lord and vassal, with their reciprocal rights and duties. Church councils (e.g., Valence, 855) condemned the judicial duel, a defective means of settling litigation—though churchmen sometimes were involved in them—and the tournament, or mock battle [Second Lateran (1139), c.14; *Conciliorum oecumenicorum decreta* (Bologna-Freiburg 1962) 176], a favorite pastime of knights when they were not engaged in serious combat.

Peace and Truce of God. From the late 10th century the Church proclaimed the PEACE OF GOD as a means of checking the excesses of private warfare (Councils of Charroux, 989; Narbonne, 990; etc.). Through the Truce of God (Council of Elne, 1027) knights were asked to pledge themselves not to attack the weak and defenseless, such as widows, orphans, merchants, and unarmed clergy, and to refrain from the use of arms on holydays and during sacred seasons of the year such as Lent and Advent.

Crusades. The Church's concern for the pacification of western Europe and the improvement of morality received new meaning when in 1095 Pope URBAN II summoned the nobles to liberate the Holy Land (*see* CRUSADES). Let those, he said, who hitherto have lived as brigands and mercenaries become true knights by devoting themselves to a cause that is just and promises an eternal reward. In making his plea the Pope was pointing to a spiritual ideal that he considered especially suitable to those who professed to be knights. In so doing he was imparting a religious significance to the code of chivalry.

Initiation Ceremony. The spiritualization of chivalry is reflected in the liturgy devised by the Church for the ceremony of initiation into the order of knighthood. In the late 12th and 13th century the vigil of arms, the ritual bath, and the blessing of the sword were common practices, though not essential to the making of a knight. While watching his arms reposing upon the altar, the future knight was expected to meditate upon the honor that he was to receive and the obligations that it entailed. The bath symbolized his purification and was likened to a second baptism. Various liturgical manuscripts, such as the late 13th-century pontifical of William DURANTI THE ELDER, contain blessings for the sword with which the initiate girded himself. The blessing reminded him that he should use his weapon for the defense of the Church and the protection of the weak. By surrounding the rite of initiation with religious symbolism and endowing it with a quasi-sacramental character, the Church fostered the idea that the knight was a man consecrated to the fulfillment of God's work on earth.

Contemporary Theories. The fullest exposition of the nature and functions of Christian knighthood is found in the writings of 12th- and 13th-century thinkers. In his *Liber de vita christiana,* written in the late 11th century, BONIZO OF SUTRI stressed the knight's duty to keep faith with his lord, to abstain from pillage, to protect the poor and the weak, and to champion orthodoxy against heresy and schism. To these obligations Urban II added that of defending the Christian people against the infidels.

Early in the 12th century BERNARD OF CLAIRVAUX wrote his *Liber de laude novae militiae* in justification of the newly formed Order of the Temple, whose members tried to combine the ideals of monasticism and chivalry. Bernard sharply contrasted the life of the TEMPLARS (the *militia Christi*) with that of contemporary lay knights (the *militia saecularis . . . non militia, sed malitia*). Condemning the latter for their "insane appetite for glory and insatiable greed for land," the abbot of Clairvaux leaves one with the impression that only the Templars could be considered true knights.

Later in the century JOHN OF SALISBURY in his *Policraticus* expressed the view that knights constituted an order instituted by God for the service of both the Church and the State. The knight should be the guardian of justice, obedient to God, Church, and prince. The contemporary Stephen of Fougères set forth similar ideas in his *Livre des manières.*

At the close of the 13th century, in his *Libre del orde de cauayleria,* Raymond LULL propounded a conception of chivalry drawn from both secular and religious sources. He believed that the knight should embody the virtues most admired by soldiers as well as those exalted by the Church. Lull described in some detail the religious ceremonies that ought to attend admission to knighthood, and he explained the symbolism of knightly accoutrements.

Effects. The Church made unceasing efforts to permeate the code of chivalry with Christian principles both by conciliar legislation and by instruction. By upholding the idea that the true knight must wield his sword only in the cause of right and justice, the Church appealed to the highest sentiments of western European nobility. The crusading movement and the MILITARY ORDERS were manifestations of this ideal. On the other hand the pages of medieval chronicles reveal that knights frequently were motivated by worldly rather than religious ends. Yet by giving a spiritual meaning to the institution of chivalry the Church tempered much of the brutality, frivolity, and artificiality of feudal and courtly society.

Bibliography: L. GAUTIER, *La Chevalerie* (Paris 1884). S. PAINTER, *French Chivalry* (Baltimore 1940). M. BLOCH, *Feudal Society,* tr. L. A. MANYON (Chicago 1961). G. COHEN, *Histoire de la chevalerie en France au moyen âge* (Paris 1949).

[J. F. O'CALLAGHAN]

"The Challenge," 15th/16th century Italian illustration depicting an act of chivalry. (Archive Photos, Inc.)

CHLODULF OF METZ, ST.

Bishop; d. May 8 *c.* 663 or 696. Chlodulf (Clodulf, Clou), son of Arnulf of Metz and brother-in-law of (St.) BEGGA; became bishop of Metz in 652 or 656. There he trained TRUDO of Brabant. The discrepancy in his death dates results from the attempt to give him the 40-year episcopate that a ninth- or tenth-century catalogue attributed to him. But although a passage from the *Miracles* of St. GERTRUDE OF NIVELLES says that he was alive at her death on March 16, 659, and his name is among those who witnessed a document of Numerius of Trier *c.* 663, it was Chlodulf's successor at Metz who signed the charter of Drausius of Soissons for the monastery of Sainte-Marie on June 25, 667. Chlodulf's vita (*Acta Sanctorum* June 2:127–132) is ninth-century and unhistorical. The celebration of his feast on June 8 may stem from a mistake in months in the Roman Martyrology. His bones are in the former Benedictine church, Lay-Saint-Christophe, near Nancy, and in St. Arnuf's, Metz.

Feast: June 8.

Bibliography: *Monumenta Germaniae Historica: Scriptores* 2:264, 267, 269. *Bibliotheca hagiograpica latina antiquae et mediae aetatis* (Brussels 1898–1901) 1:1735. J. DEPOIN, ''Grandes figures monacales des temps mérovingiens,'' *Revue Mabillon* 11 (1921) 245–258; 12 (1922) 13–25, 105–118. J. L. BAUDOT and L. CHAUSSIN, *Vies des saints et des bienhereux selon l'ordre du calendrier avec l'historique des fêtes* (Paris 1935–56) 6:147–148. A. BUTLER, *The Lives of the Saints,* ed. H. THURSTON and D. ATTWATER (New York 1956) 2:503. R. AIGRAIN, *Catholicisme* 2:1262–63.

[G. J. DONNELLY]

CHMIELOWSKI, ALBERT, ST.

Baptized Adam, artist and founder of the Brothers (and Sisters) of the Third Order of St. Francis Servants of the Poor; b. Igolomia (near Krakow), Miechów District of southern Poland, Aug. 20, 1845; d. Krakow, Poland, Dec. 25, 1916. In 1863, the aristocratic Adam Chmielowski abandoned his study of agriculture to join an uprising against the Russian occupation. Wounded and taken prisoner, Adam's left leg was amputated. He escaped prison and fled to France where he studied engineering for a year, then art, before a general amnesty permitted his return to Poland as an artist (1874). Adam's paintings increasingly turned to religious themes; one of his most famous works, *Ecce Homo* (Jesus before Pontius Pilate), led Adam to a spiritual metamorphosis.

After a decade as a successful artist, he entered the Jesuits (1880), although he left to become a Franciscan tertiary. Chmielowski worked first in the countryside, and then in Krakow, gradually abandoning his painting and turning his studio into a homeless shelter. Inspired by another former freedom fighter, St. Rafał KALINOWSKI, Adam took the name Albert (1887), donned a simple grey habit, and pledged religious vows (1888) before Cardinal Archbishop Albin Dunajewski. Thereafter the former socialite lived a life of poverty and organized shelters, soup kitchens, and other charitable institutions. Chmielowski's work and personality attracted followers who formed the nucleus of the Albertine Brothers (1888) and Sisters (1891), congregations that now serve the poor of Poland, Argentina, Italy, and the United States. In 1938, Brother Albert, who had founded 21 refuges in Poland, was posthumously awarded Poland's highest honor for his work among the destitute. Pope John Paul II, who both beatified (June 22, 1983 at Krakow) and canonized (Nov. 12, 1989 at Rome) Saint Albert, wrote a play about him in 1949 called *Our God's Brother* that was released as a motion picture in 1998.

Feast: June 17.

Bibliography: A. CASIERI, *Fratel Alberto, al secolo Adamo Chmielowski* (Rome 1989). W. KLUZ, *Adam Chmielowski, Brat Albert,* 2d. ed. (Krakow 1982). K. MICHALSKI, *Brat Albert,* 4th ed. (Krakow 1986). A. OKOŃSKA, *Adam Chmielowski: Brat Albert,* 2d. ed. (Warsaw 1999). *Acta Apostolicae Sedis* 77 (1985): 461–463.

[K. I. RABENSTEIN]

CHOICE

The act of the WILL that is concerned with means to an END; as such, it is distinct from the act of deliberation that precedes it and from the act of execution that follows it. (For a discussion of the interrelationships between these acts, *see* HUMAN ACT.) This article discusses the teachings of various philosophers concerning choice and is divided into two parts: the first is devoted to ancient and medieval thought on the subject, the second to modern and contemporary views.

Ancient and Medieval Thought. According to ARISTOTLE, when one wishes an end, which he sees as his GOOD, his choice must necessarily be concerned with the means to that end, that is, with the actions that will attain it, insofar as these lie in his power. ''Wish relates to the end, choice [προαίρεσις, meaning preference] to the means; for instance, we wish to be healthy, but we choose the acts which will make us healthy . . .; for, in general, choice seems to relate to the things that are in our own power'' (*Eth. Nic.* 1111b 27–29). From this he deduces that choice in man must be voluntary: ''The end, then, being what we wish for, the means what we deliberate about and choose, actions concerning means must be according to choice and voluntary'' (*ibid.* 1113b 3–5).

St. AUGUSTINE, reflecting on the concept of choice within the context of Christian revelation, sees it as being vitiated by sin; in his view, it was a perfection of man before original sin, a perfection that can be restored only by the gift of divine grace. ''From the bad use of free will, there originated the whole train of evil, which, with its concatenation of miseries, convoys the human race from its depraved origin, as from a corrupt root, on to the destruction of the second death, which has no end, those only being excepted who are freed by the grace of God'' (*Civ.* 13.14).

According to the doctrine of St. THOMAS AQUINAS, ''choice is substantially not an act of the reason but of the will; for choice is accomplished in a certain movement of the soul toward the good which is chosen. Consequently, it is evidently an act of the appetitive power'' (*Summa Theologiae* 1a2ae, 13.1). Aquinas follows Aristotle's teaching on choice's being concerned with means to an end: ''Just as intention regards the end, so choice regards the means'' (*ibid.* 13.4). He likewise sees in man's faculty of choice the proper explanation of his freedom, or FREE WILL: ''Man does not choose of necessity. . . . Now the reason why it is possible not to choose or to choose, may be gathered from a twofold power in man. For man can will and not will, act and not act; and again he can will this or that, and do this or that. . . . Man chooses, not of necessity, but freely'' (*ibid.* 13.6). Most scholastics are in basic agreement with this teaching. The Franciscan school generally accords more autonomy and primacy to the will, and thus sees free choice more as the will's prerogative than something it obtains from its dependency on the intellect (cf. Duns Scotus, *Opus Oxon.* 1.1.4.16). Jesuit writers generally follow Thomistic doctrine, although they dispute over the precise relationship that obtains between choice and the last practical judgment (*see* St. Robert Bellarmine, *De gratia et libero arbitrio* 3.8; G. Vázquez, in *Summa Theologiae* 1a2ae, 44.3).

Modern and Contemporary Thought. R. DESCARTES makes the important point that liberty of choice is not to be confused with indifference toward various alternatives, which he sees more as a defect of knowledge than as a perfection of the will: ''In order that I should be free it is not necessary that I should be indifferent as to the choice of one or the other of two contraries; but contrariwise the more I lean to the one . . . the more freely do I choose and embrace it'' (*Meditat.* 4.5). G. W. LEIBNIZ associates choice with the will's being induced to act by the element of goodness in what it chooses. ''The will is never prompted to action save by the representation of the good, which prevails over the opposite representations. . . . For that very reason the choice is free and independent of necessity, because it is made between several possibles, and the will is determined only by the preponderating goodness of the object'' (*Theodicy, Essays on the Justice of God* 1.45).

Thinkers in the British empiricist tradition locate liberty or freedom in man's ability to choose, which they regard as being without external constraint or coercion. This is stated quite clearly by D. HUME: ''By liberty . . . we can only mean a power of acting or not acting, according to the determination of the will; that is, if we choose to remain at rest, we may; if we choose to move, we also may'' (*An Enquiry Concerning Human Understanding* 8.73). J. LOCKE further discusses the case of choice with respect to an end. ''Liberty, it is plain, consists in the power to do, or not to do; to do, or forbear doing, as we will. . . . In most cases, a man is not at liberty to forbear the act of volition. . . . Yet there is a case wherein a man is at liberty in respect of willing; and that is the choosing of a *remote* good as an end to be pursued. Here a man may suspend the act of his choice from being determined for or against the thing proposed, till he has examined whether it be really of a nature, in itself and consequences, to make him happy or not'' (*An Essay Concerning Human Understanding* 2.21.57).

For I. KANT and the German idealist tradition that followed him, freedom of choice is derived from the exigencies of the practical reason and from moral law; thus choice is nothing more than man's autonomy in legislating for himself. In Kant's view, freedom does not consist in being able to choose one alternative or the other, but in the will's not being passively determined; will is a law unto itself independent of any quality in the object presented to it. ''The principle of autonomy then is: 'Always so to choose that the same volition shall comprehend the maxims of our choice as a universal law''' (*Fundamental Principles of the Metaphysic of Morals* 2).

William JAMES accepts free choice as a pragmatic option, although he argues that man has an immediate awareness of his ability to choose. For those who have scruples about introspective aspects of consciousness he writes: ''Let there be no such consciousness; let all our thoughts of movements be of sensational constitution; still in the emphasizing, choosing, and espousing of one of them rather than another, in the saying to it, 'be thou the reality to me,' there is ample scope for our inward initiative to be shown. Here, it seems to me, the true line between the passive materials and the activity of the spirit should be drawn'' (*Principles of Psychology* ch. 26).

It is among the existentialist thinkers, however, that choice has received the greatest emphasis as a philosophical concept. For S. A. KIERKEGAARD, choice is so fundamental that without it there can be no such thing as good or evil. ''My either/or does not in the first instance denote the choice between good and evil, it denotes the choice whereby one chooses good *and* evil/ or excludes them. . . . It is, therefore, not so much a question of choosing between willing the good *or* the evil, as of choosing to *will,* but by this in turn the good and the evil are posited'' [*Either/Or,* ed. R. Bretall, *A Kierkegaard Anthology* (New York 1946) 107]. M. Heidegger is even more emphatic; in his view, both the present state and the ultimate potentiality of *Dasein* (that is, of human existence) are rooted in the attitude toward choice. ''Dasein makes no choices, . . . and thus snares itself in inauthenticity. This process can be reversed only if Dasein specifically brings itself back to itself from its lostness in the 'they.' . . . This must be accomplished by making up for not choosing. But 'making up' for not choosing signifies choosing to make this choice—deciding for a potentiality-for-Being, and making this decision from one's own Self. In choosing to make this choice, Dasein makes possible, first and foremost, its authentic potentiality-for-Being'' [*Being and Time,* tr. J. Macquarrie and E. Robinson (London 1962) 312–313]. (*See* EXISTENTIALISM).

See Also: FREE WILL; FREEDOM; VOLUNTARITY; VOLUNTARISM.

Choir of Sisters of Mercy, London. (©Hulton-Deutsch Collection/CORBIS)

Bibliography: M. J. ADLER, ed., *The Great Ideas: A Syntopicon of Great Books of the Western World,* 2 v. (Chicago 1952) 2:1071–1101, 1309. G. PEDRAZZINI and G. MASI, *Enciclopedia filosofica,* 4 v. (Venice-Rome 1957) 4:333–337. W. H. ROBERTS, *The Problem of Choice* (New York 1948). J. GRENIER, *La Choix* (Paris 1941). R. Z. LAUER, "St. Thomas's Theory of Intellectual Causality in Election," *New Scholasticism* 28 (1954) 299–319. H. RENARD, "The Functions of Intellect and Will in the Act of Free Choice," *The Modern Schoolman* 24 (1947) 85–92.

[W. A. WALLACE]

CHOIR

Although the most common meaning of choir is a group of singers performing during a liturgical function, the term has come to mean also the place in the church from which they sing. The choir in this second sense was located, if the singers were clerics, directly behind or to the side of the altar, or between the altar and the nave if the architecture demanded it. Sometimes it was hidden from view by elaborately ornamented screens. Later, a balcony in the rear of the church served as the choir loft, especially for choirs of lay men and women. A trend toward returning the choir to the apse or nave began after promulgation of the *Constitution on the Liturgy* by Vatican Council II (1963).

Middle Ages. The earliest records of Christian worship show that the community, men and women, sang as a body in response to the ministers. The practice of having male cantors act as soloists undoubtedly was one taken over from the synagogues. There is evidence that even as late as St. Ambrose's time women alternated with the men in psalm-singing, but the general movement toward prohibiting women from singing in liturgical services seems to have reached a peak in the 6th century. This prohibition destroyed the unity of the congregation and led to the use of a select group of clerical singers (*see* SCHOLA CANTORUM).

The history of the choir in the Middle Ages revolves around the great monasteries and, later, the cathedral schools. The growth and development of polyphony increasingly demanded trained singers and tightly organized choir structure. Accurate information about the performance of early polyphony is scarce, but there is reason to believe that it was solo-polyphony rather than choir-polyphony. The medieval structure of the choir was maintained: the precentor, or leader; the succentor, or assistant; the first cantors, or rulers, who intoned and guided the chant and often sang the solo passages at the lectern; and the men and boys who formed the body of singers.

Origin of the Renaissance Choir. Before the 15th century one cannot speak of a choir in the generally accepted sense. The monastic choir was really a congregation of monks with a few specialists; the cathedral choir also was a group of relatively unskilled canons and a few soloists. The rise of private chapels (e.g., those of the Dukes of Burgundy, Berry, Orléans, and Savoy in France, and of St. George's at Windsor, St. Stephen's at Westminster, and the Royal Household), but especially the rivalry among college chapels (such as at Queen's College, Oxford; Eton College; and King's College, Cambridge, in England), brought a new professionalism into church music. For the first time small groups of trained singers were performing the polyphonic repertoire. At the turn of the 15th century and for the first part of the 16th, the average choir consisted of 15 to 20 members. Even in 1586 the papal choir had only 21 members, made up chiefly of young boys. As late as the 17th century, when clarity of tone was the chief aim, the choir was still generally small in size. Women often appear in contemporary illustrations of 17th-century choral groups, but these groups, also small in size, did not perform at church services.

The polyphony of the Renaissance is not easily performed by modern choirs, which generally lack the high male countertenor voices to sing alto parts. Another characteristic of the polyphonic choir was the *castrati* voice. From the 16th to the 18th century in Italy the practice of castration to preserve the boyish character of the voice was common. The *castrati,* highly paid and much in demand, had great range and power, combining the special timbre that came from the adult male lungs and chest with the soprano voice. The most famous choirs were the Sistine choir in Rome and the Venetian choir at St. Marks. The Sistine choir established the *a cappella* tradition; the Venetian choir developed the use of opposing sonorities and instrumental accompaniment (*cori spezzati*).

Subsequent History of the Choir. The history of the choir during the baroque and later periods of music is largely a reflection of the history of music in general.

First page of the holographic copy of the "Sixty-seventh Psalm" written by American composer Charles Ives.

The Roman tradition continued to dominate, but it was affected by the colossal (e.g., the multiple choirs of Benevoli). During the late baroque, however, there was a growth in small parish choirs, as well as in a special repertory for them. These choirs were always accompanied by organ (or instruments) and sang only the Ordinary of the Mass. Major cathedrals, on the other hand, possessed well-trained choirs of some size that performed on Sundays and special occasions. Members of cathedral choirs were often the singers and instrumentalists who formed the local opera company; their repertory consisted mostly of the newly composed baroque and classical Masses. Under the influence of the CAECILIAN MOVEMENT, there was a return to the A CAPPELLA style, and interest was renewed in the 16th-century repertory. A whole new repertory of compositions for small parish choirs was written by the post-Caecilians; these works imitated in an academic fashion the 16th-century style but retained organ accompaniment. Large choirs continued to flourish at the major churches, especially in Austria and Germany; and the concerted Masses of the neoclassical period continued to be the standard repertory.

The 20th Century. With the motu proprio on sacred music of 1903, a search began for trained choral groups to perform the difficult Gregorian chants and polyphonic works. The establishment of boys' choirs, inspired by such examples as Montserrat in Spain, led to cathedral and parish church choral organizations, which in some instances became very capable. The lack of real solfeggio instruction, however, opened the way for a repertory tailored to rote learning, making little or no demand on reading ability or ear training. The resulting paucity of art in choir loft and sanctuary was generally made worse by a dearth of male voices and inadequate rehearsal. Capable, well-trained choir directors were scarce, as was money to pay them adequately. The amateurish approach quickly proved destructive of good church music.

In the mid-20th century choirs were again receiving the benefit of skilled directors and organists, and the repertory of choir music began to show the influence of professional work. At the same time, the change from Latin to the vernacular in the liturgy created new problems for the church choir; for not only are there repertory difficulties, but choirs, far from being obviated, have been restored in an important role. The choir has today been given new settings for the Proper of the Mass, and it shares with the congregation the singing of the hymns, canticles, psalms, and the Ordinary of the Mass.

Bibliography: A. JACOBS, ed., *Choral Music* (Baltimore 1963).

[C. A. PELOQUIN/R. G. WEAKLAND]

CHOISEUL DU PLESSIS PRASLIN, GILBERT DE

Bishop; b. Paris 1613; d. Paris Dec. 31, 1689. He was a doctor at the Sorbonne by 1640; he was consecrated bishop of Comminges in 1644 then transferred to Tournai in 1671. Choiseul, a model pastor, visited every corner of his diocese, reformed his clergy, and founded many schools and seminaries. He showed a deep love for his flock by raising money to feed the poor during a famine and by ministering personally to victims of the plague. Choiseul was one of the first to champion the Jansenists of PORT-ROYAL against their critics both at Rome and at the court. He was one of 11 French bishops who petitioned the pope "to allow this important dispute . . . to continue a little longer." One biographer claims that Choiseul gave Jansenist ideas an important foothold in the diocese of Tournai, particularly among the clergy (F. Desmons, 372). Choiseul's sympathies for a sect condemned by Rome probably account also for his belligerent defense of the "Gallican Liberties." In his place Bishop Bossuet drafted the famous Articles of 1682 largely because Choiseul, the former head of the committee, had wanted to claim still greater autonomy for the French Church. Choiseul's important writings include *Memoires touchant la religion* (3 v. Paris 1681–85), *Lettre pastorale sur le culte de la Vierge* (Tournai 1907); *Les Psaumes, cantiques et hymnes de l'Église, traduit en français,* many editions of which are without place or date of publication.

Bibliography: M. H. LAURENT, *Dictionnaire d'histoire et de géographie ecclésiastiques,* ed. A. BAUDRILLART et al. (Paris 1912–) 12:757–758. R. METZ, *Lexikon für Theologie und Kirche,* ed. J. HOFER and K. RAHNER (2d, new ed. Freiburg 1957–65) 2:1075–76. F. DESMONS, *Gilbert de Choiseul, évêque de Tournai, 1671–89* (Tournai 1907).

[J. Q. C. MACKRELL]

CHOLMOGORY, ABBEY OF

Former Russian monastery dedicated to the Assumption of the Blessed Virgin, situated on one of the islands forming an arm of the Northern Dvina River about 70 miles from where it empties into the White Sea, in Archangel oblast, Russia, in the archeparchy of Archangel. From the 14th century the site had been a trading center for merchants from Novgorod, and in the 16th century it was frequented also by English merchants of the Moscow Company. About 1355 Ivan Ivanovich, Archbishop of Novgorod, stationed an agent there to collect the tithes. A monastery was situated there from about the same period, and the monks maintained themselves by trade in fish and salt. The town of Cholmogory developed independently of the monastery in the late 16th century. Almost nothing can be learned of the abbey's history because of present conditions. In 1691 the Transfiguration Cathedral was built nearby. The Russian poet Lomonosov (d. 1765) was born in Cholmogory.

Bibliography: *Bol'shaia sovetskaia entsiklopediia,* ed. V. V. KUIBYSHEVA et al., 65 v. (Moscow 1927–47) 46:283. *Masaryhkův slovník naučnӯ,* 7 v. (Prague 1925–33) 3:490.

[J. PAPIN]

CHOPIN, FRÉDÉRIC FRANÇOIS

Romanticist composer; b. Zelazowa Wola (near Warsaw), Poland, Feb. 22, 1810; d. Paris, Oct. 17, 1849. He was the second of four talented children of Nicolas Chopin, a transplanted, vaguely Voltairean French schoolman, and Justyna Krzyzanowska, a Polish woman of refinement and piety. At age seven Frédéric first played in public and had his first piece published—a polonaise set in type in the print shop of Visitation parish, where the boy later was organist. After piano training with A. Zwyny, he studied at Warsaw Conservatory under J. K. Elsner (1769–1854), a prolific composer who fostered the boy's unusual creative impulses. Following respectable successes as composer-recitalist in lesser cities, he settled (1831) in Paris, where he was lionized by French and émigré Polish nobility (while supporting himself by giving lessons to their daughters) and accepted as peer by the ranking literary and artistic spirits. Through one of these (F. LISZT) he met and entered upon a liaison with the freethinking writer George Sand (Mme. Aurore Dudevant), in whose household he remained for the next eight years, the arrangement being terminated by a sordid family quarrel. He died two years later, after receiving the last rites with great devotion (he had left the Church more through indifference than conviction). His body was buried in Père Lachaise cemetery, between the graves of BELLINI and CHERUBINI.

However sentimentalized his image in film and fiction, Chopin was a hard-working, tough-minded perfectionist whose very personality was shaped and limited by the pressure of his genius. His musical idiom partakes of the rhythms and melancholy (Lydian) mode of Polish folk music, the *bel canto* vocalisms he had heard in Warsaw opera productions, J. S. BACH's counterpoint and MOZART's formal clarity, the configurations of DUŠEK, and the nocturne contour of the Irishman John Field. All such stimuli, however, were transformed by an act of intense parareligious self-discipline into a distinctive expression that revolutionized piano composition and performance, and in turn unleashed harmonic and melodic forces that were harnessed orchestrally by R. WAGNER and anticipated the edgeless sonorities of DEBUSSY, FAURÉ, and 20th-century atonalists.

Frédéric François Chopin. (Library of Congress)

Bibliography: F. F. CHOPIN, *Selected Correspondence,* collected and annotated by B. E. SYDOW, tr. and ed. A. HEDLEY (London 1962). M. J. E. BROWN, *Chopin: An Index of His Works in Chronological Order* (New York 1960). A. HEDLEY, *Chopin* (New York 1949); *Grove's Dictionary of Music and Musicians,* ed. E. BLOM, 9 v. (5th ed. London 1954) 2:252–267. F. LISZT, *Frederic Chopin,* tr. E. N. WATERS (New York 1963), probably the work of Carolyna von Sayn Wittgenstein. A. BOUCOURECHLIEV, *Chopin: A Pictorial Biography,* tr. E. HYAMS (New York 1963). W. KAHL, *Die Musik in Geschichte und Gegenwart,* ed. F. BLUME (Kassel-Basel 1949–) 2:1218–30. *La Revue musicale,* No. 121 (1931) and No. 229 (1955), Chopin numbers. *La rassegna musicale* (Turin, Oct. 1949), Chopin number. P. H. AZOURY, ed., *Chopin through His Contemporaries: Friends, Lovers, and Rivals* (Westport, Conn. 1999). G. BUSCH-SALMEN, "Bemerkungen zu den Flötenbearbeitungen der Werke Frédéric Chopins," *Tibia: Magazin für Holzbläser,* 20 (1995) 443–452. J. M. CHOMINSKI, "Sonaty Chopina: Twórcze nawiazanie do tradycji w Scherzu Sonaty h-moll," *Studia Muzykologiczne* (1955) 152–275. C. GRABOWSKI, "Les éditions originales françaises des ouvres de Frédéric Chopin," *Revue de Musicologie,* 82 (1996) 213–243. J. KALLBERG, *Chopin at the Boundaries: Sex, History, and Musical Genre* (Cambridge, Mass. 1999). N. MEEÙS, "Question de Méthode: La *Mazurka* Op. 7 No. 5 de Chopin," *Analyse Musicale,* 32 (1993) 58–63. W. C. PETTY, "Chopin and the Ghost of Beethoven," *19th Century Music,* 22 (1999) 281–299. W. D. SUTCLIFFE, "Chopin's Counterpoint: The Largo from the Cello Sonata, Op. 65," *Musical Quarterly,* 83 (1999) 114–133.

[M. E. EVANS]

CHORBISHOP

The title given in the Christian East to a bishop caring for people in the country. The rapid diffusion of Christianity in the first half of the 2d century "not only in the cities but also in the villages" (PLINY, *Ep. ad Traianum* 96) rendered necessary the "institution of bishops for the villages and countryside" (CLEMENT, *I ad Cor.* 42:4). Zoticus, bishop of the village of Comana in Phrygia *c.* 200, who excommunicated the Montanist Maximilla, is the first so named (EUSEBIUS, *Ecclesiastical History* 5:16); and the fact that this sect still had chorbishops in Phrygia in the 4th century (SOZOMEN, *Ibid.* 7:19) lends credence to the belief that they existed in the 2d century when MONTANISM began.

There are numerous mentions of chorbishops in the 3d century: in Bithynia, Asia, Phrygia, Antioch (EUSEBIUS, 7:30), Egypt, and Palestine (*Apost. Church Order* 16). In the religious peace that followed the persecution by the Roman Emperor DECIUS, it was possible to centralize and subordinate the smaller bishoprics under the bishop of the civil metropolis of the province. There was considerable resistance, which left its mark in the canonical legislation of the 4th century (Nicaea I, can. 8; Laodicea, can. 57; Ancyra, can. 13; Antioch, can. 10; and Neocaesarea, can. 14, which cites the example of the subordination of the 70 Disciples).

Canonical institution was given to chorbishops by the bishop of the city (Antioch, can. 10), and they were called coadministrators (Neocaesarea, can. 14); they governed their territory with the bishop's supervision (Laodicea, can. 57), but they were confined to the villages and countryside (Antioch, can. 10). Their powers included the ordination of lectors, subdeacons and exorcists on their own authority, but of deacons and priests only with the consent of the bishop (Antioch, can. 10), which was to be obtained in writing (Ancyra, can. 13). BASIL OF ANCYRA demanded this even for subdeacons (can. 87). The care of the poor was particularly their office (Neocaesarea, can. 14). The institution was opposed (Ancyra, can. 89) because they were accused of not obeying the canons of the Fathers, and it was suggested that they be replaced by priests (Laodicea, can. 57; Sardica, can. 6).

In the 8th century chorbishops could not ordain even lectors without the bishop's consent (Nicaea II, can. 14), and in the 12th century the jurist BALSAMON judged it "senseless to speak of them since they were extinct" [*Syntagma* 3 (1853) 47]. Today the institution has completely disappeared in the Orthodox Churches. Among the Chaldeans and Syrians, there is one per diocese, and he can ordain lectors and subdeacons. Among the Maronites, they serve as auxiliary bishops; among the Melkites, the term chorbishop is a purely honorary title.

In the West, there is no sign of a similar institution until the 8th century, when Pope ZACHARY in a letter to Pepin (747) ordered their subordination to the diocesan bishop in accord with the Synod of Antioch (can. 10). On the Anglo-Saxon mission this system seems to have been an adaptation of the Irish institution of bishops attached to monasteries under the abbot, in which the bishop's sole function was spiritual. The abuse whereby bishops used a chorbishop as an auxiliary to perform his duties in his absence on secular affairs was opposed in the Carolingian reform (Synods of Paris, 829; Meaux, 845). While the system grew in the 9th century, it declined in the 10th and 11th and disappeared in the 12th century.

Bibliography: F. GILLMANN, *Das Institut der Chorbischöfe im Orient* (Munich 1903). T. GOTTLOB, *Der abendländische Chorepiskopat* (Bonn 1928). V. FUCHS, *Der Ordinationstitel . . .* (Bonn 1930). P. JOANNOU, Sacra Congregazione Orientale, *Codificazione orientale, Fonti* 9, v.2, Suppl. (Rome 1964), Index s.v. "Chorepiscopus."

[P. JOANNOU/EDS.]

CHORISANTES

A fanatical sect of wandering men and women, so called because of the obscenely grotesque dance that characterized their religious frenzy. Dance madness was reported as early as the 9th century among certain monks and nuns of Syria, but in Europe the source was probably the old Germanic dances celebrating the summer solstice (*Sommerson-nenwend-Tänze*), which in the Christian Era honored the nativity of John the Baptist (Sankti Johannis Chorea). Chorisantes (called variously *Dansatores, Dansers,* and *Tänzer*) appeared sporadically in the Rhineland and in the Low Countries from the 14th to 16th centuries. Their dance frenzy occurred usually in public places, near or in churches. Since they were regarded as being under DIABOLICAL POSSESSION because of invalid baptism or of baptism administered by a priest living in concubinage, their cure was sought in EXORCISM and in pilgrimages to churches of St. Vitus (hence, St. Vitus's dance).

Bibliography: "Annales Fossenses," *Monumenta Germaniae Historica: Scriptores* (Berlin 1826–) 4:35. P. DE HERENTHALS in É. BALUZE, *Vitae paparum Avenionensium,* ed. G. MOLLAT, 4 v. (Paris 1914–27) 1:466–467. RADULPH DE RIVO, *Gesta pontificum Leodiensium* in *Gesta pontificum Tungrensium, Trajectensium, et Leodiensium,* ed. J. CHAPEAUVILLE, 3 v. (Liège 1612–16) 3:19–22. J. F. K. HECKER, *The Dancing Mania of the Middle Ages,* tr. B. G. BABINGTON (New York 1885). P. FRÉDÉRICQ, *De secten der geselaars en der dansers in de Nederlanden* (Brussels 1899). G. BAREILLE, *Dictionnaire de théologie catholique,* ed. A. VACANT et al., 15 v. (Paris 1903–50; Tables générales 1951–) 4.1:134–136.

[M. F. LAUGHLIN]

CHRISM MASS

At the Chrism Mass the bishop consecrates the chrism (used in baptism, confirmation, and the ordination of priests and bishops) and blesses the oil of catechumens (used in prebaptismal anointing, optional in the case of infants), and the oil of the sick (used for anointing in the Sacrament of the Sick).

The Mass and its texts accent the priesthood, expressing the communion of priests with their bishop. If possible, all priests should take part in it and receive Communion. It is always concelebrated by the bishop with priests from various parts of the diocese. After the homily, priests renew their commitment to priestly service. A proper preface (of the priesthood) is used and the whole congregation may receive Communion under both forms. The Mass is ordinarily on Holy Thursday morning, but if it would be difficult for clergy and people to gather then, it may be held earlier, though near Easter. The texts of the Mass and the rites for blessing the oils are given in the SACRAMENTARY of the Roman Missal with the Holy Thursday liturgy.

[J. DALLEN]

CHRIST

Title of Jesus of Nazareth. The English word Christ is derived from the Latin *Christus* Corresponding to the Greek Χριστός (anointed) that the Septuagint regularly used to translate the Hebrew word *māšîah,* from which the word MESSIAH is derived. In the Old Testament the Israelite king was called *māšîaḥ yhwh,* "the anointed one of Yahweh" (*see* ANOINTING). In the last pre-Christian century the expected savior of the Jews, who was regarded as restoring the throne of David, was called simply *hammāšîaḥ,* "the Anointed One," the Messiah, or in Greek ὁ Χριστός. When the disciples of Jesus recognized Him as the promised savior, they proclaimed Him ὁ Χριστός, "the Christ" (Mk 8.29; Acts 5.42; 9.22; etc., where the article is as necessary in English as it is in Greek). However, when the Greek-speaking pagans began to be converted to Christianity, the Jewish concept of the Messiah meant little to them, and they understood the word Χριστός as one of the Savior's names, Christ—perhaps because it sounded practically the same as the personal name Χρηστός (good, kind). Therefore, in the New Testament Χριστός is often used without the article as the Savior's name, Christ, either alone (Rom 5.6, 8; 6.4, 9; etc.) or together with the name JESUS, either in the form Christ Jesus (Acts 24.24; Rom 3.24; 6.3; etc.) or, especially, in the form Jesus Christ (Mk 1.1; Jn 1.17; Acts 2.38; Rom 1.4, 6, 8; etc.).

Bibliography: R. R. HAWTHORNE, "The Significance of the Name Christ," *Bibliotheca Sacra* 103 (1946) 215–222, 348–362, 453–463. S. V. MCCASLAND, "Christ Jesus," *Journal of Biblical Literature* 65 (1946) 377–383. *Encyclopedic Dictionary of the Bible,* tr. and adap. by L. HARTMAN (New York 1963) 360.

[L. F. HARTMAN]

CHRIST THE KING, FEAST OF

Celebration of the Savior's kingship on the last Sunday of Ordinary Time. It belongs to that class of feasts called idea-feasts, that is, it celebrates no specific event in the history of salvation but rather honors our Savior Himself under the title of king. Pius XI instituted this feast in 1925 to counteract the growing secularism and atheism of his time. Originally scheduled on the last Sunday of October, Pope Paul VI's reform of the Roman calendar transferred the feast to the last Sunday of Ordinary Time. This feast affirms the sovereignty and rule of Christ over persons, families, human society, the state, the whole universe. In particular the feast affirms the messianic kingship of Christ. Jesus is the king who has obtained His sovereignty through His blood. He is the Redeemer king. The original Feast of Christ the King is that of the Ascension. The Feast of Christ the King reinforces the themes of the Ascension, i.e., the exaltation of Christ to the right hand of the Father.

Bibliography: PIUS XI, "Quas primas" (Encyclical, Dec. 11, 1925) *Acta Apostolicae Sedis* 17 (1925) 593–610.

[W. J. O'SHEA/EDS.]

CHRISTADELPHIANS

Brothers of Christ, a sect founded by Dr. John Thomas (1805–71), an English physician who came to the U.S. in 1832. At first he associated with the Campbellites (Disciples of Christ), but disagreed with them on several doctrinal points (*see* CAMPBELL, ALEXANDER; CHRISTIAN CHURCH). He severed his ties with Campbellism in 1834. Between 1844 and 1847 Thomas developed his own theological system, which he maintained was that of primitive Christianity. Branding all existing churches as apostate, he won a few converts in the U.S., Canada, and England. The name Christadelphian was adopted during the Civil War.

Christadelphians reject the doctrine of the Trinity and the divinity of Jesus Christ. They deny eternal punishment and the existence of a personal devil. They believe that Christ will soon ascend David's throne in the Holy Land, gather the 12 tribes of Israel, and rule the world for 1,000 years. Baptism by immersion is considered the sole valid form. Only those who have heard and accepted what the sect considers divine truth will receive the gift of immortality; no others will be raised from the dead. Members of the sect try to disassociate themselves from the secular community; they do not serve in the armed forces, vote, seek public office, join labor unions, or indulge in wordly amusements. They are also opposed to smoking, divorce, and marrying outside of the sect.

Local congregations, called ecclesiae, follow a congregational polity. They employ no salaried clergy; each congregation elects its own "serving brethren" for three-year terms. They handle all liturgical and administrative duties. Christadelphians usually meet for worship in private homes or rented halls. Local congregations hold a weekly communion service on Sunday. They emphasize the study of the Bible and sometimes sponsor public lectures to interest outsiders. The sect maintains no foreign missions, seminaries, or schools, except for a few summer Bible schools. Christadelphian congregations do not recognize an overall ecclesiastical authority; they may join other ecclesiae in loose federations.

Bibliography: B. R. WILSON, *Sects and Society: A Sociological Study of the Elim Tabernacle, Christian Science, and Christadelphians* (Berkeley 1961). C. H. LIPPY, *The Christadelphians in North America* (Lewiston, N.Y. 1989).

[W. J. WHALEN/EDS.]

CHRISTE SANCTORUM DECUS ANGELORUM

An anonymous Latin hymn of five sapphic strophes addressed to Christ, in which the grace of eternal blessedness is sought through the mediation of the angels. The petitions in strophes two to four honor individual angels: Michael, angel of peace; Gabriel, angel of strength; and Raphael, angel-physician of man's health. In strophe five the grace of heaven is requested through the Virgin Mary. Julian lists four forms of the hymn: the original text found in three 11th-century manuscripts; the *Textus receptus;* the Roman Breviary text; and that of the Roman Breviary appendix. In the past, the complete hymn was used at Lauds on May 8 and on September 29. Strophes 1–3–5 and 1–4–5 were sung at Vespers and Matins on the feasts of the Archangels.

Bibliography: J. STEVENSON, ed., *The Latin Hymns of the Anglo-Saxon Church* (Surtees Society 23; Durham 1851) 116. *Analecta hymnica* 50:197–198, for text. J. JULIAN, ed., *A Dictionary of Hymnology* (New York 1957)1:229–230; 2:1556. J. MEARNS, *Early Latin Hymnaries* (Cambridge, Eng. 1913) 21. M. BRITT, ed., *The Hymns of the Breviary and Missal* (new ed. New York 1948) 288–289. J. CONNELLY, *Hymns of the Roman Liturgy* (Westminster MD 1957) 194–195, for tr. J. SZÖVÉRFFY, *Die Annalen der lateinischen Hymnendichtung* (Berlin 1964–65) 1:222, 225.

[M. I. J. ROUSSEAU]

CHRISTIAN

The VATICAN COUNCIL II documents make frequent reference to the kind of life and activity that should characterize those who bear the name "Christian" or "faithful of Christ" (cf. *Apostolicam actuositatem* 31; *Lumen gentium* 15, 42; *Gaudium et spes* 1, 22; *Sacrosanctum Concilium* 9; *Perffectae caritatis* 5). But the Council's expression of the dogmatic and ecclesiological force of the term is particularly noteworthy. That expression is guided by the basic statement: "The Church recognizes that in many ways she is linked with those who, being baptized, are honored with the name of Christian" (*Lumen gentium* 15). Several elaborations appear in the Council documents:

God has gathered together as one all those who in faith look upon Jesus as the author of salvation and the sources of unity and peace, and has established them as the Church, that for each and all she may be the visible sacrament of this saving unity (ibid. 9).

All men are culled to be part of his catholic unity of the People of God, a unity which is harbinger of the universal peace it promotes. And there belong to it or are related to it in various ways, the Catholic faithful as well as all who believe in Christ, and indeed the whole of mankind. For all men are called to salvation by the grace of God (*ibid.* 13).

Men who believe in Christ and have been properly baptized are brought into a certain, though imperfect, communion with the Catholic Church (*Unitatis redintegratio* 3).

All those justified by faith through baptism are incorporated into Christ. They therefore have a right to be honored by the title of Christian, and are properly regarded as brothers in the Lord by the sons of the Catholic Church (*ibid.*).

These statements make the original New Testament use of the term "Christian" important to ecumenism.

The term appears three times, in Acts 11.26, which notes, "it was in Antioch that the disciples were first called 'Christians'"; in Acts 26.8, which quotes King Agrippa's sarcastic reply to Paul, "A little more and your arguments would make a Christian of me"; and in 1 Pt 4.16, where believers are exhorted, "if anyone of you should suffer for being a Christian, then he is not to be ashamed of it." Χριστιανοί is a rare and later synonym for "brothers," "disciples," and "saints," and is derived from χριστός, the Greek equivalent of the Hebrew *Māšîah* (anointed). The Hellenized Latin -ίανος was suffixed to indicate that those assuming the title thus formed were of the household named, the partisans, clients, or slaves of the master or κυριός thus designated. The term Christian (χριστιανός) was formed on an analogy with Ηρωδιανός (Herodian), καισαριανός (partisan of Caesar), and the family of titles bestowed by Christians themselves on heretics, such as Βασιλεδιανοί (followers of Basilides) and Νεστοριανός (Nestorian). The name was formed from the title Christ because confession that Jesus was χριστός (cf. Peter's confession, Mt 16.17) or Lord (the common Pauline formula) epitomized the believer's faith.

The only scriptural evidence regarding the origin of the name is the notice of Acts that it was first used in Antioch, and the text can be taken to mean either that the disciples invented the term or that they accepted a name already current among their pagan neighbors. Though 1

Christians attend a worship service, c. 1982, Detroit. (©David & Peter Turnley/CORBIS)

Pt 4.16 may suggest that opprobrium attached to the name Christian, the context is the writer's advice to those convicted or liable to be convicted before a Roman magistrate, and the shame which the reader is urged to bear gladly is probably that evoked by legal condemnation, especially when such condemnation implied guilt of crimes (atheism, anthropophagy) usually associated with profession of the name by opponents of the Church. There is no clear evidence that the name Christian was bestowed by antagonists of the Church, though by the end of the century it was a title of honor among Christians, a term of opprobrium among pagans.

The meaning of the name, established in part by its derivation, is clarified by consideration of the significance of the title Messiah in Jewish tradition, according to which χριστιανοί are members of the royal household of Gods anointed; and by the Jewish doctrine of names, according to which names effectively represent persons and those taking the name become members of the house-hold. Such meanings were deepened by the theology and practice of the Church, life in Christ being inaugurated by Baptism and perfected by participation in Christ's Body and Blood. That the title Christian effectively expressed the relation between Christ and his disciples is indicated by its occurrence in Pliny's account of the trial of Christians (Ep. 96), and in the *Annals* of Tacitus (15.44).

See Also: INCORPORATION INTO THE CHURCH.

Bibliography: F. J. BICKERMAN, "The Name of Christians." *Harvard Theological Review* 42 (1949) 109–124. R. A. LIPIUS, *Über den Ursprung und den ältesten Gebrauch des Christennamens* (Jena 1873). H. B. MATTLINGLY, "The Origin of the Name *Christiani*," *Journal of Theological Studies* n.s. 9 (1958) 26–37. F. PETERSON, "Chrisianus," in *Miscellanea Giovanni Mercati* 1, *Studi e Testi* 121 (1946) 356–372. C. SPICO, "Ce que signife le titre de chrétien." *Studia theologica* 15 (1961) 68–78.

[J. PATRICK]

CHRISTIAN (THE TERM)

The term "Christian" appears but three times in the New Testament. According to Acts 11.26, "it was in Antioch that the disciples were first called 'Christians.'" In Acts 26.28 King Agrippa interrupts St. Paul's discourse with the ironic remark: "In a short while thou wouldst persuade me to become a Christian." And St. Peter, in 1 Pt 4.16, exhorts that if "one suffer as a Christian, let him not be ashamed, but let him glorify God under this name."

The Greek word Χριστιανός is a composite of the Greek title Χριστός and the Hellenized Latin suffix *-ianus* meaning "belonging to." Because of its mixed origin, the probability of its creation by Antiochean pagans, and St. Peter's allusion to the contempt surrounding it, many scholars conclude that the epithet was originally one of opprobrium. Such a conclusion, however, seems unwarranted because: (1) Latin suffixes were current in Greek and added to Greek words without opprobrius intent, e.g., Ἡρωδιανός (HERODIAN) and Καισαριανός (Caesarean), and (2) St. Luke's emphasis in Acts 11.26 was on the growth of the disciples, who were naturally designated Christians, i.e., partisans of Christ. It was only later, under Greco-Roman persecution, that the name Christian became the object of pagan hatred, while loyal Christians gloried in the title, so descriptive of their total commitment to the service of Christ.

Bibliography: E. J. BICKERMAN, "The Name of Christians," *Harvard Theological Review* 42 (Cambridge, MA 1949) 109–124. C. SPICQ, "Ce que signifie le titre de chrétien," *Studia Theologica* 15 (1961) 68–78. G. RICCIOTTI, *The Act of the Apostles,* tr. L. E. BYRNE (Milwaukee 1958) 179–180, 375. *Encyclopedic Dictionary of the Bible,* translated and adapted by L. HARTMAN (New York, 1963) 360–361.

[W. F. DICHARRY]

CHRISTIAN AND MISSIONARY ALLIANCE

Both a Protestant denomination in the evangelical tradition and a worldwide missionary society that grew out of the work of the Rev. Albert B. Simpson. A native of Canada, he served as a Presbyterian minister for 18 years, leaving the pulpit of a New York City church in 1881 to embark on an independent evangelistic program aimed at reaching the masses. Simpson at first preached in tents and halls and on street corners. In 1887 he organized twin societies at a convention in Old Orchard, Maine. The Christian Alliance emphasized home missions, while the Evangelical Missionary Alliance concentrated on the foreign field. The two associations were combined in 1897 to form the present Christian and Missionary Alliance. The founder died in 1919. Prior to 1974, it was a loose alliance of local congregations. In 1974, the alliance was formally constituted as a church denomination.

The Alliance sponsors missionaries overseas, in addition to local pastors, evangelists, and church workers in North America. Starting out in 1884 with a five-member team to the Congo, the Alliance's missionary outreach comprised more than 1,000 missionaries in 49 countries by the end of the 20th century. Alliance missionaries preach and teach worldwide and have established self-sustaining and self-governing national churches in all its mission fields.

The theology of Alliance churches is conservative, and based on a literal interpretation of the Bible. The sect practices the anointing with oil for bodily healing and proclaims that Christ's Second Coming may be imminent (*see* PAROUSIA). Local congregations or branches are identified as Alliance churches or sometimes as Alliance Gospel Tabernacles.

Bibliography: H. D. AYER, *The Christian and Missionary Alliance: An Annotated Bibliography of Textual Sources* (Lanham, Md. 2001).

[W. J. WHALEN/EDS.]

CHRISTIAN ANTHROPOLOGY

Christian anthropology is the branch of theological study that investigates the origin, nature, and destiny of humans and of the universe in which they live. Reflection upon human origins and destiny yields the doctrines of CREATION and ESCHATOLOGY. Concrete human existence is studied within its various contexts and systems—as personal and social, as unfolding within history, as rooted in networks of communities and traditions, as situated within political, economic, technological, and cultural systems, and as embedded within the material ecology of Earth and the cosmos. Christian anthropology offers perspectives on the constitutive elements and experiences of human personhood—bodiliness and spirit, freedom and limitation, solitude and companionship, work and play, suffering and death, and, in specifically theological terms, sin and grace.

A comprehensive account of the situation of the human necessitates the broad range of topics that are taken up under the rubric of Christian anthropology. On the level of the human race as a whole, the Christian tradition envisions humanity's situation as progressing through a sequence of distinct states of existence, namely, the state of being created by God, the state of fallenness brought on by the misuse of human freedom, the state of redemption made available by the missions of Christ and the Spirit in history, and the future state of eschatological fulfillment for which the human race hopes. Thus human existence in its condition as originally created passes through stages of distortion, redemption, and hope for perfection. Correspondingly, individual persons come to discover within themselves the dimensions of creatureliness, fallenness, redeemedness, and hopefulness that simultaneously constitute their humanity from a Christian perspective. The entire trajectory that begins with creation and ends with the realization of a promised eschaton makes up what is referred to in the Christian tradition as the divine ECONOMY (*oikonomia*), that is, the plan or design by which God governs, manages, administers the affairs of the created "household" (from *oikos,* "house," and *nomos,* "rule" or "law").

Christian anthropology is distinct from the secular disciplines of anthropology, such as cultural anthropology, in that it moves beyond the descriptive and empirical toward the prescriptive and the normative. In other words, Christian thought does not simply consider how people actually live, but also makes claims about how people could and ought to live. The nontheological fields of study contribute enormously to the understanding of the human, and Christian anthropology builds upon their discoveries, integrating them into an overarching vision that goes beyond the methodological boundaries of anthropology as a secular discipline.

The Human Person. The Christian tradition has from the beginning appropriated the concept of the human person as created in the image and likeness of God (Gn 1:27). The *imago Dei* has been and continues to be a cornerstone in particular of Catholic theological anthropology. From a Christian viewpoint the interpretation of this concept is decidedly christological and eschatological. That is, Jesus of Nazareth manifests in tangible and visible human form the authentic and fulfilled *imago Dei,* to which humans are called to be conformed in a gradual process that will reach its culmination only in the eschaton.

The revelation of divine personhood in Jesus Christ constitutes the norm for what human personhood is called to fully become. An understanding of divine personhood is necessarily Trinitarian, for it is only in the mutuality and reciprocity of the giving and receiving of love among the persons of the Triune God that the full scope of personhood is manifested. The fundamental elements of personhood may be designated as *receptivity* and *donativity.* Only in an authentic communion of persons (*communio personarum*) can these capabilities be realized.

Receptivity refers to the capacity and openness of a person to receive from others the gifts that they offer, birth spiritual and material, and above all the gift of their very selves. Donativity, or generativity, is the corresponding and reciprocal capacity to give to others and to make a gift of oneself to others. It is only in the pattern or rhythm of receptivity and donativity that genuine personhood can be realized.

For the Christian, the prime expression of this rhythm is found in the relationship between Jesus Christ and the God who is His Father. In His earthly life Jesus reveals the fullness of self-giving or donativity by pouring out His life for others. In the gift of the Eucharist and through His passion and death Jesus' self-giving reaches its greatest realization. At the same time, His capacity to make a gift of Himself to others is grounded in the fact that He has first received everything that He has and is from the Father. But the receptivity and donativity of the earthly Christ are grounded in the eternal rhythm of the mutual relationship between the Father and the Son, in which the Father "generates" or "begets" the Son by a complete "giving away" of Himself to the Son. So extensive is this donativity of the Father that the Son is truly "one in being" with Him. In turn, so to speak, the Son offers all that He is back to the Father, who thus "receives" His own full identity as Father precisely in this mutual relationship with the Son. And the Spirit then is realized as the Spirit "of the Father and the Son," that is, the bond of mutual giving and receiving that is so complete as to stand as a distinctly existing entity in relation to Father and Son.

If the essential dynamic of Trinitarian life and personhood is the mutual giving and receiving of the Father and the Son, so for human beings, made "in the image and likeness of God," true personhood is to be found to the extent that this same rhythm and pattern of receptivity and donativity is embraced and lived out.

The specific ordering of these capacities to one another is a crucial element of Christian anthropology. The receptive dimension of personhood is prior to the donative or generative; that is, what comes first in the order of human experience is the receiving, indeed, of existence itself. All human acts of giving or donating flow from the prior reception of capabilities, charisms, talents, opportunities—in a word, of grace. This point has been defended at crucial moments of theological development in the Christian tradition. Thus Paul is at pains to proclaim the priority of the gift of faith with respect to the merit of good works. Likewise, AUGUSTINE, in his disputations with the Pelagian movement, argued for the absolute precedence of grace received purely as gift relative to any human initiative. Again, in the controversies of the Reformation, debates concerning the relationship of justification to sanctification reflected the importance of achieving an adequate articulation of the receptive and donative elements of anthropology. The Catholic perspective, as expressed in the Council of Trent's Decree on Justification, holds for the prevenience of the grace of JUSTIFICATION while simultaneously insisting on the necessity of human cooperation in the movement toward holiness.

Contemporary theological reflection continues to address these issues. While in general there has been a greater emphasis on human agency and the categories of work, labor, and creativity in more recent anthropologies, there have also been fresh articulations of the priority of the receptive element of personhood to all human action. Thus, while the notion of the human person as "created co-creator" has gained currency as an interpretation of the *imago Dei,* so theologians such as Hans von BALTHASAR have argued for the primacy of receptivity as a counterweight to the tendency of modern ideologies to view persons primarily through what they do, what they make, what they produce. Vatican II's *Gaudium et spes* (*GS*) represents the most extensive treatment of theological anthropology in the recent teaching documents of the Catholic Church. Subsequently, Pope JOHN PAUL II, in the wide sweep of his writings, has drawn on the teaching of *GS* to highlight specific aspects of anthropology. In particular, two passages from *GS* appear with regularity in the various encyclicals and letters of John Paul. First, he frequently cites the passage at the beginning of n. 22: "It is only in the mystery of the Word made flesh that the mystery of man truly becomes clear." With similar frequency he cites the final passage of n. 24: "Man can fully discover his true self only in a sincere giving of himself."

In any given time and situation the precise interplay of these elements may vary, but, for the Christian, the Augustinian truth that humans are "made good in order to do the good" grounds the Aristotelian truth that humans "do the good in order to become good."

It is the mutual sharing of goods and of persons that establishes the possibility of *communio* within the Church as a reflection of the *communio* of the divine persons. This "gift exchange" takes place among persons in a given local church, among local churches as such, and, indeed, among the churches in the diverse cultures of the world as reflective of the unity and diversity of the universal Church. If human identity is fundamentally rooted in the reception and giving of gifts, then it becomes clear that only in a matrix or network of reciprocal relationships do individuals become persons in the fullest sense of the term. Furthermore, the identity of the Church is precisely found in *missio,* in its mission to the world, which ultimately is to broaden the circles of *communio* to their most inclusive extent, embracing the entire human family.

Nature and Grace Reconceived. Some theologians have charged that the traditional discussion of NATURE and GRACE at times led to unwarranted separation between the "order of creation" and the "order of redemption," that is, between those realities arising from creation itself and those realities brought about by the missions of the Word and the Spirit in the world. That which is created is already absolutely gratuitous; therefore, it is more appropriate to speak of "nature" as a form of grace, as "the first grace" or "the grace of creation," while those gifts that come specifically through the missions of Word and Spirit may be termed "the second grace" or "the grace of redemption."

Any number of attributes may be considered to be part of the innate makeup of human persons as created. The attempt to define human nature as such has often focused on those characteristics that are unique to the species, such as rationality, FREEDOM, and the use of SYMBOLS and language, and that differentiate the human from all other forms of created reality. More broadly, it is helpful to think of the array of "anthropological constants," that is, those universal categories that are instantiated in each particular human being in a unique constellation, such as "situatedness" in history and culture, ethnicity, and bodiliness, as well as universal categories of experience such as suffering, contingency, and moral responsibility. The categories of receptivity and donativity as discussed above do not replace this wider consideration of the makeup of the human, but they are the more relevant predicates in a specifically theological anthropology.

An additional element that is specific to human existence and nature is the presence of normative ideals of living and action, which give rise to a distinction between human nature in the empirical or descriptive sense and human nature in the normative or prescriptive sense. This distinction grounds the possibility and, indeed, the actuality that human existence will fall short of what it could and should be. This reality in turn grounds, from the Christian perspective, the human need for redemption or salvation, both from the nonmoral or "ontic" evils and suffering of a finite created order and from the specifically moral evils that arise from the sinful misuse of human capabilities.

The Christian proclaims that human existence is further qualified by the possibilities opened up through the activity of Jesus Christ and the Holy Spirit in history. Thus, the original condition of humanity as given in creation itself is enveloped in a larger horizon of divine activity that reveals the full scope of the divine economy and the destiny of the human race. Quite consistently from its beginnings the Christian tradition has articulated its understanding of the effects of these further graces in two distinct but intertwined threads of thought. The first effect of these graces is described as redeeming, healing, justifying, liberating—that is, grace effects a *freedom from* those powers and forces that enslave or bind the human capacity to act. The second effect of these graces, building upon the first, is described as divinizing, elevating, sanctifying, creating—that is, grace effects a *freedom for,* an empowerment of human beings to move toward their ultimate fulfillment of life in communion with God. The grace of Jesus Christ both overcomes the negative effects of sin and evil *and* actualizes the full range of possibilities latent in the original act of creation.

A brief survey of Christian theological history reveals the continuity of this double designation of the effects of grace. In the patristic era, Western theologies gave particular attention to grace as redeeming human existence from the condition described through the images of slavery, indebtedness, woundedness, and guilt. By comparison, Eastern theologies more readily spoke of the grace of Christ as making possible the *theosis* or divinization of the human being. Again, in the Scholastic era, THOMAS AQUINAS spoke of both *gratia sanans* (the grace that heals) and *gratia elevans* (the grace that elevates). The corresponding categories more often utilized in the period of the Reformation are *justification* (the initial establishment of a right relationship with God) and *sanctification* (the ongoing development and flourishing of that relationship). Finally, contemporary theological language more readily employs the terms "liberating" and "creating" to name this twofold gratuity brought about by Christ.

It may be observed that the twofold rhythm of grace found in the order of redemption has a certain correspondence with the receptive and donative capacities given to human beings as created. That grace which redeems, heals, justifies, and liberates more properly corresponds to the receptive dimension, in that it is gift in the absolute sense of having no connection to the merit or value of any human work or initiative. In traditional terms, it is *operative grace,* that is, "what God does in us without us." Subsequently, that grace which divinizes, elevates, sanctifies, and creates corresponds to the donative dimension, in that it more directly calls forth human action as a partner. Again, in traditional terms, this is *co-operative grace,* that is, "what God does in us with us." Thus, the maxim that "grace builds on nature" is illustrated, if receptivity and donativity are considered potentialities given to humans in creation that are fully enabled and empowered by a corresponding twofold effect of grace in the order of redemption.

It will be only from the point of view of the eschaton that the full scope of the divine *oikonomia* will be re-

Mother Pauline von Mallinckrodt, founder of the Sisters of Christian Charity.

vealed. Only at that point will the full contours of the human movement through createdness, fallenness, redeemedness, and consummation become apparent. Christian faith rests on the conviction that the resurrection of Christ represents the sign and guarantee that effectively moves human history toward its fulfillment.

See Also: MAN; PERSON.

Bibliography: H. DE LUBAC, *A Brief Catechesis on Nature and Grace* (San Francisco 1984). A. O. GRAFF, ed., *In the Embrace of God: Feminist Approaches to Theological Anthropology* (Maryknoll, N.Y. 1995). POPE JOHN PAUL II, *The Theology of the Body According to John Paul II: Human Love in the Divine Plan* (Boston 1997). J. M. LAPORTE, *Patience and Power: Grace for the First World* (Mahwah, N.J. 1988). B. LONERGAN, "Healing and Creating in History," *A Third Collection,* ed. F. E. CROWE (Mahwah, N.J. 1985). K. RAHNER, "The Order of Redemption within the Order of Creation," *The Christian Commitment* (New York 1963).

[M. W. PELZEL]

CHRISTIAN CHARITY, SISTERS OF

Also known as the Daughters of the Blessed Virgin Mary of the Immaculate Conception (abbreviation: SCC, Official Catholic Directory #0660). Founded in Germany in 1849 by Pauline von Mallinckrodt, the daughter of a

German nobleman, for the care of the blind and neglected children of Paderborn. Within 20 years the activity of the growing community had spread to include elementary and secondary education in 16 European institutions. When Bismarck's May Laws forced religious educators to close their schools in Germany, Mother Pauline was able to send her religious to North and South America, in response to requests for teaching sisters. On May 4, 1873, a group of eight arrived in the harbor of New Orleans, La. In the autumn of the following year, a group of 12 made their way across the Andes by mule into Chile in South America. Subsequently, the sisters established foundations in the U.S., South America and other parts of Europe.

The spirit of Christian charity provides the particular rule and spirit of the community, following the example of the foundress. Although founded originally for the care of needy children and orphans, the congregation has expanded its ministries to encompass all manner of apostolic work, with teaching, childcare, youth ministry, catechetics, hospital work and nursing as its chief activities. The generalate is in Rome. In the U.S., the congregation has two provinces—the Eastern Province (headquarters in Mendham, N.J.), and the Western Province (headquarters in Wilmette, Ill.).

[R. WESLEY/EDS.]

CHRISTIAN CHURCH (DISCIPLES OF CHRIST)

The Disciples of Christ form the largest religious body of purely American origin, promoting a noncreedal form of Christianity in the U.S.

The founder of the Disciples of Christ, Thomas CAMPBELL, discouraged by the opposition his efforts met in Ireland, came to the U.S. in 1807, beginning his ministry in Philadelphia as a Presbyterian. Within two years he was resisted by the presbyteries, especially after his famous *Declaration and Address*, issued "to all that love our Lord Jesus Christ in all sincerity, throughout all the churches." Its main tenet was that the Church of Christ upon earth should be one, "essentially, intentionally and constitutionally," and consists of "all those in every place that profess their faith in Christ and obedience to him in all things according to the Scriptures." The constitution of this Church of Christ, said Campbell, is not a creedal statement or confession of faith but the New Testament itself. Sectarian churches have no right to impose on their members as articles of faith anything not expressly taught in the Bible. Even inferences or deductions from the New Testament are not to be held binding on the con-

science of individuals unless they are accepted by the persons themselves. Just as in apostolic times "a manifest attachment to our Lord Jesus Christ in faith, holiness, and charity was the original criterion of Christian character," so in the united Church envisioned by Campbell, this alone should be "the foundation and cement of Christian unity." Campbell was joined by his son Alexander, who came to America (1809) to share and later carry on the work of his father. They organized the Christian Association of Washington, Pa. (1810), the first local church of the new denomination. Soon after a crisis arose on the manner of administering baptism. Deciding that the ordinance must be by immersion, father and son had themselves rebaptized by a Baptist minister. For 17 years the Christian Association operated as a branch of the BAPTISTS, until the younger Campbell's anticreedalism aroused a storm of protest.

Meanwhile the Campbellites were partially merged with another noncreedal group, called the Christians, who were founded by Barton Stone, a former Presbyterian minister. They combined forces at Lexington, Ky., in 1832. When the question of a new name arose, Stone preferred keeping "Christians," but Campbell favored "Disciples," with the result that today both titles are used. The local organization, however, is generally called a Christian Church or a Church of Christ. As members and churches multiplied, the need of organization was recognized and the first national convention was held at Cincinnati in 1849. The body flourished at home and abroad; by the end of the 19th century, the Disciples counted more than a million members and had missionaries in Asia and Africa. They even weathered the Civil War without division. A conservative group, however, gradually withdrew because of a conviction that missionary societies and instrumental music in public worship were alike unscriptural. These separatists became known as the Churches of Christ.

In 1968, the Disciples of Christ reorganized themselves into a threefold ecclesial polity known as the "three manifestations"—local, regional and general. The local church or congregation is the basic unit of church, with autonomy in its own affairs. The congregations are grouped into regions, with its own administrative machinery, support mechanisms for local congregations, and clergy licensing procedures. At the highest level, the General Assembly meets every two years. Among the best known Disciples' publications is the *Christian Century,* founded 1894.

Bibliography: B. A. ABBOTT, *The Disciples: An Interpretation* (St. Louis 1924). J. M. FLANAGAN, ed., *What We Believe* (rev. ed. St. Louis 1960). A. W. FORTUNE, *Adventuring with Disciple Pioneers* (St. Louis 1942). W. E. GARRISON and A. T. DEGROOT, *The Dis-*

ciples of Christ: A History (rev. ed. St. Louis 1958). H. E. SHORT, *Doctrine and Thought of the Disciples of Christ* (St. Louis 1951).

[J. A. HARDON/EDS.]

CHRISTIAN DOCTRINE, SISTERS OF OUR LADY OF

(Abbreviation: RCD, Official Catholic Directory #3080), a congregation begun in 1908 by Marion Gurney (Mother Marianne of Jesus) in New York, N.Y., to assist pastors in teaching religion to public school students and adults. Miss Gurney, a convert from Anglicanism, was a graduate of Wellesley College. A pioneer social service director, she was cofounder of a catechetical normal training school at St. Rose's Settlement in New York City, and secretary of the city's first Confraternity of Christian Doctrine at Good Counsel Church in 1902. The work of the congregation began in 1910 when Abp. John Farley invited the sisters to assist the underprivileged by providing cultural, educational, and recreational benefits. On Cherry Street they opened Madonna House, a settlement, nursery, and kindergarten. Volunteer and paid workers helped the sisters maintain a wide program of social services. The congregation is engaged in education, childcare, catechetics, parochial work, social services, and counseling. The congregation's headquarters is in Suffern, N.Y.

[M. C. BERRETTI/EDS.]

CHRISTIAN DOCTRINE (NANCY), SISTERS OF

A religious congregation with papal approval (1886, 1929), founded in France *c.* 1700. The sisters, who take simple perpetual vows, are known also as Vatelottes, after their founder, Abbé Jean Baptiste Vatelot, who, together with three of his own sisters, opened a school for girls in his family home at Bruley, near Toul. From this institution the congregation gradually developed in France. During the French Revolution the religious adopted secular dress in order to continue their work; they later reorganized and established their motherhouse at Nancy (1804). New foundations were made throughout eastern France, and in Belgium (1833), Luxembourg (1840), Algeria (1841), Italy (1903), and Morocco (1911). After World War II the sisters expanded to the then Belgian Congo (Zaire). The congregation is engaged primarily in the education of girls and in various forms of hospital and nursing activities.

[A. J. ENNIS/EDS.]

CHRISTIAN EDUCATION, RELIGIOUS OF

(Abbreviation: RCE, Official Catholic Directory #3410), a congregation of sisters following the Rule of St. Augustine. They were founded in 1817 by Louis François Martin Lafosse (1772–1839) to work for the restoration of the Catholic faith in Échauffour, Normandy, a small parish ruined during the French Revolution. The community began with four religious who dedicated themselves to Christian education, especially in primary and secondary schools. Success at Échauffour and extension of the mission to neighboring parishes necessitated revision of the original constitutions. Subsequent petition for establishment as a papal institute was granted by Rome in 1893, and final approval of the constitutions came in 1931. Civic approbation of the work of the congregation, an early instance of which was the invitation of the government to found a teacher's college in France in 1838, encouraged steady expansion, but the hostile policies of a later anticlerical government (1903) caused withdrawal to houses already established in England (1889) and Belgium (1902). In 1905 the sisters began their mission in the U.S. The U.S. provincial headquarters is located in Milton, MA. The generalate is in France.

[A. M. MCNAMARA/EDS.]

CHRISTIAN ENDEAVOR SOCIETY

An international, interdenominational Protestant youth organization founded by Rev. Francis Clark of the Williston Congregational Church, Portland, Maine, "to make young people more useful in the service of God and more efficient in church work thereby establishing them in their faith and the practise of the gospel." Clark, desiring to provide an avenue of expression for the religious life of young people and to give them an opportunity to perform tasks for the church, organized a local youth society, which was quickly duplicated in many Protestant congregations across the nation and beyond. An international and interdenominational organization was formed in 1885 called the United Society of Christian Endeavor, with Clark as its first president. In 1927 the official name was changed to the International Society of Christian Endeavor.

The basic principles of the society are confession of Christ, service for Christ, loyalty to the church, and Christian fellowship. Any Protestant youth organization that accepts these and adopts the name Christian Endeavor is admitted to all the privileges of the international society. Individuals are received into local societies on the basis of their commitment to the Endeavorer's pledge:

"Trusting in the Lord Jesus Christ for strength, I promise Him I will strive to do whatever He would have me do." The local societies administer courses in religious training and leadership, provide for devotional meetings and social activities, and organize welfare and other Christian causes for their members. The international society holds conventions and conferences for youths of various denominations and nationalities, unites cooperating societies in interchurch programs, and joins with its constituent churches and other religious agencies in common enterprises for the Christian cause and human welfare. Headquarters for the international society was originally located in Boston, Mass., until 1946 when it moved to Columbus, Ohio.

[T. HORGAN/EDS.]

CHRISTIAN FAMILY MOVEMENT

The Christian Family Movement (CFM) consists primarily of married couples who act together on matters affecting not only their own but other families. Its basic unit is made up of five to seven married couples, usually from the same parish. They meet regularly in each others' homes to discuss the application of Scripture to their lives and to investigate a social problem or situation. It originated out of a desire to understand and implement the role of the laity in the Church and out of a conviction that couples could assist each other in enhancing married and family life, as well as in contributing to the betterment of society. CFM's meaning and purpose found endorsement in the documents of Vatican Council II. The couples act individually or with fellow members to affect some situation locally, nationally, or even internationally. The CFM groups are concerned not only with the betterment of their own family situations but also with the life of families everywhere.

The origins of CFM were in a men's Catholic Action group started in Chicago in 1943 and transformed into a couples' organization in 1947. Two years later a national coordinating committee was formed for the exchange of ideas and experiences. Since then groups have been established in most of the dioceses of the U.S. and in Canada. Similar groups, often using the same program, have been developed in North America, Latin America, Africa, Asia, Europe, and Oceania.

From its beginning CFM adopted and used the "Jocist technique" or social inquiry method of Observe—Judge—Act (attributed to Canon Joseph CARDIJN of Belgium and the Young Catholic Workers). In this method each individual observes and gathers facts on a particular problem; the problem is judged by the group; then a prac-

tical action is agreed to be taken. The distinctive characteristic of CFM is the actions taken by its members on social issues such as international life, politics, and family life. The national organization encourages and assists in these areas principally by providing "Social Inquiry" programs. Annual programs and various publications, including the monthly bulletin *Act,* are prepared by the coordinating committee and issued from national headquarters in Evansville, Illinois.

Another characteristic of the national movement has been the generation of several new organizations. In 1966, the International Confederation of Christian Family Movements (ICCFM) was founded to coordinate CFM in some 50 nations. The Foundation for International Cooperation (FIC) grew out of a CFM inquiry on foreign students. FIC fosters student exchanges and international family-to-family visiting. The concept of creative use of leisure led to CFMV—The Christian Family Mission Vacation. CFM created the Marriage Encounter in Spain. CFM in the U.S. sponsored in 1968 a tour by more than 100 Spanish couples and chaplains, who conducted encounters for Spanish-speaking couples throughout the country. The first Marriage Encounter in English was given following a CFM convention at Notre Dame in 1967.

From its inception the movement saw itself as broadly Christian and open to all Christians. There was a small but significant Protestant membership particularly in Episcopal Church parishes. In 1968 the executive committee formally declared that CFM was indeed open to all Christians and took measures to encourage expansion in Protestant Churches. Participation by Protestants slowly increased among members, committees, leaders, and staff.

CFM is administered by a board of directors comprising official couples and contact couples from the various geographical regions across the U.S. A national office is maintained in Evansville, Ill. Records and documents of CFM are available at the library of the University of Notre Dame, Notre Dame, Indiana.

[P. AND P. CROWLEY/D. AND R. MALDOON/EDS.]

CHRISTIAN MOTHERS, ARCHCONFRATERNITY OF

Originated in various parts of France, especially in Lille, when mothers began to gather to pray with and for one another and for their children, to discuss their problems, and to advise one another regarding the Christian rearing of their children. The movement gradually solidified, and on May 1, 1850, the first conference of Christian

Mothers was held in Lille, under the leadership of Louise Josson de Bilhem, a court official. After the mothers received episcopal recognition for their growing organization, the society grew rapidly throughout France and neighboring countries. By 1963 there were six archconfraternities: Notre Dame de Sion Chapel, Paris (1850); San Agostino, Rome (1863); Church of St. Giles, Regensburg (1871); Church of St. Augustine (now known as Our Lady of the Angels), Pittsburgh, Pennsylvania. (1881); Church of St. Barbara, Cracow (1913); Abbatial Church of the Order of St. Benedict, Einsiedeln, Switzerland (1944).

The society was introduced into the United States by the Capuchin Friars and on Jan. 16, 1881, the Confraternity of Christian Mothers of St. Augustine Church, Pittsburgh, Pennsylvania, was raised to the rank of an archconfraternity with the right of affiliating other confraternities wherever the ordinary approved. Since 1881 some 3,500 confraternities have been affiliated with the Pittsburgh archconfraternity.

Bibliography: E. QUINN, *Archconfraternities, Archsodalities and Primary Unions with a Supplement on the Archconfraternity of Christian Mothers* (Catholic University of America CLS 421; Washington 1962).

[B. ROLL]

CHRISTIAN OF PRUSSIA

Cistercian missionary and first bishop of Prussia; d. Poland, Dec. 4, 1245. Christian went to preach to the pagan Prussians from the Cistercian monastery in Poland. INNOCENT III named him missionary bishop (1215), and he was consecrated in Rome. HONORIUS III, who gave strong moral support to the Cistercian mission, gave Christian the privilege of a metropolitan and the right to erect episcopal sees and to consecrate bishops. He was thus at the center of the Cistercian missionary activity in Prussia. Conrad of Masovia, who surrendered to him the Kulmerland as an independent territory, assisted him, and the KNIGHTS OF DOBRIN (*Milites Christi*), at his instigation, fought the pagan Prussians. In 1230 Christian enfeoffed the Order of TEUTONIC KNIGHTS of Kulmerland without prejudice to his episcopal rights, but the order did not respect Christian's rights. When he was captured by the Prussians in 1233, nothing was done to liberate him. His missionary aim, to convert the Prussians without destroying their national independence and to train a native clergy, was in total opposition to the desires of the Teutonic Knights, who wanted to subjugate and Germanize the Prussians. The Teutonic Knights therefore cut the Cistercians out of the mission and had it handed over by the pope to the DOMINICANS. When Christian succeeded

in ransoming himself in the winter of 1239 to 1240 he immediately resumed the fight for his rights, but without success. Shortly afterward he withdrew into a Polish Cistercian monastery. Though he became irascible in his old age, his aims were always pure and above reproach. His objective was to bring to the Prussians the "freedom of the children of God."

Bibliography: A. M. ZIMMERMANN, *Kalendarium Beneditinum: Die Heiligen und Seligen des Benediktinerorderns und seiner Zweige* (Metten 1933–38) 3:393. M. TUMLER, *Der Deutsche Orden im Werden, Wachsen und Wirken bis 1400* (Vienna 1955). A. TRILLER, *Neue deutsche Biographie* (Berlin 1953–) 3:230. H. SCHMAUCH, *Lexikon für Theologie und Kirche*, ed. J. HOFER and K. RAHNER (2d, new ed. Freiburg 1957–65) 2:1123–24. S. M. SZACHERSKA, *Opactwo cysterkie w Spetalu a Misja pruska* (Warsaw 1960). J. M. CANIVEZ, *Dictionnaire d'histoire et de géographie ecclésiastiques*, ed. A. BAUDRILLART et al. (Paris 1912–) 12:772.

[C. SPAHR]

CHRISTIAN OF STABLO

Benedictine monk and exegete, one of the foremost among the lesser figures of the CAROLINGIAN RENAISSANCE; b. Burgundy, or Aquitania, first half of 9th century; d. Stablo (Stavelot), lower Lorraine (now in Belgium) after 880. He was one of the few scholars of his day who had a practiced knowledge of Greek. His only substantial work known today, however, is a commentary on St. Matthew (*c.* 865). Although addressed to beginners, it is interesting because of its careful explanation of the grammatical Biblical sense and its attempts to illustrate the text by topical allusions. A study of the commentary illumines the 9th century's methods of compiling scriptural expositions and of monastic teaching (*see* EXEGESIS, BIBLICAL, 6). Christian set forth the historical or literal meaning, rather than the allegorical, because he held that history was the foundation of the understanding of Scripture. The explanations of difficult passages are indicative of Christian's excellence as a teacher, independent spirit, and deep knowledge of the Bible. Very little has been written about Christian, and a critical edition of his commentary is needed to take the place of Migne's (*Patrologia Latina*, 106:1259–1520) inaccurate edition. J. Lebon has located some of Christian's MSS, which should help to make a critical edition easier to prepare.

Bibliography: J. LEBON, *Revue d'histoire ecclésiastique* 9 (1908) 491–496. M. L. W. LAISTNER, "A Ninth-Century Commentator on the Gospel of Matthew," *Harvard Theological Review* 20 (1927) 129–149. C. SPICQ, *Esquisse d'une histoire de l'exégese latine au moyen âge* (Paris 1944) 49–51. M. MANITIUS, *Geschichte der lateinischen Literatur des Mittelalters* (Munich 1911–31) 1:431–433. E. DUMMLER, *Sitzungsberichte der Deutschen (Preussichen to 1948) Akademie der Wissenschaften zu Berlin* 2 (1890)

935–952. F. DRESSLER, *Lexikon für Theologie und Kirche*, ed. J. HOFER and K. RAHNER (2d, new ed. Freiburg 1957–65) 2:1124.

[J. J. MAHONEY]

CHRISTIAN PHILOSOPHY

St. AUGUSTINE was the first, it seems, to have employed the expression Christian philosophy to designate the teaching proposed to men by the Church and to distinguish it from the different wisdoms taught by the philosophers of antiquity. Before him, however, the term philosophy had been used by a number of Christian writers, ever since TATIAN, as a means of establishing contact with the speculative and practical thought that was widespread in the cultivated world in which the newborn Christianity developed. During the Middle Ages, the relationship between faith and reason was made more precise, to the extent that natural intelligence began to be seen by theologians as autonomous in the domain assigned to it by God. In modern times, philosophy claimed a growing independence, aiming at forming a body of doctrine as free from nonrational influences as possible and thus, in effect, opposing itself to the teaching of revelation. The relations between philosophy and Christianity have thus undergone changes in the course of time. It was, though, only in the mid-20th century that the notion of Christian philosophy became an object of explicit discussion. The exposition that follows reconsiders the essential definitions that explain a priori the difficulties contained in the idea of a Christian philosophy and makes as precise as possible the meaning of the debate; it then proposes a clarification, in brief résumé, of the sense of the history of philosophy that is present within Christian revelation and a concluding summary of the significance of Christian philosophy in present and future thought.

Difficulties in the Notion. A complex concept expressed by the union of a substantive and an adjective is definable only if both terms have a precise and relatively fixed signification. If, on the contrary, one or other of the terms conveys different (and nonequivocal) meanings, certain problems necessarily pose themselves by reason of the variable relationships that ensue between the two terms and thereby affect the subject of the expression taken as a whole. Thus it is profitable to examine here each of the terms that compose the expression Christian philosophy and the problems that pose themselves a priori with respect to its subject.

Philosophy. By this word one may mean (1) any doctrine that proposes a WISDOM destined to conduct men toward their end by making known the origin and destination of all things, whether that wisdom be acquired naturally or revealed by God. Again, one may mean, more precisely, (2) an ensemble of truths discoverable by the human mind left to its own devices, without, however, excluding the influence of nonrational data. It is generally admitted that Greek philosophy, even when it ended in an encounter with Christianity—to which, in the persons of its last representatives, it opposed itself—had this conception of philosophical wisdom. Finally, one may mean, in a yet stricter sense, (3) a body of doctrine that possesses the coherence and certitude proper to the sciences, as these are understood in the modern sense. Philosophy, in such an understanding, would proceed from a simple and absolutely certain point of departure to draw out the entire sequence of its propositions in a necessary order. This conception has reigned since René DESCARTES under the various forms of RATIONALISM and POSITIVISM. The ideal of philosophy as a rigorous science adequately defines this conception of philosophical knowledge.

The Adjective Christian. There must also be noted a diversity of meaning concerning the adjective Christian. This results from the manner in which the Catholic Church, on the one hand, and the disciples of Martin LUTHER, on the other, conceive the relationship between nature and grace, granting the reality of sin and of its corruptive effects. On the one hand are the efforts at synthesis that Catholicism continually promotes by reason of its teaching concerning man's intelligence—an intelligence, it holds, that original sin was unable to alter substantially and that grace sustains and restores according to need. On the other is a tendency in Lutheran thought to divorce reason from grace, which is hostile to all that might resemble, proximately or remotely, an intrusion of nature into the order of salvation by faith.

The Problem. These reflections, summary though they be, allow one to eliminate at the outset two extreme positions, both negative, concerning the notion of Christian philosophy. The first, founded on the notion of philosophy in sense (3), rejects a priori—as contradictory to the true notion of philosophy—any influence that might be considered as properly Christian. The second, founded on the notion of Christian that implies a radical corruption of human nature by sin, rejects every pretension of natural intelligence, left to itself, to collaborate usefully in the discovery of the truth concerning God and the relationship of man with God. The Word of God alone, received in its purity and nudity, is the source of truth and of salvation.

One can pass rapidly over the notion of Christian philosophy founded on the concept of philosophy in sense (1). This offers no difficulty, since it signifies simply that the gospel, which contains the life and teaching of Jesus Christ, brings to man the only true doctrine of salvation and thus the only true wisdom, the only true philosophy, understood in a very broad sense.

There remain, then, philosophy in sense (2) and the concept of a relationship between the order of nature and grace that in no way rejects a priori—as threatening the purity of the gospel message—the notion that by his natural intelligence man can discover useful truths concerning both God, as Creator and End of the universe, and the natural foundations of human life, individual and collective, that grace elevates but does not destroy. Here the problem of Christian philosophy poses itself theoretically in the following manner. If one admits that there can exist a relationship between philosophy, as a work of human intelligence, and supernatural revelation, how is one to conceive any influence of revelation on philosophy without philosophy itself being transformed either (a) into a theology in the classical sense of the word, or (b) into a hybrid discipline composed of philosophy and data borrowed from faith (and tacitly guaranteed thereby), or (c) into a partial or total secularization, through transposition into abstract or scientific terms, of the concrete and historical account of the work of salvation accomplished by and in Jesus Christ? Does there even exist a choice among these three possibilities? Is it not necessary to exclude a priori any intermediary between theology properly so-called and speculations that simply subsume, in another mode, Christian data in their totality, as did G. W. F. HEGEL, or in their parts, as EXISTENTIALISM and PERSONALISM are accused of doing? Is a positive influence of revelation, faith aside, a *Christian* influence? If the answer is no, can one speak of "Christian influence" as anything more than that of the general climate of Western civilization? If the answer is yes, then what sort of symbiosis can be established between two modes of knowledge and of relationship to God that differ as much as do faith in the revealed word and a search for truth merely in function of natural evidence and certitude? The assent of supernatural faith and natural assent doubtless can coexist in one and the same mind, but one may identify them formally only by admitting a contradiction. If, therefore, one qualifies a philosophy as "Christian," even understood in sense (2), one must show that the epithet effectively qualifies the substantive without corrupting the essence of it.

Historical Perspectives. Since its beginning, the Church has made an effort to present to men of different epochs, of different levels and types of culture, the message addressed to humanity by God in Jesus Christ. Such an effort must continue till the end of time. Since this message is the Word of God revealing supernatural mysteries, it is impossible that it not exercise a positive influence of transformation and elevation, both directly, on the conceptions and even the languages that are used to express it in a mode proper to each culture and epoch, and indirectly, on everything within a given mentality, individual or collective, that gravitates around revealed data as a center. There is thus room for theology, in the precise and classic sense of the word, which is the work pursued through the centuries to express more and more precisely (against heresies or possible false interpretations) and systematically (i.e., organized in the light of wisdom) the mysteries of salvation; and, apart from this, for other effects of the Church's effort, which are seen in the transformation and the progress achieved in solving the great philosophical problems that humanity posed for itself independently of Christianity. It is these latter effects that are principally discussed in the debate over Christian philosophy.

Leaving aside, even though they are important, the problems that have been raised concerning the passage of the revealed message from the Hebrew language and mentality to Greek and Latin cultures, the following historical survey treats the relation of that message to philosophy.

Attitude of Faith. The first attitude to be noted—after an early period of reserve, if not hostility, the echo of which is found periodically throughout the centuries—is that which utilizes philosophy as a discipline interior to faith with the intention of understanding, defining, or defending the content of faith. The philosophy first so utilized was PLATONISM or, more precisely, NEOPLATONISM in its various forms. By reducing all things to a transcendent principle and a universe of intelligible Forms, Platonism seemed to lend itself most naturally to the service expected of it, though not without making the faith run serious dangers or without undergoing, on its part, profound transformations. Philosophy interior to faith, during the first 10 centuries, may be characterized by its pastoral and monastic, i.e., basically religious, intention. It remained interior to a movement that proceeds from God's initial revelation to men back toward God, to whom the spirit of man returns guided by the Word Itself, but assimilated and, as it were, acclimated to the epoch and to the individuals at different levels of culture within it.

Scholarly Attitude. Despite the profound differences that separate the apologists, the Greek and Latin Fathers, St. Augustine, and St. Anselm, the ensemble constitute a period that is clearly distinct from SCHOLASTICISM, although not by the central attitude, which remained turned toward the comprehension and assimilation of Christian doctrine. In the earlier period, this assimilation was effected in a new style that was no longer immediately pastoral and contemplative, but scholarly and scientific, under the form of a dispute with an interlocutor, real or supposed, who was regarded as defending a contrary thesis. In the high scholastic period, especially through the influence of ALBERT THE GREAT and Thomas Aquinas, the philosophy of Aristotle came to replace that of Plato in theological teaching and to hold this position for a long time. Certainly, from the 13th century onward there begins to emerge, particularly with the masters of the faculties of arts, a purely philosophical thought—of which Latin AVERROISM is the best-known representative, even though it has been necessary to reevaluate this movement in the light of recent studies. Besides, theologians themselves contributed as much as (or more than) members of the faculties of arts to transform and advance the great themes of philosophy, notably the metaphysics of being, natural theology, psychology, and moral science.

Rationalist Attitude. It is nonetheless beginning with Descartes that a conception of philosophy appears that views itself as built on its own foundations, as purely rational, and as proceeding along lines similar to those followed by mathematics. This it attempts through the construction of a system that relies on a natural certitude as solid as the *Cogito,* a system of which the philosopher is the architect without being personally involved therein. That such an enterprise, carried on by different means, was not in fact able to break the bonds that attached it to the overall structure of the culture fashioned by Christianity is easy to show. It was, nonetheless, an effort to form a philosophical thought detached from all nonrational influences.

Changing Attitude. The rationalist conception, popularized by C. WOLFF in university circles, came to be adopted by a number of scholastics beginning in the 19th century. Against this view rose philosophers who pointed out in various and somewhat opposed ways the fictitious character of a philosopher who is at once constructor and spectator. Such thinkers were led to place in evidence the true condition of man's confrontation with philosophical truth and to make philosophy resume the path toward an ultimate end that it followed, at least since Plato, until the dawn of the modern period. The relationship of such philosophers to Christianity has shown itself to be markedly different, i.e., either more positive or more brutally negative, than that of rationalism and its various developments.

Origins of the Current Debate. In the early 20th century, many Catholic philosophers maintained that revelation exercises a control over philosophy that is negative and extrinsic, namely, by notifying a philosophy that may have come to a conclusion manifestly contrary to faith of its error. There then remains for philosophy the task of redoing its demonstrations and discovering the error. This solution implicitly presupposes the complete autonomy of the order of philosophical research and its extrinsic regulation by faith.

Gilson. This solution was questioned, indirectly, by the historical studies of É. GILSON concerned with Christian philosophy. Beginning with an examination of Cartesian thought, Gilson soon perceived that Descartes, far from constituting an absolute point of departure, could be understood only in continuity with medieval thought; for it was from this thought that he had inherited his vocabulary and a great number of his essential notions and major theses, notably in natural theology. Gilson's study of medieval thought went on to show, furthermore, that the latter was not simply a repetition of Greek thought, particularly that of Aristotle, but offered an original treatment of most of the main theses of METAPHYSICS, natural THEOLOGY, and psychology. These novelties could be understood only in terms of the unquestionable influence that revelation exercised over the work of great theologians such as St. BONAVENTURE and St. THOMAS AQUINAS. A purely extrinsic regulation would not suffice to account for the facts such as they present themselves to the historian of Christian thought.

What Gilson wished to call to the attention of historians was the necessity of revising their concepts relative to the great periods in the history of Western philosophy. Instead of gaps between antiquity, the Middle Ages, the Renaissance, and modern times, he held for a real continuity that was disguised by arbitrary and false classifications. At the same time, he found himself placing in evidence the positive and intrinsic influence of Christian revelation, and this not only on the theologians of the Middle Ages but, through them, on the whole Western philosophical tradition. The latter differed profoundly from Greek thought, he argued, only because of transformations in the major themes of philosophy attributable to Christian influences during the centuries of medieval speculation.

This position could not but provoke a theoretical discussion concerning the notion of Christian philosophy, its a priori possibility, and whether or not it implied some type of contradiction. Those holding to the scholastic tradition, and notably those defending the doctrine of Aquinas, saw no intermediary possible between a pure philosophy and theology. They conceived philosophy as concerned with a completely independent order—as had been postulated by Descartes and those who followed him—with its own point of departure that would permit the construction of a coherent system, free from doubt as well as from nonrational or religious inspiration.

Maritain. J. MARITAIN, while maintaining the essential possibility of a pure philosophy, first proposed to distinguish this from philosophy's historical states. Later he came to formulate his thesis of a moral philosophy adequately understood, which he felt could be only Christian since it must be based on knowledge of the last end of man, an end that concretely is supernatural.

Blondel. The debate over Christian philosophy could not fail also to recall the passionate polemics that were incited after 1893 by the theses of M. BLONDEL on action and on the relationship of philosophy to revelation. Also, Blondel intervened in the debate to reproach Gilson for perpetuating the equivocation against which Blondel had energetically fought in all his works. Blondel had been concerned over the impossibility of philosophy's understanding itself without discovering in its heart, in its own insufficiency, an appeal to a supernatural support. For him, philosophy is not simply controlled from without by revelation, nor is it simply to be utilized on occasion by the theologian as an instrument. It must vigorously seek, on its own ground, to do what it can for humanity, while recognizing that it must ultimately ask help from another order whose necessity it points out while admitting its gratuitous character. To let it be believed that philosophy can be sufficient of itself is to hold that the order of grace has no point of attachment in the human spirit, that nothing calls it or prepares for it, that the supernatural is introduced into nature as a foreign body into a living organism.

On the eve of World War II the situation was therefore as follows: first there were the majority of scholastic theologians, who defended a radical separation of philosophy and revelation and a conception of philosophy somewhat similar, if not identical, with that of the current rationalism; then there was Gilson, who no longer confined himself merely to the role of a historian; and finally there were Blondel and his sympathizers, for whom philosophy erred totally with respect to its true nature when it thought itself capable of closing in upon itself and of giving meaning to human life without reference to the supernatural order.

After World War II the positions were profoundly modified by developments in both philosophy and theology.

Contemporary Philosophy. Under various influences, a goodly number of philosophers have come to believe that the point of departure proposed by Descartes for philosophy, which has been taken up again and again by "system builders," is too utopian. When philosophers reflect sufficiently on the real conditions of philosophy, they find that it cannot begin with a pure subject (e.g., the *Cogito,* or a transcendental subject, of whatever nature this might be) or with a pure given, as does mathematics. Man's thought begins, and can only begin, with an initial situation that implies the presence and openness of his

being, at all its levels, to a world that makes sense from the beginning, a sense that he never ceases to interrogate in order to discover its deepest meaning. It becomes actually impossible to dissociate this initial (and ultimate) datum from the human condition.

Philosophers are turning more and more toward elucidating the real condition of the philosophical enterprise possible to man, such as it is seen to be when the illusions and mirages with which imagination and language continually cover it are dissipated. This work is a search for truth wherein the philosopher is led to reflect anew, on his own grounds, on a great number of metaphysical and anthropological problems to which revelation has also given answers that have transformed the perspectives of Western philosophy.

Contemporary Theology. Christian thought, on the other hand, has experienced a profound renewal through a return to its sources: Scripture, tradition (envisaged in all its amplitude and riches), and liturgy; and the development of Latin, Greek, and Oriental patristic thought, through the Middle Ages, to modern times. It is thus no longer possible to oppose the thought of Gilson or Blondel with the simple conception that appeared in the 1930s as the only possible view of philosophy and of its role in the immense effort pursued through almost two millennia by Christians concerned with stating or defending the content of faith.

The renewal of patristic studies in the mid-20th century brought about by Henri de LUBAC, Jean DANIELOU, and other theologians associated with "la nouvelle théologie" contributed greatly to this appreciation of the varieties of Christian philosophical thought. From a speculative point of view, the more important contribution of de Lubac et al. had to do with the debate over nature and grace (see PURE NATURE, STATE OF). Their objection to the common scholastic hypothesis that a spiritual creature could, as created, have an end other than the vision of God involved a more general complaint that scholastic theology as it developed after Aquinas held an improper notion of the autonomy of the natural order. In their view, philosophical rationalism was a natural outcome of this development. While not denying that philosophy has its own methods that are distinct from those of theology, some of these theologians held that the formal objects of philosophy and theology are not so distinct. Studies in the thought of such theologians as Augustine and Bonaventure seemed to support this line of thought.

Papal Teaching. PIUS XII, in his encyclical *HUMANI GENERIS* (1950), spoke of the philosophy that reaches unchangeable, metaphysical truth as a philosophy "acknowledged and accepted by the Church" (*HG* 29). He contrasted this attitude of the Church with two related modern errors: a philosophical pluralism become a philosophical relativism, and an agnosticism about the ability of the human mind to know metaphysical truth. This philosophy is described as "Christian" simply in the sense that it attains metaphysical truth, and thus is a sound tool for the Christian to use in understanding the faith.

The topic of Christian philosophy was taken up again by JOHN PAUL II in his encyclical *FIDES ET RATIO* (1998). John Paul affirmed that "the Church has no philosophy of her own nor does she canonize one particular philosophy in preference to others" (*FR* 49). Philosophy has its own proper principles and methods, and it would not be proper for faith to dictate to philosophy on those points. Nevertheless, because the truth that comes from revelation and the truth that is recognized by reason in its own natural light are harmonious, the Church rightly takes on the role of "servant of truth" by pointing out parts of various philosophical systems that are incompatible with truth as known by faith (*FR* 50).

Pope John Paul refashioned the debate over Christian philosophy by emphasizing the proper end of philosophy: namely, understanding ultimate truth and the meaning of life (*FR* 3). Philosophy therefore has the same end as faith, though it differs in the method it uses to achieve that end. Respecting this autonomy of philosophy, faith nevertheless influences philosophy in several ways. It purifies reason, wounded by sin and tempted to presumption. It assures philosophy that its end can be known. Most importantly, "revelation clearly proposes certain truths which might never have been discovered by reason unaided, although they are not of themselves inaccessible to reason" (*FR* 76). Philosophy does not thereby become theology: the things revealed are proper philosophical objects. But the revelation of these truths guides philosophical inquiry, especially since it displays them as pertaining to man's end, which is the goal of philosophy. Thus, for example, the revelation of God as the free and personal Creator guides the philosophy of being; the revelation of the reality of sin guides philosophical reflection on evil; and the revelation of the dignity of the person guides philosophical anthropology.

Concluding Summary. The expression Christian philosophy is thus applied in different contexts. There is, first, the fact of revelation's influence on philosophy—an undeniable influence, but one that is interpreted in various ways. It is necessary in any event to distinguish clearly the properly theological enterprise of faith's using philosophy in order the better to express itself and the influence that faith exercises in this way over philosophy and that goes beyond being a mere negative norm. There are, second, the efforts to form anew, within a civilization characterized as Christian, a philosophical order independ-

dent of Christian influence. This would constitute itself theoretically as if Christianity, in fact, did not exist: either by pretending to ignore it, or by trying to render it useless, or finally, by relegating it to another level of the intellectual life (with the secret intention, however, of meeting it again or of letting oneself be regulated negatively by it). There is, third and finally, the effort to form philosophies that, from the beginning, take into account the fact of Christianity no less than the existence of stars and planets. This would either form a system in which Christianity is reduced to the object of an abstract dialectic, or, alternatively, it would conduct its inquiry in a way that, without altering its natural character, opens philosophy to wait upon, or even to make appeal to, the order of grace.

Granted a formal distinction between the two orders of knowledge, natural and supernatural, that no Catholic philosopher would question, there remain different ways of conceiving the notion of Christian philosophy, a diversity that (at least for Catholic philosophers) depends in part on philosophers' opposed views of the nature of philosophy, but also on views that mutually complement, rather than completely exclude, one another.

See Also: EXISTENTIAL METAPHYSICS; THEOLOGY, NATURAL; GOD.

Bibliography: For a complete survey of literature, see the Chronicles of *Bulletin Thomiste* 4 (1934–36) to the present. *Christian Philosophy and the Social Sciences* (*American Catholic Philosophical Association. Proceedings of the Annual Meeting* 12; Baltimore 1936). *The Role of the Christian Philosopher* (*ibid.*, 32; 1958). M. NÉDONCELLE, *Is there a Christian Philosophy?*, tr. I. TRETHOWAN (New York 1960). C. TRESMONTANT, *The Origins of Christian Philosophy,* tr. M. PONTIFEX (New York 1963). P. DELHAYE, *Medieval Christian Philosophy,* tr. S. J. TESTER (New York 1960). R. VANCOURT, *Pensée moderne et philosophie chrétienne* (Paris 1957), Eng. in prep. É. H. GILSON, *The Christian Philosophy of St. Thomas Aquinas,* tr. L. K. SHOOK (New York 1956). J. MARITAIN, *An Essay on Christian Philosophy,* tr. E. FLANNERY (New York 1955). A. C. PEGIS, *Christian Philosophy and Intellectual Freedom* (Milwaukee 1960). J. F. QUINN, *The Historical Constitution of St. Bonaventure's Philosophy* (Toronto 1973).

[L. B. GEIGER/EDS.]

CHRISTIAN REFORMED CHURCH

Organized as a conference of protest in 1857, when two ministers and a group of laymen of the Reformed Church in America disagreed with the doctrines and policies of their church (*see* REFORMED CHURCHES IN NORTH AMERICA). They established the Holland Reformed Church, later known as the Christian Reformed Church.

The early growth of the Christian Reformed Church was erratic. Its first years were marked by schisms and

The minister at the United Reformed Church, London, England, addresses his congregation. (©Christine Osborne/CORBIS)

defections; by 1863 there remained only three pastors for the entire church. Later growth came from immigration from Holland and from the affiliation of those opposed to FREEMASONRY, which was tolerated by the Reformed Church in America. Others, who objected to what they held was doctrinal liberalism in the older church, joined the dissenters. Most members of the Christian Reformed Church come from Dutch backgrounds, but English has now replaced Dutch in worship in most of its congregations. This church has continued to wage an active campaign against secret societies and forbids dual membership in the lodge and the church. It upholds classical Calvinist theology including an emphasis on predestination (*see* CALVINISM). The creedal standards are found in three historical Reformed statements: HEIDELBERG CATECHISM (1563), the Canons of Dort (1618–19), and the Belgic Confession (1561).

Bibliography: F.S. MEAD, S.S. HILL and C.D. ATWOOD, *Handbook of Denominations in the United States, 11th ed* (Nashville 2001)

[W. J. WHALEN/EDS.]

CHRISTIAN SCHOOLS OF MERCY, SISTERS OF THE

Also known as *Sorores Scholarum Christianorum a Misericordia* (SSC), a religious congregation with papal approval (1901, 1925), founded at Cherbourg, France, in 1807 by St. Marie Madeleine POSTEL to promote Christian education. The congregation, whose members take simple perpetual vows, is governed by a superior general. The rule of St. John Baptist de LA SALLE was substituted in 1837 for that of the foundress at the request of the local vicar-general. The foundress accepted it. The motherhouse was first established at Saint-Sauveur-le-Vicomte,

Normandy, where the young community settled (1832). Despite initial setbacks, there were 150 members and 37 convents in 1846. The congregation spread from France to the Netherlands, England, Ireland, Italy, Indonesia, and the Congo. In 1862 four teachers took the habit and rule at Heiligenstadt, Eichsfeld, Germany. Since 1922 this has been an independent branch with its motherhouse at Heiligenstadt. The sisters are engaged mostly in teaching, but they also conduct orphanages, homes for the aged, and hostels, besides visiting the sick and the poor, nursing, and aiding in parishes.

Bibliography: G. GRENTE, *Une sainte normande* (Paris 1946). SISTER CALISTA, *Love Endureth All Things* (Cork 1953).

[W. J. BATTERSBY/EDS.]

CHRISTIAN SCIENCE (CHURCH OF CHRIST, SCIENTIST)

A religious body founded in 1879 by Mary Baker EDDY, whose discovery of what she named Christian Science resulted from a personal experience of prayer healing in 1866. Her *Science and Health with Key to the Scriptures,* the textbook of the Christian Science Church first published in 1875, described this experience. "I knew the Principle of all harmonious Mind-action to be God, and that cures were produced in primitive Christian healing by holy, uplifting faith; but I must know the Science of this healing, and I won my way to absolute conclusions through divine revelation, reason, and demonstration" (109).

Foundation and Growth. Mrs. Eddy did not at first expect to found a separate church or denomination, but hoped that other churches would take up the discovery and utilize it within their own systems. When they did not, she founded the Church of Christ, Scientist, at Boston, Mass., in 1879. Soon, groups of Christian Scientists sprang up in other places, and in 1892 Mrs. Eddy organized the Christian Science Mother Church, The First Church of Christ, Scientist, in Boston. Local churches throughout the world are regarded as branches of this church. Newspapers, magazines, and books attacked the new religion and its founder; it received hostile receptions in many communities. But its appeal of Christian healing made a deep impact on thousands, especially in the U.S. and other English-speaking countries, and also in western Europe, particularly Germany.

Teachings. Christian Science maintains that fundamental reality is spiritual, created by God and consistently good. Thus, the human race, as the image and likeness of God, has a birthright of harmony and perfection. The ills that beset humanity, such as sickness, sin, fear, death,

and poverty, are not part of God's spiritual creation, but result from the failure of the human mind to understand and obey God perceptively. To the degree that humans do understand God and follow His precepts unswervingly, their lives are regenerated, they experience healing, and their thinking is spiritualized. The degree to which they may not be healed is a result of their limitations in understanding and loving God. Christian Science defines God not in superhuman or anthropomorphic terms, but as "the divine Principle of all that really is"; biblical terms used directly or by implication for God, such as Life, Truth, Love, Soul, Spirit, Mind, were adopted by Mrs. Eddy. Her followers regard heaven and hell, not as localities, but as states of consciousness experienced by individuals in terms of their own spiritual progress or lack of it. The immortality of man's spiritual being is an emphatic teaching of Christian Science, while the experience of death is regarded as an illusion, not touching the real man who is spiritual.

Science and Health (497) summarized the following "religious tenets": "(1) As adherents of Truth, we take the inspired Word of the Bible as our sufficient guide to eternal Life. (2) We acknowledge and adore one supreme and infinite God. We acknowledge His Son, one Christ; the Holy Ghost or divine Comforter; and man in God's image and likeness. (3) We acknowledge God's forgiveness of sin in the destruction of sin and the spiritual understanding that casts out evil as unreal. But the belief in sin is punished so long as the belief lasts. (4) We acknowledge Jesus' atonement as the evidence of divine, efficacious Love, unfolding man's unity with God through Christ Jesus the Way-shower; and we acknowledge that man is saved through Christ, through Truth, Life, and Love as demonstrated by the Galilean Prophet in healing the sick and overcoming sin and death. (5) We acknowledge that the crucifixion of Jesus and his resurrection served to uplift faith to understand eternal Life, even the allness of Soul, Spirit, and the nothingness of matter. (6) And we solemnly promise to watch, and pray for that Mind to be in us which was also in Christ Jesus; to do unto others as we would have them do unto us; and to be merciful, just, and pure."

Organization, Services, and Publications. Mrs. Eddy's death in 1910 was a test of the plan of organization she had formulated in the church manual. It set up a five-member self-perpetuating board of directors to transact the business of the Mother Church. Branch churches throughout the world are democratically self-governed. Since 1910 the movement has grown steadily, although not at a sensational rate.

There is no clergy or official prayer book, and the order of church service is simple, identical, and uncere-

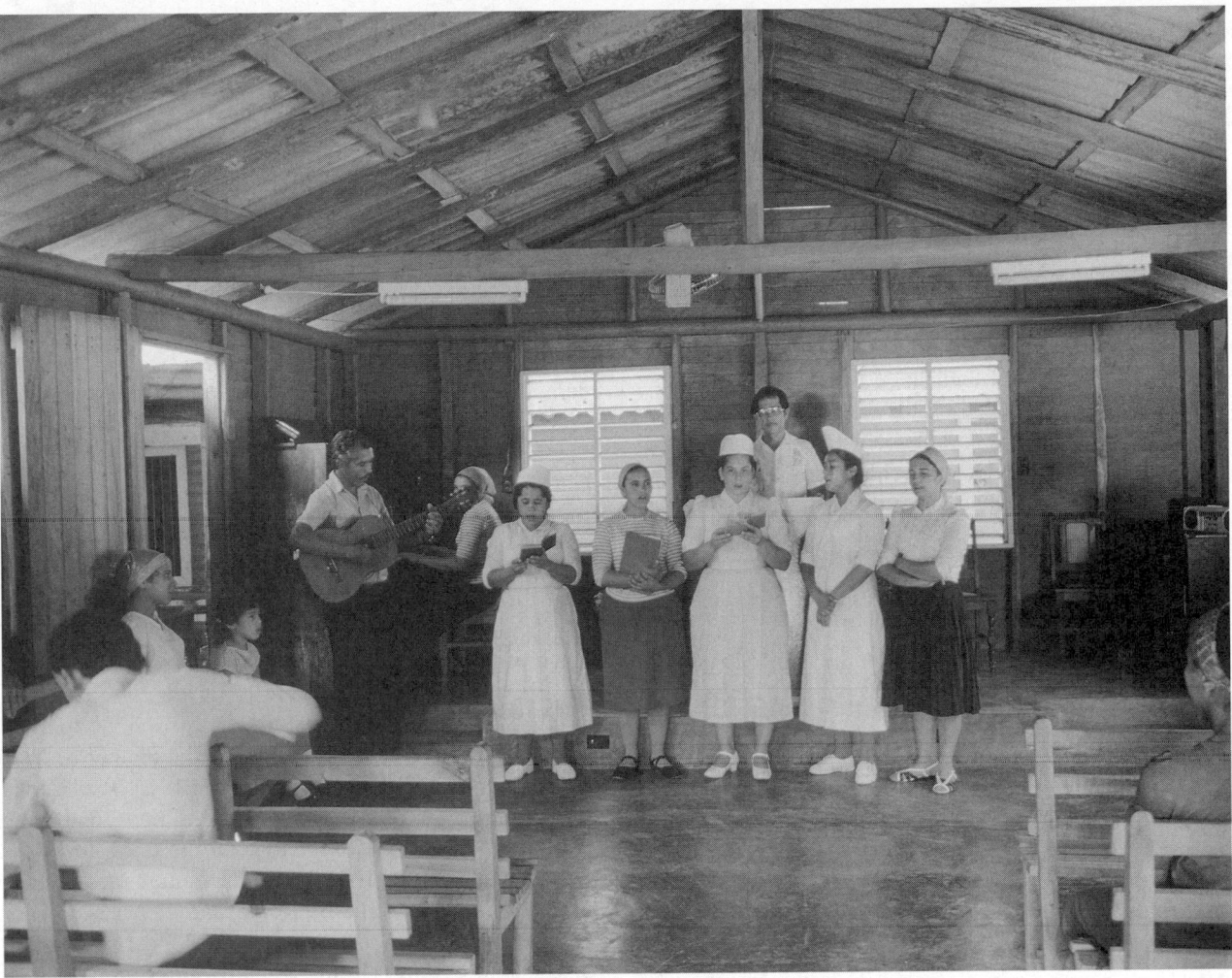

Christian Scientist Church service, Baracoa, Cuba. (©Robert van der Hilst/CORBIS)

monial. Sunday services are based on lesson-sermons, consisting of citations from the Bible and the Christian Science textbook. At the services these lesson-sermons, which have been studied in advance by church members, are read aloud by a "First and Second Reader," who are lay men or women elected for three-year terms. Hymn singing from the Christian Science Hymnal, the Lord's Prayer in common, and silent prayer, are part of the order of service. A Sunday School is held for pupils up to 20 years of age. Wednesday evening meetings include readings from the Bible and *Science and Health*, and testimonies of healing or other spiritual experiences from members of the congregation.

Although there is no clergy, there are professional practitioners of Christian Science. These men and women, whose names are registered in the church's monthly publication, the *Christian Science Journal* (1883), carry on healing work and spiritual guidance through prayer as a full-time vocation. Moreover, all

Christian Scientists try to use their understanding of God's infinite grace and His law for spiritual healing. There is no formal missionary work, but the church maintains a board of lectureship, whose members deliver public lectures on Christian Science throughout the world. Other publications include: the *Christian Science Quarterly*, which contains the lesson-sermons studied each week; the *Christian Science Sentinel*, a weekly first published in 1898, and the *Heralds of Christian Science*. In 1908, when Mrs. Eddy was in her 88th year, she directed the establishment of a daily newspaper, the *Christian Science Monitor*.

Bibliography: N. BEASLEY, *The Continuing Spirit* (New York 1956). M. B. EDDY, *Science and Health with Key to the Scriptures* (Boston 1908). D. JOHN, *The Christian Science Way of Life, with A Christian Scientist's Life* by E. D. CANHAM (Englewood Cliffs 1962). R. PEEL, *Christian Science: Its Encounter with American Culture* (New York 1958). C. P. SMITH, *Historical Sketches* (Boston

1941). F. S. MEAD, S. S. HILL and C. D. ATWOOD, *Handbook of Denominations in the United States: 11th ed* (Nashville 2001)

[E. D. CANHAM]

CHRISTIAN WAY OF LIFE (EARLY CHURCH)

In the Sermon on the Mount, Christ called His followers the salt of the earth and the light of the world (Mt 5.13–14); He admonished them to let their light shine among men by way of their good works (Mt 5.16). This admonition was preceded by the discourse on the BEATITUDES (Mt 5.3–12) and completed with a moral discourse (Mt 5.17–7.29). In the Gospels of Matthew and Mark, the eschatological atmosphere accompanying the call to repentance (*metanoia*) is stressed with the proclamation by John the Baptist that the kingdom of God is at hand (Mt 3.1–12; Mk 1.4–15). In Luke, the eschatological element is softened in favor of the history of salvation, in which conversion is offered to all through the apostolic preaching; and the promise of salvation is portrayed as realized in the Church (Lk 5.32; 15.7–10; Acts 7.38; 9.31).

Conversion and Metanoia. Conversion signifies a complete turnabout of mentality and a permanent, new way of life. The process of *metanoia* is described for the Jews in Acts (2.38–40; 3.19–21, 25–26) as the acknowledgment of their sinfulness, Baptism, remission of their sins, the gift of the Holy Spirit, their liberation, and participation in salvation. Paul speaks of the conversion of the Gentiles (*epistrephein*) as an opening of their eyes from the darkness to light, a turning from Satan to God, that they might receive the forgiveness of their sins and the call through faith among the saints (Acts 26.18).

In characterizing the way of life of the primitive Christians, the author of Acts says: "The multitude of believers had but one heart and one soul" (4.32). He describes the mutual charity exercised by the original Jerusalem community, in which the members sold their property and placed the price at the feet of the Apostles, who divided it among the members according to their need so that no one lacked anything among them (4.34). This idealized picture receives some support from the fact that the practice of a communal life is known to have been current among the QUMRAM brethren and the Sadocites. It is likewise put into perspective by St. Paul's doctrine concerning the Church as the body of Christ, in which the members, although having different functions, formed part of one sole body (Rom 12.3–8; 1 Cor 12.12; Eph 2.20–22).

The Church at Jerusalem. Although in the beginning the Apostles and earliest converts continued to pray in the temple (Acts 2.46) and follow the Jewish ritual (3.1; 5.21), they gradually became aware of themselves as a separate community or church. The term church was applied first to the Church in Jerusalem (7.38), then extended to the Christian communities at Antioch (14.27) and at Caesarea (18.22). The Church at Jerusalem was directed by the elders under the guidance of James the Just, appointed by Peter, James, and John as *episcopus,* or bishop (Eusebius, *Ecclesiastical History* 2.1.4), to whom Paul made a special visit during his stay at Jerusalem in 41 (Gal 1.18). While the widows, the poor, and the orphans among the convert Jews were cared for by the Jewish elders, the Apostles provided for the poor among the converts from Hellenism by ordaining seven deacons— Stephen, Philip, Prochorus, Nicanor, Timon, Parmenas, and the Antiochene Nicholas—thus freeing themselves for prayer and the ministry of the word.

The Lord's Day. The Jerusalem Christians assembled for prayer and the breaking of bread in their own homes (Acts 2.46), following the example of the assemblage of Apostles and Disciples awaiting the coming of the Holy Spirit in the *coenaculum,* or upper room (Acts 1.13). When Peter was released from prison, he found a large gathering at the home of Mary, the mother of John Mark, spending the night in prayer (12.12). Paul spoke to a group in the home of Lydia at Philippi (16.40) and celebrated the Eucharist at Troas on the third floor of a private home (20.9). He refers to the church in the house of Aquila and Priscilla at Rome and Ephesus (1 Cor 16.19), that of Nympha at Colossus (Col 4.15), and that of Gaius at Corinth (Rom 26.23). Besides daily gatherings for the breaking of bread and prayers of thanksgiving (Acts 2.46), the early Christians frequently spent the night of Saturday together in prayer after observing the Jewish Sabbath (Acts 20.7), gradually establishing the custom of keeping Sunday as the Lord's day (*kuriake* or *dominicum*). Acts describes the make-up of their meeting, which consisted of an instruction, the breaking of bread for the Eucharist (Acts 20.17) and the recitation of prayers (2.42). The instruction was called the didache or teaching, the exhortation or *paraklesis,* and the homily (Acts 14.22; 15.32; 20.11).

Postapostolic Documents. The Christian way of life consequent upon the apostolic preaching is described in a series of documents that appear at the turn of the second century. The epistle of CLEMENT I of Rome (*c.* 97) portrays the Church in sojourn at Corinth as a model of steadfast faith, sober and gentle piety, magnificent hospitality, and secure knowledge. Its members are praised for their obedience to God's commandments without care for rank or station, and for the respect they gave their rulers and elders. The young were trained to temperance; wives, to affectionate care for their husbands and household. All were content with the provisions Christ had made for them, and were happier in giving than in receiving. They meditated on the words of Christ, keeping His sufferings ever before their eyes. Under the outpouring of the Holy Spirit on the whole community, they experienced peace of soul, praying to God for forgiveness of inadvertent faults and vying with each other in behalf of the whole brotherhood. They mourned their shortcomings, judging their neighbors' faults their own. In virtuous citizenship, they fulfilled their duties in the fear of the Lord, whose precepts were engraved on the tablets of their hearts (*Epistole Clem.* 1, 2).

This idealized picture is offset by the history of the dissension that had broken out at Corinth and occasioned the Roman Church's letter, but the exhortations that accompany it reveal a consciousness of the Church as a strong organization whose line of authority descended from God through Christ and the Apostles to the elders of the fraternally united community (*ibid.* 42.1–5; 44.1–2). Despite the ravagings of "envy and jealousy, contention and contumacy" that accompany persecution, the letter insists on sanctification and justification, penance and conversion as leading to peace and order among men, as it characterizes God's creation of the cosmos (3.2–6.4; 13–14; 20.1–12).

Ignatius and Polycarp. According to IGNATIUS OF ANTIOCH (d. *c.* 116), the true Christian imitated Christ in His passion, achieving a complete transformation of his way of life by regeneration in God and Christ though Baptism. This is expressed in the charity that begins with the gift of self in and to the community (*Epistole ad Eph.* 10.1–3; *Smyrn.* 6.2–7) and is perfected in the Church through a consciousness of unity with Christ and one another that proceeds from, and leads back to, the Trinity by way of the Eucharist, the symbol at once of immortality (*Eph.* 20.2) and the instrument of unity between the Christians in community and of communities within the Church. In concrete terms this is accomplished by loving care for "widows and orphans, the prisoner as well as the freedman, the hungry and thirsty" (*Smyrn.* 6.2).

The organization of the Church includes the bishop, who is the "living image of the invisible God" (*Mag.* 6.1; *Tral.* 3.1); the priests, "like the college of apostles surrounding Christ" (*Phil.* 4.1), and deacons, widows, and virgins (*Smyr.* 13.1). Finally, Ignatius asserts the prerogative of marriage for Christians, entered into with the sanction of the bishop, that it may be in accord with the will of God; and he who can live in continence should do so without boasting (*Pol.* 5.1–2). This Ignatian doctrine is portrayed on a background of martyrdom, for death in and with Christ is the consummation of union with God that the Christian strives for in the practice of virtue (*Eph.* 11.1–2; *Rom.* 2.2).

To the Church at Philippi in the mid-second century, POLYCARP of Smyrna described the Christian way of life as essentially the imitation of Christ in his patience (*Epistle ad Phil.* 8.2; 9.1). Christians are to flee avarice and the love of money (2.2); and each in his station—husbands, wives, widows, deacons, and priests—must forgive injuries, practice kindness and moderation toward sinners, and pray for all, particularly rulers and magistrates (4–6). The priest in particular is described as "tenderhearted and merciful toward all, seeking the sheep who have gone astray, not neglecting widow or orphan or poor man. . .abstaining from anger, respect of persons, and unrighteous judgment, realizing that all are debtors because of sin" (6.1–3).

Hermas, Diognetus, and Justin. The practice of a moral way of life in imitation of Christ was supported by an eschatological conception of the Church that, according to the Shepherd of HERMAS, had been created before all things and was now, under the guise of a tower under construction, constituted at a time of special mercy in immediate preparation for the PAROUSIA, or Second Coming of the Savior. The Shepherd as the angel of penance describes the Church of Rome toward the middle of the second century. It is a populous assembly with a large group of the rich and numerous poor, and among both classes are many who have relapsed into pagan ways, become blasphemers, heretics, and propagandists of a false gnosis (*Sim.* 8.6–11). Hermas portrays hypocrites, ambitious clergymen, and dishonest deacons, as well as hospitable bishops, honest priests, martyrs, and the innocent. Along with a well-organized hierarchy, he speaks of itinerant apostles and teachers preaching under the inspiration of charismatic gifts, but the problem of their authenticity as faced in the Didache (11.1–12) seems all but solved (*Mand.* 10.11). For Hermas, it is moral perfection that leads to perfect knowledge (*gnosis*); hence faith without works is vain (14.4–5; 40.4; 90.2–3). The Christian is to keep the spirit of God intact within him, practicing continence, chastity in married life (29.1–11), justice, and humility while giving himself to works of supererogation (56.6–7).

In repelling the accusation of atheism and corruption brought against the Christians, the author of the letter to DIOGNETUS admits that they are persecuted by both the pagans and the Jews (5.11, 12, 16, 17), but he describes the injustice of this treatment since "Christians do not differ from other men in citizenship, in language, or in dress" (5.2). They are to be found in the Greek and barbarian cities, and conform to local usages as far as dress, food, and manner of life are concerned. They carry out all their duties as citizens. They marry like the rest of the world, but in procreating children, they do not abandon them, and although they partake of a common table, they do not share the same bed. While they pass their time on earth, they live as citizens of heaven; they obey the laws, love their enemies, and return good for evil. In a word "what the soul is to the body, Christians are to the world" (5.1–17; 6.1–10).

JUSTIN MARTYR describes the Christian Sunday (*dies solis*) as the day on which those who live in towns or the country come together for a reading of the Gospels (*commentarii apostolorum*) or of the writings of the Prophets. When the reader stops, the bishop gives an exhortation stimulating the hearers to an imitation of what has been read. Afterward all rise and pray, after which the bishop blesses the bread and the wine and water with Eucharistic prayers, and those present communicate, sending the Sacrament to those absent through the deacons. The rich make an offering either directly or through the bishop, who cares for the widows and orphans, the sick and indigent, prisoners and strangers (*1 Apol.* 67). This bread and wine is not ordinary, and cannot be received except by those who believe and have been baptized in the remission of their sins and in the regeneration of Christ (*ibid.* 65).

Reorganization. Toward the end of the second century, Eusebius describes the status of the Church as in the course of a considerable reorganization (*Ecclesiastical History* 3–4). In particular, he cites seven letters written by Bishop DIONYSIUS OF CORINTH, a contemporary of Pope Soter (166–175), to churches in Asia Minor, Crete, and Rome. In these "catholic epistles, useful to the whole church," Eusebius describes Dionysius as sending the Lacedemonians a catechesis of orthodoxy, devoted to peace and unity (4.23.2). He dispatched an exhortation to faith and conduct in keeping with the gospel to the Athenians (*ibid.*), blaming them for a falling off in fervor after the martyrdom of their bishop, Publius. In his letter to the Church of Nicomedia, he combatted the heresies of MARCION and recalled the faithful to the rule of faith (*ibid.* 4). He praised the conduct of the Church at Gortyna in Crete for its great charity and Christian observance, making special mention of its bishop, Philip. He advised Bp. Palmas of Amastris in Pontus regarding marriage and continence, and suggested that he grant pardon to sinners, even to those returning from heresy.

Dionysius cautioned Bp. Pinytos of Cnossos that the burden of continence was not to be put on all the faithful as a necessity, and that he should have in mind the weakness of the majority. In return, Pinytos, although accepting the Corinthian's counsel, suggested that he should not hesitate to feed his flock with stronger doctrine, lest they grow into immature Christians. In replying to a letter from Pope Soter, Dionysius praised highly the generosity of the Roman Church, whose fervor had been preserved down to the "persecutions of our own times" (*ibid.* 9). He assured Soter that his letter was held in esteem, and records the fact that the letter of Clement I to the Corinthians was still being read in their Church. Finally, Dionysius warned against the falsifications of both the Scriptures and the letters of bishops.

Before the turn of the century, with Tertullian in Carthage, Clement in Alexandria, Lucian in Samosata, Irenaeus in Lyons, and Hippolytus in Rome, the testimony offered by the beginnings of a great Christian literature demonstrates the unity of faith in the diversity of liturgical practice, the problems in the discipline of penance and the instruction of catechumens, and the fervor and perseverance to martyrdom during the periods of persecution, all of which were characteristic of the Early Christian way of life.

Bibliography: J. DANIÉLOU and H. I. MARROU, *The First Six Hundred Years*, tr. V. CRONIN, vol. 1 of *The Christian Centuries* (New York 1964–). J. KLEIST, ed. and tr., *The Epistles of St. Clement of Rome and St. Ignatius of Antioch* (Ancient Christian Writers, 1; 1946). P. T. CAMELOT, ed., *Ignace d'Antioche: Lettres* (Sources Chrétiennes 10; 3d ed. 1958), introd. H. I. MARROU, ed. and tr., *À Diognète* (*ibid.* 33; 1951) 118–207. J. QUASTEN, *Patrology* (Westminster, Maryland 1950–) v.1–2. G. BARDY, *La Théologie de l'Église*, v.1 (Unam Sanctam 13; Paris 1945). F. X. MURPHY, *Studia moralia*, v.1 (Rome 1963) 54–85. J. DUPONT, *Les Problems du livres des Actres* (Louvain 1950). R. MICHIELS, *Ephemerides theologicae Lovanienses* 41 (1965) 42–78. V. MONACHINO, *Gregorianum* 32 (1951) 5–49, 187–222. P. CARRINGTON, *The Early Church*, 2 v. (Cambridge, Eng. 1957) v.1. A. FLICHE and V. MARTIN, eds., *Histoire de l'église depuis les origines jusqu'à nos jours* (Paris 1935–) v.1–2.

[F. X. MURPHY]

CHRISTIANA OF LUCCA, BL.

Virgin; b. Castello di Santa Croce sull'Arno, Tuscany, Italy, 1240; d. there, Jan. 4, 1310. She was born into a poor family and was baptized Oringa, although in later life she was popularly called Christiana, perhaps in tribute to the particular reverence she had for the state of virginity. She went into the service of a noble family at Lucca, from whom she took leave to go on pilgrimage to Monte Gargano and ASSISI. On her return to Santa Croce she founded a convent there in 1279, giving it the Rule of St. AUGUSTINE. She was famed for her devotion to the Eucharist and the Blessed Virgin and was popularly acclaimed a saint. Her cult was affirmed by several popes and given official recognition in 1776.

Feast: Jan. 4; Feb. 18.

Bibliography: *Acta Sanctorum* Jan. 1 (1863) 650–662. M. BACIOCCHI DE PÉON, *La vergine Oringa* (Florence 1926). P. PACCHIANI, *La vergine santacrocese* (San Miniato 1939).

[J. L. GRASSI]

CHRISTIFIDELES LAICI

Apostolic exhortation of Pope JOHN PAUL II, "The Lay Members of Christ's Faithful People," issued Dec. 30, 1988, following the seventh ordinary assembly of the Synod of Bishops (Oct. 1–30, 1987) whose theme was the "Vocation and Mission of the Laity in the Church and in the World Twenty Years after the Second Vatican Council." The text comprises an introduction (nos. 1–7) and five chapters: "The Dignity of the Lay Faithful in the Church as Mystery," (nos. 8–17), "The Participation of the Lay Faithful in the Life of Church as Communion" (nos. 18–31), "The Coresponsibility of the Lay Faithful in the Church as Mission" (nos. 32–44), "Good Stewards of God's Varied Grace" (nos. 45–56), and "The Formation of the Lay Faithful in the Lay State" (nos. 57–64). The exhortation ends with an appeal to the intercession of the Virgin Mary.

Christifideles laici builds on the scriptural images of the vineyard (Mt 20:1) and of the vine and the branches (Jn 15:5). According to John Paul, the 1987 synod's significance might well consist in its recognition of the Lord's call to go into the vineyard, addressed to everyone (no. 64). The vineyard represents the whole world that is to be transformed (no. 1). The biblical phrase, "I am the vine, you are the branches," "lends itself to a consideration of fruitfulness and life. . . . Bearing fruit is an essential demand of life in Christ and life in the church" (no. 32). The pope's intent is to promote the gift and responsibility the lay faithful have in the communion and mission of the church (no. 2). It is, therefore, essential to view them in the "context of the church as communion" (no. 18) in which each layperson "offers a totally unique contribution on behalf of the whole body" (no. 20).

The foundation for the dignity and mission of the lay faithful is the "radical newness of the Christian life that comes from baptism" (no. 10). Accepting the synod's call to describe the lay faithful in positive terms (rather than as those who are simply not priests and not consecrated religious), the pope insists that only by acknowledging the richness of the mystery of baptism can a basic description of the laity be achieved (no. 9). The call to holiness is universal and is rooted in baptism; in fact, "the vocation to holiness" is an essential element of the new life of baptism (no. 17). It is the vocation and mission of the lay faithful—precisely as church members—to proclaim the gospel (no. 33) and to take an active, responsible role in the world's "re-evangelization" (no. 64).

The biblical theme of fruitfulness is re-emphasized in the pope's discussion of lay formation, the objective of which is the ongoing discovery of a person's vocation along with "the ever-greater willingness to live it" (no. 58). The pope accents the necessity of total and ongoing formation (no. 57).

The distinctive feature of the lay state is found in its "secular character" (no. 55). The vocation of the lay faithful "properly concerns their situation in the world" (no. 15). Two temptations are to be avoided: (1) being so greatly interested in "church services and tasks" that the lay faithful do not become "actively engaged in their responsibilities" in the world; (2) "legitimizing the unwarranted separation of faith from life" (no. 2). Formation of the laity should be integrated, not presenting "spiritual" life and "secular" life as two parallel lines of their existence (no. 59). The pope adds that faith is not "entirely thought out, not faithfully lived" if it does not affect a person's culture (no. 59).

Discussing the role of women in church and society, the pope quotes a synod recommendation which said the church needs to "recognize all the gifts of men and women for her life and mission, and put them into practice" (no. 49). The many provisions of the revised Code of Canon Law on the participation of women in the church's life and mission need to be more widely known and "realized with greater timeliness and determination" (no. 51). The first step in promoting women's full participation in church and society is to openly acknowledge their personal dignity (no. 49).

The church's pastors need to "acknowledge and foster" the ministries, offices, and roles of the lay faithful "founded in baptism, confirmation and matrimony." The pope notes that in the synod "a critical judgment was voiced" about using the word "ministry" too indiscriminately so that the common priesthood and ministerial priesthood either are confused or equated (no. 23). The ministries, offices, and roles of the lay faithful in the church should be "exercised in conformity to their specific lay vocation" (ibid.). A discussion of the charisms, the gifts of the Spirit, follows the discussion of ministries, offices, and roles (no. 24).

Some other concerns discussed in the exhortation include the aged, associations and movements, culture, the family, men's roles, parishes, public and political life, small Christian communities, spirituality, work, and youth.

Bibliography: For the text of *Christifideles laici,* see: *Acta Apostolicae Sedis* 81 (1989): 393–521 (Latin); *Origins* 18, no. 35 (Feb. 9, 1989): 561–595 (English); *The Pope Speaks* 34 (1989): 103–168 (English). For commentaries and summaries of *Christifideles laici,* see: R. W. OLIVER, *The Vocation of the Laity to Evangelization: An Ecclesiological Inquiry into the Synod on the Laity* (1987), *Christifideles Laici* (1989), and Documents of the NCCB, 1987–96 (Rome 1997). P. COUGHLAN, *The Hour of the Laity: Their Expanding Role* (Philadelphia 1989).

[D. GIBSON]

CHRISTINA OF HAMM, BL.

Flourished 15th century, Westphalia, Germany. According to W. Rolevinck in *Fasciculus temporum* (1482) 12 witnesses testified that a young girl named Stine, who had recently been baptized in 1464, had borne the stigmata (*see* STIGMATIZATION) in her hands, feet, and side. She was honored with a popular cult. Her feast day was probably adopted from that of Christina of Stommeln.

Feast: June 22.

Bibliography: K. HONSELMANN, *Lexikon für Theologie und Kirche*[2] 2:1129. A. SCHÜTTE, *Handbuch der deutschen Heiligen* (Cologne 1941) 88.

[M. G. MCNEIL]

CHRISTINA OF MARKYATE, ST.

Recluse, daughter of Auti and Beatrix, gentlefolk of Huntingdon, England; d. *c.* 1155. As a child she took a private vow of virginity on a visit to the Abbey of St. Albans. At the age of 16 she incurred the emnity of Ralph Flambard, bishop of Durham and former chancellor of England, by repulsing his immoral advances; in revenge he had her betrothed to one of his friends, Burhtred. Upon Christina's refusal to marry, her parents used flattery, ridicule, magic, and physical violence to force her hand. The Augustinian prior of Huntingdon was induced to use his authority to change her mind, and on failing, he brought her before Bp. Robert Bloet of Lincoln, who at first decided in her favor but revoked his decision after a bribe. Encouraged by Ralph d'Escures, archbishop of Canterbury, and abetted by the hermit Eadwine, Christina took refuge with Alwen, a recluse at Flamstead, where she stayed for two years. A disagreement caused her to join Roger, a hermit at Caddington, with whom she stayed for four years. Upon Roger's death, Archbishop THURSTAN OF YORK wished to make her superior of a convent in York, but she settled at Markyate. There Abbot Geoffrey of St. Albans, where her brother Gregory was a monk, built a convent for her. She exercised a beneficent influence over the abbot and his community. She was celebrated for her prophetic insight and wonder-working, and was revered by King Henry II and Pope ADRIAN IV. For Adrian she made three miters and sandals. Her Psalter is preserved at Hildesheim.

Feast: Dec. 26.

Bibliography: *The Life of Christina of Markyate, a Twelfth-Century Recluse*, ed. and tr. C. H. TALBOT (Oxford 1959, rep. Toronto 1998). O. PÄCHT et al., *The St. Albans Psalter* (London 1960).

[C. H. TALBOT]

CHRISTINA OF SPOLETO, BL.

Widow, Augustinian; b. Augustina Camozzi at Porlezza on Lake Lugano, Switzerland, c. 1435; d. Spoleto, Italy, Feb. 13, 1456. The daughter of a reputable physician, Augustina married and was widowed very young and then lived a worldly, disorderly life for several years. Converted, she entered the Third Order Regular of St. Augustine (*see* AUGUSTINIAN NUNS) at Verona, taking the name Christina. Her extremely penitential life forced Christina to change her residence frequently to remain unknown and to avoid veneration by others. Her remains, formerly in the church of S. Nicolò, now rest in S. Gregorio Maggiore, Spoleto. Gregory XVI confirmed her cult Sept. 6, 1834.

Feast: Feb. 13.

Bibliography: N. CONCETTI, "De beata Christina a Spoleto," *Analecta Augustiniana* 5 (1913–14) 457–465. W. HÜMPFNER, *Lexicon für Theologie und Kirche*, ed. J. HOFER and K. RAHNER, 10 v. (2d, new ed. Freiburg 1957–65); suppl., *Das Zweite Vatikanische Konzil: Dokumente und Kommentare*, ed. H. S. BRECHTER et al., pt. 1 (1966) 2:1129.

[M. G. MCNEIL]

CHRISTINA OF STOMMELN, BL.

Beguine; b. Stommeln, near Cologne, Germany, 1242; d. there, Nov. 6, 1312. At 13 she left her prosperous peasant family (Bruso), and became a BEGUINE in Cologne. When her singular devotions and austerities disquieted her companions, she left the Beguine convent and returned to Stommeln. In 1267 she came under the direction of the Swedish Dominican Peter of Dacia (d. 1288), who kept a record of her experiences, the sensational nature of which has led some scholars to conjecture hallucinations or hysteria. Throughout her ordeals, however, Christina's firm faith and purity were evident. After the departure of Peter of Dacia in 1269, she corresponded with him through her parish priest, who added his own comments. Her relics were translated first to Niedeggen and then to Jülich, where they are still venerated. Pius X approved her cult in 1908.

Feast: Nov. 6.

Bibliography: *Acta Sanctorum* June 5:231–387. PETRUS DE DACIA, *De gratia naturam ditante, sive, De virtutibus Christinae Stumbelensis*, critical edition by M. ASZTALOS with English abstract (Stockholm 1982); *Vita Christinae Stumbelensis*, ed. J. PAULSON (Göteborg 1896, rep. Frankfurt am Main 1985). C. RUHRBERG, *Der literarische Körper der Heiligen: Leben und Viten der Christina von Stommeln* (Tübingen 1995). A. BUTLER, *The Lives of the Saints*, ed. H. THURSTON and D. ATTWATER, 4 v. (New York 1956) 4:277–279. J. TORSY, *Lexikon für Theologie und Kirche*, ed. J. HOFER and K. RAHNER, 10 v. (2d, new ed. Freiburg 1957–65) 2:1129.

[M. J. FINNEGAN]

CHRISTMAS AND ITS CYCLE

The solemnity of Christmas, December 25, celebrates the birth of Christ. Christmas is the second major feast of the Christian liturgical year in importance after Easter, and commemorates the INCARNATION or coming of Christ in the flesh, one aspect of the Paschal Mystery. Christmas is a holy day of obligation for Roman Catholics. The Christmas season starts with Evening Prayer I of Christmas Eve, includes the feast of the Holy Family, the solemnity of Mary, Mother of God, and the solemnity of Epiphany, and concludes with the feast of the Baptism of the Lord, which begins the first week of the Year, or Ordinary Time.

HISTORY

The earliest mention of the Nativity of Christ on December 25 can be found in the *Chronograph* of Philocalus, a Roman almanac whose source material can be dated to 336. The Nativity can be found on two chronological lists: one of the consuls of Rome, the other of the death dates of Christian martyrs where the date appears at the head of the calendar, suggesting that it may have been marked as a feast among Christians in Rome.

The true birth date of Christ is unknown. The worldwide census reported in Luke 2.1–2 cannot be substantiated. By the late second century different groups of Christians held divergent ideas on the date of Christ's birth: January 6 or 10 (identified by Adoptionists as the date of his baptism as well), April 19 or 20, May 20, or November 18 (Clement of Alexandria, *Stromateis* I, 146.) The *De Pascha Computus* in 243 claimed that Christ was born on March 28. Sextus Julius Africanus, writing prior to 221, placed the dates of the annunciation and of the passion of Christ on March 25, which would point to a December 25 birth date. Origen (In *Lev. Hom.* VIII) stated that "only sinners" celebrate the birthdays of their kings such as Herod or Pharaoh; Christians customarily celebrated the death dates of their martyrs as their "birthday into heaven."

With no evidence for the exact date of Christ's birth, and no clear proof of the date at which the feast began to be celebrated, nor its rationale, liturgical historians have developed two noncompetitive theories. The theory held by the majority is known as the History of Religions hypothesis. In its more conservative form this theory suggests that the origins of the Nativity feast may be found in a series of striking parallels between the heliocentric religion of the late Roman Empire and the Christmas feast: 1) December 25 was the date of the winter solstice on the Julian calendar. As solar monotheism made inroads into Roman culture, the solstice was celebrated as the birthday of the sun god: first MITHRAS, a private cult

Christmas mass at the Church of the Nativity, Bethlehem. (©Hulton-Deutsch Collection/CORBIS)

of male devotees imported from Persia, and later *Sol Invictus*, who was placed at the head of the pantheon of official Roman state gods by the emperor Aurelian in 274 as a symbolic representation of centralized imperial power. 2) Since the Nativity feast was instituted no earlier than 243, and no later than 336, this would have coincided with the rise of imperial solar worship. 3) Patristic sermons and texts of this period both in the East and the West employed numerous analogies between Christ and the sun: the rising sun as a symbol of his resurrection, Christ as the sun of justice (Mal 3.20), and Christ as the "true Sun" as distinguished from the non-Christian worship of the sun, a "mere creature" and not the Creator. The more extreme form of this hypothesis claims that Christmas represents an appropriation by Christians of the Roman feast of the birth of the Invincible Sun at the winter solstice, a christianization or "baptizing" of the civil feast. Such a move might have been intended to set up a distraction for Christians to keep them from participating in the Roman feast and the excesses of the Satur-

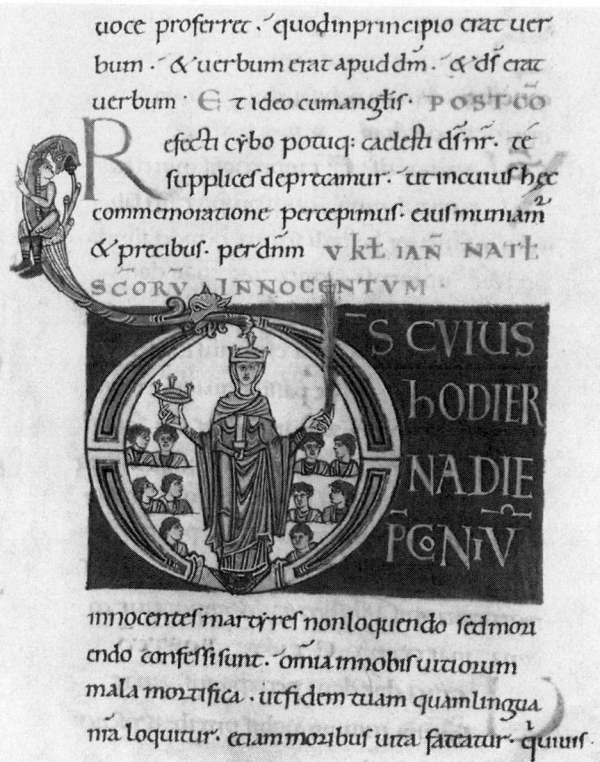

The miniature for the Feast of St. John the Evangelist, illumination from the "Berthold Missal" of the Abbey of Weingarten in Swabia, 1200–1232 (Morgan MS 710, folio 5).

nalia, which preceded it, or the civil New Year, which followed it, or perhaps to co-opt secular cultural customs in order to strengthen the newly legitimized Christian religion. However, early Christians consistently defined their own identity in opposition to their cultural surroundings, particularly in regard to other religions. Even in the mid-fifth century Leo I the Great (d. 461) scolded Christians who turned to bow to the rising sun before entering the basilica of St. Peter. (*Patrologia Latina* 54:218) This suggests that any influence of Roman worship practices upon Christians would have been strongly denied, yet the analogy between Christ and the sun clearly owed much to the cultural climate and state ideology of late imperial Rome.

A corollary of the History of Religions hypothesis holds that the main reason for the relatively rapid spread of the feast in the second half of the fourth and the fifth centuries was due to its use as an occasion for aggressive polemics on the part of Nicene Christian theologians and preachers against Arian and other variant Christian theological schools of thought, or against non-Christians. The Eastern fathers connected with the institution of the Christmas feast in the East after 380 (the Cappadocians and John Chrysostom) were also anti-Arian crusaders.

Leo the Great preached a series of ten Christmas sermons in Rome in which he both attacked various Christian and non-Christian groups, and employed numerous analogies between the sun and Christ, or between the "darkness" of his opponents and the "light" of orthodox Christians. Ironically, the Arians themselves could have interpreted the feast of Christ's birth to support their christological positions, which would suggest a date of origin later than the condemnation of Arianism in 325 at the Council of NICAEA. The link between Christmas and patristic polemics is considered plausible due to the precarious situation of the Christian church and the deteriorating state of the empire.

The earliest assertion that Christmas had replaced a pre-existing feast of the birth of the sun can be found in a marginal note on a 12th-century manuscript by Dionysius Bar-Salibi. The earliest modern scholar to espouse the theory in its extreme form was H. Usener in 1889, supported by H. Lietzmann. F. J. Dölger's theories on parallels between Christianity and Roman sun worship tended to support the theory. B. Botte's 1932 monograph summarized the evidence for a moderate form of the hypothesis, which is commonly accepted today, particularly among European scholars.

The minority thesis for the origins of Christmas, the Calculation Hypothesis, suggests that its roots are to be found less in the relation of Christianity to its surrounding secular cultural context than in shifts of thought occurring with the Christian community itself. In this theory, the date of Christmas was determined in relation to March 25, the supposed date of Christ's crucifixion in a number of early texts. The anniversary of the creation of the world was believed to coincide with the spring equinox, and so Christ the true sun was generated at the same time. The Hebrew patriarchs were supposed to have lived a full number of years, since the perfection of God was not believed to permit the imperfection of fractions, thus they were customarily believed to have died on their birthday. In the case of Christ, if his date of death was March 25, and the Annunciation is marked on the 25th, a full nine months later would give a birth date of December 25, or January 6 in the East where the ANNUNCIATION was celebrated on April 6.

While evidence exists for the significance of intricate symbolic number structures and the construction of symbolic relations among various religious phenomena in the church fathers, there are some weaknesses in this argument. There is no clear reason why the conception date of Christ would have been substituted for the birth date as in the case of the patriarchs. Such highly conceptual systems may have appealed to a well-educated elite but might not provide sufficient grounds for the institution of a feast to be celebrated by ordinary Christians.

This theory was first advanced by L. Duchesne in 1889, but not elaborated. H. Engberding attempted to boost its currency in 1949 by presenting a number of arguments that did not prove its tenets conclusively, though it intensified the scholarly debate before the theory fell into disinterest. In the 1980s T. Talley reviewed some of the evidence and built a more solid foundation to support the theory. Talley 1) disproved the thesis advanced by E. Norden in 1924 that January 6 was a pre-Christian solstice feast on the Egyptian calendar; 2) he discovered evidence in second-century Asian sources for a celebration of a Paschal feast that included the incarnation, on April 6, a conception date that would then point to a birth date of January 6 and would support the application of the even number of years in Christ's lifespan on earth; 3) he employed the argument from silence in Augustine's charge that the Donatists did not celebrate Epiphany (*Sermo* 202, *Patrologia Latina* 38:1033), to suggest that they might have celebrated Christmas before they split from the mainline Church in 311. The earlier the origins of Christmas, the less likely influence of solar worship, and, more specifically, the less likely was any intervention by the emperor Constantine. Since Constantine died in 337 at his Eastern capital Constantinople, which did not celebrate Christmas until the 380s, he is unlikely to have exerted any influence in its inception despite the parallels with Roman civil sun worship.

The earliest extant evidence for the celebration of the feast is found in a sermon by Optatus of Mileve in Numidia. In the early 360s he uses the gospel text of Herod's massacre of the innocents to encourage his people to stand fast in the face of the persecution taking place under the emperor Julian. The feast was known in Milan by the time of Ambrose (d. 397), who wrote several hymns, including *Intende qui regis Israel,* around Nativity themes. The letter of Pope Siricius (d. 399) to Himerius, bishop of Tarragona (*Epis.* 1.2.3., *Patrologia Latina* 13:1134) proves that Christmas was observed in Spain by 384, while the earliest certain evidence of the feast in Gaul is found in the calendar of Perpetuus, bishop of Tours (+491) (Gregory, *Hist. Francorum,* 10.31.6, *Patrologia Latina* 71: 566.)

In the East there had been a preexisting feast of the manifestation or genesis of Christ on January 6, a richer concept that in different geographic regions may have included the incarnation of Christ, the visit of the Magi, Christ's baptism in the Jordan, his first miracle at Cana, or the miracle of the multiplication of the loaves. The earliest evidence for a Christmas feast on December 25 comes from a sermon of Basil (d. 379) (*Homilia in s. Christi generationem, Patrologia Graeca* 31:1457–76). In 379 or 380 Gregory of Nazianzus preached a Christmas sermon in Constantinople (*In theophaniam oratio*

"Annunciation to the Shepherds," miniature accompanying the Propers for Christmas in a Sacramentary written at Mont-Saint-Michel in the 11th century (Morgan MS 641, fol. 2 v).

38, *Patrologia Graeca* 36:311–334); he also referred to himself as the originator (or possibly the main celebrant) of the feast (*In sancta lumina oratio, Patrologia Graeca* 36:349). John Chrysostom, preaching in Antioch in 386, seems to have encountered difficulty in persuading his congregation to accept this imported feast, since he resorts to several spurious arguments: that everyone has always known that the authentic birth date of Christ was December 25, which is confirmed by the census records from the time of Caesar Augustus, and an argument from the calculations of the respective birth dates (at the winter solstice and the summer solstice) and conception dates (at the spring equinox and autumn equinox) of Christ and John the Baptist. (*In diem natalem Domini n. J.C., Patrologia Graeca* 49:351). Paul of Emesa gave a Nativity sermon at Alexandria in the presence of St. Cyril on December 25, 432 (*De nativitate, Patrologia Graeca* 77:1433–44). In Palestine, however, the birth of Christ was celebrated on January 6 until the middle of the 7th century, when December 25 was accepted. The Armenians alone never accepted December 25. Under pressure from Rome some of the Eastern Catholic churches accepted the Christmas feast in the 16th century.

By the early Middle Ages Christmas marked the beginning of the calendar and was celebrated as a civil holi-

Shrine of the Manger in the Grotto of the Nativity, Bethlehem.

day in which fasting was forbidden. On Christmas Day 800, at the third Mass, Pope Leo III crowned Charlemagne emperor of the western Christian empire.

In 11th century France, the custom of enacting a Christmas play or trope appears in the liturgy, similar to that of Easter. One form of a play involved a dialogue with the shepherds based on Luke 2; plays from other countries depict the animals in the stable conversing. By the late Middle Ages many folklore customs and legends appear that claim that on Christmas Eve all of creation stops, or animals kneel, or plants bow, in honor of the Savior. Evil forces were thought to have no power to harm on Christmas.

In areas of Europe in which the Reformation took hold, Christmas celebrations took on a more muted tone and were forbidden in England during the Puritan period until 1660. In North America Christmas celebrations took on a festive and colorful character in the French and Spanish settlements. New England, due to its Puritan ethos, did not celebrate Christmas until the influx of Irish and German immigrants brought a wealth of Christmas customs such as the manger scene, carols, festive lights, and the liturgical observance of the feast.

LITURGY

The prolonged anti-Arian campaign, and later the anti-Nestorian movement, may have affected the contents of the feast. For Augustine, Christmas was a *memoria*, a commemoration of a historical event, not a mystery feast such as Easter. Less than fifty years later Leo the Great, who opposed the Arians as well as the Manichaeans, spoke of Christmas as a *mysterion*, a mystery feast or sacrament. Thus Christmas had become, in the first half of the fifth century, the liturgical celebration of the mystery of the Incarnation (see Gaillard).

Three Masses. The Feast of Christmas has three traditional Masses: at midnight, at dawn, and during the day, in addition to a vigil mass. Though this multiple liturgy is first mentioned by Gregory the Great (*Homil. 8 in evang.*, *Patrologia Latina* 76:1103) it must have developed earlier.

The earliest record of a Mass at midnight occurs in the diary of Egeria for January 6 (ed. J. Wilkinson). In addition to this Mass celebrated in Bethlehem, another Mass was offered in the morning at the church on Calvary. This custom soon spread to Rome. Perhaps it was Sixtus III (+440) who introduced it, when after the Council of Ephesus he rebuilt the Liberian Basilica (St. Mary Major) with a replica of the grotto of Bethlehem behind the main altar. (Relics of the true crib were acquired in the 7th century, and in 1586 the entire reproduction was removed to the Sistine Chapel of the basilica.) The station for the Mass at midnight has always been at this altar of the crib. The formulary is first found in the Gelasian Sacramentary (5–9; ed. L. C. Mohlberg, 7–8).

The Mass at dawn may also have been instituted in imitation of the liturgy at Palestine. Egeria describes a procession from Bethlehem back to Jerusalem with a gathering at the Holy Sepulchre at dawn. Though it is not known whether a Mass followed (a page is missing at this point), the Psalms repeated during the procession appear in the Gradual of the Roman Missal. The documents, beginning with the oldest Gregorian sacramentaries (ed. L. C. Mohlberg, 2) list St. Anastasia as the station for the second Mass. In the 6th century the cult of the Byzantine martyr Anastasia was localized in this church, named either for its founder or for the Anastasis in Jerusalem. Out of respect for the nearby Byzantine colony, the Bishop of Rome celebrated Mass here at dawn on the feast of the martyr, December 25. The Mass was the memorial of the saint, with a commemoration of Christmas. When the influence of Byzantium waned, the station was preserved and the Mass became one of Christmas with a commemoration of the martyr. From indirect evidence in the Gelasian Sacramentary, however, it has been argued that the Christmas Mass antedates that of St. Anastasia.

The third Mass, the oldest and principal Mass, was celebrated in the Basilica of St. Peter. The station was transferred to St. Mary Major by Gregory VII (1073–1085) to eliminate the inconvenience of returning to St. Peter's after the earlier Masses (*Ordo Rom.* 11.17; *Patrologia Latina* 78:1032).

Originally, the three Masses were stational and therefore celebrated only by the pope. But the multiple liturgies spread with the Roman Sacramentaries to the titular churches of the city, and then beyond Rome. In the Carolingian period the three masses were made mandatory, no longer as stational liturgies, but as three separate liturgies celebrated at different times on one day in one church.

In the 1997 Lectionary the readings for the three Christmas Masses, and the Vigil Mass, are invariable over the three yearly cycles. The vigil mass uses the gospel of Matthew 1.1–25, the extensive genealogy of Christ followed by the annunciation to Joseph, although the short form uses only the latter. The Mass at Midnight begins the readings with the prophetic text of Isaiah 9.1–6 on the Messiah who will free the people from war and oppression. The gospel reading is Luke 2.1–14, the narrative of Jesus' birth in Bethlehem and the annunciation to the shepherds. For the Mass at dawn the gospel is Luke 2:15–20, the visitation by the shepherds. The Mass during the day uses John 1.1–18, the more theological approach to the incarnation of Christ the Word of God. Each of these three Christmas liturgies uses a text from Isaiah as the first reading, and the mass during the day uses the beginning of the book of Hebrews as the second reading. The dominant scriptural themes progress with the time of day: from the theme of expectation, to the narrative of Christ's birth, to the proclamation to the shepherds and their presence and witness, to the overarching eternal plan of God whose keynote can be found in the profound prologue of the gospel of John.

Some of the eight prayer formulas from the Leonine Sacramentary, as well as other ancient sources, have been taken over in the current Roman Missal or have inspired new prayer formulas. The opening prayer for Mass during the day is taken from the Leonine Sacramentary and presents Leo the Great's theme of the "admirable exchange:" that Christ became human so that through his weakness humanity may share in his glory. The opening prayer for Mass at midnight, taken from the Gelasian Sacramentary, echoes the historically significant theme of darkness and light, presenting Christ by implication as the true sun. The second preface for Christmas echoes the controversies between Nicene and Arian Christians in the fourth century: "Christ is your Son before all ages, yet now he is born in time . . ."

The Christmas cycle. In the Leonine Sacramentary Christmas concludes the sanctoral cycle, but in the Würzburg Lectionary (7th century) it is found at the head of the temporal calendar. Christmas had become the beginning of the yearly cycle of feasts. Then, like Easter, it became the center of a season with a period of preparation (Advent), a vigil, an octave, and the related feasts of Epiphany and the Presentation of the Lord.

Vigil. The vigil of Christmas is found in the Würzburg Lectionary. Among the nine Christmas prayer formularies of the Leonine Sacramentary, two are obviously for the vigil (ed. L. C. Mohlberg, 1240, 1253).

Saints' feasts. Since ancient times, certain saints, called *comites Christi* by Durandus (*Rationale divinorum off.* 7.42.1) have been commemorated on the days following December 25. They are mentioned in Gregory of Nyssa (*Oratio funebris in laudem fratris Basilii, Patrologia Graeca* 46:789) and are found in all the Sacramentaries.

A feast of St. Stephen on December 26 is mentioned by Gregory of Nyssa (*In sanctum Stephanum, Patrologia Graeca* 46:701, 721), the *Breviarium Syriacum* (ed. B. Mariani, Rome 1956, 1:27), and in the Calendar of Carthage (H. Leclercq, *Dictionnaire d'archéologie chrétienne et de liturgie* 8:1:654). It is found in the Würzburg Lectionary and in the early Gregorian Sacramentaries. The Byzantine and Armenian rites, however, have the feast on December 27. The Leonine Sacramentary has it on August 3, but some of the texts (694, 696) contain explicit references to Christmas. Another text (701) suggests that August 3 was the dedication of the Basilica of St. Stephen.

A Feast of St. John the Evangelist is found on December 27 in the Roman books, while many Oriental and Gallican books (such as the *Breviarium Syriacum*) list SS. James and John. The Calendar of Carthage has St. John the Baptist with St. James, but this must be considered in error (*Dictionnaire d'archéologie chrétienne* 8.1:645).

Eastern sources have a commemoration of SS. Peter and Paul on December 28 (*Breviarium Syriacum*) or of Peter with James and John on December 27 and Paul on December 28 (Gregory of Nyssa, *In laudem fratris Basilii, Patrologia Graeca* 46:789). Because the feast of these two apostles was fixed at an early date in Rome on June 29, they are not commemorated after Christmas in the West.

A feast of the Holy Innocents is found in most documents on December 28. Originally festive, under Gallican influence the commemoration acquired aspects of mourning (purple vestments, omission of the *Te Deum, Gloria,* and *Alleluia*), all of which were suppressed in 1961.

The feasts of St. Thomas Becket (d. 1170) on December 29 and St. Sylvester (d. 336) on December 31 (in the *Chronograph* of Philocalus of 354) are optional memorials in the present sanctoral calendar.

Octave. January 1 has had at various times a Mass against pagan practices, a Mass of the Virgin Mary, and a Mass of the octave of Christmas.

The oldest of these is the *Missa ad prohibendum ab idolis,* which bears witness to the survival of pre-Christian practices (Righetti 2:42). St. Augustine (*Sermo* 198; *Patrologia Latina* 38:1024–26) attacked such practices and exhorted the faithful to prayer and penance. The Second Council of Tours (567) and the Fifth Council of Toledo (633) ordered penance on this day (c.17, Hefele-Leclercq 3:188, and c.11, *ibid.* 3:269). This Mass, however, fell into disuse in the 6th and 7th centuries. The Gregorian Sacramentary preserved the Secret and Postcommunion prayers, which were used in the Tridentine Mass.

A Mass in honor of the Virgin Mary on January 1 was also known at Rome (B. Botte, "La première fête mariale"). The Byzantine and Syrian liturgies have a feast of the Virgin Mary on December 26. The Roman Mass may have been inspired by local circumstances and may have originated as the dedication of S. Maria Antiqua, formerly the station on January 1. It is possible that a pre-Christian legend in which a dragon devoured a vestal virgin on this spot in the Roman Forum on January 1 may have suggested a feast in honor of the Virgin who conquered the devil. The antiphons used in the office for this day were probably inherited from the Byzantine monks who once served S. Maria Antiqua. The formulary was *vultum tuum,* the common of virgins, with proper orations and a preface derived from St. Augustine. At first the Gospel was from the same common (Mt 13.44–52), later the text of Lk 2.21–32 was used. Though this Mass persisted in some places in the Middle Ages, it fell into disuse as other feasts of the Virgin Mary developed. According to Botte this Mass can be considered the oldest Marian feast in the Roman liturgy (*ibid.*).

The Gelasian and Gregorian Sacramentaries have a formulary "in octabas Domini," for the octave of the Lord. Originally, the only reference to the Circumcision was in the Gospel, logically chosen from Lk 2.21–32. This text also included the Presentation until a proper feast of this event developed. The station, formerly at S. Maria ad Martyres, was transferred to S. Maria in Trastevere by Callistus II (1119–24). The Circumcision became the primary object of this feast day, first in Spain, then in Gaul, and finally in Rome (Righetti 22:43). From the 15th century Roman books have the title "Feast of the Circumcision." The earlier title "Octave of the Nativity" was restored in 1961.

At present this is celebrated as the Solemnity of Mary, Mother of God, and is a holy day of obligation in the United States, except when it falls on a Saturday or a Monday. The readings for Mass, invariable for all three cycles, include the gospel reading from Lk 2.16–21, which concludes with a reference to Jesus' circumcision and naming on the eighth day following his birth. At the discretion of the local bishop the Mass for the World Day of Prayer for Peace may be celebrated on this day.

Holy Family. Previously celebrated on the Sunday after Epiphany, this was moved in 1969 to the Sunday within the octave of Christmas to bring the mystery of the Holy Family into closer temporal proximity with the feast of the Nativity. In those years when no Sunday occurs during the octave, the feast is celebrated on December 30 with just one reading before the gospel. The readings provided vary among the three cycles; the gospel readings include Mt 2.13–15, 19–23 (the flight into Egypt), Lk 2.22–40 (the presentation of Jesus in the temple), and Lk 2.41–52 (Jesus in the temple at age 12).

The second Sunday after Christmas (falling between January 2 and 5) replaces the feast of the Holy Name. Dating back to 1528 and made a feast of the universal church in 1721, the feast of the Holy Name was suppressed in the 1969 calendar.

Epiphany. The Feast of the Epiphany, first celebrated in Rome in the second half of the 4th century, traditionally falls on January 6. In those countries where it is not a holy day of obligation it can be celebrated on the Sunday that falls between January 2 and 8 (*see* EPIPHANY).

European Christmas Customs. The use of the manger scene in church and home derives ultimately from the grotto in Bethlehem and its reproduction in St. Mary Major. It owes its popularity to St. Francis of Assisi, who organized a live manger scene in 1223 in the Italian town of Greccio. In many regions the figure of the Christ child is solemnly placed in the manger scene after the first Mass.

While a fir tree was commonly brought into the house in the winter even in pre-Christian times, some Christian commentators have suggested the origin of the decorated Christmas tree in the "Paradise tree," first found in Strasbourg in 1605. This tree, decorated with apples, served as a prop in Christmas mystery plays about Adam and Eve and later came to symbolize the Tree of Life.

The term "carol," formerly designating a Christmas song of a popular nature as opposed to a more solemn hymn, is now generally used of all Christmas songs. The first hymns using the themes of the Nativity of Christ were composed in the late 4th and early 5th centuries. Christmas carols were also popularized in late medieval Italy by the Franciscans, and their popularity spread throughout Europe (*see* CAROL).

Exchanging of gifts, in harmony with the significance of Christmas, may have been influenced by a similar custom (*strenae*) among non-Christians on January 1. Gifts are exchanged by the French on January 1, among the Spanish and Italians on January 6, and by other nationalities on December 25. In most parts of Europe it is the Christ Child who brings the gifts. After the Reformation the day itself was personified, and the figure of Father Christmas was later combined with St. Nicholas, the patron of children, to become Santa Claus. In Italy gifts are brought by the old woman Befana (from "Epiphany") and in Spain by the Three Kings.

Pastoral issues. Some of the contemporary pastoral issues linked with the liturgical celebration of Christmas include: 1) how to serve the relatively large numbers attending Christmas liturgies, which includes many non-Catholics or marginal Christians; 2) the high incidence of holiday depression, particularly among those with few family ties; 3) the often intense commercial pressure characteristic of the period before Christmas, which can obscure the religious meaning of the feast for Christians; 4) the preemptive anticipation of Christmas by means of Christmas concerts, pageants and other festivities throughout Advent; 5) the fact that the climatic winter symbolism characteristic of the Northern hemisphere, which largely determines the character of Christmas cultural celebrations, particularly in poetry and music, is completely reversed in the Southern hemisphere.

Bibliography: S. K. ROLL, *Toward the Origins of Christmas* (Kampen, 1995); T. J. TALLEY, *The Origins of the Liturgical Year* (Collegeville, 1991); A.J. MARTIMORT ed. *The Church at Prayer IV: The Liturgy and Time* (Collegeville, 1986); H. AUF DER MAUR, *Feiern im Rhythmus der Zeit* (Regensburg, 1983):165–176; R. E. BROWN, *The Birth of the Messiah* (New York, 1979); L. FENDT, "Der heutige Stand der Forschung über das Weihnachtsfest am 25.12 und über Epiphanie," *Theologische Literaturzeitung* 78 (1953): 1–10; B. BOTTE, *Les origines de Noël et de l'Épiphanie* (Louvain, 1932); ibid., "La premiére fête mariale de la liturgie romaine," *Ephemerides Liturgicae* 47 (1933): 425–430; F. J. DÖLGER, "Sol salutis. Gebet und Gesang im christlichen Altertum," (Münster, 1925); J. GAILLARD, "Noël: memoria ou mystère?" *La Maison-Dieu* 15/59 (1959): 37–59; J. GUNSTONE, *Christmas and Epiphany. Studies in Christian Worship* (London, 1967); F. X. WEISER, *Handbook of Christian Feasts and Customs* (New York, 1958); T. A. KROSNICKI, "The Christmas Cycle in the Roman Missal of Paul VI," *American Ecclesiastical Review* 165:4 (December 1971): 271–281; A. NOCENT, *The Liturgical Year: Advent, Christmas, Epiphany* (Collegeville, 1977); J. WILKINSON, *Egeria's Travels* (Jerusalem, 1981.)

[S. K. ROLL]

CHRISTOCENTRISM

In its most simple meaning, "Christocentrism" indicates that the humanity assumed by the Son of God is in all its mysteries, from the incarnation to the ascension into heaven, efficacious for the salvation of humankind and for the radical renewal of creation. Christ is therefore the only Redeemer and absolute exemplar.

In the New Testament. The New Testament is the primary source of our profession that Christ is the beginning, the center and the eschatological goal of human existence and of the universe. The Letter to the Philippians states that in his divinity and in his resurrected humanity Christ saves and recapitulates all things (2.6–11). Other letters of Paul confirm this: Eph. 1.10 (Christ sums up all in himself); Col. 1.15–16 (he is the image of the invisible God, the firstborn of all creation; . . . in him all things in heaven and on earth were created); Colossians 1.20 (through him God was pleased to reconcile to himself all things, whether on earth or in heaven). The witness of John's Book of Revelation cannot be ignored: 23.13 (Christ is the beginning and the end, alpha and omega). According to the prologue of the Gospel of St. John (1.1–14), all things exist through the eternal Word of God who became flesh and came to what was his own (1.11). Indeed, all authority in heaven and on earth has been given to him (Mt. 5.18).

Christocentrism acquired its eschatological character in the New Testament. According to his good will, God the Father "dispensed in the fullness of times to reestablish all things in Christ, both those in the heavens and those on the earth" (Eph. 1.10). In the words of the Letter to the Philippians, "at the name of Jesus every knee must bend, in heaven and on earth and under the earth, and every tongue must confess that Jesus Christ is Lord, to the glory of God the father" (2.10–11).

In the Patristic Era. For St. Clement, Christ is the cosmic Word. According to St. Ignatius of Antioch, Christ descended to the underworld to free his disciples. It is in this cosmic context that the former phrase of the Creed "descended into hell" came to express the faith that Christ visited the lower world to free those who awaited him there. According to St. Irenaeus, all things are therefore recapitulated in Christ. By this, he meant that even before the beginning of the world all human beings and creatures were preordained for the Logos Christ who recreates and renews his creation.

Christian art from its earliest period in the catacombs and in basilicas celebrated Christ as Pantocrator, the universal creator who sustains, renews, and recapitulates all creation. Some of the more famous mosaics of the "Pantocrator" in domes or in triumphal arcs must be mentioned: Hagia Sophia, Salonika, Greece; San Vitale, Ravenna, Italy; San Apollinare in Classe, Ravenna, Italy; 12th to 13th century immense Byzantine mosaic in the Cathedral of Monreale, Sicily; St. Paul-Outside-the-Walls, Rome; and, the 4th-century basilica of Santa Maria in Domnica, Rome, Italy. The defense of the Christological dogmas of Nicea, Chalcedon and Constantinople III inspired much of this art and devotion to Christ. His Christocentric primacy is represented in the mosaics of those times.

In Theology. Saint Bonaventure and others occasionally speak of Christ as center simply in terms of his divinity: the Son of God being at the center of the Trinity. More commonly, Christocentrism involves a focus on the mystery of the incarnation. Spirituality from the earliest centuries has been Christocentric, and the imitation of Christ is the oldest form of Christocentrism. Christ is the center of salvation, for the sacred humanity of the Word made man is the "pivotal hinge" of salvation (*caro cardo salutis*).

Christ is by the very character of the incarnation theocentric and anthropocentric at the same time. K. Rahner maintained that in terms of historical transcendentality, the primacy of Christ is Christocentrism. He held further that the free incarnation of the Logos creates the order of grace and of nature as his own.

Special interest in Christocentrism was inspired by Franciscan Scotists beginning in the 16th century. They maintained that even after sin, the incarnation of the Son of God is divinely willed previous to any reference to the fall of humankind. The reason for their position was simple: nothing may constrain God to will to do something on behalf of sinful human beings. Only the eternal and infinite love of the triune God is the motive for his redemptive acts. Thus the Incarnation of the Son of God is willed not primarily in reference to the sin of humankind, but for the sake of Christ's cosmic primacy and for his renewal of humankind and creation. Questions raised in the 19th century concerning certain aspects of the Scotistic doctrine of redemption and of the incarnation of the Son of God as independent from the motive of human sin [cf. Hilary of Paris' *Cur Deus Homo* (1867)] were addressed by R. Garrigou-Lagrange, G.M. Roschini and J.F. Bonnefoy, among others.

The Second Vatican Council described the promotion of unity in quasi-sacramental terms: "The promotion of unity belongs to the innermost mission of the Church, because it is in Christ in the nature of a sacrament or sign and instrument of the intimate union with God and of the unity of all mankind" (*Gaudium et spes*, n. 42). This unity is thoroughly Christocentric. The declaration of the Congregation for the Doctrine of the Faith "On the Unicity and Salvific Universality of Jesus Christ and the Church" (*Dominus Iesus*), issued on Aug. 6, 2000, reprises this theme. Picking up also on *Lumen gentium* 48, it illustrates the unity of the Church with Christ and defends the unicity of the relationship which Christ and the Church have with the Kingdom of God (nn. 18–19). In truth, Christocentrism and the Church are truly inseparable.

In the Liturgy. In implementing the liturgical renewal of the Second Vatican Council and reducing the number of Christ's feasts, Pope Paul VI nevertheless maintained that every liturgical celebration and every prayer of the People of God is truly the prayer of Christ and of his people. Christ is the center of the Church's liturgy, from the beginning of the advent season to the last Sunday of the year when his solemnity as King of the Universe is celebrated. He is the priest and the head of his people. He prays in them, as their God, and he is the object of the prayer of his people (cf. Apostolic Constitution *Laudis canticum*, 1970, nn.7–8).

Bibliography: P. BENOIT, *Pré-existence et Incarnation in Rev-Biblique* 77 (1970) 5–29. B. D. CHILTON, *God in Strength: Jesus' Announcement of the Kingdom* (Studien zum Neuen Testament und seiner Umwelt, Series B; Louvain 1979). O. CULLMANN, *Christ and Time* (Philadelphia 1964). M. DE JONGE, *Jesus as Prophet and King in the Fourth Gospel* A(nalecta Lovaniensia biblica et orientalia, Series V; Louvain 1973). J. A. FITZMYER, *A Christological Catechism: New Testament Answers* (New York 1982); *The Biblical Commission and Christology*, in *Theological Studies* 46 (1985) 407–75. International Theological Commission, *Quaestio de Iesu Christo* (Vatican 1980); International Theological Commission, *La conscience que Jesus avait de lui même et de sa mission*, in *Gregorianum* 57 (1986) 415–27; J. MOUROUX, *The Mystery of Time* (New York 1964). F. X. PANCHERI, *Il Primato universale di Cristo*, in *Problemi e figure della Scuola Scotista del Santo* (Padua 1966). B. PRZEWOZNY, *Church as the Sacrament of the Unity of All Mankind* (Rome 1979). J. T. SANDERS, *The New Testament Christological Hymns: Their Historical Religious Background* (Cambridge 1971).

[B. J. PRZEWOZNY]

CHRISTOLOGY

In traditional systematic theology, Christology is the study of the Person and attributes of Christ, in particular the union in Him of divine and human natures. The study was motivated by a solidly practical interest for the worship of Christ is the life of the Church. Consequently the Church has ever been under the necessity of explaining, both to its own faithful and to those without, how worship of Jesus, a man, can be combined with monotheism.

In the unsystematic fashion characteristic of Sacred Scripture, the authors of the New Testament had bequeathed to the primitive Christian community a double premise, viz, that Christ as a Person was indivisibly one and that He was simultaneously fully divine and fully human. The necessity of showing how these two affirmations could be held together in synthesis (the central problem of Christology) was not immediately felt. Confronted with the crude dissents of Ebionitism and Docetism, the Apostolic Fathers and the apologists simply repeated the gospel message either word for word or in carefully chosen equivalent terms.

Toward the close of the 2nd century, a new group of thinkers, steeped in Greek philosophy, entered into the life of the Church and rapidly propelled Christology into its most decisive epoch. Later historians (e.g., A. von Harnack, O. Cullmann) profess to find at this juncture a major setback for authentic Christianity, charging that the Hellenic influence diverted faith from its true object and turned the Church down the path of sterile speculation. In rebuttal it can be shown (1) that the passionate theological debates that raged from the 3rd to the 7th century could have been avoided only by a universal agreement to refrain from thinking about the central Figure of Christian worship and (2) that, given the right to think and the possibility of thinking incorrectly (a possibility that was repeatedly verified in fact), the Church was compelled to ponder ever more profoundly the gospel message in order to produce an apt reply to each freshly appearing heretical subtlety. The epoch opened in 318, when Arius published his daring conclusion that the Son was not God but merely a creature. There followed: Apollinarianism, which sought to mutilate the humanity of Christ by denying Him a rational soul; Nestorianism, which beheld in the Incarnation a merely affective, extrinsic union between two persons, one divine and the other human; monophysitism, which coupled belief in the one Person of Christ with the contention that He therefore possessed only one nature; and monothelitism, which confessed two natures in Christ while denying Him two wills. To list those who struggled in the orthodox cause against these mischievous heresies would be to reproduce almost the entire roster of the Fathers of the Church. The outstanding champions, however, were St. Athanasius, St. Cyril of Alexandria, Pope St. Leo the Great, and St. Sophronius in Jerusalem. Under their respective leadership the Ecumenical Councils of Nicaea I (325), Ephesus (431), Chalcedon (451), and Constantinople III (680) fashioned the dogmatic definitions that to this day remain the clearest expression of the Church's faith in its Lord.

Medieval Christology strove to make explicit and to systematize the theological truths latent in the earlier dogmatic pronouncements. Christ's several kinds of knowledge, His possession of various types of grace, and the freedom of His human will received large attention. The attempt to interpret metaphysically the HYPOSTATIC union aroused much dispute among the schools. These preoccupations of the medieval scholastic theologians formed the basis of Catholic works on Christology until the mid-20th century.

Since then Christology has undergone a paradigm shift. No longer simply explicating the hypostatic union, it seeks to recapitulate the entire development of the Christological tradition in order to mediate Christ's redemptive significance in the contemporary cultural context.

See Also: JESUS CHRIST (IN THEOLOGY); JESUS CHRIST, ARTICLES ON; THEOLOGY; THEOLOGY,

HISTORY OF; THEOLOGY, INFLUENCE OF GREEK PHILOSOPHY ON.

Bibliography: *Dictionnaire de théologie catholique,* ed. A. VACANT et al., 15 v. (Paris 1903–50; Tables générales 1951–), Tables générales 2:2548–2655. A. MICHEL, *Dictionnaire de théologie catholique,* ed. A. VACANT et al., 15 v. (Paris 1903–50; Tables générales 1951–) 7.2:1445–1539. A. GRILLMEIER *Lexikon für Theologie und Kirche,* ed. J. HOFER and K. RAHNER, 10 v. (Freiburg 1957–65) 2:1156–66. G. SEVENSTER et al., *Die Religion in Geschichte und Gegenwart,* 7 v. (Tübingen 1957–65) 1:1745–89. W. SUNDAY, *Christologies Ancient and Modern* (New York 1910). H. M. RELTON, *Studies in Christian Doctrine* (New York 1960). H. M. DIEPEN, *Douze dialogues de christologie ancienne* (Rome 1960). K. RAHNER, ''Current Problems in Christology,'' *Theological Investigations,* tr. C. ERNST, v. 1 (Baltimore 1961) 149–200. T. E. CLARKE, ''Some Aspects of Current Christology'' in J. E. O'NEILL, ed., *The Encounter with God* (New York 1962) 33–58. B. LEEMING, ''Reflections on English Christology'' in A. GRILLMEIER and H. BACHT, *Das Konzil von Chlakedon: Geschichte und Gegenwart,* 3 v. (Würzburg 1951–54) 3:695–718.

[J. J. WALSH/W. P. LOEWE]

CHRISTOLOGY, CONTROVERSIES ON (PATRISTIC)

The disputes concerning the nature of Jesus Christ, true God and true man, that troubled the theological development of the early Church. Reflection on the nature of Christ was intimately connected with His soteriological activity and with His office or function as Lord (*Kyrios*). Paul, in Rom 1.3, had spoken of Christ as at once ''according to the spirit'' and ''according to the flesh''; and the apostolic Fathers insisted that He was preexistent, unbegotten, and the head of creation. But there is little evidence for an interest in the manner in which the divine spirit and the human nature were joined together in Christ. Against the Gnostics and Ebionites, the apostolic Fathers insisted on a true divine spirit and a true body in Christ (Ignatius of Antioch, *Eph.* 3.2, 8.2; *Smyr.* 4.1), and Irenaeus considered the denial of this assertion heretical.

Apologists. In the 2d century the APOLOGISTS insisted that Jesus Christ was the visible form of the divine Logos, a statement that made sense within the sphere of the popular Hellenistic philosophy. Whereas IGNATIUS OF ANTIOCH had spoken of the historical Christ as the Logos through whom God had broken His eternal silence (*Mag.* 8.2), the apologists identified the Logos with the preexistent cosmic principle of God's wisdom and power (1 Cor 1.24). Irenaeus, in conflict with the Gnostics, opposed their DOCETISM with a theology of the INCARNATION, basing his thought on the tradition represented by Theophilus of Antioch, Justin Martyr, and Ignatius (*Eph.* 20.1). Irenaeus insisted that out of boundless love Jesus Christ became like unto men as a man so that He might fulfill in men that which He was Himself. This divinization of man required that Christ be at once true God and true man.

Tertullian. TERTULLIAN taught that the oneness of the Father and the Son required a oneness in substance that underlay the difference in persons in the Trinity. His corporeal concepts, tied in with time and quantity, however, involved his explanation in SUBORDINATIONISM; but his terminology regarding one Person in two substances, or natures, as well as the distinction of the three Persons in one substance in the Trinity, proved invaluable in the later Western Christological development. His intention was to combat MONARCHIANISM, which denied the diversity of Persons in the one God, as well as various forms of Adoptionism and Modalism. The Roman type of ADOPTIONISM that saw Christ raised to divinity in His Baptism was combated by the popes before 200; and CALLISTUS, with the condemnation of Sabellius, included a repudiation of the MODALISM of Noëtus and Praxeas in Asia Minor, who considered the three functions of the Father, Son, and Spirit in the history of salvation as mere manifestations or modes of the Godhead. This theory was rejected also by HIPPOLYTUS OF ROME. A further development of Modalism manifested itself in PATRIPASSIANISM, or the theory that if Father and Son were one in substance, the Father must have suffered for mankind.

Homoousios. Under the influence of the Neoplatonist teaching on the divine emanations, CLEMENT OF ALEXANDRIA and ORIGEN considered Christ in His cosmic function and tended to explain the Savior as the head of creation; as seen from a worldly viewpoint, Christ was eternal and therefore divine, but from God's viewpoint, He was rather the first of all creation. Two further tendencies manifested themselves among the followers of Origen: GREGORY THAUMATURGUS insisted on the oneness in nature of Son and Father; DIONYSIUS (DENIS) OF ALEXANDRIA, in opposing Libyan Modalism, asserted that Father and Son were of the same divine nature. Since the word HOMOOUSIOS, or consubstantial, had been used by PAUL OF SAMOSATA in a Monarchian sense, it was looked upon with suspicion by the Alexandrians, and after 268 it was rejected also by the Antiochians. LUCIAN OF ANTIOCH, influenced by Aristotelian logic and pursuing the conviction that the begotten Son could not be of the same being as the unbegotten Godhead, considered the Logos as joined to the divinity on a moral or even on an ethical principle. His pupil ARIUS was condemned at the Council of NICAEA I (325), where the doctrine that the Son was true God, of the same substance as the Father (homoousios), was clarified and the difference between creation out of nothing and the eternal generation of Persons in the Godhead was clearly recognized. In the politically dominated theological disputes of the next 40 years, ATHANASIUS of Alexandria played a leading part, insisting on the validity of the Nicene definition.

After the splintering of the Arianizing sects into Anomoean and Homoean groups (the Son is not like the Father; the Son is similar to the Father), Meletius of Antioch (c. 363) and the Cappadocian Fathers insisted on the consubstantiality of the three divine Persons, and by differentiating between *ousia* (substance) and *hypostasis* (person or individual) avoided the tendency to find subordination in the Trinity. *See* MELETIAN SCHISM. Under the influence of the Aristotelian concept of the unity of matter and form and in opposition to the Gnostic separation of Christ into the divine Savior and His earthly form, the APOLLINARISTS denied that Christ had a human soul, and EUSTATHIUS OF ANTIOCH claimed that the divinity dwelt in the humanity in order to justify the concept of the *Logos-sarx* unity.

Nestorianism. The Antiochene theologians led by DIODORE OF TARSUS rejected the Arian concept of the creation of the Logos, but maintained that a distinction had to be made between the flesh capable of suffering and the impassible Logos. THEODORE OF MOPSUESTIA insisted that the Logos had assumed a complete manhood. Christ must have had a human soul, since His redemptive act as the God-man freed man's soul from sin, and He led man eventually through the Resurrection to a fulfillment of human nature that was based and modeled on His own human and divine experience. To emphasize this teaching, Nestorius of Constantinople decided to call Mary the Mother of Christ rather than the THEOTOKOS, or Mother of God, in order to stress the validity of the true human nature.

In combating this manifestation of Nestorianism, CYRIL OF ALEXANDRIA, on commission from Pope Celestine I, presided over the Council of EPHESUS (431) and condemned the teaching of Nestorius. But Cyril's extreme statement of the Alexandrian position in his 12 anathemas had to be modified by a letter of Union signed by himself and JOHN OF ANTIOCH in 433.

Monophysitism. Cyril held that the divine and human substance (or natures in an abstract sense) were complete and unconfused in Christ; they could be separated only in thought, by theoretical concepts, since the concrete Christ was the divine Logos incarnated as the God-man. Cyril's insistence that Christ had to be an individual was accepted in such literal fashion by EUTYCHES that at the Synod of Constantinople (448) he was forced to admit that one nature resulted from the union of the divinity and humanity in Christ. This crude MONOPHYSITISM was condemned at the Council of Chalcedon (451), where, in consequence of the teaching in the *Tome* of Pope LEO I and the precise theological terminology achieved by a group of theologians including THEODORET OF CYR, it was asserted that Christ was "of two natures without mixture, or confusion." This definition was rejected by Nestorius, who considered the distinction between *hypostasis* (person) and *ousia* (nature) as confused, and by the Monophysites, who said that to deny that Christ was of one nature led to a logical conclusion that there were two complete and therefore individual natures in the God-man.

With the condemnation of the THREE CHAPTERS at the Council of CONSTANTINOPLE II (553), the Chalcedonian definition took on its stabilized form early in BYZANTINE THEOLOGY. Cyril's doctrine that in Christ there is one nature (*mia physis*) was interpreted to mean that there is one individual or substantial being, and John the Grammarian clarified the fact that in the hypostatic unity the human nature is inalterably united to the divine Person. However, the founding of national churches in Egypt, Syria, and Armenia exaggerated the Monophysite position.

Monothelitism. The Emperor HERACLIUS attempted to win back the Monophysites to unity by speaking of one energy or action in Christ, but this resulted in the controversies over MONOTHELITISM and Monergism. MAXIMUS THE CONFESSOR clarified these doctrines by insisting that in Christ there are two wills and two energies, representing, respectively, the fully coordinated divine and human natures. JOHN DAMASCENE combined the dythelitism (two wills) doctrine with the Chalcedonian idea of the *enhypostasis,* or one Person with two natures, to reassert the Leonine teaching of the communication of idioms. This doctrine was used subsequently by the medieval Scholastic theologians in their teaching on the relations between the natures and person in Christ and on the relations of the natures with each other (*see* SCHOLASTICISM).

In the West, a new type of Adoptionism was discussed in 7th-century Spain, and was condemned by Charlemagne in several Carolingian synods. The later scholastics argued over the personality of Christ, and this problem has been resurrected in contemporary discussions concerning the ego of Christ. Protestant theology from Luther, Calvin, and Zwingli to Hegel, Strauss, Ritschl, and M. Köhler has been more concerned with the religious, ethical, and historical implications of Christology than with the explanation of the union between the divine and human nature. Many contemporary non-Catholics accept some type of subordinationism in their Christological thinking.

Bibliography: A. MICHEL, *Dictionnaire de théologie catholique,* ed. A. VACANT et al. (Paris 1903–50; Tables générales 1951–) Tables générales 2:2642–45. A. GRILLMEIER and H. BACHT, *Das Konzl von Chalkedon: Geschichte und Gegenwart* (Wurzburg

1951–54) v. 1–3. W. ELERT, *Der Ausgang der altkirchlichen Christologie* (Berlin 1957). R. V. SELLERS, *Two Ancient Christologies* (London 1940). B. M. XIBERTA Y ROQUETA, "Un conflicto entre dos Cristologias," *Miscellanea Giovanni Mercati*, 6 v. (Rome 1946) 1:327–354. E. R. HARDY and C. C. RICHARDSON, eds., *Christology of the Later Fathers* (Philadelphia 1954). P. GALTIER, *Gregorianium* (Rome 1959) 54–66. A. GRILLMEIER, "Der Neu-Chalkedonismus," *Histoisches Jahrbuch der Görres-Gesellschaft* 77 (Munich 1958) 151–166. B. SKARD, *Die Inkarnation* (Stuttgart 1958). G. WINGREN, *Man and the Incarnation,* tr. R. MACKENZIE (Philadelphia 1959). *Handbuch der Dogmengeschichte* 3.1, ed. M. SCHMAUS and A. GRILLMEIER (Freiburg 1965).

[F. X. MURPHY]

CHRISTOPHER, ANTIPOPE

Pontificate: *c.* September 903–January 904. He probably died in early 904. Christopher was a priest of St. Damasus, one of the 25 title churches (i.e., ancient parishes) of Rome, and nothing specific is known of his career until he evidently led an internal coup against Pope Leo V (903–04). Leo had been in office for 30 days, and was imprisoned; Christopher was made pope. Christopher was nevertheless only in office four months before his successor, Sergius III (904–911), marched on Rome with the help of Duke Alberic I of Spoleto (died *c.* 925). Christopher was deposed and jailed. According to Herimannus Augiensis he finished out his days as a monk, but Vulgarius reports that Sergius had both Christopher and Leo strangled in prison. Christopher's only surviving bull is a confirmation of privileges to the monastery of Corbie, which was later referred to by Pope Leo IX (1049–54) in his confirmation of the same privileges.

The years between the 870s and 1000 were the worst in history for the papacy. Charlemagne's empire had virtually disintegrated, and Rome and the Papal States were vulnerable to attack from Muslim-controlled Sicily (and southwest Italy). The Byzantines still had outposts and clients on the Adriatic, and Lombard territory to the north was in reality a collection of semi-autonomous city-states and duchies. In this confusion, the Roman military elite routinely made and unmade popes for its own purposes. Our sources are poor, but Christopher's coup appears to have been part of a split within the group in Rome that opposed Pope Leo because he was a non-Roman. Christopher's name was generally included in lists of popes into the modern period. Nonetheless, since his election was irregular, and since Leo V now seems to have survived as long as Christopher, he is today universally considered an antipope.

Bibliography: L. DUCHESNE, ed. *Liber Pontificalis* (Paris 1886–92; repr. 1955–57) 2.235. P. JAFFÉ, *Regesta pontificum Romanorum* (Leipzig 1885–88; repr. Graz 1956) 1.444–45. E. DÜMMLER, *Auxilius und Vulgarius* (Leipzig 1866) 60, 135. FLODOARD OF REIMS, *De triumphis Christi sanctorumque Palaestinae* 12.7, in J. P. MIGNE, ed. *Patrologia Latina* (Paris 1884–64) 135.831. HERIMANNUS AUGIENSIS, *Chronicon* 904, in *Monumenta Germaniae historica, Scriptores*, 5.111. MARIANNUS SCOTTUS, *Chronicon*, in *Monumenta Germaniae historica, Scriptores*, 5.487. B. PLATINA, *De vita Christi ac omnium pontificum* 121, ed. G. GAIDA, in *Rerum italicarum scriptores* 3.1, ed. L. A. MURATORI (Città di Castello and Bologna 1913–32) 163. H. K. MANN, *The Lives of the Popes in the Early Middle Ages* (London 1902–32) 4.111–18, 130, 136. G. BARDY, *Dictionnaire d'histoire et de géographie ecclésiastiques* (Paris 1953) 12.778–79. J. N. D. KELLY, *The Oxford Dictionary of Popes* (New York 1986) 119.

[P. M. SAVAGE]

CHRISTOPHER, ST.

Possibly a martyr, whose cult was widely spread in the East and West at an early date (feast, July 25). As early as 452 a church in Bithynia was dedicated in his honor. The Roman Martyrology states that a Christopher was martyred in Lycia under King Decius. According to the legendary *passio*, Christopher was called Reprobus before his baptism and was a Canaanite of great stature and strength. Legend states that when he discovered the devil's fear of Christ, he became a Christian. The story of Christopher's bearing the Christ child upon his shoulders while fording a river does not appear in the earliest accounts and is doubtless an accretion based upon the saint's name, "Christbearer." A drop of the martyr's blood was said to have healed a wound that the persecuting King suffered while attempting to execute Christopher. As a result of this miracle the King became a Christian. This gave rise to the popular medieval belief that anyone who looked upon the saint's image would be free from harm that day; hence the custom of putting up images of the saint opposite the church door. He is also the patron of travelers.

Bibliography: *Acta Sanctorum* July 6:125–149. A. BUTLER, *The Lives of the Saints,* ed. H. THURSTON and D. ATTWATER, 4 v. (New York 1956) 3:184–187. D. WOOD, "St. Christopher, Bishop Peter of Attalia, and the Cohors Marmaritarum: A Fresh Examination," *Vigiliae Christianae* 48 (1994): 170–186. J. SCHWARTZ, "A propos de l'iconographie orientale de s. Christophe," *Le Museon: Revue des Etudes orientales* 67 (1954): 93–98.

[E. DAY]

CHRISTOPHER MACCASSOLI, BL.

Franciscan; b. Milan, *c.* 1415–20; d. Vigevano, Italy, 1485. Born of a noble family, he joined the Franciscan Observants in 1435 and, after his ordination, was assigned to preaching. He was guardian of Abbiategrasso in 1477 and was transferred later to Vigevano, where he enlarged the friary and distinguished himself by his virtues. He was buried in the chapel of St. Bernardine in the Franciscan church. There a painting done in 1503 represents him with SS. Clare and Bernardine of Siena, before the Virgin and Child. ALOYSIUS GONZAGA attested to his holiness. His remains were discovered in 1588; in 1638 his name was inserted in the Franciscan martyrology. In 1717 the above-mentioned painting was placed over the main altar of the Franciscan church. The relics were relocated in 1743, and in 1810 the reliquary and painting were transferred to the cathedral. The diocesan process for his beatification continued from 1877 to 1884, and in 1890 Leo XIII permitted an Office and Mass to be celebrated in his honor in the Diocese of Vigevano and among the FRANCISCANS.

Feast: March 11.

Bibliography: "Acta ordinis causae sanctorum ordinis nostri," *Acta Ordinis Minorum* 9 (1890) 117–119. P. M. SEVESI, *B. Cristoforo Macassoli* (Varese 1941). A. BUTLER, *The Lives of the Saints,* ed. H. THURSTON and D. ATTWATER, 4 v. (New York 1956) 1:563.

[J. CAMBELL]

CHRISTOPHER OF ROMANDIOLA, BL.

Companion of St. Francis, known also as Christopher of Cahors or of Romagnola; b. Romandiola, Italy, *c.* 1172; d. Cahors, France, Oct. 31, 1272. When FRANCIS OF ASSISI was passing through Romandiola in 1215, Christopher, a country parish priest, decided to become his disciple, and he was a member of the first group of FRANCISCANS sent to Aquitaine. The lives of these early Franciscan missionaries, who spent their time in prayer and the service of the sick and outcast, especially lepers, made a profound impression. They made many converts, and numerous houses were built for them. Christopher was a simple, devout man, not a preacher in the official sense of the word—*non erat officio praedicator*—and it seems certain that he was never minister provincial of the province of Aquitaine. He was present at the provincial chapter of Arles held in 1224 by John Bonnelli. The cult of Bl. Christopher was confirmed by Pope PIUS X in 1905.

Feast: Oct. 25.

Bibliography: L. DE CHERANCÉ, *Le Bx. Christophe de Cahors* (Paris 1907). A. BÉGUET, "Provincialat du Bx. Christophe de Cahors," *Archivum Franciscanum historicum* 4 (1911) 619–621. *Vita e culto del B. Christoforo di Romagna* (Rome 1905). *Analecta Franciscana* 3: 161–173. W. FORSTER, *Lexikon für Theologie und Kirche,* ed. J. HOFER and K. RAHNER, 10 v. (2d, new ed. Freiburg 1957–65) 2:1168–69. A. BUTLER, *The Lives of the Saints,* ed. H. THURSTON and D. ATTWATER, 4 v. (New York 1956) 4:200.

[T. C. CROWLEY]

CHRISTOPHERS, THE

Founded in 1945 by James Keller, MM (1900–1977), is the name of a movement that attempts to stimulate people in all walks of life to recognize their abilities and use them to raise the standards in all aspects of daily living through print and electronic media. There are no membership lists, meetings, or dues. The movement is supported by voluntary donations. Persons are reached through the weekly television series, *Christopher Closeup,* which promotes a universal message of hope and inspiration; through *Christopher News Notes,* sent free upon request to more than a million individuals worldwide ten times a year; through radio and television programs scheduled by radio and television stations worldwide; through the many Christopher books and videos; and through a syndicated column entitled "Light One Candle." The Christopher motto, "Better to light one candle than to curse the darkness," reflects St. Paul's admonition: "Be not overcome by evil, but overcome evil with good" (Rom 12.21).

Past and present directors of the Christophers include James Keller (1945–1969), Richard Armstrong (1969–1978), John Catoir (1978–1995), Thomas J. McSweeney (1995–2000), and James P. Lisante (2000–).

[J. KELLER/EDS.]

CHRODEGANG OF METZ, ST.

Bishop, who introduced Roman liturgy into the Frankish Church and wrote a rule for the common life of cathedral clergy; b. Hesbaye, Brabant, 712; d. Metz, March 6, 766. After being educated in the abbey school of SAINT-TROND, he went to the court of CHARLES MARTEL and became his chancellor. He was consecrated bishop of METZ in 742 but continued to hold his civil office under PEPIN III, mayor of the Palace. In 748 Chrodegang founded the Benedictine Abbey of GORZE. Later he founded the Abbey of LORSCH. In 753 Pepin, now king of the FRANKS, sent the bishop to Rome to offer refuge in France to Pope STEPHEN II, who was besieged by the LOMBARDS. Stephen gave Chrodegang the personal title of archbishop and appointed him papal legate to the kingdom of the Franks. In this capacity Chrodegang presided over the meeting held at Quiercysur-Oise (754) and persuaded the Frankish lords to go to war against Aistulf, the Lombard king, in order to win back the papal lands. He also had a prominent voice in all the reforming councils of the period, proving during his 23-year episcopate that he was the true successor to BONIFACE as the reformer of the Frankish Church. Chrodegang was one of those responsible for the introduction of the ROMAN RITE and GRE-

GORIAN CHANT into the Frankish Church (*see* GALLICAN RITES). Apparently he observed the Roman practice on his early visit to Rome and sent chanters to learn it. The school of chant they established in Metz upon their return became widely known (*see* CAROLINGIAN REFORM).

Chrodegang formed the clergy of his cathedral church of St. Stephen into a community that lived in cloister. The rule he wrote for them was based on the BENEDICTINE RULE and consisted of a preface and 34 chapters. The clergy were to chant the Divine Office in common and to eat and sleep within the cloister. Every day a chapter of the rule was to be read in common, and from this the gathering itself began to be called "chapter." These canons regular did not take a vow of poverty. It is to the credit of Chrodegang's spiritual leadership that he could induce clergy, not bound by monastic vow, to undertake a quasi-monastic observance. Thus Chrodegang is one of the founders of the historic institution of Canons Regular (*see* CANONS, CHAPTER OF). His rule spread to other churches near Metz, and it was known in England and Italy—perhaps even in the Diocese of Rome.

Feast: March 6.

Bibliography: CHRODEGANG OF METZ, *Regula canonicorum*, ed. W. SCHMITZ (Hanover 1889). *Monumenta Germaniae Historica: Scriptores* 2:267–268; 10:552–572. *Saint Chrodegang, communications présentées au Colloque tenu à Metz à l'occasion du douzième centenaire de sa mort* (Metz 1967). É MORHAIN, "Origine . . . de la *Regula canonicorum* de saint C.," *Miscellanea Pio Paschini*, 2 v. (Rome 1948–49) 1:173–185. G. HOCQUARD, *Catholicisme* 2:1094–96. J. C. DICKINSON, *The Origins of the Austin Canons* (London 1950).

[C. E. SHEEDY]

CHROMATIUS OF AQUILEIA, ST.

Fourth-century bishop and spiritual director; d. Aquileia, 407. As a priest under Bishop Valerian of Aquileia (369–387), he was associated with the group of ascetics that included RUFINUS OF AQUILEIA and St. JEROME. Chromatius probably assisted at the anti-Arian Council of Aquileia (381) presided over by St. AMBROSE OF MILAN, who was also present at the election of Chromatius and consecrated him bishop in 387 or 388. Chromatius appealed to Emperor Honorius in favor of St. JOHN CHRYSOSTOM when the latter was deposed at the Synod of the OAK (403). Jerome dedicated his Latin translation of the Book of Solomon to Chromatius; Rufinus likewise dedicated his continuation of the Church history of Eusebius to him.

Chromatius intervened in the quarrel between the two former friends, counseling Rufinus not to respond to Jerome's attacks. Of Chromatius's *tractatus*, one on the Eight Beatitudes, seventeen on the Gospel of St. Matthew, and the *Prefatio orationis Dominicae* in the Gelasian Sacramentary have been preserved. R. Étaix has claimed eight further sermons on St. Matthew's Gospel preserved among the works of John Chrysostom for Chromatius, and J. Lemarié believes he has discovered a corpus of fragments that are the notes Chromatius collected before the compilation of his *tractatus* on St. Matthew.

Feast: Dec. 2.

Bibliography: *Chromatius episcopus*, ed. CENTRO DI ANTICHITÀ ALTOADRIATICHE (Udine 1989). *Corpus Christianorum* 9 (1957) 371–447, ed. A. HOSTE, with bibliog. *Varietas indivisa: teologia della Chiesa locale*, ed. P. BERTOLLA and A. MORETTI (Brescia 1983). P. DE PUNIET, "Les Trois homélies catéchétiques du Sacramentaire Gélasien," *Revue d'histoire ecclésiastique* 5 (1904) 505–521; 6 (1905) 15–32, 304–318. P. PASCHINI, "Chromatius d'Aquilée et le commentaire Pseudo-Hiéronymien . . . ," *Revue Bénédictine* 26 (1909) 469–475. R. ÉTAIX, "Tractatus in Matheum," *ibid.* 70 (1960) 469–503. G. TRETTEL, *Mysterium e sacramentum in S. Cromazio* (Trieste 1979). C. TRUZZI, *Zeno, Gaudenzio e Cromazio: testi e contenuti della predicazione cristiana per le chiese di Verona, Brescia e Aquileia* (Brescia 1985). J. LEMARIÉ, "Homélies inédites," *ibid.* 72 (1962) 201–277; 73 (1963) 100–107, 181–243; "Trois nouveaux témoins de l'homélie VIII et une homélie de Noël," *ibid.* 74 (1964) 147–155.

[G. ORLANDI]

CHRONICLER, BIBLICAL

The name given to the Biblical author who produced the historical corpus comprising the books of 1 and 2 Chronicles, Ezra, and Nehemiah. These books give a religious history from the beginning of the world to the reforms of Nehemiah and Ezra in the postexilic Jewish community. They set forth the reign of David as the ideal for which the restored theocratic state should again confidently strive, in view of God's promises through the Prophets and their partial fulfillment in the restoration of the Jewish community.

THE WORK AS A WHOLE

Originally this was copied as one literary work in the Hebrew textual tradition. Because of its size, however, it came to be written on two scrolls, with 1 and 2 Chronicles as one book on the first scroll, and Ezra and Nehemiah as one book on the second. An unknown editor made the continuity of the scrolls evident by repeating the beginning of Ezra (Ezr 1.1–3a) at the end of Chronicles (2 Chr 36.22–23), thus also closing the latter on a happy note.

The greater bulk of the work in its Greek translation—the Greek alphabet wrote vowels as well as consonants, whereas ancient Hebrew wrote only consonants—led to a further division of the work into the four books of our present Bibles. This fourfold division passed from the Septuagint into the Vulgate and thence into the modern versions. It even made its way into the transmission of the Hebrew text, beginning with a manuscript dating from A.D. 1448.

Canonicity. Palestinian Jews placed the Chronicler's work at the end of the Writings, their third major division of the Bible. By a strange inversion of historical sequence, Ezra-Nehemiah precedes the book(s) of Chronicles. This fact supports the supposition that Chronicles was accepted at a later period among the inspired books, perhaps because its matter was already found in a somewhat different form in the earlier books of Samuel and Kings. Chronicles seems to have won acceptance by New Testament times, however, at least if Jesus' allusion in Mt 23.35 to the deaths of Abel (Gn 4.8) and Zechariah (2 Chr 24.21–22) is to be taken as a reference to the first and last murders mentioned in the Scriptures and so to the whole sweep of the Jewish Bible. It is possible that the Chronicler's idealization of David and of the theocratic community may have influenced the Pharisees to accept Chronicles into the canon.

In the Septuagint and later translations, the four books appear in their normal order as supplements to, and continuation of, the earlier histories of Samuel and Kings.

Despite the variations of its position in the canon, the Chronicler's work has never been wanting from the canonical lists of Judaism and Christianity, if one excepts the earliest hesitation of the Syrian Church, which did not at first include 1 and 2 Chronicles in its translation of the Bible. The long history of acceptance of these books culminated in the declaration of the Council of Trent that they are among the books to be received by the faithful as "sacred and canonical" (H. Denzinger, *Enchiridion symbolorum*, ed. A. Schönmetzer 150–102).

Text and Versions. In general the Hebrew text of the Chronicler's work has been well preserved in transmission, despite the fact that many proper names and possibly some numbers have been garbled. The SEPTUAGINT version is faithful to the traditional Hebrew text, sometimes so slavishly as to simply transliterate Hebrew words into Greek characters. Only the Old Latin version has value as an independent witness to the original text, since it is seemingly based on a Greek version that followed a Hebrew textual tradition other than the one represented in the Masoretic Text. The later versions—the VULGATE, the Aramaic Targum, and the Syriac Peshitto—are less useful for textual criticism, the last named being sometimes a mere paraphrase of the Hebrew original.

Date of the Chronicler's Work. When they come to assigning dates for the Chronicler's work, authors vary widely, partly because they cannot agree on the work's unity of authorship. The most frequently accepted limits for the Chronicler's activity are the late 5th century B.C. (when the most recent events narrated took place) and the early years of Alexander's domination of Syria-Palestine, 333 to 323 B.C. (since these books show little Greek influence). Within these outer limits opinion fluctuates, although many scholars now favor a date near 400 B.C. for the work's appearance in its final form.

Other dates assigned may serve to illustrate the disagreements which exist: D. N. Freedman (441) says that the Chronicler, a monarchist, composed the basic work about 515 B.C. and that later a clericalist author added the Ezra-Nehemiah memoirs (and certain other sections) to the work toward the end of the 5th century B.C. W. F. Albright (95) accepts a date shortly after 400 B.C. and sees Ezra himself as the Chronicler. A. M. Brunet (*Dictionnaire de la Bible*, supplement ed. L. Pirot et al. 6:1256) dates the work to the end of the 4th century B.C., about the time of Alexander the Great. C. C. Torrey, M. Noth, and R. H. Pfeiffer place the work well within the Greek period, Pfeiffer (580) dating it about 250 B.C.

Unity of Authorship and Identity of the Chronicler. Disagreement in dating the Chronicler is inevitably linked with disagreement over the literary unity of his work. However, strong arguments favor this unity. Not only does 2 Chr 36.22–23 repeat Ezr 1.1–3a, but the same spirit and themes can be found throughout the historiography. There is the same attachment throughout to the Jewish community and its legitimate civil and religious institutions; the same special love for the Temple and its cultic organization; the same special attention given to the lesser cultic ministers, particularly the Levites; the same concern for genealogies; and—perhaps the strongest argument of all—the same stylistic features of vocabulary, grammar, composition, and use of sources.

To these literary evidences of a single authorship can be added the traditional view of the rabbinic literature, the Church Fathers, and early commentators, who generally accepted these books as the work of one man, Ezra. The Babylonian Talmud says in fact (*Baba Bathra* 15a) that Ezra wrote his own book and the genealogies of Chronicles, beginning his own genealogy, which was completed by Nehemiah. Suspect though it is in points, this testimony reflects the ancient view that the leading reformer of postexilic Judaism was largely responsible for the four Biblical books in question.

In modern times, J. W. Rothstein (1927), G. von Rad (1934), and A. C. Welch (1939), among others, have seen two strata (Deuteronomist and Priestly) in the Chroni-

NEW CATHOLIC ENCYCLOPEDIA

cler's work. K. Galling (1954) and D. N. Freedman (1961) have also seen successive editions in the work. But M. Noth (1943) and W. Rudolph (1955) have returned to the idea of a basic unity of authorship for the work as a whole, and W. F. Albright (95), basing his opinion in part on the observation of C. C. Torrey that the style and point of view of the Ezra memoirs are those of the entire work of the Chronicler, supports the earlier tradition that Ezra is indeed the author.

FIRST AND SECOND CHRONICLES

Although Chronicles was originally one work, it was first divided into two books in the Septuagint, a practice followed by subsequent versions and even by the Hebrew textual tradition since 1448.

Title. Palestinian Jews (and Hebrew printed Bibles) called these books (*sēper*) *dibrê hayyāmîm* [literally (the book of) the words of the days], a title idiomatically equivalent to ''happenings of the times'' or ''annals.'' Greek-speaking Jews in their Septuagint (followed by the Vulgate and some modern editions) referred to these books by the name παραλειπόμενα (Paralipomenon), which Jerome (*Ep. 53, Ad Paulinum, Patrologia Latina*, ed. J. P. Migne, 22.548) and Theodoret (*Quaest. in libros Regum et Paralipomenon, Patrologia Graeca* 80:801) understood as designating the books' content, ''things omitted'' (from previous Biblical histories). Some scholars, however, prefer to translate παραλειπόμενα as ''things transmitted.'' J. P. Audet [*Journal of Theological Studies* 1 (1950) 154] proposes ''things left aside'' (for later translation from an Aramaic Targum).

The modern name for these books, ''Chronicles,'' goes back to Jerome's *Prologus Galeatus* (*Patrologia Latina* 28:554), in which he writes of these books that they form a ''χρονικόν [chronicle] of the whole of divine history.'' In his translation of the Bible M. Luther took up the term and called the books *Die Chronika,* and the name, thus popularized, is now generally accepted by the modern versions.

Contents of Chronicles. The Books of Chronicles have four clearly defined sections. (1) In 1 Chr ch. 1–9 a series of genealogies traces descent from Adam to the descendants of David and Solomon who were dwelling again in Jerusalem after the Edict of Cyrus in 538 B.C. (2) In 1 Chr. 10–29 the reign of DAVID, as it is described in his civil and religious organization of the kingdom, is idealized. (3) In 2 Chr ch. 1–9 the story of SOLOMON emphasizes his wisdom, which is particularly evident in his building and dedicating the Temple at Jerusalem. (4) In 2 Chr ch. 10–36 an account is given of the successors of David and Solomon; but the rulers of the schismatic Northern Kingdom of Israel are ignored, and even of the kings of Juda only the three ''good,'' i.e., reforming, kings—Josaphat (Jehoshaphat; *c.* 873–*c.* 849), Hezekiah and Josiah—are treated at length. The evil conduct of the other kings, the priests, and the people eventually brought about the destruction of Jerusalem and the nation (2 Chr 36.13–16). Here the story of Chronicles ends, to be completed by the Chronicler in Ezra-Nehemiah.

Sources. In the composition of his work the Chronicler had recourse to many earlier writings, most of which he mentioned explicitly. Although he often adapted these documents to suit his own purposes, they still retained considerable historical value.

Biblical Sources. Among the sources used by the Chronicler are clearly some of the earlier books of the Bible, which he had in a form substantially identical with their present text. Although the Chronicler did not cite any of them by their known titles, he drew upon the following: (1) the Pentateuch (e.g., Gn 10.22–29 in 1 Chr 1.17–23); (2) Joshua (e.g., Jos 19.1–8 in 1 Chr 4.28–33); (3) 1 and 2 Sm (e.g., 1 Sm 31.1–13 in 1 Chr 10.1–12; 2 Sm 5.1–10 in 1 Chr 11.1–9); (4) 1 and 2 Kings (e.g., 1 Kgs 8.1–52 in 2 Chr 5.2–6.40; 2 Kgs 16.2–20 in 2 Chr 28.1–26); and (5) Ps [e.g., Ps 104(105).1–15 in 1 Chr 16.8–22; Ps 95(96) in 1 Chr 16.23–33; Ps 105(106). 1, 47–48 in 1 Chr 16.34–36)]. This list of Old Testament citations is by no means complete.

Sources Explicitly Mentioned. Certain royal, prophetic, and other sources are mentioned in the Books of Chronicles.

The royal sources are: (1) The Book of the Kings of Israel and Judah (1 Chr 9.1; 2 Chr 27.7; 35.27; 36.8); (2) The Book of the Kings of Judah and Israel (2 Chr 25.26; 28.26; 32.32; 16.11); (3) The History of Jehu, the son of Hanani, which is inserted into the Book of the Kings of Israel (2 Chr 20.34); (4) The History of the Kings of Israel (2 Chr 33.18); and (5) The Midrash of the Book of Kings (2 Chr 24.27). Probably all these royal sources are in reality the same work.

The prophetic sources are: (1) The History of Samuel the Seer (1 Chr 29.29); (2) The History of Nathan the Prophet (1 Chr 29.29; 2 Chr 9.29); (3) The History of Gad the Seer (1 Chr 29.29); (4) The Prophecy of Ahijah the Shilonite (2 Chr 9.29); (5) The Visions of Iddo the Seer (2 Chr 9.29; 12.15); (6) The History of Shemaiah the Prophet (2 Chr 12.15); (7) The Midrash of the Prophet Iddo (2 Chr 13.22); (8) The History of Uzziah by the Prophet Isaiah, the son of Amos (2 Chr 26.22); (9) The Vision of the Prophet Isaiah, the son of Amos (2 Chr 32.32); and (10) The History of His [Manasseh's] Seers (2 Chr 33.19). Scholars dispute whether any, most, or all, of these sources belong to the same work that includes the royal sources.

Other sources are: (1) Family Records of Gad (1 Chr 5.17); (2) The Book of Chronicles of King David (1 Chr 27.24); (3) David's Exact Specifications for the Temple and Its Furnishings (1 Chr 28.19); (4) The Prescriptions of David and Solomon for the Levites (2 Chr 35.4); and (5) Jeremiah's Lamentation over Josiah (2 Chr 35.25).

Use of the Sources. The manner in which the Chronicler used his sources can be seen from a comparison of his work with the earlier Biblical books. With his own specific purposes in mind he repeated, omitted, rewrote, shortened, and expanded his source materials. Some examples follow: (1) repetition, e.g., 1 Sm 31.1–13 in 1 Chr 10.1–12; (2) omissions, e.g., of David's troubles with Saul, his adultery with Bathsheba, and his murder of her husband; and of the revolt of Absalom and the dynastic intrigues at Solomon's accession; (3) rewriting of material, e.g., 2 Sm 24.1 in 1 Chr 21.1; (4) shortening, e.g., 2 Kgs 18.13–19.37 in 2 Chr 32.1–23; and (5) expansion, e.g., 2 Kgs 23.21–23 in 2 Chr 35.1–19.

Evaluation of the Sources. As in so many other matters affecting the Chronicler's work scholars differ in their assessing of his sources. It is evident that he knew and used the earlier Biblical books, from Genesis to Kings, and Psalms. Whether he used additional materials is in dispute. Torrey and Pfeiffer think that he probably did not. In the parts of his work that are not clearly derived from Biblical sources, they say, the spirit and language is that of the Chronicler himself, showing that these parts do not derive from other source materials. Torrey (*Ezra Studies* 223) even says that "there is no internal evidence, anywhere, of an intermediate source between our Old Testament books and the Chronicler." And he explains the numerous explicit references to source material as fabrication of the Chronicler in his need to "parade authorities." However, this argument based on stylistic and thematic consistency is not convincing if one considers that the Chronicler need not have reproduced his sources slavishly and that in fact he did not do so, even when he clearly drew from earlier Biblical books. Note, for instance, how 2 Chr 1.3–6 expands upon 1 Kgs 3.4.

More probably, then, as Brunet (*Dictionnaire de la Bible,* supplement ed. 6:1241) and others maintain, the Chronicler's references point to one or more sources distinct from our canonical books. (Some even think that it was not the Biblical Books of Samuel and Kings that the Chronicler used, but their sources.) Finally, some authors reduce the Chronicler's non-Biblical sources to one, identified as the Midrash on the Book of Kings (2 Chr 24.27).

Historical Worth. The free use that the Chronicler makes of his sources has called into question the histori-cal worth of his narrative. For example, in 2 Chr 13.3 the monstrous figures of 400,000 men in the army of Judah under Abijah and of 800,000 men in the opposing army of Jeroboam I are obviously of no historical value; according to 2 Chr 8.1–2 Hiram, King of Tyre, gave to Solomon certain cities that were in reality given by Solomon to Hiram (1 Kgs 9.10); and David paid only 50 silver shekels for the threshing floor of Ornan (2 Sm 24.24), not 600 shekels of gold as stated in 1 Chr 21.25.

These and similar examples are best understood in the light of the Chronicler's chief interest—the theological significance of his material. It is this interest that leads him to exaggerate the size of the armies so that God's victory might be more striking. This same interest impels him to exalt Solomon by having Hiram give him the cities and to stress beyond its worth the value of the site purchased by David as the spot for his altar and eventually the Temple. Allowance must be made, then, for the Chronicler's handling of materials to achieve his theological purposes, but once this is done, the books of Chronicles become valuable historical references. In some instances, e.g., in 2 Chr 11.5–12, they preserve reliable historical details not available elsewhere.

EZRA-NEHEMIAH

Like Chronicles, which they continue, these two books were originally one work and they first became separate works in the Septuagint. Even in the current Hebrew Bibles the Book of Nehemiah follows the Book of Ezra on the same page with merely the usual paragraph division.

Titles. The first of the two books is named for the Priest-Scribe EZRA, whose name (Heb. and Aram. *'ezrā,* transcribed in Greek as Ἔζ[δ]ρας or Ἔζ[δ]ρα[ς] means "help." In the Vulgate and some other Catholic Bibles the book is known also as 1 Esdras. The second book is named for NEHEMIAH (Heb. *neḥemyâ* transcribed in Greek as Νεεμίας), whose name means "Yahweh consoles." This work is known in the Vulgate and some other Catholic Bibles also as 2 Esdras.

In the Septuagint, the apocryphal book Ἔσδρας A, the Vulgate's 3 Esdras, precedes the canonical books of Ezra and Nehemiah, which together constitute the Septuagint's Ἔσδρας B. The nomenclature is further complicated by the apocryphal *Apocalypse of Esdras,* which is known in the Vulgate as 4 Esdras. Finally, Protestant editions of the apocrypha refer to the Vulgate's 3 and 4 Esdras as 1 and 2 Esdras. The accompanying table shows the correspondences.

Contents. In Ezra ch. 1–6 the story of the chosen people is continued where Chronicles left off. These chapters tell of the edict of restoration issued by Cyrus the Great in 538 B.C., of the first return under Sassabasar, of early attempts to reconstruct the Temple, and of its final completion and dedication in the time of Zerubbabel and JOSHUA, son of Josedec. This leads to the story of Ezra's mission and his reforms as told in Ezra ch. 7–11. In Nehemiah ch. 1–7 an account is given of the building of the walls and the city of Jerusalem by Nehemiah. The rest of the Book of Nehemiah (ch. 8–13) narrates the covenant concluded under Ezra's direction, gives census lists, and tells of the dedication of the city's wall and of Nehemiah's reforms during his second administration of Juda.

Sources. The following materials were available to the Chronicler as he composed his work.
1. The Memoirs of Ezra (Ezr 7.27–9.15)
2. The Memoirs of Nehemiah (Neh 1.1–7.5; 11.1–2; 12.27–13.31)
3. Aramaic documents
    a. A document in Ezr 4.7–23 embodying the protest of Rehum to Artaxerxes I, King of Persia, about the rebuilding of Jerusalem's walls (Ezr 4.11–16) and the King's answer (Ezr 4.17–22)
    b. A document in Ezr 4.24–6.18 that contains the letter of Thathanai to Darius I, King of Persia, about the rebuilding of the Temple at Jerusalem (Ezr 5.7–17) and the King's answer (Ezr 6.3–12)
    c. The decree of Artaxerxes commissioning Ezra to reorganize Temple worship at Jerusalem (Ezr 7.12–26)
4. Official documents in Hebrew
    a. Cyrus's edict of liberation of 538 B.C. (Ezr 1.2–4), which differs from the Aramaic form of the decree in Artaxerxes' letter to Thathanai (Ezr 6.3–5).
    b. A list of those first returning from Babylon (Ezr 2.1–70; Neh 7.6–72)
    c. A list of those returning with Ezra (Ezr 8.1–14)
    d. A list of those promising to give up foreign wives (Ezr 10.18–44)
    e. A list of those who helped repair the walls of Jerusalem (Neh 3.1–32)
    f. A list of those signing the covenant agreement (Neh 10.1–28; the provisions of the pact are in Neh 10.29–40)
    g. A list of the inhabitants of Jerusalem and vicinity in Nehemia's time (Neh 11.3–36)
    h. Lists of priests and Levites (Neh 12.1–26).

Historical Worth. Since the Books of Ezra and Nehemiah form the major source for the history of Judah in the postexilic period down to the late 5th century B.C., it is important to know whether, and to what extent, they are reliable.

Some scholars, such as Torrey and Pfeiffer, treat the Chronicler's documentation with skepticism. Others are more inclined to find his sources reliable. Admittedly, as in the Books of Chronicles, the author is motivated chiefly by theological interests. Consequently he gives a decidedly Jewish tone to Ezra's commission from Artaxerxes, in which the Mosaic Law is referred to as the "wisdom" of God (Ezr 8.25). The Chronicler's rewording may be seen also in the two accounts of Cyrus's edict of 538 B.C. (Ezr 1.2–4; 6.3–5). But fundamentally there is no adequate reason to impugn the basic authenticity of these or other documents that he employs.

Despite this confidence in the Chronicler's materials, however, it is not easy for the modern scholar to reconstruct the age about which the Chronicler writes, since the documentation in these books is obviously not in chronological order. Note, for example, how the patch that is Ezr 4.24 joins the later episode of Ezr 4.7–23 to the earlier situation in Ezr 5.1–6.22; logically (and chronologically) Ezr 5.1–6.22 should have followed Ezr 4.5.

But this is not the only disturbance of historical sequence. The order of Ezra's and Nehemiah's ministries is another case in point. If the ministry of Ezra began in the 7th year of Artaxerxes I (465–424 B.C.), as Ezr 7.7 states, there would be no coordination between Ezra's ministry and that of Nehemiah, contrary to Neh 8.9; 10.1. A date in the reign of Artaxerxes II (404–358 B.C.) would make him much later than Nehemiah. A plausible solution—that the "7th year" of Artaxerxes in Ezr 7.7 should be read as the "37th year" of Artaxerxes I—resolves the difficulty and results in a Nehemiah-Ezra sequence of activity.

Other historical difficulties remain to plague the interpreter, but in spite of them modern opinion favors the basic reliability of the Chronicler's work.

THE MESSAGE OF THE CHRONICLER

The Chronicler's major interest was in the history of the theocracy embodied in the Davidic dynasty and in the restored Jewish community of the postexilic period. The genealogies of 1 Chronicles ch. 1–9 are merely introductory, leading swiftly to David and his accomplishments.

Ideal Theocracy in the Davidic Dynasty. David's dynasty had proved to be, even before the Exile, the only legitimate one, the only one enjoying divine favor. And so the Chronicler ignored the history of the Northern Kingdom of Israel. Not all of David's descendants, however, proved worthy of him. In fact, only three—the reforming kings Jehoshaphat (2 Chr 17.7–9; 19.4–11), Hezekiah (2 Chr ch. 29–32), and Josiah (2 Chr 34.1–33)—received favorable comment from the Chronicler. But even these three were not sufficient to ward off

Yahweh's displeasure with His people, who had spurned the oracles of His Prophets (2 Chr 36.15–17; Neh 9.30). Chastened by the experience of the Exile, God's people returned to the Holy Land and rebuilt Jerusalem and its Temple. This return, which is described in Ezra-Nehemiah, was the partial fulfillment of the prophetic promises (Jer 29.10 in 2 Chr 36.22 and Za 8.11–12 in Ezr 9.8, 13; Neh 9.31).

The Ideal Postexilic Community. Since the community had no Davidic ruler when the Chronicler wrote, it had to prepare for one by becoming the ideal community. This goal obliged it to a greater fidelity to God's word as contained in the Mosaic Law (Ezr 9.10–14) and to greater exactitude in worship. To inculcate this ideal of the perfect community, the Chronicler sought to legitimize the liturgical usages of his own day, and so he linked them to David (1 Chr ch. 23–29). Great importance was given also to Solomon's Temple and its ministers, particularly the Levites and the singers (2 Chr 5.11–13).

Thus constituted as a holy people, the Jews, who had been reduced to the service of a foreign king (Neh 9.36–37), turned in hopeful expectation to the next intervention of Yahweh their true King (Ezr 9.13; Neh 9.32).

Bibliography: A. M. BRUNET, "La Théologie du Chroniste:-Théocratie et messianisme," *Sacra Pagina* 1 (1954) 384–397; *Dictionnaire de la Bible*, supplement ed. L. PIROT et al. (Paris 1928–) 6:1220–61. A. LEFÈVRE, *ibid.* 6:393–424. R. H. PFEIFFER, G. A. BUTTRICK, ed., *The Interpreter's Dictionary of the Bible* 1:572–580; 2:215–219. H. CAZELLES, *Catholicisme* 2:1098–1102; 4:428–434; *Les Livres des Chroniques* (2d ed. BJ; 1961). M. REHM, *Lexikon für Theologie und Kirche*, ed. J. HOFER and K. RAHNER, 10 v. (2d, new ed. Freiburg 1957–65) 2:1184–85. H. SCHNEIDER, *ibid.* 3:1101–02; 7:868–869. K. GALLING, *Die Religion in Geschichte und Gegenwart*, 7 v. (3d ed. Tübingen 1957–65) 1:1803–06; 2:694–697; 4:1396–98; *Die Bücher der Chronik, Esra, Nehemia* (Göttingen 1954). *Encyclopedic Dictionary of the Bible*, tr. and adap. by L. HARTMAN (New York 1963) from A. VAN DEN BORN, *Bijbels Woordenboek* 361–368. M. NOTH, *Überlieferungsgeschichtliche Studien I* (2d ed. Tübingen 1957). W. RUDOLPH, *Chronikbücher (Handbuch zum Alten Testament*, ed. O. EISSFELDT (Tübingen 1934–) ser.1, no.21; 1955). A. C. WELCH, *The Work of the Chronicler* (London 1939). C. C. TORREY, *Ezra Studies* (Chicago 1910); *The Chronicler's History of Israel* (New Haven 1954). W. F. ALBRIGHT, *The Biblical Period from Abraham to Ezra* (pa. New York 1963). D. N. FREEDMAN, "The Chronicler's Purpose," *The Catholic Biblical Quarterly* 23 (1961) 436–442. R. NORTH, "Theology of the Chronicler," *Journal of Biblical Literature* 82 (1963) 369–381.

[N. J. MCELENEY]

CHRONOGRAPHER OF 354

The designation given by T. Mommsen to the unknown compiler of a calendarlike reference work prepared for general use in Rome. The original compiler

Emperor Constantine II, drawing from Chronographer of 354 (Vat. Cod. Barber. XXXI, 39, fol. 13).

stopped at the year 354, but subsequently some additions brought it down to the year 496. Although the document is preserved only in fragments, scholars have succeeded in reconstructing almost completely this important source for the history of the ancient Church.

The contents of the work are: (1) a calendar in two parts, part one containing astronomical and astrological data, and part two a civil listing of pagan feasts and games, dates for the meetings of the Senate, and birthdays of the emperors. The calendar was composed by the calligrapher Furius Dionysius Philocalus (or Filocalus) and elaborately illustrated with miniatures. (2) Annals from the time of Caesar to the year 359 (added later by a copyist). (3) A list of the consuls from A.U.C. 245 to A.D. 354—the most complete list found in extant literary sources. (4) An Easter table from 312 to 411. (5) A list of the urban prefects at Rome for the years 254 to 354. (6) A *Depositio episcoporum* (list of the death dates of the popes from 254 to 352), and a *Depositio Martyrum* (list of Roman martyrs and martyrs venerated at Rome), the oldest extant martyrology. (7) A list of the bishops of Rome from St. Peter to Liberius—the earliest form of the Liber pontificalis. (8) Annals from the time of Caesar to 403, and from 455 to 496. (9) A world chronicle to the year 354, based on that of HIPPOLYTUS OF ROME. (10) A chronicle of the city of Rome to the death of the Emperor Licinius (324), written in 334 and closely connected with the world chronicle just mentioned. (11) A description of the 14 regions of the city of Rome.

Bibliography: Editions. T. MOMMSEN, ed., *Monumenta Germaniae Historica: Auctores antiquissimi* 9.1 (Berlin 1892) 13–196; *Gesammelte Schriften* 8 v. (Berlin 1905–13) 7:536–579. Studies. O. BARDENHEWER, *Geschichte der altkirchlichen Literatur*, 5 v. (Freiburg 1913–32) 3:558–560. O. SEECK, *Paulys Realenzyklopädie der klassischen Altertumswissenschaft* 3.2 (Stuttgart 1899) 2477–81. H. LECLERCQ, ''Kalendaria,'' *Dictionnaire d'archéologie chrétienne et de liturgie*, ed. F. CABROL, H. LECLERCQ, and H. I. MARROU, 15 v. (Paris 1907–53) 8.1:624–667; ''Chronographe de 354,'' *ibid.* 3.1:1555–60. C. NORDENFALK, *Der Kalender vom Jahre 354 und die lateinische Buchmalerei des IV. Jahrhunderts* (Göteborg 1936). H. STERN, *Le Calendrier de 354: Étude sur son texte et sur ses illustrations* (Paris 1952).

[M. R. P. MCGUIRE]

CHRONOLOGY, MEDIEVAL

The science of chronology, as it applies to the Middle Ages, treats of the method of reckoning time by year or era. This article discusses the subject in its Christian orientation as it applies to the East and to the West.

THE CHRISTIAN EAST

In addition to Olympiads, regnal years, consulates, and other civil and political eras that continued to be used as chronological indexes, the Christian East had its own methods of determining chronology, viz, according to world eras, and cycles.

World eras. These were formed on the basis of three factors: (1) the idea that the world would last 6 millenniums, corresponding to the 6 days of Genesis, the coming of Christ occurring in the middle of the 6th millennium; (2) the need to find a Friday coinciding with the paschal moon as a date for the Passion; (3) the belief that the paschal cycles of the moon must have a proleptic connection with Creation. Hence arose the various cycles and the various eras.

The Lunar Cycle of Anatolius and the World Era of Julius Africanus. ANATOLIUS of Laodicea established a 19-year lunar cycle, constructed on the new moon (*neomenia*) of the vernal equinox (March 22), beginning in 258, equivalent in the world era of JULIUS Africanus –5501 (the minus signs indicates years before the birth of Christ) to 5759. By taking into account the precyclic year, which supposed 11 epacts from its beginning, the cycle through complete revolutions (303 x 19) rejoins the first year of the world era. In addition, the chronology of the Passion according to Africanus, *13 lunae*, March 23 through 31, is in agreement with the cycle of Anatolius for that same year (2d of the cycle).

The World Era of Alexandria. When the Alexandrines moved the equinox back to March 21, they changed the cycle by constructing it on the new moon of the first of the year (Thoth 1 = August 29). The inaugural year, 304, the 9th year of the cycle of Anatolius, was eight years later than his. In the 5th century, Panodorus adapted a world era to this cycle: –5493, placing the Incarnation in 5494 (= 1) and the Passion in 5526 (–34). Annianos, his rival lowered it to –5492, fixing the Incarnation at March 25, 5501, and the Resurrection at March 25, 5534 (= 42), March 25 also being the day of Creation. This Alexandrine era was favored by ecclesiastical writers. Its year began on March 25, sometimes on September 1 on the occasion of the indiction.

Protobyzantine Era. Constantinople reformed its computation in 353 by adjusting the cycle according to the equinoctial *neomenia*, March 21. Accordingly, with the addition of the precyclic year, this cycle began nine years earlier than that of Anatolius. The latter was to have begun again in 353. The new cycle, therefore, had its beginning in 344. The world era that followed was eight years earlier than that of Africanus, therefore, –5509. The birth of Christ was placed at 5507 (= –3) and the Passion at 5540 (= 31). The year began March 21.

Byzantine Era. This was constructed by subtracting a year from the cycle and from the protobyzantine era to make these agree with the indiction. The era was therefore –5508. It made its first appearance in 630 with the computist Georgios, who nevertheless retained the Alexandrine chronology for Christ. This latter was finally abandoned and the Passion reestablished at the year 91 (5539 of the era). The year had its beginning on September 1.

Other World Eras. The Era of Malalas: –5565; birth of Christ: 5967 (= –2); Passion: 6000 (= 31). The Era of Abdisho (Nestorian): –5491; birth of Christ: 5490 (=–2). The Georgian Era: –5604, constructed on the basis of the protobyzantine cycle of 344.

Particular eras. Era of Diocletian: 284, Thoth 1 (August 29). The years of the reign of this emperor, first used to date Easter, were later used to fix the dates of documents and events. The Armenian Era (undetermined years)–July 11, 522; the Little Armenian Era (fixed years)–starting point, Aug. 11, 1084. The Era of the Ascension (used by John Malalas and the *Chronicon paschale*, as well as by the Nestorian Syrians): beginning date, the year 31.

Cycles. (1) Lunar cycles (19 years) and solar cycles (28 years), were used in synchronism. It is well to note whether the Alexandrine or Byzantine cycle is employed (see table in Grumel, 266–267). (2) Paschal cycles of 532 years, product of 10 x 28 (see Grumel): (*a*) The Georgian paschal cycle (532 years) was called protobyzantine cycle of 344. (*b*) The Ethiopian paschal cycle was called the years of Mercy or of Grace—it began with the era of Diocletian, Aug. 19, 284. (3) INDICTIONS, which were periods of 15 years.

Bibliography: M. CHAINE, *La Chronologie des temps chrétiens de l'Egypte et de l'Ethiopie* (Paris 1925). V. GARDTHAUSEN, *Griechische Palaeographie*, 2 v. (2d ed. Leipzig 1911–13) v. 2. F. K. GINZEL, *Handbuch der mathematischen und technischen Chronologie*, 3 v. (Leipzig 1906–14; repr. 1958) v. 3. W. KUBITSCHEK, *Paulys Realenzyklopädie der klassischen Altertumswissenschaft*, ed. G. WISSOWA et al. 1.1 (Stuttgart 1893) 606–652. L. KOEP, *Reallexikon für Antike und Christentum* (Stuttgart 1941) 3:52–60. D. LEBEDEV, ''Iz istorii drevnich paschalnich ciklov,'' *Vizantiiskii vremennik*, ser. 1, v. 18 (1911) 146–249. H. LIETZMANN, *Zeitrechnung der romischen Kaiserzeit, des Mittelalters und der Neuzeit fur die Jahre 1–2000 nach Christus* (3d ed. Berlin 1956). E. MAHLER, *Chronologische Vergleichungs-Rabellen nebst einer Ableitung zu den Grundzugen der Chronologie* (Vienna 1888). A. MENTZ, *Beitrage zur Osterfestberechnung bei den Byzantinern* (Konigsberg 1906). P. V. NEWGEBUER, *Hilfstafeln zur technischen Chronologie* (Kiel 1937). F. RUHL, *Chronologie des Mittelalters und der Neuzeit* (Berlin 1897). E. SCHWARTZ, *Christliche unde judische Ostertafeln* (Berlin) 1905); *Paulys Realenzyklopädie der klassischen Altertumswissenschaft*, ed. G. WISSOWA et al., 3.2 (Stuttgart 1899) 2460–77. V. GRUMEL, *La Chronologie* (Paris 1958).

[V. GRUMEL]

THE WEST IN THE MIDDLE AGES

The solar calendar of approximately 365¼ days (12 months), which Julius Caesar introduced in 46 B.C., continued in use in the Middle Ages, remaining unchanged in fact until 1582 when it was revised by a commission appointed by Pope Gregory XIII.

Reckoning of years. Throughout this period, however, various methods of reckoning years were employed: (1) Byzantine, counting from the year 5508 B.C. (creation); a method originated in the 7th century and used by the Greeks and the Orthodox Church until 1700. (2) Regnal Year, from the year of office of an authority, such as emperor, pope, king, or magistrate. (3) INDICTION, a fiscal reckoning of years from 312 (Constantine's triumph), which was widely uses in chanceries, liturgical books, etc., at times in association with other reckonings. (4) Spanish, from 38 B.C., the date of the conquest of Span by Augustus; it was used in Spain, Portugal, and Visigothic Gaul for most of the Middle Ages, but Catalonia abandoned it in favor of (5) in 1180. (5) Christian Era, the dating of years from the birth of Christ (*anno Domini, Incarnationis*, etc.), a usage that rose incidentally from the Easter COMPUTUS of DIONYSIUS EXIGUUS (526); its gradual adoption in Europe was due largely to Bede's *De ratione temporum* (715; *Patrologia Latina* [Paris 1878–90] 90:295–578).

The Beginning of the year. For the beginning of the year itself various styles, generally based on major Christian festivals, were employed: (1) Byzantine (September 1), agreeing with the beginning of the Byzantine fiscal year (Indiction) and common outside of Byzantium in Byzantine parts of Italy, e.g., Bari. (2) Venetian (March 1), used in Venice until 1797. (3) Circumcision (January 1), corresponding to the beginning of the Roman and, since 1582, the modern civil year; it was widely used in Spain and Portugal and in several other places, e.g., Benevento. (5) Florentine Annunciation beginning with March 25 *after* the Nativity; originating at Arles in the late 9th century, it spread to Burgundy and northern Italy, eventually becoming peculiar to Pisa. (6) Gallican or Easter, a reckoning from the movable feast of Easter (March 11–April 25), introduced in France by Philip II Augustus (1180–1223) and used also in parts of the Rhineland and in the Low Countries, e.g., in Liege until 1333. (7) Bedan or Nativity, dating from Christmas Day (December 25). It was used by Anglo-Saxon and Norman kings until *c.* 1220, by the Empire until *c.* 1245, by the papal chancery from 962 to 1088, and at various other places, e.g., at Liege and Louvian, from 1333.

Within each month the Julian fashion of numbering the days in one continuous series (Nones, Ides, Kalends) became quite common but never fully replaced the practice of reckoning by liturgical days: e.g., ''in vigilia sancti Lucae'' (October 17); ''in Dominica *Dum clamarem*'' (10th Sunday after Pentecost, so called from the opening words of the Introit); ''This day is call'd the feast of Crispian'' (October 25). Hence a handbook, such as that of Grotefend or Cappelli or Cheney, is indispensable.

Bibliography: *L'Art de verifier les dates . . .*, 42 v. (Paris 1818–44). R. L. POOLE, *Medieval Reckonings of Time* (London 1918); *Studies in Chronology and History* (Oxford 1934). A. GIRY, *Manuel de diplomatique* (new ed. Paris 1925). A. CAPPELLI, *Cronologia, cronografia e calendario perpetuo* (2d ed. Milan 1930). H. GROTEFEND, *Taschenbuch der Zeitrechnung des deutschen Mittelalters und der Neuzeit*, ed. T. ULRICH (10th ed. Hanover, Ger. 1960). C. R. CHENEY, ed., *A Handbook of Dates for Students of English History* (London 1945; repr. 1961). J. AUGUSTI Y CASANOVAS et al., eds., *Manuel de cronologia espanola y universal* (Madrid 1952).

[L. E. BOYLE]

CHRYSANTHUS AND DARIA, SS.

Martyrs; d. *c.* 300. Their passion, probably written in Rome in the sixth or seventh century, is anachronistic and has little historical value. According to it, Chrysanthus was a rich young man from Alexandria who came to Rome and was baptized. Daria, a priestess of Minerva, was sent to him, but he converted her and they entered a continent marriage and converted many pagans, including the tribune Claudius and 62 soldiers who were martyred and buried in an abandoned aqueduct. For their apostolate, Chrysanthus and Daria were buried alive in a sandpit on the Via Sataria. Christians visiting their tomb were sealed in on the orders of Numerianus (d. 284). GREGORY OF TOURS, who knew of the last episode, said that Pope DAMASUS composed for the crypt an epitaph; this, however, has not been discovered. A later inscription for Chrysanthus and Daria says that their shrine was restored after the GOTHS devastated it in 539. These martyrs seem to be genuine, but their stories appear to have been brought together because they were buried in the Via Salaria or because they were listed together in martyrologies. Oil from the lamps of the shrine was brought to the Frankish Queen Theodelinda. Chrysanthus and Daria appear in sixth-century mosaics in RAVENNA, and their tomb is mentioned in *ITINERARIA* of the seventh century. In 844 their relics were brought to PRÜM and from there to Münstereifel, where they are still venerated. The martyrologies list them on various dates.

Feast: Oct. 25.

Bibliography: G. REITTER, *Sankt Chrysanthen: das alte Wahlfahrtsheiligtum in Osttirol u. seine europ. Kultzusammenhänge* (Innsbruck 1976). P. ALLARD, *Dictionnaire d'archéologie chrétienne et de liturgie*, ed. F. CABROL, H. LECLERCQ, and H. I. MARROU (Paris 1907–53) 3.1:1560–68. A. P. FRUTAZ, *Lexikon für Theologie und Kirche*, ed. J. HOFER and K. RAHNER (Freiburg 1957–65) 2:1192–93. J. DUBOIS, *Catholicisme* 2:1112–13.

[M. J. COSTELLOE]

CHRYSOBERGES, ANDREW

Byzantine Dominican scholar, archbishop of Rhodes; d. Famagusta, Cyprus, 1451. He was one of three Greek brothers who became Catholics and DOMINICANS under the influence of Demetrius CYDONES and the controversy over HESYCHASM. He is first mentioned in 1410 as professor of philosophy at the Dominican convent in Padua. At the Council of CONSTANCE he joined the Greek ambassadors in persuading the conciliar fathers and Pope MARTIN V of Greek readiness for union. On Feb. 12, 1418, he became master of theology, and between 1418 and 1425 he was in Constantinople and Caffa. On Feb. 12, 1420, he was made a member of the papal household, and on July 9, master of the Sacred Palace. In 1426 Pope Martin sent him to Constantinople with the Greek ambassadors returning from Rome to treat of union and appointed him vicar-general of the whole Societas Fratrum Peregrinantium et Unitorum. Chrysoberges returned to Rome before May 9, 1427, and in 1428 to 1429 he was in Poland-Lithuania on a papal mission.

Although nominated bishop of Sutri (Feb. 23, 1429), he either refused or resigned the office. He acted for Martin V with the Greek envoys, who in 1430 drew up the agreement for a council of union in Italy that was in effect realized only at Ferrara-Florence in 1438. EUGENE IV made Chrysoberges archbishop of Rhodes on May 2, 1432, and sent him to Basel to mitigate that Council's conciliarism [*See* CONCILIARISM (HISTORY OF)]. He was unsuccessful but encouraged the papal party there and visited Emperor Sigismund of Hungary on his return trip. At the Council of Florence he delivered the reply to Cardinal BESSARION's opening eulogy, and spoke in the debate on purgatory and on the addition of the *filioque* to the Creed. After the promulgation of union, he visited his archdiocese, was sent to Cyprus to investigate Greek complaints of Latin intolerance (Nov. 5, 1441), and brought into the Church certain Chaldeans and Maronites, who later confirmed the union in Rome (Aug. 7, 1445). He was made archbishop of Nicosia (April 19, 1447) and apostolic legate for Cyprus and the Aegean Islands (July 30, 1447). A letter of his to Bessarion (*c.* 1437–38) has been preserved [E. Candal, ed., *Orientalia Christiana periodica* 4 (1938) 329–371], as has an unedited treatise to JOSEPH OF METHONE against the encyclical of Mark EUGENICUS.

Bibliography: R. COULON, *Dictionnaire d'histoire et de geéographie ecclésiastiques*, ed. A. BAUDRILLART et al. (Paris 1912) 2:1696–1700. H. G. BECK, *Kirche und theologische Literatur im byzantinischen Reich* (Munich 1959) 742–743. R. J. LOENERTZ, *Catholicisme. Hier, aujourd'hui et demain* ed. G. JACQUEMET (Paris 1947–) 2:1114–15; *Archivum Fratrum Praedicatorum* 9 (1939) 5–61. M. H. LAURENT, *Échos d'Orient* (1935) 414–438. J. GILL, *The Council of Florence* (Cambridge, Eng. 1959).

[J. GILL]

CHRYSOGONUS, ST.

Apparently suffered martyrdom *c.* 304 *ad Aquas Gradatas,* near Aquileia; venerated in northern Italy. His cult was brought to Rome, where his name was introduced into the Canon of the Mass. According to his legendary *Passio,* prefixed to that of St. ANASTASIA, he was a Roman officer who became her spiritual father and continued to direct her by letter even after his imprisonment for the faith. He was beheaded under Diocletian in Aquileia. In Rome there is an early Christian church known as the *titulus Chrysogoni,* mentioned in an inscription of 521 and in the synods of Rome in 499 and 595. The legend of the saint apparently grew out of an attempt to identify the founder of the Roman church with the martyr of Aquileia.

Feast: Nov. 24.

Bibliography: V. L. KENNEDY, *The Saints of the Canon of the Mass* (Rome 1938). A. BUTLER, *The Lives of the Saints*, ed. H. THURSTON and D. ATTWATER (New York 1956) 4:418–419.

[M. J. COSTELLOE]

CHRYSOSTOM OF SAINT-LÔ, JOHN

Franciscan spiritual director and writer; b. Saint-Fremond, near Bayeux, France, 1594; d. Paris, March 26, 1646. He entered the Third Order Regular of St. Francis at the age of 16 and rapidly advanced to high positions within the order. In 1622 he was definitor of the province of France, in 1625 definitor general, in 1634 provincial of the province of France, and in 1640 provincial of the province of Saint-Yves. He was confessor to Marie de Médicis and Anne of Austria and was esteemed highly by Louis XIII and Cardinal Richelieu. Among Chrysostom's personal friends were St. Vincent de Paul, Jean Jacques Olier, and Charles de Condren. His writings were probably more extensive than the few short works that survive. These include *Divers traités spirituels et méditatifs* (Paris 1651), *Exercises de piété et de perfection* (Caen 1654), and *La Sainte désoccupation* (2d ed. Paris 1890). His greatest influence, however, was as a spiritual director, and as such he is remembered as a leading figure in French spirituality of the 17th century. He was the leading figure of the school of Norman mystics associated with the hermitage of Caen, and his disciples included St. John Eudes, Jean de Bernieres-Louvigny, Marie de Vallées, Henri Boudon, and others notable in the history of spirituality.

Bibliography: H. BOUDON, *L'Homme intérieur* (Paris 1684), also in *Oeuvres de Boudon,* ed. J. P. MIGNE (Paris 1856) 2:1127–1342. M. A. SOURIAU, *Deux mystiques normands au XVIIᵉ siècle* (Paris 1913), G. GUILLOT, *Les Pères pénitents a St. Lô* (St. Lô 1914). R. HEURTEVANT, *Dictionnaire de spiritualité ascétique et mystique. Doctrine et histoire*, ed. M. VILLER et al. (Paris 1932–) 2:881–885. É. LONGPRÉ, *Catholicisme. Hier, aujourd'hui et demain*, G. JACQUEMET (Paris 1947–) 2:1117–19.

[J. C. WILLKE]

CHTHONIC DIVINITIES, WORSHIP OF

This category of divinities in ancient Greek religion comprises the Earth (in Greek Xθών), or Gaia (Ge); the fertility goddesses who emanated from her, especially the Mother Goddesses of Asia Minor; and the dead, who often figure as spirits of fertility. S. Eitrem [*Opferritus und Voropfer der Griechen und Römer* (Christiania 1914)] attempted to show—and M. Nilsson concurred (1:135)—that the introductory ceremonies of the normal

John Chrysostom of Saint-Lô.

Greek sacrifice offered to the celestial gods indicated an important phenomenon. Inasmuch as the celestial divinities allowed themselves to be associated in the cult of the dead, they were very probably regarded as the dead with whom the spirits of the place were identified. This would mean that a remnant of the animistic-agrarian form of religion going back to pre-Greek culture was preserved as an essential element in the cult of the Olympian gods. At the stage of archaic Greek religion represented by Homer, the dead were mere wraiths who did not even have a cult. However, the employment of a cleft or fissure for channeling an offering in liquid form from the top of the grave or altar into the earth is confirmed by archeology of shaft graves of Mycenae and by the discovery of such altars in ancient Crete. Unquestionably, in ancient Crete and in the Minoan culture in general, the motherly earth was no longer viewed only as a vague personification or an abstractly conceived fertility power, the receiver of chthonic cult, but, on the contrary, as the Mistress of Life, active in the fruitful earth itself.

The close union also of the Olympian gods with an element that falls within the earthly sphere was especially striking not only in the case of the sea god, Poseidon, the Earth-Shaker, the husband of Dao (i.e., Demeter, the Earth-Goddess), but especially in the case of Hermes, the god of stone piles, who, perhaps even in his office as guide of the dead, was called Chthonios. Zeus himself was associated as Chthonios at Athens in certain sacrifices to Gaia, and was therefore the object of a chthonic cult in practice, although not perhaps by formal rite. The earliest children of Gaia, the Titans and Giants, had a continued life only in myth. The Titans conquered by Zeus were chthonic gods through their confinement, at first in Tartarus as a place of punishment and then, after their pardon by Zeus, through their abode in Elysium, the land of the dead on the rim of the earth. The worship of fertility demons frequently had an important place in the complex of cults of rural areas.

Bibliography: H. J. ROSE, *Handbook of Greek Mythology* (6th ed. New York 1958) 17–101. M. P. NILSSON, *Geschichte der griechischen Religion* v.1. U. VON WILAMOWITZ-MOELLENDORFF, *Der Glaube der Hellenen,* 2 v. (Berlin 1931–32) v.1. H. SCHWABL, "Weltschöpfung," *Paulys Realencyklopädie der klassischen Altertumswissenschaft,* Suppl 9 (1962) 1433–1582, esp. 1440ff.

[K. PRÜMM]

CHUR, MONASTERY OF

Former Premonstratensian abbey, Graubünden canton, Switzerland, Diocese of Chur (patron, St. Lucius). It is improbable that the Benedictine foundation dated from St. LUCIUS, but possibly a small clerical community, living on the site, became Benedictine *c.* 800. Before 1149, Conrad of Biberegg, Bishop of Chur, committed the monastery to the PREMONSTRATENSIANS from Roggenburg and relocated the nuns of the original double monastery at St. Hilary, not far from the abbey. Churwalden in the Engadine was a daughterhouse. In 1529 the abbot Theodul Schlegl was martyred by the Calvinists, and the abbey was suppressed in 1538. The community found refuge at Bendern in Liechtenstein. In 1624 Chur was restored, though most of its possessions were lost. Although legally it was once again an abbey *sui juris* by 1717, it remained practically a dependent house of Roggenburg. In 1806 the last abbot surrendered the monastery to the bishopric of Chur, which now uses the abbey as its diocesan seminary.

Bibliography: C. L. HUGO, *S. Ordinis Praemonstratensis annales,* 2 v. (Nancy 1734–36) 2:103–112. L. H. COTTINEAU, *Répertoire topobibliographique des abbayes et prieurés,* 2 v. (Mâcon 1935–39) 1:831. N. BACKMUND, *Monasticon Praemonstratense,* 3 v. (Straubing 1949–56) 1:68–70. M. H. VICAIRE and N. BACKMUND, *Dictionnaire d'histoire et de géographie ecclésiastiques,* ed. A. BAUDRILLART et al. (Paris 1912–) 13:213–221. G. VASELLA, *St-Luziuskirche* (Munich 1955).

[N. BACKMUND]

CHURCH, ARTICLES ON

The Church is considered in the *Encyclopedia* under a variety of aspects: theological, institutional, historical.

The principal articles concerning the theology of the Church are CHURCH, I (IN THE BIBLE) and CHURCH, II (THEOLOGY OF); see also COMMUNIO. For discussion of the theological discipline that concerns the Church, *see* ECCLESIOLOGY. In the area of dogmatic theology, the major areas are membership in the Church (COMMUNION OF SAINTS; INCORPORATION IN CHRIST; INCORPORATION INTO THE CHURCH [MEMBERSHIP]; MYSTICAL BODY; SOCIETY [CHURCH AS]; VOTUM), the character of the Church (e.g., MARKS OF THE CHURCH; APOSTOLICITY; VISIBILITY OF THE CHURCH), and the structure and offices of the Church (e.g., TEACHING AUTHORITY OF THE CHURCH [MAGISTERIUM]; INFALLIBILITY; LAITY, THEOLOGY OF; COUNCILS, GENERAL [ECUMENICAL], THEOLOGY OF).

The Church as an institution is covered in a wide variety of articles concerning canon law. There are also sets of articles dealing with the papacy (e.g., PAPACY; POPES, ELECTION OF; POPE; PRONOUNCEMENTS, PAPAL AND CURIAL; *LIBER PONTIFICALIS*), the Roman Curia (e.g., CURIA, ROMAN; EVANGELIZATION OF PEOPLES, CONGREGATION FOR THE; PONTIFICAL BIBLICAL COMMISSION), bishops (e.g., EPISCOPAL CONFERENCES; BISHOP [IN THE CHURCH]), and laity (e.g., LAITY, FORMATION AND EDUCATION OF; *CHRISTIFIDELES LAICI*; CHRISTIAN FAMILY MOVEMENT). Religious orders receive special attention, with general articles on the orders (e.g., BENEDICTINES; BENEDICTINE SPIRITUALITY; SULPICIANS; CANONS REGULAR OF ST. AUGUSTINE) and separate articles on individual congregations and religious houses; see also MONASTICISM; POVERTY CONTROVERSY; HERMITS, etc.

Many of the articles in the *Encyclopedia* deal with the history of the Church in some way. The biographies of popes, martyrs, and founders of religious orders, for example, provide indispensable information about the Church in their times and places. Other biographies, such as those of influential writers, musicians, or scientists, are included in the *Encyclopedia* because of the influence of such persons in the Church. The entries dealing with individual countries are principally accounts of the Church, or of Christianity in general, in those countries. For more on this topic, see MISSIOLOGY, ARTICLES ON. The history of the Church is treated most explicitly in four articles: CHURCH, HISTORY OF, I (EARLY); CHURCH, HISTORY OF, II (MEDIEVAL); CHURCH, HISTORY OF, III (EARLY MODERN: 1500–1789); CHURCH, HISTORY OF, IV (LATE MODERN: 1789–2002).

[G. F. LANAVE]

CHURCH, I (IN THE BIBLE)

The important considerations about the Church from a biblical viewpoint are the original terms used for it, its adumbrations in the OT, and the development of its notion in the NT.

Original Terms. The English word "church," like the German *Kirche,* is derived ultimately, through the Gothic, from the Greek τὸ κυριακόν, "thing or place pertaining to the Lord." The words for church in the Romance languages, such as the French *église* and the Italian *chièsa,* come from the Latin *ecclesia,* an exact transliteration of the Greek ἐκκλησία.

In the profane Greek ἐκκλησία designated an assembly of the people as a political force; it was used in this meaning in Acts 19.32, 39, 41; its meaning in 1 Cor 11.18 was colored by its profane signification. In the Septuagint (LXX) ἐκκλησία designated an assembly convoked for religious purposes (e.g., Dt 23.2–3; 1 Kgs 8.5, 14, 22; Ps 21 [22].26). It is used 81 times to translate the Hebrew term *qāhāl,* and four times derivatives of *qāhāl* (1 Sm 19.20, conjectured; Neh 5.7; Ps 25[26].12; 67[68].27). *Qāhāl* was used in most cases to designate a religious assembly, a usage especially of the DEUTERONOMISTS, the Biblical CHRONICLER, and the Book of PSALMS. The word *qāhāl* was translated also by other words in the LXX, in particular by συναγωγή, which, however, more frequently translated *'ēdâ,* "a gathering." There is little doubt that both the assonance and the similarity in meaning of *qāhāl* and ἐκκλησία, "that which is called forth," influenced the translators who produced the LXX.

In the NT ἐκκλησία is found 61 times in the Pauline corpus (including Hebrews), 23 times in Acts, 20 times in Revelation, and 11 in the remaining books. The meaning in each case must be derived from the context.

It was altogether natural that Jesus, in establishing a new COVENANT and hence a new people of God having continuity with the ancient one, would have designated this people with a biblical name for a religious assembly; in Aramaic He would have used *'edtâ'* or *keniŝtâ',* (both translated into Greek as συναγωγή), or *qehalâ',* in Greek ἐκκλησία. Only when the break between Christians and Jews became definitive did ἐκκλησία become a purely Christian term and συναγωγή (SYNAGOGUE) a Jewish term.

Adumbrations in the Old Testament. From its beginnings mankind was called to live in society (Gn 1.27; 2.18), to multiply itself, to subdue and to have dominion over the earth (Gn 1.28), and to live in familiarity with God (Gn 2.8–25). But sin was committed by man and broke this special relationship to God; yet God promised mercy to a sinful mankind (Genesis ch. 3). As a result of sin, men manifested hatred for one another (Gn 4.8; 6.11), showed inordinate pride (Gn 11.8–9), and lost familiarity with their Creator (Gn 3.8; 4.14).

The process of the formation of God's people commenced with the election of Abraham, which was sealed with a *berît,* "covenant." The covenant was renewed and made more particular with some of Abraham's descendants during the Exodus from Egypt under Moses (Exodus ch. 19–24). The Israelites were not always faithful to God. This infidelity showed itself during the Exodus (Ex 32.1–6), notwithstanding God's special care of them (Exodus ch. 16–17), and more brazenly later on. Instead of being God's faithful spouse, Israel acted like an adulterous wife (Hosea ch. 1–3; 9.1; Ezekiel ch. 16); it violated God's laws and belied the covenant (Is 1.2–9; 5.1–7). The Prophets often predicted that only a portion of the people, the faithful and holy remnant of Israel, would be the beneficiary of the divine promises (Is 4.3; Am 3.12; 9.8–10; Jer 3.14–18). Then God would conclude a new covenant with His people (Jer 31.31–34; Ez 11.14–21). These two ideas, the faithful remnant and the new covenant, were reaffirmed during the centuries following the Babylonian Exile, and they nourished the messianic hopes of Israel (Is 54.9–10; Zec 2.11–17; 9.7; Hg 1.12; 2.2–5; 1 Mc 2.49–64); they also held an important place in the teaching of the QUMRAN COMMUNITY.

Development of the Concept in the New Testament. While the new and ultimate covenant was ratified by Jesus' death and Resurrection, and hence the Church began at that time, only gradually was the nature of the new community manifested as separate from Judaism and as having its own proper structure.

In the Acts of the Apostles. After the Ascension, the Apostles, whom Jesus had chosen and to whom He "had given commandments through the Holy Spirit" (Acts 1.2), together with the disciples, remained in Jerusalem awaiting the coming of the Spirit; they elected Matthias as successor of Judas Iscariot at the urging of Peter to fill out the member of the TWELVE (Acts 1.12–26). After the coming of the Spirit they began immediately to preach to the Jews and to baptize (Acts 2.4–41; 4.2), though they met opposition (Acts 4.1; 5.17–18; 9.1; 12.1–5). The first members of the Jerusalem church voluntarily shared their possessions (Acts 4.34–5.11). Gradually the Apostles assigned to other members of the community certain duties; the deacons were given charge of charitable works, preaching, and baptizing (Acts 6.1–6; 8.5, 12–13, 31–38). Nevertheless, a certain type of IMPOSITION OF HANDS in order to receive the Holy Spirit was a work of the Apostles alone (Acts 8.14–18). "The communion of the breaking of the bread" was a central rite (Acts 2.42, 46; 20.7, 11). At an early date non-Jews were admitted to the

The Procession of the Church to the Cross, full-page miniature in a late-10th-century Reichenau manuscript of the "Song of Songs" in the Staatliche Bibliothek, Bamberg (MS Bibl. 22, fol. 4 v).

Birth of the Church, detail of a full-page miniature for the Book of Genesis, Bible Moralisée composed in Paris, c. 1250, Austrian National Library at Vienna (Codex 1179), with the participation of the Father (standing) and the Holy Ghost (dove-shaped flames).

Church (Acts 10.44–48); outside of Palestine, especially at Antioch, the work also of proselytizing Gentiles met with success and it was at Antioch that "the disciples were first called Christians" (Acts 11.19–26). (*See* CHRISTIAN [THE TERM].) Jewish dietary laws and circumcision did not bind the converts from paganism (Acts 11.1–18), though minor restrictions were imposed on some churches by an Apostolic decision (Acts 15.23–29; *see* JERUSALEM, COUNCIL OF). With the conversion of Paul, a former persecutor of Christians, the tempo of proselytism among non-Jews was accelerated and the tensions between the Jewish and non-Jewish elements in the Church increased (Acts 15.1–2, 35; 21.20–25). The Apostles and their converts from Judaism, however, including Paul, continued to assist at the services in the Temple in Jerusalem (Acts 3.1; 5.42; 21.26). The preaching of the Apostles and other ministers centered on Jesus, who was crucified, was raised from the dead, was to reign as King over the new Israel (Acts 2.22–39; 13.16–41), and whose subjects would rise as Jesus had (Acts 23.6; 26.23). St. Luke's record of the expansion of the Church under the guidance of the Holy Spirit ceased when the good news had reached as far as Rome (Acts 1.8; 28.28–31).

In the Pauline Corpus. The content of Paul's letters should now be examined for their teaching about the Church. The Apostle of the Gentiles, more than any other NT author, gave his personal reflections on the Church's nature. In the vision on the road to Damascus he received the revelation of the mysterious identity between Christ and the Church (Acts 9.4–5) and his later experiences forced him to delve more deeply into this mystery.

According to Paul the universal Church was composed of various local churches whose members were "saints," chosen by God (1 Cor 1.2). There was authority in the Church: Peter (Gal 1.18; 2.6–14); the Twelve and Paul himself (1 Cor 15.1–11); Timothy, Titus, and the "bishops" (1 Tm 1.3–5; 3.2; Ti 1.7; Phil 1.1; Acts 20.28; *see* BISHOP [IN THE BIBLE]); elders or PRESBYTERS (Ti 1.5; 1 Tm 5.17); and DEACONS (Phil 1.1). There were also those possessing various CHARISMS, among whom the Prophets had a special place; in their activity the charismatics were not to cause disorder (1 Cor 14.33, 40). The members of the Church lived in the expectation of the PAROUSIA of Jesus (1 Thes 1.10; 1 Cor 11.26) and the resurrection of the just (1 Thes 4.13–18; 1 Corinthians ch. 15), but the time of the Parousia was not known (1 Thes 5.1–3; 2 Thes 2.1–8). The communities were to live according to the traditions that Paul had passed on to them (1 Cor 11.2, 23–24; 15.1–3; Gal 1.6–10); the traditions were rooted in the life and teaching of Jesus (1 Cor 7.10; 11.23; 2 Cor 4.5) and concerned belief (1 Cor 15.1–4), rites such as baptism and the Lord's Supper (Gal 3.26–27; Eph 4.5; 1 Cor 11.23–24), and ways of acting

(1 Cor 7.10). Baptism united the believer to the dead and risen Lord Jesus (Rom 6.3–11); and the partaking of the bread effected unity (1 Cor 10.16–17). Baptism and the profession of faith went together (Gal 3.26–27); faith came from hearing and accepting the proclamation of Christ's word (Rom 10.17). (*See* BAPTISM [IN THE BIBLE].)

Paul described the Church as God's plantation, the growth of which depended upon God's aid (1 Cor 3.6–9), as God's building whose foundation was Christ (1 Cor 3.9–15), and as God's sanctuary (1 Cor 3.16). The Church was "the pillar and mainstay of truth" (1 Tm 3.15), a new creation (2 Cor 5.17; Gal 6.15), the spouse of Christ (2 Cor 11.2–3; Eph 5.22–33), the new covenant (1 Cor 11.25), and the kingdom of God's beloved Son (Col 1.13). The Church was made up of those who were in Christ, who were Christ's, and who were the body of Christ (1 Cor 10.16–17; 12.12; Rom 12.4–8).

The description of the Church as the MYSTICAL BODY OF CHRIST is considered by many to have been the most characteristic feature in Paul's consideration of the Church. There was a development in the Apostle's thought on this theme between the composition of 1 Corinthians (*c.* 57) and that of Colossians and Ephesians (*c.* 62). In the latter Epistles Christ was described as the head of His body (Col 1.18; Eph 5.22–24, 29–30) and the Church was called the plenitude of Christ's fullness (Eph 1.22–23), notions that were not explicitly noted in the earlier letters (1 Cor 6.15–17; 10.14–22; 12.12–31; Rom 12.4–8). The idea of the many united in the one of 1 Corinthians and Romans was conducive to the more developed idea of the body as Christ in His fullness. The Church's ministries were given by Christ "in order to perfect the saints for a work of ministry, for building up the body of Christ, until we all attain to the unity of the faith and of the deep knowledge of the Son of God, to perfect manhood, to the mature measure of the fullness of Christ" (Eph 4.11–13). The members of the Church were to be "imitators of God" (Eph 5.1) and were to "grow up in all things in . . . Christ" (Eph 4.15). Moved as they were by the Spirit to know and confess Jesus as the Christ (1 Cor 12.3), Christ's members shared in His powers, indeed in the very principle of His life (Col 2.19; Eph 4.15–16). The Apostles were in a special sense His ministers and the dispensers of His and God's mysteries (1 Cor 4.1).

Charity was to reign in the Church; as a concrete expression of this principle, Paul organized the collection on behalf of the Jerusalem church among the believers in the Greek territories (1 Cor 16.1–4; 2 Corinthians ch., 8–9; Rom 15.26–27). This was but one way of emphasizing the fact that the Church's members formed one people (Gal 3.24–29) who were children of the one God and

Father (Eph 4.1–6); thus there were among them no human divisions but all were reconciled one to another (Eph 2.11–22), Greeks and barbarians, masters and slaves, men and women (1 Cor 12.13; Col 3.11). As Christ could not be divided, neither could the Church (1 Cor 1.12–13; 3.4). Yet there were sinners in the Church, some of whom were to be expelled, though the hope of pardon was not taken away (1 Corinthians ch. 5).

In the Synoptic Gospels. The first Gospel's teaching concerning the Church was for the most part contained within the teaching concerning the kingdom of heaven. It was to have modest beginnings (Mt 13.31–33) about which men would argue (Mt 13.37–43). Entrance into it was difficult (Mt 7.13–14; 11.12), since obedience and renouncement were necessary (Mt 7.21; 12.50). It was predicted in the OT (Mt 13.35). The wise and proud would not enter into the kingdom (Mt 5.3–10; 11.25; 13.10–15), but sinners and Gentiles would (Mt 8.10–12; 9.9–13; 21.28–32). The last point was treated at some length in the Gospel because of the need to solve the problem that the religious Jews had generally rejected the life and teachings of Jesus, although He was the authentic fulfillment of the OT. The solution was contained in the parables and lessons recalling Israel's former infidelity (Mt 20.1–16; 21.28–32, 33–46; 22.1–10). The OT foretold that many of the Jews would renounce their privileges because of their obstinacy (Mt 21.42; 23.34–39); the benefits would then be given to those who had a modicum of belief (Mt 5.3–12; 13.12; 25.29).

Alone among the evangelists Matthew used the word ἐκκλησία (Mt 16.18; 18.17). The three uses of the word show the communitarian interests of the evangelist and of the Judeo-Christian Church whose preoccupations he reflected; it was a Church aware that it was the new chosen people, the beginning on Earth of the Kingdom of God. It therefore put particular insistence upon Peter's role (Mt 16.16–18) and the duties of the sacred community's members (Matthew ch. 18). The new kingdom was inaugurated with the death and Resurrection of Jesus (Mt 27.50–53; 28.16–20); yet it would reach a milestone in its life with the fall of Jerusalem in A.D. 70 (Matthew ch. 24). The community was to be governed by the authority constituted by Jesus (Mt 16.16–18; 18.15–18); it was to have sacramental rites, baptism (Mt 28.19) and the Eucharist (Mt 26.26–29). Its authorities were to proclaim the teaching of Jesus to the whole world (Mt 28.20). While the Church was the kingdom of heaven on Earth, inaugurated and ruled by Christ, the Church was not completely identical with the kingdom of the Father (cf. Mt 13.37–43 with 13.43 and 25.34). The concept of the Church presented in St. Mark's Gospel added nothing to the data found in Matthew.

The doctrine concerning the kingdom of God on Earth in St. Luke's Gospel was the same as that found in the other two Synoptic Gospels, but more than they, Luke emphasized its universalistic characteristics (Lk 4.25–27; 24.47). While Matthew used the more Hebraic phrase "kingdom of heaven" as a title for the Church, Luke and Mark used "kingdom of God," a sign that their works were addressed primarily to non-Jewish elements within the Church.

In the Johannine Literature. In the theology of St. John, Jesus was King of a kingdom that was "not of this world" (Jn 18.36). The members of the kingdom were born, "not of blood, nor of the will of the flesh, nor of the will of men, but of God" (Jn 1.13; cf. 3.3–8; 1 Jn 2.29–3.1–2, 9; 4.7; 5.1, 4, 18); they were by belief SONS OF GOD (Jn 1.12; 1 Jn 5.1). Their birth was through water and the Spirit (Jn 3.5). The Christian abided in Christ and in God (Jn 6.57; 15.4–7; 1 Jn 2.6, 24, 27–28; 3.6; 4.16). The Christian was to eat the flesh and drink the blood of Jesus (Jn 6.52–57). While emphasis certainly was given in the fourth Gospel to the relationship of the individual Christian to Jesus, the allegory of the Good Shepherd (Jn 10.1–18) and that of the Vine and the Branches (Jn 15.1–7) brought out the community aspects of John's teaching concerning believers. In the fourth Gospel the Apostles were given the power to forgive sins (Jn 20.22–23). Peter was constituted the shepherd of Jesus' flock (Jn 21.15–17), which should be universally one (Jn 10.16; 17.11). The Apostles would have the duty of carrying on the mission given by the Father to Jesus (Jn 20.21).

The suffering and ultimately triumphant Church was the main subject of the Revelation. The principal figures of the Church were the WOMAN CLOTHED WITH THE SUN and fighting with the dragon, Satan (Rv ch. 12), and the Temple and its environs (Rv 11.1–13). Warnings against various communal sins and defects were given in the letters to the seven churches of Asia Minor (Rv 1.9–3.22).

In the Other NT Literature. According to the doctrine found in the Epistle to the Hebrews, Christians did not have on Earth a permanent city but were to seek that which was to come (Heb 13.14), to which heavenly state each was called but which, to a certain degree, was already possessed (Heb 3.1; 6.4–5). The Christians' sole high priest was already in heaven interceding for them (Heb 5.1–10; 9.11–14). Christians were brothers one to another (Heb 3.1, 12), sanctified by Jesus into one brotherhood with Him (Heb 2.11–18); they were "partakers of Christ" (Heb 3.14), His house (Heb 3.6), and had been purified in His blood (Heb 9.18–28). Unlike the wandering Jews of the Exodus they were a caravan traveling in obedience toward the true, i.e., perfect, Promised Land (Heb 3.1–4.13).

In 1 Peter many figures were used to describe Christ and His Church: a cornerstone, a precious stone chosen by God, a spiritual house, "a holy priesthood, to offer spiritual sacrifices acceptable to God through Jesus Christ," "a chosen race, a royal priesthood, a holy nation, a purchased people" that should proclaim "the perfections of him who has called you out of darkness into his marvelous light," a people that had now obtained mercy (1 Pt 2.4–10). The "presbyters" were to "tend the flock of God, . . . governing not under constraint, but willingly" (1 Pt 5.1–2). Younger members of the Church were to be subject to the presbyters (5.5).

In 2 Peter the faithful were warned against false teachers and unsound interpreters of Sacred Scripture (2 Pt 2.1–3, 3.16); the Parousia would occur suddenly but it was now delayed for the Lord did not wish "that any should perish but that all should turn to repentance" (3.9).

According to Jude, the Church's members were the "called who have been loved in God the Father and preserved for Christ Jesus" (Jude 1.1); they were to be wary of false teachers.

According to James, the Church was made up of the poor who were "heirs of the kingdom which God has promised to those who love him" (Jas 2.5). There was, moreover, a special ritual for the sick that was reserved to the presbyters, who were to assemble and pray over the sick man, "anointing him with oil in the name of the Lord" (Jas 5.14–15). The prayer of faith would cure him and the Lord would raise him, and if he were guilty of sins, he would be forgiven. (*See* ANOINTING OF THE SICK, I [THEOLOGY OF].)

Bibliography: *Encyclopedic Dictionary of the Bible,* tr. and adap. by L. HARTMAN (New York 1963), from A. VAN DEN BORN, *Bijbels Woordenboek* 376–385. A. MÉDEBIELLE, *Dictionnaire de la Bible,* suppl. ed. L. PIROT et al. (Paris 1928–) 2:487–691. K. L. SCHMIDT,*Theologisches Wörterbuch zum Neuen Testament,* ed. G. KITTEL (Stuttgart 1935–) 3:502–539. L. CERFAUX, *The Church in the Theology of St. Paul,* tr. G. WEBB and A. WALKER (New York 1959). J. A. T. ROBINSON, *The Body: A Study in Pauline Theology* (London 1952). M. BLACK, *The Scrolls and Christian Origins* (New York 1961). *L'Église dans la Bible: Recherches de philosophie et de théologie publiées par les facultés S. J. de Montréal* (Studia 13; Bruges 1962). D. M. STANLEY, "Reflections on the Church in the N.T.," *Catholic Biblical Quarterly* 25 (1963) 387–400. B. M. AHERN, "The Concept of the Church in Biblical Thought," *Proceedings of the Society of Catholic College Teachers of Sacred Doctrine* 7 (1961) 32–61. P. BENOIT, *Exégèse et théologie,* 2 v. (Paris 1961) 2:107–177, 232–317; "Qumrân et le NT," *New Testament Studies* 7 (1960–61) 276–296. J. GNILKA, "Die Kirche des Matthäus und die Gemeinde von Qumran," *Biblische Zeitschrift* 7 (1963) 43–63.

[J. J. O'ROURKE]

CHURCH, II (THEOLOGY OF)

The Church is not only a receiver of divine revelation, but, as the MYSTICAL BODY OF CHRIST, it is bound up with revelation itself. The Church is God's handiwork, what God has wrought and is doing explicitly in the mystery of SALVATION; it is at the same time the tool through which God works to bring humankind the divine light and love that is salvation. The Church is a phenomenon with multiple dimensions: human and divine, visible and invisible, juridical and mystical, immanent and transcendent, earthbound and destined for heaven. In this world the Church is neither wholly alien nor wholly at home. It is both a means and an end: both a divine tool put to work for human salvation, and, at the same time, even in its pilgrim state, an anticipated realization in the obscurity of faith of the final glorious company of the heavenly Church.

This article sets forth in a general way, without excluding or minimizing other modes of systematization, the theology of the Church centered on the biblical and traditional theme of COMMUNION (*koinonia*). The Church is in its deepest being the communion of life between the Father and humankind in his Son Jesus Christ, the Redeemer and glorious Lord of life, through the gift of their one Spirit of love. As a result of this primary communion, descending vertically from the initiative of the Father's love communicated to the Son in their one Spirit, there comes into being a lateral, or horizontal, communion among human beings who, as adoptive sons and daughters of the Father in Jesus Christ, the one true Son, are by that fact brothers and sisters one of another in the same community of life and love. The Church as a communion of life with the Father in Christ necessarily entails the Church as a communion of life with the brothers and sisters in the same Christ, in each instance through the Spirit, the common love of the Father and of the Son. It is in Jesus, the one and only Son made human, that the vertical communion in sonship and the horizontal communion in brother and sisterhood meet and join in the mystery of the Church. The Church is a sacramental communication of the Father's love for human beings in Christ. It is a communion of brother and sisterhood with Christ in a sacramental faith and love, administered and directed by the episcopal order, which is itself a lesser communion of ministerial office and function, sacramentally established and commissioned by Christ to provide himself and his work with a continuing vicarious presence in time and space. The Church is a community of life that requires all remaining history to develop and to achieve its full realization when, at the Second Coming, the Body of the Church will rise in its total glory and will enter, escorted by its head, into the blessings of the Father, who will be "all in all" (1 Cor 15.28).

In the unknown span of time between the two comings of Christ, the Christian brother and sisterhood undertakes its pilgrim journey. All that must be done in the Lord on the way of Christian history—the worship of the Triune God, the patient Christianization of the world, the endless struggle against sin and demoniac forces, including the fight against social injustice—is gradually and perseveringly achieved, in the measure assigned in the economy of God, only in and with the whole brother and sisterhood, of all ages and places, acting in concert in the one Spirit of Christ. To act as brother and sister in the Spirit of Christ is the style of life and the law of action of the Christian in the communion of the Church.

New Testament. The Church is communion with the Father in Christ through the Gift of the Spirit.

Wellspring of the Church. The Church is the assembly of the Father, the Body of Christ and the temple of the Holy Spirit. In the Church people are enabled to share together in the most personal goods of the Triune God (2 Cor 13.13)—the gifts of the Father (Rom 12.3) and of the Son (Eph 4.7) and of the Spirit (Rom 12.11). The eternal plan of the Triune God lies at the origin of the Church (Eph 1.3–14). The Church's wellspring is the Father (Rom 11.36), who in unflawed love has sent the Son with the fullness of the Spirit to the sinful human beings of this fallen and estranged world (Rom 5.8; 8.32; 2 Cor 5.19; Gal 4.4–7; Eph 2.4–10; Ti 3.4–7; 1 Jn 4.9–16; Jn 3.16–17, 34–36; 6.58; 17.3, 18–25); it is the Father who has inspired the Son made human with the Spirit of love to save the world from sin, death, and the demon (Heb 9.14) and, as the glorious head of his Body the Church (Eph 1.22), to give all human beings in himself and his Body "access to the Father in the one Spirit" (Eph 2.18; see 2.19–22; Heb 10.19–20).

Visible Continuum of Christ's Mission. In establishing his Church, Christ, the while remaining wholly dependent on the loving designs of the Father (Jn 5.30; 6.38–40; 1 Cor 15.23–28), gave his own saving mission a visible continuum in history, a sacramental and social ministry in the Spirit (2 Cor 3.3, 8), charging his APOSTLES to supply a vicarious and ministerial presence to his person and his work, achieved once and for all (Heb 7.27; 9.26–28; 10.10) and ratified once and for all in his own Body-Person in its passage from death to a glorious life (Acts 2.33–36; Phil 2.9–11). The actual forms that these ministries took emerged gradually amid much variety in the early Christian centuries. Through these ministries, the eternal loving resolve of the Father to make human beings sharers in the divine life took shape within the apostolic Church commissioned by Christ (Jn 20.21; 17.18; 15.9; Acts ch. 2). The Apostles trace their office and mission to the loving will of the Father embodied in the work

A crowd gathers to celebrate Mass, Valletta, Malta. (©Paul Almasy/CORBIS)

of the incarnate Word (1 Cor 1.1; 2 Cor 1.1; Gal 1.1; Col 1.1). St. Paul is "by God's will an apostle of Jesus Christ" (Eph 1.1), and he is an Apostle in the power of Christ's Spirit (1 Thes 1.5; 1 Cor 2.4–5).

It is the role of the apostolic Church, as the receiver of Christ's mandate and as the qualified servant of his word and work in the Spirit, to introduce human beings into the life of the Triune God, baptizing them in the name of the Father and of the Son and of the Holy Spirit (Mt 28.19). The entire existence of the Church, in this present age and until its final destiny in the next world, is suspended from, and caught up into, the movement of life that joins the Father and the Son in their personal love, the Spirit. The Church in its pilgrim form exists in order to inaugurate and to sustain the divine life in human beings. The Church considered as the communion of the saints shares in that same divine life in its real beginnings here below, humble but victoriously hopeful. St. John writes: "What we have seen and heard, we announce it to you in order that you may be in communion with us. As for our communion, it is with the Father and with his son Jesus Christ" (1 Jn 1.3). That "we are in communion with one another" (1 Jn 1.7) is possible and true only because we are in communion with the Father and with his Son through the Gift of their one Spirit (1 Jn 4.13-16).

Pledge of the Spirit. The Son, commissioning his Apostles before his visible withdrawal from the world, pledges his own Spirit to them (Jn 16.7) and in them to the whole Church, as the Love of the Father and of himself, under the formality of what St. THOMAS AQUINAS calls "the prime Gift" (*Summa theologiae* 1a, 38.2) and "the Love transporting us into the heavenly world" (ST 3a, 57.1 ad 3). The very atmosphere or breath of the Church's life is the Spirit of love, making the life of the Church not intermittent reality but enduring existence, notwithstanding the abiding weakness of the people who are the human actors in the Church's pilgrimage. The supernatural world of the Church is in Christ and in his Spirit a kind of descent into time of the timeless life movement of the Triune God, catching the Body of the faithful up into the universe of the intradivine intimacy.

Having Part with Christ. If human beings are to share in the life of the Triune God, they must "have part with" (Jn 13.8) Jesus Christ, who is in the fullest sense the historical epiphany of the living God in the world of human beings (Jn 1.14; Heb 2.14–17; Col 2.17) and the total and fontal principle of the communion of human beings with the Father (Heb 2.10; 5.9; 6.20; 10.20; 1 Cor 15.20–23; 15.45–49; 2 Cor 1.19–22). The ecclesia of God the Father is the ecclesia of God in Jesus Christ (1 Thes 2.14). In the words of St. Thomas: "In Christ spiritual good is not restricted or partial, but is absolutely entire, so that he is the entire good of the Church, nor is he together with others anything greater than he is by himself" (ST 3a, suppl., 95.3 ad 4). Christ, the beloved Son and the FIRSTBORN (Col 1.13, 15), has come from the Father to share with human beings his divine life as Son, which he holds from the Father (Jn 1.16; 5.26; 6.57; 1 Jn 5.11–12), and thus to bring human beings into the family life of God as the adopted sons of the Father in himself, the one Son (Gal 4.4; Rom 8.29–30). "God can be depended on, and it was he who called you to communion with his own Son, Jesus Christ our Lord" (1 Cor 1.9).

The reality of "having part with" Christ, of being "partners with Christ" (Heb 3.14), entails the most intimate association between the One who in love shares his sonship with human beings and the Many who in him share in the one new life of adoptive sonship; moreover, it necessarily brings about the most close communion between all those who are fellow shareholders in "the common salvation" (Jude 3) of Jesus Christ the glorious Lord. This reality of communion commands a law of living, a style or deportment of life, incumbent on the Church as a whole and on each member singly. "The status of the new creature is defined as communion with God, thanks to Christ" [C. Spicq, *Dieu et l'Homme selon le N.T.* (Paris 1961) 216]; "the anthropology of the NT is a matter of *koinonia* with Christ" (*ibid.* 218), a *koinonia* that, centered in Christ, ascends to the Father through their Spirit and that reaches outward to embrace the totality of those who are one in the embodied communion of Christ's ecclesia. Stig Hanson, commenting on the parties and factions that plagued the Church of Cor-

inth (see 1 Cor 1.10–13), says: "Factions and ejkkhsiva are, in principle, contrasts. In the former case, it is the ego that is the main thought, in the latter, we. In a faction it is the individual who is the basic principle; the Church, on the other hand, aims at totality" [*The Unity of the Church in the NT: Colossians and Ephesians* (Uppsala 1946) 74]. The law of communion is the acting "We" of the brotherhood under God the Father in Christ through the Gift of their Spirit. "The identity of the Spirit of Christ in all the members of his Body, the Church, is what grounds and makes possible the Christian We" [H. Möhlen, *Der Heilige Geist als Person* (Münster in Westfalen 1963) 193].

This communion of brothers and sisters in Christ is realized in the Spirit only through the sacraments of "our common faith" (Titus 1.4), i.e., through Baptism (Rom 6.4; Col 2.12; Eph 4.4–6), and supremely through the Eucharist, which is the most real communion with the dead and risen Christ and in him with one another (1 Cor 10.17). At the altar of the Lord Christians are made in the full sense fellows of Christ, sharers in his passage from death to new life, and co- sharers with all who are their fellow communicants. Here is the primordial communication of all the blessings of the new covenant. "In this Sacrament the whole mystery of our salvation is contained" (St. Thomas, ST 3a, 83.4); "the Eucharist contains the Sacred in an absolute sense" (ST 3a, 73.1 ad 3). As the sacramental representation of the one sacrifice of the new covenant, it is the fullest presence and communication in Christ's body and blood of the Father's love in the Spirit for his people of the new alliance, and the surest and fullest anticipation of the heavenly banquet in the life to come (Jn 6.54; Mk 14.25).

Multiple Levels. Such a sharing in the life and destiny of the incarnate Son finds expression in St. Paul in a series of verbs compounded with σύν ("with") that scan the whole moving sweep of the Church's communion with Christ its head. These verbs delineate the content and the stages of the sharing of Christ's Church Body and of his members in his passage from history to its term, from death to total glorious life in the Father. The σύν verbs mark the simultaneous multiple levels of the new life shared in Christ, its dynamism, and its movement and growth toward its final achievement when Christ will come to judge the living and the dead and to hand over the kingdom to his Father (Col 3.4; 1 Cor 15.24–28).

There is a dying and a living with Christ (Rom 6.8), a suffering with Christ (Rom 8.17), a crucifixion with Christ (Rom 6.6), a burial with Christ (Rom 6.4; Col 2.12), a glorification with Christ (Rom 8.17), an inheritance with Christ (Rom 8.17), a reigning with Christ (2 Tm 2.12). Suffering with Christ is the necessary prelude and the sure pledge of the coming glory in him (Phil 3.10–11; Rom 8.17; 1 Pt 4.13); suffering serves as a fundamental law for the upbuilding of the whole Body. "The 'We-for-Christ' (2 Cor 12.10; Phil 1.29; see Col 1.24) must match the 'Christ-for-us.' We must hold firmly that the saving function of the Church consists chiefly in representing and realizing a communion with the dying and rising Redeemer" (V. Warnach, "Liebe," *op. cit.* 2:810).

Role of the Spirit. Just as the Father's love has given the Son to the world of human beings, so too the Father "lavishes the Spirit" (Gal 3.5) on the Church in order to bring to achievement the work of Christ. "Who would deny," says St. Basil, "that the saving designs with respect to humankind which have been realized by our great God and Savior Jesus Christ in accord with the goodness of God are fulfilled by the grace of the Spirit?" (*De Spiritu Sancto* 16.39; *Patrologia Graeca* 32:140) The Spirit is "the gift of God" (Acts 8.20; see Acts 2.38; Rom 5.5; Jn 14.16) of which human beings are made "partakers" (Heb 6.4) in order to become sharers in the sonship of Christ (Rom 8.14–17; Gal 4.6). It is the role of the Spirit to Christianize the Church and all its members, to make them fellows of Christ in his life and truth (1 Cor 12.13; Eph 2.22; Jn 15.26; 16.14–15; Phil 3.3), to keep the whole Church faithful to its origins in the historical Christ and to its destiny in the Christ to come, to hold the members of each and every age in a concert of loving service of the whole Body, to keep the Body one in Christ by communicating its varied graces and gifts to the good estate of the whole (1 Cor 12.7).

"Communion with Christ leads necessarily to communion with Christians, to communion of the members, one with another" (F. Hauck, *Theological Dictionary of the New Testament* 3:807). See Phlm 17; 2 Cor 8.4; Rom 12.13; 15.26–27; Gal 6.6; Phil 1.7; 4.14–15; Heb 10.33; 13.16. Dependence on the love and life of Christ means interdependence in love on one another in Christ. The new life in Christ is not an isolated gift enclosed within a multitude of discrete selves; it lives only insofar as it is lived together in the one Spirit of love by all those who are partakers of the salvation of the new alliance (1 Cor 12.25; Rom 12.5; Eph 3.6; 4.25). The joint holding and sharing of the new life in Christ shows itself as a Christian grace, i.e., as an inward-outward grace. It is embodied in prayer and almsgiving, in compassion, sympathy, and heartfelt mutual assistance, in an interchange of the spiritual and temporal works of mercy, between Christian and Christian, between local church and local church, between the Jewish and gentile world in Christ. Brotherly and sisterly love, the great gift of the Spirit (1 Cor 12.31–13.3), is, with its expansive and assimilative rhythm, the mark of communion in the Church (Jn 15.1–17; 1 Jn 3.14–18; 4.11–12; 4.19–21). C. H.

Dodd writes of the NT *koinonia*: "All the experiences and activities of the whole Church are in some sort communicated to the individual believer; and in turn the due activity of each part enables the Body to grow and build itself up (Eph 4.16)" [*The Johannine Epistles* (New York 1946) 7]. This lateral communion in its various forms is one that the Patristic writers and the scholastic theologians especially stressed.

Patristic Period. The Biblical theme of communion as applied to the Church in all the varied manifestations, sacramental and social, of its total moving life is a central theme of Patristic thought, if not always verbally, at least in reality. See, e.g., L. Hertling, *Communio: Chiesa e papato nell'antichità cristiana* (Rome 1961); W. Elert, *Abendmahl und Kirchengemeinschaft in der alten Kirche hauptsächlich des Ostens* (Berlin 1954); J. Korbacher, "Die Kirche als Gemeinschaft," *Ausserhalb der Kirche kein Heil* (Munich 1963) 52–79; A. Demoustier, "L'Ontologie de l'église selon saint Cyprien," *Recherches de science religieuse* 52 (1964) 554–588; M. Pellegrino, "Le Sens ecclésial du martyre," *Revue des sciences religieuses* 35 (1961) 151–175.

This section presents, without pressing too much considerations of chronology, certain selected aspects of Patristic thought on the Church as communion.

Ecclesia Mater. Karl Delahaye has studied the use that the Fathers of the first three centuries made of the theme of the Church's motherhood to symbolize the role of the whole Church as the bearer of Christ's salvation to humankind [*Erneuerung der Seelsorgsformen aus der Sicht der frühen Patristik* (Freiburg 1958) 7], and in this careful investigation he has made clear the strong sense that the Fathers had of the entire Church Body as one communion of all the faithful in Christ, jointly sharing in Christ's light and life and jointly communicating Christ's truth and grace to human beings. Because "the Church is the great We of the faithful" (Delahaye, 135) in Christ and in His Spirit, then all the faithful together are enabled and required to serve in unison the handing on of the "common salvation" (Jude 3) to all.

The Patristic imagery of the Church as mother strongly emphasizes "the responsibility of all the faithful for all others in the life of the community, their effective and genuine participation, their authentic and living collaboration in the duties of the community in the midst of this world" (Delahaye, 190). Every division of labor within the Church's total mediatorial activity has its meaning and justification only from within the total Church as the one communion of sanctification and sanctity. "Hierarchy and community, each in its own proper way, are the authorized and mandated bearers of the Church's pastoral activity; hence they are the subjects of that activity" (*ibid.* 191).

The early Church considers all the saints without exception as both subject and object of the Church's saving work. The Church as mother is the communion of the saints, comprising all those who are joined to Christ in faith and Baptism. Since her motherhood is grounded on her inward mysterious union with Christ, then all who have entered into this communion with Christ share in the Church's motherhood. Under the aspect of her pastoral activity the Church as the communion of the saints is always at the same time a saving community. (*ibid.* 142–143.)

God realizes these saving designs "toward all and with all. Hence all must take part in it and work together in communicating it" (*ibid.* 179).

In the imagery of the Church's maternity there is expressed the belief that God charges the whole Church, the structured communion of the saints and each member according to one's role and gift, to work together in preserving and in communicating the treasures of life that each shares in the one Spirit and that the one Spirit moves each to share with others. The whole Body of the Church is in its common life, to borrow a word that St. Ignatius of Antioch applied to the Church of Smyrna, ἁγιοφόρα, a fruitful "bearer of holy things" (Smyrn. introd.). For the Patristic writers, the basic reason why the whole Church must act in concert in communicating the good news of Christ and the new life in Christ is the whole Church's ontological unity of life in Christ through communion in the one Spirit (see Delahaye, 149–150) and through communion in his Eucharistic body and blood. As Ignatius of Antioch wrote, "the union is both according to the Spirit and according to the flesh" (*Magn.* 13.2). Much later Pope Martin I (d. 655) expressed the thought in a letter to the Church of Carthage: "Whatever is ours is yours in accordance with our undivided sharing in the one Spirit" (*Epist.* 4; *Patrologia Latina* 87:147).

St. Augustine. It is appropriate to set forth in some detail certain reflections of St. AUGUSTINE on the mystery of the Church as a community of life with the Triune God and with the whole company of Christian believers in the same Trinity. Although not all of St. Augustine's speculations may be finally acceptable, still his vast achievement and perduring influence in the history of ecclesiology, particularly of the Western Church, warrant special consideration.

Discoursing on blasphemy against the Holy Spirit (see Mt 12.31), Augustine describes the Holy Spirit in the intra-Trinitarian life of God as "the community of the Father and of the Son" (Serm. 71.12.18; *Patrologia Latina* 38:454) and then continues:

> It is through that which is common to the Father and to the Son that they have wished us to have

communion both with one another and with themselves; it is through that Gift which both have in common, i.e., through the Holy Spirit, God and the Gift of God, that they have wished to gather us together into one (*ibid.*).

The unity of communion within the Church is then the reflection of the communion of life within the Triune God, and in each case, although in vastly different ways, the communion is ascribed to the Holy Spirit, who is "the community of the Father and of the Son" and who "in his various workings [in the Church] is not another Spirit, different from himself, but one and the same" (*Serm.* 71.16.26; PL 38:459-460). Referring to 1 Cor 12.11, St. Augustine writes that the Spirit is "the one who divides and apportions, but who is himself undivided, because he is one and the same" (Epist. 187.6.20; PL 33:839). "To whom in the Trinity does communion in this society [the Church] pertain, if it is not to the Spirit who is common to the Father and to the Son?" (*Serm.* 71.18.29; PL 38:461). "He is the Spirit of the adoption of sons, in whom we cry 'Abba Father'" (*Serm.* 71.17.28; PL 38:460–461); "the society by which we are made the only Body of God's only Son is the Spirit's role" (*ibid.*); "that society of the sons of God and of the members of Christ that is to exist in all nations" (*ibid.*).

> The society of the unity of the Church of God, outside of which there is no forgiveness of sins, is, so to speak, the proper work of the Holy Spirit—the Father and the Son, to be sure, working together with Him—because the Holy Spirit Himself is in a certain sense the society of the Father and of the Son. (*Serm.* 71.20.33; PL 38:463.)

Fritz Hofmann says of the role of the Holy Spirit in the ecclesiology of St. Augustine: "Donum, caritas, and communio stand in the center of the ecclesia Spiritus, precisely because the Holy Spirit Himself is essentially donum, caritas, and communio" [*Der Kirchenbegriff des hl. Augustinus* (Munich 1933) 136].

The Church as a mystery of communion in the Trinity comprises in the outreach of its love all those who are sharers in the same divine life. The vertical (descending-ascending) communion becomes indissolubly a comprehensive lateral communion of all the members of the Body of Christ in the one Spirit. St. Augustine expresses the indivisibility of the total communion in love in the following way:

> The sons of God are the Body of the one and only Son of God. Therefore whoever loves the sons of God loves the Son of God, and whoever loves the Son of God loves the Father; nor can anyone love the Father unless he loves the Son; and whoever loves the Son also loves the sons of God. What

sons of God? The members of the Son of God. It is through love that He becomes one of His own members, it is through love that He enters into the unity of the Body of Christ; and there will be only one Christ loving Himself. When the members love one another, the Body loves itself. When you love the members of Christ, you love Christ; when you love Christ, you love the Son of God; when you love the Son of God, you love the Father too. Love then is indivisible. Choose to love one, and all the others follow your choice. (*In epist. Ioh.* 10.3; PL 35:2055-56.)

Just as God says to his sons, "Love itself makes me present to you" (*ibid.* 10.4; PL 35:2057), so too, although in an infinitely lesser way, each member of the Body in the communion of love that is the Church is present to all the others in the one Spirit of Christ, who gives to that communion in himself as Gift the reality of its undivided love. In the Spirit of Christ each Christian is present to the whole Church, and the Church is present to each Christian.

Just as in the human body there are "different functions, but a common life" (*Serm.* 267.4.4; PL 38:1231), so too in the Church Body of Christ, by virtue of the one Spirit, "each one has his own role to enact, but all alike live together" (*ibid.*). "The services of the members are variously apportioned, but the one Spirit holds them all together" (*Serm.* 268.2; PL 38:1232). The Spirit, therefore, pours into the hearts of the saints a "holy and indivisible charity" (*Epist.* 98.5; *Corpus scriptorum ecclesiaticorum latinorum* 34.2:526) and gives to the varied graces and gifts of the Body's many members a saving and serving presence to the whole Body.

> The many gifts that are proper to each one are divided for the common good among all the members of Christ by the Gift that is the Holy Spirit. For not every one has all of them, but some have these and others those, although all have the Gift Himself by whom the gifts proper to each one are apportioned, i.e., the Holy Spirit (*Trin.* 15.19.34; PL 42:1084).

St. Augustine writes of "the showing forth of the Spirit in view of the common good" (1 Cor 12.7): "If you love unity, then whoever has anything in the unity of the Church, has it for you" (*In evang. Ioh.* 32.8; *Corpus Christianorum* 36:304).

For St. Augustine, as for the Patristic writers in general, communion with Christ meant indissolubly communion with his Eucharistic body in his Church Body. "For St. Augustine the sacred mystery of the Eucharist stands sovereignly in the midpoint of the inner and outer life of the Church" (Hofmann, 390). "The Eucharist is the Sacrament of the Mystical Body itself joined with its head;

the whole essence of the Church, which consists in the unity of the members one with another, in the unity of the Body with the head, and in the unity of the totus Christus, realized through the mediation of the God-Man, with God, is set forth in the Eucharist in a sacramental but real way" (Hofmann, 412). Alluding to 1 Cor 10.17, Augustine writes: "O Sacrament of mercy! O sign of unity! O bond of charity! Whoever wishes to live has both where he may live and the wherewithal he may live. Let him draw near and believe; let him be made one Body in order to be given life" (*In evang. Ioh.* 26.13; Corpus Christianorum 36:266); "let them become the Body of Christ if they wish to live from the Spirit of Christ" (*ibid.*). Christ "wishes this food and drink to be understood as the common life of that Body and its members which is holy Church" (*In evang. Ioh.* 26.15; CorpChrist 36:267). Not only is the Eucharist the supreme sacramental realization of the common life of the entire Church Body in its total unity; it is also the sacrifice of the entire Church Body in the sacrament of the Lord's saving Passion. In the Eucharist the Church Body of the Lord is made one sacrifice in and with the sacrificial death of the unique priest Jesus Christ.

> The whole redeemed city, i.e., the congregation and society of the saints, is offered as a universal sacrifice to God through the great priest who offered Himself in the Passion for us that we might be the Body of so great a head. This is the sacrifice of Christians: "the many, one Body in Christ." In the mystery of the altar so familiar to the faithful the Church celebrates that sacrifice wherein is made clear to the Church that it itself is offered in the very reality that it offers (*Civ.* 10.6; CorpChrist 47:279).

Christ "wished the sacrifice of the Church to be the daily sacrament [of His own sacrifice on the cross], and the Church, since it is the Body of the head, learns how to offer itself through Him" (*Civ.* 10.20; Corp Christ 47:294). The whole Church, one in a communion of sacrificial love that the Spirit keeps alive, offers itself and its works of charity and mercy in the sacrament of the Lord's Passion.

For St. Augustine's speculations on the theme of *ecclesia mater* or the communion of the saints as the strictly active factor in the saving and sanctifying activity of the Church, see Hofmann, 263-275; K. Adam, *Die kirchliche Sündenvergebung nach dem hl. Augustin* (Paderborn 1917) 991-13.

Patristic Orientations. Not only St. Augustine but also the Patristic writers in general looked on the Church in its entirety and in all its local realizations as a common life centered in Christ and in his salvation. It is a communion of life that is the work of the numerically one and same Spirit of Christ, dwelling in Christ in fullness and in his Body derivatively; a brotherly and sisterly communion of those who in the one Spirit live together a life of one faith, one hope, and one love; a sacramental communion that finds its supreme sign and realization in the center of the sacramental cult of the Church, i.e., the Eucharist, containing the one sacrifice of the new alliance and the one food of the new people on its pilgrimage; an active expansive communion communicating its new life to all those who are called to share in it; a moving dynamic communion that looks to the next world and to the "peace of the heavenly city," i.e., "the perfectly ordered and harmonious society of those who find their joy in God and in one another in God" (St. Augustine, *Civ.* 19.13; CorpChrist 48:679). In the early Church the "We" of Church communion had its first ground in the one faith, authoritatively professed in the "We believe" and "We confess" with which the doctrinal decrees of the synods so often began. Orthodoxy is "homodoxy," as St. Basil the Great says, speaking of "the communion of those who hold one and the same faith" (*Epist.* 28.3; *Patrologia Graeca* 32:309). W. Elert writes of the Church as a communion in faith:

> The subject of the "We believe" is the Church . . . . The We begins with the Apostles and reaches without any break up to the present. The baptismal creed, the *regula fidei,* and dogma are professions of faith, and in their harmony there is expressed the unity of the Church as unanimity (*op. cit.* 53–54; see 62–63).

Preaching on the anniversary of his elevation to the pontificate, St. Leo the Great said: "Beloved, in the unity of faith and Baptism we share an undivided common life." (*Serm.* 4.1; PL 54:148). To give one or two further examples of the centrality of the Sacrament of the Eucharist in the Patristic understanding of the Church as communion, St. Cyril of Alexandria writes:

> We have been made one Body together in Christ, fed with the one flesh, and sealed unto unity with the one Holy Spirit, and since Christ is indivisible (for He has never been divided), we are all one in Him . . . . See how we all are one in Christ and in the Holy Spirit, both according to the Body and according to the Spirit. (*Dial. Trin.* 1; PG 75:697).

And in an old Gallican commentary on the Creed, dating from the 6th or 7th century but reflecting much earlier convictions, one reads: "There is found holy communion with the Father and the Son and the Holy Spirit, where each Sunday all the faithful ought to communicate" [see text in *Journal of Theological Studies* 21 (1920) 109].

In the mind of the Patristic writers the episcopal order with its authoritative mission and its special sacra-

mental powers and graces exists to beget, sustain, and foster the Christian communion of the Church, in its totality and in its parts, with a fidelity to its Christian origins and to its final destiny of Christian fullness (see Delahaye, 190–191; Hertling, 16–45). The hierarchical order is a ministry commissioned by Christ to serve the communion of Christian faith, and to ward off the disunion of heresy, by authoritatively handing on the message of faith; to serve the community of Christian charity, and to ward off the disunion of SCHISM , by guiding and orientating the varied expression of its common life of mutual dedication and service in the Lord; and above all to serve the community of sacramental life, wherein faith and love find their prime stay and embodiment, by administering the Eucharistic cult, by admitting to or denying Eucharistic communion (*see* EXCOMMUNICATION), and by administering the penitential procedures which issued in full Eucharistic communion (*see* PENANCE, SACRAMENT OF). Hence the Church is a juridically ordered communion. St. Cyprian speaks of those who "receive the Eucharist by right of communion" (*De dom: orat.*18, *Corpus scriptorum ecclesiasticorum latinorum* 3.1:280; see *Epist.* 57.2, CSEL 3.2:652), a right of which the bishop was the judge. The local Church finds in its bishop, as the representative of Christ, the qualified center and criterion of its communion, competent to teach, to rule, and to sanctify (see St. Ignatius of Antioch, *Smyrn.* 8; *Eph.* 4). The whole Church has in the episcopal order with its Roman center the criterion of its total communion [*see* COUNCILS, GENERAL (ECUMENICAL), THEOLOGY OF]. Finally the prime bishop of Rome is the center of communion for the whole Church: St. Ambrose, writing to the Emperors Gratian, and Theodosius Valentinian, (381), affirms that from Rome "are spread abroad to all the Churches the rights of the communion that must be revered" (*Epist.* 11.4; PL 16:946).

The ancient Church had no elaborate theory of communion; rather it was a sacramental reality lived from day to day in the ordered brother and sisterhood of the whole believing Church and of its local realizations.

St. Thomas Aquinas. "St. Thomas's whole teaching on the Church is to be divided into his teaching on the principles of the Church's being and life, on the organs of the Church's life, and on the realization of the Church's life" [M. Grabmann, *Die Lehre des heiligen Thomas von Aquin von der Kirche als Gotteswerk* (Regensburg 1903) 68]. In St. Thomas's ecclesiology the Church's life of grace, which is a sharing in the Trinitarian life, is necessarily a social life: "the principle of supernatural life, divine grace, is intrinsically characterized by a social tendency, a certain inclination toward communication" (*ibid.* 78). Hence St. Thomas writes: "In the spiritual life we enjoy society not only with human beings but also with God'' (*In 3 sent.* 37.2 sol. 2). At times St. Thomas describes the life of grace in a way that clearly signifies its social aspect, and, it is to be noted, in a context indicating that the Holy Spirit is the ultimate ground of the social orientation of the life of grace. For example, in a discussion of schism, which is a sin directly opposed to the unity of the Church as a communion in love, St. Thomas argues that schism offends against the Holy Spirit in the sense that it is ''a spiteful hatred of fraternal grace of the grace of God growing in the world'' (*Summa Theologiae* 2a2ae, 14.2); schism means ''hatred of the fraternal grace by which the members of the Church are joined together'' (*ibid.* ad 4). The Christian brother and sisterhood of grace that is the Church is directly attacked when the charity of the Spirit that moves human beings to live together in Christ, one of another, in the family of God the Father, is despised and rejected.

Grabmann further notes that ''just as the grace of Christ has within it a certain social tendency, a power of expansion, so too is it a characteristic of this grace to manifest itself, to incorporate itself, so to speak'' (*op. cit.* 91). In his treatise on the evangelical law (ST 1a2ae, 106–109), St. Thomas delineates the movement of the grace of the Christian witness as it embodies itself, sacramentally and socially, in the Church of that witness. Everything in the Church, whose prime center of force and of life is the grace of the Spirit of Christ, is either an embodiment of the grace of the Spirit, or a disposition and a way toward this grace (see ST 1a2ae, 106.1; 108.1). Because ''the grace of the Holy Spirit is manifested in faith working through love'' (ST 1a2ae, 108.1), and because ''the new law, which is the law of liberty comprises the moral precepts of the natural law, and the articles of faith and the sacraments of grace'' (*Quodl.* 4.8.2), the Church is an inward-outward communion of life in the grace of the Spirit, a communion realized through a living faith and through the sacraments of faith (see ST 3a, 64.2 ad 3).

Power of the Spirit. St. Thomas assigns to the activity of the Holy Spirit a primordial role in the Church as one body of believers and worshipers who live together a common life, sacramental and social, in Christ with the Father. The Holy Spirit, who is immanently present in all the members, is ''the ultimate and principal perfection of the whole Mystical Body'' (*In 3 sent.* 13.2.2 sol. 2); ''all the members of the Mystical Body have as their final ground of perfection the Holy Spirit, who is numerically one in all of them'' (*ibid.* ad 1); ''in the spiritual life our every movement must come from the Spirit'' (*In epist. ad Gal.* 5 lect. 7). ''Just as the result of the mission of the Son was to lead to the Father, so the effect of the mission of the Holy Spirit is to lead the faithful to the Son'' (*In Joann.* 14 lect. 6). ''Through the Spirit we are united

to Christ in a union of faith and of love and are made members of the Church'' (*ibid.* 6 lect. 7); ''there is in the Church an unbroken union [between Christ and his members] by reason of the Holy Spirit, who, numerically one and the same, fills and unites the whole Church'' (*De ver.* 29.4). Christ ''unites us one to another and to God through his Spirit, whom he gives to us'' (*In epist. ad Rom.* 12 lect. 2).

Furthermore St. Thomas stresses the Spirit's primary role in the Church insofar as it is a lateral communion of member with member and with the whole Body, a presence in charity of one to another and to the whole, a reciprocal communication of life and service. Thus he speaks of ''the power of the Holy Spirit who through the unity of love communicates the blessings of Christ's members with one another'' (ST 3a, 82.6 ad 3; see 3a, 68.9 ad 2; *In 3 sent.* 25.1.2). ''The diversity of roles and functions in the Church'' (ST 2a2ae, 183.2), which is essential to the reality of the Church as a horizontal communion, does not ''hamper the unity of the Church, which is achieved through unity of faith and love and mutual service'' (*ibid.* ad 1), precisely because ''the harmonious interplay of the various members in the Body of Christ is assured by the power of the Holy Spirit, who vivifies the Body of the Church'' (*ibid.* ad 3). ''One falls away from this unity of the Spirit when one seeks what is exclusively one's own'' (*ibid.*). Hence it is the role of the indwelling Spirit (1) to dissipate the exclusiveness and partiality that disserves the good of the other and of the whole Body and (2) to move the member parts to seek their own good only in the whole and in the movement of the whole Body toward its final perfection.

Schism. In his treatment of the sin of schism, St. Thomas says that ''schism is per se opposed to the unity of ecclesiastical love'' (ST 2a2ae, 39.1 ad 3), a love ''which does not simply unite one person with another in the spiritual bond of love, but also joins the whole Church in the unity of the Spirit'' (ST 2a2ae, 39.1). One must consider two aspects of this unity of the whole Church in the Spirit of love, i.e., ''the connection or communion of the members of the Church with one another; and the relation of all the members of the Church to one head,'' the one head being ''Christ, whose vicar in the Church is the supreme pontiff'' (*ibid.*). ''And hence they are called schismatics who refuse to obey the supreme pontiff, and who refuse to live a common life with the members of the Church subject to the pontiff'' (*ibid.*). Here one sees how St. Thomas conceives the role of the hierarchy in the life of the Church as a communion with Christ and with one another in love in the Body of Christ. The hierarchical order is a ministerial, vicarious service of the sacramental common life in faith and love, under the headship of Christ and the quickening of the Spirit.

"The ministers of the Church [are] in a certain sense the instruments of that life-giving influence which the head exercises on his members" (ST 3a, suppl., 36.3 ad 2). One may cite here the passage in *C. graec.* (2.32) in which St. Thomas associates the roles of the Spirit and of the supreme pontiff in assimilating the Church to Christ its head.

> Christ Himself, the Son of God, dedicates His Church to His service and authentically seals it with the Holy Spirit as with His own mark and stamp . . . . And in like fashion the vicar of Christ, as a faithful servant, by his primacy and foresight keeps the whole Church subject to Christ.

Dependence on the Whole. It has often been noted (see Grabmann, 181) that Cajetan, commenting on St. Thomas's teaching on schism, has excellently elaborated on St. Thomas's doctrine on the Church's unity of communion, particularly as it is understood in the lateral or horizontal sense. Cajetan writes:

> The faithful are moved by the Holy Spirit to the works of the spiritual life, i.e., to believe, to hope, and to love, to sanctify and to be sanctified, to obey and to command, to enlighten, etc. . . .in such a way that they do all these things as parts of one whole . . . . And therefore [the Spirit] moves each faithful to act inwardly and outwardly as part of the one whole and for the sake of the one whole and in accordance with that one whole . . . . And hence it is that . . . there is a connection of part to part in a congregation numerically one that is ruled first and chiefly by the Holy Spirit (ST 2a2ae, 39.1).

This spiritual unity of the numerically one Church is an effect of charity because "it is through charity that the Holy Spirit moves each single faithful to wish to be part of the one catholic communion that He vivifies" (*ibid.*). All the faithful according to Cajetan, whatever be their office or act, hierarchical or not, extraordinary or simple, act as parts in and of a totality, of a united whole numerically one; all, therefore, act in dependence on the whole, and all act in charity for the good estate of the whole. It must be noted that the dependence of the part on the whole is here one of communion, i.e., the part finds a measure, a perspective, an aid, and a finality in the existence and functioning of the whole.

Eucharist. Faithful to the Patristic tradition, St. Thomas held in closest association, in the ontology of the Church, Eucharistic communion and ecclesiastical communion, with the sacramental body of Christ being the supreme sign and ground of the communion of the Mystical Body. "The universal spiritual good of the whole Church is contained substantially in the Sacrament of the Eucharist" (ST 3a, 65.3 ad 1; see 3a, 73.1 ad 3; 3a, 83.4). In ST 3a, 73.4 St. Thomas quotes the saying of St. John Damascene that the Eucharist "is called Communion, and truly is, because through it we communicate with Christ . . . and because through it we communicate with and are joined to one another" (*De fide orth.* 4.13; PG 94:1153). "The Eucharist is called the Sacrament of charity" (ST 3a, 73.3 ad 3; see 3a, 78.3 ad 6), an ecclesial charity that leads to a communion of life with the Father and with the brothers and sisters in Christ as head of the Body. "The Eucharist is the Sacrament of the Church's entire unity" (ST 3a, 83.4 ad 3); "the unity of the Mystical Body is the fruit of the true body received sacramentally" (ST 3a, 82.9 ad 2); "the effect of this Sacrament . . . is the union of the Christian people with Christ" (ST 3a, 74.6; see the Council of Florence, Denzinger 1320). What the scholastic theologians called the *res*, or reality, of this sacrament, i.e., the ultimate grace effected, is "the Mystical Body of Christ, which is the society of the saints" (ST 3a, 80.4). The Eucharist is the sacrament of the wayfaring Church on earth in its itinerary toward the heavenly Jerusalem, "the true Church, our mother toward which we are tending, the exemplar of the militant Church" (*In epist. ad Eph.* 3 lect. 3). "The Sacrament does not immediately lead us into glory, but it gives us the power to reach glory" (ST 3a, 79.2 ad 1); the tendency of the Eucharist is toward heaven and "the society of the saints where there will be peace and full and perfect unity" (*ibid. corp.*). The Eucharist is *the* Sacrament that forms and realizes the wayfaring Church as a communion of life in the Son with his Father and with his brothers and sisters, in the sense that it purifies the Church from sin, which is the root of separation from God and of segregation from each other, and that it conveys the fullest beginnings of the Christian life, both in soul and in body, which is communion. "In strict theology, the principal effect of the Eucharist is the upbuilding of the Church as a communion of life" [J. M. R. Tillard, *L'Eucharistie, Pâque de l'église* (Paris 1964) 231]; that is, of the Church as a communion of Christian life in the conditions of this world and turned toward its full consummation as communion in the heavenly Church.

Modern Era. From the later Middle Ages until relatively modern times there is discernible in much theological writing a tendency to focus on the Church as the divinely authorized social and juridic means of communicating Christ's salvation to human beings, without at the same time considering the Church so conceived in an intimate association with the reality of the Church as the whole company of the faithful and the communion of the saints. The symbiosis of the Church as means and the Church as end, and the interplay of life and energies between the two in a total common life, did not often find a full and harmonious exposition. The defensive reaction to movements such as CONCILIARISM, PROTESTANTISM, GALLICANISM, JANSENISM, and FEBRONIANISM conspired to put theological stress on the Church as the institutional means of salvation with its unique mission and powers and with its social stance of complete independence over against the encroachment of the secular state.

Furthermore, during this period, the general absence of a separate treatise of dogmatic ecclesiology, as distinct from an apologetic treatment, did not favor the development of a rounded ecclesiology of communion. The doctrinal elements that were needed to come together to form a balanced dogmatic ecclesiology were studied in relative isolation from one another; hence, what was often lacking was "the connection of the mysteries one with another and with human beings' last end" (Denzinger 3016). For example, the mission of the Holy Spirit was not sharply related to the total Church, and in general pneumatology, apart from the inhabitation of the Spirit in the individual soul, was not much developed. The single sacraments were not usually seen within the perspective of the total prime sacrament of the Church; and the Eucharist in particular was less attended to in its intimate relationship with the whole Church Body of Christ, as the sacramental sacrifice and the sacramental food of the whole Body on its pilgrimage to the heavenly Jerusalem. Hence a more clericalized and less genuinely popular liturgy was the result.

The ecclesial dimension of Christian anthropology was less emphasized than was desirable; as a result the individual Christian was less seen as one who believes, hopes, and loves in the one faith, hope, and love of the whole Church; and the call of all to sanctity in the one holy Church was less emphasized in favor of specialization in this field. Theological writing on the tradition, the apostolate, and the liturgical life of the Church did not sufficiently stress the responsibility and the participation of all the faithful, baptized and confirmed in Christ, in these aspects of the Church's total life. Moreover eschatology tended to be more individual than collective in its theological presentation.

The 19th Century. The beginnings in theology of a renewed consideration of the Church as a communion of supernatural life in Christ wherein all share and all should contribute their share were seen in the 19th century. Among the representatives of this newer direction must be mentioned J. A. MÖHLER (1796–1838), whose brilliant work, at times perhaps overly influenced by the philosophical categories of a romantic vitalism, always tended to conceive the Church as a total living communion, "a communion in the Holy and of the saints" [*Die Einheit in der Kirche,* J. R. Geiselmann (Cologne 1957)

315]. For an assessment of Möhler's development and achievement in this respect, see Geiselmann's commentaries in his edition of Möhler's works: *Die Einheit* 613–619 and *Symbolik* (Cologne 1961) 2:609–686. See in addition M. Himes, *Ongoing Incarnation: Johann Adam Möhler and the Beginnings of Modern Ecclesiology* (New York 1997).

It is appropriate also to recall here the *De ecclesia Christi* (2 v. Regensburg 1853, 1856), which was the joint work of Carlo PASSAGLIA (1812–87) and Klemens SCHRADER (1820–75); from this work, left unfinished, one may instance the authors' reflections on "the social charity" of the Church, i.e., on "the charity of communion, the charity of the Body, and the Christian communion of the Church" (lib. 3:412; see 411-418, 461, 574-575, 581-586), on the Trinitarian origin and destiny of this communion in love (lib. 3:418), and on the sacraments as expressions of this charity of communion (lib. 3:419). M. J. SCHEEBEN (1835–88) contributed much of lasting value on "the organic unity of the teaching body with the body of the faithful in the Catholic Church" (*Theologische Erkenntnislehre; Dogmatik* 1, 13, no. 168, see nos. 168–186); Scheeben speaks in a way reminiscent of the early Patristic writers of "the whole Church . . . in the communion of the simple faithful as mater fidei" (*ibid.* no. 184). The lay theologian Friedrich Pilgram (1819–90) made the theme of communion the very center of his valuable, if complicated, study on the Church [*Physiologie der Kirche* (Mainz 1860]. Finally there are the observations of Hermann SCHELL (1850–1906) in his *Dogmatik* 3.1 (Paderborn 1892) 382–386, where the concept of the Church as a community of life with the Triune God and with one another in Christ is elaborated; as Schell says, "God does not separate and isolate, but associates and joins together in a living union, because He is triune" (386).

Early 20th Century. The work of theologians Y. CONGAR, H. de LUBAC, R. GUARDINI, C. JOURNET, and many others in areas such as Patristics, Liturgy, Ecumenism, and Biblical Studies paved the way for the ecclesiological developments that would be expressed in the documents of Vatican II. The teaching of modern popes, especially PIUS XII, paralleled these developments. For example, Pius XII's focus on the sharing of the whole Church in the apostolate and in particular on the missionary role and spirit of the Church as compassing all the faithful without exception [see, e.g., Pius XII, *Fidei donum, Acta Apostolicae Sedis* 49 (1957) 237–238] indicates clearly the participation of all the faithful in the total common life of the Church and in its major activities. Plus XII's encyclicals *MYSTICI CORPORIS* (June 29, 1943) and *MEDIATOR DEI* (Nov. 20, 1947) manifest an intensified sense of the whole Church as one worshiping and saving community in Christ through the Spirit. See, for instance, the definition of the liturgy in *Mediator Dei* (Denzinger 3841); and in *Mystici corporis* one reads: "We must all cooperate with Christ in this work of salvation—'all of us who from One and through One are saved and save'" [*Acta Apostolica Sedis* 35 (1943) 221].

Vatican II and Beyond. The word "communion" appears frequently throughout the documents of Vatican II as a way of speaking about the Church. The term appears 27 times in the English text of *Lumen gentium* alone, and eight times in the "Preliminary Note of Explanation" to that document, intended to clarify that the Church is a "hierarchical communion." The mystery of the Church is presented as rooted in the Trinity. The universal Church is described as "a people made one from the unity of the Father and of the Son and of the Holy Spirit"; a people "established by Christ as a communion of life, love, and truth"; one holy community, sacerdotal and prophetic, in which "all the faithful scattered throughout the world lead a common life with the rest in the Holy Spirit" and in which all "both labor and pray that the fullness of the world be transformed into the people of God, the Body of the Lord, and the temple of the Holy Spirit." The English text of *Unitatis redintegratio* uses "communion" 22 times, and introduces the concepts of "full communion" and "imperfect communion" to express the relationship between the Catholic Church and other Christian churches.

The concept of communion at Vatican II has also other ecumenical and theological uses. "Communion" stresses that the Church most basically consists in webs of relationships with God and with others. The institutional and juridical dimensions, while essential, exist always in the service of communion. Great emphasis is placed on local churches as communities of people bonded in love through Christ and gathered around the Eucharist in the presence of their bishop. This focus on the local church produces much fruit in the Council's teachings on ecumenism, authority, mission, liturgy, and the role of the laity. It represents a reaching beyond St. Thomas Aquinas's stress on the universal Church to the life and thought of the Church of the first millennium. Whether the council retains a clear priority of the universal Church in relation to local churches, or whether it emphasizes more strictly a dynamic simultaneity, remains a subject of debate.

Also a matter of debate is whether what is now called "communion ecclesiology" was the central guiding concept of the Church at Vatican II during the actual time the council was taking place. It is not unreasonable, however, to claim that communion ecclesiology functions at the start of a new century as the dominant category for interpreting the council in both official and theological circles. The Extraordinary Synod of 1985 called communion "the central and fundamental idea of the council's documents." Scholars as diverse as W. Kasper and L. Boff find in "communion" the primary category for speaking of the Church. J. Ratzinger has referred to communion ecclesiology as the "one basic ecclesiology." Pope JOHN PAUL II ardently promoted communion ecclesiology in a wide variety of writings.

See Also: COMMUNION OF SAINTS; ECCLESIOLOGY; KINGDOM OF GOD; MISSIONS, DIVINE; MYSTICAL BODY OF CHRIST; SACRAMENTS, ARTICLES ON; SOCIETY (CHURCH AS); TRINITY, HOLY; UNITY OF FAITH; UNITY OF THE CHURCH; CHURCH, ARTICLES ON.

Bibliography: *Dictionnaire de théologie catholique,* ed. A. VACANT et al. (Paris 1903–50) Tables générales 1:1110–30. R. SCHNACKENBURG et al., *Lexikon für Theologie und Kirche,* ed. J. HOFER and K. RAHNER (Freiburg 1957–65) 6:167–186. J. SCHMID et al., *Handbuch theologischer Grundbegriffe,* ed. H. FRIES, 2 v. (Munich 1962–63) 1:790–822. G. W. H. LAMPE, ed., *A Patristic Greek Lexicon* (Oxford 1961–) fasc. 3, 762–764. M. J. LE GUILLOU, *Le Christ et l'église* (Paris 1963); *Mission et unité,* 2 v. (Paris 1960). J. HAMER, *L'Église est une communion* (Paris 1962). F. MALMBERG, *Ein Leib-Ein Geist,* tr. R. E. TORFS (Freiburg 1960). H. MöHLEN, *Una mystica persona* (Munich 1964). H. SEESEMANN, *Der Begriff koinwniva im Neuen Testament* (Giessen 1933). J.-M. R. TILLARD, *L'Eucharistie, Pâque de l'église* (Paris 1963); *L'évêque de Rome* (Paris 1982); *Église d'Églises. L'Ecclésiologie de communion* (Paris 1987); *Chair de l'église, chair du Christ. Aux sources de l'ecclésiologie de communion* (Paris 1992); *L'Église locale: Ecclésiologie de communion et catholicité* (Paris 1995). J. KOMONCHAK, "Conceptions of Communion Past and Present," *Cristianesimo nella storia* 16 (1995) 321–40. J. ZIZIOULAS, *Being as Communion: Studies in Personhood and the Church* (Crestwood, NY 1985). M. VOLF, *After Our Likeness: The Church as the Image of the Trinity* (Grand Rapids MI 1998). S. WOOD, *Spiritual Exegesis and the Church in the Theology of Henri de Lubac* (Grand Rapids MI 1998). D. DOYLE, *Communion Ecclesiology: Vision and Versions* (Maryknoll NY 2000). P. PHAN, ed, *The Gift of the Church: A Textbook on Ecclesiology* (Collegeville MN 2000).

[F. X. LAWLOR/D. M. DOYLE]

CHURCH, HISTORY OF, I (EARLY)

The Christian Church took its rise with Christ's commission to the Apostles; "Go out into the whole world and preach my gospel to every creature." The historical fulfillment of that command began on the first Pentecost when, as Christ had promised (Acts 1. 5), the Holy Spirit descended on the Apostles and disciples, and Peter preached to the "devout Jews from every nation . . . Parthians, Medes, Elamites, inhabitants of Mesopotamia, Judea, Cappadocia, Pontus, Asia, Phrygia, Pamphilia, Egypt, and the parts of Libya about Cyrene, visitors from Rome, Jews also and proselytes, Cretans and Arabians"

(Acts 2.5–11). Calling upon them to repent and be baptized in the name of Jesus Christ for the forgiveness of their sins (Acts 2.38), "he added that day about 3,000 souls" (Acts 2.41).

The idealization of the picture drawn by LUKE is not overdone. The primitive Christian community, although considered at first but another sect within the Jewish milieu, proved unique in its theological teaching, and more particularly in the zeal of its members, who served as witnesses to Christ "in all Judea and Samaria and even to the ends of the earth" (Acts 1.8). While Christianity arose in the milieu of the religious life of late Judaism, and at first manifested an enthusiastic piety and messianic character similar to that of such sects as the Damascus and Qumran communities, the Christian *kerygma* did not stop at the border of Judea, but penetrated the surrounding world that was unified and dominated by the Greek language and the Hellenic civilization.

Early Expansion. In Palestine, Greek was understood and used in business; among the Jews living in the Diaspora, it became their native tongue; and with the Greek language a world of concepts, categories of thought, metaphors, and subtle connotations entered late Jewish ideology. It was particularly to the Hellenized portion of the Jewish people that the first Christian preachers turned. After the martyrdom of Stephen, his fellow deacons, including Philip, Nikanor, Prochoros, Timon, Parmenas, and Nicolaos seem to have scattered through Palestine, Syria, and the East and begun the missionary activity of the next generation.

The new sect received the name of Christians (*Christianoi*) at Antioch (Acts 11.26), a Greek city; and after his conversion, Paul addressed himself in Greek to the Jews gathered in the synagogues in the principal cities of the Mediterranean world. PAUL was a thoroughly educated Jew, a Pharisee of the Pharisees in his own words, who in his travels addressed himself first to the Hellenized Jews, then to the Gentiles. Paul's powerful grasp of the central mystery of salvation in Christ, the Son of God, prevented the new religion from being infected by the Hellenistic mystery cults or from being absorbed into one of the Jewish or Gnostic sects. His theological insight was basic for the preservation of the mystery of redemption in and through the Church as the body of Christ.

There is little reliable evidence concerning the missionary travels of the Apostles; but by the year 65 the Christian message had penetrated into Syria, Asia Minor, Greece, and Rome. The movement was recognized, however imperfectly, by the Roman authorities, as is witnessed by TACITUS (*Ann.* 15.44) and Suetonius (*Claud.* 29.1); and Christians were apparently blamed by the Emperor Nero for the burning of Rome. In the persecution that followed, Peter and Paul suffered martyrdom.

Doctrinal Development. The theological evolution that accompanied the spread of the Christian *kerygma* was greatly influenced by developments in the late Jewish apocalypses, apocrypha, and eschatological literature and has been characterized as Judeo-Christian, its original impetus having been given by the community at Jerusalem. It was also strongly marked by the liturgical writings of Qumran, the angelological and eschatological doctrines of several dynamic Jewish sects, and the dualism of the Essenes. However, the collections of the *Logia,* or sayings, of Jesus and the *Evangelia* quickly found their way into Greek, and the Christian writers of the apostolic age adopted the literary forms of the epistle and of the *praxeis* or acts in use among the secularist philosophers and their disciples. The next generation (*see* APOSTOLIC FATHERS) added other literary forms, adapting the diatribe, especially, to Christian use.

With the adaptation of literary forms there was an assimilation of methods of propaganda and manner of expression current mainly among the Cynics, Stoics, Pythagoreans, and Epicureans, who spread philosophical and religious tracts among the ordinary people. James, for example, in his Epistle, used the Orphic concept of "the wheel of birth" (3.6), and the Didache employed the Pythagorean device (also used by Hesiod) of the Two Ways in a moral context.

There was conflict between the Judaizers and Hellenists in the explanation and development of the Christian message, as is evident from the Pauline warnings against aberrations from the traditional faith given to him as to the other Apostles by Christ; this conflict is emphasized in the testimony of the Pseudo-Barnabas and the Clementine literature.

In Paul's first letter to Timothy there is an indication of the organization of the Church of Asia with a college of presbyters and a president bearing the title and office of *episcopus,* or bishop, and deacons. Some of the earliest Christian communities were seemingly monarchically organized, such as that under James in Jerusalem; but it is obvious that the faithful had a voice in the community life of prayer and witness to Christ, while the charismatic gifts of preaching, comforting the afflicted, and healing were held in great respect.

Clement I of Rome and Ignatius. By the turn of the 2d century, the Christian Church had emerged as a widespread entity united by a common faith and a communion of spiritual interests. The letter of the Church at Rome to the Church at Corinth, although predominantly a moral exhortation to unity and obedience, reveals a consciousness of the Church as a strong, clear, ecclesiastical organization whose line of authority descended from God through Christ and the Apostles to the elders of the fraternally united community (*Epist. Clem.* 42.1–5; 44.1–2). Utilizing the holiness code of the Old Testament synagogic teaching, it imposed a Christocentric theology of virtues on the Christian community advocating imitation of Christ in His patience and long suffering (13.2–4) and guaranteeing man's full deliverance in the resurrection (24–26). Though apparently written by CLEMENT I of Rome, the letter gives no direct evidence as to the structural organization of the Church in either Rome or Corinth.

In the letters of IGNATIUS OF ANTIOCH (d. *c.* 116) to the Churches of Asia Minor and to Polycarp of Smyrna, a monarchical type of episcopal government prevails. Ignatius witnesses to a shift of spiritual interest from the Pauline preoccupation with Mosaic law and original justice, to the Greek concern about fate and the value of existence. While the Judaic influence seems to have persisted in the QUARTODECIMAN controversy centered in Asia Minor, in Rome and the Mediterranean cities there was a gradual development of theological consciousness that considered the Church a transcendent entity.

The Shepherd of HERMAS in the treatise on penance described the Roman Church as a fairly populous assembly (*c.* 140) containing a segment of the rich as well as numerous poor. Many in both classes had relapsed into pagan ways of blasphemy and idolatry; they are described as hypocrites in concert with ambitious clergymen and dishonest deacons. But the majority are referred to as hospitable bishops, zealous priests, martyrs, and the innocent. The Church itself is well organized, with a hierarchy of bishops, priests, and deacons. Considerable emphasis was placed on the achievement of *gnosis,* or a superior knowledge of the triune mystery, particularly in relation to Baptism and the Eucharist. This was a direct offshoot of the rabbinic preoccupation with the "marvelous and true mysteries" that the one God "reveals to the hearts of his servants" as expressed in the Qumran theology (DSD 11.3; 15–16; DSH 7.1–7).

Persecution. Tacitus described the Neronian persecution of the primitive Christians as due "not so much to their having set fire to the city, as to their hatred of the human race" (*Annal.* 15.44). This *odium humani generis* was equivalent to the Greeks' *misanthropia,* a charge originally leveled against the Jews (Diodorus, *Hist.* 24), and subsequently used against the Christians because of their particular customs and refusal to participate in Roman civic and religious rites. Josephus listed these accusations as the adoring of a donkey's head, ritual murder, and incest (*Contra Apion.* 79).

While the recognition of Christianity as a separate religion took place only gradually, there seems to have been a persecution under Domitian (81–96), apparently connected with messianic troubles and millenarianism, in which the senator Flavius Clemens was put to death for "atheism and Jewish practices" (Suetonius, *Domit.* 15) and Domitilla was exiled to Pandateria (Eusebius, *Historia Ecclesiastica* 3.18.4). The letter of Clement I (1.1) speaks of the misfortunes of the Roman Church at this time, and the Book of Revelation (1.9; 2.3–13) refers to the persecution of the Churches in Asia Minor.

Accusations. Whereas Paul had called for obedience to the imperial authorities, Revelation registers hostility to the empire. This attitude is reflected also in the *Sibylline Oracles* and the *Ascension of Isaia.* Under Nerva, peace returned. Trajan (98–117), in reply to the governor of Bithynia, Pliny the Younger, decided that Christians were not to be sought out; but when denounced as guilty of crimes (*flagitia*), they were to be condemned if they refused to abjure. He also cautioned, however, against false and anonymous denunciations, indicating that pressure for persecution came not so much from the government as from people who were intolerant of those bearing the name of Christians (*Epist.* 96.2–3). It is this decision, and not a governmental proscription, that was misinterpreted as indicating the existence of an *institutum Neronianum* by TERTULLIAN. The most famous martyr of this period was Ignatius of Antioch. Under Hadrian (117–138) the Christians enjoyed comparative peace; but during the reigns of Antoninus Pius and Marcus Aurelius, they were the object of attack by intellectuals such as Fronto (Min. Felix, *Octav.* 9.16; 31.1–2), Lucian (*Life of Peregrinus*), and Crescens the Cynic (fl. 152). Galen, who visited Rome in 162 and 166, accused the Christians of fanaticism and credulity; but the great indictment was launched by the philosopher CELSUS, who considered them charlatans and vagrants dangerous to the civic ideals of the Roman state. This was the basic accusation behind the persecutions.

The Apologists. By the mid-2d century, the new religion had attracted a number of educated men who used their literary competence in defending Christianity against the charges of atheism and idolatry, and began to assess the philosophical and moral thought of their contemporaries in the light of the Judeo-Christian teachings. They are known as the APOLOGISTS; but only a few of their writings have survived. They continued the catechetical approach of the older Apostles; this they combined with the propagandist methods of their contemporaries. JUSTIN MARTYR (*c.* 100–160) supplied both Jewish and pagan audiences with a "rule of faith" and a description of the rites of Baptism and the Eucharist while encouraging a conversion from pagan immorality to the Christian way of life. The *Letter to Diognetus* described the divine economy of salvation and claimed that Christians in the empire differed in no way from their contemporaries in marriage and family life, in civic custom, and the observance of the laws; but they avoided idolatry, strove to serve as models of moral excellence, and prayed for the preservation of the empire.

Reorganization and Expansion. In the last decades of the 2d century, there was evidence (*c.* 180) of a great reorganization of the Church and its missionary and catechetical endeavors. Christian unity was emphasized by the Roman Church in its controversy with the Church of Asia Minor over the date of Easter, which continued from the reign of ANICETUS (154–166) to that of VICTOR I (189–198). IRENAEUS OF LYONS stated that Polycarp of Smyrna had visited Rome, but had failed to reach agreement on the question (Eusebius, *Historia Ecclesiastica* 5.24.16). While Polycrates of Ephesus acknowledged the apostolic foundation of the Roman Church by Peter and Paul, he insisted that the customs of the Church in Asia had equal apostolic backing.

Synods and Unity. The practice of holding synods to settle ecclesiastical problems seems to have begun in Asia Minor in the middle of the 2d century and was apparently based on a precedent of civil practice. Evidence supplied by Dionysius of Corinth in his so-called Catholic Epistles displays the interchange of doctrinal and disciplinary interests between the churches in Greece and Asia Minor. Testimony preserved by Eusebius (*Hist. eccl.* 5.25) indicates that the churches of Palestine, Pontus, Osrhoene, and Gaul, in synods, registered their agreement with the decision of a Roman synod under Victor that Easter should be celebrated only on a Sunday. Finally Irenaeus gave a list of the popes from Peter to Eleutherius (174–189) and described the efforts made by the early heretics to obtain Roman sanction for their doctrines, while Tertullian claimed that communion with the Roman See was regarded as communion with the whole Church (*Adv. Prax.* 1). He was the first churchman to utilize the so-called Petrine text (Mt 16.18); yet the institution of the papacy had achieved a definitive form by the end of the 2d century: it was the center of unity. Rival claims to occupy the apostolic see by HIPPOLYTUS (217–235) and NOVATIAN (251) were disallowed by the other Churches, and these men were considered antipopes.

In the dispute over the rebaptism of heretics that involved the churches of North Africa and Rome after the Decian (251) and Valerian (257) persecutions, Cyprian of Carthage acknowledged that the primacy had been given to Peter, and he saw in the *cathedra* of Peter a source of unity, while he still claimed the independence of individual bishops as successors to the Apostles. Despite difficulties with Novatian, Pope Stephen (254–257) asserted the validity of the Roman practice, and although

a synod at Carthage (256) upheld Cyprian, no attempt was made to sever communion with Rome.

Local Churches. By the 3d century there were flourishing Christian communities in Gaul at Lyons, Vienne, Marseilles, Arles, Toulouse, Paris, and Bordeaux. Cyprian of Carthage wrote to the churches of León-Astorga and Mérida in Spain (*Epist.* 67) and mentioned the community at Saragossa. There were 19 bishops at the Synod of Elvira (*c.* 306). In Germany churches at Cologne, Trier, Metz, Mainz, and Strassburg have left testimony in archeological remains, and the spread of Christianity along the trade routes of the Danubian provinces of Rhaetia, Noricum, and Pannonia is attested by the martyrs of the Diocletian persecution. North Africa was clearly a well-established Christian center based on Carthage in the late 2d century, and the Church in Egypt had developed with its center at Alexandria in the same epoch.

In Asia Minor there were synods in Phrygia between 172 and 180 that dealt with the errors of MONTANISM (Eusebius, *Hist. eccl.* 5.16), and the satirist Lucian complained of Christians in Pontus (*c.* 170: *Alexander* 25). ARMENIA received Christian missionaries in the 3d century, and Antioch in western Syria had a Church of apostolic origin from which missionaries Christianized the East. The house-church at DURA-EUROPOS testifies to the presence of Christianity (3d century) in eastern Syria; and Edessa, modern Urfa, and Osrhoene were likewise early recipients of the gospel, though the stories of ADDAI AND MARI are legendary. TATIAN and Bardesanes preached there (*c.* 170); and the Christian message spread to Mesopotamia and Adiabene in Assyria, to Parthia and to Persia, particularly under King Sapor I (241–272). A synod at Bostra testified to Christianity in Arabia (*c.* 244), and there is evidence, however questionable, for its spread as far east as India.

Final Persecutions. The development of the Christian way of life and its expansion continued to meet grave difficulties from within because of doctrinal disputes, and from without, through sporadic outbursts of persecution. Under Marcus Aurelius (161–180), a Stoic philosopher, a series of physical calamities disturbed the empire in the form of famine, pestilence, and barbarian incursions. The people blamed them on the failure of the Christians to worship the pagan gods. A persecution broke out, the severity of which is indicated by the apologists Athenagoras, Melito, and Miltiades. Justin Martyr was put to death, apparently in Rome, with six companions; and a number of martyrs are recorded in Lyons (177), including Blandina, Photinus, and Ponticus (Eusebius, *Hist. eccl.* 5.1–2). A letter from the Church at Lyons to that at Vienne described the persecution. After a period of peace, Septimius Severus (193–211) put down a series of Jewish insurrections and turned against the Christians, particularly in Egypt, where Leonides, the father of Origen, was martyred, and in Carthage, the place of the martyrdom of Felicitas and PERPETUA (March 7, 203).

Caracalla (211–217) allowed his mother, Julia Domna, to propagate the mystery cults of the East, particularly sun worship, and Mithraism became an official cult of the army. This caused great difficulty for Christian soldiers and officials. Severus Alexander (222–235) showed clemency, influenced by his mother, Julia Mammaea, who heard Origen lecture at Antioch. But with Maximinus Thrax (237–238), Decius (249–251), and Valerian (253–260), systematic and severe persecutions of the Christians were carried out. Under DIOCLETIAN (284–305) and GALERIUS a final attempt was made to destroy Christianity at its roots. The effort was not supported by the elder Constantius I in Gaul and the West, and it failed.

Conversion of Constantine. While the nature and manner of Constantine's conversion is controverted, there is no question about the fact. With the Battle of the Milvian Bridge and the taking of Rome (313), Christianity was accepted as a legitimate religion and rapidly reached a favored status in the empire, although it was not the religion of the vast majority. Determined to use the religious factor as a unifying force within the state, Constantine evidently employed Bp. Hosius of Córdoba as a counselor and accepted appeals in regard to the Donatist problems in North Africa. He instructed the Bishop of Rome, Miltiades (311–314), to hold a synod at the Lateran, followed by others at Arles (314) and elsewhere, to resolve the situation, and resorted to force only later. With the rise of ARIANISM, he convoked the Council of NICAEA I (325), which defined the doctrine of the homoousios or consubstantiality of the Father and the Son. Nicaea I determined also that in the ecclesiastical organization, the sees of Rome, Alexandria, and Antioch held special status as patriarchal dioceses. Other sees, such as Carthage, Ephesus, Caesarea in Palestine, Caesarea in Cappadocia, Heraclea in Thrace, and Arles in Gaul also assumed metropolitan status for surrounding sees; and the general organization of the Church was patterned on that of the civil dioceses.

Constantine came to consider himself the providentially appointed guardian of the Church; Eusebius referred to him as an *Isapostolos* (the same as an Apostle). He started a vast building program in Rome that included the Vatican, Pauline, and Lateran Basilicas; in Jerusalem, evidently under the instigation of Helena; and at Antioch and Treves. Eventually he transferred the seat of his government to Byzantium, which he rebuilt as the Christian city of CONSTANTINOPLE. His baptism on his deathbed by

EUSEBIUS OF NICOMEDIA, however, gave encouragement to the so-called semi-Arian bishops, and under the sons of Constantine turmoil marked theological disputes. There was a series of synods and counter synods that involved such champions of orthodoxy as ATHANASIUS OF ALEXANDRIA, HILARY OF POITIERS, and Pope LIBERIUS in a sequence of painful exiles.

Basil of Caesarea died (379) just as the orthodox cause was about to succeed at the Council of CONSTANTINOPLE I (381) under THEODOSIUS I (379–395), who made Christianity the official religion of the empire. Pagan opposition had reached a final climax under JULIAN THE APOSTATE (361–363); but with the removal of the statue of Victory from the Senate, despite the protest of the pagan prefect Symmachus, and with the renunciation of the title *Pontifex Maximus* by Gratian (375–383), the power of the pagan priesthood was broken. Laws had to be passed to prevent the complete dismantling of the pagan temples.

Asceticism and Spirituality. The papacy of Damasus (366–384) and the close of the 4th century saw the rapid rise of a spiritual movement that affected men such as Jerome, Gregory of Nazianzus, Gregory of Nyssa, and Chromatius of Aquileia, and that received a definite ascetic and mystical advancement with the writings of EVAGRIUS PONTICUS. MONASTICISM had developed and spread quickly in Egypt, Syria, and Asia Minor, and was stimulated in Italy and Gaul particularly by Athanasius through his *Life of Anthony the Hermit*. Pilgrimages to the Holy Land and to Rome, with the development of the cult of the holy places and of the martyrs, took on enormous proportions and influenced the rise of a popular literature that paralleled the spiritual and theological writings of Ephraem of Edessa, John CASSIAN, DIDYMUS THE BLIND, and EPIPHANIUS OF CONSTANTIA (Salamis). The *Lausiac History of Palladius,* the *Apophthegmata Patrum,* the *Historia monachorum,* and the *Peregrinatio ad Loca sancta* of Aetheria, encouraged ascetical and monastic interests.

Patristic Theology. The conversion of Augustine brought a new theological development in the West that, particularly through Ambrose of Milan and Rufinus of Aquileia, had been closely dependent on the Eastern Fathers. Augustine dealt with PELAGIANISM and DONATISM, as well as with the problems posed by the Trinity, truth, education, grace, marriage, virginity, and concupiscence. In the East, JOHN CHRYSOSTOM proved an indefatigable homilist, commenting on St. Paul and the whole of Scripture in a popular and practical fashion. JEROME translated the Old Testament from Hebrew, provided a guide to the *hebraica veritas,* and utilized the works of Origen and Eusebius of Caesarea to put Scripture study, exegesis, and Christian literature on a firm basis. He encouraged an ascetical movement in Rome, and he became involved in the first phase of the Origenistic controversy that was precipitated by Epiphanius of Salamis. This occasioned difficulties between Jerome and Rufinus, as well as with Bp. John of Jerusalem, and eventually enabled THEOPHILUS OF ALEXANDRIA to depose John Chrysostom from the See of Constantinople, at the Synod of the OAK.

Two Theologies in the East. By the start of the 5th century, two principal theologies had emerged: that of Alexandria with its insistence on the divinity of Christ, and an allegorical interpretation of the Scriptures in the pursuit of man's divinization in Christ; and that of Antioch, devoted to a literal interpretation of Scripture and an insistence on man's perfection through the humanity of Christ in the Resurrection. The differences led to the Christological controversies of the 5th and 6th centuries and the Councils of EPHESUS (431), CHALCEDON (451), and CONSTANTINOPLE II (553), which made vigorous efforts to clarify the problems presented by the two natures and one person in Christ. These councils also proved occasions for the expression of the latent rivalries among the sees of Alexandria, Antioch, and Constantinople. The preeminence of the latter had been asserted at Constantinople I as based on its civil status as the new Rome; it was challenged at Ephesus when CYRIL OF ALEXANDRIA ousted NESTORIUS of Constantinople as a heretic; and its validity was denied by LEO I after Chalcedon. The interference of the emperors, particularly in the affairs of the Eastern Church, brought conflict with the patriarchs and a general if reluctant acknowledgment of the primacy of the bishop of Rome, to whom appeals in both doctrinal and disciplinary matters were regularly made.

Leo the Great. Pope Leo I (440–461) followed a tradition handed down at least from Siricius (384–399), through Innocent I (401–417), Celestine (422–432), and Sixtus III (432–440) in giving the Church's organization a legal determination. He felt himself the vicar of Christ in the person of Peter and entertained a "care for all the churches"; he made liturgical, moral, and doctrinal decisions for the East as well as the West. His *Tome to Flavian* helped clarify the Christological issue at Chalcedon, and in collaboration with Marcian and Pulcheria, then with Emperor Leo I (457–474), he attempted to stem the rise of MONOPHYSITISM in Egypt and Syria. He defended Rome and Italy from the depredations of the HUNS under Attila, and the VANDALS under Gaiseric. In dealing with the emperors, he was conscious that he was a citizen of the empire; hence he deferred to their authority, yet felt that that same authority was entrusted to the civil ruler for the enhancement of the Christian religion. This issue was further clarified by Pope Gelasius I (492–496), who spoke of the "world as governed by two sovereignties, the papal authority and the imperial power that come from God, the supreme sovereign."

Monophysitism. With the rebellion of TIMOTHY AELURUS and Peter Mongus in Alexandria and Peter the Fuller in Antioch, Monophysitism gradually assumed a deep political as well as doctrinal and spiritual character. The great Monophysite teachers, such as SEVERUS OF ANTIOCH (512–518) and PHILOXENUS OF MABBUGH, were not actually heretics in doctrine since they followed Cyril of Alexandria literally. Their power came from their literary competence and the emphasis they placed on the spiritual doctrine of the divinization of man in Christ; they were aided by the persecution of the imperial government, which they used to influence the lower clergy, the monks, and the people.

The Emperor ZENO issued his *Henoticon* (484) to clarify the Christological issue but merely succeeded in occasioning the ACACIAN SCHISM between Rome and Constantinople. This was continued under Emperor Anastasius I (491–518) despite the efforts of popes Anastasius II (496–498) and Symmachus (498–514) to achieve a reconciliation. The Roman intervention was complicated by the rise of the Ostrogothic kingdom of Italy under THEODORIC THE GREAT and the rivalry of the Roman factions, one of whom elected Symmachus, while the anti-Byzantine party selected the deacon Laurentius and appealed to the Ostrogoths for support. Three synods in Rome (*c.* 502) settled the election in favor of Symmachus, and despite a campaign of calumny on the part of the Laurentians, Theodoric accepted Symmachus as the true pope.

Age of Justinian. In 518 JUSTIN I became emperor. He was Latin and Catholic, and with his nephew Justinian he made peace with Rome, condemned the Monophysite factions, and supported Pope Hormisdas (514–523), whose decree condemning both EUTYCHES and Nestorius and asserting the validity of Leo's *Tome* and the Council of Chalcedon was made the touchstone of orthodoxy. Pope John I (523–526) was dispatched to Constantinople by Theodoric as an emissary; but despite an honorable reception, his mission failed, and he was maltreated by the king on his return. The philosopher Boethius and his intimates were also put to death in an anti-Byzantine outbreak.

JUSTINIAN I (527–565), a theologian and also an administrator, legislator, and autocrat, attempted to wipe out paganism and closed the University of Athens (529). He passed disabling legislation against Jews and heretics and attempted to introduce some Christian concepts into the Justinian code. At the suggestion of the deacon, later Pope Pelagius, he condemned Origenism (*see* ORIGEN AND ORIGENISM) as a possible solution to doctrinal troubles among the Palestinian monks. His close adviser Theodore Ascidas suggested the condemnation of the THREE CHAPTERS as a countermeasure. Together with the Monophysite cause generally, Ascidas received the support of the Empress THEODORA (1), who appeared to counter her husband's religious policies while living an edifying private life with him.

In 532 Justinian called a colloquy of Severian Monophysite and orthodox bishops; he pursued a vigorous policy of suppression of apparent Nestorianism, attempted to appease the Monophysite monks with the Theopaschite formula, and finally brought Pope VIGILIUS (532–555) to the capital and convoked the Council of Constantinople II, which redefined the Christological doctrine in what has been termed a Neochalcedonian fashion. The pope refused to attend the council after suffering ignominious treatment; he had issued his own *Judicatum* or *Verdict on the Three Chapters* in 548; during the council he put out his *Constitutum,* which condemned the writings of the three incriminated theologians *prout sonant* (as they read) but refrained from condemning them in person. The council (7th session) condemned the pope and separated itself from the *sedens* but not the *sedes* (the occupant, but not the See of Rome); and in December 553 the emperor finally forced the aged pope to accede to the condemnation of the Three Chapters with his *Constitutum II,* in which he repudiated his former stand.

On the death of Vigilius, to counter the theological rebellion of the Western bishops, Justinian selected Pelagius I (556–561) as pope despite his previous opposition to the council. Pelagius found the West in turmoil, supported in part by the *In Defense of the Three Chapters* of FACUNDUS OF HERMIANE and the exiled African bishops. Schisms broke out in Milan and Aquileia. Justinian had given Vigilius a Pragmatic Sanction for the adjustment of civil affairs in Italy; and the pope became the protector of the population against tax gatherers, the depredations of the soldiery, and the Lombard invasions. In his last years, the emperor favored the aphthartodocetic heresy attributed to JULIAN OF HALICARNASSUS. But his suppressive measure against the Monophysites had had little effect. They were countered by the organizational efforts of James BARADAI; and gradually Egypt and Syria became disaffected against the empire on both religious and nationalist issues.

In Gaul the conversion of CLOVIS (481–511), under the influence of his wife, the Burgundian princess Clotilda, brought the whole nation into the Church (as AVITUS OF VIENNE remarked) and checked the spread of Arianism by the Ostrogoths. The tomb of St. Martin of Tours became a national pilgrimage center. Despite the interference of the kings in ecclesiastical affairs, more than 30 synods were held between 511 and 614. Among the more outstanding churchmen of this period were Remigius of Reims (d. 535), the great preacher CAESARIUS OF ARLES (d. 542), GERMAIN of Paris (d. 576), and the historian GREGORY OF TOURS (d. 594), as well as the poet Venantius FORTUNATUS of Poitiers (d. 601). The Gothic peoples, whose conversion had been effected by Bishop ULFILAS and by his translation of the Bible into Gothic, were gradually brought over from forms of Arianism to Catholicism.

Britain had been evangelized early; but the invasions of the Angles, Saxons, and Celts brought back paganism except in small sections of Wales and Cornwall. Although Palladius had been sent to Ireland by Pope Celestine in 431, the conversion of the island was due to St. PATRICK, who had studied at Lérins and Auxerre and returned to Ireland *c.* 432. The Irish Church was organized on a monastic basis, and Irish monks set out from foundations such as that of St. COMGALL at Bangor to Scotland, England, Gaul, Germany, and Italy, where they became an important aid in the development of the Church in the 6th and succeeding centuries.

Pope JOHN III (561–574) made a strenuous effort to protect Rome and Naples from the Lombards, who had conquered Ravenna; and BENEDICT I (575–579) had to wait a full year before receiving imperial confirmation of his election from Constantinople. His successor, PELAGIUS II (579–590), turned to the Franks for protection against the Lombards and supported Leander of Seville when he converted King Reccared and the Arian VISIGOTHS to Catholicism.

Gregory the Great. BENEDICT OF NURSIA had laid the foundations of Benedictine monasticism with his monastery at MONTE CASSINO (*c.* 529) and evidently was encouraged by Pope AGAPETUS (535–536) in the composing of his rule, which displays pedagogical wisdom and well-balanced asceticism in leading the monks to a perfect following of Christ. Benedictine monasticism received a great stimulus from GREGORY I THE GREAT (590–604), who had served both as prefect of the city of Rome and as papal *apocrisiarius* in Constantinople before being elected pope. Despite war and pestilence brought to Italy through the depredations of the Lombards and the continued schism in Milan, he initiated a far-sighted program of reform. He reformed church music and the liturgy, and as his tombstone proclaimed, as the *Consul Dei,* he made efforts to bring the Germanic peoples closer to the papacy and sent Augustine of Canterbury and his companions as missionaries to the British Isles. He protested the use of the title Ecumenical Patriarch for the archbishop of Constantinople. His pastoral and exegetical writings helped to preserve a modicum of ecclesiastical culture for succeeding ages. His *Liber regulae pastoralis* was translated into Greek during his own lifetime and into Anglo-Saxon by Alfred the Great. His *Moralia* is a practical handbook of pastoral morality, in the form of a commentary on the Book of Job. His exegesis of the Gospels and of Ezekiel, as well as his *Dialogues* on the lives and miracles of the Italian saints, though replete with legends, filled a great ascetical and spiritual need; and his 848 letters contain a major portion of the history of his age. While CASSIODORUS (d. *c.* 580), at his retreat in Vivarium, Calabria, preserved theological and literary learning through his *Institutiones divinarum et saecularium lectionum* and his *Historia tripartita ecclesiastica,* Gregory, as the *servus servorum Dei,* created the moral, doctrinal, and pastoral atmosphere that prevailed in the early Middle Ages.

The first period of Church history came to a natural close with Gregory. The reasons for the rise and spread of the Christian Church have challenged the ingenuity and competence of historians, particularly in modern times; but the problem is impossible to solve without an acknowledgment of the intervention of divine providence in the course of human events; it is equally insolvable without a realization that the Church, while divine in its origin and objective, is governed by human beings whose perceptions and ambitions frequently trail far behind the grace and inspiration needed to give finality to the achievement of the kingdom of God on earth.

Bibliography: L. DUCHESNE, *Early History of the Christian Church,* 3 v. (London 1909–24); *L'Église au VIᵉ siècle* (Paris 1925). K. BIHLMEYER and H. TÜCHLE, *Kirchengeschichte,* 3 v. (17th ed. Paderborn 1962); *Church History,* v.1, *Christian Antiquity,* tr. by V. MILLS (Westminster MD 1958). J. DANIÉLOU and H. I. MARROU, *The First Six Hundred Years,* v. 1 of *The Christian Centuries* (New York 1964). K. BAUS, in H. JEDIN, *Handbuch der Kirchengeschichte* (Freiburg 1962). E. CASPAR, *Geschichte de Papsttums von den Anfängen bis zur Höhe der Weltherrschaft* (Tübingen 1930–33) v.1. T. G. JALLAND, *The Church and the Papacy* (Society for Promoting Christian Knowledge; 1944). A. FLICHE and U. MARTIN, eds., *Histoire de l'église depuis les origines jusqu'à nos jours* (Paris 1935–) v.1–5. EUSEBIUS, *Historia ecclesiastica* Eng. tr. H. J. LAWLOR and J. E. OULTON, 2 v. (Society for Promoting Christian Knowledge; London 1927–28). S. LE NAIN DE TILLEMONT, *Mémoires pour servir à l'histoire ecclésiastique des six premiers siècles* (Paris 1693–1712). P. HUGHES, *A History of the Church,* 3 v. (rev. ed. New York 1947–49). P. CARRINGTON, *The Early Christian Church,* 2 v. (London 1957–60).

[F. X. MURPHY]

CHURCH, HISTORY OF, II (MEDIEVAL)

The history of the Western Church in the Middle Ages falls, as does the general history of Europe, into two main phases. In the first (600–1050), Catholic Christianity, hitherto a community within or coextensive with the Roman Empire, converted the new races that had overrun the ancient civilization. It was itself, however, hampered and pinioned by the imperfectly developed social and economic conditions of pagan and feudal Europe and remained only partially organized. In the second phase (1050–1500), the Church in all its organs and activities shared in the adolescence and maturity of medieval civilization; for almost five centuries Europe was a single cultural unit under a uniform religious organization that was dominated by the PAPACY. Each of these two phases can be subdivided almost equally. In the first period, from the death of Gregory the Great (604) to the coronation of Charlemagne (800), the papacy slipped its allegiance to the Eastern emperor, only to fall under the shadow of the Frankish monarchy; and the initiative in missionary, devotional, and even theological matters passed to the newly converted peoples of the northwest of Europe. In the second period, from 800 to *c.* 1050, the Church was absorbed into feudal society and the papacy was powerless, first in the hands of the Roman faction and then under the control of the German monarchy. In the third, from the accession of Leo IX (1049) to the death of Boniface VIII (1303), the papacy asserted and developed its claim to supremacy in spiritual matters and endeavored, for a time with success, to regulate the politics of Europe as well. Concurrently, the flowering of medieval civilization presented a religious and Catholic culture in all its aspects, intellectual, artistic, and social. In the fourth period, from 1303 to the height of the Italian Renaissance, a series of catastrophes befell Europe and the papacy; a new spirit of nationalism divided the peoples; and a moral decline afflicted many of the institutions of the Church.

First Period: 603 to 800. GREGORY THE GREAT stood on the threshold of the medieval centuries, looking back to the days when Church and Empire were coincident and looking forward to the time when the papacy would dominate the Western world. He was also the last pope for many centuries to impose his will and set his mark on western Europe outside Italy. He was followed by a long succession of short-lived, generally meritorious but mediocre popes who were hard pressed to maintain their ground in an Italy abandoned by imperial forces and a prey to the Lombard invaders. At the same time, they were called upon to defend the orthodox faith endangered both by old and new heresies and by that violence of Eastern emperors that culminated in the capture and subsequent death of Pope MARTIN I. Gregory I, lacking imperial protection, had already taken over the civil and military administration of Rome, and during the next 50 years the pope came to control the various territories between Ravenna and Terracina, enfolding the nucleus of

Mater Ecclesia buttressing the shelter of a group of clergy and a group of laymen, miniature on a late-11th-century Exultet Roll written and illuminated at Monte Cassino.

the patrimony of St. Peter, that came to be known as the STATES OF THE CHURCH and remained in being until 1870. The popes thus became, by accident and of necessity, temporal sovereigns of a small and vulnerable slice of territory with no natural frontiers. For more than 1,000 years this helped to give them status, independence, and financial support, though proving at the same time to be a source of political entanglement and temptation that distracted them from their essential purpose.

Meanwhile a series of theological issues in the Eastern Church, such as MONOTHELITISM and the controversy over ICONOCLASM, joined with personal antagonisms in separating the Eastern and Western Churches, especially after the rise of Muḥammad and the Islamic invasions. These, by reducing the Eastern Empire and by virtually eliminating the ancient patriarchates, united the emperor and the patriarch of Constantinople, often his creature, in hostility toward the claims of Rome. When at last (754)

Pope STEPHEN II, hard pressed by the LOMBARDS, appealed for help to the powerful King of the Franks, PEPIN III, a contact was made that led to a close alliance with the Frankish monarchy and the eventual coronation (800) of CHARLEMAGNE as emperor and protector of the papacy.

Missionary Activity. During this same time, Christianity extended its frontiers. The mission of AUGUSTINE OF CANTERBURY to England spread slowly in Kent, Essex, and the Thames Valley, while the conversion of Northumberland and Mercia was due to AIDAN from Celtic IONA and to CUTHBERT OF LINDISFARNE from beyond the Cheviots. The fusion of England's churches under Roman obedience at WHITBY, followed by the mission of Archbishop THEODORE OF CANTERBURY and the reorganization of the Church in England, ushered in the golden age of Northumbria and Wessex (*see* ENGLAND, THE CATHOLIC CHURCH IN). During the same period, COLUMBAN and his disciples and converts founded monasteries and preached the faith in eastern France and what is now Switzerland. More influential were the Anglo-Saxon missionaries of the early 8th century, WILLIBRORD, the apostle of Frisia (The Netherlands), and Wynfrith or St. BONIFACE, the apostle of Germany, who, besides his labors and successes in Hesse, Württemberg, and Bavaria, where he reorganized the existing Christians, did much to rejuvenate the flagging Frankish Church. Willibrord, Boniface, and Boniface's relative WILLIBALD all visited Rome and worked under the direct instruction of popes. In consequence, the German and Frisian Churches and their derivatives stood, like the Anglo-Saxon Church, in direct relationship with Rome, a circumstance that was to be of greatest significance in the later history of the papacy. In time, missionaries from England and from Germany also went to the Scandinavian countries, which were not wholly Christianized until the 11th century. To the northeast of Italy the Slavs of Moravia were converted in the late 9th century by the Byzantine brothers Constantine (CYRIL) and Methodius, working under papal patronage, though part of the territory evangelized by them later joined the ORTHODOX CHURCH. It was not until the 10th century that missionaries, preceding and accompanying the German pressure eastward, converted the Magyars and Poles, and not until the 12th and early 13th centuries that Poles and Germans together colonized and converted the tribes on the eastern shores of the Baltic.

Invasions. But there were losses to set against these gains. The armies of Islam, besides submerging the ancient Eastern churches and beating on the gates of Constantinople, overran the scattered Christian churches of North Africa and then conquered Visigothic Spain, one of the most cultured communities of Christendom, in less than three years (711–713). Washing past the Pyrenees at either end, they were only halted (732) near Poitiers, 12 years after their armies in the East had been thrown back from the walls of Constantinople. Later, the Hungarians or Magyars swept across central Europe as far as the Elbe and Burgundy, while in the north the Scandinavian raids on Britain, Ireland, and the coasts of Frisia and France, beginning shortly before 800, continued for more than a century. During part of this age, European Christendom was confined to what was little more than a wide corridor extending from Italy to the British Isles.

Second Period: 800 to 1050. A period of reconstruction began under the Frankish monarchs, culminating in the long reign of Charlemagne (768–814), who ultimately united almost all Continental Christians under his empire. Protector of the pope and, as such, crowned emperor by the pope, Charlemagne continued and developed the regime of his predecessors as divinely ordained governor and administrator of the Church of God. He ap-

A 14th-century manuscript illumination depicting a pope with clergy assembled on the left and monarchs on the right. (©Historical Picture Archive/CORBIS)

pointed bishops, settled liturgical affairs, and even pronounced upon theological issues, with the aid of a group of able clerics, among whom the Anglo-Saxon ALCUIN was preeminent. ADOPTIONISM, the question of ICONOCLASM and the FILIOQUE controversy were all dealt with at AACHEN, though the papacy was recognized as the ultimate source of authority and orthodoxy. When Charlemagne died, his son, Louis I the Pious at first continued and even extended his control of the Church, but the division of the empire and Louis's own faults and misfortunes allowed the bishops of the court, the heirs of the CAROLINGIAN REFORM, to assert their powers. For a generation they controlled the Continental Church north of the Alps, the scene being dominated by Archbishop HINCMAR OF REIMS (845–888). It was the age of the FALSE DECRETALS, the predestinarian and Eucharistic controversies, of PASCHASIUS RADBERTUS, RABANUS MAURUS and RATRAMNUS, and also of GOTTSCHALK OF ORBAIS and JOHN SCOTUS ERIGENA. A long series of complaisant and mediocre popes was broken by NICHOLAS I (858–867), the greatest pope between Gregory I and Leo IX. Nicholas, in his reestablishment of authority over the Frankish hierarchy, including Hincmar, in his steadfast refusal to countenance the divorce of Lothair II and in his treatment of the first phase of the *affaire* PHOTIUS, asserted in exemplary fashion and maintained in practice the plenary supremacy of the Roman See. If Nicholas's firmness seems at times to have become intransigence, this is attributable to his secretary, the enigmatic ANASTASIUS THE LIBRARIAN. His successor, ADRIAN II, maintained his position, but the collapse of the Carolingian Empire in 885 and the eclipse of the papacy heralded an epoch of political anarchy and weakness, in which the papal office reached a degree of degradation without parallel in the history of the Church.

Monastic Centuries. The five centuries after 600 have been called monastic, in the sense that the higher intellectual, spiritual, missionary, and administrative life of the Church was largely in the hands of monks, who were by and large the only teachers and writers of the age. In the 7th century, Irish monachism was still active, both in the Celtic homelands and in Continental foundations such as Columban's LUXEUIL and BOBBIO; but the future lay with the traditional Mediterranean type of community, which gradually accepted the BENEDICTINE RULE to the exclusion of all others. The monasteries became large landowning establishments, particularly in the German lands, where they were often centers of colonization and missionary activity, as well as seats of bishoprics. Charlemagne and Louis the Pious attempted to impose uniformity of discipline and strict observance of the rule on all monks of the Empire under BENEDICT OF ANIANE. But the organization was wanting, and the union dissolved; henceforth, however, all monks of France and Germany took St. Benedict as patron. The prevailing decadence that ensued was broken by the CLUNIAC REFORM (909), which gradually built up a vast and uniform congregation, strictly dependent on the abbot of Cluny.

Feudalization of the Church. The disappearance of the Carolingian Empire implied the final separation of France and Germany. In France decomposition into numerous feudal fiefs was rapid, and for two centuries the monarchy was in eclipse. In Germany the five (later six) great duchies came into being, one of the dukes being king of all. In 962 OTTO I the Saxon, known as Otto the Great, demanded and received the imperial crown from the pope, who alone had the right to bestow it. For nearly a century the papacy, when not a pawn of Roman intrigue, was treated as a religious appanage of the monarchs of Germany. As emperors or kings, these rulers regarded the papacy as their supreme ecclesiastical benefice. This attitude reflected the practice of more than two centuries throughout Europe, the regime of the PROPRIETARY CHURCH. During this period the old concept of the individual church as a corporation, with property and rights, and of the bishop as supporting and disposing of his clergy, had disappeared. The church was now a chattel, the parochial cure a benefice, and both were in the control of the lord, who appropriated much of the income and bestowed the office of priest, with its residual emoluments, on a clerk of his choice. Bishoprics and abbeys could be treated in the same way, while on the other hand bishops and even the papacy could own churches within or without the diocese of their title. Under such a regime the concept of a spiritual office was low. A church or a bishopric could be bought; a priest, tied by quasi-feudal obligations, might share the common rights of society, marry, or at least share domestic life with a consort and children and pass on his benefice to a son. Thus any program of reform demanded a chaste clergy and the canonical election of bishops without any payment for office.

Third Period: 1050 to 1303. The wind of reform began to blow in north Italy and in the monastic world. St. ROMUALD and St. JOHN GUALBERT, both Cluniac monks, founded strict new orders, the CAMALDOLESE and VALLOMBROSANS. PETER DAMIAN, a disciple of Romuald, was the fiercest preacher of reform. In France WILLIAM OF SAINT-BÉNIGNE, a Cluniac, reformed houses in Burgundy, north Italy, and Normandy; and there were other centers in Flanders and Lorraine. Men from all these centers, particularly Lorraine, worked for a reform of the papacy, using the ancient Canon Law (including the False Decretals and other unauthentic pieces) to exalt the office. LEO IX, a Lorrainer, appointed by Emperor Henry III in 1048, was the first pope of the new age. He traversed Germany and France, holding synods and deposing simoniacs, the first pope for two centuries to seize the reins firmly and to display papal authority in action throughout Europe. He was less well advised in his choice of the extremist Cardinal HUMBERT OF SILVA CANDIDA for the mission of 1054 to Constantinople, which led to the disastrous breach of relations that displayed, though it did not cause, the total lack of understanding between East and West. Leo's successors continued to press reform, and in 1059 a conciliar decree assigned the right of papal election to the cardinals (*see* PAPAL ELECTION DECREE). This circumvented royal control, but the crucial moment came in 1073 with the election of the archdeacon Hildebrand as GREGORY VII. The new pope developed his control of the Church, sending legates, deciding episcopal elections, and holding synods, moving firmly against clerical unchastity and simony. He did more. From an intensive study of Canon Law, he extracted a program of papal supremacy that included papal unaccountability and the right to excommunicate and depose a king or emperor. This right he asserted in 1075 when Emperor HENRY IV was excommunicated and deposed for appointing a rival archbishop at Milan. Faced with rebellion and a rival, Henry appeared as a penitent at Canossa and was absolved by the pope, who allowed spiritual duty to outweigh political wisdom. Henry vanquished his rival, whom the pope supported, and was again excommunicated and deposed (1080). He created an antipope, however, and Gregory was driven into exile, dying at Salerno in 1085. The great issue between priesthood and kingship had been joined.

Gregory VII was one of the greatest of the popes. Basing himself soundly on traditional and papal action in the past, he drove principles to their extreme conclusions and acted fearlessly and drastically when justice seemed to him to demand it. He created the centralized, politically minded papacy of the later Middle Ages; indeed, the scope of papal action in the modern world derives from his exposition of traditional doctrine. Whether in both act and word he carried firmness into harshness and spiritual truth into political design will always be debated, but the papacy could not now retreat; his ideas and ideals (*see* GREGORIAN REFORM) inspired popes and bishops in the century that followed. Pope PASCHAL II extended Gregorian practice; URBAN II seized the moral leadership of Europe by preaching the first CRUSADE; and GELASIUS II, after a period of confusion, settled the INVESTITURE struggle by the CONCORDAT OF WORMS (1122). Meanwhile, the reconquest of Spain, marked by the capture of Toledo (1085), added to Christendom a nation born of a crusade and reorganized by the papacy, a land that was soon to be a focus of new learning and thought.

The 12th Century. The 12th century saw the progress of Gregorian ideas throughout Europe. Canonical elections, clerical celibacy, legatine visitations and councils, appeals to Rome, papal protection of exempt religious houses, and assertions of the freedom of the Church were universal. The extraordinary development of intellectual activity and organizational ability throughout Europe and the emergence of numerous new and centralized religious orders accelerated the study and circulation of CANON LAW and perfected the ecclesiastical machinery of justice and administration at papal and diocesan level. It was then that the Cathedral Chapter, the bishop's curia, the archdeaconry, and the rest were set up all over Europe. At the same time there was an unparalleled expansion of the canonical and monastic life. Large and small communities of the regular "black canons," or CANONS REGULAR OF ST. AUGUSTINE, appeared. Later the more monastic "white canons," or PREMONSTRATENSIANS of St. NORBERT, covered northern and central Europe. The traditional Benedictine "black monks" and Cluniacs continued to increase, especially at the periphery of Christendom, while the new "white" CISTERCIANS, with their institute of lay brothers, enjoyed a vogue of spectacular proportions. The building of cathedrals, monasteries, and parish churches was equally remarkable. Beginning in France early in the 11th century, a new style of Romanesque architecture and sculpture was developed

and spread to Spain, north Italy, south Germany, and later, in its distinctive Norman form, to England after the Conquest. Earlier buildings were torn down to make way for larger ones, and half way through the 12th century the common use of stone vaulting and the pointed arch led to the new Gothic style that, as the techniques of design and construction improved, created masterpieces such as the cathedrals of Chartres, Amiens, and Reims; of Canterbury, Durham, and Lincoln; of Bamberg; and of Seville. These have never been surpassed in majesty of appearance or beauty of appointments. MANUSCRIPT ILLUMINATION, the art par excellence of the cloister, reached a new height of achievement. This material and artistic expansion was matched by literary and devotional development. The output of sermons, treatises, commentaries, chronicles, biographies, and letters rose steeply, as may be seen by a glance at such collections as Migne's *Patrology.* Furthermore, quality matched quantity. Such writers as ANSELM OF CANTERBURY, Peter ABELARD, BERNARD OF CLAIRVAUX, JOHN OF SALISBURY, WILLIAM OF MALMESBURY, OTTO OF FREISING, ADAM OF SAINT-VICTOR, and a hundred others put MEDIEVAL LATIN LITERATURE high among the achievements of European civilization. Though the "monastic centuries" ended *c.* 1150, it was the age that in great part "monachized" the sentiment and devotion of Western Christendom; i.e., monastic practices and ideals, such as liturgical elaborations, particular festivals, special psalmody, communal life, and vowed poverty, came to be applied to the secular clergy and even to devout lay folk, with the institution of lay brethren, oblates, and confraters. And the founding of a religious house became a good work beyond all others for a landowner.

These activities were accomplished by a society that, for its numbers, gave birth to an unexampled number of saints and edifying prelates. Popes such as Leo IX, Gregory VII, and Eugene III; bishops such as LANFRANC, Anselm of Canterbury, IVO OF CHARTRES, and Norbert at Magdeburg; monks and canons such as STEPHEN HARDING, Bernard of Clairvaux, AELRED OF RIEVAULX, and GILBERT OF SEMPRINGHAM; and women such as MARGARET, QUEEN OF SCOTLAND—all are names taken almost at random as representative of a great multitude. Especially outstanding among them was Bernard, who for 30 years was the spiritual director and ombudsman of the Church and the Doctor of his age; he was at once the last of the Fathers and the source of many elements in the devotional life of succeeding ages. No one in private place has ever held such a position of influence and esteem in the history of the Church.

The 12th century ended on a less buoyant note. The renaissance of letters was fading, the new religious orders had lost their first fervor, there were fewer men of genius and sanctity. There were internal clashes of authority and the beginnings of heresy in Italy and France. The cathedral schools were losing ground to the nascent universities, but SCHOLASTICISM had not yet unfolded its wings. The growing towns in Lombardy, Flanders, and south Germany were restless and uncared for. The papacy, at odds for years with FREDERICK BARBAROSSA and his claims to Sicily, had become entangled in anti-imperial diplomacy.

Innocent III. Then at last, after a run of elderly, short-lived popes, the cardinals in 1198 chose the young Roman canonist who took the name of Pope INNOCENT III. With extraordinary energy and breadth of view the new pope picked up the threads of government and resolved to devote his pontificate to the Crusade, to the defeat of heresy, and to reform. To the control and reform of the Church as understood by Gregory VII, Innocent added the supervision of Christendom and the claim to act and to rectify in the political sphere when justice or the good of nations demanded. In other words, the power and prestige of the papacy were in intention directed toward the purification of the Church and the well-being of the commonwealth. Innocent's unremitting work, seen in his correspondence and his decretals, was crowned by the Fourth LATERAN COUNCIL, the first Western council to rival the ancient gatherings in catholicity and scope. Touching every aspect and degree of Church life, it is notable above all as the first council to legislate for the general body of the faithful in its prescription of paschal Communion and annual parochial confession.

Nevertheless, Innocent had to deal with several difficult matters in which his success was incomplete: the growth of heresy, the Crusade, and German and English affairs. The heretical Cathari in Languedoc and Toulouse demanded attention; and after the attempts of preachers had failed, the pope launched a Crusade of northern French barons, who massacred and ravaged, replacing the papal project of peaceful settlement by military conquest. Innocent's Eastern Crusade ended in the deplorable sack of Constantinople and the establishment of a LATIN EMPIRE, which Innocent, in this too much a man of his age, rejoiced to see. In England, his stern action against the wayward and violent King John was hastily replaced by his support of the externally penitent king. In Germany, after more than one change of front, he supported the young King Frederick II, a child of sorrow for the papacy. In all these fields the pope suffered a great disadvantage in conducting shifting politics at weeks' or months' distance from the scene of action, but in each, also, he misjudged the human agents concerned. Against these failures of policy, it is only fair to set his merit in having recognized the sanctity and value of FRANCIS OF ASSISI

and St. DOMINIC. His pontificate was the summit of the medieval papacy, and all too short.

Mendicant Orders. The foundation of the two first orders of friars did more than any political or conciliar action to rejuvenate the Church. Francis of Assisi, one of the most original and arresting personalities in European history, the harbinger of a new age with his emotional and aesthetic delicacy and his capacity for self-surrender, probably never wished to found the order that so exactly met the needs and aspirations of his day. Dominic, with a clear and more conventional aim and a genius for organization, supplied the framework later adopted by all the friars. It has been said, with some inaccuracy, that Francis made the Preachers friars while Dominic made the Minors an order. Both groups had a phenomenal success and inspired many imitators, of whom the CARMELITES, AUGUSTINIANS, and later the SERVITES were the only bodies of European importance. As centralized, supranational institutes, at once favored and exploited by the papacy, they were a source of spiritual and missionary strength for the Church of the 13th century, to which each order gave a pope, a Doctor, and many notable bishops. Above all, the laity of the cities and towns profited by their preaching and direction and, later, by the consequences of their theological wisdom.

The 13th Century. The century following Innocent III and the Fourth Lateran Council was the high summer of the medieval Church. Universal centralization, given depth by the legislation of the council and the teaching of the new universities and administered by a hierarchy more competent and in general more zealous than at any previous epoch, brought about a new growth of religion at the parish level as well as in the cathedral towns and schools. Dioceses were now fully organized and parishes cared for, while in the material sphere churches were built and rebuilt on a scale and with a magnificence never to be surpassed. At the center, Innocent III was followed in the papacy by a series of able, mature lawyers who carried on and developed his program; but they were men of lesser genius and narrower vision, and it seemed to contemporaries that they monopolized power and exploited the Church. The appointment of bishops—removed from monarchs and restored to canonical electors by the Gregorians—was now claimed by the papacy in an increasing number of situations and finally in all cases by Urban V (1363). Election became a costly business for the bishop-elect. Similarly, PROVISION to benefices, great or small, throughout the Church, was increasingly claimed by or restricted to the pope: in 1265 Clement IV had asserted the principle that was gradually put into practice more and more. Papal provision, like papal appointment of bishops, brought cash as well as patronage to the Roman Curia, while bishops lost many of their assets as patrons and churches suffered from foreign or absentee incumbents. Above all, papal taxation, begun indirectly toward the end of the 12th century, increased rapidly and actual direct taxation began in 1199. Before the middle of the 13th century, first fruits on bishoprics (i.e., one year's revenue) and tenths on all clergy were regularly levied, in addition to the fees payable by exempt houses for particular favors and for costs in litigation. Under INNOCENT IV this exploitation was accompanied by a rigorous use of all means of control and every source of revenue, such as legatine visitations and the visits of bishops (AD LIMINA) to Rome. The pontificate of Innocent IV has been taken as the moment when the papacy first seemed to fleece rather than to feed its flock.

In the realm of politics, Innocent IV used weapons of excommunication and interdict ruthlessly and methodically against FREDERICK II, and the pope was obeyed by most of the German bishops. The excommunication and deposition of the emperor in 1245, followed by his death in 1250, are usually taken to mark the end of the long struggle and the victory of the papacy over the empire, and they were also the principal business of the First Council of LYONS in 1245.

The same epoch—the 13th century—saw the University of PARIS reach the height of its fame with a series of eminent doctors: WILLIAM OF AUVERGNE, ALEXANDER OF HALES, BONAVENTURE, ALBERT THE GREAT, THOMAS AQUINAS, ROBERT KILWARDBY, JOHN PECKHAM, and the enigmatic master of arts SIGER OF BRABANT. Their careers coincided with the final translation, reception, and criticism of the whole Aristotelian corpus by the theologians and with the appearance, under Siger, of heterodox integral Aristotelian teaching that provoked the Paris condemnations of 1270 and 1277. These marked the end or at least the suspension of the endeavor to make Aristotle the exclusive master of thought, though not before Aquinas had rethought the philosopher and produced a system of Christian philosophical and theological doctrine, and an answer to the old problem of clarifying the relationship of reason to revelation, of nature to grace.

The end of the 13th century was a period of harshness and embitterment. The campaign against heresy was now conducted by the INQUISITION, equipped with extraordinary powers and with the operating machinery of secret delation and examination assisted by torture, in which the accused was consistently at a legal disadvantage. The rivalry between the Preachers and the Minors (not yet called DOMINICANS and FRANCISCANS), exacerbated by the condemnation of 1277, molded theological teaching into schools coincident with the various orders of friars. Within the Minors the tension between those who claimed to follow the rule and those who accepted the many papal interpretations and relaxations—alleviated for a time by the moderation and spiritual wisdom of St. Bonaventure—was now becoming a schism between FRANCISCAN SPIRITUALS and Franciscan Conventuals, while the wider tension between clerics and secular powers was moving from Germany to England and France, where strong monarchs and a mounting spirit of nationalism were resisting papal claims to tax and to provide. In the Roman Curia the small number of cardinals gave national and family feuds an undesirable influence, and several papal elections became long and bitter contests. An attempt to escape from these resulted in the strange election of an inexperienced hermit as Pope CELESTINE V, and the confusion caused by his incompetence and resignation led to the election of Benedetto Gaetani as BONIFACE VIII (1294–1303). With Boniface papal claims to supremacy in the political sphere rose to their highest point. Thwarted in his attempt to prevent the taxation of clergy by kings, he became involved in an exchange of threats with PHILIP IV (the Fair) of France. The pope claimed the right to supervise and condemn royal policies and acts, and if need be to excommunicate and depose. The king and his ministers retorted with charges of simony, immorality, and heresy, and threatened Boniface with a general council. The pope's bull UNAM SANCTAM, a masterly exposition of extreme papal claims, was followed by his temporary capture by Nogaret at Anagni and his death a few months later.

Fourth Period: 1303 to 1500. Boniface's successor died after a brief pontificate, and the French archbishop of Bordeaux succeeded him as Pope CLEMENT V. Dominated by the French king, who demanded a posthumous trial of Boniface VIII, Clement temporized but yielded to Philip in suppressing the TEMPLARS, whose wealth the king coveted and whose conviction was secured by calumny and barbarous torture. By his creation of numerous French cardinals, Clement also ensured a series of French popes and settled the papal court at Avignon in 1308, thus occasioning the AVIGNON PAPACY. His successor, the septuagenarian JOHN XXII (1316–34), was the most remarkable pope of the century. A financial and administrative genius, he reorganized papal finances, greatly increasing the yield from direct taxation; he reformed the papal Curia and reshaped the diocesan pattern in France. Quarrelsome and obstinate, he forced the Emperor LOUIS IV the Bavarian into hostility, thereby depriving the papacy of its Italian revenue and creating an asylum for those who were enemies of the pope on other counts. These enemies included the bitter secularist MARSILIUS OF PADUA; the creator of NOMINALISM, WILLIAM OF OCKHAM; and the rebellious minister general of the Franciscans, MICHAEL OF CESENA, who refused to accept the pope's condemnation of the teaching that Christ on earth owned no property. This opinion, passionately held by the Franciscan Spirituals and many other Franciscans, led them to accuse the pope of heresy, a charge that was redoubled when John XXII gratuitously aired his opinion that souls, however pure, failed to enjoy the fullness of the BEATIFIC VISION immediately after death. This aberration was condemned by John's successor, BENEDICT XII, a Cistercian, memorable for his reforming constitutions for monks and canons. The residence at Avignon did not end until GREGORY XI returned to Rome in 1377.

The "Babylonian Captivity" at Avignon has been the object of bitter invective from the days of the contemporary Petrarch to our own. But during the past few decades, opinion has changed. The worst charges of vicious living and subservience to the French monarchy cannot be maintained. The Avignon popes were on the whole respectable and personally devout and not without a care for the wider needs of the Church. Apart from the complaisance of Clement V, few of their failings can be directly attributed to their place of residence. On the other hand, there is no doubt that during the decades at Avignon the luxury and venality of the Curia became a scandal and that the financial exactions and centralization of administration became excessive. The sense that the papacy exploited the Church grew, with the added bitterness that the exploitation was for financial, not for high political, ends, while the French monopoly of places and power and the neglect of Roman interests, spiritual and temporal, undoubtedly angered contemporaries.

There were other aggravating circumstances in this period of discontent. The catastrophic plagues of 1348–49 and the previous outbreak of the Hundred Years' War between England and France demoralized western Europe and accelerated its division into mutually hostile nations. At the same time, the intellectually disturbing effects of Nominalism and the ruthless attacks on the papacy and ecclesiastical government by Marsilius and Ockham provided a background of theory for political actions such as the English antipapal statutes of PROVISORS and PRAEMUNIRE (1351, 1353).

Western Schism and Basel. The return of the papacy to Rome was followed within a few months by an unforeseeable disaster even more damaging to religion. This was the election in 1378 of two popes in succession by the same small body of factious cardinals; the WESTERN SCHISM had begun. Though Roman tradition and modern scholarship agree on the probable validity of the first election (of Pope URBAN VI), contemporaries had no means of arriving at certainty; within a few weeks each party was furnished with cardinals, a curia, and a palace (at Rome and at Avignon), and Europe split into two

camps. France, the Iberian Peninsula, and Scotland were in one; the Empire, Hungary, the Netherlands, and England, in the other; Italy was divided. All attempts at a solution by means of resignation or conference failed; both papal lines were perpetuated, and an agreement by the cardinals of both parties to call a council at PISA in 1409 resulted in the election of a third and certainly illegitimate pope, or antipope, JOHN XXIII. Meanwhile, the opinion that only a general council could provide a solution for such a crisis was strengthened by arguments then gaining strength in academic circles at Paris, that such a council was a sovereign power superior to the pope (*see* CONCILIARISM). The vicious circle was at last broken by the Emperor SIGISMUND, who persuaded John XXIII to convoke a council at CONSTANCE (1414), which in course of time deposed him, accepted the resignation of the Roman pope, and declared the Avignon claimant deposed. Then a Colonna cardinal was elected (1417) pope as MARTIN V. Previously, the council had condemned and burned John Hus and passed the decree *Frequens,* which stated that a council should meet after five years, with decennial councils in perpetuity. Martin V successfully restored and improved the papal financial and administrative machinery and with equal success resisted reform of the papal Curia and its abuses. He yielded to opinion, however, by convoking another council, which he did not live to see. This Council, at BASEL, largely composed of academicians maintaining conciliar supremacy, successfully resolved the quarrel between Catholics and HUSSITES in Bohemia, and passed several thoroughgoing decrees against papal reservation of benefices and Curial avarice. Pope EUGENE IV, a patient conservative, awaited his hour; and when the Eastern Emperor approached both him and the council, asking for assistance and promising reunion, the pope overbid the council by transferring its sessions to Ferrara to meet Greek convenience. He was successful in achieving an artificial union with the Greeks at the succeeding Council of FLORENCE (1438–39), thereby securing the general esteem that the Council failed to diminish even after "deposing" him and electing an antipope. The gathering at Basel expired in 1449 and with it the "conciliar era," though threats of a council continued to alarm popes until the ghost was laid at Trent. It was symptomatic of the return to traditional forms of Church government that two eminent men, conciliarists in their early career, should become staunch papalists. NICHOLAS OF CUSA, who in his thought turned back to Neoplatonism, was one; the other, Cardinal Juan de TORQUEMADA, was a harbinger of the Thomist revival of the following century. Meanwhile, Eugene IV had skillfully made terms with the various governments and, by making some concessions, had retained far more power for the papacy than the nations at Basel had desired, with the single exception of France.

There, the epoch had given birth to GALLICANISM, which transferred all powers of appointment and taxation from pope to king, while admitting the spiritual supremacy of Rome. This arrangement, reasserted in the PRAGMATIC SANCTION of Bourges (1439), was constantly attacked by the papacy but remained the Magna Carta of Gallicanism for more than three centuries.

By mid-15th century conciliarism was dead, and the papacy had ostensibly recovered its status. The 40 years of unparalleled doubt and division had, however, done immense harm in lowering the spiritual prestige of the papal office and in calling into question its usefulness, its necessity, and its rights. Following hard upon the residence at Avignon, they did more than anything to prepare the ground for the great revolution of the 16th century.

Wyclif and Hus. Meanwhile, heresy had appeared again in a form that was to have only partial success in its early version but was to be absorbed later into the program of mature Protestantism. John WYCLIF, a leading realist philosopher at Oxford, turned to theology and found the Church in the invisible society of the predestined. He denied the transubstantiation of the Eucharistic elements; questioned the powers of pope, bishop, and priest; and took the Bible as the only rule of faith, preaching poverty and a married ministry. Censured and silenced by Archbishop William COURTENAY, he died in communion with the Church; and his disciples, called LOLLARDS, were driven underground by persecution. By a strange turn of events, his teaching was carried to Bohemia, where it served as the basis and confirmation of the message of John HUS, a popular preacher and national leader. Hus and his disciple JEROME OF PRAGUE were condemned and burned at Constance. Their followers, who combined a puritan zeal with nationalist enthusiasm in a country that had recently risen to a notable place in European culture, rose in armed defense of their cause, of which reception of the Eucharist under both species was a shibboleth, giving them their name (UTRAQUISTS). They successfully resisted a crusade of the Emperor Sigismund, and the Council of Basel was constrained to make a compromise in the Compacts of Prague, which in fact granted little save the optional use of the chalice. Such as it was, the arrangement gave the Hussites an uneasy place within the Catholic Church for almost a century. Though only partially successful and compounded of many elements, not all of them religious, the Hussite movement marked a point of no return. It was the first attempt of a professedly Christian body to break away from Rome in the later Middle Ages; and though it is difficult to establish direct contact between the Wyclif-Hus evangel and the first writings of Martin LUTHER, the identity of ideas between it and the fully developed program of the great Reformer is unmistakable.

Devotio Moderna. The period from 1300 to 1500 was not wholly one of discord and disaster. There were many notable instances of sanctity, with reformers such as BERNARDINE OF SIENA and ANTONINUS of Florence and women such as CATHERINE OF SIENA, BRIDGET and CATHERINE OF SWEDEN, and FRANCES OF ROME. Above all, it was an age of mystical experience and writing. The Dominican school of the Rhineland, originating with Meister ECKHART and developed by TAULER and HENRY SUSO, lay behind the teaching of the great Flemish mystic, RUYSBROECK, and in its main lines, wholly traditional in essence, though colored by Neoplatonic language, was to pass to Spain and become classical. The practical aspects of DOMINICAN SPIRITUALITY served as food for countless families of devout women in Rhenish and Flemish convents. In England, joined to the traditional Bernardine-Victorine teaching, it appeared in the works of the unknown master of the *CLOUD OF UNKNOWING* and Walter HILTON, while Richard ROLLE and the exquisite JULIAN OF NORWICH stood apart as preachers of their own experience. How deeply religious faith still saturated all kinds of men may be seen in DANTE and Petrarch in Italy, and in England in Chaucer and his contemporaries William Langland and the poet of *The Pearl*.

Still more extensive was the movement of the contemporary BRETHREN OF THE COMMON LIFE, who owed their way of life to the inspiration of Gerard GROOTE (1340–89) and whose spirit has been preserved for all subsequent generations by THOMAS À KEMPIS in his *IMITATION OF CHRIST*. The Brethren gave to generations of their countrymen a solid religious education, pure morals, and a simple devotion that anticipated the puritan sentiment of a later age; an orthodox faith with a minimum of speculation and liturgical display.

Renaissance. When the Council of Basel expired (1449), the papacy had entered a new phase; the brilliant and artistic activity of Italy was inspiring secular attitudes, and in Europe as a whole an age of authority and absolutism was about to begin. The Roman Curia and in particular the College of Cardinals, in which members of the leading families of Italy were dominant, shared to the full in the luxury and refinement of the age, while the popes entered into the shifting power politics of the day. In the past many popes had been diplomats and some had been warriors, but never before had the papacy stood in the forefront of European diplomacy in the guise of a secular power, the military ally or enemy of other states, a participant in the struggle for supremacy and territorial gain. In an age of individualism and *virtù,* a succession of pontiffs stood out as intensely human, egoistic sovereigns, who used their near relatives as faithful agents, and bought or rewarded their services with ecclesiastical as well as secular honors. The age from 1447 to 1550 was one of papal nepotism and patronage of the arts. Pope NICHOLAS V was the first to harness the Italian RENAISSANCE to the papal chariot; henceforward for more than a century, Rome, which itself was poor in artistic talent, was the mecca of architects, sculptors, and painters, whose works remain for the world to visit in ST. PETER'S BASILICA, the SISTINE CHAPEL, and the galleries of the Vatican palace. The converted conciliarist and brilliant, if slightly raffish, literary genius Aeneas Sylvius (Pope PIUS II, 1458–64) was the quintessence of his age; he was also the last of the medieval popes in his valiant but unavailing attempt to rouse a crusade. His sucessors devoted their attention to war and alliances in Italy. SIXTUS IV, a Franciscan, lived (it was said) on war and advanced his disreputable nephews, clerical and lay, to further his policy; he also planned the decoration of the chapel that bears his name. Under his rule the papal court rivaled the splendors of Florence. Under INNOCENT VIII, ALEXANDER VI, and JULIUS II the papacy, outwardly magnificent and skillfully steered in the Italian maelstrom, countenanced around it a degree of wordly display and spiritual emptiness that contemporaries at once admired and deplored. For more than a century the cry for reform in head and members of the Church had been heard—and not least frequently in Italy itself, where the tragic career of SAVONAROLA had revealed so many of the religious, social, and political ills of the time.

Yet there were still many examples of sanctity in the century of JOAN OF ARC, FRANCIS OF PAOLA, and CATHERINE OF GENOA. In France and in England, at the end of the century, LEFÈVRE D'ÉTAPLES and John COLET were inaugurating the study of Pauline teaching and the human life of Christ that was to seem to many a new and truer basis of religion than a piety of indulgences and monastic observance. The critical scholarship that was beginning to reveal the Gospels and the early Church in a new light, the discoveries that had opened a new half-world, the diffusion of thought that printing was beginning to make possible—all this and much else, was heralding a new age; but in 1500 no one could have foreseen what shape reform would take, if indeed it were to come.

Bibliography: The whole period is covered by *Histoire del'Église,* ed. originally A. FLICHE and V. MARTIN, now by J. B. DUROSELLE and E. JARRY (Paris 1935) v.5–15. The sections by É. AMANN and A. FLICHE are particularly valuable. Of the older historians, A. HAUCK, *Kirchengeschichte Deutschlands,* 5 v. (8th ed. Berlin 1954), covers France to 900 and Germany and Central Europe to 1428 and is still unrivaled for breadth of scope and wealth of documentation. H. K. MANN, *The Lives of the Popes in the Early Middle Ages,* 18 v. (London 1902–32). G. MOLLAT, *Les Papes d'Avignon* (9th ed. Paris 1950), Eng. tr. J. LOVE (New York 1963). L. PASTOR, *History of the Popes,* tr. F. I. ANTROBUS et al., 40 v. (London 1936–61), various editions. M. CREIGHTON, *A History of the Papacy from the Great Schism to the Sack of Rome,* 6 v. (new ed. New York 1897), is still valuable. C. J. HEFELE, *Histoire des conciles,* ed. and tr. H. LECLERCQ, 10 v. (Paris 1907–13), 1911 has many useful notes. **Early Middle Ages.** R. W. and A. J. CARLYLE, *A History of Mediaeval Political Theory in the West,* 6 v. (Edinburgh 1903–36; repr. New York 1953). L. DUCHESNE, *Les Premiers temps de l'état pontifical* (3d ed. Paris 1912), Eng. tr. A. H. MATHEW (London 1908). E. CASPAR, *Geschichte de Papsttums von den Anfängen bis zur Höhe der Weltherrschaft* (Tübingen 1939–33). K. S. LATOURETTE, *A History of the Expansion of Christianity* (New York 1937–45) v.2. W. LEVISON, *England and the Continent in the Eighth Century* (Oxford 1946). F. DVORNIK, *The Making of Central and Eastern Europe* (London 1949). H. X. ARQUILLIÈRE, *L'Augustinisme politique* (2d ed. Paris 1955). W. ULLMANN, *The Growth of Papal Government in the Middle Ages* (2d ed. New York 1962). **Gregorian Reform.** A. FLICHE, *La Réforme grégorienne,* 3 v. (Louvain 1924–37). Z. N. BROOKE, *Cambridge Medieval History* (London-New York 1911–36) 5:51–166. P. FOURNIER and G. LEBRAS, *Histoire des collections canoniques en occident depuis les fausses décretales jusqu'au Décret de Gratien* (Paris 1931–32). J. P. WHITNEY, *Hildebrandine Essays* (Cambridge, Eng. 1932). H. X. ARQUILLIÈRE, *Saint Grégoire VII: Essai sur sa conception du pouvoir pontifical* (Paris 1934). *Studi gregoriani* (Rome 1947–). **12th Century.** E. VACANDARD, *Vie de Saint Bernard,* 2 v. (Paris 1895; 3d ed. 1902). C. H. HASKINS, *The Renaissance of the Twelfth Century* (Cambridge, Mass. 1927; repr. 1933). G. PARÉ et al., *La Renaissance du XIIe siècle: Les Écoles et l'enseignement* (Paris 1933). J. GUIRAUD, *Histoire de l'Inquisition au moyen-âge,* 2 v. (Paris 1935–38). H. RASHDALL, *The Universities of Europe in the Middle Ages,* ed. F. M. POWICKE and A. B. EMDEN, 3 v. (new ed. Oxford 1936). É. DE MOREAU, *Histoire de l'Église en Belgique* (2d ed. Brussels 1945-). J. F. LEMARIGNIER et al., *Institutions ecclésiastiques,* v.3 of *Histoire des institutions françaises au moyen-âge,* ed. F. LOT and R. FAWTIER (Paris 1957-). J. LECLERCQ et al., *Histoire de la spiritualité chrétienne,* v.2 (Paris 1961). H. C. LEA, *The Inquisition of the Middle Ages,* with introd. by W. ULLMANN (London 1963). **13th Century.** A. LUCHAIRE, *Innocent III,* 6 v. (Paris 1906–08), a classic, but a political, not a religious study; supplement with Fliche-Martin v.10 (1950). H. GRUNDMANN, *Religiöse Bewegungen im Mittelalter* (2d ed. Hildesheim 1961); "Neue Beiträge zur Geschichte der religiösen Bewegungen im Mittelalter," *Archiv für Kulturgeschichte* 37 (1955) 129–182. G. BARRACLOUGH, *Papal Provisions* (Oxford 1935). M. H. VICAIRE, *Saint Dominic and His Times,* tr. K. POND (New York 1965). **14th Century.** N. VALOIS, *La France et le grand schisme d'Occident,* 4 v. (Paris 1896–1902). J. HALLER, *Papsttum und Kirchenreform* (Berlin 1903). J. RIVIÈRE, *Le Problème de l'église et de l'état au temps de Philippe le Bel* (Paris 1926). W. E. LUNT, *Papal Revenues in the Middle Ages,* 2 v. (New York 1934); *Financial Relations of the Papacy with England,* 2v. (Cambridge, Mass. 1939–62). B. TIERNEY, *Foundations of the Conciliar Theory* (Cambridge, Eng. 1955). G. DE LAGARDE, *La Naissance de l'esprit laïque au déclin du moyen-âge,* 5v. (new ed. Louvain 1956–63). **15th Century.** P. IMBART DE LA TOUR, *Les Origines de la Réforme,* 4 v. (Paris 1905–35) v.2, re-ed. Y. LANHERS (Melun 1946). N. VALOIS, *Le Pape et le Concile, 1418–1450,* 2 v. (Paris 1909). V. MARTIN, *Les Origines du gallicanisme,* 2 v. (Paris 1939). A. RENAUDET, *Préréforme et humanisme à Paris* (2d ed. Paris 1953). H. JEDIN, *History of the Council of Trent,* tr. E. GRAF (St. Louis 1957–60) v.1. J. LORTZ, *Die Reformation in Deutschland,* 2 v. (4th ed. Freiburg 1962), Fr. tr. (Paris 1956). J. GILL, *The Council of Florence* (Cambridge, Eng. 1959).

[M. D. KNOWLES]

CHURCH, HISTORY OF, III (EARLY MODERN: 1500–1789)

In the early modern age, the Church faced the gravest crisis it had yet experienced in the West, the Protestant REFORMATION. After suffering the loss of a considerable part of Europe, Catholicism managed by a great effort of self-reform to emerge strengthened and purified of many of the abuses that had in part caused and furthered PROT-ESTANTISM. The new energies were used in answering the missionary challenges posed by Africa, Asia, and the Americas, in consolidating the position of the Church in those parts of Europe that had remained within the old unity, in quelling grave theological quarrels within its own fold, and in maintaining the Church's autonomy within absolutistic European states. Before the end of this period, the Church was faced with yet a new challenge, the rise of disbelief and secularism. The following survey will be divided into two periods: the first (1500–1648) will treat of the Protestant Reformation, the COUNTER REFORMATION, Catholicism within the various European nations, and the missionary expansion of the Church; the second period (1648–1789) will treat of the internal theo-logical problems and Church-State quarrels, and the situ-ation of the Church throughout the world at the end of the *ancien régime*.

"March of the Holy League in the Place de Greve, Paris," *1590.* (©Archivo Iconografico, S.A./CORBIS)

THE CHURCH, 1500 TO 1648

Although certain movements and currents of thought, while more prominent in one period, are com-mon to both the first and the second period, the end of the THIRTY YEARS' WAR does mark in many respects a turning point in the history of the Church, for by 1648 both the Reformation and the Counter Reformation ceased to win any large number of new adherents.

Eve of the Reformation. The general situation of the Church on the eve of the Reformation was one of seeming great prestige and power but of internal apathy and hollowness. The cry for reform in head and members had not been satisfactorily heeded. The papacy had suf-fered a grievous loss of prestige in the period at Avignon and in the Great Schism. By 1500 the popes seemed to be more Renaissance princelings than spiritual fathers of Christendom. While, as rulers of an Italian state, they were necessarily concerned with the independence and government of their territories, the temptation to use the papacy to advance their families was too often over-whelming. In ALEXANDER VI (1462–1503), JULIUS II (1503–13), and LEO X (1513–21), the Church had succes-sively at its head a man of immoral private life, a warrior, and a pleasure-seeker. The tone of the papal court may be judged by the attempt on the life of Leo X in 1517 in which some of his own cardinals were involved. The rep-utation of the Roman CURIA for rapaciousness at the ex-pense of the Christian flock was of long standing. Absenteeism, pluralism, and lack of pastoral interest characterized the episcopacy in varying degrees; the same was true of other members of the upper clergy (e.g., the canons and the pastors of wealthy parishes). The lower clergy suffered above all from inadequate spiritual, intellectual, and moral formation, which often resulted in ignorance of even basic Christian doctrine and in the growth of concubinage. In the religious orders, despite the existence of some exemplary reformed cloisters, apa-thy and spiritual torpor appeared to be dominant. Al-though the devout Christian laity still followed their appointed leaders, the abuses and excessive privileges of the clergy were fostering an anticlericalism, which, while not new, was growing. A dessicated theology remote from pastoral concerns, an externalism in sacramental practice, and a proliferation of devotional practices often peripheral to the central message of Christianity were component parts of the spiritual malaise that gripped the Church. A spiritual hunger was felt—unconsciously by some, consciously by the more educated clerics and lay-men—for the spiritual treasures of the Sacred Scriptures and for a theology and practice of the Sacraments cen-tered upon their nature as signs of faith and sources of grace for the Christian community. The Reformers seemed to many to provide the answer to their longing for a deeply thought and lived Christianity. But when the new formulations denied or excluded part of divinely entrusted teaching, the Church could only reject those theses of Protestantism that it felt were a narrowing down or impoverishment of the riches of the Christian message. If the Reformers rediscovered basic Christian principles hidden in what was without doubt a dry, decadent, and tired scholasticism, their formulations of these were outside the central stream of Christian tradition and were linked with denials of other doctrines and practices that formed an inseparable part of the inheritance of both the Eastern and the Western Churches.

The Reformation. The Reformation took four main forms: LUTHERANISM, CALVINISM, Radicalism, and ANGLICANISM.

Lutheranism. The Lutheran Reformation, which spread from Saxony throughout much of Germany and into the Scandinavian and Baltic lands, was the result of an Augustinian monk's struggle to find peace of soul for a conscience tortured by doubts about salvation. Martin LUTHER, in his reading of St. Paul, felt that he had discovered the absolutely central truth of Christianity, viz, that God forgives man his sins or justifies him by faith alone without any other activity on man's part (*see* JUSTIFICATION). In other words, only God is active in the process of salvation; man's only reply, which has bearing upon his salvation, is his faith in his Redeemer, Jesus Christ. Good works are the fruit of justification, but are of no avail to salvation. The exclusiveness of this formulation, which had necessarily to rule out free will, forced the Church to reject it. While the Lutheran churches in varying degrees conserved more of ancient practices than the Calvinist and Radical, other denials also made the Lutheran answer impossible for the Church to accept. The hierarchical constitution of the Church was rejected. All Christians were to be considered priests without distinction. Scripture alone was to be the rule of faith without an authoritative interpreter. The Sacraments were reduced to two, Baptism and the Eucharist, while both the sacrificial character of the Mass was denied and an already rejected theory of the Eucharistic presence was introduced, that of consubstantiation.

Calvinism. The Calvinist Reformation, which spread from Switzerland to France, the Low Countries, and parts of Germany, England, and Scotland, derived from the Lutheran and a somewhat more radical type of reform that had been taking place in certain southern German and especially Swiss cities. In Switzerland the chief early leader of this radical reform was ZWINGLI in Zurich. John CALVIN, a Frenchman, who became the reformer of Geneva, accepted the cardinal doctrines of Luther: justification by faith alone and the all-sufficiency of Sacred Scripture, but he presented them in a more highly organized and systematic form and shifted the emphasis from the forgiveness of the sinning creature to the transcendency of the forgiving God. Calvinism required a far more austere way of life and worship than Lutheranism. The rejections of traditional Catholic doctrine were the same as those of Luther, while the rejection of traditional Catholic practices were more radical than those of Luther, who was willing to retain such of them as did not violate the doctrine of justification by faith alone. In one doctrinal respect, the manner of the Eucharistic presence, Calvinism differed irreconcilably from Lutheranism. While Luther steadfastly maintained the reality of Christ's presence in the Eucharist through consubstantiation, Calvin admitted only a presence of Christ in the believing communicant.

The Radical Reformation. The Radical Reformation is a term used to designate various sectarian movements that arose after the beginning of the Lutheran Reformation. No single doctrine characterized the adherents of the many, sometimes tiny, groups who are called radical, but rather they manifest a tendency to go farther than Lutheranism or Calvinism. The Low Countries, Germany, Bohemia, and Poland were the main centers. Three subjects especially interested the radical: the Eucharistic presence, which some interpreted as purely symbolic (SACRAMENTARIANS); infant baptism, which some rejected (ANABAPTISTS or BAPTISTS); and the Incarnation, which some denied (SOCINIANS, UNITARIANS). These movements, always small, were mostly suppressed by both Catholics and Protestants, but some few of them survived the Reformation era or were later revived.

Anglicanism. The Anglican Reformation, which was confined to the British Isles, differs in many respects from the Continental Reformation. In England, rather than a theological leader such as Luther or Calvin, it was more the monarch and parliament who defined the shape and form of the new ecclesiastical structure. Under HENRY VIII the English Church was separated from Rome, but Catholic practice and doctrine were retained almost without alteration. During the short reign of his son, Edward VI, liturgy and doctrine were, however, altered in a Protestant sense. Following the also brief reign of MARY TUDOR, during which the ties with Rome were restored, the definitive establishment of a church comprising both Catholic and Protestant elements was accomplished by and under ELIZABETH I. The uniqueness of Anglicanism lay in this attempt to synthesize Protestantism and much of the old Catholic tradition. Only the Anglican Church has, besides the confession of faith of the THIRTY-NINE ARTICLES, a liturgical book, the Book of COMMON PRAYER, as the basis for its beliefs. The Prayer Book is essentially a combined Breviary, Missal, and ritual, retaining many Catholic practices but with Protestant elements, especially in connection with the Eucharist and the Eucharistic service. The Thirty-Nine Articles are an attempt to fuse Catholic and Protestant doctrines in formulations broad enough to be acceptable to both. The Eucharistic service of the Prayer Book eliminated reference to its sacrificial character. Those who wished a more profound Protestantization in the Calvinist sense eventually became known as PURITANS and managed briefly in the 17th century to gain political and ecclesiastical power. Those who wished to remain fully Catholic were reduced to a tiny persecuted minority compromised in their political allegiance by the futile attempt of PIUS V to depose Queen Elizabeth. By severing its link with Rome, the English Church broke communion with the Catholic Church.

Thus, despite the rich scriptural piety of the Lutherans and their warm devotion to their Savior, the profound awe before the transcendent God and the austere sobriety of life of the Calvinists, the traditionalism and sober piety of the Anglicans, and the commitment to a totally Christian life of some of the radical Protestants, the Church had necessarily to oppose Protestantism and to attempt to answer Protestant negations.

The Catholic Reaction. In the beginning the reply to Protestantism was a defensive reaction. Basic tenets of Lutheran doctrine were solemnly condemned by the papal bull *Exsurge, Domine* (1520). In the previous year the Universities of Cologne and Louvain had issued condemnations, as did the Sorbonne in 1521. In reply to the flood of Lutheran publications, scores of Catholic theologians entered the fray to publish refutations. The quality of these works was quite uneven. Luther and his followers had the advantage of promoting a new movement that promised a long-awaited reform. The Catholic theologians, none of whom had the theological and literary genius of Luther, seemed to be defending the *status quo.* Moreover, until the Council of TRENT, there was, at least on certain points, some confusion as to what was the traditional Catholic position. Nevertheless a great deal of preparatory work, which was later to prove valuable at Trent, was done by these theologians, not only in Germany but throughout Europe. In Germany there were such men as Johann ECK, one of Luther's first and most passionate opponents; Johannes COCHLAEUS, responsible for a Catholic view of Luther enduring for centuries; the erudite Johannes Fabri of Vienna; the humanistic catechist Frederich NAUSEA, and many others, especially among members of the religious orders. At Louvain, Luther, by his own admission, found his most powerful opponent in Jacobus LATOMUS. Elsewhere in Europe also much was written against the new doctrines. In England, for example, ironically Henry VIII, as well as John FISHER and

Thomas MORE, wrote against Luther. Out of hundreds only a few additional names can be mentioned, such as Alfonso de Castro (Spain), Josse Clichtove (France), and Ambrose Catharinus (Italy). If the work of these men, often quite unappreciated in its time, in defending Catholic doctrine was flawed by anything, it was that they were speaking as individuals without the authority of the entire Church. Only an ecumenical council would at that time be heeded as speaking with the necessary authority, but such a council required convocation by the pope. For too long, the papacy hesitated to call a council mainly because it feared a resurgence of CONCILIARISM.

The Convoking of a Council. After the brief pontificate of the last non-Italian pope, Adrian VI (1522–23), one of the rare high prelates to admit the responsibility of the Church for the rupture of religious unity, CLEMENT VII (1523–34) ascended the papal throne. An indecisive pope, his fear of conciliarism, of the Emperor CHARLES V, and of a possible deposition because of his illegitimate birth caused him to refuse to summon the council that Christendom was clamoring for. His successor PAUL III (1534–49), while guilty of lavish NEPOTISM and not himself a reformer, nevertheless by his encouragement of reforms of the religious orders, by his nomination of reform-minded cardinals, and above all by successfully bringing the Council of Trent into being, effectively if belatedly placed the papacy behind the movement of Catholic reform.

It was not easy to convoke a council in a period of warfare between France and the Empire and of threatening war within the Empire itself. Attempts to convoke a council at Mantua and Vicenza failed. Moreover, in the 1540s the Emperor decided to attempt to seek his own religious agreement in Germany by means of theological conversations. These failed because the theological rift proved to be too deep. Moreover, political considerations were involved, and neither side seems really to have believed in the sincerity of the other. To Catholics, Protestants were obstinate formal heretics and the despoilers of the goods of the Church; to Protestants, Catholics were the defenders of corrupt doctrine and of entrenched abuses and interests. The meager, unwilling, brief, and fruitless appearance of Protestants at Trent in 1552 manifested their view that the demands for a free council on German soil had not been met. By a "free" council the Protestants meant one free of papal control. This demand could not be granted. Trent, however, the city where most of the council was held, was in fact part of the Empire. While the popes never appeared personally at the council, they presided through legates over its sessions, during which, it should be noted, debate was free.

The Council of Trent. The Council of Trent met in three periods separated by suspensions under three different popes. The first period (1545–48), under Paul III, produced the Catholic reply to the most profound doctrinal problem that the Reformers had raised, the manner of man's justification, along with decrees on the canonical Scriptures, the Vulgate, and original sin. It had been decided to treat reform and doctrine *pari passu* as a compromise to satisfy the curialist party, who wished to treat only of doctrine, and the imperialist party (that is, those bishops subject to the emperor, whether German, Spanish, or Italian), who wished to treat only of reform. The latter feared to further alienate the Protestants. If the reform decrees at times were timid, it should be remembered that the papacy felt that the reform of the Curia was its prerogative. Moreover, what seemed to be abuses to some were viewed as legitimate exceptions to law by others. After treating the Sacraments in general, the council was transferred to Bologna by the legates in 1547, partly because of an outbreak of a contagious fever at Trent and partly because of the desire of the papacy to have the council more under its control. Some of the imperialist bishops protested and refused to follow. Though the council discussed future decrees on the Sacraments at Bologna, no promulgations were made before it was suspended in 1549.

JULIUS III (1550–55) reconvoked the Council of Trent for its second period (1551–52), during which decrees on the Sacraments were promulgated, including the Catholic doctrine on the manner of the Eucharistic presence. The outbreak of war in the Empire caused the suspension of the Council in 1552. After the 3-week reign of Pope Marcellus II (1555), the fiery, reform-minded PAUL IV (1555–59) succeeded to the papal throne. Wanting in moderation, jealous of papal power, and too ready to brand innocent men as heretics, he refused to summon the council back into session. After his fortunately brief reign, a pope favorable to reform through the council, PIUS IV (1559–64), was elected. Pius IV brought the last period of the council (1562–63) to a successful conclusion and confirmed its decrees. Through his extremely able legate, G. MORONE, the council was enabled to surmount its final and most dangerous crisis, which had been brought about by the tensions between the curialist and imperialist parties, to whom were added also in this last session the French. Doctrinally, the most important decisions of these sessions concerned the sacrificial character of the Mass. From the standpoint of discipline the greatest achievement was the creation of a system of schools (seminaries) for the moral, intellectual, and spiritual formation of diocesan priests.

The Council of Trent furnished in the doctrinal order a much needed clarification of the divine economy of salvation in its decrees on original sin, justification, the Sacraments, and the Mass. A positive body of doctrine was thus created that would not only answer Protestant denials but also set the tone for Catholic theology, spirituality, and even culture for the succeeding centuries. If certain lines were drawn concerning Catholic belief, nevertheless the possibility of future discussions of doctrine even on the above-mentioned topics was not ruled out. The failure of the council to mention any of the Protestant Reformers by name has been taken to indicate that it did not wish to rule out the possibility of future conversations. The disciplinary reforms were somewhat disjointed in form and incomplete, but still a model of the ideal pastor, both bishop and priest, was provided, which would be imitated gradually but with increasing effectiveness. The institution of seminaries was of the highest importance in the achievement of this end.

Catholic Reform. Not all reform in the Church, however, was due to Trent. A movement of self-reform reaching back into the Middle Ages had been growing steadily even before the Reformation and without reference to it. It was especially concentrated in Spain and Italy. In Spain its early leaders were the Archbishop of Granada, Fernando de Talavera y Mendoza (1428–1507), and the Cardinal-Archbishop of Toledo, Francisco XIMÉNEZ DE CISNEROS (1436–1517). In Italy, before and independently of the Reformation, groups of priests interested in self-reform and more zealous pastoral care had been arising here and there. Of this type was the Roman confraternity, the Oratory of DIVINE LOVE, which was founded some years before the outbreak of the Reformation and which became a seed-bed of future Catholic reformers. Some of these groups developed into new societies of clerics regular, such as the THEATINES (1524), founded by St. Cajetan of Tiene and others, including the future Paul IV; the BARNABITES, founded by St. Antonio Maria Zaccaria (1530); and finally the SOMASCAN FATHERS, founded by St. Jerome Emiliani (1540). The important educational order of nuns, the URSULINES, was founded by St. Angela Merici and approved by Paul III (1544). There were also a number of reforming bishops in Italy, of whom the most outstanding was Gian Matteo GIBERTI of Verona (1495–1543). The number of reforming bishops grew after Trent.

The Jesuits. While the JESUITS are often identified with the Counter Reformation, that is, the militant Catholicism of the post-Tridentine Church, their roots are fully in the earlier Catholic movement of self-reform. In fact, the spirituality and structure of the society were developed in complete independence of the struggle against Protestantism. Beginning as a group of pilgrims to the Holy Land gathered around Ignatius of Loyola as their leader, the first Jesuits had put themselves at the disposition of the pope. After the pilgrimage had proved impossible and they had come into contact with the new clerics regular in northern Italy, a religious society called the Company of Jesus was developed by Ignatius and approved by Paul III in 1540. The originality of the new group did not consist only in its distinctive IGNATIAN SPIRITUALITY, with its emphasis on a considered commitment to Christ, or in the mobility of the society, with its revolutionary dispensation from Divine Office in choir. It was both the paramilitary character with which its soldier-founder endowed the society and, above all, the very close link between the order and the papacy that were new. The Jesuits were to be the spiritual soldiers of the papacy, tied by bonds of unquestioning obedience to the pope. Since the members were bound to observe poverty and not to seek ecclesiastical preferment, the papacy had at its disposal an increasingly vast international body of selfless supporters. When they defended the papacy they could not be accused of furthering their own personal interests—an accusation that had been raised, not always unjustly, against the curialists and others. Thus, in an age when the papacy was both denied and discredited, the Jesuits were an example of unselfish devotion to the primacy of Peter.

While the Jesuits, whose growth was extraordinary, began as part of the movement of Catholic internal reform, and while their widespread missionary activities were of great importance, they came soon to be associated with the Counter Reformation. In Germany St. Peter CANISIUS (1521–97) through his diplomatic activity, his example and preaching, his catechisms, and above all through the foundation of colleges, aided immeasurably the revival of Catholicism there. In the face of the widespread decay of the universities, which until the second half of the 17th century did not flourish in Catholic countries as they had in medieval times (except briefly in Spain), the Jesuit school system was of great importance in maintaining to some degree the prestige of Catholic intellectual activity. But while the Jesuit colleges developed an estimable form of Christian humanism, though not without borrowing something from the similar tendencies of renaissance humanism and MELANCHTHON, their openness to new subjects of study was timid. The higher education given by the Jesuits was exclusively for those entering the priesthood. The Catholic universities, perhaps recoiling from the fact that the Reformation had been in some measure the creation of academicians, remained closed to subjects of secular interests and either died of atrophy or became ultimately the secular universities of the modern world. Within this period then, until the advent of the teaching brothers, a high quality of teaching was not to be found in the universities but rather in the colleges of the Jesuits, in the houses of study of religious orders, and especially in the seminaries in France, which were highly successful in elevating the standards of the clergy.

Reforms in Religious Orders. In addition to completely new religious orders, the Catholic reform brought about a number of revivals in the older orders, which occasionally led to the foundation of new branches of congregations. A strict new congregation of the CAMALDOLESE Benedictines was founded by Paolo Giustiani (1476–1528). The generals of the AUGUSTINIANS, GILES OF VITERBO and especially Girolamo SERIPANDO, were both reformers of their order. The FRANCISCANS, the target of much pre-Reformation and Reformation satire, were hampered in their attempts to reform by fears of yet another split in the order, which was already divided into two branches—the Conventuals and the Observants. In a fresh attempt to return to the spirit of St. Francis, a third branch, the Capuchins, came into existence and thrived, despite the handicaps of a founder, Matteo da BASCIO (*ca.* 1495–1552), who left his new foundation, and of a fourth vicar-general, Bernadino OCHINO (1497–1564), who became a Protestant. The Capuchins were officially separated from the Conventuals in 1619. Under the aegis of TERESA OF AVILA (1515–82) a new reformed branch of the CARMELITES, the Discalced, was formed both for women and for men [St. JOHN OF THE CROSS (1542–91)]. Gradually reforms were brought about in the other orders.

Reforming Popes. The papacy of the period immediately after Trent produced three strong figures, PIUS V, GREGORY XIII, and SIXTUS V, who all aided in accelerating the rate of the centralization of Church government. This trend was not new, but it received additional force from the critical situation in which the Church found itself. Pius V (1566–72), the first saintly pope of the modern era, reformed the college of cardinals, the Curia, and the religious orders, and was also the first pope belonging completely to the age of the Counter Reformation. Such anachronistic gestures as the attempted deposition of Elizabeth I of England, however, were ultimately harmful. The milder Gregory XIII (1572–85) furthered the Jesuits, the missions, education (especially priestly), and both the Catholic internal reform and the Counter Reformation. To him the Gregorian calendar is due, and also an increase in the number of permanent papal diplomatic missions. The most important reorganization of the Curia, however, took place under Sixtus V (1585–90). In 1588 the cardinals were organized into 15 congregations, some concerned with the government of the papal states, others with the government of the entire Church. The Congregation of the Roman and Universal Inquisition (renamed Congregation for the Doctrine of the Faith, 1965), which had originated in 1542 under Paul III as a commission of cardinals, achieved its final form at this time. New regulations for the AD LIMINA visits and reports of bishops, another step in the increasing centralization of the Church, were issued in this pontificate. Sixtus also effected a number of reforms in the papal states and may be called the father of Rome as a baroque city.

Papal Decline. The lesser figures who occupied the papal throne until the middle of the 17th century were characterized by their interest in the beautification of Rome and in the government of the papal states. Nepotism on the part of the popes themselves was not absent, nor were curial abuses. The longer reigns were those of CLEMENT VIII (1592–1605), PAUL V (1605–21), URBAN VIII (1623–44), and INNOCENT X (1644–55). Just as the last major papal attempt to declare a monarch deposed had been unsuccessfully made under Pius V, so also under Paul V a last and equally ineffective attempt was made to place an entire state, Venice, under interdict. Further grave Church-state conflicts were soon to come, but even before them the political weakness of the papacy became more evident. Thus, Innocent X's protest against the religious provisions of the Peace of WESTPHALIA went unheard.

Outside the papal states in this period, the rest of Italy was also generally in political and economic decline, with part of the country under Spanish rule (Naples, Sicily, Milan, and Sardinia). Ecclesiastically, however, the decrees of Trent were accepted in the various states, and reforms were carried out both within the religious orders and by reforming bishops. One of the most striking of these last was Charles BORROMEO (1538–84), the reformer of the See of Milan. A nephew of Pius IV, he was one of the rare examples of a happy outcome of nepotism.

The Wars of Religion. If Italy remained in relative peace during the last half of the 16th and the first half of the 17th centuries, much of the rest of Europe was involved in the wars often called (somewhat incorrectly) the Wars of Religion, including those in France, the revolt of the Spanish Netherlands, and the Thirty Years' War.

France. In France the wars of religion (1562–98) were really a series of eight small wars divided by truces and periods of peace. The principal and original cause was the struggle for and against Calvinism, but such motives as the dynastic question, the struggle between feudal conceptions of the monarchy and an absolutist, centralizing view, and foreign intervention come to play important roles also. With the acceptance of Catholicism by HENRY IV, the issuance of the Edict of NANTES (1598) specifying the conditions for the coexistence in France of Protestant communities and Catholicism, and the peace with Spain (Vervins 1598), order was reestablished in France. The effect of the wars, however, was to put off the necessary internal Catholic reform. While the French government refused to accept officially the decrees of Trent, the doctrinal decrees were accepted by all without question. Despite the high degree of control over the Church that the Concordat of 1516 gave the French monarchy, many reforms were effected, especially through the influence of such saintly men as FRANCIS DE SALES (1567–1622), Pierre de BÉRULLE (1575–1629), Charles de CONDREN (1588–1641), Jean Jacques OLIER (1608–1), John EUDES (1601–80), and VINCENT DE PAUL (1581–1660). All of these fostered the moral, spiritual, and intellectual training of priests, especially through the new system of seminaries.

Revolt of the Spanish Netherlands. The revolt of the Spanish Netherlands is sometimes classed as a religious war between the Dutch, who were principally Calvinists, and Catholic Spain. The desire of the Dutch, however, to shake off the political and economic domination of a foreign power was equally important. In Spain itself the excessive control of the Church by the state in a period when the monarchy was entering a time of continual degeneration could scarcely encourage the religious revival that had begun with Ximenes. Spanish missionary activity, on the other hand, continued to flourish.

The Thirty Years' War. The third great religious war, the Thirty Years' War (1618–48), was fought principally on the territory of the Empire. While religious causes, especially the law that forbade the secularizing of ecclesiastical property, were not absent, political causes were or became the major factors. At the end of the war Catholic France was fighting with Lutheran Sweden against the Catholic Emperor. The Peace of Westphalia, so unsatisfactory to the papacy, marked the end of the Counter Reformation considered as an attempt to regain territories lost to Protestantism. It also marked the end of any large shifts of allegiance from one religious body to the other. When, somewhat later, the Electors of Saxony wished to be elected also kings of Poland, they became Catholic, but their Saxon subjects remained Lutheran, and their Polish subjects remained Catholic.

Catholicism in the British Isles. In the British Isles the dwindling persecuted Catholic minority suffered not only because they refused to accept Anglicanism but also because they were accused of political disloyalty. Their lot was aggravated by the fact that England's chief foreign enemy was Catholic Spain. After the death of Elizabeth, under Mary Stuart's son JAMES I (1603–25), who had been raised a Protestant, the situation of Catholics did not improve, but their treatment under Charles I (1625–49) was slightly milder. The Civil War, however, brought in the Protector, Oliver CROMWELL, a much more determined opponent of Catholicism than the Tudor or Stuart monarchs. Catholics in Scotland, which was united to England in personal union from 1603, fared no better, but a small number survived as in England. In Ireland, completely under English rule from 1602, despite persecution under extremely severe penal laws, and apart from the plantations, almost the entire population remained faithful to Catholicism.

Catholicism in Eastern Europe. In Eastern Europe the Catholic reform was introduced gradually. The religious situation of Poland mirrored the confused political order, but under the aegis of Cardinal Stanislas HOSIUS (1504–79) and the Jesuits, a strong Catholic revival took place toward the end of the 16th and the beginning of the 17th century. An important reunion of Eastern Christians, the Ruthenians, was effected by the Union of BREST (1595–96) and also by the Union of Užhorod (1646). In Hungary the Catholic reform and Counter Reformation were fostered especially by Cardinal Peter PÁZMÁNY (1570–1637).

Missionary Activity. The enthusiastic missionary activity of the 16th and 17th centuries was paralleled only by the preaching of the gospel in the first centuries. The impetus to this revived activity came from the explorations and discoveries that had begun in the 15th century. Of the newly discovered lands, or the hitherto scarcely known lands, including North and South America, the East and Far East, only Africa remained largely untouched by the missionaries, whose activities Rome began to coordinate (from 1622) under the Congregation for the PROPAGATION OF THE FAITH. An essential difference between the evangelization of the Western and the Eastern worlds was the fact that in North and South America, the missionaries, mostly members of the new and old religious orders, accompanied Spanish and Portuguese conquerors and colonists, whereas in the East the missionaries, also chiefly from the religious orders, sought to evangelize old established civilizations. This occasioned two quite different methods. In the New World, the old existing civilizations were destroyed, and in most of South and Central America an Iberian cultural and ecclesiastical order was established. Thus the first see, Santo Domingo, was established in 1511, and by 1582 there were 15 more. The missionaries fought with varying degrees of success to prevent the exploitation of the natives by their own countrymen. In Paraguay, the Jesuits organized model communities (REDUCTIONS) of native Christians. Eventually governmental opposition and an excessive paternalism caused these experiments to fail. The greatest single weakness of the Spanish and Portuguese missionary effort in Central and South America was the failure to foresee early the need for a native clergy. Consequently, in the 18th century there was a dearth of clergy and a decline of missionary zeal, although evangelization did not cease completely (e.g., California).

In the East and the Far East, the missionaries faced different problems. There, after the early heroic exploits of St. Francis XAVIER in India, China, and Japan, a number of missionaries, especially Matteo RICCI, J. Adam SCHALL, and Roberto de NOBILI, began to propose the adaptation of Christianity to certain of the cultural and intellectual features of the centuries-old civilizations of China and India. Other missionaries violently opposed such accommodations, and the problem was referred to Rome (*see* CHINESE RITES CONTROVERSY). For nearly a century it was debated until the last disapproval of adaptation was given by Rome in 1742. Interorder rivalries and national interests had envenomed the quarrels. Along with the already-noted decline of missionary fervor in the 18th century, the outcome of the rites controversy marked the virtual end of missionary activity in the East until the 19th century. The Philippines, a Spanish possession, however, presented an exception. The attempt to Christianize Japan had failed even before the rites controversy. There violent persecutions (1614–46) almost completely destroyed the missionaries' efforts, although small secret groups of Christians (Old Christians) continued on without priests. A final and lamentable result of the rites controversy was that it, along with the other grave theological dissensions, helped to discredit Christianity among the intellectual classes during the late 17th and the 18th century.

THE EUROPEAN CHURCH, 1648–1789

The history of the Church in the century and a half before the French Revolution is dominated by a series of dissensions on doctrinal matters within the Church, above all the quarrels over JANSENISM, QUIETISM, and FEBRONIANISM, and of dissensions between the papacy and the Catholic states, principally over GALLICANISM, JOSEPHINISM, and the suppression of the Jesuits. These quarrels contributed to the profoundly weakened state and seeming apathy of the Church at the end of the *ancien régime,* with whose fate its own seemed inexorably bound. It was not until the 19th and 20th centuries that the Church recovered its vigor both in thought and action.

Theology and Theological Quarrels. The trends and schools of theology from the 16th century on become exceedingly diverse. Whereas the medieval theologians had in the main been universal theologians, treating in their works of the whole of theology, later theologians became specialists in such recognized branches of theology as dogmatic or speculative, moral, ascetic, or positive. Although the traditional purely speculative method still was carried on by schoolmen such as BÁÑEZ, JOHN OF ST. THOMAS, and SUÁREZ, their efforts represented the work of theologians living to some degree in the past. The important new dimension in theology was the historical or positive theology, which derived from the methods of the humanists, such as ERASMUS. While an effort was made to integrate positive and speculative theology (e.g., Melchior CANO), theology became quite fragmentized, and no theologian of the status of the great patristic and medieval theologians emerged to produce a new synthesis. The interest in historical theology had results important for the growth of the historical sciences both ecclesiastical and secular. In this regard, the work of the BOLLAND-ISTS in hagiography and of the Benedictines of the Congregation of St. Maur are especially notable (*see* MAURISTS). In Biblical criticism, however, the work of Richard Simon, who was well ahead of his time, was condemned. Similarly, the condemnation of Galileo GALILEI implied a conflict between Christianity and science and had unfortunate consequences. The quarrel with Protestantism often brought forth only a defensive and negative theology; worse yet, internal theological quarrels exhausted the energies of the best theologians. These same quarrels were in no little part also responsible for the growth of disbelief and indifference to religion, which, in turn, presented new problems to the Church.

Jansenism. The gravest of these quarrels centered around the Augustinian doctrine of nature and grace and its practical applications. A theologian of Louvain, Cornelius JANSEN (1585–1638), and a French ecclesiastic, Jean DUVERGIER DE HAURANNE (1581–1643), dreamed of a revival of patristic theology and practice beginning with the doctrine of grace. For them scholasticism and the humanistic theology of some Jesuit theologians were abhorrent, and Calvin had, in their view, grasped Augustine's teaching even if he expressed himself badly. Thus, Jansenism was in a sense a crypto-Calvinism. The Jansenists, however, never wished to leave the Church, but rather hoped to have their doctrine accepted by the Church or at least tolerated by it. This explains, in part, the persistence of Jansenism even into the 19th century. Jansen produced his great theoretical work of doctrine in the *Augustinus* (1640), published two years after his death.

Meanwhile, Duvergier de Hauranne, now abbot of Saint-Cyran, had spread enthusiasm for their views in France, especially into the large ARNAULD family, many of whom were or became religious and whose activities were centered around the Cistercian convents of Port-Royal-des-Champs near Paris and PORT-ROYAL in Paris. Schools established by the Jansenists (*petites écoles*) fostered Jansenist doctrine, as well as new methods of pedagogy. Jansenism was almost immediately condemned by Rome, but the Jansenists, led by Antoine Arnauld (1612–94), refused to accept the condemnation as valid for what Jansen had actually taught and for what they actually held. An endless quarrel ensued about the right of the Church to judge and condemn error in a concrete case. The Jansenists admitted only a *de iure* right and denied

that the condemned doctrine was *de facto* in Jansen's writings. A new leader, Pasquier QUESNEL (1634–1719), emerged toward the end of the 17th century. Repeated condemnations and harassments failed to drive Jansenism from the French Church, where it continued clandestinely until the 19th century. French Jansenism had always been more interested in the moral rigorism that seemed to follow from Jansen's thought rather than his doctrinal elaboration, and toward the end of its history Jansenism was more a symbol of protest against ecclesiastical and political authority than a theological doctrine. A still-existing schismatic church was founded as the result of the Jansenist quarrel at Utrecht in 1723 (*see* UTRECHT, SCHISM OF).

Quietism. The quarrel over Quietism was smaller and less grave than the Jansenist quarrel. The father of Quietism was a Spaniard resident in Italy, Miguel de MOLINOS (1628–1717), although his thought was not entirely original. Molinos's *Spiritual Guide* (1675), translated into five languages, proposed a doctrine of total passivity in the face of divine action in the soul. Molinos was condemned and imprisoned, but similar ideas on the spiritual life were put forth by an unstable French woman, Mme. J. M. GUYON. It was FÉNELON (later archbishop of Cambrai), however, who, having become Mme. Guyon's confessor, became the chief spokesman for Quietism in France. The touchstone of Quietism was the belief that the soul might reach such a state of pure love that not only would it be indifferent to its own perfections and the practices of virtue, but it might even cease to will its own salvation. This doctrine of the exclusive action of God on the soul has affinities with Luther's teaching, but Luther never drew the Quietist conclusions. Fénelon's doctrine, attacked by BOSSUET, was condemned by Rome in 1699. Although Fénelon submitted, he denied that he had preached the condemned teaching. Unlike Jansenism, Quietism died out immediately and completely. Both Jansenism and Quietism, however, indirectly encouraged the growth of disbelief by the public spectacles that had been made of doctrinal differences within the Church. As a result, even within the Church a certain mistrust of mystical tendencies became evident.

Febronianism. The dissatisfaction of some German ecclesiastics with papal centralization manifested itself in several ways in the 18th century. The most important of these was the work of an auxiliary bishop of Trèves, Johann Nikolaus von HONTHEIM (1701–90). His work, published beginning in 1763 under the pseudonym of Febronius and often called simply the *Febronius,* foresaw a revival of conciliarism in an extreme form in which the papacy would be stripped of the powers that Hontheim claimed it had usurped. The *Febronius* was soon translated from Latin into other languages and achieved considerable popularity. It was condemned, and Hontheim retracted, but in a quite ambiguous manner. The work gave expression to the desire on the part of certain churchmen to be free from papal and curial control. In this it was not far removed from Gallicanism, which was, however, a political attempt to be free of these same controls.

Church-State Quarrels. This period witnessed a number of disagreements between the papacy and various Catholic states.

Gallicanism. The term Gallicanism is used to cover a number of theories of ecclesiatical government, all generally in various degrees hostile to or suspicious of Rome. All of these were present in France in the 17th century— from the purely ecclesiastical theories of authority vested in all the faithful or the clergy as a whole or the entire episcopate to political Gallicanism. The latter doctrine in its extreme form made the monarch in effect head of the Church in his country. In France it was the attempt by LOUIS XIV to extend his powers over the Church, which led in the 1680s almost to schism. Louis, since about 1670, had been attempting to increase his already extensive regalian rights, both temporal and spiritual. Meeting some opposition, he inspired the calling of an extraordinary meeting of the general assembly of the clergy. While Bossuet's opening address on the unity of the Church was credited with avoiding a break with Rome, it was he who drew up the summary of Gallican doctrine called the Four Articles of 1682. Royal edict forced the acceptance of these on the French Church. For about 15 years the papacy refused to institute Louis's appointments to the French dioceses until a large number became vacant. Finally, concessions were made on both sides, but the monarchy gave up the prescribed acceptance of the Gallican Articles. Gallicanism, while partially defeated, did not, however, die out. The state church of the Revolution was the last attempt in France to give it concrete form.

Josephinism. Not unlike the policies of Louis XIV were those of the Hapsburg Emperor JOSEPH II (1765–90) in his Austrian domains. Even his pious mother, MARIA THERESA, had, in fact, involved herself in strictly ecclesiastical matters. Moreover, due reforms were not effected by the ecclesiastical authorities themselves. In a certain sense, however, Joseph went further than Louis by attempting to make the Church a department of the state and above all by interfering in what were beyond question strictly ecclesiastical affairs, such as the curricula of seminaries, and even the liturgy. His attitude toward the Church was more than a little influenced by the ENLIGHTENMENT and enlightened despotism. An attempt by Pius VI in 1782 by a personal visit to Vienna to change the Emperor's views did not succeed. Joseph's brother Leo-

pold, his successor briefly as emperor, attempted similar reforms in the Grand Duchy of Tuscany. The Jansenist Bishop S. RICCI of Pistoia and Prato aided him, and a synod at Pistoia in 1786 drew up a list of reforms partly Jansenist, partly enlightened. The other Tuscan bishops refused, however, to follow Ricci.

While the failure to effect reforms was in part responsible for the lethargic situation of the Church in the Catholic countries in the 18th century, the method of reform proposed by the enlightened despots would have disastrously compromised the independence of the Church. The Constitutional Church of the French Revolution disintegrated when power was assumed by nonbelievers.

Suppression of the Jesuits. The most unhappy Church-state quarrel of the 18th century was the suppression of the Jesuits. Opposition to the Jesuits had arisen from many quarters—from the Jansenists, the Gallicans, and the thinkers and rulers of the Enlightenment. The Jesuits were accused, in most cases unjustly, of having acquired excessive power and wealth. They were, moreover, the religious society with the greatest loyalty to the papacy. They were suppressed by Portugal in 1759, France in 1764, and Spain in 1767, but the Catholic powers were not content until they obtained a complete suppression from Rome. This they succeeded in getting from CLEMENT XIV in 1773. Only in Russia did the society survive until its restoration in 1814.

The Papacy, 1648–1789. The political prestige of the papacy continued to decline in the period from 1648 to 1789. No longer were the popes arbiters in international disputes. Generally, in fact, they were excluded from the major international conferences. They failed also to supply the necessary leadership or to effect reforms in their own states. In the religious domain, on the other hand, they successfully resisted Jansenism and Quietism and restrained Gallicanism and Febronianism. In dealing with the enlightened despots and their followers, especially in the matter of the Jesuits, however, they failed. The most notable papal figures during this period were INNOCENT XI (1676–89), BENEDICT XIV (1740–58), and Pius VI (1775–99), who died a prisoner of the French.

Catholicism in Non-Catholic Lands. Generally speaking, the position of Catholics in Protestant lands improved somewhat during the 18th century. This was in part due to the Enlightenment with its ideal of tolerance. In the United Provinces, the existence of Catholics was tolerable although complicated by the Jansenist Church of Utrecht. In Scandinavia there were scarcely any Catholics except for a few, mostly foreigners, in Sweden. In Great Britain there was gradual progress toward greater toleration, but Catholics remained very few in number and still were not emancipated. Ireland also was beginning to progress toward emancipation (Relief Bill of 1778).

The Church Under the Old Regime. A brief survey of the situation of the Church in France on the eve of the Revolution offers a view of the virtues and failings of the Church in the Catholic lands. The struggle between Church and state had sunk from the level of the monarchy to quarrels between the Jansenist lawyers of the *Parlements* and the Church. The episcopacy, while not composed of unworthy men, was often nonresident and almost entirely drawn from the nobility. Most of the bishops were to leave France en masse when the Revolution threatened. The lower clergy, well-educated and often devoted, nevertheless resented their inability to rise in the ecclesiastical hierarchy. The monasteries had vast possessions but had experienced a sharp drop in vocations, and some were almost empty. The abuses of COMMENDATION had continued. Among the laity, the educated classes were imbued with the spirit of the Enlightenment, and some had ceased to believe; the working classes, mostly still agrarian, remained for the most part attached to Catholicism.

Bibliography: K. SCHOTTENLOHER *Bibliographie zur deutschen Geschichte im Zeitalter der Glaubensspaltung, 1517–85* (Leipzig 1933–40; repr. Stuttgart 1956–58). H. JEDIN, *Handbuch der Kirchengeschichte* (Freiburg 1962–); Eng. tr. *Handbook of Church History,* ed. H. JEDIN and J. DOLAN (New York 1965) v.4, bibliog. H. JEDIN, *History of the Council of Trent,* tr. E. GRAF (St. Louis 1957–60). *New Cambridge Modern History* (2d ed. London-New York 1957) v.2, 5, 7. A. FLICHE and V. MARTIN, eds., *Histoire de l'église depuis les origines jusqu'à nos jours* (Paris 1935) v.16–19, bibliog. L. PASTOR, *The History of the Popes from the Close of the Middle Ages* (London-St. Louis 1938–61). J. LORTZ, *Die Reformation in Deutschland,* 2 v. (4th ed. Freiburg 1962). P. HUGHES, *The Reformation in England* (5th ed. New York 1963). J. T. MCNEILL, *The History and Character of Calvinism* (New York 1954). A. MARTIMORT, *Le Gallicanisme de Bossuet* (Paris 1953). J. ORCIBAL, *Les Origines du jansénisme,* 5 v. (Louvain 1947–62). G. SCHNÜRER, *Katholische Kirche und Kultur im Zeitalter des Barock* (Paderborn 1937); *Katholische Kirche und Kultur im 18. Jahrhundert* (Paderborn 1941). F. MAASS, ed., *Der Josephinismus: Quellen zu seiner Geschichte in Österreich, 1760–1850,* 5 v. (Fontes rerum Austriacarum II.71–75; Vienna 1951–61). K. BIHLMEYER and H. TÜCHLE, *Kirchengeschichte* (17th ed. Paderborn 1962); Eng tr. by V. MILLS, *Church History* (Westminster MD 1958), bibliog. K. S. LATOURETTE, *A History of the Expansion of Christianity* (New York 1937–45) v.3. H. TÜCHLE, *Reformation und Gegenreformation (Geschichte der Kirche* 3; Einsiedeln 1965). O. CHADWICK, *The Reformation* (The Pelican History of the Church 3; Baltimore 1964). G. R. CRAGG, *The Church and the Age of Reason: 1648–1789 (ibid.* 4; New York 1961). S. NEILL, *History of Christian Missions (ibid.* 6; 1964).

[W. S. BARRON]

CHURCH, HISTORY OF, IV (LATE MODERN: 1789–2002)

The centuries from the Age of Revolutions (the French and Industrial Revolutions at the end of the 18th century) to the opening of the third millennium ushered in profound economic, social, and political changes. Although the effect of these developments has been uneven, with the passage of time almost every corner of the world has felt their impact. The widespread technological innovations flowing from the scientific revolution, giving rise to urbanization and secularization, influenced religion in general and the Roman Catholic Church in particular.

The Church has found some external changes beneficial, others harmful. Western civilization, increasingly secularized in its ideals and practices, has continued to drift away from the Church that was largely instrumental in creating it and to which it had been intimately united for centuries. The problem of adjusting to the radically new conditions of civilization remains critical. Throughout this entire period persecutions have persisted, never more violent and destructive than in the 20th century. Despite this, indeed partly because of it, the Church has become a more spiritual and more closely knit organization, under the primacy of the popes. In civil society nationalism swelled to ominous proportions; it has been extolled as a kind of religion, but its fruits have often been hatred and bloodshed. Ecclesiastical particularism, on the other hand, shrank to minimal proportions with the disappearance of GALLICANISM, FEBRONIANISM, and JOSEPHINISM, which in the 18th century had been the bane of the universal Church. Inner threats to unity in the form of heresies and schisms were few and gained few adherents. Religious indifferentism within the fold and leakage of individuals from it have, however, been sources of great concern. Counterbalancing these losses there have been great numerical gains as the Church spread worldwide as the result of large-scale emigration from Catholic Europe and of unparalleled missionary activity.

The more important developments and the most characteristic trends are outlined here. (For the ecclesiastical history of individual nations, see the articles on each country of the world.)

From 1789 to 1815. France has for centuries played a significant role in the Church's life, but never before or since has it monopolized the stage to the extent it did between the outbreak of the FRENCH REVOLUTION and the downfall of NAPOLEON I. As a political and social upheaval, the Revolution was of major importance in world history; from the religious viewpoint it was scarcely of less moment for the Church, both in France and elsewhere. Fittingly, therefore, this event is selected as inau-

Congress of Vienna, held after the Napoleonic Wars in 1814 to decide the reconstruction of Europe, painting by Johann Baptist Isabey. (©Bettmann/CORBIS)

gurating a turning point in the Church's history. After abolishing clerical privileges, nationalizing Church properties, and suppressing religious orders, the Constitutional Assembly enacted the CIVIL CONSTITUTION OF THE CLERGY, which created a schism and split France religiously into two hostile camps. As time went on, leadership in the revolution fell into the hands of men bitterly hostile to the Church, more intent on destroying than reforming it. An attempt was made to dechristianize the country by violent persecution, wholesale iconoclasm, reorganization of the calendar, imprisonment and deportation of the clergy, separation of Church and state, and propagation of a series of naturalistic, patriotic cults as substitutes for Christianity. As their crowning attack on religion, the revolutionists stripped Pope Pius VI of his temporal power, seized him, and marched him captive to southern France, where he died a prisoner.

Victorious revolutionary armies swept into the Low Countries, Germany, Switzerland, and Italy, where they imposed the French innovations. Throughout the 19th century the aspirations of the revolution kept spreading through Europe and the New World. The French Revolution afforded, then, a preview of what was in store for the Church. Reconciliation with the principles of 1789 posed for the Church a major problem that was not solved completely a century later. Even this span of years did not suffice to close the rift in French society opened during the revolutionary decade. The heirs of the great revolution were the republicans, liberals, and anticlericals of the 19th century. Loyal Catholics tended to link democracy with godlessness; in good part their politics were conservative and monarchist. They resisted the RALLIEMENT and formed the backbone of ACTION FRANÇAISE.

When Napoleon Bonaparte gained control of revolutionary France, he turned it into a military dictatorship and an instrument of his boundless ambitions. After his military genius had subjected most of western Europe, he introduced into the conquered territories the ideology of the revolution, whose devotee he claimed to be. Napoleon, a man of little or no Christian faith, utilized religion to promote his state policies. Since political considerations counseled the restoration of religious peace in France, he concluded with the Holy See the CONCORDAT OF 1801, which regulated Church-state relations for a century, and which served as a model for numerous other concordats during the 19th century. Many of the benefits accorded to the Church by the Concordat of 1801 were withdrawn as soon as they were given, by Bonaparte's unilateral action in publishing the Organic Articles. In Italy Napoleon arranged a concordat on similar terms. He was mainly responsible for the vast secularization of ecclesiastical territories in Germany. Had Napoleon attained his goals, Paris would have replaced Rome as the center of the Church and the pope would have become his chaplain. When the First Consul decided to become emperor, he humiliated Pius VII by inviting him to Paris to attend the coronation ceremony in Notre Dame as simply a spectator who had to watch the emperor crown himself. In retaliation for the Holy See's refusal to ally with France and to join the Continental Blockade, the Emperor seized the STATES OF THE CHURCH and held Pius VII captive (1809–14) until military reversals sent Bonaparte to exile in Elba.

Ecclesiastical Restoration. Following the Battle of Waterloo came a period of restoration for the Church, as well as for European governments. At the Congress of Vienna, attended by Cardinal CONSALVI, the papal secretary of state, the victorious powers undertook to revive, as far as possible, the *ancien régime*. In their endeavor to stabilize conservative monarchical governments in power, they disposed of thrones and territories on the principle of legitimacy. Political considerations predominated; but the Church, particularly the papacy, became a major beneficiary. The statesmen at Vienna were well aware that the absolutist rulers who had weakened the Church in the 17th and 18th centuries had unwittingly undermined their own thrones in the process, as events after 1789 demonstrated. The conclusion was that throne and altar are best united. A much more benign attitude toward religion came into vogue. As a result, the allied powers that had watched unmoved when Pius VII was deprived of his temporal power and detained as a prisoner decreed the return of most of the States of the Church. Not all the decisions at Vienna were of this tenor, to be sure. Catholic Belgium was united with Holland and subjected to the Protestant House of Orange. Most of Poland passed to Russia. German lay rulers, generally Protestants, were allowed to retain their recently acquired ecclesiastical principalities.

In this changed atmosphere, Pius VII restored the JESUITS throughout the world in 1814, soon after his release from Fontainebleau; he was able to take this step without objection from the royal courts that had exerted strong pressure on Clement XIV to suppress the Jesuits in 1773. The situation allowed the badly disrupted Church to reorganize itself in Europe and in the mission fields. It was very significant that the papacy, the authority of which had been much weakened since the mid-17th century, took the lead in this process. From this point date the upswing in papal spiritual power, the pronounced trend toward centralization of ecclesiastical administrative power in Rome, and the unquestioned exercise of papal primacy of jurisdiction throughout the Church; these were among the most significant developments of the century. The CONCORDATS and other agreements that were concluded by the Holy See were an important part of this reorganization.

Not surprisingly, the Church regarded the Restoration regime with favor, just as it had looked askance at the French Revolution and what it represented. The alliance of throne and altar had serious disadvantages that became more apparent in succeeding decades. After 1815 the Church was identified in many minds with the reactionary Restoration; the reorganization of the States of the Church along the lines of the *ancien régime* did nothing to dispel this notion. Metternich, the leading exponent of the political Restoration, hoped that this edifice would be an enduring one; yet revolutionary outbreaks in Latin America in the 1820s and in Europe in 1830 soon weakened its foundation. It could not withstand the explosions of nationalistic and constitutional furies of 1848, promoted by the liberals, to whom belonged the future.

Church and Liberalism. LIBERALISM and its manifold relations with the Church provided main themes for 19th-century ecclesiastical history. Liberalism is a broad but vague term that defies precise definition; its connotations varied in different countries and in different decades. In general the liberal outlook favored a minimum of restrictions on individual liberty in private and public life and defended a maximum of freedom for the individual in his social, economic, and religious existence and in his relations to the state. This viewpoint was rooted in rationalism; it was based, therefore, on an ideology sharply at variance with the Catholic one. The liberals upheld the ideals of the French Revolution and abhorred those of the Restoration. The trend in the 19th century was toward constitutional regimes, popular sovereignty, broadening of the suffrage, complete religious liberty, equality for all citizens, abolition of established churches and of clerical privileges, separation of Church and State, and assumption by the government of functions formerly exercised by the Church. Thus the civil power came to claim control over marriage, charitable endeavors, public welfare, and education. The tendency was to view the Church as a society within the state, part of it and subject to it like other societies, inferior to the state even in the religious sphere. This trend found its strongest supporters among the liberals, who looked upon the Church's conservatism as a major obstacle to their victory. Religious and philosophical propositions fundamental to doctrinaire liberalism attracted the ire of the Church in the *Mirari Vos,* SYLLABUS OF ERRORS, *QUANTA CURA,* and other notable papal pronouncements (*see* CHURCH AND STATE).

A group of Catholic liberals (or democratic Catholics), particularly in France, quickly foresaw the perils to the Church in aligning itself with forces destined for proximate oblivion. Hugues Félicité de LAMENNAIS was the pioneer in seeking an accommodation with the new order developing out of the French Revolution. His program advocated freedom of education, of association, and of the press. Still more revolutionary to the Church of his day was his advocacy of complete religious liberty and complete separation of Church and state. Among his principal disciples, Lamennais counted GERBET, Gousset, GUÉRANGER, LACORDAIRE, MONTALEMBERT, and ROHRBACHER. In some respects Lamennais was a man of prophetic vision. Unfortunately he advanced his proposals in exaggerated fashion and mixed them with a good deal of unsound theology. The conservative GREGORY XVI solemnly condemned them in *Mirari vos* (1832) and *Singulari nos* (1834). In France the hierarchy and the majority of the laity sided with the pope, and the cause of liberal Catholicism accordingly suffered a serious but not universal setback. Thus, in Belgium, Catholics joined forces with liberals to win independence in 1830 and to draft a liberal constitution. Daniel O'CONNELL, who led the successful struggle in Great Britain for Catholic EMANCIPATION (1829), and who then started an unsuccessful drive to repeal Ireland's legislative union with England, represented a decidedly liberal outlook.

Liberals, drawing their strength mainly from the middle class, came to control several countries, particularly from mid-19th century to World War I. In Spain, Portugal, Italy, France, and Latin America their rule was hostile to the Church and characterized by ANTICLERICALISM, sometimes of the most extreme type. In Germany, Austria, and Switzerland they supported the KULTURKAMPF.

Political Organization of Catholics. A striking modern innovation was been the organization of Catholics for political purposes. The Catholic Association, started in Ireland by Daniel O'Connell to win emancipation, was a pioneer. With the growth of representative government and of political parties, along with the need for Catholics to band together to further their rights, Catholic political parties were formed in several western European countries, notably in Belgium, the Netherlands, France, Germany, Austria, Switzerland, and Italy. These groups were not always professedly confessional; this was true of the best known of them, the Center party in Germany, which was succeeded after World Was II by the Christian Democratic party. Christian Democracy became more prominent after 1918. In France after 1945 the Mouvement Républicaine Populaire became important.

Political Developments after 1918. Following World War I, a series of national and international political upheavals confronted the Church with new and delicate problems of the first magnitude to replace the ones associated with liberalism. Exaggerated nationalism was a major factor in the outbreak of two world conflicts a quarter of a century apart, separated by a great economic crisis, and followed by the division of the globe into two violently hostile ideological groups with an ''iron curtain'' between them and by the increasing importance and independence of non-Western peoples in Africa and Asia. Western Europe became less prominent in the Church, although the gradient of this descent by no means paralleled the steepness of the political, economic, and intellectual declines. Particularly significant was the rise of fascism in Italy under Benito Mussolini. This dictatorial regime laid to rest the ROMAN QUESTION; yet it kept relations with the Holy See in a state of uneasy tension for two decades. National Socialism, under Adolf Hitler, was much more hostile to religion ideologically and subjected the Church in Germany to severe persecution. More important for the Church in the long run was the rise of socialism and communism.

Socialism and Communism. The spread of the industrial revolution, along with the shortcomings of prevailing liberalism, impelled the formulation of plans to reorganize society that were far more radical and sweeping than those propounded by the French Revolution. Progress in preventing and controlling diseases resulted in rapid population increases. Technological innovations sped the multiplication of factories, one of the effects of which was urbanization. To the industrial centers came masses of poorly educated persons who settled in squalid slums. There the labor of men, women, and children was ruthlessly exploited by a greedy middle class, indifferent to the welfare of their employees and intent on accumulating for themselves maximum profits under a capitalistic system that favored fierce, open competition, minimal state control of individualism, and slight governmental efforts at social legislation. The disparity in wealth and political power between the minority who owned the means of production and the proletarian majority of wage earners was glaring and became ever more irritating. Socialism arose as a solution to the evils connected with private property. In general the Socialists aimed to improve society on the basis of public ownership of the means of production, but they differed widely among themselves in principles and, still more, in the application of them. In addition to contriving theories, Socialists became active in politics and in the labor movement. Socialist political parties rose to prominence in several European countries in the second half of the 19th century and continued to be important thereafter.

Some Socialists were Christians, but very many of them ignored Christianity or attacked it. Neither Claude Henri de SAINT-SIMON (1760–1825), the father of French socialism, nor his leading disciples considered themselves Christians. Pierre Proudhon (1809–65) assailed all religions, and Mikhail Bakunin (1814–76) preached atheism. Communism evolved out of the theories of Karl MARX (1818–83) and Friedrich ENGELS (1820–95), as a completely materialistic and militantly atheistic system. Pius IX, Leo XIII, and succeeding popes condemned the basic errors in socialism and communism. In return, both of these groups regarded the Church as their most stalwart foe and entered into bitter struggle against it. For huge numbers in the working class, socialism served as a substitute for Christianity or as a religion in itself; it caused large-scale defections from Catholicism and, even more, from Protestantism. After World War I, Communists established themselves in the Union of Soviet Socialist Republics. Subsequent to World War II, they came to rule several countries in Eastern Europe as well as China. Persecution of all religion, particularly of the Catholic religion, was the usual aftermath of these victories.

Social Catholicism. Catholics recognized the implications of the French Revolution much more quickly than they did those of the industrial revolution. They became actively concerned about the political and religious aspects of liberalism long before they became fully aware of the novelty, magnitude, and complexity of the problems treated by economic liberalism. Socialism thereby gained a considerable headstart on Catholicism in attempting to solve the social question. After its beginnings in predominantly Protestant Great Britain late in the 18th century, the industrial revolution spread to the Continent, reaching different countries in different decades. The material distress and moral abandonment of the industrial proletariat became known quickly and roused sympathy and the desire to alleviate them. Poverty was a problem older than Christianity. It was widely believed that the traditional method of private charity, applied on an enlarged scale, was the proper and sufficient solution. Only gradually did it become clear that SOCIAL JUSTICE as well as charity was involved and that structural changes in the social order were required. Eventually a program in conformity with Catholic teachings was framed and put into practice. By that time, unfortunately, the industrialized proletariat of western Europe had become in great part alienated from the Church. The dechristianization of this group was branded by Pius IX as "the great scandal of the 19th century." The result was that an entire generation or more passed its life out of contact with the Church. Valiant efforts were made later to regain them, but even the heroic sacrifices of the WORKER PRIESTS met with partial success at best.

Catholics did not meet the problem simultaneously everywhere, nor were their responses the same in all lands. German Catholics were among the first to resolve the question, although the industrial revolution penetrated Germany after reaching France and Belgium. Adolf KOLPING and Bishop Wilhelm von KETTELER acted as pioneers around mid-century, and the Center party was an early advocate of enlightened social legislation. As a result, German Catholics did not desert the Church en masse as did Protestant industrial workers, who flocked to the Social Democratic party and adopted its socialist, irreligious ideas. French Catholics, on the other hand, remained wedded to social conservatism, and French bishops and priests were slow in displaying interest in or comprehension of the problem; for some time they disapproved labor unions. Belgium also was tardy in meeting the new situation. The Church in Great Britain and the United States escaped the calamitous results visited upon France and Belgium, even though men of farsighted social vision, such as Cardinal MANNING of Westminster and Cardinal GIBBONS of Baltimore, were not common.

Pius IX was preoccupied with liberalism's political and doctrinal aspects rather than with its social and economic consequences. In *Quanta cura,* however, he outlined the program that Leo XIII developed much more fully in *RERUM NOVARUM* (1891), the first thorough papal pronouncement on the subject. With this famous encyclical, the papacy assumed the leadership in supplying the Catholic solution. Succeeding popes have on many occasions amplified Leo XIII's teachings and applied Catholic principles to new situations, most notably in the encyclicals *QUADRAGESIMO ANNO* (1931), *MATER ET MAGISTRA* (1961), *LABOREM EXERCENS* (1981), and *CENTESIMUS ANNUS* (1991) (*see* SOCIAL THOUGHT, PAPAL).

The Popes. To such an extent has the recent life of the Church centered in Rome that an understanding of the development of the papal office and of the course of papal history is essential for a comprehension of Church history. One of the most remarkable phenomena in the entire history of the Church is the rapid change in papal fortunes subsequent to 1815. After a period of declining prestige and effectiveness that extended from mid-17th century and reached its nadir in the misfortunes of Pius VI and Pius VII, the papacy took advantage of the changed external situation and asserted effectively its spiritual authority over the universal Church to a degree never before equaled. Once the stormy revolutionary era closed with Napoleon's downfall, authority tended to be centralized increasingly in Rome. This trend, which became more pronounced after mid-century, reached its culmination in 1870 at VATICAN COUNCIL I, when the papal prerogatives of primacy of jurisdiction and INFALLIBILITY were solemnly defined. Especially from the time of Pius IX, the popes have been active to an unprecedented extent in the exercise of their teaching authority. Papal temporal power, on the other hand, kept declining, until in 1870 it disappeared with the loss of the States of the Church. The LATERAN PACTS (1929) resurrected this power on a very limited scale when they solved the Roman Question by creating the State of VATICAN CITY. (For the historical development of the papal office, *see* PAPACY.)

Following Pius VI (1775–99) and Pius VII (1800–23) came Leo XII (1823–29), Pius VIII (1829–30), Gregory XVI (1831–46), Pius IX (1846–78), Leo XIII (1878–1903), Pius X (1903–14), Benedict XV (1914–22), Pius XI (1922–39), Pius XII (1939–58), John XXIII (1958–63), Paul VI (1963–78), John Paul I (1978), and John Paul II (1978–). As a group the popes of the 19th and 20th centuries have been dedicated, industrious leaders, whose intellectual and spiritual qualifications were outstanding. (For the history of these pontificates, see the article on each pope.)

Clergy. Wide variations, quantitatively and qualitatively, can be observed in the inner, more important, phase of the Church's life in various parts of the world. On the whole there has been a decided improvement in the caliber of the clergy. The loss of ecclesiastical wealth, clerical privileges, and lofty social status, along with the democratic spirit of the recent period, have changed for the better the character of the hierarchy; it has become more plebeian but more knowledgeable and more intent on fulfilling its duties as the shepherd of souls. The day has passed when the upper strata of society monopolized bishoprics, canonries, and other higher posts, which were too often esteemed as sinecures. Much more attention has focused on ameliorating and standardizing the intellectual and spiritual training of priests in seminaries. The Holy See has made the seminary system the object of continual solicitude and of watchful supervision (*see* DEUS SCIENTIARUM DOMINUS). Priests of the 20th century have been better prepared than their predecessors in the 19th century to meet the problems created by vast economic, social, and intellectual upheavals. Pastoral vision in the 19th century had too often been narrow, and pastoral methods adjusted themselves slowly to a rapidly changing society.

Religions Institutes. One of the most conspicuous indications of the restored vitality of the 19th-century Church was the extraordinary progress made by religious orders and congregations. Only the 13th century can be compared with the 19th in this respect. Yet the century opened very inauspiciously for religious. The age of the Enlightenment had been one of decline for the orders, whose most conspicuous loss came in 1773 with the suppression of the Jesuits. So much religious property was seized and so many orders were dissolved in whole or in part after 1789 that most institutes had to make a fresh start after 1815. Subsequently the growth of existing orders and of new foundations was been steady, despite several attempts by anticlericals to stunt it in Germany and in Latin countries, notably in France. Some older orders never regained their former importance or numbers; others succeeded in doing so only to later suffer decline. Monastic orders, which were hardest hit by secularization, were the slowest to recover. Thus the Benedictines verged on extinction for a while, but after mid-19th century they began to prosper once more. The Dominicans and Capuchins diminished greatly in numbers until a reversal set in late in the 19th century. The Vincentians declined to a few hundred, increased in the 1960s, and subsequently declined again. There were only a few dozen Christian Brothers left at the opening of the 19th century, but membership swelled in the mid 1960s. However, they proved no more able to sustain this growth than the Jesuits, who witnessed a similar resurgence and decline. Older orders of women, such as the Ursulines, Visitation Nuns, and the Daughters of Charity of St. Paul, went through similar experiences.

Numerous new congregations appeared, more so in the 19th than in the 20th century. Most frequently they originated in France, Italy, or Spain, but much of the growth of the larger ones occurred outside these borders, even outside Europe. In the vast majority of cases these new institutes engaged in the active apostolate, predominantly in education, hospital work, and missionary endeavors. Several groups were founded explicitly for work in the missions. To an unprecedented extent, religious women traveled to foreign missions. The trend favored centralized, mobile, international organizations.

Among the new congregations for men, those that became best known include the Assumptionists, Blessed Sacrament Fathers, Claretians, Consolata Missionary Fathers, Divine Word Society, Holy Cross Congregation, Holy Ghost Fathers, Immaculate Heart of Mary Congregation (Scheut Fathers), La Salette Missionaries, Mariannhill Missionaries, Marianists, Marist Fathers, Montfort

Fathers, Oblates of Mary Immaculate, Oblates of St. Francis de Sales, Sacred Hearts Missionaries (of Issoudun), Sacred Heart of Jesus Priests (of Saint-Quentin), Sacred Hearts Fathers, Salvatorians, Stigmatine Fathers, Verona Fathers, Viatorians, and Xaverian Missionary Fathers. Members of John Bosco's Silesians and Silsesian Sisters have spread throughout the globe.

Societies of men who live a common life without vows included the African Missions Society, Pallottines, Pontifical Institute for Foreign Missions, Precious Blood Society, and White Fathers. The Columban Fathers and St. Patrick's Missionary Society were founded in Ireland; the Mill Hill Missionaries, in England; and the Josephite Fathers, Maryknoll Missionaries, and Paulists, in the United States. The Missionary Society of St. James the Apostle was the creation of Cardinal Richard Cushing of Boston.

Several congregations of brothers were founded. Among the more prominent ones were the Brothers of Christian Instruction of Ploërmel (La Mennais Brothers), Brothers of Christian Instruction of St. Gabriel, Charity Brothers, Immaculate Conception Brothers, Lourdes Brothers, Mercy Brothers, Our Lady Mother of Mercy Brothers, Sacred Heart Brothers, and Xaverian Brothers. The Marist Brothers grew to a membership exceeding 10,000. Ireland was the place of foundation of the Irish Christian Brothers, Patrician Brothers, and Presentation Brothers.

Congregations of women far exceeded those of men in the number of new foundations and in total membership. Women came to constitute a higher percentage of all religious than in earlier centuries. The number of groups of Benedictine sisters alone is large; so are the numerous groups of Charity, Dominican, Franciscan, Good Shepherd, Notre Dame, Precious Blood, Providence, and Sacred Heart Sisters. The Society of the Sacred Heart, founded by St. Madeleine Sophie BARAT, became famous for its educational work. The School Sisters of Notre Dame blossomed into a much larger organization. The Little Sisters of the Poor greatly endeared themselves by their care of the aged and impoverished. The Mercy Sisters, founded in Ireland by Mother Catherine MCAULEY, became the largest ever established in the English-speaking world (see articles on each of the above congregations).

Secular institutes represent a new direction in the religious life that has become more prominent in the mid-20th century.

Laity. Leakage and dechristianization processes have drained large numbers of the faithful. The careful surveys of religious practice that were made in the mid-20th century usually confirmed widely held opinions about the sizable, sometimes alarmingly high, percentage of nominal Catholics. Yet the laity have become more prominent in the life of the Church. After World War I, this became one of the most significant phenomena in the Church (see CATHOLIC ACTION). Much attention has been devoted to the lay state as a special vocation and to a type of spirituality best suited to this state (see LAITY, FORMATION AND EDUCATION OF; LAY SPIRITUALITY).

Catholic Organizations. The multiplication of flourishing Catholic organizations was another striking feature of this period. Some arose to foster particular devotions, others to promote the Church's rights, to aid the poor and the sick, to cultivate social life, or to unite Catholic workers, tradesmen, professional persons, war veterans, students, teachers, colleges, hospitals, etc. Prominent among these associations were the HOLY NAME SOCIETY, the LEGION OF MARY, and the National Federation of SODALITIES OF OUR LADY. The vast expansion of missionary activity, now dependent on private charity for material subsistence, has given great importance to mission aid societies, such as the Society for the PROPAGATION OF THE FAITH, the Pontifical Association of the Holy Childhood, and the Missionary Union of the Clergy. Antoine Frédéric OZANAM initiated the work of the Society of ST. VINCENT DE PAUL, the charitable undertakings of which branched into numerous countries (see CHARITY, WORKS OF; CATHOLIC CHARITIES U.S.A.). Pax Romana and the NEWMAN APOSTOLATE were intended for students and intellectuals. The GÖRRES-GESELLSCHAFT fostered Catholic scholarship. Catholic political parties have been noted above. Catholics formed their own labor unions in addition to numerous other organizations devoted to the causes of education, access among rural Catholics, and betterment of the lives of Catholics in general. Leading fraternal organizations in the United States included the KNIGHTS OF COLUMBUS, CATHOLIC DAUGHTERS OF AMERICA, and DAUGHTERS OF ISABELLA. Other countries have Catholic organizations suited to their own needs and desires. The National Catholic Welfare Conference was formed to coordinate the efforts of American Catholics to carry out the Church's social program (see UNITED STATES CONFERENCE OF CATHOLIC BISHOPS).

Devotions. Traditional forms of piety did not vanish, but new trends and emphases appeared. JANSENIST PIETY, with its moral rigorism, gave way gradually to a more sentimental type of devotion, associated with Italian Catholicity, that stressed external practices and frequentation of the Sacraments. This interior transformation of Catholic inner life north of the Alps has been termed "the real triumph of ultramontanism," more so than the definition of papal infallibility. Late in the 19th century another trend developed and gained momentum in the following decades. Catholic spirituality became predominantly Christocentric in its orientation. Evidence of this appeared in the widespread devotion of the SACRED HEART. The 19th century has been called "the century of the Sacred Heart," but this devotion still retained its popularity in the 20th century. Pius XI extended the feast of the Sacred Heart to the universal Church. Christocentric also are the devotion to the PRECIOUS BLOOD and still more to the Eucharist, manifest in the common practice of perpetual adoration, the development of EUCHARISTIC CONGRESSES and of frequent COMMUNION. Relaxation of the requirements for Eucharistic fast served to increase this practice; but this modification was in line with the general trend observable in the laws concerning FAST AND ABSTINENCE, CENSURES, and other disciplinary regulations.

Devotion to the Blessed Virgin Mary on a worldwide scale also was characteristic of the period (*see* MARY, BLESSED VIRGIN, DEVOTION TO). It was promoted by the solemn definitions of the doctrines of the IMMACULATE CONCEPTION (1854) and the ASSUMPTION OF MARY (1950), and by progress in the study of MARIOLOGY. As a result of the visions of St. Catherine LABOURÉ, devotion to the MIRACULOUS MEDAL gained many adherents. The apparitions to St. Bernadette SOUBIROUS has made LOURDES one of the most frequented SHRINES in the world. FÁTIMA and, to a lesser extent, LA SALETTE also have become goals of international PILGRIMAGES.

A third characteristic trend in 20th-century lay piety was its Biblical orientation. Relatively few Catholics in the 19th century read the Bible with any regularity, and the Modernist crisis early in the 20th century deterred ecclesiastical authorities from seeking to alter this situation. BIBLICAL THEOLOGY received more attention in later decades. Catholic scholars worked with greater freedom after the appearance of Pius XII's encyclical *DIVINO AF-FLANTE SPIRITU* (1943) and they produced numerous scholarly works. The availability of good vernacular translations of the Sacred Scriptures and of worthwhile popular literature on the subject, as well as the urging of the hierarchy, gave great impetus to this movement.

The LITURGICAL MOVEMENT progressed during the 19th century after the pioneer efforts of Dom GUÉRANGER, and in the following century it became one of the most impressive developments in the Church, one that promoted notably the role of the laity in liturgical services and that increased interest in the liturgy.

Intellectual Life. The Church confronted an enormous task of ever-increasing magnitude in solving the religious problems posed by discoveries in the natural sciences and in many other fields of learning and by new directions in thought and letters. An explosion of discoveries in physics, chemistry, geology, astronomy, and biology vastly expanded knowledge about the natural world. These findings raised numerous questions about traditional religious beliefs, and the reconciliation of science with faith. So successful was the method of the natural sciences that many became convinced that that was the sole adequate method. Enormously influential were the writings of Charles DARWIN on evolution, popularized by Thomas Huxley; they were accepted enthusiastically by scientists and thinkers and came to be applied to widely diverse fields. Their impact on religion was great and for some time destructive. Scientific investigations into the workings of the mind by psychiatrists and psychologists resulted in great advances in the understanding of man, but they also led to mechanistic, deterministic views and supplied many with substitutes for Christianity.

Modern philosophers have been much interested in religion, and their writings have had a profound influence on theology, more on Protestant than on Catholic theology. Many leading thinkers ceased to believe in Christianity, and some were openly anti-Christian. Their philosophical systems differed widely among themselves, but they tended directly or indirectly to portray Christianity as irrelevant or harmful (*see* RELIGION, PHILOSOPHY OF; AGNOSTICISM; ATHEISM; RATIONALISM; EXISTENTIALISM; HEGELIANISM; HUMANISM, SECULAR; IDEALISM; KANTIANISM; LOGICAL POSITIVISM; MATERIALISM; MECHANISM; MONISM; NATURALISM; PANTHEISM; POSITIVISM; RELATIVISM; UTILITARIANISM).

The Bible was subjected to an enormous amount of critical attention, especially in Germany. Basic to the outlook of many of the more prominent critics was a denial of all supernatural faith and a habitual contesting of the truth of Sacred Scripture. The problem of the historical Jesus gave rise to dozens of theories. David STRAUSS and Joseph Ernest RENAN, who published two of the best-known 19th-century lives of Christ, were sceptics and passed on to their readers their own disbelief in the Gospel narratives. Historical study of the origins and early development of the Church was another favorite field for scrutiny and resulted in a number of theories derogatory to Catholic claims. The comparative study of religion was a well-tilled field, but its products proved injurious, in many cases, to belief in Christianity as the sole road ordained by God for salvation. Literature served often to disseminate in wide circles these new ideologies, in the form of novels, plays, and poems impregnated with naturalistic outlooks and disdainful of Christian standards.

Catholic scholarship was for some decades ill-prepared to surmount these challenges. The closing of numerous Catholic universities, theological faculties, and monastic schools during the Revolutionary and Napoleonic periods and the disastrous infiltration of the Enlightenment and Kantian ideas into Catholic thought, even in seminaries, left Catholicism at a low intellectual ebb. Recovery was slow until mid-19th century; after that, progress was rapid and continuous. Signs of renewal became apparent first in France early in the 19th century, with the influential, if not profound, writings of François de CHATEAUBRIAND, whose *Genius of Christianity* (1802) was a sensational success, and those of Joseph de MAISTRE and Louis de BONALD. APOLOGETICS was cultivated extensively, most notably toward mid-century by John Henry NEWMAN, Victor DECHAMPS, and Jaime BALMES. Church history, patrology, and the history of dogma also received much study at this time, especially in Germany, where Johann MÖHLER, Johannes Ignaz von DÖLLINGER, and Carl von HEFELE were outstanding. German emphasis on historical theology caused tensions, however, with the theologians in Rome, who were traditionally attached to scholasticism.

The key problem of conciliating faith and reason produced several solutions, not all of them acceptable. Thus HERMESIANISM, as evolved by Georg HERMES, TRADITIONALISM, ONTOLOGISM, and the systems advocated by Franz von BAADER, Anton GUNTHER, and Jakob FROHSCHAMMER met official Roman disapproval. Vatican Council I supplied an impetus to ecclesiastical scholarship. The renewal of SCHOLASTICISM and THOMISM gained strong encouragement from Leo XIII in 1879 in his encyclical *AETERNI PATRIS* (*see* NEOSCHOLASTICISM AND NEOTHOMISM). When AMERICANISM, REFORMKATHOLIZISMUS, and, more important, MODERNISM appeared around the turn of the 20th century, the exercise of the papal magisterial power sufficed to quell them speedily. The same fate befell new theological trends in France after World War II subsequent to the publication of *HUMANI GENERIS* (1950). Heterodox movements after 1789 that resulted in lasting group separations from the Church were rare. Deutschkatholizismus, initiated by Johann RONGE and Johann CZERSKI, the OLD CATHOLICS, the LOS-VON-ROM movement, and the Polish National Catholic Church were the most sizable schisms, but their followings were relatively limited even at the height of their popularity. After 1918 Catholic ecclesiastical scholarship, centering in western Europe, became very active and prominent and moved out of the position of secondary rank it occupied earlier. The Catholic press spread its influence throughout the world.

Expansion. Emigration and missionary evangelization after 1789 established the Church in almost every corner of the globe and greatly increased its numbers. Millions of emigrants from Catholic countries in Europe were the main factors in building the Church in the United States, Canada, Australia, and New Zealand; they also augmented the Catholic populations converted earlier in Latin America.

By 1789 the missions were in a sad state after a century of stagnation and decline, hastened by the heavy loss of personnel when the Jesuits were suppressed in 1773. During the next four decades and longer, this situation deteriorated further as the religious orders suffered dissolutions, confiscations, and diminution of numbers. It has been estimated that in 1800 the vast territories in both hemispheres entrusted to the Congregation for the PROPAGATION OF THE FAITH had only about 500 priests (about half of them natives), a few dozen sisters, and somewhere between 1,400,000 and 5,000,000 faithful. Not until the pontificate of Gregory XVI was it possible to begin improving matters. After 1878 progress was remarkable. So extraordinary were the subsequent activity and accomplishments that these decades constitute one of the most flourishing periods in all mission history. No similar length of time recorded anywhere near as many converts. Mainly responsible for this growth was the revival of the religious orders. Gregory XVI, the leading mission pope of his century, and all his successors helped enormously by taking keen interest in the missions and by assuming a far more active leadership than their predecessors did or could (*see* PAPACY). The huge expenditures involved in evangelization have been met by the charitable contributions of the laity, who have carried the material burdens once assumed by the Catholic governments of Spain, Portugal, and France. External factors helped. Travel became easier and safer. China, Japan, and Siam reopened their doors to foreigners. Places such as inner Africa ceased to be inaccessible.

Almost all missionaries until the 20th century came from Europe; they suffered, not always without justification, from having their work regarded as merely one phase of European colonialism. Their reluctance in some areas to prepare native clergies gave added substance to the charge; but their outlook was severely disapproved by Rome and has disappeared. With the multiplication of precise papal directives, the attention focused on mission science, and the improvements in special training given to missionaries, the proper function and activity of the missions came to be more perfectly understood and practiced (*see* MISSION THEOLOGY; MISSIOLOGY). Disadvantageous also to the missions was the tarnished image of Christianity furnished by the arrogance, greed, immorality, and religious indifference of many transplanted colonial officials, merchants, and adventurers. By mid-20th century European prestige had dimmed, and a blaze of anti-Europeanism had erupted, fed by rising nationalisms and demands for independence. Missionaries also faced serious competition. Protestants began to spread the gospel with great zeal and success in the 19th century. Islam became a serious rival in Africa and elsewhere, and in lands where anti-Catholic or atheist ideologies gained political mastery, Christian missionaries were persecuted and expelled.

Despite all this, statistics leave no doubt about the tremendous progress of the missions. By 1957 there were some 30,000 priests, 8,000 brothers, and 60,000 sisters—about half of them native—in the territories allotted to Propaganda alone, not counting the areas dependent on the Congregation for the Oriental Church, the Consistorial Congregation (in North Africa), or the Congregation for Extraordinary Ecclesiastical Affairs (Portuguese possessions). There were also 4,000 native seminarians and 150,000 catechists and teachers. One in six of the 683 territories under Propaganda was confided to native bishops, a development that progressed rapidly under Pius XI and his successors. About 50 million Catholics inhabited mission lands. Nearly half of them were in Africa, the scene of the most spectacular gains, since the total in 1800 approximated 50,000, and in 1900, 500,000.

Reunion. UNITY OF FAITH and UNITY OF THE CHURCH are ideals which the Catholic Church has always sought. For centuries it worked to mend the break with the Orthodox churches, and on a few occasions the attempts seemed to verge on success. Practical, as well as theological, considerations heightened the urgency in the 20th century to promote these aims; they resulted in a far greater readiness to engage in interfaith dialogue. Interfaith movements became extremely prominent and well-received. Catholics and Anglicans utilized the MALINES CONVERSATIONS (1921–26) to try to resolve their differences. Important attempts to restore Christian unity were undertaken by the Protestant World Council of Churches and the Second Vatican Council. Through the decrees and efforts of the council as well as the Unitas association, the UNA SANCTA movement, and many other ventures, Catholics demonstrated a growing spirit of cooperativeness. The sincerity with which the task was faced improved the relations between religious bodies that were intolerant of one another in the not too distant past.

The Contemporary Church. The Catholic Church entered the contemporary age with the election of Giovanni Roncalli as JOHN XXIII (Oct. 28, 1958), who saw the need for some updating or *aggiornamento* of the church as well as its *aperturismo,* or opening up to the outside world. Perceiving synods and councils as the constitutional means to institute change, he called the 21st Church Council to effect the necessary *aggiornamento.* John's vision was global and catholic as he selected Cardinal Augustin BEA to head a new Secretariat for Promoting Christian Unity. It prepared the way for the

participation of observers in the council of other Christian communities, the promotion of ecumenism within the Roman Catholic Church, as well as proposing a statement against the age-old discrimination against the Jews. John set the example by meeting with the non-Catholic observers and receiving the Archbishop of Canterbury.

John also sought an accommodation with the Eastern bloc, drawing a distinction between communism as an atheistic creed with which the Church could not compromise, and communism as a social, political, and economic reality, which had to be confronted. Rather than continuing the Church's anticommunist crusade, he was prepared to adopt a pragmatic approach to the communist regimes, letting Moscow know that the Vatican sought improved relations. Later he reached agreements with a series of communist governments, enabling the Church to secure the liberation of a number of ecclesiastics from eastern Europe while filling a number of vacant bishoprics there. In turn, the Yugoslav government permitted the public funeral of Cardinal Alojzije STEPINAC. Other dividends ensued as the Soviet Union permitted the participation of the bishops from Eastern Europe in the Church Council.

During this pontificate the Church did not neglect social questions. On May 15, 1961, *MATER ET MAGISTRA,* on the Church as mother and teacher of all nations, was issued, emphasizing the Church role in social progress. In John's view *Rerum Novarum* represented a compendium of Catholic social and economic teaching, insisting that work was not another commodity, but a specifically human activity, and while private property was a right, it entailed social obligations. While the Church could not accept communism or socialism, the objectives of which did not transcend material well-being and preached atheism, it recognized the lawfulness of state and public ownership of productive goods, especially those which exercise great power. Indeed, *Mater et magistra* assigned an extraordinary responsibility to the state for providing social security, accepting the welfare state as an expression of the common good, while welcoming the increase in social relationships among nations, peoples, and classes.

Two years later, April 11, 1963, John XXIII issued the wide ranging encyclical, *PACEM IN TERRIS* which was widely heralded in the secular press. Addressed not only to Catholics, the pope called for all people of good will to work together for universal peace. To achieve that goal, government and social structures must be grounded on principles of truth, justice, charity, freedom, and the dignity of the human person. *Pacem in terris* discussed four major themes: relation between authority and conscience, human rights, disarmament, and the quest for the common good. It identified three "signs of the times," characteristic of modern society: the progressive improvement in economic and social conditions of working people; the emerging prominence of women in public life; and the collapse of colonialism and rise of independent nations.

During this pontificate the Church called for the cooperation of Catholics with Christians who were separated from the Holy See, and even with those who were non-Christians. John's global vision reflected in his calling of the council, his social encyclicals, and his support of international organizations also provided broad support for the work of the missions. In November 1959, on the 40th anniversary of Benedict XV's *Maximum Illud* on the missions, *Princeps Pastorum* on the same subject was issued. It announced that by 1959 there were 68 Asian and 25 African bishops, noting that while the history of the Church had historically been associated with Western civilization, it belonged to no one culture and had to welcome and assimilate anything that redounds to the honor of the human mind. There was a missionary component in *Mater et Magistra*, which depicted the Church as the mother and teacher of all nations.

When the first session of the Second Vatican Council closed (Dec. 8, 1962), the expectations aroused had not been fulfilled for no decrees had been approved. John proved unable to see the council to its conclusion; he died on June 3, 1963. He had been awarded the International Peace Prize of the Eugenio Balzan Foundation in March 1963, and had been selected *Time* magazine's "Man of the Year" for 1962. Yet not all concurred with his decisions. Likewise his reconciliation with Jews, Protestants, Muslims, and even non-believers, and his advancement of the social question spawned critics as well as acclaim. Some decried his opening the floodgates of change. Consciously or unconsciously, this pontificate set in motion changes that led to profound reform in the Church.

On June 21, 1963, the conclave elected as the new pope the Cardinal Archbishop of Milan, Giovanni Battista Enrico Antonio Maria Montini; he assumed the name Paul VI. Following his election he announced that the council would be continued, calling for its resumption on Sept. 29, 1963. The *aggiornamento* or updating of the Church remained his objective, citing the need to revise the canon law and reform the curia while revealing his commitment to the social justice enunciated in his predecessors' encyclicals. Thus he made it clear that the main program for the Church would be the completion, followed by implementation, of the council's decisions.

Prior to convoking the second session, Paul outlined new directives for the council including the admissions of lay Catholics and an extended invitation to non-Catholic observers. At its opening he recalled the council's goals including Church renewal, Christian unity, and dialogue in the modern world. During this second session (from Sept. 29 to Dec. 4, 1963), Paul struggled to get the Roman curia and the council to work together. He wanted the bishops to exercise their rights to govern the Church with him, while fostering conditions for ecumenical encounters with non-Catholics. Among its achievements were: proclamation of the constitution on the liturgy, *Sacrosanctum concilium,* and the decree on the means of social communication, *Inter mirifica.* In reforming the liturgy, the Church fathers sought to adapt institutions which were subject to change to the needs or the age and to foster unity among those who believe in Christ.

In December there emerged a tentative agenda for the third session, scheduled to convene in mid-September, 1964, making provision to have some women attend as auditors. By November 21, when the third session closed, three important decrees had been approved, including *Lumen gentium,* exploring the relationship of the pope, the bishops, the priests, and the laity within the church; *Orientalium ecclesiarum,* on the Catholic Eastern Churches; and *Unitatis redintegratio,* on Ecumenism. There were other issues confronting the church, including the reform of canon law, mixed marriages, birth control, and cultural diversity. Soon after the opening of the fourth session (Sept.14, 1965), Paul established a Synod of Bishops to collaborate with him in the governance of the Church. On Oct. 28, 1965, he promulgated five important council documents: one on the role of bishops in the Church, another on the renewal of religious life, a third on the training of priests, a fourth on Christian education, and *Nostra aetate,* on the Church's attitude toward non-Christian religions. Within the last document it was stipulated that the Church reproves every form of persecution and "deplores all hatreds, persecutions, displays of anti-Semitism leveled at any time or from any source against the Jews." On Dec. 8, 1965, the council closed.

Within the next decade the difficulties of the postconciliar age proved almost as troubling as those confronted in the council. Paul recognized that the documents promulgated could not affect change in the Church unless they were implemented, and therefore established postconciliar commissions to continue its work, as well as yearly meeting in Rome to continue the dialogue. The papal directive to the Postconciliar Central Commission at the end of January provided suggestions for coordinating postconciliar activities and interpreted its decrees.

In January 1967 there was established a Council on the Laity which sought to integrate the laity into the

Church's official organizations and activities. Subsequently, there was provided canonical form to the diaconate, implementing this ministry called for by the council. Meanwhile, Paul issued the encyclical *Populorm progressio* (March 26, 1967). Deemed by some the Church's *magna carta* for justice and peace, it revealed concern for those attempting to escape the ravages of hunger and poverty, pleading for social justice for the impoverished masses of the third world. A subsequent encyclical *Sacerdotalis caelibatus* (June 24, 1967) upheld the Church's traditional position of priestly celibacy. Sharing the Council's conviction that the Church had to draw closer to the world, Paul indicated there was a wrong and right way to do so. In his words the Church was in the world, not of the world, but for the world. The limits to conciliation with the modern world were evident in the pronouncement on birth control provided in *Humane vitae* (On the Regulation of Birth, July 1968), which condemned as unlawful the use of means which directly prevent conception. This position unleashed criticism within and outside the Church, particularly in North America and Europe. Paul convened an Extraordinary Synod at the end of 1969, encouraging it to explore the relationship between papal primacy and episcopal collegiality. In 1970 he ruled that bishops should submit their resignations when they reached the age of 75, and that cardinals after their 80th year could no longer take part in a conclave. Paul died at Castel Gandolo on Aug. 6, 1978, having brought the council to a successful conclusion and continued the Church's reconciliation with the modern world.

On Aug. 26, 1978, Cardinal Albino Luciani, the Patriarch of Venice, was elected pope and was the first to assume a double name, John Paul, indicating his determination to continue the work of the two previous Church leaders. He did not have time to do so. The challenge of the papacy proved burdensome, taxing his stamina and undermining his health. He died after a pontificate of only 33 days. In the second conclave of 1978, divisions prevented the election of a pope until October 16, when Cardinal Karol Wojtyła, Archbishop of Kraków, was elected the first Slavic pope and first non-Italian since Hadrian VI of Utrecht in 1522.

Wojtyła continued the work of the council. He reiterated that in the Christian view human relations should not be governed by the individualistic logic of profit; the earth is to be utilized for the well-being of humanity. He continued the social program of the Church; in September 1981 he released an encyclical, *LABOREM EXERCENS* (On Human Work), defending the right of workers to organize and calling for a new economic order which avoided the excesses of unrestrained capitalism and ideological Marxism.

At the beginning of June 1979 John Paul returned to his homeland—the first of three visits (1979, 1983, and 1987), before the opening of Eastern Europe. The visit from June 2 to June 11 was religious, but had political overtones. This tour altered the mentality of fear that prevailed in Poland and much of the Eastern bloc, forecasting a united Christian Europe. John Paul expressed his views on the role of the Church in the world in his first encyclical, released in March 1979, *REDEMPTOR HOMINIS* (The Redeemer of Man), and repeated them in his second encyclical *DIVES IN MISERICORDIA* of December 1980.

In 1984 the Church agreed to a revision of the Lateran Accords and the Italian Concordat that had been concluded between Pope Pius XI and the Mussolini government in 1929. By the terms of the new agreement, the Vatican recognized the separation of Church and state in Italy. Meanwhile, diplomatic relations with the United States were established. Early in 1984, President Reagan announced that William A. Wilson of California, would be appointed the first U.S. ambassador to the Holy See.

Foreseeing the inevitable collapse of communism and a greater role for the Church in Eastern Europe, the pope in a 1985 encyclical (*SLAVORUM APOSTOLI*) called for European unity with Christianity as its spiritual center. In 1987 the Warsaw government pledged to reopen a dialogue with the Catholic Church. It did so in July 1989, becoming the first of the communist-bloc nations to establish diplomatic relations with the Holy See and facilitating the dramatic changes that occurred from 1989 to 1992. By 1991 the Communist system in the Soviet Union had crumbled. Near the end of 1991, a Synod of European bishops, from both the East and West, met to assess the opportunities presented by the political changes on the continent and to promote a new evangelization of Europe.

During the last years of the 20th century, John Paul II took the lead in focusing on the Church's global mission, traveling more than all the previous popes combined, and targeting the developing world which housed more than half the world's Catholics. In 1992 he visited Santo Domingo for the opening of the Fourth Latin American Bishops Conference. Reiterating the church's "preferential option for the poor" as called for by the Latin American bishops at their meeting in Medellin, Columbia and Puebla, Mexico, the pope cautioned the Latin American clergy not to forget their spiritual mission while battling economic, social, and political injustices. He underlined that the Church's mission was religious rather than political. In September 1993, the pope challenged moral relativism, which he perceived as a great threat to western civilization, in the encyclical *VERITATIS SPLENDOR* (The Splendor of Truth).

During the course of 1993, John Paul apologized for the Roman Catholic Church's collaboration in the enslavement of African men, women, and children. Subsequently, at the opening of the new millennium, the Vatican issued a document entitled *Memory and Reconciliation: The Church and the Mistakes of the Past* which catalogued the Church's historical failures including the excesses of the Crusades, the Inquisition, and anti-Judaism. Regret for anti-Judaism in the Church was repeated by the pope during his March 2000 visit to the Holocaust Museum in Jerusalem.

At the same time, the Church sought to expand its global perspective. Catholicism had to become more universalized, with a different approach to the ancient cultures of non-European peoples, John Paul II explained. The pope pursued this policy through the creation of new cardinals throughout his pontificate. By the end of 1994, the Italians, once the dominant element in the college, were whittled down to 20 out of 120 cardinal electors.

Conclusion. Numerically the Church has progressed both absolutely and relatively. The 130 or so million Catholics in 1789 had increased to about 545 million by 1961 and jumped to more than one billion at the opening of the new millennium, constituting some 18 percent of the global population. In 1999, the Church growth rate was 1.6 percent, slightly higher than the general population growth of 1.4 percent. However, this Church expansion was uneven, increasing mostly in Africa, Asia, and the Americas while suffering a decline in Europe. Thus, while Europe accounted for 37 percent of the world's Catholics at the death of Paul VI (1978), at the opening of the third millennium its share had declined to 27 percent. Meanwhile, the Catholic population of the Americas had come to constitute some one-half of the world's total, and during that same time the percentage of African Catholics doubled from 6 percent to 12 percent, and Asian Catholics increased from 7.6 percent to 10.4 percent of the global Catholic population.

Periodic renewal is necessary if the Church, as the Bride of Christ, is to remain ever young and fair despite 19 centuries of age. During the 20th century, *aggiornamento* was the great opportunity and challenge; the chief instrument for carrying it to successful completion was Vatican Council II.

Bibliography: *Revue d'histoire ecclésiastique,* fullest bibliogs. For literature, esp. in Eng., see *Catholic Periodical Index* (New York-Haverford, Pa. 1930–). *Index to Religious Periodical Literature* (since 1949) (Princeton 1953–). *Guide to Catholic Literature,* ed. W. ROMIG et al. (Detroit-Grosse Pointe, MI-Haverford, PA 1888–). Universal Church from Age of Revolutions through Pius XII. O. CHADWICK, *The Popes and European Revolution* (Oxford 1981). H. DANIEL-ROPS, *The Church in an Age of Revolution 1789–1870,* tr. J. WARRINGTON (Garden City, NY 1967). C. CLAUDIA, ed., *The Papal Encyclicals, 1958–1981* (Raleigh, NC 1981). R. AUBERT, *The Church in a Secularized Society,* (New York 1978); *The Church in the Industrial Age* (New York 1981). T. MCCARTHY, *The Catholic Tradition: The Church in the Twentieth Century* (Chicago 1998). L. CHATELLIER, *The Religion of the Poor: Rural Missions in Europe and the Formation of Modern Catholicism,* tr. B. PEARCE (New York 1997). T. MCCARTHY, *The Catholic Tradition* (Chicago 1994). L. KURTZ *The Politics of Heresy: The Modernist Crisis in Roman Catholicism* (Berkeley 1986). J. LEFLON, *La Crise révolutionnaire, 1789–1846* (Paris 1949). R. AUBERT, *Le Pontificat de Pie IX* (2d ed. Paris 1964). K. S. LATOURETTE, *Christianity in a Revolutionary Age: A History of Christianity in the Nineteenth and Twentieth Centuries,* 5 v. (New York, 1958–62). F. MOURRET, *A History of the Catholic Church,* tr. N. THOMPSON, 8 v. (St. Louis 1931–57) v. 7 and 8 (1775–1878); v. 9 (1878–1903), in Fr. only, *Histoire générale de l'Église* (Paris 1924). A. BOULENGER, *Histoire générale de l'Église,* v.8–9 (Paris 1943–50). G. KRÜGER, ed., *Handbuch der Kirchengeschichte,* 4 v. (Tübingen 1909–12), v.4 by H. STEPHAN and H. LEUBE, *Die Neuzeit* (2d ed. Tübingen 1931). F. J. MONTALBAN et al., *Historia de la Iglesia Católica,* v.4 (1648–1951) (Biblioteca de autores cristianos 76; Madrid 1951). L. A. VEIT, *Die Kirche im Zeitalter des Individualismus 1648–1932,* 2 v. (Freiburg 1931–33). K. BIHLMEYER and H. TÜCHLE, *Kirchengeschichte* (17th ed. Paderborn 1962) v.3, excellent bibliog. N. C. EBERHARDT, *Summary of Catholic History,* 2 v. (St. Louis 1961), v.2. J. LORTZ, *History of the Church,* ed. and tr. E. G. KAISER from 4th Ger. ed. (Milwaukee 1938); *Geschichte der Kirche in ideengeschichtlicher Betrachtung,* 2 v. (21st rev. and enl. ed. Münster 1962–64), v.2; also in 1-vol. ed. (1964). C. POULET, *A History of the Catholic Church,* tr. S. A. RAEMERS, 2 v. (4th ed. St. Louis 1934–35), v.2. W. GURIAN and M. A. FITZSIMONS, eds., *The Catholic Church in World Affairs* (Notre Dame, IN 1954). E. E. Y. HALES, *The Catholic Church in the Modern World* (New York 1958; pa. 1960). J. N. MOODY, ed., *Church and Society, 1789–1950* (New York 1953). Universal Church from Vatican II to Present. A. FLANNERY, ed., *Vatican Council II: The Conciliar and Post Conciliar Documents* (Grand Rapids, MI 1992). T. WESTOW, *Introducing Contemporary Catholicism* (Philadelphia 1967). E. O. HANSON, *The Catholic Church in World Politics* (Princeton, NJ 1987). G. GUTIERREZ, *A Theology of Liberation* (Maryknoll, NY 1973); J. E. SMITH, *Humanae Vitae, A Generation Later* (Washington D.C. 1991). J. HITCHCOCK, *Catholicism and Modernity: Confrontation or Capitulation* (New York 1979). T. J. REESE, *Inside the Vatican: The Politics and Organization of the Catholic Church* (Cambridge, MA 1996). G. MILLER and W. STANCIL, *Catholicism at the Millennium* (Kansas City 2001). D. JODOCK, ed., *Catholicism Contending with Modernity* (New York 2000). T. BOKENKOTTER, *Church and Revolution: Catholics in the Struggle of Democracy and Social Justice* (New York 1998). R. MCBRIEN, *Report on the Church: Catholicism after Vatican II* (San Francisco 1992). A. DULLES, *The Reshaping of Catholicism* (San Francisco 1988). M. J. LEDDY, *In the Eye of the Catholic Storm: The Church Since Vatican II* (Toronto 1992). T. FITZGERALD, ed., *The Changing Face of the Church* (Chicago 1998). T. RAUSCH, *Catholicism at the Dawn of the Third Millennium* (Collegeville, MN 1996). J. EGAN, *Restoration and Renewal: The Church in the Third Millennium* (Kansas City 1995). J. DEEDY, ed., *The Catholic Church in the Twentieth Century* (Collegeville, MN 2000). J. HITCHCOCK, *Catholicism and Modernity: Confrontation or Capitulation* (New York 1979). Popes and Papacy. O. CHADWICK, *A History of the Popes, 1830–1914* (Oxford 1998). P. HEBBLEWAITE, *The Year of Three Popes* (New York 1979). P. GRANFIELD, *The Papacy in Transition* (New York 1980). M. MARTIN, *The Keys of This Blood: The Struggle for World Dominion Between Pope John Paul II, Mikail Gorbachev, and the Capitalist*

West (New York 1990). JOHN PAUL II, *Crossing the Threshold of Hope,* ed., V. MESSORI (New York 1994). R. CAMP, *The Papal Ideology of Social Reform* (Leiden 1969). M. MILLER, *The Divine Right of the Papacy in Recent Ecumenical Theology* (Rome 1980). P. PASCHINI and V. MONACHINO, eds., *I papi nella storia,* 2 v. (Rome 1961), v.2. Missions. S. DELACROIX, ed. *Histoire universelle des missions catholiques* (Paris 1956–59) v.3–4. K. S. LATOURETTE, *A History of the Expansion of Christianity* (New York 1937–45) v.4–7. A. MULDERS, *Missionsgeschichte* (Regensburg 1960). A. FREITAG, *The Universe Atlas of the Christian World* (London 1963), tr. from Fr. H. EMMERICH, *Atlas missionum a Sacra Congregatione de Propaganda Fide dependentium* (Vatican City 1958). Church in Various Countries. M. E. DE FRANCISCIS, *Italy and the Vatican: The 1984 Concordant between Church and State* (New York 1989). A. C. JEMOLO, *Church and State in Italy, 1850–1950,* tr. D. MOORE (Philadelphia 1961). W. DAIM, *The Vatican and Eastern Europe,* tr. A. GODE (New York 1970). R. C. MONTICONE, *The Catholic Church in Communist Poland, 1945–1985* (New York 1986). A. GILL, *Rendering unto Caesar: The Catholic Church and the State in Latin America* (Chicago 1998). M. TANGEMAN, *Mexico at the Crossroads: Politics, the Church, and the Poor* (New York 1995). M. BURDICK, *For God and Fatherland: Religion and Politics in Argentina* (Albany, NY 1995). A. GREENE, *The Catholic Church in Haiti* (East Lansing, MI 1994). M. PENA, *Theologies and Liberation in Peru* (Philadelphia 1995). R. J. GELB, *Politics and Religious Authority: American Catholics Since the Second Vatican Council* (Westport, CT 1994). M. GLAZIER and T. J. SHELLEY, eds., *The Encyclopedia of American Catholic History* (Collegeville, MN 1997). Statistics. *Bilan du Monde. Annuario Pontifica.*

[J. F. BRODERICK/F. J. COPPA]

Miniature painting from a Breviary showing the Church as a ship filled with saints, Christ crucified on the mast, and the symbols of the four evangelists at upper corners and sides, c. 1450–1475.

CHURCH, SYMBOLS OF

The images of dwelling, garden, and woman, and their derivatives, are the most widely used symbols of the Church.

Basic Symbols. In the New Testament the image of the Church as a dwelling or building that is also a temple is exemplified in Eph 2.20–22: "You are built upon the foundation of the apostles and prophets with Christ Jesus himself as the chief corner stone. In him the whole structure is closely fitted together and grows into a temple holy in the Lord, in him you too are being built together into a dwelling place for God in the Spirit." The Church is represented by the larger metaphor of the city of God in Heb 12.22. In this city, which is the eschatological Jerusalem, the tree of life of the Garden or Paradise is found (Rv 22.1–2).

The symbol woman appears in the New Testament under the aspect of bride and of mother. The city is compared to a bride in Rv 21.2: "And I saw the holy city, New Jerusalem, coming down out of heaven from God, made ready as a bride adorned for her husband." The similitude of mother is applied to the heavenly Jerusalem in Gal 4.26. The fusion of these symbols, especially that of bride and groom, begins to take place in the Old Testament (Isaiah ch. 61–62). The image of the Church as "body" has reference to the system of bridal symbolism; the Church is Christ's Body at the same time that she is His Bride, according to the principle that husband and wife are one flesh (Eph 5.23–32). *See* CHURCH, II (THEOLOGY OF).

In Christian antiquity these Biblical Church symbols were developed with poetic ingenuity through literary and pictorial images. In Hellenistic art, the vine had symbolized mystic union with a lifegiving deity. As an ornament in synagogues it represented Israel, God's vineyard, according to Is 5.1–7 (the vineyard song), Ez 19.1–14 (allegory of the vine branch), and Ps 79(80).9–19 (restoration of the Lord's vineyard). In the light of passages such as Jn 15.1–17 (Christ as true vine) and Mt 21.33–41 (parable of the vine-dressers), Christian art saw the pre-Christian meaning of this symbol fulfilled in the Church. Related to the vine as Church symbols are the wreath, the fountain, and the tree of life.

Often appearing together with the vine and its related symbols is the figure of a woman in the early Christian attitude of prayer, the "orant." This image may stand for an individual member of the Church (living or departed), especially its most representative member, the Virgin Mary. The main concern, however, is with the use of the image to symbolize the whole concept of the Church. As soon as churches were built they became symbols of the Church as the community of the faithful "so gathered in God's house as to become God's House" (St. Augustine, *Patrologia Latina*. 43:241). The symbolism of dwelling, garden, and woman was developed extensively in patristic literature. The Church was seen to be foreshadowed by Jerusalem and the Temple, Paradise and the garden of Ct 4.12 (the lover and his garden), and by the various figures of woman in the Bible, especially Mary to whom the Church is "most similar" (St. Augustine, *Patrologia Latina* 38:1064). The bridal symbolism gave rise to an extensive system of ecclesiology that borrowed ideas from Hellenistic astrology and mysticism and presented the Church as moon (female) receiving light and life from Christ as sun (male).

Other Symbols. The ark as an image of the Church was sanctioned by 1 Pet 3.20, where Baptism is equated with the saving power of Noah's ark. The ship symbol is probably of independent origin, from the *Testamentum Nephtali* and Lk 5.3, where Christ teaches from the boat. The ark and the ship are sometimes contrasted and sometimes fused in another important system of early ecclesiology through which the cross (as "saving wood" and as mast of Peter's Bark) soon came to stand for the Church. Throughout the Middle Ages, Church symbolism inspired by elaborate allegorical interpretation of the Bible was translated into artistic forms. The development reached its climax in the medieval cathedral, which was conceived as a mirror of the universe in which "all things prefigure Christ and His Church" (Anastasius of Sinai, *Patrologia Graeca* 89:894).

With the decline of the Middle Ages, Church allegories tended to become fanciful and didactic. For example, the Church was represented as a chariot drawn by the symbols of the Evangelists and by the Fathers of the Church. The symbol "woman" developed into allegorical representations of Mother Church with cross, banner, or crown, often contrasted with the Synagogue personified. A second area of great development was in Madonna pictures. Only in the East did the full meaning of the "orant" survive, especially in the iconography of the Ascension and in the type of Our Lady of the Sign. As God's dwelling, identified through garden symbols with Paradise, and through liturgical references with Jerusalem, Spouse, and Mother, the church building retained its symbolic meaning in the West, even during the centuries when theology lost touch with symbols. Within the framework of 20th-century Church renewal, traditional symbolism has provided a source of new insights into the nature of the Church. Contemporary church architecture, for example, has been affected by a reconsideration of the concept of "the Church incarnate."

Bibliography: Consult pertinent articles in H. LECLERCQ, *Dictionnaire d'archéologie chrétienne et de liturgie*, ed. F. CABROL, H. LECLERCQ and H. I. MARROU, 15 v. (Paris 1907–53) 15.2:1756–1811. *Reallexikon für Antike und Christentum*, ed. T. KLAUSER [Stuttgart 1941 (1950)–].K. KÜNSTLE, *Ikonographie der christlichen Kunst*, 2 v. (Freiburg 1926–28). C. LEONARDI, *Ampelos: Il simbolo della vite nell'arte pagano e paleocristiana* (Rome 1947). W. LOWRIE, *Art in the Early Church* (New York 1947), illus. L. OUSPENSKY and W. LOSSKY. *The Meaning of Icons*, tr. G. E. H. PALMER and E. KADLOUBOVSKI (Boston 1956). R. BRUNET, *Dictionnaire de spiritualité ascétique et mystique. Doctrine et histoire*, ed., M. VILLER et al. (Paris 1932) 4:384–401. R. SCHWARZ, *The Church Incarnate: The Sacred Function of Christian Architecture*, tr. C. HARRIS (Chicago 1958). J. DANIÉLOU, *From Shadows to Reality: Studies in the Biblical Typology of the Fathers*, tr. W. HIBBERD (Westminster, MD 1960). *Primitive Christian Symbols*, tr. D. ATTWATER (Baltimore 1964). P.S. MINEAR, *Images of the Church in the New Testament* (Philadelphia 1960). H. RAHNER, *Our Lady and the Church*, tr. S. BULLOUGH (New York 1961); *Symbole der Kirche, Die Ekklesiologie der Väter* (Salzburg 1964). Y. M. J. CONGAR, *The Mystery of the Temple*, tr. R. F. TREVETT (Westminster, MD 1962).

[D. WINZEN]

CHURCH AND STATE

This article presents in four parts a chronological survey of the relations between Church and State in Western civilization. The doctrinal aspects of these relations are related more fully in other articles (*see* FREEDOM OF RELIGION), as are historical and legal aspects that have particular reference to the New World and especially to the United States [*see* CHURCH AND STATE IN THE U.S. (LEGAL HISTORY); FREEDOM OF RELIGION (IN U.S. CONSTITUTION].

THE CHURCH IN THE ROMAN EMPIRE

In the ancient Near East and the Mediterranean world religious and civil functions were inseparable. The state was supreme in the religious as well as in the civil sphere, and its subjects or citizens were normally required to participate in public worship. Nonconformance was regarded as a form of treason or sacrilege. When AKHNATON made his Aton cult the official religion of Egypt, the worship of Amon was proscribed and the nonconforming priesthood of Amon was persecuted. Even in the Greek city-states, acceptance of the gods of the state and participation in the official cults were likewise prescribed. The famous trials of ANAXAGORAS and SOCRATES at Athens on the charge of impiety indicated that the most enlightened Greek state could demand religious conformity—although in these two instances religion was used as a pretext for attack by political enemies. However, it should be noted that PLATO assigned a central role to religion in the ideal state he described in the *Laws* and that he advocated the death penalty for persistent atheism.

The policy of ancient imperial states toward the religions of conquered peoples was, in general, based on toleration. The great Persian kings CYRUS and DARIUS even aided the Jewish exiles to return from Babylonia and to reestablish the worship of Yahweh in Jerusalem. There were important exceptions, however, to the policy of toleration. The Assyrians, as is evident from their own records and from the Bible, tended to impose the worship of their militant god Ashur on conquered peoples, and AN-TIOCHUS IV EPIPHANES, king of Syria, instituted formal persecution against those Jews who would not conform to his program of Hellenization. Some centuries later, the Sassanid kings of the New Persian Empire persecuted Christians, Manichaeans, and all others who would not accept or participate in the official Zoroastrian religion of the state. In practice, the acceptance of the religion of the conqueror or the toleration of the religions of conquered peoples presented no serious problems to adherents of polytheism, as the conquered could incorporate the worship of foreign divinities—or even the worship of a divine king himself—into their own cults. The Jews, on the other hand, as the chosen people of Yahweh, were committed to His worship alone. Owing in part to the historical circumstances of their association with Rome from the days of Judas Maccabee and in part to the general Roman policy toward subject ethnic groups, the Jews were granted special immunities out of respect for their religious beliefs and practices. Above all, under the early empire, they were freed from the obligation of participating in the imperial cult.

In summary, before the rise of Christianity, the official religion of a state was an essential and inseparable element in its structure and functioning. The problem of the relations of the religions of subject peoples and the ruling state had arisen, but in practice it was not a serious one except in the case of the Jews, whose uncompromising and exclusive monotheism constituted a unique phenomenon in a polytheistic world [*see* MONOTHEISM (IN THE BIBLE)]. The Romans never attempted to understand JUDAISM; they tolerated it, but with restrictions against proselytism.

Primitive Christianity and the Roman State. In the Jewish conception of the state, the religious and the civil were inseparably combined. The Jewish state was a kind of religious community, a THEOCRACY, in which institutions and law were religious in origin, being

founded in Scripture and interpreted and applied according to the spirit of Scripture. Given this background, subjection to a foreign—and pagan—power was particularly difficult to endure. Hence the question put to Christ regarding the payment of tribute to Rome was motivated in part by a desire to impugn his Jewish patriotism and in part to expose him to a charge of disloyalty to Rome. His answer, "Render, therefore, to Caesar the things that are Caesar's, and to God the things that are God's" (Mk 12.17; see also Rom 13.7), marked the beginning of a new epoch in the history of the relations between religion and the state. For the first time, a formal distinction was made between the obligations owed to God and those owed to the state, with a clear declaration that man has the duty to fulfill the obligations owed to both. St. Paul's teachings on civil AUTHORITY and civil obedience merely applied concretely the principle enunciated by Our Lord. Subsequent Christian teachings, and their elaboration, on the relations of Church and State have necessarily been based on this same principle as their ultimate foundation.

The conflict between Christianity and the Roman state was occasioned by the nonparticipation of Christians generally in public and private life, and, above all, by their refusal to worship the emperor. The imperial cult had been instituted by Augustus and was promoted, by his successors as a means, strengthened and sanctioned by religion, for developing loyalty and unity throughout the Roman Empire. When, about the middle of the 1st century A.D., the Roman authorities became aware that Christianity was not identical with Judaism and that increasing numbers of non-Jews were joining the new religion, Christians, like other non-Jewish citizens or subjects, were expected to participate in various aspects of Roman public and private life and, above all, in the imperial cult. The hope of an Imminent Second Coming (*see* PAROUSIA), a strong spirit of pacifism among some, and the general deep religious fervor of the first two or three generations of Christians were all factors in developing and maintaining an attitude of aloofness toward the life around them, but the main cause of this aloofness was paganism itself. Every aspect of public and private life was permeated with pagan rites and customs. It was practically impossible for a Christian to serve even as a petty magistrate without having to take an active part in pagan ceremonies, and military service required an oath to the divine emperor and worship of the imperial standards and other rites. It is against this background that one should interpret the statement of St. Paul that "our citizenship is in heaven" (Phil 3.20), and should understand the consolation that it offered to those who first heard it.

Sometime between the principates of Nero (A.D. 54–68) and Trajan (A.D. 98–117), Christianity was condemned as a religion inimical to the state, and refusal to worship the emperor or to participate in official sacrifices was regarded as an act of treason against the state. From this period to the Edict of GALERIUS (311) and the agreement on religious policy reached by CONSTANTINE and Licinius (the so-called Edict of MILAN of 313), Christianity was proscribed by the Roman state. In practice, however, there were long intervals in which the law against the Christians was not enforced, at least on a universal basis. The rank and file of Christians, although often attacked or ridiculed, were not officially persecuted, and some Christians occupied important posts in the imperial service.

Meanwhile, the Church grew steadily in numbers, especially in the East, and developed a complicated and strong hierarchical organization. It became a great sacred corporation, although one not recognized by the state, that was regarded as a menace to imperial unity as symbolized in the imperial cult and in other official acts of pagan public worship. The elaborately organized persecutions of DECIUS and of DIOCLETIAN and Galerius were directed especially against the leaders of the Church and ecclesiastical organization, with the hope that Christianity might be eliminated by destroying its higher and lower clergy. Despite the severities of the age of persecutions, Christian martyrs and apologists constantly maintained that they were loyal citizens and that they were bound by the precepts of their religion to render obedience to civil authority. They could and did pray *for* the emperor, but they could not pray *to* the emperor, because they had to reserve their worship for their Lord and Savior Jesus Christ, to whom the emperor himself belonged and from whom he derived his power (*Martyr. Polycarpi* 8.2; 9.2; 10.1; Tertullian, *Apol.* 4).

From Constantine to the Death of Theodosius the Great (A.D. 313–395). Constantine's extension of freedom of worship to Christians, which signified that Christianity was recognized officially as a *religio licita* beside paganism, was a revolutionary act that marked a great turning point in the history of the early Church and in universal history as well. By his legislation, Constantine continued to strengthen the position of Christianity. This policy was continued by his successors with the exception of JULIAN, whose persecution of Christianity was brought to an abrupt end by his death. Finally, in the last quarter of the 4th century, THEODOSIUS THE GREAT made Christianity the official religion of the Empire and suppressed public pagan worship.

The Relation of the Church to the Christian Empire. The Church had emerged triumphant from its long struggle with the pagan Roman state and its pagan emperors, but its precise relations with the Christian Empire and Christian emperors remained to be worked out. By the

age of Constantine, the Church had become a highly organized universal sacred society, conscious of its divine origin and divine mission. As is clear from the writings of the ante-Nicene and post-Nicene Fathers, it regarded itself as the new PEOPLE OF GOD and its leaders, the bishops, as the successors not only of the Apostles appointed by Christ to rule His Church, but also of their prototypes, the Prophets of the Old Testament, as spokesmen of God. The Church, accordingly, in keeping with its divine foundation and its concern with the things of God, considered itself supreme in the theological and spiritual sphere and as possessing its own rights and privileges within that sphere. On the other hand, and in keeping with the doctrine laid down by Christ Himself, it recognized fully the supremacy of the state and its rulers in political or civil affairs.

The Christian emperors inherited the lofty absolutism of their office from their pagan predecessors, who were supreme in religious affairs, as was symbolized by the title *pontifex maximus*. This title was relinquished by GRATIAN only in A.D. 382. Constantine considered that he was emperor by divine election and that he not only had the duty to promote the new religion that he had adopted but also the right to interfere directly in religious affairs in the interest of imperial order and unity. Thus he took for granted that he could summon ecclesiastical councils and even suggest the actions that should be taken. In any event, he considered that it was his duty to put into effect, by force if necessary, conciliar decrees. In their joy at deliverance from persecution, the Christian bishops did not perceive that Constantine's handling of the Donatist affair was to be ominous for the future (*see* DONATISM). Their joy over the imperial support received at the Council of NICAEA I, however, was soon ended when Constantine exiled ATHANASIUS, the great champion of orthodoxy, and favored the Arians.

From this time forward, it became clear that the emperor would be a defender of the faith, but that in practice this would mean the faith to which he himself subscribed. It became evident also that an emperor could and would regard himself as superior to all bishops, including the pope, in matters ecclesiastical. Arianism, in fact, owed much of its success to the official support it received from The Emperors CONSTANTIUS and VALENS and the Empress Justina, regent of her son VALENTINIAN II. Athanasius (for the second and third time), HILARY OF POITIERS, HOSIUS OF CÓRDOBA, LUCIFER OF CAGLIARI, EUSEBIUS OF VERCELLI, and Pope LIBERIUS were all exiled by Constantius, an ardent promoter of Arianism as the official religion of the state. Athanasius was exiled again by Julian the Apostate and by Valens.

Divergence between Eastern and Western Theories. Two main Christian attitudes or, rather, theories of the relations of Church and State began to take definite shape from the age of Constantine. In the West the idea of the two societies, the ecclesiastical and the civil, with their respective rights and privileges, was maintained and developed. In the East, EUSEBIUS OF CAESAREA advanced the view that as the empire was becoming Christian the two societies were merging into a single Christian society with the emperor as its head. He thus laid the foundations for what has been called CAESAROPAPISM in practice, if not in theory. It was only natural, accordingly, that the Germanic kings who were converted to Arian Christianity should regard themselves as heads of the Church in their realms. At Constantinople and in the Arian kingdom, the Church thus became in many respects a department of government.

Despite the opposition of Athanasius and other Eastern Fathers to Eusebius's concept of the merging of the two societies and, above all, to the supremacy of the emperor in the field of religion, this concept received constant imperial support and elaboration until it culminated under JUSTINIAN THE GREAT, who regarded himself as "priest-emperor." In the West, St. AMBROSE was the first great and successful champion of the rights of the Church, and he defended these rights with the vehemence and courage of an Old Testament Prophet. He maintained that the Church has certain sacred and inviolable rights, that it possesses jurisdiction over all Christians, and that the state cannot exercise jurisdiction over strictly ecclesiastical affairs (*see* his *Enarr. in Ps.* 37.43; *Epist.* 21.4). In his *Sermon against Auxentius* (36), he declared that the emperor had no title more honorable than "son of the Church" and that "the emperor is within the Church and not over it" (*imperator enim intra Ecclesiam, non supra Ecclesiam est*). For the massacre of Thessalonica, he required the powerful Emperor Theodosius the Great to acknowledge his guilt publicly, thus demonstrating that the Church had the right and the duty to insist that even an emperor obey the Christian moral law.

From the Death of Theodosius to the Accession of Justinian (A.D. 395–527). Following the death of Theodosius, the two halves of the empire remained separated until Justinian made the recovery of the West one of the major policies of his reign (his conquests in the West were largely temporary only). Beginning with the sack of Rome by Alaric (410), Roman authority in the West disintegrated steadily. The deposition of Romulus Augustus (476) marked the formal end of a Roman rule that for decades had been nominal only. Meanwhile, the bishops of the West, and especially the popes, developed the theory of the relations of Church and State much further; and they gave it the definitive form that became the inheritance of the Middle Ages.

St. AUGUSTINE in his various writings, but above all in his *De civitate Dei*, dealt in a comprehensive manner with the idea of the two societies. Unlike Eusebius, he emphasized their different character and their continued separation. Despite his fear regarding the dangers of interference by the state in religious affairs, he felt obliged, because of the violence of the Donatists, to call upon the imperial government for help. This action set a fateful precedent for the future.

In the period after Augustine, the popes, as Roman civil authority crumbled in he West, were forced to assume an increasingly important political role as the protectors and defenders of the Christian communities against the evils resulting from the Germanic invasions. At the same time, they had to defend the rights and the freedom of the Church in the East as well as in the West against the State-Church theory of the Byzantine emperors and Germanic Arian kings—and the application of the theory in practice. Popes LEO THE GREAT (440–461), SIMPLICIUS (468–483), FELIX III (II) (483–492), GELASIUS I (492–496), and SYMMACHUS (498–514) were understandably deferential in the communications that they addressed to the Roman emperors at Constantinople, for in their civil capacity they were really subjects of these exalted rulers. However, they all showed an uncompromising firmness in maintaining the rights, freedom, and supremacy of the Church in the spiritual sphere.

The theory of the two powers was given its clearest and most definitive form by Gelasius in his letter to the Emperor Anastasius:

> There are two [powers], August Emperor, by which this world is chiefly governed. The two powers are the *auctoritas sacrata pontificum* and the *regalis potestas*. Of the two the charge of the priests [*sacerdotes*] is heavier, in that they have to render an account in the Divine judgment for even the kings of men. For you know, most gracious son, that, though you preside over humankind by virtue of your office, you bow your neck piously to those who are in charge of things divine and from them you ask the things of your salvation; and hence you realize that, in receiving the heavenly mysteries and making proper arrangement for them, you must in the order of religion submit yourself rather than control, and in those matters you are dependent on their judgment and do not desire them to be subject to your will. For if, as far as the sphere of civil order is concerned, the bishops themselves, recognizing that the imperial office has been conferred upon you by Divine disposition, obey your laws . . . with what zeal, I ask you, should you not obey those who are deputed to dispense the sacred mysteries? [*Epist.* 12.2; tr. Ziegler; see also *Tract.* 4.11.]

This exposition on the two powers served as the foundation for the medieval theological and political teaching on the two swords.

See Also: ARIANISM.

Bibliography: H. RAHNER, *Kirche und Staat im frühen Christentum: Dokumente aus acht Jahrhunderten und ihre Deutung* (Munich 1961); et al., "Kirche und Staat," *Staatslexikon,* ed. GÖRRES-GESSELSCHAFT (6th ed. Freiburg 1957–63) 4: 991–1050, esp. 991–997, 1005–16, and 1046–47, bibliog. DANIÉLOU-MARROU, *Christian Century* v.1, ch. 7, 11, 14–19, 25–26, 31, 33. R. W. and A. J. CARLYLE, *A History of Mediaeval Political Theory in the West,* v.1, *The Second Century to the Ninth* (London 1927), esp. 81–193. K. F. MORRISON, "Rome and the City of God: An Essay on the Constitutional Relationships of Empire and Church in the Fourth Century," *Transactions of the American Philosophical Society,* NS 54.1 (1964) 3–55, with valuable bibliog., 53–54. E. CRANZ, "De civitate Dei XV, 2, and Augustine's Idea of Christian Society," *Speculum* 25 (1950) 215–225; "The Development of Augustine's Ideas on Society before the Donatist Controversy," *Harvard Theological Review* 47 (1954) 255–316. P. R. L. BROWN, "St. Augustine's Attitude to Religious Coercion," *Journal of Roman Studies* 54 (1964) 106–116. A. K. ZIEGLER, "Pope Gelasius I and His Teaching on the Relation of Church and State," *Catholic Historical Review* 27 (1942) 3–28, a study of basic importance.

[M. R. P. MCGUIRE]

THE MIDDLE AGES

Both in practice and in theory, the relationship between Church and State did not remain static over the 1,000 years of the Middle Ages but changed as social conditions, levels of learning, and traditions of thought also underwent change.

Early Middle Ages. It was the common assumption in the early Middle Ages that there was only one Christian society, one "congregation of the faithful," and the great problem was to balance the authority of the two chief offices, the princely office, or *regnum,* and the priestly office, or *sacerdotium,* which God had established to rule over it.

Developments in the East. In the medieval Eastern, or BYZANTINE, Empire, where strong imperial rule was unbroken by invasions and where ancient, especially Hellenistic, traditions were congenial with ideas of a sacred kingship, the emperors exercised the dominance over both Church and State that gave rise to the term CAESAROPAPISM. Emperor JUSTINIAN I (517–565) expressly counted among his responsibilities "the dignity and honor of the clergy" and "the true doctrines of the Godhead" (*Corpis iuris civilis, Novellae* 6). To maintain the clergy's dignity and honor, the emperors set the qualifications for ordinations, created bishoprics and changed their boundaries and status, appointed and even forced the resignation of patriarchs, supervised the monasteries and corrected abuses that recurred within them. Concern

for true doctrine led them to summon councils, supervise their proceedings, and enforce their decisions. ZENO in his *Henotikon* (482), HERACLIUS in his *Ekthesis* (638), and other emperors attempted to settle dogmatic disputes even without conciliar support. The Patriarch Antonius, writing between 1394 and 1397 to Prince Vasili I of Russia, maintained that the Christian emperors "from the beginning established and confirmed true religion" and that it was unthinkable and impossible to have a Church without an emperor. Not only Byzantium but also the Eastern peoples that learned from Byzantium accepted a similar princely tutelage over the Church. The Russian Primary Chronicle, for example, describes how the Prince of Kiev, Iaroslav the Wise (1016–54), built and endowed churches, appointed and supported priests, looked to their education and "bade them teach the people . . . and to go often into the churches."

This submissiveness in the East of the *sacerdotium* to the *regnum* permitted the prince to make free use of the wealth, administrative skills, and immense moral power of the Church; and this close cooperation was of inestimable value for harrassed peoples on Europe's frontier, struggling to survive against a barbarian sea. The priesthood in turn, largely freed from profane distractions, could devote itself to the sumptuous liturgy and rich mystical life characteristic of the Eastern churches. But submissiveness to princes also weakened contacts with sister churches and the universal Church, promoted a certain isolationism, facilitated schism, and compromised somewhat the prophetic liberty of the Church, in that it hampered it in its duty to denounce evil when tolerated or perpetrated by princes. Czar Ivan the Terrible could murder a patriarch, and Peter the Great could abolish the office altogether, with impunity.

The Church in the West. In the Latin West, the relations between the princely and sacerdotal powers developed under very different conditions. Up to the 11th century the low cultural level of the West, not fully relieved even by the CAROLINGIAN RENAISSANCE in the 9th century, was not conducive to original speculation on the nature of Christian society. Those pre-Carolingian and Carolingian writers who touched on kingship— ISIDORE OF SEVILLE, the unknown Irish author of the *De duodecim abusivis saeculi* (written probably between 630 and 650), Kathvulf (author of an address to Charlemagne), SMARAGDUS OF SAINT-MIHIEL, JONAS OF ORLÉANS, Sedulius Scotus and HINCMAR OF REIMS—attempted no profound analysis of the nature of royal authority, and their assumptions may be described as vaguely Gelasian: the king had a right to rule, but priests must advise him for his own spiritual welfare. The coronation of CHARLEMAGNE (800) also brought a revival of royal pretensions to dominance over the Church. Charlemagne himself, in a letter to LEO III, limited the pope's duties to praying "like Moses" for the emperor's victories, while he took charge of all other functions in the government of the Church, including the task of fortifying it "with the knowledge of the faith."

In the same period, amid a long-lasting vacuum of effective lay power, popes and bishops were developing a spirit of self-reliance and independence, as they exercised leadership not only in religious matters but in many secular affairs as well. GREGORY I (590–604), for example, had to arrange for the economic support and military security of Rome. In the early 8th century, GREGORY II and GREGORY III vigorously rejected the iconoclastic policies of the Byzantine Emperor LEO III and denounced imperial interference in dogmatic questions. The DONATION OF CONSTANTINE, a crude but effective forgery redacted probably about 750, was tantamount to a papal declaration of independence from Byzantine authority (Constantine had supposedly given the whole Western Empire to the pope), and offered justification for the momentous papal decision to seek a new champion in the Frankish monarch. The donation of the Frankish king PEPIN III, promised in 754 and completed in 756, further established the popes' claim to the temporal sovereignty over central Italy, the "patrimony of St. Peter," although throughout the Carolingian age the Frankish kings remained the effective rulers of the area.

Another expression of clerical independence were the Pseudo-Isidorian decretals, a collection of largely forged papal letters redacted probably between 847 and 852 in France and primarily intended to defend French bishops against mounting lay oppression (*see* FALSE DECRETALS). Pseudo-Isidore emphasized clerical immunities and papal authority, but he does not seem to have envisioned a true priestly or papal theocracy. More forceful than Pseudo-Isidore in expressing the supremacy of the *sacerdotium* and papacy was the strong-willed Pope NICHOLAS I (858–867), whose letters contain, apparently for the first time, the unambigous assertion that the emperor derived his power not directly from God but from the Church and priesthood.

The early Middle Ages thus developed a broad spectrum of opinion concerning the proper distribution of power in Christian society, but a full confrontation of opposing views did not occur until the 11th century, until the great quarrel between the papacy and the HOLY ROMAN EMPIRE known as the INVESTITURE STRUGGLE.

High Middle Ages. By the middle of the 11th century, a group of reformers, led by Cardinal HUMBERT OF SILVA CANDIDA, author of the highly influential *Libri III adversus simoniacos* (1054–58), by LEO IX, NICHOLAS II, and above all by the great Hildebrand, GREGORY VII, had concluded that lay domination over the Church, and in particular lay control of clerical appointments, was flooding the Church with unworthy prelates, undermining clerical morality, and placing in jeopardy the salvation of Christians. These reformers demanded a full "liberty of the Church," which implied not only freedom from lay interference in clerical elections but also the immunity of the clergy from the law, courts, discipline, and even taxes of lay rulers. Emperor HENRY IV (1056–1106) resisted this program, which would have emasculated his power, but he was excommunicated and deposed (1076) and was forced to do a humiliating penance at Canossa (1077). The Concordat of WORMS (1122) patched together a compromise with respect to clerical appointments, but left unresolved the fundamental issue as to who, pope or emperor, exercised supreme authority over the medieval Christian commonwealth, the *Respublica Christiana.*

The Papalists. The essence of Gregorian thought, which dominated papal policy for the rest of the Middle Ages, seems to have been this: the priesthood, responsible for guiding the individual Christian to personal reform, was also responsible for actively leading the Christian commonwealth to the reform of its public morals, customs, and even institutions. The papacy, through its universal authority, provided unity and direction in this work of regenerating Christian society. Kings had to follow the leadership of priests and to place their swords at their service; to oppose them was to merit reprimand, excommunication, and even deposition. Despite these exalted views of priestly leadership, it does not appear that Gregory VII was a true theocratic "monist," in the sense of maintaining that all authority derived from the priesthood. In his letters, Gregory expressed only an Augustinian disdain for the office and works of kings and no claim that the priesthood was the source of their power. MANEGOLD OF LAUTENBACH, one of the ablest of Gregorian publicists, justified Gregory's deposition of Henry not because the pope could make and unmake emperors at will, but because Henry had violated a kind of SOCIAL CONTRACT made with his subjects and had in fact deposed himself.

From the investiture controversy to the AVIGNON PAPACY (1305), the period of their maximum prestige and power, the popes continued to pursue, with some success, these Gregorian ideals. The theory of papal hegemony was also strengthened. St. BERNARD OF CLAIRVAUX, in a famous analogy, likened the priestly and regal power to the two swords mentioned in Lk 22.38 and held that both belonged to the Church and were to be employed in its service. The great development in the study of Canon Law, which the investiture controversy itself had stimulated, added a new precision, rigor, and systematic spirit to the papalist argument (*see* CANON LAW, HISTORY OF).

Canonists—decretists from the 12th century and, still more, decretalists in the 13th—contended that the pope, as vicar of God, must necessarily include royal authority within his plenitude of power and that a Christian society with two heads would be some sort of monster. To these ideas the papal publicists GILES OF ROME (d. 1316) and AUGUSTINE OF ANCONA (d. 1328) gave the most extreme expression, attributing to the pope dominion over all men, Christian and pagan, and ownership of all their possessions.

The popes of the epoch—notably INNOCENT III, INNOCENT IV, ALEXANDER IV, and BONIFACE VIII —remained in their public utterances distinctly more restrained than their enthusiastic theorists. Innocent III (1198–1216), for example, though often expressing exalted views on papal power, also, in the decretal *Novit,* written in 1204 to PHILIP II OF FRANCE, disclaimed all intent of diminishing royal jurisdiction or of judging concerning fiefs. Even the bull *UNAM SANCTAM* (1302) of Boniface VIII, the most famous papal pronouncement on Church-State relations in the Middle Ages, was essentially a summons to Christian unity through obedience to the pope, but the document, oddly anachronistic in the allegorical and imprecise arguments used, left vague the extent of the obedience demanded.

Historians still disagree as to whether these medieval popes really envisioned a kind of theocratic "world monarchy" under absolute papal power. Certainly the popes welcomed and echoed the sweeping claims of their supporters, but they were also realistic men. They seem to have used these grandiose speculations not to define the primary aims of papal policy, but as useful arguments in the achievement of the more limited and more practical goals of maintaining ecclesiastical liberty, Christian unity, and papal leadership in spiritually significant affairs.

Development of the Concept of the State. In the 12th and 13th centuries, the papacy faced an ever-stronger lay challenge to its hegemony from such powerful rulers as the Emperors FREDERICK I and FREDERICK II and the kings HENRY II and Edward I of England and PHILIP IV of France. Moreover, the renewed study of Roman law in the 12th century and the recovery of Aristotle's *Politics* in the 13th contributed strongly to what some historians call an emergent "lay spirit." Roman law attributed an unlimited SOVEREIGNTY to a prince who drew his power directly from the community, and Aristotle located the basis for political authority in the very nature of man. In this creative period, medieval political thinkers were in fact fashioning the modern idea of the state; establishing its autonomy; and, through their acute constitutional speculations, exploring the management of its power.

In the face of this naturalistic and lay challenge to the religious premises of all prior medieval political thought, THOMAS AQUINAS, with characteristic prudence, attempted to defend in new terms the traditional Gelasian notion of a balance of spiritual and secular power. For Thomas, nature and the natural law established the autonomy of, but also limited, the sovereignty of princes. Revealed or divine law established the autonomy of, but also limited, the sovereignty of popes. God alone was truly sovereign, and both the natural and divine laws, and the State and Church they established, drew their authority from His sovereign will, from what Thomas calls the eternal law of the universe.

Close to Thomas in his ideal of balance, but far more explicit in defending the autonomy of kings and rebuking papal pretensions to sovereignty over them, was JOHN OF PARIS, author of the *Tractatus de potestate regia et papali* (1302). The *De monarchia* of DANTE ALIGHIERI (written between 1310 and 1316) used Aristotelian naturalism to show the necessity of a universal empire and used Aristotelian logic to refute the allegorical use of scriptural figures (two swords, sun and moon, etc.) that papalists had enlisted to support their claims. Far more radical challenges to papal authority were presented by the Englishman WILLIAM OF OCKHAM (d. 1349) and especially by MARSILIUS OF PADUA, author of the *Defensor pacis* (1324). Marsilius, a true theoretical monist in that he conceded unlimited power to the community and to the prince who represented it, denied all substance to clerical authority and totally subjected priesthood and papacy to the prince's regulation, supervision, and discipline.

Late Middle Ages. The last two centuries of the Middle Ages were marked by the progressive disintegration of the medieval Christian commonwealth, brought about by the declining power and prestige of the papacy and the growing power of princes, who were able through their own enactments and through CONCORDATS with the papacy to gain ever-wider powers over their territorial churches. Political thought in this period was occupied more by the argument over CONCILIARISM —concerning the relation of popes and general councils—than by questions of Church and State. But such conciliarist thinkers as CONRAD OF GELNHAUSEN, HENRY HEINBUCHE OF LANGENSTEIN, Francesco ZABARELLA, Jean GERSON, and NICHOLAS OF CUSA, in attempting to make the pope subject to the corporate community of the Church, in conceding to the princes a position of prominence within that community, also contributed, if indirectly, to the growing lay power over territorial churches. More directly favoring state power was the great heretic John WYCLIF (d. 1384), who denied to the unregenerate clergy all rights of dominion and ownership and looked to the lay magistrate for leadership in reform.

The great medieval effort to build a commonwealth of Christian peoples and princes bound together by obedience to the pope and under his supreme guidance thus ended in failure. The popes themselves were perhaps too slow in recognizing that active world leadership carried grave risks of demeaning secular involvements and a degrading fiscalism and that many of their own ideals of social order and welfare could be achieved and were better achieved by the lay states that they had hoped to tutor. But that effort was not without value for the achievement in medieval Europe of a higher level of political order and an intensified political consciousness, and it also remains a rich and instructive chapter within the larger history of the Church's continuing quest to bear effective Christian witness within a complex and changing world.

Bibliography: E. BARKER, *Social and Political Thought in Byzantium* (Oxford 1957). A. MICHEL, *Die Kaisermacht in der Ostkirche, 843–1204* (Darmstadt 1959). M. PACAUT, *La Théocratie: L'Église et le pouvoir au moyen âge* (Paris 1957). W. ULLMAN, *Medieval Papalism: The Political Theories of the Medieval Canonists* (London 1949); *The Growth of Papal Government in the Middle Ages* (2d ed. New York 1962). B. TIERNEY, *The Crisis of Church and State, 1050–1300* (Englewood Cliffs, N.J. 1964). G. TELLENBACH, *Church, State and Christian Society at the Time of the Investiture Contest,* tr. R. F. BENNETT (Oxford 1959). A. STICKLER, *Sacerdotium et regnum nei decretalisti e primi decretalisti* (Turin 1953). F. KEMPF, *Papsttum und Kaisertum bei Innocenz III* (Rome 1954). J. M. POWELL, *Innocent III, Vicar of Christ or Lord of the World?* (Boston 1963).

[D. J. HERLIHY]

THE PERIOD OF CONFESSIONAL STATES

The monarchical consolidation of power in the nation-states of western Europe was achieved at the expense of the anachronistic claims of the papacy to temporal sovereignty. By the early 1500s, several princes, imbued with the secular philosophy of MARSILIUS OF PADUA and Niccoló MACHIAVELLI, warred with the STATES OF THE CHURCH. Popes of the RENAISSANCE, as much secular as spiritual princes, engaged actively in diplomacy, sometimes compromising claims to temporal sovereignty in order to win allies. The HOLY ROMAN EMPIRE was fraught with heresy, confederative tendencies, and nationalism. Germans, Czechs, and Swiss resented Spanish and Italian interference. There were strong anticlerical traditions in England and France.

Momentous forces let loose by the CRUSADES, recurring epidemics of the plague, nascent capitalism, overseas exploration, and the rise of the merchant-professional middle class played havoc with traditional political, social, and economic institutions. Great ecclesiastics were humbled by greater kings. Laymen often replaced bishops and abbots in government when the temporal claims of the papacy were opposed by nationalistic monarchs in struggles over lay investiture, ecclesiastical courts, clerical taxation, and similar issues. The prestige of the papacy had suffered through serious religious controversies from the Babylonian captivity to the rise of CONCILIARISM. Effective leadership and spirituality were lacking in some Renaissance popes and bishops. Reform movements of the 15th century fell short of the achievements of those of earlier periods.

Theories of the Reformers. Into this maelstrom the Protestant REFORMATION injected disquieting ideas that attacked papal temporal and spiritual sovereignty. Certain secular princes supported the Reformers against the pope in order to realize private political aims. The effect of the Reformation, therefore, was to encourage nationalism and ABSOLUTISM through the removal of papal restraints and the emphasis on ERASTIANISM. Conversely, without help from antipapal princes, the Reformers probably could not have survived against the awesome papal weapons of EXCOMMUNICATION, interdict, INQUISITION, and the INDEX OF FORBIDDEN BOOKS.

Luther. Martin LUTHER was deeply concerned about the relation of Church and State, but he was inconsistent in his views. Strongly nationalistic, he resented Italian domination of the Church and Spanish interference in the Empire. Similar-minded German princes sustained him and promoted his doctrines. He originally advocated the separation of Church and State, holding that all authority originated with God and passed through Him to princes, whose power on earth was superior to ecclesiastical authority. Practical problems forced him to alter this theory, however. He condoned civil control over religion in connection with the Saxon visitation of 1527, arguing that the Elector's syndics should supervise preaching, suppress Catholicism, and punish schismatics such as the ANABAPTISTS. Luther also supported the Leagues of Torgau and Schmalkalden, which forcefully advanced his doctrines. He favored the aristocracy against the peasants in 1525, thereby supporting pragmatically the civil authorities and furthering LUTHERANISM and German nationalism. He often stated theoretically that neither bishops nor princes should impose decrees or laws against the convictions of conscience, but he argued practically for theocratic absolutism. He denied papal supremacy and rejected episcopal authority as unscriptural. His advocacy of passive obedience to lawful temporal jurisdiction encouraged the 17th-century doctrine of the DIVINE RIGHT OF KINGS.

Calvin. John CALVIN of Geneva also taught the strict separation of civil and ecclesiastical power but later found it impractical to enforce it except at the cost of impairing the success of his tenets. Calvin's *Institutes* (1535) illustrate how well trained he was in theology and law and how easily he made the transition from Genevan minister to dictatorial head of the theocratic city-state. He considered the function of civil government to be simply the preservation of law and the enforcement of religion and personal piety according to his doctrines. All civil offices were divinely ordained so that it was unlawful and immoral to rebel against the state unless the state violated God's will (as Calvin interpreted it). Accordingly, civil obedience was a moral duty; and civil disobedience against immoral princes, a right. Calvin's doctrine of jusitifiable rebellion through magistrates was employed by his followers in Holland, Scotland, England, and France during the next century. His politicoecclesiastical system operated as an aristocratic theocracy headed by him and assisted by the consistory, composed of ministers and elders, which functioned as the coordinating body between magistrates and ministers. Although Calvin may have originally preached that Church and State were exclusive societies, the former admonishing citizens to moral and spiritual perfection and the latter enforcing uniformity by punishing sinners, in effect the temporal and ecclesiastical officers worked together to further CALVINISM.

Zwingli. Huldrych ZWINGLI of Zurich, who wished to expel foreign influence and suppress aristocratic oligarchy, was a modern-day prophet-avenger. He hoped to establish divine law as revealed in Scriptures through the forcible implementation of civil authority. Each community or state, he said, should determine its religion and enforce it strictly through civil officers. Denying altogether the authority of the pope and bishops, Zwingli advocated the fullest cooperation between civil and ecclesiastical officers in ruling a government operated according to Christian precepts.

English Developments. Whereas Lutheranism and Calvinism were as much social and economic as religious movements, ANGLICANISM was from the first almost entirely political. The long history of Anglo-papal controversy after the Conquest of 1066 culminated in HENRY VIII's Act of Supremacy (1534), severing the link between England and Rome by making him supreme head of the Church *in* England. Not until the Acts of Supremacy and Uniformity (1559) under ELIZABETH I, however, did Anglicanism become doctrinally the Church *of* England. The English Church and Parliament established an episcopalian ecclesiastical polity under the primacy of the monarch. Erastianism became a cardinal policy of Anglicanism, the crown-in-convocation ruling the Church. Puritanism, rooted in Calvinism, sprang up quickly. Most PURITANS accepted Episcopalianism, hoping, however, to increase lay participation in ecclesiastical affairs. Some separatist Puritans in England and Scotland favored PRESBYTERIANISM with its kirk sessions, synods, and general assemblies; John KNOX and

George Buchanan in Scotland and Thomas CARTWRIGHT in England were its chief theorists. Other separatists were CONGREGATIONALISTS, advocating the doctrinal and governmental autonomy of each parish.

Caesaropapism found its exponents and opponents in 17th-century England. The principal Anglican apologist was Richard HOOKER, who in *The Laws of Ecclesiastical Polity* (1594) defended episcopalianism against the incursions of Presbyterians. He favored monarchy that should be fully, albeit passively, obeyed. Divine-right monarchy, sanctioned directly by God (not by the pope, councils, or popular will) and invested with spiritual and temporal power flowered under the early Stuarts. Their struggles with Parliament were essentially constitutional (absolute versus mixed monarchy), but their quarrel was also vitally concerned with issues such as that of FUNDAMENTALISM versus ARMINIANISM. Many parliamentarians favored the governmental enforcement of "true religion"; others wanted a strict separation of Church and State. Thomas HOBBES argued that absolute monarchy, sovereign in civil and ecclesiastical affairs, was the best form of government. Revolution against it was therefore unthinkable, and religious uniformity was preferable to sectarianism. John LOCKE later maintained that separation of Church and State was essential and that religious toleration would develop from noninterference by the government, whose authority lay outside questions of conscience. Yet neither he nor Hobbes included Catholics among the tolerated because they were allegedly subject to external papal authority.

Catholic Response. The vehement attacks against hierocratic doctrine by the Reformers and their magisterial supporters demanded firm answers, but the Emperor CHARLES V and the popes from PAUL III to PIUS IV differed over what the answers should be. Rome considered doctrinal issues vital, whereas Charles wished to promote Catholic-Protestant talks aimed at resolving political disunity. Charles had already compromised the Church's position in the Peace of AUGSBURG (1529) and in concessions to Lutheran princes before Paul III convened the Council of TRENT (1545–63), which was in itself an admission that the pope alone could not solve the great issues. Charles disliked the choice of Trent as a site; and when the Council adjourned to Bologna in 1547, he prohibited Germans from going there. The Spaniards, remembering Spanish-papal disputes in Italy, were also unhappy. Meanwhile, Charles authorized unorthodox religious practices to placate the Reformers. Although the Council made no dogmatic pronouncement on papal infallibility, it did buttress papal authority by denying that princes could interfere with the Inquisition, excommunication, papal bulls, and ecclesiastical courts. Political problems involving the Holy See nevertheless arose soon afterward respecting England, Holland, and France. In addition, PHILIP II of Spain accepted papal help to suppress the Dutch Calvinists and the Anglicans; the pope lost prestige when both ventures failed.

Gallicanism. GALLICANISM in France posed a serious problem from the 15th century to the FRENCH REVOLUTION. The clergy had fallen increasingly under monarchical control since the reign of Philip IV (d. 1314), and caesaropapism became entrenched legally through the Pragmatic Sanction of Bourges (1438) and the Concordat of Bologna (1516), through which the king obtained the right to appoint hierarchs, subject only to *pro forma* papal approval. Naturally, FRANCIS I and his successors nominated hierarchs sympathetic to royal policy, whether or not it coincided with the interests of the Church. Gallicanism encouraged the evolution of a virtual French national Church dominated by the monarch, whose supervision of churchmen and Church property was coextensive with the degree of royal absolutism; this reached its apogee under LOUIS XIV (d. 1715).

Political theorists about the turn of the 17th century avidly supported Gallicanism. Pierre PITHOU (d. 1596), for instance, argued that papal decrees had no force in France without the *placet* of the French bishops meeting in council. Edmond RICHER (d. 1633) maintained that the authority of ecumenical councils was superior to papal authority.

Theoretical Developments. About the same time two illustrious Catholic authors, the Jesuits Robert BELLARMINE (d. 1621) and Francisco SUÁREZ (d. 1617), upheld papal spiritual supremacy but denied the pope's right to interfere in temporal affairs. Bellarmine advocated the separation of Church and State and rejected the temporal power of the pope except to prevent the implementation of laws threatening the Church's rights or to depose heretical monarchs, but he later rescinded this view of the *potestas indirecta*. Suárez likewise made a distinction between papal temporal and spiritual jurisdiction, but he held it lawful for the pope to interfere in a state's religious policy because princes were subject to divine law, which superseded civil law. He also urged freedom of conscience, even for pagans and heretics.

Decline of Papal Power. Secular authorities no longer took papal temporal power seriously after the middle of the 17th century, and religious persecution waned. Princes dismissed, for instance, the pope's objections to the Peace of WESTPHALIA in 1648. Persecution in the Holy Roman Empire and England became uncommon. Henry IV (d. 1610), converted from Calvinism to Catholicism, issued the Edict of NANTES (1598) in the hope of resolving the long struggle between Catholics and HUGUENOTS. RICHELIEU and MAZARIN tolerated the Huguenots because they were important to the French economy, although they were attacked occasionally for political reasons. Louis XIV continued the lenient policy until 1685, when he revoked the edict, saddening INNOCENT XI, who privately urged toleration by Louis and JAMES II of England. The persecution of Huguenots and Jansenists was a manifestation of divine-right absolutism aimed at regulating French life, though Louis also felt it his moral duty to suppress heresy. He frequently interfered in Church government even to the point of isolating French bishops from contact with Rome, espousing bizarre doctrines, and confiscating the revenues of vacant episcopal sees. In 1682, with Louis's approval, more than 70 French bishops rejected papal infallibility, reiterated Gallican liberties, and maintained that ecumenical councils had a higher order of authority than the pope.

The Age of Enlightenment. The ideas of the 18th-century ENLIGHTENMENT embodied a conception of a mechanistic universe regulated by immutable physical laws. RATIONALISM, DEISM, and the social contract theory of government gave a materialistic explanation of the origin of matter and of the political and social order that challenged the teachings of the Catholic Church and, indirectly, the authority of Christ's vicar. Since rationalist political theorists maintained that the stale evolved from practical necessity and was dependent on popular will, the pope was excluded from any association with civil power.

Febronianism and Josephinism. It is surprising, however, that the principal opposition to the authority of the Holy See came not from the rationalists but from the Catholic exponents of FEBRONIANISM and JOSEPHINISM, two closely related theories that developed in Germany and Austria. Bishop John Nikolaus von HONTHEIM of Trier (d. 1790), writing under the pseudonym Febronius, held that the popes had usurped primacy and were no more powerful than other bishops, a general Church council alone being authoritative. Moreover, neither papal nor conciliar decrees were binding in a country unless its ruler sanctioned them. Febronius recanted in 1778, but his ideas were widely adopted by German bishops, including the three ecclesiastical electors. At the Congress of EMS (1786) these bishops demanded privileges of episcopal independence that infringed upon papal primacy, in effect emulating Gallicanism in what amounted to the government of a separate German Catholic Church. Febronianism and its Austrian counterpart, Josephinism, thrived during Prussia's and Austria's supremacy under FREDERICK II (the Great) and MARIA THERESA. The Empress put the clergy and Church property under state control and rejected papal or episcopal decrees of which she disapproved. Her successor, JOSEPH II, appointed bishops without papal approbation, altered diocesan boundaries, changed the liturgy and Church calendar, suppressed women's religious orders, and closed hundreds of convents. Leopold II of Tuscany, his brother, made similar changes.

The First Secular States: the United States and France. Secularization in the Enlightenment led in part to the creation of secular states in France and the United States. Blaming the Church for evils that oppressed the lower classes, the French revolutionaries first confiscated Church property and later subordinated ecclesiastics to the state through the CIVIL CONSTITUTION OF THE CLERGY (1790). Many clergy, however, refused to acknowledge allegiance to what amounted to a French national Church in the face of PIUS VI's declaration that the constitution was heretical and that he would excommunicate clergy who submitted to it. The constitution therefore created schisms within France and between it and the papacy that were not healed until NAPOLEON I, for political reasons, signed with PIUS VII the CONCORDAT OF 1801.

Puritanism in America had admitted the close connection of ministerial and magisterial authority during the 17th century in the northern and mid-Atlantic colonies. But Congregationalism had found widespread support and the ''saints'' had gradually given ground. In most colonies the principle of Church and State separation had been commonly accepted by the mid-18th century so that, with the winning of American independence and the acceptance of a constitution, there was no question that the separation principle was firmly established. The first American Catholic bishop, John CARROLL, and others that followed him supported the principle as well as religious toleration for all.

Bibliography: O. F. VON GIERKE, *Political Theories of the Middle Ages,* tr. F. W. MAITLAND (Cambridge, Eng. 1900; pa. Boston 1958). F. GAVIN, *Seven Centuries of the Problem of Church and State* (New York 1938) 68–128. C. C. ECKHARDT, *The Papacy and World Affairs as Reflected in the Secularization of Politics* (Chicago 1937). R. G. GETTELL, *History of Political Thought* (New York 1924), esp. ch. 6, 8–13, 18. F. MOURRET, *A History of the Catholic Church,* tr. N. THOMPSON, 8 v. (St. Louis 1930–57) v.6, 7, *passim.* C. POULET, *A History of the Catholic Church,* tr. from 4th Fr. ed. by S. A. RAEMERS, 2 v. (St. Louis 1934–35), v.2, *passim.* H. DANIEL-ROPS, *The Church in the Seventeenth Century,* tr. J. BUCKINGHAM (London 1963). C. D. CREMEANS, *The Reception of Calvinistic Thought in England* (Urbana, Ill. 1949). G. DONALDSON, *The Scottish Reformation* (Cambridge, Eng. 1960). J. T. ELLIS, *Perspectives in American Catholicism* (Baltimore 1963) 1–39. A. SIMPSON, *Puritanism in Old and New England* (Chicago 1955).

[M. J. HAVRAN]

CHURCH AND STATE SINCE 1789

Scholars are inclined to stress the relationships among the political movements of the late 18th century and to include them under a comprehensive title—the democratic revolution (*see* DEMOCRACY). In Europe and in North and South America these movements had a common element in the rejection of absolutist pretensions and hereditary privilege. There were similar demands for checks on executive power through popular representation, assertions of popular sovereignty and the natural equality of man, and appeals to individual rights of conscience, speech, and assembly.

Extension of Liberal Constitutionalism. If the proponents of change had a common base, they were faced with different situations. In England, the theory of Constitutionalism had already been accepted; there remained the tasks of extending civil liberties to unpopular minorities such as Catholics and Jews and of broadening the base of political participation. On the Continent, entrenched institutions and social groups provided determined resistance that was only gradually overcome in the course of the 19th century. In the United States the social structure offered no such resistance to ideas and institutions that had been maturing during the colonial period.

Implicit in the constitutional theory was the distinction between the state, with its specific centrally coordinated activities, and society, with its manifold uncentralized relationships. The Constitution of the United States made this distinction explicit in its concept of reserved and delegated powers and in its first 10 amendments. In Continental Europe there remained considerable ambiguity in this field both on the theoretical level, where a Rousseauist monism had some influence, and in the tendency of the state to continue the control of religion characteristic of the Old Regime. A clear example of the latter was the Civil Constitution of the Clergy (1790).

In broadest terms the 18th-century political revolutions can be considered as efforts to reestablish constitutionalism, or the limitation of governmental authority by private right, in opposition to theories of obedience to the state that had developed since the Renaissance. Medieval precedents could be cited to justify such efforts. But when proposed in the 18th century, constitutionalism had to face the problem that the Protestant Reformation had strengthened the tendency to consider a common religion as the necessary cement for a cohesive community structure. Various Christian churches had been established in many states through arrangements that afforded protection and support to a privileged religion over which the state exercised considerable control.

American Developments. As religion weakened as a social bond in the 18th century, ''reason,'' ''nature,'' and patriotism were appealed to as substitutes (*see* DEISM; RATIONALISM). When specific circumstances made religious pluralism necessary, it was accepted. Thus, a combination of Catholic leadership and a Protestant majority led to the TOLERATION ACTS in Maryland (1639, 1649); the royal charter for Rhode Island (1663) accepted the principle of religious liberty, though it was circumscribed in practice; and William PENN's Frame of Government in Pennsylvania (1682) made his colony the freest in religious matters. This trend toward separation of Church and State was greatly extended by the American Revolution: Thomas Jefferson authored Virginia's Act for Establishing Religious Freedom (1786), which affirmed the neutrality of the state in matters of faith.

When the Bill of Rights was appended to the U.S. Constitution (1791), the opening words of the First Amendment declared: "Congress shall make no law respecting an establishment of religion, or prohibiting the free exercise thereof." The decisive factor in this solution was pragmatic: in no other way could the thirteen states, four of which had established churches and all of which had a mosaic of religious variations, be formed into a single nation. In only one other nation, Belgium, was full religious liberty written into the constitution at the foundation of the state. There, as in the United States, special circumstances made Catholics favorable to constitutional limitations on government and to freedom of religion.

Objections of Catholic Theorists. The doctrine of popular sovereignty associated with these developments met objection from Catholic theorists on the ground that it denied that God was the source of all authority. They also found disestablishment unpalatable on the premise that Church and State are independent societies, with the Church superior because of its end. Asserting the "indirect power" of the Church, they maintained that the state must support it when its aid is needed or when the temporal and spiritual converge (e.g., in education, marriage). With a variety of nuances this position continued to dominate Catholic thinking throughout the 19th century. The struggle to preserve the States of the Church strengthened this position, for the temporal power was incompatible with a theory of separation. Nor did the cause of separation recommend itself since many of its proponents wished to strip the Church of all public influence.

Theoretical objections, however, did not impede the gradual extension of liberal constitutionalism. On the practical level, circumstances determined the reaction of most Catholics to the disappearance of the confessional state. In areas where they were a minority, as in England, Canada, Australia, New Zealand, Scandinavia, Switzerland, the Netherlands, and in some German and eastern European states, Catholics welcomed any steps that extended religious freedom. The same attitude prevailed where Catholics were a majority but the governing power was non-Catholic, as in Ireland and Poland.

Attempts at Accommodation. Even where religious liberty conferred the greatest benefits, as in the United States, few developed a consistent theory to explain their preference. Those who did so were mostly Europeans and were known as Liberal Catholics. Faced with the necessity of making some accommodation with reality, the majority accepted the formula of "thesis-hypothesis." The "thesis," or ideal, was asserted to be the situation in which civil society would recognize only the true religion and would value it as the foundation of public order; the "hypothesis" was applied to situations in which the Church would accept the actual circumstances of divided religious loyalty and would demand only the right to preach the gospel freely, to rule and guide the baptized, to organize private and public religious worship, and to possess property. Even the outstanding Liberal Félix DUPANLOUP, Bishop of Orléans, appealed to this distinction to explain the apparent rigidity of the SYLLABUS OF ERRORS of PIUS IX (1864). The favorable response he drew from bishops in all countries testified to the popularity of this partial accommodation to the disappearance of the confessional state.

Use of Concordats. The proponents of indirect power and of the thesis-hypothesis formula had some difficulty in explaining the CONCORDATS that became a prominent feature of ecclesiastical policy in the 19th century. Patterned on the arrangements made by Napoleon I with PIUS VII for France (1801) and Italy (1803), the concordats bound the Church and specific governments to mutual reciprocal obligations. Both in the negotiations and in the texts, these had the appearance of contractual engagements between sovereigns. They afforded no support to the assumption of superiority of the ecclesiastical power required by the thesis.

Liberal Catholics. The Liberal Catholics made a more explicit attempt to adjust to the condition in which the Church could no longer count on the coercive power of the state to support its mission. The term Liberal Catholic lacks precision; those whom it designates were not liberal in the sense that they raised the banner of personal autonomy against authority in institutionalized religion. Nor were they genuinely philosophical in their approach to political problems. They began with the conviction that privilege was dead and that the Church could count only on the free assent of its members. They did not consider the passing of the confessional state a tragedy. They welcomed it as a boon that had already proved its worth in Belgium and the United States. They were impressed by Daniel O'CONNELL's use of the parliamentary process to gain Catholic EMANCIPATION, and contrasted the advantages of religious liberty with the deadening dependence of the Church on arbitrary power in the old regimes.

Nearly everywhere their views met resistance, notably in Rome. Early Liberal Catholics, such as Félicité de LAMENNAIS, were strong advocates of papal power, which they viewed as a necessary counterweight to the national state's control of religion. But GREGORY XVI's *Mirari vos* (1832), and particularly the determination of PIUS IX to oppose all political forms that posed a threat to the continued existence of the Papal States, caused the Liberal Catholics to drift from the ULTRAMONTANISM that had been their hallmark. In the crisis leading to the disappearance of the temporal power, the term ultramontanist came to be applied to those supporters of the papal position who rejected all accommodation with representative institutions and individual liberties.

Growth of Catholic Institutions. While circumstances were adding to the difficulties of Catholics who wished to accept the new political order, there was a remarkable growth of Catholic institutions in democratic and liberal states. Conflicts over education led to the establishment of Catholic schools; interest in social questions increased the number of welfare institutions and stimulated the formation of Catholic workingman's associations; political conflicts, such as the KULTURKAMPF in Bismarck's Germany, contributed to the strengthening of viable Catholic political parties. Even dramatic breaks with tradition, such as the unilateral denunciation of the concordat by Republican France (1905), ultimately diverted Catholic energies into social and apostolic tasks. As decision-making in government broadened to include some participation by the majority of citizens, compacts with heads of states no longer provided sufficient guarantees for the vitality or even the safety of the Church. In this context, Catholic social organizations were to provide new methods of achieving the Church's mission.

Reorientation of Papal Policy. LEO XIII did not provide a new theoretical basis for Church-State relations. But he did give a new approach to modern political problems. He made strenuous efforts to detach French Catholics from their loyalty to monarchical government (*Au milieu des sollicitudes*); he praised the religious situation in the United States (*Longinqua*); he emphasized the God-given gift of liberty of the human person (*LIBERTAS*); and he declared that the people had the right to choose their rulers freely, though not to confer the right to rule (*Diuturnum*). PIUS X made no notable contribution in this field, though he did remove the ROMAN QUESTION from the arena of world politics and improved relations with Italy by modifying the *NON EXPEDIT*. BENEDICT XV removed the latter entirely and allowed Italian Catholics to form the Populari party on a nonconfessional basis.

Threat of Totalitarianism. The immediate consequence of World War I was a great expansion of the areas in which the form of the state was democratic with constitutions guaranteeing civil rights and full freedom of worship. Benedict XV and PIUS XI entered into cordial relations with most of these and negotiated concordats that accepted religious pluralism. But the collapse of the Czarist regime in Russia gave birth to a Soviet totalitarian state that was avowedly hostile to religion. The March on Rome (1922) established a Fascist state in Italy that became increasingly totalitarian. In 1933 Hitler came to power in Germany and established a dictatorship incompatible with Christianity. Dictatorships replaced democratic systems in several smaller states.

Pius XI made a determined effort to protect the rights of the Church with the LATERAN PACT and concordat with Mussolini (1929) and a concordat with Hitler (1933). But the principles of these regimes made it impossible for the Church to operate normally, and Pius XI condemned their basic tenets in *Non abbiamo bisogno* on Italian Fascism (1931), *Mit brennender sorge* against German National Socialism (1937), and *DIVINI REDEMPTORIS* against atheistic Communism (1937). Troubles with other dictatorships underlined the relatively favorable position of the Church in the democracies.

Papal Teaching on Democracy and Freedom of Religion. This experience was reflected in the wartime messages of PIUS XII, especially that of Christmas 1944 (*Benignitas et humanitas*). In it the pope rejected absolutism in all its forms. While insisting on the right of peoples to choose their form of government, the pope noted that men "are demanding a system of government more consistent with the dignity and liberty of the citizen" [*Acta Apostolicae Sedis* 37 (1945) 13]. The Church shared this interest and believed that citizens should be an active participants in social life. The pope contrasted the masses with a "people worthy of the name," free to hold opinions, to express them, and to use them for the common good. Later, in an address (*Ci riesce*) to the national convention of Italian jurists (1953), Pius XII maintained that in the new international community with states professing a variety of religions, false religions and moral error could be tolerated to promote the common good. The state is not bound to repress error in all circumstances; the common good is the decisive element.

A comprehensive statement on the historic issues of Church and State is found in JOHN XXIII's *PACEM IN TERRIS*, which was intended to be a guide for the 2d session of VATICAN COUNCIL II. Throughout the document, the distinction between society and the state is explicit. Equally clear is the right of conscience: "Every human being has the right to honor God according to the dictates of an upright conscience, and the right to profess his religion privately and publicly" (14). Error does not destroy human rights (158). Among essential human rights based on "the dignity of the human person" is "the right to take an active part in public affairs and to contribute one's part to the common good of the citizens" (26). This is not in conflict with the principle that "authority comes from God," which can be accommodated to democracy (52). Fundamentally, "every civil authority must take pains to promote the common good of all without preference for any single citizen or civic group" (56). The basic function of government is to preserve rights: "For to safeguard the inviolable rights of the human person and to facilitate the fulfillment of duties, should be the essential office of every public authority" (60). The description of the government that best corresponds to "the innate demands of human nature" (68–77) reads like a sketch of American democracy. Throughout, liberty becomes a basic norm of political life (see SOCIAL THOUGHT, PAPAL).

The teaching of Pope John had been foreshadowed by a number of European and American theologians who described the confessional state as the product of historical circumstances rather than an ideal toward which Catholics were bound to strive. Their work was assisted by a growing awareness of the vocation of the laity in representing the Church in the temporal order and in the emphasis on autonomous bodies of laymen in CATHOLIC ACTION. In the United States John Courtney MURRAY, SJ attempted a restatement of the Gelasian formula. The Christian is both a child of God and a member of the human community as a citizen of the state. In each capacity he is endowed with a set of rights. Harmony between Church and State must be achieved in the human person. It is democratic man, conscious of his freedom and his social obligations, who must assure the primacy of the spiritual in human society. It is by his witness to the faith that the mission of the Church is furthered.

As a member of the subcommission of the Secretariat for Christian Unity that dealt with the church-state issues at the second Vatican Council Murray was a principal architect of the council's Declaration on Religious Freedom (Dignitatis humanae). Murray developed a doctrine of human freedom that showed that the position taken by the council did not contradict earlier papal teaching. In commenting the Declaration, Murray singled out its endorsement of three important doctrinal tenets: religious freedom is a human right (personal and collective); the function and right of the state in religious matters is limited; and the freedom of the Church is the fundamental principle defining the relations between the Church and the sociopolitical order. Together with the council's Pastoral Constitution on the Church in the Modern World (Gaudium et spes), Dignitatis humanae resolved a long standing ambiguity that seemed to posit a double standard freedom for the Church when Catholics are in a minority; privilege for the Church and intolerance for other religions when Catholics are in a majority. (W. M. Abbott, Documents of Vatican II, 672–673). Gaudium et spes stated explicitly that the Church is not bound to any political system. "In their proper spheres," the constitution continues, "the political community and the Church are mutually independent and self-governing," but their concern to serve the personal and social wellbeing of the same beings is best achieved with mutual cooperation (GS 76).

The archbishop of Kraków, Karol Wojtyła, took special interest in the text of Gaudium et spes at Vatican II and later, as Pope John Paul II, addressed the issues of Church and state on numerous occasions. Many of his statements were made in defense of religious freedom and the rights of the Church in the new democracies that emerged after the breakup of the Soviet bloc and the demise of communist regimes. His most systematic and comprehensive presentation of norms and principles guiding Church-state relations appeared in the encyclical Centesimus annus, commemorating the hundredth anniversary of Rerurm novarum. John Paul presented it as a "rereading" of Pope Leo's encyclical which, he says, was written to address political, socioeconomic issues that arose in the 19th century and resulted in "a new conception of society and of the State, and consequently of authority itself" (n. 4). The task of the Church is not to promote a particular model of government, but teach principles that insure the common good and the wellbeing of the human person. The Church's "contribution to the political order is precisely her vision of the dignity of the person revealed in all its fullness in the mystery of the Incarnate Word" (nn. 43, 47). John Paul's approach to Church-state relations recognizes that political institutions are conditioned by historical circumstances and that it is the duty of both Church and state to promote and insure the dignity and rights of the human person.

Bibliography: H. A. ROMMEN, *The State in Catholic Thought* (St. Louis 1945); *The Natural Law,* tr. T. A. HANLEY (St. Louis 1947). A. C. JEMOLO, *Church and State in Italy, 1850–1950,* tr. D. MOORE (Philadelphia 1960). J. N. MOODY, ed., *Church and Society* (New York 1953). J. C. MURRAY, *We Hold These Truths* (New York 1960). J. MARITAIN, *Man and the State* (Chicago 1951). L. STURZO, *Church and State,* tr. B. B. CARTER (London 1939; Notre Dame, Ind. 1962). J. N. MOODY and J. G. LAWLER, eds., *The Challenge of Mater et Magistra* (New York 1963). G. WEIGEL, *Witness to Hope: The Biography of Pope John Paul II* (New York 1999).

[J. N. MOODY/EDS.]

CHURCH AND STATE (CANON LAW)

It has long been part of the study of canon law to explore the relationships between the Church and the diverse civil governments within whose territories the Church seeks to fulfill its mission. Treatises on the public law of the Church have traditionally been divided into *ius publicum internum,* the study of the internal constitution, structures, procedures, and power of the Church, and *ius publicum externum,* the study of the external relationships between the Church and the civil legal systems that the Church encounters throughout the world.

Ius publicum externum, or the canonical study of church-state relationships, is in turn divided into the *theoretical* study of the optimal relationship between ecclesial and civil society and the *practical* study of the *de facto* accommodation between the Church and the civil government in a particular nation. The theory underwent remarkable development during the Second Vatican Council and was given renewed expression in the Declaration on Religious Freedom. In many nations, the practical working out of relationships between Church and State takes the form of concordats entered into between the Holy See and individual civil governments that seek to protect, by mutual agreement, the interests of the Church and the state in matters of common concern, such as religious liberty, marriage, education, healthcare, ownership of property, public religious expression, appointment of ecclesiastical officials, and the punishment of certain crimes.

In the United States, where no formal concordat exists with any ecclesiastical authority, church-state relationships are worked out in federal and state legislatures and courts, notably in the Supreme Court of the United States. Input from the Church in the development of the law of church and state in the United States is through scholarly research and writing, effective influencing of legislation, expert witnesses in court cases to which the Church is a party, and the filing of *amicus curiae* (friend-of-the-court) briefs in other relevant federal and state litigation.

Code of Canon Law. Relevant to working out church-state relationships in each nation are a number of canons in the 1983 Code of Canon Law that refer or pertain to civil law. Forty canons make explicit reference to civil law. The references vary from declarations of the Church's total independence from the civil law, to exhortations to follow the provisions of civil law so as not to occasion harm to the Church, to "canonization" of the civil law, where prescriptions of civil law are said to have the same effect at canon law as at civil law.

The most sweeping declaration of independence is in the area of property law where the Church claims the right to acquire, possess, administer, and dispose of temporal goods, in pursuit of ends proper to the Church, independently of civil power (c. 1254). A relic of an earlier

age, and historically understandable in the light of centuries of struggle against secular rulers who unjustly deprived the Church of property, the claim continues to spawn occasional conflict. Pursuant to the claim, the Code of Canon Law contains 57 canons regulating church-related property (cc. 1254–1310) in general, and an additional section of canons regulating the property of religious institutes (cc. 634–640). One particularly troublesome specification of the claim concerns last wills and testaments, where the Church claims the right to insist upon fulfillment of dispositions to the Church in wills that are civilly invalid for failure to fulfill required formalities (c. 1299). In recognition of modern realities, however, the fulfillment of civil law formalities in the making of wills is urged and, in the case of members of religious institutes, required (c. 668n1). The Church's claim to independence in property matters is further moderated by placing canonical obligations on administrators of church property to observe prescriptions of civil law (c. 1284n2), to see that ownership of ecclesiastical property is safeguarded through civilly valid methods (c. 1284n2), and to utilize civilly effective means of establishing various diocesan funds (c. 1274).

Based on the sacramental nature of marriage between baptized persons, the Church also claims independence from civil laws regulating the essential aspects of marriage. The Church acknowledges competence in the state to regulate only the "merely civil effects" of marriage, such as dowry and change of name (c. 1059). Permission of a local ordinary is required, however, except in case of necessity, to assist at a marriage that would not be recognized by the civil law (c. 1071n1).

As to the "canonization" of civil law, the code affirms, as a general principle, that civil laws to which the law of the Church defers are to be observed in canon law with the same effects as in civil law, to the extent that they are not contrary to divine law or to particular provisions of canon law (c. 22). The most far-reaching instance of such "canonization" is in regard to the law of contracts (c. 1290), although restrictive canonical provisions governing alienation (transfer of ownership) and the more important acts of administration often create conflict. With only a few exceptions, the code also defers to civil law in regard to the adoption of children (c. 110), the designation and authority of guardians of minor children (c. 98n2), the emancipation of a minor for purposes of acquiring an independent legal domicile (c. 105n1), the kind of legal action to be taken to recover possession of property (c. 1500), and prescription as a means of acquiring or losing a right or freeing oneself from an obligation (c. 197, 1268). In the remuneration of employees and other persons who render service to the Church, civil laws are to be observed in regard to just wage, conditions of employment, health, disability and retirement benefits, unemployment insurance, and social security (cc. 1286, 231n2).

Other references to civil law in the Code of Canon Law concern the qualifications of members of a diocesan finance council (c. 492), renunciation by religious of the right to own property (c. 668n4), structuring a process of conciliation or arbitration for the resolution of a dispute between private parties (c. 1714), judicial involvement in arbitration proceedings (c. 1716), authenticity of a mandate for marriage by proxy (c. 1105), and enactment by episcopal conferences of particular law regarding betrothals (c. 1062n1).

Some provisions in the Code of Canon Law that make no reference to civil law may, nonetheless, have church-state implications in some nations. Thus, for example, the requirement that teachers of theological disciplines in institutes of higher learning have a mandate from ecclesiastical authority (c. 812) may have implications in the United States for accreditation and government funding of Catholic colleges and universities.

Bibliography: J. P. BEAL et al., eds., *New Commentary on the Code of Canon Law* (New York 2000). T. F. DONOVAN, *The Status of the Church in American Civil Law and Canon Law* (Wash., D.C. 1966). S. A. EUART, *Church-State Implications in the United States of Canon 812 of the 1983 Code of Canon Law* (Wash., D.C. 1988). A. J. MAIDA and N. P. CAFARDI, *Church Property, Church Finances, and Church-Related Corporations* (St. Louis 1984). J. J. MCGRATH, *Catholic Institutions in the United States: Canonical and Civil Law Status* (Wash., D.C. 1968). A. OTTAVIANI, *Institutiones Iuris Publici Ecclesiastici*, v. 2 *Ecclesia et Status* (Vatican City 1960). P. CIPROTTI, "Le 'Leggi Civili' nel Nuovo Codice di Diritto Canonico," *Apollinaris* 57 (1984) 281–293. E. M. TETLOW, "The New Code of Canon Law and Church-State Relations," *Loyola Law Review* 29 (1983) 1113–1155.

[R. T. KENNEDY]

CHURCH AND STATE IN THE UNITED STATES (LEGAL HISTORY)

The United States law of FREEDOM OF RELIGION has evolved from many historical circumstances and often conflicting ideologies. The Church-State arrangements of the Colonial period were to require a new pattern when full union was finally attained. By a process of legislation and judicial decisions, continual adjustments were made to accommodate the needs and to meet the demands of a nation becoming ever more pluralistic in religion. The study of Church and State in American law indicates that there is wide latitude for the solution of conflicts and problems still to come.

1. Colonial Period (1607 to 1776)

Church-State understandings in the United States had their origins in the Colonial period between 1607 and 1776. The law of this period reflected a growing spirit of freedom and grew out of the colonists' adjustment to New World opportunities. The colonists had always to reckon with the Church of England and the religious policy of the mother country. Great diversity came out of the experience in the three major regions, the Southern, Middle, and New England Colonies, which were to some extent distinct cultural groups. Certain legal landmarks in each of the colonies of these regions will be pointed out and an account taken of the forces behind them. Restrictions on dissenters from the varying versions of establishment had great implications even for Catholics, and these will be noted.

Virginia. The Church of England was officially maintained in Virginia from the very beginning. The 1606 Virginia Company Charter urged the colony to foster Christianity "according to the rites and doctrine of the Church of England." The Royal Charter of 1624 in the era of Archbishop William LAUD carried forward the design of Anglicanism without regard for Dissenters. Novelties of doctrine were opposed and the assembly passed laws applying Canon Law. The colonial government regulated the building of chapels and appointment of ministers and ritual. It was in this environment that the first Lord Baltimore unsuccessfully attempted a settlement and saw the need of locating elsewhere. Catholics were soon disfranchised. Comprehensive legislation on these matters was passed in 1642.

The 17th century was marked by a successful move toward local vestry control of parishes. This involved conflict with the governor. Following the lead of a predecessor, William Berkeley insisted on examining credentials of ministers to make certain that they had the approval of the bishop of London. However, he won the power of presentation of ministers only in Jamestown; elsewhere parish vestries, in the hands of the planter gentry, controlled appointment.

Puritans were unable seriously to modify this order of things even during the Commonwealth period. When Berkeley returned as governor in 1661, he made further provisions for the enforcement of Anglican liturgy; legal illegitimacy was imputed to children of parents outside this rite of matrimony. Fines were levied on those failing to meet church obligations, and assessments were collected for support of the church. Quakers, Puritans, and Catholics were unwelcome during this era. Giles Brent, the wealthy Catholic planter, as an exception held a seat in the assembly.

The DECLARATION OF RIGHTS OF 1689 compelled Virginia to give legal status to congregations that were not strictly in the Anglican tradition. Huguenots and German Lutherans organized churches between 1700 and 1730 with legal incorporation. The Hanover Presbytery legally placed itself under the Philadelphia Synod. Dissenters in time established their churches in this manner, but their practice of having itinerant preachers created legal difficulties that had to be remedied by other legislation. Francis MAKEMIE first won a certificate to preach as a Presbyterian. In time itinerant preachers came to enjoy the same legal right, and Samuel Davies among Baptists played a leading role in widening practices of toleration when his appeal to the royal government was upheld.

Methodists and Baptists, however, experienced *de facto* intolerance at the hands of local officials. Instances of imprisonment for alleged disturbance of peace and verbal attacks on the Church of England shortly before the Revolution created a rallying point for opposition to establishment. General taxes on nonconformists for the support of the Church of England now became a major issue. The laity from within the Church indirectly supported this trend when they opposed what was called the "Parson's Cause." They resented the clergy's claim to greater income in the face of the losses from fluctuation in tobacco prices. They now became militant in the traditional cause against a resident bishop, who would claim more taxes and the very ecclesiastical power which the lay vestries had long retained. It was only with the Revolution, however, that the new form of the Protestant Episcopal Church brought what the laity wanted. Other denominations likewise had their remaining disabilities removed by this turn of events.

Carolinas. The Church of England was established in the Carolinas, even though dissenters soon constituted a majority of the inhabitants. The ecclesiastical law of England was applied by the Charter of 1663, and the lord proprietors soon made declarations in which religious freedom was promised. Charles II, however, gave them discretionary power in limiting it in the interest of the establishment and civil order.

The Fundamental Constitution of 1670, attributed to John LOCKE, showed greater toleration while retaining establishment. All save atheists were allowed, although tax benefits went only to the Church of England. The freedom granted to non-Christians was intended to aid the conversion of the native peoples. A law of 1696 specifically excluded Catholics from full citizenship and religious freedom. This occurred in a period of Quaker influence; a governor of that faith took office in 1694. As in Virginia, Protestant dissenters struggled for full freedom in the 18th century in the face of a more firmly established Church of England. The assembly began to supervise them strictly, and they were for a time disfran-

chised by a law of 1704. Assemblymen had to conform to the Anglican communion ritual. Dissenting ministers were not recognized and were excluded from congregations petitioning them. Joseph Boone, however, appealed successfully to the Crown and the Fundamental Constitution. Particularly in North Carolina, which became a separate colony in 1691, Quakers fought against the established church and the Vestry Act of 1704. It was some time before they were relieved of disabilities implied in oath requirements. Marriages before non-Anglican clergymen were not legal in North Carolina until 1766.

Georgia. The Charter of George II in 1732 assured all inhabitants except Catholics "a free exercise of Religion . . . ," and Quakers were allowed to substitute an affirmation for the usual oaths. The trustees in their "Design" encouraged European Protestant settlers and shortly offered material support to clergy who would minister to new communities. When the colony was put under direct royal control in 1752, formal establishment of the Church of England came about. Its parishes received support and stipends for their clergy.

Massachusetts. The founders of Massachusetts Bay brought with them the belief that the true church was the individual congregation. A group of such churches could, however, be viewed collectively as within the Church of England. The New Englanders, following the teaching of William Ames and in opposition to Thomas CARTWRIGHT, rejected the idea that the congregation existed by authority of the Church of England.

A second principle produced what has been called a "Bible State," or theocracy in Massachusetts. The Hebraic concept of covenant as a relationship between the soul and God found legal application. Persons who enjoyed such a relationship were the only full citizens, or saints. Their status was verified by the elders of the local congregation. Such covenanted souls and congregations collectively formed a covenanted state. The civil magistrates and judges ruled as the counterpart of the congregation elders. While clergymen were not civil officials, they were their authentic guides in fashioning laws, which all assumed would conform to the Bible. Such godly magistrates were guardians both of public morals and church discipline. Because religious and civil authority both derived immediately from the rule of divine revelation in the Bible, the commonwealth was properly called a theocracy.

Using to advantage the vague language of the Massachusetts Bay Company Charter, the founders through the general court limited the control and full benefits to settlers "such as are members of some of the Churches. . . ." Four years later, in 1635, such churches had to be approved by the general court. Within three years assessments were levied for the support of these congregations. Fines were soon imposed for nonattendance, and in 1646 the Act Against Heresy listed punishments that would be meted out for denial of justification, immortality of the soul, and of other orthodox beliefs.

Adjustment of authority was made within this framework of law. The clergy as learned divines were earnestly consulted by all magistrates to see that the actions of the latter conformed to the directives of Holy Scripture. Nathaniel Ward wrote a code of laws for this purpose in 1641. Controversy over the manner of forming and approving true congregational churches led to the Cambridge Platform; and a general court act of 1651 put down the WESTMINSTER CONFESSION of Faith as a criterion of orthodoxy. Thus an aristocracy of magistrates and church elders was preserved by the balance of authority that these prescriptions established.

Judicial decisions fell harshly upon dissenters from these laws. The magistrates expelled Anne Hutchinson for the heresy of antinomianism and Roger WILLIAMS for his notion of separation of Church and State. Quakers were executed when they defied decrees of expulsion, and the Salem witchcraft trials at the end of the 17th century were the result of this legal system. Catholics were singled out by specific laws as being even more unwelcome than Quakers. The Christmas festival was forbidden as a manifestation of popery.

Reaction against such harshness, the pressures of a growing secularization and religious diversity, forced concessions. The Half-Way Covenant as a law relaxed requirement for church membership and full citizenship. The strict rule of baptism for children only of parents in full communion no longer held. Forms of "communion in spirit" were applied as norms. Anglicans were increasingly receiving the Lord's Supper, and in time their churches were legally recognized. Yet Congregationalism combined with other sects in stopping the spread and influence of these churchmen lest an Anglican establishment be imposed on New England. The Declaration of Rights of 1689 urged Massachusetts to extend freedom to all Christians except Catholics. Financial support of Congregationalism became the bone of contention. The Five Mile Act of 1727 allowed Anglicans to apply their assessment to one of their churches or ministers provided they were within that distance. The 18th century saw gradual extension of this practice even to the benefit of Anabaptists. Incidental inequities were a continual object of attack by Baptists, Presbyterians, and others through the Revolution.

The Plymouth settlement, founded before Massachusetts and joined to it in 1691, did not strive so strenuously for theocracy. The MAYFLOWER COMPACT made no specific provision for theocracy, although Puritans predominated in drafting it and applying it to civil life. Laws gave civil officials power to keep peace in the churches and promote attendance at worship without specifying any sect. Financial support of some clergy was enforced. In 1671 freemen came to be limited to those of orthodox belief. Quakers were unwelcome as were Catholics, and oaths created a problem for both groups.

Connecticut. New Haven, which was joined to Connecticut in 1662, was a pure theocracy. Under the leadership of John Davenport and the Fundamental Agreement of 1639, unorthodox views were suppressed. Those who were not Congregational Church members had to apply for a certificate if they would remain in the colony and then they were without full citizenship. All settlers were put under the government of magistrates who were pillars of the church. These men chose a governor who had a similar standing.

Connecticut was not so strict a theocracy. Thomas HOOKER, who formed its principles, disagreed with John Winthrop's aristocratic theory of magistracy. Church membership was not a requirement for citizenship. The assembly was therefore more open. The governor, possessed of less authority than in Massachusetts, was required to have church standing. The substance of theocracy was found in the authority of the assembly over church discipline. It chartered Congregational and all other churches, and in disputes it might sit as a quasi-ecclesiastical court. After 1656 Connecticut was guided by Massachusetts' Half-Way Covenant and its own Saybrooke Platform of 1708 in relaxing requirements for congregations and membership. Assessments of all for the support of the official Congregational Church prevailed throughout the period.

The religious homogeneity of Connecticut in the 17th century had minimized the difficulty of dissent, but this condition of homogeneity soon changed. However, Quakers once viewed as unwelcome now found some protection. A law of 1708 made further concessions to liberty when Anglican Churches were authorized. In the Act of 1727 to protect dissenters, one provision allowed Anglicans to apply their religious assessment to their own ministers and churches. After 1750 Presbyterians and others were given a similar benefit.

New Hampshire. When John Wheelwright was banished from Massachusetts, he successfully established the foundations of what would become in 1679 the independent colony of New Hampshire. The Agreement of 1639 put down no religious requirement for citizenship, officeholding, and voting. Massachusetts agreed to this and admitted New Hampshire delegates to its general court. At the same time New Hampshire early on passed laws of assessment for the support of the clergy without specifying to what sect they must belong.

Beginning in 1680 steps were taken to make a royal colony of New Hampshire. Past practices continued. Except for a few intervals before 1700 the mother country effectively formed a policy that protected, and at times favored, the Church of England. Freedom of Protestants was decreed and dissenter churches were not opposed.

Rhode Island. The only truly radical departure from the prevailing conviction that Church and State should be united was made by Rhode Island. Roger Williams, its founder and guiding genius, argued against Massachusetts laws within the framework of Calvinistic theology. Rhode Island's first charter contained only customary statements on religious freedom. A fundamental code was soon drawn up that denied civil magistrates authority over spiritual matters. Persons of all religious persuasions were granted citizenship, and no levy of taxes for the support of any church was permitted. In his oversimplified analysis the church must stand before the law as any other corporation, free of any complicated characteristics that might put it beyond the nation or with a purely spiritual existence. Williams's own adjustments of theory to practice were confined to the task of dealing with Quakers and others where freedom of conscience might disrupt public order. In 1662 Charles II approved the original charter. The 18th century saw departures from the full measure of toleration. In 1729 Roman Catholics were disfranchised. Jews were disbarred on religious grounds from public office.

New York. The 1638 Articles of Colonization made it clear that Dutch companies were responsible for promoting the Dutch Reformed Religion. This arrangement, however, never resulted in a very strict establishment, and dissenters were generally respected.

These conditions continued to a great extent when the Catholic Duke of York, later King James II, took over control with his laws of 1665. Liberty of conscience was specifically granted and the Catholic governor, Thomas Dongan, reasserted more forcefully in 1683 the provision for religious freedom for Christians. An attempt was made in 1693 to compel appointment of Anglican ministers only, but these efforts failed. Dissenting congregations and their clergy were recognized. The Presbyterian Francis Mackemie and others were allowed to preach throughout the province.

Concessions were made to Quakers regarding oathtaking in 1734, but no concessions ever clearly freed Moravians. Catholics were specifically denied benefits of toleration, and instructions from the Crown and the governors reinforced this measure.

New Jersey. Both East and West Jersey came under the force of New York law between 1702 and 1738. Before this time official "Concessions" of the lord proprietors gave toleration to Scotch Presbyterians, Quakers, and Dutch Reformed; and in 1693 to other Christians, except Catholics. No full establishment was found after 1738, when New Jersey became a royal colony.

Pennsylvania. The proprietary form of colonial charter provided the foundation upon which Pennsylvania developed, free of an established religion. As an exercise of personal power Charles II repaid an old debt of money, services, and friendship to Admiral William PENN through the admiral's son of the same name. Young William's deep involvement with the Quakers, who were laboring under legal disabilities, made it natural to seek in the charter issued to him in 1681 a remedy for his religious troubles. Its only reference to the Church of England was an assurance to its adherents that they might freely petition and receive preachers.

The year following the issue of the charter brought a fuller public statement of the colony's legal structure. In keeping with the "Holy Experiment" characterization he had given the colony, Penn's Frame of Government clearly acknowledged God as the author and end of society. Liberty was assured to any believer in Him. The Sabbath and Scriptures were to be honored. When Penn's first colonial assembly met, representatives saw fit to require that voters and officeholders profess Christianity. No reservations were made in reference to Roman Catholics.

In 1693 William and Mary annulled all the Pennsylvania laws, but the colonial assembly immediately passed them anew. Apparently their legality needed to be established since the legality of Stuart provisions may have been questioned. Certainly the broad provision for freedom in Pennsylvania would have been narrowed if the Declaration of Rights of 1689 had been applied to it. As it was, public worship, even by Roman Catholics, continued all through the Colonial period. Unlike practices in England, one need not take the oath of supremacy nor perform prescribed acts of worship in the Church of England.

The oath, however, was required in connection with voting and officeholding in Pennsylvania. William Penn failed in his own efforts to relieve Americans of this burden, particularly to the consciences of Quakers and Catholics. Under pressure, the first assembly passed in 1696 "A New Act of Settlement," which practically had the effect of excluding many Quakers and all Catholics from voting and holding public office. It was not until 1725 that Quakers obtained relief, when the Crown finally ceased to disallow action in their favor by the assembly.

Benefits of this law were extended to other societies in 1743 and in 1772 to any person who objected to the practice of oaths. Oaths and declarations against Catholic doctrines were demanded of immigrants and do not seem to have been removed during the Colonial period, although they may not have been applied consistently.

Delaware. A Swedish Lutheran Church was established in the period before the Dutch attached the colony of Delaware to New Netherlands in 1663. Initially part of Pennsylvania when English rule began, it continued after 1701 as a separate colony to have a toleration similar to that in Pennsylvania. Oaths in particular were mitigated to the advantage of immigrants and others during the next 20 years. Church property rights were recognized. Neither benefits, however, came to Catholics.

Maryland. The Maryland Charter of 1634 freed George Calvert, First Lord Baltimore, and his colonists from requirements of the Church of England. The general references to religion in the charter and his own instructions secured freedom of conscience for all—probably including non-Christians. The Maryland TOLERATION ACT in the ordinance of 1639 made this freedom even more certain. The act of 1649 gave special force to the Christian's claim to toleration. This legislation was repealed in 1654 when the Puritans came to power, but was restored again when Cecil Calvert, Second Lord Baltimore, recovered full control as proprietor in 1660.

George Calvert had two legal controversies with the Jesuits during this early period of the colony. He refused to exempt laymen on church property from civil law and its courts. A Jesuit title to land received from the native peoples was successfully challenged, and legislation against mortmain followed.

An Act for the Establishment of the Protestant Religion was passed by the assembly following the overthrow of the Stuarts by William and Mary. Catholic proprietary government was thereafter illegal. In 1700 taxes for support of the Church of England were voted. Benedict Leonard Calvert won back proprietary rights after he had conformed to the Church of England in 1714.

The governor's powers of presentation and induction of clergy were a source of continual controversy. Attempts at obtaining a resident bishop, or a permanent commissary to supervise the clergy, failed. As late as 1769 the governor prevented the clergy of the Church of England from holding a convention to deal with their affairs.

While concessions to Quakers and other Protestants came in the 18th century, penalties continued to be imposed on Catholics. There was an Act to Prevent the Growth of Popery that ruled out public officeholding and public worship. Catholic immigrants found obstacles in coming to Maryland, and possession by a Catholic widow of children by a Protestant husband was declared unlawful.

Bibliography: H. S. SMITH et al., *American Christianity: An Historical Interpretation with Representative Documents,* 2 v. (New York 1960–63) 1:1–416. A. P. STOKES, *Church and State in the United States,* 3 v. (New York 1950) 1:151–358. S. H. COBB, *The Rise of Religious Liberty in America* (New York 1902). E. H. DAVIDSON, *The Establishment of the English Church in the Continental American Colonies* (Durham, North Carolina 1936).

[T. O. HANLEY]

2. The Disestablishment Period (1776 to 1834)

By the time of the American Revolution, physical persecution of religious dissenters had ended, and a measure of toleration existed. Yet ten of the original 13 colonies—the exceptions were Rhode Island, Pennsylvania, and Delaware—continued to prefer and support one religion, over all others. The church that by law enjoyed that status was spoken of as the established church, or establishment, of that state. The erosion of the preferential position of the established church is traced from the Revolution to the mid-19th century when, for the first time in world history, Church and State were completely divorced.

No Federal Establishment. Before proceeding, it is important to note that there has never been a Federally established church. In the Articles of Confederation, there is only one reference to religion. Each state is guaranteed the assistance of its sister states if attacked "on account of religion." The Articles only maintained the status quo.

When the Constitutional Convention met in Philadelphia in 1787, the practical needs of the situation as much as the political and philosophical theories of the day demanded that only timid reference, if any, be made to religion. By 1789, the states were on their way to religious freedom. To interfere with this current by establishing a Federal church would have jeopardized the new Union. The New England colonies generally supported a Congregational Church, while the Middle Atlantic and southern colonies possessed Episcopal establishments. Even if the founding fathers had not believed in separation of Church and State, which church was to be established? The only way Episcopal and Congregational churches could federate with Presbyterians, Baptists, and smaller groups was on a basis of Church-State separation. Article 6, proscribing a religious test of office, was the offspring of this innocuous neutralism. European political states traditionally required their officers to follow the state religion. The American colonies were no exceptions. Almost all of them enacted some religious prerequisite to holding public office. Even though the new states had not yet effected disestablishment at home, they included Article 6 in the proposed Constitution. It read: "No religious test shall ever be required its a qualification to any office or public trust under the United States."

In the state conventions called to ratify the Constitution, a desire for even stronger guarantees of religious liberty was voiced by the delegates. Whether a state still retained its own establishment or not, its delegates announced the tenor of the times: the Federal government, if only to preclude encroachment on the privileges of the state establishment, should not establish Federal religion. The Federal government was not to be antagonistic to religion, but was rather to remain impartial in that matter and to attend to its civil business.

Responding to this public sentiment, the First Congress drafted a Bill of Rights, ratified by the states in 1791, which in part declared negatively that "Congress shall make no law respecting an establishment of religion, or prohibiting the free exercise thereof." Both Article 6 and the religious guarantees of the First Amendment applied only to the Federal government [*Barron v. Mayor of Baltimore,* 7 Peters 243 (1833).] It was easier to breach centuries of history and bar a Federal religion where none yet existed than to dislodge existing establishments in the states. Thus the states of the Union that had not already done so were to spend the next half-century attaining this Federal standard of Church-State relationship.

Reasons for Disestablishment. The states granted religious freedom of their own volition, since the Federal government was without jurisdiction over a state's internal affairs [*Permoli v. New Orleans,* 3 How. 588 (1845).] The disestablishment of state churches was the result of several factors: (1) The argument voiced by establishment proponents that religion and ultimately the state would die out without the continued support of the government was rebutted dramatically by the growth of religion in the free soil of Rhode Island and Pennsylvania. (2) With the ease resulting from their wealth and legally secured position, the established churches had become stagnant and stilted, had obtained few converts, and lacked a fervent congregation that would energetically oppose disestablishment. (3) As immigration to the New World increased and the dissenting churches gained more converts, the established groups became the political minority. (4) And the Bill of Rights, even though legally inapplicable to the states, added impetus to the disestablishment process by emphasizing individual liberties. Catholic agitation during this period, while unequivocal, should not be over-emphasized. At the time of the Constitutional Convention, less than two percent of the churches in the United States were Catholic.

New England States. With the exception of Rhode Island, the New England states supported the Congregational Church and were more reluctant to disestablish than the states to the south.

Connecticut. Connecticut operated for more than 40 years after the Revolution under the royal charter of 1662, which designated the state church as the Congregational. Disestablishment was not achieved until 1818, after a long and bitter politico-religious struggle. Here, as in Massachusetts, the established Congregational ministry had retained tremendous political, social, and economic influence long after the Federal Constitution was ratified. With the Toleration Act of 1784, the first glimpse of disestablishment was visible. The act removed many disabilities, and established a "certificate" scheme whereby a dissenter was excused from contributing to the established church if he executed a paper declaring that he regularly attended a dissenting church. The dissenter might then pay his tax to his own body, but he was still required to support some one religion.

The political agitation was intense. Congregational members had always aligned themselves with the Federalist Party. The dissenters joined the liberal Jeffersonian Republican Party. As in all the New England states, the Baptists, both for reasons of religious belief and practical advantage, pressed the cause of separation. In 1816, compulsory church attendance was repealed. In 1817, Oliver Wolcott, a liberal coalition candidate, won the gubernatorial election, ending a Congregational monopoly of that post. A constitutional convention was called for the following year. After recognizing the individual's freedom to enjoy religious profession and worship, the new constitution declared that "no person shall be compelled to join or support, nor by law be classed with or associated to any congregation, church or religious association." The Methodists secured a charter for Wesleyan University in 1831, and the disestablishment was completed.

Massachusetts. Though not as slow as Connecticut in adopting a state constitution, Massachusetts was slower in bringing about a financial disestablishment of the Congregational Church. The state constitution of 1780 contained an important and inclusive Declaration of Rights (Moehlman, 40). But an abrupt and absolute break with the past was not conceivable, so the constitution went on to provide for the support of the Protestant ministry and for compulsory attendance at some religious instruction. The proposed constitutional amendment of 1820 to overturn these vestiges of the establishment was defeated by nearly two to one. The end of the establishment did not come until 1833, when a comprehensive amendment to the constitution was ratified by an overwhelming vote (Moehlman, 67).

New Hampshire. The colonial attitude was akin to that of Massachusetts, since New Hampshire was a part of it until 1679. The Bill of Rights of 1784 acknowledged the right of conscience, but permitted the several towns of the state "to make adequate provision at their own expense, for the support and maintenance of public Protestant teachers of piety, religion, and morality." Protection of the law was extended only to Christians (Moehlman, 50). Legal status was granted the Baptists in 1804, the Universalists the following year, and the Methodists in 1807. The Toleration Act of 1819 retained the requisite that public teachers and public officials be Protestant, but it did abolish mandatory support for the establishment, thereby mollifying the dissenters. An amendment of 1877 decreed that "no person is disqualified to hold office by reason of his religious opinion."

Rhode Island. From the beginning, Rhode Island guaranteed religious freedom to all its citizens. The success of Roger Williams' "Lively Experiment" was a constant rebuke to those proponents of a union of Church and State who argued that one would collapse without the other. For a time a slight "blemish" appeared on Rhode Island's record of religious freedom. In some printed editions of its charter, Roman Catholics were excepted from the "liberty to choose and be chosen officers in the Colony." This restriction was foreign to the spirit of the colony, and both Thorning and Stokes argue that it was inserted without legislative authorization, possibly a result of a clerical error. It remained in the laws of Rhode Island until 1783. The constitution of 1842 guaranteed religious and civil liberties to all citizens (Moehlman, 72).

Middle Atlantic States. Unlike New England, there was never a firmly intrenched establishment in any of the Middle Atlantic states, though New York and New Jersey did favor the Church of England.

New York. In the years preceding the Revolution, the general policy of the New York government was to favor the established Church of England as much as possible without severely alienating dissenters. By the first state constitution, enacted in 1777, the Act of Establishment of 1683 was repealed (Moehlman, 48). "Religious profession and worship, without discrimination," were assured to all citizens. No religious test was prescribed for any state officer, with the exception that ministers of the gospel were denied the right to hold public office. Quakers were allowed to affirm an oath rather than swear to it, and they were permitted to substitute a money payment for military service. The first constitutional revision in 1821 did little to change the clauses regarding religion. The disability of public office was removed from the ministry in the amendment of 1846. In New York, the disestablished church was guaranteed at all times continuous

possession of lands granted them during the establishment period, a reversal of the Virginia precedent.

New Jersey. Close political ties with liberal New York, plus the mild and tolerant spirit of the Quakers in the state legislature, leavened the whole course of New Jersey's attainment of religious freedom. The state's first constitution, adopted two days before the Declaration of Independence was announced, exempted all persons from mandatory attendance at religious services and the obligation of maintaining a church or ministry. Only Protestants, however, "were capable of being elected into any office of profit or trust, or being a member of either branch of the Legislature" (Moehlman, 48). This situation continued until 1844, when a new constitution was enacted granting civil liberties equally to all the citizenry (Moehlman, 72).

Pennsylvania. Under the enlightened William Penn, Pennsylvania grew without an establishment. His Charter of Liberties and Privileges, granted in 1701, guaranteed freedom of worship to all theists and the right to hold office to all Christians. This liberal bent was continued in the Pennsylvania constitution of 1776, but the religious test of office found in the charter was retained. Each member of the house of representatives was required to attest before being seated: "I do believe in one God, the creator and governor of the universe, the rewarder of the good and punisher of the wicked. And I do acknowledge the Scriptures of the Old and New Testament to be by Divine inspiration." This admitted Roman Catholics to full rights and was in this respect more liberal than contemporaneous constitutions of its sister states. The reference to the New Testament was, of course, distasteful to the Jewish community in Philadelphia, and in 1783 they petitioned that it be dropped. This was done in 1790, but the test of belief in God was retained.

Delaware. Delaware gained independence from Pennsylvania in 1701, and taking its lead from its parent state, it never had an established church. Religious freedom, therefore, was always the rule; complete civil freedom was not so immediate. In its constitution of 1776, Delaware, like Pennsylvania, required an oath of all elected officials to provide that the state should be governed by orthodox Christians (Moehlman, 52). Contrariwise to Pennsylvania, however, Delaware abolished any religious test of office in 1792, completely separating the state from religion.

The South. All the southern states established the Church of England. The contrast between the conduct of Virginia and that of South Carolina during the Revolution is notable.

Maryland. The position of Roman Catholics in Maryland at the time of the Revolution was more secure than in the other colonies because of the strong Catholic influence in the early years of the colony and the weak position of the Maryland establishment, the Anglican Church.

The declaration of rights adopted as part of its new constitution of 1776 recognized that "all persons, professing the Christian religion are equally entitled to protection of their religious liberty." The Quakers, Dunkers, and Mennonites, opposed to taking judicial oaths, were allowed "to affirm" and were "admitted as witnesses in all criminal cases not capital." This was extended to capital cases in 1798. Charles Carroll of Carrollton, the Catholic patriot, was one of those voting in favor of the article authorizing the state legislature to "lay a general and equal tax, for the support of the Christian religion." Finally, a "declaration of a belief in the Christian religion" was required by the constitution for admission to any office of trust or profit (Moehlman, 41). The Jew and the freethinker were still under disabilities. There were only a few Jews in the state, and the legislature did not act to remove the restriction until 1826. The religious test of office, which has since been struck down by the United States Supreme Court *Torcaso v. Watkins,* 367 U.S. 488 (1961), was then unacceptable only to a small number of agnostics and atheists, since a declaration of belief in the existence of God was still necessary.

Virginia. Thomas Jefferson, James Madison, George Mason, the Baptists, and the Presbyterians united to disestablish the conservative Episcopalian Church of Virginia and to light the path to religious freedom in the United States. The Declaration of Rights, passed three weeks before the Declaration of Independence, and the Bill for Establishing Religious Freedom combined to assure members of all faiths complete religious and civil liberties by 1785. This influenced immeasureably the course of the Federal and sister states' governments.

North Carolina. The Carolina Charter of 1663 specially recognized the Church of England, but it provided for a measure of toleration so long as nonconformity did not interfere with the civil authority. North Carolina was second only to Virginia in adopting a constitution, guaranteeing complete religious freedom (Moehlman, 44). The constitution restricted public office to those acknowledging "the being of God [and] the truth of the Protestant religion [and] the divine authority of the Old and New Testament," thereby excluding Roman Catholics and Jews. Clergymen were not permitted to hold office.

In 1835, at Raleigh, the word Protestant was changed to Christian in deference to the Roman Catholics. In fact, however, the Protestant requirement had not been enforced, for Thomas Burke, who became governor in 1781, and William Gaston, who was appointed to the North Carolina supreme court in 1833, were both Catholics. The Jewish disability was enforced, for there was little pressure to remove the bar since most of the Jewish population in the United States was found in the large cities to the north. The constitution of 1868 removed this last restriction to total religious freedom (Moehlman, 108).

South Carolina. South Carolina had established the Anglican Church. By the constitution of 1778, all theists were "freely tolerated," but that document further declared that "the Christian Protestant religion shall be deemed, and is hereby constituted . . . the established religion of this State." Despite the existence of a preferred religion, the dissenters' onerous task of supporting an establishment was removed. Only Protestants could hold public office. Any religious society holding property was permitted to retain it. This law was very beneficial to the Anglican Church, the prior establishment, since it had been the donee of much official largesse.

The state exercised a Connecticut-like control over religious activities. The election of a pastor or clergyman was prescribed by the constitution to be by majority vote of the congregation. The elected minister was further required to subscribe to a declaration anticipating his official and unofficial conduct during his tenure.

By the constitution of 1790, dissenters, previously only "tolerated," were guaranteed the "free exercise and enjoyment of religious profession and worship, without discrimination or preference." The Roman Catholics and other non-Protestant groups were enfranchised. The document was a drastic departure from the narrowly Protestant constitution of 12 years earlier (Moehlman, 45). By 1868, only those who denied the existence of a Supreme Being were ineligible to hold public office.

Georgia. The Georgia Charter of 1732 secured by James Oglethorpe stipulated that all office holders be Protestant, and "that all . . . persons, except papists, shall have a free exercise of religion." The derogatory term "papist" was deleted by the constitution of 1777 and freedom of worship was extended to all citizens. As was frequently the case, the clergy were unable to hold office. There was no religious test for voting, but the Protestant prerequisite of membership in the state legislature was retained. The 1789 constitution removed all religious restrictions upon service in public office. Thus Georgia from early times was provided with religious freedom.

In conclusion, though the Federal government was forbidden to establish a preferred religion, remnants of the state establishments existed well into the 19th century. For the first time in history, State and Church were independent of each other. The pace of disestablishment is notable, but more notable is the historic result.

Bibliography: P. W. COONS, *The Achievement of Religious Liberty in Connecticut* (New Haven 1936). J. DE L. FERGUSON, *The Relation of the State to Religion in New York and New Jersey During the Colonial Period* (New Brunswick, Connecticut 1912). L. HÜHNER, *The Struggle for Religious Liberty in North Carolina* (Baltimore 1907). J. C. MEYER, *Church and State in Massachusetts from 1740 to 1833* (Cleveland 1930). C. H. MOEHLMAN, *The American Constitutions and Religion* (Berne, Indiana 1938). J. F. THORNING, *Religious Liberty in Transition* (Washington 1931). A. P. STOKES, *Church and State in the United States* (New York 1950). A. W. WERLINE, *Problems of Church and State in Maryland during the 17th and 18th Century* (South Lancaster, Massachusetts 1948).

[M. J. MULLANEY, JR.]

3. Period Of Conflict (1834 to 1900)

The 19th century was an era of conflict on the religious front in the United States. Resentment against immigrants brought forth American NATIVISM in the form of such movements as the KU KLUX KLAN and KNOW-NOTHINGISM. The amazing growth of the Catholic parochial system was a response to the problems of the era.

At the start of this period only a few effects of state establishment of religion still remained. The most obnoxious was the religious test for public office. In spite of the Federal and state guarantees of religious freedom, the churches in the 19th century encountered several new types of difficulty with the government. A proposed constitutional amendment (Blaine Amendment) that sought to deprive religious-affiliated schools of state financial aid had a lasting effect in many states. The Mormon Church and its practice of polygamy came under direct attack. A series of disputes reached the courts as a result of schisms that split the churches into warring factions. Religious practices in public schools were both approved and forbidden by the various state courts. Problems arose concerning the holding of church property and the incorporation of churches. Amid all this conflict there was, strangely enough, a 20-year period in which the United States and the Vatican had diplomatic relationship.

Religious Tests for Public Office. The founding fathers of the United States thought that a necessary prerequisite for securing the freedom of religion in this country was the inclusion in the constitution of a clause prohibiting any religious test as a requirement for holding public office. The proposal was made originally in 1787 at the Constitutional Convention by Charles Pinckney of South Carolina. There was considerable debate on the subject at the convention; but it was finally drafted into Article 6 of the United States Constitution, and passed easily, North Carolina being the only state that voted against it. Article 6 of the United States Constitution states that elected officials shall be bound by oath or affirmation to support the Constitution, and then continues, ". . . but no religious test shall ever be required as a qualification to any office or public trust under the United States."

Although this provision in the United States Constitution was almost unanimously approved by the original 13 states, they were very slow to incorporate similar provisions in their own state constitutions. Most of the states were still feeling the effects of religious establishment and consequently limited public office to those who professed the "Protestant religion," those who were "Christians," those who believed in the "Old and New Testament" and other such conditions. Five of the original states had provisions in their constitutions limiting holders of public office to those who professed a belief in the Protestant religion (Georgia, New Hampshire, New Jersey, North Carolina and South Carolina). Georgia was the first of the five to remove this requirement, in 1789, when its constitution was changed to read that no religious test for public office would be required. New Jersey and New Hampshire did not follow suit until 1844 and 1877 respectively. North Carolina changed "Protestant" to "Christian" in 1835, and in 1868, revised it to "belief in God." This requirement is still a part of the North Carolina constitution. South Carolina replaced the qualification "Protestant" by that of belief in a supreme being in 1868, and the law still exists. Maryland and Delaware originally required officeholders to be Christians. Delaware removed this restriction in 1792. Maryland changed the requirement to belief in God in 1826, and it held until 1961, when the United States Supreme Court declared it unconstitutional (*Torcaso v. Watkins* 367 U.S. 488). Pennsylvania early required a belief in both the Old and New Testaments, but it was changed in 1790 to "belief in God" and is still retained (1965). The slow pace at which the original states proceeded to remove religious tests can be attributed to the fact that they were free to retain or modify their laws of religious liberty as they chose.

However, the new states to gain admission to the Union had to have their constitutions approved by Congress, and Congress after the beginning of the 19th century required that states have adequate guarantees of religious freedom. Consequently only four states admitted to the Union after the original states have any kind of religious restriction for public officeholders (Arkansas, Mississippi, Tennessee, Texas). These four require officeholders to hold a belief in God or in a supreme being. As of 1965 the constitutions of these states still retain this requirement. Most of the states admitted to the Union during the 19th and the early 20th century have some specific constitutional provision forbidding any religious test for public office. Some, though not specifically referring to public office, forbid a religious test in guaranteeing civil or political rights to all. A few states have made no mention of a religious test in their constitutions.

By 1912, with the admission of the 48th state to the union, the states specifically prohibiting any religious test included Alabama, Arizona, Delaware, Georgia, Idaho, Illinois, Indiana, Iowa, Kansas, Louisiana, Maine, Minnesota, Missouri, Nebraska, New Hampshire, New Jersey, New Mexico, New York, Ohio, Oregon, Rhode Island, Utah, Vermont, Virginia, Washington, West Virginia, Wisconsin, and Wyoming. States forbidding a religious test to guarantee civil and/or political rights included Michigan, Montana, Oklahoma, and South Dakota. States whose constitutions made no mention of any form of religious test were California, Colorado, Connecticut, Florida, Kentucky, Nevada, and North Dakota. Those requiring a belief in God or a supreme being included Arkansas, Maryland, Mississippi, North Carolina, Pennsylvania, South Carolina, Tennessee, and Texas. One state, Massachusetts, obliges the people in choosing their officials to pay attention to principles of piety.

The Blaine Amendment. On Dec. 14, 1875, James Gillespie Blaine, a congressman from Maine, presented a proposed amendment of the United States Constitution to the House of Representatives. The proposed amendment sought primarily to prevent the states from directly or indirectly devoting any public money or land to schools having any religious affiliation. As proposed, the amendment read:

> No state shall make any law respecting an establishment of religion, or prohibiting the free exercise thereof; and no religious test shall ever be required as a qualification to any office or public trust under any State. No public property, and no public revenue of nor any loan of credit by or under the authority of the United States, or any State, Territory, District or municipal corporation, shall be appropriated to, or made or used for, the support of any school, educational or other institution, under the control of any religious or anti-religious sect, organization, or denomination, or wherein the particular creed or tenets shall be read or taught in any school or institution supported in whole or in part by such revenue or loan of credit; and no such appropriation or loan of credit shall be made to any religious or anti-religious sect, organization or denomination, or to promote its interests or tenets. This article shall not be construed to prohibit the reading of the Bible in any school or institution, and it shall not have the effect to impair rights of property already vested. Congress shall have power, by appropriate legislation, to provide for the prevention and punishment of violation of this article.

The issue was debated in Congress, and discussion centered on the questions of states rights to determine their educational policies, and the privilege of a religious people to secure their teachings in schools attended by their children. The proposal failed to win the necessary two-thirds majority in the Senate and was never put to the states for ratification.

Since the amendment's original failure, it has been reintroduced 20 times; but only once was it reported on by the committee to which it was referred. Even this report recommended that the resolution should not be passed. But its effect has been felt in subsequent amendments or revisions of many state constitutions. Between 1877 and 1913, more than 30 state constitutions forbade financial aid to parochial schools. The provisions adopted vary greatly in detail. Some use the same language as the Blaine amendment; others say the same thing in different words. However, they all have the same purpose, of preventing the use of public school funds by private sectarian schools.

Only eight states had any constitutional provision on this matter before the Blaine amendment was introduced. These provisions were very limited in scope, usually prohibiting aid to theological and religious seminaries. The states were Wisconsin (1848), Michigan (1850), Indiana (1851), Oregon (1857), Minnesota (1857), Kansas (1858), Nebraska (1866), and Illinois (1870).

States that early responded to the Blaine amendment and incorporated some similar provision in their own constitutions before 1880 included Pennsylvania (1873); Missouri, Alabama, and Nebraska (1875); Texas and Colorado (1876); Georgia, Minnesota, and New Hampshire (1877); California and Louisiana (1879); and Nevada (1880). Other states were to follow in the next 20 years: Florida (1885); Idaho, Montana, North Dakota, South Dakota, and Wyoming (1889); Mississippi and Kentucky (1890); New York (1894); South Carolina and Utah (1895); and Delaware (1897). The three states admitted to the Union after 1900 joined in adopting similar provisions in their constitutions: Oklahoma (1907), New Mexico (1911), and Arizona (1912). Several states that have since 1900 adopted new constitutions have retained provisions on this matter that appeared in their earlier constitutions: New Hampshire, Louisiana, Massachusetts, and Alabama.

The articles on each state in this encyclopedia contain the provisions still in effect in each state.

The Mormon Church. In 1852 the Mormon Church decreed that the practice of polygamy was in accord with its doctrine. The practice, was permitted only to people of good moral character who could afford a large family. It was never widespread even among the Mormons. But opposition to it was strong. Many non-Mormons clamored for some type of legislation to suppress and prohibit the practice.

Congress responded in 1862 with the passage of the Anti-Polygamy Act (12 Stat. 501) making polygamy in any United States territory a crime, and prescribing a penalty of up to five years imprisonment for violations of the act. The law was difficult to enforce because it was hard to get evidence of plural marriages; the Mormon Temple officials secretly retained the records of such services. It was hard to get convictions also because the juries hearing the cases were often composed primarily of Mormons. One case of violation of the act did reach the United States Supreme Court [*Reynolds v. U.S.*, 98 U.S. 145 (1878)]. The Court upheld the conviction of Reynolds, reasoning that freedom of religion does not extend so far as to condone overt acts that may be disruptive of the social order.

In 1882 Congress passed the Edmunds Act (22 Stat. 30), making it a crime to cohabit with two women at once. To secure enforcement it was further provided that in a prosecution under this act no one could serve as a juror unless he swore that he never practiced polygamy or that he disapproved of such practice. The act also excluded polygamists from voting or holding public office in any territory. Prosecution under this law was much more successful than under the previous one.

Congress followed in 1887 with the Edmunds-Tucker Act (24 Stat. 635), which further restricted the privileges of people practicing polygamy. It permitted the vote only to those who would swear an oath against polygamy, and required all marriage ceremonies to be registered. It annulled laws that indirectly supported the practice, such as those affording inheritance rights to illegitimate children, laws limiting prosecution for adultery to cases in which there is a complaint by the wife, and laws that provided for elective judgeships in order to afford judicial support to the practice. This act also dissolved the corporation of the Mormon Church and seized all its property except that used for worship. Shortly after passage of this act the Mormon church officially disavowed polygamy and advised its members to abide by the laws of the United States in regard to it.

Shortly thereafter, in 1896, Utah was admitted to the Union with a constitutional provision forbidding the practice of polygamy. Four other Western states subsequently admitted to the Union also forbade the practice in their constitutions (Oklahoma, Idaho, Arizona, and New Mexico).

Religious Practices in Public Schools. The 19th century saw the advent of the public school system in the United States under the leadership of Horace Mann. Gradually, parochial schools of most denominations were absorbed into the public school system; the major exception was the Catholic school system. When parochial schools were merged with the public schools, there was not an immediate desecularization; religious practices and instruction were common in the early public schools. Since the Protestant religion was predominant at this time, most public schools incorporated the Protestant teaching in their curriculum. Catholics objected to this practice and accordingly thought it expedient to continue their own schools with their own religious instruction.

Gradually antireligious and nonreligious elements of the population began to work for the discontinuance of religious instruction in the public schools, and they soon succeeded. Toward the end of the 19th century the public school system was conducted by the state, divorced from all church control, and given over exclusively to the dissemination of secular information.

Though public schools were no longer to be controlled by any religious factions, vestiges of sectarian influence still remained in many states. Many schools retained the practices of saying prayers, singing hymns, and reading the Bible.

The several court decisions in the 19th and early 20th centuries concerning the propriety of Bible reading in public schools had conflicting results; a minority of the decisions prohibited such practices. Wisconsin [*State v. School District of Edgeton*, 44 N.W. 967 (1890)], Nebraska [*State v. Scheve*, 91 N.W. 846 (1902)], Illinois [*People v. Board of Education* 92 N.E. 251 (1910)], and Louisiana [*Herold v. Board of School Division* (1915)] were the four states to disallow Bible reading in public schools. Illinois excluded the Bible entirely; Nebraska and Wisconsin barred it only so far as it was sectarian and not when it was used to teach moral ethics. Louisiana barred it as giving preference to Christians over Jews. Twelve other states in which the question reached the courts decided in favor of allowing the reading of the Bible; they were Colorado, Georgia, Iowa, Kansas, Kentucky, Maine, Massachusetts, Michigan, Minnesota, Ohio, Pennsylvania, and Texas.

Similar inconsistent results occurred when the courts were asked to decide whether the holding of religious services and Sunday schools in the public school buildings was proper. Some courts prohibited such use, stating that school buildings can be used only for educational purposes and thereby excluding religious services. Other courts upheld the decisions of the school officials in these matters, whether the school officials allowed or disallowed the use.

The propriety of the practice of employing Roman Catholic nuns as teachers in the public schools also came to the courts for determination. Objectors pointed out that the wearing of religious garb with crucifixes and rosaries had a sectarian influence on the education in such schools. Statutes forbidding the wearing of religious garb were upheld in both Pennsylvania [*Commonwealth v. Herr* (1910) 78 Atl. 68] and New York [*O'Connor v. Hendrick* (1906) 77 N.E. 612].

In the late 19th century, antireligious feelings concerning public schools brought pressure to bear on legislation. As a result, from 1876 to 1912 nine of the ten states admitted to the Union were required as a condition of admission to agree that provision be made for the establishment of public schools free from sectarian control.

Tenure of Church Property. Early in the 19th century most of the property of the Catholic Church was held or administered by lay trustees. This was the result of an interplay of several factors including Old World customs, Protestant influence, and practical necessity.

Since priests were scarce in the early colonies, small communities desiring to establish a church had to rely on traveling missionaries. The only practical method of caring for church property in the absence of priests was to entrust its care to the lay members of the church. Also, many of the early Catholics in the United States had come from continental Europe, where a similar lay trustee system worked well in a civil-law framework. Problems were to arise, however, under the new system of law in the United States. Finally, since the Protestant sects were in a majority in the United States and since they were organized on a basis of lay control, the Catholics were inclined to trust in lay organization.

The lay trusteeship form of control of church property in the United States was the cause of great dissension and conflict within the Church for 50 years. Trustees attempted to secure a voice in spiritual affairs of the Church. Cases occurred in which they refused to accept the services of lawfully appointed priests and attempted to name priests of their choice. Often these differences resulted in civil court cases and occasionally went to Rome for settlement. (*See* TRUSTEEISM.)

In 1829 the First Provincial Council of Baltimore attempted to put an end to such internal disorders and dissension by decreeing that in the future no church could be built unless it were assigned to the bishop of the diocese in which it was to be built. The decree cited the ills of the trustee system and obviously meant to abolish this system in the future. It was immediately carried out.

Bishop as Absolute Owner. Under this system the bishop holds absolute title to the property and administers it in his individual name. This was a useful system for some time in that it proved better than the lay trustee system. However, certain difficulties arose in regard to the transfer of property at the death of the bishop, as well as

in regard to improper use or disposition of the property by the bishop during his life. Attempts were made by the provincial councils of 1837, 1840, and 1843 to guarantee continuance of property in the church's hands by requiring the bishops holding title to make valid wills in favor of fellow bishops. Many courts aided the Church in this matter by declaring that the bishop mentioned in a conveyance held the property only as trustee for the members of the Church, even though no trust is expressed in the instrument. By virtue of this interpretation the property would not descend to the heirs of a bishop not having a will, nor could he dispose of it by will since the beneficiary of the trust would be the equitable owner. By the same token, under this interpretation, the property cannot be reached for satisfaction of a bishop's personal debts as it could were he the absolute title holder. An important case in which this result was reached was *Mannix v. Purcell* [46 Ohio St. 102 (1888)].

As a result of the troubles involved in this system, the Third Plenary Council (1884) decreed that the method of making the bishop the absolute owner of church property was to be used only as a last resort. On July 29, 1911, the Congregation of the Council forbade the method entirely.

Bishop as Trustee. Under this system of property ownership the legal title is vested in the trustee (bishop) and the equitable title is vested in the *cestui que trust* (members of the congregation). The bishop holds title for the benefit of the congregation. As legal owner of the property the bishop is free to administer it according to the canons of the Church. He can delegate control of the property to administrators while retaining the right of supervision over the administration. Other advantages of the system include the protection of the property of the Church. The property of the Church cannot be reached by creditors of the bishop, and neither is there a problem of testate or intestate succession since the members of the Church are the equitable owners.

Most courts have minimized the importance of the bishop as trustee and classify him as a passive, silent trustee with little power, thereby giving the members of the congregation considerable voice in deciding what use or disposition is to be made of the property. (See *Arts v. Guthrie* 37 N.W. 395.) This is the only objection to this form of church property ownership, and in recent times such interference by a congregation is rare.

Bishop as a Corporation Sole. Some states in the United States provide for a system of church property ownership called the corporation sole. By this system the bishop and his successors are incorporated by law and are afforded perpetuity. The corporation consists of one person, the bishop. At his death the corporation does not cease but is merely in abeyance until a successor is appointed, the successor then becoming the new corporation sole. The corporation sole holds absolute title to its property. The bishop, though he is the corporation, does not hold title. This means that the property does not descend to the bishop's heirs, nor can it be reached by the bishop's creditors. The property is transferred to the succeeding bishop.

This type of ownership existed in the colonial days wherever established religions existed, e.g., in Maine, Massachusetts, and Virginia. With the disappearance of the establishments, the corporation sole disappeared until the late 19th century, when a few states provided for it by statute. Other states have created quasi corporation soles through court decisions without legislation authority.

Corporation Aggregate. Two types of corporation aggregate appeared: the trustee corporation and the congregational corporation. The trustee corporation is an outgrowth of the lay trustee system. To remedy the faults inherent in the lay trustee system, churches sought special charters incorporating the trustees. Later most states provided for such incorporation in their general statutes. In this form of property ownership the legal title is vested in the incorporated trustees, and the equitable title is in the unincorporated society. Death of a trustee has no effect on the life of the corporation, and title to property after such a death is never in abeyance.

The congregational corporation is composed of all the members of the parish. Together they form a single legal entity. The title of property is vested in the body corporate. Officers are elected (often called trustees), but they do not hold title to the property. They merely are entrusted with the management of the business affairs of the corporation and as such are agents of the corporation. Their discretion is similar to that vested in the board of directors of an ordinary business corporation.

These types of aggregate corporations began to appear with regularity in the second half of the 19th century as various states passed laws permitting their establishment. Prior to this time religious societies were not allowed to be incorporated except by special charter. This system was criticized because favoritism to certain churches was becoming manifest.

Schisms and the Courts. A schism has been defined as a division or separation in a church or denomination of Christians occasioned by diversity of opinion [*Nelson v. Benson* 69 Ill. 29 (1873)]. Such schisms have occurred with considerable frequency in the history of the churches of the United States, with comparatively few of them involving the Roman Catholic Church. Usually when a schism occurs a dispute arises concerning the property of the church. Both factions seek to have title to and use of the property. The resolution of such disputes has often been placed in the hands of the civil courts of the United States. The courts have struggled with the difficult problems involved, the primary difficulty arising from the fact that solution depends on the type of church involved. The large number and variety of denominations with varying forms of government make it impossible to find a solution that is applicable to all such disputes.

A study of the case law in this area shows that courts of the several states have given uniform treatment to these problems according to the type of church involved. In the only United States Supreme Court decision on this matter, the Court summarizes the various types of cases that have occurred and classifies them according to three categories [*Watson v. Jones* 80 U.S. 679 (1871)].

Specific Trust. A type of controversy arises when a schism occurs in a church that holds property deeded to it with an express stipulation that it be used to spread some specific form of doctrine or belief. In such a case it is the duty of the court to see that the property is not diverted to any other than the specified use. The court has to decide which faction of the church still adheres to the tenets or beliefs specified in the deed. This solution will often depend on the type of church involved. Is the church totally independent of any higher form of government or is it part of a national church by which it is governed? If the church is totally independent, the court must decide for itself which faction is adhering to the specified beliefs. There is no higher church government to rely on. If the church is a part of a larger organization, the court enforces the decision of the highest tribunal of the church. Accepting this decision, the civil court has merely to decree that one faction is entitled to the use of the property according to the terms of the deed. This result will follow even if the recognized faction is a minority of the original local congregation [*Wilson v. Pres. Church of John's Island* 2 Rich. Eq 192 (1846) S.C.].

Independent Congregation. Another type of controversy arises when a schism occurs in a religious congregation that owes no fealty to a higher authority or any other ecclesiastical association. The property that is the subject of the controversy has not been specifically entrusted. Such an organization is entirely independent and governs itself either by the will of a majority of its members or by such other local organism as the majority may have instituted for the purpose of ecclesiastical government. The rules to be followed in these cases are the ordinary principles governing voluntary associations. Whatever form of government is set up by the congregation must be followed. If the majority is to rule, the courts will abide by this, even if the majority has made a complete reversal from the doctrines to which it originally adhered. If certain officers are vested with control of the church, then whatever faction is headed by these officers will be entitled to the property. No inquiry may be made into the doctrine or beliefs of the various factions of the church. In *Shannon v. Frost* [3 B. Monro 253 (1842)], a Kentucky court showed its reluctance to interfere with the decision of the majority of an independent Baptist Church by stating: "The judicial eye cannot penetrate the will of the church for the forbidden purpose of vindicating the alleged wrongs of excised members." The court refused to allow the minority to use the house of worship, basing the decision on the decision of the majority. A Vermont court, in *Smith v. Nelson* [18 Vt. 511 (1846)], stated that in a review of church proceedings they cannot be treated differently from any other voluntary association.

In a 1903 Texas case involving a church of this type, the court correctly stated that the question of a higher church government cannot be a test, since the society is independent of all such higher ecclesiastical control, and can, by majority vote, conduct its government as it pleases (*Gibson v. Morris* 73 S.W. 85).

Associated Church. Another type of case, and the type under which most of the court cases seem to fit, is that of property normally acquired and intended for general use of a religious congregation that is itself part of a large and general organization of some religious denomination, with which it is more or less intimately connected by religious views and ecclesiastical government.

Most early cases were in agreement as to how disputes over property should be handled in such a case. Often a majority of a local congregation would attempt to break away from the general association and attempt to retain rights to its property. The courts recognized that although the dissenting group might be a majority of the local congregation, consideration must be given to the church government of the association of which the local congregation is a part.

A church originally formed as a branch of an associated church, subordinated to the government of that church, cannot break away from that form of government and discipline without losing the character or identity that confers rights to property [*Miller v. Gable* (1845) 2 Denio (New York) 492]. The portion of a church that separates itself from the old organization to form a new one cannot validly claim property belonging to the old organization if the old organization retains its original framework, tenets, and beliefs [*Gibson v. Armstrong* (1847) 46 Ken. 481]. Any majority of a local congregation that organizes resistance to the legitimate authority of its ecclesiastical

superiors is not a true congregation and is not entitled to use of the church property [*Winebrenner v. Colder* (1862) 43 Pa. 244].

In a case in which a majority of a congregation withdrew from a presbytery of the Protestant church and denounced its teachings, the court held that the title to church property should remain with that portion of the congregation adhering to the tenets and discipline of the larger organization to whose use the property was originally dedicated. This is true even though the remaining faithful are a minority [*Ferraria v. Vascanelles* 23 Ill. Repts. 403 (1860)].

These cases indicate that a minority of a local Methodist Episcopal congregation that adheres to its conference or of a local Presbyterian Church that adheres to its presbytery is entitled to the property in such a dispute. It has likewise been decided that a Roman Catholic congregation that has placed itself under authority of its archbishop cannot divorce itself from such authority and still keep title to property acquired by it [*Dochkus v. Lithuanian Benefit Society of St. Anthony* (1903) 206 Pa. 25].

The Supreme Court case of *Watson v. Jones* (81 U.S. 679) involved a division in a local congregation in Kentucky, part of the Presbyterian Church. In deciding in favor of the group still recognized by the Protestant presbytery, the Court stated:

> In this class of cases we think the rule of action which should govern the civil courts, founded in a broad and sound view of the relations of church and state under our system of laws, and supported by a preponding weight of judicial authority is, that, whenever the questions of discipline, or of faith, or ecclesiastical rule, custom, or law have been decided by the highest of these church judicatories to which the matter has been carried, the legal tribunals must accept such decisions as final, and as binding on them, in their application to the case before them.

The court based its decision on two principles. It feared that freedom of religion would be subverted if an aggrieved party could appeal to the secular courts after the church judicatory had decided against him. Second, the court reasoned that ecclesiastical courts and scholars were better equipped with the knowledge proper for deciding questions of this nature.

Generally speaking, United States civil courts have refused to hear cases concerning purely ecclesiastical matters; rather, they accept the holding of the ecclesiastical judicatories. Also, if a civil court should choose to hear such a case, it will only do so after the aggrieved person has exhausted all possible appeals in the particular church judicatory structure [*German Reformed Church v. Seibert* 3 Barr 282 Pa. (1846)].

Diplomatic Representation at the Vatican. Prior to 1846 there were a few isolated instances in which the idea was proposed that the United States send a diplomatic representative to the Vatican. However, in 1846 with the election of Pius IX to succeed Gregory XVI as pope, the idea gained new impetus since this election was greatly favored in the United States; Pius IX was considered a liberal who would strive for reforms and greater freedoms.

In June 1847 the American consul at Rome in a dispatch to the secretary of state proposed that formal diplomatic relations be established between the United States and the government of the Vatican. This proposal was made after high officials of the Vatican government and the Pope himself expressed the desire that such diplomatic relations be started.

In December 1847, President James K. Polk in his message to Congress proposed the opening of such diplomatic relations, giving as reasons the political events occurring in the papal states and protection of United States commercial interests there. In Congress the proposal met with some opposition, but easily passed (137 to 15 in the House and 36 to 7 in the Senate). The opposition argued that under the United States Constitution the government could play no part in ecclesiastical matters and that the United States had no actual commercial interests to protect in the Vatican. Some feared that the President was making the proposal merely as a political move, to secure the vote of the Roman Catholic population.

With the passage of this proposal, Jacob T. Martin, a convert to Roman Catholicism, was named the first chargé d'affaires to the Vatican in 1848. Martin's instructions from the secretary of state read:

> There is one consideration which you ought always to keep in view in your intercourse with the Papal authorities. Most, if not all Governments which have Diplomatic Representatives at Rome are connected with the Pope as the head of the Catholic Church. In this respect the Government of the United States occupies an entirely different position. It possesses no power whatever over the question of religion. All denominations of Christians stand on the same footing in this country,— and every man enjoys the inestimable right of worshiping his God according to the dictates of his own conscience—Your efforts, therefore, will be devoted exclusively to the cultivation of the most friendly civil relations with the Papal Government, and to the extension of the commerce between the two countries. You will carefully avoid even the appearance of interfering in ecclesiastical questions, whether these relate to the United States or any other portion of the world. It might be proper, should you deem it advisable, to make these views known, on some suitable occasion, to the Papal Government; so that there may be no mistake or misunderstanding on this subject.

The diplomatic relationship thus created lasted for 20 years, until 1867. During these years six different chargés d'affaires represented the United States in the Papal States. There was no interruption of the friendly feelings that existed between the two governments. Most of the matters arising were unrelated episodes that called for no sustained policy on the part of either country. Some of the more important incidents that arose included the alleged recognition of the Southern Confederacy by the Vatican; the question of the status of Monsignor Cajeton Bedini, who came to the United States as apostolic delegate; the protection of Vatican property by the United States legation during Garibaldi's entrance into Rome; and the refusal of the Washington Monument Association in 1852 of a block of marble for the monument sent by the Pope.

The matter that caused the most concern and eventually the cessation of United States diplomatic representation at the Vatican revolved around the institution of Protestant services conducted for American citizens within the Vatican. Such worship apparently seemed to the papacy inconsistent with the idea of Rome as the center of the one, true, universal, Church. To enable the American chapel, set up outside the legation, to continue their Protestant services, the American minister in 1866 placed the arms of the American legation over the building used as a chapel. The American minister insisted that this arrangement was satisfactory to the papal authorities. Nevertheless, as a result of this difficulty, which had been greatly exaggerated, the Congress refused to appropriate money for continuance of the United States representative at the Vatican. Thus the mission ceased to exist without ever having been formally discontinued. No formal message of explanation was ever sent to the Vatican.

Bibliography: L. C. FEIERTAG, *American Public Opinion on the Diplomatic Relations between the U.S. and the Papal States, 1847–1867* (Washington 1933). L. F. STOCK, *United States Ministers to the Papal States,* v.1 (Washington 1933). P. J. DIGNAN, *A History of the Legal Incorporation of Catholic Church Property in the U.S., 1784–1932* (Washington 1933). C. J. BARTLETT, *The Tenure of Parochial Property in the U.S.* (Catholic University of America Canon Law Studies 31; 1926). C. F. ZOLLMANN, *American Church Law* (St. Paul 1933). A. P. STOKES, *Church and State in the U.S.,* 3 v. (New York 1950). J. J. MCGRATH, "Canon Law and American Church Law: A Comparative Study," *Jurist* 18 (1958) 260–78. R. A. BILLINGTON, *The Protestant Crusade, 1800–1860* (New York 1938).

[J. C. POLKING]

4. Search for Solution (1900 to 2001)

The First Amendment to the United States Constitution provides in part that "Congress shall make no law respecting an establishment of religion or prohibiting the free exercise thereof.'' These 16 words were rarely commented upon from 1791 through the end of World War II. Since the late 1940s, and even more so since 1970, the Supreme Court of the United States has expended an extraordinary amount of time attempting to ascertain the meaning of these words. The more the Court has attempted to explicate its meaning, the more elusive the guarantee of religious liberty.

As interpreted by the Supreme Court of the United States before the Civil War, the guarantee of religious liberty of the First Amendment applied to action by the Federal government, but not to action by state governments [*Barron v. Baltimore*, 7 Peters 243 (1833); *see* FREEDOM OF RELIGION, IN U.S. CONSTITUTION].

14th Amendment. The 14th Amendment was one of three Constitutional amendments adopted in the wake of the Civil War. The 14th Amendment states, in part, that ''[n]o state shall . . . deprive any person of life, liberty, or property, without due process of law; nor deny to any person within its jurisdiction the equal protection of the laws.'' Although the 14th Amendment was ratified in 1868, its relation to the protection of religious liberty was rarely explored during the remainder of the 19th century. In 1875, President Ulysses S. Grant delivered a speech to the Army of the Tennessee in which he objected to any governmental support of sectarian schools and urged his listeners to ''[k]eep the church and state forever separate.'' Later that year, Grant urged the passage of a constitutional amendment requiring states to establish free public schools and forbidding states to use any school funds for the direct or indirect benefit of any religiously-affiliated school. Grant's proposal was modified shortly thereafter, and was called the Blaine Amendment, after James G. Blaine, a Republican hoping to win the 1876 Presidential nomination. Although the Blaine Amendment was overwhelmingly adopted by the House of Representatives in 1876, a similar proposal failed to pass the Senate by the required two-thirds vote. From 1875 to 1907, the proposed amendment was introduced before Congress over 20 times, but never received as more support than it did in 1876. However, Congress required all states entering the Union after 1876 to include a provision in the state's constitution mandating the creation of a nonsectarian public school system.

At the beginning of the 20th century, the 1st Amendment guarantee of religious liberty was rarely invoked against actions of the Federal government, and the guarantees of the 14th Amendment, which protected individuals from some actions of the state governments, had not been used in a religious liberty case. In 1917, when the United States entered World War I, Congress enacted a selective service law that included some exemptions for conscientious objectors. The exemption was attacked as an unconstitutional establishment of religion, but was upheld by the Supreme Court [*Arver v. United States*, 245 U.S. 366 (1918)]. A decade later, the Supreme Court interpreted the naturalization law to require denying naturalization to one who refused to swear an oath pledging his support of the United States government in future wars [*United States v. Macintosh*, 283 U.S. 605 (1931)]. That the applicant refused to so swear for religious reasons did not persuade a majority of the Court. The Court later determined that Congress did not require the swearing of such an oath, and abandoned its holding in *Macintosh* [*Girouard v. United States*, 328 U.S. 61 (1946)].

In 1925, the Supreme Court decided two cases involving claims of religious liberty. In *Pierce v. Society of Sisters*, the Supreme Court held a violation of the due process clause of the 14th Amendment an Oregon law that made it unlawful for parents to send their children to private or parochial school [268 U.S. 510 (1925)]. Although the implications of the *Pierce* decision have been interpreted in a variety of ways, all commentators have agreed that the decision gives to parents the right to send their children to religious schools. The Court also upheld New York's ''kosher'' law against a challenge that the law violated the 14th Amendment. The complainants argued that the words ''kosher'' and ''orthodox Hebrew religious requirements'' were too vague and indefinite [*Hygrade Provision Company v. Sherman*, 266 U.S. 497]. Five years later, the Supreme Court held constitutional a Louisiana law requiring school boards to purchase all books for schoolchildren, even those attending religiously-affiliated schools [*Cochran v. Louisiana State Board of Education*, 281 U.S. 370 (1930)].

In 1940, the Supreme Court concluded that the free exercise guarantee of the 1st Amendment applied to state action through the due process guarantee of the 14th Amendment [*Cantwell v. Connecticut*, 310 U.S. 296 (1940)]. Seven years later, the Court incorporated into the due process clause of the 14th Amendment the 1st Amendment clause barring laws respecting an establishment of religion [*Everson v. Board of Education*, 330 U.S. 1 (1947)].

Defining Religion. The Supreme Court has decided over 70 cases on the proper relation between religion and government since the mid-20th century. It has never offered a constitutional definition of religion. During the 19th century, the Court offered a definition, one premised on a belief in a deity and on the distinction between a religion and a cult [*Davis v. Beason*, 133 U.S. 333 (1890)]. As the United States became more religiously diverse in the 20th century, this relatively narrow definition was rejected. When Congress adopted the Selective Service and Training Act (1940), courts were required to interpret the provision granting conscientious objector status to those opposed to war in any form by reason of religious training and belief. Divergent interpretations of that language led Congress to amend the Act in 1948 by stating: "Religious training and belief in this connection means an individual's belief in a relation to a Supreme Being involving duties superior to those arising from any human relation, but does not include essentially political, sociological, or philosophical views or a merely personal moral code." During the Vietnam War, the Court twice interpreted that provision. It first held that the provision should be broadly interpreted to include those whose belief system was sincere and was parallel to the belief system of those who clearly fit the exemption [*United States v. Seeger*, 380 U.S. 163 (1965)]. Five years later, the Court held that the statutory language fit one who denied his beliefs were religious, for religion was to be given an extremely broad definition [*Welsh v. United States*, 398 U.S. 333 (1970)]. Three members of the Court dissented from the holding, claiming that the statutory provision was interpreted well beyond any sound interpretation of religion. In constitutional interpretation, the Court has alluded to the issue of the definition of religion only twice: In the Amish schooling case, discussed below, the Court noted the distinction between religious reasons and "philosophical and personal" reasons, and that only the former was protected by the 1st Amendment. In an unemployment compensation case, the Court merely noted that the free exercise clause granted special protection to beliefs rooted in religion.

Freedom of Religious Exercise. In the 1930s and 1940s, the Supreme Court weighed the individual's claim to religious liberty against the interest of the state in a variety of contexts, many of which involved members of the Jehovah's Witnesses.

Proselytizing. In the 1930s and 1940s members of the Jehovah's Witnesses pressed a number of claims alleging violations of their constitutional rights. In a number of cases, the Supreme Court used various provisions of the 1st Amendment to strike down state statutes which limited the proselytizing efforts of the Jehovah's Witnesses. In *Cantwell v. Connecticut*, the Court held unconstitutional, as a violation of the free exercise clause, a criminal conviction for soliciting without a permit money for a religious cause. The majority opinion, by Justice Owen Roberts, followed an injunction first stated in *Reynolds v. United States*, 98 U.S. 145 (1879), the Mormon polygamy case: "[Free exercise] embraces two concepts—freedom to believe and freedom to act. The first is absolute, but in the nature of things, the second cannot be." The Court then cautioned that the government can-

not unduly infringe the right to free exercise even when attaining a permissible end. In *Murdock v. Pennsylvania*, [319 U.S. 105 (1943)] and *Follett v. McCormick*, [321 U.S. 573 (1944)] the Supreme Court held violative of the free exercise clause of the 1st Amendment the imposition of a license and bookseller's taxes on Jehovah's Witnesses who offered religious books and pamphlets for sale. In 1989, a badly divided Supreme Court held that a Texas law exempting from its sales tax periodicals published or distributed by a religious faith that consisted solely of religious content violated the Establishment Clause [*Texas Monthly v. Bullock*, 489 U.S. 1 (1989)]. The plurality opinion of the Court limited the *Murdock* and *Follett* cases to their facts, which means those cases cannot be understood to prohibit the government from taxing the sale of religious publications. The Court also held unconstitutional a local ordinance prohibiting the door-to-door distribution of handbills [*Martin v. City of Struthers*, 319 U.S. 141 (1943)]. The Court did hold constitutional the conviction of Sarah Prince for violating the child labor laws of Massachusetts, which Prince claimed violated her free exercise rights. Prince permitted her niece, for whom she was the custodian, to join her in selling *Watchtower,* the magazine of the Jehovah's Witnesses. Prince's free exercise right to proselytize and sell Watchtower did not include the right to bring her niece with her while she proselytized [*Prince v. Massachusetts*, 321 U.S. 158 (1944)].

Flag Salute. A few weeks after the *Cantwell* decision, the Court decided the first flag-salute case [*Minersville School District v. Gobitis*, 310 U.S. 586 (1940)]. Justice Felix Frankfurter, speaking for eight of the nine members of the Court, upheld the constitutionality of a Pennsylvania law that required all public school pupils to salute the flag. As Jehovah's Witnesses, the Gobitis children refused to salute the flag on religious grounds, as instructed by their parents. The challenge to the law on free exercise grounds was rejected by the Court, which concluded that the state's interest in the promotion of national unity was sufficient to justify the law. The lone dissenter was Chief Justice Harlan Fiske Stone, who concluded that the state's justification for the law was insufficient when balanced against the individual interest in the free exercise of religion. The *Gobitis* opinion was released on June 3, 1940, at a time when World War II was raging in Europe, but before the United States had entered the War. Shortly after the decision in *Gobitis* was released for publication, and apparently in part because of the decision, anti-Jehovah's Witness hysteria gripped the country. Elite reaction to the *Gobitis* opinion was largely negative.

Three years later, the Court reversed itself [*West Virginia Board of Education v. Barnette*, 319 U.S. 624

(1943)]. The Court's opinion was written by Justice Robert H. Jackson, who had been appointed to the Court in 1941, after the Court issued its decision in *Gobitis*. Five other members of the Court joined Jackson's opinion, including several Justices who had joined the majority opinion in *Gobitis*. Jackson's opinion is a ringing, eloquent endorsement of the centrality of individual liberty in American constitutional law: "If there is any fixed star in our constitutional constellation, it is that no official, high or petty, can prescribe what shall be orthodox in matters of politics, nationalism, religion, or other matters of opinion or force citizens to confess by word or act their faith therein." For the majority, freedom of speech could be restricted only if there was a grave and immediate danger to paramount community interests. The refusal by schoolchildren to salute the American flag did not create such a danger to the state or community.

Church Property Disputes. In the early 1950s, the New York legislature attempted to transfer control of Saint Nicholas Cathedral in New York City from members of the Russian Orthodox church who deferred to the authority of the Patriarch in Moscow to those who saw the Patriarch as a puppet of the Soviet government. The Supreme Court, in an opinion by Justice Stanley Reed, held that this legislative effort violated the church's right to self-governance [*Kedroff v. St. Nicholas Cathedral*, 344 U.S. 94 (1952)]. From the late 1960s until the end of the decade of the 1970s, the Supreme Court decided several cases involving church property disputes. Doctrinal changes by several Protestant churches in the late 1960s led to religious disputes between local and national church bodies, and within local churches themselves. Those ecclesiological disputes resulted in litigation concerning the rightful owner of the local church. After several attempts to craft a constitutional rule concerning the resolution of church property disputes, the Supreme Court in 1979 declared constitutionally permissible the resolution of disputes based on "neutral principles of law" [*Jones v. Wolf*, 443 U.S. 595 (1979)]. The problem with the "neutral principles" approach, as noted by Justice Lewis Powell, dissenting in *Jones*, is that this rule of law fails to account for the fact that religious organizations are organized as much by religious as legal precepts. Because the neutral principles rule bars courts from acknowledging the existence of those religious precepts, courts will award title to church property contrary to the precepts that undergird the religious organization, particularly hierarchical religious organizations.

Sunday Legislation. In the early 1960s, those who worshiped the Sabbath on Saturday claimed that Sunday Closing Laws violated their religious liberty. A Sabbatarian who closed his business on Saturday for religious reasons and on Sunday because state law demanded he do so suffered adverse economic consequences compared with someone whose business remained open on Saturdays. In 1961, the Court upheld the constitutionality of Sunday closing laws against challenges on both free exercise and establishment clause grounds [*Braunfeld v. Brown*, 366 U.S. 599 (1961)]. The opinion of Chief Justice Earl Warren conceded that the Sunday closing law indirectly operated to make the practice of religion by Sabbatarians more expensive than those whose day of rest was Sunday, but concluded that the Sunday closing laws were designed primarily to achieve legitimate secular goals. An exemption to Sabbatarians might adversely affect those secular goals by granting an economic advantage to Sabbatarians over their competitors, complicate enforcement of the Sunday closing law, inject religion into decisions concerning employment, and undermine a common day of rest. The dissenters concluded that the free exercise of religion could be infringed only to prevent a grave and imminent danger of substantive evil, and the justification of a common day of rest was a mere convenience that could not outweigh the religious liberty interest of Sabbatarians. The inequities permitted by the Court in *Braunfeld* eased as the states began repealing their Sunday closing laws. At the turn of the century, the number of Sunday closing laws were few, and rarely enforced.

The abolition of Sunday closing laws led to a different problem. Connecticut abolished its Sunday closing law in 1977. In response, Caldor, Inc., opened its stores for business on Sunday. Connecticut adopted, after abolishing its Sunday closing law, a provision barring a private employer from requiring any employee to work on the employee's Sabbath as a condition of employment. Thornton was a manager with Caldor, and a Presbyterian who refused to work on Sunday, his Sabbath. He was demoted to a clerical position by Caldor, resigned, and claimed he was fired in violation of Connecticut law. The Supreme Court held that the Connecticut law violated the establishment clause, because it had the primary effect of impermissibly advancing a particular religious practice [*Estate of Thornton v. Caldor, Inc.*, 472 U.S. 703 (1985)].

Unemployment Compensation. Two years later, the Court held that South Carolina could not exclude from its unemployment compensation program a claimant, who for religious reasons, refused to take a job that required her to work on Saturdays, her Sabbath [*Sherbert v. Verner*, 374 U.S. 398 (1963)]. The Court characterized the law as requiring the claimant to "choose between following the precepts of her religion and forfeiting benefits, on the one hand, and abandoning one of the precepts of her religion in order to accept work, on the other hand." This was impermissible, because the law effectively penalized the exercise of her religious beliefs. The Court held that the state could infringe the religious liberty of the claimant, Adell Sherbert, only if it had a compelling interest. The state's interest in administrative convenience and preventing fraudulent claims did not rise to the level of a compelling interest. The Court's opinion, by Justice William Brennan, also concluded that this case was distinguishable from *Braunfeld*. A concurring opinion by Justice Potter Stewart argued that the Court had painted itself into a corner, for its interpretation of the free exercise clause in *Sherbert* was directly in conflict with its interpretation of the establishment clause. Justice Stewart claimed that the Court's interpretation of the establishment clause required South Carolina to deny Adell Sherbert unemployment benefits, and the Court's interpretation of the free exercise required South Carolina to grant Adell Sherbert unemployment benefits. Justice Stewart concluded that the Court's mechanistic interpretation of the establishment clause was unsound as a matter of history and wrong as a matter of constitutional interpretation.

In three subsequent unemployment compensation cases decided in the 1980s, the Supreme Court extended the holding of *Sherbert v. Verner*. The Court first held that the state could not deny unemployment compensation benefits to a Jehovah's Witness who left his job at a munitions factory based on his religious objections to war. That the claimant had not been fired, but had left his job voluntarily made no constitutional difference to the Court [*Thomas v. Review Board*, 450 U.S. 707 (1981)]. It then held impermissible the decision to refuse unemployment compensation to a claimant who was fired because, after working for his employer for two years, became a Seventh-day Adventist and then refused to work on Friday night or on Saturday, his Sabbath [*Hobbie v. Unemployment Appeals Comm'n of Florida*, 480 U.S. 136 (1987)]. Finally, the Court held that unemployment benefits were improperly denied to a claimant who refused to work on Sundays because he was a Christian. The Court concluded that it did not matter that the claimant was not a member of any particular Christian church or organization. The issue was whether the claimant's refusal to work was based on a sincerely held religious belief [*Frazee v. Illinois Department of Employment Sec.*, 489 U.S. 829 (1989)]. The extent to which the unemployment compensation cases stated a general rule of constitutional law was placed in great doubt after the Court's decision in *Employment Division v. Smith*, 494 U.S. 872 (1990), discussed below.

The Amish and Compulsory Schooling. The State of Wisconsin made it a criminal offense for parents to violate the State's compulsory school-attendance law mandating that children attend school until age 16. Amish parents, pursuant to their religious beliefs, removed their children from school after they completed the eighth grade. The Supreme Court, with only Justice William O. Douglas dissenting in part, held that the Wisconsin law violated the free exercise rights of Amish parents [*Wisconsin v. Yoder*, 406 U.S. 205 (1972)]. The Court, following the doctrine stated in *Sherbert v. Verner*, held that the right to free exercise could be infringed only upon a showing by the state that the justification for its action was compelling. The Court noted that the Amish were "productive and very law-abiding members of society," and that the Amish alternative to formal schooling, vocational training, had enabled them to survive as a highly self-sufficient community in the United States for over 200 years. The state's interest in educating Amish schoolchildren was not compelling, but merely "highly speculative." That the state's compulsory school-attendance law was neutral on its face, for it was not directed at the Amish or any other religious group, did not make the law constitutional, because the law clearly created an undue burden on the religious practices of the Amish. Justice Douglas dissented on the ground that the Court failed to account for the interests of the children themselves, who might disagree with their parents and opt to attend high school.

Native Americans and Free Exercise. Unlike the Jehovah's Witnesses in the 1940s, Native American religious practices have not fared well before the Supreme Court. In 1986, the Court held that the assignment of a Social Security number to a Native American child by the Social Security Administration did not violate the Free Exercise rights of the child or her parents [*Bowen v. Roy*, 476 U.S. 693 (1986)]. Two years later, the Supreme Court held that the Free Exercise Clause did not bar the government from permitting the harvesting of timber or the construction of a road on federal land, even though part of that land had traditionally been used by three Native American tribes for religious worship. The majority concluded that, because the federal government's decision did not burden the religious exercise by the complaining tribes, it did not have to address whether the government's interest in harvesting the timber and building the road constituted a compelling governmental interest [*Lyng v. Northwest Indian Cemetery Protective Association*, 485 U.S. 439 (1988)]. Shortly thereafter, the Supreme Court drastically altered its free exercise jurisprudence in another case concerning Native American religious exercise, *Employment Div. v. Smith*, 494 U.S. 872 (1990).

Retrenchment. The continuing validity of the standards set forth in *Sherbert* and *Yoder* was called into doubt by the Supreme Court's decision in *Employment Division v. Smith*. Before *Smith*, the standard for determining a violation of the free exercise clause was to determine 1) whether the governmental action burdened the exercise of religion, and if so, 2) whether the government's reason for burdening the exercise of religion was justified by a compelling governmental interest. In *Smith*, the Court rejected that test, concluding that if the law was a neutral and generally applicable law, it did not offend the free exercise clause of the 1st Amendment even if application of that law might burden an individual's exercise of religion. In *Smith*, the issue was the constitutionality of Oregon's criminal law prohibiting the possession or use of peyote, when applied to a Native American who used peyote when engaged in religious worship. Because the criminal law was a valid and neutral law generally applicable to anyone who possessed or used peyote, the incidental effect of the law's application to someone using peyote for religious reasons did not mandate a constitutional exemption from the law. The majority, in an opinion by Justice Antonin Scalia, distinguished *Sherbert* and *Yoder*. *Sherbert* was limited to a peculiar constitutional rule concerning unemployment compensation, and *Yoder* was reinterpreted to mean that a neutral and valid generally applicable law was unconstitutional only if it violated both the free exercise clause and some other constitutional right. The Court called *Yoder*-type cases "hybrid" cases, and concluded that the issue in *Smith* was not such a case.

The academic reaction to *Smith* was widespread and largely negative. Three years after the decision was issued, Congress adopted the Religious Freedom Restoration Act (1993) (RFRA), which attempted by statute to restore the test enunciated in *Sherbert* and *Yoder*. In 1997, the Supreme Court held RFRA unconstitutional, as a violation of § 5 of the 14th Amendment [*City of Boerne v. Flores*, 521 U.S. 507 (1997)]. Several states have adopted "mini-RFRAs," which protect religious liberty as a matter of state law. The constitutionality of those "mini-RFRAs" has not been tested in most states.

The Relation of Free Exercise and Free Speech. The exercise of religion often involves speech. The Supreme Court has wrestled with the relation of the free exercise, free speech and establishment clauses in several cases during the 1980s and 1990s. The University of Missouri at Kansas City allowed registered student groups to use generally available facilities for meetings. In the late 1970s, UMKC refused to allow a registered religious group named Cornerstone to use its facilities after the Board of Curators prohibited the use of University property for religious worship or religious teaching. The Court held that barring a registered student group from using a generally available facility because the group was religious constituted impermissible discrimination on the basis of content of the group's speech (i.e., that its speech was religious in nature). Further, the University's "equal access" policy, granting to registered groups the right to use open rooms, did not raise establishment clause concerns, because the University did not place its imprimatur of approval on the religious activities of Cornerstone, nor did it attempt to advance religion by creating an open forum [*Widmar v. Vincent*, 454 U.S. 263 (1981)].

Shortly after *Widmar*, Congress adopted the Equal Access Act (1984), which prohibited high schools from refusing access to religious and philosophical groups if the school granted access to other noncurricular groups. The Court held the Equal Access Act constitutional in *Board of Education v. Mergens*, 496 U.S. 296 (1990). In 1993, the Supreme Court held that a school district violated the free speech clause of First Amendment by denying a church access to school premises to show a film after school hours solely because the film dealt with a subject from a religious standpoint, and allowing church access to school premises would not have been an establishment of religion [*Lamb's Chapel v. Center Moriches Union Free School District*, 508 U.S. 384 (1993)]. In *Good News Club v. Milford Central School*,, 121 S.Ct. 2093 (2001), a closely divided Supreme Court held that the refusal of a public school district to permit a religious organization to use its facilities after school hours because the organization was teaching moral lessons from a Christian perspective through live storytelling and prayer constituted viewpoint discrimination in violation of the free speech clause. The Court determined apposite the decision in *Lamb's Chapel*, because the only difference between the two cases was the inconsequential distinction that in the former case, religious and moral lessons were taught through films, in the latter case, those lessons were taught through storytelling and prayers.

The Court returned to the issue of the relation of religion and speech in two cases in 1995. In *Capitol Square Review & Advisory Board v. Pinette*, 515 U.S. 753 (1995), the issue concerned the constitutionality of the government's refusal to allow the unattended display of a cross in a public forum. A closely divided Court held that private religious speech was fully protected by the free speech clause of the 1st Amendment. The board's refusal to allow the display of the cross was unconstitutional. The dissenters argued that the establishment clause should be interpreted to create strong presumption against the installation of unattended religious symbols on public property. In *Rosenberger v. Rectors and Visitors of the University of Virginia*, 515 U.S. 819 (1995), the University of Virginia refused to pay for the printing costs of paper printed by a recognized student organization because the paper "primarily promotes or manifests a particular belie[f] in or about a deity or an ultimate reality." This, the University claimed, violated the establishment clause. The divided Court held that, because the

University's decision discriminated against the student organization on the basis of the viewpoint of the organization (e.g., that there is a God), the University violated the free speech clause. Paying for the printing costs of the paper did not violate the establishment clause because the University's reimbursement scheme was neutral toward religion, neither advancing nor inhibiting religion by its action in paying for the printing costs of a paper distributed by a student organization recognized by the University. The dissenters claimed that the establishment clause required some justification beyond "evenhandedness." Direct funding of sectarian activities were inconsistent with the establishment clause, even if the funding was undertaken as a matter of evenhandedness.

The Court remains closely divided on the interpretation of the free exercise clause, and on the application of the free speech clause to religious speech. It appears unlikely that this division will heal any time soon.

Religious Establishment. Since the Supreme Court first applied the establishment clause in 1947 to state as well as federal action, it has regularly attempted to mark the proper boundary between religion and government interaction. As discussed more fully below, the Court has rarely reached consensus about the proper interpretation of the establishment clause. This has meant a bewildering array of cases and "tests" about the establishment clause. Those who read the Court's establishment clause decisions often leave befuddled and frustrated, for the members of the Court begin with widely differing premises, which often lead the Justices to diametrically opposed positions.

The more the Supreme Court has decided establishment clause cases, the wider the circle of types of cases it has decided. For most of the last half-century, however, the Court has focused on the interaction between government and religion in the field of education, both public education and religious education. Those parents who send their children to public schools are often of many different faiths, or of no religious faith. From 1947 to the present, the Supreme Court has issued a number of rulings attempting to demarcate the constitutional boundaries imposed on public school officials when claims of religious establishment are raised. For those parents who send their children to religious schools, the recurring question is the extent to which the state may pay, either directly or indirectly, for any costs attributable to that religious education. The result, after more than 50 years of trying, is a muddle. The Supreme Court, as discussed below, has offered a number of different "tests" concerning the meaning of religious establishments, and the current state of the law is largely a mess.

Public Transportation. The first modern case decided by the Supreme Court is *Everson v. Board of Educa-*

tion, 330 U.S. 1 (1947). A New Jersey township school board, acting pursuant to state law, reimbursed parents for the costs in sending their children to local parochial schools on municipal buses. A severely divided Court held that, though the actions of the school board were subject to the constraints of the establishment clause, the reimbursement scheme did not violate that clause. Both the majority, in an opinion by Justice Hugo Black, and the dissent, in an opinion by Justice Wiley Rutledge, agreed that the clause against an establishment of religion was intended to erect "a wall of separation between Church and State." The unanimous adoption of Thomas Jefferson's "separationist" standard (which he crafted while President in a Jan. 1, 1802, letter to the Danbury Baptist Association) masked the marked disagreement about the application of the "wall of separation" to the township's reimbursement scheme. The five-man majority concluded that spending tax monies to pay for the transportation of schoolchildren to parochial schools was part of a general program aiding all children to make their way to school. For the majority, these services were "indisputably marked off from the religious function" of the schools. Consequently, the government was not supporting the religious schools, but merely helping parents get their children, regardless of their religion, to school. The four dissenters concluded that paying the transportation costs to and from parochial school aided those parents and children "in a substantial way" to obtaining religious training, which they concluded was barred by the establishment clause.

The central difficulty with *Everson* was the implicit conflict between the claim that "absolute" separation was required between church and state, and the conclusion that the public transportation of schoolchildren was a permissible welfare measure. The effort by the majority to avoid this conflict by focusing on the fact that the benefit was not to the parochial school, but to the child attending the parochial school (the "child benefit" theory), merely removed the conflict one step. Arguably, the parochial school was the ultimate beneficiary even though the money was given to the parents of the schoolchildren rather than to the school itself. Justice Rutledge made this very argument in dissent in *Everson*, claiming that "it cannot be said that the cost of transportation is no part of the cost of education or of the religious instruction given." Consequently, concluded the dissent, the reimbursement scheme violated the required separation of church and state. The five-to-four division of the Court in *Everson* was a harbinger of what was to come.

Released Time. One year later the Court held unconstitutional the released time program in existence in the Champaign, Illinois, school district. Public school students were given religious instruction for between 30-45 minutes per week in their schools if their parents requested such instruction. Those who were not given religious instruction left their classrooms for secular instruction elsewhere. Again speaking for the Court, Justice Black held the program unconstitutional. Justice Black concluded that the public school system could not be used to aid religion [*Illinois* ex rel. *McCollum v. Board of Education*, 333 U.S. 203 (1948)]. The only dissenter, Justice Stanley Reed, concluded that, based on custom and particular historical practices (e.g., military chaplains, prayer in public schools), this aid to religion was consistent with the principle of religious liberty. Justice Reed also criticized the Court's reliance on the "wall of separation of church and state" metaphor, claiming that "[a] rule of law should not be drawn from a figure of speech."

Four years later, the Court softened its position on released time, holding constitutional a New York City program in which public school children were released from their schools to attend religious instruction off school property during the school day [*Zorach v. Clauson*, 343 U.S. 306 (1952)]. Justice Douglas's majority opinion included the statement, "We are a religious people whose institutions presuppose a Supreme Being," and held that the principle of separation was modified by the principle of neutrality toward religion. Otherwise, the principle of separation led to hostility between religion and the state. Justice Black dissented, finding no difference between the Illinois and New York programs.

The Court, with the exception of a couple of church property cases discussed above, then remained silent concerning religion for nearly a decade. After holding constitutional Sunday closing laws against both free exercise and establishment clause challenges, the Court held impermissible a Maryland constitutional requirement that public officials declare a belief a God, on the ground that the provision was a religious test for office [*Torcaso v. Watkins*, 367 U.S. 488 (1961)]. Within two years, the Court created a firestorm with its decisions in two public school prayer cases.

State prescribed prayer. New York Regents recommended that public schoolchildren recite the following prayer at the beginning of the school day: "Almighty God, we acknowledge our dependence upon Thee, and we beg thy blessings upon us, our parents, our teachers, and our country." For the Court, Justice Black held the recommended prayer violative of the establishment clause because it was composed by state officials and was designed to advance religious beliefs [*Engel v. Vitale*, 370 U.S. 421 (1962)]. The next year, the Court held unconstitutional an officially sponsored reading of the Bible and the recitation of the Lord's Prayer at the beginning of the public school day [*Abington School District v.*

Schempp, 374 U.S. 203 (1963)]. Although both decisions relied heavily on Jefferson's "wall of separation" metaphor as the touchstone for understanding the meaning of the establishment clause, the Court suggested a more particularized approach to determining the constitutionality of government actions challenged pursuant to that clause. In his opinion for the Court in *Schempp*, Justice Tom Clark held that the government's action must have 1) a secular purpose and 2) a primary effect that neither advanced nor inhibited religion.

The Court's decisions were largely unpopular with the public and with Congress. A number of efforts to overturn the school prayer decisions by constitutional amendment have been initiated by members of Congress since 1963. All have been unsuccessful. The public clamor for reversal of school prayer decisions subsided over time, which may be attributed in part to grudging acceptance of the decision and to the fact that public school officials in some areas of the United States refused to acknowledge the decisions, and continued to condone the saying of school prayers into the 1970s.

The Supreme Court did not return to the issue of prayers in public schools for nearly two decades. In 1980, the Court held that the posting of the Ten Commandments in public school classrooms violated the establishment clause because there existed no secular purpose in doing so [*Stone v. Graham*, 449 U.S. 39 (1980)]. Five years later, the Supreme Court held unconstituitional an Alabama law authorizing a moment of silence "for meditation and voluntary prayer" at the beginning of the public school day. The Court noted that the sole purpose for the law was the nonsecular purpose of returning voluntary prayer to the public school [*Wallace v. Jaffree*, 472 U.S. 38 (1985)]. Five members of the Court concluded that some moment of silence laws were constitutional, although they disagreed about the constitutionality of Alabama's law. A number of states have since adopted moment of silence statutes that meet the secular purpose standard. In 1992, the Court barred invocation and benediction prayers at public school graduation ceremonies if they were part of the official school graduation ceremony [*Lee v. Weisman*, 505 U.S. 577 (1992)]. The majority opinion in *Lee* was written by Justice Anthony Kennedy. Justice Kennedy's opinion suggested that because the graduation prayers bore the imprint of the government, and because students in effect were obliged to attend graduation, the saying of those prayers required students to participate in a religious exercise, which the establishment clause forbids. The emphasis by the Court on the official nature of the prayers led some student groups to attempt to eliminate any official sanction for an invocation and a benediction by placing the authority to include prayers at graduation with the graduating class rather than school officials. The Court appeared to respond in part to this effort in *Santa Fe Independent School District v. Doe*, 530 U.S. 290 (2000), in which it held unconstitutional a public school district policy concerning student-led prayers given before high school football games. The Court's opinion, written by Justice Kennedy, concluded that though nothing in the Constitution forbade a public school student from praying voluntarily before, during or after school, if the government affirmatively sponsors the practice of prayer, it violates the establishment clause.

Evolution and Public Schools. In 1925, John Scopes was convicted for teaching the theory of evolution in public school contrary to Tennessee state law, although it was almost certain that Scopes did not teach evolution. The trial was a circus, taking place over eight days, but culminating in a mere one hour of testimony. The conviction was reversed based on a legal fiction, but the "lesson" of the trial, according to the press, was that the forces of progress (secular modernism) had routed the forces of superstition (religious fundamentalism). Although the trial ended most efforts in the states to adopt anti-evolution laws, textbook publishers began reducing or even eliminating references to evolution in biology textbooks to avoid controversy. The issue would not arise again until the 1960s. In *Epperson v. Arkansas*, 393 U.S. 97 (1968), the Supreme Court held unconstitutional Arkansas' anti-evolution statute, calling it a "quixotic prohibition." Those opposed to the teaching of evolution responded to *Epperson* by lobbying local and state boards of education to require biology textbooks to label evolution a theory and to require the teaching of creationism if evolution was taught in the public school. The State of Louisiana passed a law barring the teaching of evolution unless the school also taught creation science. In *Edwards v. Aguillard*, 482 U.S. 578 (1987), the Supreme Court held that this law lacked a secular purpose, and thus violated the establishment clause.

Governmental Aid and Private and Parochial Schools. The importance of education in the modern world has been clear to governmental bodies for some time. Since World War II, both the federal and state governments have passed laws attempting to enhance the learning of children in both public and private schools, from the elementary through graduate studies. Laws that provide money either to students who attend (or hope to attend) a religiously affiliated school, or to the school itself, have been regularly challenged since the late 1960s. The Court has been a model of inconsistency, first creating nearly insuperable barriers to governmental aid that affects religious educational institutions, and then relaxing those barriers. It has largely done so through a multi-pronged establishment clause test, the so-called *Lemon* test.

The Lemon Test. In 1971, the Supreme Court held that state laws providing salary supplements to teachers in religious schools and reimbursing religious schools for some costs attributable to the teaching of secular subjects violated the establishment clause [*Lemon v. Kurtzman*, 403 U.S. 602 (1971)]. The Court, in an opinion by Chief Justice Warren Burger, retreated from the separationist standard first enunciated in *Everson*, noting that the language of the religion clauses "is at best opaque," and that "the line of separation, far from being a 'wall,' is a blurred, indistinct, and variable barrier depending on all the circumstances of a particular relationship." In place of the wall of separation, the Court offered a three-pronged test of constitutionality: 1) the law must have a secular purpose; 2) the principal or primary effect of the law must neither advance nor inhibit religion; and 3) the statute must not foster an excessive entanglement by government with religion. The first two prongs of this test were taken from *Schempp*, the second school prayer case; the last prong was taken from *Walz v. Tax Commission*, 397 U.S. 664 (1970), which held constitutional a property tax exemption to religious organizations for its property used for religious worship. Because the proper governmental oversight of the programs created an excessive entanglement because government and religion, the state laws were unconstitutional. Although the Court retreated from the separationist standard, and attempted to replace it with a standard of religious "neutrality," or religious "accommodation," the *Lemon* test was a severe challenge to those who believed the relation between government and religious educational institutions was too strained and hostile.

Including its decision in *Everson*, the Supreme Court has decided at least 20 cases concerning the constitutionality of aid that may, directly or indirectly, assist religious schools. The result is a foray into a byzantine world. The Court initially made a distinction between aid that flowed to religious institutions involved in higher education, and aid to religious elementary and high schools. Because the former were not considered "pervasively sectarian," aid to religiously affiliated colleges and universities was permissible because there was little fear of excessive entanglement between religion and government [*Tilton v. Richardson*, 403 U.S. 672 (1971); *Hunt v. McNair*, 413 U.S. 734 (1973); *Roemer v. Board of Public Works*, 426 U.S. 736 (1976)]. Students in religious elementary and high schools could be lent textbooks by the state (*Board of Education v. Allen*, 392 U.S. 236 (1968)), but not globes, maps, or audio-visual equipment [*Meek v. Pittenger*, 421 U.S. 349 (1975); *Wolman v. Walter*, 433 U.S. 229 (1977)]. In 2000, a divided Court overruled *Meek* and *Wolman*, permitting governmental agencies to lend educational materials and equipment to private and religious schools [*Mitchell v. Helms*, 530 U.S. 793 (2000)]. Although there is some evidence that the Court has retreated on the higher education/compulsory education dichotomy, some Justices continue to argue for its strict enforcement. Parents may take a tax deduction for educational expenses incurred in sending their children to school (*Mueller v. Allen*, 463 U.S. 388 (1983), and a handicapped student may use state tuition funds to attend a higher religious institution (*Witters v. Washington Department of Services For the Blind*, 474 U.S. 481 (1986), but parents cannot receive tuition tax credits for sending their children to religious schools (*Committee for Public Education v. Nyquist*, 413 U.S. 756 (1973). The government may not pay for teachers to provide remedial education for poor children if it takes place at the religious school (*Aguilar v. Felton*, 473 U.S. 402 (1986), but may pay for an on-premises sign language interpreter who aids a deaf child attending a religious school [*Zobrest v. Catalina Hills School District*, 509 U.S. 1 (1993)]. An issue the Supreme Court has studiously avoided for a number of years is the constitutionality of a voucher system, in which the state issues an educational voucher that may be redeemed by students at either a public or private school. State and lower federal courts addressing this issue have reached contrary results, and until the Supreme Court speaks, the constitutionality of educational vouchers is unclear.

Additional Approaches to Interpreting the Establishment Clause. In 1789, each House of Congress hired a chaplain to pray at the opening of the legislative day. In 1983, the Supreme Court decided a case concerning the constitutionality of the State of Nebraska's practice of opening each legislative day with a prayer by a chaplain paid by the State. It held that the "unique history" of the practice of hiring government-paid chaplains led it to conclude that the practice did not violate the law because the founders did not believe that the practice violated the 1st Amendment. The Court ignored the *Lemon* test in favor of this "historical practices" test, which the dissenters claimed was because application of *Lemon* would have resulted in a contrary result [*Marsh v. Chambers*, 463 U.S. 783 (1983)]. The next year, in a concurring opinion, Justice Sandra Day O'Connor suggested a revised test for the establishment clause, the "endorsement" test. This test focuses attention on the fact that the important issue was whether the government's action had made adherence to religion relevant to the person's standing in the community [*Lynch v. Donnelly*, 465 U.S. 668 (1984)]. In 1989, the Court's jurisprudence disintegrated. The issues before the Court were whether 1) the placement of a créche on the Grand Staircase of the Allegheny County Courthouse and 2) the placement of a menorah next to a Christmas tree and a sign saluting liberty on public property next to the City-County building were impermissible establishments of religion. No opinion garnered a majority of the Court. Varying coalitions held that the former was unconstitutional but the latter was constitutional. The constitutional difference between the two displays was either because the créche solely promoted a religious message, and the menorah, tree and sign saluting liberty promoted a secular message (opinion of Justice Harry Blackmun) or because the créche solely promoted a religious message, and the menorah, tree and sign promoted a message of pluralism and freedom of belief during the holiday season and did not endorse Judaism or religion in general (opinion of Justice O'Connor). The opinion of Justice Brennan concluded that both displays favored religion, and the establishment clause forbade any governmental action that favored religion over non-religion. The opinion of Justice Kennedy concluded that both displays were constitutional, because the government did not coerce anyone to support or participate in any religion or its exercise [*County of Allegheny v. American Civil Liberities Union*, 492 U.S. 573 (1989)].

The Supreme Court has never overturned the *Lemon* test, although it has been the subject of repeated criticism by Justices and legal commentators. The endorsement test suggested by Justice O'Connor has been incorporated by some Justices into the "primary effect" prong of *Lemon*, and used independently of *Lemon* by Justice O'Connor and other justices. To determine whether some action of government is an endorsement of religion, the proper perspective is that of the reasonable observer, who is understood to be a well-informed observer. A minority of Justices consider coercion the proper test of an establishment clause violation. For those Justices, the establishment clause is violated only when the government attempts to coerce an individual's religious liberty. A different minority of Justices urge a return to the wall of separation, particular in cases in which aid flows to one or more religious organizations. The former group is more "accommodationist" in its treatment of the relation of government and religion, and the latter is more "separationist" in its understanding of that relationship.

The establishment clause has become one of those fissures in American society that gave rise to the phrase "culture wars." Like much of society, the Court is badly divided about the fundamental principles that guide interpretation of the establishment clause. This division among the Court, which will probably continue for some time, makes clarity in this area of law extremely unlikely.

Bibliography: A general overview of these and other issues of church-state relations is found in M. S. ARIENS and R. A. DESTRO, *Religious Liberty in a Pluralistic Society* (1996). The classic history of the relation between religion and government remains: A. P. STOKES, *Church and State in America* 3 v. (1950). A number of studies of the history and the theory of the religion clauses was written in the 1980s. They include: G. V. BRADLEY, *Church-State Relationships in America* (1987); D. DREISBACH, *Real Threat and Mere Liberty: Religious Liberty and the First Amendment* (1987); and J. T. NOONAN, JR., *The Believer and the Powers That Are* (1987). A critical study of the Supreme Court's efforts in this doctrinal area is: S. D. SMITH, *Foreordained Failure* (1995). Two general histories of religion in America are: M. E. MARTY, *Pilgrims in Their Own Land: 500 Years of Religion in America* (1984) and S. E. AHLSTROM, *A Religious History of the American People* (1972).

[M. ARIENS]

CHURCH ARCHITECTURE, HISTORY OF

Part 1: Introduction

A vast array of literature surrounds the study of church architecture, embracing a range of interests from archaeology, anthropology, sociology, and aesthetics, to the evolution of consciousness and theology. This entry presents in 11 parts systematic summaries of the history of church architecture from the early Christian period to the eve of Vatican II.

1. OVERVIEW

In the following section five concomitants of architectural development are presented as an introduction to the subject: (1) social and cultural considerations, (2) exigencies of liturgical ritual and function, (3) symbol and meaning in architectural conception, (4) technique and structural possibilities, and (5) concepts of form.

Social and cultural considerations. Church architecture services the worship of a community, and its construction depends on a patronage that utilizes the collective resources of the worshiping community. Consequently its artistic realization is not independent.

Social Aspect. Both the architect and church architecture in particular are bound to an immediate need of society. A church is not initiated by an architect's will to form but rather by a congregation's will to build. The creative act of the architect must recognize both the will and needs of his patrons. In modern times the most common social impediment to the production of a significant ecclesiastical structure occurs when a patron refuses to allow the architect to express the identity of the congregation in and through the architect's own will to form. Under such circumstances the architect is asked to relinquish his special abilities to create architectural form and instead act as a skillful transmitter of the congregation's collective will toward a form of established acceptability. This obstacle dominated 19th-century church architec-

ture and was promoted by J. RUSKIN in his *Lamp of Obedience:* "We want no new style of architecture. . . . It does not matter one marble splinter whether we have an old or new architecture. . . . The forms of architecture already known to us are good enough and far better than any of us." The result of the 19th-century Gothic revival was a church architecture of questionable artistic value.

The effort to make the architect's vision that of society reduces the educated artistic sensibility of the architect to a position of servitude to the less-educated sensibility of the congregation or pastor. The proper relationship between socio-cultural determination and architectural formation is one of mutual specification. One of the aphorisms about architecture is that "as we shape our buildings, likewise do our buildings shape us." Among significant churches of the 20th century that have helped to restructure society's view of acceptable religious architecture are F. L. Wright's Unity Temple, A. PERRET's Le Raincy, Mies van der Rohe's Illinois Institute of Technology Chapel, and Le Corbusier's Notre Dame du Haut (Ronchamp).

Cultural Aspect. This interdependency between architecture and society has led many to regard architecture as a mirror of a society's cultural progress. For V. Hugo, for example, "Architecture is the book of human history . . . the handwriting of humanity." Monuments of religious architecture (all but synonymous with the general development of architecture for thousands of years) are most useful in tracing the origins, growth, and decline of various cultures in history. The validity of this measure rests on the assumption that a given culture has interrelated parallels in the development of its art, architecture, literature, economics, politics, philosophy, and theology. The effort to document these interrelationships has promoted some excellent though sometimes controversial studies. Among these are E. Panofsky's *Gothic Architecture and Scholasticism* (Latrobe 1951), which sheds new light on the relationship between medieval scholasticism and the visual articulation of Gothic structures, and V. Scully's *The Earth, the Temple and the Gods* (1962), which explores the influence of mythical cult and belief upon the location, orientation, and nature of Minoan, Mycenaean, and Greek temples. Cultural-architectural monographs are rare, and a definitive study of the cultural evolution of church structures has not as yet been written.

Exigencies of liturgical ritual and function. The questions that arise from the relating of ritual to church architecture are to what extent and how architectural form is, and ought to be, determined by liturgical function. Different periods have varied in their attitude toward this issue; in certain periods one finds a relatively high degree of ritual specification of form, such as in the Romanesque and in the baroque, whereas other periods show a low degree of ritual specification, as in churches of the Renaissance and 19th-century revivalism. The architectural significance of ecclesiastical structures is not necessarily dependent upon the degree of ritual determination; the Renaissance preference for centralized form promoted an architecture of merit, but its primary concern was not liturgical function. In some circumstances preoccupation with formalism produced conflicts with ritual use; the transept seating arrangement of H. H. Richardson's Trinity Church is an example.

Church architecture in the 20th century has actively addressed itself to the problem of ritual determination of form. The majority of mid-20th-century liturgical conferences on sacred art have supported the thesis that an adequate analysis of function accompanied by a genuine insight into sacred purpose will aid in the production of a significant church architecture. The idea is a vestige of the functionalist revolution that occurred in architectural thinking after the turn of the century. It emerged as a reaction against lingering public affection for outmoded revivalist styles and against the construction of churches that engaged naïve symbolic "shape-isms." Contemporary ritual functionalism is an attempt to liberate church architecture from traditional misconceptions of what churches ought to look like, and, in theory, it seeks to distinguish itself from older concepts of functionalism. The difference between the traditional Vitruvian notion of *utilitas* and the new notion of utility appears in the thesis that ritual accommodation is a sufficient aesthetic criterion for the production of a church structure. G. Santayana states this position for architecture in general: "Architecture . . . has all its forms suggested by practical demands. Use requires all our buildings to assume certain determinate forms." This view demands study of liturgy in order to avoid an erroneous conception of ritually determined form. It assumes that the ritually specified form carries the religious meaning of the building and is in itself symbolic. Although church form has always reflected functional patterns, older church structures depended upon mosaic, sculpture, and stained glass to provide religious symbolism. A. Aalto's church at Vuoksenniska, Imarta, Finland (1956–58), a good example of ritual functionalism, does not. It is starkly white and devoid of traditional images; the uniqueness of its form is derived from a spatial interpretation of a sectioned seating arrangement in which each area forms a volume of its own by closure of folding doors. This church forsakes the traditional three-entry system common to the Latin-cross plan and provides five entry-ways, each giving access to a defined area; the front entry is used only when full congregational participation is intended, at which time the dynamics of the total space is experienced.

Ritual Functionalism and Typology. The seemingly permanent and immutable fundamental ways of organizing ritual action are the general concern of ecclesiastical typology, which offers two systems of ritual arrangement: one is the longitudinal plan in which the congregation forms a linear procession toward a terminally located sacred object; the second is the centripetal plan in which the congregation groups around a centrally located sacred object. Both types have conceptual value and have determined architectural form for centuries.

The temple of Khonsu at Karnak utilized an impeded processional way. Axial movement is suggested by symmetrical rows of columns, centrally placed doorways, and longitudinal arrangement of spaces. The processional way is impeded in its arrangement by the diminishment of size and light intensity of the chambers in the direction toward the sacred terminus. This arrangement was eminently suitable for the resident god Amon, who was physically unapproachable except by the most purified of mortals and for a caste system of worshipers who were restricted to their own specific areas. The basilica of St. Paul utilized a single spatial procession that was not impeded: the church is a nave opening directly onto the terminal sanctuary; longitudinal movement is accentuated by the symmetrical rows of columns, the decoration of the clerestory walls, and the perspective view natural to such an arrangement; axial movement is direct and only slightly modulated by the visually restricting action of the triumphal arch. The basilica arrangement ritually reflects the oneness of the *ecclesia* and the public nature of Christ. The climax of processional movement in both Khonsu and St. Paul's occurs at the end of the longitudinal axis and also at the end of the architectural space.

The mastaba of Queen Merneith of Egypt utilizes the centripetal arrangement: the central sarcophagus of the Queen was placed within a larger wooden chamber around which a brick chamber was constructed; outside were the subsidiary graves of the court, with the entire ensemble bounded by a wall. The design, best described as a "box-in-a-box," reflects the social-religious position of the queen as sole inheritor of an after-life that the court wished to share. The centripetal arrangement of S. Costanza in Rome has the altar centrally located in a dome-covered chamber; an ambulatory forms a dark lower periphery of space, while the inner core explodes in light and in height, giving way to the arrangement a hierarchy of impressions natural to centripetal schemes. In contrast to the longitudinal plan, the space of centripetal arrangements does not end at the terminal object but continues around it.

Although early civilizations tended to keep these two systems separate, their merging did occur with increasing frequency beginning with the Roman Empire. The motivation for this was the desire to incorporate domical centripetal arrangements, which were regarded as symbolic of cosmic authority, with the traditional longitudinal temple plan. To combine the two disparate systems required ingenuity. The Pantheon clearly exemplifies the combination: the longitudinal processional movement began at a forecourt and terminated in the rear rotunda apse that was to receive the statue of the Emperor Hadrian; onto this central spine a great circular domed rotunda was imposed, which, by virtue of its geometric genesis and oculus as the sole light source, instituted a vertical climax at its central point; this vertical axis, if allowed to dominate, would make Hadrian's niche anticlimactic. But subordination was avoided through the use of a longitudinal series of marble roundels set into the portico pavement; these roundels reinforced the processional movement. Also, the use of an interior colonnade negated the centripetal action of the side niches, and the break in the entablature over Hadrian's niche gave visual emphasis to the termination of the longitudinal movement.

Summary of Christian Adaptation of Roman architecture. Christian architecture was the direct heir to these Roman architectural practices. Christianity favored a merging of the longitudinal and centripetal plans, which served the public nature of the Mass and complemented the concept of Christ as Pantokrator. While the West kept a predilection for the pure basilica plan, the East favored the domical-basilica plan. The architects of Hagia Sophia in Istanbul achieved a real fusion of the two systems by placing the side nave arcades directly in line with the face of the central dome supports; the visual force of the complete structural system of the dome could not then be seen in a way that would promote the dome as climax. Furthermore, with the lateral extension of the nave under the dome curtailed and two half-dome areas engaged with the central dome, a forced longitudinal movement toward the altar was successfully contrived. In St. Mark's, Venice, in order to modulate the cruciform plan and its obvious crossing climax (and also to reduce the overwhelming presence of the five domes), the architects resorted to a one-story arcade that directs visual and physical movement longitudinally past the central crossing and toward the altar.

In the church of St-Front, Périgueux, there is no modulation of the cruciform plan as at St. Mark's. As a result, it is the crossing that becomes a climax, and the altar area is an anticlimax. The architects of the Angoulême cathedral simply placed a series of domes in longitudinal arrangement, thus preserving the identity of both systems in a rather simple fashion.

Dispute over the processional plan versus the centripetal plan occurred during the Renaissance. The tradi-

tionalists advocated the Latin-cross or basilica plan and opposed the central plan, which could not satisfactorily situate the altar in terms of what they considered a proper ritual accommodation of clergy and laity. In spite of the deficiencies for ritual use presented by the centripetal plan, the Renaissance favored it. Architectural form as a geometric symbol of the nature of God and man took precedence over ritual considerations. Bramante's Tempietto and his design for St. Peter's are such symbolic exercises in pure centrality. Mannerism later merged the two systems by grafting a longitudinal plan onto a centripetal plan, as in St. Peter's.

The baroque achieved a mutation of longitudinal action and centripetal action through the use of elliptical forms, which are geometrically originated at two source points, thus giving axial extension to domical structures. Borromini's S. Carlo alle Quattro Fontane is conceived as a single spatial experience; here vault and walls are not kept distinct but are merged in one great undulating movement toward the altar. Probably the most extreme interpenetration of the systems occurred in B. Neumann's church of Vierzehnheiligen; the single dome was abolished altogether and replaced with three spatial ovals of different size disposed longitudinally. These ovals are engaged by two circular spaces at the transept; the plane arrangement is modulated by the ceiling arrangement of intersecting transverse ovals; each one provides a spatial forecourt immediately preceding the two altars. The transept crossing is not defined by a traditional dome but by a trough where the elliptical domes meet so that the transept crossing is not focal. The elliptical movement and counter movements are merged with the walls; when seen in conjunction with the lavish rococo decoration and natural light system that fractures precise visual division of objects, Vierzehnheiligen becomes a complex and sensual spatial totality. The 19th century returned to the longitudinal type in its imitated Gothic and Romanesque churches. Churches showed a succession of styles, beginning with the Egyptian restricted longitudinal plan and ending in a Renaissance central plan, whose succession may be viewed as a single great process. R. Schwarz considers this "sacred way" in the light of D. LENZ's 19th-century efforts to recapitulate the history of salvation on the walls of the church (*The Church Incarnate,* 145–153).

The 20th century uses both the longitudinal and centripetal arrangements as equally valid ways to solve contemporary ritual needs. The desire to make churches communal and intimate in character has resulted in the use of opposing longitudinal movements (St. Clement's, Alexandria, Va.), elliptical-longitudinal movement (Church of Resurrection, St. Louis), partial centripetal-longitudinal movement (Church of Christ the King, Seattle), and full centripetal movement in various shaped containers from square (Chapel of St. James the Fisherman, Wellfleet, Mass.), to round (St. Louis Priory), or octagonal (Blessed Sacrament Church, Holyoke, Mass.).

Typology Theory. A theoretical approach to ecclesiastical typology emerged when Renaissance theorists attempted to categorize church plans in accordance with symbolic values. In 1547, for example, Serlio recorded nine basic variations of centripetal arrangements in the fifth of his *Five Books on Architecture.* Subsequent centuries produced commentaries debating the merits of the Renaissance system (central type) and the Early Christian–Gothic system (longitudinal type). In the 20th century, typology underwent major revitalization in the thought of the German architect R. Schwarz. His *The Church Incarnate* presents a typology based upon a symbolic interpretation of the physiological nature of man.

There are many contemporary critics who seek to banish typology as a valid method of architectural analysis; they see in it the inherent danger that architecture will become regarded as a kind of suprapersonal activity operating according to rigid laws derived from functional, constructional, or visual schemes. Bruno Zevi suggests that "functionalism is not a rigid inflexible and mathematically calculable norm. . . . Even in confronting what would appear to be the most restrictive practical problems, the architect is not the tool of the type of building; he interprets and represents its functions spatially." The accuracy of this view is demonstrated by the brief account of the longitudinal and the centripetal in history showing that neither system accounts for the variation of forms in which they are contained. Although typology is a factor that cannot be overlooked since it provides useful insight regarding basic configuration, it is of value only when constantly reinterpreted in the light of the architectural spirit of the times.

Strict ritual functionalism has not been endorsed by architects and critics as an adequate theory, since they see the essence of architecture elsewhere: for E. Lutyens architecture begins where function ends; for A. Gaudí it is the ordering of light; for A. Perret it is the sense of line and form; and for Le Corbusier it is the play of volumes in light. Functionalism alone does not satisfy the love for design. At best, liturgical use suggests a proper programmatic attitude that may result in an intelligent horizontal placement of elements; of itself it cannot specify a necessary vertical extension of these elements, that is to say, the very quality and quantity of the spatial container. For the realizing of this, the architect must resort to his creative propensity to form.

Symbol and meanings in architectural conception. The use of symbol or other modes of conceptualization may give to ritual utility visible form that is expressive of the supernatural. Symbolism, myth, analogies of proportion, light, number, or other factors might be employed in architectural conception. These influence the disposition of structure and are of particular importance in church architecture. Important modes of significative conceptualization that have influenced church architecture are presented here beginning with the pagan temple and briefly surveying influences up to the present day.

Symbol in Mythical Consciousness. The use of symbol is determined by the attitude that man's consciousness takes in response to reality. Various authors (E. CASSIRER, M. ELIADE, H. Frankfort, G. van der Leeuw) observe that ancient civilizations and primitive peoples made use of a form of mental activity, called mythical, in which consciousness was wholly specified in the moment of confrontation with things; in both experience as well as expression, myth is bound to the substantive (immediate impressions) and lacks the category of the abstract (mediate impressions). Mythical consciousness does not differentiate between concept and reality (the subjective and the objective), since things are accepted for what they are experienced as being. For mythical consciousness the sense of the sacred stems from the immediacy of object-enthrallment; things, whether animate or inanimate, that sufficiently stimulate the psyche of man beyond the normal experience of events might be regarded as having a life of their own and even as being sacred. The mythical mind does not separate what a thing is experienced as being from the place where it was experienced as being; both share in the same existential actuality. Thus space is not regarded abstractly but is comprehended by an emotional identification with it.

Sacred Place in Temple Architecture. For the mind of the primitive, the location-form-deity relationship is not arbitrary or referential but necessary and presentational. Mythical consciousness does not structure an architecture of mediate symbolism but structures the reality itself. Where the 20th-century mind sees representation, a myth tends to experience real identity; the architecture does not stand for sacredness but is identified with sacredness. C. Yavis's study of Greek altars documents the origins of certain cult localities as an evolution from immediate manifestation (momentary deification), to site deification, altar deification, and anthropomorphic image deification, until final enclosure by the temenos wall and construction of the temple. A similar evolution occurred in other civilizations: in Mesopotamia, as at Eridu, temples went through successive reconstructions layered on top of one another because that one specific locality was where the god was first revealed.

Myth does not determine space by objective measurement but by an emotional identification of a place with the sacred. H. Nissen observes that the Romans allocated space by divining the wills of the gods, and that once the lines were drawn, the space was immediately occupied by a god; not only was this true for the cosmos, but every articulated region, city, house, room, field, and vineyard had its own spirit, who consequently gained an individuality and a specific name by which man could invoke him. The word "temple" means a space cut or marked out. The god Terminus occupied the boundary stones of Rome, and, at the festival of Terminalia, thresholds were crowned with garlands and sprinkled with sacrificial blood. The Greek propylon (entry gate) assumed the typological form common to temples because it was conceived as an entrance to a temple inhabited by boundary gods. As locality participated in the location of the god, so too did architectural form. H. Frankfort observes that the Mesopotamian ziggurat is the cosmic mountain that connects earth to heaven and from which all life springs; R. Edwards discovers the pyramid form as being the primeval hill of creation upon which Atum-Ra sat when he made all things to appear out of the waters of chaos; V. Scully's and J. Lockyear's examinations of Greek and Egyptian temples, respectively, illustrate that the location-orientation of sacred structures is a necessary embodiment of a geophysical and astronomical identity of the deities.

Mythical consciousness regards architecture as an immediate symbol of the sacred; all things, from column to floor, have real identifications that go beyond utility. Architecture is not unique in this regard since myth constantly merges daily existence and ritual existence into a single homogeneous reality. The understanding of the full symbolic system of temple architecture requires a perception of myth's coalescence of all aspects of existence into a single mythical landscape or interconnected panorama. Immediate symbolism by nature is temporary and transitory and cannot be fully documented by history.

Myth does not exclude the rational but apparently precedes it. The growth of the rational (following the maturation of language, according to E. Cassirer) did not terminate myth; the mythical and the rational co-exist in the development of culture as two modes of dealing with reality. Reason's liberation from myth occurred with the advent of Greek scientific philosophy. The philosophic search for a first principle, in the Aristotelian system, resolved itself into the two non-imagery (abstract) concepts of "matter" and "form." With the Greek philosophers the intellect gained force over myth—things became subject to logic in an appeal to reason. Greek architecture was quick to respond to the process of reason: the Doric, Ionic, and Corinthian columns underwent logical development according to a seemingly abstract idea or type; the temples reached an apogee in architectonics in their optical refinements and integral proportional systems. However, reason was unable to achieve a purely mediate symbolic architecture since the Greek religions were bound to myth.

The Christian Transformation. Christianity transformed the nature of sacred architecture for Western man. An important difference appears in the context of the Eucharistic celebration, which was not confined to a particular place. Mythical cult centers had been generally places of unique manifestations of the deity, and worship was bound to a specific locality. Christianity, however, has no one cult center restricted to locality (with the exception of certain shrines and fixed devotional places such as Lourdes). Unlike mythical sacredness, neither the locality nor the form of Christian architecture shares a real identity with Christ. Church architecture in Christianity was relatively free to develop a symbolic system of its own.

Medieval. Christian architecture did not immediately produce a system of meanings integrated with architectural form. In early centuries Christians adopted Roman forms of building, especially the basilica type, which was suitable for communal assembly; the celebration of the Eucharist and hearing the Gospels, wherever it might be, was in itself meaningful. Gradually painting, mosaic, and relief sculpture were employed as referential explicatives and signs of belief. These, however, did not radically affect the architectural conception. Elaborate philosophic and theological speculation eventually came to affect the very architectural conception in efforts to incorporate meanings into the structure.

Crucial for architecture was the Pythagorean-Platonic philosophy that saw number as immutable measure in all things. Pythagoras discovered that musical tones can be physically measured and that the musical consonances were determined by the ratios of small whole numbers. This occasioned the belief that audible-visual harmonics pervaded the cosmos. Plato added the clarification that cosmic order and harmony are contained in certain numbers (*Timaeus*). St. Augustine found support for this thesis in the Solomonic text "thou hast ordered all things in measure, number and weight" (Wis 11.20). In his *De Musica*, Augustine proposed that numerical ratios are but the echoes of the perfection of God. In music these ratios are audible; in architecture they are visible. The most admirable ratio is 1:1 since here the unity of relationship is equal and perfect; then came 1:2, 2:3, 3:4. Through the contemplation of the visible configurations of architecture, the mind is led to proportion, from proportion to number, and from number to the idea of God. This thesis of perfect ratio became the first purely mediate religious symbol in Western church architecture.

Boethius agreed with Augustine that the artist can do his best only if he follows number and not intuition.

It appears that number symbolism did not have extensive architectural influence until the Gothic period. During the 12th century, the school of Chartres fell heir to the Augustinian number system modified by the inclusion of Euclidian geometry through Arabic sources. Because THIERRY OF CHARTRES insisted upon a geometric interpretation of the nature of God, his contemporaries accused him of changing theology into geometry. Others of the school (WILLIAM OF CONCHES, ABELARD) attributed a mathematical action to God: the Holy Spirit ordered matter and the cosmos was regulated by ratios, and these ratios were best incorporated by man in architecture. God was regarded as divine Architect and Musician who gave to the cosmos its laws of harmonic proportion.

Concomitant with the emergence of number symbolism was light symbolism. St. Augustine found numerous biblical references to light and proposed in the *City of God* that luminosity is the measure of the splendor of being. PSEUDO-DIONYSIUS saw the world as one created, animated, and unified by a supra-essential light. In his *Celestial Hierarchy* creation is described as an act of illumination; the beings (angels, men, rocks) emerge in a hierarchy corresponding to their amount of light. The notion of the cosmos as a procession of spheres leading to a luminous God was advanced by the 9th- and 10th-century Arabian philosophers Alkindi (al- KINDĪ), AL-FARABI, and AVICENNA. In the 11th century, Alhazen discovered the laws of spherical light diffusion and optics. This led certain philosophers (e.g., AVICEBRON) to attempt unification of a metaphysics of light-emanation with the physical laws of light-emanation. All these lines of thought came into the Western world along with the commentaries on Aristotle during the 11th and 12th centuries.

Meanwhile, western Europe had maintained an unbroken continuity in its preoccupation with light. The writings of Pseudo-Dionysius were popular and played a critical role in the thought of Abbot Suger, who was instrumental in the reconstruction of the chevet of the Abbey of Saint-Denis as a light source: "Once the new rear part is joined to the part in front, the church shines with its middle part brightened for bright is that which is brightly coupled with the bright and bright is the noble edifice which is pervaded by the new light." ROBERT GROSSETESTE (1175–1253), bishop of Lincoln, sought to combine number symbolism and light symbolism. He saw in light the vehicle by which the traditional Aristotelian concepts of matter and form are united. Form, an ally of light, is a perfect unity and is represented by the number one; matter by the number two; the accord of form

and matter by the number three; the composite itself by the number four. These numbers give rise to proportions that describe a being's nature, namely, 1:2, 1:3, 1:4, 2:3, 3:4, and will be the source of structuring harmony. In architecture it is the division of planes into these proportions that reveals the nature of divinity; man may then contemplate God through these harmonies. A good documentation of medieval number and light symbolism may be found in G. Lesser, *Gothic Cathedrals and Sacred Geometry,* and O. von Simpson, *The Gothic Cathedral.* The best available commentary concerning the scholastic attitude toward number, light, and aspects of the beautiful in its theological relationships is E. de Bruyne, *Études d'ésthétique médiévale.*

Renaissance. The Renaissance no less than the High Middle Ages looked to traditional number symbolism; L. B. ALBERTI, A. Palladio, and Serlio attempted to discover and express in mathematical ratios the visible-audible cosmic harmonics. For them the regulation of all parts of a church according to these ratios could manifest something of the nature of God. Man, made in the image of God, embodied the harmonies of the cosmos. This led to the use of the Vitruvian figure inscribed in a square and circle as the symbol of the geometric-mathematical proportion common to microcosm and macrocosm. The basilica plan was regarded as impure since its mathematical content did not correspond to ideal architectural form; instead, the Renaissance favored the circle (central plan) in which geometric pattern generates the form with all its parts; this provides a most lucid, absolute, and immutable architecture. By the dividing and relating of all parts through measure, an architectural frame of reference was instituted by which man could contemplate the idea of an absolute and immutable God. R. Wittkower in *Architectural Principles in the Age of Humanism* explores in detail the Renaissance treatment of number symbolism.

Number symbolism is based on a rationalized ideal expressed in mathematical terms that transcends the subjective and transitory nature of man. This classical system was disrupted by the mannerists, who saw man as subject to the chaos of his emotions more than to divine harmonics. This occasioned a shift of emphasis in religious symbolic patterns from the ideal world of God to the personal subjective world of man. The results were seen in secular works more than in major church structures (e.g., Palazzo del Té). Mannerism is manifested in the illogical use of classical motifs as symbolic of earthly dissonance and opposed to divine consonance.

Baroque to Modern. The baroque merged classical geometry with the intense inner experience of man. Light and geometry were no longer the model for contemplating God; they became the experiential means of recognizing the existence of God and the reality of the Church through the activity of one's emotions. Architects forsook the purely architectonic symbolism of the Renaissance and depended more on the integration of iconography (in painting and sculpture) with architecture. This wedding of pictorial symbolism and architecture is well illustrated in Bernini's church of S. Andrea al Quirinale, Rome. The plan is worked out according to a series of intersecting circles of which the front courtyard segments extend outward; in the interior the geometric spaces are dynamic. The interior is divided into three distinct registers: the lower area, windowless, is executed in warm earth colors to symbolize the world of man; then the entablature separates earth from heaven and is the realm of sculptured angels who act as messengers of God; finally the dome, representing heaven, is executed in white and pervaded by light from the oculus in which the Holy Spirit (dove) floats. Man cannot contemplate this panorama disinterestedly. The way to heaven is by the purified flesh; the way is idealized in the white marble statue of St. Andrew that is placed so as to fracture the continuity of the entablature and thus join earth to heaven. The church is properly experienced only when the carefully calculated process of imagery and architecture are perceived. Baroque architecture in its classical phase employed a sophisticated literary type of representational symbolism in response to the teaching function of the reformed Church.

With the advent of the rococo, the engagement of subjective passions remained. With the exception of B. Neumann's brilliant geometric and psychological conception for the church of Vierzehnheiligen, few rococo churches illustrate an architectural symbolic system; meanings were carried by representational sculpture and painting.

The 17th and 18th centuries were periods of transition. With the rise of science, the classical attitude toward cosmic harmonics quickly lost public favor; the dissemination of Cartesian rationalism shifted emphasis from universally valid rules of order to the authority of the perceiving subject. Architecture witnessed this transition in the argument that ensued over the laws of harmonic proportion. Certain architects, such as H. Wotton, P. de l'Orme, F. Blondel, and O. Scamozzi, maintained the soundness of mathematical ratios in architecture. Others, such as C. Perrault, T. Temanza, and G. Guarini, defended the eye of man as the important judge of proportion. As the classical system of world order and aesthetics was abandoned, so too was the classical system of number symbolism; church architecture could no longer promote an immutable measure in order to present the ideal nature of God.

In 18th-century neoclassicism, church architecture became the vehicle of an applied aesthetics derived from sources other than religion. In the 19th-century revivalisms, church architecture became a sign of religious sentiment for the past. Symbolism was firmly bound to literary association, as expounded by J. M. Neale and B. Webb (see bibliog.): "We enter. The triple breadth of Nave and Aisles, the triple height of Pier arch, Triforium, and Clerestory; the triple length of Choir Transcepts and Nave, again set forth the Holy Trinity. And what besides is there which does not tell of our Blessed Saviour? And that does not point out 'Him First' in the two-fold Western Door, 'Him Last' in the distant Altar: 'Him Midst,' in the great Rood: 'Him Without End' in the monogram carved on boss and corbel, in the Holy Lamb, in the Lion of the Tribe of Judah, in the Mystic Fish?'' A. PUGIN held that redemption by the sacrifice of the cross was the visual basis for the form of Christian architecture.

Twentieth Century. Symbolic determination of church architecture has been widely discussed in the 20th century. The postwar directives of the German bishops (1947) supported a literary architectural symbolism by suggesting that "the portals of the church, and especially the main portal, should by their impressive design suggest to the faithful the symbolism of church portals as representing the gates of heaven." This view has occasioned the construction of contemporary churches adopting a naïve type of symbolism (e.g., Harrison and Abramovitch's fish-shaped First Presbyterian Church at Stamford, Conn.) With the advent of technology, a church, more than any other type of building, offers the least programmatic restrictions and therefore the greatest opportunity for architects to explore pure forms. In order to temper the tendency toward whimsical symbolic forms, some architects have sought a guide to meaningful architectural symbolism in the nature of communal worship. S. Davis, for example, observes that "the church building is an image of the mystical body, and our churches should be fashioned in the likeness of the assembly and express its mystery." R. Schwarz, who greatly influenced postwar church building in Europe, noted: "Church architecture is not cosmic mythology—rather it is the representation of Christian life, a new embodiment of the spiritual. To build does not mean to solve mathematical problems nor to create pleasing spaces; it means to place great communal forms before God." The desire to give the church structure immediate symbolic expression by reference to the communal action of the mystical body has shifted the basis of church architecture away from programmed symbolism. Preprogrammed architectural symbolism becomes either referential (literary), as it did in the 19th century, or it becomes subject to rules of right making, as it did in the Renaissance. Today architects, artists, and theorists do not willingly accept a referential pictorial symbol or literary device in architectural conception in order to present some "content" (meanings). There has been a shift in artistic sensibility toward the immediate existential experience of the art image, which is seen in itself as symbol (e.g., the work of art that may not be representational). The symbol has become more an event than a representational form. This shift liberates symbolic context from the confinement of referential styles and allows the artist to exercise his creative intuition more fully. The quest for communal forms of architecture immediately significative of the mystical body of Christ and the search for aniconic (i.e., nonrepresentational) art forms suitably integrated in this architectural signification are signs of a new consciousness in the structuring of religious art.

Note on Multivalent Systems. Symbolism and meanings in architecture are usually multivalent. The Gothic style is a particularly fine example of a multiple meaning system in architecture; form followed symbol as much as function. Various studies have discovered the many symbolic modes at work. Besides the symbolism of number and light mentioned above, a number of other meanings are discoverable. É. Mâle, in *A Study in Medieval Iconography and Its Sources of Inspiration,* finds that symmetry was regarded as the expression of the mysterious inner harmony controlling the cosmos; he also explored the influence of the "Mirrors" of Vincent of Beauvais on the sculpture and stained-glass program of many churches. E. Panofsky, in *Gothic Architecture and Scholasticism,* relates the articulation of cathedrals to the scholastic working habit, which is founded on the belief that the world is a unified, ordered, and indivisible hierarchy. In a different manner, W. Worringer's *Form in Gothic* accounts for parallels between the sensual lucidity and the organic harmony of the Gothic "will to form" and scholastic transcendentalism. P. Fingesten's *Topographical and Anatomical Aspects of the Gothic Cathedral* traces the topography of Gothic cathedrals to ch. 21 of the Apocalypse and to the subsequent interpretation of the cathedral as a magic city upon a magic mountain; he also documents the commonly held view that the planar relationships of cathedrals are based upon the human body as observed in Vitruvius—"For without symmetry and proportion no temple can have a regular plan; that is, it must have an exact proportion worked out after the fashion of the members of a finely shaped body." He noted the recurrence of this concept in the observations of William Durandus (13th century): "The arrangement of a material church resembleth that of the human body: the chancel, or place where the altar is representeth the head: the transepts, the hands and arms, and the remainder, towards the west the rest of the body." He extended this notion to include the idea that the skeletal structure represents the womb and rib cage of Mary sheltering the Christ, a theory that he bases on the anatomical discoveries of the times. P. Frankl presents an exhaustive study of the referential writings related to the Gothic in his monumental *Literary Sources of the Gothic.* The symbolic meanings of a particular period can be known only through a complete survey of the theological, mystical, and popular beliefs of the day, and a careful analysis of the source writings connected with individual monuments. The observations presented in this section have suggested some of the important known meanings manifest in ecclesiastical architecture.

Technique and structural abilities. Knowledge of the precise workings of structure took centuries to develop. The ancient civilizations approximated structure through practical experimentation; the posts and beams of ancient temples were often oversized in relation to their minimal necessary strength. The approximation of structural proportion through building experience continued well into the Gothic period; the height of the Beauvais Cathedral was finally determined by the point at which the structural system could no longer support the addition of stones without their falling.

It is only since mid-19th century that a true science of structure has been developed. The determination of the precise nature of structural types through a theoretical analysis of their systems of stress critically transformed the character of church architecture. The contemporary architect has complete freedom in the creative planning of spatial containers that have not as yet been built but can be built with complete assurance of safety and stability. F. Candela's chapel of Las Lomas, Cuernavaca, Mexico, is a structurally derived shape whose form reflects its systems of stress; this type of structure was not possible *c.* 1850. Consequently the history of church architecture exhibits a polarity in the nature of its forms, which results principally from the cataclysmic emergence of scientific structures. The ancients exhibit a minimum number of forms with a maximum degree of refinements, whereas the moderns exhibit a maximum number of forms with a minimum degree of refinement. The evolution of church architecture has witnessed a change in attention from the detail of the form to that of the form itself.

Significance of Structure. Although structure is a major aspect in church architecture, it is not necessarily the vehicle of a church's significance. Building as a technique neither favors nor inhibits structural refinement; it is merely a means to enclosure. In certain periods technical inventiveness is integrally associated with the recognition of certain styles. This occurs in Roman, Gothic, late baroque, and the modern periods. In other periods architecture reached an apogee of development within pre-existing structural techniques. This occurred in the Greek, Early Christian-Romanesque, Renaissance, and the classic baroque periods. Certain buildings gain a pre-eminence because of their structural avant-gardism. A partial list of examples would include the Great Pyramid, Hagia Sophia in Constantinople, Durham, Chartres, and Reims cathedrals, King's College Chapel, Brunelleschi's dome of the cathedral of Florence, Guarini's S. Lorenzo, Gaudí's Colonia Güell Chapel, A. Perret's Le Raincy, O. Bartning's Stahlkirche, M. Breuer's abbey church of St. John the Baptist, O. Niemeyer's church of St. Francis, and F. Candela's church of La Virgen Milagrosa. Others derive their historic significance from refinements of space, materials, and traditional structural systems. Typical examples are Luxor Temple, the Pantheon, S. Apollinare Nuovo, St. Michael's at Hildesheim, Pazzi Chapel, S. Lorenzo Sacristy, S. Carlo alle Quattro Fontane, Vierzehnheiligen, Illinois Institute of Technology Chapel, church of Maria Königin, church of Santa Anna, and the chapel of Notre Dame du Haut.

Structural Determinism. The 20th century has been preoccupied with the nature of structure. The origin of this may be traced in part to the rationalism found in the writings of E. Viollet-le-Duc. His work formed the immediate heritage of many early 20th-century structural innovators. A. Perret maintained that "structure is the mother tongue of the architect . . . . Anyone who hides structure deprives himself of architecture's only legitimate and beautiful ornament. Anyone who hides a pilaster commits an error; anyone who puts up a false one commits a crime." Church architecture is especially susceptible to structural exhibitionism since it is physically more flexible and less inhibiting than other structures. The physical demands of liturgy are not as rigid as are the functional demands of laboratories, schools, etc.; the adaptation of structure to churches permits a greater freedom of structural expression. Consequently, structure is often given a leading role as expressive form. O. Niemeyer's, F. Candela's, and E. Torroja's imaginative use of thin-shell reinforced concrete has produced a rich vocabulary of forms that are of marked contrast to the traditional cubic shapes.

The forcefulness present in the unadorned pure structure has led many historians and critics to favor a technological viewpoint in the study of churches. Technical progress is viewed as artistic progress; technical significance, as artistic significance; technical history, as architectural history. Thus Gothic architecture is applauded for its general structural predilection, whereas the Renaissance loses favor for its lack of technical progress. This viewpoint is based on a misconception that identifies architectural significance with technical inno-

vations. The science of structure contributes to technical methods of spatial qualification but of itself cannot determine the total reality of space. A. Raymond has pointed out that "the basis of design must be function and engineering; but function and engineering only is a brutality." The absolute insistence on macrostructure alone is bound to fail when faced with even the simplest nonstructural space-covering elements, such as doors and windows. This is apparent in E. Torroja's Pont de Suert Church and F. Candela's chapel of Nuestra Señora de la Soledad, which, although brilliantly conceived in regard to macrostructural purity, are naïve in their auxiliary attributes. Structural determinism achieves significance only when related to "the eternal and universal sense of line and form" (Perret). Moreover, the science of structures cannot of itself determine its forms or systems. Torroja, in *Philosophy of Structures,* declares that the birth of structural form is not rational but intuitive, and that mathematical calculations serve only to prove that what the creative intellect has imagined will, in fact, stand. Thus, engineering is architecture not according to a predetermination by immutable laws of statics but according to its service to the architect's creation of form.

Use of Structure in Churches. Structure has been used in church architecture in four distinct ways. The first three are concerned with a relationship between structure as support and wall as enclosure. (1) The structure is actualized by the wall, and, while it may manifest itself in projections and decorations, it is the wall that carries primacy of visual importance. Renaissance architects were especially fond of this idea, which has been used throughout the history of Christian building. The term "mural wall system" describes wall systems of this type, which have surfaces suitable for painting, fresco, mosaic, and sculpture; it is seen in Early Christian architecture. (2) The structure becomes a visible skeleton that assumes primacy, in which case the wall enclosure must find a suitable subsidiary means of expression. The Gothic and modern periods are especially characterized by this approach. The term "baldachino" has been frequently used to describe such structures, but the term is limited since it refers properly to vaulting systems. (3) The structure is freed of the enclosing wall and forms a visual pattern that modulates the visual impression of the wall. The column in front of the wall is a well-known example of this. (4) Finally, structure in church architecture may be an "all-over" distribution of the wall itself. Such a system is proper to the 20th century, deriving from the new structural ability of shell construction. A shell construction is a working membrane that provides both structural strength and total space enclosure. In E. Torroja's church of the Ascension and O. Niemeyer's chapel of Las Lomas, wall, roof, and structural strength is the form itself. Certain architects (e.g., R. Schwarz) have regarded this method of construction as the most perfect, since the whole structure is permeated by the same form.

Structure as Expression. Structure as a means of expression vacillates between the polarities of denial and assertion of supports. The denial of a sense of structure is evident in the solution of the ritual space of Hagia Sophia by way of a visual annihilation of the dome's structural supports. At times structural members become so excessively light that consciousness cannot grasp mass-support relationships; today this frequently occurs when baldachinos are hung with piano wire so that a great monolithic element appears to float without support, as in M. Breuer's abbey church of St. John. Excessive cantilever also appears to be denied; the concept of dynamic balance intensified by modern prestressing techniques may also serve to frustrate natural psycho-physiological responses.

The second pole is that of structural assertion. This tendency seeks to visually intensify the operation of structure as visual element in churches. The structure is often overdesigned; joints thicken; pins and bolts are made larger than calculations warrant or more visible than their importance demands; materials are left brutally in their natural constructional stage (e.g., concrete that displays its framework as a surface presence). The priory of St. Anselm (Tokyo), the church of St. Anthony the Abbot (Italy), the monastery of La Tourette (France), and a host of contemporary churches engage to some degree in constructional assertion; the emphasis is by far the most forceful in 20th-century church construction.

The contemporary search for positive structural expression is part of a general quest for technological honesty. The importance of this honesty in achieving genuine form has been stressed by many notable architects whose churches are witness to the force of their insights (e.g., A. Gaudí, A. Perret, O. Bartning, R. Schwarz).

Considerations on form. The criteria considered above are subsumed in a larger search for formal laws that will determine the disposition of architectural elements in order to create the beautiful. By far the most prevalent concept in Western thought has been that the beauty of architecture is found in order. This sensibility was applied to all the arts and is generally associated with the concept of God as a God of order. Classical theories of the beautiful in architecture are generally concerned with seeing the beautiful either in certain geometric forms or in numerical ratios; these fixed ratios and forms were considered eternally and absolutely beautiful. In classical architectural theory, beauty is a presentation to man's senses of a principle that is based on intellectual penetration rather than experiential response. In theories of architectural form from antiquity through the Renais-

sance, the tendency was to identify beauty of form with an abstract conceptualization of harmonic order that can be objectified in an art work. *See* AESTHETICS; ART (PHILOSOPHY).

Transition from Classical Theory to Modern Theory. Extensive opposition to the classical manner appeared in the latter part of the 17th century and in the 18th century in England. Beauty not found in order, or in certain geometric forms, emerged in English "Romantic" landscape architecture as a result of Europe's extended contact with the Orient. By 1720 the term "picturesque," meaning a roughness or sudden variation joined to irregularity, was accepted as an art principle. The desire for unexpected visual stimulation in the landscape led to the use of Greek, Gothic, and Chinese structures; especially appropriate were church forms. The English philosophers of the mid-18th century found the source of much delight in the inner senses of man, which operate without the aid of reason in comprehending the beautiful. The result of their enquiry assumed two directions: some rejected classical canons; others modulated classical canons in accord with the new sensibility. Burke argued against reason and disputed the importance of proportion and order in accounting for the beautiful; for him beauty was a social quality connected with man's response in beholding the world of life around him. In contrast, Hutcheson proposed that beauty is found in a compound relationship between unity (order) and variety; Hogarth found in a precise serpentine line the physical basis of the beautiful object, and in variety, the principal attribute of beauty. Variety itself, especially in its purest of forms in the serpentine line, is a kind of invariable and presents aspects of the classical sensibility.

The 18th-century interest in variety and the response of man's inner senses did not lead to a revolution in church architecture. The classical sensibility dominated because of the authority issuing from the French taste during Boileau's period. This influence is seen in England in the styles of Inigo Jones and Christopher Wren. The practice of the arts, including architecture, was governed by the canons of correct taste (order, elegance, and grace). Sir J. Reynolds, head of the British Academy, was able to incorporate the new sensibility with the old. He defended classical canons and introduced the new-found human element by using Hume's association of ideas to give a firm basis for the picturesque; he explicitly counted among the principles of architecture "that of affecting the imagination by means of association of ideas—thus we have naturally a veneration for antiquity; whatever building brings to our remembrance ancient customs and manners, such as the Castles of the Barons of Chivalry, is sure to give delight." Revivalism of any past style became a formal law of building and had great impact on church architecture for two centuries. The only pure style of architecture that emerged concurrently with the appearance of the picturesque was the French rococo. This style combined the classical manner with novel curvilinear formations. The rococo represents an intense but brief excursion away from the laws of antiquity. M. A. Laugier's *Essay on Greek Architecture*, archeological expeditions of Stuart and Revert, and Winckelmann's dictum that Greek art represents noble simplicity and quiet grandeur were witnesses to a resurgence of the classical canons of right making in the second half of the 18th century.

The 18th century also introduced the philosophy of the beautiful as a discipline separate from philosophy in general; Baumgarten named the science of aesthetics in his *Aesthetica* (1750). During the next 100 years in Germany a succession of thinkers (LESSING, Winckelmann, KANT, GOETHE, Schiller, FICHTE, SCHELLING, HEGEL, SCHLEIERMACHER, SCHOPENHAUER, NIETZSCHE) struggled with the problems of aesthetics; interest centered on the role of the senses and of the emotions, the role of reason, the nature of the aesthetic object, the validity of rules of art, the freedom inherent in the creative process, and the relationship of society and the aesthetic object. Speculative aesthetics attempted to fabricate an idea of architecture from what it seems or ought to be within the wider frame of a particular aesthetic system.

German speculative aesthetics, which spread internationally, placed architectural theory in a compromising position. Architecture was not considered in its own nature, but rather as a residue of a larger speculative system. Church architecture, except for the symbolic-emotive connotations of its past styles, was considered even less. The result of a century of intense aesthetic thought was the placement of architecture in a dependent position between the classical mode (represented by Greek and Renaissance styles) and the Romantic mode (represented by Gothic, rococo, and medieval styles).

A transformation occurred *c.* 1870; the speculative school of aesthetics gave way to the scientific empirical method. G. Fechner pioneered experimental aesthetics in 1876; rather than using a philosophic system to describe the facts, Fechner began with factual data in order to describe a system. In his researches and those that followed, the rise of the new sciences of physiology, psychiatry, psychology, biology, sociology, and ethnology furnished new material and diverse points of view from which facts could be compared and described. The empirical acceptance of reality influenced architectural theory. In the 20th century a number of formal considerations emerged as important in architectural developments; these provide a kind of phenomenology of architecture that greatly influenced church architecture in the postwar rebuilding.

Space. The concept of space as a primary attribute of architecture did not fully develop until the late 19th century. Renaissance theorists described architecture in terms of structure, form, and proportion. Certain authors, such as B. Zevi, have attempted to discover an implicit concept of space in the writings of Plato, Aristotle, Vitruvius, Alberti, Serlio, Michelangelo, and others, but this seems to be an overzealous attempt to discover space as a primary element in past architecture theory. The majority of historians attribute spatial consciousness first to the German art critics and aestheticians. Hegel referred to buildings in general as "limiting and enclosing a defined space" and to the Gothic in particular as "the concentration of essential soul-life which thus encloses itself in spatial relations." In particular, the art studies of H. WÖLFFLIN were based upon spatial terminology, and it is probably through his followers that the idea became disseminated in the Western world. An awareness of the primacy of space became basic in the thought of many noted architects and critics soon after the turn of the century, and it has manifested itself consistently up to the present day in the thought of, e.g., G. Scott (1914), O. Spengler (1918), L. Moholy-Nagy (1928), J. Focillon (1934), R. Schwarz (1938), and B. Zevi (1964).

The practical emergence of a spatially predicated architecture occurred after the turn of the century. Even before the spatial emphasis achieved any usable kind of conception, F. L. Wright provided the first monumental work using it in the Unity Temple, Chicago, in 1906. Developed in complete isolation from the events of continental Europe, Wright's use of cantilevered balconies forming interpenetrating spaces made of him a native architectural prophet. Wright's observation that the interior space should be expressed on the exterior as the space enclosed, distinguishes him from such of his contemporaries as A. Perret, who followed a rationalistic logic of structures, or P. Behrens, who developed an expressionistic use of industrial materials characteristic of the new technology. Germany, the birthplace of spatial philosophy, was the first to acclaim the revolutionary significance of Wright. In 1908 H. Berlage said of Wright that "the art of the masterbuilder lies in this: the creation of space, not the sketching of façades." It was in Europe that Wright was received and it was there, between 1905 and 1930, that practical experiments in space continued. The cubists fractured objects in space; the futurists dynamically related objects in space; the purists placed geometric objects in space. Various artists probed architecture in their canvases: Mondrian painted a number of compositions called "façades" in a process of searching for equilibrium between horizontal and vertical; Malevich named several of his abstract rectangular works "architectonics"; the "Elementarists" or constructivists drew on the aesthetic potential inherent in building techniques. In 1910 a monograph on F. L. Wright, published in Holland, led some historians to see a real connection between the spatial concern of the de Stijl group and the American master, but without sufficient documentation. The members of de Stijl explored aspects of pure space; for Mondrian, "space determination, and not space expression, is the pure plastic way to express the universal reality." The de Stijl group considered architecture to be a series of intersecting and overlapping planes, which, in certain relationships, could determine an infinitely discontinuous space of complete resolution. Their theory was put into practice immediately in Rietveld's Schroeder House and Mies van der Rohe's brick country houses of the 1920s, especially in his Barcelona Pavilion of 1929. This last work greatly influenced the spatial consciousness of architects the world over.

Church architecture resisted the advancement of spatial determination during those eventful years, and the appearance of the International Style in the 1930s partially interrupted the development of spatial consciousness. But in 1941, with the publication of S. Giedion's *Space, Time and Architecture* and the postwar rebuilding, space sensibility widened to international acceptance. Since then it has affected radically both the production and interpretation of architecture. In regard to it, B. Zevi's *Architecture as Space* (1957) is very meaningful to a study of churches in history. Zevi's underlying theme is that the history of architecture is the history of the attending to the single space, and this particularly in relation to church structures, with the exception of the 20th century.

Time. Modern spatial awareness is radically different from that of antiquity since the dimension of time has become in the 20th century a conscious factor in architectural formation. Whereas Le Corbusier saw baroque space as theoretically fixed to a single position from which the spatial interpenetrations are best viewed, he found his own work making a new demand: movement in time is required to experience it since he observed that space is "the foot that walks, the eye that sees, the head that turns." According to S. Giedion, it is not relevant to view spatial structures such as RONCHAMP from a single viewpoint; the church is a hollowed out vessel in all directions so that no one cross-section or series of cross-sections reveals the spatial interpenetrations of interior and of exterior except through an experiential movement in time. Giedion, a major proponent of space-time consciousness, further demands that time does not simply refer to movement of the observer, but means a mode of consciousness. The conscious apprehension of space in time heightens perception of the process of life much as does the sensible apprehension of light and sound.

Church architecture alive to spatial consciousness is a suitable container for the action of the *ecclesia* since it provides greater occasion for man to discover himself.

Mass, Enclosure, and Form. At its outer limits, architectural space is bounded by mass, or material enclosure, which presents a total configuration called form. Form gives to man objects and relationships; space gives to man only relationships. The former is easier to comprehend than the latter. In antiquity thinking about architectural form was largely object-directed. The laws of measure or proportion and the immutable relationships of geometry were the great discovery that the ancients objectified in architecture. In time the canons of form became a sort of dogma in architecture, and architecture became its life-sustaining vehicle. For the medievalists and humanists, formal measure and geometric proportion had meaning in the total spirit of their times; by the 19th century their doctrines of form had lost their relation to the world and had become little more than stylistic historical motifs. In the 20th century, the power of form was regenerated by certain artists; meanings embodied in form were revitalized according to a new sensibility. Le Corbusier, who, along with A. Ozenfant, founded purism in 1918, advocated the reduction of all buildings to basic geometric shapes of cube, cylinder, square, etc., placed in space. For Le Corbusier, architecture was understood as "the wise, correct and magnificent play of volumes in light." His contemporary H. Luckhardt, echoing of Platonic formalism, said: "Pure form is that form which, detached from all that is decorative, is freely fashioned out of the basic elements of the straight line, curve and free form, and will serve the purpose of any expression—be it a religious building or a factory." These observations, made *c.* 1915 to 1925, were a reaction against the pseudo-architecture of the revivalisms and an enthusiasm for the machined products of the new industrial age.

Purism. The emergence of the International Style marked the advent of 20th-century formalism. Although advocating volume as the first principle of architecture, its adherents conceived of architecture in terms of plane surfaces bounding a volume. Space was regarded as geometrically bounded. As a result, the integrity of the geometric surface was to be maintained at all costs; smooth-faced stucco, glass, and polished metals were advocated. The highly regarded volume was the simple box made as open as possible through extensive glazing. In Mies van der Rohe, whose later philosophy (*c.* 1930) was expressed in the dictum that "less is more," the International Style gained its greatest proponent. The governing principle of formal purism is that anything superfluous should be rejected from architecture, and that architectural expression should be sought in the fewest possible elements. Space became simply conceived as a cubic area bounded by glass walls articulated by a steel skeleton. Miesian philosophy is represented in his chapel at the Illinois Institute of Technology and in his adherents' works, e.g., R. Jones' St. Patrick's, Oklahoma City, and P. Schweikher's First Universalist Church, Chicago.

Formal purism is characterized by simplicity of volume, linear austerity of exterior and interior walls, and precision in construction. This kind of architecture held virtual sway in America from *c.* 1945 to 1955, but since then it has declined. The application of the Miesian "universal space" to houses, office buildings, and churches may provide interesting technical and artistic solutions, but it is often inadequate for human functions. Its lack of flexibility and the inability to accommodate the variety of human needs, which it subordinates to a rectilinear geometry and abstraction, accounts for the weakening of its influence as a major architectural philosophy.

Plasticism. While the International Style ran its course, another style was developing under the influence of Le Corbusier. He attempted to manipulate a variety of forms in space to create a rich interplay among all the elements of architecture (form, mass, function) in dynamic balance. By the 1950s he was able to construct mature works in what has subsequently been called "plasticism" in architecture. Plasticism is generally understood as a quality of three-dimensional or volumetric relationships in contrast to two-dimensional or linear relationships. Although all architecture is three-dimensional as a form, it is only when elements are so disposed to make apparent the three-dimensional relationships between the elements that the term plasticity can be properly applied. To a large degree plasticity in architecture represents a method of giving to volume-mass relationships greater richness, diversity, and flexibility than the method advocated by the purists. Plasticity in architecture is not the unique possession of Le Corbusier; it was manifest in the works of A. Gaudí. Although many architects were showing plastic sensibility concurrently with Le Corbusier, it was Le Corbusier who brought plasticity into the mainstream of modern architecture. Contemporary critics regard plasticity as potentially the most vital of all architectural tendencies and point to Le Corbusier's Notre Dame du Haut, Ronchamp, as tangible proof of "the fitness of plastic architecture to create the great symbols of our civilization, real landmarks of our time."

The conflict between advocates of space consciousness and those of plastic formalism is centered on the difference in their concepts of the function of mass. Some say mass should act as the reciprocal agent of space. Accordingly, the architectural exterior immediately signifies the interior and, in a sense, acts as a membrane between inside and outside space. Shell construction presents the apogee of this achievement. However, some deny that the exterior alone specifies interior space, but rather that it signifies the potential inherent in mass and its configurations. Thus R. Schwarz observed that the decisive point is whether "the boundary [enclosing structure] is the correct 'behavior' of the inside when it reaches the outside."

The Status Today. Obviously form and space are not the only considerations involved in church architecture; others are light, texture, sound, detail, construction, etc., any one of which may become a major factor in production or interpretation. As an art and as a working method, architecture does not attribute to any single one of these elements absolute primacy. Architecture succeeds only when elements are presented in suitable relations. In this regard, E. Saarinen observed: "From an ashtray to a city plan everything is architecture. In working out a design you always keep thinking of the next largest thing; the ashtray in its relation to the table top; the chair in its relation to the room; the building in its relation to the city." This is the most meaningful formal consideration that can be applied to church architecture in the 20th century. Contemporary architecture theory does not recognize the existence of an autonomous manner of working that produces an independent style called "church architecture"; the architect's quest is to relate space, form, construction, function, and all other elements into meaningful patterns of relationships. The modern architect, schooled in space and form, structure and function, does not stress the object but relation. There is no law dictating suitable relationships except that found in the total configuration itself. He is hesitant to accept any law that claims to determine the suitability of relationships within a work before the fact of architectural creation.

Bibliography: For the history and theory of specific periods, see bibliog. following sections 2, 3, 4, etc. This bibliography presents a select guide to handbooks and dictionaries on the subject and history of architecture in general; select histories of modern architecture in general (specialized studies on modern church architecture follow sections 10, 11, and 12); select literature relevant to theory, form, and interpretation of architecture. **General handbooks and dictionaries.** For a useful guide to literature alphabetized by periods, see bibliog. in *Encyclopedia of World Art* (New York 1959) 1:693–710. E. E. VIOLLET-LE-DUC, *Dictionnaire raisonné de l'architecture française du XIᵉ au XVIᵉ siècle,* 10 v. (Paris 1858–68), illus., includes applied arts. J. BURCKHARDT and W. LÜBKE, *Geschichte der neueren Baukunst,* 10 v. (Stuttgart 1882–1927), illus. G. DEHIO and G. BEZOLD, *Die kirchliche Baukunst des Abendlandes,* 2 v. (Stuttgart 1887–1901, illus., atlas, bibliog. R. STURGIS, ed., *A Dictionary of Architecture and Building, Biographical, Historical, and Descriptive. . . ,* 3 v. (New York 1901–02), illus., line dwgs., bibliog. F. M. SIMPSON, *A History of Architectural Development,* 5 v. (new ed. London 1954), a new rev. ed. based on method and technique of the orig. ed. (1905–11). F. BENOIT, *L'Architecture. . . ,* 4 v. (Paris 1911–34), antiquity and the

Interior of a Romanesque church, Arezzo, Tuscany, Italy.
(©Massimo Listri/CORBIS)

East and West up to Gothic, indexes. G. WASMUTH, *Lexikon der Baukunst,* 5 v. (Berlin 1929–37), illus. with plates, portrs., maps, plans, diagr. B.F. FLETCHER, *A History of Architecture on the Comparative Method* (New York 1961) illus. D. WARE and B. BEATTY, *A Short Dictionary of Architecture* (New York 1945). T. F. HAMLIN, *Architecture through the Ages* (rev. ed. New York 1953), useful 1 v. hist. J. E. GLOAG, *Guide to Western Architecture* (New York 1958), useful summary guide. *The Great Ages of World Architecture* (New York 1961—), series of concise monographs, select bibliog., each v. well illus.: W. L. MACDONALD, *Early Christian and Byzantine Architecture* (1962), H. SAALMAN, *Medieval* (1962), R. BRANNER, *Gothic* (1961), H. A. MILLON, *Baroque and Rococo* (1961), V. J. SCULLY, *Modern* (1961). N. PEVSNER, *An Outline of European Architecture* (7th ed. Baltimore, Md. 1963), illus., bibliog., useful concise history. H. R. HITCHCOCK, *World Architecture: An Illustrated History* (New York 1964). E. SHORT, *A History of Religious Architecture* (rev. ed. New York 1936). **General histories of modern architecture.** B. ZEVI, *Storia dell' architettura moderna* (2d ed. Turin 1953), covers U.S. and Europe, illus., bibliog., useful indexing. A. WHITTICK, *European Architecture in the Twentieth Century,* 2 v. (London 1950–53), illus., bibliog. H. R. HITCHCOCK, *Architecture: 19th and 20th Centuries* (2d ed. History of Art No. Z15; 1963). J. JOEDICKE, *A History of Modern Architecture* (New York 1959). *Encyclopedia of Modern Architecture,* ed. G. HATJE and W. PEHNT, 1 v. illus. **Theory, form, and interpretation.** P. ABRAHAM, *Viollet-le-Duc et le rationalisme médiéval* (Paris 1934). R. L. ACKOFF, *Aesthetics of the 20th-Century Architecture* (Salt Lake City, Utah 1948). L. B. ALBERTI, *De re aedificatoria* (Florence 1485), Eng. *Ten Books on Architecture,* tr. J. LEONI (London 1955). G. BACHELARD, *Poetics of Space,* tr. M. JOLAS (New York 1964). R. BANHAM, *Theory and Design in the First Machine Age* (London

1959). A. BLUNT, *Artistic Theory in Italy, 1450–1600* (Oxford 1940; pa. 1950). C. F. BRAGDON, *Organic Architecture and the Language of Form* (Chicago 1917); *A Primer of Higher Space, the Fourth Dimension, to Which is Added Man the Square, a Higher Space Parable* (London 1939). E. DE BRUYNE, *Études d'esthétique médiéval,* 3 v. (Bruges 1946). E. CASSIRER, *The Philosophy of Symbolic Forms,* tr. R. MANHEIM, 3 v. (New Haven, Conn. 1953–57), esp. v. 2 *Mythical Thought.* S. CHERMAYEFF, "Structure and Aesthetic Experience," *Magazine of Art* 39 (1946). A. CHANG IH TIAO, *The Existence of Intangible Content in Architectonic Form Based upon the Practicality of Lao tzu's Philosophy* (Princeton, N.J. 1956). P. COLLINS, *Changing Ideals in Modern Architecture, 1750–1950* (London 1965); *Concrete: The Vision of a New Architecture: A Study of A. Perret and His Precursors* (New York 1959). R. A. CRAM, *Architecture in Its Relation to Civilization* (Boston, Mass. 1918). T. H. CREIGHTON, ed., *Building for Modern Man* (Princeton, N.J. 1949). D. DAVIDSON and H. ALDERSMITH, *The Great Pyramid: Its Divine Message* (London 1924; 1961). G. DURANDUS, *Symbolism of Churches and Church Ornaments* (Leeds 1843), with an intro. essay by J. M. NEALE and B. WEBB. I. E. S. EDWARDS, *Pyramids of Egypt* (London 1949). E. P. EVANS, *Animal Symbolism in Ecclesiastical Architecture* (London 1896). P. FINGESTEN, "Topographical and Anatomical Aspects of the Gothic Cathedral," *Journal of Aesthetics and Art Criticism* 20.1 (1961) 3–23. H. FRANKFORT et al., *The Intellectual Adventure of Ancient Man* (Chicago, Ill. 1946). H. FRANKFORT, *Kingship and the Gods: A Study of Near Eastern Religion as the Integration of Society and Nature* (Chicago, Ill. 1948). R. FRY, *Vision and Design* (London 1920). S. GIEDION, *The Eternal Present,* v. 1 *The Beginnings of Art* (New York 1962), v. 2 *The Beginnings of Architecture* (1964); *Space, Time and Architecture* (3d ed. New York 1956). W. GROPIUS, *Scope of Total Architecture* (London 1956). P. HAMMOND, ed., *Towards a Church Architecture* (London 1962). L. HAUTECOEUR, *Mystique et architecture: Symbolisme du cercle et de la coupole* (Paris 1954). J. HUDNUT *Architecture and the Spirit of Man* (Cambridge, Mass. 1949). E. O. JAMES, *From Cave to Cathedral* (New York 1965). C. LE CORBUSIER, *Le Modulor: Essai sur une mesure harmonique* (Boulogne 1950); *Vers une architecture* (Paris 1924). G. LESSER, *Gothic Cathedrals and Sacred Geometry,* 2 v. (London 1957). W. R. LETHABY, *Architecture, Nature and Magic* (London 1956). É. MÂLE, *Religious Art in France, XIII Century: A Study in Mediaeval Iconography and Its Sources of Inspiration,* tr. D. NUSSEY (New York 1913); repr. as *The Gothic Image* (1958). R. D. MARTIENSSEN, *The Idea of Space in Greek Architecture* (Johannesburg 1956). P. A. MICHÉLIS, "Space-Time and Contemporary Architecture," *Journal of Aesthetics* 8 (1949–50). L. MOHOLY-NAGY, *The New Vision,* tr. D. M. HOFFMANN (4th ed. *Documents of Modern Art* 3; 1949). L. MUMFORD, *Art and Technics* (London 1952). R. NEUTRA, *Survival through Design* (New York 1954). H. NISSEN, *Das Templum* (Berlin 1869). N. PEVSNER, *Pioneers of Modern Design* (2d ed. New York 1949). S. PRENTICE, *The Heritage of the Cathedral* (New York 1936). W. N. PUGIN, *The True Principles of Pointed or Christian Architecture* (London 1841). F. R. S. RAGLAND, *The Temple and the House* (London 1964). H. READ, *Icon and Idea* (Cambridge, Mass. 1955). P. RUDOLF, "The Six Determinants of Architectural Form," *Architectural Record* 120 (Oct. 1956). J. RUSKIN, *The Seven Lamps of Architecture* (London 1849), and later eds. A. B. SAARINEN, ed., *Eero Saarinen on His Work* (New Haven, Conn. 1962). E. SAARINEN, *Search for Form* (New York 1948). M. SALVADOR and R. HELLER, *Structure in Architecture* (Englewood Cliffs, N.J. 1963). P. H. SCHOLFIELD, *The Theory of Proportion in Architecture* (Cambridge, Eng. 1958). R. SCHWARZ, *The Church Incarnate,* tr. C. HARRIS (Chicago, Ill. 1958). G. SCOTT, *The Architecture of Humanism: A Study in the History of Taste* (2d ed. London 1924). V. J. SCULLY, *The Earth, The Temple*

The early-christian church of SS. Cosmas and Damian at Caliari, Sardinia, formerly the Basilica of St. Saturnius, built between the 6th and the 12th centuries. (Alinari-Art Reference/Art Resource, NY)

and the Gods (New Haven, Conn. 1962). R. K. SEASOLTZ, *The House of God* (New York 1963). S. SERLIO, *Regole generali di architettura sopra le cinque maniere degli edifici* (Venice 1537–51). C. SIEGEL, *Structure and Form in Modern Architecture* (New York 1962). E. B. SMITH, *Architectural Symbolism of Imperial Rome and the Middle Ages* (Princeton, N.J. 1956); *The Dome: A Study in the History of Ideas* (Princeton, N.J. 1950). L. H. SULLIVAN, *Kindergarten Chats* (rev. ed. New York 1947). P. THIRY et al., *Churches and Temples* (New York 1953). R. S. J. TYRWHITT, *Christian Art and Symbolism* (London 1872). H. WÖLFFLIN, *Renaissance and Baroque,* tr. K. SIMON, from orig. Ger. ed. of 1888 (London 1964). W. WORRINGER, *Form in Gothic,* ed. and tr. H. READ (London 1927; rev. ed. New York 1964). F. L. WRIGHT, *The Future of Architecture* (New York 1953). VITRUVIUS POLLIO, *De architectura libri decem* (Leipzig 1899). C. G. YAVIS, *Greek Altars, Origins and Typology* (St. Louis 1949). B. ZEVI, *Architecture as Space* (New York 1957); *Towards an Organic Architecture* (London 1950).

[D. R. WALL]

Part 2: Early Christian

Spanning long centuries and distant provinces, Early Christian architecture embraces a lively variety of building types and styles, which gave direction to church architecture far into the Middle Ages and even beyond. The term ''Early Christian'' includes the architecture of the Church across the entire breadth of the Roman Empire, from earliest times down to the 6th century in the East, where it was supplanted by Byzantine, and down to the 9th century in the West, where it gradually gave way to Carolingian and then Romanesque styles of architecture.

Efforts to trace the origins of Early Christian architecture have demonstrated its dependence on many forms of late Roman building; elements of domestic architecture, business buildings, classical *heroa,* and imperial palace architecture were all clearly borrowed by the Christian architect. The earliest known Christian church, that of DURA- EUROPOS (*c.* 240), is no more than a tradi-

St-Philibert-de-Grandlieu, Brittany, France, development of the chevet: (a) first reconstruction, 826–829, (b) second reconstruction (lower crypt area), 840–847, (c) second reconstruction (upper nave area), showing devotional chapels arranged ladderwise or "enéchelon."

tional Roman home converted to church purposes. After the emancipation of the Church by Constantine, however, Christians required a more spacious building of greater dignity, and the basilica, or Roman business hall, was the logical choice. To Constantine himself belongs the credit for setting the pace by the grand series of basilicas he erected in Rome, in his newly founded Constantinople, and in the Holy Land.

Basilica. The Constantinian basilica consisted of a succession of contrasting spatial units along a strong horizontal, east-west axis. Entering from the street, one passed first into a rectangular courtyard surrounded by porticoes, with a fountain for washing in the center. Beyond this one entered the Eucharistic hall of the basilica proper, a timber-roofed construction consisting of a nave flanked by aisles and lighted by a clerestory above. There the long succession of columns carried the eye strongly to the sanctuary at the end of the nave, beyond which lay the apse housing the bishop's throne and the presbytery. If the basic elements were old, their Christian intent shaped them into a distinctive new style of architecture.

Made of brick, the Early Christian basilica presented a plain appearance on the exterior, contrasting sharply with the fine colonnades that surrounded pagan temples. Unlike the temple, the church was designed for the sake of its interior spaces where it housed the assembly of the faithful. The interior was therefore often richly furnished. The 4th-century mosaic exposed beneath the present cathedral of Aquileia features a profusion of vine decorations, medallions of the seasons, birds feeding, and sea motifs. Marble columns, ornate marble sanctuary barriers, mosaics in the apse, and coffered ceilings created an effect of splendor that for Eusebius was the perfect image of "the great temple which the Word, the great Creator of the universe, built throughout the whole world beneath the sun, forming again the spiritual image on earth of those vaults beyond the vaults of heaven" (*Ecclesiastical History* 10.4.69).

The Early Christian basilica was primarily a house for the liturgy. The long sweep of its colonnades enhanced the beauty of the elaborate liturgical processions—the entrance and exit of bishop and clergy and the processions of the faithful for Offertory and Communion. Chancel barriers marked off in simple, functional fashion distinct areas reserved for the celebration of the Eucharist, for the lesser clergy and honor guards (*soleaschola*), and for the offering of gifts and receiving of Communion (*senatorium and matroneum*). Beyond the sanctuary lay the presbytery and throne, where the bishop presided at the fore-mass and where he stood to preach to his people. Add to this the lights, the banners, the vestments, the direct participation of the faithful in chant and procession,

Kariye Cami, a former Byzantine Church and monastery converted by the Turks to a museum, Istanbul, Turkey. (©Wolfgang Kaehler/ CORBIS)

and the vision of the Early Christian architect begins to come to life.

The geographical spread of Early Christian architecture demonstrated the wide adaptability of the basilica. In the Latin province of Africa (the basilica of St. Cyprian outside Carthage, for example) it was used much the same as at Rome. The remains of the church show the plan with great clarity: the apse, from which Augustine is known to have preached, and the altar almost in the center of the nave. In Syria, on the other hand, altar and presbytery were reversed, though still retaining the fundamental basilica plan. The throne for the bishop and the benches for his clergy were located on a raised dais in the center of the nave; there the readings and instructions of the fore-mass took place in the midst of the community. The altar stood at the head of the church in the apse. Only further east in Mesopotamia, never solidly part of the Roman Empire, did the architect abandon basilica forms in favor of native temple plans.

In style, too, the Syrian architect reworked basilica forms with great imagination. Building in heavy stone blocks, he designed massive churches with powerful, squat arches, deeply carved architraves, and towered fa-çades strangely foreshadowing the Romanesque. Syria, one of the liveliest centers of the early Church, was the home of some of the first great monastic complexes as men gathered from all sides to receive the spiritual direction of famous ascetics. Thus the monastery of Qalat Sem'an (*c.* 480) grew up at the site of St. Simeon's famous column near Aleppo.

Other buildings. In addition to the basilica, the Church required other buildings of religious use, notably the MARTYRIUM and BAPTISTERY. The martyrium was a memorial shrine marking a holy site, whether it be the place of a martyr's burial (as at St. Peter's in Rome) or the place of some saving event (as at the holy places in Palestine). In distinction from the basilica, it was designed as a central-plan building, round, polygonal, or cruciform. Behind the basilica of Calvary, for example, stood the great rotunda of the Anastasis, centered on the spot of Our Lord's burial and Resurrection (*see* SEPULCHER, HOLY). Especially common at places of pilgrimage in the East, the martyrium was heir to the architectural traditions of pagan *heroa* and Jewish memorial shrines and became in turn the parent of the centralized vaulted designs of Byzantine architecture.

Medieval Romanesque church of San Martin, Fromista, Spain, 11th century. (©Manuel Bellver/CORBIS)

In the West, on the other hand, the central-plan structure was reserved generally for baptisteries or mortuary buildings. It is significant that the most famous martyrium in the West, the shrine of St. Peter, took the form rather of a transverse hall, or transept, at the end of the basilica, with an apse to mark the Apostle's grave. Thus, whereas in the East the architect turned more and more to exploit the possibilities of a vertical, domed space, in the West the horizontal basilica space remained standard.

Though Byzantine architecture was not without some impact on Early Christian architecture in the West, these effects were more in furnishings than in structure. The ciborium over the altar and the ambos for reading seem to have come from the East in the 7th century; and in the 8th century there was a notable increase in the use of images in reaction against ICONOCLASM. Other developments modified the chancel arrangement during the same centuries. Provision for the veneration of relics directly beneath the altar required the raising of the sanctuary for the installation of crypt and *confessio;* meanwhile, the increased sophistication of church music resulted in the augmenting of the choir space before the altar.

The enormous building activity of the 4th century all over the Mediterranean world was largely arrested, where not actually undone, in the West by the successive invasions of Visigoths and Vandals in the 5th century. And while the Eastern Empire proved stronger against the barbarian, it too suffered the destruction of the vast majority of its Early Christian monuments during the Arab invasions of the 7th century. Nevertheless, in the West,

church architecture continued to follow Early Christian patterns far into the Middle Ages, and the churches of Rome proved especially influential in this respect. For it is to Rome that the pilgrim turned once Palestine had fallen to the Arabs, and in Rome he found a second Holy Land. In Rome stood the churches of SS. Peter and Paul, princes of the Apostles; St. Mary Major, with its shrine of the Nativity; Sta. Croce, with relics of the cross sent by St. Helena; and the Lateran, the pope's own basilica. Hence the architect's standard claim to fame in the Middle Ages is that he had built *more Romano,* after the pattern of the Early Christian churches of Rome.

See Also: ART, EARLY CHRISTIAN, 1, 2; ST. PETER'S BASILICA; CATACOMBS; BASILICA.

Bibliography: W. GERBER, *Altchristliche Kulturbauten Istriens und Dalmatiens* (Dresden 1912). H. C. BUTLER, *Early Churches in Syria: Fourth to Seventh Centuries,* ed. E. B. SMITH (Princeton, N.J. 1929). R. KRAUTHEIMER, *Corpus Basilicarum Christianarum Romae* (Vatican City 1937—); "The Beginning of Early Christian Architecture," *Review of Religion* 3 (Jan. 1939) 127–148. J. W. CROWFOOT, *Early Churches in Palestine* (London 1941). M. ARMELLINI, *Le chiese di Roma dal secolo IV al XIX,* ed. C. CECCHELLI, 2 v. (new ed. Rome 1942). A. BERTHIER et al., *Les Vestiges du christianisme antique dans la Numidie centrale* (Algiers 1943). K. J. CONANT, *A Brief Commentary on Early Medieval Church Architecture* (Baltimore, Md. 1942). A. GRABAR, *Martyrium,* 3 v. (Paris 1943–46). J. LASSUS, *Sanctuairies chrétiens de Syrie* (Paris 1947). W. L. MACDONALD, *Early Christian and Byzantine Architecture* (New York 1962). G. A. SOTERIOU, "Hai palaiochristianikai basilikai tēs Hellados," *Archaiologikē Ephēmeris* (1929) 159–248. T. F. MATHEWS, "An Early Roman Chancel Arrangement and Its Liturgical Functions," *Rivista di archeologia cristiana* 38 (1962).

[T. F. MATHEWS]

Part 3: Byzantine

Although the term "Byzantine" is sometimes extended to include all the architecture of the Christian East from earliest times, it is more proper to restrict the term to the architectural style born of Justinian's empire in the 6th century. A style of great permanence, Byzantine architecture enjoyed nearly a millennium of living continuity and had periods of conspicuous creativity in the 6th century and again from the 9th century to the 11th century. From its hub in the capital city of Constantinople, it radiated over a wide area, following the spread of the Byzantine liturgy, with rich variations, especially in Greece and Russia.

The complex history of Byzantine architecture revolves about a single architectural motif, the dome, and this principally in its religious use, though it had applications in civic and palace architecture as well. Once established, this motif was interpreted over and over in everchanging combinations. Precedent for the religious use of the dome was abundant in late Roman and Early Christian architecture. Particularly influential must have been the centrally planned baptisteries, martyria, and memorial buildings, such as S. Costanza in Rome, built as a tomb for Constantine's daughter, and the Anastasis Rotunda in Jerusalem. This latter circular building marked the site of Our Lord's Resurrection, the most important pilgrimage place in Christendom, and Emperor Justinian undertook its enlargement and restoration. But the Byzantine use of the dome quickly left all precedent behind and established a style that was quite new both in its aesthetic and in its technical accomplishment.

Early works. The first masterworks of Byzantine architecture appear in Ravenna, the main stronghold of Justinian's rule in Italy. In S. Vitale (526–547) the essential themes of the new aesthetic are clearly enunciated. Basically the church consists of a central octagonal dome surrounded by an aisle and a gallery. But the classical ordering of spaces yields to a new fluidity. Each face of the octagonal core expands into the aisle and gallery in a semicircular apse with triple arcades on both levels. The main entrance, which is not on the axis but oblique, presents one with a complex view of overlapping and interpenetrating volumes. The controlled lighting on three levels lends a sense of unsubstantiality to the building, a feeling that is augmented by the handling of wall surfaces, where varicolored marble, mosaic, and inlaid work mask the strength of the vaults and supporting members. Even the capitals are transformed, the classical plastic treatment of the acanthus giving way to a flat relief in which contrasts of light and shadow take precedence. The use of the elevated dome at S. Vitale represents only one of a wide variety of early Byzantine plans. At SS. Sergius and Bacchus in Constantinople the octagonal central space was made to relate to a rectangular surrounding aisle, while at Hagia Eirene in the same city the central domed space was enlarged in an oval direction by large, major apses on the east and west. Elsewhere the dome unit itself might be multiplied, as at St. John of Ephesus, where a cross plan was crowned with a dome in the center and domes on each of the arms. In every case the architects of the 6th century strained the ancient Roman masonry techniques to accommodate a new spirit, a distinctive Byzantine aesthetic.

But in technique, too, the early Byzantine architect soon surpassed his Roman predecessor. Most important in this respect was the building of HAGIA SOPHIA (532–537), where dome construction reached a triumph not approached again until the Renaissance. The architects not only chose to elevate a huge dome to unprecedented height (it spanned 103 feet, and its apex reached to about 163 feet), but they invented for its support the first large-scale use of pendentive vaults. The pendentive,

The Gothic Church of St. Anne, Vilnius, Lithuania. (©Cory Langley)

a spherical triangular segment of vault, made a graceful transition from the circle of the dome above to the square of the piers below, carrying the weight of the dome more securely at the same time. Used only timidly in antiquity, it was now exploited to the full. The influence of Hagia Sophia on subsequent Byzantine architecture was decisive. As the principal church of the capital city, it set a pattern for all the provinces. The central dome was thus established beyond question, and the Early Christian basilica type disappeared almost entirely from Byzantine architecture, except in Greece and Macedonia.

Later works. Upon the death of Justinian (565), his empire withered as fast as it had sprung up, and church architecture, always dependent on imperial patronage, likewise waned. To the east the empire faced the threat of Islam; within, it suffered the turmoil of the iconoclast wars that destroyed many of the monuments of the first golden age (*see* ICONOCLASM). With the restoration of stability in the middle of the 9th century, however, a second golden age began, and a new church type emerged that

Cologne Cathedral, High Gothic style, Cologne, Germany, engraving by Munchen. The foundation stone was laid in 1248 and consecration took place in 1322, but the structure was not completed until 1880. (©Hulton Getty/Liaison Agency)

was destined for a much more extensive diffusion than the earlier types. The new church type, pioneered in the now destroyed Nea Ecclesia (*c.* 860) and Pharos (*c.* 880) churches of Constantinople, was generally more modest in dimensions and monastic in orientation rather than imperial. It consisted of a barrel-vaulted cross inscribed in a rectangle, with a dome over the center generally elevated on a drum. Apses were multiplied on the eastern end, and minor domes multiplied in the angles between the arms of the cross. The overall effect was one of new elegance, with emphasis on the vertical line and the decorative detail.

On the exterior, the plain brick of the earlier style gave way to alternating bands of brick and stone and even tile, and the flat wall surfaces were enlivened with tall, narrow niches. On the interior, the victory of the orthodox acceptance of images over iconoclasm secured for the icon a role of great importance. The *regula*, or colonnade

separating the sanctuary from the nave, was hung with icons and gradually transformed into an *iconostasis* (*see* ICON). At this time too, the iconography of the interior took on a definitive system, arranging the divine hierarchy in descending importance from the image of Christ Pantocrator in the dome through choirs of angels, ranks of Patriarchs and Apostles, down to saints honored by feasts of the Church calendar in the lowest levels. Thus the entire fabric of the medieval church became a symbol of the whole supernatural cosmos. The church was "an earthly heaven in which the God of heaven lives and moves about, it contains in figure the crucifixion, burial and resurrection of Christ" (Pseudo-Germanus of Constantinople; *Patrologia Graeca.*

Spread outside Byzantium. Although the Latin occupation of Constantinople (1204–58) terminated the second golden age of Byzantine architecture within the capital, the tradition had long since passed to the spiritual heirs of Constantinople. The nations of the Balkan peninsula and Russia were the principal beneficiaries, though nations farther east, such as Armenia, were sometimes indebted to the Byzantine. Greece preserved and enriched this architectural inheritance throughout the Middle Ages. The monastic centers of Daphni and Stiris in the 11th century, and later Athos and Mistra, built important original monuments. Characteristic of the Greek development, as seen in the church of the Convent of the Assumption, Daphni, is the alternation of squared stone and brick, the fine masonry details, and the almost classical concern for the external proportions of the building.

The Russians too, after their conversion, looked to Constantinople as the parent church. As the story goes, it was the beauty of the liturgy at Hagia Sophia that first attracted to the faith Vladimir of Kiev, first Christian king of Russia (980–1015). His ambassadors related to him that "there is no such splendor or beauty anywhere on earth; we cannot describe it to you. Only this we know, that God dwells there among men and that their liturgy surpasses the worship of all other places." Byzantine architecture in Russia carries this kind of emotional overtone. Where the Bulgarians had elevated their domes on slender drums, the Russians both elevated and expanded their domes, eventually developing the picturesque onion shapes usually associated with Russia. The church was conceived as a compact grouping of vertical volumes capped by a cluster of shining domes. Later translating these forms into wooden structures in brilliant colors, the Russians succeeded in combining the Byzantine with the northern spirit.

Even in the West, Byzantine architecture has had considerable impact. The Mediterranean islands as far as Sicily, the monastery towns of southern Italy, and the great trading center of Venice are all rich in the Byzantine tradition. In Sicily, Cefalù, Monreale, and Palermo are all important for their Byzantine mosaics. In Venice, the cathedral of St. Mark borrowed from St. John of Ephesus the arrangement of several major domes distributed in a cross, whence this plan becomes part of the 12th-century tradition of Romanesque architecture in southern France.

See Also: HAGIA SOPHIA.

Bibliography: A. VAN MILLINGEN, *Byzantine Churches in Constantinople* (London 1912). G. MILLET, *L'École grecque dans l'architecture byzantine* (Paris 1916). O. M. DALTON, *East Christian Art* (Oxford 1925). E. H. SWIFT, *Hagia Sophia* (New York 1940). O. G. VON SIMSON, *Sacred Fortress* (Chicago, Ill. 1948). G. H. HAMILTON, *The Art and Architecture of Russia* (Pelican History of Art No. 26; New York 1954). J. A. HAMILTON, *Byzantine Architecture and Decoration* (2d ed. London 1956). G. DOWNEY, *Constantinople in the Age of Justinian* (Norman, Okla. 1960). W. L. MACDONALD, *Early Christian and Byzantine Architecture* (New York 1962). P. VERZONE, *Encyclopedia of World Art* (New York 1959) 2:758'785.

The Gothic Notre-Dame Cathedral, Pierre Chambiges, architect, Senlis, France, ca. 1240. (©Vanni Archives/CORBIS)

R. KRAUTHEIMER, *Early Christian and Byzantine Architecture* (Pelican History of Art; New York 1965).

[T. F. MATHEWS]

Part 4: Romanesque

Romanesque was the major medieval style in western European architecture from about 950 to 1150. Based on the principle of the Roman round arch, Romanesque architecture introduced to medieval church-building structural concepts of unprecedented monumental scale and originality. Its origins lay in the so-called proto-Romanesque structures of the preceding two centuries, notably in the imperial abbeys of the Carolingian renaissance and the Asturian and Mozarabic buildings of northern Spain. Since the most characteristic Romanesque monuments appeared between 1050 and 1150, the century from 950 to 1050 is generally regarded as a formative period.

From 950 to 1050. The adventuresome spirit that created the Romanesque style emerged in an atmosphere of general optimism in Western Christendom after the passing of the millennium. Within the newly stabilized framework of medieval culture, the character of Romanesque architecture was shaped by the pervasive influ-

Nave of the Romanesque-Gothic cathedral at Cremona. (Alinari-Art Reference/Art Resource, NY)

ences of feudalism and monasticism. The decentralization of Europe into independent feudal states led to such a variety of distinctive regional idioms that some scholars prefer to define Romanesque as a group of related styles rather than a single style. However, through the powerful unifying force of monasticism, Romanesque became an international style, whose dissemination throughout western Europe was guaranteed by the arteries of communication opened by the great pilgrimages and the early CRUSADES.

The builders of the abbey churches of the 11th and 12th centuries created a basic architectural vocabulary of compact masses animated by the vertical thrusts of exterior towers and interior vaults. These fortresslike structures tended to be conceived as additive complexes of quasi-independent components in an expanded basilica plan with ambulatory and radiating chapels. During its two centuries of experimentation with problems of structural articulation and vaulting techniques, Romanesque

architecture produced a wide range of local variants within the framework of one international style.

Lombard-Catalan architecture, extending from northern Italy to French Catalonia and northern Spain, was one of the first Romanesque styles to concentrate on the practical problems of vaulting. Dominated by a basically utilitarian approach, the architecture of the Lombard-Catalan region developed in simple vaulted structures based on a direct revival of Roman techniques. The earliest and best-preserved buildings of the formative period, St.-Martin-du-Canigou (1001–26) in the French Pyrenees and the Spanish pilgrimage church of Sta María at Ripoll (1020–38), are covered by heavy unribbed tunnel vaults carried on simple piers. Although their interior spaces were dark and crudely inarticulate, the exterior elevations were decorated with typical Lombard devices of delicate blind arcading. The mature phase of Lombard-Catalan architecture was reached with the introduction of domed-up, ribbed groin vaults in the nave of

The cupolas of the Cathedrale-St.-Front rise above the town of Perigueux, France. (©John Heseltine/CORBIS)

Sant'Ambrogio at Milan in the last quarter of the 11th century. These low, broad Milanese vaults, with their application of heavy ribs and alternating supports in compound piers, introduced a new structural articulation of the nave into double bays, but the cautious omission of clerestory windows resulted in a heavy, dark interior, characteristic of the Mediterranean area.

The later Romanesque architecture that developed in the wealthy Tuscan communes of central Italy was structurally more conservative, adopting only the decorative features of the northern Lombard style, while ignoring its innovations in vaulting. The 12th-century cathedral basilicas at Pisa and Lucca are distinguished chiefly by their ornate exterior overlay of marble veneers and decorative arcading.

In Germany the initial phase of Romanesque took the form of an ambitious Ottonian revival of CAROLINGIAN architecture. The monastic foundations of Gernrode

Abbey (*c.* 980) and St. Michael at Hildesheim (*c.* 1001–33) adopted the earlier double-ended plan with its western apse and multiple exterior towers. More concerned with aesthetic articulation than with technical problems, the builders of these early churches developed a system of alternating supports forming double bays in a nave still covered by a conservative, trussed timber ceiling. Under later Lombard influence, the 12th-century German cathedrals along the Rhine, e.g., Speyer, Mainz, and Worms, show groin vaulting applied to the nave and elaborate Lombard decorative motifs to the exterior walls.

From 1050 to 1150. The major developments of mature Romanesque architecture occurred in France. One of the most impressive and characteristic types appeared in the series of monumental abbey churches in Tours, Conques, Limoges, and Toulouse, along the pilgrimage roads to SANTIAGO DE COMPOSTELA in northwestern Spain. Modeled after the famous shrine of St. James (*c.*

The "Malatesta Temple" at Rimini, Renaissance architecture, façade by Leon Battista Alberti, designed 1450. (Alinari-Art Reference/Art Resource, NY)

1075–1150), the French pilgrimage church consisted of a huge Latin-cross plan, which included a spacious aisled transept and an elaborate ambulatory with radiating chapels to accommodate the cult of the relics. In its most typical example, St.-Sernin at Toulouse, the dark, windowless nave is covered by a series of barrel vaults articulated by heavy transverse ribs and dynamically buttressed by quadrant vaults over the triforium gallery.

Under the patronage of the powerful Cluniac Order, the Burgundian churches of eastern France created one of the most original and experimental developments in Romanesque architecture. In its sophisticated efforts to solve the problem of admitting light to a vaulted interior, Burgundian architecture evolved a complex style that incorporated both Lombard and Norman influences. The nave of St.-Philibert at Tournus (vaulted 1066–1120), which is covered by parallel, transverse barrel vaults carried by heavy cross walls springing directly from heavy masonry columns, is a typical example of the eccentric experimental direction of the Burgundian Romanesque style. At Vézelay, the church of La Madeleine (1104–32) illustrates the development of an equally radical vaulted nave in its application of ponderous, unribbed cross vaults over large oblong bays. The huge third abbey church at Cluny (1088–1130), with its double, towered transept, ambulatory with multiple radiating chapels and long covered narthex, was the masterpiece of Romanesque architecture. Cluny III incorporated the most pronounced "half-Gothic" features of Burgundian style in the remarkably tall proportions of its nave, its thin, light barrel vaults buttressed by transverse ribs carried down into compound piers, and its use of the stilted, double-centered arch in the nave arcade. Following the Burgundian tendency to push Roman vaulting methods beyond their structural limits, the architect of St.-Lazare at Autun (c. 1120–32) adopted the Cluniac stilted arch in a daring system of pointed barrel vaults over the nave.

Two distinctive types of Romanesque hall church were created in western France. In Poitou the barrel-vaulted churches of Notre-Dame-la-Grande at Poitiers (*c.* 1130–45) and St.-Savin-sur-Gartempe (*c.* 1060–1115) have aisles and nave of almost the same height, while in Aquitaine the hall church developed under Byzantine influence as a single-nave structure covered by a series of domes on pendentives, e.g., the cathedrals in Angoulême (*c.* 1105–25) and at Périgueux (*c.* 1120).

Most conservative were the French Romanesque buildings of the southern provinces. The isolated region of Auvergne developed a unique feature in its high tower-like transept, e.g., Notre-Dame-du-Port at Clermont-Ferrand; whereas the 12th-century churches of Provence, St.-Gilles-du-Gard and St.-Trophime at Arles, preserved late Roman elements in the fluted columns, the Corinthian capitals, and the flat architraves of their façades.

The energetic Norman style, with its predilection for severe monumentality, logical articulation, and dynamic vertical momentum, produced the most progressive structural innovations in Romanesque vaulting. The Norman churches of the 11th century, e.g., Jumièges (1040–67) and St.-Étienne at Caen (1066–77), adopted the conservative Ottonian timber-roofed nave divided into double bays by alternating piers with salient shafts rising through the whole height of the wall. With the application of low-sprung, sexpartite, ribbed vaults over the huge double bays in St.-Étienne and Ste.-Trinité at Caen (*c.* 1115), the structural function of the proto-Gothic rib was realized as a skeletal framework that could carry a lighter fabric of masonry in the vaults. Norman architecture was introduced in England by Edward the Confessor at Westminster and was established after the conquest (1066) as a more massive, squared-off version of French Romanesque. While such English cathedrals as Durham (1093; 1128–33) applied heavy ribbed vaults to the nave, other Norman churches, e.g., Ely and Peterborough, retained timber coverings.

In the royal domain of the Île-de-France, the adoption and modification of the innovations of Norman proto-Gothic and the Burgundian ''half-Gothic'' Romanesque led to the creation of the first Gothic style in the abbey church of Saint-Denis (1137–44). Gothic then spread to the new town cathedrals of the later 12th century, while Romanesque survived in provincial examples well into the 13th century.

See Also: CISTERCIANS, ART AND ARCHITECTURE OF; CLUNIAC ART AND ARCHITECTURE.

Bibliography: K. J. CONANT, *Carolingian and Romanesque Architecture, 800–1200* (Pelican History of Art No. Z13; New York 1959). H. SAALMAN, *Medieval Architecture: European Architecture, 600–1200* (New York 1962). A. W. CLAPHAM, *Romanesque*

The Church of S. Andrea della Valle, baroque style, with façade designed by Carlo Rainaldi, built 1661–1665, Rome. (Alinari-Art Reference/Art Resource, NY)

Architecture in Western Europe (Oxford 1936). A. K. PORTER, *Medieval Architecture: Its Origins and Development* (New York 1909). R. C. DE LASTEYRIE DU SAILLANT, *L'Architecture religieuse en France à l'époque romane* (2d ed. Paris 1929). P. FRANKL, *Die frühmittelalterliche und romanische Baukunst* (Potsdam 1926).

[S. EDWARDS]

Part 5: Gothic

A transition and change in construction systems, predominantly in ecclesiastical building, originated in northern France in the first half of the 12th century and produced the Gothic style of architecture that dominated Europe well into the 15th century (in some areas it was continued in the 16th century and even later). The Gothic style, developed first in monastic churches and the great cathedrals of northern France, was also adopted in the structuring of less ambitious parish churches. Although not confined to church architecture alone, it flourished and found its best expression in ecclesiastical building; its verticality did not lend itself easily to domestic building and its openness was not suitable for military architecture.

Gothic architecture is characterized by its ribbed vaulting, buttressing, and high piers. The weight and

Nossa Senhora da Graca, baroque style, Evora, Portugal, 16th century. (©Vanni Archive/CORBIS)

thrust of the vaulting is carried downward with the aid of extended (flying) buttresses, without needing heavy masonry walls (as in Romanesque). Hence the nave walls are an open skeletal frame free to receive large expanses of STAINED GLASS. The exaggerated elongation of rising supporting members, which culminate in pointed arches, and the brilliant surfaces of light elevate the experience within to an otherworldliness where gravity seems overcome and natural light seems transformed. The exterior of Gothic structure achieves a similar transformation by disguising horizontals with steeply pointed elements and by multiplying vertical terminals with subtle gradations that fuse with the atmosphere.

Theories on Gothic. Gothic ecclesiastical architecture has been viewed in many different and conflicting ways, none of them complete or perfectly accurate in itself. The French tend to be technical in their approach to the Gothic style (Eugène Emmanuel Viollet-le-Duc, Camile Enlart). Germanic thought categorizes Gothic as a mystical expression of religious symbolism (Hans Sedlmayr) or of Neoplatonism (Hans Jantzen). The English view Gothic as a social manifestation of their own national character (A. N. W. PUGIN, John RUSKIN). Americans have been inclined to concentrate on developments of style (A. K. Porter, Robert Branner). Other writers have,

of course, presented different views, linking religious experience with construction (Henry ADAMS) or seeing in the perfection of Gothic architecture a parallel with medieval scholastic thought (Erwin Panofsky). *See* SCHOLASTICISM, 1, MEDIEVAL. But no workable, satisfactory, and definitive statement of the Gothic style of architecture has yet been advanced. Nor have the causes of its formation been fully explained, and it seems clear that no single point of view will suffice.

Some of the older, more blatantly unsatisfactory notions about the origin and meaning of Gothic architecture have, fortunately, long been abandoned. It is no longer accepted that the style began in the overlapping branches of Teutonic forests (Pseudo-Raphael Letter, between 1503 and 1510) or that it was Saracen in origin (Christopher Wren, 1713). But the very name ''Gothic'' betrays the derogatory connotations the style had for those Renaissance writers who first named it.

The ''why'' of the origin of Gothic architecture is not easily explained. Although the single-mindedness of a purely functional approach must be avoided, it seems equally unavoidable that the Gothic style originated amidst technical considerations. Over a given span, a pointed arch *is* more stable than a round arch. More important, because a pointed arch can be readily stilted by varying the point from which the arcs are swung, irregular spaces could be vaulted at uniform heights. The Île-de-France builders of the 1140s and 1150s were certainly aware of this. The rib vault, all too often seen simply as the *fons et origo* of the Gothic style, was unquestionably essential to it. The frankly insoluble problem is not whether the rib is a true supporting member whenever it appears in a vault, but what the medieval builder thought he was doing and why. And even if the Gothic style developed, as Paul Frankl maintains, from the vault downward, as designers attempted to give a visual unity from floor to keystone, it was a question of aesthetics no less than a question of construction.

But it must not be forgotten that aims, means, and results cannot be completely isolated one from another. The constructional means of voiding walls, however and for whatever reason achieved, made possible great areas of stained glass. The stories presented in these windows were exclusively nonstructural, ecclesiastical considerations, although the window plane itself formed a part of the wall. The mystical light of the Gothic church, so important at the very birth of the style, is perhaps more important to the character of the style than any number or combination of pointed arches. Because of the combined effect of the arches, the soaring shafts, the skeletal system of structure, the decorative moldings, the tracery screens, the finely cut sculpture, and the stained glass, one looking

Façade of the Baroque Hospital de Nuestra Señora de la Paz, Seville, Spain. (©Philipa Lewis; Edifice/CORBIS)

at Gothic architecture cannot help but repeat with Abbot SUGER (after Ovid, *Metamorphoses* 2.5), *materiam opusque superabat effectus.*

Origin and development. Gothic architecture first appeared in the form of the chevet of Suger's BENEDIC-TINE abbey church at SAINT-DENIS, outside of Paris, between 1140 and 1144. It was the effect, especially that of light, that was new or ''Gothic'' at Saint-Denis. Certain of the arch profiles came from the north, from Normandy, as did the concept of the rib vault, which made possible uniformly vaulted irregular spaces. The idea of openness, of voiding the wall, probably came from Romanesque Normandy also (e.g., transept arms of Notre-Dame at Jumièges; La Trinité and Saint-Étienne at Caen). Pointed arches and a regular sequence of piers came from the south, from Romanesque Burgundy (e.g., Autun, CLUNY, Parayle-Monial). Thus it was the collocation of older Romanesque features in a new and ordered concept that gave rise to the Gothic style of architecture in the hitherto relatively barren Île-de-France.

The degree to which the new chevet at Saint-Denis, with its regularity of plan, spacious chapels, and flood of light, satisfied the general religious needs of the time as opposed merely to manifesting Suger's overt interest in light (see his *De Administratione* ch. 28) is apparent in the number of ''copies'' of the plan during the following decade (e.g., the cathedrals of Noyon and Senlis, the abbey church of Saint-Germain-des-Prés). The problem of elevation was yet another matter, there being no readily available way to adapt older, heavier Romanesque schemes to meet the new desire for voided walls (light) and great height. During the second half of the 12th century, a great number of experiments took place in the architecture of northern France. The result was a variety of buildings related by colossal size and four-part interior elevations—main arcade, vaulted tribune, triforium passage, and small clerestory (e.g., Saint-Remi at Reims, 1170–80; south transept arm of Soissons, 1176–90). There were, nonetheless, obvious differences of effect and appearance among these buildings. For example, Paris and Laon both were begun *c.* 1160, but the decorative plasticity of the latter contrasts sharply with the planar quality of the former.

Classic Gothic plan. The solution of various problems, such as alternation of supports under six-part vaults and the logical codification of the desire for colossal buildings, came with the reconstruction of the cathedral of Chartres after a fire on June 9 and 10, 1194. Here the

Baroque bell towers of Santa Prisca Church, Taxco, Mexico, 1751–1758. (©Charles & Josette Lenars/CORBIS)

first fully competent use of the flying buttress made possible an immense building with a simplified interior elevation of three stories, namely, main arcade, triforium passage, and gigantic clerestory. The regular vaulting system with one four-part nave bay vault for each four-part vault of the side aisle, the aisled transept arms, and the chevet with ambulatory and radiating chapels together formed what must be termed the "classic" Gothic plan, especially as it appeared completely regularized at Reims (begun after a fire, May 6, 1210). Space for pilgrims in great naves and five or more radiating chapels for altars and relics—the plan was adopted for monastic use, e.g., Cistercian abbey church at Longpont, consecrated 1227—large areas of stained glass with the legends of the Church and its saints, and complex exterior sculpture programs completed the High Gothic architectural ensemble.

Gothic outside France. Outside France before *c.* 1250, the Gothic style developed along individual, regional lines, and there seems to have been little interest in building strictly *in more francigeno.* England, despite the work of the Frenchman Guillaume de Sens at Canterbury in the 1170s, perfected a style emphasizing longitudinal rather than vertical fusion (e.g., Salisbury, begun

1220; and coloristic, decorative effects (e.g., chevet at Lincoln, begun 1192). The flat chevets in England indicate the strong monastic orientation of the cathedrals in that country as well as the impact of the Cistercians.

In Italy, the Gothic style grew along very non-French lines. The large, open volume of such a building as the Dominican church of Santa Maria Novella in Florence (begun *c.* 1278) reflects the acoustical needs of a preaching order. The Gothic quality or character of this church lies mainly in the use of pointed arches, for the piers are purely Romanesque.

Germany and Spain, however, were much more receptive to French ideas and forms. The cathedral of Cologne (begun 1248) was modeled after those of Amiens and Beauvais and is extraordinarily French in character. By *c.* 1260 both León and Toledo in Spain had been influenced from France, the former by Reims (in plan) and Amiens (in elevation), the latter by Le Mans (mainly in plan and chevet buttressing system). However, it is both misleading and inaccurate to attempt to reduce the development of Gothic architecture in Europe after 1250 to expressions of French architecture, save in those special cases where a French architect can be isolated (e.g., Étienne de Bonneuil at the cathedral of Uppsala, Sweden,

Church of the Holy Ghost, designed by the Finnish architect Alvar Aalto (1898–1976), Wolfsburg, Germany. (©Adam Woolfitt/ CORBIS)

1287). The appearance of *Hallenkirchen* in Germany (e.g., St. Martin at Landshut, begun 1387) owes nothing to France, despite earlier similar constructions in Poitou (e.g., Poitiers, begun 1162) and Anjou (e.g., hospital of Saint-Jean, Angers, 1170s).

Indeed, after the middle of the 13th century, French influence on the architecture of western Europe began to be less precise, the occasional mention of a church being built *in more francigeno* notwithstanding (e.g., Bruckhard von Hall, *c.* 1280, in reference to the then decade-old church at Wimpfen im Tal). In short, a desire for decorative effects began to overshadow interest in construction. Whether one chooses Hans Jantzen's term "the diaphanous wall" or Paul Frankl's notion of "surface texture," the effect is the same. The collapse in 1284 of the 156-foot-tall vaults of the chevet at Beauvais (begun 1225) cannot be blamed for a return to less ambitious buildings. The main problem posed by the Gothic system of construction, that of maintaining great vaulted areas with external flying buttresses, had been essentially solved at Amiens by 1250 and presented no new challenge to the builder after that time. In Paris, during the decade from 1240 to 1250, the appearance of small, elegant buildings such as Ste.-Chapelle (consecrated 1248) and the nave of

Saint-Denis (begun 1243) reflect the stylistic interests of LOUIS IX (the Saint) and his court. The voided walls of such French buildings as Saint-Urbain at Troyes (begun *c.* 1262), with screens of delicate tracery, together with the widespread use of the glazed triforium (e.g., nave of Saint-Denis; the chevet of Amiens) mark a new age in medieval architecture.

Save in Italy, there seems to have been a general interest throughout Europe in openness, in lightness, and in decorative effect—in extending the concept of plasticity to its utmost. This interest manifests itself in such widely scattered buildings as the cathedral of Prague (begun 1344; triforium level and clerestory after 1374), Aachen Minster (begun 1355), La Trinité at Vendôme, France (in the nave, begun 1306), and the reconstructed and redecorated chevet of Gloucester (begun 1337).

Flamboyant Gothic. The fantastic vaulting patterns of the late Gothic, especially the fan vaults of England (e.g., King's College Chapel, Cambridge, begun 1446), spiral piers (e.g., chevet aisles, Brunswick, 1469), hanging keystones and pendent bosses (e.g., chapel of St. Catherine, Stephansdom, Vienna, begun 1340 or 1359), and complex tracery screens on façades (e.g., Saint-

Bell tower, Catholic Mission, San Diego California. (©Richard Cummins/CORBIS)

Maclou, Rouen, built 1500–14) all deny the clarity of earlier Gothic. But whether these architectural forms are termed flamboyant in France, *Sondergotik* in Germany, or Perpendicular in England, each in its own way was the ultimate statement of an experiment carried on from the very onset of the Gothic style.

One should not depreciate these late Gothic structures as decadent. They are among the finest expressions of the fertile medieval imagination. Rather, it remains to explain their rich fantasy of forms and effects. This cannot be done simply, but a parallel can at least be suggested with the growing inquisitiveness of the 14th- and 15th-century European mind and the ever-increasing preoccupation with the bizarre, as can be seen in the widespread popularity of the *danse macabre* (see DANCE OF DEATH) and the *ARS MORIENDI*.

Other Gothic Buildings. By comparison with the number of great cathedrals and abbey churches that have survived from the Gothic period, relatively few subsid-

iary structures such as cloisters, refectories, and hospitals (*hôtel-Dieu*) remain. However, such buildings as the hospital of Saint-Jean at Angers (1170s), the archiepiscopal chapel at Reims (*c.* 1210–15), the Synodal Hall at Sens (between 1222 and 1241, but over-restored), and the Capitular Hall at Westminster Abbey (*c.* 1245–50) demonstrate at least palely the wide variety of building types needed by the medieval Church and the inventiveness of the Gothic designer-builder in meeting this need.

Bibliography: Theoretical Studies. P. FRANKL *The Gothic: Literary Sources and Interpretations through Eight Centuries* (Princeton, N.J. 1960), the most comprehensive study of the subject; contains analyses, esp. those of H. JANTZEN from *Kunst der Gotik* (Hamburg 1957) Eng. *High Gothic,* tr. J. PALMES (New York 1962), H. SEDLMAYR from *Die Entstehung der Kathedrale* (Zurich 1950), E. PANOFSKY from *Gothic Architecture and Scholasticism* (Latrobe, Pa. 1951). Surveys. R. BRANNER, *Gothic Architecture* (New York 1961) short. E. LAMBERT et al., *Encyclopedia of World Art* (New York 1959) 6:467–539, with extensive bibliog. 645–648. G. DEHIO and G. VON BEZOLD, *Die kirchliche Baukunst des Abendlandes,* 7 v. (Stuttgart 1897–1901), 2 v. text, 5 v. drawings. P. FRANKL, *Gothic Architecture,* tr. D. PEVSNER (Pelican History of Art No. Z19; New York 1963), emphasizes the period after 1300. Some fine writing and thought is to be found in H. FOCILLON, *Art d'Occident* (Paris 1938), Eng. *The Art of the West in the Middle Ages,* ed. J. BONY, tr. D. KING, 2 v. (New York 1963). France. E. E. VIOLLET-LE-DUC, *Dictionnaire raisonné de l'architecture française du XIe au XVIe siècle,* 10 v. (Paris 1854–68). R. C. DE LASTEYRIE DU SAILLANT, *L'Architecture religieuse en France à l'époque gothique,* 2 v. (Paris 1926–27). E. GALL, *Die Vorstufen in Nordfrankreich,* v. 1 of *Die gotische Baukunst in Frankreich und Deutschland* (2d ed. Braunschweig 1955). There exist some excellent monographs, e.g., C. SEYMOUR, *Notre-Dame of Noyon in the Twelfth Century* (New Haven, Conn. 1939), but the studies of the Societé française d'Archéologie since 1834 in the *Congrès archéologique de France* and in the *Bulletin monumental* form the best general source of monograph studies on Fr. medieval architecture. A model regional study is R. BRANNER, *Burgundian Gothic Architecture* (London 1960). England. F. BOND, *Gothic Architecture in England* (London 1905); *An Introduction to English Church Architecture from the 11th to the 16th Century,* 2 v. (London 1913). G. F. WEBB, *Architecture in Britain: The Middle Ages* (Pelican History of Art No. Z12; New York 1956). J. BONY, "French Influences on the Origins of English Gothic Architecture," *Journal of the Warburg and Courtauld Institutes* 12 (1949) 1–15. Germany, Spain, and Italy. G. DEHIO, *Geschichte der deutschen Kunst,* 4 v. (Berlin 1923–34). L. TORRES BALBÁS, *Arquitectura gótica* (Ars Hispaniae 7; Madrid 1952). É. LAMBERT, *L'Art gothique en Espagne aux XIIe et XIIIe siècles* (Paris 1931). C. ENLART, *Origines françaises de l'architecture gothique en Italie* (Paris 1894). Technical Studies. R. WILLIS, "On the Construction of the Vaults of the Middle Ages," *Transactions of the Royal Institute of British Architects* 1.2 (1842) 1–69. J. FITCHEN, *The Construction of Gothic Cathedrals* (New York 1961). E. LEFÈVRE-PONTALIS, "L'Origine des arcs-boutants," *Congrès archéologique de France* 82 (1919) 367–396. M. AUBERT, "Les Plus anciennes croisées d'ogives," *Bulletin monumental* 93 (1934) 5–67, 137–237; "La Construction au moyen-âge," *ibid.* 119 (1961) 7–42. J. BILSON, "The Beginnings of Gothic Architecture," *Journal of the Royal Institute of British Architects,* ser. 3, v. 6 (1898–99) 259–289, the Eng. viewpoint. The best studies of the architects themselves are L. F. SALZMAN, *Building in England, down to 1540* (New York 1952) 1–29; N. PEVSNER, "The

Church in Alfred, Maine, photograph by Bluford Muir. (©CORBIS)

Term *Architect* in the Middle Ages,'' *Speculum* 17 (1942) 549–562 and P. DU COLOMBIER, *Les Chantiers des cathédrales* (Paris 1953).

[C. F. BARNES, JR.]

Part 6. Renaissance

Renaissance architecture, so far as churches are concerned, began in Italy in the 1420s. It is generally accepted that a Renaissance church is not Gothic in style, but beyond this it is more difficult to establish agreement. Until recently, there tended to be a tacit assumption that the deliberate revival of the forms of imperial Roman architecture presupposed an abandonment of a specifically Christian architecture, which corresponded to Gothic forms. This argument was advanced, with great force, in the mid-19th century by PUGIN and RUSKIN. It is, however, demonstrably false.

Brunelleschi. The first systematic attempts at a renaissance of Roman forms in architecture were made by F. Brunelleschi and paralleled the revived interest in Latin letters displayed by his humanist contemporaries and predecessors. Brunelleschi's reputation was founded on the engineering feat of the dome of Florence Cathedral, which is a marriage between Gothic vaulting and Roman domical forms. This was a special case; but Brunelleschi's two churches in Florence, S. Lorenzo and Sto Spirito, both dating from the 1430s and 1440s, were deliberately imitated from such Early Christian basilicas as S. Paolo in ROME. The proportional system of Brunelleschi's churches is based on simple mathematical relationships, but their actual shapes, as well as the decorative forms used, are those of basilicas built in the Christian Roman Empire. Brunelleschi also built S. Maria degli Angeli in Florence, left unfinished in 1437. The shape of this church is that known as a central plan, that is, a regular geometrical figure rather than a cruciform shape. Here the shape is an octagon with a chapel on each of the eight sides. These shapes clearly recall those of the so-called Temple of Minerva Medica in Rome, so that once more the reference to antiquity is quite explicit. Brunelleschi thus revived the two main types of Early Christian churches: the large, Latin-cross basilica type, suitable for parish churches, and the smaller, centrally planned type that, in early Christian times, was normally reserved for baptisteries and commemorative buildings known as *martyria* (*see* MARTYRIUM).

Brunelleschi did not, so far as is known, formulate his theories explicitly; nor is there any other information

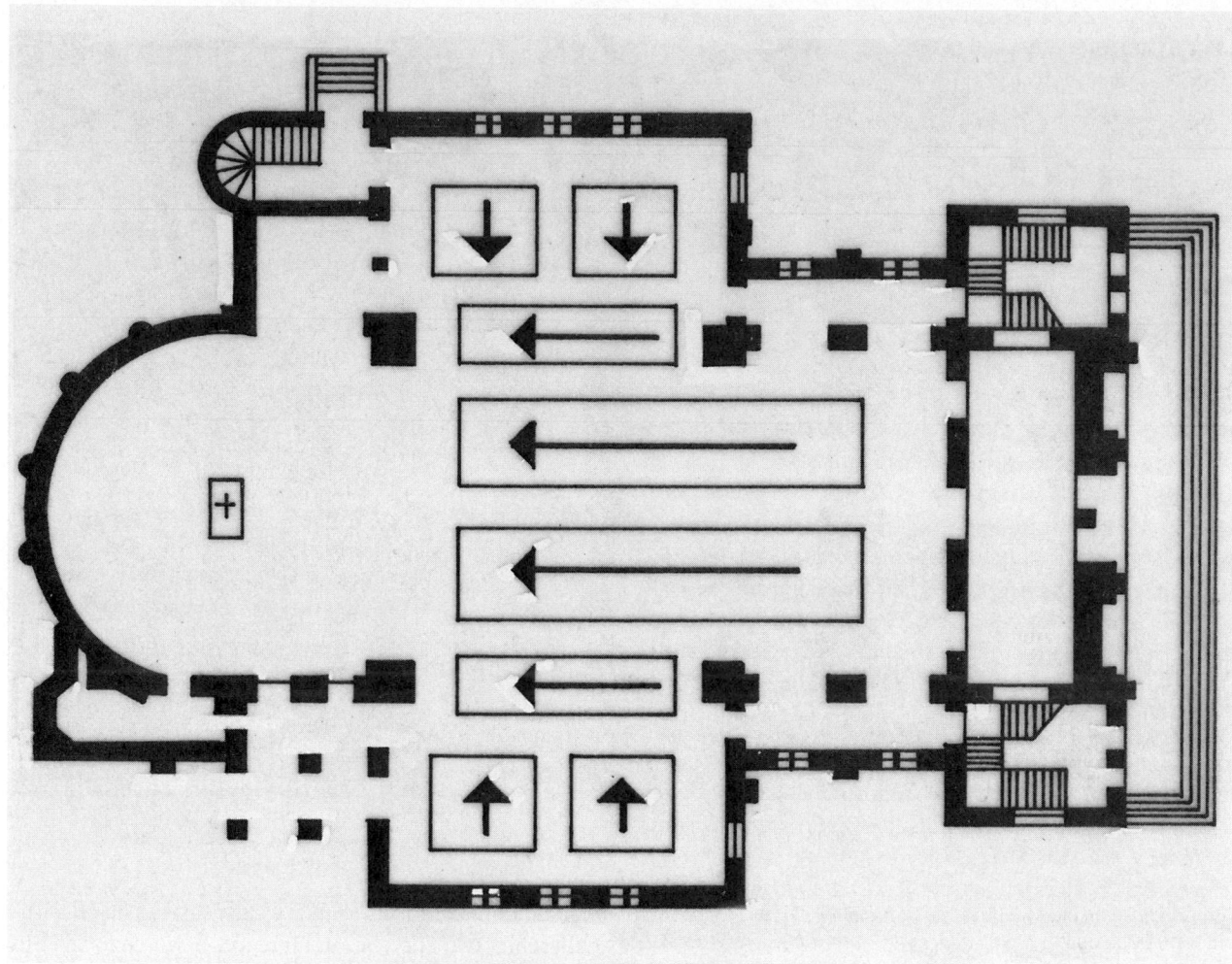

H.H. Richardson's Trinity Church, Boston, 1872–77, illustrating a transept seating arrangement.

about his views on church architecture. There is, however, a great deal of direct evidence in the form of writings by most of the major Italian architects of the 15th and 16th centuries, and their words make it quite clear that they regarded certain classical forms as specifically suited to the building of Christian temples (the use of *templum* for "church" is hardly evidence of paganism). It has been shown by Wittkower that the architectural forms employed between Brunelleschi's time and the Counter Reformation correspond to new, Platonic, theological ideas:

> The belief in the correspondence of microcosm and macrocosm, in the harmonic structure of the universe, in the comprehension of God through the mathematical symbols of centre, circle and sphere—all these closely related ideas which had their roots in antiquity and belonged to the undisputed tenets of mediaeval philosophy and theology, acquired new life in the Renaissance, and found visual expression in the Renaissance

church. . . . For the men of the Renaissance this architecture with its strict geometry, the equipoise of its harmonic order, its formal serenity and, above all, with the sphere of the dome, echoed and at the same time revealed the perfection, omnipotence, truth and goodness of God. (Wittkower, 29.)

Alberti and Bramante. These ideas can be traced in the work of L. B. ALBERTI, both in his treatise on architecture (written *c.* 1443–52) and in his two churches in Mantua. The earlier of these, S. Sebastiano, was designed about 1460 and is the earliest example of a Greek-cross plan, although one side has a porch that gives it a directional axis. This type of central plan can be traced back to the time of Constantine and, beyond that, to Roman tombs. In his second Mantuan church, Sant'Andrea, designed about 1470, Alberti repeated the Roman-basilica type used by Brunelleschi in Florence, but Alberti's forms are more classically Roman in spirit, and his church is covered by an enormous barrel vault of a purely antique type.

Leonardo da Vinci never built anything, but he made many drawings of churches of the centrally planned type. At least three churches were actually built in this form at the end of the 15th and beginning of the 16th centuries: at Prato, where the church by Giuliano da Sangallo is a combination of Brunelleschi's forms with the plan of Alberti's S. Sebastiano; and two others, at Todi and Montepulciano. These latter, together with Sant'Eligio in Rome, were all profoundly influenced by Bramante (who had already built two churches in Milan), and specifically by Bramante's projects for the rebuilding of St. Peter's. There seems little doubt that the foundation medal, struck in 1506, represents St. Peter's as a Greek-cross building with a vast dome over it; and although this project was repeatedly modified, it proved an ideal form for several other churches, of which the most beautiful is S. Biagio at Montepulciano, begun by Antonio da Sangallo the Elder in 1518.

Bramante is said to have written a treatise, but it is not extant. Some idea of his theories can be gained, however, from the projects for St. Peter's and from the writings of Serlio, who was the pupil of a pupil of Bramante. Several other treatises give a good idea of the practice of Renaissance architects and of their view that the form of a building should be suited to its purpose. Serlio, for example, said that several shapes are possible for churches, but the circular (rather than the cruciform) is the most perfect: "Many and diverse forms of ancient and modern Temples are to be seen in all parts of Christendom . . . but because the circular form is the most perfect of them all I will commence with it" (prologue to book 5). The idea that Renaissance architects equated the ideals of symmetry, clarity, and harmony in church building with the perfections of God was most clearly stated by Palladio in his *Quattro Libri* of 1570, even though both of his own churches in Venice were cruciform. In book four he said:

> We read that the men of Antiquity, in the building of their temples, set themselves to observe Decorum, which is one of the most beautiful elements of Architecture. And we, who know not false gods, in order to observe Decorum in the form of temples, will choose the most perfect and excellent, which is the circle; for it alone is simple, uniform, equal, strong, and adapted to its purpose. Thus, we should make our temples circular . . . most apt to demonstrate the Unity, the infinite Essence, the Uniformity and Justice of God.

It should be noted, however, that Palladio was born in 1508 and was thus 62 years old when his treatise was published. This was after the Council of Trent, which is-

Trinity Church, Gothic Revival style, New York City. (©Bettmann/CORBIS)

sued a decree on music in 1562 and on images in 1563, but made no special reference to architecture. The Counter Reformation ideals of church building were stated at length by Charles BORROMEO, in his *Instructiones Fabricae Ecclesiasticae* of 1577, in which he advocated the cruciform plan. Palladio's theories reflect the early 16th century, the period now called the High Renaissance, about 1510 to 1520, rather than the Counter Reformation. The architectural ideals changed in accordance with theology; and in the 16th century it did not occur to anyone to condemn Palladio's architecture as pagan, as Ruskin did 300 years later.

Only a small number of churches were built in accordance with these ideals, and what should have been the greatest of them all, Bramante's St. Peter's, was so profoundly modified that, in its present form, it is largely a baroque building (*see* ST. PETER'S BASILICA). Apart from churches already mentioned, there are some others, mostly small, in various Italian cities. Vignola built Sant'Andrea in Via Flaminia and, far more important for later generations, Il Gesù, as the mother church of the Society of Jesus. Both are in Rome, as is the most beautiful of all centrally planned churches, the tiny *martyrium* built in 1502 by Bramante himself in the courtyard of S. Pietro

Crystal Cathedral, Garden Grove, California, 1977–1980. (©Bettmann/CORBIS)

in Montorio, on the spot that traditionally marks the place of St. Peter's martyrdom.

Bibliography: Sources. L. B. ALBERTI, *De re aedificatoria* (Florence 1485), Eng. *Ten Books on Architecture,* tr. J. LEONI (London 1955). S. SERLIO, *Regole generali di architettura . . .* (Venice 1537–51), and his later books, some pub. in France. Serlio was partly tr. into Eng. in 1611 but never completed. A. PALLADIO, *I quattro libri dell'architettura,* 4 v. in 1 (Venice 1570), Eng. *The Architecture of A. Palladio in Four Books,* tr. N. DUBOIS, 2 v. (3d ed. London 1742). All text translations are by P. Murray. Literature. P. MURRAY, *The Architecture of the Italian Renaissance* (New York 1963), a general survey with bibliog. R. WITTKOWER, *Architectural Principles in the Age of Humanism* (3d ed. London 1962), most important modern work. G. SCOTT, *The Architecture of Humanism* (2d ed. London 1924), and later reprints. H. WÖLFFLIN, *Renaissance und Barock* (4th ed. Munich 1926), Eng. *Renaissance and Baroque,* tr. K. SIMON from the original Ger. ed. of 1888 (London 1964).

[P. MURRAY]

Part 7: Baroque

The formation of the baroque in church architecture took place in Rome toward the end of the 16th century; the diffusion of the baroque style followed in Italy during the 16th and 17th centuries, and finally it spread to France, Flanders, Spain, and the countries of central Europe.

Church architecture in the 17th and 18th centuries in western Europe is characterized, in Roman Catholic countries, by an integration of urban planning, architecture, sculpture, painting, and the decorative arts to a degree rivaled only, perhaps, by the Gothic. Acting to counter the effects of the Protestant Reformation, the reformatory orders of the 16th century restored to the Church confidence in the self-regenerative forces within Catholicism.

Artists and architects presented mysteries of the Church through interrelated illusionistic sensual displays

St. John the Evangelist Church, Hopkins, Minnesota, 1970–1971. (©G.E. Kidder Smith/CORBIS)

that encouraged identification with the subject portrayed. The architect of the Renaissance, in contrast, because of the relation of the Renaissance to classical antiquity and Neo- platonic thought, approached the mysteries through mathematics and the intellect. As a result, the ideas and forms of Renaissance architects, and those of painters and sculptors as well, remained more abstract, isolated, discrete, and independent.

Development in Rome. The baroque began in Rome, where the Counter Reformation movements of the 16th century culminated in the building of a series of major longitudinal plan churches: the Gesù (1568) by the Jesuits; the Chiesa Nuova (1575) by followers of St. Philip Neri; and S. Andrea della Valle (1591) by the Theatines.

The plan of the Gesù with its wide nave, chapels but no side aisles, and short transepts provided an ideal preaching space. It was sufficiently successful for hundreds of churches with similar plans to be built in the succeeding century and a half and was probably responsible for the inclusion of a nave when St. Peter's was completed (1607–14) according to the designs of Carlo Maderno (1556–1629).

Maderno. Maderno drew heavily on the works of his predecessor Giacomo della Porta (1533–1602), who completed most of the projects Michelangelo left unfinished and was himself responsible for the façade of the Gesù and the plan and section of S. Andrea della Valle. Della Porta exploited both Michelangelo's emphasis on the vertical and his tendency to concentrate supporting members (in opposition to Renaissance horizontality and uniformly distributed supports). Della Porta, however, eliminated the conflicting elements that were the source of disturbing tensions and intriguing ambiguities in Michelangelo's work.

Maderno accepted Della Porta's interpretation of Michelangelo, but in addition he brought a richer play of

Saint Mary's Cathedral, Gothic style, Gdansk, Poland. (©Steve Raymer/CORBIS)

mass and light and shadow to the otherwise planal surfaces of Roman architects and conceived architecture as part of a larger context. In individual buildings he included more plastic elements—half and fully round columns, the giant order, and more varied decorative sculptural features—and within a complex included more of the surroundings.

Maderno's new ideas can be first seen in the façade of S. Susanna (1597–1603), where he achieved dramatic emphasis on the central portal through (1) pilasters and columns arranged in a rhythmical sequence, culminating at the central portal, (2) successive stepping forward of the wall surface toward the center, increasing thereby the impression of mass of the wall, and (3) successive increase in size and relief of decorative detail from extremities to the central opening. Maderno also designed the buildings on either side of the church to make the façade become part of a much larger scheme—a focal point in an intentionally neutral setting.

In terms of urban design, Maderno was the first to develop some of the ideas implied by Domenico Fontana (1543–1607) and SIXTUS V (1585–90) when they planned straight avenues linking the major pilgrimage centers and culminating in centrally placed obelisks. For Fontana and

Sixtus V the buildings lining the avenues were secondary; the circulation route and the foci, as they represented the pilgrimage centers, were essential. Maderno likewise conceived the church as part of an environment that included the background against which the church façade would be seen. After the initial successes of the baroque, the city could no longer be thought of as a conglomerate of isolated churches, palaces, and other buildings, but only as a formally and visually related whole.

In the nave of St. Peter's (1607–14), Maderno also altered the traditional Renaissance way of conceiving of space and structure. In a Renaissance church (cf. S. Spirito, Florence, Brunelleschi; Sant'Andrea, Mantua, Alberti), structure served to define spatial units as discrete cells that, added together, composed the whole. Maderno, on the other hand, by widening and heightening the nave, admitting light through the vault and through domes in the side aisles, reducing the mass and width of the nave piers, and enlarging openings between chapels, sought to emphasize spatial unity across the nave from outer wall to outer wall, as well as from narthex to crossing and diagonally.

Borromini, Cortona, and Bernini. Maderno's achievements in the rhythmical manipulation of mass and

The apse of an early Christian church against the Temple of Artemis (c. 300 B.C.), Sardis, Turkey, 4th century A.D. (©Roger Wood/CORBIS)

spatial interaction for dramatic emphasis were continued by his pupil and successor, Francesco Borromini (1599–1667), the painter-architect Pietro da Cortona (1596–1669), and the sculptor, painter, and architect Giovanni Lorenzo BERNINI (1598–1680). These men initiated the full baroque. By 1640 each of the three had completed major works in Rome: Bernini—S. Bibiana reconstruction (1624–26), St. Peter's baldachino (1624–33); Cortona—SS. Martina and Luca (begun 1634); Borromini—S. Carlo alle Quattro Fontane (1638–41). Their achievements from the 1640s through the 1660s influenced all architecture in Italy and Sicily, and much of the architecture in France, Spain, and Belgium for the remainder of the century.

In accord with the precepts laid down by St. Charles BORROMEO in his *De fabrica ecclesiae,* the large Roman churches of the late 16th and the early 17th century were longitudinal cross-shaped plans serving to focus attention on the main altar. To Charles Borromeo the central plan was "less used by Christians than the longitudinal plan."

In contrast, in the full baroque there is a decisive return to the central plan, which, however, by treating the wall as an active sculptural surface, maintained and heightened the dramatic focus on the main altar: SS. Martina and Luca; S. Carlo alle Quattro Fontane; S. Ivo, Rome (Borromini, 1642–1650); S. Agnese, Rome (Borromini and Carlo Rainaldi, begun 1652); S. M. della Salute, Venice (Baldassare Longhena, begun 1631); S. M. Egiziaca, Naples (Cosimo Fanzago, 1651–1717); S. Tomaso di Villanova, Castel Gandolfo (Bernini, 1658–61); S. Andrea al Quirinale, Rome (Bernini, 1658–62); S. M. dell'Assunzione, Ariccia (Bernini, 1661–64); S. M. di Monte Santo, Rome (Rainaldi and Bernini, 1662–75); S. M. de'Miracoli, Rome (Rainaldi, 1662–79).

Diffusion in Italy and other European countries. The temporal power of the papacy declined in the last half of the 17th century, and with it Rome's artistic rule. By the end of the century Venice, Genoa, the Piedmont, and Naples became major artistic centers.

Guarino Guarini (1624–83), a Theatine priest who was a follower of Borromini working in Turin in the Piedmont, made the most significant contribution of the last half of the century when, in the SS. Sindone (1667–92) and S. Lorenzo (1666–79), he designed domes that admitted light through spaces left open between intersecting and superimposed arches.

In the early 18th century in Italy in the major centers two separate currents may be discerned. One is a classicizing continuation of the late baroque developing out of late Bernini and the Bernini school (for example, Carlo Fontana, 1634–1714); the other, a freer new current (the rococo) developing most probably from Borromini, emphasizing skeletal structure, verticality, spatial unity, and abundance of light (for example, the late works of Filippo Juvarra [1678–1736] in Turin).

France. In France architecture of the 17th and 18th centuries has been labeled "classic" because of its greater dependence on both the principles of the High Renaissance and the architecture of Andrea Palladio. Baroque classicism is a rational, reserved, and specifically French phenomenon that influenced most north European countries. French architects were not, however, insensitive to the discoveries of the Italian baroque and in restrained and subtle ways capitalized on the dramatic culmination that in both countries was achieved through subordination of parts to the whole, interactions and interpenetration of spaces, and vertical continuity of both structure and mass.

The baroque first appears in France in church buildings that reflect Italian precedent, such as the church of the Sorbonne, Paris, begun in 1635 by Jacques Lemercier (1580 or 1585–1654), who studied in Rome from *c.* 1607 to 1614, and St. Paul–St. Louis, Paris, begun in 1627 by E. Martellange (1569–1641) and completed by François Derand (1588–1644). François Mansart (1598–1666) was the unquestioned master of the mid-17th century in France. From his earliest church (Ste. M. de la Visitation, begun 1632) to his unexecuted project for the Bourbon Mausoleum at Saint-Denis (1664), Mansart shows better than any of his contemporaries the spatial and structural unity of the baroque while both preserving and enhancing the scrupulous purity of the High Renaissance. Mansart's major church, the Val-de-Grâce (begun 1645 but completed later by Lemercier), best shows his cool, restrained, and precise interiors with crisp and finely detailed sculptural decoration executed completely in pale limestone.

The Dôme des Invalides, Paris (1680–91), by Jules Hardouin Mansart (*c.* 1646–1708), is perhaps the best late 17th-century example exhibiting both a continued dependence on the High Renaissance central plan and a sophisticated integration of the spaces of the arms with the domed central space culminating in a frescoed double dome that is illuminated from hidden sources.

Flanders and Spain. Flemish architecture, due to its political ties with Spain and thereby to Italy, was more positively fluid and sensuous than in France and less dependent on the High Renaissance–Palladian tradition.

Jacques Francart (1577–1651; Béguinage church, Malines, 1629) and Peter Huyssens (1577–1637; St. Charles Borromeo, Antwerp, 1615), in collaboration with the painter Peter Paul Rubens (1577–1640), established an important center from which full baroque ideas were to flow in northern Europe. Notable mid-century examples include S. Michel, Louvain, 1650, by Willem Hesius and the Abbey of Averbode, 1662, by Jan van den Eynde.

In Spain, as in Italy, the late baroque developed in two major directions, one free and curvilinear (e.g., SS. Justo y Pastor, Madrid, by Bonavia, 1739–46), indebted to Borromini and Guarini (who built the Theatine church in Lisbon), and the other a rectilinear version (e.g., cathedral, Saragossa, begun 1680, later altered), growing out of both the late 16th-century tradition in Spain and the influence of Bernini. However, there was in Spain a greater emphasis on dramatic spatial and light culminations and on surface texture. José Churriguera (1665–1725) gave his name to an entire style characterized by heavily ornate stucco decoration (Granada, Charterhouse, sacristy interior, 1742–47).

Central Europe. The unstable political situation reflected in the Thirty Years' War was followed by the threat of the expanding Ottoman Empire, and it was not until the Turks were crushed at Vienna in 1683 that energies could be devoted to rebuilding the country. The full baroque with an Italianate flavor appeared in central Europe after 1680, but it was not until the 18th century that independent work was produced. Chief among the late 17th-century architects were Fischer von Erlach (1656–1723), Jakob Prandtauer (1660–1726), and Lukas von Hildebrandt (1668–1745). Fischer and Hildebrandt were court architects; Prandtauer's buildings were chiefly monastic. Particularly noteworthy are Fischer's Collegiate Church in Salzburg (1696) and the Karlskirche, Vienna (1716), Hildebrandt's Piaristen Church, Vienna (designed 1698), and Prandtauer's Abbey of MELK (begun 1702).

Bibliography: General Histories. A. E. BRINCKMANN, *Die Baukunst des 17. und 18. Jahrhunderts in den romanischen Ländern* (Berlin 1915). V. GOLZIO, *Il seicento e il settecento* (Turin 1950). S. F. KIMBALL, *Creation of the Rococo* (Philadelphia, Pa. 1943). H. A. MILLON, *Baroque and Rococo Architecture* (New York 1961). W. WEISBACH, *Die Kunst des Barock* (Berlin 1924). Italy. R. WITTKOWER, *Art and Architecture in Italy, 1600–1750* (Pelican History of Art No. Z16; New York 1958). A. BLUNT, *Artistic Theory in Italy, 1450–1600* (Oxford 1940). C. BORROMEO, *Arte sacra*, ed. and tr. C. CASTIGLIONI and C. MARCORA (Milan 1952). G. DELOGU, *L'architettura italiana del seicento e del settecento* (Florence 1935). T. H. FOKKER, *Roman Baroque Art* . . . (London 1938). É. MÂLE, *L'Art religieux de la fin du XVIe siècle du XVIIe siècle et du XVIIIe siècle* (2d ed. Paris 1951). L. PASTOR, *The History of the Popes From the Close of the Middle Ages*, v. 20–40. J. WEINGARTNER, *Römische Barockkirchen* (Munich 1930). France. R. T. BLOMFIELD, *A History of French Architecture from the Reign of Charles*

VIII till the Death of Mazarin, 2 v. (London 1911); *A History of French Architecture, 1661–1774,* 2 v. (London 1921). A. BLUNT, *Art and Architecture in France, 1500–1700* (Pelican History of Art No. Z4; New York 1953). L. HAUTECOEUR, *Histoire de l'architecture classique en France,* 7 v. in 9 (Paris 1943–57). P. MOISY, *Les Églises des Jésuits de l'ancienne assistance de France,* 2 v. (Rome 1958). Spain and Portugal. G. KUBLER and M. SORIA, *Art and Architecture in Spain and Portugal and Their American Dominions, 1500–1800* (Pelican History of Art No. Z17; New York 1959). Central Europe. E. HEMPEL, *Baroque Art and Architecture in Central Europe* (Baltimore, Md. 1965). J. BOURKE, *Baroque Churches of Central Europe* (London 1958). W. HAGER, *Die Bauten des Deutschen Barocks* (Jena 1942). W. HEGE and G. BARTHEL, *Barockkirchen in Altbayern und Schwaben* (Munich 1938; 3d ed. 1953). N. LIEB, *Barockkirchen zwischen Donau und Alpen* (Munich 1953). N. POWELL, *From Baroque to Rococo* (New York 1959). H. SEDLMAYR, *Österreichische Barockarchitektur 1690–1740* (Vienna 1930). M. WACKERNAGEL, *Die Baukunst des 17. und 18. Jahrhunderts in den germanischen Ländern* (Berlin 1919). Urban history. L. MUMFORD, *The City in History* (New York 1961).

[H. A. MILLON]

Part 8: Eighteenth-Century Europe

European church building of the 18th century manifested those mutations of the classical theme, of both form and style, that had already been established in the high baroque of the 17th century. The dramatic, calculated manipulation of longitudinal and central church plans, the often daring disposition of interior space, the sweeping, formalized modeling of exterior form so characteristic of baroque construction formed a movement that flowed easily into the new century. Initially the unbaroque Palladianism of Italy continued strong in England, while France never quite deserted its formal classical structure. This century saw the mainstream of BAROQUE merge into the extravagance of rococo, which, toward the end, was submerged by the rise of neoclassicism.

Although the 17th century had been one of much intellectual ferment and scientific inquiry, religion itself, despite those differences that disturbed its European community, had not been seriously challenged. In the new century, churches continued to be built—Palladian or Georgian in England, formally classical in France, and rococo in much of the rest of Europe, although there were exceptions to the general rule. The period of the Enlightenment in France preceded the antireligious storms of the end of the century.

Georgian. The life of Sir Christopher Wren, perhaps the last great architect of the Renaissance tradition, spanned the turn of the century. In ST. PAUL'S CATHEDRAL, London (1675–1710), and in his many smaller churches, he influenced the future development of the classical church in both England and America. These churches with their ingenious plans (often a combination of longitudinal and central types), their rich but simple detailing, and their superb towers and spires were eminently suitable to Protestant (Anglican) congregations of the Georgian era. Nicholas Hawksmoor (1661–1736), Thomas Archer (1668–1743), and James Gibbs (1682–1764) continued the Wren theme in a succession of churches remarkable for a restrained interplay of baroque form and space and native English classicality allied with Palladianism.

The standard Georgian church, of which Gibbs's St. Martin-in-the-Fields, London (1722–26), is a typical example, usually has a columnar portico with tower and spire above, and it is most often based on a longitudinal plan; a galleried interior also is not uncommon. A good American example of the type is St. Michael's, Charleston, S.C. (1752–61). The Georgian church has been favored so long by public taste that it is still being erected today.

Rococo. The rococo style induced a general lightening of baroque pomp. Church buildings became more light, airy, and decorative, fluid in form and ambiguous in plan; they are ornamental and buoyant to the point of theatricality or fantasy. In France, where the style originated, rococo art was secular rather than ecclesiastical; and it may be seen best in Germany and Austria, where the new monastery and town churches demonstrated the almost pyrotechnical abilities of such architects as the brothers Asam and J. B. Neumann (1687–1772). The latter's church of Vierzehnheiligen (1743–72) in Franconia, florid and sinuous as it is, is like a splendid sonata, its flowing calculated melody based on subtle oval configurations of a longitudinal plan.

The Protestant Frauenkirche (1726–40) at Dresden (now destroyed) with its oval dome and central plan was a rather more restrained but equally sculpturesque rococo composition.

The rococo also flourished strongly in Spain and Portugal, notably in the work of José de Churriguera (1650–1725) and his followers; the Churrigueresque manner is characterized by an omnipresent rich ornamentation, encrusting and hiding the structure beneath it. The sacristy of the Cartuja (1727–64) at Granada and the façade of the cathedral of SANTIAGO DE COMPOSTELA (1738–49) are good examples; here again construction is lost in thickets of florid ornament. The style was also popular in the New World, as in the sanctuary at Ocotlán, Mexico (c. 1745). Color is added to the polyphonic intricacy of the sculptured detail.

Italy had ceased to be an important architectural center, but the late baroque of that country was still vigorous enough to produce a fine domed church, the Superga (1717–31), near Turin, designed by Filippo Juvara

(1676?–1736), which, although baroque in both composition and execution, has a certain grand simplicity of treatment that makes it one of the best of baroque churches. Although the Italian rococo is charming, as a rule its productions are in no way outstanding.

Neoclassicism. Contemporary with the Enlightenment, an architectural neoclassicism, characterized by a renewed interest in and a closer study of the arts of antiquity (especially those of ancient Greece), made its appearance in France. Even before 1750, the rather severe façade of St.-Sulpice in Paris, constructed (1733–49) after the design of J. N. Servandoni (1695–1766), prefigures the developing preoccupation with the past, while it graphically demonstrates the limited adherence of French architects to the baroque.

The church of Ste.-Geneviève (1755–92) in Paris, secularized at the time of the French Revolution and renamed the Panthéon, is perhaps the finest religious building of the century. Its designer J. G. Soufflot (1713–80) was influenced by the new cult of antiquity, which demanded an architectural sobriety that was the very antithesis of the rococo. The Panthéon with its logical central plan and monumental Roman detail manifests certainly the spirit of the new movement, if not the letter. Soufflot was also sympathetic to English work since his dome has obviously been influenced by that of St. Paul's by Wren.

Soufflot was also acquainted with Gothic architecture, as is evident in the general lightness of construction of the Panthéon. In this final noble religious structure of the century, one may note how various were the sources that fed the broad neoclassical development that continued into the next century. Its dome sums up the grandest phase of 18th-century church building and also provides its epitaph. For the French Revolution, which took from Ste.-Geneviève its ecclesiastical status, plunged all of Europe into a turmoil hardly conducive to church building.

In conclusion, the age of the rococo was not a period of great religious buildings despite the presence of some admirable productions. The 18th-century church gives pleasure; it entertains the aesthetic sensibilities, if not the soul, but it rarely edifies or induces profound religious feeling.

Bibliography: S. SITWELL, *Southern Baroque Art* (London 1924). A. L. MAYER, "Liturgie und Barock," *Jahrbuch für Liturgiewissenschaft* 15 (1941) 67–154. S. F. KIMBALL, *The Creation of the Rococo* (Philadelphia, Pa. 1943). L. HAUTECOEUR, *Histoire de l'architecture classique en France*, 5 v. in 7 (Paris 1943–57). M. WHIFFEN, *Stuart and Georgian Churches* (London 1948). P. KELEMAN, *Baroque and Rococo in Latin America* (New York 1951). S. P. DORSEY, *Early English Churches in America* (New York 1952). H. S. MORRISON, *Early American Architecture* (New York 1952). J. N. SUMMERSON, *Architecture in Britain 1530–1830* (4th ed. Pelican History of Art No. Z3; New York 1963). R. WITTKOWER, *Art and Architecture in Italy, 1600–1750* (Pelican History of Art No. Z16; New York 1958). G. KUBLER and M. SORIA, *Art and Architecture in Spain and Portugal and Their American Dominions, 1500–1800* (ibid. Z17; New York 1959). J. BOURKE, *Baroque Churches of Central Europe* (2d ed. London 1962). N. POWELL, *From Baroque to Rococo* (New York 1959). H. A. MILLON, *Baroque and Rococo Architecture* (New York 1961).

[J. D. VAN TRUMP]

Part 9: Nineteenth-Century Europe

The 19th century, which saw a series of profound changes in Western civilization, as well as its worldwide extension, was also a great church-building age. Many churches were erected to serve the needs of the new urban centers created by the industrial revolution. Contemporary scientific thought was often no friend of religion, but numerous religious revivals—notably the Anglican and Roman Catholic in England—occurred during the period. The century evolved many building types to serve a vast new democratic population and yet remained faithful to the Church.

European architecture at the dawn of the new century was still largely classical, but this final broad deposit of the Renaissance tradition contained within itself strong currents moving outward to form new styles; a complex intermingling of innovations and revivals created a maze of stylistic trends. It was a century of unbridled architectural eclecticism.

The cultural romanticism that historically accompanied the democratic age threatened the classical traditions and eventually weakened them. A preoccupation with the medieval past, already manifested in 18th-century thought, increasingly informed the art and literature of the new century. In architecture the Romanesque and particularly the Gothic revivals were the result of this ferment, but styles remote in time or place—Indian, Chinese, or Japanese—were also favored by the romantics.

Greek revival. The still-dominant classicism at the beginning of the century produced a full-fledged Greek revival that had generally run its course in Europe by 1830, although it did not lose favor in America until 1850. More Greco-Roman than Greek was the church of La Madeleine in Paris, built between 1806 and 1842, after the designs of Pierre Vignon (1763–1828). Originally intended to be a secular Temple de la Gloire, it was converted by Napoleon into a church—the Panthéon situation in reverse.

The severe temple form of La Madeleine also became fashionable for churches elsewhere in Europe and in America; a rigorous adherence to Greek orders—especially the Doric—was generally maintained. Possibly the best Greek revival church in England is W. and W. H. Inwood's St. Pancras in London (1819–22), which is a fine design based on the Erechtheion in Athens. In America, Greek temple forms also prevailed. Perhaps the most successful classical church of the new century in the United States was the domed Roman Catholic cathedral of the Assumption in Baltimore, which with the exception of the later added portico was built between 1805 and 1821 according to the design of B. H. Latrobe (1764–1820). It bears some relation to the work of Sir John Soane in England. As the Greek revival waned, the classicists largely shifted their interest to the Renaissance, but classicism assumed a minor role in the later 19th century as a revived church "style."

Gothic revival. The Gothic revival, unquestionably the most pervasive of the revival styles, had received considerable impetus in England from the Cambridge Camden (later the Ecclesiological) Society, founded in 1839. Of considerable influence also was the work of A. C. and A. W. N. PUGIN, a father and son with a passion for the medieval past and vast knowledge of its Gothic ornament. The classicists did not give up without a struggle, but after the new Houses of Parliament (1840–c. 1865) were detailed by A. W. N. Pugin in the late Gothic and Tudor manner, the Gothic, if it did not entirely win the day, became a potent force in Western architecture. Although much used, the revived Gothic was not quite as important on the Continent as it was in England.

It was naturally adaptable to the building of churches and firmly lodged itself in all English-speaking countries. Moreover, it had a strong literary cast, as can be seen in the influence wielded by the *Ecclesiologist* (founded 1841), the magazine of the Ecclesiological Society, and the books written by many revivalist architects. John RUSKIN (1819–1900) advanced his own Italianate version of the revival. The movement was aided in England by the revivals in both the Anglican and Roman Catholic religious bodies. As in the 14th and 15th centuries, the Gothic again became an international style.

The Gothic revival, through many mutations until its eventual disappearance about the time of World War II, interested a large number of architects. The Pugins reinforced their writing with their practice; they and the Ecclesiologists influenced a notable group of designers, of whom the most original was William Butterfield (1814–1900) and the most popular was Sir George Gilbert Scott (1811–78). The former's All Saints, Margaret Street, London (1849–59) manipulated the Gothic in a fresh if harsh manner, while the latter's Nicholaikirche in Hamburg (1845–63) was an impressive archeological project done with a contemporary flair.

Men of the century were devoted to the archeological restoration of medieval monuments. Eugène Viollet-le-Duc (1814–79) and Sir G. G. Scott were famous for their activities in this field. During the course of the century, many Gothic cathedrals and churches throughout Europe were restored and completed, a notable instance being Cologne Cathedral (1824–80). Meanwhile, on the side of modern technology, cast iron began to be used in churches, as at Saint-Eugène in Paris (1854–55) by L. A. Boileau (1812–96).

Romanesque revival. A Romanesque revival paralleled the Gothic and produced a pre-Gothic style in which Byzantine and Renaissance elements were sometimes mixed. The new style was aptly christened by the Germans as the "Rundbogenstil." This round-arched style is to be found throughout much of Europe and in surprising vernacular manifestations in America. Later in the century, the American architect H. H. Richardson (1834–86) worked in a highly personal Romanesque manner; his best work is Trinity Church, Boston (1873–77), which recalls the Spanish lantern churches of the 12th century. Romanesque-Byzantine style characterized the Sacré-Coeur, Paris (begun in 1874 and largely finished by 1900), by Paul Abadie (1812–44), while Westminster Roman Catholic cathedral, London (1895–1903) by J. F. Bentley (1839–1902) is an impressive building in the Byzantine style.

In America, the two principal early practitioners in the Gothic style were Richard Upjohn (1802–78), whose Trinity Church, New York (1839–46), was inspired by English precedent, and James Renwick, Jr. (1818–95), whose St. Patrick's Cathedral, New York (1858–79) was derived from French sources. The work of both architects was influential on church building in the United States.

All the revival styles of the 19th century were continued well into the 20th century, until they were replaced by the modern ideas following World War II. Perhaps the fantastic, highly original Gothic-derived church of the Sagrada Familia in Barcelona may be taken as the logical outcome of the Gothic revival. It was designed by Antonio Gaudí (1852–1926), who took over its construction in 1884. It is still unfinished; but it is probably, as H. R. Hitchcock has said, the grandest ecclesiastical monument that was produced in the late 19th century.

Bibliography: A. C. PUGIN, *Examples of Gothic Architecture,* 3 v. (2d ed. London 1838–40; repr. 1930–40). A. W. N. PUGIN, *Contrasts: Or, a Parallel between the Noble Edifices of the Fourteenth and Fifteenth Centuries, and Similar Buildings of the Present Day, Showing the Decay of Taste* (London 1836); *An Apology for the Revival of Christian Architecture in England* (London 1843). J. RUSKIN, *The Seven Lamps of Architecture* (London 1907; repr. 1932); *Stones of Venice,* ed. L. M. PHILLIPS, 3 v. (New York 1921–27). C. L. EASTLAKE, *A History of the Gothic Revival* (London 1872). G. W. SHINN, *King's Handbook of Notable Episcopal Churches in the United States* (Boston, Mass. 1889). K. M. CLARK, *The Gothic Revival* (3d ed. New York 1962). B. F. L. CLARKE, *Church Builders of* *the Nineteenth Century* (New York 1938). T. F. HAMLIN, *Greek Revival Architecture in America* (New York 1944). D. R. GWYNN, *Lord Shrewsbury, Pugin and the Catholic Revival* (London 1946). G. W. O. ADDLESHAW and F. ETCHELLS, *The Architectural Setting of Anglican Worship* (London 1948). H. M. CASSON, *An Introduction to Victorian Architecture* (New York 1948). J. N. SUMMERSON, *Heavenly Mansions* (New York 1950). R. TURNOR, *Nineteenth-Century Architecture in Britain* (London 1950). H. S. GOODHART-RENDEL, *English Architecture since the Regency* (London 1953). H. R. HITCHCOCK, *Early Victorian Architecture in Britain,* 2 v. (New Haven, Conn. 1954); *Architecture: Nineteenth and Twentieth Centuries* (2d ed. Pelican History of Art; 1963). P. FERRIDAY, ed., *Victorian Architecture* (Philadelphia, Pa. 1964).

[J. D. VAN TRUMP]

Part 10: Twentieth-Century Europe (1900s–1960s)

Twentieth-century church architecture in Europe was caught in the process of development involving concepts of form, materials, and techniques, as well as cultural changes and growing liturgical awareness. Church architecture in 20th-century Europe was a product of a liturgical and secular renewal, which elaborated in various stages a fresh concept of the Church and of the church building as an ecclesiastical edifice. It employed the most advanced stylistic resources and building techniques. These made possible a new breadth and centripetal articulation of the church interior. A surge of vitality and unprecedented structural ability combined with a rejuvenation of the liturgy through the LITURGICAL MOVEMENT.

The new building materials (iron, concrete, glass) did not of themselves lead to a new church architecture: in France, Anatole de Baudot (1834–1915) had used reinforced concrete, but the new building materials remained at the outset simply a scaffolding for the traditional styles of architecture (St.-Eugène, Paris, 1854, done in cast iron; St.-Jean-de-Montmartre, 1894–1902, with moulded vaults). Open steel construction was used by Astruc in Notre-Dame du Travail in Paris (1899–1901), but it was not until the 1920–24 period that new stylistic use of these building materials was made. The advance occurred when Auguste PERRET designed Notre-Dame du Raincy near Paris, rightly termed the first stylistically modern church in Europe. The altar stands somewhat free on a raised stage, and steel columns support a concrete roof. The exterior walls have abstract light-absorbing ornamentation. Karl Moser, inspired by the Raincy church, created the church of St. Antonius in Basel as early as 1927.

Unfinished concrete was then introduced as a stylistic element and was adopted and developed, despite many difficulties, by Hans Herkommer and Dominikus Böhm

in Germany. In 1928 Otto Bartning erected the first steel church (Evangelical) with stained glass in Cologne. The suitability of new building materials for sacred edifices remained a subject of controversy for a long time.

European architecture began to develop during the period immediately prior to World War II; despite many challenges, the Liturgical Movement gave birth to new growth, especially in Germany. Since the war and right up to Vatican II, church architecture has been given a deeper theological basis and has experienced a great renewal in every European country.

Liturgical Movement. Opportunely, the Liturgical Movement, whose initial impulse had been given in the 19th century, had gathered momentum. It had gained impetus with the new Missal of the Benedictine Anselm Schott, who was interested as early as 1884 in the participation of the laity in the Mass. With the additional influence of Pius X, fresh vitality appeared in the liturgy after World War I. Six million Schott Missals had been printed by 1955. A new attitude and liturgical worship service had sprung up in French and Belgian monasteries, and the awakening extended into Germany as well as in such places as Maria Laach and Beuron.

A liturgical trend in church architecture can be detected from about 1910 in the work of Böhm. Even before World War I he had planned chapels to house the often neglected and marginalized baptismal font, and he moved side altars as far from the principal sanctuary space as possible, to focus attention on the main altar. During World War I, together with the Benedictine-oriented architect Martin Weber, he drafted the first square church interior (1915). The church, which was to be built in Neu-Ulm, was to have apses for the side altars. The architects placed the baptismal font in the middle of the entrance hall, and brought the altar closer to the people on a raised, circular island. The bell tower on the side was incorporated into the design of the main structure.

Problems of transition. Architectural forms and designs were strongly influenced by RAVENNA but modified by contemporary trends. German and Austrian architects (e.g., Otto Wagner) had begun to show concern for more space and a gradual abandonment of overloading. The progress represented by their plans and projects can be properly appreciated only when one reflects on the state of affairs that existed: in central Europe, neo-Gothic was considered to be the one proper form of architecture for sacred edifices. Accordingly, the Catholic cathedral of Cologne, the tower of a Protestant cathedral at Ulm, and the basilicas in Lourdes and Lisieux had all been finished in neo-Gothic style. In 1912 the Cologne hierarchy allowed only neo-Romanesque and neo-Gothic structures for ecclesiastical building. It was in 1927 that the Association for Christian Art in Cologne spoke out against the dominance of the old style, and even then it considered reinforced concrete a building material unsuitable for churches. As traditional styles lost popularity, new building materials developed their own potentialities and suggested new designs for churches. In the transitional period, Böhm developed the technique of laid-on hard wall plaster, especially in vaulting, and created the church of St. Engelbert, Cologne-Riehl (1930). Reinforced concrete, steel, iron, and glass became legitimate building materials between 1925 and 1927. They rendered new ceiling solutions possible and reduced the structural confusion between supporting and space- enclosing elements, between wall and ceiling, thrust and load. The new wide interior with modern design and glass walls began to prevail. A new transparency was added to the breadth of the interior, materializing what Otto Wagner of Vienna had advocated as early as 1895.

In the midst of this transition stood Böhm (1880–1955). His first important designs were executed in 1922 for churches in Dettingen and Vaals (Holland). The latter design, for a Benedictine abbey church, places the tabernacle for the first time in the choir wall; the altar had on it only a cross and candles and was placed in a central location to accommodate the *circumstantes*. He also designed the St. John Baptist church in Neu-Ulm (1926), with its distinct baptismal chapel that influenced later building. After creating the design for Mainz-Bischofsheim (1926), he entered the "Opfergang" competition for the Frauenfriedenskirche in Frankfurt am Main. In this, the largest church architecture competition of the 20th century, Böhm won first prize among 650 competitors, although his design was never realized. His plan called for an enclosed space "with sheer presence" in which the community is led to the impressive place of sacrifice, emphasized by the lighting arrangement. The concept of the altar as central to the Mass had triumphed.

Growth in Germany. New church architecture prevailed in Germany more extensively than in other European countries prior to World War II. Advanced stylistic elements were demonstrated in the Corpus Christi Church in Aachen (1929–30), designed by Rudolf Schwarz (1897–1961). He based his design on the ground plan of the Frankfurt design, on which he had worked as a collaborator with Böhm. The period from 1925 to 1927 was the moment of greatest innovation and stylistic power in German ecclesiastical architecture; churches were built in Bavaria with money that Cardinal Faulhaber had collected in the United States. Such fruitful results were made possible by the earlier work of J. van Acken, by the Liturgical Movement, and by the renewal thought of a portion of the Christians in Germany after World War I. In 1927 *Der Verfall der kirchlichen Kunst* had

been published in Germany. This work, by the Swiss artist Alexandre Cingria, had been published in French in 1917 as *La Decadence de l'art sacré*. It had been welcomed by P. Claudel, who expressed the hope for an encounter between creative imagination, joyous sensuous appeal, and Christianity. Pertinent as his insight was, it was dimmed in the general preoccupation with industrial development and natural science.

In Germany the questions of theology, ideals, form, and material continued to be the subjects of lively discussion. Serious reflection and a new religious attitude influenced architects of many European countries and others in America. Protestants also made intensive efforts to find a genuine church architecture: Otto Bartning was a leader in both his writing and designs. New ideas were being tried by Hans Döllgast, Hans Herkommer, Clemens Holzmeister, J. Krahn, Michael Kurz, Otto-Orlando Kurz, Alfons Leitl, Rudolph Schwarz, Hans Schwippert, and Thomas Wechs.

Meanwhile the Liturgical Movement received impetus from the abbeys of Maria Laach and Beuron, the Quickborn Youth Movement, and such individuals as R. Guardini, J. Jungmann, K. Kramp, and Bishop Landersdorfer. However, it was not unified and gave few direct impulses to church architecture. One feature that resulted from it, however, was a Christocentric emphasis in church plans in which the altar was detached from the choir wall and set on a raised "stage." As early as 1919, Weber and Böhm had proposed, without success, that altars be erected without tabernacles. Frankfurt am Main developed many remarkable churches after 1925. In the church of the Holy Spirit by Weber (1930), the altar was moved toward the middle of the church, so that it could be surrounded by the faithful, and the tabernacle was put onto a pillar. The trend in religious life and preaching was to accent essentials and to eliminate superfluities and accretions. Thus more attention was given to the altar, the font, and the confessional; side altars and statues of the saints were eliminated. The Stations of the Cross were assigned a less conspicuous place. The church was conceived as the spatial envelope for the altar, on which the Eucharist is celebrated, and not any longer the static site of the tabernacle.

Between 1927 and 1933 an impressive series of church designs emerged, such as those by Böhm for Leverkusen-Küppersteg, Hindenburg in Upper Saxony, München-Gladbach, Norderney, and Dülmen. Böhm also transferred the site of the choir, hitherto far off to one side in the west, to the chancel. His leading successor was Schwarz, who defended Böhm's ideas in lectures and writings; he proceeded to design interiors of imposing breadth and height. From 1933, the beginning of the Nazi regime, church architecture declined, and was throttled completely during World War II.

There followed a complete change in the European picture. Between 1933 and 1950, churches were built in Switzerland (chiefly in Basel, Lucerne, and Zurich), designed by Hermann Baur of Basel and F. Metzger of Zurich. These were more centralized churches that brought the congregation closer to the altar. Switzerland became the leader for the whole of Europe.

Church architecture experienced a revival after 1950, since many churches had been destroyed and the many new communities needed churches. Between 1950 and 1965, about 8,000 churches, Catholic and Protestant, were either built or remodeled, and others that had been slightly damaged were renovated.

A Deeper Theological Basis. The oppression of Christians from 1933 to 1945 had chastened and ennobled some of the Christian communities. Not only did they pray the Mass along with the priest, as had been the goal of efforts prior to 1933, but in addition the laity became more conscious of their status (1 Pt 2.5, 9; Rev 1.6; 5.10; 20.6), and their concept of the Church was deepened. The altar was moved even further into the middle of the church, as it had been in primitive Christian worship; the faithful were grouped around the altar on all four sides; and, in the mystery of the Eucharist, stress was laid upon the commemorative sacrifice and the Consecration. Renewed attention was directed to the Trinity and the entire economy of salvation embracing all of time to Judgment Day.

The long rectangular ground plan was almost completely supplanted by short rectangular, square, parabolic, rhomboidal, circular, polygonal, L- shaped, and T-shaped ground plans.

Unlike the basilicas of early Christian churches, 20th-century structures developed on the basis of theological rather than secular considerations. Concepts of the relationship of the assembly to the altar have helped determine the planning of sanctuary and congregational space; the attempt has been to realize liturgical worship within the framework of expanded artistic possibilities.

In the 1960s leading up to Vatican II and beyond, the character of the church building as a community assembly room began to be stressed. Since 1965 celebration of Mass facing the people became the universal norm; the tabernacle has come to be housed more frequently in a chapel; and an area with ambo has been created for the liturgy of the Word. Often a slightly elevated seat is placed behind the altar for the priest. This new attitude, derived from the 1965 decrees of VATICAN II, was realized in the church of St. Helen, Munich, designed by

Hansjakob Lill, the first church in this style since the council. Until about 1950 to 1955, a strictly architectonic cubic interior with large flat surfaces had dominated modern church architecture; but after a few years, perhaps following the precedent of RONCHAMP, a tendency toward organic forms of spatial articulation began to be manifested. Walls and ceiling assumed a flexibility in flowing contours and a great variety of form and combination of materials. The danger arose that church architecture might degenerate into industrial art, and it stimulated discussion of a crisis in church architecture (1963–65). On the other hand, the freedom of articulation enabled remarkable structures to be erected, with the result that Catholic church architecture has attracted and challenged architects and has come to play a leading part in architecture as a whole. It has also engaged the interest of the decorative arts.

Austria. Because of financial difficulties and the strong hold of tradition, the development of a new church architecture in Austria proceeded very slowly. Peter Behrens (1868–1940), summoned from Düsseldorf to Vienna, gave it its first impetus. Apart from a few churches by Holzmeister (b. 1886) and Robert Kramreiter (b. 1905), a disciple of Böhm, examples of new church architecture were few. Innovations began on a large scale only around 1954, even though the Liturgical Movement had been promoted since 1922 by Canon Pius PARSCH (Klosterneuburg). Notable buildings that have been designed include: the church of Christ the King (Gloggnitz, 1963) by C. Holzmeister; Klagenfurt seminary church by K. Holey; structures in Salzburg (1955) and Vienna (1957) by the Group 4 architects; a parish church (Neu-Arzl, Innsbruck, 1961) by J. Lackner; a structural steel church (Donawitz, 1954) by K. Lebwohl and K. Weber; Fatima Church (Graz, 1954) by G. Lippert; Holy Family Church (Kapfenberg-Hafendorf, 1963) by K. Schwanzer; and the chapel of Catholic University (Vienna, 1963) by O. Uhl.

Italy. Italy was more tradition- bound than Austria, but new forces similar to those in Austria began to stir from 1954 onward. The Bologna National Church Architecture Congress was held in 1955 and presided over by Cardinal Lercaro, a promoter of liturgy and art. In 1956 the Centro di Studio e Informazione per l'Architettura Sacra was founded, and a journal was initiated. A study center was established in Milan, where Cardinal Montini (later Pope Paul VI) promoted church building. Consequently, new Italian church architecture flourished in the industrial centers around Bologna and Milan, while Rome remained traditional. The 1957 competition for design of the shrine of the "Weeping Madonna" in Syracuse attracted a large number of talented architects, some of whom produced impressive designs. Church architecture in Italy moved forward aggressively; representative of its progress was the "highway church" of S. Giovanni a Campi Bisenzio, near Florence, designed by G. Michelucci.

Spain. Twentieth-century Spain had in Miguel Fisac a leading architect, the first in Europe to promote "dynamic" church architecture, which was later carried forward in France by Le Corbusier and in Germany by Hans Schädel. The Dominican church of Alcobendas in Madrid, designed by Fisac, is impressive from the liturgical point of view. By the 1960s there had been erected about 30 new churches, mostly rectangular in plan. The university church in Córdoba and the church of St. Rita in Madrid were both erected on a centripetal plan.

France. A number of French painters toward the end of the 19th century (and more in the 20th century) were active leaders in Christian art: O. Redon, P. Puvis de Chavannes, M. Denis, G. Desvallières, and G. Rouault. Church edifices with new building materials were erected in the suburbs of Paris, but the real advancement came in 1922 with the Raincy church designed by A. Perret (*see* RAINCY, NOTRE-DAME DU). Besides being revolutionary in concept, it included windows by Denis and sculpture by E. A. Bourdelle. Many new churches were built in France after World War I, though liturgical and architectural progress was slow. The architect Maurice Novarina designed the church of Notre-Dame de Toutes Graces at ASSY (1938–50). Though less aesthetic on the whole than the later chapel by H. Matisse at Vence, it is exceptional for its decorative elements; it was an effort, inspired by the Dominicans, especially P. COUTURIER, to create a renaissance of sacred art. Jewish and other non-Catholic artists, including atheists and communists, were engaged to produce works along with the Catholic artist G. Rouault. The Assy church includes work by P. Bonnard, M. Chagall, F. Léger, J. Lipchitz, J. Lurçat, and H. Matisse (see W. Rubin, *Modern Sacred Art and the Church of Assy,* New York 1961). Among Novarina's other structures are the parish church at Le Fayet (1939), that at Vongy (1938), and the more significant Sacred Heart Church at Audincourt (1952), which includes a mosaic façade and baptistery stained glass by J. Bazaine, and both stained glass and a choir tapestry by Léger. The stained glass here and elsewhere represented an improvement in the ability of modern architecture to engage the decorative artist (see D. Grosman, in *Das Münster* 9 [1958] 9–10). Architecture had been progressing toward a climax in France for several years in the works of P. BELLOT: Our Lady of Peace, Suresnes, 1934; Benedictine convent, Vauves, 1935; and Immaculate Conception Church, Audincourt, 1935.

After 1939, many circular churches were designed, especially by G. H. Pingusson, for the worker parishes in the "Zone"; the first such designs were realized in Bouts, Corny, and Orsay. A significant thrust forward occurred when Le Corbusier completed the pilgrimage church at RONCHAMP (Notre-Dame du Haut, 1953–55). An astonishing architectural and engineering accomplishment was the ovoid Pius X Basilica at Lourdes (1956–58), designed by Le Donné, P. Vago, and P. Pinsard.

Belgium and Holland. In Belgium, too, a new church architecture has made significant progress since the mid-1950s. Designs for liturgical appurtenances and sacred vessels in particular showed an interesting appropriateness, promoted by the Benedictine Abbey of St. Andrew, Bruges in its journal, *Art d'Église.* In Holland the various Christian confessions have exercised an influence on new church styles, though not to the same extent as in Germany.

Bibliography: H. SCHNELL, *Zur Situation der christlichen Kunst der Gegenwart* (Munich 1962). X. VON HORNSTEIN, *St. Antonius, Basel* (Munich 1936). A. HOFF et al., *Dominikus Böhm* (Munich 1962). R. SCHWARZ, *The Church Incarnate: The Sacred Function of Christian Architecture,* tr. C. HARRIS (Chicago, Ill. 1958); *Von der Bebauung der Erde* (Heidelberg 1949); *Kirchenbau* (Heidelberg 1960). J. VAN ACKEN, *Christozentrische Kirchenkunst* (2d ed. Gladbeck i. W. 1923). O. BARTNING, *Vom neuen Kirchbau* (Berlin 1919); *Vom Raum der Kirche* (Bramsche bei Osnabrück 1958). H. BAUR et al., *Kirchenbauten* (Zurich 1956). For modern Swiss church architecture, see the periodicals *Das Werk* and *Das Münster.* R. HESS, *Neue kirchliche Kunst in der Schweiz* (Zurich 1962). For current reports on German, European, and other church architecture, see *Das Münster,* ed. H. SCHNELL, 6 issues yearly, well illus., the only German pub. in this field, with Eng., Fr., and Span. résumés. For up to 1937, see *Die christliche Kunst* (Munich 1904–37) and the yearbooks of the *Deutsche Gesellschaft für christliche Kunst* (Munich, to 1937, 1951–56). R. GROSCHE, "Überlegungen zur Theorie des Kirchenbaues," *Das Münster* 13 (1960) 344–349. H. SCHNELL, "Der neue Kirchenbau und die Konzilsberatungen," *Theologie und Glaube* 53 (1963) 292–299; "Zur Konstitution des II. Vatikanischen Konzils über Liturgie und Kunst," *Das Münster* 17 (1964) 60–64. General surveys of German church architecture since 1948, in A. HENZE and T. FILTHAUT, *Contemporary Church Art,* ed. M. LAVANOUX, tr. C. HASTINGS (New York 1956), new ed. and illus. as *Neue kirchliche Kunst* (Recklinghausen 1958). R. JASPERT, ed., *Handbuch moderner Architektur* (Berlin 1957), with contributions by W. WEYRES on Catholic church architecture, and by G. LANGMAACK on Protestant. W. WEYRES, *Neue Kirchen im Erzbistum Köln 1945–56* (Düsseldorf 1957). W. WEYRES and O. BARTNING, eds., *Kirchen: Handbuch für den Kirchenbau* (Munich 1959), most comprehensive survey next to *Das Münster.* Exhibition catalogs by H. SCHNELL et al., *Arte liturgica in Germania: 1945–55* (Munich 1956); *Kirchenbau der Gegenwart in Deutschland* (Munich 1960). C. HOLZMEISTER, *Kirchenbau ewig neu* (Innsbruck 1951). R. KRAMREITER and P. PARSCH, *Neue Kirchendunst im Geist der Liturgie* (Vienna 1939). E. WIDDER, *Zeichen des Heils: Kirchenkunst der Gegenwart in Österreich* (Linz 1963). *Das Münster* 8.3–4 (1955) 17.7–8 (1964), special issues. *Der grosse Entschluss* (1946—), monthly, each issue contains a brief contribution by H. MUCK on contemporary Christian art. *Chiesa e quartiere* (Bologna 1957—), quarterly, ed. G. GRESLERI, esp. on northern Italy. *Dieci anni di archittetura sacra in Italia: 1945–1955,* ed. L. GHERARDI (Bologna 1956). *Fede e arte* (Rome 1953—), ed. G. FALLANI. *Can-*

celleria, Vatican art journal. F. MORALES, *Arquitectura religiosa de Miguel Fisac* (Madrid 1960). Survey in A. FERNANDEZ ARENAS, *Iglesias nuevas en España* (Barcelona 1963), illus. *L'Art sacré* (1935–), monthly. *Art chrétien* (1934–), quarterly, illus. surveys of new churches in individual dioceses, with bibliogs. P. RÉGAMEY, *Religious Art in the Twentieth Century* (New York 1963). *Art d'Église* (Bruges 1927–), trimestrally, on Belgian and European Christian art. U. Hård af Segerstad, *Nya kyrkor i Skandinavien* (Stockholm 1962). Surveys on European Churches in F. PFAM-MATER, *Betonkirchen* (Einsiedeln 1948). J. PICHARD, *Modern Church Architecture,* tr. E. CALLMANN (New York 1960). G. E. KID-DER-SMITH, *The New Churches of Europe* (New York 1964). *Christliche Kunst der Gegenwart* (Salzburg 1956–), biennial.

[H. SCHNELL/EDS.]

Part 11: United States (Colonial to 1960s)

In this entry, the history of church architecture in the United States is discussed according to three main periods: colonial and missionary times, the 19th century, and the early the 20th century. Where appropriate, references are also made to historical developments in Canadian church architecture.

Colonial and missionary times. Church architecture in early America shows different influences in the three major areas of European settlement: Canada, which was settled by the French; the Southwest, colonized by the Spanish; and the Atlantic Coast, built up by the English. Gradually, in these sections, indigenous styles evolved.

Spanish Influence. The first Mass in the New World was celebrated in 1494; and as the colonists spread westward, missionary, priests also went, building churches over a period of 300 years in Mexico and regions now known as Florida, Texas, New Mexico, Arizona, Kansas, and California. Influences in Mexico of Spanish baroque, Gothic, Aztec, and Miztec produced buildings of simple basilican form, with thick stone or adobe walls and rich interior decoration. The monastery church in Huejotzingo (1544–71) is an example, but by 1700 the mixture of indigenous styles had produced the flamboyant richness of churches such as Santo Domingo at San Cristobal las Casas, with domes, elaborately carved façade, and ornate interiors. In California, Arizona, and New Mexico, owing to the poverty of the people, the use of adobe for construction limited building to that of squat boxlike structures with low bell towers and roofs of thatch on poles, reflecting the building tradition of the Pueblo Indians. As Spanish baroque influence increased, forms became more elaborate and sanctuary walls more ornate; but there was no counterpart to the elaborate stone carving of Mexican churches. Thus began the mission styles whose later development included churches in California at Carmel, San Francisco (Mission Dolores), and San Juan Bautista; these are buildings with a long history of demolition and

restoration, whose formal influence is still felt on the West Coast.

French Influence. Missionaries in New France built early churches of wood, stone, straw, and poles, from Quebec to the Great Lakes and southward; but by the 18th century they too had developed a style. It originated in the dependence on local materials and climate, in the building craft of Normandy, and in the architectural taste of the Île-de-France. A typical example is the small church of St. Laurent, Île d'Orleans (1708), with its Latin-cross plan, steeply pitched roof, low stone walls, roundheaded windows and doors, and a two-level wooden belfry. This development was attributable also to the efforts of the famed Bishop Laval of Quebec (1622–1708) and the architects Claude Baillief (1635–98) and Jean Baillargé (1726–1805). While New France was still a mission, Laval had many churches built, and from examples such as Lachenaie (1724) grew the restrained exteriors and exuberantly decorated interiors that became popular in 18th- and 19th-century Canada.

English Colonies along the Atlantic Coast. Catholics numbered few among the early settlers, most of whom were either Anglicans or members of dissenting Protestant sects seeking religious freedom. Their buildings reflected their differences in attitude and worship. The Anglicans, keeping a firm tie with the Eucharistic liturgy of the motherland, retained the English hierarchical plan with nave, rood-screen, chancel, choir, table, and lectern. The dissenters, on the other hand, gathered around the pulpit or lectern in an almost square space, emphasizing communal worship and the Word. Anglican churches, like those of England, were of stone or brick, with a bell tower as in St. Luke's, Smithfield, Va. (1682); but the meeting houses were usually clapboarded timber structures, such as the Old Ship Meeting House at Hingham, Mass. (1681), generating a style identified only with America. Later the styles overlapped; St. Paul's, Wickford, R.I., was an Anglican meeting house, and the Old South Meeting House in Boston had a very English (Gibbsian) spire. The establishment of Maryland by Lord Baltimore (a convert to Catholicism) gave immigrant Catholics a base in the colonies, but the successive enactment and repeal of tolerance laws, with alternating freedom and oppression, gave this minority little opportunity for substantial church building. Survival was more urgent, and their first real contribution had to wait 150 years. James Gibbs, in *A Book of Architecture* (1728), spread the formal ideas of English Georgian churches rapidly in North America. The carefully proportioned spires, classical portico, Palladian details, roundheaded windows, and ornate lightsome interiors inspired, among others, Christ Church, Philadelphia (Anglican, 1729–54);

the First Baptist Meeting House, Providence, R.I. (1778); and the Anglican cathedral in Quebec (1804). The last mentioned was modeled on St.-Martin-in-the-Fields, London, a contrast with the French Gothic tendencies of Catholics in New France.

The Nineteenth Century. A wide range of stylistic directions flourished after the American Revolution. Presidents Washington and Jefferson advocated the use of classical Roman and Greek forms in architecture. Gibbs' Georgian flourished in New England with the advent of design manuals, such as carpenters' notebooks by Asher Benjamin and others. At mid-century the Gothic revival stimulated by the work of Augustus Welby PUGIN in England became the accepted ecclesiastical style. H. H. Richardson countered this with a short-lived eclectic Romanesque period in Victorian times. Meanwhile, the steel frame shaped Chicago's secular buildings away from the style of the church, and modern architecture and the skyscraper were born. Vast immigration increased the number of Catholics and the demand for churches. Great Catholic architects emerged.

In 1806 Bp. John Carroll consecrated Benjamin Latrobe's Catholic cathedral at Baltimore, a classical building modeled on the Pantheon, and described by historian Henry Russell Hitchcock as the first masterpiece of American architecture. Bishop Carroll, choosing the most talented architect available, departed from Georgian precedent to develop a liturgical solution in which the choir formed a crescent behind the altar and the great dome united the people spatially with the priest. Many Catholic cathedrals followed with the rapid growth of the Church, and the early ones were decidedly neoclassical with occasional Georgian exceptions. Plans compromised between the architecture of the Anglican Church and the meeting house. The altar, sometimes placed against an end wall lacking even an apse, but clearly visible, reflected, perhaps, the desire for lay participation voiced by Bp. A. MARÉCHAL of Baltimore in 1822 and the earlier plea by John Carroll for use of the vernacular in the Mass (1778). Examples are at Bardstown, Ky., by John Rogers (1816); Old St. Louis Cathedral (1818) by Morton and Laveille; Letourneau's Old St. Peter's, Detroit (1841); and Henry Walters' St. Peter in Chains, Cincinnati (1845). But styles varied across the country, from Pedro Huizar's Mission San Jose in San Antonio, Tex. (1800; Spanish baroque), and the square wooden Russian church at Fort Ross, Calif. (1828), to the Egyptian revival of Minard Lafever's "Whalers' Church" at Sag Harbor, N.Y. (1844); from the "paste-board" Gothic of Notre Dame, Montreal, by James O'Donnell (1829) to the serene classical temple of the First Presbyterian Church at Princeton, N.J. (1836).

Maximilian Godefroy's neo-Gothic chapel for St. Mary's Seminary in Baltimore (1806), contemporary with Latrobe's great cathedral, was the small beginning of a great and widespread stylistic development. In 1846 Richard Upjohn's Anglican Trinity Church, and James Renwick's Grace Church, both in New York, established Gothic as the ecclesiastical style of the day, thus following the English example of Pugin; Upjohn's "rural architecture" provided models for Gothic chapels as far west as California. Further, the Oxford Movement in 1833 and the Cambridge ecclesiologists in 1841 in England stimulated a new interest in the richness of medieval liturgy. The first Catholic response was in SS. Peter and Paul, Brooklyn, N.Y. (1848), by Patrick KEELY, who designed hundreds of churches, including Holy Cross Cathedral, Boston (1867). In 1858 James Renwick built St. Patrick's, New York. The ultimate leader of the movement was Ralph Adams Cram, whose churches from 1890 to 1936, including St. Thomas (Episcopal), New York (1907), the chapel at West Point Military Academy (1907), and the redesign of St. John the Divine Cathedral, New York, illustrated his faith in English Perpendicular Gothic as the perfect frame for the liturgy. The soaring pinnacles and vaults of Gothic, with its long narrow nave, rood-screen, and deep chancel with the choir before the altar, became the symbol of High-Church building in America. Its influence was felt even in such structures as the Jewish temple in Cincinnati (1866).

The great H. H. Richardson established a rival Victorian trend in his neo-Romanesque Trinity Church at Boston (1873), which returned to the semicircular choir around the altar, and his Albany cathedral project of 1882, a trend that Cram denounced as being Low-Church but that many Catholic architects later followed. Toward the century's end, Catholic churches tended in many stylistic directions, Renaissance, Italianate, colonial revival, etc., perhaps because of two factors: (1) the great influx (5 million between 1815 and 1860) of Catholic immigrants of diverse nationalities demanded many new buildings in which costs and expediency took precedence over liturgy or architecture; (2) the activities of nativist groups (the infamous Know-Nothings, etc.) in persecution of religious foreigners generated in the immigrants the desire to be accepted as established citizens and to conform, in architecture, to local fashion. Powerful architecture was readily seen as a status symbol.

The Twentieth century. Frank Lloyd Wright's Unity Temple, Chicago (1906), can be considered America's first modern church, for it departed from axial planning and used nonderivative forms in poured concrete. The First Church of Christ Scientist, Berkeley, Calif. (1912), by Bernard Maybeck, despite Gothic elements, was avant-garde in its space arrangement, its hollow columns containing service ducts, and its creative use of industrial materials. Popular taste, however, had been affected by the neoclassical styles of the Chicago World's Fair (1893) and the plastic baroque of the San Diego exposition (1915), both of which added to the 19th-century stylistic heritage. Early 20th-century Catholic cathedrals were thus Gothic, Romanesque, Renaissance, Byzantine, baroque, and eclectic, the range including Halifax, Nova Scotia, by Cram; Seattle, Wash., by Maginnis and Walsh; St. Louis, Mo., by Barnett, Haynes, and Barnett; St. Paul, Minn., by Masqueray; and Los Angeles, Calif., by Maginnis and Walsh. The early Christian basilica inspired McKim, Mead, and White's Madison Square Presbyterian Church in New York City (1906) and St. John's Catholic Church at North Cambridge, Mass., by Maginnis and Walsh (1905).

The Early Liturgical Movement. A major factor in rescuing church building from the expensive romance with the past was a rising consciousness of the role of liturgy in community worship. The 1903 and 1905 encyclical letters of Pope St. Pius X encouraging greater lay participation in the Mass received little architectural response in America, except in a few remodeled churches of the Paulist Fathers. The later recognition of liturgical study and reform as the key to a new church architecture owes much to the work of the Benedictines in Collegeville, Minn., beginning with Dom Virgil MICHEL, who in 1925 had studied new directions in Europe. The LITURGICAL ARTS SOCIETY, New York, founded in 1928, and the annual liturgical weeks, begun in Chicago in 1940, also helped to develop architecture that recognized the pastoral nature of the liturgy. In addition, the Immigration Bill of 1921 curtailed the influx of European Catholics and allowed the Church more time to reexamine its social, liturgical and architectural situation.

Early response among architects emphasized the visual primacy and accessibility of the altar and the elimination of excessive ornament, as in Barry Byrne's church of Christ the King, Tulsa, Okla. (1927), where the sanctuary projects into a short but wide, column-free nave. This contrasted with the monumentality of the National Shrine of the Immaculate Conception (1928–62) and the neo-Renaissance Trinity College chapel (1928), both by Maginnis and Walsh, in Washington, D.C.

Postwar Years. After World War II there was an urgent demand for churches. New techniques were tried, and experiments in form were launched by a host of talented young architects. Even in the war years, new directions emerged. The elimination of all touches of antiquarianism occurred in three new churches built in 1940 and 1941. Paul Thiry's church of Our Lady of the Lake, Seattle, Wash. (1941), and the Saarinens' Taberna-

cle Church of Christ, Columbus, Ind. (1941), relied on an austere organization of light and proportions in modern structural materials. Even more radical was Paul Schweikher's Third Unitarian Church in Chicago (1940), a brick box whose formal origins were more secular than ecclesiastical. The latter foreshadowed sophisticated developments of the "rectangular box" church in Mies van der Rohe's serene Episcopal Chapel of brick, steel, and glass at the Illinois Institute of Technology, Chicago (1951); Schweikher's own First Universalist Church, Chicago (1956); and Ralph Rapson's Lutheran Chapel for the Deaf, St. Paul, Minn. (1961). Early attempts to ensure maximum lay participation resulted in St. Mark's, Burlington, Vt. (1943), by Freeman, French, and Freeman, a Greek-cross plan with seats on three sides of the altar, the choir on the fourth. A similar early attempt was St. Clement's (Episcopal), Alexandria, Va. (1947), by Joseph Saunders, which has seats on two sides of an axis linking the entry, font, altar, and pulpit. Fan-shaped plans focusing on the sanctuary were used in Joseph Murphy's Church of the Resurrection, St. Louis, Mo., (1954), Maynard Lyndon's Christian Science Church, Los Angeles, Calif. (1956), and Paul Thiry's semicircular church of Christ the King, Seattle, Wash. (1957). All of these exploited the plasticity and freedom of concrete construction. The altar was completely surrounded by seats in Olaf Hammarstrom's square wooden church (Episcopal, 1954) at Wellfleet, Mass., and in C. F. Wright's octagonal church of the Blessed Sacrament at Holyoke, Mass. (1954). Finally, the church became a circular tent at St. Peter's, Linda del Mar, Calif. (1962), by Mario Ciampi, and at the Benedictine priory church, St. Louis, Mo. (1963), by Hellmuth, Obata, and Kassabaum. The latter, a pyramid of parabolic shells, flooding the sanctuary with light, presents a new nonhistoricist symbolism, but poses visual and acoustic difficulties for preachers. New ways of enclosing worship space generated a new concern with formal symbolism. Frank Lloyd Wright's Unitarian church in Madison, Wis. (1951), had a roof modeled on "hands in the attitude of prayer." Barry Byrne's St. Francis Xavier Church in Kansas City, Mo. (1951), and the Stamford, Conn., Presbyterian Church by Max Abramovitz (1958) were shaped like the fish-symbol of the early Christians. Victor Lundy's church designs have been likened to "petals of a giant tropical wallflower" and a "bird about to take flight." Light, as a shaper of space, determined the sophisticated square geometry of Philip Johnson's synagogue in Port Chester, New York (1957), and Louis Kahn's magnificent Unitarian church in Rochester, N.Y. (1962). The desire for an atmosphere conducive to meditation produced Saarinen's small, cylindrical, brick chapel at the Massachusetts Institute of Technology (1959). Form took precedence over liturgy in Walter Netsch's Air Force Academy chapel, Colo.

(1962), where 150-foot spires of aluminum and stained glass enclose a long rectangular nave for Protestants, with Jewish and Catholic chapels beneath. In contrast to this, and earlier, was Max Abramovitz's Interfaith Center at Brandeis University, Waltham, Mass. (1959), where three concrete chapels almost similar in plan, grouped around a pool, emphasize at once the common and different aspects of three modes of worship.

Liturgical Renewal. The diverse forms of the 1950s gave way to more liturgy-conscious designs in the 1960s. A considerable amount of interdenominational study began, helped by the writings of Rudolf Schwarz (Germany), Peter Hammond (England), and Father H. A. Reinhold (U.S.). The 1957 liturgical directives of the Catholic Archdiocese of Superior, Wis., modeled on a 1947 publication by the bishops of Germany, raised new questions about liturgical planning in the light of modern theology and directly influenced the design of St. Anthony's Superior (1960), by Thorsov and Cerny. There the concrete nave was short and wide; the choir stood beside the sanctuary; the pulpit became a simple lectern near the altar; and the font, symbolic of entrance, stood in an ample narthex, which also contained confessionals.

Liturgy was the chief determinant in the planning also of St. Patrick's, Oklahoma City (1960), by Robert Jones, where the glass-walled nave extends visually into a high surrounding concrete-walled atrium providing for overflow congregations. The influence of liturgy in planning is noticeable also in Pietro Belluschi's Episcopal church of the Redeemer, Baltimore, Md. (1960), an elegant cruciform wood structure, whose modern form has vague echoes of the Gothic; Belluschi's Benedictine priory in Portsmouth, R.I. (1962); and Robert Olwell's shallow-domed, circular Greek Orthodox church in Oakland, Calif. (1962).

In Canada, the church of St. Maurice, Duvernay, Quebec (1963), by Roger d'Astons, and the church of the Canadian Martyrs, St. Boniface, Manitoba (1962), by J. Gaboury, show innovation: the celebrant of the Mass faces the people, the choir is near the sanctuary, and there is a separate altar of reservation. St. Rose of Lima Church, Ste. Rose du Lac, Manitoba (1962), by Green, Blankenstein, and Russell, groups people on three sides of the altar in a small square space, an arrangement that follows the new trend in Europe.

Marcel Breuer's Benedictine abbey church at St. John's, Collegeville, Minn., the first modern church to rival the scale and majesty of the 19th-century neo-Gothic cathedrals, grew from strictly liturgical considerations. Its vast folded-concrete structure encloses a sanctuary that visually unites the crescent choir with the congregation. The traditional communion rail is replaced by stations at the head of processional aisles; the ambos, central altar, and abbot's seat are all well positioned to symbolize their liturgical roles. Church architecture in the early 1960s included such widely contrasting types as the Episcopal and Catholic cathedrals in San Francisco. The neo-Norman Grace Cathedral (Episcopal), with its golden replica of Ghiberti's famous baptistery door in Florence and its altar now moved to a central position, was completed in 1964. Belluschi and Nervi's new Catholic cathedral has a diamond-shaped, column-free plan with central altar. Its great prestressed, marble-clad concrete roof-walls twist up to 180 feet in space to form a Greek-cross skylight. The San Francisco cathedral represents an approach far different from the long medieval plan (1954) for the new Baltimore Catholic cathedral by Maginnis and Walsh.

The *Constitution on the Sacred Liturgy* issued by Vatican Council II has since become a prerequisite to the design of Catholic churches. The emphasis on the liturgy of the Word as a clearly defined part of the Mass, the clarification of the choir's role, the stress on the significance of Mass with the celebrant facing the people at Mass, and above all the pastoral and ecumenical overtones mark it as the single document that may ultimately lead to a clearly ordered 20th-century church architecture.

Bibliography: H. S. MORRISON, *Early American Architecture* (New York 1952). W. ANDREWS, *Architecture, Ambition and Americans* (New York 1955; pa. New York 1964); *Architecture in America* (New York 1960). T. F. HAMLIN, *Greek Revival Architecture in America* (New York 1944); *Benjamin Henry Latrobe* (New York 1955). H. R. HITCHCOCK, *Architecture: 19th and 20th Centuries,* (2d ed. Pelican History of Art No. Z15; Baltimore, Md. 1963); *Architecture of H. H. Richardson and His Times* (New York 1936). A. GOWANS, *Church Architecture in the New France* (New Brunswick 1955); *Looking at Architecture in Canada* (Toronto 1958). F. W. KERVICK, *Architects in America of Catholic Tradition* (Rutland, Vt. 1962). D. D. EGBERT and C. W. MOORE, "Religious Expression in American Architecture" in *Religious Perspectives in American Culture,* ed. J. W. SMITH and A. L. JAMISON (Religion in American Life 2; Princeton, N.J. 1961) 361–411. A. CHRIST-JANER and M. M. FOLEY, *Modern Church Architecture* (New York 1962). K. BAER, *Architecture of the California Missions* (Berkeley, Calif. 1958). R. NEWCOMB, *Architecture of the Old Northwest Territory* (Chicago, Ill. 1950); *Spanish-Colonial Architecture in the United States* (New York 1937). G. KUBLER, *The Religious Architecture of New Mexico* (Colorado Springs, Colo. 1940; repr. Chicago, Ill. 1962). J. A. BAIRD, *The Churches of Mexico* (Berkeley, Calif. 1962). T. B. WHITE, ed., *Philadelphia Architecture in the 19th Century* (Philadelphia, Pa. 1953). A. EMBURY, *Early American Churches* (Garden City, N.Y. 1914). R. K. SEASOLTZ, *The House of God* (New York 1963). R. TRAQUAIR, *The Old Architecture of Quebec* (Toronto 1947). A. GOWANS, *Images of American Living* (Philadelphia, Pa. 1964). J. K. SHEAR, ed., *Religious Buildings for Today* (New York 1957). P. THIRY et al., *Churches and Temples* (New York 1953). W. H. HUNTER, *Century of Baltimore Architecture* (Baltimore, Md. 1957). W. W. WATKIN, *Planning and Building the Modern Church* (New York 1951). S. P. DORSEY, *Early English Churches in America, 1607–1807* (New York 1952). R. H. HOWLAND and E. P. SPEN-

CER, *The Architecture of Baltimore* (Baltimore, Md. 1953). H. D. EBERLEIN, *The Architecture of Colonial America* (Boston, Mass. 1915). P. DUELL, *Mission Architecture . . .* (Tucson, Ariz. 1919). M. SCHUYLER, *American Architecture,* ed. W. H. JORDY and R. COE, 2 v. (Cambridge, Mass. 1961). R. A. CRAM, *My Life in Architecture* (Boston, Mass. 1936); *American Church Building of Today* (New York 1929). B. F. L. CLARKE, *Anglican Cathedrals Outside the British Isles* (London 1958). R. C. BRODERICK, *Historic Churches of the United States* (New York 1958). H. W. ROSE, *The Colonial Houses of Worship in America* (New York 1963). P. HAMMOND, *Liturgy and Architecture* (New York 1961). Periodicals, etc. *Documents for Sacred Architecture* (Collegeville, Minn. 1957). *Liturgical Arts,* 1931—. C. D. MAGINNIS, "The Movement for a Vital Christian Architecture and the Obstacles: The Roman Catholic View," *Christian Art,* 4 v. (Boston 1907–08) 1:22–26. W. E. ANTHONY, "The Church of St. Paul the Apostle, New York," *ibid.* 3:101–117. M. SCHUYLER, "Italian Gothic in New York," *Architectural Record* 26 (1909) 46–54; "The Works of Cram, Goodhue and Ferguson," *ibid.* 29 (1911) 1–112.

[P. J. QUINN/EDS.]

CHURCH MEMBERSHIP, U.S.

Numerical summaries of religious affiliation in the United States, besides being of statistical interest, also are valuable as indices of the relative strength, distribution, and culture of various religious populations. In addition, changes over time in the membership and configuration of religious groups help to provide an indication of shifts in the direction of American religious observance and practice. Figures for religious affiliation, then, are an important resource in the social scientific study of religion in the United States.

Sources. An immediate difficulty in assessing American church membership is the absence of a single source for religious demographics. While the federal government issued a series of census reports on religious affiliation in 1890, 1906, 1916, 1926, and 1936, the practice was abandoned after that time following protests to the Department of Commerce that the gathering of such information violated the separation of Church and State.

For Christian churches, the best single source of data after 1936 is annual *Yearbook of American and Canadian Churches* (prior to 1973, the *Yearbook of American Churches*) published by the National Council of Churches of Christ in the U.S.A. The 2001 edition of this yearbook provides listings for approximately 180 different religious denominations. While the *Yearbook* gives a taxative numerical list of religious data including membership, clergy, churches and Sunday schools, it is limited by its reliance on denominational reporting. Figures for a single religious group over a short time span sometimes exhibit wide fluctuations, suggesting that the manner of data collection and reporting is inconsistent. Additional-

ly, some denominations fail to report annually, resulting in the listing of statistics that, in some cases, are more than ten years old. Finally, different bodies define membership differently and even the utilization of two categories for membership does not entirely solve this problem.

For Catholics, the annual *Official Catholic Directory* supplies relatively accurate numbers. This is the result of fairly thorough data collection by individual dioceses and a standard mode of aggregation by the directory's publishers. However, many loosely affiliated Catholics, especially recent immigrants, who fail to register with local parishes remain unrepresented. This problem is of growing concern given the continuing influx of immigrants from Latin America, most of whom come from traditionally Catholic backgrounds.

Estimates of Jewish religious membership must be taken from the *American Jewish Yearbook*. Here, however, affiliation is defined somewhat differently than in the previously mentioned sources. Data on Jewish religious affiliation is much more a "culture count," since the data is approximated from various sources and is not based on the membership rolls of local synagogues. As significant is the failure of the *Yearbook* to indicate affiliation by the major religious groupings of Reconstructionist, Reform, Conservative, and Orthodox. Essentially, the figures provided indicate involvement in some form of Jewish activity, rather than index membership in explicitly religious organizations.

Affiliation figures for other non-Christian groups are estimates at best. While Islam is one of America's fastest growing religions, the absence of any central agency for record-keeping makes data collection difficult. A further problem involves the question of whether organizations like the Nation of Islam are considered to be Muslim for demographic purposes. Similarly, although the American Hindu population has increased dramatically in recent years as a result of immigration, accurate numerical data are hard to obtain. This makes assessment of the entire religious configuration of America extremely difficult.

One recent source is worthy of mention. The result of a nationwide survey of 113,000 Americans conducted in 1990, the National Survey of Religious Identification (NSRI) is the most comprehensive recent study of religious affiliation in the United States. However, its usefulness in spotting religious trends will be limited until there is at least another survey collected in the same manner to provide multiple data points for comparison.

General Observations. To a significant degree, the general contours of American religion have changed relatively little since the mid-1960s. Major denominations continue to be important elements in the religious landscape in the early twenty-first century. In terms of numbers, Roman Catholicism continues to be the largest religious denomination in the United States. The Southern Baptist Convention is the second largest group, as it was in 1965, though by a wider margin than was the case at that time. Among Protestants, other major groups over the last half century have been the American Baptists, Lutheran Church Missouri Synod, United Methodists, Presbyterian Church in the U.S.A., Episcopalians, and United Church of Christ. With the exception of the Missouri Synod Lutherans, all of these are liberal or centrist churches, sometimes referred to as "mainline" denominations. While strictly speaking not Protestant in origin or theology, the Church of Jesus Christ of the Latter Day Saints has also been a major American denomination for over half a century. Two Eastern Orthodox groups also have had significant membership during these years. These are the Orthodox Church in America, largely Slavic in origin, and the Greek Orthodox Archdiocese of North and South America.

Among non-Christian groups, Jews remained the largest at the beginning of the twenty-first century, as they were at the middle of the twentieth. Their actual numbers are hard to determine, however, for several reasons. There was a generally decline in the American Jewish population during the last half of the twentieth century. Moreover, the issue of whether Jewish numbers are determined by ethnic criteria or religious observance exercises a significant impact on ranking. Finally, the rapid growth of Islam in America threatens the Jewish numerical superiority, although accurate numbers here are also difficult to obtain. In all probability, at the beginning of the twenty-first century Judaism continues to be the largest non-Christian religion in the United States, followed by Islam, Hinduism and Buddhism.

Religious Shifts. At the same time, the relative position of various groups within the American religious constellation continues to change. This serves as an index of shifts in the religious perspectives and preferences of the population as a whole.

The Roman Catholic Church continues to exhibit a pattern of growth, with about 62 million members in 2000, compared with about 49.6 million in 1980, and 44.8 million in 1965. Studies suggest that much of this is due to the influx of immigrants from traditionally Catholic countries in Latin America. The higher birth rate within such immigrant communities from lower socioeconomic groups has enhanced this trend.

Within the ranks of American Protestantism, the most obvious growth has been among conservative churches. From a total membership of around 10.4 million in 1965, for example, Southern Baptists had grown to some 15.7 million by 2000. Similarly, the Seventh Day Adventists increased from 346 thousand in 1965 to nearly 840 thousand in 2000, more than doubling their membership. The Church of the Nazarene likewise grew from 342 to 623 thousand during the same period, while the relatively small Church of God (Anderson, Indiana) increased from 144 to 234 thousand.

Arguably, the most dramatic growth in the latter part of the twentieth century was by the Church of Jesus Christ of the Latter Day Saints. With about 1.79 million members in 1965, it had grown to 2.54 million by 1980, and 4.42 million in 2000. This was largely the result of intense missionary activity by the church throughout the United States.

There has also been a notable rise in membership in two Eastern Orthodox bodies. The Orthodox Church in America with 750 thousand members in 1965 increased to 1 million by 2000, while the Greek Orthodox Archdiocese grew from 1.55 to 1.95 million during the same period. In the former case, conversion was a major factor while increased immigration accounted for much of the increase in the latter.

This gain in conservative Christianity has been paralleled by a decline in liberal and centrist groups. The United Methodist Church, for example, has gone from 10.2 million members in 1965 to 8.4 million in 2000, and similar decline can be seen in the Presbyterian Church (U.S.A.). Most dramatically, the Episcopal Church went from around 3.3 million members in 1962 to around 1.6 million in 2000. Other groups experiencing decline have been the American Baptists, Disciples of Christ, and United Church of Christ. Over the course of less than half a century, these denominations, mostly characterized as "mainline," have become significantly less numerically powerful.

Outside the Christian sector, a similar conservative trend is demonstrated by significant changes in America's Jewish and Islamic populations. Decreases in the Jewish population continued throughout the second half of the twentieth century, with a decline of about 10 percent between 1990 and 2001 alone, resulting in around 2.8 million adherents. This largely is accounted for by a declining birth rate and rising number of intermarriages, now over 50 percent. What growth has occurred has been in the Orthodox sector.

During this same period of ten years, however, the American Muslim population grew from an estimated 527 thousand to 1.1 million, a 109 percent increase. In 2001, Muslims accounted for approximately .5 percent of the U.S. religious population. While the estimated number of Jews is still considerably greater, such demographic trends make it likely that Islam will overtake Judaism as America's second largest religious group (after Christianity) during the twenty-first century.

Demographic Differences by Denomination. Within American Christianity, different denominations exhibit varying patterns of attendance, church size, and geographic concentration. These are useful indicators of differing modes of organization and group culture.

In 2001, conservative denominations led in percentage of members attending church weekly. Mormons were first with 71 percent, followed by Assemblies of God (69 percent), Pentecostals (66 percent) and Baptists (50 percent). Conversely, among Episcopalians, only around 30 percent were weekly attenders. Weekly attendance by Roman Catholics was around 48 percent, reflecting the significant gap between those who identify themselves as members of this community and those who practice regularly.

The number of churches and congregants per church varies widely among the ten religious bodies with the most churches in the United States. In 1990, the Southern Baptists led with nearly 38 thousand churches, followed closely by the United Methodists with 37 thousand. Catholics ranked third with around 22 thousand churches, followed by the Churches of Christ, Presbyterian Church (U.S.A.), Assemblies of God, Evangelical Lutheran Church in America, Mormons, Jehovah's Witnesses, and Episcopalians. However, Catholics ranked first in the number of congregants per church with 2, 380. Southern Baptists came in second with 499 and Evangelical Lutherans with 479, while Jehovah's Witnesses (161) and Churches of Christ (128) had the smallest congregations. Especially noteworthy in these numbers is the marked difference between the Roman Catholic pattern of smaller numbers of large parishes compared with Protestantism's dramatically smaller congregational size even in denominations with relatively large numbers of churches and adherents. These likely reflect in part the relative differences in emphases between Catholicism's sacramental focus and the more word-dominant Protestant orientation.

That America's religious populations are not randomly distributed geographically is clear from the numerical data. Catholics, in 1990, were the largest religious body in 36 states. These tended to be clustered in the Northeast, New England, the Midwest, Great Plains, and West Coast, with Rhode Island having the highest percentage of Catholic population (63 percent). Southern Baptists tend to be strongest in the Southern and Middle Border states. Their density is highest in Mississippi, with one citizen in three a church member. Methodists were largely to be found in the Plains States, as well as the Midwest, Northeast, and New England. Only in West Virginia, however, were they the largest denomination, with 10 percent of the population. The Evangelical Lutheran Church in America was strongest in the Upper Midwest, and was the largest religious group in North Dakota (28 percent of the population). Mormons were concentrated in the Inter-Mountain West and West Coast states, with 71 percent of Utah's citizens, and 27 percent of Idaho's, members of this church.

This geographic distribution of religious populations reflects both patterns of immigration and denominational history. American Catholic immigrants, though mainly from rural backgrounds, disproportionately settled in urban centers in the late nineteenth and early twentieth centuries, fueling the nation's industrial development. Their concentration in the Midwest, Northeast, and New England reflects this early pattern. Similarly, Scandinavian immigrants tended to settle in states like Wisconsin, Minnesota, and the Dakotas, resuming the agricultural vocations they had previously undertaken. The concentration of Evangelical Lutherans in this region reflects the ethnic character of the denominations that merged into that church in 1988.

The Southern Baptist Convention was formed in 1845 when American Baptists split along geographical lines on the issue of abolition. This church's name reflects its regional homeland, still a center of its strength. The Mormon migration to Utah in the nineteenth century to avoid persecution made the Inter-Mountain West a locus of church activity. This is seen today in Mormon concentrations in the western part of the Inter-Mountain West, California, and the Pacific Northwest. A large number of United Church of Christ congregations (as distinct from members) in Hawaii is a legacy of intense missionary activity by that church in Polynesia during the nineteenth century.

Geographic clustering is also reflected in the population distribution of America's two most numerous non-Christian religions. Muslims were most frequently found in New York and New Jersey in the East, Ohio, Illinois and Michigan in the Midwest, California in the West and Florida in the South. This distribution in part reflects settlement patterns of Arabs for economic reasons in the late nineteenth and twentieth centuries as well as a desire to locate in climates comparable to those of the Middle East and South Asia. American Jews, on the other hand, were most prevalent in the Northeast, especially New York, New Jersey, Pennsylvania, and Massachusetts, Florida and Maryland in the South, Illinois in the Midwest, and California in the West. The essentially urban character of this religious group is indicated by the fact that the metropolitan areas of New York, Los Angeles, Miami, and

Chicago together accounted for over 50 percent of the American Jewish population. Here again, the relatively greater opportunities for immigrants in urban America during the late nineteenth and early twentieth centuries account for much of the Jewish pattern of settlement in the urban areas of states with large commercial and industrial bases.

Conclusions. Numerical data regarding religious populations in the United States both provide summary indices about specific American faith communities and indicate the general contours of religion in the nation as a whole. Geographic density, church size, and attendance data point out how individual religious groups are organized and give indications about their histories and patterns of initial settlement and expansion. Indirectly, they also help to demonstrate how theological tenets are expressed in concrete demographic arrangements.

Viewed longitudinally, membership data provide a useful indication of shifts within the American religious ecology. Here, the most obvious trend of the second half of the twentieth century and beginning of the twenty-first was the growing strength of conservative religious groups, and the concomitant diminution of ''mainline'' centrist and liberal denominations. Within the Protestant sector, the growth of evangelical and Pentecostal churches like the Southern Baptists and Assemblies of God were illustrative of this conservative impulse. During the same period, more liberal denominations such as the United Church of Christ and Episcopal Church suffered significant declines. The substantial rise in membership within the Church of Jesus Christ of the Latter Day Saints also testified to this trend. Increasing American religious conservatism, too, was indicated in the losses within the liberal sector of Judaism, as well as the dramatic gains made by Islam in the second half of the twentieth century. Data gathered in the 1990s suggest that these will continue to be the directions of religion in the United States well into the twenty-first century.

Bibliography: The results of the National Survey of Religious Identification are published in B. KOSMIN and S. LACHMAN, *One Nation under God: Religion in Contemporary American Society* (New York 1993). Glenmary Research Center, *Churches and Church Membership in the United States, 1990* (Atlanta 1992).

[F. M. PERKO]

CHURCH OF THE BRETHREN (DUNKERS)

Also known as Schwarzenau Brethren, German Baptists, and historically, as Taufer, Tunkers, Dompelaars, and Dunkards. The Brethren immerse the kneeling candidate for baptism three times forward in the water; their popular name is derived from the German word *tunken* which means to dip or immerse.

The Brethren movement originated in 1708 at Schwarzenau, Germany, as part of the Pietistic-Anabaptist protest against the established Lutheran and Reformed churches (*see* PIETISM; ANABAPTISTS). Seeking less formalism and dogma and more warmth in religion, they emphasized study of the Bible and right living. Their leader, Alexander Mack, Sr. (1679–1735), was baptized by trine immersion and in turn baptized seven companions in the same manner. When the early Brethren were persecuted in their homeland, some fled to Holland and eventually to the Germantown area in Pennsylvania; others came directly from Germany to America. The first Dunkers came to American shores in 1719, and Mack himself arrived with additional families in 1729.

In the 19th century, the Schwarzenau Brethren movement split into three groups. The first was the Old German Baptist Brethren or Old Order Brethren who objected to the liberalism of the other Brethren and established their own organization in 1881. They oppose missions, Sunday schools, a salaried ministry, and church-operated schools, and still wear plain garb. The Old German Baptist Brethren are found principally in Ohio and Indiana. A second group of Brethren, known as the Progressive Brethren, objecting to certain traditions and to the church's alleged disinterest in education, left in 1882. Calling themselves the Brethren Church, they preferred an Arminian to a Calvinist theology. In 1939 the Progressive Brethren split into two groupings. The splinter group called themselves the Fellowship of Grace Brethren Churches and favored Calvinism. The third group were the moderates who were left after the Old Order and the Progressive broke away. They are known as the Church of the Brethren.

Until recently most Brethren remained farmers; the largest concentration of adherents is still in Pennsylvania. They oppose participation in war, oaths, and secret societies. For many years the Brethren spoke only German and until around 1900 wore a distinctive, plain garb; the women were expected to wear veils in church. They reject creeds and follow only the New Testament. Parts of the Old Testament are rejected since they uphold war, slavery, divorce, and the idea of revenge. Its headquarters and publishing house are in Elgin, Ill.

The church follows a theology similar to that of the mainstream Protestant denominations. Although it baptizes by trine immersion, it now receives into its fellowship Christians who have been baptized in other ways. It recognizes four ordinances: baptism, the Lord's Supper, anointing of the sick, and imposition of hands on Christian workers. The love feast, observed once or twice a year, includes an evening fellowship meal, the foot-washing rite, and communion; many congregations hold additional communion services at other times. Voting delegates from each congregation meet for the annual conference, the church's highest authority. The church belongs to the National and World Councils of Churches.

Bibliography: H. A. KENT, *250 Years Conquering Frontiers: A History of the Brethren Church* (Winona Lake, Ind. 1958). F. MALLOTT, *Studies in Brethren History* (Elgin, Ill. 1954). D. F. DURN-BAUGH, comp. and tr., *European Origins of the Brethren: A Source Book on the Beginnings of the Church of the Brethren in the Early Eighteenth Century* (Elgin, Ill. 1958, 1986). D. F. DURNBAUGH, *Brethren Beginnings: The Origin of the Church of the Brethren in Early Eighteenth-Century Europe* (Philadelphia 1992). C. F. BOW-MAN, *Brethren Society: The Cultural Transformation of a "Peculiar People"* (Baltimore 1995). D. F. DURNBAUGH, *Fruit of the Vine: A History of the Brethren, 1708–1995* (Elgin, Ill. 1997).

[W. J. WHALEN/EDS.]

CHURCH OF THE NAZARENE

One of the largest of the HOLINESS CHURCHES formed (1908) as a separate church by the union of several small pentecostal groups. Although most of these were originally METHODIST congregations or missions founded under Methodist auspices, holiness evangelists of the Ohio Yearly Meeting of Friends were influential also in originating the Church of the Nazarene.

The principal bodies involved in the 1908 merger were the Church of the Nazarene, with headquarters at Los Angeles, Calif.; the Association of Pentecostal Churches of America, centered at Brooklyn, N.Y.; and the Pentecostal Mission of Nashville, Tenn. Missions to the unchurched in the slums of newly urbanized America were one of the first fruits of the holiness movement in this country. The Peoples' Evangelical Church at Providence, R.I., founded in 1887, became the nucleus for the Central Evangelical Holiness Association formed in 1890 of holiness missions in industrial towns in Massachusetts and Rhode Island. About the same time William Hoople and Charles BeVier established the Utica Avenue Tabernacle in Brooklyn, uniting first with other New York congregations and then with the New England group to form (1896) the Association of Pentecostal Churches. The years 1888 to 1894 saw the holiness advocates steadily losing ground in Methodism. Phineas Bresee, removed as presiding elder by Bp. John H. Vincent in 1892, established a mission at Peniel Hall, Los Angeles, in 1894. Further difficulties led to its separation from Methodism and the founding (1895) of the Church of the Nazarene. The Pentecostal Mission at Nashville, led by B. F. Haynes and J. O. McClurkan, began negotiations for

union with the Church of the Nazarene in 1901. Other independent congregations in the South, including the New Testament Church of Christ formed by Robert L. Harris, and the Holiness Association of Texas, both originally Methodist, merged in 1905 to form the Holiness Church of Christ. In 1907 the Church of the Nazarene and the Brooklyn Association churches united and in 1908 union was completed with several small southern bodies, including the Holiness Church of Christ. The Nashville group joined the others only in 1915 after protracted negotiations. The Middle West then became the scene of intense missionary work and rapid growth in membership. Differences over the meaning of baptism and other issues led to the secession of Seth C. Rees and a California congregation in 1917, and financial problems led to much greater centralization after 1923. The Church of the Nazarene established (1904) a Spanish-speaking mission in Los Angeles, the precursor of many home missions to minority groups. Its foreign mission work began in Africa (1907) and was extended to Mexico (1919) and Peru (1917) and later to most parts of the world.

The Church of the Nazarene claims to be the largest denomination in the Wesleyan-Arminian theological tradition. The original creedal statement drawn up at Los Angeles in 1895 stressed the Unity and Trinity of God, the inspiration and sufficiency of the Scriptures, man's fallen nature, Christ's atonement, the work of the Holy Spirit in conversion, and sanctification by faith. In the tradition of the holiness movement, Nazarene theologians have emphasized the crisis and process of sanctification, seeing it as an instantaneous experience, a second religious crisis after conversion, in which the Christian is cleansed from inner sin by the sanctifying baptism with the Holy Spirit. Nazarene services, whether "evangelistic" or "worship" services, are always open to demonstrations of praise or zeal; their ritual and sacramental observances are simple and allow for freedom of spirit.

In its tradition, the Church of the Nazarene is democratic. Congregations retain a large measure of independence, although its missionary, educational, and publishing activities have been centralized since 1911. In polity, as in worship, it is close to Methodism; its superintendents are similar to Methodist bishops. The Church of the Nazarene has always been opposed to use of liquor, tobacco, and dancing, as well as various other kinds of worldliness and adornment.

Bibliography: C. T. CORBETT, *Our Pioneer Nazarenes* (Kansas City, Mo. 1958). T. L. SMITH, *Called unto Holiness* (Kansas City, Mo. 1962). W. PURSIKER, *Conflicting Concepts in Holiness* (Kansas City, Mo. 1958); G. V. NOTE, *The People Called Nazarenes: Who We Are and What We Believe* (Kansas City, Mo. 1983).

[R. K. MACMASTER/EDS.]

CHURCH PROPERTY

The history of Church property is considered here according to the following periods: (1) the first three centuries (to 313); (2) the Christian Roman Empire (313–c. 500); (3) the Middle Ages (c. 500–1500); (4) the modern world (c. 1500 to the present).

First Three Centuries (to 313). To maintain its worship and its charitable activities, the Christian Church from its origins acquired, administered, and distributed property. Even before the death of Christ, the Apostles had accepted donations (Lk 8.3) and had kept a common purse (Jn 12.6). Christ Himself had directed His Apostles to be unstinting in their charity (Lk 6.29–30) and told them that they in turn could expect to be supported by those to whom they ministered (Mt 10.10; Lk 10.7). After Pentecost, the first converts in Jerusalem sold their possessions (Acts 2.45), gave the price to the Apostles, and "distribution was made to each according as anyone had need" (Acts 4.34–35). This passage was frequently cited with admiration by later ecclesiastical writers, but the communistic regimen it describes seems in fact to have been limited to the Church in Jerusalem. Christians in Antioch (Acts 11.29) and in the provinces of Galatia (1 Cor 16.1–2), Macedonia (2 Cor 8.1), and Achaia (2 Cor 9.2) evidently retained private means, as they were exhorted to be generous in giving help to their impoverished brethren in Jerusalem. The same passages, however, leave no doubt that the obligation to support their own and sister churches rested upon all Christians. Tertullian (*Apol.* 38), writing in 198, described how Christians often paid to their churches a regular voluntary tax (*stipes*) proportionate to their wealth. This *stipes* was probably analogous to the *qorbānîm* paid by Jews to their synagogues.

Ecclesiastical possessions initially consisted of movables—the sacred vessels used in worship, the liturgical oblations made by the faithful at the Christian services, and the charitable donations in kind and money to be distributed among the poor. Tertullian mentions an *arca,* or treasury, in which the community's valuables were kept.

It is uncertain when the churches first acquired real property. Christians seem to have worshiped in private homes and buried their dead in private cemeteries until about 200. In the *Life* (ch. 49) of Alexander Severus (d. 235), attributed to Lampridius and preserved in the *Augustan History,* a Christian community is mentioned as the collective owner of its place of worship. The edict of Emperor GALLIENUS in 257–258 (Eusebius, *Hist. Eccl.* 7.13), ending a persecution of the Christians, stipulated that their cemeteries should be restored to them. In a discussion of Church property from the first half of the 3d century, ORIGEN (*Patrologia Graeca* 13:1696–97) used technical terms—*dispensator,* or administrator, of real

properties, *redditus* or ground rents—that make it almost certain that churches by then possessed income-producing lands. By the late 3d and early 4th centuries, similar references to ecclesiastical property became clearer and more numerous, leaving no doubt that the churches were landlords even before the conversion of Emperor CONSTANTINE I.

The precise juridical title by which the often persecuted churches held their properties has long puzzled historians. In 1864 G. B. de ROSSI ingeniously suggested that the churches enjoyed the status of Roman funeral colleges (*collegia tenuiorum*), to which Roman law conceded the capacity to own property. Rossi's thesis has been much criticized, chiefly because the Christian churches greatly differed from the funeral colleges in their internal organization and purpose. Recent research, however, has tended to favor his interpretation. The Roman state, viewing the churches from the outside and having little accurate knowledge of their internal constitution and purposes, may well have considered them analogous to the familiar *collegia tenuiorum* and, between persecutions, conceded them a right to hold property. It is also likely that ecclesiastical possessions were assimilated to the sacred property, the *res sacrae et religiosae* of Roman law (Gaius, *Inst.* 2.2–9), which meant that they could not be alienated or restored to secular purposes.

The Apostles were initially responsible for the administration of ecclesiastical possessions of the Church of Jerusalem, though they appointed seven DEACONS to relieve them of the burden (Acts 6.1–6). According to later sources, full authority over the possessions of each church fell to its bishop. JUSTIN MARTYR (1 *Apol.* 67.12), writing about 150, described the "president" or bishop of the community as receiving and distributing the donations of the faithful. St. CYPRIAN (*De Lapsis,* 6) condemned bishops who used Church property for their private interests. In other words, well before the conversion of Constantine, supreme and unrestricted authority over a church's property rested with its bishop, although his personal possessions were sharply differentiated from those of his church.

The Apostles and the bishops were aided in administering property by the deacons, already mentioned in Acts 6.9. The deacons had similar responsibilities according to the DIDACHE (A.D. 80–90; 15.1–2) and the writings of IGNATIUS OF ANTIOCH (A.D. 110–117; *Ad Trallesios,* 2–3). The 4th-century *Legend* of St. LAWRENCE, the deacon of the Church of Rome martyred in about 268, recounts how a pagan judge ordered the saint to produce the treasures he, as deacon, was known to possess (he foiled his persecutors by producing the Church's poor).

By the 3d century, Origen mentioned a still more specialized officer: the *dispensator* or *oikonomos*, responsible for the administration of real property.

Donations and revenues maintained worship, supported Church officials, and aided the poor. St. Paul had insisted upon the right of those who ministered to churches to be supported by them (1 Cor 9.13–14), and widows too were to be maintained by the churches (1 Tm 6.3–18). Justin Martyr (1 *Apol.* 67) mentions as recipients of aid orphans, captives, travelers, and the poor.

No estimate can be given of the extent of Church property in this early period, but undoubtedly it remained small. Still, the fact that these often persecuted churches were able to acquire and manage property, maintain a budget, and support their religious and charitable services within a hostile social milieu is no small tribute to their dedication, energy, and precocious administrative skill.

Christian Roman Empire (313–c. 500). The so-called Edict of Milan (313) and the official establishment (380) of the Christian Church within the empire affected its property holdings in three ways. Ecclesiastical wealth, particularly in land, grew enormously. The historic patrimony of the Church, functioning as a major factor in economic and social history, must be considered the product of the 4th and 5th centuries. Church property also acquired a clarified, standardized, and privileged juridical status throughout the empire. And the churches themselves developed more specialized and effective administrative offices and techniques in managing their enlarged endowments.

Through the generosity of the Christian emperors and the growing numbers of the faithful, the patrimonies of such ancient and honored churches as ROME, ALEXANDRIA, ANTIOCH, CARTHAGE, and Milan soon reached prodigious size. The Roman church owned lands and estates scattered over the Mediterranean world from Syria and Egypt to Gaul. On the other hand, churches in such newly Christianized areas as Gaul seem to have possessed only modest holdings. No estimate can yet be made as to the extent of ecclesiastical land. It undoubtedly varied among regions, but it was substantial in its totality.

By the 5th century, the churches were also fully recognized as corporate persons before the law, able to acquire and manage property without impediments or restrictions. Their holdings were also privileged. The emperors of the early 4th century exempted them from the property tax (*Codex Theodosianus* 16.2.15), from the *annona* or grain requisition (*Codex Theodosianus* 11.1.1), and from the obligatory services or *corvées* known as the *munera sordida*. These and other privileges, many of which are preserved in Book 16 of the Theodosian Code, served as a precedent and model for the Church's later claims to tax immunities and exemptions.

While the bishop's personal possessions were rigorously distinct from those of his church, he still exercised almost absolute control over his church's holdings. He directly administered all ecclesiastical properties within his diocese and collected all the revenues from them. This almost modern system of financial administration—based upon a unified patrimony, single budget, and salaried clergy within each diocese—reflected the favorable economic conditions of the late empire, notably the still lively commercial exchange and abundance of money.

Although he was the supreme administrator, the bishop was supposed to conform to a growing number of regulations set by councils, emperors, and popes, concerning his use of property. According to the Council of Antioch (ch. 24 and 25; A.D. 332–341), bishops were forbidden to alienate their church's holdings. In a famous decretal of 494, Pope GELASIUS I (*Ep.* 14.27) advised the bishops of Lucania to retain one-fourth of their revenues for themselves and to spend one-fourth for the clergy, one-fourth for buildings, and one-fourth for charity (for *clerus, cultus,* and *caritas*). Churches in Gaul and Spain followed slightly different formulas for allocating revenues, these having been defined by the councils of Agde (ch. 36; A.D. 506) and Braga (ch 7; A.D. 563). But churches everywhere devoted a substantial part of their revenues to social and charitable services, in fact, completely relieving the state of responsibility for them. The social service of the churches has been and is one of the major justifications for ecclesiastical wealth.

Administrative offices also developed greatly under the Christian Empire. From the 4th century, the ARCHDEACON assumed the role of the bishop's chief lieutenant in property administration, and he continued to fulfill this function in the Middle Ages. Widely in the East and occasionally in the West, the *oikonomos* also served as property administrator. Another clerical official, the *defensor ecclesiae* is mentioned in 452 (*Novellae* of Valentinian, 35 in *Codex Theodosianus*), and such "defenders" were still the chief administrators of the patrimony of the Roman Church under GREGORY I the Great (590–604); 14 of them are mentioned in his letters. Lay *defensores,* responsible for defending churches in lawsuits and suggestive of the later medieval *advocatus,* are cited in 407 (*Codex Theodosianus* 16.2.38) but disappear after 438; their historical importance is that they represent an early penetration of laymen into the ecclesiastical administration.

The 4th century witnessed also the first protests concerning ecclesiastical wealth. On moral and religious grounds, critics such as LUCIFER OF CAGLIARI were already condemning the luxurious living of many clergymen. The pagan AMMIANUS MARCELLINUS (*Rer. gest.* 27.3.14) similarly castigated clerical affluence. Even the Christian emperors, faced with mounting fiscal needs, curtailed some of the ecclesiastical tax exemptions in the 5th century (*Codex Theodosianus* 16.2.40; 5.3.6; *Corpus iuris civilis, Codex Iustinianus* 1.2.11), though the privileged status of Church property was never fully abrogated. The age of the Christian Roman Empire, in other words, bequeathed to the Middle Ages not only a large and well administered ecclesiastical endowment, but also the tenacious social and moral problems connected with it.

Middle Ages (*c.* 500–*c.* 1500). The patrimony of the churches was profoundly affected by the new economic, social, political, and intellectual conditions of the Middle Ages, and in its turn it greatly influenced the course of medieval history. The decline of commercial exchange and the growing scarcity of money in the early Middle Ages no longer permitted the support of the clergy of each diocese through salaries paid by the bishop. Just as lay lords had to maintain their dependents through direct grants of land (fiefs), so the bishops from at least the early 6th century were distributing from their formerly unified patrimonies grants of land, called *beneficia* or *precaria.* The recipient of a benefice enjoyed the usufruct, or income, from the property granted him; but he could not alienate it, and with his death it was supposed to revert to the bishop. The ecclesiastical patrimony also was divided through the need to establish and support rural churches as Christianity, originally urban, spread through the countryside. From about the 4th century in Italy and from the 5th in Africa, Gaul, and Spain, local churches were acquiring and holding their separate patrimonies. Like the benefice, the endowments of local churches remained under the bishop's supreme, if often remote, supervision.

From the 5th century too, monasteries held their own separate endowment. From the 7th century on, many of the great monasteries were able to obtain from kings, emperors, popes, and the bishops themselves partial or complete exemptions from episcopal supervision. From the 9th century, even the bishop's own cathedral clergy acquired a distinct endowment. The portion of the church's lands set aside for the support of the chapter was called a *mensa,* or table. The canons might keep it integral, living a common life by the income it provided; or they might divide it among themselves as separate prebends or livings. Exactly comparable to this separate table, and likewise dating from the early 9th century, were the portions, similarly called *mensae,* set aside from monastic patrimonies for the support of the monks (as distinct from the abbot). Similarly too, the monks might keep their

mensa unified. But by the late Middle Ages the practice developed of providing separate livings for the great monastic officers (the obedientiaries) and even for the monks themselves. This clearly abusive practice was hard to reconcile with the Benedictine ideal of individual poverty.

Feudalism. An even more serious threat to episcopal authority was the extension, in the early Middle Ages, of the PROPRIETARY CHURCH. This was a church owned by a layman (frequently its founder), who exercised a quasi-episcopal authority over it. He supervised and managed its endowment, appointed the priest who served in it, and often collected fees for the spiritual services performed. The proprietary or private church was once thought to be a specifically Germanic institution, but it is now recognized as common to Latins, Germans, and even Greeks, and is peculiarly a product of the economic and juridical conditions of the early Middle Ages.

The development of the tenurial system of FEUDALISM also confused ecclesiastical and lay property and often subordinated churches to laymen or lay interests. Bishops were inevitably drawn into the feudal hierarchy; they gave and received fiefs to such an extent that historians sometimes speak of a "feudalization" of the Church and its endowment in the early Middle Ages. Laymen also came to exercise extraordinary authority in the administration of supposedly ecclesiastical property. The lay *advocatus* or *avoué,* for example, of the Carolingian Age, acted as a kind of policeman upon ecclesiastical estates, defended the churches in lawsuits with outsiders, and often claimed exorbitant payments for his services.

Because so much of the ecclesiastical revenue was diverted to laymen, it is difficult to calculate exactly the extent of Church property in the Middle Ages, although a rough estimate can be made. In the age of the barbarian kingdoms (6th and 7th centuries), the churches and monasteries effectively owned—in the sense of claiming the major portion of rents—about 10 percent of the land, and exercised a shadowy lordship over considerably more. Under the Carolingian rulers, Church property seems to have grown considerably, reaching 33 percent, probably its peak, by the late 9th century. The chaos of the 10th century was accompanied by extensive pillaging of the Church's property, reducing it by the early 11th century to about 20 percent. The great religious revival of the 11th century, which climaxed in the GREGORIAN REFORM, effected a partial recovery, raising the percentage to about a quarter of Europe's cultivated lands. From the mid-12th century, the portion of ecclesiastical property became largely stabilized and even slightly declined, reflecting growing lay opposition to its continued growth and, perhaps, a cooling of ardor among the faithful. In the later Middle Ages, after the black death (1348), the increase of lay piety brought another increase, but HOSPITALS and confraternities (many of which remained under effective lay control), rather than churches or monasteries, benefited.

Successes and Failures. The history of ecclesiastical property is intimately connected with both the successes and failures of the medieval Church. Ecclesiastical estates made a major contribution to the economic growth of Europe, particularly in the early Middle Ages. In a barbarous and socially chaotic period, ecclesiastical managers were literate, disciplined, relatively enlightened, and able to take advantage of the administrative continuity and enlarged resources that community ownership made possible. Monks such as the CISTERCIANS were the great practitioners of farming in the Middle Ages. On the other hand, these same characteristics of ecclesiastical management—discipline, conservatism, rigidity, and engagement with other concerns—were to prove obstructive to economic progress in the more stable society and buoyant economy of later periods. Meanwhile, monasteries served as early centers of credit in the countryside, and the military-religious order of the TEMPLARS, founded in the course of the CRUSADES, was a pioneer in banking. The history of medieval banking and taxation is, in fact, inextricable from the history of ecclesiastical finance. Moreover, the Church's rich endowment alone provided for the medieval community its hospitals, orphanages, and social services. And it can never be forgotten that ecclesiastical wealth made possible those magnificent achievements of medieval culture—the CATHEDRALS, universities, and systems of thought they engendered.

But ecclesiastical wealth also cast shadows over the moral and spiritual life of the medieval Church. There was acute maldistribution of ecclesiastical revenues; inadequate support for the lower clergy led many of them to exploit their sacramental powers for material profit; extravagant revenues went to the great prelates and abbots; and there was a growing institutional paralysis in correcting the imbalance. The splintering of the ecclesiastical endowment and the erosion of episcopal authority introduced chaos into property administration. Up to the 11th century, lay owners of private churches and lay overlords and vassals were chiefly responsible for diverting the revenues from the priests who served the people to other uses. The Gregorian Reform of the 11th century sought with no little success to free the Church from this pernicious lay domination. Meanwhile, the private churches themselves survived. Many were acquired and retained by monasteries, which monopolized their revenues and appointed miserably paid vicars to serve in them. Laymen often retained rights of advowson or presentation over parochial churches, assuring them of a

strong and not always beneficent influence over clerical appointments. Furthermore, by the late Middle Ages the practice was widespread of delivering monasteries and abbeys to laymen *in commendam;* the laymen were supposed to protect the interests of the commended institutions, but they often ruined them. The increase in the number of commended abbeys seemed a resuscitation of the private church, and the familiar evils associated with this were resuscitated too (*see* COMMENDATION).

While the Gregorian Reform curtailed without entirely eliminating direct lay control over the Church, episcopal supervision continued to be obstructed and ecclesiastical discipline threatened by the unrestrained growth of exempt monasteries, chantries, collegiate churches, and hospitals. Since the bishop was unable and often unwilling to maintain discipline, such characteristic abuses as pluralism (the simultaneous holding of several benefices) and absenteeism proliferated; income was thereby diverted from the support of the people's ministers to those who contributed nothing to their spiritual welfare.

Unfortunately, the growth of papal taxation must be recognized as a major factor in this breakdown of clerical discipline. To be sure, the medieval PAPACY was slow to emerge as a financial power, and the amount of its revenues has often been grossly exaggerated. As late as the 12th century, papal income from all over Europe seems to have amounted to a paltry 810 silver marks, whereas at the same time, Normandy and England together provided their common ruler 85,000 marks. Papal revenues on the eve of the Reformation amounted to only 450,000 ducats—well below the contemporary income of the Kingdom of Naples.

The Holy See, which assumed primary responsibility for financing the crusading movement while simultaneously pursuing a great-power policy in Europe, was for most of the Middle Ages severely strapped for funds. But rather than curtail its aspirations, it took to exploiting its spiritual authority for fiscal ends. The age of papal fiscalism was the period of the AVIGNON PAPACY (1305–77). and its greatest architect was Pope JOHN XXII (1316–34). Papal taxation developed with extraordinary rapidity and complexity. The popes imposed a variety of claims whenever a benefice changed hands: the *spolia* or the inheritances of bishops who died intestate; vacancies or revenues from unoccupied benefices; ANNATES or common services, from one third to one half of the first year's revenue of a benefice; expectancies or fees paid for appointment to benefices not yet vacant. Exemptions and dispensations from canonical obligations, chancery fees, TITHES, and traffic in INDULGENCES were exploited in unseemly fashion for revenue. Many of these claims the

Holy See had to dispute or share with bishops and even kings, and given the difficulties of collection, only a small portion of the revenues ever reached Rome. But the mounting fiscalism weighed heavily upon the lower clergy, angered laymen who resented the flow of bullion to Rome, promoted an often virulent anti-clericalism, undermined episcopal authority, and disrupted ecclesiastical discipline.

The Critics. With growing abuses came growing criticisms. Such thoroughly orthodox writers as PETER DAMIAN in the 11th century, BERNARD OF CLAIRVAUX and PETER CANTOR in the 12th century, DOMINIC in the 13th century and ALVARO PELAYO in the 14th century were unsparing in their denunciations of lax clerical morality associated with excessive clerical wealth. In the tradition of secular letters, the goliards and other satirists of the 12th century, later humanists such as ERASMUS, pilloried the fiscal interests and devices of the Roman Curia. Ominously, ecclesiastical wealth attracted the violent strictures of heretics: the ALBIGENSES, WALDENSES, Franciscan SPIRITUALS, LOLLARDS, and HUSSITES. John WYCLIF (d. 1384) categorically denied the Church's right to own property and called for the lay magistracy to secularize ecclesiastical holdings and reform the Church. His ideas anticipated by 150 years the essential program of the REFORMATION.

Ominously too, the ever more powerful secular states of the late Middle Ages encroached upon Church property. The effort of PHILIP IV to tax the clergy of France led directly to his famous dispute with Pope BONIFACE VIII and the papal humiliation at Anagni (1303). By the late Middle Ages most of the powerful kings of Europe were able to extract ''free gifts'' from their clergy almost at will, to limit papal taxation within their frontiers, and to inhibit the export of specie to Rome. The popes had little choice but to enter into concordats with the lay rulers, as with Francis I of France in 1516, and thus concede to the lay lords a practical supremacy over their territorial churches (*see* GALLICANISM). The Reformation, in its attack on ecclesiastical property and undermining of Church unity, only brought to a climax trends that had long been in evidence.

Modern World (*c.* 1500 to the Present). The history of Church property in the modern age is largely the account of a radical transformation in the Church's financial basis and fiscal administration. Much of this story concerns the progressive SECULARIZATION OF CHURCH PROPERTY by the Protestant princes, enlightened despots, French revolutionists, and liberals of the 19th century. The Church itself, in the COUNTER REFORMATION, attempted to correct the abuses and institutional paralysis that had bred such disasters. The common effort

of the reforming popes of the 16th century, of the Council of TRENT, and of such model bishops as St. Charles BORROMEO of Milan was to restore the bishops' disciplinary authority over churches, religious institutions, and clerics within his diocese, and thus to correct the longstanding misuse of Church revenues. This aspect of the Catholic reformation enjoyed real success, but neither the reforming popes nor the Council of Trent was able to limit the baneful influence that the Catholic princes exerted over their territorial churches (*see* JOSEPHINISM; CHURCH AND STATE). By the 18th century, maldistribution of revenues, inadequate support of the lower clergy, a careerist and spiritually lukewarm upper clergy—the classical syndrome of abuses—had come again to disfigure the churches of the old regime and to invite the condemnations and secularizations of the revolutionary period.

The collapse of the old regime in the revolutionary and liberal epochs, the gradual emancipation of the churches from the tutelage of princes, even the secularization of their historic patrimonies, proved in many ways an unexpected blessing. The churches had to seek out a new basis for their economic support, and more and more the continuing donations of the faithful, rather than property, rents, or obligatory tithes, have provided it. The Church in the United States probably provides the best example of the new fiscal basis of ecclesiastical life. The yearly budgets of some American dioceses, with gigantic educational and charitable as well as religious activities to support, run to tens of millions of dollars. While no exact figures are available, only a minute part of these huge operating revenues comes from rents or investments. The American churches have, to be sure, acquired large physical possessions in buildings and land, but little additional revenue is provided by them. The Church in America could not live without the weekly freewill offerings of the faithful. It is not an exaggeration to say that the fiscal basis of the modern American Church, dependent as it is upon the continuing and free donations from the faithful, more nearly resembles that of the pre-Constantinian Church than that of the Middle Ages. That the Church should have become a great landlord in the medieval past is understandable. A bastion of organized social life in a tumultuous age, it had little choice but to assume the responsibilities of property management. Its stewardship was on the whole good, and civilization was served by it, but the role caused frequent and deep injury to its spiritual life. The modern Church, on the other hand, must rely for its support primarily upon the free donations, the good will, and the love of its members, and this has proved a liberation.

Bibliography: A. FLICHE and V. MARTIN, eds. *Histoire de l'église depuis les origines jusqu'à nos jours* (Paris 1935—) all volumes. J. GAUDEMET, *L'Église dans l'Empire romain* (Paris

1958). É. LESNE, *Histoire de la propriété ecclésiastique en France,* 6 v. (Lille 1910–43); *L'Origine des menses dans le temporel des églises et des monastères de France au IXᵉ siècle* (Mémoires et travaux pub. par des professeurs des Facultés catholiques de Lille 7; Lille 1910). A. PÖSCHL, *Bischofsgut und Mensa episcopalis: Ein Beitrag zur Geschichte des kirchlichen Vermögensrechtes,* 3 v. (Bonn 1908–12). H. LECLERCQ, *Dictionnaire d'archéologie chrétienne et de liturgie,* 15 v. (Paris 1907–53) 14.2:1906–24. G. KRÜGER, *Die Rechtsstellung der vorkonstantinischen Kirchen* (Stuttgart 1935). G. B. DE ROSSI, *La Roma sotterranea cristiana,* 3 v. (Rome 1864–77). G. G. COULTON, *Getting and Spending,* v. 3 of *Five Centuries of Religion* (Cambridge, Eng. 1923—). D. HERLIHY, "Church Property on the European Continent, 701–1200," *Speculum* 36 (1961) 81–105. V. PFAFF, "Die Einnahmen der römischen Kurie am Ende des XII. Jhts.," *Vierteljahrsschrift für Sozial- und Wirtschaftsgeschichte* 40 (1953) 97–118. M. MONACO, *La situazione della Reverenda Camera Apostolica nell'anno 1525* (Rome 1960). H. J. BYRNE, "The Financial Structure of the Church in the United States," *The Catholic Church, U.S.A.,* ed. L. J. PUTZ (Chicago 1956) 93–108.

[D. HERLIHY]

CHYLINSKI, RAFAŁ MELCHOIR, BL.

Baptized Melchoir, Conventual Franciscan priest and musician; b. Buk in Wysoczka near Poznán, Poland, Jan. 8, 1694; d. Łagiewniki near Łodz, Poland, Dec. 2, 1741. Melchoir completed three years of military service and exited as an officer. Although he had studied with the JESUITS, he entered the Conventual Franciscans at Krakow (1715). He received the name Rafał (Raphael) and studied theology and philosophy. Because of a shortage of priests, his studies were cut short, and he was ordained in 1717. After being assigned to nine parishes in different cities, he was appointed to Łagiewniki, Poland, where he remained, except for a short period, until his death thirteen years later.

Chylinski's simple, powerful preaching, commitment to the Sacrament of Reconciliation, and life of self-sacrifice drew people of all classes. He enhanced liturgical worship by playing the harp, lute, and mandolin. For twenty months (1736–37), he ministered to victims of a Warsaw flood and the resultant epidemic without considering the risk to his own health. Before his death at age forty-seven, he became known as the patron of the poor, whom he would supply from his own resources. His body rests in the Franciscan church at Łagiewniki and has becomme a pilgrimage site. He was beatified by John Paul II, June 9, 1991, in Warsaw, Poland.

Feast: Dec. 2 (Franciscans).

Bibliography: L. J. BERNATEK, *Rafał Chylinski: studium z dziejów zycia religijnego w epoce saskiej* (Warsaw 1971); *Błogosławiony Rafał Chylinski z Łagiewnik* (Niepokalanów 1991).

[K. I. RABENSTEIN]

CIASCA, AGOSTINO

Orientalist; b. Polignano a Mare, Italy, May 7, 1835; d. Rome, Feb. 6, 1902. His baptismal name was Pasquale; he received the name Agostino when he entered the Order of St. Augustine in 1856. He made his religions profession in March 1857 and was ordained in 1858. Ciasca was outstanding for his proficiency in Oriental languages, especially Arabic and Coptic. In 1866 he obtained the chair of Hebrew in the College of Propaganda. He assisted at the VATICAN COUNCIL I as a theologian and as interpreter for the Oriental bishops. In 1879 he participated in a pontifical mission to Egypt and Syria. He examined and corrected the Syrian Breviary and acquired many important MSS, mostly Christian Arabic. In 1891 he was created titular archbishop of Larissa with the appointment to the office of prefect of the Vatican Secret Archives. He presided at the Ruthenian Synod of Lemburg in 1891. In 1892 he was named prosecretary and later secretary (1893) of the Congregation of the Propaganda, during which time he helped organize some Catholic missions to the Congo. He was elevated to the cardinalate June 19, 1899.

Among his scholarly contributions may be mentioned *Examen critico-apologeticum super constitutionem dogmaticam de Fide Catholica editam in sessione tertia SS. Oecumenici Concilii Vaticani* (1872), *I papiri Copti del Museo Borgiano della S.C. de Propaganda Fide tradotti e commentati* (1881), his publication of a very ancient Coptic version of the OT "Sacrorum Bibliorum Fragmenta Copto-Sahidica Musei Borgiani" (2 v. 1885–89), and his discovery and publication (1888) of a valuable Arabic version of the DIATESSARON of TATIAN.

Bibliography: D. A. PERINI, *Studio Bio-bibliografico sul Cardinale Agostino Ciasca* (Rome 1903); *Bibliographia Augustiniana* (Florence 1929–38) 1:229–231. A. PALMIERI, *Dictionnaire de théologie catholique,* ed. A. VACANT et al. (Paris 1903–50) 2.2:2472–73. G. HOFFMAN, *Lexikon für Theologie und Kirche,* ed. J. HOFER and K. RAHNER (2d, new ed. Freiburg 1957–65) 2:1201.

[B. A. LAZOR]

CIBORIUM

A word of which the etymology is disputed, was the name given in early times to a pillared canopy, of Byzantine origin, erected over the altar. In the late Middle Ages it was applied to a small sacrament house with a gabled top in which the Blessed Sacrament was reserved. Finally, in the 16th century, it was used to designate the vessel in which the Blessed Sacrament was reserved for the Communion of the faithful. This vessel is but a developed form of the PYX, which, in the 13th century, acquired a foot under the cylindrical container. At first the ciborium was small, containing but a few consecrated hosts for the sick. After the Council of Trent, Communion of the faithful became less infrequent, and was given from previously consecrated Hosts kept in the tabernacle. The ciborium then had to be made larger, and was given the shape of a cup, often with a conical lid.

Bibliography: J. BRAUN, *Das chrisliche Altargerät* (Munich 1932).

[C. W. HOWELL/EDS.]

CIBOT, PIERRE MARTIAL

Jesuit missionary and scientist; b. Limoges, Aug. 14, 1727; d. Beijing, Aug. 8, 1780. He is noted chiefly for his many contributions to the memoirs composed by the missionaries in Beijing and published under the title *Mémoires concernant l'histoire, les sciences, les arts, les moeurs, les usages etc. de Chinois* (16 v. Paris 1776–89). Cibot entered the Society of Jesus in 1743, and in 1758 he was sent to Beijing, where he remained at the court until his death. A zealous missionary and an eager, intelligent student with wide scientific interests, he wrote on a great variety of subjects. Often accused of using his imagination too much in his writings and of sometimes being unreliable, he nevertheless contributed much interesting information on on customs, institutions, trees, plants, etc., of China. His work on the chronology of the Chinese Empire was strongly assailed by learned contemporaries, but modern science has become somewhat favorable to his thesis.

Bibliography: L. PFISTER, *Notices biographiques et bibliographiques sur les Jésuites de l'ancienne mission de Chine 1552–1773* (Shanghai 1932–34) 2:896–902, with detailed bibliog. A. DE BIL, *Dictionnaire d'histoire et de géographie ecclésiastiques*, ed. A. BAUDRILLART et al. (Paris 1912–) 12:826. J. BRUCKER, *Dictionnaire de théologie catholique*, ed. A. VACANT et al. (Paris 1903–50) 2.2:2473. H. M. BROCK, *The Catholic Encyclopedia*, ed. C. G. HERBERMANN et al. (New York 1907–14) 3:767–768. C. SOMMERVOGEL et al., *Bibliothèque de la Compagnie de Jésus* (Brussels-Paris 1890-1932) 2:1167–69.

[M. J. BARRY]

CICERO, MARCUS TULLIUS

Orator, statesman, and greatest man of letters of antiquity; b. Arpinum, Italy, Jan. 3, 106 B.C.; d. Formiae, Dec. 7, 43. He was of middle-class origin, and he received an excellent education at Rome that was completed by philosophical and rhetorical studies at Athens and Rhodes. He distinguished himself as an orator and served as quaestor in 75, as praetor in 66, and as consul in 63. His greatest political triumph was the unmasking and suppression of the conspiracy of Cataline. As an opponent of Caesar he was exiled in 58 to 57, but through Pompey's efforts he was able to return to Rome. In 51 to 50 he served as a governor of Cilicia. In the civil war he supported Pompey and the senate. Following the assassination of Caesar, he courageously defended the senatorial cause against Mark Antony. He perished as a victim, with the acquiescence of Octavian, of Antony's hatred.

Cicero was a man of peace, innately conservative in politics, who found himself deeply involved in the violence that marked the last years of the Republic. Owing to the preservation of most of his voluminous writings, especially of his letters, his life is better known than that of any other ancient personality, with the possible exception of St. AUGUSTINE.

Cicero's chief extant works comprise orations, rhetorical compositions, and philosophical treatises, cast in the form of dialogues, and letters. His orations and letters, apart from their high literary place in oratory and epistolography, are invaluable sources for the history of the late Republic. His rhetorical works are primarily concerned with the theory of oratory and give precious information on the earlier Roman orators. His extant philosophical dialogues cover political theory and religion as well as philosophical themes as ordinarily understood. They are: *De Republica* (preserved only in part), *De legibus, Academica, De finibus bonorum et malorum, Tusculanae disputationes, De natura deorum, De divinatione, De senectute, De amicitia, Paradoxa Stoicorum,* and *De officiis.* His *De consolatione* and the *Hortensius,* which exercised such a great influence on the young Augustine, have been lost.

Cicero was not an original thinker, but as an eclectic he expounded in a beautiful literary style the basic ideas of the chief Greek schools of philosophy. In epistemology he followed the New Academy; in ethics, chiefly the Stoics. He rejected both the materialism of the Epicureans and the popular religious beliefs in the gods, but believed in a divine providence and the immortality of the soul. Cicero is the undisputed master of Latin prose style and the creator of Latin philosophical language. He was the first, for example, to employ such basic terms as *essentia, qualitas,* and *materia* in their philosophical sense.

Cicero's influence on subsequent Latin prose style was immediate and very significant because of his central place beside VERGIL in the ancient school tradition. Since the ancient Christian writers were trained chiefly in pagan schools, it is only natural that they should reflect Ciceronian influence in both thought and style. Cicero's treatment of Greco-Roman philosophy and religion furnished Christian apologists with arguments that were all the more effective because they were based on a universally acknowledged authority. MINUCIUS FELIX, ARNOBIUS THE ELDER, and LACTANTIUS drew heavily on Cicero's *De natura deorum, De divinatione,* and other works. Lactantius, because of his indebtedness to Cicero for his content and style, has been called the "Christian Cicero."

St. AMBROSE's *De officiis* shows the obvious influence of Cicero in its title and in its division into three books, but in actual content it is much less dependent on its model than is usually assumed. St. JEROME's dream and the style of his treatises and letters furnish ample testimony for his familiarity with the great Roman writer. The reading of the *Hortensius,* as already noted, marked a turning point in the life of the young Augustine. Later, Augustine found Cicero and Varro invaluable sources for his apologetic in the *De civitate Dei.* His definition of the pagan state, for example, is taken from Cicero. Book four of his *De doctrina Christiana,* a treatise on Christian rhetoric, is based essentially on Cicero's theory of rhetoric and education. BOETHIUS reflects Ciceronian influence in his style of writing rather than in his thought.

The influence of Cicero continued throughout the Middle Ages, but it was confined largely to the knowledge and use of a limited number of his philosophical works, his rhetorical treatise *De inventione,* and the *Auctor ad Herennium,* which was regarded as a Ciceronian production. Few scholars in the Middle Ages were as familiar with Cicero as Lupus of Ferrières, JOHN OF SALISBURY, and Peter of Blois. From the beginning of the Renaissance, with the recovery and study of his extant works, Cicero became the universally recognized, and for a time the exclusive, master of Latin prose style.

The cultivation of Ciceronian Latin in the European school tradition exercised a marked effect on the development of vernacular prose style in general. In the late 19th century Pope LEO XIII gave Ciceronian Latin a basic place in his reform of papal chancery style; his own encyclicals, especially, and those of his successors exhibit the deliberate use of Ciceronian language and stylistic devices. Ciceronian thought exercised some influence throughout the modern period, but his influence in modern times has been primarily in the field of rhetorical theory and style.

Bibliography: G. C. RICHARDS, *The Oxford Classical Dictionary,* ed. M. CARY et al. (Oxford 1949) 188–191, with bibliog. K. BÜCHNER, "M. Tullius Cicero, der Redner (29)," *Paulys Realenzkopädie der klassischen Altertumswissenschaft,* ed. G. WISSOWA et al. 7A.1 (1939) 827–1274. C. BECKER, *Reallexikon für Antike und Christentum,* ed. T. KLAUSER (Stuttgart 1941–50) 3:86–127, with bibliog. J. W. DUFF, *A Literary History of Rome from the Origins to the Close of the Golden Age,* ed. A. M. DUFF (3d ed. London 1953) 255–290, with bibliog. 501–503. J. E. SANDYS *History of Classical Scholarship* (Cambridge, Eng.), v.1 (3d ed. 1921), v.2, 3 (2d ed.

1906–08); repr. (New York 1958), indices s.v. "Cicero." M. MANITIUS, *Geschischte der lateinischen Literatur des Mittelaters* (Munich 1911–31) indices s.v. "Cicero." G. HIGHET, *The Classical Tradition* (New York 1949), index s.v. "Cicero." R. R. BOLGAR, *The Classical Heritage and Its Beneficiaries* (Cambridge, Eng. 1954), index s.v. "Cicero." H. HAGENDAHL, *Latin Fathers and the Classics* (Göteborg 1958), index s.v. "Cicero." M. VAN DE BRUWAINE, *La Théologie de Cicéron* (Louvain 1937). T. A. DOREY, ed., *Cicero* (London 1965).

[M. R. P. MCGUIRE]

CICOGNANI, AMLETO GIOVANNI

Vatican secretary of state and apostolic delegate to the United States; b. Brisighella, Italy, Feb. 24, 1883; d. Rome, Dec. 17, 1973. After attending the seminary at Faenza, Italy, he was ordained to the priesthood in 1905 and was sent to study at Rome, receiving doctorates in theology and canon law. Almost immediately he began a lifelong career of service to the Holy See. He first served with the Congregation for the Sacraments (1910–14) and then in the Consistorial Congregation (1914–28). In 1928 Pius XI appointed him assessor of the Congregation for Oriental Churches and in 1929 he became secretary of the Commission for Revision of Oriental Canon Law. In addition to his administrative duties, he taught canon law at the Juridical Pontifical Institute of Sant'Apollinare and served as chaplain to university students.

In 1933 Cicognani was appointed titular archbishop of Laodicea in Phrygia and named apostolic delegate to the United States, a post he held until 1958. During this period he traveled widely throughout the United States and saw extensive growth of the U.S. Catholic Church. During World War II he made special efforts to minister to Catholic prisoners of war held by the United States. Cicognani's tenure in Washington ended in 1958 when John XXIII raised him to the college of cardinals, a rank his older brother Gaetano already held.

Cicognani became secretary of the Oriental Congregation in Jan. of 1961 and the following August was appointed successor to Cardinal Domenico Tardini as secretary of state, an office he held until he resigned because of age in 1969. From March 24, 1972 until his death, he was dean of the college of cardinals. At the Second Vatican Council he served as president of the Commission for the Oriental Churches. Among his writings are *Sanctity in America* (1939), a book on Americans who had been proposed for beatification, and *Canon Law* (1925; Eng. tr. 1934), at the time considered one of the authoritative treatments of the subject.

[T. EARLY]

CICONIA, JOHANNES

Walloon musician and theorist of the *Ars nova;* b. Liège, Belgium, *c.* 1335–40; d. Padua, Italy, December 1411. In 1350 he was in Avignon, France, as favorite of Clement VI's niece, Alienor de Cominges-Turenne, and in 1358 he was in the employment of Cardinal ALBORNOZ, then papal legate for Italy, who granted him a canonry at Cesena and obtained one from Urban V at St. John the Evangelist, Liège, previously requested by Clement's niece. After Albornoz's death (1367) Ciconia returned to his native land and in 1372 took up his Liège canonry. Finally, in 1401, he returned to Padua as canon and precentor at St. John Church. Trained in the French musical tradition, in both his own country and Avignon, he became acquainted early with Italian music, and his first works, Italian madrigals and ballatas, testify to his knowledge of the art of Jacopo da Bologna and the Lombard court composers. On returning to Liège, he wrote some Masses in the Avignon style, blending French structures with the allurements of Italian melody, with which his French songs are imbued. At Padua he composed Masses and motets for special occasions and at the end some ballatas in which archaisms mingle with the innovations of the musical dialectic that was to usher in the polyphony and resonances of the *quattrocento.* Ciconia's known works, all preserved in their original codices in Padua, Rome, Trent, and other cities, are: four madrigals and 11 ballatas on Italian texts; two French songs (virelay and ballade); two canons, one on a Latin text, the other, French; 11 Mass parts; and 13 motets. His five-book theoretical work, *Nova Musica,* has never been published.

Bibliography: Modern reprints of his music appear in *Denkmäler der Tonkunst in Österreich* (1893– ; repr. Graz 1959–) 7, 14, and 61; *Polyphonia Sacra,* ed. C. VAN DEN BORREN (University Park, Pa. 1963). S. CLERCX (-LEJEUNE), *Johannes Ciconia: Un musicien liégeois et son temps,* 2 v. (Brussels 1960) bibliog. xi–xxii. H. BESSELER, *Die Musik in Geschichte und Gegenwart,* ed. F. BLUME (Kassel-Basel 1949–) 2:1423–1434; "Johannes Ciconia, Begründer der Chorpolyphonie," *International Congress on Sacred Music, Proceedings 1950* (Rome 1952). E. DANNEMANN, *Grove's Dictionary of Music and Musicians,* ed. E. BLOM, 9 v. (5th ed. London 1954) 2:295–296. M. F. BUKOFZER, "The Beginnings of Choral Polyphony," *Studies in Medieval and Renaissance Music* (New York 1950) 176–189. J. CICONIA, "De proportionibus," *Greek and Latin Music Theory,* O. B. ELLSWORTH, ed. and tr., v. 9 (Lincoln, Nebr. 1993) 412–446. J. CICONIA, "Nova musica, liber primus de consonantiis," *Greek and Latin Music Theory,* O. B. ELLSWORTH, ed. and tr., v. 9 (Lincoln, Nebr. 1993) 42–232. J. CICONIA, "Nova musica, liber secundus de speciebus," *Greek and Latin Music Theory,* O. B. ELLSWORTH, ed. and tr., v. 9 (Lincoln, Nebr. 1993) 234–336. J. CICONIA, "Nova musica, liber tertius de proportionibus," *Greek and Latin Music Theory,* O. B. ELLSWORTH, ed. and tr., v. 9 (Lincoln, Nebr. 1993) 338–360. J. CICONIA, "Nova musica, liber quartus de accidentibus," *Greek and Latin Music Theory,* O. B. ELLSWORTH, ed. and tr., v. 9 (Lincoln, Nebr. 1993) 362–410. S. CLERCX-LEJEUNE and D. FALLOWS, "Johannes Ciconia," in *The New Grove Dictionary of Music and Musicians,* ed. S. SADIE, v. 4 (New York 1980) 391–394. A. KREUTZIGER-HERR, "Johannes Ciconia (ca. 1370–1412): Komponieren in einer Kultur des Wortes" (Ph.D. diss. Hamburg 1990). D. M. RANDEL, ed., *The Harvard Biographical Dictionary of Music* (Cambridge, Mass. 1996) 161–162.

[S. CLERCX-LEJEUNE]

CIENFUEGOS, ÁLVARO

Theologian; b. Anguerina, Spain, Feb. 27, 1657; d. Rome, Aug. 19, 1739. After studying philosophy in Salamanca, he entered the Society of Jesus in 1676 and studied theology in the same city. He taught philosophy at Compostela (1688–91) and theology at Salamanca.

Charles of Austria named Cienfuegos his envoy to Portugal and retained him as an advisor. At the end of the war of 1714, Charles VI, then emperor, called him to Venice and in 1720 succeeded in having him named cardinal. In 1722 he was consecrated bishop of Catania and in 1724 archbishop of Monreal. Cienfuegos had to renounce his archbishopric when the Bourbons occupied the kingdom of the two Sicilies. He was then given the see of Fünfkirchen by the emperor (1735), although he continued to live in Rome as the emperor's legate and held important posts in Roman congregations until his death.

As a theologian he was considered to have sharp and brilliant ingenuity. His principal theological works are: the *Aenigma Theologicum,* 2 v. (Vienna 1717), and the *Vita abscondita* (Rome 1728). The first, on the Trinity, does not give any new solutions, although the author appears to believe it does. Cienfuegos's doctrine on the Eucharist, contained in the second work, had more of a hearing. According to him, the sacramental Christ supernaturally exercises acts of the sensitive life, but immediately after the Consecration this activity is suspended until the mingling of the two species, which is a symbol of the Resurrection. The sacrificial immolation properly consists in this suspension. Communion really unites the faithful to the soul of Christ; even though the species are dissolved, the communicant is, like a motor, an instrument of the Word. Franzelin comments: "Certainly this opinion is so constructed that a cautious theologian would be frightened by its singularity" (*De Eucharistia,* th. 16).

Cienfuegos also wrote the *Heroica vida, virtudes y milagros dal grande San Francisco de Borja* (Madrid 1702). Although it is difficult reading, it is better documented than earlier biographies.

Bibliography: C. SOMMERVOGEL et al., *Bibliothèque de la Compagnie de Jésus* (Brussels-Paris 1890–1932) 2:1182–85. H.

HURTER, *Nomenclator literarius theologiae catholicae* (3d ed. Innsbruck 1903–13) 4:1020–26. H. DUTOUQUET, *Dictionnaire de théologie catholique*, ed. A VACANT et al. (Paris 1903–50) 2:2511–13. A. PEREZ GOYENA, ''Teólogos antifranceses en la Guerra de Sucesión,'' *Razón y Fe* 91.2 (1930) 326–338.

[J. M. DALMAU]

CIENFUEGOS, JOSÉ IGNACIO

Chilean bishop and enlightened reformer; b. 1762; d. Talca, 1845. He was ordained in 1785 and stationed in Talca until 1813. As a member of the education commission of the new national regime in Chile, he effected his most important action, the union of the Tridentine Seminary with the National Institute, the new foundation planned by the Creole junta. The consolidation of the seminary with the basic college for humanistic, philosophic, and scientific studies, intended for laymen, opened the way for the new enlightened and liberal ideas among future secular priests. The fusion of these institutions was characteristic of Josephinism, current throughout America during the period of independence.

Cienfuegos was banished to the Juan Fernandez Islands at the time of the Spanish reconquest, but returned in 1817, when independence was finally achieved. He was president of the Senate and on various occasions was governor of the bishopric of Santiago, owing to the confidence that the political heads of the new state had in him. In 1821, as plenipotentiary, he went to the Holy See and brought about the mission of Juan Muzi to Chile; it failed and the legislative reforms of the Church were consolidated. Muzi accused Cienfuegos of usurping episcopal jurisdiction since Bp. RODRÍGUEZ ZORRILLA had been expelled by O'Higgins, but Cienfuegos went to Rome again in 1827 and succeeded in vindicating himself. Nevertheless, he had cooperated with the ecclesiastical reforms and proposed the selection of parish priests by the people in accord with the parochial tendencies then in vogue.

He became titular bishop of Rétimo in 1828 and bishop of Concepción in 1830. In 1837 he gave up his diocese and retired to Talca, where he died. Among his charitable works are his donations to the hospital and the Institute of Talca, and the foundation of a chair of theology. He published a *Catechism of Christian Doctrine* (Geneva 1829), with commentary, which shows the moral seriousness that characterized his pastoral work. Among the Chilean clergy he is the chief representative of the so-called Catholic Enlightenment.

Bibliography: L. F. PRIETO DEL RÍO, *Diccionario biográfico del clero secular de Chile* (Santiago de Chile 1922).

[M. GÓNGORA]

CIEPLAK, JAN

Bishop; b. Dabrowa Górniczna, Poland, Aug. 17, 1857; d. Jersey City, N.J., Feb. 17, 1926. After his mother's death (1859), Cieplak was reared by his maternal grandmother and by two priests. In 1869 he entered the Gymnasium at Kielce, and in 1873 began to study for the priesthood in the Latin rite. He pursued higher studies in St. Petersburg (1878) and was ordained (1881). In 1882 he became professor at the Catholic academy in St. Petersburg. He was consecrated bishop of Evaria and appointed auxiliary bishop of Mogilev (1908). After the Russian Revolution he became archbishop of Achrida and apostolic administrator of Mohilev in place of the imprisoned Archbishop Ropp (1919). Accused of conspiring with the papal nuncio in Warsaw, Cieplak was arrested as a counterrevolutionary and sentenced to death (1923). His sentence, however, was commuted through the intervention of the Holy See, the U.S. and British governments, and Edmund WALSH, SJ. In 1924 Cieplak was transferred from Butyrki prison to Lubianka, and was soon after deposited penniless at the Latvian border. From Riga he went to Poland and then to Rome. In 1925 he began an extended tour of the United States, where in the course of three months he visited 375 parishes and 800 institutions in 25 dioceses. He was named archbishop of Vilna (then in Poland), but died as he was preparing to go there. His cause for beatification has been introduced, and the *decretum super scripta* was issued in 1960.

Bibliography: F. DOMANSKI, *The Great Apostle of Russia: The Servant of God Archbishop John Baptist Cieplak* (Chicago 1953). J. LEDIT, *Archbishop Jan Baptist Cieplak* (Montreal 1963).

[J. PAPIN]

CILICIA OF THE ARMENIANS, PATRIARCHATE OF

The Catholic patriarchate of the Armenian Catholic Church, based in Beirut, Lebanon, established 1742 by Pope Benedict XIV with jurisdiction over Armenian Eastern Catholics in the then Ottoman Empire. The patriarchate derives from the episcopacy of St. GREGORY THE ILLUMINATOR (315).

Cilicia, with its Cilician Gates, has long been a link between Asia Minor and Syria. It was under the HITTITES, the Persians (*c.* 500 B.C.), ALEXANDER THE GREAT (333 B.C.), and Rome (103 B.C.), who rid its coast of pirates (62 B.C.) and made it part of the Diocese of the East (A.D. 297). Invaded by Arabs from 639 and retaken by the Byzantine Nicephorus II Phocas (965), it became a principality under Armenians who had fled the SELJUK Turks

(1080). It was an ally of the Latin crusaders and became a kingdom (1199), which went to the Lusignans of CYPRUS (1342) and then fell to the Mamelukes (1375). By 1522 Cilicia was part of the Ottoman Empire.

St. PAUL was born in Tarsus, a capital of Cilicia and one of nine Cilician sees represented at the Council of Nicaea I (325). To the original two ecclesiastical provinces of Cilicia under the Patriarchate of ANTIOCH, Tarsus with five suffragans and Anazarbus with nine suffragans, Seleucia with 23 suffragans was added in Constantine's time. MOPSUESTIA also was an important city of Cilicia. Some 15 of the ancient sees of Cilicia still exist as titular sees. Remains of basilicas have been discovered in the region, which had early Christian martyrs.

In the aftermath of the Ecumenical Council of CHALCEDON, Cilicia was divided into JACOBITES and MELKITES, and the Arab conquest caused more harm to the Church there. Pope Gregory VII corresponded with the Armenian CATHOLICOS Gregory II before the Crusades. LEO II's coronation as king of Lesser Armenia by a papal legate (1199) restored unity with Rome until 1375. Latin crusaders had established Latin sees in Cilicia; and a Dominican organization worked for union with Rome from 1328 but had to be abandoned. Sis, capital of Cilicia to 1375, had a catholicos (1293–1441), who moved to Echmiadzin. Echmiadzin's position as head of the Armenian National Church, which it still obtains, was eventually recognized by the Catholicos of Sis, who was acknowledged by Echmiadzin as a subordinate "patriarch." This Armenian Catholicos-Patriarch of Sis, who presided over 15 dioceses and 285,000 souls in 1914, fled Turkey (1921) by moving to Alep and Lebanon (1928). Several councils in Sis (1251, 1307, 1342) and Adana (1316) dealt with the matter of recognizing the primacy of Rome. Sis was also the seat of a Jacobite bishop and, from 1292 to 1387, of the Jacobite patriarch.

In 1740 Abraham (Peter) Ardzivean, Catholic bishop of Alep, was elected Catholicos-Patriarch of Sis and in 1742 received the pallium in Rome; but he had to reside in Lebanon. The primatial archbishopric for Armenian Catholics established in Istanbul (1830) was united with the Patriarchate of Cilicia (1867) following a jurisdictional dispute over six new sees created in Turkey (1850), and the patriarch moved to Istanbul (1867–1928). Reorganization of the patriarchate (1928) after the persecution following World War I established the patriarch in Beirut.

Bibliography: R. ROBERSON, *The Eastern Christian Churches: A Brief Survey,* (6th ed. Rome 1999).

[J. A. DEVENNY/EDS.]

Domenico Cimarosa.

CIMAROSA, DOMENICO

Composer best known for his comic operas; b. Aversa (near Naples), Dec. 17, 1749; d. Venice, Jan. 11, 1801. He received his musical training at a Franciscan free school in Naples and then at the Conservatorio Santa Maria di Loreto (1761–72). His first opera, *Le Stravaganze del Conte*, was produced in 1772. Despite rivals in the field of Neapolitan opera (notably PAISIELLO) Cimarosa was soon writing both comic and serious operas for various theaters throughout Italy. In 1787 he accepted an invitation to become chamber composer to Catherine II in St. Petersburg, but he left there in 1791 for the court of Leopold II in Vienna. There he wrote his best-known work, *Il Matrimonio segreto* (1792), a masterpiece of genuine buffo style, which received 67 consecutive performances the following year in Naples. Cimarosa helped welcome French revolutionary troops into Naples in 1799; on the return of the Bourbons he was sentenced to death, then pardoned. Setting out again for Russia, he fell sick in Venice and died shortly after. In addition to 75 operas, he wrote many motets and concerted Masses, several oratorios, cantatas, and shorter vocal and instrumental compositions, all of them largely forgotten.

Bibliography: R. VITALE, *Domenico Cimarosa* (Aversa 1929). M. TIBALDI CHIESA, *Cimarosa e il suo tempo* (Milan 1939). COMITATO NAZIONALE PER LE CELEBRAZIONI CIMAROSIANE 1949,

Per il bicentenario della nascita di Domenico Cimarosa, ed. F. DE FILIPPIS (Aversa 1949). D. J. GROUT, *A Short History of Opera* 2 v. (New York 1965). H. WIRTH, *Die Musik in Geschichte und Gegenwart*, ed. F. BLUME 2: 1442–49. *Baker's Biographical Dictionary of Musicians*, ed. N. SLONIMSKY (New York 1958) 294–295. T. BARFOOT, "Domenico Cimarosa," in *International Dictionary of Opera* 2 v. ed. C. S. LARUE (Detroit 1993) 259–262; "*Il Matrimonio Segreto* [*The Secret Marriage*]," ibid., 826–827. J. E. JOHNSON, *Domenico Cimarosa (1749–1801)* (Ph.D. diss. Cardiff University, 1976); "Domenico Cimarosa," in *The New Grove Dictionary of Music and Musicians*, ed. S. SADIE (New York 1980) 398-403. D. M. RANDEL, ed., *The Harvard Biographical Dictionary of Music* (Cambridge, Mass. 1996) 162-163. N. SLONIMSKY, ed. *Baker's Biographical Dictionary of Musicians*, (New York 1992) 334–335.

[R. W. LOWE]

CIMATTI, MARIA RAFFAELLA, BL.

Baptized Santa Cimatti, virgin of the Congregation of Hospital Sisters of Mercy; b. Celle di Faenza near Ravenna, Emilia-Romagna, Italy, June 6, 1861,; d. Alatri, Italy, June 23, 1945. Santina, as she was called by her family of modest means, was the eldest of six children, three of whom died in childhood. When her mother was widowed (1882), Santina helped to raise and educate her younger brothers: Venerable Vincenzo Cimatti (1879–1965), who became the first Salesian missionary in Japan (1925); and another, who also became a Salesian priest.

Until her brothers and mother were safely settled, she responded to her vocation by teaching catechism and working with children. Then, she joined the Hospital Sisters of Mercy in Rome (1889), professed her initial vows (1891), and received the name Sister Maria Raffaella. Thereafter she devoted herself to the care of the sick and poor, first as a pharmacy assistant at Alatri, and later at Frosinone. She was elected superior of the house at Frosinone (1921–28), then superior of Alatri (1928–40). Renouncing her position in 1940 after fifty years of religious life, she spent the majority of her time in prayer. At the age of eighty-three, she became known as the "Angel of the Sick" for the comfort she gave the wounded of the Second World War. Her courage in personally confronting the German Field Marshal Kesselring prevented massive bombing of Alatri. Her cause for canonization was opened in 1962. Pope John Paul II beatified Maria Raffaella (May 12, 1996) "as a humble religious who constitutes a shining example of femininity plainly realized in self-giving."

Feast: June 23.

Bibliography: *Acta Apostolicae Sedis*, 12 (1996): 551–53. *L'Osservatore Romano*, no. 20 (1996): 1; no. 21 (1996): 4–5.

[K. I. RABENSTEIN]

CINCINNATI, ARCHDIOCESE OF

Metropolitan see of the Province of Cincinnati (*Cincinnatensis*); comprising 19 counties in southwest Ohio, an area of 8,543 square miles, with a 20 percent Catholic population. The province, encompasses five suffragan sees: Cleveland, Columbus, Toledo, Youngstown, and Steubenville. Cincinnati was designated a diocese on June 19, 1821—two years after the first permanent church was built on the northern edge of town—and an archdiocese on July 19, 1850. The diocese originally included the entire state of Ohio, plus Michigan and the Old Northwest. The latter became part of the Diocese of Detroit, erected in 1833. The northern reaches of Ohio became the Diocese of Cleveland in 1847 and the southeastern section the Diocese of Columbus in 1868. Toledo became a diocese in 1910, Youngstown in 1943 and Steubenville in 1944.

Early history. The territory was included in the immense Quebec diocese until Cincinnati became part of the prefecture apostolic of the new American republic in 1785. It was folded into the first U.S. see, Baltimore, in 1789, a year after colonists from Massachusetts made the first permanent settlement in Ohio at Marietta. French Catholics settled at Gallipolis in southeastern Ohio, where Peter Joseph Didier, OSB, served them for a few years until he left the colony in discouragement. The few Catholics who settled in the area looked to the occasional missionary journeys of priests from Kentucky for the sacraments. Among those priests was Edward Dominic FENWICK, O.P., one of the founders of the first Dominican house in the U.S., near Springfield, Ky.

Diocese. Pope Pius VII recognized the needs of the increasing Catholic population in Ohio by erecting the Diocese of Cincinnati and appointing Fenwick as its first bishop.

Fenwick. Bishop Benedict Flaget consecrated Fenwick at St. Rose Priory in Washington County, Ky., on Jan. l3, 1822. The new bishop took up residence in a small rented house in Cincinnati on March 23, 1822. He moved the only church building in the community from what is today Liberty and Vine Streets (the current site of St. Francis Seraph Church) to Sixth and Sycamore Streets (the current site of St. Francis Xavier Church). He changed its name from Christ Church to St. Peter's Cathedral.

When this change of location caused controversy with members of the congregation who had built the church, the bishop demanded the transfer of the property title to himself. Later, the Congregation for the Propagation of the Faith in Rome settled a problem concerning the property acquired by Dominican priests working in

Ohio and held in the name of the Dominican Order. The Congregation ordered a separation of diocesan and Dominican property. The agreement signed in 1828 provided that Fenwick was to hold diocesan property in the name of the diocese and willed to his successor in the see of Cincinnati. This practice of holding diocesan property in the name of the bishop, which spread throughout the Old Northwest, was largely responsible for the fact that TRUSTEEISM never became a serious problem for the Church in those states.

Fenwick went to Europe in 1823 to secure money and personnel for the 6,000 Catholics of his diocese, mostly German but many of them Swiss or Irish. He obtained substantial contributions from Pope Leo XII, from the Lyons Association of the Propagation of the Faith, and from collections in Belgium, Holland, and England.

When he returned with five recruits for the Diocese of Cincinnati—four priests and one French Sister of Mercy—he found that a new episcopal residence had been built in his absence. He dedicated a new St. Peter's Cathedral at Sixth and Sycamore on Dec. 17, 1826 and opened a theological seminary, St. Francis Xavier, next door with an enrollment of ten students on May 11, 1829.

In Baltimore in 1829 for the First Provincial Council, Fenwick secured the services of four Dominican Sisters for Somerset and four Sisters of Charity of Emmitsburg for Cincinnati. Fenwick's regular missionary journeys on horseback throughout the diocese resulted in numerous conversions and the establishment of many parishes in missions—St. Martin's in Brown County in 1830 and St. Stephen's in Hamilton in 1831. His success provoked attacks in the Protestant press and pulpit. In response, Fenwick founded a weekly newspaper for the Diocese. *The Catholic Telegraph* began publishing in October 1831 and remains the oldest continuously published Catholic newspaper in the United States. Ill health caused Fenwick to ask Rome four times for a coadjutor bishop, but he never got one. Fenwick died in Wooster, Ohio, on Sept. 26, 1832 during a mission trip through Ohio and the Northwest.

Purcell. Pope Gregory XVI named John Baptist PURCELL, president of Mount St. Mary College in Emmitsburg, Md., as the second bishop of Cincinnati on May 12, 1833. He was consecrated in Baltimore on Oct. 13, 1833, attended the Second Provincial Council of BALTIMORE, then traveled west to his diocese by stage and steamboat. Bishop Flaget installed him at St. Peter's Cathedral on Nov. 14, 1833.

Purcell's first concern was to follow the will of his predecessor regarding the division of diocesan and Dominican property. Following his negotiations with the

Dominicans, seven of the 16 churches in Ohio were named as diocesan, nine as Dominican property. The new bishop also lost no time in beginning the series of annual missionary visitations for which his episcopate was noted, and which were responsible for a considerable part of the steady growth of Catholicism in the diocese. He made seven European trips between 1838 and 1869 to help supply the vocational and financial needs of the diocese. On Nov. 2, 1845, he consecrated a new Cathedral at Eighth and Plum Streets under the patronage of St. Peter in Chains.

Archdiocese. Cincinnati was raised to the rank of metropolitan see in 1850. Archbishop Purcell received the pallium when he visited Rome the following year. The new archbishop frequently defended the immigrant church against nativist attacks in debates and appearances in Protestant churches in the early 1850s. But on the secession controversy that preceded the Civil War, the archdiocese remained officially silent. With the outbreak of hostilities, Purcell and *The Catholic Telegraph* became strongly Unionist. The Catholic population largely supported Lincoln's administration and helped to supply the military needs of the North. Women religious made their contribution in nursing service—Sisters of Charity, Sisters of Mercy and Franciscan Sisters. Sister of Charity Anthony O'Connell was known as "angel of the battlefield" for her works of mercy among the troops. Part of the House of Mercy became a hospital and prisoner-of-war encampment. Catholic loyalty during the war years did much to overcome earlier anti-Catholic sentiment among nativist non-Catholics.

Like Fenwick before him, Purcell was a tireless traveler within his own vast diocese and in Europe, making seven trips abroad in search of money and people. Both men and women religious orders responded generously. The Jesuits, Franciscans, Precious Blood Fathers, Passionists, and Marianists established houses and institutions in the archdiocese in response to his efforts. Women religious orders that answered his call included the Sisters of Notre Dame de Namur, Precious Blood Sisters, Ursuline Sisters, Good Shepherd Sisters, Notre Dame Sisters of Mauhausen, Little Sisters of the Poor and the Sisters of the Poor of St. Francis.

Unfortunately, Purcell's name was tainted by the "Purcell failure" that rocked the archdiocese near the end of his long tenure. When the panic of 1837 weakened state banks, Father Edward Purcell, brother of the bishop, began an informal banking operation based at the cathedral. Catholic immigrants, largely ignorant of financial matters and mistrusting banks, turned in increasing numbers to "Father Purcell's Bank." Following the great national panic of 1873, a run on the money deposited with

Purcell depleted available funds. An examination found the bank to be insolvent, largely because of Father Purcell's inefficient operation. All of the resources of the bank were assigned to Edward B. Mannix, together with diocesan property estimated as sufficient to cover all liabilities. The estimates were wrong. There was not enough money to go around. Litigation kept the issue alive in state and federal courts from 1880 to 1905. Voluntary contributions from the priests and people of the archdiocese—and from other dioceses throughout the U.S.—helped to pay the bank's creditors.

Although their bitter critics acknowledged that neither Archbishop Purcell nor his brother profited from the failed bank, nevertheless the Purcell failure did great harm to the archdiocese. Its effects included losses and consequent hardships for many poor depositors, abandonment of the faith by many scandalized Catholics, temporary difficulty in effecting conversions to the faith, the closing of the seminary for a time, and the inability to promote the material growth of the archdiocese until the eve of World War I.

On Jan. 3, 1880, as the scandal enveloped the archdiocese, Rome appointed Bishop William H. ELDER of Natchez as coadjutor with right of succession. Purcell's ill health and advanced age (80) caused him to turn over the administration of the diocese to Elder in April 1880, three years before his death on July 4, 1883.

Elder. Burdened with the need to resolve the continuing lawsuits and bring healing to the archdiocese, Elder labored under the shadow of the Purcell failure for his entire episcopate. Nevertheless, he managed to orchestrate a significant reorganization of the archdiocesan administration. He established a chancery, canonical courts, advisory bodies, and compulsory annual reports from ecclesiastical institutions. He also established 32 new parishes and missions and, in 1890, St. Gregory's minor seminary. Slowed by age and physical infirmities in his 80s, he requested a coadjutor. On April 27, 1903, Rome appointed Cincinnati native Henry Moeller, bishop of Columbus, as coadjutor with right of succession.

Moeller. Moeller became archbishop upon Elder's death on Oct. 31, 1904. The new archbishop, who had been associated with the administrative work of the archdiocese, continued the important work of reorganization. Early in his tenure the final resolution of litigation related to the Purcell failure cleared the way for growth of parishes and institutions. He presided over the founding of the Fenwick Club, a hotel and center for Catholic men; St. Rita's School for the Deaf; a diocesan bureau of Catholic Charities; and the establishment in Cincinnati of the national headquarters for Catholic Charities and the Catholic Students Mission Crusade. In 1906, Moeller appoint-

ed the first archdiocesan Superintendent of Schools and organized the first board of education. At his death on Jan. 5, 1925, Moeller's work to extend the diocesan school system was well under way.

McNicholas. A quarter-century of extraordinary growth began with the appointment of Bishop John T. MCNICHOLAS, O.P., of Duluth, Minn., to the see of Cincinnati on July 15, 1925. The period saw 50 new parishes established, the number of high schools increased to 28, a doubling in the number of priests working the archdiocese, numerous mission chapels constructed in rural areas and administered by seminary professors until they required parochial status, and more than 100 diocesan priests educated in postgraduate programs in order to staff the diocesan agencies and educational institutions. New religious orders came to the archdiocese, including the Home Missionary Society for the United States (Glenmary). Seeing the need for organized youth activities on a diocesan basis, McNicholas established the Catholic Youth Organization (CYO) and the National Federation of Catholic College Students and developed the Fort Scott Camps. He undertook an apostolate for African Americans, building or converting 12 parishes for its work and founding two high schools for its special needs. He created an annual Holy Name parade at which Catholic men demonstrated their faith each October. In 1936, McNicholas welcomed to Cincinnati a future pope, Cardinal Eugenio Pacelli (Pius XII), for the dedication of Cardinal Pacelli School at Our Lord Christ the King parish. Because of the decay in the basin of the city where it was located, McNicholas abandoned St. Peter in Chains and created St. Monica's Church as a pro-cathedral in 1937. McNicholas became a strong voice of the American church, often influencing the stance of the U.S. bishops with his many public statements and radio broadcasts. The approach of the centenary of the archdiocese found McNicholas in poor health. His death on April 22, 1950 prevented his celebration of this event and of his 25th year as archbishop.

Alter. The appointment of Bishop Karl J. Alter of Toledo, Ohio, to Cincinnati continued a period of marked progress as he saw the church through the dynamic postwar and early post-Vatican II periods. A boom in population and the curtailment of construction during the depression and war years had left a backlog of building for the archdiocese to do. Alter directed a program of 350 archdiocesan and parish projects costing a total of $60 million. The most notable single work was the remodeling and reconstruction of the Cathedral of St. Peter in Chains and its reconstitution as the cathedral of the archdiocese—a project that sparked the renewal of downtown Cincinnati. The restored cathedral was rededicated in November 1957 before the largest assemblage of the hierarchy and clergy in the history of the archdiocese. A second major project was the completion of St. Gregory preparatory seminary, in part made necessary by a fire that destroyed the south wing on the night of Good Friday, 1956. Alter participated in the preparation of Vatican II and attended all of the sessions. He began the implementation of its documents and its spirit with great enthusiasm. He established a presbyter council, an archdiocesan pastoral council and parish councils, and formed commissions for ecumenism, poverty and human rights.

As the stresses of the 1960s reached Cincinnati, Alter wrote pastoral letters on inter-racial justice, the removal of discrimination in employment, voting rights and education. He supported Project Commitment, a major program on race relations. Organized by lay men and women with Protestant and Jewish participation, the project proved to be a valuable effort for inter-racial peace following Martin Luther King's murder. A leader in the national church on socio-economic issues, Alter in 1968 responded to the national urban crisis by pledging $1.25 million to help fund Catholic and ecumenical programs on race and poverty. The archdiocese under Alter also supported the creation of the Metropolitan Area Religious Coalition of Cincinnati, an inter-faith social justice organization of which the archdiocese remains the biggest funding source. A strong supporter of ecumenism, Alter presided in January 1967 at the first ecumenical service ever held at the Cathedral of St. Peter in Chains. He retired on July 23, 1969 and died on Aug. 23, 1977, outliving his successor. Both commanding and pastoral, Alter is remembered as the last great ''prince'' of the old style in the Cincinnati hierarchy.

Leibold. Pope Paul VI named Bishop Paul F. Leibold of Evansville, a native of Dayton and a former auxiliary bishop of Cincinnati, to succeed Alter. He was installed on July 23, 1969. At a time of perplexing change and confusion in the church and in the world, Leibold devoted his episcopacy to education, social action and ecumenism. He encouraged the organization of the Black Catholic Caucus and named members of the caucus to the Archdiocesan Pastoral Council. His greatest achievement was the Sixth Synod of the Archdiocese, held in 1971. Unlike previous diocesan synods, which were limited to priests, this synod also involved religious and lay men and women of the archdiocese. After a year of preparation, over 3,000 delegates gathered in assembly and voted upon documents that provided new guidelines for the life of the archdiocese. Leibold accepted these documents in an October 1971 Mass celebrating the 150th anniversary of the archdiocese. But Leibold died unexpectedly on June 1, 1972 and never lived to see the synod implemented.

Bernardin. Bishop Joseph L. BERNARDIN, the 44-year-old general secretary of the National Conference of Catholic Bishops, became the youngest archbishop in the United States upon his installation as archbishop of Cincinnati on Nov. 21, 1972. In contrast to the historical situation enjoyed by many of his predecessors, it was not a time of great growth for the church in the U.S. Mass attendance was in decline. Many priests and religious left active ministry. The minor seminary, St. Gregory's, closed. Bernardin responded to the changing circumstances with great skill. He was an efficient and effective administrator who consolidated most of the offices of the archdiocese in a single building. Even as Archbishop of Cincinnati, his quiet voice of reason made him a major figure in the church nationally and internationally. He was president of the National Conference of Catholic Bishops from 1974 to 1977. In 1974, 1977, 1980 and 1983 his fellow U.S. bishops named him a delegate to the World Synod of Bishops in Rome. Pope John Paul II, who as a cardinal had visited Bernardin in Cincinnati in 1976, appointed him archbishop of Chicago on July 10, 1982 and created him a cardinal the following year. Bernardin's last years were a model of grace under pressure. When a former seminarian from Cincinnati—a young man dying of AIDS—in 1993 accused Bernardin of sexually abusing him while archbishop of Cincinnati, the cardinal defended himself with disarming simplicity and a refusal to counterattack. After the accuser recanted his allegation the following year, Bernardin privately celebrated Mass with him in a liturgy of forgiveness and reconciliation. Less than two years later, Bernardin died on Nov. 14, 1996 after a very public and courageous battle with cancer.

Pilarczyk. Daniel E. Pilarczyk, auxiliary bishop and director of educational services for the archdiocese, was installed as archbishop on Dec. 20, 1982. He provided steady leadership in the local and national church at a time of uncertainty. Facing the new reality of relatively fewer priests and more faithful, Pilarczyk has fostered long-range planning processes, encouraged cooperation among parishes and expanded the concept of church ministry, especially in parishes. A former seminary professor of theology and rector, the Dayton, Ohio native strengthened seminary and other ministry training programs. The decline in priestly vocations was turned around during his tenure. Pilarczyk also has strongly supported Catholic schools, especially in the inner-city where the Catholic Inner-City School Education Fund raises more than $1 million a year for scholarships. One of his chief interests is adult faith formation, which he has fostered through *The Catholic Telegraph,* the official archdiocesan newspaper, and an initiative to add faith formation to all meetings throughout the archdiocese. Pilarczyk was vice president (1986–1989) and president (1989–1992) of the National Conference of Catholic Bishops. He has written more than 11 books aimed at general audiences, and is highly regarded throughout the country for his theological acumen.

Institutional Development. The Archdiocese of Cincinnati held formal synods in 1865, 1886, 1898, 1920, 1954, and 1971. Decrees affecting the development of the parochial system of education became patterns for similar legislation in other dioceses in the U.S. The provincial councils of 1855, 1858, 1861, 1882 and 1889 enacted legislation to secure conformity throughout the province in disciplinary or procedural concerns.

The archdiocese has had nine auxiliary bishops: Sylvester H. Rosecrans (1862–68); Joseph H. Albers (1929–37), later bishop of Lansing, Mich.; George J. Rehring (1937–1950), later bishop of Toledo, Ohio; Clarence G. Issenbaum (1954–1957), later bishop of Columbus, Ohio; Paul F. Leibold (1958–1965), later bishop of Evansville and archbishop of Cincinnati; Edward A. McCarthy, (1965–1969), later archbishop of Miami; Nicholas T. Elko (1971–1985); Daniel E. Pilarczyk, (1974–1982), later archbishop of Cincinnati; James A. Garland (1985–1992), later bishop of Marquette, Mich.; and Carl K. Moeddel (1993–).

Educational Development. Even in the early missionary years of Cincinnati the objective was a school in every parish. This was realized to a considerable degree in the 16 parishes established during Fenwick's episcopacy. It became the common practice under Purcell to open church and school simultaneously. Purcell's success in bringing teaching communities to the archdiocese is one of the most significant factors in the developing parochial school system. The Sister of Notre Dame de Namur began their work in 1940, the Franciscan Fathers and Brothers in 1844, the Ursulines in 1845, the Brothers of Mary in 1849, the Sisters of Mercy in 1858, the Sisters of the Sacred Heart in 1869, the Franciscan Sisters in 1876, and the Sisters of Christian Charity in 1881. By the end of Purcell's episcopate, the parochial school system was so generally established that his successor, Elder, could promulgate regulations for compulsory attendance at Catholic schools. During the same period, schools were attached to orphanages and convents as well.

The need for control and organization at the archdiocesan level caused Moeller to establish an archdiocesan Superintendent of Schools. The first report from this office in 1908 listed 27,233 students in attendance at 110 schools. Almost a hundred years later, at the beginning of the 21st century, the Catholic school system in Cincinnati remains strong. Although the archdiocese is only the 26th largest diocese in the U.S., its school system is the ninth largest—41,106 students in 114 elementary schools and 12,051 students in 22 high schools in the 2001–2002 school year.

In higher education, the archdiocese established a teachers college in 1928. Although primarily intended for teaching communities of sisters, the program attracted lay teachers, seminarians, and priests as well. The Athenaeum of Ohio was incorporated in 1928 with a board headed by the archbishop for the supervision of all Catholic colleges, seminaries, high schools and other institutions of higher learning. Today the Athenaeum has three divisions: Mount St. Mary's Seminary of the West, the Lay Pastoral Ministry Program (LPMP), and Special Studies. LPMP, founded in 1975 as a pioneering center for lay education and formation for ministry, is the biggest of the three programs. Special Studies includes formation for the diaconate.

Other Catholic institutions of higher learning in the archdiocese include Xavier University (operated by the Jesuits), the University of Dayton (Marianists), the College of Mount St. Joseph (Sisters of Charity of Cincinnati), and Chatfield College (Sisters of St. Ursuline of Brown County).

Bibliography: E. A. CONNAUGHTON, *A History of Educational Legislation and Administration in the Archdiocese of Cincinnati* (Washington 1946). J. H. LAMOTT, *History of the Archdiocese of Cincinnati, 1821–1921* (New York 1921). V. F. O'DANIEL, *The Right Reverend Edward Dominic Fenwick, O.P., First Bishop of Cincinnati* (Washington 1920). K. J. ALTER, *The Mind of an Archbishop: A Study of Man's Essential Relationship to God, Church, Country and Fellow Men,* ed. M. E. REARDON (Paterson 1960). J. BERNARDIN, *The Gift of Peace: Personal Reflections* (Chicago 1997).

[A. STRITCH/D. ANDRIACCO]

CIPITRIA Y BARRIOLA, CÁNDIDA MARÍA DE JESÚS, BL.

Baptized Juana Josefa, foundress of the Daughters of Jesus (Hijas de Jesús); b. Berrospe, Andoáin, Guipúzcoa, Spain, May 31, 1845; d. Salamanca, Spain, Aug. 9, 1912. As the daughter of a weaver, Juana Cipitria was virtually uneducated, yet in Salamanca she founded the Daughters of Jesus for the purpose of educating girls (Dec. 8, 1871). The congregation began after Juana (later Mother Cándida María de Jesús) had gathered like-minded women to assist with a series of charitable and educational programs she had started under the guidance of Jesuit Father Miguel Herranz. His influence can also be seen in the order's constitution (approved by Leo XIII, 1902), which is based on that of St. IGNATIUS OF LOYOLA. Her various foundations demonstrate her commitment to incarnating social justice and her appreciation of contemplation. The

Daughters of Jesus now operate schools, medical dispensaries, retreat houses, and social service centers in many countries around the globe, including Argentina, Colombia, Japan, the Philippines, Spain, and the United States. Mother Cándida was declared venerable July 6, 1993, and beatified by Pope John Paul II, together with her religious sister María Antonia BANDRÉS Y ELOSEGUI, May 12, 1996.

Bibliography: M. MARCOS, *Del Tormes al río Azul* (Salamanca 1932).

[K. I. RABENSTEIN]

CIRCUMCISION

The cutting off of the prepuce of the male. While there are instances of similar operations performed on females (e.g., the cutting off of the internal labia), the term circumcision is usually limited to males. Circumcision is a very ancient practice common to various peoples of primitive agriculture, but not among those of truly primitive culture. Among these peoples living in such disparate locales as Africa, America, and Australia, it seems to have been a rite connected in some way with puberty and the entrance into the adult or married state and probably related to fertility rites.

Its use by the Israelites is well known. Great emphasis was placed upon it as a sign of orthodoxy, especially in postexilic times. Allusions to this rite in the Bible confirm some of the primitive characteristics of this practice. The mention, for instance, in Ex 4.25 and Jos 5.2 of flint knives used in the operation points to the antiquity of the practice. The enigmatic action of Moses' wife Zipporah and her reference to a "spouse of blood" (Ex 4.25–26), as also the incident with the men of Shechem recorded in Gn 34.14–17, could refer to the connection of this rite with marriage.

The origin of the practice among the Israelites cannot be clearly determined. Some scholars are of the opinion that the Israelites received it from the Egyptians, since it was practiced in Egypt in the time of the Old Kingdom. Others disagree with this view, holding for a common source for both the Egyptians and the Israelites rather than a direct transmission. According to this view, the Israelites would have accepted the practice from the Canaanites as they settled among them in Palestine. It would appear that these people did practice circumcision, since the Israelites refer to the Philistines as the uncircumcised (e.g., 1 Sm 14.6), but they never thus distinguish the other peoples with whom they were in contact in Palestine.

Whatever its origin, this rite had a special religious significance for the Israelites. It was practiced as a sign

"The Circumcision," 1500, oil on canvas painting by the Italian artist Marco Marziale, painted for the high altarpiece of S. Silvestro.

of the relationship with God stemming from the covenant made with Abraham. It is not clear just when the rite took on such a significance. The principal texts describing its origin with this significance all belong to the Pentateuchal PRIESTLY WRITERS (Gn 17.10–14; Ex 12.43–48; Lv 12.3). The fact that the practice does not appear in the other Israelite law codes suggests that this was a family ceremony adopted from the practices of the neighboring peoples. Probably in the beginning its connection with matrimonial rites was maintained, but gradually it received a more lofty religious significance, especially when the rite began to be administered immediately after birth rather than at puberty. Then, when the people found themselves in exile among those who did not practice such a rite, circumcision would have become the distinctive mark of the man who belonged both to Israel and to Yahweh.

The metaphorical usage of the concept of circumcision seems to strengthen the hypothesis that circumcision

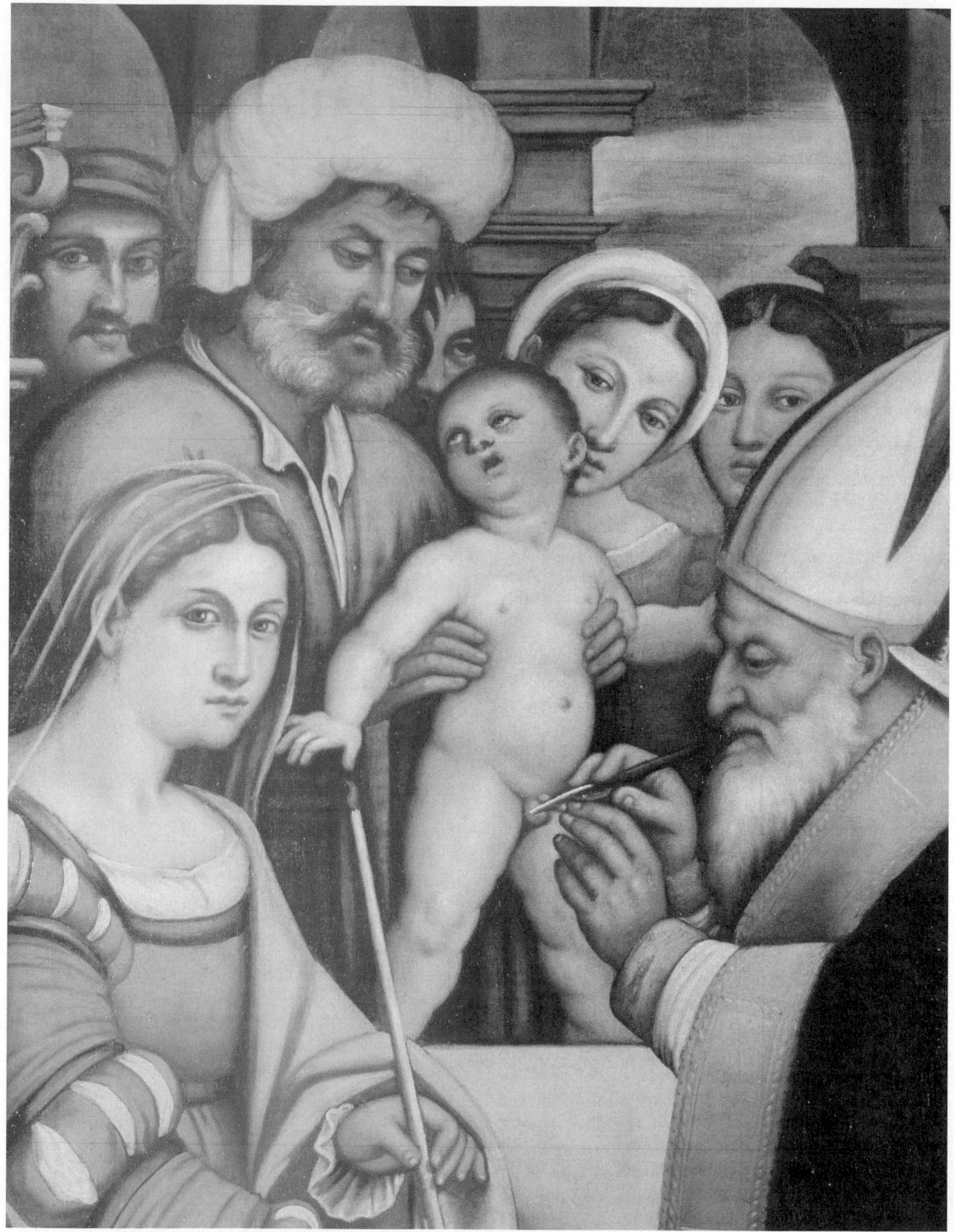

"Circumcision of Jesus Christ," 1701, *painting by L. Candido.* (©Elio Ciol/CORBIS)

in Israel was connected with the rite of marriage. In such places as Dt 10.16; 30.6; Jer 4.4; 6.10; 9.25; Lv 26.41; and Ex 6.12, 30, reference is made to "uncircumcised" lips, heart, and ears as organs that do not fulfill their function; they can do so only when they are, metaphorically speaking, circumcised.

Toward the end of the OT period, circumcision occupied a very important place in the religious life of the people. ANTIOCHUS IV EPIPHANES energetically opposed the practice with cruel punishments (1 Mc 1.63–64; 2 Mc 6.10), and to cling to this rite was the test of Jewish faith.

In modern-day Judaism circumcision is still practiced by both Orthodox and Reform elements. The male infants are circumcised on the 8th day after birth, even if it is a Sabbath or Day of Atonement. Among the Orthodox the rite is carried out by a functionary called a *mohel* (circumciser). The Reform Jews allow the rite to be performed by a physician; contrary to the practice of the Orthodox, they do not require it for adult proselytes.

Circumcision of Jesus. Christ's circumcision is briefly described in Lk 2.21: "And when eight days were fulfilled for his circumcision, his name was called Jesus, the name given him by the angel before he was conceived in the womb."

In the 1st century the Jews did not bring their children to the Temple or to the synagogue for the rite of circumcision; it was performed in the midst of the assembled family at home with great ceremony. It was at this time that the child was given his name. It seems that the circumcision of Christ took place in Bethlehem, because of the obligation imposed on the Jews by sacerdotal prescription to have their sons circumcised on the 8th day after birth; this obligation was so strict that it superseded the ordinance of the Sabbath rest. Only when a child was so weak that the operation would endanger his life could the ceremony be postponed. Since the father of the household usually was the minister of circumcision, it would seem that St. Joseph performed this ceremony for Christ. The prescriptions of the law mentioned in Gn 17.12 and Lv 12.3 were followed, since there is no other indication in the Gospels of any specific divine command to Mary and Joseph. The Gospel stresses that the newly born Savior of the world is the appointed heir of the promises made to Abraham, and that this is confirmed by the rite of circumcision; on this same occasion He is given the name Jesus to indicate His role as Savior.

The practice of administering circumcision on the 8th day after birth, and not as a puberty rite, specified the act among the Jews as a religious rite. It was thus more easily recognized as the religious act by which the child became a member of the people of God and heir of the messianic promises made to Abraham. In St. Luke's mind in describing the circumcision of Christ, since salvation is from the Jews, the Savior of the world must be the descendant of Abraham. It is through faith in Christ, who was Himself circumcised, that the new Israel is grafted onto the root of Abraham.

The early Christians had difficulty with the practice of circumcision within the context of the controversy over the necessity for Gentile converts to observe the prescriptions of the Mosaic Law. St. Paul clearly saw the error of attributing any efficacy to such practices since it would mitigate the universality of the salvific effect on Christ's sacrifice (Gal 5.6; 6.15). Those who urged such requirements he called "enemies of the cross of Christ" (Phil 3.18).

Bibliography: R. DE VAUX, *Ancient Israel, Its Life and Institutions* (New York 1961) 46–48. *Encyclopedic Dictionary of the Bible* (New York 1963) 389–390. F. R. LEHMANN and K. GALLING, *Die Religion in Geschichte und Gegenwart* (3d ed. Tübingen 1957–65) 1:1090–91. S. H. BLANK and M. JOSEPH, *Universal Jewish Encyclopedia* (New York 1939–44) 3:211–216.

[S. M. POLAN/R. L. FOLEY]

CIRCUMINCESSION

This article briefly considers first the positive foundations of the doctrine and then its theological formulation.

Positive Foundations. By the term circumincession theology understands the mutual immanence and penetration of the three divine PERSONS. *Circuminsessio (circum-in-sedere:* to sit around) stresses rather the passive, somewhat static aspect of the doctrine, whereas *circumincessio (circum-incedere:* to go, to move around) looks at it from the dynamic angle of movement. The earliest usage was of a corresponding Greek word, περιχώρησις, by St. Gregory of Nazianzus (middle of fourth century), not in a Trinitarian but in a Christological context, to signify the mutual immanence of the two natures in Christ (*Epist.* 101; *Patrologia Graeca,* 37:182; *See* PERICHORESIS; CHRISTOLOGICAL). In its present Trinitarian meaning it was first used by St. John Damascene in the eighth century (*De fide orth.* 1.8; *Patrologia Graeca,* 94:829). However, the doctrine itself has deep roots in Scripture: ". . . believe in the works, that you may know and believe that the Father is in me and I in the Father" (John 10.38; 14.11; 17.21). These three Johannine texts have traditionally been understood by Catholic (J. Knabenbauer, A. Wikenhauser, J. Leal) and Protestant (C. Barret, W. Hendriksen) exegetes in the sense of a mutual divine immanence between Father and Son. Explicit scriptural basis for the mutual penetration of the Holy

Spirit and the other two Persons is lacking (1 Corinthians 2.10, often quoted, is inconclusive).

Formulation. St. Thomas (*Summa Theologiae* 1a, 42.5) admirably synthesizing the two conceptions, Latin and Greek, explains circumincession by the unicity of the divine nature (Latin) as well as by the very origin of the Persons (Greek).

The divine nature, numerically one, is conceived by Latin theology as the common ground (in its theory with a certain unavoidable logical priority over the Persons) where Father, Son and Holy Spirit meet. The common bond of the only divine essence, which is equally possessed by all three, necessarily links all three. Besides this unity of nature, there is a perfect fusion of personal rational activities: the three Persons cannot but think, decide and act together, with all these divine acts flowing down the very same channel of the divine nature.

The Greek background is different: less static, more vital and dynamic. For a Greek the primary datum is not nature but Person, throbbing with life, communicable life. Each Divine Person is irresistibly drawn, by the very constitution of His being, to the other two. Branded in the very depths of each one of them is a necessary outward impulse, a centrifugal force, urging Him to give Himself fully to the other two, to pour Himself out into the divine receptacle of the other two. It is a "reciprocal irruption" (Cyril of Alex., *In Jo.* 1.5; *Patrologia Graeca,* 73:81), or unceasing circulation of life. Thus, each Person being necessarily in the other two, unity is achieved not so much on account of the unicity of a single passive nature but rather because of this irresistible impulse in each Person, which mightily draws them to one another.

One has here two different explanations, substantially identical, yet rich and colorful in their variety, of the same divine circumincession. Probably the best formulation of this mysterious reality is that given in the West by the 11th Council of Toledo (675), which, with an unmistakable oriental ring, teaches that the mutual relations, binding the Persons and referring them to one another, are the deepest root of the doctrine (H. Denzinger, *Enchiridion Symbolorum* 532). In the beatific vision "it will be granted to the eyes of the human mind, strengthened by the light of glory, to contemplate the Father, the Son, and the Holy Spirit in an utterly ineffable manner, to assist throughout eternity at the processions of the Divine Persons, and to rejoice with a happiness like to that with which the holy and undivided Trinity is happy" ("Mystici Corporis Christi," *Acta Apostolicae Sedis* 80).

See Also: TRINITY, HOLY, ARTICLES ON; NATURE; PERSON (IN THEOLOGY); PROCESSIONS, TRINITARIAN; RELATIONS, TRINITARIAN.

Bibliography: A. CHOLLET, *Dictionnaire de théologie catholique,* ed. A. VACANT et al., 15 v. (Paris 1903–50) 2.2:2527–32. M. SCHMAUS, *Lexikon für Theologie und Kirche,* eds., J. HOFER and K. RAHNER, 10 v. (2d, new ed. Freiburg 1957–65) 8:274–276. T. DE RÉGNON, *Études de théologie positive sur la Sainte Trinité,* 4 v. (Paris 1892–98). A. DENEFFE, "Perichoresis, circumincessio, circuminsessio," *Zeitschrift für katholische Theologie,* 47 (1923) 497–532. L. PRESTIGE, "περιχωρέω and περιχώρησις in the Fathers," *Journal of Theological Studies,* 29 (1928) 242–252. *Patrologia Graeca,* ed., J. P. MIGNE, 161 v. (Paris 1857–66). PIUS XII, "Mystici Corporis Christi," *Acta Apostolicae Sedis* 35 (1943) 193–248.

[A. M. BERMEJO]

CIRCUMSTANCES, MORAL

A HUMAN ACT is moral insofar as it is subject to reason. That which specifies a human action as morally good or bad is whatever makes an action to be the kind of act that it is, and this is determined by the object of the act. The object of a moral act is that to which the action tends by its very nature. For example, the object of murder is the taking of the life of an innocent person. It is the object, so understood, that primarily specifies an action as morally good or bad. This moral object makes the action to be good or bad as such.

No action, however, is performed in the abstract. Every human act in the concrete order is done under particular circumstances. Circumstances may therefore affect the morality of an action and add something to the moral quality that it has by reason of its object. The latter concerns the abstract nature of the act, that is, what kind of action it is morally, while the circumstances concern the individuality of the action, that is, the act as it exists here and now. But since many individuating conditions or circumstances are involved in any human action, we must restrict circumstances to those that have a moral bearing on the action. For example, the action of murder is by its object morally evil; the circumstance of using a dagger is relevant whereas the circumstance of the murderer's wearing a necktie is not. A moral circumstance, therefore, is an individuating condition that, though it is something over and beyond the nature of the action itself, nevertheless modifies in some real way the moral quality of the act.

Aristotle first treated moral circumstances in an explicit manner, in the context of ignorance: an agent's ignorance of this or that circumstance could introduce an involuntary aspect into a given action and, to the extent that it does, it lessens responsibility (*Eth. Nic.* 111a 3–8). St. Thomas Aquinas, taking Cicero into account as well as Aristotle, treated moral circumstances in terms of seven questions that can be asked about a moral action, and noted which circumstances are the most important (*Summa theologiae* 1a2ae, 7.3–4).

Classification of Circumstances. Some circumstances affect the very doing of the action. *When* the action takes place refers to the relevance this or that period of time has in the performance of an act, e.g., whether it is done by day or night, during war or peace, and so on. *Where* the action takes place can affect its morality; murder in a cathedral adds an additional moral evil to murder itself. *How* the action occurs concerns the manner in which the action is carried out, e.g., a person saves the life of another by acting with courage.

Other circumstances relate to causes that bring about the action. *Why* the action takes place refers to the motive or purpose a person has in performing an action; it is the extrinsic end for which the action is done. *Who* is doing the action refers to the agent himself who performs the act, and this circumstance is significant when some quality of his person affects the moral character of what he does. *By what means* the action is carried out refers to the instrumental moral cause used to accomplish the action; it makes a difference, for example, whether a murderer chooses a painful means to commit his crime.

Another circumstance concerns the effect of the action with regard primarily to its *quantitative* aspect. Stealing is an action morally wrong by its object; stealing a large amount of money is a circumstance aggravating the malice of the act.

Moral Consequences of Circumstances. It is clear that circumstances add varying degrees of moral good and evil to a voluntary act to the extent that a person is aware of them. The primary and essential morality of a human action, however, is taken from the object and not from any of the circumstances. The moral kind of an act cannot be changed by any circumstance attending its performance. The taking of the life of an innocent person is murder and as such is morally evil; accompanying circumstances will not alter this primary specification. However, granted the primary moral worth of the action, circumstances may clearly contribute additional morality to it. Sometimes circumstances affect the morality of the action only in degree, that is, they increase or diminish its goodness or malice. Stealing is bad by object; stealing a rare object increases the malice of the action but it adds no additional kind of evil to the act. Giving money for a charitable cause is a good action in itself; giving a large amount that one can afford increases the goodness of the action.

Sometimes circumstances add a new kind of morality to an act. In the example of murder in a cathedral, the evil action of murder, through circumstance of place, involves the profanation of a consecrated place of worship and hence the additional evil of sacrilege. However, it is the circumstance of end, the purpose in doing the act, that

matters most in this regard and, indeed, is the most important circumstance of all precisely because it can, more than any other circumstance, add a new moral quality to an action. The motive an agent has can change an act morally good by object into a morally evil act. Telling the truth is a morally good action by object, but to tell the truth about someone with the intention of injuring him turns an action still good by object into a bad one. However, the reverse effect does not occur, namely, that a good intention should turn an act evil by object into one that is morally good. The reason for this is that the morality of an act is based essentially on its specification by its object. No motive the agent has in mind, regardless of how noble it may be, can change what is essentially evil into something good. In a word, no end or motive, no matter how good, can morally justify an essentially evil means; for example, one cannot use murder, morally evil by object, as a means to any end, no matter how good.

Many contemporary Catholic theologians take the position that circumstances sometimes can make actions legitimate that are evil *ex objecto*. Such acts they term "prima facie evil," "physical evil," "ontic evil," "premoral evil," "nonmoral evil," but not necessarily "moral evil" (sin). Nonmoral evil does not become moral evil until it is taken up into the agent's intention; that is to say, it does not become moral evil if it is done for a proportionately good reason. The final moral evaluation of an act must take into consideration all the circumstances, especially the personally intended end. Accordingly, these theologians justify certain actions that are evil *ex objecto* in certain circumstances, for instance abortion to save the life of the mother, masturbation for fertility testing, therapeutic sterilization. This means that these Catholic theologians reject the concept of "intrinsically evil acts," i.e., actions which are judged morally evil or sinful prior to a consideration of the circumstances in which they are done. In his 1993 encyclical *VERITATIS SPLENDOR* (no. 79ff.), Pope John Paul II explicitly rejected such a position.

Bibliography: THOMAS AQUINAS, *Summa theologiae* 1a2ae, 18. D. M. PRÜMMER, *Manuale theologiae moralis*, ed. E. M. MÜNCH, 3 v. (10th ed. Barcelona 1945–46) 1:75–86. J. A. OESTERLE, *Ethics: The Introduction to Moral Science* (Englewood Cliffs, NJ 1957) 103–110. J. FUCHS, "The Absoluteness of Moral Terms," *Gregorianum* 52 (1971) 415–458. R. MCCORMICK, *Ambiguity in Moral Choice* (Milwaukee 1973).

[J. A. OESTERLE/J. F. DEDEK/EDS.]

CIRER CARBONNEL, FRANCINAINA, BL.

Known in religion as Francinaina de los Dolores de María, also known as Francinaina de Sencelles, foundress of the Sisters of Charity; b. Sencelles, Mallorca, Balearic Islands, Spain, June 1, 1781; d. Sencelles, Mallorca, Feb. 27, 1855. When Cirer's wealthy family refused her permission to become a nun, she led a life of poverty, consecration to prayer, and obedience to the will of God as a lay woman. Even after the deaths of all her family members, she remained in her home, caring for the sick, engaging in spiritual exercises, and offering her possessions for the work of her parish and the relief of the poor. Nevertheless her holiness drew others to her. On Dec. 23, 1850 at age 70, she provided her home and the funds to found the Sisters of Charity in Sencelles. She pronounced her vows with two companions on Dec. 7, 1951 and continued her works of charity and evangelization until her death. Today her tomb in the Sisters of Charity convent in Sencelles is a place of pilgrimage. Pope John Paul II declared Francinaina venerable in 1983 and beatified her, Oct. 1, 1989.

Feast: Feb. 27.

Bibliography: J. LLABRÉS I MARTORELL, *La beata Francinaina de Sencelles* (Mallorca 1989, 2d ed. Mallorca 1990). B. C. LLULL, *Francisca Ana Cirer. Una vida evangélica* (Mallorca 1971). B. OLIVER, *Sor Francina-Aina dels Dolors (La Tia Xiroia de Sencelles)* (Mallorca 1970). T. SUAU PUIG, *Sor Francinaina Cirer, una vida para los demas* (Mallorca 1992). *Acta Apostolicae Sedis* (1989): 1030.

[K. I. RABENSTEIN]

CISNEROS, GARCÍA DE

Benedictine abbot of the abbey of MONTSERRAT, monastic reformer, and ascetical writer; b. Cisneros, diocese of Léon (Castile), 1455 or 1456; d. Montserrat, Nov. 27, 1510. Cousin of Cardinal Francisco XIMÉNEZ and only son of a poor but proud nobleman, García early gave up the possibility of social privilege to enter the austere Castilian monastery of San Benito de Valladolid in 1475. Chosen as subprior in 1488, he played a prominent role in Valladolid's efforts to centralize and reform monastic observance in the newly united Spain of Ferdinand and Isabella. When called to initiate the observance of Valladolid in the Catalan monastery shrine of Our Lady of Montserrat, he found himself favoring the independence of that monastery and accepted papal permission to become its abbot for life. He succeeded in winning Valladolid's recognition of his adaptations for the venerable pilgrimage center. In 1500 he published *Directorio de las horas canónicas* (*Directory of the Canonical Hours*) for community prayer at Montserrat; the *Constitutions* of 1501 established the monastery's character and observances for the next two centuries. His most famous work (also 1500), *Ejercitatorio de la vida espiritual* (*Exercises*

for the Spiritual Life), is a skillful compilation drawn from Devotio Moderna sources and intended for both monks and pilgrims (such as St. Ignatius would be in 1522) as a practical, systematic guide toward contemplation. He was an important link between medieval, monastic piety and the psychological, analytical systems of St. Ignatius of Loyola and the Spanish mystics later in the century.

Bibliography: *Obras completas,* ed. C. BARAUT (Montserrat 1965), bibliog. E. A. PEERS, *Studies of the Spanish Mystics,* v. 2 (London 1930; repr. 1960) 3–37, 401–407. G. COLOMBÁS, *Un reformador benedictino en tiempo de los reyes católicos: García Jiménez de Cisneros, abad de Montserrat* (*Scripta et documenta* 5; Montserrat 1955), biog. and bibliog.

[P. EDWARDS]

CISTERCIAN NUNS

Under this title are included several groups of cloistered nuns who, in their history and tradition, are associated with the CISTERCIANS. The first Cistercian monastery for women was organized at Tart, near CÎTEAUX, *c.* 1120. Other foundations followed throughout Europe; many were Benedictine convents that adopted the Cistercian reform. In the beginning the monks had rejected any legal relationship with the nuns. A century later Cîteaux incorporated a group of convents, although most remained under diocesan jurisdiction. The incorporated convents were subject to the Cistercian general chapter and were directed by neighboring abbots who assigned chaplains and furnished occasional economic assistance. The convent of Helfta (1258), Eisleben, Saxony, under Abbess Gertrude of Hackeborn (1251–92), developed a rich mystical tradition, represented by St. GERTRUDE (THE GREAT) and MECHTILD OF MAGDEBURG. Cîteaux's continuing reluctance to assume full responsibility occasioned the emergence of several prominent convents as organizers and leaders of other communities. Thus, Tart in the 13th century headed a group of 18 convents and convoked annual chapters for the abbesses. About the same time a similar and still more extensive Spanish organization was controlled by the royal Abbey of Las Huelgas, near Burgos, founded (1187) by King Alfonso VIII of Castile (1158–1214).

The Hundred Years' War, the Reformation, and subsequent secularization and warfare destroyed hundreds of convents. Surviving ones often abandoned their rural isolation and sought permanent refuge within walled cities. The 17th century witnessed a number of local reforms; many of these reformed nuns adopted the name Bernardines. Famous among the Cistercian convents of that period was PORT-ROYAL, outside Paris. It was reformed by

Angélique ARNAULD and became a stronghold of JAN-SENISM under the influence of the Abbé de Saint-Cyran (*see* DUVERGIER DE HAURANNE, JEAN). A later reform movement, that of the Trappistines, began during the period of the French Revolution when Dom Augustin established (1796) the convent La Sainte Volonté de Dieu near Riédra, Switzerland. In the 19th century, when the revived Cistercian Order found itself divided into Strict and Common Observances, both groups of monks renewed their associations with many Cistercian convents. The nuns of both observances lead cloistered and contemplative lives.

Cistercian Nuns of the Common Observance. Official Catholic Directory #0680; known also as Cistercians of the Original Observance, *Sacer Ordo monialium Cisterciensium* (OCist) or as Bernardines. The headquarters of the order is in Rome. In the U.S., the Swiss convent of Frauenthal established a monastery Valley of Our Lady Monastery (formerly known as St. Ida's Convent), in Prairie du Sac, Wisconsin in 1957.

Cistercian Nuns of the Strict Observance. Official Catholic Directory #0670; known also as Trappistines, the *Ordo monialium Cisterciensium strictioris observantiae* (OCSO) has its generalate in Rome, and five foundations in the U.S. Mount St. Mary's Abbey (Wrentham, MA), Our Lady of the Mississippi Abbey (Dubuque, IA), Santa Rita Abbey (Sonoita, AZ), Our Lady of the Redwoods Abbey (Whitethorn, CA); Our Lady of the Angels Monastery (Crozet, VA).

Bibliography: A. J. LUDDY, *The Cistercian Nuns* (Dublin 1931). Y. ESTIENNE, *Les Trappistines cisterciennes de la stricte observance* (Paris 1937). J. BOUTON, "L'Établissement des moniales cisterciennes," *XXIV e Congrès de l'Assoc. Bourguignonne des Sociétés savantes* (Dijon 1953) 37–70. E. G. KRENIG, "Mittelalterliche Frauenklöster nach den Konstitutionen von Cîteaux," *Analecta Sacri Ordinis Cisterciensis* 10 (1954) 1–105. M. HEIMBUCHER, *Die Orden und Kongregationen der katholischen Kirche,* 2 v. (3rd ed. Paderborn 1932–34) 1:356–362, 373.

[L. J. LEKAI/EDS.]

CISTERCIAN RITE

This entry discusses the history and development of the pre-Vatican II Cistercian Rite, and its form of the Divine Office and Mass.

Divine Office. The Cistercian Office is basically that of the Rule of St. Benedict. Before the founding of Cîteaux this Office had become so overlaid with additional psalms, little offices, litanies, processions, and commemorations that the monks were spending the greater part of their day in choir and had little or no time for manual labor. In the first half of the 12th century the Cister-

cians swept aside these accretions and boasted of having returned to the balanced monastic day that St. Benedict had intended. Yet the second half of the century witnessed the same process of elaboration of the choral service. First an office of the dead was to be said in choir on most days, then a daily office of Our Lady; processions were multiplied, and common commemorations introduced. Only in the 20th century was this process brought to a halt and measures taken to reform the Office to its historical simplicity.

Traditionally, on ferial days Vigils (Matins) had two nocturns, each with six psalms, the first nocturn containing either three lessons or one short lesson. On Sundays and feasts there were three nocturns, the first two each containing six psalms and four lessons, the third having three canticles and four lessons. Lauds and the Little Hours were similar in structure to those of the Roman rite. Vespers had only four psalms, and these were always ferial, that is, they did not vary for feasts. Compline began with a 15-minute reading in the cloister, consisting of Psalms 4, 90, and 133 every day, and lacked the familiar Confiteor, Nunc Dimittis, and *In Manus Tuas* of the Roman rite. Proper to the Cistercians were a commemoration of Our Lady before the hours, and the well-known Cistercian *SALVE REGINA* after Compline.

Mass. Since the Rule of St. Benedict did not give detailed instructions for the celebration of Mass, the first Cistercians appeared simply to have taken the rite of the ecclesiastical province of Lyons in which they were first situated, together with some Cluniac usages from Molesmes. In their desire for uniformity they made this rite obligatory for all houses, no matter where located. The early Cistercian Mass was characterized by simplicity. There were two categories of high Mass: the Sunday-feast-day Mass with deacon and subdeacon, and the ferial-day Mass with only one minister, either a deacon or a subdeacon. The dalmatic and tunic were not worn. Incense was used on Sundays and feasts, only at the Offertory. There were no acolytes, merely a server who came up from the choir when needed. Holy Communion was still being distributed at that time under both species, and the profound bow had not yet given way to the genuflection. Later centuries saw progressive embellishment in the form of added candles, incense, dalmatic and tunic, pontifical Masses, and a greater variety of chants. When at the end of the 16th century Pius V published his reformed Roman Missal, the ancient religious orders, although not required to adopt it, were invited to do so. The Cistercians, after much internal dissension, finally accepted the rubrics of the 1570 Missal.

Bibliography: P. GUIGNARD, *Les Monuments primitifs de la règle cistercienne* (Dijon 1878). H. SÉJALON, ed., *Nomasticon cistercienne* (new ed. Solesmes 1892). A. MALET, *La Liturgie*

Œlt fydus nitidum: vefter præfulgidus ozdo.
Jam penitus toto clarus in oabe micat.
Sanctus 7 exemptus: þmaqz ab ozigine liber.
Nullus in hunc quicqz iuris habere folet.

Anno milleno centeno bis minus vno.
Sub pfe Roberto cepit Lifterci⁹ ozdo.

Paschal II approving Cistercian Order, woodcut by Peter Metlinger, 1491.

cistercienne (Westmalle 1921). A. A. KING, *Liturgies of the Religious Orders* (Milwaukee 1955) 62–156. L. J. LEKAI, *The White Monks* (Okauchee, Wis. 1953) 171–186. C. WADDELL, "The pre-Cistercian background of Cîteaux and the Cistercian liturgy," in E. R. ELDER, *Goad and Nail: Studies in Medieval Cistercian History* (Kalamazoo, Mich. 1985) 109–132.

[T. BOYD/EDS.]

CISTERCIANS

The Order of Cîteaux (Ocist, Official Catholic Directory #0340), a Roman Catholic monastic order based on the Rule of St. Benedict, originated in 1098, and was named after the first establishment, Cîteaux, in Burgundy, France (Latin *Cistercium*).

History

Cîteaux was founded by (St.) ROBERT OF MOLESME (d. 1111). As Benedictine abbot of MOLESME he had failed to achieve real monastic reform, so he left that abbey with 21 of his adherents, and in 1098 founded CÎTEAUX in a wooded wilderness near Dijon. The purpose of the new establishment was the instituting of a life of poverty, simplicity, and eremitical solitude, under the guidance of the Rule of St. Benedict in its strictest interpretation. Such a program was no novelty at the end of the 11th century, but Cîteaux found itself exposed to the hostile criticism of neighboring monasteries. In July 1099, through the intervention of higher ecclesiastical authority, Molesme enforced the return of Robert; (St.) Alberic (1099–1109) succeeded him at Cîteaux. In 1100 Pope Paschal II approved the new foundation and placed Cîteaux under papal protection. According to tradition, it was under Alberic that the monks adopted their distinctive white or gray habit under a black scapular; hence the popular name, White Monks.

After Alberic's death the Englishman (St.) STEPHEN HARDING, an organizer of broad vision and experience, was elected abbot (1109–33). Although there were still many problems to be solved, a sound program and able leadership assured the survival of Cîteaux. The first regulations, passed either under Alberic or Stephen, revealed Cîteaux's uniqueness, for unlike other reformed Benedictine houses, the statutes rejected all feudal revenues, and based the monastic economy on the manual labor of the monks themselves, assisted by lay brothers. Other measures simplified the overgrown monastic liturgy then customary in Benedictine houses, and prescribed austere simplicity both in church vestments and in church furnishings.

Expansion. As early as 1113 a small band of monks was ready to leave Cîteaux for the foundation of her first "daughter," La Ferté. Yet, the dramatic growth and extraordinary popularity of the order was due to (St.) BERNARD, who in 1113, with about 30 companions, applied for admission at Cîteaux. It was his example and magnetic personality that drew thousands of others to Cîteaux, and to the rapidly multiplying new establishments. La Ferté was followed by the foundation of PONTIGNY in 1114, and in 1115 Bernard became the founder and first abbot of CLAIRVAUX. It was largely through Bernard's international fame that the order spread with unprecedented rapidity throughout foreign lands as well as France. In 1120 Cistercians founded their first establishment in Italy, in 1123 they settled in Germany, in 1128 in England, in 1130 in Austria, in 1132 in Spain, and foundations in all other countries of Western Christendom followed. Bernard was personally responsible for the organization of 65 new houses in France and abroad. At his death in 1153 the order possessed more than 300 monasteries, and toward the end of the same century the number exceeded 500. The rise of the MENDICANT OR-

DERS reduced monastic vocations considerably, but growth continued at a slower pace until, before the Reformation, there were 742 Cistercian houses, with 246 abbeys in France alone. At the peak of their popularity, the monastic population of many abbeys amounted to several hundred, although these figures included a large number of lay brothers.

As another result of Bernard's example, the order gradually became involved in activities beyond the scope of a purely contemplative life. Abbots served as papal diplomats, others combated Albigensian heretics, participated in the Crusades, and served as missionaries in Eastern Europe and in the Baltic lands. Cistercians were responsible for the organization of several military orders in Spain. The greatest of them, CALATRAVA, was founded in 1158, and, in spiritual matters, was under the control of the Abbey of MORIMOND. An increasing number of monks were engaged in pastoral activities, and by the 16th century most houses took care of the spiritual needs of the surrounding population. All this was a departure from the original ideals of Cîteaux, although each incident occurred as a response to a particular contemporary need, or as an act of obedience to higher authorities.

Decline. The decline of the order, well in evidence in the 15th century, was caused not so much by external engagements nor by the impact of the Renaissance, as by outside intervention originating during the Avignon papacy. The right of monastic communities to elect their abbots was superseded by a commendatory system (*see* COMMENDATION), in which abbots were appointed either by the pope or by secular rulers. Such appointees were not members of the order but usually secular prelates who received the title for other than monastic virtues. Commendatory abbots rarely lived in their monasteries and were concerned mostly with the collection of abbatial revenues. The result was devastating. Lacking the guidance and control of their abbots, the communities became impoverished, discipline deteriorated, churches and monasteries became dilapidated, and eventually many houses were virtually deserted. The damage was particularly severe in Italy and France, where by the end of the 16th century nearly all abbeys were *in commendam.* The subsequent religious and civil wars of the Reformation era threatened the order with annihilation. Within a few decades Cistercians disappeared in England and Scotland, in the Scandinavian countries, and in the greater part of Germany. Meanwhile, the central administration of the order broke down and each abbey struggled alone for bare survival.

Reform. Nevertheless, the 16th century witnessed vigorous attempts at reform, which, in the absence of initiative from Cîteaux, originated on a local or regional basis and resulted in the formation of more or less independent congregations, each differing in customs and discipline. One such reform was that of the FEUILLANTS, initiated by Jean de la BARRIÈRE (1544–1600), abbot of Les Feuillants in France. The congregation united a number of monasteries in France and Italy, was approved in 1586 by Sixtus V, and became entirely independent; it was noted for extraordinary severity of discipline. The Feuillants, however, failed to survive the French Revolution. Still more significant was the reform of the Strict Observance, for it resulted in a permanent schism within the order. This movement combined the efforts of several reformed communities in France early in the 17th century, and aimed at the restoration of the initial discipline of Cîteaux. The reform was spreading on a voluntary basis when, between 1623 and 1635, Cardinal François de La Rochefoucauld (1558–1645), as visitor of the order, repeatedly attempted to enforce the same discipline over all houses in France. His violent measures encountered embittered resistance on the part of the reluctant Common Observance. The same method was adopted by Cardinal Armand RICHELIEU, who in 1635, enforced his own election as abbot of Cîteaux. At the time of his death (1642) only 30 monasteries belonged to the reform, but by the end of the same century the Strict Observance was followed in 60 houses. Because of its leaders' Gallican bent the Strict Observance received no support from the papacy; instead, a more moderate reform of the Common Observance was launched by Alexander VII in 1666.

Although the ENLIGHTENMENT undermined the foundations of monasticism, the fatal blow was struck in 1791 by the French revolutionary government. In that year all Cistercian establishments in France were dissolved and later, in the wake of Napoleon's armies, nearly all abbeys were secularized elsewhere in Europe. The end of the revolutionary area found only a dozen surviving houses, scattered throughout the Hapsburg Empire.

La Trappe. After the Bourbon restoration, the Strict Observance was successfully revived by former members of La Trappe, hence their popular name, TRAPPISTS. The Common Observance was reorganized in Italy under papal auspices, and having made considerable gains elsewhere, by 1891 numbered 30 monasteries with nearly 1,000 monks. During the 19th century the difference between the two observances became more pronounced. The Trappists insisted on a strictly contemplative life according to the interpretation of the reformer of La Trappe, the Abbé Armand-Jean de Rance (1626–1700), while the Common Observance assumed an increasing load of teaching and pastoral duties. The final break took place in 1892, when the Trappist congregation became independent as the Order of Cistercians of the Strict Observance, while the Common Observance has been known as the Sacred Order of Cistercians.

The growth of both groups continued in the 20th century, and establishments were made in nearly every Christian land. The end of World War II found Eastern and Central Europe under communist control. The satellite governments, with the exception of the Polish, suppressed all Cistercian houses, among them the most populous congregation of the order, the Hungarian.

U.S. Foundations. The first house of the Sacred Order of Cistercians in the United States, Our Lady of Spring Bank, in Okauchee, Wisconsin, was founded in 1928 by Austrian monks. The same group added to its possessions in 1935 a small residence, Our Lady of Gerowvall, in Paulding, Mississippi. In 1955 refugees from Hungary established Our Lady of Dallas monastery near Dallas, Texas. The latter is a teaching community, furnishing a part of the faculty of the diocesan University of Dallas.

Constitution

The founders of Cîteaux had no intention of establishing a new order. It was called, in its early years, simply the "New Monastery," one among many reformed communities, all following, more or less closely, the Rule of St. Benedict. The peculiar significance of Cîteaux lay in the fact that in a time of crisis, when the great CLUNY had lost much of its luster, and Oriental ideas had infiltrated the Western monastic world, the New Monastery reaffirmed in uncompromising terms the authority of the BENEDICTINE RULE. The problem of a distinct central organization, i.e., the foundation of an order, emerged only when Cîteaux had established her first daughterhouses.

Charta Caritatis. The document aiming at the maintenance of uniform customs and discipline for all houses, known as the *Charta Caritatis* or Charter of Charity, was the work of Stephen Harding. The precise date of its composition, and the exact nature of the text has been a much debated question. Undoubtedly, during the course of the 12th century, the initial document was repeatedly revised and modified before it reached its final form. An early version of the charter, approved by Pope Callixtus II in 1119, already had incorporated the basic concept of the Cistercian constitution. It represented a compromise between the isolated independence of the earliest Benedictine houses, and the excessive centralization of the congregation of Cluny. While insisting on uniformity of liturgy and discipline, the charter granted extensive autonomy to individual establishments under the surveillance of the abbot responsible for the foundation, who was expected to visit such affiliations annually. The abbot of Cîteaux claimed no jurisdiction over the whole order. Both legislative and judicial power was entrusted to the general chapter composed of all abbots, meeting annually at Cîteaux. The abbot of Cîteaux convoked the chapter and presided over the gathering, but except for the direct affiliations of Cîteaux, he could act only as an agent of the chapter. Cîteaux itself was subject to annual visitation, made jointly by the abbots of her first four daughters, La Ferté, Pontigny, Clairvaux, and Morimond, the so-called protoabbots. In time of material need, mutual assistance was decreed.

Modifications. The first major modification of the Charter of Charity occurred in 1265, when Pope Clement IV issued the apostolic constitution *Parvus Fons.* This document, in an attempt to curb the influence of the protoabbots and to expedite the proceedings of the chapters, created an advisory council of 25 abbots, the *definitorium.* As the attendance at the general chapters decreased, however, this advisory council came to exercise a decisive influence over the chapters. Another papal constitution, the *Fulgens Sicut Stella,* issued in 1335 by the Cistercian Benedict XII, further modified the charter. It decreed the formal scholastic education of young monks, and put fiscal administration on a business basis. The turbulent era shortly before and after the Reformation witnessed the breakdown of central administration. Independent reform congregations refused to obey orders from Cîteaux and, especially in Italy and Spain, adopted mendicant customs and discipline, remaining Cistercian in name only. For the same reason, chapters were no longer held annually. Nicholas Boucherat I (1571–84), abbot of Cîteaux, in an attempt to fill the gap, assumed the title of abbot general. The same title has been used by all his successors, although the abbot's legal position has not been altered.

During the course of the 17th century, central control was reestablished over France, Belgium, the German-speaking countries, and Poland. Even the Strict Observance had to submit to Cîteaux's authority. In 1666 a new constitution by Pope Alexander VII, *In Suprema,* enforced a moderate reform of uniform discipline that remained in effect until the French Revolution. After the dissolution of Cîteaux in 1791, attempts to restore the unity of the scattered remains of the order were fruitless until 1869, when a general chapter finally initiated an effective reorganization. The modern Cistercian constitution calls for chapters in every fifth year, while in the chapterless years the *definitorium* holds meetings. The abbot general, considered the legal heir of the abbot of Cîteaux, is elected for life by the general chapter, and resides in Rome. The abbey of Cîteaux was successfully revived by the Trappists in 1898, but their abbot general, too, resides in Rome.

Cultural Contributions

The basis of Cistercian piety was the Rule of St. Benedict, but the greatest contribution of Bernard and his school to medieval spirituality was the revival of a mysticism having the sacred humanity of Christ and the Blessed Virgin as its center of devotion. The most eminent of Bernard's followers were WILLIAM OF SAINT-THIERRY (d. 1148), GUERRIC OF IGNY (d. 1157), St. AELRED of Rievaulx (d. 1167), ISAAC OF STELLA (d. 1169), GILBERT OF HOLLAND (d. 1172), and later ADAM OF PERSEIGNE (d. 1221).

Letters. Early Cistercian monastic training did not emphasize education. Those, however, who had received their education before entering the order continued their literary activity. Stephen Harding (d. 1134) composed a lucid and well-documented history of early Cîteaux, the *Exordium Parvum*. Otto of Freising (d. 1158) was certainly the greatest historian of his century. Toward the end of the 12th century, Conrad of Eberbach compiled a collection of Cistercian legends, the *Exordium Magnum*. Caesar of Heisterbach (d. 1240) was responsible for an even more popular book of similar nature, the *Dialogus Miraculorum*. SCHOLASTICISM was eventually adopted under the influence of the mendicants. A general house of studies in Paris, the Bernardinum, founded in 1245, was followed by a number of other colleges elsewhere. Teaching in secondary schools became the profession of several communities in Austria and Hungary, when under governmental pressure they took over abandoned Jesuit schools after the suppression of the Society of Jesus in 1773.

Arts. The characteristic mark of early Cistercian art was austere simplicity (*see* CISTERCIAN ART AND ARCHITECTURE). The best-preserved example of this style is Fontenay in France. By the middle of the 13th century the rules of simplicity were much relaxed. Royaumont near Paris, Fountains and RIEVAULX in England, and MELROSE in Scotland, are only a few examples of many splendid monuments of the most elaborate Gothic. The Renaissance added little to the existing monastic plants, but the era of Baroque was characterized by a feverish building activity, especially in Southern Germany and Austria. The history of economy praises Cistercians as the most accomplished agriculturists of the Middle Ages. Their spectacular achievements in clearing forests and reclaiming wasteland, however, were results not of revolutionary techniques, but rather of the intelligent employment of hundreds of lay brothers under central direction. In the middle of the 13th century the sharply declining number of lay brother vocations ended the era of Cistercian prosperity.

Bibliography: Sources. P. GUIGNARD, *Les Monuments primitifs de la règle cistercienne* (Dijon 1878). H. SÈJALON, *Nomasticon cisterciense, editio nova* (Solesmes 1892). J. CANIVEZ, *Statuta Capitulorum Generalium Ordinis Cisterciensis, ab anno 1116 ad annum 1786*, 8 v. (Louvain 1933–41). J. TURK, *Cistercii Statuta Antiquissima* (Rome 1949). B. GRIESSER, *Exordium Magnum Cisterciense* (Rome 1961). B. LUCET, *La Codification cistercienne de 1202 et son évolution ultérieure* (Rome 1964). General. L. JANAUSCHEK, *Origines Cistercienses*, v. 1 (Vienna 1877). H. ROSE, *Die Baukunst der Cistercienser* (Munich 1916). G. MüLLER, *Vom Cistercienser Orden* (Bregenz 1927). M. AUBERT, *L'Architecture cistercienne en France*, 2 v. (Paris 1943). A. DIMIER, *Recueil de plans d'églises cisterciennes*, 2 v. (Paris 1949). J. B. MAHN, *L'Ordre cistercien et son gouvernement, des origines au milieu du XIIIᵉ siècle* (new ed. Paris 1951). J. CANIVEZ, *Dictionnaire d'histoire et de géographie ecclésiastiques*, ed. A. BAUDRILLART et al. (Paris 1912–) 12:852–997. *Menologium Cisterciense* (Westmalle 1952). L. J. LEKAI, *The White Monks* (Okauchee, Wis. 1953). A. A. KING, *Cîteaux and Her Elder Daughters* (London 1954). C. BOCK, *Les Codifications du droit cistercien* (Westmalle 1955). L. BOUYER, *The Cistercian Heritage*, tr. E. A. LIVINGSTONE (Westminster, Md. 1958). V. HERMANS, *Commentarium cisterciense historico-practicum in Codicis Canones de Religiosis* (Rome 1961). A. DIMIER and J. PORCHER, *L'Art cistercien* (Abbaye Ste-Marie de la Pierre-Qui-Vire 1962). H. DANIEL-ROPS, *Bernard of Clairvaux*, tr. E. ABBOTT (New York 1964). The following periodicals are dedicated exclusively to Cistercian history and spirituality: *Cistercienser-Chronik* (1889–). *Collectanea Ordinis Cisterciensium Reformatorum* (1934–). *Analecta Sacri Ordinis Cisterciensis* (1945–). *Cîteaux. Commentarii cistercienses* (Belgium 1950–). For further bibliography see: U. CHEVALIER, *Répertoire des sources historiques du moyen-âge. Topobibliographie*, 2 v. (Paris 1894–1903) 1:721–722. M. HEIMBUCHER, *Die Orden und Kongregationen der katholischen Kirche*, 2 v. (3d ed. Paderborn 1932–34) 1:330–356. L. H. COTTINEAU, *Répertoire topobibliographique des abbayes et prieurés*, 2 v. (Mâcon 1935–39) 1:787–790.

[L. J. LEKAI/EDS.]

CISTERCIANS, ART AND ARCHITECTURE OF

The Cistercians occupy an important place in the history of art primarily because of their architecture. They excelled as well in manuscript illumination and stained glass, but the few surviving specimens of these types of work pale when compared with the immense array of monasteries they constructed during the 12th and 13th centuries all over Europe and even in Cyprus and Syria.

Architecture. The Cistercian buildings, and especially their churches, were distinguished by structural simplicity and lack of ornamentation, which were the result of the principles laid down by the founders of CÎTEAUX as the basis of their reform of the order. As Étienne Gilson pointed out, "Cistercian architecture forms an integral part of Cistercian spirituality and cannot be separated from it" (*Les Arts du Beau* [Paris 1963]). The aim of the Cistercian reform was a return to the full observance of the Rule of St. Benedict, which over the centuries had changed and slackened, particular-

Exterior detail of projecting corbel on Cistercian Rievauix Abbey, 13th century, Helmsley, River Rye, Yorkshire, England. (©Adam Woolfitt/CORBIS)

went on to add the following well-known passage: "What are these ridiculous monsters, this deformed beauty and this beautiful deformity, doing in the cloisters under the eyes of monks occupied by their reading? What are these filthy apes, ferocious lions, monstrous centaurs doing there? . . . Good God! Even if one is not ashamed of these stupidities, one should at least regret the expenditure of money they involve."

The noble and austere architecture that is so esteemed by the Cistercians sprang from their rules and the *Apologia* of St. Bernard. After a long period of fidelity to the Roman architectural style, their master workmen adopted the Gothic style and contributed to its expansion all over Europe, where numerous examples of their work are still to be found. To name some of the most typical churches: in France, Fontenay, LE THORONET and Silvacane; in Germany, EBERBACH and EBRACH; in England, FOUNTAINS and RIEVAULX; in Austria, HEILIGENKREUZ; in Belgium, VILLERS; in Spain, Poblet and Santes Creus; in Italy, FOSSANOVA and Casamari; in Poland, Mogila and Wachock; in Portugal, ALCOBAÇA; in Sweden, Varnhem; and in Switzerland, Bonmont and HAUTERIVE. Ultimately even the Cistercians succumbed to the malady of building immense churches decorated with sculpture and painting. When baroque art became the rage, in Germany, Austria, and Switzerland they went so far as to reconstruct their monasteries in accordance with the taste of the times, or they simply added rococo decoration to already existing buildings. All of this was a far cry from the architecture of the first Cistercians, which, as Henri Focillon said, "is still an ancient witness to a very great spiritual revolution" (*Art of the West in the Middle Ages* [Greenwich, Conn. 1963]).

Manuscript illumination. The oldest manuscripts from the scriptorium of Cîteaux are filled with ornamented letters and illumination work of a high artistic level, as in a copy of the Bible that was begun under the direction of Stephen Harding during the first years of the foundation and completed in 1109, and the *Moralia in Job* of St. Gregory the Great, which dates from 1111. But a short time later, *c.* 1150 and under the influence of St. Bernard, a decree of the general chapter ruled that only one color was to be used for the initial letters. The copyists then devoted all their care to the quality of the parchment used, to the outline of the letters, and to the arrangement of the text on the page, the only ornamentation being the beautiful initial letters in monochrome. Nothing was allowed to interfere with the beautiful arrangement of the calligraphy. Soon, however, the prohibitive rule was forgotten and illuminations reappeared.

Stained glass. A statute of the general chapter decreed that the windows should be of clear glass, without

ly with regard to simplicity and poverty. The Cistercians desired to be poor with Christ, who was poor. As a result they decided to reject everything that might imply luxury or diminish poverty, whether in divine worship, clothing, or food. In their architecture they renounced stone bell towers, paintings, and sculpture for their churches, feeling that these might distract the religious from their prayer and meditation. All this was vigorously expressed by St. Bernard in the famous *Apologia* addressed to his friend WILLIAM OF SAINT-THEIRRY, a Benedictine abbot. In this essay, which reads like a pamphlet, the saint protested against the extravagant splendor of the Cluny churches, their excessive size, their sumptuous decoration, and especially the ornamentation of the capitals in both the cloisters and the churches. He admitted that the representation of scenes from the Bible or the lives of the saints can serve for the instruction and edification of the faithful; "but," he said, "of what use is that for men vowed to poverty, for monks, for spiritual men?" He either cross or color. The Cistercian master glassworkers then hit upon the idea of tracing all sorts of foliated scrolls, rosettes, interlacing designs, and arabesques onto the glass with the lead in which the glass was set. Very beautiful effects were produced by this technique. Unfortunately, very few specimens of this type of glasswork have survived. The finest are to be found in France in the churches of Bénisson-Dieu in the Diocese of Lyon, of OBAZINE in the Diocese of Tulle, and of Bonlieu in the Diocese of Limoges. However, at the end of the 13th century the Cistercians came to employ representational windows.

Bibliography: General. M. A. DIMIER, *Recueil de plans d'églises cisterciennes*, 2 v. (Paris 1949), v. 1, text; v. 2, plates. F. VAN DER MEER, *Atlas de l'ordre cistercien des origines jusqu'à la Révolution française, avec une introduction aux images cisterciennes* (Amsterdam 1965). M. AUBERT, *L'Architecture cistercienne en France*, 2 v. (2d ed. Paris 1947). M. A. DIMIER and J. PORCHER, *L'Art cistercien, France* (La Pierre-qui-Vire 1962). H. P. EYDOUX, *L'Architecture des églises cisterciennes d'Allemagne* (Paris 1952); "L'Abbatiale de Moreruela et l'architecture des églises cisterciennes d'Espagne," *Cîteaux in de Nederlanden* 5 (1954) 173–207. J. BILSON, "The Architecture of the Cistercians, with Special Reference to Some of Their Earlier Churches in England," *Archaeological Journal* 66 (1909) 185–280. P. CLEMEN and C. GURLITT, *Die Klosterbauten der Cistercienser in Belgien* (Berlin 1916). L. FRACCARO DE LONGHI, *L'architettura delle chiese cistercensi italiane* (Milan 1958). Illumination. C. OURSEL, *Minatures cisterciennes, 1109–1134* (Mâcon 1960), 40 color pl. L. BONNAY, "Église d'Obazine (Corrèze): Vitraux du XIIᵉ siécle," *Bulletin scientifique et archéologique de la Corrèze* 2 (1879) 199–211, 4 diagrams.

[M. A. DIMIER]

CÎTEAUX, ABBEY OF

Chief abbey of the Cistercian Order, founded in 1098 in the Diocese of Chalon-sur-Saône (today the Diocese of Dijon), 23 kilometers south of Dijon, Burgundy, France. The Latin variants of the abbey's name are *Novum monasterium, Cisterium, Cistellum.* The first monks came from the Benedictine abbey of MOLESME with their abbot, ROBERT OF MOLESME, in order to observe the BENEDICTINE RULE in its primitive simplicity. Land was donated by Raynard, Viscount of Beaune; Eudes I, Duke of Burgundy, was the great benefactor of Cîteaux. In 1099 Abbot Robert returned to Molesme but was succeeded by Albertic (1099–1109), who received from Pope Paschal II approbation of the *Instituta monachorum cisterciensium de Molismo venientium.* Under Alberic's successor, STEPHEN HARDING (1109–33), the abbey experienced some difficult years at first because it was impoverished and lacked recruits, but in 1112 BERNARD OF CLAIRVAUX entered Cîteaux with his 30 companions. As early as 1113 the Abbey of LA FERTÉ was founded; in 1114, PONTIGNY; in 1115, the Abbeys of

CLAIRVAUX and MORIMOND. In 1119 Pope Callistus II approved the *Charta caritatis,* once attributed to Stephen Harding. It is the fundamental document of the order of Cîteaux, calling for autonomy of each abbey, annual canonical VISITATION, and an annual general chapter at Cîteaux, which chapter was to be the supreme authority in the order. The abbey grew prosperous; the domain was large, and the monks and conversi (lay brothers) cultivated many granges. At the death of Abbot Stephen (1134), the CISTERCIANS had 75 abbeys spread throughout every country of Europe. The first three abbots were entered in the Cistercian menology as "blessed." In 1164 conflict erupted between Cîteaux and its first four daughter abbeys. A bull of Pope Clement IV, *Parvus fons* (1265), ended the quarrel by modifying the constitution. During the 14th century the abbey was hard hit by the BLACK DEATH and the Hundred Years' War: in 1360, 1364, and 1392 the religious had to seek refuge in Dijon. Then COMMENDATION resulted in relaxation of spiritual life as well as in financial difficulties. The WESTERN SCHISM caused a division within the order, and it became apparent that reform was necessary. In 1589 and 1595, during the Wars of Religion, the abbey was pillaged and burned. It was no longer possible for the annual chapter to meet, and a period of decadence followed. Abbot Nicolas Boucherat (1605–25) visited the abbeys to reform them, but his ideas was accepted by only a few: ORVAL, Clairvaux, La Charmoye, and Châtillon. As a result a conflict that lasted 40 years erupted between the reformed abbeys and those that had rejected reform (*see* TRAPPISTS). In 1636 Cîteaux was plundered by imperial troops. During the French Revolution (1791) the abbey was sold, and the surviving 12th-century buildings were destroyed. In 1841 Arthur Young, a disciple of F. Fourier, established a phalanstery at Cîteaux, and in 1846 the Abbé Joseph Rey opened a school for juvenile delinquents. In 1898 the reformed Cistercians repurchased the Abbey, and since that time they have occupied the large residence, constructed in 1772 by Lenoir le Romain, the first building of the grandiose plan that was interrupted by the French Revolution.

Bibliography: Sources. WILLIAM OF MALMESBURY, *Gesta regum anglorum* 4:334–337, in *Patrologia Latina,* ed. J. P. MIGNE, 217 v. (Paris 1878–90) 179:1286–90. ORDERICUS VITALIS, *Historia ecclesiastica* 3.8.25, in *Patrologia Latina* 188:640–642. C. HENRIQUEZ, *Regula, constitutiones et privilegia ordinis cistertiensis* (Antwerp 1630). P. GUIGNARD, *Les Monuments primitifs de la règle cistercienne* (Dijon 1878). J. M. CANIVEZ, ed., *Statuta capitulorum generalium ordinis cisterciensis,* 8 v. (Louvain 1933–41). B. GRIESSER, *Exordium Magnum Cisterciense* (Rome 1961). J. MARILIER, *Chartes et documents concernant l'abbaye de Cîteaux, 1098–1182* (Rome 1961). Literature. L. H. COTTINEAU, *Répertoire topobibliographique des abbayes et prieurés,* 2 v. (Mâcon 1935–39) 1:787–790. BEAUNIER, *Abbayes et prieurés de l'ancienne France,* ed. J. M. BESSE, v.12 (Paris 1941) 306–308. J. B. MAHN, *L'Ordre Cistercien et son gouvernement, des origines au milieu du XIIIᵉ siècle, 1098–1265* (new ed. Paris 1951). M. A. DIMIER, *Recueil* *de plans d'églises cisterciennes,* 2 v. (Paris 1949) 1:99. J. M. CA-NIVEZ, *Dictionnaire d'histoire et de géographie ecclésiastiques,* ed. A. BAUDRILLART et al. (Paris 1912–) 12:852–874. L. J. LEKAI, *The White Monks* (Okauchee, Wis. 1953). A. A. KING, *Cîteaux and Her Elder Daughters* (London 1954). J. WINANDY, "Les Origines de Cîteaux et les travaux de M. Lefèvre," *Revue Bénédictine* 67 (1957) 49–76. J. B. VAN DAMME, "Autour des origines cisterciennes," *Colectanea ordinis Cisterciensium Reformatorum* 20 (1958) 37–60, 153–168, 374–390; 21 (1959) 70–86, 137–156, C. OURSEL, *Miniatures cisterciennes* (Mâcon 1960). ,

[M. A. DIMIER]

CITTADINI, CATERINA, BL.

Foundress of the Ursuline Sisters of Somasca; b. Sept. 28, 1801, Bergamo, Italy, d. May 5, 1857, Somasca, Diocese of Bergamo. After the death of Caterina's mother Margherita Lanzani, in 1808, her father, Giovanni Battista, placed her and her sister Giuditta (b. 1803) in the convent orphanage of Bergamo when he was called to military service. There they received an intensely Christian formation and attained teaching diplomas. While living with two priestly cousins in Calolzio (1823–25), the sisters were provided additional spiritual direction, recognized religious vocations, and were guided to found a new religious order in Somasca.

In 1926, with financial help from their cousin Fr. Antonio Cittadini, the sisters moved to a rented house in Somasca, where they purchased a building in October that would become a boarding school for poor children and the motherhouse for the Ursuline Sisters. Much admired for the fervor and commitment Caterina exhibited while continuing to teach in the public elementary school, the sisters' boarding school soon filled and a second private school was established (1836). Caterina's influence was spread by her graduates who returned to their home towns to erect similar schools and extend the charity taught by the Cittadinis.

Her life was not without suffering. Following the death of Giuditta (1840) and her spiritual director (1841), Caterina herself fell gravely ill (1842). Miraculously cured, she again taught in the public school until retiring in 1845 to dedicate herself entirely to the boarding school, orphanage, and developing religious community for which she wrote a constitution in 1844. Although Pius IX permitted the community to erect a private oratory with a Tabernacle (1850), the bishop initially denied approval for the establishment of religious order in 1851 and 1854. Shortly after her death, the institute and its rule were approved by the bishop (Dec. 14, 1857), and later by the Vatican (July 8, 1927). Today the Ursulines of Somasca labor in Belgium, Bolivia, Brazil, India, Indonesia, Italy, the Philippines, and Switzerland.

Following the conclusion of the diocesan process for beatification in Bergamo (1967–78), the cause was opened in Rome (Jan. 2, 1979). Pope John Paul II declared her venerable (Dec. 17, 1996), approved the miraculous healing of Samuele Piovani attributed to her intercession (Dec. 20, 1999), and beatified her (April 29, 2001).

Feast: May 5.

Bibliography: *L'Osservatore Romano,* Eng. Ed. 18 (2001), 1, 6–8; 19 (2001), 7, 10.

[K. I. RABENSTEIN]

CIVEZZA, MARCELLINO DA

Franciscan missiologist and historian of the 19th century; b. Civezza, Italy, May 29, 1822; d. Leghorn, 1906. Although his family name was Ranise, he commonly used the name of his native Ligurian village. He entered the Franciscan Order in 1831 and was ordained in 1845. Very early, Civezza manifested a gift for research and writing. In 1856 the general of the Franciscan Order, Bernardino de Montefranco, commanded Civezza to write a history of the Franciscan missions. The first five volumes, with the title *Storia universale delle missioni francescane,* appeared in rapid order between 1857 and 1861. Then the series lagged. In 1875 the then general of the Franciscan Order, Bernardino de Portogruaro, not only insisted that Civezza complete his history of the missions but also made it possible for him to spend several years visiting the main libraries and archives of Europe and arranged to have friars in America, especially Ubaldo Pandolfi, send him needed documents and maps. Volume six was published in 1881 and the last volume, nine, in 1895. In all, Civezza published more than 100 works besides innumerable magazine articles. Most of these are of ephemeral value, but his source studies on the life of St. Francis were epoch-making, while *Saggio di bibliografia geografica, storica, etnografica sanfrancescana* (Prato 1879), *Il romano pontificato nella storia d'Italia* (3 v., Florence, 1886–87), and his studies on the life of Dante have permanent value. Most important is his history of the Franciscan missions from the time of St. Francis, a survey of magnificent proportions, even though it has occasional weaknesses because preliminary monographic studies were not available.

Bibliography: R. PRATESI, "Il P. Marcellino da Civezza, O. F. M.: Vita e scritti," *Archivum Franciscanum historicum* 43 (1950) 243–334.

[L. G. CANEDO]

CIVIL CONSTITUTION OF THE CLERGY

An organic law adopted by the Constituent Assembly (July 12, 1790) to impose a new organization on the Church in France. It began a serious conflict between the FRENCH REVOLUTION and the Catholic Church.

Genesis of the Law. When the Estates-General met in 1789, it was generally recognized in France that civil administrative reorganization and ecclesiastical reform were needed. Ambition to recast the political constitution necessarily implied modification of the Church's status; for under the ancient régime, Church and State were so intimately bound that one could not be touched without disturbing the other.

The Constituent Assembly voted abolition of the privileges of the nobles and clergy (Aug. 4, 1789); seizure of ecclesiastical possessions to balance the government's financial deficit (Nov. 2); and suppression of religious houses, or at least the release of religious from their vows (February of 1790). These first measures introduced such profound changes in the traditional structure of the Church that other steps had to be taken to prevent shackling the exercise of religion and alarming the people. The Revolution, moreover, needed the support of the *curés* known as "patriots." It envisioned, therefore, supplying a religious foundation for the moral unity of the nation. An Ecclesiastical Committee, appointed (Aug. 20, 1789) by the *Constituante,* presented a plan nine months later to reorganize the French Church.

This plan was not inspired by the antireligious ideas of the ENLIGHTENMENT, save perhaps in its tacit provision to suppress the religious congregations. It proceeded in places from the theses of RICHER and from the JANSENISM in vogue among the lower clergy and the legal profession. It reflected, above all, the defiance of GALLICANISM toward Rome and the resolve of the Jacobins to submit the religion of the nation exclusively to State authority. Here the assembly members were copying the royal absolutism that they sought to overthrow. The new constitution was termed civil because, according to its authors, it dealt only with matters pertaining to temporal power. The Constituent Assembly considered it beneath its dignity to consult in advance the views of the clergy or to negotiate with the Holy See. During the long, bitter discussion (May 29–July 12) and in numerous controversial writings, Catholic deputies tried vainly to have their colleagues seek papal assent, without which the law would be unacceptable. PIUS VI hoped that at least the king would refuse to acquiesce in the vote of the Assembly. Louis XVI, however, approved the Constitution (August 24) to avoid worse troubles.

Contents of the Law. The Civil Constitution was a document of considerable length, in four sections that dealt with: (1) ecclesiastical offices, (2) appointments to benefices, (3) payment of ministers of religion and (4) obligations of ecclesiastics as public functionaries.

Ecclesiastical boundaries were drawn to coincide with the new administrative divisions, with one diocese per *département,* one parish for 6,000 souls. This reduced the number of dioceses from 135 to 85, grouped in ten metropolitan districts. The sole ecclesiastical functionaries recognized were bishops, pastors (*curés*) and curates (*vicaires*). The law suppressed chapters and ignored religious congregations, which later laws were to destroy.

Bishops and pastors had to be elected by the populace, with voting power restricted to "active" citizens, Catholics and non-Catholics, who paid the required taxes. A newly elected bishop did not need to solicit from the pope even his spiritual investiture; but he was required to seek canonical investiture from the first or oldest bishop of the metropolitan district (*métropole*). Bishops were to administer dioceses with a council of *vicaires.*

Ecclesiastical functionaries of the Catholic religion alone were to be paid by the State, since the clergy no longer possessed landed properties after nationalization. They had to provide religious services gratuitously and remain in residence unless authorized to absent themselves from their posts.

Defenders of the legislation emphasized during the debates that the Civil Constitution left to Catholicism the dignity of being the national religion, with other "religious opinions" granted mere tolerance; also that it ended grave abuses and restored certain usages of the primitive Church. But adversaries objected that the Holy See would never accept a modification of ecclesiastical boundaries drawn up unilaterally, an elective procedure that permitted Protestants and unbelievers to choose Catholic bishops and pastors, or the separation introduced between bishops and the pope, who alone could give to a bishop his episcopal character and his jurisdiction over a diocese.

The Civil Constitution was, therefore, doubly vicious in that it was imposed on Catholics and severed the unity between pope and bishops that is essential to the Catholic religion. French bishops were unanimous, save for LOMÉNIE DE BRIENNE, TALLEYRAND-PÉRIGORD and five others, in censoring very firmly the principles of the Constitution and in proclaiming their attachment to the successor of St. Peter. After eight months of delays and consultations, Pius VI published two briefs (March 10 and April 13, 1791) condemning the law outright and forbidding the faithful to participate in its application.

Results. Before the papal condemnation, the Assembly had put into effect a law, concerning which it wanted no compromise. It proved this by enjoining (Nov. 27, 1790) all bishops, pastors and functionary priests to take an oath of fidelity to the Civil Constitution under pain of deposition. To replace those refusing to take the oath (the refractory clergy or nonjurors), the Assembly also expedited the election of new bishops, commonly termed constitutional bishops or jurors, but stigmatized by the pope as schismatics and intruders.

Clergy and faithful divided into two rival Churches. The Constitutional Church, the sole legal one, stood for the State; the Refractory Church, the sole orthodox one, sided with the papacy. Their forces were in balance. On one side were the clergy whose patriotism and attachment to their parishioners impelled them to submit to the law. They represented more than one-third of the clergy and enjoyed the support of the public authorities. On the other side were those clergy faithful to Roman orthodoxy, numbering all but three of the bishops in charge of dioceses and a majority of the priests. At first this latter group was not prominent, but it grew stronger when the judgments of the Holy See on the affairs of France became known.

This division caused discord and then civil war; to a large extent it modified the course of the Revolution. The pope, almost the entire French episcopate, many priests and religious men and women turned against the Revolution, which was accused of seeking to subvert the Church. The revolutionary assemblies, especially the Legislative Assembly, accused the refractory clergy of accepting aristocrats and foreigners as accomplices. According to a decree of Nov. 20, 1791, ecclesiastics who had not taken the oath were "suspect of revolt against the law" and against the Fatherland, and should be deported. At least 30,000 ecclesiastics fled or were driven from France. Those who remained in the country, particularly after the outbreak of war between revolutionary France and the rest of Europe, risked life as well as liberty. Henceforth the Catholic clergy, whose support was responsible for the first successes of the Revolution, joined the front rank of its adversaries. Religious difficulties complicated all the political crises confronting the Convention and the Directory during the period.

The Constitutional Church succeeded in establishing itself and for three years strove, after a fashion, to replace the Catholic Church amid populations attached to the traditional religion. For a number of reasons the attempt proved vain. Revolutionary governments abandoned the constitutionals. Under the terror the dechristianizers attacked all clerics, jurors and nonjurors alike, and all cults. Then on Feb. 21, 1795, the Thermidorian Convention adopted a regime separating the State from the Churches, thereby abandoning the Civil Constitution.

Internal decadence infected the Constitutional Church, which counted dubious, ambitious, or corrupt elements. GRÉGOIRE and other of its bishops showed dauntless courage and undeniable integrity at the height of persecution; but Bishop GOBEL OF PARIS and numerous others defected, seriously harming their cause. Catholics in France very often demonstrated their favor for the refractory "good priests" in preference to the jurors. Outside France, Catholics manifested solidarity with the émigré CLERGY faithful to orthodoxy.

NAPOLEON, as First Consul, showed himself eager to re-establish religious peace as a necessary preliminary to domestic concord. As a result, he signed with PIUS VII the CONCORDAT OF 1801, which implied a rejection of the Civil Constitution and resulted eventually in the submission to the Holy See of the last Constitutionals.

Bibliography: Sources. J. H. STEWART, *A Documentary Survey of the French Revolution* (New York 1951), contains an Eng. tr. of the Civil Constitution, the papal condemnation, *Charitas* and other closely related documents. Literature. L. SCIOUT, *Histoire de la Constitution civile du clergé*, 4 v. (Paris 1872–81). A. MATHIEZ, *Rome et le clergé français sous la Constituante* (Paris 1911). C. CONSTANTIN, *Dictionnaire de théologie catholique*, ed., A. VACANT et al., 15 v. (Paris 1903–50) 3.2:1537–1604. A. LATREILLE, *L'Église catholique et la Révolution française*, 2 v. (Paris 1946–50). J. LEFLON, *La Crise révolutionnaire 1789–1846* (*Histoire de l'église depuis les origines jusqu'à nos jours*, eds., A. FLICHE and V. MARTIN, 20; 1949). L. CARRET, *Dictionnaire de droit cannonique*, ed. R. NAZ, 7 v. (Paris 1935–65) 4:429–453.

[A. LATREILLE]

CIVIL DISOBEDIENCE

Civil disobedience is a term that has been employed in various senses, but usually signifies disobedience to civil law for the purpose of dramatizing the injustice of a law or to call the public's attention to a special grievance. The term came back into vogue in 1955 when Martin Luther King, Jr., led a boycott in Birmingham, Alabama to protest a law requiring segregation of Black passengers in public buses. By urging citizens to flaunt the law, he and his followers focused attention on the prevailing discrimination in the South and fueled anew the debate about what it is and when it is justified.

Legal theorists, even positivists, do not exclude the political or moral right in certain circumstances to disobey civil law. Still not all such violations constitute "civil disobedience." According to Rawls (364–365) civil disobedience is based not on moral obligation or divine right, but on a theory of society, the conception that society is a "scheme of cooperation among equals." In this view, civil disobedience, as distinguished from other forms of opposition to law, is "a public, nonviolent, conscientious yet political act contrary to law with the aim of bringing about a change in the law or policies of the government." One invokes neither a personal morality (such as opposition to all war) nor group interest (such as higher wages for cotters), but "the commonly shared conception of justice that underlies the political order." The civilly disobedient actor seeks to touch the "public's sense of justice." To do this, Rawls insists, the disobedience must be open, not covert. And it must be nonviolent, rather than militant (for militance attacks the legal and political order as a whole).

The broader view of civil disobedience, as in Henry David THOREAU's 1848 essay *Civil Disobedience* (Bedau 27–48), embraces what Rawls calls "conscientious refusal," which may be grounded on discrete religious concerns rather than shared principles of justice, and may include "conscientious evasion," where the actor seeks to conceal, rather than proclaim, his deliberate violation of law (*see also* Zinn).

Civil disobedience, in brief, is a facet of a global revolution away from rigid and unjust laws toward a fuller recognition of the dignity of the human person. It must be employed when a law commands a person to violate his conscience; it may be employed profitably in other instances, but only with caution, delicacy, and respect for law in general. Neither Catholic tradition or such human-rights documents of the Church as *PACEM IN TERRIS* and *Gaudium et spes* (74) maintain that there is a moral right in all circumstances to disobey an "unjust law"—public order, the avoidance of scandal, etc. may sometimes dictate obeying it.

Bibliography: A. FORTAS, *Concerning Dissent and Civil Disobedience* (New American Library pa. New York 1968). H. A. BEDAU, ed., *Civil Disobedience* (New York, 1969). J. RAWLS, *A Theory of Justice* (Cambridge, Mass. 1971). H. ZINN, *Disobedience and Democracy* (New York 1968). R. DWORKIN, "On Not Prosecuting Civil Disobedience," *New York Review of Books* (June 6, 1968) 14ff. R. A. MCCORMICK, SJ, "Notes on Moral Theology," *Theological Studies* 27.4 (December 1966) 633–638; *Theological Studies* 29.4 (December 1968) 685–697.

[J. B. SHEERIN/J. A. BRODERICK]

CIVIL RELIGION

Civil religion in America today refers to a national faith that has a creed and moves the people of the nation on occasion to stand in judgment on its laws when they perceive that those laws violate what the creed affirms. It also moves people to rejoice in their nation-state when they experience it as realizing the values of the creed.

The term "civil religion" comes from ROUSSEAU's *Social Contract* (Book 4, ch. 8), where it was used to refer to a set of beliefs that support the political authority of the State. In Rousseau's analysis, these included belief in the existence of God, life to come, the reward of virtue, and the punishment of vice, with the added dictum of the "exclusion of religious intolerance." In his essay, Rousseau, as social philosopher, was recommending a way to civic harmony through supporting civic authority, a development of the ancient *pietas* (Marty, 1974).

Bellah's Theory. In 1967 the American sociologist Robert N. Bellah extracted the term from Rousseau's work and gave it a new meaning. In Bellah's use, it refers to something more specifically religious in the sense of transcending the law of the land yet capable of passing judgment on it. He introduced the term as a concept for sociological analysis of a phenomenon he thought could be distinguished from several others. At that time, he said: "While some have argued that Christianity is the national faith and others, that church and synagogue celebrate only the generalized religion of the 'American Way of Life,' few have realized that there actually exists alongside of and rather clearly differentiated from the churches an elaborate and well-institutionalized civil religion in America" (Bellah, 1967). The main tenets of this faith he extracts from the *Declaration of Independence* and the *Constitution.* The central elements are the belief that God created all people as equal and endowed them with certain inalienable rights (Bellah, 1976, 168). The critical quality of this religion, he claims, is that people who believe in it can call upon it as a framework from which to judge the nation when it violates the rights of people or fails to protect them in time of unrest. Thus, the test of the depth of the institutionalization of America's civil religion in the mid-1960s was to be its response to the civil-rights movement and the antiwar movement (Bellah, 1967). Writing again about civil religion in 1974, Bellah entitled his book *The Broken Covenant.* Here he speaks as prophet to a nation failing to fulfill its promise. He expresses the hope, however, that scholars who find flaws in the American system will do what Max WEBER and Émile DURKHEIM, who preceded them in the analysis of the relationship between religion and society, did, namely, use the lecture platform to clarify the present reality and to warn their colleagues about imminent dangers their analyses reveal. Their scientific observations thereby provide social service (Bellah, 1976). To make his point clear, he refers to the behaviors of Jefferson and Lincoln as foremost spokesmen of American civil religion, reiterating "the right of revolution should the state attempt to destroy the God-given rights of the individuals" (Bellah, 1976, 167–168).

For Bellah, "civil religion at its best is a genuine apprehension of universal and transcendent religious reality as seen in or, one could almost say, as revealed through the experience of the American people." Political theorists and activists who have taken a position on separation of Church and State are disturbed by Bellah's passion and, for this reason, question his objectivity as a sociologist, claiming that the intent of his analysis is to bring about a condition of critical self-examination from the perspective of religious symbol and fervor, while they believe that the failures of State are better addressed from the perspective of cool reason and secular values (Smith; Wilson, 1971). This focus is but one dimension of the debate that currently surrounds civil religion.

The Sociological Debate. Writings of social scientists and ethicists preceded the debate by providing the books that incorporated the themes that later were analyzed as civil religion (de Tocqueville, Dewey, Tuveson, Smith). It is possible, as Prof. Mary L. Schneider of Michigan State Univ. suggests, to extract from the debate at least five definitions that provide different focuses on religion and the State or society. The first became popular in the mid-1950s, when America's common religion was described as emerging from actual life, ideals, values, ceremonies, and loyalties of the people. The suggestion was made that, out of its own ethos and history, a people can come to worship its own heritage (Warner, Williams). A second theme took the form of religious nationalism. In this perspective, the State becomes the object of religious adoration and glorification. This is a main aspect of classical *pietas*, wherein religion and patriotism are one (Dohen). Stress on the value of liberty as provided for in a democracy without dependence on a transcendent deity or even on a spiritualized nation is described as the focus found in Dewey's *Common Faith*; here, democracy is religion (Williams). A fourth theme is Protestant nationalism, without there being any zealous or idolatrous element to it; it simply is the fusion of Protestantism and Americanism, its moralism, individualism, pragmatism, values, and the like. This perspective characterizes any number of works, but is particularly evident in Winthrop Hudson (Ahlstrom; Cuddihy).

All of these emphases, analyses, and commentaries are not the phenomenon that Bellah seeks to isolate for analysis. The fifth theme, then, is the one that characterizes his own work. Civil religion is a normative reality; it is essentially prophetic and stands over and against the folk ways of the people. It judges idolatrous tendencies of particular forms of Christianity and Judaism. In the words of Bellah, "it is of the essence of the American civil religion that it 'challenges institutional authority'" (Bellah, 1976). He locates in civil religion the prophetic function of calling the nation, including its civic leaders,

to account whenever they fail to provide the members their rights as people "created equal." He includes, therefore, among the martyrs of the republic Abraham Lincoln and Martin Luther King, Jr. Bellah predicted a crisis of conscience for the nation at the time of the Vietnam War. When this did not occur, it did not disconfirm, for him, his analysis but indicated that the covenant was broken, although hope never fails. When his own writings carried the prophetic above the analytic function, his social-science colleagues chided him for his lack of objectivity (Fenn, Hammond). However, religionists espoused his cause and made him the central figure of major bicentennial celebrations (Boardman and Fuchs). The debate continued, then, with two new focuses: (1) is the covenant really broken? (Novak); (2) has the focus of civil religion moved from the nation to the world society? (Neal).

While essayists were debating the reality or emergent quality of civil religion (Bourg, Richey, and Jones), some survey analysts were attempting to measure the verbalized opinions and attitudes from samples of significant size and diversity to determine whether any variable could be found with consistency that might be claimed to carry this conception of civil religion through the social consciousness of acting communities of American people. To date that research is indecisive. In some cases, the sample is too narrowly encompassed to preclude the Protestant nationalism concept (Hoge). At other times, the items are too general to conclude that civic piety is not also being measured (Christenson and Wimberley). This lack of conclusiveness is agreed to by the researchers themselves. In the late 1970s, they invited more empirical studies with better measures and samples before anything decisive could be claimed as causally connected with civil religion, or before it could be stated that civil religion can be differentiated for analysis from any of the other concepts connected with national patriotism, with which it is so closely connected experientially (Wimberley, Cole and Hammond). To get evidence that would be convincing for the existence of the civil-religion hypothesis, one would have to find a substantial number of non-church-related believers as well as church-related ones. At the present time, the items used provide high association with church attendance but correspondingly low association with socially concerned non-church-attenders. There should be no significant difference if civil religion is an independent variable. Other research, assuming the civic-piety definitions of civil religion, examines its presence in new religious expression of the 1970s (Robbins).

Theological Interest. The intellectual and religious interest in the idea of civil religion is directly associated with a new political consciousness in modern theological speculation (*see* POLITICAL THEOLOGY). Theologians show the need of new reflection on religion and State now that their attention has been drawn to the growing problems of a world economy that outstrips the power of the State, and the corresponding need for associations of some type capable of seriously addressing the ethical and social problems generated by new centers of power (Baum, Neal, 1977). This political emphasis is dialectically related to the Churches' affirming the value of their plurality and social commentators' allocating religion to the private sphere with high public approval in established states only (Bell, Berger, Greeley). The emergence of more effective power centers in Third-World concentrations in the international struggle for survival brings the question of the object of civil religion into the forefront of Catholic reflection and analysis. In this context, the traditional association of Catholicism with the affirmation of hierarchy and of Protestantism with congregationalism, shifts interest to the Judaic theme of exodus and covenant for a movement-perspective for historian, social scientist, and religionist simultaneously. From this fact derive the contemporary debates about civil religion.

Bibliography: S. AHLSTROM, "The American National Faith: Humane Yet All Too Human," in J. M. ROBISON, ed., *Religion and the Humanizing of Man* (Council on the Study of Religion, Waterloo, Ont. 1973). G. BAUM, *Religion and Alienation* (New York 1975). R. N. BELLAH, "Civil Religion in America," *Daedalus* 96 (1967) 1–21; "American Civil Religion in the 1970's," in R. E. RICHEY and D. G. JONES, eds., *American Civil Religion* (New York 1974) 255–572; *The Broken Covenant* (New York 1975); "Response to the Panel on Civil Religion," *Sociological Analysis* 37 (Summer 1976) 153–159; "Comment on 'Bellah and the New Orthodoxy'," *Sociological Analysis* 37 (summer 1976) 167–168. P. L. BERGER, *The Sacred Canopy: Elements of a Sociological Theory of Religion* (Garden City, N.Y. 1967). J. BERNARDIN, "Civil Religion," *Origins* 5 (1975–76) 113, 115–117. C. J. BOURG, "A Symposium on Civil Religion," *Sociological Analysis* 37 (Summer 1976) 141–159. C. CHERRY, ed., *Today's New Israel: Religious Interpretations of American Destiny* Englewood Cliffs, N.J. 1971). J. A. CHRISTENSON and R. C. WIMBERLEY, "Who Is Civil Religious?" *Sociological Analysis* 39 (Spring, 1978) 77–83. W. A. COLE and P. E. HAMMOND, "Religious Pluralism, Legal Development, and Societal Complexity: Rudimentary Forms of Civil Religion," *Journal for the Scientific Study of Religion* 13 (June, 1974) 177–189. J. M. CUDDIHY, *No Offense: Civil Religion and Protestant Taste* (New York 1978). J. DEWEY, *A Common Faith*. Terry Lectures (New Haven 1934). D. DOHEN, *Nationalism and American Catholicism* (New York 1967). A. GREELEY, *The Denominational Society* (Glenview, Ill. 1972). P. E. HAMMOND, "The Sociology of American Civil Religion: A Bibliographic Essay," *Sociological Analysis* 37 (Summer, 1976) 169–182. D. R. HOGE, "Theological Views of America among Protestants," *Sociological Analysis* 37 (Summer, 1976) 127–139. W. S. HUDSON, *Nationalism and Religion in America: Concepts of American Destiny and Mission* (New York 1970). B. KATHAN and N. FUCHS, *Civil Religion in America: A Bibliography* (New Haven 1976). M. MARTY, *The New Shape of American Religion* (New York 1959); "Two Kinds of Civil Religion," in R. E. RICHEY and D. G. JONES, *American Civil Religion* (New York 1974) 139–157. S. E. MEAD, "The Nation with the Soul of a Church," *Church History* 36 (Sept., 1967) 262–283. M. A. NEAL, "Civil Religion, Theology and Politics in America," in *America in Theological Perspective* (New York 1976); "Civil Religion and the Development of Peoples," *Journal of Religious Education* (March–April, 1976); "Rationalization or Religion: When is Civil Religion Not Religion But Merely Civil?" in *A Socio-Theology of Letting Go* (New York 1977) 9–31. R. NEUHAUS, *Time Toward Home: the American Experiment as Revelation* (New York 1975). M. NOVAK, *Choosing Our King: Powerful Symbols in Presidential Politics* (New York 1974). T. ROBBINS et al., "The Last Civil Religion: Reverend Moon and the Unification Church." *Sociological Analysis* 37 (Summer 1976) 111–125. E. A. SMITH, ed., *The Religion of the Republic* (Philadelphia 1971). E. L. TUVESON, *Redeemer Nation: The Idea of America's Millennial Role* (Chicago 1968). W. L. WARNER, *American Life: Dream and Reality* (Chicago 1957). R. WILLIAMS, *American Society* (New York 1970). J. F. WILSON, "A Historian's Approach to Civil Religion," in R. E. RICHEY and D. G. JONES, *American Civil Religion* (New York 1974) 115–138; "The Status of 'Civil Religion' in America," in E. A. SMITH, ed., *Civil Religion* (Philadelphia 1971) 1–21. R. C. WIMBERLEY, "Testing the Civil Religion Hypothesis," *Sociological Analysis* 37 (Winter, 1976) 341–351. M. L. SCHNEIDER, "A Catholic Perspective on American Civil Religion," in T. M. MCFADDEN, ed., *America in Theological Perspective* (New York 1976) 123–139.

[M. A. NEAL]

CIVILTÀ CATTOLICA, LA

With the blessing of Pope Pius IX, the Jesuit biweekly *La Civiltà Cattolica* was founded in 1850 by Carlo Maria Curci, SJ. It soon became Italy's most prestigious Catholic periodical, defending the pope and the Church against their philosophical and political opponents. In particular, it played an important role in the struggle against MODERNISM in the early 1900s. Pius IX was convinced that in order to combat the liberal and agnostic ideas propagated by European journalism in the mid-19th century, the Church needed a journal of its own, which would defend the values of the traditional "Catholic civilization." Although the Jesuit superior at the time, Father Johannes ROOTHAAN, had misgivings about involving the society in political matters, the Jesuits complied with the pope's wish. After a few months in Naples, the journal moved to Rome, under the editorial control of a staff of Jesuit writers who consulted frequently with the Vatican. In 1868, this formula of a "college of writers" was confirmed by pontifical statute.

From the beginning, the magazine's tone was sharp and combative in defense of the faith and the papacy, during a historical period when both were perceived to be under siege in Italy. Among the early causes enjoined by *La Civiltà Cattolica* was the refusal of Pius IX to concede temporal power in the face of Italy's political unification movement. In the 20th century, it ran articles attacking the errors of liberalism, Modernism, and socialism, taking an uncompromising line even against more open positions within the Church. Although favorable to some of the religious positions of fascism in Italy, the magazine voiced increasing criticism of its totalitarian policies. In 1938, the magazine condemned Nazism as neopagan, anti-Christian, and imperialistic. In the post-World War II period, the journal called for Catholic unity at the Italian polls to counter the political threat posed by Socialist and Communist parties. In the 1960s, four writers from the Jesuit "Civiltà" college were chosen by the Vatican to review thousands of confidential Holy See documents dating from 1939–45 and pertaining to the question of whether Pope Pius XII had done enough to help Jews suffering from Nazi persecution.

With the Second Vatican Council the magazine began a more tolerant dialogue with modern culture. It also widened its sphere of editorial interest, writing on such varied topics as the existence of hell, the vivisection of animals, cinema, and literature. In the 1990s, it had a circulation of about 16,000 in more than 100 countries. Although never an official publication of the Holy See, its articles were reviewed before publication at the Vatican—by the pope himself until Pope John XXIII's pontificate, and subsequently by other high officials of the Secretariat of State. The stated policy was that articles would "harmonize" with the Vatican's positions and the church's teachings. Articles touching on theology, faith, and morality received additional review by the Congregation for the Doctrine of the Faith. Sometimes "trial balloons" were floated in the magazine's pages on sensitive international questions, such as the Palestinian-Israeli conflict, offering Vatican diplomats an opportunity to gauge reactions to ideas or proposals before they were officially adopted by the Holy See.

[J. THAVIS]

CLAIRVAUX, ABBEY OF

Former CISTERCIAN abbey founded in 1115 as the third daughter abbey of CÎTEAUX, in the Diocese of Langres (now the Diocese of Troyes) in the Aube Valley near Bar-sur-Aube, Champagne, France (Latin, *Claravallis*). Its first abbot was BERNARD OF CLAIRVAUX, and the first religious were, for the most part, relatives who had entered Cîteaux with Bernard. Land for the abbey was donated by his cousin, Josbert of La Ferté. The abbey prospered rapidly. Its property was increased by donations and acquisitions and included as many as 12 granges and two wine cellars. Meanwhile Bernard attracted numerous recruits, and Clairvaux, which numbered as many as 700 residents, was soon able to found other abbeys: Trois-Fontaines in Champagne in 1118; Fontenay in Burgundy in 1119, Foigny in Thiérache in 1121; and Igny in Champagne. In 38 years Bernard

founded 68 abbeys, which in turn founded others; by the end of the 15th century there were 350 abbeys descending from Clairvaux. Bernard assembled an important library and placed much emphasis on studies. The writings—particularly sermons—of several monks of Clairvaux have been preserved, namely, those of GEOFFREY OF CLAIRVAUX, GUERRIC OF IGNY, GILBERT OF HOLLAND, and Henry of Clairvaux. In 1244, abbot Stephen de LEXINTON founded the college of St. Bernard near the University of Paris.

Clairvaux became a school for sanctity. One of its monks became Pope EUGENE III, 12 were made cardinals, more than 30 became bishops, and many were abbots. Although Clairvaux escaped commendatory abbots, it nevertheless experienced a period of decline and financial difficulty during the 15th and 16th centuries. In 1615, Abbot Denis Largentier reformed the abbey, introducing the Strict Observance, but this was abandoned by his nephew and successor, Claude Largentier. During the French Revolution, the abbey was sold, and in 1808 it was converted into the central prison. None of the buildings erected by Bernard remains. The structure used by the conversi, dating from the end of the 12th century, still stands, but all other existing buildings were constructed during the 18th century. The abbey church was destroyed between 1812 and 1819.

Bibliography: Sources. *Chronicon Clarevallense* in *Patrologia Latina*, ed. J. P. MIGNE, 217 v. (Paris 1878–90) 185:1247–52. J. WAQUET, *Recueil des chartes de l'abbaye de Clairvaux*, fasc. 1 (Troyes 1950). J. M. CANIVEZ, ed., *Statuta capitulorum generalium ordinis cisterciensis*, 8 v. (Louvain 1933–41). Literature. A. WILMART, "L'Ancienne bibliothèque de Clairvaux," *Collectanea ordinis Cisterciensium Reformatorum* 11 (1949) 101–127, 301–319. L. H. COTTINEAU, *Répertoire topobibliographique des abbayes et prieurés*, 2 v. (Mâcon 1935–39) 1:799–800. BEAUNIER, *Abbayes et prieurés de l'ancienne France*, ed. J. M. L. BESSE, 12 v. (Paris 1905–41) 12:308–344. J. M. CANIVEZ, *Dictionnaire d'histoire et de géographie ecclésiastiques*, ed. A. BAUDRILLART et al. (Paris 1912–) 12:1050–61. M. A. DIMIER, *Recueil de plans d'églises cisterciennes Grignan*, 2 v. (Paris 1949) 1:100–101; *Saint Bernard, pêcheur de Dieu* (Paris 1953); "Saint Bernard, Fondateur de monastères," *Collectio ordinis Cisterciensium Reformatorum* 15 (1953) 45–60, 130–139; 16 (1954) 122–128, 192–203. A. A. KING, *Cîteaux and Her Elder Daughters* (London 1954) 207–328.

[M. A. DIMIER]

CLAIRVOYANCE, SPIRITUAL

An intellectual occult phenomenon in which a person is able to sense, feel, or know something about a person or thing or is able to receive or send knowledge to a person at a distance of time or space without using any ordinary medium of communication is spiritual clairvoyance. It remains to be seen whether or not there is a natural explanation for certain types of clairvoyance, whether by means of some type of extrasensory perception, a kind of wave that radiates from brain to brain, or some occult energy or force that emanates from one soul to another. Since clairvoyance has been manifested by persons under the influence of the devil, by canonized saints, and by persons suffering from pathological states, this phenomenon may proceed from diabolical, supernatural, or natural causes as yet unknown. If it is irrevocably established that a type of clairvoyance, such as the reading of hearts and minds, is a true miracle, then neither the devil nor a purely natural cause could be offered as an explanation.

Under the general name of clairvoyance other special phenomena may be listed. Telepathy is the sensation or knowledge of something at a distance or the communication of knowledge at a distance, with no known means of communication intervening. There has been no positive and certain explanation of its cause. Telesthesia is the ability to see, sometimes as in a vision, events or persons who are at a great distance; it is recorded of SWEDEN-BORG, who claimed to have seen in his mind's eye the burning of Göteborg. Cryptoscopy is the ability to read a letter enclosed in its envelope, to read a book without opening the cover, or to see what is happening on the other side of a wall or closed door. This feat is said to have occurred in the strange case of Mollie Fancher, born in Brooklyn, N.Y., in 1848 (Thurston, 294–325).

Psychometry is a kind of retrospective clairvoyance in which a person can witness or relive events that have happened in the past, sometimes centuries ago. Such clairvoyance was claimed for Bridey Murphy and for the Misses Moberly and Jourdain [cf. C. A. E. Moberly and E. F. Jourdain, *An Adventure,* ed. Joan Evans (New York 1955)]. Occult divination, or second sight, is the ability to see clearly and often in detail some event that will happen in the future, sometimes in a manner similar to a prophetic vision. The reading of hearts is a special insight by which one individual is able to know the secrets of another person, even when the second person is unwilling that those secrets be known. St. John VIANNEY is an outstanding example of this phenomenon among the saints. Hierognosis is the ability to recognize immediately either holiness or evil in any person, place, or thing. This phenomenon, like true reading of hearts, transcends the natural order and cannot be explained by natural or diabolical causes. It was manifested in the lives of Catherine EMMERICH and SS. CATHERINE OF SIENA and FRANCES OF ROME.

Bibliography: H. THURSTON, *The Physical Phenomena of Mysticism,* ed. J. H. CREHAN (Chicago 1952). Z. ARADI, *The Book of Miracles* (New York 1956). J. G. ARINTERO, *The Mystical Evolution in the Development and Vitality of the Church,* tr. J. AUMANN, 2 v. (St. Louis 1949–51). A. F. POULAIN, *The Graces of Interior Prayer,* tr. L. L. YORKE SMITH (St. Louis 1950). J. MARÉCHAL, *Studies in the Psychology of the Mystics,* tr. A. THOROLD (London 1927). R. OMEZ, *Psychical Phenomena,* tr. R. HAYNES (New York 1958).

[J. AUMANN]

CLARA, JERÓNIMO EMILIANO

Pastor, Argentine defender of the rights of the Church; b. Villa del Rosario, province of Córdoba, Nov. 12, 1827; d. Córdoba, Dec. 29, 1892. He was ordained in 1850 and was a parish priest, chaplain, canon, archdeacon of the cathedral of Córdoba; vice rector at the Colegio of Monserrat; rector of the seminary in that same city; and capitular vicar in *sede vacante* in 1883 and 1884. In 1877 he founded the Institute of Daughters of Mary Immaculate, which still exists. In 1883 and 1884 he was the most intrepid and determined opponent of the anti-religious laws promulgated in Buenos Aires to destroy the influence of the Church, expressing his position in pastoral letters against secular education and civil matrimony. Córdoba society supported Clara wholeheartedly and followed his example. Some professors of the University of Córdoba supported their pastor so forcefully that they were dismissed from their posts. Among them were Rafael García Montaña, Nicéforo Castellano, and Nicolás Berrotarán. The government urged the ecclesiastical cabildo of Córdoba to oust Clara from the post of capitular vicar, but the request was denied. He was then taken prisoner by order of the national government and was kept imprisoned until Juan C. Tissera took possession of the See of Córdoba in December 1884. In Salta, Bp. Buenaventura Rizo Patron emulated Clara's example, and other vicars did the same.

Bibliography: F. COMPANY, *El Vicario Clara: Sus ideales, sus trabajos, su lucha* (Buenos Aires 1955).

[G. FURLONG]

CLARE GAMBACORTA, BL.

Widow, Dominican reformer; b. Pisa, 1362; d. there, April 17, 1419. At birth she was named Tora; she was the daughter of Pietro Gambacorta, ruler of Pisa (1369–93), and the sister of (Bl.) PETER OF PISA. At the age of 12 she accepted a political marriage, but was widowed at 15. Urged by (St.) CATHERINE OF SIENA to abandon secular life, she joined the POOR CLARES the next year, receiving the name Clare. She was immediately removed by her family and imprisoned. Released by her father after five months, she was allowed to join the DOMINICANS and was free eventually to found a community of strict observance. In 1382, she and five companions established the convent of S. Domenico in Pisa. Her virtues attracted vocations of quality, won the affection of Pisans, and, together with her insistent pleadings, influenced the reform of the Dominican Order. Clare's father and two brothers were killed in an uprising in 1393; one of them met death at the door of the monastery when, to protect the nuns, she had to refuse him refuge. She heroically pardoned the murderers. A special fragrance, noted on her person in life, was observed at her death and renewed, 13 years later, when her body was exhumed, at which time her tongue was found incorrupt. Pius VIII approved her cult in 1830. Clare's spirit as well as her fidelity to the strict observance still mark the community she founded.

Feast: April 17.

Bibliography: Archives, Monastero S. Domenico, Pisa. N. ZUCCHELLI, *La B. Chiara Gambacorta* (Pisa 1914). D. TONCELLI, *La. B. Chiara Gambacorta* (Pisa 1920). M. E. MURPHY, *Blessed Clara Gambacorta* (Fribourg 1928). A. BUTLER, *The Lives of the Saints*, rev. ed. H. THURSTON and D. ATTWATER (New York 1956) 2:117–119. T. MCGLYNN, *This Is Clara of Pisa* (Pisa 1962).

[T. MCGLYNN]

CLARE OF ASSISI, ST.

Founder of the Order of Saint Clare; b. Assisi, Italy, 1193/94, d. Monastery of San Damiano outside the walls of Assisi, Aug. 11, 1253. Clare was born to Ortulana and Favarone di Offreducio, a noble Umbrian household. Attracted to the gospel message of FRANCIS OF ASSISI, and with his assistance and that of Guido, bishop of Assisi, on Palm Sunday 1211/12, Clare left her home with a companion and was received by Francis as a penitent at the Portiuncula in lower Assisi. During Holy Week, she stayed at the Benedictine Monastery of San Paolo in Bastia until Francis, Bernard, and Philip brought her to the beguine-like house of Sant'Angelo on the slope of Mount Subasio. There her sister Catherine, later canonized as AGNES OF ASSISI, joined her despite the attempts of the Offreducio family to impede both daughters from exchanging their aristocratic privileges for the simple life exemplified by Francis and his early brotherhood.

Before 1215, when the Fourth Lateran Council forbade the establishment of new religious orders, Francis provided Clare with a simple Form of Life and persuaded her to accept the title of abbess in an effort to legitimize the enclosed life of the Poor Ladies of San Damiano. According to tradition, before his death Pope Innocent III granted Clare the privilege to follow the poor Christ without owning property.

While recent scholars may question the authenticity of the document known as the *Privilege of Poverty*, it is undisputed that Clare's life energy was spent establishing a way for religious women to live as Francis did: *sine proprio*, without property. Spanning the terms of five popes, she tried to incorporate her radical form of life into the existing ecclesial patterns for monastic women. Neither the rules written for her and the Poor Ladies of San Damiano by Pope Gregory IX in 1219 nor by Pope Innocent IV in 1247 provided for her vision of communal poverty or her desire for her sisters to benefit from the ministries of Francis's brothers. Ultimately, Clare became the first woman to write a religious Form of Life which, while she was on her deathbed, received papal approbation (from Innocent IV). Her form of life dismantled established monastic practices for women by embracing members from all societal classes, providing for participation in governance, moderating the interpretation of the enclosure, and describing the role of abbess as that of sister and servant. At the same time, Clare held firmly to the monastic rhythm of the liturgy of the hours, the importance of silence, and manual work.

Clare became known for healing those in need, as well as for saving the city of Assisi from Saracen attacks in 1240 and 1241. Her spirituality flowed from her imitation of the humanity of Christ and her compassion for the crucified Christ extended to the suffering and poor. Her canonization proceedings began in November 1253; she was canonized on Aug. 12, 1255. In 1260, her body was moved inside Assisi to the Church of San Giorgio. Her body is interred in the Basilica of Santa Chiara, the proto-monastery of the POOR CLARES. Clare was declared the patron of television because of her 1252 vision of the Christmas liturgy at the Basilica of Santa Francesco; she is also a patron of needleworkers. In iconography she is often represented with her Rule, the Gospel, the Eucharist, a crucifix, or a lily.

Feast: Aug. 11.

Bibliography: Z. LAZZERI, ed., "Process of Canonization," *Archivum Franciscanum historicum* 13 (1920) 403–507. R. ARMSTRONG, *Clare of Assisi: Early Documents* (St. Bonaventure, N.Y. 1993). M. BARTOLI, *Clare of Assisi* (Quincy, Ill. 1993). M. CARNEY, *The First Franciscan Woman: Clare of Assisi and her Form of Life* (Quincy, Ill. 1993). I. PETERSON, *Clare of Assisi: A Biographical Study* (Quincy, Ill. 1993). W. MALECZEK, "Questions About the Authenticity of the Privilege of Poverty of Innocent III and the Testament of Clare of Assisi," *Greyfriars Review Supp.* (1998) 1–80. M. ALBERZONI, "San Damiano in 1228: A Contribution to the 'Clare Question,'" tr. E. HAGMAN, *Greyfriars Review* 13, no.1 (1999).

[I. PETERSON]

CLARE OF MONTEFALCO, ST.

Augustinian nun; b. Montefalco (province of Perugia) *c.* 1268; d. Montefalco, Aug. 17, 1308. Despite her youth, in 1275 Clare of Montefalco entered the enclosure where her older sister, Joanna, was living a type of religious life with other pious women. In 1290 the local bishop officially recognized the group as a monastic community and placed them under the Rule of St. AUGUSTINE. When Joanna, who had been the superior, died in November of 1291, Clare was elected to succeed her. Her spirituality centered on the passion of Christ, and she was often favored with mystical visions. She also showed a practical concern for the poor and preserved her community from the errors of a quietist sect of the day in Umbria. After her death, the nuns, moved by her statement that she had the cross of Christ in her heart, opened her heart and found formations resembling the instruments of Christ's passion. A canonical investigation was soon undertaken by the bishop's representative, Berengario di Donadio, who wrote the first *Life*. In 1624 Urban VIII granted permission to use an office and Mass in her honor to the Augustinians and the diocese of Spoleto. Leo XIII canonized her in 1881. Beautiful 14th- century frescos adorn a chapel in her shrine at Montefalco. Her iconography often includes the opened heart with the instruments of the passion.

Feast: Aug. 17.

Bibliography: Sources. *Acta Sanctorum* Aug. 3: 676–688. B. DI DONADIO, *Vita Sancte Clare de Cruce,* ed. A. SEMENZA (Città del Vaticano 1943); *St. Clare of the Cross of Montefalco,* tr. M. O'CONNELL and ed. J. E. ROTELLE (Villanova 1999). E. MENESTÒ, *Il processo di canonizzazione di Chiara da Montefalco* (Regione dell'Umbria 1984). Literature. *Bibliotheca sanctorum* 3:1217–24. *La spiritualità di S. Chiara da Montefalco: Atti del I convegno di studio, Montefalco, 8–10 agosto 1985,* ed. S. NESSI (Montefalco 1986). R. SALA, *S. Chiara della Croce: La mistica Agostiniana di Montefalco* (Rome 1977). *S. Chiara da Montefalco e il suo tempo: Atti del quarto convegno di studi storici ecclesiastici, Spoleto, 28–30 dicembre 1981,* ed. C. LEONARDI and E. MENESTÒ (Perugia 1985).

[K. A. GERSBACH]

CLARE OF RIMINI, BL.

Franciscan tertiary, mystic; b. Rimini, Italy, 1262 or 1282; d. Rimini, Feb. 10, 1320 or 1346. Born of the wealthy Agolanti(?) family, Clare married young and lived scandalously until at the age of 34 she received the grace of conversion. She then joined the FRANCISCAN THIRD ORDER and after the death of her second husband gave herself to rigorous penance, prayer, and the service of the poor. Living with several companions near the POOR CLARE convent, which she had established, she observed the Rule of St. CLARE OF ASSISI but without enclosure, in order not to hinder her works of charity. Her mystical experiences, to which her iconography sometimes refers,

centered on the Passion and the wounded side and heart of Christ. Although Pius VI confirmed her cult (1784), her feast is not in the Franciscan calendar.

Feast: Feb. 10

Bibliography: L. WADDING, *Scriptores Ordinis Minorum* (3d ed. Quaracchi-Florence 1931–) 7:394–400. LÉON DE CLARY, *Lives of the Saints and Blessed of the Three Orders of St. Francis* (Taunton, Eng. 1885–87). A. BUTLER, *The Lives of the Saints,* rev. ed. H. THURSTON and D. ATTWATER (New York 1956) 1:297–298.

[M. F. LAUGHLIN]

CLARENBAUD OF ARRAS

French scholastic, representative of the school of Chartres; fl. 1130 to 1170. He studied at Paris under HUGH OF SAINT-VICTOR and THIERRY OF CHARTRES probably in the late 1130s. From at least 1152 until 1156 he was provost of the church of Arras. "Summoned" to direct the schools by Walter II of Mortagne, Bishop of Laon from 1155 to 1174, he went to Laon, probably in 1160. He did not teach there for long, but returned to Arras, where he was made archdeacon by Andrew, bishop of Arras (1161–73). He is known to have been alive in the 1170s, for he possessed some relics of St. Thomas BECKET, who died in 1170.

Although Clarenbaud taught philosophy, he is best known for his theological writings. Many monks turned to him, complaining that they were unable to understand the commentary on Boethius's *De Trinitate* written by GILBERT DE LA PORRÉE. At their repeated and "sacred requests" he agreed to write a commentary of his own, relying mainly on the lectures of his two "venerable teachers." In his lucid and polished commentary on *De Trinitate,* he severely criticized ABELARD and Gilbert de la Porrée. He accused Abelard of SABELLIANISM and claimed that he had read "many childish, ridiculous and damnable things" in Abelard's *Theologia* (*De Trin.* 1.38). More frequently he criticized Gilbert not only for errors and heresies, but also for a deliberately involved and obscure style. He strongly rejected Gilbert's assertion that the divine persons "differ by number," and admitted only a certain "otherness" among the persons (*De Trin.* 3.35–36).

At a later date Clarenbaud wrote a commentary on the third of Boethius's tracts, *De hebdomadibus,* and a *Tractatulus* on the opening chapter of Genesis. In all his writings he relied heavily on Thierry of Chartres without simply plagiarizing him. In addition to a polished style and lucid presentation of doctrine, Clarenbaud's writings reveal a vast knowledge of Christian and non-Christian literature.

Since for Clarenbaud ignorance of creation leads to heresies, he carefully analyzed the notion of creation as a transition from nonbeing to being. The first movement of created being marks the beginning of time. Creatures are composed of primeval matter and seminal causes. Primeval matter is absolute potency (*possibilitas absoluta*), itself formless, containing every nature in a possible state. A seminal cause is a hidden power implanted by God in the four elements. Only God, or "Absolute Necessity," can operate on primeval matter, giving it forms that determine the nature of "defined potency" (*possibilitas definita*). From Absolute Necessity descends "the necessity of combination or concatenation" (*necessitas concatenationis*). Thus all things existed in the divine wisdom in undeveloped simplicity. They unfold and descend from the eternally One in a predetermined order and are, as it were, produced in concatenated and interwoven steps. He points out that St. AUGUSTINE and PYTHAGORAS present the same doctrine in different terms.

Bibliography: N. M. HARING, *Life and Works of Clarembald of Arras* (Studies and Texts 10; Toronto 1965). W. JANSEN, *Der Kommentar des Clarenbaldus von Arras zu Boethius 'De Trinitate'* (Breslauer Studien zur historischen Theologie 8; Breslau 1926) 26–105. É. H. GILSON, *History of Christian Philosophy in the Middle Ages* (New York 1955) 149–150, 623. A. TOGNOLO, *Enciclopedia filosofica* (Venice-Rome 1957) 1:1074.

[N. M. HARING]

CLARENDON, CONSTITUTIONS OF

A list of allegedly ancestral customs put forward by King HENRY II of England in January 1164 at a council held near Salisbury. Relations between the king and Abp. Thomas Becket had been strained by Becket's refusal to hand over for punishment by the king "criminous clerks" convicted in the church courts. Instead, Becket proposed degradationn to the lay state which would render them in the future liable to trial by the royal courts. Henry, at a council at Westminster (1163), required the bishops to swear to observe the ancient customs of the kingdom in this and other matters. They demurred, but Becket finally agreed, commanding the others to follow. The king at Clarendon insisted upon solemn submission to written provisions. Of these, six clauses were innocuous. Six others clearly ran counter to Canon Law: clauses six and eight forbade clergy to leave the country or appeal to Rome without royal permission; clauses five, six, and ten limited the bishops' powers of excommunication; and clause 12 regulated the royal control of episcopal elections. Four others defined in the king's favor questions of jurisdiction, including the punishment of criminous clerks. Historians agree that as a whole the constitutions were a fair statement of royal practice under Henry I, but that several clauses were incompatible with the freedom of the Church as defined by current Canon Law. On the issue of criminous clerks, opinion is divided as to both the canonical validity and the practical justification of the archbishop's claim, which was subsequently upheld by Pope ALEXANDER III. The archbishop yielded; his subsequent remorse and resistance are recorded elsewhere.

See Also: BECKET, THOMAS, ST.

Bibliography: Text. W. STUBBS, *Select Charters* (Oxford 1929) 163–167. *English Historical Documents*, ed. D. C. DOUGLAS (New York 1953–) 2:718–722. A. L. POOLE, *From Domesday Book to Magna Carta* (Oxford 1955) 205–207. H. G. RICHARDSON and G. O. SAYLES, *The Governance of Medieval England* (Edinburgh 1963) 303–318.

[M. D. KNOWLES]

CLARENI

A group of radical FRANCISCAN SPIRITUALS, cofounded by the Franciscans Peter of Macerata and Peter of Fossombrone when the former obtained from Pope CELESTINE V in authorization (1294) for his group to separate from the Franciscan Order and become hermits, or CELESTINES, directly under the Rule of St. Francis. Macerata was thereafter called Liberato; his associate, ANGELUS CLARENUS. When BONIFACE VIII annulled Celestine's concession on April 8, 1295, this group of Celestines or more properly, Clareni, moved to Achaia for two years and then to southern Thessaly and finally had to return to Italy c. 1304. Upon the death of Liberato (1307), Angelus succeeded as head of the group, which was at first settled along the banks of the Chiarino River. When the bull *Sancta Romana* of JOHN XXII (Dec. 30, 1317) refused autonomy to any of the groups that it called FRATICELLI (including the Clareni)—in an attempt to preserve the unity of the FRANCISCANS—the Clareni reluctantly joined the main group of (Benedictine) Celestines and moved to the Subiaco area. In 1334, alarmed by the Roman INQUISITION investigating the extremism of the Clareni, Angelus moved to Basilicata, Italy, where he died (1337). But the Clareni, then located in several places throughout Italy, refused to disband, even in the face of inquisitorial proceedings, the death of Angelus, and the confirmation of their suppression (1341). Their life continued to be difficult; e.g., at the end of the 14th century Florence framed laws to expel them from the city.

At a time difficult to pinpoint, there appeared the *Societas pauperum hermitarum quondam fr. Angeli de Clarino,* an orthodox Congregation of Clareni under episcopal jurisdiction. This group obtained a bull from Boniface IX (1389–1404), confirming its orthodoxy, and thus ending its persecution. The Clareni of St. Maria de Valle Ceraso, near Treia, were recognized as orthodox in 1437 and 1439; a bull of Eugene IV did the same for those of Narni (1446); and a year later a bull of Nicholas V cleared the name of the Clareni in nine dioceses of central Italy. In 1473 Sixtus IV subordinated them to the Franciscan minister general, and in 1475 they were exempted from episcopal jurisdiction. In September 1483 their chapter adopted the Franciscan rule, but the Clareni remained a separate Franciscan family under their own vicar. Their Roman residence was San Geronimo (1473–1524), then San Bartolomeo on the Island. United to the Franciscan Observants in 1512, they formed a separate province of San Geronimo (1518–36) and of San Bartolomeo (1536–68), when the rites and statutes of the Clareni were abolished, and the group finally merged with the Observants.

Bibliography: G. L. POTESTA, *Angelo Clareno: Dai poveri eremiti ai fraticelli* (Rome 1990). D. L. DOUIE, *The Nature and the Effect of the Heresy of the Fraticelli* (Manchester, Eng. 1932).

[J. CAMBELL]

CLARET, ANTHONY MARY, ST.

Archbishop, founder of the Claretians; b. Sallent, Spain, Dec. 23, 1807; d. Frontfroid, France, Oct. 24, 1870. A weaver's son, he worked in his youth as a weaver and a designer in the textile mills of Barcelona. In 1835 he was ordained for the Diocese of Vich, and after 1840 he became one of Spain's most popular preachers. In his preaching he centered everything on devotion to the Eucharist and the Immaculate Heart of Mary. He founded a congregation of preachers called the Sons of the Immaculate Heart of Mary (*see* CLARETIANS). In 1850 he was appointed to the much-neglected Archdiocese of Santiago in Cuba. Immediately he set about reforming the seminary and his clergy and began extensive visitations of his vast territory. His greatest efforts were directed against the widespread concubinage and illegitimacy on the island. He also encouraged sound farming methods and credit unions among the poor so as to create material conditions favorable to good Christian family life. In 1857 he returned to Spain to become the confessor of Queen Isabella II. The frequent royal tours of the country afforded him an occasion to resume his earlier preaching. Claret was also impressed by the power of the popular press. In Catalonia and Madrid, he founded societies to publish and distribute free Catholic literature, much of which he himself had written. His position at the royal court excited the suspicion and hostility of the anticlerical liberals, and consequently he became the victim of vicious calumny in the radical press. During the revolution of 1868 Claret, forced to leave Spain, went to Rome where he participated in Vatican Council I. On May 31, 1870, he spoke before the council in defense of papal infallibility. Claret died at the Cistercian Monastery of Frontfroid, France. He was beatified by Pius XI on Feb. 25, 1934 and canonized by Pius XII on May 7, 1950.

Feast: Oct. 24 (formerly Oct. 23).

Bibliography: A. M. CLARET, *Escritos autobiográficos y espirituales* (Madrid 1959, rep. 1981); *Autobiografía*, ed. J. M. VIÑAS (Barcelona 1975) and Eng. tr. J. DAVIES (Chicago 1976). *El Apóstol claretiano seglar*, ed. J. BERMEJO (Barcelona 1979). A. CABRÉ RUFATT, *Evangelizador de dos mundos* (Barcelona 1983). FR. CODINACHS I VERDAGUER, *Pobre i a peu* (Barcelona 1997). C. FERNÁNDEZ, *El padrito* (Madrid 1972); *El Beato Padre Antonio María Claret* (Madrid 1941); *El confesor de Isabel II y sus actividades en Madrid* (Madrid 1964). J. M. GARCIA-CASCALES, *Antonius M. Claret* (4th ed. Vienna 1970). F. GUTIÉRREZ, *Azorín y San Antonio María Claret* (Madrid 1979). J. M. LOZANO, *El Corazón de María en San Antonio María Claret* (Madrid 1963); *The Claretians*, tr. J. DARIES (Chicago 1980); *Anthony Claret: A Life at the Service of the Gospel* (Chicago 1985). F. ROYER, *St. Anthony Claret* (New York 1957). D. SARGENT, *Assignments of Antonio Claret* (New York 1948).

[T. P. JOYCE]

CLARET DE LA TOUCHE, LOUISE

Visitandine and mystic; b. Saint-Germain-en-Laye, March 15, 1868; d. Vische, May 14, 1915. Her health was fragile. At 11 she made a vow of virginity, and on Nov. 20, 1890, entered the Visitation at Romans. While there were no sensible visions recorded in her life, she experienced many mystical graces. These are difficult to isolate in character because she recorded them as they occurred from day to day and no synthesis has yet been made of them.

In 1902 she records that Christ said to her: "Margaret Mary showed my heart to the world; you will show it to priests." About 1913 opposition arose to her promulgation of this message and as a result she was detached from her community. Under the authority of Monsignor Filipello, she made a new foundation at Vische in March 1914, which, while following the rule of the Visitation, practiced greater exterior austerity and recited the full office. This community is now known as Bethany of the Sacred Heart and sponsors L'Alliance Sacerdotale, which encourages priests to study and imitate the mercy of the Sacred Heart. In 1933 an informative process was opened by the bishop of Ivrée.

Bibliography: *Messagère de l'amour infini: Mère Louise Marguerite Claret de la Touche* (Paris 1937), an anonymous work with a preface by R. P. HÉRIS.

[J. VERBILLION]

CLARETIANS

Popular name for the Missionary Sons of the Immaculate Heart of Mary (abbreviated: CMF, Official Catholic Directory #0360), a religious congregation of simple vows founded in 1849 by (St.) Anthony Mary CLARET in Vich, Spain, for the ministry of preaching.

Foundation and Development. When anticlericalism in Spain after 1835 led to the suppression of all but a few Dominican and Franciscan monasteries, a group of diocesan clergy in Catalonia, led by Anthony Claret, took up the work of the suppressed religious, who had had almost exclusive charge of catechizing and popular preaching. Claret realized that the necessity of forming a community in which the preachers could practice the evangelical counsels and the common life without formally professing religious vows or even promises, at that time prohibited by law. Thus he and five young Catalan diocesan priests formed the first community on July 16, 1849, at the diocesan seminary of Vich.

The community, left without a written rule when Claret was appointed archbishop of Santiago, Cuba, in 1850, had a difficult time for the next few years. Confusion arose as to the founder's purpose in establishing the association, and as new members entered, much of the earlier missionary zeal and fervor waned. In 1857, at the insistence of José Xifré, who became the second superior general (1857–99), Claret drew up a constitution of 15 chapters that became the core of the Claretian rule; in it the active ministry of preaching is emphasized. In 1859 the constitutions were approved by the Spanish government; the following year they received the decree of praise from the Holy See.

At first only priests were admitted into the community after a year of probation. They were bound neither by vows nor promises and were free to leave without formality at any time. After the general chapter of 1862, however, all members were required to pronounce private vows of obedience, chastity, and poverty in a public ceremony after a year of novitiate. At the same time they were to make an oath of perseverance in the community and promise not to accept any honor outside the community without the express permission of the superiors or the command of the Holy See. The revised constitutions received the definitive approbation and confirmation of Pius IX on May 8, 1870. The community was also raised to the status of a religious congregation and all members were required to make a public profession of simple vows. After the constitutions were revised in accordance with the 1917 Code of Canon Law, Pius XI solemnly approved them on July 16, 1924.

Ministry. The earliest work of the Claretians was to continue the popular preaching begun by Claret. This preaching had always centered on devotion to the Holy Eucharist and to the Immaculate Heart of Mary. After 1862 the ministry of the Claretians was extended to include teaching in diocesan seminaries and the direction of parishes. By the time of their founder's death (1870), Claretians had been sent to their first foreign mission in North Africa. In 1885 the vicariate of Fernando Po, in Spanish Guinea (Africa), was entrusted to the Claretians. In 1963 they had missions in Spanish and Portuguese Guinea, Colombia, Panama, China, the Philippine Islands, and Japan. In the field of scholarship, Claretians have distinguished themselves especially for their studies in the Canon Law for religious and in Mariology. In 1920 a quarterly dealing with canonical questions related to the religious life, *Commentarium pro Religiosis,* was founded at Rome. In 1951 another journal, *Ephemerides Mariologicae,* was initiated by the general government of the congregation to further Marian studies.

U.S. Foundations. The Claretians were first invited to the U.S. in 1902 to preach to the Spanish-speaking in Brownsville, Tex.; from there they soon spread to San Antonio, Tex., and Los Angeles, Calif. To them Bp. John Forest entrusted his Cathedral of San Fernando in San Antonio, and from this center they spread out through central Texas, preaching and founding parishes and missions for the Spanish-speaking. In 1907 the Claretians were established at San Fernando Mission, Los Angeles, but the following year they transferred to San Gabriel Mission. In the earliest years the Claretians confined their labors almost exclusively to the Spanish-speaking of Texas, Arizona, and California. In 1922 when there were nine American communities, the general government separated them from the Mexican province and formed an independent American province.

In 1925 the Claretians went to Chicago, Ill., where they erected the National Shrine of St. Jude, and in 1929 the League of St. Jude, to foster devotion to the Apostle. The league also fosters vocations and supports Claretian seminaries; it publishes two Catholic monthlies of general interest, *U.S. Catholic* and *Today,* and a devotional magazine, *Immaculate Heart Crusader.* In 1932 a special branch of the league was added for the Chicago Police Department, ministering to the special needs of policemen and placing them under the protection of St. Jude. This Claretian initiative led other cities, such as Milwaukee, Wis., Indianapolis, Ind., and Grand Rapids, Mich., to adopt St. Jude as patron of their Catholic police organizations, though they are not affiliated with the Claretian League.

In 1926 Rev. Joseph Maiztegui, a consultor on the government of the American province, was appointed vicar apostolic of Darien, Panama, which was made dependent on the American province for its missionaries. From the U.S., missions were established in the Philippine Islands (1947) and in Japan (1951). In 1954 the American province of the Claretians was divided into the Eastern province, centered in Chicago and having jurisdiction over two communities in Canada; and the Western province, centered in Los Angeles.

By the end of the 20th century, the Claretians had foundations in 58 countries in five continents. In addition to their original charism of preaching, the congregation is heavily involved in parishes, missionary outreach, publishing, and ministering to refugees and immigrants. The generalate is in Rome.

Bibliography: A. M. CLARET, *Escritos autobiográficos* (Madrid 1959). M. IZQUIERDO GALLO, *Historia sucinta de la Congregación de Misioneros Hijos del Corazón de María, 1849–1973* (Madrid 1975). J. M. LOZANO, *Una vida al servicio del evangelic: Antonio Maria Claret* (Barcelona 1985).

[T. P. JOYCE/EDS.]

CLARITUS, BL.

Monastic founder; b. Florence, Italy, *c.* 1300; d. convent of Chiarito, Florence, May 25, 1348. He was a member of the noble Voglia family, and although he had received orders, he married. After a miraculous answer to an appeal to St. Zenobius (early 5th-century bishop of Florence), he returned to the clerical state, founding *c.* 1343 the convent of Chiarito (Regina Coeli), where his wife, Nicolosia, became a nun. He prescribed the Rule of St. AUGUSTINE for the community and devoted himself to ministering to its needs until his death. His tomb, in the convent, and his crucifix, also on display there, were objects of popular veneration. Pope LEO XI, while he was still archbishop of Florence, recognized the cult of Claritus. His body is now in the church of the Dominican sisters, Al Sodo (in Florence-Castello).

Feast: May 6.

Bibliography: *Acta Sanctorum* May 6:160–164. *Bollettino storico Agostiniano* 1 (1924) 15–20. R. VAN DOREN, *Dictionnaire d'istoire et de géographie ecclésiastiques* 12:1068. A. MERCATI and A. PELZER, *Dizionario ecclesiastico* 1:637. W. HUMPFNER, *Lexikon für Theologie und Kirche*[2] 2:1215.

[B. J. COMASKEY]

CLARKE, MOTHER MARY FRANCES

Foundress of the Sisters of Charity of the Blessed Virgin Mary, and of Clarke College, Dubuque, Iowa; b.

Mother Mary Frances Clarke.

Dublin, Ireland, March 2, 1803; d. Dubuque, Dec. 4, 1887. She was the daughter of Cornelius and Catherine (Hyland) Clarke. Mary and three young Irish girls arrived as missionary teachers in Philadelphia, Pa., in 1833. After meeting with Rev. Terence J. Donaghoe, her lifelong mentor, she founded her order in November 1833. Bishop John Hughes requested Mother Clarke to settle in the New York diocese; but since it was already well staffed, she responded instead to requests by Bp. Jean Mathias Pierre LORAS and Pierre DE SMET, SJ, to serve the Diocese of Dubuque. Her sisters, the first in Iowa, were transferred to Dubuque in 1843; and Donaghoe, director of the order, was made diocesan vicar-general. That same year the order founded St. Mary's Female Academy (later Clarke College). After the death of Donaghoe in 1869, Mother Clarke made application for pontifical status, and a decree of final approbation was issued in 1885. She died after governing for 54 years, leaving schools that were pioneers in the late-19th-century movement for women's colleges.

Bibliography: M. L. DORAN, *In the Early Days: Annals, 1833–87* (St. Louis 1925).

[M. ST. V. BERRY]

CLARKE, SAMUEL

Philosopher and divine; b. Norwich, England, Oct. 11, 1675; d. Leicester, May 17, 1729. Educated at Caius College, Cambridge, he became an ardent disciple of Isaac Newton. In 1697 he published a Latin translation of Rohault's *Traité de Physique*, an established textbook of Cartesian physics, adding notes to explain the ideas of Newton's *Principia*. In 1706 he published a Latin translation of Newton's *Optics*. His correspondence with G. W. LEIBNIZ apart, his most important work is the two sets of Boyle lectures he delivered in 1704 and 1705, published together (1719) under the title *A Discourse concerning the Being and Attributes of God, the Obligation of Natural Religion, and the Truth and Certainty of the Christian Revelation.* . . . In natural theology he used a method "as near mathematical as the nature of such a discourse would allow." His proofs of the existence of God were well known in 18th-century England and were treated by D. HUME as the standard ones. When Leibniz criticized some of Newton's ideas—about space and his mechanistic physics—for the theological and philosophical conclusions he saw in them, Clarke defended his master and published the correspondence in *A Collection of Papers Which Passed between the Late Learned Mr Leibnitz and Dr Clarke relating to the Principles of Natural Philosophy and Religion* (1717). Clarke wrote also a number of theological works, notably, *The Scripture Doctrine of the Trinity* (1712), for which he was severely criticized on account of his Arian and Latitudinarian ideas. He ranks among the foremost rationalist theologians of his time.

See Also: BRITISH MORALISTS.

Bibliography: *Works,* 4 v. (London 1738–42) preface, B. HOADLY. *The Clarke-Leibniz Correspondence*, ed. H. G. ALEXANDER (New York 1956). L. STEPHENS, *The Dictionary of National Biography from the Earliest Times to 1900* (London 1885–1900; repr. with corrections, 1908–09, 1921–22, 1938) 4:443–446. M. A. HOSKIN, "Mining All Within: Clarke's Notes to Rohault's *Traité de Physique*," *The Dignity of Science*, ed. J. A. WEISHEIPL (Washington 1961) 217–227.

[E. A. SILLEM]

CLARUS, ST.

Abbot; b. near Vienne, in Dauphiné, France, beginning of the seventh century; d. *c.* 660. He became a monk at Saint-Ferréol, then abbot of Saint-Marcel (*c.* 625). His virtues gained for him the admiration of Cadeoldus, bishop of Vienne, who charged him with the spiritual direction of the hermits at Sainte-Blandine. The ancient cult of Clarus was confirmed by PIUS X in 1903. He is the patron saint of tailors.

Feast: Jan. 1.

Bibliography: *Bibliotheca hagiograpica latina antiquae et mediae aetatis* (Brussels 1898–1901)1:1825. M. BLANC, *Vie et le culte de s. Claire,* 2 v. (Toulon 1898). J. L. BAUDOT and L. CHAUSSIN, *Vies des saints et des bienhereux selon l'ordre du calendrier avec l'historique des fêtes* (Paris 1935–56) 1:15. R. AIGRAIN, *Catholicisme* 2:1160. W. BÖHNE, *Lexikon für Theologie und Kirche,* ed. J. HOFER and K. RAHNER (Freiburg 1957–65) 2:1216. R. VAN DOREN, *Dictionnaire d'histoire et de géographie ecclésiastiques,* ed. A. BAUDRILLART et al. (Paris 1912) 12:1030.

[B. F. SCHERER]

CLAUDEL, PAUL LOUIS CHARLES MARIE

French poet and dramatist; b. Villeneuve-sur-Fèreen-Tardenois (Champagne), Aug. 6, 1868; d. Paris, Feb. 23, 1955. Claudel was not, as is commonly thought, of the peasantry of Champagne. His family, originally from the Vosges and Ile-de-France, were in public administration on his father's side; his mother came from one of those rural middle-class families, the Cerveaux, whose rise in status was promoted by the Revolution of 1789. The Cerveaux, who are important in the Claudelian psychology, are reflected in Toussaint Turelure, the principal character in *L'Otage* (1910) and *Pain dur* (1914); but if Paul Claudel was not "un paysan" (for his diplomatic career kept him constantly away from his native heath), he was nonetheless marked by his home region, even to its accent: that famous manner of grinding out his words between his teeth.

Roots and Early Formation. This background was important with respect both to his poetic genius and to his spiritual attitude, two qualities strongly bound together. The soil of Champagne, its rustic tales, and the local history and family tradition fed the imagination of the dramatic poet, and their influence is especially notable in one of his masterpieces, *L'Annonce faite à Marie* (1912).

It was particularly in the house at Villeneuve, the site of his vacations—although the family moved when he was two to Bar-le-Duc, where his father had been named to a new post—that the "child perched among the apples" in the top of an old tree discovered the world and foresaw, yearned for, a connection among all things, a complete meaning, "a catholic order." It was there also that at the age of 13 he witnessed the death of his maternal grandfather Cerveaux, a doctor, so ravaged by cancer that he died while suffering hallucinations.

With Villeneuve as its center, the family moved about as the father received various assignments, and the child passed from one school to another. The Claudels and the Cerveaux were Catholic by tradition, and there were several priests in the family, but the family maintained a respectful indifference. Young Paul received only as much religious instruction as was needed to prepare him for his first Communion (1880), and he soon abandoned all religious observances. He was 14 when his mother and the three children, at the insistence of the eldest daughter Camille, who was to become the very talented pupil (and a victim of the mental cruelty) of the sculptor Rodin, took up residence in Paris.

Paul Claudel entered the lycée Louis-le-Grand, where he won a first prize in oratory and, on that occasion, was "kissed on the brow" by RENAN. There he came under the influence of, and accepted as a disheartening reality, a philosophy that placed absolute confidence in science, at that time authoritative and triumphant. He spoke later of the "sad Eighties," of the "materialistic prison," and of "the state of suffocation and despair" he experienced as a student (1889) at L'École de Droit et des Sciences Politiques de Paris. For although the dogmatism of "science" seemed indisputable to young Claudel, there still remained within him the overpowering need to satisfy the urge he had experienced from earliest youth—to understand the "why" of life.

Literary and Religious Stirrings. In June 1886, after having been introduced to great literature—Aeschylus, Dante, Shakespeare—by his sister Camille, he read *Les Illuminations* and *Une Saison en enfer* by Arthur Rimbaud. In his own words, this was a "capital event," because the works of a "miserable poet" revealed to him that, in spite of the dominant philosophy, the universe was not a machine, obedient to the "laws" of nature, but that a limitless realm of the spiritual—in truth, of the supernatural—was a reality. In this frame of mind he went to Notre Dame de Paris for the Christmas services of the same year. In the famous story of his conversion he called his attitude "superlative dilettantism." He followed the high Mass with but moderate interest; he went again the next afternoon to hear Vespers. It was then, "near the second pillar by the entrance to the choir, on the night, in the direction of the Sacristy," that dilettantism dissolved in grace: "In one instant my heart was touched, and I believed."

A four-year struggle followed; the faith was there, but so were the convictions of his ingrained philosophy, intact and irreconcilable. On that first evening the convert opened a Bible belonging to his sister Camille and chanced upon a chapter in the Book of Wisdom. That voice "so sweet and so uncompromising" engaged him in a colloquy that lasted until his death. Some serious reading—Pascal, Bossuet, *The Imitation of Christ*, Aristotle, St. Thomas—contributed to the complete cleansing of his spirit: "I was before Thee as a fighter who yields." The final victory for God was won on Christmas Day in 1890 when Paul Claudel made his second Communion.

Paul Claudel.

One cannot neglect these preliminaries, however anecdotal they may seem, because they set the course, simultaneously and organically, for a long life and prodigious work.

Full Religious Transformation. In the interval between the first touch of grace in 1886 and the decisive "capitulation" of 1890, Claudel wrote a play, a work of genius—making allowances for the fumblings of a 20-year-old author—and particularly indicative of his fundamental need: *Tête d'or.* He had already produced *Premiers vers* and had had a close association with Mallarmé, with whose pure aestheticism he was not satisfied. However, with *Tête d'or,* "a drama of the conquest of the earth," about a hunger for power that collides with the mystery of death, he found his own voice: "Here am I—foolish, ignorant—an inexperienced man before the unknown! O being, young and fresh! Who are you? What are you doing?" This question by the first person on stage, Cébès, and the inability of his friend Simon Agnel, nicknamed "tête d'or" because of his flaming locks, to reply to it, express the duality and the confusion of the young Claudel, and, at the same time, give us a clue to the continuous unfolding of Claudel's poetic and catholic creation and its fundamental unity.

This unfolding can be called a "development"—as Claudel said of the Church—following his experiences of the inner life. He has been accused—and not always without reason, on the artistic level—of repeatedly turning his works to the ends of moral enlightenment. From *La Jeune fille Violaine* (1892) to the final *L'Annonce faite à Marie* (1948) on the theme of sacrifice, one can count five versions of the same drama. There are two versions of *Tête d'or;* there were two versions also of *La Ville* (1890), its sequel, a work concerned with the temptations of a "paradise on earth"; and two of *L'Échange* (1894), a conflict between the desire for freedom, represented by an American actress, and the "passion for service," represented by a woman who was sold to a trader by her husband. There are also two versions of *Père humilié,* the last book of the trilogy that includes *L'Otage* and *Le Pain dur,* in which the upstart Toussaint Turelure forces marriage on the aristocratic Sygne de Coufontaine in exchange for the liberty of Pope Pius VII; and *Protée,* a lyric farce. There are also three versions of *Partage de midi* (1905), an echo of a serious emotional upset, of which the two versions of *Soulier de satin* (1921), truly the Claudelian "whole," became the amplified orchestration and the idealized transformation.

Claudel's veritable obsession to revise his work was motivated at first by the necessity for self-enlightenment, for reworking the first spontaneous creation into a perspective that would lend it a sense of the supernatural and the providential. However, his conviction that he was bound to use his gifts as an apostolate and to channel them toward moral enlightenment is not a sufficient explanation for the extent to which he felt compelled to revise.

In this respect, another keystone in Claudel's thought and art, a gauge of the mutual fructification of poetry and the faith within him, is to be found in his *L'Art poétique* (1907). The two treatises of which it is made up, *De la Connaissance de temps* and *De la Co-naissance au monde et de soi-même*, are based on the argument of Holy Writ that "things visible are only for the purpose of leading us to an understanding of things invisible." Accordingly, by analogy and metaphor, the poetic word echoes the divine word, permits the deciphering and ordering of the "holy truth," and becomes a religious act. No less than his dramatic works, the lyrics of Claudel, especially *Cinq grandes odes* (1910) and *La Cantate à trois voix* (1911), thus have some of the characteristics of a glimpse of the cosmos been rendered intelligible through the vision of faith. Yet both are firmly planted in the soil, not only through their concrete language and their "native tang," but also by all Claudel put there from his own experience: his taste for violent adventure, for extreme hazard, for the "savage mystic." This aspect of Claudel's psychology contrasts strikingly with his exemplary and fruitful career as a diplomat.

Public Career. Claudel took first place (1870) in a course on foreign affairs, and after some time in L'École des Langues Orientales in Paris he made his diplomatic debut as French vice-consul in New York (1893), then served as acting consul at Boston (1894). He was later assigned to China—Shanghai, Fuzhou, Beijing, Tianjin—until 1908. These were among his most productive years, the years of *Connaissance de l'est* (1900). He kept both irons in the fire—his diplomatic duties and his literary productivity—without diverting a single hour from the former to the benefit of the latter. Furthermore, he feared that his poetry might be injurious to his public career and published his work quietly, almost confidentially. He was recognized as a genius at once, but he long remained well known only to the literary coterie. In the course of a sojourn in France, in 1900, he made retreats at the Abbeys of Solesmes and Ligugé, but he felt himself "mysteriously rejected" (*Partage de midi* carries some evidence of this).

In 1905 he married Reine Sainte-Marie Perrin, who bore him five children. He was consul at Prague (1908), consul-general at Frankfurt (1911) and Hamburg (1913), *chargé* of the Economic Mission at Rome, minister plenipotentiary to Brazil (1917) and to Copenhagen (1919), and ambassador to Japan (1922), to Washington (1927), and to Brussels (1933). After retirement (1935), he divided his residence between the chateau at Brangues (Isère) and Paris, where he died, full of years, work, and honors. A most unusual honor was accorded when a reading of his poetry was given by the artists of the Théâtre Hébertot de Paris before Pius XII, with Claudel present, on April 29, 1950.

Claudel's recognition by the general public was long delayed; his theatrical successes date only from World War II, and his election to the French Academy, from 1946, but his influence on the elite goes back a long way, and the most recalcitrant (foremost among them André Gide) toward the severity of Claudel's Catholicism have acclaimed, and still acclaim, the imposing work that stands as witness of that Catholicism.

In addition to the works cited above, the following must be mentioned: for the theater, *le Livre de Christophe Colomb* (1933), *Jeanne au bûcher* (1939); for poetry, *Corona benignitatis anni Dei* (1915), *Ode jubilaire pour le sixième centenaire de la mort de Dante* (1919), *Cent phrases pour éventails* (1942); for prose, *Le Chemin de la Croix* (1915), *Correspondance avec Jacques Rivière* (1926), *Positions et propositions*, 2 v. (1928–34), *Conversations dans le Loir-et-Cher* (1929), *Introduction à l'Apocalypse* (1946), *L'Oeil écoute* (1946), and *Correspondance avec André Gide* (1949).

Bibliography: *Oeuvres complètes*, ed. R. MALLET et al. (Paris 1950–), the first 9 v. ed. under direction of Claudel, 23 v. pub. to

1964. J. RIVIÈRE, "Paul Claudel, poète chrétien," *Études* 3 (Paris 1911) 61–129. F. DE MIOMANDRE, *Claudel et Suarès* (Brussels 1907). J. DE TONQUÉDEC, *L'Oeuvre de Paul Claudel* (Paris 1917). P. LASSERRE, *Les Chapelles littéraires* (Paris 1920). E. SAINTE-MARIE PERRIN, *Introduction à l'oeuvre de Paul Claudel* (Paris 1926). F. LEFÈVRE, *Les Sources de Paul Claudel* (Paris 1927). J. BENOIST-MÉCHIN and G. BLAIZOT, *Bibliographie des oeuvres de Paul Claudel* (Paris 1931). P. PETIT, "Bibliographie claudélienne," *La Vie intellectuelle* (Dec. 1931–Feb. 1932). J. MADAULE, *Le Génie de Paul Claudel* (Paris 1933); *Le Drame de Paul Claudel* (Paris 1936). E. FRICHE, *Études claudéliennes* (Porrentruy, Switz. 1943). C. CHONEZ, *Introduction à Paul Claudel* (Paris 1947). F. MAURIAC, *Répose à Paul Claudel* (Paris 1947). L. BARJON, *Paul Claudel* (Paris 1953). S. FUMET, *Claudel* (Paris 1958). P. A. LESORT, *Paul Claudel par lui-même* (Paris 1963). G. C. RAWLINSON, *Recent French Tendencies from Renan to Claudel* (London 1917). F. CASNATI, *Paul Claudel e i suoi drammi* (Como 1921). H. HATZFELD, *Paul Claudel und Romain Roland* (Munich 1921). E. R. CURTIUS, *Die literarischen Wegbereiter des neuen Frankreichs* (Potsdam 1923); *Französischer Geist im zwanzigsten Jahrhundert* (Bern 1952). R. GROSCHE, *Paul Claudel* (Hellerau, Ger. 1930). H. DIECKMAN, *Die Kunstanschauung Paul Claudels* (Munich 1931). E. FRANCIA, *Paul Claudel* (Brescia 1947). M. RYAN, *Introduction to Paul Claudel* (Westminster, Md. 1951). J. VILA SELMA, *André Gide y Paul Claudel frente a frente* (Madrid 1952). H. U. VON BALTHASAR, epilogue to Claudel's *Der seidene Schuh* (Salzburg 1959).

[L. ESTANG]

CLAUDIANUS, MAMERTUS

Gallic writer of the 5th century; b. Lyon; d. *c.* 474. A monk and a priest, he collaborated with his brother, Saint Mamertus, bishop of Vienne. His principal work, *De statu animae,* is dedicated to his friend SIDONIUS APOLLINARIS. It is a refutation of FAUSTUS OF RIEZ and his theory of the corporeal soul. Book one establishes the spirituality of the soul on a rational basis; book two makes an appeal to the arguments of authorities: the Greek and Latin philosophers, the Fathers of the Church, and the Bible; book three refutes the arguments of Faustus. Though a hymn and a lectionary are lost, Mamertus's letters to the rhetor Sapaudus and to Sidonius Apollinaris have been preserved; none of the poems attributed to him were his. Mamertus was formed by the ancient thought, particularly that of Plato and Neoplatonism. He seems also to have reflected Augustinian views and to have influenced the early scholastics and Descartes.

Bibliography: *Opera,* ed. A. ENGELBRECHT, *Corpus scriptorium ecclesiasticorum latinorum* 11; 1885. F. BOEMER, *Der lateinische Neuplatonismus und Neupythagoreismus und Claudius Mamertus* (Leipzig 1936). A. JÜLICHER, *Paulys Realenzyklopädie der klassischen Altertumswissenschaft,* ed. G. WISSOWA et al. (1899) 2660–61. J. MADOZ, ed., *Liciniano de Carthagena* (Madrid 1948) 35–53. P. COURCELLE, *Les Lettres grecques en occident* (rev. ed. Paris 1948) 223–235. W. SCHMID, *Reallexikon für Antike und Christentum,* ed. T. KLAUSER (Stuttgart 1950–) 3:169–179. N. K. CHADWICK, *Poetry and Letters in Early Christian Gaul* (London

1955) 207–210. É. AMANN, *Dictionnaire de théologie catholique,* ed. A. VACANT et al. (Paris 1903–50) 9.2:1809–11.

[P. ROCHE]

CLAUDIUS OF CONDAT, ST.

Also known as Claudius of Besançon; bishop and abbot; b. possibly Franche-Comté, early seventh century; d. Condat, France, June 6, 696. The accounts of his life are largely legendary, but it appears that he was already well advanced in years and had introduced the BENEDICTINE RULE at Condat as abbot before he was called to serve as bishop of Besançon. Several years before his death, he resigned his see and retired to the monastic life at Condat. He was later mistakenly identified by ORDERICUS with another Claudius of Besançon, who was present at the councils of Epao (517) and Lyons (529). After his death the abbey was dedicated to his memory, and in 1213 the monks discovered his remains. The church became a place of pilgrimage for the local inhabitants, but the relics were lost during the French Revolution.

Feast: June 6.

Bibliography: *Acta Sanctae Sedis* June 1:634–696. *Bibliotheca hagiographica latina antiquae et mediae aetatis* (Brussels 1898–1901) 1:1840–47. *Saint Claude, vie et présence,* ed. G. DUHEM et al. (Paris 1960). R. VAN DOREN, *Dictionnaire d'histoire et de géographie ecclésiastiques,* ed. A. BAUDRILLART et al. (Paris 1912) 12:1072. G. BARDY, *Catholicisme* 2:1171–72. A. M. ZIMMERMANN, *Kalendarium Benedictinum,* (Metten 1933–38) 2:279–281.

[P. BLECKER]

CLAUDIUS OF TURIN

Bishop and exegete; b. probably near Seo de Urgel, Spain; d. Turin, Italy, toward the end of 827. He received his education among the clerics of Felix of Urgel, one of the main figures of the Adoptionist heresy (*see* ADOPTIONISM). Toward the end of the 8th century he went to Lyons, attracted by the reputation of the school of LEIDRADUS. There he received most of his theological and scriptural formation. He became a priest in the court of Louis the Pious in Aquitaine, and when the latter became emperor, Claudius followed him to Aachen. His teaching in the schools of both cities gave him material for his numerous Biblical commentaries. In 817 or 818 he was elevated to the bishopric of Turin. As bishop he attacked the cult of images, as can be seen in his *Liber de imaginibus,* long attributed to AGOBARD OF LYONS; an *Excerptum* of this work is preserved. It was on this excerpt that his opponents DUNGAL and JONAS OF ORLÉANS based their attacks against him. Claudius's Biblical commentaries belong to the collectanea type: they constitute true Biblical CATENAE. He contributed to the formation of this type of commentary, which was generally followed in Carolingian and later medieval times. His commentaries are: Genesis (808 or 811), a Chronicle (814), Matthew (815), Galatians (815), Ephesians-Philippians (816), Romans (812–820), 1 and 2 Corinthians (820), Exodus (821), Numbers (823 or sometime before—lost), Leviticus (823), Ruth-Kings—Questions on Kings (824), and Josue-Judges (825–826). He probably prepared commentaries on all of the Pauline Epistles, but none of the introductory letters are known to be extant. Many of his works are unedited and some are attributed to other authors: Genesis and Kings, for example, appears as pseudo- EUCHERIUS OF LYONS. The following commentaries attributed to ATTO OF VERCELLI certainly belong to Claudius: Colossians, Titus, Philemon, and Hebrews. The homilies found in various Breviaries and dictionaries under Claudius's name are extracts from his exegetical works.

Bibliography: *Patrologia Latina*, ed. J. P. MIGNE (Paris 1878–90) 104:199–250, 615–928; 50:893–1208; 105:459–464; 134:609–644, 699–834. *Monumenta Germaniae Historica: Epistolae* (Berlin 1826–) 4:586–613. F. STEGMÜLLER, *Repertorium biblicum medii aevi* (Madrid 1949–61) 2: no. 1949–75. J. B. HABLITZEL, *Historisches Jahrbuch der Görres-Gesellschaft* 27 (1906) 74–85; 38 (1917) 539–548. M. MANITIUS, *Geschichte der lateinischen Literatur es Mittelalters* (Munich 1911–31) 1:390–396. G. BOFFITTO, "Il codice Vallicelliano C 3," *Atti Acc. Sc. Torino* 33 (1898) 250–285. E. RIGGENBACH in *Forschungen z. Geschichte d. Neutestamentlichen Kanons u. d. altkirchl. Literatur*, v.8.1, ed. T. ZAHN (Leipzig 1907). A. SOUTER, *The Earliest Latin Commentaries on the Epistles of St. Paul* (Oxford 1927). P. BELLET, "Claudio de Turín, autor de los comentarios *In Genesim et Regum* del Pseudo Euquerio," *Estudios biblicos* 9 (1950) 209–223; in *Colligere fragmenta: Festschrift Alban Dold* (Beuron 1952) 140–143; "El *Liber de imaginibus sanctorum*, bajo el nombre de Agobardo de Lyon, obra de Claudio de Turín," *Analecta Sacra Tarraconensia* 26 (1953) 151–194. A. BIGELMAIR, *Lexikon für Theologie und Kirche*, ed. J. HOFER and K. RAHNER (2d, new ed. Freiburg 1957–65) 2:1220.

[P. BELLET]

CLAUDIUS AND COMPANIONS, SS.

Claudius, Asterius, Neon, Domnina, and Theonilla, saints and martyrs of Aegaeae in Cilicia in 285; commemorated in the Western MARTYROLOGIES on August 23 and in the Greek SYNAXARIES on October 30 and January 27. Two late Latin recensions of their acts are still extant; both of them are different in detail from the two abbreviated accounts of their martyrdom in the Synaxary of Constantinople and the Menology of Basil. According to the Latin texts, "three brothers and two women with an infant" were brought before Lysias, the governor of

the province. After the interrogation, torture, and condemnation of Claudius, Asterius, and Neon, Domnina was stripped and beaten to death. Theonilla was cruelly tortured and slain by having burning coals heaped on her stomach. Neither the Synaxary of Constantinople nor the Menology of Basil mention Domnina. This fact, and the incongruities in the second part of the Latin acts, led Pio Franchi de' Cavalieri to suspect that the deaths of the two women were later added by two different hands to explain what had happened to them. Nothing is said about the child. If the accounts of the martyrdom of the women belong to the original protocol, the child must have been Domnina's since Theonilla declared that she had been a widow for 23 years.

Bibliography: P. FRANCHI DE' CAVALIERI, "Su gli atti dei SS. Claudio, Asterio e Neone," *Note Agiografiche* 5 (*Studi e Testi* 27; 1915) 107–126.

[M. J. COSTELLOE]

CLAVER, PETER, ST.

Jesuit missionary, called the Saint of the Slaves; b. Verdu, Spain, 1580; d. Cartagena, Colombia, 1654. Very little is known of his early years. He entered the Society of Jesus in 1602. In 1605, while studying for his degree in philosophy in the San Sion College of Mallorca, he was befriended by (St.) Alphonsus RODRÍGUEZ, who encouraged him in his apostolic zeal and in his later missionary work in the New World. He continued his theological studies in Barcelona until 1610, when he was sent to Cartagena, which was then a very important port of entry to the Indies, teeming with merchants and slave traders. In Cartagena he met Alonso de Sandoval, who was deeply concerned with helping the slaves who, captured in Africa, were landed in America chained together in misery and fear of the unknown. Two important books by Sandoval are fundamental to any knowledge of the fate of African slaves in the Indies. The first, and less known, was published in 1627, *Naturaleza, policía sagrada y profana, costumbres, ritos y supersticiones de todos los Etíopes*. The second, published in 1641, was *De instauranda aethiopum salute*. Sandoval's indignation was soon shared by Claver.

In 1616 Claver was sent to Bogotá, where he was the first member of the Society of Jesus to be ordained. After Sandoval's transfer to another mission, Claver returned to Cartagena, probably on the recommendation of Sandoval, who must have early recognized his zeal and compassion. Claver was not only a missionary but a doctor and teacher. He greeted the incoming slave ships with his small host of interpreters. Carrying on high the holy cross, he went into the infested holds where during the long voyages epidemics and despair had taken their toll. Braving the horrible odors, the sickly atmosphere, and anxiety, Claver not only brought these slaves spiritual comfort but cured their sores, bandaged their wounds, and sometimes carried the disabled ones on his own shoulders. He first befriended the so-called savages, winning their confidence before starting on their catechization. He converted more than 300,000 by 1615.

During his lifetime he was already considered a saint. The stories of his miracles were passed from place to place through that mysterious primitive form of communication known only to those kept in bondage. In his last years, Claver suffered a paralysis that kept him at the mercy of a surly slave who vented on him his resentment and evil nature. While suffering all these trials in Christian resignation, he learned that his friend Alfonso Rodriguez was being considered for canonization, and in 1639 he learned of URBAN VIII's bull condemning slave traffic. Claver was canonized in 1888 by Pope LEO XIII.

Feast: Sept. 9.

Bibliography: A. VALTIERRA, *Peter Claver: Saint of the Slaves* (Westminster, MD 1960). M. BRICEÑO JÁUREGUI, *Miguel Antonio Caro y San Pedro Claver* (Bogotá 1981).

[H. VIVAS SALAS]

Woodcut of St. Peter Claver.

CLAVIGERO, FRANCISCO JAVIER

Mexican Jesuit teacher and scholar, best known for writing the first popular work on the Aztecs; b. Veracruz, Mexico, Sept. 9, 1731; d. Bologna, Italy, April 2, 1787. Clavigero spent his earliest years in the Mixteca, the western part of the modern state of Oaxaca, where his father was royal agent. In February 1748 he entered the Society of Jesus in Puebla. He was ordained in October 1754. Late in 1756 he was sent to Mexico City to teach the Native Mexicans at San Gregorio's, a school adjoining the famed Jesuit school of St. Peter and St. Paul. Here he deepened his enthusiasm for pre-Columbian Mexican history. In March 1762 Clavigero was transferred to another native school in Puebla, where he remained until appointed professor of philosophy at Morelia in the summer of 1763. Heeding the call of the Jesuit general to modernize the curriculum of studies in the Jesuit schools, he taught courses in the new physics of Isaac Newton. In so doing he won lasting fame as a pioneer in the intellectual reform of 18th-century Mexico. When the Jesuits were banished from the Spanish Empire in June 1767, Clavigero went to Bologna and at first occupied his leisure hours in the study of Aztec civilization. He was distressed by the misinformation European books contained about the Americas in general and Mexico in particular.

He determined to refute these errors by portraying Mexico as it really was. The result was the *Ancient History of Mexico* (1780–81), which for its systematic arrangement, clear style, and sympathetic interest in Aztec civilization was praised by historians and won him international renown. His work strongly influenced the study of Aztec civilization for many decades, and it is still held in high repute, despite shortcomings and the fact that much progress has been made in Aztec studies since Clavigero's time. He also wrote a *History of [Lower] California* (1789). After the suppression of the Jesuits in 1773, Clavigero spent the rest of his life as a diocesan priest in Bologna.

Bibliography: E. J. BURRUS, "Jesuit Exiles: Precursors of Mexican Independence," *Mid America* 36 (1954) 161–175. J. LE RIVEREND BRUSONE, "La historia antigua del padre Francisco Javier Clavijero," in *Estudios de historiografía de la Nueva España*, by H. DÍAZ THOMAS et al. (Mexico City 1945).

[C. E. RONAN]

CLAVIUS, CHRISTOPHER

Jesuit mathematician and astronomer, and one of the principal collaborators in the Gregorian calendar reform (1577–82); b. Bamberg, 1537?; d. Rome, Feb. 6, 1612. He entered the Jesuit Order in 1555, studied at Coimbra under P. Nunes, and taught mathematics at the Collegio Romano from 1565.

Christopher Clavius, 18th-century engraving.

"The Correspondence of Father Christopher Clavius, S.J.," *Archivum historicum Societatis Jesu* 8 (1939) 193–222. G. V. COYNE, M. A KOSKIN, and O. PEDERSEN, eds., *Gregorian Reform of the Calendar: Proceedings of the Vatican Conference to Commemorate Its 400th Anniversary 1582–1982* (Vatican City 1983).

[J. B. EASTON]

CLEMENCY

Clemency is a virtue whose act is to moderate punishment. In a spirit of leniency it would lessen PUNISHMENT as far as the demands of justice permit. Clemency does not seek to mitigate punishment contrary to the order of justice or the dictates of right reason. Rather, considering the circumstances of fact, person, manner, place, etc., it judges that right reason does not require the guilty one to be punished as severely as the words of the law or custom would otherwise demand. To be good, the act must proceed from a virtuous motive. The mitigation of punishment because of sentimental considerations, fear, or bribery would not be an act of clemency, except in material sense.

Clemency is related to severity as EPIKEIA is to legal justice. But it differs from epikeia. In the latter there is a diminution of penalty because it is supposed that the mind of the legislator did not intend the severity expressed in the words of the law to be applied to a given case; this is probable where there are notably extenuating circumstances. Clemency, however, brings about the diminution because the one whose duty it is to impose the penalty has a certain tenderness or consideration toward the offender and is therefore unwilling to inflict punishment to the full extent of his authority.

Clemency and mildness are the same as far as the virtue of temperance moderates the feelings and their external expression; but in spite of a certain affinity, they differ, clemency being a virtue proper to superiors while mildness is something that should be common to all. Cruelty, which is a savage readiness to inflict punishment, is the direct opposite of clemency.

Bibliography: THOMAS AQUINAS, *Summa Theologica*, 2a2ae, 157.4. H. D. NOBLE, *Dictionnaire de spiritualité asce et mystique. Doctrine et histoire,* ed. M. VILLER et al. (Paris 1932–) 2.1:944–947. L. DESBRUS, *Dictionnaire de théologie catholique,* ed. A. VACANT et al., 15 v. (Paris 1903–50; Tables générales 1951–) 3.1:45–47.

[W. HERBST]

In addition to his defense and explanation of the calendar, *Novi calendarii romani apologia . . .* (Rome 1595), Clavius wrote on all branches of mathematics. He is noted for his pedagogical skill, rather than as a creative mathematician. His *Euclides Elementorum . . .* (1574 and many later editions), with its detailed commentaries and supplementary material, became the standard text in the schools. The first six books were translated into Chinese under the direction of his student Matteo RICCI. His *Opera Mathematica* (5 v. Mainz 1611–12) contains, among other works, his practical arithmetic (first pub. 1583), practical geometry (1604), algebra (1608), and commentaries on the sphere of JOHN DE SACROBOSCO (1570) and Theodosius (1586).

Clavius corresponded with the leading scholars of the day, and his letters confirming Galileo's discoveries with the telescope were very influential.

Bibliography: C. SOMMERVOGEL, *Bibliotèque de la Compagnie de Jésus,* 11 v. (Brussels-Paris 1890–1932) 2:1212–24. E. LAMALLE, *Neue deutsche Biographie* (Berlin 1953–) 3:279. J. E. HOFMANN, *Geschichte der Mathematik* v. 1 (1953). E. C. PHILLIPS,

CLEMENS NON PAPA, JACOBUS

Renaissance composer; b. Ypres, Flanders, *c.* 1510; d. Dixmuide?, *c.* 1555. In 1544, then a priest, he was appointed choirmaster at St. Donatien, Bruges, but was dismissed the following year. Writers in the 17th century place his activity at Antwerp, Ypres, and finally Dixmuide, where he is said to have died. His final work, the motet *Hic est vere martir*, was copied in 1555, and it is likely that death interrupted composition of his *Souterliedekens* (Little Psalter Songs), completed and published by Susato (Antwerp 1556). A lament on his death by Jakob Vaet appeared in 1558. He was published under the name Jacques Clément until he began using Clemens non Papa in 1546—to distinguish himself, so it is thought, from an Ypres poet, Jacobus Papa. His works include 15 Masses, 231 motets, many French and Flemish songs, and *Souterliedekens*, three-part settings of the Psalms in Flemish, employing popular tunes of the day. His clear and expressive style influenced such composers as Orlando di LASSO.

Bibliography: *Opera omnia*, ed. K. P. BERNET KEMPERS, *Corpus mensurablis musicae*, ed. American Institute of Musicology 4 (Rome 1951–), 21 v. planned. K. P. BERNET KEMPERS, *Jacobus Clemens non Papa und seine Motetten* (Augsburg 1929). *Die Musik in Geschichte und Gegenwart*, ed. F. BLUME (Kassel-Basel 1949–) 2:1476–80. "Zum Todesjahr des Clemens non Papa," *Karl Gustav Fellerer zum 60 Geburtstag*, ed. H. DRUX et al. (Studien zur Musikgeschichte des Rheinlandes 2; Cologne 1962). E. LOWINSKY, *Secret Chromatic Art in the Netherlands Motet*, tr. C. BUCHMAN (New York 1946). G. REESE, *Music in the Renaissance* (rev. ed. New York 1959). E. S. BEEBE, "Mode, Structure, and Text Expression in the Motets of Jacobus Clemens non Papa: A Study of Style in Sacred Music" (Ph.D. diss. Yale University, 1976). W. ELDERS, "Clemens (non Papa,)" in *The New Grove Dictionary of Music and Musicians, vol. 4*, ed. S. SADIE 476–480, (New York 1980). D. M. RANDEL, ed., *The Harvard Biographical Dictionary of Music* (Cambridge, Massachusetts 1996) 164. N. SLONIMSKY, ed. *Baker's Biographical Dictionary of Musicians, Eighth Edition* (New York 1992) 339.

[M. PICKER]

CLEMENS WENZESLAUS

Archbishop of Trier, Duke of Saxony; b. Hubertusberg Castle, Saxony, Sept. 28, 1739; d. Marktoberdorf, Swabia, July 27, 1812. He was the youngest son of Friedrich August II, King of Poland and Elector of Saxony. Clemens first pursued a military career, but after a serious illness (1761) deserted it for an ecclesiastical one. Because of his noble rank, his advance in the Church was rapid. He was prince-bishop of Freising and Regensburg (1763–68), coadjutor (1764) and then bishop (1768) of Augsburg. In 1768 he became archbishop and elector of Trier, the last to hold these two offices. In addition he was coadjutor (1772) and prince provost (1778) of Ellwangen. Clemens Wenzeslaus possessed laudable priestly qualities, and with the help of influential advisers he inaugurated reforms in monastic and devotional life, and

sought to improve primary and secondary schools. His reforms were those advocated by the leaders of the ENLIGHTENMENT who aimed to improve the Church. Clemens forced Johann von HONTHEIM, his auxiliary bishop, to retract the writings he had published under the pseudonymn Febronius; yet the archbishop participated in the Congress of EMS. He was adverse to extreme views and represented a moderate episcopalism. Ferdinand von Duminique, his minister after 1782, utilized his family ties in gaining for Trier the support of France and Austria. The financial and economic policies of Clemens promoted the prosperity of his subjects. In 1794 he fled from the armies of the French Revolution to Augsburg.

Bibliography: H. RAAB, *Clemens Wenzeslaus von Sachsen und seine Zeit (1739–1812)* (Freiburg 1962–); *Lexikon für Theologie und Kirche*, ed. J. HOFER and K. RAHNER (2d, new ed. Freiburg 1957–65) 2:1231. L. JUST, *Neue deutsche Biographie* (Berlin 1953–) 3:282–283.

[V. CONZEMIUS]

CLEMENT, CAESAR

Priest of the English Mission; place and date of birth unknown; d. Aug. 28, 1626. He was the grandson of John Clement and the illegitimate son of Thomas Clement. He sought admission into the English College at Rome in February 1578, but was refused as too young. He was admitted in September 1579, took the missionary oath in 1584, and was ordained in December of the following year. It is not known at which Italian university or when he received the D.D. He was sent to England at the end of 1587 but no record of his life there exists. He is next heard of as Dean of St. Guddule's, Brussels, and as vicar-general of the Spanish army in the Netherlands. He was greatly attached to his aunt, Margaret Clement, prioress of St. Ursula's convent, Louvain, from 1570, whom he aided in the foundation of St. Monica's Convent, Louvain, in 1609. In 1612 he was commissioned by Rome to accompany Robert Chambers in the visitation of Douai College so as to settle the administrical disturbances there. There is no account of his later years.

Bibliography: *The Dictionary of National Biography from the Earliest Times to 1900* (London 1885–1900; repr. with corrections, 1908–09, 1921–22, 1938) 4:448. J. GILLOW, *A Literary and Biographical History or Bibliographical Dictionary of the English Catholics from 1534 to the Present Time* (London-New York 1885–1902; repr. New York 1961) 1:496.

[E. E. REYNOLDS]

CLEMENT I, POPE, ST.

Pontificate: 92 to 99 (or 68 to 76). Accurate biographical data on Clement of Rome are meager. His iden-

St. Pope Clement I in a detail of an 11th-century fresco in the subterranean basilica of St. Clement, Rome.

tity with the Clement mentioned in Phil 4.3 or with the consul Titus Flavius Clemens, put to death for his faith by Emperor Domitian, is conjectural. There is no extant evidence to support the view that he was a convert from Judaism. Because of divergent notices in such early Christian writers as TERTULLIAN (*De Praescriptione* 32) and IRENAEUS (*Adv. Haer.* 3.3.3), and because of Epiphanius's efforts (*Panarion* 27.6) to reconcile the conflicting data, Clement's traditional third place (following Linus and Cletus) in the list of Peter's successors is not certain. His pontificate is usually assigned to the last decade of the 1st century. Accounts of his martyrdom are legendary, based on the *Passio S. Clementis,* written in either the 4th or 5th century.

First Epistle. In spite of biographical uncertainties, Clement of Rome is an important Apostolic Father whose eminence is founded on the *First Epistle of Clement to the Corinthians.* The text of the epistle nowhere claims Clement as its author; it states merely that the Church of Rome is writing to the Church of Corinth. Irenaeus (*loc. cit.*), however, maintained that Clement was the author of that letter. He notes that during the episcopacy of Clement, the Church of Rome wrote a most fitting letter to the Church of Corinth. Eusebius (*Hist. Eccl.* 4.23.11) quotes a letter written by DIONYSIUS, Bishop of Corinth, to Pope Soter shortly after the middle of the 2d century that clearly links the sending of the epistle with Clement. His name has thus been associated with the letter since early Christian antiquity and its authenticity is not questioned. The letter was considered inspired and was read in many churches of the subapostolic era. It has long been studied for evidence of the sojourn and martyrdom of Peter and Paul in Rome, for its dogmatic and juridical contents (the distinction between clergy and laity, the illicitness of depriving duly appointed officials of their office), and for references to the moral code and liturgy of the early Church in Rome.

Historical Background. The historical background of the epistle is still in need of clarification. Corinth was the administrative seat of the Roman province of Achaia and as a commercial center attracted large numbers of Greeks, Jews, and other peoples. In the course of his second missionary journey, St. Paul founded a flourishing Christian community there. Even during his lifetime strife and factions, among other disorders, caused serious problems for the community (1 Cor 1.11–16). Apparently, similar conditions developed in the days of Clement during the last decade of the 1st century.

Structure. In structure, the epistle consists of an introduction (1–3), two main sections (4–36 and 37–61), and a brief conclusion (62–65). After calling attention to the once flourishing Christian community, Clement deplores the present factions and exhorts the community to penance, piety, humility, and hospitality, adding numerous quotations and examples from Scripture to each admonition. After reminding the Corinthians of the harmony in all creation and of God's goodness and omnipotence, he ends the first section with remarks on the resurrection and judgment and an exhortation to faith and good works. Stoic thought is an element in this doctrine, which, however, may have come from the OT SAPIENTIAL BOOKS.

The second main section deals directly with the quarrel in the local Church. God requires order and obedience from all creatures, consequently obedience and discipline are necessary in the Church. Just as there were definite offices and duties established by God in the Old Law, so too Christ chose Apostles, who in turn appointed bishops and deacons to continue His work. The contentious elements among the Corinthians, the younger members, are exhorted to do penance as well as to be submissive.

The conclusion summarizes the exhortations and expresses the hope that the envoys who delivered the letter will return with the good news that peace has been reestablished. There is no evidence that the Church of Corinth appealed to the Church of Rome for an authoritative decision, nor does the tone of the epistle indicate that it is an official reply to a situation formally presented for action and solution. In fact, the letter clearly states that it gives counsel (58.2) and is making a request (59.2).

Salutation. The salutation of the epistle, "The Church of God which sojourns in Rome to the Church of God which sojourns in Corinth," echoes in its very wording the preoccupation of the subapostolic age with the imminence of the PAROUSIA, the second coming of Christ as judge. In a spirit of fraternal solidarity, the Church in Rome appeals to the Christian community in Corinth to restore peace and harmony, using language that is hortatory rather than peremptory. Since Clement wrote in the name of the community and not in his own name, many scholars conclude that the monarchical episcopate did not exist in Rome at that time and that a communal structure was likely. Furthermore, he uses *episkopoi* (overseers) and *presbyteroi* (elders) as equivalent terms, suggesting that those offices had not attained firm lines in Rome. Clement's allusions to Stoic philosophy and his citation of the phoenix as a natural proof of resurrection, show that the Roman community did not completely shun pagan culture.

The so-called Second Epistle of Clement to the Corinthians is not a letter, but rather a homily, written perhaps at Corinth by an unknown author, probably near the middle of the 2d century.

Feast: Nov. 23.

Bibliography: T. LENSCHAU, *Paulys Realenzyklopädie der klassischen Altertumswissenschaft*, ed. G. WISSOWA et al., suppl. 4 (1924) 1033–34. H. CAMPENHAUSEN, *Kirchliches Amt und geistliche Vollmacht* (Tübingen 1953). E. MOLLAND, *Die Religion in Geschichte und Gegenwart*, 7 v. (3d ed. Tübingen 1957–65) 1:1836–38. A. STUIBER, *Reallexikon für Antike und Christentum*, ed. T. KLAUSER (Stuttgart 1941 [1950]–) 3:188–197; *Lexikon für Theologie und Kirche*, ed. J. HOFER and K. RAHNER, 10 v. (2d, new ed. Freiburg 1957–65) 2:1222–23. B. ALTANER, *Patrology*, tr. H. GRAEF from 5th German ed. (New York 1960) 99–103. J. QUASTEN, *Patrology*, 4 v. (Westminster, Md. 1950–86) 1:42–58. W. W. JAEGER, *Early Christianity and Greek Paideia* (Cambridge, Mass. 1961). H. JEDIN, *Handbuch der Kirchengeschichte*, 6 v. (Freiburg 1962–) 1:164, 173, 178–179. C. ANDRESEN, *Reallexikon für Antike und Christentum*, ed. T. KLAUSER (Stuttgart 1941 [1950]–) 6:111–113. D. HAGNER, *The Use of the Old and New Testament in Clement of Rome* (Leiden 1973). B. BOWE, *A Church in Crisis: Ecclesiology and Paraenesis in Clement of Rome* (Philadelphia 1988). J. JEFFERS, *Conflict at Rome: Social Order and Hierarchy in Early Christianity* (Minneapolis 1991). K. P. DONFRIED, "The Theology of Sacred Clement," *Studies in Early Christianity* 2 (1993) 23–37.

[H. DRESSLER]

CLEMENT II, POPE

Pontificate: Dec. 24, 1046 (election, Rome); Dec. 25, 1046 (consecration), to Oct. 9, 1047 (at the abbey of St. Thomas de Foglia, near Pesaro, buried at Bamberg cathedral, Bamberg, Germany); b. Suidger of noble Saxon descent; educated as a canon at the cathedral of Halberstadt, he became a chaplain of Archbishop Hermann of Hamburg-Bremen in 1032 and imperial court chaplain in 1035. At the nomination of Emperor Henry III, he was consecrated as bishop of Bamberg, Christmas, 1040. After the councils of Sutri and Rome in late 1046 and the deposition or abdication of Pope GREGORY VI because of simony, Henry III nominated him as successor. He was elected Pope Clement II December 24, but retained his office as bishop of Bamberg. Immediately upon his consecration on Christmas Day he crowned Henry emperor. Agnes, his consort and mother of Emperor Henry IV, was crowned empress. Clement II is the first of several "German" popes who pushed the aims of ecclesiastical reform in the city of Rome. He held a reforming synod in January 1047, issuing decrees against simony and accompanied Henry III to southern Italy. After a summer spent in Rome, he died on a journey north at the Abbey of St. Thomas near Pesaro. An exhumation in 1942 revealed an abnormally high lead content in his bones, thus lending credence to the ancient rumor that he was poisoned. Because of the brevity of his pontificate it cannot be fairly evaluated. His is the only papal tomb north of the Alps, and the treasury of the Cathedral of Bamberg preserves his pontifical vestments.

Bibliography: W. GOEZ, "Papa qui et episcopus," *Archivum Historiae Pontificiae* 8 (1970) 27–59. L. GÖLLER, A. DECHANT, *Clemens II, der Papst aus Bamberg* (Bamberg 1997). E. V. GUTTENBERG, ed., *Das Bistum Bamberg* (Berlin 1937). K. HAUCK, "zum Tode Papst Clemens' II," *Jahrbuch für fränkische Landesforschung* 19 (1959) 265–274. H-P. LAQUA, "Clemente II," *Dizionario biografico degli Italiani* 26 (1982) 178–181. J. LAUDAGE, "Clemens II," *Lexikon der Päpste und des Papsttums* (Freiburg-Basel-Vienna 2001), 50f. S. MÜLLER-CHRISTENSEN, *Das Grab des Papstes Clemens II. im Dom zu Bamberg* (Munich 1960). M. PARISSE, "Clément II," *Dictionnaire Historique de la Papauté*, ed. P. LEVILLAIN (Paris 1994) 362. R. TIMMEL and G. ZIMMERMANN, "Bischof Suidger von Bamberg—Papst Clemens II," *Fränkische Lebensbilder* 10 (1982) 1–19. G. ZIMMERMANN, "Bambergs Zeichenhaftigkeit für die Reichskirche des 11. Jahrhunderts," *Historischer Verein Bamberg für die Pflege der Geschichte des ehemaligen Fürstbistums* 133 (1997) 83–92. H. WOLTER, *Die Synoden im Reichsgebiet und in Reichsitalien von 916–1056* (Paderborn 1988) 379–404.

[U.-R. BLUMENTHAL]

CLEMENT III, POPE

Pontificate: Dec. 19, 1187 (at Pisa), to March 29, 1191 (at Rome); b. Paolo Scolari at Rome to an upper-class family. Educated at Santa Maria Maggiore, where he was elevated to subdeacon in 1176 and subsequently to archpriest. On Sept. 21, 1179 Pope ALEXANDER III named him cardinal-deacon of Santi Sergio e Bacco, in 1180 cardinal-priest of Santa Pudenziana. From 1181 to his election as pope in 1187 he was cardinal-bishop of Palestrina (Preneste). The assumptions of the electors proved correct. The elderly cardinal was indeed able to reach an agreement with the Roman Commune and to overcome divisions in the college of cardinals. After his triumphal entry into Rome in early February 1188, he concluded a peace treaty with the Roman senate that restored papal sovereignty and with it regalian as well as fiscal rights in the city as well and the surrounding regions. Moreover, the senate promised an annual oath of fealty, since it now regarded the pope as its defender against Hohenstaufen claims. Clement III in his turn recognized the autonomy of the Roman Commune and granted it annual financial contributions. However, the pope never succeeded in fulfilling one of his obligations under the treaty: the destruction of the walls of the Roman rival Tusculum.

Clement III was equally successful in his negotiations with the Hohenstaufen Emperor FREDERICK I BARBAROSSA in connection with the Third Crusade, which was planned in response to Saladin's capture of Jerusalem (1187). In the treaty of Strasbourg (April 1189) Barbarossa returned the papal states to the pope with the exception of the former lands of Mathilda of Tuscany. In return Clement promised to crown Barbarossa's son Henry VI emperor, but it was a promise he did not keep. Instead he supported the claims of Tancred of Lecce to succeed to the Sicilian throne (January 1189), when Henry claimed that crown through his wife Constance. The pope feared that Rome and the Papal States would be surrounded by imperial lands both north and south. It attests to his skills as a diplomat that he nonetheless maintained good relations with Emperor Frederick Barbarossa and even managed to persuade King Philip Augustus of France and King Richard Lionheart of England to depart on crusade in the summer of 1190 after the sudden death of Barbarossa in Asia Minor on the way to the Holy Land.

The short and complicated reign of Clement III also brought progress in papal administration and expansion in papal influence. Cardinal Albinus of Albano began to compile census lists and other important documents that benefited the papacy, a work later completed by Cencius Camerarius who became pope as HONORIUS III. Willingness to expand papal influence is also reflected in the decretals of Clement III especially with regard to matrimonial law and to oaths, even if a fair number of them are now correctly attributed to his successor, CELESTINE III. He freed the Scottish Church from the jurisdiction of the archbishop of York and formally canonized the Danish Bishop KJELD (Ketil) of Viborg (1188), Bishop OTTO I of Bamberg (1189), STEPHEN OF MURET, founder of the Order of Grandmont (1189), and the Irish Archbishop Malachie O'Morgair (1190).

Bibliography: P. CZENDES, "Die Anfänge der Kanzlei Heinrich VI. und die Verhandlungen mit der Kurie 1188/89," *Mitteilungen des Instituts für österreichische Geschichtsforschung* 82 (1974) 403–411. R. FOREVILLE, "Clément III," *Dictionnaire d'histoire et de géographie ecclésiastiques*, ed. A. BAUDRILLART et al. (Paris 1912) 12, 1096–1109. H. HALLER, "Heinrich VI und die römische Kurie," *Mitteilungen des Instituts für österreichische Geschichtsforschung* 35 (1914) 385–454, 545–669. W. HOLTZMANN, "La Collectio Seguntina et les décrétales de Célestin III," *Revue d'histoire ecclésiastique* 50 (1955) 400–453. H. HOUBEN, "Philipp von Heinsberg, Heinrich VI und Montecassino. Mit einem Exkurz zum Todesdatum Papst Clemens' III," *Quellen und Forschungen aus italienischen Archiven und Bibliotheken* 68 (1988), 52–73. W. MALECZEK, "Clemens III," *Lexikon des Mittelalters* 2 (1981–1983) 2140–2141. J. PETERSOHN, "Der Vertrag des Römischen Senats mit Papst Clemens III (1188) und das Pactum Friedrich Barbarossas mit den Römern," *Mitteilungen des Instituts für österreichische Geschichtsforschung* 82 (1974) 289–337; "Kaiser, Papst und Praefectura Urbis zwischen Alexander III. und Innozenz III.," *Quellen und Forschungen aus Italienischen Archiven und Bibliotheken* 60 (1980) 168–181; "Clement III," *Dizionario biografico degli Italiani* 26 (1982) 188–192. V. PFAFF, "Papst Clemens III (1187–1191)," *Zeitschrift der Savigny–Stiftung für Rechtsgeschichte, Kanonistische Abteilung* 97 (1980) 261–316. C. REISINGER, *Tankred von Lecce* (Cologne 1992). L. VONES, "Clément III," *Dictionnaire historique de la papauté* (1994) 64–366. P. ZERBI, *Papato, Impero e "Respublica Christiana" dal 1187 al 1198,* Milano 2d ed. 1980. K. ZEILLINGER, "Clemens III," *Lexikon der Päpste und des Papsttums* (2001) 52.

[U.–R. BLUMENTHAL]

CLEMENT III, ANTIPOPE

Pontificate: June 25, 1080–Sept. 8, 1100. Known earlier as Guibert (or Wibert) of Ravenna, he was born between 1020 and 1030 in Parma; his family was related to the counts of Canossa. Guibert died at Città Castellana on Sept. 8, 1100. He was at the German court by 1055, and was named imperial chancellor for Italy (1058–63) with the backing of the empress Agnes. An independent thinker who was more opposed to Hildebrand-Gregory than to reform, Guibert was at the Synod of Sutri (January 1059), which excommunicated the antipope BENEDICT X (1058–59). Yet he later became a driving force behind the election of Peter Cadalus as Antipope HONORIUS II (1061–64), rival to ALEXANDER II (1061–73). Nothing much is known of Guibert from then until 1072, when King Henry IV (1056–1106) named him bishop of Ravenna. Pope Alexander II was not enthusiastic, since Guibert supported Honorius, but he accepted Guibert after his archdeacon, Hildebrand, compelled Guibert to take an oath of allegiance. Not long after Hildebrand was elected Pope Gregory VII (1073–85), and Guibert became one of the most visible leaders of the opposition to the Gregorian reform program.

Guibert attended Gregory's first Lenten synod (March 1074) and participated in passing decrees against simony and lax behavior among the clergy. But since Guibert declined to attend the following year in spite of an oath to do so, Gregory suspended him in 1075. In February 1075 he excommunicated Guibert along with the other bishops who had adopted a resolution deposing the pope at a synod in Worms (January 1076). Guibert was again excommunicated at the Lenten synod of 1078, probably because he had presided over a synod of Lom-

bard bishops and abbots that excommunicated Gregory (Pavia, April 1076). Finally, when Henry summoned his German and Lombard bishops to a meeting at Brixen in June 1080, the bishops deposed Gregory yet again and elected Guibert as pope. Henry immediately recognized the election.

Four years later Henry marched into Rome and controlled the city, forcing Gregory to flee to the Castel Sant' Angelo. At this point, the people and clergy of Rome elected Guibert pope; he took the name Clement III and was consecrated at the Lateran on Palm Sunday, March 24, 1084. A week later on Easter, with Gregory still in the Castel Sant' Angelo, Clement solemnly crowned Henry emperor in St. Peter's. Soon however, Gregory had made his way to Salerno, and the troops of his Norman ally Robert Guiscard forced both Henry and Clement to leave Rome. Clement went to Ravenna, where he became archbishop in spite of the great support he still had among the people and clergy of Rome (13 of the cardinals still recognized him). Indeed he was back in Rome functioning as pope during the reigns of Victor III (1086–87) and Urban II (1088–99). He was also able to broaden slightly his support in German and Italian territories, and at various times had the obedience of England, Hungary, Serbia, Croatia, Portugal, and Denmark. He even pursued negotiations toward union with Metropolitan John II of Kiev as well as with the eastern emperor and the patriarch of Constantinople. Nonetheless, in the 1190s Henry IV's influence in Rome declined, while support for Pope Urban II steadily increased.

In 1098 Clement was forced out of Rome by the Pierleoni family. Clement and his supporters only controlled the Castel Sant' Angelo, and were forced to abandon that on Aug. 24, 1098. With Henry's troops withdrawn from Italy, Clement's only area of influence was around his diocese of Ravenna. After Paschal II (1099–1118) was elected, Clement prepared to press his claim to the papacy at Albano, but he was forced to withdraw by Norman troops loyal to the pope. He reached Città Castellana and died there less than a year later. Clement's Roman supporters set up three successive antipopes—Theoderic (1100), Albert (1101), and Sylvester IV (1105–11), but these men (with the possible exception of Sylvester) never had the backing of Henry IV, who would soon reach a compromise with the reformers and keep his right to invest bishops with their ring and staff.

Clement was an intelligent and principled man who sought his own course in politically complex times. Though he relied on Henry's support, he was more than a pawn of imperial policy. Obviously well educated, Clement was responsible for some of the most articulate opposition to the Gregorian reformers, whose methods he opposed more than their goals. Clement, for instance, legislated against clerical marriage (Nicolaitism) and simony at a synod in Rome (1089) and supported communial for his clergy. Unlike the majority of Gregorian reformers, however, Clement maintained that the sacraments of schismatic priests and his opponent's ordinations were valid. Clement's position was more politically attractive to those caught between the two parties. In much the same way, he allowed his cardinals more influence, thus forcing Urban II to do the same in order to keep their loyalty. As a result, the College of Cardinals increased in importance during this period.

Bibliography: L. DUCHESNE, ed. *Liber Pontificalis* (Paris 1886–92; repr. 1955–57) 2.282–95. P. JAFFÉ, *Regesta pontificum Romanorum* (Leipzig 1885–88; repr. Graz 1956) 1.649–655; 2.713. *Decretum Wiberti*, and *Altercatio inter Urbanum et Clementem*, in *Monumenta Germaniae historica, Libelli de lite* 1.621–26 and 2.169–72. O. KÖHNCKE, *Wibert von Ravenna* (Leipzig 1888). P. KEHR, "Zur Geschichte Wiberts von Ravenna (Clemens III)," *Sitzungsberichte der Preussischen Akademie der Wissenschaften zu Berlin* (1921) 355–371, 973–988. K. JORDAN, "Die Stellung Wiberts in der Publistik des Investiturstreites," *Mitteilungen des Instituts für österreichische Geschichtsforschung* 62 (1954) 155–64. F. X. SEPPELT, *Geschichte der Päpste von den Anfängen bis zur Mitte des zwanzigsten Jahrhunderts* (Munich 1956) 3.93–134. K. REINDEL, *Lexikon für Theologie und Kirche* (Freiburg 1965) 10.1087–88. W. ULLMANN, *A Short History of the Papacy in the Middle Ages* (London 1972). T. STRUVE, *Lexikon des Mittelalters* (Munich 1983) 2.2139–40 for extensive bibliography. J. ZIESE, *Wibert von Ravenna, der Gegenpapst Clemens III, 1084–1100* (Stuttgart 1982). I. HEIDRICH, *Ravenna unter Erzbischof Wibert, 1073–1100* (Sigmaringen 1984). J. N. D. KELLY, *The Oxford Dictionary of Popes* (New York 1986) 156–57. I. S. ROBINSON, *The Papacy 1073–1198: Continuity and Innovation* (Cambridge 1990). G. TELLENBACH, *The Church in Western Europe from the Tenth to the Early Twelfth Century* (Cambridge 1993) 230–64. I. S. ROBINSON, *Henry IV of Germany, 1156–1106* (Cambridge 1999).

[P. M. SAVAGE]

CLEMENT IV, POPE

Pontificate: Feb. 5, 1265 to Nov. 29, 1268; b. Guy Fulcodi, Saint-Gilles (Rhône), toward the end of the 12th century. Guy was a lawyer in the service of the counts of the Toulouse and a consultant of King LOUIS IX. After the death of the his wife (*c.* 1256), he was ordained and served as archdeacon of Le Puy. His advancement in the Church was meteoric: he became bishop of Le Puy Oct. 19, 1257; archbishop of Narbonne, 1259; cardinal bishop of Sabina, 1261; and papal legate to England, Wales, and Ireland. He was elected pope at Perugia—*in absentia*. During much of his pontificate, Clement, in collaboration with France, participated in the political affairs of Italy and Germany. He abetted the cause of Charles of Anjou, the brother of St. Louis. In a bull (Nov. 4, 1265) Clement confirmed Charles in the Kingdom of Sicily. The Ange-

vin was crowned in St. Peter's (1266) by cardinals appointed by the pope. Moreover, Clement helped considerably in the financing of Charles's expedition against Manfred who was defeated at Benevento and slain Feb. 26, 1266. Clement and Charles disagreed over the king's failure to fulfill the agreement made at his coronation. On several occasions Clement upbraided him for his rapacity, greed, and the cruelty that he exercised toward his new subjects.

Difficulty again arose in the Kingdom of Sicily when Conradin, the son of Conrad IV, was persuaded to invade Italy and assert his hereditary claims. Clement, not wishing to have another Hohenstaufen neighbor, sent letters to Abp. Wernher of Cologne and to other ecclesiastical princes in Germany, excommunicating all who would abet Conradin's candidacy for the vacant ecclesiastical post in April 1267. In Lombary and Sicily, Ghibellines rose in Conradin's support, but the problem was decided in favor of the Angevins when Charles defeated and captured Conradin in 1268 (*see* GUELFS AND GHIBELLINES). Ghibelline resistance collapsed, and savage reprisals culminated in the execution of Conradin. Clement actively supported the "crusade" in Prussia, Livonia, and Courland. He also vigorously assisted Alfonso X of Castile against the Moors of Spain and Africa. Although often criticized for his centralizing and financial policies, particularly his extension of the usage of reserving benefices to the Holy See, Clement was primarily concerned in lessening the influence of local nobles and kings in the important matter of the appointment of bishops.

Bibliography: E. JORDAN, *Les Registres de Clement IV* (Paris 1904). A. POTTHAST, *Regesta pontificum romanorum inde ab a. 1198 ad a. 1304* (Berlin 1874–75; repr. Graz 1957) 2:1542–1650. J. HEIDEMANN, *Papst Clemens IV: Das Vorleben des Pastes und sein Legationregister* (Münster 1903). E. HORN, "Le Rôle politique de Clement IV," *Compte rendu de l'Académie des sciences morales et politiques* (1925) 273–300. H. K. MANN, *The Lives of the Popes in the Early Middle Ages from 590 to 1304* (London 1902–32) 15. C. NICOLAS, *Un Pape Saint-Gillois: Clément IV dans le monde et dans l'Église* (Nimes 1910). J. HALLER, *Das Papsttum* (2d ed. Stuttgart 1950–53) 4:314–359, 451–464. J. N. D. KELLY, *Oxford Dictionary of Popes* (New York 1986) 196. A. KIESEWTTER, *Lexikon für Theologie und Kirche* (Freiburg 1996) 2:1220–1221. M. MIGLIO, "Una ricognizione dlla tomba di Clement IV," *Rivista Storica di Lazio* 4 (1996) 5:25–40.

[J. J. SMITH]

CLEMENT V, POPE

Pontificate: June 5, 1305, to April 20, 1314; b. Bertrand de Got, in Villandraut (Gironde) in the mid-13th century; d. Roquemaure (Gard). Clement V had a successful ecclesiastical career up to his accession to the papacy. Having studied canon and Roman law in Orléans and Bologna, he was consecrated bishop of Comminges in March 1295 and archbishop of Bordeaux in December 1299. After a protracted conclave, in Perugia, he was elected pope by a majority of 10 of the 15 votes. The cardinals' difficulties in reaching a consensus eventually facilitated his election, since the former archbishop of Bordeaux had developed good relations with both Pope BONIFACE VIII and King PHILIP IV OF FRANCE. Besides, many cardinals knew Bertrand well from his services in the papal curia. His candidacy was supported by Philip IV, a fact that inflamed rumors about French interference in the conclave and the pope's compliance with French interests.

The pro-French bias that is usually attributed to Clement V stems, to some degree, from his family roots in Gascony. Such an assumption, the origins of which go back to the 14th century, overlooks the fact that Gascony was dependent on England and that the former archbishop of Bordeaux was the senior prelate in the continental domain of Edward I. Indeed, analysis of Clement's pontificate clearly evinces his strong support of the kings of England, both in their internal crises and in their belligerent policy in Scotland. This course eventually placed the pope at odds with most barons and prelates of England and impaired his ability to arbitrate in Christendom.

Clement's policy in France, as well, offers a rather complex picture: the pope may have given vociferous support to Philip IV, but he implemented an independent policy based on his own scale of priorities. In the most crucial events of Philip's reign, such as the trials of the TEMPLARS and Pope Boniface, Clement succeeded in sabotaging the original plans of Philip IV, while protecting papal aims. Given the circumstances dictated by the king of France in the Templars affair, Clement perceived the abolition of the order by apostolic decision to be the only way to protect ecclesiastical immunity. Yet, both the avoidance of a clear verdict on the guilt of the order and the transfer of Templar wealth to the Hospital clearly contradicted the French king's original expectations. Moreover, the pope had to moderate the zeal of Philip IV in attacking his predecessor Boniface VIII more than once. In a clear *do ut des,* Clement succeeded in protecting the memory of Boniface and voiding the charges of heresy brought against him. Yet, he exonerated Philip of the outrage at Anagni and conditionally absolved its main protagonist, Guillaume de Nogaret (1311). The canonization of CELESTINE V (1313)—Boniface's predecessor, who had resigned the papacy and whose mysterious death was also charged to Boniface's account—reflects yet another papal concession to Capetian demands.

By trying to navigate a middle course between papal and royal interests, Clement prevented an open conflict

Pope Clement V with others, from the "Decretale Clementinae," 15th-century manuscript illumination. (©Archivo Iconografico, S.A./CORBIS)

with the king of France that might have put an end to the dearest goal of his pontificate: the crusade. Clement's belief in the *Gesta Dei per Francos* led to the assignment of Church resources to the Capetian treasury and fostered the nomination of royal protégés to leading ecclesiastical positions. In joining forces with the kings of England and France, Clement attempted to safeguard the papal monarchy in the framework of the limitations posed by the emergence of the national state. In this regard, Clement V paved the way for the papacy in the modern era, when ecclesiastical prerogatives were no longer unquestionably acknowledged; they became, rather, a subject of painful bargaining between the king and the clergy, and then between the king, the clergy, and the pope. From an ecclesiastical perspective, the consequences of Clement's alliance with the western kings were hardly satisfactory. Papal taxation covered the growing needs of royal treasuries while papal provisions became a convenient compensation for royal clerks. The curia thus lost both income from and influence in the national churches.

In Italy, Clement's policy was aimed at advancing papal authority, a rather difficult goal to achieve from the Comtat-Venaissin. Papal diplomacy tried to maintain the delicate political equilibrium among rival factions while preventing any one of them from gaining preeminence. Although Clement never abandoned his design to return to Rome, the negotiations for a peace treaty between England and France, coupled with the pope's deteriorating health, ultimately dictated his permanent absence from the Apostolic See. Until 1309, when Clement fixed his residence in Avignon, the papal curia was itinerant. During his whole pontificate, the pope did not reside in Avignon for more than 160 days, a fact that does not support reference to Clement V as the first pope of Avignon. On the other hand, papal nominations to the College of Cardinals paved the way for the Avignon papacy and, especially, its protracted absence from Italy; they also substantiated the nepotistic bias attributed to Clement V. Of the 24 cardinals whom he nominated, 23 were from France—9 of them from Languedoc—and 6 of these were the pope's relatives.

As a whole, papal policy in the Church was conducted along the centralizing lines established during the previous century, which gave the Roman pontiff full control, by PROVISION or reservation, of all churches, parsonages, dignities, and other ecclesiastical benefices. Although Clement V has often been criticized for his lack of initiative, there was hardly an issue concerning the Church that escaped his attention. Clement analyzed in depth the Church's fragile balance with the rulers of Christendom as well as the different facets of ecclesiastical life, in both the secular and monastic orders, and the ties between the exempt orders and the secular clergy, and the FRANCISCAN SPIRITUALS and the Conventuals (*see* FRANCISCANS, FIRST ORDER). The result, in the form of a juridical document, the *CLEMENTINAE*, gives ample proof of the pope's legal skills. As the seventh book of the DECRETALS, the *Clementinae* complemented the legislative process that had begun in the 13th century, the classic era of Canon Law.

Being a man of letters, Clement encouraged the founding of universities at Orléans, Dublin, and Perugia and supported those of Bologna and Toulouse. At the Council of VIENNE (1311–12), he promoted chairs of Hebrew, Arabic, and "Chaldean" at the universities of Paris, Bologna, Oxford, and Salamanca and in the papal curia.

Bibliography: *Regestum Clementis papae V,* 9 v. in 8 (Rome 1885–92). *Tables des registres de Clément V,* ed. Y. LANHERS and C. VOGEL, 2 v. (Paris 1948–57). E. BALUZE, *Vitae paparum Avenionensium,* ed. G. MOLLAT, 4 v. (Paris 1914–27). G. MOLLAT, *The Popes at Avignon, 1305–1378,* tr. J. LOVE (New York 1963). S. MENACHE, *Clement V* (Cambridge 1998). H. FINKE, *Papsttum und Untergang des Templerordens,* 2 v. (Münster 1907). H. G. RICHARDSON, "Clement V and the See of Canterbury," *English Historical Review* 56 (1941) 97–103. W. BOWSKY, "Clement V and the Emperor-Elect," *Medievalia et Humanistica* 12 (1958) 52–69. J. H. DENTON, "Pope Clement V's Early Career as a Royal Clerk," *English Historical Review* 83 (1968) 303–314. N. HOUSLEY, "Pope Clement V and the Crusaders of 1309–10," *Journal of Medieval History* 8 (1982) 29–43. C. T. WOOD, "Celestine V, Boniface VIII and the Authority of Parliament," *Journal of Medieval History* 8 (1982) 45–62. B. GUILLEMAIN, "Il papato sotto la pressione del re di Francia," *Storia della chiesa* 11 (1994) 177–232.

[S. MENACHE]

CLEMENT VI, POPE

Pontificate: May 7, 1342, to Dec. 6, 1352; b. Pierre Roger, Corrèze, France, *c.* 1291; d. Avignon. A Benedictine of CHAISE-DIEU since 1301, he received a doctorate in theology before becoming abbot of FÉCAMP and Chaise-Dieu. He was bishop of Arras (1328), archbishop of Sens (1329) and of Rouen (1330), and cardinal priest (1338). His learning, eloquence, amiable manner, and diplomatic skill won him the favor of King Philip VI of France and Pope JOHN XXII. Having been elected successor to Pope BENEDICT XII, he was crowned May 19, 1342, at Avignon (*see* AVIGNON PAPACY).

During his pontificate the Church became markedly centralized. In 1344 he decreed that all churches, dignities, offices, and ecclesiastical benefices were subject to papal PROVISION. The bishops objected but to no avail. Edward III of England retaliated in 1345 by seizing all benefices in his country held by foreigners. Philip VI followed his example in 1347, and the pope's remonstrances resulted only in an exception being made for cardinals, the curialists, and the pope's official family. By contrast, there were almost no difficulties in Aragon over the conferring of benefices. Conflicts there with Pedro IV centered upon the seizure of the estates of deceased bishops and the exercise of ecclesiastical jurisdiction. But in the political arena, the kingdom of Majorca was reunited to the crown despite Clement's objections. Clement opposed the FRANCISCAN SPIRITUALS.

In spite of his diplomatic skill, Clement never succeeded in ending the hostilities of the Hundred Years' War. Likewise, in Italy he had only disappointments, e.g., the revolution in Rome of COLA DI RIENZI, the regicide of the husband of Jeanne I of Sicily. Within the Empire, Clement ended the long quarrel between the Church and Emperor Louis IV of Bavaria by deposing him and favoring the election of Charles IV of Luxembourg as emperor (1347).

Clement was buried at Chaise-Dieu, where his tomb still remains. Political enemies, especially PETRARCH, vilified his memory, reproaching him for the ostentatious pomp of his court, which was the most sophisticated court of the day. The incriminations against his moral conduct are unfounded.

Bibliography: CLEMENT VI, *Lettres closes, patentes et curiales se rapportant à la France,* ed. E. DÉPREZ et al. (Paris 1901–);

Lettres . . . intéressant les pays autres que la France, ed. E. DÉ-PREZ and G. MOLLAT (Paris 1960–). É. BALUZE, *Vitae paparum Avenionensium,* ed. G. MOLLAT, 4 v. (Paris 1914–27). G. MOLLAT, *The Popes at Avignon,* 1305–1378, tr. J. LOVE (New York 1963); *Comptes rendus des séances de l'Académie des inscriptions et belles-lettres* (1957) 412–419; *Mélanges d'archéologie et d'histoire* 71 (1959) 377–380; *ibid.* 73 (1961) 375–389; *Journal des savants* (1959) 16–27; *ibid.* (1963) 191–195; *ibid.* (1960) 122–129; *Revue d'histoire ecclésiastique* 55 (1960) 5–24. A. PÉLIS-SIER, *Clement VI le Magnifique, premier pape limousin* (Brive, France 1951). R. J. LOENERTZ, "Ambassadeurs grecs auprès du pape C. VI," *Orientalia Christiana periodica* 19 (1953) 178–196. H. S. OFFLER, "A Political *Collatio* of Pope C. VI, O.S.B.," *Revue Bénédictine* 65 (1955) 126–144. A. H. BURNE, *The Crecy War* (New York 1955). F. GIUNTA, "Sulla politica orientale di C. VI," *Studi di storia medievale e moderna in onore di ettore Rota,* ed. P. VAC-CARI, and P. F. PALUMBO (Rome 1958) 149–162. J. N. D. KELLY, *Oxford Dictionary of Popes* (New York 1986) 291. P. HUTTON, "Clement VI," *The Dictionary of Art* (New York 1996) 7:411. A. PARAVICINI BAGLIANI, "Clemente VI e il giubileo del 1350," *Storia dei Giubilei,* 1:270–277.

[G. MOLLAT]

Silver coin depicting Pope Clement VI, Vatican Library, Rome.

CLEMENT VII, POPE

Pontificate: Nov. 19, 1523, to Sept. 25, 1534; b. Giulio de'Medici, Florence, May 26, 1478; d. Rome. He was the illegitimate son of Giuliano de'Medici and Antonia del Cittadino, member of the Gorini family. Giulio, born a month after the Pazzi conspiracy, in which his father was slain, was raised by his grandfather, Lorenzo de' Medici (the Magnificent), Florentine merchant prince and statesman. After Lorenzo's death (1492) Giulio remained with the family. During the period of Medici exile (1494–1512) he visited several European cities with his cousins Giuliano and Giovanni, and then took up residence in Rome.

Ecclesiastical Offices. On May 9, 1513, Giulio was appointed archbishop of Florence by his cousin Giovanni, who had become LEO X two months before. Because of the impediment of illegitimacy, he was granted a dispensation *super defectu natalium.* On September 22 of that same year he was raised to the cardinalate, after a document was published stipulating that his parents had been betrothed *per sponsalia de praesenti* and declaring him legitimate. He was appointed vice chancellor, March 9, 1517, and was chiefly responsible for determining the political policies of the Pope. He was active at the later session of the Fifth Lateran Council (1512–17) and was the first to apply the new decrees in his own diocese of Florence. In 1515 he was present at the meeting of Leo X and CHARLES V at Bologna. At the death of Leo X (1521) he came to Rome, and while a strong candidate for the papal throne, he lost the election to ADRIAN VI.

Troubled Pontificate. In a conclave that lasted six weeks (Oct. 8 to Nov. 19, 1523) Giulio was chosen to succeed Adrian VI. He faced the problems of curtailing the progress of the Protestant revolt, the political rivalries of Francis I, King of France, and the young Emperor Charles V, the question of the annulment of the marriage of HENRY VIII, King of England, and the need of general Church reform.

Lutheran Movement. Shortly after his accession, Clement sent Lorenzo CAMPEGGIO as papal legate to the Diet of Nuremberg (1524) to assure the emperor that he supported the Edict of Worms (1521). He conferred with Charles V on means of conciliating the Lutherans but opposed calling a general council of the Church, which the emperor favored. Clement met the emperor twice at Bologna for discussion, but could not agree on the means of solving the Lutheran question.

Hapsburg-Valois Rivalry. The contest between Francis I and Charles V to dominate Europe included the control of Italy. Clement attempted to maintain a status quo that would prevent the success of either one. He supported the imperialist cause that ended in the Battle of Pavia, February 24, 1525, where the Spanish commanders, the Constable de Bourbon and the Marquis de Pescara, defeated the French and took Francis I as a prisoner to Madrid. In the Treaty of Madrid (Jan. 14, 1526) Francis surrendered his claims in Italy. On May 22, 1526, Clement entered the League of Cognac with Francis I, the Sforza of Milan, Florence, and Venice to check the growing power of Charles. This led to the humiliation of the sack of Rome by mutinous imperial mercenary forces (1527) and the virtual imprisonment of Clement in the

"Pope Clement VII," painting by Sebastiano del Piombo in the Gallerie Nazionale di Capodimonte, Naples, 1527.

CASTEL SANT' ANGELO for more than seven months. Upon his release he fled to Orvieto, and then to Viterbo, and reentered Rome on Oct. 6, 1528. In a period of peace Charles received the imperial crown from Clement in Bologna on Feb. 24, 1530. In February 1532 Clement again met the emperor at Bologna to discuss the formation of a league of Italian states. In October 1533 Clement met with Francis I at Marseilles, where he officiated at the marriage of his niece, Catherine de Médicis, and the king's son (later Henry II, 1547 to 1559). In these interviews he failed to reconcile the two rulers.

The Marriage of Henry VIII. In 1527 Henry VIII requested an annulment of his 18-year-old marriage to CATHERINE OF ARAGON, alleging his scruples over its validity. Clement, mindful that Catherine was the aunt of Charles V, his captor, and hoping that the king's interest in Anne Boleyn would wane, adopted a policy of delay. He sent Lorenzo Campeggio to London to act as colegate with Cardinal Thomas WOLSEY in the inquiries, with instructions to keep the proceedings from solution. Not until March 23, 1534, did the papal tribunal declare the validity of Henry's marriage to Catherine. Meanwhile, the king had married Anne (1533), and his parliament had begun its series of acts that effected the schism

and the loss of England from the Catholic fold. [*See* REFORMATION, PROTESTANT (IN THE BRITISH ISLES).]

Church Reform. Clement was hindered from serious consideration of the pressing need for reform. The first five years of his reign were filled with the Hapsburg-Valois wars and the threatening developments of Lutheranism. The last six years were troubled by the increased seriousness of the Protestant revolt, the opposition of Francis I to a general council, and the rapid development of the events of Henry VIII's attempted annulment toward a complete break with Rome. Motions toward reform, however, were already under way in the activities of the Oratory of DIVINE LOVE in northern Italy and the appearance of future religious founders: Cajetan (Gaetano da Thiene) and Gian Pietro Carafa (Paul IV, 1555–59, Theatines), Jerome Emiliani (Somaschi), Anthony Zaccaria (Barnabites), Matteo di Bassi (Capuchins), Ignatius of Loyola (Jesuits), Angela Merici (Ursulines), and others. Clement's successor approved these groups and inaugurated the Council of Trent.

Like his predecessors Alexander VI, Julius II, and Leo X, Clement was a patron of the arts and encouraged such artists as Raphael and Sebastiano del Piombo. He was likewise enmeshed in Italian political affairs and immersed in Renaissance culture. He commissioned Michelangelo to prepare tombs for two members of his family. His tomb is in the church of S. Maria sopra Minerva in Rome. Baccio Bandinelli constructed his tomb; Giovanni di Baccio Bigio made his statue.

The verdict of history on the pontificate of Clement has not been favorable as he left an impoverished papacy and a Church burdened by schism. Clement's weakness and indecision, which contributed to the growth of the Protestant revolt, are accentuated by the position of his reign between those of two reform popes, Adrian VI and Paul III.

Bibliography: H. M. VAUGHAN, *The Medici Popes* (New York 1908). P. CRABITES, *Clement VII and Henry VIII* (London 1936). P. HUGHES, *The Reformation in England,* (5th, rev. ed. New York 1963) v. 1. *Bullarium Romanum* (Magnum), ed. H. MAINARDI and C. COCQUELINES, 18 folio v. (Rome 1733–62) 6:26–172. H. M. FÉRET, *Catholicisme* 2:1191–93. P. BALAN, *Clemente VII e l'Italia dé suoi tempi* (Milan 1887). L. PASTOR, *The History of the Popes from the Close of the Middle Ages* (London-St. Louis 1938–61) v. 9–10. R. MOLS, *Dictionnaire d'histoire et de géographie ecclésiastiques,* ed. A. BAUDRILLART et al. (Paris 1912) 12:1175–1244, bibliog. A. FLICHE and V. MARTIN, eds., *Histoire de l'église depuis les origines jusqu'à nos jours* (Paris 1935–) v.17. H. HEMMER, *Dictionnaire de théologie catholique,* ed. A. VACANT et al., 15 v. (Paris 1903–50; Tables générales 1951–) 3.1:72–76. H. LUTZ, *Lexikon für Theologie und Kirche,* ed. J. HOFER and K. RAHNER, 10 v. (2d, new ed. Freiburg 1957–65) 2:1226. E. P. RODOCANACHI, . . .*Les Pontificats d'Adrien VI et de Clément VII* (Paris 1933). H. M. VAUGHAN, *The Medici Popes* (Port Washington, N.Y. 1971). A. CHASTEL, *The Sack of Rome, 1527* (Princeton 1983). J. HOOK, *The Sack of Rome*

(London 1972). *Epistolae ad Principles. Leo X–Pius IV (1513–1565),* ed. L. NANNI (Vatican City 1993). J. HOOK, "Clement VII, the Colonna and Charles V." *European Studies Review* 2 (1972) 281–99. M. MERIAM BULLARD, *Filippo Strozzi and the Medici* (Cambrige 1980).

[W. J. STEINER]

CLEMENT VII, ANTIPOPE

Pontificate, Sept. 20, 1378, to Sept. 16, 1394; b. Robert of Geneva, at Geneva, 1342; d. Avignon. Robert was the son of Count Amadeus III and Marie de Boulogne. He was indirectly related to the Valois and was a cousin to the king of France through his mother's lineage. As a young man, Robert served both as the chancellor of Amiens and as the canon of Paris. By 1361 he had been appointed bishop of Thérouanne and seven years later he was made bishop of Cambrai. In May 1371, Robert was elevated to the cardinalate by Pope GREGORY XI, the last pope of the AVIGNON PAPACY. A short time later, Robert emerged as a capable leader when he was charged with the task of pacifying the Papal States in Italy. Building on the fragile political legacy of Cardinal Gil de Albornoz, Robert used diplomacy to neutralize the Visconti, came to terms with the British mercenary John Hawgood (Hawkwood), and eventually took command of the Breton free companies. In the process of isolating Florence, Robert also proved himself to be a fearsome military leader, and he is credited with leading horrible massacres particularly in Cesena in February 1377.

On March 27, 1378 Pope Gregory XI died. Under intense pressure from the Roman populace, the assembled cardinals elected an Italian, Bartolomeo Prignano, as his successor. By most counts, Bartolomeo, URBAN VI, was an agreeable choice and it would appear that even Robert himself favored the new pontiff. In his letter dated April 14, 1378, Robert wrote to the Emperor Charles IV, describing Bartolomeo as "my very familiar friend when he was of lesser estate." Towards the end of May, however, Robert's preference for Pope Urban began to fade. The new pope proved to be a strong advocate for moral reform, and he subjected the cardinals to abusive attacks for their worldliness. Naturally, the cardinals resented Urban's high-handed criticisms and by August 2, 13 cardinals, with Robert of Geneva among them, called for his abdication. On Sept. 20, 1378 the discontented cardinals, including the three Italians, assembled at Fondi. They nullified the election of the irascible Bartolomeo Prignano, and elected Robert of Geneva as their new pope. Robert's coronation took place on October 31, and the WESTERN SCHISM of which he was the first antipope, began.

Opening section of the Bull of Pope Urban VI excommunicating the antipope Clement VII, from an official transcript dated February 13, 1383.

Robert took the name Clement VII and he wasted no time in securing allies against Urban. As a French nominee, most of the cardinals favored him, and Queen Joanna of Naples emerged as a strong advocate for his cause. Clement was, however, unable to gain sole possession of the papacy. In April 1379 his troops were crushed at Marino, and the hope of removing Urban by force quickly faded. Undeterred by his military defeat, Clement retired to Naples. While there, he encouraged Louis of Anjou, son of the French King, to take up arms on his behalf by offering the Papal States, a 'Kingdom of Adria,' as a fief to be conquered. Yet, Clement's failure to find popularity among the citizenry of Naples combined with his inability to secure a place in Italy forced him to move his court consisting of 500 cardinals back to Avignon. Sanguine, Clement continued his bid for legitimacy through letters and embassies. The cardinals who supported Clement published a *declaratio* in which they justified his election. The Urbanists replied both with supporting documentation for the legitimacy of their pope and with the corroborating witness of St. CATHERINE OF SWEDEN. St. CATHERINE OF SIENA, who was at Rome during the time, also backed Urban. On the other side, St. VINCENT FERRER and St. COLETTE provided strong support for the

Clement. Thus even the best attempts to gain absolute unanimity on moral grounds resulted in a stalemate.

In November 1379, Clement gained a powerful ally in Charles V of France. Yet, both Clement and Urban were obliged to continue their propaganda campaigns and within only a few years Europe was split into two roughly equal allegiances. Those areas that were loyal to France, Brittany, Arras, Cambrai, Thérouanne, and Tournai followed Clement. Both Scotland and Sicily (October 1379) can be added to the list and so can, albeit much later, Castile (1380), Aragon (1387) and Navarre (1390). In the orient, Clement also found support from Cyprus, Corfu, Albania and Pelopponesus. Urban, however, retained the support of England and those areas under English influence, *e.g.*, Guienne and Aquitaine, Flanders, Utrecht, and Liège. Portugal also remained with Urban as did the eastern and Nordic countries: Hungary, Poland, Denmark, and Scandinavia. Finally, Urban also appears to have had some support from the German king Wenceslas.

Clement's wide base of support was expensive to maintain and the costs of patronage, military campaigns, and numerous diplomatic missions also drained his treasury. In order to offset his expenses, Clement resorted to heavy borrowing and exacting taxes on the clergy. His unpopular financial policy, however, was not enough to end his reign. Both he and his opponent continued a flurry of activity, which included violence as well as anathemas and excommunications, in order to gain sole control of the papacy. There seemed to be only two solutions: (1) the *via cessionis*, whereby one or both of the claimants would be induced to resign and (2) the *via concilli* by which both rivals would be superseded by a general council. The first option was patently unrealistic, although on Oct. 29, 1393, Clement did order the celebration of the mass that was offered to end schism. The other option, conciliarism, was favored by some of the intellectuals at the University of Paris. Its two most notable advocates were Conrad of Gelnhausen and Henry of Langenstien, but their idea of a general council to determine the legitimate pope begged the question of who would call such a council.

No solution to the Schism was in sight when Clement died of apoplexy on the morning of Sept. 16, 1394 in Avignon. He was succeeded by Antipope BENEDICT XIII.

Bibliography: J. N. D. KELLY, *Oxford Dictionary of Popes* (Oxford 1986) 228–230. *The New Cambridge Medieval History* v. 6 (Cambridge 2000). Y. RENOUARD, *The Avignon Papacy* (London 1970) 69–73. G. MOLLAT, *Dictionnaire d'histoire et de géographie ecclésiastiques,* ed. A. BAUDRILLART et al. (Paris 1912–) 12:1174–75, lists sources extensively. L. PASTOR, *The History of the Popes from the Close of the Middle Ages* (London-St. Louis 1938–61) 1:134–174. F. X. SEPPELT, *Geschichte der Päpste von den Anfängen bis zur Mitte des 20 Jh.* (Munich 1957) 4:172, 196, 198–209, 211, 216–219, 222–223. For additional bibliog. *see* WESTERN SCHISM.

[J. A. SHEPPARD]

CLEMENT VIII, POPE

Pontificate: Jan. 30, 1592, to March 5, 1605; b. Ippolito Aldobrandini, Fano, Italy, Feb. 24, 1536. Of an old and distinguished Florentine family, the fourth son of Silvestro ALDOBRANDINI and Lisa Deti, Ippolito studied law at Padua, Perugia, and Bologna, where he received the doctorate. Under Pius V, a family benefactor, he became consistorial advocate in 1568, and auditor of the Rota in 1570. Rapidly promoted under Sixtus V, he became datary, only becoming a priest in 1581. In December 1585 he was made cardinal priest of the titular church of St. Pancratius. He was consecrated as a bishop only after his election as pope. In January 1586 he became grand penitentiary. His public prominence was furthered when, as legate extraordinary, he successfully mediated the dispute over the Polish throne to the satisfaction of both King Sigismund III and Emperor Rudolf II. During three conclaves, from 1590 to 1591, he received support, but he was elected in 1592 when the influence of Philip II in papal elections had begun to wane.

A lifetime friend of St. Philip NERI, Clement was known for his high moral integrity and devout character, as well as for industry and attention to detail. As pope he was an example of kindliness and charity in his frequent visits to Roman churches and his care for the poor, sick, and imprisoned; in his legislation he aimed at improving conditions within the papal territories. With piety and pastoral zeal he worked tirelessly for the improvement of the Church, and its spiritual growth, striving for the removal of abuses and scandals.

Of primary importance was Clement's enlightened policy regarding the Church in France. He reversed the former pro-Spanish policy of the papacy in the Wars of Religion by absolving HENRY IV and recognizing him as legitimate king in France. This reconciliation was followed by papal toleration of the Edict of NANTES (1598) and the implementation of the Tridentine decrees that brought about the rejuvenation of the French Church. Henry's support in 1597 allowed Clement to claim successfully, against the opposition of Spain and the Empire, that the Duchy of Ferrara had devolved to papal jurisdiction after the death of Duke Alphonso II without legitimate heir. The incorporation of Ferrara into the Papal State bolstered its economic and fiscal position. Moreover, Clement was able to bring about peace between France and Spain in 1598 and also between France and Savoy.

Clement also attempted to improve the situation of the English Catholics. While dealing with the ARCHPRIEST CONTROVERSY and internal disputes within the English mission, he supported and strengthened the English colleges on the Continent and established the Scottish college in Rome. His hopes for reconciliation with the English court proved futile. Although James VI of Scotland had seemed amenable to a settlement with the papacy, after his succession to the English throne was secured, James proved recalcitrant.

Considered one of the last Counter-Reformation popes, Clement assisted the work of St. FRANCIS DE SALES in Geneva and furthered Catholic reform in Poland and Germany. He received the reunion of the metropolitan of Kiev and a number of Ruthenian bishops in 1595 following the Union of BREST. Clement failed in his efforts to inaugurate an effective league of Christian princes against the Ottoman Turks, but he furthered the foreign missions by establishing central commissions whose work anticipated that of the Congregation for the Propagation of the Faith.

In a series of decrees he promoted the reform of religious houses and the fidelity of bishops and clergy to the dictates of Trent. He ordered a new and corrected edition of the Vulgate, and also new editions of the Pontifical (1596), the Ceremonial (1600), the Breviary (1602), and the Missal (1604). He raised to the cardinalate Cesare Baronius, Robert Bellarmine, Francesco Tarugi, Francisco de Toledo, Silvio Antoniano, and his two nephews Cinzio and Pietro Aldobrandini. His excellent choice of advisers more than compensated for his occasional lack of decisiveness. In 1600 he proclaimed a Jubilee Year.

During Clement's reign a serious theological controversy arose over Luis de MOLINA's theory of the efficacy of divine grace. Confronted by a heated dispute between the Jesuits and the Dominicans, Clement established a commission to investigate the problem, the famous CONGREGATIO DE AUXILIIS. While Clement personally presided at the debates before the commission, he refrained from pronouncement, and the matter was settled only after his death.

His remains rest in the Basilica of S. Maria Maggiore under a monument erected by the Borghese family.

Bibliography: L. PASTOR, *The History of the Popes from the Close of the Middle Ages,* (London–St. Louis 1938–61) v.23 and 34. *Bullarium Romanum* (Magnum), ed. H. MAINARDI and C. COCQUELINES, 18 folio v. (Rome 1733–62) v.9–11. R. MOLS, *Dictionnaire d'histoire et de géographie ecclésiastiques,* ed. A. BAUDRILLAT et al. (Paris 1912–) 12:1249–97. J. DE LA SERVIÈRE, *Dictionnaire de théologie catholique,* ed. A. VACANT et al., 15 v. (Paris 1903–50; Tables générales 1951–) 3.1:76–86. A. F. ARTAUD DE MONTOR, *The Lives and Times of the Popes,* ed. and tr. C. ARTAUD DE MONTOR, 10 v. (New York 1910–11) 5:221–260. G. LABROT, *Image de Rome. Une Arme pur la Contre-Reforme, 1534–1677* (Seyssel 1987). J. FREIBERG, *The Lateran in 1600. Christian Concord in Counter-Reformation Rome* (Cambridge 1995). W. V. HUDSON, ''Religion and Society in Early Modern Italy—Old Questions, New Insights'' *American Historical Review* (June 1996) vol. 101, n.3, 783–804. G. LUTZ ed., *Das Papsttum die Christenheit und die Staaten Europas 1592–1605* (Tubingen 1994). M. C. ABROMSON, *Painting in Rome during the Papacy of Clement VIII* (New York 1981).

[J. C. WILLKE]

CLEMENT VIII, ANTIPOPE

Pontificate (Avignon obedience): June 10, 1423 to July 26, 1429. Born 1369 or 1370 in Teruel into a noble Aragonese family as Gil Sanchez Muñoz y Carbón; his parents were Pedro II Sanchez Muñoz y Liñán, the Baron of Escriche, and Catalina Sanchez de Carbón. He died Dec. 28, 1446. Sanchez Muñoz was a doctor of canon law (Montpellier 1365) who served in the household of cardinal deacon Pedro de Luna. There he became a friend and trusted advisor of the future antipope. After de Luna was named BENEDICT XIII (1394–1417), Sanchez Muñoz became a member of the curia at Avignon, and in 1396 was an envoy to the Archbishop of Valencia, an important position meant to maintain Spanish support for Avignon and ostensibly to further discussions that might end the schism. Eventually, Sanchez Muñoz became provost of Valencia and archpriest of Teruel. When Benedict XIII died, three of his four remaining cardinals elected Sanchez Muñoz pope on June 10, 1423. He took the name Clement VIII, a clear reference to CLEMENT VII (1378–94), who began the Great Schism when he moved the papacy back to Avignon.

In a noteworthy aside to the Great Schism, the fourth of Benedict's cardinals, Jean Carrier, did not attend the conclave because he was serving in Armagnac as Benedict's vicar-general. When he returned to Peñíscola in December 1423, Carrier declared that the election of Clement VIII had been invalid (he made accusations of simony in regard to the conferral of benefices). As a result, Clement excommunicated him, and Carrier went on to elect his own antipope (Nov. 12, 1425): Bernard Garnier, a sacrist from Rodez, who took the name Benedict XIV. Nothing of substance is known of Benedict XIV's career; we do not even have a date for his death. Some secondary works claim that Carrier himself went on to take the name Benedict XIV. Inasmuch as no power in Europe recognized either of these Benedict XIVs, the name does not appear on most lists of antipopes. Clement VIII is thus generally considered the last antipope of the Great Schism.

For his part, Clement had no secure power base of his own, and thus the Roman pope MARTIN V (1417–31), was eventually able to secure his abdication. The closest Clement came to support was the Aragonese king Alfonso V (1416–1458), who would not publicly denounce the antipope because he found Clement's claim a useful bargaining chip in his effort to secure control of Naples. Nonetheless, Clement's claim lacked credibility even in Aragón, because while Alfonso was in Italy, Queen Maria was regent and actively supported Martin, as did the majority of Aragonese bishops. She went so far as to censure the antipope and to blockade Peñíscola. Alfonso temporarily lifted these measures in 1423, but only as a ploy meant to put pressure on Martin. Finally, when his claims in Naples appeared secure, Alfonso sent a personal delegation to Clement to convince the antipope that he should recognize Martin. The delegation was headed by Alfonso de Borja, who would become Pope CALLISTUS III (1455–58). Clement abdicated on July 26, 1429; this was confirmed on August 13 in St. Mateo by Martin's legate, Pierre de Foix. There was no obvious ill will between pope and former antipope, and on Aug. 26, 1429 Martin named Sanchez Muñoz bishop of Majorca. He remained at this position until his death on Dec. 28, 1446. As he had requested, the tiara he used as bishop continues to hang over his tomb in the Cathedral of Palma.

Bibliography: J. D. MANSI, *Sacrorum conciliorum nova et amplissima collectio* (Florence and Venice 1759–98; repr. Graz 1960–61) 28.1117–41. MARTIN DE ALPARTIL, *Chronica actitatorum temporibus domini Benedicti XIII*, ed. F. EHRLE (Paderborn 1906). A. DEGERT, ''La fin du Schisme d'Occident,'' in *Mélanges Léonce Couture* (Toulouse 1902) 223–42. S. PUIG Y PUIG, *Pedro de Luna: Ultimo papa de Aviñón, 1387–1430* (Barcelona 1920) 363–453, 606–17. R. MOLS, *Dictionnaire d'histoire et de géographie ecclésiastiques* (Paris 1953) 12.1245–49. M. GARCIA MIRALLES, *La personalidad de Gil Sanchez Muñoz y la solución del cisma de occidente* (Teruel 1954). V. A. ÁLVAREZ PALENZUELA, *Extinción del Cisma de Occidente: La legación del cardenal Pedro de Foix en Aragón, 1425–1430* (Madrid 1977). W. BRANDMÜLLER, *Lexikon des Mittelalters* (Munich 1979) 2.2145–46. J. N. D. KELLY, *The Oxford Dictionary of Popes* (New York 1986) 240–41. J. GOÑI, *Diccionario de Historia Eclesiastica de España, Suplemento I* (Madrid 1987) 158–62 for additional bibliography; also 128–158 for an overview of the schism with an emphasis on Spain.

[P. M. SAVAGE]

CLEMENT IX, POPE

Pontificate: June 20, 1667, to Dec. 9, 1669; b. Giulio Rospigliosi, Pistoia, Jan. 28, 1600. He came of an ancient family from Lombardy. He studied first at Rome with the Jesuits, then at the University of Pisa. A man of talents, Rospigliosi was an author of verses and a successful playwright. His dramas on religious themes, influenced by Calderón, were quite successful, and he is credited with developing comic opera as an individual form. Through the favor of URBAN VIII he rose from referendary (1632)

to become nuncio to Spain (1644–53) and titular archbishop of Tarsus. ALEXANDER VII made him his secretary of state (1657) and cardinal priest of S. Sisto. The two chief problems of his pontificate were the stubborn Jansenists and the oncoming Ottomans. Four Jansenist bishops—Caulet de Pamiers, Buzenvol de Beauvais, Pavillon d'Alet, Henri Arnauld d'Angers—had refused to give their acceptance to the formulary of Alexander VII (1665), and these were supported by many others. They had written pastorals that had been condemned and in general had showed themselves recalcitrant. The French authorities, alarmed over the possibility of schism, persuaded the four bishops to sign their acceptance of Alexander's bull. Clement permitted them to do this without any explicit retraction of their pastoral letters. The bishops signed, with reservations carefully kept from the pope, and an uneasy peace (*Pax Clementina*) settled on France. Since the Jansenists had deceived the pope, the peace was not lasting. (*See* JANSENISM; HERESY, HISTORY OF.)

The Ottomans, who had been attacking Crete since 1645, were engaged in reducing Candia, the last Christian stronghold on that island kingdom. Clement did everything to help the beleaguered Venetians. He failed to secure the aid of Louis XIV and in sadness learned that Candia had fallen on Sept. 5, 1669. Clement was a good shepherd. He reduced taxes and was charitable to the poor, solicitous for the spiritual welfare of his flock, and interested in missionary expansion. He was kind to CHRISTINA OF SWEDEN, who returned to Rome after an absence of more than two years in her homeland. During his reign he canonized Mary Magdalene de' PAZZI and PETER OF ALCANTARA, and declared ROSE OF LIMA blessed.

Bibliography: L. PASTOR, *The History of the Popes From the Close of the Middle Ages* (London–St. Louis 1938–61) 31:314–430. A. F. ARTAUD DE MONTOR, *The Lives and Times of the Popes*, 10 v. (New York 1910–11) 6:106–115. H. BREMOND, *Histoire littéraire du sentiment réligieux en France depuis la fin des guerres de religion jusqu'd nos jours*, 12 v. (Paris 1911–36) 4:241–242. N. J. ABERCROMBIE, *The Origins of Jansenism* (Oxford 1936). *Bullarium Romanum* (Magnum), ed. H. MAINARDI and C. COCQUELINES, 18 folio v. (Rome 1733–62) 17:512–839. R. MOLS, *Dictionnaire d'histoire et de géographie ecclésiastiques*, ed. A. BAUDRILLAT et al. (Paris 1912–) 12:1297–1313, with bibliog. J. DE LA SERVIÈRE, *Dictionnaire de théologie catholique*, ed. A. VACANT et al., 15 v. (Paris 1903–50; Tables générales 1951–) 3:86–94, with bibliog. R. CHALUMEAU, *Catholicisme* 2:1195. A. NIGRO, *La collezione Rospigliosi* (Rome 1999).

[J. S. BRUSHER]

CLEMENT X, POPE

Pontificate: April 29, 1670 to July 22, 1676; b. Emilio Bonaventura Altieri, Rome, July 13, 1590. From

"Pope Clement X," tomb/monument by Ercole Ferrata, (1610–85), St. Peter's Basilica, Rome. (Alinari-Art Reference/Art Resource, NY)

a family of ancient Roman nobility, he obtained a doctorate in law in 1611 and worked for a time with John Baptist Pamfili (later Innocent X). At the urging of his elder brother, John Baptist, he became a cleric and in 1623 served as auditor to Lancellotti in the nunciature in Poland. On his return to Italy in 1627, Emilio replaced his brother as bishop of Camerino. INNOCENT X in 1644 appointed him nuncio to Naples, where his diplomatic acumen was tested during the revolution of Tommaso Aniello in 1647. In 1652 he returned to his see, and two years later by appointment of ALEXANDER VII he became secretary of the Congregation of Bishops and Regulars and a consultor of the Inquisition. Clement IX made him superintendent of the Exchequer and, a month before his death, raised him to the cardinalate. In the next conclave, prolonged by a conflict of interests among the Spanish and French cardinals for more than four months, Emilio was elected as he approached 80. He adopted Cardinal Paluzzi degli Albertoni as cardinal nephew and entrusted him with administration to an excess that irritated Romans.

During his reign of six years, Clement, who was in his eighties, brought order to papal finances, took great interest in agricultural conditions, assembled a special congregation for Polish affairs, and regulated by his decree of June 21, 1670, the relationship between bishops and religious orders.

He canonized Cajetan, Philip Benitius, Francis Borgia, Louis Bertrand, and Rose of Lima, and beatified Pius V, John of the Cross, and the martyrs of Gorkom in Holland. His most conspicuous foreign policies centered on resistance to LOUIS XIV' demands on the *regale* (royal right to revenues of vacant sees), pressed by Cardinal César d'Estrees (*see* GALLICANISM), and his large financial aid to Poland in its struggle against Turkish invasion. He celebrated the Holy Year 1675 and is remembered in Rome for the erection of the Palazzo Altieri, the fountains in the piazza of St. Peter, and the statues on the bridge of Sant' Angelo.

Bibliography: L. PASTOR, *The History of the Popes from the Close of the Middle Ages* (London-St. Louis 1938–61) 31:431–508. F. X. SEPPELT, *Geschichte der Päpste von den Anfängen bis zur Mitte des 20 Jh.,* v.5 (Leipzig 1931–41). J. DE LA SERVIÈRE, *Dictionnaire de théologie catholique,* ed. A. VACANT et al., 15 v. (Paris 1903–50; Tables générales 1951–) 3:94–98. R. MOLS, *Dictionnaire d'histoire et de géographie ecclésiastiques,* ed. A. BAUDRILLART et al. (Paris 1912–) 12:1313–26. G. HANOTAUX, *Recueil des Instructions Données aux Ambassadeurs et Ministres de France,* 3 v. (Paris 1888–). *Bullarium Romanum* (Magnum), ed. H. MAINARDI and C. COCQUELINES, 18 folio v. (Rome 1733–62) 18. J. DULUMEAU, *Catholicism between Luther and Voltaire* (London 1977). A. D. WRIGHT, *The Early Modern Papacy: From the Council of Trent to the French Revolution (1564–1789)* (London 2000).

[S. V. RAMGE]

CLEMENT XI, POPE

Pontificate: Nov. 23, 1700, to March 19, 1721; b. Giovanni Francesco Albani, Urbino, Italy, July 23, 1649. Of a noble Umbrian family, he was educated at the Roman College, where he became expert in the classics and admitted into the famed Academy of Queen Christina of Sweden. The study of theology and law followed, and in 1677, at the age of 28, he became associated with the Papal Curia as governor of Rieti and, later, of the Sabine province and Orvieto. In 1687 he was appointed secretary of briefs, in 1690 created cardinal deacon, and ordained in September 1700. When more senior candidates in the conclave of 1700 proved unacceptable, Cardinal Albani, only 51 and highly regarded for his virtuous life and his experience in government, was elected pope after 46 days of deliberation.

European Diplomacy. It was his misfortune to reign while the prestige of the papacy was diminishing in the political life of Europe, and this explains many of the problems of the pontificate. The chief European powers were at war during much of his pontificate (War of the Spanish Succession, 1701–14). Neutrality proved difficult, since almost every decision Clement made in international affairs was challenged by one of the monarchs involved. Shortly after his election, he approved the selection of the French Philip of Anjou as king of Spain, but when the Austrians invaded the Papal States and threatened Rome in 1709, Clement was forced to favor the cause of the Austrian Hapsburg claimant to the Spanish throne. In the proceedings of the Treaty of Utrecht (1713), not only was the pope ignored, but one of the papal dominions, Sicily, was transferred to Savoy. Similarly, the treaty opposed the pope by granting the title of king of Prussia to the elector of Brandenburg and by discounting the claims of the son of James II to the English throne. On the other hand, Clement was successful in a project that gave him great consolation—arousing Spain and Austria to take defensive measures against the Turks.

Church-State Relations. No less complicated were Clement's problems in Church-State relations, with Spain after Philip V was rejected and with France during the closing years of Louis XIV's rule and the Regency period. Some historians believe that the pope lacked vigor and decisiveness in handling the major problems that confronted him. He seems to have been timorous by nature; he loved peace and harmony, and hence was slow to press for immediate solutions. He was, however, realistic enough to appreciate the fact that the power of the papacy was waning, and therefore persuasion and negotiation were more necessary. Thus he wrestled for years with the Jansenist-Gallican party in France and showed extraordinary patience with the highly controversial archbishop of Paris, Cardinal Louis de NOAILLES. In condemnation of JANSENISM he issued the bulls *Vineam Domini* (1705) and *UNIGENITUS* (1713), the latter being a detailed study of the doctrine of the Jansenist Pasquier QUESNEL. *Unigenitus* proved to be a source of contention in France for the next 30 years, but eventually it was accepted as official policy in Church and State. Equally controversial was Clement's decision in the CHINESE RITES CONTROVERSY, when he curtailed the use of local Chinese customs in the Jesuit missions. The decision was reached after lengthy discussions in commissions and after long study by the pope himself. Furthermore, the implementation of the new policy by his representatives in China lacked discretion and was the cause of severe tensions in the missions, and the persecution of Chinese Christians.

The foreign missions were close to Clement's heart, a mark of his burning desire to further the Church's interests. He encouraged missionary work in northern Germany and in the Philippines, and he promoted new missionary colleges in Rome. His pastoral concern for the clergy and faithful was felt more directly in Rome and in the papal dominions. He encouraged bishops to reside in their sees and recommended to all the clergy the annual retreat, and in particular the Spiritual Exercises of St. Ignatius. His generosity to the poor was exemplary, and he provided broad support for the arts and scholarship. And with all his administrative duties, he remained a scholar, striving always to enlarge the collections of the Vatican Library and to preserve the cultural treasures of Rome. Clement composed the Breviary Office in honor of St. Joseph, and decreed the feast of the Immaculate Conception of the BVM obligatory for Christiandom. His letters, briefs, and homilies were collected and published by his nephew, Cardinal Annibale ALBANI (2 v. Rome 1729).

Bibliography: L. PASTOR, *The History of the Popes from the Close of the Middle Ages* (London-St. Louis 1938–61) v. 33. A. FLICHE and V. MARTIN, eds., *Histoire de l'église depuis les origines jusqu'à nos jours* (Paris 1935–) v. 19.1–2. L. NINA, *Le Finánze pontificie sotto Clemente XI* (Milan 1928). A. ALDOBRANDINI, *La guerra di successione di Spagna negli stati dell'Alta Italia dal 1702 al 1705 e la politica di Clemente XI dal carteggio di Mons* (Rome 1931). A. CORNARO, *Lexikon für Theologie und Kirche,* ed. J. HOFER and K. RAHNER, 10 v. (2d, new ed. Freiburg 1957–65) 2:1227–28. C. JOHNS, *Rome in the Age of Clement XI* (New York 1993). A. LE ROY, *La France et Rome de 1700 à 1715* (Paris 1892).

[C. B. O'KEEFE]

CLEMENT XII, POPE

Pontificate: July 12, 1730, to Feb. 6, 1740; b. Lorenzo Corsini, Florence, April 7, 1652. His family was influential in Florence for centuries and included in its record the 14th-century bishop of Fiesole, St. ANDREW CORSINI.

"Pope Clement XI," painting by Carlo Maratta.

After studies at the Roman College, Lorenzo proceeded to the University of Pisa to study law. Upon the death of his father, this eldest son of the family surrendered his rights of inheritance and entered the service of the Church, where his merit was recognized. Corsini became in turn titular bishop of Nicomedia (1690), nuncio to Vienna (1691), governor of the CASTEL SANT' ANGELO (1696), cardinal deacon of S. Susanna (1706), and later cardinal priest of S. Pietro in Vincoli and cardinal bishop of Frascati. While still a cardinal, Corsini emerged as a patron of art and scholarship. His long experience in church administration and his excellent life brought him to the papacy. At 79 he was experienced and wise, but he suffered much from gout and poor eyesight that deteriorated to the point of blindness in 1732. In spite of his physical debility Clement proved to be a vigorous leader, showing good executive judgment in his choice of capable officials. He sentenced the venal Cardinal Niccolò Coscia, who had abused the confidence of his predecessor, BENEDICT XIII, to ten years' imprisonment. Among the measures Clement took to improve the bad state of finances in the papal kingdom was the restoration of the state lottery, which had been suppressed by Benedict XIII. With the money brought in by his many financial measures Clement was able to spend considerable sums to alleviate the distress of areas afflicted by natural disas-

Monument of Pope Clement XII, bronze and marble sculptural group by Giovanni Battista Maini, 18th century, Basilica of St. John Lateran, Rome. (Alinari-Art Reference/Art Resource, NY)

ter, as well as carry out a building program that included the erection of the famous Fontana di Trevi and improvements of the venerable basilica of St. John Lateran. He also established a papal printing press.

His dealings with foreign powers were troubled. When Antonio Farnese, Duke of Parma and Piacenza, died in 1731 without a son, Don Carlos, son of King Philip V of Spain, claimed the duchies and took them over without regard for the pope's suzerainty. Clement protested in vain and preserved a prudent neutrality in the war in which Don Carlos also drove the Austrians out of Sicily.

Clement continued the policy of his predecessors with regard to the Jansenists. He demanded full submission to Clement XI's bull *UNIGENITUS* (1713). In this matter he had the satisfaction of receiving the submission of the Benedictine Congregation of St. Maur (*see* MAURISTS). While JANSENISM was dying, other movements were growing in this fourth decade of the 18th century. The Freemasons, who were making great progress throughout Europe, founded lodges in Italy during Clement's pontificate. In 1738 Clement condemned Freemasonry and forbade Catholics to belong to Masonic lodges under pain of excommunication. In the bull *In Eminenti*

the pope expressed his reasons: the Freemasons are men of all sects and religions, bound together by natural morality; this bond is secret with an oath enforced by exaggerated penalties.

Perhaps Clement's greatest glory was his unceasing interest in missionary activity. He began by helping missionary seminaries. He founded a seminary for training priests of the Greek rite at Ullano in southern Italy. He helped the Maronites of Lebanon by sending the distinguished Lebanese scholar and Vatican librarian, Joseph Assemani, to preside over a national synod. He sent Franciscans to Abyssinia to work for the union of that kingdom with the Holy See. In the Far East he continued the policy of his predecessors in opposing the so-called Chinese and Malabar rites.

In the interests of justice, Clement overruled his representative at Ancona, the once powerful and famous minister of Spain, Cardinal Giulio ALBERONI, who in 1739 annexed the small republic of San Marino to the Papal States. Clement heeded the protests of the mountain folk and restored their freedom.

Bibliography: L. PASTOR, *The History of the Popes from the Close of the Middle Ages,* (London-St. Louis 1938–61) 34:301–510. A. F. ARTAUD DE MONTOR, *The Lives and Times of the Popes,* 10 v. (New York 1910–11) 6:246–268. *Bullarium Romanum* (Magnum), ed., H. MAINARDI and C. COCQUELINES, 18 folio v. (Rome 1733–62) v.23–24. J. DE LA SERVIÈRE, *Dictionnaire de théologie catholique,* ed. A. VACANT et al., 15 v. (Paris 1903–50; Tables générales 1951–) 3.1:111–115. R. MOLS, *Dictionnaire d'histoire et de géographie ecclésiastiques,* ed. A. BAUDRILLAT et al. (Paris 1912–) 12: 1361–81, bibliog. R. CHALUMEAU, *Catholicisme* 2:1197. W. J. CALLAHAN and D. HIGGS, eds., *Church and State in Catholic Europe of the Eighteenth Century* (Cambridge 1979). A. D. WRIGHT, *The Early Modern Papacy: From the Council of Trent to the French Revolution, 1564–1789* (London 2000). M. CARAVALE and A. CARACCIOLO, *Lo stato pontificio de Martino V a Pio IX* (Turin 1978).

[J. S. BRUSHER]

CLEMENT XIII, POPE

Pontificate: July 6, 1758, to Feb. 2, 1769; b. Carlo della Torre Rezzonico, Venice, March 7, 1693. His family, which originated at Como in central Italy, emigrated to Genoa and then to Venice (1640), where the family name was inscribed in the Golden Book of nobility (1687).

Ecclesiastical Career. Carlo was educated in humanities and philosophy at the Jesuit college at Bologna, and received his doctorate in theology and Canon Law at the University of Padua; in 1714 he entered the Accademia ecclesiastica at Rome to prepare for a career of diplomacy. Two years later he was ordained, began service as a prothonotary, and was immediately appointed by Clement XI governor of Rieti, then of Fano (1721). Benedict XIII called him to Rome (1725) as a member of the Consulta, and after four years selected him as an auditor of the Rota for Venice. His diligence in this office is reflected in the *Decisiones S. Rotae Romanae coram R. P. D. Carolo Rezzonico,* 3 v. (Rome 1759). He was created a cardinal deacon by Clement XII (Dec. 20, 1737) with the title of S. Niccolò in Carcere (changed to cardinal priest of S. Maria in Ara Coeli, then to S. Marco), and on March 11, 1743, he succeeded Pietro Ottoboni in the See of Padua; his consecration was performed by Benedict XIV in the church of the SS. Apostoli. His efforts for the improvement of his clergy made his episcopate imitative of those of Charles Borromeo and Gregory Barbarigo. The latter, his predecessor in the bishopric of Padua (1667–97), was a relative through his mother, Vittoria Barbarigo; Gregory was beatified by Clement, Sept. 20, 1761. Rezzonico held a synod (1746) and spent large sums of his own wealth in enlarging and improving the seminary. At Padua he was regarded as *il santo,* and at Rome diplomatic agents wrote of his conscientiousness, candor, affability, benevolence, and generosity, although some commented on his *talento mediocre.*

Papal Election. The conclave of 53 days that brought the tiara to Rezzonico opened on May 15, 1758, and became an electoral contest among the *Anziani* (elders), the imperialists, the supporters of the Bourbons, and the *Zelanti,* who sought a candidate who would bring vigor to the office. A deadlock resulting from the *exclusiva* used by the Bourbon party against Cardinal Cavalchini ended when Cardinal Spinelli, leader of the *Zelanti,* and the imperial Cardinal Roth of Constance proposed Rezzonico as a compromise candidate; his name was fourteenth on the list of those acceptable to Vienna. His coronation occurred July 16. Surprised and humbled by the high office, Clement faced the problems inherited from his predecessor, Benedict XIV. One urgent problem was the anti-Romanism of the rulers of Europe, which expressed itself in the FEBRONIANISM of Johann Nikolaus von HONTHEIM and the deism of the ENCYCLOPEDISTS. Its particular expression, however, was the "family pact" of the Bourbon courts of France, Spain, Naples, and Parma to destroy the Jesuits, who were at a high point in their influence with 23,000 members, 800 residences, 700 colleges, and 270 missions.

The Jesuit Question. The extinction of the Jesuits became the *affaire célèbre* that harassed the new pontiff, who, inclined to timidity and indecision, relied upon his curial advisers: first, Cardinal Spinelli and the Secretary of State, Alberico Archinto, both inimical to the society, then Cardinal Luigi Torrigiani, successor to Archinto (1758) and a strong defender of the Jesuits. Clement's

nephew, Carlo Rezzonico, created a cardinal, Oct. 2, 1758, had neither skill nor interest in diplomacy.

Portugal. The reign of Joseph I (1750–77) was dominated by his chief minister, Sebastião José de Carvalho e Mello, Marquis of POMBAL, who considered the Jesuits an obstacle to his plans for strengthening the monarchy and exploiting the colonies. Under Benedict XIV he had accused them of opposing the Hispano-Portuguese Treaty (Jan. 8, 1750) that partitioned Paraguay, of organizing the natives for rebellion, and of practicing illicit trade (including slaves) at Maranhão and Gran Pará. On Sept. 20, 1757, he dismissed Jesuit confessors from court and obtained from Benedict the appointment of Cardinal Francesco Saldanha as visitor of Jesuit houses. When the king was wounded by gunshot (Sept. 3, 1758), the Jesuits were included in accusations made at the trial proceedings that sent José Mascarenhas, Duke of Aviero, the Marquis da Távora, and members of his family and household to a cruel execution for treason and regicide (Jan. 12, 1759). By royal edict (January 19) Jesuits were confined to their houses, their property confiscated and a list of their transgressions in the colonies (*Relacão abreviada*) was sent to Rome and circulated. Clement's brief of August 18, appealing for canonical procedures in the handling of the Jesuits, and his two subsequent letters were rejected as "unauthorized." On September 17 the deportation of approximately 1,100 Jesuits to Civitavecchia began; there they found refuge and kindness from the pope. Two hundred and fifty other Jesuits (superiors and foreigners) were imprisoned in the subterranean dungeons of São Juliao, São Jorge, and Belem until the death of Joseph (1777), when 60 survivors were freed. Diplomatic relations were severed when the papal nuncio Filippo ACCIAIOLI was expelled, and the Portuguese ambassador Almada was recalled from Rome (July 7, 1760). The break was made more dramatic when the Jesuit Gabriel Malagria, already indicted in the Távora trial, was declared a heretic by the Inquisition, strangled, and burned in a solemn auto-da-fé (Sept. 21, 1761); Clement regarded him as a martyr. The breach between Rome and Lisbon continued throughout Clement's pontificate.

France. The unwise speculation of the procurator of the mission of Martinique, Antoine de La Valette (1709–67), brought the Jesuits of the Paris province to bankruptcy and also to the attention of Parlement, which in May 1761, examined the constitutions of the society, and advocated a vicar-general for the Jesuits of France, appointed by the Crown and independent of the generalate in Rome. The Parlement also compiled the *Extraits des assertions dangereuses et pernicieuses,* where passages from Jesuit writings, were misused to proclaim the society a menace to the state. Louis XV, at the behest of Clement, consulted the Assembly of the French Clergy

(December 1761): 45 bishops against six approved the constitutions as they were; of the others, the Jansenist bishop Fitz James of Soissons asked for the suppression of the Jesuits; 27 absent bishops voted favorably on the constitutions. The king, fearful of Parlement and influenced by his mistress, Mme. de Pompadour, and her adviser, Étienne François de Choiseul, ignored the votes of the bishops and petitioned Rome for a special vicar-general, but was refused. On this occasion Clement remarked to Lorenzo RICCI, the Jesuit general, "Sint ut sunt aut non sint" (Let them be as they are or not be). His appeal to the king was without effect, and in a final *arrêt* of the Paris Parlement (Aug. 6, 1762), the society was suppressed and declared "nonexistent" by Louis in November 1764. In protest Clement wrote a solemn bull, *Apostolicum pascendi munus* (Jan. 9, 1765), restating papal approval of the Jesuits, praising their achievements, and declaring this affront to the society to be equally an affront to the Church.

Spain, Naples, and Parma. Charles III (1759–88), regarded as an enlightened despot and the greatest of the Spanish Bourbons, was at first apparently friendly to the Jesuits, though surrounded by ministers who sought their destruction. Among these ministers were the Irishman Richard Wall, Minister of Foreign Affairs; his successor, Marqués de Grimaldi (1763); Manuel de Roda y Arrieta, Minister of Justice; Pedro Campomanés, fiscal; Count Pedro Pablo Aranda, president of the Council of Castile; and José Moniño (Count Florida Blanca), ambassador to Rome. Moreover Charles still received the advice of Bernardo TANUCCI, who had been his chief minister when he was king of Naples (1738–59), and now served his son, King Ferdinand IV. The queen mother, Elizabeth Farnese, stayed their influence on the king, but after her death (July 10, 1766) Charles acknowledged the Jesuits as the authors of pamphlets urging insurrection, as conspirators for his deposition on the grounds of illegitimate birth, and as the principal opponents to the canonization of Ven. Juan de PALAFOX Y MENDOZA, Bishop of Mexico (d. 1659), whose cause Charles favored. In a session of the Extraordinary Council of Jan. 29, 1767, the Jesuits were declared instigators of rebellion and by a royal decree (February 27) were banished from Spain and its colonies. In a letter to Clement (March 31) Charles announced that the reasons for his action were locked in the royal breast; Clement's reply urging clemency and justice was unheeded. On the night of April 2–3 Jesuits were expelled from their houses and hustled into ships to sail to Civitavecchia; their property was voided to the state, and a yearly pension of 100 pesetas, to be forfeited upon leaving the Papal States, was promised to each member of the society. Because of the diplomatic indignity of this act and the impossibility of settling so great a number of ex-

iles (5,100 Jesuits would converge from the ports of Spain; 2,600 of all nationalities from the colonies), the pope's officials refused their embarkation. Under Joseph PIGNATELLI's leadership, the Jesuits settled in Corsica until 1768 when they were received into the Papal States and the cities of northern Italy.

Charles's edict was duplicated in the other countries controlled by the Spanish Bourbons. In the name of the young King Ferdinand IV of Naples (1759–1825) the regent Tanucci forbade the reading of the *Apostolicum pascendi munus,* and on Feb. 8, 1768, issued the decree of expulsion; 1,400 Jesuits were marched over the frontier into the Papal States. Pinto de Fonseca, Grandmaster of the Knights of Malta, a feudatory of Naples, expelled 20 Jesuits from the island, April 23, 1768. On Jan. 16, 1768, François du Tillot, Marquis of Fellino and chief minister of Duke Ferdinand of Parma, Piacenza, and Guastalla (1765–1802), ordered a commission to investigate monastic charters. Clement, as traditional suzerain of the Duchy of Parma, protested in a brief known as the *Monitorium,* which was rejected, and on February 8 in retaliation 170 Jesuits were exiled. The Bourbon courts supported Parma; France occupied Avignon and Venaissin; Naples invaded Pontecorvo and Benevento. The crisis reached its summit when in January of the next year the ambassadors of France, Spain, and Naples placed a formal demand for the suppression of the society. To forestall action, Clement called a special consistory to decide the fate of the Jesuits, but the day before its scheduled meeting (February 3), an apoplectic stroke ended his trials. He was buried in St. Peter's Basilica and Canova created his funeral monument.

Pastor and Patron. The pastoral interest that won him praise as bishop of Padua marked his government of Rome and the Papal States. Nonetheless, his pontificate has been seen by many to mark the final abandonment of reform within the Catholic enlightenment. Still, during the great drought of 1763 and 1764 Clement instituted a *monte dell' abbondanza,* bought grain and oil, and built shelters for the thousands who crowded into Rome; he also attempted to drain the Pontine marshes, but was unsuccessful (1762). In his name the Holy Office condemned the *Histoire du peuple de Dieu . . .* by the Jesuit Isaac Joseph Berruyer (Dec. 2, 1758), *Encyclopédie* by Denis Diderot et al. (Sept. 3, 1759), *De l'Esprit* by Claude Adrien Helvétius (Jan. 31, 1759; in that year it was condemned also by the Sorbonne and publicly burned), *Exposition de la doctrine chrétienne . . .* by François Philippe Mésenguy (1677–1763), called the "Second Quesnel" (June 14, 1761), *Emile ou Traité de l'Éducation* by Jean Jacques ROUSSEAU (Sept. 9, 1762; condemned also by Parlement), and *De statu ecclesiae et* *legitima potestate Romani pontificis* by Febronius (Feb. 27, 1764).

Arts and scholarship were favored during this pontificate. The completion of the Villa Albani was entrusted to Niccolò Savi (1763), and of the Fontana di Trevi to Giuseppe Pannini (1762). The painters Anton Raphael Mengs (1728–79) and Giovanni Piranesi received Clement's patronage, although they shared the dismay of artists when Clement ordered coverings for the ''indecent'' statues of antiquity in the Villa Albani and Vatican and commissioned Stefano Pozzi to paint over the nudities of the frescoes in the Sistine Chapel. St. Paul's-Outside-the-Walls, the Quirinal Palace, and the Castel Gandolfo were adorned. The VATICAN LIBRARY was enriched with Oriental MSS, many formerly owned by the Assemani; the *Illyricum sacrum,* 8 v. (1751–90) by Daniele FARLATI, SJ, and the *Inscriptiones romanae infimi aevi* of Pier Luigi Galletti, OSB, 3 v. (1760) had his support; and Giuseppe GARAMPI, prefect of the Archives, was sent twice (1761, 1764) to Germany on diplomatic missions and was appointed secretary of the ciphers (1766).

Clement advanced the devotion to the Sacred Heart by granting a Mass and Office for Poland, as requested by King Augustus III, and for the Archconfraternity of the Sacred Heart in Rome (Jan. 26, 1765). The Immaculate Conception was declared the principal patronal feast for Spain (Nov. 8, 1760) and the title ''mater immaculata'' was added to the litanies; the Preface of the Trinity was ordered for all Sunday Masses. On the anniversary of his coronation (Aug. 16, 1767) Clement canonized JOSEPH CALASANCTIUS, JOSEPH CUPERTINO, Jerome EMILIANI, Jane Frances de CHANTAL, JOHN CANTIUS, and SERAFINO OF ASCOLI. He beatified the Trinitarian Simon de ROJAS (May 19, 1766) and the Capuchin BERNARD OF CORLEONE (April 29, 1768), and declared many venerable.

Bibliography: *Bullarium Romanum Continuatio,* ed. A. BARBÈRI et al. (Rome 1835–57) v.3. G. X. DE RAVIGNAN, *Clément XIII et Clément XIV* (2d ed. Paris 1856). L. PASTOR, *The History of the Popes From the Close of the Middle Ages* (London–St. Louis 1938–61) 36, 37. J. SARRAILH, *L'Espagne éclairée de la seconde moitié du XVIIIᵉ siècle* (Paris 1954). F. ROUSSEAU, *Le Règne de Charles III d'Espagne, 1759–1788,* 2 v. (Paris 1907). A. FERRER DEL RÍO, *Historia del reinado de Carlos III en España,* 4 v. (Madrid 1856). M. DANVILA Y COLLADO, *Reinado de Carlos III,* 6 v. (Madrid 1890–96). J. L. D'AZEVEDO, *O Marquêz de Pombal e a sua época* (2d ed. Lisbon 1922). O. BUSCH, ''Pombal und die Jesuiten,'' *Stimmen der Zeit* (Freiburg 1915–) 164 (1958–59) 466–470. M. CHEKE, *Dictator of Portugal: A Life of the Marquis of Pombal, 1699–1782* (London 1938); *The Cardinal de Bernis* (New York 1959). L. DOLLOT, *Bernis et Choiseul* (Paris 1941). S. J. DE CARVALHO E MELLO, *Pombal, Choiseul et d'Aranda: L'Intrigue des trois cabinets* (Paris 1830). C. LO SORDO, *Tanucci e la Reggenza al tempo di Ferdinando IV* (Bari 1912). S. F. SMITH, ''The Suppression of the Society of Jesus,'' *Month* 99 (1902) 113–130, 346–368, 497–517, 626–650; 100 (1902) 20–34, 126–152, 258–273. E. ROTA, *Le origini del Risorgimento, 1700–1800,* 2 v. (2d ed. Milan 1948). E. DAMMIG, *Il movimento giansenista a Roma nella seconda metà del secolo XVIII* (*Studi e Testi* 119; Rome 1945). L. KOCH, *Jesuiten-Lexikon: Die Gesellschaft Jesu einst und jetzt* (Paderborn 1934) 991–993. R. MOLS, *Dictionnaire d'histoire et de géographie ecclésiastiques,* ed. A. BAUDRILLAT et al. (Paris 1912–) 12:1381–1410, bibliog. J. DE LA SERVIÈRE, *Dictionnaire de théologie catholique,* ed. A. VACANT et al., 15 v. (Paris 1903–50; Tables générales 1951–) 3.1:115–124. H. RAAB, *Lexikon für Theologie und Kirche,* ed. J. HOFER and K. RAHNER, 10 v. (2d, new ed. Freiburg 1957–65) 2:1229. H. GROSS, *Rome in the Age of Enlightenment* (Cambridge 1990). H. DANIEL-ROPS, *The Church in the Eighteenth Century* (Garden City, N.Y. 1966). D. K. VAN KLEY, *The Jansenists and the Expulsion of the Jesuits from France* (London 1975).

[E.D. MCSHANE]

CLEMENT XIV, POPE

Pontificate: May 19, 1769, to Sept. 22, 1774; b. Giovanni Vincenzo Antonio Ganganelli, at Sant' Arcangelo, near Rimini (Legation of Ravenna), Oct. 31, 1705. His father, Lorenzo, was a surgeon; his mother, Angela Serafina, was a descendant of the distinguished family of Mazza in Pesaro. After his education with the Jesuits at Rimini and the Piarists at Urbino, Ganganelli entered the novitiate of the Conventual Franciscans at Mondaino (May 1723), taking Lorenzo as his name in religion; he was solemnly professed on May 18, 1724. At the completion of his studies at the College of St. Bonaventure in Rome, he received a doctorate in theology (1731) and taught philosophy and theology at the convents of Ascoli, Milan, and Bologna. In May 1740 he was appointed rector of St. Bonaventure's through the recommendation of a Jesuit to Cardinal Annibale Albani, patron of the college. At Milan he printed a theological defense (*Diatriba theologica,* 1743) with a dedication to St. Ignatius of Loyola and a foreword of praise for the Society of Jesus. He was chosen first consultor of the Holy Office (1746), and twice (1753, 1759) refused the nomination to the generalship of his order. On Sept. 24, 1759, Clement XIII created him a cardinal with the title of S. Lorenzo in Panisperna (later changed to SS. Apostoli), calling him a Jesuit in the clothes of a Franciscan. It has been claimed that he was recommended to Clement either by Lorenzo RICCI, the Jesuit general, because of his avowed esteem for Jesuits, or by Cardinal Giuseppe Spinelli because of Ganganelli's concealed dislike for ''Gesuitismo.'' Throughout the nine years before his elevation to the papacy, Ganganelli's manner was devout, frugal, unostentatious, and impenetrable. A reserve and fear of being influenced in his judgments made him usually reluctant to declare his mind. By some diplomats this was regarded as a sign of astuteness and keen wit, by others, as a mark of insincerity and deceit, e.g., Bernard TANUCCI, who

Pope Clement XIV announcing dissolution of Society of Jesus to ambassador of Spain, 18th-century engraving.

complained that Ganganelli rode keeping his feet in two stirrups. That he was already veering toward the Bourbon courts appears in his opposition to the pro-Jesuit policies of the papal secretary of state Cardinal Luigi Torrigiani; in his defense of the Bourbon Duke Ferdinand of Parma's stand against the *Monitorium* of Clement XIII (1768); and in his intimacy with Manuel de Roda y Arrieta, the anti-Jesuit Spanish minister.

The Conclave of 1769. The conciliation of Portugal, nine years in virtual schism, and of the Bourbon courts of France, Spain, Naples, and Parma, who had demanded the suppression of the Jesuits at the end of the reign of Clement XIII, was the issue of this conclave, which convened on February 15. The 43 electors split into three parties: the *Zelanti,* pro-Jesuit and advocating a strong stand against the Powers; the Crown Cardinals, seeing the peace of the Church possible only through the sacrifice of the Jesuits; and the Indifferents or Undeclared. The requirements of strict secrecy and seclusion set down in the

bulls of Julius II (*Cum tam divino,* Jan. 14, 1505), Pius IV (*In eligendis,* Oct. 9, 1562), Gregory XV (*Aeterni Patris,* Nov. 15, 1621), and Clement XII (*Apostolatus officium,* Oct. 5, 1732) were transgressed. Cardinals François de BERNIS, Paul d'Albert Lynes, and Domenico Orsini d'Aragona were in open and frequent communication with the French ambassador Marquis d'Aubeterre and the Spanish ambassador Abp. Thomas Azpuru. They were instructed to use the *exclusiva* against all "unenlightened" candidates. In a list sent to the courts, the cardinals were divided into classes and judged as very good, good, bad, and very bad. Ganganelli, the only regular cleric in the conclave, was placed in the first class, and rated "good" (Spain), "very good" (Choiseul), and "there are letters which say he is a Jesuit" (Tanucci). In the conclave Ganganelli "trimmed his sails to the wind" on the question of the Jesuits. On one occasion he remarked that there should be no more thought of abolishing the Society of Jesus "than of overturning St. Peter's." Yet when asked his opinion on its possible suppression he said that if the precepts of Canon Law were observed, it was possible, perhaps profitable. The idea of a written or oral promise to suppress the society as a condition for election was proposed by D'Aubeterre and Azpuru, and again by the Spanish Cardinal Francisco de Solis when he arrived at the conclave (April 27), but it was rejected. The claim that Ganganelli made such a simoniacal bargain is unproved and held by no historian except Crétineau-Joly. When the crown candidate, Antonio Sersale, Archbishop of Naples, failed to win the support of the *Zelanti,* attention moved to Ganganelli, who was elected with only one opposing vote (his own, which was cast for Cardinal Carlo Rezzonico) on May 19. The Bourbons rejoiced; Charles III of Spain called the election a miracle worked by St. Francis and Ven. Juan de PALAFOX Y MENDOZA.

Peace by Concession. The inscription on the first medal struck by Clement, *Fiat pax in virtute tua,* revealed his eagerness to come to terms with secular powers. To the "exemplary Catholic Charles III," he wrote (Nov. 30, 1769) an acknowledgment of his indebtedness and devotion and promised that there would be "shortly a plan for the complete dissolution of the society." He also appointed the former nuncio to Madrid, Opizio Pallavicini, as his secretary of state, and reintroduced the process of beatification for Juan de Palafox. A settlement with Portugal came with the appointment (Nov. 26, 1769) of a nuncio, Innocenzo Conti, pleasing to the Marquis of POMBAL; a red hat for Pombal's brother, Paulo de Carvalho e Mendoza, who died (Jan. 17, 1770) three days before the announcement of this honor (Clement gave it to another of the minister's favorites, João Cosme da Cunha, Bishop of Evora); and the confirmation of eight of Pombal's episcopal nominations. The reading of the bull *In coena Domini* (so called because from 1364 it was published annually at Rome on Maundy Thursday, and cited reserved censures), which had been used by Clement XIII to announce the excommunication of duke Ferdinand of Parma (1768), was omitted in 1770, and dropped completely after 1774. He further pleased the duke by granting a dispensation for his marriage to his cousin Amelia, daughter of Empress Maria Theresa. In a letter to Louis XV, Clement promised that the Jesuit issue would be terminated "avec satisfaction reciproque" (October 1769).

Suppression of the Jesuits. Clement delayed decisive action regarding the Jesuits for four years. He met the formal petition for their extinction, made by the courts of Portugal, Spain, and France (July 22, 1769) with alternative proposals such as a complete reform of the society, or its gradual dissolution by allowing no election of a general after the death of Lorenzo Ricci, but he finally yielded before the unrelenting harassment of Cardinal de Bernis and José Moniño, who succeeded Azpuru as

Spanish ambassador (July 4, 1772). As preliminary steps, documents were gathered for a *motu proprio,* and a program to diminish the prestige of the Jesuits in Rome and the Papal States was begun. Bishops were advised to withhold their permission to preach or hear confessions; Jesuits were removed from their colleges in Frascati, Macerata, Modena, Bologna, Ferrara, Ravenna; a visitation of the Irish College and the Roman Seminary was entrusted to Cardinal Marefoschi, of the Jesuit houses in Bologna to Cardinal Malvezzi; Jesuit exiles from Portugal were deprived of the pensions granted by Clement XIII. On December 13, after renewed threats of schism and attempts to bribe his only confidant, the Conventual friar Bontempi, the pope appointed Francesco Saverio Zelada, titular bishop of Petra, to collaborate with Moniño in the preparation of the brief of suppression. The resulting document, *Dominus ac Redemptor,* was signed by Clement on June 9, 1773 (though dated July 21). Already more than half of the members of the society were exiled; this brief extinguished the remaining 11,000 Jesuits, 266 colleges, 103 seminaries, and 88 residences. On September 23, Ricci was imprisoned for questioning in the Castel Sant'Angelo, together with his assistants of Spain, Italy, Portugal, Germany, and Poland.

The Brief *Dominus ac Redemptor.* The reception of this brief was varied. Festivities were ordered in Lisbon, but there was disappointment in France and Spain that the document was not a solemn bull. Maria Theresa accepted it regretfully and allowed Jesuits to remain in their houses as secular priests; Frederick II of Prussia and Catherine II of Russia forbade its promulgation, thereby insuring the survival of the society. At the end of the pontificate of Clement XIII, the territories of Avignon and Venaissin had been taken by the French, and Pontecorvo and Benevento invaded by Naples; these were now returned to papal jurisdiction.

In the brief, Clement proclaims his duty in the interest of peace to sacrifice things most dear to himself. Just as past pontiffs had suppressed the Templars (1312), the Humiliati (1571), the Reformed Conventuals (1626), the Order of SS. Ambrose and Barnabas (1643), the Order of St. Basil of Armenia (1650), and the Jesuati (1668), so he had examined the Society of Jesus and found that at its birth seeds of strife and jealousy germinated within it, and against other orders, the secular clergy, and princes. Since it could no longer be fruitful or useful and hindered the peace of the Church, he, for the reasons given, and for others "reserved in our heart," dissolved, suppressed, extinguished, and abolished the said society. The members "whom We love with a paternal love" were thus free from the weight of oppression. Novices were to be released; scholastics were permitted to remain in their houses for a year, and being liberated from their vows might embrace a new state of life; priests might enter other religious orders or place themselves under the jurisdiction of a bishop. All appeals or attempts to defend the society were prohibited. It is to be noted that the brief does not condemn the constitutions of the order, nor any specified member, nor the orthodoxy of any Jesuit doctrine (*Bullarium Romanum Continuatio* 4:619–629). According to a letter of June 29, 1774, Clement retracted *Dominus ac Redemptor* and instructed his confessor to transmit it to the next pope (Pius VI). The letter is found in P. P. Wolf, *Allgemeine Geschichte der Jesuiten . . . ,* 4 v. (Zurich 1789–92) v. 3, but its authenticity remains disputed.

Other Affairs. During the long struggle over the Jesuit question, Clement received Marc Simeon, patriarch of the Nestorians, and six of his bishops into union with Rome (1771); condemned Abbé Jean Martin de Prades's abridgment of Claude Fleury's *Histoire ecclesiastique* (March 1, 1770), the philosophical works of Julien Offray de La Mettrie (Feb. 15, 1770), and some lesser works of Voltaire (Nov. 29, 1771); favored the Carmel of Saint-Denis after it received Louise of France (Thérèse de Saint Augustin), daughter of Louis XV (1770); and brought new hope for Catholic emancipation in England by abandoning the support of the exiled Stuarts and negotiating with William Henry, duke of Gloucester, brother of King George III, for the appointment of Giovanni Battista Caprara as papal nuncio (1772). He patronized the arts and letters by commissioning Raphael Mengs to decorate the Vatican Museum, by acquiring antiquities for the Museo Clementino, by increasing the papal coin collection, by encouraging literati, and by decorating the 14-year-old prodigy Mozart with the order of the Golden Spur (1770). Clement canonized no one, but he beatified Francesco Caracciolo (June 4, 1769) and Paolo Burali of Arezzo (May 13, 1772); he confirmed the cultus (not solemn beatification) of Antonio Primaldi and his 840 companions executed at the capture of Otranto by the Ottomans (1480), of Tommaso Bellaci (d. 1447), of Bonaventura of Potenza (d. 1711), of Giuliana Puricelli (of Busto Arsizio, d. 1501), of Bernhard von Baden (d. 1458), of Giovanni Scopelli (of Reggio Emelia, d. *c.* 1491), and of Giovanni Bottegoni (of Bastone, d. 1240); and he declared the heroicity of the virtues of the Oratorians Giovanni Battista Villani and Antonio Grassi, of John of St. William, of Charles of Sezze, and of Pedro de Betancur, founder of the Bethlehemites of Guatemala. Clement had a deep regard for St. Paul of the Cross and reconfirmed the rule of the Passionists in *Suprem apostolatus* (Nov. 15, 1769) and approved the rule of the Passionist nuns (Feb. 9, 1771).

The last year of Clement's life was one of depression, fear of assassination, and torment caused by a scorbutic skin ailment. After his death the rapid decomposition of the body, which required that the face be covered with a mask for the solemn exequies at St. Peter's, fortified rumors of poison. An autopsy by Clement's physicians, Natale Saliceti and Pasquale Adinolfi, indicated death from natural causes; more recent medical interpretations of their reports ascribe death to edema and possible gastric carcinoma.

Clement's policy of appeasement and his ambiguous behavior have brought a generally adverse judgment of his pontificate and little praise to himself. In Pastor's *Lives* (published posthumously) he is called "one of the weakest and most unhappy of the long line of popes, and yet one most deserving of sympathy, for though filled with the best intentions he failed in almost everything, being quite unfitted to deal with the extraordinarily difficult situation." During his pontificate the prestige of the papacy reached one of the lowest levels in centuries (38:550; for the debate over this volume, see bibliography).

Bibliography: *Bullarium Romanum Continuatio,* ed. A. BARÈRI et al. (Rome 1835–57) v.4. *Clementis XIV . . . epistolae et brevia selectiora . . . ,* ed. A. THEINER (Paris 1852). *Lettere interesanti del pontefice Clemente XIV Ganganelli,* ed. L. A. CARACCIOLI, 5 v. (Venice 1776–79), Fr. tr., 2 v. (Paris 1776), interpolated and untrustworthy; Eng. tr., 2 v. (London 1777). *Lettere, bolle e discorsi di Ganganelli,* ed. C. FREDIANI (Florence 1845). G. C. CORDARA, *De suis ac suorum rebus . . . usque ad occasum Societatis Jesu commentarii . . . ,* ed. G. ALBERTOTTI and A. FAGGIOTTO (*Miscellanea di storia italiana,* ser. 3, v. 22; Turin 1933); *De suppressione Societatis Jesu commentarii,* ed. G. ALBERTOTTI (Padua 1925), extracts and comments in J. J. I. VON DÖLLINGER, *Beiträge zur politischen, kirchlichen und Kultur-Geschichte der 6 letzten Jahrhunderte,* 3 v. (Regensburg 1862–82) 3:1–74. J. CRÉTINEAU-JOLY, *Clément XIV et les Jésuites* (Paris 1847); *Le Pape Clément XIV: Lettre au Père Augustin Theiner* (Paris 1853). A. THEINER, *Geschichte des Pontificats Clemens XIV,* 2 v. (Leipzig-Paris 1853), favorable to Clement. I. DE RÉCALDE, *Le Bref "Dominus ac Redemptor"* (Paris 1920), hostile to Jesuits. F. MASSON, *Le Cardinal de Bernis depuis son ministère, 1758–1794* (Paris 1884). S. F. SMITH, "The Suppression of the Society of Jesus," *Month* 100 (1902) 517–536, 581–591; 101 (1903) 48–61, 179–197, 259–277, 383–403, 498–516, 604–623; 102 (1903) 46–63, 170–184. F. BERTOLINI, *Clemente XIV e la soppressione dei gesuiti* (Rome 1886). A. GALLASSI, "La malattia e morte di Clemente XIV," *Revista di storia delle scienze* 48 (1950) 153–165. L. GUALINO, *Storia medica dei romani pontefici* (Turin 1934) 69–97, 109–113. A. VON REUMONT, *Ganganelli, Papst Clement XIV, seine Briefe und seine Zeit* (Berlin 1847). P. DUDON, "De la suppression de la Compagnie de Jésus, 1758–1773," *Revue des questions historiques* 132 (Paris 1938) 75–107. L. PASTOR, *The History of the Popes from the Close of the Middle Ages* (London–St. Louis 1938–61) v. 38. For dispute between the Conventual Franciscans and the Jesuits over the documents used by Pastor, see L. CICCHITTO, "Il Pontefice Clemente XIV . . . della *Storia dei Papi di L. von Pastor,*" *Miscellanea Francescana* 34 (1934) 198–231. G. KRATZ and P. LETURIA, *Intorno al "Clemente XIV" del Barone von Pastor* (Rome 1935). E. PRÉCLIN, *Dictionnaire d'histoire et de géographie ecclésiastiques,* ed. A. BAUDRILLAT et al. (Paris 1912–) 12:1411–23. H. RAAB, *Lexikon* *für Theologie und Kirche,* ed. J. HOFER and K. RAHNER, 10 v. (2d, new ed. Freiburg 1957–65) 2:1229–30. R. CHALUMEAU, *Catholicisme* 2:1199–1200. L. KOCH, *Jesuiten-Lexikon: Die Gesellschaft Jesu einst und jetzt* (Paderborn 1934) 994–996. S. SOLERO, A. MERCATI and A. PELZER, *Dizionario ecclesiastico,* 3 v. (Turin 1954–58) 1:649–650. J. DE LA SERVIÈRE, *Dictionnaire de théologie catholique,* ed. A. VACANT et al., 15 v. (Paris 1903–50; Tables générales 1951–) 3.1:124–134. O. CHADWICK, *The Popes and the European Revolution* (Cambridge 1981). A. D. WRIGHT, *The Early Modern Papacy: From the Council of Trent to the French Revolution, 1564–1789* (London 2000). M. CARAVALE and A. CARACCIOLO, *Lo stato pontificio de Martino V a Pio IX* (Turin 1978).

[E. D. MCSHANE]

CLEMENT OF ALEXANDRIA

Titus Flavius Clemens, 3d-century Father of the Church, after ORIGEN, the principal representative of the early theological School of ALEXANDRIA.

Life. Of the two traditions for Clement's birthplace extant in Epiphanius's time, modern authors prefer Athens, even though Clement spent most of his life in Alexandria. Clement, a convert to Christianity, traveled extensively to seek instruction from famous Christian teachers, until he came to Egypt. There he attached himself to one whom Eusebius (*Hist. eccl.* 5.11.2) assumed to be PANTAENUS, the earliest of the Alexandrian teachers known to us and one of Origen's masters.

Eusebius (*Hist. eccl.* 6.6) asserts that Clement succeeded Pantaenus as head of the catechetical School of Alexandria and places Origen among Clement's disciples. But modern historians offer serious objections to these assertions. As J. Munck observes, the Christian instruction given by Clement probably never had an official character, but remained a private enterprise, in keeping with the pedagogic practice of other philosophers in those days. Such institutions ended when their founders ceased teaching. The fact that Origen never cites Clement in his writings is a reason for doubting that he had studied under Clement, despite their obvious intellectual affinity.

Clement's activities in Alexandria were interrupted by the persecution of Septimius Severus in 202 or 203, and he left Egypt apparently never to return. About 211 Alexander, Bishop of Cappadocia, sent a priest named Clement with a letter to the Church of Antioch: "I am sending you, my lords and brothers, this letter through the intermediary of Clement, the blessed priest, an esteemed and virtuous man whom you already know. His presence here, through the providence and vigilance of the Master, has strengthened and enhanced the Church of the Lord" (Eusebius, *Hist. eccl.* 6.11.6). It is possible that this refers to Clement of Alexandria, for Bishop Alexander was his friend and admirer, and Clement had dedicated one of his

Clement of Alexandria, 12th-century Byzantine fresco painting. (© Archivo Iconografico, S.A./CORBIS)

works to him (*Hist. eccl.* 6.13.3). In a letter addressed to Origen in 215 or 216, the same Alexander, having meanwhile become bishop of Jerusalem, mentions some deceased teachers, including Pantaenus and "holy Clement who has been my master and has helped me," thus giving rise to the conjecture that Clement had taken refuge in Cappadocia and that he was dead by the time Alexander wrote to Origen.

Eusebius is apparently relying on the letter from Alexander to the Church at Antioch when he designates Clement as a priest in his *Chronicle,* but a passage in the *Paedagogus* (1.6.37) often cited to prove Clement's priesthood can no longer be advanced after O. Stählin's textual correction.

Writings. Clement was a cultured Greek philosopher and scholar, though his erudition was often secondhand; a Christian apologist and exegete; a theologian and mystic. His open mind and enthusiasm are reflected in a varied literary output, original and daring in content, refined and elegant in style. The absence of method and synthesis in his work was often calculated, but it disconcerts the modern reader.

Protrepticus, following the meaning of the word, is an "exhortation" to conversion and an apology for

Christianity, addressed to pagans. The work reveals close links with the earlier Christian apologetic, whose terms and types of argument Clement uses, but with a personal touch and uncommon warmth. Clement criticizes Greek religion (he supplies valuable details on the "mysteries") and Greek philosophical doctrines about God (ch. 2–5). He maintains that the best philosophers and poets of old had caught glimpses of the truth (ch. 6–7); but this truth is revealed through the Hebrew prophets and above all by the Logos, who calls men to faith and conversion, and whose role in the world Clement extols in remarkable language (ch. 8–12).

Paedagogus, a sequel to the *Protrepticus,* is addressed to the baptized. Clement portrays Christ the Educator as He trains the Christian in a moral way of life. Book 1 presents the pedagogy of the Word and introduces the reader to a thoroughly evangelical spirituality that stamps the ethics of Clement with a truly Christian character. Books 2 and 3 form a treatise on practical morality and describe in detail the Christians' daily life, mixing together moral precepts and rules of decency and hygiene. This combination of Christian casuistry and etiquette parallels Stoic literature and employs long excerpts borrowed from Musonius, the teacher of EPICTETUS. The Stoic influence gives a highly rational character to Clement's presentation of morality: man must follow "nature" or "reason" (*logos*), which for Clement meant at the same time following the divine Logos.

After the "exhortation" to conversion and moral "pedagogy" at the outset of the *Paedagogus,* Clement calls attention to a third stage in the action of the Logos: doctrinal instruction. Historians debate whether Clement had contemplated a trilogy that would add a dogmatic work to the *Protrepticus* and *Paedagogus* and whether the *Stromata* should be considered an imperfect attempt in this direction.

Stromata (tapestries—a term used for a work of very free composition comparable to an anthology or miscellany), in eight books, is the most important of Clement's extant writings, and is a veritable mine of ideas, but it defies analysis. The absence of a plan and the deliberate obscurity of style make for difficult reading. Certain principal themes dominate the whole: the relations between Christianity and hellenism, and between faith and philosophy; the elaboration of a Christian gnosis to confront the "false gnosis"; and the search for ways to know God and achieve union with Him. The only definite chronological indication is that Book 1 was written after the death of the Emperor Commodus in 192 (cf. *Strom.* 1.21.139–147).

Quis dives salvetur? (What rich man will be saved?), a homily, is a delicately expressive commentary on Mk 10.17–31. *Eclogae Propheticae,* exegetical notes, and the *Excerpta ex Theodoto,* annotated extracts from Gnostic writings, are collections of materials assembled by Clement in preparation for further work. Of other writings only fragments survive, especially in the case of the *Hypotyposes,* a long exegetical work on the Old and New Testaments.

Doctrine. In his *Stromata* Clement deals extensively with the problem of the relation of Christianity to Greek culture and philosophy. In Christian thought he opened an optimistic and liberal approach to secular knowledge, laying the foundations for a Christian humanism and introducing philosophy to its role as "the servant of theology." He considered Plato the best of philosophers (1.42.1); but far from being a confirmed Platonist, Clement exemplifies the eclecticism of his time. If Platonism serves to clarify his conception of man's union with God, it is Stoicism that permeates his ethic. He admits that by philosophy he means "what each of the different schools has said that is good" (1.37.6). As such, philosophy is a gift of God (1.37.1); it is partial but nonetheless real truth (6.83.2). It forms a propaedeutic to faith for the unbeliever (1.28.1; 7.20.2; cf. 1.28.3), a useful exercise for the believer (1.20.2), and a necessary aid to a deeper scientific penetration of the faith (1.35.2). Still, faith can spring up in a soul and lead it to salvation without philosophy (*ibid.* 2 and 4).

Clement affirms the autonomy and transcendence of faith and Christian truth. On occasion he goes back to the less fortunate themes of the older Christian apologetic, which claimed that the truths known by the pagan philosophers had been "stolen" by lesser angels or borrowed from the Bible, and thus he insists on the "barbarian" origin of Greek philosophy (1.66–1.81; 148).

The influence of Greek philosophy contributed greatly to the intellectualist tendency of Clement's ethic and spirituality, and to his desire to fashion an authentically Christian gnosis. Knowledge and contemplation are in the foreground of the spiritual life: the perfect Christian is a gnostic. But Clement dissociates himself sharply from unorthodox GNOSTICISM. Every Christian is, in a real sense, perfect from the moment of his Baptism (*Paed.* 1.25–31). Gnosis is not in conflict with faith, but is faith's perfection and flowering: "Gnosis is faithful, and faith is gnostic" (*Strom.* 2.16.2; cf. 5.1.3). "Faith, to all intents and purposes, is a condensed gnosis of essential truths, but gnosis is the strong and solid demonstration of the truths accepted by faith . . . leading to an unshakable certainty and a scientific understanding" (*ibid.* 7.57.3). In opposition to the Gnostics, and while clearly underlining the role and necessity of grace (*ibid.* 2.5.4–5; 3.57.2), Clement insists that free choice is a condition of salvation (*ibid.* 2.115.2). Likewise the Platonic dualism that crops up sometimes in his spirituality does not prevent him from defending the essential goodness of the body, worldly goods, and marriage.

On the other hand, Clement draws closer to the Gnostics when he introduces into the Christian gnosis the knowledge of revelations secretly transmitted from the time of the Apostles or hidden in Scripture under symbols discoverable only by an allegorizing exegesis whose method he derives from PHILO JUDAEUS. This esotericism sometimes leads the author of the *Stromata* to place the favored Christian who is a gnostic in opposition to a mere believer.

Völker, however, has clearly shown that Clement's gnosis is as much an ethic as an intellectual quest. It leads to the ἀπάθεια, apathy (*Strom.* 6.71–79) and the ἀγάπη or love (*ibid.* 7.57.4) that assimilate and unite the soul to God. By thus sketching the states of mystical ascent and by orienting his spiritual doctrine toward contemplation, Clement, together with Philo and Origen, exercised a profound influence on the whole of Greco-Christian spirituality.

Clement's contribution to speculative theology is of minor importance; at times it is unfortunate, as when he seems to favor a kind of DOCETISM. Only occasionally in his theology does he mention the place of the Church (*Strom.* 7.89; 7.107), Baptism (*Paed.* 1.26), and the Eucharist (*ibid.* 42–43) in the process of salvation. But he witnesses to what might be termed a pastoral approach to theology in the third century that was actual and effective. He depicts the life of the intelligent Christian family in its ascent toward union with God. For this reason, too, his contribution to the development of Christian thought is far from negligible.

Bibliography: J. QUASTEN, *Patrology* (Westminster, Md.) 2:5–36. J. MUNCK, *Untersuchungen über Klemens von Alexandria* (Stuttgart 1933). M. SPANNEUT, *Le Stoïcisme des Pères de l'Église* (Paris 1957). E. F. OSBORN, *The Philosophy of Clement of Alexandria* (Cambridge, Eng. 1957). F. QUATEMBER, *Die christliche Lebenshaltung des Klemens von Alexandrien nach seinem Paedogogus* (Vienna 1945). C. MONDÉSERT, *Clément d'Alexandrie: Introduction à l'étude de sa pensée religieuse à partir de l'Écriture* (Paris 1944). P. T. CAMELOT, *Foi et Gnose: Introduction à l'étude de la connaissance mystique chez Clément d'Alexandrie* (Paris, 1945). W. VÖLKER, *Der wahre Gnostiker nach Clemens Alexandrinus* (Texte und Untersuchungen zur Geschichte der altchristlichen Literatur 57; 1952), with important bibliog.

[M. SPANNEUT]

CLEMENT OF IRELAND, ST.

Irish grammarian and master of the palace school under CHARLEMAGNE and Louis I the Pious; b. Ireland,

mid-eighth century; d. on the Continent, after 828. He was probably at the Carolingian court before 796 when ALCUIN became abbot of Saint-Martin's, Tours, and Clement succeeded him as head of the PALACE SCHOOL. Irish influence on the studies there was attacked by THEODULF OF ORLÉANS, ALCUIN, and EINHARD, but Clement retained his position at least until 826, when he was present at court at the baptism of the Danish King Harold. Modestus of Fulda and the future emperor, LOTHAIR I, were among Clement's pupils. An entry in a WÜRZBURG necrology—*IV Kal. Junii Clementis Magistri Palatini*—suggests that he may have died there on pilgrimage to the tomb of St. KILIAN OF WÜRZBURG. Clement wrote (*c.* 817–20) an *Ars grammatica,* dedicated to Lothair, which is valuable for its extensive quotations from earlier authors. It contains three parts: *De philosophia* (the grammatical part proper), *De metris,* and *De barbarismo;* the entire text was first published in *Philologus* (Supplementband 20; 1928).

Feast: Mar. 20.

Bibliography: M. CAPPUYNS, *Dictionnaire d'histoire et de géographie ecclésiastiques,* ed. A. BAUDRILLART et al. (Paris 1912) 12:1430.

[T. Ó FIAICH]

CLEMENT THE BULGARIAN, ST.

Also known as Clement of Ochrida (Kliment Ohridski), bishop of Velitsa (probably near Ochrida, Yugoslavia); b. Macedonia; d. Ochrida, July 27, 916. He was a pupil of SS. CYRIL AND METHODIUS, whom he accompanied on their mission to Moravia. Expelled from Moravia under the pressure of the German bishops after Methodius's death in 885, he found refuge, along with many colleagues, among the Bulgars. He was sent to Devol in western Bulgaria (now Albania), where he established a mission and school, and in 893 or 894 he was consecrated bishop of Velitsa. He is buried in the monastery of St. Panteleimon at Ochrida, which he founded. He also founded three churches, which still survive. Clement was one of the fathers of Slavonic literature; his works include liturgical texts translated from the Greek, homilies and lives of saints, and probably the surviving *Life and Encomium of St. Cyril.* Not all are yet published.

Feast: July 17 (West); July 27 (Eastern Church).

Bibliography: THEOPHYLACT OF OCHRID, *Vita* in *Patrologia Graeca,* ed. J. P. MIGNE (Paris 1858–66) 126:1194–1240. L. N. TUNNICKIJ, *Monumenta ad SS. Cyrilli et Methodii successorum vitas resque gestas pertinentia* I (Zagorsk 1918, rep. London 1972); *Svjatoj Kliment episkop Slověnskij* (Zagorsk 1913), rep. as *Der hl. Clemens* (Munich 1970). I. SNEGAROV, *Bŭlgarskijat pŭrvoučitel ' Sv. Kliment Okhridski* (Sofia 1927). V. VELINOVA, *Kliment Okhridski:*

uchiteliat i tvoretsut (Sofiia 1995). V. STEFANIC, *Dictionnaire d'histoire et de géographie ecclésiastiques*, ed. A. BAUDRILLART et al. (Paris 1912) 12:1086–87. A. MILEV, *Teofilakt Ohridski, Žitie na Kliment Ohridski* (Sofia 1955) 33–88. F. DVORNIK, *Les Slaves, Byzance et Rome au IXᵉ siècle* (Paris 1926). F. GRIVEC, *Konstantin und Method: Lehrer der Slaven* (Wiesbaden 1960).

[R. BROWNING]

CLEMENTINAE

The accepted title of the authentic collection of legislation of Pope Clement V (1305–14) and of the Council of Vienne (1311–12), which was promulgated by John XXII in 1317. In the troubled period after the deaths of Boniface VIII (1303) and Benedict XI (1304), Clement had issued a number of important decretals, some of which were presented for approval at the last session of Vienne (May 6, 1312). This collection was enlarged afterward by the inclusion of the legislation of the Council and of at least two later constitutions of Clement (*Romani principes* and *Pastoralis cura,* both after Aug. 24, 1313); it was published, possibly as Liber Septimus, at a consistory in Monteux (Carpentras, southern France) on March 21, 1314. Promulgation in the usual manner (i.e., by sending copies to certain universities, principally Bologna) was interrupted by Clement's death on April 20, although the bull of promulgation, *Cum nuper,* had been drawn up, if not sent out. It was left to John XXII, his successor after a three-year vacancy, to complete the formal procedure of promulgation on Oct. 25, 1317.

John in his bull does not use the title Liber Septimus; indeed, the great decretalist JOANNES ANDREAE, when writing in 1326 what was to become the *GLOSSA ORDINARIA,* refused the title to the work on the grounds that a proper Liber Septimus should include all decretals appearing after the LIBER SEXTUS of 1298: he preferred *Constitutiones Clementis V* or *Clementinae.* With the exception of one decretal of Boniface VIII (*Super cathedram*), which had been abrogated by Benedict XI and restored by Vienne (*Corpus iuris canonici clementinae* 3.7.2), and of one of Urban IV also reinstated at Vienne (*Corpus iuris canonici clementinae* 3.16), all the legislation in the *Clementinae* appears as *Clemens V in concilio Viennensi* in most manuscripts. How much is Clementine in origin, as distinct from conciliar, is not at all clear; just as Clement's legislation previous to the Council certainly was approved there, so also he may have had a mandate to issue other constitutions afterward as though they were issued from the Council.

Unlike the Decretals of GREGORY IX and the Liber Sextus, the *Clementinae* were not exclusive, and did not abrogate all other legislation between 1298 (Sext) and 1317. Divided along the lines of the Decretals and Sext into five books, 52 titles, and 106 chapters, they are cited accordingly, thus: *Corpus iuris canonici clementinae* 3.7.2. Commentaries appeared as early as 1319 with the *apparatus* of William of Mont Lauzun, followed by an *apparatus* of Gesselin de Cassanges (1323) and glosses by Joannes Andreae (1326), etc. There are a number of printed editions of the Clementines, notably that in the official *CORPUS IURIS CANONICI* of 1582; the latter is repeated, with critical notes, in the edition of A. Friedberg (Leipzig 1881).

Bibliography: F. EHRLE, "Aus den Acten des Vienner Concils," H. DENIFLE and F. EHRLE, eds., *Archiv für Literatur-und Kirchengeschichte des Mittelalters,* 7 v. (Freiburg 1888) 4: 439–464. G. MOLLAT, *Dictionnaire de droit canonique,* ed. R. NAZ, 7 v. (Paris 1935–65) 4:635–640. E. MÜLLER, *Das Konzil von Vienne, 1311–1312* (Münster 1934) 396–408, 671–706. J. F. VON SCHULTE, *Die Geschichte der Quellen und der Literatur des kanonischen Rechts,* 3 v. in 4 pts. (Stuttgart 1875–80; repr. Graz 1956) 2:45–50. A. M. STICKLER, *Historia iuris canonici latini: v.1, Historica fontium* (Turin 1950) 264–268.

[L. E. BOYLE]

CLENOCK, MAURICE (CLYNNOG)

First rector of the English College, Rome; b. Caernarvonshire, Wales, *c.* 1525; drowned at sea, 1580 or 1581. He earned the D.D. and B.C.L. degrees at Oxford, where he lectured in civil law. Later he was almoner and secretary to Cardinal Reginald Pole, and chancellor of the prerogative court at Canterbury. He was nominated to the See of Bangor in 1558, but the death of Mary Tudor prevented his consecration. He retired in exile to Louvain, where he studied theology and advocated the restoration of English Catholicism by foreign military intervention. At Milan in 1558 he published a book of Christian doctrine in Welsh titled *Athravaeth Gristnogavl.* In 1565 and from 1576 to 1577 he was warden of the hospice for exiled English dons in Rome and was closely concerned with the negotiations that transformed it into a seminary. He became its first rector but was dismissed in 1579 through the appeals of the English students to the pope, who alleged his partiality for Welshmen. The seminary was then entrusted to the Society of Jesus.

Bibliography: *Dictionary of Welsh Biography* (London 1959) 78–80. J. GILLOW, *A Literary and Biographical History or Bibliographical Dictionary of the English Catholics from 1534 to the Present Time* (London-New York 1885–1902; repr. New York 1961) 1:501–505.

[J. M. CLEARY]

CLEOPAS

One of the two disciples to whom Christ appeared on the road to EMMAUS after His Resurrection (Lk 24.18). Except for his part in the account of the Resurrection appearance found in Lk 24.13–35, nothing is known with certainty of this disciple, for the name does not recur in the New Testament. However, the Greek name Cleopas (Κλεοπᾶς, a shortened form of Κλεόπατρος) may have been used as a substitute for Clopas (Κλωπᾶς), probably an Aramaic name of uncertain meaning (cf. the *qlwp'* found at PALMYRA). If the equivalence of the two names is accepted, the way is opened for the identification of the Cleopas named by St. Luke with the Clopas who was the husband (or possibly, though less likely, the father) of one of the Marys present at the Crucifixion in St. John's account (19.25), although there is no positive basis for such identification. If the enumeration "his [Jesus'] mother and his mother' sister, Mary of Clopas [Μαρία ἡ τοῦ Κλωπᾶ], and Mary Magdalene" (Jn 19.25) is to be taken as identifying Mary of Clopas with "his mother's sister," Clopas and Mary, his wife, would be related to Jesus and Mary. Such an identification is possible only if "sister" is taken in the broad Semitic sense of a female relative; otherwise it would entail the unlikely supposition of two sisters named Mary. Tradition has sometimes identified Clopas with Alphaeus, the father of James (Mt 10.3; Mk 3.18; Lk 6.15; Acts 1.13), but there is no sure basis for this. *See* JAMES (SON OF ALPHAEUS), ST.

Bibliography: *Encyclopedic Dictionary of the Bible*, tr. and adap. by L. HARTMAN (New York 1963) 395. E. JACQUIER, *Dictionnaire de la Bible*, ed. F. VIGOUROUX (Paris 1895–1912) 1.1:418–419. F. PRAT, *Jesus Christ: His Life, His Teaching, and His Work*, tr. J. J. HEENAN, 2 v. (Milwaukee 1950) 1:132–138, 500–510.

[J. A. LEFRANÇOIS]

CLERICAL DRESS (CANON LAW)

For the first three centuries of the Christian era clerics used no special dress when engaged in divine services. About the beginning of the 4th century, a distinction began to be made between the everyday wear of the clergy and the vestments used by them in sacred functions. SS. Athanasius (295–373), Jerome (*c.* 342–420), and John Chrysostom (*c.* 345–407), among others, made mention in their writings of special garb to be used by clerics in the performance of liturgical actions. This is especially true with reference to the orarion, or primitive stole. Councils of the same and succeeding periods, e.g., the Council of Laodicea, 343 to 381, referred quite often to a special clerical vesture for use in sacred functions.

History. Special clerical dress for use outside the sanctuary did not exist much before the 6th century. The garb worn by clerics was the old Roman dress, i.e., a tunic without sleeves (*collobium*) and a long white coat with sleeves (*dalmatica* or *tunica manicata et talaris*). For several centuries there was no other evident distinction observed between the ordinary apparel of the cleric and the laity save that inherent in the fact that the former was more constrained to wear that which was more modest and grave, and becoming his state in life. It seems that the use of a specific clerical dress in daily wear came about as a result of the fact that the clergy gradually came to be composed chiefly of philosophers and ascetics, men who all along had worn a distinctive garb, the PALLIUM. Prior to the early 6th century various members of the clergy had tried without success to introduce the pallium as a specific garb for clerics in place of the birrus, the common tunic worn by members of the secular clergy and by Christians generally.

Even as to the color of the garb, centuries passed before any definite regulations were laid down. The Council of Trent (1545–63) required merely that "clerics always wear a dress conformable to their order, that by the propriety of their outward apparel they may show forth the inward uprightness of their morals" (sess. 14, *de ref.,* c.6). Nothing was mentioned about the color. Reliable authors state that black has been the color of the cleric's garb only since the 17th century. In the Eastern Catholic Churches, the subrhason (cassock) may be of any color; the rhason, worn over it in public, must be black. Pope Sixtus V (1585–90) called the dress demanded by the Council of Trent the *vestis talaris* or CASSOCK. From his time onward clerics were obliged to wear the cassock at all times as their distinctive dress. By approved custom, however, the interpretation prevailed that what was prescribed by Pope Sixtus was the wearing of the cassock at least for sacred and public functions.

Norms and Practice in the U.S. In the U.S., the Third Plenary Council of Baltimore (1884) decreed that clerics were to wear the Roman collar and cassock at home and in the church, while outside the rectory they were to wear the Roman collar together with a coat of black or somber color, the length of which reached the knees. A contrary custom evolved regarding coat length, and the suit-coat, ending between the waist and the knees became the usual street attire of clerics. This prescription was never revoked, and was normative for the Church in the United States both from the time of the promulgation of the 1917 Code of Canon Law (CIC 17) and throughout the time extending up until the promulgation of the 1983 Code of Canon Law.

Although the issue of clerical dress was not raised directly in any of the conciliar documents, it was discussed particularly during the preparation of the decree,

Presbyterorum Ordinis. Despite the fact that the 1917 Code remained operative, there was a gradual relaxation in practice that seemed to be acknowledged by the 1983 Code when it states: "Clerics are to wear suitable ecclesiastical garb in accord with the norms issued by the conference of bishops and in accord with legitimate local customs" (c. 284). This canon, general in its scope, called for adaptation by countries and dioceses.

Complementary legislation to canon 284 was promulgated on one November 1999 by the National Conference of Catholic Bishops: "The National Conference of Catholic Bishops, in accord with the prescriptions of can. 284, hereby decrees that without prejudice to the provisions of can. 288, clerics are to dress in conformity with their sacred calling. In liturgical rites, clerics shall wear the vesture prescribed in the proper liturgical books. Outside liturgical functions, a black suit and Roman collar are the usual attire for priests. The use of the cassock is at the discretion of the cleric. In the case of religious clerics, the determinations of their proper institutes or societies are to be observed with regard to wearing the religious habit." Canon 288 exempted permanent deacons from wearing distinctive clerical street dress. However, all clerics are free to wear the cassock at their discretion; those of religious institutes or societies are free to wear distinctive habits according to their proper law and customs. With canon 284 and the U. S. complementary legislation as a guide, diocesan bishops are free to issue particular legislation according to local circumstances and conditions.

Bibliography: J. BINGHAM, *The Antiquities of the Christian Church,* 2 v. (London 1856). H. J. MCCLOUD, *Clerical Dress and Insignia of the Roman Catholic Church* (Milwaukee 1948). B. GANTER, *Clerical Attire* (Catholic University of America Canon Law Studies 361; Washington, DC 1955). J. CODY, *Clerical Dress of Priests* (Catholic University of America Canon Law Studies; Washington, DC 2001).

[J. A. SHIELDS/J. CODY]

CLERICALISM

Since the Middle Ages the adjective clerical has designated that which relates to clerics and the clergy. In the 19th century the French and Italians created a noun out of the term and imparted to it a new meaning whereby clerical signified a Catholic, cleric or lay, who with more or less success defended the rights of the Church, particularly those of the pope as temporal sovereign. Enemies of the Church and defenders of Italian unity attributed to these clericals a system, which *c.* 1865 they labelled clericalism. The aim of this system, it was claimed, was to make civil governments on the national and local levels submit to the desires of popes, bishops, and priests. English journalists adopted the neologism *c.* 1883; but anti-Roman polemics had previously enriched its vocabulary with terms almost synonymous, such as priestdom, priestcraft, priestridden, monkish, and popery. Subsequent decades enlarged the connotations of clericalism, so that it served to designate every excessive intervention of a religion in public affairs, or every attempt at domination over a state by a religion. Attention will be confined here to the clericalism attributed wrongly or rightly to the Church by anticlericals and by Catholics themselves.

For anticlericals, clericalism has proved a useful word for polemical purposes. Under the pretext of remedying an abuse, anticlericals have often attacked the Church. One phrase has become famous: "Le cléricalisme, voilà l'ennemi!" ("Clericalism! That is the enemy."). Léon Gambetta, who coined it (May 4, 1877), claimed to be citing his friend Peyrat. Peyrat did not, however, use precisely these words, but: "Le catholicisme, c'est là l'ennemi!" [L. Capéran, *Histoire contemporaine de la laïcité française* 3 v. (Paris 1957) 1:60, 63]. In the Chamber of Deputies in 1901 René Viviani denied that there could be a difference between the most sincere Catholic and the clerical. Politicians pretended that they wanted to single out not good pastors or their flocks but JESUITS, the CONGREGATION, the Vatican (understood as a foreign power), and international religious congregations accumulating properties in mortmain.

Catholics, on the other hand, were not astonished that the Church was the object of persecution. The success of a persecution utilizing such an equivocal notion did, however, move Catholics to a self-examination. In their reaction against an invasion of laicism they questioned whether or not the successors of Gregory VII had gone too far; whether the revocation of the Edict of NANTES (1685), so widely acclaimed by the French hierarchy, had not been an injustice; whether in defense of its immunities a well-protected clergy had not cloaked its egotism; whether many clerics were not dreaming about a new Constantine who would facilitate their ministerial work; whether the French clergy had not been too complaisant toward NAPOLEON III, who was so adroit in making use of them; whether it was important religiously to prefer a monarchical to a republican regime; and whether pastors did not display too pronounced a tendency to act like "parish captains." In brief, clericalism has existed in the past and continues to exist. Even if it disappears, the tendency expressed by it will very likely endure.

See Also: ANTICLERICALISM; LAICISM.

Bibliography: J. LECLER, *The Two Sovereignties* (New York 1952), tr. from Fr.; *Catholicisme* 2:1235–39. F. MÉJAN, *La Laïcité* *de l'État* (Paris 1956). C. A. WHITTUCK, *Encyclopedia of Religion and Ethics,* ed. J. HASTINGS, 13 v. (Edinburgh 1908–27) 3:689–693.

[C. BERTHELOT DU CHESNAY]

CLERICIS LAICOS

Constitution of BONIFACE VIII (Feb. 24, 1296), whereby, under sentence of excommunication reserved to the Apostolic See, ecclesiastics were forbidden to pay taxes, under any pretext, to lay rulers without express leave of the pope, and whereby lay authorities were enjoined from imposing and receiving such taxes and from seizing goods deposited in churches. The constitution, defended by Boniface as a reaffirmation of existing canons (*Corpus iuris canonici* X 3.49.4, 7), with the addition of penalties against transgressors, was the result of clerical complaints, in particular from the lower clergy of England, against the financial exactions of Edward I and Philip IV the Fair. Its promulgation caused serious problems between Boniface and Philip and strained relations between the English clergy, especially Abp. ROBERT OF WINCHELSEA and Edward. Ultimately the constitution was a failure. Benedict XI modified it; Clement V revoked it.

Bibliography: G. DIGARD et al., eds., *Les Registres de Boniface VIII,* 4 v. (Paris 1884–1939) 1:584–585, No. 1567. T. S. R. BOASE, *Boniface VIII* (London 1933). L. SANTIFALLER, "Zur Original-Überlieferung der Bulle Papst Bonifaz VIII. 'Clericis Laicos' von 1296 Februar 25," *Studia Gratiana* 11 (1967) 69–90. E. J. SMYTH, "*Clericis Laicos* and the Lower Clergy in England," in G. G. STECKLER and D. L. DAVIS, eds., *Studies in Mediaevalia and Americana: Essays in Honor of William Lyle Davis, SJ* (Spokane 1973) 77–87. T. M. IZBICKI, "*Clerici Laicos* and the Canonists," in JAMES R. SWEENEY and STANLEY CHODOROW, eds., *Popes, Teachers and Canon Law in the Middle Ages* (Ithaca, NY 1989) 179–90.

[E. J. SMYTH]

CLERK, JOHN

Henrician bishop of Bath and Wells; b. place and date unknown; d. St. Botolph's, Aldgate, Jan. 3, 1541. He took his B.A. at Cambridge in 1499 and his M.A. in 1502. He later took a doctor's degree in law at Bologna. He received rapid preferment and in 1519 became archdeacon of Colchester, then dean of Windsor, a judge in Star Chamber, Thomas Wolsey's chaplain, and dean of the king's chapel. In 1521 he was sent as ambassador to Rome and presented Henry VIII's *The Defense of the Seven Sacraments,* prefaced by an "Oratio" of his own, to Leo X. On Leo's death Clerk was employed to further Wolsey's aspirations to the papal throne, but he could not get enough support. He was unsuccessful again two years later on the death of Adrian VI. In 1523 Clerk was nominated bishop of Bath and Wells. Three years later he was sent to France to attempt to negotiate a marriage between Francis I and Princess Mary Tudor. The following year he was in Rome, and in 1529 he was a counselor for Queen Catherine in the divorce proceedings. His last task was that of appeasing the Duke of Cleves after Henry's farcical marriage with the Duke's daughter, Anne. On his return trip he fell sick at Dunkirk and died a few months later in England.

Bibliography: W. HUNT, *The Dictionary of National Biography from the Earliest Times to 1900* (London 1885–1900; repr. with corrections, 1908–09, 1921–22, 1938) 4:495–496. S. H. CASSAN, *Lives of the Bishops of Bath and Wells,* 2 v. (London 1829). P. HUGHES, *The Reformation in England* (5th, rev. ed. New York 1963).

[M. M. CURTIS]

CLERKS REGULAR OF THE MOTHER OF GOD

Clerks Regular of the Mother of God is a religious order, also known as *Ordo Clericorum Regularium Matris Dei* (CRMD, OMD), whose members are known also as Religious of the Mother of God, or Leonardini. It was founded by St. John LEONARDI in the church of the Madonna of the Rose, Lucca, Italy, Sept. 1, 1573, to combat Protestantism and to promote the Counter Reformation as advocated by the Council of Trent. In accordance with the founder's wish, members have charge of parishes, preach, teach Christian doctrine to youths, direct Catholic organizations, promote devotion to the Eucharist and to the Blessed Virgin, and perform a variety of other pastoral works. Members were called Reformed Priests of the Blessed Virgin until 1580, when the founder transferred their headquarters to the church of S. Maria Corteorlandini. When Bp. Alessandro Guidiccioni approved the institute canonically (1583), it took the name Congregation of Secular Clerics of the Blessed Virgin. Clement VIII gave it papal approbation in 1595.

Despite opposition from Protestants and from the leaders of the Republic of Lucca, who claimed to detect in the new organization religious and political dangers to the state, the congregation survived and prospered. In 1601 St. John Leonardi established in Rome the convent of S. Maria in Portico (now Campitelli). The first general chapter there (1603) elected Leonardi superior general for life, and approved the constitution elaborated by him during the preceding three decades. Clement VIII approved this constitution in 1604. In 1621 Gregory XV designated the institute a religious order with solemn vows, and with all the privileges of other orders. The

Interior sanctuary of S. Maria in Campitelli, Rome, mother church of the Clerks Regular of the Mother of God.

Leonardi united in 1614 with the PIARISTS at the urging of Cardinal Giustiniani, but the two groups separated in 1617 because the pastoral nature of the former proved incompatible with the scholastic character of the latter. From this time Leonardi's institute took the definitive name of Clerks Regular of the Mother of God.

As the order spread in Italy from Lucca to Genoa, Milan, Rome, southern Italy, and Sicily, it flourished. In Lucca its school produced the leading citizens of the upper and middle classes. The Leonardini were active in all forms of the apostolate and in literary movements. Among the outstanding members of the order were Ippolito Marracci (d. 1675), author of about 100 works on the Immaculate Conception, and his brother Ludovico (d. 1700), an Arabic scholar; Bartolomeo Beverini (d. 1686), theologian, historian, and man of letters; Massimiliano Dezza (d. 1704), preacher at the court of Vienna; Sebastiano Paoli (d. 1751), orator and man of letters; and Giovanni MANSI (d. 1779), theologian.

Suppressions in the Napoleonic period and in the late 19th century by the Italian government practically destroyed the order, which had no houses outside Italy. Throughout the 19th century the order continued to lead a precarious existence. Conditions became more promising from the mid-20th century onwards. The congregation is found principally in Italy and France.

Bibliography: F. FERRAIRONI, *Tre Secoli di storia dell'Ordine Religioso della Madre di Dio* (Rome 1939). V. PASCUCCI, *S. Giovanni Leonardi* (Rome 1963).

[P. PIERONI/EDS.]

CLERMONT-TONNERRE, ANNE ANTOINE JULES DE

Cardinal, archbishop of Toulouse; b. Paris, Jan. 1, 1749; d. Toulouse, Feb. 21, 1830. He was born into an illustrious family, studied at the Seminary of Saint-Sulpice, and received a doctorate from the Sorbonne. In 1774 he became vicar-general of the archdiocese of Besançon, and in 1781 bishop of Châlons-sur-Marne. He was elected a deputy to the Estates General (1789). Upon refusing the oath of loyalty to the CIVIL CONSTITUTION OF THE CLERGY, he went into exile (1791) in Belgium and Germany. After the CONCORDAT OF 1801, he resigned his see and returned to retirement in France. Louis XVIII named him a peer of France (1814). Since his former see was not reestablished, Clermont-Tonnerre was promoted to that of Toulouse (1820), and to the cardinalate (1822). In his diocese he restored discipline, reorganized seminaries, founded a missionary society, published a Ritual, and fought for the restoration of all the Church's rights. Notably he opposed the regulations on minor seminaries (1828). He attended the 1829 conclave in Rome, despite a serious accident on the way there, which led ultimately to his death.

Bibliography: É. FRANCESCHINI, *Dictionnaire de biographie française* (Paris 1929–) 8:1515–16. C. LAPLATTE, *Dictionnaire d'histoire et de géographie ecclésiastiques,* ed. A. BAUDRILLART et al. (Paris 1912–) 12:319–322. G. CAYRE, *Histoire des évêques et archevêques de Toulouse* (Toulouse 1873). *L'Épiscopat français depuis le Concordat jusqu'à la Séparation (1802–1905)* (Paris 1907).

[R. LIMOUZIN-LAMOTHE]

CLIFFORD, RICHARD

Civil servant, bishop of London; d. Aug. 20, 1421. No firm evidence survives concerning his parentage and education. He was not styled master before 1397 or regularly afterward, and this scholastic title may have been used in error or as a compliment. Most authorities assert Clifford's descent from the baronial house of Westmorland; his father may have been the Lollard courtier Sir Lewis Clifford. As a retainer of the Black Prince and his wife, Lewis could have introduced his son to King Richard II. Richard Clifford was known as a "king's clerk" from 1380, when he received the first of numerous benefices. He was one of the royal chaplains arrested by the Lords Appellant in 1388 but was soon released. He was appointed keeper of the great wardrobe (1390) and keeper of the privy seal (1397), an office he retained even after Richard II's deposition.

In 1400 the new king, Henry IV, refused to allow Clifford's PROVISION to the see of Bath and Wells but did assent to his transfer to that of WORCESTER (1401) and to his translation to the see of London (1407). Clifford had resigned the privy seal soon after his consecration as bishop and thereafter took little part in secular government except for an embassy to Germany (1402). He was one of the episcopal assessors at Sir John Oldcastle's trial as a Lollard heretic (1413). He served in Henry V's embassy to the Council of CONSTANCE and was its spokesperson, favoring the election of Pope MARTIN V. The unsupported statement of Thomas WALSINGHAM in his *Historia Anglicana* (*Rerum Britannicarum medii aevi scriptores,* 2:320) that Clifford himself was considered as a candidate for the papacy is hard to credit in view of his comparatively undistinguished career. He was buried in St. Paul's, London.

Bibliography: T. A. ARCHER, *The Dictionary of National Biography from the Earliest Times to 1900* (London 1885–1900; repr. with corrections, 21 v., 1908–09, 1921–22, 1938) 4:525–526. A. B. EMDEN, *A Biographical Register of the University of Oxford to A.D. 1500* (Oxford 1957–59) 1:440–441.

[R. L. STOREY]

CLITHEROW, MARGARET, BL.

The "pearl of York," English martyr; b. *c.* 1556; d. March 25, 1586 (feast, March 25). Her father, Thomas Middleton, was a prosperous chandler and sheriff of York. He died soon after his term of office (1564–65). In 1571 Margaret married John Clitherow, a rich and prominent butcher in York. Margaret had been brought up a Protestant; but John, although he conformed to the new faith, belonged to a Catholic family and had a brother who was a priest. Two or three years after her marriage, Margaret became a Catholic, although her husband, by then a chamberlain of York, was necessarily becoming more resolute in his Protestantism. By this time the Clitherows had two children, Henry and Anne; their third child, William, was born in prison during one of Margaret's internments for her faith. After her release she returned to her home, The Shambles, and her duties, looking after the butcher's shop and teaching her children. (She had taught herself to read in prison.) Soon, however, she decided that she was no longer qualified to teach her elder son, so she sent him abroad to Douai for a Catholic education and employed a tutor, Mr. Stapleton, for her two other children and those of her Catholic neighbors. Her husband turned a blind eye to this and to her other more dangerous practice of harboring priests.

Margaret, however, was becoming known as a fearless and outspoken Catholic. The government, perturbed by the persistence of the old faith in Yorkshire, urged the Council of the North to take strong measures and make an example of the leading Catholics. On March 10, 1586, the Council summoned John Clitherow to explain his son's absence abroad. While John was testifying, they sent a search party to his house. Stapleton escaped; there were no signs of any priests, vestments, or chalices. The Clitherow children revealed nothing when questioned, but a Flemish boy was frightened into betraying where the vestments were hidden. Margaret and her household were arrested. Charged with harboring priests and attending Mass, Margaret refused to plead, saying, "Having made no offence, I need no trial." Had she pleaded, her own children might have been forced to give evidence against her, and this she was determined to prevent. The punishment for refusing to plead was *peine forte et dure,* and reluctantly Judge Clinch pronounced it: "You must . . . be stripped naked, laid down, your back upon the ground and as much weight laid up on you as you are able to bear and so to continue for three days . . . and on the third day to be pressed to death.'' Margaret was not allowed to see her children again. In prison she sewed a loose shift, for she was determined not to die naked. On March 25 the sentence was carried out. She died within a quarter of an hour, but her body was left for six hours in the press.

Feast: March 25.

Bibliography: A contemporary memoir by her confessor, John Mush, appears in J. MORRIS, ed., *The Troubles of Our Catholic Forefathers Related by Themselves,* 3 v. (London 1872–77). A. BUTLER, *The Lives of Saints,* ed. H. THURSTON and D. ATTWATER, 4 v. (New York, 1956). M. T. MONRO, *Blessed Margaret Clitherow* (New York 1947). J. GILLOW, *A Literary and Biographical History or Bibliographical Dictionary of the English Catholics from 1534 to the Present Time,* 5 v. (London–New York 1885–1902; reprinted New York 1961).

[G. FITZHERBERT]

CLOISTER, CANONICAL RULES FOR

Cloister, from the Latin *claustra,* a bar or enclosure, describes the physical space reserved in all houses of religious institutes for solitude and prayer. From a theological perspective, cloister witnesses to the contemplative nature of the Church in her intimacy with God through recollection and silence, the withdrawal from the world so necessary and present in every Christian vocation (*Venite seorsum* I). Cloister is enjoined on both contemplative and apostolic religious institutes through norms prescribed in Church law.

Code of Canon Law. Canon 667 §1 prescribes cloister for all houses of religious institutes in accord with their character and mission. Norms for the observance of cloister are to be determined in the proper law of each institute with some part of the religious house reserved for the members alone. The norm reflects Pope Paul VI's apostolic exhortation *Evangelica testificatio* 46, reminding all religious of the vital need for silence in their search for intimacy with God. Canon 667 §2 regulates a stricter (*strictior*) cloister for monasteries ordered to the contemplative life. In keeping with *Perfectae caritatis* 16, the cloister should be adjusted to the conditions of time and place and all obsolete practices abolished. Canon 667 §3 provides for monasteries of nuns. Those monasteries entirely ordered to the contemplative life must observe papal cloister, i.e., cloister in accord with norms issued by the Apostolic See. The Congregation for Institutes of Consecrated Life and Societies of Apostolic Life revised the norms governing papal cloister; these were approved by Pope John Paul II and published on May 13, 1999, in the instruction *Verbi sponsa.* Monasteries of nuns that are

not ordered entirely to the contemplative life are to observe cloister adapted to their proper character and defined in the constitutions; this latter form is referred to as constitutional cloister. Canon 667 §4 gives the diocesan bishop the faculty for a just cause to enter the cloister of monasteries of nuns situated in his diocese. He also has the faculty, for a grave cause and with the consent of the superior, of permitting others to be admitted to the cloister and permitting the nuns to leave it for a truly necessary period of time.

Code of Canons of the Eastern Churches. Canon 477 §1 provides that enclosure shall be observed in monasteries as prescribed in the typicon or proper law of the monastery. In individual instances and for a grave reason, the superior has the right to admit into the enclosure persons of the gender other than those who may enter in accord with the typicon. Canon 477 §2 provides that the parts of the monastery subject to the law of enclosure shall be clearly indicated, and Canon 477 §3 leaves to the superior of a monastery *sui iuris,* with the consent of the council and after notifying the local hierarch, to prescribe precisely the boundaries of the enclosure or to change them for just reasons. Canon 541 provides that the statutes of orders and congregations shall determine the norms for enclosure in accord with their own character. Superiors, even local ones, possess the right to permit something different for a just cause in individual instances.

[R. MCDERMOTT]

CLONMACNOIS, MONASTERY OF

Former monastic foundation in County Offaly, Ireland (Gaelic, Clúain moccu Nois). St. Ciarán (or Kieran) founded it in 545; it was exceeded in influence only by ARMAGH, and it in turn outshone Armagh in learning and sanctity. Its *paruchia* extended over about half of Ireland, and students flocked there, even from abroad. From its scriptorium came some of the most valuable manuscripts Ireland possesses: *Chronicon Scotorum, Annals of Tigernach,* Rawlinson B 502, and *Lebor na hUidre.* It successfully resisted domination by secular princes, and in the 8th and 9th centuries it was a reforming influence in a period of general decline. In the 10th century its abbots began to exercise episcopal jurisdiction, thus originating the Diocese of Clonmacnois. Referred to as the Westminster Abbey of Ireland (with countless royal tombs), it invited marauding attacks from its beginnings until its final razing at the hands of the English in 1552. Some idea of the magnitude of this monastic city may still be gained from the surviving ruins: two round towers, eight churches, three large sculptured IRISH CROSSES, a castle, and

The ruins of Clonmacnois Monastery, County Offaly, Ireland. (©Michael St. Maur Shell/CORBIS)

over 200 inscribed tombstones, all of which have been the subjects of an imposing list of studies.

Bibliography: J. R. GARSTIN, "On the Identification of a Bronze Shoe-shaped Object as Part of the Head of an Ancient Irish Crozier," *Proceedings of the Royal Irish Academy* ser. 2, 1 (1879) 261–264. *Clonmacnois, Kings County,* extract from the 75th annual report of the Commissioners of Public Works in Ireland (Dublin 1906–07). J. F. KENNEY, *The Sources for the Early History of Ireland:* v. 1, *Ecclesiastical* (New York 1929) 1:376–383. R. A. MACALISTER, "Story of Clonmacnois," *Proceedings of the Belfast Natural History and Philosophical Society* ser. 2, 1 (1935–40) 9–11. F. O. BRIAIN, *Dictionnaire d'histoire et de géographie ecclésiastiques,* ed. A. BAUDRILLART et al. (Paris 1912–) 13:10–14. J. RYAN, "The Abbatial Succession at Clonmacnois," *Essays and Studies Presented to Professor Eoin MacNeill,* ed. J. RYAN (Dublin 1940) 490–507. E. H. L. SEXTON, *Descriptive and Bibliographical List of Irish Figure Sculptures of the Early Christian Period* (Portland, Maine 1946) 101–114. H. G. LEASK, *Irish Churches and Monastic Buildings,* 3 v. (Dundalk, Ire. 1955–60).

[C. MCGRATH]

CLORIVIÈRE, JOSEPH PIERRE PICOT DE

Soldier, priest; b. Brittany, France, Nov. 4, 1768; d. Washington, D.C., Sept. 29, 1826. He was the son of Mi-chel Alain Picot and Renée Jeanne Roche, and for many years was called simply Joseph Picot de Limoëlan. He studied at the College of Rennes and the Royal Military School in Paris. He was assigned to the Régiment d'Angoulême, but resigned his commission early in 1791 and from then until 1799 was associated with the counter-revolutionists, taking an active part in the abortive plot to assassinate Napoleon on Dec. 24, 1800. He escaped to Savannah, Georgia, and henceforth was known as Joseph Picot de Clorivière. In 1808 he entered St. Mary's Seminary in Baltimore; he was ordained Aug. 1, 1812. Charleston, South Carolina, with many refugees from Santo Domingo, needed a French priest, and he was sent there to assist Simon Felix GALLAGHER. In 1814 he went to France, and on his return to Charleston he found that Gallagher and the vestry of the church had replaced him with another priest and would not honor his appointment from Abp. John Carroll. Archbishops Carroll, Leonard Neale, and Ambrose Maréchal in turn upheld him against the trustees and interdicted the church. To restore peace, Maréchal sent Benedict Fenwick, SJ, to Charleston in 1818, and Clorivière was appointed chaplain at the Visitation Convent in Georgetown, Washington, D.C. He also helped in founding St. Joseph's School in the District of

Columbia. He was generous to the Visitation Convent and is considered its second founder.

Bibliography: D. H. DARRAH, *Conspiracy in Paris: The Strange Career of Joseph Picot de Limoëlan* (New York 1953). P. K. GUILDAY, *The Life and Times of John England,* 2 v. (New York 1927). G. P. and R. H. LATHROP, *A Story of Courage: Annals of the Georgetown Convent of the Visitation of the Blessed Virgin Mary* (Cambridge, Mass. 1895).

[R. C. MADDEN]

CLOTILDE, ST.

Frankish queen; b. Lyons or Vienne, *c.* 470; d. Tours, June 3, 545. She was the daughter of the Burgundian King Chilperic, and although a Catholic, was sought in marriage (492) by the pagan CLOVIS. Their children, and eventually Clovis himself, received Baptism at the hands of St. REMIGIUS OF REIMS. Clotilde was widowed in 511. In 523 she urged her sons to war against King Sigismund of Burgundy to avenge her father's death years earlier. She retired to the burial shrine of St. MARTIN OF TOURS. Clotilde was buried with Clovis at St. GENEVIÈVE IN PARIS. In the Middle Ages her cult was extensive and her relics were prized. In 1793 her body was cremated in order to avoid profanation, and the ashes were retained in Paris.

Feast: June 3.

Bibliography: A. BERNET, *Sainte Clotilde: marraine de la France* (Monaco 1997). F. OPPENHEIMER, *Frankish Themes and Problems* (London 1952). J. M. WALLACE-HADRILL, *The Long-Haired Kings* (London 1962). G. BARDY, *Catholicisme* 2:1259–60. A. DUMAS *Dictionnaire de biographie française* (Paris 1929—) 9:34–35.

[R. H. SCHMANDT]

CLOUD, ST.

Known also as Chlodovald or Clodoald; d. 7(?) Sept. 560. He was a grandson of CLOVIS and youngest son of Chlodomer, king of Orléans. Clovis's widow CLOTILDE reared the three sons of Chlodomer after he was killed in an attack on the Burgundian kingdom (524). To acquire Chlodomer's kingdom, his brothers Childebert I and Chlothar I murdered two nephews, but Cloud escaped and voluntarily renounced royalty by entering religion. He led an edifying life, founded a monastery at Novigentum near Paris, and died a priest. Miracles occurred at his tomb and by 811 his foundation was known as Saint-Cloud.

Feast: Sept. 7.

Bibliography: *Acta Sanctae Sedis* Sept. 3:91–101. *Bibliotheca hagiograpica latina antiquae et mediae aetatis* (Brussels 1898–1901) 1732–34. GREGORIUS TURONENSIS, *Historiarum libri,* 3:6, 18, ed. B. KRUSCH and W. LEVISON, *Monumenta Germaniae Historica: Scriptores rerum Merovingicarum* 1:101–103, 117–120. *Vita sancti Chlodovaldi,* ed. B. KRUSCH, *ibid.* 2:349–357. Literature. O. M. DALTON, ed. and tr., *The History of the Franks by Gregory of Tours,* 2 v. (Oxford 1927) 1:98–100.

[W. GOFFART]

CLOUD OF UNKNOWING

Of unknown authorship, the *Cloud of Unknowing* is generally considered the greatest spiritual classic to issue from the mystical movement of the 14th century in England. It is a treatise on the contemplative life written for the instruction of a disciple who has already passed through the preparatory stages of discursive prayer and now finds himself in a state of deprivation and darkness, "as it were a cloud of unknowing." The *Cloud* is evidently the work of a priest and theologian at home in both patristic thought and contemporary controversy and speculation. The anonymous author stresses the primacy of the will (as the faculty for loving) over intellect in the work of contemplation: "By love He may be gotten and holden; but by thought neither." He synthesizes with masterly skill traditional doctrine (especially of the Dionysian and Victorine line) and argues with the closely reasoned thought characteristic of Thomistic theology. His skill in working scriptural language and images into the very texture of his prose is a feature of his markedly original and forceful prose style. Manuscript evidence assigns the *Cloud* to the late 14th century and to an East Midland dialect.

Bibliography: P. HODGSON, ed., *The Cloud of Unknowing and The Book of Privy Counselling* (Early English Text Society, 218, London 1944); ed., *Deonise hid Diuinite and Other Treatises* (Early English Text Society, 231, London 1955); "Walter Hilton and 'The Cloud of Unknowing': A Problem of Authorship Reconsidered," *Modern Language Review* 50 (1955) 395–406. J. MCCANN, ed., *The Cloud of Unknowing* (London 1952). E. UNDERHILL, ed., *A Book of Contemplation, the Which Is Called The Cloud of Unknowing* (London 1946). D. KNOWLES, *The English Mystical Tradition* (New York 1961). C. PEPLER, *The English Religious Heritage* (St. Louis 1958). J. P. H. CLARK, "The Cloud of Unknowing," in *An Introduction to the Medieval Mystics of Europe* (Albany, N.Y. 1984) 273–291. K. EMERY, JR., "The Cloud of Unknowing and Mystica Theologia," in *The Spirituality of Western Christendom, II,* (Kalamazoo, Mich. 1984) 46–70. R. W. ENGLERT, "Of Another Mind: Ludic Imagery and Spiritual Doctrine in the Cloud of Unknowing," *Studia Mystica* 8 No. 1 (1985) 3–12. M. J. WILL, "Dionysian Neoplatonism and the Theology of the Cloud Author," *Downside Review* 110 (1992) 98–109 [Pt. 1] 184–194 [Pt. 2]. N. K. POKORN, "The Language and Discourse of The Cloud of Unknowing," *Literature and Theology* 11 (1997) 408–421.

[M. E. EATON/EDS.]

CLOVIS I

Born *c.* 465; died 511. A member of the Merovingian family, Clovis was the founder of the kingdom of the Franks over which he ruled from 481 or 482 until 511. The ground work for Clovis' successful reign was prepared by his father, Childeric I, king of the Salian Franks, whose realm was centered around Tournai. As indicated in a letter sent by REMIGIUS, bishop of Reims, to Clovis about the time he succeeded his father, Childeric was recognized not only as leader of the Salian Franks but also as a legally constituted official who exercised authority over the non-Frankish population of the Roman province of Belgica II and enjoyed the support of the Christian episcopacy in that area even though he was a pagan. Childeric and his Frankish followers saw their ancient Germanic ways of life modified by their adoption of many aspects of Roman civilization.

The main source for Clovis' reign, the *History of the Franks* written by GREGORY OF TOURS, presents his career in terms of two interrelated themes: his spectacular military victories over a variety of enemies in Gaul and his conversion from paganism to orthodox Christianity, developments that together elevated him to heroic stature. Such a picture contains considerable truth, but requires some refinement. A careful reading of all the evidence suggests that Clovis continued the ways of earlier leaders of the Salian Franks, including especially his father. He pursued their policy of extending Frankish control over and settlement in an ever larger area of the Roman Empire south and west of the lower Rhine. Like them, his successes in expanding the area of Frankish control resulted in his rule over ever-increasing numbers of Gallo-Romans inhabiting that area. Like them, he readily adopted Roman ways as a means of making his authority more effective. What distinguished his reign was the scale of his achievements along lines already plotted by his Frankish predecessors.

In 507 Clovis invaded the Visigothic kingdom and won a decisive victory at Vouillé near Poitiers which allowed him to claim almost all Visigothic territory in Gaul; only the intervention of Theoderic, king of the Ostrogoths, kept Clovis from extending the Frankish frontier to the Mediterranean. The annexation of Gaul south of the Loire confronted Clovis with the challenge of ruling a population still powerfully influenced by Roman civilization. His victory over the Visigoths marked the apogee of Clovis' career. A symbolic recognition of his achievements awaited him when he reached Tours on his return from his victory over the Visigoths; there he was met by an embassy from the Roman emperor Anastasius which had come to seek an alliance with Clovis against the Ostrogoths and to bestow on him with impressive

Clovis I, king of the Franks, drawing.

pomp an honorary consulship. Through his military conquests the petty kingdom he inherited had become the major power in Gaul, ranking alongside and soon to surpass such other Germanic successor states to the Roman Empire as the Ostrogothic, the Visigothic, the Burgundian, and the Vandal kingdoms.

Conversion to Christianity. A significant factor in Clovis' success was his conversion to orthodox Christianity. How this came about is far from clear. In his *History of the Franks* Gregory of Tours attributed Clovis' abandonment of paganism in part to the persuasive influence of Queen CLOTILDE, who was an orthodox Christian. Clovis' decision to allow the baptism of his two oldest sons points to her role in shaping the king's religious views. Especially decisive in Gregory's account was Clovis' conviction that his victory over the Alemanni at Tolbiac was caused by the intervention of the God of Clotilde on the side of the Franks; that conviction convinced the king to seek baptism from Bishop Remigius of Reims. According to Gregory, many of Clovis' warriors willingly followed their king's example. The evidence related to the conversion leaves no doubt that there were religious factors involved in Clovis' final decision. It is equally clear that political considerations related to his rule over the Gallo-Roman population of his growing kingdom played a decisive role in Clovis' acceptance of orthodox Christianity. He was certainly aware of the important role bishops played in late antiquity in directing Gallo-Roman society and of the value of episcopal support for anyone wishing to rule in Gaul. It was also obvious that the bishops of Gaul and their followers were committed to orthodox Christianity and opposed to the Arianism of the ruling regimes in the rival kingdoms of the Bungundians and the Visigoths. Although some evidence suggests that Clovis may have toyed with accepting Arian Christianity as a means of winning diplomatic advantage in his dealings with the Arian rulers of the Ostrogoths, Visigoths, and Burgunds, the political advantage of accepting orthodox Christianity in terms of his role as ruler of the kingdom of the Franks was obvious, especially when he faced his crucial confrontation with the Visigoths. As it turned out, the decision of Clovis and his Frankish followers to accept the religion of the Gallo-Roman population became a decisive factor in making Frankish rule acceptable to an indigenous population much larger in number than those who were of Frankish origin and in stabilizing the new regime that replaced Roman rule in Gaul.

Clovis' Rule. While the surviving record portrays Clovis chiefly as a successful warrior and as a champion of the true religion, his career had another dimension no less important. Clovis was an effective ruler who laid the foundations for a monarchical system that survived for at least two and one half centuries. That regime was based partly on military force which Clovis used ruthlessly to dispose of those who opposed him. But more crucial to his regime than brute force was Clovis' ability to merge Frankish and Roman political usages into a system that was acceptable to the population he governed, especially its elite segments.

While still a warlord, Clovis began to assume symbols of power that added a Roman dimension to his rule. Clovis' regime left undisturbed most of the traditional Roman local administrative system. Throughout most of his vast kingdom royal power was represented locally by counts whose jurisdiction extended over the territory once defined by the Roman city *civitas* and whose functions included recruiting military forces, administering justice, enforcing royal orders, and collecting taxes. Both Frankish and Gallo-Roman nobles were appointed to the office of count.

Especially important in the coalescence of the two cultural worlds was the religious establishment which Clovis skillfully exploited to serve his ends. The key figures in the Church were the bishops, who not only played a decisive role in directing religious life in Gaul but also who with the support of the Roman imperial regime had since the 4th century been expanding their role in keeping alive the idea of public service, especially in the cities. The episcopal office was increasingly monopolized by powerful aristocratic families whose interests were advanced by the power, wealth, and prestige attached to the office. Clovis encouraged bishops to expand their involvement in directing local affairs. The king's chief concern was to assure that only members of aristocratic families loyal to the king gained episcopal office, an objective that led him to take a keen interest in the selection of bishops. The bishops reciprocated by lending their considerable support to the newly converted champion of orthodox Christianity. They became the chief agents in the Frankish kingdom supporting charity, urban improvement, education, patronage of art and letters, all endeavors that contributed to sustaining the Roman heritage and in softening the violent, barbaric aspects of Clovis' regime. Beyond encouraging individual bishops to play a vital role in his kingdom, Clovis sought to use their collective presence as a force to shape a "national" church that would serve under royal direction to institute a common religious life throughout his realm. In 511 he summoned a synod of bishops at Orleans and defined an agenda aimed at regulating various aspects of religious life in a uniform fashion, including especially fortifying the authority of bishops and protecting the material resources of the Church. No less important than his collaboration with the episcopacy in sustaining royal authority among the Gallo-Roman population was the acceptance by Clovis and his Frankish followers of the forms of piety that were deeply rooted in Gallo-Roman society, especially the cult of saints and of relics. Clovis reflected this aspect of religious life especially in his reverence for the cult of St. Martin of Tours. His entire religious policy played an important role in bringing the Christian establishment into support for the new regime and in providing a conduit through which the conquerors and the conquered could find a common ground.

On Nov. 27, 511, Clovis died at the age of 45 after a 30-year reign. He was buried in Paris, which during the last years of his reign became the chief city in his kingdom. He left behind four sons, the eldest illegitimate and the other three children of Queen Clotilde. A division of the kingdom as if it were private property was arranged, which provided each son with a share of Clovis' realm; the model provided by this division was destined to cause unending trouble for future Frankish kings. But that fact in no way subtracts from the accomplishments of Clovis, who made the Franks masters of Gaul and a power to be reckoned with in the larger world of the early 6th century. At the same time Clovis played a significant role in establishing a political and religious order which provided a framework in which the Germanic and Roman worlds could join hands in shaping a new civilization in western Europe.

See Also: ARIANISM; FRANKS; MEROVINGIANS; VANDALS; VISIGOTHS.

Bibliography: Sources: *Gregorii Episcopi Turonensis Historiarum Libri X,* Bk. 2, chs. 27–43, ed. B. KRUSCH, *Monumenta Germaniae Historica, Scriptore rerum Merowingicarum* 1 (Hannover 1937) 71–94, English translation as *Gregory of Tours, History of the Franks,* Bk. 2, chs. 27–43, trans. with intro. L. THROPE (Harmondsworth, Eng. 1974) 139–158. *Die Gesetze des Merowingerreiches 478–714,* v. 1: *Pactus legis Salicae: Recensiones Merovingicae,* ed. K.A. ECKHARDT (*Germanenrechte, Texte und Übersetzungen* 1; Göttingen 1955), English translations as *Laws of the Salian and Ripuarian Franks,* trans. T. J. RIVERS (New York, 1986), and as *The Laws of the Salian Franks,* ed. K. FISHER DREW (*Middle Ages Series;* Philadelphia 1991). *Concilia Gallia, A. 551–A.695,* ed. C. DE CLERCQ, *Corpus Christianorum, Series Latina* 148A (Turnhout 1965) 3–19. *Epistolae Merowingii et Karolini aevi,* ed. W. GUNDLACH, *Monumenta Germaniae Historica, Epistolae* 3 (Berlin 1982) 112–113 (letter of Bishop Remigius of Reims to Clovis). Literature: W. VON DEN STEINEN, *Clodwigs Übergang zum Christentum: eine quellenkritische Studie* (Darmstadt 1963). G. TESSIER, *La baptême de Clovis: 25 décembre 496(?),* (Paris 1964). I. GOBRY, *Clovis le Grand* (Paris 1995). B. CHEVALLIER *Clovis, un roi européen,* (Paris 1996). M. ROUCHE, *Clovis,* (Paris 1996). P. DELORME and L. DE GOUSTINE, *Clovis, 496–1996: Enquête sur le XVème centenaire* (Paris 1996). P. CHAUME and É. MENSION–RIGAU, *Baptême de Clovis, baptême de la France: De la religion d'État à la laïcité d'État* (Paris 1996). *Clovis, histoire et mémoire. Actes du Colloque international d'histoire de Reims, 19–25 septembre 1996,* ed. M. ROUCHE, 2 v. (Paris 1997). J. W. CURRIER, *Clovis, King of the Franks* (Milwaukee, WI 1997). R. MUSSOT–GOULARD *Clovis, "Que sais-je?"* (Paris 1997). G. BORDONOVE, *Clovis et les Mérovingiens (Les rois qui on fait le France. Les Préecurseurs* 1; Paris 1998).

[R. E. SULLIVAN]

CLUNIAC ART AND ARCHITECTURE

During the 250 years after their foundation, the monastic houses of Cluny became the most important and widespread in Europe, comprising some 1,450 priories and some 10,000 monks in England and on the Continent as far east as Poland. Very active in the arts, the Cluniacs were responsible for bringing to fruition the Romanesque style, especially in France. The practicing of St. BENEDICT's precept of prayer and work (*ora et labora*) virtually guaranteed the order great church and cloister architecture. Music was essential also; ODO, a former precentor at Tours and the first great abbot at Cluny (927–49), firmly established the inseparable musical and spiritual traditions of the Cluniacs (*see* CLUNIAC REFORM). PETER THE VENERABLE, the last great 12th-century abbot at Cluny (1122–57), gave an intellectual and artistic interpretation to *labora:* "It is more noble to set one's hand to the pen than to the plow, to trace divine letters upon the page than furrows upon the fields." It was during his abbacy that Cluniac art reached its zenith.

Architecture. The most important single Cluniac manifestation of Romanesque style was the great church of SS. Peter and Paul constructed at Cluny under Abbots HUGH OF CLUNY (1049–1109) and Peter the Venerable between its official founding, Sept. 30, 1088, and its formal dedication by Pope Innocent II, Oct. 25, 1130. Work continued until about 1450 on the western towers, long after Cluniac power had diminished. The church itself was destroyed, save for the south arm of the western transept, between 1798 and 1823. Cluny III, so termed in contradistinction to two earlier churches of the 10th century that it superseded, was the largest church in Europe save St. Peter's in Rome and was the principal expression of Benedictine Romanesque monastic architecture.

Built on the plan of a double-armed archiepiscopal cross, Cluny III was over 600 feet in length, including a Gothic narthex completed about 1225, and reached an interior vaulted height of 100 feet for the first time in medieval architecture. This feat duly impressed a chronicler in 1120, who wrote, ". . . and suddenly [as one enters the nave] a giant basilica surges up. . . ." As capital church of the Cluniac congregation of Benedictines, Cluny III was able to hold all the monks of the order; in 1132 there were 1,212 monks assembled in procession in the church. Medieval visitors were no less impressed by its workmanship than by its size; later visitors were equally awed by its total effect: "If you see its majesty a hundred times, you are overwhelmed on each occasion" (Mabillon, 1682).

The *chevet* of the great church had five isolated chapels radiating from an ambulatory, a distinguishing feature of later Cluniac Romanesque architecture. It is seen in Saint-Étienne at Nevers, consecrated 1097, and Paray-le-Monial, 1104, each of which has three chapels. But at Cluny concentration focused on the great altar whose top is preserved in the Musée Ochier, Cluny, and from which for nearly 700 years song and incense rose daily to the large "Christ in Glory" fresco in the apse. This painting is now destroyed, but a contemporary reflection may be seen in Abbot Hugh's chapel in the Cluniac grange at nearby Berzé-la-Ville (*c.* 1100). The mosaic floors with images of the saints led past two transepts (a rare feature for the time), each with lateral chapels, to the great five-aisled nave. The central nave aisle, 33 feet wide and 100 feet high under its pointed, ribbed barrel vault (part of which collapsed in 1125 but was rebuilt by 1130), was flanked by compound piers eight feet in diameter. It consisted of a main arcade, a false triforium having no lateral passage in the wall, and a clerestory. The pointed arches used at Cluny III for the first time on such a scale in medieval architecture may have reflected, as did the cusping of the triforium arcade, Islamic influences from Spain, one of whose monarchs, Alfonso el Bravo (d. 1109), was married to Hugh's niece Constance and contributed annually 200 ounces of gold to the abbey. The basic concept, however, was neither Spanish nor Islamic. The architects of Cluny III were Gunzo, a retired abbot of Baume, who served as designer (μηχιανίκος), and Hérzelo, a former canon of Liège, who served as builder (ἀρχιτέκτων). As K. J. Conant has demonstrated, the design was based on several systems of musical numbers, notably the Pythagorean series of 2, 3, 4, 6, 8, 9, and 12. Further, since Gunzo is known to have been a musician (*psalmista praecipuus*), it is not impossible that the design should have been related to GREGORIAN CHANT, an essential part of Cluniac ritual and one demanding vaulted churches for acoustical reasons.

A number of buildings reflect the interior disposition of Cluny III, especially the nave of Autun cathedral (*c.* 1125) and the Cluniac priory churches of Paray-le-Monial and La Charité-sur-Loire (consecrated 1107), but there never existed a Cluniac school of architecture in the sense that Cistercian churches of the 12th century unquestionably relate to a single concept. (*See* CISTERCIAN ART AND ARCHITECTURE.) Cluniac influence may account for the general uniformity found in the great churches of the pilgrimage roads, such as Sainte-Foi at Conques and Saint-Martial at Limoges, the latter a Cluniac dependency; but, despite discernible interdependent relationships and groupings among the some 325 Cluniac churches remaining at least in part (for example, the *en échelon* apse plan of Cluny II and Payerne, Switzerland, after 1050), Conant is correct in saying that the "Cluniacs were more zealous for uniformity in customs, discipline, and liturgy than in architecture."

Sculpture. Cluniac sculpture developed from manuscript illustrations, the expected source in an intellectual order. St. Benedict's Rule required each monk to read one book during Lent, and the library at Cluny possessed some 570 volumes in the 12th century. Nowhere is the relationship between manuscript illustration and sculpture more clearly seen than by comparing the cloister plaques at Moissac (*c.* 1100) with manuscripts known to have been at the Cluniac abbey. However, the most artistically complete treatment of iconographic themes is to be found at Cluny III itself. The now-destroyed "Christ in Glory" with symbols of the EVANGELISTS of the central west tympanum (carved *c.* 1115; destroyed 1810) was "painted like a manuscript page" and was the first large sculptural expression of this theme, the forerunner of many such portals extending in time well into the Gothic period (Carennac, *c.* 1130; Charlieu porch, *c.* 1145; Last Judgment at Beaulieu, *c.* 1135; central narthex tympanum at Vézelay, by 1135).

Cluniac capitals were often Corinthianesque in form, especially after 1090, and the order found place also for such Islamic motifs as pointed arches (Cluny III; Paray-le-Monial; Vézelay) and cusping (Cluny III; La Charité-sur-Loire; Chalais, *c.* 1150). Cluny did not, then, invent Romanesque themes or inaugurate stylistic features, but it did give the former a coherency and the latter a fullness that neither had previously.

This consummate combining of theme and style is most evident in the ambulatory capitals surviving from the *chevet* of Cluny III, consecrated Oct. 25, 1095, by Pope Urban II (Musée Ochier, Cluny). The illustrated themes provided the first important series of allegorical capitals in Romanesque art. Inspired by the writings of Radulphus Glaber, they included the four seasons, the cardinal virtues, the four trees (a new subject), and the four rivers of paradise. Two capitals from the ambulatory represented the eight tones of the chant; they indicate a link between Cluniac liturgy and art. These personifications of the musical tones, based on a late 11th-century *tonarius* manuscript from Saint-Martial at Limoges (Paris, Bibl. Nat., MS lat. 1118), are among the finest of all early Romanesque capitals and demonstrate fully how the Cluniacs gave sculptural substance to musical and allegorical themes.

St. BERNARD OF CLAIRVAUX (d. 1153) disliked Cluniac "ostentatiousness" in art, but even he acknowledged its "endless varieties of forms . . . fashioned with marvelous subtlety of art" (*Apologia ad Guillelmum, c.* 1125). Through the enrichment of decoration with meaningful and systematic symbolism, the Cluniacs made one of their most important contributions to the development of medieval art.

Bibliography: J. EVANS, *The Romanesque Architecture of the Order of Cluny* (Cambridge, Eng. 1938); *Cluniac Art of the Romanesque Period* (Cambridge, Eng. 1950), the two best gen. introds. to Cluniac art and architecture, with extensive bibliogs. K. J. CONANT, "Mediaeval Academy Excavations at Cluny, VIII: Final Stages of the Project," *Speculum* 29 (1954) 1–43, author's many earlier *Speculum* articles are cited on p. 1; "New Results in the Study of Cluny Monastery," *Journal of the Society of Architectural History* 16 (October 1957) 3–11; "Mediaeval Academy Excavations at Cluny, IX: Systematic Dimensions in the Buildings," *Speculum* 38 (1963) 1–45, good illus.; *Carolingian and Romanesque Architecture, 800 to 1200* (*Pelican History of Art* Z13; Baltimore 1959). M. AUBERT, "Église abbatiale de Cluny," *Congrès archéologique de France* 98 (1935) 503–22, a good description, but dating of the sculpture too late. F. DESHOULIÈRES, "Le Rôle de Cluny," *Bulletin monumental* 94 (1945) 413–34, indicates the specific Cluniac contributions of Romanesque architecture.

[C. F. BARNES, JR.]

CLUNIAC REFORM

One of the most significant monastic movements of the high Middle Ages. It is necessary first of all to clarify the notion of "Cluny" and of the reform movement that sprang from it. Cluny as such is a mere abstraction, given different meanings at various times and places. If the reform is limited to the period extending from its foundation (909) to the death of St. HUGH OF CLUNY (1109), it denotes a monastic evolution (expressed by the various successive Customaries), and an administrative evolution brought on by rapid territorial expansion. The reform was centered in one place: the Abbey of CLUNY. It is a mistake to attribute to the Order of Cluny or to the Abbey of Cluny the reforming activity carried out by the great abbots of Cluny as individuals, and the reverse also is true.

History of the Reform. The Abbey of Cluny was not founded as a reforming agency. Originally, Cluniac monasticism drew its inspiration from the Rule of St. Benedict and the legislation of BENEDICT OF ANIANE. Because of specific historical circumstances, alien to the mentality of its founders, Cluny rapidly became the center of a vast movement of reform that continued until the 12th century. The popes and feudal authorities alike entrusted to the abbots of Cluny the reform of older monasteries and the foundation of new houses. There is, however, no trace of a "will to power" prejudicial to contemporary monastic congregations independent of the Cluniac movement. Following G. Tellenbach, J. Leclercq has noted that the influence of the Cluniacs, first in Aquitaine and later over a wider area, was the result of a flexible method of adaptation to various feudal milieus and to concrete circumstances at various monasteries, which interested princes and lay lords in monastic reform and reduced to a minimum the obstacle that political frontiers might have created. The spread of the Cluniac reform was spontaneous in most instances. Cluny did not try to gain possession of churches belonging to laymen. This fact is worth noting, since the feudal Church had fallen into lay hands. Beginning with ODO OF CLUNY (d. 949), the expansion of the Cluniac Order accelerated, and Cluny benefited from the changing conditions in feudal society. Enjoying temporal immunity from the time of its foundation, it received canonical exemption only in 931 (Bull of John XI), and exemption from episcopal authority, c. 998 to 999 (Gregory V granting the privilege confirmed and clarified by John XIX in 1027; later by his successors, notably Gregory VII). The monasteries attached to Cluny enjoyed the same temporal and spiritual independence, except in certain specific cases such as those of Saint-Martin-des-Champs and SAINT-BERTIN. Henceforth Cluniac monasteries were the property of the Apostolic See, which defended and protected them in jurisdictional conflicts, notably those instigated by the bishops of Mâcon, in whose territory Cluny was situated. The strong organizing personalities of ODILO and Hugh assured a certain juridical unity among the monasteries, but the ties of each community varied from strict subjection to sim-

ple affiliation or mere adoption of the Cluniac Customary (which did not necessarily imply juridical dependence). This unity consisted in a federation, independent of sectionalism and of political and territorial structures, lay and ecclesiastic. Its members (abbeys and priories with their dependencies) were united to a central authority, the abbot of Cluny, by bonds of varying degrees of closeness and according to a meticulously ordered hierarchy.

Nature of the Reform. The Cluniac reform, without deviating from its initial purpose, dedicated itself also to tasks of the temporal and political order. The abbots, especially Odo, Odilo, and Hugh, gave to this objective the loyal support of personal service and moral influence, without loss of independence. This is evidenced in the diplomatic missions they carried out on behalf of German emperors, Capetian kings, and popes, notably during the INVESTITURE STRUGGLE. And yet the trust in Cluny engendered in the world's great leaders did not hinder its human and spiritual influence, of which there are abundant contemporary records.

The Cluniac reform consisted first of all in the establishment of a monasticism based on *Consuetudines*, to which *Statuta* were later added. Only secondarily did it lend support to the renovation undertaken by ecclesiastical and lay authorities regarding simony and unworthy clerics; and in so doing it promoted an effective and general recognition of papal supremacy. The Order of Cluny was never a specialized entity organized to combat the decadence of the Church or to withstand the Empire, even when Cluniac monks became popes, cardinals, and bishops. Other movements of reform received their inspiration from Cluny. Suffice it to cite the *Ordo monasterii sancti Benigni* of Dijon, organized before 1069, which was based literally on the Customaries of BERNARD (*c.* 1070) and Udalric (*c.* 1080–83). The *Ordo* of Dijon was later adopted at FÉCAMP, as well as at FRUTTUARIA, which introduced its reform into Germany.

The End of Reform. After more than two centuries of unparalleled expansion, Cluniac monasticism was weakened in part by its internal structure and by the order's excessive expansion, temporal power, and the absence of a centralized governing body. It has been calculated that at the height of its development the order had 1,184 houses, situated in several provinces. PETER THE VENERABLE (d. 1157) understood the need for adaptation required by economic and social change; and at successive general chapters statutes were passed. But in the same era the new order of Cîteaux seemed to be a return to Cluny's primitive simplicity; and with the rapid development of the CISTERCIAN movement, the Cluniac reform came to an end. In the centuries that followed, Cluny itself was in need of reform.

Exterior of Abbey of Cluny, Tour des Fromages, Burgundy region, France. (©Paul Almasy/CORBIS)

Bibliography: G. DE VALOUS, *Dictionnaire d'histoire et de géographie ecclésiastiques*, ed. A. BAUDRILLART et al. (Paris 1912–) 13:35–178. J. LECLERCQ, "Pour une histoire de la vie à Cluny," *Revue d'histoire ecclésiastique* 57 (1962) 385–408, 783–812. G. SCHREIBER, "Gregor VII, Cluny, Cîteaux, Prémontré zur Eigenkirche, Parochie, Seelsorge," *Zeitschrift der Savigny-Stiftung für Rechtsgeschichte, Kanonistische Abteilung* 34 (1947) 31–171. K. HALLINGER, *Gorze-Kluny*, 2 v. (Rome 1950–51). J. WOLLASCH et al., *Neue Forschungen über Cluny und die Cluniacenser*, ed. G. TELLENBACH (Freiburg 1959). C. VIOLANTE, "Il monachesimo cluniacense di fronte al mondo politico ed ecclesiastico (secoli X e XI)," *Spiritualità cluniacense* (Todi 1960) 153–242. J. F. LEMARIGNIER, "Les Institutions ecclésiastiques en France de la fin du Xe au milieu du XIIe siècle," *Institutions ecclésiastiques*, v.3 of *Histoire des institutions françaises au moyen âge*, ed. F. LOT and R. FAWTIER (Paris 1957–62).

[R. GRÉGOIRE]

CLUNY, ABBEY OF

A Benedictine abbey of primary importance in the reform of the Church in the Middle Ages, located in the Rhône Valley (Burgundy), Diocese of Mâcon, department of Saône-et-Loire.

Foundation and Buildings. On Sept. 2, 909, Duke William of Aquitaine offered Bl. BERNO the territory of Cluny on which he planned to build a monastery under the patronage of SS. Peter and Paul and which he exempted from all temporal authority except that of the Holy See. The successive stages of the buildings at Cluny have been the subject of intensive study by K. J. Conant. Berno replaced the original oratory with a church begun in 910 (Cluny I); this church, razed by MAJOLUS, was replaced by Cluny II, which was dedicated in 981. The monastery was rebuilt by ODILO. Under HUGH, Cluny III was an immense church completed *c.* 1113, and dedicated by INNOCENT II in 1130. Its main altar had been consecrated by URBAN II in 1095. This sumptuous basilica influenced the Romanesque architecture of Burgundy (PARAY-LE-MONIAL, etc.) and the monumental sculpture of France and Spain in the 12th century. Six centuries later, during the tenure of Frederick Jerome de la Rochefoucauld (1747–57), the monastery was partially replaced by structures still in existence. The old basilica was almost totally destroyed during the 1798 to 1823 period.

Abbots and Monks. The list of abbots has been carefully established by G. de Valous [*Dictionnaire d'histoire et de géographie ecclésiastiques*, ed. A. Baudrillart et al. 13 (1956) 40–135]. Several of these had a hand in the making of medieval Europe. ODO OF CLUNY (927–942), Berno's successor, was the first of a series of abbots who during two centuries enabled Cluny to play its important role. Majolus (948–994), Odilo (994–1049), and Hugh (1049–109) were saints who epitomized the Cluniac ideal. Besides being counselors to the German emperors and diplomats in the service of popes and kings, the abbots of Cluny strove to create an authentic monastic spirit in their concern for the interests of the Church and the needs of the time. Many monasteries introduced internal reforms and adopted Cluniac customs; priories were founded and gradually united by the adoption of common observance in essential matters. Together these formed an *Ordo cluniacensis*, which progressively became an order (i.e., a grouping of monasteries under the sole authority of the abbot of Cluny) under Odilo, Hugh, and their successors (*see* CLUNIAC REFORM). Until the 12th century, the growth of the Cluniac properties was rapid. Cluniac "provinces" were established in France, Germany, England, Italy, and Spain, totaling 1,184 houses at the peak of the order's development (beginning of 12th century). Enjoying canonical exemption and temporal immunity, they were subject only to the Apostolic See.

Under Pons de Melgueil (1109–22) a less glorious period began, even though the prestige of Cluny remained great. PETER THE VENERABLE (1122–57) engaged in a series of animated discussions with BERNARD OF CLAIRVAUX concerning Cluniac observance. Despite the fact that the statutes were reformed in 1132, the vitality of Cluny diminished, especially because of difficult economic conditions. Subsequent abbots, chosen often from the great feudal families (Clermont, Anjou, Alsace, etc.), engaged in national or local struggles, and at the end of the 13th century, the order became completely national and French. Unfortunately the popes, with a view to remedying the deplorable state of the Curia's finances, conceded Cluniac priories *in commendam*, and certain abbots preferred to reside in Avignon rather than at Cluny. Jean de Bourbon (1456–85) was the last regular abbot. The commendatory abbots left a part of the government in the hands of vicars-general, but Cluny declined rapidly despite efforts at reform, especially in the 17th century. The order was divided into the Old Observance and the Strict Observance. On Feb. 19, 1790, Cluny came to an end juridically. The number of monks living in the Abbey of Cluny varied. There were 76 at the time of Odilo's election (994); more than 400 at the beginning of the 12th century; 140 during the abbacy of Eymard Gouffier (1518–28); 72 in 1635; and 36 in 1725.

Legislation and Observance. At the time Cluny's foundation, Berno introduced the usages of Baume, i.e., the Rule of St. BENEDICT as adapted by the legislation of BENEDICT OF ANIANE (*see* BENEDICTINE RULE). At the beginning of the 11th century, the first customary appeared. It was a liturgical directory founded on usage, not on law. Several redactions, even for Cluny itself, are known. Under Abbot Odilo: the *Antiquiores consuetudines (B)*, c. 1000 to 1015; and the *Consuetudines Farfenses*, c. 1030 to 1049. During the tenure of Hugh: the *Consuetudines Bernardi*, c. 1070; and the *Consuetudines Udalrici*, c. 1080 to 1083. The *Consuetudines* are descriptive rather than regulatory and do not contain the entire observance. When the needs of the order demanded, as they did during the terms of Peter the Venerable (1132) and Jean de Bourbon (1458), the *Statuta* were revised. Religious observance varied during the eight centuries of the abbey's existence. The daughter abbeys, moreover, were not required to follow the same observances as Cluny, for the customary was essentially flexible and devoid of legalism.

Cultural and Liturgical Life. Cluny's influence was not the result merely of the strong personalities of its abbots. Its monastic spirit was due to the hundreds of monks who generously consented to live the Cluniac observance of prayer and work, and whom Callistus II, in 1120, called "the mirror of monastic observance in modern times" (*Patrologia Latina*, ed. J. P. Migne, 180:1164 D). The cultural and artistic activity of Cluny surpassed that of all other monastic centers, with the exception of MONTE CASSINO (*see* CLUNIAC ART AND ARCHITECTURE). Texts cited by J. Leclercq show that Cluny joined a profound spirituality with broad culture. The library had 570 volumes in the 12th century; and Cluniac writings reveal essentially biblical, patristic, and historical orientation, which attached importance to the authors of classical antiquity.

The primacy of the liturgy in Cluniac observance did not impede individual work and private prayer. Most of the additional liturgical offices that brought on Cluny the accusation of "ritualism" had accumulated prior to Cluny. The customaries and statutes provided for many mitigations and dispensations (especially with regard to the monks entrusted with conventual functions). The weekly liturgy was essentially the same as that of the Rule of St. Benedict, with various supplements and with an amount of solemnity measured by the importance of a feast. The temporal and sanctoral cycles were related to the Roman rite, with local and monastic usages. A long and sometimes exhausting liturgy seems not to have excluded an air of joy and contentment.

Bibliography: L. H. COTTINEAU, *Répertoire topobibliographique des abbayes et prieurés*, 2 v. (Mâcon 1935–39) 1:816–25, with bibliog. K. J. CONANT, "Mediaeval Academy Excavations at Cluny, VIII: Final Stages of the Project," *Speculum* 29 (1954) 1–43; "Mediaeval Academy Excavations at Cluny, IX: Systematic Dimensions in the Buildings," *ibid.* 38 (1963) 1–45; "New Results in the Study of Cluny Monastery," *Journal of the Society of Architectural History* 16 (October 1957) 3–11; "Measurements and Proportions of the Great Church at Cluny," *Beiträge zu Kunstgeschichte und Archäologie des Frühmittelalters* 22 (1960) 230–38. P. SCHMITZ, "La Liturgie de Cluny," *Spiritualità cluniacense* (Todi 1960) 83–99. J. LECLERCQ, "Spiritualité et culture à Cluny," *ibid.* 101–51, with bibliography; *Aux Sources de la spiritualité occidentale* (Paris 1964). K. HALLINGER, ed., *Corpus consuetudinum monasticarum* (Siegburg 1963–), ed. of Cluniac customaries. For additional bibliography, *see* CLUNIAC REFORM.

[R. GRÉGOIRE]

COADY, MOSES MICHAEL

Educator; b. East Margaree, Nova Scotia, Canada, Jan. 3, 1882; d. Antigonish, Nova Scotia, July 28, 1959. He was the son of Michael J. and Sara Jane (Tompkins) Coady. After studying at St. Francis Xavier University, Antigonish, where he received his B.A. in 1905, he went to Rome and began studies for the priesthood at the Urban College there, later receiving the Ph.D. (1907) and D.D. (1910) degrees. He was ordained in Rome (1910); on returning to Canada, he taught in St. Francis Xavier High School and University (1910–25) and was professor of education at St. Francis Xavier University (1925–28). He later studied education at the Catholic University of America, Washington, D.C., and in 1928 became the first director of St. Francis Xavier University's extension department. In 1927 he was appointed by the federal government to organize maritime shore fishermen into cooperatives. In his capacity as director of the extension department, he launched a highly successful program of adult education among the fishermen and promoted cooperatives and credit unions, all of which improved the economic conditions of the fishermen of the Maritime Provinces. In recognition of his work in the Antigonish movement, he was the recipient of numerous awards and was raised to the dignity of domestic prelate (1946) by Pius XII. He served as president of the Canadian Association for Adult Education from 1949 to 1951. His book, *Masters of Their Own Destiny* (New York 1939), is an account of the Antigonish Movement through economic cooperation. It had three editions and was translated into French (Gardenville, Quebec, 1948).

[J. T. FLYNN]

COCCHETTI, ANNUNCIATA, BL.

Religious, foundress of the Sisters of St. Dorothy of Cemmo; b. Rovato, Lombardy, Italy, May 9, 1800; d. Cemmo, Val Camonica, Lombardy, Italy, March 23, 1882. After the death of her parents, Annunciata was raised by her devout grandmother, a noblewoman. She received her education from the Ursulines until their suppression by Napoleon, then from tutors in her home. Annunciata lived with her uncle in Milan for six years following the death of her grandmother in 1823. In 1831, she joined Erminia Panzerini at Cemmo, where they taught girls. With the help of Bishop Girolamo Verzeri, Annunciata founded the Sisters of Saint Dorothy of Cemmo (1840). After receiving training as a religious in Venice, she returned to Cemmo to govern the community until her death. Pope John Paul II beatified her on April 21, 1991.

Bibliography: A. ZUCCHETTI, *Il pane sul muricciolo: beata Annunciata Cocchetti, fondatrice delle Suore Dorotee di Cemmo* (Milan 1990). *Acta Apostolicae Sedis* (1991): 564.

[K. I. RABENSTEIN]

COCHLAEUS, JOHANNES (JOHANN DOBENECK)

Priest, humanist, theologian, and opponent of Luther; b. Wendelstein, near Nuremberg, 1479; d. Breslau, Jan. 10, 1552. He came of peasant origin. He studied humanism first at Nuremberg and then more intensively at the University of Cologne (1504–07) with Ulrich Von HUTTEN. As rector of the Latin school of St. Lawrence in Nuremberg (1510–15), he published noted textbooks and improved methods of instruction. He studied law at Bologna (1515–17), took a degree in scholastic theology at Ferrara in 1517, although he preferred the humanist method, and was ordained while in Rome (1517–19). At Frankfurt in 1520 he entered the reformation controversies, granting need of reform and trying, with Girolamo Aleandro, to reconcile Martin LUTHER. When Luther spurned debate, Cochlaeus began to write the first of his

many polemical tracts, to which Luther answered but once. In his nearly 200 writings Cochlaeus was always zealous and often persuasive, but too frequently his learning was inadequate or clouded with invective. Such was his *Commentaria de actis et scriptis Martini Lutheri* (1549), long famous among Catholics but now discredited. Valuable for reference is his *Historia Hussitarum XII libri* (1549). Some of his works ended on the Index, because of his *argumentum ad absurdum* against "Scripture alone." He gave his services to Cardinal ALBRECHT OF BRANDENBURG (1526) and became chaplain and secretary to Duke GEORGE OF SAXONY from 1528 to 1539. With them he attended the famous diets and helped refute the AUGSBURG CONFESSION (1530).

Bibliography: M. SPAHN, *Johannes Cochlaeus* (Berlin 1898), a catalogue of his works. H. JEDIN, *Des Johannes Cochlaeus Streitschrift De libero arbitrio hominis* (Breslau 1927). A. HERTE, *Das Katholische Lutherbild im Bann der Lutherkommentare des Cochlaeus,* 3 v. (Münster 1943). R. BÄUMER, *Lexikon für Theologie und Kirche* ed. J. HOFER and K. RAHNER (2d, new ed. Freiburg 1957–65) 2:1243–44. H. LIEBING, *Die Religion in Geschichte und Gegenwart* (3d ed. Tübingen 1957–65) 1:1842.

[J. T. GRAHAM]

CODDE, PIETER (CODDAEUS)

Archbishop of Sebaste *in partibus,* seventh vicar apostolic of the Dutch Mission; b. Amsterdam, Nov. 27, 1648; d. Utrecht, Dec. 18, 1710. He came of an aristocratic family; he pursued his studies at Malines and Louvain. In Paris he joined the Congregation of the Oratory before he was ordained in 1672. He became the vicar-general of Utrecht in 1683 and succeeded Johannes van Neercassel as vicar apostolic five years later. In 1689 he was consecrated archbishop of Sebaste. The Jesuits of the mission and some secular priests stigmatized his doctrine and practices as Jansenistic. At Rome in 1701 Codde wrote three statements in his defense *Declaratio, Responsiones, De morte Christi pro omnibus,* but three years later he was condemned by a decree of the Inquisition and deprived of spiritual jurisdiction. He furthermore refused to sign the anti-Jansenistic formula of Alexander VII without restriction. This question of Jansenism occasioned the schism of Utrecht in 1723. Some friends attempted to persuade Codde that the pope had exceeded his rights, but he refused to reassume the exercise of his functions, while at the same time he persevered in his protests against his dismissal from office.

Bibliography: P. POLMAN, ed., *Romeinse Bronnen,* v.3, 4 (The Hague 1952, 1955). L. J. ROGIER, *Geschiedenis van het Katholicisme in Noord-Nederland,* 2 v. (Amsterdam 1945–46) 2:268–348. A. C. DE VEER, *Dictionnaire d'histoire et de géographie* *ecclésiastiques* ed. A. BAUDRILLART et al. (Paris 1912–) 13:184–188.

[P. POLMAN]

CODE OF CANONS OF THE EASTERN CHURCHES

The Code of Canons of the Eastern Churches (*Codex Canonum Ecclesiarum Orientalium*, or CCEO), promulgated by John Paul II on Oct. 18, 1990, is the first complete code of the Eastern Catholic Churches. After Vatican Council II had declared that the Eastern and Western Churches are of equal rank (*Orientalium ecclesiarum* 3), the promulgation of a separate Eastern code of equal title and dignity with the 1983 Western Code of CANON LAW (CIC) meant to supersede the principle, *praestantia ritus latini* (the superiority of the Latin rite), which had been invoked in the Church especially since Benedict XIV declared it in the apostolic constitution *Etsi pastoralis* (May 26, 1742) and his encyclical *Allatae sunt* (June 26, 1755). When John Paul II chose to present the new Eastern code to a general congregation of the Synod of Bishops and, thus, to the entire Church (Oct. 25, 1990), he declared that CCEO, together with CIC and *Pastor bonus* (June 28, 1988) governing the Roman Curia, formed one *Corpus Iuris Canonici* in the universal Church (*Acta Apostolicae Sedis* 83:490). This gave entirely new meaning to the expression *Corpus Iuris Canonici*, formerly associated with Gratian's Decree together with other Latin canonical collections. As John Paul II promulgated CCEO and thereby finished the process mandated by Vatican II of revising the Latin and Eastern codes enacted earlier in the twentieth century, the pope also completed what might well be considered in the Church the century of the codes.

Origins and Background. The apostolic constitution *Sacri canones* (ActApS 82:1033–1044), by which John Paul II promulgated CCEO, traces the historical background to the new Eastern code. The very title *Sacri canones* means to pinpoint the origins of CCEO in the sacred canons confirmed by Nicea II (787) as a first code for all the Eastern Churches. Those 765 canons, together with another 21 promulgated later, still constitute the fundamental code in force in the Orthodox Churches and it is essentially in the light of the sacred canons that CCEO norms are to be received and interpreted (cf. c. 2). Given this bridge with the sacred canons of the first millennium, *Sacri canones* in fact proposes CCEO as a vehicle for future ecumenical dialogue.

In the centuries that followed the Great Schism (1054), when the universal Church was often identified with the Latin Church and the superiority of its rite was invoked, a certain Latinization of the Eastern rites occurred. At Vatican I (1869–70), the call for the sake of disciplinary uniformity to adopt one code in the Catholic Church was supported by the Preparatory Commission for the Missions and the Eastern Churches, although the proposal encountered strong opposition from Eastern fathers who defended the *varietas* of the Eastern rites. An historical turning point for deciding this question would come with the apostolic letter *Orientalium dignitas* (Nov. 30, 1890), in which Leo XIII declared that the variety of Eastern liturgy and discipline was a resplendent ornament that only affirmed the unity of the entire Church.

After the promulgation of the 1917 Latin code, a project for codifying Eastern canon law was formally proposed (July 25, 1927) by the Congregation for the Eastern Church and a circular letter was sent (Jan. 5, 1929) to the Eastern patriarchs asking for their suggestions and collaboration. On Nov. 23, 1929, Pius XI established the Commission of Cardinals for the Preparatory Studies of the Eastern Codification, under the presidency of Cardinal Pietro Gasparri. As a proposed point of departure for the Commission's work, Cardinal Gasparri conceived of one *Codex Ecclesiae Universalis*, in which the characteristic discipline of the Eastern Churches would be duly considered. However, in an audience (March 1, 1930) that ultimately determined the route the Eastern codification would take, Pius XI replied that the Eastern Churches were to have a separate code. This was to remove any suspicion of Latinization and avoid the impression of imposing Latin discipline on the Easterners, who were to make their own norms even though they could draw upon the 1917 Latin code as a kind of exemplar. The Commission worked six years to produce eight schemata that were submitted to Eastern hierarchs as well as other consultative bodies for their observations.

Following the death of Cardinal Gasparri, Pius XI established (July 17, 1935) the Pontifical Commission for the Redaction of the "Code of Eastern Canon Law," under the presidency of Cardinal Aloysius Sincero. By placing the title "Code of Eastern Canon Law" (CICO) in quotes, the pope meant to indicate it as the best choice until a better title could be found. The Redaction Commission was to determine, on the basis of the schemata and the observations made regarding them, the actual text of the Eastern canons. More than twelve years later, in January of 1948, the Redaction Commission presented to Pius XII, himself a former member of the same Commission, the draft of CICO. Composed of 2,666 canons and divided into 24 titles, like other collections of a genuine Eastern tradition, CICO nevertheless was modeled to a great extent upon the 1917 Latin code. From 1949–57, three-fifths of these canons (ten titles) were promulgated in the form of motu proprios: *Crebrae allatae* (ActApS 41:89–119) dealt with marriage law; *Sollicitudinem nostram* (ActApS 42:5–120) outlined procedural law; *Postquam apostolicis litteris* (ActApS 44:65–150) concerned religious life, temporal goods and the definition of terms; and *Cleri sanctitati* (ActApS 49:433–603) treated interritual questions and set norms governing physical and moral persons. With the death of Pius XII and the subsequent convocation of Vatican II by John XXIII, the other 1095 canons (14 titles), though ready for promulgation, remained in the archives of the Redaction Commission.

On Jan. 25, 1959, John XXIII not only convoked Vatican II but also called for the canonical discipline of the Church to be updated. It soon became clear that this revision was necessary in the Latin as well as the Eastern Catholic Churches. Before a project was undertaken to revise the Eastern legislation, Vatican II promulgated (Nov. 21, 1964) *Orientalium ecclesiarum*, which already introduced changes in the relatively new, but incomplete, CICO.

Preparation. On June 10, 1972, Paul VI established the Pontifical Commission for the Revision of the Code of Eastern Canon Law (PCCICOR), composed of members and consultors appointed from both the Eastern and Latin Churches. Eastern non-Catholics were also invited to collaborate in the revision as observers. The task of PCCICOR was to prepare, especially in the light of the decrees of Vatican II, a reform of CICO, with respect to those parts already promulgated in four motu proprios as well as the parts that remained unpublished. The proceedings of PCCICOR (1972–90) are reported in its official organ *Nuntia*, which, though indispensable for tracing the legislative history of CCEO canons, does not presume to be exhaustive. The more detailed minutes of PCCICOR and other unpublished material are now with the Pontifical Council for the Interpretation of Legislative Texts.

For the work of reform, the consultors were divided into ten study groups (*coetus*) that were to follow a series of Guidelines for the Revision of the Code of Eastern Canon Law (*Nuntia* 3:18–24), approved by PCCICOR at its First Plenary Assembly (March 18–23, 1974). Apart from the *Coetus Centralis*, which oversaw the work and harmonized the overall formulation of the canons, each of the study groups drafted a schema of canons with respect to a particular subject matter that would be treated by the new Eastern code. Eight schemas were subsequently produced and sent to consultative bodies for their observations. Special study groups then considered and responded to these observations by way of a *denua recognitio* (further review). By the beginning of 1984, PCCICOR set up the *Coetus de coordinatione* to carry out

"a systematic co-ordination of all the schemas of the future Code of Eastern Canon Law" (*Nuntia* 21:66). The 1986 Schema of the Code of Eastern Canon Law (SCICO) that followed was also sent to PCCICOR members for their suggestions and proposals. These proposals were considered and answered by the *Coetus de expensione observationum*, constituted by PCCICOR specifically for that purpose (*Nuntia* 28). At working sessions of the Second Plenary Assembly of PCCICOR (Nov. 3–14, 1988), members again examined the entire SCICO before voting favorably on each of its thirty titles. Once the changes approved by PCCICOR were made to SCICO and its text further improved, the *Schema novissimum* was presented to John Paul II on Jan. 28, 1989. After the Holy Father reviewed the *Schema novissimum*, some final changes were made to the canons before promulgation (*Nuntia* 31:37–45).

Title and Scope. Although Pius XI had intended the title "Code of Eastern Canon Law" to be temporary, more than fifty years passed before the title "Code of Canons of the Eastern Churches" was chosen (Nov. 9, 1988) for the Eastern codification. When the Second Plenary Assembly of PCCICOR debated the choice, it was pointed out that Cardinal Sincero, President of the Redaction Commission, had proposed substantially the same title since it conformed more with Eastern canonical collections and reflected the esteem in which the sacred canons were held. PCCICOR also chose CCEO over CICO to avoid giving the impression that the Eastern code was of lower rank or simply an appendix to the Latin CIC (cf. *Nuntia* 29:30–34).

CCEO canon 1 indicates that the Eastern code generally affects all and only the Eastern Catholic Churches. This explains why John Paul II promulgated CCEO alone, since he is the only hierarch who could promulgate laws common to all twenty-one Eastern Catholic Churches *sui iuris*. Besides CCEO, the "common law" (cf. c. 1493) of these Churches is found in the laws common to the entire Church (e.g. *Pastor bonus*). CCEO does not legislate regarding the Roman CURIA nor are its dicasteries ever mentioned. In a broad application of the guideline of subsidiarity approved by PCCICOR, CCEO has left the making of particular law to the Churches *sui iuris*. This explains in part why CCEO (1546 canons) has fewer canons than CIC (1752 canons), which contains more detailed, particular law regarding the Latin Church.

Contents. Unlike CIC, which is divided into five books, CCEO is composed of thirty titles in accord with Eastern canonical tradition. Although certain CCEO titles are substantially similar to parallel areas in CIC, they are not always identical. For example, among the corresponding norms regarding lay persons, CCEO recognizes three categories of the Christian faithful by defining the secular state of lay persons as distinct from those in holy order or those who are religious (cf. 399). When compared to CIC, other CCEO titles are significantly different or even unique. While CIC texts served as references for the formulation of some CCEO norms, it cannot be said that CCEO is merely a copy of CIC with some terminological or other minor adjustments made to reflect the different structure of the Eastern Catholic Churches.

Substantially similar to CIC are the following CCEO titles: Preliminary canons (cc. 1–6); I The Rights and Obligations of all the Christian Faithful (cc. 7–26); III The Supreme Authority of the Church (cc. 42–54); XI Lay Persons (cc. 399–409); XIX Persons and Juridic Acts (cc. 909–935); XX Offices (cc. 936–978); XXI The Power of Governance (cc. 979–995); XXIII The Temporal Goods of the Church (cc. 1007–1054); XXIV Trials in General (cc. 1055–1184); XXV The Contentious Trial (cc. 1185–1356); XXVI Certain Special Processes (cc. 1357–1400); XXIX Law, Custom and Administrative Acts (cc. 1488–1539); XXX Prescription and the Computation of Time (cc. 1540–1546).

Significantly different or even unique CCEO titles are: II Churches *sui iuris* and Rites (cc. 27–41), containing definitions for both "Church *sui iuris*" and "rite" (cc. 27–28) and more developed and detailed norms regarding ascription to these Churches (cc. 29–38); IV Patriarchal Churches (cc. 55–150): CCEO recognizes in the patriarchal, major archiepiscopal and metropolitan Churches *sui iuris* an intermediate level (between the local bishop and the bishop of Rome) of Church hierarchy and attributes to the patriarchal Churches, within their territories, the highest degree of autonomy in self-government (cf. cc. 78 and 110); V Major Archiepiscopal Churches (cc. 151–154), to which the norms on patriarchal Churches generally apply (cf. c. 152); VI Metropolitan Churches and Other Churches *Sui Iuris* (cc. 155–176), which have relatively less autonomy; VII Eparchies and Bishops (cc. 177–310), in which norms are established for the election of bishops in the patriarchal Churches (cc. 181–187 §1); VIII Exarchies and Exarchs (cc. 311–321); IX Assemblies of Hierarchs of Several Churches *Sui Iuris* (c. 322), constituting a separate title, are comparable to Latin episcopal conferences; X Clerics (cc. 323–398), where it is affirmed that the state of married clerics, sanctioned by the early Church and the Eastern Churches, "is to be held in honor" (cf. c. 373); XII Monks and Other Religious and Members of Other Institutes of Consecrated Life (cc. 410–572), in which CCEO highlights the monastic life and intends to foster consecrated life in general by recognizing it in six institutional (monasteries, orders, congregations, societies of common life, secular institutes, and ascetic institutes) and three individual (virgins, widows and ascetics) forms; XIII Associations of the Christian Faithful (cc. 573–583); XIV Evangelization of Peoples (cc. 584–594); XV The Ecclesiastical Magisterium (cc. 595–666); XVI Divine Worship and Especially the Sacraments (cc. 667–895), containing characteristic CCEO norms on marriage that will affect its validity: canonical form, which requires the intervention of a priest assisting and blessing (c. 828 §2), can only be dispensed by the Roman Apostolic See or the patriarch in his territory (c. 835); marriages based on a condition cannot be celebrated (c. 826); and, regarding impediments, abduction refers to women or men (c. 806), affinity also applies in the collateral line to the second degree (c. 809 §1), public propriety arises from attempted civil marriages (c. 810, 3°), and the impediment of spiritual relationship has been retained in CCEO (c. 811); XVII Baptized Non-Catholics Coming into Full Communion with the Catholic Church (cc. 896–901), unique to CCEO; XVIII Ecumenism or Fostering the Unity of Christians (cc. 902–908), which, unlike the one CIC canon 755, represents a distinct title and theme that belong by nature to CCEO; XXII Recourses against Administrative Decrees (cc. 996–1006); XXVII Penal Sanctions in the Church (cc. 1401–1467), where CCEO, applying an approved PCCICOR guideline, has abolished *latae sententiae* penalties because they do not correspond to genuine Eastern traditions and constitute no real deterrent; XXVIII Procedure for Imposing Penalties (cc. 1468–1487), in which CCEO, having abolished *latae sententiae* penalties, establishes as a general rule (c. 1402) that a canonical penalty must be imposed by a penal trial (*ferendae sententiae* penalties).

Relationship to CIC. When John Paul II presented the Eastern code to the universal Church, he implied the interrelationship of CCEO and CIC by referring to them as integral parts of one *Corpus Iuris Canonici*. In fact, this interrelationship is codified in CCEO canon 1, which states that Eastern canons also affect the Latin Church where it is expressly (explicitly/implicitly) established. There are nine CCEO canons (37; 41; 207; 322 §1; 432; 696 §§1–2; 830 §1; 916 §5; and 1465) which explicitly regard the Latin Church. Implicit references to the Latin Church arise in CCEO, for example, due to the use of the expression "Church *sui iuris*," since the Latin Church is also one (cf. CIC c. 111 §2). Although this expression appears 243 times in CCEO, its scope must be examined in each case to determine whether or not it means to include the Latin Church, given that the legislator has made one set of laws for the Latin Church and a different one for the Eastern Churches. While the reference to Church *sui iuris* in CCEO undoubtedly intends only the major archiepiscopal (c. 151), metropolitan (c. 155) or other Eastern Churches (c. 174) *sui iuris*, the same expression includes the Latin Church where CCEO refers to the establishment of a common: clerical formation program (c. 330 §2), catechetical commission (c. 622 §1), or ecclesiastical tribunal (c. 1068 §1). CCEO norms may also implicitly concern the Latin Church because of the nature of the matter (*ex natura rei*). These cases may involve the different CCEO marriage norms (mentioned above) in the context of interecclesial marriages, the Eastern canons (29–38) regarding ascription and transfer to a Church *sui iuris*, or norms also to be considered when admitting Eastern faithful to the novitiate of a Latin religious institute (cf. CCEO cc. 40 §2; 452).

Another example of the interrelationship of CCEO and CIC is that parallel passages of one or other of the codes can serve as an interpretative resource in resolving ambiguities in the other. However, as both CCEO canon 1499 and CIC canon 17 indicate, parallel passages are only one such resource to be considered along with the purpose and circumstances of the law as well as the mind of the legislator. Nor can parallel passages of one code simply be regarded as supplementary law to the other since the legislator has promulgated two distinct codes. Moreover, when parallel passages are compared, they are also to be assessed in accord with the canonical sources from which they have come (CCEO c. 2; CIC c. 6 §2). Most importantly, such interpretative recourse can in no way condition the power of the legislator to interpret laws authentically (CCEO c. 1498; CIC c. 16).

A further interrelationship of the codes is established by CIC canon 19, but not by the parallel CCEO canon 1501. The Latin canon states that individual cases involving a lacuna in the law (except penal law) are to be decided having considered, among other things, laws made in similar circumstances. Therefore, where CCEO contains laws to govern similar matters treated in CIC, the Eastern norms can serve to fill gaps in the Latin law. Since the legislator promulgated CCEO nearly eight years after CIC, it may well be that he had certain lacunae in CIC in mind when enacting CCEO. However, the interpretative principle established by CIC canon 19 can only be invoked in individual cases since the legislator alone has the authority to intervene and remedy such legislative gaps definitively.

CCEO can also serve as supplementary law to CIC if the legislator has expressly provided for such a possibility. When Latin Catholics agree to trial by arbitration, for example, CIC canon 1714 allows them to choose the procedural norms to be followed. Since CCEO canons 1168–1184 provide detailed rules in this regard, the Latin faithful may opt to follow these characteristic Eastern norms to avoid a trial.

Although CCEO and CIC are not so separate and distinct as to be unrelated, giving final definition to their interrelationship as integral parts of the one *Corpus Iuris Canonici* of the universal Church is a future task for canonists. Subject to the authority of the legislator, canonical science will need further to articulate and define the ways in which the interrelationship of the codes in the one *Corpus* has been established while, at the same time, respecting the integrity of each code and, in turn, the entire body of law. Within the perspective of the *varietas Ecclesiarum* (variety of Churches) that make up the one Catholic Church, such investigation will be vital if CCEO and CIC are truly to form and animate the one body of canon law of the universal Church.

Bibliography: J. ABBASS, *Two Codes in Comparison* (Rome 1997). "The Interrelationship of the Latin and Eastern Codes." *Jurist* 58 (1998) 1–40. A. AL-AHMAR, A. KHALIFFE and D. LETOURNEAU, eds. *Acta symposii internationalis circa Codicem Canonum Ecclesiarum Orientalium* (Kaslik, Lebanon 1996). K. BHARANIKULANGARA, *Il Diritto Canonico Orientale nell'ordinamento ecclesiale* (Vatican City 1995). J. CHIRAMEL and K. BHARANIKULANGARA, eds. *The Code of Canons of the Eastern Churches: A Study and Interpretation* (Alwaye, India 1992). R. COPPOLA, ed. *Atti del congresso internazionale: Incontro fra canoni d'Oriente e d'Occidente*. 3 vols. (Bari 1994). J. D. FARIS, *The Eastern Catholic Churches: Constitution and Governance According to the "Code of Canons of the Eastern Churches"* (Brooklyn, N.Y. 1992). F. R. MCMANUS, "The Code of Canons of the Eastern Catholic Churches." *Jurist* 53 (1993) 22–61. G. NEDUNGATT, *A Companion to the Eastern Code* (Rome 1994). *The Spirit of the Eastern Code* (Rome/Bangalore 1993). Pontifical Commission for the Revision of the Code of Eastern Canon Law. *Nuntia*. 31 nn. (Rome 1975–1990). V. POSPISHIL, *Eastern Catholic Church Law*. 2d ed. (Staten Island, N.Y. 1996). I. ŽUŽEK, *Understanding the Eastern Code* (Rome 1997).

[J. ABBAS]

CODRINGTON, THOMAS

Preacher to James II; place and date of birth unknown; d. Saint-Germain, France, 1691? He was probably the son of Edward Codrington of Sutton Mandeville, Wiltshire, England, who was presented for recusancy (1645 and 1669), together with his sons, Bonaventure and Thomas, secular priests who worked in England. He was educated at Douai, where he was ordained and became a prominent professor of humanities. Later, having been invited to Rome, he there became chaplain and secretary to Cardinal Philip HOWARD. In July 1684 he returned to England, and he became one of the preachers in ordinary and chaplains to James, Duke of York, later King James II. In Rome he had joined a German institute of secular priests. John Morgan and he were appointed procurators to introduce the community into England. The rule was published in 1697, but elicited much opposition and was attacked by the Rev. John Sargeant in "A Letter to Our Worthy Brethren of the New Institute." This opposition proved fatal to the institute, which was ordered suppressed by Bishop Giffard in 1703. Codrington was preacher to James II at £60 per annum during his reign and followed him into exile at Saint-Germain, France.

Bibliography: *The Victoria History of the County of Wiltshire,* ed. R. B. PUGH and E. CRITTALL (London 1953) v.3, for the Codrington family. T. COOPER, *The Dictionary of National Biography from the Earliest Times to 1900* (London 1885–1900; repr. with corrections, 1908–09, 1921–22, 1938) 4:666. J. GILLOW, *A Literary and Biographical History or Bibliographical Dictionary of the English Catholics from 1534 to the Present Time* (London-New York 1885–1902; repr. New York 1961) 1:520–522.

[H. S. REINMUTH, JR.]

CODY, JOHN PATRICK

Cardinal archbishop of Chicago; b. St. Louis, Mo., Dec. 24, 1907; d. Chicago, Ill., April 25, 1982. He was ordained a priest Dec. 8, 1931. While a seminarian at the NORTH AMERICAN COLLEGE in Rome (1926–32), Cody earned doctorates in philosophy and theology and later a doctorate in canon law. From 1933 to 1938 he served on the staff of the Secretariat of State under Giovanni Battista Montini (later PAUL VI).

In 1938 Archbishop John J. GLENNON of St. Louis appointed him his secretary and, two years later, chancellor, a post he held until 1950. Consecrated bishop on July 2, 1947, Cody served as auxiliary to the archbishop of St. Louis, Joseph E. RITTER, until 1954 when he became coadjutor to the bishop of St. Joseph, Missouri, succeeding to that see in the following year when Bishop Charles H. Leblond resigned. He was transferred in 1956 to the newly united diocese of Kansas City-St. Joseph as coadjutor to Archbishop Edwin Vincent O'HARA, who died in the same year. In 1960 he was appointed both to the National Catholic Welfare Council's Episcopal Commission for the Liturgical Apostolate and to the Preparatory Commission for Studies and Seminaries of the Second Vatican Council. During the council he was a member of the Commission on Seminaries, Studies, and Catholic Education.

Named coadjutor to the archbishop of New Orleans, Joseph F. RUMMEL, in 1961, and Apostolic Administrator of the archdiocese the following year, Cody became the archbishop following Rummel's death on Nov. 8, 1964. Rummel had ordered in 1961 that all Catholic schools of the archdiocese be desegregated by September of 1962, and Cody executed this mandate, refusing to yield to segregationists who threatened a boycott of schools and collections. In this way he gained national recognition for his firm stand on racial justice, which was regarded as a model for educators in the South.

After the death of Cardinal Albert MEYER, Cody was installed as the sixth archbishop of Chicago, on Aug. 24, 1965. In the consistory of June 26, 1967, Cody was created cardinal priest of the title of Santa Cecilia. He was attached to the Congregations for the Clergy and for the Evangelization of Peoples and to the Council for the Execution of the Constitution on the Sacred Liturgy and was later transferred to the new Congregation for Divine Worship.

After Vatican II. Cody executed the decrees of the Second Vatican Council according to the norms issued by the postconciliar commissions and devoted particular attention to the clergy. In a major administrative reorganization, he divided the archdiocese, first into seven vicariates under vicars delegate and later into twelve vicariates under urban vicars nominated by the clergy. Early in 1967 he announced a master plan, called Project: Renewal, to raise money for the modernization of parishes and schools. With a portion of the funds he himself directed the renovation of the Cathedral of the Holy Name, which had become structurally unsound and liturgically outdated. He compelled old and ineffective pastors to retire and kept a close watch over priests from elsewhere residing in the archdiocese. In 1966 he permitted the establishment of the independent Association of Chicago Priests, which made constructive suggestions at first but then more radical demands until finally, in 1971, by a close vote, it censured the archbishop and his auxiliaries for not having presented its views at the spring meeting of the National Council of Catholic Bishops in Detroit. At the end of that year, he established the long-planned Presbyteral Senate but subsequently found it sometimes to be more an adversary than an advisory body.

Cody's decision to close four inner-city schools in the summer of 1975 provoked vociferous protests both in newspapers and to the Apostolic Delegate and the pope. In 1978 the Association of Chicago Priests, by now much shrunken in size, complained to the Congregation of the Clergy about his governance of the archdiocese and requested an official visitation; a year later it appealed directly to the pope himself. Apparently some of the priests who had been embittered by his treatment of them brought the U.S. Attorney for the Northern District of Illinois allegations of improper use of tax-exempt church funds, and on September 10, 1981, the *Sun-Times* revealed that a federal grand jury was investigating whether the cardinal had illegally diverted as much as $1 million to enrich his "stepcousin" (the stepdaughter of his maternal aunt), a lifelong friend, or her children. These "slanderous and nasty innuendos," as Cody termed the attacks, hastened the decline of his health, ultimately resulting in a fatal heart attack.

Large of stature, Cody was jovial, affable, sociable, and genial, but also choleric, jealous of his power, reluctant to consult others or delegate authority, sensitive to injuries or slights, inclined to defer major decisions to the last minute, and wont to fail to answer letters or requests that displeased him. He faced problems unknown to his predecessors, such as numerous defections of priests and a decline in priestly vocations as well as in the ranks of teaching sisters and brothers, a diminution of respect for episcopal authority, a falling off of church attendance, and public criticism, ridicule, and denigration, even from priests. On the other hand, he was esteemed by most of the black clergy and laity. The sad conclusion of his brilliant career dramatized the troubled transition of the Church in the postconciliar age.

Bibliography: C. W. DAHM, *Power and Authority in the Catholic Church: Cardinal Cody in Chicago* (Notre Dame, Ind. 1981). H. C. KOENIG, ed., *Caritas Christi Urget Nos. A History of the Offices, Agencies, and Institutions of the Archdiocese of Chicago*, 2 v. (Chicago 1981).

[R. TRISCO]

COEFFETEAU, NICOLAS

Theologian; b. Château-du-Loir, 1574; d. Paris, April 21, 1623. He joined the Dominican Order in 1588. After receiving his doctorate in theology at Paris (1590), he taught theology, was prior, and served as regent of studies at the Priory of St. Jacques in the same city for nine years. He was also vicar of the French congregation of his order. In 1608 Henry IV chose him as court preacher. Paul V named Coeffeteau coadjutor bishop of Metz in 1617, and he was designated bishop of Marseilles in 1621. In all these capacities he proved himself a staunch defender of the faith against Calvinism. He was a prolific writer, so much so that he is considered one of the creators of French prose. Chief among his works are *Merveilles de la saincte eucharistie* (Paris 1606), *Defense de la saincte eucharistie et présence réelle du Corps de Jésus Christ* (Paris 1607), *Pro sacra monarchia ecclesiae* (Paris 1623), and *Tableau des passions humaines* (Paris 1620).

Bibliography: J. QUÉTIF and J. ÉCHARD, *Scriptores Ordinis Praedicatorum* (New York 1959) 2.1:434–435. H. HURTER, *Nomenclator literarius theologiae catholicae* (Innsbruck 1903–13) 3:715–718. R. COULON, *Dictionnaire de théologie catholique*, ed. A. VACANT et al. (Paris 1903–50) 3.1:267–271. H. M. FÉRET, *Catholicisme* 2:1278–79.

[J. H. MILLER]

COFFIN, EDWARD

Jesuit controversialist; b. Exeter, 1570 or 1571; d. Saint-Omer, France, April 17, 1626. He entered the English College, Rome, in 1588, was ordained in Rome (1593), and was sent to England (1594); he joined the Society of Jesus (1598) while on the mission. On his way to make his novitiate in Flanders, he was captured by the Dutch near Antwerp and sent back to England as a prisoner. He spent the next five years in jail, but on the accession of James I (1603) he was released and exiled. For nearly 20 years he was confessor at the English College, Rome. Near the end of his life he set out again for the English mission but got no farther than Saint-Omer. He wrote a number of books, including several controversial works against the English Protestants. He edited and contributed a lengthy introduction to Robert PERSONS' posthumous reply to William Barlow, bishop of Lincoln, *A Discussion of the Answere of M. William Barlow, 1612*.

Bibliography: T. COOPER, *The Dictionary of National Biography from the Earliest Times to 1900* (London 1885–1900; repr. with corrections, 1908–09, 1921-22, 1938) 4:671–672. *Publications of the Catholic Record Society* (London 1905–) v.37. C. SOMMERVOGEL et al., *Bibliothèque de la Compagnie de Jésus* (Brussels-Paris 1890–1932) 2:1270–71. J. GILLOW, *A Literary and Biographical History or Bibliographical Dictionary of the English Catholics from 1534 to the Present Time* (London-New York 1885–1902; repr. New York 1961) 1:522–523.

[A. F. ALLISON]

COGITATIVE POWER

The cogitative power (or sense) is a power of knowledge that acts in a roundabout, discursive way. The name is borrowed from the Latin *vis cogitativa,* which in turn refers to *cogitatio*—rational, or discursive, thought in contrast to INTUITION, CERTITUDE, and immediate knowledge. This power is also less commonly called the DISCURSIVE POWER. It plays a role in human knowledge similar to that of the ESTIMATIVE POWER in brute animals.

History of the Notion. The first distinctive use of the term was that proposed by AVICENNA. He developed a notion of distinct powers of knowledge that are distinguished from one another by their formal objects. On this basis, he distinguished the following "internal senses," COMMON SENSE, phantasy, IMAGINATION or cogitative power, MEMORY, and reminiscence (*Liber canonis* 1.1.6.5; *De anima* 1.5; 2.1; 4.1, 3). The cogitative power was distinguished from the other powers by its manner of acting in the composition and separation of images.

A different theory was evolved by AVERROËS. He regarded Avicenna's theory as not founded on the Aristotelian text, and thus he referred the knowledge of good and evil to NATURE and imagination (*Destructio Destructionum,* disp. 2). He held that INTELLECT and sense are distinguished completely, but also that the internal

SENSES approach intellect to some extent. The external senses grasp the object according to external accidents as presented here and now. The imagination grasps the same object, according to its permanent qualities, as abstracted from the here and now. The cogitative grasps the object as a particular SUBSTANCE, abstracting from the accidents. Finally, the intellect grasps the universal substance, abstracting from all particularity (*Collegit,* 2.20; *In 3 anim.* comm. 6, 7, 20, 33, 57).

Since Avicenna's *De anima* was the first work to make these notions known to the Latin West, his version of the internal senses was first adopted by such authors as ALEXANDER OF HALES, JOHN OF LA ROCHELLE, and St. BONAVENTURE. However, St. ALBERT THE GREAT also made use of Averroës.

St. THOMAS AQUINAS adopted most of the basic ideas of Avicenna concerning the internal senses, but he also considered the explanations and criticisms of Averroës. Notable are St. Thomas's refusal to accept the real distinction between the phantasy and imagination, and his transfer of the term cogitative to the human estimative; in both of these considerations he seems to have been influenced by Averroës. Basically, his reason for asserting that man possesses this cogitative power is that he learns concrete good and evil by a kind of comparison of many individual instances (*Summa Theologiae* 1a, 78.4). St. Thomas himself made only brief references to the evidence for this. Contemporary thinkers, such as Rudolf Allers, adduce material both from the slow and uncertain way in which an individual learns, and from the relativity of human opinions about good and evil, as shown, for example, by anthropologists.

Existence and Nature. Some philosophers have professed to find the notion of the cogitative difficult if not contradictory. Knowledge of good, it is said, is knowledge of a relation, and only intellect can know a relation. A first and immediate answer is accepted by all Thomists. For "to know good" is quite different from knowing goodness. The cogitative knows a concrete good; it cannot know goodness and relation as abstract and universal (John of St. Thomas, *Curs. phil.* 3:260–65).

For this reason, the knowledge or judgment of the cogitative cannot be called free except by denomination, in the sense of "free in its cause, not in itself." For, as is commonly held by Thomists, only a power that can grasp its formal object as such in ABSTRACTION is able to reflect on its own act and on itself.

Exclusively in Man. First, then, the cogitative power can be found only in man. Secondly, its special mode of operation is due to the fact that it is a sense power of a rational nature, that is, under some influence from reason

(*Summa Theologiae* 1a, 78.4). In general, all Thomists accept this position.

Moreover, an influence implies some kind of causality. There is the order of formal causality, and in this way, the QUIDDITY of the cogitative power is ordered to the quiddity of the intellect. Then, too, there is the order of FINAL causality, according to which the cogitative power subserves the purposes of intellect and will. So much is agreed on by all Thomists. It is in the order of EFFICIENT CAUSALITY that differences arise. Most Thomists, and E. Hugon would here be typical, hold that there is a permanent influence of intellect upon the cogitative as power, prior to activity. Others regard this proffered explanation as obscure. They hold that an efficient influence can be found only in the act of the cogitative.

Impressed Species. Another question often raised, also from a systematic viewpoint, is the way that the cogitative is put into act. According to the general Thomistic theory of cognitive powers, such a power cannot be put into act except through an intrinsic inherent determination, called the "impressed species" (*see* SPECIES, INTENTIONAL). Apart from minor variations, Thomists generally explain the impressed species of the cogitative thus: An external sensation (or an act of the imagination) is joined with the act of CONSCIOUSNES to impress a particular determination upon the cogitative. By the external sense (or imagination) an object is made present; by the CENTRAL SENSE, the knowing subject is cognitively present. The simultaneous impression of these two acts upon the cogitative provides the concrete relation, which is judged good or evil partly by the very nature of the power, partly by reason and EXPERIENCE.

Acts of the Cogitative. It is clear that in the very beginning of human life, one cannot act from prior experience. Thus, if there are any evaluative judgments at this level, they must be of a purely sensory nature. In this sense man has an estimative power. But as a child gains some experiences, he can begin to relate and compare. In the beginning he cannot do this actively, but he can only accept those instances of good and evil that occur in his environment. Because a baby's environment is mostly a human one, the learning of sensory good and evil is rational—that is, at first with the rationality of the family and the culture, and only considerably later with the person's own rationality.

Experience gradually leads to complex memories. Memory depends on attention, and at this early stage this can be only what appeals to APPETITE. Thus the cogitative power is actively involved with the construction of elaborated phantasms from which the intellect in time draws its concepts and forms its judgments and reasonings (*see* KNOWLEDGE, PROCESS OF). In this account, the cogitative power is associated with the formation of phantasms according to its nature as evaluative.

Some Thomists, among whom A. da Castronovo would be typical, offer a different account of the functioning of the cogitative power, basing this on St. Thomas's commentary on Aristotle's *De anima*. There St. Thomas follows Averroës in stating that the cogitative power knows "an individual as standing under a common nature" (*In 2 de anim.* 13, 398). Many interpret this text, possibly in the light of a tradition stemming from the dubious *De principio individuationis,* to mean that the cogitative power comes to know individuals, and to recognize that they have a common nature. Thus it prepares for the intellect a PHANTASM of a number of individuals from which the intellect can legitimately abstract a common nature because it is already known to be there. This knowledge is possible because of the previously mentioned influence of the intellect upon the cogitative power as power.

Cogitative as Particular Reason. From one point of view, all human action is a doing (*agere*) and as such falls under the virtue of PRUDENCE. One of the tasks of prudence is to judge about an action insofar as that action has a relation to the agent himself and his interior attitudes. In this connection judgments are made about what is suitable and reasonable. This "particular reason" is just what the cogitative power grasps, and so the power itself is sometimes called "particular reason." The intellect directs the cogitative power to make such concrete evaluations as here and now, for this man, express a general VALUE JUDGMENT. Since the operations of principal and INSTRUMENTAL CAUSALITY are one action (though the causes are two), the action of intellect and cogitative power in the particular evaluation are also one action of judging (*In 6 eth.* 4, 7, 9; *Summa Theologiae* 2a2ae, 47.3 and ad 3).

From still another point of view, the universal knowledge and the particular sense cognition are comparable as form and matter-form composite. In other words, the principle must be particularized and embodied in a concrete judgment of good and evil.

These considerations point out a way in which we can understand how the judgment of the cogitative is what it is—a discursive judgment of human good or evil—by its union with the intellect of man. For the matter form unity of two acts into one composite activity explains why that single activity shows aspects of reason on the one hand (discursiveness, direct relation to the universal, some transcendence of the order of mere sense pleasure and even utility), and on the other shows aspects of sense (particularity, concreteness, contingence).

See Also: SENSES; SENSATION; ESTIMATIVE POWER; FACULTIES OF THE SOUL.

Bibliography: M. A. GAFFNEY, *Psychology of the Interior Senses* (St. Louis 1942). G. P. KLUBERTANZ, *The Discursive Power: Sources and Doctrine of the Vis Cogitativa According to St. Thomas Aquinas* (St. Louis 1952). J. PEGHAIRE, "A Forgotten Sense, the Cogitative, According to St. Thomas Aquinas," *Modern Schoolman* 20 (1943) 123–140, 210–229. R. ALLERS, "The Vis Cogitativa and Evaluation," *New Scholasticism* 15 (1941) 195–221. A. DE CASTRONOVO, "La cogitativa in S. Tommaso," *Doctor Communis* 12 (1959) 99–244. C. FABRO, "Knowledge and Perception in Aristotelic-Thomistic Psychology," *New Scholasticism* 12 (1938) 337–365. R. HAIN, "De vi cogitativa et de instinctu hominis," *Revue de l'Université d'Ottawa* 3.2 (1933) 41–62. T. V. MOORE, "The Scholastic Theory of Perception," *New Scholasticism* 7 (1933) 222–238. H. A. WOLFSON, "The Internal Senses in Latin, Arabic, and Hebrew Philosophic Texts," *Harvard Theological Review* 28 (1935) 69–133.

[G. P. KLUBERTANZ]

COGLEY, JOHN

Editor and author; b. in Chicago, March 16, 1916; d. in Santa Barbara, Cal., March 28, 1976. He attended parochial schools, the Servite preparatory seminary, and Loyola University in Chicago. During the Depression he joined the Catholic Worker movement, led by Dorothy DAY and Peter MAURIN. For four years he was in charge of its St. Joseph House of Hospitality, Chicago, and edited the *Chicago Catholic Worker.* A nonpacifist despite his Catholic Worker connection, Cogley served in the Air Force from 1942 to 1945. After the war he was cofounder and coeditor of *Today*, the national Catholic student magazine. After a stint in Switzerland, studying theology at the Catholic University of Fribourg, he returned to the United States, and in 1949 he became executive editor of *COMMONWEAL*, the lay-edited journal of opinion where he was to remain as an editor for five years and as a columnist for another ten.

In 1955 Cogley left *Commonweal* to join the Fund for the Republic (now the Center for the Study of Democratic Institutions). His first task was to head a study of blacklisting in the entertainment industry, producing a two-volume critical study of the widespread practice. Becoming a permanent member of the center, Cogley headed up the project on "Religious Institutions in a Free Society" with John Courtney MURRAY and Reinhold NIEBUHR as consultants, and later the Center's study on "The American Character." In 1960 he served as church-state advisor in the Kennedy presidential campaign, playing a leading role in briefing Kennedy before the crucial Houston ministers' confrontation. In 1964 he took a leave from the center to live in Rome for a year while expanding an *Encyclopedia Brittanica* article into a book, *Religion in a Secular Age* (New York 1968), and at the same time covering the proceedings of VATICAN COUNCIL II for Religious News Service. In 1965 he left the Center for the Study of Democratic Institutions to join the *New York Times* as religious news editor. In 1967 for reasons of health he returned to Santa Barbara and the center, where he become a senior fellow and founding editor of the successful *Center Magazine*. In 1972 he published *Catholic America*, a popular history of the Catholic church in this country. Among his other writings was a regular syndicated column for the Catholic diocesan press and later for the *National Catholic Reporter*.

After *Humanae vitae,* Pope Paul's encyclical on contraception, Cogley gave up writing his regular weekly column, feeling that it was not right for him to be considered a Catholic writer when he could no longer support papal positions. In *A Canterbury Tale* (New York 1976), his memoirs, he later wrote: "It was now clear to me that by the time of *Humanae vitae* I no longer accepted the papal claim to infallibility. . . . After 1968 and that fatal encyclical, I began to look more to the Episcopal Church." In September 1973 he joined the Episcopal church. He was ordained deacon in the Episcopal Diocese of California but died before he could become a priest.

Bibliography: *New York Times Biographical Edition* 7 (1976) 337.

[J. O'GARA]

COGNITION, SPECULATIVE-PRACTICAL

"Speculative" and "practical" are terms used as modifiers in philosophy to denote distinctive cognitive qualities about the objects they modify. Speculative generally has reference to TRUTH that is sought for its own sake and considered in itself, whereas practical has reference to truth that is sought for the sake of doing or making something other. According to St. AUGUSTINE, speculative is derived from *speculo,* meaning mirror [Trin. 1.15.8; *Patrologia Latina,* ed. J. P. Migne, 217 v., indexes 4 v. (Paris 1878–90) 42:1067–68]; St. THOMAS AQUINAS adopts the same etymology, noting that the term does not come from *specula,* meaning watchtower (St. Thomas Aquinas, *Summa theologiae,* 2a2ae, 180.3 ad 2). Practical is derived from the Greek πρᾶξις—meaning a doing, an action, or a mode of action—and from πρακτικός—meaning fit for or concerned with action. In their root significations, therefore, speculative refers to seeing or beholding as in a reflection; and practical, to performing deeds or acts.

Philosophical Usage. Speculative and practical have long been used to indicate modalities in cognitive facul-

ties, intellectual habits, ways of life, and felicity. Common distinctions are those between the speculative and the practical intellect, between speculative and practical sciences, between speculative (contemplative) and practical (active) life, or between the happiness associated with the contemplative life and that associated with the active life.

The reason for this usage is that anything that can be identified by its characteristic manner of knowing can be described in terms of a distinction that is proper to the mode of being known, i.e., knowledge itself. Since the distinction between speculative and practical pertains primarily and essentially to modes of human knowledge, the terms designate a real and essential distinction of acts and habits of human knowledge. When applied to the intellect, to life, and to felicity, the terms do not imply an essential distinction, but only some accidental relation to intellectual acts or habits. Thus, the intellect of man is not really divided into a speculative part and a practical part, even though the mind does perform acts and acquire habits that are speculative or practical. Acts and habits of the intellect that are designated as speculative or practical, on the other hand, are really distinct entities and qualities. Inasmuch as these distinct entities are attributed to the intellect, the intellect is denominated in one act or quality as speculative, in another act or quality as practical. Similarly, speculative or practical may be attributed to the whole of human life, since, as rational, a man's life can be characterized by the modality of the acts and habits that predominate in it. That such a distinction is accidental and the elements not mutually exclusive is obvious, for no human being can live a life that is exclusively either speculative or practical. Although every human life contains a mixture of contemplation and action, still the speculative or the practical mode may so dominate a particular life that it can be characterized as either contemplative or active. The same general conclusion, *servando servandis,* follows with regard to felicity.

Intellectual Habits. Three ways of distinguishing intellectual habits as speculative or practical have long been recognized; these are (1) by reason of object, (2) by reason of mode, and (3) by reason of end.

By reason of object some knowledge can be only speculative, because some things that are knowable cannot involve acting or doing. The mind can discover the order, intelligibility, essence, and causes of natural things; but mind does not make or direct such order, intelligibility, essence, or causes. The mind can attain to such truth, consider it, and reflect upon it; but it does not make the truth itself. Other objects of knowledge and science are operable; i.e., the human mind can give order to, direct, make, or do them. The mind can design and direct the construction of a building, the writing of a poem, or the performance of a virtuous act. Such operables can be the object of a practical science or of prudence or of the arts and thus pertain to practical knowledge.

By reason of a mode some intellectual habits are speculative and some are practical. The speculative process—with its first principles ordered to truth alone, its movement toward truth by way of resolution, and its term in the consideration of truth—differs essentially from the practical process with its first principles of operation ordered to doing or making, its movement toward operation by way of composition, and its term in the actual directing of operation.

By reason of end the speculative and the practical are most perfectly determined. "The speculative has for its end the truth which it considers; the practical orders the truth to operation as to an end (St. Thomas, *In Boeth. de Trin.* 5.1). Thus speculative knowledge is perfected in the actual consideration of truth and practical knowledge is perfected in actually directing an operation of making or doing.

Other Applications. Although divine knowledge is sometimes distinguished into speculative and practical, this distinction is analogical because it designates divine knowledge according to a human manner of knowing. In itself divine knowledge is eminently both speculative and practical. The same is true of THEOLOGY.

Human knowledge that is ordered to operation but is enjoyed simply for the consideration of its truth is sometimes called speculative; this, however, is only by reason of the intention of the knower and not by reason of the object, mode, and end of the knowledge itself.

Objects other than human intellectual acts and habits may similarly be called speculative or practical if they indirectly reflect the essential meaning as a sign, an instrument, an effect, or a similarity, or if they are otherwise analogically related to the basic signification.

See Also: KNOWLEDGE; SCIENCE (SCIENTIA); HABIT.

Bibliography: J. PETRIN, *Connaissance spéculative et connaissance pratique: Fondements de leur distinction* (Ottawa 1948). W. A. WALLACE, *The Role of Demonstration in Moral Theology* (Washington 1962). S. E. DOLAN, "Resolution and Composition in Speculative and Practical Discourse," *Laval Théologique et Philosophique* 6 (1950) 9–62. H. PICHETTE, "Considerations sur quelques principes fondamentaux de la doctrine du spéculatif et du pratique," *ibid.* 1 (1945) 52–70. L. WAKEFIELD, "Practical Knowledge," *Reality* 1 (1950) 105–113. M. LABOURDETTE, "Savoir spéculatif et savoir pratique," *Revue thomiste* 44 (1938) 564–568.

[A. D. LEE]

COGOLLUDO, DIEGO LÓPEZ DE

Franciscan missionary and author; b. and d. dates unknown. He joined the Franciscan Order in 1629 at his native city, Alcala de Henares, Spain. In 1634 he arrived in Yucatán, where he learned Maya from Juan Coronel, then served in various pueblos, and taught philosophy and theology at Mérida. He was elected provincial in 1663 and probably died before the end of his three-year term. His *Historia de Yucatán*, written between 1647 and 1656 and published posthumously by Francisco de Ayeta, treats of both civil and religious matters and includes data on native religion and custom. In addition to using the works of others, including Bernal Díaz, Herrera, Torquemada, Las Casas, Remesal, Lizana, Sánchez de Aguilar, and Cárdenas Valencia, Cogolludo consulted the documents preserved in the governmental and Franciscan archives of Yucatán and, when possible, the private papers of prominent citizens. He had not, however, access to Landa's *Relación* or the *Relaciones de Yucatán*. His failure to meet modern standards of historical scholarship in the use of his sources is an inevitable reflection of the outlook and standards of his time. Although he could be naively credulous, he displayed, on occassion, fine critical sense. The enduring value of Cogolludo's work rests on the success of his efforts to collect and preserve much valuable historical material.

Bibliography: D. L. DE COGOLLUDO, *Historia de Yucatán*, 2 v. (5th ed. Mexico City 1957), prologue by J. I. RUBIO MAÑÉ. E. B. ADAMS, *A Bio-Bibliography of Franciscan Authors in Colonial Central America* (Washington 1953).

[E. B. ADAMS]

COHEN, HERMANN (AUGUSTINE MARY OF THE BLESSED SACRAMENT)

Jewish convert who became a Carmelite priest after a career as a pianist; b. Hamburg, Germany, Nov. 10, 1820; d. Berlin, Jan. 20, 1870. As a child prodigy, he was brought to Paris by his mother at the age of 11 and became a student of Franz Liszt. He grew up in the artists' circle in Paris and was a special protégé of Georges Sand; he soon gave piano recitals and concerts of his own. Until he was 27 Cohen led an irresponsible artist's life, traveling throughout Europe and gambling. While playing the organ in the church of Saint-Valère in Paris as a favor to a friend, he experienced during Benediction of the Blessed Sacrament a sudden desire to change his life and become a Catholic. Two years later he entered the Discalced Carmelite novitiate at Le Broussey near Bordeaux and was ordained after four years. He became a renowned

Coimbra University Library, Coimbra, Portugal. (©Peter M. Wilson/CORBIS)

preacher in France, and when he returned to Paris for the first time his opening statement in the pulpit of Saint-Sulpice was: "My first words from this Christian pulpit must be words of repentance for the scandals I once committed in this city." He founded the Carmelite desert at Tarasteix at the foot of the Pyrenees and led the first group of Carmelites to return to London since the Reformation. When the Franco-Prussian War broke out, it became politically difficult for him to remain in France, and he returned to Berlin where he died of smallpox in the prison camp of Spandau while ministering to the prisoners.

Bibliography: C. SYLVAIN, *Life of the Reverend Father Hermann,* tr. F. RAYMOND-BARKER (New York 1925). ÉLISÉE DE LA NATIVITÉ, *Catholicisme. Hier aujourd'hui et demain,* ed. G. JACQUEMET (Paris 1947–) 5:662–663.

[P. T. ROHRBACH]

COIMBRA, UNIVERSITY OF

A Portuguese university of medieval origin under the jurisdiction of the ministry of higher education. Founded in 1290 by King Dinis, the University of Coimbra is among the oldest European universities in the world. It was originally established in Lisbon, where it remained until 1308. Subsequent years, however, found the University shifting back and forth between Coimbra and Lisbon, as circumstances demanded: 1308 to 1338, Coimbra; 1338 to 1354, Lisbon; 1354 to 1377, Coimbra; 1377 to 1537, Lisbon. In 1537 the University was permanently established in Coimbra. These continual changes were not unusual in a period when educational installations and equipment were naturally still rudimentary. Although another university was founded in Évora in 1559 under Jesuit direction and continued in óperation until 1759, it lacked Faculties of Medicine and Civil and Canon Law, leaving Coimbra the center of Portuguese cultural life until the 20th century, when the Universities of Lisbon and Oporto were founded in 1911.

Early History. Until 1290 education in Portugal had been limited to the primary and secondary levels offered in parish, MONASTIC and CATHEDRAL SCHOOLS. Famous among the monastic schools were the Cistercian monastery of Alcobaça and the Augustinian monastery of Santa Cruz de Coimbra, whose pupil Fernando de Bulhões, later known as St. Anthony, became a Doctor of the Church. Previous to this time Portuguese students in pursuit of higher learning were obliged to go either to the

University of BOLOGNA in Italy, PARIS in France, or SALAMANCA in Spain. To avoid the inconveniences of travel abroad, King Dinis founded the first Portuguese university, which Pope Nicholas IV confirmed, granting the new institution, among other privileges, the *ius ubique docendi* and ecclesiastical immunity.

The University was composed of four Faculties: Medicine, Civil Law, Canon Law and Arts, which included the trivium and the quadrivium. There was no Faculty of Theology, which the Church, with the intention of preserving unity of faith, reserved to the University of Paris. Doctors and lawyers, however, could now be educated in their own country, a fact that led to their increase in number and to an educational self sufficiency that the University has preserved throughout the centuries.

As a cultural center, in the 14th century the University probably devoted time to the study of astronomy, thus preparing the way for the geographical discoveries for which Portugal is renowned. In the 15th century Prince Henry, a famous leader of the maritime enterprises, became the protector of the University, now deeply committed to the study of mathematics. It was not until the 15th century that theology was introduced into the course of studies.

In 1537, when King John III established the University permanently in Coimbra, he undertook a complete reform of studies, not sparing any effort to place the University of Coimbra among the most famous institutions of the Renaissance. The professors included both outstanding Portuguese and foreign scholars, among them the Portuguese mathematician Pedro Nunes and the Spaniards Martin Azpilcueta, a famous canonist and the learned anatomist Guevara. Erasmus also was invited to the University. Among the students who have left their names to posterity is Luis de Camões, author of the *Lusíadas,* the Portuguese national epic. King John III initiated the foundation of the Coimbra University colleges, the majority of which belonged to religious orders, to enable their members to attend the University. These colleges increased in number until religious orders were suppressed in Portugal in 1834, when they totaled 23. To this day the buildings are used for various purposes and contribute in large part to Coimbra's architectural distinction as a university city.

Decline and Restoration. The early period of University splendor, enhanced by King John III's protection, was followed by one of decline, to which two major factors contributed: (1) Spanish domination toward the end of the 16th century, which came to an end in 1640 with the restoration of independence; and (2) the subsequent period of political conflict, in which both students and professors took part and which terminated with the peace of 1668. Despite the unrest, however, the University had its notable professors, among them the well-known Jesuit scholastic philosopher Francisco SUÁREZ. The University's greatest decline, in comparison with other European universities, was noted in mathematics and experimental sciences. This was remedied, however, by the large-scale reform undertaken in 1772 by the Marques de Pombal, minister to King Joseph I.

Pombal's reform was preceded by the expulsion of the Jesuits from Portugal, who since 1555 had influenced or directed University education. The reform, which had the support of the founder of the Oratorians, Philip NERI, among other things substituted St. Augustine for Aristotle, qualitative for quantitative physics and created the Faculty of Mathematics and the Faculty of Philosophy, the latter including natural history, experimental physics and chemistry. It relegated metaphysics to the background and provided for properly equipped facilities in line with the new educational orientation, for example, the observatory for astronomy and the botanical gardens, both of which are still worthy of admiration. The Faculty of Theology continued to function until early in the 20th century, when it was replaced by the Faculty of Letters.

Bibliography: H. RASHDALL, *The Universities of Europe in the Middle Ages,* eds., F. M. POWICKE and A. B. EMDEN, 3 v. (new ed. Oxford 1936). M. BRANDÃO and M. LOPES D'ALMEIDA, *A Universidade de Coimbra: Esbôço da sua História* (Coimbra, Port. 1937).

[S. DIAS ARNAUT]

COLA DI RIENZO

Roman revolutionary; b. Rome, Italy, 1313 or 1314; d. Campidoglio Palace, Rome, Oct. 8, 1354. He was born into humble surroundings (an anonymous contemporary biographer says that his father, Lorenzo, was a tavern keeper and his mother a washerwoman and water carrier) and was orphaned at an early age. Until he was 20 years old he lived at Anagni, and in 1333 or 1334 he returned to Rome. There he devoted himself to the study of the classics and of Roman antiquities; he also began to study law. In 1343 he was sent to Avignon by the popular government of the 13 *boni homines* to inform Pope CLEMENT VI of the pitiable state of the city and beg him to declare 1350 a HOLY YEAR. The personality and eloquence of the Roman politician greatly impressed the pope, who named him a notary of the papal camera in Rome on April 13, 1344.

While at Avignon he met PETRARCH and found in him a man who shared his own ideals. In 1344 he returned, not without difficulty, to Rome and there began his public career. He created a sensation by the allegorical images and messianic tone of his speeches, set against the background of a continued deterioration of affairs in the city. Supported by the popular elements of the city, as well as by the gentry and the wealthy merchants, he staged a *coup d'état* on Pentecost Sunday, May 20, 1347. Rienzo assumed broad governmental powers and proclaimed new ordinances intended to restore the material and spiritual well-being of the city, reduce the privileged position of the nobility, and guarantee security and justice for all classes of the population. He applied himself with decision to implementing this program, took the title of tribune, and surrounded himself with a sumptuous ceremonial that, together with the extravagant claims he then began to make, tended to aggravate the political situation in Rome and to increase the opposition of its citizens. A series of contretemps embittered his relations with the pope and the Roman townspeople, until he was forced (December 15) to resign and withdraw to CASTEL SANT' ANGELO. Pursued by the papal authorities, he sought refuge in 1348 among the hermits of Maiella near Mt. Merrone. Incited by his reading and conversations with the sense of an almost prophetic mission, he traveled to the court of Emperor Charles IV in Prague (July 1350), but was imprisoned as an excommunicate. In 1352 he was transferred to Avignon and subjected to a lengthy trial by the INQUISITION, which ended in his absolution and liberation. INNOCENT VI decided to use Rienzo in preparing the ground for Cardinal ALBORNOZ in his efforts to reestablish papal authority at Rome, for he could hold the lower classes in check and lead the opposition to the nobility. On Aug. 1, 1354, at the head of an army of mercenaries, Rienzo entered Rome amid wild acclaim, bearing the title of senator conferred on him by the papal legate. A series of unpopular and arbitrary acts, however, together with violence and extortion that were associated with his rule, turned the people against him and he was killed in the course of a popular riot. The personality of Cola di Rienzo is a controversial subject even today, and varying and sometimes contradictory interpretations of his career make it difficult to judge its precise significance.

Bibliography: COLA DI RIENZO, *Briefwechsel* . . . , ed. K. BURDACH and P. PIUR, 5 v. in 6 (Berlin 1912–29). *La vita di Cola di Rienzo,* ed. A.M. GHISALBERTI (Florence 1928). F. A. GREGOROVIUS, *History of the City of Rome in the Middle Ages,* tr. from 4th Ger. ed. by A. HAMILTON, 8 v. in 13 (London 1894–1902). R. MORGHEN, *Cola di Rienzo, senatore, 1354,* ed. L. GATTO (Rome 1956). E. DUPRÉ THESEIDER, *Roma dal comune di popolo alla signoria pontificia, 1252–1377* (Bologna 1952); *I papi di Avignone, e la questione romana* (Florence 1939). H. VIELSTEDT, *Cola di Rienzo: Die Geschichte des Volkstribunen* (Berlin 1936). G. VINAY, ''Cola di Rienzo e la crisi dell'universalismo medievale,'' *Convivium* NS 2 (1948) 96–107. G. SEIBT, *Anonimo Romano* (Stuttgart 1992). F. PETRARCH, *The Revolution of Cola di Rienzo* (New York 1986). J. WRIGHT, trans., *The Life of Cola di Rienzo* (Toronto 1975).

[M. MONACO]

COLE, HENRY

Confessor of the faith; b. Godshill, Isle of Wight, *c.* 1500; d. Fleet Prison, Feb. 1580. He was educated at Winchester College and New College, Oxford, and received a bachelor of civil law degree on March 3, 1530. He traveled abroad, residing mainly at Padua. Upon acknowledging Henry VIII head of the church in England, he received several ecclesiastical prebends. After he became doctor of civil law (Oxford 1540) he was elected (1542) warden of New College and rector of Newton Longueville, Buckinghamshire. As an ardent reformer during the reign of Edward VI, he later regretted this and between 1548 and 1551 gradually resigned all his preferments. At Queen Mary's accession, he publicly adhered to Roman Catholicism and was appointed archdeacon of Ely in 1553, and canon of Westminster and provost of Eton College in 1554. Cole was chosen by the queen to preach the sermon before the execution of Thomas Cranmer (1556). He was a delegate of Cardinal Pole for the visitation of Oxford (1556), was elected dean of St. Paul's and judge of the Archiepiscopal Court of Audience (1557). Cardinal Pole appointed him executor of his will. Under Queen Elizabeth, Cole was one of eight leading Catholics appointed to take part in the disputation at Westminster in 1559. He was heavily fined for his defense of the faith and deprived of all his preferments. He was committed to the Tower on May 20, 1560, but was transferred to the Fleet in June. Here he died, after nearly 20 years imprisonment.

Bibliography: J. GILLOW, *A Literary and Biographical History or Bibliographical Dictionary of English Catholics from 1534 to the Present Time* (London-New York 1885–1902; repr. New York 1961) 1:529–532. H. TOOTELL, *Dodd's Church History of England,* ed. M. A. TIERNEY (London 1839–43) v.2, 3. A. À WOOD, *Athenae Oxonienses,* ed. P. BLISS (London 1813–20) v.1. P. HUGHES, *The Reformation in England,* 3 v. in 1 (5th, rev. ed. New York 1963).

[J. D. HANLON]

COLEMAN, EDWARD, BL.

Controversialist, intrigant, and victim of the Popish Plot; b. Suffolk, sometime before 1650; d. Tyburn, London, Dec. 3, 1678. Coleman, a Puritan and a Cambridge graduate, became a Catholic about 1670, certainly before 1673, and shortly thereafter assumed the office of secretary to Mary of Modena, wife of James, Duke of York and the king's brother. In this capacity Coleman engaged in frequent correspondence with civil and ecclesiastical authorities at the French court concerning aid for a Catholic revival in England under the leadership of the newly converted Duke of York, and conducted able polemical exchanges with Edward Stillingfleet and Gilbert Burnet. When in September 1678 Titus Oates made his revelation of a "popish plot," Coleman confidently accepted arrest and interrogation (*see* OATES PLOT). To the arraignment of high treason, on the testimony of Oates and William Bedloe that he had conspired with a French Jesuit, several Irish cutthroats, and the royal physician, to murder the king and foment rebellion against Parliament, he replied that he had indeed discussed foreign subsidies for influencing parliamentary elections and reinstating the Duke of York in the Admiralty, but that none of this corresponded to the perjured charges made against him. He was nevertheless found guilty and executed as a traitor.

Bibliography: J. GILLOW, *A Literary and Biographical History or Bibliographical Dictionary of the English Catholics from 1534 to the Present Time* (London-New York 1885–1902; repr. New York 1961) 1:532–536. For a résumé of Oates's charges, see H. FOLEY, ed., *Records of the English Province of the Society of Jesus,* 7 v. (London 1877–82) 5.1:97–109. D. OGG, *England in the Reign of Charles II,* 2 v. (Oxford 1934). J. W. EBSWORTH, *The Dictionary of National Biography from the Earliest Times to 1900* (London 1885–1900; repr. with corrections, 21 v. 1908–09, 1921–22, 1938) 4:744–745.

[R. I. BRADLEY]

COLEMAN, WALTER

Franciscan, missionary, and poet; b. Cannock, Staffordshire, date unknown; d. London, England, 1645. Coleman (Colman) was certainly the younger son of Walter Coleman (b. *c.* 1566) and his wife, Dorothy, of Cannock, Staffordshire, a community whose 400 inhabitants were described in 1604 as virtually all Catholic. He entered the English College, Douai, Sept. 19, 1616. Later he was educated in France. He went back to England for a time, but returned to Douai, where he entered the English Franciscans of the Strict Observance in 1625, receiving the religious name Christopher à Santa Clara. He was sent to England as a missionary and imprisoned, probably in late 1627, but later released. He spent several more years as a missionary and was then rearrested, imprisoned at length, and finally brought to trial at the Old Bailey with six other priests in Dec. 1641. He was sentenced to death, but Charles I, at the behest of the French ambassador, commuted the sentence; Coleman was returned to prison at Newgate, where he died after a lengthy illness. In 1633 he published a poem in 262 stanzas, entitled *La Dance Machabre,* or *Death's Duell,* a rare work that has been virtually unnoticed by literary historians; its dedication to Queen Henrietta Maria is in French.

Bibliography: *The Victoria History of the County of Stafford,* ed. L. M. MIDGLEY (London 1959), for references to the Coleman family. E. H. BURTON and T. L. WILLIAMS, eds., *The Douay College*

Diaries (*Publications of the Catholic Record Society* 10; 1911). T. COOPER, *The Dictionary of National Biography from the Earliest Times to 1900,* 63 v. (London 1885–1900) 4:852. J. GILLOW, *A Literary and Biographical History or Bibliographical Dictionary of the English Catholics from 1534 to the Present time,* 5 v. (London-New York 1885–1902; repr. New York 1961) 1:536–538.

[H. S. REINMUTH, JR.]

COLERIDGE, HENRY JAMES

Editor and writer; b. Ottery St. Mary, Devonshire, Sept. 20, 1822; d. Roehampton, April 13, 1893. He was a great-nephew of Samuel Taylor Coleridge; the son of John Taylor Coleridge, a judge of the Queen's Bench; and the brother of Lord Coleridge, the Lord Chief Justice of England. After attending Eton, he followed J. H. Newman's footsteps at Oxford as a scholar of Trinity College who became a fellow at Oriel. He took Anglican orders in 1848 and was one of the cofounders of the *Guardian,* the organ of the High Church party. One of the second generation of the Tractarians (*see* TRACTARIANISM), he was refused appointment as tutor at Oriel because of his devotion to Newman, just after Newman was received into the Church. Coleridge himself was received in 1852, went to Rome, where he studied for the priesthood at the Accademia dei Nobili, and was ordained (1856). The following year he entered the Jesuit novitiate at Roehampton; his superiors quickly availed themselves of his exceptional talent, and in 1865 he was appointed editor of the recently founded (1864) *Month.* During the 16 years of his editorship, the journal became a leading Catholic publication. He was also editor of the *Messenger* (1877–81). He was a thorough scholar, and in order to raise the level of Catholic education, he founded the Quarterly series, to which he contributed, among other works, *The Public Life of Our Lord* (1872), *The Life and Letters of St. Francis Xavier* (1872), *The Life and Letters of St. Teresa* (1881–88), and *The Story of the Gospels Harmonized for Meditation* (1884). In all he wrote some 20 books. Always an ardent student of the New Testament, he devoted himself to this interest in his later years, even after his health broke in 1890. He spent the last two years of his life, a period of great suffering, at the novitiate where he had begun his Jesuit life.

Bibliography: J. PATTERSON and R. F. CLARKE in *Month* (1893) 153–181.

[D. WOODRUFF]

COLERIDGE, SAMUEL TAYLOR

Poet, philosopher, critic, seminal thinker; b. Ottery St. Mary, Devon, Oct. 20, 1772; d. Highgate, London,

July 25, 1834. He was the youngest son and ninth child of Rev. John Coleridge, vicar of Ottery and master of the grammar school there, by his second wife, Anne (nee Bowdon). While studying at Christ's Hospital (1782–91), the young Coleridge was known as an eccentric but gregarious virtuoso, and formed an important friendship with Charles Lamb (1775–1834).

Career and Works. Coleridge entered Jesus College, Cambridge (1792), as exhibitioner and sizar; but after a brilliant and tempestuous beginning, he joined the Dragoons (1793). After release from military service, he met (June 1794) his future brother-in-law Robert Southey (1774–1843); he never seriously resumed his university career. In Bristol in 1795 Coleridge and Southey sought unsuccessfully the means to found an ideal community in the United States. In the same year he married Sarah Fricker, by whom he had four children. At that time Coleridge began to establish his reputation as a poet and journalist. He met Unitarian intellectuals and for a time intended to become a Unitarian minister, but by 1802 the Trinitarian doctrine had become the basis for his theological reflections.

Coleridge settled at Nether Stowey, Somerset, in 1796 and was joined in 1797 by William and Dorothy (1771–1855) Wordsworth. In 1796 and in 1797 Coleridge had published collections of his poems. In 1798 his poetic gifts flowered in *The Rime of the Ancient Mariner* and *Kubla Khan,* in some of his other contributions to the volume *Lyrical Ballads,* which he published jointly with Wordsworth, and in his "conversation poems." His visit to Germany in 1798 to 1799 enabled him to master the German language and gave him his first acquaintance with Immanuel Kant and German philosophy. In 1800 he moved to Keswick, Cumberland, to be near the Wordsworths and Sara Hutchinson (1775–1835). In April 1804, hoping to halt the deterioration of his health and escape from marital unhappiness, he went to the Mediterranean, where for a time he was private secretary to the governor of Malta, and then acting public secretary. He also traveled in Sicily and Italy. Coleridge returned to England in July 1806—ill, addicted to opium, estranged from his wife, uncertain of his future—relying upon the Wordsworths for comfort and direction. At Grasmere he wrote his periodical, *The Friend* (1809–10, 28 numbers). His alienation from the Wordsworths, which had been deepening since 1807, was never repaired after 1812. Coleridge was in London and Bristol from 1811 to early 1815, working intermittently as a journalist and lecturer; he was in poor health and spirits, and was looked after by new friends, until he finally resolved to break his drug addiction.

The renewal of Coleridge's powers was marked by his collection of poems, *Sibylline Leaves,* and his *Bio-*

Samuel Taylor Coleridge.

graphia Literaria of 1815. In April 1816 he took up residence with Dr. James Gillman in Highgate, London, where he remained until his death. Coleridge's early Highgate years were his most prolific: in 1816 he produced the *Christabel* volume and *The Statesman's Manual;* in 1817, the second *Lay Sermon, Biographia Literaria,* and *Sibylline Leaves;* in 1818, *On Method,* a much-enlarged *Friend,* and two pamphlets on the factory children; and in 1818 to 1819, an important series of literary lectures and the *Philosophical Lectures* (ed. K. Coburn, 1949). Coleridge never completed his philosophical-theological *opus maximum,* and published only two more books, *Aids to Reflection* (1825) and *Church and State* (1830), but he issued collective editions of his poems in three volumes (1828, 1829, 1834).

Coleridge's daughter and his nephew H. N. Coleridge (1798–1843) prepared new editions of his work after his death, and collected and edited much of his unpublished writings. The work of accurate editing, long deferred by the difficulties of the task, should be fulfilled with the edition of the *Notebooks* (ed. K. Coburn 4 v. New York and London 1957– ; 11 v. planned), *Collected Letters* (ed. E. L. Griggs, 6 v. Oxford 1956– ; 6 v. planned), and the *Collected Coleridge* (K. Coburn, gen. ed; 4 v. New York 1966; about 23 v. planned).

His Influence. Coleridge's poetry at its best is characterized by sensitive craftsmanship, a symbolic rather than descriptive thrust, and a way of making myth out of his interior life and the actual world. The strength of his criticism arises from his acute introspective understanding of the psychology and ontology of poetry. Imagination, a way of mind that he distinguished sharply from fancy, is the supreme realizing activity in which a person becomes unified. His *Biographia Literaria,* though allusive and difficult, laid the foundations for the complex critical revolution of the 20th century; Coleridge's splendid critique of Wordsworth's unique genius has not been superseded; and the fragmentary records of his Shakespeare lectures have been influential.

Coleridge's philosophy has Platonic and Kantian origins, but transcends both in establishing an organic (or dynamic or polar) framework in which he sees life as the interpenetration of opposites. J. S. MILL regarded Coleridge and BENTHAM as "the two great seminal minds of England in their age" and recognized that in all his thinking Coleridge "expresses the revolt of the human mind against the philosophy of the 18th century," i.e., mechanical MATERIALISM. Unity was always Coleridge's theme; and life, his guiding analogy. In the absence of a central philosophical work from Coleridge, his reputation and influence as philosopher and theologian depend on scattered passages in his various writings and on the recollection of his lectures and conversation. His philosophy has a strong ethical bias: "My metaphysics are merely the referring of the mind to its own consciousness for truths indispensable to its own happiness." Reason and understanding correspond in the ethical field to imagination and fancy in the poetical, and faith is "the personal realization of the reason by its union with the will." An admirer of the CAROLINE DIVINES and CAMBRIDGE PLATONISTS, he was familiar also with the work of Johann Eichhorn (1752–1827) and F. D. E. SCHLEIERMACHER, as well as that of the contemporary English biblical scholars; he greeted with enthusiasm the emerging historical and anthropological analysis of the Bible (*see* BIBLE, VI). In the posthumously published *Confessions of an Inquiring Spirit* (1840) he sought, in an age of "Bibliolatry," to establish the invulnerability of the Bible, not by avoiding criticism, but by insisting on broader and deeper understanding of Scripture. He had an important influence on the New England transcendentalists (*see* TRANSCENDENTALISM, LITERARY); and his theological influence in England is acknowledged by Thomas Arnold (1795–1842), Thomas Carlyle, J. C. Hare (1795–1855), F. D. MAURICE, and John Henry NEWMAN, among others.

Bibliography: *Complete Works,* ed. W. G. T. SHEED, 7 v. (2d ed. New York 1884), crabbed and incomplete; *Inquiring Spirit,* ed. K. COBURN (New York 1951), best gen. introd. to his thought; *Poetical Works,* ed. J. D. CAMPBELL (New York 1903), ed. E. H. COLERIDGE (Oxford 1912), standard but needs revision; *Biographia Literaria,* ed. J. SHAWCROSS, 2 v. (Oxford 1907), useful nn., but text superseded by the Everyman ed. by G. WATSON (New York 1956). J. D. CAMPBELL, *Samuel Taylor Coleridge: A Narrative of the Events of His Life* (New York 1894), the best biog. E. K. CHAMBERS, *Samuel Taylor Coleridge: A Biographical Study* (Oxford 1938), useful. F. W. BATESON, ed., *The Cambridge Bibiliographies of English Literature,* 5 v. (Cambridge, Eng. 1940–57) v. 3, 5, best cumulative bibliog. J. H. MUIRHEAD, *Coleridge as Philosopher* (New York 1930). C. R. SANDERS, *Coleridge and the Broad Church Movement* (Durham, N.C. 1942). B. WILLEY, *Nineteenth Century Studies* (New York 1949). A. H. HOUSE, *Coleridge* (New York 1953). J. D. BOULGER, *Coleridge as a Religious Thinker* (New York 1961).

[G. WHALLEY]

COLET, JOHN

Dean of St. Paul's, major figure in early Tudor humanism; b. London, 1467?; d. Sept. 16, 1519. He was the son of Sir Henry Colet, enormously wealthy and twice Lord Mayor of London; he was the only one of 11 sons and as many daughters to survive childhood. Educated probably at St. Anthony's School, London, and Magdalen College, Oxford, he may have begun Greek with Grocyn and LINACRE, who had just returned from their Italian studies. Doubtless stimulated by their accounts of Italian HUMANISM, Colet went to Italy in 1493 and there studied Canon and civil law, Greek, philosophy, and Sacred Scriptures. He did not meet FICINO but did correspond with him (Jayne), and the work of Ficino, PICO DELLA MIRANDOLA, and other Italian NEOPLATONISTS was a strong influence on his own thought. He apparently returned to Oxford about 1496 and resumed his studies for the degree of doctor of divinity (which he probably received in 1504); between 1496 and 1499 he was ordained, carried further his philosophical and scriptural studies, and wrote commentaries. In 1499 he met ERASMUS, and the two greatly influenced each other. In 1509 he became dean of ST. PAUL's, London.

Soon after his return from Italy he lectured on the Epistles of St. Paul at Oxford; the lectures on 1 Corinthians made a very strong impact because of their new stress on Paul and their concern with Paul's writings in the context of early Christianity. Colet's interest, then, was moral and historical, not allegorical or speculative. In these lectures, fortunately extant, "Paul and Colet together have much to say about fifteenth-century evils" (Harbison), and here were "the roots of Colet's later famous sermons as Dean of St. Paul's castigating clerical abuses and advocating a Christian pacifism" (*see* PREACHING, I). Though he published very little (like others of his generation of humanists, such as Grocyn and Linacre), Colet communicated through his conversation and correspondence, and one can see the power of his influence upon friends like Erasmus and Thomas MORE, and perhaps also on TYNDALE, who is likely to have heard him at Oxford and in London. And, finally, his foundation of St. Paul's School the year before his death enabled him to build a living memorial of many of his educational ideals, a memorial that played a significant role in the development of Tudor education. About 1510 Colet wrote a Latin grammar—his accidence (*Aeditio*) for the syntax by William Lily —and this work was frequently reprinted both separately and as part of what was popularly known as Lily's grammar. The later official textbook of Henry VIII, compiled after Lily's death, built upon not only Colet and Erasmus but also Melanchthon and others.

Bibliography: Works, ed. and tr. J. H. LUPTON, 5 v. (London 1867–76). F. SEEBOHM, *The Oxford Reformers . . .* (3d ed. London 1887). J. H. LUPTON, *A Life of John Colet* (new ed. London 1909; repr. Hamden, CT 1961). D. ERASMUS, *Opus epistolarum,* ed. P. S. ALLEN et al., 12 v. (Oxford 1906–58) 4:1211; *The Epistles of Erasmus . . . ,* ed. and tr. *F. M. NICHOLS,* 3 v. (New York 1901–18; repr. 1962). P. A. DUHAMEL, "The Oxford Lectures of John Colet," *Journal of the History of Ideas* 14 (1953) 493–510. E. H. HARBISON, *The Christian Scholar in the Age of the Reformation* (New York 1956). E. W. HUNT, *Dean Colet and His Theology* (London 1956). V. J. FLYNN, "The Grammatical Writings of William Lily, ?1468–?1523," *Papers of the Bibliographical Society of America* 37 (1943) 85–113. For the full story of Lily's Latin grammar and that of Henry VIII see C. G. ALLEN in *The Library,* 5th ser. 9 (1954) 85–100; 14 (1959) 49–53. P. B. O'KELLY, *John Colet's Commentary on I Cor.* (Doctoral diss. unpub. Harvard U. 1960). L. MILES, *John Colet and the Platonic Tradition* (La Salle, IL 1961), largely superseded by JAYNE. C. S. MEYER, "John Colet's Significance for the English Reformation," *Concordia Theological Monthly* 34 (1963) 410–418; *John Colet Bibliog.* (privately printed; Concordia Seminary, St. Louis, MO 1963). S. R. JAYNE, *John Colet and Marsilio Ficino* (Oxford 1963). A. B. EMDEN, *A Biographical Register of the Scholars of the University of Oxford to A.D. 1500,* 3 v. (Oxford 1957–59) 1:462–464. J. GLEASON, *John Colet* (Berkeley 1989). J. B. TRAPP *Erasmus, Colet and More* (London 1991).

[R. J. SCHOECK]

COLETTE, ST.

Foundress of Colettine Poor Clares; b. Nicolette Boylet (or Boellet) at Calcye, near CORBIE, Jan. 13, 1381; d. Ghent, March 6, 1447. Born in answer to her parents' prayer, she lived a life marked by the unusual. At age 21 she became a recluse, after three unsuccessful attempts at the religious life, and for several years lived in rigorous penance. During this time her mission to reform the POOR CLARES was made clear to her. She sought permission from antipope BENEDICT XIII, at Avignon, who received her into the Second Order of St. Francis, dispensed her from a novitiate, and appointed her abbess general. In 1408, with the help of Bl. Henry de la Baume, she began the work of restoring the primitive Rule of St. Clare

John Colet.

(1253), imposing absolute poverty and perpetual fast. Many existing convents of the Urbanist Clares were reformed and some 20 new ones established during her lifetime. In 1412 the Franciscan Conventuals in northern France and Belgium established a reformed branch called Coletans. Never numerous, they were suppressed in 1517. Iconography shows Colette as an abbess, barefooted, usually with a lamb at her feet. She was canonized in 1807.

Feast: March 6.

Bibliography: C. VAN CORSTANJE et al., eds., *Vita Sanctae Coletae* (Leiden 1981). M. FRANCIS, *Walled in Light* (New York 1959, rep. Chicago 1985). E. LOPEZ, *Culture et sainteté: C. de Corbie* (Saint-Etienne 1994). P. DE VAUX, *Vie de soeur C.,* tr. E. LOPEZ (Saint-Etienne 1994). M. RICHARDS, "Community and Poverty in the Reformed order of St. Clare in the Fifteenth Century" *Journal of Religious History* 19 (June 1995) 10–25.

[M. F. LAUGHLIN]

COLGAN, JOHN

Irish Franciscan hagiographer; b. Priest-town, near Carndonagh, County Donegal, *c.* 1592; d. St. Anthony's College, Louvain, Jan. 15, 1658. There is no definite information about Colgan's early years. He left Ireland for

Spain or Belgium about 1612, and having done courses in philosophy and theology, was ordained about 1618. He entered the Franciscan Order at St. Anthony's College, Louvain, on April 26, 1620. A letter in Irish written by Colgan on Dec. 26, 1628 gives the impression that he had at that time been teaching for a period in Germany and indicates that he was being transferred to Mainz as lector of theology.

Sometime before June 1634, Colgan returned to St. Anthony's College, Louvain, where he was appointed lector in theology and master of novices. He also joined wholeheartedly in a scheme, which was then under way at St. Anthony's College, for the collection and publication of manuscript material dealing with the ecclesiastical history of Ireland and the lives of the Irish saints. This scheme grew out of a meeting between two Irish Franciscans, Hugh Ward and Patrick Fleming, and an Irish secular priest, Thomas Messingham, at Paris in 1623. Messingham was preparing a volume on the lives of the Irish saints, and Ward and Fleming decided to join with him in the project. The agreement reached with Messingham fell through, and Ward and Fleming continued on their own. It was their intention to gather, at St. Anthony's College, copies of the lives of the Irish saints to be found in the libraries of Europe, and Ward sent Brother Michael O'Clery to Ireland in 1626 to make copies of the material in the old books there. Many other Irish Franciscans took an active part in the work, and there is evidence to show that in 1628 Colgan was already interested in the project, since he was then inquiring about documents that could be copied from libraries in Central Europe.

Patrick Fleming was killed in Bohemia in 1631, and four years later Hugh Ward died. It fell to Colgan to direct the historical publications that they had had in mind. He set about his task by putting the finishing touches to Ward's work and by preparing for the printers manuscripts and copies of manuscripts that had been brought together at Louvain. He sought out new material, and if there was no biography available for some particular saint, Colgan compiled one from various scattered references.

Although he applied himself diligently to the task of preparing the lives of Irish saints for publication, poor health and lack of sufficient money thwarted his efforts. However, in 1645 he succeeded in having the first volume of the *Acta Sanctorum* published at Louvain; it contained the lives of Irish saints whose feast days fell in January, February, and March. A generous grant of money from Hugh O'Reilly, Archbishop of Armagh, covered the cost of printing. His *Triadis Thaumaturgae Acta,* appeared in 1647, containing the lives of SS. Patrick, Brigid, and Colmcille. Archbishop Thomas Fleming

of Dublin met the expenses of this volume. Both volumes were illustrated with copious notes and valuable appendices.

In 1651 Colgan had been appointed commissary of the three Irish Franciscan colleges at Louvain, Prague, and Vielun (Poland), but because of failing health he found it necessary to ask his superiors to relieve him of this office in February of 1652. In 1655 he published at Antwerp a book of about 200 pages dealing with the life, writings, and fatherland of John Duns Scotus. He was an ardent defender of the Irish birth of Scotus. At the time of his death Colgan had a third volume on the Irish saints in an advanced stage of preparation; it contained the lives of those saints whose feast days fell in the months of April, May, and June, but the necessary financial support to have it printed was not forthcoming. It was his intention to publish seven or eight folio volumes in all, and three of these were to be devoted to the Irish apostolate abroad.

Bibliography: J. COLGAN, *Triadis Thaumaturgae* (Dublin 1996). R. SHARPE, *Medieval Irish Saints' Lives: An Introduction to Vitae Sanctorum Hiberniae* (Oxford 1991). C. PLUMMER, ed., *Vitae Sanctorum Hiberniae* (Dublin 1997).

[C. GIBLIN]

COLIN, FREDERIC LOUIS

Missionary, founder of the Canadian College in Rome; b. Lignières, France, Jan. 14, 1835; d. Montreal, Canada, Nov. 27, 1902. Although admitted to the École Normale Supérieure of Paris, he entered the Sulpician seminary of Issy (1855) and was ordained in Paris, Dec. 17, 1859. He was sent to Montreal (1862), where he served as missionary, curate, and professor and director of the major seminary. From 1881 until his death, he was superior of the Sulpicians in Canada. He distinguished himself in the field of education, founding the philosophy seminary in Montreal (1892), and playing a major part in establishing what later became the University of Montreal (1876). At the suggestion of Cardinal Edward H. Howard, Colin organized and founded the Canadian College in Rome, where the first students were enrolled in 1888.

Bibliography: H. GAUTHIER, *Sulpitiana* (Montreal 1926).

[J. LANGIS]

COLIN, JEAN CLAUDE MARIE, VEN.

Founder of the MARIST FATHERS and MARIST SISTERS; b. Saint-Bonnet-le-Troncy, near Lyons, France, Aug. 7, 1790; d. La Neylière (Rhône), Nov. 15, 1875.

During his boyhood his ambition was to lead a religious life as a solitary. He was ordained (1816) after studies in the seminary at Lyons, where he became interested in the plan for a society of Mary promoted by a fellow seminarian, Jean Claude Courveille. On the day after his ordination he and 11 others signed a promise to strive for the creation of this society. In 1817 Colin and Jean Marie Chavoin founded the Marist Sisters. While working as assistant to his brother Pierre in Cerdon (Ain), Colin composed the first rule of the Marist Fathers and received from Pius VII in 1822 a letter encouraging him to proceed with the formation of this congregation. When Colin was assigned to the Diocese of Belley, restored in 1822, the bishop placed him in charge of the missionary Marists of the diocese (1825–29) and head of the minor seminary (1829–45). Aspirant Marist priests elected Colin superior (1830). After the Holy See approved the congregation (1836) subsequent to Colin's acceptance of Western Oceania as a mission, Colin became superior general (1836–54). As head of the institute, he promoted mission and educational works at home and sent more than 100 missionaries to the Pacific area. Colin revealed enterprise and prudence as superior general and in his dealings with ecclesiastical and civil officials in Oceania he displayed diplomatic talent. By 1854 the Marists had 280 priests and brothers. Upon completing his term as superior general Colin spent his remaining years at La Neylière, where he completed the final text of the congregation's constitutions (1869), which were approved by Rome (1873). The decree introducing his cause for beatification was issued in 1908, and the decree on the validity of his process in 1926.

Bibliography: *Le Très Révérend Père Colin,* 6 v. Lyon 1895–98). P. MULSANT, *Le Vénérable Père Jean-Claude Colin* (Paris 1925); *L'Âme du vénérable Père Colin* (Lyons 1933). J. BONNEFOUX, *Dictionnaire de spiritualité ascétique et mystique. Doctrine et histoire,* ed. M. VILLER et al. (Paris 1932–) 2:1078–85. J. COSTE and G. LESSARD, eds., *Origines maristes, 1786–1836,* 4 v. (Rome 1960–66).

[S. W. HOSIE]

COLL GUITART, FRANCISCO, BL.

Dominican priest, founder of the Dominican Sisters of the Annunciation; b. Gombreny (Gombrèn) near Gerona (Catalonian Pyrenees), Spain, May 18, 1812; d. Barcelona, Spain, April 2, 1875. Coll was the youngest of ten children of a wool carder who died when Coll was four. Even while studying at the seminary of Vich (1823–30), he devoted himself to the catechesis of children. He also taught grammar to pay for his education. He joined the Dominicans at Gerona (1830), where he was professed and ordained to the diaconate. When the friars were ex-

claustrated by the government (1835), Coll continued to live as a Dominican and was ordained priest (March 28, 1836) with the consent of his superiors. After serving as a parish priest (1836–39), Coll preached throughout Catalonia for several decades, giving popular missions and offering spiritual direction, like his friend St. Anthony Mary CLARET, whom he aided in forming the Apostolic Fraternity of priests. Named director of the secular order of Dominicans (1850), Coll reopened the former Dominican friary, cared for the cholera victims during the 1854 outbreak, and founded the Dominican Sisters of the Annunciation (1856) to provide for the religious formation of youth in poor and neglected regions. From 1869 until his death, Coll suffered from increasing physical problems caused by a stroke, including blindness and the loss of mental acuity. Nevertheless, the Dominicans, upon returning to Spain in 1872, found that Coll had carefully maintained the order's spirit and work throughout its suppression. Coll's mortal remains are venerated in the motherhouse of La Annunciata (Vich), which had grown to 300 members in 50 houses by the time of his death. Coll was beatified in the first ceremony presided over by John Paul II, April 29, 1979.

Feast: May 19 (Dominicans).

Bibliography: L. GALMÉS MÁS, *Francisco Coll y Guitart, O.P., vida y obra* (Barcelona 1976). *Acta Apostolicae Sedis* (1979) 1505–08. *L'Osservatore Romano,* Eng. ed. 19 (1979): 6–7.

[K. I. RABENSTEIN]

COLL Y PRAT, NARCISO

Archbishop of Caracas, Venezuela, during the War of Independence; b. Cornellá de Ter, Gerona, Spain, 1754; d. Madrid, Dec. 28, 1822. He was a doctor of law, both civil and Canon; professor at the University of Cervera, Spain; and member of the Academy of Fine Arts of Barcelona. He took possession of the archbishopric of Caracas on July 31, 1810, just as there had been established a new political regime that would proclaim absolute independence from Spain the next year. That independence cost long years of warfare, during which Republicans and Royalists were alternately in power. In addition to the calamities of war, a terrible earthquake destroyed large parts of cities and towns. In Caracas alone, more than 10,000 persons died, almost a third of the population. In the face of the misery and helplessness of the populace, the archbishop showed extraordinary charity. As a Spaniard and appointee of the king, he was loyal to the Spanish authorities; but he also showed respect and obedience to the Republican authorities. Above all, with the authorities of either, he always tried to be a good pastor, preventing cruelty, interceding on behalf of those

Narciso Coll Y Prat.

persecuted by either faction, and helping those in need, while at the same time maintaining religious services, religious discipline, and the piety of the faithful. Bolívar recognized the virtues of the archbishop and therefore retained him in his position. On the other hand, the Spanish authorities considered Coll lax in his behavior toward the Republicans, and he was recalled by the king. On Dec. 8, 1816, he returned to Spain to answer the charges of disloyalty made by the Spanish leader Morillo. To justify himself, he wrote two extensive *Memoriales,* to which he attached numerous supporting documents. In 1822 he was appointed bishop of Palencia, Spain, but he died without assuming the office.

Bibliography: N. COLL Y PRAT, *Memoriales sobre la independencia de Venezuela* (Caracas 1960). P. LETURIA, *Relaciones entre la Santa Sede e Hispanoamérica,* 3 v. (*Analecta Gregoriana,* 101–103; Rome 1959–60). N. E. NAVARRO, *Anales eclesiásticos Venezolanos* (2d ed. Caracas 1951).

[P. P. BARNOLA]

COLLATIO

A term having several meanings in ecclesiastical contexts, especially the following: (1) The light meal permitted on days of fasting in addition to the full meal. (2) The lives of the Fathers, especially as arranged for public reading in monastic establishments of the Middle Ages; a usage deriving, perhaps, from the *Collationes Patrum* of John CASSIAN. (3) A sermon or exposition of a passage from Scripture, the religious rule, or a patristic writing, common in houses of friars in the 13th and 14th centuries (e.g., the *Collationes in Hexaemeron* of St. BONAVENTURE); sometimes only an outline or plan is meant. (4) In some 13th-century scholastic circles, the inductive stage of philosophical investigation. (5) Formerly in Canon Law, the act of conferring an ecclesiastical benefice or office (*collatio tituli*) on a designated person or presentee, whether by right ordinary jurisdiction (e.g., a bishop) or of a prerogative arising out of a lawful title, custom, or privilege (e.g., patronage). *See* 1917 *Codex iuris canonici* (Rome 1918; repr. Graz 1955) cc. 1431–47.

Bibliography: J. LECLERCQ, "Recherches sur l'anciens sermons monastiques," *Revue Mabillon* 36 (1946) 1–14. J. G. BOUGEROL, *Introduction à l'étude de Saint Bonaventure* (Paris 1962) 178–192. M. D. CHENU, "Notes de lexicographie philosophique médiévale," *Revue des sciences philosophiques et théologiques* 16 (1927) 435–446. E. F. REGATILLO, *Institutiones iuris canonici* (6th ed. Santander 1961) 1:228–245. G. BARRACLOUGH, *Papal Provisions* (Oxford 1935); "Praxis Beneficiorum," *Zeitschrift der Savigny-Stiftung für Rechtsgeschichte, Kanonistische Abteilung* 27 (1938) 94–134. G. MOLLAT, *Dictionnaire de droit canonique,* ed. R. NAZ (Paris 1935–65) 2:413–431. N. DEL RE, A. MERCATI and A. PELZER, *Dizionario ecclesiastico* (Turin 1954–58) 1:663. F. L. CROSS, *The Oxford Dictionary of the Christian Church* (London 1957) 310. A. STURM, *Lexikon für Theologie und Kirche,* ed. J. HOFER and K. RAHNER (Freiberg 1957–65) 3:3.

[L. E. BOYLE]

COLLEGE THEOLOGY SOCIETY

The College Theology Society was founded in 1953 and originally called the Society of Catholic College Teachers of Sacred Doctrine. The present name, "College Theological Society" was adopted at the 1967 annual meeting.

An association of college and university teachers, the College Theology Society serves to promote the teaching of theology, especially on the undergraduate level; to foster communication and exchange of information and experience relative to the study of religion through publications sponsored by the Society and through national and regional meetings; and to integrate religious studies into the rest of the undergraduate curriculum.

Although full membership is open to all who teach religious thought on the college or university level or who have been awarded a graduate degree in the field, the Society has historically drawn a significant majority of its members from Catholic institutions. While maintaining its roots in the Roman Catholic tradition, the Society has become ecumenical in its membership and outlook.

The adoption of a new name mirrored the changes that took place in the academic study of religion at Catholic colleges in the 1960s. Religious studies, as well as that branch of the discipline that concerns itself particularly with Christian theology, were increasingly recognized as bona fide academic pursuits that have a legitimate place in the liberal arts curriculum. As college curricula changed in the 1960s and 1970s, so also did the College Theology Society—a change concretely illustrated by the adoption of its new name at the 1967 annual meeting. Today the Society reflects a broad range of academic inquiry, although its principal focus remains Christian theology. Its membership includes non-Catholic as well as Catholic teachers in public and religiously affiliated institutions.

Publications have been a strong component of the Society's efforts. An annual publication, distributed to members but also marketed as a trade book, is built around papers presented at the annual convention. A semiannual journal, *Horizons,* begun in 1974, has proven to be exceptionally successful. With an editorial office at Villanova University and partially supported by assistance from that institution, the journal features scholarly articles, book reviews, opportunities for readers' comments on contemporary issues, and studies on effective college teaching.

[T. M. MCFADDEN/EDS.]

COLLEGIALITY, EPISCOPAL

The term collegiality came into vogue about the time of the Second Vatican Council. Found in the Dogmatic Constitution on the Church it was used to describe the Church's mode of life, especially governance: "Together with its head, the Roman Pontiff, and never without this head, the episcopal order is the subject of supreme and full power over the universal Church" (*Lumen gentium* 22). Conciliar documents regularly interchanged the term *collegium* (college), with the related terms *ordo* (order), *corpus* (body), and *fraternitas* (brotherhood). The meaning of the term was warmly debated, and in order to safeguard against misunderstanding the Council offered *societas stabilis* as a synonym (*Lumen gentium* 19).

Doctrinal History. In the 4th and 5th centuries *collegium* was a common term, designating the apostolic community, as well as the community of bishop-presbyter (priest) and of the bishops among themselves.

During the 14th–19th centuries, even among those decidedly dedicated to papal primacy, the concept of the collegial character of the episcopacy played a prominent role.

However, from the 12th century on a distinction between *ordo* and *jurisdictio* intensified to the point of becoming a separation. This was complicated by an undue emphasis on the cultic (and priestly) dimension of both the Church and its ordained minister or office (equated terminologically with priest), as well as a decidedly individualistic approach to priesthood and Eucharist. The ordained minister (priest, bishop) was related to the *corpus verum* (the Eucharistic Body of Christ) on the basis of ordination by the Sacrament of Holy Orders, to the *corpus mysticum* (the ecclesial Body of Christ) on the basis of appointment by (episcopal or papal) jurisdiction (cf. de Lubac). Scholastic theology declined to acknowledge that episcopal ordination belongs to the Sacrament of Holy Orders and attributed it solely to papal jurisdictional empowerment. Consequently the episcopal college came to be regarded as merely the jurisdictional creation of the papacy.

The Teaching Restored. *Lumen gentium* in the final draft emphatically restored the ancient understanding of collegiality as the juridical as well as moral communion of the bishops among themselves and in union with the pope, for the shepherding of the universal Church. Thus the paragraph from Chapter III of the Constitution, quoted at the beginning of this article, also states "one is constituted a member of the episcopal body by virtue of sacramental consecration and by hierachical communion with the head and members of the body" (*Lumen gentium* 22). At the time of the Council Joseph Ratzinger emphasized that "conciliarity is something that belongs to the essence of the Church; however it has worked historically, the conciliar principle lies at the heart of the Church and ever presses from within towards realization" (Ratzinger 180).

When the Dogmatic Constitution on the Church was published, a prefatory note was appended, reportedly at the direction of Pope Paul VI, by way of explanation of the terms in Chapter III. The purpose of the *Nota explicativa,* drafted by the Theological Commission, was to set forth in more technical language how certain points in the text are to be understood. It clarifies the meaning of the term "college," the manner by which one becomes a member, the significance of "hierarchical communion," and the relation of the collegial authority of the bishops and the primacy of the Pope (W. Abbot, *Documents of Vatican II,* p. 98). The *Nota,* although a part of the *acta* of the Council, does not belong to the official text of the Constitution.

See Also: BISHOP (SACRAMENTAL THEOLOGY OF); BISHOP, DIOCESAN (CANON LAW); APOSTOLIC

SUCCESSION; EPISCOPAL CONFERENCES; PRIMACY OF THE POPE.

Bibliography: G. ALBERIGO, *Lo sviluppo della dottrina sui poteri nella chiesa universale* (Rome 1964). R. AUBERT, ed., *Le Concile et les Conciles* (Paris 1960). J. COLSON, *L'épiscopat catholique* (Paris 1963). Y. CONGAR, "Konzil als Versammlung und grundsatzliche Konziliarität der Kirche," in H. VORGRIMLER, ed., *Gott in Welt II* (Freiburg 1964) 135–165 (contains many sources). Y. CONGAR, ed., *La collégialité épiscopale* (Paris 1964). V. FAGIOLI and G. CONCETTI, eds., *La Collegialità episcopale per il futuro della Chiesa* (Florence 1969). J. GUYOT, *Études sur le sacrement de l'ordre* (Paris 1957). O. KARRER, *Um die Einheit der Christen* (Frankfurt 1953). H. KÜNG, ed., *Papal Ministry in the Church. Concilium 64* (New York 1971). J. LECUYER, *Études sur la collégialité épiscopale* (Lyons 1964). M. J. LE GUILLOU, "L'Expérience orientale de la collégialité épiscopale et ses requêtes," *Istina* 10 (1964) 111–124. H. DE LUBAC, *Corpus mysticum* (rev. ed., Paris 1949). K. RAHNER, *Bishops: Their Status and Function,* tr. E. QUINN (London 1964). K. RAHNER and J. RATZINGER, *The Episcopate and the Primacy,* tr. K. BARKER et al. (New York 1962). J. RATZINGER, *Das neue Volk Gottes* (Düsseldorf 1970). P. RUSCH, "Die kollegiale Struktur des Bischofsamtes," *Zeitschrift für katholische Theologie* 86 (Vienna 1964) 197–216. O. SEMMELROTH, "Die Lehre von der kollegialen Hirtengewalt über die Gesamtkirche," *Scholastik* 39 (1964) 161–179. D. M. STANLEY, "The New Testament Basis for the Concept of Collegiality," *Theological Studies* 25 (Woodstock, Md. 1964) 197–216. W. DE VRIES, "Der Episkopat auf den Synoden vor Nicäa," *Theologische-praktische Quartalschrift* 111 (Linz 1963) 263–275; "Die kollegiale Struktur der Kirche in den ersten Jahrhunderten," *Una sancta* 19 (Meitingen-Augsburg 1964) 296–317.

[R. KRESS/EDS.]

COLLIER, PETER FENELON

Pioneer U.S. Catholic subscription book and magazine publisher; b. Myshall, Ireland, Dec. 12, 1849; d. New York City, April 24, 1909; son of Robert C. and Catherine (Fenelon) Collier. Coming to the United States in 1866, the family settled in Dayton, Ohio, where Peter worked in the railroad shops. In 1868 he entered the seminary of the Cincinnati archdiocese but soon left and moved to New York City. There he worked as a book salesman for the Catholic publishing firm of J. and D. Sadlier and later as a salesman for the firm of P. J. Kenedy. In 1875, with a capital of $300, he set up his own firm, which quickly achieved success in selling Catholic and Irish-national books for small monthly payments. He then branched out into general reference publishing.

Encouraged by the success of his book business and to promote it further, Collier began in 1888 a magazine, *Once a Week,* which had an initial sale of 50,000 copies and grew to 200,000 in two years. In 1895 the name was changed to *Collier's Weekly,* which at the time of its demise in December 1956 had more than four million subscribers. As the "father of the subscription book industry," Collier first brought the works of standard authors, encyclopedias, and reference books to the average family. After his death the business was continued by his son Robert, who died in 1918; the following year the controlling interest in the Collier company was taken over by the Crowell Publishing Company, and in 1939 the name was changed to the Crowell-Collier Publishing Company.

[J. F. CARROLL]

COLLINS, DOMINIC, BL.

Irish martyr and Jesuit lay brother; b. Youghal, Ireland, 1566 or 1567; d. there or at Cork, Oct. 29, 1602. Collins was born of a noble family; both his father and brother served as mayor of Youghal. After studying under the Jesuits in his hometown, Dominic went to France in 1586. There he worked in an inn for three years before entering the service of Philip Emmanuel of Lorraine, who eventually made him commander of cavalry. Dominic was rewarded with the military governorship of Lapena after he captured its castle. He served in the Spanish army from 1594 until 1598 when he entered the Society of Jesus at Santiago de Compostela. After his profession as a lay brother (Feb. 4, 1601), he was chosen as companion to Father James Archer, who was then about to return to Ireland. Dominic sailed there in the Spanish fleet, landing at Castlehaven in 1602. He was at Dunboy during the siege, not as a combatant, but as one concerned with the spiritual and temporal needs of the besieged who chose him to treat for terms with the English. Taken prisoner on June 18, 1602, he was offered his liberty and bribed with a position of honor on the condition he renounce his faith and swear allegiance to ELIZABETH I. Following a lengthy interrogation and many attempts at persuasion, Br. Dominic was condemned to death on July 9. He was detained in Cork Prison until his execution by hanging. All contemporary accounts state that he died at Cork. Such details as disemboweling and quartering are found only in later (Jesuit) sources. Br. Dominic was beatified with 16 other Irish martyrs on Sept. 27, 1992.

Feast: Oct. 30 (Jesuits).

See Also: IRISH CONFESSORS AND MARTYRS.

Bibliography: Archives (unpublished) of the Society of Jesus, Rome. E. HOGAN, *Distinguished Irishmen of the Sixteenth and Seventeenth Centuries* (London 1894). J. N. TYLENDA, *Jesuit Saints and Martyrs* (Chicago 1998) 357–59.

[F. FINEGAN]

COLLINS, JOSEPH BURNS

Leader in catechetics in the U. S.; b. Waseca, Minnesota, Sept. 7, 1897; d. Washington, D.C., Jan. 23, 1975. After attending school in Waseca, Collins went on to study at St. Mary's College in Winona, Minnesota, the St. Paul Seminary in Saint Paul, and the Urban University in Rome, receiving an S.T.D. in 1924. He was ordained for the Diocese of Winona in Rome on May 17, 1924. Returning to the United States, he taught philosophy at St. Mary's College and the College of St. Teresa in Winona, 1925–1930. He did post-graduate work at Johns Hopkins University and was awarded a Ph.D. in 1934. He taught one year at Notre Dame College of Maryland and at Sulpician Seminary in Washington, D.C., 1933–1937. His acquaintance and association with the Sulpician Fathers at St. Mary's Seminary in Baltimore led him to join the Society of Priests of Saint Sulpice in 1935. In 1937 Collins began teaching at The Catholic University of America. He became a regular faculty member in 1939 and taught moral theology and catechetics there until his retirement in 1968.

Early in his career Collins became interested in the CONFRATERNITY OF CHRISTIAN DOCTRINE as a practical solution to the problems and task of catechizing children and adults. In 1942 he became the director of the National Center for the CCD, a post he held for 25 years. Following his resignation as director in 1967, he remained at the National Center as Assistant Director and later as a consultant until his death. As director of the National Center for the CCD in the years from 1942 to 1967, Collins was an important and influential figure in catechetics in the United States. For 24 years (1942–66) he edited the bimonthly aid for catechists, *Our Parish Confraternity*. In 1964, under his leadership, the National Center began to publish the quarterly catechetical journal, *The Living Light*.

Collins authored or edited 14 books and countless articles that appeared in publications such as *The Register, Our Sunday Visitor, American Ecclesiastical Review* and the *New Catholic Encyclopedia*. Among his more important books are *Kergymatic Renewal and the CCD, Updating the CCD High School of Religion, CCD Methods and Modern Catechetics*; and *Some Guidelines for a New American Catechism*.

His long and dedicated service in the field of catechetics was recognized and rewarded in 1964 by Pope Paul VI with the Pro Ecclesia et Pontifice Medal. He also received the Benemerenti Medal in 1965. He was working on a history of the CCD at the time of his death. The first chapters were published in the *American Ecclesiasti-cal Review* 168 (1974) 695–706; 169 (1975) 48–67; 237–255; 610–620; 690–702.

[T. E. KRAMER]

COLLINS, THOMAS AQUINAS (RAYMOND)

Dominican priest, Scripture scholar; b. July 17, 1915, Lowell, Mass., the son of Jeremiah F. Collins and Mary R. (Sullivan) Collins; d. Oct. 8, 2000, Washington, D.C. After receiving an A.B. from Providence College in 1938, Collins studied for the priesthood at the Dominican Pontifical Faculties in River Forest, Ill., and Washington, D.C. He was ordained to the priesthood in Washington, D.C., on June 8, 1945. He studied at the Ecole Biblique in Jerusalem from 1946 to 1948 and received an S.S.B. from the Pontifical Biblical Commission in 1949. He was part of the first wave of Catholic biblical scholars to emerge in the aftermath of Pope Pius XII's 1943 encyclical, *DIVINO AFFLANTE SPIRITU*. From 1950 to 1958 he was Old Testament Professor at the Dominican Pontifical Faculty in Washington. He then completed his doctoral studies at the University of Ottawa, receiving an S.T.D. in 1959. That same year he joined the faculty at Providence College, teaching Biblical Studies and serving as chairman of the Theology Department. He was the founder of the Summer School of Sacred Theology and directed that program from 1964 to 1969. He continued to direct the Biblical Studies portion of that program until his retirement in 1986.

Collins was president of the Catholic Biblical Association from 1955 to 1956 and subsequently served for many years on the Board of Trustees. In 1977 he joined the editorial board of *Biblical Archeology Review*. For 12 years (1971–1982) he lectured at and co-directed the Biblical Institute at Trinity College in Burlington, Vt. He also taught and served as co-director at the annual Sinsinawa Biblical Institute in Sinsinawa, Wisc., from 1975 to 1983. His publications include "The Cajetan Controversy," *AER* 128 (Feb. 1953); "Theology and Sacred Scripture," in *Theology, Philosophy, and History as Integrating Disciplines in the Catholic College of Liberal Arts* (Washington, D.C. 1953); "Cardinal Cajetan's Fundamental Biblical Principles," *CBQ* 17 (July 1955); "Changing Styles in Johannine Studies," in *The Bible in Current Catholic Thought* (1962); "Archeology and the Bible," *The Bible Today* 6 (April 1963); "Toward a Biblical Theology of Mary," *Marian Studies* 25 (Spring 1973); and "The Truth of the Bible Debate," in *Biblical Studies in Contemporary Thought* (1975).

[T. KEEGAN]

839

Hieronymus Colloredo.

COLLIUS, FRANCESCO (COLLIO)

Theologian; b. Milan, exact date not known; d. Milan, 1640. He entered the Milanese congregation of the Oblates of St. Charles, and later served as grand penitentiary for the diocese of Milan. Three authentic works are ascribed to him: *Conclusiones in sacra theologia numero MCLXV una cum variorum doctorum opinionibus* (Milan 1609), *De sanguine Christi libri quinque in quibus de illius natura, effusionibus ac miraculis copiose disseritur* (Cologne 1612; Milan 1617), and the *De animabus paganorum* (Milan 1622). The last work manifests the author's preoccupation with the problem of whether the souls of well-known Biblical and pagan personages of antiquity have attained salvation.

Bibliography: B. HEURTEBIZE, *Dictionnaire de théologie catholique,* ed. A. VACANT et al. (Paris 1903–50) 3.1:369.

[G. M. GRABKA]

COLLOREDO, HIERONYMUS

Prince archbishop of Salzburg; b. Vienna, May 31, 1732; d. there May 20, 1812. This second son of Prince Rudolph Joseph studied at the Collegium Germanicum at Rome, became a canon of the cathedral at Salzburg (1747), prior of Kremsier in Moravia (1761), bishop of Gurk (1762), and after a drawn-out election prince bishop of Salzburg (1772). His main interest was his principality, whose well-being he sought to promote in every way. He raised the level of elementary education, patronized literary and artistic efforts, summoned German professors, and sent young noblemen to foreign universities. In Church history, however, he made a place for himself not as a secular ruler but as the prince archbishop of enlightened ideas. The program he developed in his famous pastoral letter of May 29, 1782, was met with complete approval by Emperor Joseph II and was translated into French and Italian. His reforms were aimed at a simple Christianity, purified of all incidentals and externals. They failed partly through opposition from conservative classes, but mostly because they were effected in haste and without sympathetic understanding of the mentality of the people. Colloredo did not vie for popular favor and even in exile sought to protect his episcopal rights as against the emperor. He was buried in St. Stephen's Cathedral.

Bibliography: J. C. ALLMAYER-BECK, *Neue deutsche Biographie* (Berlin 1953–) 3:327–328. J. MACK, *Die Reform- und Aufklärungsbestrebungen unter Colloredo* (Munich 1912). J. SCHÖTTL, *Kirchliche Reformen des Salzburger Erzbischofs Hieronymus v. Colloredo im Zeitalter der Aufklärung* (Hirschenhausen 1939). E. WOLF, *Die Religion in Geschichte und Gegenwart* (3d ed. Tübingen 1957–65) 1:1851. F. LOIDL, *Lexikon für Theologie und Kirche,* ed. J. HOFER and K. RAHNER (2d, new ed. Freiburg 1957–65) 3:5–6.

[F. MAASS]

COLMAN, SS.

Five of numerous Irish saints of the name from the sixth and seventh centuries.

Colman of Cloyne, bishop, patron of Diocese of Cloyne, Ireland; b. 530 (Annals of Inisfallen); d. 606. A bard, he was a late vocation to the priesthood. His life centered in County Cork, where he founded his principal church at Cloyne, with another important foundation at Kilmaclenine. His cultus was approved in 1903.

Feast: Nov. 24.

Colman of Dromore, bishop, patron of Diocese of Dromore, Ireland, early sixth century. He is one of the early important but obscure Irish saints. His life and work centered in County Down. He appears to have studied under St. Caylan at Nendrum on Strangford Lough, and may have founded his church at Dromore *c.* 514. Devotion to Colman spread to Scotland and Wales, where several churches were dedicated to him.

Feast: June 7 or Oct. 29.

Colman Elo (Eala, of Lynally, of Lann Elo), monastic founder; b. County Tyrone, Ireland, *c.* 555; d. 611

(Annals of Ulster) or 613 (Annals of Inisfallen). His principal monastery was at Lynally, County Offaly. He was a friend of COLUMBA OF IONA and stayed at IONA on one of his visits to Scotland. Several Scottish churches were dedicated in his honor.

Feast: Sept. 26.

Colman of Lindisfarne, third Irish bishop-abbot of LINDISFARNE, England; d. *c.* 670. Colman opposed the anti-Celtic decisions of the Synod of WHITBY in 664. Hence he and the Irish monks and some of the English monks left Lindisfarne for IONA, and then for the island of Inishbofin off the west coast of Ireland. From there, the English monks founded Mayo abbey on the Irish mainland.

Feasts: Feb. 18 and Aug. 8.

Colman Macduach (of Kilmacduagh), patron of the Diocese of Kilmacduagh, Ireland; b. Kiltartan, County Clare, seventh century. Having studied on the Aran Islands, he lived as a hermit in the Burren district of the Irish mainland opposite these islands. Later he founded a great monastery at Kilmacduagh, but in his old age he returned to the Burren hills to found Oughtmama.

Feast: Oct. 29 throughout Ireland.

Bibliography: Of Cloyne. J. C., "St. Colman of Cloyne," *Journal of the Cork Historical and Archaeological Society* 16 (1910) 132–142. A. BUTLER, *The Lives of the Saints*, ed. H. THURSTON and D. ATTWATER (New York 1956) 4:419. Of Dromore. *Acta Sanctae Sedis* June 2:24–29. A. BUTLER, *The Lives of the Saints*, ed. H. THURSTON and D. ATTWATER (New York 1956) 2:493–494. J. F. KENNEY, *The Sources for the Early History of Ireland* (New York 1929) 466. Elo. J. F. KENNEY, *The Sources for the Early History of Ireland* (New York 1929) 400. C. PLUMMER, *Bethada náem nÉrenn*, 2 v. (Oxford 1922) 1:168–182; 2:162–176; comp., *Vitae sanctorum Hiberniae*, 2 v. (Oxford 1910) 1:258–273. F. Ó BRIAIN, *Dictionnaire d'histoire et de géographie ecclésiastiques*, ed. A. BAUDRILLART et al. (Paris 1912) 13:257–258. A. BUTLER, *The Lives of the Saints*, ed. H. THURSTON and D. ATTWATER (New York 1956) 3:654. Of Lindisfarne. BEDE, *Ecclesiastical History* 3.25, 26; 4.4. J. F. KENNEY, *The Sources for the Early History of Ireland* (New York 1929) 463–464. F. Ó BRIAIN, *Dictionnaire d'histoire et de géographie ecclésiastiques*, ed. A. BAUDRILLART et al. (Paris 1912) 13:256. D. D. C. POCHIN MOULD, *The Irish Saints* (Dublin 1964) 89–90. A. BUTLER, *The Lives of the Saints*, ed. H. THURSTON and D. ATTWATER (New York 1956) 1:369–370. Macduach. J. FAHEY, *The History and Antiquities of the Diocese of Kilmacduagh* (Dublin 1893). J. F. KENNEY, *The Sources for the Early History of Ireland* (New York 1929) 456. A. BUTLER, *The Lives of the Saints*, ed. H. THURSTON and D. ATTWATER (New York 1956) 4:218.

[D. D. C. POCHIN MOULD]

COLOGNE

City in west central Germany, North Rhineland-Westphalia, on both sides of the Rhine. It is the seat of

Cologne Cathedral, High Gothic tracery. (©Kevin R. Morris/ CORBIS)

the most important German archbishopric (*Coloniensis*), whose history, as that of the city, dates from Roman times.

The City. The son-in-law of Emperor Augustus, M. Vipsanius Agrippa, settled the Ubii, from the right bank of the Rhine, between the Rhine and the Maas. The *oppidum Ubiorum* with its military camp and colony of veterans (*c.* 12 B.C.) was to become, with its shrines (*ara Ubiorum*), the capital of *Germania*; but, after the Roman defeat in the Teutoburg Forest (A.D. 9), the frontier *oppidum* remained. Thanks to Agrippina the Younger, who was born there and became the wife of Emperor Claudius, it obtained the city privileges (A.D. 50); and, thereafter called *Colonia Claudia Ara Agrippinensis*, it was the capital of *Germania inferior*, with many buildings, a glass and pottery industry, and (from the 4th century) Christian churches. Constantine built the first permanent bridge across the Rhine there.

Under the Franks (from *c.* 400) Cologne became a royal residence, soon famous for its many churches.

The main façade of Cologne Cathedral. (Hulton/Archive Photos)

Under Charlemagne it was the point from which Saxony was conquered and evangelized. In the division of the Carolingian Empire (843) it went to the Middle Kingdom (Lotharingia); when Lotharingia was divided (870), Cologne went to the East Frankish kingdom, later the German Empire.

The Ottonians and the archbishop rulers of the city favored its development as a trade center, and it had expanded several times by 1200. From *c.* 1100 the burghers struggled for independence of the archbishop and in 1288 won complete freedom. Thereafter the archbishops resided in Bonn, and Cologne became a free imperial city. In 1396 the burghers drew up a democratic constitution. From the 11th to the 16th century, Cologne, the largest and richest city of the empire, had a thriving trade with Scandinavia, Poland, and Russia, as well as with Flanders and England. It was a leading city in the Hanseatic League.

Riches encouraged achievements in art, especially ecclesiastical. Through its possession of relics of the Three Magi (from 1164), Cologne became a major pilgrimage center. The city seal of 1150, the oldest in Germany, bears the inscription *Sancta Colonia Sanctae Romanae Ecclesiae Fidelis Filia.* Even after the departure of the archbishop, Cologne remained the seat of di-

ocesan administration and the most important ecclesiastical center of Germany. In the city were the cathedral domain and those of ten collegiate churches and three Benedictine abbeys, besides 19 parishes and cloisters of most religious orders. The *studia generalia* of Dominicans and Franciscans prepared the way for the university of 1388. The city vigorously prevented inroads of the Reformation, banning Lutheranism until 1794. At the end of the 16th century began a gradual decline, following the opening of new routes for world trade and religious and political changes in Germany. Cologne remained a medieval city until *c.* 1800; in the face of new ideas the traditionalist burghers remained passive. The archbishop elector resided elsewhere, and there was no baroque prince to fashion changes.

After conquest by France (1794–1814), Cologne was incorporated in Protestant Prussia, little to the city's liking. A steady growth began *c.* 1850, attributable primarily to local forces, and Cologne became the economic and cultural center of west Germany, the crossroads of European transport routes, and the center of political and social Catholicism. Large-scale expansion and building took place under Mayor Konrad Adenauer (1917–33). In 1933 Cologne was the third largest German city, 75 per cent of whose 750,000 residents were Catholic. In the last Reichstag election (March 1933) Hitler received less than 30 per cent of the votes.

In World War II, Cologne was especially hard hit. From May of 1942 to March of 1945 methodical Allied bombing completely destroyed the inner city, doing irreparable ruin to one of Europe's most beautiful cities and claiming 25,000 lives. Most of the people fled, but in May of 1945 some 40,000 still lived in the ruins. One church out of 104 was undamaged.

The Archbishopric. Christian origins date from *c.* 200. The first historically known bishop, Maternus, attended the Councils of Rome (313) and Arles (314). The see survived the Frankish conquest, but to *c.* 600 the episcopal list has many gaps. CUNIBERT (623–*c.* 660) raised Cologne's status. Pope Zacharias gave St. BONIFACE Cologne as a metropolitanate (745); but the Frankish episcopacy and nobility thwarted the plan, fearing for their independence, and Mainz was chosen instead.

Under Charlemagne the metropolitan system of Germany developed. Cologne became a metropolitanate (785) with the suffragans LIÈGE, Utrecht, and the new Saxon sees of Münster, Osnabrück, Minden, and for a while Bremen. The borders of the vast archbishopric (23 deaneries and in Westphalia on the Rhine, Ruhr, and Wupper Rivers) and of the ecclesiastical province were almost unchanged through the Middle Ages. Utrecht became an archdiocese, and several deaneries went to the new See of Roermond in 1559. Protestant Minden was suppressed as a see in 1648. From the 12th century the archbishop yielded authority to the ten archdeacons (provosts and deans freely elected by their respective chapters). Four of them especially, the cathedral provost of Cologne and the provosts of Bonn, Xanten, and Soest, won jurisdictional rights that survived the centralizing tendencies of the Council of Trent.

The list of great medieval prelates begins with BRUNO OF COLOGNE (Bruno I, 953–965), brother and collaborator of Otto I the Great, who as duke of Lotharingia was the first united episcopal and secular authority. His successors developed a principality whose borders partly coincided with those of the archdiocese. From the 11th century the archbishops were archchancellors of the Italian part of the empire. They also won the right to crown German kings and belonged to the influential electors of the king; the Golden Bull of Charles IV (1356) made them definitely part of the privileged group of seven electors.

HERIBERT (999–1021) was the friend and chancellor of Otto III. Pilgrim (1021–36), Herman II (1036–56), and ANNO OF COLOGNE (Anno II, 1056–75, for a while vice regent of the empire) sponsored church and cloister reform. Instead of royal nomination, election by the cathedral chapter (most of whom belonged to the Rhenish nobility) determined episcopal appointment after the Concordat of Worms (1122); from the 13th century, 8 of 24 canonries were reserved for clergy of bourgeois origin. Imperial influence continued to be strong, however. Frederick I Barbarossa had two of his chancellors archbishops, the talented RAINALD OF DASSEL (1156–67), who conceived and directed the antipapal imperial policy of the Emperor, and Philip of Heinsberg (1167–91), who acquired the duchy of Westphalia. In following years the emperor's power waned. Even Cologne's archbishops (except ENGELBERT, 1216–25, vice regent of the empire) followed a predominantly territorial policy; the fall of the Hohenstaufen encouraged the archbishops, especially Conrad of Hochstaden (1238–61), to consolidate a large state in northwest Germany. But a coalition of neighboring princes, allied with the city of Cologne, brought their plan to naught (1288). The constitution of the Electorate (1463) conceded some rule to the cathedral chapter, counts, knights, and cities. Hermann V von Wied (1515–47), a good sovereign, favored the Reformation and so met opposition from his chapter, the university, and the city of Cologne; he resigned under pressure from the Emperor. Gebhard TRUCHSESS VON WALDBURG (1577–83) became Lutheran and sought to make the archbishopric a secular electorate. In the "War of Cologne" the Emperor and his allies assured the continuation of Ca-

tholicism in northwest Germany and a Catholic majority in the college of electors.

When Duke Ernst of Bavaria became archbishop (1583–1612), he began a series of Wittelsbach electors, who while protecting the Church used their position on the Rhine to further Wittelsbach policies. Ernst and his successors, Ferdinand (1612–50), Maximilian Heinrich (1650–88), Joseph Clemens (1688–1723), and Clemens August (1723–61), also held several neighboring bishoprics. They devoted themselves mostly to politics and art (baroque churches and castles). Only Ferdinand, who took a personal interest in reform and the revival of Church life, was a distinguished ecclesiastic. Spiritual administration was in the hands of good auxiliary bishops and general vicars.

Maximilian Friedrich von Königsegg-Rothenfels (1761–84) supported the ENLIGHTENMENT and in the Nuntiature Controversy defended his episcopal rights against the centralization of Rome. Maximilian Franz of Austria, youngest son of Maria Theresa and last Elector of Cologne (1781–1801), who favored the same course, took part in the anticurial EMS congress (1786). He was also an outstanding prelate and regent, surpassing most of his predecessors in conscientiousness and zeal. When the French invaded (1794), he fled to the right bank of the Rhine.

The part of the see on the left bank of the Rhine became French and was placed under the Diocese of AACHEN founded by Napoleon (1801); church goods were secularized. On the right bank, where the episcopal administration of Cologne continued, the secularization of 1803, which initiated the end of the HOLY ROMAN EMPIRE, took place.

After French domination, the archbishopric of Cologne was restored (1821), with Prussian consent. But it had been reduced in area and had as suffragans Münster, Paderborn, and TRIER. The Prussian regime's mistrust of Catholics led to strained relations, but it lessened after 1840, under Frederick William IV. The prudent Ferdinand August von SPIEGEL (1824–36) reorganized the archdiocese, dividing it into 44 deaneries. His many accomplishments were clouded by his indulgence in the question of mixed marriages (see COLOGNE, MIXED MARRIAGE DISPUTE IN), which laid the basis for the arrest of his successor, Clemens August von DROSTE ZU VISCHERING (1835–45). Johannes von GEISSEL (1846–64), cardinal in 1850, made gains for Church freedom and Catholic organizations. In 1848 he presided at the first conference of all German bishops in Würzburg, and in 1860 held a provincial council. Paulus MELCHERS (1866–85), opponent of papal infallibility at VATICAN COUNCIL I, headed Prussian bishops in the KULTURKAMPF, was arrested

(1874) and in exile in the Netherlands from 1876. In 1885 he resigned, in the interest of a settlement, and became a cardinal in the Roman Curia (d. 1895). Philipp Krementz (1885–99), cardinal in 1893, repaired the damage of the Kulturkampf.

Most of the industrial area of the Ruhr, Rhine, and Wupper lay in the Archdiocese of Cologne. Population migration and concentration in the large cities posed serious problems of pastoral care. Associations developed with success; the most important Catholic organizations in all Germany (trade unions, Borromeo societies, the association for Catholic Germany [Volksverein], and the mission center) had headquarters in the archdiocese, as did interdenominational Christian trade unions, which Abp. Antonius Fischer (1902–12) defended against integrationist attempts. Centers of pastoral care were established for immigrant Polish workers in the Ruhr. Karl Joseph Schulte (1920–41), cardinal in 1921, who fostered scholarship and modern techniques in pastoral care, was a confirmed opponent of National Socialism; he died during a bombing raid. The Prussian Concordat (1929) introduced changes in ecclesiastical organization. The extensive archdiocese of 3,500,000 Catholics ceded 29 deaneries with 1,000,000 Catholics to the new See of Aachen in 1930. Paderborn became an archbishopric. As suffragans Cologne has had since then Aachen, Limburg, Münster, Osnabrück, Trier, and (since 1957) Essen.

Art. From Roman and early Christian times there survive many burial monuments, high quality glass, a mosaic of Dionysius (*c.* 200), and remains of the city wall. St. Ursula and St. Gereon date from cemetery edifices over tombs of the martyrs; St. Gereon was an oval monument. St. Kunibert and St. Maria im Kapitol (7th century) were built in Frankish times. Recent excavations reveal a 6th-century church under the cathedral, with some of the richest tombs of Frankish princes.

From late Carolingian days come large church edifices, which were later copied. Excavations beneath the Gothic cathedral show that the earlier cathedral (to 870) was the first large German church with two transepts. St. Pantaleon (*c.* 980) had a wider nave with monumental work on the west side. St. Maria im Kapitol (mid-11th century, as is St. Georg) had a round three-apse choir damaged in World War II. The Gero cross in the cathedral (*c.* 970) is the first German monumental sculpture. From the same period and later come pieces of smaller sculpture, ivory carvings, and MS illumination, showing Byzantine influence.

The artistic peak was reached with late Romanesque in which most of the churches of Cologne were built (*c.* 1150–*c.* 1250). Classical proportions and colors, three-apse choirs, the marked division of inner and outer walls,

and rich detail mark the style of this period. Exuberant later forms reflect the characteristic joy of the style: the choir (*c.* 1190) and decagon (1219–27) of St. Gereon; the choir (to 1172) of Great St. Martin; the west part (1188) of St. Georg; St. Cecilia (1160–70); the restoration and new choir of Holy Apostles (1200–20); St. Andreas (after 1200); St. Kunibert (1200–47); the new choir of St. Severin (to 1237); and the Overstolzenhaus and gates of the city fortress (early 13th century). Of the same high quality are the sculpture (figures in St. Maria im Kapitol) and painting (frescoes in St. Maria Lyskirchen *c.* 1250 and glass paintings in St. Kunibert *c.* 1230). Especially precious is the gold work, influenced by that of the Maas, in the costly shrines for relics; the most famous is that of the Three Magi (1180–1220), the largest sarcophagus in Europe, with gold work, whose classical figures anticipate the sculpture of Gothic cathedrals. Other masterpieces are the shrines of SS. Heribert, Maurinus, Albinus, Aetherius, and Anno and many smaller reliquaries and liturgical vessels.

The most important Gothic structure is the cathedral, dedicated to St. Peter and the Blessed Virgin, which brought the school of north French cathedrals to completion. It is a five-nave basilica with a three-nave transept, a three-story design with high walls broken by pillars and large windows, which was begun in 1248; the choir was consecrated in 1322. Construction, discontinued in the 16th century, was completed in the 19th century after Romanticists rediscovered Gothic and Cologne's cathedral was seen as a national German monument. Other Gothic churches are the Franciscan Church (13th century), St. Ursula (choir 1287), the Church of the Brothers of St. Anthony (1384), the Carthusian Church (1393), and St. Andreas (choir 1420); and among secular edifices, the Hansa hall (1360) and the tower (*c.* 1410) of the town hall, and Gürzenich banqueting palace (1437–44). Many statues and paintings, especially anguished Crucifixions and loving Madonnas, show the influence of mysticism. After 1350, Cologne's art became more statuesque and corporeal.

Glass paintings and frescoes of the cathedral were the first work of the Cologne school of painting, the longest-lived of any German school (*c.* 1300–*c.* 1530), of a constantly high quality. It was distinguished by lyrical lines, light and bright colors, and pious thoughtful themes. Although open to outside influences, the school stuck to its own tradition. Of the masters of the 15th century, only Stephen Lochner (d. 1451) is known (thanks to Dürer); Lochner was the artist of the altar of Cologne's patron saints in the cathedral. Others are known by their most important works: the master of the Veronica, the master of the Life of Mary, the master of the Holy Fami-

844

NEW CATHOLIC ENCYCLOPEDIA

ly, etc. Barthel Bruyn (d. 1555), the last of the Cologne school, committed himself freely to Renaissance ways.

Other works of the Renaissance, influenced from the Netherlands, are the vestibule of the town hall (1567–71) and the choir screens in St. Pantaleon and St. Maria im Kapitol (1502–23).

Cologne had few outstanding baroque buildings: the Jesuit Church of the Assumption (1618––27) with strong traces of Gothic; St. Maria on Schnurgasse (1643–1716); and several secular buildings, few of which have survived. The sculpture of J. F. Helmont was destroyed in World War II. Baroque gold work was of high quality: the Engelbert shrine in the cathedral (1633), monstrances, chalices, reliquaries, and rich vestments.

The destruction of Cologne's art began after secularization (1803), when many churches were wrecked. The worst came in Word War II. Although almost all churches were damaged, many have been restored; movable objects survived the war best. Many works, dispersed following secularization, came into museums: Darmstadt, Munich, Nürnberg, and London. Of the works left in Cologne, many are in churches and others are in city museums: Roman-Germanic Museum, Schnütgen Museum (medieval sculpture and objects), Wallraf-Richartz Museum (Cologne school of painting; also important Dutch works, German and French masters of the 19th century, and a large modern collection), and the museum of applied arts. The archiepiscopal museum contains church art from the Middle Ages to the baroque age.

Bibliography: General. *Kunstdenkmäler der Rheinprovinz,* ed. P. CLEMEN, 6–7 (Düsseldorf 1906–38). *Handbuch des Erzbistums Köln* (25th ed. Cologne 1958). *Regesten der Erzbischöfe von Köln,* ed. R. KNIPPING et al (Bonn 1902–61). Periodicals. *Annalen des Historischen Vereins für den Niederrhein* (1855–). *Jahrbuch des Kölnischen Geschichtsvereins* (1913–). *Kölner Domblatt* (1948–). Studies. M. BRAUBACH, *Kurköln* (Münster 1949); *Kurfürst Maximilian Franz* (Vienna 1961). H. SCHMITZ, *Colonia Claudia Ara Agrippinensium* (Cologne 1956); *Rheinische Kirchen im Wiederaufbau,* ed. W. NEUSS (München-Gladbach 1951). *Studien zur Kölner Kirchengeschichte,* ed. the Archiepiscopal historical archives (1952–). A. STELZMANN, *Illustrierte Geschichte der Stadt Köln* (Cologne 1958). *Geschichte des Erzbistums Köln* v.1 ed. W. NEUSS and F. W. OEDIGER (Cologne 1964). H. REINERS, *Die Kölner Malerschule* (München-Gladbach 1925). H. VOGTS, *Köln im Spiegel seiner Kunst* (Cologne 1950). A. VERBEEK, *Kölner Kirchen* (Cologne 1959). H. SCHNITZLER, *Rheinische Schatzkammer,* 2 v. (Düsseldorf 1957–59). H. RODE, *Kunstführer Köln* (2d ed. Cologne 1963). R. HAASS et al., *Lexicon für Theologie und Kirche,* 6:383–396. A. FRANZEN, *Dictionnaire d'histoire et de géographie ecclésiastiques* 13:275–311. *Annuario Pontificio* (1965) 218–219. W. LIPGENS, *Ferdinand August Graf Spiegel und das Verhältnis von Kirche und Staat 1789–1835,* 2 v. (Münster 1965).

[R. LILL]

COLOGNE, MIXED MARRIAGE DISPUTE IN

The Cologne dispute, which found its external climax in the arrest of Abp. Clemens von DROSTE ZU VISCHERING of Cologne (Nov. 20, 1837), was the first great controversy over the liberation of the Catholic Church in Germany from state tutelage. Its immediate occasion was the mixed marriage question and the teaching of Georg HERMES, professor of theology at the University of Bonn. The deeper causes were the opposition between the ecclesiastical policy of Prussia, which since the secularization of the Catholic Church in Germany and the end of the Holy Roman Empire (1806) had forced the Church into a largely dependent relationship, and the movement for Church freedom, supported principally by the lower clergy and the laity. This movement had been gaining strength since the 1820s. Prussia's policy was similar to that of the other German states.

When Prussia applied its legislation on mixed marriages to the Catholic regions in the Rhineland and Westphalia that had been acquired in 1815, great discontent resulted. In his brief of March 25, 1830, Pius VIII went to great lengths to accommodate Prussia by permitting priests to render passive assistance at mixed marriages that did not have the guarantees customarily required by the Church, but the government of Frederick William III wanted more. After giving considerable counterpledges, it induced Abp. Ferdinand von SPIEGEL of Cologne to sign a secret agreement (June 19, 1834) that made solemn consecration of mixed marriages possible even in cases in which the non-Catholic party refused to allow the children to be educated as Catholics. The three suffragan bishops of Cologne gave their assent. One of them, Joseph von Hommer of Trier, recanted before his death (November 1836) and informed the Roman Curia of the arrangement. At first the Curia was content with a diplomatic protest. Many priests and laymen, however, disapproved of the complaisance of the bishops; their complaints were disseminated in the press outside of Prussia.

Hermes made the first attempt to reconcile Catholic theology with German idealist philosophy, but his doctrine was condemned by Gregory XVI for its rationalist tendencies (Sept. 26, 1835). The papal decree was not fully implemented in Prussia because the government supported the Hermesian professors. When Droste became archbishop of Cologne in 1836, he at once took sharp, and in part illegal, measures against the Hermesians on the Catholic Theology Faculty at the University of Bonn. As a champion of the seminaries and an opponent of training candidates for the priesthood in universities, he wanted also to strike at the Faculty as such. When the professors turned to the state for help, the archbishop was soon in grave difficulty.

In the spring of 1837 Droste took up the mixed-marriage question, in which the government was clearly in the wrong, and demanded an exact observance of the papal brief of 1830. Neither promises nor threats could change him. Thereupon the government had him arrested in the false charge of engaging in revolutionary activities. Gregory XVI defended Droste and solemnly protested against this act of violence in his allocution of Dec. 10, 1837. The bishops of Munster and Paderborn then renounced the convention of 1834. When Abp. Martin von DUNIN of Gnesen and Posen demanded in 1838 that the Church's law concerning mixed marriage be respected, he too was arrested.

It was not so much the arrest of the rigid, unpopular Droste as the press reaction to the movement for Church freedom that stirred up the Catholics and helped them attain a common conviction on Church policy. The greatest effect was achieved by Johann von GÖRRES, who in his polemic masterpiece *Athanasius* (January 1838) supported Droste, demanded freedom for the Church, and denounced the police-state principles of the Prussian bureaucracy. Numerous other polemical works followed and so aroused public opinion that, for the first time in 19th-century German history, it became a significant factor in establishing government policy. Settlement of the conflict took place only under Frederick William IV (1840–61), who desired the close cooperation of the state with both the Catholic and Lutheran churches. Dunin returned to his see. Droste was released from custody and received a personal apology from the king; but at Prussia's request the pope assigned the administration of his archbishopric to his coadjutor, Johannes von GEISSEL (September 1841). In a simultaneous agreement with Rome, the government left the handling of the mixed-marriage question to the bishops and granted other important concessions. Thus the *placet* was abolished. Bishops were permitted unrestricted communications with the pope. Selections of bishops were to be free, except that the king could strike undesirable names from the list of candidates. Also it was agreed to set up a section for Catholic affairs in the ministry of education. With this settlement there began in Prussia a period of peace in matters of ecclesiastical policy that lasted until the KULTURKAMPF. After the Cologne conflict the group that supported Church freedom and close ties to Rome assumed more and more the leadership of German Catholicism.

Bibliography: G. GOYAU, *L'Allemagne religieuse: Le Catholicisme, 1800–48,* 2 v. (Paris 1905) 2:142–201. H. SCHRÖRS, *Die Kölner Wirren: Studien zu ihrer Geschichte* (Berlin 1927). H. BASTGEN, *Forschungen und Quellen zur Kirchenpolitik Gregors XVI,* 1 v. I (Paderborn 1929); *Die Verhandlungen zwischen dem Berliner Hof und dem Hl. Stuhl über die konfessionell gemischten Ehen* (Paderborn 1936). J. GRISAR, "Die Allokution Gregors XVI," vom 10., Dez. 1837 in *Greggorio XV Miscellanea Commemorativa,* 2 v. (Rome 1948) 2:441–560; "Das Kölner Ereignis nach den Berichten italienischer Dilpomaten," *Historisches Jahrbuch der Görres-Gesellschaft* 74 (1955) 727–39. A. THOMAS, "Bichoff Hommer von Trier und seine Stellung zu Mischehenfrage," *Trierer theologische Zeitschrift* (Trier 1945–) 58 (1949) 76–90, 358–73. F. SCHNABEL, *Deutsche Geschichte im 19. Jahrhundert* v.4 (3d ed. Freiburg 1955) 106–64. R. LILL, *Die Beilegung der Kölner Wirren 1840-1842* (Düsseldorf 1962). E. HEGEL, *Lexikon für Theologie und Kirche,* ed. J. HOFER and K. RAHNER, 10 v. (2d new ed. Freiburg 1957–65) 6:394–95. W. LIPGENS, *Ferdinand August Graf Speigel und das Verhältnis von Kirche und Staat 1789–1835,* 2 v. (Münster 1965).

[R. LILL]

COLOGNE, SCHOOL OF

Prior to the Council of Trent a group of Catholic theologians known as the school of Cologne developed a theory of double justice designed to bridge the gap between the reformers and the Church. A. PIGGE, J. Gropper, and G. SERIPANDO had much in common in their presentation of this unorthodox doctrine. Although Gasparo CONTARINI came into contact with the school merely by attempting to clarify the issues raised by it, he nonetheless came under its influence.

Pigge distorted the traditional teaching on original sin and treated justification in a corresponding way by ascribing to man the vicarious justice of Christ. Gropper, putting Pigge's statements into a systematized framework, placed them before the Ratisbon Conference of 1541, convinced that the members would recognize in them a suitable basis for discussion with the Protestants. When Gropper's document was rejected, the Augustinian Seripando defended both men from accusations of heresy.

Then Seripando formulated their thought for the Council of Trent. Because he failed to distinguish concupiscence from original sin, while he admitted the intrinsic character of sanctifying grace, he yet maintained that only when God applies exteriorly to the soul the merits of Jesus can a man become truly a child of God. In his turn, Contarini spoke indiscriminately of "iustitia nobis donata et imputata," inclining subtilely toward a doctrine of double perfection by attributing the efficient causality of justification to the Holy Spirit.

Despite the sincerity of the efforts of these theologians, they missed their mark by projecting an Ockamism channeled to them through the voluntarism of Biel. The lengthy investigation of their views at Trent, however, indicates the esteem in which they were held by their peers.

The Tridentine declaration that sanctifying grace is the only formal cause of man's justice put an end to the theory of double justice.

See Also: IMPUTATION OF JUSTICE AND MERIT; JUSTICE, DOUBLE; JUSTICE OF MEN; JUSTIFICATION; GRACE, ARTICLES ON.

Bibliography: J. RIVIÈRE, *Dictionnaire de théologie catholique,* ed. A. VACANT et al. (Paris 1903–50) 8.2:2182–84. B. HEURTEBIZE, *ibid.* 3.2:1615–16. A. HUMBERT *ibid.* 6.2:1880–85. È. AMANN, *ibid.* 12.2:2094–2104. J. MERCIER, *ibid.* 14.2:1923–40. H. RONDET, *Gratia Christi* (Paris 1948) 244–258, 261, 263. R. W. GLEASON, *Grace* (New York 1962) 94–95, 213–218.

[K. HARGROVE]

COLOMAN, ST.

Irish pilgrim; b. Ireland, late tenth century; d. Stockerau, near Vienna, Austria, July 17, 1012. He may have been the son of Maolsheachlainn II, High-King of Ireland (980–1002 and 1014–22). While traveling secretly as a pilgrim to the Holy Land, he was arrested as a spy on July 16, 1012, and after being tortured he was hanged on the following day. Subsequently, many miracles were reported where his body had been buried and on Oct. 13, 1014, Margrave Henry I had it transferred to MELK, where he now rests in the Benedictine abbey church. Throughout Austria, Hungary, and southern Germany scores of churches are dedicated to him, and he is invoked as protector of farm animals and patron of marriageable girls. Several villages in Austria and Germany also bear his name. Iconographically he is shown with pilgrim staff and a rope or withe about his neck. He is one of the patrons of Austria, but he was superseded as national patron by St. LEOPOLD III in 1663.

Feast: Oct. 13.

Bibliography: *Acta Sanctae Sedis* Oct. 6:357–362; Suppl., 13 Oct.:149–152. *Monumenta Germaniae Historica: Scriptores* 4:674–681. J. URWALEK, *Der königliche Pilger St. Colomann* (Vienna 1880). *Bibliotheca hagiograpica latina antiquae et mediae aetatis* (Brussels 1898–1901) 1:1881–82. C. JUHAIZ, *S. Koloman der einstige Schutzpatron Niederösterreichs* (Linz 1916). L. GOUGAUD, *Les Saints irlandais hors d'Irlande* (Louvain 1936) 47–50. M. NIEDERKORN-BRUCK, *Der heilige Koloman: der erste Patron Niederösterreichs* (Vienna 1992). F. Ó. BRIAIN, *Dictionnaire d'histoire et de géographie ecclésiastiques,* ed. A. BAUDRILLART et al. (Paris 1912) 13:256–257.

[T. ÖFIAICH]

COLOMBIA, THE CATHOLIC CHURCH IN

The Republic of Colombia has coastlines on both the North Pacific Ocean and the Caribbean Sea. Its land borders Venezuela and Brazil on the east, Ecuador and Peru on the south and Panama on the northwest. From northern coastal plains, the terrain rises to highlands in the central region and thence south to the rugged Andes mountains. In the east the land drops to a lowlands region. The third largest country in South America, Colombia is exceptionally rich in minerals: it is the largest producer of gold in South America; it stands fifth in the world in the production of platinum; and it has practically a world monopoly in the mining of emeralds. Other natural resources include silver, rock salt, coal, hydrocarbons, iron ore and copper. In 1991 a major petroleum reserve was discovered in the region. The variety of climates—from the tropical coast to the more temperate highlands—favors the cultivation of many agricultural products, which include coffee, bananas, tobacco, cotton and sugar cane. Despite being illegal, Cannabis and coca are also widely cultivated and processed into marijuana and cocaine for export.

Once known as the New Kingdom of Granada, the region was renamed Columbia upon its independence from Spain in 1819. At the Congress of Angostura it combined with Venezuela and Ecuador as Gran Colombia. When the tripartite union was dissolved in 1831, the state took the name of New Granada until 1858, when it became Confederación Granadina. From 1863 to 1886, it was the United States of Colombia, and from then on, simply Colombia. An effort by multiple guerilla groups to unseat the region's stable democratic government has continued since the 1960s, fueled by Colombia's powerful drug lords.

The Early Church. The region was originally inhabited by Chibcha tribes, who were displaced after the arrival of Spanish explorers on the Caribbean coast and the colonization of the region as the New Kingdom of Granada. Beginning with the Franciscans in 1508, missionaries carried the faith to the most remote parts of Colombia. These missions used the reduction system to adapt the Chibcha to community life through instruction in animal husbandry, agriculture and crafts. This system stimulated new industries, perfected existing ones, opened roads for commerce, imported tools and brought in trained craftsmen to teach new trades. The missionaries erected the church in which the converted congregated, built hospitals and ran schools in which were taught reading, writing, arithmetic, chant and above all Christian doctrine (*see* MISSION IN COLONIAL AMERICA, I). Along with these efforts, the missionaries became the defenders of the Chibcha people, who were otherwise mistreated and exploited without mercy by *encomenderos* seeking slave labor for their plantations.

The first Franciscan mission was formally established in 1550 with the erection of the Custody of San

Capital: Bogotá.
Size: 439,829 sq. miles.
Population: 39,685,660 in 2000.
Languages: Spanish.
Religions: 35,716,900 Catholics (90%), 120,000 Muslims (.3%), 1,985,460 Protestants (5%), 475,000 follow indigenous faiths (1%), 1,388,300 without religious affiliation.

Archdioceses	Suffragans
Barranquilla	Riohacha, Santa Marta, Valledupar
Bogotá	Facatativá, Girardot, Granada en Colombia, San José de Guaviare, Villavicencio, Zipaquirá
Bucaramanga	Barrancabermeja, Málaga-Soatá, Soccoro y San Gil
Cali	Buenaventura, Buga, Cartago, Palmira
Cartagena	Magangué, Montelíbano, Montería, Sincelejo
Ibagué	Espinal, Florencia, Garzón, Líbano-Honda, Neiva
Manizales	Armenia, La Dorada-Guaduas, Pereira
Medellín	Caldas, Girardota, Jericó, Sonsón-Rionegro
Nueva Pamplona	Arauca, Cúcuta, Ocaña, Tibú
Popayán	Ipiales, Mocoa-Sibundoy, Pasto, Tumaco
Santa Fe de Antioquia	Apartadó, Istmina-Tadó, Quibdó, Santa Rosa de Osos
Tunja	Chiquinquirá, Duitama-Sagamoso, Garagoa, Yopal.

There are seven apostolic vicariates and four apostolic prefectures in the country.

Juan Bautista. The Dominicans arrived in 1529, founding a convent in Cartagena in 1549 and one the following year in Santafé. The Mercedarians established a convent in Cali in 1537, while the Augustinian Hermits erected a convent in Santafé in 1575 and organized the province of Nuestra Señora de la Gracia in 1597. In the instructions written by Archbishop Zapata de Cárdenas in 1576 for the use of the clergy, he stated that the clergy should establish in the reductions a house for the sick close to the church, where natives could be attended in their illnesses. For the maintenance of the hospitals, farms were to be worked and the profits used to support the ill and the nurses. The Chibcha were to contribute chickens or other birds. Two native nurses were to be provided to prepare the food and care for the patients. Homes for the aged, widows and orphans were also to be founded.

Many obstacles were encountered in the propagation of the faith in Colombia, partly stemming from the sophistication of the Christian doctrine and the fact that Christian morality conflicted with Chibcha customs, such as polygamy and idolatry. The preaching of the gospel among native tribes sparked serious resistance on the part of both caciques and witch doctors on the one hand and hypocritical Spanish slave owners on the other. A further difficulty was the linguistic diversity among the tribes: when missionaries succeeded in mastering the language of one community, the language of the next would again confound their efforts to communicate the word of God. There were also rivalries among the religious orders prejudicial to the preaching of the gospel and interference of civil authorities in purely ecclesiastical matters because of the ecclesiastical patronage.

Concurrent with the development of the missions was the development of the hierarchy: Santa Marta and Cartagena were erected in 1534, Popayán in 1546 and Santafé de Bogotá in 1564. The first bishop of Santa Marta chosen by the king of Spain was Alonso de Tobes, of the Colegio de San Bartolomé in Salamanca. When his appointment was confirmed in Rome, he had been dead for more than two weeks, so it was the Dominican Tomás Toro who held the seat of Cartagena for the first time (1534–36). Another Cartagenan bishop, Dionisio de Sanctis (1574–78), authored the first Amerindian catechism. Juan del Valle, a great defender of the native peo-

ple, was the first bishop of Popayán. The Franciscan Juan de los Barrios was the bishop of Santa Marta and the first archbishop of Santafé de Bogotá. To Archbishop Barrios the city owes its first hospital, which began operation in 1564 in his house. After a century of service it was entrusted to the Hospitallers of St. John of God and eventually became known as the Hortúa.

When Bishop Barrios arrived in Santafé in 1553, he found far too few clergy to minister effectively to the extensive diocese. He asked Spain for help, but at his death there were still no more than 50 religious and 20 members of the secular clergy, almost all Spaniards. In 1563 the Dominican fathers established a professorship of Latin in the convent of Santafé, where a few Creoles prepared for the priesthood. Archbishop Barrios ordained the first Creole and the first mestizo of New Granada. In 1573 Zapata de Cárdenas encountered a serious shortage

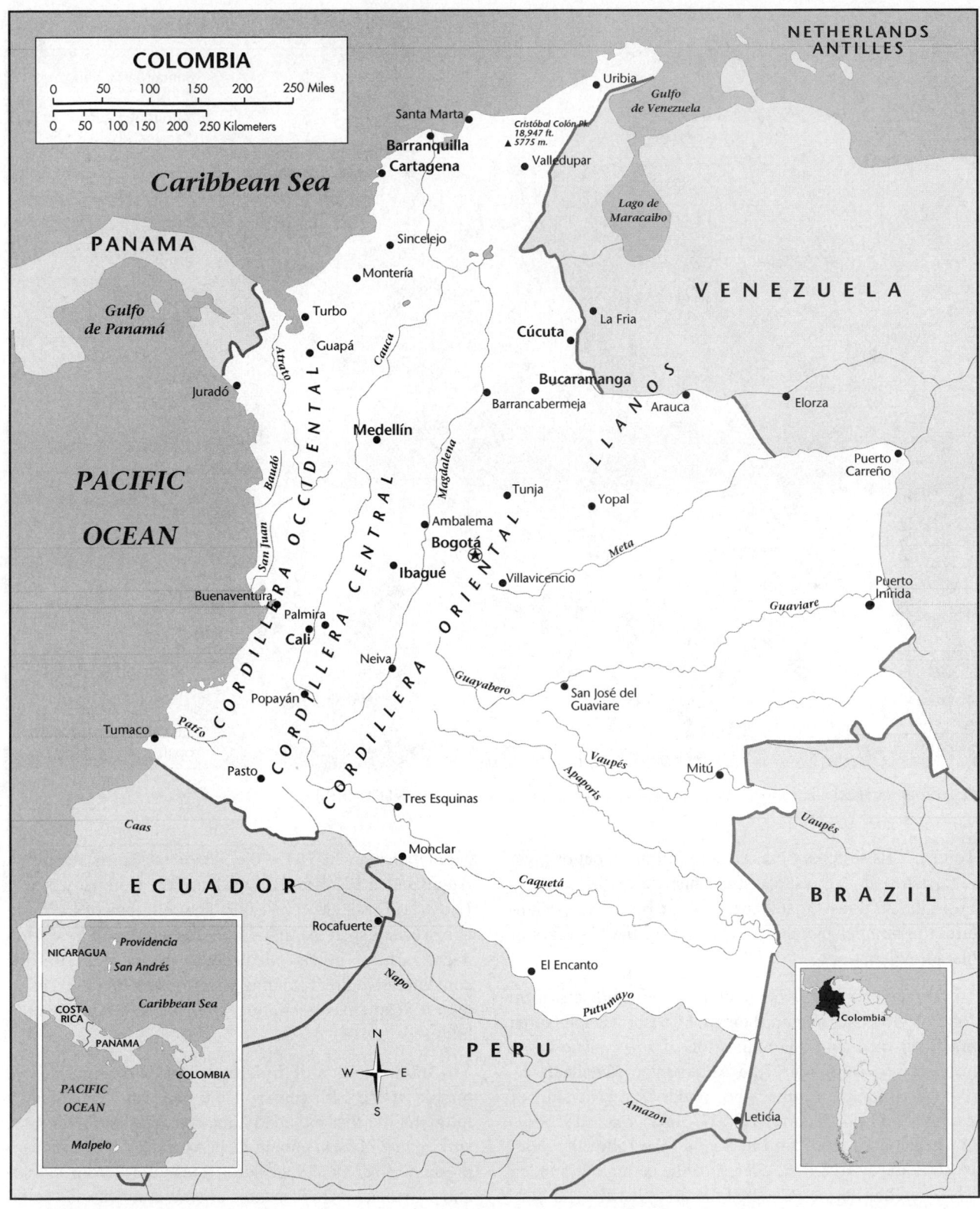

COLOMBIA

0   50   100   150   200   250 Miles

0   50   100   150   200   250 Kilometers

NETHERLANDS
ANTILLES

Uribia

*Gulfo
de Venezuela*

Santa Marta

Cristóbal Colón Pk.
18,947 ft.
▲ 5775 m.

Barranquilla

Cartagena

Valledupar

Caribbean Sea

PANAMA

*Gulfo
de Panamá*

Sincelejo

Montería

*Lago de
Maracaibo*

V E N E Z U E L A

Turbo

Guapá

La Fria

Cúcuta

Juradó

Bucaramanga

Atrato

Cauca

Barrancabermeja

Arauca

Elorza

Medellín

Baudó

San Juan

PACIFIC

Magdalena

OCEAN

Tunja

Yopal

Ambalema

CORDILLERA OCCIDENTAL

Buenaventura

CORDILLERA CENTRAL

Palmira

Cali

Neiva

Popayán

Patía

Tumaco

Pasto

Caas

Puerto
Carreño

Bogotá

Ibagué

Villavicencio

Meta

L L A N O S

Puerto
Inírida

Guaviare

CORDILLERA ORIENTAL

Guayabero

San José del
Guaviare

Vaupés

Apaporis

Mitú

Tres Esquinas

Uaupés

Uaupés

Monclar

Caquetá

B R A Z I L

E C U A D O R

Rocafuerte

Napo

El Encanto

Putumayo

PERU

Amazon

Leticia

NICARAGUA

Providencia

San Andrés

COSTA
RICA

Caribbean Sea

PANAMA

COLOMBIA

*PACIFIC
OCEAN*

Malpelo

N
W   E
S

Colombia

of clergy even though the Dominicans already had a chair of art and theology. Conferring orders on the Saturdays of the four ember days, Zapata ordained Creoles and mes-tizos over the protests of local authorities, priests and the regular clergy. He also founded, in 1582, the first semi-nary of Santafé, one of the first in America, San Luis de

Santa Catalina Catholic Church, Islade Providencia, Colombia. (©Richard Bickel/CORBIS)

Tolosa. This seminary was of short duration but of great importance in the ecclesiastical history of the country. From the 20 priests that Zapata had on his arrival at Santafé, the number increased to 93 during the ten years of his administration.

By the end of the 16th century the Hospitallers of St. John of God had erected their first house, wherein some practiced medicine under the title of *protomédicos*. At turn of the 17th century the Augustinian Recollects arrived, as did the Jesuits who, under the leadership of Archbishop Lobo Guerrero (1599–1608), opened schools in Cartagena in 1603 and in Santafé the following year. In 1605 the Jesuits took charge of the seminary founded by the archbishop, established the first pharmacy in Santafé and erected their province in 1610. By 1600 female religious were also present in Colombia, among them convents of Santa Clara (founded 1573) and Franciscan Conceptionists (1583). Other orders followed, the Discalced Carmelites in 1606; the Order of Santa Inés de

Montepulciano in 1645; the Recollect Tertiaries of St. Augustine in 1739; and the Order of the Company of Our Lady (La Enseñanza) in 1783. The religious of La Enseñanza established the first school for women in New Granada, while others dedicated themselves to the contemplative life, founding vocations among the daughters of Spaniards and among Creoles and Chibcha populations.

Intellectual and Spiritual Development. By the middle of the 17th century Colombia had an exuberant religious life that included a metropolitan see with three suffragan dioceses, numerous parishes and doctrines, appropriate canonical legislation emanating from synods and provincial councils, and clergy in convents and seminaries. The Colegio Seminario de San Bartolomé was founded in 1605 and after many vicissitudes, became the Seminario Conciliar of San José; in 1653 the Colegio Mayor de Nuestra Señora del Rosario came into being, while another seminary was founded in Popayán. Idolatry

Children carry an effigy of Christ through the streets during a children's procession to mark Holy Week. Popayan, Colombia. (©Jeremy Horner/CORBIS)

was almost completely uprooted, and thousands of Chibcha were converted and instructed in the Catholic faith. Among the most important missionary figures of colonial times were St. Louis BERTRAND and St. Peter CLAVER, the apostle of the Africans; the Augustinian, Francisco Romero, author of *Llanto Sagrado* (1693); and the Jesuits Alonso de Sandoval (1576–1652), José Gumilla (1686–1750) and Juan Ribero (1681–1736).

In addition to spiritual needs, the Church influenced the intellectual life of the colonial era, as an intellectual culture developed around the schools, seminaries and universities. The first press, introduced in Colombia by the Jesuits, went into operation in 1738 and printed mainly catechisms and small books of devotion. Soon groups of writers were formed who gave glory to the Church through their written works: priests and religious penned the first chronicles of conquest and colonization, cultivated the sacred science, became outstanding in the humanities, and were poets, dramatists and noted orators. The *doctrineros* in their chapels and the friars in their convents also furthered cultural advancement, while the educational mission rested in the hands of the Church, supported by the throne. In these educational centers, instruction was given mainly to the children of Spaniards,

but also to native Colombians. The Botanical Expedition founded by the archbishop-viceroy Antonio CABALLERO Y GÓNGORA in 1783 had the learned priest José Celestino MUTIS as director and the technical assistance of various priests.

Independence and the Church. During the 18th century the region was transferred from the viceroyalty of Peru to that of New Granada, and the seat of power for not only Colombia but also Venezuela, Ecuador and Panama was transferred to Bogotá. Following the Battle of Boyacá in 1819 Colombia declared its independence from Spain. Together with Venezuela, the region was renamed the United States of Colombia by Simón Bolívar, who went on in 1822 to unite not only the United States of Colombia but also New Granada, Panama and Ecuador as the Republic of Gran Colombia. This union collapsed within eight years, and in 1832 Colombia and Panama promulgated a joint independent constitution. Continued temporary alliances between the regions culminated in the formation of the Republic of Colombia in 1886; the "War of the Thousand Days," waged with U.S. backing from 1899 to 1902, divided Panama and Colombia politically.

During the colonial period the Church acquired great wealth from legacies, foundations and chaplaincies, which it used for religious services and the support of convents. However, it was subject to the *patronato* system, which allowed the Spanish crown to interfere in ecclesiastical appointments, and other areas of Church administration. After Colombia broke with the Spanish crown in 1819, the new state assumed the right of patronage in the Law of 1824, although this was never acknowledged by the Holy See. After efforts to establish diplomatic relations with the Holy See proved unsuccessful, the government enacted a constitutional separation of Church and State in 1853, while continuing to allow Roman Catholicism the position of official religion. At this point the persecution of the Church began. Properties accumulated during the colonial era were confiscated by the state and passed into the hands of individuals. In 1887 and 1892 concordats were negotiated curtailing the *patronato*. The president of the republic could intervene in only two ways in the appointment of bishops: in recommending candidates to the Holy See or in vetoing for civil or political reasons those chosen for appointments. In compensation for those properties confiscated by the State during the 19th century, the government began appropriating an annual sum as remuneration for the Church.

The Modern Church. In 1948 Colombia suffered an economic downturn, which resulted in violence that moved from urban to rural areas of the country. In 1953

Catedral Primada de Colombia, Bogota. (The Purcell Team/CORBIS)

a military government assumed power and stabilized the country to the point where democratic rule could be restored. Beginning in the 1960s a proliferation of small guerrilla groups initiated a reign of terror in an effort to overthrow the government and institute their own right- or left-wing policies, among which was the redistribution of land. As in other South American countries, some Church leaders were involved in a revolution of their own, through LIBERATION THEOLOGY, a view of the role of the Church as advocating programs benefiting the poorer classes while disapproving of the violent means employed by guerrillas. Although such actions often made clergy the focus of attacks by the Colombian military, Church leaders attempted frequent mediation between rebel and government officials as a way to end the bloodshed. Efforts at mediation by both Church leaders and the government—in 1990 with the ultra-radical M-19 guerillas and in 1998 with the National Liberation Army (ELN)—saw some success, although violence by other groups continued, and in June of 1999 the ELN had returned to the offensive by kidnapping over 120 churchgoers in Cali. In 1999 a death squad sponsored by the AUC guerilla group murdered 27 Catholics attending a baptismal mass in northern Colombia, as part of a new trend in terrorism that left hundreds dead by the year's end.

In 1991 the government promulgated a new constitution, under which the Church was no longer named as the religion of the state. However, it continued to command a privileged position as the faith of the majority of Colombians, and was authorized to provide the educational needs of rural communities where state-run schools were lacking. In addition, only Catholic priests were allowed to serve as chaplains. All churches remained exempt from taxation in Colombia, and Catholic-run private schools were also extended this privilege. In their roles as the majority church, Catholic leaders remained an active presence as an advocate for Columbian society, in 1996 speaking out on proposed legislation to legalize abortion. In the wake of both this proposal and the legalization of euthanasia earlier in the decade, Pope John Paul II advised Colombian bishops to work against what he termed "the painful problem of accelerated family disintegration."

Into the 21st Century. By 2000 there were 3,295 parishes tended by 5,050 diocesan and 2,265 religious priests. Other religious included approximately 790 brothers and 17,990 sisters, many of whom aided in teaching and operating the 1,660 primary and 1,230 secondary Catholic schools in Colombia. In addition, the first Catholic television station in the country was launched in February of 2000. An historic Catholic emblem, the famous sanctuary of Nuestra Señora de Chiquinquira, remained a popular pilgrimage attracting participants of all social classes as well as people from neighboring countries. In 1997 a timely pilgrimage was held by several thousand Colombians who, accompanying a giant cross, traveled 800 miles through the region's most violence-plagued regions as part of the "Way of the Cross for Peace and Life." The problem of displaced populations following the flight from violence-torn rural areas was of increasing concern to the Church in the new millennium.

Bibliography: J. M. GROOT, *Historia eclesiástica y civil de la Nueva Granada*, 5 v. (2d ed. Bogotá 1889–93). M. G. ROMERO, *Fray Juan de los Barrios y la evangelización del Nuevo Reino de Granada* (Bogotá 1960). A. LEE LOPEZ, "Clero indígena en el arzobispado de Santa Fé en el siglo XVI," *Boletín de historia y antigüedades*, 50 (1963) 1–86. J. A. SALAZAR, *Los estudios eclesiásticos superiors en el Nuevo Reino de Granada, 1563–1810* (Madrid 1946).

[M. G. ROMERO/EDS.]

COLOMBIÈRE, CLAUDE DE LA, ST.

Missionary priest of the Society of Jesus; ascetical writer; b. Saint-Symphorien d'Ozen (near Grenoble, between Lyons and Vienne), Dauphiné, France, Feb. 2, 1641; d. Paray-le-Monial, France, Feb. 15, 1682. Born of noble parentage, Claude entered the Society of Jesus at Avignon (Oct. 25, 1659). Thereafter he taught grammar and literature at Trinity College, Lyons (1661–66), then took up theological studies in Paris at Clermont College. The year after his ordination (April 6, 1669), he returned to Lyons to teach rhetoric (1670–73). He began his tertianship (final year of spiritual formation for the Jesuits) following a year-long assignment as preacher in the Jesuit church of Lyons.

Having taken final vows, in 1675, Colombière was named superior of the Jesuit house at Paray-le-Monial, where he demonstrated academic brilliance and became the spiritual director of St. Margaret Mary ALACOQUE. Thereafter he was a zealous apostle of devotion to the Sacred Heart of Jesus, first celebrated privately by the two saints on June 21, 1675. This devotion, centered on the humanity of Christ, was aimed at countering JANSENISM. In October of 1676, Colombière was sent to London, England, as chaplain to Mary Beatrice d'Este, the duchess of York, wife of the future King James II. From England he continued his spiritual direction of St. Margaret Mary by letter. Imprisoned as a conspirator in the fictitious OATES PLOT to overthrow King Charles II, Colombière was spared death because of his position in the household of the duchess of York and the protection of King Louis XIV; however, Columbière was banished (1679).

Columbière returned to Lyons where he was spiritual director to the young Jesuits, then repaired to Paray-le-Monial, where he died. He was buried in the Jesuit chapel at Paray-le-Monial; a church was built over the same spot in 1685. He was beatified by Pius XI, June 16, 1929, and canonized by John Paul II in Rome, May 31, 1992. Patron of toy makers and turners.

Feast: Feb. 15.

Bibliography: C. DE LA COLOMBIÈRE, *Escritos espirituales del Beato Claudio de la Colombière, S.J.* (Bilbao, Spain 1979); *Oeuvres du R. P. Claude de la Colombière* (Avignon 1832; Paris 1864), which includes "Pious Reflections," "Meditations on the Passion," and "Retreat and Spiritual Letters." G. GUITTON, *Le bienheureux Claude La Colombière: apôtre du Sacré-Cœur, 1641–1682: d'après ses œuvres (sermons et correspondance) et de nombreux documents inédits . . .* (Paris 1981); *Perfect Friend: The Life of Blessed Claude La Colombière, SJ*, tr. W. J. YOUNG (St. Louis 1956). R. H. LAVIGNE, *The Life of St. Claude de la Colombiere: Spiritual director of St. Margaret Mary* (Boston 1992); *Special messenger* (Boston 1978). W. LÜBEN, *Der ehrwürdige diener Gottes p. Claudius de la Colombière* (New York 1884). J. N. TYLENDA, *Jesuit Saints & Martyrs* (Chicago 1998) 44–47.

[K. I. RABENSTEIN]

COLONNA

Powerful family of Rome from the Middle Ages to the twentieth century. The history of the family from 1100 to 1562 was that of the Colonna-led Ghibelline struggle against the papacy, the Orsini, and other Guelf families. This article provides some general observations to establish a historical setting, a comparison of the Colonna and Orsini families, a description of the Ghibelline-Guelf conflict, and a history of the family after 1562.

Historical context. When the Colonna began opposing the papacy in the twelfth century, FEUDALISM was a major institution, with emphasis on land and family loyalty. The nobles had their own armies, made war and peace, and held court to decide the innocence or guilt of their people. Ambitious, energetic nobles sought wealth and power by acquiring more land. Another method of achieving wealth was by obtaining higher offices in the Church, and it became common practice to have younger sons become churchmen. Such appointees reflected the influences of the time. Some were inspiring religious leaders; others were interested in the new learning of the Renaissance. Cardinals were not always ordained; they served as administrators in the STATES OF THE CHURCH, performing services that laymen supply today.

Powerful nobles could, and sometimes did, challenge a ruler. There was, however, an important difference in ROME, resulting from the dual role of the PAPACY during the medieval period in both spiritual and temporal affairs and the difficulty of separating the two roles. The Colonna and other Ghibelline families did not oppose the pope as a religious ruler; they objected to his temporal power, or his being a sovereign in civil affairs. There had been an attempt to revive the civil competence of the Roman Senate, but in 1188 ecclesiastical jurisdiction was established over the Senate. However, in the thirteenth century more nobles became senators, and the Senate was no longer ecclesiastically dominated. Yet the Ghibellines could still arouse the people to revolt with the cry, "The People and Colonna." (*See* GUELFS AND GHIBELLINES.)

Colonna-Orsini. More than 100 years ago G. MORONI pointed out (14:278; 49:146) that the Colonna family always had its own interests as well as the emperor's at heart; the ORSINI, in turn, thought of their family as well as of the papacy. Both families had property in Rome and in the countryside. Their first houses in Rome were like fortresses, guarded by their men. Both first possessed a few villages, then in the thirteenth century a dozen or more with one village becoming the chief family seat, for example, Palestrina for the Colonna. Both families produced about the same number of cardinals over the years, but the Orsini possessed the greater number before 1562. In the sixteenth century both acquired the special honor of having the head of the family at papal functions with the title "prince in attendance at the papal throne."

The Colonna struggle for power was not one of slow even gains or of long periods of success. After a victory came defeat. Houses in Rome were destroyed or seized, and villages were captured. Absence from Rome was often necessary, but the Colonna returned, rebuilt, and again became influential.

Ghibelline-Guelf conflict. From 1100 until the modern era that began in 1562, the Ghibelline-Guelf conflict passed through six periods.

From 1100 to 1200. The ancestors of the Colonna were the TUSCULANI. *Pietro de Colonna* (1064–1118?) was the first member to use this name. Writers differ about the origin of the name. It may have derived from his possible home in the district of Rome near Trajan's Column or in the village of Colonna, 16 miles from Rome. Early in the twelfth century he tried to capture Cave, which belonged to the papacy. In defeat he lost two villages. About 1167 the Colonna, assisted by troops belonging to FREDERICK I BARBAROSSA, defeated the Romans near Monte Porzio. After 1168 the Orsini and SAVELLI destroyed the Colonna and Conti houses in Rome. In 1191 the Romans destroyed Tuscolo. The first cardinal in the family, the Benedictine *Giovanni,* created 1192 or 1193 (d. *c.* 1214), served as legate in several countries.

From 1200 to 1288. The Colonna family was stronger in the thirteenth than in the twelfth century, having three branches: Palestrina, Gallicano, and Gelazzano. In Rome it had fortified the mausoleum of Augustus and dominated the district near the church of the Holy Apostles. *Giovanni,* created cardinal in 1212 (d. 1244), was legate to the Holy Land during the Fifth CRUSADE. He brought back a part of the column at which Christ was scourged and placed it in his titular church, St. Praxedes, where it may still be seen. Changing sides, he became a supporter of Emperor FREDERICK II against the pope. While the Holy See was vacant (1241–43), Senator Matteo Russo Orsini defeated the Colonna and captured their stronghold, the mausoleum. For more than 30 years the Colonna seemed unimportant. Then they won recognition from Pope NICHOLAS III, an Orsini, who created *Giacomo* cardinal in 1278 (d. 1318) as a kind of peace offering between the two families.

From 1288 to 1298. It might be said that Pope NICHOLAS IV (1288–92), who had been bishop of Palestrina, adopted the Colonna, so much did he favor them. He made *Pietro* a cardinal in 1288 (d. 1326). For the first time the family had two members in the college of cardinals. During a rebellion in 1290 the people called *Sciarra Colonna* (d. 1329) their Caesar. Alarmed at such power, Pope BONIFACE VIII, a Guelf of the GAETANI family, decided to restrict it. In the altercation that followed, family feeling bound Cardinal Giacomo to his nephews Sciarra, *Stefano* (d. after 1347), and Cardinal Pietro, rather than to the pope. When Stefano's men seized the papal treasury as it was being brought from Anagni to Rome, Boniface insisted on its restoration and the cession of the towns of Palestrina, Colonna, and Zagarolo. The cardinals agreed about the treasury but refused to give up the property. Excommunications and war followed. With Orsini support, Palestrina was captured. The Colonna fled. Eventually they reached France. There the new pope, CLEMENT V, reinstated the Colonna cardinals, and they remained in AVIGNON until their deaths.

Cardinal Giacomo's sister, Bl. *Margaret Colonna,* belonged to the POOR CLARES and was venerated for centuries after her death in 1290. She is representative of the religious members of her family—the monks, abbots, and bishops, who are less well known than the cardinals and the aggressive members.

From 1303 to 1417. In 1303 Sciarra returned to Rome with King PHILIP IV of France's representative, Nogaret. Their violent treatment of Boniface VIII probably hastened his death. Stefano supported Emperor HENRY VII when he went to Rome in 1312, but he then changed to the side of the papacy and opposed Emperor Louis IV the Bavarian's coronation in Rome. Sciarra, however, supported Louis and was at his coronation in St. Peter's in 1328; Sciarra then left Rome and died in exile. Pope JOHN XXII rewarded Stefano by making his son *Giovanni* cardinal in 1327 (d. 1348), the only Colonna churchman created cardinal during the AVIGNON PAPACY (1305–78). Cardinal Giovanni proved to be an able judge in civil cases; he was a learned man and a friend of PETRARCH. The Colonnas fought bravely against COLA DI RIENZO, several members of the family being killed. After Rienzo's death, they helped to restore order in Rome. An example of Colonna generosity was shown at the time of the Black Death, when the Romans toiled up the Capitoline Hill to St. Mary in Aracoeli to pray for the end of the plague. Cardinal Giovanni Colonna arranged for the building of the first steps up the Capitoline Hill (1348), the only public construction in Rome between 1305 and 1378.

Among the learned Colonna was GILES OF ROME (d. 1316), an AUGUSTINIAN who studied under Thomas Aquinas and became the general of the order in 1292. Some writers state that Boniface VIII created him a cardinal in 1302, but there was no public announcement.

Three Colonna cardinals were created during the WESTERN SCHISM: *Agapito* (d. 1380), who had served as nuncio to Emperor Charles IV and peace envoy to Castile and Portugal, was created cardinal in 1378 along with his brother *Stefano* (d. 1379), and *Oddo,* later Pope MARTIN V, became cardinal in 1405.

From 1417 to 1500. Pope Martin V (1417–31) increased the power and wealth of his family by giving it property, especially Paliano, which became the seat of an important branch. Queen Joanna II of Naples bestowed fiefs on Martin's two brothers. In 1426 Martin created his nephew *Prospero* cardinal (d. 1463), but he withheld the announcement until 1430. When Martin V died, Cardinal Prospero and his brothers tried to keep a part of the treasury, but the new pope, EUGENE IV, made them give it up. The Colonna rebelled in 1434, forcing the pope to leave Rome. In a second rebellion in 1437, however, the Orsini and others defeated the Colonna and destroyed Palestrina. Cardinal Prospero was excommunicated and exiled, though Pope NICHOLAS V later absolved and reinstated him. Prospero's Ghibelline politics were only one of his interests; another was his appreciation of learning. During the last three years of the reign of Pope SIXTUS IV (1471–84), there was another Colonna-papacy conflict. The Orsini supported Girolamo RIARIO, the pope's nephew, and the Colonna opposed him. The Colonna suffered reverses and defeat: the imprisonment of *Giovanni,* who had been created cardinal in 1480 (d. 1508); the imprisonment of *Lorenzo,* during which he died or was killed; the confiscation of the Colonna palace, the loss of vil-

lages, and banishment. After the death of Pope Sixtus, the Roman people rose against Riario and welcomed the return of the Colonna. The position of the family was shown when King Charles VIII of France went to Rome on his way to Naples in 1495. *Prospero* (d. 1523) and *Fabrizio* (d. 1520) Colonna, great generals, rode in the cavalcade that received the king. Cardinal Giovanni was one of five cardinals who were admitted to his audiences.

From 1500 to 1562. In 1501 Cesare BORGIA defeated the Colonna; confiscations and exile followed. Pope JULIUS II (1503–13) sought to conciliate the Colonna by restoring their palace and other possessions, marrying his niece to a Colonna, and bestowing on the head of the family the honor of being the "prince in attendance at the papal throne." Such acts did not satisfy *Pompeo Colonna* (d. 1532), who had been forced to become a churchman by his family. When Julius was seriously ill in 1511, Pompeo gathered his supporters on the Capitoline to plot against the temporal power of the papacy. The pope's recovery, however, prevented any action. Pope LEO X created Pompeo a cardinal in 1517. The cardinal and *Ascanio Colonna* (d. 1559) displayed their position and wealth by a lavish entertainment given when Pope CLEMENT VII spent the night in their palace after making his official visit to St. John Lateran in 1523. Clement appointed Pompeo vice-chancellor, but the cardinal continued to favor the empire; for example, he gave a banquet to celebrate the imperial victory over France at Pavia in 1525. To punish the pope for making a treaty against Emperor Charles V, the cardinal, together with *Vespasiano* and Ascanio Colonna, sacked the Vatican in 1526. The cardinal was not with the invaders in the siege of Rome in 1527. When he saw the resulting sad state of Rome, he showed compassion for the pope and other people, many of whom he took into his chancellery palace. In 1530 he became viceroy of Naples.

Marco Antonio II (d. 1584), Ascanio's son, fought the family's last battles against the papacy. Pope PAUL IV (1555–59) resented the control of Naples by Spain and the independence of Roman nobles. His restrictions on the nobles and their reaction led him to demand surrender of the Orsini and Colonna castles. The Orsini complied; the Colonna did not and fled to Naples. Their estates were declared forfeited and given to the pope's eldest nephew in May of 1556. In September the Duke of Alba, the Spanish general, and Marco Antonio began to march toward Rome. Their victories and nearness to Rome by July of 1557 led to a negotiated peace. Spain insisted that all Colonna possessions be restored. All were returned, except Paliano, which was not ceded until 1562. The year 1562 marked the end of the long Colonna-papacy struggle, which dated from 1100. The decline of feudalism, the weakening of the imperial idea with the rise of the national states, and the preoccupation of the new states in other affairs—hence the lack of support for the Ghibellines in Italy—all made the old struggle meaningless.

Modern era. In 1562 a new period began for the Colonna. Less than 13 years after Marco Antonio's march against the papacy, Pope PIUS V asked him (1570) to command the papal fleet in the war against the Turks. He immediately set to work to prepare the galleys. When the pope made an alliance with Venice and Spain, Don Juan became the general of the expedition and Marco Antonio lieutenant. The latter's part in the Battle of LEPANTO (1571) made him a hero, and, against his wishes, he was awarded a triumphal march in Rome.

The large number of Colonna cardinals after 1562 indicates the high favor the family enjoyed with the papacy after that time: during 462 years of enmity (1100–1562) there had been 11 Colonna cardinals; in only 241 years of good relations (1562–1803, the death of the last cardinal) there were 12 Colonna cardinals, and there were often two of them sitting at the same time in the college of cardinals. The sixteenth- and seventeenth-century Colonna cardinals were: (1) *Marco Antonio IV,* cardinal 1565 (d. 1597), the nephew of Marco Antonio of Lepanto fame, an excellent administrator as archbishop of Taranto and Salerno, who attended the Council of TRENT, was appointed head of the Commission on the Vulgate, and became librarian at the Vatican; (2) *Ascanio,* cardinal 1586 (d. 1608), son of Marco Antonio of Lepanto, who won esteem because of his character and knowledge and served as viceroy of Catalonia; (3) *Girolamo,* cardinal 1628 (d. 1666), an excellent administrator of the Diocese of Bologna, who represented the king of Spain in Rome and spent his last years in Spain; and (4) *Federico Baldeschi,* cardinal 1673 (d. 1691), who was adopted by the Colonna family in order to have a cardinal. During the eighteenth century, Colonna cardinals were: (5) *Carlo,* cardinal 1706 (d. 1739); (6) *Prospero,* cardinal 1739 (d. 1743); (7) *Girolamo,* cardinal 1743 (d. 1763); and (8) *Prospero,* cardinal 1743 (d. 1765); (9) *Marco Antonio,* cardinal 1759 (d. 1803), the nephew of Cardinal Girolamo, who fulfilled his duties so well that he was a model for both lay and ecclesiastical princes; (10) *Antonio Branciforte,* cardinal 1766 (d. 1783), son of a Sicilian noble, nuncio to France and Venice; (11) *Pietro Pamphili,* cardinal 1766 (d. 1780), grandson of Olimpia Pamphili, brother of Cardinal Marco Antonio, nuncio to France; (12) *Niccolò Colonna di Stigliano,* cardinal 1785 (d. 1796), of Neapolitan nobility, nuncio to Spain.

After 1562 two popes, Sixtus V and Gregory XVI, confirmed the honor—shared only by the Orsini and Colonna—of being officially in attendance at papal functions. Protests came from the Savelli, the Conti, and in

1623 from the conservators, but to no avail. The honor or right was still exercised in the twentieth century.

In the seventeenth century the Colonna sold several of their properties, including Palestrina, to other Roman families. The present palace in Rome near the church of the Holy Apostles dates back to the seventeenth and eighteenth centuries, and a portion stands on the site of the palace built by Martin V in the early fifteenth century and of houses from a still earlier period. There is reason to believe that the family has lived in this district for seven centuries, and perhaps longer.

See Also: COLONNA, VITTORIA.

Bibliography: P. LITTA et al., *Famiglie celebri italiane,* 14 v. (Milan 1819–1923) v. 4. G. MORONI, *Dizionario de erudizione storico-ecclesiastica,* 103 v. (Venice 1840–61) 4:61–62; 14:277–310; 55:233–243, for "Principe assistente al soglio pontificio." L. PASTOR, *The History of the Popes from the Close of the Middle Ages,* 40 v. (London-St. Louis 1938–61) 1:282–328; 4:379–384; 5:229–231, 247–248, 451–455; 6:103–104; 9:275–341, 367–461; 14:90–174; 18:369–434. P. COLONNA, *I Colonna* (Rome 1927). L. CÀLLARI, *I palazzi di Roma* (3d ed. Rome 1944). P. PASCHINI, *I Colonna* (Rome 1955). G. MOLLAT et al., *Dictionnaire d'histoire et de géographie ecclésiastiques* (Paris 1912–) 13:328–340. H. K. WEINERT and F. BOCK, *Lexikon für Theologie und Kirche,* 10 v. (Freiburg 1957–65) 3:8–12.

[M. L. SHAY]

COLONNA, VITTORIA

Poet; b. Marino, near Rome, 1490; d. Rome, Feb. 27, 1547. In 1509 she married Ferrante d'Avalos, Marquis of Pescara. After his death (1525) from wounds received fighting for the emperor at the battle of Pavia, she passionately celebrated his memory in verses that won her contemporary renown but are now less admired; they are mostly sonnets in the Petrarchan tradition of Christianized Platonism. Very devout and deeply concerned for the reform of the Church, Vittoria divided the rest of her life between religious seclusion in various convents (at Orvieto, Viterbo, and Rome) and the cultivation of friendships with people—churchmen, scholars, and artists—who shared her own spiritual aspirations. She actively supported the Franciscan Capuchin reform and, until his apostasy, was in touch with Bernadino OCHINO; she knew Cardinals Reginald POLE and Gasparo CONTARINI and various members of the circle of Juan de VALDÉS. During her stay at Viterbo (1541–44), she was drawn most into contact with Pole and other Catholic reformers who were trying to continue Contarini's efforts to find a *via media* between Catholic teaching on grace and the Lutheran position (*see* JUSTICE, DOUBLE). Her purely religious poetry (the *Rime spirituali*) belongs to these later years. Her most famous friendship, however, was with MICHELANGELO, who celebrated her beauty, both physical and spiritual, in many poems similar to her own in their Christian-Platonist inspiration, though far more powerful and intense. She was a minor poet, but she has an honorable place in the history of Italian spirituality.

Bibliography: Works. V. COLONNA, *Le Rime,* ed. P. E. VISCONTI (Rome 1840); *Carteggio,* ed. E. FERRERO and G. MÜLLER, suppl. D. TORDI (2d ed. Turin 1892). L. BALDACCI, ed., *Lirici del Cinquecento* (Florence 1957). Studies. G. TOFFANIN, *Il Cinquecento* (4th ed. Milan 1950). ''V. C.,'' *Italia francescana,* series 2., 22 (1947) 1–134.

[K. FOSTER]

COLORADO, CATHOLIC CHURCH IN

According to the Official Catholic Directory FY 2000 approximately 14 percent of the population of Colorado—about 553,000 of a total population for four million—are Catholics. They are served by 199 parishes, 102 missions, and assorted pastoral centers distributed into three dioceses: the archdiocese of Denver, Pueblo, and Colorado Springs.

Early History. Colorado became a territory of the United States in 1861 and a state in 1876, but its Catholic history began much earlier. Spanish explorers and missionaries traversed the southern and western part of the state in the 16th century. In the 17th century French fur traders penetrated to the mountain areas, and France claimed the land east of the mountains. This section was transferred to the U.S. by the Louisiana Purchase (1803). In 1821 the western part of Colorado became Mexican territory. This section was ceded to the U.S. in 1848. The gold rush of 1859 brought thousands of prospectors to the area. Congress established the Colorado territory in 1861. The steady growth of population and the establishment of towns to serve the mining region, as well as the building of railroads and the settlement of farming communities, led to the admittance of Colorado to the Union in 1876.

Spanish Franciscans established missions in the southern and western part of the state in the 18th century. When Mexican rule superseded Spanish, the Franciscans were replaced by Mexican diocesan clergy. After the acquisition of the territory by the U.S., the southern Colorado missions were served by priests from New Mexico. The area north of the Arkansas River and east of the mountains was included in the Vicariate Apostolic of Kansas.

Hispanic villagers from Northern New Mexico moved into the San Luis Valley in 1851. They established

Vittoria Colonna, reproduced from a facsimile of a chalk drawing by Michelangelo.

settlements at San Luis de la Culebra, the oldest permanent community in Colorado, in 1851; San Pedro was founded in 1852, San Acacio in 1853, and Conejos in 1854. Priests from Abiquiu, New Mexico, celebrated Mass regularly in the Conejos Valley until Bishop John B. Lamy of Santa Fe established Our Lady of Guadalupe Parish in Conejos in 1857. A secular priest, Father Montaño, served as pastor until 1860, when Father Jose Miguel Vigil succeeded him. Father Miguel Rolly served as pastor from 1866 until December 1871, when he was replaced by Father Salvador Personé, S. J.

Personé's pastoral care included some 3000 parishioners, scattered among 25 settlements. He traveled from village to village, including, Pinos, which featured a chapel, and Rincones, which only had a small altar, offering Mass, hearing confessions, and celebrating first communions. Father Alejandro Leone, S.J., and Brother Prisco Caso, S.J., arrived in the San Luis Valley in February 1872, where they took up the itinerant mantle from Personé, traveling great distances to celebrate Mass and administer the sacraments.

Growth. The Colorado Gold Rush of the mid-19th century sparked population growth and led to the establishment of a Catholic diocese in Colorado. After prospectors discovered gold in the Rocky Mountains near

Archdiocese/Diocese	Year Created
Archdiocese of Denver	1941
Diocese of Colorado Springs	1984
Diocese of Pueblo	1941

Denver in July 1858, miners flooded into the region. Since the area north of the Arkansas River and east of the mountains was included in the Kansas and Nebraska Territories, it fell within the purview of John B. Miége, vicar apostolic of Indian Territory. In May 1860, Miége journeyed from his headquarters at Leavenworth, Kansas Territory, to the Colorado goldfields. His purpose was to investigate the situation in the goldfields and to build a church for the many Catholics who had journeyed to the central Rockies, and he was angered by what he saw as the invasion of Native American lands by greedy whites. Miége established a parish and promised to send a priest to the Catholics who worked the goldfields around Denver. Finding that he was unable to spare a priest for the new parish in Denver, Miége convinced the Holy See to transfer responsibility for Colorado to the Diocese of Santa Fe.

To fill the Denver post, in October 1860 Bishop Lamy sent his close friend Joseph P. MACHEBEUF (1812–1889), accompanied by a young French priest, Jean Raverdy (1831–1889). Machebeuf had served as a missionary on American frontiers for more than 20 years, but Raverdy was only recently ordained. In Denver, the duo found an incomplete church building and a parish discouraged by their long wait for a priest. Ten Catholic families greeted the priests, though more than 200, including non-Catholics, attended Sunday Mass on a regular basis. In early 1861, Machebeuf struck out in search of Catholics in the goldfields, leaving Raverdy to offer Masses and to learn English. Machebeuf's buggy served as a rectory and chapel on wheels. On his tour, Machebeuf established parishes at Arapahoe City, Golden, and Central City and visited the principal mining towns.

The Central City parish was the largest of the goldfield congregations, with some 200 parishioners. The parish shared worship space with other Christian groups. After several months, Machebeuf determined that Central City parishioners were wealthy enough to build their own church. The parishioners, however, were not as quick to part with their money as the priest had hoped. When pledges did not come rolling in, Machebeuf locked parishioners in the shared city church one Sunday, and would not unlock the doors until he was satisfied with the level of pledges. The tactic worked and Central City soon boasted a new Catholic church building. Another of

Machebeuf's innovative techniques concerned farming. During his years in New Mexico, he learned how to farm lands that received little rainfall. He transferred this knowledge to the Colorado soil, irrigating some of the land he purchased for the Church and grew vegetables and grain.

A Colorado Diocese. Staffing problems continued to plague the church in Colorado. Machebeuf and Raverdy functioned without much assistance, relying on Bishop Lamy and his successor, Bishop Jean B. Salpointe, to send priests as best they could. In 1868, when the Holy See responded positively to his request that Colorado be separated from the Diocese of Santa Fe and formed into a new ecclesiastical jurisdiction, Machebeuf was appointed vicar apostolic of Colorado. Before his ordination as a bishop, Machebeuf made a tour of the East Coast and upper Midwest, hoping to raise funds for the purchase of land and to acquire new priests for his vicariate. He met with little success. On his return, however, Coloradans feted their new bishop with a parade and reception. A year later, Machebeuf made a European tour with the same purposes in mind. He returned from Europe with five new priests, only one of them English-speaking, and a loan to cover the vicariate's debts. The English-speaking priest was assigned to the Denver parish, while the others were sent to the Hispanic parishes in southern Colorado's San Luis and Arkansas valleys. By 1870, Catholic churches in Colorado could seat 8,575 parishioners in 14 parishes. Catholics by far outnumbered other Christians. Much of the demographic growth in the region resulted from the migration of some 8,000 New Mexicans during the 1860s, most of whom were Catholics. By 1890, more than half of the Christians in Colorado (47,111 of 86,837) were Catholics.

The arrival of Jesuits in 1871 greatly alleviated Machebeuf's personnel problems. They took over the southern Colorado parishes, freeing up Machebeuf's recruits to minister in Denver and the surrounding mining areas. Machebeuf and his small retinue of priests even managed to build three Catholic schools by 1870. While rival Protestants saw these Catholic schools as a tool for Catholic conversions, Catholics viewed them as vital for keeping the flock intact. St. Mary's Academy for girls opened in 1863 in Denver. With daughters of the territory's most prestigious families in attendance, Protestant as well as Catholic, the school was an immediate success. Catholics also opened a high school for boys in the 1860s in Denver. The Sisters of Charity from Cincinnati, Ohio, under the leadership of the famous Sister Blandina Segale, built and staffed a Catholic school in Trinidad, St. Joseph's Academy. The Sisters also taught at a public school in Trinidad, until the school board requested that they no longer wear their habits in the classroom. The sisters resigned and established a parish school free of government restrictions.

The vicariate apostolic became the Diocese of Denver in 1887, with Machebeuf serving as the first ordinary and Bishop Nicholas Chrysostom Matz, his coadjutor. Matz, born in Munster, Lorraine, had come to Colorado shortly after his ordination in 1874. Bishop Matz succeeded Machebeuf upon his death in July 1889 and served as diocesan bishop for 28 years (1889–1917). Matz oversaw the diocese's first synod in 1890, the construction of Our Lady of the Immaculate Conception Cathedral, and the establishment of St. Thomas Seminary, under the direction of the Vincentian Fathers, in 1908. In 1912, St. Frances Cabrini founded an orphanage on a Rocky Mountain peak near Denver. The state's fluctuating mining-based economy caused financial hardships for the diocese during the Matz era, as did increased anti-Catholicism and conflicts among German and Irish Catholics.

Bishop John Henry Tihen who had been bishop of Lincoln was transferred to Denver when Matz died in 1917. Tihen also dealt with growing anti-Catholicism, led by the Ku Klux Klan. Increased diocesan support for the *Denver Catholic Register* helped counter the anti-Catholic sentiment. As with his successors, Tihen focused on education, particularly the enlargement of St. Thomas Seminary and the addition of a college for women, Loretto Heights Academy, in 1918. The school, directed by the Sisters of Loretto, became Loretto Heights College and in 1994 became Teikyo Loretto Heights, losing its Roman Catholic affiliation. Three new hospitals, an orphanage, and a home for the elderly were also built under his leadership, and the cathedral was consecrated in 1921. When age and illness prompted Tihen to resign in 1931 Urban J. Vehr replaced him. Vehr ably guided the diocese for the next 36 years, the first 10 years as bishop and, after Denver was made a metropolitan see, as archbishop (1942–1967). He was succeeded by the Most Reverends James V. Casey (1967–1986), formerly the auxiliary bishop in Lincoln, J. Francis Stafford (1986–1996), formerly auxiliary bishop in Baltimore, and Charles J. Chaput, O.F.M.Cap. (1997–) who had been bishop of Rapid City. Archbishop Stafford resigned the see when Pope John Paul II appointed him President of the Pontifical Council for the Laity in Rome, August 1996.

At the time that Denver was designated an archdiocese, the diocese of Pueblo was formed with the Most Reverend Joseph Clement Willging as its first bishop (1941–1959). The new diocese included some of the oldest Catholic settlements in the state (San Luis, 1851; and Conejos, 1858). The diocese of Pueblo boasted an im-

Interior of the Holy Ghost Catholic Church, Denver. (©Richard Cummins/CORBIS)

pressive increase in the number of Catholic during the years of Bishop Willging and his successor, Charles A. Buswell (1959–1979). Upon Bishop Buswel's retirement, he was succeeded by Arthur N. Tafoya (1980–). Continued growth of Colorado's Catholic population led in 1984 to the creation of a third diocese in the state with the see city in Colorado Springs with Bishop Richard C. Hanifen as the first bishop. At the time of his appointment Bishop Hanifen was auxiliary bishop in Denver.

Bibliography: A. C. COCHRAN, *Miners, Merchants, and Missionaries: The Roles of Missionaries and Pioneer Churches in the Colorado Gold Rush and Its Aftermath, 1858–1870.* (Metuchen, N.J. and London: American Theological Library Association, 1980). J. M. ESPINOSA, trans. and ed., "The Opening of the First Jesuit Mission in Colorado: Conejos Parish," *Mid-America* 18 (1936), 272–75. H. R. LAMAR, ed. "Colorado" entry. *The New Encyclopedia of the American West* (New Haven 1998), 241–44. J. B. MIÉGE, "An Early Episcopal Visitation of Colorado: 1860. Letters of the Rt. Rev. John Baptist Miége, S.J., D.D., annotated by Rev. W. J. HOWLETT, ed. T. F. O'CONNOR, *Mid-America* 18 (1936) 266–71. D. SCOTT, "Go Tell It in the Rockies: Denver's Vibrant Catholicism," *Crisis: Politics, Culture, and the Church* 19:6 (June 2001), 12–18.

[E. M. GOODROW/D. S. MCDONALD]

COLOSSAE

The oldest of the three major cities (with Laodicea and Hierapolis) in the Lycus Valley, in the southwestern part of ancient Phrygia. It was mentioned by both Herodotus and Xenophon. Although it was on one of the routes from Antioch in Pisidia to EPHESUS, it does not seem that Paul visited the Christian community there (Col. 1.6–8). It had been evangelized by the Colossian Epaphras (Col 1.6–8; 4.12–13). Jewish, Greek, and ancient Phrygian elements composed the population; the Christians were mainly of Gentile origin. The city was abandoned in the 8th century, and the site has not yet been excavated.

Bibliography: S. E. JOHNSON, "Laodicea and Its Neighbors," *The Biblical Archaeologist* 13 (1950) 1–18. H. LECLERCQ, *Dictionnaire d'archéologie chrétienne et de liturgie*, ed. F. CABROL, H. LECLERCQ, and H. I. MARROU, 15 v. (Paris 1907–53) 3.2:2339–42. *Encyclopedic Dictionary of the Bible*, tr. and adap. by L. HARTMAN (New York 1963), from A. VAN DEN BORN, *Bijbels Woordenboek* 407–08.

[E. H. MALY]

COLOSSEUM

The Colosseum in Rome, Italy, was originally called the Amphitheatrum Flavianum. Since its construction (A.D. 72–80) this gigantic amphitheater has been regarded both as a symbol of Rome's power and as one of the world's greatest wonders. The structure, built of travertine blocks upon the site of Nero's Golden House by the Emperors Vespasian and Titus, is an ellipse 1,719 feet in circumference and 159 feet in height, with an arena 282 by 177 feet. In its best preserved section it is four stories high. The first three stories are formed by arcades with pillars of Doric, Ionic, and Corinthian orders respectively; the fourth is a tier of blind arcading, broken by alternate panels and windows. The interior had three tiers of marble seats for about 50,000 spectators. Beneath the sanded arena was an elaborate structure of rooms, vaults, passageways, and drains.

The intricate system of substructures beneath the arena seems to indicate that it could be flooded for mock naval battles. There were efficient devices for the drainage of the entire interior, which have been in part restored. Surrounding the arena was a low wall surmounted by a railing high enough to protect the audience from wild animals and combatants. The primary purpose of the huge arena was entertainment, such as gladiatorial fights, naval clashes, and wild beast fights. While it has been venerated as the scene of numerous Christian martyrdoms since the 17th century, this late tradition has been seriously questioned by recent scholars, especially the Bollandist H. DELEHAYE, as the ancient Christian sources make no mention of such martyrdoms.

Because of earthquakes and its use as a stone quarry, the Colosseum continued to deteriorate until Pope BENEDICT XIV (1740–58) forbade further demolition. Because of periodic stories of buried treasure in the Colosseum, Pope PIUS IX, in 1864, gave permission for excavations. Nothing of intrinsic value was found. However, the excavations did give R. Lanciani an opportunity to examine the foundations of the vast structure. He found that the substructures were arched like those of the structure above the ground, and that underneath them was a very thick bed of concrete. Further excavations were begun in 1938. The outbreak of World War II in the following year suspended the work, which resumed at the end of the war. An eight-year restoration of the Colosseum in 1992 was part of a project of sprucing up the city of Rome for the new millennium. Archaeological excavations continue to be carried out in the elaborate system of labyrinths beneath.

Bibliography: G. LUGLI, *The Flavian Amphitheatre: the Colosseum* (Rome 1971). P. QUENNELL, *The Colosseum* (New York 1971). M. L. CONFORTO and A. M. REGGIANI, *Anfiteatro flavio: immagine, testimonianze, spettacoli* (Rome 1988). R. LUCIANI, *The Colosseum: Architecture, History, and Entertainment in the Flavian Amphitheatre, Ancient Rome's Most Famous Building* (Novara, Italy 1990).

[T. J. ALLEN/EDS.]

COLOSSIANS, EPISTLE TO THE

This letter follows the regular structure of Pauline letters: greeting (1:1–2); thanksgiving and prayer (1:3–23); exposition (1:24–3:4); exhortation (3:5–4:6); messages and closing (4:7–18). The letter includes some blocks of traditional material: a hymn (1:15–20); baptismal catechesis (2:6–15); lists of vices and virtues (3:5–17); and a household code (3:18–4:1).

The precise situation that the letter addresses is not easy to determine. The Colossian Christians seem to have been converts from paganism. This is borne out by the references, both direct and indirect, to their former Gentile status (1:12–13, 27; 2:13), by the mention of vices that were more proper to paganism than to Judaism (3:5–7), and by the general failure to make use of arguments from the Old Testament. However, the frequent mention of Judaizing tendencies must also be accounted for. The di-

Ancient Amphitheatre Flavian or Colosseum, Rome, March, 1980. (AP/Wide World Photos)

etary and cultic scruples described in 2:16–17, 20–21 must have at least a partially Jewish background. To explain these apparent inconsistencies, it is assumed that Judaizing elements in Asia Minor had made their influence felt among the Christian communities. It is known that the Jewish population in Asia Minor had grown ever since the Hellenistic conquest. It is clear from the Acts of the Apostles that, while many of these Jews accepted Christianity, there was a decided tendency among them to resist the abandonment of any of their Jewish practices. It is suggested by some that there existed, especially in this area, a syncretistic Judaism that had been influenced by the philosophy and mysticism of a Hellenized Asia Minor. Such a Jewish heterodoxy would account for the type of speculation, asceticism, and mysticism attacked in Colossians. Specific Gnostic elements, such as characterized later groups, are not present here, and the possible Gnosticizing tendency (2:8, 18) can be explained on the basis of similar tendencies found in both Jewish and Gentile circles even before this time (*see* GNOSIS).

Specific ethical recommendations, the *Haustalfen*, made toward the close of the letter, may have been occasioned by particular circumstances in the Colossian community. Especially encouraged is the proper Christian attitude of wives and husbands, children and parents to one another (3:18–21). And receiving more than the usual attention is the attitude of slaves and masters to one another (3.22–4.1).

Doctrine. In response to these dangers the author presented some profound statements, which can be summed up under three headings: (1) Christ, (2) the Church, and (3) the Christian.

Christ. No higher christology is found anywhere in the New Testament than in 1:5–20. Preexistence, equality with the Father, a cosmic dimension both in creation and in Redemption through Him, and absolute superiority over all creatures—these are all boldly stated of Jesus Christ. To sum up and to explain all this, the letter refers to the πλήρωμα (fullness) that God has made to dwell in him (1:9). Its meaning is much discussed. Many scholars see Christ as containing within himself everything that God is. Others see it rather in relation to the universe, so that Christ possesses the fullness of any excellence found in it. Because of this fullness Christ is the perfect mediator between God and humans.

The absolute superiority of Christ over the angels (1:6) is such that He has despoiled them of any power they may have had over man before this (through the regime of the Law) and has made their inferiority to himself publicly manifest (2:5). In relation to the hurch Christ is the "head," an attribute that is His in the order of time by reason of His being "the firstborn from the dead" (1:8) and in the order of grace by reason of His reconciliation of all things to himself (1:20).

The Church. In this epistle the church, too, takes on new dimensions. It refers here, as in Ephesians, not only to the local gathering of Christians (4:6) but primarily to the universal church, which is more clearly seen to be organically connected with Christ; he is now, for the first time, explicitly called its head, and the Church is his body (1:8, 24). The realism of the assertion has been emphasized in recent exegesis. This is not a mere figure of speech, nor does it signify simply a social entity, in which case the Church would be merely a body of "Christians" who are named after Christ. It is the body of Christ inasmuch as its members are united through baptism to the physical but resurrected body of Christ and as a consequence are really his own members.

The Christian. The connatural emergent of this theology of Christ and the Church is the meaning it has for the Christian. Here, too, the epistle offers profound insights. Central is the Christian's relation to Christ already mentioned. The assimilation to Christ is described here in a way that recalls Rom 6:3–11; the Christian repeats sacramentally in baptism the saving acts of Christ (Col 2:12). For this reason it can be said that the Christians receives of the fullness of Christ (2:10). So real is this resulting union that the writer could say that the Christian is filling up in the flesh of his or her own body "what is lacking of the sufferings of Christ" (1:24); it is Christ who is suffering in the Christian.

All of this is possible only through the saving work of Christ. It was his body, subjected to that state in which sinful man finds himself, that was the place where reconciliation of mankind was effected through death (1:22). For if the Christian does die to sin and rise to life, it is because he or she dies, is buried, and rises "with Christ," i.e., is joined to Christ (2:12). When God brought His Son to life, He brought the Christian along with him (2:13). Once this is understood, then it is evident how useless are those humanely devised practices that presume to possess within themselves the power to save (2:16–23), including a false asceticism (2:20–22). This does not mean that the author condemned all asceticism or mortification. In almost the same breath that he attacked the erroneous practices he also encouraged a life of mortification that is "in Christ" (3:5). Here Christians meet once again the familiar tension between the indicative and the imperative in the Christian life, between "you have put on Christ" and "put on Christ." In Baptism a renovation has already taken place, a complete incorporation into the resurrected Christ. It is now for the Christian to live in accord with this new life, to "strip off the old person and its deeds, and put on the new" (3:9–10; see also 2:11).

Authenticity. Debate about the authenticity of the letter has focused on two areas: language and theology. Some characteristically Pauline terms, e.g., "righteousness," "to believe," "law," and "to save," do not occur in Colossians. Moreover, the christology, eschatology, and ecclesiology show some marked differences from the undisputed Pauline letters. Christological statements that have no parallel in Paul include the following: Christ is the mystery of God (1:27; 2:2–3); believers have been raised with Christ (2:12); Christ forgives sins (1:13–14; 3:13); Christ is victorious over the principalities and powers (2:15). Whereas Paul expected the parousia in the near future (1 Thes 4:15; 1 Cor 7:26), there is a lessening of expectation in Colossians (2:12; 3:1), but in the undisputed letters resurrection is a future expectation (1 Cor 6:14; 2 Cor 4:14).

The chief difference in ecclesiology between Colossians and the undisputed Pauline writings is that, whereas in the Pauline writings the term "church" usually designates the local church in a specific way, in Colossians the church is a universal entity, the body of which Christ is the head (1:18, 14; 2:19; 3:15). The weight of these and other differences from the genuine letters has persuaded many modern scholars that Paul did not write Colossians (E. Lohse, J. Gnilka, W. A. Meeks, E. Käeman, J. A. Fitzmyer, M. Y. MacDonald), although the authenticity of the letter is still defended by some (R. P. Martin, G. B. Caird, C. F. D. Moule). The issues raised in the community suggest that the letter was written after Paul's lifetime, between A.D. 70 and A.D. 80, by someone who knew the Pauline tradition.

Bibliography: M. P. HORGAN, *The Letter to the Colossians, The New Jerome Biblical Commentary* (Englewood Cliffs, New Jersey 1990) 876–82. J. KNOX, "Philemon and the Authenticity of Colossians," *Journal of Religion* 18 (1938) 144–60. J. E. CROUCH, *The Origin and Intention of the Colossian Haustafel* (Göttingen 1973). R. DEICHGRÄBER, *Gotteshymnus und Christushymnus in der* *frühen Christenheit* (Göttingen 1967). E. LOHSE. *Colossians and Philemon* (Philadelphia 1971). R. P. MARTIN, *Colossians and Philemon* (London 1981). M. Y. MACDONALD, *Colossians. Ephesians* (SacPag 17; Collegeville Liturgical 2000). For additional bibliography, *see* CAPTIVITY EPISTLES.

[E. H. MALY/M. P. HORGAN]

COLUMBA OF IONA, ST.

Irish ascetic and monastic founder; b. Gartan, Donegal *c.* 521; d. Iona, June 9, 597. Columba, of the royal O'Neill dynasty, was educated at Clonard under St. Finnian of Moville, and at Glasnevin near Dublin. He was ordained in 551 and established a monastery at Derry. In 563 he migrated to the island of Iona (Hy) and established a monastic center for missions among the Picts and Northumbrians, as well as for scholarly pursuit. He apparently visited the Irish mainland on one or two occasions, and in the Assembly of Druim-Cetta (575) he acted as a peacemaker. He is credited with the authorship of poems in both Latin (*Altus Prosator*) and early Gaelic. The "cathach" psalter, the oldest known manuscript of the Gallican Psalter, may be in his handwriting. Columba left no written rule, but his *Vita* by ADAMNAN OF IONA gives a description of the manner of life of the monks. He is variously called Colm, Colum, Columbkille, Columcille, Columbus, and Combs.

Feast: June 9.

Bibliography: ADAMNAN OF IONA, *Life of Columba*, ed. and tr. A. O. and M. O. ANDERSON (New York 1962); tr. R. SHARPE (Harmondsworth, Middlesex, England 1991). M. A. FITZGERALD, *The World of Colmcille* (Dublin 1997). D. FORRISTAL, *Colum Cille* (Dublin 1997). M. HERBERT, *Iona, Kells, and Derry: The History and Hagiography of the Monastic Familia of Columba* (Oxford 1988). B. LACEY, *Colum Cille and the Columban Tradition* (Dublin 1997). M. O'DONNELL, *The Life of Colum Cille*, ed. B. LACEY (Dublin 1998). L. WHITESIDE, *In Search of Columba* (Blackrock Co., Dublin 1997). *Lives of the Scottish Saints*, tr. W. M. METCALFE (Felinfach 1990). *The Prophecies of St. Malachy and St. Columbkille*, ed. H. E. CARDINALE and W. COSLETT QUIN (Gerrards Cross 1969). J.F. KENNEY, *The Sources for the Early History of Ireland*, v. 1 *Ecclesiastical* (New York 1929) 1:422–442.

[J. RYAN]

COLUMBA OF RIETI, BL.

Patroness of Perugia, Italy; b. Angelella Guadagnoli, Rieti, Feb. 2, 1467; d. Perugia, May 20, 1501. Her name was changed to Columba when a dove flew over the font at her christening. Refusing the marriage arranged by her parents, she made a vow of virginity and entered upon a solitary life. At the age of 19, having become a Dominican tertiary, she left her seclusion, journeying to Viterbo,

Narni, Foligno, and eventually to turbulent Perugia, where she founded the convent of St. Catherine (1490). Civil rulers and members of the hierarchy came to consult her; her influence as a peacemaker was remarkable. She practiced severe penances and endured painful illnesses and calumnies. She was particularly devoted to St. CATHERINE OF SIENA. When Columba was dying, the civil magistrates came to visit her, and the expenses of her funeral were defrayed by the city of Perugia. Her cult was confirmed in 1627.

Feast: May 20.

Bibliography: *Année Dominicaine*, 23 v. (Lyons 1883–1909) May 2:527–544. A. BAGLIONI, *Colomba da Rieti, la seconda Caterina da Siena* (Rome 1967). M. D. DE GANAY, *Les Bienheureuses Dominicaines* (4th ed. Paris 1924) 305–354. R. FRASCISCO, A. MERCATI and A. PELZER, *Dizionario ecclesiastico*, 3 v. (Turin 1954–58) 1:668. A. BUTLER, *The Lives of the Saints*, ed. H. THURSTON and D. ATTWATER, 4 v. (New York 1956) 2:359–361. A. WALZ, *Lexikon für Theologie und Kirche*, ed. J. HOFER and K. RAHNER, 10 v. (2d, new ed. Freiburg 1957–65) 3:13.

[M. J. FINNEGAN]

COLUMBA AND POMPOSA, SS.

Virgin martyrs; b. Córdoba, Spain, *c.* 830 and *c.* 840; d. there, Sept. 17 and 19, 853. Columba and her sister built the double monastery of Tabanos, from which came several of the first martyrs of CÓRDOBA. Columba was martyred after she confessed Christ and denounced the prophet Mohammed before the Islamic authorities. Christians recovered her relics from the Guadalquivir River and buried them in a basilica outside Córdoba. EULOGIUS makes of her vita an exemplum of the virtues practiced in the monastic life. The youthful Pomposa slipped out of a monastery built by her parents and repeated Columba's words before the *cadi*. She was slain immediately. Her body also was recovered from the river and buried at the feet of Columba. Both were included in the Roman martyrology in 1583.

Feasts: Sept. 17 (St. Columba) and Sept. 19 (St. Pomposa).

Bibliography: EULOGIUS, *Memoriale sanctorum* 3.10, 11 in *Patrologia Latina*, 217 v. (Paris 1878–90) 115:806–813. E. P. COLBERT, *The Martyrs of Córdoba* (Washington 1962) 850–859.

[E. P. COLBERT]

COLUMBAN, ST.

Also known as Columbanus or Columba the Younger, Irish monk, abbot of LUXEUIL and BOBBIO; b. Leinster, Ireland, *c.* 543; d. Bobbio, Italy, Nov. 23, 615.

Columbanus studied at the school of St. Sinell (a disciple of St. Finnian of Clonard) at Cleenish in Lough Erne and entered the monastery and school of St. Comgall at BANGOR, where sanctity and scholarship were combined. In 591, after 30 years of teaching during which he composed a commentary on the Psalter and poems for his students, he was sent by St. Comgall with 12 companions to do missionary work on the continent of Europe. Invited by the Merovingian King Childebert, he settled in Burgundy and founded three monasteries, Annegray, Luxeuil, and Fontaines, whence there originated some 200 monastic foundations for which he composed a *Regula monachorum* and a *Regula coenobialis*. Vigorously attacking the degenerate local clergy, the immoral court, and undesirable local customs, he introduced the strict Irish system of Penance, contributing two PENITENTIALS himself. He had difficulty with the local bishops over the date for celebrating Easter (*see* EASTER CONTROVERSY) and wrote to Pope GREGORY I for support, using the term *totius Europae* for the first time to express the Irish concept of the West as a Christian cultural unit. Expelled from BURGUNDY by King Theuderic whom he censured for living in concubinage, Columbanus passed through Neustria at the request of King Clothar and settled near Zurich, whence he was driven out by the local population for his attack on paganism. He crossed the Alps and founded a monastery at Bobbio; from there his influence spread all over Europe, although his successors mitigated some of the rigors of Irish MONASTICISM with Benedictine elements. His letters, rules, and poetry form part of the great tradition of Irish Latin literature and had a lasting effect on the culture of the Middle Ages. His body is buried in a crypt of the Church of St. Columbanus at Bobbio.

Feast: Nov. 23, Nov. 21 (Roman Martyrology).

Bibliography: *S. Columbani Opera*, ed. G. S. M. WALKER (*Scriptores Latini Hiberniae* 2; Dublin 1957). G. METLAKE, *Life and Writings of St. Columbanus* (Felinfach, Lampeter, Dyfed 1993). T. Ó FIAICH, *Columbanus in his Own Words* (Dublin 1974). JONAS OF BOBBIO, *Vita sancti Columbani*, ed. B. KRUSCH (*Monumenta Germaniae Historica: Scriptores rerum Germanicarum* 35; 1905), tr. as *Life of St. Columban*, ed. D. C. MUNRO (Felinfach 1993). M. M. DUBOIS, *Saint Columban* (Paris 1950). J. O'CARROLL, tr., "The Chronology of St. Columban," *Irish Theological Quarterly* 24 (1957) 76–95. F. MACMANUS, *Saint Columban* (New York 1962). L. BIELER and D. A. BINCHY, eds., *The Irish Penitentials* (*Scriptores Latini Hiberniae* 5; Dublin 1963). *Columbanus and Merovingian Monasticism*, ed. H. B. CLARKE and M. BRENNAN (Oxford 1981). *Columbanus: Studies on the Latin Writings*, ed. M. LAPIDGE (Woodbridge, Suffolk, England 1997). J. F. KENNEY, *The Sources for the Early History of Ireland* (New York 1929) 1:186–205.

[J. RYAN]

COLUMBAN FATHERS

Columban Fathers is the popular name for the St. Columban's Foreign Mission Society (SSC), founded in Ireland in October 1916. An influential committee, organized by the missionary Edward J. GALVIN and Rev. John Blowick, a Maynooth professor, requested the Irish hierarchy to approve the foundation of a seminary to train secular priests as missionaries for China; the bishops authorized the project, and Benedict XV approved it. The seminary (major) was opened January 1918, at Dalgan Park, Galway; in March it was placed under the patronage of the Congregation for the Propagation of the Faith. On June 29, 1918, 17 priests took the oath of membership in this new society which chose St. COLUMBAN, Irish missionary (d. 615), as its patron. It became a pontifical society in 1924.

At the invitation of Abp. Jeremiah Harty, the Columban Fathers established their first house in the U.S. at Omaha, Nebr., on Dec. 14, 1918. In 1920, two Columban Fathers went to Australia, where a year later Abp. Daniel Mannix of Melbourne blessed the first Columban house in his archdiocese. In 1929 Columban Fathers went to the Philippines in response to an appeal from Archbishop O'Doherty of Manila. In China the first area assigned to the Columban Fathers (1920) was Hanyang, where Galvin became first vicar apostolic in 1927, and bishop in 1946. The Communists expelled the bishop and the missionaries in 1952. In 1928 the society received a district in Jiangxi province, then the headquarters of the Communists. Father Patrick Cleary was consecrated the first bishop of Hanzhong, Jiangxi, in 1939. When Communism triumphed in China, at least 90 Columban Fathers were forced to depart from their mission stations where there were almost 56,000 Chinese Catholics.

The general headquarters of the society are located at Dublin, Ireland. The U.S. headquarters are at St. Columbans, Nebraska.

Bibliography: Archives, St. Columbans, Nebr. P. CROSBIE, *March Till They Die* (Westminster, Md. 1956). R. REILLY, *Christ's Exile: Life of Bishop Edward J. Galvin* (Dublin 1958). B. T. SMYTH, ed., *But Not Conquered* (Westminster, Md. 1958). F. HERLIHY, *Now Welcome Summer* (Dublin 1948).

[D. A. BOLAND/EDS.]

COLUMBUS, CHRISTOPHER

Italian, Cristoforo Colombo and Spanish, Cristóbal Colón, seaman, chartmaker, navigator, discoverer of America; b. Genoa, Italy, September–October 1451; d. Valladolid, Spain, May 20, 1506. Christopher, Bartholomew, and Diego, sons of Domenico Colombo and his wife, Susanna Fontanarossa, became wool carders but not master weavers like their father and grandfathers. Christopher went to sea at 14, without schooling. His will of 1498 refers to Genoa as "that noble and powerful city by the sea." Throughout life, Columbus attempted to emulate St. Christopher, "the Christ bearer." Ardent in religious devotion, he desired to spread the Christian faith more than he wished for personal glory, wealth, and distinction. He had rare ability to acquire knowledge through observation and experience; he demonstrated superlative competence as a seaman and navigator during his four famous voyages. Little is known of his life prior to 1486. He served in a Genoese privateer; he made one or more voyages to Chios in the Aegean Sea. He survived the sinking of a ship in battle, off Cape St. Vincent, Portugal, Aug. 13, 1476. Although wounded, he seized a large oar and used it for partial support in swimming to the Portuguese coast. After being cared for in the Genoese colony of Lisbon, he became a chartmaker with his brother Bartholomew. He made a voyage to Iceland, and visited Galway, Ireland. Castilian Spanish was the language of the educated in Portugal when the Columbus brothers were establishing themselves as chartmakers. The writings of Christopher are in Castilian with Portuguese spellings, or in Latin learned after he began to think in Spanish. As an agent for Genoese merchants he visited Genoa and lived in Madeira for a time. In command of a merchant vessel, he made at least one voyage to equatorial west Africa. He married Doña Felipa Perestrello e Moniz, whose brother held the hereditary captaincy of the island of Porto Santo, near Madeira. Their son Diego was born *c.* 1480. She died before Columbus went to Spain and was buried in the Moniz family chapel in Lisbon's church of the Carmo.

The Indies. Portugal led Europe in sea exploration and a chartmaker in Lisbon could be familiar with Portuguese progress. Christopher studied geography, and three of his books have been preserved: *Imago Mundi* by PETER OF AILLY of Cambrai, written *c.* 1410, printed *c.* 1480; *Historia Rerum Ubique Gestarum* by Aeneas Sylvius Piccolomini (PIUS II, 1458–64) written 1440, printed 1477; and the Far Eastern travels of Marco Polo, also in Latin. Both brothers read and reread these books. Christopher made some 2,000 marginal notes and filled the blank pages at the ends of the volumes. He conceived the idea of sailing westward to Asia. The "Fixed Idea" of Columbus was based on faith in his own ability as a seaman-navigator, combined with a gross underestimate of the distance involved. The size of the earth had been debated for 1,800 years. According to PTOLEMY (A.D. 145) the distance from Cape St. Vincent to easternmost China spanned 180° or halfway around the globe. Enthusiasm helped Columbus to prefer the earlier estimate of

Christopher Columbus.

Marinus of Tyre, viz, 225°. The Venetian traveler Marco Polo placed China and Japan farther east. Columbus argued that a degree on the equator measured 45.2 nautical miles, the smallest estimate ever made. Columbus obtained partial support from P. Toscanelli of Florence in 1481, when the latter estimated that Japan was only 3,000 miles west of the Canary Islands. Christopher calculated that 2,400 miles was the distance, and placed the coast of Japan in the longitude of San Juan, Puerto Rico. He asked the King of Portugal to send him westward to Asia, but Portuguese geographers advised that the voyage would require fully 100 days.

Preparations for the Voyage. Unsuccessful in his effort to engage the support of King John II of Portugal, Columbus sought help elsewhere.

Columbus in Spain. Upon arriving at Palos from Portugal in 1485, Christopher left his son Diego with the Franciscan friars at La Rabida. Bartholomew continued chartmaking in Lisbon. The head of the Franciscans in Seville, Antonio de Marchena (*see* PÉREZ, JUAN), was favorably impressed by the ideas of Columbus, and the latter was able to explain them to Queen ISABELLA at Córdoba, in May 1486. At that time the sovereigns were engaged in war against the Moorish Kingdom of Granada.

Columbus at Salamanca. Twice in Spain, and once in Portugal, royal commissions considered the advisability of financing an expedition for Columbus. Father Hernando de Talavera, later archbishop of Granada, headed the best known commission, December 1486, in Salamanca. It should be remembered that there was no accurate way to determine longitude prior to 1765. In 1486, neither the size of the earth nor the longitude of Japan was known. The commission reported that the earth was considerably larger than Columbus believed, that the distance to Japan was far greater than he estimated, and that available ships could not carry sufficient food and water for a voyage of that length. On these three points the commission was correct, but the members were favorably impressed by the dignity and earnestness of Columbus himself. The consensus in Spain then was that a degree on the equator measured 55.9 nautical miles; an underestimate of about 6.83 per cent in the size of the earth. By contrast, Columbus underestimated by about 24.67 per cent.

The popular "Columbus Myth" describes the Salamanca meeting as an attempt by Columbus to convince university professors, mostly churchmen, that the earth is round. The University of Salamanca was not involved. Spain had no capital at that time, and the royal commission met in that city because the court was there. The shape of the earth was not in question. Ever since men first built ships and put out from land it had been known that the earth is a sphere. The masts and spars of an approaching vessel appear over the horizon before the hull is seen. In heading away, a ship goes "hull down" before the masts disappear. Vessels often pass each other "hull down" at sea. Lookouts go to the masthead to see objects not visible from the deck. This explains the use of fires on headlands or lights on towers as aids to navigation. Lighthouses were in use for 2,100 years before the meeting at Salamanca.

Delays. The report of the Talavera Commission was delayed, and Columbus wrote King John II of Portugal. He was invited to return there, and he wrote in his copy of *Imago Mundi* that he was in Lisbon in December 1488 when Bartholomew Dias returned after discovering the Cape of Good Hope. With the route to India around Africa thus open to him, the King of Portugal lost interest in Columbus's idea. Columbus probably supported himself by selling books and charts in Seville. Bartholomew Columbus failed to interest King Henry VII of England in 1489. Although unsuccessful also in France, Bartholomew was retained at Fontainbleau as a chartmaker by the King's sister, Anne de Beaujeu, until he learned of his brother's discovery. Christopher suffered genuine distress after the unfavorable report of the Commission. Determined to go to France, he traveled first to La Rabida.

Father Juan Pérez wrote to Queen Isabella and secured for Christopher another summons to court. His proposals were considered again, and referred to the Royal Council of Castile. Immediately after Columbus marched in the triumphal procession entering Granada on Jan. 2, 1492, his plan was rejected.

Queen Isabella's Decision. On the day that Christopher left court, one of King Ferdinand V of Castile's Aragonese advisers, Luis de Santangel, persuaded Isabella to reconsider. Columbus was recalled and had another interview with Isabella. She won her husband's approval. Santangel argued that the enterprise required little risk while offering great possibilities. Probably the character of Columbus won for him the support of the Queen and of many able men. The Franciscan Father Juan Pérez assisted in making the agreements with the crown.

The First Voyage. With a total of 90 men embarked, the ship *Santa Maria* and the caravels *Pinta* and *Nina* sailed from Palos on Friday, Aug. 3, 1492. They departed the Canary Islands on September 9. With favorable weather and winds, they were beyond the position where land was expected on October 10, and the crew complained. Columbus promised to turn back if land was not sighted in 2 or 3 days. San Salvador Island was discovered on Oct. 12, 1492; latitude 24° 00' north, longitude 74° 30' west; 33 days and 3,066 nautical miles from the Canaries. After exploring northeastern Cuba, Columbus crossed the Windward Passage to the north shore of Hispaniola, where the *Santa Maria* was wrecked on Christmas morning. Forty men were left in a fort on shore called "Navidad." With a number of natives and some gold, Columbus started his return passage in the *Nina,* from Samana Bay on Jan. 16, 1493. Heading northeast, Columbus weathered severe storms, stopped in the Azores, and was driven into Lisbon. After calling on the King of Portugal, Columbus reached Palos a few hours ahead of the *Pinta* on March 15, 1493.

News of the discovery spread rapidly in Spain and Italy, slowly elsewhere. Columbus visited the court at Barcelona, was ordered to prepare another expedition, and was confirmed in the title Admiral of the Ocean Sea. While recognizing his discovery, many educated men doubted that he had reached the Indies in 33 days from the Canaries.

Second Voyage. The second departure was on Oct. 13, 1493. A high mountainous island sighted Sunday, November 3 was named Dominica. Skirting the Leeward Islands, inside the Caribbean, via the Mona Passage, all 17 vessels reached Navidad safely on November 28. Columbus was shocked by the discovery that all of the garrison were dead, and influenced by the necessity of returning ships to Spain, he hastily chose for the new town of "Isabela" a site that lacked natural advantages. A better anchorage was available 20 miles east at Puerto Plata. Throughout the first voyage crews had been healthy, but hard work, exposure to mosquitos, rain, and strange diets made 300 men ill soon after work began at Isabela. Medicaments were exhausted; the doctor worn out. Columbus was not an experienced administrator; his errors were repeated, however, by the English in Virginia a century later, and by other colonizers. Columbus explored part of the southern coast of Cuba in May, circled Jamaica, and returned along the southern coast of Hispaniola, reaching Isabela on Sept. 29, 1494. His brother Bartholomew had arrived, and there was a letter from the sovereigns suggesting that he return to Spain to advise them. Although suffering from arthritis, Columbus remained while discontent increased in the colony. He sailed March 10, and reached Cadiz June 11, 1496.

Third Voyage. Departure was from the Cape Verde Islands July 4, 1498. Sighting Trinidad July 31, the admiral entered the Gulf of Paria, where he recognized that the volume of fresh water proved that the land to the South and West was part of a continent. Worried about conditions in Hispaniola, Columbus failed to seek the pearl fisheries after learning of them and seeing some pearls. Instead he left the coast near Margarita Island, heading for the colony. With the hope of improving matters, the admiral asked for a chief justice from Spain. Francisco de Bobadilla arrived while Christopher and Bartholomew were absent from Santo Domingo City; he listened to the malcontents and sent the brothers home in chains without hearing them. The sovereigns released Columbus, but King Ferdinand was preoccupied with diplomacy and did not study the colonial problem.

Fourth Voyage. This departure was from the Canaries May 26, 1502. Reaching Martinique June 15, the admiral headed for Santo Domingo with the hope of exchanging his flagship for a better vessel. Columbus recognized that a hurricane was imminent, asked for shelter in the Ozama River, suggested that all vessels be held in port until the storm passed. Disregarding the warning, 25 ships sailed; 20 ships and 500 men were lost. Denied shelter, the admiral rode out the storm at sea. He then spent nine months exploring the coast of Central America from Honduras to a point about 125 miles east of Porto Bello. He suffered from malaria, and bad weather, tropical rain, sickness, and difficulties with the natives affected all hands. Shipworms damaged the hulls of his vessels, and he was forced to run them aground in Saint Ann's Bay, Jamaica. Diego Méndez crossed to Cape Tiburon against wind and current, and made his way to Governor Ovando, but Ovando left the admiral and his men marooned for 370 days. Bartholomew and the admiral's

younger son, Ferdinand, were on this voyage. Nearly half the men mutinied, and mistreated the natives, and the latter almost ceased to supply food. Columbus knew that a total eclipse of the moon was expected on the night of Feb. 29, 1504. Summoning the native chiefs to a conference, the admiral told them that the God of the Christians would make a sign with the moon to show his disapproval of their failure to supply food to the stranded white men. The eclipse was persuasive. Rescued June 29, he reached Spain Nov. 7, 1504, a few weeks before Isabella's death, and died two years later. His remains rest in the cathedral of Santo Domingo City. Those of his son Don Diego, the second Admiral of the Ocean Sea, are in the cathedral of Seville. The will of Columbus commended the family, including Beatriz Enríquez de Harana, mother of Ferdinand (b. 1488), to Diego's benevolence.

Achievements of Columbus. In the most famous voyages of modern history Columbus set an example for Europe, raising standards as a seaman, as a navigator, and as an explorer. Before the development of celestial navigation he demonstrated a degree of skill in "dead reckoning" that would be highly creditable to the best navigators of the 1960s. He exhibited outstanding practical seamanship in fair weather and during storms. Although he had spent only a few years in the Caribbean area, his observations of weather conditions enabled him to predict an impending hurricane. He gave Spain an empire and extended Christian civilization. As an administrator he made mistakes, but few men have done better under similar primitive conditions in colonization.

Bibliography: J. WINSOR, *Christopher Columbus* (5th ed. Boston 1892); ed., *Narrative and Critical History of America,* 8 v. (Boston 1884–89) 2:1–128. R. Academia de la historia, Madrid, *Bibliografía Colombina: Enumeración de libros y documentos concernientes a Cristóbal Colón y sus viajes* (Madrid 1892). *Raccolta di documenti e studi pubblicati dalla R. Commissione Colombiana,* 14 v. (Rome 1892–94). J. B. THACHER, *Christopher Columbus: His Life, His Work, His Remains,* 3 v. (New York 1903–04). F. COLÓN, *The Life of the Admiral Christopher Columbus,* ed. and tr. B. KEEN (New Brunswick, N.J. 1959). S. E. MORISON, *Admiral of the Ocean Sea: A Life of Christopher Columbus,* 2 v. (Boston 1942); *Christopher Columbus, Mariner* (Boston 1955); ed. and tr., *Journals and Other Documents on the Life and Voyages of Christopher Columbus* (New York 1963). A. BALLESTEROS Y BERETTA, *Cristóbal Colón y el descubrimiento de América,* 2 v. (Barcelona 1945). L. HANKE, *Bartolomé de las Casas* (Philadelphia 1952). *Studi Colombiana,* 3 v. (Genoa 1952). C. SANZ, *Bibliotheca Americana vetustissima: Ultimas adiciones,* 2 v. (Madrid 1960).

[J. B. HEFFERNAN]

COLUMBUS, DIOCESE OF

The Diocese of Columbus (*Columbensis*) embraces 23 counties in central and southern Ohio and is geographically the largest in the state. The boundaries form a triangle stretching from the rich farmlands around Ada and Kenton in the northwest to the rolling, wooded hills of Zoar in the northeast to Portsmouth on the Ohio River in the south and include Columbus, the capital city of the state. As established by Pope Pius IX on March 3, 1868, the diocese included the 31 counties lying east and south of Marion County, but excluding those portions of four counties lying west of the Scioto River and south of Franklin County. In 1944, 13 counties of the diocese along the Ohio River were formed into the new Diocese of Steubenville and five counties from the Archdiocese of Cincinnati, along with the partial counties lying west of the Scioto, were added on the west.

The initial Catholic population was about 40,000, 5% of the total population of 790,000. The early Catholic people were descendants of German, Irish, and English settlers of Pennsylvania and Maryland along with new immigrants from Ireland and Germany, numerous converts, and scattered pockets of French immigrants. They were concentrated in Perry County, site of St. Joseph Church near Somerset (the first Catholic parish in the state), and elsewhere along Zane's Trace and the National Road. From the 1880s through the 1910s large numbers of Eastern European immigrants came to the eastern part of the diocese, as well as to Columbus, to work in the mines and factories. Early in the 20th century a parish was established and St. Katherine Drexel's Sisters of the Blessed Sacrament came to the diocese to evangelize the many African Americans who had moved to Columbus from the South. Later in the century numerous Spanish-speaking people, notably from Mexico and Guatemala, made their homes in the diocese. The population of the diocese has grown through the immigration of people from many areas of the country, many of whom were attracted to jobs in government, services, trade, and manufacturing offered by the strong central Ohio economy. At the beginning of the 21st century, registered Catholics numbered about 210,000 in a total population of 2.3 million. The largest concentrations were in the Columbus suburbs.

The Diocese of Columbus has had ten ordinaries. Bishop Sylvester Rosecrans (1868–1878) had been the first auxiliary bishop in the country, in Cincinnati. Bishop John A. Watterson (1878–1899), former president of Mt. St. Mary's College, Emmitsburg, was known throughout the country for his scholarship and eloquence. Bishop Henry Moeller (1900–1903) became archbishop of Cincinnati. Bishop James J. Hartley (1903–1944), a son of the diocese, shunned publicity but accomplished much. Bishop Michael J. Ready (1944–1957), before coming to Columbus, had been general secretary of the National Catholic Welfare Conference. Bishop Clarence G. Issenmann (1957–1965) subsequently became bishop of Cleveland. Bishop John J. Carberry (1965–1968) later was cardinal archbishop of St. Louis. Bishop Clarence E. Elwell (1968–1973) was an educator and author of textbooks. Bishop Edward J. Herrmann (1973–1982) initiated Operation Feed, one of the most successful, ongoing, public food drives in the country. He was succeeded by Bishop James A. Griffin, a priest of Cleveland.

The early years of the diocese were marked by the poverty of its people. St. Joseph Cathedral, prominently located on East Broad Street not far from the Ohio Statehouse, was begun in 1868 and dedicated in 1878, but its construction debt was not retired until 1906. The bishops also struggled to find priests, especially after Bishop Rosecrans had to close his St. Aloysius Seminary in 1876 and Eastern Europeans began flooding into the diocese, creating a need for many multilingual priests. The situation improved after Bishop Hartley founded St. Charles, a preparatory school and minor seminary, in 1923, but the diocese was not self-sufficient in priests until the 1930s.

Columbus is home to the Pontifical College Josephinum, which developed from an orphanage founded by Rev. Joseph Jessing, a priest of the diocese. The diocese has had a close relationship with the Dominican Fathers and Sisters through the years, beginning with the earliest missionaries. At Somerset they operated at various times a girls' academy, a priory, a novitiate, a house of studies, a secular college, and Rosary Press, in addition to a parish school. In Columbus they staff many elementary and high schools. The Dominican Fathers minister in a number of parishes and the Sisters operate Ohio Dominican College.

[D. SCHLEGEL]

ISBN 0-7876-4007-7

90000

9 780787 640071